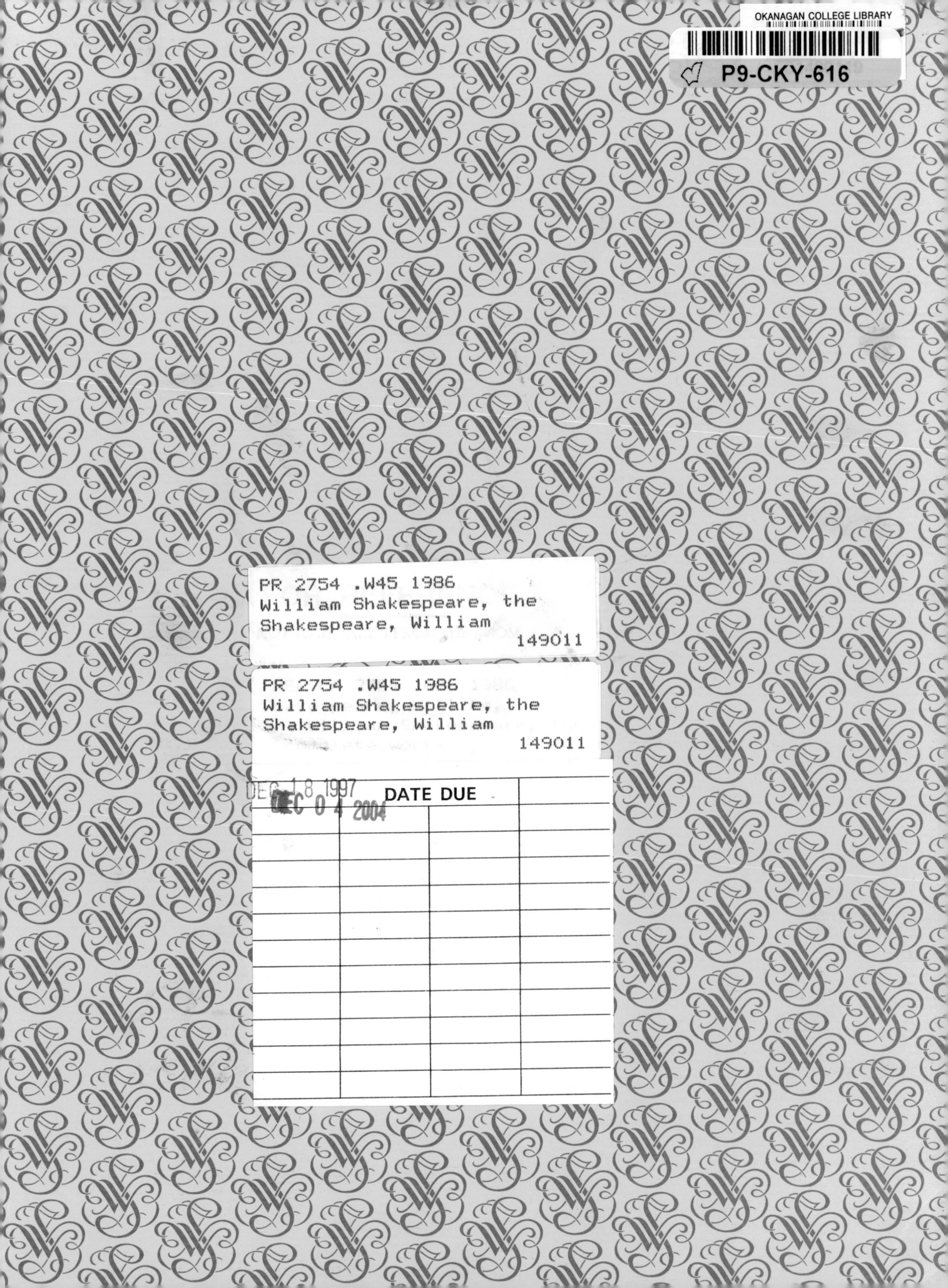

WILLIAM SHAKESPEARE

THE

COMPLETE
WORKS

ORIGINAL-SPELLING
EDITION

Martin Droeshout's sculpsit London.

Martin Droeshout's engraving of Shakespeare, first published on the title-page of the First Folio (1623)

To the Reader

This Figure, that thou here seest put,
It was for gentle Shakespeare cut;
Wherein the Grauer had a strife
With Nature, to out-doo the life:
O, could he but haue drawne his wit
As well in brasse, as he hath hit

His face; the Print would then surpasse
All, that was euer writ in brasse.
But, since he cannot, Reader, looke
Not on his Picture, but his Booke.

B.I.

WILLIAM SHAKESPEARE

THE COMPLETE WORKS

ORIGINAL-SPELLING EDITION

General Editors
STANLEY WELLS AND GARY TAYLOR

Editors
STANLEY WELLS, GARY TAYLOR
JOHN JOWETT, AND WILLIAM MONTGOMERY

With Introductions by
STANLEY WELLS

*and an Essay on Shakespeare's Spelling and
Punctuation by*
VIVIAN SALMON

CLARENDON PRESS · OXFORD

1986

Oxford University Press, Walton Street, Oxford OX2 6DP
Oxford New York Toronto
Delhi Bombay Calcutta Madras Karachi
Petaling Jaya Singapore Hong Kong Tokyo
Nairobi Dar es Salaam Cape Town
Melbourne Auckland
and associated companies in
Beirut Berlin Ibadan Nicosia

OXFORD is a trade mark of Oxford University Press

Published in the United States
by Oxford University Press, New York

British Library Cataloguing in Publication Data
Shakespeare, William
[Works] William Shakespeare: the complete works—
Original-spelling ed.
I. [Works]   II. Title   III. Wells, Stanley. 1930-
IV. Salmon, Vivian
822.3'3   PR2754
ISBN 0-19-812919-X

Library of Congress Cataloging in Publication Data
Shakespeare, William, 1564–1616.
William Shakespeare, the complete works.
I. Wells, Stanley W., 1930-   .   II. Taylor, Gary.   III. Title.
PR2754.W45 1986   822.3'3   86-8476
ISBN 0-19-812919-X

Computerized typesetting by Oxford University Press
Printed in Great Britain
at the University Printing House, Oxford
by David Stanford
Printer to the University

WILLIAM SHAKESPEARE

THE COMPLETE WORKS

with a General Introduction, and Introductions to individual works, by
STANLEY WELLS

The Complete Works has been edited collaboratively under the General Editorship of Stanley Wells and Gary Taylor. Each editor has undertaken prime responsibility for certain works, as follows:

STANLEY WELLS *The Two Gentlemen of Verona*; *The Taming of the Shrew*; *Titus Andronicus*; *Venus and Adonis*; *The Rape of Lucrece*; *Love's Labour's Lost*; *Much Ado About Nothing*; *As You Like It*; *Twelfth Night*; The Sonnets and 'A Lover's Complaint'; Various Poems (printed); *Othello*; *Macbeth*; *Antony and Cleopatra*; *The Winter's Tale*

GARY TAYLOR *1 Henry VI*; *Richard III*; *The Comedy of Errors*; *A Midsummer Night's Dream*; *Henry V*; *Hamlet*; *Troilus and Cressida*; Various Poems (manuscript); *Sir Thomas More* (passages attributed to Shakespeare); *All's Well That Ends Well*; *King Lear*; *Pericles*; *Cymbeline*

JOHN JOWETT *Romeo and Juliet*; *Richard II*; *King John*; *1 Henry IV*; *The Merry Wives of Windsor*; *2 Henry IV*; *Julius Caesar*; *Measure for Measure*; *Timon of Athens*; *Coriolanus*; *The Tempest*

WILLIAM MONTGOMERY *The First Part of the Contention*; *Richard Duke of York*; *The Merchant of Venice*; *All is True*; *The Two Noble Kinsmen*

American Advisory Editor · S. Schoenbaum
Textual Adviser · G. R. Proudfoot
Music Adviser · F. W. Sternfeld
Editorial Assistant · Christine Avern-Carr

ACKNOWLEDGEMENTS

THE preparation of a volume such as this would be impossible without the generosity that scholars can count on receiving from their colleagues, at home and overseas. Among those to whom we are particularly grateful are: R. E. Alton; John F. Andrews; Peter Beal; Thomas L. Berger; David Bevington; J. W. Binns; Peter W. M. Blayney; Fredson Bowers; A. W. Braunmüller; A. F. Brissenden; Susan Brock; J. P. Brockbank; Robert Burchfield; Lou Burnard; Lesley Burnett; John Carey; Janet Clare; Thomas Clayton; T. W. Craik; Norman Davis; Alan Dessen; E. E. Duncan-Jones; K. Duncan-Jones; R. D. Eagleson; Philip Edwards; G. Blakemore Evans; Jean Fuzier; Hans Walter Gabler; Philip Gaskell; A. J. Gurr; Antony Hammond; Richard Hardin; G. R. Hibbard; Myra Hinman; R. V. Holdsworth; E. A. J. Honigmann; T. H. Howard-Hill; MacD. P. Jackson; Harold Jenkins; John Kerrigan; Randall McLeod; Nancy Maguire; Giorgio Melchiori; Peter Milward; Kenneth Muir; Stephen Orgel; Kenneth Palmer; John Pitcher; Eleanor Prosser; S. W. Reid; Marvin Spevack; R. K. Turner; E. M. Waith; Michael Warren; Paul Werstine; G. Walton Williams; Laetitia Yeandle. Vivian Salmon wishes to acknowledge the assistance of Gary Taylor in preparing the textual and bibliographical portions of her essay.

We are conscious also of a great debt to the past: to our predecessors R. B. McKerrow and Alice Walker, who did not live to complete an Oxford Shakespeare but whose papers have been of invaluable assistance, and to the long line of editors and other scholars, from Nicholas Rowe onwards, whose work is acknowledged in *William Shakespeare: A Textual Companion*.

We gratefully acknowledge assistance from the staff of the following libraries and institutions: the Beinecke Library, Yale University; the Birmingham Shakespeare Library; the Bodleian Library, Oxford; the British Library; the English Faculty Library, Oxford; the Folger Shakespeare Library; Lambeth Palace Library; St. John's College, Cambridge; the Shakespeare Centre, Stratford-upon-Avon; the Shakespeare Institute, University of Birmingham; Trinity College, Cambridge; the Victoria and Albert Museum; Westminster Abbey Library.

Many debts of gratitude have also been incurred to persons employed in a variety of capacities by Oxford University Press. Among those with whom we have worked especially closely are Linda Agerbak, Sue Dommett, Oonagh Ferrier, Paul Luna, Jamie Mackay, Louise Pengelley, Graham Roberts, Maria Tsoutsos, and Patricia Wilkie. John Bell started it all, Kim Scott Walwyn made sure we finished it, and from beginning to end Christine Avern-Carr's meticulous standards of accuracy have been exemplary.

S.W.W. G.T.
J.J. W.L.M.

CONTENTS

THE WORKES OF WILLIAM SHAKSPERE

CONTENTS

ILLUSTRATIONS

GENERAL INTRODUCTION

THIS volume contains all the known plays and poems of William Shakespeare, a writer, actor, and man of the theatre who lived from 1564 to 1616. He was successful and admired in his own time; major literary figures of the subsequent century, such as John Milton, John Dryden, and Alexander Pope, paid tribute to him, and some of his plays continued to be acted during the later seventeenth and earlier eighteenth centuries; but not until the dawn of Romanticism, in the later part of the eighteenth century, did he come to be looked upon as a universal genius who outshone all his fellows and even, some said, partook of the divine. Since then, no other secular imaginative writer has exerted so great an influence over so large a proportion of the world's population. Yet Shakespeare's work is firmly rooted in the circumstances of its conception and development. Its initial success depended entirely on its capacity to please the theatre-goers (and, to a far lesser extent, the readers) of its time; and its later, profound impact is due in great part to that in-built need for constant renewal and adaptation that belongs especially to those works of art that reach full realization only in performance. Shakespeare's power over generations later than his own has been transmitted in part by artists who have drawn on, interpreted, and restructured his texts as others have drawn on the myths of antiquity; but it is the texts as they were originally performed that are the sources of his power, and that we attempt here to present with as much fidelity to his intentions as the circumstances in which they have been preserved will allow.

Shakespeare's Life: Stratford-upon-Avon and London

Shakespeare's background was commonplace. His father, John, was a glover and wool-dealer in the small Midlands market-town of Stratford-upon-Avon who had married Mary Arden, daughter of a prosperous farmer, in or about 1557. During Shakespeare's childhood his father played a prominent part in local affairs, becoming bailiff (mayor) and justice of the peace in 1568; later his fortunes declined. Of his eight children, four sons and one daughter survived childhood. William, his third child and eldest son, was baptized in Holy Trinity Church, Stratford-upon-Avon, on 26 April 1564; his birthday is traditionally celebrated on 23 April—St. George's Day. The only other member of his family to take up the theatre as a profession was his youngest brother, Edmund, born sixteen years after William. He became an actor and died at the age of twenty-seven: on the last day of 1607 the sexton of St. Saviour's, Southwark, noted 'Edmund Shakspeare A player Buried in yᵉ Church wᵗʰ a forenoone knell of yᵉ great bell, xxs.' The high cost of the funeral suggests that it may have been paid for by his prosperous brother.

John Shakespeare's position in Stratford-upon-Avon would have brought certain privileges to his family. When young William was four years old he could have had the excitement of seeing his father, dressed in furred scarlet robes and wearing the alderman's official thumb-ring, regularly attended by two mace-bearing sergeants in buff, presiding at fairs and markets. A little later, he would have begun to attend a 'petty school' to acquire the rudiments of an education that would be continued at the King's New School, an established grammar school with a well-qualified master, assisted by an usher to help with the younger pupils. We have no lists of the school's pupils in Shakespeare's time, but his father's position would have qualified him to attend, and the school offered the kind of education that lies behind the plays and poems. Its boy pupils, aged from about eight to fifteen, endured an arduous routine. Classes began early in the morning: at six, normally; hours were long, holidays infrequent. Education was centred on Latin; in the upper forms, the speaking of English was forbidden. A scene (Sc. 13) in *The Merry Wiues of Windsor* showing a schoolmaster taking a boy named William through his Latin grammar draws on the officially approved textbook, William Lily's *Shorte introduction of grammar*, and, no doubt, on Shakespeare's memories of his youth.

From grammar the boys progressed to studying works of classical and neo-classical literature. They might read anthologies of Latin sayings and Aesop's *Fables*, followed by the fairly easy plays of Terence and Plautus (on whose *Menaechmi* Shakespeare was to base *The Comedie of Errors*). They might even act scenes from Latin plays. As they progressed, they would improve their command of language by translating from Latin into English and back, by imitating approved models of style, and by studying manuals of composition, the ancient rules of rhetoric, and modern rules of letter-writing. Putting their training into practice, they would compose formal epistles, orations, and declamations. Their efforts at composition would be stimulated, too, by their reading of the most admired authors. Works that Shakespeare wrote throughout his career show the abiding influence of Virgil's *Aeneid* and of Ovid's *Metamorphoses* (both in the original and in Arthur Golding's translation of 1567). Certainly he developed a taste for books, both classical and modern: his plays show that he continued to read seriously and imaginatively for the whole of his working life.

After Shakespeare died, Ben Jonson accused him of knowing 'small Latine, *and lesse* Greeke'; but Jonson took pride in his classical knowledge: a boy educated at an Elizabethan grammar school would be more thoroughly trained in classical rhetoric and Roman (if not Greek) literature than most present-day holders of a university degree in classics. Modern languages would not normally be on the curriculum. Somehow Shakespeare seems to have picked up a working knowledge of French—which he expected audiences of *Henry V* to understand—and of Italian (the source of *Othello*, for instance, is an Italian tale that had not been published in translation when he wrote his play). We do not know whether he ever travelled outside England.

Shakespeare must have worked hard at school, but there was a life beyond the classroom. He lived in a beautiful and fertile part of the country, with rivers and fields at hand. He had the company of brothers and sisters. Each Sunday the family would go to Stratford's splendid parish church, as the law required; his father, by virtue of his dignified status, would sit in the front pew. There Shakespeare's receptive mind would be impressed by the sonorous phrases of the Bible, in either the Bishops' or the Geneva version, the Homilies, and the Book of Common Prayer. From time to time travelling players would visit Stratford. Shakespeare's father would have the duty of licensing them to perform; probably his son first saw plays professionally acted in the Guildhall below his schoolroom.

Shakespeare would have left school when he was about fifteen. What he did then is not known. One of the earliest legends about him, recorded by John Aubrey around 1681, is that 'he had been in his yonger yeares a Schoolmaster in the Countrey'. John Cottom, who was master of the Stratford school between 1579 and 1581 or 1582, and may have taught Shakespeare, was a Lancashire man whose family home was close to that of a landowner, Alexander Houghton. Both Cottom and Houghton were Roman Catholics, and there is some reason to believe that John Shakespeare may have retained loyalties to the old religion. When Houghton died, in 1581, he mentioned in his will one William Shakeshafte, apparently a player. The name is a possible variant of Shakespeare; conceivably Cottom found employment in Lancashire for his talented pupil as a tutor who also acted. If so, Shakespeare was soon back home. On 28 November 1582 a bond was issued permitting him to marry Anne Hathaway of Shottery, a village close to Stratford. She was eight years his senior, and pregnant. Their daughter, Susanna, was baptized on 26 May 1583, and twins, Hamnet and Judith, on 2 February 1585. Though Shakespeare's professional career (described in the next section of this Introduction) was to centre on London, his family remained in Stratford, and he maintained his links with his birthplace till he died and was buried there.

One of the unfounded myths about Shakespeare is that all we know about his life could be written on the back of a postage stamp. In fact we know a lot about some of the less exciting aspects of his life, such as his business dealings and his tax debts (as may be seen from the list of Contemporary Allusions, pp. xxxix–xli). Though we cannot tell how often he visited Stratford after he moved to London, clearly he felt that he belonged where

1. The Shakespeare coat of arms, from a draft dated 20 October 1596, prepared by Sir William Dethick, Garter King-of-Arms

he was born. His success in his profession may be reflected in his father's application for a grant of arms in 1596, by which John Shakespeare acquired the official status of gentleman. In August of that year William's son, Hamnet, died, aged eleven and a half, and was buried in Stratford. Shakespeare was living in the Bishopsgate area of London, north of the river, in October of the same year, but in the following year showed that he looked on Stratford as his real home by buying a large house, New Place. It was demolished in 1759.

In October 1598 Richard Quiney, whose son was to marry Shakespeare's daughter Judith, travelled to London to plead with the Privy Council on behalf of Stratford Corporation, which was in financial trouble because of fires and bad weather. He wrote the only surviving letter addressed to Shakespeare; as it was found among Quiney's papers, it was presumably never delivered. It requested a loan of £30—a large sum, suggesting confidence in his friend's prosperity. In 1601 Shakespeare's father died, and was buried in Stratford. In May of the following year Shakespeare was able to invest £320 in 107 acres of arable land in Old Stratford. In the same year John Manningham, a London law student, recorded a piece of gossip that gives us a rare contemporary anecdote about the private life of Shakespeare and of Richard Burbage, the leading tragedian of his company:

Vpon a tyme when Burbidge played Rich. 3 there was a Citizen greue soe farr in liking wth him, that before shee went from the play shee appointed him to come that night unto hir by the name of Ri. the 3. Shakespeare overhearing their conclusion went before, was intertained, and at his game ere Burbidge came. Then message being brought that Rich. the 3.^{d} was at the dore, Shakespeare caused returne to be made that William the Conquerour was before Rich. the 3.

In 1604 Shakespeare was lodging in north London with a Huguenot family called Mountjoy; in 1612 he was to testify in a court case relating to a marriage settlement on

2. Shakespeare's monument, designed by Gheerart Janssen, in Holy Trinity Church, Stratford-upon-Avon

the daughter of the house. The records of the case provide our only transcript of words actually spoken by Shakespeare; they are not characterful. In 1605 Shakespeare invested £440 in the Stratford tithes, which brought him in £60 a year; in June 1607 his elder daughter, Susanna, married a distinguished physician, John Hall, in Stratford, and there his only grandchild, their daughter Elizabeth, was baptized the following February. In 1609 his mother died there, and from about 1610 his increasing involvement with Stratford along with the reduction in his dramatic output suggests that he was withdrawing from his London responsibilities and spending more time at New Place. Perhaps he was deliberately devoting himself to his family's business interests; he was only forty-six years old: an age at which a healthy man was no more likely to retire then than now. If he was ill, he was not totally disabled, as he was in London in 1612 for the Mountjoy lawsuit. In March 1613 he bought a house in the Blackfriars area of London for £140: it seems to have been an investment rather than a home. Also in 1613 the last of his three brothers died. In late 1614 and 1615 he was involved in disputes about the enclosure of the land whose tithes he owned. In February 1616 his second daughter, Judith, married Thomas Quiney, causing William to make alterations to the draft of his will, which he signed on 25 March. His widow was entitled by law and local custom to part of his estate; he left most of the remainder to his elder daughter, Susanna, and her husband. He died on 23 April, and was buried two days later in a prominent position in the chancel of Holy Trinity Church. A monument was commissioned, presumably by members of his family, and was in position by 1623. The work of Gheerart Janssen, a stonemason whose shop was not far from the Globe Theatre, it incorporates a half-length effigy which is one of the only two surviving likenesses of Shakespeare with any strong claim to authenticity.

As this selective survey of the historical records shows, Shakespeare's life is at least as well documented as those of most of his contemporaries who did not belong to great families; we know more about him than about any other dramatist of his time except Ben Jonson. The inscription on the Stratford landowner's memorial links him with Socrates and Virgil; and in the far greater memorial of 1623, the First Folio edition of his plays, Jonson links this 'Starre of Poets' with his home town as the 'Sweet swan of Auon'. The Folio includes the second reliable likeness of Shakespeare, an engraving by Martin Droeshout which, we must assume, had been commissioned and approved by his friends and colleagues who put the volume together. In the Folio it faces the lines signed 'B.I.' (Ben Jonson) which we print beneath it. Shakespeare's widow died in 1623, and his last surviving descendant, Elizabeth Hall (who inherited New Place and married first a neighbour, Thomas Nash, and secondly John Bernard, knighted in 1661), in 1670.

Shakespeare's Professional Career

We do not know when Shakespeare joined the theatre after his marriage, or how he was employed in the mean time. In 1587 an actor of the Queen's Men—the most successful company of the 1580s—died as a result of manslaughter shortly before the company visited Stratford. That Shakespeare may have taken his place is an intriguing speculation. Nor do we know when he began to write. It seems likely (though not certain) that he became an actor before starting to write plays; at any rate, none of his extant writings certainly dates from his youth or early manhood. One of his less impressive sonnets—No. 145—apparently plays on the name 'Hathaway' ('I hate, from hate away she threw'), and may be an early love poem; but this is his only surviving non-dramatic work that seems at all likely to have been written before he became a playwright. Possibly his earliest efforts in verse or drama are lost; just possibly some of them survive anonymously. It would have been very much in keeping with contemporary practice if he had worked in collaboration with other writers at this stage in his career. *1 Henry VI* is the only early play that we feel confident enough to identify as collaborative, but other writers' hands have also been plausibly suspected in *The First Part of the Contention* (*2 Henry VI*), *Richard Duke of Yorke* (*3 Henry VI*), and the opening scenes, in particular, of *Titus Andronicus*.

The first printed allusion to Shakespeare dates from 1592, in the pamphlet *Green's Groats-worth of Wit*, published as the work of Robert Greene, writer of plays and prose romances, shortly after he died. Mention of an 'vpstart Crow' who 'supposes he is as well able to bombast out a blanke verse as the best of you' and who 'is in his owne conceit the onely Shake-scene in a countrey' suggests rivalry; though parody of a line from *Richard Duke of Yorke* (*3 Henry VI*) shows that Shakespeare was already known on the London literary scene, the word 'vpstart' does not suggest a long-established author.

It seems likely that Shakespeare's earliest surviving plays date from the late 1580s and the early 1590s: they include comedies (*The Two Gentlemen of Verona* and *The Taming of the Shrew*), history plays based on English chronicles (*The First Part of the Contention, Richard Duke of Yorke*), and a pseudo-classical tragedy (*Titus Andronicus*). We cannot say with any confidence which company (or companies) of players these were written for;

3. Henry Wriothesley, 3rd Earl of Southampton (1573-1624), at the age of twenty: a miniature by Nicholas Hilliard

Titus Andronicus, at least, seems to have gone from one company to another, since according to the title-page of the 1594 edition it had been acted by the Earl of Derby's, the Earl of Pembroke's, and the Earl of Sussex's Men. Early in his career, Shakespeare may have worked for more than one company. A watershed in his career was the devastating outbreak of plague which closed London's theatres almost entirely from June 1592 to May 1594. This seems to have turned Shakespeare's thoughts to the possibility of a literary career away from the theatre: in spring 1593 appeared his witty narrative poem *Venus and Adonis*, to be followed in 1594 by its tragic counterpart, *The Rape of Lucrece*. Both carry dedications over Shakespeare's name to Henry Wriothesley, third Earl of Southampton, who, though aged only twenty in 1593, was already making a name for himself as a patron of poets. Patrons could be important to Elizabethan writers; how Southampton rewarded Shakespeare for his dedications we do not know, but the affection with which Shakespeare speaks of him in the dedication to *Lucrece* suggests a strong personal connection and has encouraged the belief that Southampton may be the young man addressed so lovingly in Shakespeare's Sonnets.

Whether Shakespeare began to write the Sonnets at this time is a vexed question. Certainly it is the period at which his plays make most use of the formal characteristics of the sonnet: *Loues labors lost* and *Romeo and Iuliet*, for example, both incorporate sonnets into their structure; but *Henry V*, probably dating from 1599, has a sonnet as an Epilogue, and in *All's Well that Ends Well* (*c.*1604) a letter is cast in this form. Allusions within the

Sonnets suggest that they were written over a period of at least three years. At some later point they seem to have been rearranged into the order in which they were printed. Behind them—if indeed they are autobiographical at all—lies a tantalizingly elusive story of Shakespeare's personal life. Many attempts have been made to identify the poet's friend, the rival poet, and the dark woman who is both the poet's mistress and the seducer of his friend; none has achieved any degree of certainty.

After the epidemic of plague dwindled, a number of actors who had previously belonged to different companies amalgamated to form the Lord Chamberlain's Men. In the first official account that survives, Shakespeare is named, along with the famous comic actor Will Kemp and the tragedian Richard Burbage, as payee for performances at court during the previous Christmas season. The Chamberlain's Men rapidly became the leading dramatic company, though rivalled at first by the Admiral's Men, who had Edward Alleyn as their leading tragedian. Shakespeare stayed with the Chamberlain's (later King's) Men for the rest of his career as actor, playwright, and administrator. He is the only prominent playwright of his time to have had so stable a relationship with a single company.

With the founding of the Lord Chamberlain's Men, Shakespeare's career was placed upon a firm footing. It is not the purpose of this Introduction to describe his development as a dramatist, or to attempt a thorough discussion of the chronology of his writings. The Introductions to individual works state briefly what is known about when they were composed, and also name the principal literary sources on which Shakespeare drew in composing them. The works themselves are arranged in a conjectural order of composition. There are many uncertainties about this, especially in relation to the early plays. The most important single piece of evidence is a passage in a book called *Palladis Tamia: Wits Treasury*, by a minor writer, Francis Meres, published in 1598. Meres wrote:

As *Plautus* and *Seneca* are accounted the best for Comedy and Tragedy among the Latines, so *Shakespeare* among yᵉ English is the most excellent in both kinds for the stage; for Comedy, witnes his *Gĕtlemĕ of Verona*, his *Errors*, his *Loue labor's lost*, his *Loue labours wonne*, his *Midsummers night dreame*, & his *Merchant of Venice*: for Tragedy his *Richard the 2., Richard the 3. Henry the 4. King Iohn, Titus Andronicus* and his *Romeo* and *Iuliet*.

Some of the plays that Meres names had already been published or alluded to by 1598; but for others (including the lost *Loues labours won*), he supplies a date by which they must have been written. Meres also alludes to Shakespeare's 'sugred Sonnets among his priuate friends', which suggests that some, if not all, of the poems printed in 1609 as Shakespeare's Sonnets were circulating in manuscript by this date. Works not mentioned by Meres that are believed to have been written by 1598 are the three plays concerned with the reign of Henry VI, *The Taming of the Shrew*, and the narrative poems.

Shakespeare seems to have had less success as an actor than as a playwright. We cannot name for certain any of the parts that he played, though seventeenth-century traditions have it that he played Adam in *As you Like it*, and Hamlet's Ghost—and more generally that he had a penchant for 'kingly parts'. Ben Jonson listed him first among the 'principall Comœdians' in *Euery Man In His Humour*, acted in 1598, when he reprinted it in the 1616 Folio, and Shakespeare is also listed among the performers of Jonson's tragedy *Seianus* in 1603. He was certainly one of the leading administrators of the Chamberlain's Men. Until 1597, when their lease expired, they played mainly in the Theatre, London's first important playhouse, situated north of the River Thames in Shoreditch, outside the jurisdiction of the City fathers, who exercised a repressive influence on the drama. It had been built in 1576 by James Burbage, a joiner, the tragedian's father. Then they seem to have played mainly at the Curtain until some time in 1599. Shakespeare was a member of the syndicate

4. King James I
(1566–1625): a portrait
(1621) by Daniel Mytens

responsible for building the first Globe theatre, in Southwark, on the south bank of the Thames, out of the dismantled timbers of the Theatre in 1599. Initially he had a ten-per-cent financial interest in the enterprise, fluctuating as other shareholders joined or withdrew. It was a valuable share, for the Chamberlain's Men won great acclaim and made substantial profits. After Queen Elizabeth died, in 1603, they came under the patronage of the new king, James I; the royal patent of 19 May 1603 names Shakespeare along with other leaders of the company. London was in the grip of another severe epidemic of plague which caused a ban on playing till the following spring. The King's processional entry into London had to be delayed; when at last it took place, on 15 March 1604, each of the company's leaders was granted four and a half yards of scarlet cloth for his livery as one of the King's retainers; but the players seem not to have processed. Their association with the King was far from nominal; during the next thirteen years—up to the time of Shakespeare's death—they played at court more often than all the other theatre companies combined. Records are patchy, but we know, for instance, that they gave eleven plays at court between 1 November 1604 and 31 October 1605, and that seven of them were by Shakespeare: they included older plays—*The Comedie of Errors, Loues labors lost*—and more recent ones—*Othello* and *Measure, for Measure. The Merchant of Venice* was played twice.

Some measure of Shakespeare's personal success during this period may be gained from the ascription to him of works not now believed to be his; *Locrine* and *Thomas Lord Cromwell* were published in 1595 and 1602 respectively as by 'W.S.'; in 1599 a collection of poems, *The Passionate Pilgrime*, containing some poems certainly by other writers, appeared under his name; so, in 1606 and 1608, did *The London Prodigall* and *A Yorkshire Tragedy*. Since Shakespeare's time, too, many plays of the period, some published, some surviving only in manuscript, have been attributed to him. In modern times, the most plausible case has been made for parts, or all, of *Edward III*, which was entered in the registers of the Stationers' Company (a normal, but not invariable, way of setting in motion the publication process) in 1595 and published in 1596. It was first ascribed to Shakespeare in 1656. Certainly it displays links with some of his writings, but authorship problems are particularly acute during the part of his career when this play seems to have been written, and we cannot feel confident of the attribution.

In August 1608 the King's Men took up the lease of the smaller, 'private' indoor theatre, the Blackfriars; again, Shakespeare was one of the syndicate of owners. The company took possession in 1609; the Blackfriars served as a winter home; in better weather, performances continued to be given at the Globe. By now, Shakespeare was at a late stage in his career. Perhaps he realized it; he seems to have been willing to share his responsibilities as the company's resident dramatist with younger writers. *Timon of Athens*, tentatively dated around 1604-5, seems on internal evidence to be partly the work of Thomas Middleton (c.1570-1627). Another collaborative play, very successful in its time, was *Pericles* (c.1608), in which Shakespeare probably worked with George Wilkins, an unscrupulous character who gave up his brief career as a writer in favour of a longer one as a tavern (or brothel) keeper. But Shakespeare's most fruitful collaboration was with John Fletcher, his junior by fifteen years. Fletcher was collaborating with Francis Beaumont on plays for the King's Men by about 1608. Beaumont stopped writing plays when he married, in about 1613, and it is at this time that Fletcher seems to have collaborated with Shakespeare. A lost play, *Cardenio*, acted by the King's Men some time before 20 May 1613, was plausibly ascribed to Shakespeare and Fletcher in a document of 1653; *All is True* (*Henry VIII*), first acted about June 1613, is generally agreed on stylistic evidence to be another fruit of the same partnership; and *The Two Noble Kinsmen*, also dated 1613, which seems to be the last play in which Shakespeare had a hand, was ascribed to the pair on its publication in 1634. One of Shakespeare's last professional tasks seems to have been the minor one of devising an *impresa* for the Earl of Rutland to bear at a tournament held on 24 March 1613 to celebrate the tenth anniversary of the King's accession. An *impresa* was a paper or pasteboard shield painted with an emblematic device and motto which would be carried and interpreted for a knight by his squire; such a ceremony is portrayed in *Pericles* (Sc. 6). Shakespeare received forty-four shillings for his share in the work; Richard Burbage was paid the same sum 'for paynting & making it'.

The Drama and Theatre of Shakespeare's Time

Shakespeare came upon the theatrical scene at an auspicious time. English drama and theatre had developed only slowly during the earlier part of the sixteenth century; during Shakespeare's youth they exploded into vigorous life. It was a period of secularization; previously, drama had been largely religious in subject matter and overtly didactic in treatment; as a boy of fifteen, Shakespeare could have seen one of the last performances of a great cycle of plays on religious themes at Coventry, not far from his home town. 1576 saw the building in London of the Theatre, to be rapidly followed by the Curtain: England's first important, custom-built playhouses. There was a sudden spurt in the development of all aspects of theatrical art: acting, production, playwriting, company organization, and administration. Within a few years the twin arts of drama and theatre entered upon a period of achievement whose brilliance remains unequalled.

The new drama was literary and rhetorical rather than scenic and spectacular: but its mainstream was theatrical too. Its writers were poets. Prose was only beginning to be used in plays during Shakespeare's youth; a playwright was often known as a 'poet', and most of the best playwrights of the period wrote with distinction in other forms. Shakespeare's most important predecessors and early contemporaries, from whom he learned much, were John Lyly (c.1554-1606), pre-eminent for courtly comedy and elegant prose, Robert Greene (1558-92), who helped particularly to develop the scope and language of romantic comedy, and Christopher Marlowe (1564-93), whose 'mighty line' put heroism excitingly on the stage and who shares with Shakespeare credit for establishing the English history play as a dramatic mode. As Shakespeare's career progressed, other dramatists displayed their talents and, doubtless, influenced and stimulated him. George Chapman (c.1560-1634) emerged as a dramatist in the mid-1590s and succeeded in both comedy and tragedy. He was deeply interested in classical themes, as was Ben Jonson (1572-1637), who became Shakespeare's chief rival. Jonson was a dominating personality, vocal about his accomplishments (and about Shakespeare, who, he said, 'wanted arte'), and biting as a comic satirist. Thomas Dekker (c.1572-1632) wrote comedies that are more akin to Shakespeare's in their romantic warmth; the satirical plays of John Marston (c.1575-1634) are more sensational and cynical than Jonson's. Thomas Middleton brought a sharp wit to the portrayal of contemporary London life, and developed into a great tragic dramatist. Towards the end of Shakespeare's career, Francis Beaumont (1584-1616) and John Fletcher (1579-1625) came upon the scene; the affinity between Shakespeare's late tragicomedies and some of Fletcher's romances is reflected in their collaboration.

The companies for which these dramatists wrote were organized mainly from within. They were led by the sharers: eight in the Lord Chamberlain's Men at first, twelve by the end of Shakespeare's career. Collectively they owned the joint stock of play scripts, costumes, and properties; they shared both expenses and profits. All were working members of the company. Exceptionally, the sharers of Shakespeare's company owned the Globe theatre itself; more commonly, actors rented theatres from financial speculators such as Philip Henslowe, financier of the Admiral's Men. Subordinate to the sharers were the 'hired men'—lesser actors along with prompters ('bookholders'), stagekeepers, wardrobe keepers ('tiremen'), musicians, and money-collectors ('gatherers'). Even those not employed principally as actors might swell a scene at need. The hired men were paid by the week. Companies would need scribes to copy out actors' parts and to make fair copies from the playwrights' foul papers (working manuscripts), but they seem mainly to have been employed part-time. The other important group of company members is the apprentices. These were boys or youths each serving a formal term of apprenticeship to one of the sharers. They played female and juvenile roles.

The success of plays in the Elizabethan theatres depended almost entirely on the actors. They had to be talented, hard-working, and versatile. Plays were given in a repertory system on almost every afternoon of the week except during Lent. Only about two weeks could be allowed for rehearsal of a new play, and during that time the company would be regularly performing a variety of plays. Lacking printed copies, the actors worked from

5. Richard Burbage: reputedly a self-portrait

'parts' written out on scrolls giving only the cue lines from other characters' speeches. The bookholder, or prompter, had to make sure that actors entered at the right moment, properly equipped. Many of them would take several parts in the same play: doubling was a necessary practice. The strain on the memory was great, demanding a high degree of professionalism. Conditions of employment were carefully regulated: a contract of 1614 provides that an actor and sharer, Robert Dawes (not in Shakespeare's company), be fined one shilling for failure to turn up at the beginning of a rehearsal, two shillings for missing a rehearsal altogether, three shillings if he was not 'ready apparrelled' for a performance, ten shillings if four other members of the company considered him to be 'ouercome with drinck' at the time he should be acting, and one pound if he simply failed to turn up for a performance without 'lycence or iust excuse of sicknes'.

There can be no doubt that the best actors of Shakespeare's time would have been greatly admired in any age. English actors became famous abroad; some of the best surviving accounts are in letters written by visitors to England: the actors were literally 'something to write home about', and some of them performed (in English) on the Continent. Edward Alleyn, the leading tragedian of the Admiral's Men, renowned especially for his performances of Marlowe's heroes, made a fortune and founded Dulwich College. All too little is known about the actors of Shakespeare's company and the roles they played, but many testimonies survive to Richard Burbage's excellence in tragic roles. According to an elegy written after he died, in 1619,

> No more young Hamlett, ould Heironymoe.
> Kind Leer, the greued Moore, and more beside,
> That liued in him, haue now for ever dy'de.

There is no reason to suppose that the boy actors lacked talent and skill; they were highly trained as apprentices to leading actors. Most plays of the period, including Shakespeare's,

6. The hall of the Middle Temple, London

have far fewer female than male roles, but some women's parts—such as Rosalind (in *As you Like it*) and Cleopatra—are long and important; Shakespeare must have had confidence in the boys who played them. Some of them later became sharers themselves.

The playwriting techniques of Shakespeare and his contemporaries were intimately bound up with the theatrical conditions to which they catered. Theatre buildings were virtually confined to London. Plays continued to be given in improvised circumstances when the companies toured the provinces and when they acted at court (that is, wherever the sovereign and his or her entourage happened to be—in London, usually Whitehall or Greenwich). In 1602, *Twelfe Night* was given in the still-surviving hall of one of London's Inns of Court, the Middle Temple. Acting companies could use guildhalls, the halls of great houses or of Oxford and Cambridge colleges, the yards of inns. (In 1608, *Richard II* and *Hamlet* were even performed by ships' crews at sea off the coast of Sierra Leone.) Many plays of the period require no more than an open space and the costumes and properties that the actors carried with them on their travels. Others made more use of the expanding facilities of the professional stage.

Permanent theatres were of two kinds, known now as public and private. Most important to Shakespeare were public theatres such as the Theatre, the Curtain, and the Globe. Unfortunately, the only surviving drawing (reproduced overleaf) portraying the interior of a public theatre in any detail is of the Swan, not used by Shakespeare's company. Though theatres were not uniform in design, they had important features in common. They were large wooden buildings, usually round or polygonal; the Globe, which was about 100 feet in diameter and 36 feet in height, could hold over three thousand spectators. Between the outer and inner walls—a space of about 12 feet—were three levels of tiered benches extending round most of the auditorium and roofed on top; after the Globe burnt down, in 1613, the roof, formerly thatched, was tiled. The surround of benches was broken on the lowest level by the stage, broad and deep, edged with palings, which jutted forth at a height of about 5 feet into the central yard, where spectators ('groundlings') could stand. Actors entered mainly, perhaps entirely, from openings in the wall at the back of the stage. At least two doors, one on each side, could be used; stage directions frequently call for characters to enter simultaneously from different doors, when the dramatic situation requires them to be meeting, and to leave 'seuerally' (separately) when they are parting. The depth of the stage meant that characters could enter through the stage doors some moments before other characters standing at the front of the stage might be expected to notice them.

Also in the wall at the rear of the stage there appears to have been some kind of central aperture which could be used for the disclosing and putting forth of Desdemona's bed (*Othello*, Sc. 15) or the concealment of the spying Polonius (*Hamlet*, Sc. 11) or of the sleeping Lear (*The Historie of King Lear*, Sc. 20). Behind the stage wall was the tiring-house—the actors' dressing area.

On the second level the seating facilities for spectators seem to have extended even to the back of the stage, forming a balcony which at the Globe was probably divided into five bays. Here was the 'lords' room', which could be taken over by the actors for plays in which action took place 'above' (or 'aloft'), as in Romeo's wooing of Iuliet or the death of Mark Anthony. It seems to have been possible for actors to move from the main stage to the upper level during the time taken to speak a few lines of verse, as we may see in *The Merchant of Venice* (909-15) or *Iulius Cæsar* (2262-4). Somewhere above the lords' room was a window or platform known as 'the top'; Ioane le Pucell appears there briefly in *1 Henry VI* (Sc. 16), and in *The Tempest*, Prospero is seen 'on the top (inuisible)' (3.3).

Above the stage, at a level higher than the second gallery, was a canopy, probably

7. The Swan Theatre: a copy, by Aernout van Buchel, of a drawing made about 1596 by Johannes de Witt, a Dutch visitor to London

supported by two pillars (which could themselves be used as hiding places) rising from the stage. One function of the canopy was to shelter the stage from the weather; it also formed the floor of one or more huts housing the machinery for special effects and its operators. Here cannon-balls could be rolled around a trough to imitate the sound of thunder, and fire crackers could be set off to simulate lightning. And from this area actors could descend in a chair operated by a winch. Shakespeare uses this facility mainly in his late plays: in *Cymbeline* for the descent of Iupiter (5.4), and, probably, in *Pericles* for the descent of Diana (Sc. 21) and in *The Tempest* for Iuno's appearance in the masque (4.1). On the stage itself was a trap which could be opened to serve as Ophelia's grave (*Hamlet*, Sc. 18) or as Maluolio's dungeon (*Twelfe Night*, Sc. 16).

Somewhere in the backstage area, perhaps in or close to the gallery, must have been a space for the musicians who played a prominent part in many performances. No doubt then, as now, a single musician was capable of playing several instruments. Stringed instruments, plucked (such as the lute) and bowed (such as viols), were needed. Woodwind instruments included recorders (called for in *Hamlet*, Sc. 9) and the stronger, shriller hautboys (ancestors of the modern oboe); trumpets and cornetts were needed for the many flourishes and sennets (more elaborate fanfares) played especially for the comings and goings of royal characters. Sometimes musicians would play on stage: entrances for trumpeters and drummers are common in battle scenes. More often they would be heard but not seen; from behind the stage (as, perhaps, at the opening of *Twelfe Night* or in the concluding dance of *Much adoe about Nothing*), or even occasionally under it (*Anthonie, and Cleopatra*, Sc. 28). Some actors were themselves musicians: the performers of the Clowne (in *Twelfe Night*) and Ariel (in *The Tempest*) must sing and, probably, accompany themselves on lute and tabor (a small drum slung around the neck). Though traditional music has survived for some of the songs in Shakespeare's plays (such as Ophelia's mad songs, in *Hamlet*), we have little music which was certainly composed for them in his own time. The principal exception is two songs for *The Tempest* by Robert Johnson, a fine composer who was attached to the King's Men.

Shakespeare's plays require few substantial properties. A 'state', or throne on a dais, is sometimes called for, as are tables and chairs and, occasionally, a bed, a pair of stocks (*King Lear*, Sc. 7/2.2), a cauldron (*Macbeth*, 4.1), a rose brier (*1 Henry VI*, Sc. 12), and a bush (*Two Noble Kinsmen*, 5.3). No doubt these and other such objects were pushed on and off the stage by attendants in full view of the audience. We know that Elizabethan companies spent lavishly on costumes, and some plays require special clothes; at the beginning of *2 Henry IV*, Rumour enters 'painted full of tongues'; regal personages, and supernatural figures such as Hymen in *As you Like it* (Sc. 22) and the goddesses in *The Tempest* (4.1) must have been distinctively costumed; presumably a bear-skin was needed for *The Winters Tale* (3.3). Probably no serious attempt was made at historical realism. The only surviving contemporary drawing of a scene from a Shakespeare play, illustrating *Titus Andronicus* (reproduced on the following page), shows the characters dressed in a mixture of Elizabethan and classical costumes, and this accords with the often anachronistic references to clothing in plays with a historical setting. The same drawing also illustrates the use of head-dresses, of varied weapons as properties—the guard to the left appears to be wearing a scimitar—of facial and bodily make-up for Aron, the Moor, and of eloquent gestures. Extended passages of wordless action are not uncommon in Shakespeare's plays. Dumb shows feature prominently in earlier Elizabethan plays, and in Shakespeare the direction 'alarum' or 'alarums and excursions' may stand for lengthy and exciting passages of arms. Even in one of Shakespeare's latest plays, *Cymbeline*, important episodes are conducted in wordless mime (see, for example, 5.2-4).

8. A drawing, attributed to Henry Peacham, illustrating Shakespeare's *Titus Andronicus*

Towards the end of Shakespeare's career his company regularly performed in a private theatre, the Blackfriars, as well as at the Globe. Like other private theatres, this was an enclosed building, using artificial lighting, and so more suitable for winter performances. Private playhouses were smaller than the public ones—the Blackfriars held about 600 spectators—and admission prices were much higher—a minimum of sixpence at the Blackfriars against one penny at the Globe. Facilities at the Blackfriars must have been essentially similar to those at the Globe since some of the same plays were given at both theatres. But the sense of social occasion seems to have been different. Audiences were more elegant (though not necessarily better behaved); music featured more prominently.

It seems to have been under the influence of private-theatre practice that, from about 1609 onwards, performances of plays customarily marked the conventional five-act structure by a pause, graced with music, after each act. Previously, though dramatists often showed awareness of five-act structure (as Shakespeare conspicuously does in *Henry V*, with a Chorus before each act), public performances seem to have been continuous, making the scene the main structural unit. None of the editions of Shakespeare's plays printed in his lifetime (which do not include any written after 1609) marks either act or scene divisions. The innovation of act-pauses threw more emphasis on the act as a unit, and made it possible for dramatists to relax their observance of what has come to be known as 'the law of re-entry', according to which a character who had left the stage at the end of one scene would not normally make an immediate reappearance at the beginning of the next. Thus, if Shakespeare had been writing *The Tempest* before 1609, it is unlikely that Prospero and Ariel, having left the stage at the end of Act 4, would have instantly reappeared at the start of Act 5. We attempt to reflect this feature of Shakespeare's dramaturgy by making no special distinction between scene-breaks and act-breaks except in those later plays in which Shakespeare seems to have observed the new convention (and in *Titus Andronicus*, *Measure, for Measure*, and *Macbeth*, since the texts of these plays apparently reflect theatre practice after they were first written, and in *The Comedie of Errors*, a neo-classically structured play in which the act-divisions appear to be authoritative, and to represent a private performance). In our modern-spelling edition we give the act and scene divisions, for ease of reference; but here our primary division is by scenes, as a more accurate reflection of Shakespeare's practice.

Dramatic conventions changed and developed considerably during Shakespeare's career.

Throughout it, they favoured self-evident artifice over naturalism. This is apparent in Shakespeare's dramatic language, with its soliloquies (sometimes addressed directly to the audience), its long, carefully structured speeches, its elaborate use of simile, metaphor, and rhetorical figures of speech (in prose as well as verse), its rhyme, and its patterned dialogue. It is evident in some aspects of behaviour and characterization: Oberon and Prospero have only to declare themselves invisible to become so; disguises can be instantly donned with an appearance of impenetrability, and as rapidly abandoned; some characters—Rumour at the opening of *2 Henry IV*, Time in *The Winters Tale*, even the Gardeners in *Richard II*—clearly serve a symbolic rather than a realistic function: and supernatural manifestations are common. The calculated positioning of characters on the stage may help to make a dramatic point, as in the scene in *The Two Gentlemen of Verona* (Sc. 14) in which the disguised Iulia overhears her faithless lover's serenade to her rival, Siluia; or, more complexly, that in *Troylus and Cressida* (Sc. 18) in which Troylus and Vlisses observe Diomed's courtship of Cressid while they are themselves observed by the cynical Thersites. Not uncommonly, Shakespeare provokes his spectators into consciousness that they are watching a play, as when Cassius, in *Iulius Cæsar*, looks forward to the time when the conspirators' 'lofty scene' will be 'acted ouer | In States vnborne, and Accents yet vnknowne' (1200-2); or, in *Troylus and Cressida*, when Troylus, Cressid, and Pandarus reach out from the past tense of history to the present tense of theatrical performance in a ritualistic anticipation of what their names will come to signify (1745-79).

Techniques such as these are closely related to the non-illusionistic nature of the Elizabethan stage, in which the mechanics of production were frequently visible. Many scenes take place nowhere in particular. Awareness of place was conveyed through dialogue and action rather than through scenery; location could change even within a scene (as, for example, in *2 Henry IV*, where movement of the dying King's bed across the stage establishes the scene as 'some other Chamber': 2457). Sometimes Shakespeare uses conflicting reactions to an imagined place as a kind of shorthand guide to character: to the idealistic Gonzalo, Prospero's island is lush, lusty, and green; to the cynical Antonio, 'tawny' (*The Tempest*, 629-32): such an effect would have been dulled by scenery which proved one or the other right.

In some ways, the changes in Shakespeare's practice as his art develops favour naturalism: his verse becomes freer, metaphor predominates over simile, rhyme and other formalistic elements are reduced, the proportion of prose over verse increases to the middle of his career (but then decreases again), some of his most psychologically complex character portrayals—Coriolanus, Cleopatra—come late. But his drama remains rooted in the conventions of a rhetorical, non-scenic (though not unspectacular) theatre: the supernatural looms largest in his later plays—*Macbeth*, *Pericles*, *Cymbeline*, and *The Tempest*. *The Tempest* draws no less self-consciously on the neo-classical conventions of five-act structure than *The Comedie of Errors*, and Prospero's narration to Miranda (1.2) is as blatant a piece of dramatic exposition as Egeon's tale in the opening scene of the earlier play. Heroines of the late romances—Marina (in *Pericles*), Perdita (in *The Winters Tale*), and Miranda (in *The Tempest*)—are portrayed with less concern for psychological realism than those of the romantic comedies—Viola (in *Twelfe Night*) and Rosalind (in *As you Like it*)—and the revelation to Leontes at the end of *The Winters Tale* is both more improbable and more moving than the similar revelation made to Egeon at the end of *The Comedie of Errors*.

The theatre of Shakespeare's time was his most valuable collaborator. Its simplicity was one of its strengths. The actors of his company were the best in their kind. His audiences may not have been learned, or sophisticated, by modern standards; according to some accounts, they could be unruly; but they conferred popularity upon plays which for emotional power, range, and variety, for grandeur of conception and subtlety of execution, are among the most demanding, as well as the most entertaining, ever written. If we value Shakespeare's plays, we must also think well of the theatrical circumstances that permitted, and encouraged, his genius to flourish.

The Early Printing of Shakespeare's Plays

For all its literary distinction, drama in Shakespeare's time was an art of performance; many plays of the period never got into print: they were published by being acted. It is lucky for us that, so far as we know, all Shakespeare's finished plays except the collaborative *Cardenio* reached print. None of his plays that were printed in his time survives in even a fragment of his own handwriting; the only literary manuscript plausibly ascribed to him is a section of *Sir Thomas Moore*, a play not printed until the nineteenth century. The only works of Shakespeare that he himself seems to have cared about putting into print are the narrative poems *Venus and Adonis* and *The Rape of Lucrece*. A major reason for this is Shakespeare's exceptionally close involvement with the acting company for which he wrote. There was no effective dramatic copyright; acting companies commonly bought plays from their authors—as a resident playwright, Shakespeare was probably expected to write about two each year—and it was in the companies' interests that their plays should not get into print, when they could be acted by rival companies. Nevertheless, by one means and another, and in one form and another, about half of Shakespeare's plays were printed singly in his lifetime, almost all of them in the flimsy, paperback format of a quarto—a book made from sheets of paper that had been folded twice, and normally costing sixpence. Some of the plays were pirated: printed, that is, in unauthorized editions, from texts that seem to have been put together from memory by actors or even, perhaps, by spectators, perhaps primarily to create scripts for other companies, perhaps purely for publication. These are the so-called 'bad' quartos: bad not because they were, necessarily, badly printed, but because they did not descend in a direct line of written transmission from their author's manuscript. The reported texts of *The First Part of the Contention* and *Richard Duke of Yorke* (usually known by the titles under which they were printed in the First Folio—*2 Henry VI* and *3 Henry VI*) appeared in 1594 and 1595 respectively; they seem to have been made on the basis of London performances so that the plays could be acted by a company other than the one for which they were written. Also in 1594 appeared *The Taming of A Shrew*, perhaps better described as an imitation of Shakespeare's *The Taming of the Shrew* (the titles may have been regarded as interchangeable) than as a detailed reconstruction of it. The 1597 *Richard III* is perhaps the best of the reported texts; it seems to have been assembled from the company's collective memory, perhaps because they did not have access to the official prompt-book. The text of *Romeo and Iuliet* printed in the same year seems to have been put together by a few actors exploiting a popular success. The 1600 quarto of *Henry V* probably presents a text made for a smaller company of actors than that for which it had been written. *The Merry Wiues of Windsor* of 1602 seems to derive largely from the memory of the actor who played the Host of the Garter Inn—perhaps a hired man no longer employed by Shakespeare's company. Worst reported of all is the 1603 *Hamlet*, which also appears to derive from the memory of one or more actors in minor roles. Last printed of the 'bad' quartos is *Pericles*, of 1609.

The reported texts have many faults. Frequently they garble the verse and prose of the original—'To be, or not to be, I there's the point', says the 1603 *Hamlet*; usually they abbreviate—the 1603 *Hamlet* has about 2,200 lines, compared to the 3,800 of the good quarto; sometimes they include lines from plays by other authors (especially Marlowe);

> *Ham.* To be, or not to be, I there's the point,
> To Die, to sleepe, is that all? I all:
> No, to sleepe, to dreame, I mary there it goes,
> For in that dreame of death, when wee awake,
> And borne before an euerlasting Iudge,
> From whence no passenger euer retur'nd,
> The vndiscouered country, at whose sight
> The happy smile, and the accursed damn'd.
> But for this, the ioyfull hope of this,
> Whol'd beare the scornes and flattery of the world,
> Scorned by the right rich, the rich curssed of the poore?
> The widow being oppressed, the orphan wrong'd,
> The taste of hunger, or a tirants raigne,
> And thousand more calamities besides,
> To grunt and sweate vnder this weary life,
> When that he may his full *Quietus* make,
> With a bare bodkin, who would this indure,
> But for a hope of something after death?
> Which puzles the braine, and doth confound the sence,
> Which makes vs rather beare those euilles we haue,
> Than flie to others that we know not of.
> I that, O this conscience makes cowardes of vs all,
> Lady in thy orizons, be all my sinnes remembred.

9. 'To be or not to be' as it appeared in the 'bad' quarto of 1603

sometimes they include passages clearly cobbled together to supply gaps in the reporter's memory. For all this, they are not without value in helping us to judge how Shakespeare's plays were originally performed. Their stage directions may give us more information about how the plays were staged than is available in other texts: for instance, the reported text of *Hamlet* has the direction '*Enter Ofelia playing on a Lute, and her haire downe singing*'—far more vivid than the good Quarto's '*Enter Ophelia*', or even the Folio's '*Enter Ophelia distracted*'. Because these are post-performance texts, they may preserve, in the midst of corruption, authentically Shakespearian changes made to the play after it was first written and not recorded elsewhere. A particularly interesting case is *The Taming of the Shrew*: the play as printed in the Folio, in what is clearly, in general, the more authentic text, abandons early in its action the framework device which makes the story of Katherine and Petruchio a play within the play; the quarto continues this framework through the play, and provides an amusing little episode rounding it off. These passages may derive from ones written by Shakespeare but not printed in the Folio: we print them as Additional Passages at the end of the play. In general, we draw more liberally than most previous editors on the reported texts, in the belief that they can help us to come closer than before to the plays as they were acted by Shakespeare's company as well as by others.

Although in general it was to the advantage of the companies that owned play scripts not to allow them to be printed, some of Shakespeare's plays were printed from authentic manuscripts during his lifetime, and even while they were still being performed by his company; these are the 'good' quartos. First came *Titus Andronicus*, printed in 1594 from Shakespeare's own papers, probably because the company for which he wrote it had been disbanded. In 1597 *Richard II* was printed from Shakespeare's manuscript, minus the politically sensitive episode (Sc. 13) in which Richard gives up his crown to Bullingbrooke: a clear instance of censorship, whether self-imposed or not. The first play to be published in Shakespeare's name is *Loues labors lost*, in 1598. Several other quartos printed from good manuscripts appeared around the same time: *1 Henry IV* (probably from a scribal transcript) in 1598, and *A Midsommer nights dreame*, *The Merchant of Venice*, *2 Henry IV*, and *Much adoe About Nothing* (all from Shakespeare's papers) in 1600. In 1604 appeared a text of *Hamlet* printed from Shakespeare's own papers and declaring itself to be 'Newly imprinted and enlarged to almost as much againe as it was, according to the true and perfect Copie': surely an attempt to replace a bad text by a good one. *King Lear* followed, in 1608, in a badly printed quarto whose status has been much disputed, but which we believe to derive from Shakespeare's own manuscript. In 1609 came *Troylus and Cressida*, probably from Shakespeare's own papers, in an edition which in the first-printed copies claims to present the play 'As it was acted by the Kings Maiesties seruants at the Globe', but in later-printed ones declares that it has never been 'stal'd with the Stage'. The only new play to appear between Shakespeare's death and the publication of the Folio in 1623 was *Othello*, printed in 1622 apparently from a transcript of Shakespeare's own papers.

It is clear that publishers found Shakespeare a valuable property—some of these quartos were several times reprinted—and easy to understand why some of his plays were pirated. It is less easy to see why Shakespeare and his colleagues released reliable texts of some plays for publication but not others. As a shareholder in the company to which the plays belonged, Shakespeare himself must have been a partner in its decisions, and it is difficult to believe that he was so lacking in personal vanity that he was happy to be represented in print by garbled texts; but he seems to have taken no interest in the progress of his plays through the press. Even some of those printed from authentic manuscripts—such as the 1604 *Hamlet*—are badly printed, and certainly not proof-read by the author; none of them bears an author's dedication or shows any sign of having been prepared for the press in the way that, for instance, Ben Jonson clearly prepared some of his plays. John Marston, introducing the printed text of his play *The Malcontent* in 1604, wrote: 'onely one thing afflicts mee, to thinke that Scenes inuented, meerely to be spoken, should be inforciuely published to be read'. Perhaps Shakespeare was similarly afflicted.

In 1616, the year of Shakespeare's death, Ben Jonson published his own collected plays in a handsome Folio. It was the first time that an English writer for the popular stage had been so honoured (or had so honoured himself), and it established a precedent by which Shakespeare's fellows could commemorate their colleague and friend. Principal responsibility for this ambitious enterprise was undertaken by John Heminges and Henry Condell, both long-established actors with Shakespeare's company; latterly, Heminges had been its business manager. They, along with Richard Burbage, had been the colleagues whom Shakespeare remembered in his will: he left each of them 26s. 8d. to buy a mourning ring. Although the Folio did not appear until 1623, they may have started work on it soon after Shakespeare died: big books take a long time to prepare. And they undertook their task with serious care. Most importantly, they printed eighteen plays that had not so far appeared in print, and which might otherwise have vanished. They omitted (so far as we can tell) only *Pericles*—perhaps because it was collaborative—*Cardenio* (which has vanished), perhaps for the same reason, and the mysterious *Loues labors wonne* (see p. 349). And they went to considerable pains to provide good texts. They had no previous experience as editors; they may have had help from others (including Ben Jonson, who wrote commendatory verses for the Folio): anyhow, although printers find it easier to set from print than from manuscript, they were not content simply to reprint quartos whenever they were available. In fact they seem to have made a conscious effort to identify and to avoid making use of the quartos now recognized as bad. In their introductory epistle addressed 'To the great Variety of Readers', they declare that the public has been 'abus'd with diuerse stolne, and surreptitious copies, maimed, and deformed by the frauds and stealthes of iniurious imposters'. But now these plays are 'offer'd to your view cur'd, and perfect of their limbes; and all the rest, absolute in their numbers, as he conceiued thē'.

None of the quartos believed by modern scholars to be unauthoritative was used unaltered as copy for the Folio. As men of the theatre, Heminges and Condell had access to prompt-books, and they made considerable use of them. For some plays, such as *Titus Andronicus* (which includes a whole scene not present in the quarto), and *A Midsommer nights dreame*, the printers had a copy of a quarto (not necessarily the first) marked up with alterations made as the result of comparison with a theatre manuscript. For other plays (the first four to be printed in the Folio—*The Tempest*, *The Two Gentlemen of Verona*, *The Merry Wiues of Windsor*, and *Measure, for Measure*—along with *The Winters Tale*) they employed a professional scribe, Ralph Crane, to transcribe papers in the theatre's possession. For others, such as *Henry V* and *All's Well that Ends Well*, they seem to have had authorial papers; and for yet others, such as *Macbeth*, a prompt-book. We cannot always be sure of the copy used by the printers, and sometimes it may have been mixed: for *Richard III* they seem to have used pages of the third quarto mixed with pages of the sixth quarto combined with passages in manuscript; a copy of the third quarto of *Richard II*, a copy of the fifth quarto, and a theatre manuscript all contributed to the Folio text of that play; the annotated third quarto of *Titus Andronicus* was supplemented by the 'fly' scene (3.2) which Shakespeare appears to have added after the play was first composed. Dedicating the Folio to the brother Earls of Pembroke and Montgomery, Heminges and Condell claimed that, in collecting Shakespeare's plays together, they had 'done an office to the dead, to procure his Orphanes, Guardians' (that is, to provide noble patrons for the works he had left behind), 'without ambition either of selfe-profit, or fame: onely to keepe the memory of so worthy a Friend, & Fellow aliue, as was our SHAKESPEARE'. Certainly they deserve our gratitude.

The Modern Editor's Task

It will be clear from all this that the documents from which even the authoritative early editions of Shakespeare's plays were printed were of a very variable nature. Some were his own papers in a rough state, including loose ends, duplications, inconsistencies, and vaguenesses. At the other extreme were prompt-books representing the play as close to the state in which it appeared in Shakespeare's theatre as we can get; and there were various intermediate states. For those plays of which we have only one text—those first printed in the Folio, along with *Pericles* and *The Two Noble Kinsmen*—the editor is at least not faced with the problem of alternative choices. The surviving text of *Macbeth* gives every sign of being an adaptation: if so, there is no means of recovering what Shakespeare originally wrote. The scribe seems to have entirely expunged Shakespeare's stage directions from *The Two Gentlemen of Verona*: we must make do with what we have. Other plays, however, confront the editor with a problem of choice. Pared down to its essentials, it is this: should he offer his readers a text which is as close as possible to what Shakespeare originally wrote, or should he aim to formulate a text presenting the play as it appeared when performed by the company of which Shakespeare was a principal shareholder in the theatres that he helped to control and on whose success his livelihood depended? The problem exists in two different forms. For some plays, the changes made in the more theatrical text (always the Folio, if we discount the bad quartos) are relatively minor, consisting perhaps in a few reallocations of dialogue, the addition of music cues to the stage directions, and perhaps some cuts. So it is with, for example, *A Midsommer nights dreame* and *Richard II*. More acute—and more critically exciting—are the problems raised when the more theatrical version appears to represent, not merely the text as originally written after it had been prepared for theatrical use, but a more radical revision of that text made (in some cases) after the first version had been presented in its own terms. At least five of Shakespeare's plays exist in these states: they are *2 Henry IV, Hamlet, Troylus and Cressida, Othello,* and *King Lear*.

The editorial problem is compounded by the existence of conflicting theories to explain the divergences between the surviving texts of these plays. Until recently, it was generally believed that the differences resulted from imperfect transmission: that Shakespeare wrote only one version of each play, and that each variant text represents that original text in a more or less corrupt form. As a consequence of this belief, editors conflated the texts, adding to one passages present only in the other, and selecting among variants in wording in an effort to present what the editor regarded as the most 'Shakespearian' version possible. *Hamlet* provides an example. The 1604 quarto was set from Shakespeare's own papers (with some contamination from the reported text of 1603). The Folio includes about 80 lines that are not in the quarto, but omits about 230 that are there. The Folio was clearly influenced by, if not printed directly from, a theatre manuscript. There are hundreds of local variants. Editors invariably conflate the two texts, assuming that the absence of passages from each was the result either of accidental omission or of cuts made in the theatre against Shakespeare's wishes; they also reject a selection of the variant readings. It is at least arguable that this produces a version that never existed in Shakespeare's time. We believe that the 1604 quarto represents the play as Shakespeare first wrote it, before it was performed, and that the Folio represents a theatrical text of the play after he had revised it. Given this belief, it would be equally logical to base an edition on either text: one the more literary, the other the more theatrical. Both types of edition would be of interest; each would present within its proper context readings which editors who conflate the texts have to abandon.

It would be extravagant in a one-volume edition to present double texts of all the plays that exist in significantly variant form. The theatrical version is, inevitably, that which comes closest to the 'final' version of the play. We have ample testimony from the theatre at all periods, including our own, that play scripts undergo a process of, often, considerable modification on their way from the writing table to the stage. Occasionally, dramatists resent this process; we know that some of Shakespeare's contemporaries resented cuts made in some of their plays. But we know too that plays may be much improved by intelligent cutting, and that dramatists of great literary talent may benefit from the discipline of the theatre. It is, of course, possible that Shakespeare's colleagues occasionally overruled him, forcing him to omit cherished lines, or that practical circumstances—such as the incapacity of a particular actor to do justice to every aspect of his role—necessitated adjustments that Shakespeare would have preferred not to make. But he was himself, supremely, a man of the theatre. We have seen that he displayed no interest in how his plays were printed: in this he is at the opposite extreme from Ben Jonson, who was still in mid-career when he prepared the collected edition of his works. We know that Shakespeare was an actor and shareholder in the leading theatre company of its time, a major financial asset to that company, a man immersed in the life of that theatre and committed to its values. The concept of the director of a play did not exist in his time; but someone must have exercised some, at least, of the functions of the modern director, and there is good reason to believe that that person must have been Shakespeare himself, for his own plays. The very fact that those texts of his plays that contain cuts also give evidence of more 'literary' revision suggests that he was deeply involved in the process by which his plays came to be modified in performance. For these reasons, this edition chooses, when possible, to print the more theatrical version of each play. In some cases, this requires the omission from the body of the text of lines that Shakespeare certainly wrote; there is, of course, no suggestion that these lines are unworthy of their author; merely that, in some if not all performances, he and his company found that the play's overall structure and pace were better without them. All such lines are printed as Additional Passages at the end of the play.

In all but one of Shakespeare's plays the revisions are local—changes in the wording of individual phrases and lines—or else they are effected by additions and cuts. Essentially, then, the story line is not affected. But in *King Lear* the differences between the two texts are more radical. It is not simply that the 1608 quarto lacks over 100 lines that are in the Folio, or that the Folio lacks close on 300 lines that are in the Quarto, or that there are over 850 verbal variants, or that several speeches are assigned to different speakers. It is rather that the sum total of these differences amounts, in this play, to a substantial shift in the presentation and interpretation of the underlying action. The differences are particularly apparent in the military action of the last two acts. We believe, in short, that there are two distinct plays of *King Lear*, not merely two different texts of the same play; so we print edited versions of both the Quarto ('*The Historie of . . .*') and the Folio ('*The Tragedie of . . .*').

Though the editor's selection, when choice is available, of the edition that should form the basis of his text is fundamentally important, many other tasks remain. Elizabethan printers could do meticulously scholarly work, but they rarely expended their best efforts on plays, which—at least in quarto format—they treated as ephemeral publications. Moreover, dramatic manuscripts and heavily annotated quartos must have set them difficult problems. Scribal transcripts would have been easier for the printer, but scribes were themselves liable to introduce error in copying difficult manuscripts, and also had a habit of sophisticating what they copied—for example, by expanding colloquial contractions—in ways that would distort the dramatist's intentions. On the whole, the Folio is a rather well-printed volume; there are not a great many obvious misprints; but for all that, corruption is often discernible. A few quartos—notably *A Midsommer nights dreame* (1600)—are exceptionally well printed, but others, such as the 1604 *Hamlet*, abound in obvious error, which is a sure sign that they also commit hidden corruptions. Generations of editors have tried to correct the texts; but possible corruptions are still being identified, and new attempts at correction are often made. The preparation of this edition has required a minutely detailed examination of the early texts. At many points we have adopted emendations suggested by previous editors; at other points we offer original readings; and occasionally we revert to the original text at points where it has often been emended.

The present edition follows the spelling, punctuation, and other 'incidentals'—capitalization, italicization, etc.—of the earliest edition of each work, or, where more than one edition survives, of that which we regard as being closest to Shakespeare's manuscript. Where necessary, a brief note at the end of the introduction to each work indicates our view of the authority of the incidentals of the edition we follow. When we have emended the text, or added directions, we have attempted to adopt incidentals characteristic of the text used as copy, or, where possible, of the manuscript underlying it. We do not claim in general that our edition recaptures the spelling and other authorial characteristics of the manuscripts underlying the printed editions, a task which, in view of the changes made by compositors and scribes, we regard as impossible except in isolated instances. Nevertheless, this edition does offer Shakespeare's text in a form which his contemporaries would have recognized, and which reflects the conventions of his own period; and in some texts, especially those originally printed from Shakespeare's working papers, it brings us close to the manuscripts.

Original-spelling editions of Shakespeare have rarely been attempted. Ever since the seventeenth century Shakespeare's texts have commonly been presented according to the printing conventions of the time at which they were published; almost all edited texts have been modernized to some degree. This fact reflects Shakespeare's popularity as a read poet and performed dramatist. Although there have been occasional attempts to act his plays in pronunciation characteristic of his time, performance cannot possibly reflect the spelling and punctuation of the early editions. But the modernizing process requires an act of interpretation which interposes the judgement of the editor between the text as originally printed and the modern reader. For example, to an Elizabethan reader some spellings could signify either of two basic meanings which modern English distinguishes by differences in spelling: in Shakespeare's time 'loose' and 'lose' were not distinguished; neither were 'I' and 'ay', 'then' and 'than', 'born' and 'borne', 'lest' and 'least', 'of' and 'off', 'on' and 'one', 'to' and 'too', 'human' and 'humane', 'travel' and 'travail', and so on. Usually a modernizing editor will have no doubt as to which meaning is intended, but at times an arbitrary decision is unavoidable. In *Macbeth*, for instance, faced with

> Blood hath bene shed ere now, i'th'olden time
> Ere humane Statute purg'd the gentle Weale

he must decide whether to print 'human' or 'humane'. Again in *Macbeth*, modernization of the Folio's 'weyward Sisters' to 'weird sisters' takes away the range of senses that might be conveyed by 'weyward'. Similarly in *The Tempest*, when Gonzalo and Alonso have complained of fatigue after wandering around the island, Antonio says 'they are oppress'd with trauaile', where 'trauaile' might equally well be rendered in modern English as either 'travel' or 'travail'.

The process of selection is also one of limitation, for it reduces the potential range of meanings that the words would have suggested at a time when they were not differentiated. This process may be particularly damaging in passages of deliberate word-play. When Richard II is asked if he will resign the throne, he replies 'I, no; no, I: for I must nothing bee'. The resonances available to a reader for whom 'I' could mean 'ay' are inevitably reduced by an editor who is obliged to select one or other interpretation.

Elizabethan spelling was not fully phonetic, but in some words it reflected pronunciation more closely than our own. Not all rhymes in early texts are conveyed by the spelling: for example, in Folio *Henry V* 'Charge' rhymes with 'George' (1070-1), and in *Venus and Adonis* (1593; ll. 422-4), 'chat' with 'gate'. Here, the modernizing editor (like the old-spelling editor) can do nothing to suggest the rhyme; but at other points he has to choose between retaining a spelling that is no longer current and obscuring a rhyme; so in the couplet of Sonnet 34:

> Ah but those teares are pearle which thy loue sheds,
> And they are ritch, and ransome all ill deeds.

At many other points, too, the spelling of early texts reflects pronunciation in a way that adds significance. It may, for instance, indicate scansion where modern spelling would obscure it:

> The spirit that I haue seene
> May be a deale, and the deale hath power
> T'assume a pleasing shape . . .
> (*Hamlet*, Q2, sig. G1)

It may point word-play, as when Talbot puns on 'dauphin' and 'dolphin': 'Dolphin or Dog-fish' (*1 Henry VI* 522). And, more generally, it may do more than a modern-spelling editor can to convey what Shakespeare's verse sounded like to its original audiences.

The original punctuation of the early texts, too, may provide evidence that the modernizing process obscures. In Shakespeare's time, light punctuation often reflected a fluidity of syntax greater than that of modern literary English. Even editors fully aware of this may have difficulty in conveying the effect of the original text while also using acceptable modern punctuation. This is not to claim that the original text is necessarily fully expressive in its own right; rather that its punctuation permits readers to see, as it were, the raw material that lies behind modernized texts in order to make their own judgements about its significance, without editorial intervention. In the 1604 quarto of *Hamlet*, a climactic speech of Laertes is punctuated only with commas:

> It is heere *Hamlet*, thou art slaine,
> No medcin in the world can doe thee good,
> In thee there is not halfe an houres life,
> The treacherous instrument is in my hand
> Vnbated and enuenom'd, the foule practise
> Hath turn'd it selfe on me, loe heere I lie
> Neuer to rise againe, thy mother's poysned,
> I can no more, the King, the Kings too blame.
>
> (sig. O1)

A modern editor would almost inevitably introduce a far less breathless scheme of punctuation; one recent edition breaks the speech up into nine separate sentences; yet it might be argued that the quarto's light punctuation is dramatically effective, that it follows Shakespeare's manuscript, and that it represents his conception of how the speech should be delivered. Individual punctuation marks, too, pose problems: in Elizabethan usage the question mark could have the force of the modern exclamation mark; a modernizing editor often has to make a purely arbitrary decision about which mark to use.

Shakespeare's plays provide a mass of evidence about the state of the language in his time, because of the wide range of situations, and types of speaker, portrayed. Even in our modernized edition we retain some early spellings (in normalized form) to indicate speech that is regional or otherwise idiosyncratic. But readers interested in the language of Shakespeare and his contemporaries need an edition of his works which obscures the original evidence as little as possible. For this reason we make only the most essential changes to the basic texts, and we note our alterations in the *Textual Companion*. Spellings recorded in the *Oxford English Dictionary* are left unaltered, and only the most actively misleading punctuation is changed; hyphenations of the original texts are preserved, and we have set the text so that no new hyphens are introduced across line-breaks. Readers with less specialized interests, too, may welcome an opportunity to read, and to quote from, texts that represent as closely as possible what Shakespeare wrote with the dialogue printed in the form in which it first appeared. Such a text poses problems for the reader unfamiliar with the orthography, punctuation, and printing practices of Shakespeare's time, and for this reason we include an essay by Professor Vivian Salmon, a scholar with a special expertise in the linguistic aspects of Shakespeare's works, who aims to explain some matters over which difficulties may arise.

The editor is faced with a special problem by the stage directions of the early editions, especially in preparing a one-volume edition where some degree of uniformity may be considered desirable. Early texts are often deficient in directions for essential action, even in such basic matters as when characters enter and when they depart. Generations of editors have tried to supply such deficiencies, not always systematically. We try to remedy the deficiencies, always bearing in mind the conditions of Shakespeare's stage. At many points the requisite action is apparent from the dialogue; at other points precisely what should happen, or the precise point at which it should happen, is in doubt—and, perhaps, was never clearly determined even by the author. We use broken brackets—e.g. ⌈He kneels⌉—to identify dubious action or placing. Inevitably, this is to some extent a matter of individual interpretation; and, of course, modern directors may, and often do, depart from the original directions, both explicit and implicit. Our modern-spelling edition is somewhat freer with the wording of directions in the original editions than the present, original-spelling edition, in which changes have been kept to a minimum. Readers interested in the precise directions of the original texts on which ours are based will find them reproduced in our *Textual Companion*.

Theatre is an endlessly fluid medium. Each performance of a play is unique, differing from others in pace, movement, gesture, audience response, and even—because of the fallibility of human memory—in the words spoken. It is likely too that in Shakespeare's time, as in ours, changes in the texts of plays were consciously made to suit varying circumstances: the characteristics of particular actors, the place in which the play was performed, the anticipated reactions of his audience, and so on. The circumstances by which Shakespeare's plays have been transmitted to us mean that it is impossible to recover exactly the form in which they stood either in his own original manuscripts or in those manuscripts, or transcripts of them, after they had been prepared for use in the theatre. Still less can we hope to pinpoint the words spoken in any particular performance. Nevertheless, it is in performance that the plays lived and had their being. Performance is the end to which they were created, and in this edition we have devoted our efforts to recovering and presenting texts of Shakespeare's plays as they were acted in the London playhouses which stood at the centre of his professional life.

CONTEMPORARY ALLUSIONS TO SHAKESPEARE

MANY contemporary documents, some manuscript, some printed, refer directly to Shakespeare and to members of his family. The following list (which is not exhaustive) briefly indicates the nature of the principal allusions to him and to his closest relatives. It does not include publication records of his plays (given in the *Textual Companion*), the appearances of his name on title-pages, unascribed allusions to his works, commendatory poems, epistles, and dedications printed elsewhere in the edition, or records of performances except for that of 1604–5, in which Shakespeare is named. The principal documents are discussed, and most of them reproduced, in S. Schoenbaum's *William Shakespeare: A Documentary Life* (1975).

26 April 1564	Baptism of 'Gulielmus filius Iohannes Shakspere' in Stratford-upon-Avon
27 November 1582	Entry of marriage licence at Worcester 'inter Wᵐ Shaxpere et Annõ whateley'
28 November 1582	Marriage licence bond issued in Worcester for 'Willm Shagspere' and 'Anne Hathwey'
26 May 1583	Baptism of 'Susanna daughter to William Shakspere' in Stratford-upon-Avon
2 February 1585	Baptism of 'Hamnet & Iudeth sonne & daughter to Williã Shakspere' in Stratford-upon-Avon
1589	Reference to William Shakespeare in an earlier lawsuit brought by his parents against John Lambert concerning property at Wilmcote, near Stratford-upon-Avon
1592	Robert Greene's reference in *Greene's Groatsworth of Wit* to 'an vpstart Crow' who 'is in his owne conceit the onely Shake-scene in a countrey' (see p. xviii); Henry Chettle's (oblique) reference in *Kind-Harts Dreame* to Shakespeare's 'vprightnes of dealing, and fatious [= facetious?] grace in writting'.
1594	Reference to Shakespeare as author of *Lucrece* in Henry Willobie's *Willobie his Avisa*
1595	Allusion to 'Sweet Shakespeare' as author of *Lucrece* in William Covell's *Polimanteia*
15 March 1595	Shakespeare named as joint payee of the Lord Chamberlain's Men for performances at court
1596	A petition by William Wayte (in London) for sureties of the peace against 'Willm̃ Shakspere' and others
11 August 1596	Burial of 'Hamnet filius William Shakspere' in Stratford-upon-Avon
October, 1596	Two draft grants of arms to John Shakespeare
4 May 1597, etc.	Documents recording William Shakespeare's purchase of New Place, Stratford-upon-Avon

15 November 1597	'William Shackspeare' of Bishopsgate ward, London, listed as not having paid taxes due in February
1598	Shakespeare one of the 'principall Comœdians' in Ben Jonson's *Every Man in his Humour* (according to a list printed in the 1616 Jonson Folio)
1598	Sale by 'mr shaxspere' of a load of stone in Stratford-upon-Avon
1598	Appearance of Shakespeare's name on title-pages of the second quartos of *Richard II* and *Richard III* and of the first (surviving) quarto of *Love's Labour's Lost*. (Later title-page ascriptions are not listed.)
1598	Praise of Shakespeare as author of *Venus and Adonis* and *Lucrece* in Richard Barnfield's *Poems in Divers Humours*
1598	Francis Meres's references in *Palladis Tamia* (see p. xix)
4 February 1598	'Wᵐ Shackespe' listed as holder of corn and malt in Stratford-upon-Avon
1 October 1598	'William Shakespeare' named as tax defaulter in Bishopsgate ward, London
15 October 1598	Letter from Richard Quiney asking 'mr Wᵐ Shackespe' for a loan of £30
1598–9	'Willm̃ Shakespeare' named in Enrolled Subsidy Account (London)
1598–1601	References to Shakespeare in *The Pilgrimage to Parnassus* and *The Return from Parnassus, Parts 1 and 2*, acted at St. John's College, Cambridge
1599	Draft of grant permitting John Shakespeare to impale his arms with those of the Arden family
16 May 1599	The newly built Globe theatre mentioned (in a London inventory) as being in the occupation of 'William Shakespeare and others'
6 October 1599	'Willmus Shakspere' named as owing money to the Exchequer (London)
6 October 1600	'Willmus Shakspeare' named as owing money to the Exchequer (London)
c.1601	References to Shakespeare as author of *Venus and Adonis*, *Lucrece*, and *Hamlet* in a manuscript note by Gabriel Harvey
8 September 1601	Burial of John Shakespeare in Stratford-upon-Avon
1602	Reconveyance of New Place to William Shakespeare
1602	Reference to 'Shakespear yᵉ Player' in York Herald's complaint
13 March 1602	John Manningham's diary entry of an anecdote about Burbage and Shakespeare (see pp. xv–xvi)
1 May 1602	Shakespeare paid William and John Combe £320 for land in Old Stratford
28 September 1602	Shakespeare bought a cottage in Chapel Lane, Stratford-upon-Avon
1603	Shakespeare listed among 'The principall Tragœdians' in Ben Jonson's *Sejanus*
1603	Shakespeare (and others) called on to lament the death of Queen Elizabeth in Henry Chettle's *A Mourneful Dittie, entituled Elizabeths Losse*
17 and 19 May 1603	Shakespeare named in documents conferring the title of King's Men on the former Lord Chamberlain's Men
c.1604	Shakespeare sued Philip Rogers of Stratford-upon-Avon for debt
1604	Anthony Scoloker, in *Diaphantus, or the Passions of Love*, mentions the popularity of *Hamlet* and refers to '*Friendly Shakespeare's Tragedies*'
15 March 1604	Shakespeare and his fellows granted scarlet cloth for King James's entry into London (see p. xx)
24 October 1604	Shakespeare recorded as owner of a cottage and garden in Rowington Manor
1604–5	'Shaxberd' named as author of several plays performed at court

1605	Passing reference to Shakespeare in William Camden's *Remaines of a greater Worke concerning Britaine*'
4 May 1605	Augustine Phillips (actor) bequeathes 'to my fellowe William Shakespeare a xxx[s] peece in gould'
24 July 1605	Shakespeare pays £440 for an interest in a lease of tithes in the Stratford-upon-Avon area
1607	Commendatory allusion to Shakespeare in William Barksted's *Myrrha, the Mother of Adonis*
5 June 1607	Marriage of Susanna Shakespeare to John Hall in Stratford-upon-Avon
9 September 1608	Burial of Shakespeare's mother, 'Mary Shaxspere wydowe', in Stratford-upon-Avon
1608–9	Documents recording Shakespeare's lawsuit for debt against John Addenbrooke of Stratford-upon-Avon
11 September 1611	Shakespeare subscribes to the cost of a bill for repairing highways
1612	Praise of 'the right happy and copious industry of M. *Shake-speare*' (and others) in John Webster's epistle to *The White Devil*
1612	Shakespeare testifies in Stephen Belott's suit against Christopher Mountjoy, in London (see pp. xvi–xvii)
*c.*1613	Leonard Digges, in a manuscript note, compares Shakespeare to Lope de Vega
28 January 1613	John Combe of Stratford-upon-Avon bequeathes £5 to 'mr William Shackspere'
10 March 1613	Shakespeare buys a gatehouse in Blackfriars for £140
31 March 1613	Payment to Shakespeare and Richard Burbage of 44 shillings for an *impresa* for the Earl of Rutland (see p. xxi)
1614	Passing reference to Shakespeare in an epistle by Richard Carew printed in the second edition of Camden's *Remaines*
5 September 1614, etc.	Documents recording Shakespeare's involvement in disputes concerning enclosures in the Stratford-upon-Avon area
*c.*1615	Complimentary reference to Shakespeare in a manuscript poem by Francis Beaumont
1615	Passing reference to Shakespeare by Edward Howes in fifth edition of John Stow's *Annales*
26 April 1615	Shakespeare engaged in litigation concerned with the Blackfriars gatehouse
10 February 1616	Marriage of Judith Shakespeare to Thomas Quiney in Stratford-upon-Avon
25 March 1616	Shakespeare's will drawn up in Stratford-upon-Avon
25 April 1616	Burial of William Shakespeare in Stratford-upon-Avon (his monument records that he died on 23 April)
8 August 1623	Burial of Anne Shakespeare in Stratford-upon-Avon
16 July 1649	Burial of Shakespeare's daughter, Susanna Hall, in Stratford-upon-Avon
9 February 1662	Burial of Shakespeare's daughter, Judith Quiney, in Stratford-upon-Avon
1670	Death of Shakespeare's last direct descendant, his granddaughter Elizabeth, who married Thomas Nash in 1626 and John (later Sir John) Bernard in 1649

THE SPELLING AND PUNCTUATION
OF SHAKESPEARE'S TIME

It has always been customary for actors to deliver the lines which Shakespeare wrote in the pronunciation of their own time; it would, of course, be difficult for them to do otherwise, since we do not know precisely how Shakespeare and his contemporaries spoke; and even if we did, the effect of listening to a performance in Elizabethan English would be comparable to listening to one in a regional dialect of the present day. Though Shakespeare's language is distinguished for us by time rather than place, the occasional attempt to pronounce his lines as he may have heard them has produced in listeners more bafflement and amusement than comprehension or appreciation. The situation is different with the printed word; although it is also customary (and has been since the seventeenth century) to modernize the spelling and punctuation of the texts printed in the lifetime of Shakespeare and his near contemporaries, the original version is much more accessible to the modern reader than to the listener, and has more to offer for the full appreciation of the meaning of the original Elizabethan or Jacobean text.

Readers confronted with an old-spelling text for the first time may be deterred by its unfamiliar appearance; and several questions will occur to them which, it is hoped, this essay will help to answer. They may be surprised that the spelling differs in so many respects from that of modern English; while certain differences might reasonably be expected in early works in manuscript, it will no doubt seem strange that, even after a century of printing since Caxton's time, spelling was not yet that of the present day, or indeed, that of English since the Restoration period. Why, and in what ways, does it differ? The modern reader will want to know whose spelling this is: is it Shakespeare's? that of a scribe who copied his rough drafts? that of the printing-house compositors who set the work into type? or that of a printer's proof-reader? Even a cursory glance will show that the spelling is by no means consistent, and a word appearing in one form in a given line may appear with a different spelling only a few lines later—or even within the same line. Modern readers will undoubtedly be puzzled by the punctuation, which often seems to bear no relation to current practice. Finally, they will find capitals and italics used, once again, in a largely unfamiliar system—if, indeed, they can find any system at all in the text.

The major differences between Elizabethan and modern spelling are explained by the historical development of English orthography. In the Middle Ages, writers normally represented in their spelling the sounds of the dialect which they themselves spoke; there was no generally accepted standard of orthography, most official documents intended for national distribution being written in Latin or Anglo-French. With the reign of Henry V (1387-1422), there came a radical change. Perhaps for patriotic reasons, in order to unite the nation behind him in his wars against the French, Henry encouraged the use of English in official documents. Most of these emanated from Chancery, which was at that period the government secretariat; from the later 1420s officials developed a standard form of spelling which, being to a large extent based on the pronunciation of the central Midlands, would have been fairly readily comprehensible in all the English regions. This form of spelling became more and more firmly established during the fifteenth century, although in private correspondence regional spelling still existed; and when William Caxton set up his printing press in Westminster in 1476, one might have expected that the ready dissemination of multiple copies of a single text, all with the same spelling, would have led to a generally accepted written standard and to the adoption by printers of a consistent spelling practice.

Surprisingly, this did not happen at once. Caxton, who although English by birth had spent a long time as a merchant in Bruges, had to import foreign compositors when he brought his printing press to Westminster. Unfamiliar with the English language, they sometimes adopted uncritically what might have been obsolescent, regional or idiosyncratic spellings in their copy; they also introduced foreign spelling conventions (e.g. *gh* in *ghost*) and—apparently—were happy to adopt almost any reasonable spelling which might be necessitated by exigencies of the printing house. But when native speakers of English were trained as compositors, it became easier to introduce a standard spelling, and as early as 1530 we find a manual (now surviving only in fragments) giving directions how 'one may lerne to . . . spel & to rede & how one shuld wryte englysh treu[ly]'. This text was accompanied by playing cards designed 'to tech þe pleyers to spell'. It is clear that John Rastell, who printed this text, advocated a standard spelling system, and those fragments which survive show his concern to distinguish between the vowels in *seek, breed, bleed, speed; bed, red, leg,* by spelling the former set with a '*dowbull ee*' and the latter with 'þe syngull .e.'; and likewise to decide 'when þe one & þe oþer shuld be wrytyn'. Similarly, he provides rules for printing with single or double *o*. What he does not discuss (at least in the fragments which survive) is the possibility of an orthographic distinction between two long vowels current in early Tudor English (though now lost) which were at that time represented by *e*. Later in the sixteenth century printers introduced the digraphs *ea* and *ee*, as in *read* and *reed*, *seam* and *seem*, to distinguish between the two sounds; they also introduced an orthographic distinction between the two long vowels represented by *o*, i.e. *oa* and *oo*, as in *road* and *rood* where, although the vowel sounds have changed, they remain distinct. These orthographic conventions are used by Shakespeare's printers, but not altogether consistently. There was a further alternation, also not completely resolved in Shakespeare's time, between spellings like *compleat* and *complete*, *yoake* and *yoke*, where final *e* was taken as indicating the length, though not the exact quality, of the preceding vowel. Shakespeare's plays appeared, then, at a time when printers, although apparently aiming at a standard form of spelling, had not yet finally succeeded in establishing one.

What eventually helped to establish a national standard of spelling—perhaps even more successfully than the sixteenth-century printers—was the influence of schoolmasters. So irregular was the spelling of the mid-sixteenth century thought to be that a number of scholars attempted to create an entirely new spelling system, which would represent more accurately the sounds of English as spoken in and near the capital. One of these reformers, John Hart, advocated the introduction of a new phonetic alphabet (1551-70); another, William Bullokar, proposed the retention of existing letters of the alphabet but in combination with numerous diacritics such as vowel accents (1580-5). The system he produced was aesthetically unattractive, while Hart's, though pleasant to look at, was difficult to read. Consequently, a different approach was proposed by two schoolmasters, Richard Mulcaster, Head in turn of Merchant Taylors' and St Paul's schools, and Edmund Coote, master of the 'free school' at Bury St Edmunds, who both suggested regularization, rather than a more radical reform of English spelling. Mulcaster's book, *The Elementarie* (1582), was large and no doubt expensive; Coote's was a small handbook, probably within the reach of most would-be literates, and therefore printed in edition after edition in the seventeenth century. In *The English Schoolemaister* (1596), Coote admitted that 'many writers disagreed' on the appropriate way to spell, some arguing that an English word derived from a foreign source such as Latin or French should attempt to imitate the orthography of that source (rather than the English pronunciation) as far as possible. Both Mulcaster and Coote published lengthy word lists in their books (giving preferred spellings) which provided models which printers could (and no doubt did) imitate. But since Shakespeare himself was already at work as a poet and playwright when Coote's textbook was published, it would not be surprising if the spelling of his drafts was neither consistent nor standard: the schoolmasters' precepts would have been published only after he had become confirmed in the orthographic practices of his youth.

Certain orthographic differences between Elizabethan and modern English are immediately obvious because they occur with great frequency; in some cases it is a question of the form or use of individual letters; in others it is a question of the spelling of individual words. One graphic distinction which has not been retained in this present edition is that between the two forms of *s*. The printers of the first editions of Shakespeare's works employed two forms which were based ultimately on manuscript tradition. Some scripts made a distinction between *s* in final position ('s') and *s* occurring elsewhere in a word ('ſ')—i.e. the long *s* which is still to be seen on, for example, seventeenth- and eighteenth-century funerary monuments. Such a distinction had originally been made in manuscript for the sake of legibility; similar alternatives had occurred with some other letters, e.g. *r*. Although such positional variants often survive in individual handwriting at the present day, they have not been retained in printing. The occurrence of 'ſ' in the original Shakespearian text is worthy of note because it could be mistaken for 'f'; consequently, the original use of 'ſ' has been preserved in the notes to *William Shakespeare: A Textual Companion*. But the distinction between the two forms has no relevance to meaning or pronunciation, and hence has not been preserved in this edition (except in the diplomatic transcript of *Pericles*).

The other problems relating to individual letters concern the use of *u/v* and *i/j*, where the present edition retains the usage of Shakespeare's printers. Apart from some attempts at regularization by fifteenth-century Chancery scribes, it was customary to select either *u* or *v*, *i* or *j*, not according to the sounds they represented but to the position in which they occurred in the word; *v* was written initially, *u* elsewhere, whether the sound denoted was the consonant *v* or the vowel *u*. This usage originated in classical Latin, where *v* did not represent a distinctive sound, but was the form of *u* or *uu* (i.e. 'double *u*') used in inscriptions on stone. About AD 800 the pronunciation of *uu* (i.e. *w*) in certain positions changed to the consonant *v*, and continued in use in French (a descendant of Latin), although in Old English it was merely the sound denoted by *f* occurring between two vowels. From French it was introduced into English in the Middle Ages, when *v* became established as a component of many English words, like *valley* and *value*, which were derived from French. It was the Italian printer Arrighi who in 1524 first distinguished between *u* and *v* by sound, rather than by position; but the printing trade has always been deeply conservative, and the new system took some time to establish itself. The Italians were followed, first by French, and then by English printers; but *V* continued to be used as a capital form of both *u* and *v* throughout the seventeenth century—as in the names LVCRECE and TARQVIN in *Lucrece*.

Similarly, *i* and *j* were originally positional variants, since the sound *j* (as in *judged*) was, like *v*, not found in the classical Latin from which our alphabet, and the 'roman' type face, is derived. The symbol *j* was the form taken by *i* as the last element of a Roman numeral (e.g. *iij*) where it was adopted purely for reasons of legibility. Like *u* and *v* it was first adopted by continental printers in the sixteenth century. An English printer, Thomas Dawkes, writing in 1685, comments: 'the first Book where I find this distinction of j Consonant and the v Consonant from the i Vowel and u Vowel, (in the Small Letters, but not at that time observed among the Capitals) is . . . [in] 1633. and the first Book, wherein I find it universally observed with us in *England*, in both Capitals & Small Letters, is . . . Printed at *Cambridge*, 1634'. These developments can be seen in *The Two Noble Kinsmen*, the last of Shakespeare's plays to be printed (1634), which mixes the two conventions, and also in the later items in the section of 'Commendatory Poems and Prefaces'. The older conventions occur throughout the Quartos and the First Folio text, and hardly need exemplification. For the most part these conventions, once familiar, create no real difficulties of interpretation. But occasionally they result in ambiguities: 'proud' could be modernized to 'proud' or 'proved'; 'loud', to 'loud' or 'loved'. In the word 'Lieutenant' the medial *u* could, in Shakespeare's time, be pronounced either as a 'u' (as in modern American usage) or as a 'v' (as in modern British). Similarly, in the French dialogue in *Henry V* 2337, the spelling 'distinie' may be interpreted as 'distinje' (i.e. *distingué*, in modern French; not *destinée*). And the form 'Troian' could represent either 'Trojan', or the alternative pronunciation 'Troyan'. The most familiar of such ambiguities concerns the pronunciation of the names of two of Shakespeare's villains: 'Iago' (modern Spanish 'Iago') and 'Iachimo' (modern Italian 'Giacomo'). Nevertheless, the number of words affected by such ambiguities is small.

More important are the differences of spelling in individual words, which are of three kinds. First, there are differences which are due to scribal conventions in the early seventeenth century, not to any major difference in pronunciation between the relevant words and their modern English equivalents. Secondly, there are differences in spelling which reflect a genuine difference in pronunciation; and thirdly, there are differences where the modern and Elizabethan pronunciation is approximately the same, but where the earlier spelling is a more faithful representation of the sound. To the first type belong some major differences which strike the modern reader at a glance; most noticeable of these is the frequent occurrence of final *e* which is lost in modern English and appears to have had no phonetic realization in Shakespeare's time. In some cases, an unnecessary *e* is added to words which would otherwise consist of only two letters, e.g. *bee, wee, mee, yee* (a preference for a minimum of three which still survives in Modern English, except for prepositions and pronouns). In other cases, final *e* represents the 'reduced' form of an inflection in earlier English, for example, *walken* > *walke* (= 'walk'), where *e* is derived from the unstressed infinitive inflection *en*. By about 1400, final *e* (pronounced like *a* in Modern English *China*) had disappeared in the spoken form, but survived, traditionally, in the written form. A function did, however, develop in due course; because it was associated with the lengthening of short vowels in the preceding syllable in certain grammatical forms in Middle English, it became regarded as an indicator of a long vowel or diphthong in sixteenth-century English, and as such it still survives: compare *hat, hate; not, note*. As Mulcaster remarks, *e* is a 'letter of maruellous vse in the writing of our tung . . . most times it is writen to great purpos, euen where it semeth idle . . . I call that E, qualifying, whose absence or presence, somtime altereth the vowell' and he compares *made* and *mad, stripe* and *strip*, and several others. But *e* survived where it had no such function; for example, in *passe, nedelesse, discusse*. Of such spellings Mulcaster has no explanation; he merely remarks 'When the vowell sitteth hard vpon the ſ, in the end, ſ, is dubled frenchlike . . . Where custom . . . causeth the dubling' and, of course, final *e* also. Shakespeare's printers retained this non-functional spelling, which disappeared by about 1650. Doubled consonants in general, as in *sitt, pitty, linnen, mannor, dogge, comming, widdow*, also came to be regarded as functional, in marking a preceding vowel as short—an orthographic device which has usually survived in modern English where the spelling would otherwise indicate a preceding long vowel e.g. *sit, sitting*, compared with *siting*. In the early seventeenth century, these purely orthographic doubled consonants, relics of Old English phonetically doubled consonants—now occurring only in compounds like *book-case*—were still retained by printers, and eventually dropped where it was obvious that they had no specific function. One particular example of non-functional doubled consonants (in this case $c + k$) is found until the early nineteenth century in words like *musick* and *frolick*, where *k* appears now only before inflections beginning with a vowel, e.g. *frolicking*. But the Shakespeare texts sometimes display differences in the use of doubled consonants in an unexpected way— e.g. with single *l*, instead of double, in *cal, shal, dwel, smel* etc.

Other very noticeable spelling differences which do not affect pronunciation include the common use of *ie* instead of *y* in final position. Of this spelling, Mulcaster remarks 'When ... [i] is it self the last letter ... it is qualified by the e, as *manie, merie, tarie, carie*, where the verie pen, will rather end in the e, then in the naked i'. Mulcaster distinguished between *ie*, where *i* 'soundeth gentlie' and *i* which sounds 'sharp and loud' where it is to be written by 'hauing no, e, after it, as neding no qualification, *deny, cry, defy*'. Possibly the spelling *ie* was modelled on the similar common French suffix. At all events, the custom of using *y* in final position when it represents a stressed vowel must have led to the general adoption of *y*, rather than *ie*, in all such final positions; *i* and *y* were interchangeable because, in Middle English, they were merely variant graphs (like 's' and 'ſ') representing the same sound, when there was a tendency for scribes to use *y* for legibility in certain positions, or as a consistent replacement for *i* in certain forms of handwriting.

Other variant spellings where an archaic form is used by Shakespeare's printers include *au* rather than *a*, e.g. *auncient* for *ancient, daunce* for *dance*, where the variant forms represent different pronunciations in the dialects of French from which such words were imported into Middle English; *ee* and *ea, oo* and *oa, e/o* and final *e* where as already noted, the sixteenth-century orthographic distinction between two pronunciations of *e* and two of *o* had not been completely established; or *u* and *w* (compare *prowd, howr, perswade*) where *w* was, as its name suggests, merely the equivalent of 'double' *u*. A very few unusual spellings appearing in the Shakespeare texts depend on 'false etymology'; for example, *despight* (French *dépit*) by false analogy with *light*, where *gh* originally represented a sound now lost for native English speakers except in Scottish *loch* and place and personal names like *Tulloch*. An example of this false etymology survives in modern English *sprightly*, from French *esprit*; others which have been lost include Shakespeare's *abhominable*, as though from Latin *homo* 'man' (as Holofernes supposes, at *Loues labors lost* 1627–8), rather than (correctly) from *omen*.

More interesting differences in spelling between the Shakespeare texts and present-day English are those which reflect a genuine difference of pronunciation in the late sixteenth and early seventeenth century. There are too many to list here, but the most important of them include *ar* where modern English has *er*, e.g. *marchant* rather than *merchant*. Although this particular example is now lost, the pronunciation still survives in forms like *clerk* and *Derby*. A sound-change in late Middle English of *er* to *ar* is now retained only sporadically: whereas Shakespeare's *marchant* has been replaced by *merchant*, French *ferme* (as at *Historie of King Lear* 1190) is Modern English *farm, merveille* (as at *Henry the Fift* 530, 'meruailous') is Modern English *marvel*. A second example is the common phonetic development of final 'excrescent' *t* or *d* in words ending in *n* or *l*, for example, *orphant* (*All is true* 1893), *margent* and *vilde*. Some still survive in modern English, e.g. *pheasant* from French *faisan, peasant* from *paysan*, and also following other consonants e.g. *against* and *betwixt*. A third example of differences in both spelling and pronunciation is Shakespearian *burthen* for *burden*, *murther* for *murder*, *Bermoothes* (*Tempest* 296) for *Bermuda*, where—once again—the replacement of the sound denoted by *th* by that represented by *d* is a fairly common phenomenon. Conversely, the Shakespearian text occasionally illustrates the reverse situation e.g. *fardingale* (*Shrew* 1935) for *farthingale*. Variation between *e* and *i* is exemplified in *diuell* for *devil*, *sildome* (*All's Well* 1656) for *seldom*. Changes of a different kind include the loss of an intervocalic *v* as in *e'er*, *e'en*, *ne'er* and *se'nnight*, now only occurring in fossilized forms like *ne'er-do-well* and *Hallowe'en*. Such elisions must often be presumed even when they are not indicated orthographically. Alternatively, intervocalic *v* is sometimes associated with loss of one of the adjacent vowels, so that *euen* could be spelled *e'en* or *eu'n*. Gabriel Harvey, urging a reform of the spelling system, wrote of words like *heauen* and *seuen* that he 'would as well in Writing as in speaking, haue them vsed as *Monosyllaba*, thus: *heaun*, *seaun*', and complained that his contemporaries absurdly wrote '*euen* for *eun*, *Diuel* for *Diul*'. For all these words—and comparable ones like *giuen*—the early Shakespeare editions do occasionally signal the elision, but more generally they fail to mark it, even when the metre clearly requires it; modern readers are particularly prone to overlook such elisions, because they are no longer in use (though the pronunciation of *devil* as a monosyllable survives in modern Scots *deal*). In addition, there are a few oddities like *ioynter* (*Shrew* 1174), where the more recent re-spelling on the model of the original French, *jointure*, has resulted in a change of pronunciation as well.

A third kind of spelling difference between modern English and the Shakespeare text is the recording in the latter of certain features of pronunciation which are common to both, but not realized orthographically in modern English. A large number of such occurrences relate to the loss of the medial vowel in trisyllabic words, for example, in *business* and *medicine*. These losses are probably noted by Shakespeare's printers because they are metrically important, e.g. *sland'rous*, *desp'rate*, but, as the modern equivalents show, such spellings were merely occasional and ephemeral. Also occasional in spelling, though surviving in pronunciation, was the loss of consonants in clusters, as in *Wensday* and *hansome* (*Much adoe* 2074, 2662), which are closer to modern pronunciation than modern spelling is; also closer are forms like *dreampt* (*Romeo* 509, *Cæsar* 971), where *p* represents the transitional consonant occurring in normal utterance between *m* and *t*.

Other differences include a few cases where the early spelling represents the same pronunciation as the modern one, but where the current spelling has been remodelled to appear closer to its ultimate source e.g. *cabidge* (*Merry Wiues* 113), *vertue* (cf. Latin *virtus*). On the other hand, some spellings in the text are closer to the French source than their modern equivalents e.g. *soudain*, Modern *sudden*, *battaile*, Modern *battle*. In some respects, sixteenth-century English was closer to French than it is now, both in spelling and pronunciation and also in shared vocabulary and idioms; thus, the Elizabethan expression *in fine*—meaning 'in conclusion'—becomes much more intelligible once we recognize it as the French *en fin*.

Finally, there is the linguistically interesting case of spellings like *Yedward* (*Hystorie of Henry the fourth* 236) for *Edward* and *yerewhile* (*As you Like it* 1827) for *erewhile*. These indicate the development of a glide before certain vowels, such as is currently heard now in Southern English between *the* and *only*, and is preserved in spelling in place-names like *Yeovil* and *Yaxley*. In the seventeenth century, the forms *yerb* for *herb* and *yerth* for *earth* were apparently quite common (though they never appear in Shakespeare's works), but were condemned by grammarians as 'vulgar' and have disappeared from the standard language; although the glide 'w', which developed in comparable circumstances between back vowels, is preserved in the pronunciation of *one* and *once*, in the dialect form *wuts* for *oats*, and in the juncture between two back vowels, (for example, *to all* in modern Southern English).

Perhaps most immediately obvious to the modern student of an old-spelling edition is the recording in print of certain unstressed forms which we now tend to reproduce only in informal correspondence, although we normally make use of them in conversation. These unstressed forms, as in *he'll* (where '*ll* = 'will'), result from the isochronous nature of English speech; we tend to speak in rhythmical units, with stressed syllables occurring at roughly regular intervals, and unstressed syllables—perhaps as many as four or five— uttered rapidly between the beats. The items which are normally stressed are nouns, verbs, adjectives and adverbs; the remaining items—prepositions, articles, conjunctions and pronouns—develop unstressed forms where the vowel either disappears altogether, or is reduced to the unstressed vowel found in the second syllable of *China*. These 'grammatical' words can also occur in stressed position, when, for example, *am* as sentence initial retains its original vowel ('Am I?'). While the system of unstressed forms appears to have existed in Elizabethan English, and even earlier, the evidence of the Shakespearian texts shows that it differed in many respects from the comparable system at the present day. The texts also show that notation of the full range of such forms was less common in Shakespeare's early plays, although they had been extensively recorded in 'domestic' drama of the mid to late sixteenth century. There is little doubt that unstressed forms must have been used by actors in Shakespeare's early plays, but the dramatist seems to have been less adventurous or careful about recording them than he was in his later work.

Many unstressed forms, such as *he'll*, will be familiar to the modern reader already, but others require comment. First, in the auxiliary verbs, there is a set of forms associated with *thou*: *thou art/wert* is reduced to *thou'rt*, *thou hast* to *thou'st*, and *have* to *ha* e.g. *let's ha't*. The pronouns differ more radically from Modern English. *He* is sometimes printed as *a*, to indicate the sound of the second vowel in *China*, for which no specific letter-form exists. *Thou, thy, she, we, ye,* and *they* lose the final vowel or diphthong, producing forms like *th'art, sh'adulterates* (*King Iohn* 931), *w'are, y'are, y'haue, th'are. His* is reduced to *s* in e.g. *in's, all's, to's; us* (as in Modern English *let's*) to *s*, e.g. *cram's* (*Winters Tale* 140), *upon's*; and *it* to *t*, e.g. *'tis, 'twas, on't, know't.* Unstressed *them* is replaced by *'em*, as in *call 'em*, from an archaic pronoun *hem* 'them'. The prepositions *in, on, of, to* show unstressed forms in e.g. *i'th, o'th, o' lantern, t'aduance;* the conjunctions *as* and *so* are reduced to *s*, e.g. *that's, s'incapeable* (*Coriolanus* 2626), and the definite article *the* to *th* e.g. *th'other, th'affection.* Where two normally unstressed forms occur in immediate proximity one of them remains in its regular form e.g. *on't, thou'rt* or *th'art*.

The reproduction in the printed text of these unstressed forms is possibly the most reliable evidence of Shakespeare's own spelling; otherwise the question remains—whose spelling is represented in the Quartos and Folio? In the absence of acknowledged manuscripts in Shakespeare's own hand, we have nothing with which to compare the printed texts; the only possible evidence is that of the manuscript of *Sir Thomas Moore*. It has been argued, and this edition accepts, that a small section, in what is known as 'Hand D', is actually in Shakespeare's handwriting. If so, it is clear that his spelling was far from consistent; for example, 'Hand D' spells 'Sheriff' as '*Shreiff*', '*shreef*', '*shreeue*', '*Shreiue*', and '*Shreue*' within five lines, and *More* as *Moor* and *Moore*. Whether or not 'Hand D' was Shakespeare, this kind of inconsistency is by no means atypical. For example, the few autograph manuscripts of Philip Massinger (1583-1640)—a younger dramatist, who might be expected to have been more influenced by the increasing tendency toward standardization—show that he spelled *you'll* in five different ways (*youl, you'l, youle, youll, you'll*), and other words in at least three ways (*guarded, imposed, mischief, should,* etc.). Some of the evidence that

'Hand D' is indeed Shakespeare's hand lies in certain peculiarities of spelling which are common to the printed Shakespeare texts and this manuscript, for example, *scilens* for *silence*; but that evidence is not, in itself, totally convincing, since we know so little about Shakespeare's spelling preferences, or those of his contemporaries.

Although this is the only surviving manuscript which may be in Shakespeare's hand, there is evidence that a few of the printed texts are at only one remove from his own drafts, and may therefore represent fairly closely his own spelling habits. The texts in this volume which probably reflect Shakespeare's orthography most faithfully are *Titus Andronicus*, *Venus and Adonis* and *The Rape of Lucrece*, *Loues labors lost*, *A Midsommer nights dreame*, *Romeo and Iuliet*, *Richard the second*, *Merchant of Venice*, *The second part of Henry the fourth*, *Much adoe*, *Hamlet*, *Troylus and Cressida*, and *The Historie of King Lear*, all printed during Shakespeare's lifetime from manuscripts (apparently) in his own handwriting. *The Comedie of Errors*, *Henry the Fift*, and *All's Well that Ends Well* were also apparently printed from such manuscripts, but not until 1623; so too were *Henry the Sixt* and *Timon of Athens*, though in their case late printing is compounded by collaborative authorship.

It may be asked, however, why the printer did not always use Shakespeare's own drafts—his 'foul papers'—as his copy, and reproduce them exactly. One very good reason is that foul papers—as the term implies—were usually untidy and illegible, and printers preferred cleaner, more readable manuscripts which had already been (in modern parlance) 'copy-edited'. We know the identity of one professional scrivener who copied dramatic texts in this way, Ralph Crane. In 1621 he published a volume of verse, the *Induction* to which provides some useful information about his professional activities. He made transcripts of several dramatic works, and from these we are able to assess his spelling habits and, even more importantly, the possibility that it was Crane who wrote out the fair copies for William Jaggard, the Folio printer, of five comedies by Shakespeare. Close comparison of Crane's spelling and punctuation habits with those found in *The Tempest*, *The Two Gentlemen of Verona*, *The Merry Wiues of Windsor*, *Measure, for Measure* and *The Winters Tale* indicates that he wrote the fair copies for them. A complete account of the evidence for Crane's intervention, and of the nature of Crane's orthography, is not possible here, but certain spellings are regularly preferred here and in the Crane transcripts, e.g. *ei*, not *ie*, as in *feirce*; *nck*, not *nk*, as in *thinck*; *s* or *sse*, not *ss*, as in *profes* and *progresse*; *lly* not *ly*, as in *principally*. He also preferred *ow* to *ou* in *lowd*, *prowd*; *oa* to *o* in *doated*, *yoak*; *ea* to *e* in *compleate*; *tearmes* and *ique* to *ic* in *politique*, *heroique*; and he had regular preferences in the use of doubled consonants, although he seems to have been indifferent to certain other variables such as *au* or *a* in words like *ancient*. There is little doubt that Crane's spelling is reflected in the Folio edition of these plays. A number of other texts were apparently set from manuscripts prepared by other scribes, whose identities are as yet unknown: in this volume *King Iohn*, *The Hystorie of Henry the fourth*, *Iulius Cæsar*, *As you Like it*, *Twelfe Night*, the Sonnets, *Macbeth*, *Coriolanus*, *Cymbeline* and *All is true* probably reflect the habits of scribes more than of Shakespeare.

Other texts are even further removed from Shakespeare's manuscripts. For *Pericles* we are almost entirely dependent upon a manuscript reflecting someone's memories of a performance; the same is true of parts of *Richard the Third* (1426.1–c.1575, 3094–end) and *The First Part of the Contention* (779–817.4). For the rest of *Richard the Third* our text is based upon such a memorial transcription corrected in part by a manuscript prepared by an unknown scribe. Such texts may reflect the practice of Shakespeare's period, but they obviously tell us nothing about the practice of Shakespeare himself.

If the intervention of a professional scribe removes us one stage away from Shakespeare's own manuscript, the introduction of compositorial spelling habits removes us even further.

It is at least probable that a compositor would follow fairly closely a clearly written copy such as Crane's, but it is by no means evident that he always did so, particularly when his copy was spelt in a manner seriously at variance with his own preferred conventions, or perhaps those of his printing-house. If it seems strange that a compositor was free to alter his copy, there is no question but that he did so. The most important early manual of the English printing trade, Joseph Moxon's *Mechanick Exercises on the Whole Art of Printing* (1683-4) tells us that '*the carelesness of some good Authors, and the ignorance of other Authors, has forc'd* Printers *to introduce a Custom, which among them is look'd upon as a task and duty incumbent on the* Composer, *viz. to discern and amend the bad* Spelling *and* Pointing *of his* Copy, *if it be English; But if it be in any Forrain Language, the Author is wholy left to his own Skill and Judgement in* Spelling *and* Pointing.' We can see this process at work in Shakespeare's period. It is, for example, possible to compare an extant manuscript in an author's own hand, with the printed version of his work: one such manuscript, of part of a translation of *Orlando Furioso*, is by Sir John Harington, from which the first edition (1591) was printed by Richard Field. Field—who also printed *Venus and Adonis* (1593) and *Lucrece* (1594)—altered both spelling and punctuation so drastically that numerous changes of spelling, and more than forty alterations in punctuation, occur in sixty-four lines of *Orlando*. Likewise, where a Shakespeare play was first published in Quarto form, and it can be shown that the Folio text was practically a reprint (as with *Titus Andronicus*, *Loues labors lost*, *A Midsommer nights dreame*, etc), there are substantial spelling and punctuation differences which could only have been due to the compositor. Similar changes occur in quarto reprints of early quartos, and later reprints of the First Folio itself. On the other hand, the inverse of Moxon's rule—that the compositor made no effort to improve the orthography and pointing of passages in a foreign language—means that we may be particularly close to Shakespeare's own handwriting in the language lesson in *Henry the Fift* Sc. 12. (Certainly, the apparent errors in that scene suggest that Shakespeare's handwriting was prone to certain kinds of misreading, also often suspected elsewhere in the canon.)

The final question to be asked about the source of Quarto and Folio spelling is—could it have been affected not only by the compositor but by the proof-reader? Proof-readers generally concerned themselves with the correction of error: either substantive errors (omission, interpolation, or substitution of words) or typographical ones (turned letters, wrong fount types, irregular inking, irregularities of layout). But they also occasionally interfered with spellings: for instance, in Folio *Othello*, the proof-reader altered 'Leiutenant' (an acceptable period spelling) to 'Lieutenant'. Likewise, in *The Historie of King Lear* accredited spellings like 'wosted' (1022), 'clamarous' (1028), and 'past' (1292) were proof-corrected to 'worsted' and 'clamorous' and 'pâst'; in *The Tragedie of King Lear*, 'holly' (1087) became 'holy', by the same process. Occasionally, too, when a necessary correction of wording had to be inserted, the proof-corrector (or the compositor) might alter the spelling of adjacent words, in order to cause as little disturbance as possible to the line or paragraph or page. But in general, the proof-reader would have influenced the spelling of only a small proportion of words in any text; when he did intervene, he usually brought spellings into greater conformity with a developing 'standard' usage, closer to our own modern conventions, and further from the occasional eccentricities of authorial orthography.

It must be concluded that the individual compositor was mainly responsible for the text, and this fact in part explains why spelling is so inconsistent, varying from page to page, not only within a single word like *speare/spear*, but also in the spelling of sets of phonetically analogous words. Such variety is neatly illustrated by the printers' habit of using 'catchwords', by which the first word of a new page is indicated at the bottom of the preceding page. Usually catchword and text agree, but not always. For instance, at *Troylus and Cressida* (E4v), we find 'mary' in the catchword and 'marry' in the text. Although the author was no doubt responsible for much orthographical inconsistency—as 'Hand D' demonstrates—he can hardly be blamed for both spellings of such words.

Even if an author were consistent, his efforts might be vitiated if (as often happens) his manuscript was set into type by a variety of different compositors. For instance, detailed analysis of the spelling and punctuation of the First Folio has shown that up to eight compositors were at work on that book, all with different spelling (and punctuation) habits. These individual habits are especially noticeable in three words of very frequent occurence, *do/doe*, *go/goe*, and *here/heere*; but they affect many other words too. The division of work between compositors depended upon the sequence and distribution of the manufacturing process, and can sometimes be very complicated; anyone interested in current hypotheses about the shares of compositors in the texts printed here will find this information in *William Shakespeare: A Textual Companion*. Elizabethan printing techniques influenced spellings in other ways, too. Compositors needed to 'justify' line lengths so as to produce a regular right-hand margin, in passages of prose; when setting verse, they often tried to fit lines into a single type-line, rather than producing an unsightly turn-over. If the spelling of his copy, or his own spelling preferences, would produce too long or too short a line, he felt free to insert extra letters (such as a final *e* or a doubled consonant), to omit letters, or to use an abbreviation such as &, y^t ('that'), y^e ('the'), *and the tilde* (*a line over a vowel indicating an omitted nasal, e.g. frõ*). A compositor might also occasionally find himself 'out of sorts', i.e. with an inadequate supply of the types required for his text; in those circumstances he might substitute another reasonably appropriate letter for the one which he found in his manuscript.

Spelling was also influenced by the shape of individual pieces of type. For instance, in this italic setting of the playwright's own name, taken from the First Folio—

Shakeſpeare.

—both the 'k' and the medial 'ſ' are kerned: that is, elements of the letter extend off above or below other letters in the line. If we removed the medial 'e' between these two consonants, the forward kern of the 'k' would collide with the backward kern of the 'ſ', and result in bending or breakage of the types. Such accidents could be prevented by inserting a filler: in this case, either an 'e' or a hyphen. Similar expedients could affect other words, particularly in italic founts, where the number of kerning letters was greater than in roman.

This catalogue of the agents and causes of interference makes it clear that Shakespeare's own orthography has been obscured and overlaid in the printed texts. Nevertheless, Shakespeare's own spelling does sometimes clearly survive the process of transmission from manuscript into print. As already noted, passages in a foreign language were probably disturbed very little; elisions and syncopations also probably originated with the author. For the general pattern of Shakespearian orthography, the early quartos printed from his own manuscripts are the most reliable guides. More specifically, for a few words we can be virtually certain of Shakespeare's spelling. Thus, the very unusual spelling of *silence* with an initial *sc* occurs in two early Shakespeare quartos, prepared by different printers: often in *The second parte of Henry the fourth*, once in *Troylus and Cressida* (1703). In the latter instance, the spelling was sophisticated by a proof-reader, who 'corrected' the anomalous *sc* to *s*; we can be sure that a similar fate overtook many other occurrences of the odd spelling—and, in general, the more unusual a spelling the more likely that it originated

The Tragedie of Hamlet

Lord. The King, and Queene, and all are comming downe.

Ham. In happy time.

Lord. The Queene desires you to vse some gentle entertainment   3
to *Laertes*, before you fall to play.   4

Ham. Shee well instructs me.   5

Hora. You will loose my Lord.

Ham. I doe not thinke so, since he went into France, I haue bene
in continuall practise, I shall winne at the ods; thou would'st not
thinke how ill all's heere about my hart, but it is no matter.   9

Hora. Nay good my Lord.

Ham. It is but foolery, but it is such a kinde of gamgiuing, as
would perhapes trouble a woman.

Hora. If your minde dislike any thing, obay it. I will forstal their
repaire hether, and say you are not fit.

Ham. Not a whit, we desie augury, there is speciall prouidence in
the fall of a Sparrowe, if it be, tis not to come, if it be not to come,   16
it will be now, if it be not now, yet it well come, the readines is all,
since no man of ought he leaues, knowes what ist to leaue betimes,
let be.

A table prepard, Trumpets, Drums and officers with Cushions,
King, Queene, and all the state, Foiles, daggers,
and Laertes.

King. Come *Hamlet*, come and take this hand from me.

Ham. Giue me your pardon sir, I haue done you wrong,
But pardon't as you are a gentleman, this presence knowes,
And you must needs haue heard, how I am punnisht
With a sore distraction, what I haue done
That might your nature, honor, and exception
Roughly awake, I heare proclame was madnesse,   29
Wast *Hamlet* wronged *Laertes*? neuer *Hamlet*.
If *Hamlet* from himselfe be tane away,
And when hee's not himselfe, dooes wrong *Laertes*,
Then *Hamlet* dooes it not, *Hamlet* denies it,
Who dooes it then? his madnesse. Ift be so,
Hamlet is of the faction that is wronged,
His madnesse is poore *Hamlets* enimie,
Let my disclaiming from a puipos'd euill,
Free me so farre in your most generous thoughts
That I haue shot my arrowe ore the house

And

10. Features of the printing of Shakespeare's time illustrated in this page from the 1604 quarto of *Hamlet* include: fully justified lines (such as line 3); variable spelling: 'heere' in line 9, 'heare' in line 29; the use of italic type for proper names (e.g. *Laertes*, line 4) and for the stage direction; the layout of stage directions; catchwords (the bottom line); abbreviated speech-prefixes; capitalization of common nouns (*Cushions* and *Foiles* in the stage direction, 'Sparrowe' in line 16); light punctuation (such as the many commas in Hamlet's long speech where we should use full stops); ligatures (e.g. 'instructs', line 5); 'v' for initial 'u' and long s (e.g. 'use', line 3).

with the author rather than the compositor. Thus, all three occurrences of the word *summit* in the Shakespeare canon take the form *somnet* (*Hamlet* 600, 2134; *The Tragedie of King Lear* 2264), an anomalous spelling not recorded elsewhere by the *Oxford English Dictionary* and—as yet—not noted by scholars in any other works of the period. For other words Shakespeare's spelling is apparently less anomalous, but we can be reasonably sure of it none the less. For instance, in all of the early quarto editions in which it appears *culled* is spelled *culd* (*Titus Andronicus* 1443; *Loues labors lost* 1474, 1690; *Romeo and Iuliet* 2356); the alternative form *cull'd* appears only much later, in the 1623 Folio, where it conforms to that edition's strong preference for the apostrophe in elided past participial inflections: *Henry the Sixt* 2206 (probably not by Shakespeare), *King Iohn* 2244 (set from a scribal manuscript), and *Henry the fift* 1026. For other words, we can identify Shakespearian spellings by other means. Compositors in general are more likely to interfere with common words, for which they have settled conventions, than for rare or unfamiliar ones. Thus, both *mobled* (*Hamlet* 1434-6) and *arint* (*Historie of King Lear* 1736) appear to be Warwickshire dialect words, which Shakespeare introduced into literary English; the spellings of both words are almost certainly authorial. In other cases, we can infer a manuscript spelling because the compositor has apparently misread the word, allowing us to reconstruct the manuscript form which misled him. Thus, although the authoritative 1604 quarto edition of *Hamlet* three times has *mobled*, in the Folio a compositor by contrast set *inobled*, which is clearly an error: the unfamiliarity of the word apparently led him to misinterpret the three strokes of *m* as the three strokes of *in*. The 1623 compositor's error thus confirms the testimony of the 1604 edition, that Shakespeare spelled the word *mobled*. It is to be hoped that the availability of a critical old-spelling edition, in conjunction with the *Textual Companion*, will make it easier to identify such patterns of Shakespearian orthography.

A potential problem for the modern reader of old-spelling texts is the use of punctuation marks, which seems to be both inconsistent and occasionally even completely random. Again, it is clear from the discrepancies between manuscripts and printed texts, or between first editions and reprints, that printers did not follow copy in punctuation any more than in spelling, so that it is dangerous to place too much reliance on punctuation (as some scholars have done) as an indication of the author's directions for dramatic pauses at— sometimes—unexpected places in the text. With spelling it is possible to make some headway in isolating Shakespeare's own practice, because we can analyse the treatment of individual words in different kinds of editions; but no such method can identify for us which particular pieces of punctuation are authorial.

In 1600, pauses could be marked by full stop, comma, colon and semicolon. Both the comma (replacing from about 1530 the *virgule* or short stroke) and the semicolon were sixteenth-century innovations, the latter being first recorded in an English text in the late 1530s, but not used regularly until the second half of the century. In medieval manuscripts punctuation marks did indeed indicate pause (and sometimes intonation), for the benefit of those reading aloud to a (usually) illiterate audience; by the early seventeenth century, the commonest marks had come to indicate, rather, the grammatical structure of the sentence, for improved comprehension by an increasingly literate readership. Naturally enough, pause and grammatical structure often coincided, and even at the present day it is not always possible to differentiate between them as a reason for punctuation. In the early seventeenth century, it was apparently the case that if the author's manuscript was lightly punctuated (as was 'Hand D' in *Sir Thomas Moore*) the compositor felt free to insert additional punctuation, some compositors being obviously more eager to do so than others. In general, the later the edition the heavier its punctuation, so that plays printed in the

Folio (1623) are much further from the author's pointing than the quartos of the 1590s. The difference may be observed particularly in *Titus Andronicus*, where Sc. 7 is added in the Folio to a text originally printed in 1594; the same thing happens in *Richard the second*, where 1976-2140.1 are taken from the Folio, and the remainder of the text from the quarto edition of 1597. In other cases it can be shown that certain compositors favoured particular punctuation marks: for instance, one compositor who helped set up the Folio had a special fondness for semicolons, which can be seen in parts of *All is true*; and the two compositors of the Sonnets differ in their manner of punctuating the ends of quatrains. We can therefore draw few specific interpretative conclusions about Shakespeare's practice from the punctuation which we find in the printed text, unless it is so abnormal that we might suspect that the compositor could do no more than follow an incomprehensible copy.

Conventions for the use of question and exclamation marks seem to have been different in Shakespearian texts; sentences such as 'Will I liue' (*Shrew* 721) are followed by a question mark, although in fact they are intended as exclamations. Likewise, exclamations beginning with an interrogative word as in 'How lovely it is!' might also be followed by question marks, possibly because the exclamation mark, at least in its modern form, was a fairly recent innovation, described by John Hart in 1569 as the 'admiratiue', and by Shakespeare (*Winters Tale* 2697) as a 'note of admiration'.

The apostrophe (or 'apostraphus', *Loues labors lost* 1197) was derived, as its name indicates, from Greek classical usage; not until the later sixteenth century was it found in English texts, where it was used by the 'more learned' printers like Richard Field, as Alexander Hume remarks in his manuscript grammar of English (*c.*1612). Hume points out that the apostrophe marks the omission of a vowel within a word, especially in verse e.g. *grug'd*, *dispatch'd*, or the omission of a vowel between two words, e.g. *th'ingrate*, *I s'it*, (*I see it*); and Thomas Campion, in his *Obseruations in the Art of English Poesie* (1602), points out the necessity of such elisions 'to auoid the hollowness and gaping in our verse, as *to* and *the*, *t'inchaunt*, *th'inchaunter*, or may be vsd at pleasure, as for *let vs*, to say *let's*'. Writing a grammar of English in the 1620s, Ben Jonson describes an apostrophe as 'an affection of words coupled, and joyned together' and 'the rejecting of a Vowell from the beginning, or ending of a Word'; but he regrets that 'through the negligence of Writers and Printers' it is often omitted. He gives several examples in his grammar, and frequently uses the apostrophe himself in his dramatic works, whether combining both 'omitted' vowel and an apostrophe, as in *to'vndoe*, *glory'inough*, or omitting the vowel altogether, as in *th'outward* and *to't*.

Examples of Shakespeare's usage in marking unstressed pronouns and prepositions have already been given; and other cases where he frequently denotes elision are in past participles and past tenses, although a syllable often remains because of the phonetic context, as in modern English *wanted*, *wicked*, and *assuredly*. But in other cases, where modern pronunciation insists upon two syllables, Elizabethan pronunciation allowed for either one or two: thus, *crooked* could be written (and apparently pronounced, if we are to trust the verse) as *crook'd* or *crookt* (*Richard Duke of Yorke* 2843, *The second part of Henry the fourth* 2638, *Cymbeline* 1226). The adjectives *ag'd* and *learn'd* could also be monosyllabic. Shakespearian examples of elision include such forms as *look'd*, *mark'd*, and the vowel in the verb inflection *est*, where he writes, for example, *liu'st*. It is clear that Elizabethan English had a choice, for metrical reasons, which is not now open to us, so that Shakespeare could use, for example, *desir'd* or *desired* as he needed; sometimes the spelling, rather than the apostrophe, indicated which form was metrically appropriate (e.g. *talkt*). The early editions are for the most part reliable in indicating orthographically whether *ed* or *est* should be syllabic, with certain recurring exceptions: if the stem of a verb ended with a vowel or a silent consonant (e.g. *follow*) the inflection was normally spelled out in full, even when elided; the same licence also often applied when the word occurred at the end of a verse line.

The early appearance of genitive *'s* is found in Crane's transcripts, e.g. *odd's, it's* (not *its*), and with names ending in a vowel. At other times the apostrophe is used illogically: we find for example, *applau'd*, and other verbs with final *s, d* or *t* as well as *dos't, go'st* and *endu'rd*. Sometimes grammatically illogical forms are logical, from a printer's point of view. For certain frequently combined letters, especially if one or more of the letters is kerned— ct, fi, fl, ff, ffi, ffl, fi, fl, ft, ffi, ffl—printers made use of a ligature: a single piece of type which contained more than one letter. Except where they may affect pronunciation (as in the vowel combinations æ and œ), such ligatures have not been reproduced in this edition, though they are indicated in the textual notes of *William Shakespeare: A Textual Companion*. But such typographical conventions do account for odd forms like *accur'ſt* and *expre'ſt*, where in the early editions the two final letters *ſt* were printed from a single piece of type, so that the apostrophe was inserted before (rather than after) the ſ.

Other punctuation marks of some interest, because they seem to denote that the text has been transmitted through a professional scribe, are parentheses and hyphens. It is clear from his signed transcripts that Crane used parentheses very frequently, particularly in marking off vocatives and exclamations e.g. *what* (*the dickins*); and he frequently used single hyphens in what he took (incorrectly) to be compound words, e.g. *viza-ments, put-off, tall-fellowes*. Although we can never be certain about individual instances, it is clear from the early editions closest to Shakespeare's manuscripts that Shakespeare himself made relatively little use of parentheses, hyphens, or apostrophes.

Three conventions of Elizabethan punctuation may actively confuse a modern reader. First, brackets were sometimes treated as the equivalent of commas or dashes: that is, a parenthesis can be opened without ever being closed (*Cymbeline* 2861), or closed without being opened (2495). Second, Shakespeare and his contemporaries made extensive use of proverbs and sententiae, and adopted the 'gnomic pointing' common in medieval manuscripts to draw attention to them. The most popular method was to place double inverted commas at the beginning of the sententiae, as can be seen frequently in *Lucrece* and occasionally in *Hamlet* and *Troylus and Cressida*: to a modern reader, this looks like the opening of a quotation which never ends. Alternatively, double commas might be placed before the sententiae (*Troylus and Cressida* 427, 429), or single inverted commas (*Hamlet* 2573-6); or the phrase might be set off in a distinct typeface (Preface to *Othello*); or italics and double inverted commas could be combined (*Troylus and Cressida* 433; *The second part of Henry the fourth* 609). Also worth comment is the occasional use of a comma where later editors feel the need for a hyphen, e.g. *actiue, valiant* and *well, aimd* (*The Hystorie of Henry the fourth* 2586, 593). Shakespeare probably intended these to be understood as compounds: *actiue-valiant* and *well-aimd*. The use of commas in such cases may result from compositorial error, for if the manuscript was unpunctuated the compositor would have to decide for himself how to interpret the juxtaposition of the two words. This task would have been made more difficult by the frequent identity of form in Elizabethan English of adjectives and adverbs (compare Modern English *fast*). On the other hand, it seems to us more likely that Shakespeare himself in such cases used a comma as the equivalent of a hyphen: in *Hamlet* he wrote that peace should 'stand a Comma tweene their amities' (3310), in which most commentators understand 'Comma' to mean 'connecting link'. Although the interpretation of that passage, and of such commas in compounds, will no doubt remain a matter of dispute, in accordance with their generally conservative policy in these matters the editors have left such commas intact in this edition, to enable readers and scholars to decide for themselves their significance.

Finally, the modern reader will note differences from current practice in the use of italics and capitals. It was usual in the manuscript tradition to employ different forms of script to emphasize a word; in particular, the native Elizabethan 'secretary' hand incorporated items in the more legible 'italic' recently introduced from Italy. Shakespeare's printers used italics for several reasons; for personal names like *Tranio* and *Ouid*, place-names like *Florence*, and animal names like *Meriman*, *Siluer* and *Clowder*; for quotations from other languages, e.g. *Paucas pallabris*; for emphasis, e.g. *Alce Madam* or *Ione Madam* (*The Taming of the Shrew*), where it is clear that the personal names must be stressed by the actor; and to make formal distinctions, as with letters or songs. Very rarely, an unusual word, such as a recent borrowing from Latin, might be printed in italics, e.g. *interim* (*Henry V* 2765, etc.). But for all these features practice varied between printers, and between different compositors employed by the same printers.

In the use of capitals, printed texts continue the manuscript tradition of denoting paragraphs, sentences and proper nouns by initial capitals. But Shakespeare's printers (especially in the Folio) are moving in the direction of capitalizing all nouns; by the eighteenth century the system was roughly what it is now in German today. It is difficult to discern any consistent practice in capitalization of the Quartos and the Folio; practice varied considerably between individual compositors.

No brief account of late sixteenth- and early seventeenth-century spelling can attempt to deal with a related but highly controversial issue—the extent to which it accurately represented the pronunciation of Shakespeare and his contemporaries. Some attempt was obviously made at a phonetic representation, both by the dramatist and his printers, where national, regional and foreign forms of English were concerned; otherwise, the printed text was a conventionalized spelling system representing whatever standardized form of English was acceptable and comprehensible on the London stage. Even if we knew how to reproduce it now, the effect might be no more than comic; but to follow as closely as possible the printed word which Shakespeare knew is an altogether different matter. Once aware of the spelling conventions, present-day readers can judge for themselves the meaning of the forms which Shakespeare and his fellow actors found appropriate in a printed text, unaffected by the cumulative modernizations of generations of editors, and it is hoped that literary critics, linguists and the general reader will appreciate the opportunity to study the texts as they appeared to their predecessors nearly four centuries ago. Seeing the body of Shakespeare's work in the orthography of his own era should, if nothing else, remind us that Shakespeare is of an age, as well as for all time.

VIVIAN SALMON

COMMENDATORY POEMS AND PREFACES (1599–1640)

Ad Gulielmum Shakespeare

Honie-tong'd *Shakespeare* when I saw thine issue
I swore *Apollo* got them and none other,
Their rosie-tainted features cloth'd in tissue,
Some heauen born goddesse said to be their mother:
Rose-cheekt *Adonis* with his amber tresses,
Faire fire-hot *Venus* charming him to loue her,
Chaste *Lucretia* virgine-like her dresses,
Prowd lust-stung *Tarquine* seeking still to proue her:
Romeo Richard; more whose names I know not,
10 Their sugred tongues, and power attractiue beuty
Say they are Saints althogh that Sts they shew not
For thousands vowes to them subiectiue dutie:
They burn in loue thy childrē *Shakespear* het thē,
Go, wo thy Muse more Nymphish brood beget them.

Iohn Weeuer, *Epigrammes* (1599)

A neuer writer, to an euer reader. Newes

*Eternall reader, you haue heere a new play, neuer stal'd with the Stage, neuer clapper-clawd with the palmes of the vulger, and yet passing full of the palme comicall; for it is a birth of y*ᵗ *braine, that neuer vnder-tooke any thing commicall, vainely: And were but the vaine names of commedies changde for the titles of Commodities, or of Playes for Pleas; you should see all those grand censors, that now stile them such vanities, flock to them for the maine grace of their grauities:
especially this authors Commedies, that are so fram'd to the*
10 *life, that they serue for the most common Commentaries, of all the actions of our liues, shewing such a dexteritie, and power of witte, that the most displeased with Playes, are pleasd with his Commedies. And all such dull and heauy-witted worldlings, as were neuer capable of the witte of a Commedie, comming by report of them to his representations, haue found that witte there, that they neuer found in them-selues, and haue parted better wittied then they came: feeling an edge of witte set vpon them, more then euer they dreamd they had braine to grinde it on. So much and such sauored salt of witte*
20 *is in his Commedies, that they seeme (for their height of pleasure) to be borne in that sea that brought forth* Venus. *Amongst all there is none more witty then this: And had I time I would comment vpon it, though I know it needs not, (for so much as will make you thinke your testerne well bestowd) but for so much worth, as euen poore I know to be*

stuft *in it. It deserues such a labour, as well as the best Commedy in* Terence *or* Plautus. *And beleeue this, that when hee is gone, and his Commedies out of sale, you will scramble for them, and set vp a new English Inquisition. Take this for a warning, and at the perrill of your pleasures losse, and* 30 *Iudgements, refuse not, nor like this the lesse, for not being sullied, with the smoaky breath of the multitude; but thanke fortune for the scape it hath made amongst you. Since by the grand possessors wills I beleeue you should haue prayd for them rather then beene prayd. And so I leaue all such to bee prayd for (for the states of their wits healths)*
that will not praise it.
Vale.

Anonymous, in *Troylus and Cressida* (1609)

To our English Terence, Mʳ. Will: Shake-speare

Some say (good *Will* which I, in sport, do sing)
Had'st thou not plaid some Kingly parts in sport,
Thou hadst bin a companion for a *King*;
And, beene a King among the meaner sort.
Some others raile; but, raile as they thinke fit,
Thou hast no rayling; but, a raigning Wit:
  And honesty *thou sow'st*, which they do reape;
  So, to increase their Stocke which they do keepe.

Iohn Dauies, *The Scourge of Folly* (1610)

To Master W. Shakespeare

Shakespeare, that nimble *Mercury* thy braine,
Lulls many hundred *Argus*-eyes asleepe,
So fit, for all thou fashionest thy vaine,
At th'*horse-foote* fountaine thou hast drunk full deepe,
Vertues or vices theame to thee all one is:
Who loues chaste life, there's *Lucrece* for a Teacher:
Who list read lust there's *Venus* and *Adonis*,
True modell of a most lasciuious leatcher.
Besides in plaies thy wit windes like *Meander*:
Whence needy new-composers borrow more   10
Then *Terence* doth from *Plautus* or *Menander*.
But to praise thee aright I want thy store:
  Then let thine owne works thine owne worth vpraise,
  And help t'adorne thee with deserued Baies.

Thomas Freeman, *Runne and a Great Cast* (1614)

Inscriptions vpon the Shakespeare Monument, Stratford vpon Auon

IVDICIO PYLIVM, GENIO SOCRATEM, ARTE MARONEM,
TERRA TEGIT, POPVLVS MÆRET, OLYMPVS HABET.

STAY PASSENGER, WHY GOEST THOV BY SO FAST?
READ IF THOV CANST, WHOM ENVIOVS DEATH HATH PLAST,
WITH IN THIS MONVMENT SHAKSPEARE WITH WHOME
QVICK NATURE DIDE: WHOSE NAME DOTH DECK Yˢ TOMBE
FAR MORE THEN COST: SITH ALL, Yᵗ HE HATH WRITT,
LEAVES LIVING ART, BVT PAGE, TO SERVE HIS WITT.

OBIIT ANO DOⁱ 1616
ÆTATIS, 53. DIE 23 AP.

———

On the death of William Shakespeare

Renowned *Spenser* lie a thought more nigh
To learned *Chauser*, and rare *Beaumount* lie
A little neerer *Spenser*, to make roome,
For *Shakespeare* in your three-fold, foure-fold Tombe;
To lodge all foure in one bed make a shift,
Vntill Doomes-day, for hardly will a fift
Betwixt this day and that by Fate be slaine,
For whom your Curtaines need be drawne againe.
But if precedencie in death doth barre,
A fourth place in your sacred Sepulchre,
Vnder this carved Marble of thine owne,
Sleepe rare Tragedian *Shakespeare*, sleepe alone;
Thy unmolested peace, unshared Cave,
Possesse as Lord, not Tennant of thy Grave.
That unto us, or others it may be,
Honour hereafter to be laid by thee.

William Basse (*c.*1616–22), in Shakespeare's
Poems (1640)

———

The Stationer to the Reader
(in *The Tragœdy of Othello*, 1622)

*To set forth a booke without an Epistle, were like to the old
English prouerbe, A blew coat without a badge, & the
Author being dead, I thought good to take that piece of worke
vpon mee: To commend it, I will not, for that which is good,
I hope euery man will commend, without intreaty: and I am
the bolder, because the Authors name is sufficient to vent his
worke. Thus leauing euery one to the liberty of iudgement: I
haue ventered to print this Play, and leaue it to the generall
censure.*

Yours,
Thomas Walkley.

The Epistle Dedicatorie
(in *Comedies, Histories, & Tragedies*, 1623)

TO THE MOST NOBLE
AND
INCOMPARABLE PAIRE
OF BRETHREN

WILLIAM
Earle of Pembroke, &c. Lord Chamberlaine to the
Kings most Excellent Maiesty.

AND

PHILIP
Earle of Montgomery, &c. Gentleman of his Maiesties
Bed-Chamber. Both Knights of the most Noble Order
of the Garter, and our singular good
LORDS.

Right Honourable,

*Whilst we studie to be thankful in our particular, for the
many fauors we haue receiued from your L.L we are falne
vpon the ill fortune, to mingle two the most diuerse things
that can bee, feare, and rashnesse; rashnesse in the enterprize,
and feare of the success. For, when we valew the places your
H.H. sustaine, we cannot but know their dignity greater, then
to descend to the reading of these trifles: and, while we name
them trifles, we haue depriu'd our selues of the defence of our
Dedication. But since your L.L. haue beene pleas'd to thinke
these trifles some-thing, heeretofore; and haue prosequuted
both them, and their Authour liuing, with so much fauour:
we hope, that (they out-liuing him, and he not hauing the
fate, common with some, to be exequutor to his owne writings)
you will vse the like indulgence toward them, you haue done
vnto their parent. There is a great difference, whether any
Booke choose his Patrones, or finde them: This hath done
both. For, so much were your L.L. likings of the seuerall
parts, when they were acted, as before they were published,
the Volume ask'd to be yours. We haue but collected them,
and done an office to the dead, to procure his Orphanes,
Guardians; without ambition either of selfe-profit, or fame:
onely to keepe the memory of so worthy a Friend, & Fellow
aliue, as was our SHAKESPEARE, by humble offer of his playes,
to your most noble patronage. Wherein, as we haue iustly
obserued, no man to come neere your L.L. but with a kind of
religious addresse; it hath bin the height of our care, who
are the Presenters, to make the present worthy of your H.H.
by the perfection. But, there we must also craue our abilities
to be considerd, my Lords. We cannot go beyond our owne
powers. Country hands reach foorth milke, creame, fruites,
or what they haue: and many Nations (we haue heard) that
had not gummes & incense, obtained their requests with a
leauened Cake. It was no fault to approch their Gods, by what
meanes they could: And the most, though meanest, of things
are made more precious, when they are dedicated to Temples.*

50 *In that name therefore, we most humbly consecrate to your*
H.H. these remaines of your seruant Shakespeare; *that what*
delight is in them, may be euer your L.L. the reputation his,
& the faults ours, if any be committed, by a payre so carefull
to shew their gratitude both to the liuing, and the dead, as
is

> Your Lordshippes most bounden,
> IOHN HEMINGE.
> HENRY CONDELL.

To the great Variety of Readers

From the most able, to him that can but spell: There you
are number'd. We had rather you were weighd. Especially,
when the fate of all Bookes depends vpon your capacities:
and not of your heads alone, but of your purses. Well! It
is now publique, & you wil stand for your priuiledges wee
know: to read, and censure. Do so, but buy it first. That
doth best commend a Booke, the Stationer saies. Then,
how odde soeuer your braines be, or your wisedomes,
make your licence the same, and spare not. Iudge your
10 sixe-pen'orth, your shillings worth, your fiue shillings
worth at a time, or higher, so you rise to the iust rates,
and welcome. But, what euer you do, Buy. Censure will
not driue a Trade, or make the Iacke go. And though
you be a Magistrate of wit, and sit on the Stage at
Black-Friers, or the *Cock-pit*, to arraigne Playes dailie,
know, these Playes haue had their triall alreadie, and
stood out all Appeales; and do now come forth quitted
rather by a Decree of Court, then any purchas'd Letters
of commendation.
20   It had bene a thing, we confesse, worthie to haue bene
wished, that the Author himselfe had liu'd to haue set
forth, and ouerseen his owne writings; But since it hath
bin ordain'd otherwise, and he by death departed from
that right, we pray you do not envie his Friends, the
office of their care, and paine, to haue collected & publish'd
them; and so to haue publish'd them, as where (before)
you were abus'd with diuerse stolne, and surreptitious
copies, maimed, and deformed by the frauds and stealthes
of iniurious impostors, that expos'd them: euen those,
30 are now offer'd to your view cur'd, and perfect of their
limbes; and all the rest, absolute in their numbers, as he
conceiued thē. Who, as he was a happie imitator of
Nature, was a most gentle expresser of it. His mind and
hand went together: And what he thought, he vttered
with that easinesse, that wee haue scarse receiued from
him a blot in his papers. But it is not our prouince, who
onely gather his works, and giue them you, to praise
him. It is yours that reade him. And there we hope, to
your diuers capacities, you will finde enough, both to
40 draw, and hold you: for his wit can no more lie hid, then
it could be lost. Reade him, therefore; and againe, and
againe: And if then you doe not like him, surely you are
in some manifest danger, not to vnderstand him. And so
we leaue you to other of his Friends, whom if you need,
can bee your guides: if you neede them not, you can

leade your selues, and others. And such Readers we wish
him.

> Iohn Heminge, Henrie Condell, in *Comedies, Histories,*
> *& Tragedies* (1623)

To the memory of my beloued,
The AVTHOR
MR. WILLIAM SHAKESPEARE:
AND
what he hath left vs

To draw no enuy (Shakespeare) *on thy name,*
  Am I thus ample to thy Booke, and Fame:
While I confesse thy writings to be such,
  As neither Man, *nor* Muse, *can praise too much.*
'Tis true, and all mens suffrage. But these wayes
  Were not the paths I meant vnto thy praise:
For seeliest Ignorance on these may light,
  Which, when it sounds at best, but eccho's right;
Or blinde Affection, which doth ne're aduance
  The truth, but gropes, and vrgeth all by chance;   10
Or crafty Malice, might pretend this praise,
  And thinke to ruine, where it seem'd to raise.
These are, as some infamous Baud, or Whore,
  Should praise a Matron. What could hurt her more?
But thou art proofe against them, and indeed
  Aboue th'ill fortune of them, or the need.
I, therefore will begin. Soule of the Age!
  The applause! delight! the wonder of our Stage!
My Shakespeare, *rise; I will not lodge thee by*
  Chaucer, *or* Spenser, *or bid* Beaumont *lye*   20
A little further, to make thee a roome:
  Thou art a Moniment, without a tombe,
And art aliue still, while thy Booke doth liue,
  And we haue wits to read, and praise to giue.
That I not mixe thee so, my braine excuses;
  I meane with great, but disproportion'd Muses:
For, if I thought my iudgement were of yeeres,
  I should commit thee surely with thy peeres,
And tell, how farre thou didst our Lily *out-shine,*
  Or sporting Kid, *or* Marlowes *mighty line.*   30
And though thou hadst small Latine, *and lesse* Greeke,
  From thence to honour thee, I would not seeke
For names; but call forth thund'ring Æschilus,
  Euripides, *and* Sophocles *to vs,*
Paccuuius, Accius, *him of* Cordoua *dead,*
  To life againe, to heare thy Buskin tread,
And shake a Stage: Or, when thy Sockes were on,
  Leaue thee alone, for the comparison
Of all, that insolent Greece, *or haughtie* Rome
  Sent forth, or since did from their ashes come.
Triúmph, my Britaine, *thou hast one to showe,*   40
  To whom all Scenes of Europe *homage owe.*
He was not of an age, but for all time!
  And all the Muses still were in their prime,
When like Apollo *he came forth to warme*
  Our eares, or like a Mercury *to charme!*

Nature her selfe was proud of his designes,
  And ioy'd to weare the dressing of his lines!
Which were so richly spun, and wouen so fit,
50 *As, since, she will vouchsafe no other Wit.*
The merry Greeke, tart Aristophanes,
  Neat Terence, witty Plautus, now not please;
But antiquated, and deserted lye
  As they were not of Natures family.
Yet must I not giue Nature all: Thy Art,
  My gentle Shakespeare, must enioy a part.
For though the Poets matter, Nature be,
  His Art doth giue the fashion. And, that he,
Who casts to write a liuing line, must sweat,
60 *(Such as thine are) and strike the second heat*
Vpon the Muses anuile: turne the same,
  (And himselfe with it) that he thinkes to frame;
Or for the lawrell, he may gaine a scorne,
  For a good Poet's made, as well as borne.
And such wert thou. Looke how the fathers face
  Liues in his issue, euen so, the race
Of Shakespeares minde, and manners brightly shines
  In his well torned, and true-filed lines:
In each of which, he seemes to shake a Lance,
70 *As brandish't at the eyes of Ignorance.*
Sweet Swan of Auon! what a sight it were
  To see thee in our waters yet appeare,
And make those flights vpon the bankes of Thames,
  That so did take Eliza, and our James!
But stay, I see thee in the Hemisphere
  Aduanc'd, and made a Constellation there!
Shine forth, thou Starre of Poets, and with rage,
  Or influence, chide, or cheere the drooping Stage;
Which, since thy flight frō hence, hath mourn'd like night,
80 *And despaires day, but for thy Volumes light.*

Ben Ionson, in *Comedies, Histories, & Tragedies*
(1623)

Vpon the Lines and Life of the Famous
Scenicke Poet, Master WILLIAM
SHAKESPEARE

Those hands, which you so clapt, go now, and wring
You *Britaines* braue; for done are *Shakespeares* dayes;
His dayes are done, that made the dainty Playes,
Which made the Globe of heau'n and earth to ring.
Dry'de is that veine, dry'd is the *Thespian* Spring,
Turn'd all to teares, and *Phœbus* clouds his rayes:
That corp's, that coffin now besticke those bayes,
Which crown'd him *Poet* first, then *Poets* King.
If *Tragedies* might any *Prologue* haue,
10 All those he made, would scarse make one to this:
Where *Fame*, now that he gone is to the graue
(Deaths publique tyring-house) the *Nuncius* is.
  For though his line of life went soone about,
  The life yet of his lines shall neuer out.

Hugh Holland, in *Comedies, Histories, & Tragedies*
(1623)

TO THE MEMORIE
of the deceased Authour Maister
W. SHAKESPEARE

Shake-speare, at length thy pious fellowes giue
The world thy Workes: thy Workes, by which, out-liue
Thy Tombe, thy name must; when that stone is rent,
And Time dissolues thy Stratford Moniment,
Here we aliue shall view thee still. This Booke,
When Brasse and Marble fade, shall make thee looke
Fresh to all Ages: when Posteritie
Shall loath what's new, thinke all is prodegie
That is not Shake-speares; eu'ry Line, each Verse
Here shall reuiue, redeeme thee from thy Herse. 10
Nor Fire, nor cankring Age, as Naso said,
Of his, thy wit-fraught Booke shall once inuade.
Nor shall I e're beleeue, or thinke thee dead
(Though mist) vntill our bankrout Stage be sped
(Impossible) with some new straine t'outdo
Passions of Iuliet, and her Romeo;
Or till I heare a Scene more nobly take,
Then when thy half-Sword parlying Romans spake.
Till these, till any of thy Volumes rest
Shall with more fire, more feeling be exprest, 20
Be sure, our Shake-speare, thou canst neuer dye,
But crown'd with Lawrell, liue eternally.

Leonard Digges, in *Comedies, Histories, & Tragedies*
(1623)

To the memorie of M. W. Shake-speare

Wee wondred (Shake-speare) that thou went'st so soone
From the Worlds-Stage, to the Graues-Tyring-roome.
Wee thought thee dead, but this thy printed worth,
Tels thy Spectators, that thou went'st but forth
To enter with applause. An Actors Art,
Can dye, and liue, to acte a second part.
That's but an Exit of Mortalitie;
This, a Re-entrance to a Plaudite.

Iames Mabbe, in *Comedies, Histories, & Tragedies*
(1623)

The Names of the Principall Actors
in all these Playes

William Shakespeare.	*Samuel Gilburne.*
Richard Burbadge.	*Robert Armin.*
John Hemmings.	*William Ostler.*
Augustine Phillips.	*Nathan Field.*
William Kempe.	*Iohn Vnderwood.*
Thomas Poope.	*Nicholas Tooley.*
George Bryan.	*William Ecclestone.*
Henry Condell.	*Ioseph Taylor.*
William Slye.	*Robert Benfield.*
Richard Cowly.	*Robert Goughe.*
Iohn Lowine.	*Richard Robinson.*
Samuell Crosse.	*Iohn Shancke.*
Alexander Cooke.	*Iohn Rice.*

In *Comedies, Histories, & Tragedies* (1623)

An Epitaph on the admirable Dramaticke Poet,
W. SHAKESPEARE

What neede my Shakespeare for his honour'd bones,
The labour of an Age, in piled stones
Or that his hallow'd Reliques should be hid
Vnder a starre-ypointing Pyramid?
Deare Sonne of Memory, great Heire of Fame,
What needst thou such dull witnesse of thy Name?
Thou in our wonder and astonishment
Hast built thy selfe a lasting Monument:
For whil'st to th' shame of slow-endevouring Art
Thy easie numbers flow, and that each hart,
Hath from the leaves of thy unvalued Booke,
Those Delphicke Lines with deepe Impression tooke
Then thou our fancy of her selfe bereaving,
Dost make us Marble with too much conceiving,
And so Sepulcher'd in such pompe dost lie
That Kings for such a Tombe would wish to die.

Iohn Milton (1630), in *Comedies, Histories, & Tragedies*
(1632)

Vpon the Effigies of my worthy
Friend, the Author Master William
Shakespeare, and his Workes

Spectator, this Lifes Shaddow is; To see
The truer image and a livelier he
Turne Reader. But, observe his Comicke vaine,
Laugh, and proceed next to a Tragicke straine,
Then weepe; So when thou find'st two contraries,
Two different passions from thy rapt soule rise,
Say, (who alone effect such wonders could)
Rare Shake-speare to the life thou dost behold.

Anonymous, in *Comedies, Histories, & Tragedies* (1632)

On Worthy Master Shake-
speare and his Poems

A Mind reflecting ages past, whose cleere
And equall surface can make things appeare
Distant a Thousand yeares, and represent
Them in their lively colours just extent.
To out run hasty time, retrive the fates,
Rowle backe the heavens, blow ope the iron gates
Of death and Lethe, where (confused) lye
Great heapes of ruinous mortalitie.
In that deepe duskie dungeon to discerne
A royall Ghost from Churles; By art to learne
The Physiognomie of shades, and give
Them suddaine birth, wondring how oft they live.
What story coldly tells, what Poets faine
At second hand, and picture without braine
Senselesse and soulelesse showes. To give a Stage
(Ample and true with life) voyce, action, age,
As Plato's yeare and new Scene of the world

Them unto us, or us to them had hurld.
To raise our auncient Soveraignes from their herse
Make Kings his subjects, by exchanging verse 20
Enlive their pale trunkes, that the present age
Ioyes in their joy, and trembles at their rage:
Yet so to temper passion, that our eares
Take pleasure in their paine; And eyes in teares
Both weepe and smile; fearefull at plots so sad,
Then laughing at our feare; abus'd, and glad
To be abus'd, affected with that truth
Which we perceive is false; pleas'd in that ruth
At which we start; and by elaborate play
Tortur'd and tickled; by a crablike way 30
Time past made pastime, and in ugly sort
Disgorging up his ravaine for our sport—
—While the Plebeian Impe, from lofty throne,
Creates and rules a world, and workes upon
Mankind by secret engines; Now to move
A chilling pitty, then a rigorous love:
To strike up and stroake downe, both joy and ire;
To steere th'affections; and by heavenly fire
Mould us anew. Stolne from our selves—
This and much more which cannot bee exprest, 40
But by himselfe, his tongue and his owne brest,
Was Shakespeares freehold, which his cunning braine
Improv'd by favour of the nine fold traine.
The buskind Muse, the Commicke Queene, the graund
And lowder tone of Clio; nimble hand,
And nimbler foote of the melodious paire,
The Silver voyced Lady; the most faire
Calliope, whose speaking silence daunts.
And she whose prayse the heavenly body chants.
These joyntly woo'd him, envying one another 50
(Obey'd by all as Spouse, but lov'd as brother)
And wrought a curious robe of sable grave
Fresh greene, and pleasant yellow, red most brave,
And constant blew, rich purple, guiltlesse white
The lowly Russet, and the Scarlet bright;
Branch't and embroydred like the painted Spring
Each leafe match't with a flower, and each string
Of golden wire, each line of silke; there run
Italian workes whose thred the Sisters spun;
And there did sing, or seeme to sing, the choyce 60
Birdes of a forraine note and various voyce.
Here hangs a mossey rocke; there playes a faire
But chiding fountaine purled: Not the ayre
Nor cloudes nor thunder, but were living drawne
Not out of common Tiffany or Lawne,
But fine materialls, which the Muses know
And onely know the countries where they grow.
Now when they could no longer him enjoy
In mortall garments pent; death may destroy
They say his body, but his verse shall live 70
And more then nature takes, our hands shall give.
In a lesse volumne, but more strongly bound
Shakespeare shall breath and speake, with Laurell crown'd
Which never fades. Fed with Ambrosian meate
In a well-lyned vesture rich and neate.

So with this robe they cloath him, bid him weare it
For time shall never staine, nor envy teare it.

'The friendly admirer of his Endowments', I.M.S.,
in *Comedies, Histories, & Tragedies* (1632)

————

Vpon Master WILLIAM SHAKESPEARE, the *Deceased Authour, and his* POEMS

Poets are borne not made, when I would prove
This truth, the glad rememberance I must love
Of never dying *Shakespeare*, who alone,
Is argument enough to make that one.
First, that he was a Poet none would doubt,
That heard th' applause of what he sees set out
Imprinted; where thou hast (I will not say
Reader his Workes for to contrive a Play
To him twas none) the patterne of all wit,
10 Art without Art unparaleld as yet.
Next Nature onely helpt him, for looke thorow
This whole Booke, thou shalt find he doth not borrow,
One phrase from Greekes, nor Latines imitate,
Nor once from vulgar Languages Translate,
Nor Plagiari-like from others gleane,
Nor begges he from each witty friend a Scene
To peece his Acts with, all that he doth write,
Is pure his owne, plot, language exquisite,
But oh! what praise more powerfull can we give
20 The dead, then that by him the Kings men live,
His Players, which should they but have shar'd the Fate,
All else expir'd within the short Termes date;
How could the Globe have prospered, since through want
Of change, the Plaies and Poems had growne scant.
But happy Verse thou shalt be sung and heard,
When hungry quills shall be such honour bard.
Then vanish upstart Writers to each Stage,
You needy Poetasters of this Age,
Where *Shakespeare* liv'd or spake, Vermine forbeare,
30 Least with your froth you spot them, come not neere;
But if you needs must write, if poverty
So pinch, that otherwise you starve and die,
On Gods name may the Bull or Cockpit have
Your lame blancke Verse, to keepe you from the grave:
Or let new Fortunes younger brethren see,
What they can picke from your leane industry.
I doe not wonder when you offer at
Blacke-Friers, that you suffer: tis the fate
Of richer veines, prime judgements that have far'd
40 The worse, with this deceased man compar'd.
So have I seene, when Cesar would appeare,
And on the Stage at halfe-sword parley were,
Brutus and *Cassius*: oh how the Audience,
Were ravish'd, with what wonder they went thence,
When some new day they would not brooke a line,
Of tedious (though well laboured) *Cataline*;
Sejanus too was irkesome, they priz'de more
Honest *Iago*, or the jealous Moore.

And though the Fox and subtill Alchimist,
Long intermitted could not quite be mist, 50
Though these have sham'd all the Ancients, and might raise,
Their Authours merit with a crowne of Bayes.
Yet these sometimes, even at a friends desire
Acted, have scarce defrai'd the Seacoale fire
And doore-keepers: when let but *Falstaffe* come,
Hall, Poines, the rest you scarce shall have a roome
All is so pester'd: let but *Beatrice*
And *Benedicke* be seene, loe in a trice
The Cockpit Galleries, Boxes, all are full
To heare *Malvoglio* that crosse garter'd Gull. 60
Briefe, there is nothing in his wit fraught Booke,
Whose sound we would not heare, on whose worth looke
Like old coynd gold, whose lines in every page,
Shall passe true currant to succeeding age.
But why doe I dead *Shakespeares* praise recite,
Some second *Shakespeare* must of *Shakespeare* write;
For me tis needlesse, since an host of men,
Will pay to clap his praise, to free my Pen.

Leonard Digges (before 1636), in Shakespeare's
Poems (1640)

————

In remembrance of Master *William Shakespeare.*
ODE

I.

Beware (delighted Poets!) when you sing
To welcome Nature in the early Spring;
    Your num'rous Feet not tread
The Banks of Avon; for each Flowre
(As it nere knew a Sunne or Showre)
    Hangs there, the pensive head.

2.

Each Tree, whose thick, and spreading growth hath made,
Rather a Night beneath the Boughs, than Shade,
    (Unwilling now to grow)
Lookes like the Plume a Captive weares, 10
Whose rifled *Falls* are steept i' th teares
    Which from his last rage flow.

3.

The piteous River wept it selfe away
Long since (Alas!) to such a swift decay;
    That reach the Map; and looke
If you a River there can spie;
And for a River your mock'd Eie,
    Will finde a shallow Brooke.

Sir William D'avenant, *Madagascar, with other Poems* (1637)

An Elegie on the death of that famous Writer and Actor,
M. William Shakspeare

I dare not doe thy Memory that wrong,
Vnto our larger griefes to give a tongue;
Ile onely sigh in earnest, and let fall
My solemne teares at thy great Funerall;
For every eye that raines a showre for thee,
Laments thy losse in a sad Elegie.
Nor is it fit each humble Muse should have,
Thy worth his subject, now th' art laid in grave;
No its a flight beyond the pitch of those,
10 Whose worthles Pamphlets are not sence in Prose.
Let learned *Iohnson* sing a Dirge for thee,
And fill our Orbe with mournefull harmony:
But we neede no Remembrancer, thy Fame
Shall still accompany thy honoured Name,
To all posterity; and make us be,
Sensible of what we lost in losing thee:
Being the Ages wonder whose smooth Rhimes,
Did more reforme than lash the looser Times.
Nature her selfe did her owne selfe admire,
20 As oft as thou wert pleased to attire
Her in her native lusture, and confesse,
Thy dressing was her chiefest comlinesse.
How can we then forget thee, when the age
Her chiefest Tutor, and the widdowed Stage
Her onely favorite in thee hath lost,
And Natures selfe what she did bragge of most.
Sleepe then rich soule of numbers, whilst poore we,
Enjoy the profits of thy Legacie;
And thinke it happinesse enough we have,
30 So much of thee redeemed from the grave,
As may suffice to enlighten future times,
With the bright lustre of thy matchlesse Rhimes.

Anonymous (before 1638), in Shakespeare's
Poems (1640)

———

To *Shakespeare*

Thy Muses sugred dainties seeme to us
Like the fam'd Apples of old Tantalus:
For we (admiring) see and heare thy straines,
But none I see or heare, those sweets attaines.

To *the same*

Thou hast so us'd thy *Pen,* (or *shooke thy Speare*)
That Poets startle, nor thy wit come neare.

Thomas Bancroft, *Two Bookes of Epigrammes, and*
Epitaphs (1639)

To *Mr. William Shake-spear*

Shake-speare, we must be silent in thy praise,
'Cause our encomion's will but blast thy Bayes,
Which envy could not, that thou didst so well;
Let thine own histories prove thy Chronicle.

Anonymous, in *Witts Recreations* (1640)

———

To the Reader

I here presume (under favour) to present to your view,
some excellent and sweetely composed Poems, of Master
William Shakespeare, *Which in themselves appeare of the*
same purity, the Authour himselfe then living avouched; they
had not the fortune by reason of their Infancie in his death,
to have the due accommodatiō of proportionable glory, with
the rest of his everliving Workes, yet the lines of themselves
will afford you a more authentick approbation than my
assurance any way can, to invite your allowance, in your
perusall you shall finde them Seren, cleere and eligantly 10
plaine, such gentle straines as shall recreate and not perplexe
your braine, no intricate or cloudy stuffe to puzzell intellect,
but perfect eloquence; such as will raise your admiration to
his praise: this assurance I know will not differ from your
acknowledgement. And certaine I am, my opinion will be
seconded by the sufficiency of these ensuing Lines; I have
beene somewhat solicitus to bring this forth to the perfect
view of all men; and in so doing, glad to be serviceable for
the continuance of glory to the deserved Author in these his
Poems. 20

John Benson, in Shakespeare's *Poems* (1640)

———

Of Mr. *William Shakespeare*

What, lofty *Shakespeare,* art againe reviv'd?
And *Virbius* like now show'st thy selfe twise liv'd,
Tis *Benson's* love that thus to thee is showne,
The labours his, the glory still thine owne.
These learned Poems amongst thine after-birth,
That makes thy name immortall on the earth,
Will make the learned still admire to see,
The Muses gifts so fully infus'd on thee.
Let Carping *Momus* barke and bite his fill,
And ignorant *Davus* slight thy learned skill: 10
Yet those who know the worth of thy desert,
And with true judgement can discerne thy Art,
Will be admirers of thy high tun'd straine,
Amongst whose number let me still remaine.

John Warren, in Shakespeare's *Poems* (1640)

THE TWO GENTLEMEN OF VERONA

THE accomplished elegance of the lyrical verse in *The Two Gentlemen of Verona*, as well as the skilful, theatrically effective prose of Launce's monologues, demonstrates that Shakespeare had already developed his writing skills when he composed this play. Nevertheless—and although the earliest mention of it is by Francis Meres in 1598—it may be his first work for the stage; for its dramatic structure is comparatively unambitious, and while some of its scenes are expertly constructed, those involving more than, at the most, four characters betray an uncertainty of technique suggestive of inexperience. It was first printed in the 1623 Folio.

The friendship of the 'two gentlemen'—Valentine and Protheus—is strained when both fall in love with Siluia. Protheus has followed Valentine from Verona to Milan, leaving behind his beloved Iulia, who in turn follows him, disguised as a boy. At the climax of the action Valentine displays the depth of his friendship by offering Siluia to Protheus. The conflicting claims of love and friendship illustrated in this plot had been treated in a considerable body of English literature written by the time Shakespeare wrote his play, probably in the late 1580s. John Lyly's didactic fiction *Euphues* (1578) was an immensely popular example; and Lyly's earliest plays, such as *Campaspe* (1584) and *Endimion* (1588), influenced Shakespeare's style as well as his subject matter. Shakespeare was writing in a fashionable mode, but his story of Protheus and Iulia is specifically (though perhaps indirectly) indebted to a prose fiction, *Diana*, written in Spanish by the Portuguese Jorge de Montemayor and first published in 1559. Many other influences on the young dramatist may be discerned: his idealized portrayal of Siluia and her relationship with Valentine derives from the medieval tradition of courtly love; Arthur Brooke's long poem *The Tragicall Historye of Romeus and Iuliet* (1562) provided some details of the plot; and the comic commentary on the romantic action supplied by the page-boy Speed and the more rustic clown Launce has dramatic antecedents in English plays such as Lyly's early comedies.

Though the play was probably acted in Shakespeare's time, its first recorded performance is in 1762, in a rewritten version at Drury Lane. Later performances have been sparse, and the play has succeeded best when subjected to adaptation, increasing its musical content, adjusting the emphasis of the last scene so as to reduce the shock of Valentine's donation of Siluia to Protheus, and updating the setting. It can be seen as a dramatic laboratory in which Shakespeare first experimented with conventions of romantic comedy which he would later treat with a more subtle complexity, but it has its own charm. If the whole is not greater than the parts, some of the parts—such as Launce's brilliant monologues, and the delightful scene (Sc. 14) in which Protheus serenades his new love with 'Who is Siluia?' while his disguised old love, Iulia, looks wistfully on—are wholly successful. And Launce's dog, Crab, has the most scene-stealing non-speaking role in the canon: this is an experiment that Shakespeare did not repeat.

The Folio text apparently derives from a transcript betraying the characteristics of the scrivener Ralph Crane; the original stage directions are exceptionally sparse and laconic.

THE NAMES OF THE ACTORS

DUKE of Millaine

SILUIA, his daughter

PROTHEUS, a gentleman of Verona

LAUNCE, his 'clownish seruant'

VALENTINE, a gentleman of Verona

SPEED, his 'clownish seruant'

THURIO, 'a foolish riuall to Valentine'

ANTONIO, 'father to Protheus'

PANTHINO, 'seruant to Antonio'

IULIA, 'beloued of Protheus'

LUCETTA, 'waighting-woman to Iulia'

HOST, 'where Iulia lodges'

EGLAMOURE, 'Agent for Siluia in her escape'

OUT-LAWS 'with Valentine'

Seruants, Musitians

The Two Gentlemen of Verona

Sc. 1 *Enter Valentine and Protheus*
(1.1) VALENTINE
Cease to perswade, my louing *Protheus*;
Home-keeping youth, haue euer homely wits,
Wer't not affection chaines thy tender dayes
To the sweet glaunces of thy honour'd Loue,
I rather would entreat thy company,
To see the wonders of the world abroad,
Then (liuing dully sluggardiz'd at home)
Weare out thy youth with shapelesse idlenesse.
But since thou lou'st; loue still, and thriue therein,
10   Euen as I would, when I to loue begin.
PROTHEUS
Wilt thou be gone? Sweet *Valentine* adew,
Thinke on thy *Protheus*, when thou (hap'ly) seest
Some rare note-worthy obiect in thy trauaile.
Wish me partaker in thy happinesse,
When thou do'st meet good hap; and in thy danger,
(If euer danger doe enuiron thee)
Commend thy grieuance to my holy prayers,
For I will be thy beades-man, *Valentine*.
VALENTINE
And on a loue-booke pray for my successe?
PROTHEUS
20   Vpon some booke I loue, I'le pray for thee.
VALENTINE
That's on some shallow Storie of deepe loue,
How yong *Leander* crost the *Hellespont*.
PROTHEUS
That's a deepe Storie, of a deeper loue,
For he was more then ouer-shooes in loue.
VALENTINE
'Tis true; for you are ouer-bootes in loue,
And yet you neuer swom the *Hellespont*.
PROTHEUS
Ouer the Bootes? nay giue me not the Boots.
VALENTINE
No, I will not; for it boots thee not.
PROTHEUS   What?
VALENTINE
To be in loue; where scorne is bought with grones:
Coy looks, with hart-sore sighes: one fading moments
30   mirth,
With twenty watchfull, weary, tedious nights;
If hap'ly won, perhaps a haplesse gaine;
If lost, why then a grieuous labour won;
How euer: but a folly bought with wit,
Or else a wit, by folly vanquished.
PROTHEUS
So, by your circumstance, you call me foole.
VALENTINE
So, by your circumstance, I feare you'll proue.

PROTHEUS
'Tis Loue you cauill at, I am not Loue.
VALENTINE
Loue is your master, for he masters you;
And he that is so yoked by a foole,   40
Me thinkes should not be chronicled for wise.
PROTHEUS
Yet Writers say; as in the sweetest Bud,
The eating Canker dwels; so doting Loue
Inhabits in the finest wits of all.
VALENTINE
And Writers say; as the most forward Bud
Is eaten by the Canker ere it blow,
Euen so by Loue, the yong, and tender wit
Is turn'd to folly, blasting in the Bud,
Loosing his verdure, euen in the prime,
And all the faire effects of future hopes.   50
But wherefore waste I time to counsaile thee
That art a votary to fond desire?
Once more adieu: my Father at the Road
Expects my comming, there to see me ship'd.
PROTHEUS
And thither will I bring thee *Valentine*.
VALENTINE
Sweet *Protheus*, no: Now let vs take our leaue:
To *Millaine* let me heare from thee by Letters
Of thy successe in loue; and what newes else
Betideth here in absence of thy Friend:
And I likewise will visite thee with mine.   60
PROTHEUS
All happinesse bechance to thee in *Millaine*.
VALENTINE
As much to you at home: and so farewell.   *Exit*
PROTHEUS
He after Honour hunts, I after Loue;
He leaues his friends, to dignifie them more;
I leaue my selfe, my friends, and all for loue:
Thou *Iulia*, thou hast metamorphis'd me:
Made me neglect my Studies, loose my time;
Warre with good counsaile; set the world at naught;
Made Wit with musing, weake; hart sick with thought.
    Enter Speed
SPEED
Sir *Protheus*: 'saue you: saw you my Master?   70
PROTHEUS
But now he parted hence to embarque for *Millain*.
SPEED
Twenty to one then, he is ship'd already,
And I haue plaid the Sheepe in loosing him.
PROTHEUS
Indeede a Sheepe doth very often stray,
And if the Shepheard be awhile away.

3

SPEED
    You conclude that my Master is a Shepheard then,
       and I a Sheepe?
PROTHEUS I doe.
SPEED
    Why then my hornes are his hornes, whether I wake
       or sleepe.
PROTHEUS A silly answere, and fitting well a Sheepe.
80 SPEED This proues me still a Sheepe.
PROTHEUS True: and thy Master a Shepheard.
SPEED Nay, that I can deny by a circumstance.
PROTHEUS It shall goe hard but ile proue it by another.
SPEED The Shepheard seekes the Sheepe, and not the
    Sheepe the Shepheard; but I seeke my Master, and my
    Master seekes not me: therefore I am no Sheepe.
PROTHEUS The Sheepe for fodder follow the Shepheard,
    the Shepheard for foode followes not the Sheepe: thou
    for wages followest thy Master, thy Master for wages
90   followes not thee: therefore thou art a Sheepe.
SPEED Such another proofe will make me cry baa.
PROTHEUS But do'st thou heare: gau'st thou my Letter to
    Iulia?
SPEED I Sir: I (a lost-Mutton) gaue your Letter to her (a
    lac'd-Mutton) and she (a lac'd-Mutton) gaue mee (a
    lost-Mutton) nothing for my labour.
PROTHEUS Here's too small a Pasture for such store of
    Muttons.
SPEED If the ground be ouer-charg'd, you were best sticke
100   her.
PROTHEUS Nay, in that you are astray: 'twere best pound
    you.
SPEED Nay Sir, lesse then a pound shall serue me for
    carrying your Letter.
PROTHEUS You mistake; I meane the pound, a Pinfold.
SPEED
    From a pound to a pin? fold it ouer and ouer,
    'Tis threefold too little for carrying a letter to your
       louer.
PROTHEUS But what said she?
SPEED (*nods, then saies*) I.
110 PROTHEUS Nod-I, why that's noddy.
SPEED You mistooke Sir: I say she did nod; and you aske
    me if she did nod, and I say I.
PROTHEUS And that set together is noddy.
SPEED Now you haue taken the paines to set it together,
    take it for your paines.
PROTHEUS No, no, you shall haue it for bearing the letter.
SPEED Well, I perceiue I must be faine to beare with you.
PROTHEUS Why Sir, how doe you beare with me?
SPEED Marry Sir, the letter very orderly, hauing nothing
120   but the word noddy for my paines.
PROTHEUS Beshrew me, but you haue a quicke wit.
SPEED And yet it cannot ouer-take your slow purse.
PROTHEUS Come, come, open the matter in briefe; what
    said she.
SPEED Open your purse, that the money, and the matter
    may be both at once deliuered.
PROTHEUS (*giuing money*) Well Sir: here is for your paines:
    what said she?

SPEED Truely Sir, I thinke you'll hardly win her.
PROTHEUS Why? could'st thou perceiue so much from 130
    her?
SPEED Sir, I could perceiue nothing at all from her; no,
    not so much as a ducket for deliuering your letter: and
    being so hard to me, that brought your minde; I feare
    she'll proue as hard to you in telling your minde. Giue
    her no token but stones, for she's as hard as steele.
PROTHEUS What said she, nothing?
SPEED No, not so much as take this for thy pains: to
    testifie your bounty, I thank you, you haue testern'd
    me; in requital whereof, henceforth, carry your letters 140
    your selfe; And so Sir, I'le commend you to my Master.
                                 ⌈*Exit*⌉
PROTHEUS
    Go, go, be gone, to saue your Ship from wrack,
    Which cannot perish hauing thee aboarde,
    Being destin'd to a drier death on shore:
    I must goe send some better Messenger,
    I feare my *Iulia* would not daigne my lines,
    Receiuing them from such a worthlesse post.   *Exit*

        Enter Iulia and Lucetta   **Sc. 2**
IULIA   **(1.2)**
    But say *Lucetta* (now we are alone)
    Would'st thou then counsaile me to fall in loue?
LUCETTA
    I Madam, so you stumble not vnheedfully.   150
IULIA
    Of all the faire resort of Gentlemen,
    That euery day with par'le encounter me,
    In thy opinion which is worthiest loue?
LUCETTA
    Please you repeat their names, ile shew my minde,
    According to my shallow simple skill.
IULIA
    What thinkst thou of the faire sir *Eglamoure*?
LUCETTA
    As of a Knight, well-spoken, neat, and fine;
    But were I you, he neuer should be mine.
IULIA
    What think'st thou of the rich *Mercatio*?
LUCETTA
    Well of his wealth; but of himselfe, so, so.   160
IULIA
    What think'st thou of the gentle *Protheus*?
LUCETTA
    Lord, Lord: to see what folly raignes in vs.
IULIA
    How now? what meanes this passion at his name?
LUCETTA
    Pardon deare Madam, 'tis a passing shame,
    That I (vnworthy body as I am)
    Should censure thus on louely Gentlemen.
IULIA
    Why not on *Protheus*, as of all the rest?
LUCETTA
    Then thus: of many good, I thinke him best.
IULIA Your reason?

LUCETTA

170 I haue no other but a womans reason:
I thinke him so, because I thinke him so.

IULIA

And would'st thou haue me cast my loue on him?

LUCETTA

I: if you thought your loue not cast away.

IULIA

Why he, of all the rest, hath neuer mou'd me.

LUCETTA

Yet he, of all the rest, I thinke best loues ye.

IULIA

His little speaking, shewes his loue but small.

LUCETTA

Fire that's closest kept, burnes most of all.

IULIA

They doe not loue, that doe not shew their loue.

LUCETTA

Oh, they loue least, that let men know their loue.

IULIA

180 I would I knew his minde.

LUCETTA (giuing Protheus Letter)
Peruse this paper Madam.

IULIA

To Iulia: say, from whom?

LUCETTA

That the Contents will shew.

IULIA

Say, say: who gaue it thee?

LUCETTA

Sir Valentines page: & sent I think from Protheus;
He would haue giuen it you, but I being in the way,
Did in your name receiue it: pardon the fault I pray.

IULIA

Now (by my modesty) a goodly Broker:
Dare you presume to harbour wanton lines?
190 To whisper, and conspire against my youth?
Now trust me, 'tis an office of great worth,
And you an officer fit for the place:
There: take the paper:
          She giues Lucetta the Letter
                    see it be return'd,
Or else returne no more into my sight.

LUCETTA

To plead for loue, deserues more fee, then hate.

IULIA

Will ye be gon?

LUCETTA   That you may ruminate.   Exit

IULIA

And yet I would I had ore-look'd the Letter;
It were a shame to call her backe againe,
And pray her to a fault, for which I chid her.
200 What 'foole is she, that knowes I am a Maid,
And would not force the letter to my view?
Since Maides, in modesty, say no, to that,
Which they would haue the profferer construe, I.
Fie, fie: how way-ward is this foolish loue;
That (like a testie Babe) will scratch the Nurse,
And presently, all humbled kisse the Rod?

How churlishly, I chid Lucetta hence,
When willingly, I would haue had her here?
How angerly I taught my brow to frowne,
When inward ioy enforc'd my heart to smile?   210
My pennance is, to call Lucetta backe
And aske remission, for my folly past.
What hoe: Lucetta.
          Enter Lucetta

LUCETTA   What would your Ladiship?

IULIA

Is't neere dinner time?

LUCETTA   I would it were,
That you might kill your stomacke on your meat,
And not vpon your Maid.
          ⌈She drops and picks vp the Letter⌉

IULIA   What is't that you
Tooke vp so gingerly?

LUCETTA Nothing.

IULIA Why didst thou stoope then?

LUCETTA

To take a paper vp, that I let fall.   220

IULIA

And is that paper nothing?

LUCETTA

Nothing concerning me.

IULIA

Then let it lye, for those that it concernes.

LUCETTA

Madam, it will not lye where it concernes,
Vnlesse it haue a false Interpreter.

IULIA

Some loue of yours, hath writ to you in Rime.

LUCETTA

That I might sing it (Madam) to a tune:
Giue me a Note, your Ladiship can set

IULIA

As little by such toyes, as may be possible:
Best sing it to the tune of Light o' Loue.   230

LUCETTA

It is too heauy for so light a tune.

IULIA

Heauy? belike it hath some burden then?

LUCETTA

I: and melodious were it, would you sing it.

IULIA

And why not you?

LUCETTA   I cannot reach so high.

IULIA

Let's see your Song:
          ⌈She tries to take the Letter⌉
                    How now Minion?

LUCETTA

Keepe tune there still; so you will sing it out:
And yet me thinkes I do not like this tune.

IULIA You doe not?

LUCETTA

No (Madam) tis too sharpe.

IULIA

You (Minion) are too saucie.   240

LUCETTA

Nay, now you are too flat;

And marre the concord, with too harsh a descant:

There wanteth but a Meane to fill your Song.

IULIA

The meane is dround with your vnruly base.

LUCETTA

Indeede I bid the base for *Protheus.*

IULIA

This babble shall not henceforth trouble me;

Here is a coile with protestation:

She teares the Letter and drops the pieces

Goe, get you gone: and let the papers lye:

You would be fingring them, to anger me.

LUCETTA *(aside)*

250   She makes it strãge, but she would be best pleas'd

To be so angred with another Letter.   *Exit*

IULIA

Nay, would I were so angred with the same:

Oh hatefull hands, to teare such louing words;

Iniurious Waspes, to feede on such sweet hony,

And kill the Bees that yeelde it, with your stings;

Ile kisse each seuerall paper, for amends:

She picks vp some of the pieces of paper

Looke, here is writ, kinde *Iulia*: vnkinde *Iulia*,

As in reuenge of thy ingratitude,

I throw thy name against the bruzing-stones,

260   Trampling contemptuously on thy disdaine.

And here is writ, *Loue wounded Protheus.*

Poore wounded name: my bosome, as a bed,

Shall lodge thee till thy wound be throughly heal'd;

And thus I search it with a soueraigne kisse.

But twice, or thrice, was *Protheus* written downe:

Be calme (good winde) blow not a word away,

Till I haue found each letter, in the Letter,

Except mine own name: That, some whirle-winde

beare

Vnto a ragged, fearefull, hanging Rocke,

270   And throw it thence into the raging Sea.

Loe, here in one line is his name twice writ:

Poore forlorne Protheus, passionate Protheus:

To the sweet Iulia: that ile teare away:

And yet I will not, sith so prettily

He couples it, to his complaining Names;

Thus will I fold them, one vpon another;

Now kisse, embrace, contend, doe what you will.

Enter Lucetta

LUCETTA

Madam: dinner is ready: and your father staies.

IULIA Well, let vs goe.

LUCETTA

280   What, shall these papers lye, like Tel-tales here?

IULIA

If you respect them; best to take them vp.

LUCETTA

Nay, I was taken vp, for laying them downe.

Yet here they shall not lye, for catching cold.

IULIA

I see you haue a months minde to them.

LUCETTA

I (Madam) you may say what sights you see;

I see things too, although you iudge I winke.

IULIA Come, come, wilt please you goe.   *Exeunt*

Enter Antonio and Panthino   Sc. 3

ANTONIO   (1.3)

Tell me *Panthino*, what sad talke was that,

Wherewith my brother held you in the Cloyster?

PANTHINO

'Twas of his Nephew *Protheus*, your Sonne.   290

ANTONIO

Why? what of him?

PANTHINO   He wondred that your Lordship

Would suffer him, to spend his youth at home,

While other men, of slender reputation

Put forth their Sonnes, to seeke preferment out.

Some to the warres, to try their fortune there;

Some, to discouer Islands farre away:

Some, to the studious Vniuersities;

For any, or for all these exercises,

He said, that *Protheus*, your sonne, was meet;

And did request me, to importune you   300

To let him spend his time no more at home;

Which would be great impeachment to his age,

In hauing knowne no trauaile in his youth.

ANTONIO

Nor need'st thou much importune me to that

Whereon, this month I haue bin hamering.

I haue consider'd well, his losse of time,

And how he cannot be a perfect man,

Not being tryed, and tutord in the world:

Experience is by industry atchieu'd,

And perfected by the swift course of time: 310

Then tell me, whether were I best to send him?

PANTHINO

I thinke your Lordship is not ignorant

How his companion, youthfull *Valentine*,

Attends the Emperour in his royall Court.

ANTONIO I know it well.

PANTHINO

'Twere good, I thinke, your Lordship sent him thither,

There shall he practise Tilts, and Turnaments;

Heare sweet discourse, conuerse with Noble-men,

And be in eye of euery Exercise

Worthy his youth, and noblenesse of birth.   320

ANTONIO

I like thy counsaile: well hast thou aduis'd:

And that thou maist perceiue how well I like it,

The execution of it shall make knowne;

Euen with the speediest expedition,

I will dispatch him to the Emperors Court.

PANTHINO

To morrow, may it please you, *Don Alphonso*,

With other Gentlemen of good esteeme

Are iournying, to salute the *Emperor*,
And to commend their seruice to his will.

ANTONIO

330 Good company: with them shall *Protheus* go:
          Enter Protheus with a Letter. He does not see
          Antonio and Panthino
     And in good time: now will we breake with him.

PROTHEUS Sweet Loue, sweet lines, sweet life,
     Here is her hand, the agent of her heart;
     Here is her oath for loue, her honors paune;
     O that our Fathers would applaud our loues
     To seale our happinesse with their consents.
     Oh heauenly *Iulia*.

ANTONIO

     How now? What Letter are you reading there?

PROTHEUS

     May't please your Lordship, 'tis a word or two
340 Of commendations sent from *Valentine*;
     Deliuer'd by a friend, that came from him.

ANTONIO

     Lend me the Letter: Let me see what newes.

PROTHEUS

     There is no newes (my Lord) but that he writes
     How happily he liues, how well-belou'd,
     And daily graced by the Emperor;
     Wishing me with him, partner of his fortune.

ANTONIO

     And how stand you affected to his wish?

PROTHEUS

     As one relying on your Lordships will,
     And not depending on his friendly wish.

ANTONIO

350 My will is something sorted with his wish:
     Muse not that I thus sodainly proceed;
     For what I will, I will, and there an end:
     I am resolu'd, that thou shalt spend some time
     With *Valentinus*, in the Emperors Court:
     What maintenance he from his friends receiues,
     Like exhibition thou shalt haue from me,
     To morrow be in readinesse, to goe,
     Excuse it not: for I am peremptory.

PROTHEUS

     My Lord I cannot be so soone prouided,
360 Please you deliberate a day or two.

ANTONIO

     Look what thou want'st shalbe sent after thee:
     No more of stay: to morrow thou must goe;
     Come on *Panthino*; you shall be imployd,
     To hasten on his Expedition.

          Exeunt Antonio and Panthino

PROTHEUS

     Thus haue I shund the fire, for feare of burning,
     And drench'd me in the sea, where I am drown'd.
     I fear'd to shew my Father *Iulias* Letter,
     Least he should take exceptions to my loue,
     And with the vantage of mine owne excuse
370 Hath he excepted most against my loue.
     Oh, how this spring of loue resembleth

The vncertaine glory of an Aprill day,
Which now shewes all the beauty of the Sun,
And by and by a clowd takes all away.
          Enter Panthino

PANTHINO

     Sir *Protheus*, your Father call's for you,
          He is in hast, therefore I pray you go.

PROTHEUS

     Why this it is: my heart accords thereto,
          And yet a thousand times it answer's no.   *Exeunt*

          Enter Valentine and Speed   Sc. 4

SPEED (*offering Valentine a Gloue*)   (2.1)
     Sir, your Gloue.

VALENTINE   Not mine: my Gloues are on.

SPEED

     Why then this may be yours: for this is but one.   380

VALENTINE

     Ha? Let me see: I, giue it me, it's mine:
     Sweet Ornament, that deckes a thing diuine,
     Ah *Siluia*, *Siluia*.

SPEED Madam *Siluia*: Madam *Siluia*.

VALENTINE How now Sirha?

SPEED Shee is not within hearing Sir.

VALENTINE Why sir, who bad you call her?

SPEED Your worship sir, or else I mistooke.

VALENTINE Well: you'll still be too forward.

SPEED And yet I was last chidden for being too slow.   390

VALENTINE Goe to, sir, tell me: do you know Madam
     Siluia?

SPEED Shee that your worship loues?

VALENTINE Why, how know you that I am in loue?

SPEED Marry by these speciall markes: first, you haue
     learn'd (like Sir *Protheus*) to wreath your Armes like a
     Male-content: to rellish a Loue-song, like a *Robin-
     redbreast*: to walke alone like one that had the
     pestilence: to sigh, like a Schoole-boy that had lost his
     A.B.C. to weep like a yong wench that had buried her   400
     Grandam: to fast, like one that takes diet: to watch,
     like one that feares robbing: to speake puling, like a
     beggar at Hallow-Masse: You were wont, when you
     laughed, to crow like a cocke; when you walk'd, to
     walke like one of the Lions: when you fasted, it was
     presently after dinner: when you look'd sadly, it was
     for want of money: And now you are Metamorphis'd
     with a Mistris, that when I looke on you, I can hardly
     thinke you my Master.

VALENTINE Are all these things perceiu'd in me?   410

SPEED They are all perceiu'd without ye.

VALENTINE Without me? they cannot.

SPEED Without you? nay, that's certaine: for without you
     were so simple, none else would: but you are so without
     these follies, that these follies are within you, and shine
     through you like the water in an Vrinall: that not an
     eye that sees you, but is a Physician to comment on
     your Malady.

VALENTINE But tell me: do'st thou know my Lady *Siluia*?

SPEED Shee that you gaze on so, as she sits at supper?   420

VALENTINE Hast thou obseru'd that? euen she I meane.

SPEED Why sir, I know her not.

VALENTINE Do'st thou know her by my gazing on her, and yet know'st her not?

SPEED Is she not hard-fauour'd, sir?

VALENTINE Not so faire (boy) as well fauour'd.

SPEED Sir, I know that well enough.

VALENTINE What dost thou know?

SPEED That shee is not so faire, as (of you) well-fauourd.

430 VALENTINE I meane that her beauty is exquisite, but her fauour infinite.

SPEED That's because the one is painted, and the other out of all count.

VALENTINE How painted? and how out of count?

SPEED Marry sir, so painted to make her faire, that no man counts of her beauty.

VALENTINE How esteem'st thou me? I account of her beauty.

SPEED You neuer saw her since she was deform'd.

440 VALENTINE How long hath she beene deform'd?

SPEED Euer since you lou'd her.

VALENTINE I haue lou'd her euer since I saw her, and still I see her beautifull.

SPEED If you loue her, you cannot see her.

VALENTINE Why?

SPEED Because Loue is blinde: O that you had mine eyes, or your owne eyes had the lights they were wont to haue, when you chidde at Sir *Protheus*, for going vngarter'd.

450 VALENTINE What should I see then?

SPEED Your owne present folly, and her passing deformitie: for hee beeing in loue, could not see to garter his hose; and you, beeing in loue, cannot see to put on your hose.

VALENTINE Belike (boy) then you are in loue, for last morning you could not see to wipe my shooes.

SPEED True sir: I was in loue with my bed, I thanke you, you swing'd me for my loue, which makes mee the bolder to chide you, for yours.

460 VALENTINE In conclusion, I stand affected to her.

SPEED I would you were set, so your affection would cease.

VALENTINE Last night she enioyn'd me, to write some lines to one she loues.

SPEED And haue you?

VALENTINE I haue.

SPEED Are they not lamely writt?

VALENTINE No (Boy) but as well as I can do them: Peace, here she comes.

Enter Siluia

470 SPEED (*aside*) Oh excellent motion; oh exceeding Puppet: Now will he interpret to her.

VALENTINE
Madam & Mistres, a thousand good-morrows.

SPEED (*aside*) Oh, 'giue ye-good-eu'n: heer's a million of manners.

SILUIA
Sir *Valentine*, and seruant, to you two thousand.

SPEED (*aside*) He should giue her interest: & she giues it him.

VALENTINE
As you inioynd me; I haue writ your Letter
Vnto the secret, nameles friend of yours:
Which I was much vnwilling to proceed in,   480
But for my duty to your Ladiship.
He giues her a Letter

SILUIA
I thanke you (gentle Seruant) 'tis very Clerkly-done.

VALENTINE
Now trust me (Madam) it came hardly-off:
For being ignorant to whom it goes,
I writ at randome, very doubtfully.

SILUIA
Perchance you think too much of so much pains?

VALENTINE
No (Madam) so it steed you, I will write
(Please you command) a thousand times as much:
And yet—

SILUIA
A pretty period: well: I ghesse the sequell;   490
And yet I will not name it: and yet I care not.
And yet, take this againe:
She offers him the Letter
                         and yet I thanke you:
Meaning henceforth to trouble you no more.

SPEED (*aside*)
And yet you will: and yet, another yet.

VALENTINE
What meanes your Ladiship? Doe you not like it?

SILUIA
Yes, yes: the lines are very queintly writ,
But (since vnwillingly) take them againe.
She presses the Letter vpon him
Nay, take them.

VALENTINE   Madam, they are for you.

SILUIA
I, I: you writ them Sir, at my request,
But I will none of them: they are for you: 500
I would haue had them writ more mouingly.

VALENTINE
Please you, Ile write your Ladiship another.

SILUIA
And when it's writ: for my sake read it ouer,
And if it please you, so: if not: why so.

VALENTINE
If it please me, (Madam?) what then?

SILUIA
Why if it please you, take it for your labour;
And so good-morrow Seruant.   *Exit*

SPEED (*aside*)
Oh Iest vnseene: inscrutible: inuisible,
As a nose on a mans face, or a Wethercocke on a steeple:
My Master sues to her: and she hath taught her Sutor,   510
He being her Pupill, to become her Tutor.

8

Oh excellent deuise, was there euer heard a better?
That my master being scribe, to himselfe should write
the Letter?

VALENTINE How now Sir? What, are you reasoning with
your selfe?

SPEED Nay: I was riming: 'tis you yᵗ haue the reason.

VALENTINE To doe what?

SPEED To be a Spokes-man from Madam *Siluia*.

VALENTINE To whom?

520 SPEED To your selfe: why, she woes you by a figure.

VALENTINE What figure?

SPEED By a Letter, I should say.

VALENTINE Why she hath not writ to me?

SPEED What need she, when shee hath made you write
to your selfe? Why, doe you not perceiue the iest?

VALENTINE No, beleeue me.

SPEED No beleeuing you indeed sir: But did you perceiue
her earnest?

VALENTINE She gaue me none, except an angry word.

530 SPEED Why she hath giuen you a Letter.

VALENTINE That's the Letter I writ to her friend.

SPEED And yᵗ letter hath she deliuer'd, & there an end.

VALENTINE I would it were no worse.

SPEED Ile warrant you, 'tis as well:
For often haue you writ to her: and she in modesty,
Or else for want of idle time, could not againe reply,
Or fearing els some messẽger, yᵗ might her mind
discouer
Her self hath taught her Loue himself, to write vnto
her louer.
All this I speak in print, for in print I found it. Why
540 muse you sir, 'tis dinner time.

VALENTINE I haue dyn'd.

SPEED I, but hearken sir: though the Cameleon Loue can
feed on the ayre, I am one that am nourish'd by my
victuals; and would faine haue meate: oh bee not like
your Mistresse, be moued, be moued.   *Exeunt*

Sc. 5   *Enter Protheus and Iulia*
(2.2) PROTHEUS
Haue patience, gentle *Iulia*.

IULIA
I must where is no remedy.

PROTHEUS
When possibly I can, I will returne.

IULIA
If you turne not: you will return the sooner:
She giues him a ring
550 Keepe this remembrance for thy *Iulia's* sake.

PROTHEUS
Why then wee'll make exchange; Here, take you this.
He giues her a ring

IULIA
And seale the bargaine with a holy kisse.
⌈*They kisse*⌉

PROTHEUS
Here is my hand, for my true constancie:
And when that howre ore-slips me in the day,

Wherein I sigh not (*Iulia*) for thy sake,
The next ensuing howre, some foule mischance
Torment me for my Loues forgetfulnesse:
My father staies my comming: answere not:
The tide is now; (*Iulia weeps*) nay, not thy tide of
teares,
That tide will stay me longer then I should,   560
Iulia, farewell: *Exit Iulia*
what, gon without a word?
I, so true loue should doe: it cannot speake,
For truth hath better deeds, then words to grace it.
Enter Panthino

PANTHINO
Sir *Protheus*: you are staid for.

PROTHEUS   Goe: I come, I come:
Alas, this parting strikes poore Louers dumbe.   *Exeunt*

Enter Launce with his dog Crab   Sc. 6

LAUNCE (*to the audience*) Nay, 'twill bee this howre ere I   (2.3)
haue done weeping: all the kinde of the *Launces*, haue
this very fault: I haue receiu'd my proportion, like the
prodigious Sonne, and am going with Sir *Protheus* to
the Imperialls Court: I thinke *Crab* my dog, be the   570
sowrest natured dogge that liues: My Mother weeping:
my Father wayling: my Sister crying: our Maid
howling: our Catte wringing her hands, and all our
house in a great perplexitie, yet did not this cruell-
hearted Curre shedde one teare: he is a stone, a very
pibble stone, and has no more pitty in him then a
dogge: a Iew would haue wept to haue seene our
parting: why my Grandam hauing no eyes, looke you,
wept her selfe blinde at my parting: nay, Ile shew you
the manner of it. This shooe is my father: no, this left   580
shooe is my father; no, no, this left shooe is my mother:
nay, that cannot bee so neyther: yes; it is so, it is so:
it hath the worser sole: this shooe with the hole in it,
is my mother: and this my father: a veng'ance on't,
there 'tis: Now sir, this staffe is my sister: for, looke
you, she is as white as a lilly, and as small as a wand:
this hat is *Nan* our maid: I am the dogge: no, the
dogge is himselfe, and I am the dogge: oh, the dogge
is me, and I am my selfe: I; so, so: now come I to my
Father; Father, your blessing: now should not the   590
shooe speake a word for weeping: now should I kisse
my Father; well, hee weepes on: Now come I to my
Mother: Oh that she could speake now, like a mou'd
woman: well, I kisse her: why there 'tis; heere's my
mothers breath vp and downe: Now come I to my
sister; marke the moane she makes: now the dogge all
this while sheds not a teare: nor speakes a word: but
see how I lay the dust with my teares.
Enter Panthino

PANTHINO *Launce*, away, away: a Boord: thy Master is
ship'd, and thou art to post after with oares; what's   600
the matter? why weep'st thou man? away asse, you'l
loose the Tide, if you tarry any longer.

LAUNCE It is no matter if the tide were lost, for it is the
vnkindest Tide, that euer any man tide.

PANTHINO What's the vnkindest tide?

LAUNCE Why, he that's tide here, *Crab* my dog.

PANTHINO Tut, man: I meane thou'lt loose the flood, and
in loosing the flood, loose thy voyage, and in loosing
thy voyage, loose thy Master, and in loosing thy Master,
610   loose thy seruice, and in loosing thy seruice:—

Launce stops Panthinos mouth

why dost thou stop my mouth?

LAUNCE For feare thou shouldst loose thy tongue.

PANTHINO Where should I loose my tongue?

LAUNCE In thy Tale.

PANTHINO In thy Taile.

LAUNCE Loose the Tide, and the voyage, and the Master,
and the Seruice, and the tide: why man, if the Riuer
were drie, I am able to fill it with my teares: if the
winde were downe, I could driue the boate with my
620   sighes.

PANTHINO Come: come away man, I was sent to call thee.

LAUNCE Sir: call me what thou dar'st.

PANTHINO Wilt thou goe?

LAUNCE Well, I will goe.   *Exeunt*

Sc. 7   *Enter Valentine, Siluia, Thurio, and Speed*
(2.4)   SILUIA Seruant.

VALENTINE Mistris.

SPEED (*to Valentine*) Master, Sir *Thurio* frownes on you.

VALENTINE I Boy, it's for loue.

SPEED Not of you.

630   VALENTINE Of my Mistresse then.

SPEED 'Twere good you knockt him.

SILUIA (*to Valentine*) Seruant, you are sad.

VALENTINE Indeed, Madam, I seeme so.

THURIO Seeme you that you are not?

VALENTINE Hap'ly I doe.

THURIO So doe Counterfeyts.

VALENTINE So doe you.

THURIO What seeme I that I am not?

VALENTINE Wise.

640   THURIO What instance of the contrary?

VALENTINE Your folly.

THURIO And how quoat you my folly?

VALENTINE I quoat it in your Ierkin.

THURIO My Ierkin is a doublet.

VALENTINE Well then, Ile double your folly.

THURIO How?

SILUIA What, angry, Sir *Thurio*, do you change colour?

VALENTINE Giue him leaue, Madam, he is a kind of
Camelion.

650   THURIO That hath more minde to feed on your bloud,
then liue in your ayre.

VALENTINE You haue said Sir.

THURIO I Sir, and done too for this time.

VALENTINE I know it wel sir, you alwaies end ere you
begin.

SILUIA A fine volly of words, gentlemē, & quickly shot off.

VALENTINE 'Tis indeed, Madam, we thank the giuer.

SILUIA Who is that Seruant?

VALENTINE Your selfe (sweet Lady) for you gaue the fire,

Sir *Thurio* borrows his wit from your Ladiships lookes,   660
and spends what he borrowes kindly in your company.

THURIO Sir, if you spend word for word with me, I shall
make your wit bankrupt.

VALENTINE I know it well sir: you haue an Exchequer of
words, and I thinke, no other treasure to giue your
followers: For it appeares by their bare Liueries that
they liue by your bare words.

SILUIA No more, gentlemen, no more: Here comes my
father.

Enter the Duke

DUKE

Now, daughter *Siluia*, you are hard beset.   670

Sir *Valentine*, your father is in good health,

What say you to a Letter from your friends

Of much good newes?

VALENTINE   My Lord, I will be thankfull,

To any happy messenger from thence.

DUKE

Know ye *Don Antonio*, your Countriman?

VALENTINE

I, my good Lord, I know the Gentleman

To be of worth, and worthy estimation,

And not without desert so well reputed.

DUKE Hath he not a Sonne?

VALENTINE

I, my good Lord, a Son, that well deserues   680

The honor, and regard of such a father.

DUKE You know him well?

VALENTINE

I knew him as my selfe: for from our Infancie

We haue conuerst, and spent our howres together,

And though my selfe haue beene an idle Trewant,

Omitting the sweet benefit of time

To cloath mine age with Angel-like perfection:

Yet hath Sir *Protheus* (for that's his name)

Made vse, and faire aduantage of his daies:

His yeares but yong, but his experience old: 690

His head vn-mellowed, but his Iudgement ripe;

And in a word (for far behinde his worth

Comes all the praises that I now bestow,)

He is compleat in feature, and in minde,

With all good grace, to grace a Gentleman.

DUKE

Beshrew me sir, but if he make this good

He is as worthy for an Empresse loue,

As meet to be an Emperors Councellor:

Well, Sir: this Gentleman is come to me

With Commendation from great Potentates,   700

And heere he meanes to spend his time a while,

I thinke 'tis no vn-welcome newes to you.

VALENTINE

Should I haue wish'd a thing, it had beene he.

DUKE

Welcome him then according to his worth:

Siluia, I speake to you, and you Sir *Thurio*,

For *Valentine*, I need not cite him to it,

I will send him hither to you presently.   *Exit*

VALENTINE
This is the Gentleman I told your Ladiship
Had come along with me, but that his Mistresse
710 Did hold his eyes, lockt in her Christall lookes.
SILUIA
Be-like that now she hath enfranchis'd them
Vpon some other pawne for fealty.
VALENTINE
Nay sure, I thinke she holds them prisoners stil.
SILUIA
Nay then he should be blind, and being blind
How could he see his way to seeke out you?
VALENTINE
Why Lady, Loue hath twenty paire of eyes.
THURIO
They say that Loue hath not an eye at all.
VALENTINE
To see such Louers, *Thurio*, as your selfe,
Vpon a homely obiect, Loue can winke.
SILUIA
720 Haue done, haue done: here comes yᵉ gentleman.
    Enter Protheus
VALENTINE
Welcome, deer *Protheus*: Mistris, I beseech you
Confirme his welcome, with some speciall fauor.
SILUIA
His worth is warrant for his welcome hether,
If this be he you oft haue wish'd to heare from.
VALENTINE
Mistris, it is: sweet Lady, entertaine him
To be my fellow-seruant to your Ladiship.
SILUIA
Too low a Mistres for so high a seruant.
PROTHEUS
Not so, sweet Lady, but too meane a seruant
To haue a looke of such a worthy Mistresse.
VALENTINE
730 Leaue off discourse of disabilitie:
Sweet Lady, entertaine him for your Seruant.
PROTHEUS
My dutie will I boast of, nothing else.
SILUIA
And dutie neuer yet did want his meed.
Seruant, you are welcome to a worthlesse Mistresse.
PROTHEUS
Ile die on him that saies so but your selfe.
SILUIA
That you are welcome?
PROTHEUS   That you are worthlesse.
   ⌜*Enter a Seruant*⌝
⌜SERUANT⌝
Madam, my Lord your father wold speak with you.
SILUIA
I wait vpon his pleasure: ⌜*Exit the Seruant*⌝
        Come Sir *Thurio*,
Goe with me: once more, new Seruant welcome;
740 Ile leaue you to confer of home affaires,
When you haue done, we looke too heare from you.

PROTHEUS
Wee'll both attend vpon your Ladiship.
        Exeunt Siluia and Thurio
VALENTINE
Now tell me: how do al from whence you came?
PROTHEUS
Your frends are wel, & haue thẽ much cõmended.
VALENTINE
And how doe yours?
PROTHEUS   I left them all in health.
VALENTINE
How does your Lady? & how thriues your loue?
PROTHEUS
My tales of Loue were wont to weary you,
I know you ioy not in a Loue-discourse.
VALENTINE
I *Protheus*, but that life is alter'd now,
I haue done pennance for contemning Loue,   750
Whose high emperious thoughts haue punish'd me
With bitter fasts, with penitentiall grones,
With nightly teares, and daily hart-sore sighes,
For in reuenge of my contempt of loue,
Loue hath chas'd sleepe from my enthralled eyes,
And made them watchers of mine owne hearts sorrow.
O gentle *Protheus*, Loue's a mighty Lord,
And hath so humbled me, as I confesse
There is no woe to his correction,
Nor to his Seruice, no such ioy on earth: 760
Now, no discourse, except it be of loue:
Now can I breake my fast, dine, sup, and sleepe,
Vpon the very naked name of Loue.
PROTHEUS
Enough; I read your fortune in your eye:
Was this the Idoll, that you worship so?
VALENTINE
Euen She; and is she not a heauenly Saint?
PROTHEUS
No; But she is an earthly Paragon.
VALENTINE
Call her diuine.
PROTHEUS   I will not flatter her.
VALENTINE
O flatter me: for Loue delights in praises.
PROTHEUS
When I was sick, you gaue me bitter pils,   770
And I must minister the like to you.
VALENTINE
Then speake the truth by her; if not diuine,
Yet let her be a principalitie,
Soueraigne to all the Creatures on the earth.
PROTHEUS
Except my Mistresse.
VALENTINE   Sweet: except not any,
Except thou wilt except against my Loue.
PROTHEUS
Haue I not reason to prefer mine owne?
VALENTINE
And I will help thee to prefer her to:
Shee shall be dignified with this high honour,

780 To beare my Ladies traine, lest the base earth
Should from her vesture chance to steale a kisse,
And of so great a fauor growing proud,
Disdaine to roote the Sommer-swelling flowre,
And make rough winter euerlastingly.

PROTHEUS
Why *Valentine*, what Bragadisme is this?

VALENTINE
Pardon me (*Protheus*) all I can is nothing,
To her, whose worth, makes other worthies nothing;
Shee is alone.

PROTHEUS   Then let her alone.

VALENTINE
Not for the world: why man, she is mine owne,
790 And I as rich in hauing such a Iewell
As twenty Seas, if all their sand were pearle,
The water, Nectar, and the Rocks pure gold.
Forgiue me, that I doe not dreame on thee,
Because thou seest me doate vpon my loue:
My foolish Riuall that her Father likes
(Onely for his possessions are so huge)
Is gone with her along, and I must after,
For Loue (thou know'st is full of iealousie.)

PROTHEUS But she loues you?

VALENTINE
I, and we are betroathd: nay more, our mariage
800   howre,
With all the cunning manner of our flight
Determin'd of: how I must climbe her window,
The Ladder made of Cords, and all the means
Plotted, and 'greed on for my happinesse.
Good *Protheus* goe with me to my chamber,
In these affaires to aid me with thy counsaile.

PROTHEUS
Goe on before: I shall enquire you forth:
I must vnto the Road, to dis-embarque
Some necessaries, that I needs must vse,
810 And then Ile presently attend you.

VALENTINE Will you make haste?

PROTHEUS I will.   *Exit Valentine*
Euen as one heate, another heate expels,
Or as one naile, by strength driues out another,
So the remembrance of my former Loue
Is by a newer obiect quite forgotten,
Is it mine eye, or *Valentines* praise?
Her true perfection, or my false transgression?
That makes me reasonlesse, to reason thus?
820 Shee is faire: and so is *Iulia* that I loue,
(That I did loue, for now my loue is thaw'd,
Which like a waxen Image 'gainst a fire
Beares no impression of the thing it was.)
Me thinkes my zeale to *Valentine* is cold,
And that I loue him not as I was wont:
O, but I loue his Lady too-too much,
And that's the reason I loue him so little.
How shall I doate on her with more aduice,
That thus without aduice begin to loue her?
830 'Tis but her picture I haue yet beheld,

And that hath dazeled my reasons light:
But when I looke on her perfections,
There is no reason, but I shall be blinde.
If I can checke my erring loue, I will,
If not, to compasse her Ile vse my skill.   *Exit*

Enter Speed, and Launce with his dog Crab   Sc. 8
                                                (2.5)
SPEED *Launce*, by mine honesty welcome to *Milan*.

LAUNCE Forsweare not thy selfe, sweet youth, for I am
not welcome. I reckon this alwaies, that a man is neuer
vndon till hee be hang'd, nor neuer welcome to a place,
till some certaine shot be paid, and the Hostesse say   840
welcome.

SPEED Come-on you mad-cap: Ile to the Ale-house with
you presently; where, for one shot of fiue pence, thou
shalt haue fiue thousand welcomes: But sirha, how did
thy Master part with Madam *Iulia*?

LAUNCE Marry after they cloas'd in earnest, they parted
very fairely in iest.

SPEED But shall she marry him?

LAUNCE No.

SPEED How then? shall he marry her?   850

LAUNCE No, neither.

SPEED What, are they broken?

LAUNCE No; they are both as whole as a fish.

SPEED Why then, how stands the matter with them?

LAUNCE Marry thus, when it stands well with him, it
stands well with her.

SPEED What an asse art thou, I vnderstand thee not.

LAUNCE What a blocke art thou, that thou canst not? My
staffe vnderstands me?

SPEED What thou saist?   860

LAUNCE I, and what I do too: looke thee, Ile but leane,
and my staffe vnderstands me.

SPEED It stands vnder thee indeed.

LAUNCE Why, stand-vnder: and vnder-stand is all one.

SPEED But tell me true, wil't be a match?

LAUNCE Aske my dogge, if he say I, it will: if hee say no,
it will: if hee shake his taile, and say nothing, it will.

SPEED The conclusion is then, that it will.

LAUNCE Thou shalt neuer get such a secret from me, but
by a parable.   870

SPEED 'Tis well that I get it so: but *Launce*, how saist thou
that my master is become a notable Louer?

LAUNCE I neuer knew him otherwise.

SPEED Then how?

LAUNCE A notable Lubber: as thou reportest him to bee.

SPEED Why, thou whorson Asse, thou mistak'st me.

LAUNCE Why Foole, I meant not thee, I meant thy Master.

SPEED I tell thee, my Master is become a hot Louer.

LAUNCE Why, I tell thee, I care not, though hee burne
himselfe in Loue. If thou wilt, goe with me to the   880
Alehouse: if not, thou art an Hebrew, a Iew, and not
worth the name of a Christian.

SPEED Why?

LAUNCE Because thou hast not so much charity in thee
as to goe to the Ale with a Christian: Wilt thou goe?

SPEED At thy seruice.   *Exeunt*

Sc. 9   *Enter Protheus solus*
(2.6)   PROTHEUS
          To leaue my *Iulia*; shall I be forsworne;
          To loue faire *Siluia*; shall I be forsworne;
          To wrong my friend, I shall be much forsworne.
890   And eu'n that Powre which gaue me first my oath
          Prouokes me to this three-fold periurie.
          Loue bad mee sweare, and Loue bids me for-sweare;
          O sweet-suggesting Loue, if thou hast sin'd,
          Teach me (thy tempted subiect) to excuse it.
          At first I did adore a twinkling Starre,
          But now I worship a celestiall Sunne:
          Vn-heedfull vowes may heedfully be broken,
          And he wants wit, that wants resolued will,
          To learne his wit, t'exchange the bad for better;
900   Fie, fie, vnreuerend tongue, to call her bad,
          Whose soueraignty so oft thou hast preferd,
          With twenty thousand soule-confirming oathes.
          I cannot leaue to loue; and yet I doe:
          But there I leaue to loue, where I should loue.
          Iulia I loose, and *Valentine* I loose,
          If I keepe them, I needs must loose my selfe:
          If I loose them, thus finde I by their losse,
          For *Valentine*, my selfe: for *Iulia*, *Siluia*.
          I to my selfe am deerer then a friend,
910   For Loue is still most precious in it selfe,
          And *Siluia* (witnesse heauen that made her faire)
          Shewes *Iulia* but a swarthy Ethiope.
          I will forget that *Iulia* is aliue,
          Remembring that my Loue to her is dead.
          And *Valentine* Ile hold an Enemie,
          Ayming at *Siluia* as a sweeter friend.
          I cannot now proue constant to my selfe,
          Without some treachery vs'd to *Valentine*.
          This night he meaneth with a Corded-ladder
920   To climbe celestiall *Siluia's* chamber window,
          My selfe in counsaile his competitor.
          Now presently Ile giue her father notice
          Of their disguising and pretended flight:
          Who (all inrag'd) will banish *Valentine*:
          For *Thurio* he intends shall wed his daughter,
          But *Valentine* being gon, Ile quickely crosse
          By some slie tricke, blunt *Thurio's* dull proceeding.
          Loue lend me wings, to make my purpose swift
          As thou hast lent me wit, to plot this drift.   *Exit*

Sc. 10   *Enter Iulia and Lucetta*
(2.7)   IULIA
930   Counsaile, *Lucetta*, gentle girle assist me,
          And eu'n in kinde loue, I doe coniure thee,
          Who art the Table wherein all my thoughts
          Are visibly Character'd, and engrau'd,
          To lesson me, and tell me some good meane
          How with my honour I may vndertake
          A iourney to my louing *Protheus*.
             LUCETTA
          Alas, the way is wearisome and long.

IULIA
          A true-deuoted Pilgrime is not weary
          To measure Kingdomes with his feeble steps,
          Much lesse shall she that hath Loues wings to flie,   940
          And when the flight is made to one so deere,
          Of such diuine perfection as Sir *Protheus*.
LUCETTA
          Better forbeare, till *Protheus* make returne.
IULIA
          Oh, know'st y^u not, his looks are my soules food?
          Pitty the dearth that I haue pined in,
          By longing for that food so long a time.
          Didst thou but know the inly touch of Loue,
          Thou wouldst as soone goe kindle fire with snow
          As seeke to quench the fire of Loue with words.
LUCETTA
          I doe not seeke to quench your Loues hot fire,   950
          But qualifie the fires extreame rage,
          Lest it should burne aboue the bounds of reason.
IULIA
          The more thou dam'st it vp, the more it burnes:
          The Current that with gentle murmure glides
          (Thou know'st) being stop'd, impatiently doth rage:
          But when his faire course is not hindered,
          He makes sweet musicke with th'enameld stones,
          Giuing a gentle kisse to euery sedge
          He ouer-taketh in his pilgrimage.
          And so by many winding nookes he straies   960
          With willing sport to the wilde Ocean.
          Then let me goe, and hinder not my course:
          Ile be as patient as a gentle streame,
          And make a pastime of each weary step,
          Till the last step haue brought me to my Loue,
          And there Ile rest, as after much turmoile
          A blessed soule doth in *Elizium*.
LUCETTA
          But in what habit will you goe along?
IULIA
          Not like a woman, for I would preuent
          The loose encounters of lasciuious men: 970
          Gentle *Lucetta*, fit me with such weedes
          As may beseeme some well reputed Page.
LUCETTA
          Why then your Ladiship must cut your haire.
IULIA
          No girle, Ile knit it vp in silken strings,
          With twentie od-conceited true-loue knots:
          To be fantastique, may become a youth
          Of greater time then I shall shew to be.
LUCETTA
          What fashion (Madam) shall I make your breeches?
IULIA
          That fits as well, as tell me (good my Lord)
          What compasse will you weare your Farthingale?   980
          Why eu'n what fashion thou best likes (*Lucetta*.)
LUCETTA
          You must needs haue thē with a cod-peece (Madam.)

IULIA

Out, out, (*Lucetta*) that wilbe illfauourd.

LUCETTA

A round hose (Madam) now's not worth a pin
Vnlesse you haue a cod-peece to stick pins on.

IULIA

Lucetta, as thou lou'st me let me haue
What thou think'st meet, and is most mannerly.
But tell me (wench) how will the world repute me
For vndertaking so vnstaid a iourney?
990   I feare me it will make me scandaliz'd.

LUCETTA

If you thinke so, then stay at home, and go not.

IULIA Nay, that I will not.

LUCETTA

Then neuer dreame on Infamy, but go:
If *Protheus* like your iourney, when you come,
No matter who's displeas'd, when you are gone:
I feare me he will scarce be pleas'd with all.

IULIA

That is the least (*Lucetta*) of my feare:
A thousand oathes, an Ocean of his teares,
And instances of infinite of Loue,
1000   Warrant me welcome to my *Protheus*.

LUCETTA

All these are seruants to deceitfull men.

IULIA

Base men, that vse them to so base effect;
But truer starres did gouerne *Protheus* birth,
His words are bonds, his oathes are oracles,
His loue sincere, his thoughts immaculate,
His teares, pure messengers, sent from his heart,
His heart, as far from fraud, as heauen from earth.

LUCETTA

Pray heau'n he proue so when you come to him.

IULIA

Now, as thou lou'st me, do him not that wrong,
1010   To beare a hard opinion of his truth:
Onely deserue my loue, by louing him,
And presently goe with me to my chamber
To take a note of what I stand in need of,
To furnish me vpon my longing iourney:
All that is mine I leaue at thy dispose,
My goods, my Lands, my reputation,
Onely, in lieu thereof, dispatch me hence:
Come; answere not: but to it presently,
I am impatient of my tarriance.   *Exeunt*

Sc. 11   *Enter Duke, Thurio, and Protheus*
(3.1)   DUKE
1020   Sir *Thurio*, giue vs leaue (I pray) a while,
We haue some secrets to confer about.   *Exit Thurio*
Now tell me *Protheus*, what's your will with me?

PROTHEUS

My gracious Lord, that which I wold discouer,
The Law of friendship bids me to conceale,
But when I call to minde your gracious fauours
Done to me (vndeseruing as I am)
My dutie pricks me on to vtter that

Which else, no worldly good should draw from me:
Know (worthy Prince) Sir *Valentine* my friend
This night intends to steale away your daughter: 1030
My selfe am one made priuy to the plot.
I know you haue determin'd to bestow her
On *Thurio*, whom your gentle daughter hates,
And should she thus be stolne away from you,
It would be much vexation to your age.
Thus (for my duties sake) I rather chose
To crosse my friend in his intended drift,
Then (by concealing it) heap on your head
A pack of sorrowes, which would presse you downe
(Being vnpreuented) to your timelesse graue.   1040

DUKE

Protheus, I thank thee for thine honest care,
Which to requite, command me while I liue.
This loue of theirs, my selfe haue often seene,
Haply when they haue iudg'd me fast asleepe,
And oftentimes haue purpos'd to forbid
Sir *Valentine* her companie, and my Court.
But fearing lest my iealous ayme might erre,
And so (vnworthily) disgrace the man
(A rashnesse that I euer yet haue shun'd)
I gaue him gentle lookes, thereby to finde   1050
That which thy selfe hast now disclos'd to me.
And that thou maist perceiue my feare of this,
Knowing that tender youth is soone suggested,
I nightly lodge her in an vpper Towre,
The key whereof, my selfe haue euer kept:
And thence she cannot be conuay'd away.

PROTHEUS

Know (noble Lord) they haue deuis'd a meane
How he her chamber-window will ascend,
And with a Corded-ladder fetch her downe:
For which, the youthfull Louer now is gone,   1060
And this way comes he with it presently.
Where (if it please you) you may intercept him.
But (good my Lord) doe it so cunningly
That my discouery be not aimed at:
For, loue of you, not hate vnto my friend,
Hath made me publisher of this pretence.

DUKE

Vpon mine Honor, he shall neuer know
That I had any light from thee of this.

PROTHEUS

Adiew, my Lord, Sir *Valentine* is comming.   *Exit*
          Enter Valentine

DUKE

Sir *Valentine*, whether away so fast?   1070

VALENTINE

Please it your Grace, there is a Messenger
That stayes to beare my Letters to my friends,
And I am going to deliuer them.

DUKE Be they of much import?

VALENTINE

The tenure of them doth but signifie
My health, and happy being at your Court.

DUKE

Nay then no matter: stay with me a while,

I am to breake with thee of some affaires
That touch me neere: wherein thou must be secret.
1080 'Tis not vnknown to thee, that I haue sought
To match my friend Sir *Thurio*, to my daughter.
VALENTINE
I know it well (my Lord) and sure the Match
Were rich and honourable: besides, the gentleman
Is full of Vertue, Bounty, Worth, and Qualities
Beseeming such a Wife, as your faire daughter:
Cannot your Grace win her to fancie him?
DUKE
No, trust me, She is peeuish, sullen, froward,
Prowd, disobedient, stubborne, lacking duty,
Neither regarding that she is my childe,
1090 Nor fearing me, as if I were her father:
And may I say to thee, this pride of hers
(Vpon aduice) hath drawne my loue from her,
And where I thought the remnant of mine age
Should haue beene cherish'd by her child-like dutie,
I now am full resolu'd to take a wife,
And turne her out, to who will take her in:
Then let her beauty be her wedding dowre:
For me, and my possessions she esteemes not.
VALENTINE
What would your Grace haue me to do in this?
DUKE
1100 There is a Lady of *Verona* heere
Whom I affect: but she is nice, and coy,
And naught esteemes my aged eloquence.
Now therefore would I haue thee to my Tutor
(For long agone I haue forgot to court,
Besides the fashion of the time is chang'd)
How, and which way I may bestow my selfe
To be regarded in her sun-bright eye.
VALENTINE
Win her with gifts, if she respect not words,
Dumbe Iewels often in their silent kinde
1110 More then quicke words, doe moue a womans minde.
DUKE
But she did scorne a present that I sent her.
VALENTINE
A woman somtime scorns what best cõtents her.
Send her another: neuer giue her ore,
For scorne at first, makes after-loue the more.
If she doe frowne, 'tis not in hate of you,
But rather to beget more loue in you.
If she doe chide, 'tis not to haue you gone,
For why, the fooles are mad, if left alone.
Take no repulse, what euer she doth say,
1120 For, get you gon, she doth not meane away.
Flatter, and praise, commend, extoll their graces:
Though nere so blacke, say they haue Angells faces,
That man that hath a tongue, I say is no man,
If with his tongue he cannot win a woman.
DUKE
But she I meane, is promis'd by her friends
Vnto a youthfull Gentleman of worth,
And kept seuerely from resort of men,
That no man hath accesse by day to her.

VALENTINE
Why then I would resort to her by night.
DUKE
I, but the doores be lockt, and keyes kept safe,   1130
That no man hath recourse to her by night.
VALENTINE
What letts but one may enter at her window?
DUKE
Her chamber is aloft, far from the ground,
And built so sheluing, that one cannot climbe it
Without apparant hazard of his life.
VALENTINE
Why then a Ladder quaintly made of Cords
To cast vp, with a paire of anchoring hookes,
Would serue to scale another *Hero's* towre,
So bold *Leander* would aduenture it.
DUKE
Now as thou art a Gentleman of blood   1140
Aduise me, where I may haue such a Ladder.
VALENTINE
When would you vse it? pray sir, tell me that.
DUKE
This very night; for Loue is like a childe
That longs for euery thing that he can come by.
VALENTINE
By seauen a clock, ile get you such a Ladder.
DUKE
But harke thee: I will goe to her alone,
How shall I best conuey the Ladder thither?
VALENTINE
It will be light (my Lord) that you may beare it
Vnder a cloake, that is of any length.
DUKE
A cloake as long as thine will serue the turne?   1150
VALENTINE
I my good Lord.
DUKE   Then let me see thy cloake,
Ile get me one of such another length.
VALENTINE
Why any cloake will serue the turn (my Lord.)
DUKE
How shall I fashion me to weare a cloake?
I pray thee let me feele thy cloake vpon me.
He lifts Valentines cloake and findes a Letter and a
    rope-ladder
What Letter is this same? what's here? to *Siluia*?
And heere an Engine fit for my proceeding,
Ile be so bold to breake the seale for once.
(*Reads*)
My thoughts do harbour with my Siluia nightly,
    And slaues they are to me, that send them flying.   1160
Oh, could their Master come, and goe as lightly,
    Himselfe would lodge where (senceles) they are lying.
My Herald Thoughts, in thy pure bosome rest-them,
    While I (their King) that thither them importune
Doe curse the grace, that with such grace hath blest them,
    Because my selfe doe want my seruants fortune.
I curse my selfe, for they are sent by me,
    That they should harbour where their Lord should be.

15

What's here?

1170   *Siluia, this night I will enfranchise thee.*
        'Tis so: and heere's the Ladder for the purpose.
        Why *Phaeton* (for thou art *Merops* sonne)
        Wilt thou aspire to guide the heauenly Car?
        And with thy daring folly burne the world?
        Wilt thou reach stars, because they shine on thee?
        Goe base Intruder, ouer-weening Slaue,
        Bestow thy fawning smiles on equall mates,
        And thinke my patience, (more then thy desert)
        Is priuiledge for thy departure hence.

1180   Thanke me for this, more then for all the fauors
        Which (all too-much) I haue bestowed on thee.
        But if thou linger in my Territories
        Longer then swiftest expedition
        Will giue thee time to leaue our royall Court,
        By heauen, my wrath shall farre exceed the loue
        I euer bore my daughter, or thy selfe.
        Be gone, I will not heare thy vaine excuse,
        But as thou lou'st thy life, make speed from hence.
                                                    Exit

        VALENTINE
        And why not death, rather then liuing torment?
1190   To die, is to be banisht from my selfe,
        And *Siluia* is my selfe: banish'd from her
        Is selfe from selfe. A deadly banishment:
        What light, is light, if *Siluia* be not seene?
        What ioy is ioy, if *Siluia* be not by?
        Vnlesse it be to thinke that she is by
        And feed vpon the shadow of perfection.
        Except I be by *Siluia* in the night,
        There is no musicke in the Nightingale.
        Vnlesse I looke on *Siluia* in the day,
1200   There is no day for me to looke vpon.
        Shee is my essence, and I leaue to be
        If I be not by her faire influence
        Foster'd, illumin'd, cherish'd, kept aliue.
        I flie not death, to flie his deadly doome,
        Tarry I heere, I but attend on death,
        But flie I hence, I flie away from life.
                Enter Protheus and Launce
        PROTHEUS Run (boy) run, run, and seeke him out.
        LAUNCE So-hough, Soa hough—
        PROTHEUS What seest thou?
1210   LAUNCE Him we goe to finde, there's not a haire on's
        head, but 'tis a *Valentine.*
        PROTHEUS *Valentine?*
        VALENTINE No.
        PROTHEUS Who then? his Spirit?
        VALENTINE Neither.
        PROTHEUS What then?
        VALENTINE Nothing.
        LAUNCE Can nothing speake?
                He threatens Valentine
        Master, shall I strike?
1220   PROTHEUS Who wouldst thou strike?
        LAUNCE Nothing.
        PROTHEUS Villaine, forbeare.
        LAUNCE Why Sir, Ile strike nothing: I pray you—

PROTHEUS
    Sirha, I say forbeare: friend *Valentine,* a word.
VALENTINE
    My eares are stopt, & cannot hear good newes,
    So much of bad already hath possest them.
PROTHEUS
    Then in dumbe silence will I bury mine,
    For they are harsh, vn-tuneable, and bad.
VALENTINE
    Is *Siluia* dead?
PROTHEUS   No, *Valentine.*
VALENTINE
    No *Valentine* indeed, for sacred *Siluia,*   1230
    Hath she forsworne me?
PROTHEUS   No, *Valentine.*
VALENTINE
    No *Valentine,* if *Siluia* haue forsworne me.
    What is your newes?
LAUNCE Sir, there is a proclamation, y^t you are vanished.
PROTHEUS
    That thou art banish'd: oh that's the newes,
    From hence, from *Siluia,* and from me thy friend.
VALENTINE
    Oh, I haue fed vpon this woe already,
    And now excesse of it will make me surfet.
    Doth *Siluia* know that I am banished?
PROTHEUS
    I, I: and she hath offer'd to the doome   1240
    (Which vn-reuerst stands in effectuall force)
    A Sea of melting pearle, which some call teares;
    Those at her fathers churlish feete she tenderd,
    With them vpon her knees, her humble selfe,
    Wringing her hands, whose whitenes so became them,
    As if but now they waxed pale, for woe:
    But neither bended knees, pure hands held vp,
    Sad sighes, deepe grones, nor siluer-shedding teares
    Could penetrate her vncompassionate Sire;
    But *Valentine,* if he be tane, must die.   1250
    Besides, her intercession chaf'd him so,
    When she for thy repeale was suppliant,
    That to close prison he commanded her,
    With many bitter threats of biding there.
VALENTINE
    No more: vnles the next word that thou speak'st
    Haue some malignant power vpon my life:
    If so: I pray thee breath it in mine eare,
    As ending Antheme of my endlesse dolor.
PROTHEUS
    Cease to lament for that thou canst not helpe,
    And study helpe for that which thou lament'st,   1260
    Time is the Nurse, and breeder of all good;
    Here, if thou stay, thou canst not see thy loue:
    Besides, thy staying will abridge thy life:
    Hope is a louers staffe, walke hence with that
    And manage it, against despairing thoughts:
    Thy letters may be here, though thou art hence,
    Which, being writ to me, shall be deliuer'd
    Euen in the milke-white bosome of thy Loue.
    The time now serues not to expostulate,

1270 Come, Ile conuey thee through the City-gate.
And ere I part with thee, confer at large
Of all that may concerne thy Loue-affaires:
As thou lou'st *Siluia* (though not for thy selfe)
Regard thy danger, and along with me.

VALENTINE
I pray thee *Launce*, and if thou seest my Boy
Bid him make haste, and meet me at the North-gate.

PROTHEUS
Goe sirha, finde him out: Come *Valentine*.

VALENTINE
Oh my deere *Siluia*; haplesse *Valentine*.
Exeunt Protheus and Valentine

LAUNCE I am but a foole, looke you, and yet I haue the
1280 wit to thinke my Master is a kinde of a knaue: but
that's all one, if he be but one knaue: He liues not
now that knowes me to be in loue, yet I am in loue,
but a Teeme of horse shall not plucke that from me:
nor who 'tis I loue: and yet 'tis a woman; but what
woman, I will not tell my selfe: and yet 'tis a Milke-
maid: yet 'tis not a maid: for shee hath had Gossips:
yet 'tis a maid, for she is her Masters maid, and serues
for wages. Shee hath more qualities then a Water-
Spaniell, which is much in a bare Christian:
He takes out a paper
1290 Heere is the Cate-log of her Conditions. *Inprimis*. Shee
can fetch and carry: why a horse can doe no more;
nay, a horse cannot fetch, but onely carry, therefore
is shee better then a Iade. *Item*. She can milke, looke
you, a sweet vertue in a maid with cleane hands.
Enter Speed
SPEED How now Signior *Launce*? what newes with your
Mastership?
LAUNCE With my Mastership? why, it is at Sea.
SPEED Well, your old vice still: mistake the word: what
newes then in your paper?
1300 LAUNCE The black'st newes that euer thou heard'st.
SPEED Why man? how blacke?
LAUNCE Why, as blacke as Inke.
SPEED Let me read them?
LAUNCE Fie on thee Iolt-head, thou canst not read.
SPEED Thou lyest: I can.
LAUNCE I will try thee: tell me this: who begot thee?
SPEED Marry, the son of my Grand-father.
LAUNCE Oh illiterate loyterer; it was the sonne of thy
Grand-mother: this proues that thou canst not read.
1310 SPEED Come foole, come: try me in thy paper.
LAUNCE (*giuing Speed the paper*) There: and S. *Nicholas* be
thy speed.
SPEED Inprimis she can milke.
LAUNCE I that she can.
SPEED Item, she brewes good Ale.
LAUNCE And thereof comes the prouerbe: (*Blessing of your
heart, you brew good Ale.*)
SPEED Item, she can sowe.
LAUNCE That's as much as to say (*Can she so?*)
1320 SPEED Item she can knit.
LAUNCE What neede a man care for a stock with a wench,
when she can knit him a stocke?

SPEED Item, she can wash and scoure.
LAUNCE A speciall vertue: for then shee neede not be
wash'd, and scowr'd.
SPEED Item, she can spin.
LAUNCE Then may I set the world on wheeles, when she
can spin for her liuing.
SPEED Item, she hath many namelesse vertues.
LAUNCE That's as much as to say *Bastard-vertues*: that   1330
indeede know not their fathers; and therefore haue no
names.
SPEED Here followes her vices.
LAUNCE Close at the heeles of her vertues.
SPEED Item, shee is not to be broken with fasting in
respect of her breth.
LAUNCE Well: that fault may be mended with a breakfast:
read on.
SPEED Item, she hath a sweet mouth.
LAUNCE That makes amends for her soure breath.   1340
SPEED Item, she doth talke in her sleepe.
LAUNCE It's no matter for that; so shee sleepe not in her
talke.
SPEED Item, she is slow in words.
LAUNCE Oh villaine, that set this downe among her vices;
to be slow in words, is a womans onely vertue: I pray
thee out with't, and place it for her chiefe vertue.
SPEED Item, she is proud.
LAUNCE Out with that too: it was *Eues* legacie, and cannot
be t'ane from her.   1350
SPEED Item, she hath no teeth.
LAUNCE I care not for that neither: because I loue crusts.
SPEED Item, she is curst.
LAUNCE Well: the best is, she hath no teeth to bite.
SPEED Item, she will often praise her liquor.
LAUNCE If her liquor be good, she shall: if she will not, I
will; for good things should be praised.
SPEED Item, she is too liberall.
LAUNCE Of her tongue she cannot; for that's writ downe
she is slow of: of her purse, shee shall not, for that ile   1360
keepe shut: Now, of another thing shee may, and that
cannot I helpe. Well, proceede.
SPEED Item, shee hath more haire then wit, and more
faults then haires, and more wealth then faults.
LAUNCE Stop there: Ile haue her: she was mine, and not
mine, twice or thrice in that last Article: rehearse that
once more.
SPEED Item, she hath more haire then wit.
LAUNCE More haire then wit: it may be. Ile proue it: The
couer of the salt, hides the salt, and therefore it is more   1370
then the salt; the haire that couers the wit, is more
then the wit; for the greater hides the lesse: What's
next?
SPEED And more faults then haires.
LAUNCE That's monstrous: oh that that were out.
SPEED And more wealth then faults.
LAUNCE Why that word makes the faults gracious: Well,
ile haue her: and if it be a match, as nothing is
impossible—
SPEED What then?   1380

LAUNCE Why then, will I tell thee, that thy Master staies
    for thee at the *North gate.*

SPEED For me?

LAUNCE For thee? I, who art thou? he hath staid for a
    better man then thee.

SPEED And must I goe to him?

LAUNCE Thou must run to him; for thou hast staid so
    long, that going will scarce serue the turne.

SPEED Why didst not tell me sooner? 'pox of your loue

1390   Letters.   *Exit*

LAUNCE Now will he be swing'd for reading my Letter;
    An vnmannerly slaue, that will thrust himselfe into
    secrets: Ile after, to reioyce in the boyes correctiõ.
                                    Exit

Sc. 12   *Enter Duke and Thurio*

(3.2) DUKE

    Sir *Thurio*, feare not, but that she will loue you,
    Now *Valentine* is banish'd from her sight.

THURIO

    Since his exile she hath despis'd me most,
    Forsworne my company, and rail'd at me,
    That I am desperate of obtaining her.

DUKE

    This weake impresse of Loue, is as a figure

1400   Trenched in ice, which with an houres heate
    Dissolues to water, and doth loose his forme.
    A little time will melt her frozen thoughts,
    And worthlesse *Valentine* shall be forgot.

        Enter Protheus

    How now sir *Protheus*, is your countriman
    (According to our Proclamation) gon?

PROTHEUS Gon, my good Lord.

DUKE

    My daughter takes his going grieuously?

PROTHEUS

    A little time (my Lord) will kill that griefe.

DUKE

    So I beleeue: but *Thurio* thinkes not so:

1410   *Protheus*, the good conceit I hold of thee,
    (For thou hast showne some signe of good desert)
    Makes me the better to confer with thee.

PROTHEUS

    Longer then I proue loyall to your Grace,
    Let me not liue, to looke vpon your Grace.

DUKE

    Thou know'st how willingly, I would effect
    The match betweene sir *Thurio*, and my daughter?

PROTHEUS I doe my Lord.

DUKE

    And also, I thinke, thou art not ignorant
    How she opposes her against my will?

PROTHEUS

1420   She did my Lord, when *Valentine* was here.

DUKE

    I, and peruersly, she perseuers so:
    What might we doe to make the girle forget
    The loue of *Valentine*, and loue sir *Thurio*?

PROTHEUS

    The best way is, to slander *Valentine*,
    With falsehood, cowardize, and poore discent:
    Three things, that women highly hold in hate.

DUKE

    I, but she'll thinke, that it is spoke in hate.

PROTHEUS

    I, if his enemy deliuer it.
    Therefore it must with circumstance be spoken
    By one, whom she esteemeth as his friend.   1430

DUKE

    Then you must vndertake to slander him.

PROTHEUS

    And that (my Lord) I shall be loath to doe:
    'Tis an ill office for a Gentleman,
    Especially against his very friend.

DUKE

    Where your good word cannot aduantage him,
    Your slander neuer can endamage him;
    Therefore the office is indifferent,
    Being intreated to it by your friend.

PROTHEUS

    You haue preuail'd (my Lord) if I can doe it
    By ought that I can speake in his dispraise,   1440
    She shall not long continue loue to him:
    But say this weede her loue from *Valentine*,
    It followes not that she will loue sir *Thurio*.

THURIO

    Therefore, as you vnwinde her loue from him;
    Least it should rauell, and be good to none,
    You must prouide to bottome it on me:
    Which must be done, by praising me as much
    As you, in worth dispraise, sir *Valentine*.

DUKE

    And *Protheus*, we dare trust you in this kinde,
    Because we know (on *Valentines* report)   1450
    You are already loues firme votary,
    And cannot soone reuolt, and change your minde.
    Vpon this warrant, shall you haue accesse,
    Where you, with *Siluia*, may conferre at large.
    For she is lumpish, heauy, mellancholly,
    And (for your friends sake) will be glad of you;
    Where you may temper her, by your perswasion,
    To hate yong *Valentine*, and loue my friend.

PROTHEUS

    As much as I can doe, I will effect:
    But you sir *Thurio*, are not sharpe enough: 1460
    You must lay Lime, to tangle her desires
    By walefull Sonnets, whose composed Rimes
    Should be full fraught with seruiceable vowes.

DUKE

    I, much is the force of heauen-bred Poesie.

PROTHEUS

    Say that vpon the altar of her beauty
    You sacrifice your teares, your sighes, your heart:
    Write till your inke be dry: and with your teares
    Moist it againe: and frame some feeling line,
    That may discouer such integrity:
    For *Orpheus* Lute, was strung with Poets sinewes,   1470

Whose golden touch could soften steele and stones;
Make Tygers tame, and huge *Leuiathans*
Forsake vnsounded deepes, to dance on Sands.
After your dire-lamenting Elegies,
Visit by night your Ladies chamber-window
With some sweet Consort; To their Instruments
Tune a deploring dumpe: the nights dead silence
Will well become such sweet complaining grieuance:
This, or else nothing, will inherit her.

DUKE
1480   This discipline, showes thou hast bin in loue.

THURIO
And thy aduice, this night, ile put in practise:
Therefore, sweet *Protheus*, my direction-giuer,
Let vs into the City presently
To sort some Gentlemen, well skil'd in Musicke.
I haue a Sonnet, that will serue the turne
To giue the on-set to thy good aduise.

DUKE About it Gentlemen.

PROTHEUS
We'll wait vpon your Grace, till after Supper,
And afterward determine our proceedings.

DUKE
1490   Euen now about it, I will pardon you.
              Exeunt Thurio and Protheus at one doore, and
                            the Duke at another

Sc. 13   *Enter certaine Out-lawes*
(4.1)   1. OUT-LAW
Fellowes, stand fast: I see a passenger.

2. OUT-LAW
If there be ten, shrinke not, but down with 'em.
            Enter Valentine and Speed

3. OUT-LAW
Stand sir, and throw vs that you haue about 'ye.
If not: we'll make you sit, and rifle you.

SPEED (*to Valentine*)
Sir we are vndone; these are the Villaines
That all the Trauailers doe feare so much.

VALENTINE (*to the Out-lawes*) My friends.

1. OUT-LAW
That's not so, sir: we are your enemies.

2. OUT-LAW Peace: we'll heare him.

1500 3. OUT-LAW I by my beard will we: for he is a proper
man.

VALENTINE
Then know that I haue little wealth to loose;
A man I am, cross'd with aduersitie:
My riches, are these poore habiliments,
Of which, if you should here disfurnish me,
You take the sum and substance that I haue.

2. OUT-LAW Whether trauell you?

VALENTINE To Verona.

1. OUT-LAW Whence came you?

1510 VALENTINE From *Millaine*.

3. OUT-LAW Haue you long soiourn'd there?

VALENTINE
Some sixteene moneths, and longer might haue staid,
If crooked fortune had not thwarted me.

1. OUT-LAW
What, were you banish'd thence?

VALENTINE   I was.

2. OUT-LAW   For what offence?

VALENTINE
For that which now torments me to rehearse;
I kil'd a man, whose death I much repent,
But yet I slew him manfully, in fight,
Without false vantage, or base treachery.

1. OUT-LAW
Why nere repent it, if it were done so;
But were you banisht for so small a fault?   1520

VALENTINE
I was, and held me glad of such a doome.

2. OUT-LAW Haue you the Tongues?

VALENTINE
My youthfull trauaile, therein made me happy,
Or else I had beene often miserable.

3. OUT-LAW
By the bare scalpe of *Robin Hoods* fat Fryer,
This fellow were a King, for our wilde faction.

1. OUT-LAW
We'll haue him: Sirs, a word.
        The Out-lawes confer

SPEED (*to Valentine*)   Master, be one of them:
It's an honourable kinde of theeuery.

VALENTINE Peace villaine.

2. OUT-LAW
Tell vs this: haue you any thing to take to?   1530

VALENTINE Nothing but my fortune.

3. OUT-LAW
Know then, that some of vs are Gentlemen,
Such as the fury of vngouern'd youth
Thrust from the company of awfull men.
My selfe was from *Verona* banished,
For practising to steale away a Lady,
An heire and neere alide vnto the Duke.

2. OUT-LAW
And I from *Mantua*, for a Gentleman,
Who, in my moode, I stab'd vnto the heart.

1. OUT-LAW
And I, for such like petty crimes as these.   1540
But to the purpose: for we cite our faults,
That they may hold excus'd our lawlesse liues;
And partly seeing you are beautifide
With goodly shape; and by your owne report,
A Linguist, and a man of such perfection,
As we doe in our quality much want—

2. OUT-LAW
Indeede because you are a banish'd man,
Therefore, aboue the rest, we parley to you:
Are you content to be our Generall?
To make a vertue of necessity,   1550
And liue as we doe in this wildernesse?

3. OUT-LAW
What saist thou? wilt thou be of our consort?
Say I, and be the captaine of vs all:
We'll doe thee homage, and be rul'd by thee,
Loue thee, as our Commander, and our King.

1. OUT-LAW

But if thou scorne our curtesie, thou dyest.

2. OUT-LAW

Thou shalt not liue, to brag what we haue offer'd.

VALENTINE

I take your offer, and will liue with you,
Prouided that you do no outrages
1560   On silly women, or poore passengers.

3. OUT-LAW

No, we detest such vile base practises.
Come, goe with vs, we'll bring thee to our Crewes,
And show thee all the Treasure we haue got;
Which, with our selues, all rest at thy dispose.

                                        Exeunt

Sc. 14   *Enter Protheus*
(4.2)   PROTHEUS

Already haue I bin false to *Valentine*,
And now I must be as vniust to *Thurio*,
Vnder the colour of commending him,
I haue accesse my owne loue to prefer.
But *Siluia* is too faire, too true, too holy,
1570   To be corrupted with my worthlesse guifts;
When I protest true loyalty to her,
She twits me with my falsehood to my friend;
When to her beauty I commend my vowes,
She bids me thinke how I haue bin forsworne
In breaking faith with *Iulia*, whom I lou'd;
And notwithstanding all her sodaine quips,
The least whereof would quell a louers hope:
Yet (Spaniel-like) the more she spurnes my loue,
The more it growes, and fawneth on her still;
1580   But here comes *Thurio*; now must we to her window,
And giue some euening Musique to her eare.
            Enter Thurio with Musitians

THURIO

How now, sir *Protheus*, are you crept before vs?

PROTHEUS

I gentle *Thurio*, for you know that loue
Will creepe in seruice, where it cannot goe.

THURIO

I, but I hope, Sir, that you loue not here.

PROTHEUS

Sir, but I doe: or else I would be hence.

THURIO

Who, *Siluia*?

PROTHEUS   I, *Siluia*, for your sake.

THURIO

I thanke you for your owne: Now Gentlemen
Let's tune: and too it lustily a while.
            *Enter the Host, and Iulia as a boy. They speake
            apart*

1590   HOST Now, my yong guest; me thinks your' allycholly; I
        pray you why is it?

IULIA Marry (mine *Host*) because I cannot be merry.

HOST Come, we'll haue you merry: ile bring you where
        you shall heare Musique, and see the Gentleman that
        you ask'd for.

IULIA But shall I heare him speake.

HOST I that you shall.

IULIA That will be Musique.

HOST Harke, harke.

IULIA Is he among these?

HOST I: but peace, let's heare'm.   1600

                        Song

        Who is Siluia? what is she?
            That all our Swaines commend her?
        Holy, faire, and wise is she,
            The heauen such grace did lend her,
        That she might admired be.

        Is she kinde as she is faire?
            For beauty liues with kindnesse:
        Loue doth to her eyes repaire,
            To helpe him of his blindnesse: 1610
        And being help'd, inhabits there.

        Then to Siluia, let vs sing,
            That Siluia is excelling;
        She excels each mortall thing
            Vpon the dull earth dwelling.
        To her let vs Garlands bring.

HOST How now? are you sadder then you were before;
        How doe you, man? the Musicke likes you not.

IULIA You mistake: the Musitian likes me not.

HOST Why, my pretty youth?   1620

IULIA He plaies false (father.)

HOST How, out of tune on the strings.

IULIA Not so: but yet so false that he grieues my very
        heart-strings.

HOST You haue a quicke eare.

IULIA I, I would I were deafe: it makes me haue a slow
        heart.

HOST I perceiue you delight not in Musique.

IULIA Not a whit, when it iars so.

HOST Harke, what fine change is in the Musique.   1630

IULIA I: that change is the spight.

HOST You would haue them alwaies play but one thing.

IULIA I would alwaies haue one play but one thing. But
        Host, doth this Sir *Protheus*, that we talke on, often
        resort vnto this Gentlewoman?

HOST I tell you what *Launce* his man told me, he lou'd
        her out of all nicke.

IULIA Where is *Launce*?

HOST Gone to seeke his dog, which to morrow, by his
        Masters command, hee must carry for a present to his   1640
        Lady.

IULIA Peace, stand aside, the company parts.

PROTHEUS

Sir *Thurio*, feare not you, I will so pleade,
That you shall say, my cunning drift excels.

THURIO

Where meete we?

PROTHEUS   At Saint *Gregories* well.

THURIO   Farewell.
            Exeunt Thurio and the Musitians

Enter Siluia, aboue

PROTHEUS

Madam: good euen to your Ladiship.

SILUIA

I thanke you for your Musique (Gentlemen)
Who is that that spake?

PROTHEUS

One (Lady) if you knew his pure hearts truth,
1650   You would quickly learne to know him by his voice.

SILUIA Sir *Protheus*, as I take it.

PROTHEUS

Sir *Protheus* (gentle Lady) and your Seruant.

SILUIA

What's your will?

PROTHEUS   That I may compasse yours.

SILUIA

You haue your wish: my will is euen this,
That presently you hie you home to bed:
Thou subtile, periur'd, false, disloyall man:
Think'st thou I am so shallow, so conceitlesse,
To be seduced by thy flattery,
That has't deceiu'd so many with thy vowes?
1660   Returne, returne, and make thy loue amends:
For me (by this pale queene of night I sweare)
I am so farre from granting thy request,
That I despise thee, for thy wrongfull suite;
And by and by intend to chide my selfe,
Euen for this time I spend in talking to thee.

PROTHEUS

I grant (sweet loue) that I did loue a Lady,
But she is dead.

IULIA (*aside*)   'Twere false, if I should speake it;
For I am sure she is not buried.

SILUIA

Say that she be: yet *Valentine* thy friend
1670   Suruiues; to whom (thy selfe art witnesse)
I am betroth'd; and art thou not asham'd
To wrong him, with thy importunacy?

PROTHEUS

I likewise heare that *Valentine* is dead.

SILUIA

And so suppose am I; for in his graue
Assure thy selfe, my loue is buried.

PROTHEUS

Sweet Lady, let me rake it from the earth.

SILUIA

Goe to thy Ladies graue and call hers thence,
Or at the least, in hers, sepulcher thine.

IULIA (*aside*) He heard not that.

PROTHEUS

1680   Madam: if your heart be so obdurate:
Vouchsafe me yet your Picture for my loue,
The Picture that is hanging in your chamber:
To that ile speake, to that ile sigh and weepe:
For since the substance of your perfect selfe
Is else deuoted, I am but a shadow;
And to your shadow, will I make true loue.

IULIA (*aside*)

If 'twere a substance you would sure deceiue it,
And make it but a shadow, as I am.

SILUIA

I am very loath to be your Idoll Sir;
But, since your falsehood shall become you well   1690
To worship shadowes, and adore false shapes,
Send to me in the morning, and ile send it:
And so, good rest.   *Exit*

PROTHEUS   As wretches haue ore-night
That wait for execution in the morne.   *Exit*

IULIA *Host*, will you goe?

HOST By my hallidome, I was fast asleepe.

IULIA Pray you, where lies Sir *Protheus*?

HOST Marry, at my house: Trust me, I thinke 'tis almost
day.

IULIA

Not so: but it hath bin the longest night   1700
That ere I watch'd, and the most heauiest.   *Exeunt*

Enter Eglamore   Sc. 15
                                         (4.3)
EGLAMOURE

This is the houre that Madam *Siluia*
Entreated me to call, and know her minde:
Ther's some great matter she'ld employ me in.
Madam, Madam.

        Enter Siluia ⌈*aboue*⌉

SILUIA   Who cals?

EGLAMOURE   Your seruant, and your friend;
One that attends your Ladiships command.

SILUIA

Sir *Eglamore*, a thousand times good morrow.

EGLAMOURE

As many (worthy Lady) to your selfe:
According to your Ladiships impose,
I am thus early come, to know what seruice   1710
It is your pleasure to command me in.

SILUIA

Oh *Eglamoure*, thou art a Gentleman:
Thinke not I flatter (for I sweare I doe not)
Valiant, wise, remorse-full, well accomplish'd.
Thou art not ignorant what deere good will
I beare vnto the banish'd *Valentine*:
Nor how my father would enforce me marry
Vaine *Thurio* (whom my very soule abhors.)
Thy selfe hast lou'd, and I haue heard thee say
No griefe did euer come so neere thy heart,   1720
As when thy Lady, and thy true-loue dide,
Vpon whose Graue thou vow'dst pure chastitie:
Sir *Eglamoure*: I would to *Valentine*
To *Mantua*, where I heare, he makes aboad;
And for the waies are dangerous to passe,
I doe desire thy worthy company,
Vpon whose faith and honor, I repose.
Vrge not my fathers anger (*Eglamoure*)
But thinke vpon my griefe (a Ladies griefe)
And on the iustice of my flying hence,   1730

To keepe me from a most vnholy match,
Which heauen and fortune still rewards with plagues.
I doe desire thee, euen from a heart
As full of sorrowes, as the Sea of sands,
To beare me company, and goe with me:
If not, to hide what I haue said to thee,
That I may venture to depart alone.

EGLAMOURE
Madam, I pitty much your grieuances,
Which, since I know they vertuously are plac'd,
1740   I giue consent to goe along with you,
Wreaking as little what betideth me,
As much, I wish all good befortune you.
When will you goe?

SILUIA   This euening comming.

EGLAMOURE
Where shall I meete you?

SILUIA   At *Frier Patrickes* Cell,
Where I intend holy Confession.

EGLAMOURE
I will not faile your Ladiship:
Good morrow (gentle Lady.)

SILUIA
Good morrow, kinde Sir *Eglamoure.*   *Exeunt*

Sc. 16   *Enter Launce and his dog Crab*
(4.4)
    LAUNCE (*to the audience*) When a mans seruant shall play
1750   the Curre with him (looke you) it goes hard: one that
I brought vp of a puppy: one that I sau'd from
drowning, when three or foure of his blinde brothers
and sisters went to it: I haue taught him (euen as one
would say precisely, thus I would teach a dog) I was
sent to deliuer him, as a present to Mistris *Siluia*, from
my Master; and I came no sooner into the dyning-
chamber, but he steps me to her Trencher, and steales
her Capons-leg: O, 'tis a foule thing, when a Cur cannot
keepe himselfe in all companies: I would haue (as one
1760   should say) one that takes vpon him to be a dog
indeede, to be, as it were, a dog at all things. If I had
not had more wit then he, to take a fault vpon me that
he did, I thinke verily hee had bin hang'd for't: sure
as I liue he had suffer'd for't: you shall iudge: Hee
thrusts me himselfe into the company of three or foure
gentleman-like-dogs, vnder the Dukes table: hee had
not bin there (blesse the marke) a pissing while, but
all the chamber smelt him: out with the dog (saies
one) what cur is that (saies another) whip him out
1770   (saies the third) hang him vp (saies the Duke.) I hauing
bin acquainted with the smell before, knew it was Crab;
and goes me to the fellow that whips the dogges: friend
(quoth I) you meane to whip the dog: I marry doe I
(quoth he) you doe him the more wrong (quoth I) 'twas
I did the thing you wot of: he makes me no more adoe,
but whips me out of the chamber: how many Masters
would doe this for his Seruant? nay, ile be sworne I
haue sat in the stockes, for puddings he hath stolne,
otherwise he had bin executed: I haue stood on the
1780   Pillorie for Geese he hath kil'd, otherwise he had sufferd
for't: (*to Crab*) thou think'st not of this now: nay, I

remember the tricke you seru'd me, when I tooke my
leaue of Madam *Siluia*: did not I bid thee still marke
me, and doe as I do; when did'st thou see me heaue
vp my leg, and make water against a Gentlewomans
farthingale? did'st thou euer see me doe such a tricke?

     Enter Protheus, with Iulia as a boy

PROTHEUS (*to Iulia*)
Sebastian is thy name: I like thee well,
And will imploy thee in some seruice presently.

IULIA
In what you please, ile doe what I can.

PROTHEUS
I hope thou wilt. How now you whorson pezant,   1790
Where haue you bin these two dayes loytering?

LAUNCE Marry Sir, I carried Mistris *Siluia* the dogge you
bad me.

PROTHEUS And what saies she to my little Iewell?

LAUNCE Marry she saies your dog was a cur, and tels you
currish thanks is good enough for such a present.

PROTHEUS But she receiu'd my dog?

LAUNCE No indeede did she not: Here haue I brought him
backe againe.

PROTHEUS What, didst thou offer her this from me?   1800

LAUNCE I Sir, the other Squirrill was stolne from me by
the Hangman boyes in the market place, and then I
offer'd her mine owne, who is a dog as big as ten of
yours, & therefore the guift the greater.

PROTHEUS
Goe, get thee hence, and finde my dog againe,
Or nere returne againe into my sight.
Away, I say: stay'st thou to vexe me here;
                     Exit Launce with Crab
A Slaue, that still an end, turnes me to shame:
Sebastian, I haue entertained thee,
Partly that I haue neede of such a youth,   1810
That can with some discretion doe my businesse:
For 'tis no trusting to yond foolish Lowt;
But chiefely, for thy face, and thy behauiour,
Which (if my Augury deceiue me not)
Witnesse good bringing vp, fortune, and truth:
Therefore know thou, for this I entertaine thee.
Go presently, and take this Ring with thee,
Deliuer it to Madam *Siluia*;
She lou'd me well, deliuer'd it to me.

IULIA
It seemes you lou'd not her, to leaue her token: 1820
She is dead belike?

PROTHEUS   Not so: I thinke she liues.

IULIA
Alas.

PROTHEUS Why do'st thou cry alas?

IULIA
I cannot choose but pitty her.

PROTHEUS
Wherefore should'st thou pitty her?

IULIA
Because, me thinkes that she lou'd you as well
As you doe loue your Lady *Siluia*:
She dreames on him, that has forgot her loue,

You doate on her, that cares not for your loue.
'Tis pitty Loue, should be so contrary:
1830 And thinking on it, makes me cry alas.
PROTHEUS
Well: giue her that Ring, and therewithall
This Letter: (*pointing*) that's her chamber: Tell my
    Lady,
I claime the promise for her heauenly Picture:
Your message done, hye home vnto my chamber,
Where thou shalt finde me sad, and solitarie.   *Exit*
IULIA
How many women would doe such a message?
Alas poore *Protheus*, thou hast entertain'd
A Foxe, to be the Shepheard of thy Lambs;
Alas, poore foole, why doe I pitty him
1840 That with his very heart despiseth me?
Because he loues her, he despiseth me,
Because I loue him, I must pitty him.
This Ring I gaue him, when he parted from me,
To binde him to remember my good will:
And now am I (vnhappy Messenger)
To plead for that, which I would not obtaine;
To carry that, which I would haue refus'd;
To praise his faith, which I would haue disprais'd.
I am my Masters true confirmed Loue,
1850 But cannot be true seruant to my Master,
Vnlesse I proue false traitor to my selfe.
Yet will I woe for him, but yet so coldly,
As (heauen it knowes) I would not haue him speed.
        Enter Siluia
Gentlewoman, good day: I pray you be my meane
To bring me where to speake with Madam *Siluia*.
SILUIA
What would you with her, if that I be she?
IULIA
If you be she, I doe intreat your patience
To heare me speake the message I am sent on.
SILUIA From whom?
IULIA
1860 From my Master, Sir *Protheus*, Madam.
SILUIA Oh: he sends you for a Picture?
IULIA I, Madam.
SILUIA *Vrsula*, bring my Picture there,
        ⌈*An Attendant brings a Picture*⌉
Goe, giue your Master this: tell him from me,
One *Iulia*, that his changing thoughts forget
Would better fit his Chamber, then this Shadow.
IULIA
Madam, please you peruse this Letter;
        She giues Siluia a Letter
Pardon me (Madam) I haue vnaduis'd
Deliuer'd you a paper that I should not;
        She takes backe the Letter and giues Siluia another
        Letter
1870 This is the Letter to your Ladiship.
SILUIA
I pray thee let me looke on that againe.
IULIA
It may not be: good Madam pardon me.

SILUIA
There, hold: I will not looke vpon your Masters lines:
I know they are stuft with protestations,
And full of new-found oathes, which he will breake
As easily, as I doe teare his paper.
        She teares the Letter
IULIA
Madam, he sends your Ladiship this Ring.
        She offers Siluia a ring
SILUIA
The more shame for him, that he sends it me;
For I haue heard him say a thousand times,
His *Iulia* gaue it him, at his departure: 1880
Though his false finger haue prophan'd the Ring,
Mine shall not doe his *Iulia* so much wrong.
IULIA She thankes you.
SILUIA What sai'st thou?
IULIA
I thanke you Madam, that you tender her:
Poore Gentlewoman, my Master wrongs her much.
SILUIA Do'st thou know her?
IULIA
Almost as well as I doe know my selfe.
To thinke vpon her woes, I doe protest
That I haue wept a hundred seuerall times.   1890
SILUIA
Belike she thinks that *Protheus* hath forsook her?
IULIA
I thinke she doth: and that's her cause of sorrow.
SILUIA Is she not passing faire?
IULIA
She hath bin fairer (Madam) then she is,
When she did thinke my Master lou'd her well;
She, in my iudgement, was as faire as you.
But since she did neglect her looking-glasse,
And threw her Sun-expelling Masque away,
The ayre hath staru'd the roses in her cheekes,
And pinch'd the lilly-tincture of her face,   1900
That now she is become as blacke as I.
SILUIA How tall was she?
IULIA
About my stature: for at *Pentecost*,
When all our Pageants of delight were plaid,
Our youth got me to play the womans part,
And I was trim'd in Madam *Iulias* gowne,
Which serued me as fit, by all mens iudgements,
As if the garment had bin made for me:
Therefore I know she is about my height,
And at that time I made her weepe a good,   1910
For I did play a lamentable part.
(Madam) 'twas *Ariadne*, passioning
For *Thesus* periury, and vniust flight;
Which I so liuely acted with my teares:
That my poore Mistris moued therewithall,
Wept bitterly: and would I might be dead,
If I in thought felt not her very sorrow.
SILUIA
She is beholding to thee (gentle youth)
Alas (poore Lady) desolate, and left;

1920 I weepe my selfe to thinke vpon thy words:
Here youth: there is my purse; I giue thee this
For thy sweet Mistris sake, because thou lou'st her.
Farewell.   *Exit*

IULIA
And she shall thanke you for't, if ere you know her.
A vertuous gentlewoman, milde, and beautifull.
I hope my Masters suit will be but cold,
Since she respects my Mistris loue so much.
Alas, how loue can trifle with it selfe:
Here is her Picture: let me see, I thinke
1930 If I had such a Tyre, this face of mine
Were full as louely, as is this of hers;
And yet the Painter flatter'd her a little,
Vnlesse I flatter with my selfe too much.
Her haire is *Aburne*, mine is perfect *Yellow*;
If that be all the difference in his loue,
Ile get me such a coulour'd Perrywig:
Her eyes are grey as glasse, and so are mine.
I, but her fore-head's low, and mine's as high:
What should it be that he respects in her,
1940 But I can make respectiue in my selfe?
If this fond Loue, were not a blinded god.
Come shadow, come, and take this shadow vp,
For 'tis thy riuall: O thou sencelesse forme,
Thou shalt be worship'd, kiss'd, lou'd, and ador'd;
And were there sence in his Idolatry,
My substance should be statue in thy stead.
Ile vse thee kindly, for thy Mistris sake
That vs'd me so: or else by *Ioue*, I vow,
I should haue scratch'd out your vnseeing eyes,
1950 To make my Master out of loue with thee.   *Exit*

Sc. 17   *Enter Eglamoure*
(5.1) EGLAMOURE
The Sun begins to guild the westerne skie,
And now it is about the very houre
That *Siluia*, at Fryer *Patricks* Cell should meet me,
She will not faile; for Louers break not houres,
Vnlesse it be to come before their time,
So much they spur their expedition.
        Enter Siluia
See where she comes: Lady a happy euening.

SILUIA
Amen, Amen: goe on (good *Eglamoure*)
Out at the Posterne by the Abbey wall;
1960 I feare I am attended by some Spies.

EGLAMOURE
Feare not: the Forrest is not three leagues off,
If we recouer that, we are sure enough.   *Exeunt*

Sc. 18   *Enter Thurio, Protheus, and Iulia as a boy*
(5.2) THURIO
Sir *Protheus*, what saies *Siluia* to my suit?

PROTHEUS
Oh Sir, I finde her milder then she was,
And yet she takes exceptions at your person.

THURIO
What? that my leg is too long?

PROTHEUS
No, that it is too little.

THURIO
Ile weare a Boote, to make it somewhat rounder.

IULIA (*aside*)
But loue will not be spurd to what it loathes.

THURIO
What saies she to my face?   1970

PROTHEUS
She saies it is a faire one.

THURIO
Nay then the wanton lyes: my face is blacke.

PROTHEUS
But Pearles are faire; and the old saying is,
Blacke men are Pearles, in beauteous Ladies eyes.

IULIA (*aside*)
'Tis true, such Pearles as put out Ladies eyes,
For I had rather winke, then looke on them.

THURIO
How likes she my discourse?

PROTHEUS
Ill, when you talke of war.

THURIO
But well, when I discourse of loue and peace.

IULIA (*aside*)
But better indeede, when you hold your peace.   1980

THURIO
What sayes she to my valour?

PROTHEUS
Oh Sir, she makes no doubt of that.

IULIA (*aside*)
She needes not, when she knowes it cowardize.

THURIO
What saies she to my birth?

PROTHEUS
That you are well deriu'd.

IULIA (*aside*)
True: from a Gentleman, to a foole.

THURIO
Considers she my Possessions?

PROTHEUS
Oh, I: and pitties them.

THURIO Wherefore?

IULIA (*aside*)
That such an Asse should owe them.   1990

PROTHEUS
That they are out by Lease.

IULIA   Here comes the Duke.
        Enter the Duke

DUKE
How now sir *Protheus*; how now *Thurio*?
Which of you saw *Eglamoure* of late?

THURIO
Not I.

PROTHEUS Nor I.

DUKE   Saw you my daughter?

PROTHEUS   Neither.

DUKE
Why then she's fled vnto that pezant, *Valentine*;

24

And *Eglamoure* is in her Company:
'Tis true: for Frier *Laurence* met them both
As he, in pennance wander'd through the Forrest:
Him he knew well: and guesd that it was she,
2000   But being mask'd, he was not sure of it.
Besides she did intend Confession
At *Patricks* Cell this euen, and there she was not.
These likelihoods confirme her flight from hence;
Therefore I pray you stand not to discourse,
But mount you presently, and meete with me
Vpon the rising of the Mountaine foote
That leads toward *Mantua*, whether they are fled:
Dispatch (sweet Gentlemen) and follow me.   *Exit*

THURIO
Why this it is, to be a peeuish Girle,
2010   That flies her fortune when it followes her:
Ile after; more to be reueng'd on *Eglamoure*,
Then for the loue of reck-lesse *Siluia*.   ⌈*Exit*⌉

PROTHEUS
And I will follow, more for *Siluias* loue
Then hate of *Eglamoure* that goes with her.   ⌈*Exit*⌉

IULIA
And I will follow, more to crosse that loue
Then hate for *Siluia*, that is gone for loue.   ⌈*Exit*⌉

Sc. 19   *Enter the Out-lawes with Siluia captiue*
(5.3)   I. OUT-LAW
Come, come be patient: We must bring you to our
          Captaine.

SILUIA
A thousand more mischances then this one
Haue learn'd me how to brooke this patiently.

2020   2. OUT-LAW Come, bring her away.

I. OUT-LAW
Where is the Gentleman that was with her?

3. OUT-LAW
Being nimble footed, he hath out-run vs.
But *Moyses* and *Valerius* follow him:
Goe thou with her to the West end of the wood,
There is our Captaine: Wee'll follow him that's fled,
The Thicket is beset, he cannot scape.

          Exeunt the Second and Third Out-lawes

I. OUT-LAW (*to Siluia*)
Come, I must bring you to our Captains caue.
Feare not: he beares an honourable minde,
And will not vse a woman lawlesly.

SILUIA (*aside*)
2030   O *Valentine*: this I endure for thee.   *Exeunt*

Sc. 20   *Enter Valentine*
(5.4)   VALENTINE
How vse doth breed a habit in a man?
This shadowy desart, vnfrequented woods
I better brooke then flourishing peopled Townes:
Here can I sit alone, vn-seene of any,
And to the Nightingales complaining Notes
Tune my distresses, and record my woes.
O thou that dost inhabit in my brest,
Leaue not the Mansion so long Tenant-lesse,

Lest growing ruinous, the building fall,
And leaue no memory of what it was,   2040
Repaire me, with thy presence, *Siluia*:
Thou gentle Nimph, cherish thy for-lorne swaine.
What hallowing, and what stir is this to day?
These are my mates, that make their wills their Law,
Haue some vnhappy passenger in chace;
They loue me well: yet I haue much to doe
To keepe them from vnciuill outrages.
Withdraw thee *Valentine*: who's this comes heere?
          He stands aloofe.
          Enter Protheus, Siluia, and Iulia as a boy

PROTHEUS
Madam, this seruice I haue done for you
(Though you respect not aught your seruant doth)   2050
To hazard life, and reskew you from him,
That would haue forc'd your honour, and your loue,
Vouchsafe me for my meed, but one faire looke:
(A smaller boone then this I cannot beg,
And lesse then this, I am sure you cannot giue.)

VALENTINE (*aside*)
How like a dreame is this? I see, and heare:
Loue, lend me patience to forbeare a while.

SILUIA
O miserable, vnhappy that I am.

PROTHEUS
Vnhappy were you (Madam) ere I came:
But by my comming, I haue made you happy.   2060

SILUIA
By thy approach thou mak'st me most vnhappy.

IULIA (*aside*)
And me, when he approcheth to your presence.

SILUIA
Had I beene ceazed by a hungry Lion,
I would haue beene a breakfast to the Beast,
Rather then haue false *Protheus* reskue me:
Oh heauen be iudge how I loue *Valentine*,
Whose life's as tender to me as my soule,
And full as much (for more there cannot be)
I doe detest false periur'd *Protheus*:
Therefore be gone, sollicit me no more.   2070

PROTHEUS
What dangerous action, stood it next to death
Would I not vndergoe, for one calme looke:
Oh 'tis the curse in Loue, and still approu'd
When women cannot loue, where they're belou'd.

SILUIA
When *Protheus* cannot loue, where he's belou'd:
Read ouer *Iulia's* heart, (thy first best Loue)
For whose deare sake, thou didst then rend thy faith
Into a thousand oathes; and all those oathes
Descended into periury, to loue me,
Thou hast no faith left now, vnlesse thou'dst two,   2080
And that's farre worse then none: better haue none
Then plurall faith, which is too much by one:
Thou Counterfeyt, to thy true friend.

PROTHEUS   In Loue,
Who respects friend?

SILUIA   All men but *Protheus*.

PROTHEUS

Nay, if the gentle spirit of mouing words
Can no way change you to a milder forme;
Ile wooe you like a Souldier, at armes end,
And loue you 'gainst the nature of Loue: force ye.

SILUIA

Oh heauen.

PROTHEUS (*assailing her*) Ile force thee yeeld to my desire.

VALENTINE (*comming forward*)

2090   Ruffian: let goe that rude vnciuill touch,
Thou friend of an ill fashion.

PROTHEUS   *Valentine.*

VALENTINE

Thou cõmon friend, that's without faith or loue,
For such is a friend now: treacherous man,
Thou hast beguil'd my hopes; nought but mine eye
Could haue perswaded me: now I dare not say
I haue one friend aliue; thou wouldst disproue me:
Who should be trusted, when ones right hand
Is periur'd to the bosome? *Protheus*
I am sorry I must neuer trust thee more,
2100   But count the world a stranger for thy sake:
The priuate wound is deepest: oh time, most accurst:
'Mongst all foes that a friend should be the worst?

PROTHEUS My shame and guilt confounds me:

Forgiue me *Valentine*: if hearty sorrow
Be a sufficient Ransome for offence,
I tender't heere: I doe as truely suffer,
As ere I did commit.

VALENTINE   Then I am paid:

And once againe, I doe receiue thee honest;
Who by Repentance is not satisfied,
2110   Is nor of heauen, nor earth; for these are pleas'd:
By Penitence th'Eternalls wrath's appeas'd:
And that my loue may appeare plaine and free,
All that was mine, in *Siluia*, I giue thee.

IULIA

Oh me vnhappy.
She falls to the ground

PROTHEUS   Looke to the Boy.

VALENTINE   Why, Boy?

Why wag: how now? what's the matter? look vp:
speak.

IULIA O good sir, my master charg'd me to deliuer a ring
to Madam *Siluia*: wᶜ (out of my neglect) was neuer
done.

PROTHEUS Where is that ring? boy?

2120   **IULIA** Heere 'tis: this is it.
She giues Protheus the ring

PROTHEUS How? let me see.

Why this is the ring I gaue to *Iulia*.

IULIA

Oh, cry you mercy sir, I haue mistooke:
She offers Protheus another ring
This is the ring you sent to *Siluia*.

PROTHEUS

But how cam'st thou by this ring? at my depart
I gaue this vnto *Iulia*.

IULIA

And *Iulia* her selfe did giue it me,
And *Iulia* her selfe hath brought it hither.

PROTHEUS How? *Iulia*?

IULIA

Behold her, that gaue ayme to all thy oathes,   2130
And entertain'd 'em deepely in her heart.
How oft hast thou with periury cleft the roote?
Oh *Protheus*, let this habit make thee blush.
Be thou asham'd that I haue tooke vpon me,
Such an immodest rayment; if shame liue
In a disguise of loue?
It is the lesser blot modesty findes,
Women to change their shapes, then men their minds.

PROTHEUS

Then men their minds? tis true: oh heuen, were man
But Constant, he were perfect; that one error   2140
Fils him with faults: makes him run through all
th'sins;
Inconstancy falls-off, ere it begins:
What is in *Siluia's* face, but I may spie
More fresh in *Iulia's*, with a constant eye?

VALENTINE Come, come: a hand from either:

Let me be blest to make this happy close:
'Twere pitty two such friends should be long foes.
Iulia and Protheus ioin hands

PROTHEUS

Beare witnes (heauen) I haue my wish for euer.

IULIA

And I mine.
Enter the Out-lawes with the Duke and Thurio as
captiues

OUT-LAWS   A prize: a prize: a prize.

VALENTINE

Forbeare, forbeare I say: It is my Lord the *Duke*.   2150
The Out-lawes release the Duke and Thurio
(*To the Duke*) Your Grace is welcome to a man
disgrac'd,
Banished *Valentine*.

DUKE   Sir *Valentine*?

THURIO

Yonder is *Siluia*: and *Siluia's* mine.

VALENTINE

Thurio giue backe; or else embrace thy death:
Come not within the measure of my wrath:
Doe not name *Siluia* thine: if once againe,
Verona shall not hold thee: heere she stands,
Take but possession of her, with a Touch—
I dare thee, but to breath vpon my Loue.

THURIO

Sir *Valentine*, I care not for her, I: 2160
I hold him but a foole that will endanger
His Body, for a Girle that loues him not:
I claime her not, and therefore she is thine.

DUKE

The more degenerate and base art thou
To make such meanes for her, as thou hast done,
And leaue her on such slight conditions.

Now, by the honor of my Ancestry,
I doe applaud thy spirit, *Valentine*,
And thinke thee worthy of an Empresse loue:
2170 Know then, I heere forget all former greefes,
Cancell all grudge, repeale thee home againe,
Plead a new state in thy vn-riual'd merit,
To which I thus subscribe: Sir *Valentine*,
Thou art a Gentleman, and well deriu'd,
Take thou thy *Siluia*, for thou hast deseru'd her.

VALENTINE
I thank your Grace, yᵉ gift hath made me happy:
I now beseech you (for your daughters sake)
To grant one Boone that I shall aske of you.

DUKE
I grant it (for thine owne) what ere it be.

VALENTINE
2180 These banish'd men, that I haue kept withall,
Are men endu'd with worthy qualities:
Forgiue them what they haue committed here,
And let them be recall'd from their Exile:
They are reformed, ciuill, full of good,
And fit for great employment (worthy Lord.)

DUKE
Thou hast preuaild, I pardon them and thee:
Dispose of them, as thou knowst their deserts.
Come, let vs goe, we will include all iarres,
With Triumphes, Mirth, and rare solemnity.

VALENTINE
And as we walke along, I dare be bold   2190
With our discourse, to make your Grace to smile.
What thinke you of this Page (my Lord?)

DUKE
I think the Boy hath grace in him, he blushes.

VALENTINE
I warrant you (my Lord) more grace, then Boy.

DUKE What meane you by that saying?

VALENTINE
Please you, Ile tell you, as we passe along,
That you will wonder what hath fortuned:
Come *Protheus*, 'tis your pennance, but to heare
The story of your Loues discouered.
That done, our day of marriage shall be yours,   2200
One Feast, one house, one mutuall happinesse.

Exeunt

FINIS

THE TAMING OF THE SHREW

The Taming of the Shrew was first published in the 1623 Folio, but a related play, shorter and simpler, with the title *The taming of A Shrew*, had appeared in print in 1594. The exact relationship of these plays is disputed. *A Shrew* has sometimes been regarded as the source for *The Shrew*; some scholars have believed that both plays derive independently from an earlier play, now lost; it has even been suggested that Shakespeare wrote both plays. In our view Shakespeare's play was written first, not necessarily on the foundation of an earlier play, and *A Shrew* is an anonymous imitation, written for publication in the hope of capitalizing on the success of Shakespeare's play. The difference between the titles is probably no more significant than the fact that *The Winters Tale* is even now often loosely referred to as *A Winter's Tale*, or *The Comedie of Errors* as *A Comedy of Errors*.

The plot of *The Taming of the Shrew* has three main strands. First comes the Induction showing how a drunken tinker, Christopher Slie, is made to believe himself a lord for whose entertainment a play is to be presented. This resembles an episode in *The Arabian Nights*, in which Caliph Haroun al Raschid plays a similar trick on Abu Hassan. A Latin version of this story was known in Shakespeare's England; it may also have circulated by word of mouth. Second comes the principal plot of the play performed for Slie, in which the shrewish Katherine is wooed, won, and tamed by the fortune-hunting Petruchio. This is a popular narrative theme; Shakespeare may have known a ballad called 'A merry Iest of a Shrewde and Curste Wyfe, Lapped in Morrelle's Skin, for Her Good Behauyour', printed around 1550. The third strand of the play involves Lucentio, Gremio, and Hortensio, all of them suitors for the hand of Katherine's sister, Bianca. This is based on the first English prose comedy, George Gascoigne's *Supposes*, translated from Ludovico Ariosto's *I Suppositi* (1509), acted in 1566, and published in 1573. In *The Taming of the Shrew* as printed in the 1623 Folio Christopher Slie fades out after Act 1, Scene 1 (Sc. 3); in *The Taming of A Shrew* he makes other appearances, and rounds off the play. These episodes may derive from a version of Shakespeare's play different from that preserved in the Folio; we print them as Additional Passages.

The adapting of Shakespeare's play that seems to have occurred early in its career foreshadows its later history on the stage. Seven versions appeared during the seventeenth and eighteenth centuries, culminating in David Garrick's *Catharine and Petruchio*, first performed in 1754. This version, omitting Christopher Slie and concentrating on the taming story, held the stage almost unchallenged until late in the nineteenth century. In various incarnations *The Taming of the Shrew* has always been popular on the stage, but its reputation as a robust comedy verging on farce has often obscured its more subtle and imaginative aspects, brutalizing Petruchio and trivializing Kate. The Induction, finely written, establishes a fundamentally serious concern with the powers of persuasion to change not merely appearance but reality, and this theme is acted out at different levels in both strands of the subsequent action.

The Folio text seems in many ways close to Shakespeare's working papers, but they may have been wholly or partially transcribed.

THE NAMES OF THE ACTORS

In the Induction

CHRISTOPHER SLIE, begger and tinker

A HOSTES

A LORD

BARTHOLOMEW, his page

HUNTSMEN

SERUANTS

PLAYERS

In the play within the play

BAPTISTA Minola, a gentleman of Padua

KATHERINE, his elder daughter

BIANCA, his yonger daughter

PETRUCHIO, a gentleman of Verona, suitor of Katherine

GRUMIO }
CURTIS } his seruants

GREMIO, a rich old man of Padua, suitor of Bianca

HORTENSIO, another suitor, who disguises him selfe as Litio, a teacher

LUCENTIO, from Pisa, who disguises him selfe as Cambio, a teacher

TRANIO }
BIONDELLO } his seruants

VINCENTIO, father of Lucentio

A PEDANT, from Mantua

A WIDOW

A TAILOR

A HABERDASHER

An OFFICER

SERUINGMEN (among them NATHANIEL, PHILIP, JOSEPH, and PETER)

Other seruants of Baptista and Petruchio

The Taming of the Shrew

Sc. 1
(Ind. 1)

Enter Christophero Sly the Begger, and Hostes

SLIE Ile pheeze you infaith.

HOSTES A paire of stockes you rogue.

SLIE Y'are a baggage, the *Slies* are no Rogues. Looke in the Chronicles, we came in with *Richard Conqueror*: therefore *Paucas pallabris*, let the world slide: *Sessa*.

HOSTES You will not pay for the glasses you haue burst?

SLIE No, not a deniere: go by S. *Ieronimie*, goe to thy cold bed, and warme thee.

HOSTES I know my remedie, I must go fetch the Headborough.   *Exit*

10

SLIE Third, or fourth, or fift Borough, Ile answere him by Law. Ile not budge an inch boy: Let him come, and kindly.

> *Falles asleepe.*
>
> *Winde hornes. Enter a Lord from hunting, with his traine*

LORD

Huntsman I charge thee, tender wel my hounds,
Breath *Meriman*, the poore Curre is imbost,
And couple *Clowder* with the deepe-mouth'd brach,
Saw'st thou not boy how *Siluer* made it good
At the hedge corner, in the couldest fault,
I would not loose the dogge for twentie pound.

1. HUNTSMAN

20

Why *Belman* is as good as he my Lord,
He cried vpon it at the meerest losse,
And twice to day pick'd out the dullest sent,
Trust me, I take him for the better dogge.

LORD

Thou art a Foole, if *Eccho* were as fleete,
I would esteeme him worth a dozen such:
But sup them well, and looke vnto them all,
To morrow I intend to hunt againe.

1. HUNTSMAN I will my Lord.

LORD *(seeing Slie)*

What's heere? One dead, or drunke? See doth he breath?

2. HUNTSMAN

30

He breath's my Lord. Were he not warm'd with Ale,
This were a bed but cold to sleep so soundly.

LORD

Oh monstrous beast, how like a swine he lyes.
Grim death, how foule and loathsome is thine image:
Sirs, I will practise on this drunken man.
What thinke you, if he were conuey'd to bed,
Wrap'd in sweet cloathes: Rings put vpon his fingers:
A most delicious banquet by his bed,
And braue attendants neere him when he wakes,
Would not the begger then forget himselfe?

1. HUNTSMAN

40

Beleeue me Lord, I thinke he cannot choose.

2. HUNTSMAN

It would seem strange vnto him when he wak'd.

LORD

Euen as a flatt'ring dreame, or worthles fancie.
Then take him vp, and manage well the iest:
Carrie him gently to my fairest Chamber,
And hang it round with all my wanton pictures:
Balme his foule head in warme distilled waters,
And burne sweet Wood to make the Lodging sweete:
Procure me Musicke readie when he wakes,
To make a dulcet and a heauenly sound:
And if he chance to speake, be readie straight   50
(And with a lowe submissiue reuerence)
Say, what is it your Honor wil command:
Let one attend him with a siluer Bason
Full of Rose-water, and bestrew'd with Flowers,
Another beare the Ewer: the third a Diaper,
And say wilt please your Lordship coole your hands.
Some one be readie with a costly suite,
And aske him what apparrel he will weare:
Another tell him of his Hounds and Horse,
And that his Ladie mournes at his disease,   60
Perswade him that he hath bin Lunaticke,
And when he sayes he is, say that he dreames,
For he is nothing but a mightie Lord:
This do, and do it kindly, gentle sirs,
It wil be pastime passing excellent,
If it be husbanded with modestie.

1. HUNTSMAN

My Lord I warrant you we wil play our part
As he shall thinke by our true diligence
He is no lesse then what we say he is.

LORD

Take him vp gently, and to bed with him,   70
And each one to his office when he wakes.

> *Seruingmen carrie Slie out*
>
> *Sound trumpets*

Sirrah, go see what Trumpet 'tis that sounds,

> *Exit Seruingman*

Belike some Noble Gentleman that meanes
(Trauelling some iourney) to repose him heere.

> *Enter Seruingman*

How now? who is it?

SERUINGMAN   An't please your Honor, Players
That offer seruice to your Lordship.

> *Enter Players*

LORD

Bid them come neere: Now fellowes, you are welcome.

PLAYERS We thanke your Honor.

LORD

Do you intend to stay with me to night?

31

A PLAYER

80   So please your Lordshippe to accept our dutie.

LORD

With all my heart. This fellow I remember,
Since once he plaide a Farmers eldest sonne,
'Twas where you woo'd the Gentlewoman so well:
I haue forgot your name: but sure that part
Was aptly fitted, and naturally perform'd.

ANOTHER PLAYER

I thinke 'twas *Soto* that your honor meanes.

LORD

'Tis verie true, thou didst it excellent:
Well you are come to me in happie time,
The rather for I haue some sport in hand,
90   Wherein your cunning can assist me much.
There is a Lord will heare you play to night;
But I am doubtfull of your modesties,
Least (ouer-eying of his odde behauiour,
For yet his honor neuer heard a play)
You breake into some merrie passion,
And so offend him: for I tell you sirs,
If you should smile, he growes impatient.

A PLAYER

Feare not my Lord, we can contain our selues,
Were he the veriest anticke in the world.

LORD (*to a Seruingman*)

100   Go sirra, take them to the Butterie,
And giue them friendly welcome euerie one,
Let them want nothing that my house affoords.

Exit one with the Players

(*To a Seruingman*) Sirra go you to Bartholmew my
    Page,
And see him drest in all suites like a Ladie:
That done, conduct him to the drunkards chamber,
And call him Madam, do him obeisance:
Tell him from me (as he will win my loue)
He beare himselfe with honourable action,
Such as he hath obseru'd in noble Ladies
110   Vnto their Lords, by them accomplished,
Such dutie to the drunkard let him do:
With soft lowe tongue, and lowly curtesie,
And say: What is't your Honor will command,
Wherein your Ladie, and your humble wife,
May shew her dutie, and make knowne her loue.
And then with kinde embracements, tempting kisses,
And with declining head into his bosome
Bid him shed teares, as being ouer-ioyed
To see her noble Lord restor'd to health,
120   Who for this seuen yeares hath esteemed him
No better then a poore and loathsome begger:
And if the boy haue not a womans guift
To raine a shower of commanded teares,
An Onion wil do well for such a shift,
Which in a Napkin (being close conuei'd)
Shall in despight enforce a waterie eie:
See this dispatch'd with all the hast thou canst,
Anon Ile giue thee more instructions.

Exit a seruingman

I know the boy will wel vsurpe the grace,
Voice, gate, and action of a Gentlewoman: 130
I long to heare him call the drunkard husband,
And how my men will stay themselues from laughter,
When they do homage to this simple peasant.
Ile in to counsell them: haply my presence
May well abate the ouer-merrie spleene,
Which otherwise would grow into extreames.   *Exeunt*

Enter aloft Slie the drunkard with attendants,   **Sc. 2**
    some with apparel, Bason and Ewer, & other   **(Ind. 2)**
    appurtenances, & Lord

SLIE For Gods sake a pot of small Ale.

1. SERUINGMAN

Wilt please your Lordship drink a cup of sacke?

2. SERUINGMAN

Wilt please your Honor taste of these Conserues?

3. SERUINGMAN

What raiment wil your honor weare to day.   140

SLIE I am *Christophero Sly*, call not mee Honour nor
Lordship: I ne're drank sacke in my life: and if you
giue me any Conserues, giue me conserues of Beefe:
nere ask me what raiment Ile weare, for I haue no
more doublets then backes: no more stockings then
legges: nor no more shooes then feet, nay sometime
more feete then shooes, or such shooes as my toes
looke through the ouer-leather.

LORD

Heauen cease this idle humor in your Honor.
Oh that a mightie man of such discent,   150
Of such possessions, and so high esteeme
Should be infused with so foule a spirit.

SLIE What would you make me mad? Am not I *Christopher
Slie*, old Slies sonne of Burton-heath, by byrth a Pedler,
by education a Cardmaker, by transmutation a Beare-
heard, and now by present profession a Tinker. Aske
Marrian Hacket the fat Alewife of Wincot, if shee know
me not: if she say I am not xiiii.d. on the score for
sheere Ale, score me vp for the lyingst knaue in
Christendome. What I am not bestraught: here's—   160

3. SERUINGMAN

Oh this it is that makes your Ladie mourne.

2. SERUINGMAN

Oh this is it that makes your seruants droop.

LORD

Hence comes it, that your kindred shuns your house
As beaten hence by your strange Lunacie.
Oh Noble Lord, bethinke thee of thy birth,
Call home thy ancient thoughts from banishment,
And banish hence these abiect lowlie dreames:
Looke how thy seruants do attend on thee,
Each in his office readie at thy becke.
Wilt thou haue Musicke?   *Musick*
        Harke Apollo plaies,   170
And twentie caged Nightingales do sing.
Or wilt thou sleepe? Wee'l haue thee to a Couch,
Softer and sweeter then the lustfull bed
On purpose trim'd vp for Semiramis.

Say thou wilt walke: we wil bestrow the ground.
Or wilt thou ride? Thy horses shal be trap'd,
Their harnesse studded all with Gold and Pearle.
Dost thou loue hawking? Thou hast hawkes will
    soare
Aboue the morning Larke. Or wilt thou hunt,
180 Thy hounds shall make the Welkin answer them
And fetch shrill ecchoes from the hollow earth.

I. SERUINGMAN

Say thou wilt course, thy gray-hounds are as swift
As breathed Stags: I fleeter then the Roe.

2. SERUINGMAN

Dost thou loue pictures? we wil fetch thee strait
Adonis painted by a running brooke,
And Citherea all in sedges hid,
Which seeme to moue and wanton with her breath,
Euen as the wauing sedges play with winde.

LORD

Wee'l shew thee _Io_, as she was a Maid,
190 And how she was beguiled and surpriz'd,
As liuelie painted, as the deede was done.

3. SERUINGMAN

Or _Daphne_ roming through a thornie wood,
Scratching her legs, that one shal sweare she bleeds,
And at that sight shal sad Apollo weepe,
So workmanlie the blood and teares are drawne.

LORD

Thou art a Lord, and nothing but a Lord:
Thou hast a Ladie farre more Beautifull,
Then any woman in this waining age.

I. SERUINGMAN

And til the teares that she hath shed for thee,
200 Like enuious flouds ore-run her louely face,
She was the fairest creature in the world,
And yet shee is inferiour to none.

SLIE

Am I a Lord, and haue I such a Ladie?
Or do I dreame? Or haue I dream'd till now?
I do not sleepe: I see, I heare, I speake:
I smel sweet sauours, and I feele soft things:
Vpon my life I am a Lord indeede,
And not a Tinker, nor Christopher Slie.
Well, bring our Ladie hither to our sight,
210 And once againe a pot o'th smallest Ale.

2. SERUINGMAN

Wilt please your mightinesse to wash your hands:
Oh how we ioy to see your wit restor'd,
Oh that once more you knew but what you are:
These fifteene yeeres you haue bin in a dreame,
Or when you wak'd, so wak'd as if you slept.

SLIE

These fifteene yeeres, by my fay, a goodly nap,
But did I neuer speake of all that time.

I. SERUINGMAN

Oh yes my Lord, but verie idle words,
For though you lay heere in this goodlie chamber,
220 Yet would you say, ye were beaten out of doore,

And raile vpon the Hostesse of the house,
And say you would present her at the Leete,
Because she brought stone-Iugs, and no seal'd quarts:
Sometimes you would call out for Cicely Hacket.

SLIE I, the womans maide of the house.

3. SERUINGMAN

Why sir you know no house, nor no such maid
Nor no such men as you haue reckon'd vp,
As _Stephen Slie_, and old _Iohn Naps_ of Greete,
And _Peter Turph_, and _Henry Pimpernell_,
And twentie more such names and men as these,   230
Which neuer were, nor no man euer saw.

SLIE

Now Lord be thanked for my good amends.

ALL Amen.

SLIE I thanke thee, thou shalt not loose by it.
      Enter Bartholomew the Page, as Lady, with
      Attendants

BARTHOLOMEW

How fares my noble Lord?

SLIE   Marrie I fare well,
For heere is cheere enough. Where is my wife?

BARTHOLOMEW

Heere noble Lord, what is thy will with her?

SLIE

Are you my wife, and will not cal me husband?
My men should call me Lord, I am your good-man.

BARTHOLOMEW

My husband and my Lord, my Lord and husband   240
I am your wife in all obedience.

SLIE

I know it well, (_to the Lord_) what must I call her?

LORD   Madam.

SLIE _Alce_ Madam, or _Ione_ Madam?

LORD

Madam, and nothing else, so Lords cal Ladies.

SLIE

Madame wife, they say that I haue dream'd,
And slept aboue some fifteene yeare or more.

BARTHOLOMEW

I, and the time seeme's thirty vnto me,
Being all this time abandon'd from your bed.

SLIE

'Tis much, seruants leaue me and her alone:
           Exeunt ⌐Lord and⌐ attendants
Madam vndresse you, and come now to bed.   250

BARTHOLOMEW

Thrice noble Lord, let me intreat of you
To pardon me yet for a night or two:
Or if not so, vntill the Sun be set.
For your Physitians haue expressely charg'd,
In perill to incurre your former malady,
That I should yet absent me from your bed:
I hope this reason stands for my excuse.

SLIE I, it stands so that I may hardly tarry so long: But
I would be loth to fall into my dreames againe: I wil
therefore tarrie in despight of the flesh & the blood.   260

Enter a Messenger

MESSENGER

Your Honors Players hearing your amendment,
Are come to play a pleasant Comedie,
For so your doctors hold it very meete,
Seeing too much sadnesse hath congeal'd your blood,
And melancholly is the Nurse of frenzie,
Therefore they thought it good you heare a play,
And frame your minde to mirth and merriment,
Which barres a thousand harmes, and lengthens life.

SLIE

Marrie I will let them play it, is not a Comontie,
270   A Christmas gambold, or a tumbling tricke?

BARTHOLOMEW

No my good Lord, it is more pleasing stuffe.

SLIE

What, houshold stuffe.

BARTHOLOMEW   It is a kinde of history.

SLIE

Well, we'l see't: Come Madam wife sit by my side,
And let the world slip, we shall nere be yonger.
Bartholomew sits

Sc. 3   *Flourish. Enter Lucentio, and his man Tranio*
(1.1)   LUCENTIO

Tranio, since for the great desire I had
To see faire *Padua*, nurserie of Arts,
I am arriu'd for fruitfull *Lumbardie*,
The pleasant garden of great *Italy*,
And by my fathers loue and leaue am arm'd
280   With his good will, and thy good companie,
My trustie seruant well approu'd in all,
Heere let vs breath, and haply institute
A course of Learning, and ingenious studies.
Pisa renowned for graue Citizens
Gaue me my being, and my father first
A Merchant of great Trafficke through the world:
Vincentio come of the *Bentiuolij*,
Vincentio's sonne, brought vp in *Florence*,
It shall become to serue all hopes conceiu'd
290   To decke his fortune with his vertuous deedes:
And therefore *Tranio*, for the time I studie,
Vertue and that part of Philosophie
Will I applie, that treats of happinesse,
By vertue specially to be atchieu'd.
Tell me thy minde, for I haue *Pisa* left,
And am to *Padua* come, as he that leaues
A shallow plash, to plunge him in the deepe,
And with sacietie seekes to quench his thirst.

TRANIO

Me Pardonato, gentle master mine:
300   I am in all affected as your selfe,
Glad that you thus continue your resolue,
To sucke the sweets of sweete Philosophie.
Onely (good master) while we do admire
This vertue, and this morall discipline,
Let's be no Stoickes, nor no stockes I pray,
Or so deuote to *Aristotles* checkes

As *Ouid* be an out-cast quite abiur'd:
Balke Lodgicke with acquaintaince that you haue,
And practise Rhetoricke in your common talke,
Musicke and Poesie vse, to quicken you,   310
The Mathematickes, and the Metaphysickes
Fall to them as you finde your stomacke serues you:
No profit growes, where is no pleasure tane:
In briefe sir, studie what you most affect.

LUCENTIO

Gramercies *Tranio*, well dost thou aduise,
If *Biondello* thou wert come ashore,
We could at once put vs in readinesse,
And take a Lodging fit to entertaine
Such friends (as time) in *Padua* shall beget.
But stay a while, what companie is this?   320

TRANIO

Master some shew to welcome vs to Towne.
Enter Baptista with his two daughters, Katerina &
Bianca, Gremio a Pantelowne, Hortentio suter to
Bianca. Lucentio Tranio, stand by

BAPTISTA

Gentlemen, importune me no farther,
For how I firmly am resolu'd you know:
That is, not to bestow my yongest daughter,
Before I haue a husband for the elder:
If either of you both loue *Katherina*,
Because I know you well, and loue you well,
Leaue shall you haue to court her at your pleasure.

GREMIO

To cart her rather. She's to rough for mee,
There, there *Hortensio*, will you any Wife?   330

KATHERINE (*to Baptista*)

I pray you sir, is it your will
To make a stale of me amongst these mates?

HORTENSIO

Mates maid, how meane you that? No mates for you,
Vnlesse you were of gentler milder mould.

KATHERINE

I'faith sir, you shall neuer neede to feare,
I-wis it is not halfe way to her heart:
But if it were, doubt not, her care should be,
To combe your noddle with a three-legg'd stoole,
And paint your face, and vse you like a foole.

HORTENSIO

From all such diuels, good Lord deliuer vs.   340

GREMIO And me too, good Lord.

TRANIO (*aside to Lucentio*)

Husht master, heres some good pastime toward;
That wench is starke mad, or wonderfull froward.

LUCENTIO (*aside to Tranio*)

But in the others silence do I see,
Maids milde behauiour and sobrietie.
Peace *Tranio*.

TRANIO (*aside to Lucentio*)

Well said Mr, mum, and gaze your fill.

BAPTISTA

Gentlemen, that I may soone make good
What I haue said, *Bianca* get you in,

350 And let it not displease thee good *Bianca*,
For I will loue thee nere the lesse my girle.

KATHERINE A pretty peate, it is best
Put finger in the eye, and she knew why.

BIANCA
Sister content you, in my discontent.
(*To Baptista*) Sir, to your pleasure humbly I subscribe:
My bookes and instruments shall be my companie,
On them to looke, and practise by my selfe.

LUCENTIO (*aside to Tranio*)
Harke *Tranio*, thou maist heare *Minerua* speak.

HORTENSIO
Signior *Baptista*, will you be so strange,
360 Sorrie am I that our good will effects
Bianca's greefe.

GREMIO   Why will you mew her vp
(Signior *Baptista*) for this fiend of hell,
And make her beare the pennance of her tongue.

BAPTISTA
Gentlemen content ye: I am resolud:
Go in *Bianca*.   *Exit Bianca*
And for I know she taketh most delight
In Musicke, Instruments, and Poetry,
Schoolemasters will I keepe within my house,
Fit to instruct her youth. If you *Hortensio*,
370 Or signior *Gremio* you know any such,
Preferre them hither: for to cunning men,
I will be very kinde, and liberall
To mine owne children, in good bringing vp,
And so farewell: *Katherina* you may stay,
For I haue more to commune with *Bianca*.   *Exit*

KATHERINE Why, and I trust I may go too, may I not?
What shall I be appointed houres, as though (belike) I
knew not what to take, and what to leaue? Ha.   *Exit*

GREMIO You may go to the diuels dam: your guifts are
380 so good heere's none will holde you: Their loue is not
so great *Hortensio*, but we may blow our nails together,
and fast it fairely out. Our cakes dough on both sides.
Farewell: yet for the loue I beare my sweet *Bianca*, if I
can by any meanes light on a fit man to teach her that
wherein she delights, I will wish him to her father.

HORTENSIO So will I signiour *Gremio*: but a word I pray:
Though the nature of our quarrell yet neuer brook'd
parle, know now vpon aduice, it toucheth vs both: that
we may yet againe haue accesse to our faire Mistris,
390 and be happie riuals in *Bianca's* loue, to labour and
effect one thing specially.

GREMIO What's that I pray?

HORTENSIO Marrie sir to get a husband for her Sister.

GREMIO A husband: a diuell.

HORTENSIO I say a husband.

GREMIO I say, a diuell: Think'st thou *Hortensio*, though
her father be verie rich, any man is so verie a foole to
be married to hell?

HORTENSIO Tush *Gremio*: though it passe your patience &
400 mine to endure her lowd alarums, why man there bee
good fellowes in the world, and a man could light on
them, would take her with all faults, and mony enough.

GREMIO I cannot tell: but I had as lief take her dowrie
with this condition; To be whipt at the hie crosse euerie
morning.

HORTENSIO Faith (as you say) there's small choise in rotten
apples: but come, since this bar in law makes vs friends,
it shall be so farre forth friendly maintain'd, till by
helping *Baptistas* eldest daughter to a husband, wee set
his yongest free for a husband, and then haue too't   410
afresh: Sweet *Bianca*, happy man be his dole: hee that
runnes fastest, gets the Ring: How say you signior
Gremio?

GREMIO I am agreed, and would I had giuen him the best
horse in *Padua* to begin his woing that would
thoroughly woe her, wed her, and bed her, and ridde
the house of her. Come on.
                Exeunt ambo. Manet Tranio and Lucentio

TRANIO
I pray sir tel me, is it possible
That loue should of a sodaine take such hold.

LUCENTIO
Oh *Tranio*, till I found it to be true,   420
I neuer thought it possible or likely.
But see, while idely I stood looking on,
I found the effect of Loue in idlenesse,
And now in plainnesse do confesse to thee
That art to me as secret and as deere
As *Anna* to the Queene of Carthage was:
Tranio I burne, I pine, I perish *Tranio*,
If I atchieue not this yong modest gyrle:
Counsaile me *Tranio*, for I know thou canst:
Assist me *Tranio*, for I know thou wilt.   430

TRANIO
Master, it is no time to chide you now,
Affection is not rated from the heart:
If loue haue touch'd you, naught remaines but so,
Redime te captum quam queas minimo.

LUCENTIO
Gramercies Lad: Go forward, this contents,
The rest wil comfort, for thy counsels sound.

TRANIO
Master, you look'd so longly on the maide,
Perhaps you mark'd not what's the pith of all.

LUCENTIO
Oh yes, I saw sweet beautie in her face,
Such as the daughter of *Agenor* had,   440
That made great *Ioue* to humble him to her hand,
When with his knees he kist the Cretan strond.

TRANIO
Saw you no more? Mark'd you not how hir sister
Began to scold, and raise vp such a storme,
That mortal eares might hardly indure the din.

LUCENTIO
Tranio, I saw her corrall lips to moue,
And with her breath she did perfume the ayre,
Sacred and sweet was all I saw in her.

TRANIO (*aside*)
Nay, then 'tis time to stirre him frõ his trance:

450 (*To Lucentio*) I pray awake sir: if you loue the Maide,
Bend thoughts and wits to atcheeue her. Thus it
    stands:
Her elder sister is so curst and shrew'd,
That til the Father rid his hands of her,
Master, your Loue must liue a maide at home,
And therefore has he closely meu'd her vp,
Because she will not be annoy'd with suters.

LUCENTIO
Ah *Tranio*, what a cruell Fathers he:
But art thou not aduis'd, he tooke some care
To get her cunning Schoolemasters to instruct her.

TRANIO
460 I marry am I sir, and now 'tis plotted.

LUCENTIO
I haue it *Tranio*.

TRANIO   Master, for my hand,
Both our inuentions meet and iumpe in one.

LUCENTIO
Tell me thine first.

TRANIO   You will be schoole-master,
And vndertake the teaching of the maid:
That's your deuice.

LUCENTIO   It is: May it be done?

TRANIO
Not possible: for who shall beare your part,
And be in *Padua* heere *Vincentio*'s sonne,
Keepe house, and ply his booke, welcome his friends,
Visit his Countrimen, and banquet them?

LUCENTIO
470 *Basta*, content thee: for I haue it full.
We haue not yet bin seene in any house,
Nor can we be distinguish'd by our faces,
For man or master: then it followes thus;
Thou shalt be master, *Tranio* in my sted:
Keepe house, and port, and seruants, as I should,
I will some other be, some *Florentine*,
Some *Neapolitan*, or meaner man of *Pisa*.
'Tis hatch'd, and shall be so: *Tranio* at once
Vncase thee: take my Coulord hat and cloake,
480 When *Biondello* comes, he waites on thee,
But I will charme him first to keepe his tongue.

TRANIO So had you neede:
                ⌐They exchange cloathes⌐
In breefe Sir, sith it your pleasure is,
And I am tyed to be obedient,
For so your father charg'd me at our parting:
Be seruiceable to my sonne (quoth he)
Although I thinke 'twas in another sense,
I am content to bee *Lucentio*,
Because so well I loue *Lucentio*.

LUCENTIO
490 *Tranio* be so, because *Lucentio* loues,
And let me be a slaue, t'atchieue that maide,
Whose sodaine sight hath thral'd my wounded eye.
                Enter Biondello
Heere comes the rogue. Sirra, where haue you bin?

BIONDELLO Where haue I beene? Nay how now, where
are you? Maister, ha's my fellow *Tranio* stolne your
cloathes, or you stolne his, or both? Pray what's the
newes?

LUCENTIO
Sirra come hither, 'tis no time to iest,
And therefore frame your manners to the time.
Your fellow *Tranio* heere to saue my life,   500
Puts my apparrell, and my count'nance on,
And I for my escape haue put on his:
For in a quarrell since I came a-shore,
I kil'd a man, and feare I was descried:
Waite you on him, I charge you, as becomes:
While I make way from hence to saue my life:
You vnderstand me?

BIONDELLO   I sir, ne're a whit.

LUCENTIO
And not a iot of *Tranio* in your mouth,
Tranio is chang'd into *Lucentio*.

BIONDELLO
The better for him, would I were so too.   510

TRANIO
So could I 'faith boy, to haue the next wish after,
That *Lucentio* indeede had *Baptistas* yongest daughter.
But sirra, not for my sake, but your masters, I aduise
You vse your manners discreetly in all kind of
    companies:
When I am alone, why then I am *Tranio*:
But in all places else, your master *Lucentio*.

LUCENTIO *Tranio* let's go:
One thing more rests, that thy selfe execute,
To make one among these wooers: if thou ask me
    why,
Sufficeth my reasons are both good and waighty.   520
                                Exeunt

The Presenters aboue speake

I. SERUINGMAN
My Lord you nod, you do not minde the play.

SLIE Yes by Saint Anne do I, a good matter surely: Comes
there any more of it?

BARTHOLOMEW My Lord, 'tis but begun.

SLIE 'Tis a verie excellent peece of worke, Madame Ladie:
would 'twere done.
                They sit and marke

                Enter Petruchio, and his man Grumio   Sc. 4
PETRUCHIO   (1.2)
Verona, for a while I take my leaue,
To see my friends in *Padua*; but of all
My best beloued and approued friend
Hortensio: & I trow this is his house: 530
Heere sirra *Grumio*, knocke I say.

GRUMIO Knocke sir? whom should I knocke? Is there any
man ha's rebus'd your worship?

PETRUCHIO Villaine I say, knocke me heere soundly.

GRUMIO Knocke you heere sir? Why sir, what am I sir,
that I should knocke you heere sir.

PETRUCHIO
Villaine I say, knocke me at this gate,
And rap me well, or Ile knocke your knaues pate.

GRUMIO
My M^r is growne quarrelsome: I should knocke you
    first,
540 And then I know after who comes by the worst.

PETRUCHIO Will it not be?
'Faith sirrah, and you'l not knocke, Ile ring it,
Ile trie how you can *Sol*, *Fa*, and sing it.
    He rings him by the eares. ⌈*Grumio kneeles*⌉

GRUMIO Helpe masters helpe, my master is mad.

PETRUCHIO Now knocke when I bid you: sirrah villaine.
    Enter Hortensio

HORTENSIO How now, what's the matter? My olde friend
Grumio, and my good friend *Petruchio*? How do you all
at *Verona*?

PETRUCHIO
Signior *Hortensio*, come you to part the fray?
550 *Con tutto il core ben trobatto*, may I say.

HORTENSIO *Alla nostra casa ben venuto molto honorato signior
mio Petruchio.*
Rise *Grumio* rise, we will compound this quarrell.
    Grumio rises

GRUMIO Nay 'tis no matter sir, what he leges in Latine.
If this be not a lawfull cause for me to leaue his seruice,
looke you sir: He bid me knocke him, & rap him
soundly sir. Well, was it fit for a seruant to vse his
master so, being perhaps (for ought I see) two and
thirty, a peepe out?
560 Whom would to God I had well knockt at first,
Then had not *Grumio* come by the worst.

PETRUCHIO
A sencelesse villaine: good *Hortensio*,
I bad the rascall knocke vpon your gate,
And could not get him for my heart to do it.

GRUMIO Knocke at the gate? O heauens: spake you not
these words plaine? Sirra, Knocke me heere: rappe me
heere: knocke me well, and knocke me soundly? And
come you now with knocking at the gate?

PETRUCHIO
Sirra be gone, or talke not I aduise you.

HORTENSIO
570 *Petruchio* patience, I am *Grumio's* pledge:
Why this a heauie chance twixt him and you,
Your ancient trustie pleasant seruant *Grumio*:
And tell me now (sweet friend) what happie gale
Blowes you to *Padua* heere, from old *Verona*?

PETRUCHIO
Such wind as scatters yongmen throgh ye world,
To seeke their fortunes farther then at home,
Where small experience growes. But in a few,
Signior *Hortensio*, thus it stands with me,
Antonio my father is deceast,
580 And I haue thrust my selfe into this maze,
Happily to wiue and thriue, as best I may:
Crownes in my purse I haue, and goods at home,
And so am come abroad to see the world.

HORTENSIO
Petruchio, shall I then come roundly to thee,
And wish thee to a shrew'd ill-fauour'd wife?
Thou'dst thanke me but a little for my counsell:
And yet Ile promise thee she shall be rich,
And verie rich: but th'art too much my friend,
And Ile not wish thee to her.

PETRUCHIO
Signior *Hortensio*, 'twixt such friends as wee, 590
Few words suffice: and therefore, if thou know
One rich enough to be *Petruchio's* wife:
(As wealth is burthen of my woing dance)
Be she as foule as was *Florentius* Loue,
As old as *Sibell*, and as curst and shrow'd
As *Socrates Zentippe*, or a worse:
She moues me not, or not remoues at least
Affections edge in me, were she as rough
As are the swelling *Adriaticke* seas.
I come to wiue it wealthily in *Padua*: 600
If wealthily, then happily in *Padua*.

GRUMIO (*to Hortensio*) Nay looke you sir, hee tels you flatly
what his minde is: why giue him Gold enough, and
marrie him to a Puppet or an Aglet babie, or an old
trot with ne're a tooth in her head, though she haue
as manie diseases as two and fiftie horses. Why nothing
comes amisse, so monie comes withall.

HORTENSIO
Petruchio, since we are stept thus farre in,
I will continue that I broach'd in iest,
I can *Petruchio* helpe thee to a wife 610
With wealth enough, and yong and beautious,
Brought vp as best becomes a Gentlewoman.
Her onely fault, and that is faults enough,
Is, that she is intollerable curst,
And shrow'd, and froward, so beyond all measure,
That were my state farre worser then it is,
I would not wed her for a mine of Gold.

PETRUCHIO
Hortensio peace: thou knowst not golds effect,
Tell me her fathers name, and 'tis enough:
For I will boord her, though she chide as loud 620
As thunder, when the clouds in Autumne cracke.

HORTENSIO
Her father is *Baptista Minola*,
An affable and courteous Gentleman,
Her name is *Katherina Minola*,
Renown'd in *Padua* for her scolding tongue.

PETRUCHIO
I know her father, though I know not her,
And he knew my deceased father well:
I wil not sleepe *Hortensio* til I see her,
And therefore let me be thus bold with you,
To giue you ouer at this first encounter, 630
Vnlesse you wil accompanie me thither.

GRUMIO I pray you Sir let him go while the humor lasts.
A my word, and she knew him as wel as I do, she
would thinke scolding would doe little good vpon him.
Shee may perhaps call him halfe a score Knaues, or

so: Why that's nothing; and he begin once, hee'l raile
in his rope trickes. Ile tell you what sir, and she stand
him but a litle, he wil throw a figure in her face, and
so disfigure hir with it, that shee shal haue no more
640   eies to see withall then a Cat: you know him not sir.
HORTENSIO
      Tarrie *Petruchio*, I must go with thee,
      For in *Baptistas* keepe my treasure is:
      He hath the Iewel of my life in hold,
      His yongest daughter, beautiful *Bianca*,
      And her with-holds from me and other more,
      Suters to her, and riuals in my Loue:
      Supposing it a thing impossible,
      For those defects I haue before rehearst,
      That euer *Katherina* wil be woo'd:
650   Therefore this order hath *Baptista* tane,
      That none shal haue accesse vnto *Bianca*,
      Til *Katherine* the Curst, haue got a husband.
GRUMIO *Katherine* the curst,
      A title for a maide, of all titles the worst.
HORTENSIO
      Now shal my friend *Petruchio* do me grace,
      And offer me disguis'd in sober robes,
      To old *Baptista* as a schoole-master
      Well seene in Musicke, to instruct *Bianca*,
      That so I may by this deuice at least
660   Haue leaue and leisure to make loue to her,
      And vnsuspected court her by her selfe.
            Enter Gremio with a paper, and Lucentio disguised
            as a schoole-master
GRUMIO Heere's no knauerie. See, to beguile the olde
      folkes, how the young folkes lay their heads together.
      Master, master, looke about you: Who goes there? ha.
HORTENSIO
      Peace *Grumio*, it is the riuall of my Loue.
      Petruchio stand by a while.
GRUMIO
      A proper stripling, and an amorous.
            Petruchio, Hortensio and Grumio stand aside
GREMIO (*to Lucentio*)
      O very well, I haue perus'd the note:
      Hearke you sir, Ile haue them verie fairely bound,
670   All bookes of Loue, see that at any hand,
      And see you reade no other Lectures to her:
      You vnderstand me. Ouer and beside
      Signior *Baptistas* liberalitie,
      Ile mend it with a Largesse. Take your paper too,
      And let me haue them verie wel perfum'd;
      For she is sweeter then perfume it selfe
      To whom they go to: what wil you reade to her.
LUCENTIO
      What ere I reade to her, Ile pleade for you,
      As for my patron, stand you so assur'd,
680   As firmely as your selfe were still in place,
      Yea and perhaps with more successefull words
      Then you; vnlesse you were a scholler sir.
GREMIO
      Oh this learning, what a thing it is.

GRUMIO (*aside*)
      Oh this Woodcocke, what an Asse it is.
PETRUCHIO Peace sirra.
HORTENSIO
      Grumio mum: (*Comming forward*) God saue you signior
            Gremio.
GREMIO
      And you are wel met, Signior *Hortensio*.
      Trow you whither I am going?
      To *Baptista Minola*,
      I promist to enquire carefully   690
      About a schoolemaster for the faire *Bianca*,
      And by good fortune I haue lighted well
      On this yong man: For learning and behauiour
      Fit for her turne, well read in Poetrie
      And other bookes, good ones, I warrant ye.
HORTENSIO
      'Tis well: and I haue met a Gentleman
      Hath promist me to helpe me to another,
      A fine Musitian to instruct our Mistris,
      So shal I no whit be behinde in dutie
      To faire *Bianca*, so belou'd of me.   700
GREMIO
      Belou'd of me, and that my deeds shal proue.
GRUMIO (*aside*) And that his bags shal proue.
HORTENSIO
      Gremio, 'tis now no time to vent our loue,
      Listen to me, and if you speake me faire,
      Ile tel you newes indifferent good for either.
      Heere is a Gentleman whom by chance I met
      Vpon agreement from vs to his liking,
      Will vndertake to woo curst *Katherine*,
      Yea, and to marrie her, if her dowrie please.
GREMIO So said, so done, is well: 710
      Hortensio, haue you told him all her faults?
PETRUCHIO
      I know she is an irkesome brawling scold:
      If that be all Masters, I heare no harme.
GREMIO
      No, sayst me so, friend? What Countreyman?
PETRUCHIO
      Borne in *Verona*, old *Antonios* sonne:
      My father dead, his fortune liues for me,
      And I do hope, good dayes and long, to see.
GREMIO Oh sir, such a life with such a wife, were strange:
      But if you haue a stomacke, too't a Gods name,
      You shal haue me assisting you in all.   720
      But will you woo this Wilde-cat?
PETRUCHIO   Will I liue?
GRUMIO
      Wil he woo her? I: or Ile hang her.
PETRUCHIO
      Why came I hither, but to that intent?
      Thinke you, a little dinne can daunt mine eares?
      Haue I not in my time heard Lions rore?
      Haue I not heard the sea, puft vp with windes,
      Rage like an angry Boare, chafed with sweat?
      Haue I not heard great Ordnance in the field?

And heauens Artillerie thunder in the skies?
730 Haue I not in a pitched battell heard
Loud larums, neighing steeds, & trumpets clangue?
And do you tell me of a womans tongue?
That giues not halfe so great a blow to heare,
As wil a Chesse-nut in a Farmers fire.
Tush, tush, feare boyes with bugs.

GRUMIO For he feares none.

GREMIO *Hortensio* hearke:
This Gentleman is happily arriu'd,
My minde presumes for his owne good, and ours.

HORTENSIO
740 I promist we would be Contributors,
And beare his charge of wooing whatsoere.

GREMIO
And so we wil, prouided that he win her.

GRUMIO
I would I were as sure of a good dinner.

    Enter Tranio braue, as Lucentio, and Biondello

TRANIO Gentlemen God saue you. If I may be bold tell me
I beseech you, which is the readiest way to the house
of Signior *Baptista Minola?*

BIONDELLO He that ha's the two faire daughters: ist he
you meane?

TRANIO Euen he *Biondello.*

GREMIO
750 Hearke you sir, you meane not her to—

TRANIO
Perhaps him and her sir, what haue you to do?

PETRUCHIO
Not her that chides sir, at any hand I pray.

TRANIO
I loue no chiders sir: *Biondello*, let's away.

LUCENTIO (*aside*)
  Well begun *Tranio.*

HORTENSIO   Sir, a word ere you go:
Are you a sutor to the Maid you talke of, yea or no?

TRANIO
And if I be sir, is it any offence?

GREMIO
No: if without more words you will get you hence.

TRANIO
Why sir, I pray are not the streets as free
For me, as for you?

GREMIO   But so is not she.

TRANIO
760 For what reason I beseech you.

GREMIO
For this reason if you'l kno,
That she's the choise loue of Signior *Gremio.*

HORTENSIO
That she's the chosen of signior *Hortensio.*

TRANIO
Softly my Masters: If you be Gentlemen
Do me this right: heare me with patience.
Baptista is a noble Gentleman,
To whom my Father is not all vnknowne,
And were his daughter fairer then she is,

She may more sutors haue, and me for one.
Faire *Laedaes* daughter had a thousand wooers, 770
Then well one more may faire *Bianca* haue;
And so she shall: *Lucentio* shal make one,
Though *Paris* came, in hope to speed alone.

GREMIO
What, this Gentleman will out-talke vs all.

LUCENTIO
Sir giue him head, I know hee'l proue a Iade.

PETRUCHIO
Hortensio, to what end are all these words?

HORTENSIO
Sir, let me be so bold as aske you,
Did you yet euer see *Baptistas* daughter?

TRANIO
No sir, but heare I do that he hath two:
The one, as famous for a scolding tongue, 780
As is the other, for beauteous modestie.

PETRUCHIO
Sir, sir, the first's for me, let her go by.

GREMIO
Yea, leaue that labour to great *Hercules*,
And let it be more then *Alcides* twelue.

PETRUCHIO
Sir vnderstand you this of me (insooth)
The yongest daughter whom you hearken for,
Her father keepes from all accesse of sutors,
And will not promise her to any man,
Vntill the elder sister first be wed.
The yonger then is free, and not before. 790

TRANIO
If it be so sir, that you are the man
Must steed vs all, and me amongst the rest:
And if you breake the ice, and do this feete,
Atchieue the elder: set the yonger free,
For our accesse, whose hap shall be to haue her,
Wil not so gracelesse be, to be ingrate.

HORTENSIO
Sir you say wel, and wel you do conceiue,
And since you do professe to be a sutor,
You must as we do, gratifie this Gentleman,
To whom we all rest generally beholding. 800

TRANIO
Sir, I shal not be slacke, in signe whereof,
Please ye we may contriue this afternoone,
And quaffe carowses to our Mistresse health,
And do as aduersaries do in law,
Striue mightily, but eate and drinke as friends.

GRUMIO *and* BIONDELLO
Oh excellent motion: fellowes let's be gon.

HORTENSIO
The motions good indeed, and be it so,
Petruchio, I shal be your *Ben venuto.*   *Exeunt*

    Enter Katherina and Bianca, her hands bound   **Sc. 5
                               (2.1)**

BIANCA
Good sister wrong me not, nor wrong your self,
To make a bondmaide and a slaue of mee, 810

That I disdaine: but for these other goods,
Vnbinde my hands, Ile pull them off my selfe,
Yea all my raiment, to my petticoate,
Or what you will command me, wil I do,
So well I know my dutie to my elders.

KATHERINE
Of all thy sutors heere I charge thee tel
Whom thou lou'st best: see thou dissemble not.

BIANCA
Beleeue me sister, of all the men aliue,
I neuer yet beheld that speciall face,
820   Which I could fancie, more then any other.

KATHERINE
Minion thou lyest: Is't not *Hortensio*?

BIANCA
If you affect him sister, heere I sweare
Ile pleade for you my selfe, but you shal haue him.

KATHERINE
Oh then belike you fancie riches more,
You wil haue *Gremio* to keepe you faire.

BIANCA
Is it for him you do enuie me so?
Nay then you iest, and now I wel perceiue
You haue but iested with me all this while:
I prethee sister Kate, vntie my hands.

KATHERINE (*strikes her*)
830   If that be iest, then all the rest was so.
       Enter Baptista

BAPTISTA
Why how now Dame, whence growes this insolence?
Bianca stand aside, poore gyrle she weepes:
Go ply thy Needle, meddle not with her.
(*To Katherine*) For shame thou Hilding of a diuellish
   spirit,
Why dost thou wrong her, that did nere wrong thee?
When did she crosse thee with a bitter word?

KATHERINE
Her silence flouts me, and Ile be reueng'd.
       Flies after Bianca

BAPTISTA
What in my sight? *Bianca* get thee in.   *Exit Bianca*

KATHERINE
What will you not suffer me: Nay now I see
840   She is your treasure, she must haue a husband,
I must dance bare-foot on her wedding day,
And for your loue to her, leade Apes in hell.
Talke not to me, I will go sit and weepe,
Till I can finde occasion of reuenge.   *Exit*

BAPTISTA
Was euer Gentleman thus greeu'd as I?
But who comes heere.
     Enter Gremio, Lucentio as a schoole-master, in the
     habit of a meane man, Petruchio with Hortensio as
     a musitian, Tranio as Lucentio, with Biondello his
     boy bearing a Lute and Bookes

GREMIO Good morrow neighbour *Baptista*.

BAPTISTA Good morrow neighbour *Gremio*: God saue you
   Gentlemen.

PETRUCHIO
And you good sir: pray haue you not a daughter,   850
Cal'd *Katerina*, faire and vertuous.

BAPTISTA
I haue a daughter sir, cal'd *Katerina*.

GREMIO
You are too blunt, go to it orderly.

PETRUCHIO
You wrong me signior *Gremio*, giue me leaue.
(*To Baptista*) I am a Gentleman of *Verona* sir,
That hearing of her beautie, and her wit,
Her affability and bashfull modestie:
Her wondrous qualities, and milde behauiour,
Am bold to shew my selfe a forward guest
Within your house, to make mine eye the witnesse   860
Of that report, which I so oft haue heard,
And for an entrance to my entertainment,
I do present you with a man of mine (*presenting*
   Hortensio)
Cunning in Musicke, and the Mathematickes,
To instruct her fully in those sciences,
Whereof I know she is not ignorant,
Accept of him, or else you do me wrong.
His name is *Litio*, borne in *Mantua*.

BAPTISTA
Y'are welcome sir, and he for your good sake.
But for my daughter *Katerine*, this I know,   870
She is not for your turne, the more my greefe.

PETRUCHIO
I see you do not meane to part with her,
Or else you like not of my companie.

BAPTISTA
Mistake me not, I speake but as I finde,
Whence are you sir? What may I call your name.

PETRUCHIO
Petruchio is my name, *Antonio*'s sonne,
A man well knowne throughout all Italy.

BAPTISTA
I know him well: you are welcome for his sake.

GREMIO
Sauing your tale *Petruchio*, I pray
Let vs that are poore petitioners speake too?   880
Bacare, you are meruaylous forward.

PETRUCHIO
Oh, Pardon me signior *Gremio*, I would faine be
   doing.

GREMIO
I doubt it not sir. But you will curse your wooing.
(*To Baptista*) Neighbor: this is a guift very gratefull, I
am sure of it, to expresse the like kindnesse my selfe,
that haue beene more kindely beholding to you then
any: Freely giue vnto you this yong Scholler (*presenting
Lucentio*), that hath beene long studying at *Rhemes*, as
cunning in Greeke, Latine, and other Languages, as
the other in Musicke and Mathematickes: His name is   890
Cambio: pray accept his seruice.

BAPTISTA A thousand thankes signior *Gremio*: Welcome
good *Cambio*. (*To Tranio*) But gentle sir, me thinkes you

walke like a stranger, may I be so bold, to know the
cause of your comming?

TRANIO

Pardon me sir, the boldnesse is mine owne,
That being a stranger in this Cittie heere,
Do make my selfe a sutor to your daughter,
Vnto *Bianca*, faire and vertuous:
900 Nor is your firme resolue vnknowne to me,
In the preferment of the eldest sister.
This liberty is all that I request,
That vpon knowledge of my Parentage,
I may haue welcome 'mongst the rest that woo,
And free accesse and fauour as the rest.
And toward the education of your daughters:
I heere bestow a simple instrument,
And this small packet of Greeke and Latine bookes:
If you accept them, then their worth is great.

BAPTISTA

910 *Lucentio* is your name, of whence I pray.

TRANIO

Of *Pisa* sir, sonne to *Vincentio*.

BAPTISTA

A mightie man of *Pisa*, by report
I know him well: you are verie welcome sir:
(*To Hortensio*) Take you the Lute, (*to Lucentio*) and
    you the set of bookes.
You shall go see your Pupils presently.
Holla, within.
        Enter a Seruant
                Sirrah, leade these Gentlemen
To my daughters, and tell them both
These are their Tutors, bid them vse them well,
            Exit Seruant with Lucentio and Hortensio,
                ⌜*Biondello following*⌝
(*To Petruchio*) We will go walke a little in the
    Orchard,
920 And then to dinner: you are passing welcome,
And so I pray you all to thinke your selues.

PETRUCHIO

Signior *Baptista*, my businesse asketh haste,
And euerie day I cannot come to woo,
You knew my father well, and in him me,
Left solie heire to all his Lands and goods,
Which I haue better'd rather then decreast,
Then tell me, if I get your daughters loue,
What dowrie shall I haue with her to wife.

BAPTISTA

After my death, the one halfe of my Lands,
930 And in possession twentie thousand Crownes.

PETRUCHIO

And for that dowrie, Ile assure her of
Her widdow-hood, be it that she suruiue me
In all my Lands and Leases whatsoeuer,
Let specialties be therefore drawne betweene vs,
That couenants may be kept on either hand.

BAPTISTA

I, when the speciall thing is well obtain'd,
That is her loue: for that is all in all.

PETRUCHIO

Why that is nothing: for I tell you father,
I am as peremptorie as she proud minded:
And where two raging fires meete together,   940
They do consume the thing that feedes their furie.
Though little fire growes great with little winde,
Yet extreme gusts will blow out fire and all:
So I to her, and so she yeelds to me,
For I am rough, and woo not like a babe.

BAPTISTA

Well maist thou woo, and happy be thy speed:
But be thou arm'd for some vnhappie words.

PETRUCHIO

I to the proofe, as Mountaines are for windes,
That shakes not, though they blow perpetually.
        Enter Hortensio with his head broke

BAPTISTA

How now my friend, why dost thou looke so pale?   950

HORTENSIO

For feare I promise you, if I looke pale.

BAPTISTA

What, will my daughter proue a good Musitian?

HORTENSIO

I thinke she'l sooner proue a souldier,
Iron may hold with her, but neuer Lutes.

BAPTISTA

Why then thou canst not break her to the Lute?

HORTENSIO

Why no, for she hath broke the Lute to me:
I did but tell her she mistooke her frets,
And bow'd her hand to teach her fingering,
When (with a most impatient diuellish spirit)
Frets call you these? (quoth she) Ile fume with them: 960
And with that word she stroke me on the head,
And through the instrument my pate made way,
And there I stood amazed for a while,
As on a Pillorie, looking through the Lute,
While she did call me Rascall, Fidler,
And twangling Iacke, with twentie such vilde
    tearmes,
As had she studied to misuse me so.

PETRUCHIO

Now by the world, it is a lustie Wench,
I loue her ten times more then ere I did,
Oh how I long to haue some chat with her.   970

BAPTISTA (*to Hortensio*)

Wel go with me, and be not so discomfited.
Proceed in practise with my yonger daughter,
She's apt to learne, and thankefull for good turnes:
Signior *Petruchio*, will you go with vs,
Or shall I send my daughter *Kate* to you.

PETRUCHIO

I pray you do.   *Exeunt all but Petruchio*
        Ile attend her heere,
And woo her with some spirit when she comes,
Say that she raile, why then Ile tell her plaine,
She sings as sweetly as a Nightinghale:
Say that she frowne, Ile say she lookes as cleere   980

As morning Roses newly washt with dew:
Say she be mute, and will not speake a word,
Then Ile commend her volubility,
And say she vttereth piercing eloquence:
If she do bid me packe, Ile giue her thankes,
As though she bid me stay by her a weeke:
If she denie to wed, Ile craue the day
When I shall aske the banes, and when be married.
But heere she comes, and now *Petruchio* speake.

    Enter Katerina

990 Good morrow *Kate*, for thats your name I heare.

KATHERINE

Well haue you heard, but something hard of hearing:
They call me *Katerine*, that do talke of me.

PETRUCHIO

You lye infaith, for you are call'd plaine *Kate*,
And bony *Kate*, and sometimes *Kate* the curst:
But *Kate*, the prettiest *Kate* in Christendome,
Kate of *Kate*-hall, my super-daintie *Kate*,
For dainties are all *Kates*, and therefore *Kate*
Take this of me, *Kate* of my consolation,
Hearing thy mildnesse prais'd in euery Towne,
1000 Thy vertues spoke of, and thy beautie sounded,
Yet not so deeply as to thee belongs,
My selfe am moou'd to woo thee for my wife.

KATHERINE

Mou'd, in good time, let him that mou'd you hether
Remoue you hence: I knew you at the first
You were a mouable.

PETRUCHIO   Why, what's a mouable?

KATHERINE

A ioyn'd stoole.

PETRUCHIO   Thou hast hit it: come sit on me.

KATHERINE

Asses are made to beare, and so are you.

PETRUCHIO

Women are made to beare, and so are you.

KATHERINE

No such Iade as you, if me you meane.

PETRUCHIO

1010 Alas good *Kate*, I will not burthen thee,
For knowing thee to be but yong and light.

KATHERINE

Too light for such a swaine as you to catch,
And yet as heauie as my waight should be.

PETRUCHIO

Shold be, should: buzze.

KATHERINE   Well tane, and like a buzzard.

PETRUCHIO

Oh slow-wing'd Turtle, shal a buzard take thee?

KATHERINE

I for a Turtle, as he takes a buzard.

PETRUCHIO

Come, come you Waspe, y'faith you are too angrie.

KATHERINE

If I be waspish, best beware my sting.

PETRUCHIO

My remedy is then to plucke it out.

KATHERINE

I, if the foole could finde it where it lies.   1020

PETRUCHIO

Who knowes not where a Waspe does weare his
     sting?
In his taile.

KATHERINE   In his tongue?

PETRUCHIO   Whose tongue.

KATHERINE

Yours if you talke of tales, and so farewell.

PETRUCHIO

What with my tongue in your taile. Nay, come
     againe,
Good *Kate*, I am a Gentleman.

KATHERINE   That Ile trie.

    She strikes him

PETRUCHIO

I sweare Ile cuffe you, if you strike againe.

KATHERINE So may you loose your armes,
If you strike me, you are no Gentleman,
And if no Gentleman, why then no armes.

PETRUCHIO

A Herald *Kate*? Oh put me in thy bookes.   1030

KATHERINE What is your Crest, a Coxcombe?

PETRUCHIO

A comblesse Cocke, so *Kate* will be my Hen.

KATHERINE

No Cocke of mine, you crow too like a crauen.

PETRUCHIO

Nay come *Kate*, come: you must not looke so sowre.

KATHERINE

It is my fashion when I see a Crab.

PETRUCHIO

Why heere's no crab, and therefore looke not sowre.

KATHERINE There is, there is.

PETRUCHIO Then shew it me.

KATHERINE Had I a glasse, I would.

PETRUCHIO

What, you meane my face.

KATHERINE   Well aym'd of such a yong one.   1040

PETRUCHIO

Now by S. George I am too yong for you.

KATHERINE

Yet you are wither'd.

PETRUCHIO   'Tis with cares.

KATHERINE   I care not.

PETRUCHIO

Nay heare you *Kate*. Insooth you scape not so.

KATHERINE

I chafe you if I tarrie. Let me go.

PETRUCHIO

No, not a whit, I finde you passing gentle:
'Twas told me you were rough, and coy, and sullen,
And now I finde report a very liar:
For thou art pleasant, gamesome, passing courteous,
But slow in speech: yet sweet as spring-time flowers.
Thou canst not frowne, thou canst not looke a
     sconce,   1050

Nor bite the lip, as angry wenches will,
Nor hast thou pleasure to be crosse in talke:
But thou with mildnesse entertain'st thy wooers,
With gentle conference, soft, and affable.
Why does the world report that *Kate* doth limpe?
Oh sland'rous world: *Kate* like the hazle twig
Is straight, and slender, and as browne in hue
As hazle nuts, and sweeter then the kernels:
Oh let me see thee walke: thou dost not halt.

KATHERINE

1060   Go foole, and whom thou keep'st command.

PETRUCHIO

Did euer *Dian* so become a Groue
As *Kate* this chamber with her princely gate:
O be thou *Dian*, and let her be *Kate*,
And then let *Kate* be chaste, and *Dian* sportfull.

KATHERINE

Where did you study all this goodly speech?

PETRUCHIO

It is *extempore*, from my mother wit.

KATHERINE

A witty mother, witlesse else her sonne.

PETRUCHIO

Am I not wise?

KATHERINE   Yes, keepe you warme.

PETRUCHIO

Marry so I meane sweet *Katherine* in thy bed:
1070   And therefore setting all this chat aside,
Thus in plaine termes: your father hath consented
That you shall be my wife; your dowry greed on,
And will you, nill you, I will marry you.
Now *Kate*, I am a husband for your turne,
For by this light, whereby I see thy beauty,
Thy beauty that doth make me like thee well,
Thou must be married to no man but me,

    Enter Baptista, Gremio, Tranio as Lucentio

For I am he am borne to tame you *Kate*,
And bring you from a wilde *Kate* to a *Kate*
1080   Conformable as other houshold *Kates*:
Heere comes your father, neuer make deniall,
I must, and will haue *Katherine* to my wife.

BAPTISTA Now Signior *Petruchio*, how speed you with my
daughter?

PETRUCHIO How but well sir? how but well?
It were impossible I should speed amisse.

BAPTISTA

Why how now daughter *Katherine*, in your dumps?

KATHERINE

Call you me daughter? now I promise you
You haue shewd a tender fatherly regard,
1090   To wish me wed to one halfe Lunaticke,
A mad-cap ruffian, and a swearing Iacke,
That thinkes with oathes to face the matter out.

PETRUCHIO

Father, 'tis thus, your selfe and all the world
That talk'd of her, haue talk'd amisse of her:
If she be curst, it is for pollicie,
For shee's not froward, but modest as the Doue,

Shee is not hot, but temperate as the morne,
For patience shee will proue a second *Grissell*,
And Romane *Lucrece* for her chastitie:
And to conclude, we haue greed so well together,   1100
That vpon sonday is the wedding day.

KATHERINE

Ile see thee hang'd on sonday first.

GREMIO Hark *Petruchio*, she saies shee'll see thee hang'd
first.

TRANIO

Is this your speeding? nay thē godnight our part.

PETRUCHIO

Be patient gentlemen, I choose her for my selfe,
If she and I be pleas'd, what's that to you?
'Tis bargain'd twixt vs twaine being alone,
That she shall still be curst in company.
I tell you 'tis incredible to beleeue   1110
How much she loues me: oh the kindest *Kate*,
Shee hung about my necke, and kisse on kisse
Shee vi'd so fast, protesting oath on oath,
That in a twinke she won me to her loue.
Oh you are nouices, 'tis a world to see
How tame when men and women are alone,
A meacocke wretch can make the curstest shrew:
Giue me thy hand *Kate*, I will vnto *Venice*
To buy apparell 'gainst the wedding day;
Prouide the feast father, and bid the guests,   1120
I will be sure my *Katherine* shall be fine.

BAPTISTA

I know not what to say, but giue me your hāds,
God send you ioy, *Petruchio*, 'tis a match.

GREMIO *and* TRANIO

Amen say we, we will be witnesses.

PETRUCHIO

Father, and wife, and gentlemen adieu,
I will to *Venice*, sonday comes apace,
We will haue rings, and things, and fine array,
And kisse me *Kate*, we will be married a sonday.

    Exeunt Petruchio and Katherine seuerally

GREMIO

Was euer match clapt vp so sodainly?

BAPTISTA

Faith Gentlemen now I play a marchants part,   1130
And venture madly on a desperate Mart.

TRANIO

Twas a commodity lay fretting by you,
'Twill bring you gaine, or perish on the seas.

BAPTISTA

The gaine I seeke, is quiet in the match.

GREMIO

No doubt but he hath got a quiet catch:
But now *Baptista*, to your yonger daughter,
Now is the day we long haue looked for,
I am your neighbour, and was suter first.

TRANIO

And I am one that loue *Bianca* more
Then words can witnesse, or your thoughts can
    guesse.   1140

GREMIO
    Yongling thou canst not loue so deare as I.
TRANIO
    Gray-beard thy loue doth freeze.
GREMIO   But thine doth frie,
    Skipper stand backe, 'tis age that nourisheth.
TRANIO
    But youth in Ladies eyes that florisheth.
BAPTISTA
    Content you gentlemen, I wil cōpound this strife.
    'Tis deeds must win the prize, and he of both
    That can assure my daughter greatest dower,
    Shall haue my *Biancas* loue.
    Say signior *Gremio*, what can you assure her?
GREMIO
1150   First, as you know, my house within the City
    Is richly furnished with plate and gold,
    Basons and ewers to laue her dainty hands:
    My hangings all of *tirian* tapestry:
    In Iuory cofers I haue stuft my crownes:
    In Cypres chests my arras counterpoints,
    Costly apparell, tents, and Canopies,
    Fine Linnen, Turky cushions bost with pearle,
    Vallens of Venice gold, in needle worke:
    Pewter and brasse, and all things that belongs
1160   To house or house-keeping: then at my farme
    I haue a hundred milch-kine to the pale,
    Sixe-score fat Oxen standing in my stalls,
    And all things answerable to this portion.
    My selfe am strooke in yeeres I must confesse,
    And if I die to morrow this is hers,
    If whil'st I liue she will be onely mine.
TRANIO
    That only came well in: sir, list to me,
    I am my fathers heyre and onely sonne,
    If I may haue your daughter to my wife,
1170   Ile leaue her houses three or foure as good
    Within rich *Pisa* walls, as any one
    Old Signior *Gremio* has in *Padua*,
    Besides, two thousand Duckets by the yeere
    Of fruitfull land, all which shall be her ioynter.
    What, haue I pincht you Signior *Gremio*?
GREMIO
    Two thousand Duckets by the yeere of land,
    My Land amounts not to so much in all:
    That she shall haue, besides an Argosie
    That now is lying in Marcellus roade:
1180   What, haue I choakt you with an Argosie?
TRANIO
    Gremio, 'tis knowne my father hath no lesse
    Then three great Argosies, besides two Galliasses
    And twelue tite Gallies, these I will assure her,
    And twice as much what ere thou offrest next.
GREMIO
    Nay, I haue offred all, I haue no more,
    And she can haue no more then all I haue,
    If you like me, she shall haue me and mine.

TRANIO
    Why then the maid is mine from all the world.
    By your firme promise, *Gremio* is out-vied.
BAPTISTA
    I must confesse your offer is the best,   1190
    And let your father make her the assurance,
    Shee is your owne, else you must pardon me:
    If you should die before him, where's her dower?
TRANIO
    That's but a cauill: he is olde, I young.
GREMIO
    And may not yong men die as well as old?
BAPTISTA Well gentlemen,
    I am thus resolu'd, on sonday next, you know
    My daughter *Katherine* is to be married:
    (*To Tranio*) Now on the sonday following, shall *Bianca*
    Be Bride to you, if you make this assurance: 1200
    If not, to Signior *Gremio*:
    And so I take my leaue, and thanke you both.
GREMIO
    Adieu good neighbour: *Exit Baptista*
                      now I feare thee not:
    Sirra, yong gamester, your father were a foole
    To giue thee all, and in his wayning age
    Set foot vnder thy table: tut, a toy,
    An olde Italian foxe is not so kinde my boy.   *Exit*
TRANIO
    A vengeance on your crafty wither'd hide,
    Yet I haue fac'd it with a card of ten:
    'Tis in my head to doe my master good: 1210
    I see no reason but suppos'd *Lucentio*
    Must get a father, call'd suppos'd *Vincentio*,
    And that's a wonder: fathers commonly
    Doe get their children: but in this case of woing,
    A childe shall get a sire, if I faile not of my cunning.
                                          Exit

    Enter Lucentio with bookes, as Cambio, Hortentio   Sc. 6
    with a lute, as Litio, and Bianca   (3.1)
LUCENTIO
    Fidler forbeare, you grow too forward Sir,
    Haue you so soone forgot the entertainment
    Her sister *Katherine* welcom'd you withall.
HORTENSIO
    But wrangling pedant, this *Bianca* is,
    The patronesse of heauenly harmony: 1220
    Then giue me leaue to haue prerogatiue,
    And when in Musicke we haue spent an houre,
    Your Lecture shall haue leisure for as much.
LUCENTIO
    Preposterous Asse that neuer read so farre,
    To know the cause why musicke was ordain'd:
    Was it not to refresh the minde of man
    After his studies, or his vsuall paine?
    Then giue me leaue to read Philosophy,
    And while I pause, serue in your harmony.
HORTENSIO
    Sirra, I will not beare these braues of thine.   1230

BIANCA
Why gentlemen, you doe me double wrong,
To striue for that which resteth in my choice:
I am no breeching scholler in the schooles,
Ile not be tied to howres, nor pointed times,
But learne my Lessons as I please my selfe,
And to cut off all strife: heere sit we downe,
(*To Hortensio*) Take you your instrument, play you the
    whiles,
His Lecture will be done ere you haue tun'd.

HORTENSIO
You'll leaue his Lecture when I am in tune?

LUCENTIO
1240   That will be neuer, tune your instrument.
      Hortensio tunes his lute. Lucentio opens a booke

BIANCA Where left we last?

LUCENTIO Heere Madam:
   (*Reads*)   *Hic Ibat Simois, hic est sigeia tellus,*
        Hic steterat Priami regia Celsa senis.

BIANCA Conster them.

LUCENTIO *Hic Ibat,* as I told you before, *Simois,* I am
Lucentio, *hic est,* sonne vnto Vincentio of Pisa, *Sigeia
tellus,* disguised thus to get your loue, *hic steterat,* and
that Lucentio that comes a wooing, *priami,* is my man
1250   Tranio, *regia,* bearing my port, *celsa senis* that we might
beguile the old Pantalowne.

HORTENSIO Madam, my Instrument's in tune.

BIANCA Let's heare, (*Hortensio playes*) oh fie, the treble
iarres.

LUCENTIO Spit in the hole man, and tune againe.
      Hortensio tunes his lute againe

BIANCA Now let mee see if I can conster it. *Hic ibat simois,*
I know you not, *hic est sigeia tellus,* I trust you not, *hic
steterat priami,* take heede he heare vs not, *regia* presume
not, *Celsa senis,* despaire not.

HORTENSIO
Madam, tis now in tune.

1260   LUCENTIO   All but the base.

HORTENSIO
The base is right, 'tis the base knaue that iars.
(*Aside*) How fiery and forward our Pedant is,
Now for my life the knaue doth court my loue,
Pedascule, Ile watch you better yet.

BIANCA (*to Lucentio*)
In time I may beleeue, yet I mistrust.

LUCENTIO
Mistrust it not, for sure *Aeacides*
Was *Aiax* cald so from his grandfather.

BIANCA
I must beleeue my master, else I promise you,
I should be arguing still vpon that doubt,
1270   But let it rest, now *Litio* to you:
Good master take it not vnkindly pray
That I haue beene thus pleasant with you both.

HORTENSIO (*to Lucentio*)
You may go walk, and giue me leaue a while,
My Lessons make no musicke in three parts.

LUCENTIO
Are you so formall sir, well I must waite
(*Aside*) And watch withall, for but I be deceiu'd,
Our fine Musitian groweth amorous.

HORTENSIO
Madam, before you touch the instrument,
To learne the order of my fingering,
I must begin with rudiments of Art,   1280
To teach you gamoth in a briefer sort,
More pleasant, pithy, and effectuall,
Then hath beene taught by any of my trade,
And there it is in writing fairely drawne.
      He giues a paper

BIANCA
Why, I am past my gamouth long agoe.

HORTENSIO
Yet read the gamouth of *Hortentio.*

BIANCA (*reads*)
    Gamouth I am, the ground of all accord:
      A re, to plead *Hortensio*'s passion:
    Bee me, Bianca take him for thy Lord
      C fa vt, that loues with all affection: 1290
    D sol re, one Cliffe, two notes haue I,
    E la mi, show pitty or I die,
Call you this gamouth? tut I like it not,
Old fashions please me best, I am not so nice
To change true rules for odd inuentions.
    Enter a Messenger

MESSENGER
Mistresse, your father prayes you leaue your books,
And helpe to dresse your sisters chamber vp,
You know to morrow is the wedding day.

BIANCA
Farewell sweet masters both, I must be gone.

LUCENTIO
Faith Mistresse then I haue no cause to stay.   1300
    Exeunt Bianca, Messenger, Lucentio

HORTENSIO
But I haue cause to pry into this pedant,
Methinkes he lookes as though he were in loue:
Yet if thy thoughts *Bianca* be so humble
To cast thy wandring eyes on euery stale:
Seize thee that List, if once I finde thee ranging,
Hortensio will be quit with thee by changing.   *Exit*

    Enter Baptista, Gremio, Tranio as Lucentio,   Sc. 7
    Katherine, Bianca, and others, attendants   (3.2)

BAPTISTA (*to Tranio*)
Signior *Lucentio,* this is the pointed day
That *Katherine* and *Petruchio* should be married,
And yet we heare not of our sonne in Law:
What will be said, what mockery will it be?   1310
To want the Bride-groome when the Priest attends
To speake the ceremoniall rites of marriage?
What saies *Lucentio* to this shame of ours?

KATHERINE
No shame but mine, I must forsooth be forst

To giue my hand oppos'd against my heart
Vnto a mad-braine rudesby, full of spleene,
Who woo'd in haste, and meanes to wed at leysure:
I told you I, he was a franticke foole,
Hiding his bitter iests in blunt behauiour,
1320   And to be noted for a merry man,
Hee'll wooe a thousand, point the day of marriage,
Make friends, inuite them, and proclaime the banes,
Yet neuer meanes to wed where he hath woo'd:
Now must the world point at poore *Katherine*,
And say, loe, there is mad *Petruchio*'s wife
If it would please him come and marry her.

TRANIO
Patience good *Katherine* and *Baptista* too,
Vpon my life *Petruchio* meanes but well,
What euer fortune stayes him from his word,
1330   Though he be blunt, I know him passing wise,
Though he be merry, yet withall he's honest.

KATHERINE
Would *Katherine* had neuer seen him though.

Exit weeping

BAPTISTA
Goe girle, I cannot blame thee now to weepe,
For such an iniurie would vexe a very saint,
Much more a shrew of thy impatient humour.

Enter Biondello

BIONDELLO Master, master, newes, olde newes, and such
newes as you neuer heard of.
BAPTISTA Is it new and olde too? how may that be?
BIONDELLO Why, is it not newes to heare of *Petruchio*'s
1340   comming?
BAPTISTA Is he come?
BIONDELLO Why no sir.
BAPTISTA What then?
BIONDELLO He is comming.
BAPTISTA When will he be heere?
BIONDELLO When he stands where I am, and sees you
there.
TRANIO But say, what to thine olde newes?
BIONDELLO Why *Petruchio* is comming, in a new hat and
1350   an old ierkin, a paire of old breeches thrice turn'd; a
paire of bootes that haue beene candle-cases, one
buckled, another lac'd: an olde rusty sword tane out
of the Towne Armory, with a broken hilt, and
chapelesse: with two broken points: his horse hip'd
with an olde mothy saddle, and stirrops of no kindred:
besides possest with the glanders, and like to mose in
the chine, troubled with the Lampasse, infected with
the fashions, full of Windegalls, sped with Spauins,
raied with the Yellowes, past cure of the Fiues, starke
1360   spoyl'd with the Staggers, begnawne with the Bots,
Waid in the backe, and shoulder-shotten, neere leg'd
before, and with a halfe-chekt Bitte, & a headstall of
sheepes leather, which being restrain'd to keepe him
from stumbling, hath been often burst, and now
repaired with knots: one girth six times peec'd, and a
womans Crupper of velure, which hath two letters for
her name, fairely set down in studs, and heere and
there peec'd with packthred.
BAPTISTA Who comes with him?
BIONDELLO Oh sir, his Lackey, for all the world Caparison'd   1370
like the horse: with a linnen stock on one leg, and a
kersey boot-hose on the other, gartred with a red and
blew list; an old hat, & the humor of forty fancies
prickt in't for a feather: a monster, a very monster in
apparell, & not like a Christian foot-boy, or a gentlemans
Lacky.

TRANIO
'Tis some od humor pricks him to this fashion,
Yet oftentimes he goes but meane apparel'd.

BAPTISTA
I am glad he's come, howsoere he comes.
BIONDELLO Why sir, he comes not.   1380
BAPTISTA Didst thou not say hee comes?
BIONDELLO Who, that *Petruchio* came?
BAPTISTA I, that *Petruchio* came.
BIONDELLO No sir, I say his horse comes with him on his
backe.
BAPTISTA Why that's all one.
BIONDELLO   Nay by S. *Iamy*,
I hold you a penny,
A horse and a man
Is more then one,   1390
And yet not many.

Enter Petruchio and Grumio, fantastically dressed

PETRUCHIO Come, where be these gallants? who's at
home?
BAPTISTA You are welcome sir.
PETRUCHIO And yet I come not well.
BAPTISTA And yet you halt not.

TRANIO
Not so well apparell'd as I wish you were.

PETRUCHIO
Were it not better I should rush in thus:
But where is *Kate*? where is my louely Bride?
How does my father? gentles methinkes you frowne,   1400
And wherefore gaze this goodly company,
As if they saw some wondrous monument,
Some Commet, or vnusuall prodigie?

BAPTISTA
Why sir, you know this is your wedding day:
First were we sad, fearing you would not come,
Now sadder that you come so vnprouided:
Fie, doff this habit, shame to your estate,
An eye-sore to our solemne festiuall.

TRANIO
And tell vs what occasion of import
Hath all so long detain'd you from your wife,   1410
And sent you hither so vnlike your selfe?

PETRUCHIO
Tedious it were to tell, and harsh to heare,
Sufficeth I am come to keepe my word,
Though in some part inforced to digresse,
Which at more leysure I will so excuse,
As you shall well be satisfied with all.

But where is *Kate*? I stay too long from her,
The morning weares, 'tis time we were at Church.

TRANIO

See not your Bride in these vnreuerent robes,
1420 Goe to my chamber, put on clothes of mine.

PETRUCHIO

Not I, beleeue me, thus Ile visit her.

BAPTISTA

But thus I trust you will not marry her.

PETRUCHIO

Good sooth euen thus: therefore ha done with words,
To me she's married, not vnto my cloathes:
Could I repaire what she will weare in me,
As I can change these poore accoutrements,
'Twere well for *Kate*, and better for my selfe.
But what a foole am I to chat with you,
When I should bid good morrow to my Bride
1430 And seale the title with a louely kisse.
                                    Exit ⌜with Grumio⌝

TRANIO

He hath some meaning in his mad attire,
We will perswade him be it possible,
To put on better ere he goe to Church.
                                    ⌜Exit with Gremio⌝

BAPTISTA

Ile after him, and see the euent of this.   *⌜Exeunt⌝*

Sc. 8   *⌜Enter Lucentio as Cambio and Tranio as Lucentio⌝*
(3.3)   TRANIO

But sir, to Loue concerneth vs to adde
Her fathers liking, which to bring to passe
As I before imparted to your worship,
I am to get a man what ere he be,
It skills not much, weele fit him to our turne,
1440 And he shall be *Vincentio* of *Pisa*,
And make assurance heere in *Padua*
Of greater summes then I haue promised,
So shall you quietly enioy your hope,
And marry sweet *Bianca* with consent.

LUCENTIO

Were it not that my fellow schoolemaster
Doth watch *Bianca*'s steps so narrowly:
'Twere good me-thinkes to steale our marriage,
Which once perform'd, let all the world say no,
Ile keepe mine owne despite of all the world.

TRANIO

1450 That by degrees we meane to looke into,
And watch our vantage in this businesse,
Wee'll ouer-reach the grey-beard *Gremio*,
The narrow prying father *Minola*,
The quaint Musician, amorous *Litio*,
All for my Masters sake *Lucentio*.
            Enter Gremio
Signior *Gremio*, came you from the Church?

GREMIO

As willingly as ere I came from schoole.

TRANIO

And is the Bride & Bridegroom coming home?

GREMIO

A bridegroome say you? 'tis a groome indeed,
A grumbling groome, and that the girle shall finde. 1460

TRANIO

Curster then she, why 'tis impossible.

GREMIO

Why hee's a deuill, a deuill, a very fiend.

TRANIO

Why she's a deuill, a deuill, the deuils damme.

GREMIO

Tut, she's a Lambe, a Doue, a foole to him:
Ile tell you sir *Lucentio*; when the Priest
Should aske if *Katherine* should be his wife,
I, by goggs woones quoth he, and swore so loud,
That all amaz'd the Priest let fall the booke,
And as he stoop'd againe to take it vp,
This mad-brain'd bridegroome tooke him such a cuffe, 1470
That downe fell Priest and booke, and booke and
    Priest,
Now take them vp quoth he, if any list.

TRANIO

What said the vicar when he rose againe?

GREMIO

Trembled and shooke: for why, he stamp'd and
    swore,
As if the Vicar meant to cozen him:
But after many ceremonies done,
Hee calls for wine, a health quoth he, as if
He had beene aboord carowsing to his Mates
After a storme, quaft off the Muscadell,
And threw the sops all in the Sextons face: 1480
Hauing no other reason,
But that his beard grew thinne and hungerly,
And seem'd to aske him sops as hee was drinking:
This done, hee tooke the Bride about the necke,
And kist her lips with such a clamorous smacke,
That at the parting all the Church did eccho:
And I seeing this, came thence for very shame,
And after mee I know the rout is comming,
Such a mad marryage neuer was before:
        Musicke playes
Harke, harke, I heare the minstrels play.   1490
    Enter Petruchio, Kate, Bianca, Hortensio as Litio,
    Baptista, Grumio, and others, attendants

PETRUCHIO

Gentlemen & friends, I thank you for your pains,
I know you thinke to dine with me to day,
And haue prepar'd great store of wedding cheere,
But so it is, my haste doth call me hence,
And therefore heere I meane to take my leaue.

BAPTISTA

Is't possible you will away to night?

PETRUCHIO

I must away to day before night come,
Make it no wonder: if you knew my businesse,
You would intreat me rather goe then stay:
And honest company, I thanke you all,   1500
That haue beheld me giue away my selfe

To this most patient, sweet, and vertuous wife,
Dine with my father, drinke a health to me,
For I must hence, and farewell to you all.

TRANIO
Let vs intreat you stay till after dinner.

PETRUCHIO
It may not be.

GREMIO   Let me intreat you.

PETRUCHIO
It cannot be.

KATHERINE   Let me intreat you.

PETRUCHIO
I am content.

KATHERINE   Are you content to stay?

PETRUCHIO
I am content you shall entreat me stay,
1510   But yet not stay, entreat me how you can.

KATHERINE
Now if you loue me stay.

PETRUCHIO   Grumio, my horse.

GRUMIO I sir, they be ready, the Oates haue eaten the
horses.

KATHERINE
Nay then, doe what thou canst, I will not goe to day,
No, nor to morrow, not till I please my selfe,
The dore is open sir, there lies your way,
You may be iogging whiles your bootes are greene:
For me, Ile not be gone till I please my selfe,
'Tis like you'll proue a iolly surly groome,
1520   That take it on you at the first so roundly.

PETRUCHIO
O Kate content thee, prethee be not angry.

KATHERINE
I will be angry, what hast thou to doe?
Father, be quiet, he shall stay my leisure.

GREMIO
I marry sir, now it begins to worke.

KATHERINE
Gentlemen, forward to the bridall dinner,
I see a woman may be made a foole
If she had not a spirit to resist.

PETRUCHIO
They shall goe forward Kate at thy command,
Obey the Bride you that attend on her.
1530   Goe to the feast, reuell and domineere,
Carowse full measure to her maiden-head,
Be madde and merry, or goe hang your selues:
But for my bonny Kate, she must with me:
Nay, looke not big, nor stampe, nor stare, nor fret,
I will be master of what is mine owne,
Shee is my goods, my chattels, she is my house,
My houshold-stuffe, my field, my barne,
My horse, my oxe, my asse, my any thing,
And heere she stands, touch her who euer dare,
1540   Ile bring mine action on the proudest he
That stops my way in Padua: Grumio
Draw forth thy weapon, we are beset with theeues,

Rescue thy Mistresse if thou be a man:
Feare not sweet wench, they shall not touch thee
        Kate,
Ile buckler thee against a Million.
                Exeunt Petruchio, Katherina, and Grumio

BAPTISTA
Nay, let them goe, a couple of quiet ones.

GREMIO
Went they not quickly, I should die with laughing.

TRANIO
Of all mad matches neuer was the like.

LUCENTIO
Mistresse, what's your opinion of your sister?

BIANCA
That being mad her selfe, she's madly mated.   1550

GREMIO
I warrant him Petruchio is Kated.

BAPTISTA
Neighbours and friends, though Bride & Bridegroom
        wants
For to supply the places at the table,
You know there wants no iunkets at the feast:
Lucentio, you shall supply the Bridegroomes place,
And let Bianca take her sisters roome.

TRANIO
Shall sweet Bianca practise how to bride it?

BAPTISTA
She shall Lucentio: come gentlemen lets goe.   Exeunt

Enter Grumio   Sc. 9
                                                    (4.1)
GRUMIO Fie, fie on all tired Iades, on all mad Masters, &
all foule waies: was euer man so beaten? was euer   1560
man so raide? was euer man so weary? I am sent
before to make a fire, and they are comming after to
warme them: now were not I a little pot, & soone hot;
my very lippes might freeze to my teeth, my tongue to
the roofe of my mouth, my heart in my belly, ere I
should come by a fire to thaw me, but I with blowing
the fire shall warme my selfe: for considering the
weather, a taller man then I will take cold: Holla, hoa
Curtis.

        Enter Curtis

CURTIS Who is that calls so coldly?   1570

GRUMIO A piece of Ice: if thou doubt it, thou maist slide
from my shoulder to my heele, with no greater a run
but my head and my necke. A fire good Curtis.

CURTIS Is my master and his wife comming Grumio?

GRUMIO Oh I Curtis I, and therefore fire, fire, cast on no
water.

CURTIS Is she so hot a shrew as she's reported.

GRUMIO She was good Curtis before this frost: but thou
know'st winter tames man, woman, and beast: for it
hath tam'd my old master, and my new mistris, and   1580
my selfe fellow Curtis.

CURTIS Away you three inch foole, I am no beast.

GRUMIO Am I but three inches? Why thy horne is a foot
and so long am I at the least. But wilt thou make a

fire, or shall I complaine on thee to our mistris, whose hand (she being now at hand) thou shalt soone feele, to thy cold comfort, for being slow in thy hot office.

CURTIS I prethee good *Grumio*, tell me, how goes the world?

1590 GRUMIO A cold world *Curtis* in euery office but thine, & therefore fire: do thy duty, and haue thy dutie, for my Master and mistris are almost frozen to death.

CURTIS There's fire readie, and therefore good *Grumio* the newes.

GRUMIO Why Iacke boy, ho boy, and as much newes as wilt thou.

CURTIS Come, you are so full of conicatching.

GRUMIO Why therefore fire, for I haue caught extreme cold. Where's the Cooke, is supper ready, the house
1600 trim'd, rushes strew'd, cobwebs swept, the seruingmen in their new fustian, the white stockings, and euery officer his wedding garment on? Be the Iackes faire within, the Gils faire without, the Carpets laide, and euerie thing in order?

CURTIS All readie: and therefore I pray thee newes.

GRUMIO First know my horse is tired, my master & mistris falne out.

CURTIS How?

GRUMIO Out of their saddles into the durt, and thereby
1610 hangs a tale.

CURTIS Let's ha't good *Grumio*.

GRUMIO Lend thine eare.

CURTIS Heere.

GRUMIO (*cuffing him*) There.

CURTIS This 'tis to feele a tale, not to heare a tale.

GRUMIO And therefore 'tis cal'd a sensible tale: and this Cuffe was but to knocke at your eare, and beseech listning: now I begin, Inprimis wee came downe a fowle hill, my Master riding behinde my Mistris.

1620 CURTIS Both of one horse?

GRUMIO What's that to thee?

CURTIS Why a horse.

GRUMIO Tell thou the tale: but hadst thou not crost me, thou shouldst haue heard how her horse fel, and she vnder her horse: thou shouldst haue heard in how miery a place, how she was bemoil'd, how hee left her with the horse vpon her, how he beat me because her horse stumbled, how she waded through the durt to plucke him off me: how he swore, how she prai'd, that
1630 neuer prai'd before: how I cried, how the horses ranne away, how her bridle was burst: how I lost my crupper, with manie things of worthy memorie, which now shall die in obliuion, and thou returne vnexperienc'd to thy graue.

CURTIS By this reckning he is more shrew than she.

GRUMIO I, and that thou and the proudest of you all shall finde when he comes home. But what talke I of this? Call forth *Nathaniel, Ioseph, Nicholas, Phillip, Walter, Sugersop* and the rest: let their heads bee slickely
1640 comb'd, their blew coats brush'd, and their garters of an indifferent knit, let them curtsie with their left

legges, and not presume to touch a haire of my Masters horse-taile, till they kisse their hands. Are they all readie?

CURTIS They are.

GRUMIO Call them forth.

CURTIS (*calling*) Do you heare ho? you must meete my maister to countenance my mistris.

GRUMIO Why she hath a face of her owne.

CURTIS Who knowes not that?   1650

GRUMIO Thou it seemes, that cals for company to countenance her.

CURTIS I call them forth to credit her.

    Enter foure or fiue seruingmen

GRUMIO Why she comes to borrow nothing of them.

NATHANIEL Welcome home *Grumio*.

PHILLIP How now *Grumio*.

IOSEPH What *Grumio*.

NICK Fellow *Grumio*.

NATHANIEL How now old lad.

GRUMIO Welcome you: how now you: what you: fellow   1660
you: and thus much for greeting. Now my spruce companions, is all readie, and all things neate?

NATHANIEL All things is readie, how neere is our master?

GRUMIO E'ne at hand, alighted by this: and therefore be not—Cockes passion, silence, I heare my master.

    Enter Petruchio and Kate

PETRUCHIO
Where be these knaues? What no man at doore
To hold my stirrop, nor to take my horse?
Where is *Nathaniel, Gregory, Phillip*.

ALL SERUANTS Heere, heere sir, heere sir.

PETRUCHIO
Heere sir, heere sir, heere sir, heere sir.   1670
You logger-headed and vnpollisht groomes:
What? no attendance? no regard? no dutie?
Where is the foolish knaue I sent before?

GRUMIO
Heere sir, as foolish as I was before.

PETRUCHIO
You pezant, swain, you horson malt-horse drudg
Did I not bid thee meete me in the Parke,
And bring along these rascal knaues with thee?

GRUMIO
Nathaniels coate sir was not fully made,
And *Gabrels* pumpes were all vnpinkt i'th heele:
There was no Linke to colour *Peters* hat,   1680
And *Walters* dagger was not come from sheathing:
There were none fine, but *Adam, Rafe*, and *Gregory*,
The rest were ragged, old, and beggerly,
Yet as they are, heere are they come to meete you.

PETRUCHIO
Go rascals, go, and fetch my supper in.

    Exeunt Seruants

(*Sings*)   *Where is the life that late I led?*
        Where are those?

Sit downe *Kate*, and welcome. Soud, soud, soud, soud.
    Enter seruants with supper

Why when I say? Nay good sweete *Kate* be merrie.
1690 Off with my boots, you rogues: you villaines, when?
(*Sings*)   *It was the Friar of Orders gray,*
                As he forth walked on his way.
Out you rogue, you plucke my foote awrie,
(*Kicking a seruant*) Take that, and mend the plucking
          of the other.
Be merrie *Kate*: (*Calling*) Some water heere: what
          hoa.
          Enter one with water
Where's my Spaniel *Troilus*? Sirra, get you hence,
And bid my cozen *Ferdinand* come hither:
One *Kate* that you must kisse, and be acquainted
          with.
(*Calling*) Where are my Slippers? Shall I haue some
          water?
1700 Come *Kate* and wash, & welcome heartily:
          ⌈*A seruant drops water*⌉
You horson villaine, will you let it fall?
KATHERINE
Patience I pray you, 'twas a fault vnwilling.
PETRUCHIO
A horson beetle-headed flap-ear'd knaue:
Come *Kate* sit downe, I know you haue a stomacke,
Will you giue thankes, sweete *Kate*, or else shall I?
What's this, Mutton?
1. SERUINGMAN   I.
PETRUCHIO   Who brought it?
PETER   I.
PETRUCHIO
'Tis burnt, and so is all the meate:
What dogges are these? Where is the rascall Cooke?
How durst you villaines bring it from the dresser
1710 And serue it thus to me that loue it not?
There, (*throwing foode*) take it to you, trenchers, cups,
          and all:
You heedlesse iolt-heads, and vnmanner'd slaues.
What, do you grumble? Ile be with you straight.
          He chases the Seruants away
KATHERINE
I pray you husband be not so disquiet,
The meate was well, if you were so contented.
PETRUCHIO
I tell thee *Kate*, 'twas burnt and dried away,
And I expressely am forbid to touch it:
For it engenders choller, planteth anger,
And better 'twere that both of vs did fast,
1720 Since of our selues, our selues are chollericke,
Then feede it with such ouer-rosted flesh:
Be patient, to morrow't shalbe mended,
And for this night we'l fast for companie.
Come I wil bring thee to thy Bridall chamber.   *Exeunt*
          Enter Seruants seuerally
NATHANIEL *Peter* didst euer see the like.
PETER He kils her in her owne humor.
          Enter Curtis a Seruant
GRUMIO Where is he?
CURTIS In her chamber,

Making a sermon of continencie to her,
And railes, and sweares, and rates, that shee (poore
          soule)   1730
Knowes not which way to stand, to looke, to speake,
And sits as one new risen from a dreame.
Away, away, for he is comming hither.   *Exeunt*
          Enter Petruchio
PETRUCHIO
Thus haue I politickely begun my reigne,
And 'tis my hope to end successefully:
My Faulcon now is sharpe, and passing emptie,
And til she stoope, she must not be full gorg'd,
For then she neuer lookes vpon her lure.
Another way I haue to man my Haggard,
To make her come, and know her Keepers call: 1740
That is, to watch her, as we watch these Kites,
That baite, and beate, and will not be obedient:
She eate no meate to day, nor none shall eate.
Last night she slept not, nor to night she shall not:
As with the meate, some vndeserued fault
Ile finde about the making of the bed,
And heere Ile fling the pillow, there the boulster,
This way the Couerlet, another way the sheets:
I, and amid this hurlie I intend,
That all is done in reuerend care of her,   1750
And in conclusion, she shal watch all night,
And if she chance to nod, Ile raile and brawle,
And with the clamor keepe her stil awake:
This is a way to kil a Wife with kindnesse,
And thus Ile curbe her mad and headstrong humor:
He that knowes better how to tame a shrew,
Now let him speake, 'tis charity to shew.   *Exit*

          Enter Tranio as Lucentio and Hortensio as Litio   Sc. 10
TRANIO   (4.2)
Is't possible friend *Lisio*, that mistris *Bianca*
Doth fancie any other but *Lucentio*,
I tel you sir, she beares me faire in hand.   1760
HORTENSIO
Sir, to satisfie you in what I haue said,
Stand by, and marke the manner of his teaching.
          They stand aside.
          Enter Bianca and Lucentio as Cambio
LUCENTIO
Now Mistris, profit you in what you reade?
BIANCA
What Master reade you, first resolue me that?
LUCENTIO
I reade that I professe, the Art to loue.
BIANCA
And may you proue sir Master of your Art.
LUCENTIO
While you sweet deere proue Mistresse of my heart.
          They stand aside
HORTENSIO
Quicke proceeders marry, now tel me I pray,
You that durst sweare that your Mistris *Bianca*
Lou'd none in the World so wel as *Lucentio*.   1770

TRANIO

    Oh despightful Loue, vnconstant womankind,

    I tel thee *Lisio* this is wonderfull.

HORTENSIO

    Mistake no more, I am not *Lisio*,

    Nor a Musitian as I seeme to bee,

    But one that scorne to liue in this disguise,

    For such a one as leaues a Gentleman,

    And makes a God of such a Cullion;

    Know sir, that I am cal'd *Hortensio*.

TRANIO

    Signior *Hortensio*, I haue often heard

1780   Of your entire affection to *Bianca*,

    And since mine eyes are witnesse of her lightnesse,

    I wil with you, if you be so contented,

    Forsweare *Bianca*, and her loue for euer.

HORTENSIO

    See how they kisse and court: Signior *Lucentio*,

    Heere is my hand, and heere I firmly vow

    Neuer to woo her more, but do forsweare her

    As one vnworthie all the former fauours

    That I haue fondly flatter'd her withall.

TRANIO

    And heere I take the like vnfained oath,

1790   Neuer to marrie with her, though she would intreate,

    Fie on her, see how beastly she doth court him.

HORTENSIO

    Would all the world but he had quite forsworn.

    For me, that I may surely keepe mine oath,

    I wil be married to a wealthy Widdow,

    Ere three dayes passe, which hath as long lou'd me,

    As I haue lou'd this proud disdainful Haggard,

    And so farewel signior *Lucentio*,

    Kindnesse in women, not their beauteous lookes

    Shal win my loue, and so I take my leaue,

1800   In resolution, as I swore before.   *Exit*

TRANIO

    Mistris *Bianca*, blesse you with such grace,

    As longeth to a Louers blessed case:

    Nay, I haue tane you napping gentle Loue,

    And haue forsworne you with *Hortensio*.

BIANCA

    Tranio you iest, but haue you both forsworne mee?

TRANIO

    Mistris we haue.

LUCENTIO   Then we are rid of *Lisio*.

TRANIO

    I'faith hee'l haue a lustie Widdow now,

    That shalbe woo'd, and wedded in a day.

BIANCA God giue him ioy.

1810 TRANIO I, and hee'l tame her.

BIANCA He sayes so *Tranio*.

TRANIO

    Faith he is gone vnto the taming schoole.

BIANCA

    The taming schoole: what is there such a place?

TRANIO

    I mistris, and *Petruchio* is the master,

    That teacheth trickes eleuen and twentie long,

    To tame a shrew, and charme her chattering tongue.

        Enter Biondello

BIONDELLO

    Oh Master, master I haue watcht so long,

    That I am dogge-wearie, but at last I spied

    An ancient Angel comming downe the hill,

    Wil serue the turne.

TRANIO   What is he *Biondello*?   1820

BIONDELLO

    Master, a Marcantant, or a pedant,

    I know not what, but formall in apparrell,

    In gate and countenance surely like a Father.

LUCENTIO And what of him *Tranio*?

TRANIO

    If he be credulous, and trust my tale,

    Ile make him glad to seeme *Vincentio*,

    And giue assurance to *Baptista Minola*.

    As if he were the right *Vincentio*.

    Take in your loue, and then let me alone.

            Exeunt Lucentio and Bianca

      Enter a Pedant

PEDANT

    God saue you sir.

TRANIO   And you sir, you are welcome,   1830

    Trauaile you farre on, or are you at the farthest?

PEDANT

    Sir at the farthest for a weeke or two,

    But then vp farther, and as farre as Rome,

    And so to Tripolie, if God lend me life.

TRANIO

    What Countreyman I pray?

PEDANT   Of *Mantua*.

TRANIO

    Of *Mantua* Sir, marrie God forbid,

    And come to Padua carelesse of your life.

PEDANT

    My life sir? how I pray? for that goes hard.

TRANIO

    'Tis death for any one in Mantua

    To come to Padua, know you not the cause?   1840

    Your ships are staid at Venice, and the Duke

    For priuate quarrel 'twixt your Duke and him,

    Hath publish'd and proclaim'd it openly:

    'Tis meruaile, but that you are but newly come,

    You might haue heard it else proclaim'd about.

PEDANT

    Alas sir, it is worse for me then so,

    For I haue bils for monie by exchange

    From Florence, and must heere deliuer them.

TRANIO

    Wel sir, to do you courtesie,

    This wil I do, and this I wil aduise you.   1850

    First tell me, haue you euer beene at Pisa?

PEDANT

    I sir, in Pisa haue I often bin,

    Pisa renowned for graue Citizens.

TRANIO

    Among them know you one *Vincentio*?

PEDANT

    I know him not, but I haue heard of him:
    A Merchant of incomparable wealth.

TRANIO

    He is my father sir, and sooth to say,
    In count'nance somewhat doth resemble you.

BIONDELLO (*aside*) As much as an apple doth an oyster, &
1860   all one.

TRANIO

    To saue your life in this extremitie,
    This fauor wil I do you for his sake,
    And thinke it not the worst of all your fortunes,
    That you are like to Sir *Vincentio.*
    His name and credite shal you vndertake,
    And in my house you shal be friendly lodg'd,
    Looke that you take vpon you as you should,
    You vnderstand me sir: so shal you stay
    Til you haue done your businesse in the Citie:
1870   If this be court'sie sir, accept of it.

PEDANT

    Oh sir I do, and wil repute you euer
    The patron of my life and libertie.

TRANIO

    Then go with me, to make the matter good,
    This by the way I let you vnderstand,
    My father is heere look'd for euerie day,
    To passe assurance of a dowre in marriage
    'Twixt me, and one *Baptistas* daughter heere:
    In all these circumstances Ile instruct you,
    Go with me to cloath you as becomes you.   *Exeunt*

Sc. 11   *Enter Katherina and Grumio*
(4.3) GRUMIO
1880   No, no forsooth I dare not for my life.

KATHERINE

    The more my wrong, the more his spite appears.
    What, did he marrie me to famish me?
    Beggers that come vnto my fathers doore,
    Vpon intreatie haue a present almes,
    If not, elsewhere they meete with charitie:
    But I, who neuer knew how to intreat,
    Nor neuer needed that I should intreate,
    Am staru'd for meate, giddie for lacke of sleepe:
    With oathes kept waking, and with brawling fed,
    And that which spights me more then all these
1890   wants,
    He does it vnder name of perfect loue:
    As who should say, if I should sleepe or eate
    'Twere deadly sicknesse, or else present death.
    I prethee go, and get me some repast,
    I care not what, so it be holsome foode.

GRUMIO What say you to a Neats foote?

KATHERINE

    'Tis passing good, I prethee let me haue it.

GRUMIO

    I feare it is too chollericke a meate.
    How say you to a fat Tripe finely broyl'd?

KATHERINE

1900   I like it well, good Grumio fetch it me.

GRUMIO

    I cannot tell, I feare 'tis chollericke.
    What say you to a peece of Beefe and Mustard?

KATHERINE

    A dish that I do loue to feede vpon.

GRUMIO

    I, but the Mustard is too hot a little.

KATHERINE

    Why then the Beefe, and let the Mustard rest.

GRUMIO

    Nay then I wil not, you shal haue the Mustard
    Or else you get no beefe of Grumio.

KATHERINE

    Then both or one, or any thing thou wilt.

GRUMIO

    Why then the Mustard without the beefe.

KATHERINE

    Go get thee gone, thou false deluding slaue,   1910
      Beats him
    That feed'st me with the verie name of meate.
    Sorrow on thee, and all the packe of you
    That triumph thus vpon my misery:
    Go get thee gone, I say.
      Enter Petruchio, and Hortensio with meate

PETRUCHIO

    How fares my Kate, what sweeting all a-mort?

HORTENSIO

    Mistris, what cheere?

KATHERINE   Faith as cold as can be.

PETRUCHIO

    Plucke vp thy spirits, looke cheerfully vpon me.
    Heere Loue, thou seest how diligent I am,
    To dresse thy meate my selfe, and bring it thee.
    I am sure sweet Kate, this kindnesse merites thankes.   1920
    What, not a word? Nay then, thou lou'st it not:
    And all my paines is sorted to no proofe.
    Heere take away this dish.

KATHERINE   I pray you let it stand.

PETRUCHIO

    The poorest seruice is repaide with thankes,
    And so shall mine before you touch the meate.

KATHERINE I thanke you sir.

HORTENSIO

    Signior *Petruchio*, fie you are too blame:
    Come Mistris Kate, Ile beare you companie.

PETRUCHIO (*aside*)

    Eate it vp all *Hortensio*, if thou lou'st mee:
    (*To Katherine*) Much good do it vnto thy gentle heart: 1930
    Kate eate apace; and now my honie Loue,
    Will we returne vnto thy Fathers house,
    And reuell it as brauely as the best,
    With silken coats and caps, and golden Rings,
    With Ruffes and Cuffes, and Fardingales, and things:
    With Scarfes, and Fannes, & double change of
        brau'ry,
    With Amber Bracelets, Beades, and all this knau'ry.
    What hast thou din'd? The Tailor staies thy leasure,
    To decke thy bodie with his ruffling treasure.

Enter Tailor with a gowne

1940 Come Tailor, let vs see these ornaments.
Lay forth the gowne.

Enter Haberdasher with a cap

What newes with you sir?

HABERDASHER

Heere is the cap your Worship did bespeake.

PETRUCHIO

Why this was moulded on a porrenger,
A Veluet dish: Fie, fie, 'tis lewd and filthy,
Why 'tis a cockle or a walnut-shell,
A knacke, a toy, a tricke, a babies cap:
Away with it, come let me haue a bigger.

KATHERINE

Ile haue no bigger, this doth fit the time,
And Gentlewomen weare such caps as these.

PETRUCHIO

1950 When you are gentle, you shall haue one too,
And not till then.

HORTENSIO (*aside*)   That will not be in hast.

KATHERINE

Why sir I trust I may haue leaue to speake,
And speake I will. I am no childe, no babe,
Your betters haue indur'd me say my minde,
And If you cannot, best you stop your eares.
My tongue will tell the anger of my heart,
Or els my heart concealing it wil breake,
And rather then it shall, I will be free,
Euen to the vttermost as I please in words.

PETRUCHIO

1960 Why thou saist true, it is a paltrie cap,
A custard coffen, a bauble, a silken pie,
I loue thee well in that thou lik'st it not.

KATHERINE

Loue me, or loue me not, I like the cap,
And it I will haue, or I will haue none.

⌈*Exit Haberdasher*⌉

PETRUCHIO

Thy gowne, why I: come Tailor let vs see't.
Oh mercie God, what masking stuffe is heere?
Whats this? a sleeue? 'tis like a demi cannon,
What, vp and downe caru'd like an apple Tart?
Heers snip, and nip, and cut, and slish and slash,
1970 Like to a Cizor in a barbers shoppe:
Why what a deuils name Tailor cal'st thou this?

HORTENSIO (*aside*)

I see shees like to haue nor cap nor gowne.

TAILOR

You bid me make it orderlie and well,
According to the fashion, and the time.

PETRUCHIO

Marrie and did: but if you be remembred,
I did not bid you marre it to the time.
Go hop me ouer euery kennell home,
For you shall hop without my custome sir:
Ile none of it; hence, make your best of it.

KATHERINE

1980 I neuer saw a better fashion'd gowne,

More queint, more pleasing, nor more commendable:
Belike you meane to make a puppet of me.

PETRUCHIO

Why true, he meanes to make a puppet of thee.

TAILOR She saies your Worship meanes to make a puppet
of her.

PETRUCHIO

Oh monstrous arrogance: Thou lyest, thou thred,
    thou thimble,
Thou yard three quarters, halfe yard, quarter, naile,
Thou Flea, thou Nit, thou winter cricket thou:
Brau'd in mine owne house with a skeine of thred:
Away thou Ragge, thou quantitie, thou remnant,   1990
Or I shall so be-mete thee with thy yard,
As thou shalt thinke on prating whil'st thou liu'st:
I tell thee I, that thou hast marr'd her gowne.

TAILOR

Your worship is deceiu'd, the gowne is made
Iust as my master had direction:
Grumio gaue order how it should be done.

GRUMIO

I gaue him no order, I gaue him the stuffe.

TAILOR

But how did you desire it should be made?

GRUMIO Marrie sir with needle and thred.

TAILOR

But did you not request to haue it cut?   2000

GRUMIO Thou hast fac'd many things.

TAILOR I haue.

GRUMIO Face not mee: thou hast brau'd manie men,
braue not me; I will neither bee fac'd nor brau'd. I say
vnto thee, I bid thy Master cut out the gowne, but I
did not bid him cut it to peeces. Ergo thou liest.

TAILOR (*showing a paper*) Why heere is the note of the
fashion to testify.

PETRUCHIO Reade it.

GRUMIO The note lies in's throate if he say I said so.   2010

TAILOR (*reads*) Inprimis, a loose bodied gowne.

GRUMIO Master, if euer I said loose-bodied gowne, sow
me in the skirts of it, and beate me to death with a
bottome of browne thred: I said a gowne.

PETRUCHIO Proceede.

TAILOR (*reads*) With a small compast cape.

GRUMIO I confesse the cape.

TAILOR (*reads*) With a trunke sleeue.

GRUMIO I confesse two sleeues.

TAILOR (*reads*) The sleeues curiously cut.   2020

PETRUCHIO I there's the villanie.

GRUMIO Error i'th bill sir, error i'th bill? I commanded
the sleeues should be cut out, and sow'd vp againe,
and that Ile proue vpon thee, though thy little finger
be armed in a thimble.

TAILOR This is true that I say, and I had thee in place
where thou shouldst know it.

GRUMIO I am for thee straight: take thou the bill, giue
me thy meat-yard, and spare not me.

HORTENSIO God-a-mercie *Grumio*, then hee shall haue no   2030
oddes.

PETRUCHIO

Well sir in breefe the gowne is not for me.

GRUMIO You are i'th right sir, 'tis for my mistris.

PETRUCHIO (*to the Tailor*)

Go take it vp vnto thy masters vse.

GRUMIO (*to the Tailor*) Villaine, not for thy life: Take vp
my Mistresse gowne for thy masters vse.

PETRUCHIO Why sir, what's your conceit in that?

GRUMIO Oh sir, the conceit is deeper then you think for:
Take vp my Mistris gowne to his masters vse. Oh fie,
2040 fie, fie.

PETRUCHIO (*aside*)

Hortensio, say thou wilt see the Tailor paide:
(*To the Tailor*) Go take it hence, be gone, and say no
more.

HORTENSIO (*aside to the Tailor*)

Tailor, Ile pay thee for thy gown to morrow,
Take no vnkindnesse of his hastie words:
Away I say, commend me to thy master.   *Exit Tailor*

PETRUCHIO

Well, come my *Kate*, we will vnto your fathers,
Euen in these honest meane habiliments:
Our purses shall be proud, our garments poore:
For 'tis the minde that makes the bodie rich.
2050 And as the Sunne breakes through the darkest clouds,
So honor peereth in the meanest habit.
What is the Iay more precious then the Larke
Because his feathers are more beautifull?
Or is the Adder better then the Eele,
Because his painted skin contents the eye.
Oh no good *Kate*: neither art thou the worse
For this poore furniture, and meane array.
If thou account'st it shame, lay it on me,
And therefore frolicke, we will hence forthwith,
2060 To feast and sport vs at thy fathers house,
Go call my men, and let vs straight to him,
And bring our horses vnto Long-lane end,
There wil we mount, and thither walke on foote,
Let's see, I thinke 'tis now some seuen a clocke,
And well we may come there by dinner time.

KATHERINE

I dare assure you sir, 'tis almost two,
And 'twill be supper time ere you come there.

PETRUCHIO

It shall be seuen ere I go to horse:
Looke what I speake, or do, or thinke to doe,
2070 You are still crossing it, sirs let't alone,
I will not goe to day, and ere I doe,
It shall be what a clock I say it is.

HORTENSIO (*aside*)

Why so this gallant will command the sunne.   *Exeunt*

Sc. 12
(4.4)   *Enter Tranio as Lucentio, and the Pedant drest like*
     Vincentio, booted and bare-headed

TRANIO

Sir, this is the house, please it you that I call.

PEDANT

I what else, and but I be deceiued,

Signior *Baptista* may remember me
Neere twentie yeares a goe in *Genoa*.

TRANIO

Where we were lodgers, at the *Pegasus*.
Tis well, and hold your owne in any case
With such austeritie as longeth to a father.   2080
     Enter Biondello

PEDANT

I warrant you: but sir here comes your boy,
'Twere good he were school'd.

TRANIO

Feare you not him: sirra *Biondello*,
Now doe your dutie throughlie I aduise you:
Imagine 'twere the right *Vincentio*.

BIONDELLO Tut, feare not me.

TRANIO

But hast thou done thy errand to *Baptista*.

BIONDELLO

I told him that your father was at *Venice*,
And that you look't for him this day in *Padua*.

TRANIO (*giuing money*)

Th'art a tall fellow, hold thee that to drinke,   2090
Here comes *Baptista*: set your countenance sir.
     Enter Baptista and Lucentio as Cambio

TRANIO

Signior *Baptista* you are happilie met:
(*To the Pedant*) Sir, this is the gentleman I told you of,
I pray you stand good father to me now,
Giue me *Bianca* for my patrimony.

PEDANT

Soft son: (*to Baptista*) sir by your leaue, hauing com
     to *Padua*
To gather in some debts, my son *Lucentio*
Made me acquainted with a waighty cause
Of loue betweene your daughter and himselfe:
And for the good report I heare of you,   2100
And for the loue he beareth to your daughter,
And she to him: to stay him not too long,
I am content in a good fathers care
To haue him matcht, and if you please to like
No worse then I, vpon some agreement
Me shall you finde readie and willing
With one consent to haue her so bestowed:
For curious I cannot be with you
Signior *Baptista*, of whom I heare so well.

BAPTISTA

Sir, pardon me in what I haue to say,   2110
Your plainnesse and your shortnesse please me well:
Right true it is your sonne *Lucentio* here
Doth loue my daughter, and she loueth him,
Or both dissemble deeply their affections:
And therefore if you say no more then this,
That like a Father you will deale with him,
And passe my daughter a sufficient dower,
The match is made, and all is done,
Your sonne shall haue my daughter with consent.

TRANIO

I thanke you sir, where then doe you know best   2120

We be affied and such assurance tane,
As shall with either parts agreement stand.

BAPTISTA
Not in my house *Lucentio,* for you know
Pitchers haue eares, and I haue manie seruants,
Besides old *Gremio* is harkning still,
And happilie we might be interrupted.

TRANIO
Then at my lodging, and it like you,
There doth my father lie: and there this night
Weele passe the businesse priuately and well:
2130 Send for your daughter by your seruant here,
My Boy shall fetch the Scriuener presentlie,
The worst is this that at so slender warning,
You are like to haue a thin and slender pittance.

BAPTISTA
It likes me well: *Cambio* hie you home,
And bid *Bianca* make her readie straight:
And if you will tell what hath happened,
Lucentios Father is arriu'd in *Padua,*
And how she's like to be *Lucentios* wife.
⌜*Exit Lucentio*⌝

BIONDELLO
I praie the gods she may with all my heart.

TRANIO
2140 Dallie not with the gods, but get thee gone.
⌜*Exit Biondello*⌝
Signior *Baptista,* shall I leade the way,
Welcome, one messe is like to be your cheere,
Come sir, we will better it in *Pisa.*

BAPTISTA I follow you.   *Exeunt*

Sc. 13   *Enter Lucentio and Biondello*
(4.5) BIONDELLO *Cambio.*
LUCENTIO What saist thou *Biondello.*
BIONDELLO You saw my Master winke and laugh vpon
    you?
LUCENTIO *Biondello,* what of that?
2150 BIONDELLO Faith nothing: but has left mee here behinde
    to expound the meaning or morrall of his signes and
    tokens.
LUCENTIO I pray thee moralize them.
BIONDELLO Then thus: *Baptista* is safe talking with the
    deceiuing Father of a deceitfull sonne.
LUCENTIO And what of him?
BIONDELLO His daughter is to be brought by you to the
    supper.
LUCENTIO And then.
2160 BIONDELLO The old Priest at Saint *Lukes* Church is at your
    command at all houres.
LUCENTIO And what of all this.
BIONDELLO I cannot tell, except they are busied about a
    counterfeit assurance: take you assurance of her, *Cum
    priuilegio ad Impremendum solum,* to th' Church take the
    Priest, Clarke, and some sufficient honest witnesses:
    If this be not that you looke for, I haue no more to
        say,
    But bid *Bianca* farewell for euer and a day.

LUCENTIO Hear'st thou *Biondello.*
BIONDELLO I cannot tarry: I knew a wench maried in an   2170
    afternoone as shee went to the Garden for Parseley to
    stuffe a Rabit, and so may you sir: and so adew sir,
    my Master hath appointed me to goe to Saint *Lukes* to
    bid the Priest be readie t'attend against you come with
    your appendix.   *Exit*

LUCENTIO
I may and will, if she be so contented:
She will be pleas'd, then wherefore should I doubt:
Hap what hap may, Ile roundly goe about her:
It shall goe hard if *Cambio* goe without her.   *Exit*

        Enter Petruchio, Katherine, Hortentio, and seruants   Sc. 14
PETRUCHIO   (4.6)
Come on a Gods name, once more toward our
        fathers: 2180
Good Lord how bright and goodly shines the Moone.

KATHERINE
The Moone, the Sunne: it is not Moonelight now.

PETRUCHIO
I say it is the Moone that shines so bright.

KATHERINE
I know it is the Sunne that shines so bright.

PETRUCHIO
Now by my mothers sonne, and that's my selfe,
It shall be moone, or starre, or what I list,
Or ere I iourney to your Fathers house:
Goe on, and fetch our horses backe againe,
Euermore crost and crost, nothing but crost.

HORTENSIO (*to Katherine*)
Say as he saies, or we shall neuer goe.   2190

KATHERINE
Forward I pray, since we haue come so farre,
And be it moone, or sunne, or what you please:
And if you please to call it a rush Candle,
Henceforth I vowe it shall be so for me.

PETRUCHIO
I say it is the Moone.

KATHERINE
I know it is the Moone.

PETRUCHIO
Nay then you lye: it is the blessed Sunne.

KATHERINE
Then God be blest, it is the blessed sun,
But sunne it is not, when you say it is not,
And the Moone changes euen as your minde: 2200
What you will haue it nam'd, euen that it is,
And so it shall be still for *Katherine.*

HORTENSIO
Petruchio, goe thy waies, the field is won.

PETRUCHIO
Well, forward, forward, thus the bowle should run,
And not vnluckily against the Bias:
But soft, Company is comming here.
        Enter old Vincentio
(*To Vincentio*) Good morrow gentle Mistris, where
        away:

Tell me sweete *Kate*, and tell me truely too,
Hast thou beheld a fresher Gentlewoman:
2210 Such warre of white and red within her cheekes:
What stars do spangle heauen with such beautie,
As those two eyes become that heauenly face?
Faire louely Maide, once more good day to thee:
Sweete *Kate* embrace her for her beauties sake.

HORTENSIO A will make the man mad to make the woman
of him.

KATHERINE
Yong budding Virgin, faire, and fresh, & sweet,
Whether away, or where is thy aboade?
Happy the Parents of so faire a childe;
2220 Happier the man whom fauourable stars
Alots thee for his louely bedfellow.

PETRUCHIO
Why how now *Kate*, I hope thou art not mad,
This is a man old, wrinckled, faded, withered,
And not a Maiden, as thou saist he is.

KATHERINE
Pardon old father my mistaking eies,
That haue bin so bedazled with the sunne,
That euery thing I looke on seemeth greene:
Now I perceiue thou art a reuerent Father:
Pardon I pray thee for my mad mistaking.

PETRUCHIO
2230 Do good old grandsire, & withall make known
Which way thou trauell'st, if along with vs,
We shall be ioyfull of thy companie.

VINCENTIO
Faire Sir, and you my merry Mistris,
That with your strange encounter much amasde me:
My name is call'd *Vincentio*, my dwelling *Pisa*,
And bound I am to *Padua*, there to visite
A sonne of mine, which long I haue not seene.

PETRUCHIO
What is his name?

VINCENTIO   *Lucentio* gentle sir.

PETRUCHIO
Happily met, the happier for thy sonne:
2240 And now by Law, as well as reuerent age,
I may intitle thee my louing Father,
The sister to my wife, this Gentlewoman,
Thy Sonne by this hath married: wonder not,
Nor be not grieu'd, she is of good esteeme,
Her dowrie wealthie, and of worthie birth;
Beside, so qualified, as may beseeme
The Spouse of any noble Gentleman:
Let me imbrace with old *Vincentio*,
And wander we to see thy honest sonne,
2250 Who will of thy arriuall be full ioyous.
              He embraces Vincentio

VINCENTIO
But is this true, or is it else your pleasure,
Like pleasant trauailors to breake a Iest
Vpon the companie you ouertake?

HORTENSIO
I doe assure thee father so it is.

PETRUCHIO
Come goe along and see the truth hereof,
For our first merriment hath made thee iealous.
                    Exeunt all but Hortentio

HORTENSIO
Well *Petruchio*, this has put me in heart;
Haue to my Widdow, and if she be froward,
Then hast thou taught *Hortentio* to be vntoward.   *Exit*

Enter Biondello, Lucentio and Bianca, Gremio is out   Sc. 15
before   (5.1)

BIONDELLO Softly and swiftly sir, for the Priest is ready.

LUCENTIO I flie *Biondello*; but they may chance to neede   2261
thee at home, therefore leaue vs.

BIONDELLO Nay faith, Ile see the Church a your backe,
and then come backe to my masters as soone as I can.
              Exeunt Lucentio, Bianca, and Biondello

GREMIO
I maruaile *Cambio* comes not all this while.
        Enter Petruchio, Kate, Vincentio, Grumio with
        Attendants

PETRUCHIO
Sir heres the doore, this is *Lucentios* house,
My Fathers beares more toward the Market-place,
Thither must I, and here I leaue you sir.

VINCENTIO
You shall not choose but drinke before you go,
I thinke I shall command your welcome here;   2270
And by all likelihood some cheere is toward.
        Knock

GREMIO They're busie within, you were best knocke
lowder.
        Knock againe. Pedant lookes out of the window

PEDANT What's he that knockes as he would beat downe
the gate?

VINCENTIO Is Signior *Lucentio* within sir?

PEDANT He's within sir, but not to be spoken withall.

VINCENTIO What if a man bring him a hundred pound or
two to make merrie withall.

PEDANT Keepe your hundred pounds to your selfe, hee   2280
shall neede none so long as I liue.

PETRUCHIO (*to Vincentio*) Nay, I told you your sonne was
well beloued in *Padua*: (*to the Pedant*) doe you heare
sir, to leaue friuolous circumstances, I pray you tell
signior *Lucentio* that his Father is come from *Pisa*, and
is here at the doore to speake with him.

PEDANT Thou liest his Father is come from *Padua*, and
here looking out at the window.

VINCENTIO Art thou his father?

PEDANT I sir, so his mother saies, if I may beleeue her.   2290

PETRUCHIO (*to Vincentio*) Why how now gentleman: why
this is flat-knauerie to take vpon you another mans
name.

PEDANT Lay hands on the villaine, I beleeue a meanes to
cosen some bodie in this Citie vnder my countenance.
        Enter Biondello

BIONDELLO (*aside*) I haue seene them in the Church
together, God send 'em good shipping: but who is here?

mine old Master *Vincentio*: now wee are vndone and
brought to nothing.

2300 VINCENTIO (*to Biondello*) Come hither crackhempe.

BIONDELLO I hope I may choose Sir.

VINCENTIO Come hither you rogue, what haue you forgot
mee?

BIONDELLO Forgot you, no sir: I could not forget you, for
I neuer saw you before in all my life.

VINCENTIO What, you notorious villaine, didst thou neuer
see thy Masters father, *Vincentio*?

BIONDELLO What my old worshipfull old master? yes marie
sir see where he lookes out of the window.

2310 VINCENTIO Ist so indeede.

He beates Biondello

BIONDELLO Helpe, helpe, helpe, here's a mad man will
murder me.   *Exit*

PEDANT Helpe, sonne, helpe signior *Baptista*.   *Exit aboue*

PETRUCHIO Preethe *Kate* let's stand aside and see the end
of this controuersie.

They stand aside.

*Enter Pedant with Seruants, Baptista, Tranio as
Lucentio*

TRANIO (*to Vincentio*) Sir, what are you that offer to beate
my seruant?

VINCENTIO What am I sir: nay what are you sir: oh
immortall Goddes: oh fine villaine, a silken doublet, a

2320 veluet hose, a scarlet cloake, and a copataine hat: oh
I am vndone, I am vndone: while I plaie the good
husband at home, my sonne and my seruant spend all
at the vniuersitie.

TRANIO How now, what's the matter?

BAPTISTA What is the man lunaticke?

TRANIO Sir, you seeme a sober ancient Gentleman by
your habit: but your words shew you a mad man:
why sir, what cernes it you, if I weare Pearle and gold:
I thank my good Father, I am able to maintaine it.

2330 VINCENTIO Thy father: oh villaine, he is a Saile-maker in
Bergamo.

BAPTISTA You mistake sir, you mistake sir, praie what do
you thinke is his name?

VINCENTIO His name, as if I knew not his name: I haue
brought him vp euer since he was three yeeres old,
and his name is *Tranio*.

PEDANT Awaie, awaie mad asse, his name is *Lucentio*, and
he is mine onelie sonne and heire to the Lands of me
signior *Vincentio*.

2340 VINCENTIO *Lucentio*: oh he hath murdred his Master; laie
hold on him I charge you in the Dukes name: oh my
sonne, my sonne: tell me thou villaine, where is my
son *Lucentio*?

TRANIO Call forth an officer:

Enter an Officer

Carrie this mad knaue to the Iaile: father *Baptista*, I
charge you see that hee be forth comming.

VINCENTIO Carrie me to the Iaile?

GREMIO Staie officer, he shall not go to prison.

BAPTISTA Talke not signior *Gremio*: I saie he shall goe to

2350 prison.

GREMIO Take heede signior *Baptista*, least you be
conicatcht in this businesse: I dare sweare this is the
right *Vincentio*.

PEDANT Sweare if thou dar'st.

GREMIO Naie, I dare not sweare it.

TRANIO Then thou wert best saie that I am not *Lucentio*.

GREMIO Yes, I know thee to be signior *Lucentio*.

BAPTISTA Awaie with the dotard, to the Iaile with him.

Enter Biondello, Lucentio and Bianca

VINCENTIO Thus strangers may be haild and abusd: oh
monstrous villaine.   2360

BIONDELLO Oh we are spoil'd, and—yonder he is, denie
him, forsweare him, or else we are all vndone.

*Exeunt Biondello, Tranio and Pedant as fast as
may be*

LUCENTIO (*to Vincentio*) Pardon sweete father.

Kneele

VINCENTIO Liues my sweete sonne?

BIANCA (*to Baptista*) Pardon deere father.

BAPTISTA
How hast thou offended, where is *Lucentio*?

LUCENTIO
Here's *Lucentio*, right sonne to the right *Vincentio*,
That haue by marriage made thy daughter mine,
While counterfeit supposes bleer'd thine eine.

GREMIO
Here's packing with a witnesse to deceiue vs all.   2370

VINCENTIO
Where is that damned villaine *Tranio*,
That fac'd and brau'd me in this matter so?

BAPTISTA
Why, tell me is not this my *Cambio*?

BIANCA
Cambio is chang'd into *Lucentio*.

LUCENTIO
Loue wrought these miracles. *Biancas* loue
Made me exchange my state with *Tranio*,
While he did beare my countenance in the towne,
And happilie I haue arriued at the last
Vnto the wished hauen of my blisse:
What *Tranio* did, my selfe enforst him to;   2380
Then pardon him sweete Father for my sake.

VINCENTIO Ile slit the villaines nose that would haue sent
me to the Iaile.

BAPTISTA But doe you heare sir, haue you married my
daughter without asking my good will?

VINCENTIO Feare not *Baptista*, we will content you, goe
to: but I will in to be reueng'd for this villanie.   *Exit*

BAPTISTA And I to sound the depth of this knauerie.

Exit

LUCENTIO Looke not pale *Bianca*, thy father will not frown.

Exeunt Lucentio and Bianca

GREMIO
My cake is dough, but Ile in among the rest,   2390
Out of hope of all, but my share of the feast.   *Exit*

KATHERINE (*comming forward*) Husband let's follow, to see
the end of this adoe.

PETRUCHIO First kisse me *Kate*, and we will.

KATHERINE What in the midst of the streete?

PETRUCHIO What art thou asham'd of me?

KATHERINE No sir, God forbid, but asham'd to kisse.

PETRUCHIO

Why then let's home againe: Come Sirra let's awaie.

KATHERINE

Nay, I will giue thee a kisse, now praie thee Loue
staie.
They kisse

PETRUCHIO

2400 Is not this well? come my sweete *Kate*.
Better once then neuer, for neuer to late.   *Exeunt*

Sc. 16   *Enter Baptista, Vincentio, Gremio, the Pedant,*
(5.2)   *Lucentio, and Bianca, Petruchio, Katherine, and*
          Hortentio, Tranio, Biondello, Grumio, and Widdow:
          The Seruingmen with Tranio bringing in a Banquet

LUCENTIO

At last, though long, our iarring notes agree,
And time it is when raging warre is done,
To smile at scapes and perils ouerblowne:
My faire *Bianca* bid my father welcome,
While I with selfesame kindnesse welcome thine:
Brother *Petruchio*, sister *Katerina*,
And thou *Hortentio* with thy louing *Widdow*,
Feast with the best, and welcome to my house,
2410 My Banket is to close our stomakes vp
After our great good cheere: praie you sit downe,
For now we sit to chat as well as eate.
They sit

PETRUCHIO

Nothing but sit and sit, and eate and eate.

BAPTISTA

Padua affords this kindnesse, sonne *Petruchio*.

PETRUCHIO

Padua affords nothing but what is kinde.

HORTENSIO

For both our sakes I would that word were true.

PETRUCHIO

Now for my life *Hortentio* feares his Widow.

WIDDOW

Then neuer trust me if I be affeard.

PETRUCHIO

You are verie sencible, and yet you misse my sence:
2420 I meane *Hortentio* is afeard of you.

WIDDOW

He that is giddie thinks the world turns round.

PETRUCHIO Roundlie replied.

KATHERINE Mistris, how meane you that?

WIDDOW Thus I conceiue by him.

PETRUCHIO

Conceiues by me, how likes *Hortentio* that?

HORTENSIO

My Widdow saies, thus she conceiues her tale.

PETRUCHIO Verie well mended: kisse him for that good
Widdow.

KATHERINE

He that is giddie thinkes the world turnes round,
2430 I praie you tell me what you meant by that.

WIDDOW

Your housband being troubled with a shrew,
Measures my husbands sorrow by his woe:
And now you know my meaning.

KATHERINE

A verie meane meaning.

WIDDOW   Right, I meane you.

KATHERINE

And I am meane indeede, respecting you.

PETRUCHIO To her *Kate*.

HORTENSIO To her *Widdow*.

PETRUCHIO

A hundred marks, my *Kate* does put her down.

HORTENSIO That's my office.

PETRUCHIO

Spoke like an Officer: ha to the lad.   2440
Drinkes to Hortentio

BAPTISTA

How likes *Gremio* these quicke witted folkes?

GREMIO

Beleeue me sir, they But together well.

BIANCA

Head and but, an hastie witted bodie,
Would say your Head and But were head and horne.

VINCENTIO

I Mistris Bride, hath that awakend you?

BIANCA

I, but not frighted me, therefore Ile sleepe againe.

PETRUCHIO

Nay that you shall not since you haue begun:
Haue at you for a better iest or too.

BIANCA

Am I your Bird, I meane to shift my bush,
And then pursue me as you draw your Bow.   2450
You are welcome all.
Exit Bianca with Katherine and Widdow

PETRUCHIO

She hath preuented me, here signior *Tranio*,
This bird you aim'd at, though you hit her not,
Therefore a health to all that shot and mist.

TRANIO

Oh sir, *Lucentio* slipt me like his Gray-hound,
Which runs himselfe, and catches for his Master.

PETRUCHIO

A good swift simile, but something currish.

TRANIO

'Tis well sir that you hunted for your selfe:
'Tis thought your Deere does hold you at a baie.

BAPTISTA

Oh, oh *Petruchio*, *Tranio* hits you now.   2460

LUCENTIO

I thanke thee for that gird good *Tranio*.

HORTENSIO

Confesse, confesse, hath he not hit you here?

PETRUCHIO

A has a little gald me I confesse:
And as the Iest did glaunce awaie from me,
'Tis ten to one it maim'd you too out right.

BAPTISTA
  Now in good sadnesse sonne *Petruchio*,
  I thinke thou hast the veriest shrew of all.

PETRUCHIO
  Well, I say no: and therefore sir assurance,
  Let's each one send vnto his wife,
2470 And he whose wife is most obedient,
  To come at first when he doth send for her,
  Shall win the wager which we will propose.

HORTENSIO Content, what's the wager?

LUCENTIO Twentie crownes.

PETRUCHIO Twentie crownes,
  Ile venture so much of my Hawke or Hound,
  But twentie times so much vpon my Wife.

LUCENTIO A hundred then.

HORTENSIO Content.

2480 PETRUCHIO A match, 'tis done.

HORTENSIO Who shall begin?

LUCENTIO That will I.
  Goe *Biondello*, bid your Mistris come to me.

BIONDELLO I goe.   *Exit*

BAPTISTA
  Sonne, Ile be your halfe, *Bianca* comes.

LUCENTIO
  Ile haue no halues: Ile beare it all my selfe.
    Enter Biondello
  How now, what newes?

BIONDELLO   Sir, my Mistris sends you word
  That she is busie, and she cannot come.

PETRUCHIO
  How? she's busie, and she cannot come:
  Is that an answere?

2490 GREMIO   I, and a kinde one too:
  Praie God sir your wife send you not a worse.

PETRUCHIO
  I hope better.

HORTENSIO   Sirra *Biondello*,
  Goe and intreate my wife to come to me forthwith.
                                    Exit Biondello

PETRUCHIO
  Oh ho, intreate her, nay then shee must needes come.

HORTENSIO
  I am affraid sir, doe what you can
    Enter Biondello
  Yours will not be entreated: Now, where's my wife?

BIONDELLO
  She saies you haue some goodly Iest in hand,
  She will not come: she bids you come to her.

PETRUCHIO
  Worse and worse, she will not come: Oh vilde,
2500 Intollerable, not to be indur'd:
  Sirra *Grumio*, goe to your Mistris,
  Say I command her come to me.   *Exit Grumio*

HORTENSIO
  I know her answere.

PETRUCHIO   What?

HORTENSIO   She will not.

PETRUCHIO
  The fouler fortune mine, and there an end.
    Enter Katerina

BAPTISTA
  Now by my hollidam here comes *Katerina*.

KATHERINE (*to Petruchio*)
  What is your will sir, that you send for me?

PETRUCHIO
  Where is your sister, and *Hortensios* wife?

KATHERINE
  They sit conferring by the Parler fire.

PETRUCHIO
  Goe fetch them hither, if they denie to come,
  Swinge me them soundly forth vnto their husbands: 2510
  Away I say, and bring them hither straight.
                                    Exit Katerina

LUCENTIO
  Here is a wonder, if you talke of wonders.

HORTENSIO
  And so it is: I wonder what it boads.

PETRUCHIO
  Marrie peace it boads, and loue, and quiet life,
  An awfull rule, and right supremicie:
  And to be short, what not, that's sweete and happie.

BAPTISTA
  Now faire befall thee good *Petruchio*;
  The wager thou hast won, and I will adde
  Vnto their losses twentie thousand crownes,
  Another dowrie to another daughter,   2520
  For she is chang'd as she had neuer bin.

PETRUCHIO
  Nay, I will win my wager better yet,
  And show more signe of her obedience,
  Her new built vertue and obedience.
    Enter Kate, Bianca, and Widdow
  See where she comes, and brings your froward Wiues
  As prisoners to her womanlie perswasion:
  Katerine, that Cap of yours becomes you not,
  Off with that bable, throw it vnderfoote.
    Katherine throws downe her Cap

WIDDOW
  Lord let me neuer haue a cause to sigh,
  Till I be brought to such a sillie passe.   2530

BIANCA
  Fie what a foolish dutie call you this?

LUCENTIO
  I would your dutie were as foolish too:
  The wisdome of your dutie faire *Bianca*,
  Hath cost me a hundred crownes since supper time.

BIANCA
  The more foole you for laying on my dutie.

PETRUCHIO
  Katherine I charge thee tell these head-strong women,
  What dutie they doe owe their Lords and husbands.

WIDDOW
  Come, come, your mocking: we will haue no telling.

PETRUCHIO
  Come on I say, and first begin with her.

2540   WIDDOW She shall not.

PETRUCHIO

     I say she shall, and first begin with her.

KATHERINE

     Fie, fie, vnknit that threatning vnkinde brow,

     And dart not scornefull glances from those eies,

     To wound thy Lord, thy King, thy Gouernour.

     It blots thy beautie, as frosts doe bite the Meads,

     Confounds thy fame, as whirlewinds shake faire

         budds,

     And in no sence is meete or amiable.

     A woman mou'd, is like a fountaine troubled,

     Muddie, ill seeming, thicke, bereft of beautie,

2550   And while it is so, none so dry or thirstie

     Will daigne to sip, or touch one drop of it.

     Thy husband is thy Lord, thy life, thy keeper,

     Thy head, thy soueraigne: One that cares for thee,

     And for thy maintenance, commits his body

     To painfull labour, both by sea and land:

     To watch the night in stormes, the day in cold,

     Whil'st thou ly'st warme at home, secure and safe,

     And craues no other tribute at thy hands,

     But loue, faire lookes, and true obedience;

2560   Too little payment for so great a debt.

     Such dutie as the subiect owes the Prince,

     Euen such a woman oweth to her husband:

     And when she is froward, peeuish, sullen, sowre,

     And not obedient to his honest will,

     What is she but a foule contending Rebell,

     And gracelesse Traitor to her louing Lord?

     I am asham'd that women are so simple,

     To offer warre, where they should kneele for peace:

     Or seeke for rule, supremacie, and sway,

2570   When they are bound to serue, loue, and obay.

     Why are our bodies soft, and weake, and smooth,

     Vnapt to toyle and trouble in the world,

     But that our soft conditions, and our harts,

     Should well agree with our externall parts?

     Come, come, you froward and vnable wormes,

     My minde hath bin as bigge as one of yours,

     My heart as great, my reason haplie more,

     To bandie word for word, and frowne for frowne;

     But now I see our Launces are but strawes:

     Our strength as weake, our weakenesse past compare,   2580

     That seeming to be most, which we indeed least are.

     Then vale your stomackes, for it is no boote,

     And place your hands below your husbands foote:

     In token of which dutie, if he please,

     My hand is readie, may it do him ease.

PETRUCHIO

     Why there's a wench: Come on, and kisse mee *Kate*.

         They kisse

LUCENTIO

     Well go thy waies olde Lad for thou shalt ha't.

VINCENTIO

     Tis a good hearing, when children are toward.

LUCENTIO

     But a harsh hearing, when women are froward.

PETRUCHIO Come *Kate*, wee'le to bed,   2590

     We three are married, but you two are sped.

     'Twas I wonne the wager, though (*to Lucentio*) you

         hit the white,

     And being a winner, God giue you good night.

         Exit Petruchio with Katherine

HORTENSIO

     Now goe thy wayes, thou hast tam'd a curst Shrow.

LUCENTIO

     Tis a wonder, by your leaue, she wil be tam'd so.

         Exeunt

FINIS

ADDITIONAL PASSAGES

The Taming of A Shrew, printed in 1594 and believed to derive from Shakespeare's play as performed, contains episodes continuing and rounding off the Christopher Slie framework which may echo passages written by Shakespeare but not printed in the Folio. They are given below.

A. The following exchange occurs at a point for which there is no exact equivalent in Shakespeare's play. It could come at the end of Sc. 5. The 'fool' of the first line is Sander, the counterpart of Grumio.

     Then Slie speakes

SLIE *Sim*, when will the foole come againe?

LORD Heele come againe my Lord anon.

SLIE Gis some more drinke here, souns wheres the Tapster, here *Sim* eate some of these things.

LORD So I doo my Lord.

SLIE Here *Sim*, I drinke to thee.

LORD My Lord heere comes the plaiers againe.

SLIE O braue, heers two fine gentlewomen.

B. This passage comes between Sc. 12 and Sc. 13. If it originates with Shakespeare, it implies that Grumio accompanies Petruchio at the beginning of Sc. 13.

SLIE *Sim* must they be married now?

LORD I my Lord.

     Enter Ferando and Kate and Sander

SLIE Looke *Sim* the foole is come againe now.

C. Slie interrupts the action of the play-within-play. This
is at line 2362.1 of Shakespeare's play.

> *Phylotus and Valeria runnes away.*
> *Then Slie speakes*

SLIE I say wele haue no sending to prison.

LORD My Lord this is but the play, theyre but in iest.

SLIE I tell thee *Sim* wele haue no sending to prison thats
flat: why *Sim* am not I *Don Christo Vary*? Therefore I
say they shall not go to prison.

LORD No more they shall not my Lord, they be run away.

SLIE Are they run away *Sim*? thats well, then gis some
more drinke, and let them play againe.

LORD Here my Lord.

> *Slie drinkes and then falls asleepe*

D. Slie is carried off between Sc. 15 and Sc. 16.

> *Exeunt Omnes*
>
> *Slie sleepes*

LORD

Whose within there? come hither sirs my Lords
Asleepe againe: go take him easily vp,
And put him in his one apparell againe,
And lay him in the place where we did find him,
Iust vnderneath the alehouse side below,
But see you wake him not in any case.

BOY

It shall be don my Lord come helpe to beare him hence.

> *Exit*

E. The conclusion.

> *Then enter two bearing of Slie in his owne apparrell*
> *againe, and leaues him where they found him, and*
> *then goes out.*
> *Then enter the Tapster*

TAPSTER

Now that the darkesome night is ouerpast,
And dawning day apeares in cristall sky,
Now must I hast abroad: but soft whose this?
What *Slie* oh wondrous hath he laine here allnight,
Ile wake him, I thinke he's starued by this,
But that his belly was so stuft with ale,
What how *Slie*, Awake for shame.

SLIE *Sim* gis some more wine: whats all the plaiers gon:
am not I a Lord?

TAPSTER

A Lord with a murrin: come art thou dronken still?   10

SLIE

Whose this? *Tapster*, oh Lord sirra, I have had
The brauest dreame to night, that euer thou
Hardest in all thy life.

TAPSTER

I marry but you had best get you home,
For your wife will course you for dreming here to night.

SLIE

Will she? I know now how to tame a shrew,
I dreamt vpon it all this night till now,
And thou hast wakt me out of the best dreame
That euer I had in my life, but Ile to my
Wife presently and tame her too   20
And if she anger me.

TAPSTER

Nay tarry *Slie* for Ile go home with thee,
And heare the rest that thou hast dreamt to night.

> *Exeunt Omnes*

THE FIRST PART OF THE
CONTENTION
(2 HENRY VI)

WHEN Shakespeare's history plays were gathered together in the 1623 Folio, seven years after he died, they were printed in the order of their historical events, each with a title naming the king in whose reign those events occurred. No one supposes that this is the order in which Shakespeare wrote them; and the Folio titles are demonstrably not, in all cases, those by which the plays were originally known. The three concerned with the reign of Henry VI are listed in the Folio, simply and unappealingly, as the *First*, *Second*, and *Third Parts of King Henry the Sixt*, and these are the names by which they have continued to be known. Versions of the *Second* and *Third* had appeared long before the Folio, in 1594 and 1595; their head titles read *The First Part of the Contention of the two Famous Houses of Yorke and Lancaster with the Death of the Good Duke Humphrey* and *The True Tragedie of Richard Duke of Yorke and the good King Henry the Sixt*. These are, presumably, full versions of the plays' original titles, and we revert to them in preference to the Folio's historical listing.

A variety of internal evidence suggests that the Folio's *Part One* was composed after *The First Part of the Contention* and *Richard Duke of Yorke*, so we depart from the Folio order, though a reader wishing to read the plays in their narrative sequence will read *Henry VI, Part One* before the other two plays. The dates of all three are uncertain, but *Part One* is alluded to in 1592, when it was probably new. *The First Part of the Contention* probably belongs to 1590-1.

The play draws extensively on English chronicle history for its portrayal of the troubled state of England under Henry VI (1421-71). It dramatizes the touchingly weak King's powerlessness against the machinations of his nobles, especially Richard, Duke of Yorke, himself ambitious for the throne. Richard engineers the Kentish rebellion, led by Iack Cade, which provides some of the play's liveliest episodes; and at the play's end Richard seems poised to take the throne.

Historical events of ten years (1445-55) are dramatized with comparative fidelity within a coherent structure that offers a wide variety of theatrical entertainment. Though the play employs old-fashioned conventions of language (particularly the recurrent classical references) and of dramaturgy (such as the horrors of severed heads), its bold characterization, its fundamentally serious but often ironically comic presentation of moral and political issues, the powerful rhetoric of its verse, and the vivid immediacy of its prose have proved highly effective in its rare modern revivals.

Our text is based on the Folio, probably printed from an authorial draft. The First Quarto (1594) is probably based on memories of the play in performance; we have accepted from it a number of clarifications of staging and of narrative development.

THE NAMES OF THE ACTORS

Of the Kings Partie

KING Henry the Sixt

QUEENE Margaret

William de la Pole, Marquesse, later Duke, of SUFFOLKE, the
    Queenes louer

Duke Humfrey of GLOSTER, the Lord Protector, Vnckle of the King

Dame ELIANOR Cobham, the Duchesse of Gloster

CARDINALL Beauford, Bishop of Winchester, Vnckle of Gloster
    and Great Vnckle of the King

Duke of BUCKINGHAM

Duke of SOMERSET

Old Lord CLIFFORD

YONG CLIFFORD, his sonne

Of the Duke of Yorkes Partie

Duke of YORKE

EDWARD, Earle of March ⎫
                ⎬ his sonnes
Crook-backe RICHARD ⎭

Earle of SALISBURY

Earle of WARWICKE, his sonne

The Petitions and the Combat

2. or 3. PETITIONERS

Thomas Horner, an ARMORER

PETER Thumpe, his Man

3. NEIGHBORS, who drinke to Horner

3. PRENTICES, who drinke to Peter

The Coniuration

Sir Iohn HUME ⎫
           ⎬ Priests
Iohn SOUTHWELL ⎭

Margerie Iordan, a WITCH

Roger BULLINGBROOKE, a Coniurer

Asnath, a SPIRIT

The False Miracle

Symon SIMPCOXE

His WIFE

The MAIOR of Saint Albones

His Brethren

A BEADLE of Saint Albones

Townes-men of Saint Albones

Elianors Penance

Glosters SERUANTS

2. SHERIFFES of London

Sir Iohn STANLEY

HERALD

The Murther of Gloster

2. MURTHERERS

COMMONS

The Murther of Suffolke

CAPTAINE of a Ship

MASTER of that Ship

The Masters MATE

Water WHITMORE

2. GENTLEMEN

The Cade Rebellion

Iacke CADE, a Kentishman seduc'd by the Duke of Yorke to make
    Commotion

Dicke the BUTCHER ⎫

Smith the WEAUER ⎪

A Sawyer ⎬ Cades followers

IOHN ⎪

REBELLS ⎭

Emanuell, the CLEARKE of Chattam ⎫

Sir Humfrey STAFFORD ⎪

His BROTHER ⎪

Lord SAY ⎬ Those who die at the
                   Rebells Hands
Lord SCAYLES ⎪

Mathew Goffe ⎪

A SARGIANT ⎭

3. or 4. CITIZENS of London

Alexander IDEN, an Esquire of Kent, who kills Cade

Others

VAUX, a messenger

A POST

MESSENGERS

A SOULDIER

Attendants, Guards, Seruants, Souldiers, Faulkners

The First Part of the Contention
of the Two Famous Houses of Yorke & Lancaster

*Flourish of Trumpets: Then Hoboyes. Enter at one
doore, King Henry the sixt, and Humphrey Duke of
Gloster, the Duke of Sommerset, the Duke of
Buckingham, Cardinall Bewford, ⌈and others⌉.
Enter at the other doore, the Duke of Yorke, and the
Marquess of Suffolke, and Queene Margaret, and
the Earles of Salisbury and Warwicke*

SUFFOLKE (*kneeling before the King*)
As by your high Imperiall Maiesty,
I had in charge at my depart for France,
As Procurator to your Excellence,
To marry Princes *Margaret* for your Grace;
So in the Famous Ancient City, *Toures*,
In presence of the Kings of *France*, and *Sicill*,
The Dukes of *Orleance, Calaber, Britaigne*, and *Alanson*,
Seuen Earles, twelue Barons, & twenty reuerend
    Bishops
I haue perform'd my Taske, and was espous'd,
10 And humbly now vpon my bended knee,
In sight of England, and her Lordly Peeres,
Deliuer vp my Title in the Queene
To your most gracious hands, that are the Substance
Of that great Shadow I did represent:
The happiest Gift, that euer Marquesse gaue,
The Fairest Queene, that euer King receiu'd.

KING
Suffolke arise. Welcome Queene *Margaret*,
I can expresse no kinder signe of Loue
Then this kinde kisse:
    Kisses her
                O Lord, that lends me life,
20 Lend me a heart repleate with thankfulnesse:
For thou hast giuen me in this beauteous Face
A world of earthly blessings to my soule,
If Simpathy of Loue vnite our thoughts.

QUEENE
Th'excess of loue I beare vnto your grace,
Forbids me to be lauish of my tongue,
Least I should speake more then beseemes a woman:
Let this suffice, my blisse is in your liking,
And nought can make poore *Margaret* miserable,
Vnlesse the frowne of mightie Englands King.

KING
30 Her sight did rauish, but her grace in Speech,
Her words yclad with wisedomes Maiesty,
Makes me from Wondring, fall to Weeping ioyes,
Such is the Fulnesse of my hearts content.
Lords, with one cheerefull voice, Welcome my Loue.

LORDS (*kneel*)
Long liue Qu. *Margaret*, Englands happines.

QUEENE We thanke you all.

Florish. ⌈*All rise*⌉

SUFFOLKE (*to Gloster*)
My Lord Protector, so it please your Grace,
Heere are the Articles of contracted peace,
Betweene our Soueraigne, and the French King
    Charles,
For eighteene moneths concluded by consent. 40

GLOSTER (*reades*) Inprimis, *It is agreed betweene the French
K. Charles, and William de la Pole Marquesse of Suffolke,
Ambassador for Henry King of England, That the said
Henry shal espouse the Lady Margaret, daughter vnto
Reignier King of Naples, Sicillia, and Ierusalem, and Crowne
her Queene of England, ere the thirtieth of May next
ensuing.*
    Item, *It is further agreed betwene them, That the Dutchy
of Aniou, and the County of Main, shall be released and
deliuered to the King her fa.* 50

    ⌈*Gloster lets the paper fall*⌉

KING
Vnkle, how now?

GLOSTER   Pardon me gracious Lord,
Some sodaine qualme hath strucke me at the heart,
And dim'd mine eyes, that I can reade no further.

KING (*to the Cardinall*)
Vnckle of Winchester, I pray read on.

CARDINALL (*reades*) Item, *It is further agreed betweene them,
that the Duchy of Aniou and the County of Mayne, shall
be released and deliuered to the King her father, & she sent
ouer of the King of Englands owne proper cost and charges
without dowry.*

KING
They please vs well, (*to Suffolke*) Lord Marquesse
    kneele downe, 60
    Suffolke kneels
We here create thee first Duke of *Suffolke*,
And girt thee with the sword.
    Suffolke rises
                Cosin of Yorke,
We here discharge your grace from being Regent
I'th parts of *France*, till terme of 18. months
Be full expirde. Thankes vnckle *Winchester*,
Gloster, Yorke, and *Buckingham, Somerset,
Salsbury*, and *Warwicke*.
We thanke you all for this great fauour done,
In entertainment to my Princely Queene,
Come let vs in, and with all speed prouide 70
To see her Coronation be performde.
    Exit King, Queene, and Suffolke. ⌈*Duke Humfrey
         of Gloster staies*⌉ *all the rest*

GLOSTER
Braue Peeres of England, Pillars of the State,

To you Duke *Humfrey* must vnload his greefe:
Your greefe, the common greefe of all the Land.
What? did my brother *Henry* spend his youth,
His valour, coine, and people in the warres?
Did he so often lodge in open field,
In Winters cold, and Summers parching heate,
To conquer France, his true inheritance?
80 And did my brother *Bedford* toyle his wits,
To keepe by policy what *Henrie* got:
Haue you your selues, *Somerset*, *Buckingham*,
Braue *Yorke*, *Salisbury*, and victorious *Warwicke*,
Receiud deepe scarres in France and Normandie:
Or hath mine Vnckle *Beauford*, and my selfe,
With all the Learned Counsell of the Realme,
Studied so long, sat in the Councell house,
Early and late, debating too and fro
How France and Frenchmen might be kept in awe,
90 And had his Highnesse in his infancie,
Crowned in Paris in despight of foes,
And shall these Labours, and these Honours dye?
Shall *Henries* Conquest, *Bedfords* vigilance,
Your Deeds of Warre, and all our Counsell dye?
O Peeres of England, shamefull is this League,
Fatall this Marriage, cancelling your Fame,
Blotting your names from Bookes of memory,
Racing the Charracters of your Renowne,
Defacing Monuments of Conquer'd France,
100 Vndoing all as all had neuer bin.
CARDINALL
Nephew, what meanes this passionate discourse?
This peroration with such circumstance?
For France, 'tis ours; and we will keepe it still.
GLOSTER
I Vnckle, we will keepe it, if we can:
But now it is impossible we should.
Suffolke, the new made Duke that rules the rost,
Hath giuen the Dutchy of *Aniou* and *Mayne*,
Vnto the poore King *Reignier*, whose large style
Agrees not with the leannesse of his purse.
SALISBURY
110 Now by the death of him that dyed for all,
These Counties were the Keyes of *Normandie*:
But wherefore weepes *Warwicke*, my valiant sonne?
WARWICKE
For greefe that they are past recouerie.
For were there hope to conquer them againe,
My sword should shed hot blood, mine eyes no teares.
Aniou and *Maine*? My selfe did win them both:
Those Prouinces, these Armes of mine did conquer,
And are the Citties that I got with wounds,
Deliuer'd vp againe with peacefull words?
120 *Mort Dieu.*
YORKE
For Suffolkes Duke, may he be suffocate,
That dims the Honor of this Warlike Isle:
France should haue torne and rent my very hart,
Before I would haue yeelded to this League.
I neuer read but Englands Kings haue had

Large summes of Gold, and Dowries with their wiues,
And our King *Henry* giues away his owne,
To match with her that brings no vantages.
GLOSTER
A proper iest, and neuer heard before,
That Suffolke should demand a whole Fifteenth,   130
For Costs and Charges in transporting her:
She should haue staid in France, and steru'd in France
Before—
CARDINALL
My Lord of Gloster, now ye grow too hot,
It was the pleasure of my Lord the King.
GLOSTER
My Lord of Winchester I know your minde.
'Tis not my speeches that you do mislike:
But 'tis my presence that doth trouble ye,
Rancour will out, proud Prelate, in thy face
I see thy furie: If I longer stay,   140
We shall begin our ancient bickerings:
But ile begone, and giue thee leaue to speake.
Lordings farewell, and say when I am gone,
I prophesied, France will be lost ere long.
Exit Humfrey of Gloster
CARDINALL
So, there goes our Protector in a rage:
'Tis knowne to you he is mine enemy:
Nay more, an enemy vnto you all,
And no great friend, I feare me to the King;
Consider Lords, he is the next of blood,
And heyre apparant to the English Crowne: 150
Had *Henrie* got an Empire by his marriage,
And all the wealthy Kingdomes of the West,
There's reason he should be displeas'd at it:
Looke to it Lords, let not his smoothing words
Bewitch your hearts, be wise and circumspect.
What though the common people fauour him,
Calling him, *Humfrey the good Duke of Gloster*,
Clapping their hands, and crying with loud voyce,
Iesu maintaine your Royall Excellence,
With God preserue the good Duke *Humfrey*:   160
I feare me Lords, for all this flattering glosse,
He will be found a dangerous Protector.
BUCKINGHAM
Why should he then protect our Soueraigne?
He being of age to gouerne of himselfe.
Cosin of Somerset, ioyne you with me,
And altogether with the Duke of Suffolke,
Wee'l quickly hoyse Duke *Humfrey* from his seat.
CARDINALL
This weighty businesse will not brooke delay,
Ile to the Duke of Suffolke presently.   *Exit Cardinall*
SOMERSET
Cosin of Buckingham, though *Humfries* pride   170
And greatnesse of his place be greefe to vs,
Yet let vs watch the haughtie Cardinall,
His insolence is more intollerable
Then all the Princes in the Land beside,
If Gloster be displac'd, hee'l be Protector.

BUCKINGHAM

    Or thou, or I Somerset will be Protector,

    Despite Duke *Humfrey*, or the Cardinall.

                  Exit Buckingham, and Somerset

SALISBURY

    Pride went before, Ambition followes him.

    While these do labour for their owne preferment,

180 Behooues it vs to labor for the Realme.

    I neuer saw but Humfrey Duke of Gloster,

    Did beare him like a Noble Gentleman:

    Oft haue I seene the haughty Cardinall,

    More like a Souldier then a man o'th'Church,

    As stout and proud as he were Lord of all,

    Sweare like a Ruffian, and demeane himselfe

    Vnlike the Ruler of a Common-weale.

    Warwicke my sonne, the comfort of my age,

    Thy deeds, thy plainnesse, and thy house-keeping,

190 Hath wonne the greatest fauour of the Commons,

    Excepting none but good Duke Humfrey.

    And Brother Yorke, thy Acts in Ireland,

    In bringing them to ciuill Discipline:

    Thy late exploits done in the heart of France,

    When thou wert Regent for our Soueraigne,

    Haue made thee fear'd and honor'd of the people,

    The reuerence of mine age, and *Neuels* name,

    Is of no litle force if I command,

    Ioyne we together for the publike good,

200 In what we can, to bridle and suppresse

    The pride of Suffolke, and the Cardinall,

    With Somersets and Buckinghams Ambition,

    And as we may, cherish Duke Humfries deeds,

    While they do tend the profit of the Land.

WARWICKE

    So God helpe Warwicke, as he loues the Land,

    And common profit of his Countrey.

YORKE

    And so sayes Yorke, (*aside*) for he hath greatest cause.

SALISBURY

    Then lets away, and looke vnto the maine.

WARWICKE

    Vnto the maine? Oh Father, *Maine* is lost,

    That *Maine*, which by maine force Warwicke did

210   winne,

    And would haue kept, so long as breath did last:

    Main-chance father you meant, but I meant *Maine*,

    Which I will win from France, or else be slaine.

         Exit Warwicke, and Salisbury. Manet Yorke

YORKE

    Aniou and *Maine* are giuen to the French,

    Paris is lost, the state of *Normandie*

    Stands on a tickle point, now they are gone:

    Suffolke concluded on the Articles,

    The Peeres agreed, and *Henry* was well pleas'd,

    To change two Dukedomes for a Dukes faire daughter.

220 I cannot blame them all, what is't to them?

    'Tis thine they giue away, and not their owne.

    Pirates may make cheape penyworths of their pillage,

    And purchase Friends, and giue to Curtezans,

    Still reuelling like Lords till all be gone,

    While as the silly Owner of the goods

    Weepes ouer them, and wrings his haplesse hands,

    And shakes his head, and trembling stands aloofe,

    While all is shar'd, and all is borne away,

    Ready to sterue, and dare not touch his owne.

    So Yorke must sit, and fret, and bite his tongue,   230

    While his owne Lands are bargain'd for, and sold:

    Me thinkes the Realmes of England, France, & Ireland,

    Beare that proportion to my flesh and blood,

    As did the fatall brand *Althæa* burnt,

    Vnto the Princes heart of *Calidon*:

    Aniou and *Maine* both giuen vnto the French?

    Cold newes for me: for I had hope of France,

    Euen as I haue of fertile Englands soile.

    A day will come, when Yorke shall claime his owne,

    And therefore I will take the *Neuils* parts,   240

    And make a shew of loue to proud Duke *Humfrey*,

    And when I spy aduantage, claime the Crowne,

    For that's the Golden marke I seeke to hit:

    Nor shall proud Lancaster vsurpe my right,

    Nor hold the Scepter in his childish Fist,

    Nor weare the Diadem vpon his head,

    Whose Church-like humors fits not for a Crowne.

    Then Yorke be still a-while, till time do serue:

    Watch thou, and wake when others be asleepe,

    To prie into the secrets of the State,   250

    Till *Henrie* surfet in the ioyes of loue,

    With his new Bride, & Englands deere bought Queen,

    And *Humfrey* with the Peeres be falne at iarres:

    Then will I raise aloft the Milke-white-Rose,

    With whose sweet smell the Ayre shall be perfum'd,

    And in my Standard beare the Armes of Yorke,

    To grapple with the house of Lancaster,

    And force perforce Ile make him yeeld the Crowne,

    Whose bookish Rule, hath pull'd faire England downe.

                      Exit Yorke

    Enter Duke Humfrey of Gloster and his wife Elianor   **Sc. 2**

                                            (1.2)

ELIANOR

    Why droopes my Lord like ouer-ripen'd Corn,   260

    Hanging the head at Ceres plenteous load?

    Why doth the Great Duke *Humfrey* knit his browes,

    As frowning at the Fauours of the world?

    Why are thine eyes fixt to the sullen earth,

    Gazing on that which seemes to dimme thy sight?

    What seest thou there? King *Henries* Diadem,

    Inchac'd with all the Honors of the world?

    If so, Gaze on, and grouell on thy face,

    Vntill thy head be circled with the same.

    Put forth thy hand, reach at the glorious Gold.   270

    What, is't too short? Ile lengthen it with mine,

    And hauing both together heau'd it vp,

    Wee'l both together lift our heads to heauen,

    And neuer more abase our sight so low,

    As to vouchsafe one glance vnto the ground.

GLOSTER

    O *Nell*, sweet *Nell*, if thou dost loue thy Lord,

Banish the Canker of ambitious thoughts:
And may that houre, when I imagine ill
Against my King and Nephew, vertuous *Henry*,
280 Be my last breathing in this mortall world.
My troublous dreame this night, doth make me sad.

ELIANOR

What dream'd my Lord? tell me, and Ile requite it
With sweet rehearsall of my mornings dreame.

GLOSTER

Me thought this staffe mine Office-badge in Court
Was broke in twaine: by whom, I haue forgot,
But as I thinke, it was by'th Cardinall,
And on the peeces of the broken Wand
Were plac'd the heads of *Edmond* Duke of Somerset,
And *William de la Pole* first Duke of Suffolke.
290 This was my dreame, what it doth bode God knowes.

ELIANOR

Tut, this was nothing but an argument,
That he that breakes a sticke of Glosters groue,
Shall loose his head for his presumption.
But list to me my *Humfrey*, my sweete Duke:
Me thought I sate in Seate of Maiesty,
In the Cathedrall Church of Westminster,
And in that Chaire where Kings & Queens are crownd,
Where *Henrie* and Dame *Margaret* kneel'd to me,
And on my head did set the Diadem.

GLOSTER

300 Nay *Elinor*, then must I chide outright:
Presumptuous Dame, ill-nurter'd *Elianor*,
Art thou not second Woman in the Realme?
And the Protectors wife belou'd of him?
Hast thou not worldly pleasure at command,
Aboue the reach or compasse of thy thought?
And wilt thou still be hammering Treachery,
To tumble downe thy husband, and thy selfe,
From top of Honor, to Disgraces feete?
Away from me, and let me heare no more.

ELIANOR

310 What, what, my Lord? Are you so chollericke
With *Elianor*, for telling but her dreame?
Next time Ile keepe my dreames vnto my selfe,
And not be check'd.

GLOSTER

Nay be not angry, I am pleas'd againe.

Enter Messenger

MESSENGER

My Lord Protector, 'tis his Highnes pleasure,
You do prepare to ride vnto S. *Albons*,
Where as the King and Queene do meane to Hawke.

GLOSTER

I go. Come *Nel* thou wilt ride with vs?

ELIANOR

Yes my good Lord, Ile follow presently.

Exit Humfrey of Gloster with the Messenger

320 Follow I must, I cannot go before,
While Gloster beares this base and humble minde.
Were I a Man, a Duke, and next of blood,
I would remoue these tedious stumbling blockes,

And smooth my way vpon their headlesse neckes.
And being a woman, I will not be slacke
To play my part in Fortunes Pageant.
(*Calling within*) Where are you there? Sir *Iohn*; nay
    feare not man,
We are alone, here's none but thee, & I.

Enter Hume

HUME

Iesus preserue your Royall Maiesty.

ELIANOR

What saist thou? Maiesty: I am but Grace.   330

HUME

But by the grace of God, and *Humes* aduice,
Your Graces Title shall be multiplied.

ELIANOR

What saist thou man? Hast thou as yet confer'd
With *Margerie Iordane* the cunning Witch of Eye,
With *Roger Bollingbrooke* the Coniurer?
And will they vndertake to do me good?

HUME

This they haue promised, to shew your Highnes
A Spirit rais'd from depth of vnder ground,
That shall make answere to such Questions,
As by your Grace shall be propounded him.   340

ELIANOR

It is enough, Ile thinke vpon the Questions:
When from Saint *Albones* we doe make returne,
Wee'le see these things effected to the full.
Here *Hume*, (*giuing him money*) take this reward,
    make merry man
With thy Confederates in this weightie cause.

Exit Elianor

HUME

Hume must make merry with the Duchesse Gold:
Marry and shall: but how now, Sir *Iohn Hume*?
Seale vp your Lips, and giue no words but Mum,
The businesse asketh silent secrecie.
Dame *Elianor* giues Gold, to bring the Witch: 350
Gold cannot come amisse, were she a Deuill.
Yet haue I Gold flyes from another Coast:
I dare not say, from the rich Cardinall,
And from the great and new-made Duke of Suffolke;
Yet I doe finde it so: for to be plaine,
They (knowing Dame *Elianors* aspiring humor)
Haue hyred me to vnder-mine the Duchesse,
And buzze these Coniurations in her brayne.
They say, A craftie Knaue do's need no Broker,
Yet am I *Suffolke* and the Cardinalls Broker.   360
Hume, if you take not heed, you shall goe neere
To call them both a payre of craftie Knaues.
Well, so it stands: and thus I feare at last,
Humes Knauerie will be the Duchesse Wracke,
And her Attainture, will be *Humphreyes* fall:
Sort how it will, I shall haue Gold for all.   *Exit*

Enter three or foure Petitioners, Peter the Armorers   Sc. 3
Man being one   (1.3)

I. PETITIONER My Masters, let's stand close, my Lord

68

Protector will come this way by and by, and then wee
may deliuer our Supplications in the Quill.

370   2. PETITIONER Marry the Lord protect him, for hee's a
good man, Iesu blesse him.

Enter Suffolke, and Queene

⌈1. PETITIONER⌉ Here a comes me thinkes, and the Queene
with him: Ile be the first sure.

He goes to meet Suffolke and the Queene

2. PETITIONER Come backe foole, this is the Duke of
Suffolk, and not my Lord Protector.

SUFFOLKE (*to 1. Petitioner*)

How now fellow: would'st any thing with me?

1. PETITIONER I pray my Lord pardon me, I tooke ye for
my Lord Protector.

QUEENE ⌈*seeing his Supplication she reades*⌉ To my Lord
380   Protector? Are your Supplications to his Lordship? Let
me see them:

⌈*She takes the 1. Petitioners Supplication*⌉

what is thine?

1. PETITIONER Mine is, and't please your Grace, against
Iohn Goodman, my Lord Cardinals Man, for keeping my
House, and Lands, and Wife and all, from me.

SUFFOLKE Thy Wife too? that's some Wrong indeede. ⌈*To
2. Petitioner*⌉ What's yours?

He takes the Supplication

What's heere? (*Reades*) Against the Duke of Suffolke,
for enclosing the Commons of Melforde. ⌈*To 2. Petitioner*⌉
390   How now, Sir Knaue?

2. PETITIONER Alas Sir, I am but a poore Petitioner of our
whole Towneship.

PETER ⌈*offering his Petition*⌉ Against my Master *Thomas
Horner*, for saying, That the Duke of Yorke was rightfull
Heire to the Crowne.

QUEENE What say'st thou? Did the Duke of Yorke say,
hee was rightfull Heire to the Crowne?

PETER That my M^r was? No forsooth: my Master said,
That he was, and that the King was an vsurer.

400   QUEENE An vsurper thou wouldst say.

PETER I forsooth an vsurper.

SUFFOLKE (*calling within*) Who is there?

Enter Seruant

Take this fellow in, and send for his Master with a
Purseuant presently: (*to Peter*) wee'le heare more of
your matter before the King.   *Exit seruant with Peter*

QUEENE (*to the Petitioners*)

And as for you that loue to be protected
Vnder the Wings of our Protectors Grace,
Begin your Suites anew, and sue to him.

Teare the Supplication

Away, base Cullions: *Suffolke* let them goe.

410   ALL PETITIONERS Come, let's be gone.   *Exeunt*

QUEENE

My Lord of Suffolke, say, is this the guise?
Is this the Fashions in the Court of England?
Is this the Gouernment of Britaines Ile?
And this the Royaltie of *Albions* King?
What, shall King *Henry* be a Pupill still,
Vnder the surly *Glosters* Gouernance?

Am I a Queene in Title and in Stile,
And must be made a Subiect to a Duke?
I tell thee *Poole*, when in the Citie *Tours*
Thou ran'st a-tilt in honor of my Loue,   420
And stol'st away the Ladies hearts of France;
I thought King *Henry* had resembled thee,
In Courage, Courtship, and Proportion:
But all his minde is bent to Holinesse,
To number *Aue-Maries* on his Beades:
His Champions, are the Prophets and Apostles,
His Weapons, holy Sawes of sacred Writ,
His Studie is his Tilt-yard, and his Loues
Are brazen Images of Canonized Saints.
I would the Colledge of the Cardinalls   430
Would chuse him Pope, and carry him to Rome,
And set the Triple Crowne vpon his Head;
That were a State fit for his Holinesse.

SUFFOLKE

Madame be patient: as I was cause
Your Highnesse came to England, so will I
In England worke your Graces full content.

QUEENE

Beside the haught Protector, haue we *Beauford*
The imperious Churchman; *Somerset*, *Buckingham*,
And grumbling *Yorke*: and not the least of these,
But can doe more in England then the King.   440

SUFFOLKE

And he of these, that can doe most of all,
Cannot doe more in England then the *Neuils*:
Salisbury and *Warwick* are no simple Peeres.

QUEENE

Not all these Lords do vex me halfe so much,
As that prowd Dame, the Lord Protectors Wife:
She sweepes it through the Court with troups of
     Ladies,
More like an Empresse, then Duke *Humphreyes* Wife:
Strangers in Court, doe take her for the Queene:
She beares a Dukes Reuenewes on her backe,
And in her heart she scornes our Pouertie: 450
Shall I not liue to be aueng'd on her?
Contemptuous base-borne Callot as she is,
She vaunted 'mongst her Minions t'other day,
The very trayne of her worst wearing Gowne,
Was better worth then all my Fathers Lands,
Till *Suffolke* gaue two Dukedomes for his Daughter.

SUFFOLKE

Madame, my selfe haue lym'd a Bush for her,
And plac't a Quier of such enticing Birds,
That she will light to listen to their Layes,
And neuer mount to trouble you againe.   460
So let her rest: and Madame list to me,
For I am bold to counsaile you in this;
Although we fancie not the Cardinall,
Yet must we ioyne with him and with the Lords,
Till we haue brought Duke *Humphrey* in disgrace.
As for the Duke of Yorke, this late Complaint
Will make but little for his benefit:

So one by one wee'le weed them all at last,
And you your selfe shall steere the happy Helme.
    Sound a Sennet. ⌈*Enter King Henry, and the Duke*
    of Yorke and the Duke of Somerset on both sides of
    the King, whispering with him, and enter Duke
    Humphrey of Gloster, Dame Elnor, the Duke of
    Buckingham, the Earle of Salsbury, the Earle of
    Warwicke, and the Cardinall of Winchester⌉

KING

470   For my part, Noble Lords, I care not which,
    Or *Somerset*, or *Yorke*, all's one to me.

YORKE

    If *Yorke* haue ill demean'd himselfe in France,
    Then let him be denay'd the Regent-ship.

SOMERSET

    If *Somerset* be vnworthy of the Place,
    Let *Yorke* be Regent, I will yeeld to him.

WARWICKE

    Whether your Grace be worthy, yea or no,
    Dispute not that, *Yorke* is the worthyer.

CARDINALL

    Ambitious *Warwicke*, let thy betters speake.

WARWICKE

    The Cardinall's not my better in the field.

BUCKINGHAM

480   All in this presence are thy betters, *Warwicke*.

WARWICKE

    Warwicke may liue to be the best of all.

SALISBURY

    Peace Sonne, (*to Buckingham*) and shew some reason
    Buckingham
    Why *Somerset* should be preferr'd in this?

QUEENE

    Because the King forsooth will haue it so.

GLOSTER

    Madame, the King is old enough himselfe
    To giue his Censure: These are no Womens matters.

QUEENE

    If he be old enough, what needs your Grace
    To be Protector of his Excellence?

GLOSTER

    Madame, I am Protector of the Realme,
490   And at his pleasure will resigne my Place.

SUFFOLKE

    Resigne it then, and leaue thine insolence.
    Since thou wert King; as who is King, but thou?
    The Common-wealth hath dayly run to wrack,
    The Dolphin hath preuayl'd beyond the Seas,
    And all the Peeres and Nobles of the Realme
    Haue beene as Bond-men to thy Soueraigntie.

CARDINALL (*to Gloster*)

    The Commons hast thou rackt, the Clergies Bags
    Are lanke and leane with thy Extortions.

SOMERSET (*to Gloster*)

    Thy sumptuous Buildings, and thy Wiues Attyre
500   Haue cost a masse of publique Treasurie.

BUCKINGHAM (*to Gloster*)

    Thy Crueltie in execution

Vpon Offendors, hath exceeded Law,
And left thee to the mercy of the Law.

QUEENE (*to Gloster*)

    Thy sale of Offices and Townes in France,
    If they were knowne, as the suspect is great,
    Would make thee quickly hop without thy Head.
                Exit Humfrey of Gloster
    The Queene lets fall her Fanne
(*To Elianor*)
    Giue me my Fanne: what, Mynion, can ye not?
    She giues the Duchesse a box on the eare
    I cry you mercy, Madame: was it you?

ELIANOR

    Was't I? yea, I it was, prowd French-woman:
    Could I come neere your Beautie with my Nayles,   510
    Ide set my ten Commandements in your face.

KING

    Sweet Aunt be quiet, 'twas against her will.

ELIANOR

    Against her will? good King, looke to't in time,
    Shee'le pamper thee, and dandle thee like a Baby:
    Though in this place most Master weare no Breeches,
    She shall not strike Dame *Elianor* vnreueng'd.
                    Exit Elianor

BUCKINGHAM (*aside to the Cardinall*)

    Lord Cardinall, I will follow *Elianor*,
    And listen after *Humfrey*, how he proceedes:
    Shee's tickled now, her Furie needs no spurres,
    Shee'le gallop farre enough to her destruction.   520
                 Exit Buckingham
    Enter Humfrey of Gloster

GLOSTER

    Now Lords, my Choller being ouer-blowne,
    With walking once about the Quadrangle,
    I come to talke of Common-wealth Affayres.
    As for your spightfull false Obiections,
    Proue them, and I lye open to the Law:
    But God in mercie so deale with my Soule,
    As I in dutie loue my King and Countrey.
    But to the matter that we haue in hand:
    I say, my Soueraigne, *Yorke* is meetest man
    To be your Regent in the Realme of France.   530

SUFFOLKE

    Before we make election, giue me leaue
    To shew some reason, of no little force,
    That *Yorke* is most vnmeet of any man.

YORKE

    Ile tell thee, *Suffolke*, why I am vnmeet.
    First, for I cannot flatter thee in Pride:
    Next, if I be appointed for the Place,
    My Lord of Somerset will keepe me here,
    Without Discharge, Money, or Furniture,
    Till France be wonne into the Dolphins hands:
    Last time I danc't attendance on his will,   540
    Till Paris was besieg'd, famisht, and lost.

WARWICKE

    That can I witnesse, and a fouler fact
    Did neuer Traytor in the Land commit.

SUFFOLKE Peace head-strong *Warwicke*.

WARWICKE

Image of Pride, why should I hold my peace?

Enter Armorer and Peter his Man, guarded

SUFFOLKE

Because here is a man accus'd of Treason,

Pray God the Duke of Yorke excuse himselfe.

YORKE

Doth any one accuse *Yorke* for a Traytor?

KING

What mean'st thou, *Suffolke*? tell me, what are these?

SUFFOLKE

550   Please it your Maiestie, this is the man

He indicates Peter

That doth accuse his Master (*indicating the Armorer*) of

High Treason;

His words were these: That *Richard*, Duke of *Yorke*,

Was rightfull Heire vnto the English Crowne,

And that your Maiestie was an Vsurper.

KING (*to the Armorer*) Say man, were these thy words?

ARMORER And't shall please your Maiestie, I neuer sayd

nor thought any such matter: God is my witnesse, I

am falsely accus'd by the Villaine.

PETER ⌈*raising his hands*⌉ By these tenne bones, my Lords,

560   hee did speake them to me in the Garret one Night, as

wee were scowring my Lord of Yorkes Armor.

YORKE

Base Dunghill Villaine, and Mechanicall,

Ile haue thy Head for this thy Traytors speech:

(*To the King*) I doe beseech your Royall Maiestie,

Let him haue all the rigor of the Law.

ARMORER Alas, my Lord, hang me if euer I spake the

words: my accuser is my Prentice, and when I did

correct him for his fault the other day, he did vow

vpon his knees he would be euen with me: I haue good

570   witnesse of this; therefore I beseech your Maiestie, doe

not cast away an honest man for a Villaines accusation.

KING (*to Gloster*)

Vnckle, what shall we say to this in law?

GLOSTER

This doome, my Lord, if I may iudge by case:

Let *Somerset* be Regent o're the French,

Because in *Yorke* this breedes suspition;

(*Indicating the Armorer and Peter*)

And let these haue a day appointed them

For single Combat, in conuenient place,

For he (*indicating the Armorer*) hath witnesse of his

seruants malice:

This is the Law, and this Duke *Humfreyes* doome.

KING

580   Then be it so. (*To Somerset*) My Lord of *Somerset*,

We make you Regent o're the Realme of *France*,

There to defend our rights gainst forraine foes.

SOMERSET

I humbly thanke your Royall Maiestie.

ARMORER

And I accept the Combat willingly.

PETER ⌈*to Gloster*⌉ Alas, my Lord, I cannot fight; for Gods

sake pitty my case: the spight of man preuayleth

against me. O Lord haue mercy vpon me, I shall neuer

be able to fight a blow: O Lord my heart.

GLOSTER

Sirrha, or you must fight, or else be hang'd.

KING

Away with them to Prison: and the day   590

Of Combat, be the last of the next moneth.

Come *Somerset*, wee'le see thee sent away.

Flourish. Exeunt

Enter the Witch, Hume and Southwell two Priests,   Sc. 4

and Bullingbrooke a Coniurer   (1.4)

HUME Come my Masters, the Duchesse I tell you expects

performance of your promises.

BULLINGBROOKE Master *Hume*, we are therefore prouided:

will her Ladyship behold and heare our Exorcismes?

HUME I, what else? feare you not her courage.

BULLINGBROOKE I haue heard her reported to be a Woman

of an inuincible spirit: but it shall be conuenient, Master

Hume, that you be by her aloft, while wee be busie   600

below; and so I pray you goe in Gods Name, and leaue

vs.   *Exit Hume*

(*To the Witch*) Mother *Iordan*, be you prostrate, and

grouell on the Earth;

She lies downe vpon her face.

⌈*Enter Elianor aloft*⌉

Iohn Southwell reade you, and let vs to our worke.

ELIANOR Well said my Masters, and welcome all: To this

geere, the sooner the better.

⌈*Enter Hume aloft*⌉

BULLINGBROOKE

Patience, good Lady, Wizards know their times:

Deepe Night, darke Night, the silent of the Night,

The time of Night when Troy was set on fire,   610

The time when Screech-owles cry, and Bandogs

howle,

And Spirits walke, and Ghosts breake vp their Graues;

That time best fits the worke we haue in hand.

Madame, sit you, and feare not: whom wee rayse,

Wee will make fast within a hallow'd Verge.

Here doe the Ceremonies belonging, and make the

Circle, Southwell reades, Coniuro te, &c. It

Thunders and Lightens terribly: then the Spirit

Asnath riseth

SPIRIT *Ad sum.*

WITCH *Asnath*,

By the eternall God, whose name and power

Thou tremblest at, answere that I shall aske:

For till thou speake, thou shalt not passe from hence.   620

SPIRIT

Aske what thou wilt; that I had sayd, and done.

BULLINGBROOKE (*reades*)

First of the King: What shall of him become?

SPIRIT

The Duke yet liues, that *Henry* shall depose:

But him out-liue, and dye a violent death.

As the Spirit speakes ⌈Southwell⌉ writes the
answeres downe

BULLINGBROOKE (*reades*)

Tell me what fate awaits the Duke of Suffolke?

SPIRIT

By Water shall he dye, and take his end.

BULLINGBROOKE (*reades*)

What shall betide the Duke of Somerset?

SPIRIT

Let him shun Castles, safer shall he be
Vpon the sandie Plaines, then where Castles mounted
stand.

630   Haue done, for more I hardly can endure.

BULLINGBROOKE

Discend to Darknesse, and the burning Lake:
False Fiend auoide.

Thunder and Lightning. The Spirit sinkes downe
againe

Enter the Duke of Yorke and the Duke of
Buckingham with their Guard, and Sir Humfrey
Stafford, and breake in

YORKE

Lay hands vpon these Traytors, and their trash:
⌈*Bullingbrooke, Southwell, and Iordan are taken*
Prisoner. Buckingham takes the Writings from
Bullingbrooke and Southwell⌉

(*To Iordan*) Beldam I thinke we watcht you at an
ynch.

(*To Elianor*) What Madame, are you there? the King &
Commonweale
Are deepe indebted for this peece of paines;
My Lord Protector will, I doubt it not,
See you well guerdon'd for these good deserts.

ELIANOR

Not halfe so bad as thine to Englands King,

640   Iniurious Duke, that threatest where's no cause.

BUCKINGHAM

True Madame, none at all:
⌈*He raises the Writings*⌉
                        what call you this?
(*To his Men*) Away with them, let them be clapt vp
close,
And kept asunder: (*to Elianor*) you Madame shall with
vs.
Stafford take her to thee.

Exit Stafford ⌈and others⌉ to Elianor ⌈and
Hume⌉, aboue

Wee'le see your Trinkets here all forth-comming.
All away.

Exit below Iordan, Southwell, and
Bullingbrooke, guarded, and aboue ⌈Hume and⌉
Elianor, guarded by Stafford ⌈and others. Manet
Yorke and Buckingham⌉

YORKE

Lord *Buckingham*, me thinks you watcht her well:
A pretty Plot, well chosen to build vpon.
Now pray my Lord, let's see the Deuils Writ.
⌈*Buckingham giues him the Writings*⌉

What haue we here?
He Reades the Writings
                        Why this is iust,   650
Aio Æacidã Romanos vincere posse.
These Oracles are hardely attain'd,
And hardly vnderstood. Come, come my Lorde,
The King is now in progresse towards Saint *Albones*,
With him, the Husband of this louely Lady:
Thither goes these Newes, as fast as Horse can carry
them:
A sorry Breakfast for my Lord Protector.

BUCKINGHAM

Your Grace shal giue me leaue, my Lord of York,
To be the Poste, in hope of his reward.

YORKE (*returning the Writings to Buckingham*)

At your pleasure, my good Lord.   ⌈*Exit Buckingham*⌉
(*Calling within*)   Who's within there, hoe?   660
Enter a Seruingman
Inuite my Lords of Salisbury and Warwick
To suppe with me to morrow Night. Away.

Exeunt seuerally

Enter the King, Queene with her Hawke on her fist,   Sc. 5
Gloster the Protector, Cardinall, and Suffolke, with   (2.1)
Faulkners hallowing

QUEENE

Beleeue me Lords, for flying at the Brooke,
I saw not better sport these seuen yeeres day:
Yet by your leaue, the Winde was very high,
And ten to one, old *Ioane* had not gone out.

KING (*to Gloster*)

But what a point, my Lord, your Faulcon made,
And what a pytch she flew aboue the rest:
To see how God in all his Creatures workes,
Yea Man and Birds are fayne of climbing high.   670

SUFFOLKE

No maruell, and it like your Maiestie,
My Lord Protectors Hawkes doe towre so well,
They know their Master loues to be aloft,
And beares his thoughts aboue his Faulcons Pitch.

GLOSTER

My Lord, 'tis but a base ignoble minde,
That mounts no higher then a Bird can sore:

CARDINALL

I thought as much, hee would be aboue the Clouds.

GLOSTER

I my Lord Cardinall, how thinke you by that?
Were it not good your Grace could flye to Heauen?

KING

The Treasurie of euerlasting Ioy.   680

CARDINALL (*to Gloster*)

Thy Heauen is on Earth, thine Eyes & Thoughts
Beat on a Crowne, the Treasure of thy Heart,
Pernitious Protector, dangerous Peere,
That smooth'st it so with King and Common-weale.

GLOSTER

What, Cardinall? Is your Priest-hood growne
peremptorie?

Tantæne animis Cœlestibus iræ,
Church-men so hot? Good Vnckle hide such mallice
With some Holynesse: can you doe it?

SUFFOLKE
No mallice Sir, no more then well becomes
690   So good a Quarrell, and so bad a Peere.

GLOSTER
As who, my Lord?

SUFFOLKE   Why, as you, my Lord,
An't like your Lordly Lords Protectorship.

GLOSTER
Why *Suffolke*, England knowes thine insolence.

QUEENE
And thy Ambition, *Gloster*.

KING   I prythee peace,
Good Queene, and whet not on these furious Peeres,
For blessed are the Peace-makers on Earth.

CARDINALL
Let me be blessed for the Peace I make
Against this prowd Protector with my Sword.
      ⌐Gloster and the Cardinall speake priuately to one
      another⌐

GLOSTER
Faith holy Vnckle, would't were come to that.

CARDINALL
Marry, when thou dar'st.

700 GLOSTER   Dare. I tell thee Priest,
Plantagenets could neuer brooke the dare.

CARDINALL
I am Plantagenet as well as thou,
And sonne to Iohn of Gaunt.

GLOSTER In Bastardie.

CARDINALL I scorne thy words.

GLOSTER
Make vp no factious numbers for the matter,
In thine owne person answere thy abuse.

CARDINALL
I, where thou dar'st not peepe: and if thou dar'st,
This Euening, on the East side of the Groue.

KING
How now, my Lords?

710 CARDINALL (*alowd*)   Beleeue me, Cousin *Gloster*,
Had not your man put vp the Fowle so suddenly,
We had had more sport. (*Aside to Gloster*) Come with
      thy two-hand Sword.

GLOSTER (*alowd*) True Vnckle,
(*Aside to the Cardinall*)
Are ye aduis'd? The East side of the Groue.

CARDINALL (*aside to Gloster*)
I am with you.

KING   Why how now, Vnckle *Gloster*?

GLOSTER
Talking of Hawking; nothing else, my Lord.
(*Aside to the Cardinall*) Now by Gods Mother, Priest,
      Ile shaue your Crowne for this,
Or all my Fence shall fayle.

CARDINALL (*aside to Gloster*)   *Medice teipsum*,
Protector see to't well, protect your selfe.

KING
The Windes grow high, so doe your Stomacks, Lords: 720
How irkesome is this Musick to my heart?
When such Strings iarre, what hope of Harmony?
I pray my Lords let me compound this strife.
      Enter one crying a Miracle

GLOSTER What meanes this noyse?
Fellow, what Miracle do'st thou proclayme?

ONE
A Miracle, a Miracle.

SUFFOLKE
Come to the King, tell him what Miracle.

ONE (*to the King*)
Forsooth, a blinde man at Saint *Albones* Shrine,
Within this halfe houre hath receiu'd his sight,
A man that ne're saw in his life before.   730

KING
Now God be prays'd, that to beleeuing Soules
Giues Light in Darknesse, Comfort in Despaire.
      *Enter the Maior of Saint Albones and his brethren
      with Musicke, bearing the man Simpcoxe that had
      bene blind, betweene two in a chaire. Enter
      Simpcoxes Wife ⌐and other Townes-men⌐ with them*

CARDINALL
Here comes the Townes-men, on Procession,
To present your Highnesse with the man.
      ⌐The Townes-men kneele⌐

KING
Great is his comfort in this Earthly Vale,
Although by sight his sinne be multiplyed.

GLOSTER (*to the Townes-men*)
Stand by, my Masters, bring him neere the King,
His Highnesse pleasure is to talke with him.
      They ⌐rise and⌐ beare Simpcoxe before the King

KING (*to Simpcoxe*)
Good-fellow, tell vs here the circumstance,
That we for thee may glorifie the Lord.   740
What, hast thou beene long blinde, and now restor'd?

SIMPCOXE
Borne blinde, and't please your Grace.

WIFE   I indeede was he.

SUFFOLKE What Woman is this?

WIFE His Wife, and't like your Worship.

GLOSTER Hadst thou been his Mother,
Thou could'st haue better told.

KING (*to Simpcoxe*)   Where wert thou borne?

SIMPCOXE
At Barwick in the North, and't like your Grace.

KING
Poore Soule, Gods goodnesse hath beene great to thee:
Let neuer Day nor Night vnhallowed passe,
But still remember what the Lord hath done.   750

QUEENE (*to Simpcoxe*)
Tell me, good-fellow, cam'st thou here by Chance,
Or of Deuotion, to this holy Shrine?

SIMPCOXE
God knowes of pure Deuotion, being call'd
A hundred times, and oftner, in my sleepe,

By good Saint *Albon*: who said; *Symon*, come;
Come offer at my Shrine, and I will helpe thee.

WIFE
Most true, forsooth: and many time and oft
My selfe haue heard a Voyce, to call him so.

CARDINALL (*to Simpcoxe*)
What, art thou lame?

SIMPCOXE   I, God Almightie helpe me.

SUFFOLKE
How cam'st thou so?

760 SIMPCOXE   A fall off of a Tree.

WIFE (*to Suffolke*)
A Plum-tree, Master.

GLOSTER   How long hast thou beene blinde?

SIMPCOXE
O borne so, Master.

GLOSTER   What, and would'st climbe a Tree?

SIMPCOXE
But that in all my life, when I was a youth.

WIFE (*to Gloster*)
Too true, and bought his climbing very deare.

GLOSTER (*to Simpcoxe*)
'Masse, thou lou'dst Plummes well, that would'st
      venture so.

SIMPCOXE
Alas, good Master, my Wife desir'd some Damsons,
And made me climbe, with danger of my Life.

GLOSTER ⌈aside⌉
A subtill Knaue, but yet it shall not serue:
(*To Simpcoxe*) Let me see thine Eyes; winck now, now
      open them,
770 In my opinion, yet thou seest not well.

SIMPCOXE Yes Master, cleare as day, I thanke God and
Saint *Albone*.

GLOSTER
Say'st thou me so: (*pointing*) what Colour is this
      Cloake of?

SIMPCOXE
Red Master, Red as Blood.

GLOSTER   Why that's well said:
(*Pointing*) And his cloake?

SIMPCOXE   Why thats greene.

GLOSTER (*pointing*)   And what colours
His hose?

SIMPCOXE   Yellow maister, yellow as gold.

GLOSTER
And what colours my gowne?

SIMPCOXE   Blacke sir, Coale-Black, as Iet.

KING
Why then, thou know'st what Colour Iet is of?

SUFFOLKE
And yet I thinke Ieat did he neuer see.

GLOSTER
780 But cloakes and gownes before this day a many.

WIFE
Neuer before this day, in all his life.

GLOSTER Tell me sirrha, whats my name?

SIMPCOXE Alasse maister I know not.

GLOSTER (*pointing*) Whats his name?

SIMPCOXE I know not.

GLOSTER (*pointing*) Nor his?

SIMPCOXE No truly sir.

GLOSTER (*pointing*) Nor his name?

SIMPCOXE No indeed maister.

GLOSTER Whats thine owne name?   790

SIMPCOXE *Symon Simpcoxe*, and it please you maister.

GLOSTER
Then Symon, sit thou there, the lying'st knaue
In Christendom. If thou hadst bene born blind,
Thou might'st aswell haue knowne our names, as
      thus
To name the seuerall colours we doo weare.
Sight may distinguish colours, but sodeinly
To nominate them all, it is impossible.
Saint Albone here hath done a Miracle,
Would you not thinke his cunning to be great,
That could restore this Cripple to his legs againe.   800

SIMPCOXE Oh maister that you could.

GLOSTER (*to the Maior and his Brethren*)
My Maisters of saint Albones, haue you not
Beadles in your Towne, and things call'd whippes?

MAIOR
We haue my Lord, and if it please your grace.

GLOSTER Then send for one presently.

MAIOR (*to a Townes-man*)
Sirrha, go fetch the Beadle hither straight.   *Exit one*

GLOSTER
Bring me a stoole.
      A stoole is brought
(*To Simpcoxe*)   Now sirrha, If you meane
To saue your selfe from whipping, leape me ore
This stoole and runne away.

SIMPCOXE   Alasse maister
I am not able euen to stand alone,   810
You go about to torture me in vaine.
      Enter a Beadle with Whippes

GLOSTER
Well sirrha, we must haue you finde your legges.
(*To the Beadle*) Whip him till he leape ouer that same
      stoole.

BEADLE I will my Lord,
(*To Simpcoxe*) Come on sirrha, off with your doublet
      quickly.

SIMPCOXE Alas maister what shall I do, I am not able to
stand.
      *After the Beadle hath hit him one girke, he leapes
      ouer the stoole and runnes away, and ⌈some of⌉ the
      Townes-men run after him, crying, A miracle, a
      miracle*

KING
O God, seest thou this, and bear'st so long?

QUEENE
It made me laugh, to see the Villaine runne.

GLOSTER ⌈to the Beadle⌉
Follow the Knaue, and take this Drab away.   820

WIFE
Alas Sir, we did it for pure need.
      ⌈*Exit the Beadle with the Wife*⌉

GLOSTER ⌈to the Maior⌉
  Let thē be whipt through euery Market Towne,
  Till they come to Barwick, from whence they came.
                    Exit Mayor ⌈and remaining Townes-men⌉

CARDINALL
  Duke *Humfrey* ha's done a Miracle to day.

SUFFOLKE
  True: made the Lame to leape and flye away.

GLOSTER
  But you haue done more Miracles then I:
  You made in a day, my Lord, whole Townes to flye.
                    Enter Buckingham

KING
  What Tidings with our Cousin *Buckingham*?

BUCKINGHAM
  Such as my heart doth tremble to vnfold:
830 A sort of naughtie persons, lewdly bent,
  Vnder the Countenance and Confederacie
  Of Lady *Elianor*, the Protectors Wife,
  The Ring-leader and Head of all this Rout,
  Haue practis'd dangerously against your State,
  Dealing with Witches and with Coniurers,
  Whom we haue apprehended in the Fact,
  Raysing vp wicked Spirits from vnder ground,
  Demanding of King *Henries* Life and Death,
  And other of your Highnesse Priuie Councell.
840 And heres the answere the diuel did make to them.
                    Buckingham giues the Writings to the King

⌈KING⌉ (*reades*)
  First of the King: What shall of him become?
  The Duke yet liues, that Henry *shall depose:*
  But him out-liue, and dye a violent death.
  Gods will be done in all. Well, to the rest:
  (*Reades*) Tell me what fate awaits the Duke of
        Suffolke?
  By Water shall he dye, and take his end.

SUFFOLKE ⌈aside⌉
  By water must the Duke of Suffolke die?
  It must be so, or else the diuel doth lie.

⌈KING⌉ (*reades*)
  What shall betide the Duke of Somerset?
850 *Let him shunne Castles, safer shall he be*
  Vpon the sandie Plaines, then where Castles mounted
        stand.

CARDINALL (*to Gloster*)
  And so my Lord Protector, by this meanes
  Your Lady is forth-comming, yet at London.
  (*Aside to Gloster*) This Newes I thinke hath turn'd
        your Weapons edge;
  'Tis like, my Lord, you will not keepe your houre.

GLOSTER
  Ambitious Church-man, leaue to afflict my heart:
  Sorrow and griefe haue vanquisht all my powers;
  And vanquisht as I am, I yeeld to thee,
  Or to the meanest Groome.

KING
860 O God, what mischiefes work the wicked ones?
  Heaping confusion on their owne heads thereby.

QUEENE
  Gloster, see here the Tainctture of thy Nest,
  And looke thy selfe be faultlesse, thou wert best.

GLOSTER
  Madame, for my selfe, to Heauen I doe appeale,
  How I haue lou'd my King, and Common-weale:
  And for my Wife, I know not how it stands,
  Sorry I am to heare what I haue heard.
  Noble shee is: but if shee haue forgot
  Honor and Vertue, and conuers't with such,
  As like to Pytch, defile Nobilitie;   870
  I banish her my Bed, and Companie,
  And giue her as a Prey to Law and Shame,
  That hath dis-honor'd *Glosters* honest Name.

KING
  Well, for this Night we will repose vs here:
  To morrow toward London, back againe,
  To looke into this Businesse thorowly,
  And call these foule Offendors to their Answeres;
  And poyse the Cause in Iustice equall Scales,
  Whose Beame stands sure, whose rightful cause
        preuailes.   *Flourish. Exeunt*

                    Enter Yorke, Salisbury, and Warwick   Sc. 6
YORKE   (2.2)
  Now my good Lords of Salisbury & Warwick,   880
  Our simple Supper ended, giue me leaue,
  In this close Walke, to satisfie my selfe,
  In crauing your opinion of my Title,
  Which is infallible, to Englands Crowne.

SALISBURY
  My Lord, I long to heare it out at full.

WARWICKE
  Sweet *Yorke* begin: and if thy clayme be good,
  The *Neuills* are thy Subiects to command.

YORKE Then thus:
  Edward the third, my Lords, had seuen Sonnes:
  The first, *Edward* the Black-Prince, Prince of Wales;   890
  The second, *William* of Hatfield; and the third,
  Lionel, Duke of Clarence; next to whom,
  Was *Iohn* of Gaunt, the Duke of Lancaster;
  The fift, was *Edmond Langley*, Duke of Yorke;
  The sixt, was *Thomas* of Woodstock, Duke of Gloster;
  William of Windsor was the seuenth, and last.
  Edward the Black-Prince dyed before his Father,
  And left behinde him *Richard*, his onely Sonne,
  Who after *Edward* the third's death, raign'd as King,
  Till *Henry Bullingbrooke*, Duke of Lancaster,   900
  The eldest Sonne and Heire of *Iohn* of Gaunt,
  Crown'd by the Name of *Henry* the fourth,
  Seiz'd on the Realme, depos'd the rightfull King,
  Sent his poore Queene to France, from whence she
        came,
  And him to Pumfret; where, as well you know,
  Harmelesse *Richard* was murthred traiterously.

WARWICKE (*to Salisbury*)
  Father, the Duke of Yorke hath told the truth;
  Thus got the House of *Lancaster* the Crowne.

YORKE

Which now they hold by force, and not by right:

910 For *Richard*, the first Sonnes Heire, being dead,

The Issue of the next Sonne should haue reign'd.

SALISBURY

But *William* of Hatfield dyed without an Heire.

YORKE

The third Sonne, Duke of Clarence, from whose Line

I clayme the Crowne, had Issue *Phillip*, a Daughter,

Who married *Edmond Mortimer*, Earle of March:

Edmond had Issue, *Roger*, Earle of March;

Roger had Issue, *Edmond*, *Anne*, and *Elianor*.

SALISBURY

This *Edmond*, in the Reigne of *Bullingbrooke*,

As I haue read, layd clayme vnto the Crowne,

920 And but for *Owen Glendour*, had beene King;

Who kept him in Captiuitie, till he dyed.

But, to the rest.

YORKE   His eldest Sister, *Anne*,

My Mother, being Heire vnto the Crowne,

Married *Richard*, Earle of Cambridge, who was Sonne

To *Edmond Langley*, *Edward* the thirds fift Sonne;

By her I clayme the Kingdome: she was Heire

To *Roger*, Earle of March, who was the Sonne

Of *Edmond Mortimer*, who marryed *Phillip*,

Sole Daughter vnto *Lionel*, Duke of Clarence.

930 So, if the Issue of the elder Sonne

Succeed before the younger, I am King.

WARWICKE

What plaine proceedings is more plain then this?

Henry doth clayme the Crowne from *Iohn* of Gaunt,

The fourth Sonne, *Yorke* claymes it from the third:

Till *Lionels* Issue fayles, *Iohns* should not reigne.

It fayles not yet, but flourishes in thee,

And in thy Sonnes, faire slippes of such a Stock.

Then Father *Salisbury*, kneele we together,

And in this priuate Plot be we the first,

940 That shall salute our rightfull Soueraigne

With honor of his Birth-right to the Crowne.

SALISBURY *and* WARWICKE (*kneeling*)

Long liue our Soueraigne *Richard*, Englands King.

YORKE

We thanke you Lords:

⌈*Salisbury and Warwicke rise*⌉

but I am not your King,

Till I be Crown'd, and that my Sword be stayn'd

With heart-blood of the House of *Lancaster*:

And that's not suddenly to be perform'd,

But with aduice and silent secrecie.

Doe you as I doe in these dangerous dayes,

Winke at the Duke of Suffolkes insolence,

950 At *Beaufords* Pride, at *Somersets* Ambition,

At *Buckingham*, and all the Crew of them,

Till they haue snar'd the Shepheard of the Flock,

That vertuous Prince, the good Duke *Humfrey*:

'Tis that they seeke; and they, in seeking that,

Shall finde their deaths, if *Yorke* can prophecie.

SALISBURY

My Lord, breake off; we know your minde at full.

WARWICKE

My heart assures me, that the Earle of Warwick

Shall one day make the Duke of Yorke a King.

YORKE

And *Neuill*, this I doe assure my selfe,

Richard shall liue to make the Earle of Warwick   960

The greatest man in England, but the King.   *Exeunt*

Sound Trumpets. Enter the King and State, with   Sc. 7

Guard, to banish the Duchesse: King Henry, and   (2.3)

the Queene, Duke Humphrey of Gloster, the Duke of

Suffolke ⌈*and the Duke of Buckingham, the*

Cardinall,⌉ *and, led with the Officers, Dame Elnor*

Cobham, the Witch, the two Priests Southwell and

Hume, and the Coniurer Roger Bullingbrooke. Then

enter to them the Duke of Yorke, and the Earls of

Salsbury ⌈*and Warwicke*⌉

KING (*to Elianor*)

Stand forth Dame *Elianor Cobham*, *Glosters* Wife:

She comes forward

In sight of God, and vs, your guilt is great,

Receiue the Sentence of the Law for sinnes,

Such as by Gods Booke are adiudg'd to death.

(*To the Witch, Southwell, Hume, and Bullingbrooke*)

You foure from hence to Prison, back againe;

From thence, vnto the place of Execution:

The Witch in Smithfield shall be burnt to ashes,

And you three shall be strangled on the Gallowes.

⌈*Exit Witch, Southwell, Hume, and*

Bullingbrooke, guarded⌉

(*To Elianor*) You Madame, for you are more Nobly

borne,

Despoyled of your Honor in your Life,   970

Shall, after three dayes open Penance done,

Liue in your Countrey here, in Banishment,

With Sir *Iohn Stanly*, in the Ile of Man.

ELIANOR

Welcome is Banishment, welcome were my Death.

GLOSTER

Elianor, the Law thou seest hath iudged thee,

I cannot iustifie whom the Law condemnes:

⌈*Exit Elianor, guarded*⌉

Mine eyes are full of teares, my heart of griefe.

Ah *Humfrey*, this dishonor in thine age,

Will bring thy head with sorrow to the graue.   980

(*To the King*) I beseech your Maiestie giue me leaue to

goe;

Sorrow would sollace, and mine Age would ease.

KING

Stay *Humfrey*, Duke of Gloster, ere thou goe,

Giue vp thy Staffe, *Henry* will to himselfe

Protector be, and God shall be my hope,

My stay, my guide, and Lanthorne to my feete:

And goe in peace, *Humfrey*, no lesse belou'd,

Then when thou wert Protector to thy King.

QUEENE

990 I see no reason, why a King of yeeres
Should be to be protected like a Child,
God and King *Henry* gouerne Englands Healme:
Giue vp your Staffe, Sir, and the King his Realme.

GLOSTER

My Staffe? Here, Noble *Henry*, is my Staffe:
As willingly doe I the same resigne,
As erst thy Father *Henry* made it mine;
And euen as willing at thy feete I leaue it,
As others would ambitiously receiue it.
   He lays the Staffe at Henrys feete
Farewell good King: when I am dead, and gone,
May honorable Peace attend thy Throne.   *Exit Gloster*

QUEENE

1000 Why now is *Henry* King, and *Margaret* Queen,
And *Humfrey*, Duke of Gloster, scarce himselfe,
That beares so shrewd a mayme: two Pulls at once;
His Lady banisht, and a Limbe lopt off.
   She picks vp the Staffe
This Staffe of Honor raught, there let it stand,
Where it best fits to be, in *Henries* hand.
   She giues the Staffe to Henry

SUFFOLKE

Thus droupes this loftie Pyne, & hangs his sprayes,
Thus *Elianors* Pride dyes in her youngest dayes.

YORKE

Lords, let him goe. Please it your Maiestie,
This is the day appointed for the Combat,
1010 And ready are the Appellant and Defendant,
The Armorer and his Man, to enter the Lists,
So please your Highnesse to behold the fight.

QUEENE

I, good my Lord: for purposely therefore
Left I the Court, to see this Quarrell try'de.

KING

A Gods Name see the Lysts and all things fit,
Here let them end it, and God defend the right.

YORKE

I neuer saw a fellow worse bestead,
Or more afraid to fight, then is the Appellant,
The seruant of this Armorer, my Lords.
   *Enter at one doore the Armourer and his
   neighbours, drinking to him so much that he is
   drunken, and he enters with a drum before him, and
   his staffe with a sand-bag fastened to it, and at the
   other doore, Peter his man with a drum and sand-
   bagge, and Prentises drinking to him*

1020 1. NEIGHBOR (*offering drinke to the Armorer*) Here neighbor
Hornor, I drink to you in a cup of Sacke. And feare
not neighbor, you shall do well inough.

2. NEIGHBOR (*offering drinke to the Armorer*) And here
neighbor, heres a cup of Charneco.

3. NEIGHBOR (*offering drinke to the Armorer*) Heres a pot of
good double beere, neighbor drinke and be merry, and
feare not your man.

ARMORER ⌈*accepting the offers of drinke*⌉ Let it come, yfaith
ile pledge you all, and a figge for Peter.

1. PRENTICE (*offering drinke to Peter*) Here Peter I drinke   1030
to thee, and be not affeard.

2. PRENTICE (*offering drinke to Peter*) Here Peter, heres a
pinte of Claret-wine for thee.

3. PRENTICE (*offering drinke to Peter*) And heres a quart for
me, and be merry Peter, and feare not thy maister,
fight for credit of the Prentises.

PETER ⌈*refusing the offers of drinke*⌉ I thanke you all: drinke,
and pray for me, I pray you, for I thinke I haue taken
my last Draught in this World. Here *Robin*, and if I
dye, I giue thee my Aporne; and *Will*, thou shalt haue   1040
my Hammer: and here *Tom*, take all the Money that I
haue. O Lord blesse me, I pray God, for I am neuer
able to deale with my Master, hee hath learnt so much
fence already.

SALISBURY Come leaue your drinking, and fall to blowes.
(*To Peter*) Sirrha, whats thy name?

PETER Peter forsooth.

SALISBURY Peter, what more?

PETER *Thumpe*.

SALISBURY Thumpe, then see that thou thumpe thy   1050
maister well.

ARMORER Masters, I am come hither as it were vpon my
Mans instigation, to proue him a Knaue, and my selfe
an honest man: and touching the Duke of Yorke, I will
take my death, I neuer meant him any ill, nor the
King, nor the Queene: and therefore *Peter* haue at thee
with a downe-right blow.

YORKE

Dispatch, this Knaues tongue begins to double.
   *Sound Trumpets, Alarum to the Combattants. They
   fight, and Peter hits the Armorer on the head and
   strikes him downe*

ARMORER Hold *Peter*, hold, I confesse, I confesse Treason.
   He dies

YORKE (*to an Attendant, pointing at the Armorer*) Take away   1060
his Weapon: (*To Peter*) Fellow thanke God, and the
good Wine in thy Masters waӳ.

PETER ⌈*kneeling*⌉ O God, haue I ouercome mine Enemie in
this presence? O *Peter*, thou hast preuayl'd in right.

KING (*to Attendants, pointing at the Armorer*)
Go take hence that Traitor from our sight,
For by his death we do perceiue his guilt,
And God in iustice hath reuealed to vs,
The truth and innocence of this poore fellow,
Which he had thought to haue murther'd wrongfully.
(*To Peter*) Come fellow, follow vs for thy reward.   1070
   *Sound a flourish. Exeunt, some carrying
   Horners Body*

Enter Duke Humfrey of Gloster and his men, in   Sc. 8
mourning cloakes   (2.4)

GLOSTER

Thus sometimes hath the brightest day a Cloud:
And after Summer, euermore succeedes
Barren Winter, with his wrathfull nipping Cold;
So Cares and Ioyes abound, as Seasons fleet.
Sirs, what's a Clock?

SERUANT Tenne, my Lord.

GLOSTER

Tenne is the houre that was appointed me,
To watch the comming of my punisht Duchesse:
Vnneath may shee endure the Flintie Streets,
1080　To treade them with her tender-feeling feet.
Sweet *Nell*, ill can thy Noble Minde abrooke
The abiect People, gazing on thy face,
With enuious Lookes laughing at thy shame,
That erst did follow thy prowd Chariot-Wheeles,
When thou didst ride in triumph through the streets.
But soft, I thinke she comes, and Ile prepare
My teare-stayn'd eyes, to see her Miseries.

　　　Enter Dame Elnor Cobham bare-foote, and a white
　　　sheete about her, with a waxe candle in her hand,
　　　and verses written on her backe and pind on, and
　　　accompanied with the ⌈*2. Sheriffes*⌉ *of London, and*
　　　Sir Iohn Standly, and Officers, with billes and
　　　holbards

SERUANT (*to Gloster*)

So please your Grace, wee'le take her from the Sherifes.

GLOSTER

No, stirre not for your liues, let her passe by.

ELIANOR

1090　Come you, my Lord, to see my open shame?
Now thou do'st Penance too. Looke how they gaze,
See how the giddy multitude doe point,
And nodde their heads, and throw their eyes on thee.
Ah *Gloster*, hide thee from their hatefull lookes,
And in thy Closet pent vp, rue my shame,
And banne thine Enemies, both mine and thine.

GLOSTER

Be patient, gentle *Nell*, forget this griefe.

ELIANOR

Ah *Gloster*, teach me to forget my selfe:
For whilest I thinke I am thy married Wife,
1100　And thou a Prince, Protector of this Land;
Me thinkes I should not thus be led along,
Mayl'd vp in shame, with Papers on my back,
And follow'd with a Rabble, that reioyce
To see my teares, and heare my deepe-fet groanes.
The ruthlesse Flint doth cut my tender feet,
And when I start, the enuious people laugh,
And bid me be aduised how I treade.
Ah *Humfrey*, can I beare this shamefull yoake?
Trowest thou, that ere Ile looke vpon the World,
1110　Or count them happy, that enioyes the Sunne?
No: Darke shall be my Light, and Night my Day.
To thinke vpon my Pompe, shall be my Hell.
Sometime Ile say, I am Duke *Humfreyes* Wife,
And he a Prince, and Ruler of the Land:
Yet so he rul'd, and such a Prince he was,
As he stood by, whilst I, his forlorne Duchesse,
Was made a wonder, and a pointing stock
To euery idle Rascall follower.
But be thou milde, and blush not at my shame,
1120　Nor stirre at nothing, till the Axe of Death
Hang ouer thee, as sure it shortly will.

For *Suffolke*, he that can doe all in all
With her, that hateth thee and hates vs all,
And *Yorke*, and impious *Beauford*, that false Priest,
Haue all lym'd Bushes to betray thy Wings,
And flye thou how thou canst, they'le tangle thee.
But feare not thou, vntill thy foot be snar'd,
Nor neuer seeke preuention of thy foes.

GLOSTER

Ah *Nell*, forbeare: thou aymest all awry.
I must offend, before I be attainted:　　1130
And had I twentie times so many foes,
And each of them had twentie times their power,
All these could not procure me any scathe,
So long as I am loyall, true, and crimelesse.
Would'st haue me rescue thee from this reproach?
Why yet thy scandall were not wipt away,
But I in danger for the breach of Law.
Thy greatest helpe is quiet, gentle *Nell*:
I pray thee sort thy heart to patience,
These few dayes wonder will be quickly worne.　　1140

　　　Enter a Herald

HERALD I summon your Grace to his Maiesties Parliament,
holden at Bury, the first of this next Moneth.

GLOSTER

And my consent ne're ask'd herein before?
This is close dealing. Well, I will be there.　*Exit Herald*
My *Nell*, I take my leaue: and Master Sherife,
Let not her Penance exceed the Kings Commission.

⌈1.⌉ SHERIFE

And't please your Grace, here my Commission stayes:
And Sir *Iohn Stanly* is appointed now,
To take her with him to the Ile of Man.

GLOSTER

Must you, Sir *Iohn*, protect my Lady here?　　1150

STANLEY

So am I giuen in charge, may't please your Grace.

GLOSTER

Entreat her not the worse, in that I pray
You vse her well: the World may laugh againe,
And I may liue to doe you kindnesse, if
You doe it her. And so Sir *Iohn*, farewell.

　　　⌈*Gloster begins to leaue*⌉

ELIANOR

What, gone my Lord, and bid me not farewell?

GLOSTER

Witnesse my teares, I cannot stay to speake.

　　　　　　　　Exit Gloster and his men

ELIANOR

Art thou gone to? all comfort goe with thee,
For none abides with me: my Ioy, is Death;
Death, at whose Name I oft haue beene afear'd,　　1160
Because I wish'd this Worlds eternitie.
Stanley, I prethee goe, and take me hence,
I care not whither, for I begge no fauor;
Onely conuey me where thou art commanded.

STANLEY

Why, Madame, that is to the Ile of Man,
There to be vs'd according to your State.

ELIANOR

    That's bad enough, for I am but reproach:
    And shall I then be vs'd reproachfully?

STANLEY

    Like to a Duchesse, and Duke *Humfreyes* Lady,
1170   According to that State you shall be vs'd.

ELIANOR

    Sherife farewell, and better then I fare,
    Although thou hast beene Conduct of my shame.

⌈1.⌉ SHERIFE

    It is my Office, and Madame pardon me.

ELIANOR

    I, I, farewell, thy Office is discharg'd: ⌈*Exit Sherifes*⌉
    Come *Stanley*, shall we goe?

STANLEY

    Madame, your Penance done, throw off this Sheet,
    And goe we to attyre you for our Iourney.

ELIANOR

    My shame will not be shifted with my Sheet:
    No, it will hang vpon my richest Robes,
1180   And shew it selfe, attyre me how I can.
    Goe, leade the way, I long to see my Prison.   *Exeunt*

Sc. 9   *Sound a Senet. Enter to the Parlament. Enter two*
(3.1)   *Heralds before, then the Duke of Buckingham, and*
         the Duke of Suffolke, and then the Duke of Yorke,
         and the Cardinall of Winchester, and then the King
         and the Queene, and then the Earle of Salisbury,
         and the Earle of Warwicke ⌈*with Attendants*⌉

KING

    I muse my Lord of Gloster is not come:
    'Tis not his wont to be the hindmost man,
    What e're occasion keepes him from vs now.

QUEENE

    Can you not see? or will ye not obserue
    The strangenesse of his alter'd Countenance?
    With what a Maiestie he beares himselfe,
    How insolent of late he is become,
    How prowd, how peremptorie, and vnlike himselfe.
1190   We know the time since he was milde and affable,
    And if we did but glance a farre-off Looke,
    Immediately he was vpon his Knee,
    That all the Court admir'd him for submission.
    But meet him now, and be it in the Morne,
    When euery one will giue the time of day,
    He knits his Brow, and shewes an angry Eye,
    And passeth by with stiffe vnbowed Knee,
    Disdaining dutie that to vs belongs.
    Small Curres are not regarded when they grynne,
1200   But great men tremble when the Lyon rores,
    And *Humfrey* is no little Man in England.
    First note, that he is neere you in discent,
    And should you fall, he is the next will mount.
    Me seemeth then, it is no Pollicie,
    Respecting what a rancorous minde he beares,
    And his aduantage following your decease,
    That he should come about your Royall Person,
    Or be admitted to your Highnesse Councell.

    By flatterie hath he wonne the Commons hearts:
    And when he please to make Commotion,   1210
    'Tis to be fear'd they all will follow him.
    Now 'tis the Spring, and Weeds are shallow-rooted,
    Suffer them now, and they'le o're-grow the Garden,
    And choake the Herbes for want of Husbandry.
    The reuerent care I beare vnto my Lord,
    Made me collect these dangers in the Duke.
    If it be fond, call it a Womans feare:
    Which feare, if better Reasons can supplant,
    I will subscribe, and say I wrong'd the Duke.
    My Lord of Suffolke, Buckingham, and Yorke,   1220
    Reproue my allegation, if you can,
    Or else conclude my words effectuall.

SUFFOLKE

    Well hath your Highnesse seene into this Duke:
    And had I first beene put to speake my minde,
    I thinke I should haue told your Graces Tale.
    The Duchesse, by his subornation,
    Vpon my Life, began her diuellish practises:
    Or if he were not priuie to those Faults,
    Yet by reputing of his high discent,
    As next the King, he was successiue Heire,   1230
    And such high vaunts of his Nobilitie,
    Did instigate the Bedlam braine-sick Duchesse,
    By wicked meanes to frame our Soueraignes fall.
    Smooth runnes the Water, where the Brooke is deepe,
    And in his simple shew he harbours Treason.
    The Fox barkes not, when he would steale the Lambe.
    (*To the King*) No, no, my Soueraigne, *Glouster* is a man
    Vnsounded yet, and full of deepe deceit.

CARDINALL (*to the King*)

    Did he not, contrary to forme of Law,
    Deuise strange deaths, for small offences done?   1240

YORKE (*to the King*)

    And did he not, in his Protectorship,
    Leuie great summes of Money through the Realme,
    For Souldiers pay in France, and neuer sent it?
    By meanes whereof, the Townes each day reuolted.

BUCKINGHAM (*to the King*)

    Tut, these are petty faults to faults vnknowne,
    Which time will bring to light in smooth Duke
        Humfrey.

KING

    My Lords at once: the care you haue of vs,
    To mowe downe Thornes that would annoy our Foot,
    Is worthy prayse: but shall I speake my conscience,
    Our Kinsman *Gloster* is as innocent,   1250
    From meaning Treason to our Royall Person,
    As is the sucking Lambe, or harmelesse Doue:
    The Duke is vertuous, milde, and too well giuen,
    To dreame on euill, or to worke my downefall.

QUEENE

    Ah what's more dangerous, then this fond affiance?
    Seemes he a Doue? his feathers are but borrow'd,
    For hee's disposed as the hatefull Rauen.
    Is he a Lambe? his Skinne is surely lent him,
    For hee's enclin'd as is the rauenous Wolfe.

1260   Who cannot steale a shape, that meanes deceit?
      Take heed, my Lord, the welfare of vs all,
      Hangs on the cutting short that fraudfull man.
           Enter Somerset

SOMERSET ⌜*kneeling before the King*⌝
      All health vnto my gracious Soueraigne.

KING
      Welcome Lord *Somerset*: What Newes from France?

SOMERSET
      That all your Interest in those Territories,
      Is vtterly bereft you: all is lost.

KING
      Cold Newes, Lord *Somerset*: but Gods will be done.
          ⌜*Somerset rises*⌝

YORKE (*aside*)
      Cold Newes for me: for I had hope of France,
      As firmely as I hope for fertile England.
1270   Thus are my Blossomes blasted in the Bud,
      And Caterpillers eate my Leaues away:
      But I will remedie this geare ere long,
      Or sell my Title for a glorious Graue.
          Enter Gloucester

GLOSTER ⌜*kneeling before the King*⌝
      All happinesse vnto my Lord the King:
      Pardon, my Liege, that I haue stay'd so long.

SUFFOLKE
      Nay *Gloster*, know that thou art come too soone,
      Vnlesse thou wert more loyall then thou art:
      I doe arrest thee of High Treason here.

GLOSTER ⌜*rising*⌝
      Well *Suffolkes* Duke, thou shalt not see me blush,
1280   Nor change my Countenance for this Arrest:
      A Heart vnspotted, is not easily daunted.
      The purest Spring is not so free from mudde,
      As I am cleare from Treason to my Soueraigne.
      Who can accuse me? wherein am I guiltie?

YORKE
      'Tis thought, my Lord, that you tooke Bribes of France,
      And being Protector, stay'd the Souldiers pay,
      By meanes whereof, his Highnesse hath lost France.

GLOSTER
      Is it but thought so? What are they that thinke it?
      I neuer rob'd the Souldiers of their pay,
1290   Nor euer had one penny Bribe from France.
      So helpe me God, as I haue watcht the Night,
      I, Night by Night, in studying good for England,
      That Doyt that ere I wrested from the King,
      Or any Groat I hoorded to my vse,
      Be brought against me at my Tryall day.
      No: many a Pound of mine owne proper store,
      Because I would not taxe the needie Commons,
      Haue I dis-pursed to the Garrisons,
      And neuer ask'd for restitution.

CARDINALL
1300   It serues you well, my Lord, to say so much.

GLOSTER
      I say no more then truth, so helpe me God.

YORKE
      In your Protectorship, you did deuise
      Strange Tortures for Offendors, neuer heard of,
      That England was defam'd by Tyrannie.

GLOSTER
      Why 'tis well known, that whiles I was Protector,
      Pittie was all the fault that was in me:
      For I should melt at an Offendors teares,
      And lowly words were Ransome for their fault:
      Vnlesse it were a bloody Murtherer,
      Or foule felonious Theefe, that fleec'd poore passengers,   1310
      I neuer gaue them condigne punishment.
      Murther indeede, that bloodie sinne, I tortur'd
      Aboue the Felon, or what Trespas else.

SUFFOLKE
      My Lord, these faults are easie, quickly answer'd:
      But mightier Crimes are lay'd vnto your charge,
      Whereof you cannot easily purge your selfe.
      I doe arrest you in his Highnesse Name,
      And here commit you to my good Lord Cardinall
      To keepe, vntill your further time of Tryall.

KING
      My Lord of Gloster, 'tis my speciall hope,   1320
      That you will cleare your selfe from all suspence,
      My Conscience tells me you are innocent.

GLOSTER
      Ah gracious Lord, these dayes are dangerous:
      Vertue is choakt with foule Ambition,
      And Charitie chas'd hence by Rancours hand;
      Foule Subornation is predominant,
      And Equitie exil'd your Highnesse Land.
      I know, their Complot is to haue my Life:
      And if my death might make this Iland happy,
      And proue the Period of their Tyrannie,   1330
      I would expend it with all willingnesse.
      But mine is made the Prologue to their Play:
      For thousands more, that yet suspect no perill,
      Will not conclude their plotted Tragedie.
      Beaufords red sparkling eyes blab his hearts mallice,
      And *Suffolks* cloudie Brow his stormie hate;
      Sharpe *Buckingham* vnburthens with his tongue,
      The enuious Load that lyes vpon his heart:
      And dogged *Yorke*, that reaches at the Moone,
      Whose ouer-weening Arme I haue pluckt back,   1340
      By false accuse doth leuell at my Life.
      (*To the Queene*) And you, my Soueraigne Lady, with
        the rest,
      Causelesse haue lay'd disgraces on my head,
      And with your best endeuour haue stirr'd vp
      My liefest Liege to be mine Enemie:
      I, all of you haue lay'd your heads together,
      My selfe had notice of your Conuenticles,
      And all to make away my guiltlesse Life.
      I shall not want false Witnesse, to condemne me,
      Nor store of Treasons, to augment my guilt: 1350
      The ancient Prouerbe will be well effected,
      A Staffe is quickly found to beat a Dogge.

CARDINALL (*to the King*)

  My Liege, his rayling is intollerable.

  If those that care to keepe your Royall Person

  From Treasons secret Knife, and Traytors Rage,

  Be thus vpbrayded, chid, and rated at,

  And the Offendor graunted scope of speech,

  'Twill make them coole in zeale vnto your Grace.

SUFFOLKE (*to the King*)

  Hath he not twit our Soueraigne Lady here

1360 With ignominious words, though Clarkely couch't?

  As if she had suborned some to sweare

  False allegations, to o'rethrow his state.

QUEENE

  But I can giue the loser leaue to chide.

GLOSTER

  Farre truer spoke then meant: I lose indeede,

  Beshrew the winners, for they play'd me false,

  And well such losers may haue leaue to speake.

BUCKINGHAM (*to the King*)

  Hee'le wrest the sence, and hold vs here all day.

  Lord Cardinall, he is your Prisoner.

CARDINALL (*to some of his Attendants*)

  Sirs, take away the Duke, and guard him sure.

GLOSTER

1370 Ah, thus King *Henry* throwes away his Crutch,

  Before his Legges be firme to beare his Body.

  Thus is the Shepheard beaten from thy side,

  And Wolues are gnarling, who shall gnaw thee first.

  Ah that my feare were false, ah that it were;

  For good King *Henry*, thy decay I feare.

               Exit Gloster, with the Cardinals men

KING

  My Lords, what to your wisdomes seemeth best,

  Doe, or vndoe, as if our selfe were here.

QUEENE

  What, will your Highnesse leaue the Parliament?

KING

  I *Margaret*: my heart is drown'd with griefe,

1380 Whose floud begins to flowe within mine eyes;

  My Body round engyrt with miserie:

  For what's more miserable then Discontent?

  Ah Vnckle *Humfrey*, in thy face I see

  The Map of Honor, Truth, and Loyaltie:

  And yet, good *Humfrey*, is the houre to come,

  That ere I prou'd thee false, or fear'd thy faith.

  What lowring Starre now enuies thy estate?

  That these great Lords, and *Margaret* our Queene,

  Doe seeke subuersion of thy harmelesse Life.

1390 Thou neuer didst them wrong, nor no man wrong:

  And as the Butcher takes away the Calfe,

  And binds the Wretch, and beats it when it strayes,

  Bearing it to the bloody Slaughter-house;

  Euen so remorselesse haue they borne him hence:

  And as the Damme runnes lowing vp and downe,

  Looking the way her harmelesse young one went,

  And can doe naught but wayle her Darlings losse;

  Euen so my selfe bewayles good *Glosters* case

  With sad vnhelpefull teares; and with dimn'd eyes,

Looke after him, and cannot doe him good: 1400

So mightie are his vowed Enemies.

His fortunes I will weepe, and 'twixt each groane,

Say, who's a Traytor? *Gloster* he is none.

             Exit ⌈with Salsbury and Warwicke⌉

QUEENE

Free Lords: cold Snow melts with the Sunnes hot

  Beames:

Henry, my Lord, is cold in great Affaires,

Too full of foolish pittie: and *Glosters* shew

Beguiles him, as the mournefull Crocodile

With sorrow snares relenting passengers;

Or as the Snake, roll'd in a flowring Banke,

With shining checker'd slough doth sting a Child,   1410

That for the beautie thinkes it excellent.

Beleeue me Lords, were none more wise then I,

And yet herein I iudge mine owne Wit good;

This *Gloster* should be quickly rid the World,

To rid vs from the feare we haue of him.

CARDINALL

That he should dye, is worthie pollicie,

But yet we want a Colour for his death:

'Tis meet he be condemn'd by course of Law.

SUFFOLKE

But in my minde, that were no pollicie:

The King will labour still to saue his Life,   1420

The Commons haply rise, to saue his Life;

And yet we haue but triuiall argument,

More then mistrust, that shewes him worthy death.

YORKE

So that by this, you would not haue him dye.

SUFFOLKE

Ah *Yorke*, no man aliue, so faine as I.

YORKE (*aside*)

'Tis *Yorke* that hath more reason for his death.

(*Alowd*) But my lord Cardinall, and you my Lord of

  Suffolke,

Say as you thinke, and speake it from your Soules:

Wer't not all one, an emptie Eagle were set,

To guard the Chicken from a hungry Kyte,   1430

As place Duke *Humfrey* for the Kings Protector?

QUEENE

So the poore Chicken should be sure of death.

SUFFOLKE

Madame 'tis true: and wer't not madnesse then,

To make the Fox surueyor of the Fold?

Who being accus'd a craftie Murtherer,

His guilt should be but idly posted ouer,

Because his purpose is not executed.

No: let him dye, in that he is a Fox,

By nature prou'd an Enemie to the Flock,

Before his Chaps be stayn'd with Crimson blood,   1440

As *Humfrey*, prou'd by Reasons, to my Liege.

And doe not stand on Quillets how to slay him:

Be it by Gynnes, by Snares, by Subtletie,

Sleeping, or Waking, 'tis no matter how,

So he be dead; for that is good conceit,

Which mates him first, that first intends deceit.

QUEENE

  Thrice Noble *Suffolke*, 'tis resolutely spoke.

SUFFOLKE

  Not resolute, except so much were done,

  For things are often spoke, and seldome meant,

1450 But that my heart accordeth with my tongue,

  Seeing the deed is meritorious,

  And to preserue my Soueraigne from his Foe,

  Say but the word, and I will be his Priest.

CARDINALL

  But I would haue him dead, my Lord of Suffolke,

  Ere you can take due Orders for a Priest:

  Say you consent, and censure well the deed,

  And Ile prouide his Executioner,

  I tender so the safetie of my Liege.

SUFFOLKE

  Here is my Hand, the deed is worthy doing.

1460 QUEENE And so say I.

YORKE

  And I: and now we three haue spoke it,

  It skills not greatly who impugnes our doome.

          Enter a Poste

POST

  Great Lords, from Ireland am I come amaine,

  To signifie, that Rebels there are vp,

  And put the Englishmen vnto the Sword.

  Send Succours (Lords) and stop the Rage betime,

  Before the Wound doe grow vncurable;

  For being greene, there is great hope of helpe.   ⌈*Exit*⌉

CARDINALL

  A Breach that craues a quick expedient stoppe.

1470 What counsaile giue you in this weightie cause?

YORKE

  That *Somerset* be sent as Regent thither:

  'Tis meet that luckie Ruler be imploy'd,

  Witnesse the fortune he hath had in France.

SOMERSET

  If *Yorke*, with all his farre-fet pollicie,

  Had beene the Regent there, in stead of me,

  He neuer would haue stay'd in France so long.

YORKE

  No, not to lose it all, as thou hast done.

  I rather would haue lost my Life betimes,

  Then bring a burthen of dis-honour home,

1480 By staying there so long, till all were lost.

  Shew me one skarre, character'd on thy Skinne,

  Mens flesh preseru'd so whole, doe seldome winne.

QUEENE

  Nay then, this sparke will proue a raging fire,

  If Wind and Fuell be brought, to feed it with:

  No more, good *Yorke*; sweet *Somerset* be still.

  Thy fortune, *Yorke*, hadst thou beene Regent there,

  Might happily haue prou'd farre worse then his.

YORKE

  What, worse then naught? nay, then a shame take all.

SOMERSET

  And in the number, thee, that wishest shame.

CARDINALL

  My Lord of Yorke, trie what your fortune is: 1490

  Th'vnciuill Kernes of Ireland are in Armes,

  And temper Clay with blood of Englishmen.

  To Ireland will you leade a Band of men,

  Collected choycely, from each Countie some,

  And trie your hap against the Irishmen?

YORKE

  I will, my Lord, so please his Maiestie.

SUFFOLKE

  Why, our Authoritie is his consent,

  And what we doe establish, he confirmes:

  Then, Noble *Yorke*, take thou this Taske in hand.

YORKE

  I am content: Prouide me Souldiers, Lords,   1500

  Whiles I take order for mine owne affaires.

SUFFOLKE

  A charge, Lord *Yorke*, that I will see perform'd.

  But now returne we to the false Duke *Humfrey*.

CARDINALL

  No more of him: for I will deale with him,

  That henceforth he shall trouble vs no more:

  And so breake off, the day is almost spent.

  Lord *Suffolke*, you and I must talke of that euent.

YORKE

  My Lord of Suffolke, within foureteene dayes

  At Bristow I expect my Souldiers,

  For there Ile shippe them all for Ireland.   1510

SUFFOLKE

  Ile see it truly done, my Lord of Yorke.

          Exeunt. Manet Yorke

YORKE

  Now *Yorke*, or neuer, steele thy fearfull thoughts,

  And change misdoubt to resolution;

  Be that thou hop'st to be; or what thou art,

  Resigne to death, it is not worth th'enioying:

  Let pale-fac't feare keepe with the meane-borne man,

  And finde no harbor in a Royall heart.

  Faster thē Spring-time showres, comes thoght on

      thoght,

  And not a thought, but thinkes on Dignitie.

  My Brayne, more busie then the laboring Spider,   1520

  Weaues tedious Snares to trap mine Enemies.

  Well Nobles, well: 'tis politikely done,

  To send me packing with an Hoast of men:

  I feare me, you but warme the starued Snake,

  Who cherisht in your breasts, will sting your hearts.

  'Twas men I lackt, and you will giue them me;

  I take it kindly: yet be well assur'd,

  You put sharpe Weapons in a mad-mans hands.

  Whiles I in Ireland nourish a mightie Band,

  I will stirre vp in England some black Storme,   1530

  Shall blowe ten thousand Soules to Heauen, or Hell:

  And this fell Tempest shall not cease to rage,

  Vntill the Golden Circuit on my Head,

  Like to the glorious Sunnes transparant Beames,

  Doe calme the furie of this mad-bred Flawe.

And for a minister of my intent,
I haue seduc'd a head-strong Kentishman,
Iohn Cade of Ashford,
To make Commotion, as full well he can,
1540 Vnder the Title of *Iohn Mortimer.*
In Ireland haue I seene this stubborne *Cade*
Oppose himselfe against a Troupe of Kernes,
And fought so long, till that his thighes with Darts
Were almost like a sharpe-quill'd Porpentine:
And in the end being rescued, I haue seene
Him capre vpright, like a wilde Morisco,
Shaking the bloody Darts, as he his Bells.
Full often, like a shag-hayr'd craftie Kerne,
Hath he conuersed with the Enemie,
1550 And vndiscouer'd, come to me againe,
And giuen me notice of their Villanies.
This Deuill here shall be my substitute;
For that *Iohn Mortimer*, which now is dead,
In face, in gate, in speech he doth resemble.
By this, I shall perceiue the Commons minde,
How they affect the House and Clayme of *Yorke.*
Say he be taken, rackt, and tortured;
I know, no paine they can inflict vpon him,
Will make him say, I mou'd him to those Armes.
1560 Say that he thriue, as 'tis great like he will,
Why then from Ireland come I with my strength,
And reape the Haruest which that coistrill sow'd.
For *Humfrey*, being dead, as he shall be,
And *Henry* put apart: the next for me.   *Exit*

Sc. 10 ⌐*Then the Curtaines being drawne, Duke Humphrey*
(3.2)   *is discouered in his bed, and two men lying on his*
        brest and smothering him in his bed⌐
    1. MURTHERER (*to 2. Murtherer*)
    Runne to my Lord of Suffolke: let him know
    We haue dispatcht the Duke, as he commanded.
    2. MURTHERER
    Oh, that it were to doe: what haue we done?
    Didst euer heare a man so penitent?
        Enter Suffolke
    1. MURTHERER Here comes my Lord.
    SUFFOLKE
1570 Now Sirs, haue you dispatcht this thing?
    1. MURTHERER I, my good Lord, hee's dead.
    SUFFOLKE
    Why that's well said. Goe, get you to my House,
    I will reward you for this venturous deed:
    The King and all the Peeres are here at hand.
    Haue you layd faire the Bed? Is all things well,
    According as I gaue directions?
    1. MURTHERER 'Tis, my good Lord.
    SUFFOLKE
    Then draw the curtaines close: away, be gone.
        Exeunt ⌐*Murtherers, drawing the Curtaines*⌐
        Sound Trumpets, then enter the King, the Queene,
        Cardinall, Somerset, with Attendants
    KING ⌐*to Suffolke*⌐
    Goe call our Vnckle to our presence straight:

Say, we intend to try his Grace to day,   1580
If he be guiltie, as 'tis published.
SUFFOLKE
Ile call him presently, my Noble Lord.   *Exit*
KING
Lords take your places: and I pray you all
Proceed no straiter 'gainst our Vnckle *Gloster,*
Then from true euidence, of good esteeme,
He be approu'd in practise culpable.
QUEENE
God forbid any Malice should preuayle,
That faultlesse may condemne a Noble man:
Pray God he may acquit him of suspition.
KING
I thanke thee *Meg*, these wordes content mee much.   1590
    Enter Suffolke
How now? why look'st thou pale? why tremblest
    thou?
Where is our Vnckle? what's the matter, *Suffolke?*
SUFFOLKE
Dead in his Bed, my Lord: *Gloster* is dead.
QUEENE Marry God forfend.
CARDINALL
Gods secret Iudgement: I did dreame to Night,
The Duke was dumbe, and could not speake a word.
    King sounds
QUEENE
How fares my Lord? Helpe Lords, the King is dead.
SOMERSET
Rere vp his Body, wring him by the Nose.
QUEENE
Runne, goe, helpe, helpe: Oh *Henry* ope thine eyes.
SUFFOLKE
He doth reuiue againe, Madame be patient.   1600
KING
Oh Heauenly God.
QUEENE   How fares my gracious Lord?
SUFFOLKE
Comfort my Soueraigne, gracious *Henry* comfort.
KING
What, doth my Lord of Suffolke comfort me?
Came he right now to sing a Rauens Note,
Whose dismall tune bereft my Vitall powres:
And thinkes he, that the chirping of a Wren,
By crying comfort from a hollow breast,
Can chase away the first-conceiued sound?
Hide not thy poyson with such sugred words,
    ⌐*He begins to rise: Suffolke offers to assist him*⌐
Lay not thy hands on me: forbeare I say,   1610
Their touch affrights me as a Serpents sting.
Thou balefull Messenger, out of my sight:
Vpon thy eye-balls, murderous Tyrannie
Sits in grim Maiestie, to fright the World.
Looke not vpon me, for thine eyes are wounding;
Yet doe not goe away: come Basiliske,
And kill the innocent gazer with thy sight:
For in the shade of death, I shall finde ioy;
In life, but double death, now *Gloster's* dead.

QUEENE

1620 Why do you rate my Lord of Suffolke thus?
     Although the Duke was enemie to him,
     Yet he most Christian-like laments his death:
     And for my selfe, Foe as he was to me,
     Might liquid teares, or heart-offending groanes,
     Or blood-consuming sighes recall his Life;
     I would be blinde with weeping, sicke with grones,
     Looke pale as Prim-rose with blood-drinking sighes,
     And all to haue the Noble Duke aliue.
     What know I how the world may deeme of me?
1630 For it is knowne we were but hollow Friends:
     It may be iudg'd I made the Duke away,
     So shall my name with Slanders tongue be wounded,
     And Princes Courts be fill'd with my reproach:
     This get I by his death: Aye me vnhappie,
     To be a Queene, and Crown'd with infamie.

KING

     Ah woe is me for Gloster, wretched man.

QUEENE

     Be woe for me, more wretched then he is.
     What, Dost thou turne away, and hide thy face?
     I am no loathsome Leaper, looke on me.
1640 What? Art thou like the Adder waxen deafe?
     Be poysonous too, and kill thy forlorne Queene.
     Is all thy comfort shut in Glosters Tombe?
     Why then Queene *Margaret* was neere thy ioy.
     Erect his Statue, and worship it,
     And make my Image but an Ale-house signe.
     Was I for this nye wrack'd vpon the Sea,
     And twice by aukward winds from Englands banke
     Droue backe againe vnto my Natiue Clime.
     What boaded this? but well fore-warning winds
1650 Did seeme to say, seeke not a Scorpions Nest,
     Nor set no footing on this vnkinde Shore.
     What did I then? But curst the gentle gusts,
     And he that loos'd them forth their Brazen Caues,
     And bid them blow towards Englands blessed shore,
     Or turne our Sterne vpon a dreadfull Rocke:
     Yet Æolus would not be a murtherer,
     But left that hatefull office vnto thee.
     The pretty vaulting Sea refus'd to drowne me,
     Knowing that thou wouldst haue me drown'd on shore
1660 With teares as salt as Sea, through thy vnkindnesse.
     The splitting Rockes cowr'd in the sinking sands,
     And would not dash me with their ragged sides,
     Because thy flinty heart more hard then they,
     Might in thy Pallace, perish *Margaret*.
     As farre as I could ken thy Chalky Cliffes,
     When from thy Shore, the Tempest beate vs backe,
     I stood vpon the Hatches in the storme:
     And when the duskie sky, began to rob
     My earnest-gaping-sight of thy Lands view,
1670 I tooke a costly Iewell from my necke,
     A Hart it was bound in with Diamonds,
     And threw it towards thy Land: The Sea receiu'd it,
     And so I wish'd thy body might my Heart:
     And euen with this, I lost faire Englands view,
     And bid mine eyes be packing with my Heart,

And call'd them blinde and duskie Spectacles,
For loosing ken of *Albions* wished Coast.
How often haue I tempted Suffolkes tongue
(The agent of thy foule inconstancie)
To sit and witch me as *Ascanius* did,   1680
When he to madding *Dido* would vnfold
His Fathers Acts, commenc'd in burning Troy.
Am I not witcht like her? Or thou not false like him?
Aye me, I can no more: Dye *Margaret*,
For *Henry* weepes, that thou dost liue so long.
     Noyse within. Enter Warwicke and Salisbury, and
       many Commons

WARWICKE (*to the King*)

It is reported, mighty Soueraigne,
That good Duke *Humfrey* Traiterously is murdred
By Suffolke, and the Cardinall *Beaufords* meanes:
The Commons like an angry Hiue of Bees
That want their Leader, scatter vp and downe,   1690
And care not who they sting in his reuenge.
My selfe haue calm'd their spleenfull mutinie,
Vntill they heare the order of his death.

KING

That he is dead good Warwick, 'tis too true,
But how he dyed, God knowes, not *Henry*:
Enter his Chamber, view his breathlesse Corpes,
And comment then vpon his sodaine death.

WARWICKE

That shall I do my Liege; Stay Salsburie
With the rude multitude, till I returne.
            ⌐*Exit Warwicke at one doore, Salisbury and*
                           Commons at another⌐

KING

O thou that iudgest all things, stay my thoghts: 1700
My thoughts, that labour to perswade my soule,
Some violent hands were laid on *Humfries* life:
If my suspect be false, forgiue me God,
For iudgement onely doth belong to thee:
Faine would I go to chafe his palie lips,
With twenty thousand kisses, and to draine
Vpon his face an Ocean of salt teares,
To tell my loue vnto his dumbe deafe trunke,
And with my fingers feele his hand, vnfeeling:
But all in vaine are these meane Obsequies: 1710
     ⌐*Enter Warwicke who drawes the Curtaines and*
       shows ⌐ *Gloster dead in his bed. Bed put forth*
And to suruey his dead and earthy Image,
What were it but to make my sorrow greater?

WARWICKE

Come hither gracious Soueraigne, view this body.

KING

That is to see how deepe my graue is made,
For with his soule fled all my worldly solace:
For seeing him, I see my life in death.

WARWICKE

As surely as my soule intends to liue
With that dread King that tooke our state vpon him,
To free vs from his Fathers wrathfull curse,
I do beleeue that violent hands were laid   1720
Vpon the life of this thrice-famed Duke.

SUFFOLKE

A dreadfull Oath, sworne with a solemn tongue:
What instance giues Lord Warwicke for his vow.

WARWICKE

See how the blood is setled in his face.
Oft haue I seene a timely-parted Ghost,
Of ashy semblance, meager, pale, and bloodlesse,
Being all descended to the labouring heart,
Who in the Conflict that it holds with death,
Attracts the same for aydance 'gainst the enemy,
Which with the heart there cooles, and ne're
1730   returneth,
To blush and beautifie the Cheeke againe.
But see, his face is blacke, and full of blood:
His eye-balles further out, than when he liued,
Staring full gastly, like a strangled man:
His hayre vprear'd, his nostrils stretcht with strugling:
His hands abroad display'd, as one that graspt
And tugg'd for Life, and was by strength subdude.
Looke on the sheets his haire (you see) is sticking,
His well proportion'd Beard, made ruffe and rugged,
1740 Like to the Summers Corne by Tempest lodged:
It cannot be but he was murdred heere,
The least of all these signes were probable.

SUFFOLKE

Why Warwicke, who should do the D. to death?
My selfe and *Beauford* had him in protection,
And we I hope sir, are no murtherers.

WARWICKE

But both of you were vowed D. Humfries foes,
(*To the Cardinall*)
And you (forsooth) had the good Duke to keepe:
Tis like you would not feast him like a friend,
And 'tis well seene, he found an enemy.

QUEENE

1750 Than you belike suspect these Noblemen,
As guilty of Duke *Humfries* timelesse death.

WARWICKE

Who finds the Heyfer dead, and bleeding fresh,
And sees fast-by, a Butcher with an Axe,
But will suspect, 'twas he that made the slaughter?
Who finds the Partridge in the Puttocks Nest,
But may imagine how the Bird was dead,
Although the Kyte soare with vnbloudied Beake?
Euen so suspitious is this Tragedie.

QUEENE

Are you the Butcher, *Suffolk*? where's your Knife?
1760 Is *Beauford* tearm'd a Kyte? where are his Tallons?

SUFFOLKE

I weare no Knife, to slaughter sleeping men,
But here's a vengefull Sword, rusted with ease,
That shall be scowred in his rancorous heart,
That slanders me with Murthers Crimson Badge.
Say, if thou dar'st, prowd Lord of Warwickshire,
That I am faultie in Duke *Humfreyes* death.
                  ⌈*Exit Cardinal assisted by Somerset*⌉

WARWICKE

What dares not *Warwick*, if false *Suffolke* dare him?

QUEENE

He dares not calme his contumelious Spirit,
Nor cease to be an arrogant Controller,
Though *Suffolke* dare him twentie thousand times.   1770

WARWICKE

Madame be still: with reuerence may I say,
For euery word you speake in his behalfe,
Is slander to your Royall Dignitie.

SUFFOLKE

Blunt-witted Lord, ignoble in demeanor,
If euer Lady wrong'd her Lord so much,
Thy Mother tooke into her blamefull Bed
Some sterne vntutur'd Churle; and Noble Stock
Was graft with Crab-tree slippe, whose Fruit thou art,
And neuer of the *Neuils* Noble Race.

WARWICKE

But that the guilt of Murther bucklers thee,   1780
And I should rob the Deaths-man of his Fee,
Quitting thee thereby of ten thousand shames,
And that my Soueraignes presence makes me milde,
I would, false murd'rous Coward, on thy Knee
Make thee begge pardon for thy passed speech,
And say, it was thy Mother that thou meant'st,
That thou thy selfe wast borne in Bastardie;
And after all this fearefull Homage done,
Giue thee thy hyre, and send thy Soule to Hell,
Pernicious blood-sucker of sleeping men.   1790

SUFFOLKE

Thou shalt be waking, while I shed thy blood,
If from this presence thou dar'st goe with me.

WARWICKE

Away euen now, or I will drag thee hence:
Vnworthy though thou art, Ile cope with thee,
And doe some seruice to Duke *Humfreyes* Ghost.
                  Exeunt Suffolke and Warwicke

KING

What stronger Brest-plate then a heart vntainted?
Thrice is he arm'd, that hath his Quarrell iust;
And he but naked, though lockt vp in Steele,
Whose Conscience with Iniustice is corrupted.
          All the Commons within, cries, downe with
          Suffolke, downe with Suffolk

QUEENE What noyse is this?   1800
          Enter Suffolke and Warwicke, with their Weapons
          drawne

KING

Why how now Lords? Your wrathfull Weapons
          drawne,
Here in our presence? Dare you be so bold?
Why what tumultuous clamor haue we here?

SUFFOLKE

The trayt'rous *Warwick*, with the men of Bury,
Set all vpon me, mightie Soueraigne.
          The Commons againe cries, downe with Suffolke,
          downe with Suffolke. And then enter from them,
          the Earle of Salsbury

SALISBURY (*to the Commons, within*)

Sirs stand apart, the King shall know your minde.

(*To the King*) Dread Lord, the Commons send you
    word by me,
Vnlesse Lord *Suffolke* straight be done to death,
Or banished faire Englands Territories,
1810   They will by violence teare him from your Pallace,
And torture him with grieuous lingring death.
They say, by him the good Duke *Humfrey* dy'de:
They say, in him they feare your Highnesse death;
And meere instinct of Loue and Loyaltie,
Free from a stubborne opposite intent,
As being thought to contradict your liking,
Makes them thus forward in his Banishment.
They say, in care of your most Royall Person,
That if your Highnesse should intend to sleepe,
1820   And charge, that no man should disturbe your rest,
In paine of your dislike, or paine of death;
Yet notwithstanding such a strait Edict,
Were there a Serpent seene, with forked Tongue,
That slyly glyded towards your Maiestie,
It were but necessarie you were wak't:
Least being suffer'd in that harmefull slumber,
The mortall Worme might make the sleepe eternall.
And therefore doe they cry, though you forbid,
That they will guard you, where you will, or no,
1830   From such fell Serpents as false *Suffolke* is;
With whose inuenomed and fatall sting,
Your louing Vnckle, twentie times his worth,
They say is shamefully bereft of life.
COMMONS (*within*) An answer from the King, my Lord of
    Salisbury.
SUFFOLKE
'Tis like the Commons, rude vnpolisht Hindes,
Could send such Message to their Soueraigne:
But you, my Lord, were glad to be imploy'd,
To shew how queint an Orator you are.
1840   But all the Honor *Salisbury* hath wonne,
Is, that he was the Lord Embassador,
Sent from a sort of Tinkers to the King.
COMMONS (*within*) An answer from the King, or wee will
    all breake in.
KING
Goe *Salisbury*, and tell them all from me,
I thanke them for their tender louing care;
And had I not beene cited so by them,
Yet did I purpose as they doe entreat:
For sure, my thoughts doe hourely prophecie,
1850   Mischance vnto my State by *Suffolkes* meanes.
And therefore by his Maiestie I sweare,
Whose farre-vnworthie Deputie I am,
He shall not breathe infection in this ayre,
But three dayes longer, on the paine of death.
                ⌈*Exit Salisbury*⌉
QUEENE ⌈*kneeling*⌉
Oh *Henry*, let me pleade for gentle *Suffolke*.
KING
Vngentle Queene, to call him gentle *Suffolke*.
No more I say: if thou do'st pleade for him,
Thou wilt but adde encrease vnto my Wrath.

Had I but sayd, I would haue kept my Word;
But when I sweare, it is irreuocable: 1860
(*To Suffolke*) If after three dayes space thou here bee'st
    found,
On any ground that I am Ruler of,
The World shall not be Ransome for thy Life.
Come *Warwicke*, come good *Warwicke*, goe with mee,
I haue great matters to impart to thee.
       Exit King and Warwicke with Attendants,
      ⌈*drawing the curtaines*⌉. *Manet the Queene and*
                       Suffolke
QUEENE ⌈*rising*⌉
Mischance and Sorrow goe along with you,
Hearts Discontent, and sowre Affliction,
Be play-fellowes to keepe you companie:
There's two of you, the Deuill make a third,
And three-fold Vengeance tend vpon your steps.   1870
SUFFOLKE
Cease, gentle Queene, these Execrations,
And let thy *Suffolke* take his heauie leaue.
QUEENE
Fye Coward woman, and soft harted wretch,
Hast thou not spirit to curse thine enemies.
SUFFOLKE
A plague vpon them: wherefore should I cursse them?
Could curses kill, as doth the Mandrakes grone,
I would inuent as bitter searching termes,
As curst, as harsh, and horrible to heare,
Deliuer'd strongly through my fixed teeth,
With full as many signes of deadly hate,   1880
As leane-fac'd enuy in her loathsome caue.
My tongue should stumble in mine earnest words,
Mine eyes should sparkle like the beaten Flint,
My haire be fixt an end, as one distract:
I, euery ioynt should seeme to curse and ban,
And euen now my burthen'd heart would breake
Should I not curse them. Poyson be their drinke.
Gall, worse then Gall, the daintiest that they taste:
Their sweetest shade, a groue of Cypresse Trees:
Their cheefest Prospect, murd'ring Basiliskes: 1890
Their softest Touch, as smart as Lyzards stings:
Their Musicke, frightfull as the Serpents hisse,
And boading Screech-Owles, make the Consort full.
All the foule terrors in darke seated hell—
QUEENE
Enough sweet Suffolke, thou torment'st thy selfe,
And these dread curses like the Sunne 'gainst glasse,
Or like an ouer-charged Gun, recoile,
And turne the force of them vpon thy selfe.
SUFFOLKE
You bad me ban, and will you bid me leaue?
Now by this ground that I am banish'd from,   1900
Well could I curse away a Winters night,
Though standing naked on a Mountaine top,
Where byting cold would neuer let grasse grow,
And thinke it but a minute spent in sport.
QUEENE
Oh, let me intreat thee cease, giue me thy hand,

That I may dew it with my mournfull teares:
Nor let the raine of heauen wet this place,
To wash away my wofull Monuments.
　　　⌈*She kisses his palm*⌉
Oh, could this kisse be printed in thy hand,
1910　That thou might'st thinke vpon these lips by the Seale,
Through whom a thousand sighes are breath'd for
　　　thee.
So get thee gone, that I may know my greefe,
'Tis but surmiz'd, whiles thou art standing by,
As one that surfets, thinking on a want:
I will repeale thee, or be well assur'd,
Aduenture to be banished my selfe:
And banished I am, if but from thee.
Go, speake not to me; euen now be gone.
Oh go not yet. Euen thus, two Friends condemn'd,
1920　Embrace, and kisse, and take ten thousand leaues,
Loather a hundred times to part then dye;
Yet now farewell, and farewell Life with thee.

SUFFOLKE
Thus is poore Suffolke ten times banished,
Once by the King, and three times thrice by thee.
'Tis not the Land I care for, wer't thou thence,
A Wildernesse is populous enough,
So Suffolke had thy heauenly company:
For where thou art, there is the World it selfe,
With euery seuerall pleasure in the World:
1930　And where thou art not, Desolation.
I can no more: Liue thou to ioy thy life;
My selfe no ioy in nought, but that thou liu'st.
　　　Enter Vaux

QUEENE
Whether goes *Vaux* so fast? What newes I prethee?

VAUX
To signifie vnto his Maiesty,
That Cardinal *Beauford* is at point of death:
For sodainly a greeuous sicknesse tooke him,
That makes him gaspe, and stare, and catch the aire,
Blaspheming God, and cursing men on earth.
Sometime he talkes, as if Duke *Humfries* Ghost
1940　Were by his side: Sometime, he calles the King,
And whispers to his pillow, as to him,
The secrets of his ouer-charged soule,
And I am sent to tell his Maiestie,
That euen now he cries alowd for him.

QUEENE
Go tell this heauy Message to the King.　　*Exit Vaux*
Aye me! What is this World? What newes are these?
But wherefore greeue I at an houres poore losse,
Omitting Suffolkes exile, my soules Treasure?
Why onely Suffolke mourne I not for thee?
1950　And with the Southerne clouds, contend in teares?
Theirs for the earths encrease, mine for my sorrowes.
Now get thee hence, the King thou know'st is
　　　comming,
If thou be found by me, thou art but dead.

SUFFOLKE
If I depart from thee, I cannot liue,

And in thy sight to dye, what were it else,
But like a pleasant slumber in thy lap?
Heere could I breath my soule into the ayre,
As milde and gentle as the Cradle-babe,
Dying with mothers dugge betweene his lips.
Where from thy sight, I should be raging mad,　　1960
And cry out for thee to close vp mine eyes:
To haue thee with thy lippes to stop my mouth:
So should'st thou eyther turne my flying soule,
Or I should breathe it so into thy body,
　　　⌈*He kisseth her*⌉
And then it liu'd in sweete Elizium.
By thee to dye, were but to dye in iest,
From thee to dye, were torture more then death:
Oh let me stay, befall what may befall.

QUEENE
Away: Though parting be a fretfull corosiue,
It is applyed to a deathfull wound.　　　　　　　1970
To France sweet Suffolke: Let me heare from thee:
For wheresoere thou art in this worlds Globe,
Ile haue an *Iris* that shall finde thee out.

SUFFOLKE
I go.

QUEENE　And take my heart with thee.
　　　⌈*She kisseth him*⌉

SUFFOLKE
A Iewell lockt into the wofulst Caske,
That euer did containe a thing of worth,
Euen as a splitted Barke, so sunder we:
This way fall I to death.

QUEENE　　　　　　　　This way for me.
　　　　　　　　　　　　　　　Exeunt seuerally

　　　Enter the King, Salisbury, and Warwicke, and then　Sc. 11
　　　the Curtaines be drawne, and the Cardinall is　　(3.3)
　　　discouered in his bed, rauing and staring as if he
　　　were madde

KING (*to the Cardinall*)
How fare's my Lord? Speake *Beauford* to thy
　　　Soueraigne.

CARDINALL
If thou beest death, Ile giue thee Englands Treasure,　1980
Enough to purchase such another Island,
So thou wilt let me liue, and feele no paine.

KING
Ah, what a signe it is of euill life,
Where death's approach is seene so terrible.

WARWICKE
Beauford, it is thy Soueraigne speakes to thee.

CARDINALL
Bring me vnto my Triall when you will.
Dy'de he not in his bed? Where should he dye?
Can I make men liue where they will or no?
Oh torture me no more, I will confesse.
Aliue againe? Then shew me where he is,　　　　1990
Ile giue a thousand pound to looke vpon him.
He hath no eyes, the dust hath blinded them.
Combe downe his haire; looke, looke, it stands vpright,

Like Lime-twigs set to catch my winged soule:
Giue me some drinke, and bid the Apothecarie
Bring the strong poyson that I bought of him.

KING

Oh thou eternall mouer of the heauens,
Looke with a gentle eye vpon this Wretch,
Oh beate away the busie medling Fiend,
2000   That layes strong siege vnto this wretches soule,
And from his bosome purge this blacke dispaire.

WARWICKE

See how the pangs of death do make him grin.

SALISBURY

Disturbe him not, let him passe peaceably.

KING

Peace to his soule, if Gods good pleasure be.
Lord Card'nall, if thou think'st on heauens blisse,
Hold vp thy hand, make signall of thy hope.
        The Cardinall dies
He dies and makes no signe: Oh God forgiue him.

WARWICKE

So bad a death, argues a monstrous life.

KING

Forbeare to iudge, for we are sinners all.
2010   Close vp his eyes, and draw the Curtaine close,
And let vs all to Meditation.
                Exeunt, ⌐drawing the Curtaines. The Bed is
                                        remoued⌐

Sc. 12   *Alarmes within, and the chambers be discharged,*
(4.1)   *like as it were a fight at sea. And then enter the*
           Captaine of the ship and the Maister, and the
           Maisters Mate and Water Whitmore, ⌐and others⌐;
           with them, as their prisoners, the Duke of Suffolke
           disguised, and 2. Gentlemen

CAPTAINE

The gaudy blabbing and remorsefull day,
Is crept into the bosome of the Sea:
And now loud houling Wolues arouse the Iades
That dragge the Tragicke melancholy night:
Who with their drowsie, slow, and flagging wings
Cleape dead-mens graues, and from their misty Iawes,
Breath foule contagious darknesse in the ayre:
Therefore bring forth the Souldiers of our prize,
2020   For whilst our Pinnace Anchors in the Downes,
Heere shall they make their ransome on the sand,
Or with their blood staine this discolour'd shore.
Maister, (*pointing at 1. Gentleman*) this Prisoner freely
        giue I thee,
(*To the Mate*) And thou that art his Mate, make boote
        of this:
        Points at 2. Gentleman
(*To Whitmore*) The other (*pointing at Suffolke*) Water
        Whitmore is thy share.

1. GENTLEMAN (*to the Master*)

What is my ransome Master, let me know.

MASTER

A thousand Crownes, or else lay down your head.

MATE (*to 2. Gentleman*)

And so much shall you giue, or off goes yours.

CAPTAINE (*to both the Gentlemen*)

What thinke you much to pay 2000. Crownes,
And beare the name and port of Gentlemen?   2030

⌐WHITMORE⌐

Cut both the Villaines throats, ⌐*to Suffolke*⌐ for dy you
        shall:
The liues of those which we haue lost in fight,
⌐   ⌐
Be counter-poys'd with such a pettie summe.

1. GENTLEMAN (*to the Master*)

Ile giue it sir, and therefore spare my life.

2. GENTLEMAN (*to the Mate*)

And so will I, and write home for it straight.

WHITMORE (*to Suffolke*)

I lost mine eye in laying the prize aboord,
And therefore to reuenge it, shalt thou dye,
And so should these, if I might haue my will.

CAPTAINE

Be not so rash, take ransome, let him liue.   2040

SUFFOLKE

Looke on my George, I am a Gentleman,
Rate me at what thou wilt, thou shalt be payed.

WHITMORE

And so am I: my name is *Water Whitmore*.
        Suffolke starteth
How now? why starts thou? What doth thee affright?

SUFFOLKE

Thy name affrights me, in whose sound is death:
A cunning man did calculate my birth,
And told me that by Water I should dye:
Yet let not this make thee be bloody-minded,
Thy name is *Gualtier*, being rightly sounded.

WHITMORE

Gualtier or *Water*, which it is I care not,   2050
Neuer yet did base dishonour blurre our name,
But with our sword we wip'd away the blot.
Therefore, when Merchant-like I sell reuenge,
Broke be my sword, my Armes torne and defac'd,
And I proclaim'd a Coward through the world.

SUFFOLKE

Stay *Whitmore*, for thy Prisoner is a Prince,
The Duke of Suffolke, *William de la Pole*.

WHITMORE

The Duke of Suffolke, muffled vp in ragges?

SUFFOLKE

I, but these ragges are no part of the Duke.
Ioue sometime went disguisde, and why not I?   2060

CAPTAINE

But Ioue was neuer slaine as thou shalt be.

SUFFOLKE

Obscure and lowsie Swaine, King *Henries* blood,
The honourable blood of Lancaster
Must not be shed by such a iadie Groome:
Hast thou not kist thy hand, and held my stirrop?
Bare-headed plodded by my foot-cloth Mule,
And thought thee happy when I shooke my head.
How often hast thou waited at my cup,
Fed from my Trencher, kneel'd downe at the boord,
When I haue feasted with Queene *Margaret*?   2070

Remember it, and let it make thee Crest-falne,
I, and alay this thy abortiue Pride:
How in our voyding Lobby hast thou stood,
And duly wayted for my comming forth?
This hand of mine hath writ in thy behalfe,
And therefore shall it charme thy riotous tongue.

WHITMORE
Speak Captaine, shall I stab the forlorn Swain.

CAPTAINE
First let my words stab him, as he hath me.

SUFFOLKE
Base slaue, thy words are blunt, and so art thou.

CAPTAINE
2080   Conuey him hence, and on our long boats side,
Strike off his head.

SUFFOLKE   Thou dar'st not for thy owne.

CAPTAINE
Poole.

⌈SUFFOLKE⌉ Poole?

CAPTAINE   I kennell, puddle, sinke, whose filth and dirt
Troubles the siluer Spring, where England drinkes:
Now will I dam vp this thy yawning mouth,
For swallowing the Treasure of the Realme.
Thy lips that kist the Queene, shall sweepe the ground:
And thou that smil'dst at good Duke Humfries death,
Against the senselesse windes shalt grin in vaine,
Who in contempt shall hisse at thee againe.
2090   And wedded be thou to the Hagges of hell,
For daring to affye a mighty Lord
Vnto the daughter of a worthlesse King,
Hauing neyther Subiect, Wealth, nor Diadem:
By diuellish policy art thou growne great,
And like ambitious Sylla ouer-gorg'd,
With gobbets of thy Mothers bleeding heart.
By thee Aniou and Maine were sold to France.
The false reuolting Normans thorough thee,
Disdaine to call vs Lord, and Piccardie
2100   Hath slaine their Gouernors, surpriz'd our Forts,
And sent the ragged Souldiers wounded home.
The Princely Warwicke, and the Neuils all,
Whose dreadfull swords were neuer drawne in vaine,
As hating thee, are rising vp in armes.
And now the House of Yorke thrust from the Crowne,
By shamefull murther of a guiltlesse King,
And lofty proud incroaching tyranny,
Burnes with reuenging fire, whose hopefull colours
Aduance our halfe-fac'd Sunne, striuing to shine;
2110   Vnder the which is writ, Inuitis nubibus.
The Commons heere in Kent are vp in armes,
And to conclude, Reproach and Beggerie,
Is crept into the Pallace of our King,
And all by thee: (to Whitmore) away, conuey him
hence.

SUFFOLKE
O that I were a God, to shoot forth Thunder
Vpon these paltry, seruile, abiect Drudges:
Small things make base men proud. This Villaine
heere,

Being Captaine of a Pinnace, threatens more
Then Bargulus the strong Illyrian Pyrate.
Drones sucke not Eagles blood, but rob Bee-hiues: 2120
It is impossible that I should dye
By such a lowly Vassall as thy selfe.
Thy words moue Rage, and not remorse in me.

⌈CAPTAINE⌉
But my deeds, Suffolke, soone shall staie thy Rage.

SUFFOLKE
I go of Message from the Queene to France:
I charge thee waft me safely crosse the Channell.

CAPTAINE Water:

WHITMORE
Come Suffolke, I must waft thee to thy death.

SUFFOLKE
Pene gelidus timor occupat artus,
It is thee I feare.   2130

WHITMORE
Thou shalt haue cause to feare before I leaue thee.
What, are ye danted now? Now will ye stoope.

I. GENTLEMAN (to Suffolke)
My gracious Lord intreat him, speak him fair.

SUFFOLKE
Suffolkes Imperiall tongue is sterne and rough:
Vs'd to command, vntaught to pleade for fauour.
Farre be it, we should honor such as these
With humble suite: no, rather let my head
Stoope to the blocke, then these knees bow to any,
Saue to the God of heauen, and to my King:
And sooner dance vpon a bloody pole,   2140
Then stand vncouer'd to the Vulgar Groome.
True Nobility, is exempt from feare:
More can I beare, then you dare execute.

CAPTAINE
Hale him away, and let him talke no more.

SUFFOLKE
Come Souldiers, shew what cruelty ye can,
That this my death may neuer be forgot.
Great men oft dye by vilde Bezonions.
A Romane Sworder, and Bandetto slaue
Murder'd sweet Tully. Brutus Bastard hand
Stab'd Iulius Cæsar, Sauage Islanders   2150
Pompey the Great, and Suffolke dyes by Pyrats.
                    Exit Whitmore with Suffolke

CAPTAINE
And as for these whose ransome we haue set,
It is our pleasure one of them depart:
(To 2. Gentleman)
Therefore come you with vs, and (to his men, pointing
        at I. Gentleman) let him go.
                        Exit Captaine, and the rest. Manet the first
                                                    Gentleman
        Enter Whitmore with Suffolkes head and body

WHITMORE
There let his head, and liuelesse bodie lye,
Vntill the Queene his Mistris bury it.   Exit

I. GENTLEMAN
O barbarous and bloudy spectacle,

His body will I beare vnto the King:
If he reuenge it not, yet will his Friends,
2160   So will the Queene, that liuing, held him deere.

Exit with Suffolkes head and body

Sc. 13   *Enter 2. Rebels ⌈with long staues⌉*
(4.2)   1. REBELL Come and get thee a sword, though made of a
Lath, they haue bene vp these two dayes.

2. REBELL They haue the more neede to sleepe now then.

1. REBELL I tell thee, *Iacke Cade* the Cloathier, meanes to
dresse the Common-wealth and turne it, and set a new
nap vpon it.

2. REBELL So he had need, for 'tis thred-bare. Well, I say,
it was neuer merrie world in England, since Gentlemen
came vp.

2170   1. REBELL O miserable Age: Vertue is not regarded in
Handy-crafts men.

2. REBELL The Nobilitie thinke scorne to goe in Leather
Aprons.

1. REBELL Nay more, the Kings Councell are no good
Workemen.

2. REBELL True: and yet it is said, Labour in thy Vocation:
which is as much to say, as let the Magistrates be
labouring men, and therefore should we be Magistrates.

1. REBELL Thou hast hit it: for there's no better signe of
2180   a braue minde, then a hard hand.

2. REBELL I see them, I see them: There's *Bests* Sonne,
the Tanner of Wingham.

1. REBELL Hee shall haue the skinnes of our enemies, to
make Dogges Leather of.

2. REBELL And Dicke the Butcher.

1. REBELL Then is sin strucke downe like an Oxe, and
iniquities throate cut like a Calfe.

2. REBELL And Smith the Weauer.

1. REBELL Argo, their thred of life is spun.

2190   2. REBELL Come, come, let's fall in with them.

Drumme. Enter Cade, Dicke the Butcher, Smith the
Weauer, and a Sawyer, with infinite numbers, ⌈all
with long staues⌉

CADE Wee *Iohn Cade*, so tearm'd of our supposed Father.

BUTCHER (*to his Fellowes*) Or rather of stealing a Cade of
Herrings.

CADE For our enemies shall falle before vs, inspired with
the spirit of putting down Kings and Princes. Command
silence.

BUTCHER Silence.

CADE My Father was a *Mortimer.*

BUTCHER (*to his Fellowes*) He was an honest man, and a
2200   good Bricklayer.

CADE My mother a *Plantagenet.*

BUTCHER (*to his Fellowes*) I knew her well, she was a
Midwife.

CADE My wife descended of the *Lacies.*

BUTCHER (*to his Fellowes*) She was indeed a Pedlers
daughter, & sold many Laces.

WEAUER (*to his Fellowes*) But now of late, not able to
trauell with her furr'd Packe, she washes buckes here
at home.

2210   CADE Therefore am I of an honorable house.

BUTCHER (*to his Fellowes*) I by my faith, the field is
honourable, and there was he borne, vnder a hedge:
for his Father had neuer a house but the Cage.

CADE Valiant I am.

WEAUER (*to his Fellowes*) A must needs, for beggery is
valiant.

CADE I am able to endure much.

BUTCHER (*to his Fellowes*) No question of that: for I haue
seene him whipt three Market dayes together.

CADE I feare neither sword, nor fire.   2220

WEAUER (*to his Fellowes*) He neede not feare the sword,
for his Coate is of proofe.

BUTCHER (*to his Fellowes*) But me thinks he should stand
in feare of fire, being burnt i'th hand for stealing of
Sheepe.

CADE Be braue then, for your Captaine is Braue, and
Vowes Reformation. There shall be in England, seuen
halfe peny Loaues sold for a peny: the three hoop'd
pot, shall haue ten hoopes, and I wil make it Fellony
to drink small Beere. All the Realme shall be in   2230
Common, and in Cheapside shall my Palfrey go to
grasse: and when I am King, as King I will be.

ALL CADES FOLLOWERS God saue your Maiesty.

CADE I thanke you good people. There shall bee no mony,
all shall eate and drinke on my score, and I will
apparrell them all in one Liuery, that they may agree
like Brothers, and worship me their Lord.

BUTCHER The first thing we do, let's kill all the Lawyers.

CADE Nay, that I meane to do. Is not this a lamentable
thing, that of the skin of an innocent Lambe should be   2240
made Parchment; that Parchment being scribeld ore,
should vndoe a man. Some say the Bee stings, but I
say, 'tis the Bees waxe: for I did but seale once to a
thing, and I was neuer mine owne man since. How
now? Who's there?

Enter some, bringing forth the Clearke of Chattam

WEAUER The Clearke of Chattam: hee can write and reade,
and cast accompt.

CADE O monstrous.

WEAUER We tooke him setting of boyes Copies.

CADE Here's a Villaine.   2250

WEAUER Ha's a Booke in his pocket with red Letters in't.

CADE Nay then he is a Coniurer.

BUTCHER Nay, he can make Obligations, and write Court
hand.

CADE I am sorry for't: The man is a proper man of mine
Honour: vnlesse I finde him guilty, he shall not die.
Come hither sirrah, I must examine thee: What is thy
name?

CLEARKE *Emanuell.*

BUTCHER They vse to writ y^t on the top of Letters: 'Twill   2260
go hard with you.

CADE Let me alone: (*To the Clearke*) Dost thou vse to write
thy name? Or hast thou a marke to thy selfe, like an
honest plain dealing man?

CLEARKE Sir I thanke God, I haue bin so well brought vp,
that I can write my name.

ALL CADES FOLLOWERS He hath confest: away with him:
he's a Villaine and a Traitor.

CADE Away with him I say: Hang him with his Pen and
2270   Inke-horne about his necke.
                              Exit one with the Clearke
        Enter a Messenger
MESSENGER Where's our Generall?
CADE Heere I am thou particular fellow.
MESSENGER Fly, fly, fly, Sir *Humfrey Stafford* and his brother
    are hard by, with the Kings Forces.
CADE Stand villaine, stand, or Ile fell thee downe: he shall
    be encountred with a man as good as himselfe. He is
    but a Knight, is a?
MESSENGER No.
CADE To equall him I will make my selfe a knight
2280   presently;
        Kneeles and Knights himselfe
    Rise vp Sir *Iohn Mortimer*.
        Rises
    Now haue at him.
        Enter Sir Humfrey Stafford, and his Brother, with
        Drum and Soldiers
STAFFORD (*to Cades followers*)
    Rebellious Hinds, the filth and scum of Kent,
    Mark'd for the Gallowes: Lay your Weapons downe,
    Home to your Cottages: forsake this Groome.
    The King is mercifull, if you reuolt.
BROTHER (*to Cades followers*)
    But angry, wrathfull, and inclin'd to blood,
    If you go forward: therefore yeeld, or dye.
CADE (*to his followers*)
    As for these silken-coated slaues I passe not,
2290   It is to you good people, that I speake,
    Ouer whom (in time to come) I hope to raigne:
    For I am rightfull heyre vnto the Crowne.
STAFFORD
    Villaine, thy Father was a Playsterer,
    And thou thy selfe a Sheareman, art thou not?
CADE
    And *Adam* was a Gardiner.
BROTHER   And what of that?
CADE
    Marry, this: *Edmund Mortimer* Earle of March,
    Married the Duke of *Clarence* daughter, did he not?
STAFFORD I sir.
CADE
    By her he had two children at one birth.
2300 BROTHER That's false.
CADE
    I, there's the question; But I say, 'tis true:
    The elder of them being put to nurse,
    Was by a begger-woman stolne away,
    And ignorant of his birth and parentage,
    Became a Bricklayer, when he came to age.
    His sonne am I, deny it and you can.
BUTCHER
    Nay, 'tis too true, therefore he shall be King.
WEAUER Sir, he made a Chimney in my Fathers house, &
    the brickes are aliue at this day to testifie: therefore
2310   deny it not.

STAFFORD (*to Cades followers*)
    And will you credit this base Drudges Wordes,
    That speakes he knowes not what.
ALL CADES FOLLOWERS
    I marry will we: therefore get ye gone.
BROTHER
    Iacke Cade, the D. of York hath taught you this.
CADE (*aside*)
    He lyes, for I inuented it my selfe.
    (*Alowd*) Go too Sirrah, tell the King from me, that for
    his Fathers sake *Henry* the fift, (in whose time, boyes
    went to Span-counter for French Crownes) I am content
    he shall raigne, but Ile be Protector ouer him.
BUTCHER And furthermore, wee'l haue the Lord *Sayes* 2320
    head, for selling the Dukedome of *Maine*.
CADE And good reason: for thereby is England main'd
    and faine to go with a staffe, but that my puissance
    holds it vp. Fellow-Kings, I tell you, that that Lord *Say*
    hath gelded the Commonwealth, and made it an
    Eunuch: & more then that, he can speake French, and
    therefore hee is a Traitor.
STAFFORD
    O grosse and miserable ignorance.
CADE Nay answer if you can: The Frenchmen are our
    enemies: go too then, I ask but this: Can he that speaks 2330
    with the tongue of an enemy, be a good Councellour,
    or no?
ALL CADES FOLLOWERS No, no, and therefore wee'l haue
    his head.
BROTHER (*to Stafford*)
    Well, seeing gentle words will not preuayle,
    Assaile them with the Army of the King.
STAFFORD
    Herald away, and throughout euery Towne,
    Proclaime them Traitors that are vp with *Cade*,
    That those which flye before the battell ends,
    May euen in their Wiues and Childrens sight,   2340
    Be hang'd vp for example at their doores:
    And you that be the Kings Friends follow me.
          Exit ⌈the Staffords and their Souldiers⌉
CADE
    And you that loue the Commons, follow me:
    Now shew your selues men, 'tis for Liberty.
    We will not leaue one Lord, one Gentleman:
    Spare none, but such as go in clouted shooen,
    For they are thrifty honest men, and such
    As would (but that they dare not) take our parts.
BUTCHER They are all in order, and march toward vs.
CADE
    But then are we in order, when we are   2350
    Most out of order. Come, march forward.   ⌈*Exeunt*⌉

    Alarums to the fight, ⌈excursions⌉ wherein both the   Sc. 14
    Staffords are slaine. Enter Cade, Dicke the Butcher   (4.3)
    and the rest
CADE Where's Dicke, the Butcher of Ashford?
BUTCHER Heere sir.
CADE They fell before thee like Sheepe and Oxen, & thou

behaued'st thy selfe, as if thou hadst beene in thine
owne Slaughter-house: Therfore thus will I reward
thee, the Lent shall bee as long againe as it is. Thou
shalt haue License to kill for a hundred lacking one.

BUTCHER I desire no more.

2360 CADE And to speake truth, thou deseru'st no lesse.

⌈*He apparrells himselfe in the Staffords Armour*⌉

This Monument of the victory will I beare, and the
bodies shall be dragg'd at my horse heeles, till I do
come to London, where we will haue the Maiors sword
born before vs.

BUTCHER If we meane to thriue, and do good, breake open
the Gaoles, and let out the Prisoners.

CADE Feare not that I warrant thee. Come, let's march
towards London.

Exeunt, ⌈*dragging the Staffords bodies*⌉

Sc. 15   *Enter the King* ⌈*reading*⌉ *a Supplication, and the*
(4.4)   *Queene with Suffolkes head, the Duke of*
Buckingham, and the Lord Say ⌈*with others*⌉

QUEENE ⌈*aside*⌉
Oft haue I heard that greefe softens the mind,
2370 And makes it fearefull and degenerate,
Thinke therefore on reuenge, and cease to weepe.
But who can cease to weepe, and looke on this.
Heere may his head lye on my throbbing brest:
But where's the body that I should imbrace?

BUCKINGHAM (*to the King*)
What answer makes your Grace to the Rebells
Supplication?

KING
Ile send some holy Bishop to intreat:
For God forbid, so many simple soules
Should perish by the Sword. And I my selfe,
Rather then bloody Warre shall cut them short,
2380 Will parley with *Iacke Cade* their Generall.
But stay, Ile read it ouer once againe.
He reades

QUEENE (*to Suffolkes head*)
Ah barbarous villaines: Hath this louely face,
Rul'd like a wandering Plannet ouer me,
And could it not inforce them to relent,
That were vnworthy to behold the same.

KING
Lord *Say, Iacke Cade* hath sworne to haue thy head.

SAY
I, but I hope your Highnesse shall haue his.

KING (*to the Queene*)
How now Madam? Still lamenting and mourning
Suffolkes death?
2390 I feare me (*Loue*) if that I had beene dead,
Thou wouldest not haue mourn'd so much for me.

QUEENE
No my Loue, I should not mourne, but dye for thee.
Enter a Messenger ⌈*in haste*⌉

KING
How now? What newes? Why com'st thou in such
haste?

MESSENGER
The Rebels are in Southwarke: Fly my Lord:
Iacke Cade proclaimes himselfe Lord *Mortimer*,
Descended from the Duke of *Clarence* house,
And calles your Grace Vsurper, openly,
And vowes to Crowne himselfe in Westminster.
His Army is a ragged multitude
Of Hindes and Pezants, rude and mercilesse: 2400
Sir *Humfrey Stafford*, and his Brothers death,
Hath giuen them heart and courage to proceede:
All Schollers, Lawyers, Courtiers, Gentlemen,
They call false Catterpillers, and intend their death.

KING
Oh gracelesse men: they know not what they do.

BUCKINGHAM
My gracious Lord, retire to Killingworth,
Vntill a power be rais'd to put them downe.

QUEENE
Ah were the Duke of Suffolke now aliue,
These Kentish Rebels would be soone appeas'd.

KING
Lord *Say*, the Traitors rabble hateth thee,   2410
Therefore away with vs to Killingworth.

SAY
So might your Graces person be in danger.
The sight of me is odious in their eyes:
And therefore in this Citty will I stay,
And liue alone as secret as I may.
Enter another Messenger

2. MESSENGER (*to the King*)
Iacke Cade hath almost gotten London-bridge.
The Citizens flye and forsake their houses:
The Rascall people, thirsting after prey,
Ioyne with the Traitor, and they ioyntly sweare
To spoyle the City, and your Royall Court.   2420

BUCKINGHAM (*to the King*)
Then linger not my Lord, away, take horse.

KING
Come *Margaret*, God our hope will succor vs.

QUEENE ⌈*aside*⌉
My hope is gone, now Suffolke is deceast.

KING (*to Say*)
Farewell my Lord, trust not the Kentish Rebels.

BUCKINGHAM (*to Say*)
Trust no body for feare you be betraid.

SAY
The trust I haue, is in mine innocence,
And therefore am I bold and resolute.
Exeunt ⌈*Say at one doore, the rest at another*⌉

Enter the Lord Skayles vpon the Tower walls   Sc. 16
walking. Enter three or four Citizens below   (4.5)

LORD SCAYLES How now, is *Iacke Cade* slaine?

1. CITIZEN No my Lord Scayles, nor likely to be slaine,
for he and his men haue wonne the bridge, killing all   2430
those that did withstand them. The Lord Mayor craueth
ayde of your honor from the Tower, to defend the Citie
from the Rebels.

LORD SCAYLES
    Such aide as I can spare, you shall command,
    But I am troubled here with them my selfe,
    The Rebels haue assay'd to win the Tower,
    Get you to Smythfield, there to gather head,
    And thither will I send you Mathew Goffe,
    Fight for your King, your Country, and your liues,
2440   And so farewell, for I must hence againe.
                Exeunt, Scayles aboue, Citizens below

Sc. 17   *Enter Iacke Cade, the Weauer, the Butcher and the*
(4.6)   *rest, and Cade strikes his sword vpon London stone*
CADE Now is *Mortimer* Lord of this City, and heere sitting
    vpon London Stone, I charge and command, that of
    the Cities cost the pissing Conduit run nothing but
    Clarret Wine this first yeare of our raigne. And now
    henceforward it shall be Treason for any, that calles
    me otherwise then Lord *Mortimer*.
        Enter a Soldier running
SOULDIER Iacke Cade, Iacke Cade.
CADE Sounes, knocke him downe there.
        They kill him
BUTCHER If this Fellow be wise, hee'l neuer call yee *Iacke*
2450   *Cade* more, I thinke he hath a very faire warning.
      ⌈*He takes a paper from the souldiers body, and*
      reades it⌉
    My Lord, there's an Army gathered together in
    Smithfield.
CADE Come, then let's go fight with them: but first, go
    on and set London Bridge a fire, and if you can, burne
    downe the Tower too. Come, let's away.
                Exeunt omnes

Sc. 18   *Alarums.* ⌈*Excursions, wherein*⌉ *Mathew Goffe is*
(4.7)   *slain, and all the rest of his men with him.*
     Then enter Iacke Cade, with his Company, among
     them the Butcher, the Weauer, and Iohn, a Rebell
CADE So sirs: now go some and pull down the Sauoy:
    others to'th Innes of Court, downe with them all.
BUTCHER I haue a suite vnto your Lordship.
CADE Bee it a Lordshippe, thou shalt haue it for that
2460   word.
BUTCHER Onely that the Lawes of England may come out
    of your mouth.
IOHN (*aside to his Fellowes*) Masse 'twill be sore Law then,
    for he was thrust in the mouth with a Speare, and 'tis
    not whole yet.
WEAUER (*aside to Iohn*) Nay *Iohn*, it wil be stinking Law,
    for his breath stinkes with eating toasted cheese.
CADE I haue thought vpon it, it shall bee so. Away, burne
    all the Records of the Realme, my mouth shall be the
2470   Parliament of England.
IOHN (*aside to his Fellowes*) Then we are like to haue biting
    Statutes vnlesse his teeth be pull'd out.
CADE And hence-forward all things shall be in Common.
        Enter a Messenger
MESSENGER My Lord, a prize, a prize, heeres the Lord *Say*,

which sold the Townes in France. He that made vs pay
one and twenty Fifteenes, and one shilling to the pound,
the last Subsidie.
     Enter a Rebell, with the Lord Say
CADE Well, hee shall be beheaded for it ten times: (*to Say*)
    ah thou Say, thou Surge, nay thou Buckram Lord, now
    art thou within point-blanke of our Iurisdiction Regall.   2480
    What canst thou answer to my Maiesty, for giuing vp
    of Normandie vnto Mounsieur *Basimecu*, the Dolphine
    of France? Be it knowne vnto thee by these presence,
    euen the presence of Lord *Mortimer*, that I am the
    Beesome that must sweepe the Court cleane of such
    filth as thou art: Thou hast most traiterously corrupted
    the youth of the Realme, in erecting a Grammar
    Schoole: and whereas before, our Fore-fathers had no
    other Bookes but the Score and the Tally, thou hast
    caused printing to be vs'd, and contrary to the King,   2490
    his Crowne, and Dignity, thou hast built a Paper-Mill.
    It will be prooued to thy Face, that thou hast men
    about thee, that vsually talke of a Nowne and a Verbe,
    and such abhominable wordes, as no Christian eare
    can endure to heare. Thou hast appointed Iustices of
    Peace, to call poore men before them, about matters
    they were not able to answer. Moreouer, thou hast put
    them in prison, and because they could not reade, thou
    hast hang'd them, when (indeede) onely for that cause
    they haue beene most worthy to liue. Thou dost ride   2500
    on a foot-cloth, dost thou not?
SAY What of that?
CADE Marry, thou ought'st not to let thy horse weare a
    Cloake, when honester men then thou go in their Hose
    and Doublets.
BUTCHER And worke in their shirts to, as my selfe for
    example, that am a butcher.
SAY You men of Kent.
BUTCHER What say you of Kent.
SAY
    Nothing but this: 'Tis *bona terra, mala gens*.   2510
CADE *Bonum terum*, sounds whats that?
BUTCHER He speakes French.
⌈1. REBELL⌉ No tis Dutch.
⌈2. REBELL⌉ No tis outtalian, I know it well inough.
SAY
    Heare me but speake, and beare mee wher'e you will:
    Kent, in the Commentaries *Cæsar* writ,
    Is term'd the ciuel'st place of all this Isle:
    Sweet is the Country, because full of Riches,
    The People Liberall, Valiant, Actiue, Wealthy,
    Which makes me hope you are not void of pitty.   2520
    I sold not *Maine*, I lost not *Normandie*,
    Yet to recouer them would loose my life:
    Iustice with fauour haue I alwayes done,
    Prayres and Teares haue mou'd me, Gifts could neuer.
    When haue I ought exacted at your hands?
    But to maintaine the King, the Realme and you,
    Large gifts haue I bestow'd on learned Clearkes,
    Because my Booke preferr'd me to the King,
    And seeing Ignorance is the curse of God,

2530 Knowledge the Wing wherewith we flye to heauen.
Vnlesse you be possest with diuellish spirits,
You cannot but forbeare to murther me:
This Tongue hath parlied vnto Forraigne Kings
For your behoofe.
CADE Tut, when struck'st thou one blow in the field?
SAY
Great men haue reaching hands: oft haue I struck
Those that I neuer saw, and strucke them dead.
REBELL O monstrous Coward! What, to come behinde
Folkes?
SAY
2540 These cheekes are pale for watching for your good.
CADE Giue him a box o'th'eare, and that wil make 'em
red againe.
          ⌈One of the Rebells strikes Say⌉
SAY
Long sitting to determine poore mens causes,
Hath made me full of sicknesse and diseases.
CADE Ye shall haue a hempen Caudle then, & the helth
oth hatchet.
BUTCHER (to Say) Why dost thou quiuer man?
SAY
The Palsie, and not feare prouokes me.
CADE Nay, he noddes at vs, as who should say, Ile be
2550 euen with you. Ile see if his head will stand steddier
on a pole, or no: Take him away, and behead him.
SAY
Tell me: wherein haue I offended most?
Haue I affected wealth, or honor? Speake.
Are my Chests fill'd vp with extorted Gold?
Is my Apparrell sumptuous to behold?
Whom haue I iniur'd, that ye seeke my death?
These hands are free from guiltlesse bloodshedding,
This breast from harbouring foule deceitfull thoughts.
O let me liue.
2560 CADE (aside) I feele remorse in my selfe with his words:
but Ile bridle it: he shall dye, and it bee but for pleading
so well for his life. (Alowd) Away with him, he ha's a
Familiar vnder his Tongue, he speakes not a Gods
name. Goe, take him away I say, to the standerd in
Cheapeside, and strike off his head presently, and then
go to milende-greene, breake into his Sonne in Lawes
house, Sir Iames Cromer, and strike off his head, and
bring them both vppon two poles hither.
ALL CADES FOLLOWERS It shall be done.
SAY
2570 Ah Countrimen: If when you make your prair's,
God should be so obdurate as your selues:
How would it fare with your departed soules,
And therefore yet relent, and saue my life.
CADE Away with him, and do as I command ye:
          Exeunt ⌈the Butcher and⌉ one or two, with the
                                                  Lord Say
the proudest Peere in the Realme, shall not weare a
head on his shoulders, vnlesse he pay me tribute: there
shall not a maid be married, but she shall pay to me
her Maydenhead ere they haue it: Married men shall
hold of mee in Capite. And we charge and command,

that their wiues be as free as heart can wish, or tongue   2580
can tell.
          Enter a Rebell
REBELL O Captaine, London bridge is a fire.
CADE Runne to Billingsgate, and fetche pitch and flaxe
and quench it.
          Enter the Butcher and a Sargiant
SARGIANT Iustice, iustice, I pray you sir, let me haue
iustice of this fellow here.
CADE Why what has he done?
SARGIANT Alasse sir he has rauisht my wife.
BUTCHER (to Cade) Why my Lord he would haue rested
me, and I went and entred my Action in his wiues   2590
proper house.
CADE Dicke follow thy sute in her common place, (to the
Sargiant) you horson villaine, you are a Sargiant, youle
take any man by the throate for twelue pence, and rest
a man when hees at dinner, and haue him to prison
ere the meate be out of his mouth. (To the Butcher) Go
Dicke take him hence, cut out his toong for cogging,
hough him for running, and to conclude, brane him
with his owne mace.   Exit Butcher with the Sargiant
REBELL My Lord, when shall we go to Cheapside, and   2600
take vp commodities vpon our billes?
CADE Marry presently. He that will lustily stand to it,
shall go with me, and take vp these commodities
following: item, a gowne, a kirtle, a petticoate, and a
smocke.
ALL CADES FOLLOWERS O braue.
          Enter two with the Lord Sayes head, and sir Iames
          Cromers, vpon two poles
CADE But is not this brauer: let them kisse one another:
For they lou'd well when they were aliue.
          ⌈The two heads are made to kisse⌉
Now part them againe, least they consult about the
giuing vp of some more Townes in France. Soldiers,   2610
deferre the spoile of the Citie vntill night: for with these
borne before vs, in steed of Maces, will we ride through
the streets, & at euery Corner haue them kisse. Away.
          ⌈Exit two with the heads. The others begin to
                                                  follow⌉
Vp Fish-streete, downe Saint Magnes corner, kill and
knocke downe, throw them into Thames:
          Sound a parley
What noise is this? Dare any be so bold to sound
Retreat or Parley when I command them kill?
          Enter Buckingham, and old Clifford
BUCKINGHAM
I heere they be, that dare and will disturb thee:
Know Cade, we come Ambassadors from the King
Vnto the Commons, whom thou hast misled,   2620
And heere pronounce free pardon to them all,
That will forsake thee, and go home in peace.
CLIFFORD
What say ye Countrimen, will ye relent
And yeeld to mercy, whil'st 'tis offered you,
Or let a rebbel leade you to your deaths.
Who loues the King, and will imbrace his pardon,
Fling vp his cap, and say, God saue his Maiesty.

Who hateth him, and honors not his Father,
Henry the fift, that made all France to quake,
2630 Shake he his weapon at vs, and passe by.
          They ⌈fling vp their caps and⌉ forsake Cade
ALL CADES FOLLOWERS God saue the King, God saue the
King.
CADE What Buckingham and Clifford are ye so braue?
(*To the Rabble*) And you base Pezants, do ye beleeue
him, will you needs be hang'd with your Pardons about
your neckes? Hath my sword therefore broke through
London gates, that you should leaue me at the White-
heart in Southwarke. I thought ye would neuer haue
giuen out these Armes til you had recouered your
2640 ancient Freedome. But you are all Recreants and
Dastards, and delight to liue in slauerie to the Nobility.
Let them breake your backes with burthens, take your
houses ouer your heads, rauish your Wiues and
Daughters before your faces. For me, I will make shift
for one, and so Gods Cursse light vppon you all.
ALL CADES FOLLOWERS Wee'l follow *Cade*, wee'l follow *Cade*.
          They runne to Cade againe
CLIFFORD
Is *Cade* the sonne of *Henry* the fift,
That thus you do exclaime you'l go with him.
Will he conduct you through the heart of France,
2650 And make the meanest of you Earles and Dukes?
Alas, he hath no home, no place to flye too:
Nor knowes he how to liue, but by the spoile,
Vnlesse by robbing of your Friends, and vs.
Wer't not a shame, that whilst you liue at iarre,
The fearfull French, whom you late vanquished
Should make a start ore-seas, and vanquish you?
Me thinkes alreadie in this ciuill broyle,
I see them Lording it in London streets,
Crying *Villiago* vnto all they meete.
2660 Better ten thousand base-borne *Cades* miscarry,
Then you should stoope vnto a Frenchmans mercy.
To France, to France, and get what you haue lost:
Spare England, for it is your Natiue Coast:
Henry hath mony, you are strong and manly:
God on our side, doubt not of Victorie.
ALL CADES FOLLOWERS A Clifford, a Clifford, wee'l follow
the King, and Clifford.
          They forsake Cade
CADE (*aside*) Was euer Feather so lightly blowne too & fro,
as this multitude? The name of Henry the fift, hales
2670 them to an hundred mischiefes, and makes them leaue
mee desolate. I see them lay their heades together to
surprize me. My sword make way for me, for heere is
no staying: (*alowd*) in despight of the diuels and hell,
haue through the verie middest of you, and heauens
and honor be witnesse, that no want of resolution in
mee, but onely my Followers base and ignominious
treasons, makes me betake mee to my heeles.
          He runs through them with his staffe, and flies
                                        away
BUCKINGHAM
What, is he fled? Go some and follow him,

And he that brings his head vnto the King,
Shall haue a thousand Crownes for his reward.   2680
          Exeunt some Rebells after Cade
(*To the remaining Rebells*)
Follow me souldiers, wee'l deuise a meane,
To reconcile you all vnto the King.   *Exeunt omnes*

Sound Trumpets. Enter King, Queene, and Somerset   Sc. 19
on the Tarras   (4.8)
KING
Was euer King that ioy'd an earthly Throne,
And could command no more content then I?
No sooner was I crept out of my Cradle,
But I was made a King, at nine months olde.
Was neuer Subiect long'd to be a King,
As I do long and wish to be a Subiect.
          Enter Buckingham and Clifford ⌈on the Tarras⌉
BUCKINGHAM (*to the King*)
Health and glad tydings to your Maiesty.
KING
Why Buckingham, is the Traitor *Cade* surpris'd?   2690
Or is he but retir'd to make him strong?
          Enter below Multitudes with Halters about their
          Neckes
CLIFFORD
He is fled my Lord, and all his powers do yeeld,
And humbly thus with halters on their neckes,
Expect your Highnesse doome of life, or death.
KING
Then heauen set ope thy euerlasting gates,
To entertaine my vowes of thankes and praise.
(*To the Multitudes below*)
Souldiers, this day haue you redeem'd your liues,
And shew'd how well you loue your Prince &
          Countrey:
Continue still in this so good a minde,
And *Henry* though he be infortunate,   2700
Assure your selues will neuer be vnkinde:
And so with thankes, and pardon to you all,
I do dismisse you to your seuerall Countries.
ALL CADES FORMER FOLLOWERS God saue the King, God
saue the King.   ⌈*Exeunt Multitudes, below*⌉
          Enter a Messenger ⌈on the Tarras⌉
MESSENGER (*to the King*)
Please it your Grace to be aduertised,
The Duke of Yorke is newly come from Ireland,
And with a puissant and a mighty power
Of Gallow-glasses and stout Irish Kernes,
Is marching hitherward in proud array,   2710
And still proclaimeth as he comes along,
His Armes are onely to remoue from thee
The Duke of Somerset, whom he tearmes a Traitor.
KING
Thus stands my state, 'twixt Cade and Yorke distrest,
Like to a Ship, that hauing scap'd a Tempest,
Is straight way calmd, and boorded with a Pyrate.
But now is Cade driuen backe, his men dispierc'd,
And now is Yorke in Armes, to second him.

I pray thee Buckingham go and meete him,
2720 And aske him what's the reason of these Armes:
Tell him, Ile send Duke *Edmund* to the Tower,
And *Somerset* we will commit thee thither,
Vntill his Army be dismist from him.

SOMERSET

My Lord, Ile yeelde my selfe to prison willingly,
Or vnto death, to do my Countrey good.

KING (*to Buckingham*)

In any case, be not to rough in termes,
For he is fierce, and cannot brooke hard Language.

BUCKINGHAM

I will my Lord, and doubt not so to deale,
As all things shall redound vnto your good.

KING

2730 Come wife, let's in, and learne to gouern better,
For yet may England curse my wretched raigne.

                    Flourish. Exeunt

Sc. 20   *Enter Cade*
(4.9) CADE Fye on Ambitions: fie on my selfe, that haue a
sword, and yet am ready to famish. These fiue daies
haue I hid me in these Woods, and durst not peepe
out, for all the Country is laid for me: but now am I
so hungry, that if I might haue a Lease of my life for
a thousand yeares, I could stay no longer. Wherefore
or a Bricke wall haue I climb'd into this Garden, to see
if I can eate Grasse, or picke a Sallet another while,
2740 which is not amisse to coole a mans stomacke this hot
weather: and I think this word Sallet was borne to do
me good: for many a time but for a Sallet, my braine-
pan had bene cleft with a brown Bill; and many a time
when I haue beene dry, & brauely marching, it hath
seru'd me insteede of a quart pot to drinke in: and now
the word Sallet must serue me to feed on.

       ⌐*Cade lies downe picking of hearbes and eating them.*⌐
       Enter Iden ⌐*and 5. of his men*⌐

IDEN

Lord, who would liue turmoyled in the Court,
And may enioy such quiet walkes as these?
This small inheritance my Father left me,
2750 Contenteth me, and worth a Monarchy.
I seeke not to waxe great by others waining,
Or gather wealth I care not with what enuy:
Sufficeth, that I haue maintaines my state,
And sends the poore well pleased from my gate.

         ⌐*Cade rises to his knees*⌐

CADE (*aside*) Sounes, heere's the Lord of the soile come to
seize me for a stray, for entering his Fee-simple without
leaue. (*To Iden*) A Villaine, thou wilt betray me, and
get a 1000. Crownes of the King by carrying my head
to him, but Ile make thee eate Iron like an Ostridge,
2760 and swallow my Sword like a great pin ere thou and I
part.

IDEN

Why rude Companion, whatsoere thou be,
I know thee not, why then should I betray thee?
Is't not enough to breake into my Garden,

And like a Theefe to come to rob my grounds:
Climbing my walles inspight of me the Owner,
But thou wilt braue me with these sawcie termes?

CADE Braue thee? I by the best blood that euer was
broach'd, and beard thee to. Looke on mee well, I haue
eate no meate these fiue dayes, yet come thou and thy   2770
fiue men, and if I doe not leaue you all as dead as a
doore naile, I pray God I may neuer eate grasse more.

IDEN

Nay, it shall nere be said, while England stands,
That *Alexander Iden* an Esquire of Kent,
Tooke oddes to combate a poore famisht man.
Oppose thy stedfast gazing eyes to mine,
See if thou canst out-face me with thy lookes:
Set limbe to limbe, and thou art farre the lesser:
Thy hand is but a finger to my fist,
Thy-legge a sticke compared with this Truncheon,   2780
My foote shall fight with all the strength thou hast,
And if mine arme be heaued in the Ayre,
Thy graue is digg'd already in the earth:
As for words, whose greatnesse answer's words,
Let this my sword report what speech forbeares.
(*To his men*) Stand you all aside.

CADE By my Valour: the most compleate Champion that
euer I heard. (*To his sword*) Steele, if thou turne the
edge, or cut not out the burly bon'd Clowne in chines
of Beefe, ere thou sleepe in thy Sheath, I beseech God   2790
on my knees thou mayst be turn'd to Hobnailes.

       ⌐*Cade stands:*⌐ *Heere they Fight, and Cade fals downe*

O I am slaine, Famine and no other hath slaine me,
let ten thousand diuelles come against me, and giue
me but the ten meales I haue lost, and I'de defie them
all. Wither Garden, and be henceforth a burying place
to all that do dwell in this house, because the
vnconquered soule of *Cade* is fled.

IDEN

Is't *Cade* that I haue slain, that monstrous traitor?
Sword, I will hallow thee for this thy deede,
And hang thee o're my Tombe, when I am dead.   2800
Ne're shall this blood be wiped from thy point,
But thou shalt weare it as a Heralds coate,
To emblaze the Honor that thy Master got.

CADE *Iden* farewell, and be proud of thy victory: Tell Kent
from me, she hath lost her best man, and exhort all
the World to be Cowards: For I that neuer feared any,
am vanquished by Famine, not by Valour.   *Dyes*

IDEN

How much thou wrong'st me, heauen be my iudge;
Die damned Wretch, the curse of her that bare thee:
And ⌐*stabbing him againe*⌐ as I thrust thy body in with
     my sword,   2810
So wish I, I might thrust thy soule to hell.
Hence will I dragge thee headlong by the heeles
Vnto a dunghill, which shall be thy graue,
And there cut off thy most vngracious head,
Which I will beare in triumph to the King,
Leauing thy trunke for Crowes to feed vpon.

                   Exit with the body

Sc. 21   *Enter Yorke, and his Army of Irish, with Drum and*
(5.1)   *Colours*

YORKE

From Ireland thus comes York to claim his right,
And plucke the Crowne from feeble *Henries* head.
Ring Belles alowd, burne Bonfires cleare and bright
2820   To entertaine great Englands lawfull King.
Ah *Sancta Maiestas*! who would not buy thee deere?
Let them obey, that knowes not how to Rule.
This hand was made to handle nought but Gold.
I cannot giue due action to my words,
Except a Sword or Scepter ballance it.
A Scepter shall it haue, haue I a sword,
On which Ile tosse the Fleure-de-Luce of France.
        Enter Buckingham
(*Aside*) Whom haue we heere? Buckingham to
        disturbe me?
The king hath sent him sure: I must dissemble.

BUCKINGHAM

2830   Yorke, if thou meanest wel, I greet thee well.

YORKE

Humfrey of Buckingham, I accept thy greeting.
Art thou a Messenger, or come of pleasure.

BUCKINGHAM

A Messenger from *Henry*, our dread Liege,
To know the reason of these Armes in peace.
Or why, thou being a Subiect, as I am,
Against thy Oath, and true Allegeance sworne,
Should raise so great a power without his leaue?
Or dare to bring thy Force so neere the Court?

YORKE (*aside*)

Scarse can I speake, my Choller is so great.
2840   Oh I could hew vp Rockes, and fight with Flint,
I am so angry at these abiect tearmes.
And now like *Aiax Telamonius*,
On Sheepe or Oxen could I spend my furie.
I am farre better borne then is the king:
More like a King, more Kingly in my thoughts.
But I must make faire weather yet a while,
Till *Henry* be more weake, and I more strong.
(*Alowd*) Buckingham, I prethee pardon me,
That I haue giuen no answer all this while:
2850   My minde was troubled with deepe Melancholly.
The cause why I haue brought this Armie hither,
Is to remoue proud Somerset from the King,
Seditious to his Grace, and to the State.

BUCKINGHAM

That is too much presumption on thy part:
But if thy Armes be to no other end,
The King hath yeelded vnto thy demand:
The Duke of Somerset is in the Tower.

YORKE

Vpon thine Honor is he Prisoner?

BUCKINGHAM

Vpon mine Honor he is Prisoner.

YORKE

2860   Then Buckingham I do dismisse my Powres.
Souldiers, I thanke you all: disperse your selues:

Meet me to morrow in S. Georges Field,
You shall haue pay, and euery thing you wish.
                        Exit souldiers
(*To Buckingham*) And let my Soueraigne, vertuous
        Henry,
Command my eldest sonne, nay all my sonnes,
As pledges of my Fealtie and Loue,
Ile send them all as willing as I liue:
Lands, Goods, Horse, Armor, any thing I haue
Is his to vse, so Somerset may die.

BUCKINGHAM

Yorke, I commend this kinde submission,   2870
We twaine will go into his Highnesse Tent.
        Enter King and Attendants

KING

Buckingham, doth Yorke intend no harme to vs
That thus he marcheth with thee arme in arme?

YORKE

In all submission and humility,
Yorke doth present himselfe vnto your Highnesse.

KING

Then what intends these Forces thou dost bring?

YORKE

To heaue the Traitor Somerset from hence,
And fight against that monstrous Rebell *Cade*,
Who since I heard to be discomfited.
        Enter Iden with Cades head

IDEN

If one so rude, and of so meane condition   2880
May passe into the presence of a King:
⌈*Kneeling*⌉ Loe, I present your Grace a Traitors head,
The head of *Cade*, whom I in combat slew.

KING

The head of *Cade*? Great God, how iust art thou?
Oh let me view his Visage being dead,
That liuing wrought me such exceeding trouble.
Tell me my Friend, art thou the man that slew him?

IDEN ⌈*rising*⌉

I wus, an't like your Maiesty.

KING

How art thou call'd? And what is thy degree?

IDEN

Alexander Iden, that's my name,   2890
A poore Esquire of Kent, that loues his King.

BUCKINGHAM (*to the King*)

So please it you my Lord, 'twere not amisse
He were created Knight for his good seruice.

KING

Iden, kneele downe,
        Iden kneeles and the King Knights him
                        rise vp a Knight:
        Iden rises
We giue thee for reward a thousand Markes,
And will, that thou henceforth attend on vs.

IDEN

May *Iden* liue to merit such a bountie,
And neuer liue but true vnto his Liege.   ⌈*Exit*⌉

Enter Queene and Somerset

KING

See Buckingham, Somerset comes wi'th' Queene,

2900   Go bid her hide him quickly from the Duke.

QUEENE

For thousand Yorkes he shall not hide his head,

But boldly stand, and front him to his face.

YORKE

How now? is Somerset at libertie?

Then Yorke vnloose thy long imprison'd thoughts,

And let thy tongue be equall with thy heart.

Shall I endure the sight of Somerset?

False King, why hast thou broken faith with me,

Knowing how hardly I can brooke abuse?

King did I call thee? No: thou art not King:

2910   Not fit to gouerne and rule multitudes,

Which dar'st not, no nor canst not rule a Traitor.

That Head of thine doth not become a Crowne:

Thy Hand is made to graspe a Palmers staffe,

And not to grace an awefull Princely Scepter.

That Gold, must round engirt these browes of mine,

Whose Smile and Frowne, like to *Achilles* Speare

Is able with the change, to kill and cure.

Heere is a hand to hold a Scepter vp,

And with the same to acte controlling Lawes:

2920   Giue place: by heauen thou shalt rule no more

O're him, whom heauen created for thy Ruler.

SOMERSET

O monstrous Traitor! I arrest thee Yorke

Of Capitall Treason 'gainst the King and Crowne:

Obey audacious Traitor, kneele for Grace.

YORKE (*to an Attendant*)

Sirrah, call in my sonnes to be my bale:

                         Exit Attendant

I know ere they will haue me go to Ward,

They'l pawne their swords for my infranchisement.

QUEENE ⌐*to Buckingham*⌐

Call hither *Clifford*, bid him come amaine,

To say, if that the Bastard boyes of Yorke

2930   Shall be the Surety for their Traitor Father.

                      Exit ⌐*Buckingham*⌐

YORKE

O blood-bespotted Neopolitan,

Out-cast of *Naples*, Englands bloody Scourge,

The sonnes of Yorke, thy betters in their birth,

Shall be their Fathers baile, and bane to those

That for my Surety will refuse the Boyes.

    Enter the Duke of Yorkes sonnes, Edward the Earle

    of March, and crook-backe Richard, ⌐*at the one*

    doore, with Drumme and soldiers⌐

See where they come, Ile warrant they'l make it good.

    ⌐*At the other doore,*⌐ *enter Clifford* ⌐*and his sonne,*

    with Drumme and souldiers⌐

QUEENE

And here comes *Clifford* to deny their baile.

CLIFFORD (*kneeling to the King*)

Health, and all happinesse to my Lord the King.

    He rises

YORKE

I thanke thee *Clifford*: Say, what newes with thee?

Nay, do not fright vs with an angry looke: 2940

We are thy Soueraigne *Clifford*, kneele againe;

For thy mistaking so, We pardon thee.

CLIFFORD

This is my King Yorke, I do not mistake,

But thou mistakes me much to thinke I do,

(*To the King*) To Bedlem with him, is the man growne

    mad.

KING

I Clifford, a Bedlem and ambitious humor

Makes him oppose himselfe against his King.

CLIFFORD

He is a Traitor, let him to the Tower,

And chop away that factious pate of his.

QUEENE

He is arrested, but will not obey: 2950

His sonnes (he sayes) shall giue their words for him.

YORKE (*to Edward and Richard*) Will you not Sonnes?

EDWARD

I Noble Father, if our words will serue.

RICHARD

And if words will not, then our Weapons shal.

CLIFFORD

Why what a brood of Traitors haue we heere?

YORKE

Looke in a Glasse, and call thy Image so.

I am thy King, and thou a false-heart Traitor:

Call hither to the stake my two braue Beares,

That with the very shaking of their Chaines,

They may astonish these fell-lurking Curres,   2960

(*To an Attendant*)

Bid Salsbury and Warwicke come to me.

                    Exit Attendant

    Enter the Earles of Warwicke, and Salisbury, ⌐*with*

    Drumme and souldiers⌐

CLIFFORD

Are these thy Beares? Wee'l bate thy Bears to death,

And manacle the Berard in their Chaines,

If thou dar'st bring them to the bayting place.

RICHARD

Oft haue I seene a hot ore-weening Curre,

Run backe and bite, because he was with-held,

Who being suffer'd with the Beares fell paw,

Hath clapt his taile, betweene his legges and cride,

And such a peece of seruice will you do,

If you oppose your selues to match Lord Warwicke.   2970

CLIFFORD

Hence heape of wrath, foule indigested lumpe,

As crooked in thy manners, as thy shape.

YORKE

Nay we shall heate you thorowly anon.

CLIFFORD

Take heede least by your heate you burne your selues.

KING

Why Warwicke, hath thy knee forgot to bow?

Old Salsbury, shame to thy siluer haire,

Thou mad misleader of thy brain-sicke sonne,

What wilt thou on thy death-bed play the Ruffian?
And seeke for sorrow with thy Spectacles?
2980   Oh where is Faith? Oh, where is Loyalty?
If it be banisht from the frostie head,
Where shall it finde a harbour in the earth?
Wilt thou go digge a graue to finde out Warre,
And shame thine honourable Age with blood?
Why art thou old, and want'st experience?
Or wherefore doest abuse it, if thou hast it?
For shame in dutie bend thy knee to me,
That bowes vnto the graue with mickle age.

SALISBURY

My Lord, I haue consider'd with my selfe
2990   The Title of this most renowned Duke,
And in my conscience, do repute his grace
The rightfull heyre to Englands Royall seate.

KING

Hast thou not sworne Allegeance vnto me?

SALISBURY I haue.

KING

Canst thou dispense with heauen for such an oath?

SALISBURY

It is great sinne, to sweare vnto a sinne:
But greater sinne to keepe a sinfull oath:
Who can be bound by any solemne Vow
3000   To do a murd'rous deede, to rob a man,
To force a spotlesse Virgins Chastitie,
To reaue the Orphan of his Patrimonie,
To wring the Widdow from her custom'd right,
And haue no other reason for this wrong,
But that he was bound by a solemne Oath?

QUEENE

A subtle Traitor needs no Sophister.

KING (to an Attendant)

Call Buckingham, and bid him arme himselfe.

                                    Exit Attendant

YORKE (to the King)

Call Buckingham, and all the friends thou hast,
I am resolu'd for death or dignitie.

CLIFFORD

The first I warrant thee, if dreames proue true.

WARWICKE

3010   You were best to go to bed, and dreame againe,
To keepe you from the Tempest of the field.

CLIFFORD

I am resolu'd to beare a greater storme,
Then any thou canst coniure vp to day:
And that Ile write vpon thy Burgonet,
Might I but know thee by thy houshold Badge.

WARWICKE

Now by my Fathers badge, old *Neuils* Crest,
The rampant Beare chain'd to the ragged staffe,
This day Ile weare aloft my Burgonet,
As on a Mountaine top, the Cedar shewes,
3020   That keepes his leaues inspight of any storme,
Euen to affright thee with the view thereof.

CLIFFORD

And from thy Burgonet Ile rend thy Beare,

And tread it vnder foot with all contempt,
Despight the Bearard, that protects the Beare.

YONG CLIFFORD

And so to Armes victorious Father,
To quell the Rebels, and their Complices.

RICHARD

Fie, Charitie for shame, speake not in spight,
For you shall sup with Iesu Christ to night.

YONG CLIFFORD

Foule stygmaticke that's more then thou canst tell.

RICHARD

If not in heauen, you'l surely sup in hell.   3030

                                    Exeunt seuerally

Alarmes to the battaile, and then enter the Duke of   Sc. 22
Somerset and Richard fighting, and Richard kils   (5.2)
him ⌈*vnder the signe of the Castle in saint Albones*⌉

RICHARD So lye thou there:
For vnderneath an Ale-house paltry signe,
The Castle in S. *Albons*, Somerset
Hath made the Wizard famous in his death:
Sword, hold thy temper; Heart, be wrathfull still:
Priests pray for enemies, but Princes kill.

                Exit ⌈*with Somersets body. The signe is*
                                    remoued⌉

⌈*Alarme again, and*⌉ *enter the Earle of Warwicke*   Sc. 23
alone   (5.3)

WARWICKE

Clifford of Cumberland, 'tis Warwicke calles:
And if thou dost not hide thee from the Beare,
Now when the angrie Trumpet sounds alarum,
And dead mens cries do fill the emptie ayre,   3040
Clifford I say, come forth and fight with me,
Proud Northerne Lord, Clifford of Cumberland,
Warwicke is hoarse with calling thee to armes.

    Clifford speakes within

Warwicke stand still, and stir not till I come.

    Enter Yorke

WARWICKE

How now my Noble Lord? What all a-foot.

YORKE

The deadly handed Clifford slew my Steed:
But match to match I haue encountred him,
And made a prey for Carrion Kytes and Crowes
Euen of the bonnie beast he lou'd so well.

    Enter Clifford

WARWICKE (to Clifford)

Of one or both of vs the time is come.   3050

YORKE

Hold Warwick: seek thee out some other chace
For I my selfe must hunt this Deere to death.

WARWICKE

Then nobly Yorke, 'tis for a Crown thou fightst:
(*To Clifford*) As I intend Clifford to thriue to day,
It greeues my soule to leaue thee vnassail'd.

                                    Exit Warwicke

YORKE

  Clifford, since we are singled here alone,

  Be this the day of doome to one of vs,

  For know my heart hath sworne immortal hate

  To thee, and all the house of Lancaster.

CLIFFORD

3060   And here I stand, and pitch my foot to thine,

  Vowing not to stir, till thou or I be slaine.

  For neuer shall my heart be safe at rest,

  Till I haue spoyld the hatefull house of Yorke.

    Alarmes, and they fight, and Yorke kils Clifford

YORKE

  Now Lancaster sit sure, thy sinowes shrinke,

  Come fearefull Henry grouelling on thy face,

  Yeelde vp thy Crowne vnto the Prince of Yorke.

                        Exit Yorke

    Alarmes, then enter yoong Clifford alone

YONG CLIFFORD

  Shame and Confusion all is on the rout,

  Feare frames disorder, and disorder wounds

  Where it should guard. O Warre, thou sonne of hell,

3070   Whom angry heauens do make their minister,

  Throw in the frozen bosomes of our part,

  Hot Coales of Vengeance. Let no Souldier flye.

  He that is truly dedicate to Warre,

  Hath no selfe-loue: nor he that loues himselfe,

  Hath not essentially, but by circumstance

  The name of Valour.

    He sees his fathers body

                    O let the vile world end,

  And the premised Flames of the Last day,

  Knit earth and heauen together.

  Now let the generall Trumpet blow his blast,

3080   Particularities, and pettie sounds

  To cease. Was't thou ordained (deere Father)

  To loose thy youth in peace, and to atcheeue

  The Siluer Liuery of aduised Age,

  And in thy Reuerence, and thy Chaire-dayes, thus

  To die in Ruffian battell? Euen at this sight,

  My heart is turn'd to stone: and while 'tis mine,

  It shall be stony. Yorke, not our old men spares:

  No more will I their Babes, Teares Virginall,

  Shall be to me, euen as the Dew to Fire,

3090   And Beautie, that the Tyrant oft reclaimes,

  Shall to my flaming wrath, be Oyle and Flax:

  Henceforth, I will not haue to do with pitty.

  Meet I an infant of the house of Yorke,

  Into as many gobbits will I cut it

  As wilde *Medea* yong *Absirtis* did.

  In cruelty, will I seeke out my Fame.

  Come thou new ruine of olde Cliffords house:

    He takes his fathers body vp on his backe

  As did *Æneas* old *Anchyses* beare,

  So beare I thee vpon my manly shoulders:

3100   But then, *Æneas* bare a liuing loade;

  Nothing so heauy as these woes of mine.

                  Exit with the body

    ⌐*Alarmes againe, and then enter three or foure,*   **Sc. 24**

    bearing the Duke of Buckingham wounded to his   **(5.4)**

    Tent⌐. *Alarmes still. Enter King, Queene, and others*

QUEENE

  Away my Lord, you are slow, for shame away.

KING

  Can we outrun the Heauens? Good *Margaret* stay.

QUEENE

  What are you made of? You'l nor fight nor fly:

  Now is it manhood, wisedome, and defence,

  To giue the enemy way, and to secure vs

  By what we can, which can no more but flye.

    Alarum a farre off

  If you be tane, we then should see the bottome

  Of all our Fortunes: but if we haply scape,

  (As well we may, if not through your neglect)   3110

  We shall to London get, where you are lou'd,

  And where this breach now in our Fortunes made

  May readily be stopt.

    Enter yong Clifford

YONG CLIFFORD (*to the King*)

  But that my hearts on future mischeefe set,

  I would speake blasphemy ere bid you flye:

  But flye you must: Vncureable discomfite

  Reignes in the hearts of all our present parts.

  Away for your releefe, and we will liue

  To see their day, and them our Fortune giue.

  Away my Lord, away.   *Exeunt* 3120

    Alarum. Retreat. Enter Yorke, his sonnes Edward   **Sc. 25**

    and Richard, and Soldiers, with Drum & Colours   **(5.5)**

YORKE (*to Edward and Richard*)

  How now boyes, fortunate this fight hath bene,

  I hope to vs and ours, for Englands good,

  And our great honour, that so long we lost,

  Whilst faint-heart Henry did vsurpe our rights:

  Of Salsbury, who can report of him,

  That Winter Lyon, who in rage forgets

  Aged contusions, and all brush of Time:

  And like a Gallant, in the brow of youth,

  Repaires him with Occasion. This happy day

  Is not it selfe, nor haue we wonne one foot,   3130

  If Salsbury be lost.

RICHARD   My Noble Father:

  Three times to day I holpe him to his horse,

  Three times bestrid him: Thrice I led him off,

  Perswaded him from any further act:

  But still where danger was, still there I met him,

  And like rich hangings in a homely house,

  So was his Will, in his old feeble body.

    Enter Salisbury and Warwicke

EDWARD (*to Yorke*)

  See noble father, where they both do come,

  The onely props vnto the house of Yorke.

SALISBURY

  Now by my Sword, well hast thou fought to day: 3140

  By'th'Masse so did we all. I thanke you *Richard*.

God knowes how long it is I haue to liue:
And it hath pleas'd him that three times to day
You haue defended me from imminent death.
Well Lords, we haue not got that which we haue,
'Tis not enough our foes are this time fled,
Being opposites of such repayring Nature.

YORKE

I know our safety is to follow them,
For (as I heare) the King is fled to London,
3150　To call a present Court of Parliament:

Let vs pursue him ere the Writs go forth.
What sayes Lord Warwicke, shall we after them?

WARWICKE

After them: nay before them if we can:
Now by my hand (Lords) 'twas a glorious day.
Saint Albons battell wonne by famous Yorke,
Shall be eterniz'd in all Age to come.
Sound Drummes and Trumpets, and to London all,
And more such dayes as these, to vs befall.

⌐Flourish.⌐ Exeunt

FINIS

ADDITIONAL PASSAGES

A. We adopt the Quarto version of the Queene's initial speech, lines 24–9; the Folio version, which follows, is probably the author's original draft.

QUEENE

Great King of England, & my gracious Lord,
The mutuall conference that my minde hath had,
By day, by night; waking, and in my dreames,
In Courtly company, or at my Beades,
With you mine *Alder liefest* Soueraigne,
Makes me the bolder to salute my King,
With ruder termes, such as my wit affoords,
And ouer ioy of heart doth minister.

B. For 631–2.2 Q substitutes the following. Q may here report a revision made in rehearsal to cover the Spirit's descent.

The Spirit sinkes downe againe

BULLINGBROOKE

Then downe I say, vnto the damned poule,
Where Pluto in his firie Waggon sits,
Ryding amidst the singde and parched smoakes,
The Rode of *Dytas* by the Riuer Stykes.
There howle and burne for euer in those flames.
Rise *Iordaine* rise, and staie thy charming Spels.
Sounes, we are betraide.

C. The entire debate on Duke Humfrey's death in Sc. 9 is handled differently by the Quarto from the Folio. We retain the Folio version of the debate, but the Quarto version may represent authorial revision. The following Q lines, roughly corresponding to 1500–11.1, are of particular interest because they supply Buckingham with speeches for this latter part of the scene.

[YORKE]

Let me haue some bands of chosen soldiers,
And Yorke shall trie his fortune gainst those kernes.

QUEENE

Yorke thou shalt. My Lord of Buckingham,
Let it be your charge to muster vp such souldiers
As shall suffise him in these needfull warres.

BUCKINGHAM

Madame I will, and leauie such a band

As soone shall ouercome those Irish Rebels,
But Yorke, where shall those soldiers staie for thee?

YORKE

At Bristow, I wil expect them ten daies hence.

BUCKINGHAM

Then thither shall they come, and so farewell.　10

Exet Buckingham.

YORKE

Adieu my Lord of Buckingham.

QUEENE

Suffolke remember what you haue to do.
And you Lord Cardinall concerning Duke Humphrey,
Twere good that you did see to it in time,
Come let vs go, that it may be performde.

Exet omnis. Manet Yorke

D. We adopt the Quarto version of the confrontation between Clifford and Yorke at 3056–66.1; the Folio version, an edited text of which follows, is probably the author's original draft.

CLIFFORD

What seest thou in me Yorke? Why dost thou pause?

YORKE

With thy braue bearing should I be in loue,
But that thou art so fast mine enemie.

CLIFFORD

Nor should thy prowesse want praise & esteeme,
But that 'tis shewne ignobly, and in Treason.

YORKE

So let it helpe me now against thy sword,
As I in iustice, and true right expresse it.

CLIFFORD

My soule and bodie on the action both.

YORKE

A dreadfull lay, addresse thee instantly.

CLIFFORD

La fin Corrone les oeuures.　10

Alarmes, and they fight, and Yorke kils Clifford

YORKE

Thus Warre hath giuen thee peace, for yᵘ art still,
Peace with his soule, heauen if it be thy will

Exit Yorke

RICHARD DUKE OF YORKE

(3 HENRY VI)

THE play printed in the 1623 Folio as *The third Part of Henry the Sixt, with the death of the Duke of Yorke* was described on the title-page of its first, unauthoritative publication in 1595 as *The true Tragedie of Richard Duke of Yorke, and the death of good King Henrie the Sixt, with the whole Contention betweene the two Houses Lancaster and Yorke*. It is clearly a continuation of *The First Part of the Contention*, taking up the story where that play had ended, with the aspirations of Richard, Duke of Yorke to the English throne, and was probably composed immediately afterwards.

The final scenes of *The First Part of the Contention* briefly introduce two of Yorke's sons, Edward (the eldest) and Richard (already described as a 'foule indigested lumpe, | As crooked in . . . manners as [in] shape'). They, along with their brothers Edmund, Earle of Rutland, and George (later Duke of Clarence), figure more prominently in *Richard Duke of Yorke*. The first scenes show Yorke apparently fulfilling his ambition, as Henry VI weakly cedes his rights to the throne after his death; but Queene Margaret leads an army against Yorke, and, when he is captured, personally taunts him with news of the murder of his youngest son, stabs Yorke to death, and commands that his head be 'set on Yorke Gates'. (This powerful scene includes the line 'Oh Tygres Heart, wrapt in a Womans Hide', paraphrased by Robert Greene before September 1592, which establishes the upward limit of the play's date.)

Though Richard of Yorke dies early in the action, the remainder of the play centres on his sons' efforts (aided by Warwicke's politic schemings) to avenge his death and to establish the dominance of Yorkists over Lancastrians. The balance of power shifts frequently, and the brothers' alliance crumbles, but finally Queene Margaret, with her French allies, is defeated and captured, and Richard of Yorke's surviving sons avenge their father's death by killing her son, Edward, before her eyes. Richard of Gloster starts to clear his way to the throne by murdering 'Good King Henry' in the Tower, and the play ends with the new King Edward IV exulting in his 'Countries peace, and Brothers loues' while Richard makes clear to the audience that Edward's self-confidence is ill-founded.

Though the play is loud and strife-ridden with war, power politics, and personal ambition, a concern with humane values emerges in the subtle and touching continuing portrayal of the quietist Henry VI, a saintly fool who meditates on the superiority of humble contentment to regal misery in an emblematic scene (Sc. 9) that epitomizes the tragedy of civil strife.

Richard Duke of Yorke, like *The First Part of the Contention*, draws extensively on English chronicle history. Historically, the period of the action covers about sixteen years (1455 to 1471), but events are telescoped and rearranged; for instance, the opening scenes move rapidly from the Battle of St Albans (1445) to Yorke's death (1450); the future Richard III was only three years old, and living abroad, at the time of this opening battle in which he takes an active part; and Richard's murder of Henry owes more to legend than to fact.

Our text is based on the Folio, probably printed from an early authorial draft. The Octavo (1595) seems to derive from memories of performances; we accept some of its clarifications and improvements.

THE NAMES OF THE ACTORS

Of the Kings Partie

KING HENRY the Sixt

QUEENE MARGARET

PRINCE EDWARD, their sonne

Duke of SOMERSET

Duke of EXETER

Earle of NORTHUMBERLAND

Earle of WESTMERLAND

Lord CLIFFORD

Stafford

SOMERUILE

Henry, young Earle of Richmond

A SOULDIER who hath killed his Father

A HUNTSMAN who guards King Edward

The Diuided House of Neuil

Earle of WARWICKE, first of Yorkes Partie, later of Lancasters

Marquesse of MOUNTAGUE, his brother, of Yorkes Partie

Earle of OXFORD, their brother in law, of Lancasters Partie

Lord HASTINGS, their brother in law, of Yorkes Partie

Of the Duke of Yorkes Partie

Richard Plantagenet, Duke of YORKE

EDWARD, Earle of March, his sonne, later Duke of Yorke and KING EDWARD the Fourth

LADY GRAY, a widow, later Edwards wife and Queene

Earle RIUERS, her brother

GEORGE, Edwards brother, later Duke OF CLARENCE

RICHARD, Edwards brother, later Duke OF GLOSTER

Edmund, Earle of RUTLAND, Edwards brother

Rutlands TUTOR, a Chaplaine

SIR IOHN Mortimer, Yorkes vnckle

Sir Hugh Mortimer, his brother

Duke of NORFOLKE

Sir William Stanley

Earle of Pembrooke

Sir Iohn MOUNTGOMERIE

A NOBLE MAN

2. KEEPERS

3. WATCHMEN, who guard King Edwards Tent

LIEUTENANT of the Tower

The French

KING LEWIS

Lady BONA, his sister in law

Lord Bourbon, the French High Admirall

Others

A SOULDIER who hath killed his sonne

Maior of Couentry

MAIOR of Yorke

Brethren of Yorke

Souldiers, Messengers, and Attendants

The true Tragedie of Richard Duke of Yorke, and the good King Henry the Sixt

Sc. 1
(1.1)

A Chayre of State. Alarum. Enter Richard
Plantagenet Duke of Yorke, his sonnes Edward and
Crookeback Richard, Norfolke, Mountague,
Warwicke, ⌈with Drumme⌉ and Souldiers, ⌈all with
white Roses in their hats⌉

WARWICKE
    I wonder how the King escap'd our hands?

YORKE
    While we pursu'd the Horsmen of yᵉ North,
    He slyly stole away, and left his men:
    Whereat the great Lord of Northumberland,
    Whose Warlike eares could neuer brooke retreat,
    Chear'd vp the drouping Army, and himselfe,
    Lord *Clifford* and Lord *Stafford* all a-brest
    Charg'd our maine Battailes Front: and breaking in,
    Were by the Swords of common Souldiers slaine.

EDWARD
10 Lord *Staffords* Father, Duke of *Buckingham*,
    Is either slaine or wounded dangerous.
    I cleft his Beauer with a down-right blow:
    That this is true (Father) behold his blood.
        He shewes a bloody sword

MOUNTAGUE ⌈*to Yorke*⌉
    And Brother, here's the Earle of Wiltshires blood,
        He shewes a bloody sword
    Whom I encountred as the Battels ioyn'd.

RICHARD (*to Somersets head, which he shewes*)
    Speake thou for me, and tell them what I did.

YORKE
    Richard hath best deseru'd of all my sonnes:
    (*To the head*) But is your Grace dead, my Lord of
        Somerset?

NORFOLKE
    Such hape haue all the line of *Iohn of Gaunt*.

RICHARD
20 Thus do I hope to shake King *Henries* head.
        ⌈*He holds aloft the head, then throwes it downe*⌉

WARWICKE
    And so doe I, victorious Prince of *Yorke*.
    Before I see thee seated in that Throne,
    Which now the House of *Lancaster* vsurpes,
    I vow by Heauen, these eyes shall neuer close.
    This is the Pallace of the fearefull King,
    And this (*pointing to the Chayre of State*) the Regall
        Seat: possesse it *Yorke*,
    For this is thine, and not King *Henries* Heires.

YORKE
    Assist me then, sweet *Warwick*, and I will,
    For hither we haue broken in by force.

NORFOLKE
30 Wee'le all assist you: he that flyes, shall dye.

YORKE
    Thankes gentle *Norfolke*, stay by me my Lords,
    And Souldiers stay and lodge by me this Night.
        They goe vp vpon the State

WARWICKE
    And when the King comes, offer him no violence,
    Vnlesse he seeke to thrust you out perforce.
        ⌈*The Souldiers withdraw*⌉

YORKE
    The Queene this day here holds her Parliament,
    But little thinkes we shall be of her counsaile,
    By words or blowes here let vs winne our right.

RICHARD
    Arm'd as we are, let's stay within this House.

WARWICKE
    The bloody Parliament shall this be call'd,
    Vnlesse *Plantagenet*, Duke of *Yorke*, be King,   40
    And bashfull *Henry* depos'd, whose Cowardize
    Hath made vs by-words to our enemies.

YORKE
    Then leaue me not my Lords: be resolute,
    I meane to take possession of my Right.

WARWICKE
    Neither the King, nor he that loues him best,
    The prowdest hee that holds vp *Lancaster*,
    Dares stirre a Wing, if *Warwick* shake his Bells.
    Ile plant *Plantagenet*, root him vp who dares:
    Resolue thee *Richard*, clayme the English Crowne.
        ⌈*Yorke sits in the Chayre.*⌉
        Flourish. Enter King Henry, Clifford,
        Northumberland, Westmerland, Exeter, and the rest,
        ⌈*all with red Roses in their hats*⌉

KING HENRY
    My Lords, looke where the sturdie Rebell sits,   50
    Euen in the Chayre of State: belike he meanes,
    Backt by the power of *Warwicke*, that false Peere,
    To aspire vnto the Crowne, and reigne as King.
    Earle of Northumberland, he slew thy Father,
    And thine, Lord *Clifford*, & you both haue vow'd
        reuenge
    On him, his sonnes, his fauorites, and his friends.

NORTHUMBERLAND
    If I be not, Heauens be reueng'd on me.

CLIFFORD
    The hope thereof, makes *Clifford* mourne in Steele.

WESTMERLAND
    What, shall we suffer this? lets pluck him down,
    My heart for anger burnes, I cannot brooke it.   60

KING HENRY
    Be patient, gentle Earle of Westmerland.

CLIFFORD

Patience is for Poultroones, such as he (*indicating
    Yorke*):
He durst not sit there, had your Father liu'd.
My gracious Lord, here in the Parliament
Let vs assayle the Family of *Yorke*.

NORTHUMBERLAND

Well hast thou spoken, Cousin be it so.

KING HENRY

Ah, know you not the Citie fauours them,
And they haue troupes of Souldiers at their beck?

EXETER

But when the Duke is slaine, they'le quickly flye.

KING HENRY

70 Farre be the thought of this from *Henries* heart,
To make a Shambles of the Parliament House.
Cousin of Exeter, frownes, words, and threats,
Shall be the Warre that *Henry* meanes to vse.
(*To Yorke*) Thou factious Duke of Yorke descend my
    Throne,
And kneele for grace and mercie at my feet,
I am thy Soueraigne.

YORKE   I am thine.

EXETER

For shame come downe, he made thee Duke of Yorke.

YORKE

It was mine Inheritance, as the Earledome was.

EXETER

Thy Father was a Traytor to the Crowne.

WARWICKE

80 *Exeter* thou art a Traytor to the Crowne,
In following this vsurping *Henry*.

CLIFFORD

Whom should hee follow, but his naturall King?

WARWICKE

True *Clifford*, and that's *Richard* Duke of Yorke.

KING HENRY (*to Yorke*)

And shall I stand, and thou sit in my Throne?

YORKE

It must and shall be so, content thy selfe.

WARWICKE (*to King Henry*)

Be Duke of Lancaster, let him be King.

WESTMERLAND

He is both King, and Duke of Lancaster,
And that the Lord of Westmerland shall maintaine.

WARWICKE

And *Warwick* shall disproue it. You forget,
90 That we are those which chas'd you from the field,
And slew your Fathers, and with Colours spread
Marcht through the Citie to the Pallace Gates.

NORTHUMBERLAND

Yes *Warwicke*, I remember it to my griefe,
And by his Soule, thou and thy House shall rue it.

WESTMERLAND (*to Yorke*)

Plantagenet, of thee and these thy Sonnes,
Thy Kinsmen, and thy Friends, Ile haue more liues
Then drops of bloud were in my Fathers Veines.

CLIFFORD (*to Warwicke*)

Vrge it no more, lest that in stead of words,

I send thee, *Warwicke*, such a Messenger,
As shall reuenge his death, before I stirre.   100

WARWICKE ⌈*to Yorke*⌉

Poore *Clifford*, how I scorne his worthlesse Threats.

YORKE ⌈*to King Henry*⌉

Will you we shew our Title to the Crowne?
If not, our Swords shall pleade it in the field.

KING HENRY

What Title hast thou Traytor to the Crowne?
Thy Father was as thou art, Duke of Yorke,
Thy Grandfather *Roger Mortimer*, Earle of March.
I am the Sonne of *Henry* the Fift,
Who made the Dolphin and the French to stoupe,
And seiz'd vpon their Townes and Prouinces.

WARWICKE

Talke not of France, sith thou hast lost it all.   110

KING HENRY

The Lord Protector lost it, and not I:
When I was crown'd, I was but nine moneths old.

RICHARD

You are old enough now, and yet me thinkes you
    loose:
(*To Yorke*) Father teare the Crowne from the Vsurpers
    Head.

EDWARD (*to Yorke*)

Sweet Father doe so, set it on your Head.

MOUNTAGUE (*to Yorke*)

Good Brother, as thou lou'st and honor'st Armes,
Let's fight it out, and not stand cauilling thus.

RICHARD

Sound Drummes and Trumpets, and the King will flye.

YORKE Sonnes peace.

⌈NORTHUMBERLAND⌉

Peace thou, and giue King *Henry* leaue to speake.   120

KING HENRY

Ah *Yorke*, why seekest thou to depose me?
Are we not both *Plantagenets* by birth,
And from two brothers lineallie discent?
Suppose by right and equitie thou be king,
Think'st thou, that I will leaue my Kingly Throne,
Wherein my Grandsire and my Father sat?
No: first shall Warre vnpeople this my Realme;
I, and their Colours often borne in France,
And now in England, to our hearts great sorrow,
Shall be my Winding-sheet. Why faint you Lords?   130
My Title's good, and better farre then his.

WARWICKE

Proue it *Henry*, and thou shalt be King.

KING HENRY

Henry the Fourth by Conquest got the Crowne.

YORKE

'Twas by Rebellion against his King.

KING HENRY ⌈*aside*⌉

I know not what to say, my Titles weake:
(*To Yorke*) Tell me, may not a King adopt an Heire?

YORKE What then?

KING HENRY

And if he may, then am I lawfull King:
For *Richard*, in the view of many Lords,

140 Resign'd the Crowne to *Henry* the Fourth,
Whose Heire my Father was, and I am his.

YORKE
He rose against him, being his Soueraigne,
And made him to resigne his Crowne perforce.

WARWICKE
Suppose, my Lords, he did it vnconstrayn'd,
Thinke you 'twere preiudiciall to his Crowne?

EXETER
No: for he could not so resigne his Crowne,
But that the next Heire should succeed and reigne.

KING HENRY
Art thou against vs, Duke of Exeter?

EXETER
His is the right, and therefore pardon me.

YORKE
150 Why whisper you, my Lords, and answer not?

EXETER ⌈*to King Henry*⌉
My Conscience tells me he is lawfull King.

KING HENRY ⌈*aside*⌉
All will reuolt from me, and turne to him.

NORTHUMBERLAND (*to Yorke*)
Plantagenet, for all the Clayme thou lay'st,
Thinke not, that *Henry* shall be so depos'd.

WARWICKE
Depos'd he shall be, in despight of all.

NORTHUMBERLAND
Thou art deceiu'd: 'tis not thy Southerne power
Of Essex, Norfolke, Suffolke, nor of Kent,
Which makes thee thus presumptuous and prowd,
Can set the Duke vp in despight of me.

CLIFFORD
160 King *Henry*, be thy Title right or wrong,
Lord *Clifford* vowes to fight in thy defence:
May that ground gape, and swallow me aliue,
Where I shall kneele to him that slew my Father.

KING HENRY
Oh *Clifford*, how thy words reuiue my heart.

YORKE
Henry of Lancaster, resigne thy Crowne:
What mutter you, or what conspire you Lords?

WARWICKE
Doe right vnto this Princely Duke of Yorke,
Or I will fill the House with armed men,
And ouer the Chayre of State, where now he sits,
170 Write vp his Title with vsurping blood.
        He stampes with his foot, and the Souldiers shew
        themselues

KING HENRY
My Lord of Warwick, heare me but one word,
Let me for this my life time reigne as King.

YORKE
Confirme the Crowne to me and to mine Heires,
And thou shalt reigne in quiet while thou liu'st.

KING HENRY
I am content: *Richard Plantagenet*
Enioy the Kingdome after my decease.

CLIFFORD
What wrong is this vnto the Prince, your Sonne?

WARWICKE
What good is this to England, and himselfe?

WESTMERLAND
Base, fearefull, and despayring *Henry*.

CLIFFORD
How hast thou iniur'd both thy selfe and vs?   180

WESTMERLAND
I cannot stay to heare these Articles.

NORTHUMBERLAND Nor I.

CLIFFORD
Come Cousin, let vs tell the Queene these Newes.

WESTMERLAND (*to King Henry*)
Farwell faint-hearted and degenerate King,
In whose cold blood no sparke of Honor bides.
                    ⌈*Exit with his Souldiers*⌉

NORTHUMBERLAND (*to King Henry*)
Be thou a prey vnto the House of *Yorke*,
And dye in Bands, for this vnmanly deed.
                    ⌈*Exit with his Souldiers*⌉

CLIFFORD (*to King Henry*)
In dreadfull Warre may'st thou be ouercome,
Or liue in peace abandon'd and despis'd.
                    Exit ⌈*with his Souldiers*⌉

WARWICKE (*to King Henry*)
Turne this way *Henry*, and regard them not.   190

EXETER (*to King Henry*)
They seeke reuenge, and therefore will not yeeld.

KING HENRY
Ah *Exeter*.

WARWICKE   Why should you sigh, my Lord?

KING HENRY
Not for my selfe Lord *Warwick*, but my Sonne,
Whom I vnnaturally shall dis-inherite.
But be it as it may: (*to Yorke*) I here entayle
The Crowne to thee and to thine Heires for euer,
Conditionally, that heere thou take thine Oath,
To cease this Ciuill Warre: and whil'st I liue,
To honor me as thy King, and Soueraigne:
And nor by Treason nor Hostilitie,   200
To seeke to put me downe, and reigne thy selfe.

YORKE
This Oath I willingly take, and will performe.

WARWICKE
Long liue King *Henry*: (*to Yorke*) *Plantagenet* embrace
        him.
        ⌈*Yorke descends:*⌉ *Henry and Yorke embrace*

KING HENRY (*to Yorke*)
And long liue thou, and these thy forward Sonnes.

YORKE
Now *Yorke* and *Lancaster* are reconcil'd.

EXETER
Accurst be he that seekes to make them foes.
        Senet. Here Yorkes Traine comes downe from the
        State

YORKE (*to King Henry*)
Farewell my gracious Lord, Ile to my Castle.
        Exeunt Yorke, Edward, and Richard ⌈*with*
                                Souldiers⌉

WARWICKE

And Ile keepe London with my Souldiers.

Exit ⌈with Souldiers⌉

NORFOLKE

And I to Norfolke with my followers.

Exit ⌈with Souldiers⌉

MOUNTAGUE

210 And I vnto the Sea, from whence I came.

Exit ⌈with Souldiers⌉

KING HENRY

And I with griefe and sorrow to the Court.

⌈*King Henry and Exeter turne to leaue.*⌉

Enter Margaret the Queene and Prince Edward

EXETER

Heere comes the Queene, whose Lookes bewray her
    anger:

Ile steale away.

KING HENRY   *Exeter* so will I.

QUEENE MARGARET

Nay, goe not from me, I will follow thee.

KING HENRY

Be patient gentle Queene, and I will stay.

QUEENE MARGARET

Who can be patient in such extreames?

Ah wretched man, would I had dy'de a Maid?

And neuer seene thee, neuer borne thee Sonne,

Seeing thou hast prou'd so vnnaturall a Father.

220 Hath he deseru'd to loose his Birth-right thus?

Hadst thou but lou'd him halfe so well as I,

Or felt that paine which I did for him once,

Or nourisht him, as I did with my blood;

Thou would'st haue left thy dearest heart-blood there,

Rather then haue made that sauage Duke thine Heire,

And dis-inherited thine onely Sonne.

PRINCE EDWARD

Father, you cannot dis-inherite me:

If you be King, why should not I succeede?

KING HENRY

Pardon me *Margaret*, pardon me sweet Sonne,

230 The Earle of Warwick and the Duke enforc't me.

QUEENE MARGARET

Enforc't thee? Art thou King, and wilt be forc't?

I shame to heare thee speake: ah timorous Wretch,

Thou hast vndone thy selfe, thy Sonne, and me,

And giu'n vnto the House of *Yorke* such head,

As thou shalt reigne but by their sufferance.

To entayle him and his Heires vnto the Crowne,

What is it, but to make thy Sepulcher,

And creepe into it farre before thy time?

Warwick is Chancelor, and the Lord of Callice,

240 Sterne *Falconbridge* commands the Narrow Seas,

The Duke is made Protector of the Realme,

And yet shalt thou be safe? Such safetie findes

The trembling Lambe, inuironned with Wolues.

Had I beene there, which am a silly Woman,

The Souldiers should haue toss'd me on their Pikes,

Before I would haue granted to that Act.

But thou preferr'st thy Life, before thine Honor.

And seeing thou do'st, I here diuorce my selfe,

Both from thy Table *Henry*, and thy Bed,

Vntill that Act of Parliament be repeal'd,   250

Whereby my Sonne is dis-inherited.

The Northerne Lords, that haue forsworne thy
    Colours,

Will follow mine, if once they see them spread:

And spread they shall be, to thy foule disgrace,

And the vtter ruine of the House of *Yorke*.

Thus doe I leaue thee: (*To Prince Edward*) Come
    Sonne, let's away,

Our Army is ready; come, wee'le after them.

KING HENRY

Stay gentle *Margaret*, and heare me speake.

QUEENE MARGARET

Thou hast spoke too much already:

⌈*To Prince Edward*⌉   get thee gone.

KING HENRY

Gentle Sonne *Edward*, thou wilt stay with me?   260

QUEENE MARGARET

I, to be murther'd by his Enemies.

PRINCE EDWARD (*to King Henry*)

When I returne with victorie from the field,

Ile see your Grace: till then, Ile follow her.

QUEENE MARGARET

Come Sonne away, we may not linger thus.

Exit with Prince Edward

KING HENRY

Poore Queene, how loue to me, and to her Sonne,

Hath made her breake out into termes of Rage.

Reueng'd may she be on that hatefull Duke,

Whose haughtie spirit, winged with desire,

Will cost my Crowne, and like an emptie Eagle,

Tyre on the flesh of me, and of my Sonne.   270

The losse of those three Lords torments my heart:

Ile write vnto them, and entreat them faire;

Come Cousin, you shall be the Messenger.

EXETER

And I, I hope, shall reconcile them all.

Flourish. Exeunt

Enter Richard, Edward, and Mountague   Sc. 2
                                                (1.2)
RICHARD

Brother, though I bee youngest, giue mee leaue.

EDWARD

No, I can better play the Orator.

MOUNTAGUE

But I haue reasons strong and forceable.

Enter the Duke of Yorke

YORKE

Why how now Sonnes, and Brother, at a strife?

What is your Quarrell? how began it first?

EDWARD

No Quarrell, but a slight Contention.   280

YORKE About what?

RICHARD

About that which concernes your Grace and vs,

The Crowne of England, Father, which is yours.

YORKE

Mine Boy? not till King *Henry* be dead.

RICHARD

Your Right depends not on his life, or death.

EDWARD

Now you are Heire, therefore enioy it now:
By giuing the House of *Lancaster* leaue to breathe,
It will out-runne you, Father, in the end.

YORKE

I tooke an Oath, that hee should quietly reigne.

EDWARD

290 But for a Kingdome any Oath may be broken:
I would breake a thousand Oathes, to reigne one yeere.

RICHARD (*to Yorke*)

No: God forbid your Grace should be forsworne.

YORKE

I shall be, if I clayme by open Warre.

RICHARD

Ile proue the contrary, if you'le heare mee speake.

YORKE

Thou canst not, Sonne: it is impossible.

RICHARD

An Oath is of no moment, being not tooke
Before a true and lawfull Magistrate,
That hath authoritie ouer him that sweares.
Henry had none, but did vsurpe the place.

300 Then seeing 'twas he that made you to depose,
Your Oath, my Lord, is vaine and friuolous.
Therefore to Armes: and Father doe but thinke,
How sweet a thing it is to weare a Crowne,
Within whose Circuit is *Elizium*,
And all that Poets faine of Blisse and Ioy.
Why doe we linger thus? I cannot rest,
Vntill the White Rose that I weare, be dy'de
Euen in the luke-warme blood of *Henries* heart.

YORKE

Richard ynough: I will be King, or dye.
(*To Mountague*) Brother, thou shalt to London

310   presently,
And whet on *Warwick* to this Enterprise.
Thou *Richard* shalt to the Duke of Norfolke,
And tell him priuily of our intent.
You *Edward* shall to *Edmund Brooke* Lord *Cobham*,
With whom the Kentishmen will willingly rise.
In them I trust: for they are Souldiors,
Wittie, courteous, liberall, full of spirit.
While you are thus imploy'd, what resteth more?
But that I seeke occasion how to rise,

320 And yet the King not priuie to my Drift,
Nor any of the House of *Lancaster*.

         Enter a Messenger

But stay, what Newes? Why comm'st thou in such
         poste?

MESSENGER

The Queene, with all the Northerne Earles and Lords,
Intend here to besiege you in your Castle.
She is hard by, with twentie thousand men:
And therefore fortifie your Hold, my Lord.

YORKE

I, with my Sword. What? think'st thou, that we feare
         them?
Edward and *Richard*, you shall stay with me,
My Brother *Mountague* shall poste to London.
Let Noble *Warwicke*, *Cobham*, and the rest,   330
Whom we haue left Protectors of the King,
With powrefull Pollicie strengthen themselues,
And trust not simple *Henry*, nor his Oathes.

MOUNTAGUE

Brother, I goe: Ile winne them, feare it not.
And thus most humbly I doe take my leaue.   *Exit*
         *Enter Sir Iohn Mortimer, and his Brother, Sir
         Hugh*

YORKE

Sir *Iohn*, and Sir *Hugh Mortimer*, mine Vnckles,
You are come to Sandall in a happie houre.
The Armie of the Queene meane to besiege vs.

SIR IOHN

Shee shall not neede, wee'le meete her in the field.

YORKE What, with fiue thousand men?   340

RICHARD

I, with fiue hundred, Father, for a neede.
A Woman's generall: what should we feare?
         A March sounds afarre off

EDWARD

I heare their Drummes: let's set our men in order,
And issue forth, and bid them Battaile straight.

YORKE ⌜*to Sir Iohn and Sir Hugh*⌝

Fiue men to twentie: though the oddes be great,
I doubt not, Vnckles, of our Victorie.
Many a Battaile haue I wonne in France,
When as the Enemie hath beene tenne to one:
Why should I not now haue the like successe?

         Exeunt

         Alarmes, and then enter the young Rutland, and his   Sc. 3
         Tutor a Chaplaine   (1.3)

RUTLAND

Ah, whither shall I flye, to scape their hands?   350
         Enter Clifford with Souldiers
Ah Tutor, looke where bloody *Clifford* comes.

CLIFFORD (*to the Tutor*)

Chaplaine away, thy Priesthood saues thy life.
As for the Brat of this accursed Duke,
Whose Father slew my Father, he shall dye.

TUTOR

And I, my Lord, will beare him company.

CLIFFORD Souldiers, away with him.

TUTOR

Ah *Clifford*, murther not this innocent Child,
Least thou be hated both of God and Man.

         Exit, guarded

         ⌜*Rutland falls to the ground*⌝

CLIFFORD

How now? is he dead alreadie?
Or is it feare, that makes him close his eyes?   360
Ile open them.

RUTLAND ⌈reuiuing⌉
    So looks the pent-vp Lyon o're the Wretch,
    That trembles vnder his deuouring Pawes:
    And so he walkes, insulting o're his Prey,
    And so he comes, to rend his Limbes asunder.
    Ah gentle *Clifford*, kill me with thy Sword,
    And not with such a cruell threatning Looke.
    Sweet *Clifford* heare me speake, before I dye:
    I am too meane a subiect for thy Wrath,
370 Be thou reueng'd on men, and let me liue.
CLIFFORD
    In vaine thou speak'st, poore Boy: My Fathers blood
    Hath stopt the passage where thy words should enter.
RUTLAND
    Then let my Fathers blood open it againe,
    He is a man, and *Clifford* cope with him.
CLIFFORD
    Had I thy Brethren here, their liues and thine
    Were not reuenge sufficient for me:
    No, if I digg'd vp thy fore-fathers Graues,
    And hung their rotten Coffins vp in Chaynes,
    It could not slake mine ire, nor ease my heart.
380 The sight of any of the House of *Yorke*,
    Is as a furie to torment my Soule:
    And till I root out their accursed Line,
    And leaue not one aliue, I liue in Hell.
    Therefore—
RUTLAND
    Oh let me pray, before I take my death:
    ⌈Kneeling⌉ To thee I pray; sweet *Clifford* pitty me.
CLIFFORD
    Such pitty as my Rapiers point affords.
RUTLAND
    I neuer did thee harme: why wilt thou slay me?
CLIFFORD
    Thy Father hath.
RUTLAND   But 'twas ere I was borne.
390 Thou hast one Sonne, for his sake pitty me,
    Least in reuenge thereof, sith God is iust,
    He be as miserably slaine as I.
    Ah, let me liue in Prison all my dayes,
    And when I giue occasion of offence,
    Then let me dye, for now thou hast no cause.
CLIFFORD
    No cause? thy Father slew my Father: therefore dye.
        He stabs him
RUTLAND
    Dij faciant laudis summa sit ista tuæ.   *He dyes*
CLIFFORD
    Plantagenet, I come *Plantagenet*:
    And this thy Sonnes blood cleauing to my Blade,
400 Shall rust vpon my Weapon, till thy blood
    Congeal'd with this, doe make me wipe off both.
                    Exit with body ⌈*and Souldiers*⌉

Sc. 4   *Alarum. Enter Richard, Duke of Yorke*
(1.4) YORKE
    The Army of the Queene hath got the field:

    My Vnckles both are slaine, in rescuing me;
    And all my followers, to the eager foe
    Turne back, and flye, like Ships before the Winde,
    Or Lambes pursu'd by hunger-starued Wolues.
    My Sonnes, God knowes what hath bechanced them:
    But this I know, they haue demean'd themselues
    Like men borne to Renowne, by Life or Death.
    Three times did *Richard* make a Lane to me,   410
    And thrice cry'de, Courage Father, fight it out:
    And full as oft came *Edward* to my side,
    With Purple Faulchion, painted to the Hilt,
    In blood of those that had encountred him:
    And when the hardyest Warriors did retyre,
    Richard cry'de, Charge, and giue no foot of ground,
    ⌈   ⌉
    And cry'de, A Crowne, or else a glorious Tombe,
    A Scepter, or an Earthly Sepulchre.
    With this we charg'd againe: but out alas,   420
    We bodg'd againe, as I haue seene a Swan
    With bootlesse labour swimme against the Tyde,
    And spend her strength with ouer-matching Waues.
        A short Alarum within
    Ah hearke, the fatall followers doe pursue,
    And I am faint, and cannot flye their furie:
    And were I strong, I would not shunne their furie.
    The Sands are numbred, that makes vp my Life,
    Here must I stay, and here my Life must end.
        Enter Margaret the Queene, Clifford,
        Northumberland, the young Prince Edward, and
        Souldiers
    Come bloody *Clifford*, rough *Northumberland*,
    I dare your quenchlesse furie to more rage:
    I am your Butt, and I abide your Shot.   430
NORTHUMBERLAND
    Yeeld to our mercy, proud *Plantagenet*.
CLIFFORD
    I, to such mercy, as his ruthlesse Arme
    With downe-right payment, shew'd vnto my Father.
    Now *Phaeton* hath tumbled from his Carre,
    And made an Euening at the Noone-tide Prick.
YORKE
    My ashes, as the Phœnix, may bring forth
    A Bird, that will reuenge vpon you all:
    And in that hope, I throw mine eyes to Heauen,
    Scorning what ere you can afflict me with.   440
    Why come you not? what, multitudes, and feare?
CLIFFORD
    So Cowards fight, when they can flye no further,
    So Doues doe peck the Faulcons piercing Tallons,
    So desperate Theeues, all hopelesse of their Liues,
    Breathe out Inuectiues 'gainst the Officers.
YORKE
    Oh *Clifford*, but bethinke thee once againe,
    And in thy thought ore-run my former time:
    And if thou canst, for blushing, view this face,
    And bite thy tongue, that slanders him with
        Cowardice,
    Whose frowne hath made thee faint and flye ere this. 450

CLIFFORD

I will not bandie with thee word for word,
But buckle with thee blowes twice two for one.
⌈*He drawes his Sword*⌉

QUEENE MARGARET

Hold valiant *Clifford*, for a thousand causes
I would prolong a while the Traytors Life:
Wrath makes him deafe; speake thou *Northumberland*.

NORTHUMBERLAND

Hold *Clifford*, doe not honor him so much,
To prick thy finger, though to wound his heart.
What valour were it, when a Curre doth grinne,
For one to thrust his Hand betweene his Teeth,
460 When he might spurne him with his Foot away?
It is Warres prize, to take all Vantages,
And tenne to one, is no impeach of Valour.
                  They ⌈*fight, and*⌉ *take Yorke*

CLIFFORD

I, I, so striues the Woodcocke with the Gynne.

NORTHUMBERLAND

So doth the Connie struggle in the Net.

YORKE

So triumph Theeues vpon their conquer'd Booty,
So True men yeeld with Robbers, so o're-matcht.

NORTHUMBERLAND (*to the Queene*)

What would your Grace haue done vnto him now?

QUEENE MARGARET

Braue Warriors, *Clifford* and *Northumberland*,
Come make him stand vpon this Mole-hill here,
470 That raught at Mountaines with out-stretched Armes,
Yet parted but the shadow with his Hand.
(*To Yorke*) What, was it you that would be Englands
            King?
Was't you that reuell'd in our Parliament,
And made a Preachment of your high Descent?
Where are your Messe of Sonnes, to back you now?
The wanton *Edward*, and the lustie *George*?
And where's that valiant Crook-back Prodigie,
Dickie, your Boy, that with his grumbling voyce
Was wont to cheare his Dad in Mutinies?
480 Or with the rest, where is your Darling, *Rutland*?
Looke *Yorke*, I stayn'd this Napkin with the blood
That valiant *Clifford*, with his Rapiers point,
Made issue from the Bosome of thy Boy:
And if thine eyes can water for his death,
I giue thee this to drie thy Cheekes withall.
Alas poore *Yorke*, but that I hate thee deadly,
I should lament thy miserable state.
I prythee grieue, to make me merry, *Yorke*.
What, hath thy fierie heart so parcht thine entrayles,
490 That not a Teare can fall, for *Rutlands* death?
Why art thou patient, man? thou should'st be mad:
And I, to make thee mad, doe mock thee thus.
Stampe, raue, and fret, that I may sing and dance.
Thou would'st be fee'd, I see, to make me sport:
Yorke cannot speake, vnlesse he weare a Crowne.
(*To her men*) A Crowne for *Yorke*; and Lords, bow
            lowe to him:
Hold you his hands, whilest I doe set it on.

She puts a paper Crowne on Yorkes head

I marry Sir, now lookes he like a King:
I, this is he that tooke King *Henries* Chaire,
And this is he was his adopted Heire.   500
But how is it, that great *Plantagenet*
Is crown'd so soone, and broke his solemne Oath?
As I bethinke me, you should not be King,
Till our King *Henry* had shooke hands with Death.
And will you pale your head in *Henries* Glory,
And rob his Temples of the Diademe,
Now in his Life, against your holy Oath?
Oh 'tis a fault too too vnpardonable.
Off with the Crowne;
            ⌈*She knocks it from his head*⌉
                        and with the Crowne, his Head,
And whilest we breathe, take time to doe him dead.   510

CLIFFORD

That is my Office, for my Fathers sake.

QUEENE MARGARET

Nay stay, let's heare the Orizons hee makes.

YORKE

Shee-Wolfe of France, but worse then Wolues of
            France,
Whose Tongue more poysons then the Adders Tooth:
How ill-beseeming is it in thy Sex,
To triumph like an Amazonian Trull,
Vpon their Woes, whom Fortune captiuates?
But that thy Face is Vizard-like, vnchanging,
Made impudent with vse of euill deedes,
I would assay, proud Queene, to make thee blush.   520
To tell thee whence thou cam'st, of whom deriu'd,
Were shame enough, to shame thee, wert thou not
            shamelesse.
Thy Father beares the type of King of Naples,
Of both the Sicils, and Ierusalem,
Yet not so wealthie as an English Yeoman.
Hath that poore Monarch taught thee to insult?
It needes not, nor it bootes thee not, prowd Queene,
Vnlesse the Adage must be verify'd,
That Beggers mounted, runne their Horse to death.
'Tis Beautie that doth oft make Women prowd,   530
But God he knowes, thy share thereof is small.
'Tis Vertue, that doth make them most admir'd,
The contrary, doth make thee wondred at.
'Tis Gouernment that makes them seeme Diuine,
The want thereof, makes thee abhominable.
Thou art as opposite to euery good,
As the *Antipodes* are vnto vs,
Or as the South to the *Septentrion*.
Oh Tygres Heart, wrapt in a Womans Hide,
How could'st thou drayne the Life-blood of the Child,   540
To bid the Father wipe his eyes withall,
And yet be seene to beare a Womans face?
Women are soft, milde, pittifull, and flexible;
Thou, sterne, obdurate, flintie, rough, remorselesse.
Bidst thou me rage? why now thou hast thy wish.
Would'st haue me weepe? why now thou hast thy will.
For raging Wind blowes vp incessant showers,
And when the Rage allayes, the Raine begins.

These Teares are my sweet *Rutlands* Obsequies,
550 And euery drop cryes vengeance for his death,
'Gainst thee fell *Clifford*, and thee false French-woman.

NORTHUMBERLAND
Beshrew me, but his passions moue me so,
That hardly can I check my eyes from Teares.

YORKE
That Face of his, the hungry Caniballs
Would not haue toucht, would not haue stayn'd with
            blood:
But you are more inhumane, more inexorable,
Oh, tenne times more then Tygers of Hyrcania.
See, ruthlesse Queene, a haplesse Fathers Teares:
This Cloth thou dipd'st in blood of my sweet Boy,
560 And I with Teares doe wash the blood away.
Keepe thou the Napkin, and goe boast of this,
And if thou tell'st the heauie storie right,
Vpon my Soule, the hearers will shed Teares:
Yea, euen my Foes will shed fast-falling Teares,
And say, Alas, it was a pittious deed.
There, take the Crowne, and with the Crowne, my
            Curse,
And in thy need, such comfort come to thee,
As now I reape at thy too cruell hand.
Hard-hearted *Clifford*, take me from the World,
570 My Soule to Heauen, my Blood vpon your Heads.

NORTHUMBERLAND
Had he been slaughter-man to all my Kinne,
I should not for my Life but weepe with him,
To see how inly Sorrow gripes his Soule.

QUEENE MARGARET
What, weeping ripe, my Lord *Northumberland*?
Thinke but vpon the wrong he did vs all,
And that will quickly drie thy melting Teares.

CLIFFORD
Heere's for my Oath, heere's for my Fathers Death.
            He stabs Yorke

QUEENE MARGARET
And heere's to right our gentle-hearted King.
            She stabs Yorke

YORKE
Open thy Gate of Mercy, gracious God,
My Soule flyes through these wounds, to seeke out
580   thee.   ⌈*He dyes*⌉

QUEENE MARGARET
Off with his Head, and set it on Yorke Gates,
So *Yorke* may ouer-looke the Towne of Yorke.
            Flourish. Exeunt with Yorkes body

Sc. 5   *A March. Enter Edward and Richard,* ⌈*with drum*
(2.1)   *and Souldiers*⌉

EDWARD
I wonder how our Princely Father scap't:
Or whether he be scap't away, or no,
From *Cliffords* and *Northumberlands* pursuit?
Had he been ta'ne, we should haue heard the newes;
Had he beene slaine, we should haue heard the newes:
Or had he scap't, me thinkes we should haue heard

The happy tidings of his good escape.
How fares my Brother? why is he so sad?   590

RICHARD
I cannot ioy, vntill I be resolu'd
Where our right valiant Father is become.
I saw him in the Battaile range about,
And watcht him how he singled *Clifford* forth.
Me thought he bore him in the thickest troupe,
As doth a Lyon in a Heard of Neat,
Or as a Beare encompass'd round with Dogges:
Who hauing pincht a few, and made them cry,
The rest stand all aloofe, and barke at him.
So far'd our Father with his Enemies,   600
So fled his Enemies my Warlike Father:
Me thinkes 'tis prize enough to be his Sonne.
            ⌈*Three sunnes appeare in the aire*⌉
See how the Morning opes her golden Gates,
And takes her farwell of the glorious Sunne.
How well resembles it the prime of Youth,
Trimm'd like a Yonker, prauncing to his Loue?

EDWARD
Dazle mine eyes, or doe I see three Sunnes?

RICHARD
Three glorious Sunnes, each one a perfect Sunne,
Not seperated with the racking Clouds,
But seuer'd in a pale cleare-shining Skye.   610
            ⌈*The three sunnes begin to ioyne*⌉
See, see, they ioyne, embrace, and seeme to kisse,
As if they vow'd some League inuiolable.
Now are they but one Lampe, one Light, one Sunne:
In this, the Heauen figures some euent.

EDWARD
'Tis wondrous strange, the like yet neuer heard of.
I thinke it cites vs (Brother) to the field,
That wee, the Sonnes of braue *Plantagenet*,
Each one alreadie blazing by our meedes,
Should notwithstanding ioyne our Lights together,
And ouer-shine the Earth, as this the World.   620
What ere it bodes, hence-forward will I beare
Vpon my Targuet three faire shining Sunnes.

RICHARD
Nay, beare three Daughters: by your leaue, I speake it,
You loue the Breeder better then the Male.
            Enter one blowing
But what art thou, whose heauie Lookes fore-tell
Some dreadfull story hanging on thy Tongue?

MESSENGER
Ah, one that was a wofull looker on,
When as the Noble Duke of Yorke was slaine,
Your Princely Father, and my louing Lord.

EDWARD
Oh speake no more, for I haue heard too much.   630

RICHARD
Say how he dy'de, for I will heare it all.

MESSENGER
Enuironed he was with many foes,
And stood against them, as the hope of Troy
Against the Greekes, that would haue entred Troy.

But *Hercules* himselfe must yeeld to oddes:
And many stroakes, though with a little Axe,
Hewes downe and fells the hardest-tymber'd Oake.
By many hands your Father was subdu'd,
But onely slaught'red by the irefull Arme
640 Of vn-relenting *Clifford*, and the Queene:
Who crown'd the gracious Duke in high despight,
Laugh'd in his face: and when with griefe he wept,
The ruthlesse Queene gaue him, to dry his Cheekes,
A Napkin, steeped in the harmelesse blood
Of sweet young *Rutland*, by rough *Clifford* slaine:
And after many scornes, many foule taunts,
They tooke his Head, and on the Gates of Yorke
They set the same, and there it doth remaine,
The saddest spectacle that ere I view'd.

EDWARD
650 Sweet Duke of Yorke, our Prop to leane vpon,
Now thou art gone, wee haue no Staffe, no Stay.
Oh *Clifford*, boyst'rous *Clifford*, thou hast slaine
The flowre of Europe, for his Cheualrie,
And trecherously hast thou vanquisht him,
For hand to hand he would haue vanquisht thee.
Now my Soules Pallace is become a Prison:
Ah, would she breake from hence, that this my body
Might in the ground be closed vp in rest:
For neuer henceforth shall I ioy againe:
660 Neuer, oh neuer shall I see more ioy.

RICHARD
I cannot weepe: for all my bodies moysture
Scarse serues to quench my Furnace-burning hart:
Nor can my tongue vnloade my hearts great burthen,
For selfe-same winde that I should speake withall,
Is kindling coales that fires all my brest,
And burnes me vp with flames, that tears would
    quench.
To weepe, is to make lesse the depth of greefe:
Teares then for Babes; Blowes, and Reuenge for mee.
Richard, I beare thy name, Ile venge thy death,
670 Or dye renowned by attempting it.

EDWARD
His name that valiant Duke hath left with thee:
His Dukedome, and his Chaire with me is left.

RICHARD
Nay, if thou be that Princely Eagles Bird,
Shew thy descent by gazing 'gainst the Sunne:
For Chaire and Dukedome, Throne and Kingdome say,
Either that is thine, or else thou wer't not his.
    March. Enter Warwicke, Marquesse Mountacute,
    ⌈*with drum, ancient, and souldiers*⌉

WARWICK
How now faire Lords? What faire? What newes
    abroad?

RICHARD
Great Lord of Warwicke, if we should recompt
Our balefull newes, and at each words deliuerance
680 Stab Poniards in our flesh, till all were told,
The words would adde more anguish then the wounds.
O valiant Lord, the Duke of Yorke is slaine.

EDWARD
O Warwicke, Warwicke, that *Plantagenet*
Which held thee deerely, as his Soules Redemption,
Is by the sterne Lord *Clifford* done to death.

WARWICKE
Ten dayes ago, I drown'd these newes in teares.
And now to adde more measure to your woes,
I come to tell you things sith then befalne.
After the bloody Fray at Wakefield fought,
Where your braue Father breath'd his latest gaspe, 690
Tydings, as swiftly as the Postes could runne,
Were brought me of your Losse, and his Depart.
I then in London, keeper of the King,
Muster'd my Soldiers, gathred flockes of Friends,
And verie well appointed as I thought,
Marcht toward S. Albons, to intercept the Queene,
Bearing the King in my behalfe along:
For by my Scouts, I was aduertised
That she was comming with a full intent
To dash our late Decree in Parliament, 700
Touching King *Henries* Oath, and your Succession:
Short Tale to make, we at S. Albons met,
Our Battailes ioyn'd, and both sides fiercely fought:
But whether 'twas the coldnesse of the King,
Who look'd full gently on his warlike Queene,
That robb'd my Soldiers of their heated Spleene,
Or whether 'twas report of her successe,
Or more then common feare of *Cliffords* Rigour,
Who thunders to his Captaines, Blood and Death,
I cannot iudge: but to conclude with truth, 710
Their Weapons like to Lightning, came and went:
Our Souldiers like the Night-Owles lazie flight,
Or like an idle Thresher with a Flaile,
Fell gently downe, as if they strucke their Friends.
I cheer'd them vp with iustice of our Cause,
With promise of high pay, and great Rewards:
But all in vaine, they had no heart to fight,
And we (in them) no hope to win the day,
So that we fled: the King vnto the Queene,
Lord *George*, your Brother, Norfolke, and my Selfe, 720
In haste, post haste, are come to ioyne with you:
For in the Marches heere we heard you were,
Making another Head, to fight againe.

EDWARD
Where is the Duke of Norfolke, gentle Warwick?
And when came *George* from Burgundy to England?

WARWICKE
Some six miles off the Duke is with his Soldiers,
And for your Brother he was lately sent
From your kinde Aunt Dutchesse of Burgundie,
With ayde of Souldiers to this needfull Warre.

RICHARD
'Twas oddes belike, when valiant Warwick fled; 730
Oft haue I heard his praises in Pursuite,
But ne're till now, his Scandall of Retire.

WARWICKE
Nor now my Scandall *Richard*, dost thou heare:
For thou shalt know this strong right hand of mine,

Can plucke the Diadem from faint *Henries* head,
And wring the awefull Scepter from his Fist,
Were he as famous, and as bold in Warre,
As he is fam'd for Mildnesse, Peace, and Prayer.

RICHARD
I know it well Lord Warwick, blame me not,
740   'Tis loue I beare thy glories make me speake:
But in this troublous time, what's to be done?
Shall we go throw away our Coates of Steele,
And wrap our bodies in blacke mourning Gownes,
Numb'ring our Aue-Maries with our Beads?
Or shall we on the Helmets of our Foes
Tell our Deuotion with reuengefull Armes?
If for the last, say I, and to it Lords.

WARWICKE
Why therefore Warwick came to seek you out,
And therefore comes my Brother *Mountague*:
750   Attend me Lords, the proud insulting Queene,
With *Clifford*, and the haught Northumberland,
And of their Feather, many moe proud Birds,
Haue wrought the easie-melting King, like Wax.
(*To Edward*) He swore consent to your Succession,
His Oath enrolled in the Parliament.
And now to London all the crew are gone,
To frustrate both his Oath, and what beside
May make against the house of Lancaster.
Their power (I thinke) is thirty thousand strong:
760   Now, if the helpe of Norfolke, and my selfe,
With all the Friends that thou braue Earle of March,
Among'st the louing Welshmen can'st procure,
Will but amount to fiue and twenty thousand,
Why Via, to London will we march,
And once againe, bestride our foaming Steeds,
And once againe cry Charge vpon our Foes,
But neuer once againe turne backe and flye.

RICHARD
I, now me thinks I heare great Warwick speak;
Ne're may he liue to see a Sun-shine day,
770   That cries Retire, if Warwicke bid him stay.

EDWARD
Lord Warwicke, on thy shoulder will I leane,
And when thou failst (as God forbid the houre)
Must *Edward* fall, which perill heauen forefend.

WARWICKE
No longer Earle of March, but Duke of Yorke:
The next degree, is Englands Royall Throne:
For King of England shalt thou be proclaim'd
In euery Burrough as we passe along,
And he that throwes not vp his cap for ioy,
Shall for the Fault make forfeit of his head.
780   King *Edward*, valiant *Richard*, *Mountague*:
Stay we no longer, dreaming of Renowne,
But sound the Trumpets, and about our Taske.

RICHARD
Then *Clifford*, were thy heart as hard as Steele,
As thou hast shewne it flintie by thy deeds,
I come to pierce it, or to giue thee mine.

EDWARD
Then strike vp Drums, God and S. George for vs.

Enter a Messenger

WARWICKE How now? what newes?

MESSENGER
The Duke of Norfolke sends you word by me,
The Queene is comming with a puissant Hoast,
And craues your company, for speedy counsell.   790

WARWICKE
Why then it sorts, braue Warriors, let's away.
⌈*March.*⌉ *Exeunt Omnes*

⌈*Yorkes head thrust out, aboue.*⌉   Sc. 6
Flourish. Enter Henry the King, Margaret the   (2.2)
Queene, Clifford, Northumberland and Yong Prince
Edward, with Drumme and Trumpettes

QUEENE MARGARET
Welcome my Lord, to this braue town of Yorke,
Yonders the head of that Arch-enemy,
That sought to be incompast with your Crowne.
Doth not the obiect cheere your heart, my Lord.

KING HENRY
I, as the rockes cheare them that feare their wrack,
To see this sight, it irkes my very soule:
With-hold reuenge (deere God) 'tis not my fault,
Nor wittingly haue I infring'd my Vow.

CLIFFORD
My gracious Liege, this too much lenity   800
And harmfull pitty must be layd aside:
To whom do Lyons cast their gentle Lookes?
Not to the Beast, that would vsurpe their Den.
Whose hand is that the Forrest Beare doth licke?
Not his that spoyles her yong before her face.
Who scapes the lurking Serpents mortall sting?
Not he that sets his foot vpon her backe.
The smallest Worme will turne, being troden on,
And Doues will pecke in safegard of their Brood.
Ambitious Yorke, did leuell at thy Crowne,   810
Thou smiling, while he knit his angry browes.
He but a Duke, would haue his Sonne a King,
And raise his issue like a louing Sire.
Thou being a King, blest with a goodly sonne,
Did'st yeeld consent to disinherit him:
Which argued thee a most vnlouing Father.
Vnreasonable Creatures feed their young,
And though mans face be fearefull to their eyes,
Yet in protection of their tender ones,
Who hath not seene them euen with those wings,   820
Which sometime they haue vs'd with fearfull flight,
Make warre with him that climb'd vnto their nest,
Offering their owne liues in their yongs defence?
For shame, my Liege, make them your President:
Were it not pitty that this goodly Boy
Should loose his Birth-right by his Fathers fault,
And long heereafter say vnto his childe,
What my great Grandfather, and Grandsire got,
My carelesse Father fondly gaue away.
Ah, what a shame were this? Looke on the Boy,   830
And let his manly face, which promiseth
Successefull Fortune steele thy melting heart,
To hold thine owne, and leaue thine owne with him.

KING HENRY

Full well hath *Clifford* plaid the Orator,
Inferring arguments of mighty force:
But *Clifford* tell me, did'st thou neuer heare,
That things ill got, had euer bad successe.
And happy alwayes was it for that Sonne,
Whose Father for his hoording went to hell:
840 Ile leaue my Sonne my Vertuous deeds behinde,
And would my Father had left me no more:
For all the rest is held at such a Rate,
As brings a thousand fold more care to keepe,
Then in possession any iot of pleasure.
Ah Cosin Yorke, would thy best Friends did know,
How it doth greeue me that thy head is heere.

QUEENE MARGARET

My Lord cheere vp your spirits, our foes are nye,
And this soft courage makes your Followers faint:
You promist Knighthood to our forward sonne,
850 Vnsheath your sword, and dub him presently.
Edward, kneele downe.
            Prince Edward kneeles

KING HENRY

Edward Plantagenet, arise a Knight,
And learne this Lesson; Draw thy Sword in right.

PRINCE EDWARD (*rising*)

My gracious Father, by your Kingly leaue,
Ile draw it as Apparant to the Crowne,
And in that quarrell, vse it to the death.

CLIFFORD

Why that is spoken like a toward Prince.
            Enter a Messenger

MESSENGER

Royall Commanders, be in readinesse,
For with a Band of thirty thousand men,
860 Comes Warwicke backing of the Duke of Yorke,
And in the Townes as they do march along,
Proclaimes him King, and many flye to him,
Darraigne your battell, for they are at hand.

CLIFFORD (*to King Henry*)

I would your Highnesse would depart the field,
The Queene hath best successe when you are absent.

QUEENE MARGARET (*to King Henry*)

I good my Lord, and leaue vs to our Fortune.

KING HENRY

Why, that's my fortune too, therefore Ile stay.

NORTHUMBERLAND

Be it with resolution then to fight.

PRINCE EDWARD (*to King Henry*)

My Royall Father, cheere these Noble Lords,
870 And hearten those that fight in your defence:
Vnsheath your Sword, good Father: Cry S. George.
            *March. Enter Edward, Warwicke, Richard, George,
            Norfolke, Mountague, and Soldiers*

EDWARD

Now periur'd *Henry*, wilt thou kneel for grace?
And set thy Diadem vpon my head?
Or bide the mortall Fortune of the field.

QUEENE MARGARET

Go rate thy Minions, proud insulting Boy,

Becomes it thee to be thus bold in termes,
Before thy Soueraigne, and thy lawfull King?

EDWARD

I am his King, and he should bow his knee:
I was adopted Heire by his consent.

GEORGE (*to Queene Margaret*)

Since when, his Oath is broke: for as I heare,   880
You that are King, though he do weare the Crowne,
Haue caus'd him by new Act of Parliament,
To blot our brother out, and put his owne Sonne in.

CLIFFORD And reason too,

Who should succeede the Father, but the Sonne.

RICHARD

Are you there Butcher? O, I cannot speake.

CLIFFORD

I Crooke-back, here I stand to answer thee,
Or any he, the proudest of thy sort.

RICHARD

'Twas you that kill'd yong Rutland, was it not?

CLIFFORD

I, and old Yorke, and yet not satisfied.   890

RICHARD

For Gods sake Lords giue signall to the fight.

WARWICKE

What say'st thou *Henry*, wilt thou yeeld the Crowne?

QUEENE MARGARET

Why how now long-tongu'd Warwicke, dare you
      speake?
When you and I, met at S. *Albons* last,
Your legges did better seruice then your hands.

WARWICKE

Then 'twas my turne to fly, and now 'tis thine.

CLIFFORD

You said so much before, and yet you fled.

WARWICKE

'Twas not your valor *Clifford* droue me thence.

NORTHUMBERLAND

No, nor your manhood that durst make you stay.

RICHARD

Northumberland, I hold thee reuerently,   900
Breake off the parley, for scarse I can refraine
The execution of my big-swolne heart
Vpon that *Clifford*, that cruell Child-killer.

CLIFFORD

I slew thy Father, cal'st thou him a Child?

RICHARD

I like a Dastard, and a treacherous Coward,
As thou didd'st kill our tender Brother Rutland,
But ere Sunset, Ile make thee curse the deed.

KING HENRY

Haue done with words (my Lords) and heare me speake.

QUEENE MARGARET

Defie them then, or els hold close thy lips.

KING HENRY

I prythee giue no limits to my Tongue,   910
I am a King, and priuiledg'd to speake.

CLIFFORD

My Liege, the wound that bred this meeting here,
Cannot be cur'd by Words, therefore be still.

RICHARD

    Then Executioner vnsheath thy sword:

    By him that made vs all, I am resolu'd,

    That *Cliffords* Manhood, lyes vpon his tongue.

EDWARD

    Say *Henry*, shall I haue my right, or no:

    A thousand men haue broke their Fasts to day,

    That ne're shall dine, vnlesse thou yeeld the Crowne.

WARWICKE (*to King Henry*)

920   If thou deny, their Blood vpon thy head,

    For Yorke in iustice put's his Armour on.

PRINCE EDWARD

    If that be right, which Warwick saies is right,

    There is no wrong, but euery thing is right.

RICHARD

    Who euer got thee, there thy Mother stands,

    For well I wot, thou hast thy Mothers tongue.

QUEENE MARGARET

    But thou art neyther like thy Sire nor Damme,

    But like a foule mishapen Stygmaticke,

    Mark'd by the Destinies to be auoided,

    As venome Toades, or Lizards dreadfull stings.

RICHARD

930   Iron of Naples, hid with English gilt,

    Whose Father beares the Title of a King,

    (As if a Channell should be call'd the Sea)

    Sham'st thou not, knowing whence thou art

        extraught,

    To let thy tongue detect thy base-borne heart.

EDWARD

    A wispe of straw were worth a thousand Crowns,

    To make this shamelesse Callet know her selfe:

    Helen of Greece was fayrer farre then thou,

    Although thy Husband may be *Menelaus*;

    And ne're was *Agamemnons* Brother wrong'd

940   By that false Woman, as this King by thee.

    His Father reuel'd in the heart of France,

    And tam'd the King, and made the Dolphin stoope:

    And had he match'd according to his State,

    He might haue kept that glory to this day.

    But when he tooke a begger to his bed,

    And grac'd thy poore Sire with his Bridall day,

    Euen then that Sun-shine brew'd a showre for him,

    That washt his Fathers fortunes forth of France,

    And heap'd sedition on his Crowne at home:

950   For what hath broach'd this tumult but thy Pride?

    Had'st thou bene meeke, our Title still had slept,

    And we in pitty of the Gentle King,

    Had slipt our Claime, vntill another Age.

GEORGE (*to Queene Margaret*)

    But when we saw, our Sunshine made thy Spring,

    And that thy Summer bred vs no increase,

    We set the Axe to thy vsurping Roote:

    And though the edge hath something hit our selues,

    Yet know thou, since we haue begun to strike,

    Wee'l neuer leaue, till we haue hewne thee downe,

960   Or bath'd thy growing, with our heated bloods.

EDWARD (*to Queene Margaret*)

    And in this resolution, I defie thee,

    Not willing any longer Conference,

    Since thou deniest the gentle King to speake.

    Sound Trumpets, let our bloody Colours waue,

    And either Victorie, or else a Graue.

QUEENE MARGARET Stay *Edward*.

EDWARD

    No wrangling Woman, wee'l no longer stay,

    These words will cost ten thousand liues this day.

    ⌈*Flourish. March. Exeunt Edward and his Men*

      at one doore, Queene Margaret and her Men at

          another doore⌉

       Alarum. Excursions. Enter Warwicke   Sc. 7

WARWICKE   (2.3)

    Fore-spent with Toile, as Runners with a Race,

    I lay me downe a little while to breath: 970

    For strokes receiu'd, and many blowes repaid,

    Haue robb'd my strong knit sinewes of their strength,

    And spight of spight, needs must I rest a-while.

      Enter Edward running

EDWARD

    Smile gentle heauen, or strike vngentle death,

    For this world frownes, and *Edwards* Sunne is clowded.

WARWICKE

    How now my Lord, what happe? what hope of good?

      Enter George ⌈*running*⌉

GEORGE

    Our hap is losse, our hope but sad dispaire,

    Our rankes are broke, and ruine followes vs.

    What counsaile giue you? whether shall we flye?

EDWARD

    Bootlesse is flight, they follow vs with Wings,   980

    And weake we are, and cannot shun pursuite.

      Enter Richard ⌈*running*⌉

RICHARD

    Ah Warwicke, why hast yᵘ withdrawn thy selfe?

    Thy Brothers blood the thirsty earth hath drunk,

    Broach'd with the Steely point of *Cliffords* Launce:

    And in the very pangs of death, he cryde,

    Like to a dismall Clangor heard from farre,

    Warwicke, reuenge; Brother, reuenge my death.

    So vnderneath the belly of their Steeds,

    That stain'd their Fetlockes in his smoaking blood,

    The Noble Gentleman gaue vp the ghost.   990

WARWICKE

    Then let the earth be drunken with our blood:

    Ile kill my Horse, because I will not flye:

    Why stand we like soft-hearted women heere,

    Wayling our losses, whiles the Foe doth Rage,

    And looke vpon, as if the Tragedie

    Were plaid in iest, by counterfetting Actors.

    (*Kneeling*) Heere on my knee, I vow to God aboue,

    Ile neuer pawse againe, neuer stand still,

    Till either death hath clos'd these eyes of mine,

    Or Fortune giuen me measure of Reuenge.   1000

EDWARD (*kneeling*)

    Oh Warwicke, I do bend my knee with thine,

    And in this vow do chaine my soule to thine:

    And ere my knee rise from the Earths cold face,

I throw my hands, mine eyes, my heart to thee,
Thou setter vp, and plucker downe of Kings:
Beseeching thee (if with thy will it stands)
That to my Foes this body must be prey,
Yet that thy brazen gates of heauen may ope,
And giue sweet passage to my sinfull soule.
          ⌜They rise⌝

1010   Now Lords, take leaue vntill we meete againe,
        Where ere it be, in heauen, or in earth.

RICHARD
        Brother, giue me thy hand, and gentle Warwicke,
        Let me imbrace thee in my weary armes:
        I that did neuer weepe, now melt with wo,
        That Winter should cut off our Spring-time so.

WARWICKE
        Away, away: once more sweet Lords farwell.

GEORGE
        Yet let vs altogether to our Troopes,
        And giue them leaue to flye, that will not stay:
        And call them Pillars that will stand to vs:
1020   And if we thriue, promise them such rewards
        As Victors weare at the Olympian Games.
        This may plant courage in their quailing breasts,
        For yet is hope of Life and Victory:
        Foreslow no longer, make we hence amaine.   Exeunt

Sc. 8   ⌜Alarmes.⌝ Excursions. Enter Richard ⌜at one dore⌝
(2.4)   and Clifford ⌜at the other⌝

RICHARD
        Now Clifford, I haue singled thee alone,
        Suppose this arme is for the Duke of Yorke,
        And this for Rutland, both bound to reuenge,
        Wer't thou inuiron'd with a Brazen wall.

CLIFFORD
        Now Richard, I am with thee heere alone,
1030   This is the hand that stabb'd thy Father Yorke,
        And this the hand, that slew thy Brother Rutland,
        And here's the heart, that triumphs in their death,
        And cheeres these hands, that slew thy Sire and
              Brother,
        To execute the like vpon thy selfe,
        And so haue at thee.
              They Fight, Warwicke comes and rescues Richard.
              Clifford flies

RICHARD
        Nay Warwicke, single out some other Chace,
        For I my selfe will hunt this Wolfe to death.   Exeunt

Sc. 9   Alarum. Enter King Henry alone
(2.5)   KING HENRY
        This battell fares like to the mornings Warre,
              When dying clouds contend, with growing light,
1040   What time the Shepheard blowing of his nailes,
              Can neither call it perfect day, nor night.
        Now swayes it this way, like a Mighty Sea,
              Forc'd by the Tide, to combat with the Winde:
        Now swayes it that way, like the selfe-same Sea,
              Forc'd to retyre by furie of the Winde.

Sometime, the Flood preuailes; and than the Winde:
Now, one the better: then, another best;
Both tugging to be Victors, brest to brest:
Yet neither Conqueror, nor Conquered.
So is the equall poise of this fell Warre.   1050
Heere on this Mole-hill will I sit me downe,
To whom God will, there be the Victorie:
For Margaret my Queene, and Clifford too
Haue chid me from the Battell: Swearing both,
They prosper best of all when I am thence.
Would I were dead, if Gods good will were so;
For what is in this world, but Greefe and Woe.
Oh God! me thinkes it were a happy life,
To be no better then a homely Swaine,
To sit vpon a hill, as I do now,   1060
To carue out Dialls queintly, point by point,
Thereby to see the Minutes how they runne:
How many makes the Houre full compleate,
How many Houres brings about the Day,
How many Dayes will finish vp the Yeare,
How many Yeares, a Mortall man may liue.
When this is knowne, then to diuide the Times:
So many Houres, must I tend my Flocke;
So many Houres, must I take my Rest:
So many Houres, must I Contemplate: 1070
So many Houres, must I Sport my selfe:
So many Dayes, my Ewes haue bene with yong:
So many weekes, ere the poore Fooles will Eane:
So many yeares, ere I shall sheere the Fleece:
So Minutes, Houres, Dayes, Weekes, Monthes, and
        Yeares,
Past ouer to the end they were created,
Would bring white haires, vnto a Quiet graue.
Ah! what a life were this? How sweet? how louely?
Giues not the Hawthorne bush a sweeter shade
To Shepheards, looking on their silly Sheepe,   1080
Then doth a rich Imbroider'd Canopie
To Kings, that feare their Subiects treacherie?
Oh yes, it doth; a thousand fold it doth.
And to conclude, the Shepherds homely Curds,
His cold thinne drinke out of his Leather Bottle,
His wonted sleepe, vnder a fresh trees shade,
All which secure, and sweetly he enioyes,
Is farre beyond a Princes Delicates:
His Viands sparkling in a Golden Cup,
His bodie couched in a curious bed,   1090
When Care, Mistrust, and Treason waits on him.
        Alarum. Enter ⌜at one doore⌝ a souldier with a dead
        man in his armes. King Henry stands aloofe

SOULDIER
Ill blowes the winde that profits no body,
This man whom hand to hand I slew in fight,
May be possessed with some store of Crownes,
And I that (haply) take them from him now,
May yet (ere night) yeeld both my Life and them
To some man else, as this dead man doth me.
        ⌜He remoues the dead mans helmet⌝
Who's this? Oh God! It is my Fathers face,

Whom in this Conflict, I (vnwares) haue kill'd:
1100 Oh heauy times! begetting such Euents.
From London, by the King was I prest forth,
My Father being the Earle of Warwickes man,
Came on the part of Yorke, prest by his Master:
And I, who at his hands receiu'd my life,
Haue by my hands, of Life bereaued him.
Pardon me God, I knew not what I did:
And pardon Father, for I knew not thee.
My Teares shall wipe away these bloody markes:
And no more words, till they haue flow'd their fill.
          He weepes

KING HENRY
1110 O pitteous spectacle! O bloody Times!
Whiles Lyons Warre, and battaile for their Dennes,
Poore harmlesse Lambes abide their enmity.
Weepe wretched man: Ile ayde thee Teare for Teare,
And let our hearts and eyes, like Ciuill Warre,
Be blinde with teares, and break ore-charg'd with griefe.
          Enter ⌈at another doore⌉ an other souldier, with a
          dead man ⌈in his armes⌉

2. SOULDIER
Thou that so stoutly hath resisted me,
Giue me thy Gold, if thou hast any Gold:
For I haue bought it with an hundred blowes.
          ⌈*He remoues the dead mans helmet*⌉
But let me see: Is this our Foe-mans face?
1120 Ah, no, no, no, it is mine onely Sonne.
Ah Boy, if any life be left in thee,
Throw vp thine eye: (*weeping*) see, see, what showres
          arise,
Blowne with the windie Tempest of my heart,
Vpon thy wounds, that killes mine Eye, and Heart.
O pitty God, this miserable Age!
What Stratagems? how fell? how Butcherly?
Erreoneous, mutinous, and vnnaturall,
This deadly quarrell daily doth beget?
O Boy! thy Father gaue thee life too soone,
1130 And hath bereft thee of thy life too late.

KING HENRY
Wo aboue wo: greefe, more thē common greefe!
O that my death would stay these ruthfull deeds:
O pitty, pitty, gentle heauen pitty:
The Red Rose and the White are on his face,
The fatall Colours of our striuing Houses:
The one, his purple Blood right well resembles,
The other his pale Cheekes (me thinkes) presenteth:
Wither one Rose, and let the other flourish:
If you contend, a thousand liues must wither.

1. SOULDIER
1140 How will my Mother, for a Fathers death
Take on with me, and ne're be satisfi'd?

2. SOULDIER
How will my Wife, for slaughter of my Sonne,
Shed seas of Teares, and ne're be satisfi'd?

KING HENRY
How will the Country, for these woful chances,
Mis-thinke the King, and not be satisfied?

1. SOULDIER
Was euer sonne, so rew'd a Fathers death?

2. SOULDIER
Was euer Father so bemoan'd his Sonne?

KING HENRY
Was euer King so greeu'd for Subiects woe?
Much is your sorrow; Mine, ten times so much.

1. SOULDIER (*to his Fathers body*)
Ile beare thee hence, where I may weepe my fill.   1150
          Exit ⌈at one doore⌉ with the body of his Father

2. SOULDIER (*to his Sonnes body*)
These armes of mine shall be thy winding sheet:
My heart (sweet Boy) shall be thy Sepulcher,
For from my heart, thine Image ne're shall go.
My sighing brest, shall be thy Funerall bell;
And so obsequious will thy Father be,
Een for the losse of thee, hauing no more,
As *Priam* was for all his Valiant Sonnes,
Ile beare thee hence, and let them fight that will,
For I haue murthred where I should not kill.
          Exit ⌈at another doore⌉ with the body
                              of his Sonne

KING HENRY
Sad-hearted-men, much ouergone with Care;   1160
Heere sits a King, more wofull then you are.
          Alarums. Excursions. Enter Edward the Prince

PRINCE EDWARD
Fly Father, flye: for all your Friends are fled.
And Warwicke rages like a chafed Bull:
Away, for death doth hold vs in pursuite.
          ⌈*Enter Queene Margaret*⌉

QUEENE MARGARET
Mount you my Lord, towards Barwicke post amaine:
Edward and *Richard* like a brace of Grey-hounds,
Hauing the fearfull flying Hare in sight,
With fiery eyes, sparkling for very wrath,
And bloody steele graspt in their yrefull hands
Are at our backes, and therefore hence amaine.   1170
          ⌈*Enter Exeter*⌉

EXETER
Away: for vengeance comes along with them.
Nay, stay not to expostulate, make speed,
Or else come after, Ile away before.

KING HENRY
Nay take me with thee, good sweet Exeter:
Not that I feare to stay, but loue to go
Whether the Queene intends. Forward, away.   *Exeunt*

          A lowd alarum. Enter Clifford Wounded, ⌈with an   **Sc. 10**
          arrow in his necke⌉   **(2.6)**

CLIFFORD
Heere burnes my Candle out; I, heere it dies,
Which whiles it lasted, gaue King *Henry* light.
O Lancaster! I feare thy ouerthrow,
More then my Bodies parting with my Soule: 1180
My Loue and Feare, glew'd many Friends to thee,
And now I fall, thy tough Commixture melts,
Impairing *Henry*, strength'ning misproud Yorke;

The common people swarme like summer flies,
And whether flye the Gnats, but to the Sunne?
And who shines now, but *Henries* Enemies?
O Phœbus! had'st thou neuer giuen consent,
That *Phaeton* should checke thy fiery Steeds,
Thy burning Carre neuer had scorch'd the earth.
1190 And *Henry*, had'st thou sway'd as Kings should do,
Or as thy Father, and his Father did,
Giuing no ground vnto the house of Yorke,
They neuer then had sprung like Sommer Flyes:
I, and ten thousand in this lucklesse Realme,
Had left no mourning Widdowes for our death,
And thou this day, had'st kept thy Chaire in peace.
For what doth cherrish Weeds, but gentle ayre?
And what makes Robbers bold, but too much lenity?
Bootlesse are Plaints, and Curelesse are my Wounds:
1200 No way to flye, nor strength to hold out flight:
The Foe is mercilesse, and will not pitty:
For at their hands I haue deseru'd no pitty.
The ayre hath got into my deadly Wounds,
And much effuse of blood, doth make me faint:
Come *Yorke*, and *Richard*, *Warwicke*, and the rest,
I stab'd your Fathers bosomes; Split my brest.
    ⌈He swownes.⌉
        Alarum & Retreat. Enter Edward, Warwicke,
        Richard, and Soldiers, ⌈*Montague*,⌉ & *George*

EDWARD
Now breath we Lords, good fortune bids vs pause,
And smooth the frownes of War, with peacefull lookes:
Some Troopes pursue the bloody-minded Queene,
1210 That led calme *Henry*, though he were a King,
As doth a Saile, fill'd with a fretting Gust
Command an Argosie to stemme the Waues.
But thinke you (Lords) that Clifford fled with them?

WARWICKE
No, 'tis impossible he should escape:
(For though before his face I speake the words)
Your Brother *Richard* markt him for the Graue.
And wheresoere he is, hee's surely dead.
        Clifford grones
⌈EDWARD⌉
Whose soule is that which takes hir heauy leaue?
⌈RICHARD⌉
A deadly grone, like life and deaths departing.
⌈EDWARD⌉ ⌈*to Richard*⌉
See who it is.
        ⌈*Richard goes to Clifford*⌉
1220   And now the Battailes ended,
If Friend or Foe, let him be gently vsed.
RICHARD
Reuoke that doome of mercy, for 'tis *Clifford*,
Who not contented that he lopp'd the Branch
In hewing Rutland, when his leaues put forth,
But set his murth'ring knife vnto the Roote,
From whence that tender spray did sweetly spring,
I meane our Princely Father, Duke of Yorke.
WARWICKE
From off the gates of Yorke, fetch down ye head,

Your Fathers head, which *Clifford* placed there:
In stead whereof, let this supply the roome,   1230
Measure for measure, must be answered.
EDWARD
Bring forth that fatall Schreechowle to our house,
That nothing sung but death, to vs and ours:
        ⌈*Clifford is dragged forward*⌉
Now death shall stop his dismall threatning sound,
And his ill-boading tongue, no more shall speake.
WARWICKE
I thinke his vnderstanding is bereft:
Speake *Clifford*, dost thou know who speakes to thee?
Darke cloudy death ore-shades his beames of life,
And he nor sees, nor heares vs, what we say.
RICHARD
O would he did, and so (perhaps) he doth,   1240
'Tis but his policy to counterfet,
Because he would auoid such bitter taunts
Which in the time of death he gaue our Father.
GEORGE
If so thou think'st, vex him with eager Words.
RICHARD
Clifford, aske mercy, and obtaine no grace.
EDWARD
Clifford, repent in bootlesse penitence.
WARWICKE
Clifford, deuise excuses for thy faults.
GEORGE
While we deuise fell Tortures for thy faults.
RICHARD
Thou didd'st loue Yorke, and I am son to Yorke.
EDWARD
Thou pittied'st Rutland, I will pitty thee.   1250
GEORGE
Where's Captaine *Margaret*, to fence you now?
WARWICKE
They mocke thee *Clifford*, sweare as thou was't wont.
RICHARD
What, not an Oath? Nay then the world go's hard
When *Clifford* cannot spare his Friends an oath:
I know by that he's dead, and by my Soule,
If this right hand would buy but two houres life,
That I (in all despight) might rayle at him,
This hand should chop it off: & with the issuing Blood
Stifle the Villaine, whose vnstanched thirst
Yorke, and yong Rutland could not satisfie.   1260
WARWICKE
I, but he's dead. Of with the Traitors head,
And reare it in the place your Fathers stands.
And now to London with Triumphant march,
There to be crowned Englands Royall King:
From whence, shall Warwicke cut the Sea to France,
And aske the Ladie *Bona* for thy Queene:
So shalt thou sinow both these Lands together,
And hauing France thy Friend, thou shalt not dread
The scattred Foe, that hopes to rise againe:
For though they cannot greatly sting to hurt,   1270
Yet looke to haue them buz to offend thine eares:

First, will I see the Coronation,
And then to Britanny Ile crosse the Sea,
To effect this marriage, so it please my Lord.

EDWARD
Euen as thou wilt sweet Warwicke, let it bee:
For in thy shoulder do I builde my Seate;
And neuer will I vndertake the thing
Wherein thy counsaile and consent is wanting:
Richard, I will create thee Duke of Gloucester,
1280   And *George* of Clarence; *Warwicke* as our Selfe,
Shall do, and vndo as him pleaseth best.

RICHARD
Let me be Duke of Clarence, *George* of Gloster,
For Glosters Dukedome is too ominous.

WARWICKE
Tut, that's a foolish obseruation:
Richard, be Duke of Gloster: Now to London,
To see these Honors in possession.
                    Exeunt. ⌈*Yorkes head is remoued*⌉

Sc. 11   *Enter 2. Keepers, with Crosse-bowes in their hands*
(3.1)   1. KEEPER
Vnder this thicke growne brake, wee'l shrowd our
        selues:
For through this Laund anon the Deere will come,
And in this couert will we make our Stand,
1290   Culling the principall of all the Deere.

2. KEEPER
Ile stay aboue the hill, so both may shoot.

1. KEEPER
That cannot be, the noise of thy Crosse-bow
Will scarre the Heard, and so my shoot is lost:
Heere stand we both, and ayme we at the best:
And for the time shall not seeme tedious,
Ile tell thee what befell me on a day,
In this selfe-place, where now we meane to stand.

1. KEEPER
Heere comes a man, let's stay till he be past.
        They stand aloofe.
        Enter Henry the King disguisde, with a Prayer
        booke

KING HENRY
From Scotland am I stolne euen of pure loue,
1300   To greet mine owne Land with my wishfull sight:
No *Harry*, *Harry*, 'tis no Land of thine,
Thy place is fill'd, thy Scepter wrung from thee,
Thy Balme washt off, wherewith thou wast Annointed:
No bending knee will call thee *Cæsar* now,
No humble suters prease to speake for right:
No, not a man comes for redresse of thee:
For how can I helpe them, and not my selfe?

1. KEEPER (*to 2. Keeper*)
I, heere's a Deere, whose skin's a Keepers Fee:
This is the quondam King; Let's seize vpon him.

KING HENRY
1310   Let me embrace the sower Aduersitie,
For Wise men say, it is the wisest course.

2. KEEPER (*to 1. Keeper*)
Why linger we? Let vs lay hands vpon him.

1. KEEPER (*to 2. Keeper*)
Forbeare a-while, wee'l heare a little more.

KING HENRY
My Queene and Son are gone to France for aid:
And (as I heare) the great Commanding Warwicke
Is thither gone, to craue the French Kings Sister
To wife for *Edward*. If this newes be true,
Poore Queene, and Sonne, your labour is but lost:
For Warwicke is a subtle Orator:
And *Lewis* a Prince soone wonne with mouing words: 1320
By this account then, *Margaret* may winne him,
For she's a woman to be pittied much:
Her sighes will make a batt'ry in his brest,
Her teares will pierce into a Marble heart:
The Tyger will be milde, whiles she doth mourne;
And *Nero* will be tainted with remorse,
To heare and see her plaints, her Brinish Teares.
I, but shee's come to begge, Warwicke to giue:
Shee on his left side, crauing ayde for *Henrie*;
He on his right, asking a wife for *Edward*.   1330
Shee Weepes, and says, her *Henry* is depos'd:
He Smiles, and says, his *Edward* is instaul'd;
That she (poore Wretch) for greefe can speake no
        more:
Whiles Warwicke tels his Title, smooths the Wrong,
Inferreth arguments of mighty strength,
And in conclusion winnes the King from her,
With promise of his Sister, and what else,
To strengthen and support King *Edwards* place.
O *Margaret*, thus 'twill be, and thou (poore soule)
Art then forsaken, as thou went'st forlorne.   1340

2. KEEPER (*comming forward*)
Say, what art thou that talk'st of Kings & Queens?

KING HENRY
More then I seeme, and lesse then I was born to:
A man at least, for lesse I should not be:
And men may talke of Kings, and why not I?

2. KEEPER
I, but thou talk'st, as if thou wer't a King.

KING HENRY
Why so I am (in Minde) and that's enough.

2. KEEPER
But if thou be a King, where is thy Crowne?

KING HENRY
My Crowne is in my heart, not on my head:
Not deck'd with Diamonds, and Indian stones:
Nor to be seene: my Crowne, is call'd Content,   1350
A Crowne it is, that sildome Kings enioy.

2. KEEPER
Well, if you be a King crown'd with Content,
Your Crowne Content, and you, must be contented
To go along with vs. For (as we thinke)
You are the king King *Edward* hath depos'd:
And we his subiects, sworne in all Allegeance,
Will apprehend you, as his Enemie.

KING HENRY
But did you neuer sweare, and breake an Oath.

2. KEEPER
No, neuer such an Oath, nor will not now.

KING HENRY

1360   Where did you dwell when I was K. of England?

2. KEEPER

Heere in this Country, where we now remaine.

KING HENRY

I was annointed King at nine monthes old,
My Father, and my Grandfather were Kings:
And you were sworne true Subiects vnto me:
And tell me then, haue you not broke your Oathes?

1. KEEPER

No, for we were Subiects, but while you wer king.

KING HENRY

Why? Am I dead? Do I not breath a Man?
Ah simple men, you know not what you sweare:
Looke, as I blow this Feather from my Face,
1370   And as the Ayre blowes it to me againe,
Obeying with my winde when I do blow,
And yeelding to another, when it blowes,
Commanded alwayes by the greater gust:
Such is the lightnesse of you, common men.
But do not breake your Oathes, for of that sinne,
My milde intreatie shall not make you guiltie.
Go where you will, the king shall be commanded,
And be you kings, command, and Ile obey.

1. KEEPER

We are true Subiects to the king, King *Edward*.

KING HENRY

1380   So would you be againe to *Henrie*,
If he were seated as king *Edward* is.

1. KEEPER

We charge you in Gods name & in the Kings,
To go with vs vnto the Officers.

KING HENRY

In Gods name lead, your Kings name be obeyd,
And what God will, that let your King performe,
And what he will, I humbly yeeld vnto.   *Exeunt*

Sc. 12   *Enter King Edward, Richard Duke of Gloster,*
(3.2)   *George Duke of Clarence, Lady Gray*

KING EDWARD

Brother of Gloster, at S. Albons field
This Ladyes Husband, Sir *Richard Grey*, was slaine,
His Lands then seiz'd on by the Conqueror,
1390   Her suit is now, to repossesse those Lands,
Which wee in Iustice cannot well deny,
Because in Quarrell of the House of *Yorke*,
The worthy Gentleman did lose his Life.

RICHARD OF GLOSTER

Your Highnesse shall doe well to graunt her suit:
It were dishonor to deny it her.

KING EDWARD

It were no lesse, but yet Ile make a pawse.

RICHARD OF GLOSTER (*aside to George*) Yea, is it so:
I see the Lady hath a thing to graunt,
Before the King will graunt her humble suit.

GEORGE OF CLARENCE (*aside to Richard*)

1400   Hee knowes the Game, how true hee keepes the winde?

RICHARD OF GLOSTER (*aside to George*) Silence.

KING EDWARD (*to Lady Gray*)

Widow, we will consider of your suit,
And come some other time to know our minde.

LADY GRAY

Right gracious Lord, I cannot brooke delay:
May it please your Highnesse to resolue me now,
And what your pleasure is, shall satisfie me.

RICHARD OF GLOSTER (*aside to George*)

I Widow? then Ile warrant you all your Lands,
And if what pleases him, shall pleasure you:
Fight closer, or good faith you'le catch a Blow.

GEORGE OF CLARENCE (*aside to Richard*)

I feare her not, vnlesse she chance to fall.   1410

RICHARD OF GLOSTER (*aside to George*)

God forbid that, for hee'le take vantages.

KING EDWARD (*to Lady Gray*)

How many Children hast thou, Widow? tell me.

GEORGE OF CLARENCE (*aside to Richard*)

I thinke he meanes to begge a Child of her.

RICHARD OF GLOSTER (*aside to George*)

Nay whip me then: hee'le rather giue her two.

LADY GRAY (*to King Edward*) Three, my most gracious Lord.

RICHARD OF GLOSTER (*aside*)

You shall haue foure, and you'le be rul'd by him.

KING EDWARD (*to Lady Gray*)

'Twere pittie they should lose their Fathers Lands.

LADY GRAY

Be pittifull, dread Lord, and graunt it them.

KING EDWARD (*to Richard and George*)

Lords giue vs leaue, Ile trye this Widowes wit.

RICHARD OF GLOSTER ⌈*aside to George*⌉

I, good leaue haue you, for you will haue leaue,   1420
Till Youth take leaue, and leaue you to the Crutch.
          Richard and George stand aloofe

KING EDWARD (*to Lady Gray*)

Now tell me, Madame, doe you loue your Children?

LADY GRAY

I, full as dearely as I loue my selfe.

KING EDWARD

And would you not doe much to doe them good?

LADY GRAY

To doe them good, I would sustayne some harme.

KING EDWARD

Then get your Husbands Lands, to doe them good.

LADY GRAY

Therefore I came vnto your Maiestie.

KING EDWARD

Ile tell you how these Lands are to be got.

LADY GRAY

So shall you bind me to your Highnesse seruice.

KING EDWARD

What seruice wilt thou doe me, if I giue them?   1430

LADY GRAY

What you command, that rests in me to doe.

KING EDWARD

But you will take exceptions to my Boone.

LADY GRAY

No, gracious Lord, except I cannot doe it.

KING EDWARD
    I, but thou canst doe what I meane to aske.
LADY GRAY
    Why then I will doe what your Grace commands.
RICHARD OF GLOSTER (*to George*)
    Hee plyes her hard, and much Raine weares the
        Marble.
GEORGE OF CLARENCE
    As red as fire? nay then, her Wax must melt.
LADY GRAY (*to King Edward*)
    Why stoppes my Lord? shall I not heare my Taske?
KING EDWARD
    An easie Taske, 'tis but to loue a King.
LADY GRAY
1440   That's soone perform'd, because I am a Subiect.
KING EDWARD
    Why then, thy Husbands Lands I freely giue thee.
LADY GRAY (*cursies*)
    I take my leaue with many thousand thankes.
RICHARD OF GLOSTER (*to George*)
    The Match is made, shee seales it with a Cursie.
KING EDWARD (*to Lady Gray*)
    But stay thee, 'tis the fruits of loue I meane.
LADY GRAY
    The fruits of Loue, I meane, my louing Liege.
KING EDWARD
    I, but I feare me in another sence.
    What Loue, think'st thou, I sue so much to get?
LADY GRAY
    My loue till death, my humble thanks, my prayers,
    That loue which Vertue begges, and Vertue graunts.
KING EDWARD
1450   No, by my troth, I did not meane such loue.
LADY GRAY
    Why then you meane not, as I thought you did.
KING EDWARD
    But now you partly may perceiue my minde.
LADY GRAY
    My minde will neuer graunt what I perceiue
    Your Highnesse aymes at, if I ayme aright.
KING EDWARD
    To tell thee plaine, I ayme to lye with thee.
LADY GRAY
    To tell you plaine, I had rather lye in Prison.
KING EDWARD
    Why then thou shalt not haue thy Husbands Lands.
LADY GRAY
    Why then mine Honestie shall be my Dower,
    For by that losse, I will not purchase them.
KING EDWARD
1460   Therein thou wrong'st thy Children mightily.
LADY GRAY
    Herein your Highnesse wrongs both them & me:
    But mightie Lord, this merry inclination
    Accords not with the sadnesse of my suit:
    Please you dismisse me, eyther with I, or no.
KING EDWARD
    I, if thou wilt say I to my request:
    No, if thou do'st say No to my demand.

LADY GRAY
    Then No, my Lord: my suit is at an end.
RICHARD OF GLOSTER (*to George*)
    The Widow likes him not, shee knits her Browes.
GEORGE OF CLARENCE
    Hee is the bluntest Wooer in Christendome.
KING EDWARD (*aside*)
    Her Looks doth argue her replete with Modesty,   1470
    Her Words doth shew her Wit incomparable,
    All her perfections challenge Soueraigntie,
    One way, or other, shee is for a King,
    And shee shall be my Loue, or else my Queene.
    (*To Lady Gray*) Say, that King *Edward* take thee for his
        Queene?
LADY GRAY
    'Tis better said then done, my gracious Lord:
    I am a subiect fit to ieast withall,
    But farre vnfit to be a Soueraigne.
KING EDWARD
    Sweet Widow, by my State I sweare to thee,
    I speake no more then what my Soule intends,   1480
    And that is, to enioy thee for my Loue.
LADY GRAY
    And that is more then I will yeeld vnto:
    I know, I am too meane to be your Queene,
    And yet too good to be your Concubine.
KING EDWARD
    You cauill, Widow, I did meane my Queene.
LADY GRAY
    'Twill grieue your Grace, my Sonnes should call you
        Father.
KING EDWARD
    No more, then when my Daughters call thee Mother.
    Thou art a Widow, and thou hast some Children,
    And by Gods Mother, I being but a Batchelor,
    Haue other-some. Why, 'tis a happy thing,   1490
    To be the Father vnto many Sonnes:
    Answer no more, for thou shalt be my Queene.
RICHARD OF GLOSTER (*to George*)
    The Ghostly Father now hath done his Shrift.
GEORGE OF CLARENCE
    When hee was made a Shriuer, 'twas for shift.
KING EDWARD (*to Richard and George*)
    Brothers, you muse what Chat wee two haue had.
        Richard and George come forward
RICHARD OF GLOSTER
    The Widow likes it not, for shee lookes very sad.
KING EDWARD
    You'ld thinke it strange, if I should marrie her.
GEORGE OF CLARENCE
    To who, my Lord?
KING EDWARD   Why *Clarence*, to my selfe.
RICHARD OF GLOSTER
    That would be tenne dayes wonder at the least.
GEORGE OF CLARENCE
    That's a day longer then a Wonder lasts.   1500
RICHARD OF GLOSTER
    By so much is the Wonder in extremes.

KING EDWARD

Well, ieast on Brothers: I can tell you both,
Her suit is graunted for her Husbands Lands.
    Enter a Noble man

NOBLE MAN

My gracious Lord, *Henry* your Foe is taken,
And brought as Prisoner to your Pallace Gate.

KING EDWARD

See that he be conuey'd vnto the Tower:
(*To Richard and George*)
And goe wee Brothers to the man that tooke him,
To question of his apprehension.
(*To Lady Gray*) Widow goe you along: ⌈*To Richard and*
    George⌉ Lords vse her honourablie.
            Exeunt. Manet Richard

RICHARD OF GLOSTER

1510 I, *Edward* will vse Women honourably:
Would he were wasted, Marrow, Bones, and all,
That from his Loynes no hopefull Branch may spring,
To crosse me from the Golden time I looke for:
And yet, betweene my Soules desire, and me,
The lustfull *Edwards* Title buryed,
Is *Clarence, Henry,* and his Sonne young *Edward,*
And all the vnlook'd-for Issue of their Bodies,
To take their Roomes, ere I can place my selfe:
A cold premeditation for my purpose.

1520 Why then I doe but dreame on Soueraigntie,
Like one that stands vpon a Promontorie,
And spyes a farre-off shore, where hee would tread,
Wishing his foot were equall with his eye,
And chides the Sea, that sunders him from thence,
Saying, hee'le lade it dry, to haue his way:
So doe I wish the Crowne, being so farre off,
And so I chide the meanes that keepes me from it,
And so (I say) Ile cut the Causes off,
Flattering me with impossibilities:

1530 My Eyes too quicke, my Heart o're-weenes too much,
Vnlesse my Hand and Strength could equall them.
Well, say there is no Kingdome then for *Richard*:
What other Pleasure can the World affoord?
Ile make my Heauen in a Ladies Lappe,
And decke my Body in gay Ornaments,
And 'witch sweet Ladies with my Words and Lookes.
Oh miserable Thought! and more vnlikely,
Then to accomplish twentie Golden Crownes.
Why Loue forswore me in my Mothers Wombe:

1540 And for I should not deale in her soft Lawes,
Shee did corrupt frayle Nature with some Bribe,
To shrinke mine Arme vp like a wither'd Shrub,
To make an enuious Mountaine on my Back,
Where sits Deformitie to mocke my Body;
To shape my Legges of an vnequall size,
To dis-proportion me in euery part:
Like to a Chaos, or an vn-lick'd Beare-whelpe,
That carryes no impression like the Damme.
And am I then a man to be belou'd?

1550 Oh monstrous fault, to harbour such a thought.

Then since this Earth affoords no Ioy to me,
But to command, to check, to o're-beare such,
As are of better Person then my selfe:
Ile make my Heauen, to dreame vpon the Crowne,
And whiles I liue, t'account this World but Hell,
Vntill my mis-shap'd Trunke, that beares this Head,
Be round impaled with a glorious Crowne.
And yet I know not how to get the Crowne,
For many Liues stand betweene me and home:
And I, like one lost in a Thornie Wood,   1560
That rents the Thornes, and is rent with the Thornes,
Seeking a way, and straying from the way,
Not knowing how to finde the open Ayre,
But toyling desperately to finde it out,
Torment my selfe, to catch the English Crowne:
And from that torment I will free my selfe,
Or hew my way out with a bloody Axe.
Why I can smile, and murther whiles I smile,
And cry, Content, to that which grieues my Heart,
And wet my Cheekes with artificiall Teares,   1570
And frame my Face to all occasions.
Ile drowne more Saylers then the Mermaid shall,
Ile slay more gazers then the Basiliske,
Ile play the Orator as well as *Nestor,*
Deceiue more slyly then *Vlisses* could,
And like a *Synon,* take another Troy.
I can adde Colours to the Camelion,
Change shapes with *Proteus,* for aduantages,
And set the murtherous *Macheuill* to Schoole.
Can I doe this, and cannot get a Crowne?   1580
Tut, were it farther off, Ile plucke it downe.   *Exit*

⌈*2.*⌉ *Chayres of State. Flourish. Enter Lewis the*   Sc. 13
French King, his Sister Bona, his Admirall, call'd   (3.3)
Bourbon: Prince Edward, Queene Margaret, and the
Earle of Oxford. Lewis goes vp vpon the State, sits,
and riseth vp againe

KING LEWIS

Faire Queene of England, worthy *Margaret,*
Sit downe with vs: it ill befits thy State,
And Birth, that thou should'st stand, while *Lewis*
    doth sit.

QUEENE MARGARET

No, mightie King of France: now *Margaret*
Must strike her sayle, and learne a while to serue,
Where Kings command. I was (I must confesse)
Great Albions Queene, in former Golden dayes:
But now mischance hath trod my Title downe,
And with dis-honor layd me on the ground,   1590
Where I must take like Seat vnto my fortune,
And to my humble State conforme my selfe.

KING LEWIS

Why say, faire Queene, whence springs this deepe
    despaire?

QUEENE MARGARET

From such a cause, as fills mine eyes with teares,
And stops my tongue, while heart is drown'd in cares.

KING LEWIS

What ere it be, be thou still like thy selfe,
And sit thee by our side.
        Seats her by him
                        Yeeld not thy necke
To Fortunes yoake, but let thy dauntlesse minde
Still ride in triumph, ouer all mischance.
1600   Be plaine, Queene *Margaret*, and tell thy griefe,
It shall be eas'd, if France can yeeld reliefe.

QUEENE MARGARET

Those gracious words reuiue my drooping thoughts,
And giue my tongue-ty'd sorrowes leaue to speake.
Now therefore be it knowne to Noble *Lewis*,
That *Henry*, sole possessor of my Loue,
Is, of a King, become a banisht man,
And forc'd to liue in Scotland a Forlorne;
While prowd ambitious *Edward*, Duke of Yorke,
Vsurpes the Regall Title, and the Seat
1610   Of Englands true anoynted lawfull King.
This is the cause that I, poore *Margaret*,
With this my Sonne, Prince *Edward*, *Henries* Heire,
Am come to craue thy iust and lawfull ayde:
And if thou faile vs, all our hope is done.
Scotland hath will to helpe, but cannot helpe:
Our People, and our Peeres, are both mis-led,
Our Treasure seiz'd, our Souldiors put to flight,
And (as thou seest) our selues in heauie plight.

KING LEWIS

Renowned Queene, with patience calme the Storme,
1620   While we bethinke a meanes to breake it off.

QUEENE MARGARET

The more wee stay, the stronger growes our Foe.

KING LEWIS

The more I stay, the more Ile succour thee.

QUEENE MARGARET

O, but impatience waiteth on true sorrow.
        Enter Warwicke
And see where comes the breeder of my sorrow.

KING LEWIS

What's hee approacheth boldly to our presence?

QUEENE MARGARET

Our Earle of Warwicke, *Edwards* greatest Friend.

KING LEWIS

Welcome braue *Warwicke*, what brings thee to France?
        Hee descends. Shee ariseth

QUEENE MARGARET (aside)

I now begins a second Storme to rise,
For this is hee that moues both Winde and Tyde.

WARWICKE (to King Lewis)

1630   From worthy *Edward*, King of Albion,
My Lord and Soueraigne, and thy vowed Friend,
I come (in Kindnesse, and vnfayned Loue)
First, to doe greetings to thy Royall Person,
And then to craue a League of Amitie:
And lastly, to confirme that Amitie
With Nuptiall Knot, if thou vouchsafe to graunt
That vertuous Lady *Bona*, thy faire Sister,
To Englands King, in lawfull Marriage.

QUEENE MARGARET (aside)

If that goe forward, *Henries* hope is done.

WARWICKE (Speaking to Bona)

And gracious Madame, in our Kings behalfe,   1640
I am commanded, with your leaue and fauor,
Humbly to kisse your Hand, and with my Tongue
To tell the passion of my Soueraignes Heart;
Where Fame, late entring at his heedfull Eares,
Hath plac'd thy Beauties Image, and thy Vertue.

QUEENE MARGARET

King *Lewis*, and Lady *Bona*, heare me speake,
Before you answer *Warwicke*. His demand
Springs not from *Edwards* well-meant honest Loue,
But from Deceit, bred by Necessitie:
For how can Tyrants safely gouerne home,   1650
Vnlesse abroad they purchase great allyance?
To proue him Tyrant, this reason may suffice,
That *Henry* liueth still: but were hee dead,
Yet here Prince *Edward* stands, King *Henries* Sonne.
Looke therefore *Lewis*, that by this League and Mariage
Thou draw not on thy Danger, and Dis-honor:
For though Vsurpers sway the rule a while,
Yet Heau'ns are iust, and Time suppresseth Wrongs.

WARWICKE

Iniurious *Margaret*.

PRINCE EDWARD   And why not Queene?

WARWICKE

Because thy Father *Henry* did vsurpe,   1660
And thou no more art Prince, then shee is Queene.

OXFORD

Then *Warwicke* disanulls great *Iohn* of Gaunt,
Which did subdue the greatest part of Spaine;
And after *Iohn* of Gaunt, *Henry* the Fourth,
Whose Wisdome was a Mirror to the wisest:
And after that wise Prince, *Henry* the Fift,
Who by his Prowesse conquered all France:
From these, our *Henry* lineally descends.

WARWICKE

Oxford, how haps it in this smooth discourse,
You told not, how *Henry* the Sixt hath lost   1670
All that, which *Henry* the Fift had gotten:
Me thinkes these Peeres of France should smile at that.
But for the rest: you tell a Pedigree
Of threescore and two yeeres, a silly time
To make prescription for a Kingdomes worth.

OXFORD

Why *Warwicke*, canst thou speak against thy Liege,
Whom thou obeydest thirtie and six yeeres,
And not bewray thy Treason with a Blush?

WARWICKE

Can *Oxford*, that did euer fence the right,
Now buckler Falsehood with a Pedigree?   1680
For shame leaue *Henry*, and call *Edward* King.

OXFORD

Call him my King, by whose iniurious doome
My elder Brother, the Lord *Aubrey Vere*
Was done to death? and more then so, my Father,
Euen in the downe-fall of his mellow'd yeeres,

When Nature brought him to the doore of Death?
No *Warwicke*, no: while Life vpholds this Arme,
This Arme vpholds the House of *Lancaster*.

WARWICKE And I the House of *Yorke*.

KING LEWIS
1690 Queene *Margaret*, Prince *Edward*, and *Oxford*,
Vouchsafe at our request, to stand aside,
While I vse further conference with *Warwicke*.
            Queen Margaret ⌈comes down from the State and⌉
            with Prince Edward and Oxford stands aloofe

QUEENE MARGARET
Heauens graunt, that *Warwickes* wordes bewitch him
   not.

KING LEWIS
Now *Warwicke*, tell me euen vpon thy conscience
Is *Edward* your true King? for I were loth
To linke with him, that were not lawfull chosen.

WARWICKE
Thereon I pawne my Credit, and mine Honor.

KING LEWIS
But is hee gracious in the Peoples eye?

WARWICKE
The more, that *Henry* was vnfortunate.

KING LEWIS
1700 Then further: all dissembling set aside,
Tell me for truth, the measure of his Loue
Vnto our Sister *Bona*.

WARWICKE   Such it seemes,
As may beseeme a Monarch like himselfe.
My selfe haue often heard him say, and sweare,
That this his Loue was an eternall Plant,
Whereof the Root was fixt in Vertues ground,
The Leaues and Fruit maintain'd with Beauties Sunne,
Exempt from Enuy, but not from Disdaine,
Vnlesse the Lady *Bona* quit his paine.

KING LEWIS (*to Bona*)
1710 Now Sister, let vs heare your firme resolue.

BONA
Your graunt, or your denyall, shall be mine.
(*Speaks to Warwicke*)
Yet I confesse, that often ere this day,
When I haue heard your Kings desert recounted,
Mine eare hath tempted iudgement to desire.

KING LEWIS (*to Warwicke*)
Then *Warwicke*, thus: our Sister shall be *Edwards*.
And now forthwith shall Articles be drawne,
Touching the Ioynture that your King must make,
Which with her Dowrie shall be counter-poys'd:
(*To Queene Margaret*)
Draw neere, Queene *Margaret*, and be a witnesse,
1720 That *Bona* shall be Wife to the English King.
            Queene Margaret, Prince Edward ⌈and Oxford⌉ come
            forward

PRINCE EDWARD
To *Edward*, but not to the English King.

QUEENE MARGARET
Deceitfull *Warwicke*, it was thy deuice,
By this alliance to make void my suit:
Before thy comming, *Lewis* was *Henries* friend.

KING LEWIS
And still is friend to him, and *Margaret*.
But if your Title to the Crowne be weake,
As may appeare by *Edwards* good successe:
Then 'tis but reason, that I be releas'd
From giuing ayde, which late I promised.
Yet shall you haue all kindnesse at my hand,   1730
That your Estate requires, and mine can yeeld.

WARWICKE (*to Queene Margaret*)
Henry now liues in Scotland, at his ease;
Where hauing nothing, nothing can he lose.
And as for you your selfe (our quondam Queene)
You haue a Father able to maintaine you,
And better 'twere, you troubled him, then France.

QUEENE MARGARET
Peace, impudent and shamelesse Warwicke, Peace,
Proud setter vp, and puller downe of Kings,
I will not hence, till with my Talke and Teares
(Both full of Truth) I make King *Lewis* behold   1740
Thy slye conueyance, and thy Lords false loue,
            Post blowing a horne Within
For both of you are Birds of selfe-same Feather.

KING LEWIS
Warwicke, this is some poste to vs, or thee.
            Enter the Poste

POST (*Speakes to Warwick*)
My Lord Ambassador, these Letters are for you.
Sent from your Brother Marquesse *Montague*.
(*To Lewis*) These from our King, vnto your Maiesty.
(*To Queene Margaret*)
And Madam, these for you: from whom, I know not.
            They all reade their Letters

OXFORD (*to Prince Edward*)
I like it well, that our faire Queene and Mistris
Smiles at her newes, while *Warwicke* frownes at his.

PRINCE EDWARD
Nay marke how *Lewis* stampes as he were netled.   1750
I hope, all's for the best.

KING LEWIS
Warwicke, what are thy Newes? And yours, faire
   Queene.

QUEENE MARGARET
Mine such, as fill my heart with vnhop'd ioyes.

WARWICKE
Mine full of sorrow, and hearts discontent.

KING LEWIS
What? has your King married the Lady *Grey*?
And now to sooth your Forgery, and his,
Sends me a Paper to perswade me Patience?
Is this th'Alliance that he seekes with France?
Dare he presume to scorne vs in this manner?

QUEENE MARGARET
I told your Maiesty as much before: 1760
This proueth *Edwards* Loue, and Warwickes honesty.

WARWICKE
King *Lewis*, I heere protest in sight of heauen,
And by the hope I haue of heauenly blisse,
That I am cleere from this misdeed of *Edwards*;
No more my King, for he dishonors me,

But most himselfe, if he could see his shame.
Did I forget, that by the House of Yorke
My Father came vntimely to his death?
Did I let passe th'abuse done to my Neece?
1770   Did I impale him with the Regall Crowne?
Did I put *Henry* from his Natiue Right?
And am I guerdon'd at the last, with Shame?
Shame on himselfe, for my Desert is Honor.
And to repaire my Honor lost for him,
I heere renounce him, and returne to *Henry*.
(*To Queene Margaret*) My Noble Queene, let former
    grudges passe,
And henceforth, I am thy true Seruitour:
I will reuenge his wrong to Lady *Bona*,
And replant *Henry* in his former state.

QUEENE MARGARET
1780   Warwicke, these words haue turn'd my Hate, to Loue,
And I forgiue, and quite forget old faults,
And ioy that thou becom'st King *Henries* Friend.

WARWICKE
So much his Friend, I, his vnfained Friend,
That if King *Lewis* vouchsafe to furnish vs
With some few Bands of chosen Soldiours,
Ile vndertake to Land them on our Coast,
And force the Tyrant from his seat by Warre.
'Tis not his new-made Bride shall succour him.
And as for *Clarence*, as my Letters tell me,
1790   Hee's very likely now to fall from him,
For matching more for wanton Lust, then Honor,
Or then for strength and safety of our Country.

BONA (*to King Lewis*)
Deere Brother, how shall *Bona* be reueng'd,
But by thy helpe to this distressed Queene?

QUEENE MARGARET (*to King Lewis*)
Renowned Prince, how shall Poore *Henry* liue,
Vnlesse thou rescue him from foule dispaire?

BONA (*to King Lewis*)
My quarrel, and this English Queens, are one.

WARWICKE
And mine faire Lady *Bona*, ioynes with yours.

KING LEWIS
And mine, with hers, and thine, and *Margarets*.
1800   Therefore, at last, I firmely am resolu'd
You shall haue ayde.

QUEENE MARGARET
Let me giue humble thankes for all, at once.

KING LEWIS (*to the Post*)
Then Englands Messenger, returne in Poste,
And tell false *Edward*, thy supposed King,
That *Lewis* of France, is sending ouer Maskers
To reuell it with him, and his new Bride.
Thou seest what's past, go feare thy King withall.

BONA (*to the Post*)
Tell him, in hope hee'l proue a widower shortly,
Ile weare the Willow Garland for his sake.

QUEENE MARGARET (*to the Post*)
1810   Tell him, my mourning weeds are layde aside,
And I am ready to put Armor on.

WARWICKE (*to the Post*)
Tell him from me, that he hath done me wrong,
And therefore Ile vn-Crowne him, er't be long.
(*Giuing money*) There's thy reward, be gone.   *Exit Post*

KING LEWIS
But *Warwicke*, thou and Oxford, with fiue thousand
    men
Shall crosse the Seas, and bid false *Edward* battaile:
And as occasion serues, this Noble Queen
And Prince, shall follow with a fresh Supply.
Yet ere thou go, but answer me one doubt:
What Pledge haue we of thy firme Loyalty?   1820

WARWICKE
This shall assure my constant Loyalty,
That if our Queene, and this young Prince agree,
Ile ioyne mine eldest daughter, and my Ioy,
To him forthwith, in holy Wedlocke bands.

QUEENE MARGARET
Yes, I agree, and thanke you for your Motion.
(*To Prince Edward*) Sonne *Edward*, she is Faire and
    Vertuous,
Therefore delay not, giue thy hand to Warwicke,
And with thy hand, thy faith irreuocable,
That onely *Warwickes* daughter shall be thine.

PRINCE EDWARD
Yes, I accept her, for she well deserues it,   1830
And heere to pledge my Vow, I giue my hand.
He giues his hand to Warwicke

KING LEWIS
Why stay we now? These soldiers shalbe leuied,
And thou Lord Bourbon, our High Admirall
Shall waft them ouer with our Royall Fleete.
I long till *Edward* fall by Warres mischance,
For mocking Marriage with a Dame of France.
    Exeunt. Manet Warwicke

WARWICKE
I came from *Edward* as Ambassador,
But I returne his sworne and mortall Foe:
Matter of Marriage was the charge he gaue me,
But dreadfull Warre shall answer his demand.   1840
Had he none else to make a stale but me?
Then none but I, shall turne his Iest to Sorrow.
I was the Cheefe that rais'd him to the Crowne,
And Ile be Cheefe to bring him downe againe:
Not that I pitty *Henries* misery,
But seeke Reuenge on *Edwards* mockery.   *Exit*

Enter Richard of Gloster, George of Clarence,   Sc. 14
Somerset, and Mountague   (4.1)

RICHARD OF GLOSTER
Now tell me Brother *Clarence*, what thinke you
Of this new Marriage with the Lady *Gray*?
Hath not our Brother made a worthy choice?

GEORGE OF CLARENCE
Alas, you know, tis farre from hence to France,   1850
How could he stay till *Warwicke* made returne?

SOMERSET
My Lords, forbeare this talke: heere comes the King.

Flourish. Enter King Edward, Lady Grey his
Queene, Pembrooke, Stafford, Hastings: foure stand
on one side ⌈of the king⌉, and foure on the other

RICHARD OF GLOSTER And his well-chosen Bride.

GEORGE OF CLARENCE
I minde to tell him plainly what I thinke.

KING EDWARD
Now Brother of Clarence, how like you our Choyce,
That you stand pensiue, as halfe malecontent?

GEORGE OF CLARENCE
As well as *Lewis* of France, or the Earle of Warwicke,
Which are so weake of courage, and in iudgement,
That they'le take no offence at our abuse.

KING EDWARD
1860 Suppose they take offence without a cause:
They are but *Lewis* and *Warwicke*, I am *Edward*,
Your King and *Warwickes*, and must haue my will.

RICHARD OF GLOSTER
And you shall haue your will, because our King:
Yet hastie Marriage seldome proueth well.

KING EDWARD
Yea, Brother *Richard*, are you offended too?

RICHARD OF GLOSTER
Not I: no: God forbid, that I should wish them
 seuer'd,
Whom God hath ioyn'd together: I, and 'twere pittie,
To sunder them, that yoake so well together.

KING EDWARD
Setting your skornes, and your mislike aside,
1870 Tell me some reason, why the Lady *Grey*
Should not become my Wife, and Englands Queene?
And you too, *Somerset*, and *Mountague*,
Speake freely what you thinke.

GEORGE OF CLARENCE
Then this is my opinion: that King *Lewis*
Becomes your Enemie, for mocking him
About the Marriage of the Lady *Bona*.

RICHARD OF GLOSTER
And *Warwicke*, doing what you gaue in charge,
Is now dis-honored by this new Marriage.

KING EDWARD
What, if both *Lewis* and *Warwick* be appeas'd,
1880 By such inuention as I can deuise?

MOUNTAGUE
Yet, to haue ioyn'd with France in such alliance,
Would more haue strength'ned this our Commonwealth
'Gainst forraine stormes, then any home-bred Marriage.

HASTINGS
Why, knowes not *Mountague*, that of it selfe,
England is safe, if true within it selfe?

MOUNTAGUE
But the safer, when 'tis back'd with France.

HASTINGS
'Tis better vsing France, then trusting France:
Let vs be back'd with God, and with the Seas,
Which he hath giu'n for fence impregnable,
1890 And with their helpes, onely defend our selues:
In them, and in our selues, our safetie lyes.

GEORGE OF CLARENCE
For this one speech, Lord *Hastings* well deserues
To haue the Heire of the Lord *Hungerford*.

KING EDWARD
I, what of that? it was my will, and graunt,
And for this once, my Will shall stand for Law.

RICHARD OF GLOSTER
And yet me thinks, your Grace hath not done well,
To giue the Heire and Daughter of Lord *Scales*
Vnto the Brother of your louing Bride;
Shee better would haue fitted me, or *Clarence*:
But in your Bride you burie Brotherhood. 1900

GEORGE OF CLARENCE
Or else you would not haue bestow'd the Heire
Of the Lord *Bonuill* on your new Wiues Sonne,
And leaue your Brothers to goe speede elsewhere.

KING EDWARD
Alas, poore *Clarence*: is it for a Wife
That thou art malecontent? I will prouide thee.

GEORGE OF CLARENCE
In chusing for your selfe, you shew'd your
 iudgement:
Which being shallow, you shall giue me leaue
To play the Broker in mine owne behalfe;
And to that end, I shortly minde to leaue you.

KING EDWARD
Leaue me, or tarry, *Edward* will be King, 1910
And not be ty'd vnto his Brothers will.

LADY GRAY
My Lords, before it pleas'd his Maiestie
To rayse my State to Title of a Queene,
Doe me but right, and you must all confesse,
That I was not ignoble of Descent,
And meaner then my selfe haue had like fortune.
But as this Title honors me and mine,
So your dislikes, to whom I would be pleasing,
Doth cloud my ioyes with danger, and with sorrow.

KING EDWARD
My Loue, forbeare to fawne vpon their frownes: 1920
What danger, or what sorrow can befall thee,
So long as *Edward* is thy constant friend,
And their true Soueraigne, whom they must obey?
Nay, whom they shall obey, and loue thee too,
Vnlesse they seeke for hatred at my hands:
Which if they doe, yet will I keepe thee safe,
And they shall feele the vengeance of my wrath.

RICHARD OF GLOSTER (*aside*)
I heare, yet say not much, but thinke the more.
 Enter the Poste from France

KING EDWARD
Now Messenger, what Letters, or what Newes from
 France?

POST
My Soueraigne Liege, no Letters, & few words, 1930
But such, as I (without your speciall pardon)
Dare not relate.

KING EDWARD
Goe too, wee pardon thee: therefore, in briefe,

Tell me their words, as neere as thou canst guesse
　　them.
What answer makes King *Lewis* vnto our Letters?

POST

At my depart, these were his very words:
Goe tell false *Edward*, thy supposed King,
That *Lewis* of France is sending ouer Maskers,
To reuell it with him, and his new Bride.

KING EDWARD

1940　Is *Lewis* so braue? belike he thinkes me *Henry*.
But what said Lady *Bona* to my Marriage?

POST

These were her words, vtt'red with mild disdaine:
Tell him, in hope hee'le proue a Widower shortly,
Ile weare the Willow Garland for his sake.

KING EDWARD

I blame not her; she could say little lesse:
She had the wrong. But what said *Henries* Queene?
For I haue heard, that she was there in place.

POST

Tell him (quoth she) my mourning Weedes are done,
And I am readie to put Armour on.

KING EDWARD

1950　Belike she minds to play the Amazon.
But what said *Warwicke* to these iniuries?

POST

He, more incens'd against your Maiestie,
Then all the rest, discharg'd me with these words:
Tell him from me, that he hath done me wrong,
And therefore Ile vncrowne him, er't be long.

KING EDWARD

Ha? durst the Traytor breath out so prowd words?
Well, I will arme me, being thus fore-warn'd:
They shall haue Warres, and pay for their
　　presumption.
But say, is *Warwicke* friends with *Margaret*?

POST

1960　I, gracious Soueraigne, they are so link'd in friendship,
That yong Prince *Edward* marryes *Warwicks* Daughter.

GEORGE OF CLARENCE

Belike, the elder; *Clarence* will haue the younger.
Now Brother King farewell, and sit you fast,
For I will hence to *Warwickes* other Daughter,
That though I want a Kingdome, yet in Marriage
I may not proue inferior to your selfe.
You that loue me, and *Warwicke*, follow me.

　　　　　Exit Clarence, and Somerset followes

RICHARD OF GLOSTER

Not I: ⌈*aside*⌉ my thoughts ayme at a further matter:
I stay not for the loue of *Edward*, but the Crowne.

KING EDWARD

1970　*Clarence* and *Somerset* both gone to *Warwicke*?
Yet am I arm'd against the worst can happen:
And haste is needfull in this desp'rate case.
Pembrooke and *Stafford*, you in our behalfe
Goe leuie men, and make prepare for Warre;
They are alreadie, or quickly will be landed:
My selfe in person will straight follow you.

　　　　　Exeunt Pembrooke and Stafford

But ere I goe, *Hastings* and *Mountague*
Resolue my doubt: you twaine, of all the rest,
Are neer'st to *Warwicke*, by bloud, and by allyance:
Tell me, if you loue *Warwicke* more then me;　　1980
If it be so, then both depart to him:
I rather wish you foes, then hollow friends.
But if you minde to hold your true obedience,
Giue me assurance with some friendly Vow,
That I may neuer haue you in suspect.

MOUNTAGUE

So God helpe *Mountague*, as hee proues true.

HASTINGS

And *Hastings*, as hee fauours *Edwards* cause.

KING EDWARD

Now, Brother *Richard*, will you stand by vs?

RICHARD OF GLOSTER

I, in despight of all that shall withstand you.

KING EDWARD

Why so: then am I sure of Victorie.　　1990
Now therefore let vs hence, and lose no howre,
Till wee meet *Warwicke*, with his forreine powre.

　　　　　Exeunt

Enter Warwicke and Oxford in England, with　Sc. 15
French Souldiors　　　　　(4.2)

WARWICKE

Trust me, my Lord, all hitherto goes well,
The common sort by numbers swarme to vs.
　　　　　Enter Clarence and Somerset
But see where *Somerset* and *Clarence* comes:
Speake suddenly, my Lords, are wee all friends?

GEORGE OF CLARENCE Feare not that, my Lord.

WARWICKE

Then gentle *Clarence*, welcome vnto *Warwicke*,
And welcome *Somerset*: I hold it cowardize,
To rest mistrustfull, where a Noble Heart　　2000
Hath pawn'd an open Hand, in signe of Loue;
Else might I thinke, that *Clarence*, *Edwards* Brother,
Were but a fained friend to our proceedings:
But come sweet *Clarence*, my Daughter shall be thine.
And now, what rests? but in Nights Couerture,
Thy Brother being carelessely encamp'd,
His Souldiors lurking in the Townes about,
And but attended by a simple Guard,
Wee may surprize and take him at our pleasure,
Our Scouts haue found the aduenture very easie:　　2010
That as *Vlysses*, and stout *Diomede*,
With sleight and manhood stole to *Rhesus* Tents,
And brought from thence the Thracian fatall Steeds;
So wee, well couer'd with the Nights black Mantle,
At vnawares may beat downe *Edwards* Guard,
And seize himselfe: I say not, slaughter him,
For I intend but onely to surprize him.
You that will follow me to this attempt,
Applaud the Name of *Henry*, with your Leader.
　　　　　They all cry, Henry
Why then, let's on our way in silent sort,　　2020
For *Warwicke* and his friends, God and Saint *George*.

　　　　　Exeunt

Sc.16
(4.3)

Enter three Watchmen to guard Edward the Kings
Tent

1. WATCH
Come on my Masters, each man take his stand,
The King by this, is set him downe to sleepe.

2. WATCH What, will he not to Bed?

1. WATCH
Why, no: for he hath made a solemne Vow,
Neuer to lye and take his naturall Rest,
Till *Warwicke*, or himselfe, be quite supprest.

2. WATCH
To morrow then belike shall be the day,
If *Warwicke* be so neere as men report.

3. WATCH
2030   But say, I pray, what Noble man is that,
That with the King here resteth in his Tent?

1. WATCH
'Tis the Lord *Hastings*, the Kings chiefest friend.

3. WATCH
O, is it so? but why commands the King,
That his chiefe followers lodge in Townes about him,
While he himselfe keepes in the cold field?

2. WATCH
'Tis the more honour, because more dangerous.

3. WATCH
I, but giue me worship, and quietnesse,
I like it better then a dangerous honor.
If *Warwicke* knew in what estate he stands,
2040   'Tis to be doubted he would waken him.

1. WATCH
Vnlesse our Halberds did shut vp his passage.

2. WATCH
I: wherefore else guard we his Royall Tent,
But to defend his Person from Night-foes?

Enter Warwicke, George Duke of Clarence, Oxford,
Somerset, and French Souldiors, silent all

WARWICKE
This is his Tent, and see where stand his Guard:
Courage my Masters: Honor now, or neuer:
But follow me, and *Edward* shall be ours.

1. WATCH Who goes there?

2. WATCH Stay, or thou dyest.

Warwicke and the rest cry all, Warwicke,
Warwicke, and set vpon the Guard, who flye,
crying, Arme, Arme, Warwicke and the rest
following them

Sc. 17
(4.4)

The Drumme playing, and Trumpet sounding. Enter
Warwicke, Somerset, and the rest, bringing Edward
the King out in his Gowne, sitting in a Chaire:
Richard of Gloster and Hastings flyes ouer the
Stage

SOMERSET What are they that flye there?

WARWICKE
2050   *Richard* and *Hastings*: let them goe, heere is the Duke.

KING EDWARD
The Duke? Why *Warwicke*, when wee parted,
Thou call'dst me King.

WARWICKE   I, but the case is alter'd.

When you disgrac'd me in my Embassade,
Then I degraded you from being King,
And come now to create you Duke of Yorke.
Alas, how should you gouerne any Kingdome,
That know not how to vse Embassadors,
Nor how to be contented with one Wife,
Nor how to vse your Brothers Brotherly,
Nor how to studie for the Peoples Welfare,   2060
Nor how to shrowd your selfe from Enemies?

KING EDWARD (*seeing George*)
Yea, Brother of Clarence, art thou here too?
Nay then I see, that *Edward* needs must downe.
Yet *Warwicke*, in despight of all mischance,
Of thee thy selfe, and all thy Complices,
Edward will always beare himselfe as King:
Though Fortunes mallice ouerthrow my State,
My minde exceeds the compasse of her Wheele.

WARWICKE
Then for his minde, be *Edward* Englands King,

Warwicke takes off Edwards Crowne

But *Henry* now shall weare the English Crowne,   2070
And be true King indeede: thou but the shadow.
My Lord of Somerset, at my request,
See that forthwith Duke *Edward* be conuey'd
Vnto my Brother Arch-Bishop of Yorke:
When I haue fought with *Pembrooke*, and his fellowes,
Ile follow you, and tell what answer
Lewis and the Lady *Bona* send to him.
Now for a-while farewell good Duke of Yorke.

They begin to leade Edward out forcibly

KING EDWARD
What Fates impose, that men must needs abide;
It boots not to resist both winde and tide.   2080

Exeunt some with Edward

OXFORD
What now remaines my Lords for vs to do,
But march to London with our Soldiers?

WARWICKE
I, that's the first thing that we haue to do,
To free King *Henry* from imprisonment,
And see him seated in the Regall Throne.   *Exeunt*

Enter Riuers, and Lady Gray, Edwards Queene   **Sc. 18**
(4.5)

RIUERS
Madam, what makes you in this sodain change?

LADY GRAY
Why Brother *Riuers*, are you yet to learne
What late misfortune is befalne King *Edward*?

RIUERS
What? Losse of some pitcht battell against *Warwicke*?

LADY GRAY
No, but the losse of his owne Royall person.   2090

RIUERS Then is my Soueraigne slaine?

LADY GRAY
I almost slaine, for he is taken prisoner,
Either betrayd by falshood of his Guard,
Or by his Foe surpriz'd at vnawares:
And as I further haue to vnderstand,

Is new committed to the Bishop of Yorke,
Fell Warwickes Brother, and by that our Foe.

RIUERS

These Newes I must confesse are full of greefe,
Yet gracious Madam, beare it as you may,
2100 Warwicke may loose, that now hath wonne the day.

LADY GRAY

Till then, faire hope must hinder liues decay:
And I the rather waine me from dispaire
For loue of *Edwards* Off-spring in my wombe:
This is it that makes me bridle passion,
And beare with Mildnesse my misfortunes crosse:
I, I, for this I draw in many a teare,
And stop the rising of blood-sucking sighes,
Least with my sighes or teares, I blast or drowne
King *Edwards* Fruite, true heyre to th'English Crowne.

RIUERS

2110 But Madam, where is Warwicke then become?

LADY GRAY

I am informed that he comes towards London,
To set the Crowne once more on *Henries* head,
Guesse thou the rest, King *Edwards* Friends must
     downe.
But to preuent the Tyrants violence,
(For trust not him that hath once broken Faith)
Ile hence forthwith vnto the Sanctuary,
To saue (at least) the heire of *Edwards* right:
There shall I rest secure from force and fraud:
Come therefore let vs flye, while we may flye,
2120 If Warwicke take vs, we are sure to dye.   *Exeunt*

Sc. 19   *Enter Richard of Gloster, Lord Hastings, and Sir*
(4.6)   *William Stanley ⌈with Souldiers⌉*

RICHARD OF GLOSTER

Now my Lord *Hastings*, and Sir *William Stanley*
Leaue off to wonder why I drew you hither,
Into this cheefest Thicket of the Parke.
Thus stands the case: you know our King, my Brother,
Is prisoner to the Bishop here, at whose hands
He hath good vsage, and great liberty,
And often but attended with weake guard,
Comes hunting this way to disport himselfe.
I haue aduertis'd him by secret meanes,
2130 That if about this houre he make this way,
Vnder the colour of his vsuall game,
He shall heere finde his Friends with Horse and Men,
To set him free from his Captiuitie.

          Enter King Edward, and a Huntsman with him

HUNTSMAN

This way my Lord, for this way lies the Game.

KING EDWARD

Nay this way man, see where the Huntsmen stand.
Now Brother of Gloster, Lord Hastings, and the rest,
Stand you thus close to steale the Bishops Deere?

RICHARD OF GLOSTER

Brother, the time and case, requireth hast,
Your horse stands ready at the Parke-corner.

2140 KING EDWARD But whether shall we then?

HASTINGS To Lyn my Lord,
And shipt from thence to Flanders.

RICHARD OF GLOSTER ⌈*aside*⌉

Wel guest beleeue me, for that was my meaning.

KING EDWARD

Stanley, I will requite thy forwardnesse.

RICHARD OF GLOSTER

But wherefore stay we? 'tis no time to talke.

KING EDWARD

Huntsman, what say'st thou? Wilt thou go along?

HUNTSMAN

Better do so, then tarry and be hang'd.

RICHARD OF GLOSTER

Come then away, lets ha no more adoo.

KING EDWARD

Bishop farwell, sheeld thee from *Warwickes* frowne,
And pray that I may re-possesse the Crowne.   *Exeunt* 2150

          Flourish. Enter Warwicke and George of Clarence,   Sc. 20
          ⌈with the Crowne,⌉ and then King Henry the sixt,   (4.7)
          and Oxford, and Somerset ⌈with⌉ young Henry Earle
          of Richmond, and Mountague, and the Lieutenant
          of the Tower

KING HENRY

M. Lieutenant, now that God and Friends
Haue shaken *Edward* from the Regall seate,
And turn'd my captiue state to libertie,
My feare to hope, my sorrowes vnto ioyes,
At our enlargement what are thy due Fees?

LIEUTENANT

Subiects may challenge nothing of their Sou'rains:
But, if an humble prayer may preuaile,
I then craue pardon of your Maiestie.

KING HENRY

For what, Lieutenant? For well vsing me?
Nay, be thou sure, Ile well requite thy kindnesse,   2160
For that it made my prisonment, a pleasure:
I, such a pleasure, as incaged Birds
Conceiue; when after many moody Thoughts,
At last, by Notes of Houshold harmonie,
They quite forget their losse of Libertie.
But *Warwicke*, after God, thou set'st me free,
And chiefely therefore, I thanke God, and thee,
He was the Author, thou the Instrument.
Therefore that I may conquer Fortunes spight,
By liuing low, where Fortune cannot hurt me,   2170
And that the people of this blessed Land
May not be punisht with my thwarting starres,
Warwicke, although my Head still weare the Crowne,
I here resigne my Gouernment to thee,
For thou art fortunate in all thy deeds.

WARWICKE

Your Grace hath still beene fam'd for vertuous,
And now may seeme as wise as vertuous,
By spying and auoiding Fortunes malice,
For few men rightly temper with the Starres:
Yet in this one thing let me blame your Grace,   2180
For chusing me, when *Clarence* is in place.

GEORGE OF CLARENCE
No *Warwicke*, thou art worthy of the sway,
To whom the Heau'ns in thy Natiuitie,
Adiudg'd an Oliue Branch, and Lawrell Crowne,
As likely to be blest in Peace and Warre:
And therefore I yeeld thee my free consent.

WARWICKE
And I chuse *Clarence* onely for Protector.

KING HENRY
Warwick and *Clarence*, giue me both your Hands:
Now ioyne your Hands, & with your Hands your
    Hearts,
2190   That no dissention hinder Gouernment:
I make you both Protectors of this Land,
While I my selfe will lead a priuate Life,
And in deuotion spend my latter dayes,
To sinnes rebuke, and my Creators prayse.

WARWICKE
What answeres *Clarence* to his Soueraignes will?

GEORGE OF CLARENCE
That he consents, if *Warwicke* yeeld consent,
For on thy fortune I repose my selfe.

WARWICKE
Why then, though loth, yet must I be content:
Wee'le yoake together, like a double shadow
2200   To *Henries* Body, and supply his place;
I meane, in bearing weight of Gouernment,
While he enioyes the Honor, and his ease.
And *Clarence*, now then it is more then needfull,
Forthwith that *Edward* be pronounc'd a Traytor,
And all his Lands and Goods be confiscate.

GEORGE OF CLARENCE
What else? and that Succession be determined.

WARWICKE
I, therein *Clarence* shall not want his part.

KING HENRY
But with the first, of all your chiefe affaires,
Let me entreat (for I command no more)
2210   That *Margaret* your Queene, and my Sonne *Edward*,
Be sent for, to returne from France with speed:
For till I see them here, by doubtfull feare,
My ioy of libertie is halfe eclips'd.

GEORGE OF CLARENCE
It shall bee done, my Soueraigne, with all speede.

KING HENRY
My Lord of Somerset, what Youth is that,
Of whom you seeme to haue so tender care?

SOMERSET
My Liege, it is young *Henry*, Earle of Richmond.

KING HENRY
Come hither, Englands Hope:
    King Henry layes his Hand on Richmonds Head
                    If secret Powers
Suggest but truth to my diuining thoughts,
2220   This prettie Lad will proue our Countries blisse.
His Lookes are full of peacefull Maiestie,
His Head by nature fram'd to weare a Crowne,
His Hand to wield a Scepter, and himselfe

Likely in time to blesse a Regall Throne:
Make much of him, my Lords; for this is hee
Must helpe you more, then you are hurt by mee.
    Enter a Poste

WARWICKE What newes, my friend?

POSTE
That *Edward* is escaped from your Brother,
And fled (as hee heares since) to Burgundie.

WARWICKE
Vnsauorie newes: but how made he escape?   2230

POSTE
He was conuey'd by *Richard*, Duke of Gloster,
And the Lord *Hastings*, who attended him
In secret ambush, on the Forrest side,
And from the Bishops Huntsmen rescu'd him:
For Hunting was his dayly Exercise.

WARWICKE
My Brother was too carelesse of his charge.
(*To King Henry*) But let vs hence, my Soueraigne, to
    prouide
A salue for any sore, that may betide.
        Exeunt. Manet Somerset, Richmond, and
                                    Oxford

SOMERSET (*to Oxford*)
My Lord, I like not of this flight of *Edwards*:
For doubtlesse, *Burgundie* will yeeld him helpe,   2240
And we shall haue more Warres befor't be long.
As *Henries* late presaging Prophecie
Did glad my heart, with hope of this young *Richmond*:
So doth my heart mis-giue me, in these Conflicts,
What may befall him, to his harme and ours.
Therefore, Lord *Oxford*, to preuent the worst,
Forthwith wee'le send him hence to Brittanie,
Till stormes be past of Ciuill Enmitie.

OXFORD
I: for if *Edward* re-possesse the Crowne,
'Tis like that *Richmond*, with the rest, shall downe.   2250

SOMERSET
It shall be so: he shall to Brittanie.
Come therefore, let's about it speedily.   *Exeunt*

    Flourish. Enter King Edward, Richard of Gloster,   Sc. 21
    Hastings, ⌈with a troope of Hollanders⌉   (4.8)

KING EDWARD
Now Brother *Richard*, Lord *Hastings*, and the rest,
Yet thus farre Fortune maketh vs amends,
And sayes, that once more I shall enterchange
My wained state, for *Henries* Regall Crowne.
Well haue we pass'd, and now re-pass'd the Seas,
And brought desired helpe from Burgundie.
What then remaines, we being thus arriu'd
From Rauenspurre Hauen, before the Gates of Yorke,   2260
But that we enter, as into our Dukedome?
    ⌈*Hastings*⌉ *knockes at the Gates of Yorke*

RICHARD OF GLOSTER
The Gates made fast? Brother, I like not this.
For many men that stumble at the Threshold,
Are well fore-told, that danger lurkes within.

KING EDWARD

Tush man, aboadments must not now affright vs:
By faire or foule meanes we must enter in,
For hither will our friends repaire to vs.

HASTINGS

My Liege, Ile knocke once more, to summon them.
He knockes.
Enter on the Walls, the Maior of Yorke, and his
Brethren

MAIOR

My Lords, we were fore-warned of your comming,
2270   And shut the Gates, for safetie of our selues;
For now we owe allegeance vnto *Henry.*

KING EDWARD

But, Master Maior, if *Henry* be your King,
Yet *Edward,* at the least, is Duke of Yorke.

MAIOR

True, my good Lord, I know you for no lesse.

KING EDWARD

Why, and I challenge nothing but my Dukedome,
As being well content with that alone.

RICHARD OF GLOSTER *(aside)*

But when the Fox hath once got in his Nose,
Hee'le soone finde meanes to make the Body follow.

HASTINGS

Why, Master Maior, why stand you in a doubt?
2280   Open the Gates, we are King *Henries* friends.

MAIOR

I, say you so? the Gates shall then be opened.
They descend

RICHARD OF GLOSTER

A wise stout Captaine, and soone perswaded.

HASTINGS

The good old man would faine that all were wel,
So 'twere not long of him: but being entred,
I doubt not I, but we shall soone perswade
Both him, and all his Brothers, vnto reason.
Enter, below, the Maior, and two Aldermen

KING EDWARD

So, Master Maior: these Gates must not be shut,
But in the Night, or in the time of Warre.
What, feare not man, but yeeld me vp the Keyes,
Takes his Keyes
2290   For *Edward* will defend the Towne, and thee,
And all those friends, that deine to follow mee.
March. Enter Mountgomerie, with Drumme and
Souldiers

RICHARD OF GLOSTER

Brother, this is Sir *Iohn* Mountgomerie,
Our trustie friend, vnlesse I be deceiu'd.

KING EDWARD

Welcome Sir *Iohn*: but why come you in Armes?

MOUNTGOMERIE

To helpe King *Edward* in his time of storme,
As euery loyall Subiect ought to doe.

KING EDWARD

Thankes good *Mountgomerie*: but we now forget

Our Title to the Crowne, and onely clayme
Our Dukedome, till God please to send the rest.

MOUNTGOMERIE

Then fare you well, for I will hence againe,   2300
I came to serue a King, and not a Duke:
Drummer strike vp, and let vs march away.
The Drumme begins to march

KING EDWARD

Nay stay, Sir *Iohn,* a while, and wee'le debate
By what safe meanes the Crowne may be recouer'd.

MOUNTGOMERIE

What talke you of debating? in few words,
If you'le not here proclaime your selfe our King,
Ile leaue you to your fortune, and be gone,
To keepe them back, that come to succour you.
Why shall we fight, if you pretend no Title?

RICHARD OF GLOSTER *(to King Edward)*

Why Brother, wherefore stand you on nice points?   2310

KING EDWARD

When wee grow stronger, then wee'le make our
      Clayme:
Till then, 'tis wisdome to conceale our meaning.

HASTINGS

Away with scrupulous Wit, now Armes must rule.

RICHARD OF GLOSTER

And fearelesse minds clyme soonest vnto Crowns.
Brother, we will proclaime you out of hand,
The bruit thereof will bring you many friends.

KING EDWARD

Then be it as you will: for 'tis my right,
And *Henry* but vsurpes the Diademe.

MOUNTGOMERIE

I, now my Soueraigne speaketh like himselfe,
And now will I be *Edwards* Champion.   2320

HASTINGS

Sound Trumpet, *Edward* shal be here proclaim'd:
⌜*To Mountgomerie*⌝
Come, fellow Souldior, make thou proclamation.
Flourish

⌜MOUNTGOMERIE⌝ *Edward the Fourth, by the Grace of God,*
King of England and France, and Lord of Ireland,
And whosoe're gainsayes King Edwards right,
By this I challenge him to single fight.
Throwes downe his Gauntlet

ALL Long liue *Edward* the Fourth.

KING EDWARD

Thankes braue *Mountgomery,* and thankes vnto you all:
If fortune serue me, Ile requite this kindnesse.
Now for this Night, let's harbor here in Yorke: 2330
And when the Morning Sunne shall rayse his Carre
Aboue the Border of this Horizon,
Wee'le forward towards *Warwicke,* and his Mates;
For well I wot, that *Henry* is no Souldier.
Ah froward *Clarence,* how euill it beseemes thee,
To flatter *Henry,* and forsake thy Brother?
Yet as wee may, wee'le meet both thee and *Warwicke.*
Come on braue Souldiors: doubt not of the Day,
And that once gotten, doubt not of large Pay.   *Exeunt*

Sc. 22
(4.9)

Flourish. Enter Henry the King, Warwicke,
Mountague, George of Clarence, and Oxford

WARWICKE

2340 What counsaile, Lords? *Edward* from Belgia,
With hastie Germanes, and blunt Hollanders,
Hath pass'd in safetie through the Narrow Seas,
And with his troupes doth march amaine to London,
And many giddie people flock to him.

KING HENRY

Let's leuie men, and beat him backe againe.

GEORGE OF CLARENCE

A little fire is quickly trodden out,
Which being suffer'd, Riuers cannot quench.

WARWICKE

In Warwickshire I haue true-hearted friends,
Not mutinous in peace, yet bold in Warre,
2350 Those will I muster vp: and thou Sonne *Clarence*
Shalt stirre in Suffolke, Norfolke, and in Kent,
The Knights and Gentlemen, to come with thee.
Thou Brother *Mountague*, in Buckingham,
Northampton, and in Leicestershire, shalt find
Men well enclin'd to heare what thou command'st.
And thou, braue *Oxford*, wondrous well belou'd
In Oxfordshire, shalt muster vp thy friends.
My Soueraigne, with the louing Citizens,
Like to his Iland, gyrt in with the Ocean,
2360 Or modest *Dyan*, circled with her Nymphs,
Shall rest in London, till we come to him:
Faire Lords take leaue, and stand not to reply.
Farewell my Soueraigne.

KING HENRY

Farewell my *Hector*, and my *Troyes* true hope.

GEORGE OF CLARENCE

In signe of truth, I kisse your Highnesse Hand.
He kisses King Henrys hand

KING HENRY

Well-minded *Clarence*, be thou fortunate.

MOUNTAGUE

Comfort, my Lord, and so I take my leaue.
⌈*He kisses King Henrys hand*⌉

OXFORD

And thus I seale my truth, and bid adieu.
⌈*He kisses King Henrys hand*⌉

KING HENRY

Sweet *Oxford*, and my louing *Mountague*,
2370 And all at once, once more a happy farewell.   ⌈*Exit*⌉

WARWICKE

Farewell, sweet Lords, let's meet at Couentry.
Exeunt seuerally

Sc. 23
(4.10)

⌈*Enter King Henry and Exeter*⌉

KING HENRY

Here at the Pallace will I rest a while.
Cousin of *Exeter*, what thinkes your Lordship?
Me thinkes, the Power that *Edward* hath in field,
Should not be able to encounter mine.

EXETER

The doubt is, that he will seduce the rest.

KING HENRY

That's not my feare, my meed hath got me fame:
I haue not stopt mine eares to their demands,
Nor posted off their suites with slow delayes,
My pittie hath beene balme to heale their wounds,   2380
My mildnesse hath allay'd their swelling griefes,
My mercie dry'd their water-flowing teares.
I haue not been desirous of their wealth,
Nor much opprest them with great Subsidies,
Nor forward of reuenge, though they much err'd.
Then why should they loue *Edward* more then me?
No *Exeter*, these Graces challenge Grace:
And when the Lyon fawnes vpon the Lambe,
The Lambe will neuer cease to follow him.
Shout within, A Lancaster, ⌈A Yorke⌉

EXETER

Hearke, hearke, my Lord, what Shouts are these?   2390
Enter King Edward, Richard of Gloster and
Souldiers

KING EDWARD

Seize on the shamefac'd *Henry*, beare him hence,
And once againe proclaime vs King of England.
You are the Fount, that makes small Brookes to flow,
Now stops thy Spring, my Sea shall suck them dry,
And swell so much the higher, by their ebbe.
Hence with him to the Tower, let him not speake.
Exit some with King Henry and Exeter
And Lords, towards Couentry bend we our course,
Where peremptorie *Warwicke* now remaines:
The Sunne shines hot, and if we vse delay,
Cold biting Winter marres our hop'd-for Hay.   2400

RICHARD OF GLOSTER

Away betimes, before his forces ioyne,
And take the great-growne Traytor vnawares:
Braue Warriors, march amaine towards Couentry.
Exeunt

Enter Warwicke, the Maior of Couentry, two
Messengers, and others vpon the Walls

Sc. 24
(5.1)

WARWICKE

Where is the Post that came from valiant *Oxford*?
⌈*Messenger 1. comes forward*⌉
How farre hence is thy Lord, mine honest fellow?

MESSENGER 1.

By this at Dunsmore, marching hitherward.

WARWICKE

How farre off is our Brother *Mountague*?
Where is the Post that came from *Mountague*?
⌈*Messenger 2. comes forward*⌉

MESSENGER 2.

By this at Daintry, with a puissant troope.
Enter Someruile ⌈to them, aboue⌉

WARWICKE

Say *Someruile*, what sayes my louing Sonne?   2410
And by thy guesse, how nigh is *Clarence* now?

SOMERUILE

At Southam I did leaue him with his forces,
And doe expect him here some two howres hence.

A March afarre off

WARWICKE

Then *Clarence* is at hand, I heare his Drumme.

SOMERUILE

It is not his, my Lord, here Southam lyes:

The Drum your Honor heares, marcheth from
   Warwicke.

WARWICKE

Who should that be? belike vnlook'd for friends.

SOMERUILE

They are at hand, and you shall quickly know.
   *Flourish. Enter, below, King Edward, Richard of
   Gloster, and Souldiers*

KING EDWARD

Goe, Trumpet, to the Walls, and sound a Parle.
   ⌈*Sound a parle*⌉

RICHARD OF GLOSTER

2420   See how the surly *Warwicke* mans the Wall.

WARWICKE

Oh vnbid spight, is sportfull *Edward* come?

Where slept our Scouts, or how are they seduc'd,

That we could heare no newes of his repayre.

KING EDWARD

Now *Warwicke*, wilt thou ope the Citie Gates,

Speake gentle words, and humbly bend thy Knee,

Call *Edward* King, and at his hands begge Mercy,

And he shall pardon thee these Outrages?

WARWICKE

Nay rather, wilt thou draw thy forces hence,

Confesse who set thee vp, and pluckt thee downe,

2430   Call *Warwicke* Patron, and be penitent,

And thou shalt still remaine the Duke of Yorke.

RICHARD OF GLOSTER

I thought at least he would haue said the King,

Or did he make the least against his will?

WARWICKE

Is not a Dukedome, Sir, a goodly gift?

RICHARD OF GLOSTER

I, by my faith, for a poore Earle to giue,

Ile doe thee seruice for so good a gift.

WARWICKE

'Twas I that gaue the Kingdome to thy Brother.

KING EDWARD

Why then 'tis mine, if but by *Warwickes* gift.

WARWICKE

Thou art no *Atlas* for so great a weight:

2440   And Weakeling, *Warwicke* takes his gift againe,

And *Henry* is my King, *Warwicke* his Subiect.

KING EDWARD

But *Warwickes* King is *Edwards* Prisoner:

And gallant *Warwicke*, doe but answer this,

What is the Body, when the Head is off?

RICHARD OF GLOSTER

Alas, that *Warwicke* had no more fore-cast,

But whiles he thought to steale the single Ten,

The King was slyly finger'd from the Deck:

⌈*To Warwicke*⌉ You left poore *Henry* at the Bishops
   Pallace,

And tenne to one you'le meet him in the Tower.

KING EDWARD

'Tis euen so, ⌈*to Warwicke*⌉ yet you are *Warwicke* still.   2450

RICHARD OF GLOSTER

Come *Warwicke*, take the time, kneele downe, kneele
   downe:

Nay when? strike now, or else the Iron cooles.

WARWICKE

I had rather chop this Hand off at a blow,

And with the other, fling it at thy face,

Then beare so low a sayle, to strike to thee.

KING EDWARD

Sayle how thou canst, haue Winde and Tyde thy
   friend,

This Hand, fast wound about thy coale-black hayre,

Shall, whiles thy Head is warme, and new cut off,

Write in the dust this Sentence with thy blood,

Wind-changing *Warwicke* now can change no more.   2460
   *Enter Oxford, ⌈and souldiers⌉ with Drumme and
   Colours*

WARWICKE

Oh chearefull Colours, see where *Oxford* comes.

OXFORD

Oxford, Oxford, for Lancaster.
   ⌈*Oxford and his Men passe ouer the stage and
   exeunt into the City*⌉

RICHARD OF GLOSTER (*to King Edward*)

The Gates are open, let vs enter too.

KING EDWARD

So other foes may set vpon our backs.

Stand we in good array: for they no doubt

Will issue out againe, and bid vs battaile;

If not, the Citie being but of small defence,

Wee'le quickly rowze the Traitors in the same.

WARWICKE ⌈*to Oxford, within*⌉

Oh welcome *Oxford*, for we want thy helpe.
   *Enter Mountague, ⌈and souldiers⌉ with Drumme and
   Colours*

MOUNTAGUE

Mountague, Mountague, for Lancaster.   2470
   ⌈*Mountague and his Men passe ouer the stage
   and exeunt into the City*⌉

RICHARD OF GLOSTER

Thou and thy Brother both shall buy this Treason

Euen with the dearest blood your bodies beare.

KING EDWARD

The harder matcht, the greater Victorie,

My minde presageth happy gaine, and Conquest.
   *Enter Somerset, ⌈and souldiers⌉ with Drumme and
   Colours*

SOMERSET

Somerset, Somerset, for Lancaster.
   ⌈*Somerset and his Men passe ouer the stage and
   exeunt into the City*⌉

RICHARD OF GLOSTER

Two of thy Name, both Dukes of Somerset,

Haue sold their Liues vnto the House of *Yorke*,

And thou shalt be the third, and this Sword hold.
   *Enter George of Clarence, with Drumme and
   Colours*

WARWICKE

And loe, where *George* of Clarence sweepes along,

2480 Of force enough to bid his Brother Battaile:

With whom, an vpright zeale to right preuailes

More then the nature of a Brothers Loue.

GEORGE OF CLARENCE

Clarence, Clarence, for *Lancaster*.

KING EDWARD

Et tu Brute, wilt thou stab *Cæsar* too?

(*To a Trumpet*) A parlie sirra to *George* of Clarence.

Sound a Parlie, and Richard of Gloster and George

of Clarence whispers togither

WARWICKE

Come *Clarence*, come: thou wilt, if *Warwicke* call.

GEORGE OF CLARENCE

Father of Warwick, know you what this meanes?

⌈*He takes his red Rose out of his hat, and throwes it*

at Warwicke⌉

Looke here, I throw my infamie at thee:

I will not ruinate my Fathers House,

2490 Who gaue his blood to lyme the stones together,

And set vp *Lancaster*. Why, trowest thou, *Warwicke*,

That *Clarence* is so harsh, so blunt, vnnaturall,

To bend the fatall Instruments of Warre

Against his Brother, and his lawfull King.

Perhaps thou wilt obiect my holy Oath:

To keepe that Oath, were more impietie,

Then *Iephthah*, when he sacrific'd his Daughter.

I am so sorry for my Trespas made,

That to deserue well at my Brothers hands,

2500 I here proclayme my selfe thy mortall foe:

With resolution, wheresoe're I meet thee,

(As I will meet thee, if thou stirre abroad)

To plague thee, for thy foule mis-leading me.

And so, prowd-hearted *Warwicke*, I defie thee,

And to my Brothers turne my blushing Cheekes.

(*To King Edward*) Pardon me *Edward*, I will make amends:

(*To Richard*) And *Richard*, doe not frowne vpon my faults,

For I will henceforth be no more vnconstant.

KING EDWARD

Now welcome more, and ten times more belou'd,

2510 Then if thou neuer hadst deseru'd our hate.

RICHARD OF GLOSTER (*to George*)

Welcome good *Clarence*, this is Brother-like.

WARWICKE (*to George*)

Oh passing Traytor, periur'd and vniust.

KING EDWARD

What *Warwicke*, wilt thou leaue the Towne, and fight?

Or shall we beat the Stones about thine Eares?

WARWICKE ⌈*aside*⌉

Alas, I am not coop'd here for defence:

(*To King Edward*) I will away towards Barnet presently,

And bid thee Battaile, *Edward*, if thou dar'st.

KING EDWARD

Yes *Warwicke*, *Edward* dares, and leads the way:

Lords to the field: Saint *George*, and Victorie.

Exeunt, below, King Edward and his companie.

March. Warwicke and his companie descends

and followes

Alarum, and Excursions. Enter King Edward   Sc. 25

bringing forth Warwicke wounded   (5.2)

KING EDWARD

So, lye thou there: dye thou, and dye our feare,   2520

For *Warwicke* was a Bugge that fear'd vs all.

Now *Mountague* sit fast, I seeke for thee,

That *Warwickes* Bones may keepe thine companie.

Exit

WARWICKE

Ah, who is nigh? come to me, friend, or foe,

And tell me who is Victor, *Yorke*, or *Warwicke*?

Why aske I that? my mangled body shewes,

My blood, my want of strength, my sicke heart

shewes,

That I must yeeld my body to the Earth,

And by my fall, the conquest to my foe.

Thus yeelds the Cedar to the Axes edge,   2530

Whose Armes gaue shelter to the Princely Eagle,

Vnder whose shade the ramping Lyon slept,

Whose top-branch ouer-peer'd *Ioues* spreading Tree,

And kept low Shrubs from Winters pow'rfull Winde.

These Eyes, that now are dim'd with Deaths black

Veyle,

Haue beene as piercing as the Mid-day Sunne,

To search the secret Treasons of the World:

The Wrinkles in my Browes, now fill'd with blood,

Were lik'ned oft to Kingly Sepulchers:

For who liu'd King, but I could digge his Graue?   2540

And who durst smile, when *Warwicke* bent his Brow?

Loe, now my Glory smear'd in dust and blood.

My Parkes, my Walkes, my Mannors that I had,

Euen now forsake me; and of all my Lands,

Is nothing left me, but my bodies length.

Why, what is Pompe, Rule, Reigne, but Earth and

Dust?

And liue we how we can, yet dye we must.

Enter Oxford and Somerset

SOMERSET

Ah *Warwicke*, *Warwicke*, wert thou as we are,

We might recouer all our Losse againe:

The Queene from France hath brought a puissant

power.   2550

Euen now we heard the newes: ah, could'st thou flye.

WARWICKE

Why then I would not flye. Ah *Mountague*,

If thou be there, sweet Brother, take my Hand,

And with thy Lippes keepe in my Soule a while.

Thou lou'st me not: for, Brother, if thou didst,

Thy teares would wash this cold congealed blood,

That glewes my Lippes, and will not let me speake.

Come quickly *Mountague*, or I am dead.

SOMERSET

Ah *Warwicke*, *Mountague* hath breath'd his last,

And to the latest gaspe, cry'd out for *Warwicke*:   2560

And said, Commend me to my valiant Brother.

And more he would haue said, and more he spoke,

Which sounded like a Cannon in a Vault,

That mought not be distinguisht: but at last,

I well might heare, deliured with a groane,
Oh farewell *Warwicke*.

WARWICKE

Sweet rest his Soule: flye Lords, and saue your selues,
For *Warwicke* bids you all farewell, to meet in Heauen.
                                        He dyes

OXFORD

Away, away, to meet the Queenes great power.
                    Here they beare away Warwickes Body. Exeunt

Sc. 26
(5.3)
*Flourish. Enter King Edward in triumph, with
Richard of Gloster, George of Clarence, and
⌐souldiers⌐*

KING EDWARD

2570
Thus farre our fortune keepes an vpward course,
And we are grac'd with wreaths of Victorie:
But in the midst of this bright-shining Day,
I spy a black suspicious threatning Cloud,
That will encounter with our glorious Sunne,
Ere he attaine his easefull Westerne Bed:
I meane, my Lords, those powers that the Queene
Hath rays'd in Gallia, haue arriu'd our Coast,
And, as we heare, march on to fight with vs.

GEORGE OF CLARENCE

A little gale will soone disperse that Cloud,
2580
And blow it to the Source from whence it came,
Thy very Beames will dry those Vapours vp,
For euery Cloud engenders not a Storme.

RICHARD OF GLOSTER

The Queene is valued thirtie thousand strong,
And *Somerset*, with *Oxford*, fled to her:
If she haue time to breathe, be well assur'd
Her faction will be full as strong as ours.

KING EDWARD

We are aduertis'd by our louing friends,
That they doe hold their course toward Tewksbury.
We hauing now the best at Barnet field,
2590
Will thither straight, for willingnesse rids way,
And as we march, our strength will be augmented:
In euery Countie as we goe along,
Strike vp the Drumme, cry courage, and away.
                    ⌐*Flourish. March.*⌐ *Exeunt*

Sc. 27
(5.4)
*Flourish. March. Enter Margaret the Queene, young
Prince Edward, Somerset, Oxford, and Souldiers*

QUEENE MARGARET

Great Lords, wise men ne'r sit and waile their losse,
But chearely seeke how to redresse their harmes.
What though the Mast be now blowne ouer-boord,
The Cable broke, the holding-Anchor lost,
And halfe our Saylors swallow'd in the flood?
Yet liues our Pilot still. Is't meet, that hee
2600
Should leaue the Helme, and like a fearefull Lad,
With tearefull Eyes adde Water to the Sea,
And giue more strength to that which hath too much,
Whiles in his moane, the Ship splits on the Rock,
Which Industrie and Courage might haue sau'd?

Ah what a shame, ah what a fault were this.
Say *Warwicke* was our Anchor: what of that?
And *Mountague* our Top-Mast: what of him?
Our slaught'red friends, the Tackles: what of these?
Why is not *Oxford* here, another Anchor?
And *Somerset*, another goodly Mast?   2610
The friends of France our Shrowds and Tacklings?
And though vnskilfull, why not *Ned* and I,
For once allow'd the skilfull Pilots Charge?
We will not from the Helme, to sit and weepe,
But keepe our Course (though the rough Winde say no)
From Shelues and Rocks, that threaten vs with Wrack.
As good to chide the Waues, as speake them faire.
And what is *Edward*, but a ruthlesse Sea?
What *Clarence*, but a Quick-sand of Deceit?
And *Richard*, but a raged fatall Rocke?   2620
All these, the Enemies to our poore Barke.
Say you can swim, alas 'tis but a while:
Tread on the Sand, why there you quickly sinke,
Bestride the Rock, the Tyde will wash you off,
Or else you famish, that's a three-fold Death.
This speake I (Lords) to let you vnderstand,
If case some one of you would flye from vs,
That there's no hop'd-for Mercy with the Brothers *Yorke*,
More then with ruthlesse Waues, with Sands and Rocks.
Why courage then, what cannot be auoided,   2630
'Twere childish weakenesse to lament, or feare.

PRINCE EDWARD

Me thinkes a Woman of this valiant Spirit,
Should, if a Coward heard her speake these words,
Infuse his Breast with Magnanimitie,
And make him, naked, foyle a man at Armes.
I speake not this, as doubting any here:
For did I but suspect a fearefull man,
He should haue leaue to goe away betimes,
Least in our need he might infect another,
And make him of like spirit to himselfe.   2640
If any such be here, as God forbid,
Let him depart, before we neede his helpe.

OXFORD

Women and Children of so high a courage,
And Warriors faint, why 'twere perpetuall shame.
Oh braue young Prince: thy famous Grandfather
Doth liue againe in thee; long may'st thou liue,
To beare his Image, and renew his Glories.

SOMERSET

And he that will not fight for such a hope,
Goe home to Bed, and like the Owle by day,
If he arise, be mock'd and wondred at.   2650

QUEENE MARGARET

Thankes gentle *Somerset*, sweet *Oxford* thankes.

PRINCE EDWARD

And take his thankes, that yet hath nothing else.
                    Enter a Messenger

MESSENGER

Prepare you Lords, for *Edward* is at hand,
Readie to fight: therefore be resolute.

OXFORD

  I thought no lesse: it is his Policie,
  To haste thus fast, to finde vs vnprouided.

SOMERSET

  But hee's deceiu'd, we are in readinesse.

QUEENE MARGARET

  This cheares my heart, to see your forwardnesse.

OXFORD

  Here pitch our Battaile, hence we will not budge.
     Flourish, and march. Enter King Edward, Richard
     of Gloster, George of Clarence, and Souldiers

KING EDWARD (*to his followers*)

2660
  Braue followers, yonder stands the thornie Wood,
  Which by the Heauens assistance, and your strength,
  Must by the Roots be hew'ne vp yet ere Night.
  I need not adde more fuell to your fire,
  For well I wot, ye blaze, to burne them out:
  Giue signall to the fight, and to it Lords.

QUEENE MARGARET (*to her followers*)

  Lords, Knights, and Gentlemen, what I should say,
  My teares gaine-say: for euery word I speake,
  Ye see I drinke the water of my eye.
  Therefore no more but this: *Henry* your Soueraigne

2670
  Is Prisoner to the Foe, his State vsurp'd,
  His Realme a slaughter-house, his Subiects slaine,
  His Statutes cancell'd, and his Treasure spent:
  And yonder is the Wolfe, that makes this spoyle.
  You fight in Iustice: then in Gods Name, Lords,
  Be valiant, and giue signall to the fight.
     Alarum, Retreat, Excursions. Exeunt

Sc. 28
(5.5)
     Flourish. Enter King Edward, Richard of Gloster,
     and George of Clarence with Queene Margaret,
     Oxford and Somerset, guarded

KING EDWARD

  Now here a period of tumultuous Broyles.
  Away with *Oxford*, to Hames Castle straight:
  For *Somerset*, off with his guiltie Head.
  Goe beare them hence, I will not heare them speake.

OXFORD

2680
  For my part, Ile not trouble thee with words.
                ⌈*Exit Oxford, guarded*⌉

SOMERSET

  Nor I, but stoupe with patience to my fortune.
               ⌈*Exit Somerset, guarded*⌉

QUEENE MARGARET

  So part we sadly in this troublous World,
  To meet with Ioy in sweet Ierusalem.

KING EDWARD

  Is Proclamation made, That who finds *Edward*,
  Shall haue a high Reward, and he his Life?

RICHARD OF GLOSTER

  It is, and loe where youthfull *Edward* comes.
     Enter Edward the Prince, guarded

KING EDWARD

  Bring forth the Gallant, let vs heare him speake.
  What? can so young a Thorne begin to prick?

Edward, what satisfaction canst thou make,
For bearing Armes, for stirring vp my Subiects,   2690
And all the trouble thou hast turn'd me to?

PRINCE EDWARD

  Speake like a Subiect, prowd ambitious *Yorke*.
  Suppose that I am now my Fathers Mouth,
  Resigne thy Chayre, and where I stand, kneele thou,
  Whil'st I propose the selfe-same words to thee,
  Which (Traytor) thou would'st haue me answer to.

QUEENE MARGARET

  Ah, that thy Father had beene so resolu'd.

RICHARD OF GLOSTER

  That you might still haue worne the Petticoat,
  And ne're haue stolne the Breech from *Lancaster*.

PRINCE EDWARD

  Let *Æsop* fable in a Winters Night,   2700
  His Currish Riddles sorts not with this place.

RICHARD OF GLOSTER

  By Heauen, Brat, Ile plague ye for that word.

QUEENE MARGARET

  I, thou wast borne to be a plague to men.

RICHARD OF GLOSTER

  For Gods sake, take away this Captiue Scold.

PRINCE EDWARD

  Nay, take away this scolding Crooke-backe, rather.

KING EDWARD

  Peace wilfull Boy, or I will charme your tongue.

GEORGE OF CLARENCE (*to Prince Edward*)

  Vntutor'd Lad, thou art too malapert.

PRINCE EDWARD

  I know my dutie, you are all vndutifull:
  Lasciuious *Edward*, and thou periur'd *George*,
  And thou mis-shapen *Dicke*, I tell ye all,   2710
  I am your better, Traytors as ye are,
  And thou vsurp'st my Fathers right and mine.

KING EDWARD

  Take that, the likenesse of this Rayler here.
     King Edward stabs Prince Edward

RICHARD OF GLOSTER

  Sprawl'st thou? take that, to end thy agonie.
     Richard stabs Prince Edward

GEORGE OF CLARENCE

  And ther's for twitting me with periurie.
     George stabs Prince Edward, ⌈*who dyes*⌉

QUEENE MARGARET

  Oh, kill me too.

RICHARD OF GLOSTER Marry, and shall.
     Offers to kill her

KING EDWARD

  Hold, *Richard*, hold, for we haue done too much.

RICHARD OF GLOSTER

  Why should shee liue, to fill the World with words.
     Queene Margaret swownes

KING EDWARD

  What? doth shee swowne? vse meanes for her recouerie.

RICHARD OF GLOSTER (*aside to George*)

  Clarence excuse me to the King my Brother: 2720

Ile hence to London on a serious matter,
Ere ye come there, be sure to heare some newes.

GEORGE OF CLARENCE (*aside to Richard*) What? what?

RICHARD OF GLOSTER (*aside to George*) The Tower, the Tower.
                                                              Exit

QUEENE MARGARET
Oh *Ned*, sweet *Ned*, speake to thy Mother Boy.
Can'st thou not speake? O Traitors, Murtherers!
They that stabb'd *Cæsar*, shed no blood at all:
Did not offend, nor were not worthy Blame,
If this foule deed were by, to equall it.

2730 He was a Man; this (in respect) a Childe,
And Men, ne're spend their fury on a Childe.
What's worse then Murtherer, that I may name it?
No, no, my heart will burst, and if I speake,
And I will speake, that so my heart may burst.
Butchers and Villaines, bloudy Caniballes,
How sweet a Plant haue you vntimely cropt:
You haue no children (Butchers) if you had,
The thought of them would haue stirr'd vp remorse,
But if you euer chance to haue a Childe,

2740 Looke in his youth to haue him so cut off,
As deathsmen you haue rid this sweet yong Prince.

KING EDWARD
Away with her, go beare her hence perforce.

QUEENE MARGARET
Nay, neuer beare me hence, dispatch me heere:
Here sheath thy Sword, Ile pardon thee my death:
What? wilt thou not? Then *Clarence* do it thou.

GEORGE OF CLARENCE
By heauen, I will not do thee so much ease.

QUEENE MARGARET
Good *Clarence* do: sweet *Clarence* do thou do it.

GEORGE OF CLARENCE
Did'st thou not heare me sweare I would not do it?

QUEENE MARGARET
I, but thou vsest to forsweare thy selfe.

2750 'Twas Sin before, but now 'tis Charity.
What wilt yᵘ not? Where is that diuels butcher,
Hard fauor'd *Richard*? *Richard*, where art thou?
Thou art not heere; Murther is thy Almes-deed:
Petitioners for Blood, thou ne're put'st backe.

KING EDWARD
Away I say, I charge ye beare her hence.

QUEENE MARGARET
So come to you, and yours, as to this Prince.
                                    Exit Queene, guarded

KING EDWARD Where's *Richard* gone.

GEORGE OF CLARENCE
To London all in post, ⌈*aside*⌉ and as I guesse,
To make a bloody Supper in the Tower.

KING EDWARD
2760 He's sodaine if a thing comes in his head.
Now march we hence, discharge the common sort
With Pay and Thankes, and let's away to London,
And see our gentle Queene how well she fares,
By this (I hope) she hath a Sonne for me.   *Exit*

Enter King Henry the sixt reading a booke, and   Sc. 29
Richard Duke of Gloster, with the Lieutenant on the   (5.6)
Walles

RICHARD OF GLOSTER
Good day, my Lord, what at your Booke so hard?

KING HENRY
I my good Lord: my Lord I should say rather,
'Tis sinne to flatter, Good was little better:
Good Gloster, and good Deuill, were alike,
And both preposterous: therefore, not Good Lord.

RICHARD OF GLOSTER (*to the Lieutenant*)
Sirra, leaue vs to our selues, we must conferre.   2770
                                    Exit Lieutenant

KING HENRY
So flies the wreaklesse shepherd from yᵉ Wolfe:
So first the harmlesse Sheepe doth yeeld his Fleece,
And next his Throate, vnto the Butchers Knife.
What Scene of death hath *Rossius* now to Acte?

RICHARD OF GLOSTER
Suspition alwayes haunts the guilty minde,
The Theefe doth feare each bush an Officer.

KING HENRY
The Bird that hath bin limed in a bush,
With trembling wings misdoubteth euery bush;
And I the haplesse Male to one sweet Bird,
Haue now the fatall Obiect in my eye,   2780
Where my poore yong was lim'd, was caught, and
   kill'd.

RICHARD OF GLOSTER
Why what a peeuish Foole was that of Creet,
That taught his Sonne the office of a Fowle,
And yet for all his wings, the Foole was drown'd.

KING HENRY
I *Dedalus*, my poore Boy *Icarus*,
Thy Father *Minos*, that deni'de our course,
The Sunne that sear'd the wings of my sweet Boy,
Thy Brother *Edward*, and thy Selfe, the Sea
Whose enuious Gulfe did swallow vp his life:
Ah, kill me with thy Weapon, not with words,   2790
My brest can better brooke thy Daggers point,
Then can my eares that Tragicke History.
But wherefore dost thou come? Is't for my Life?

RICHARD OF GLOSTER
Think'st thou I am an Executioner?

KING HENRY
A Persecutor I am sure thou art,
If murthering Innocents be Executing,
Why then thou art an Executioner.

RICHARD OF GLOSTER
Thy Son I kill'd for his presumption.

KING HENRY
Hadst thou bin kill'd, when first yᵘ didst presume,
Thou had'st not liu'd to kill a Sonne of mine: 2800
And thus I prophesie, that many a thousand,
Which now mistrust no parcell of my feare,
And many an old mans sighe, and many a Widdowes,
And many an Orphans water-standing-eye,

Men for their Sonnes, Wiues for their Husbands,
Orphans, for their Parents timeles death,
Shall rue the houre that euer thou was't borne.
The Owle shriek'd at thy birth, an euill signe,
The Night-Crow cry'de, aboding lucklesse time,
Dogs howl'd, and hiddeous Tempests shook down
2810   Trees:
The Rauen rook'd her on the Chimnies top,
And chatt'ring Pies in dismall Discords sung:
Thy Mother felt more then a Mothers paine,
And yet brought forth lesse then a Mothers hope,
To wit, an indigested and deformed lumpe,
Not like the fruit of such a goodly Tree.
Teeth had'st thou in thy head, when thou was't
    borne,
To signifie, thou cam'st to bite the world:
And if the rest be true, which I haue heard,
2820   Thou cam'st—
RICHARD
Ile heare no more: dye Prophet in thy speech,
    Stabbes him
For this (among'st the rest) was I ordain'd.
KING HENRY
I, and for much more slaughter after this,
O God forgiue my sinnes, and pardon thee.   *Dyes*
RICHARD OF GLOSTER
What? will the aspiring blood of Lancaster
Sinke in the ground? I thought it would haue
    mounted.
See how my sword weepes for the poore Kings death.
O may such purple teares be alway shed
From those that wish the downfall of our house.
2830   If any sparke of Life be yet remaining,
Downe, downe to hell, and say I sent thee thither.
    Stabs him againe
I that haue neyther pitty, loue, nor feare.
Indeed 'tis true that *Henrie* told me of:
For I haue often heard my Mother say,
I came into the world with my Legges forward.
Had I not reason (thinke ye) to make hast,
And seeke their Ruine, that vsurp'd our Right?
The Midwife wonder'd, and the Women cri'de
O Iesus blesse vs, he is borne with teeth,
2840   And so I was, which plainly signified,
That I should snarle, and bite, and play the dogge:
Then since the Heauens haue shap'd my Body so,
Let Hell make crook'd my Minde to answer it.
I had no father, I am like no father,
I haue no Brother, I am like no Brother:
And this word [Loue] which Gray-beards call Diuine,
Be resident in men like one another,
And not in me: I am my selfe alone.
Clarence beware, thou kept'st me from the Light,
2850   But I will sort a pitchy day for thee:
For I will buzze abroad such Prophesies,
That *Edward* shall be fearefull of his life,
And then to purge his feare, Ile be thy death.

Henry and his Son are gone, thou *Clarence* art next,
And by one and one I will dispatch the rest,
Counting my selfe but bad, till I be best.
Ile throw thy body in another roome,
And Triumph *Henry*, in thy day of Doome.

    Exit with the body

⌈*A Chayre of State.*⌉ *Flourish. Enter King Edward,*   Sc. 30
Lady Gray his Queene, George of Clarence, Richard   (5.7)
of Gloster, Hastings, Nurse with the infant Prince
Edward, and Attendants
KING EDWARD
Once more we sit in Englands Royall Throne,
Re-purchac'd with the Blood of Enemies: 2860
What valiant Foe-men, like to Autumnes Corne,
Haue we mow'd downe in tops of all their pride?
Three Dukes of Somerset, threefold Renownd,
For hardy and vndoubted Champions:
Two *Cliffords*, as the Father and the Sonne,
And two Northumberlands: two brauer men,
Ne're spurr'd their Coursers at the Trumpets sound.
With them, the two braue Beares, *Warwick &*
    Montague,
That in their Chaines fetter'd the Kingly Lyon,
And made the Forrest tremble when they roar'd.   2870
Thus haue we swept Suspition from our Seate,
And made our Footstoole of Security.
(*To Lady Gray*)
Come hither *Besse*, and let me kisse my Boy:
    The Nurse brings forth the infant Prince. King
    Edward kisses him
Yong *Ned*, for thee, thine Vnckles, and my selfe,
Haue in our Armors watcht the Winters night,
Went all afoote in Summers scalding heate,
That thou might'st repossesse the Crowne in peace,
And of our Labours thou shalt reape the gaine.
RICHARD OF GLOSTER (*aside*)
Ile blast his Haruest, and your head were laid,
For yet I am not look'd on in the world.   2880
This shoulder was ordain'd so thicke, to heaue,
And heaue it shall some waight, or breake my backe,
Worke thou the way, and thou shalt execute.
KING EDWARD
Clarence and *Gloster*, loue my louely Queene,
And kis your Princely Nephew Brothers both.
GEORGE OF CLARENCE
The duty that I owe vnto your Maiesty,
I Seale vpon the lips of this sweet Babe.
    He kisses the infant Prince
LADY GRAY
Thankes Noble *Clarence*, worthy brother thanks.
RICHARD OF GLOSTER
And that I loue the tree frõ whence yᵘ sprang'st:
Witnesse the louing kisse I giue the Fruite,   2890
    He kisses the infant Prince
(*Aside*) To say the truth, so *Iudas* kist his master,
And cried all haile, when as he meant all harme.

KING EDWARD

 Now am I seated as my soule delights,
 Hauing my Countries peace, and Brothers loues.

GEORGE OF CLARENCE

 What will your Grace haue done with *Margaret*,
 Reynard her Father, to the King of France
 Hath pawn'd the Sicils and Ierusalem,
 And hither haue they sent it for her ransome.

KING EDWARD

 Away with her, and waft her hence to France:
 And now what rests, but that we spend the time　　　2900
 With stately Triumphes, mirthfull Comicke shewes,
 Such as befits the pleasure of the Court.
 Sound Drums and Trumpets, farwell sowre annoy,
 For heere I hope begins our lasting ioy.

       ⌈*Flourish.*⌉ *Exeunt omnes*

FINIS

ADDITIONAL PASSAGES

A. Our text adopts the Octavo version of lines 120–5; the Folio alternative follows. See the Textual Note to 120–4.

KING HENRY

 Peace thou and giue King *Henry* leaue to speake.

WARWICKE

 Plantagenet shall speake firste: Heare him Lords,
 And be you silent and attentiue too,
 For he that interrupts him, shall not liue.

KING HENRY ⌈*to Yorke*⌉

 Think'st thou, that I will leaue my Kingly Throne,

B. For 2675.1–2692 the Octavo substitutes the following abridged version, which may represent the authorized prompt-book (see the textual notes):

ALL THE LANCASTER PARTIE

 Saint *George* for *Lancaster*.

  Alarmes to the battell, ⌈*the House of*⌉ *Yorke flies, then*
  the chambers be discharged. Then enter King Edward,
  George of Clarence & Richard of Gloster & the rest, &
  make a great shout, and crie for Yorke, for Yorke, and
  then Queene Margaret is taken, & Prince Edward, &
  Oxford & Sumerset and then flourish and enter all
  againe

KING EDWARD

 Now here a period of tumultuous broiles,
 Awaie with Oxford to *Hames* castll straight,
 For *Summerset* off with his guiltie head.
 Goe beare them hence, I will not heare them speake.

OXFORD

 For my part Ile not trouble thee with words.

       Exit Oxford, guarded

SOMERSET

 Nor I, but stoope with patience to my death.

      Exit Somerset, guarded

KING EDWARD (*to Prince Edward*)

 Edward what satisfaction canst thou make,
 For stirring vp my subiects to rebellion?

PRINCE EDWARD

 Speake like a subiect proud ambitious Yorke.　　　10

TITUS ANDRONICUS

SHAKESPEARE'S first, most sensation-packed tragedy appeared in print in 1594, and a performance record dating from January of that year appears to indicate that it was then a new play. But according to its title-page it had been acted by three companies, one of which was bankrupt by the summer of 1593; and the play's style, too, suggests that it was written earlier. Shakespeare seems to have added a scene after the play's earliest performances, for Act 3, Scene 2 was first printed in the 1623 Folio. The 1594 performance record may refer to the revised play, not the original, or to the play's first London performance after plague had closed the theatres from June 1592.

By convention, Elizabethan tragedies treated historical subjects, and *Titus Andronicus* is set in Rome during the fourth century BC; but its story (like that of Shakespeare's other early tragedy, *Romeo and Iuliet*) is fictitious. Whether Shakespeare invented it is an open question: the same tale is told in both a ballad and a chap-book which survive only in eighteenth-century versions but which could derive from pre-Shakespearian originals. Even if Shakespeare knew these works, they could have supplied only a skeletal narrative. His play's spirit and style owe much to Ovid's *Metamorphoses*, one of his favourite works of classical literature, which he actually brings on stage in Act 4, Scene 1. Ovid's tale of the rape of Philomela was certainly in Shakespeare's mind as he wrote, and the play's more horrific elements owe something to the Roman dramatist Seneca.

In its time, *Titus Andronicus* was popular, perhaps because it combines sensational incident with high-flown rhetoric of a kind that was fashionable around 1590. It tells a story of double revenge. Tamora, Queene of the Gothes, seeks revenge on her captor, Titus, for the ritual slaughter of her son Alarbus; she achieves it when her other sons, Chiron and Demetrius, rape and mutilate Titus' daughter, Lauinia. Later, Titus himself seeks revenge on Tamora and her husband, Saturninus, after Tamora's black lover, Aron, has falsely led him to believe that he can save his sons' lives by allowing his own hand to be chopped off. Though he is driven to madness, Titus, with his brother Marcus and his last surviving son, Lucius, achieves a spectacular sequence of vengeance in which he cuts Tamora's sons' throats, serves their flesh baked in a pie to their mother, kills Lauinia to save her from her shame, and stabs Tamora to death. Then, in rapid succession, Saturninus kills Titus and is himself killed by Lucius, who, as the new Emperor, is left with Marcus to bury the dead, to punish Aron, and 'To heale Romes harmes, and wipe away her woe'.

In *Titus Andronicus*, as in his early history plays, Shakespeare is at his most successful in the expression of grief and the portrayal of vigorously energetic evil. The play's piling of horror upon horror can seem ludicrous, and the reader may be surprised by the apparent disjunction between terrifying events and the measured verse in which characters react; but a few remarkable modern productions have revealed that the play may still arouse pity as well as terror in its audiences.

Our text is (with the exception of 3.2) based on the 1594 Quarto, apparently set from Shakespeare's own draft.

THE NAMES OF THE ACTORS

SATURNINUS, eldest sonne of the late Emperour of Rome; later Emperour

BASSIANUS, his brother

TITUS ANDRONICUS, a Romaine nobleman, Generall against the Gothes

LUCIUS
QUINTUS
MARTIUS
MUTIUS
} sonnes of Titus

LAUINIA, daughter of Titus

Young Lucius (PUER), sonne of Lucius

MARCUS ANDRONICUS, Tribune of the people, brother of Titus

PUBLIUS, his sonne

SEMPRONIUS
VALENTINE
} kinsemen of Titus

A CAPTAINE

EMILLIUS

TAMORA, Queene of the Gothes, later wife of Saturninus

ALARBUS
DEMETRIUS
CHIRON
} her sonnes

ARON, a Moore, her louer

A NURSE

A CLOWNE

Senatours, Tribunes, Romaines, Gothes, Souldiers, and Attendants

The most Lamentable Romaine Tragedie of
Titus Andronicus

1.1
(Sc. 1)

⌈*Flourish.*⌉ *Enter the Tribunes and Senatours aloft:*
And then enter below Saturninus and his followers
at one dore, and Bassianus and his followers ⌈*at the*
other, with Drum and Colours⌉

SATURNINE

Noble *Patricians*, Patrons of my Right,
Defend the iustice of my cause with armes.
And Countrimen my louing followers,
Plead my successiue Title with your swords:
I am his first borne sonne, that was the last
That ware the Imperiall Diademe of Rome,
Then let my Fathers honours liue in me,
Nor wrong mine age with this indignitie.

BASSIANUS

Romaines, friends, followers, fauourers of my Right,
10 If euer *Bassianus Ceasars* sonne,
Were gratious in the eyes of Royall Rome,
Keepe then this passage to the Capitoll,
And suffer not dishonour to approch,
The Imperiall seate to vertue consecrate,
To iustice, continence, and Nobillitie:
But let desert in pure election shine,
And Romaines fight for freedome in your choice.
⌈*Enter*⌉ *Marcus Andronicus* ⌈*aloft*⌉ *with the Crowne*

MARCUS

Princes that striue by factions and by friends,
Ambitiously for Rule and Emperie,
20 Know that the people of Rome for whom we stand
A speciall Partie, haue by common voice,
In election for the Romaine Empery
Chosen *Andronicus*, surnamed *Pius*:
For many good and great deserts to Rome,
A Nobler man, a brauer Warriour,
Liues not this day within the Cittie walls.
Hee by the Senate is accited home,
From weary warres against the barbarous *Gothes*,
That with his sonnes a terrour to our foes,
30 Hath yoakt a Nation strong, traind vp in Armes.
Tenne yeares are spent since first he vndertooke
This cause of Rome, and chastised with armes
Our enemies pride: Fiue times he hath returnd
Bleeding to Rome, bearing his valiant sonnes,
In Coffins from the field.
And now at last laden with honours spoiles,
Returnes the good *Andronicus* to Rome,
Renowned *Titus* flourishing in Armes.
Let vs intreat by honour of his name,
40 Whom worthily you would haue now succeeded,
And in the Capitall and Senates Right,
Whom you pretend to honour and adore,
That you withdraw you, and abate your strength,

Dismisse your followers, and as suters should,
Pleade your deserts in peace and humblenes.

SATURNINE

How faire the Tribune speakes to calme my thoughts.

BASSIANUS

Marcus Andronicus, so I doe affie,
In thy vprightnes and integritie,
And so I loue and honour thee and thine,
Thy Noble brother *Titus* and his sonnes,   50
And her to whom my thoughts are humbled all,
Gratious *Lauinia*, Romes rich ornament,
That I will here dismisse my louing friends:
And to my fortunes and the peoples fauour,
Commit my cause in ballance to be waid.
⌈*Exit his Soldiers and followers*⌉

SATURNINE

Friends that haue beene thus forward in my right,
I thanke you all, and here dismisse you all,
And to the loue and fauour of my Countrie,
Commit my selfe, my person, and the cause:
⌈*Exit his Soldiers and followers*⌉
(*To the Tribunes and Senatours*)
Rome be as iust and gratious vnto me,   60
As I am confident and kinde to thee.
Open the gates and let me in.

BASSIANUS

Tribunes and me a poore Competitor.
⌈*Flourish.*⌉ *They goe vp into the Senate house.*
Enter a Captaine

CAPTAINE

Romaines make way, the good *Andronicus*,
Patron of vertue, Romes best Champion:
Succesfull in the battailes that he fights,
With honour and with fortune is returnd,
From where he circumscribed with his sword,
And brought to yoake the enemies of Rome.
Sound Drums and Trumpets, and then enter Martius
and Mutius two of Titus sonnes, and then ⌈*men*
bearing Coffins⌉ *couered with black, then Lucius and*
Quintus, two other sonnes, then Titus Andronicus
⌈*in his Chariot*⌉, *and then Tamora the Queene of*
Gothes and her sonnes Alarbus Chiron and
Demetrius, with Aron the More, and others as
many as can be, then set downe the ⌈*Coffins*⌉, *and*
Titus speakes

TITUS

Haile Rome, victorious in thy mourning weeds,   70
Lo as the Barke that hath dischargd his fraught,
Returnes with pretious lading to the bay,
From whence at first shee wayd her anchorage;
Commeth *Andronicus*, bound with Lawrell bowes,

To resalute his Countrie with his teares,
Teares of true ioy for his returne to Rome,
Thou great defender of this Capitoll,
Stand gratious to the rights that we entend.
Romaines, of fiue and twenty valiant sonnes,
80   Halfe of the number that king *Priam* had,
Behold the poore remaines aliue and dead:
These that suruiue, let Rome reward with loue:
These that I bring vnto their latest home,
With buriall amongst their auncestors.
Here *Gothes* haue giuen me leaue to sheath my sword,
Titus vnkinde, and careles of thine owne,
Why sufferst thou thy sonnes vnburied yet,
To houer on the dreadfull shore of stix,
Make way to lay them by their brethren.
          They open the Tombe
90   There greete in silence as the dead are wont,
And sleepe in peace, slaine in your Countries warres:
O sacred Receptacle of my ioyes,
Sweete Cell of vertue and Nobilitie,
How many sonnes hast thou of mine in store,
That thou wilt neuer render to me more.

LUCIUS
Giue vs the prowdest prisoner of the *Gothes*,
That we may hew his limbs and on a pile,
Ad manes fratrum, sacrifice his flesh:
Before this earthy prison of their boanes,
100 That so the shadows be not vnappeazde,
Nor we disturbde with prodegies on earth.

TITUS
I giue him you the Noblest that suruiues,
The eldest sonne of this distressed Queene.

TAMORA ⌐kneeling⌐
Stay Romaine brethren, gratious Conquerour,
Victorious *Titus*, rue the teares I shed,
A mothers teares in passion for her sonne:
And if thy sonnes were euer deare to thee,
Oh thinke my sonne to be as deare to mee.
Sufficeth not that we are brought to Rome
110 To beautifie thy triumphs, and returne
Captiue to thee, and to thy Romaine yoake:
But must my sonnes be slaughtered in the streets,
For valiant dooings in their Countries cause?
O if to fight for king and common-weale,
Were pietie in thine, it is in these:
Andronicus, staine not thy tombe with bloud.
Wilt thou draw neere the nature of the Gods?
Draw neere them then in being mercifull,
Sweete mercie is Nobilities true badge,
120 Thrice Noble *Titus*, spare my first borne sonne.

TITUS
Patient your selfe Madam, and pardon me,
These are their brethren, whom your *Gothes* beheld
Aliue and dead, and for their brethren slaine,
Religiously they aske a sacrifice:
To this your sonne is markt, and die he must,
T'appease their groning shadowes that are gone.

LUCIUS
Away with him, and make a fire straight,
And with our swords vpon a pile of wood,
Lets hew his limbs till they be cleane consumde.
               Exit Titus sonnes with Alarbus

TAMORA ⌐rising⌐
O cruell irreligeous pietie.   130

CHIRON
Was neuer Sythia halfe so barbarous.

DEMETRIUS
Oppose not Sythia to ambitious Rome,
Alarbus goes to rest and we suruiue,
To tremble vnder *Titus* threatning looke,
Then Madam stand resolud, but hope withall,
The selfe same Gods that armde the Queene of Troy
With opportunitie of sharpe reuenge
Vpon the Thracian Tyrant in his Tent,
May fauour *Tamora* the Queene of Gothes,
(When Gothes were Gothes, and *Tamora* was Queene,) 140
To quit her bloodie wrongs vpon her foes.
     Enter Quintus, Marcus, Mutius and Lucius the
     sonnes of Andronicus againe with bloudie swords

LUCIUS
See Lord and father how we haue performd
Our Romane rights, *Alarbus* limbs are lopt,
And intrals feede the sacrifising fire,
Whose smoke like incense doth perfume the skie,
Remaineth nought but to interre our brethren,
And with lowd larums welcome them to Rome.

TITUS
Let it be so, and let *Andronicus*,
Make this his latest farewell to their soules.
     ⌐*Flourish.*⌐ *Then sound Trumpets, and lay the*
     ⌐*Coffins*⌐ *in the Tombe*
In peace and honour rest you here my sonnes,   150
Roomes readiest Champions, repose you here in rest,
Secure from worldly chaunces and mishaps:
Here lurks no treason, here no enuie swels,
Here grow no damned drugges, here are no stormes,
No noyse, but silence and eternall sleepe,
In peace and honour rest you here my sonnes.
          Enter Lauinia

LAUINIA
In peace and honour, liue Lord *Titus* long,
My Noble Lord and father liue in fame:
Lo at this Tombe my tributarie teares,
I render for my brethrens obsequies: 160
(*Kneeling*) And at thy feete I kneele, with teares of ioy
Shed on this earth, for thy returne to Rome,
O blesse me here with thy victorious hand,
Whose fortunes Roomes best Citizens applaud.

TITUS
Kinde Rome that hast thus louingly reserude,
The Cordiall of mine age to glad my hart,
Lauinia liue, outliue thy fathers daies,
And fames eternall date for vertues praise.
          ⌐*Lauinia rises*⌐

MARCUS ⌜aloft⌝

    Long liue Lord *Titus* my beloued brother,

170   Gratious triumpher in the eies of Rome.

TITUS

    Thanks gentle Tribune, Noble brother *Marcus*.

MARCUS

    And welcome Nephews from succesfull wars

    You that suruiue, and you that sleepe in fame:

    Faire Lords, your fortunes are alike in all,

    That in your Countries seruice drew your swords,

    But safer triumph is this funerall pompe,

    That hath aspirde to *Solons* happines,

    And triumphs ouer chaunce in honours bed.

    Titus Andronicus, the people of Rome,

180   Whose friend in iustice thou hast euer beene,

    Send thee by mee their Tribune and their trust,

    This Palliament of white and spotles hue,

    And name thee in election for the Empire,

    With these our late deceased Emperours sonnes.

    Be *Candidatus* then and put it on,

    And helpe to set a head on headles Roome.

TITUS

    A better head her glorious bodie fits,

    Than his that shakes for age and feeblenes:

    What should I don this Roabe and trouble you?

190   Be chosen with Proclamations to daie,

    To morrow yeeld vp rule, resigne my life,

    And set abroad new busines for you all.

    Roome I haue beene thy souldier fortie yeares,

    And led my Countries strength succesfullie,

    And buried one and twentie valiant sonnes

    Knighted in Field, slaine manfullie in Armes,

    In right and seruice of their Noble Countrie:

    Giue me a staffe of Honour for mine age,

    But not a scepter to controwle the world,

200   Vpright he held it Lords that held it last.

MARCUS

    Titus thou shalt obtaine & aske the Emperie.

SATURNINE

    Proud and ambitious Tribune canst thou tell.

TITUS

    Patience Prince *Saturninus*.

SATURNINE   Romaines doe me right.

    Patricians draw your swords and sheath them not,

    Till *Saturninus* be Romes Emperour:

    Andronicus would thou were shipt to hell,

    Rather than robbe me of the peoples harts.

LUCIUS

    Prowd *Saturnine*, interrupter of the good,

    That noble minded *Titus* meanes to thee.

TITUS

210   Content thee Prince, I will restore to thee

    The peoples harts, and weane them from themselues.

BASSIANUS

    Andronicus I doo not flatter thee,

    But honour thee and will doo till I die:

    My faction if thou strengthen with thy friends

    I will most thankefull be, and thanks to men

    Of Noble minds, is honourable meede.

TITUS

    People of Rome, and peoples Tribunes here,

    I aske your voyces and your suffrages,

    Will yee bestow them friendly on *Andronicus*.

TRIBUNES

    To gratifie the good *Andronicus*,   220

    And gratulate his safe returne to Rome,

    The people will accept whom he admits.

TITUS

    Tribunes I thanke you, and this sute I make,

    That you create our Emperours eldest sonne,

    Lord *Saturnine*: whose vertues will I hope,

    Reflect on Rome as Tytãs Raies on earth,

    And ripen iustice in this Common weale:

    Then if you will elect by my aduise,

    Crowne him and say, *Long liue our Emperour*.

MARCUS

    With voyces and applause of euery sort,   230

    Patricians and *Plebeans*, we create

    Lord *Saturninus* Romes great Emperour,

    And say *Long liue our Emperour* Saturnine.

      ⌜*A long Flourish till they come downe.*

      Marcus inuests Saturnine in the white Palliament

      and hands him a scepter⌝

SATURNINE

    Titus Andronicus, for thy fauours done,

    To vs in our election this day,

    I giue thee thankes in part of thy deserts,

    And will with deeds requite thy gentlenes:

    And for an onset *Titus* to aduance,

    Thy name and honourable familie,

    Lauinia will I make my Empresse,   240

    Romes Royall Mistris, Mistris of my hart,

    And in the sacred Pãthean her espouse:

    Tell me *Andronicus* doth this motion please thee.

TITUS

    It doth my worthie Lord, and in this match,

    I hold me highly Honoured of your Grace,

    And here in sight of Rome to *Saturnine*,

    King and Commander of our common weale,

    The wide worlds Emperour, doe I consecrate

    My sword, my Chariot, and my Prisoners,

    Presents well worthy Romes imperious Lord: 250

    Receiue them then, the tribute that I owe,

    Mine honours Ensignes humbled at thy feete.

SATURNINE

    Thankes Noble *Titus* Father of my life,

    How proude I am of thee and of thy gifts

    Rome shall record, and when I doe forget

    The least of these vnspeakeable deserts,

    Romans forget your Fealtie to me.

TITUS (*to Tamora*)

    Now Madam are you prisoner to an Emperour.

    To him that for your honour and your state,

    Will vse you Nobly, and your followers.   260

SATURNINE

    A goodly Lady trust me of the hue,

    That I would choose were I to choose a new:

    Cleare vp faire Queene that cloudy countenance,

    Though chance of war hath wrought this change of

        chear

    Thou comst not to be made a scorne in Rome.

    Princely shall be thy vsage euerie waie.

    Rest on my word, and let not discontent,

    Daunt all your hopes, Madam he comforts you,

    Can make you greater than the Queene of *Gothes*,

270   *Lauinia* you are not displeasde with this.

LAUINIA

    Not I my Lord, sith true Nobilitie,

    Warrants these words in Princely curtesie.

SATURNINE

    Thanks sweete *Lauinia*, Romans let vs goe,

    Raunsomles here we set our prisoners free,

    Proclaime our Honours Lords with Trumpe and Drum.

          ⌈*Flourish. Exeunt Saturnine, Tamora, Demetrius,*

                  Chiron, and Aron the moore⌉

BASSIANUS

    Lord *Titus* by your leaue, this maid is mine.

TITUS

    How sir, are you in earnest then my Lord?

BASSIANUS

    I Noble *Titus* and resolude withall,

    To doo my selfe this reason and this right.

MARCUS

280   *Suum cuique* is our Romane iustice,

    This Prince in iustice ceazeth but his owne.

LUCIUS

    And that he will, and shall if *Lucius* liue.

TITUS

    Traitors auaunt, where is the Emperours gard?

MUTIUS

    Brothers, helpe to conuay her hence away,

    And with my sword Ile keepe this doore safe.

              Exeunt Bassianus, Marcus, Quintus and

                  Martius with Lauinia

    (*To Titus*) My Lord you passe not here.

TITUS   What villaine boy,

    Barst me my way in Rome?

        He attacks Mutius

MUTIUS   Helpe *Lucius*, helpe.

        Titus kils him

LUCIUS (*to Titus*)

    My Lord you are vniust, and more than so,

    In wrongfull quarrell you haue slaine your sonne.

TITUS

290   Nor thou, nor he, are any sonnes of mine,

    My sonnes would neuer so dishonour me,

    Traitor restore *Lauinia* to the Emperour.

LUCIUS

    Dead if you will, but not to be his wife,

    That is anothers lawfull promist loue.

              Exit ⌈*with Mutius body*⌉

Enter aloft Saturnine the Emperour with Tamora

and Chiron and Demetrius her two sonnes and

Aron the moore

TITUS

    Follow my Lord, and Ile soone bring her backe.

SATURNINE

    No *Titus*, no, the Emperour needes her not,

    Nor her, nor thee, nor any of thy stocke:

    Ile trust by leysure, him that mocks me once,

    Thee neuer, nor thy traiterous hawtie sonnes,

    Confederates all thus to dishonour mee.   300

    Was none in Rome to make a stale

    But *Saturnine*? Full well *Andronicus*

    Agree these deeds, with that prowd bragge of thine,

    That saidst I begd the Empire at thy hands.

TITUS

    O monstrous, what reprochfull words are these?

SATURNINE

    But goe thy waies, goe giue that changing piece,

    To him that florisht for her with his sword:

    A valiant sonne in law thou shalt inioy,

    One fit to bandie with thy lawlesse sonnes,

    To ruffle in the Common-wealth of Rome.   310

TITUS

    These words are rasors to my wounded hart.

SATURNINE

    And therfore louely *Tamora* Queene of Gothes,

    That like the statelie *Phebe* mongst her Nymphs,

    Dost ouershine the gallanst Dames of Rome,

    If thou be pleasde with this my sodaine choise,

    Behold I choose thee *Tamora* for my Bride,

    And will create thee Emperesse of Rome.

    Speake Queene of Gothes dost thou applaud my

        choise?

    And here I sweare by all the Romane Gods,

    Sith Priest and holy water are so neere,   320

    And tapers burne so bright, and euery thing

    In readines for *Hymeneus* stand,

    I will not resalute the streets of Rome,

    Or clime my Pallace, till from forth this place,

    I lead espowsde my Bride along with mee.

TAMORA

    And here in sight of heauen to Rome I sweare,

    If *Saturnine* aduaunce the Queene of Gothes,

    Shee will a handmaide be to his desires,

    A louing Nurse, a Mother to his youth.

SATURNINE

    Ascend faire Queene Panthean: Lords accompany   330

    Your Noble Emperour and his louelie Bride,

    Sent by the Heauens for Prince *Saturnine*,

    Whose wisdome hath her Fortune conquered,

    There shall wee consummate our spousall rites.

                  Exeunt all but Titus

TITUS

    I am not bid to wait vpon this bride,

    Titus when wert thou wont to walke alone,

    Dishonoured thus and challenged of wrongs.

Enter Marcus and Titus sonnes, Lucius, Quintus
and Martius, ⌈carrying Mutius body⌉

MARCUS

O *Titus* see: O see what thou hast done
In a bad quarrell slaine a vertuous sonne.

TITUS

340 No foolish Tribune, no: No sonne of mine,
Nor thou, nor these, confederates in the deede,
That hath dishonoured all our Familie,
Vnworthy brother, and vnworthy sonnes.

LUCIUS

But let vs giue him buriall as becomes,
Giue *Mucius* buriall with our bretheren.

TITUS

Traitors away, he rests not in this toombe:
This monument fiue hundreth yeares hath stood,
Which I haue sumptuouslie reedified:
Here none but souldiers and Romes seruitors
350 Repose in fame: None basely slaine in braules.
Burie him where you can he comes not here.

MARCUS

My Lord this is impietie in you,
My Nephew *Mutius* deedes doo plead for him,
He must be buried with his brethren.

⌈QUINTUS *and* MARTIUS⌉

And shall or him wee will accompanie.

TITUS

And shall. What villaine was it spake that word?

⌈QUINTUS⌉

He that would vouch it in any place but here.

TITUS

What would you burie him in my despight?

MARCUS

No Noble *Titus*, but intreat of thee
360 To pardon *Mutius* and to bury him.

TITUS

Marcus: Euen thou hast stroke vpon my Crest.
And with these boyes mine honour thou hast
          wounded,
My foes I doe repute you euerie one,
So trouble me no more, but get you gone.

⌈MARTIUS⌉

He is not with himselfe, let vs withdraw.

⌈QUINTUS⌉

Not I till *Mutius* bones be buried.

          The brother and the sonnes kneele

MARCUS

Brother, for in that name doth nature pleade.

⌈QUINTUS⌉

Father, and in that name doth nature speake.

TITUS

Speake thou no more, if all the rest will speede.

MARCUS

370 Renowmed *Titus*, more than halfe my soule.

LUCIUS

Deare father, soule and substance of vs all.

MARCUS

Suffer thy brother *Marcus* to interre,

His Noble Nephew here in vertues nest,
That died in honour and *Lauinias* cause.
Thou art a Romane, be not barbarous:
The Greeks vpon aduise did burie *Ayax*
That slew himselfe: and wise *Laertes* sonne,
Did gratiouslie plead for his Funeralls:
Let not young *Mutius* then that was thy ioy,
Be bard his entrance here.

TITUS   Rise *Marcus*, rise,   380
The dismalst day is this that ere I saw,
To be dishonoured by my sonnes in Rome:
Well burie him, and burie me the next.

          they put Mutius in the tombe

LUCIUS

There lie thy bones sweete *Mutius* with thy friends,
Till wee with Trophees doo adorne thy tombe:

ALL ⌈BUT TITUS⌉ (*kneeling*)

No man shed teares for Noble *Mutius*,
He liues in fame, that dide in vertues cause.

                    Exit ⌈all but Marcus and Titus⌉

MARCUS

My Lord to step out of these dririe dumps,
How comes it that the subtile Queene of *Gothes*,
Is of a sodaine thus aduaunc'd in Rome.   390

TITUS

I know not *Marcus*, but I know it is.
(Whether by deuise or no, the heauens can tell.)
Is shee not then beholding to the man,
That brought her for this high good turne so farre.

⌈MARCUS⌉

Yes, and will Nobly him remunerate.

          ⌈*Flourish.*⌉ *Enter the Emperour Saturnine, Tamora*
          and her two sonnes Chiron and Demetrius, with
          Aron the Moore at one doore.
          Enter at the other doore Bascianus and Lauinia,
          with ⌈Lucius, Quintus, and Martius⌉

SATURNINE

So *Bascianus*, you haue plaid your prize,
God giue you ioy sir of your gallant Bride.

BASSIANUS

And you of yours my Lord, I say no more,
Nor wish no lesse, and so I take my leaue.

SATURNINE

Traitor, if Rome haue law, or we haue power,   400
Thou and thy faction shall repent this Rape.

BASSIANUS

Rape call you it my Lord to ceaze my owne,
My true betrothed loue, and now my wife:
But let the lawes of Rome determine all,
Meane while am I possest of that is mine.

SATURNINE

Tis good sir, you are verie short with vs.
But if we liue, weele be as sharpe with you.

BASSIANUS

My Lord what I haue done as best I may,
Answere I must, and shall doo with my life,
Onely thus much I giue your Grace to know,   410
By all the dueties that I owe to Rome,

This Noble Gentleman Lord *Titus* here,
Is in opinion and in honour wrongd,
That in the rescue of *Lauinia*,
With his owne hand did slay his youngest sonne,
In zeale to you, and highly moude to wrath,
To be controwld in that he frankelie gaue.
Receaue him then to fauour *Saturnine*,
That hath exprest himselfe in all his deeds,
420 A father and a friend to thee and Rome.

TITUS
Prince *Bascianus* leaue to pleade my deeds,
Tis thou, and those, that haue dishonoured me,
⌐He kneeles⌐
Rome and the righteous heauens be my iudge,
How I haue loude and honoured *Saturnine*.

TAMORA (*to Saturnine*)
My worthy Lord, if euer *Tamora*,
Were gratious in those Princelie eies of thine,
Then heare me speake indifferently for all:
And at my sute (sweete) pardon what is past.

SATURNINE
What Madam be dishonoured openly,
430 And baselie put it vp without reuenge.

TAMORA
Not so my Lord, the Gods of Rome forfend,
I should be Authour to dishonour you.
But on mine honour dare I vndertake,
For good Lord *Titus* innocence in all,
Whose furie not dissembled speakes his griefes:
Then at my sute looke gratiouslie on him,
Loose not so noble a friend on vaine suppose,
Nor with sowre looks afflict his gentle hart.
(*Aside to Saturnine*)
My Lord: Be rulde by me, be wonne at last,
440 Dissemble all your griefes and discontents,
You are but newlie planted in your Throne,
Least then the people, and Patricians too,
Vpon a iust suruay take *Titus* part,
And so supplant you for ingratitude,
Which Rome reputes to be a hainous sinne,
Yeeld at intreats: and then let me alone,
Ile find a day to massacre them all,
And race their faction and their familie,
The cruell father, and his traiterous sonnes,
450 To whom I sued for my deare sonnes life,
And make them know what tis to let a Queene,
Kneele in the streets and begge for grace in vaine.
(*Aloude*) Come, come sweete Emperour, (come
                Andronicus:)
Take vp this good old man, and cheare the hart,
That dies in tempest of thy angrie frowne.

SATURNINE
Rise *Titus* rise, my Empresse hath preuaild.

TITUS (*rising*)
I thanke your Maiestie, and her my Lord,
These words, these looks, infuse new life in me.

TAMORA
Titus I am incorporate in Rome,

A Roman now adopted happilie,   460
And must aduise the Emperour for his good,
This day all quarrels die *Andronicus*.
And let it be mine honour good my Lord,
That I haue reconciled your friends and you.
For you Prince *Bassianus* I haue past
My word and promise to the Emperour,
That you will be more milde and tractable.
And feare not Lords, and you *Lauinia*,
By my aduise all humbled on your knees,
You shall aske pardon of his Maiestie.   470
    ⌐*Bassianus*,⌐ *Lauinia, Lucius, Quintus and Martius*
    kneele

⌐LUCIUS⌐
Wee doo, and vowe to Heauen and to his Highnes,
That what wee did, was mildlie as we might,
Tendring our sisters honour and our owne.

MARCUS ⌐*kneeling*⌐
That on mine honour here doo I protest.

SATURNINE
Away, and talke not, trouble vs no more.

TAMORA
Nay, nay sweet Emperor, we must all be friends,
The Tribune and his Nephews kneele for grace,
I will not be denied, sweete hart looke backe.

SATURNINE
Marcus, for thy sake, and thy brothers here,
And at my louelie *Tamoras* intreats,   480
I doo remit these young mens hainous faults,
Stand vp:
    Marcus, Bassianus, Lauinia and Titus sonnes stand
        Lauinia though you left me like a Churle,
I found a friend, and sure as death I swore,
I would not part a Batchiler from the Priest.
Come if the Emperours Court can feast two Brides,
You are my guest *Lauinia* and your friends:
This daie shall be a loue-daie *Tamora*.

TITUS
To morrow and it please your Maiestie,
To hunt the Panther and the Hart with me,
With horne and hound, weele giue your grace bon
    iour.   490

SATURNINE
Be it so *Titus* and gramercie too.   ⌐*Flourish. Exeunt*⌐

⌐*Enter Aron alone*⌐   2.1

ARON
Now climeth *Tamora* Olympus toppe,
Safe out of fortunes shot, and sits aloft,
Secure of thunders cracke or lightning flash,
Aduaunc'd aboue pale enuies threatning reach,
As when the golden sunne salutes the morne,
And hauing gilt the Ocean with his beames,
Gallops the Zodiacke in his glistering Coach,
And ouer-looks the highest piering hills.
So *Tamora*.   500
Vpon her wit doth earthly honour wait,

And vertue stoops and trembles at her frowne.
Then *Aron* arme thy hart, and fit thy thoughts,
To mount aloft with thy Emperiall Mistris,
And mount her pitch, whom thou in triumph long
Hast prisoner held, fettred in amourous chaines,
And faster bound to *Arons* charming eies,
Than is *Prometheus* tide to *Caucasus*.
Away with slauish weedes and seruile thoughts,
510 I will be bright and shine in pearle and golde,
To wait vpon this new made Emperesse.
To wait said I? to wanton with this Queene,
This Goddesse, this Semerimis, this Nymph,
This Syren that will charme Romes *Saturnine*,
And see his shipwracke, and his Common-weales.
Hollo, what storme is this?
          Enter Chiron and Demetrius brauing
DEMETRIUS
Chiron thy yeares wants wit, thy wits wants edge,
And manners to intrude where I am grac'd,
And may for ought thou knowest affected bee.
CHIRON
520 *Demetrius*, thou dost ouerweene in all,
And so in this, to beare me downe with braues,
Tis not the difference of a yeare or two
Makes me lesse gratious, or thee more fortunate:
I am as able and as fit as thou,
To serue, and to deserue my Mistris grace,
And that my sword vpon thee shall approue,
And plead my passions for *Lauinias* loue.
ARON (*aside*)
Clubs, Clubs, these louers will not keepe the peace.
DEMETRIUS
Why boy, although our mother (vnaduizd)
530 Gaue you a daunsing Rapier by your side,
Are you so desperate growne to threat your friends:
Goe too: haue your lath glued within your sheath,
Till you know better how to handle it.
CHIRON
Meane while sir, with the little skill I haue,
Full well shalt thou perceiue how much I dare.
DEMETRIUS
I boy, grow yee so braue?
          they drawe
ARON   Why how now Lords?
So neere the Emperours Pallace dare yee drawe,
And maintaine such a quarrell openlie?
Full well I wote the ground of all this grudge,
540 I would not for a million of gold,
The cause were knowne to them it most concernes,
Nor would your Noble Mother for much more,
Be so dishonoured in the Court of Rome.
For shame put vp.
DEMETRIUS   Not I till I haue sheathd,
My Rapier in his bosome, and withall
Thrust those reprochfull speeches downe his throat,
That he hath breathd in my dishonour here.
CHIRON
For that I am prepard, and full resolude,

Fowle spoken Coward, that thundrest with thy
          tongue,
And with thy weapon nothing darst performe.   550
ARON Away I say.
Now by the Gods that warlike *Gothes* adore,
This pettie brabble will vndoo vs all:
Why Lords, and thinke you not how dangerous
It is to iet vpon a Princes right?
What is *Lauinia* then become so loose,
Or *Bascianus* so degenerate,
That for her loue such quarrels may be brocht,
Without controulement, iustice, or reuenge.
Young Lords beware, and should the Empresse know,   560
This discords ground, the musicke would not please.
CHIRON
I care not I, knew shee and all the world,
I loue *Lauinia* more than all the world.
DEMETRIUS
Yongling learne thou to make some meaner choise,
Lauinia is thine elder brothers hope.
ARON
Why are ye mad? or know yee not in Rome,
How furious and impatient they bee,
And cannot brooke competitors in loue?
I tell you Lords, you doo but plot your deaths,
By this deuise.
CHIRON   *Aron*, a thousand deaths   570
Would I propose, to atchiue her whom I loue.
ARON
To atchiue her how?
DEMETRIUS   Why makes thou it so strange?
Shee is a woman, therefore may be woode,
Shee is a woman, therefore may be woonne,
Shee is *Lauinia*, therefore must be loude.
What man, more water glideth by the mill
Than wots the Miller of, and easie it is,
Of a cut loafe to steale a shiue we know:
Though *Bascianus* be the Emperours brother,
Better than he haue worne *Vulcans* badge.   580
ARON (*aside*)
I and as good as *Saturninus* may.
DEMETRIUS
Then why should he dispaire that knows to court it,
With words, faire looks, and liberalitie.
What hast not thou full often stroke a Doe,
And borne her cleanlie by the Keepers nose?
ARON
Why then it seemes some certaine snatch, or so
Would serue your turnes.
CHIRON   I so the turne were serued.
DEMETRIUS
Aron thou hast hit it.
ARON   Would you had hit it too,
Then should not we be tirde with this adoo.
Why harke ye, harke ye, and are you such fooles   590
To square for this: would it offend you then
That both should speede.
CHIRON Faith not me.

DEMETRIUS Nor me so I were one.

ARON

  For shame be friends, and ioine for that you iar,

  Tis pollicie and stratageme must doo

  That you affect, and so must you resolue,

  That what you cannot as you would atchiue,

  You must perforce accomplish as you may:

600 Take this of mee, *Lucrece* was not more chast

  Than this *Lauinia*, *Bascianus* loue.

  A speedier course than lingring languishment

  Must we pursue, and I haue found the path:

  My Lords a solemne hunting is in hand,

  There will the louelie Romane Ladies troope:

  The forrest walks are wide and spatious,

  And many vnfrequented plots there are,

  Fitted by kinde for rape and villanie:

  Single you thither then this daintie Doe,

610 And strike her home by force, if not by words,

  This waie or not at all, stand you in hope.

  Come, come, our Empresse with her sacred wit

  To villanie and vengeance consecrate,

  Will we acquaint with all what we intend,

  And shee shall file our engines with aduise,

  That will not suffer you to square your selues,

  But to your wishes hight aduaunce you both.

  The Emperours Court is like the house of fame,

  The Pallace full of tongues, of eies, and eares:

620 The woods are ruthles, dreadfull, deafe, and dull:

  There speake, and strike braue boies, and take your

    turns,

  There serue your lust, shadowed from heauens eie,

  And reuell in *Lauinias* treasurie.

CHIRON

  Thy counsell Lad smels of no cowardize.

DEMETRIUS

  Sit fas aut nefas, till I finde the streame,

  To coole this heate, a charme to calme these fits,

  Per Stigia, per manes Vehor.　　　　　　*Exeunt*

2.2　　　*Enter Titus Andronicus, and his three sonnes*

(Sc. 2)　　*(Quintus, Lucius and Martius), and Marcus,*

    making a noise with hounds & hornes

TITUS

  The hunt is vp the Morne is bright and gray,

  The fields are fragrant, and the woods are greene,

630 Vncouple here, and let vs make a bay,

  And wake the Emperour, and his louelie Bride,

  And rowze the Prince, and ring a Hunters peale,

  That all the Court may eccho with the noise.

  Sonnes let it be your charge, as it is ours,

  To attend the Emperours person carefullie:

  I haue beene troubled in my sleepe this night,

  But dawning day new comfort hath inspirde.

    Here a crie of Hounds, and wind hornes in a peale:

    then enter Saturninus, Tamora, Bassianus, Lauinia,

    Chiron, Demetrius, and their Attendants

  Many good morrowes to your Maiestie,

  Madam to you as many, and as good,

  I promised your Grace a Hunters peale.　　　　640

SATURNINE

  And you haue rung it lustilie my Lords,

  Somewhat too earlie for new married Ladies.

BASSIANUS

  Lauinia, how say you?

LAUINIA　　　　　　　　　I say no:

  I haue been broad awake, two howres & more.

SATURNINE

  Come on then, horse and Chariots let vs haue,

  And to our sport: (*To Tamora*) Madam, now shall ye

    see,

  Our Romane hunting.

MARCUS　　　　　　　　I haue Dogges my Lord,

  Will rouze the prowdest Panther in the Chase,

  And clime the highest promontarie topp.

TITUS

  And I haue horse will follow where the game　　650

  Makes way, and runne like swallowes ore the plaine.

DEMETRIUS (*aside*)

  Chiron we hunt not we, with horse nor hound

  But hope to plucke a daintie Doe to ground.　　*Exeunt*

    Enter Aron alone, with gold　　　　**2.3**

ARON　　　　　　　　　　　　　　　　　**(Sc. 3)**

  He that had wit, would thinke that I had none,

  To burie so much gold vnder a tree,

  And neuer after to inherit it.

  Let him that thinks of me so abiectlie,

  Know that this gold must coine a stratageme,

  Which cunninglie effected will beget,

  A verie excellent peece of villanie:　　　　　660

  And so repose sweet gold for their vnrest,

  That haue their almes out of the Empresse Chest.

    He hides the gold.

    Enter Tamora alone to the Moore

TAMORA

  My louelie *Aron*, wherefore lookst thou sad,

  When euerie thing doth make a gleefull bost?

  The birds chaunt melodie on euerie bush,

  The snakes lies rolled in the chearefull sunne,

  The greene leaues quiuer with the cooling winde,

  And make a checkerd shadow on the ground:

  Vnder their sweet shade, *Aron* let vs sit,

  And whilst the babling eccho mocks the hounds,　　670

  Replying shrillie to the well tun'd hornes,

  As if a double hunt were heard at once,

  Let vs sit downe and marke their yellowing noyse:

  And after conflict such as was supposde

  The wandring Prince and *Dido* once inioyed,

  When with a happie storme they were surprisde,

  And curtaind with a counsaile-keeping Caue,

  We may each wreathed in the others armes,

  (Our pastimes done,) possesse a golden slumber,

  Whiles hounds and hornes, and sweete mellodious

    birds　　　　　　　　　　　　　　　　680

Be vnto vs as is a Nurces song
Of Lullabie, to bring her Babe a sleepe.

ARON

Maddam, though *Venus* gouerne your desires,
Saturne is dominator ouer mine:
What signifies my deadlie standing eie,
My silence, and my clowdie melancholie,
My fleece of wollie haire that now vncurles,
Euen as an Adder when shee doth vnrowle,
To doo some fatall execution.

690 No Maddam, these are no veneriall signes,
Vengeance is in my hart, death in my hand,
Blood and reuenge are hammering in my head.
Harke *Tamora* the Empresse of my soule,
Which neuer hopes more heauen than rests in thee,
This is the daie of doome for *Bassianus*,
His *Philomel* must loose her tongue to daie,
Thy sonnes make pillage of her chastitie,
And wash their hands in *Bascianus* blood.
Seest thou this letter? *(giuing a letter)* take it vp I pray
thee,

700 And giue the king this fatall plotted scrowle.
Now question me no more we are espied,
Here comes a parcell of our hopefull bootie,
Which dreads not yet their liues destruction.
     Enter Bascianus, and Lauinia

TAMORA *(aside to Aron)*
Ah my sweete *Moore*, sweeter to me than life.

ARON *(aside to Tamora)*
No more great Empresse, *Bascianus* comes,
Be crosse with him, and Ile goe fetch thy sonnes
To backe thy quarrels what so ere they bee.   *Exit*

BASSIANUS
Who haue we here? Romes Royall Empresse,
Vnfurnisht of her well beseeming troope?
710 Or is it *Dian* habited like her,
Who hath abandoned her holie groues,
To see the generall hunting in this Forrest?

TAMORA
Sawcie controwler of my priuate steps,
Had I the powre that some say *Dian* had,
Thy temples should be planted presentlie,
With hornes as was *Acteons*, and the hounds,
Should driue vpon thy new transformed limbes,
Vnmannerly intruder as thou art.

LAUINIA
Vnder your patience gentle Empresse,
720 Tis thought you haue a goodly gift in horning,
And to be doubted that your *Moore* and you,
Are singled forth to trie experiments:
Ioue sheeld your husband from his hounds to day,
Tis pittie they should take him for a Stag.

BASSIANUS
Beleeue me Queene your swarte Cymerion,
Doth make your honour of his bodies hue,
Spotted, detested, and abhominable.
Why are you sequestred from all your traine,

Dismounted from your snow white goodly steede,
And wandred hither to an obscure plot,   730
Accompanied but with a barbarous *Moore*,
If foule desire had not conducted you?

LAUINIA
And being intercepted in your sport,
Great reason that my Noble Lord be rated
For sausines, *(to Bassianus)* I pray you let vs hence,
And let her ioy her Rauen culloured loue,
This valie fitts the purpose passing well.

BASSIANUS
The King my brother shall haue note of this.

LAUINIA
I, for these slips haue made him noted long,
Good King to be so mightily abused.   740

TAMORA
Why haue I patience to indure all this.
     Enter Chiron and Demetrius

DEMETRIUS
How now deare soueraigne, and our gratious Mother,
Why doth your highnes looke so pale and wan?

TAMORA
Haue I not reason thinke you to looke pale,
These two haue ticed me hither to this place,
A barren, detested vale you see it is,
The trees though summer yet forlorne and leane,
Ouercome with mosse and balefull misselto.
Here neuer shines the sunne, here nothing breeds,
Vnlesse the nightly Owle or fatall Rauen: 750
And when they showd me this abhorred pit,
They told me here at dead time of the night,
A thousand feends, a thousand hissing snakes,
Ten thousand swelling toades, as manie vrchins,
Would make such fearefull and confused cries,
As any mortall body hearing it
Should strait fall mad, or els die suddainely.
No sooner had they told this hellish tale,
But strait they told me they would binde me here,
Vnto the body of a dismall Ewghe,   760
And leaue me to this miserable death.
And then they calde me foule adulteresse,
Laciuious Goth, and all the bitterest tearmes,
That euer eare did heare to such effect.
And had you not by wondrous fortune come,
This vengeance on me had they executed:
Reuenge it as you loue your Mothers life,
Or be yee not hence forward cald my Children.

DEMETRIUS
This is a witnes that I am thy son.
     stab Bassianus

CHIRON
And this for me struck home, to shew my strength.   770
     Stab Bassianus, who dies.
     ⌈*Tamora turnes to Lauinia*⌉

LAUINIA
I come *Semeramis*, nay barbarous *Tamora*,
For no name fits thy nature but thy owne.

TAMORA (*to Chiron*)
Giue me the poynard, you shall know my boies,
Your Mothers hand shall right your Mothers wrong.

DEMETRIUS
Stay Madame here is more belongs to her,
First thrash the corne, then after burne the straw:
This minion stood vpon her chastitie,
Vpon her Nuptiall vow, her loyaltie,
And with that quainte hope, braues your mightenes,
780   And shall she carrie this vnto her graue.

CHIRON
And if she doe, I would I were an Euenuke,
Drag hence her husband to some secret hole,
And make his dead trunke pillow to our lust.

TAMORA
But when yee haue the honie ye desire,
Let not this waspe out liue vs both to sting.

CHIRON
I warrant you maddame we will make that sure:
Come Mistris now perforce we will enioy,
That nice preserued honestie of yours.

LAUINIA
Oh *Tamora*, thou bearest a womans face.

TAMORA
790   I will not heare her speake awaie with her.

LAUINIA
Sweet Lords intreat her heare me but a word.

DEMETRIUS (*to Tamora*)
Listen faire Maddame let it be your glory
To see her teares, but be your hart to them:
As vnrelenting Flint to drops of raine.

LAUINIA
When did the Tigers young ones teach the dam,
Oh doe not learne her wrath: she taught it thee,
The Milke thou suckst from her did turne to Marble,
Euen at thy teat thou hadst thy tyrranie,
Yet euerie Mother breeds not sonnes a like,
(*To Chiron*) Doe thou intreat her shew a womans
800   pittie.

CHIRON
What wouldst thou haue me proue my selfe a
          bastard?

LAUINIA
Tis true the Rauen doth not hatch a Larke,
Yet haue I hard, Oh could I finde it now,
The Lion moued with pittie did indure,
To haue his Princelie pawes parde all away:
Some say that Rauens foster forlorne children,
The whilst their owne birds famish in their nests:
Oh be to me though thy hard hart say no,
Nothing so kinde but something pittifull.

TAMORA
810   I know not what it meanes, away with her.

LAUINIA
Oh let me teach thee: for my Fathers sake,
That gaue thee life when well he might haue slaine
          thee,
Be not obdurate, open thy deafe yeares.

TAMORA
Hadst thou in person nere offended mee,
Euen for his sake am I pittilesse.
Remember boyes I powrd forth teares in vaine,
To saue your brother from the sacrifice,
But fearce *Andronicus* would not relent,
Therefore away with her, and vse her as you will,
The worse to her the better lou'd of mee.   820

LAUINIA
Oh *Tamora* be calld a Gentle Queene,
And with thine owne hands kill me in this place,
For tis not life that I haue begd so long,
Poore I was slaine when *Bascianus* dide.

TAMORA
What begst thou then fond woman let me goe?

LAUINIA
Tis present death I beg, and one thing more,
That woman-hood denies my tong to tell,
Oh keepe me from there worse than killing lust,
And tumble me into some lothsome pit,
Where neuer mans eye may behold my bodie,   830
Doe this and be a charitable murderer.

TAMORA
So should I rob my sweet sonnes of their fee,
No let them satisfie their lust on thee.

DEMETRIUS (*to Lauinia*)
Away for thou hast staide vs here too long.

LAUINIA
No grace, no womanhood, ah beastly creature,
The blot and enemie to our generall name,
Confusion fall

CHIRON
Nay then Ile stop your mouth, (*to Demetrius*) bring
          thou her husband,
This is the hole where *Aron* bid vs hide him.
          Demetrius and Chiron cast Bassianus body into the
          pit ⌈and couer the mouth of it with branches⌉, then
          exeunt dragging Lauinia

TAMORA
Farewell my sons, see that you make her sure,   840
Nere let my hart know merry cheare indeede,
Till all the *Andronicie* be made away:
Now will I hence to seeke my louely *Moore*,
And let my spleenfull sonnes this Trull defloure.   *Exit*
          Enter Aron with Quintus and Martius, two of Titus
          sonnes

ARON
Come on my Lords the better foot before,
Straight will I bring you to the lothsome pit,
Where I espied the Panther fast a sleepe.

QUINTUS
My sight is verie dull what ere it bodes.

MARTIUS
And mine I promise you, were it not for shame,
Well could I leaue our sport to sleepe a while.   850
          He falls into the pit

QUINTUS
What art thou fallen what subtill hole is this,

Whose mouth is couered with rude growing briers,
Vpon whose leaues are drops of new shed blood,
As fresh as morning dew distild on flowers,
A verie fatall place it seemes to mee,
Speake brother hast thou hurt thee with the fall?

MARTIUS
Oh brother with the dismalst obiect hurt,
That euer eie with sight made hart lament.

ARON (aside)
Now will I fetch the King to finde them here,
860   That he thereby may haue a likely gesse,
How these were they, that made away his brother.
                                                      Exit

MARTIUS
Why dost not comfort me and help me out
From this vnhallowd, and bloodstained hole.

QUINTUS
I am surprised with an vncouth feare,
A chilling sweat oreruns my trembling ioynts,
My hart suspects more than mine eie can see.

MARTIUS
To proue thou hast a true diuining hart,
Aron, and thou looke downe into this den,
And see a fearefull sight of blood and death.

QUINTUS
870   Aron is gone, and my compassionate hart,
Will not permit mine eyes once to behold,
The thing where at it trembles by surmise:
Oh tell me who it is, for nere till now,
Was I a child to feare I know not what.

MARTIUS
Lord Bassianus lies bereied in blood,
All on a heape like to a slaughtered Lambe,
In this detested darke blood drinking pit.

QUINTUS
If it be darke how dost thou know tis hee.

MARTIUS
Vpon his bloody finger he doth weare
880   A pretious ring, that lightens all this hole:
Which like a taper in some monument,
Doth shine vpon the dead mans earthy cheekes,
And shewes the ragged intrals of this pit:
So pale did shine the Moone on Piramus,
When he by night lay bathd in Maiden blood,
O Brother help me with thy fainting hand,
If feare hath made thee faint as me it hath,
Out of this fell deuouring receptacle,
As hatefull as Cocitus mistie mouth.

QUINTUS
890   Reach me thy hand, that I may helpe thee out,
Or wanting strength to doe thee so much good,
I may be pluckt into the swallowing wombe,
Of this deepe pit, poore Bassianus graue:
I haue no strength to plucke thee to the brinck,

MARTIUS
Nor I no strength to clime without thy help.

QUINTUS
Thy hand once more, I will not loose againe,

Till thou art here a loft or I belowe:
Thou canst not come to me, I come to thee.
        He falls into the pit.
        Enter Saturnine the Emperour ⌈with attendants⌉ and
        Aron, the Moore

SATURNINE
Along with me, Ile see what hole is here,
And what he is that now is leapt into it.   900
        He speakes into the pit
Say who art thou that lately didst descend,
Into this gaping hollow of the earth.

MARTIUS
The vnhappie sonnes of old Andronicus,
Brought hither in a most vnluckie houre,
To finde thy brother Bassianus dead.

SATURNINE
My brother dead, I know thou dost but iest,
He and his Ladie both are at the lodge,
Vpon the north side of this pleasant chase,
Tis not an houre since I left them there.

MARTIUS
We know not where you left them all a liue,   910
But out alas, here haue we found him dead.
        Enter Tamora, Titus Andronicus, and Lucius

TAMORA Where is my Lord the King?

SATURNINE
Here Tamora, though gripde with killing griefe.

TAMORA
Where is thy brother Bassianus?

SATURNINE
Now to the bottome dost thou search my wound,
Poore Bassianus here lies murthered.

TAMORA
Then all too late I bring this fatall writ,
The complot of this timelesse Tragedie,
And wonder greatly that mans face can fold,
In pleasing smiles such murderous tyrranie.   920
        She giueth Saturnine a letter. Saturninus reads the
        letter

SATURNINE
And if wee misse to meete him handsomelie,
Sweet huntsman, Bassianus tis we meane,
Doe thou so much as dig the graue for him,
Thou knowst our meaning looke for thy reward,
Among the Nettles at the Elder tree,
Which ouer shades the mouth of that same pit,
Where we decreed to burie Bassianus,
Doe this and purchase vs thy lasting friends.
Oh Tamora was euer heard the like,
This is the pit, and this the Elder tree,   930
Looke Sirs if you can finde the huntsman out,
That should haue murthered Bassianus here.

ARON
My gratious Lord here is the bag of gold.

SATURNINE (to Titus)
Two of thy whelps, fell curs of bloody kinde,
Haue here bereft my brother of his life:
Sirs drag them from the pit vnto the prison,

There let them bide vntill we haue deuisd,
Some neuer hard of tortering paine for them.

TAMORA

What are they in this pit, Oh wondrous thing!
940   How easily murder is discouered.

    Attendants drag Quintus, Martius, and Bassianus
    body from the pit

TITUS (*kneeling*)

High Emperour, vpon my feeble knee,
I beg this boone, with teares not lightly shed,
That this fell fault of my accursed sonnes,
Accursed, if the fault be proud in them.

SATURNINE

If it be proude, you see it is apparant,
Who found this letter, *Tamora* was it you?

TAMORA

Andronicus himselfe did take it vp.

TITUS

I did my Lord, yet let me be their baile,
For by my Fathers reuerent toombe I vowe,
950   They shall be ready at your highnes will,
To answere their suspition with their liues.

SATURNINE

Thou shalt not baile them, see thou follow me.
Some bring the murthered body, some the murtherers,
Let them not speake a word the guilt is plaine,
For by my soule, were there worse end than death,
That end vpon them should be executed.   ⌈*Exit*⌉

TAMORA

Andronicus I will intreat the King,
Feare not thy sonnes, they shall doe well enough.

TITUS ⌈*rising*⌉

Come *Lucius* come, stay not to talke with them.
                              Exeunt

2.4   *Enter the Empresse sonnes Chiron and Demetrius*
(Sc. 4)   *with Lauinia, her handes cut off, and her tongue*
    cut out, & rauisht

DEMETRIUS

960   So now go tell and if thy tongue can speake,
Who twas that cut thy tongue and rauisht thee.

CHIRON

Write downe thy minde bewray thy meaning so,
And if thy stumpes will let thee play the scribe.

DEMETRIUS

See how with signes and tokens she can scrowle.

CHIRON (*to Lauinia*)

Goe home, call for sweet water wash thy hands.

DEMETRIUS

She hath no tongue to call, nor hands to wash,
And so lets leaue her to her silent walkes.

CHIRON

And twere my cause, I should goe hang my selfe.

DEMETRIUS

If thou hadst hands to helpe thee knit the corde.
              Exeunt Chiron and Demetrius
   ⌈*Winde Hornes.*⌉ *Enter Marcus from hunting, to*
   Lauinia

MARCUS

Who is this, my Neece that flies away so fast,   970
Cosen a word, where is your husband:
If I doe dreame would all my wealth would wake me.
If I doe wake some Plannet strike me downe,
That I may slumber an eternall sleepe.
Speake gentle Neece, what sterne vngentle hands,
Hath lopt, and hewde, and made thy body bare,
Of her two branches those sweet Ornaments,
Whose cyrcling shadowes, Kings haue sought to
    sleepe in,
And might not gaine so great a happines
As halfe thy loue: Why dost not speake to me?   980
Alas, a crimson Riuer of warme blood,
Like to a bubling Fountaine stirde with winde,
Doth rise and fall betweene thy Rosed lips,
Comming and going with thy honie breath.
But sure some *Tereus* hath deflowred thee,
And lest thou shouldst detect him cut thy tongue.
Ah now thou turnst awaie thy face for shame,
And notwithstanding all this losse of blood,
As from a Conduit with three issuing spouts,
Yet doe thy cheekes looke red as *Titans* face,   990
Blushing to be encountred with a Clowde.
Shall I speake for thee, shall I say tis so.
Oh that I knew thy hart, and knew the beast,
That I might raile at him to ease my minde.
Sorrow concealed like an Ouen stoppt,
Doth burne the hart to cinders where it is.
Faire *Philomele*, why she but lost her tongue,
And in a tedious sampler sowed her minde.
But louely Neece, that meane is cut from thee,
A craftier *Tereus*, Cosen hast thou met,   1000
And he hath cut those prettie fingers off,
That could haue better sowed than *Philomel*.
Oh had the monster seene those Lillie hands,
Tremble like aspen leaues vpon a Lute,
And make the silken strings delight to kisse them,
He would not then haue tucht them for his life.
Or had he heard the heauenly Harmonie,
Which that sweete tongue hath made,
He would haue dropt his knife and fell a sleepe,
As *Cerberus* at the Thracian Poets feete.   1010
Come let vs goe, and make thy father blind,
For such a sight will blind a fathers eie.
One houres storme will drowne the fragrant meades,
What will whole months of teares thy fathers eies?
Doe not drawe backe, for we will mourne with thee,
Oh could our mourning ease thy miserie.   *Exeunt*

                    ❂

Enter the Iudges Tribunes and Senatours with Titus   3.1
two sonnes Martius and Quintus bound, passing   (Sc. 5)
⌈*ou*ʳ⌉ *the Stage to the place of execution, and Titus*
going before pleading

TITUS

Heare me graue Fathers, Noble Tribunes stay,
For pittie of mine age, whose youth was spent

In dangerous warres, whilst you securelie slept.
1020 For all my blood in Roomes great quarrell shed,
For all the frostie nights that I haue watcht,
And for these bitter teares which now you see,
Filling the aged wrincles in my cheeks,
Be pittifull to my condemned sonnes,
Whose soules is not corrupted as tis thought.
For two and twentie sonnes I neuer wept,
Because they died in honours loftie bed,
        Andronicus lieth downe, and the Iudges passe
        by him
For these two, Tribunes, in the dust I write
My harts deepe languor, and my soules sad teares:
1030 Let my teares staunch the earths drie appetite,
My sonnes sweete blood will make it shame and blush:
                        ⌈*Exeunt all but Titus*⌉
O earth I will befriend thee more with raine,
That shall distill from these two auntient ruines,
Than youthfull Aprill shall with all his showres.
In summers drought, Ile drop vpon thee still,
In winter with warme teares Ile melt the snow,
And keepe eternall springtime on thy face,
So thou refuse to drinke my deare sonnes blood.
        Enter Lucius with his weapon drawne
Oh reuerent *Tribunes*, Oh gentle aged men
1040 Vnbinde my sonnes, reuerse the doome of death,
And let me say, (that neuer wept before)
My teares are now preuailing Oratours.
LUCIUS
Oh Noble Father you lament in vaine,
The *Tribunes* heare you not, no man is by,
And you recount your sorrowes to a stone.
TITUS
Ah *Lucius*, for thy brothers let me plead,
Graue *Tribunes*, once more I intreat of you.
LUCIUS
My gratious Lord, no *Tribune* heares you speak.
TITUS
Why tis no matter man, if they did heare
1050 They would not marke me, if they did marke,
They would not pittie me, yet pleade I must.
Therefore I tell my sorrowes to the stones,
Who though they cannot answere my distresse,
Yet in some sort they are better than the *Tribunes*,
For that they will not intercept my tale:
When I doe weepe, they humblie at my feete
Receiue my teares, and seeme to weepe with me,
And were they but attired in graue weeds,
Rome could afford no *Tribunes* like to these:
A stone is soft as waxe, *Tribunes* more hard than
1060   stones:
A stone is silent, and offendeth not,
And *Tribunes* with their tongues doome men to death.
But wherefore standst thou with thy weapon drawne?
LUCIUS
To rescue my two brothers from their death,
For which attempt the Iudges haue pronouncst,
My euerlasting doome of banishment.

TITUS ⌈*rising*⌉
O happie man, they haue befriended thee:
Why foolish *Lucius*, dost thou not perceiue
That Rome is but a wildernes of tygers?
Tygers must pray, and Rome affords no pray   1070
But me and mine, how happie art thou then,
From these deuourers to be banished.
But who comes with our brother *Marcus* here?
        Enter Marcus with Lauinia
MARCUS
Titus, prepare thy aged eies to weepe,
Or if not so, thy Noble hart to breake:
I bring consuming sorrow to thine age.
TITUS
Will it consume mee? Let me see it then.
MARCUS This was thy Daughter.
TITUS Why *Marcus* so shee is.
LUCIUS (*falling on his knees*) Ay mee, this Obiect kils mee.   1080
TITUS
Faint-harted-boy, arise and looke vpon her,
        ⌈*Lucius rises*⌉
Speake *Lauinea*, what accursed hand,
Hath made thee handles in thy fathers sight?
What foole hath added water to the sea?
Or brought a faggot to bright burning Troy?
My griefe was at the height before thou camst,
And now like *Nylus* it disdaineth bounds.
Giue me a sword Ile choppe off my hands too,
For they haue fought for Rome, and all in vaine:
And they haue nurst this woe, in feeding life: 1090
In bootlesse praier haue they beene held vp,
And they haue serude me to effectles vse.
Now all the seruice I require of them,
Is that the one will helpe to cut the other,
Tis well *Lauinia* that thou hast no hands,
For hands to doe Rome seruice is but vaine.
LUCIUS
Speake gentle sister, who hath martred thee.
MARCUS
Oh that delightfull engine of her thoughts,
That blabd them with such pleasing eloquence,
Is torne from forth that prettie hollow cage,   1100
Where like a sweete mellodious bird it sung,
Sweete varied notes inchaunting euerie eare.
LUCIUS
Oh say thou for her, who hath done this deed?
MARCUS
Oh thus I found her straying in the Parke,
Seeking to hide her selfe, as doth the Deare
That hath receaude some vnrecuring wound.
TITUS
It was my Deare, and he that wounded her,
Hath hurt me more than had he kild me dead:
For now I stand as one vpon a rocke,
Inuirond with a wildernes of sea,   1110
Who markes the waxing tide, grow waue by waue,
Expecting euer when some enuious surge,
Will in his brinish bowels swallow him.

This way to death my wretched sonnes are gone,
Here stands my other sonne a banisht man,
And here my brother weeping at my woes:
But that which giues my soule the greatest spurne
Is deare *Lauinia*, dearer than my soule.
Had I but seene thy picture in this plight,
1120　　It would haue madded me: what shall I doo,
Now I behold thy liuelie bodie so?
Thou hast no hands to wipe away thy teares,
Nor tongue to tell me who hath martred thee:
Thy husband he is dead, and for his death
Thy brothers are condemnde, and dead by this.
Looke *Marcus*, Ah sonne *Lucius* looke on her,
When I did name her brothers, then fresh teares
Stood on her cheeks, as doth the honie dew,
Vpon a gathred Lillie almost withered.

MARCUS

Perchance shee weepes because they kild her
1130　　　　husband,
Perchance, because shee knowes them innocent.

TITUS

If they did kill thy husband then be ioyfull,
Because the Law hath tane reuenge on them.
No, no, they would not doo so fowle a deede,
Witnes the sorrow that their sister makes.
Gentle *Lauinia*, let me kisse thy lips,
Or make some signe how I may doe thee ease:
Shall thy good Vncle, and thy brother *Lucius*,
And thou, and I, sit round about some Fountaine,
1140　　Looking all downewards to behold our cheekes,
How they are staind like meadowes yet not drie,
With mierie slime left on them by a flood?
And in the fountaine shall wee gaze so long,
Till the fresh tast be taken from that clearenes,
And made a brine pit with our bitter teares?
Or shall we cut away our hands like thine?
Or shall we bite our tongues? and in dumbe showes
Passe the remainder of our hatefull daies?
What shall we doe? Let vs that haue our tongues,
1150　　Plot some deuise of further miserie,
To make vs wonderd at in time to come.

LUCIUS

Sweete father cease your teares, for at your grief
See how my wretched sister sobs and weepes.

MARCUS

Patience deare niece, good *Titus* dry thine eies.

TITUS

Ah *Marcus*, *Marcus*, Brother well I wote,
Thy napkin cannot drinke a teare of mine,
For thou poore man, hast drownd it with thine owne.

LUCIUS

Ah my *Lauinia*, I will wipe thy cheekes.

TITUS

Marke *Marcus*, marke, I vnderstand her signes,
1160　　Had shee a tongue to speake, now would shee say
That to her Brother, which I said to thee.
His napking with his true teares all bewet,
Can doe no seruice on her sorrowfull cheekes,

Oh what a simpathie of woe is this,
As farre from helpe, as Lymbo is from blisse.

　　　Enter Aron the Moore alone

ARON

Titus Andronicus, My Lord the Emperour,
Sends thee this word, that if thou loue thy sonnes,
Let *Marcus*, *Lucius*, or thy selfe olde *Titus*,
Or any one of you, chop off your hand
And send it to the King, he for the same,　　　　　1170
Will send thee hither both thy sonnes aliue,
And that shall be the raunsome for their fault.

TITUS

Oh gratious Emperour, Oh gentle *Aron*,
Did euer Rauen sing so like a Larke,
That giues sweete tidings of the Sunnes vprise?
With all my hart, Ile send the Emperour my hand,
Good *Aron* wilt thou helpe to chop it off?

LUCIUS

Stay father, for that Noble hand of thine,
That hath throwne downe so many enemies,
Shall not be sent: my hand will serue the turne,　　1180
My youth can better spare my bloud than you,
And therefore mine shall saue my brothers liues.

MARCUS

Which of your hands hath not defended Rome,
And reard aloft the bloudie Battleaxe,
Wrighting destruction on the enemies Castle?
Oh none of both, but are of high desert:
My hand hath beene but idle, let it serue
To raunsome my two Nephews from their death,
Then haue I kept it to a worthie ende.

ARON

Nay come agree whose hand shall goe along,　　　　1190
For feare they die before their pardon come.

MARCUS

My hand shall goe.

LUCIUS　　　　　　　By heauen it shall not goe.

TITUS

Sirs striue no more, such withred hearbs as these
Are meete for plucking vp, and therefore mine.

LUCIUS

Sweete father, if I shall be thought thy sonne,
Let me redeeme my brothers both from death.

MARCUS

And for our fathers sake, and mothers care,
Now let me show a brothers loue to thee.

TITUS

Agree betweene you, I will spare my hand.

LUCIUS

Then Ile goe fetch an Axe.

MARCUS　　　　　　　　　But I will vse the Axe.　　1200
　　　　　　　Exeunt Lucius and Marcus

TITUS

Come hither *Aron*, Ile deceiue them both,
Lend me thy hand, and I will giue thee mine.

ARON (*aside*)

If that be calde deceit, I will be honest,
And neuer whilst I liue deceiue men so:

But Ile deceiue you in another sort,
And that youle say ere halfe an houre passe.
    He cuts off Titus hand.
    Enter Lucius and Marcus againe

TITUS
Now stay your strife, what shall be, is dispatcht.
Good *Aron* giue his Maiestie my hand,
Tell him it was a hand that warded him
1210 From thousand dangers, bid him burie it,
More hath it merited, that let it haue:
As for my sonnes, say I account of them,
As iewels purchasde at an easie price,
And yet deare too, because I bought mine owne.

ARON
I goe *Andronicus*, and for thy hand,
Looke by and by to haue thy sonnes with thee.
(*Aside*) Their heads I meane: Oh how this villanie,
Doth fat me with the verie thoughts of it.
Let fooles doe good, and faire men call for grace,
1220 *Aron* will haue his soule blacke like his face.   *Exit*

TITUS
Oh here I lift this one hand vp to heauen,
And bow this feeble ruine to the earth,
    He kneeles
If any power pitties wretched teares,
To that I call: (*to Lauinia, who kneeles*) what wouldst
    thou kneele with mee?
Doe then deare hart, for heauen shall heare our
    praiers,
Or with our sighs wele breath the welkin dimme,
And staine the sunne with fogge, as sometime clowds,
When they doe hug him in their melting bosomes.

MARCUS
Oh Brother speake with possibilitie,
1230 And doe not breake into these deepe extreames.

TITUS
Is not my sorrows deepe hauing no bottome?
Then be my passions bottomlesse with them.

MARCUS
But yet let reason gouerne thy lament.

TITUS
If there were reason for these miseries,
Then into limits could I binde my woes:
When heauen doth weepe, doth not the earth
    oreflow?
If the winds rage, doth not the sea waxe mad,
Threatning the welkin with his bigswolne face?
And wilt thou haue a reason for this coile?
1240 I am the sea. Harke how her sighs doth blow:
Shee is the weeping welkin, I the earth:
Then must my sea be mooued with her sighs,
Then must my earth with her continuall teares,
Become a deluge: ouerflowed and drownd:
For why, my bowels cannot hide her woes,
But like a drunkard must I vomit them.
Then giue me leaue, for loosers will haue leaue,
To ease their stomacks with their bitter tongues.

    Enter a messenger with two heads and a hand
MESSENGER
Worthy *Andronicus*, ill art thou repaid,
For that good hand thou sentst the Emperour: 1250
Here are the heads of thy two Noble sonnes,
And heres thy hand in scorne to thee sent backe:
Thy griefe, their sports: Thy resolution mockt:
That woe is me to thinke vpon thy woes,
More than remembrance of my fathers death.
    ⌈*He sets downe the heads and hand. Exit*⌉

MARCUS
Now let hote Aetna coole in Cycilie,
And be my hart an euerburning hell:
These miseries are more than may be borne.
To weepe with them that weepe doth ease some
    deale,
But sorrow flowted at, is double death.   1260

LUCIUS
Ah that this sight should make so deepe a wound
And yet detested life not shrinke thereat:
That euer death should let life beare his name,
Where life hath no more interest but to breath.
    Lauinia kisses Titus

MARCUS
Alas poore hart, that kisse is comfortlesse,
As frozen water to a starued snake.

TITUS
When will this fearefull slumber haue an end?

MARCUS
Now farewell flattrie, die *Andronicus*,
Thou dost not slumber, see thy two sonnes heads,
Thy warlike hand, thy mangled Daughter heere: 1270
Thy other banisht sonne with this deere sight,
Strucke pale and bloodlesse, and thy brother I,
Euen like a stony image cold and numme.
Ah now no more will I controwle thy greefes,
Rent off thy siluer haire, thy other hand,
Gnawing with thy teeth, and be this dismall sight
The closing vp of our most wretched eies:
Now is a time to storme, why art thou still?

TITUS Ha, ha, ha.

MARCUS
Why dost thou laugh? It fits not with this houre.   1280

TITUS
Why I haue not another teare to shed;
Besides this sorrow is an enemie,
And would vsurpe vpon my watrie eies,
And make them blinde with tributarie teares.
Then which way shall I find Reuenges Caue,
For these two heads doe seeme to speake to mee
And threat me, I shall neuer come to blisse,
Till all these mischiefes be returnd againe,
Euen in their throats that hath commited them.
Come let me see what taske I haue to doe,   1290
    ⌈*He and Lavinia rise*⌉
You heauie people cirkle me about,
That I may turne mee to each one of you,
And sweare vnto my soule to right your wrongs,

Marcus, Lucius and Lauinia cirkle Titus. He
pledges them

The vow is made. Come brother take a head,
And in this hand the other will I beare,
And *Lauinia* thou shalt be imployde,
Beare thou my hand sweet wench betweene thine
    Armes:
As for thee boy, goe get thee from my sight,
Thou art an Exile, and thou must not stay,
1300   Hie to the *Gothes* and raise an armie there,
And if yee loue me as I thinke you doe,
Lets kisse and part for we haue much to doe.
    They kisse. Exeunt. Manet Lucius

LUCIUS

Farewell *Andronicus* my Noble Father,
The woefulst man that euer liude in Rome:
Farewell proud Rome till *Lucius* come againe,
He loues his pledges dearer than his life:
Farewell *Lauinia* my Noble sister,
O would thou wert as thou to fore hast beene,
But now nor *Lucius* nor *Lauinia* liues,
1310   But in obliuion and hatefull greefes:
If *Lucius* liue, he will requite your wrongs,
And make proud *Saturnine* and his Emperesse,
Beg at the gates like *Tarquin* and his Queene.
Now will I to the *Gothes* and raise a powre,
To bee reuengd on Rome and *Saturnine*.   *Exit Lucius*

3.2
(Sc. 6)   *A Banket. Enter Titus Andronicus, Marcus, Lauinia,*
    and the Boy (young Lucius)

    TITUS

So, so, now sit, and looke you eate no more
Then will preserue iust so much strength in vs
As will reuenge these bitter woes of ours.
    ⌈*They sit*⌉
Marcus vnknit that sorrow-wreathen knot:
1320   Thy Neece and I (poore Creatures) want our hands
And cannot passionate our tenfold griefe,
With foulded Armes. This poore right hand of mine,
Is left to tirranize vppon my breast,
Who when my hart all mad with misery,
Beats in this hollow prison of my flesh,
Then thus I thumpe it downe.
    He beats his breast
(*To Lauinia*) Thou Map of woe, that thus dost talk in
    signes,
When thy poore hart beates with outragious beating,
Thou canst not strike it thus to make it still?
1330   Wound it with sighing girle, kil it with grones:
Or get some little knife betweene thy teeth,
And iust against thy hart make thou a hole,
That all the teares that thy poore eyes let fall
May run into that sinke, and soaking in,
Drowne the lamenting foole, in Sea salt teares.

MARCUS

Fy brother fy, teach her not thus to lay
Such violent hands vppon her tender life.

TITUS

How now! Has sorrow made thee doate already?

Why *Marcus*, no man should be mad but I:
What violent hands can she lay on her life: 1340
Ah, wherefore dost thou vrge the name of hands,
To bid *Æneas* tell the tale twice ore
How Troy was burnt, and he made miserable?
O handle not the theame, to talke of hands,
Least we remember still that we haue none,
Fie, fie, how Frantiquely I square my talke
As if we should forget we had no hands:
If *Marcus* did not name the word of hands.
Come, lets fall too, and gentle girle eate this,
Heere is no drinke? Harke *Marcus* what she saies,   1350
I can interpret all her martir'd signes,
She saies, she drinkes no other drinke but teares
Breu'd with her sorrow, mesh'd vppon her cheekes:
Speechlesse complayner, I will learne thy thought:
In thy dumb action, will I be as perfect
As begging Hermits in their holy prayers.
Thou shalt not sighe nor hold thy stumps to heauen,
Nor winke, nor nod, nor kneele, nor make a signe,
But I (of these) will wrest an Alphabet,
And by still practice, learne to know thy meaning.   1360

PUER

Good grandsire leaue these bitter deepe laments,
Make my Aunt merry, with some pleasing tale.

MARCUS

Alas, the tender boy in passion mou'd,
Doth weepe to see his grandsires heauinesse.

TITUS

Peace tender Sapling, thou art made of teares,
And teares will quickly melt thy life away.
    Marcus strikes the dish with a knife
What doest thou strike at *Marcus* with thy knife.

MARCUS

At that that I haue kil'd my Lord, a Fly.

TITUS

Out on the murderour: thou kil'st my hart,
Mine eyes are cloi'd with view of Tirranie: 1370
A deed of death done on the Innocent
Becoms not *Titus* brother: get thee gone,
I see thou art not for my company.

MARCUS

Alas (my Lord) I haue but kild a flie.

TITUS

But? How: if that Flie had a father, brother?
How would he hang his slender gilded wings
And buz lamenting dirges in the ayer,
Poore harmelesse Fly,
That with his pretty buzing melody,
Came heere to make vs merry, and thou hast kil'd
    him.   1380

MARCUS

Pardon me sir, it was a blacke illfauour'd Fly,
Like to the Empresse Moore, therefore I kild him.

TITUS O, o, o,
Then pardon me for reprehending thee,
For thou hast done a Charitable deed:
Giue me thy knife, I will insult on him,
Flattering my selfe, as if it were the Moore,

Come hither purposely to poyson me.
He takes a knife and strikes
There's for thy selfe, and thats for *Tamira*: Ah sirra,
1390   Yet I thinke we are not brought so low,
But that betweene vs, we can kill a Fly,
That comes in likenesse of a Cole-blacke Moore.

MARCUS
Alas poore man, griefe ha's so wrought on him,
He takes false shadowes, for true substances.

TITUS
Come, take away: *Lauinia*, goe with me,
Ile to thy closset, and goe read with thee
Sad stories, chanced in the times of old.
Come boy, and goe with me, thy sight is young,
And thou shalt read, when mine begin to dazell.
                          Exeunt

4.1   *Enter Lucius sonne and Lauinia running after him,*
(Sc. 7)   *and the Boy flies from her with his Bookes vnder*
         his Arme. Enter Titus and Marcus

PUER
1400   Help Grandsier helpe, my Aunt *Lauinia*,
Followes me euerie where I know not why.
Good Vnckle *Marcus* see how swift shee comes,
Alas sweet Aunt I know not what you meane.
    ⌜*He drops his Bookes*⌝

MARCUS
Stand by me *Lucius*, doe not feare thine Aunt.

TITUS
She loues thee boy too well to doe thee harme.

PUER
I when my Father was in Rome she did.

MARCUS
What meanes my Neece *Lauinia* by these signes.

TITUS
Feare her not *Lucius*, somewhat doth she meane.
⌜MARCUS⌝
See *Lucius* see, how much she makes of thee:
1410   Some whither would she haue thee goe with her.
A boy, *Cornelia* neuer with more care,
Red to her sonnes than she hath red to thee,
Sweet Poetrie and Tullies Oratour:
Canst thou not gesse wherefore she plies thee thus.

PUER
My Lord I know not I, nor can I gesse,
Vnlesse some fit or frenzie do possesse her:
For I haue heard my Grandsier say full oft,
Extremitie of greeues would make men mad.
And I haue red that *Hecuba* of Troy,
1420   Ran mad for sorrow, that made me to feare,
Although my Lord I know my Noble Aunt,
Loues me as deare as ere my Mother did,
And would not but in furie fright my youth,
Which made me downe to throwe my bookes and flie
Causeles perhaps, but pardon me sweet Aunt,
And Maddam if my Vnckle *Marcus* goe,
I will most willinglie attend your Ladyship.

MARCUS *Lucius* I will.
    Lauinia turnes the bookes ouer with her stumpes
TITUS
How now *Lauinia*, *Marcus* what meanes this?
Some booke there is that she desires to see: 1430
Which is it gyrle of these, open them boy,
(*To Lauinia*) But thou art deeper read and better skild,
Come and take choise of all my Lybrarie,
And so beguile thy sorrow, till the heauens
Reueale the damn'd contriuer of this deede.
Why lifts she vp her Armes in sequence thus?

MARCUS
I thinke she meanes that there were more than one
Confederate in the fact, I more there was:
Or else to heauen, she heaues them for reuenge.

TITUS
Lucius what booke is that shee tosseth so.   1440

PUER
Grandsier tis Ouids Metamorphosis,
My Mother gaue it me.

MARCUS   For loue of her thats gone,
Perhaps shee culd it from among the rest.

TITUS
Soft so busilie she turnes the leaues,
Help her, what would she finde? *Lauinia* shal I read?
This is the tragicke tale of *Philomel*,
And treats of *Tereus* treason and his rape,
And rape I feare, was roote of thy annoie.

MARCUS
See brother see, note how she coats the leaues.

TITUS
Lauinia wert thou thus surpriz'd sweet gyrle?   1450
Rauisht and wrongd as *Philomela* was,
Forcd in the ruthlesse Vast and gloomie woods;
See, see, I such a place there is where we did hunt,
(O had we neuer, neuer hunted there,)
Patternd by that the Poet here describes,
By nature made for murthers and for rapes.

MARCUS
O why should nature build so fowle a den,
Vnlesse the Gods delight in Tragedies.

TITUS
Giue signes sweet gyrle, for here are none but friends,
What Romaine Lord it was durst doe the deed?   1460
Or slonke not *Saturnine* as *Tarquin* erst,
That left the Campe to sinne in *Lucrece* bed.

MARCUS
Sit downe sweet Neece, brother sit downe by mee,
    They sit
Appollo, Pallas, Ioue or *Mercurie*,
Inspire me that I may this treason finde,
My Lord looke here, looke here *Lauinia*,
This sandie plot is plaine, guide if thou canst
This after me,
    He writes his name with his staffe and guides it
    with feete and mouth
            I here haue writ my name,
Without the help of any hand at all.

1470 Curst be that hart that forcd vs to this shift:
Write thou good Neece, and here display at last,
What God will haue discouered for reuenge,
Heauen guide thy pen to print thy sorrowes plaine,
That we may know the traytors and the truth,
Shee takes the staffe in her mouth, and guides it
with her stumps and writes
Oh doe yee read my Lord what she hath writ.
⌈TITUS⌉ *Stuprum, Chiron, Demetrius.*

MARCUS
What, what, the lustfull sonnes of *Tamora*,
Performers of this haynous bloody deede.

TITUS
Magni Dominator poli,
1480 *Tam lentus audis scelera, tam lentus vides?*

MARCUS
Oh calme thee gentle Lord, although I know
There is enough written vpon this earth,
To stir a mutinie in the mildest thoughts,
And arme the mindes of infants to exclaimes,
My Lord kneele downe with me, *Lauinia* kneele,
And kneele sweet boy, the Romaine Hectors hope
All kneele
And sweare with me as with the wofull feere,
And father of that chast dishonoured Dame,
Lord *Iunius Brutus* sware for *Lucrece* rape,
1490 That we will prosecute by good aduice
Mortall reuenge vpon these Traiterous *Gothes*,
And see their blood or die with this reproch.
They rise

TITUS
Tis sure enough, and you knew how,
But if you hunt these Beare whelpes then beware,
The Dam will wake and if she winde yee once,
Shee's with the Lion deepely still in league,
And luls him whilst shee plaieth on her backe.
And when he sleepes, will shee doe what she list.
You are a young huntsman *Marcus*, let alone,
1500 And come I will goe get a leafe of brasse,
And with a gad of steele will write these words,
And lay it by: the angry northen wind
Will blow these sands like *Sibels* leaues abroad,
And wheres our lesson then, boy what say you?

PUER
I say my Lord that if I were a man,
Their mothers bed-chamber should not be safe,
For these base bond-men to the yoake of Rome.

MARCUS
I thats my boy, thy father hath full oft,
For his vngratefull Countrie done the like.

PUER
1510 And Vnkle so will I, and if I liue.

TITUS
Come goe with me into mine Armorie,
Lucius Ile fit thee, and withall my boy
Shall carrie from me to the Empresse sonnes,
Presents that I intend to send them both:
Come, come, thoult doe my message wilt thou not?

PUER
I with my dagger in their bosomes Grandsier.

TITUS
No boy not so, Ile teach thee another course,
Lauinia come, *Marcus* looke to my house,
Lucius and Ile goe braue it at the Court,
I marrie will we sir, and weele be waited on.   1520
Exeunt all but Marcus

MARCUS
O heauens, can you heare a good man grone
And not relent, or not compassion him?
Marcus attend him in his extasie,
That hath more scars of sorrow in his hart,
Than foe-mens marks vpon his battred shield,
But yet so iust, that he will not reuenge,
Reuenge the heauens for olde *Andronicus*.   *Exit*

Enter Aron, Chiron, and Demetrius at one doore,   4.2
and at the other doore young Lucius, and another   (Sc. 8)
with a bundle of weapons, and verses writ vpon
them

CHIRON
Demetrius, her's the sonne of *Lucius*,
He hath some message to deliuer vs.

ARON
I some mad message from his mad Grandfather.   1530

PUER
My Lords, with all the humblenes I may,
I greete your Honours from *Andronicus*;
(*Aside*) And pray the Romane Gods confound you
both.

DEMETRIUS
Gramarcie Louelie *Lucius*, whats the news.

PUER (*aside*)
That you are both discipherd, thats the newes,
For villaines markt with rape. (*Aloude*) May it please
you,
My Grandsier well aduisde hath sent by me,
The goodliest weapons of his Armorie,
To gratefie your honourable youth
The hope of Rome, for so he bid me say: 1540
His attendant giues the weapons
And so I doe, and with his gifts present
Your Lordships, that when euer you haue neede,
You may be armed and appointed well,
And so I leaue you both: (*Aside*) Like bloudie villaines.
Exit with attendant

DEMETRIUS
What's here? a scrole, and written round about,
Let's see,
Integer vitae scelerisque purus,
Non eget mauri iaculis nec arcu.

CHIRON
O tis a verse in *Horace* I know it well,
I read it in the Grammer long agoe.   1550

ARON
I iust, a verse in *Horace*, right you haue it,
(*Aside*) Now what a thing it is to be an Asse.

Her's no sound ieast, the olde man hath found their
    gilt,
And sends them weapons wrapt about with lines,
That wound beyond their feeling to the quicke:
But were our wittie Empresse well a foote,
Shee would applaud *Andronicus* conceit,
But let her rest in her vnrest a while.
(*To Chiron and Demetrius*)
And now young Lords, wast not a happie starre,
1560 Led vs to Rome strangers, and more than so
Captiues, to be aduaunced to this height:
It did me good before the Pallace gate,
To braue the *Tribune* in his brothers hearing.

DEMETRIUS
But me more good to see so great a Lord,
Baselie insinuate and send vs gifts.

ARON
Had he not reason Lord *Demetrius*,
Did you not vse his daughter very friendlie?

DEMETRIUS
I would we had a thousand Romane Dames
At such a bay, by turne to serue our lust.

CHIRON
1570 A charitable wish, and full of loue.

ARON
Here lacks but your mother for to say Amen.

CHIRON
And that would she for twenty thousand more.

DEMETRIUS
Come let vs goe and pray to all the Gods,
For our beloued mother in her paines.

ARON
Pray to the deuills, the Gods haue giuen vs ouer.
    Trumpets sound

DEMETRIUS
Why do the Emperours trumpets flourish thus.

CHIRON
Belike for ioy the Emperour hath a sonne.

DEMETRIUS
Soft who comes here.
    Enter Nurse with a blackamoore childe

NURSE   God morrow Lords,
O tell me did you see *Aron* the *Moore*.

ARON
1580 Well, more or lesse, or nere a whit at all,
Here *Aron* is, and what with *Aron* now.

NURSE
Oh gentle *Aron* we are all vndone,
Now helpe, or woe betide thee euermore.

ARON
Why what a catterwalling dost thou keepe,
What dost thou wrap and fumble in thy armes?

NURSE
O that which I would hide from heauens eye,
Our Empresse shame and stately Romes disgrace,
Shee is deliuered Lords she is deliuered.

ARON
To whome.

NURSE   I meane she is brought a bed.

ARON
Well god giue her good rest, what hath he sent her? 1590

NURSE
A diuell.

ARON   Why then she is the deuils Dam,
A ioyfull issue.

NURSE
A Ioyles, dismall, blacke, and sorrowfull issue,
Here is the babe as loathsome as a toade,
Amongst the fairefast breeders of our clime,
The Empresse sends it thee, thy stampe, thy seale,
And bids thee christen it with thy daggers point.

ARON
Zounds ye whore, is blacke so base a hue?
Sweete blowse you are a beautious blossome sure.

DEMETRIUS Villaine what hast thou done?   1600

ARON That which thou canst not vndoe.

CHIRON Thou hast vndone our mother.

ARON Villaine I haue done thy mother.

DEMETRIUS
And therein hellish dog thou hast vndone her,
Woe to her chaunce, and damde her loathed choice,
Accurst the offspring of so foule a fiend.

CHIRON
It shall not liue.

ARON   It shall not die.

NURSE
Aron it must, the mother wils it so.

ARON
What must it Nurse? then let no man but I,
Doe execution on my flesh and blood.   1610

DEMETRIUS
Ile broach the tadpole on my Rapiers point,
Nurse giue it me, my sword shall soone dispatch it.

ARON
Sooner this sword shall plow thy bowels vp,
    He takes the childe and drawes his sworde
Stay murtherous villaines will you kill your brother?
Now by the burning tapors of the skie,
That shone so brightly when this boy was got,
He dies vpon my Semitars sharpe point,
That touches this my first borne sonne and heire:
I tell you yonglings, not *Enceladus*,
With all his threatning band of *Typhons* broode, 1620
Nor great *Alcides*, nor the God of warre,
Shall ceaze this pray out of his fathers hands:
What, what, yee sanguine shallow harted boies,
Yee whitelimde walles, yee ale-house painted signes,
Cole-blacke is better than another hue,
In that it scornes to beare another hue:
For all the water in the Ocean,
Can neuer turne the swans blacke legs to white,
Although shee laue them howrely in the flood:
Tell the Empresse from mee I am of age   1630
To keepe mine owne, excuse it how shee can.

DEMETRIUS
Wilt thou betray thy Noble Mistris thus.

ARON
My Mistris is my Mistris, this my selfe,

The vigour, and the picture of my youth:
This before all the world doe I preferre,
This mauger all the world will I keepe safe,
Or some of you shall smoke for it in Rome.

DEMETRIUS
By this our mother is for euer shamde.

CHIRON
Rome will despise her for this foule escape.

NURSE
1640   The Emperour in his rage will doome her death.

CHIRON
I blush to thinke vpon this ignomie.

ARON
Why ther's the Priuiledge your beautie bears:
Fie trecherous hue, that will betraie with blushing
The close enacts and counsels of thy hart:
Her's a young Lad framde of another leere,
Looke how the blacke slaue smiles vpon the father,
As who should say, olde Lad I am thine owne.
Hee is your brother Lords, sensiblie fed
Of that selfe bloud that first gaue life to you,
1650   And from y^t wombe where you imprisoned were,
Hee is infraunchised, and come to light:
Nay hee is your brother by the surer side,
Although my seale be stamped in his face.

NURSE
Aron, what shall I say vnto the Empresse.

DEMETRIUS
Aduise thee Aron, what is to be done,
And we will all subscribe to thy aduise:
Saue thou the childe, so wee may all be safe.

ARON
Then sit we downe and let vs all consult,
My sonne and I will haue the winde of you:
1660   Keepe there, now talke at pleasure of your safetie.
      They sit

DEMETRIUS *(to the Nurse)*
How many women saw this childe of his?

ARON
Why so braue Lords, when we doe ioine in league
I am a Lambe, but if you braue the *Moore*,
The chafed Bore, the mountaine Lionesse,
The Ocean swels not so as Aron stormes:
(To the Nurse) But saie againe, how manie saw the
    childe.

NURSE
Cornelia the Midwife, and my selfe,
And no one els but the deliuered Empresse.

ARON
The Empresse, the Midwife, and your selfe,
1670   Two may keepe counsell when the third's away:
Goe to the Empresse, tell her this I said.
      He kils her
Weeke, weeke, so cries a Pigge prepared to the spit.

DEMETRIUS
What meanst thou Aron, wherfore didst thou this?

ARON
O Lord sir, tis a deede of pollicie,

Shall shee liue to betraie this gilt of ours?
A long tongude babling Gossip, No Lords, no:
And now be it knowne to you my full intent.
Not farre, one *Muliteus* my Countriman
His wife but yesternight was brought to bed,
His childe is like to her, faire as you are: 1680
Goe packe with him, and giue the mother gold,
And tell them both, the circumstance of all,
And how by this their childe shall be aduaunst,
And be receiued for the Emperours Heire,
And substituted in the place of mine,
To calme this tempest whirling in the Court,
And let the Emperour dandle him for his owne.
Harke yee Lords, you see I haue giuen her Phisicke,
And you must needs bestow her Funerall,
The fields are neere, and you are gallant Groomes: 1690
This done, see that you take no longer daies,
But send the Midwife presentlie to mee.
The Midwife and the Nurse well made away,
Then let the Ladies tattle what they please.

CHIRON
Aron, I see thou wilt not trust the aire
With secrets.

DEMETRIUS   For this care of *Tamora*,
Her selfe, and hers, are highlie bound to thee.
      Exeunt Chiron and Demetrius with
        the Nurses body

ARON
Now to the *Gothes* as swift as swallow flies,
There to dispose this treasure in mine armes,
And secretlie to greete the Empresse friends: 1700
Come on you thicke-lipt-slaue, Ile beare you hence,
For it is you that puts vs to our shifts:
Ile make you feede on berries, and on roots,
And fat on curds and whay, and sucke the Goate,
And cabbin in a Caue, and bring you vp,
To be a warriour and commaund a Campe.
      Exit with the childe

Enter Titus, olde Marcus, his sonne Publius, young   **4.3**
Lucius, and other gentlemen (Sempronius, Caius),   **(Sc. 9)**
with bowes, and Titus beares the arrowes with
letters on the ends of them

TITUS
Come *Marcus*, come, kinsemen this is the way,
Sir boy let me see your Archerie,
Looke yee draw home inough and tis there straight,
Terras Astreá reliquit,   1710
Be you remembred *Marcus*, shees gone, shees fled,
Sirs take you to your tooles, you Cosens shall
Goe sound the ocean, and cast your nets,
Happilie you may catch her in the sea,
Yet ther's as little iustice as at land:
No *Publius* and *Sempronius*, you must doe it,
Tis you must dig with mattocke and with spade,
And pierce the inmost Center of the earth,
Then when you come to *Plutoes* Region,
I pray you deliuer him this petition,   1720

Tell him it is for iustice and for aide,
And that it comes from olde *Andronicus*
Shaken with sorrowes in vngratefull Rome.
Ah Rome, well, well, I made thee miserable,
What time I threw the peoples suffrages
On him that thus doth tyrrannize ore mee.
Goe get you gone, and pray be carefull all,
And leaue you not a man of warre vnsearcht,
This wicked Emperour may haue shipt her hence,
1730 And kinsemen then we may goe pipe for iustice.
MARCUS
O *Publius*, is not this a heauie case
To see thy Noble Vnkle thus distract?
PUBLIUS
Therefore my Lords it highly vs concernes,
By daie and night t'attend him carefullie:
And feede his humour kindly as we may,
Till time beget some carefull remedie.
MARCUS
Kinsmen his sorrowes are past remedie
But ⌈   ⌉
Ioine with the *Gothes*, and with reuengefull warre,
1740 Take wreake on Rome for this ingratitude,
And vengeance on the traitour *Saturnine*.
TITUS
Publius how now, how now my Masters,
What haue you met with her?
PUBLIUS
No my good Lord, but *Pluto* sends you word,
If you will haue reuenge from hell you shall,
Marrie for Iustice shee is now imploid,
He thinks with *Ioue* in heauen, or some where else,
So that perforce you must needs staie a time.
TITUS
He doth me wrong to feede me with delaies,
1750 Ile diue into the burning lake belowe,
And pull her out of *Acaron* by the heeles.
Marcus we are but shrubs, no Cedars wee,
No big-boand-men framde of the *Cyclops* size,
But mettall *Marcus*, steele to the verie backe,
Yet wrung with wrongs more than our backs can
      beare:
And sith ther's no iustice in earth nor hell,
We will sollicite heauen and moue the Gods,
To send downe Iustice for to wreake our wrongs:
Come to this geare, you are a good Archer *Marcus*,
      He giues them the Arrowes
1760 *Ad Iouem*, thats for you, here *ad Apollinem*,
Ad Martem, thats for my selfe,
Here boy to *Pallas*, here to *Mercurie*,
To *Saturn, Caius*, not to *Saturnine*,
You were as good to shoote against the winde.
Too it boy, *Marcus* loose when I bid,
Of my word I haue written to effect,
Ther's not a God left vnsollicited.
MARCUS
Kinsemen, shoot all your shafts into the Court,
Wee will afflict the Emperour in his pride.

TITUS
Now Masters draw,
      They shoot
                  Oh well said *Lucius*,   1770
Good boy in *Virgoes* lappe, giue it *Pallas*.
MARCUS
My Lord, I aime a mile beyond the Moone,
Your letter is with *Iubiter* by this.
TITUS
Ha, ha, *Publius, Publius*, what hast thou done?
See, see, thou hast shot off one of *Taurus* hornes.
MARCUS
This was the sport my Lord, when *Publius* shot
The Bull being galde, gaue *Aries* such a knocke,
That downe fell both the Rams hornes in the Court,
And who should finde them but the Empresse villaine:
Shee laught, and tolde the *Moore* hee should not
      choose,   1780
But giue them to his Master for a present.
TITUS
Why there it goes, God giue his Lordship ioy.
      *Enter the Clowne with a basket and two pidgeons
      in it*
Newes, newes from heauen, *Marcus* the Poast is come.
Sirra what tidings, haue you any letters,
Shall I haue iustice, what saies *Iubiter*?
CLOWNE Ho the Gibbetmaker? Hee saies that he hath
taken them downe againe, for the man must not be
hangd till the next weeke.
TITUS
But what saies *Iubiter* I aske thee?
CLOWNE Alas sir, I know not *Iubiter*, I neuer dranke with   1790
him in all my life.
TITUS
Why villaine art not thou the Carrier.
CLOWNE I of my pidgeons sir, nothing els.
TITUS Why didst thou not come from heauen?
CLOWNE From heauen, alas sir, I neuer came there, God
forbid I should be so bolde, to presse to heauen in my
young daies: why I am going with my pidgeons to the
tribunall Plebs, to take vp a matter of brawle betwixt
my Vncle, and one of the Emperals men.
TITUS
Sirra come hither, make no more adoo,   1800
But giue your pidgeons to the Emperour,
By mee thou shalt haue iustice at his hands,
Hold, hold, (*giuing money*) meanewhile here's money
      for thy charges,
Giue me pen and inke. Sirra, can you with a grace
Deliuer vp a Supplication?
CLOWNE I sir.
TITUS (*writing and giuing the Clowne a paper*) Then here is
a Supplication for you, and when you come to him, at
the first approch you must kneele, then kisse his foote,
then deliuer vp your pidgeons, and then looke for your   1810
reward. Ile bee at hand sir, see you doe it brauelie.
CLOWNE I warrant you sir, let me alone.
TITUS
Sirra hast thou a knife? Come let me see it.

Here *Marcus*, fold it in the Oration,
For thou hast made it like an humble Suppliant.
And when thou hast giuen it to the Emperour,
Knocke at my doore, and tell me what he saies.

CLOWNE God be with you sir, I will.   *Exit*

TITUS

Come *Marcus* let vs goe, *Publius* follow mee.   *Exeunt*

4.4
(Sc. 10)   *Enter Saturnine the Emperour and Tamora the*
            Empresse and Chiron and Demetrius her two
            sonnes, and others, the Emperour brings the
            Arrowes in his hand that Titus shot at him

SATURNINE

1820   Why Lords what wrongs are these, was euer seene,
        An Emperour in Rome thus ouer-borne,
        Troubled, confronted thus, and for the extent
        Of egall iustice, vsde in such contempt.
        My Lords you know as know the mightfull Gods,
        How euer these disturbers of our peace
        Buz in the peoples eares, there nought hath past
        But euen with law against the wilfull sonnes
        Of old *Andronicus*. And what and if
        His sorrowes haue so ouerwhelmde his witts?
1830   Shall we be thus afflicted in his wreakes,
        His fits, his frencie, and his bitternes?
        And now he writes to heauen for his redresse,
        See heres to *Ioue*, and this to *Mercurie*.
        This to *Apollo*, this to the God of warre:
        Sweete skrowles to flie about the streets of Rome,
        Whats this but libelling against the Senate,
        And blazoning our vniustice euerie where,
        A goodly humor is it not my Lords?
        As who would say in Rome no iustice were.
1840   But if I liue his fained extasies
        Shall be no shelter to these outrages,
        But he and his shall know that iustice liues
        In *Saturninus* health, whome if he sleepe,
        Hele so a wake as he in furie shall,
        Cut off the proud'st conspiratour that liues.

TAMORA

        My gratious Lord, my louely *Saturnine*,
        Lord of my life, commander of my thoughts,
        Calme thee and beare the faults of *Titus* age,
        The'ffects of sorrow for his valiant sonnes,
1850   Whose losse hath pearst him deepe and skard his hart,
        And rather comfort his distressed plight,
        Than prosecute the meanest or the best
        For these contempts: (*aside*) why thus it shall become
        Hie witted *Tamora* to glose with all.
        But *Titus* I haue touched thee to the quicke:
        Thy life blood out, if *Aron* now be wise,
        Then is all safe, the Anchor in the port.
            Enter Clowne
        How now good fellow wouldst thou speake with vs?

CLOWNE Yea forsooth & your Mistriship be Emperiall.

1860 TAMORA Empresse I am, but yonder sits the Emperour.

CLOWNE Tis he, God and Saint *Steuen* giue you Godden,
        I haue brought you a letter and a couple of pigeons
        here.

            Saturnine reads the letter

SATURNINE (*to an attendant*)
        Goe take him away and hang him presently?

CLOWNE How much money must I haue.

TAMORA Come sirra you must be hanged.

CLOWNE Hangd be Lady, then I haue brought vp a neck
        to a faire end.   *Exit* ⌜*with attendant*⌝

SATURNINE

        Dispightfull and intollerable wrongs,
        Shall I endure this monstrous villanie?   1870
        I know from whence this same deuise proceeds.
        May this be borne as if his traitorous sonnes,
        That dide by law for murther of our brother,
        Haue by my meanes bin butchered wrongfully.
        Goe dragge the villaine hither by the haire,
        Nor age, nor honour, shall shape priueledge,
        For this proud mocke, Ile be thy slaughter man,
        Sly franticke wretch, that holpst to make me great,
        In hope thy selfe should gouerne Rome and me.
            Enter Nũtius Emillius

SATURNINE

        What newes with thee *Emillius*?   1880

EMILLIUS

        Arme my Lords, Rome neuer had more cause,
        The *Gothes* haue gathered head and with a power
        Of high resolued men, bent to the spoile,
        They hither march amaine, vnder conduct
        Of *Lucius*, sonne to old *Andronicus*,
        Who threats in course of this reuenge, to doe
        As much as euer *Coriolanus* did.

SATURNINE

        Is warlike *Lucius* Generall of the *Gothes*,
        These tidings nip me, and I hang the head
        As flowers with frost, or grasse beat downe with
            stormes.   1890
        I now begins our sorrowes to approch,
        Tis he the common people loue so much,
        My selfe hath often heard them say,
        When I haue walked like a priuate man,
        That *Lucius* banishment was wrongfullie,
        And they haue wisht that *Lucius* were their
            Emperour.

TAMORA

        Why should you feare, is not your Citie strong?

SATURNINE

        I but the Citizens fauour *Lucius*,
        And will reuolt from me to succour him.

TAMORA

        King Be thy thoughts imperious like thy name, 1900
        Is the sunne dimde, that Gnats doe flie in it,
        The Eagle suffers little birds to sing,
        And is not carefull what they meane thereby,
        Knowing that with the shadow of his winges,
        He can at pleasure stint their melodie.
        Euen so maiest thou the giddie men of Rome,
        Then cheare thy spirit for know thou Emperour,
        I will inchaunt the old *Andronicus*,
        With words more sweete and yet more dangerous
        Then baites to fish, or honniestalkes to sheepe, 1910

When as the one is wounded with the bait,
The other rotted with delicious feede.

SATURNINE

But he will not intreat his sonne for vs.

TAMORA

If *Tamora* intreat him than he will,
For I can smooth and fill his aged eares,
With golden promises, that were his hart
Almost impregnable, his old yeares deafe,
Yet should both eare and hart obay my tongue.
(*To Emillius*) Goe thou before to be our Ambassador,
1920   Say that the Emperour requests a parlie,
Of warlike *Lucius*, and appoint the meeting,
Euen at his Fathers house the old *Andronicus*.

SATURNINE

Emillius doe this message honourably,
And if he stand on hostage for his saftie,
Bid him demaund what pledge will please him best.

EMILLIUS

Your bidding shall I doe effectually.   *Exit*

TAMORA

Now will I to that old *Andronicus*,
And temper him with all the Art I haue,
To plucke proude *Lucius* from the warlike *Gothes*.
1930   And now sweet Emperour be blith againe,
And burie all thy feare in my deuises.

SATURNINE

Then goe incessantly and plead to him.
                    Exeunt seuerally

5.1
(Sc. 11)   ⌜*Flourish.*⌝ *Enter Lucius with an Armie of Gothes*
                with Drums and Souldiers

LUCIUS

Approued warriours, and my faithfull friends,
I haue receaued letters from great Rome,
Which signifies what hate they beare their Emperour,
And how desirous of our sight they are.
Therefore great Lords bee as your titles witnes,
Imperious, and impatient of your wrongs,
And wherein Rome hath done you any skath,
1940   Let him make treable satisfaction.

A GOTH

Braue slip sprong from the great *Andronicus*,
Whose name was once our terrour, now our comfort,
Whose high exployts and honourable deeds,
Ingratefull Rome requites with foule contempt,
Be bold in vs weele follow where thou leadst,
Like stinging Bees in hottest summers day,
Led by their Master to the flowred fields,
And be aduengde on cursed *Tamora*.

GOTHS

And as he saith, so say we all with him.

LUCIUS

1950   I humblie thanke him and I thanke you all,
But who comes here led by a lustie *Gothe*?
       Enter a Goth leading of Aron with his child in his
       Armes

GOTH

Renowmed *Lucius* from our troupes I straid,
To gaze vpon a ruinous Monasterie,
And as I earnestly did fixe mine eye,
Vpon the wasted building suddainely,
I heard a child crie vnderneath a wall,
I made vnto the noise, when soone I heard,
The crying babe controld with this discourse:
Peace tawnie slaue, halfe me, and halfe thy Dame,
Did not thy hue bewray whose brat thou art,   1960
Had nature lent thee but thy mothers looke,
Villaine thou mightst haue bin an Emperour.
But where the bull and Cow are both milke white,
They neuer doe beget a coleblacke Calfe:
Peace Villaine peace, euen thus he rates the babe,
For I must beare thee to a trustie *Goth*,
Who when he knowes thou art the Empresse babe,
Will hold thee dearely for thy mothers sake.
With this my weapon drawen I rusht vpon him
Surprisde him suddainely, and brought him hither   1970
To vse as you thinke needefull of the man.

LUCIUS

Oh worthie *Goth* this is the incarnate diuell,
That robd *Andronicus* of his good hand,
This is the Pearle that pleasd your Empresse eye,
And her's the base fruit of her burning lust,
(*To Aron*) Say wall-eyd slaue whither wouldst thou
      conuay,
This growing image of thy fiendlike face,
Why doost not speake? what deafe, what not a word?
A halter Souldiers, hang him on this tree,
And by his side his fruite of Bastardie.   1980

ARON

Touch not the boy, he is of Roiall bloud.

LUCIUS

Too like the sier for euer being good,
First hang the child that he may see it sprall,
A sight to vex the fathers soule withall.
Get me a ladder.
      ⌜*A Goth brings a ladder, which Aron climes*⌝

ARON   *Lucius* saue the child,
And beare it from me to the Empresse:
If thou do this, ile shew thee wondrous things,
That highly may aduantage thee to heare,
If thou wilt not, befall what may befall,
Ile speake no more, but vengeance rotte you all.   1990

LUCIUS

Say on, and if it please me which thou speakst,
Thy child shall liue, and I will see it nourisht.

ARON

And if it please thee? why assure thee *Lucius*,
Twill vexe thy soule to heare what I shall speake:
For I must talke of murthers, rapes, and massakers,
Acts of black night, abhominable deeds,
Complots of mischiefe, treason, villanies,
Ruthfull to heare, yet pitteously performde,
And this shall all be buried in my death,
Vnlesse thou sweare to me my child shall liue.   2000

LUCIUS

Tell on thy minde, I say thy child shall liue.

ARON

Sweare that he shall, and then I will begin.

LUCIUS

Who should I sweare by, thou beleeuest no God,

That graunted, how canst thou beleeue an oath.

ARON

What if I doe not, as indeed I do not,

Yet for I know thou art religious,

And hast a thing within thee called conscience,

With twenty popish tricks and ceremonies,

Which I haue seene thee carefull to obserue,

2010   Therefore I vrge thy oath, for that I know,

An ideot holds his bauble for a God,

And keepes the oath which by that God he sweares,

To that ile vrge him, therefore thou shalt vow,

By that same God, what God so ere it be

That thou adorest, and hast in reuerence,

To saue my boy, to nourish and bring him vp,

Or else I will discouer nought to thee.

LUCIUS

Euen by my God I sweare to thee I will.

ARON

First know thou, I begot him on the Empresse.

LUCIUS

2020   Oh most insatiate and luxurious woman.

ARON

Tut *Lucius*, this was but a deed of charitie,

To that which thou shalt heare of me anon,

Twas her two sonnes that murdered *Bassianus*,

They cut thy Sisters tongue, and rauisht her,

And cut her hands, and trimd her as thou sawest.

LUCIUS

Oh detestable villaine, callst thou that trimming.

ARON

Why she was washt, and cut, and trimd, and twas

Trim sport for them which had the doing of it.

LUCIUS

Oh barberous beastlie villaines like thy selfe.

ARON

2030   Indeed I was their tutor to instruct them,

That codding spirit had they from their mother,

As sure a card as euer wonne the set:

That bloodie minde I thinke they learnd of me,

As true a Dog as euer fought at head:

Well let my deeds be witnes of my worth,

I traind thy brethren to that guilefull hole,

Where the dead corpes of *Bassianus* laie:

I wrote the letter that thy Father found,

And hid the gold within that letter mentioned,

2040   Confederate with the Queene and her two sonnes.

And what not done, that thou hast cause to rue,

Wherein I had no stroke of mischiefe in it,

I plaid the cheater for thy fathers hand,

And when I had it drew my selfe a part,

And almost broke my hart with extreame laughter,

I pried me through the creuice of a wall,

When for his hand he had his two sonnes heads,

Beheld his teares and laught so hartelie,

That both mine eyes were raynie like to his:

And when I tolde the Empresse of this sport,   2050

Shee sounded almost at my pleasing tale,

And for my tidings gaue me twentie kisses.

A GOTH

What canst thou say all this and neuer blush?

ARON

I like a blacke Dog, as the saying is.

LUCIUS

Art thou not sorrie for these hainous deeds.

ARON

I that I had not done a thousand more,

Euen now I curse the day and yet I thinke

Fewe come within the compasse of my curse,

Wherein I did not some notorious ill.

As kill a man, or els deuise his death,   2060

Rauish a maide, or plot the waie to doe it,

Accuse some innocent, and forsweare my selfe,

Set deadly enmitie betweene two friends,

Make poore mens cattle breake their necks,

Set fire on barnes and haystacks in the night,

And bid the owners quench them with their teares:

Oft haue I digd vp dead men from their graues,

And set them vpright at their deare friends dore,

Euen when their sorrowes almost was forgot,

And on their skinnes as on the barke of trees,   2070

Haue with my knife carued in Romaine letters,

Let not your sorrow die though I am dead.

But I haue done a thousand dreadfull things,

As willingly as one would kill a flie,

And nothing grieues me hartelie indeede,

But that I cannot doe ten thousand more.

LUCIUS

Bring downe the Diuell for he must not die,

So sweet a death as hanging presently.

    Goths bring Aron downe the ladder

ARON

If there be Diuels would I were a Diuel,

To liue and burne in euerlasting fire,   2080

So I might haue your companie in hell,

But to torment you with my bitter tongue.

LUCIUS

Sirs stop his mouth and let him speake no more.

    Goths gag Aron.

    Enter Emillius

A GOTH

My Lord there is a messenger from Rome,

Desiers to be admitted to your presence.

LUCIUS Let him come nere.

Welcome *Emillius*, what's the newes from Rome?

EMILLIUS

Lord *Lucius*, and you Princes of the *Gothes*,

The Romaine Emperour greets you all by me,

And for he vnderstands you are in Armes,   2090

He craues a Parley at your fathers house,
Willing you to demaund your hostages,
And they shall be immediatly deliuered.

A GOTH What saies our Generall.

LUCIUS

Emillius, let the Emperour giue his pledges,
Vnto my Father and my Vnkle *Marcus*,
And we will come, away.

⌈*Flourish.*⌉ *Exeunt* ⌈*marching*⌉

5.2   *Enter Tamora and Chiron and Demetrius her two*
(Sc. 12)   *sonnes disguised*

TAMORA

Thus in this strange and sad habilliament,
I will encounter with *Andronicus*,
2100   And say I am reuenge sent from belowe,
To ioyne with him and right his hainous wrongs,
Knocke at his studie where they say he keepes,
To ruminate strange plots of diere reuenge,
Tell him reuenge is come to ioyne with him,
And worke confusion on his enemies.

They knocke and Titus ⌈*aloft*⌉ *opens his studie doore*

TITUS

Who doth molest my contemplation?
Is it your tricke to make me ope the dore,
That so my sad decrees may flie away,
And all my studie be to no effect.
2110   You are deceiude, for what I meane to doe,
See here in bloodie lines I haue set downe.
And what is written shall be executed.

TAMORA

Titus, I am come to talke with thee.

TITUS

No not a word, how can I grace my talke,
Wanting a hand to giue it action,
Thou hast the odds of me therefore no more.

TAMORA

If thou didst know me thou wouldst talk with me.

TITUS

I am not mad, I know thee well enough,
Witnes this wretched stump, witnes these crimson
lines,
2120   Witnes these trenches made by greefe and care,
Witnes the tiring day and heauie night,
Witnes all sorrow that I know thee well
For our proud Empresse, mighty *Tamora*:
Is not thy comming for my other hand.

TAMORA

Know thou sad man, I am not *Tamora*,
Shee is thy enemie, and I thy friend,
I am Reuenge sent from th'infernall Kingdome,
To ease the gnawing vulture of thy minde,
By working wreakfull vengeance on thy foes:
2130   Come downe and welcome me to this worlds light,
Conferre with me of murder and of death.
Ther's not a hollow Caue or lurking place,
No vast obscuritie or mistie vale,
Where bloodie murther or detested rape,

Can couch for feare but I will finde them out,
And in their eares tell them my dreadfull name,
Reuenge which makes the foule offender quake.

TITUS

Art thou Reuenge? and art thou sent to mee,
To be a torment to mine enemies.

TAMORA

I am, therefore come downe and welcome mee.   2140

TITUS

Doe me some seruice ere I come to thee,
Lo by thy side where Rape and Murder stands,
Now giue some surance that thou art reuenge,
Stab them, or teare them on thy Chariot wheeles,
And then Ile come and be thy wagoner,
And wherle along with thee about the Globe.
Prouide two proper palfrays, black as iet,
To hale thy vengefull waggon swift away,
And finde out murderers in their guiltie caues.
And when thy Car is loaden with their heads,   2150
I will dismount and by thy waggon wheele,
Trotte like a seruile footeman all day long,
Euen from *Hipereons* rising in the East,
Vntill his verie downefall in the Sea.
And day by day Ile do this heauie taske,
So thou destroy Rapine and Murder there.

TAMORA

These are my ministers and come with me.

TITUS

Are they thy ministers, what are they calld?

TAMORA

Rape and Murder, therefore called so,
Cause they take vengeance of such kinde of men.   2160

TITUS

Good Lord how like the Empresse sonnes they are,
And you the Empresse, but we wordlie men
Haue miserable mad mistaking eies:
Oh sweete Reuenge, now doe I come to thee,
And if one armes imbracement will content thee,
I will imbrace thee in it by and by.   *Exit* ⌈*aloft*⌉

TAMORA

This closing with him fits his Lunacie,
What ere I forge to feede his braine-sicke humors,
Doe you vphold and maintaine in your speeches,
For now he firmelie takes me for Reuenge,   2170
And being credulous in this mad thought,
Ile make him send for *Lucius* his sonne,
And whilst I at a banket hold him sure,
Ile finde some cunning practise out of hand,
To scatter and disperse the giddie *Gothes*,
Or at the least make them his enemies:
See here he comes, and I must plie my theame.

Enter Titus belowe

TITUS

Long haue I bin forlorne and all for thee,
Welcome dread Furie to my woefull house,
Rapine and Murther you are welcome too: 2180
How like the Empresse and her sonnes you are,
Well are you fitted, had you but a *Moore*,

Could not all hell afford you such a Diuell?
For well I wot the Empresse neuer wags,
But in her companie there is a *Moore*.
And would you represent our Queene a right,
It were conuenient you had such a Diuell:
But welcome as you are. What shall wee doe?

TAMORA
What wouldst thou haue vs doe *Andronicus*?

DEMETRIUS
2190   Show me a murtherer Ile deale with him.

CHIRON
Show me a villaine that hath done a rape,
And I am sent to be reuengde on him.

TAMORA
Show me a thousand that hath done thee wrong,
And I will be reuenged on them all.

TITUS (*to Demetrius*)
Looke round about the wicked streets of Rome,
And when thou findst a man that's like thy selfe,
Good murther stab him, hee's a murtherer.
(*To Chiron*) Goe thou with him, and when it is thy
        hap,
To finde another that is like to thee,
2200   Good Rapine stab him, he is a rauisher.
(*To Tamora*) Goe thou with them, and in the
        Emperours Court,
There is a Queene attended by a *Moore*,
Well shalt thou know her by thine owne proportion,
For vp and downe she doth resemble thee,
I pray thee doe on them some violent death,
They haue bin violent to me and mine.

TAMORA
Well hast thou lessond vs, this shall we doe,
But would it please thee good *Andronicus*,
To send for *Lucius* thy thrice valiant sonne,
2210   Who leades towards Rome a band of warlike *Gothes*,
And bid him come and banquet at thy house,
When he is here euen at thy solemne feast,
I will bring in the Empresse and hir sonnes,
The Emperour him selfe and all thy foes,
And at thy mercie shall they stoope and kneele,
And on them shalt thou ease thy angry hart:
What sayes *Andronicus* to this deuise.

TITUS
Marcus my brother, tis sad *Titus* calles,
        Enter Marcus
Goe gentle *Marcus* to thy nephew *Lucius*,
2220   Thou shalt enquire him out among the *Gothes*,
Bid him repaire to me and bring with him,
Some of the chiefest Princes of the *Gothes*,
Bid him encampe his Souldiers where they are.
Tell him the Emperour and the Empresse too
Feast at my house, and he shall feast with them,
This doe thou for my loue, and so let him,
As he regards his aged Fathers life.

MARCUS
This will I doe, and soone returne againe.   *Exit*

TAMORA
Now will I hence about thy busines,
And take my ministers a long with me.   2230

TITUS
Nay, nay, let rape and murder stay with me,
Or els Ile call my brother backe againe,
And cleaue to no reuenge but *Lucius*.

TAMORA (*aside to her sonnes*)
What say you boyes will you abide with him,
Whiles I goe tell my Lord the Emperour,
How I haue gouernd our determind iest,
Yeeld to his humor, smooth and speake him faire,
And tarrie with him till I turne againe.

TITUS (*aside*)
I knew them all though they supposd me mad,
And will ore reach them in their owne deuises,   2240
A paire of cursed hell hounds and their Dame.

DEMETRIUS
Maddam depart at pleasure, leaue vs here.

TAMORA
Farewell *Andronicus*, Reuenge now goes,
To lay a complot to betray thy foes.

TITUS
I know thou dost and sweet Reuenge farewell.
                                        Exit Tamora

CHIRON
Tell vs old man how shall we be imploid.

TITUS
Tut I haue worke enough for you to doe.
Publius, come hither, *Caius*, and *Valentine*.
        Enter Publius, Caius and Valentine

PUBLIUS
What is your will?

TITUS   Know you these two.

PUBLIUS
The Empresse sonnes I take them, *Chiron. Demetrius*.   2250

TITUS
Fie, *Publius* fie, thou art too much deceaude,
The one is Murder and Rape is the others name,
And therefore binde them gentle *Publius*,
Caius and *Valentine*, lay hands on them,
Oft haue you heard me wish for such an houre,
And now I finde it therefore binde them sure,
And stop their mouthes if they begin to crie.   *Exit*

CHIRON
Villaines forbeare we are the Empresse sons.

PUBLIUS
And therefore doe we what we are commanded,
        Publius, Caius and Valentine binde and gag Chiron
        and Demetrius
Stop close their mouthes let them not speak a word,   2260
Is he sure bound, looke that you bind them fast.
        Enter Titus Andronicus, with a knife, and Lauinia,
        with a Bason

TITUS
Come, come, *Lauinia* looke thy foes are bound,
Sirs stop their mouthes let them not speake to me,

But let them heare what fearefull words I vtter.
Oh villaines *Chiron* and *Demetrius*,
Here stands the spring whome you haue staind with
    mud,
This goodly sommer with your winter mixt,
You kild her husband, and for that vild fault,
Two of her brothers were condemnd to death,
2270 My hand cut off and made a merrie iest,
Both her sweete hands, hir tongue, and that more
    deare
Than hands or tongue, her spotlesse chastitie,
Inhumane traitors you constraind and forst.
What would you say if I should let you speake?
Villaines for shame you could not beg for grace.
Harke wretches how I meane to marter you,
This one hand yet is left to cut your throats,
Whiles that *Lauinia* tweene her stumps doth hold,
The bason that receaues your guiltie blood.
2280 You know your Mother meanes to feast with me,
And calles herselfe Reuenge and thinks me mad.
Harke villaines I will grinde your bones to dust,
And with your blood and it Ile make a paste,
And of the paste a coffen I will reare,
And make two pasties of your shamefull heades,
And bid that strumpet your vnhallowed Dam,
Like to the earth swallow her owne increase.
This is the feast that I haue bid her too,
And this the banket she shall surfet on,
2290 For worse than *Philomell* you vsde my daughter,
And worse than *Progne* I will be reuengd.
And now prepare your throats, *Lauinia* come,
Receaue the blood, and when that they are dead,
Let me goe grinde their bones to powder small,
And with this hatefull liquour temper it,
And in that paste let their vile heades be bakt,
Come, come, be euerie one officius,
To make this banket which I wish may proue
More sterne and bloodie than the Centaurs feast,
        He cuts their throats
2300 So now bring them in for Ile play the Cooke,
And see them readie against their Mother comes.
        Exeunt carrying the bodies

5.3   *Enter Lucius, Marcus, and the Gothes with Aron,*
(Sc. 13)   *prisoner, ⌈and an attendant with his child⌉*

LUCIUS
Vnckle *Marcus*, since tis my Fathers minde,
That I repaire to Rome I am content.

A GOTH
And ours with thine, befall what Fortune will.

LUCIUS
Good Vnckle take you in this barberous *Moore*,
This rauenous tiger, this accursed diuell,
Let him receaue no sustnance, fetter him,
Till he be brought vnto the Empresse face,
For testemonie of her foule proceedings,
2310 And see the Ambush of our friends be strong,
I feare the Emperour meanes no good to vs.

ARON
Some diuell whisper curses in my eare,
And prompt me that my tongue may vtter forth,
The venemous mallice of my swelling hart.

LUCIUS
Away inhumane dogge vnhallowed slaue.
Sirs help our vnckle to conuay him in,
        ⌈*Exeunt Gothes with Aron and his child*⌉
    Flourish
The trumpets shewe the Emperour is at hand.
    Enter Saturnine the Emperour and Tamora the
    Empresse with Emillius, Tribunes, Senators and
    others

SATURNINE
What hath the firmament mo sunnes than one?

LUCIUS
What boots it thee to call thy selfe a sunne?

MARCUS
Romes Emperour and Nephew break the Parle,   2320
These quarrels must be quietly debated,
The feast is ready which the carefull *Titus*,
Hath ordainde to an honorable end,
For peace, for loue, for league and good to Rome,
Please you therefore, draw nie and take your places.

SATURNINE *Marcus* we will.
    ⌈*Hoboyes. A Table brought in.*⌉ *They sit.*
    Enter Titus like a Cooke, placing the dishes, and
    Lauinia with a vaile ouer her face, ⌈*young Lucius,*
    and others⌉

TITUS
Welcome my gratious Lord, welcome dread Queene,
Welcome yee warlike *Gothes*, welcome *Lucius*,
And welcome all: although the cheare be poore,
Twill fill your stomacks, please you eate of it.   2330

SATURNINE
Why art thou thus attired *Andronicus*?

TITUS
Because I would be sure to haue all well,
To entertaine your highnes and your Empresse.

TAMORA
We are beholding to you good *Andronicus*.

TITUS
And if your highnes knew my hart you were,
My Lord the Emperour resolue me this,
Was it well done of rash *Virginius*
To slay his daughter with his owne right hand
Because she was enforst, stainde, and deflowrde?

SATURNINE
It was *Andronicus*.

TITUS   Your reason mighty Lord.   2340

SATURNINE
Because the girle should not suruiue her shame,
And by her presence still renewe his sorrowes.

TITUS
A reason mighty, strong, effectuall,
A patterne president, and liuelie warrant,
For me most wretched to performe the like,

Die, die, *Lauinia* and thy shame with thee,
And with thy shame thy Fathers sorrow die.
⌐*He kils her*⌐

SATURNINE
What hast thou done, vnnaturall and vnkinde.

TITUS
Kild her for whom my teares haue made me blind.
2350   I am as woefull as *Virginius* was,
And haue a thousand times more cause than he,
To doe this outrage, and it now is done.

SATURNINE
What was she rauisht, tell who did the deede.

TITUS
Wilt please you eate, wilt please your highnes feed.

TAMORA
Why hast thou slaine thine only Daughter thus?

TITUS
Not I, twas *Chiron*, and *Demetrius*,
They Rauisht her and cut away her tongue,
And they, twas they, that did her all this wrong.

SATURNINE
Goe fetch them hither to vs presently.

TITUS ⌐*reuealing the heads*⌐
2360   Why there they are both baked in this Pie,
Whereof their Mother daintilie hath fed,
Eating the flesh that shee her selfe hath bred,
Tis true, tis true, witnes my kniues sharpe point.
    He stabs the Empresse

SATURNINE
Die franticke wretch for this accursed deede.
    He kills Titus

LUCIUS
Can the sonnes eie behold his father bleede?
Ther's meede for meede, death for a deadly deede.
    He kills Saturnine. Confusion followes.
    ⌐*Enter Gothes. Lucius, Marcus and others goe aloft*⌐

MARCUS
You sad facde men, people and sons of Rome
By vprores seuerd as a flight of fowle,
Scatterd by winds and high tempestuous gusts,
2370   Oh let me teach you how to knit againe,
This scattered corne into one mutuall sheaffe,
These broken limbs againe into one bodie.

ROMANE LORD
Let Rome her selfe bee bane vnto her selfe.
And shee whome mightie kingdomes cursie too,
Like a forlorne and desperate castaway,
Doe shamefull execution on her selfe,
But if my frostie signes and chappes of age,
Graue witnesses of true experience,
Cannot induce you to attend my words,
(*To Lucius*) Speake Roomes deare friend as erst our
2380   Ancestor,
When with his solemne tongue he did discourse
To loue sicke Didoes sad attending eare,
The storie of that balefull burning night,
When subtile Greekes surprizd King Priams Troy.

Tell vs what Sinon hath bewicht our eares,
Or who hath brought the fatall engine in
That giues our Troy, our Rome the ciuill wound.
My hart is not compact of flint nor steele,
Nor can I vtter all our bitter greefe,
But flouds of teares will drowne my Oratorie,   2390
And breake my vttrance euen in the time,
When it should moue yee to attend me most,
And force you to commiseration,
Her's Romes young Captaine let him tell the tale,
While I stand by and weepe to heare him speake.

LUCIUS
Then gratious auditorie be it knowne to you,
That *Chiron* and the damn'd *Demetrius*,
Were they that murdred our Emperours brother,
And they it were that rauished our sister,
For their fell faults our brothers were beheaded,   2400
Our Fathers teares dispisde, and basely cousend,
Of that true hand that fought Romes quarrell out,
And sent her enemies vnto the graue.
Lastly my selfe vnkindely banished,
The gates shut on me and turnd weeping out,
To beg reliefe among Romes enemies,
Who drownd their enmetie in my true teares,
And opt their armes to imbrace me as a friend,
I am the turned forth be it knowne to you,
That haue preserude her welfare in my blood,   2410
And from her bosome tooke the enemies point,
Sheathing the steele in my aduentrous body.
Alas you know I am no vaunter I,
My scars can witnes dumb although they are,
That my report is iust and full of truth,
But soft, me thinkes I doe digresse too much,
Cyting my worthles praise, Oh pardon me
For when no friends are by, men praise themselues.

MARCUS
Now is my turne to speake, behold the child,
Of this was *Tamora* deliuered,   2420
The issue of an irreligious *Moore*,
Chiefe architect and plotter of these woes,
The villaine is aliue in *Titus* house,
And as he is to witnes this is true.
Now iudge what cause had *Titus* to reuenge
These wrongs vnspeakeable past patience,
Or more than any liuing man could beare,
Now haue you heard the truth, what say you
        Romaines?
Haue we done ought amisse, shew vs wherein,
And from the place where you behold vs pleading,   2430
The poore remainder of *Andronicie*,
Will hand in hand, all headlong hurle our selues,
And on the ragged stones beat forth our soules,
And make a mutuall closure of our house,
Speake Romans speake, and if you say wee Shall,
Lo hand in hand *Lucius* and I will fall.

EMILLIUS
Come come thou reuerent man of Rome,

170

And bring our Emperour gently in thy hand,
Lucius our Emperour for well I know,
2440 The common voice doe cry it shall be so.
⌈ROMANS⌉
Lucius, all haile Romes royall Emperour.
MARCUS (*to attendants*)
Goe goe into old *Titus* sorrowfull house,
And hither hale that misbelieuing *Moore*,
To be adiudgde some dyrefull slaughtring death,
As punishment for his most wicked life.   *Exeunt some*
⌈*Lucius, Marcus and the others come downe*⌉
ROMANS
Lucius all haile Romes gratious gouernour.
LUCIUS
Thankes gentle Romanes may I gouerne so,
To heale Romes harmes, and wipe away her woe,
But gentle people giue me ayme a while,
2450 For nature puts me to a heauie taske,
Stand all a loofe but vnckle draw you neare,
To shed obsequious teares vpon this trunke,
(*Kissing Titus*) Oh take this warme kisse on thy pale
cold lips,
These sorrowfull drops vpon thy blood staind face,
The last true duties of thy noble sonne.
MARCUS (*kissing Titus*)
Teare for teare, and louing kisse for kisse,
Thy brother *Marcus* tenders on thy lips,
Oh were the summe of these that I should pay,
Countlesse and infinite, yet would I pay them.
LUCIUS (*to young Lucius*)
2460 Come hither boy come, come and learne of vs
To melt in showers, thy Grandsire lou'd thee well,
Many a time hee daunst thee on his knee,
Song thee a sleepe his louing brest thy pillow,
Many a storie hath he told to thee,
And bid thee bare his prettie tales in minde,
And talke of them when he was dead and gone.
MARCUS
How manie thousand times hath these poore lips,
When they were liuing warmd themselues on thine,

Oh now sweete boy giue them their latest kisse,
Bid him farewell commit him to the graue,   2470
Doe them that kindnes and take leaue of them.
PUER (*kissing Titus*)
Oh Grandsire, Grandsire, eu'n with all my hart,
Would I were dead so you did liue againe,
O Lord I cannot speake to him for weeping,
My teares will choacke me if I ope my mouth.
Enter some with Aron
A ROMANE
You sad *Andronicie* haue done with woes,
Giue sentence on this execrable wretch,
That hath bin breeder of these dyre euents.
LUCIUS
Set him brest deepe in earth and famish him,
There let him stand and raue and crie for foode.   2480
If any one releeues or pitties him,
For the offence he dies, this is our doome,
Some stay to see him fastned in the earth.
ARON
Ah why should wrath be mute and furie dumb,
I am no babie I, that with base prayers
I should repent the euils I haue done,
Ten thousand worse than euer yet I did
Would I performe if I might haue my will,
If one good deed in all my life I did
I doe repent it from my verie soule.   2490
LUCIUS
Some louing friends conuay the Emperour hence,
And giue him buriall in his fathers graue,
My Father and *Lauinia* shall forthwith,
Be closed in our housholds monument,
As for that rauinous tiger *Tamora*,
No funerall right, nor man in mourning weede,
No mournefull bell shall ring her buriall
But throw her forth to beasts and birds to pray,
Her life was beastlie and deuoide of pittie,
And being dead let birds on her take pittie.   2500
Exeunt with the bodies

Finis the Tragedie of Titus Andronicus

ADDITIONAL PASSAGES

A. AFTER 35

The following passage, found in the First Quarto following a comma after 'field' but not included in the Second or Third Quartos or the Folio, conflicts with the subsequent action and presumably should have been deleted. (In the second line, Q1 reads 'that' for 'yᵉ'.)

> and at this day,
> To the Monument of yᵉ *Andronicy*
> Done sacrifice of expiation,
> And slaine the Noblest prisoner of the *Gothes*.

B. AFTER 283

The following passage found in the quartos and the Folio is difficult to reconcile with the apparent need for Saturninus and his party to leave the stage at 275.1–2 before entering 'above' at 294.2–4. It is omitted from our text in the belief that Shakespeare intended it to be deleted after adding the episode of Mutius' killing to his original draft, and that the printers of Q1 included it by accident.

[TITUS]
Treason my Lord, *Lavinia* is surprizde.

SATURNINUS
Surprizde, by whom?

BASSIANUS   By him that justly may,
Beare his betrothde from all the world away.

C. AFTER 1799

The following lines, found in the early texts, appear to be a draft of the subsequent six lines.

MARCUS (*to Titus*) Why sir, that is as fit as can bee to serve for your Oration, and let him deliver the pidgeons to the Emperour from you.

TITUS (*to the Clowne*) Tell mee, can you deliver an Oration to the Emperour with a grace.

CLOWNE Nay truelie sir, I could never say grace in all my life.

HENRY VI PART ONE

BY WILLIAM SHAKESPEARE AND OTHERS

THE play printed here first appeared in the 1623 Folio, as *The first Part of Henry the Sixt*; it tells the beginning of the story that is continued in *The First Part of the Contention* and in *Richard Duke of Yorke*. Although in narrative sequence it belongs before those plays, there is good reason to believe that it was written after them. It is probably the 'new' play referred to as 'harey the vj' in the record of its performance on 3 March 1592 by Lord Strange's Men. The box-office takings of £3 16s. 8d. were a record for the season, and the play was acted another fifteen times during the following ten months. Its success is mentioned in Thomas Nashe's satirical pamphlet *Pierce Penilesse*, published later in 1592. Defending the drama against moralistic attacks, Nashe claims that plays based on 'our English Chronicles' celebrate 'our forefathers valiant acts' and set them up as a 'reproofe to these degenerate effeminate dayes of ours'. By way of illustration he alludes specifically to the exploits of Lord Talbot, the principal English warrior in *Henry VI Part One*: 'How would it haue ioyed braue *Talbot* (the terror of the French) to thinke that after he had lyne two hundred yeares in his Tombe, hee should triumphe againe on the Stage, and haue his bones newe embalmed with the teares of ten thousand spectators at least (at seuerall times), who, in the Tragedian that represents his person, imagine they behold him fresh bleeding.' Nashe may have had personal reasons to puff this play: a variety of evidence suggests that Shakespeare wrote it in collaboration with at least two other authors; Nashe himself was probably responsible for Act 1. The passages most confidently attributed to Shakespeare are Scene 12, and Scene 23 to the death of Talbot in Scene 28.

A mass of material, some derived from 'English Chronicles', some invented, is packed into this play. It opens impressively with the funeral of Henry V, celebrated for unifying England and subjugating France; but his nobles are at loggerheads even over his coffin, and news rapidly arrives of serious losses in France. The rivalry displayed here between Humfrey, Duke of Gloster—Protector of the infant Henry VI—and Henry Beaufort, Bishop of Winchester, plays an important part in both this play and *The Contention*, as does the conflict between Richard Duke of Yorke, and the houses of Somerset and Suffolke; in the Temple Garden scene (Sc. 12), invented by Shakespeare, Yorke's and Somerset's supporters symbolize their respective loyalties by plucking white and red roses. Their dissension weakens England's military strength, but she has a great hero in Lord Talbot, whose nobility as a warrior is pitted against the treachery of the French, led by King Charles and Ioan la Pucell (Joan of Arc), here—following the chronicles—portrayed as a witch and a whore. Historical facts are freely manipulated: Joan was burnt in 1431, though the play's authors have her take part in a battle of 1451 in which Talbot's death is brought forward by two years. The play ends with an uneasy peace between England and France.

Our text is based on the Folio, which was probably printed from the foul papers of the collaborators, touched up in places by one of them, or by a bookkeeper, in charge of co-ordinating their contributions.

THE NAMES OF THE ACTORS

The English

KING Henry the Sixt

Duke of GLOSTER, Lord Protector, vnckle of the King

Duke of BEDFORD, Regent of France

Duke of EXETER

Bishop of WINCHESTER (later Cardinall), vnckle of the King

Duke of SOMERSET

RICHARD PLANTAGENET, later DUKE OF YORKE and Regent of France

Earle of WARWICKE

Earle of SALISBURY

Earle of SUFFOLKE

Lord TALBOT

IOHN Talbot, his sonne

Edmund MORTIMER

Sir William GLASDALE

Sir Thomas GARGRAUE

Sir Iohn FALSTAFFE

Sir William LUCY

WOODUILE, Lieutenant of the Tower of London

MAIOR of London

VERNON

BASSET

A LAWYER

A LEGATE

Messengers, Warders and Keepers of the Tower of London, Seruingmen, Officers, Captaines, Souldiers, Herald, Watch

The French

CHARLES, Dolphin of France

REIGNIER, Duke of Aniou, King of Naples

MARGARET, his daughter

Duke of ALANSON

BASTARD of Orleance

Duke of BURGONIE, vnckle of King Henry

GENERALL of the French Garrison at Burdeaux

COUNTESSE of Ouergne

M. GUNNER of Orleance

A BOY, his sonne

Ioane la PUCELL

A SHEPHEARD, father of Ioane

Porter, French Sergeant, French Sentinels, French Scout, French Herald, the Gouernour of Paris, fiends, and souldiers

The first Part of Henry the Sixt

Dead March. Enter the Funerall of King Henry the
Fift, attended on by the Duke of Bedford, Regent of
France; the Duke of Gloster, Protector; the Duke of
Exeter, Warwicke, the Bishop of Winchester, and
the Duke of Somerset

BEDFORD

Hung be yᵉ heauens with black, yield day to night;
Comets importing change of Times and States,
Brandish your crystall Tresses in the Skie,
And with them scourge the bad reuolting Stars,
That haue consented vnto *Henries* death:
King *Henry* the Fift, too famous to liue long,
England ne're lost a King of so much worth.

GLOSTER

England ne're had a King vntill his time:
Vertue he had, deseruing to command,
10 His brandisht Sword did blinde men with his beames,
His Armes spred wider then a Dragons Wings:
His sparkling Eyes, repleat with wrathfull fire,
More dazled and droue back his Enemies,
Then mid-day Sunne, fierce bent against their faces.
What should I say? his Deeds exceed all speech:
He ne're lift vp his Hand, but conquered.

EXETER

We mourne in black, why mourn we not in blood?
Henry is dead, and neuer shall reuiue:
Vpon a Woodden Coffin we attend;
20 And Deaths dishonourable Victorie,
We with our stately presence glorifie,
Like Captiues bound to a Triumphant Carre.
What? shall we curse the Planets of Mishap,
That plotted thus our Glories ouerthrow?
Or shall we thinke the subtile-witted French,
Coniurers and Sorcerers, that afraid of him,
By Magick Verses haue contriu'd his end.

WINCHESTER

He was a King, blest of the King of Kings.
Vnto the French, the dreadfull Iudgement-Day
30 So dreadfull will not be, as was his sight.
The Battailes of the Lord of Hosts he fought:
The Churches Prayers made him so prosperous.

GLOSTER

The Church? where is it? Had not Church-men
  pray'd,
His thred of Life had not so soone decay'd.
None doe you like, but an effeminate Prince,
Whom like a Schoole-boy you may ouer-awe.

WINCHESTER

Gloster, what ere we like, thou art Protector,
And lookest to command the Prince and Realme.
Thy Wife is prowd, she holdeth thee in awe,
40 More then God or Religious Church-men may.

GLOSTER

Name not Religion, for thou lou'st the Flesh,

And ne're throughout the yeere to Church thou go'st,
Except it be to pray against thy foes.

BEDFORD

Cease, cease these Iarres, & rest your minds in peace:
Let's to the Altar: Heralds wayt on vs;
        ⌐*Exeunt Warwicke, Somerset, and Heralds with*
                                              Coffin⌐

In stead of Gold, wee'le offer vp our Armes,
Since Armes auayle not, now that *Henry*'s dead,
Posteritie await for wretched yeeres,
When at their Mothers moistned eyes, Babes shall
  suck,
Our Ile be made a marrish of salt Teares,   50
And none but Women left to wayle the dead.
Henry the Fift, thy Ghost I inuocate:
Prosper this Realme, keepe it from Ciuill Broyles,
Combat with aduerse Planets in the Heauens;
A farre more glorious Starre thy Soule will make,
Then *Iulius Cæsar*, or bright—
        Enter a Messenger

MESSENGER

My honourable Lords, health to you all:
Sad tidings bring I to you out of France,
Of losse, of slaughter, and discomfiture:
Guyen, Champaigne, Roan, Rheimes, Orleance,   60
Paris, Guysors, Poictiers, are all quite lost.

BEDFORD

What say'st thou man, before dead *Henry*'s Coarse?
Speake softly, or the losse of those great Townes
Will make him burst his Lead, and rise from death.

GLOSTER (*to the Messenger*)

Is Paris lost? is Roan yeelded vp?
If *Henry* were recall'd to life againe,
These news would cause him once more yeeld the
  Ghost.

EXETER (*to the Messenger*)

How were they lost? what trecherie was vs'd?

MESSENGER

No trecherie, but want of Men and Money.
Amongst the Souldiers this is muttered,   70
That here you maintaine seuerall Factions:
And whil'st a Field should be dispatcht and fought,
You are disputing of your Generals.
One would haue lingring Warres, with little cost;
Another would flye swift, but wanteth Wings:
A third thinkes, without expence at all,
By guilefull faire words, Peace may be obtayn'd.
Awake, awake, English Nobilitie,
Let not slouth dimme your Honors, new begot;
Cropt are the Flower-de-Luces in your Armes;   80
Of Englands Coat, one halfe is cut away.   ⌐*Exit*⌐

EXETER

Were our Teares wanting to this Funerall,
These Tidings would call forth her flowing Tides.

BEDFORD

Me they concerne, Regent I am of France:
Giue me my steeled Coat, Ile fight for France.
Away with these disgracefull wayling Robes;
⌐He remoues his mourning Robe⌐
Wounds will I lend the French, in stead of Eyes,
To weepe their intermissiue Miseries.
Enter to them another Messenger, with Letters

2. MESSENGER

Lords view these Letters, full of bad mischance.
90 France is reuolted from the English quite,
Except some petty Townes, of no import.
The Dolphin *Charles* is crowned King in Rheimes:
The Bastard of Orleance with him is ioyn'd:
Reyneir, Duke of Aniou, doth take his part,
The Duke of Alanson flyeth to his side.   *Exit*

EXETER

The Dolphin crowned King? all flye to him?
O whither shall we flye from this reproach?

GLOSTER

We will not flye, but to our enemies throats.
Bedford, if thou be slacke, Ile fight it out.

BEDFORD

100 *Gloster*, why doubtst thou of my forwardnesse?
An Army haue I muster'd in my thoughts,
Wherewith already France is ouer-run.
Enter another Messenger

3. MESSENGER

My gracious Lords, to adde to your laments,
Wherewith you now bedew King *Henries* hearse,
I must informe you of a dismall fight,
Betwixt the stout Lord *Talbot*, and the French.

WINCHESTER

What? wherein *Talbot* ouercame, is't so?

3. MESSENGER

O no: wherein Lord *Talbot* was o'rethrown:
The circumstance Ile tell you more at large.
110 The tenth of August last, this dreadfull Lord,
Retyring from the Siege of Orleance,
Hauing full scarce six thousand in his troupe,
By three and twentie thousand of the French
Was round incompassed, and set vpon:
No leysure had he to enranke his men.
He wanted Pikes to set before his Archers:
In stead whereof, sharpe Stakes pluckt out of Hedges
They pitched in the ground confusedly,
To keepe the Horsemen off, from breaking in.
120 More then three houres the fight continued:
Where valiant *Talbot*, aboue humane thought,
Enacted wonders with his Sword and Lance.
Hundreds he sent to Hell; and none durst stand him:
Here, there, and euery where enrag'd, he slew.
The French exclaym'd, the Deuill was in Armes,
All the whole Army stood agaz'd on him.
His Souldiers spying his vndaunted Spirit,
A *Talbot*, a *Talbot*, cry'd out amaine,
And rusht into the Bowels of the Battaile.
130 Here had the Conquest fully been seal'd vp,

If Sir *Iohn Falstaffe* had not play'd the Coward.
He being in the Vauward, plac't behinde,
With purpose to relieue and follow them,
Cowardly fled, not hauing struck one stroake.
Hence grew the generall wrack and massacre:
Enclosed were they with their Enemies.
A base Wallon, to win the Dolphins grace,
Thrust *Talbot* with a Speare into the Back,
Whom all France, with their chiefe assembled
      strength,
Durst not presume to looke once in the face.   140

BEDFORD

Is *Talbot* slaine then? I will slay my selfe,
For liuing idly here, in pompe and ease,
Whil'st such a worthy Leader, wanting ayd,
Vnto his dastard foe-men is betray'd.

3. MESSENGER

O no, he liues, but is tooke Prisoner,
And Lord *Scales* with him, and Lord *Hungerford*:
Most of the rest slaughter'd, or tooke likewise.

BEDFORD

His Ransome there is none but I shall pay.
Ile hale the Dolphin headlong from his Throne,
His Crowne shall be the Ransome of my friend: 150
Foure of their Lords Ile change for one of ours.
Farwell my Masters, to my Taske will I,
Bonfires in France forthwith I am to make,
To keepe our great Saint *Georges* Feast withall.
Ten thousand Souldiers with me I will take,
Whose bloody deeds shall make all Europe quake.

3. MESSENGER

So you had need, for Orleance besieg'd,
The English Army is growne weake and faint:
The Earle of Salisbury craueth supply,
And hardly keepes his men from mutinie,   160
Since they so few, watch such a multitude.   ⌐Exit⌐

EXETER

Remember Lords your Oathes to *Henry* sworne:
Eyther to quell the Dolphin vtterly,
Or bring him in obedience to your yoake.

BEDFORD

I doe remember it, and here take my leaue,
To goe about my preparation.   *Exit Bedford*

GLOSTER

Ile to the Tower with all the hast I can,
To view th'Artillerie and Munition,
And then I will proclayme young *Henry* King.
Exit Gloster

EXETER

To Eltam will I, where the young King is,   170
Being ordayn'd his speciall Gouernor,
And for his safetie there Ile best deuise.   *Exit*

WINCHESTER

Each hath his Place and Function to attend:
I am left out; for me nothing remaines:
But long I will not be Iack out of Office.
The King from Eltam I intend to steale,
And sit at chiefest Sterne of publique Weale.   *Exit*

Sc. 2   *Sound a Flourish. Enter Charles, Alanson, and*
(1.2)   *Reigneir, marching with Drum and Souldiers*

CHARLES
Mars his true mouing, euen as in the Heauens,
So in the Earth, to this day is not knowne.
180 Late did he shine vpon the English side:
Now we are Victors, vpon vs he smiles.
What Townes of any moment, but we haue?
At pleasure here we lye, neere Orleance:
Otherwhiles, the famisht English, like pale Ghosts,
Faintly besiege vs one houre in a moneth.

ALANSON
They want their Porredge, & their fat Bul Beeues:
Eyther they must be dyeted like Mules,
And haue their Prouender ty'd to their mouthes,
Or pitteous they will looke, like drowned Mice.

REIGNEIR
190 Let's rayse the Siege: why liue we idly here?
Talbot is taken, whom we wont to feare:
Remayneth none but mad-brayn'd Salisbury,
And he may well in fretting spend his gall,
Nor men nor Money hath he to make Warre.

CHARLES
Sound, sound Alarum, we will rush on them.
Now for the honour of the forlorne French:
Him I forgiue my death, that killeth me,
When he sees me goe back one foot, or flye.   *Exeunt*

Sc. 3   *Here Alarum, the French are beaten back by the*
(1.3)   *English, with great losse. Enter Charles, Alanson,*
       and Reigneir

CHARLES
Who euer saw the like? what men haue I?
200 Dogges, Cowards, Dastards: I would ne're haue fled,
But that they left me 'midst my Enemies.

REIGNEIR
Salisbury is a desperate Homicide,
He fighteth as one weary of his life:
The other Lords, like Lyons wanting foode,
Doe rush vpon vs as their hungry prey.

ALANSON
Froysard, a Countreyman of ours, records,
England all Oliuers and Rowlands bred,
During the time Edward the third did raigne:
More truly now may this be verified;
210 For none but Samsons and Goliasses
It sendeth forth to skirmish: one to tenne?
Leane raw-bon'd Rascals, who would e're suppose,
They had such courage and audacitie?

CHARLES
Let's leaue this Towne, for they are hayre-brayn'd
    Slaues,
And hunger will enforce them to be more eager:
Of old I know them; rather with their Teeth
The Walls they'le teare downe, then forsake the Siege.

REIGNEIR
I thinke by some odde Gimmors or Deuice
Their Armes are set, like Clocks, still to strike on;

Else ne're could they hold out so as they doe: 220
By my consent, wee'le euen let them alone.

ALANSON   Be it so.
     Enter the Bastard of Orleance

BASTARD
Where's the Prince Dolphin? I haue newes for him.

CHARLES
Bastard of Orleance, thrice welcome to vs.

BASTARD
Me thinks your looks are sad, your chear appal'd.
Hath the late ouerthrow wrought this offence?
Be not dismay'd, for succour is at hand:
A holy Maid hither with me I bring,
Which by a Vision sent to her from Heauen,
Ordayned is to rayse this tedious Siege,   230
And driue the English forth the bounds of France:
The spirit of deepe Prophecie she hath,
Exceeding the nine Sibyls of old Rome:
What's past, and what's to come, she can descry.
Speake, shall I call her in? beleeue my words,
For they are certaine, and vnfallible.

CHARLES
Goe call her in: *Exit Bastard*
       but first, to try her skill,
Reignier stand thou as Dolphin in my place;
Question her prowdly, let thy Lookes be sterne,
By this meanes shall we sound what skill she hath.   240
     Enter ⌈the Bastard, with⌉ Ioane Puzel, armed

REIGNEIR (*as Charles*)
Faire Maid, is't thou wilt doe these wondrous feats?

PUCELL
Reignier, is't thou that thinkest to beguile me?
Where is the Dolphin? (*To Charles*) Come, come from
    behinde,
I know thee well, though neuer seene before.
Be not amaz'd, there's nothing hid from me;
In priuate will I talke with thee apart:
Stand back you Lords, and giue vs leaue a while.
     Reignier, Alanson, ⌈and Bastard⌉ stand apart

REIGNEIR ⌈*to Alanson and Bastard*⌉
She takes vpon her brauely at first dash.

PUCELL
Dolphin, I am by birth a Shepheards Daughter,
My wit vntrayn'd in any kind of Art: 250
Heauen and our Lady gracious hath it pleas'd
To shine on my contemptible estate.
Loe, whilest I wayted on my tender Lambes,
And to Sunnes parching heat display'd my cheekes,
Gods Mother deigned to appeare to me,
And in a Vision full of Maiestie,
Will'd me to leaue my base Vocation,
And free my Countrey from Calamitie:
Her ayde she promis'd, and assur'd successe.
In compleat Glory shee reueal'd her selfe: 260
And whereas I was black and swart before,
With those cleare Rayes, which shee infus'd on me,
That beautie am I blest with, which you may see.
Aske me what question thou canst possible,

And I will answer vnpremeditated:
My Courage trie by Combat, if thou dar'st,
And thou shalt finde that I exceed my Sex.
Resolue on this, thou shalt be fortunate,
If thou receiue me for thy Warlike Mate.

CHARLES

270 Thou hast astonisht me with thy high termes:
Onely this proofe Ile of thy Valour make,
In single Combat thou shalt buckle with me;
And if thou vanquishest, thy words are true,
Otherwise I renounce all confidence.

PUCELL

I am prepar'd: here is my keene-edg'd Sword,
Deckt with fiue Flower-de-Luces on each side,
The which at Touraine, in S. Katherines Church-yard,
Out of a great deale of old Iron, I chose forth.

CHARLES

Then come a Gods name, I feare no woman.

PUCELL

280 And while I liue, Ile ne're flye from a man.
            Here they fight, and Ioane le Puzel ouercomes

CHARLES

Stay, stay thy hands, thou art an Amazon,
And fightest with the Sword of *Debora*.

PUCELL

Christs Mother helpes me, else I were too weake.

CHARLES

Who e're helps thee, 'tis thou that must help me:
Impatiently I burne with thy desire,
My heart and hands thou hast at once subdu'd.
Excellent *Puzel*, if thy name be so,
Let me thy seruant, and not Soueraigne be,
'Tis the French Dolphin sueth to thee thus.

PUCELL

290 I must not yeeld to any rights of Loue,
For my Profession's sacred from aboue:
When I haue chased all thy Foes from hence,
Then will I thinke vpon a recompence.

CHARLES

Meane time looke gracious on thy prostrate Thrall.

REIGNEIR ⌈*to the other Lords, apart*⌉

My Lord me thinkes is very long in talke.

ALANSON

Doubtlesse he shriues this woman to her smock,
Else ne're could he so long protract his speech.

REIGNEIR

Shall wee disturbe him, since hee keepes no meane?

ALANSON

He may meane more then we poor men do know,
300 These women are shrewd tempters with their tongues.

REIGNEIR (*to Charles*)

My Lord, where are you? what deuise you on?
Shall we giue o're Orleance, or no?

PUCELL

Why no, I say: distrustfull Recreants,
Fight till the last gaspe: Ile be your guard.

CHARLES

What shee sayes, Ile confirme: wee'le fight it out.

PUCELL

Assign'd am I to be the English Scourge.
This night the Siege assuredly Ile rayse:
Expect Saint *Martins* Summer, *Halcyons* dayes,
Since I haue entred into these Warres.
Glory is like a Circle in the Water,   310
Which neuer ceaseth to enlarge it selfe,
Till by broad spreading, it disperse to naught.
With *Henries* death, the English Circle ends,
Dispersed are the glories it included:
Now am I like that prowd insulting Ship,
Which *Cæsar* and his fortune bare at once.

CHARLES

Was *Mahomet* inspired with a Doue?
Thou with an Eagle art inspired then.
Helen, the Mother of Great *Constantine*,
Nor yet S. *Philips* daughters were like thee.   320
Bright Starre of *Venus*, falne downe on the Earth,
How may I reuerently worship thee enough?

ALANSON

Leaue off delayes, and let vs rayse the Siege.

REIGNEIR

Woman, do what thou canst to saue our honors,
Driue them from Orleance, and be immortaliz'd.

CHARLES

Presently wee'le try: come, let's away about it,
No Prophet will I trust, if shee proue false.   *Exeunt*

    Enter Gloster, with his Seruing-men in Blew Coates   **Sc. 4**
GLOSTER   **(1.4)**

I am come to suruey the Tower this day;
Since *Henries* death, I feare there is Conueyance:
Where be these Warders, that they wait not here?   330
        ⌈*A Seruing-man*⌉ *knocketh on the gates*
Open the Gates, 'tis *Gloster* that calls.

1. WARDER ⌈*within the Tower*⌉

Who's there, that knocketh so imperiously?

GLOSTERS 1. MAN

It is the Noble Duke of Gloster.

2. WARDER ⌈*within the Tower*⌉

Who ere he be, you may not be let in.

GLOSTERS 1. MAN

Villaines, answer you so the Lord Protector?

1. WARDER ⌈*within the Tower*⌉

The Lord protect him, so we answer him,
We doe no otherwise then wee are will'd.

GLOSTER

Who willed you? or whose will stands but mine?
There's none Protector of the Realme, but I:
(*To Seruing-men*) Breake vp the Gates, Ile be your
            warrantize;   340
Shall I be flowted thus by dunghill Groomes?
        Glosters men rush at the Tower Gates

WOODUILE ⌈*within the Tower*⌉

What noyse is this? what Traytors haue wee here?

GLOSTER

Lieutenant, is it you whose voyce I heare?
Open the Gates, here's *Gloster* that would enter.

WOODUILE ⌈*within the Tower*⌉
Haue patience Noble Duke, I may not open,
My Lord of Winchester forbids:
From him I haue expresse commandement,
That thou nor none of thine shall be let in.

GLOSTER
Faint-hearted *Wooduile*, prizest him 'fore me?
350   Arrogant *Winchester*, that haughtie Prelate,
Whom *Henry* our late Soueraigne ne're could brooke?
Thou art no friend to God, or to the King:
Open the Gates, or Ile shut thee out shortly.

SERUINGMEN
Open the Gates vnto the Lord Protector,
Or wee'le burst them open, if that you come not
    quickly.
      Enter to the Protector at the Tower Gates,
      Winchester and his men in Tawney Coates

WINCHESTER
How now ambitious *Visheir*, what meanes this?

GLOSTER
Piel'd Priest, doo'st thou command me to be shut out?

WINCHESTER
I doe, thou most vsurping Proditor,
And not Protector of the King or Realme.

GLOSTER
360   Stand back thou manifest Conspirator,
Thou that contriud'st to murther our dead Lord,
Thou that giu'st Whores Indulgences to sinne,
If thou proceed in this thy insolence—

WINCHESTER
Nay, stand thou back, I will not budge a foot:
This be Damascus, be thou cursed *Cain*,
To slay thy Brother *Abel*, if thou wilt.

GLOSTER
I will not slay thee, but Ile driue thee back:
Thy Purple Robes, as a Childs bearing Cloth,
Ile vse, to carry thee out of this place.

WINCHESTER
370   Doe what thou dar'st, I beard thee to thy face.

GLOSTER
What? am I dar'd, and bearded to my face?
Draw men, for all this priuiledged place,
    All draw their Swords
Blew Coats to Tawny Coats. Priest, beware your
    Beard,
I meane to tugge it, and to cuffe you soundly.
Vnder my feet Ile stampe thy Bishops Mitre:
In spight of Pope, or dignities of Church,
Here by the Cheekes Ile drag thee vp and downe.

WINCHESTER
Gloster, thou wilt answere this before the Pope.

GLOSTER
Winchester Goose, I cry, a Rope, a Rope.
(*To his Seruing-men*)
380   Now beat them hence, why doe you let them stay?
(*To Winchester*)
Thee Ile chase hence, thou Wolfe in Sheepes array.
Out Tawney-Coates, out cloked Hypocrite.

Here Glosters men beat out the Bishops men, and
enter in the hurly-burly the Maior of London, and
his Officers

MAIOR
Fye Lords, that you being supreme Magistrates,
Thus contumeliously should breake the Peace.

GLOSTER
Peace Maior, thou know'st little of my wrongs:
Here's *Beauford*, that regards nor God nor King,
Hath here distrayn'd the Tower to his vse.

WINCHESTER (*to Maior*)
Here's *Gloster*, a Foe to Citizens,
One that still motions Warre, and neuer Peace,
O're-charging your free Purses with large Fines;   390
That seekes to ouerthrow Religion,
Because he is Protector of the Realme;
And would haue Armour here out of the Tower,
To Crowne himselfe King, and suppresse the Prince.

GLOSTER
I will not answer thee with words, but blowes.
    Here the Factions skirmish againe

MAIOR
Naught rests for me, in this tumultuous strife,
But to make open Proclamation.
Come Officer, as lowd as e're thou canst, cry.

OFFICER *All manner of men, assembled here in Armes this*
day, against Gods Peace and the Kings, wee charge and   400
command you, in his Highnesse Name, to repayre to your
seuerall dwelling places, and not to weare, handle, or vse
any Sword, Weapon, or Dagger hence-forward, vpon paine
of death.

    The skirmishes cease

GLOSTER
Bishop, Ile be no breaker of the Law:
But we shall meet, and breake our minds at large.

WINCHESTER
Gloster, wee'le meet to thy cost, be sure:
Thy heart-blood I will haue for this dayes worke.

MAIOR
Ile call for Clubs, if you will not away:
(*Aside*) This Bishop is more haughtie then the Deuill.   410

GLOSTER
Maior farewell: thou doo'st but what thou may'st.

WINCHESTER
Abhominable *Gloster*, guard thy Head,
For I intend to haue it ere long.
    Exeunt both Factions, seuerally

MAIOR (*to Officers*)
See the Coast clear'd, and then we will depart.
Good God, these Nobles should such stomacks beare,
I my selfe fight not once in fortie yeere.   *Exeunt*

    Enter the Master Gunner of Orleance, and his Boy   Sc. 5

M. GUNNER   (1.5)
Sirrha, thou know'st how Orleance is besieg'd,
And how the English haue the Suburbs wonne.

BOY

    Father I know, and oft haue shot at them,
420   How e're vnfortunate, I miss'd my ayme.

M. GUNNER

    But now thou shalt not. Be thou rul'd by me:
    Chiefe Master Gunner am I of this Towne,
    Something I must doe to procure me grace:
    The Princes spyals haue informed me,
    How the English, in the Suburbs close entrencht,
    Wont through a secret Grate of Iron Barres,
    In yonder Tower, to ouer-peere the Citie,
    And thence discouer, how with most aduantage
    They may vex vs with Shot or with Assault.
430   To intercept this inconuenience,
    A Peece of Ordnance 'gainst it I haue plac'd,
    And euen these three dayes haue I watcht, if I could
        see them.
    Now doe thou watch, for I can stay no longer.
    If thou spy'st any, runne and bring me word,
    And thou shalt finde me at the Gouernors.

BOY

    Father, I warrant you, take you no care,
            ⌈Exit M. Gunner at one doore⌉
    Ile neuer trouble you, if I may spye them.
            Exit ⌈at the other doore⌉

Sc. 6   *Enter Salisbury and Talbot aboue on the Turrets,*
(1.6)   *with others; among them, Gargraue and Glasdale*

SALISBURY

    Talbot, my life, my ioy, againe return'd?
    How wert thou handled, being Prisoner?
440   Or by what meanes got's thou to be releas'd?
    Discourse I prethee on this Turrets top.

TALBOT

    The Duke of Bedford had a Prisoner,
    Call'd the braue Lord *Ponton de Santrayle*,
    For him was I exchang'd, and ransomed.
    But with a baser man of Armes by farre,
    Once in contempt they would haue barter'd me:
    Which I disdaining, scorn'd, and craued death,
    Rather then I would be so pil'd esteem'd:
    In fine, redeem'd I was as I desir'd.
450   But O, the trecherous *Falstaffe* wounds my heart,
    Whom with my bare fists I would execute,
    If I now had him brought into my power.

SALISBURY

    Yet tell'st thou not, how thou wert entertain'd.

TALBOT

    With scoffes and scornes, and contumelious taunts,
    In open Market-place produc't they me,
    To be a publique spectacle to all:
    Here, sayd they, is the Terror of the French,
    The Scar-Crow that affrights our Children so.
    Then broke I from the Officers that led me,
460   And with my nayles digg'd stones out of the ground,
    To hurle at the beholders of my shame.
    My grisly countenance made others flye,
    None durst come neere, for feare of suddaine death.

    In Iron Walls they deem'd me not secure:
    So great feare of my Name 'mongst them were spread,
    That they suppos'd I could rend Barres of Steele,
    And spurne in pieces Posts of Adamant.
    Wherefore a guard of chosen Shot I had,
    That walkt about me euery Minute while:
    And if I did but stirre out of my Bed,
    Ready they were to shoot me to the heart.   470
    The Boy ⌈passes ouer the stage⌉ with a Linstock

SALISBURY

    I grieue to heare what torments you endur'd,
    But we will be reueng'd sufficiently.
    Now it is Supper time in Orleance:
    Here, through this Grate, I count each one,
    And view the Frenchmen how they fortifie:
    Let vs looke in, the sight will much delight thee:
    Sir *Thomas Gargraue*, and Sir *William Glasdale*,
    Let me haue your expresse opinions,
    Where is best place to make our Batt'ry next?   480
    ⌈*They looke through the Grate*⌉

GARGRAVE

    I thinke at the North Gate, for there stands Lou.

GLASDALE

    And I heere, at the Bulwarke of the Bridge.

TALBOT

    For ought I see, this Citie must be famisht,
    Or with light Skirmishes enfeebled.
    Here they shoot off chambers ⌈within⌉, and
    Salisbury and Gargraue fall downe

SALISBURY

    O Lord haue mercy on vs, wretched sinners.

GARGRAVE

    O Lord haue mercy on me, wofull man.

TALBOT

    What chance is this, that suddenly hath crost vs?
    Speake *Salisbury*; at least, if thou canst, speake:
    How far'st thou, Mirror of all Martiall men?
    One of thy Eyes, and thy Cheekes side struck off?   490
    Accursed Tower, accursed fatall Hand,
    That hath contriu'd this wofull Tragedie.
    In thirteene Battailes, *Salisbury* o'recame:
    Henry the Fift he first trayn'd to the Warres.
    Whil'st any Trumpe did sound, or Drum struck vp,
    His Sword did ne're leaue striking in the field.
    Yet liu'st thou *Salisbury*? though thy speech doth
        fayle,
    One Eye thou hast to looke to Heauen for grace.
    The Sunne with one Eye vieweth all the World.
    Heauen be thou gracious to none aliue,   500
    If *Salisbury* wants mercy at thy hands.
    Sir *Thomas Gargraue*, hast thou any life?
    Speake vnto *Talbot*, nay, looke vp to him.
    Beare hence his Body, I will helpe to bury it.
            ⌈*Exit one with Gargraues body*⌉
    Salisbury cheare thy Spirit with this comfort,
    Thou shalt not dye whiles—
    He beckens with his hand, and smiles on me:
    As who should say, When I am dead and gone,

Remember to auenge me on the French.
510 *Plantaginet* I will, and like thee, *Nero*,
Play on the Lute, beholding the Townes burne:
Wretched shall France be onely in my Name.
> *Here an Alarum, and it Thunders and Lightens*

What stirre is this? what tumult's in the Heauens?
Whence commeth this Alarum, and the noyse?
> *Enter a Messenger*

MESSENGER
My Lord, my Lord, the French haue gather'd head.
The Dolphin, with one *Ioane le Puzel* ioyn'd,
A holy Prophetesse, new risen vp,
Is come with a great Power, to rayse the Siege.
> *Here Salisbury lifteth himselfe vp, and groanes*

TALBOT
Heare, heare, how dying *Salisbury* doth groane,
520 It irkes his heart he cannot be reueng'd.
Frenchmen, Ile be a *Salisbury* to you.
Puzel or *Pussel*, Dolphin or Dog-fish,
Your hearts Ile stampe out with my Horses heeles,
And make a Quagmire of your mingled braines.
Conuey me *Salisbury* into his Tent,
And then wee'le try what these dastard Frenchmen
dare.   *Alarum. Exeunt carrying Salisbury*

Sc. 7   *Here an Alarum againe, and Talbot pursueth the*
(1.7)   *Dolphin, and driueth him: Then enter Ioane le*
           Puzel, driuing Englishmen before her, and exeunt.
           Then enter Talbot

TALBOT
Where is my strength, my valour, and my force?
Our English Troupes retyre, I cannot stay them,
A Woman clad in Armour chaseth men.
> *Enter Puzel*

Here, here shee comes. (*To Pucell*) Ile haue a bowt
530   with thee:
Deuill, or Deuils Dam, Ile coniure thee:
Blood will I draw on thee, thou art a Witch,
And straightway giue thy Soule to him thou seru'st.

PUCELL
Come, come, 'tis onely I that must disgrace thee.
> *Here they fight*

TALBOT
Heauens, can you suffer Hell so to preuayle?
My brest Ile burst with straining of my courage,
And from my shoulders crack my Armes asunder,
But I will chastise this high-minded Strumpet.
> *They fight againe*

PUCELL
Talbot farwell, thy houre is not yet come,
540 I must goe Victuall Orleance forthwith:
> *A short Alarum: then ⌈the French passe ouer the*
> *stage and⌉ enter the Towne with Souldiers*

O're-take me if thou canst, I scorne thy strength.
Goe, goe, cheare vp thy hungry-starued men,
Helpe *Salisbury* to make his Testament,
This Day is ours, as many more shall be.
> *Exit into the Towne*

TALBOT
My thoughts are whirled like a Potters Wheele,
I know not where I am, nor what I doe:
A Witch by feare, not force, like *Hannibal*,
Driues back our troupes, and conquers as she lists:
So Bees with smoake, and Doues with noysome
    stench,
Are from their Hyues and Houses driuen away.   550
They call'd vs, for our fiercenesse, English Dogges,
Now like to Whelpes, we crying runne away.
> *A short Alarum. ⌈Enter English Souldiers⌉*

Hearke Countreymen, eyther renew the fight,
Or teare the Lyons out of Englands Coat;
Renounce your Style, giue Sheepe in Lyons stead:
Sheepe run not halfe so trecherous from the Wolfe,
Or Horse or Oxen from the Leopard,
As you flye from your oft-subdued slaues.
> *Alarum. Here another Skirmish*

It will not be, retyre into your Trenches:
You all consented vnto *Salisburies* death,   560
For none would strike a stroake in his reuenge.
Puzel is entred into Orleance,
In spight of vs, or ought that we could doe.
> *⌈Exeunt Souldiers⌉*

O would I were to dye with *Salisbury*,
The shame hereof, will make me hide my head.
> *Exit Talbot. Alarum, Retreat*

> *Flourish. Enter on the Walls, Puzel, Charles the*   Sc. 8
> *Dolphin, Reigneir, Alanson, and Souldiers ⌈with*   (1.8)
> *Colours⌉*

PUCELL
Aduance our wauing Colours on the Walls,
Rescu'd is Orleance from the English.
Thus *Ioane le Puzel* hath perform'd her word.

CHARLES
Diuinest Creature, *Astrea's* Daughter,
How shall I honour thee for this successe?   570
Thy promises are like *Adonis* Garden,
That one day bloom'd, and fruitfull were the next.
France, triumph in thy glorious Prophetesse,
Recouer'd is the Towne of Orleance,
More blessed hap did ne're befall our State.

REIGNEIR
Why ring not out the Bells alowd, throughout the
    Towne?
Dolphin command the Citizens make Bonfires,
And feast and banquet in the open streets,
To celebrate the ioy that God hath giuen vs.

ALANSON
All France will be repleat with mirth and ioy,   580
When they shall heare how we haue play'd the men.

CHARLES
'Tis *Ioane*, not we, by whom the day is wonne:
For which, I will diuide my Crowne with her,
And all the Priests and Fryers in my Realme,
Shall in procession sing her endlesse prayse.
A statelyer Pyramis to her Ile reare,

Then *Rhodophe's* of *Memphis* euer was.
In memorie of her, when she is dead,
Her Ashes, in an Vrne more precious
590   Then the rich-iewel'd Coffer of *Darius*,
Transported, shall be at high Festiuals
Before the Kings and Queenes of France.
No longer on Saint *Dennis* will we cry,
But *Ioane le Puzel* shall be France's Saint.
Come in, and let vs Banquet Royally,
After this Golden Day of Victorie.   *Flourish. Exeunt*

Sc. 9   Enter ⌈*on the Walls*⌉ *a French Sergeant of a Band,*
(2.1)   *with two Sentinels*

SERGEANT
Sirs, take your places, and be vigilant:
If any noyse or Souldier you perceiue
Neere to the walles, by some apparant signe
600   Let vs haue knowledge at the Court of Guard.

⌈A SENTINEL⌉
Sergeant you shall.   *Exit Sergeant*
            Thus are poore Seruitors
(When others sleepe vpon their quiet beds)
Constrain'd to watch in darknesse, raine, and cold.
            Enter Talbot, Bedford, and Burgundy, and Souldiers,
            with scaling Ladders: Their Drummes beating a
            Dead March

TALBOT
Lord Regent, and redoubted *Burgundy*,
By whose approach, the Regions of *Artoys*,
Wallon, and *Picardy*, are friends to vs:
This happy night, the Frenchmen are secure,
Hauing all day carows'd and banquetted,
Embrace we then this opportunitie,
610   As fitting best to quittance their deceite,
Contriu'd by Art, and balefull Sorcerie.

BEDFORD
Coward of France, how much he wrongs his fame,
Dispairing of his owne armes fortitude,
To ioyne with Witches, and the helpe of Hell.

BURGONIE
Traitors haue neuer other company.
But what's that *Puzell* whom they tearme so pure?

TALBOT
A Maid, they say.

BEDFORD   A Maid? And be so martiall?

BURGONIE
Pray God she proue not masculine ere long:
If vnderneath the Standard of the French
620   She carry Armour, as she hath begun—

TALBOT
Well, let them practise and conuerse with spirits.
God is our Fortresse, in whose conquering name
Let vs resolue to scale their flinty bulwarkes.

BEDFORD
Ascend braue *Talbot*, we will follow thee.

TALBOT
Not altogether: Better farre I guesse,
That we do make our entrance seuerall wayes:

That if it chance the one of vs do faile,
The other yet may rise against their force.

BEDFORD
Agreed; Ile to yond corner.

BURGONIE   And I to this.
            ⌈*Exeunt seuerally Bedford and Burgundy, with*
                                some Souldiers⌉

TALBOT
And heere will *Talbot* mount, or make his graue.   630
Now *Salisbury*, for thee and for the right
Of English *Henry*, shall this night appeare
How much in duty, I am bound to both.
            ⌈*Talbot and his Souldiers*⌉ *scale the Walls*

⌈SENTINELS⌉
Arme, arme, the enemy doth make assault.
            English cry, S. George, A Talbot, & exeunt aboue.
            ⌈*Alarum.*⌉ *The French* ⌈*Souldiers*⌉ *leape ore the*
            walles in their shirts ⌈*and exeunt*⌉. *Enter seuerall*
            wayes, Bastard, Alanson, Reignier, halfe ready, and
            halfe vnready

ALANSON
How now my Lords? what all vnreadie so?

BASTARD
Vnready? I and glad we scap'd so well.

REIGNIER
'Twas time (I trow) to wake and leaue our beds,
Hearing Alarums at our Chamber doores.

ALANSON
Of all exploits since first I follow'd Armes,
Nere heard I of a warlike enterprize   640
More venturous, or desperate then this.

BASTARD
I thinke this *Talbot* be a Fiend of Hell.

REIGNIER
If not of Hell, the Heauens sure fauour him.

ALANSON
Here commeth *Charles*, I maruell how he sped?
            Enter Charles and Ioane le Pucell

BASTARD
Tut, holy *Ioane* was his defensiue Guard.

CHARLES (*to Pucell*)
Is this thy cunning, thou deceitfull Dame?
Didst thou at first, to flatter vs withall,
Make vs partakers of a little gayne,
That now our losse might be ten times so much?

PUCELL
Wherefore is *Charles* impatient with his friend?   650
At all times will you haue my Power alike?
Sleeping or waking, must I still preuayle,
Or will you blame and lay the fault on me?
Improuident Souldiors, had your Watch been good,
This sudden Mischiefe neuer could haue falne.

CHARLES
Duke of Alanson, this was your default,
That being Captaine of the Watch to Night,
Did looke no better to that weightie Charge.

ALANSON
Had all your Quarters been as safely kept,

660 As that whereof I had the gouernment,
We had not beene thus shamefully surpriz'd.

BASTARD

Mine was secure.

REIGNIER   And so was mine, my Lord.

CHARLES

And for my selfe, most part of all this Night
Within her Quarter, and mine owne Precinct,
I was imploy'd in passing to and fro,
About relieuing of the Centinels.
Then how, or which way, should they first breake in?

PUCELL

Question (my Lords) no further of the case,
How or which way; 'tis sure they found some place,
670 But weakely guarded, where the breach was made:
And now there rests no other shift but this,
To gather our Souldiors, scatter'd and disperc't,
And lay new Plat-formes to endammage them.

Alarum. Enter an English Souldier, crying, a Talbot,
a Talbot: the French flye, leauing their Clothes
behind

SOULDIER

Ile be so bold to take what they haue left:
The Cry of *Talbot* serues me for a Sword,
For I haue loaden me with many Spoyles,
Vsing no other Weapon but his Name.

Exit with Spoyles

Sc. 10   *Enter Talbot, Bedford, Burgundie, a Captaine, ⌈and*
(2.2)   *Souldiers⌉*

BEDFORD

The Day begins to breake, and Night is fled,
Whose pitchy Mantle ouer-vayl'd the Earth.
680 Here sound Retreat, and cease our hot pursuit.

Retreat is sounded

TALBOT

Bring forth the Body of old *Salisbury*,
And here aduance it in the Market-Place,
The middle Centure of this cursed Towne.

⌈*Exit one or more*⌉

Now haue I pay'd my Vow vnto his Soule:
For euery drop of blood was drawne from him,
There hath at least fiue Frenchmen dyed to night.
And that hereafter Ages may behold
What ruine happend in reuenge of him,
Within their chiefest Temple Ile erect
690 A Tombe, wherein his Corps shall be interr'd:
Vpon the which, that euery one may reade,
Shall be engrau'd the sacke of Orleance,
The trecherous manner of his mournefull death,
And what a terror he had beene to France.
But Lords, in all our bloudy Massacre,
I muse we met not with the Dolphins Grace,
His new-come Champion, vertuous *Ioane* of Arce,
Nor any of his false Confederates.

BEDFORD

'Tis thought Lord *Talbot*, when the fight began,
700 Rows'd on the sudden from their drowsie Beds,

They did amongst the troupes of armed men,
Leape o're the Walls for refuge in the field.

BURGONIE

My selfe, as farre as I could well discerne,
For smoake, and duskie vapours of the night,
Am sure I scar'd the Dolphin and his Trull,
When Arme in Arme they both came swiftly running,
Like to a payre of louing Turtle-Doues,
That could not liue asunder day or night.
After that things are set in order here,
Wee'le follow them with all the power we haue.   710

Enter a Messenger

MESSENGER

All hayle, my Lords: which of this Princely trayne
Call ye the Warlike *Talbot*, for his Acts
So much applauded through the Realme of France?

TALBOT

Here is the *Talbot*, who would speak with him?

MESSENGER

The vertuous Lady, Countesse of Ouergne,
With modestie admiring thy Renowne,
By me entreats (great Lord) thou would'st vouchsafe
To visit her poore Castle where she lyes,
That she may boast she hath beheld the man,
Whose glory fills the World with lowd report.   720

BURGONIE

Is it euen so? Nay, then I see our Warres
Will turne vnto a peacefull Comick sport,
When Ladyes craue to be encountred with.
You may not (my Lord) despise her gentle suit.

TALBOT

Ne're trust me then: for when a World of men
Could not preuayle with all their Oratorie,
Yet hath a Womans kindnesse ouer-rul'd:
And therefore tell her, I returne great thankes,
And in submission will attend on her.
Will not your Honors beare me company?   730

BEDFORD

No, truly, 'tis more then manners will:
And I haue heard it sayd, Vnbidden Guests
Are often welcommest when they are gone.

TALBOT

Well then, alone (since there's no remedie)
I meane to proue this Ladyes courtesie.
Come hither Captaine,

He whispers

                              you perceiue my minde.

CAPTAINE

I doe my Lord, and meane accordingly.   *Exeunt*

Enter Countesse and Porter   **Sc. 11**
                                                      (2.3)
COUNTESSE

Porter, remember what I gaue in charge,
And when you haue done so, bring the Keyes to me.

PORTER Madame, I will.   *Exit* 740

COUNTESSE

The Plot is layd, if all things fall out right,
I shall as famous be by this exploit,

As Scythian *Tomyris* by *Cyrus* death.
Great is the rumour of this dreadfull Knight,
And his atchieuements of no lesse account:
Faine would mine eyes be witnesse with mine eares,
To giue their censure of these rare reports.
    Enter Messenger and Talbot

MESSENGER
Madame, according as your Ladyship desir'd,
By Message crau'd, so is Lord *Talbot* come.

COUNTESSE
750   And he is welcome: what? is this the man?

MESSENGER
Madame, it is.

COUNTESSE   Is this the Scourge of France?
Is this the *Talbot*, so much fear'd abroad?
That with his Name the Mothers still their Babes?
I see Report is fabulous and false.
I thought I should haue seene some *Hercules*,
A second *Hector*, for his grim aspect,
And large proportion of his strong knit Limbes.
Alas, this is a Child, a silly Dwarfe:
It cannot be, this weake and writhled shrimpe
760   Should strike such terror to his Enemies.

TALBOT
Madame, I haue beene bold to trouble you:
But since your Ladyship is not at leysure,
Ile sort some other time to visit you.
    He is going

COUNTESSE (*to Messenger*)
What meanes he now? Goe aske him, whither he
    goes?

MESSENGER
Stay my Lord *Talbot*, for my Lady craues,
To know the cause of your abrupt departure?

TALBOT
Marry, for that shee's in a wrong beleefe,
I goe to certifie her *Talbot's* here.
    Enter Porter with Keyes

COUNTESSE
If thou be he, then art thou Prisoner.

TALBOT
Prisoner? to whom?

COUNTESSE   To me, blood-thirstie Lord:
770   And for that cause I trayn'd thee to my House.
Long time thy shadow hath been thrall to me,
For in my Gallery thy Picture hangs:
But now the substance shall endure the like,
And I will chayne these Legges and Armes of thine,
That hast by Tyrannie these many yeeres
Wasted our Countrey, slaine our Citizens,
And sent our Sonnes and Husbands captiuate.

TALBOT Ha, ha, ha.

COUNTESSE
Laughest thou Wretch? Thy mirth shall turne to
780   moane.

TALBOT
I laugh to see your Ladyship so fond,
To thinke, that you haue ought but *Talbots* shadow,
Whereon to practise your seueritie.

COUNTESSE Why? art not thou the man?

TALBOT I am indeede.

COUNTESSE Then haue I substance too.

TALBOT
No, no, I am but shadow of my selfe:
You are deceiu'd, my substance is not here;
For what you see, is but the smallest part,
And least proportion of Humanitie: 790
I tell you Madame, were the whole Frame here,
It is of such a spacious loftie pitch,
Your Roofe were not sufficient to contayn't.

COUNTESSE
This is a Riddling Merchant for the nonce,
He will be here, and yet he is not here:
How can these contrarieties agree?

TALBOT
That will I shew you presently.
    Winds his Horne, within Drummes strike vp, a
    Peale of Ordenance: Enter Souldiors
How say you Madame? are you now perswaded,
That *Talbot* is but shadow of himselfe?
These are his substance, sinewes, armes, and
    strength,   800
With which he yoaketh your rebellious Neckes,
Razeth your Cities, and subuerts your Townes,
And in a moment makes them desolate.

COUNTESSE
Victorious *Talbot*, pardon my abuse,
I finde thou art no lesse then Fame hath bruited,
And more then may be gatherd by thy shape.
Let my presumption not prouoke thy wrath,
For I am sorry, that with reuerence
I did not entertaine thee as thou art.

TALBOT
Be not dismay'd, faire Lady, nor misconster   810
The minde of *Talbot*, as you did mistake
The outward composition of his body.
What you haue done, hath not offended me:
Nor other satisfaction doe I craue,
But onely with your patience, that we may
Taste of your Wine, and see what Cates you haue,
For Souldiers stomacks alwayes serue them well.

COUNTESSE
With all my heart, and thinke me honored,
To feast so great a Warrior in my House.   *Exeunt*

A Rose Bryer. Enter Richard Plantagenet, Warwick,   Sc. 12
Somerset, William de la Poole the Earl of Suffolke,   (2.4)
Vernon and a Lawyer

RICHARD PLANTAGENET
Great Lords and Gentlemen, what meanes this
    silence?   820
Dare no man answer in a Case of Truth?

SUFFOLKE
Within the Temple Hall we were too lowd,
The Garden here is more conuenient.

RICHARD PLANTAGENET
Then say at once, if I maintain'd the Truth:
Or else was wrangling *Somerset* in th'error?

SUFFOLKE

 Faith I haue beene a Truant in the Law,
 And neuer yet could frame my will to it,
 And therefore frame the Law vnto my will.

SOMERSET

 Iudge you, my Lord of Warwicke, then betweene vs.

WARWICKE

830 Between two Hawks, which flyes the higher pitch,
 Between two Dogs, which hath the deeper mouth,
 Between two Blades, which beares the better temper,
 Between two Horses, which doth beare him best,
 Between two Girles, which hath the merryest eye,
 I haue perhaps some shallow spirit of Iudgement:
 But in these nice sharpe Quillets of the Law,
 Good faith I am no wiser then a Daw.

RICHARD PLANTAGENET

 Tut, tut, here is a mannerly forbearance:
 The truth appeares so naked on my side,
840 That any purblind eye may find it out.

SOMERSET

 And on my side it is so well apparrell'd,
 So cleare, so shining, and so euident,
 That it will glimmer through a blind-mans eye.

RICHARD PLANTAGENET

 Since you are tongue-ty'd, and so loth to speake,
 In dumbe significants proclayme your thoughts:
 Let him that is a true-borne Gentleman,
 And stands vpon the honor of his birth,
 If he suppose that I haue pleaded truth,
 From off this Bryer pluck a white Rose with me.
   He plucks a white Rose

SOMERSET

850 Let him that is no Coward, nor no Flatterer,
 But dare maintaine the partie of the truth,
 Pluck a red Rose from off this Thorne with me.
   He plucks a red Rose

WARWICKE

 I loue no Colours: and without all colour
 Of base insinuating flatterie,
 I pluck this white Rose with *Plantagenet*.

SUFFOLKE

 I pluck this red Rose, with young *Somerset*,
 And say withall, I thinke he held the right.

VERNON

 Stay Lords and Gentlemen, and pluck no more
 Till you conclude, that he vpon whose side
860 The fewest Roses from the Tree are cropt,
 Shall yeeld the other in the right opinion.

SOMERSET

 Good Master *Vernon*, it is well obiected:
 If I haue fewest, I subscribe in silence.

RICHARD PLANTAGENET And I.

VERNON

 Then for the truth, and plainnesse of the Case,
 I pluck this pale and Maiden Blossome here,
 Giuing my Verdict on the white Rose side.

SOMERSET

 Prick not your finger as you pluck it off,

Least bleeding, you doe paint the white Rose red,
And fall on my side so against your will. 870

VERNON

 If I, my Lord, for my opinion bleed,
 Opinion shall be Surgeon to my hurt,
 And keepe me on the side where still I am.

SOMERSET Well, well, come on, who else?

LAWYER

 Vnlesse my Studie and my Bookes be false,
 The argument you held, was wrong in law;
 In signe whereof, I pluck a white Rose too.

RICHARD PLANTAGENET

 Now *Somerset*, where is your argument?

SOMERSET

 Here in my Scabbard, meditating that
 Shall dye your white Rose in a bloody red. 880

RICHARD PLANTAGENET

 Meane time your cheeks do counterfeit our Roses:
 For pale they looke with feare, as witnessing
 The truth on our side.

SOMERSET   No *Plantagenet*:

 'Tis not for feare, but anger, that thy cheekes
 Blush for pure shame, to counterfeit our Roses,
 And yet thy tongue will not confesse thy error.

RICHARD PLANTAGENET

 Hath not thy Rose a Canker, *Somerset*?

SOMERSET

 Hath not thy Rose a Thorne, *Plantagenet*?

RICHARD PLANTAGENET

 I, sharpe and piercing to maintaine his truth,
 Whiles thy consuming Canker eates his falsehood. 890

SOMERSET

 Well, Ile find friends to weare my bleeding Roses,
 That shall maintaine what I haue said is true,
 Where false *Plantagenet* dare not be seene.

RICHARD PLANTAGENET

 Now by this Maiden Blossome in my hand,
 I scorne thee and thy fashion, peeuish Boy.

SUFFOLKE

 Turne not thy scornes this way, *Plantagenet*.

RICHARD PLANTAGENET

 Prowd *Poole*, I will, and scorne both him and thee.

SUFFOLKE

 Ile turne my part thereof into thy throat.

SOMERSET

 Away, away, good *William de la Poole*,
 We grace the Yeoman, by conuersing with him. 900

WARWICKE

 Now by Gods will thou wrong'st him, *Somerset*:
 His Grandfather was *Lyonel* Duke of Clarence,
 Third Sonne to the third *Edward* King of England:
 Spring Crestlesse Yeomen from so deepe a Root?

RICHARD PLANTAGENET

 He beares him on the place's Priuiledge,
 Or durst not for his crauen heart say thus.

SOMERSET

 By him that made me, Ile maintaine my words
 On any Plot of Ground in Christendome.
 Was not thy Father, *Richard*, Earle of Cambridge,

910 For Treason executed in our late Kings dayes?
And by his Treason, stand'st not thou attainted,
Corrupted, and exempt from ancient Gentry?
His Trespas yet liues guiltie in thy blood,
And till thou be restor'd, thou art a Yeoman.

RICHARD PLANTAGENET
My Father was attached, not attainted,
Condemn'd to dye for Treason, but no Traytor;
And that Ile proue on better men then *Somerset*,
Were growing time once ripend to my will.
For your partaker *Poole*, and you your selfe,
920 Ile note you in my Booke of Memorie,
To scourge you for this apprehension:
Looke to it well, and say you are well warn'd.

SOMERSET
Ah, thou shalt finde vs ready for thee still:
And know vs by these Colours for thy Foes,
For these, my friends in spight of thee shall weare.

RICHARD PLANTAGENET
And by my Soule, this pale and angry Rose,
As Cognizance of my blood-drinking hate,
Will I for euer, and my Faction weare,
Vntill it wither with me to my Graue,
930 Or flourish to the height of my Degree.

SUFFOLKE
Goe forward, and be choak'd with thy ambition:
And so farwell, vntill I meet thee next.   Exit

SOMERSET
Haue with thee *Poole*: Farwell ambitious *Richard*.   Exit

RICHARD PLANTAGENET
How I am brau'd, and must perforce endure it?

WARWICKE
This blot that they obiect against your House,
Shall be whipt out in the next Parliament,
Call'd for the Truce of *Winchester* and *Gloucester*:
And if thou be not then created *Yorke*,
I will not liue to be accounted *Warwicke*.
940 Meane time, in signall of my loue to thee,
Against prowd *Somerset*, and *William Poole*,
Will I vpon thy partie weare this Rose.
And here I prophecie: this brawle to day,
Growne to this faction in the Temple Garden,
Shall send betweene the Red-Rose and the White,
A thousand Soules to Death and deadly Night.

RICHARD PLANTAGENET
Good Master *Vernon*, I am bound to you,
That you on my behalfe would pluck a Flower.

VERNON
In your behalfe still will I weare the same.

950 LAWYER And so will I.

RICHARD PLANTAGENET Thankes gentles.
Come, let vs foure to Dinner: I dare say,
This Quarrell will drinke Blood another day.
                Exeunt. The Rose Bryer is remoued

Sc. 13   *Enter Mortimer, brought in a Chayre, ⌈by⌉ his*
(2.5)   *Keepers*

MORTIMER
Kind Keepers of my weake decaying Age,

Let dying *Mortimer* here rest himselfe.
Euen like a man new haled from the Wrack,
So fare my Limbes with long Imprisonment:
And these gray Locks, the Pursuiuants of death,
Argue the end of *Edmund Mortimer*,
Nestor-like aged, in an Age of Care.   960
These Eyes, like Lampes, whose wasting Oyle is spent,
Waxe dimme, as drawing to their Exigent.
Weake Shoulders, ouer-borne with burthening Griefe,
And pyth-lesse Armes, like to a witherd Vine,
That droupes his sappe-lesse Branches to the ground.
Yet are these Feet, whose strength-lesse stay is
          numme,
(Vnable to support this Lumpe of Clay)
Swift-winged with desire to get a Graue,
As witting I no other comfort haue.
But tell me, Keeper, will my Nephew come?   970

KEEPER
Richard Plantagenet, my Lord, will come:
We sent vnto the Temple, vnto his Chamber,
And answer was return'd, that he will come.

MORTIMER
Enough: my Soule shall then be satisfied.
Poore Gentleman, his wrong doth equall mine.
Since *Henry Monmouth* first began to reigne,
Before whose Glory I was great in Armes,
This loathsome sequestration haue I had;
And euen since then, hath *Richard* beene obscur'd,
Depriu'd of Honor and Inheritance.   980
But now, the Arbitrator of Despaires,
Iust Death, kinde Vmpire of mens miseries,
With sweet enlargement doth dismisse me hence:
I would his troubles likewise were expir'd,
That so he might recouer what was lost.
          Enter Richard

KEEPER
My Lord, your louing Nephew now is come.

MORTIMER
Richard Plantagenet, my friend, is he come?

RICHARD PLANTAGENET
I, Noble Vnckle, thus ignobly vs'd,
Your Nephew, late despised *Richard*, comes.

MORTIMER (*to Keepers*)
Direct mine Armes, I may embrace his Neck,   990
And in his Bosome spend my latter gaspe.
Oh tell me when my Lippes doe touch his Cheekes,
That I may kindly giue one fainting Kisse.
          He embraces Richard
And now declare sweet Stem from *Yorkes* great Stock,
Why didst thou say of late thou wert despis'd?

RICHARD PLANTAGENET
First, leane thine aged Back against mine Arme,
And in that ease, Ile tell thee my Disease.
This day in argument vpon a Case,
Some words there grew 'twixt *Somerset* and me:
Among which tearmes, he vs'd his lauish tongue,   1000
And did vpbrayd me with my Fathers death;
Which obloquie set barres before my tongue,
Else with the like I had requited him.

Therefore good Vnckle, for my Fathers sake,
In honor of a true *Plantagenet*,
And for Alliance sake, declare the cause
My Father, Earle of Cambridge, lost his Head.

MORTIMER
That cause (faire Nephew) that imprison'd me,
And hath detayn'd me all my flowring Youth,
1010 Within a loathsome Dungeon, there to pyne,
Was cursed Instrument of his decease.

RICHARD PLANTAGENET
Discouer more at large what cause that was,
For I am ignorant, and cannot guesse.

MORTIMER
I will, if that my fading breath permit,
And Death approach not, ere my Tale be done.
Henry the Fourth, Grandfather to this King,
Depos'd his Nephew *Richard*, *Edwards* Sonne,
The first begotten, and the lawfull Heire
Of *Edward* King, the Third of that Descent.
1020 During whose Reigne, the *Percies* of the North,
Finding his Vsurpation most vniust,
Endeuour'd my aduancement to the Throne.
The reason mou'd these Warlike Lords to this,
Was, for that (young K. *Richard* thus remou'd,
Leauing no Heire begotten of his Body)
I was the next by Birth and Parentage:
For by my Mother, I deriued am
From *Lionel* Duke of Clarence, the third Sonne
To King *Edward* the Third; whereas the King,
1030 From *Iohn* of Gaunt doth bring his Pedigree,
Being but fourth of that Heroick Lyne.
But marke: as in this haughtie great attempt,
They laboured, to plant the rightfull Heire,
I lost my Libertie, and they their Liues.
Long after this, when *Henry* the Fift
(Succeeding his Father *Bullingbrooke*) did reigne;
Thy Father, Earle of Cambridge then, deriu'd
From famous *Edmund Langley*, Duke of Yorke,
Marrying my Sister, that thy Mother was;
1040 Againe, in pitty of my hard distresse,
Leuied an Army, weening to redeeme,
And haue install'd me in the Diademe:
But as the rest, so fell that Noble Earle,
And was beheaded. Thus the *Mortimers*,
In whom the Title rested, were supprest.

RICHARD PLANTAGENET
Of which, my Lord, your Honor is the last.

MORTIMER
True; and thou seest, that I no Issue haue,
And that my fainting words doe warrant death:
Thou art my Heire; the rest, I wish thee gather:
1050 But yet be wary in thy studious care.

RICHARD PLANTAGENET
Thy graue admonishments preuayle with me:
But yet me thinkes, my Fathers execution
Was nothing lesse then bloody Tyranny.

MORTIMER
With silence, Nephew, be thou pollitick,
Strong fixed is the House of *Lancaster*,
And like a Mountaine, not to be remou'd.
But now thy Vnckle is remouing hence,
As Princes doe their Courts, when they are cloy'd
With long continuance in a setled place.

RICHARD PLANTAGENET
O Vnckle, would some part of my young yeeres   1060
Might but redeeme the passage of your Age.

MORTIMER
Thou do'st then wrong me, as y^t slaughterer doth,
Which giueth many Wounds, when one will kill.
Mourne not, except thou sorrow for my good,
Onely giue order for my Funerall.
And so farewell, and faire be all thy hopes,
And prosperous be thy Life in Peace and Warre.   *Dyes*

RICHARD PLANTAGENET
And Peace, no Warre, befall thy parting Soule.
In Prison hast thou spent a Pilgrimage,
And like a Hermite ouer-past thy dayes.   1070
Well, I will locke his Councell in my Brest,
And what I doe imagine, let that rest.
Keepers conuey him hence, and I my selfe
Will see his Buryall better then his Life.

Exit Keepers, with Mortimers body

Here dyes the duskie Torch of *Mortimer*,
Choakt with Ambition of the meaner sort.
And for those Wrongs, those bitter Iniuries,
Which *Somerset* hath offer'd to my House,
I doubt not, but with Honor to redresse.
And therefore haste I to the Parliament,   1080
Eyther to be restored to my Blood,
Or make myn ill th'aduantage of my good.   *Exit*

Flourish. Enter young King, Exeter, Gloster,   Sc. 14
Winchester; Somerset and Suffolk ⌐with red   (3.1)
Roses⌐, Warwick and Richard Plantagenet ⌐with
white Roses⌐. Gloster offers to put vp a Bill:
Winchester snatches it, teares it

WINCHESTER
Com'st thou with deepe premeditated Lines?
With written Pamphlets, studiously deuis'd?
Humfrey of Gloster, if thou canst accuse,
Or ought intend'st to lay vnto my charge,
Doe it without inuention, suddenly,
As I with sudden, and extemporall speech,
Purpose to answer what thou canst obiect.

GLOSTER
Presumptuous Priest, this place cõmands my patiẽce,   1090
Or thou should'st finde thou hast dis-honor'd me.
Thinke not, although in Writing I preferr'd
The manner of thy vile outragious Crymes,
That therefore I haue forg'd, or am not able
Verbatim to rehearse the Methode of my Penne.
No Prelate, such is thy audacious wickednesse,
Thy lewd, pestiferous, and dissentious prancks,
As very Infants prattle of thy pride.
Thou art a most pernitious Vsurer,
Froward by nature, Enemie to Peace,   1100
Lasciuious, wanton, more then well beseemes
A man of thy Profession, and Degree.

And for thy Trecherie, what's more manifest?
In that thou layd'st a Trap to take my Life,
As well at London Bridge, as at the Tower.
Beside, I feare me, if thy thoughts were sifted,
The King, thy Soueraigne, is not quite exempt
From enuious mallice of thy swelling heart.

WINCHESTER

1110 *Gloster*, I doe defie thee. Lords vouchsafe
To giue me hearing what I shall reply.
If I were couetous, ambitious, or peruerse,
As he will haue me: how am I so poore?
Or how haps it, I seeke not to aduance
Or rayse my selfe? but keepe my wonted Calling.
And for Dissention, who preferreth Peace
More then I doe? except I be prouok'd.
No, my good Lords, it is not that offends,
It is not that, that hath incens'd the Duke:
It is because no one should sway but hee,
1120 No one, but hee, should be about the King;
And that engenders Thunder in his breast,
And makes him rore these Accusations forth.
But he shall know I am as good.

GLOSTER As good?
Thou Bastard of my Grandfather.

WINCHESTER

I, Lordly Sir: for what are you, I pray,
But one imperious in anothers Throne?

GLOSTER

Am I not Protector, sawcie Priest?

WINCHESTER

And am not I a Prelate of the Church?

GLOSTER

1130 Yes, as an Out-law in a Castle keepes,
And vseth it, to patronage his Theft.

WINCHESTER

Vnreuerent *Glocester*.

GLOSTER   Thou art reuerent,
Touching thy Spirituall Function, not thy Life.

WINCHESTER

Rome shall remedie this.

⌈GLOSTER⌉   Roame thither then.

⌈WARWICKE⌉ (*to Winchester*)
My Lord, it were your dutie to forbeare.

SOMERSET

I, soe the Bishop be not ouer-borne:
Me thinkes my Lord should be Religious,
And know the Office that belongs to such.

WARWICKE

Me thinkes his Lordship should be humbler,
1140 It fitteth not a Prelate so to plead.

SOMERSET

Yes, when his holy State is toucht so neere.

WARWICKE

State holy, or vnhallow'd, what of that?
Is not his Grace Protector to the King?

RICHARD PLANTAGENET (*aside*)
Plantagenet I see must hold his tongue,
Least it be said, Speake Sirrha when you should:

Must your bold Verdict entertalke with Lords?
Else would I haue a fling at *Winchester*.

KING

Vnckles of *Gloster*, and of *Winchester*,
The speciall Watch-men of our English Weale,
I would preuaile, if Prayers might preuaile,   1150
To ioyne your hearts in loue and amitie.
Oh, what a Scandall is it to our Crowne,
That two such Noble Peeres as ye should iarre?
Beleeue me, Lords, my tender yeeres can tell,
Ciuill dissention is a viperous Worme,
That gnawes the Bowels of the Common-wealth.

A noyse within, Downe with the Tawny-Coats
What tumult's this?

WARWICKE   An Vprore, I dare warrant,
Begun through malice of the Bishops men.
A noyse againe, Stones, Stones.
Enter Maior

MAIOR

Oh my good Lords, and vertuous *Henry*,
Pitty the Citie of London, pitty vs: 1160
The Bishop, and the Duke of Glosters men,
Forbidden late to carry any Weapon,
Haue fill'd their Pockets full of peeble stones;
And banding themselues in contrary parts,
Doe pelt so fast at one anothers Pate,
That many haue their giddy braynes knockt out:
Our Windowes are broke downe in euery Street,
And we, for feare, compell'd to shut our Shops.
Enter in skirmish with bloody Pates Winchesters
Seruing-men in Tawny-Coats and Glosters in Blew
Coates

KING

We charge you, on allegeance to our selfe,
To hold your slaughtring hands, and keepe the Peace: 1170
⌈*The skirmish ceases*⌉
Pray' Vnckle *Gloster* mittigate this strife.

1. SERUINGMAN Nay, if we be forbidden Stones, wee'le fall
to it with our Teeth.

2. SERUINGMAN

Doe what ye dare, we are as resolute.
Skirmish againe

GLOSTER

You of my household, leaue this peeuish broyle,
And set this vnaccustom'd fight aside.

3. SERUINGMAN

My Lord, we know your Grace to be a man
Iust, and vpright; and for your Royall Birth,
Inferior to none, but to his Maiestie:
And ere that we will suffer such a Prince,   1180
So kinde a Father of the Common-weale,
To be disgraced by an Inke-horne Mate,
Wee and our Wiues and Children all will fight,
And haue our bodyes slaughtred by thy foes.

1. SERUINGMAN

I, and the very parings of our Nayles
Shall pitch a Field when we are dead.
Begin to skirmish againe

GLOSTER   Stay, stay, I say:

And if you loue me, as you say you doe,
Let me perswade you to forbeare a while.

KING

1190 Oh, how this discord doth afflict my Soule.
Can you, my Lord of Winchester, behold
My sighes and teares, and will not once relent?
Who should be pittifull, if you be not?
Or who should study to preferre a Peace,
If holy Church-men take delight in broyles?

WARWICKE

Yeeld my Lord Protector, yeeld *Winchester*,
Except you meane with obstinate repulse
To slay your Soueraigne, and destroy the Realme.
You see what Mischiefe, and what Murther too,
Hath beene enacted through your enmitie:
1200 Then be at peace, except ye thirst for blood.

WINCHESTER

He shall submit, or I will neuer yeeld.

GLOSTER

Compassion on the King commands me stoupe,
Or I would see his heart out, ere the Priest
Should euer get that priuiledge of me.

WARWICKE

Behold my Lord of Winchester, the Duke
Hath banisht moodie discontented fury,
As by his smoothed Browes it doth appeare:
Why looke you still so sterne, and tragicall?

GLOSTER

Here *Winchester*, I offer thee my Hand.

KING (*to Winchester*)

1210 Fie Vnckle *Beauford*, I haue heard you preach,
That Mallice was a great and grieuous sinne:
And will not you maintaine the thing you teach?
But proue a chiefe offendor in the same.

WARWICKE

Sweet King: the Bishop hath a kindly gyrd:
For shame my Lord of Winchester relent;
What, shall a Child instruct you what to doe?

WINCHESTER

Well, Duke of Gloster, I will yeeld to thee
Loue for thy Loue, and Hand for Hand I giue.

GLOSTER (*aside*)

I, but I feare me with a hollow Heart.
(*To the others*) See here my Friends and louing
1220   Countreymen,
This token serueth for a Flagge of Truce,
Betwixt our selues, and all our followers:
So helpe me God, as I dissemble not.

WINCHESTER

So helpe me God, (*aside*) as I intend it not.

KING

Oh louing Vnckle, kinde Duke of Gloster,
How ioyfull am I made by this Contract.
(*To Seruing-men*) Away my Masters, trouble vs no
    more,
But ioyne in friendship, as your Lords haue done.

1. SERUINGMAN Content, Ile to the Surgeons.

1230 2. SERUINGMAN And so will I.

3. SERUINGMAN And I will see what Physick the Tauerne
affords.   *Exeunt Maior and Seruing-men*

WARWICKE

Accept this Scrowle, most gracious Soueraigne,
Which in the Right of *Richard Plantagenet*,
We doe exhibite to your Maiestie.

GLOSTER

Well vrg'd, my Lord of Warwick: for sweet Prince,
And if your Grace marke euery circumstance,
You haue great reason to doe *Richard* right,
Especially for those occasions
At Eltam Place I told your Maiestie.   1240

KING

And those occasions, Vnckle, were of force:
Therefore my louing Lords, our pleasure is,
That *Richard* be restored to his Blood.

WARWICKE

Let *Richard* be restored to his Blood,
So shall his Fathers wrongs be recompenc't.

WINCHESTER

As will the rest, so willeth *Winchester*.

KING

If *Richard* will be true, not that alone,
But all the whole Inheritance I giue,
That doth belong vnto the House of *Yorke*,
From whence you spring, by Lineall Descent.   1250

RICHARD PLANTAGENET

Thy humble seruant vowes obedience,
And humble seruice, till the point of death.

KING

Stoope then, and set your Knee against my Foot,
    Richard kneeles
And in reguerdon of that dutie done,
I gyrt thee with the valiant Sword of *Yorke*:
Rise *Richard*, like a true *Plantagenet*,
And rise created Princely Duke of *Yorke*.

RICHARD DUKE OF YORKE (*rising*)

And so thriue *Richard*, as thy foes may fall,
And as my dutie springs, so perish they,
That grudge one thought against your Maiesty.   1260

ALL BUT RICHARD AND SOMERSET

Welcome high Prince, the mighty Duke of *Yorke*.

SOMERSET (*aside*)

Perish base Prince, ignoble Duke of *Yorke*.

GLOSTER

Now will it best auaile your Maiestie,
To crosse the Seas, and to be Crown'd in France:
The presence of a King engenders loue
Amongst his Subiects, and his loyall Friends,
As it dis-animates his Enemies.

KING

When *Gloster* sayes the word, King *Henry* goes,
For friendly counsaile cuts off many Foes.

GLOSTER

Your Ships alreadie are in readinesse.   1270
    Senet. Exeunt. Manet Exeter

EXETER

I, we may march in England, or in France,

Not seeing what is likely to ensue:
This late dissention growne betwixt the Peeres,
Burnes vnder fained ashes of forg'd loue,
And will at last breake out into a flame,
As festred members rot but by degree,
Till bones and flesh and sinewes fall away,
So will this base and enuious discord breed.
And now I feare that fatall Prophecie,
1280 Which in the time of *Henry*, nam'd the Fift,
Was in the mouth of euery sucking Babe,
That *Henry* borne at Monmouth should winne all,
And *Henry* borne at Windsor, should loose all:
Which is so plaine, that *Exeter* doth wish,
His dayes may finish, ere that haplesse time.   *Exit*

Sc. 15   *Enter Pucell disguis'd, with foure French Souldiors*
(3.2)   *with Sacks vpon their backs*

PUCELL
These are the Citie Gates, the Gates of Roan,
Through which our Pollicy must make a breach.
Take heed, be wary how you place your words,
Talke like the vulgar sort of Market men,
1290 That come to gather Money for their Corne.
If we haue entrance, as I hope we shall,
And that we finde the slouthfull Watch but weake,
Ile by a signe giue notice to our friends,
That *Charles* the Dolphin may encounter them.

A SOULDIER
Our Sacks shall be a meane to sack the City,
And we be Lords and Rulers ouer Roan,
Therefore wee'le knock.
            Knock

WATCH (*within*)
Che la.

PUCELL   *Peasauns la pouure gens de Fraunce,*
Poore Market folkes that come to sell their Corne.

WATCH (*opening the Gates*)
1300 Enter, goe in, the Market Bell is rung.

PUCELL (*aside*)
Now Roan, Ile shake thy Bulwarkes to the ground.
            Exeunt

Sc. 16   *Enter Charles, Bastard,* ⌈*Alanson, Reignier, and*
(3.3)   *French Souldiers*⌉

CHARLES
Saint *Dennis* blesse this happy Stratageme,
And once againe wee'le sleepe secure in Roan.

BASTARD
Here entred *Pucell*, and her Practisants:
Now she is there, how will she specifie?
Here is the best and safest passage in.

REIGNIER
By thrusting out a Torch from yonder Tower,
Which once discern'd, shewes that her meaning is,
No way to that (for weaknesse) which she entred.
            Enter Pucell on the top, thrusting out a Torch
            burning

PUCELL
1310 Behold, this is the happy Wedding Torch,

That ioyneth Roan vnto her Countreymen,
But burning fatall to the *Talbonites.*

BASTARD
See Noble *Charles* the Beacon of our friend,
The burning Torch in yonder Turret stands.

CHARLES
Now shine it like a Commet of Reuenge,
A Prophet to the fall of all our Foes.

REIGNIER
Deferre no time, delayes haue dangerous ends,
Enter and cry, the Dolphin, presently,
And then doe execution on the Watch.
            Alarum. Exeunt

            An Alarum. Enter Talbot in an Excursion   Sc. 17
TALBOT   (3.4)
France, thou shalt rue this Treason with thy teares,   1320
If *Talbot* but suruiue thy Trecherie.
Pucell that Witch, that damned Sorceresse,
Hath wrought this Hellish Mischiefe vnawares,
That hardly we escap't the Pride of France.   *Exit*

            An Alarum: Excursions. Bedford brought in sicke in   Sc. 18
            a Chayre. Enter Talbot and Burgonie without: (3.5)
            within, Pucell, Charles, Bastard, ⌈*Alanson, and*
            Reigneir⌉ *on the Walls*

PUCELL
God morrow Gallants, want ye Corn for Bread?
I thinke the Duke of Burgonie will fast,
Before hee'le buy againe at such a rate.
'Twas full of Darnell: doe you like the taste?

BURGONIE
Scoffe on vile Fiend, and shamelesse Curtizan,
I trust ere long to choake thee with thine owne,   1330
And make thee curse the Haruest of that Corne.

CHARLES
Your Grace may starue (perhaps) before that time.

BEDFORD
Oh let no words, but deedes, reuenge this Treason.

PUCELL
What will you doe, good gray-beard? Breake a Launce,
And runne a-Tilt at Death, within a Chayre.

TALBOT
Foule Fiend of France, and Hag of all despight,
Incompass'd with thy lustfull Paramours,
Becomes it thee to taunt his valiant Age,
And twit with Cowardise a man halfe dead?
Damsell, Ile haue a bowt with you againe,   1340
Or else let *Talbot* perish with this shame.

PUCELL
Are ye so hot, Sir: yet *Pucell* hold thy peace,
If *Talbot* doe but Thunder, Raine will follow.
            The English whisper together in counsell
God speed the Parliament: who shall be the Speaker?

TALBOT
Dare yee come forth, and meet vs in the field?

PUCELL
Belike your Lordship takes vs then for fooles,
To try if that our owne be ours, or no.

TALBOT

I speake not to that rayling *Hecate*,

But vnto thee *Alanson*, and the rest.

1350 Will ye, like Souldiors, come and fight it out?

ALANSON

Seignior no.

TALBOT   Seignior hang: base Muleters of France,

Like Pesant foot-Boyes doe they keepe the Walls,

And dare not take vp Armes, like Gentlemen.

PUCELL

Away Captaines, let's get vs from the Walls,

For *Talbot* meanes no goodnesse by his Lookes.

God b'uy my Lord, we came but to tell you

That wee are here.   *Exeunt French from the Walls*

TALBOT

And there will we be too, ere it be long,

Or else reproach be *Talbots* greatest fame.

1360 Vow *Burgonie*, by honor of thy House,

Prickt on by publike Wrongs sustain'd in France,

Either to get the Towne againe, or dye.

And I, as sure as English *Henry* liues,

And as his Father here was Conqueror;

As sure as in this late betrayed Towne,

Great *Cordelions* Heart was buryed;

So sure I sweare, to get the Towne, or dye.

BURGONIE

My Vowes are equall partners with thy Vowes.

TALBOT

But ere we goe, regard this dying Prince,

The valiant Duke of Bedford: (*To Bedford*) Come my

1370   Lord,

We will bestow you in some better place,

Fitter for sicknesse, and for crasie age.

BEDFORD

Lord *Talbot*, doe not so dishonour me:

Here will I sit, before the Walls of Roan,

And will be partner of your weale or woe.

BURGONIE

Couragious *Bedford*, let vs now perswade you.

BEDFORD

Not to be gone from hence: for once I read,

That stout *Pendragon*, in his Litter sick,

Came to the field, and vanquished his foes.

1380 Me thinkes I should reuiue the Souldiors hearts,

Because I euer found them as my selfe.

TALBOT

Vndaunted spirit in a dying breast,

Then be it so: Heauens keepe old *Bedford* safe.

And now no more adoe, braue *Burgonie*,

But gather we our Forces out of hand,

And set vpon our boasting Enemie.

               Exit with Burgonie

An Alarum: Excursions. Enter Sir Iohn Falstaffe,

and a Captaine

CAPTAINE

Whither away Sir *Iohn Falstaffe*, in such haste?

FALSTAFFE

Whither away? to saue my selfe by flight,

We are like to haue the ouerthrow againe.

CAPTAINE

What? will you flye, and leaue Lord *Talbot*?   1390

FALSTAFFE

I, all the *Talbots* in the World, to saue my life.   *Exit*

CAPTAINE

Cowardly Knight, ill fortune follow thee.   *Exit*

     Retreat. Excursions. Pucell, Alanson, and Charles

     flye

BEDFORD

Now quiet Soule, depart when Heauen please,

For I haue seene our Enemies ouerthrow.

What is the trust or strength of foolish man?

They that of late were daring with their scoffes,

Are glad and faine by flight to saue themselues.

     Bedford dyes, and is carryed in by two in his Chaire

An Alarum. Enter Talbot, Burgonie, and the rest of   Sc. 19

the English Souldiers   (3.6)

TALBOT

Lost, and recouerd in a day againe,

This is a double Honor, *Burgonie*:

Yet Heauens haue glory for this Victorie.   1400

BURGONIE

Warlike and Martiall *Talbot, Burgonie*

Inshrines thee in his heart, and there erects

Thy noble Deeds, as Valors Monuments.

TALBOT

Thanks gentle Duke: but where is *Pucel* now?

I thinke her old Familiar is asleepe.

Now where's the Bastards braues, and *Charles* his

     glikes?

What all amort? Roan hangs her head for griefe,

That such a valiant Company are fled.

Now will we take some order in the Towne,

Placing therein some expert Officers,   1410

And then depart to Paris, to the King,

For there young *Henry* with his Nobles lye.

BURGONIE

What wills Lord *Talbot*, pleaseth *Burgonie*.

TALBOT

But yet before we goe, let's not forget

The Noble Duke of Bedford, late decceas'd,

But see his Exequies fulfill'd in Roan.

A brauer Souldier neuer couched Launce,

A gentler Heart did neuer sway in Court.

But Kings and mightiest Potentates must die,

For that's the end of humane miserie.   *Exeunt*   1420

Enter Charles, Bastard, Alanson, Pucell ⌈and French   Sc. 20

Souldiers⌉   (3.7)

PUCELL

Dismay not (Princes) at this accident,

Nor grieue that Roan is so recouered:

Care is no cure, but rather corrosiue,

For things that are not to be remedy'd.

Let frantike *Talbot* triumph for a while,

And like a Peacock sweepe along his tayle,

Wee'le pull his Plumes, and take away his Trayne,

If Dolphin and the rest will be but rul'd.

CHARLES
    We haue been guided by thee hitherto,
1430   And of thy Cunning had no diffidence,
    One sudden Foyle shall neuer breed distrust.

BASTARD (*to Pucell*)
    Search out thy wit for secret pollicies,
    And we will make thee famous through the World.

ALANSON (*to Pucell*)
    Wee'le set thy Statue in some holy place,
    And haue thee reuerenc't like a blessed Saint.
    Employ thee then, sweet Virgin, for our good.

PUCELL
    Then thus it must be, this doth *Ioane* deuise:
    By faire perswasions, mixt with sugred words,
    We will entice the Duke of Burgonie
1440   To leaue the *Talbot*, and to follow vs.

CHARLES
    I marry Sweeting, if we could doe that,
    France were no place for *Henryes* Warriors,
    Nor should that Nation boast it so with vs,
    But be extirped from our Prouinces.

ALANSON
    For euer should they be expuls'd from France,
    And not haue Title of an Earledome here.

PUCELL
    Your Honors shall perceiue how I will worke,
    To bring this matter to the wished end.
        Drumme sounds a farre off
    Hearke, by the sound of Drumme you may perceiue
1450   Their Powers are marching vnto Paris-ward.
        Here sound an English March
    There goes the *Talbot*, with his Colours spred,
    And all the Troupes of English after him.
        Here sound a French march
    Now in the Rereward comes the Duke and his:
    Fortune in fauor makes him lagge behinde.
    Summon a Parley, we will talke with him.
        Trumpets sound a Parley

CHARLES ⌈*calling*⌉
    A Parley with the Duke of Burgonie.
        ⌈*Enter Burgonie*⌉

BURGONIE
    Who craues a Parley with the Burgonie?

PUCELL
    The Princely *Charles* of France, thy Countreyman.

BURGONIE
    What say'st thou *Charles*? for I am marching hence.

CHARLES
1460   Speake *Pucell*, and enchaunt him with thy words.

PUCELL
    Braue *Burgonie*, vndoubted hope of France,
    Stay, let thy humble Hand-maid speake to thee.

BURGONIE
    Speake on, but be not ouer-tedious.

PUCELL
    Looke on thy Country, look on fertile France,
    And see the Cities and the Townes defac't,

    By wasting Ruine of the cruell Foe.
    As lookes the Mother on her lowly Babe,
    When Death doth close his tender-dying Eyes,
    See, see the pining Maladie of France:
    Behold the Wounds, the most vnnaturall Wounds,   1470
    Which thou thy selfe hast giuen her wofull Brest.
    Oh turne thy edged Sword another way,
    Strike those that hurt, and hurt not those that helpe:
    One drop of Blood drawne from thy Countries Bosome,
    Should grieue thee more then streames of forraine
       gore.
    Returne thee therefore with a floud of Teares,
    And wash away thy Countries stayned Spots.

BURGONIE ⌈*aside*⌉
    Either she hath bewitcht me with her words,
    Or Nature makes me suddenly relent.

PUCELL
    Besides, all French and France exclaimes on thee,   1480
    Doubting thy Birth and lawfull Progenie.
    Who ioyn'st thou with, but with a Lordly Nation,
    That will not trust thee, but for profits sake?
    When *Talbot* hath set footing once in France,
    And fashion'd thee that Instrument of Ill,
    Who then, but English *Henry*, will be Lord,
    And thou be thrust out, like a Fugitiue?
    Call we to minde, and marke but this for proofe:
    Was not the Duke of Orleance thy Foe?
    And was he not in England Prisoner?   1490
    But when they heard he was thine Enemie,
    They set him free, without his Ransome pay'd,
    In spight of *Burgonie* and all his friends.
    See then, thou fight'st against thy Countreymen,
    And ioyn'st with them will be thy slaughter-men.
    Come, come, returne; returne thou wandering Lord,
    Charles and the rest will take thee in their armes.

BURGONIE ⌈*aside*⌉
    I am vanquished: these haughtie wordes of hers
    Haue batt'red me like roaring Cannon-shot,
    And made me almost yeeld vpon my knees.   1500
    (*To the others*) Forgiue me Countrey, and sweet
       Countreymen:
    And Lords accept this heartie kind embrace.
    My Forces and my Power of Men are yours.
    So farwell *Talbot*, Ile no longer trust thee.

PUCELL
    Done like a Frenchman: ⌈*aside*⌉ turne and turne
       againe.

CHARLES
    Welcome braue Duke, thy friendship makes vs fresh.

BASTARD
    And doth beget new Courage in our Breasts.

ALANSON
    Pucell hath brauely play'd her part in this,
    And doth deserue a Coronet of Gold.

CHARLES
    Now let vs on, my Lords, and ioyne our Powers,   1510
    And seeke how we may preiudice the Foe.   *Exeunt*

Sc. 21
(3.8)

⌐*Flourish.*⌐ *Enter the King, Gloucester, Winchester,*
Exeter ; Richard Duke of Yorke, Warwicke, and
Vernon, ⌐*with white Roses*⌐ ; *Suffolke, Somerset,*
and Basset, ⌐*with red Roses*⌐ : *To them, with his*
Souldiors, enter Talbot

TALBOT
My gracious Prince, and honorable Peeres,
Hearing of your arriuall in this Realme,
I haue a while giuen Truce vnto my Warres,
To doe my dutie to my Soueraigne.
In signe whereof, this Arme, that hath reclaym'd
To your obedience, fiftie Fortresses,
Twelue Cities, and seuen walled Townes of strength,
Beside fiue hundred Prisoners of esteeme ;

1520
Lets fall his Sword before your Highnesse feet :
And with submissiue loyaltie of heart
Ascribes the Glory of his Conquest got,
First to my God, and next vnto your Grace.
      ⌐*He kneeles*⌐

KING
Is this the Lord *Talbot*, Vnckle *Gloucester*,
That hath so long beene resident in France ?

GLOSTER
Yes, if it please your Maiestie, my Liege.

KING (*to Talbot*)
Welcome braue Captaine, and victorious Lord.
When I was young (as yet I am not old)
I doe remember how my Father said,

1530
A stouter Champion neuer handled Sword.
Long since we were resolued of your truth,
Your faithfull seruice, and your toyle in Warre :
Yet neuer haue you tasted our Reward,
Or beene reguerdon'd with so much as Thanks,
Because till now, we neuer saw your face.
Therefore stand vp,
      Talbot rises
                        and for these good deserts,
We here create you Earle of Shrewsbury,
And in our Coronation take your place.
                  Senet. Exeunt. Manet Vernon and Basset

VERNON
Now Sir, to you that were so hot at Sea,

1540
Disgracing of these Colours that I weare,
In honor of my Noble Lord of Yorke :
Dar'st thou maintaine the former words thou spak'st ?

BASSET
Yes Sir, as well as you dare patronage
The enuious barking of your sawcie Tongue,
Against my Lord the Duke of Somerset.

VERNON
Sirrha, thy Lord I honour as he is.

BASSET
Why, what is he ? as good a man as *Yorke*.

VERNON
Hearke ye : not so : in witnesse take ye that.
      Vernon strikes him

BASSET
Villaine, thou knowest the Law of Armes is such,

That who so drawes a Sword, 'tis present death,   1550
Or else this Blow should broach thy dearest Bloud.
But Ile vnto his Maiestie, and craue,
I may haue libertie to venge this Wrong,
When thou shalt see, Ile meet thee to thy cost.

VERNON
Well miscreant, Ile be there as soone as you,
And after meete you, sooner then you would.   *Exeunt*

⌐*Flourish.*⌐ *Enter King, Glocester, Winchester,*   Sc. 22
Exeter ; Yorke, and Warwicke, with white Roses ;   (4.1)
Suffolke, and Somerset, with red Roses ; Talbot, and
Gouernor of Paris

GLOSTER
Lord Bishop set the Crowne vpon his head.

WINCHESTER
God saue King *Henry* of that name the sixt.
      Winchester crownes the King

GLOSTER
Now Gouernour of Paris take your oath,
That you elect no other King but him ;   1560
Esteeme none Friends, but such as are his Friends,
And none your Foes, but such as shall pretend
Malicious practises against his State :
This shall ye do, so helpe you righteous God.
      Enter Falstaffe with a Letter

FALSTAFFE
My gracious Soueraigne, as I rode from Calice,
To haste vnto your Coronation :
A Letter was deliuer'd to my hands,
      ⌐*He presents the Letter*⌐
Writ to your Grace, from th'Duke of Burgundy.

TALBOT
Shame to the Duke of Burgundy, and thee :
I vow'd (base Knight) when I did meete the next,   1570
To teare the Garter from thy Crauens legge,
      He teares it off
Which I haue done, because (vnworthily)
Thou was't installed in that High Degree.
Pardon me Princely *Henry*, and the rest :
This Dastard, at the battell of *Patay*,
When (but in all) I was six thousand strong,
And that the French were almost ten to one,
Before we met, or that a stroke was giuen,
Like to a trustie Squire, did run away.
In which assault, we lost twelue hundred men.   1580
My selfe, and diuers Gentlemen beside,
Were there surpriz'd, and taken prisoners.
Then iudge (great Lords) if I haue done amisse :
Or whether that such Cowards ought to weare
This Ornament of Knighthood, yea or no ?

GLOSTER
To say the truth, this fact was infamous,
And ill beseeming any common man ;
Much more a Knight, a Captaine, and a Leader.

TALBOT
When first this Order was ordain'd my Lords,
Knights of the Garter were of Noble birth ;   1590
Valiant, and Vertuous, full of haughtie Courage,

Such as were growne to credit by the warres:
Not fearing Death, nor shrinking for Distresse,
But always resolute, in most extreames.
He then, that is not furnish'd in this sort,
Doth but vsurpe the Sacred name of Knight,
Prophaning this most Honourable Order,
And should (if I were worthy to be Iudge)
Be quite degraded, like a Hedge-borne Swaine,

1600 That doth presume to boast of Gentle blood.

KING (to Falstaffe)

Staine to thy Countrymen, thou hear'st thy doom:
Be packing therefore, thou that was't a knight:
Henceforth we banish thee on paine of death.

Exit Falstaffe

And now my Lord Protector, view the Letter
Sent from our Vnckle Duke of Burgundy.

GLOSTER

What meanes his Grace, that he hath chaung'd his
Stile?
No more but plaine and bluntly? (*To the King.*)
Hath he forgot he is his Soueraigne?
Or doth this churlish Superscription

1610 Pretend some alteration in good will?
What's heere? *I haue vpon especiall cause,*
Mou'd with compassion of my Countries wracke,
Together with the pittifull complaints
Of such as your oppression feedes vpon,
Forsaken your pernitious Faction,
And ioyn'd with Charles, the rightfull king of France.
O monstrous Treachery: Can this be so?
That in alliance, amity, and oathes,
There should be found such false dissembling guile?

KING

1620 What? doth my Vnckle Burgundy reuolt?

GLOSTER

He doth my Lord, and is become your foe.

KING

Is that the worst this Letter doth containe?

GLOSTER

It is the worst, and all (my Lord) he writes.

KING

Why then Lord *Talbot* there shal talk with him,
And giue him chasticement for this abuse.
(*To Talbot*) How say you (my Lord) are you not
content?

TALBOT

Content, my Liege? Yes: But y^t I am preuented,
I should haue begg'd I might haue bene employd.

KING

Then gather strength, and march vnto him straight:

1630 Let him perceiue how ill we brooke his Treason,
And what offence it is to flout his Friends.

TALBOT

I go my Lord, in heart desiring still
You may behold confusion of your foes. *Exit*

Enter Vernon wearing a white Rose, and Bassit
wearing a red Rose

VERNON (*to the King*)

Grant me the Combate, gracious Soueraigne.

BASSET (*to the King*)

And me (my Lord) grant me the Combate too.

RICHARD DUKE OF YORKE (*to the King, pointing to Vernon*)

This is my Seruant, heare him Noble Prince.

SOMERSET (*to the King, pointing to Basset*)

And this is mine (sweet *Henry*) fauour him.

KING

Be patient Lords, and giue them leaue to speak.
Say Gentlemen, what makes you thus exclaime,
And wherefore craue you Combate? Or with whom? 1640

VERNON

With him (my Lord) for he hath done me wrong.

BASSET

And I with him, for he hath done me wrong.

KING

What is that wrong, wherof you both complain?
First let me know, and then Ile answer you.

BASSET

Crossing the Sea, from England into France,
This Fellow heere with enuious carping tongue,
Vpbraided me about the Rose I weare,
Saying, the sanguine colour of the Leaues
Did represent my Masters blushing cheekes:
When stubbornly he did repugne the truth, 1650
About a certaine question in the Law,
Argu'd betwixt the Duke of Yorke, and him:
With other vile and ignominious tearmes.
In confutation of which rude reproach,
And in defence of my Lords worthinesse,
I craue the benefit of Law of Armes.

VERNON

And that is my petition (Noble Lord:)
For though he seeme with forged queint conceite
To set a glosse vpon his bold intent,
Yet know (my Lord) I was prouok'd by him, 1660
And he first tooke exceptions at this badge,
Pronouncing that the palenesse of this Flower,
Bewray'd the faintnesse of my Masters heart.

RICHARD DUKE OF YORKE

Will not this malice Somerset be left?

SOMERSET

Your priuate grudge my Lord of York, wil out,
Though ne're so cunningly you smother it.

KING

Good Lord, what madnesse rules in braine-sicke men,
When for so slight and friuolous a cause,
Such factious æmulations shall arise?
Good Cosins both of Yorke and Somerset, 1670
Quiet your selues (I pray) and be at peace.

RICHARD DUKE OF YORKE

Let this dissention first be tried by fight,
And then your Highnesse shall command a Peace.

SOMERSET

The quarrell toucheth none but vs alone,
Betwixt our selues let vs decide it then.

RICHARD DUKE OF YORKE

There is my pledge, accept it Somerset.

VERNON (*to the King*)

Nay, let it rest where it began at first.

BASSET (*to the King*)

    Confirme it so, mine honourable Lord.

GLOSTER

    Confirme it so? Confounded be your strife,

1680   And perish ye with your audacious prate,

    Presumptuous vassals, are you not asham'd

    With this immodest clamorous outrage,

    To trouble and disturbe the King, and Vs?

    And you my Lords, me thinkes you do not well

    To beare with their peruerse Obiections:

    Much lesse to take occasion from their mouthes,

    To raise a mutiny betwixt your selues.

    Let me perswade you take a better course.

EXETER

    It greeues his Highnesse, good my Lords, be Friends.

KING

1690   Come hither you that would be Combatants:

    Henceforth I charge you, as you loue our fauour,

    Quite to forget this Quarrell, and the cause.

    And you my Lords: Remember where we are,

    In France, amongst a fickle wauering Nation:

    If they perceyue dissention in our lookes,

    And that within our selues we disagree;

    How will their grudging stomackes be prouok'd

    To wilfull Disobedience, and Rebell?

    Beside, What infamy will there arise,

1700   When Forraigne Princes shall be certified,

    That for a toy, a thing of no regard,

    King *Henries* Peeres, and cheefe Nobility,

    Destroy'd themselues, and lost the Realme of France?

    Oh thinke vpon the Conquest of my Father,

    My tender yeares, and let vs not forgoe

    That for a trifle, that was bought with blood.

    Let me be Vmper in this doubtfull strife:

    I see no reason if I weare this Rose,

        He takes a red Rose

    That any one should therefore be suspitious

1710   I more incline to Somerset, than Yorke:

    Both are my kinsmen, and I loue them both.

    As well they may vpbray'd me with my Crowne,

    Because (forsooth) the King of Scots is Crown'd.

    But your discretions better can perswade,

    Then I am able to instruct or teach:

    And therefore, as we hither came in peace,

    So let vs still continue peace, and loue.

    Cosin of Yorke, we institute your Grace

    To be our Regent in these parts of France:

1720   And good my Lord of Somerset, vnite

    Your Troopes of horsemen, with his Bands of foote,

    And like true Subiects, sonnes of your Progenitors,

    Go cheerefully together, and digest

    Your angry Choller on your Enemies.

    Our Selfe, my Lord Protector, and the rest,

    After some respit, will returne to Calice;

    From thence to England, where I hope ere long

    To be presented by your Victories,

    With *Charles*, *Alanson*, and that Traiterous rout.

        Flourish. Exeunt. Manet Yorke, Warwick,

                Vernon, Exeter

WARWICKE

    My Lord of Yorke, I promise you the King   1730

    Prettily (me thought) did play the Orator.

RICHARD DUKE OF YORKE

    And so he did, but yet I like it not,

    In that he weares the badge of Somerset.

WARWICKE

    Tush, that was but his fancie, blame him not,

    I dare presume (sweet Prince) he thought no harme.

RICHARD DUKE OF YORKE

    And if I wist he did. But let it rest,

    Other affayres must now be managed.

        Exeunt. Manet Exeter

EXETER

    Well didst thou *Richard* to suppresse thy voice:

    For had the passions of thy heart burst out,

    I feare we should haue seene decipher'd there   1740

    More rancorous spight, more furious raging broyles,

    Then yet can be imagin'd or suppos'd:

    But howsoere, no simple man that sees

    This iarring discord of Nobilitie,

    This shouldering of each other in the Court,

    This factious bandying of their Fauourites,

    But that it doth presage some ill euent.

    'Tis much, when Scepters are in Childrens hands:

    But more, when Enuy breeds vnkinde deuision,

    There comes the ruine, there begins confusion.   *Exit* 1750

    Enter Talbot with Trumpe and Drumme and   Sc. 23

    Souldiers, before Burdeaux   (4.2)

TALBOT

    Go to the Gates of Burdeaux Trumpeter,

    Summon their Generall vnto the Wall.

        The Trumpet sounds a Parley. Enter French Generall

        aloft

    English *Iohn Talbot* (Captaine) calls you forth,

    Seruant in Armes to *Harry* King of England,

    And thus he would. Open your Citie Gates,

    Be humble to vs, call my Soueraigne yours,

    And do him homage as obedient Subiects,

    And Ile withdraw me, and my bloody power.

    But if you frowne vpon this proffer'd Peace,

    You tempt the fury of my three attendants,   1760

    Leane Famine, quartering Steele, and climbing Fire,

    Who in a moment, eeuen with the earth,

    Shall lay your stately, and ayre-brauing Towers,

    If you forsake the offer of their loue.

GENERALL

    Thou ominous and fearefull Owle of death,

    Our Nations terror, and their bloody scourge,

    The period of thy Tyranny approacheth,

    On vs thou canst not enter but by death:

    For I protest we are well fortified,

    And strong enough to issue out and fight.   1770

    If thou retire, the Dolphin well appointed,

    Stands with the snares of Warre to tangle thee.

    On either hand thee, there are squadrons pitcht,

    To wall thee from the liberty of Flight;

And no way canst thou turne thee for redresse,
But death doth front thee with apparant spoyle,
And pale destruction meets thee in the face:
Ten thousand French haue tane the Sacrament,
To vyre their dangerous Artillerie
1780 Vpon no Christian soule but English *Talbot*:
Loe, there thou standst a breathing valiant man
Of an inuincible vnconquer'd spirit:
This is the latest Glorie of thy praise,
That I thy enemy dew thee withall:
For ere the Glasse that now begins to runne,
Finish the processe of his sandy houre,
These eyes that see thee now well coloured,
Shall see thee witherd, bloody, pale, and dead.
            Drum a farre off
Harke, harke, the Dolphins drumme, a warning bell,
1790 Sings heauy Musicke to thy timorous soule,
And mine shall ring thy dire departure out.   *Exit*

TALBOT
He Fables not, I heare the enemie:
Out some light Horsemen, and peruse their Wings.
                        ⌈*Exit one or more*⌉
O negligent and heedlesse Discipline,
How are we park'd and bounded in a pale?
A little Heard of Englands timorous Deere,
Maz'd with a yelping kennell of French Curres.
If we be English Deere, be then in blood,
Not Rascall-like to fall downe with a pinch,
1800 But rather moodie mad, and desperate Stagges,
Turne on the bloody Hounds with heads of Steele,
And make the Cowards stand aloofe at bay:
Sell euery man his life as deere as mine,
And they shall finde deere Deere of vs my Friends.
God, and S. *George*, *Talbot* and Englands right,
Prosper our Colours in this dangerous fight.   *Exeunt*

Sc. 24   *Enter a Messenger that meets Yorke. Enter Yorke*
(4.3)   *with Trumpet, and many Soldiers*
RICHARD DUKE OF YORKE
Are not the speedy scouts return'd againe,
That dog'd the mighty Army of the Dolphin?
MESSENGER
They are return'd my Lord, and giue it out,
1810 That he is march'd to Burdeaux with his power
To fight with *Talbot*: as he march'd along,
By your espyals were discouered
Two mightier Troopes then that the Dolphin led,
Which ioyn'd with him, and made their march for
      Burdeaux.
RICHARD DUKE OF YORKE
A plague vpon that Villaine Somerset,
That thus delayes my promised supply
Of horsemen, that were leuied for this siege.
Renowned *Talbot* doth expect my ayde,
And I am lowted by a Traitor Villaine,
1820 And cannot helpe the noble Cheualier:
God comfort him in this necessity:
If he miscarry, farewell Warres in France.

Enter another Messenger: Sir William Lucie
LUCY
Thou Princely Leader of our English strength,
Neuer so needfull on the earth of France,
Spurre to the rescue of the Noble *Talbot*,
Who now is girdled with a waste of Iron,
And hem'd about with grim destruction:
To Burdeaux warlike Duke, to Burdeaux Yorke,
Else farewell *Talbot*, France, and Englands honor.
RICHARD DUKE OF YORKE
O God, that Somerset who in proud heart   1830
Doth stop my Cornets, were in *Talbots* place,
So should wee saue a valiant Gentleman,
By forfeyting a Traitor, and a Coward:
Mad ire, and wrathfull fury makes me weepe,
That thus we dye, while remisse Traitors sleepe.
LUCY
O send some succour to the distrest Lord.
RICHARD DUKE OF YORKE
He dies, we loose: I breake my warlike word:
We mourne, France smiles: We loose, they dayly get,
All long of this vile Traitor Somerset.
LUCY
Then God take mercy on braue *Talbots* soule,   1840
And on his Sonne yong *Iohn*, who two houres since,
I met in trauaile toward his warlike Father;
This seuen yeeres did not *Talbot* see his sonne,
And now they meete where both their liues are done.
RICHARD DUKE OF YORKE
Alas, what ioy shall noble *Talbot* haue,
To bid his yong sonne welcome to his Graue:
Away, vexation almost stoppes my breath,
That sundred friends greete in the houre of death.
Lucie farewell, no more my fortune can,
But curse the cause I cannot ayde the man.   1850
Maine, *Bloys*, *Poytiers*, and *Toures*, are wonne away,
Long all of Somerset, and his delay.
                        Exeunt. Manet Lucie
LUCY
Thus while the Vulture of sedition,
Feedes in the bosome of such great Commanders,
Sleeping neglection doth betray to losse
The Conquest of our scarse-cold Conqueror,
That euer-liuing man of Memorie,
Henrie the fift: Whiles they each other crosse,
Liues, Honours, Lands, and all, hurrie to losse.   ⌈*Exit*⌉

Enter Somerset with his Armie   Sc. 25
SOMERSET (*to a Captaine*)   (4.4)
It is too late, I cannot send them now: 1860
This expedition was by *Yorke* and *Talbot*,
Too rashly plotted. All our generall force,
Might with a sally of the very Towne
Be buckled with: the ouer-daring *Talbot*
Hath sullied all his glosse of former Honor
By this vnheedfull, desperate, wilde aduenture:
Yorke set him on to fight, and dye in shame,
That *Talbot* dead, great *Yorke* might beare the name.

⌈*Enter Lucie*⌉

CAPTAINE
    Heere is Sir *William Lucie*, who with me
1870 Set from our ore-matcht forces forth for ayde.

SOMERSET
    How now Sir *William*, whether were you sent?

LUCY
    Whether my Lord, from bought & sold L. *Talbot*,
    Who ring'd about with bold aduersitie,
    Cries out for noble Yorke and Somerset,
    To beate assayling death from his weake legions,
    And whiles the honourable Captaine there
    Drops bloody swet from his warre-wearied limbes,
    And vnaduantagd lingring lookes for rescue,
    You his false hopes, the trust of Englands honor,
1880 Keepe off aloofe with worthlesse emulation:
    Let not your priuate discord keepe away
    The leuied succours that should lend him ayde,
    While he renowned Noble Gentleman
    Yeeld vp his life vnto a world of oddes.
    Orleance the Bastard, *Charles*, and *Burgundie*,
    Alanson, *Reignard*, compasse him about,
    And *Talbot* perisheth by your default.

SOMERSET
    Yorke set him on, Yorke should haue sent him ayde.

LUCY
    And Yorke as fast vpon your Grace exclaimes,
1890 Swearing that you with-hold his leuied horse,
    Collected for this expidition.

SOMERSET
    York lyes: He might haue sent, & had the Horse:
    I owe him little Dutie, and lesse Loue,
    And take foule scorne to fawne on him by sending.

LUCY
    The fraud of England, not the force of France,
    Hath now intrapt the Noble-minded *Talbot*:
    Neuer to England shall he beare his life,
    But dies betraid to fortune by your strife.

SOMERSET
    Come go, I will dispatch the Horsemen strait:
1900 Within six houres, they will be at his ayde.

LUCY
    Too late comes rescue, he is tane or slaine,
    For flye he could not, if he would haue fled:
    And flye would *Talbot* neuer though he might.

SOMERSET
    If he be dead, braue *Talbot* then adieu.

LUCY
    His Fame liues in the world. His Shame in you.
                   Exeunt ⌈*seuerally*⌉

Sc. 26   *Enter Talbot and his Sonne Iohn*
(4.5) **TALBOT**
    O yong *Iohn Talbot*, I did send for thee
    To tutor thee in stratagems of Warre,
    That *Talbots* name might be in thee reuiu'd,
    When saplesse Age, and weake vnable limbes
1910 Should bring thy Father to his drooping Chaire.

    But O malignant and ill-boading Starres,
    Now thou art come vnto a Feast of death,
    A terrible and vnauoyded danger:
    Therefore deere Boy, mount on my swiftest horse,
    And Ile direct thee how thou shalt escape
    By sodaine flight. Come, dally not, be gone.

IOHN
    Is my name *Talbot*? and am I your Sonne?
    And shall I flye? O, if you loue my Mother,
    Dishonor not her Honorable Name,
    To make a Bastard, and a Slaue of me: 1920
    The World will say, he is not *Talbots* blood,
    That basely fled, when Noble *Talbot* stood.

TALBOT
    Flye, to reuenge my death, if I be slaine.

IOHN
    He that flyes so, will ne're returne againe.

TALBOT
    If we both stay, we both are sure to dye.

IOHN
    Then let me stay, and Father doe you flye:
    Your losse is great, so your regard should be;
    My worth vnknowne, no losse is knowne in me.
    Vpon my death, the French can little boast;
    In yours they will, in you all hopes are lost.   1930
    Flight cannot stayne the Honor you haue wonne,
    But mine it will, that no Exploit haue done.
    You fled for Vantage, euery one will sweare:
    But if I bow, they'le say it was for feare.
    There is no hope that euer I will stay,
    If the first howre I shrinke and run away:
    Here on my knee I begge Mortalitie,
    Rather then Life, preseru'd with Infamie.

TALBOT
    Shall all thy Mothers hopes lye in one Tombe?

IOHN
    I, rather then Ile shame my Mothers Wombe.   1940

TALBOT
    Vpon my Blessing I command thee goe.

IOHN
    To fight I will, but not to flye the Foe.

TALBOT
    Part of thy Father may be sau'd in thee.

IOHN
    No part of him, but will be shamd in mee.

TALBOT
    Thou neuer hadst Renowne, nor canst not lose it.

IOHN
    Yes, your renowned Name: shall flight abuse it?

TALBOT
    Thy Fathers charge shal cleare thee from yᵗ staine.

IOHN
    You cannot witnesse for me, being slaine.
    If Death be so apparant, then both flye.

TALBOT
    And leaue my followers here to fight and dye?   1950
    My Age was neuer tainted with such shame.

IOHN
    And shall my Youth be guiltie of such blame?

No more can I be seuerd from your side,
Then can your selfe, your selfe in twaine diuide:
Stay, goe, doe what you will, the like doe I;
For liue I will not, if my Father dye.

TALBOT

Then here I take my leaue of thee, faire Sonne,
Borne to eclipse thy Life this afternoone:
Come, side by side, together liue and dye,
1960   And Soule with Soule from France to Heauen flye.

                                                    Exeunt

Sc. 27   *Alarum: Excursions, wherein Talbots Sonne Iohn is*
(4.6)   *hemm'd about by French Souldiers, and Talbot*
            rescues him. ⌐*The English driue off the French*⌐

TALBOT

Saint *George*, and Victory; fight Souldiers, fight:
The Regent hath with *Talbot* broke his word,
And left vs to the rage of France his Sword.
Where is *Iohn Talbot*? (*to Iohn*) pawse, and take thy
          breath,
I gaue thee Life, and rescu'd thee from Death.

IOHN

O twice my Father, twice am I thy Sonne:
The Life thou gau'st me first, was lost and done,
Till with thy Warlike Sword, despight of Fate,
To my determin'd time thou gau'st new date.

TALBOT

1970   When frõ the *Dolphins* Crest thy Sword struck fire,
It warm'd thy Fathers heart with prowd desire
Of bold-fac't Victorie. Then Leaden Age,
Quicken'd with Youthfull Spleene, and Warlike Rage,
Beat downe *Alanson*, *Orleance*, *Burgundie*,
And from the Pride of Gallia rescued thee.
The irefull Bastard *Orleance*, that drew blood
From thee my Boy, and had the Maidenhood
Of thy first fight, I soone encountered,
And interchanging blowes, I quickly shed
1980   Some of his Bastard blood, and in disgrace
Bespoke him thus: Contaminated, base,
And mis-begotten blood, I spill of thine,
Meane and right poore, for that pure blood of mine,
Which thou didst force from *Talbot*, my braue Boy.
Here purposing the Bastard to destroy,
Came in strong rescue. Speake thy Fathers care:
Art thou not wearie, *Iohn*? How do'st thou fare?
Wilt thou yet leaue the Battaile, Boy, and flie,
Now thou art seal'd the Sonne of Chiualrie?
1990   Flye, to reuenge my death when I am dead,
The helpe of one stands me in little stead.
Oh, too much folly is it, well I wot,
To hazard all our liues in one small Boat.
If I to day dye not with Frenchmens Rage,
To morrow I shall dye with mickle Age.
By me they nothing gaine, and if I stay,
'Tis but the shortning of my Life one day.
In thee thy Mother dyes, our Households Name,
My Deaths Reuenge, thy Youth, and Englands Fame:
2000   All these, and more, we hazard by thy stay;
All these are sau'd, if thou wilt flye away.

IOHN

The Sword of *Orleance* hath not made me smart,
These words of yours draw Life-blood from my Heart.
On that aduantage, bought with such a shame,
To saue a paltry Life, and slay bright Fame,
Before young *Talbot* from old *Talbot* flye,
The Coward Horse that beares me, fall and dye:
And like me to the pesant Boyes of France,
To be Shames scorne, and subiect of Mischance.
Surely, by all the Glorie you haue wonne,   2010
And if I flye, I am not *Talbots* Sonne.
Then talke no more of flight, it is no boot,
If Sonne to *Talbot*, dye at *Talbots* foot.

TALBOT

Then follow thou thy desp'rate Syre of Creet,
Thou *Icarus*, thy Life to me is sweet:
If thou wilt fight, fight by thy Fathers side,
And commendable prou'd, let's dye in pride.   *Exeunt*

Alarum. Excursions. Enter old Talbot led by a   Sc. 28
Seruant   (4.7)

TALBOT

Where is my other Life? mine owne is gone.
O, where's young *Talbot*? where is valiant *Iohn*?
Triumphant Death, smear'd with Captiuitie,   2020
Young *Talbots* Valour makes me smile at thee.
When he perceiu'd me shrinke, and on my Knee,
His bloodie Sword he brandisht ouer mee,
And like a hungry Lyon did commence
Rough deeds of Rage, and sterne Impatience:
But when my angry Guardant stood alone,
Tendring my ruine, and assayl'd of none,
Dizzie-ey'd Furie, and great rage of Heart,
Suddenly made him from my side to start
Into the clustring Battaile of the French: 2030
And in that Sea of Blood, my Boy did drench
His ouer-mounting Spirit; and there di'de
My *Icarus*, my Blossome, in his pride.

          Enter English Souldiers with Iohn Talbots body,
          borne

SERUANT

O my deare Lord, loe where your Sonne is borne.

TALBOT

Thou antique Death, which laugh'st vs here to scorn,
Anon from thy insulting Tyrannie,
Coupled in bonds of perpetuitie,
Two *Talbots* winged through the lither Skie,
In thy despight shall scape Mortalitie.
(*To Iohn*) O thou whose wounds become hard fauourd
          death,   2040
Speake to thy father, ere thou yeeld thy breath,
Braue death by speaking, whither he will or no:
Imagine him a Frenchman, and thy Foe.
Poore Boy, he smiles, me thinkes, as who should say,
Had Death bene French, then Death had dyed to day.
Come, come, and lay him in his Fathers armes,
          Souldiers lay Iohn in Talbots armes
My spirit can no longer beare these harmes.

Souldiers adieu: I haue what I would haue,
Now my old armes are yong *Iohn Talbots* graue.
            Dyes. ⌈*Alarum.*⌉ *Exeunt, leauing the bodyes*
        Enter Charles, Alanson, Burgundie, Bastard, and
        Pucell

CHARLES

2050   Had Yorke and Somerset brought rescue in,
        We should haue found a bloody day of this.

BASTARD

        How the yong whelpe of *Talbots* raging wood,
        Did flesh his punie-sword in Frenchmens blood.

PUCELL

        Once I encountred him, and thus I said:
        Thou Maiden youth, be vanquisht by a Maide.
        But with a proud Maiesticall high scorne
        He answer'd thus: Yong *Talbot* was not borne
        To be the pillage of a Giglot Wench:
        So rushing in the bowels of the French,
2060   He left me proudly, as vnworthy fight.

BURGONIE

        Doubtlesse he would haue made a noble Knight:
        See where he lyes inherced in the armes
        Of the most bloody Nursser of his harmes.

BASTARD

        Hew them to peeces, hack their bones assunder,
        Whose life was Englands glory, Gallia's wonder.

CHARLES

        Oh no forbeare: For that which we haue fled
        During the life, let vs not wrong it dead.
            Enter Lucie ⌈*with a French Herald*⌉

LUCY

        Herald, conduct me to the Dolphins Tent,
        To know who hath obtain'd the glory of the day.

CHARLES

2070   On what submissiue message art thou sent?

LUCY

        Submission Dolphin? Tis a meere French word:
        We English Warriours wot not what it meanes.
        I come to know what Prisoners thou hast tane,
        And to suruey the bodies of the dead.

CHARLES

        For prisoners askst thou? Hell our prison is.
        But tell me whom thou seek'st?

LUCY

        But where's the great Alcides of the field,
        Valiant Lord *Talbot* Earle of Shrewsbury?
        Created for his rare successe in Armes,
2080   Great Earle of *Washford*, *Waterford*, and *Valence*,
        Lord *Talbot* of *Goodrig* and *Vrchinfield*,
        Lord *Strange* of *Blackmere*, Lord *Verdon* of *Alton*,
        Lord *Cromwell* of *Wingefield*, Lord *Furniuall* of *Sheffeild*,
        The thrice victorious Lord of *Falconbridge*,
        Knight of the Noble Order of *S. George*,
        Worthy S. *Michael*, and the *Golden Fleece*,
        Great Marshall to *Henry* the sixt,
        Of all his Warres within the Realme of France.

PUCELL

        Heere's a silly stately stile indeede:

The Turke that two and fiftie Kingdomes hath,   2090
Writes not so tedious a Stile as this.
Him that thou magnifi'st with all these Titles,
Stinking and fly-blowne lyes heere at our feete.

LUCY

Is *Talbot* slaine, the Frenchmens only Scourge,
Your Kingdomes terror, and blacke *Nemesis*?
Oh were mine eye-balles into Bullets turn'd,
That I in rage might shoot them at your faces.
Oh, that I could but call these dead to life,
It were enough to fright the Realme of France.
Were but his Picture left amongst you here,   2100
It would amaze the prowdest of you all.
Giue me their Bodyes, that I may beare them hence,
And giue them Buriall, as beseemes their worth.

PUCELL (*to Charles*)

I thinke this vpstart is old *Talbots* Ghost,
He speakes with such a proud commanding spirit:
For Gods sake let him haue them, to keepe them here,
They would but stinke, and putrifie the ayre.

CHARLES Go take their bodies hence.

LUCY

Ile beare them hence: but from their ashes shal be
        reard
A Phœnix that shall make all France affear'd.   2110

CHARLES

So we be rid of them, do with them what yᵘ wilt.
        ⌈*Exeunt Lucie and Herald with bodyes*⌉
And now to Paris in this conquering vaine,
All will be ours, now bloody *Talbots* slaine.   *Exeunt*

        SENNET. *Enter King, Glocester, and Exeter* ⌈*and*   Sc. 29
            others⌉   (5.1)

KING (*to Gloster*)

Haue you perus'd the Letters from the Pope,
The Emperor, and the Earle of Arminack?

GLOSTER

I haue my Lord, and their intent is this,
They humbly sue vnto your Excellence,
To haue a godly peace concluded of,
Betweene the Realmes of England, and of France.

KING

How doth your Grace affect their motion?   2120

GLOSTER

Well (my good Lord) and as the only meanes
To stop effusion of our Christian blood,
And stablish quietnesse on euery side.

KING

I marry Vnckle, for I always thought
It was both impious and vnnaturall,
That such immanity and bloody strife
Should reigne among Professors of one Faith.

GLOSTER

Beside my Lord, the sooner to effect,
And surer binde this knot of amitie,
The Earle of Arminacke neere knit to *Charles*,   2130
A man of great Authoritie in France,

Proffers his onely daughter to your Grace,
In marriage, with a large and sumptuous Dowrie.

KING

Marriage Vnckle? Alas my yeares are yong:
And fitter is my studie, and my Bookes,
Than wanton dalliance with a Paramour.
Yet call th'Embassadors,   ⌐Exit one or more⌐
                         and as you please,
So let them haue their answeres euery one:
I shall be well content with any choyce
2140   Tends to Gods glory, and my Countries weale.
         Enter Winchester in Cardinals habite, and three
         Ambassadors (one a Papal Legate)

EXETER *(aside)*

What, is my Lord of *Winchester* install'd,
And call'd vnto a Cardinalls degree?
Then I perceiue, that will be verified
Henry the Fift did sometime prophesie.
If once he come to be a Cardinall,
Hee'l make his cap coequall with the Crowne.

KING

My Lords Ambassadors, your seuerall suites
Haue bin consider'd and debated on,
Your purpose is both good and reasonable:
2150   And therefore are we certainly resolu'd,
To draw conditions of a friendly peace,
Which by my Lord of Winchester we meane
Shall be transported presently to France.

GLOSTER ⌐*to Ambassadors*⌐

And for the proffer of my Lord your Master,
I haue inform'd his Highnesse so at large,
As liking of the Ladies vertuous gifts,
Her Beauty, and the valew of her Dower,
He doth intend she shall be Englands Queene.

KING ⌐*to Ambassadors*⌐

In argument and proofe of which contract,
2160   Beare her this Iewell, pledge of my affection.
(To Gloster) And so my Lord Protector see them
         guarded,
And safely brought to *Douer*, wherein ship'd
Commit them to the fortune of the sea.
         Exeunt ⌐seuerally⌐. Manet Winchester and
                                      ⌐*Legate*⌐

WINCHESTER

Stay my Lord Legate, you shall first receiue
The summe of money which I promised
Should be deliuerd to his Holinesse,
For cloathing me in these graue Ornaments.

LEGATE

I will attend vpon your Lordships leysure.   ⌐*Exit*⌐

WINCHESTER

Now Winchester will not submit, I trow,
2170   Or be inferiour to the proudest Peere;
Humfrey of Gloster, thou shalt well perceiue,
That nor in birth, or for authoritie,
The Bishop will be ouer-borne by thee:
Ile either make thee stoope, and bend thy knee,
Or sacke this Country with a mutiny.   ⌐*Exit*⌐

Enter Charles ⌐reading a Letter⌐, Burgundy,   Sc. 30
Alanson, Bastard, Reignier, and Ione le Pucell   (5.2)

CHARLES

These newes (my Lords) may cheere our drooping
         spirits:
'Tis said, the stout Parisians do reuolt,
And turne againe vnto the warlike French.

ALANSON

Then march to Paris Royall *Charles* of France,
And keepe not backe your powers in dalliance.   2180

PUCELL

Peace be amongst them if they turne to vs,
Else ruine combate with their Pallaces.
         Enter Scout

SCOUT

Successe vnto our valiant Generall,
And happinesse to his accomplices.

CHARLES

What tidings send our Scouts? I prethee speak.

SCOUT

The English Army that diuided was
Into two parties, is now conioyn'd in one,
And meanes to giue you battell presently.

CHARLES

Somewhat too sodaine Sirs, the warning is,
But we will presently prouide for them.   2190

BURGONIE

I trust the Ghost of *Talbot* is not there.

⌐PUCELL⌐

Now he is gone my Lord, you neede not feare.
Of all base passions, Feare is most accurst.
Command the Conquest *Charles*, it shall be thine:
Let *Henry* fret, and all the world repine.

CHARLES

Then on my Lords, and France be fortunate.   *Exeunt*

Alarum. Excursions. Enter Ione le Pucell   Sc. 31
PUCELL   (5.3)

The Regent conquers, and the Frenchmen flye.
Now helpe ye charming Spelles and Periapts,
And ye choise spirits that admonish me,
And giue me signes of future accidents.   2200
         Thunder
You speedy helpers, that are substitutes
Vnder the Lordly Monarch of the North,
Appeare, and ayde me in this enterprize.
         Enter Fiends
This speede and quicke appearance argues proofe
Of your accustom'd diligence to me.
Now ye Familiar Spirits, that are cull'd
Out of the powerfull Regions vnder earth,
Helpe me this once, that France may get the field.
         They walke, and speake not
Oh hold me not with silence ouer-long:
Where I was wont to feed you with my blood,   2210
Ile lop a member off, and giue it you,
In earnest of a further benefit:
So you do condiscend to helpe me now.

They hang their heads
No hope to haue redresse? My body shall
Pay recompence, if you will graunt my suite.
      They shake their heads
Cannot my body, nor blood-sacrifice,
Intreate you to your wonted furtherance?
Then take my soule; my body, soule, and all,
Before that England giue the French the foyle.
      They depart
2220   See, they forsake me. Now the time is come,
That France must vale her lofty plumed Crest,
And let her head fall into Englands lappe.
My ancient Incantations are too weake,
And hell too strong for me to buckle with:
Now France, thy glory droopeth to the dust.   *Exit*

Sc. 32   *Excursions. Burgundie and Yorke fight hand to*
(5.4)   *hand. French flye. Pucell is taken*
RICHARD DUKE OF YORKE
      Damsell of France, I thinke I haue you fast,
      Vnchaine your spirits now with spelling Charmes,
      And try if they can gaine your liberty.
      A goodly prize, fit for the diuels grace.
      ⌈*To his Souldiers*⌉ See how the vgly Witch doth bend
2230   her browes,
      As if with *Circe*, she would change my shape.
PUCELL
      Chang'd to a worser shape thou canst not be.
RICHARD DUKE OF YORKE
      Oh, *Charles* the Dolphin is a proper man,
      No shape but his can please your dainty eye.
PUCELL
      A plaguing mischeefe light on *Charles*, and thee,
      And may ye both be sodainly surpriz'd
      By bloudy hands, in sleeping on your beds.
RICHARD DUKE OF YORKE
      Fell banning Hagge, Inchantresse hold thy tongue.
PUCELL
      I prethee giue me leaue to curse awhile.
RICHARD DUKE OF YORKE
2240   Curse Miscreant, when thou comest to the stake.
                                                    Exeunt

Sc. 33   *Alarum. Enter Suffolke with Margaret in his hand*
(5.5) SUFFOLKE
      Be what thou wilt, thou art my prisoner.
            Gazes on her
      Oh Fairest Beautie, do not feare, nor flye:
      For I will touch thee but with reuerend hands,
      And lay them gently on thy tender side.
      I kisse these fingers for eternall peace,
      Who art thou, say? that I may honor thee.
MARGARET
      Margaret my name, and daughter to a King,
      The King of Naples, who so ere thou art.
SUFFOLKE
      An Earle I am, and Suffolke am I call'd.
2250   Be not offended Natures myracle,

Thou art alotted to be tane by me:
So doth the Swan his downie Signets saue,
Keeping them prisoner vnderneath his wings:
Yet if this seruile vsage once offend,
Go, and be free againe, as Suffolkes friend.
      She is going
Oh stay: (*aside*) I haue no power to let her passe,
My hand would free her, but my heart sayes no.
As playes the Sunne vpon the glassie streame,
Twinkling another counterfetted beame,
So seemes this gorgeous beauty to mine eyes.   2260
Faine would I woe her, yet I dare not speake:
Ile call for Pen and Inke, and write my minde:
Fye *De la Pole*, disable not thy selfe:
Hast not a Tongue? Is she not heere to heere?
Wilt thou be daunted at a Womans sight?
I: Beauties Princely Maiesty is such,
'Confounds the tongue, and makes the senses rough.
MARGARET
      Say Earle of Suffolke, if thy name be so,
      What ransome must I pay before I passe?
      For I perceiue I am thy prisoner.   2270
SUFFOLKE (*aside*)
      How canst thou tell she will deny thy suite,
      Before thou make a triall of her loue?
MARGARET
      Why speak'st thou not? What ransom must I pay?
SUFFOLKE (*aside*)
      She's beautifull; and therefore to be Wooed:
      She is a Woman; therefore to be Wonne.
MARGARET
      Wilt thou accept of ransome, yea or no?
SUFFOLKE (*aside*)
      Fond man, remember that thou hast a wife,
      Then how can *Margaret* be thy Paramour?
MARGARET (*aside*)
      I were best to leaue him, for he will not heare.
SUFFOLKE (*aside*)
      There all is marr'd: there lies a cooling card.   2280
MARGARET (*aside*)
      He talkes at randon: sure the man is mad.
SUFFOLKE (*aside*)
      And yet a dispensation may bee had.
MARGARET
      And yet I would that you would answer me.
SUFFOLKE (*aside*)
      Ile win this Lady *Margaret*. For whom?
      Why for my King: Tush, that's a woodden thing.
MARGARET (*aside*)
      He talkes of wood: It is some Carpenter.
SUFFOLKE (*aside*)
      Yet so my fancy may be satisfied,
      And peace established betweene these Realmes.
      But there remaines a scruple in that too:
      For though her Father be the King of *Naples*,   2290
      Duke of *Aniou* and *Mayne*, yet is he poore,
      And our Nobility will scorne the match.
MARGARET
      Heare ye Captaine? Are you not at leysure?

SUFFOLKE (*aside*)
  It shall be so, disdaine they ne're so much:
  Henry is youthfull, and will quickly yeeld.
  (*To Margaret*) Madam, I haue a secret to reueale.
MARGARET (*aside*)
  What though I be inthral'd, he seems a knight
  And will not any way dishonor me.
SUFFOLKE
  Lady, vouchsafe to listen what I say.
MARGARET (*aside*)
2300 Perhaps I shall be rescu'd by the French,
  And then I need not craue his curtesie.
SUFFOLKE
  Sweet Madam, giue me hearing in a cause.
MARGARET (*aside*)
  Tush, women haue bene captiuate ere now.
SUFFOLKE Lady, wherefore talke you so?
MARGARET
  I cry you mercy, 'tis but *Quid* for *Quo*.
SUFFOLKE
  Say gentle Princesse, would you not suppose
  Your bondage happy, to be made a Queene?
MARGARET
  To be a Queene in bondage, is more vile,
  Than is a slaue, in base seruility:
  For Princes should be free.
2310 SUFFOLKE   And so shall you,
  If happy Englands Royall King be free.
MARGARET
  Why what concernes his freedome vnto mee?
SUFFOLKE
  Ile vndertake to make thee *Henries* Queene,
  To put a Golden Scepter in thy hand,
  And set a precious Crowne vpon thy head,
  If thou wilt condiscend to be my—
MARGARET   What?
SUFFOLKE His loue.
MARGARET
  I am vnworthy to be *Henries* wife.
SUFFOLKE
  No gentle Madam, I vnworthy am
2320 To woe so faire a Dame to be his wife,
  (*Aside*) And haue no portion in the choice my selfe.
  How say you Madam, are ye so content?
MARGARET
  And if my Father please, I am content.
SUFFOLKE
  Then call our Captaines and our Colours forth,
    ⌈*Enter Captaines, Colours, and Trumpets*⌉
  And Madam, at your Fathers Castle walles,
  Wee'l craue a parley, to conferre with him.
      Sound a Parley. Enter Reignier on the Walles
  See *Reignier* see, thy daughter prisoner.
REIGNIER
  To whom?
SUFFOLKE   To me.
REIGNIER   Suffolke, what remedy?
  I am a Souldier, and vnapt to weepe,
2330 Or to exclaime on Fortunes ficklenesse.

SUFFOLKE
  Yes, there is remedy enough my Lord,
  Assent, and for thy Honor giue consent,
  Thy daughter shall be wedded to my King,
  Whom I with paine haue wooed and wonne thereto:
  And this her easie held imprisonment,
  Hath gain'd thy daughter Princely libertie.
REIGNIER
  Speakes Suffolke as he thinkes?
SUFFOLKE   Faire *Margaret* knowes,
  That Suffolke doth not flatter, face, or faine.
REIGNIER
  Vpon thy Princely warrant, I descend,
  To giue thee answer of thy iust demand.   2340
SUFFOLKE
  And heere I will expect thy comming.
                    ⌈*Exit Reignier aboue*⌉
        Trumpets sound. Enter Reignier
REIGNIER
  Welcome braue Earle into our Territories,
  Command in *Aniou* what your Honor pleases.
SUFFOLKE
  Thankes *Reignier*, happy for so sweet a Childe,
  Fit to be made companion with a King:
  What answer makes your Grace vnto my suite?
REIGNIER
  Since thou dost daigne to woe her little worth,
  To be the Princely Bride of such a Lord:
  Vpon condition I may quietly
  Enioy mine owne, the Countrys *Maine* and *Aniou*,   2350
  Free from oppression, or the stroke of Warre,
  My daughter shall be *Henries*, if he please.
SUFFOLKE
  That is her ransome, I deliuer her,
  And those two Counties I will vndertake
  Your Grace shall well and quietly enioy.
REIGNIER
  And I againe in *Henries* Royall name,
  As Deputy vnto that gracious King,
  Giue thee her hand for signe of plighted faith.
SUFFOLKE
  Reignier of France, I giue thee Kingly thankes,
  Because this is in Trafficke of a King.   2360
  (*Aside*) And yet me thinkes I could be well content
  To be mine owne Atturney in this case.
  (*To Reignier*) Ile ouer then to England with this newes,
  And make this marriage to be solemniz'd:
  So farewell *Reignier*, set this Diamond safe
  In Golden Pallaces as it becomes.
REIGNIER
  I do embrace thee, as I would embrace
  The Christian Prince King *Henrie* were he heere.
MARGARET (*to Suffolke*)
  Farewell my Lord, good wishes, praise, & praiers,
  Shall Suffolke euer haue of *Margaret*.   2370
      Shee is going
SUFFOLKE
  Farwell sweet Madam: but hearke you *Margaret*,
  No Princely commendations to my King?

MARGARET

    Such commendations as becomes a Maide,
    A Virgin, and his Seruant, say to him.

SUFFOLKE

    Words sweetly plac'd, and modestlie directed,
       ⌈*Shee is going*⌉
    But Madame, I must trouble you againe,
    No louing Token to his Maiestie?

MARGARET

    Yes, my good Lord, a pure vnspotted heart,
    Neuer yet taint with loue, I send the King.

2380 SUFFOLKE And this withall.
       Kisse her

MARGARET

    That for thy selfe, I will not so presume,
    To send such peeuish tokens to a King.
       ⌈*Exeunt Reignier and Margaret*⌉

SUFFOLKE ⌈*aside*⌉

    Oh wert thou for my selfe: but *Suffolke* stay,
    Thou mayest not wander in that Labyrinth,
    There Minotaurs and vgly Treasons lurke.
    Solicite *Henry* with her wonderous praise,
    Bethinke thee on her Vertues that surmount,
    Mad naturall Graces that extinguish Art,
    Repeate their semblance often on the Seas,
2390   That when thou com'st to kneele at *Henries* feete,
    Thou mayest bereaue him of his wits with wonder.
       ⌈*Exeunt*⌉

Sc. 34   *Enter Yorke, Warwicke, Shepheard*
(5.6) RICHARD DUKE OF YORKE

    Bring forth that Sorceresse condemn'd to burne.
       ⌈*Enter Pucell, guarded*⌉

SHEPHEARD

    Ah *Ione*, this kils thy Fathers heart out-right,
    Haue I sought euery Country farre and neere,
    And now it is my chance to finde thee out,
    Must I behold thy timelesse cruell death:
    Ah *Ione*, sweet daughter *Ione*, Ile die with thee.

PUCELL

    Decrepit Miser, base ignoble Wretch,
    I am descended of a gentler blood.
2400   Thou art no Father, nor no Friend of mine.

SHEPHEARD

    Out, out: My Lords, and please you, 'tis not so:
    I did beget her, all the Parish knowes:
    Her Mother liueth yet, can testifie
    She was the first fruite of my Bach'ler-ship.

WARWICKE (*to Pucell*)

    Gracelesse, wilt thou deny thy Parentage?

RICHARD DUKE OF YORKE

    This argues what her kinde of life hath beene,
    Wicked and vile, and so her death concludes.

SHEPHEARD

    Fye *Ione*, that thou wilt be so obstacle:
    God knowes, thou art a collop of my flesh,
2410   And for thy sake haue I shed many a teare:
    Deny me not, I prythee, gentle *Ione*.

PUCELL

    Pezant auant. (*To the English*) You haue suborn'd this
      man
    Of purpose, to obscure my Noble birth.

SHEPHEARD (*to the English*)

    'Tis true, I gaue a Noble to the Priest,
    The morne that I was wedded to her mother.
    (*To Pucell*) Kneele downe and take my blessing, good
      my Gyrle.
    Wilt thou not stoope? Now cursed be the time
    Of thy natiuitie: I would the Milke
    Thy mother gaue thee when thou suck'st her brest,
    Had bin a little Rats-bane for thy sake.   2420
    Or else, when thou didst keepe my Lambes a-field,
    I wish some rauenous Wolfe had eaten thee.
    Doest thou deny thy Father, cursed Drab?
    (*To the English*) O burne her, burne her, hanging is
      too good.   *Exit*

RICHARD DUKE OF YORKE (*to guards*)

    Take her away, for she hath liu'd too long,
    To fill the world with vicious qualities.

PUCELL

    First let me tell you whom you haue condemn'd;
    Not one begotten of a Shepheard Swaine,
    But issued from the Progeny of Kings.
    Vertuous and Holy, chosen from aboue,   2430
    By inspiration of Celestiall Grace,
    To worke exceeding myracles on earth.
    I neuer had to do with wicked Spirits.
    But you that are polluted with your lustes,
    Stain'd with the guiltlesse blood of Innocents,
    Corrupt and tainted with a thousand Vices:
    Because you want the grace that others haue,
    You iudge it straight a thing impossible
    To compasse Wonders, but by helpe of diuels.
    No, misconceyued *Ione* of *Arce* hath beene   2440
    A Virgin from her tender infancie,
    Chaste, and immaculate in very thought,
    Whose Maiden-blood thus rigorously effus'd,
    Will cry for Vengeance, at the Gates of Heauen.

RICHARD DUKE OF YORKE

    I, I: (*to guards*) away with her to execution.

WARWICKE (*to guards*)

    And hearke ye sirs: because she is a Maide,
    Spare for no Faggots, let there be enow:
    Place barrelles of pitch vpon the fatall stake,
    That so her torture may be shortened.

PUCELL

    Will nothing turne your vnrelenting hearts?   2450
    Then *Ione* discouer thine infirmity,
    That warranteth by Law, to be thy priuiledge.
    I am with childe ye bloody Homicides:
    Murther not then the Fruite within my Wombe,
    Although ye hale me to a violent death.

RICHARD DUKE OF YORKE

    Now heauen forfend, the holy Maid with child?

WARWICKE (*to Pucell*)

    The greatest miracle that ere ye wrought.
    Is all your strict precisenesse come to this?

RICHARD DUKE OF YORKE

    She and the Dolphin haue bin ingling,

2460   I did imagine what would be her refuge.

WARWICKE

    Well go too, we will haue no Bastards liue,

    Especially since *Charles* must Father it.

PUCELL

    You are deceyu'd, my childe is none of his,

    It was *Alanson* that inioy'd my loue.

RICHARD DUKE OF YORKE

    Alanson that notorious Macheuile?

    It dyes, and if it had a thousand liues.

PUCELL

    Oh giue me leaue, I haue deluded you,

    'Twas neyther *Charles*, nor yet the Duke I nam'd,

    But *Reignier* King of *Naples* that preuayl'd.

WARWICKE

2470   A married man, that's most intollerable.

RICHARD DUKE OF YORKE

    Why here's a Gyrle: I think she knowes not wel

    (There were so many) whom she may accuse.

WARWICKE

    It's signe she hath beene liberall and free.

RICHARD DUKE OF YORKE

    And yet forsooth she is a Virgin pure.

    (*To Pucell*) Strumpet, thy words condemne thy Brat,

        and thee.

    Vse no intreaty, for it is in vaine.

PUCELL

    Then lead me hence: with whom I leaue my curse.

    May neuer glorious Sunne reflex his beames

    Vpon the Countrey where you make abode:

2480   But darknesse, and the gloomy shade of death

    Inuiron you, till Mischeefe and Dispaire,

    Driue you to break your necks, or hang your selues.

        Enter Winchester

RICHARD DUKE OF YORKE (*to Pucell*)

    Breake thou in peeces, and consume to ashes,

    Thou fowle accursed minister of Hell.

              ⌈*Exit Pucell, guarded*⌉

WINCHESTER

    Lord Regent, I do greete your Excellence

    With Letters of Commission from the King.

    For know my Lords, the States of Christendome,

    Mou'd with remorse of these out-ragious broyles,

    Haue earnestly implor'd a generall peace,

2490   Betwixt our Nation, and the aspyring French;

    And heere at hand, the Dolphin and his Traine

    Approacheth, to conferre about some matter.

RICHARD DUKE OF YORKE

    Is all our trauell turn'd to this effect,

    After the slaughter of so many Peeres,

    So many Captaines, Gentlemen, and Soldiers,

    That in this quarrell haue beene ouerthrowne,

    And sold their bodyes for their Countryes benefit,

    Shall we at last conclude effeminate peace?

    Haue we not lost most part of all the Townes,

2500   By Treason, Falshood, and by Treacherie,

    Our great Progenitors had conquered:

    Oh Warwicke, Warwicke, I foresee with greefe

    The vtter losse of all the Realme of France.

WARWICKE

    Be patient Yorke, if we conclude a Peace

    It shall be with such strict and seuere Couenants,

    As little shall the Frenchmen gaine thereby.

        Enter Charles, Alanson, Bastard, Reignier

CHARLES

    Since Lords of England, it is thus agreed,

    That peacefull truce shall be proclaim'd in France,

    We come to be informed by your selues,

    What the conditions of that league must be.   2510

RICHARD DUKE OF YORKE

    Speake Winchester, for boyling choller chokes

    The hollow passage of my poyson'd voyce,

    By sight of these our balefull enemies.

WINCHESTER

    Charles, and the rest, it is enacted thus:

    That in regard King *Henry* giues consent,

    Of meere compassion, and of lenity,

    To ease your Countrie of distressefull Warre,

    And suffer you to breath in fruitfull peace,

    You shall become true Liegemen to his Crowne.

    And *Charles*, vpon condition thou wilt sweare   2520

    To pay him tribute, and submit thy selfe,

    Thou shalt be plac'd as Viceroy vnder him,

    And still enioy thy Regall dignity.

ALANSON

    Must he be then as shadow of himselfe?

    Adorne his Temples with a Coronet,

    And yet in substance and authority,

    Retaine but priuiledge of a priuate man?

    This proffer is absurd, and reasonlesse.

CHARLES

    'Tis knowne already that I am possest

    With more then halfe the Gallian Territories,   2530

    And therein reuerenc'd for their lawfull King.

    Shall I for lucre of the rest vn-vanquisht,

    Detract so much from that prerogatiue,

    As to be call'd but Viceroy of the whole?

    No Lord Ambassador, Ile rather keepe

    That which I haue, than coueting for more

    Be cast from possibility of all.

RICHARD DUKE OF YORKE

    Insulting *Charles*, hast thou by secret meanes

    Vs'd intercession to obtaine a league,

    And now the matter growes to compremize,   2540

    Stand'st thou aloofe vpon Comparison.

    Either accept the Title thou vsurp'st,

    Of benefit proceeding from our King,

    And not of any challenge of Desert,

    Or we will plague thee with incessant Warres.

REIGNIER (*aside to Charles*)

    My Lord, you do not well in obstinacy,

    To cauill in the course of this Contract:

    If once it be neglected, ten to one

    We shall not finde like opportunity.

ALANSON (*aside to Charles*)

2550 To say the truth, it is your policie,
To saue your Subiects from such massacre
And ruthlesse slaughters as are dayly seene
By our proceeding in Hostility,
And therefore take this compact of a Truce,
Although you breake it, when your pleasure serues.

WARWICKE

How sayst thou *Charles*? Shall our Condition stand?

CHARLES It Shall:
Onely reseru'd, you claime no interest
In any of our Townes of Garrison.

RICHARD DUKE OF YORKE

2560 Then sweare Allegeance to his Maiesty,
As thou art Knight, neuer to disobey,
Nor be Rebellious to the Crowne of England,
Thou nor thy Nobles, to the Crowne of England.
⌐They sweare⌐
So, now dismisse your Army when ye please:
Hang vp your Ensignes, let your Drummes be still,
For heere we entertaine a solemne peace.   *Exeunt*

Sc. 35   *Enter Suffolke in conference with the King,*
(5.7)   *Glocester, and Exeter*

KING (*to Suffolke*)

Your wondrous rare description (noble Earle)
Of beauteous *Margaret* hath astonish'd me:
Her vertues graced with externall gifts,
2570 Do breed Loues setled passions in my heart,
And like as rigour of tempestuous gustes
Prouokes the mightiest Hulke against the tide,
So am I driuen by breath of her Renowne,
Either to suffer Shipwracke, or arriue
Where I may haue fruition of her Loue.

SUFFOLKE

Tush my good Lord, this superficiall tale,
Is but a preface of her worthy praise:
The cheefe perfections of that louely Dame,
(Had I sufficient skill to vtter them)
2580 Would make a volume of inticing lines,
Able to rauish any dull conceit.
And which is more, she is not so Diuine,
So full repleate with choice of all delights,
But with as humble lowlinesse of minde,
She is content to be at your command:
Command I meane, of Vertuous chaste intents,
To Loue, and Honor *Henry* as her Lord.

KING

And otherwise, will *Henry* ne're presume:
(*To Gloster*) Therefore my Lord Protector, giue consent,
2590 That *Marg'ret* may be Englands Royall Queene.

GLOSTER

So should I giue consent to flatter sinne,
You know (my Lord) your Highnesse is betroath'd
Vnto another Lady of esteeme,
How shall we then dispense with that contract,
And not deface your Honor with reproach?

SUFFOLKE

As doth a Ruler with vnlawfull Oathes,
Or one that at a Triumph, hauing vow'd
To try his strength, forsaketh yet the Listes
By reason of his Aduersaries oddes.
A poore Earles daughter is vnequall oddes,   2600
And therefore may be broke without offence.

GLOSTER

Why what (I pray) is *Margaret* more then that?
Her Father is no better than an Earle,
Although in glorious Titles he excell.

SUFFOLKE

Yes my Lord, her Father is a King,
The King of Naples, and Ierusalem,
And of such great Authoritie in France,
As his alliance will confirme our peace,
And keepe the Frenchmen in Allegeance.

GLOSTER

And so the Earle of Arminacke may doe,   2610
Because he is neere Kinsman vnto *Charles*.

EXETER

Beside, his wealth doth warrant a liberal dower,
Where *Reignier* sooner will receyue, than giue.

SUFFOLKE

A Dowre my Lords? Disgrace not so your King,
That he should be so abiect, base, and poore,
To choose for wealth, and not for perfect Loue.
Henry is able to enrich his Queene,
And not to seeke a Queene to make him rich,
So worthlesse Pezants bargaine for their Wiues,
As Market men for Oxen, Sheepe, or Horse.   2620
Marriage is a matter of more worth,
Then to be dealt in by Atturney-ship:
Not whom we will, but whom his Grace affects,
Must be companion of his Nuptiall bed.
And therefore Lords, since he affects her most,
Y^t most of all these reasons bindeth vs,
In our opinions she should be preferr'd.
For what is wedlocke forced? but a Hell,
An Age of discord and continuall strife,
Whereas the contrarie bringeth blisse,   2630
And is a patterne of Celestiall peace.
Whom should we match with *Henry* being a King,
But *Margaret*, that is daughter to a King:
Her peerelesse feature, ioyned with her birth,
Approues her fit for none, but for a King.
Her valiant courage, and vndaunted spirit,
(More then in women commonly is seene)
Will answer our hope in issue of a King.
For *Henry*, sonne vnto a Conqueror,
Is likely to beget more Conquerors,   2640
If with a Lady of so high resolue,
(As is faire *Margaret*) he be link'd in loue.
Then yeeld my Lords, and heere conclude with mee,
That *Margaret* shall be Queene, and none but shee.

KING

Whether it be through force of your report,

My Noble Lord of Suffolke: Or for that
My tender youth was neuer yet attaint
With any passion of inflaming loue,
I cannot tell: but this I am assur'd,
2650 I feele such sharpe dissention in my breast,
Such fierce alarums both of Hope and Feare,
As I am sicke with working of my thoughts.
Take therefore shipping, poste my Lord to France,
Agree to any couenants, and procure
That Lady *Margaret* do vouchsafe to come
To crosse the Seas to England, and be crown'd
King *Henries* faithfull and annointed Queene.
For your expences and sufficient charge,
Among the people gather vp a tenth.
2660 Be gone I say, for till you do returne,
I rest perplexed with a thousand Cares.
(*To Gloster*) And you (good Vnckle) banish all offence:

If you do censure me, by what you were,
Not what you are, I know it will excuse
This sodaine execution of my will.
And so conduct me, where from company,
I may reuolue and ruminate my greefe.
                                   Exit ⌈*with Exeter*⌉
GLOSTER
I greefe I feare me, both at first and last.
                                   Exit Glocester
SUFFOLKE
Thus Suffolke hath preuail'd, and thus he goes
As did the youthfull *Paris* once to Greece,   2670
With hope to finde the like euent in loue,
But prosper better than the Troian did:
Margaret shall now be Queene, and rule the King:
But I will rule both her, the King, and Realme.   *Exit*

FINIS

RICHARD III

In narrative sequence, *Richard III* follows directly after *Richard Duke of Yorke*, and that play's closing scenes, in which Richard of Gloster expresses his ambitions for the crown, suggest that Shakespeare had a sequel in mind. But he seems to have gone back to tell the beginning of the story of Henry VI's reign before covering the events from Henry VI's death (in 1471) to the Battle of Bosworth (1485). We have no record of the first performance of *Richard III* (probably in late 1592 or early 1593, outside London); it was printed in 1597, with five reprints before its inclusion in the 1623 Folio.

The principal source of information about Richard III available to Shakespeare was Sir Thomas More's *History of King Richard III* as incorporated in chronicle histories by Edward Halle (1542) and Raphael Holinshed (1577, revised in 1587), both of which Shakespeare seems to have used. His artistic influences include the tragedies of the Roman dramatist Seneca (who was born about 4 BC and died in AD 65), with their ghosts, their rhetorical style, their prominent choruses, and their indirect, highly formal presentation of violent events. (Except for the stabbing of Clarence (Sc. 4) there is no on-stage violence in *Richard III* until the final battle scenes.)

In this play, Shakespeare demonstrates a more complete artistic control of his historical material than in its predecessors: Richard himself is a more dominating central figure than is to be found in any of the earlier plays, historical events are freely manipulated in the interests of an overriding design, and the play's language is more highly patterned and rhetorically unified. That part of the play which shows Richard's bloody progress to the throne is based on the events of some twelve years; the remainder covers the two years of his reign. Shakespeare omits some important events, but invents Richard's wooing of Lady Anne over her father-in-law's coffin, and causes Queene Margaret, who had returned to France in 1476 and who died before Richard became king, to remain in England as a choric figure of grief and retribution. The characterization of Richard as a self-delighting ironist builds upon More. The episodes in which the older women of the play—the Dutchesse of Yorke, Queene Elizabeth, and Queene Margaret—bemoan their losses, and the climactic procession of ghosts before the final confrontation of Richard with the idealized figure of Richmond, the future Henry VII, help to make *Richard III* the culmination of a tetralogy as well as a masterly poetic drama in its own right. The final speech, in which Richmond, heir to the house of Lancaster and grandfather of Queen Elizabeth I, proclaims the union of 'the white rose and the red' in his marriage to Elizabeth of Yorke, provides a patriotic climax which must have been immensely stirring to the play's early audiences.

Colley Cibber's adaptation (1700) of *Richard III*, incorporating the death of Henry VI, shortening and adapting the play, and making the central role (played by Cibber) even more dominant than it had originally been, held the stage with great success until the late nineteenth century. Since then, Shakespeare's text has been restored (though usually abbreviated—next to *Hamlet*, this is Shakespeare's longest play), and the role of Richard has continued to present a rewarding challenge to leading actors.

The punctuation and spelling of this play have little authority. The first edition (Q1, 1597) was apparently compiled from memory: the Folio (1623), although more reliable verbally, was printed from annotated copies of two later reprints (Q3, 1602; Q6, 1622).

THE NAMES OF THE ACTORS

KING EDWARD the fourth

DUTCHESSE of Yorke, his mother

PRINCE EDWARD

Richard, the young Duke of YORKE } his sonnes

George, Duke of CLARENCE

RICHARD, Duke of GLOCESTER, later
   KING RICHARD } his brothers

BOY, sonne of Clarence

DAUGHTER of Clarence

QUEENE ELIZABETH, King Edwards wife

Anthony Woodeuille, Earle RYUERS, her brother

Marquesse of DORSET

Lord GREY   her sonnes

Sir Thomas VAUGHAN

GHOST of King Henry the sixt

QUEENE MARGARET, his widdow

GHOST of Prince Edward, his sonne

LADY ANNE, Prince Edwards widdow, later Richard Glocesters
   wife

Lord William HASTINGS, Lord Chamberlaine

Lord STANLEY, Earle of Derby, his friend

HENRY EARLE OF RICHMOND, later KING HENRY the seuenth,
   Stanleys Sonne-in-Law

Earle of OXFORD

Sir Iames BLUNT } followers of Richmond

Sir Walter HERBERT

Duke of BUCKINGHAM

Duke of NORFFOLKE

Sir Richard RATCLIFFE

Sir William CATESBY } followers of Richard Glocester

Sir Iames TYRREL

Two MURTHERERS

A PAGE

CARDINALL

Bishop of ELY

Iohn, a PRIEST

CHRISTOPHER, a Priest

Sir Robert BRAKENBURY, Lieutenant of the Tower of London

Lord MAIOR of London

A SCRIUENER

Hastings, a PURSUIUANT

SHERIFF

Aldermen and Cittizens

Attendants, two Bishops, Messengers, Souldiers

208

The Tragedy of King Richard the Third

Sc. 1   *Enter Richard Duke of Glocester solus*

(1.1)   RICHARD GLOCESTER

Now is the winter of our discontent,
Made glorious summer by this sonne of Yorke:
And all the cloudes that lowrd vpon our house,
In the deepe bosome of the Ocean buried.
Now are our browes bound with victorious wreathes,
Our bruised armes hung vp for monuments,
Our sterne alarmes changd to merry meetings,
Our dreadfull marches to delightfull measures.
Grim-visagde warre, hath smoothde his wrinkled front,

10   And now in steed of mounting barbed steedes,
To fright the soules of fearefull aduersaries,
He capers nimbly in a Ladies chamber,
To the lasciuious pleasing of a lute.
But I that am not shapte for sportiue trickes,
Nor made to court an amorous looking glasse,
I that am rudely stampt and want loues maiesty,
To strut before a wanton ambling Nymph:
I that am curtaild of this faire proportion,
Cheated of feature by dissembling nature,

20   Deformd, vnfinisht, sent before my time
Into this breathing world scarse halfe made vp,
And that so lamely and vnfashionable,
That dogs barke at me as I halt by them:
Why I in this weake piping time of peace
Haue no delight to passe away the time,
Vnlesse to spie my shadow in the sunne,
And descant on mine owne deformity:
And therefore since I cannot prooue a louer
To entertaine these faire well spoken daies,

30   I am determined to prooue a villaine,
And hate the idle pleasures of these daies:
Plots haue I laid, inductions dangerous,
By drunken Prophesies, libels and dreames,
To set my brother Clarence and the King
In deadly hate the one against the other.
And if King Edward be as true and iust,
As I am subtile, false, and trecherous:
This day should Clarence closely be mewed vp,
About a Prophecy which saies that G.

40   Of Edwards heires the murtherer shall be.

Enter Clarence, guarded, and Brakenbury

Diue thoughts downe to my soule, heere Clarence
     comes,
Brother, good day, what meanes this armed gard
That waites vpon your grace?

CLARENCE   His Maiesty

Tendering my persons safety hath appointed
This conduct to conuay me to the tower.

RICHARD GLOCESTER

Vpon what cause?

CLARENCE   Because my name is George.

RICHARD GLOCESTER

Alacke my Lord that fault is none of yours,
He should for that commit your Godfathers:
Belike his Maiesty hath some intent
That you should be new christened in the Tower.   50
But whats the matter Clarence may I know?

CLARENCE

Yea Richard when I know; for I protest
As yet I doe not, but as I can learne,
He harkens after Prophecies and dreames,
And from the crosse-rowe pluckes the letter G:
And saies a wisard told him that by G,
His issue disinherited should be.
And for my name of George begins with G,
It followes in his thought that I am he.
These as I learne and such like toies as these,   60
Hath moued his highnes to commit me now.

RICHARD GLOCESTER

Why this it is when men are rulde by women,
Tis not the King that sends you to the tower,
My Lady Gray his wife, Clarence tis she,
That tempts him to this harsh extremity,
Was it not she and that good man of worshippe
Anthony Woodeuile her brother there,
That made him send Lord Hastings to the tower;
From whence this present day he is deliuered?
We are not safe Clarence, we are not safe.   70

CLARENCE

By heauen I thinke there is no man secure,
But the Queenes kindred and night-walking Heralds,
That trudge betwixt the King and Mistresse Shore,
Heard ye not what an humble suppliant
Lord Hastings was for his deliuery.

RICHARD GLOCESTER

Humbly complaining to her deity,
Got my Lord Chamberlaine his liberty.
Ile tell you what, I thinke it is our way,
If we will keepe in fauour with the King,
To be her men and weare her liuery.   80
The iealous oreworne widdow and her selfe,
Since that our brother dubd them gentlewomen,
Are mighty gossips in our monarchy.

BRAKENBURY

I beseech your Graces both to pardon me:
His Maiesty hath streightly giuen in charge,
That no man shall haue priuate conference,
Of what degree soeuer with your brother.

RICHARD GLOCESTER

Euen so and please your worship Brakenbury,
You may pertake of any thing we say:
We speake no treason man, we say the King   90
Is wise and vertuous, and his noble Queene
Well stroke in yeres, faire and not iealous.

We say that Shores wife hath a pretty foote,
A cherry lippe,
A bonny eie, a passing pleasing tongue:
And that the Queenes kin are made gentlefolks.
How say you sir, can you deny all this?

BRAKENBURY

With this (my Lord) my selfe haue nought to do.

RICHARD GLOCESTER

Naught to do with Mistris Shore, I tell thee fellow,
100 He that doth naught with her, excepting one
Were best to doe it secretly alone.

BRAKENBURY What one my Lord?

RICHARD GLOCESTER

Her husband knaue, wouldst thou betray me?

BRAKENBURY

I beseech your Grace to pardon me, and do withal
Forbeare your conference with the noble Duke.

CLARENCE

We know thy charge Brakenbury and will obey.

RICHARD GLOCESTER

We are the Queenes abiects and must obey.
Brother farewell, I will vnto the King,
And whatsoeuer you will imploy me in,
110 Were it to call King Edwards widdow sister,
I will performe it to enfranchise you,
Meane time this deepe disgrace in brotherhood,
Touches me deerer then you can imagine.

CLARENCE

I know it pleaseth neither of vs well.

RICHARD GLOCESTER

Well, your imprisonment shall not be long,
I will deliuer you or lie for you,
Meane time haue patience.

CLARENCE   I must perforce; farewell.

Exit Clarence, guarded, and Brakenbury, to the
Tower

RICHARD GLOCESTER

Go treade the path that thou shalt nere returne,
Simple plaine Clarence I doe loue thee so,
120 That I will shortly send thy soule to heauen,
If heauen will take the present at our hands:
But who comes here the new deliuered Hastings?

Enter Lord Hastings from the Tower

HASTINGS

Good time of day vnto my gratious Lord.

RICHARD GLOCESTER

As much vnto my good Lord Chamberlaine:
Well are you welcome to the open aire,
How hath your Lordship brookt imprisonment?

HASTINGS

With patience (noble Lord) as prisoners must:
But I shall liue my Lord to giue them thankes
That were the cause of my imprisonment.

RICHARD GLOCESTER

130 No doubt, no doubt, and so shal Clarence too,
For they that were your enemies are his,
And haue preuaild as much on him as you.

HASTINGS

More pitty that the Eagles should be mewed,
While keihts and bussards prey at liberty.

RICHARD GLOCESTER What newes abroad?

HASTINGS

No newes so bad abroad as this at home:
The King is sickly, weake and melancholy,
And his Phisitions feare him mightily.

RICHARD GLOCESTER

Now by Saint Paul that newes is bad indeede,
Oh he hath kept an euill diet long,   140
And ouermuch consumed his royall person,
Tis very grieuous to be thought vpon:
Where is he, in his bed?

HASTINGS   He is.

RICHARD GLOCESTER

Go you before and I will follow you.   *Exit Hastings*
He cannot liue I hope, and must not die,
Till George be packt with post haste vp to heauen.
Ile in to vrge his hatred more to Clarence,
With lies well steeld with weighty arguments,
And if I faile not in my deepe intent,
Clarence hath not an other day to liue: 150
Which done, God take King Edward to his mercy,
And leaue the world for me to bussell in,
For then Ile marry Warwicks yongest daughter:
What though I kild her husband and her father,
The readiest way to make the wench amends,
Is to become her husband and her father:
The which will I, not all so much for loue,
As for another secret close intent,
By marrying her which I must reach vnto.
But yet I run before my horse to market: 160
Clarence still breathes, Edward still liues and raignes,
When they are gone then must I count my gaines.

Exit

Enter Gentlemen, bearing the Coarse of Henrie the   Sc. 2
sixt in an open Coffin, with Halberds to guard it,   (1.2)
Lady Anne being the Mourner

LADY ANNE

Set downe set downe your honourable load
If honor may be shrowded in a hearse,
Whilst I a while obsequiously lament
The vntimely fall of vertuous Lancaster:
They set the Coffin downe
Poore kei-cold figure of a holy King,
Pale ashes of the house of Lancaster,
Thou bloudlesse remnant of that royall bloud,
Be it lawfull that I inuocate thy ghost,   170
To heare the lamentations of poore Anne,
Wife to thy Edward, to thy slaughtered sonne,
Stabd by the selfesame hand that made these wounds,
Lo in these windowes that let foorth thy life,
I powre the helplesse balme of my poore eies,
O cursed be the hand that made these holes,
Cursed the Blood, that let this blood from hence:

Cursed the heart that had the heart to doe it.
More direfull hap betide that hated wretch,
180 That makes vs wretched by the death of thee:
Than I can wish to Wolues, to spiders, toades,
Or any creeping venomde thing that liues.
If euer he haue child abortiue be it,
Prodigious and vntimely brought to light:
Whose vgly and vnnaturall aspect,
May fright the hopefull mother at the view,
And that be Heyre to his vnhappinesse.
If euer he haue wife, let her be made
More miserable by the death of him,
190 Then I am made by my young Lord and thee.
Come now towards Chertsey with your holy loade,
Taken from Paules to be interred there:
⌈*The Gentlemen lift the Coffin*⌉
And still as you are weary of this waight,
Rest you whiles I lament King Henries corse.
    Enter Richard Duke of Glocester
RICHARD GLOCESTER (*to the Gentlemen*)
Stay you that beare the corse and set it downe.
LADY ANNE
What blacke magitian coniures vp this fiend,
To stop deuoted charitable deedes.
RICHARD GLOCESTER (*to the Gentlemen*)
Villaines set downe the corse, or by S. Paule,
Ile make a corse of him that disobeies.
⌈HALBERD⌉
200 My Lord, stand backe and let the coffin passe.
RICHARD GLOCESTER
Vnmanerd dog, stand thou when I command,
Aduance thy halbert higher than my brest,
Or by Saint Paul Ile strike thee to my foote,
And spurne vpon thee begger for thy boldnes.
    They set the Coffin downe
LADY ANNE (*to Gentlemen and Halberds*)
What doe you tremble, are you all afraid?
Alas, I blame you not, for you are mortall,
And mortall eies cannot endure the diuell.
(*To Richard*) Auaunt thou dreadfull minister of hell,
Thou hadst but power ouer his mortall body,
210 His soule thou canst not haue, therefore be gone.
RICHARD GLOCESTER
Sweete Saint, for Charity be not so curst.
LADY ANNE
Foule Diuell, for Gods sake hence & trouble vs not,
For thou hast made the happy earth thy hell:
Fild it with cursing cries and deepe exclaimes.
If thou delight to view thy hainous deedes,
Behold this patterne of thy butcheries.
Oh gentlemen see, see dead Henries woundes,
Ope their congeald mouthes and bleede a fresh.
Blush blush thou lumpe of foule deformity,
220 For tis thy presence that exhales this bloud,
From cold and empty veines where no bloud dwells.
Thy deed inhumane and vnnaturall,
Prouokes this deluge supernaturall.

Oh God which this bloud madest, reuenge his death,
Oh earth which this bloud drinkst, reuenge his death:
Either heauen with lightning strike the murtherer
    dead,
Or earth gape open wide and eate him quicke,
As thou doest swallow vp this good Kings bloud,
Which his hell-gouernd arme hath butchered.
RICHARD GLOCESTER
Lady you know no rules of charity,   230
Which renders good for bad, blessings for curses.
LADY ANNE
Villaine thou knowest no law of God nor man:
No beast so fierce but knowes some touch of pitty.
RICHARD GLOCESTER
But I know none, and therefore am no beast.
LADY ANNE
Oh wonderfull when Diuels tell the troth.
RICHARD GLOCESTER
More wonderfull when Angels are so angry.
Voutsafe deuine perfection of a woman,
Of these supposed Crimes to giue me leaue,
By circumstance but to acquite my selfe.
LADY ANNE
Vouchsafe defused infection of a man,   240
Of these knowne euils but to giue me leaue,
By circumstance t'accuse thy cursed selfe.
RICHARD GLOCESTER
Fairer then tongue can name thee, let me haue
Some patient leisure to excuse my selfe.
LADY ANNE
Fouler then heart can thinke thee thou canst make
No excuse currant but to hang thy selfe.
RICHARD GLOCESTER
By such despaire I should accuse my selfe.
LADY ANNE
And by despairing shalt thou stand excusde,
For doing worthy vengeance on thy selfe,
That didst vnworthy slaughter vpon others.   250
RICHARD GLOCESTER
Say that I slew them not.
LADY ANNE   Then say they were not slaine,
But dead they are, and diuelish slaue by thee.
RICHARD GLOCESTER
I did not kill your husband.
LADY ANNE   Why then he is aliue.
RICHARD GLOCESTER
Nay, he is dead, and slaine by Edwards hand.
LADY ANNE
In thy foule throat thou liest, Queene Margaret saw
Thy murd'rous faulchion smoking in his bloud,
The which thou once didst bend against her brest,
But that thy brothers beat aside the point.
RICHARD GLOCESTER
I was prouoked by her slaunderous tongue,
That laid their guilt vpon my guiltlesse shoulders.   260
LADY ANNE
Thou wast prouoked by thy bloudy minde,

That neuer dream'st on ought but butcheries,
Didst thou not kill this King.

RICHARD GLOCESTER   I grant yea.

LADY ANNE

Doest grant me hedghogge then god grant me too
Thou maiest be damnd for that wicked deede,
Oh he was gentle, milde, and vertuous.

RICHARD GLOCESTER

The better for the King of Heauen that hath him.

LADY ANNE

He is in heauen where thou shalt neuer come.

RICHARD GLOCESTER

Let him thanke me that holpe to send him thither,
270   For he was fitter for that place then earth,

LADY ANNE

And thou vnfit for any place but hell.

RICHARD GLOCESTER

Yes one place els if you will heare me name it.

LADY ANNE

Some dungeon.

RICHARD GLOCESTER   Your bedchamber.

LADY ANNE

Ill rest betide the chamber where thou liest.

RICHARD GLOCESTER

So will it Madame till I lie with you.

LADY ANNE

I hope so.

RICHARD GLOCESTER   I know so, but gentle Lady Anne,
To leaue this keene incounter of our wits,
And fall something into a slower methode:
Is not the causer of the timeles deaths,
280   Of these Plantagenets Henry and Edward,
As blamefull as the executioner.

LADY ANNE

Thou was't the cause of that accurst effect.

RICHARD GLOCESTER

Your beauty was the cause of that effect,
Your beauty that did haunt me in my sleepe:
To vndertake the death of all the world
So I might liue one houre in your sweete bosome.

LADY ANNE

If I thought that I tell thee homicide,
These nailes should rend that beauty from my cheekes.

RICHARD GLOCESTER

These eies could not indure sweet beauties wrack,
290   You should not blemish it if I stood by:
As all the world is cheered by the sonne,
So I by that, it is my day, my life.

LADY ANNE

Blacke night ouershade thy day, and death thy life.

RICHARD GLOCESTER

Curse not thy selfe faire creature, thou art both.

LADY ANNE

I would I were to be reuenged on thee.

RICHARD GLOCESTER

It is a quarrell most vnnaturall,
To be reuengd on him that loueth you.

LADY ANNE

It is a quarrell iust and reasonable,
To be reuengd on him that kill'd my husband.

RICHARD GLOCESTER

He that bereft thee Lady of thy husband,   300
Did it to helpe thee to a better husband.

LADY ANNE

His better doth not breath vpon the earth.

RICHARD GLOCESTER

He liues that loues thee better then he could.

LADY ANNE

Name him.

RICHARD GLOCESTER   Plantagenet.

LADY ANNE   Why that was hee.

RICHARD GLOCESTER

The selfesame name but one of better nature.

LADY ANNE

Where is he.

RICHARD GLOCESTER   Heere,
      Shee spits at him
                         Why doest thou spitte at me.

LADY ANNE

Would it were mortall poison for thy sake.

RICHARD GLOCESTER

Neuer came poison from so sweete a place.

LADY ANNE

Neuer hung poison on a fouler toade,
Out of my sight thou doest infect mine eies.   310

RICHARD GLOCESTER

Thine eies sweete Lady haue infected mine.

LADY ANNE

Would they were basiliskes to strike thee dead.

RICHARD GLOCESTER

I would they were that I might die at once,
For now they kill me with a liuing death:
Those eies of thine from mine haue drawen salt teares,
Shamd their aspects with store of childish drops:
I neuer sued to friend nor enemy,
My tongue could neuer learne sweete smoothing word:
But now thy beauty is proposde my fee:
My proud heart sues and prompts my tongue to speake, 320
      She lookes scornfully at him
Teach not thy lip such scorne, for it was made
For kissing Lady not for such contempt.
If thy reuengefull heart cannot forgiue,
      ⌈*He kneeles and offers her his sword*⌉
Lo here I lend thee this sharpe pointed sword:
Which if thou please to hide in this true brest,
And let the soule forth that adoreth thee:
I laie it naked to the deadly stroke,
And humbly beg the death vpon my knee.
      *He layes his brest open, she offers at it with his
      sword*
Nay, doe not pawse, for I did kill King *Henrie*,
But twas thy beauty that prouoked me: 330
Nay now dispatch twas I that stabb'd yong *Edward*,
But twas thy heauenly face that set me on:

She fals the Sword
Take vp the sword againe or take vp me.

LADY ANNE
Arise dissembler,
⌈*He rises*⌉
                        though I wish thy death,
I will not be thy executioner.

RICHARD GLOCESTER
Then bid me kill my selfe, and I will doe it.

LADY ANNE
I haue already.

RICHARD GLOCESTER   That was in thy rage:
Speake it againe, and euen with the word,
This hand which for thy loue did kill thy loue,
340   Shall for thy loue, kill a farre truer loue:
To both their deaths shalt thou be accessary.

LADY ANNE   I would I knew thy heart.

RICHARD GLOCESTER   Tis figured in my tongue.

LADY ANNE   I feare me both are false.

RICHARD GLOCESTER   Then neuer man was true.

LADY ANNE   Well, well, put vp your sword.

RICHARD GLOCESTER   Say then my peace is made.

LADY ANNE   That shalt thou know hereafter.

RICHARD GLOCESTER   But shall I liue in hope.

350   LADY ANNE   All men I hope liue so.

RICHARD GLOCESTER   Voutsafe to weare this ring.

LADY ANNE   To take is not to giue.

RICHARD GLOCESTER
Looke how my ring incompasseth thy finger,
Euen so thy breast incloseth my poore heart.
Weare both of them for both of them are thine,
And if thy poore deuoted Seruant may
But beg one fauour at thy gratious hand,
Thou doest confirme his happines for euer.

LADY ANNE   What is it?

RICHARD GLOCESTER
360   That it may please you leaue these sad designes,
To him that hath most cause to be a mourner,
And presently repaire to Crosbie House,
Where after I haue solemnly interred
At Chertsie monastery this noble King,
And wet his graue with my repentant teares,
I will with all expedient dutie see you:
For diuers vnknowne reasons, I beseech you
Grant me this boone.

LADY ANNE
With all my heart, and much it ioies me too,
370   To see you are become so penitent:
Tressill and Barkley go along with me.

RICHARD GLOCESTER
Bid me farewell.

LADY ANNE   Tis more then you deserue:
But since you teach me how to flatter you,
Imagine I haue said farewell already.
                        Exit two with Anne

RICHARD GLOCESTER
Sirs take vp the corse.

GENTLEMAN   Towards Chertsie noble Lord.

RICHARD GLOCESTER
No, to black Friers there attend my comming.
                Exeunt with Coarse. Manet Glocester
Was euer woman in this humor woed,
Was euer woman in this humor wonne:
Ile haue her, but I will not keepe her long.
What I that kild her husband and his father,   380
To take her in her hearts extreamest hate:
With curses in her mouth, teares in her eies,
The bleeding witnesse of my hatred by,
Hauing God, her conscience, and these bars against
    me:
And I no Friends to backe my suite w^tall,
But the plaine Diuell and dissembling lookes,
And yet to win her all the world to nothing. Hah
Hath she forgot already that braue Prince
Edward, her Lord whom I some three months since,
Stabd in my angry moode at Tewxbery,   390
A sweeter and a louelier gentleman,
Framd in the prodigality of nature:
Young, valiant, wise, and no doubt right royall,
The spacious world cannot againe affoord:
And will she yet abase her eyes on me
That cropt the golden prime of this sweete Prince,
And made her widdow to a wofull bed,
On me whose all not equals Edwards moity,
On me that halts, and am mishapen thus.
My Dukedome to a beggerly denier.   400
I doe mistake my person all this while,
Vpon my life she findes, although I cannot
My selfe, to be a merueilous proper man.
Ile be at charges for a looking glasse,
And entertaine a score or two of taylers,
To study fashions to adorne my body,
Since I am crept in fauour with my selfe,
I will maintaine it with some little cost:
But first Ile turne yon fellow in his graue,
And then returne lamenting to my loue.   410
Shine out faire sunne till I haue bought a glasse,
That I may see my shadow as I passe.   *Exit*

Enter Queene Elizabeth, Lord Riuers, ⌈Marquesse   Sc. 3
Dorset,⌉ and Lord Gray   (1.3)

RYUERS (*to Elizabeth*)
Haue patience Madame, theres no doubt his Maiestie
Will soone recouer his accustomed health.

GRAY (*to Elizabeth*)
In that you brooke it ill, it makes him worse,
Therefore for Gods sake entertaine good comfort,
And cheere his grace with quick and mery eyes.

QUEENE ELIZABETH
If he were dead what would betide on me.

⌈RYUERS⌉
No other harme but losse of such a Lord.

QUEENE ELIZABETH
The losse of such a Lord includes all harmes.   420

GRAY
The heauens haue blest you with a goodly sonne,
To be your comforter when he is gone.

QUEENE ELIZABETH

   Ah he is young, and his minority
   Is put vnto the trust of Rich. Glocester,
   A man that loues not me nor none of you.

RYUERS

   Is it concluded he shall be protector?

QUEENE ELIZABETH

   It is determinde, not concluded yet,
   But so it must be if the King miscarry.
        Enter Buckingham and Lord Stanley Earle of Darby

GRAY

   Here come the Lords of Buckingham and Darby.

BUCKINGHAM (*to Elizabeth*)

430   Good time of day vnto your royall grace.

STANLEY (*to Elizabeth*)

   God make your Maiesty ioyfull as you haue been.

QUEENE ELIZABETH

   The Countesse Richmond good my Lo: of Darby,
   To your good praier will scarcely say, Amen:
   Yet Darby, notwithstanding shees your wife,
   And loues not me, be you good Lo. assurde
   I hate not you for her proud arrogance.

STANLEY

   I do beseech you either not beleeue
   The enuious slaunders of her false accusers,
   Or if she be accusde on true report,
440   Beare with her weakenes which I thinke proceedes
   From wayward sicknesse, and no grounded malice.

⌈RYUERS⌉

   Saw you the King to day, my Lo: of Darby?

STANLEY

   But now the Duke of Buckingham and I
   Are come from visiting his Maiesty.

QUEENE ELIZABETH

   With likelihood of his amendment Lords?

BUCKINGHAM

   Madame good hope, his Grace speaks cheerfully.

QUEENE ELIZABETH

   God grant him health, did you confer with him.

BUCKINGHAM

   I Madame: He desires to make attonement
   Betweene the Duke of Glocester and your brothers,
450   And betweene them and my Lord chamberlaine,
   And sent to warne them to his royall presence.

QUEENE ELIZABETH

   Would all were well, but that will neuer be.
   I feare our happines is at the height.
        Enter Richard and Hastings

RICHARD GLOCESTER

   They doe me wrong and I will not endure it,
   Who are they that complaine vnto the King,
   That I forsooth am sterne and loue them not:
   By holy Paul they loue his grace but lightly,
   That fill his eares with such discentious rumors:
   Because I cannot flatter and looke faire,
460   Smile in mens faces, smoothe, deceiue and cog,
   Ducke with french nods and apish courtesie,
   I must be held a rankerous enimy.

   Cannot a plaine man liue and thinke no harme,
   But thus his simple truth must be abusde,
   With silken slie insinuating iackes?

⌈RYUERS⌉

   To whom in all this presence speakes your Grace?

RICHARD GLOCESTER

   To thee that hast nor honesty nor grace,
   When haue I iniured thee, when done thee wrong,
   Or thee or thee or any of your faction:
   A plague vpon you all. His royall Grace   470
   (Whom God preserue better then you would wish)
   Cannot be quiet scarce a breathing while,
   But you must trouble him with lewd complaints.

QUEENE ELIZABETH

   Brother of Glocester, you mistake the matter:
   The King on his owne royall disposition,
   And not prouokt by any suiter else,
   Ayming belike at your interiour hatred,
   That in your outward action shewes it selfe,
   Against my Children, brothers, and my selfe:
   Makes him to send that he may learne the ground   480
   Of your ill will and thereby to remoue it.

RICHARD GLOCESTER

   I cannot tell, the world is growen so bad
   That wrens make pray where Eagles dare not pearch,
   Since euery Iacke became a Gentleman:
   Theres many a gentle person made a Iacke.

QUEENE ELIZABETH

   Come come, we know your meaning brother Gloster
   You enuy my aduancement and my friends,
   God graunt we neuer may haue neede of you.

RICHARD GLOCESTER

   Meane time God grants that I haue neede of you,
   Our brother is imprisoned by your meanes,   490
   My selfe disgract, and the nobility
   Held in contempt, while great promotions,
   Are daily giuen to enoble those
   That scarce some two daies since were worth a noble.

QUEENE ELIZABETH

   By him that raisde me to this carefull height,
   From that contented hap which I enioyd,
   I neuer did incense his Maiesty
   Against the Duke of Clarence: but haue beene,
   An earnest aduocate to pleade for him.
   My Lord you doe me shamefull iniury,   500
   Falsely to draw me in these vile suspects.

RICHARD GLOCESTER

   You may deny that you were not the meane,
   Of my Lord Hastings late imprisonment.

RYUERS She may my Lord, for—

RICHARD GLOCESTER

   She may Lo: Ryuers, why who knowes not so?
   She may doe more Sir then denying that:
   She may helpe you to many faire preferments,
   And then deny her ayding hand therein,
   And lay those honours on your high desert,
   What may she not, she may, I marry may she.   510

RYUERS What mary may she.

RICHARD GLOCESTER

What mary may she, marry with a King,
A batchelor, and a handsome stripling too.
Iwis your Grandam had a worser match.

QUEENE ELIZABETH

My Lo: of Glocester, I haue too long borne
Your blunt vpbraidings and your bitter scoffes,
By heauen I will acquaint his Maiesty
Of those grose taunts that oft I haue endured:
I had rather be a countrey seruant maid,
Then a great Queene with this condition,   520
To be so baited, scorned, and stormed at:
    Enter old Qu. Margaret, behind
Small ioy haue I in being Englands Queene.

QUEENE MARGARET (*aside*)

And lesned be that smal, God I beseech him,
Thy honour, state, and seate is due to me.

RICHARD GLOCESTER (*to Elizabeth*)

What? threat you me with telling of the King,
Tell him and spare not, looke what I haue said,
I will auouch't in presence of the King:
I dare aduenture to be sent to th'Towre.
Tis time to speake, my paines are quite forgot.

QUEENE MARGARET (*aside*)

Out diuell I remember them too well,   530
Thou killd'st my husband Henry in the tower,
And Edward my poore sonne at Teuxbery.

RICHARD GLOCESTER (*to Elizabeth*)

Ere you were Queene, I or your husband King,
I was a packhorse in his great affaires,
A weeder out of his proud aduersaries,
A liberall rewarder of his friends:
To royalize his bloud I spent mine owne.

QUEENE MARGARET (*aside*)

I and much better bloud then his or thine.

RICHARD GLOCESTER (*to Elizabeth*)

In all which time you and your husband Gray,
Were factious for the house of Lancaster: 540
And Ryuers, so were you, was not your husband
In Margarets battaile at Saint Albones slaine:
Let me put in your mindes, if you forget
What you haue beene ere this, and what you are.
Withall, what I haue been, and what I am.

QUEENE MARGARET (*aside*)

A murtherous villaine, and so still thou art.

RICHARD GLOCESTER

Poore Clarence did forsake his father Warwicke,
I and forswore himselfe (which Iesu pardon.)

QUEENE MARGARET (*aside*) Which God reuenge.

RICHARD GLOCESTER

To fight on Edwards party for the crowne,   550
And for his meede poore Lo: he is mewed vppe:
I would to God my heart were flint like Edwards,
Or Edwards soft and pittifull like mine,
I am too childish, foolish for this world.

QUEENE MARGARET (*aside*)

Hie thee to hell for shame and leaue this world
Thou Cacodemon, there thy kingdome is.

RYUERS

My Lo: of Glocester in those busie daies,
Which here you vrge to proue vs enemies,
We followed then our Lo: our Soueraigne King,
So should we you if you should be our King.   560

RICHARD GLOCESTER

If I should be? I had rather be a pedler,
Farre be it from my heart the thought thereof.

QUEENE ELIZABETH

As little ioy my Lord as you suppose
You should enioy, were you this countries King,
As little ioy may you suppose in me,
That I enioy being the Queene thereof.

QUEENE MARGARET (*aside*)

A little ioy enioies the Queene thereof,
For I am she and altogether ioylesse.
I can no longer hold me patient:
(*Comming forward*) Heare me you wrangling Pyrats   570
    that fall out,
In sharing that which you haue pild from me:
Which of you trembles not that lookes on me?
If not, that I am Queene you bow like subiects,
Yet that by you deposde you quake like rebels:
(*To Richard*) Ah gentle villaine doe not turne away.

RICHARD GLOCESTER

Foule wrinckled witch what makst thou in my sight?

QUEENE MARGARET

But repetition of what thou hast mard,
That will I make before I let thee go:
A husband and a son thou owest to me,
(*To Elizabeth*) And thou a kingdome, (*to the rest*) all of   580
    you allegeance:
This sorrow that I haue by right is yours,
And all the pleasures you vsurpe are mine.

RICHARD GLOCESTER

The curse my noble father laid on thee,
When thou didst crowne his warlike browes with
    paper,
And with thy scornes drewst riuers from his eies,
And then to drie them gau'st the Duke a clout,
Steept in the faultlesse bloud of pretty Rutland:
His curses then from bitternes of soule
Denounst, against thee, are all fallen vpon thee,
And God, not we, hath plagde thy bloudy deede.   590

QUEENE ELIZABETH (*to Margaret*)

So iust is God to right the innocent.

HASTINGS (*to Margaret*)

O twas the foulest deede to slaie that babe,
And the most mercilesse that euer was heard of.

RYUERS (*to Margaret*)

Tyrants themselues wept when it was reported.

DORSET (*to Margaret*)

No man but prophecied reuenge for it.

BUCKINGHAM (*to Margaret*)

Northumberland then present wept to see it.

QUEENE MARGARET

What? were you snarling all before I came,
Ready to catch each other by the throat,

And turne you all your hatred now on me?
600 Did Yorkes dread curse preuaile so much with heauen,
That Henries death my louely Edwards death,
Their kingdomes losse, my wofull banishment,
Should all but answere for that peeuish brat?
Can curses pierce the clouds and enter heauen?
Why then giue way dull cloudes to my quicke curses:
Though not by war, by surfet die your King,
As ours by murder to make him a King.
(*To Elizabeth*) Edward thy sonne that now is Prince of
Wales,
For Edward my sonne that was Prince of Wales,
610 Die in his youth by like vntimely violence,
Thy selfe a Queene, for me that was a Queene,
Outliue thy glory like my wretched selfe:
Long maiest thou liue to waile thy childrens death,
And see another as I see thee now
Deckt in thy rights, as thou art stald in mine:
Long die thy happy daies before thy death,
And after many lengthened houres of griefe,
Die neither mother, wife, nor Englands Queene:
Riuers and Dorset you were standers by,
620 And so wast thou Lo: Hastings when my sonne
Was stabd with bloudy daggers, god I pray him,
That none of you may liue his naturall age,
But by some vnlookt accident cut off.
RICHARD GLOCESTER
Haue done thy charme thou hatefull withred hag.
QUEENE MARGARET
And leaue out the? stay dog for thou shalt hear me.
If heauen haue any grieuous plague in store,
Exceeding those that I can wish vpon thee:
O let them keepe it till thy sinnes be ripe,
And then hurle downe their indignation
630 On thee the troubler of the poore worlds peace:
The worme of conscience still begnaw thy soule,
Thy friends suspect for traitors while thou liuest,
And take deepe traitors for thy dearest friends:
No sleepe, close vp that deadly eye of thine,
Vnlesse it be while some tormenting dreame
Affrights thee with a hell of vgly diuels.
Thou eluish markt abortiue rooting hog,
Thou that wast seald in thy natiuity
The slaue of nature, and the sonne of hell,
640 Thou slaunder of thy heauy mothers wombe,
Thou lothed issue of thy fathers loynes,
Thou rag of honour, thou detested—
RICHARD GLOCESTER Margaret.
QUEENE MARGARET
Richard.
RICHARD GLOCESTER Ha.
QUEENE MARGARET   I call thee not.
RICHARD GLOCESTER
I crie thee mercy then, for I did thinke
That thou hadst cald me all these bitter names.
QUEENE MARGARET
Why so I did, but lookt for no reply,
O Let me make the period to my curse.

RICHARD GLOCESTER
Tis done by me, and ends in Margaret.
QUEENE ELIZABETH (*to Margaret*)
Thus haue you breathed your curse against your selfe.   650
QUEENE MARGARET
Poore painted Queene, vaine flourish of my fortune
Why strewst thou suger on that bottled spider,
Whose deadly web ensnareth thee about?
Foole foole, thou whetst a knife to kill thy selfe,
The day will come that thou shalt wish for me,
To helpe thee curse this poisenous bunchbackt toade.
HASTINGS
False boading woman, end thy frantike curse,
Lest to thy harme thou moue our patience.
QUEENE MARGARET
Foule shame vpon you, you haue all mou'd mine.
RYUERS
Were you well seru'd you would be taught your duty.   660
QUEENE MARGARET
To serue me well, you all should doe me duty,
Teach me to be your Queene, and you my subiects:
O serue me well, and teach your selues that duty.
DORSET
Dispute not with her, she is lunatique.
QUEENE MARGARET
Peace Master Marques you are malapert,
Your fire-new stampe of honour is scarse currant:
O that your young nobility could iudge,
What twere to loose it and be miserable:
They that stand high haue many blasts to shake them,
And if they fall they dash themselues to pieces.   670
RICHARD GLOCESTER
Good counsell mary, learne it learne it Marques.
DORSET
It touches you my Lo: asmuch as me.
RICHARD GLOCESTER
I and much more, but I was borne so high,
Our aiery buildeth in the Cedars top,
And dallies with the winde, and scornes the sunne.
QUEENE MARGARET
And turnes the sun to shade, alas, alas,
Witnes my son, now in the shade of death,
Whose bright outshining beames, thy cloudy wrath
Hath in eternall darkenes foulded vp:
Your aiery buildeth in our aieries nest,   680
O God that seest it, doe not suffer it:
As it was wonne with bloud, lost be it so.
⌈RICHARD GLOCESTER⌉
Peace, peace for shame, if not for charity.
QUEENE MARGARET
Vrge neither charity nor shame to me,
Vncharitably with me haue you dealt,
And shamefully my hopes by you are butcherd,
My charity is outrage, life my shame,
And in that shame, still liue my sorrowes rage.
BUCKINGHAM Haue done, haue done.
QUEENE MARGARET
O Princely Buckingham, Ile kisse thy hand   690

In signe of league and amity with thee:
Now faire befall thee and thy Noble house,
Thy garments are not spotted with our bloud,
Nor thou within the compasse of my curse.

BUCKINGHAM

Nor no one here, for curses neuer passe
The lips of those that breath them in the aire.

QUEENE MARGARET

I will not thinke but they ascend the skie,
And there awake gods gentle sleeping peace.
O Buckingham take heede of yonder dog,
　　　She points at Richard
700 Looke when he fawnes, he bites, and when he bites,
His venome tooth will räckle to the death,
Haue nought to doe with him, beware of him:
Sinne, death and hell, haue set their markes on him,
And all their ministers attend on him.

RICHARD GLOCESTER

What doth she say my Lo: of Buckingham?

BUCKINGHAM

Nothing that I respect my gratious Lord.

QUEENE MARGARET

What doest thou scorne me for my gentle counsell,
And sooth the diuell that I warne thee from:
O but remember this another day,
710 When he shall split thy very heart with sorrow,
And say poore Margaret was a prophetesse:
Liue each of you the subiects to his hate,
And he to yours, and all of you to Gods.　　　*Exit*

⌈HASTINGS⌉

My haire doth stand on end to heare her curses.

RYUERS

And so doth mine, I muse why shees at liberty.

RICHARD GLOCESTER

I cannot blame her by gods holy mother,
She hath had too much wrong, and I repent
My part thereof that I haue done to her.

QUEENE ELIZABETH

I neuer did her any to my knowledge.

RICHARD GLOCESTER

720 Yet you haue all the vantage of her wrong.
I was too hoat to doe some body good,
That is too cold in thinking of it now:
Marry as for Clarence he is well repaid,
He is franckt vp to fatting for his paines,
God pardon them that are the cause thereof.

RYUERS

A vertuous and a Christianlike conclusion,
To pray for them that haue done scathe to vs.

RICHARD GLOCESTER

So doe I euer (*Speakes to himselfe*) being well aduisde,
For had I curst, now I had curst my selfe.
　　　Enter Catesby

CATESBY

730 Madam his Maiesty doth call for you,
And for your Grace, and you my gracious Lo:

QUEENE ELIZABETH

Catesby I come, Lords will you go with mee.

RYUERS We wait vpon your grace.
　　　　　　　　　　Exeunt all but Gloster

RICHARD GLOCESTER

I doe the wrong, and first begin to braule.
The secret mischiefes that I set abroach,
I lay vnto the grieuous charge of others:
Clarence whom I indeed haue cast in darkenes,
I doe beweepe to many simple guls:
Namely to Darby, Hastings, Buckingham,
And tell them 'tis the Queene and her allies,　　740
That stirre the King against the Duke my brother.
Now they beleeue it, and withall whet me,
To be reuenged on Ryuers, Dorset, Gray:
But then I sigh, and with a piece of scripture,
Tell them that God bids vs doe good for euill:
And thus I clothe my naked villany,
With odde old ends stolne forth of holy writ,
And seeme a Saint when most I play the Diuell:
　　　Enter two murtherers
But soft here come my executioners.
How now my hardy stout resolued mates,　　750
Are you now going to dispatch this thing.

A MURTHERER

We are my Lord, and come to haue the warrant,
That we may be admitted where he is.

RICHARD GLOCESTER

Well thought vpon, I haue it here about me,
　　　He giues them the warrant
When you haue done repaire to Crosby place;
But sirs, be sudden in the execution,
Withall, obdurate, doe not heare him pleade,
For Clarence is well spoken, and perhaps,
May moue your harts to pitty if you marke him.

A MURTHERER

Tut, tut, my Lo: we will not stand to prate,　　760
Talkers are no good doers be assured:
We go to vse our hands, and not our tongues.

RICHARD GLOCESTER

Your eies drop milstones when fooles eies fall tears,
I like you lads, about your busines straight.
Go, go, dispatch.

⌈MURTHERERS⌉　　　We will my Noble Lord.
　　　Exeunt Richard at one door, the Murderers at
　　　　　　　　　　　　　　　　　　　another

　　　Enter Clarence, ⌈Brakenbury⌉　　　　Sc. 4

⌈BRAKENBURY⌉　　　　　　　　　　　　　　　　(1.4)

Why lookes your grace so heauily to day?

CLARENCE

Oh I haue past a miserable night,
So full of fearefull dreames, of vgly sights,
That as I am a christian faithfull man,
I would not spend another such a night,　　770
Though twere to buy a world of happy daies,
So full of dismall terror was the time.

⌈BRAKENBURY⌉

What was your dreame my Lord, I pray you tel me.

CLARENCE

    Me thoughts that I had broken from the Tower,
    And was imbarkt to crosse to Burgundy,
    And in my company my brother Glocester,
    Who from my cabbine tempted me to walke,
    Vpon the hatches: there we lookt toward England,
    And cited vp a thousand heauy times,
780 During the wars of Yorke and Lancaster
    That had befallen vs, as we pact along,
    Vpon the giddy footing of the hatches,
    Me thought that Glocester stumbled, and in falling,
    Stroke me that sought to stay him ouer board,
    Into the tumbling billowes of the maine.
    O Lord, me thought what paine it was to drowne,
    What dreadfull noise of waters in my eares,
    What sights of vgly death within my eies:
    Me thoughts I sawe a thousand fearefull wracks,
790 Ten thousand men, that fishes gnawed vpon,
    Wedges of gold, great ouches, heapes of pearle,
    Inestimable stones, vnualued Iewels,
    All scattred in the bottome of the Sea,
    Some lay in dead mens sculs, and in those holes,
    Where eies did once inhabite, there were crept
    As twere in scorne of eies reflecting gems,
    Which woo'd the slimy bottome of the deepe,
    And mockt the dead bones that lay scattered by.

⌈BRAKENBURY⌉

    Had you such leisure in the time of death,
800 To gaze vpon these secrets of the deepe?

CLARENCE

    Me thought I had, and often did I striue
    To yeeld the Ghost: but still the enuious floud
    Stop'd in my soule, and would not let it foorth,
    To find the emptie vast and wandering aire,
    But smothered it within my panting bulke,
    Who almost burst to belch it in the sea.

⌈BRAKENBURY⌉

    Awakt you not in this sore agony.

CLARENCE

    No, no, my dreame was lengthned after life,
    O then began the tempest to my soule.
810 I past me thought the melancholy floud,
    With that sowre ferriman, which Poets write of,
    Vnto the kingdome of perpetuall night:
    The first that there did greet my stranger soule,
    Was my great father in law renowmed Warwicke,
    Who cried alowd what scourge for periury,
    Can this darke monarchy affoord false Clarence,
    And so he vanisht, then came wandring by,
    A shadow like an angell with bright haire,
    Dabled in bloud, and he shriek'd out alowd,
820 Clarence is come, false, fleeting, periurd Clarence,
    That stabd me in the field by Teuxbery:
    Seaze on him furies, take him vnto torment,
    With that me thoughts a legion of foule fiends
    Enuirond me, and howled in mine eares
    Such hideous cries, that with the very noise
    I trembling, wakt, and for a season after

    Could not beleeue but that I was in hell,
    Such terrible impression made my dreame.

⌈BRAKENBURY⌉

    No marueile Lo: though it affrighted you,
    I am afraid (me thinkes) to heare you tell it.   830

CLARENCE

    Ah Brakenbury I haue done these things,
    That now giue euidence against my soule
    For Edwards sake, and see how he requites me.
    Keeper, I pray thee sit by me a-while,
    My soule is heauy, and I faine would sleepe.

⌈BRAKENBURY⌉

    I will my Lo: God giue your Grace good rest,
        Clarence sleepes
    Sorrowe breakes seasons, and reposing howers,
    Makes the night morning, and the noonetide night,
    Princes haue but their titles for their glories,
    An outward honour, for an inward toile,   840
    And for vnfelt imaginations,
    They often feele a world of restlesse cares:
    So that betweene their titles and lowe name,
    Theres nothing differs but the outward fame.
        Enter two murtherers

1 MURTHERER Ho, who's heere?

BRAKENBURY

    What would'st thou Fellow, and how cam'st thou
        hither?

2 MURTHERER I would speake with Clarence, and I came
hither on my legs.

BRAKENBURY What so briefe.

1 MURTHERER 'Tis better (Sir) then to be tedious. (*To 2* 850
Murderer) Let him see our commission, and talke no
more.
        Brakenbury reads

BRAKENBURY

    I am in this commanded to deliuer
    The noble Duke of Clarence to your hands,
    I will not reason what is meant hereby,
    Because I wilbe guiltles of the meaning:
    There lies the Duke a sleepe, and there the keies,
        ⌈*He throwes down the keies*⌉
    Ile to the King, and signifie to him,
    That thus I haue resignd to you my charge.

1 MURTHERER You may sir,'tis a point of wisedome. Far 860
you well.   *Exit Brakenbury*

2 MURTHERER What shall I stab him as he sleepes?

1 MURTHERER No hee'l say twas done cowardly when he
wakes.

2 MURTHERER Why he shall neuer wake vntill the great
iudgement day.

1 MURTHERER Why then hee'l say, we stabd him sleeping.

2 MURTHERER The vrging of that word Iudgement, hath
bred a kind of remorse in me.

1 MURTHERER What art thou afraid.   870

2 MURTHERER Not to kill him hauing a warrant, but to
be dãnd for killing him, from the which no warrant
can defend me.

1 MURTHERER I thought thou had'st bin resolute.

2 MURTHERER So I am, to let him liue.

1 MURTHERER Ile backe to the Duke of Glocester, and tell him so.

2 MURTHERER Nay, I pray thee stay a little, I hope this passionate humor of mine will change, it was wont to
880 hold me but while one tels xx.

⌐He tels xx⌐

1 MURTHERER How doest thou feele thy selfe now?

2 MURTHERER Some certaine dregs of conscience are yet within me.

1 MURTHERER Remember our reward when the deede's done.

2 MURTHERER Zounds he dies, I had forgot the reward.

1 MURTHERER Where's thy conscience now?

2 MURTHERER O, in the Duke of Glocesters purse.

1 MURTHERER When he opens his purse to giue vs our
890 reward, thy conscience flies out.

2 MURTHERER 'Tis no matter, let it go, theres few or none will entertaine it.

1 MURTHERER What if it come to thee againe?

2 MURTHERER Ile not meddle with it, it makes a man a coward: A man cannot steale, but it accuseth him: A man cannot sweare, but it checks him: A man cannot lie with his neighbors wife, but it detects him. 'Tis a blushing shamefast spirit, that mutinies in a mans bosome: it fils a man full of obstacles, it made me once
900 restore a pursse of gold that (by chance) I found, it beggers any man that keepes it: it is turned out of Townes and Citties for a dangerous thing, and euery man that meanes to liue wel, endeuors to trust to himselfe, and liue without it.

1 MURTHERER Zounds 'tis euen now at my elbowe perswading me not to kill the Duke.

2 MURTHERER Take the diuell in thy minde, and beleeue him not, he would insinuate with thee but to make thee sigh.
910 1 MURTHERER I am strong fram'd, he cannot preuaile with me.

2 MURTHERER Spoke like a tall man that respects thy reputation. Come shall we fall to worke?

1 MURTHERER Take him on the costard with the hilts of thy sword, and then throw him into the malmsey But in the next roome.

2 MURTHERER Oh excellent deuice, and make a sop of him.

1 MURTHERER Soft, he wakes.
920 2 MURTHERER Strike.

1 MURTHERER No, wee'l reason with him.

CLARENCE
Where art thou keeper, giue me a cup of wine.

2 MURTHERER
You shall haue wine enough my Lo: anon.

CLARENCE
In Gods name what art thou.

1 MURTHERER   A man as you are.

CLARENCE But not as I am, royall.

1 MURTHERER Nor you as we are, loyall.

CLARENCE
Thy voice is thunder, but thy lookes are humble.

1 MURTHERER
My voice is now the Kings, my lookes mine owne.

CLARENCE
How darkly, and how deadly doest thou speake:
Your eyes do menace me: why looke you pale?   930
Who sent you hither? Wherefore do you come?

2 MURTHERER
To, to, to.

CLARENCE   To murther me.

AMBO   I, I.

CLARENCE
You scarcely haue the hearts to tell me so,
And therefore cannot haue the hearts to doe it.
Wherein my friends haue I offended you?

1 MURTHERER
Offended vs you haue not, but the King.

CLARENCE
I shalbe reconcild to him againe.

2 MURTHERER
Neuer my Lo: therfore prepare to die.

CLARENCE
Are you drawne foorth among a world of men
To slay the innocent? what is my offence.   940
Where is the euidence that doth accuse me:
What lawfull quest haue giuen their verdict vp
Vnto the frowning Iudge, or who pronounst
The bitter sentence of poore Clarence death?
Before I be conuict by course of law,
To threaten me with death, is most vnlawfull:
I charge you as you hope to haue redemption,
By Christs deare bloud shed for our grieuous sinnes,
That you depart and lay no hands on me,
The deede you vndertake is damnable.   950

1 MURTHERER
What we will doe, we doe vpon command.

2 MURTHERER
And he that hath commanded, is our King.

CLARENCE
Erronious Vassailes, the great King of Kings,
Hath in the table of his law commanded,
That thou shalt doe no murder, will you then
Spurne at his edict, and fulfill a mans?
Take heede, for he holds vengeance in his hand,
To hurle vpon their heads that breake his law.

2 MURTHERER
And that same vengeance doth he hurle on thee,
For false forswearing, and for murder too: 960
Thou didst receiue the sacrament, to fight
In quarell of the house of Lancaster.

1 MURTHERER
And like a traitor to the name of God,
Didst breake that vowe, and with thy trecherous
    blade,
Vnripst the bowels of thy soueraignes sonne.

2 MURTHERER
Whom thou was't sworne to cherish and defend.

I MURTHERER

How canst thou vrge Gods dreadfull Law to vs,
When thou hast broke it in such deare degree?

CLARENCE

Alas, for whose sake did I that ill deede,
970 For Edward, for my brother, for his sake:
He sends ye not to murder me for this,
For in that sinne he is as deepe as I:
If God will be auenged for the deede,
O know you yet, he doth it publiquely,
Take not the quarrell from his powerfull arme,
He needes no indirect, or lawlesse course,
To cut off those that haue offended him.

I MURTHERER

Who made thee then a bloudy minister,
When gallant springing braue Plantagenet,
980 That Princely Nouice was stroke dead by thee?

CLARENCE

My brothers loue, the diuell, and my rage.

I MURTHERER

Thy brothers loue, our Duty and thy faults
Prouoke vs hither now to slaughter thee.

CLARENCE

If you do loue my brother, hate not me,
I am his brother, and I loue him well:
If you are hirde for meede, go backe againe,
And I will send you to my brother Glocester,
Who shall reward you better for my life,
Then Edward will for tydings of my death.

2 MURTHERER

990 You are deceiu'd, your brother Glocester hates you.

CLARENCE

Oh no, he loues me, and he holds me deare,
Go you to him from me.

I MURTHERER   I, so we will.

CLARENCE

Tell him, when that our princely father Yorke,
Blest his three sonnes with his victorious arme:
And chargd vs from his soule, to loue each other,
He little thought of this deuided friendship.
Bid Glocester thinke of this, and he will weepe.

I MURTHERER

I, milstones as he lessond vs to weepe.

CLARENCE

O doe not slaunder him for he is kind.

I MURTHERER

1000 As snow in haruest, come you deceiue your selfe,
Tis he that sends vs to destroy you heere.

CLARENCE

It cannot be, for he bewept my Fortune,
And hugd me in his armes, and swore with sobs,
That he would labour my deliuery.

I MURTHERER

Why so he doth, when he deliuers you,
From this earths thraldome, to the ioies of heauen.

2 MURTHERER

Make peace with God, for you must die my Lo:

CLARENCE

Haue you that holy feeling in your soules,
To counsell me to make my peace with God;
And are you yet to your owne soules so blinde,   1010
That you will war with God, by murdring me?
O sirs, consider, they that set you on
To doe this deede, will hate you for the deede.

2 MURTHERER (to 1 Murtherer)

What shall we doe?

CLARENCE   Relent, and saue your soules.

I MURTHERER

Relent? no, tis cowardly and womanish.

CLARENCE

Not to relent, is beastly, sauage, diuelish,
(To 2 Murtherer) My friend, I spie some pitty in thy
     lookes:
Oh if thine eye be not a flatterer,
Come thou on my side, and intreat for me,
A begging Prince, what begger pitties not?   1020
Which of you, if you were a Princes Sonne,
Being pent from Liberty, as I am now,
If two such murtherers as your selues came to you,
Would not intreat for life? as you would begge
Were you in my distresse—

2 MURTHERER Looke behinde you, my Lord.

I MURTHERER (stabbing Clarence)

Take that, and that: if all this wil not serue,
Ile drowne you in the malmesey But, within.

                    Exit with Clarence body

2 MURTHERER

A bloudy deede and desperately dispatcht,
How faine like Pilate would I wash my hands,   1030
Of this most grieuous guilty murder done.

          Enter 1. Murtherer

I MURTHERER

How now? what mean'st thou that thou help'st me
     not?
By heauen the Duke shall know how slacke you haue
     beene.

2 MURTHERER

I would he knew that I had saued his brother.
Take thou the fee, and tell him what I say,
For I repent me that the Duke is slaine.   Exit

I MURTHERER

So doe not I, go coward as thou art:
Well, Ile go hide the body in some hole,
Till that the Duke giue order for his buriall:
And when I haue my meede I will away,   1040
For this will out, and then I must not stay.   Exit

          Flourish. Enter the King sicke, the Queene, Lord   Sc. 5
          Marquesse Dorset, Riuers, Hastings, Catesby,   (2.1)
          Buckingham, ⌈and Grey⌉

KING EDWARD

Why so, now haue I done a good daies worke,
You peeres continue this vnited league,
I euery day expect an Embassage

From my redeemer to redeeme me hence:
And more in peace my soule shall part to heauen,
Since I haue made my friends at peace on earth:
Hastings and Riuers, take each others hand,
Dissemble not your hatred, sweare your loue.

RYUERS
1050   By heauen, my soule is purgd from grudging hate,
And with my hand I seale my true hearts loue.
⌈*He takes Hastings hand*⌉

HASTINGS
So thriue I as I truly sweare the like.

KING EDWARD
Take heede you dally not before your King,
Least he that is the supreme King of Kings,
Confound your hidden falshood and award
Either of you to be the others end.

HASTINGS
So prosper I, as I sweare perfect loue.

RYUERS
And I, as I loue Hastings with my heart.

KING EDWARD (*to Elizabeth*)
Madame, your selfe is not exempt from this,
1060   Nor your son Dorset, Buckingham nor you,
You haue beene factious one against the other:
Wife, loue Lo: Hastings, let him kisse your hand,
And what you doe, doe it vnfainedly.

QUEENE ELIZABETH (*giuing Hastings her hand to kisse*)
There Hastings I will neuer more remember
Our former hatred so thriue I and mine.

KING EDWARD
Dorset, imbrace him: Hastings, loue Lord Marquesse.

DORSET
This enterchange of loue, I here protest,
Vpon my part shalbe inuiolable.

HASTINGS And so sweare I.
    They embrace

KING EDWARD
1070   Now princely Buckingham seale thou this league
With thy embracements to my wiues allies,
And make me happy in your vnity.

BUCKINGHAM (*to Elizabeth*)
When euer Buckingham doth turne his hate,
Vpon your Grace, but with all duteous loue
Doth cherish you and yours, God punish me
With hate, in those where I expect most loue,
When I haue most neede to imploy a friend,
And most assured that he is a friend,
Deepe, hollow, trecherous, and full of guile
1080   Be he vnto me, this doe I begge of heauen,
When I am cold in loue to you or yours.
    They embrace

KING EDWARD
A pleasing cordiall Princely Buckingham,
Is this thy vow vnto my sickly heart:
There wanteth now our brother Glocester here,
To make the blessed period of this peace.
    Enter Ratcliffe, and Glocester

BUCKINGHAM And in good time
Here comes Sir Richard Ratcliffe, and the Duke.

RICHARD GLOCESTER
Good morrow to my soueraigne King & Queene,
And Princely peeres, a happy time of day.

KING EDWARD
Happy indeede as we haue spent the day: 1090
Brother we haue done deedes of charity:
Made peace of enmity, faire loue of hate,
Betweene these swelling wrong insenced peeres.

RICHARD GLOCESTER
A blessed labour, my most soueraigne Lord,
Among this princely heape, if any here
By false intelligence or wrong surmise,
Hold me' a foe,
If I vnwittingly or in my rage,
Haue ought committed that is hardly borne
By any in this presence, I desire   1100
To reconcile me to his friendly peace,
Tis death to me to be at enmity.
I hate it, and desire all good mens loue.
First Madam I intreate true peace of you,
Which I will purchase with my dutious seruice.
Of you my noble Coosen Buckingham,
If euer any grudge were logde betweene vs.
Of you Lo: Riuers, and Lord Gray of you,
That all without desert haue frownd on me,
Dukes, Earles, Lords, gentlemen, indeed of all: 1110
I doe not know that English man aliue,
With whom my soule is any iotte at oddes,
More then the infant that is borne to night:
I thanke my God for my humility.

QUEENE ELIZABETH
A holy day shall this be kept hereafter,
I would to God all strifes were well compounded,
My soueraigne Lord I doe beseech your Highnesse,
To take our brother Clarence to your Grace.

RICHARD GLOCESTER
Why Madame, haue I offred loue for this,
To be so flowted in this royall presence?   1120
Who knowes not that the gentle Duke is dead,
    They all start
You doe him iniury to scorne his corse.

⌈RYUERS⌉
Who knowes not he is dead? who knowes he is?

QUEENE ELIZABETH
All seeing heauen, what a world is this?

BUCKINGHAM
Looke I so pale Lo: Dorset as the rest?

DORSET
I my good L: and no one in the presence,
But his red couler hath forsooke his cheekes.

KING EDWARD
Is Clarence dead, the order was reuerst.

RICHARD GLOCESTER
But he poore man by your first order died,
And that a winged Mercury did beare,   1130

Some tardy cripple bore the countermaund,
That came too lag to see him buried:
God grant that some lesse noble, and lesse loyall,
Neerer in bloudy thoughts, but not in bloud:
Deserue not worse then wretched Clarence did,
And yet go currant from suspition.

Enter Lord Stanley Earle of Darby

STANLEY (*kneeling*)
A boone my soueraigne for my seruice done.

KING EDWARD
I pray thee peace, my soule is full of sorrow.

STANLEY
I will not rise vnlesse your highnesse heare me.

KING EDWARD
1140   Then say at once, what is it thou requests.

STANLEY
The forfeit soueraigne of my seruants life,
Who slew to day a riotous gentleman,
Lately attendant on the Duke of Norfolke.

KING EDWARD
Haue I a tongue to doome my brothers death,
And shall that tongue giue pardon to a slaue?
My brother slew no man, his fault was thought,
And yet his punishment was bitter death.
Who sued to me for him? who in my wrath,
Kneeld at my feete and bid me be aduisde?
1150   Who spoke of Brotherhood? who spoke of loue?
Who told me how the poore soule did forsake
The mighty Warwicke, and did fight for me:
Who tolde me in the field at Teuxbery,
When Oxford had me downe, he rescued me,
And said deare brother, liue and be a King?
Who told me when we both lay in the field,
Frozen almost to death, how he did lappe me
Euen in his garments, and did giue himselfe
All thin and naked to the numbcold night?
1160   All this from my remembrance brutish wrath
Sinfully pluckt, and not a man of you
Had so much grace to put it in my minde.
But when your carters, or your waighting vassailes
Haue done a drunken slaughter, and defaste
The pretious image of our deare Redeemer,
You straight are on your knees for pardon pardon,
And I vniustly too, must grant it you:
But for my brother, not a man would speake,
Nor I vngratious speake vnto my selfe,
1170   For him poore soule: The proudest of you all
Haue beene beholding to him in his life:
Yet none of you would once begge for his life:
Oh God I feare thy Iustice will take hold
On me, and you, and mine, and yours for this.
Come Hastings help me to my closet,
Ah poore Clarence.   *Exeunt some with King & Queen*

RICHARD GLOCESTER
This is the fruits of rashnes: markt you not
How that the guilty kindred of the Queene,
Lookt pale when they did heare of Clarence death?
1180   Oh they did vrge it still vnto the King,

God will reuenge it. Come Lords will you go,
To comfort Edward with our company.

BUCKINGHAM   We wait vpon your Grace.   *Exeunt*

Enter the old Dutches of Yorke, with the two   Sc. 6
children of Clarence   (2.2)

BOY
Good Granam tell vs, is our father dead?

DUTCHESSE   No boy.

DAUGHTER
Why doe you weepe so oft, and beate your breast,
And crie, Oh Clarence my vnhappy sonne?

BOY
Why doe you looke on vs and shake your head,
And call vs Orphanes, wretches, castawaies,
If that our noble father were aliue?   1190

DUTCHESSE
My prety Cosens, you mistake me both,
I doe lament the sicknesse of the King:
As loth to loose him, not your fathers death:
It were lost sorrow, to waile one thats lost.

BOY
Then you conclude my Granam he is dead,
The King mine Vnckle is too blame for this:
God will reuenge it, whom I will importune
With earnest praiers, all to that effect.

DAUGHTER   And so will I.

DUTCHESSE
Peace children, peace, the King doth loue you wel,   1200
Incapable and shallow innocents,
You cannot guesse who causde your fathers death.

BOY
Granam we can: For my good Vnckle Glocester
Tould me, the King prouoked to it by the Queene,
Deuisd impeachments to imprison him:
And when my Vnckle tould me so, he wept,
And pittied me, and kindly kist my cheeke,
Bad me rely on him as on my father,
And he would loue me dearely as his child.

DUTCHESSE
Ah that deceit should steale such gentle shapes,   1210
And with a vertuous visard hide deepe vice:
He is my sonne, I, and therein my shame:
Yet from my dugs he drew not this deceit.

BOY
Thinke you my Vnckle did dissemble Granam?

DUTCHESSE   I boy.

BOY
I cannot thinke it, hark what noise is this.

Enter the Queene with her haire about her ears

QUEENE ELIZABETH
Ah who shall hinder me to waile and weepe?
To chide my fortune, and torment my selfe?
Ile ioine with blacke despaire against my soule,
And to my selfe become an enemy.   1220

DUTCHESSE
What meanes this sceane of rude impatience.

QUEENE ELIZABETH

    To marke an act of tragicke violence:
    Edward, my Lord, thy sonne our King is dead.
    Why grow the branches, when the roote is gone?
    Why wither not the leaues, that want their sap?
    If you will liue, lament: if die, be briefe:
    That our swiftwinged soules may catch the Kings,
    Or like obedient subiects, follow him
    To his new kingdome of nere-changing night.

DUTCHESSE

1230   Ah somuch interest haue I in thy sorrow,
    As I had title in thy noble husband:
    I haue bewept a worthy husbands death,
    And liu'd with looking on his images.
    But now two mirrours of his Princely semblance,
    Are crackt in pieces by malignant death:
    And I for comfort haue but one false glasse,
    That grieues me when I see my shame in him.
    Thou art a widdow, yet thou art a mother,
    And hast the comfort of thy children left:
1240   But death hath snatcht my Husband from mine armes,
    And pluckt two crutches from my feeble hands,
    Clarence and Edward, Oh what cause haue I
    Thine being but a moity of my moane,
    To ouergo thy woes and drowne thy cries?

BOY (*to Elizabeth*)

    Ah Aunt, you wept not for our fathers death,
    How can we aide you with our kindred teares.

DAUGHTER (*to Elizabeth*)

    Our fatherlesse distresse was left vnmoand,
    Your widdow-dolour likewise be vnwept.

QUEENE ELIZABETH

    Giue me no help in lamentation,
1250   I am not barren to bring foorth complaints:
    All springs reduce their currents to mine eies,
    That I being gouernd by the watry moone,
    May send foorth plenteous teares to drowne the world:
    Ah for my husband, for my deere Lo: Edward.

CHILDREN

    Ah for our father, for our deare Lo: Clarence.

DUTCHESSE

    Alas for both, both mine Edward and Clarence.

QUEENE ELIZABETH

    What stay had I but Edward, and he is gone?

CHILDREN

    What stay had we but Clarence, and he is gone?

DUTCHESSE

    What staies had I but they, and they are gone?

QUEENE ELIZABETH

1260   Was neuer Widdow, had so deare a losse.

CHILDREN

    Were neuer Orphanes had so deere a losse.

DUTCHESSE

    Was neuer mother had so deere a losse:
    Alas, I am the mother of these Greefes,
    Their woes are parceld, mine is generall:
    She for an Edward weepes, and so doe I:
    I for a Clarence weepe, so doth not she:

These babes for Clarence weepe, and so doe I:
I for an Edward weepe, so doe not they.
Alas, you three on me threefold distrest,
Poure all your teares, I am your sorrowes nurse,   1270
And I will pamper it with lamentation.

    Enter Richard, Buckingham, Lord Stanley Earle of
    Derbie, Hastings, and Ratcliffe

RICHARD GLOCESTER (*to Elizabeth*)

    Sister haue comfort, all of vs haue cause
    To waile the dimming of our shining Starre:
    But none can helpe our harmes by wayling them.
    Madam, my Mother, I do cry you mercie,
    I did not see your Grace. Humbly on my knee,
    I craue your Blessing.

DUTCHESSE

    God blesse thee, and put meeknes in thy breast,
    Loue, Charity, Obedience, and true Dutie.

RICHARD GLOCESTER

    Amen, (*aside*) and make me die a good old man,   1280
    That is the butt-end of a Mothers blessing;
    I maruell that her Grace did leaue it out.

BUCKINGHAM

    You clowdy-Princes, & hart-sorowing-Peeres,
    That beare this heauie mutuall loade of Moane,
    Now cheere each other, in each others Loue:
    Though we haue spent our Haruest of this King,
    We are to reape the Haruest of his Sonne.
    The broken rancour of your high-swolne hartes,
    But lately splinter'd, knit, and ioyn'd together,
    Must gently be preseru'd, cherisht, and kept: 1290
    Me seemeth good, that with some little Traine,
    Forthwith from Ludlow, the young Prince be fet
    Hither to London, to be crown'd our King.

RICHARD GLOCESTER

    Then be it so; and go we to determine,
    Who they shalbe that straight shall post to Ludlow:
    Madame, and you my Sister will you go,
    To giue your censures in this waighty busines.

QUEENE ELIZABETH *and* DUTCHESSE OF YORKE

    With all our hearts.

    Exeunt manet Buckingham, and Richard

BUCKINGHAM

    My Lord who euer iourneies to the Prince,
    For Gods sake let not vs two stay at home: 1300
    For by the way Ile sort occasion,
    As index to the story we late talkt of,
    To part the Queenes proud kindred from the Prince.

RICHARD GLOCESTER

    My other selfe, my counsels consistory:
    My Oracle, my Prophet, my deare Cosen:
    I as a childe will go by thy direction:
    Towards Ludlow then, for we will not stay behinde.
    Exeunt

    Enter one Citizen at one doore, and another at the   Sc. 7
    other   (2.3)

I CITTIZEN

    Good morrow Neighbour, whither away so fast?

2 CITTIZEN

    I promise you, I scarcely know my selfe.

    Heare you the newes abroad?

1310 I CITTIZEN   Yes, that the King is dead.

2 CITTIZEN

    Ill newes birlady, seldome comes the better,

    I feare, I feare, twill prooue a giddy world.

          Enter another Cittizen

3 CITTIZEN

    Neighbours, God speed.

I CITTIZEN   Giue you good morrow sir.

3 CITTIZEN

    Doth the newes hold of good King Edwards death?

2 CITTIZEN

    I sir, it is too true, God helpe the while.

3 CITTIZEN

    Then masters looke to see a troublous world.

I CITTIZEN

    No no, by Gods good grace his sonne shall raigne.

3 CITTIZEN

    Woe to that land thats gouernd by a childe.

2 CITTIZEN

    In him there is a hope of gouernement,

1320   Which in his nonage counsell vnder him,

    And in his full and ripened yeres himselfe,

    No doubt shall then, and till then gouerne well.

I CITTIZEN

    So stoode the state when Henry the sixt

    Was crownd in Paris, but at ix. moneths olde.

3 CITTIZEN

    Stoode the state so? no, no, good friends, God wot

    For then this land was famously enricht

    With pollitike graue counsell: then the King

    Had vertuous Vnckles to protect his Grace.

I CITTIZEN

    Why so hath this, both by his father and mother.

3 CITTIZEN

1330   Better it were they all came by his father,

    Or by his father there were none at all:

    For emulation, who shall now be neerest,

    Will touch vs all too neare, if God preuent not.

    Oh full of danger is the Duke of Glocester,

    And the Queenes Sons, and Brothers, haut and proud,

    And were they to be rulde, and not to rule,

    This sickly land might solace as before.

I CITTIZEN

    Come come, we feare the worst, all will be well.

3 CITTIZEN

    When cloudes are seen, wise men put on their clokes:

1340   When great leaues fall, then winter is at hand:

    When the sunne sets, who doth not looke for night:

    Vntimely stormes, make men expect a darth:

    All may be well: but if God sort it so,

    Tis more then we deserue or I expect.

2 CITTIZEN

    Truely the hearts of men are full of feare:

    You cannot reason (almost) with a man

    That lookes not heauily, and full of dread.

3 CITTIZEN

    Before the dayes of change still is it so:

    By a diuine instinct mens mindes mistrust

    Ensuing danger, as by proofe we see,   1350

    The water swell before a boistrous storme:

    But leaue it all to God: whither away?

2 CITTIZEN

    Marry we were sent for to the Iustices.

3 CITTIZEN

    And so was I, Ile beare you company.   *Exeunt*

       Enter ⌈Cardinall⌉, young Yorke, Queene Elizabeth,   Sc. 8

       and the Dutches of Yorke   (2.4)

⌈CARDINALL⌉

    Last night I heare they lay them at Northhampton.

    At Stonistratford they do rest to night,

    To morrow or next day, they will be here.

DUTCHESSE

    I long with all my heart to see the Prince,

    I hope he is much growen since last I saw him.

QUEENE ELIZABETH

    But I heare no, they say my sonne of Yorke   1360

    Ha's almost ouertane him in his growth.

YORKE

    I mother, but I would not haue it so.

DUTCHESSE

    Why my young Cosen it is good to growe.

YORKE

    Grandam, one night as we did sit at supper,

    My Vnckle Riuers talkt how I did grow

    More then my brother. I quoth my Nunckle Glocester,

    Small herbes haue grace, groce weedes do grow apace,

    And since me thinkes I would not grow so fast:

    Because sweete flowers are slow, and weedes make

        haste.

DUTCHESSE

    Good faith, good faith, the saying did not hold   1370

    In him that did obiect the same to thee:

    He was the wretchedst thing when he was young,

    So long a growing, and so leisurely,

    That if his rule were true, he should be gratious.

⌈CARDINALL⌉

    Why so no doubt he is, my gracious Madam.

DUTCHESSE

    I hope he is, but yet let mothers doubt.

YORKE

    Now by my troth if I had beene remembred,

    I could haue giuen my Vnckles grace a flout,

    To touch his growth, neerer then he toucht mine.

DUTCHESSE

    How my yong Yorke? I pray thee let me heare it.   1380

YORKE

    Mary they say, my Vnckle grew so fast,

    That he could gnaw a crust at two houres olde:

    Twas full two yeares ere I could get a tooth.

    Granam this would haue beene a byting iest.

DUTCHESSE

    I pray thee pretty Yorke who tolde thee this.

YORKE Granam his nurse.

DUTCHESSE

His Nurse? why she was dead ere thou wast borne.

YORKE

If twere not she, I cannot tell who tolde me.

QUEENE ELIZABETH

A parlous boy, go to, you are too shrewde.

⌈CARDINALL⌉

1390 Good Madame be not angry with the childe.

QUEENE ELIZABETH

Pitchers haue eares.

        Enter ⌈Dorset⌉

⌈CARDINALL⌉   Here comes your sonne, Lo: Dorset.

What newes Lo: Marques?

⌈DORSET⌉   Such newes my Lo:

As grieues me to report.

QUEENE ELIZABETH   How doth the Prince?

⌈DORSET⌉

Well Madame, and in health.

DUTCHESSE   What is thy newes then?

⌈DORSET⌉

Lo: Riuers and Lo: Gray are sent to Pomfret,

And with them, Thomas Vaughan, prisoners.

DUTCHESSE

Who hath committed them?

⌈DORSET⌉   The mighty Dukes,

Glocester and Buckingham.

⌈CARDINALL⌉   For what offence.

⌈DORSET⌉

The summe of all I can, I haue disclosed:

1400 Why, or for what, the nobles were committed,

Is all vnknowen to me my gratious Lord.

QUEENE ELIZABETH

Ay me I see the ruine of our house,

The tyger now hath ceazd the gentle hinde:

Insulting tyranny beginnes to iet,

Vpon the innocent and awlesse throane:

Welcome destruction, Blood and massacre,

I see as in a mappe the ende of all.

DUTCHESSE

Accursed and vnquiet wrangling daies,

How many of you haue mine eies beheld?

1410 My husband lost his life to get the crowne,

And often vp and downe my sonnes were tost,

For me to ioy and weepe their gaine and losse,

And being seated and domestike broiles

Cleane ouerblowne, themselues the conquerours

Make warre vpon themselues, Brother to Brother,

Bloud to bloud, selfe against selfe, O preposterous

And frantike outrage, ende thy damned spleene,

Or let me die to looke on death no more.

QUEENE ELIZABETH (to Yorke)

Come come my boy, we will to sanctuary.

Madam, farwell.

1420 DUTCHESSE   Stay, I will go with you.

QUEENE ELIZABETH

You haue no cause.

⌈CARDINALL⌉ (to Elizabeth) My gratious Lady go,

And thither beare your treasure and your goods,

For my part, Ile resigne vnto your Grace

The seale I keepe, and so betide to me,

As well I tender you and all of yours:

Go Ile conduct you to the sanctuary.   Exeunt

        The Trumpets sound. Enter young Prince Edward,   Sc. 9
        the Dukes of Glocester, and Buckingham, Lord   (3.1)
        Cardinall, with others, including ⌈Lord Stanley Earle
        of Darby and⌉ Catesby

BUCKINGHAM

Welcome sweete Prince to London to your chamber.

RICHARD GLOCESTER (to Prince Edward)

Welcome deare Cosen my thoughts soueraigne,

The weary way hath made you melancholy.

PRINCE EDWARD

No Vnckle, but our crosses on the way   1430

Haue made it tedious, wearisome, and heauy:

I want more Vnckles here to welcome me.

RICHARD GLOCESTER

Sweete Prince, the vntainted vertue of your yeres,

Hath not yet diued into the worlds deceit:

Nor more can you distinguish of a man,

Then of his outward shew, which God he knowes,

Seldome or neuer iumpeth with the heart:

Those Vnckles which you want, were dangerous,

Your Grace attended to their sugred words,

But lookt not on the poison of their hearts: 1440

God keepe you from them, and from such false friends.

PRINCE EDWARD

God keepe me from false friends, but they wer none.

        Enter Lord Maior ⌈and his Traine⌉

RICHARD GLOCESTER

My Lo, the Maior of London comes to greete you.

MAIOR (kneeling to Prince Edward)

God blesse your grace with health and happy daies.

PRINCE EDWARD

I thanke you good my Lo: and thanke you all:

I thought my mother, and my brother Yorke,

Would long ere this haue met vs on the way:

Fie, what a slug is Hastings that he hastes not

To tell vs whether they will come, or no.

        Enter L. Hastings

BUCKINGHAM

In happie time, here comes the sweating Lo: 1450

PRINCE EDWARD (to Hastings)

Welcome my Lo: what will our mother come?

HASTINGS

On what occasion, God he knowes, not I:

The Queene your mother and your brother Yorke

Haue taken sanctuary: The tender Prince

Would faine haue come with me, to meete your Grace,

But by his mother was perforce withheld.

BUCKINGHAM

Fie, what an indirect and peeuish course

Is this of hers? Lo: Cardinall will your grace

Perswade the Queene to send the Duke of Yorke

Vnto his Princely brother presently?   1460

If she deny, Lo: Hastings go with him,
And from her iealous armes plucke him perforce.

CARDINALL

My Lo: of Buckingham, if my weake oratory
Can from his mother winne the Duke of Yorke,
Anone expect him: but if she be obdurate
To milde entreaties, God in heauen forbid
We should infringe the sacred priuiledge
Of blessed sanctuary, not for all this land,
Would I be guilty of so deepe a sinne.

BUCKINGHAM

1470 You are too sencelesse obstinate my Lo:
Too ceremonious and traditionall:
Weigh it not with the grossenes of this age.
You breake not sanctuary in seazing him:
The benefit thereof is alwaies granted
To those whose dealings haue deserude the place,
And those who haue the wit to claime the place.
This Prince hath neither claimed it, nor deserued it,
And therefore in my minde, he cannot haue it.
Then taking him from thence that longs not there,
1480 You breake thereby no priuiledge nor charter:
Oft haue I heard of sanctuary men,
But sanctuary children neuer till now.

CARDINALL

My Lo: you shall ouerrule my minde for once:
Come on Lo: Hastings will you go with me?

HASTINGS I come my Lord.

PRINCE EDWARD

Good Lords make all the speedy hast you may:

          Exit Cardinall & Hastings

Say Vnckle Glocester, if our brother come,
Where shall we soiourne till our coronation?

RICHARD GLOCESTER

Where it seemes best vnto your royall selfe:
1490 If I may councell you, some day or two,
Your highnes shall repose you at the tower:
Then where you please, and shalbe thought most fit
For your best health and recreation.

PRINCE EDWARD

I doe not like the tower of any place:
Did Iulius Cæsar build that place my Lord?

BUCKINGHAM

He did, my gratious Lo: begin that place,
Which since succeeding ages haue reedified.

PRINCE EDWARD

Is it vpon record, or els reported
Successiuely from age to age he built it?

BUCKINGHAM

1500 Vpon record my gratious liege.

PRINCE EDWARD

But say my Lo: it were not registred,
Me thinkes the truth should liue from age to age,
As twere retailde to all posterity,
Euen to the generall all-ending day.

RICHARD GLOCESTER (*aside*)

So wise, so young, they say doe neuer liue long.

PRINCE EDWARD What say you Vnckle?

RICHARD GLOCESTER

I say without characters fame liues long:
(*Aside*) Thus like the formall vice iniquity,
I morallize two meanings in one word.

PRINCE EDWARD

That Iulius Cesar was a famous man,   1510
With what his valour did t'enrich his wit,
His wit set downe to make his valure liue:
Death made no conquest of this conquerour,
For yet he liues in fame though not in life:
Ile tell you what my Cosen Buckingham.

BUCKINGHAM What my good Lord?

PRINCE EDWARD

And if I liue vntill I be a man,
Ile winne our auncient right in France againe,
Or die a souldier as I liude a King.

RICHARD GLOCESTER (*aside*)

Short summers lightly haue a forward spring.   1520

       Enter young Yorke, Hastings, Cardinall

BUCKINGHAM

Now in good time here comes the Duke of Yorke.

PRINCE EDWARD

Rich. of Yorke how fares our louing brother?

YORKE

Well my dread Lo: so must I call you now.

PRINCE EDWARD

I brother to our griefe as it is yours:
Too late he died that might haue kept that title,
Which by his death hath lost much maiesty.

RICHARD GLOCESTER

How fares our noble Cosen Lo: of Yorke?

YORKE

I thanke you gentle Vnckle, well. O my Lo:
You said that idle weedes are fast in growth:
The Prince my brother hath outgrowen me farre.   1530

RICHARD GLOCESTER

He hath my Lo:

YORKE   And therfore is he idle?

RICHARD GLOCESTER

Oh my faire Cosen, I must not say so.

YORKE

He is more beholding to you then then I.

RICHARD GLOCESTER

He may command me as my soueraigne,
But you haue power in me as a kinseman.

YORKE

I pray you Vnckle render me this dagger.

RICHARD GLOCESTER

My dagger little Cosen, with all my heart.

PRINCE EDWARD A begger brother?

YORKE

Of my kind Vnckle that I know will giue,
It being but a toy, which is no griefe to giue.   1540

RICHARD GLOCESTER

A greater gift then that, Ile giue my Cosen.

YORKE

A greater gift, O thats the sword to it.

RICHARD GLOCESTER

    I gentle Cosen, were it light enough.

YORKE

    O then I see you will part but with light gifts,

    In weightier things youle say a begger nay.

RICHARD GLOCESTER

    It is too heauy for your Grace to weare.

YORKE

    I'd weigh it lightly were it heauier.

RICHARD GLOCESTER

    What would you haue my weapon little Lord?

YORKE

    I would, that I might thanke you as you call me.

1550   RICHARD GLOCESTER How?

YORKE Little.

PRINCE EDWARD

    My Lo: of Yorke will still be crosse in talke:

    Vnckle your grace knowes how to beare with him.

YORKE

    You meane to beare me, not to beare with me:

    Vnckle, my brother mockes both you and me,

    Because that I am little like an Ape,

    He thinkes that you should beare me on your

        shoulders.

BUCKINGHAM

    With what a sharpe prodigal wit he reasons:

    To mittigate the scorne he giues his Vnckle,

1560   He pretely and aptly taunts himselfe,

    So cunning and so young is wonderfull.

RICHARD GLOCESTER (to Prince Edward)

    My Lo: wilt please you passe along,

    My selfe and my good Coosen Buckingham,

    Will to your mother, to entreate of her,

    To meete you at the tower, and welcome you.

YORKE (to Prince Edward)

    What will you go vnto the tower my Lo?

PRINCE EDWARD

    My Lo: protector needes will haue it so.

YORKE

    I shall not sleepe in quiet at the tower.

RICHARD GLOCESTER Why, what should you feare there?

YORKE

1570   Mary my Vnckle Clarence angry ghost:

    My Granam tolde me he was murdred there.

PRINCE EDWARD

    I feare no Vnckles dead.

RICHARD GLOCESTER   Nor none that liue, I hope.

PRINCE EDWARD

    And if they liue, I hope I neede not feare:

    (To Yorke) But come my Lo: and with a heauy heart

    Thinking on them, go we vnto the tower.

          A Senet. Exeunt all but Richard, Buckingham,

                     and Catesby

BUCKINGHAM (to Richard)

    Thinke you my Lo: this little prating Yorke,

    Was not incensed by his subtile mother,

    To taunt and scorne you thus opprobriously?

RICHARD GLOCESTER

    No doubt, no doubt, Oh tis a parlous boy,

    Bold, quicke, ingenious, forward, capable,   1580

    He is all the mothers, from the top to toe.

BUCKINGHAM

    Well, let them rest: Come hither Catesby, thou art

        sworne

    As deepely to effect what we intend,

    As closely to conceale what we impart.

    Thou knowest our reasons vrgde vpon the way:

    What thinkest thou? is it not an easie matter

    To make Lo: William Hastings of our minde,

    For the instalement of this noble Duke,

    In the seate royall of this famous Ile?

CATESBY

    He for his fathers sake so loues the Prince,   1590

    That he will not be wonne to ought against him.

BUCKINGHAM

    What thinkest thou then of Stanley will not he?

CATESBY

    He will doe all in all as Hastings doth.

BUCKINGHAM

    Well then no more but this: go gentle Catesby,

    And as it were farre off, sound thou Lo: Hastings,

    How he doth stand affected to our purpose,

    If thou do'st finde him tractable to vs,

    Encourage him, and tell him all our reasons:

    If he be leaden, icie, cold, vnwilling,

    Be thou so too: and so breake off y^r talke,   1600

    And giue vs notice of his inclination:

    For we to morrow hold deuided counsels,

    Wherein thy selfe shalt highly be emploied.

RICHARD GLOCESTER

    Commend me to Lo: William, tell him Catesby,

    His auncient knot of dangerous aduersaries

    To morrow are let bloud at Pomfret Castle,

    And bid my Lord for ioy of this good newes,

    Giue Mistresse Shore, one gentle kisse the more.

BUCKINGHAM

    Good Catesby goe effect this busines soundly.

CATESBY

    My good Lo: both, with all the heede I can.   1610

RICHARD GLOCESTER

    Shall we heare from you Catesby ere we sleepe?

CATESBY You shall my Lord.

RICHARD GLOCESTER

    At Crosby House there shall you finde vs both.

                    Exit Catesby

BUCKINGHAM

    My Lo: what shall we doe, if we perceiue

    Lo: Hastings will not yeeld to our complots?

RICHARD GLOCESTER

    Chop of his head, something we will determine,

    And looke when I am King, claime thou of me

    The Earledome of Hereford and all the moueables,

    Whereof the King my brother was possest.

BUCKINGHAM

    Ile claime that promise at your Graces hand.   1620

RICHARD GLOCESTER
 And looke to haue it yeelded with all kindnes:
 Come let vs suppe betimes, that afterwards
 We may digest our complots in some forme.   *Exeunt*

Sc. 10   *Enter a Messenger to the Doore of Lo: Hastings*
(3.2) MESSENGER (*knocking*)
 My Lord, my Lord.
HASTINGS ⌈*within*⌉   Who knockes.
MESSENGER   One from Lo: Stanley.
        ⌈*Enter L. Hastings*⌉
HASTINGS
 What is't a clocke?
MESSENGER   Vpon the stroke of foure.
HASTINGS
 Cannot my Lord Stanley sleepe these tedious nights?
MESSENGER
 So it appeares by that I haue to say:
 First he commends him to your noble selfe.
HASTINGS What then.
MESSENGER
1630 Then certifies your Lordship, that this Night
 He dreamt the boare had rased off his helme:
 Besides, he saies there are two councels kept,
 And that may be determined at the one,
 Which may make you and him to rewe at the other,
 Therefore he sends to know your Lordships pleasure:
 If you will presently take horse with him,
 And with all speede post with him toward the North,
 To shun the danger that his soule diuines.
HASTINGS
 Go fellow go, returne vnto thy Lord,
1640 Bid him not feare the seperated counsels:
 His honour and my selfe are at the one,
 And at the other, is my good friend Catesby:
 Where nothing can proceede that toucheth vs,
 Whereof I shall not haue intelligence.
 Tell him his feares are shallow, without instance.
 And for his dreames, I wonder he is so simple,
 To trust the mockery of vnquiet slumbers,
 To flie the boare, before the boare pursues,
 Were to incense the boare to follow vs,
1650 And make pursuite where he did meane no chase:
 Go bid thy Master rise and come to me,
 And we will both together to the tower,
 Where he shall see the boare will vse vs kindely.
MESSENGER
 Ile goe, my Lord, and tell him what you say.   *Exit*
        Enter Catesby
CATESBY
 Many good morrowes to my noble Lo:
HASTINGS
 Good morrow Catesby, you are early stirring,
 What newes what newes, in this our tottering state?
CATESBY
 It is a reeling world indeede my Lo:
 And I beleeue will neuer stand vpright,
1660 Till Richard weare the garland of the Realme.

HASTINGS
 How? weare the garland? doest thou meane the
   crowne?
CATESBY I my good Lord.
HASTINGS
 Ile haue this crowne of mine, cut from my shoulders
 Before Ile see the crowne so foule misplaste:
 But canst thou guesse that he doth aime at it.
CATESBY
 I, on my life, and hopes to find you forward
 Vpon his party for the gaine thereof,
 And thereupon he sends you this good newes,
 That this same very day, your enemies,
 The kindred of the Queene must die at Pomfret.   1670
HASTINGS
 Indeede I am no mourner for that newes,
 Because they haue beene still my aduersaries:
 But that Ile giue my voice on Richards side,
 To barre my Masters heires in true discent,
 God knowes I will not doe it to the death.
CATESBY
 God keepe your Lordship in that gratious minde.
HASTINGS
 But I shall laugh at this a tweluemonth hence,
 That they which brought me in my Masters hate,
 I liue to looke vpon their tragedy:
 Well Catesby, ere a fortnight make me older,   1680
 Ile send some packing, that yet thinke not on it.
CATESBY
 Tis a vile thing to die my gratious Lord,
 When men are vnprepard and looke not for it.
HASTINGS
 O Monstrous monstrous, and so fals it out
 With Riuers, Vaughan, Gray, and so twill doe
 With some men els, that thinke themselues as safe
 As thou, and I, who as thou knowest are deare
 To Princely Richard, and to Buckingham.
CATESBY
 The Princes both make high account of you,
 (*Aside*) For they account his head vpon the bridge.   1690
HASTINGS
 I know they doe, and I haue well deserued it.
        Enter Lord Stanley
 Come on, come on, where is your boare-speare man?
 Feare you the boare and go so vnprouided?
STANLEY
 My Lo: good morrow: good morrow Catesby:
 (*To Hastings*) You may iest on: but by the holy roode,
 I doe not like these seuerall councels I.
HASTINGS
 My Lo: I hould my life as deare as you doe yours,
 And neuer in my dayes I doe protest,
 Was it so pretious to me as it is now:
 Thinke you, but that I know our state secure,   1700
 I would be so triumphant as I am?
STANLEY
 The Lords at Pomfret when they rode from London,
 Were iocund, and supposde their states were sure,
 And they indeed had no cause to mistrust:

But yet you see how soone the day ouercast,
This sodaine stab of rancour I misdoubt,
Pray God, I say, I proue a needelesse coward:
What, shall we toward the tower? the day is spent.

HASTINGS

1710   Come, come, haue with you: Wot you what, my Lord,
To day the Lords you talkt of, are beheaded.

STANLEY

They for their truth might better weare their heads,
Then some that haue accusde them weare their hats:
But come my Lo: let vs away.
     Enter ⌈Hastings⌉ a Purssuant

HASTINGS

Go on before, Ile follow presently.
                  Exit L. Stanley, & Catesby
Well met Hastings, how goes the world with thee?

PURSIUANT

The better that your Lordship please to aske.

HASTINGS

I tell thee man tis better with me now,
Then when I met thee last where now we meete:
Then was I going prisoner to the tower,
1720   By the suggestion of the Queenes allies:
But now I tell thee (keepe it to thy selfe)
This day those enemies are put to death,
And I in better state then euer I was.

PURSIUANT

God hold it to your honors good content.

HASTINGS

Gramercy Hastings there, drinke that for me.
     He throwes him his purse
PURSIUANT God saue your Lordship.   *Exit Pursuiuant*
     Enter a priest

PRIEST

Well met, my Lord, I am glad to see your Honor.

HASTINGS

I thanke thee, good Sir Iohn, with all my heart.
I am in your debt for your last exercise:
1730   Come the next sabaoth and I will content you.
     ⌈*He whispers in his eare.*⌉
     Enter Buckingham

BUCKINGHAM

What talking with a priest, Lo: Chamberlaine,
Your friends at Pomfret they doe need the priest
Your honour hath no shriuing worke in hand.

HASTINGS

Good faith and when I met this holy man,
The men you talke of came into my minde:
What, go you toward the tower?

BUCKINGHAM

I doe, my Lord, but long I can not stay there,
I shall returne before your Lordship thence.

HASTINGS

Nay like enough, for I stay dinner there.

BUCKINGHAM (*aside*)

1740   And supper too, although thou knowest it not:
Come will you go?

HASTINGS   Ile wait vpon your Lordship.
                                 Exeunt

Enter Sir Richard Ratcliffe, with Halberds, carrying Sc. 11
the Nobles (Lo: Riuers, Gray, and Vaughan) to   (3.3)
death at Pomfret

RYUERS

Sir Richard Ratcliffe let me tell thee this:
To day shalt thou behold a subiect die,
For truth, for duty, and for loyalty.

GRAY (*to Ratcliffe*)

God blesse the Prince from all the packe of you:
A knot you are of damned bloudsuckers.

VAUGHAN (*to Ratcliffe*)

You liue, that shall cry woe for this heereafter.

RATCLIFFE

Dispatch, the limit of your liues is out.

RYUERS

O Pomfret Pomfret, Oh thou bloudy prison,
Fatall and ominous to noble peeres.
Within the guilty closure of thy wals   1750
Richard the second here was hackt to death:
And for more slaunder to thy dismall seate,
We giue to thee our guiltlesse bloud to drinke.

GRAY

Now Margarets curse is falne vpon our heads:
For standing by, when Richard stabd her sonne.

RYUERS

Then curst she Hastings, then curst she Buckingham:
Then curst she Richard. Oh remember God,
To heare her praier for them as now for vs,
And for my sister, and her princely sonnes: 1760
Be satisfied deare God with our true bloud,
Which as thou knowest vniustly must be spilt.

RATCLIFFE

Make haste, the houre of death is expiate.

RYUERS

Come Gray, come Vaughan, let vs here imbrace.
Farewell vntill we meete againe in heauen.   *Exeunt*

Enter Buckingham, Lord Stanley Earle of Darby, Sc. 12
Hastings, Bishop of Ely, Norfolke, ⌈Catesby,⌉ with (3.4)
others, at a Table

HASTINGS

Now Noble Peeres the cause why we are met,
Is to determine of the coronation:
In Gods name speake, when is the royall day?

BUCKINGHAM

Is all things ready for that solemn time?

STANLEY

It is, and wants but nomination.   1770

BISHOP OF ELY

To morrow then, I iudge a happy day.

BUCKINGHAM

Who knowes the Lo: protectors mind herein?
Who is most inward with the noble Duke.

BISHOP OF ELY

Your Grace me thinks should soonest know his mind.

BUCKINGHAM

We know each others faces: for our harts,
He knowes no more of mine, then I of yours:

Or I of his, my Lord, then you of mine:
Lo: Hastings you and he are neere in loue.

HASTINGS

I thanke his Grace, I know he loues me well:
1780 But for his purpose in the coronation:
I haue not sounded him nor he deliuerd
His gracious pleasure any way therein:
But you my Honorable Lo: may name the time,
And in the Dukes behalfe, Ile giue my voice,
Which I presume he will take in Gentle part.

Enter Gloucester

BISHOP

In happie time here comes the Duke himselfe.

RICHARD GLOCESTER

My noble L. and Cosens all, good morrow,
I haue beene long a sleeper, but I trust
My absence doth neglect no great designe,
1790 Which by my presence might haue been concluded.

BUCKINGHAM

Had not you come vpon your kew my Lo:
William L: Hastings had pronounst your part:
I meane your voice for crowning of the King.

RICHARD GLOCESTER

Than my Lo: Hastings no man might be bolder,
His Lordship knowes me well, and loues me well.
My Lo: of Elie, when I was last in Holborne:
I saw good strawberries in your garden there,
I doe beseech you send for some of them.

BISHOP OF ELY

Mary and will, my Lord, with all my heart.

Exit Bishop

RICHARD GLOCESTER

1800 Cosen of Buckingham, a word with you:
(*Aside*) Catesby hath sounded Hastings in our busines,
And findes the testy Gentleman so hoat,
That he will loose his head eare giue consent,
His Masters Child as worshipfull he termes it,
Shall loose the roialty of Englands throane.

BUCKINGHAM

Withdraw your selfe a while, Ile goe with you.

Exeunt Richard ⌈and Buckingham⌉

STANLEY

We haue not yet set downe this day of triumph,
To morrow in my iudgement is too sudden:
For I my selfe am not so well prouided,
1810 As els I would be, were the day prolonged.

Enter B. of Ely

BISHOP OF ELY

Where is my L. the Duke of Gloster,
I haue sent for these strawberies.

HASTINGS

His Grace lookes cheerfully and smooth this morning,
Theres some conceit or other likes him well,
When that he bids good morrow with such spirit.
I thinke there is neuer a man in christendome,
Can lesser hide his loue or hate then he:
For by his face straight shall you know his heart.

STANLEY

What of his heart perceiue you in his face,
By any likelihood he shewed to day?   1820

HASTINGS

Mary, that with no man here he is offended.
For were he, he had shewen it in his lookes.

STANLEY I pray God he be not.

Enter Richard ⌈and Buckingham⌉

RICHARD GLOCESTER

I pray you all, tell me what they deserue,
That doe conspire my death with diuelish plots,
Of damned witchcraft, and that haue preuaild,
Vpon my body with their hellish charmes?

HASTINGS

The tender loue I beare your grace my Lord,
Makes me most forward in this Princely presence,
To doome the offenders whatsoeuer they be: 1830
I say my Lo: they haue deserued death.

RICHARD GLOCESTER

Then be your eies the witnesse of their euill,
See how I am bewitcht, behold mine arme
Is like a blasted sapling withered vp.
And this is Edwards wife, that monstrous witch,
Consorted with that harlot strumpet Shore,
That by their witchcraft, thus haue marked me.

HASTINGS

If they haue done this deed my Noble Lo:

RICHARD GLOCESTER

If, thou protector of this damned strumpet,
Talkst thou to me of iffes? thou art a traitor.   1840
Off with his head. Now by Saint Paule I sweare,
I will not dine, vntill I see the same,
Some see it done,
The rest that loue me, rise and follow me.

Exeunt manet ⌈Catesby⌉ with the Lord Hastings

HASTINGS

Wo wo for England, not a whit for me:
For I too fond might haue preuented this:
Stanley did dreame the boare did raise our helmes,
But I did scorne it, and disdaine to flie,
Three times to day, my footecloth horse did stumble,
And started when he lookt vpon the tower,   1850
As loath to beare me to the slaughterhouse.
Oh, now I need the Priest that spake to me,
I now repent I tolde the Pursiuant,
As too triumphing, how mine enemies
To day at Pomfret bloudily were butcherd,
And I my selfe secure in grace and fauour:
Oh Margaret Margaret: now thy heauy curse,
Is lighted on poore Hastings wretched head.

⌈CATESBY⌉

Come, come, dispatch, the Duke would be at dinner:
Make a short shrift, he longs to see your head.   1860

HASTINGS

O momentary grace of mortall men,
Which we more hunt for, then the grace of God:
Who buildes his hope in th'aire of your good lookes,

Liues like a drunken sayler on a mast,
Ready with euery nod to tumble downe
Into the fatall bowels of the deepe.

⌜CATESBY⌝
Come, come, dispatch, 'tis bootlesse to exclaime.

HASTINGS
O bloody Richard: miserable England,
I prophecie the fearefull'st time to thee,
1870   That euer wretched Age hath look'd vpon.
Come leade me to the blocke, beare him my head,
They smile at me who shortly shalbe dead.   *Exeunt*

Sc. 13   *Enter Richard and Buckingham in rotten armour,*
(3.5)   *maruellous ill-fauoured*

RICHARD GLOCESTER
Come Cosen, canst thou quake and change thy colour?
Murther thy breath in middle of a word,
And then againe beginne, and stop againe,
As if thou wert distraught and mad with terror.

BUCKINGHAM
Tut I can counterfait the deepe Tragedian:
Tremble and start at wagging of a Straw:
Speake, and looke backe, and prie on euery side,
1880   Intending deepe suspition: gastly lookes
Are at my seruice like inforced smiles,
And both are ready in their offices
At any time to grace my stratagems.
            Enter Maior

RICHARD GLOCESTER (*aside to Buckingham*) Here comes the
      Maior.

BUCKINGHAM (*aside to Richard*)
Let me alone to entertaine him. (*Aloud*) Lo: Maior,

RICHARD GLOCESTER ⌜*calling as to one within*⌝ Looke to the
      drawbridge there.

BUCKINGHAM Harke, a drumme.

RICHARD GLOCESTER ⌜*calling as to one within*⌝ Catesby
      ouerlooke the wals.

BUCKINGHAM Lord Maior, the reason we haue sent.

RICHARD GLOCESTER
1890   Looke backe, defend thee, here are enemies.

BUCKINGHAM
God and our innocence defend and guard vs.
            Enter ⌜*Catesby*⌝ *with Hastings head*

RICHARD GLOCESTER
O, O, be quiet, it is Catesby.

CATESBY
Here is the head of that ignoble traitor,
The daungerous and vnsuspected Hastings.

RICHARD GLOCESTER
So deare I lou'd the man, that I must weepe:
I tooke him for the plainest harmelesse Creature,
That breathed vpon the earth, a christian,
Made him my booke, wherein my soule recorded,
The history of all her secret thoughts:
1900   So smoothe he daubd his vice with shew of vertue,
That his apparant open guilt omitted:
I meane his conuersation with Shores wife,
He liu'd from all attainder of suspect.

BUCKINGHAM
The couertst sheltred traitor that euer liu'd,
(*To the Maior*) Would you imagine, or almost beleeue,
Wert not that by great preseruation
We liue to tell it, that the subtile traitor
This day had plotted in the councell house,
To murder me, and my good Lord of Glocester.

MAIOR Had he done so?   1910

RICHARD GLOCESTER
What thinke you we are Turkes or Infidels,
Or that we would against the forme of lawe,
Proceede thus rashly in the villaines death,
But that the extreame perill of the case,
The peace of England, and our persons safety
Inforst vs to this execution.

MAIOR
Now faire befall you, he deserued his death,
And your good Graces both, haue well proceeded
To warne false traitours from the like attempts:
I neuer lookt for better at his hands,   1920
After he once fell in with Mistresse Shore.

⌜RICHARD GLOCESTER⌝
Yet had not we determined he should die,
Vntill your Lordship came to see his end,
Which now the louing haste of these our friends,
Something against our meanings haue preuented,
Because, my Lord, we would haue had you heare
The traitor speake, and timerously confesse
The maner, and the purpose of his treason,
That you might well haue signified the same
Vnto the Citizens, who happily may   1930
Misconster vs in him, and wayle his death.

MAIOR
But my good Lord, your graces word shall serue
As well as I had seene and heard him speake,
And doe not doubt, right noble Princes both,
But Ile acquaint our dutious citizens,
With all your iust proceedings in this cause.

RICHARD GLOCESTER
And to that end we wish'd your Lordship here
To auoyde the censures of the carping world.

BUCKINGHAM
Which since you come too late of our intent,
Yet witnesse what you heare we did intend,   1940
And so my good Lord Maior, we bid farwell.
            Exit Maior

RICHARD GLOCESTER
Goe after, after, coosin Buckingham,
The Maior towards Guildhall hies him in all post,
There at your meetest vantage of the time,
Inferre the bastardy of Edwards children:
Tell them how Edward put to death a Cittizen,
Onely for saying he would make his sonne
Heire to the Crowne, meaning (indeede) his house,
Which by the signe thereof was termed so.
Moreouer, vrge his hatefull luxurie,   1950
And bestiall appetite in change of lust,
Which stretcht vnto theyr seruants, daughters, wiues,

Euen where his raging eye, or sauage heart
Without controll listed to make a prey:
Nay for a neede thus farre, come neere my person,
Tell them, when that my mother went with childe
Of that insatiate Edward, noble Yorke
My princely father then had warres in Fraunce,
And by true computation of the tyme

1960 Found, that the issue was not his begot,
Which well appeared in his lineaments,
Being nothing like the noble Duke my father:
Yet touch this sparingly as it were farre off,
Because, my Lord, you know my mother liues.

BUCKINGHAM

Doubt not, my Lord, Ile play the Orator,
As if the golden fee for which I pleade
Were for my selfe: and so my Lord adue.

He offers to goe

RICHARD GLOCESTER

If you thriue well, bring them to Baynards castle,
Where you shall finde me well accompanyed,

1970 Wyth reuerend fathers and well learned Bishops.

BUCKINGHAM

I goe, and towards three or foure a clocke
Look for the news that the Guildhall affords.

Exit Buckingham

RICHARD GLOCESTER

Now will I in to take some priuy order,
To draw the brats of Clarence out of sight,
And to giue notice, that no maner person
Haue any tyme recourse vnto the Princes. *Exeunt*

Sc. 14   *Enter a Scriuener with a paper in his hand*
(3.6) SCRIUENER

Here is the indictment of the good Lord Hastings,
Which in a set hand fairely is engrosst,
That it may be to day read ouer in Paules:

1980 And marke how well the sequele hangs together,
Eleuen houres I haue spent to wryte it ouer,
For yesternight by Catesby was it sent me,
The president was full as long a doyng,
And yet within these fiue houres Hastings liued,
Vntaynted, vnexamined, free, at liberty:
Heeres a good world, the while. Whoe is so grosse
That cannot see this palpable deuice?
Yet whoe so bold but sayes he sees it not?
Bad is the world, and all will come to naught,

1990 When such ill dealing must be sene in thought. *Exit*

Sc. 15   *Enter Richard and Buckingham at seuerall Doores*
(3.7) RICHARD GLOCESTER

How now how now, what say the Cittizens?

BUCKINGHAM

Now by the holy mother of our Lord,
The Citizens are mumme, say not a word.

RICHARD GLOCESTER

Toucht you the bastardy of Edwards children?

BUCKINGHAM

I did, wyth his Contract with Lady Lucy,

And his Contract by Deputie in France,
The insatiate greedinesse of his desire,
And his enforcement of the Citie Wiues,
His tyranny for trifles, his owne bastardy,
As beyng got, your father then in Fraunce: 2000
And his resemblance, being not like the Duke.
Withall I did inferre your lineaments,
Beyng the right Idea of your father,
Both in your face and noblenesse of minde,
Laid open all your victories in Scotland:
Your discipline in warre, wisedome in peace:
Your bounty, vertue, faire humility:
Indeede left nothing fitting for your purpose
Vntoucht, or sleightly handled in discourse:
And when mine oratory grew toward ende, 2010
I bid them that did loue their countries good,
Crie, God saue Richard, Englands royall King.

RICHARD GLOCESTER And did they so?

BUCKINGHAM

No so God helpe me, they spake not a word,
But like dumbe statues or breathing stones,
Starde each on other and lookt deadly pale:
Which when I saw, I reprehended them,
And askt the Maior, what meant this wilfull silence?
His answere was, the people were not vsed
To be spoke to, but by the Recorder. 2020
Then he was vrgde to tell my tale againe:
Thus, saith the Duke, thus hath the Duke inferd:
But nothing spoke in warrant from himselfe:
When he had done, some followers of mine owne
At lower end of the Hall, hurld vp their caps,
And some ten voices cried, God saue King Richard.
And thus I tooke the vantage of those few.
Thankes gentle Cittizens and friends quoth I,
This generall applause and chearefull shoute,
Argues your wisedomes and your loue to Richard: 2030
And euen here brake off and came away.

RICHARD GLOCESTER

What tonglesse blockes were they, would they not
  speake?

⌈BUCKINGHAM⌉ No by my troth my Lo:

RICHARD GLOCESTER

Will not the Maior then, and his brethren come.

BUCKINGHAM

The Maior is here at hand, intend some feare,
Be not you spoke with, but by mighty suite:
And looke you get a praier booke in your hand,
And stand betweene two churchmen good my Lo:
For on that ground Ile build a holy descant:
And be not easily wonne to our request: 2040
Play the maides part, still answer nay, and take it.

RICHARD GLOCESTER

I goe, and if you pleade aswell for them,
As I can say nay to thee, for my selfe,
No doubt weele bring it to a happie issue.

One knocks within

BUCKINGHAM

Go, go vp to the leads, the Lord Maior knocks.

Exit Richard

Enter the Maior, Aldermen, and Citizens
Welcome, my L., I dance attendance heare,
I thinke the Duke will not be spoke withall.
          Enter Catesby
Now *Catesby* what saies your Lord to my request?
CATESBY
      He doth intreat your grace, my Noble Lord,
2050 To visit him to morrow or next daie,
      He is within with two right reuerend fathers,
      Diuinely bent to meditation,
      And in no worldly suites would he be mou'd,
      To draw him from his holy exercise.
BUCKINGHAM
      Returne good *Catesby* to the gracious Duke,
      Tell him my selfe, the Maior and Aldermen,
      In deepe designes in matter of great moment,
      No lesse importing then our generall good,
      Are come to haue some conference with his grace.
CATESBY
2060 Ile signifie so much vnto him straight.   *Exit*
BUCKINGHAM
      A ha my Lord this prince is not an Edward:
      He is not lulling on a lewd day bed,
      But on his knees at meditation:
      Not dalying with a brace of Curtizans,
      But meditating with two deepe Diuines:
      Not sleeping to ingrosse his idle body,
      But praying to inrich his watchfull soule.
      Happy were England, would this vertuous prince
      Take on his Grace the so.erainty thereof,
2070 But sure I feare we shall not winne him to it.
MAIOR
      Marry God defend his grace should say vs nay.
BUCKINGHAM
      I feare he wil, here Catesby comes againe.
          Enter Catesby
      Now Catesby, what saies his Grace?
CATESBY
      He wonders to what end, you haue assembled
      Such troupes of Cittizens to come to him,
      His grace not being warnd thereof before,
      He feares, my Lord, you meane no good to him.
BUCKINGHAM
      Sorrie I am my noble Cosen should
      Suspect me that I meane no good to him.
2080 By heauen we come to him in perfit loue,
      And so once more returne and tell his grace:
                              Exit Catesby
      When hollie and deuout religious men,
      Are at their beads, tis much to draw them thence,
      So sweet is zealous contemplation.
          Enter Richard a lofte, betweene two bishops. ⌐Enter
          Catesby below⌐
MAIOR
      See where his Grace stands tween two clergie men.
BUCKINGHAM
      Two props of vertue for a christian Prince,
      To staie him from the fall of vanitie,

And see a Booke of Prayer in his hand,
True Ornaments to know a holy man.
Famous Plantaganet, most gracious prince,   2090
Lend fauorable eare to our request,
And pardon vs the interruption
Of thy deuotion and right Christian zeale.
RICHARD GLOCESTER
      My Lord, there needs no such apologie,
      I do beseech your Grace to pardon me,
      Who earnest in the seruice of my God,
      Deferr'd the visitation of my friends,
      But leauing this, what is your graces pleasure?
BUCKINGHAM
      Euen that I hope which pleaseth God aboue,
      And all good men of this vngouerned Ile.   2100
RICHARD GLOCESTER
      I do suspect I haue done some offence,
      That seemes disgracious in the Citties eie,
      And that you come to reprehend my ignorance.
BUCKINGHAM
      You haue my Lord, would it might please your grace
      On our entreaties to amend your fault.
RICHARD GLOCESTER
      Else wherefore breath I in a Christian land?
BUCKINGHAM
      Know then it is your fault that you resigne
      The supreame seat, the throne maiesticall,
      The sceptred office of your auncestors,
      Your State of Fortune, and your Deaw of Birth,   2110
      The lineall glorie of your roiall house,
      To the corruption of a blemisht stocke:
      Whiles in the mildnesse of your sleepie thoughts,
      Which here we waken to our countries good,
      The noble Ile doth want hir proper limbes,
      Hir face defac't with scars of infamie,
      Hir Royall Stock grafft with ignoble Plants,
      And almost shouldred in the swallowing gulph,
      Of darke forgetfulnesse and deepe obliuion,
      Which to recure we hartily solicit,   2120
      Your gratious selfe to take on you the charge
      And Kingly Gouernment of this your Land,
      Not as Protector steward substitute,
      Or lowlie factor for anothers gaine:
      But as successiuelie from bloud to bloud,
      Your right of birth, your Emperie, your owne:
      For this consorted with the Citizens
      Your verie worshipfull and louing frinds,
      And by their vehement instigation,
      In this iust Cause come I to moue your grace.   2130
RICHARD GLOCESTER
      I cannot tell, if to depart in silence,
      Or bitterlie to speake in your reproofe,
      Best fitteth my degree or your condition:
      Your loue deserues my thanks, but my desert
      Vnmeritable shunes your high request,
      First if all obstacles were cut awaie,
      And that my path were euen to the crown,
      As the ripe reuenew and dew of birth,

Yet so much is my pouerty of spirit,
2140 So mightie and so many my defects,
That I would rather hide me from my greatnes,
Beeing a Barke to brooke no mightie sea,
Then in my greatnes couet to be hid,
And in the vapour of my glorie smotherd:
But God be thank'd there is no need of me,
And much I need to helpe you were there need,
The roiall tree hath left vs roiall fruit,
Which mellowed by the stealing houres of time,
Will well become the seat of maiestie,
2150 And make no doubt vs happie by his raigne,
On him I laie that you would laie on me:
The right and fortune of his happie stars,
Which God defend that I should wring from him.

BUCKINGHAM
My lord, this argues conscience in your grace,
But the respects thereof are nice and triuiall,
All circumstances well considered:
You saie that Edward is your brothers sonne,
So saie we to, but not by Edwards wife,
For first was he contract to lady *Lucy*,
2160 Your mother liues a witnesse to his vowe,
And afterward by substitute betrothed
To *Bona* sister to the king of Fraunce,
These both put off a poore petitioner
A care-crazd mother to a many Sonnes,
A beauty-waining and distressed widow,
Euen in the afternoone of her best daies
Made prise and purchase of his wanton eye,
Seduc'd the pitch and height of his degree,
To base declension and loathd bigamie,
2170 By her in his vnlawfull bed he got,
This Edward whom our maners call the prince,
More bitterlie could I expostulate,
Saue that for reuerence to some aliue
I giue a sparing limit to my tongue:
Then good my Lord, take to your royall selfe,
This proffered benefit of dignitie:
If not to blesse vs and the land withall,
Yet to draw forth your Noble Ancestrie,
From the corruption of abusing times,
2180 Vnto a lineall true deriued course.

MAIOR (*to Richard*)
Do good my Lord, your Cittizens entreat you.

BUCKINGHAM (*to Richard*)
Refuse not, mightie Lord, this proffer'd loue.

CATESBY (*to Richard*)
O make them ioifull grant their lawful suite.

RICHARD GLOCESTER
Alas, why would you heape this care on me,
I am vnfit for state and Maiestie,
I do beseech you take it not amisse,
I cannot nor I will not yeeld to you.

BUCKINGHAM
If you refuse it as in loue and zeale,
Loath to depose the child your brothers sonne,
2190 As well we know your tendernes of heart,
And gentle kind effeminate remorse,

Which wee haue noted in you to your kindred,
And egallie indeed to all estates,
Yet know, whether you accept our suite or no,
Your brothers sonne shall neuer raigne our king,
But we will plant some other in the throane,
To the disgrace and downfall of your house:
And in this resolution here we leaue you.
Come Citizens, zounds ile intreat no more.

RICHARD GLOCESTER
O do not sweare my Lord of Buckingham. 2200
        ⌐*Exeunt Buckingham and some others*⌐

CATESBY
Call him againe, sweet Prince, accept their sute.

⌐ANOTHER⌐
If you denie them, all the land will rew it.

RICHARD GLOCESTER
Will you inforce me to a world of cares:
Call them againe,   *Exit one or more*
        I am not made of stone,
But penetrable to your kind intreates,
Albeit against my conscience and my soule.
    Enter Buckingham, and the rest
Coosin of Buckingham, and sage graue men,
Since you will buckle fortune on my backe,
To beare her burthen whether I will or no,
I must haue patience to indure the lode, 2210
But if blacke scandale or foule-fac't reproch
Attend the sequell of your imposition,
Your meere inforcement shall acquittance mee
From all the impure blots and staines thereof,
For God doth knowe, and you may partly see,
How farre I am from the desire of this.

MAIOR
God blesse your grace, we see it, and will say it.

RICHARD GLOCESTER
In saying so, you shall but say the truth.

BUCKINGHAM
Then I salute you with this Royall title:
Long liue kind Richard, Englands worthie king. 2220

⌐ALL BUT RICHARD⌐ Amen.

BUCKINGHAM
To morrow may it please you to be crown'd.

RICHARD GLOCESTER
Euen when you please, for you will haue it so.

BUCKINGHAM
To morrow then we will attend your grace,
And so most ioyfully we take our leaue.

RICHARD GLOCESTER (*to the bishops*)
Come, let vs to our holy Worke againe:
Farewel my coosine, farwel gentle friends.
    Exeunt Richard and bishops aboue, the rest
                           below

Enter the Quee. mother Elizabeth, the Duchesse of   **Sc. 16**
Yorke, and Marques Dorset, at one doore, Lady   **(4.1)**
Anne Duchesse of Glocester with Clarence daughter
at another doore

DUCHESSE OF YORKE
Who meets vs heere? my neece Plantagenet,

Led in the hand of her kind Aunt of Gloster?
2230 Now, for my Life, shee's wandring to the Tower,
On pure hearts loue, to greet the tender Prince.
Daughter, well met.

LADY ANNE   God giue your Graces both,
A happie and a ioyfull time of day.

QUEENE ELIZABETH
As much to you, good Sister, whether awaie?

LADY ANNE
No farther then the Tower, and as I ghesse
Vpon the like deuotion as your selues,
To gratulate the gentle Princes there.

QUEENE ELIZABETH
Kind sister thanks, weele enter al togither,

Enter from the Tower ⌈Brakenbury⌉ the Lieutenant

And in good time here the Lieutenant comes.
2240 M. Lieutenant, pray you by your leaue,
How doth the Prince, and my young Sonne of Yorke?

BRAKENBURY
Right wel deare Madam: by your patience,
I may not suffer you to visite them,
The King hath strictlie charged the contrarie.

QUEENE ELIZABETH
The King? whose that?

BRAKENBURY   I meane the Lord protector.

QUEENE ELIZABETH
The Lord protect him from that Kinglie title:
Hath he set boundes betweene their loue and me:
I am their mother, who shall barre me from them?

DUCHESSE OF YORKE
I am their Fathers Mother, I will see them.

LADY ANNE
2250 Their aunt I am in law, in loue their mother:
Then bring me to their sights, Ile beare thy blame,
And take thy office from thee on my perill.

BRAKENBURY
No, Madame, no; I may not leaue it so:
I am bound by oath, and therefore pardon me.

Exit Lieutenant

Enter Stanlie

STANLEY
Let me but meete you Ladies one houre hence,
And Ile salute your grace of Yorke, as Mother:
And reuerente looker on, of two faire Queenes.
(*To Anne*) Come Madam, you must straight to
    Westminster,
There to be crowned, Richards royall Queene.

QUEENE ELIZABETH
2260 Ah cut my lace asunder, that my pent heart,
May haue some scope to beate, or else I swoone,
With this dead killing newes.

LADY ANNE
Despightfull tidings, O vnpleasing newes.

DORSET (*to Anne*)
Be of good cheare: (*To Elizabeth*) Mother, how fares
    your grace?

QUEENE ELIZABETH
O Dorset speake not to me, get thee gone,

Death and destruction dogges thee at thy heeles,
Thy Mothers name is ominous to children,
If thou wilt outstrip death, go crosse the seas,
And liue with Richmond, from the reach of hell,
Go hie thee, hie thee from this slaughter house,   2270
Least thou increase the number of the dead,
And make me die the thrall of Margarets cursse,
Nor Mother, Wife, nor counted Englands Queene.

STANLEY
Full of wise care is this your counsell Madam,
(*To Dorset*) Take all the swift aduantage of the
    howres,
You shall haue letters from me to my sonne,
In your behalfe, to meete you on the way,
Be not ta'ne tardie, by vnwise delaie.

DUTCHESSE OF YORKE
O ill dispersing winde of miserie,
O my accursed wombe, the bed of death,   2280
A Cocatrice hast thou hatcht to the world,
Whose vnauoided eye is murtherous.

STANLEY (*to Anne*)
Come Madam, come, I in all hast was sent.

LADY ANNE
And I in all vnwillingnes will go,
O would to God that the inclusiue verge,
Of golden mettall that must round my browe,
Were red hotte steele to seare me to the braines,
Annointed let me be with deadlie Venome,
And die, ere men can say, God saue the Queene.

QUEENE ELIZABETH
Goe, goe, poore soule, I enuie not thy glorie,   2290
To feede my humor, wish thy selfe no harme.

LADY ANNE
No, why? when he that is my husband now,
Came to me as I followed Henries course,
When scarse the bloud was well washt from his
    handes,
Which issued from my other angel husband,
And that deare saint, which then, I weeping followed,
O, when I say, I lookt on Richards face,
This was my wish, be thou quoth I accurst,
For making me so young, so olde a widow,
And when thou wedst, let sorrow haunt thy bed,   2300
And be thy wife, if any be so madde,
More miserable made by the Life of thee,
Then thou hast made me by my deare Lordes death,
Loe, ere I can repeate this curse againe,
With in so small a time, my womans hart,
Grosselie grewe captiue to his honie wordes,
And prou'd the subiecte of mine owne soules curse,
Which hitherto hath held mine eyes from rest,
For neuer yet, one houre in his bed,
Did I enioy the golden dew of sleepe,   2310
But with his timerous dreames was still awak'd,
Besides, he hates me for my father Warwicke,
And will no doubt, shortlie be rid of me.

QUEENE ELIZABETH
Poore heart adieu, I pittie thy complaining.

LADY ANNE

No more then with my soule I mourne for yours.

DORSET

Farewell, thou wofull welcomer of glorie.

LADY ANNE

Adew poore soule, that takst thy leaue of it.

DUTCHESSE OF YORKE

Go thou to Richmond, and good fortune guide thee.
⌈*Exit Dorset*⌉

Go thou to Richard, and good Angels tend thee,
⌈*Exeunt Anne, Stanley, and Clarence daughter*⌉

Go thou to sanctuarie, and good thoughts possesse
2320   thee,   ⌈*Exit Elizabeth*⌉

I to my graue where peace and rest lie with me,

Eightie odde yeares of sorrow haue I seene,

And each houres ioy wrackt with a weeke of teene.
⌈*Exit*⌉

Sc. 17   *Sound a Sennet. Enter Richard in pompe,*
(4.2)   *Buckingham, Catesby, ⌈with other Nobles⌉, and a*
              Page

KING RICHARD

Stand al apart. Coosin of Buckingham.

BUCKINGHAM My gracious Soueraigne.

KING RICHARD Giue me thy hand:
              Sound ⌈a Sennet⌉. Here he ascendeth the throne

Thus high by thy aduice

And thy assistance is king Richard seated:

But shal we weare these Glories for a day?
2330   Or shall they last, and we reioice in them.

BUCKINGHAM

Stil liue they, and for euer let them last.

KING RICHARD

Ah Buckingham, now do I plaie the touch,

To trie if thou be currant gold indeed:

Young Edward liues: thinke now what I would
              speake.

BUCKINGHAM Saie on my louing Lord.

KING RICHARD

Whie Buckingham, I saie I would be king.

BUCKINGHAM

Whie so you are my thrice renowned liege.

KING RICHARD

Ha: am I king? tis so, but Edward liues.

BUCKINGHAM

True noble prince.

KING RICHARD   O bitter consequence,
2340   That Edward stil should liue true noble prince.

Coosin, thou wast not wont to be so dul:

Shal I be plaine? I wish the bastards dead,

And I would haue it immediately performde.

What saist thou now? speake suddenlie, be briefe.

BUCKINGHAM Your grace may doe your pleasure.

KING RICHARD

Tut, tut, thou art all yce, thy kindnesse freezes,

Saie, haue I thy consent that they shal die?

BUCKINGHAM

Giue me some little breath, some pause deare lord,

Before I positiuelie speake in this:

I wil resolue you herein presently.   *Exit Buckingham*   2350

CATESBY (*to another, aside*)

The king is angrie, see, he gnawes his lip.

KING RICHARD (*aside*)

I wil conuerse with iron witted fooles

And vnrespectiue boies, none are for me

That looke into me with considerate eies:

High reaching Buckingham growes circumspect.

Boy.

PAGE My Lord.

KING RICHARD

Knowst thou not any whom corrupting gold

Will tempt vnto a close exploit of death.

PAGE

I know a discontented gentleman,   2360

Whose humble meanes match not his haughtie spirit,

Gould were as good as twentie Orators,

And will no doubt tempt him to any thing.

KING RICHARD

What is his name.

PAGE   His name my Lord is Tirrell.

KING RICHARD

I partly know the man: Go call him hither Boy,
              Exit Page

⌈*Aside*⌉ The deepe reuoluing wittie Buckingham,

No more shall be the neighbour to my counsells,

Hath he so long held out with me vntirde

And stops he nowe for breath? Well, be it so.
              Enter Lord Stanley Earle of Darby

How now, Lord Stanley, what's the neewes?   2370

STANLEY Know my louing Lord,

The Marques Dorset as I heare is fled

To Richmond, in those partes beyond the seas

Where he abides.

KING RICHARD

Come hither Catesby. (*Aside to Catesby*) Rumor it
              abroad

That Anne my wife is very grieuous sicke,

I will take order for her keeping close:

Enquire me out some meane borne gentleman,

Whom I will marrie straight to Clarence daughter,

The boy is foolish, and I feare not him: 2380

Looke how thou dreamst: I say againe giue out

That Anne my Queene is sicke and like to die.

About it, for it stands me much vpon

To stop all hopes whose growth may damadge me,
              ⌈*Exit Catesby*⌉

(*Aside*) I must be married to my brothers daughter,

Or else my kingdome stands on brittle glasse,

Murther her brothers, and then marrie her,

Vncertaine waie of gaine, but I am in

So far in bloud that sinne will plucke on sin,

Teare falling pittie dwels not in this eie.   2390
              Enter Tirrel ⌈and kneeles⌉

Is thy name Tirrill?

TIRREL

Iames Tirrell and your most obedient subiect.

KING RICHARD
  Art thou indeed?
TIRREL   Proue me my gracious Lord.
KING RICHARD
  Darst thou resolue to kill a friend of mine?
TIRREL
  Please you, but I had rather kill two enemies.
KING RICHARD
  Why there thou hast it two deepe enemies,
  Foes to my rest, and my sweet sleepes disturbers,
  Are they that I would haue thee deale vpon:
  Tirrel I meane those bastards in the tower.
TIRREL
2400 Let me haue open meanes to come to them,
  And soone ile rid you from the feare of them.
KING RICHARD
  Thou singst sweet musicke. Hearke, come hither *Tirrel*,
  Go by this token, rise and lend thine eare,
      Richard wispers in his eare
  Tis no more but so, saie it is done,
  And I will loue thee and prefer thee for it.
TIRREL I will dispatch it straight.
⌈KING RICHARD⌉
  Shal we heare from thee *Tirrel* ere we sleep?
      Enter Buckingham
⌈TIRREL⌉ Ye shall my lord.   Exit
BUCKINGHAM
  My lord, I haue considered in my mind,
2410 The late request that you did sound me in.
KING RICHARD
  Well, let that rest, Dorset is fled to Richmond.
BUCKINGHAM I heare the newes my lord.
KING RICHARD
  Stanley he is your wifes sonne. Wel looke to it.
BUCKINGHAM
  My lord, I claime the gift, my dew by promise,
  For which your honor and your faith is pawnd,
  The Earledome of Herford and the moueables,
  Which you haue promised I shall possesse.
KING RICHARD
  Stanley looke to your wife, if she conuay
  Letters to Richmond you shall answere it.
BUCKINGHAM
2420 What saies your highnes to my iust request.
KING RICHARD
  I doe remember me, Henrie the sixt
  Did prophecie that Richmond should be king,
  When Richmond was a little peeuish boy:
  A king perhaps, perhaps.
BUCKINGHAM   My lord.
KING RICHARD
  How chance the prophet could not at that time,
  Haue told me I being by, that I should kill him.
BUCKINGHAM
  My lord, your promise for the Earledome.
KING RICHARD
  Richmond, when last I was at Exeter,
  The Maior in curtesie showd me the Castle,

And called it Ruge-mount, at which name I started,   2430
Because a Bard of Ireland told me once
I should not liue long after I saw Richmond.
BUCKINGHAM My lord.
KING RICHARD I, whats a clocke?
BUCKINGHAM
  I am thus bold to put your grace in mind
  Of what you promisd me.
KING RICHARD   But whats a clocke?
BUCKINGHAM Vpon the stroke of ten.
KING RICHARD Well, let it strike.
BUCKINGHAM Whie let it strike?
KING RICHARD
  Because that like a Iacke thou keepst the stroke   2440
  Betwixt thy begging and my meditation,
  I am not in the giuing vaine to day.
BUCKINGHAM
  Whie then resolue me whether you wil or no?
KING RICHARD
  Thou troublest me, I am not in the vain.
      Exit Richard, followed by all but Buckingham
BUCKINGHAM
  And is it thus? repayes he my deepe seruice
  With such contempt, made I him king for this?
  O let me thinke on *Hastings* and be gone
  To Brecnock while my fearefull head is on.
      Exit ⌈*at another doore*⌉

      Enter Sir Iames Tirrell   Sc. 18
TIRREL   (4.3)
  The tyrranous and bloudie act is done,
  The most arch-deed of pitteous massacre,   2450
  That euer yet this land was guiltie of,
  Dighton and Forrest whom I did suborne,
  To do this peece of ruthles butcherie,
  Albeit they were flesht villains, bloudie dogs,
  Melted with tendernes and milde compassion,
  Wept like two children in their deaths sad storie:
  O thus quoth Dighton laie the gentle babes,
  Thus thus quoth Forrest girdling on another,
  Within their alablaster innocent armes,
  Their lips were foure red Roses on a stalke,   2460
  And in their summer beautie kist each other,
  A booke of praiers on their pillow laie,
  Which once quoth Forrest almost changd my mind,
  But ô the Diuell their the villaine stopt,
  When Dighton thus told on we smothered
  The most replenished sweet worke of nature,
  That from the prime creation euer she framed,
  Hence both are gone with Conscience and Remorse,
  They could not speake and so I left them both,
  To beare this tidings to the bloudie king.   2470
      Enter Ki. Richard
  And here he comes, all health my soueraigne Lord.
KING RICHARD
  Kind Tirrell am I happie in thy newes.
TIRREL
  If to haue done the thing you gaue in charge,

Beget your happinesse, be happie then
For it is done.

KING RICHARD   But didst thou see them dead?

TIRREL

I did my Lord.

KING RICHARD   And buried gentle *Tirrell?*

TIRREL

The Chaplaine of the tower hath buried them,
But where (to say the truth) I do not know.

KING RICHARD

Come to me *Tirrel* soone at after supper,
2480   When thou shalt tell the processe of their death,
Meane time but thinke how I may do thee good,
And be inheritor of thy desire,
Farewel til then.

TIRREL   I humbly take my leaue.   *Exit Tirrel*

KING RICHARD

The sonne of Clarence haue I pent vp close,
His daughter meanelie haue I matcht in mariage,
The sonnes of Edward sleepe in Abrahams bosome,
And Anne my wife hath bid this world godnight,
Now for I know the Brittaine Richmond aimes
At young Elizabeth, my brothers daughter,
2490   And by that knot lookes proudly ore the crowne,
To her go I a iollie thriuing wooer,
            Enter Ratcliffe, ⌜running⌝

RATCLIFFE   My Lord.

KING RICHARD

Good newes or bad that thou comst in so bluntly?

RATCLIFFE

Bad newes my lord, *Ely* is fled to Richmond,
And Buckingham backt with the hardie Welchmen,
Is in the field, and still his power increaseth.

KING RICHARD

Ely with Richmond troubles me more neare
Then Buckingham and his rash leuied Strength:
Come I haue learn'd that feareful commenting,
2500   Is leaden seruitor to dull delaie,
Delaie leades impotent and snaile-pact beggerie,
Then fierie expedition be my wing,
Ioues Mercurie an Herald for a king:
Go muster men, my counsaile is my shield,
We must be briefe when traitors braue the field.
                                    Exeunt

Sc. 19   *Enter old Queene Margaret sola*
(4.4)   QUEENE MARGARET

So now prosperitie begins to mellow
And drop into the rotten mouth of Death:
Here in these confines slilie haue I lurkt,
To watch the waining of mine enemies:
2510   A dire induction am I witnesse to,
And wil to Fraunce, hoping the consequence
Wil prooue as bitter, blacke and tragical.
            ⌜Enter the Dutchesse of Yorke and Queene Elizabeth⌝
Withdraw thee wretched Margaret, who comes here?

QUEENE ELIZABETH

Ah my poore princes, ah my tender babes!

My vnblowne flowers, new appearing sweets,
If yet your gentle soules flie in the ayre
And be not fixt in doome perpetual,
Houer about me with your aierie winges,
And heare your mothers lamentation.

QUEENE MARGARET *(aside)*

Houer about her, saie that right for right,   2520
Hath dimd your infant morne, to aged night.

DUTCHESSE OF YORKE

So many miseries haue craz'd my voyce,
That my woe-wearied tongue is still and mute.
Edward Plantagenet, why art thou dead?

QUEENE MARGARET *(aside)*

Plantagenet doth quit Plantagenet,
Edward for Edward, payes a dying debt.

QUEENE ELIZABETH

Wilt thou, O God, flie from such gentle lambes,
And throw them in the intrailes of the Wolfe:
When didst thou sleepe when such a deed was done?

QUEENE MARGARET *(aside)*

When holie *Harry* died, and my sweet sonne.   2530

DUTCHESSE OF YORKE

Dead life, blind sight, poore mortal liuing ghost,
Woes sceane, worlds shame, graues due by life
        vsurpt,
Breefe abstract and record of tedious dayes,
Rest thy vnrest on Englands lawful earth,
Vnlawfullie made drunke with innocents bloud.
            ⌜They⌝ sit

QUEENE ELIZABETH

Ah that thou wouldst assoone affoord a graue,
As thou canst yeeld a melancholie seate,
Then would I hide my bones, not rest them here:
Ah who hath anie cause to mourne but wee!

QUEENE MARGARET *(comming forward)*

If ancient sorrow be most reuerent,   2540
Giue mine the benefite of signorie,
And let my greefes frowne on the vpper hand,
If sorrow can admitte societie,
Tell ouer your woes againe by vewing mine,
I had an Edward, till a Richard kild him:
I had a Husband, till a Richard kild him:
(To Elizabeth) Thou hadst an Edward, till a Richard
        kild him:
Thou hadst a Richard, till a Richard kild him.

DUTCHESSE OF YORKE ⌜rising⌝

I had a Richard to, and thou didst kill him:
I had a Rutland to, thou holpst to kill him.   2550

QUEENE MARGARET

Thou hadst a Clarence to, and Richard kild him:
From forth the kennell of thy wombe hath crept,
A hel-hound that doeth hunt vs all to death,
That dogge, that had his teeth before his eyes,
To worrie lambes, and lap their gentle bloud,
That foule defacer of Gods handie worke,
That reignes in gauled eyes of weeping soules:
That excellent grand Tyrant of the earth,
Thy wombe let loose, to chase vs to our graues,

2560　O vpright, iust, and true disposing God,
　　　How doe I thanke thee, that this carnal curre,
　　　Praies on the issue of his mothers bodie,
　　　And makes her puefellow with others mone.

DUTCHESSE OF YORKE

　　　O, Harries wife triumph not in my woes,
　　　God witnes with me, I haue wept for thine.

QUEENE MARGARET

　　　Beare with me, I am hungrie for reuenge,
　　　And now I cloie me with beholding it,
　　　Thy Edward, he is dead, that kill'd my Edward,
　　　Thy other Edward dead, to quitte my Edward,
2570　Yong Yorke, he is but boote because both they
　　　Matcht not the high perfection of my losse,
　　　Thy Clarence he is dead, that stab'd my Edward,
　　　And the beholders of this franticke plaie,
　　　The adulterate Hastings, Riuers, Vａghan, Gray,
　　　Vntimelie smothred in their duskie graues,
　　　Richard yet liues, hels blacke intelligencer,
　　　Onely reserued their factor to buie soules,
　　　And send them thether, but at hand at hand,
　　　Ensues his piteous, and vnpittied end,
2580　Earth gapes, hell burnes, fiendes roare, saintes praie,
　　　To haue him suddenly conueied from hence.
　　　Cancell his bond of life, deare God I plead,
　　　That I may liue and say, the dog is dead.

QUEENE ELIZABETH

　　　O thou didst prophecie the time would come,
　　　That I should wish for thee to helpe me cursse,
　　　That botteld spider, that foule bunch-backt toade.

QUEENE MARGARET

　　　I cald thee then, vaine floorish of my fortune,
　　　I cald thee then, poore shadow, painted Queene,
　　　The presentation of, but what I was,
2590　The flattering Index of a direfull pageant,
　　　One heaued a high, to be hurld downe belowe,
　　　A mother onelie mockt with two faire babes,
　　　A dreame of what thou wast, a garish flagge,
　　　To be the aime of euerie dangerous shot,
　　　A signe of dignitie, a breath, a bubble,
　　　A Queene in ieast onelie to fill the sceane,
　　　Where is thy husband now, where be thy brothers?
　　　Where are thy two Sonnes, wherein doest thou ioye?
　　　Who sues and kneeles, and sayes God saue the
　　　　　Queene?
2600　Where be the bending peeres that flattered thee?
　　　Where be the thronging troopes that followed thee?
　　　Decline all this, and see what now thou art,
　　　For happie wife, a most distressed widow,
　　　For ioyfull Mother, one that wailes the name,
　　　For Queene, a verie caitiue crownd with care,
　　　For one being sued to, one that humblie sues,
　　　For she that scornd at me, now scornd of me,
　　　For she being feared of all, now fearing one:
　　　For she commaunding all, obeyed of none,
2610　Thus hath the course of iustice whirl'd about,
　　　And left thee but, a verie praie to time,
　　　Hauing no more, but thought of what thou wert,

To torture thee the more, being what thou art,
Thou didst vsurpe my place, and doest thou not,
Vsurpe the iust proportion of my sorrow,
Now thy proud necke, beares halfe my burthened
　　yoke,
From which, euen here, I slippe my wearie head,
And leaue the burthen of it all on thee:
Farewell Yorkes wife, and Queene of sad mischance,
These English woes, shall make me smile in France.　2620

QUEENE ELIZABETH ⌈rising⌉

O thou wel skild in curses, staie a while,
And teach me how to curse mine enemies.

QUEENE MARGARET

Forbeare to sleepe the nights, and fast the daies,
Compare dead happinesse with liuing woe,
Thinke that thy babes were sweeter then they were,
And he that slew them fouler then he is,
Bettring thy losse makes the bad causer worse,
Reuoluing this, wil teach thee how to curse.

QUEENE ELIZABETH

My words are dul, O quicken them with thine.

QUEENE MARGARET

Thy woes wil make them sharp, & pierce like mine.　2630
　　　　　　　　　　　　　　　　　Exit Margaret

DUTCHESSE OF YORKE

Why should calamitie be ful of words?

QUEENE ELIZABETH

Windie atturnies to their Client woes,
Aerie recorders of intestate ioies,
Poore breathing Orators of miseries,
Let them haue scope, though what they will impart,
Helpe nothing els, yet do they ease the hart.

DUTCHESSE OF YORKE

If so, then be not toong-tide, go with me,
And in the breath of bitter words lets smother
My damned sonne, that thy two sweet sons smotherd,
　　A march within
The Trumpet sounds, be copious in exclaimes.　　2640
　　Enter K. Richard and his Traine ⌈marching with
　　Drummes and Trumpets⌉

KING RICHARD

Who intercepts me in my expedition?

DUTCHESSE OF YORKE

O she, that might haue intercepted thee
By strangling thee in her accursed wombe,
From al the slaughters wretch, that thou hast done.

QUEENE ELIZABETH

Hidst thou that forehead with a golden crowne
Where should be branded, if that right were right,
The slaughter of the Prince that owed that Crowne,
And the dire death of my poore sonnes, and brothers:
Tel me thou villaine slaue, where are my children?

DUTCHESSE OF YORKE

Thou tode, thou tode, where is thy brother Clarence?　2650
And little Ned Plantagenet, his sonne?

QUEENE ELIZABETH

Where is the gentle *Riuers, Vaughan, Gray?*

DUTCHESSE OF YORKE Where is kind *Hastings?*

KING RICHARD (*to his Traine*)

    A flourish trumpets, strike alarum drummes,

    Let not the heauens heare these tel-tale women

    Raile on the Lords annointed. Strike I saie.

        Flourish. Alarums

    (*To the women*) Either be patient, and intreat me faire,

    Or with the clamorus report of war:

    Thus will I drowne your exclamations.

2660 DUTCHESSE OF YORKE Art thou my son?

KING RICHARD

    I, I thanke God, my father and your selfe,

DUTCHESSE OF YORKE

    Then patiently here my impatience.

KING RICHARD

    Madam I haue a touch of your condition,

    That cannot brooke the accent of reproofe.

DUTCHESSE OF YORKE

    O let me speake.

KING RICHARD   Do then, but Ile not heare.

DUTCHESSE OF YORKE

    I will be mild and gentle in my words.

KING RICHARD

    And briefe good mother for I am in hast.

DUTCHESSE OF YORKE

    Art thou so hastie? I haue staid for thee,

    God knowes in torment, and in agonie,

KING RICHARD

2670   And came I not at last to comfort you?

DUTCHESSE OF YORKE

    No by the holie roode thou knowst it well,

    Thou camst on earth to make the earth my hell,

    A greuous burthen was thy berth to me,

    Techie and waiward was thy infancie,

    Thy schoele-daies frightful, desperate, wild, and furious,

    Thy prime of Manhood, daring, bold, and venturous,

    Thy age confirmed, proud, subtile, slye, and bloudie,

    More milde, but yet more harmfull; Kinde in hatred:

    What comfortable houre canst thou name

2680   That euer grac't me in thy companie?

KING RICHARD

    Faith none but Humphrey Hewer, that cald your grace

    To breake fast once forth of my companie,

    If I be so disgracious in your eye,

    Let me march on, and not offend you Madam.

    Strike vp the Drumme.

DUTCHESSE OF YORKE   I pray thee heare me speake.

KING RICHARD

    You speake too bitterly.

DUTCHESSE OF YORKE   Heare me a word:

    For I shal neuer speake to thee againe.

KING RICHARD So.

DUTCHESSE OF YORKE

    Either thou wilt die by Gods iust ordinance,

2690   Eare from this war thou turne a conqueror,

    Or I with griefe and extreame age shall perish,

    And neuer more behold thy face againe,

    Therefore take with thee my most heauy curse,

    Which in the daie of battaile tire thee more

    Then all the compleat armor that thou wearst,

    My praiers on the aduerse partie fight,

    And there the little soules of Edwards children,

    Whisper the spirits of thine enemies,

    And promise them successe and victorie,

    Bloudie thou art, bloudie wil be thy end,   2700

    Shame serues thy life, and doth thy death attend.

                        Exit

QUEENE ELIZABETH

    Though far more cause, yet much lesse spirit to curse

    Abides in me, I saie Amen to all.

KING RICHARD

    Staie Maddam, I must talke a word with you.

QUEENE ELIZABETH

    I haue no moe sonnes of the royall bloud,

    For thee to slaughter, for my daughters Richard,

    They shalbe praying nunnes not weeping Queenes,

    And therefore leuell not to hit their liues.

KING RICHARD

    You haue a daughter cald Elizabeth,

    Vertuous and faire, roiall and gracious.   2710

QUEENE ELIZABETH

    And must she die for this? O let her liue!

    And ile corrupt her maners, staine her beautie,

    Slander my selfe as false to Edwards bed

    Throw ouer her the vale of infamie,

    So she may liue vnskard of bleeding slaughter,

    I will confesse she was not Edwards daughter.

KING RICHARD

    Wrong not her birth, she is a roiall Princesse.

QUEENE ELIZABETH

    To saue her life, ile saie she is not so.

KING RICHARD

    Her life is safest onlie in hir birth.

QUEENE ELIZABETH

    And onlie in that safetie died her brothers.   2720

KING RICHARD

    Lo at their births good stars were opposite.

QUEENE ELIZABETH

    No to their liues ill friends were contrarie.

KING RICHARD

    All vnauoided is the doome of destinie,

QUEENE ELIZABETH

    True when auoided grace makes destinie,

    My babes were destinde to a fairer death,

    If grace had blest thee with a fairer life.

KING RICHARD

    Madam, so thriue I in my enterprize

    And dangerous successe of bloody warres

    As I intend more good to you and yours,

    Then euer you or yours by me were harm'd.   2730

QUEENE ELIZABETH

    What good is couerd with the face of heauen,

    To be discouerd that can do me good.

KING RICHARD

    The aduancement of your children gentle Ladie.

QUEENE ELIZABETH

Vp to some scaffold, there to loose their heads.

KING RICHARD

Vnto the dignitie and height of Fortune,
The high imperial tipe of this earths glorie.

QUEENE ELIZABETH

Flatter my sorrowe with report of it,
Tell me what state, what dignitie, what honor,
Canst thou demise to anie child of mine.

KING RICHARD

2740   Euen all I haue, I and my selfe and all,
Will I withal endow a child of thine,
So in the Lethe of thy angrie soule,
Thou drown the sadd remembrance of those wrongs
Which thou supposest I haue done to thee.

QUEENE ELIZABETH

Be briefe, least that the processe of thy kindnes,
Last longer telling then thy kindnes date.

KING RICHARD

Then know that from my soule I loue thy daughter.

QUEENE ELIZABETH

My daughters mother thinkes yᵗ with her soule.

KING RICHARD What do you thinke?

QUEENE ELIZABETH

2750   That thou dost loue my daughter from thy soule,
So from thy soules loue didst thou loue her brothers,
And from my harts loue I do thanke thee for it.

KING RICHARD

Be not so hastie to confound my meaning,
I meane that with my soule I loue thy daughter,
And do intend to make her Queene of England.

QUEENE ELIZABETH

Well then, who dost thou meane shal be her king?

KING RICHARD

Euen he that makes her Queen, who else should bee?

QUEENE ELIZABETH

What thou?

KING RICHARD Euen so, how thinke you of it?

QUEENE ELIZABETH

How canst thou wooe her?

KING RICHARD   That would I learne of you,
2760   As one being best acquainted with her humor.

QUEENE ELIZABETH

And wilt thou learn of me?

KING RICHARD   Madam with al my hart.

QUEENE ELIZABETH

Send to her by the man that slew her brothers,
A paire of bleeding harts: thereon ingraue,
Edward and Yorke, then happelie wil she weepe,
Therefore present to her as sometimes Margaret
Did to thy father, steept in Rutlands bloud,
A handkercher, which say to her did dreyne
The purple sappe from her sweet Brothers body,
And bid her wipe her weeping eies withall,
2770   If this inducement moue her not to loue,
Send her a Letter of thy noble deeds,
Tel her thou madst awaie her Vncle Clarence,

Her Vncle Riuers, I, and for her sake
Madst quicke conueiance with her good Aunt Anne.

KING RICHARD

You mocke me Madam, this is not the waie
To win your daughter.

QUEENE ELIZABETH   There is no other waie
Vnlesse thou couldst put on some other shape,
And not be Richard that hath done all this.

KING RICHARD

Infer faire Englands peace by this alliance.

QUEENE ELIZABETH

Which she shall purchase with still lasting war.   2780

KING RICHARD

Tell her, the king that may command intreats.

QUEENE ELIZABETH

That at her hands which the kings king forbids.

KING RICHARD

Saie she shalbe a high and mightie Queene.

QUEENE ELIZABETH

To vaile the title as her mother doth.

KING RICHARD

Saie I wil loue her euerlastinglie.

QUEENE ELIZABETH

But how long shall that title euer last.

KING RICHARD

Sweetlie in force vnto her faire lyues end.

QUEENE ELIZABETH

But how long farely shall her sweet life last?

KING RICHARD

As long as heauen and nature lengthens it.

QUEENE ELIZABETH

As long as hell and Richard likes of it.   2790

KING RICHARD

Saie I her soueraign am her subiect loue.

QUEENE ELIZABETH

But she your subiect loaths such soueraintie.

KING RICHARD

Be eloquent in my behalfe to her.

QUEENE ELIZABETH

An honest tale speeds best being plainlie told.

KING RICHARD

Then plainly to her tell my louing tale.

QUEENE ELIZABETH

Plaine and not honest is to harsh a stile.

KING RICHARD

Your reasons are too shallow & too quicke.

QUEENE ELIZABETH

O no my reasons are to deepe and dead.
Too deepe and dead poore infants in their graues.

KING RICHARD

Harpe not on that string Madam, that is past.   2800

QUEENE ELIZABETH

Harpe on it still shall I till hart strings breake.

KING RICHARD

Now by my George, my Garter and my crown.

QUEENE ELIZABETH

Prophand, dishonerd, and the third vsurped.

KING RICHARD
  I sweare.

QUEENE ELIZABETH By nothing, for this is no oath.
  Thy George prophand hath lost his holie honor,
  Thy Garter blemisht pawnd his Lordlie vertue,
  Thy crown vsurpt disgrac't his kinglie Glory,
  If something thou would'st sweare to be beleeude,
  Sweare then by something that thou hast not wrongd.

KING RICHARD
  Then by my selfe.

2810 QUEENE ELIZABETH   Thy selfe, is selfe misus'd.

KING RICHARD
  Now by the world.

QUEENE ELIZABETH   Tis ful of thy foule wrongs.

KING RICHARD
  My Fathers death.

QUEENE ELIZABETH   Thy life hath y^t dishonord.

KING RICHARD
  Whie, then by God.

QUEENE ELIZABETH   Gods wrong is most of all,
  If thou didst feare, to breake an oath with him,
  The vnitie the king my husband made,
  Thou had'st not broken, nor my brothers died.
  If thou hadst feard to breake an oath by him,
  The emperiall mettall circling now thy head,
  Had grast the tender temples of my childe,
2820 And both the princes had bene breathing heere,
  Which now, two tender Bed-fellowes for dust,
  Thy broken faith, hath made the praie for wormes.
  What can'st thou sweare by now.

KING RICHARD   The time to come.

QUEENE ELIZABETH
  That thou hast wrongd in the time orepast,
  For I my selfe, haue manie teares to wash,
  Hereafter time, for time past wrongd by the,
  The children liue, whose Fathers thou hast
    slaughterd,
  Vngouernd youth, to waile it in their age,
  The parents liue, whose children thou hast butcherd,
2830 Olde barren plantes, to waile it with their age,
  Sweare not by time to come, for that thou hast,
  Misused, eare vsed, by times ill-vs'd orepast.

KING RICHARD
  As I intend to prosper and repent,
  So thriue I in my dangerous Affayres
  Of hostile armes, my selfe, my selfe confound,
  Heauen, and Fortune barre me happy houres:
  Daye yeeld me not thy light, nor night thy rest,
  Be opposite, all planets of good lucke,
  To my proceeding, if with deere heartes loue,
2840 Immaculate deuocion, holie thoughtes,
  I tender not thy beauteous princelie daughter,
  In her consistes my happines and thine,
  Without her followes to my selfe and thee,
  Her selfe, the Land, and manie a Christian soule,
  Death, desolation, ruine, and decaie,
  It cannot be auoided but by this,
  It will not be auoided but by this:

  Therefore good mother (I must call you so,)
  Be the atturney of my loue to her.
  Pleade what I will be, not what I haue bene,   2850
  Not my desertes, but what I will deserue,
  Vrge the necessitie and state of times,
  And be not pieuish, fond in great designes.

QUEENE ELIZABETH
  Shall I be tempted of the diuell thus.

KING RICHARD
  I, if the diuell tempt you to doe good.

QUEENE ELIZABETH
  Shall I forget my selfe, to be my selfe.

KING RICHARD
  I, if your selfes remembrance, wrong your selfe.

QUEENE ELIZABETH Yet thou didst kill my children.

KING RICHARD
  But in your daughters wombe, I burie them,
  Where in that nest of spicerie they will breed,   2860
  Selfes of themselues, to your recomfiture.

QUEENE ELIZABETH
  Shall I go winne my daughter to thy will.

KING RICHARD
  And be a happie mother by the deede.

QUEENE ELIZABETH
  I goe, write to me verie shortlie
  And you shal vnderstand from me her mind.

KING RICHARD
  Beare her my true loues kisse,
    He kisses her
                and so farewell.
              Exit Q. Elizabeth
  Relenting foole, and shallow changing woman.
    Enter Ratcliffe
  How now, what newes?

RATCLIFFE
  Most mightie Soueraigne on the westerne coast,
  Rideth a puissant Nauie. To our shores,   2870
  Throng manie doubtfull hollow harted friendes,
  Vnarmd, and vnresolud to beate them backe:
  Tis thought that Richmond is their admirall,
  And there they hull, expecting but the aide,
  Of Buckingham, to welcome them a shore.

KING RICHARD
  Some light-foote friend, post to the Duke of Norffolke.
  Ratcliffe thy selfe, or Catesbie, where is hee?

CATESBY
  Here my good Lord.

KING RICHARD   Catesby, flie to the Duke.

CATESBY
  I will, my Lord, with all conuenient haste.

KING RICHARD
  Ratcliffe come hither, post to Salisburie,   2880
  When thou comst thither, (*to Catesby*) dull vnmindfull
    villaine,
  Whie stay'st thou here? and goest not to the Duke.

CATESBY
  First mightie Liege, tell me your Highnesse pleasure,
  What, from your grace, I shall deliuer to him.

KING RICHARD
O, true good Catesbie, bid him leuie straight,
The greatest strength and power that he can make,
And meete me suddenlie at Salisburie.
CATESBY I goe.   *Exit*
RATCLIFFE
What may it please you, shall I do at Salisbury.
KING RICHARD
2890   Whie? what wouldst thou doe there before I goe?
RATCLIFFE
Your highnes told me I should post before.
KING RICHARD
My mind is changd.
        Enter Lord Stanley
                Stanley, what newes with you?
STANLEY
None good my Liege, to please you with the hearing,
Nor none so bad, but well may be reported.
KING RICHARD
Hoiday, a riddle, neither good, nor bad:
Why need'st thou runne so many mile about,
When thou maist tell thy tale the neerest way.
Once more, what newes?
STANLEY   Richmond is on the Seas.
KING RICHARD
There let him sinke, and be the seas on him,
2900   White liuerd runnagate, what doeth he there?
STANLEY
I know not mightie Soueraigne, but by guesse.
KING RICHARD Well, as you guesse.
STANLEY
Sturd vp by Dorset, Buckingham, and Elie,
He makes for England, here to claime the crowne.
KING RICHARD
Is the chaire emptie? is the sword vnswaied?
Is the king dead? the Empire vnpossest?
What heire of Yorke is there aliue but we?
And who is Englands King, but great Yorkes heire,?
Then tell me, what makes he vpon the seas?
STANLEY
2910   Vnlesse for that my liege, I cannot guesse.
KING RICHARD
Vnlesse for that, he comes to be your liege,
You cannot guesse, wherefore the Welshman comes,
Thou wilt reuolt, and flie to him I feare.
STANLEY
No my good Lord, therefore mistrust me not.
KING RICHARD
Where is thy power then? to beate him backe,
Where be thy tennants? and thy followers?
Are they not now vpon the Westerne shore?
Safe conducting, the rebels from their ships.
STANLEY
No my good Lord, my friendes are in the North.
KING RICHARD
2920   Cold friends to me, what doe they in the North?
When they should serue, their Soueraigne in the West.

STANLEY
They haue not bin commaunded, mightie King.
Pleaseth your Maiestie to giue me leaue,
Ile muster vp my friendes and meete your grace,
Where, and what time, your Maiestie shall please.
KING RICHARD
I, I, thou wouldest be gone, to ioyne with Richmond,
But Ile not trust thee.
STANLEY   Most mightie Soueraigne,
You haue no cause to hold my friendship doubtfull,
I neuer was, nor neuer will be false.
KING RICHARD
Go then, and muster men, but leaue behinde,   2930
Your sonne George Stanlie, looke your heart be firme,
Or else, his heads assurance is but fraile.
STANLEY
So deale with him, as I proue true to you.
                        Exit Stanley
        Enter a Messenger
MESSENGER
My gracious Soueraigne, now in Deuonshire,
As I by friendes am well aduertised,
Sir Edward Courtney, and the haughtie Prelate,
Bishop of Exceter, his elder brother,
With manie mo confederates, are in armes.
        Enter another Messenger
2. MESSENGER
In Kent, my Liege, the Guilfordes are in armes,
And euerie houre more competitors,   2940
Flocke to the Rebels, and their power growes strong.
        Enter another Messenger
3. MESSENGER
My Lord, the armie of great Buckingham.
KING RICHARD
Out on ye owles, nothing but songs off death.
        He striketh him
There, take thou that till thou bring better newes.
3. MESSENGER
The newes I haue to tell your Maiestie,
Is that by sudden floud, and fall of water,
Buckinghams armie is disperst and scattered,
And he himselfe wandred away alone,
No man knowes whether.
KING RICHARD   I crie thee mercie,
Ratcliffe reward him, for the blow I gaue him,   2950
Hath any well aduised friend proclaym'd
Reward to him that brings the Traytor in.
3. MESSENGER
Such proclamation hath bene made my lord.
        Enter another Messenger
4. MESSENGER
Sir Thomas Louel, and Lord Marques Dorset,
Tis said my liege, in Yorkeshire are in armes,
But this good comfort bring I to your Highnesse,
The Brittaine nauie is disperst by Tempest,
Richmond in Dorsetshire sent out a boate
Vnto the shore, to aske those on the Banks,

2960 If they were his assistants yea, or no:
Who answered him, they came from Buckingham,
Vpon his partie, he mistrusting them,
Hoist sale, and made his course againe for Brittaine.

KING RICHARD

March on, march on, since we are vp in armes,
If not to fight with forreine enemies,
Yet to beate downe, these rebels here at home.

Enter Catesbie

CATESBY

My liege, the Duke of Buckingham is taken,
That is the best newes, that the Earle of Richmond,
Is with a mightie power landed at Milford,
2970 Is colder tidings, yet they must be told.

KING RICHARD

Away towardes Salisburie, while we reason here,
A royall battell might be wonne and lost.
Some one take order, Buckingham be brought,
To Salisburie, the rest march on with me.

Florish. Exeunt

Sc. 20   *Enter Lord Stanley Earle of Darbie, and Sir*
(4.5)   *Christopher, a priest*

STANLEY

Sir Christapher, tell Richmond this from me,
That in the stie of this most deadlie bore,
My sonne George Stanlie is franckt vp in hold,
If I reuolt, off goes young Georges head,
The feare of that, holdes off my present aide,
2980 But tell me, where is princelie Richmond now?

SIR CHRISTOPHER

At Pembroke, or at Harford-west in Wales.

STANLEY

What men of name resort to him.

SIR CHRISTOPHER

Sir Walter Herbert, a renowned souldier,
Sir Gilbert Talbot, Sir William Stanlie,
Oxford, redoubted Pembroke, Sir Iames Blunt,
And Rice ap Thomas, with a valiant crew,
And many other of great name and worth,
And towardes London doe they bend their power,
If by the way, they be not fought withall.

STANLEY

2990 Well hye thee to thy Lord, commend me to him,
Tell him, the Queene hath heartily consented
He should espouse Elizabeth hir daughter,
My letter will resolue him of my minde.
Farewell.   *Exeunt seuerally*

Sc. 21   *Enter Buckingham with Halberds, led by a Sheriffe*
(5.1)   *to execution*

BUCKINGHAM

Will not king Richard let me speake with him.

SHERIFFE

No my good Lord, therefore be patient.

BUCKINGHAM

Hastings, and Edwards children, Gray & Riuers,
Holie king Henrie, and thy faire sonne Edward,

Vaughan, and all that haue miscarried,
By vnderhand corrupted, foule iniustice,   3000
If that your moodie discontented soules,
Doe through the cloudes, behold this present houre,
Euen for reuenge, mocke my destruction.
This is Alsoules day fellowe, is it not?

SHERIFFE It is.

BUCKINGHAM

Whie then Alsoules day, is my bodies domesday:
This is the day, which in king Edwards time,
I wisht might fall on me, when I was found,
False to his children, and his wiues allies:
This is the day, wherein I wisht to fall,   3010
By the false faith, of him whom most I trusted:
This, this Alsoules day, to my fearefull soule,
Is the determind respit of my wrongs:
That high al-seer, which I dallied with,
Hath turned my fained prayer on my head,
And giuen in earnest what I begd in iest.
Thus doeth he force the swordes of wicked men,
To turne their owne pointes, in their Maisters
    bosomes:
Thus Margarets curse, falles heauy on my necke,
When he quoth she, shall split thy hart with sorrow,   3020
Remember, Margaret was a Prophetesse,
Come leade me Officers to the blocke of shame,
Wrong hath but wrong, and blame the dew of blame.

Exeunt Buckingham with Officers

Enter Richmond with a letter, Oxford, Blunt,   Sc. 22
Herbert, and others, with drum and colours   (5.2)

HENRY EARLE OF RICHMOND

Fellowes in armes, and my most louing friendes,
Bruisd vnderneath the yoake of tyrannie,
Thus farre into the bowels of the land,
Haue we marcht on without impediment,
And here receiue we, from our Father Stanlie,
Lines of faire comfort, and incouragement,
The wretched, bloudie, and vsurping bore,   3030
That spoils your somer-fieldes, and fruitfull vines,
Swils your warme bloud like wash, and makes his
    trough,
In your inboweld bosomes, this foule swine,
Lies now euen in the centry of this Ile,
Neare to the towne of Leycester as we learne:
From Tamworth thether, is but one dayes march,
In Gods name cheerelie on, couragious friendes,
To reape the haruest of perpetuall peace,
By this one bloudie triall of sharpe warre.

OXFORD

Euerie mans conscience is a thousand swordes,   3040
To fight against this guiltie homicide.

HERBERT

I doubt not but his friendes will turne to vs.

BLUNT

He hath no friendes, but what are friendes for feare,
Which in his deerest neede will flye from him.

HENRY EARLE OF RICHMOND
All for our vantage, then in Gods name march,
True hope is swift, and flies with Swallowes wings,
Kings it makes Gods, and meaner creatures kings.

Exeunt Omnes ⌐marching⌐

Sc. 23
(5.3)   *Enter King Richard in Armes, with Norffolke,*
          Ratcliffe, ⌐Catesbie, with others⌐

KING RICHARD
Here pitch our tent, euen here in Bosworth field,

Soldiers begin to pitch ⌐a tent⌐

Whie, how now Catesbie, whie look you so sad.

⌐CATESBY⌐

3050   My hart is ten times lighter then my lookes.

KING RICHARD
My Lord of Norffolke.

NORFFOLKE   Heere most gracious Liege.

KING RICHARD
Norffolke, we must haue knockes, ha, must we not?

NORFFOLKE
We must both giue, and take, my louing Lord.

KING RICHARD
Vp with my tent, here will I lie to night,
But where to morrow, well, all is one for that:
Who hath discried the number of the Traitors.

NORFFOLKE
Sixe or seuen thousand is their vtmost power.

KING RICHARD
Whie our battalia trebles that account,
Besides, the Kings name is a tower of strength,
3060   Which they vpon the aduerse Faction want,
Vp with the tent, Come Noble gentlemen,
Let vs suruey the vantage of the ground,
Call for some men of sound direction,
Lets lacke no discipline, make no delaie,
For Lordes, to morrow is a busie day.

Exeunt ⌐at one door⌐

Sc. 24
(5.4)   *Enter ⌐at another door⌐ Richmond, Blunt, Sir*
          William Brandon, ⌐Oxford, and Dorset, &c.⌐

HENRY EARLE OF RICHMOND
The wearie sonne hath made a golden set,
And by the bright tracke of his fierie Carre,
Giues token of a goodlie day to morrow,
Sir William Brandon, you shall beare my standerd,
3070   The Earle of Pembroke keepes his regiment,
Good captaine Blunt, beare my good night to him,
And by the second houre in the morning,
Desire the Earle to see me in my tent.
Yet one thing more, good Captaine do for me:
Where is Lord Stanlie quarterd, do you know.

BLUNT
Vnlesse I haue mistane his coulers much,
Which well I am assur'd, I haue not done,
His regiment, lies halfe a mile at least,
South from the mightie power of the king.

HENRY EARLE OF RICHMOND
3080   If without perrill it be possible,

Sweet Blunt make some good meanes to speak with
     him,
And giue him from me, this most needefull Note.

BLUNT
Vpon my life my Lord, Ile vndertake it,
And so God giue you quiet rest tonight.

HENRY EARLE OF RICHMOND
Good night good Captaine Blunt.   *Exit Blunt*
                        Come Gentlemen,
Giue me some inke, and paper, in my tent,
Ile drawe the forme, and modle of our battel,
Limit each leader to his seuerall charge,
And part in iust proportion our small Power,
Let vs consult vpon to morrowes busines,   3090
In to my tent, the Dew is rawe and cold.

They withdraw into the Tent

⌐A Table brought in.⌐ *Enter king Richard, Norffolke,*   **Sc. 25**
Ratcliffe, & Catesbie, &c.   **(5.5)**

KING RICHARD What is't a clocke.

CATESBY
It's supper time my Lord, it's nine a clocke.

KING RICHARD
I will not sup to night, giue me some inke and paper,
What? is my beuer easier then it was?,
And all my armour laid into my tent?

CATESBY
It is my Liege, and all thinges are in readines.

KING RICHARD
Good Norffolke, hie thee to thy charge,
Vse carefull watch, chuse trustie centinells.

NORFFOLKE I goe my Lord.   3100

KING RICHARD
Stur with the Larke to morrow gentle Norffolke.

NORFFOLKE
I warrant you my Lord.   *Exit*

KING RICHARD   Catesby.

CATESBY   My lord.

KING RICHARD
Send out a Pursiuant at armes
To *Stanleys* regiment, bid him bring his power
Before sun rising, least his sonne George fall
Into the blind caue of eternal night.   ⌐*Exit Catesby*⌐
Fill me a bowle of wine, giue me a watch,
Saddle white Surrey for the field to morrow,
Looke that my staues be sound and not too heauy.
Ratcliffe.   3110

RATCLIFFE My lord.

KING RICHARD
Sawst thou the melancholie Lo. Northumberland?

RATCLIFFE
Thomas the Earle of Surrey and himselfe,
Much about cockshut time, from troupe to troupe
Went through the army cheering vp the soldiors.

KING RICHARD
So I am satisfied, giue me some wine,
I haue not that alacrity of spirit

Nor cheere of mind that I was wont to haue:
     The wine is brought
Set it down. Is inke and paper ready?

RATCLIFFE

It is my lord.

3120 **KING RICHARD** Leaue me. Bid my guard watch,
About the mid of night come to my tent
Ratcliffe and helpe to arme me: leaue me I say.
        Exit Ratcliffe ⌈&c. Richard writes, and
            later sleepes⌉
   Enter Lord Stanley Earle of Darby to Richmond and
   the lords in his tent

STANLEY

Fortune and victorie sit on thy helme.

HENRY EARLE OF RICHMOND

All comfort that the darke night can afford,
Be to thy person noble father in law,
Tel me how fares our louing mother?

STANLEY

I by atturney blesse thee from thy mother,
Who praies continuallie for Richmonds good,
So much for that: the silent houres steale on,
3130 And flakie darkenesse breakes within the east,
In briefe, for so the season bids vs be:
Prepare thy battell earelie in the morning,
And put thy fortune to the arbitrement,
Of bloudie strokes and mortal sharing war,
I as I may, that which I would, I cannot,
With best aduantage will deceiue the time,
And aide thee in this doubtful shocke of armes,
But on thy side I may not be too forward,
Least being seene thy brother tender George
3140 Be executed in his fathers sight.
Farewel, the leasure and the fearefull time,
Cuts off the ceremonious vowes of loue,
And ample enterchange of sweet discourse,
Which so long sundired friends should dwel vpon,
God giue vs leisure for these rights of loue,
Once more adiew, be valiant and speed well.

HENRY EARLE OF RICHMOND

Good lords conduct him to his regiment:
Ile striue with troubled thoughts to take a nap,
Least leaden slumber peise me downe to morrow,
3150 When I should mount with wings of victorie,
Once more good night kind Lords and gentlemen,
            Exeunt Stanley and the lords
   ⌈Richmond kneeles⌉
O thou whose Captaine I account my selfe,
Looke on my forces with a gracious eie:
Put in their hands thy brusing Irons of wrath,
That they may crush downe with a heauie fall,
The vsurping helmets of our aduersaries,
Make vs thy ministers of chastisement,
That we may praise thee in the victorie,
To thee I do commend my watchfull soule,
3160 Eare I let fal the windowes of mine eies,
Sleeping and waking, oh defend me still!   *He sleepes*

   Enter the ghost of young Prince Edward ⌈aboue⌉

GHOST (*to Richard*)

Let me sit heauie on thy soule to morrow,
Prince Edward, sonne to Henry the sixt.
Thinke how thou stabst me in my prime of youth,
At Teukesburie, dispaire therefore and die.
(*To Richmond*) Be cheerful Richmond for the wronged
     soules
Of Butchered princes fight in thy behalfe,
King Henries issue Richmond comforts thee.   ⌈*Exit*⌉
   Enter ⌈aboue⌉ the ghost of Henry the sixt

GHOST (*to Richard*)

When I was mortall my annointed body,
By thee was punched full of deadlie holes,   3170
Thinke on the tower and me dispaire and die,
Harrie the sixt bids thee dispaire and die.
(*To Richmond*) Vertuous and holie be thou conqueror,
Harrie that prophisied thou shouldst be king,
Comforts thee in thy sleepe liue and florish.   ⌈*Exit*⌉
   Enter ⌈aboue⌉ the Goast of Clarence

GHOST (*to Richard*)

Let me sit heauie on thy soule to morrow,
I that was washt to death with fulsome wine,
Poore Clarence by thy guile betraid to death:
To morrow in the battaile thinke on me,
And fall thy edgeles sword, dispaire and die.   3180
(*To Richmond*) Thou ofspring of the house of
     Lancester,
The wronged heires of Yorke do pray for thee,
Good angels guard thy battaile liue and florish.   ⌈*Exit*⌉
   Enter ⌈aboue⌉ the ghosts of Riuers, Gray, Vaughan

RIUERS (*to Richard*)

Let me sit heauie on thy soule to morrow,
Riuers that died at Pomfret, dispaire and die.

GRAY (*to Richard*)

Thinke vpon Graie, and let thy soule dispaire.

VAUGHAN (*to Richard*)

Thinke vpon Vaughan, and with guiltie feare,
Let fall thy pointles launce, dispaire and die.

ALL (*to Richmond*)

Awake and thinke our wrongs in Richards bosome,
Wil conquer him, awake and win the daie.   3190
            ⌈*Exeunt ghosts*⌉
   Enter ⌈aboue⌉ the ghosts of the two yong Princes

⌈**GHOSTS**⌉ (*to Richard*)

Dreame on thy Coosens smothered in the tower,
Let vs be lead within thy bosome Richard,
And weigh thee down to ruine, shame, and death,
Thy Nephewes soules bid thee dispaire and die.
(*To Richmond*) Sleepe Richmond, sleepe in peace and
     wake in ioy,
Good angels guard thee from the bores annoy,
Liue and beget a happie race of kings,
Edwards vnhappie sonnes do bid thee florish.
            ⌈*Exeunt ghosts*⌉
   Enter ⌈aboue⌉ the ghost of Hastings

GHOST (*to Richard*)

Bloudie and guiltie, guiltilie awake,

3200 And in a bloudie battaile end thy daies,
Thinke on lord Hastings then dispaire and die.
(*To Richmond*) Quiet vntroubled soule, awake, awake,
Arme, fight and conquer for faire Englands sake.

⌜*Exit*⌝

Enter ⌜*aboue*⌝ *the ghost of Lady Anne his wife*

GHOST (*to Richard*)
Richard thy wife, that wretched Anne thy wife,
That neuer slept a quiet houre with thee,
Now fils thy sleepe with perturbations,
To morrow in the battaile thinke on me,
And fall thy edgeles sword despaire and die.
(*To Richmond*) Thou quiet soule, sleepe thou a quiet
     sleepe,
3210 Dreame of successe and happie victorie,
Thy aduersaries wife doth praie for thee.   ⌜*Exit*⌝

Enter ⌜*aboue*⌝ *the Goast of Buckingham*

GHOST (*to Richard*)
The first was I that helpt thee to the crown,
The last was I that felt thy tyrrannie,
O in the battaile thinke on Buckingham,
And die in terror of thy giltinesse,
Dreame on, dreame on, of bloudie deeds and death,
Fainting, despaire, desparing yeeld thy breath,
(*To Richmond*) I died for hope ere I could lend thee aid,
But cheare thy heart, and be thou not dismaid,
3220 God and good angels fight on Richmonds side,
And Richard fals in height of all his pride.   ⌜*Exit*⌝

Richard starteth vp out of a dreame

KING RICHARD
Giue me another horse, bind vp my wounds,
Haue mercie Iesu: soft, I did but dreame,
O Coward conscience, how dost thou afflict me?
The lights burne blew, it is now dead midnight,
Cold fearefull drops stand on my trembling flesh,
What do I feare? my selfe? theres none else by,
Richard loues Richard, that is I am I,
Is there a murtherer here? no. Yes I am,
3230 Then flie, what from my selfe? great reason: whie?
Least I reuenge. My selfe vpon my selfe?
Alacke I loue my selfe, wherefore? for anie good
That I my selfe haue done vnto my selfe:
O no, alas I rather hate my selfe,
For hatefull deedes committed by my selfe,
I am a villaine, yet I lie I am not,
Foole of thy selfe speake well, foole do not flatter,
My conscience hath a thousand seuerall tongues,
And euerie tongue brings in a seueral tale,
3240 And euerie tale condemns me for a villaine,
Periurie, periurie, in the highest degree,
Murther, sterne murther, in the dyrest degree,
All seuerall sinnes, all vsde in each degree,
Throng to the barre, crying all guiltie, guiltie.
I shall dispaire, there is no creature loues me,
And if I die, no soule will pitie me:
Nay wherefore should they, since that I my selfe,
Finde in my selfe, no pitie to my selfe.

Me thought the soules of all that I had murtherd,
Came to my tent, and euery one did threat,   3250
To morrows vengeance on the head of Richard.

Enter Ratcliffe

RATCLIFFE My Lord.
KING RICHARD Zoundes, who is there?
RATCLIFFE
My Lord, tis I, the earlie village cocke,
Hath twise done salutation to the morne,
Your friendes are vp, and buckle on their armor.
KING RICHARD
O Ratcliffe, I haue dreamd a fearefull dreame,
What thinkst thou, will all our friendes proue true?
RATCLIFFE
No doubt my Lord.
KING RICHARD   Ratcliffe, I feare, I feare.
RATCLIFFE
Nay good my Lord, be not afraid of shadowes.   3260
KING RICHARD
By the Apostle Paul, shadowes to night,
Haue stroke more terror to the soule of Richard,
Then can the substance of ten thousand souldiers,
Armed in proofe, and led by shallow Richmond.
Tis not yet neere day, come, go with me,
Vnder our tents Ile plaie the ease dropper,
To see if any meane to shrinke from me.

Exeunt Richard & Ratcliffe

Enter the Lordes to Richmond sitting in his Tent

⌜LORDS⌝ Good morrow Richmond.
HENRY EARLE OF RICHMOND
Crie mercie Lordes, and watchfull gentlemen,
That you haue tane a tardie sluggard here.   3270
⌜A LORD⌝ How haue you slept my Lord?
HENRY EARLE OF RICHMOND
The sweetest sleepe, and fairest boding dreames,
That euer entred in a drowsie head,
Haue I since your departure had my Lordes,
Me thought their soules, whose bodies Richard
     murtherd,
Came to my tent, and cried on victorie,
I promise you, my soule is verie Iocund,
In the remembrance of so faire a dreame.
How farre into the morning is it Lordes?
⌜A LORD⌝
Vpon the stroke of foure.   3280
HENRY EARLE OF RICHMOND
Whie, then tis time to arme, and giue direction.

His oration to his souldiers

Much that I could saie, louing countriemen,
The leasure and inforcement of the time,
Forbids to dwell on, yet remember this,
God, and our good cause, fight vpon our side,
The praiers of holy Saints and wronged soules,
Like high reard bulwarkes, stand before our forces,
Richard except, those whome we fight against,
Had rather haue vs winne, then him they follow:
For, what is he they follow? truelie friends,   3290

A bloudie tirant, and a homicide.
One raisd in bloud, and one in bloud established,
One that made meanes to come by what he hath,
And slaughtered those, that were the meanes to helpe
    him.
A base foule stone, made precious by the foile,
Of Englands chaire, where he is falsely set,
One that hath euer bene Gods enemie.
Then if you fight against Gods enemie,
God will in iustice, ward you as his souldiers,
3300 If you doe sweate to put a tyrant downe,
You sleepe in peace, the tyrant being slaine,
If you doe fight against your countries foes,
Your countries foyzon, paies your paines the hire.
If you doe fight in safegard of your wiues,
Your wiues shall welcome home the conquerors.
If you doe free your children from the sword,
Your childrens children quits it in your age:
Then in the name of God and all these rightes,
Aduaunce your standards, drawe your willing swordes,
3310 For me, the raunsome of this bold attempt,
Shall be my could corps on the earths cold face:
But if I thriue, to gaine of my attempt,
The least of you, shall share his part thereof.
Sound drummes and trumpets bold, and cheerefullie,
God, and Saint George, Richmond, and victorie.
           ⌜*Exeunt, to the sound of drummes and*
                                  trumpets⌝

Sc. 26   *Enter King Richard, Ratcliffe, Catesby &c.*
(5.6)   KING RICHARD
    What said Northumberland, as touching Richmond.
RATCLIFFE
    That he was neuer trained vp in armes.
KING RICHARD
    He said the trueth, and what said Surrey then.
RATCLIFFE
    He smiled and said, the better for our purpose.
KING RICHARD
3320   He was in the right, and so in deede it is:
          Clocke strikes
    Tell the clocke there. Giue me a calender,
    Who saw the Sunne to day?
        ⌜*A booke is brought*⌝
RATCLIFFE   Not I my Lord.
KING RICHARD
    Then he disdaines to shine, for by the booke,
    He should haue braud the East an hower agoe,
    A blacke day will it be to some bodie.
    Ratcliffe.
RATCLIFFE
    My Lord.
KING RICHARD The Sunne will not be seene to day,
    The skie doeth frowne, and lowre vpon our armie,
    I would these dewie teares were from the ground,
3330   Not shine to day: whie, what is that to me,
    More then to Richmond? for the selfe-same heauen,
    That frownes on me, lookes sadlie vpon him.

            Enter Norffolke
NORFFOLKE
    Arme, arme, my Lord, the foe vaunts in the field.
KING RICHARD
    Come, bustle, bustle, caparison my horse,
      ⌜*Richard armes*⌝
    Call vp Lord Standlie, bid him bring his power,
                                Exit one
    I will leade forth, my souldiers to the plaine,
    And thus my battaile shall be ordered.
    My foreward shall be drawen out all in length,
    Consisting equallie of horse and foote,
    Our Archers placed strongly in the midst,   3340
    Iohn, Duke of Norffolke, Thomas Earle of Surrey,
    Shall haue the leading of this multitude,
    They thus directed, we ourself will follow,
    In the maine battle, whose puissance on both sides,
    Shall be well winged with our chiefest horse:
    This, and Saint George to boote, what thinkst thou
       Norffolke?
NORFFOLKE
    A good direction warlike soueraigne,
       He sheweth him a paper
    This paper found I on my tent this morning.
       Iocky of Norfolke be not to bould,
        For Dickon thy master is bought and sould.   3350
KING RICHARD
    A thing deuised by the enemie.
    Go gentlemen each man vnto his charge,
    Let not our babling dreames affright our soules:
    Conscience is but a word that cowards vse,
    Deuisd at first to keepe the strong in awe,
    Our strong armes be our conscience, swords our law.
    March on, ioine brauelie, let vs to it pell mell,
    If not to heauen then hand in hand to hell.
       His Oration to his army
    What shal I saie more then I haue inferd?
    Remember whom you are to cope withall,   3360
    A sort of vagabonds, rascols and runawaies,
    A scum of Brittains and base lacky pesants,
    Whom their orecloied country vomits forth,
    To desperate ventures and assurd destruction,
    You sleeping safe they bring to you vnrest,
    You hauing lands and blest with beauteous wifes,
    They would distraine the one, distaine the other,
    And who doth lead them but a paltrey fellow,?
    Long kept in Brittaine at our mothers cost,
    A milkesope, one that neuer in his life   3370
    Felt so much colde as ouer shooes in snow:
    Lets whip these stragglers ore the seas againe,
    Lash hence these ouerweening rags of France,
    These famisht beggers wearie of their liues,
    Who but for dreaming on this fond exploit,
    For want of means poore rats had hangd themselues,
    If we be conquered, let men conquer vs,
    And not these bastard Brittains whom our fathers
    Haue in their own land beaten bobd and thumpt,
    And in record left them the heires of shame.   3380

Shall these enioy our lands, lie with our wiues,
Rauish our daughters?
    Drum affarre off
                Harke I heare their drum,
Fight gentlemen of England, fight bold yeomen,
Draw archers draw your arrowes to the head,
Spur your proud horses hard, and ride in bloud,
Amaze the welkin with your broken staues,
    Enter a Messenger
What saies lord Stanley, wil he bring his power?
MESSENGER
My lord, he doth deny to come.
KING RICHARD Off with yong Georges head.
NORFFOLKE

3390   My lord, the enemie is past the marsh,
After the battaile let George Stanley die.
KING RICHARD
A thousand harts are great within my bosome,
Aduance our standards, set vpon our foes,
Our ancient word of courage, faire saint George
Inspire vs with the spleene of fierie Dragons,
Vpon them victorie sits on our helmes.   *Exeunt*

Sc. 27   *Alarum, excursions, Enter Catesby*
(5.7) **CATESBY** ⌈*calling*⌉
Rescew my lord of Norffolke, rescew, rescew,
⌈*To a soldier*⌉ The king enacts more wonders then a
    man,
Daring an opposite to euerie danger,
3400 His horse is slaine, and all on foot he fights,
Seeking for Richmond in the throat of death,
⌈*Calling*⌉ Rescew faire lord, or else the daie is lost.
    Alarums. Enter Richard
KING RICHARD
A horse, a horse, my kingdome for a horse.
CATESBY
Withdraw my lord, ile helpe you to a horse.
KING RICHARD
Slaue I haue set my life vpon a cast,
And I will stand the hazard of the die,
I thinke there be six Richmonds in the field,
Fiue haue I slaine to daie in stead of him,
A horse, a horse, my kingdome for a horse.   *Exeunt*

Sc. 28   *Alarum, Enter Richard ⌈at one door⌉ and Richmond*
(5.8)   ⌈*at another*⌉, *they fight, Richard is slain.* ⌈*Exit*
    Richmond.⌉ *Retrait and Flourish. Enter Richmond,*
    Lord Stanley Earle of Darby, with diuers other
    Lords, &c.
HENRY EARLE OF RICHMOND
3410 God and your armes be praisd victorious freends,

The daie is ours, the bloudie dog is dead.
STANLEY (*bearing the crowne*)
Couragious Richmond, wel hast thou acquit thee,
Loe here this long vsurped roialtie,
From the dead temples of this bloudie wretch,
Haue I pluckt off to grace thy browes withall,
Weare it, enioy it, and make much of it.
    ⌈*He sets the crowne on Henries head*⌉
KING HENRY
Great God of heauen saie Amen to all,
But tell me, yong George Stanley, is he liuing.
STANLEY
He is my lord, and safe in Leicester towne,
Whether if it please you we may now withdraw vs. 3420
KING HENRY
What men of name are slaine on either side?
⌈**STANLEY**⌉ (*reads*)
Iohn Duke of Norffolke, Robert Brakenbury,
Water Lord Ferrers, & sir William Brandon.
KING HENRY
Inter their bodies as becomes their births,
Proclaime a pardon to the soldiers fled,
That in submission will returne to vs,
And then as we haue tane the sacrament,
We will vnite the white rose and the red,
Smile heauen vpon this faire coniunction,
That long haue frownd vpon their enmitie,   3430
What traitor heares me and saies not Amen?
England hath long been madde and scard herselfe,
The brother blindlie shed the brothers bloud,
The father rashlie slaughterd his own sonne,
The sonne compeld ben butcher to the sire,
All that deuided Yorke and Lancaster,
Vnited in their dire deuision,
O now let Richmond and Elizabeth,
The true succeeders of each royall house,
By Gods faire ordinance conioine together,   3440
And let their heires (God if his will be so)
Enrich the time to come with smooth-faste peace,
With smiling plentie and faire prosperous daies,
Abate the edge of traitors gracious Lord,
That would reduce these bloudy daies againe,
And make poore England weepe forth streames of
    bloud,
Let them not liue to tast this lands increase,
That would with treason wound this faire lands
    peace,
Now ciuill wounds are stopt, peace liues againe,
That she may long liue heare, God saie *Amen.*   3450
    ⌈*Flourish.*⌉ *Exeunt*

FINIS

ADDITIONAL PASSAGES

The following passages are contained in the Folio text, but not the Quarto; they were apparently omitted from performances.

A. AFTER 316

These eyes, which neuer shed remorsefull teare,
No, when my Father Yorke, and *Edward* wept,
To heare the pittious moane that Rutland made
When black-fac'd *Clifford* shooke his sword at him.
Nor when thy warlike Father like a Childe,
Told the sad storie of my Fathers death,
And twenty times, made pause to sob and weepe:
That all the standers by had wet their cheekes
Like Trees bedash'd with raine. In that sad time,
My manly eyes did scorne an humble teare: 10
And what these sorrowes could not thence exhale,
Thy Beauty hath, and made them blinde with weeping.

B. AFTER 578

RICHARD
Wert thou not banished, on paine of death?

QUEENE MARGARET
I was: but I doe find more paine in banishment,
Then death can yeeld me here, by my abode.

C. AFTER 833

O God! if my deepe prayres cannot appease thee,
But thou wilt be aueng'd on my misdeeds,
Yet execute thy wrath in me alone:
O spare my guiltlesse Wife, and my poore children.

D. AFTER 1271

The Folio has Dorset and Ryuers enter with Queene Elizabeth at 1216.1.

DORSET
Comfort deere Mother, God is much displeas'd,
That you take with vnthankfulnesse his doing.
In common worldly things, 'tis call'd vngratefull,
With dull vnwillingnesse to pay a debt,
Which with a bounteous hand was kindly lent:
Much more to be thus opposite with heauen,
For it requires the Royall debt it lent you.

RYUERS
Madam, bethinke you like a carefull Mother
Of the young Prince your sonne: send straight
          for him,
Let him be Crown'd, in him your comfort liues.   10
Drowne desperate sorrow in dead *Edwards* graue,
And plant your ioyes in liuing *Edwards* Throne.

E. AFTER 1293

RYUERS
Why with some little Traine, my Lord of
          Buckingham?

BUCKINGHAM
Marrie my Lord, least by a multitude,
The new-heal'd wound of Malice should breake out,
Which would be so much the more dangerous,
By how much the estate is greene, and yet
          vngouern'd.
Where euery Horse beares his commanding Reine,
And may direct his course as please himselfe,
As well the feare of harme, as harme apparant,
In my opinion, ought to be preuented.

RICHARD GLOCESTER
I hope the King made peace with all of vs,   10
And the compact is firme, and true in me.

RYUERS
And so in me, and so (I thinke) in all.
Yet since it is but greene, it should be put
To no apparant likely-hood of breach,
Which haply by much company might be vrg'd:
Therefore I say with Noble Buckingham,
That it is meete so few should fetch the Prince.

HASTINGS And so say I.

F. AFTER 1596

And summon him to morrow to the Tower,
To sit about the Coronation.

G. AFTER 1972

Beginning Richard Glocester's speech. The Folio brings on Louell and Ratcliffe instead of Catesby at 1891.1.

KING RICHARD
Goe *Louell* with all speed to Doctor *Shaw*,
(*To Ratcliffe*) Goe thou to Fryer *Penker*, bid them both
Meet me within this houre at Baynards Castle.
                    Exit Louell and Ratcliffe

H. AFTER 2133

If not to answer, you might haply thinke,
Tongue-ty'd Ambition, not replying, yeelded
To beare the Golden Yoake of Soueraigntie,
Which fondly you would here impose on me.
If to reproue you for this suit of yours,
So season'd with your faithfull loue to me,
Then on the other side I check'd my friends.
Therefore to speake, and to auoid the first,
And then in speaking, not to incurre the last,
Definitiuely thus I answer you.   10

I. AFTER 2323

In the Folio, the characters do not exit during the
Dutchesse of Yorke's preceding speech.

QUEENE ELIZABETH

Stay, yet looke backe with me vnto the Tower.
Pitty, you ancient Stones, those tender Babes,
Whom Enuie hath immur'd within your Walls,
Rough Cradle for such little prettie ones,
Rude ragged Nurse, old sullen Play-fellow,
For tender Princes: vse my Babies well;
So foolish Sorrowe bids your Stones farewell.   *Exeunt*

J. AFTER 2726

KING RICHARD

You speake as if that I had slaine my Cosins?

QUEENE ELIZABETH

Cosins indeed, and by their Vnckle couzend,
Of Comfort, Kingdome, Kindred, Freedome, Life,
Whose hand soeuer lanch'd their tender hearts,
Thy head (all indirectly) gaue direction.
No doubt the murd'rous Knife was dull and blunt,
Till it was whetted on thy stone-hard heart,
To reuell in the Intrailes of my Lambes.
But that still vse of greefe, makes wilde greefe tame,
My tongue should to thy eares not name my Boyes,   10
Till that my Nayles were anchor'd in thine eyes:
And I in such a desp'rate Bay of death,
Like a poore Barke, of sailes and tackling reft,
Rush all to peeces on thy Rocky bosome.

K. AFTER 2778

KING RICHARD

Say that I did all this for loue of her.

QUEENE ELIZABETH

Nay then indeed she cannot choose but hate thee
Hauing bought loue, with such a bloody spoyle.

KING RICHARD

Looke what is done, cannot be now amended:
Men shall deale vnaduisedly sometimes,
Which after-houres giues leysure to repent.
If I did take the Kingdome from your Sonnes,
To make amends, Ile giue it to your daughter:
If I haue kill'd the issue of your wombe,
To quicken your encrease, I will beget   10

Mine yssue of your blood, vpon your Daughter:
A Grandams name is little lesse in loue,
Then is the doting Title of a Mother;
They are as Children but one steppe below,
Euen of your mettall, of your very blood:
Of all one paine, saue for a night of groanes
Endur'd of her, for whom you bid like sorrow.
Your Children were vexation to your youth,
But mine shall be a comfort to your Age,
The losse you haue, is but a Sonne being King,   20
And by that losse, your Daughter is made Queene.
I cannot make you what amends I would,
Therefore accept such kindnesse as I can.
Dorset your Sonne, that with a fearfull soule
Leads discontented steppes in Forraine soyle,
This faire Alliance, quickly shall call home
To high Promotions, and great Dignity.
The King that calles your beauteous Daughter Wife,
Familiarly shall call thy *Dorset*, Brother:
Againe shall you be Mother to a King: 30
And all the Ruines of distressefull Times,
Repayr'd with double Riches of Content.
What? we haue many goodly dayes to see:
The liquid drops of Teares that you haue shed,
Shall come againe, transform'd to Orient Pearle,
Aduantaging their Lone, with interest
Of ten-times double gaine of happinesse.
Go then (my Mother) to thy Daughter go,
Make bold her bashfull yeares, with your experience,
Prepare her eares to heare a Woers Tale.   40
Put in her tender heart, th'aspiring Flame
Of Golden Soueraignty: Acquaint the Princesse
With the sweet silent houres of Marriage ioyes:
And when this Arme of mine hath chastised
The petty Rebell, dull-brain'd *Buckingham*,
Bound with Triumphant Garlands will I come,
And leade thy daughter to a Conquerors bed:
To whom I will retaile my Conquest wonne,
And she shalbe sole Victoresse, *Cæsars Cæsar*.

QUEENE ELIZABETH

What were I best to say, her Fathers Brother   50
Would be her Lord? Or shall I say her Vnkle?
Or he that slew her Brothers, and her Vnkles?
Vnder what Title shall I woo for thee,
That God, the Law, my Honor, and her Loue,
Can make seeme pleasing to her tender yeares?

VENUS AND ADONIS

WITH *Venus and Adonis,* Shakespeare made his debut in print: his signature appears at the end of the formal dedication to the Earl of Southampton in which the poem is described as 'the first heire of my inuention'—though Shakespeare had already begun to make his mark as a playwright. A terrible outbreak of plague, which was to last for almost two years, began in the summer of 1592, and London's theatres were closed as a precaution against infection. Probably Shakespeare wrote his poem at this time, perhaps seeing a need for an alternative career. It is an early example of the Ovidian erotic narrative poems that were fashionable for about thirty years from 1589; the best known outside Shakespeare is Christopher Marlowe's *Hero and Leander*, written at about the same time.

Ovid, in Book 10 of the *Metamorphoses*, tells the story of Venus and Adonis in about seventy-five lines of verse; Shakespeare's poem—drawing, probably, on both the original Latin and Arthur Golding's English version (1565-7)—is 1,194 lines long. He modified Ovid's tale as well as expanding it. In Ovid, the handsome young mortal Adonis returns the love urged on him by Venus, the goddess of love. Shakespeare turns Adonis into a bashful teenager, unripe for love, who shies away from her advances. In Ovid, the lovers go hunting together (though Venus chases only relatively harmless beasts, and advises Adonis to do the same); in Shakespeare, Adonis takes to the hunt rather as a respite from Venus' remorseless attentions. Whereas Ovid's Venus flies off to Cyprus in her dove-drawn chariot and returns only after Adonis has been mortally wounded, Shakespeare's anxiously awaits the outcome of the chase. She hears the yelping of Adonis' hounds, sees a blood-stained boar, comes upon Adonis' defeated dogs, and at last finds his body. In Ovid, she metamorphoses him into an anemone; in Shakespeare, Adonis' body melts away, and Venus plucks the purple and white flower that springs up in its place.

Shakespeare's only addition to Ovid's narrative is the episode (259-324) in which Adonis' stallion lusts after a mare, so frustrating Adonis' attempt to escape Venus' embraces. But there are many rhetorical elaborations, such as Venus' speech of attempted seduction (95-174), her disquisition on the dangers of boar-hunting (613-714), her metaphysical explanation of why the night is dark (721-68), Adonis' reply (769-810), culminating in his eloquent contrast between lust and love, and Venus' lament over his body (1069-1164).

Venus and Adonis is a mythological poem whose landscape is inhabited by none but the lovers and those members of the animal kingdom—the lustful stallion, the timorous hare (679-708), the sensitive snail (1033-6), and the savage boar—which reflect their passions. The boar's disruption of the harmony that existed between Adonis and the animals will, says Venus, result in eternal discord: 'Sorrow on loue hereafter shall attend' (1136).

In Shakespeare's own time, *Venus and Adonis* was his most frequently reprinted work, with at least ten editions during his life, and another half-dozen by 1636. After this it fell out of fashion until Coleridge wrote enthusiastically about it in *Biographia Literaria* (1817). Though its conscious artifice may limit its appeal, it is a brilliantly sophisticated erotic comedy, a counterpart in verbal ingenuity to *Loues labours lost*; the comedy of the poem, like that of the play, is darkened and deepened in its later stages by the shadow of sudden death.

The text was probably printed from a fair copy made by Shakespeare; he may also have read the proofs.

Vilia miretur vulgus: mihi flauus Apollo
Pocula Castalia plena ministret aqua.

TO THE RIGHT HONORABLE HENRIE WRIOTHESLEY,
EARLE OF SOUTHAMPTON, AND BARON OF TITCHFIELD.

Right Honourable, I know not how I shall offend in dedicating my vnpolisht lines to your Lordship, nor how the worlde will censure mee for choosing so strong a proppe to support so weake a burthen, onelye if your Honour seeme but pleased, I account my selfe highly praised, and vowe to take aduantage of all idle houres, till I haue honoured you with some grauer labour. But if the first heire of my inuention proue deformed, I shall be sorie it had so noble a god-father: and neuer after eare so barren a land, for feare it yeeld me still so bad a haruest, I leaue it to your Honourable suruey, and your Honor to your hearts content, which I wish may alwaies answere your owne wish, and the worlds hopefull expectation.

Your Honors in all dutie,

William Shakespeare.

Venus and Adonis

Euen as the sunne with purple-colourd face,
Had tane his last leaue of the weeping morne,
Rose-cheekt Adonis hied him to the chace,
Hunting he lou'd, but loue he laught to scorne:
   Sick-thoughted Venus makes amaine vnto him,
   And like a bold fac'd suter ginnes to woo him.

Thrise fairer then my selfe, (thus she began)
The fields chiefe flower, sweet aboue compare,
Staine to all Nimphs, more louely then a man,
More white, and red, then doues, or roses are:
   Nature that made thee with her selfe at strife,
   Saith that the world hath ending with thy life.

Vouchsafe thou wonder to alight thy steed,
And raine his proud head to the saddle bow,
If thou wilt daine this fauor, for thy meed
A thousand honie secrets shalt thou know:
   Here come and sit, where neuer serpent hisses,
   And being set, Ile smother thee with kisses.

And yet not cloy thy lips with loth'd sacietie,
But rather famish them amid their plentie,
Making them red, and pale, with fresh varietie:
Ten kisses short as one, one long as twentie:
   A sommers day will seeme an houre but short,
   Being wasted in such time-beguiling sport.

With this she ceazeth on his sweating palme,
The president of pith, and liuelyhood,
And trembling in her passion, calls it balme,
Earths soueraigne salue, to do a goddesse good,
   Being so enrag'd, desire doth lend her force,
   Couragiously to plucke him from his horse.

Ouer one arme the lustie coursers raine,
Vnder her other was the tender boy,
Who blusht, and powted in a dull disdaine,
With leaden appetite, vnapt to toy,
   She red, and hot, as coles of glowing fier,
   He red for shame, but frostie in desier.

The studded bridle on a ragged bough,
Nimbly she fastens, (ô how quicke is loue!)
The steed is stalled vp, and euen now,
To tie the rider she begins to proue:
   Backward she pusht him, as she would be thrust,
   And gouernd him in strength though not in lust.

So soone was she along, as he was downe,
Each leaning on their elbowes and their hips:
Now doth she stroke his cheek, now doth he frown,
And gins to chide, but soone she stops his lips,

And kissing speaks, with lustful language broken,
If thou wilt chide, thy lips shall neuer open.

He burnes with bashfull shame, she with her teares
Doth quench the maiden burning of his cheekes,
Then with her windie sighes, and golden heares,
To fan, and blow them drie againe she seekes.
   He saith, she is immodest, blames her misse,
   What followes more, she murthers with a kisse.

Euen as an emptie Eagle sharpe by fast,
Tires with her beake on feathers, flesh, and bone,
Shaking her wings, deuouring all in hast,
Till either gorge be stuft, or pray be gone:
   Euen so she kist his brow, his cheeke, his chin,
   And where she ends, she doth anew begin.

Forst to content, but neuer to obey,
Panting he lies, and breatheth in her face.
She feedeth on the steame, as on a pray,
And calls it heauenly moisture, aire of grace,
   Wishing her cheeks were gardens ful of flowers,
   So they were dew'd with such distilling showers.

Looke how a bird lyes tangled in a net,
So fastned in her armes Adonis lyes,
Pure shame and aw'd resistance made him fret,
Which bred more beautie in his angrie eyes:
   Raine added to a riuer that is ranke,
   Perforce will force it ouerflow the banke.

Still she intreats, and prettily intreats,
For to a prettie eare she tunes her tale.
Still is he sullein, still he lowres and frets,
Twixt crimson shame, and anger ashie pale,
   Being red she loues him best, and being white,
   Her best is betterd with a more delight.

Looke how he can, she cannot chuse but loue,
And by her faire immortall hand she sweares,
From his soft bosome neuer to remoue,
Till he take truce with her contending teares,
   Which lõg haue raind, making her cheeks al wet,
   And one sweet kisse shal pay this comptlesse debt.

Vpon this promise did he raise his chin,
Like a diuedapper peering through a waue,
Who being lookt on, ducks as quickly in:
So offers he to giue what she did craue,
   But when her lips were readie for his pay,
   He winks, and turnes his lips another way.

Neuer did passenger in sommers heat,
More thirst for drinke, then she for this good turne,
Her helpe she sees, but helpe she cannot get,
She bathes in water, yet her fire must burne:
 Oh pitie gan she crie, flint-hearted boy,
 Tis but a kisse I begge, why art thou coy?

I haue bene wooed as I intreat thee now,
Euen by the sterne, and direfull god of warre,
Whose sinowie necke in battell nere did bow,
100 Who conquers where he comes in euerie iarre,
 Yet hath he bene my captiue, and my slaue,
 And begd for that which thou vnaskt shalt haue.

Ouer my Altars hath he hong his launce,
His battred shield, his vncontrolled crest,
And for my sake hath learnd to sport, and daunce,
To toy, to wanton, dallie, smile, and iest,
 Scorning his churlish drumme, and ensigne red,
 Making my armes his field, his tent my bed.

Thus he that ouer-ruld, I ouer-swayed,
110 Leading him prisoner in a red rose chaine,
Strong-temperd steele his stronger strength obayed,
Yet was he seruile to my coy disdaine,
 Oh be not proud, nor brag not of thy might,
 For maistring her that foyld the god of fight.

Touch but my lips with those faire lips of thine,
Though mine be not so faire, yet are they red,
The kisse shalbe thine owne as well as mine,
What seest thou in the ground? hold vp thy head,
 Looke in mine ey-bals, there thy beautie lyes,
120 Then why not lips on lips, since eyes in eyes?

Art thou asham'd to kisse? then winke againe,
And I will winke, so shall the day seeme night.
Loue keepes his reuels where there are but twaine:
Be bold to play, our sport is not in sight,
 These blew-veind violets whereon we leane,
 Neuer can blab, nor know not what we meane.

The tender spring vpon thy tempting lip,
Shewes thee vnripe; yet maist thou well be tasted,
Make vse of time, let not aduantage slip,
130 Beautie within it selfe should not be wasted,
 Faire flowers that are not gathred in their prime,
 Rot, and consume them selues in litle time.

Were I hard-fauourd, foule, or wrinckled old,
Il-nurtur'd, crooked, churlish, harsh in voice,
Ore-worne, despised, reumatique, and cold,
Thick-sighted, barren, leane, and lacking iuyce;
 Thẽ mightst thou pause, for thẽ I were not for thee,
 But hauing no defects, why doest abhor me?

Thou canst not see one wrinckle in my brow,
Mine eyes are grey, and bright, & quicke in turning: 140
My beautie as the spring doth yearelie grow,
My flesh is soft, and plumpe, my marrow burning,
 My smooth moist hand, were it with thy hand felt,
 Would in thy palme dissolue, or seeme to melt.

Bid me discourse, I will inchaunt thine eare,
Or like a Fairie, trip vpon the greene,
Or like a Nimph, with long disheueld heare,
Daunce on the sands, and yet no footing seene.
 Loue is a spirit all compact of fire,
 Not grosse to sinke, but light, and will aspire. 150

Witnesse this Primrose banke whereon I lie,
These forcelesse flowers like sturdy trees support me:
Two strẽgthles doues will draw me through the skie,
From morne till night, euen where I list to sport me.
 Is loue so light sweet boy, and may it be,
 That thou should thinke it heauie vnto thee?

Is thine owne heart to thine owne face affected?
Can thy right hand ceaze loue vpon thy left?
Then woo thy selfe, be of thy selfe reiected:
Steale thine own freedome, and complaine on theft. 160
 Narcissus so him selfe him selfe forsooke,
 And died to kisse his shadow in the brooke.

Torches are made to light, iewels to weare,
Dainties to tast, fresh beautie for the vse,
Herbes for their smell, and sappie plants to beare.
Things growing to them selues, are growths abuse,
 Seeds spring frõ seeds, & beauty breedeth beauty,
 Thou wast begot, to get it is thy duty.

Vpon the earths increase why shouldst thou feed,
Vnlesse the earth with thy increase be fed? 170
By law of nature thou art bound to breed,
That thine may liue, when thou thy selfe art dead:
 And so in spite of death thou doest suruiue,
 In that thy likenesse still is left aliue.

By this the loue-sicke Queene began to sweate,
For where they lay the shadow had forsooke them,
And Titan tired in the midday heate,
With burning eye did hotly ouer-looke them,
 Wishing Adonis had his teame to guide,
 So he were like him, and by Venus side. 180

And now Adonis with a lazie sprite,
And with a heauie, darke, disliking eye,
His lowring browes ore-whelming his faire sight,
Like mistie vapors when they blot the skie,
 Sowring his cheekes, cries, fie, no more of loue,
 The sunne doth burne my face I must remoue.

Ay, me, (quoth Venus) young, and so vnkinde,
What bare excuses mak'st thou to be gon?
Ile sigh celestiall breath, whose gentle winde,
190 Shall coole the heate of this descending sun:
    Ile make a shadow for thee of my heares,
    If they burn too, Ile quench them with my teares.

The sun that shines from heauen, shines but warme,
And lo I lye betweene that sunne, and thee:
The heate I haue from thence doth litle harme,
Thine eye darts forth the fire that burneth me,
    And were I not immortall, life were done,
    Betweene this heauenly, and earthly sunne.

Art thou obdurate, flintie, hard as steele?
200 Nay more then flint, for stone at raine relenteth:
Art thou a womans sonne and canst not feele
What tis to loue, how want of loue tormenteth?
    O had thy mother borne so hard a minde,
    She had not brought forth thee, but died vnkind.

What am I that thou shouldst contemne me this?
Or what great danger, dwels vpon my sute?
What were thy lips the worse for one poore kis?
Speake, faire, but speake faire words, or else be mute:
    Giue me one kisse, Ile giue it thee againe,
210   And one for intrest, if thou wilt haue twaine.

Fie, liuelesse picture, cold, and sencelesse stone,
Well painted idoll, image dull, and dead,
Statüe contenting but the eye alone,
Thing like a man, but of no woman bred:
    Thou art no man, though of a mans complexion,
    For men will kisse euen by their owne direction.

This said, impatience chokes her pleading tongue,
And swelling passion doth prouoke a pause,
Red cheeks, and fierie eyes blaze forth her wrong:
220 Being Iudge in loue, she cannot right her cause.
    And now she weeps, & now she faine would speake
    And now her sobs do her intendments breake.

Sometime she shakes her head, and then his hand,
Now gazeth she on him, now on the ground;
Sometime her armes infold him like a band,
She would, he will not in her armes be bound:
    And when from thence he struggles to be gone,
    She locks her lillie fingers one in one.

Fondling, she saith, since I haue hemd thee here
230 Within the circuit of this iuorie pale,
Ile be a parke, and thou shalt be my deare:
Feed where thou wilt, on mountaine, or in dale;
    Graze on my lips, and if those hils be drie,
    Stray lower, where the pleasant fountaines lie.

Within this limit is reliefe inough,
Sweet bottome grasse, and high delightfull plaine,
Round rising hillocks, brakes obscure, and rough,
To shelter thee from tempest, and from raine:
    Then be my deare, since I am such a parke,
    No dog shal rowze thee, though a thousand bark. 240

At this Adonis smiles as in disdaine,
That in ech cheeke appeares a prettie dimple;
Loue made those hollowes, if him selfe were slaine,
He might be buried in a tombe so simple,
    Foreknowing well, if there he came to lie,
    Why there loue liu'd, & there he could not die.

These louely caues, these round inchanting pits,
Opend their mouthes to swallow Venus liking:
Being mad before, how doth she now for wits?
Strucke dead at first, what needs a second striking? 250
    Poore Queene of loue, in thine own law forlorne,
    To loue a cheeke that smiles at thee in scorne.

Now which way shall she turne? what shall she say?
Her words are done, her woes the more increasing,
The time is spent, her obiect will away,
And from her twining armes doth vrge releasing:
    Pitie she cries, some fauour, some remorse,
    Away he springs, and hasteth to his horse.

But lo from forth a copp's that neighbors by,
A breeding Iennet, lustie, young, and proud, 260
Adonis trampling Courser doth espy:
And forth she rushes, snorts, and neighs aloud.
    The strong-neckt steed being tied vnto a tree,
    Breaketh his raine, and to her straight goes hee.

Imperiously he leaps, he neighs, he bounds,
And now his wouen girthes he breaks asunder,
The bearing earth with his hard hoofe he wounds,
Whose hollow wombe resounds like heauens thunder,
    The yron bit he crusheth tweene his teeth,
    Controlling what he was controlled with. 270

His eares vp prickt, his braided hanging mane
Vpon his compast crest now stand on end,
His nostrils drinke the aire, and forth againe
As from a fornace, vapors doth he send:
    His eye which scornfully glisters like fire,
    Shewes his hote courage, and his high desire.

Sometime he trots, as if he told the steps,
With gentle maiestie, and modest pride,
Anon he reres vpright, curuets, and leaps,
As who should say, lo thus my strength is tride. 280
    And this I do, to captiuate the eye,
    Of the faire breeder that is standing by.

What recketh he his riders angrie sturre,
His flattering holla, or his stand, I say,
What cares he now, for curbe, or pricking spurre,
For rich caparisons, or trappings gay:
    He sees his loue, and nothing else he sees,
    For nothing else with his proud sight agrees.

290
Looke when a Painter would surpasse the life,
In limming out a well proportiond steed,
His Art with Natures workmanship at strife,
As if the dead the liuing should exceed:
    So did this Horse excell a common one,
    In shape, in courage, colour, pace and bone.

Round hooft, short ioynted, fetlocks shag, and long,
Broad breast, full eye, small head, and nostrill wide,
High crest, short eares, straight legs, & passing strõg,
Thin mane, thicke taile, broad buttock, tender hide:
    Looke what a Horse should haue, he did not lack,
300
    Saue a proud rider on so proud a back.

Sometime he scuds farre off, and there he stares,
Anon he starts, at sturring of a feather:
To bid the wind a base he now prepares,
And where he runne, or flie, they know not whether:
    For through his mane, & taile, the high wind sings,
    Fanning the haires, who waue like feathred wings.

He lookes vpon his loue, and neighes vnto her,
She answers him, as if she knew his minde,
Being proud as females are, to see him woo her,
310
She puts on outward strangenesse, seemes vnkinde:
    Spurnes at his loue, and scorns the heat he feeles,
    Beating his kind imbracements with her heeles.

Then like a melancholy malcontent,
He vailes his taile that like a falling plume,
Coole shadow to his melting buttocke lent,
He stamps, and bites the poore flies in his fume:
    His loue perceiuing how he was inrag'd,
    Grew kinder, and his furie was asswag'd.

His testie maister goeth about to take him,
320
When lo the vnbackt breeder full of feare,
Iealous of catching, swiftly doth forsake him,
With her the Horse, and left Adonis there:
    As they were mad vnto the wood they hie them,
    Outstripping crowes, that striue to ouerfly them.

All swolne with chafing, downe Adonis sits,
Banning his boystrous, and vnruly beast;
And now the happie season once more fits
That louesicke loue, by pleading may be blest:
    For louers say, the heart hath treble wrong,
330
    When it is bard the aydance of the tongue.

An Ouen that is stopt, or riuer stayd,
Burneth more hotly, swelleth with more rage:
So of concealed sorow may be sayd,
Free vent of words loues fier doth asswage,
    But when the hearts atturney once is mute,
    The client breakes, as desperat in his sute.

He sees her comming, and begins to glow:
Euen as a dying coale reuiues with winde,
And with his bonnet hides his angrie brow,
Lookes on the dull earth with disturbed minde: 340
    Taking no notice that she is so nye,
    For all askance he holds her in his eye.

O what a sight it was wistly to view,
How she came stealing to the wayward boy,
To note the fighting conflict of her hew,
How white and red, ech other did destroy:
    But now her cheeke was pale, and by and by
    It flasht forth fire, as lightning from the skie.

Now was she iust before him as he sat,
And like a lowly louer downe she kneeles,   350
With one faire hand she heaueth vp his hat,
Her other tender hand his faire cheeke feeles:
    His tendrer cheeke, receiues her soft hands print,
    As apt, as new falne snow takes any dint.

Oh what a war of lookes was then betweene them,
Her eyes petitioners to his eyes suing,
His eyes saw her eyes, as they had not seene them,
Her eyes wooed still, his eyes disdaind the wooing:
    And all this dumbe play had his acts made plain,
    With tears which Chorus-like her eyes did rain.   360

Full gently now she takes him by the hand,
A lillie prisond in a gaile of snow,
Or Iuorie in an allablaster band,
So white a friend, ingirts so white a fo:
    This beautious combat wilfull, and vnwilling,
    Showed like two siluer doues that sit a billing.

Once more the engin of her thoughts began,
O fairest mouer on this mortall round,
Would thou wert as I am, and I a man,
My heart all whole as thine, thy heart my wound,   370
    For one sweet looke thy helpe I would assure thee,
    Thogh nothing but my bodies bane wold cure thee.

Giue me my hand (saith he,) why dost thou feele it?
Giue me my heart (saith she,) and thou shalt haue it.
O giue it me lest thy hard heart do steele it,
And being steeld, soft sighes can neuer graue it.
    Then loues deepe grones, I neuer shall regard,
    Because Adonis heart hath made mine hard.

For shame he cries, let go, and let me go,
380 My dayes delight is past, my horse is gone,
And tis your fault I am bereft him so,
I pray you hence, and leaue me here alone,
   For all my mind, my thought, my busie care,
   Is how to get my palfrey from the mare.

Thus she replies, thy palfrey as he should,
Welcomes the warme approch of sweet desire,
Affection is a coale that must be coold,
Else sufferd it will set the heart on fire,
   The sea hath bounds, but deepe desire hath none,
390 Therfore no maruell though thy horse be gone.

How like a iade he stood tied to the tree,
Seruilly maisterd with a leatherne raine,
But when he saw his loue, his youths faire fee,
He held such pettie bondage in disdaine:
   Throwing the base thong from his bending crest,
   Enfranchising his mouth, his backe, his brest.

Who sees his true-loue in her naked bed,
Teaching the sheets a whiter hew then white,
But when his glutton eye so full hath fed,
400 His other agents ayme at like delight?
   Who is so faint that dares not be so bold,
   To touch the fier the weather being cold?

Let me excuse thy courser gentle boy,
And learne of him I heartily beseech thee,
To take aduantage on presented ioy,
Though I were dũbe, yet his proceedings teach thee.
   O learne to loue, the lesson is but plaine,
   And once made perfect, neuer lost againe.

I know not loue (quoth he) nor will not know it,
410 Vnlesse it be a Boare, and then I chase it,
Tis much to borrow, and I will not owe it,
My loue to loue, is loue, but to disgrace it,
   For I haue heard, it is a life in death,
   That laughs and weeps, and all but with a breath.

Who weares a garment shapelesse and vnfinisht?
Who plucks the bud before one leafe put forth?
If springing things be anie iot diminisht,
They wither in their prime, proue nothing worth,
   The colt that's backt and burthend being yong,
420 Loseth his pride, and neuer waxeth strong.

You hurt my hand with wringing, let vs part,
And leaue this idle theame, this bootlesse chat,
Remoue your siege from my vnyeelding hart,
To loues allarmes it will not ope the gate,
   Dismisse your vows, your fained tears, your flattry,
   For where a heart is hard they make no battry.

What canst thou talke (quoth she) hast thou a tong?
O would thou hadst not, or I had no hearing,
Thy marmaides voice hath done me double wrong,
I had my lode before, now prest with bearing, 430
   Mellodious discord, heauenly tune harsh sounding,
   Eares deep sweet musik, & harts deep sore woũding.

Had I no eyes but eares, my eares would loue,
That inward beautie and inuisible,
Or were I deafe, thy outward parts would moue
Ech part in me, that were but sensible,
   Though neither eyes, nor eares, to heare nor see,
   Yet should I be in loue, by touching thee.

Say that the sence of feeling were bereft me,
And that I could not see, nor heare, nor touch, 440
And nothing but the verie smell were left me,
Yet would my loue to thee be still as much,
   For frõ the stillitorie of thy face excelling,
   Coms breath perfumd, that breedeth loue by
      smelling.

But oh what banquet wert thou to the tast,
Being nourse, and feeder of the other foure,
Would they not wish the feast might euer last,
And bid suspition double locke the dore;
   Lest iealousie that sower vnwelcome guest,
   Should by his stealing in disturbe the feast? 450

Once more the rubi-colourd portall opend,
Which to his speech did honie passage yeeld,
Like a red morne that euer yet betokend,
Wracke to the sea-man, tempest to the field:
   Sorrow to shepherds, wo vnto the birds,
   Gusts, and foule flawes, to heardmen, & to herds.

This ill presage aduisedly she marketh,
Euen as the wind is husht before it raineth:
Or as the wolfe doth grin before he barketh:
Or as the berrie breakes before it staineth: 460
   Or like the deadly bullet of a gun:
   His meaning strucke her ere his words begun.

And at his looke she flatly falleth downe,
For lookes kill loue, and loue by lookes reuiueth,
A smile recures the wounding of a frowne,
But blessed bankrout that by losse so thriueth.
   The sillie boy beleeuing she is dead,
   Claps her pale cheeke, till clapping makes it red.

And all amaz'd, brake off his late intent,
For sharply he did thinke to reprehend her, 470
Which cunning loue did wittily preuent,
Faire-fall the wit that can so well defend her:
   For on the grasse she lyes as she were slaine,
   Till his breath breatheth life in her againe.

He wrings her nose, he strikes her on the cheekes,
He bends her fingers, holds her pulses hard,
He chafes her lips, a thousand wayes he seekes,
To mend the hurt, that his vnkindnesse mard,
　　He kisses her, and she by her good will,
480　　Will neuer rise, so he will kisse her still.

The night of sorrow now is turnd to day,
Her two blew windowes faintly she vpheaueth,
Like the faire sunne when in his fresh array,
He cheeres the morne, and all the earth releeueth:
　　And as the bright sunne glorifies the skie:
　　So is her face illumind with her eye.

Whose beames vpon his hairelesse face are fixt,
As if from thence they borrowed all their shine,
Were neuer foure such lamps, together mixt,
490　Had not his clouded with his browes repine.
　　But hers, which through the cristal tears gaue light,
　　Shone like the Moone in water seene by night.

O where am I (quoth she,) in earth or heauen,
Or in the Ocean drencht, or in the fire:
What houre is this, or morne, or wearie euen,
Do I delight to die or life desire?
　　But now I liu'd, and life was deaths annoy,
　　But now I dy'de, and death was liuely ioy.

O thou didst kill me, kill me once againe,
500　Thy eyes shrowd tutor, that hard heart of thine,
Hath taught them scornfull tricks, & such disdaine,
That they haue murdred this poore heart of mine,
　　And these mine eyes true leaders to their queene,
　　But for thy piteous lips no more had seene.

Long may they kisse ech other for this cure,
Oh neuer let their crimson liueries weare,
And as they last, their verdour still endure,
To driue infection from the dangerous yeare:
　　That the star-gazers hauing writ on death,
510　May say, the plague is banisht by thy breath.

Pure lips, sweet seales in my soft lips imprinted,
What bargaines may I make still to be sealing?
To sell my selfe I can be well contented,
So thou wilt buy, and pay, and vse good dealing,
　　Which purchase if thou make, for feare of slips,
　　Set thy seale manuell, on my wax-red lips.

A thousand kisses buyes my heart from me,
And pay them at thy leisure, one by one,
What is ten hundred touches vnto thee,
520　Are they not quickly told, and quickly gone?
　　Say for non-paimēt, that the debt should double,
　　Is twentie hundred kisses such a trouble?

Faire Queene (quoth he) if anie loue you owe me,
Measure my strangenesse with my vnripe yeares,
Before I know my selfe, seeke not to know me,
No fisher but the vngrowne frie forbeares,
　　The mellow plum doth fall, the greene sticks fast,
　　Or being early pluckt, is sower to tast.

Looke the worlds comforter with wearie gate,
His dayes hot taske hath ended in the west,　　530
The owle (nights herald) shreeks, tis verie late,
The sheepe are gone to fold, birds to their nest,
　　And cole-black clouds, that shadow heauens light,
　　Do summon vs to part, and bid good night.

Now let me say goodnight, and so say you,
If you will say so, you shall haue a kis;
Goodnight (quoth she) and ere he sayes adue,
The honie fee of parting tendred is,
　　Her armes do lend his necke a sweet imbrace,
　　Incorporate then they seeme, face growes to face.　　540

Till breathlesse he disioynd, and backward drew,
The heauenly moisture that sweet corall mouth,
Whose precious tast, her thirstie lips well knew,
Whereon they surfet, yet complaine on drouth,
　　He with her plentie prest, she faint with dearth,
　　Their lips together glewed, fall to the earth.

Now quicke desire hath caught the yeelding pray,
And gluttonlike she feeds, yet neuer filleth,
Her lips are conquerers, his lips obay,
Paying what ransome the insulter willeth:　　550
　　Whose vultur thought doth pitch the price so hie,
　　That she will draw his lips rich treasure drie.

And hauing felt the sweetnesse of the spoile,
With blind fold furie she begins to forrage,
Her face doth reeke, & smoke, her blood doth boile,
And carelesse lust stirs vp a desperat courage,
　　Planting obliuion, beating reason backe,
　　Forgetting shames pure blush, & honors wracke.

Hot, faint, and wearie, with her hard imbracing,
Like a wild bird being tam'd with too much hādling,　　560
Or as the fleet-foot Roe that's tyr'd with chasing,
Or like the froward infant stild with dandling:
　　He now obayes, and now no more resisteth,
　　While she takes all she can, not all she listeth.

What waxe so frozen but dissolues with tempring,
And yeelds at last to euerie light impression?
Things out of hope, are compast oft with ventring,
Chiefly in loue, whose leaue exceeds commission:
　　Affection faints not like a pale-fac'd coward,
　　But thē woes best, whē most his choice is froward.　　570

260

When he did frowne, ô had she then gaue ouer,
Such nectar from his lips she had not suckt,
Foule wordes, and frownes, must not repell a louer,
What though the rose haue prickles, yet tis pluckt?
    Were beautie vnder twentie locks kept fast,
    Yet loue breaks through, & picks them all at last.

For pittie now she can no more detaine him,
The poore foole praies her that he may depart,
She is resolu'd no longer to restraine him,
580   Bids him farewell, and looke well to her hart,
    The which by Cupids bow she doth protest,
    He carries thence incaged in his brest.

Sweet boy she saies, this night ile wast in sorrow,
For my sick heart commands mine eyes to watch,
Tell me loues maister, shall we meete to morrow,
Say, shall we, shall we, wilt thou make the match?
    He tell's her no, to morrow he intends,
    To hunt the boare with certaine of his frends.

The boare (quoth she) whereat a suddain pale,
590   Like lawne being spred vpon the blushing rose,
Vsurpes her cheeke, she trembles at his tale,
And on his neck her yoaking armes she throwes.
    She sincketh downe, still hanging by his necke,
    He on her belly fall's, she on her backe.

Now is she in the verie lists of loue,
Her champion mounted for the hot incounter,
All is imaginarie she doth proue,
He will not mannage her, although he mount her,
    That worse then Tantalus is her annoy,
600   To clip Elizium, and to lacke her ioy.

Euen so poore birds deceiu'd with painted grapes,
Do surfet by the eye, and pine the maw:
Euen so she languisheth in her mishaps,
As those poore birds that helplesse berries saw,
    The warme effects which she in him finds missing,
    She seekes to kindle with continuall kissing.

But all in vaine, good Queene, it will not bee,
She hath assai'd as much as may be prou'd,
Her pleading hath deseru'd a greater fee,
610   She's loue; she loues, and yet she is not lou'd,
    Fie, fie, he saies, you crush me, let me go,
    You haue no reason to withhold me so.

Thou hadst bin gone (quoth she) sweet boy ere this,
But that thou toldst me, thou woldst hunt the boare,
Oh be aduisd, thou know'st not what it is,
With iauelings point a churlish swine to goare,
    Whose tushes neuer sheathd, he whetteth still,
    Like to a mortall butcher bent to kill.

On his bow-backe, he hath a battell set,
Of brisly pikes that euer threat his foes,   620
His eyes like glow-wormes shine, when he doth fret,
His snout digs sepulchers where ere he goes,
    Being mou'd he strikes, what ere is in his way,
    And whom he strikes, his crooked tushes slay.

His brawnie sides with hairie bristles armed,
Are better proofe then thy speares point can enter,
His short thick necke cannot be easily harmed,
Being irefull, on the lyon he will venter,
    The thornie brambles, and imbracing bushes,
    As fearefull of him part, through whom he rushes.   630

Alas, he naught esteem's that face of thine,
To which loues eyes paies tributarie gazes,
Nor thy soft handes, sweet lips, and christall eine,
Whose full perfection all the world amazes,
    But hauing thee at vantage (wondrous dread!)
    Wold roote these beauties, as he root's the mead.

Oh let him keep his loathsome cabin still,
Beautie hath naught to do with such foule fiends,
Come not within his danger by thy will,
They that thriue well, take counsell of their friends,   640
    When thou didst name the boare, not to dissëble,
    I feard thy fortune, and my ioynts did tremble.

Didst thou not marke my face, was it not white?
Sawest thou not signes of feare lurke in mine eye?
Grew I not faint, and fell I not downe right?
Within my bosome whereon thou doest lye,
    My boding heart, pants, beats, and takes no rest,
    But like an earthquake, shakes thee on my brest.

For where loue raignes, disturbing iealousie,
Doth call him selfe affections centinell,   650
Giues false alarmes, suggesteth mutinie,
And in a peacefull houre doth crie, kill, kill,
    Distempring gentle loue in his desire,
    As aire, and water do abate the fire.

This sower informer, this bate-breeding spie,
This canker that eates vp loues tender spring,
This carry-tale, dissentious iealousie,
That somtime true newes, somtime false doth bring,
    Knocks at my heart, and whispers in mine eare,
    That if I loue thee, I thy death should feare.   660

And more then so, presenteth to mine eye,
The picture of an angrie chafing boare,
Vnder whose sharpe fangs, on his backe doth lye,
An image like thy selfe, all staynd with goare,
    Whose blood vpon the fresh flowers being shed,
    Doth make thē droop with grief, & hang the hed.

What should I do, seeing thee so indeed?
That tremble at th'imagination,
The thought of it doth make my faint heart bleed,
670 And feare doth teach it diuination;
 I prophecie thy death, my liuing sorrow,
 If thou incounter with the boare to morrow.

But if thou needs wilt hunt, be rul'd by me,
Vncouple at the timerous flying hare,
Or at the foxe which liues by subtiltie,
Or at the Roe which no incounter dare:
 Pursue these fearfull creatures o're the downes,
 And on thy wel breathd horse keep with thy hoŭds.

And when thou hast on foote the purblind hare,
680 Marke the poore wretch to ouer-shut his troubles,
How he outruns the wind, and with what care,
He crankes and crosses with a thousand doubles,
 The many musits through the which he goes,
 Are like a laberinth to amaze his foes.

Sometime he runnes among a flocke of sheepe,
To make the cunning hounds mistake their smell,
And sometime where earth-deluing Conies keepe,
To stop the loud pursuers in their yell:
 And sometime sorteth with a heard of deare,
690 Danger deuiseth shifts, wit waites on feare.

For there his smell with others being mingled,
The hot sent-snuffing hounds are driuen to doubt,
Ceasing their clamorous cry, till they haue singled
With much ado the cold fault cleanly out,
 Then do they spend their mouth's, eccho replies,
 As if an other chase were in the skies.

By this poore wat farre off vpon a hill,
Stands on his hinder-legs with listning eare,
To hearken if his foes pursue him still,
700 Anon their loud alarums he doth heare,
 And now his griefe may be compared well,
 To one sore sicke, that heares the passing bell.

Then shalt thou see the deaw-bedabbled wretch,
Turne, and returne, indenting with the way,
Ech enuious brier, his wearie legs do scratch,
Ech shadow makes him stop, ech murmour stay,
 For miserie is troden on by manie,
 And being low, neuer releeu'd by anie.

Lye quietly, and heare a litle more,
710 Nay do not struggle, for thou shalt not rise,
To make thee hate the hunting of the bore,
Vnlike my selfe thou hear'st me moralize,
 Applying this to that, and so to so,
 For loue can comment vpon euerie wo.

Where did I leaue? no matter where (quoth he)
Leaue me, and then the storie aptly ends,
The night is spent; why what of that (quoth she?)
I am (quoth he) expected of my friends,
 And now tis darke, and going I shall fall.
 In night (quoth she) desire sees best of all.   720

But if thou fall, oh then imagine this,
The earth in loue with thee, thy footing trips,
And all is but to rob thee of a kis,
Rich prayes make true-men theeues: so do thy lips
 Make modest Dyan, cloudie and forlorne,
 Lest she should steale a kisse and die forsworne.

Now of this darke night I perceiue the reason,
Cinthia for shame, obscures her siluer shine,
Till forging nature be condemn'd of treason,
For stealing moulds from heauen, that were diuine,   730
 Wherin she fram'd thee, in hie heauens despight,
 To shame the sunne by day, and her by night.

And therefore hath she brib'd the destinies,
To crosse the curious workmanship of nature,
To mingle beautie with infirmities,
And pure perfection with impure defeature,
 Making it subiect to the tyrannie,
 Of mad mischances, and much miserie.

As burning feauers, agues pale, and faint,
Life-poysoning pestilence, and frendzies wood,   740
The marrow-eating sicknesse whose attaint,
Disorder breeds by heating of the blood,
 Surfets, impostumes, griefe, and damnd dispaire,
 Sweare natures death, for framing thee so faire.

And not the least of all these maladies,
But in one minutes fight brings beautie vnder,
Both fauour, sauour, hew, and qualities,
Whereat th'impartiall gazer late did wonder,
 Are on the sudden wasted, thawed, and donne,
 As mountain snow melts with the midday sonne.   750

Therefore despight of fruitlesse chastitie,
Loue-lacking vestals, and selfe-louing Nuns,
That on the earth would breed a scarcitie,
And barraine dearth of daughters, and of sons;
 Be prodigall, the lampe that burnes by night,
 Dries vp his oyle, to lend the world his light.

What is thy bodie but a swallowing graue,
Seeming to burie that posteritie,
Which by the rights of time thou needs must haue,
If thou destroy them not in darke obscuritie?   760
 If so the world will hold thee in disdaine,
 Sith in thy pride, so faire a hope is slaine.

So in thy selfe, thy selfe art made away,
A mischiefe worse then ciuill home-bred strife,
Or theirs whose desperat hands them selues do slay,
Or butcher sire, that reaues his sonne of life:
    Foule cankring rust, the hidden treasure frets,
    But gold that's put to vse more gold begets.

770 Nay then (quoth Adon) you will fall againe,
Into your idle ouer-handled theame,
The kisse I gaue you is bestow'd in vaine,
And all in vaine you striue against the streame,
    For by this black-fac't night, desires foule nourse,
    Your treatise makes me like you, worse & worse.

If loue haue lent you twentie thousand tongues,
And euerie tongue more mouing then your owne,
Bewitching like the wanton Marmaids songs,
Yet from mine eare the tempting tune is blowne,
    For know my heart stands armed in mine eare,
780   And will not let a false sound enter there.

Lest the deceiuing harmonie should ronne,
Into the quiet closure of my brest,
And then my litle heart were quite vndone,
In his bed-chamber to be bard of rest,
    No Ladie no, my heart longs not to grone,
    But soundly sleeps, while now it sleeps alone.

What haue you vrg'd, that I can not reproue?
The path is smooth that leadeth on to danger,
I hate not loue, but your deuise in loue,
790 That lends imbracements vnto euery stranger,
    You do it for increase, ô straunge excuse!
    When reason is the bawd to lusts abuse.

Call it not loue, for loue to heauen is fled,
Since sweating lust on earth vsurpt his name,
Vnder whose simple semblance he hath fed,
Vpon fresh beautie, blotting it with blame;
    Which the hot tyrant staines, & soone bereaues:
    As Caterpillers do the tender leaues.

Loue comforteth like sun-shine after raine,
800 But lusts effect is tempest after sunne,
Loues gentle spring doth always fresh remaine,
Lusts winter comes, ere sommer halfe be donne:
    Loue surfets not, lust like a glutton dies:
    Loue is all truth, lust full of forged lies.

More I could tell, but more I dare not say,
The text is old, the Orator too greene,
Therefore in sadnesse, now I will away,
My face is full of shame, my heart of teene,
    Mine eares that to your wanton talke attended,
810   Do burne them selues, for hauing so offended.

With this he breaketh from the sweet embrace,
Of those faire armes which bound him to her brest,
And homeward through the dark lawnd runs apace,
Leaues loue vpon her backe, deeply distrest,
    Looke how a bright star shooteth from the skye;
    So glides he in the night from Venus eye.

Which after him she dartes, as one on shore
Gazing vpon a late embarked friend,
Till the wilde waues will haue him seene no more,
Whose ridges with the meeting cloudes contend: 820
    So did the mercilesse, and pitchie night,
    Fold in the obiect that did feed her sight.

Whereat amas'd as one that vnaware,
Hath dropt a precious iewell in the flood,
Or stonisht, as night wandrers often are,
Their light blowne out in some mistrustfull wood;
    Euen so confounded in the darke she lay,
    Hauing lost the faire discouerie of her way.

And now she beates her heart, whereat it grones,
That all the neighbour caues as seeming troubled,   830
Make verball repetition of her mones,
Passion on passion, deeply is redoubled,
    Ay me, she cries, and twentie times, wo, wo,
    And twentie ecchoes, twentie times crie so.

She marking them, begins a wailing note,
And sings extemporally a wofull dittie,
How loue makes yong-men thrall, & old men dote,
How loue is wise in follie, foolish wittie:
    Her heauie antheme still concludes in wo,
    And still the quier of ecchoes answer so.   840

Her song was tedious, and out-wore the night,
For louers houres are long, though seeming short,
If pleasd themselues, others they thinke delight,
In such like circumstance, with such like sport:
    Their copious stories oftentimes begunne,
    End without audience, and are neuer donne.

For who hath she to spend the night withall,
But idle sounds resembling parasits?
Like shrill-tongu'd Tapsters answering euerie call,
Soothing the humor of fantastique wits,   850
    She sayes tis so, they answer all tis so,
    And would say after her, if she said no.

Lo here the gentle larke wearie of rest,
From his moyst cabinet mounts vp on hie,
And wakes the morning, from whose siluer brest,
The sunne ariseth in his maiestie,
    Who doth the world so gloriously behold,
    That Ceader tops and hils, seeme burnisht gold.

Venus salutes him with this faire good morrow,
860 Oh thou cleare god, and patron of all light,
From whom ech lamp, and shining star doth borrow,
The beautious influence that makes him bright,
　　There liues a sonne that suckt an earthly mother,
　　May lend thee light, as thou doest lend to other.

This sayd, she hasteth to a mirtle groue,
Musing the morning is so much ore-worne,
And yet she heares no tidings of her loue;
She harkens for his hounds, and for his horne,
　　Anon she heares them chaunt it lustily,
870 　　And all in hast she coasteth to the cry.

And as she runnes, the bushes in the way,
Some catch her by the necke, some kisse her face,
Some twin'd about her thigh to make her stay,
She wildly breaketh from their strict imbrace,
　　Like a milch Doe, whose swelling dugs do ake,
　　Hasting to feed her fawne, hid in some brake.

By this she heares the hounds are at a bay,
Whereat she starts like one that spies an adder,
Wreath'd vp in fatall folds iust in his way,
880 The feare whereof doth make him shake, & shudder,
　　Euen so the timerous yelping of the hounds,
　　Appals her senses, and her spirit confounds.

For now she knowes it is no gentle chase,
But the blunt boare, rough beare, or lyon proud,
Because the crie remaineth in one place,
Where fearefully the dogs exclaime aloud,
　　Finding their enemie to be so curst,
　　They all straine curt'sie who shall cope him first.

This dismall crie rings sadly in her eare,
890 Through which it enters to surprise her hart,
Who ouercome by doubt, and bloodlesse feare,
With cold-pale weakenesse, nums ech feeling part,
　　Like soldiers when their captain once doth yeeld,
　　They basely flie, and dare not stay the field.

Thus stands she in a trembling extasie,
Till cheering vp her senses all dismayd,
She tels them tis a causlesse fantasie,
And childish error that they are affrayd,
　　Bids thē leaue quaking, bids them feare no more,
900 　　And with that word, she spide the hunted boare.

Whose frothie mouth bepainted all with red,
Like milke, & blood, being mingled both togither,
A second feare through all her sinewes spred,
Which madly hurries her, she knowes not whither,
　　This way she runs, and now she will no further,
　　But backe retires, to rate the boare for murther.

A thousand spleenes beare her a thousand wayes,
She treads the path, that she vntreads againe;
Her more then hast, is mated with delayes,
Like the proceedings of a drunken braine, 910
　　Full of respects, yet naught at all respecting,
　　In hand with all things, naught at all effecting.

Here kenneld in a brake, she finds a hound,
And askes the wearie caitiffe for his maister,
And there another licking of his wound,
Gainst venimd sores, the onely soueraigne plaister.
　　And here she meets another, sadly skowling,
　　To whom she speaks, & he replies with howling.

When he hath ceast his ill resounding noise,
Another flapmouthd mourner, blacke, and grim, 920
Against the welkin, volies out his voyce,
Another, and another, answer him,
　　Clapping their proud tailes to the ground below,
　　Shaking their scratcht-eares, bleeding as they go.

Looke how, the worlds poore people are amazed,
At apparitions, signes, and prodigies,
Whereon with feareful eyes, they long haue gazed,
Infusing them with dreadfull prophecies;
　　So she at these sad signes, drawes vp her breath,
　　And sighing it againe, exclaimes on death. 930

Hard fauourd tyrant, ougly, meagre, leane,
Hatefull diuorce of loue, (thus chides she death)
Grim-grinning ghost, earths-worme what dost thou
　　meane?
To stifle beautie, and to steale his breath?
　　Who when he liu'd, his breath and beautie set
　　Glosse on the rose, smell to the violet.

If he be dead, ô no, it cannot be,
Seeing his beautie, thou shouldst strike at it,
Oh yes, it may, thou hast no eyes to see,
But hatefully at randon doest thou hit, 940
　　Thy marke is feeble age, but thy false dart,
　　Mistakes that aime, and cleaues an infants hart.

Hadst thou but bid beware, then he had spoke,
And hearing him, thy power had lost his power,
The destinies will curse thee for this stroke,
They bid thee crop a weed, thou pluckst a flower,
　　Loues golden arrow at him should haue fled,
　　And not deaths ebon dart to strike him dead.

Dost thou drink tears, that thou prouok'st such
　　weeping,
What may a heauie grone aduantage thee? 950
Why hast thou cast into eternall sleeping,
Those eyes that taught all other eyes to see?
　　Now nature cares not for thy mortall vigour,
　　Since her best worke is ruin'd with thy rigour.

Here ouercome as one full of dispaire,
She vaild her eye-lids, who like sluces stopt
The christall tide, that from her two cheeks faire,
In the sweet channell of her bosome dropt.
 But through the floud-gates breaks the siluer rain,
960 And with his strong course opens them againe.

O how her eyes, and teares, did lend, and borrow,
Her eye seene in the teares, teares in her eye,
Both christals, where they viewd ech others sorrow:
Sorrow, that friendly sighs sought still to drye,
 But like a stormie day, now wind, now raine,
 Sighs drie her cheeks, tears make thĕ wet againe.

Variable passions throng her constant wo,
As striuing who should best become her griefe,
All entertaind, ech passion labours so,
970 That euerie present sorrow seemeth chiefe,
 But none is best, then ioyne they all together,
 Like many clouds, consulting for foule weather.

By this farre off, she heares some huntsman hallow,
A nourses song nere pleasd her babe so well,
The dyre imagination she did follow,
This sound of hope doth labour to expell,
 For now reuiuing ioy bids her reioyce,
 And flatters her, it is Adonis voyce.

Whereat her teares began to turne their tide,
980 Being prisond in her eye: like pearles in glasse,
Yet sometimes fals an orient drop beside,
Which her cheeke melts, as scorning it should passe
 To wash the foule face of the sluttish ground,
 Who is but dronken when she seemeth drownd.

O hard beleeuing loue how strange it seemes!
Not to beleeue, and yet too credulous:
Thy weale, and wo, are both of them extreames,
Despaire, and hope, makes thee ridiculous.
 The one doth flatter thee in thoughts vnlikely,
990 In likely thoughts the other kils thee quickly.

Now she vnweaues the web that she hath wrought,
Adonis liues, and death is not to blame:
It was not she that cald him all to nought;
Now she ads honours to his hatefull name.
 She clepes him king of graues, & graue for kings,
 Imperious supreme of all mortall things.

No, no, quoth she, sweet death, I did but iest,
Yet pardon me, I felt a kind of feare
When as I met the boare, that bloodie beast,
1000 Which knowes no pitie but is still seuere,
 Then gentle shadow (truth I must confesse)
 I rayld on thee, fearing my loues decesse.

Tis not my fault, the Bore prouok't my tong,
Be wreak't on him (inuisible commaunder)
T'is he foule creature, that hath done thee wrong,
I did but act, he's author of thy slaunder.
 Greefe hath two tongues, and neuer woman yet,
 Could rule them both, without ten womens wit.

Thus hoping that Adonis is aliue,
Her rash suspect she doth extenuate, 1010
And that his beautie may the better thriue,
With death she humbly doth insinuate.
 Tels him of trophies, statues, tombes, and stories
 His victories, his triumphs, and his glories.

O Ioue quoth she, how much a foole was I,
To be of such a weake and sillie mind,
To waile his death who liues, and must not die,
Till mutuall ouerthrow of mortall kind?
 For he being dead, with him is beautie slaine,
 And beautie dead, blacke Chaos comes againe. 1020

Fy, fy, fond loue, thou art as full of feare,
As one with treasure laden, hem'd with theeues,
Trifles vnwitnessed with eye, or eare,
Thy coward heart with false bethinking greeues.
 Euen at this word she heares a merry horne,
 Whereat she leaps, that was but late forlorne.

As Faulcons to the lure, away she flies,
The grasse stoops not, she treads on it so light,
And in her hast, vnfortunately spies,
The foule boares conquest, on her faire delight, 1030
 Which seene, her eyes as murdred with the view,
 Like stars asham'd of day, themselues withdrew.

Or as the snaile, whose tender hornes being hit,
Shrinks backward in his shellie caue with paine,
And, there all smoothred vp, in shade doth sit,
Long after fearing to creepe forth againe:
 So at his bloodie view her eyes are fled,
 Into the deep-darke cabbins of her head.

Where they resigne their office, and their light,
To the disposing of her troubled braine, 1040
Who bids them still consort with ougly night,
And neuer wound the heart with lookes againe,
 Who like a king perplexed in his throne,
 By their suggestion, giues a deadly grone.

Whereat ech tributarie subiect quakes,
As when the wind imprisond in the ground,
Struggling for passage, earths foundation shakes,
Which with cold terror, doth mens minds confound:
 This mutinie ech part doth so surprise,
 That frõ their dark beds once more leap her eies. 1050

And being opend, threw vnwilling light,
Vpon the wide wound, that the boare had trencht
In his soft flanke, whose wonted lillie white
With purple tears that his wound wept, was drẽcht.
    No floure was nigh, no grasse, hearb, leaf, or weed,
    But stole his blood, and seemd with him to bleed.

This solemne sympathie, poore Venus noteth,
Ouer one shoulder doth she hang her head,
Dumblie she passions, frantikely she doteth,
1060   She thinkes he could not die, he is not dead,
    Her voice is stopt, her ioynts forget to bow,
    Her eyes are mad, that they haue wept till now.

Vpon his hurt she lookes so stedfastly,
That her sight dazling, makes the wound seem three,
And then she reprehends her mangling eye,
That makes more gashes, where no breach shuld be:
    His face seems twain, ech seuerall lim is doubled,
    For oft the eye mistakes, the brain being troubled.

My tongue cannot expresse my griefe for one,
1070   And yet (quoth she) behold two Adons dead,
My sighes are blowne away, my salt teares gone,
Mine eyes are turn'd to fire, my heart to lead,
    Heauie hearts lead melt at mine eyes red fire,
    So shall I die by drops of hot desire.

Alas poore world what treasure hast thou lost,
What face remains aliue that's worth the viewing?
Whose tongue is musick now? what cãst thou boast,
Of things long since, or any thing insuing?
    The flowers are sweet, their colours fresh, and trim,
1080   But true sweet beautie liu'd, and di'de with him.

Bonnet, nor vaile henceforth no creature weare,
Nor sunne, nor wind will euer striue to kisse you,
Hauing no faire to lose, you need not feare,
The sun doth skorne you, & the wind doth hisse you.
    But when Adonis liu'de, sunne, and sharpe aire,
    Lurkt like two theeues, to rob him of his faire.

And therefore would he put his bonnet on,
Vnder whose brim the gaudie sunne would peepe,
The wind would blow it off, and being gon,
1090   Play with his locks, then would Adonis weepe.
    And straight in pittie of his tender yeares,
    They both would striue who first should drie his
        teares.

To see his face the Lion walkt along,
Behind some hedge, because he would not fear him:
To recreate himself when he hath song,
The Tygre would be tame, and gently heare him.
    If he had spoke, the wolfe would leaue his praie,
    And neuer fright the sillie lambe that daie.

When he beheld his shadow in the brooke,
The fishes spread on it their golden gils,   1100
When he was by the birds such pleasure tooke,
That some would sing, some other in their bils
    Would bring him mulberries & ripe-red cherries,
    He fed them with his sight, they him with berries.

But this foule, grim, and vrchin-snowted Boare,
Whose downeward eye still looketh for a graue:
Ne're saw the beautious liuerie that he wore,
Witnesse the intertainment that he gaue.
    If he did see his face, why then I know,
    He thought to kisse him, and hath kild him so.   1110

Tis true, tis true, thus was Adonis slaine,
He ran vpon the Boare with his sharpe speare,
Who did not whet his teeth at him againe,
But by a kisse thought to persuade him there.
    And nousling in his flanke the louing swine,
    Sheath'd vnaware the tuske in his soft groine.

Had I bin tooth'd like him I must confesse,
With kissing him I should haue kild him first,
But he is dead, and neuer did he blesse
My youth with his, the more am I accurst.   1120
    With this she falleth in the place she stood,
    And staines her face with his congealed bloud.

She lookes vpon his lips, and they are pale,
She takes him by the hand, and that is cold,
She whispers in his eares a heauie tale,
As if they heard the wofull words she told:
    She lifts the coffer-lids that close his eyes,
    Where lo, two lamps burnt out in darknesse lies.

Two glasses where her selfe, her selfe beheld
A thousand times, and now no more reflect,   1130
Their vertue lost, wherein they late exceld,
And euerie beautie robd of his effect;
    Wonder of time (quoth she) this is my spight,
    That thou being dead, the day shuld yet be light.

Since thou art dead, lo here I prophecie,
Sorrow on loue hereafter shall attend:
It shall be wayted on with iealousie,
Find sweet beginning, but vnsauorie end.
    Nere setled equally, but high or lo,
    That all loues pleasure shall not match his wo.   1140

It shall be fickle, false, and full of fraud,
Bud, and be blasted, in a breathing while,
The bottome poyson, and the top ore-strawd
With sweets, that shall the truest sight beguile,
    The strongest bodie shall it make most weake,
    Strike the wise dũbe, & teach the foole to speake.

It shall be sparing, and too full of ryot,
Teaching decrepit age to tread the measures,
The staring ruffian shall it keepe in quiet,
1150 Pluck down the rich, inrich the poore with treasures,
 It shall be raging mad, and sillie milde,
 Make the yoong old, the old become a childe.

It shall suspect where is no cause of feare,
It shall not feare where it should most mistrust,
It shall be mercifull, and too seueare,
And most deceiuing, when it seemes most iust,
 Peruerse it shall be, where it showes most toward,
 Put feare to valour, courage to the coward.

It shall be cause of warre, and dire euents,
1160 And set dissention twixt the sonne, and sire,
Subiect, and seruill to all discontents:
As drie combustious matter is to fire,
 Sith in his prime, death doth my loue destroy,
 They that loue best, their loues shall not enioy.

By this the boy that by her side laie kild,
Was melted like a vapour from her sight,
And in his blood that on the ground laie spild,
A purple floure sproong vp, checkred with white,
 Resembling well his pale cheekes, and the blood,
1170 Which in round drops, vpõ their whitenesse stood.

She bowes her head, the new-sprong floure to smel,
Comparing it to her Adonis breath,
And saies within her bosome it shall dwell,
Since he himselfe is reft from her by death;
 She crop's the stalke, and in the breach appeares,
 Green-dropping sap, which she cõpares to teares.

Poore floure (quoth she) this was thy fathers guise,
Sweet issue of a more sweet smelling sire,
For euerie little griefe to wet his eies,
To grow vnto himselfe was his desire; 1180
 And so tis thine, but know it is as good,
 To wither in my brest, as in his blood.

Here was thy fathers bed, here in my brest,
Thou art the next of blood, and tis thy right.
Lo in this hollow cradle take thy rest,
My throbbing hart shall rock thee day and night;
 There shall not be one minute in an houre,
 Wherein I wil not kisse my sweet loues floure.

Thus weary of the world, away she hies,
And yokes her siluer doues, by whose swift aide, 1190
Their mistresse mounted through the emptie skies,
In her light chariot, quickly is conuaide,
 Holding their course to Paphos, where their queen,
 Meanes to immure her selfe, and not be seen.

FINIS

THE RAPE OF LUCRECE

DEDICATING *Venus and Adonis* to the Earl of Southampton in 1593, Shakespeare promised, if the poem pleased, to 'take aduantage of all idle houres' to honour the Earl with 'some grauer labour'. *The Rape of Lucrece*, also dedicated to Southampton, was entered in the Stationers' Register on 9 May 1594, and printed in the same year. The warmth of the dedication suggests that the Earl was by then a friend as well as a patron.

Like *Venus and Adonis*, *The Rape of Lucrece* is an erotic narrative based on Ovid, but this time the subject matter is historical, the tone tragic. The events took place in 509 BC, and were already legendary at the time of the first surviving account, by Livy in his history of Rome published between 27 and 25 BC. Shakespeare's main source was Ovid's *Fasti*, but he seems also to have known Livy's and other accounts.

Historically, Lucretia's rape had political consequences. Her ravisher, Tarquin, was a member of the tyrannical ruling family of Rome. During the siege of Ardea, a group of noblemen boasted of their wives' virtue, and rode home to test them; only Collatine's wife, Lucretia, lived up to her husband's claims, and Sextus Tarquinius was attracted to her. Failing to seduce her, he raped her and returned to Rome. Lucretia committed suicide, and her husband's friend, Lucius Junius Brutus, used the occasion as an opportunity to rouse the Roman people against Tarquinius' rule and to constitute themselves a republic.

Shakespeare concentrates on the private side of the story; Tarquin is lusting after Lucrece in the poem's opening lines, and the ending devotes only a few lines to the consequence of her suicide. As in *Venus and Adonis*, Shakespeare makes a little narrative material go a long way. At first, the focus is on Tarquin; after he has threatened Lucrece, it swings over to her. The opening sequence, with its marvellously dramatic account of Tarquin's tormented state of mind as he approaches Lucrece's chamber, is the more intense. Tarquin disappears from the action soon after the rape, when Lucrece delivers herself of a long complaint, apostrophizing night, opportunity, and time, and cursing Tarquin with rhetorical fervour, before deciding to kill herself. After summoning her husband, she seeks consolation in a painting of Troy which is described (1373-1442) in lines indebted to the first and second books of Virgil's *Aeneid* and to Book 13 of Ovid's *Metamorphoses*. After she dies, her husband and father mourn, but Brutus calls for deeds not words, and determines on revenge. The last lines of the poem look forward to the banishment of the Tarquins, but nothing is said of the establishment of a republic.

Like *Venus and Adonis*, *Lucrece*, initially popular (with six editions in Shakespeare's lifetime and another three by 1655), was later neglected. Coleridge admired it, and more recent criticism has recognized in it a profoundly dramatic quality combined with, if sometimes dissipated by, a remarkable force of rhetoric. The writing of the poem seems to have been a formative experience for Shakespeare. In it he not only laid the basis for his later plays on Roman history, but also explored themes that were to figure prominently in his later work. This is especially apparent in the portrayal of a man who 'still pursues his feare' (308), the relentless power of self-destructive evil that Shakespeare remembered when he made Macbeth, on his way to murder Duncan, speak of 'wither'd Murther' which, 'With *Tarquins* rauishing strides, towards his designe | Moues like a Ghost'.

The text was probably printed from a fair copy made by Shakespeare, who may also have read the proofs.

The loue I dedicate to your Lordship is without end: wherof this Pamphlet without beginning is but a superfluous Moity. The warrant I haue of your Honourable disposition, not the worth of my vntutord Lines makes it assured of acceptance. What I haue done is yours, what I haue to doe is yours, being part in all I haue, deuoted yours. Were my worth greater, my duety would shew greater, meane time, as it is, it is bound to your Lordship; To whom I wish long life still lengthned with all happinesse.

Your Lordships in all duety.

William Shakespeare.

THE ARGVMENT.

Lucius Tarquinius (*for his excessiue pride surnamed* Superbus) *after hee had caused his owne father in law* Seruius Tullius *to be cruelly murdred, and contrarie to the Romaine lawes and customes, not requiring or staying for the peoples suffrages, had possessed himselfe of the kingdome: went accompanyed with his sonnes and other Noble men of Rome, to besiege* Ardea, *during which siege, the principall men of the Army meeting one euening at the Tent of* Sextus Tarquinius *the Kings sonne, in their discourses after supper euery one commended the vertues of his owne wife: among whom* Colatinus *extolled the incomparable chastity of his wife* Lucretia. *In that pleasant humor they all posted to Rome, and intending by theyr secret and sodaine arriuall to make triall of that which euery one had before auouched, onely* Colatinus *finds his wife (though it were late in the night) spinning amongest her maides, the other Ladies were all found dauncing and reuelling, or in seuerall disports: whereupon the Noble men yeelded* Colatinus *the victory, and his wife the Fame. At that time* Sextus Tarquinius *being enflamed with* Lucrece *beauty, yet smoothering his passions for the present, departed with the rest backe to the Campe: from whence he shortly after priuily withdrew himselfe, and was (according to his estate) royally entertayned and lodged by* Lucrece *at* Colatium. *The same night he tretcherouslie stealeth into her Chamber, violently rauisht her, and early in the morning speedeth away.* Lucrece *in this lamentable plight, hastily dispatcheth Messengers, one to Rome for her father, another to the Campe for* Colatine. *They came, the one accompanyed with* Iunius Brutus, *the other with* Publius Valerius: *and finding* Lucrece *attired in mourning habite, demanded the cause of her sorrow. Shee first taking an oath of them for her reuenge, reuealed the Actor, and whole maner of his dealing, and withall sodainely stabbed her selfe. Which done, with one consent they all vowed to roote out the whole hated family of the* Tarquins: *and bearing the dead body to Rome,* Brutus *acquainted the people with the doer and manner of the vile deede: with a bitter inuectiue against the tyranny of the King, wherewith the people were so moued, that with one consent and a general acclamation, the* Tarquins *were all exiled, and the state gouernment changed from Kings to Consuls.*

The Rape of Lucrece

From the besiegd Ardea all in post,
Borne by the trustlesse wings of false desire,
Lust-breathed TARQVIN, leaues the Roman host,
And to Colatium beares the lightlesse fire,
Which in pale embers hid, lurkes to aspire,
 And girdle with embracing flames, the wast
 Of COLATINES fair loue, LVCRECE the chast.

Hap'ly that name of chast, vnhap'ly set
This batelesse edge on his keene appetite:
When COLATINE vnwisely did not let,
To praise the cleare vnmatched red and white,
Which triumpht in that skie of his delight:
 Where mortal stars as bright as heauẽs Beauties,
 With pure aspects did him peculiar dueties.

For he the night before in Tarquins Tent,
Vnlockt the treasure of his happie state:
What priselesse wealth the heauens had him lent,
In the possession of his beauteous mate.
Reckning his fortune at such high proud rate,
 That Kings might be espowsed to more fame,
 But King nor Peere to such a peerelesse dame.

O happinesse enioy'd but of a few,
And if possest as soone decayed and done:
As is the mornings siluer melting dew,
Against the golden splendour of the Sunne.
An expir'd date canceld ere well begunne.
 Honour and Beautie in the owners armes,
 Are weakelie fortrest from a world of harmes.

Beautie it selfe doth of it selfe perswade,
The eies of men without an Orator,
What needeth then Appologie be made
To set forth that which is so singuler?
Or why is Colatine the publisher
 Of that rich iewell he should keepe vnknown,
 From theeuish eares because it is his owne?

Perchance his bost of Lucrece Sou'raigntie,
Suggested this proud issue of a King:
For by our eares our hearts oft taynted be:
Perchance that enuie of so rich a thing
Brauing compare, disdainefully did sting
 His high pitcht thoughts that meaner men should
  vant,
 That golden hap which their superiors want.

But some vntimelie thought did instigate,
His all too timelesse speede if none of those,

His honor, his affaires, his friends, his state,
Neglected all, with swift intent he goes,
To quench the coale which in his liuer glowes.
 O rash false heate, wrapt in repentant cold,
 Thy hastie spring still blasts and nere growes old.

When at Colatium this false Lord ariued,   50
Well was he welcom'd by the Romaine dame,
Within whose face Beautie and Vertue striued,
Which of them both should vnderprop her fame.
Whẽ Vertue brag'd, Beautie wold blush for shame,
 When Beautie bosted blushes, in despight
 Vertue would staine that ore with siluer white.

But Beautie in that white entituled
From Venus doues, doth challenge that faire field,
Then Vertue claimes from Beautie, Beauties red,
Which Vertue gaue the golden age, to guild   60
Their siluer cheekes, and cald it then their shield,
 Teaching them thus to vse it in the fight,
 Whẽ shame assaild, the red should fẽce the white.

This Herauldry in LVCRECE face was seene,
Argued by Beauties red and Vertues white,
Of eithers colour was the other Queene:
Prouing from worlds minority their right,
Yet their ambition makes them still to fight:
 The soueraignty of either being so great,
 That oft they interchange ech others seat.   70

This silent warre of Lillies and of Roses,
Which TARQVIN vew'd in her faire faces field,
In their pure rankes his traytor eye encloses,
Where least betweene them both it should be kild,
The coward captiue vanquished, doth yeeld
 To those two Armies that would let him goe,
 Rather then triumph in so false a foe.

Now thinkes he that her husbands shallow tongue,
The niggard prodigall that praisde her so:
In that high taske hath done her Beauty wrong.   80
Which farre exceedes his barren skill to show.
Therefore that praise which COLATINE doth owe,
 Inchaunted TARQVIN aunswers with surmise,
 In silent wonder of still gazing eyes.

This earthly sainct adored by this deuill,
Little suspecteth the false worshipper:
"For vnstaind thoughts do seldom dream on euill.
"Birds neuer lim'd, no secret bushes feare:
So guiltlesse shee securely giues good cheare,
 And reuerend welcome to her princely guest,   90
 Whose inward ill no outward harme exprest.

For that he colourd with his high estate,
Hiding base sin in pleats of Maiestie:
That nothing in him seemd inordinate,
Saue sometime too much wonder of his eye,
Which hauing all, all could not satisfie;
　　But poorly rich so wanteth in his store,
　　That cloy'd with much, he pineth still for more.

But she that neuer cop't with straunger eies,
100 Could picke no meaning from their parling lookes,
Nor read the subtle shining secrecies,
Writ in the glassie margents of such bookes,
Shee toucht no vnknown baits, nor feard no hooks,
　　Nor could shee moralize his wanton sight,
　　More then his eies were opend to the light.

He stories to her eares her husbands fame,
Wonne in the fields of fruitfull Italie:
And decks with praises Colatines high name,
Made glorious by his manlie chiualrie,
110 With bruised armes and wreathes of victorie,
　　Her ioie with heaud-vp hand she doth expresse,
　　And wordlesse so greetes heauen for his successe.

Far from the purpose of his comming thither,
He makes excuses for his being there,
No clowdie show of stormie blustring wether,
Doth yet in his faire welkin once appeare,
Till sable Night mother of dread and feare,
　　Vppon the world dim darknesse doth displaie,
　　And in her vaultie prison, stowes the daie.

120 For then is Tarquine brought vnto his bed,
Intending wearinesse with heauie sprite:
For after supper long he questioned,
With modest Lucrece, and wore out the night,
Now leaden slumber with liues strength doth fight,
　　And euerie one to rest himselfe betakes,
　　Saue theeues, and cares, and troubled minds that
　　　wakes.

As one of which doth Tarquin lie reuoluing
The sundrie dangers of his wils obtaining:
Yet euer to obtaine his will resoluing
130 Though weake-built hopes perswade him to abstaining.
Dispaire to gaine doth traffique oft for gaining,
　　And when great treasure is the meede proposed,
　　Though death be adiũct, ther's no death supposed.

Those that much couet are with gaine so fond,
That what they haue not, that which they possesse
They scatter and vnloose it from their bond,
And so by hoping more they haue but lesse,
Or gaining more, the profite of excesse
　　Is but to surfet, and such griefes sustaine,
140 　That they proue bãckrout in this poore rich gain.

The ayme of all is but to nourse the life,
With honor, wealth, and ease in wainyng age:
And in this ayme there is such thwarting strife,
That one for all, or all for one we gage:
As life for honour, in fell battailes rage,
　　Honor for wealth, and oft that wealth doth cost
　　The death of all, and altogether lost.

So that in ventring ill, we leaue to be
The things we are, for that which we expect:
And this ambitious foule infirmitie, 150
In hauing much torments vs with defect
Of that we haue: so then we doe neglect
　　The thing we haue, and all for want of wit,
　　Make something nothing, by augmenting it.

Such hazard now must doting TARQVIN make,
Pawning his honor to obtaine his lust,
And for himselfe, himselfe he must forsake.
Then where is truth if there be no selfe-trust?
When shall he thinke to find a stranger iust,
　　When he himselfe, himselfe confounds, betraies, 160
　　To sclandrous tongues & wretched hateful daies?

Now stole vppon the time the dead of night,
When heauie sleepe had closd vp mortall eyes,
No comfortable starre did lend his light,
No noise but Owles, & wolues death-boding cries:
Now serues the season that they may surprise
　　The sillie Lambes, pure thoughts are dead & still,
　　While Lust and Murder wakes to staine and kill.

And now this lustfull Lord leapt from his bed,
Throwing his mantle rudely ore his arme, 170
Is madly tost betweene desire and dred;
Th'one sweetely flatters, th'other feareth harme,
But honest feare, bewicht with lustes foule charme,
　　Doth too too oft betake him to retire,
　　Beaten away by brainesicke rude desire.

His Faulchon on a flint he softly smiteth,
That from the could stone sparkes of fire doe flie,
Whereat a waxen torch forthwith he lighteth,
Which must be lodestarre to his lustfull eye.
And to the flame thus speakes aduisedlie; 180
　　As from this cold flint I enforst this fire,
　　So LVCRECE must I force to my desire.

Here pale with feare he doth premeditate,
The daungers of his lothsome enterprise:
And in his inward mind he doth debate,
What following sorrow may on this arise.
Then looking scornfully, he doth despise
　　His naked armour of still slaughtred lust,
　　And iustly thus controlls his thoughts vniust.

190 Faire torch burne out thy light, and lend it not
To darken her whose light excelleth thine:
And die vnhallowed thoughts, before you blot
With your vncleannesse, that which is deuine:
    Let faire humanitie abhor the deede,
    That spots & stains loues modest snow-white weed.

O shame to knighthood, and to shining Armes,
O foule dishonor to my houshoulds graue:
O impious act including all foule harmes.
200 A martiall man to be soft fancies slaue,
True valour still a true respect should haue,
    Then my digression is so vile, so base,
    That it will liue engrauen in my face.

Yea though I die the scandale will suruiue,
And be an eie-sore in my golden coate:
Some lothsome dash the Herrald will contriue,
To cipher me how fondlie I did dote:
That my posteritie sham'd with the note
    Shall curse my bones, and hold it for no sinne,
210   To wish that I their father had not beene.

What win I if I gaine the thing I seeke?
A dreame, a breath, a froth of fleeting ioy,
Who buies a minutes mirth to waile a weeke?
Or sels eternitie to get a toy?
For one sweete grape who will the vine destroy?
    Or what fond begger, but to touch the crowne,
    Would with the scepter straight be strokĕ down?

If COLATINVS dreame of my intent,
Will he not wake, and in a desp'rate rage
220 Post hither, this vile purpose to preuent?
This siege that hath ingirt his marriage,
This blur to youth, this sorrow to the sage,
    This dying vertue, this suruiuing shame,
    Whose crime will beare an euer-during blame.

O what excuse can my inuention make
When thou shalt charge me with so blacke a deed?
Wil not my tongue be mute, my fraile ioints shake?
Mine eies forgo their light, my false hart bleede?
The guilt beeing great, the feare doth still exceede;
230   And extreme feare can neither fight nor flie,
    But cowardlike with trembling terror die.

Had COLATINVS kild my sonne or sire,
Or laine in ambush to betray my life,
Or were he not my deare friend, this desire
Might haue excuse to worke vppon his wife:
As in reuenge or quittall of such strife.
    But as he is my kinsman, my deare friend,
    The shame and fault finds no excuse nor end.

Shamefull it is: I, if the fact be knowne,
Hatefull it is: there is no hate in louing, 240
Ile beg her loue: but she is not her owne:
The worst is but deniall and reproouing.
My will is strong past reasons weake remoouing:
    Who feares a sentence or an old mans saw,
    Shall by a painted cloth be kept in awe.

Thus gracelesse holds he disputation,
Tweene frozen conscience and hot burning will,
And with good thoughts makes dispensation,
Vrging the worser sence for vantage still.
Which in a moment doth confound and kill 250
    All pure effects, and doth so farre proceede,
    That what is vile, shewes like a vertuous deede.

Quoth he, shee tooke me kindlie by the hand,
And gaz'd for tidings in my eager eyes,
Fearing some hard newes from the warlike band,
Where her beloued COLATINVS lies.
O how her feare did make her colour rise!
    First red as Roses that on Lawne we laie,
    Then white as Lawne the Roses tooke awaie.

And how her hand in my hand being lockt, 260
Forst it to tremble with her loyall feare:
Which strooke her sad, and then it faster rockt,
Vntill her husbands welfare shee did heare.
Whereat shee smiled with so sweete a cheare,
    That had NARCISSVS seene her as shee stood,
    Selfe-loue had neuer drown'd him in the flood.

Why hunt I then for colour or excuses?
All Orators are dumbe when Beautie pleadeth,
Poore wretches haue remorse in poore abuses,
Loue thriues not in the hart that shadows dreadeth, 270
Affection is my Captaine and he leadeth.
    And when his gaudie banner is displaide,
    The coward fights, and will not be dismaide.

Then childish feare auaunt, debating die,
Respect and reason waite on wrinckled age:
My heart shall neuer countermand mine eie;
Sad pause, and deepe regard beseemes the sage,
My part is youth and beates these from the stage.
    Desire my Pilot is, Beautie my prise,
    Then who feares sinking where such treasure lies? 280

As corne ore-growne by weedes: so heedfull feare
Is almost choakt by vnresisted lust:
Away he steales with open listning eare,
Full of foule hope, and full of fond mistrust:
Both which as seruitors to the vniust,
    So crosse him with their opposit perswasion,
    That now he vowes a league, and now inuasion.

Within his thought her heauenly image sits,
And in the selfe same seat sits COLATINE,
₂₉₀ That eye which lookes on her confounds his wits,
That eye which him beholdes, as more deuine,
Vnto a view so false will not incline;
  But with a pure appeale seekes to the heart,
  Which once corrupted takes the worser part.

And therein heartens vp his seruile powers,
Who flattred by their leaders iocound show,
Stuffe vp his lust: as minutes fill vp howres.
And as their Captaine: so their pride doth grow,
Paying more slauish tribute then they owe.
₃₀₀   By reprobate desire thus madly led,
  The Romane Lord marcheth to LVCRECE bed.

The lockes betweene her chamber and his will,
Ech one by him inforst retires his ward:
But as they open they all rate his ill,
Which driues the creeping theefe to some regard,
The threshold grates the doore to haue him heard,
  Night-wandring weezels shreek to see him there,
  They fright him, yet he still pursues his feare.

As each vnwilling portall yeelds him way,
₃₁₀ Through little vents and cranies of the place,
The wind warres with his torch, to make him staie,
And blowes the smoake of it into his face,
Extinguishing his conduct in this case.
  But his hot heart, which fond desire doth scorch,
  Puffes forth another wind that fires the torch.

And being lighted, by the light he spies
LVCRECIAS gloue, wherein her needle sticks,
He takes it from the rushes where it lies,
And griping it, the needle his finger pricks.
₃₂₀ As who should say, this gloue to wanton trickes
  Is not inur'd; returne againe in hast,
  Thou seest our mistresse ornaments are chast.

But all these poore forbiddings could not stay him,
He in the worst sence consters their deniall:
The dores, the wind, the gloue that did delay him,
He takes for accidentall things of triall.
Or as those bars which stop the hourely diall,
  Who with a lingring staie his course doth let,
  Till euerie minute payes the howre his debt.

₃₃₀ So so, quoth he, these lets attend the time,
Like little frosts that sometime threat the spring,
To ad a more reioysing to the prime,
And giue the sneaped birds more cause to sing.
Pain payes the income of ech precious thing,
  Huge rocks, high winds, strong pirats, shelues and
     sands
  The marchant feares, ere rich at home he lands.

Now is he come vnto the chamber dore,
That shuts him from the Heauen of his thought,
Which with a yeelding latch, and with no more,
Hath bard him from the blessed thing he sought. ₃₄₀
So from himselfe impiety hath wrought,
  That for his pray to pray he doth begin,
  As if the Heauens should countenance his sin.

But in the midst of his vnfruitfull prayer,
Hauing solicited th'eternall power,
That his foule thoughts might cõpasse his fair faire,
And they would stand auspicious to the howre.
Euen there he starts, quoth he, I must deflowre;
  The powers to whom I pray abhor this fact,
  How can they then assist me in the act? ₃₅₀

Then Loue and Fortune be my Gods, my guide,
My will is backt with resolution:
Thoughts are but dreames till their effects be tried,
The blackest sinne is clear'd with absolution.
Against loues fire, feares frost hath dissolution.
  The eye of Heauen is out, and mistie night
  Couers the shame that followes sweet delight.

This said, his guiltie hand pluckt vp the latch,
And with his knee the dore he opens wide,
The doue sleeps fast that this night Owle will catch. ₃₆₀
Thus treason workes ere traitors be espied.
Who sees the lurking serpent steppes aside;
  But shee sound sleeping fearing no such thing,
  Lies at the mercie of his mortall sting.

Into the chamber wickedlie he stalkes,
And gazeth on her yet vnstained bed:
The curtaines being close, about he walkes,
Rowling his greedie eye-bals in his head.
By their high treason is his heart mis-led,
  Which giues the watch-word to his hand ful soon, ₃₇₀
  To draw the clowd that hides the siluer Moon.

Looke as the faire and fierie pointed Sunne,
Rushing from forth a cloud, bereaues our sight:
Euen so the Curtaine drawne, his eyes begun
To winke, being blinded with a greater light.
Whether it is that shee reflects so bright,
  That dazleth them, or else some shame supposed,
  But blind they are, and keep themselues inclosed.

O had they in that darkesome prison died,
Then had they seene the period of their ill: ₃₈₀
Then COLATINE againe by LVCRECE side,
In his cleare bed might haue reposed still.
But they must ope this blessed league to kill,
  And holie-thoughted LVCRECE to their sight,
  Must sell her ioy, her life, her worlds delight.

Her lillie hand, her rosie cheeke lies vnder,
Coosning the pillow of a lawfull kisse:
Who therefore angrie seemes to part in sunder,
Swelling on either side to want his blisse.
390   Betweene whose hils her head intombed is;
    Where like a vertuous Monument shee lies,
    To be admir'd of lewd vnhallowed eyes.

Without the bed her other faire hand was,
On the greene couerlet whose perfect white
Showed like an Aprill dazie on the grasse,
With pearlie swet resembling dew of night.
Her eyes like Marigolds had sheath'd their light,
    And canopied in darkenesse sweetly lay,
    Till they might open to adorne the day.

400 Her haire like goldē threeds playd with her breath,
O modest wantons, wanton modestie!
Showing lifes triumph in the map of death,
And deaths dim looke in lifes mortalitie.
Ech in her sleepe themselues so beautifie,
    As if betweene them twaine there were no strife,
    But that life liu'd in death, and death in life.

Her breasts like Iuory globes circled with blew,
A paire of maiden worlds vnconquered,
Saue of their Lord, no bearing yoke they knew,
410 And him by oath they truely honored.
These worlds in TARQVIN new ambition bred,
    Who like a fowle vsurper went about,
    From this faire throne to heaue the owner out.

What could he see but mightily he noted?
What did he note, but strongly he desired?
What he beheld, on that he firmely doted,
And in his will his wilfull eye he tyred.
With more then admiration he admired
    Her azure vaines, her alablaster skinne,
420   Her corall lips, her snow-white dimpled chin.

As the grim Lion fawneth ore his pray,
Sharpe hunger by the conquest satisfied:
So ore this sleeping soule doth TARQVIN stay,
His rage of lust by gazing qualified;
Slakt, not supprest, for standing by her side,
    His eye which late this mutiny restraines,
    Vnto a greater vprore tempts his vaines.

And they like stragling slaues for pillage fighting,
Obdurate vassals fell exploits effecting,
430 In bloudy death and rauishment delighting;
Nor childrens tears nor mothers grones respecting,
Swell in their pride, the onset still expecting:
    Anon his beating heart allarum striking,
    Giues the hot charge, & bids thē do their liking.

His drumming heart cheares vp his burning eye,
His eye commends the leading to his hand;
His hand as proud of such a dignitie,
Smoaking with pride, marcht on, to make his stand
On her bare brest, the heart of all her land;
    Whose ranks of blew vains as his hand did scale, 440
    Left their round turrets destitute and pale.

They mustring to the quiet Cabinet,
Where their deare gouernesse and ladie lies,
Do tell her shee is dreadfullie beset,
And fright her with confusion of their cries.
Shee much amaz'd breakes ope her lockt vp eyes,
    Who peeping foorth this tumult to behold,
    Are by his flaming torch dim'd and controld.

Imagine her as one in dead of night,
From forth dull sleepe by dreadfull fancie waking, 450
That thinkes shee hath beheld some gastlie sprite,
Whose grim aspect sets euerie ioint a shaking,
What terror tis: but shee in worser taking,
    From sleepe disturbed, heedfullie doth view
    The sight which makes supposed terror trew.

Wrapt and confounded in a thousand feares,
Like to a new-kild bird shee trembling lies:
Shee dares not looke, yet winking there appeares
Quicke-shifting Antiques vglie in her eyes.
"Such shadowes are the weake-brains forgeries, 460
    Who angrie that the eyes flie from their lights,
    In darknes daunts thē with more dreadfull sights.

His hand that yet remaines vppon her brest,
(Rude Ram to batter such an Iuorie wall:)
May feele her heart (poore Cittizen) distrest,
Wounding it selfe to death, rise vp and fall;
Beating her bulke, that his hand shakes withall.
    This moues in him more rage and lesser pittie,
    To make the breach and enter this sweet Citty.

First like a Trompet doth his tongue begin, 470
To sound a parlie to his heartlesse foe,
Who ore the white sheet peers her whiter chin,
The reason of this rash allarme to know,
Which he by dum demeanor seekes to show.
    But shee with vehement prayers vrgeth still,
    Vnder what colour he commits this ill.

Thus he replies, the colour in thy face,
That euen for anger makes the Lilly pale,
And the red rose blush at her owne disgrace,
Shall plead for me and tell my louing tale. 480
Vnder that colour am I come to scale
    Thy neuer conquerd Fort, the fault is thine,
    For those thine eyes betray thee vnto mine.

Thus I forestall thee, if thou meane to chide,
Thy beauty hath ensnar'd thee to this night,
Where thou with patience must my will abide,
My will that markes thee for my earths delight,
Which I to conquer sought with all my might.
   But as reproofe and reason beat it dead,
490   By thy bright beautie was it newlie bred.

I see what crosses my attempt will bring,
I know what thornes the growing rose defends,
I thinke the honie garded with a sting,
All this before-hand counsell comprehends.
But Will is deafe, and hears no heedfull friends,
   Onely he hath an eye to gaze on Beautie,
   And dotes on what he looks, gainst law or duety.

I haue debated euen in my soule,
What wrong, what shame, what sorrow I shal breed,
500 But nothing can affections course controull,
Or stop the headlong furie of his speed.
I know repentant teares insewe the deed,
   Reproch, disdaine, and deadly enmity,
   Yet striue I to embrace mine infamy.

This said, hee shakes aloft his Romaine blade,
Which like a Faulcon towring in the skies,
Cowcheth the fowle below with his wings shade,
Whose crooked beake threats, if he mount he dies.
So vnder his insulting Fauchion lies
510   Harmelesse LVCRETIA marking what he tels,
   With trembling feare: as fowl hear Faulcōs bels.

LVCRECE, quoth he, this night I must enioy thee,
If thou deny, then force must worke my way:
For in thy bed I purpose to destroie thee,
That done, some worthlesse slaue of thine ile slay,
To kill thine Honour with thy liues decaie.
   And in thy dead armes do I meane to place him,
   Swearing I slue him seeing thee imbrace him.

So thy suruiuing husband shall remaine
520 The scornefull marke of euerie open eye,
Thy kinsmen hang their heads at this disdaine,
Thy issue blur'd with namelesse bastardie;
And thou the author of their obloquie,
   Shalt haue thy trespasse cited vp in rimes,
   And sung by children in succeeding times.

But if thou yeeld, I rest thy secret friend,
The fault vnknowne, is as a thought vnacted,
"A little harme done to a great good end,
For lawfull pollicie remaines enacted.
530 "The poysonous simple sometime is compacted
   In a pure compound; being so applied,
   His venome in effect is purified.

Then for thy husband and thy childrens sake,
Tender my suite, bequeath not to their lot
The shame that from them no deuise can take,
The blemish that will neuer be forgot:
   Worse then a slauish wipe, or birth howrs blot,
    For markes discried in mens natiuitie,
    Are natures faultes, not their owne infamie.

Here with a Cockeatrice dead killing eye,   540
He rowseth vp himselfe, and makes a pause,
While shee the picture of pure pietie,
Like a white Hinde vnder the grypes sharpe clawes,
Pleades in a wildernesse where are no lawes,
   To the rough beast, that knowes no gentle right,
   Nor ought obayes but his fowle appetite.

But when a black-fac'd clowd the world doth thret,
In his dim mist th'aspiring mountaines hiding:
From earths dark-womb, some gentle gust doth get,
Which blows these pitchie vapours frō their biding: 550
Hindring their present fall by this deuiding.
   So his vnhallowed hast her words delayes,
   And moodie PLVTO winks while Orpheus playes.

Yet fowle night-waking Cat he doth but dallie,
While in his hold-fast foot the weak mouse pāteth,
Her sad behauiour feedes his vulture follie,
A swallowing gulfe that euen in plentie wanteth.
His eare her prayers admits, but his heart granteth
   No penetrable entrance to her playning,
   "Tears harden lust though marble were with
     rayning.   560

Her pittie-pleading eyes are sadlie fixed
In the remorselesse wrinckles of his face.
Her modest eloquence with sighes is mixed,
Which to her Oratorie addes more grace.
Shee puts the period often from his place,
   And midst the sentence so her accent breakes,
   That twise she doth begin ere once she speakes.

She coniures him by high Almightie Ioue,
By knighthood, gentrie, and sweete friendships oth,
By her vntimely teares, her husbands loue,   570
By holie humaine law, and common troth,
By Heauen and Earth, and all the power of both:
   That to his borrowed bed he make retire,
   And stoope to Honor, not to fowle desire.

Quoth shee, reward not Hospitalitie,
With such black payment, as thou hast pretended,
Mudde not the fountaine that gaue drinke to thee,
Mar not the thing that cannot be amended.
End thy ill ayme, before thy shoote be ended.
   He is no wood-man that doth bend his bow,
   To strike a poore vnseasonable Doe.   580

My husband is thy friend, for his sake spare me,
Thy selfe art mightie, for thine own sake leaue me:
My selfe a weakling, do not then insnare me.
Thou look'st not like deceipt, do not deceiue me.
My sighes like whirlewindes labor hence to heaue thee.
　　If euer man were mou'd with womãs mones,
　　Be moued with my teares, my sighes, my grones.

All which together like a troubled Ocean,
Beat at thy rockie, and wracke-threatning heart, 590
To soften it with their continuall motion:
For stones dissolu'd to water do conuert.
O if no harder then a stone thou art,
　　Melt at my teares and be compassionate,
　　Soft pittie enters at an iron gate.

In TARQVINS likenesse I did entertaine thee,
Hast thou put on his shape, to do him shame?
To all the Host of Heauen I complaine me.
Thou wrongst his honor, woũdst his princely name:
Thou art not what thou seem'st, and if the same, 600
　　Thou seem'st not what thou art, a God, a King;
　　For kings like Gods should gouerne eeuerything.

How will thy shame be seeded in thine age
When thus thy vices bud before thy spring?
If in thy hope thou darst do such outrage,
What dar'st thou not when once thou art a King?
O be remembred, no outragious thing
　　From vassall actors can be wipt away,
　　Then Kings misdeedes cannot be hid in clay.

This deede will make thee only lou'd for feare, 610
But happie Monarchs still are feard for loue:
With fowle offendors thou perforce must beare,
When they in thee the like offences proue;
If but for feare of this, thy will remoue.
　　For Princes are the glasse, the schoole, the booke,
　　Where subiects eies do learn, do read, do looke.

And wilt thou be the schoole where lust shall learne?
Must he in thee read lectures of such shame?
Wilt thou be glasse wherein it shall discerne
Authoritie for sinne, warrant for blame? 620
To priuiledge dishonor in thy name.
　　Thou backst reproch against long-liuing lawd,
　　And mak'st faire reputation but a bawd.

Hast thou commaund? by him that gaue it thee
From a pure heart commaund thy rebell will:
Draw not thy sword to gard iniquitie,
For it was lent thee all that broode to kill.
Thy Princelie office how canst thou fulfill?
　　When patternd by thy fault fowle sin may say,
　　He learnd to sin, and thou didst teach the way. 630

Thinke but how vile a spectacle it were,
To view thy present trespasse in another:
Mens faults do seldome to themselues appeare,
Their own transgressions partiallie they smother,
This guilt would seem death-worthie in thy brother.
　　O how are they wrapt in with infamies,
　　That frõ their own misdeeds askaunce their eyes?

To thee, to thee, my heau'd vp hands appeale,
Not to seducing lust thy rash relier:
I sue for exil'd maiesties repeale, 640
Let him returne, and flattring thoughts retire.
His true respect will prison false desire,
　　And wipe the dim mist from thy doting eien,
　　That thou shalt see thy state, and pittie mine.

Haue done, quoth he, my vncontrolled tide
Turnes not, but swels the higher by this let.
Small lightes are soone blown out, huge fires abide,
And with the winde in greater furie fret:
The petty streames that paie a dailie det
　　To their salt soueraigne, with their fresh fals hast 650
　　Adde to his flowe, but alter not his tast.

Thou art, quoth shee, a sea, a soueraigne King,
And loe there fals into thy boundlesse flood,
Blacke lust, dishonor, shame, mis-gouerning,
Who seeke to staine the Ocean of thy blood.
If all these pettie ils shall change thy good,
　　Thy sea within a puddels wombe is hersed,
　　And not the puddle in thy sea dispersed.

So shall these slaues be King, and thou their slaue,
Thou noblie base, they baselie dignified: 660
Thou their faire life, and they thy fowler graue:
Thou lothed in their shame, they in thy pride,
The lesser thing should not the greater hide.
　　The Cedar stoopes not to the base shrubs foote,
　　But low-shrubs wither at the Cedars roote.

So let thy thoughts low vassals to thy state,
No more quoth he, by Heauen I will not heare thee.
Yeeld to my loue, if not inforced hate,
In steed of loues coy tutch shall rudelie teare thee.
That done, despitefullie I meane to beare thee 670
　　Vnto the base bed of some rascall groome,
　　To be thy partner in this shamefull doome.

This said, he sets his foote vppon the light,
For light and lust are deadlie enemies,
Shame folded vp in blind concealing night,
When most vnseene, then most doth tyrannize.
The wolfe hath ceazd his pray, the poor lamb cries,
　　Till with her own white fleece her voice controld,
　　Intombes her outcrie in her lips sweet fold.

680 For with the nightlie linnen that shee weares,
He pens her piteous clamors in her head,
Cooling his hot face in the chastest teares,
That euer modest eyes with sorrow shed.
O that prone lust should staine so pure a bed,
  The spots whereof could weeping purifie,
  Her tears should drop on them perpetuallie.

But shee hath lost a dearer thing then life,
And he hath wonne what he would loose againe,
This forced league doth force a further strife,
690 This momentarie ioy breeds months of paine,
This hot desire conuerts to colde disdaine;
  Pure chastitie is rifled of her store,
  And lust the theefe farre poorer then before.

Looke as the full-fed Hound, or gorged Hawke,
Vnapt for tender smell, or speedie flight,
Make slow pursuite, or altogether bauk,
The praie wherein by nature they delight:
So surfet-taking TARQVIN fares this night:
  His tast delicious, in digestion sowring,
700 Deuoures his will that liu'd by fowle deuouring.

O deeper sinne then bottomlesse conceit
Can comprehend in still imagination!
Drunken Desire must vomite his receipt
Ere he can see his owne abhomination.
While Lust is in his pride no exclamation
  Can curbe his heat, or reine his rash desire,
  Till like a Iade, self-will himselfe doth tire.

And then with lanke, and leane discolour'd cheeke,
With heauie eye, knit-brow, and strengthlesse pace,
710 Feeble desire all recreant, poore and meeke,
Like to a banckrout begger wailes his cace:
The flesh being proud, Desire doth fight with grace;
  For there it reuels, and when that decaies,
  The guiltie rebell for remission praies.

So fares it with this fault-full Lord of Rome,
Who this accomplishment so hotly chased,
For now against himselfe he sounds this doome,
That through the length of times he städs disgraced:
Besides his soules faire temple is defaced,
720   To whose weake ruines muster troopes of cares,
  To aske the spotted Princesse how she fares.

Shee sayes her subiects with fowle insurrection,
Haue batterd downe her consecrated wall,
And by their mortall fault brought in subiection
Her immortalitie, and made her thrall,
To liuing death and payne perpetuall.
  Which in her prescience shee controlled still,
  But her foresight could not forestall their will.

Eu'n in this thought through the dark-night he
    stealeth,
A captiue victor that hath lost in gaine,   730
Bearing away the wound that nothing healeth,
The scarre that will dispight of Cure remaine,
Leauing his spoile perplext in greater paine.
  Shee beares the lode of lust he left behinde,
  And he the burthen of a guiltie minde.

Hee like a theeuish dog creeps sadly thence,
Shee like a wearied Lambe lies panting there,
He scowles and hates himselfe for his offence,
Shee desperat with her nailes her flesh doth teare.
He faintly flies sweating with guiltie feare;   740
  Shee staies exclayming on the direfull night,
  He runnes and chides his vanisht loth'd delight.

He thence departs a heauy conuertite,
Shee there remaines a hopelesse cast-away,
He in his speed lookes for the morning light:
Shee prayes shee neuer may behold the day.
For daie, quoth shee, nights scapes doth open lay,
  And my true eyes haue neuer practiz'd how
  To cloake offences with a cunning brow.

They thinke not but that euerie eye can see,   750
The same disgrace which they themselues behold:
And therefore would they still in darkenesse be,
To haue their vnseene sinne remaine vntold.
For they their guilt with weeping will vnfold,
  And graue like water that doth eate in steele,
  Vppon my cheeks, what helpelesse shame I feele.

Here shee exclaimes against repose and rest,
And bids her eyes hereafter still be blinde,
Shee wakes her heart by beating on her brest,
And bids it leape from thence, where it maie finde   760
Some purer chest, to close so pure a minde.
  Franticke with griefe thus breaths shee forth her
      spite,
  Against the vnseene secrecie of night.

O comfort-killing night, image of Hell,
Dim register, and notarie of shame,
Blacke stage for tragedies, and murthers fell,
Vast sin-concealing Chaos, nourse of blame.
Blinde muffled bawd, darke harber for defame,
  Grim caue of death, whispring conspirator,
  With close-tong'd treason & the rauisher.   770

O hatefull, vaporous, and foggy night,
Since thou art guilty of my curelesse crime:
Muster thy mists to meete the Easterne light,
Make war against proportion'd course of time.
Or if thou wilt permit the Sunne to clime
  His wonted height, yet ere he go to bed,
  Knit poysonous clouds about his golden head.

With rotten damps rauish the morning aire,
Let their exhald vnholdsome breaths make sicke
780 The life of puritie, the supreme faire,
Ere he arriue his wearie noone-tide pricke,
And let thy mustie vapours march so thicke,
 That in their smoakie rankes, his smothred light
 May set at noone, and make perpetuall night.

Were TARQVIN night, as he is but nights child,
The siluer shining Queene he would distaine;
Her twinckling handmaids to (by him defil'd)
Through nights black bosom shuld not peep again.
So should I haue copartners in my paine,
790 And fellowship in woe doth woe asswage,
 As Palmers chat makes short their pilgrimage.

Where now I haue no one to blush with me,
To crosse their armes & hang their heads with mine,
To maske their browes and hide their infamie,
But I alone, alone must sit and pine,
Seasoning the earth with showres of siluer brine;
 Mingling my talk with tears, my greef with grones,
 Poore wasting monuments of lasting mones.

O night thou furnace of fowle reeking smoke!
800 Let not the iealous daie behold that face,
Which vnderneath thy blacke all-hiding cloke
Immodestly lies martird with disgrace.
Keepe still possession of thy gloomy place,
 That all the faults which in thy raigne are made,
 May likewise be sepulcherd in thy shade.

Make me not obiect to the tell-tale day,
The light will shew characterd in my brow,
The storie of sweete chastities decay,
The impious breach of holy wedlocke vowe.
810 Yea the illiterate that know not how
 To cipher what is writ in learned bookes,
 Will cote my lothsome trespasse in my lookes.

The nourse to still her child will tell my storie,
And fright her crying babe with TARQVINS name.
The Orator to decke his oratorie,
Will couple my reproch to TARQVINS shame.
Feast-finding minstrels tuning my defame,
 Will tie the hearers to attend ech line,
 How TARQVIN wronged me, I COLATINE.

820 Let my good name, that sencelesse reputation,
For COLATINES deare loue be kept vnspotted:
If that be made a theame for disputation,
The branches of another roote are rotted;
And vndeseru'd reproch to him alotted,
 That is as cleare from this attaint of mine,
 As I ere this was pure to COLATINE.

O vnseene shame, inuisible disgrace,
O vnfelt sore, crest-wounding priuat scarre!
Reproch is stampt in COLATINVS face,
And TARQVINS eye maie read the mot a farre, 830
 "How he in peace is wounded not in warre.
 "Alas how manie beare such shamefull blowes,
 Which not thẽselues but he that giues thẽ knowes.

If COLATINE, thine honor laie in me,
From me by strong assault it is bereft:
My Honnie lost, and I a Drone-like Bee,
Haue no perfection of my sommer left,
But rob'd and ransak't by iniurious theft.
 In thy weake Hiue a wandring waspe hath crept, 840
 And suck't the Honnie which thy chast Bee kept.

Yet am I guiltie of thy Honors wracke,
Yet for thy Honor did I entertaine him,
Comming from thee I could not put him backe:
For it had beene dishonor to disdaine him,
Besides of wearinesse he did complaine him,
 And talk't of Vertue (O vnlook't for euill,)
 When Vertue is prophan'd in such a Deuill.

Why should the worme intrude the maiden bud?
Or hatefull Kuckcowes hatch in Sparrows nests?
Or Todes infect faire founts with venome mud? 850
Or tyrant follie lurke in gentle brests?
Or Kings be breakers of their owne behestes?
 "But no perfection is so absolute,
 That some impuritie doth not pollute.

The aged man that coffers vp his gold,
Is plagu'd with cramps, and gouts, and painefull fits,
And scarce hath eyes his treasure to behold,
But like still pining TANTALVS he sits,
And vselesse barnes the haruest of his wits:
 Hauing no other pleasure of his gaine, 860
 But torment that it cannot cure his paine.

So then he hath it when he cannot vse it,
And leaues it to be maistred by his yong:
Who in their pride do presently abuse it,
Their father was too weake, and they too strong
To hold their cursed-blessed Fortune long.
 "The sweets we wish for, turne to lothed sowrs,
 "Euen in the moment that we call them ours.

Vnruly blasts wait on the tender spring,
Vnholsome weeds take roote with precious flowrs, 870
The Adder hisses where the sweete birds sing,
What Vertue breedes Iniquity deuours:
We haue no good that we can say is ours,
 But ill annexed opportunity
 Or kils his life, or else his quality.

O opportunity thy guilt is great,
Tis thou that execut'st the traytors treason:
Thou sets the wolfe where he the lambe may get,
Who euer plots the sinne thou poinst the season.
880 Tis thou that spurn'st at right, at law, at reason,
   And in thy shadie Cell where none may spie him,
   Sits sin to ceaze the soules that wander by him.

Thou mak'st the vestall violate her oath,
Thou blowst the fire when temperance is thawd,
Thou smotherst honestie, thou murthrest troth,
Thou fowle abbettor, thou notorious bawd,
Thou plantest scandall, and displacest lawd.
   Thou rauisher, thou traytor, thou false theefe,
   Thy honie turnes to gall, thy ioy to greefe.

890 Thy secret pleasure turnes to open shame,
Thy priuate feasting to a publicke fast,
Thy smoothing titles to a ragged name,
Thy sugred tongue to bitter wormwood tast,
Thy violent vanities can neuer last.
   How comes it then, vile opportunity
   Being so bad, such numbers seeke for thee?

When wilt thou be the humble suppliants friend
And bring him where his suit may be obtained?
When wilt thou sort an howre great strifes to end?
900 Or free that soule which wretchednes hath chained?
Giue phisicke to the sicke, ease to the pained?
   The poore, lame, blind, hault, creepe, cry out for
     thee,
   But they nere meet with oportunitie.

The patient dies while the Phisitian sleepes,
The Orphane pines while the oppressor feedes.
Iustice is feasting while the widow weepes.
Aduise is sporting while infection breedes.
Thou graunt'st no time for charitable deeds.
   Wrath, enuy, treason, rape, and murthers rages,
910   Thy heinous houres wait on them as their Pages.

When Trueth and Vertue haue to do with thee,
A thousand crosses keepe them from thy aide:
They buie thy helpe, but sinne nere giues a fee,
He gratis comes, and thou art well apaide,
As well to heare, as graunt what he hath saide.
   My COLATINE would else haue come to me,
   When TARQVIN did, but he was staied by thee.

Guilty thou art of murther, and of theft,
Guilty of periurie, and subornation,
920 Guilty of treason, forgerie, and shift,
Guilty of incest that abhomination,
An accessarie by thine inclination,
   To all sinnes past and all that are to come,
   From the creation to the generall doome.

Misshapen time, copesmate of vgly night,
Swift subtle post, carrier of grieslie care,
Eater of youth, false slaue to false delight:
Base watch of woes, sins packhorse, vertues snare.
Thou noursest all, and murthrest all that are.
   O heare me then, iniurious shifting time,
   Be guiltie of my death since of my crime. 930

Why hath thy seruant opportunity
Betraide the howres thou gau'st me to repose?
Canceld my fortunes, and inchained me
To endlesse date of neuer-ending woes?
Times office is to fine the hate of foes,
   To eate vp errours by opinion bred,
   Not spend the dowrie of a lawfull bed.

Times glorie is to calme contending Kings,
To vnmaske falshood, and bring truth to light, 940
To stampe the seale of time in aged things,
To wake the morne, and Centinell the night,
To wrong the wronger till he render right,
   To ruinate proud buildings with thy howres,
   And smeare with dust their glitring golden towrs.

To fill with worme-holes stately monuments,
To feede obliuion with decay of things,
To blot old bookes, and alter their contents,
To plucke the quils from auncient rauens wings,
To drie the old oakes sappe, and blemish springs: 950
   To spoile Antiquities of hammerd steele,
   And turne the giddy round of Fortunes wheele.

To shew the beldame daughters of her daughter,
To make the child a man, the man a childe,
To slay the tygre that doth liue by slaughter,
To tame the Vnicorne, and Lion wild,
To mocke the subtle in themselues beguild,
   To cheare the Plowman with increasefull crops,
   And wast huge stones with little water drops.

Why work'st thou mischiefe in thy Pilgrimage, 960
Vnlesse thou could'st returne to make amends?
One poore retyring minute in an age
Would purchase thee a thousand thousand friends,
Lending him wit that to bad detters lends,
   O this dread night, would'st thou one howr come
     backe,
   I could preuent this storme, and shun thy wracke.

Thou ceaselesse lackie to Eternitie,
With some mischance crosse TARQVIN in his flight.
Deuise extreames beyond extremitie,
To make him curse this cursed crimefull night: 970
Let gastly shadowes his lewd eyes affright,
   And the dire thought of his committed euill,
   Shape euery bush a hideous shapelesse deuill.

Disturbe his howres of rest with restlesse trances,
Afflict him in his bed with bedred grones,
Let there bechaunce him pitifull mischances,
To make him mone, but pitie not his mones:
Stone him with hardned hearts harder then stones,
    And let milde women to him loose their mildnesse,
    Wilder to him then Tygers in their wildnesse.

980

Let him haue time to teare his curled haire,
Let him haue time against himselfe to raue,
Let him haue time of times helpe to dispaire,
Let him haue time to liue a lothed slaue,
Let him haue time a beggers orts to craue,
    And time to see one that by almes doth liue,
    Disdaine to him disdained scraps to giue.

Let him haue time to see his friends his foes,
And merrie fooles to mocke at him resort:
Let him haue time to marke how slow time goes
In time of sorrow, and how swift and short
His time of follie, and his time of sport.
    And euer let his vnrecalling crime
    Haue time to waile th'abusing of his time.

990

O time thou tutor both to good and bad,
Teach me to curse him that thou taught'st this ill:
At his owne shadow let the theefe runne mad,
Himselfe, himselfe seeke euerie howre to kill,
Such wretched hãds such wretched blood shuld spill.
    For who so base would such an office haue,
    As sclandrous deaths-man to so base a slaue.

1000

The baser is he comming from a King,
To shame his hope with deedes degenerate,
The mightier man the mightier is the thing
That makes him honord, or begets him hate:
For greatest scandall waits on greatest state.
    The Moone being clouded, presently is mist,
    But little stars may hide them when they list.

The Crow may bath his coaleblacke wings in mire,
And vnperceau'd flie with the filth away,
But if the like the snow-white Swan desire,
The staine vppon his siluer Downe will stay.
Poore grooms are sightles night, kings glorious day,
    Gnats are vnnoted wheresoere they flie,
    But Eagles gaz'd vppon with euerie eye.

1010

Out idle wordes, seruants to shallow fooles,
Vnprofitable sounds, weake arbitrators,
Busie your selues in skill contending schooles,
Debate where leysure serues with dull debators:
To trembling Clients be you mediators,
    For me, I force not argument a straw,
    Since that my case is past the helpe of law.

1020

In vaine I raile at oportunitie,
At time, at TARQVIN, and vnchearfull night,
In vaine I cauill with mine infamie,
In vaine I spurne at my confirm'd despight,
This helplesse smoake of words doth me no right:
    The remedie indeede to do me good,
    Is to let forth my fowle defiled blood.

Poore hand why quiuerst thou at this decree?
Honor thy selfe to rid me of this shame,
For if I die, my Honor liues in thee,
But if I liue thou liu'st in my defame;
Since thou couldst not defend thy loyall Dame,
    And wast affeard to scratch her wicked Fo,
    Kill both thy selfe, and her for yeelding so.

1030

This said, from her betombled couch shee starteth,
To finde some desp'rat Instrument of death,
But this no slaughter house no toole imparteth,
To make more vent for passage of her breath,
Which thronging through her lips so vanisheth,
    As smoake from ÆTNA, that in aire consumes,
    Or that which from discharged Cannon fumes.

1040

In vaine (quoth shee) I liue, and seeke in vaine
Some happie meane to end a haplesse life.
I fear'd by TARQVINS Fauchion to be slaine,
Yet for the selfe same purpose seeke a knife;
But when I fear'd I was a loyall wife,
    So am I now, ô no that cannot be,
    Of that true tipe hath TARQVIN rifled me.

1050

O that is gone for which I sought to liue,
And therefore now I need not feare to die,
To cleare this spot by death (at least) I giue
A badge of Fame to sclanders liuerie,
A dying life, to liuing infamie:
    Poore helplesse helpe, the treasure stolne away,
    To burne the guiltlesse casket where it lay.

Well well deare COLATINE, thou shalt not know
The stained tast of violated troth:
I will not wrong thy true affection so,
To flatter thee with an infringed oath:
This bastard graffe shall neuer come to growth,
    He shall not boast who did thy stocke pollute,
    That thou art doting father of his fruite.

1060

Nor shall he smile at thee in secret thought,
Nor laugh with his companions at thy state,
But thou shalt know thy intrest was not bought
Basely with gold, but stolne from foorth thy gate.
For me I am the mistresse of my fate,
    And with my trespasse neuer will dispence,
    Till life to death acquit my forst offence.

1070

I will not poyson thee with my attaint,
Nor fold my fault in cleanly coin'd excuses,
My sable ground of sinne I will not paint,
To hide the truth of this false nights abuses.
My tongue shall vtter all, mine eyes like sluces,
  As from a mountaine spring that feeds a dale,
  Shal gush pure streams to purge my impure tale.

By this lamenting Philomele had ended
1080 The well-tun'd warble of her nightly sorrow,
And solemne night with slow sad gate descended
To ouglie Hell, when loe the blushing morrow
Lends light to all faire eyes that light will borrow.
  But cloudie LVCRECE shames her selfe to see,
  And therefore still in night would cloistred be.

Reuealing day through euery crannie spies,
And seems to point her out where she sits weeping,
To whom shee sobbing speakes, ô eye of eyes,
Why pry'st thou throgh my window? leaue thy
  peeping,
1090 Mock with thy tickling beams, eies that are sleeping;
  Brand not my forehead with thy percing light,
  For day hath nought to do what's done by night.

Thus cauils shee with euerie thing shee sees,
True griefe is fond and testie as a childe,
Who wayward once, his mood with naught agrees,
Old woes, not infant sorrowes beare them milde,
Continuance tames the one, the other wilde,
  Like an vnpractiz'd swimmer plunging still,
  With too much labour drowns for want of skill.

1100 So shee deepe drenched in a Sea of care,
Holds disputation with ech thing shee vewes,
And to her selfe all sorrow doth compare,
No obiect but her passions strength renewes:
And as one shiftes another straight insewes,
  Somtime her griefe is dumbe and hath no words,
  Sometime tis mad and too much talke affords.

The little birds that tune their mornings ioy,
Make her mones mad, with their sweet melodie,
"For mirth doth search the bottome of annoy,
1110 "Sad soules are slaine in merrie companie,
"Griefe best is pleas'd with griefes societie;
  "True sorrow then is feelinglie suffiz'd,
  "When with like semblance it is simpathiz'd.

"Tis double death to drowne in ken of shore,
"He ten times pines, that pines beholding food,
"To see the salue doth make the wound ake more:
"Great griefe greeues most at that wold do it good;
"Deepe woes roll forward like a gentle flood,
  Who being stopt, the boŭding banks oreflowes,
1120 Griefe dallied with, nor law, nor limit knowes.

You mocking Birds (quoth she) your tunes intombe
Within your hollow swelling feathred breasts,
And in my hearing be you mute and dumbe,
My restlesse discord loues no stops nor rests:
"A woefull Hostesse brookes not merrie guests.
  Ralish your nimble notes to pleasing eares,
  "Distres likes dŭps whē time is kept with teares.

Come Philomele that sing'st of rauishment,
Make thy sad groue in my disheueld heare,
As the danke earth weepes at thy languishment: 1130
So I at each sad straine, will straine a teare,
And with deepe grones the Diapason beare:
  For burthen-wise ile hum on TARQVIN still,
  While thou on TEREVS descants better skill.

And whiles against a thorne thou bear'st thy part,
To keepe thy sharpe woes waking, wretched I
To imitate thee well, against my heart
Will fixe a sharpe knife to affright mine eye,
Who if it winke shall thereon fall and die.
  These meanes as frets vpon an instrument, 1140
  Shal tune our heart-strings to true languishment.

And for poore bird thou sing'st not in the day,
As shaming anie eye should thee behold:
Some darke deepe desert seated from the way,
That knowes not parching heat, nor freezing cold
Will wee find out: and there we will vnfold
  To creatures stern, sad tunes to change their kinds,
  Since mē proue beasts, let beasts bear gētle minds.

As the poore frighted Deare that stands at gaze,
Wildly determining which way to flie, 1150
Or one incompast with a winding maze,
That cannot tread the way out readilie:
So with her selfe is shee in mutinie,
  To liue or die which of the twaine were better,
  When life is sham'd and death reproches detter.

To kill my selfe, quoth shee, alacke what were it,
But with my body my poore soules pollution?
They that loose halfe with greater patience beare it,
Then they whose whole is swallowed in confusion.
That mother tries a mercilesse conclusion, 1160
  Who hauing two sweet babes, when death takes one,
  Will slay the other, and be nurse to none.

My bodie or my soule which was the dearer?
When the one pure, the other made deuine,
Whose loue of eyther to my selfe was nearer?
When both were kept for Heauen and COLATINE:
Ay me, the Barke pild from the loftie Pine,
  His leaues will wither, and his sap decay,
  So must my soule her barke being pild away.

1170 Her house is sackt, her quiet interrupted,
Her mansion batterd by the enemie,
Her sacred temple spotted, spoild, corrupted,
Groslie ingirt with daring infamie.
Then let it not be cald impietie,
   If in this blemisht fort I make some hole,
   Through which I may conuay this troubled soule.

Yet die I will not, till my COLATINE
Haue heard the cause of my vntimelie death,
That he may vow in that sad houre of mine,
1180 Reuenge on him that made me stop my breath,
My stained bloud to TARQVIN ile bequeath,
   Which by him tainted, shall for him be spent,
   And as his due writ in my testament.

My Honor ile bequeath vnto the knife
That wounds my bodie so dishonored,
Tis Honor to depriue dishonord life,
The one will liue, the other being dead.
So of shames ashes shall my Fame be bred,
   For in my death I murther shamefull scorne,
1190   My shame so dead, mine honor is new borne.

Deare Lord of that deare iewell I haue lost,
What legacie shall I bequeath to thee?
My resolution loue shall be thy bost,
By whose example thou reueng'd mayst be.
How TARQVIN must be vs'd, read it in me,
   My selfe thy friend will kill my selfe thy fo,
   And for my sake serue thou false TARQVIN so.

This briefe abridgement of my will I make,
My soule and bodie to the skies and ground:
1200 My resolution Husband doe thou take,
Mine Honor be the knifes that makes my wound,
My shame be his that did my Fame confound;
   And all my Fame that liues disbursed be,
   To those that liue and thinke no shame of me.

Thou COLATINE shalt ouersee this will,
How was I ouerseene that thou shalt see it?
My bloud shall wash the sclander of mine ill,
My liues foule deed my lifes faire end shall free it.
Faint not faint heart, but stoutlie say so be it,
1210   Yeeld to my hand, my hand shall conquer thee,
   Thou dead, both die, and both shall victors be.

This plot of death when sadlie shee had layd,
And wip't the brinish pearle from her bright eies,
With vntun'd tongue shee hoarslie cals her mayd,
Whose swift obedience to her mistresse hies.
"For fleet-wing'd duetie with thoghts feathers flies,
   Poore LVCRECE cheeks vnto her maid seem so,
   As winter meads when sun doth melt their snow.

Her mistresse shee doth giue demure good morrow, 1220
With soft slow-tongue, true marke of modestie,
And sorts a sad looke to her Ladies sorrow,
(For why her face wore sorrowes liuerie.)
But durst not aske of her audaciouslie,
   Why her two suns were clowd ecclipsed so,
   Nor why her faire cheeks ouer-washt with woe.

But as the earth doth weepe the Sun being set,
Each flowre moistned like a melting eye:
Euen so the maid with swelling drops gan wet
Her circled eien inforst by simpathie
Of those faire Suns set in her mistresse skie, 1230
   Who in a salt wau'd Ocean quench their light,
   Which makes the maid weep like the dewy night.

A prettie while these prettie creatures stand,
Like Iuorie conduits corall cesterns filling:
One iustlie weepes, the other takes in hand
No cause, but companie of her drops spilling.
Their gentle sex to weepe are often willing,
   Greeuing themselues to gesse at others smarts,
   And thẽ they drown their eies, or break their harts.

For men haue marble, women waxen mindes, 1240
And therefore are they form'd as marble will,
The weake opprest, th'impression of strange kindes
Is form'd in them by force, by fraud, or skill.
Then call them not the Authors of their ill,
   No more then waxe shall be accounted euill,
   Wherein is stampt the semblance of a Deuill.

Their smoothnesse, like a goodly champaine plaine,
Laies open all the little wormes that creepe,
In men as in a rough-growne groue remaine
Caue-keeping euils that obscurely sleepe. 1250
Through christall wals ech little mote will peepe,
   Though mẽ cã couer crimes with bold stern looks,
   Poore womens faces are their owne faults books.

No man inueigh against the withred flowre,
But chide rough winter that the flowre hath kild,
Not that deuour'd, but that which doth deuour
Is worthie blame, ô let it not be hild
Poore womens faults, that they are so fulfild
   With mens abuses, those proud Lords to blame,
   Make weak-made womẽ tenants to their shame. 1260

The president whereof in LVCRECE view,
Assail'd by night with circumstances strong
Of present death, and shame that might insue,
By that her death to do her husband wrong,
Such danger to resistance did belong:
   That dying feare through all her bodie spred,
   And who cannot abuse a bodie dead?

By this milde patience bid faire Lvcrece speake,
To the poore counterfaite of her complayning,
1270 My girle, quoth shee, on what occasion breake
Those tears frõ thee, that downe thy cheeks are
    raigning?
If thou dost weepe for griefe of my sustaining:
  Know gentle wench it small auailes my mood,
  If tears could help, mine own would do me good.

But tell me girle, when went (and there shee staide,
Till after a deepe grone) Tarqvin from hence,
Madame ere I was vp (repli'd the maide,)
The more to blame my sluggard negligence.
Yet with the fault I thus farre can dispence:
1280   My selfe was stirring ere the breake of day,
  And ere I rose was Tarqvin gone away.

But Lady, if your maide may be so bold,
Shee would request to know your heauinesse:
(O peace quoth Lvcrece) if it should be told,
The repetition cannot make it lesse:
For more it is, then I can well expresse,
  And that deepe torture may be cal'd a Hell,
  When more is felt then one hath power to tell.

Go get mee hither paper, inke, and pen,
1290 Yet saue that labour, for I haue them heare,
(What should I say) one of my husbands men
Bid thou be readie, by and by, to beare
A letter to my Lord, my Loue, my Deare,
  Bid him with speede prepare to carrie it,
  The cause craues hast, and it will soone be writ.

Her maide is gone, and shee prepares to write,
First houering ore the paper with her quill:
Conceipt and griefe an eager combat fight,
What wit sets downe is blotted straight with will.
1300 This is too curious good, this blunt and ill,
  Much like a presse of people at a dore,
  Throng her inuentions which shall go before.

At last shee thus begins: thou worthie Lord,
Of that vnworthie wife that greeteth thee,
Health to thy person, next, vouchsafe t'afford
(If euer loue, thy Lvcrece thou wilt see,)
Some present speed, to come and visite me:
  So I commend me, from our house in griefe,
  My woes are tedious, though my words are briefe.

1310 Here folds shee vp the tenure of her woe,
Her certaine sorrow writ vncertainely,
By this short Cedule Colatine may know
Her griefe, but not her griefes true quality,
Shee dares not thereof make discouery,
  Lest he should hold it her own grosse abuse,
  Ere she with bloud had stain'd her stain's excuse.

Besides the life and feeling of her passion,
She hoords to spend, when he is by to heare her,
When sighs, & grones, & tears may grace the fashiõ
Of her disgrace, the better so to cleare her   1320
From that suspiciõ which the world might bear her.
  To shun this blot, shee would not blot the letter
  With words, till action might becom thẽ better.

To see sad sights, moues more then heare them told,
For then the eye interpretes to the eare
The heauie motion that it doth behold,
When euerie part, a part of woe doth beare.
Tis but a part of sorrow that we heare,
  Deep sounds make lesser noise thẽ shallow foords,
  And sorrow ebs, being blown with wind of words. 1330

Her letter now is seal'd, and on it writ
At Ardea to my Lord with more then hast,
The Post attends, and shee deliuers it,
Charging the sowr-fac'd groome, to high as fast
As lagging fowles before the Northerne blast,
  Speed more then speed, but dul & slow she deems,
  Extremity still vrgeth such extremes.

The homelie villaine cursies to her low,
And blushing on her with a stedfast eye,
Receaues the scroll without or yea or no,   1340
And forth with bashfull innocence doth hie.
But they whose guilt within their bosomes lie,
  Imagine euerie eye beholds their blame,
  For Lvcrece thought, he blusht to see her shame.

When seelie Groome (God wot) it was defect
Of spirite, life, and bold audacitie,
Such harmlesse creatures haue a true respect
To talke in deeds, while others saucilie
Promise more speed, but do it leysurelie.
  Euen so this patterne of the worne-out age,   1350
  Pawn'd honest looks, but laid no words to gage.

His kindled duetie kindled her mistrust,
That two red fires in both their faces blazed,
Shee thought he blusht, as knowing Tarqvins lust,
And blushing with him, wistlie on him gazed,
Her earnest eye did make him more amazed.
  The more shee saw the bloud his cheeks replenish,
  The more she thought he spied in her som blemish.

But long shee thinkes till he returne againe,
And yet the dutious vassall scarce is gone,   1360
The wearie time shee cannot entertaine,
For now tis stale to sigh, to weepe, and grone,
So woe hath wearied woe, mone tired mone,
  That shee her plaints a little while doth stay,
  Pawsing for means to mourne some newer way.

At last shee cals to mind where hangs a peece
Of skilfull painting, made for PRIAMS Troy,
Before the which is drawn the power of Greece,
For HELENS rape, the Cittie to destroy,
1370 Threatning cloud-kissing ILLION with annoy,
　　Which the conceipted Painter drew so prowd,
　　As Heauen (it seem'd) to kisse the turrets bow'd.

A thousand lamentable obiects there,
In scorne of Nature, Art gaue liuelesse life,
Many a dry drop seem'd a weeping teare,
Shed for the slaughtred husband by the wife.
The red bloud reek'd to shew the Painters strife,
　　And dying eyes gleem'd forth their ashie lights,
　　Like dying coales burnt out in tedious nights.

1380 There might you see the labouring Pyoner
Begrim'd with sweat, and smeared all with dust,
And from the towres of Troy, there would appeare
The verie eyes of men through loop-holes thrust,
Gazing vppon the Greekes with little lust,
　　Such sweet obseruance in this worke was had,
　　That one might see those farre of eyes looke sad.

In great commaunders, Grace, and Maiestie,
You might behold triumphing in their faces,
In youth quick-bearing and dexteritie,
1390 And here and there the Painter interlaces
Pale cowards marching on with trembling paces.
　　Which hartlesse peasaunts did so wel resemble,
　　That one would swear he saw them quake & trēble.

In AIAX and VLYSSES, ô what Art
Of Phisiognomy might one behold!
The face of eyther cypher'd eythers heart,
Their face, their manners most expreslie told,
In AIAX eyes blunt rage and rigour rold,
　　But the mild glance that slie VLYSSES lent,
1400 　　Shewed deepe regard and smiling gouernment.

There pleading might you see graue NESTOR stand,
As'twere incouraging the Greekes to fight,
Making such sober action with his hand,
That it beguild attention, charm'd the sight,
In speech it seemd his beard, all siluer white,
　　Wag'd vp and downe, and from his lips did flie,
　　Thin winding breath which purl'd vp to the skie.

About him were a presse of gaping faces,
Which seem'd to swallow vp his sound aduice,
1410 All ioyntlie listning, but with seuerall graces,
As if some Marmaide did their eares intice,
Some high, some low, the Painter was so nice.
　　The scalpes of manie almost hid behind,
　　To iump vp higher seem'd to mocke the mind.

Here one mans hand leand on anothers head,
His nose being shadowed by his neighbours eare,
Here one being throng'd, bears back all boln, & red,
Another smotherd, seemes to pelt and sweare,
And in their rage such signes of rage they beare,
　　As but for losse of NESTORS golden words, 1420
　　It seem'd they would debate with angrie swords.

For much imaginarie worke was there,
Conceipt deceitfull, so compact so kinde,
That for ACHILLES image stood his speare
Grip't in an Armed hand, himselfe behind
Was left vnseene, saue to the eye of mind,
　　A hand, a foote, a face, a leg, a head
　　Stood for the whole to be imagined.

And from the wals of strong besieged TROY,
When their braue hope, bold HECTOR march'd to field, 1430
Stood manie Troian mothers sharing ioy,
To see their youthfull sons bright weapons wield,
And to their hope they such odde action yeeld,
　　That through their light ioy seemed to appeare,
　　(Like bright things staind) a kind of heauie feare.

And from the strond of DARDAN where they fought,
To SIMOIS reedie bankes the red bloud ran,
Whose waues to imitate the battaile sought
With swelling ridges, and their rankes began
To breake vppon the galled shore, and than 1440
　　Retire againe, till meeting greater ranckes
　　They ioine, & shoot their fome at SIMOIS bancks.

To this well painted peece is LVCRECE come,
To find a face where all distresse is steld,
Manie shee sees, where cares haue carued some,
But none where all distresse and dolor dweld,
Till shee dispayring HECVBA beheld,
　　Staring on PRIAMS wounds with her old eyes,
　　Which bleeding vnder PIRRHVS proud foot lies.

In her the Painter had anathomiz'd 1450
Times ruine, beauties wracke, and grim cares raign,
Her cheeks with chops and wrincles were disguiz'd,
Of what shee was, no semblance did remaine:
Her blew bloud chang'd to blacke in euerie vaine,
　　Wanting the spring, that those shrunke pipes had fed,
　　Shew'd life imprison'd in a bodie dead.

On this sad shadow LVCRECE spends her eyes,
And shapes her sorrow to the Beldames woes,
Who nothing wants to answer her but cries,
And bitter words to ban her cruell Foes. 1460
The Painter was no God to lend her those,
　　And therefore LVCRECE swears he did her wrong,
　　To giue her so much griefe, and not a tong.

Poore Instrument (quoth shee) without a sound,
Ile tune thy woes with my lamenting tongue,
And drop sweet Balme in PRIAMS painted wound,
And raile on PIRRHVS that hath done him wrong;
And with my tears quench Troy that burns so long;
    And with my knife scratch out the angrie eyes,
1470   Of all the Greekes that are thine enemies.

Shew me the strumpet that began this stur,
That with my nailes her beautie I may teare:
Thy heat of lust fond PARIS did incur
This lode of wrath, that burning Troy doth beare;
Thine eye kindled the fire that burneth here,
    And here in Troy for trespasse of thine eye,
    The Sire, the sonne, the Dame and daughter die.

Why should the priuate pleasure of some one
Become the publicke plague of manie moe?
1480 Let sinne alone committed, light alone
Vppon his head that hath transgressed so.
Let guiltlesse soules be freed from guilty woe,
    For ones offence why should so many fall?
    To plague a priuate sinne in generall.

Lo here weeps HECVBA, here PRIAM dies,
Here manly HECTOR faints, here TROYLVS sounds,
Here friend by friend in bloudie channel lies:
And friend to friend giues vnaduised wounds,
And one mans lust these manie liues confounds.
1490   Had doting PRIAM checkt his sons desire,
    TROY had bin bright with Fame, & not with fire.

Here feelingly she weeps TROYES painted woes,
For sorrow, like a heauie hanging Bell,
Once set on ringing, with his own waight goes,
Then little strength rings out the dolefull knell,
So LVCRECE set a worke, sad tales doth tell
    To pencel'd pensiuenes, & colour'd sorrow,
    She lends them words, & she their looks doth borrow.

Shee throwes her eyes about the painting round,
1500 And who shee finds forlorne, shee doth lament:
At last shee sees a wretched image bound,
That piteous lookes, to Phrygian sheapheards lent,
His face though full of cares, yet shew'd content,
    Onward to TROY with the blunt swains he goes,
    So mild that patience seem'd to scorne his woes.

In him the Painter labour'd with his skill
To hide deceipt, and giue the harmlesse show
An humble gate, calme looks, eyes wayling still,
A brow vnbent that seem'd to welcome wo,
1510 Cheeks neither red, nor pale, but mingled so,
    That blushing red, no guiltie instance gaue,
    Nor ashie pale, the feare that false hearts haue.

But like a constant and confirmed Deuill,
He entertain'd a show, so seeming iust,
And therein so ensconc't his secret euill,
That Iealousie it selfe could not mistrust,
False creeping Craft, and Periurie should thrust
    Into so bright a daie, such blackfac'd storms,
    Or blot with Hell-born sin such Saint-like forms.

The well-skil'd workman this milde Image drew   1520
For periur'd SINON, whose inchaunting storie
The credulous old PRIAM after slew.
Whose words like wild fire burnt the shining glorie
Of rich-built ILLION, that the skies were sorie,
    And little stars shot from their fixed places,
    Whẽ their glas fel, wherin they view'd their faces.

This picture shee aduisedly perus'd,
And chid the Painter for his wondrous skill:
Saying, some shape in SINONS was abus'd,
So faire a forme lodg'd not a mind so ill,   1530
And still on him shee gaz'd, and gazing still,
    Such signes of truth in his plaine face shee spied,
    That shee concludes, the Picture was belied.

It cannot be (quoth she) that so much guile,
(Shee would haue said) can lurke in such a looke:
But TARQVINS shape, came in her mind the while,
And from her tongue, can lurk, from cannot, tooke.
It cannot be, shee in that sence forsooke,
    And turn'd it thus, it cannot be I find,
    But such a face should beare a wicked mind.   1540

For euen as subtill SINON here is painted,
So sober sad, so wearie, and so milde,
(As if with griefe or trauaile he had fainted)
To me came TARQVIN armed, to beguild
With outward honestie, but yet defild
    With inward vice: as PRIAM him did cherish,
    So did I TARQVIN, so my Troy did perish.

Looke looke how listning PRIAM wets his eyes,
To see those borrowed teares that SINON sheeds,
PRIAM why art thou old, and yet not wise?   1550
For euerie teare he fals a Troian bleeds:
His eye drops fire, no water thence proceeds,
    Those roŭd clear pearls of his that moue thy pitty,
    Are bals of quenchlesse fire to burne thy Citty.

Such Deuils steale effects from lightlesse Hell,
For SINON in his fire doth quake with cold,
And in that cold hot burning fire doth dwell,
These contraries such vnitie do hold,
Only to flatter fooles, and make them bold,
    So PRIAMS trust false SINONS teares doth flatter,   1560
    That he finds means to burne his Troy with water.

Here all inrag'd such passion her assailes,
That patience is quite beaten from her breast,
Shee tears the sencelesse SINON with her nailes,
Comparing him to that vnhappie guest,
Whose deede hath made herselfe, herselfe detest,
 At last shee smilingly with this giues ore,
 Foole fool, quoth she, his wounds wil not be sore.

1570 Thus ebs and flowes the currant of her sorrow,
And time doth wearie time with her complayning,
Shee looks for night, & then shee longs for morrow,
And both shee thinks too long with her remayning.
Short time seems long, in sorrowes sharp sustayning,
 Though wo be heauie, yet it seldome sleepes,
 And they that watch, see time, how slow it creeps.

Which all this time hath ouerslipt her thought,
That shee with painted Images hath spent,
Being from the feeling of her own griefe brought,
By deepe surmise of others detriment,
1580 Loosing her woes in shews of discontent:
 It easeth some, though none it euer cured,
 To thinke their dolour others haue endured.

But now the mindfull Messenger come backe,
Brings home his Lord and other companie,
Who finds his LVCRECE clad in mourning black,
And round about her teare-distained eye
Blew circles stream'd, like Rain-bows in the skie.
 These watergalls in her dim Element,
 Foretell new stormes to those alreadie spent.

1590 Which when her sad beholding husband saw,
Amazedlie in her sad face he stares:
Her eyes though sod in tears look'd red and raw,
Her liuelie colour kil'd with deadlie cares,
He hath no power to aske her how shee fares,
 Both stood like old acquaintance in a trance,
 Met far from home, wondring ech others chance.

At last he takes her by the bloudlesse hand,
And thus begins: what vncouth ill euent
Hath thee befalne, that thou dost trembling stand?
1600 Sweet loue what spite hath thy faire colour spent?
Why art thou thus attir'd in discontent?
 Vnmaske deare deare, this moodie heauinesse,
 And tell thy griefe, that we may giue redresse.

Three times with sighes shee giues her sorrow fire,
Ere once shee can discharge one word of woe:
At length addrest to answer his desire,
Shee modestlie prepares, to let them know
Her Honor is tane prisoner by the Foe,
 While COLATINE and his consorted Lords,
1610 With sad attention long to heare her words.

And now this pale Swan in her watrie nest,
Begins the sad Dirge of her certaine ending,
Few words (quoth shee) shall fit the trespasse best,
Where no excuse can giue the fault amending.
In me moe woes then words are now depending,
 And my laments would be drawn out too long,
 To tell them all with one poore tired tong.

Then be this all the taske it hath to say,
Deare husband in the interest of thy bed
A stranger came, and on that pillow lay, 1620
Where thou wast wont to rest thy wearie head,
And what wrong else may be imagined,
 By foule inforcement might be done to me,
 From that (alas) thy LVCRECE is not free.

For in the dreadfull dead of darke midnight,
With shining Fauchion in my chamber came
A creeping creature with a flaming light,
And softly cried, awake thou Romaine Dame,
And entertaine my loue, else lasting shame
 On thee and thine this night I will inflict, 1630
 If thou my loues desire do contradict.

For some hard fauour'd Groome of thine, quoth he,
Vnlesse thou yoke thy liking to my will
Ile murther straight, and then ile slaughter thee,
And sweare I found you where you did fulfill
The lothsome act of Lust, and so did kill
 The lechors in their deed, this Act will be
 My Fame, and thy perpetuall infamy.

With this I did begin to start and cry,
And then against my heart he set his sword, 1640
Swearing, vnlesse I tooke all patiently,
I should not liue to speake another word.
So should my shame still rest vpon record,
 And neuer be forgot in mightie Roome
 Th'adulterat death of LVCRECE, and her Groome.

Mine enemy was strong, my poore selfe weake,
(And farre the weaker with so strong a feare)
My bloudie Iudge forbod my tongue to speake,
No rightfull plea might plead for Iustice there.
His scarlet Lust came euidence to sweare 1650
 That my poore beautie had purloin'd his eyes,
 And when the Iudge is rob'd, the prisoner dies.

O teach me how to make mine owne excuse,
Or (at the least) this refuge let me finde,
Though my grosse bloud be staind with this abuse,
Immaculate, and spotlesse is my mind,
That was not forc'd, that neuer was inclind
 To accessarie yeeldings, but still pure
 Doth in her poyson'd closet yet endure.

1660
Lo heare the hopelesse Marchant of this losse,
With head declin'd, and voice dam'd vp with wo,
With sad set eyes and wreathed armes acrosse,
From lips new waxen pale, begins to blow
The griefe away, that stops his answer so.
　　But wretched as he is he striues in vaine,
　　What he breaths out, his breath drinks vp again.

As through an Arch, the violent roaring tide,
Outruns the eye that doth behold his hast:
Yet in the Edie boundeth in his pride,
1670
Backe to the strait that forst him on so fast:
In rage sent out, recald in rage being past,
　　Euen so his sighes, his sorrowes make a saw,
　　To push griefe on, and back the same grief draw.

Which speechlesse woe of his poore she attendeth,
And his vntimelie frenzie thus awaketh,
Deare Lord, thy sorrow to my sorrow lendeth
Another power, no floud by raining slaketh,
My woe too sencible thy passion maketh
　　More feeling painfull, let it than suffice
1680
　　To drowne on woe, one paire of weeping eyes.

And for my sake when I might charme thee so,
For shee that was thy LVCRECE, now attend me,
Be sodainelie reuenged on my Foe.
Thine, mine, his own, suppose thou dost defend me
From what is past, the helpe that thou shalt lend me
　　Comes all too late, yet let the Traytor die,
　　"For sparing Iustice feeds iniquitie.

But ere I name him, you faire Lords, quoth shee,
(Speaking to those that came with COLATINE)
1690
Shall plight your Honourable faiths to me,
With swift pursuit to venge this wrong of mine,
For 'tis a meritorious faire designe,
　　To chase iniustice with reuengefull armes,
　　Knights by their oaths should right poore Ladies
　　　harmes.

At this request, with noble disposition,
Each present Lord began to promise aide,
As bound in Knighthood to her imposition,
Longing to heare the hatefull Foe bewraide.
But shee that yet her sad taske hath not said,
1700
　　The protestation stops, ô speake quoth shee,
　　How may this forced staine be wip'd from me?

What is the qualitie of my offence
Being constrayn'd with dreadfull circumstance?
May my pure mind with the fowle act dispence
My low declined Honor to aduance?
May anie termes acquit me from this chance?
　　The poyson'd fountaine cleares it selfe againe,
　　And why not I from this compelled staine?

With this they all at once began to saie,
Her bodies staine, her mind vntainted cleares,
1710
While with a ioylesse smile, shee turnes awaie
The face, that map which deepe impression beares
Of hard misfortune, caru'd in it with tears.
　　No no, quoth shee, no Dame hereafter liuing,
　　By my excuse shall claime excuses giuing.

Here with a sigh as if her heart would breake,
Shee throwes forth TARQVINS name: he he, she saies,
But more then he, her poore tong could not speake,
Till after manie accents and delaies,
Vntimelie breathings, sicke and short assaies,
1720
　　Shee vtters this, he he faire Lords, tis he
　　That guides this hand to giue this wound to me.

Euen here she sheathed in her harmlesse breast
A harmfull knife, that thence her soule vnsheathed,
That blow did baile it from the deepe vnrest
Of that polluted prison, where it breathed:
Her contrite sighes vnto the clouds bequeathed
　　Her winged sprite, & through her woŭds doth flie
　　Liues lasting date, from cancel'd destinie.

Stone still, astonisht with this deadlie deed,
1730
Stood COLATINE, and all his Lordly crew,
Till LVCRECE Father that beholds her bleed,
Himselfe, on her selfe-slaughtred bodie threw,
And from the purple fountaine BRVTVS drew
　　The murdrous knife, and as it left the place,
　　Her bloud in poore reuenge, held it in chase.

And bubling from her brest, it doth deuide
In two slow riuers, that the crimson bloud
Circles her bodie in on euerie side,
Who like a late sack't Iland vastlie stood
1740
Bare and vnpeopled, in this fearfull flood.
　　Some of her bloud still pure and red remain'd,
　　And som look'd black, & that false TARQVIN stain'd.

About the mourning and congealed face
Of that blacke bloud, a watrie rigoll goes,
Which seemes to weep vpon the tainted place,
And euer since as pittying LVCRECE woes,
Corrupted bloud, some waterie token showes,
　　And bloud vntainted, still doth red abide,
　　Blushing at that which is so putrified.
1750

Daughter, deare daughter, old LVCRETIVS cries,
That life was mine which thou hast here depriued,
If in the childe the fathers image lies,
Where shall I liue now LVCRECE is vnliued?
Thou wast not to this end from me deriued.
　　If children prædecease progenitours,
　　We are their ofspring and they none of ours.

Poor broken glasse, I often did behold
In thy sweet semblance, my old age new borne,
1760 But now that faire fresh mirror dim and old
Shewes me a bare-bon'd death by time out-worne,
O from thy cheekes my image thou hast torne,
   And shiuerd all the beautie of my glasse,
   That I no more can see what once I was.

O time cease thou thy course and last no longer,
If they surcease to be that should suruiue:
Shall rotten death make conquest of the stronger,
And leaue the foultring feeble soules aliue?
The old Bees die, the young possesse their hiue,
1770   Then liue sweet Lvcrece, liue againe and see
   Thy father die, and not thy father thee.

By this starts Colatine as from a dreame,
And bids Lvcrecivs giue his sorrow place,
And than in key-cold Lvcrece bleeding streame
He fals, and bathes the pale feare in his face,
And counterfaits to die with her a space.
   Till manly shame bids him possesse his breath,
   And liue to be reuenged on her death.

The deepe vexation of his inward soule,
1780 Hath seru'd a dumbe arrest vpon his tongue,
Who mad that sorrow should his vse controll,
Or keepe him from heart-easing words so long,
Begins to talke, but through his lips do throng
   Weake words, so thick come in his poor harts aid,
   That no man could distinguish what he said.

Yet sometime Tarqvin was pronounced plaine,
But through his teeth, as if the name he tore,
This windie tempest, till it blow vp raine,
Held backe his sorrowes tide, to make it more.
1790 At last it raines, and busie windes giue ore,
   Then sonne and father weep with equall strife,
   Who shuld weep most for daughter or for wife.

The one doth call her his, the other his,
Yet neither may possesse the claime they lay.
The father saies, shee's mine, ô mine shee is
Replies her husband, do not take away
My sorrowes interest, let no mourner say
   He weepes for her, for shee was onely mine,
   And onelie must be wayl'd by Colatine.

1800 O, quoth Lvcretivs, I did giue that life
Which shee to earely and too late hath spil'd.
Woe woe, quoth Colatine, shee was my wife,
I owed her, and tis mine that shee hath kil'd.
My daughter and my wife with clamors fild
   The disperst aire, who holding Lvcrece life,
   Answer'd their cries, my daughter and my wife.

Brvtvs who pluck't the knife from Lvcrece side,
Seeing such emulation in their woe,
Began to cloath his wit in state and pride,
Burying in Lvcrece wound his follies show, 1810
He with the Romains was esteemed so
   As seelie ieering idiots are with Kings,
   For sportiue words, and vttring foolish things.

But now he throwes that shallow habit by,
Wherein deepe pollicie did him disguise,
And arm'd his long hid wits aduisedlie,
To checke the teares in Colatinvs eies.
Thou wronged Lord of Rome, quoth he, arise,
   Let my vnsounded selfe suppos'd a foole,
   Now set thy long experienc't wit to schoole. 1820

Why Colatine, is woe the cure for woe?
Do wounds helpe wounds, or griefe helpe greeuous deeds?
Is it reuenge to giue thy selfe a blow,
For his fowle Act, by whom thy faire wife bleeds?
Such childish humor from weake minds proceeds,
   Thy wretched wife mistooke the matter so,
   To slaie her selfe that should haue slaine her Foe.

Couragious Romaine, do not steepe thy hart
In such relenting dew of Lamentations,
But kneele with me and helpe to beare thy part, 1830
To rowse our Romaine Gods with inuocations,
That they will suffer these abhominations,
   (Since Rome her self in thē doth stand disgraced,)
   By our strong arms frō forth her fair streets chaced.

Now by the Capitoll that we adore,
And by this chast bloud so vniustlie stained,
By heauens faire sun that breeds the fat earths store,
By all our countrey rights in Rome maintained,
And by chast Lvcrece soule that late complained
   Her wrongs to vs, and by this bloudie knife, 1840
   We will reuenge the death of this true wife.

This sayd, he strooke his hand vpon his breast,
And kist the fatall knife to end his vow:
And to his protestation vrg'd the rest,
Who wondring at him, did his words allow.
Then ioyntlie to the ground their knees they bow,
   And that deepe vow which Brvtvs made before,
   He doth againe repeat, and that they swore.

When they had sworne to this aduised doome,
They did conclude to beare dead Lvcrece thence, 1850
To shew her bleeding bodie thorough Roome,
And so to publish Tarqvins fowle offence;
Which being done, with speedie diligence,
   The Romaines plausibly did giue consent,
   To Tarqvins euerlasting banishment.

FINIS

THE COMEDIE OF ERRORS

ON the night of 28 December 1594, the Christmas revels at Gray's Inn—one of London's law schools—became so uproarious that one performance planned for the occasion had to be abandoned. Eventually 'it was thought good not to offer any thing of Account, sauing Dancing and Reuelling with Gentlewomen; and after such Sports, a Comedy of Errors (like to *Plautus* his *Menechmus*) was played by the Players. So that Night was begun, and continued to the end, in nothing but Confusion and Errors; wherevpon, it was euer afterwards called, *The Night of Errors*.'

This sounds like a reference to Shakespeare's play, first printed in the 1623 Folio, which is certainly based in large part on the Roman dramatist Plautus' comedy *Menaechmi*. As Shakespeare's shortest play, it would have been especially suited to late-night performance; there is no evidence that it was written for the occasion, but it may well have been new in 1594.

The comedy in *Menaechmi* derives from the embarrassment experienced by a man in search of his long-lost twin brother when various people intimately acquainted with that twin—including his wife, his mistress, and his father—mistake the one for the other. Shakespeare greatly increases the possibilities of comic confusion by giving the brothers (both called Antipholus) servants (both called Dromio) who themselves are long-separated twins. An added episode in which Antipholus of Ephesus' wife, Adriana, bars him from his own house in which she is entertaining his brother is based on another play by Plautus, *Amphitruo*. Shakespeare sets the comic action within a more serious framework, opening with a scene in which the twin masters' old father, Egeon, who has arrived at Ephesus in search of them, is shown under imminent sentence of death unless he finds someone to redeem him. This strand of the plot, as well as the surprising revelation that brings about the resolution of the action, is based on the story of Apollonius of Tyre which Shakespeare was to use again, many years later, in *Pericles*.

The Comedie of Errors is a kind of diploma piece, as if Shakespeare were displaying his ability to outshine both his classical progenitors and their English imitators. Along with *The Tempest*, it is his most classically constructed play: all the action takes place within a few hours and in a single place. Moreover, it seems to make use of the conventionalized arcade setting of academic drama, with three 'houses'—the Phœnix, the Porpentine, and the Priory—represented by doors and signs on stage. The working out of the complexities inherent in the basic situation represents a considerable intellectual feat. But the comedy is humanized by the interweaving of romantic elements, such as Egeon's initial plight, the love between the visiting Antipholus and his twin brother's sister, Luciana, and the entirely serious portrayal of Egeon's suffering when his own son fails to recognize him at the moment of his greatest need. From time to time the comic tension is relaxed by the presence of discursive set pieces, none more memorable than Dromio of Siracuse's description of Nell, the kitchen wench who is 'sphericall, like a globe'.

The First Folio text is probably based on Shakespeare's own papers.

THE NAMES OF THE ACTORS

Solinus, DUKE of Ephesus

Egeon, a MERCHANT of Syracuse, FATHER of the Antipholus twins

EPHESIAN ANTIPHOLUS
SYRACUSIAN ANTIPHOLUS } twin brothers, sonnes of Egeon

EPHESIAN DROMIO
SYRACUSIAN DROMIO } twin brothers, and bondmen of the Antipholus twins

ADRIANA, wife of Ephesian Antipholus

LUCIANA, her sister

NELL, Adrianas kitchin maide

Angelo, a GOLDSMITH

BALTHASAR, a merchant

A CURTIZAN

Doctor PINCH, a Schoolemaster and Coniurer

MARCHANT OF EPHESUS, a friend of Syracusian Antipholus

Another MARCHANT, Creditor of the Goldsmith

Æmilia, an ABBESSE at Ephesus

Iailor, Messenger, Headsman, Officers, and other Attendants

The Comedie of Errors

Enter the Duke of Ephesus, with the Merchant of
Siracusa, Iaylor, and other attendants

MERCHANT FATHER (*to the Duke*)

Proceed *Solinus* to procure my fall,
And by the doome of death end woes and all.

DUKE

Merchant of *Siracusa*, plead no more.
I am not partiall to infringe our Lawes;
The enmity and discord which of late
Sprung from the rancorous outrage of your Duke,
To Merchants our well-dealing Countrimen,
Who wanting gilders to redeeme their liues,
Haue seal'd his rigorous statutes with their blouds,
Excludes all pitty from our threatning lookes: 10
For since the mortall and intestine iarres
Twixt thy seditious Countrimen and vs,
It hath in solemne Synodes beene decreed,
Both by the *Siracusians* and our selues,
To admit no trafficke to our aduerse townes:
Nay more, if any borne at *Ephesus*
Be seene at *Siracusian* Marts and Fayres:
Againe, if any *Siracusian* borne
Come to the Bay of *Ephesus*, he dies:
His goods confiscate to the Dukes dispose, 20
Vnlesse a thousand markes be leuied
To quit the penalty, and ransome him:
Thy substance, valued at the highest rate,
Cannot amount vnto a hundred Markes,
Therefore by Law thou art condemn'd to die.

MERCHANT FATHER

Yet this my comfort, when your words are done,
My woes end likewise with the euening Sonne.

DUKE

Well *Siracusian*; say in briefe the cause
Why thou departedst from thy natiue home?
And for what cause thou cam'st to *Ephesus*. 30

MERCHANT FATHER

A heauier taske could not haue beene impos'd,
Then I to speake my griefes vnspeakeable:
Yet that the world may witnesse that my end
Was wrought by nature, not by vile offence,
Ile vtter what my sorrow giues me leaue.
In *Syracusa* was I borne, and wedde
Vnto a woman, happy but for me,
And by me happy; had not our hap beene bad:
With her I liu'd in ioy, our wealth increast
By prosperous voyages I often made 40
To *Epidamnum*, till my factors death,
And the great care of goods at randone left,
Drew me from kinde embracements of my spouse;
From whom my absence was not six moneths olde,
Before her selfe (almost at fainting vnder
The pleasing punishment that women beare)
Had made prouision for her following me,

And soone, and safe, arriued where I was:
There had she not beene long, but she became
A ioyfull mother of two goodly sonnes: 50
And, which was strange, the one so like the other,
As could not be distinguish'd but by names.
That very howre, and in the selfe-same Inne,
A meane born woman was deliuered
Of such a burthen Male, twins both alike:
Those, for their parents were exceeding poore,
I bought, and brought vp to attend my sonnes.
My wife, not meanely prowd of two such boyes,
Made daily motions for our home returne:
Vnwilling I agreed, alas, too soone 60
Wee came aboord.
A league from *Epidamnum* had we saild
Before the alwaies winde-obeying deepe
Gaue any Tragicke Instance of our harme:
But longer did we not retaine much hope;
For what obscured light the heauens did grant,
Did but conuay vnto our fearefull mindes
A doubtfull warrant of immediate death,
Which though my selfe would gladly haue imbrac'd,
Yet the incessant weepings of my wife, 70
Weeping before for what she saw must come,
And pitteous playnings of the prettie babes
That mourn'd for fashion, ignorant what to feare,
Forst me to seeke delayes for them and me,
And this it was: (for other meanes was none)
The Sailors sought for safety by our boate,
And left the ship then sinking ripe to vs.
My wife, more carefull for the latter borne,
Had fastned him vnto a small spare Mast,
Such as sea-faring men prouide for stormes: 80
To him one of the other twins was bound,
Whil'st I had beene like heedfull of the other.
The children thus dispos'd, my wife and I,
Fixing our eyes on whom our care was fixt,
Fastned our selues at eyther end the mast,
And floating straight, obedient to the streame,
Was carried towards *Corinth*, as we thought.
At length the sonne gazing vpon the earth,
Disperst those vapours that offended vs,
And by the benefit of his wished light 90
The seas waxt calme, and we discouered
Two shippes from farre, making amaine to vs:
Of *Corinth* that, of *Epidarus* this,
But ere they came, oh let me say no more,
Gather the sequell by that went before.

DUKE

Nay forward old man, doe not breake off so,
For we may pitty, though not pardon thee.

MERCHANT FATHER

Oh had the gods done so, I had not now
Worthily tearm'd them mercilesse to vs:

100 For ere the ships could meet by twice fiue leagues,
We were encountred by a mighty rocke,
Which being violently borne vpon,
Our helpefull ship was splitted in the midst;
So that in this vniust diuorce of vs,
Fortune had left to both of vs alike,
What to delight in, what to sorrow for,
Her part, poore soule, seeming as burdened
With lesser waight, but not with lesser woe,
Was carried with more speed before the winde,
110 And in our sight they three were taken vp
By Fishermen of *Corinth*, as we thought.
At length another ship had seiz'd on vs,
And knowing whom it was their hap to saue,
Gaue healthfull welcome to their ship-wrackt guests,
And would haue reft the Fishers of their prey,
Had not their barke beene very slow of saile;
And therefore homeward did they bend their course.
Thus haue you heard me seuer'd from my blisse,
That by misfortunes was my life prolong'd,
120 To tell sad stories of my owne mishaps.

DUKE
And for the sake of them thou sorrowest for,
Doe me the fauour to dilate at full,
What haue befalne of them and thee till now.

MERCHANT FATHER
My yongest boy, and yet my eldest care,
At eighteene yeeres became inquisitiue
After his brother; and importun'd me
That his attendant, so his case was like,
Reft of his brother, but retain'd his name,
Might beare him company in the quest of him:
130 Whom whil'st I labourd of a loue to see,
I hazarded the losse of whom I lou'd.
Fiue Sommers haue I spent in farthest *Greece*,
Roming cleane through the bounds of *Asia*,
And coasting homeward, came to *Ephesus*:
Hopelesse to finde, yet loth to leaue vnsought
Or that, or any place that harbours men:
But heere must end the story of my life,
And happy were I in my timelie death,
Could all my trauells warrant me they liue.

DUKE
140 Haplesse *Egeon* whom the fates haue markt
To beare the extremitie of dire mishap:
Now trust me, were it not against our Lawes,
Which Princes would they may not disanull,
Against my Crowne, my oath, my dignity,
My soule should sue as aduocate for thee:
But though thou art adiudged to the death,
And passed sentence may not be recal'd
But to our honours great disparagement:
Yet will I fauour thee in what I can;
150 Therefore Marchant, Ile limit thee this day
To seeke thy helth by beneficiall helpe,
Try all the friends thou hast in *Ephesus*,
Beg thou, or borrow, to make vp the summe,

And liue: if no, then thou art doom'd to die:
Iaylor, take him to thy custodie.

IAYLOR I will my Lord.

MERCHANT FATHER
Hopelesse and helpelesse doth *Egean* wend,
But to procrastinate his liuelesse end.   *Exeunt*

> *Enter ⌈from the Bay⌉ Antipholis Eraticus of*   **1.2**
> *Siracuse, a Marchant ⌈of Ephesus⌉, and Dromio of*   **(Sc. 2)**
> *Siracuse*

MARCHANT ⌈OF EPHESUS⌉
Therefore giue out you are of *Epidamnum*,
Lest that your goods too soone be confiscate: 160
This very day a *Syracusian* Marchant
Is apprehended for ariuall here,
And not being able to buy out his life,
According to the statute of the towne,
Dies ere the wearie sunne set in the West:
There is your monie that I had to keepe.

SIRACUSIAN ANTIPHOLUS (*to Dromio*)
Goe beare it to the Centaure, where we host,
And stay there *Dromio*, till I come to thee;
Within this houre it will be dinner time,
Till that Ile view the manners of the towne,   170
Peruse the traders, gaze vpon the buildings,
And then returne and sleepe within mine Inne,
For with long trauaile I am stiffe and wearie.
Get thee away.

SIRACUSIAN DROMIO
Many a man would take you at your word,
And goe indeede, hauing so good a meane.
                     Exit Dromio

SIRACUSIAN ANTIPHOLUS
A trustie villaine sir, that very oft,
When I am dull with care and melancholly,
Lightens my humour with his merry iests:
What will you walke with me about the towne,   180
And then goe to my Inne and dine with me?

MARCHANT ⌈OF EPHESUS⌉
I am inuited sir to certaine Marchants,
Of whom I hope to make much benefit:
I craue your pardon, soone at fiue a clocke,
Please you, Ile meete with you vpon the Mart,
And afterward consort you till bed time:
My present businesse cals me from you now.

SIRACUSIAN ANTIPHOLUS
Farewell till then: I will goe loose my selfe,
And wander vp and downe to view the Citie.

MARCHANT ⌈OF EPHESUS⌉
Sir, I commend you to your owne content.   *Exit*   190

SIRACUSIAN ANTIPHOLUS
He that commends me to mine owne content,
Commends me to the thing I cannot get:
I to the world am like a drop of water,
That in the Ocean seekes another drop,
Who falling there to finde his fellow forth,
(Vnseene, inquisitiue) confounds himselfe.

So I, to finde a Mother and a Brother,
In quest of them (vnhappie) loose my selfe.
    Enter Dromio of Ephesus
Here comes the almanacke of my true date:
200 What now? How chance thou art return'd so soone.
EPHESIAN DROMIO
Return'd so soone, rather approacht too late:
The Capon burnes, the Pig fals from the spit;
The clocke hath strucken twelue vpon the bell:
My Mistris made it one vpon my cheeke:
She is so hot because the meate is colde:
The meate is colde, because you come not home:
You come not home, because you haue no stomacke:
You haue no stomacke, hauing broke your fast:
But we that know what 'tis to fast and pray,
210 Are penitent for your default to day.
SIRACUSIAN ANTIPHOLUS
Stop in your winde sir, tell me this I pray?
Where haue you left the mony that I gaue you.
EPHESIAN DROMIO
Oh sixe pence that I had a wensday last,
To pay the Sadler for my Mistris crupper:
The Sadler had it Sir, I kept it not.
SIRACUSIAN ANTIPHOLUS
I am not in a sportiue humor now:
Tell me, and dally not, where is the monie?
We being strangers here, how dar'st thou trust
So great a charge from thine owne custodie.
EPHESIAN DROMIO
220 I pray you iest sir as you sit at dinner:
I from my Mistris come to you in post:
If I returne I shall be post indeede.
For she will scoure your fault vpon my pate:
Me thinkes your maw, like mine, should be your clocke,
And strike you home without a messenger.
SIRACUSIAN ANTIPHOLUS
Come *Dromio*, come, these iests are out of season,
Reserue them till a merrier houre then this:
Where is the gold I gaue in charge to thee?
EPHESIAN DROMIO
To me sir? why you gaue no gold to me?
SIRACUSIAN ANTIPHOLUS
230 Come on sir knaue, haue done your foolishnes,
And tell me how thou hast dispos'd thy charge.
EPHESIAN DROMIO
My charge was but to fetch you frõ the Mart
Home to your house, the *Phœnix* sir, to dinner;
My Mistris and her sister staies for you.
SIRACUSIAN ANTIPHOLUS
Now as I am a Christian answer me,
In what safe place you haue bestow'd my monie;
Or I shall breake that merrie sconce of yours
That stands on tricks, when I am vndispos'd:
Where is the thousand Markes thou hadst of me?
EPHESIAN DROMIO
240 I haue some markes of yours vpon my pate:
Some of my Mistris markes vpon my shoulders:

But not a thousand markes betweene you both.
If I should pay your worship those againe,
Perchance you will not beare them patiently.
SIRACUSIAN ANTIPHOLUS
Thy Mistris markes? what Mistris slaue hast thou?
EPHESIAN DROMIO
Your worships wife, my Mistris at the *Phœnix*;
She that doth fast till you come home to dinner:
And praies that you will hie you home to dinner.
SIRACUSIAN ANTIPHOLUS
What wilt thou flout me thus vnto my face
Being forbid? There take you that sir knaue.   250
    He beats Dromio
EPHESIAN DROMIO
What meane you sir, for God sake hold your hands:
Nay, and you will not sir, Ile take my heeles.
                    Exit Dromio Ep.
SIRACUSIAN ANTIPHOLUS
Vpon my life by some deuise or other,
The villaine is ore-wrought of all my monie.
They say this towne is full of cosenage:
As nimble Iuglers that deceiue the eie:
Darke working Sorcerers that change the minde:
Soule-killing Witches, that deforme the bodie:
Disguised Cheaters, prating Mountebankes;
And manie such like libertīes of sinne: 260
If it proue so, I will be gone the sooner:
Ile to the Centaur to goe seeke this slaue,
I greatly feare my monie is not safe.   *Exit*

                    ✸

Enter ⌈from the Phœnix⌉ Adriana, wife to Antipholis   2.1
Sureptus of Ephesus, with Luciana her Sister   (Sc. 3)
ADRIANA
Neither my husband nor the slaue return'd,
That in such haste I sent to seeke his Master?
Sure *Luciana* it is two a clocke.
LUCIANA
Perhaps some Merchant hath inuited him,
And from the Mart he's somewhere gone to dinner:
Good Sister let vs dine, and neuer fret;
A man is Master of his libertie:
Time is their Mʳˢ, and when they see time,   270
They'll goe or come; if so, be patient Sister.
ADRIANA
Why should their libertie then ours be more?
LUCIANA
Because their businesse still lies out adore.
ADRIANA
Looke when I serue him so, he takes it ill.
LUCIANA
Oh, know he is the bridle of your will.
ADRIANA
There's none but asses will be bridled so.
LUCIANA
Why, headstrong liberty is lasht with woe:
There's nothing situate vnder heauens eye,
But hath his bound in earth, in sea, in skie.   280

The beasts, the fishes, and the winged fowles
Are their males subiects, and at their controules:
Man more diuine, the Master of all these,
Lord of the wide world, and wilde watry seas,
Indued with intellectuall sence and soules,
Of more preheminence then fish and fowles,
Are masters to their females, and their Lords:
Then let your will attend on their accords.

ADRIANA
This seruitude makes you to keepe vnwed.

LUCIANA
290   Not this, but troubles of the marriage bed.

ADRIANA
But were you wedded, you wold bear some sway.

LUCIANA
Ere I learne loue, Ile practise to obey.

ADRIANA
How if your husband start some other where?

LUCIANA
Till he come home againe, I would forbeare.

ADRIANA
Patience vnmou'd, no maruel though she pause,
They can be meeke, that haue no other cause:
A wretched soule bruis'd with aduersitie,
We bid be quiet when we heare it crie.
But were we burdned with like waight of paine,
300   As much, or more, we should our selues complaine:
So thou that hast no vnkinde mate to greeue thee,
With vrging helpelesse patience would releeue me;
But if thou liue to see like right bereft,
This foole-beg'd patience in thee will be left.

LUCIANA
Well, I will marry one day but to trie:
        Enter Dromio Eph.
Heere comes your man, now is your husband nie.

ADRIANA
Say, is your tardie master now at hand?

EPHESIAN DROMIO Nay, hee's at too hands with mee, and
that my two eares can witnesse.

ADRIANA
Say, didst thou speake with him? knowst thou his
310   minde?

EPHESIAN DROMIO
I, I, he told his minde vpon mine eare,
Beshrew his hand, I scarce could vnderstand it.

LUCIANA
Spake hee so doubtfully, thou couldst not feele his
        meaning.

EPHESIAN DROMIO Nay, hee strooke so plainly, I could too
well feele his blowes; and withall so doubtfully, that I
could scarce vnderstand them.

ADRIANA
But say, I prethee, is he comming home?
It seemes he hath great care to please his wife.

EPHESIAN DROMIO
Why Mistresse, sure my Master is horne mad.

320   ADRIANA Horne mad, thou villaine?

EPHESIAN DROMIO
I meane not Cuckold mad, but sure he is starke mad:
When I desir'd him to come home to dinner,
He ask'd me for a thousand markes in gold:
'Tis dinner time, quoth I: my gold, quoth he:
Your meat doth burne, quoth I: my gold quoth he:
Will you come home, quoth I: my gold, quoth he;
Where is the thousand markes I gaue thee villaine?
The Pigge quoth I, is burn'd: my gold, quoth he:
My mistresse, sir, quoth I: hang vp thy Mistresse:
I know thy mistresse not, out on thy mistresse.   330

LUCIANA Quoth who?

EPHESIAN DROMIO Quoth my Master,
I know quoth he, no house, no wife, no mistresse:
So that my arrant due vnto my tongue,
I thanke him, I bare home vpon my shoulders:
For in conclusion, he did beat me there.

ADRIANA
Go back againe, thou slaue, & fetch him home.

EPHESIAN DROMIO
Goe backe againe, and be new beaten home?
For Gods sake send some other messenger.

ADRIANA
Backe slaue, or I will breake thy pate a-crosse.   340

EPHESIAN DROMIO
And he will blesse yᵗ crosse with other beating,
Betweene you, I shall haue a holy head.

ADRIANA
Hence prating pesant, fetch thy Master home.
        She beats Dromio

EPHESIAN DROMIO
Am I so round with you, as you with me,
That like a foot-ball you doe spurne me thus:
You spurne me hence, and he will spurne me hither,
If I last in this seruice, you must case me in leather.
                                                Exit

LUCIANA (*to Adriana*)
Fie how impatience lowreth in your face.

ADRIANA
His company must do his minions grace,
Whil'st I at home starue for a merrie looke: 350
Hath homelie age th'alluring beauty tooke
From my poore cheeke? then he hath wasted it.
Are my discourses dull? Barren my wit?
If voluble and sharpe discourse be mar'd,
Vnkindnesse blunts it more then marble hard.
Doe their gay vestments his affections baite?
That's not my fault, hee's master of my state.
What ruines are in me that can be found,
By him not ruin'd? Then is he the ground
Of my defeatures. My decayed faire,   360
A sunnie looke of his, would soone repaire.
But, too vnruly Deere, he breakes the pale,
And feedes from home; poore I am but his stale.

LUCIANA
Selfe-harming Iealousie; fie beat it hence.

ADRIANA
Vnfeeling fools can with such wrongs dispence:

I know his eye doth homage other-where,
Or else, what lets it but he would be here?
Sister, you know he promis'd me a chaine,
Would that alone, a loue he would detaine,
370 So he would keepe faire quarter with his bed:
I see the Iewell best enamaled
Will loose hir beautie: yet the gold bides still
That others touch, and often touching will
Weare gold, and yet no man that hath a name,
By falshood and corruption doth it shame:
Since that my beautie cannot please his eie,
Ile weepe (what's left away) and weeping die.

LUCIANA
How manie fond fooles serue mad Ielousie?

⌈*Exeunt into the Phœnix*⌉

2.2   *Enter Antipholis Erraticus of Siracuse*
(Sc. 4)   SIRACUSIAN ANTIPHOLUS
The gold I gaue to *Dromio* is laid vp
380 Safe at the *Centaur*, and the heedfull slaue
Is wandred forth in care to seeke me out.
By computation and mine hosts report
I could not speake with *Dromio*, since at first
I sent him from the Mart? see here he comes.

Enter Dromio Siracusia

How now sir, is your merrie humor alter'd?
As you loue stroakes, so iest with me againe:
You know no *Centaur*? you receiu'd no gold?
Your Mistresse sent to haue me home to dinner?
My house was at the *Phœnix*? Wast thou mad,
390 That thus so madlie thou didst answere me?

SIRACUSIAN DROMIO
What answer sir? when spake I such a word?

SIRACUSIAN ANTIPHOLUS
Euen now, euen here, not halfe an howre since.

SIRACUSIAN DROMIO
I did not see you since you sent me hence
Home to the *Centaur* with the gold you gaue me.

SIRACUSIAN ANTIPHOLUS
Villaine, thou didst denie the golds receit,
And toldst me of a Mistresse, and a dinner,
For which I hope thou feltst I was displeas'd.

SIRACUSIAN DROMIO
I am glad to see you in this merrie vaine,
What meanes this iest, I pray you Master tell me?

SIRACUSIAN ANTIPHOLUS
400 Yea, dost thou ieere & flowt me in the teeth?
Thinkst yᵘ I iest? hold, take thou that, & that.

Beats Dromio

SIRACUSIAN DROMIO
Hold sir, for Gods sake, now your iest is earnest,
Vpon what bargaine do you giue it me?

SIRACUSIAN ANTIPHOLUS
Because that I familiarlie sometimes
Doe vse you for my foole, and chat with you,
Your sawcinesse will iest vpon my loue,
And make a Common of my serious howres,
When the sunne shines, let foolish gnats make sport,

But creepe in crannies, when he hides his beames:
If you will iest with me, know my aspect,   410
And fashion your demeanor to my lookes,
Or I will beat this method in your sconce.

SIRACUSIAN DROMIO Sconce call you it? so you would
leaue battering, I had rather haue it a head, and you
vse these blows long, I must get a sconce for my head,
and Insconce it to, or else I shall seek my wit in my
shoulders, but I pray sir, why am I beaten?

SIRACUSIAN ANTIPHOLUS Dost thou not know?

SIRACUSIAN DROMIO Nothing sir, but that I am beaten.

SIRACUSIAN ANTIPHOLUS Shall I tell you why?   420

SIRACUSIAN DROMIO I sir, and wherefore; for they say,
euery why hath a wherefore.

SIRACUSIAN ANTIPHOLUS
Why first for flowting me, and then wherefore,
For vrging it the second time to me.

SIRACUSIAN DROMIO
Was there euer anie man thus beaten out of season,
When in the why and the wherefore, is neither rime
nor reason.
Well sir, I thanke you.

SIRACUSIAN ANTIPHOLUS   Thanke me sir, for what?

SIRACUSIAN DROMIO Marry sir, for this something that you
gaue me for nothing.

SIRACUSIAN ANTIPHOLUS Ile make you amends next, to   430
giue you nothing for something. But say sir, is it dinner
time?

SIRACUSIAN DROMIO No sir, I thinke the meat wants that
I haue.

SIRACUSIAN ANTIPHOLUS In good time sir: what's that?

SIRACUSIAN DROMIO Basting.

SIRACUSIAN ANTIPHOLUS Well sir, then 'twill be drie.

SIRACUSIAN DROMIO If it be sir, I pray you eat none of it.

SIRACUSIAN ANTIPHOLUS Your reason?

SIRACUSIAN DROMIO Lest it make you chollericke, and   440
purchase me another drie basting.

SIRACUSIAN ANTIPHOLUS Well sir, learne to iest in good
time, there's a time for all things.

SIRACUSIAN DROMIO I durst haue denied that before you
were so chollericke.

SIRACUSIAN ANTIPHOLUS By what rule sir?

SIRACUSIAN DROMIO Marry sir, by a rule as plaine as the
plaine bald pate of Father time himselfe.

SIRACUSIAN ANTIPHOLUS Let's heare it.

SIRACUSIAN DROMIO There's no time for a man to recouer   450
his haire that growes bald by nature.

SIRACUSIAN ANTIPHOLUS May he not doe it by fine and
recouerie?

SIRACUSIAN DROMIO Yes, to pay a fine for a perewig, and
recouer the lost haire of another man.

SIRACUSIAN ANTIPHOLUS Why, is Time such a niggard of
haire, being (as it is) so plentifull an excrement?

SIRACUSIAN DROMIO Because it is a blessing that hee
bestowes on beasts, and what he hath scanted men in
haire, hee hath giuen them in wit.   460

SIRACUSIAN ANTIPHOLUS Why, but theres manie a man
hath more haire then wit.

SIRACUSIAN DROMIO Not a man of those but he hath the
   wit to lose his haire.
SIRACUSIAN ANTIPHOLUS Why thou didst conclude hairy
   men plain dealers without wit.
SIRACUSIAN DROMIO The plainer dealer, the sooner lost;
   yet he looseth it in a kinde of iollitie.
SIRACUSIAN ANTIPHOLUS For what reason.
470 SIRACUSIAN DROMIO For two, and sound ones to.
SIRACUSIAN ANTIPHOLUS Nay not sound I pray you.
SIRACUSIAN DROMIO Sure ones then.
SIRACUSIAN ANTIPHOLUS Nay, not sure in a thing falsing.
SIRACUSIAN DROMIO Certaine ones then.
SIRACUSIAN ANTIPHOLUS Name them.
SIRACUSIAN DROMIO The one to saue the money that he
   spends in tyring: the other, that at dinner they should
   not drop in his porrage.
SIRACUSIAN ANTIPHOLUS You would all this time haue
480 prou'd, there is no time for all things.
SIRACUSIAN DROMIO Marry and did sir: namely, in no time
   to recouer haire lost by Nature.
SIRACUSIAN ANTIPHOLUS But your reason was not
   substantiall, why there is no time to recouer.
SIRACUSIAN DROMIO Thus I mend it: Time himselfe is bald,
   and therefore to the worlds end, will haue bald
   followers.
SIRACUSIAN ANTIPHOLUS I knew'twould be a bald
   conclusion:
       Enter ⌈from the Phœnix⌉ Adriana and Luciana
490 but soft, who wafts vs yonder.
ADRIANA
   I, I, *Antipholus*, looke strange and frowne,
   Some other Mistresse hath thy sweet aspects:
   I am not *Adriana*, nor thy wife.
   The time was once, when thou vn-vrg'd wouldst vow,
   That neuer words were musicke to thine eare,
   That neuer obiect pleasing in thine eye,
   That neuer touch well welcome to thy hand,
   That neuer meat sweet-sauour'd in thy taste,
   Vnlesse I spake, or look'd, or touch'd, or caru'd to thee.
500 How comes it now, my Husband, oh how comes it,
   That thou art then estranged from thy selfe?
   Thy selfe I call it, being strange to me:
   That vndiuidable Incorporate
   Am better then thy deere selfes better part.
   Ah doe not teare away thy selfe from me;
   For know my loue: as easie maist thou fall
   A drop of water in the breaking gulfe,
   And take vnmingled thence that drop againe
   Without addition or diminishing,
510 As take from me thy selfe, and not me too.
   How deerely would it touch thee to the quicke,
   Shouldst thou but heare I were licencious?
   And that this body consecrate to thee,
   By Ruffian Lust should be contaminate?
   Wouldst thou not spit at me, and spurne at me,
   And hurle the name of husband in my face,
   And teare the stain'd skin of my Harlot brow,
   And from my false hand cut the wedding ring,

   And breake it with a deepe-diuorcing vow?
   I know thou canst, and therefore see thou doe it.   520
   I am possest with an adulterate blot,
   My bloud is mingled with the crime of lust:
   For if we two be one, and thou play false,
   I doe digest the poison of thy flesh,
   Being strumpeted by thy contagion:
   Keepe then faire league and truce with thy true bed,
   I liue vnstain'd, thou vndishonoured.
SIRACUSIAN ANTIPHOLUS
   Plead you to me faire dame? I know you not:
   In *Ephesus* I am but two houres old,
   As strange vnto your towne, as to your talke,   530
   Who euery word by all my wit being scan'd,
   Wants wit in all, one word to vnderstand.
LUCIANA
   Fie brother, how the world is chang'd with you:
   When were you wont to vse my sister thus?
   She sent for you by *Dromio* home to dinner.
SIRACUSIAN ANTIPHOLUS By *Dromio*?
SIRACUSIAN DROMIO By me.
ADRIANA
   By thee, and this thou didst returne from him.
   That he did buffet thee, and in his blowes,
   Denied my house for his, me for his wife.   540
SIRACUSIAN ANTIPHOLUS
   Did you conuerse sir with this gentlewoman:
   What is the course and drift of your compact?
SIRACUSIAN DROMIO
   I sir? I neuer saw her till this time.
SIRACUSIAN ANTIPHOLUS
   Villaine thou liest, for euen her verie words,
   Didst thou deliuer to me on the Mart.
SIRACUSIAN DROMIO
   I neuer spake with her in all my life.
SIRACUSIAN ANTIPHOLUS
   How can she thus then call vs by our names?
   Vnlesse it be by inspiration.
ADRIANA
   How ill agrees it with your grauitie,
   To counterfeit thus grosely with your slaue,   550
   Abetting him to thwart me in my moode;
   Be it my wrong, you are from me exempt,
   But wrong not that wrong with a more contempt.
   Come I will fasten on this sleeue of thine:
   Thou art an Elme my husband, I a Vine:
   Whose weaknesse married to thy stronger state,
   Makes me with thy strength to communicate:
   If ought possesse thee from me, it is drosse,
   Vsurping Iuie, Brier, or idle Mosse,
   Who all for want of pruning, with intrusion,   560
   Infect thy sap, and liue on thy confusion.
SIRACUSIAN ANTIPHOLUS (*aside*)
   To mee shee speakes, shee moues mee for her theame;
   What, was I married to her in my dreame?
   Or sleepe I now, and thinke I heare all this?
   What error driues our eies and eares amisse?

Vntill I know this sure vncertaintie,
Ile entertaine the ofred fallacie.

LUCIANA

Dromio, goe bid the seruants spred for dinner.

SIRACUSIAN DROMIO (*aside*)

Oh for my beads, I crosse me for a sinner.
570 This is the Fairie land, oh spight of spights,
We talke with Goblins, Oafes and Sprights;
If we obay them not, this will insue:
They'll sucke our breath, or pinch vs blacke and blew.

LUCIANA

Why prat'st thou to thy selfe, and answer'st not?
Dromio, thou Drone, thou snaile, thou slug, thou sot.

SIRACUSIAN DROMIO (*to Antipholus*)

I am transformed Master, am not I?

SIRACUSIAN ANTIPHOLUS

I thinke thou art in minde, and so am I.

SIRACUSIAN DROMIO

Nay Master, both in minde, and in my shape.

SIRACUSIAN ANTIPHOLUS

Thou hast thine owne forme.

SIRACUSIAN DROMIO   No, I am an Ape.

LUCIANA

580 If thou art chang'd to ought, 'tis to an Asse.

SIRACUSIAN DROMIO ⌈*to Antipholus*⌉

'Tis true she rides me, and I long for grasse.
'Tis so, I am an Asse, else it could neuer be,
But I should know her as well as she knowes me.

ADRIANA

Come, come, no longer will I be a foole,
To put the finger in the eie and weepe;
Whil'st man and Master laughes my woes to scorne:
(*To Antipholus*) Come sir to dinner, *Dromio* keepe the
     gate:
Husband Ile dine aboue with you to day,
And shriue you of a thousand idle prankes:
590 (*To Dromio*) Sirra, if any aske you for your Master,
Say he dines forth, and let no creature enter:
Come sister, *Dromio* play the Porter well.

SIRACUSIAN ANTIPHOLUS (*aside*)

Am I in earth, in heauen, or in hell?
Sleeping or waking, mad or well aduisde:
Knowne vnto these, and to my selfe disguisde:
Ile say as they say, and perseuer so:
And in this mist at all aduentures go.

SIRACUSIAN DROMIO

Master, shall I be Porter at the gate?

ADRIANA

I, and let none enter, least I breake your pate.

LUCIANA

600 Come, come, *Antipholus*, we dine to late.

         Exeunt ⌈*into the Phœnix*⌉

✤

3.1   *Enter Antipholus of Ephesus, his man Dromio,*
(Sc. 5)   *Angelo the Goldsmith, and Balthaser the Merchant*

EPHESIAN ANTIPHOLUS

Good signior *Angelo* you must excuse vs all,
My wife is shrewish when I keepe not howres;
Say that I lingerd with you at your shop
To see the making of her Carkanet,
And that to morrow you will bring it home.
But here's a villaine that would face me downe
He met me on the Mart, and that I beat him,
And charg'd him with a thousand markes in gold,
And that I did denie my wife and house;
Thou drunkard thou, what didst thou meane by this? 610

EPHESIAN DROMIO

Say what you wil sir, but I know what I know,
That you beat me at the Mart I haue your hand to
     show;
If ye skin were parchment, & ye blows you gaue were
     ink,
Your owne hand-writing would tell you what I
     thinke.

EPHESIAN ANTIPHOLUS

I thinke thou art an asse.

EPHESIAN DROMIO   Marry so it doth appeare
By the wrongs I suffer, and the blowes I beare,
I should kicke being kickt, and being at that passe,
You would keepe from my heeles, and beware of an
     asse.

EPHESIAN ANTIPHOLUS

Y'are sad signior *Balthazar*, pray God our cheer
May answer my good will, and your good welcom here. 620

BALTHAZAR

I hold your dainties cheap sir, & your welcom deer.

EPHESIAN ANTIPHOLUS

Oh signior *Balthazar*, either at flesh or fish,
A table full of welcome, makes scarce one dainty dish.

BALTHAZAR

Good meat sir is cõmon that euery churle affords.

EPHESIAN ANTIPHOLUS

And welcome more common, for thats nothing but
     words.

BALTHAZAR

Small cheere and great welcome, makes a merrie
     feast.

EPHESIAN ANTIPHOLUS

I, to a niggardly Host, and more sparing guest:
But though my cates be meane, take them in good
     part,
Better cheere may you haue, but not with better hart.
But soft, my doore is lockt; (*to Dromio*) goe bid them
     let vs in.   630

EPHESIAN DROMIO (*calling*)

Maud, Briget, Marian, Cisley, Gillian, Ginn.

     ⌈*Enter Dromio Siracusa within the Phœnix*⌉

SIRACUSIAN DROMIO (*within the Phœnix*)

Mome, Malthorse, Capon, Coxcombe, Idiot, Patch,
Either get thee from the dore, or sit downe at the
     hatch:
Dost thou coniure for wenches, that y^u calst for such
     store,
When one is one too many, goe get thee from the dore.

EPHESIAN DROMIO

What patch is made our Porter? my Master stayes in
the street.

SIRACUSIAN DROMIO (*within the Phœnix*)

Let him walke from whence he came, lest hee catch
cold on's feet.

EPHESIAN ANTIPHOLUS

Who talks within there? hoa, open the dore.

SIRACUSIAN DROMIO (*within the Phœnix*)

Right sir, Ile tell you when, and you'll tell me
wherefore.

EPHESIAN ANTIPHOLUS

640 Wherefore? for my dinner: I haue not din'd to day.

SIRACUSIAN DROMIO (*within the Phœnix*)

Nor to day here you must not come againe when you
may.

EPHESIAN ANTIPHOLUS

What art thou that keep'st mee out from the howse I
owe?

SIRACUSIAN DROMIO (*within the Phœnix*)

The Porter for this time Sir, and my name is *Dromio*.

EPHESIAN DROMIO

O villaine, thou hast stolne both mine office and my
name,

The one nere got me credit, the other mickle blame:

If thou hadst beene *Dromio* to day in my place,

Thou wouldst haue chang'd thy pate for an ame, or
thy name for an asse.

Enter Nell within the Phœnix

NELL (*within the Phœnix*)

What a coile is there *Dromio*? who are those at the
gate?

EPHESIAN DROMIO

Let my Master in *Nell*.

NELL (*within the Phœnix*) Faith no, hee comes too late,

And so tell your Master.

650 EPHESIAN DROMIO   O Lord I must laugh,

Haue at you with a Prouerbe, shall I set in my staffe.

NELL (*within the Phœnix*)

Haue at you with another, that's when? can you tell?

SIRACUSIAN DROMIO (*within the Phœnix*)

If thy name be called *Nell*, *Nell* thou hast answer'd
him well.

⌈   ⌉

EPHESIAN ANTIPHOLUS (*to Nell*)

Doe you heare you minion, you'll let vs in I hope?

NELL (*within the Phœnix*)

I thought to haue askt you.

SIRACUSIAN DROMIO (*within*)   And you said no.

EPHESIAN DROMIO

So come helpe,

⌈*He and Antipholus beat the doore*⌉

well strooke, there was blow for blow.

EPHESIAN ANTIPHOLUS (*to Nell*)

Thou baggage let me in.

NELL (*within the Phœnix*)   Can you tell for whose sake?

EPHESIAN DROMIO

Master, knocke the doore hard.

NELL (*within the Phœnix*)   Let him knocke till it ake.

EPHESIAN ANTIPHOLUS

You'll crie for this minion, if I beat the doore downe. 660

NELL (*within the Phœnix*)

What needs all that, and a paire of stocks in the towne?

Enter Adriana within the Phœnix

ADRIANA (*within the Phœnix*)

Who is that at the doore yᵗ keeps all this noise?

SIRACUSIAN DROMIO (*within the Phœnix*)

By my troth your towne is troubled with vnruly boies.

EPHESIAN ANTIPHOLUS (*to Adriana*)

Are you there Wife? you might haue come before.

ADRIANA (*within the Phœnix*)

Your wife sir knaue? go get you from the dore.

Exit with Nell

EPHESIAN DROMIO (*to Antipholus*)

If you went in paine Master, this knaue wold goe sore.

GOLDSMITH (*to Antipholus*)

Heere is neither cheere sir, nor welcome, we would
faine haue either.

BALTHAZAR

In debating which was best, wee shall part with
neither.

EPHESIAN DROMIO (*to Antipholus*)

They stand at the doore, Master, bid them welcome
hither.

EPHESIAN ANTIPHOLUS

There is something in the winde, that we cannot get
in.   670

EPHESIAN DROMIO

You would say so Master, if your garments were thin.

Your cake here is warme within: you stand here in
the cold.

It would make a man mad as a Bucke to be so bought
and sold.

EPHESIAN ANTIPHOLUS

Go fetch me something, Ile break ope the gate.

SIRACUSIAN DROMIO (*within the Phœnix*)

Breake any breaking here, and Ile breake your knaues
pate.

EPHESIAN DROMIO

A man may breake a word with you sir, and words
are but winde:

I and breake it in your face, so he break it not behinde.

SIRACUSIAN DROMIO (*within the Phœnix*)

It seemes thou want'st breaking, out vpon thee hinde.

EPHESIAN DROMIO

Here's too much out vpon thee, I pray thee let me in.

SIRACUSIAN DROMIO (*within the Phœnix*)

I, when fowles haue no feathers, and fish haue no fin. 680

EPHESIAN ANTIPHOLUS

Well, Ile breake in: go borrow me a crow.

EPHESIAN DROMIO

A crow without feather, Master meane you so;

For a fish without a finne, ther's a fowle without a
fether,

(*To Dromio Siracusa*) If a crow help vs in sirra, wee'll
plucke a crow together.

EPHESIAN ANTIPHOLUS

Go, get thee gon, fetch me an iron Crow.

BALTHAZAR

    Haue patience sir, oh let it not be so,
    Heerein you warre against your reputation,
    And draw within the compasse of suspect
    Th'vnuiolated honor of your wife.
690   Once this: your long experience of her wisedome,
    Her sober vertue, yeares, and modestie,
    Plead on her part some cause to you vnknowne;
    And doubt not sir, but she will well excuse
    Why at this time the dores are made against you.
    Be rul'd by me, depart in patience,
    And let vs to the Tyger all to dinner,
    And about euening come your selfe alone,
    To know the reason of this strange restraint:
    If by strong hand you offer to breake in
700   Now in the stirring passage of the day,
    A vulgar comment will be made of it;
    And that supposed by the common rowt
    Against your yet vngalled estimation,
    That may with foule intrusion enter in,
    And dwell vpon your graue when you are dead;
    For slander liues vpon succession;
    For euer hows'd, where once it gets possession.

EPHESIAN ANTIPHOLUS

    You haue preuail'd, I will depart in quiet,
    And in despight of mirth meane to be merrie:
710   I know a wench of excellent discourse,
    Prettie and wittie; wilde, and yet too gentle;
    There will we dine: this woman that I meane
    My wife (but I protest without desert)
    Hath oftentimes vpbraided me withall:
    To her will we to dinner, (*to Angelo*) get you home
    And fetch the chaine, by this I know 'tis made,
    Bring it I pray you to the *Porpentine*,
    For there's the house: That chaine will I bestow
    (Be it for nothing but to spight my wife)
720   Vpon mine hostesse there, good sir make haste:
    Since mine owne doores refuse to entertaine me,
    Ile knocke else-where, to see if they'll disdaine me.

GOLDSMITH

    Ile meet you at that place some houre hence.

EPHESIAN ANTIPHOLUS

    Do so,   ⌐*Exit Goldsmith*⌐
        this iest shall cost me some expence.
        Exeunt ⌐*Dromio Siracusa within the Phœnix,*
           and the others into the Porpentine⌐

3.2   *Enter* ⌐*from the Phœnix*⌐ *Luciana, with Antipholus*
(Sc. 6)   *of Siracusa*

LUCIANA

    And may it be that you haue quite forgot
      A husbands office? shall *Antipholus*
    Euen in the spring of Loue, thy Loue-springs rot?
      Shall loue in building grow so ruinous?
    If you did wed my sister for her wealth,
      Then for her wealths-sake vse her with more
730   kindnesse:
    Or if you like else-where doe it by stealth,
      Muffle your false loue with some shew of blindnesse:

    Let not my sister read it in your eye:
      Be not thy tongue thy owne shames Orator:
    Looke sweet, speake faire, become disloyaltie:
      Apparell vice like vertues harbenger:
    Beare a faire presence, though your heart be tainted,
      Teach sinne the carriage of a holy Saint,
    Be secret false: what need she be acquainted?
      What simple thiefe brags of his owne attaint?   740
    'Tis double wrong to truant with your bed,
      And let her read it in thy lookes at boord:
    Shame hath a bastard fame, well managed,
      Ill deeds is doubled with an euill word:
    Alas poore women, make vs but beleeue
      (Being compact of credit) that you loue vs,
    Though others haue the arme, shew vs the sleeue:
      We in your motion turne, and you may moue vs.
    Then gentle brother get you in againe;
      Comfort my sister, cheere her, call her wife;   750
    'Tis holy sport to be a little vaine,
      When the sweet breath of flatterie conquers strife.

SIRACUSIAN ANTIPHOLUS

    Sweete Mistris, what your name is else I know not;
      Nor by what wonder you do hit of mine:
    Lesse in your knowledge, and your grace you show
      not,
    Then our earths wonder, more then earth diuine.
    Teach me deere creature how to thinke and speake:
      Lay open to my earthie grosse conceit:
    Smothred in errors, feeble, shallow, weake,
      The foulded meaning of your words deceit: 760
    Against my soules pure truth, why labour you,
      To make it wander in an vnknowne field?
    Are you a god? would you create me new?
      Transforme me then, and to your powre Ile yeeld.
    But if that I am I, then well I know,
      Your weeping sister is no wife of mine,
    Nor to her bed no homage doe I owe:
      Farre more, farre more, to you doe I decline:
    Oh traine me not sweet Mermaide with thy note,
      To drowne me in thy sisters floud of teares: 770
    Sing Siren for thy selfe, and I will dote:
      Spread ore the siluer waues thy golden haires;
    And as a bed Ile take them, and there lie:
      And in that glorious supposition thinke,
    He gaines by death, that hath such meanes to die:
      Let Loue, being light, be drowned if she sinke.

LUCIANA

    What are you mad, that you doe reason so?

SIRACUSIAN ANTIPHOLUS

    Not mad, but mated, how I doe not know.

LUCIANA

    It is a fault that springeth from your eie.

SIRACUSIAN ANTIPHOLUS

    For gazing on your beames faire sun being by.   780

LUCIANA

    Gaze wher you should, and that will cleere your
      sight.

SIRACUSIAN ANTIPHOLUS

    As good to winke sweet loue, as looke on night.

LUCIANA
Why call you me loue? Call my sister so.

SIRACUSIAN ANTIPHOLUS
Thy sisters sister.

LUCIANA   That's my sister.

SIRACUSIAN ANTIPHOLUS   No:
It is thy selfe, mine owne selfes better part:
Mine eies cleere eie, my deere hearts deerer heart;
My foode, my fortune, and my sweet hopes aime;
My sole earths heauen, and my heauens claime.

LUCIANA
All this my sister is, or else should be.

SIRACUSIAN ANTIPHOLUS
790   Call thy selfe sister sweet, for I am thee:
Thee will I loue, and with thee lead my life;
Thou hast no husband yet, nor I no wife:
Giue me thy hand.

LUCIANA   Oh soft sir, hold you still:
Ile fetch my sister to get her good will.

Exit ⌈into the Phœnix⌉

Enter ⌈from the Phœnix⌉ Dromio, Siracusia

SIRACUSIAN ANTIPHOLUS Why how now *Dromio*, where
run'st thou so fast?

SIRACUSIAN DROMIO Doe you know me sir? Am I *Dromio*?
Am I your man? Am I my selfe?

SIRACUSIAN ANTIPHOLUS Thou art *Dromio*, thou art my
800   man, thou art thy selfe.

SIRACUSIAN DROMIO I am an asse, I am a womans man,
and besides my selfe.

SIRACUSIAN ANTIPHOLUS What womans man? and how
besides thy selfe?

SIRACUSIAN DROMIO Marrie sir, besides my selfe, I am due
to a woman: One that claimes me, one that haunts
me, one that will haue me.

SIRACUSIAN ANTIPHOLUS What claime laies she to thee?

SIRACUSIAN DROMIO Marry sir, such claime as you would
810   lay to your horse, and she would haue me as a beast,
not that I beeing a beast she would haue me, but that
she being a verie beastly creature layes claime to me.

SIRACUSIAN ANTIPHOLUS What is she?

SIRACUSIAN DROMIO A very reuerent body: I such a one,
as a man may not speake of, without he say sir
reuerence, I haue but leane lucke in the match, and
yet is she a wondrous fat marriage.

SIRACUSIAN ANTIPHOLUS How dost thou meane a fat
marriage?

820 SIRACUSIAN DROMIO Marry sir, she's the Kitchin wench,
& al grease, and I know not what vse to put her too,
but to make a Lampe of her, and run from her by her
owne light. I warrant, her ragges and the Tallow in
them, will burne a *Poland* Winter: If she liues till
doomesday, she'l burne a weeke longer then the whole
World.

SIRACUSIAN ANTIPHOLUS What complexion is she of?

SIRACUSIAN DROMIO Swart like my shoo, but her face
nothing like so cleane kept: for why? she sweats a man
830   may goe ouer-shooes in the grime of it.

SIRACUSIAN ANTIPHOLUS That's a fault that water will
mend.

SIRACUSIAN DROMIO No sir, 'tis in graine, *Noahs* flood
could not do it.

SIRACUSIAN ANTIPHOLUS What's her name?

SIRACUSIAN DROMIO *Nell* Sir: but her name & three
quarters, that's an Ell and three quarters, will not
measure her from hip to hip.

SIRACUSIAN ANTIPHOLUS Then she beares some bredth?

SIRACUSIAN DROMIO No longer from head to foot, then   840
from hippe to hippe: she is sphericall, like a globe: I
could find out Countries in her.

SIRACUSIAN ANTIPHOLUS In what part of her body stands
Ireland?

SIRACUSIAN DROMIO Marry sir in her buttockes, I found it
out by the bogges.

SIRACUSIAN ANTIPHOLUS Where *Scotland*?

SIRACUSIAN DROMIO I found it by the barrennesse, hard in
the palme of her hand.

SIRACUSIAN ANTIPHOLUS Where *France*?   850

SIRACUSIAN DROMIO In her forhead, arm'd and reuerted,
making warre against her heire.

SIRACUSIAN ANTIPHOLUS Where *England*?

SIRACUSIAN DROMIO I look'd for the chalkie Cliffes, but I
could find no whitenesse in them. But I guesse, it stood
in her chin by the salt rheume that ranne betweene
France, and it.

SIRACUSIAN ANTIPHOLUS Where *Spaine*?

SIRACUSIAN DROMIO Faith I saw it not: but I felt it hot in
her breth.   860

SIRACUSIAN ANTIPHOLUS Where *America*, the *Indies*?

SIRACUSIAN DROMIO Oh sir, vpon her nose, all ore
embellished with Rubies, Carbuncles, Saphires,
declining their rich Aspect to the hot breath of Spaine,
who sent whole Armadoes of Carrects to be ballast at
her nose.

SIRACUSIAN ANTIPHOLUS Where stood *Belgia*, the
Netherlands?

SIRACUSIAN DROMIO Oh sir, I did not looke so low. To
conclude, this drudge or Diuiner layd claime to mee,   870
call'd mee *Dromio*, swore I was assur'd to her, told me
what priuie markes I had about mee, as the marke of
my shoulder, the Mole in my necke, the great Wart on
my left arme, that I amaz'd ranne from her as a witch.
And I thinke, if my brest had not beene made of faith,
and my heart of steele, she had transform'd me to a
Curtull dog, & made me turne i'th wheele.

SIRACUSIAN ANTIPHOLUS
Go hie thee presently, post to the rode,
And if the winde blow any way from shore,
I will not harbour in this Towne to night.   880
If any Barke put forth, come to the Mart,
Where I will walke till thou returne to me:
If euerie one knowes vs, and we know none,
'Tis time I thinke to trudge, packe, and be gone.

SIRACUSIAN DROMIO
As from a Beare a man would run for life,
So flie I from her that would be my wife.

Exit ⌈to the Bay⌉

SIRACUSIAN ANTIPHOLUS
There's none but Witches do inhabite heere,

And therefore 'tis hie time that I were hence:
She that doth call me husband, euen my soule
890 Doth for a wife abhorre. But her faire sister
Possest with such a gentle soueraigne grace,
Of such inchanting presence and discourse,
Hath almost made me Traitor to my selfe:
But least my selfe be guilty to selfe wrong,
Ile stop mine eares against the Mermaids song.

Enter Angelo the Goldsmith with the Chaine

GOLDSMITH
  Mr *Antipholus*.

SIRACUSIAN ANTIPHOLUS I that's my name.

GOLDSMITH
  I know it well sir, loe here's the chaine,
  I thought to haue tane you at the *Porpentine*,
  The chaine vnfinish'd made me stay thus long.

SIRACUSIAN ANTIPHOLUS (*taking the chaine*)
900 What is your will that I shal do with this?

GOLDSMITH
  What please your selfe sir: I haue made it for you.

SIRACUSIAN ANTIPHOLUS
  Made it for me sir, I bespoke it not.

GOLDSMITH
  Not once, nor twice, but twentie times you haue:
  Go home with it, and please your Wife withall,
  And soone at supper time Ile visit you,
  And then receiue my money for the chaine.

SIRACUSIAN ANTIPHOLUS
  I pray you sir receiue the money now.
  For feare you ne're see chaine, nor mony more.

GOLDSMITH
  You are a merry man sir, fare you well.   *Exit*

SIRACUSIAN ANTIPHOLUS
910 What I should thinke of this, I cannot tell:
  But this I thinke, there's no man is so vaine,
  That would refuse so faire an offer'd Chaine.
  I see a man heere needs not liue by shifts,
  When in the streets he meetes such Golden gifts:
  Ile to the Mart, and there for *Dromio* stay,
  If any ship put out, then straight away.   *Exit*

✦

4.1   *Enter another Merchant, Goldsmith, and an Officer*
(Sc. 7) MARCHANT (*to Goldsmith*)
  You know since Pentecost the sum is due,
  And since I haue not much importun'd you,
  Nor now I had not, but that I am bound
920 To *Persia*, and want Gilders for my voyage:
  Therefore make present satisfaction,
  Or Ile attach you by this Officer.

GOLDSMITH
  Euen iust the sum that I do owe to you,
  Is growing to me by *Antipholus*,
  And in the instant that I met with you,
  He had of me a Chaine, at fiue a clocke
  I shall receiue the money for the same:

Pleaseth you walke with me downe to his house,
I will discharge my bond, and thanke you too.

*Enter Antipholus Ephes., Dromio Ephes. from the
Courtizans house, the Porpentine*

OFFICER
  That labour may you saue: See where he comes. 930

EPHESIAN ANTIPHOLUS (*to Dromio*)
  While I go to the Goldsmiths house, go thou
  And buy a ropes end, that will I bestow
  Among my wife, and her confederates,
  For locking me out of my doores by day:
  But soft I see the Goldsmith; get thee gone,
  Buy thou a rope, and bring it home to me.

EPHESIAN DROMIO
  I buy a thousand pound a yeare, I buy a rope.

                           Exit Dromio

EPHESIAN ANTIPHOLUS (*to Goldsmith*)
  A man is well holpe vp that trusts to you,
  I promised your presence, and the Chaine,
  But neither Chaine nor Goldsmith came to me: 940
  Belike you thought our loue would last too long
  If it were chain'd together: and therefore came not.

GOLDSMITH
  Sauing your merrie humor: here's the note
  How much your Chaine weighs to the vtmost charect,
  The finenesse of the Gold, and chargefull fashion,
  Which doth amount to three odde Duckets more
  Then I stand debted to this Gentleman,
  I pray you see him presently discharg'd,
  For he is bound to Sea, and stayes but for it.

EPHESIAN ANTIPHOLUS
  I am not furnish'd with the present monie: 950
  Besides I haue some businesse in the towne,
  Good Signior take the stranger to my house,
  And with you take the Chaine, and bid my wife
  Disburse the summe, on the receit thereof,
  Perchance I will be there as soone as you.

GOLDSMITH
  Then you will bring the Chaine to her your selfe.

EPHESIAN ANTIPHOLUS
  No beare it with you, least I come not time enough.

GOLDSMITH
  Well sir, I will? Haue you the Chaine about you?

EPHESIAN ANTIPHOLUS
  And if I haue not sir, I hope you haue:
  Or else you may returne without your money. 960

GOLDSMITH
  Nay come I pray you sir, giue me the Chaine:
  Both winde and tide stayes for this Gentleman,
  And I too blame haue held him heere too long.

EPHESIAN ANTIPHOLUS
  Good Lord, you vse this dalliance to excuse
  Your breach of promise to the *Porpentine*,
  I should haue chid you for not bringing it,
  But like a shrew you first begin to brawle.

MARCHANT (*to Goldsmith*)
  The houre steales on, I pray you sir dispatch.

GOLDSMITH (*to Antipholus*)
    You heare how he importunes me, the Chaine.
EPHESIAN ANTIPHOLUS
970   Why giue it to my wife, and fetch your mony.
GOLDSMITH
    Come, come, you know I gaue it you euen now.
    Either send the Chaine, or send me by some token.
EPHESIAN ANTIPHOLUS
    Fie, now you run this humor out of breath,
    Come where's the Chaine, I pray you let me see it.
MARCHANT
    My businesse cannot brooke this dalliance,
    Good sir say, whe'r you'l answer me, or no:
    If not, Ile leaue him to the Officer.
EPHESIAN ANTIPHOLUS
    I answer you? What should I answer you.
GOLDSMITH
    The monie that you owe me for the Chaine.
EPHESIAN ANTIPHOLUS
980   I owe you none, till I receiue the Chaine.
GOLDSMITH
    You know I gaue it you halfe an houre since.
EPHESIAN ANTIPHOLUS
    You gaue me none, you wrong mee much to say so.
GOLDSMITH
    You wrong me more sir in denying it.
    Consider how it stands vpon my credit.
MARCHANT
    Well Officer, arrest him at my suite.
OFFICER (*to Goldsmith*)
    I do, and charge you in the Dukes name to obey me.
GOLDSMITH (*to Antipholus*)
    This touches me in reputation.
    Either consent to pay this sum for me,
    Or I attach you by this Officer.
EPHESIAN ANTIPHOLUS
990   Consent to pay thee that I neuer had:
    Arrest me foolish fellow if thou dar'st.
GOLDSMITH
    Heere is thy fee, arrest him Officer.
    I would not spare my brother in this case,
    If he should scorne me so apparantly.
OFFICER (*to Antipholus*)
    I do arrest you sir, you heare the suite.
EPHESIAN ANTIPHOLUS
    I do obey thee, till I giue thee baile.
    (*To Goldsmith*) But sirrah, you shall buy this sport as
        deere,
    As all the mettall in your shop will answer.
GOLDSMITH
    Sir, sir, I shall haue Law in *Ephesus*,
1000   To your notorious shame, I doubt it not.
            Enter Dromio Sira. from the Bay
SIRACUSIAN DROMIO
    Master, there's a Barke of *Epidamnum*,
    That staies but till her Owner comes aboord,
    And then she beares away. Our fraughtage sir,
    I haue conuei'd aboord, and I haue bought
    The Oyle, the *Balsamum*, and Aqua-vitæ.

The ship is in her trim, the merrie winde
Blowes faire from land: they stay for nought at all,
But for their Owner, Master, and your selfe.
EPHESIAN ANTIPHOLUS
    How now? a Madman? Why thou peeuish sheep
    What ship of *Epidamnum* staies for me.   1010
SIRACUSIAN DROMIO
    A ship you sent me too, to hier waftage.
EPHESIAN ANTIPHOLUS
    Thou drunken slaue, I sent thee for a rope,
    And told thee to what purpose, and what end.
SIRACUSIAN DROMIO
    You sent me for a ropes end as soone,
    You sent me to the Bay sir, for a Barke.
EPHESIAN ANTIPHOLUS
    I will debate this matter at more leisure
    And teach your eares to list me with more heede:
    To *Adriana* Villaine hie thee straight:
    Giue her this key, and tell her in the Deske
    That's couer'd o're with Turkish Tapistrie,   1020
    There is a purse of Duckets, let her send it:
    Tell her, I am arrested in the streete,
    And that shall baile me: hie thee slaue, be gone,
    On Officer to prison, till it come.
                            Exeunt. Manet Dromio
SIRACUSIAN DROMIO
    To *Adriana*, that is where we din'd,
    Where Dowsabell did claime me for her husband,
    She is too bigge I hope for me to compasse,
    Thither I must, although against my will:
    For seruants must their Masters mindes fulfill.   *Exit*

            Enter ⌈from the Phœnix⌉ Adriana and Luciana   **4.2**
ADRIANA   (Sc. 8)
    Ah *Luciana*, did he tempt thee so?   1030
        Might'st thou perceiue austeerely in his eie,
    That he did plead in earnest, yea or no:
        Look'd he or red or pale, or sad or merrily?
    What obseruation mad'st thou in this case
    Of his hearts Meteors tilting in his face.
LUCIANA
    First he deni'de you had in him no right.
ADRIANA
    He meant he did me none: the more my spight.
LUCIANA
    Then swore he that he was a stranger heere.
ADRIANA
    And true he swore, though yet forsworne hee were.
LUCIANA
    Then pleaded I for you.
ADRIANA   And what said he?   1040
LUCIANA
    That loue I begg'd for you, he begg'd of me.
ADRIANA
    With what perswasion did he tempt thy loue?
LUCIANA
    With words, that in an honest suit might moue.
    First, he did praise my beautie, then my speech.

ADRIANA
Did'st speake him faire?

LUCIANA   Haue patience I beseech.

ADRIANA
I cannot, nor I will not hold me still.
My tongue, though not my heart, shall haue his will.
He is deformed, crooked, old, and sere,
Ill-fac'd, worse bodied, shapelesse euery where:
1050 Vicious, vngentle, foolish, blunt, vnkinde,
Stigmaticall in making worse in minde.

LUCIANA
Who would be iealous then of such a one?
No euill lost is wail'd, when it is gone.

ADRIANA
Ah but I thinke him better then I say:
  And yet would herein others eies were worse:
Farre from her nest the Lapwing cries away;
  My heart praies for him, though my tongue doe
    curse.
    Enter S. Dromio running

SIRACUSIAN DROMIO
Here goe: the deske, the purse, sweet now make haste.

LUCIANA
How? hast thou lost thy breath?

SIRACUSIAN DROMIO   By running fast.

ADRIANA
1060 Where is thy Master *Dromio*? Is he well?

SIRACUSIAN DROMIO
No, he's in Tartar limbo, worse then hell:
A diuell in an euerlasting garment hath him;
On whose hard heart is button'd vp with steele:
A Feind, a Fairie, pittilesse and ruffe:
A Wolfe, nay worse, a fellow all in buffe:
A back friend, a shoulder-clapper, one that
    countermāds
The passages of allies, creekes, and narrow lands:
A hound that runs Counter, and yet draws drifoot well,
One that before the Iudgmēt carries poore soules to hel.

1070 **ADRIANA** Why man, what is the matter?

SIRACUSIAN DROMIO
I doe not know the matter, hee is rested on the case.

ADRIANA
What is he arrested? tell me at whose suite?

SIRACUSIAN DROMIO
I know not at whose suite he is arested well;
But is in a suite of buffe which rested him, that can I
    tell,
Will you send him Mistris redemption, the monie in
    his deske.

ADRIANA
Go fetch it Sister: *Exit Luciana ⌈into the Phœnix⌉*
    this I wonder at,
That he vnknowne to me should be in debt:
Tell me, was he arested on a band?

SIRACUSIAN DROMIO
Not on a band, but on a stronger thing:
1080 A chaine, a chaine, doe you not here it ring.

ADRIANA
What, the chaine?

SIRACUSIAN DROMIO
No, no, the bell, 'tis time that I were gone:
It was two ere I left him, and now the clocke strikes
    one.

ADRIANA
The houres come backe, that did I neuer here.

SIRACUSIAN DROMIO
Oh yes, if any houre meete a Serieant, a turnes backe
    for verie feare.

ADRIANA
As if time were in debt: how fondly do'st thou reason?

SIRACUSIAN DROMIO
Time is a verie bankerout, and owes more then he's
    worth to season.
Nay, he's a theefe too: haue you not heard men say,
That time comes stealing on by night and day?
If a be in debt and theft, and a Serieant in the way,
Hath he not reason to turne backe an houre in a day?   1090
    Enter Luciana ⌈from the Phœnix⌉ with the monie

ADRIANA
Go *Dromio*, there's the monie, beare it straight,
  And bring thy Master home imediately.
                              ⌈Exit Dromio⌉
Come sister, I am prest downe with conceit:
  Conceit, my comfort and my iniurie.
                    Exeunt ⌈into the Phœnix⌉

Enter Antipholus Siracusia wearing the Chaine   **4.3**

SIRACUSIAN ANTIPHOLUS   **(Sc. 9)**
There's not a man I meete but doth salute me
As if I were their well acquainted friend,
And euerie one doth call me by my name:
Some tender monie to me, some inuite me;
Some other giue me thankes for kindnesses;
Some offer me Commodities to buy.   1100
Euen now a tailor cal'd me in his shop,
And show'd me Silkes that he had bought for me,
And therewithall tooke measure of my body.
Sure these are but imaginarie wiles,
And lapland Sorcerers inhabite here.
    Enter Dromio Sir. with the monie

SIRACUSIAN DROMIO Master, here's the gold you sent me
for: what haue you got redemption from the picture of
old *Adam* new apparel'd?

SIRACUSIAN ANTIPHOLUS
What gold is this? What *Adam* do'st thou meane?

SIRACUSIAN DROMIO Not that *Adam* that kept the Paradise: 1110
but that *Adam* that keepes the prison; hee that goes in
the calues-skin, that was kil'd for the Prodigall: hee
that came behinde you sir, like an euill angel, and bid
you forsake your libertie.

SIRACUSIAN ANTIPHOLUS I vnderstand thee not.

SIRACUSIAN DROMIO No? why 'tis a plaine case: he that
went like a Base-Viole in a case of leather; the man
sir, that when gentlemen are tired giues them a sob,

and rests them: he sir, that takes pittie on decaied men,
1120 and giues them suites of durance: he that sets vp his
rest to doe more exploits with his Mace, then a Moris
Pike.

SIRACUSIAN ANTIPHOLUS What thou mean'st an officer?

SIRACUSIAN DROMIO I sir, the Serieant of the Band: he
that brings any man to answer it that breakes his
Band: one that thinkes a man alwaies going to bed,
and saies, God giue you good rest.

SIRACUSIAN ANTIPHOLUS Well sir, there rest in your
foolerie: Is there any ships puts forth to night? may
1130 we be gone?

SIRACUSIAN DROMIO Why sir, I brought you word an houre
since, that the Barke *Expedition* put forth to night, and
then were you hindred by the Serieant to tarry for the
Hoy Delay: Here are the angels that you sent for to
deliuer you.

SIRACUSIAN ANTIPHOLUS
The fellow is distract, and so am I,
And here we wander in illusions:
Some blessed power deliuer vs from hence.

Enter a Curtizan ⌈from the Porpentine⌉

CURTIZAN
Well met, well met, Master *Antipholus*:
1140 I see sir you haue found the Gold-smith now:
Is that the chaine you promis'd me to day.

SIRACUSIAN ANTIPHOLUS
Sathan auoide, I charge thee tempt me not.

SIRACUSIAN DROMIO Master, is this Mistris *Sathan*?

SIRACUSIAN ANTIPHOLUS It is the diuell.

SIRACUSIAN DROMIO Nay, she is worse, she is the diuels
dam: And here she comes in the habit of a light wench,
and thereof comes, that the wenches say God dam me,
That's as much to say, God make me a light wench:
It is written they appeare to men like angels of light,
1150 light is an effect of fire, and fire will burne: *ergo*, light
wenches will burne, come not neere her.

CURTIZAN
Your man and you are maruailous merrie sir.
Will you goe with me, wee'll mend our dinner here?

SIRACUSIAN DROMIO Master, if you do expect spoon-meate,
and bespeake a long spoone.

SIRACUSIAN ANTIPHOLUS Why *Dromio*?

SIRACUSIAN DROMIO Marrie he must haue a long spoone
that must eate with the diuell.

SIRACUSIAN ANTIPHOLUS (*to Curtizan*)
Auoid thou fiend, what tel'st thou me of supping?
1160 Thou art, as you are all a sorceresse:
I coniure thee to leaue me, and be gon.

CURTIZAN
Giue me the ring of mine you had at dinner,
Or for my Diamond the Chaine you promis'd,
And Ile be gone sir, and not trouble you.

SIRACUSIAN DROMIO
Some diuels aske but the parings of ones naile,
A rush, a haire, a drop of blood, a pin,
A nut, a cherrie-stone:
But she more couetous, wold haue a chaine:

Master be wise, and if you giue it her,
The diuell will shake her Chaine, and fright vs with it.   1170

CURTIZAN (*to Antipholus*)
I pray you sir my Ring, or else the Chaine,
I hope you do not meane to cheate me so?

SIRACUSIAN ANTIPHOLUS
Auant thou witch: Come *Dromio* let vs go.

SIRACUSIAN DROMIO
Flie pride saies the Pea-cocke, Mistris that you know.

Exit Antipholus Siracusia and Dromio Siracusia

CURTIZAN
Now out of doubt *Antipholus* is mad,
Else would he neuer so demeane himselfe,
A Ring he hath of mine worth fortie Duckets,
And for the same he promis'd me a Chaine,
Both one and other he denies me now:
The reason that I gather he is mad,   1180
Besides this present instance of his rage,
Is a mad tale he told to day at dinner,
Of his owne doores being shut against his entrance.
Belike his wife acquainted with his fits,
On purpose shut the doores against his way:
My way is now to hie home to his house,
And tell his wife, that being Lunaticke,
He rush'd into my house, and tooke perforce
My Ring away. This course I fittest choose,
For fortie Duckets is too much to loose.   *Exit*   1190

Enter Antipholus Ephes. with the Officer   **4.4**
                                                        (Sc. 10)
EPHESIAN ANTIPHOLUS
Feare me not man, I will not breake away,
Ile giue thee ere I leaue thee so much money
To warrant thee as I am rested for.
My wife is in a wayward moode to day,
And will not lightly trust the Messenger,
That I should be attach'd in *Ephesus*,
I tell you 'twill sound harshly in her eares.

Enter Dromio Eph. with a ropes end
Heere comes my Man, I thinke he brings the monie.
How now sir? Haue you that I sent you for?

EPHESIAN DROMIO
Here's that I warrant you will pay them all.   1200

EPHESIAN ANTIPHOLUS But where's the Money?

EPHESIAN DROMIO
Why sir, I gaue the Monie for the Rope.

EPHESIAN ANTIPHOLUS
Fiue hundred Duckets villaine for a rope?

EPHESIAN DROMIO
Ile serue you sir fiue hundred at the rate.

EPHESIAN ANTIPHOLUS
To what end did I bid thee hie thee home?

EPHESIAN DROMIO To a ropes end sir, and to that end am
I return'd.

EPHESIAN ANTIPHOLUS
And to that end sir, I will welcome you.

Beats Dromio

OFFICER Good sir be patient.

EPHESIAN DROMIO Nay 'tis for me to be patient, I am in   1210
aduersitie.

OFFICER Good now hold thy tongue.

EPHESIAN DROMIO Nay, rather perswade him to hold his hands.

EPHESIAN ANTIPHOLUS Thou whoreson senselesse Villaine.

EPHESIAN DROMIO I would I were senselesse sir, that I might not feele your blowes.

EPHESIAN ANTIPHOLUS Thou art sensible in nothing but blowes, and so is an Asse.

1220 EPHESIAN DROMIO I am an Asse indeede, you may prooue it by my long eares. I haue serued him from the houre of my Natiuitie to this instant, and haue nothing at his hands for my seruice but blowes. When I am cold, he heates me with beating: when I am warme, he cooles me with beating: I am wak'd with it when I sleepe, rais'd with it when I sit, driuen out of doores with it when I goe from home, welcom'd home with it when I returne, nay I beare it on my shoulders, as a begger woont her brat: and I thinke when he hath 1230 lam'd me, I shall begge with it from doore to doore.

Enter Adriana, Luciana, Courtizan, and a Schoole-
master, call'd Pinch

EPHESIAN ANTIPHOLUS
Come goe along, my wife is comming yonder.

EPHESIAN DROMIO (*to Adriana*) Mistris *respice finem*, respect your end, or rather to prophesie like the Parrat, beware the ropes end.

EPHESIAN ANTIPHOLUS Wilt thou still talke?

Beats Dromio

CURTIZAN (*to Adriana*)
How say you now? Is not your husband mad?

ADRIANA
His inciuility confirmes no lesse:
Good Doctor *Pinch*, you are a Coniurer,
Establish him in his true sence againe,
1240 And I will please you what you will demand.

LUCIANA
Alas how fiery, and how sharpe he lookes.

CURTIZAN
Marke, how he trembles in his extasie.

PINCH (*to Antipholus*)
Giue me your hand, and let mee feele your pulse.

EPHESIAN ANTIPHOLUS
There is my hand, and let it feele your eare.

He strikes Pinch

PINCH
I charge thee Sathan, hous'd within this man,
To yeeld possession to my holie praiers,
And to thy state of darknesse hie thee straight,
I coniure thee by all the Saints in heauen.

EPHESIAN ANTIPHOLUS
Peace doting wizard, peace; I am not mad.

ADRIANA
1250 Oh that thou wer't not, poore distressed soule.

EPHESIAN ANTIPHOLUS
You Minion you, are these your Customers?
Did this Companion with the saffron face
Reuell and feast it at my house to day,
Whil'st vpon me the guiltie doores were shut,
And I denied to enter in my house.

ADRIANA
O husband, God doth know you din'd at home
Where would you had remain'd vntill this time,
Free from these slanders, and this open shame.

EPHESIAN ANTIPHOLUS
Din'd at home?
(*To Dromio*)   Thou Villaine, what sayest thou?

EPHESIAN DROMIO
Sir sooth to say, you did not dine at home.   1260

EPHESIAN ANTIPHOLUS
Were not my doores lockt vp, and I shut out?

EPHESIAN DROMIO
Perdie, your doores were lockt, and you shut out.

EPHESIAN ANTIPHOLUS
And did not she her selfe reuile me there?

EPHESIAN DROMIO
Sans Fable, she her selfe reuil'd you there.

EPHESIAN ANTIPHOLUS
Did not her Kitchen maide raile, taunt, and scorne me?

EPHESIAN DROMIO
Certis she did, the kitchin vestall scorn'd you.

EPHESIAN ANTIPHOLUS
And did not I in rage depart from thence?

EPHESIAN DROMIO
In veritie you did, my bones beares witnesse,
That since haue felt the vigor of his rage.

ADRIANA (*aside to Pinch*)
Is't good to sooth him in these contraries?   1270

PINCH (*aside to Adriana*)
It is no shame, the fellow finds his vaine,
And yeelding to him, humors well his frensie.

EPHESIAN ANTIPHOLUS (*to Adriana*)
Thou hast subborn'd the Goldsmith to arrest mee.

ADRIANA
Alas, I sent you Monie to redeeme you,
By *Dromio* heere, who came in hast for it.

EPHESIAN DROMIO
Monie by me? Heart and good will you might,
But surely Master not a ragge of Monie.

EPHESIAN ANTIPHOLUS
Wentst not thou to her for a purse of Duckets.

ADRIANA
He came to me, and I deliuer'd it.

LUCIANA
And I am witnesse with her that she did.   1280

EPHESIAN DROMIO
God and the Rope-maker beare me witnesse,
That I was sent for nothing but a rope.

PINCH (*aside to Adriana*)
Mistris, both Man and Master is possest,
I know it by their pale and deadly lookes,
They must be bound and laide in some darke roome.

EPHESIAN ANTIPHOLUS (*to Adriana*)
Say wherefore didst thou locke me forth to day,
(*To Dromio*) And why dost thou denie the bagge of gold?

ADRIANA
I did not gentle husband locke thee forth.

EPHESIAN DROMIO

And gentle Mr I receiu'd no gold:

1290   But I confesse sir, that we were lock'd out.

ADRIANA

Dissembling Villain, thou speak'st false in both.

EPHESIAN ANTIPHOLUS

Dissembling harlot, thou art false in all,

And art confederate with a damned packe,

To make a loathsome abiect scorne of me:

But with these nailes, Ile plucke out those false eyes,

That would behold in me this shamefull sport.

⌈*He reaches for Adriana; she shreeks.*⌉

Enter three or foure, and offer to binde him: Hee

striues

ADRIANA

Oh binde him, binde him, let him not come neere me.

PINCH

More company, the fiend is strong within him.

LUCIANA

Aye me poore man, how pale and wan he looks.

EPHESIAN ANTIPHOLUS

1300   What will you murther me? thou Iailor thou,

I am thy prisoner, wilt thou suffer them

To make a rescue?

OFFICER   Masters let him go:

He is my prisoner, and you shall not haue him.

PINCH

Go binde his man, for he is franticke too.

They binde Dromio

ADRIANA

What wilt thou do, thou peeuish Officer?

Hast thou delight to see a wretched man

Do outrage and displeasure to himselfe?

OFFICER

He is my prisoner, if I let him go,

The debt he owes will be requir'd of me.

ADRIANA

1310   I will discharge thee ere I go from thee,

Beare me forthwith vnto his Creditor,

And knowing how the debt growes I will pay it.

Good Master Doctor see him safe conuey'd

Home to my house, oh most vnhappy day.

EPHESIAN ANTIPHOLUS Oh most vnhappie strumpet.

EPHESIAN DROMIO

Master, I am heere entred in bond for you.

EPHESIAN ANTIPHOLUS

Out on thee Villaine, wherefore dost thou mad mee?

EPHESIAN DROMIO

Will you be bound for nothing, be mad good Master,

Cry the diuell.

LUCIANA

1320   God helpe poore soules, how idlely doe they talke.

ADRIANA

Go beare him hence, sister go you with me:

Exeunt ⌈into the Phœnix⌉, Pinch and others

carrying off Antipholus Eph. and Dromio Eph.

Manet Officer, Adriana, Luciana, Courtizan

(*To the Officer*) Say now, whose suite is he arrested at?

OFFICER

One *Angelo* a Goldsmith, do you know him?

ADRIANA

I know the man: what is the summe he owes?

OFFICER

Two hundred Duckets.

ADRIANA   Say, how growes it due.

OFFICER

Due for a Chaine your husband had of him.

ADRIANA

He did bespeake a Chain for me, but had it not.

CURTIZAN

When as your husband all in rage to day

Came to my house, and tooke away my Ring,

The Ring I saw vpon his finger now,   1330

Straight after did I meete him with a Chaine.

ADRIANA

It may be so, but I did neuer see it.

Come Iailor, bring me where the Goldsmith is,

I long to know the truth heereof at large.

Enter Antipholus Siracusia, wearing the Chaine, and

Dromio Sirac., with their Rapiers drawne

LUCIANA

God for thy mercy, they are loose againe.

ADRIANA

And come with naked swords, let's call more helpe

To haue them bound againe.

OFFICER   Away, they'l kill vs.

Exeunt omnes: Runne all out, as fast as may

be, frighted. Manet Antipholus and Dromio

SIRACUSIAN ANTIPHOLUS

I see these Witches are affraid of swords.

SIRACUSIAN DROMIO

She that would be your wife, now ran from you.

SIRACUSIAN ANTIPHOLUS

Come to the Centaur, fetch our stuffe from thence: 1340

I long that we were safe and sound aboord.

SIRACUSIAN DROMIO Faith stay heere this night, they will

surely do vs no harme: you saw they speake vs faire,

giue vs gold: me thinkes they are such a gentle Nation,

that but for the Mountaine of mad flesh that claimes

mariage of me, I could finde in my heart to stay heere

still, and turne Witch.

SIRACUSIAN ANTIPHOLUS

I will not stay to night for all the Towne,

Therefore away, to get our stuffe aboord.   *Exeunt*

✿

Enter the Merchant and the Goldsmith   **5.1**

GOLDSMITH   (Sc. 11)

I am sorry Sir that I haue hindred you,   1350

But I protest he had the Chaine of me,

Though most dishonestly he doth denie it.

MARCHANT

How is the man esteem'd heere in the Citie?

GOLDSMITH

Of very reuerent reputation sir,

Of credit infinite, highly belou'd,

Second to none that liues heere in the Citie:
His word might beare my wealth at any time.

MARCHANT

Speake softly, yonder as I thinke he walkes.

Enter Antipholus Siracusia, wearing the Chaine, and
Dromio Siracusia againe

GOLDSMITH

'Tis so: and that selfe chaine about his necke,
1360   Which he forswore most monstrously to haue.
Good sir draw neere to me, Ile speake to him:
Signior *Antipholus*, I wonder much
That you would put me to this shame and trouble,
And not without some scandall to your selfe,
With circumstance and oaths, so to denie
This Chaine, which now you weare so openly.
Beside the charge, the shame, imprisonment,
You haue done wrong to this my honest friend,
Who but for staying on our Controuersie,
1370   Had hoisted saile, and put to sea to day:
This Chaine you had of me, can you deny it?

SIRACUSIAN ANTIPHOLUS

I thinke I had, I neuer did deny it.

MARCHANT

Yes that you did sir, and forswore it too.

SIRACUSIAN ANTIPHOLUS

Who heard me to denie it or forsweare it?

MARCHANT

These eares of mine thou knowst did hear thee:
Fie on thee wretch, 'tis pitty that thou liu'st
To walke where any honest men resort.

SIRACUSIAN ANTIPHOLUS

Thou art a Villaine to impeach me thus,
Ile proue mine honor, and mine honestie
1380   Against thee presently, if thou dar'st stand.

MARCHANT

I dare and do defie thee for a villaine.

They draw. Enter Adriana, Luciana, Courtezan,
& others ⌈from the Phœnix⌉

ADRIANA

Hold, hurt him not for God sake, he is mad,
Some get within him, take his sword away:
Binde *Dromio* too, and beare them to my house.

SIRACUSIAN DROMIO

Runne master run, for Gods sake take a house,
This is some Priorie, in, or we are spoyl'd.

Exeunt Antipholus Siracusia and
Dromio Siracusia to the Priorie
Enter Ladie Abbesse ⌈from the Priorie⌉

ABBESSE

Be quiet people, wherefore throng you hither?

ADRIANA

To fetch my poore distracted husband hence,
Let vs come in, that we may binde him fast,
1390   And beare him home for his recouerie.

GOLDSMITH

I knew he was not in his perfect wits.

MARCHANT

I am sorry now that I did draw on him.

ABBESSE

How long hath this possession held the man.

ADRIANA

This weeke he hath beene heauie, sower sad,
And much much different from the man he was:
But till this afternoone his passion
Ne're brake into extremity of rage.

ABBESSE

Hath he not lost much wealth by wrack at sea,
Buried some deere friend, hath not else his eye
Stray'd his affection in vnlawfull loue,   1400
A sinne preuailing much in youthfull men,
Who giue their eies the liberty of gazing.
Which of these sorrowes is he subiect too?

ADRIANA

To none of these, except it be the last,
Namely, some loue that drew him oft from home.

ABBESSE

You should for that haue reprehended him.

ADRIANA

Why so I did.

ABBESSE   I but not rough enough.

ADRIANA

As roughly as my modestie would let me.

ABBESSE Haply in priuate.

ADRIANA And in assemblies too.   1410

ABBESSE I, but not enough.

ADRIANA

It was the copie of our Conference.
In bed he slept not for my vrging it,
At boord he fed not for my vrging it:
Alone, it was the subiect of my Theame:
In company I often glanced it:
Still did I tell him, it was vilde and bad.

ABBESSE

And thereof came it, that the man was mad.
The venome clamors of a iealous woman,
Poisons more deadly then a mad dogges tooth.   1420
It seemes his sleepes were hindred by thy railing,
And thereof comes it that his head is light.
Thou saist his meate was sawc'd with thy vpbraidings,
Vnquiet meales make ill digestions,
Thereof the raging fire of feauer bred,
And what's a Feauer, but a fit of madnesse?
Thou sayest his sports were hindred by thy bralles.
Sweet recreation barr'd, what doth ensue
But moodie and dull melancholly,
Kinsman to grim and comfortlesse dispaire,   1430
And at her heeles a huge infectious troope
Of pale distemperatures, and foes to life?
In food, in sport, and life-preseruing rest
To be disturb'd, would mad or man, or beast:
The consequence is then, thy iealous fits
Hath scar'd thy husband from the vse of wits.

LUCIANA

She neuer reprehended him but mildely,
When he demean'd himselfe, rough, rude, and wildly,

(*To Adriana*) Why beare you these rebukes, and
            answer not?

ADRIANA

1440   She did betray me to my owne reproofe,
            Good people enter, and lay hold on him.

ABBESSE

            No, not a creature enters in my house.

ADRIANA

            Then let your seruants bring my husband forth.

ABBESSE

            Neither: he tooke this place for sanctuary,
            And it shall priuiledge him from your hands,
            Till I haue brought him to his wits againe,
            Or loose my labour in assaying it.

ADRIANA

            I will attend my husband, be his nurse,
            Diet his sicknesse, for it is my Office,
1450   And will haue no atturney but my selfe,
            And therefore let me haue him home with me.

ABBESSE

            Be patient, for I will not let him stirre,
            Till I haue vs'd the approoued meanes I haue,
            With wholsome sirrups, drugges, and holy prayers
            To make of him a formall man againe:
            It is a branch and parcell of mine oath,
            A charitable dutie of my order,
            Therefore depart, and leaue him heere with me.

ADRIANA

            I will not hence, and leaue my husband heere:
1460   And ill it doth beseeme your holinesse
            To separate the husband and the wife.

ABBESSE

            Be quiet and depart, thou shalt not haue him.
                                ⌈*Exit to the Priorie*⌉

LUCIANA (*to Adriana*)

            Complaine vnto the Duke of this indignity.

ADRIANA

            Come go, I will fall prostrate at his feete,
            And neuer rise vntill my teares and prayers
            Haue won his grace to come in person hither,
            And take perforce my husband from the Abbesse.

MARCHANT

            By this I thinke the Diall points at fiue:
            Anon I'me sure the Duke himselfe in person
1470   Comes this way to the melancholly vale;
            The place of death, and sorrie execution,
            Behinde the ditches of the Abbey heere.

GOLDSMITH Vpon what cause?

MARCHANT

            To see a reuerent *Siracusian* Merchant,
            Who put vnluckily into this Bay
            Against the Lawes and Statutes of this Towne,
            Beheaded publikely for his offence.

GOLDSMITH

            See where they come, we wil behold his death.

LUCIANA

            Kneele to the Duke before he passe the Abbey.

*Enter the Duke of Ephesus, and the Merchant
Father of Siracuse bare head, with the Headsman,
& other Officers*

DUKE

            Yet once againe proclaime it publikely,   1480
            If any friend will pay the summe for him,
            He shall not die, so much we tender him.

ADRIANA (*kneeling*)

            Iustice most sacred Duke against the Abbesse.

DUKE

            She is a vertuous and a reuerend Lady,
            It cannot be that she hath done thee wrong.

ADRIANA

            May it please your Grace, *Antipholus* my husbād,
            Who I made Lord of me, and all I had,
            At your important Letters this ill day,
            A most outragious fit of madnesse tooke him:
            That desp'rately he hurried through the streete,   1490
            With him his bondman, all as mad as he,
            Doing displeasure to the Citizens,
            By rushing in their houses: bearing thence
            Rings, Iewels, any thing his rage did like.
            Once did I get him bound, and sent him home,
            Whil'st to take order for the wrongs I went,
            That heere and there his furie had committed,
            Anon I wot not, by what strong escape
            He broke from those that had the guard of him,
            And with his mad attendant and himselfe,   1500
            Each one with irefull passion, with drawne swords
            Met vs againe, and madly bent on vs
            Chac'd vs away: till raising of more aide
            We came againe to binde them: then they fled
            Into this Abbey, whether we pursu'd them,
            And heere the Abbesse shuts the gates on vs,
            And will not suffer vs to fetch him out,
            Nor send him forth, that we may beare him hence,
            Therefore most gracious Duke with thy command,
            Let him be brought forth, and borne hence for helpe. 1510

DUKE ⌈*raising Adriana*⌉

            Long since thy husband seru'd me in my wars
            And I to thee ingag'd a Princes word,
            When thou didst make him Master of thy bed,
            To do him all the grace and good I could.
            Go some of you, knocke at the Abbey gate,
            And bid the Lady Abbesse come to me:
            I will determine this before I stirre.

            Enter a Messenger ⌈*from the Phœnix*⌉

MESSENGER (*to Adriana*)

            Oh Mistris, Mistris, shift and saue your selfe,
            My Master and his man are both broke loose,
            Beaten the Maids a-row, and bound the Doctor,   1520
            Whose beard they haue sindg'd off with brands of fire,
            And euer as it blaz'd, they threw on him
            Great pailes of puddled myre to quench the haire;
            My M^r preaches patience to him, and the while
            His man with Cizers nickes him like a foole:
            And sure (vnlesse you send some present helpe)
            Betweene them they will kill the Coniurer.

ADRIANA

Peace foole, thy Master and his man are here,
And that is false thou dost report to vs.

MESSENGER

1530 Mistris, vpon my life I tel you true,
I haue not breath'd almost since I did see it.
He cries for you, and vowes if he can take you,
To scorch your face, and to disfigure you:
    Cry within
Harke, harke, I heare him Mistris: flie, be gone.

DUKE (*to Adriana*)

Come stand by me, feare nothing: guard with Halberds.
    Enter Antipholus of Ephesus, and Dromio of
    Ephesus ⌐from the Phœnix⌐

ADRIANA

Ay me, it is my husband: witnesse you,
That he is borne about inuisible,
Euen now we hous'd him in the Abbey heere.
And now he's there, past thought of humane reason.

EPHESIAN ANTIPHOLUS

1540 Iustice most gracious Duke, oh grant me iustice,
Euen for the seruice that long since I did thee,
When I bestrid thee in the warres, and tooke
Deepe scarres to saue thy life; euen for the blood
That then I lost for thee, now grant me iustice.

MERCHANT FATHER (*aside*)

Vnlesse the feare of death doth make me dote,
I see my sonne *Antipholus* and *Dromio*.

EPHESIAN ANTIPHOLUS

Iustice (sweet Prince) against yᵗ Woman there:
She whom thou gau'st to me to be my wife;
That hath abused and dishonord me,

1550 Euen in the strength and height of iniurie:
Beyond imagination is the wrong
That she this day hath shamelesse throwne on me.

DUKE

Discouer how, and thou shalt finde me iust.

EPHESIAN ANTIPHOLUS

This day (great Duke) she shut the doores vpon me,
While she with Harlots feasted in my house.

DUKE

A greeuous fault: say woman, didst thou so?

ADRIANA

No my good Lord. My selfe, he, and my sister,
To day did dine together: so befall my soule,
As this is false he burthens me withall.

LUCIANA

1560 Nere may I looke on day, nor sleepe on night,
But she tels to your Highnesse simple truth.

GOLDSMITH (*aside*)

O periur'd woman! They are both forsworne,
In this the Madman iustly chargeth them.

EPHESIAN ANTIPHOLUS

My Liege, I am aduised what I say,
Neither disturbed with the effect of Wine,
Nor headie-rash prouoak'd with raging ire,
Albeit my wrongs might make one wiser mad.
This woman lock'd me out this day from dinner;
That Goldsmith there, were he not pack'd with her,

Could witnesse it: for he was with me then,   1570
Who parted with me to go fetch a Chaine,
Promising to bring it to the Porpentine,
Where *Balthasar* and I did dine together.
Our dinner done, and he not comming thither,
I went to seeke him. In the street I met him,
And in his companie that Gentleman.
    He points to the Marchant
There did this periur'd Goldsmith sweare me downe,
That I this day of him receiu'd the Chaine,
Which God he knowes, I saw not. For the which,
He did arrest me with an Officer.   1580
I did obey, and sent my Pesant home
For certaine Duckets: he with none return'd.
Then fairely I bespoke the Officer
To go in person with me to my house.
By'th'way, we met my wife, her sister, and a rabble
   more
Of vilde Confederates: Along with them
They brought one *Pinch*, a hungry leane-fac'd Villaine;
A meere Anatomie, a Mountebanke,
A thred-bare Iugler, and a Fortune-teller,
A needy-hollow-ey'd-sharpe-looking-wretch;   1590
A liuing dead man. This pernicious slaue,
Forsooth tooke on him as a Coniurer:
And gazing in mine eyes, feeling my pulse,
And with no-face (as 'twere) out-facing me,
Cries out, I was possest. Then altogether
They fell vpon me, bound me, bore me thence,
And in a darke and dankish vault at home
There left me and my man, both bound together,
Till gnawing with my teeth my bonds in sunder,
I gain'd my freedome; and immediately   1600
Ran hether to your Grace, whom I beseech
To giue me ample satisfaction
For these deepe shames, and great indignities.

GOLDSMITH

My Lord, in truth, thus far I witnes with him:
That he din'd not at home, but was lock'd out.

DUKE

But had he such a Chaine of thee, or no?

GOLDSMITH

He had my Lord, and when he ran in heere,
These people saw the Chaine about his necke.

MARCHANT (*to Antipholus*)

Besides, I will be sworne these eares of mine,
Heard you confesse you had the Chaine of him,   1610
After you first forswore it on the Mart,
And thereupon I drew my sword on you:
And then you fled into this Abbey heere,
From whence I thinke you are come by Miracle.

EPHESIAN ANTIPHOLUS

I neuer came within these Abbey wals,
Nor euer didst thou draw thy sword on me:
I neuer saw the Chaine, so helpe me heauen:
And this is false you burthen me withall.

DUKE

Why what an intricate impeach is this?
I thinke you all haue drunke of *Circes* cup: 1620

If heere you hous'd him, heere he would haue bin.
If he were mad, he would not pleade so coldly:
(*To Adriana*) You say he din'd at home, the Goldsmith
     heere
Denies that saying. (*To Dromio*) Sirra, what say you?

EPHESIAN DROMIO (*pointing at the Curtizan*)
Sir he din'de with her there, at the Porpentine.

CURTIZAN
He did, and from my finger snacht that Ring.

EPHESIAN ANTIPHOLUS
Tis true (my Liege) this Ring I had of her.

DUKE (*to Curtizan*)
Saw'st thou him enter at the Abbey heere?

CURTIZAN
As sure (my Liege) as I do see your Grace.

DUKE
1630   Why this is straunge: Go call the Abbesse hither.
I thinke you are all mated, or starke mad.
                                   Exit one to the Priorie

MERCHANT FATHER (*comming forward*)
Most mighty Duke, vouchsafe me speak a word:
Haply I see a friend will saue my life,
And pay the sum that may deliuer me.

DUKE
Speake freely *Siracusian* what thou wilt.

MERCHANT FATHER (*to Antipholus*)
Is not your name sir call'd *Antipholus*?
And is not that your bondman *Dromio*?

EPHESIAN DROMIO
Within this houre I was his bondman sir,
But he I thanke him gnaw'd in two my cords,
1640   Now am I *Dromio*, and his man, vnbound.

MERCHANT FATHER
I am sure you both of you remember me.

EPHESIAN DROMIO
Our selues we do remember sir by you:
For lately we were bound as you are now.
You are not *Pinches* patient, are you sir?

MERCHANT FATHER
Why looke you strange on me? you know me well.

EPHESIAN ANTIPHOLUS
I neuer saw you in my life till now.

MERCHANT FATHER
Oh! griefe hath chang'd me since you saw me last,
And carefull houres with times deformed hand,
Haue written strange defeatures in my face:
1650   But tell me yet, dost thou not know my voice?

EPHESIAN ANTIPHOLUS Neither.

MERCHANT FATHER *Dromio*, nor thou?

EPHESIAN DROMIO No trust me sir, nor I.

MERCHANT FATHER I am sure thou dost?

EPHESIAN DROMIO I sir, but I am sure I do not, and
whatsoeuer a man denies, you are now bound to
beleeue him.

MERCHANT FATHER
Not know my voice, oh times extremity
Hast thou so crack'd and splitted my poore tongue

In seuen short yeares, that heere my onely sonne   1660
Knowes not my feeble key of vntun'd cares?
Though now this grained face of mine be hid
In sap-consuming Winters drizled snow,
And all the Conduits of my blood froze vp:
Yet hath my night of life some memorie:
My wasting lampes some fading glimmer left;
My dull deafe eares a little vse to heare:
All these old witnesses, I cannot erre.
Tell me, thou art my sonne *Antipholus*.

EPHESIAN ANTIPHOLUS
I neuer saw my Father in my life.   1670

MERCHANT FATHER
But seuen yeares since, in *Siracusa* bay
Thou know'st we parted, but perhaps my sonne,
Thou sham'st to acknowledge me in miserie.

EPHESIAN ANTIPHOLUS
The Duke, and all that know me in the City,
Can witnesse with me that it is not so.
I ne're saw *Siracusa* in my life.

DUKE (*to Merchant Father*)
I tell thee *Siracusian*, twentie yeares
Haue I bin Patron to *Antipholus*,
During which time, he ne're saw *Siracusa*:
I see thy age and dangers make thee dote.   1680
     *Enter ⌈from the Priorie⌉ the Abbesse with
     Antipholus Siracusa, wearing the Chaine, and
     Dromio Sir.*

ABBESSE
Most mightie Duke, behold a man much wrong'd.
     All gather to see them

ADRIANA
I see two husbands, or mine eyes deceiue me.

DUKE
One of these men is *genius* to the other:
And so of these, which is the naturall man,
And which the spirit? Who deciphers them?

SIRACUSIAN DROMIO
I Sir am *Dromio*, command him away.

EPHESIAN DROMIO
I Sir am *Dromio*, pray let me stay.

SIRACUSIAN ANTIPHOLUS (*to Merchant Father*)
Egeon art thou not? or else his ghost.

SIRACUSIAN DROMIO
Oh my olde Master, who hath bound him heere?

ABBESSE
Who euer bound him, I will lose his bonds,   1690
And gaine a husband by his libertie:
Speake olde *Egeon*, if thou bee'st the man
That hadst a wife once call'd *Æmilia*,
That bore thee at a burthen two faire sonnes?
Oh if thou bee'st the same *Egeon*, speake:
And speake vnto the same *Æmilia*.

DUKE
Why heere begins his Morning storie right:
These two *Antipholus*, these two so like,
And these two *Dromio's*, one in semblance:

1700 Besides his vrging of her wracke at sea,
These are the parents to these children,
Which accidentally are met together.

MERCHANT FATHER
If I dreame not, thou art *Æmilia*,
If thou art she, tell me, where is that sonne
That floated with thee on the fatall rafte.

ABBESSE
By men of *Epidamnum*, he, and I,
And the twin *Dromio*, all were taken vp;
But by and by, rude Fishermen of *Corinth*
By force tooke *Dromio*, and my sonne from them,
1710 And me they left with those of *Epidamnum*.
What then became of them, I cannot tell:
I, to this fortune that you see mee in.

DUKE (*to Antipholus Siracusia*)
Antipholus thou cam'st from *Corinth* first.

SIRACUSIAN ANTIPHOLUS
No sir, not I, I came from *Siracuse*.

DUKE
Stay, stand apart, I know not which is which.

EPHESIAN ANTIPHOLUS
I came from *Corinth* my most gracious Lord.

EPHESIAN DROMIO And I with him.

EPHESIAN ANTIPHOLUS
Brought to this Town by that most famous Warriour,
Duke *Menaphon*, your most renowned Vnckle.

ADRIANA
1720 Which of you two did dine with me to day?

SIRACUSIAN ANTIPHOLUS I, gentle Mistris.

ADRIANA And are not you my husband?

EPHESIAN ANTIPHOLUS No, I say nay to that.

SIRACUSIAN ANTIPHOLUS
And so do I, yet did she call me so:
And this faire Gentlewoman her sister heere
Did call me brother. (*To Luciana*) What I told you then,
I hope I shall haue leisure to make good,
If this be not a dreame I see and heare.

GOLDSMITH
That is the Chaine sir, which you had of mee.

SIRACUSIAN ANTIPHOLUS
1730 I thinke it be sir, I denie it not.

EPHESIAN ANTIPHOLUS (*to Goldsmith*)
And you sir for this Chaine arrested me.

GOLDSMITH
I thinke I did sir, I deny it not.

ADRIANA (*to Ephesian Antipholus*)
I sent you monie sir to be your baile
By *Dromio*, but I thinke he brought it not.

EPHESIAN DROMIO No, none by me.

SIRACUSIAN ANTIPHOLUS (*to Adriana*)
This purse of Duckets I receiu'd from you,
And *Dromio* my man did bring them me:
I see we still did meete each others man,
And I was tane for him, and he for me,

And thereupon these errors are arose.   1740

EPHESIAN ANTIPHOLUS
These Duckets pawne I for my father heere.

DUKE
It shall not neede, thy father hath his life.

CURTIZAN
Sir I must haue that Diamond from you.

EPHESIAN ANTIPHOLUS
There take it, and much thanks for my good cheere.

ABBESSE
Renowned Duke, vouchsafe to take the paines
To go with vs into the Abbey heere,
And heare at large discoursed all our fortunes,
And all that are assembled in this place:
That by this simpathized one daies error
Haue suffer'd wrong. Goe, keepe vs companie,   1750
And we shall make full satisfaction.
Thirtie three yeares haue I but gone in trauaile
Of you my sonnes, and till this present houre
My heauie burthen nere deliuered:
The Duke my husband, and my children both,
And you the Kalenders of their Natiuity,
Go to a Gossips feast, and ioy with mee,
After so long greefe such Festiuitie.

DUKE
With all my heart, Ile Gossip at this feast.

              *Exeunt omnes ⌈to the Priorie⌉. Manet the two
                    Dromio's and two Brothers Antipholus*

SIRACUSIAN DROMIO (*to Ephesian Antipholus*)
Mast. shall I fetch your stuffe from shipbord?   1760

EPHESIAN ANTIPHOLUS
Dromio, what stuffe of mine hast thou imbarkt?

SIRACUSIAN DROMIO
Your goods that lay at host sir in the Centaur.

SIRACUSIAN ANTIPHOLUS
He speakes to me, I am your master *Dromio*.
Come go with vs, wee'l looke to that anon,
Embrace thy brother there, reioyce with him.

                    Exit the Brothers Antipholus

SIRACUSIAN DROMIO
There is a fat friend at your masters house,
That kitchin'd me for you to day at dinner:
She now shall be my sister, not my wife.

EPHESIAN DROMIO
Me thinks you are my glasse, & not my brother:
I see by you, I am a sweet-fac'd youth,   1770
Will you walke in to see their gossiping?

SIRACUSIAN DROMIO Not I sir, you are my elder.

EPHESIAN DROMIO That's a question, how shall we trie it.

SIRACUSIAN DROMIO Wee'l draw Cuts for the Signior, till
then, lead thou first.

EPHESIAN DROMIO Nay then thus:
We came into the world like brother and brother:
And now let's go hand in hand, not one before
     another.   *Exeunt ⌈to the Priorie⌉*

FINIS

313

LOUES LABORS LOST

THE 1598 edition of *Loues labors lost* is the first play text to carry Shakespeare's name on the title-page, which also refers to performance before the Queen 'this last Christmas'. The play is said to be 'Newly corrected and augmented', so perhaps an earlier edition has failed to survive. Even so, the text shows every sign of having been printed from Shakespeare's working papers, since it includes some passages in draft as well as in revised form. We print the drafts as Additional Passages. The play was probably written some years before publication, in 1593 or 1594.

The setting is Nauar—a kingdom straddling the border between Spain and France—where the young King and three of his friends vow to devote the following three years to austere self-improvement, forgoing the company of women. But they have forgotten the imminent arrival on a diplomatic mission of the Princesse of France with, as it happens, three of her ladies; much comedy derives from, first, the men's embarrassed attempts to conceal from one another that they are falling in love, and second, the girls' practical joke in exchanging identities when the men, disguised as Russians, come to entertain and to woo them. Shakespeare seems to have picked up the King's friends' names—Berowne, Dumaine, and Longauill—from leading figures in contemporary France, but to have invented the plot himself. He counterpoints the main action with events involving characters based in part on the type-figures of Italian commedia dell'arte who reflect facets of the lords' personalities. Costard, an unsophisticated, open-hearted yokel, and his girl-friend Iaquenetta are sexually uninhibited; Don Adriano de Armado, 'a refined trauailer of Spaine' who also, though covertly, loves Iaquenetta, is full of pompous affectation; and Holofernes, a schoolmaster (seen always with his admiring companion, the curate Sir Nathaniel), demonstrates the avid pedantry into which the young men's verbal brilliance could degenerate. Much of the play's language is highly sophisticated (this is, as the title-page claims, a 'Conceited Comedie'), in keeping with its subject matter. But the action reaches its climax when a messenger brings news which is communicated entirely without verbal statement. This is a theatrical masterstroke which also signals Shakespeare's most daring experiment with comic form. 'The scene begins to cloud'; in the play's closing minutes the lords and ladies seek to readjust themselves to the new situation, and the play ends in subdued fashion with a third entertainment, the songs of the owl and the cuckoo.

Loues labors lost was for long regarded as a play of excessive verbal sophistication, of interest mainly because of a series of supposed topical allusions; but a number of distinguished twentieth-century productions have revealed its theatrical mastery.

THE NAMES OF THE ACTORS

Ferdinand, KING of Nauar

BEROWNE
LONGAUILL } Lordes attending on the King
DUMAINE

Don Adriano de ARMADO, an affected Spanish Braggart
BOY (Moth), his page

PRINCESSE of France

ROSALINE
KATHERINE } Ladies attending on the Princesse
MARIA

BOYET
Two other LORDS } attending on the Princesse

CLOWNE (Costard)
IAQUENETTA, a countrey wench

Sir NATHANIEL, a Curate
PEDANT (Holofernes)
Anthony DULL, a Constable

MARCADE, a Messenger

A FORRESTER

Loues labors lost

Sc. 1
(1.1)

Enter Ferdinand K. of Nauar, Berowne, Longauill,
and Dumaine

KING

Let Fame, that all hunt after in their lyues,
Liue registred vpon our brazen Tombes,
And then grace vs, in the disgrace of death:
When spight of cormorant deuouring Time,
Thendeuour of this present breath may buy
That honour which shall bate his sythes keene edge,
And make vs heires of all eternitie.
Therefore braue Conquerours, for so you are,
That warre agaynst your owne affections,
And the hudge armie of the worldes desires,
Our late edict shall strongly stand in force,
Nauar shall be the wonder of the worlde.
Our Court shalbe a lytlle Achademe,
Still and contemplatyue in lyuing art.
You three, *Berowne, Dumaine,* and *Longauill,*
Haue sworne for three yeeres tearme, to liue with me:
My fellow Schollers, and to keepe those statutes
That are recorded in this sedule here.
Your othes are past, and now subscribe your names:
That his owne hand may strike his honour downe,
That violates the smallest branch herein.
If you are armd to do, as sworne to do,
Subscribe to your deepe othes, and keepe it to.

LONGAUILL

I am resolud, tis but a three yeeres fast:
The minde shall banquet, though the body pine,
Fat paunches haue leane pates: and daynty bits
Make rich the ribbes, but bancrout quite the wits.

He signes

DUMAINE

My louing Lord, *Dumaine* is mortefied,
The grosser manner of these worldes delyghts
He throwes vppon the grosse worlds baser slaues.
To loue, to wealth, to pompe, I pine and die,
With all these lyuing in Philosophie.

He signes

BEROWNE

I can but say their protestation ouer,
So much deare Liedge, I haue already sworne,
That is, to lyue and study heere three yeeres.
But there are other strickt obseruances:
As not to see a woman in that terme,
Which I hope well is not enrolled there.
And one day in a weeke to touch no foode:
And but one meale on euery day beside:
The which I hope is not enrolled there.
And then to sleepe but three houres in the nyght,
And not be seene to wincke of all the day,
When I was wont to thinke no harme all nyght,
And make a darke nyght too of halfe the day:

Which I hope well is not enrolled there.
O these are barraine taskes, too hard to keepe,
Not to see Ladyes, study, fast, not sleepe.

KING

Your othe is past, to passe away from these.

BEROWNE

Let me say no my liedge, and yf you please,
I onely swore to study with your grace,
And stay heere in your Court for three yeeres space.

LONGAUILL

You swore to that *Berowne,* and to the rest.

BEROWNE

By yea and nay sir, than I swore in iest.
What is the ende of study, let me know?

KING

Why that to know which else we should not know.

BEROWNE

Things hid & bard (you meane) from common sense.

KING

I, that is studies god-like recompence.

BEROWNE

Com'on then, I will sweare to study so,
To know the thing I am forbid to know:
As thus, to study where I well may dine,
   When I to feast expressely am forbid.
Or studie where to meete some Mistris fine,
   When Mistresses from common sense are hid.
Or hauing sworne too hard a keeping oth,
Studie to breake it, and not breake my troth.
If studies gaine be thus, and this be so,
Studie knowes that which yet it doth not know,
Sweare me to this, and I will nere say no.

KING

These be the stopps that hinder studie quit,
And traine our intelects to vaine delight.

BEROWNE

Why? all delightes are vaine, but that most vaine
Which with payne purchas'd, doth inherite payne,
As paynefully to poare vpon a Booke,
   To seeke the lyght of trueth, while trueth the whyle
Doth falsely blinde the eye-sight of his looke:
   Light seeking light, doth light of light beguyle:
So ere you finde where light in darknes lyes,
Your light growes darke by loosing of your eyes.
Studie me how to please the eye in deede,
   By fixing it vppon a fayrer eye,
Who dazling so, that eye shalbe his heed,
   And giue him light that it was blinded by.
Studie is lyke the heauens glorious Sunne,
   That will not be deepe searcht with sawcie lookes:
Small haue continuall plodders euer wonne,
   Saue base aucthoritie from others Bookes.

These earthly Godfathers of heauens lights,
  That giue a name to euery fixed Starre,
90 Haue no more profite of their shyning nights,
    Then those that walke and wot not what they are.
Too much to know, is to know nought but fame:
And euery Godfather can giue a name.

KING
How well hees read to reason against reading.

DUMAINE
Proceeded well, to stop all good proceeding.

LONGAUILL
He weedes the corne, & still lets grow the weeding.

BEROWNE
The Spring is neare when greene geese are a breeding.

DUMAINE
How followes that?

BEROWNE   Fit in his place and tyme.

DUMAINE
In reason nothing.

BEROWNE   Something then in rime.

KING
100 *Berowne* is like an enuious sneaping Frost,
    That bites the first borne infants of the Spring.

BEROWNE
Well, say I am, why should proude Sommer boast,
  Before the Birdes haue any cause to sing?
Why should I ioy in any abhortiue byrth?
At Christmas I no more desire a Rose,
Then wish a Snow in Mayes new fangled showes:
But like of each thing that in season growes.
So you to studie now it is too late,
Clymbe ore the house to vnlocke the little gate.

KING
110 Well, sit you out: go home *Berowne*: adue.

BEROWNE
No my good Lord, I haue sworne to stay with you.
And though I haue for barbarisme spoke more
  Then for that Angell knowledge you can say,
Yet confident Ile keepe what I haue sworne,
  And bide the pennance of each three yeeres day.
Giue me the paper, let me reade the same,
And to the strictst decrees Ile write my name.

KING (*giuing a paper*)
How well this yeelding rescewes thee from shame.

BEROWNE (*reades*) *Item*, That no woman shall come within
120 a myle of my Court. Hath this bin proclaymed?

LONGAUILL Foure dayes ago.

BEROWNE Lets see the penaltie. On payne of loosing her
tung. Who deuis'd this penaltie?

LONGAUILL Marrie that did I.

BEROWNE Sweete Lord and why?

LONGAUILL
To fright them hence with that dread penaltie.

BEROWNE
A dangerous law against gentiletie.
Item, Yf any man be seene to talke with a woman
within the tearme of three yeeres, he shall indure such

publique shame as the rest of the Court can possible 130
deuise.
This Article my liedge your selfe must breake,
  For well you know here comes in Embassie,
The French kinges daughter with your selfe to speake:
  A Maide of grace and complet maiestie,
About surrender vp of *Aquitaine*,
  To her decrepit, sicke, and bedred Father.
Therefore this Article is made in vaine,
  Or vainely comes th'admired Princesse hither.

KING
What say you Lordes? why, this was quite forgot. 140

BEROWNE
So Studie euermore is ouershot,
While it doth studie to haue what it would,
It doth forget to do the thing it should:
And when it hath the thing it hunteth most,
Tis won as townes with fire, so won so lost.

KING
We must of force dispence with this Decree,
Shee must lie heere on meere necessitie.

BEROWNE
Necessitie will make vs all forsworne
  Three thousand times within this three yeeres space:
For euery man with his affectes is borne, 150
  Not by might mastred, but by speciall grace.
If I breake fayth, this word shall speake for me,
I am forsworne on meere necessitie.
So to the Lawes at large I write my name,
  And he that breakes them in the least degree,
Standes in attainder of eternall shame.
    He signes
  Suggestions are to other as to me:
But I beleeue although I seeme so loth,
I am the last that will last keepe his oth.
But is there no quicke recreation graunted? 160

KING
I that there is, our Court you know is haunted
  With a refined trauailer of Spaine,
A man in all the worldes new fashion planted,
  That hath a mint of phrases in his braine:
On who the musique of his owne vaine tongue
  Doth rauish like inchaunting harmonie:
A man of complements whom right and wrong
  Haue chose as vmpier of their mutenie.
This childe of Fancie that *Armado* hight,
  For interim to our studies shall relate, 170
In high borne wordes the worth of many a Knight
  From tawnie Spaine lost in the worldes debate.
How you delight my Lords I know not I,
But I protest I loue to heare him lie,
And I will vse him for my Minstrelsie.

BEROWNE
Armado is a most illustrious wight,
A man of fier new wordes, Fashions owne knight.

LONGAUILL
Costard the swaine and he, shalbe our sport,
And so to studie three yeeres is but short.

Enter a Constable, Dull, with Costard the Clowne
with a letter

180 DULL Which is the Dukes owne person?

BEROWNE This fellow, What would'st?

DULL I my selfe reprehend his owne person, for I am his graces Farborough: But I would see his owne person in flesh and blood.

BEROWNE This is he.

DULL Signeour *Arme Arme* commendes you: Ther's villanie abrod, this letter will tell you more.

CLOWNE Sir the Contempts thereof are as touching me.

KING A letter from the magnifisent *Armado.*

190 BEROWNE How low so euer the matter, I hope in God for high words.

LONGAUILL A high hope for a low heauen. God grant vs patience.

BEROWNE To heare, or forbeare laughing.

LONGAUILL To heare meekely sir, and to laugh moderatly, or to forbeare both.

BEROWNE Well sir, be it as the stile shall giue vs cause to clime in the merrines.

CLOWNE The matter is to me sir, as concerning *Iaquenetta:*
200 The manner of it is, I was taken with the manner.

BEROWNE In what manner?

CLOWNE In manner and forme folowing sir all those three. I was seene with her in the Manner house, sitting with her vppon the Forme, and taken following her into the Parke: which put togeather, is in manner and forme following. Now sir for the manner, It is the manner of a man to speake to a woman, for the forme in some forme.

BEROWNE For the following sir.

210 CLOWNE As it shall follow in my correction, and God defend the right.

KING Will you heare this Letter with attention?

BEROWNE As we would heare an Oracle.

CLOWNE Such is the simplicitie of man to harken after the flesh.

KING (*reades*) *Great Deputie the welkīs Vizgerent, and sole dominatur of* Nauar, *my soules earthes God, and bodies fostring patrone:*

CLOWNE Not a worde of *Costard* yet.

220 KING *So it is*

CLOWNE It may be so: but if he say it is so, he is in telling true: but so.

KING Peace.

CLOWNE Be to me, and euerie man that dares not fight.

KING No wordes.

CLOWNE Of other mens secrets I beseech you.

KING *So it is besedged with sable coloured melancholie, I did commende the blacke oppressing humour to the most holsome phisicke of thy health-geuing ayre: And as I am*
230 *a Gentleman, betooke my selfe to walke: the time When? about the sixt houre, When Beastes most grase, Birdes best peck, and Men sit downe to that nourishment which is called Supper: So much for the time When. Now for the ground Which? which I meane I walkt vpon, it is ycliped Thy Park. Then for the place Where? where I meane, I did incounter that obseene & most propostrous euent that*

draweth frō my snowhite pen the ebon coloured Incke, which here thou viewest, beholdest, suruayest, or seest. But to the place Where? It standeth North North-east & by East from the West corner of thy curious knotted 240 *garden; There did I see that low spirited Swaine, that base Minow of thy myrth,*

(CLOWNE Mee?)

KING *That vnlettered smal knowing soule,*

(CLOWNE Mee?)

KING *That shallow vassall*

(CLOWNE Still mee?)

KING *Which as I remember, hight* Costard,

(CLOWNE O mee)

KING *Sorted and consorted contrary to thy established* 250 *proclaymed Edict and continent Cannon: with with, ô with, but with this I passion to say wherewith:*

CLOWNE With a Wench.

KING *With a childe of our Grandmother* Eue, *a female; or for thy more sweete vnderstanding a Woman: him, I (as my euer esteemed duetie prickes me on) haue sent to thee, to receiue the meede of punishment by thy sweete Graces Officer* Anthonie Dull, *a man of good reput, carriage bearing, and estimation.*

DULL Me ant shall please you? I am *Anthony Dull.* 260

KING *For* Iaquenetta *(so is the weaker vessell called) which I apprehended with the aforesayd Swaine, I keepe hir as a vessell of thy Lawes furie, and shall at the least of thy sweete notice, bring hir to tryall. Thine in all complements of deuoted and hartburning heate of duetie.*

Don Adriano de Armado.

BEROWNE This is not so well as I looked for, but the best that euer I heard.

KING I the best, for the worst. (*To Costard*) But sirra, What say you to this? 270

CLOWNE Sir I confesse the Wench.

KING Did you heare the Proclamation?

CLOWNE I do confesse much of the hearing it, but little of the marking of it.

KING It was proclaymed a yeeres imprisonment to be taken with a Wench.

CLOWNE I was taken with none sir, I was taken with a Demsel.

KING Well, it was proclaimed Damsel.

CLOWNE This was no Damsel neither sir, she was a Virgin. 280

⌈KING⌉ It is so varried to, for it was proclaimed Virgin.

CLOWNE If it were, I denie her Virginitie: I was taken with a Maide.

KING This Maide will not serue your turne sir.

CLOWNE This Maide will serue my turne sir.

KING Sir I will pronounce your sentence: You shall fast a weeke with Branne and Water.

CLOWNE I had rather pray a month with Mutton & Porridge.

KING

And *Don Armado* shall be your keeper. 290

My Lord *Berowne,* see him deliured ore,

And goe we Lordes to put in practise that,

Which each to other hath so strongly sworne.

Exeunt the King, Longauill and Dumaine

BEROWNE

    Ile lay my Head to any good mans Hat,

      These othes and lawes will proue an idle scorne.

    Surra, Come on.

CLOWNE I suffer for the trueth sir: for true it is, I was
taken with *Iaquenetta*, and *Iaquenetta* is a trew girle,
and therefore welcome the sower Cup of prosperitie,
300   afflicciõ may one day smile againe, and till then sit
thee downe sorrow.   *Exeunt*

Sc. 2   *Enter Armado and Moth his page*

(1.2) ARMADO Boy, What signe is it when a man of great spirite
growes melancholy?

BOY A great signe sir that he will looke sadd.

ARMADO Why? sadnes is one & the selfe same thing deare
imp.

BOY No no, O Lord sir no.

ARMADO How canst thou part sadnes and melancholy,
my tender Iuuenall?

310 BOY By a familier demonstration of the working, my
tough signeor.

ARMADO Why tough signeor? Why tough signeor?

BOY Why tender iuuenall? Why tender iuuenall?

ARMADO I spoke it tender iuuenal, as a congruent
apethaton apperteining to thy young dayes, which we
may nominate tender.

BOY And I tough signeor, as an appertinent title to your
olde time, which we may name tough.

ARMADO Prettie and apt.

320 BOY How meane you sir, I prettie, and my saying apt?
or I apt, and my saying prettie?

ARMADO Thou prettie because little.

BOY Little prettie, because little: wherefore apt.

ARMADO And therfore apt, because quicke.

BOY Speake you this in my praise Maister?

ARMADO In thy condigne praise.

BOY I will praise an Eele with the same praise.

ARMADO What? that an Eele is ingenious.

BOY That an Eele is quicke.

330 ARMADO I do say thou art quicke in answeres. Thou
heatst my blood.

BOY I am answerd sir.

ARMADO I loue not to be crost.

BOY (*aside*) He speakes the meer contrarie, crosses loue
not him.

ARMADO I haue promised to studie three yeeres with the
duke.

BOY You may do it in an houre sir.

ARMADO Impossible.

340 BOY How many is one thrice tolde?

ARMADO I am ill at reckning, it fitteth the spirit of a
Tapster.

BOY You are a Gentleman and a Gamster sir.

ARMADO I confesse both, they are both the varnish of a
compleat man.

BOY Then I am sure you know how much the grosse
summe of deus-ace amountes to.

ARMADO It doth amount to one more then two.

BOY Which the base vulgar do call three.

ARMADO True.   350

BOY Why sir is this such a peece of studie? Now heere is
three studied ere yele thrice wincke: and how easie it
is to put yeeres to the worde three, and studie three
yeeres in two wordes, the dauncing Horse will tell you.

ARMADO A most fine Figure.

BOY ⌈*aside*⌉ To proue you a Cypher.

ARMADO I will hereupon confesse I am in loue: and as it
is base for a Souldier to loue; so am I in loue with a
base wench. If drawing my Sword against the humor
of affection, would deliuer me from the reprobate   360
thought of it, I would take Desire prisoner, and ransome
him to anie French Courtier for a new deuisde cursie.
I thinke scorne to sigh, mee thinks I should outsweare
Cupid. Comfort mee Boy, What great men haue bin in
loue?

BOY *Hercules* Maister.

ARMADO Most sweete *Hercules*: more authoritie deare Boy,
name more; and sweete my childe let them be men of
good repute and carriage.

BOY *Sampson* Maister, he was a man of good carriage,   370
great carriage: for he carried the Towne-gates on his
backe like a Porter: and he was in loue.

ARMADO O wel knit *Sampson*, strong ioynted *Sampson*; I
do excel thee in my rapier, as much as thou didst me
in carying gates. I am in loue too. Who was *Sampsons*
loue my deare Moth?

BOY A Woman, Maister.

ARMADO Of what complexion?

BOY Of all the foure, or the three, or the two, or one of
the foure.   380

ARMADO Tell me precisely of what complexion?

BOY Of the sea-water Greene sir.

ARMADO Is that one of the foure complexions?

BOY As I haue read sir, and the best of them too.

ARMADO Greene in deede is the colour of Louers: but to
haue a loue of that colour, mee thinkes *Sampson* had
small reason for it. He surely affected her for her wit.

BOY It was so sir, for she had a greene wit.

ARMADO My loue is most immaculate white and red.

BOY Most maculate thoughts Maister, are maskt vnder   390
such colours.

ARMADO Define, define, well educated infant.

BOY My fathers wit, and my mothers tongue assist me.

ARMADO Sweet inuocation of a child, most pretty &
pathetical.

BOY   Yf she be made of white and red,

        Her faultes will nere be knowne:

      For blushing cheekes by faultes are bred,

        And feares by pale white showne:

      Then if she feare or be to blame,   400

        By this you shall not know,

      For still her cheekes possesse the same,

        Which natiue she doth owe.

A dangerous rime maister against the reason of white
& red.

ARMADO Is there not a Ballet Boy, of the King & the
Begger?

BOY The worlde was very guiltie of such a Ballet some

three ages since, but I thinke now tis not to be found:
410 or if it were, it would neither serue for the writing, nor
the tune.

ARMADO I will haue that subiect newly writ ore, that I
may example my digression by some mightie presedent.
Boy, I do loue, that Countrey girle that I tooke in the
Parke with the rational hinde *Costard*: she deserues
well.

BOY (*aside*) To be whipt: and yet a better loue then my
maister.

ARMADO Sing Boy, My spirit growes heauie in loue.

420 BOY And thats great maruaile, louing a light Wench.

ARMADO I say sing.

BOY Forbeare till this companie be past.

*Enter Costard the Clowne, Constable Dull, and
Iaquenetta a Wench*

DULL (*to Armado*) Sir, the Dukes pleasure is that you keepe
Costard safe, and you must suffer him to take no delight,
nor no penance, but a' must fast three dayes a weeke:
for this Damsell I must keepe her at the Parke, she is
alowde for the Day woman. Fare you well.

ARMADO ⌈*aside*⌉ I do betray my selfe with blushing: Maide.

IAQUENETTA Man.

430 ARMADO I will visit thee at the Lodge.

IAQUENETTA Thats hereby.

ARMADO I know where it is situate.

IAQUENETTA Lord how wise you are.

ARMADO I will tell thee wonders.

IAQUENETTA With that face.

ARMADO I loue thee.

IAQUENETTA So I heard you say.

ARMADO And so farewell.

IAQUENETTA Faire weather after you.

440 ⌈DULL⌉ Come *Iaquenetta*, away.

⌈*Exeunt Dull and Iaquenetta*⌉

ARMADO Villaine, thou shalt fast for thy offences ere thou
be pardoned.

CLOWNE Well sir I hope when I do it, I shall do it on a
full stomacke.

ARMADO Thou shalt be heauely punished.

CLOWNE I am more bound to you then your fellowes, for
they are but lightly rewarded.

ARMADO Take away this villaine, shut him vp.

BOY Come you transgressing slaue, away.

450 CLOWNE Let me not be pent vp sir, I will fast being loose.

BOY No sir, that were fast and loose: thou shalt to prison.

CLOWNE Well, if euer I do see the merry dayes of desolation
that I haue seene, some shall see.

BOY What shall some see?

CLOWNE Nay nothing M. *Moth*, but what they looke
vppon. It is not for prisoners to be too silent in their
wordes, and therfore I will say nothing: I thanke God
I haue as litle patience as an other man, & therfore I
can be quiet.   *Exeunt Moth and Costard*

460 ARMADO I do affect the verie ground (which is base) where
her shoo (which is baser) guided by her foote (which
is basest) doth tread. I shall be forsworne (which is a
great argument of falsehood) if I loue. And how can

that be true loue, which is falsely attempted? Loue is
a familiar; Loue is a Diuell. There is no euill angel but
Loue, yet was *Sampson* so tempted, and he had an
excellent strength: Yet was *Salomon* so seduced, and
he had a very good wit. *Cupids* Butshaft is too hard for
Hercules Clubb, and therefore too much oddes for a
Spaniards Rapier: The first and second cause will not   470
serue my turne: the *Passado* he respects not, the *Duella*
he regards not; his disgrace is to be called Boy, but his
glorie is to subdue men. Adue Valoure, rust Rapier, be
still Drum, for your manager is in loue; yea he loueth.
Assist me some extemporall God of Rime, for I am sure
I shall turne Sonnet. Deuise Wit, write Pen, for I am
for whole volumes in folio.   *Exit*

Enter the Princesse of Fraunce, with three attending   Sc. 3
Ladies (*Maria, Katherine, and Rosaline*) *and three*   (2.1)
Lordes (*one named Boyet*)

BOYET
Now Maddame summon vp your dearest spirrits,
Cõsider who the King your father sendes:
To whom he sendes, and whats his Embassie.   480
Your selfe, helde precious in the worldes esteeme,
To parlee with the sole inheritoure
Of all perfections that a man may owe,
Matchles *Nauar*, the plea of no lesse weight,
Then *Aquitaine* a Dowrie for a Queene.
Be now as prodigall of all Deare grace,
As Nature was in making Graces deare,
When she did starue the generall world beside,
And prodigally gaue them all to you.
PRINCESSE
Good L. *Boyet*, my beautie though but meane,   490
Needes not the painted florish of your prayse:
Beautie is bought by iudgement of the eye,
Not vttred by base sale of chapmens tongues:
I am lesse proude to heare you tell my worth,
Then you much willing to be counted wise,
In spending your Wit in the prayse of mine.
But now to taske the tasker, good *Boyet*,
You are not ignorant all telling fame
Doth noyse abroad *Nauar* hath made a Vow,
Till painefull studie shall outweare three yeeres,   500
No Woman may approch his silent Court:
Therefore to's seemeth it a needfull course,
Before we enter his forbidden gates,
To know his pleasure, and in that behalfe
Bold of your worthines, we single you,
As our best mouing faire soliciter:
Tell him, the Daughter of the King of France
On serious busines crauing quicke dispatch,
Importunes personall conference with his grace.
Haste, signifie so much while we attende,   510
Like humble visagd Suters his high will.
BOYET
Proud of imployment, willingly I go.
PRINCESS
All pride is willing pride, and yours is so: *Exit Boyet*

Who are the Votaries my louing Lordes,
That are vowfellowes with this vertuous Duke?

A LORD
L. *Longauill* is one.

PRINCESSE   Know you the man?

MARIA
I know him Maddame: at a marriage feast,
Betweene L. *Perigort* and the bewtious heire
Of *Iaques Fauconbridge* solemnized
In *Normandie* saw I this *Longauill*,
A man of soueraigne partes he is esteemd:
Well fitted in artes, glorious in armes:
Nothing becoms him ill that he would well.
The onely soyle of his fayre vertues glose,
If vertues glose will staine with any soyle,
Is a sharpe Wit matcht with too blunt a Will:
Whose edge hath power to cut, whose will still wils
It should none spare, that come within his power.

PRINCESSE
Some merrie mocking Lord belike, ist so?

MARIA
They say so most, that most his humors know.

PRINCESSE
Such short liued wits do wither as they grow.
Who are the rest?

KATHERINE
The young *Dumaine*, a well accomplist youth,
Of all that Vertue loue, for Vertue loued.
Most power to do most harme, least knowing ill:
For he hath wit to make an ill shape good,
And shape to win grace though he had no wit.
I saw him at the Duke *Alansões* once,
And much too little of that good I saw,
Is my report to his great worthines.

ROSALINE
An other of these Studentes at that time,
Was there with him, if I haue heard a trueth.
Berowne they call him, but a merrier man,
Within the limit of becomming mirth,
I neuer spent an houres talke withall.
His eye begets occasion for his wit,
For euery obiect that the one doth catch,
The other turnes to a mirth-moouing iest,
Which his fayre tongue (conceites expositer)
Deliuers in such apt and gracious wordes,
That aged eares play treuant at his tales,
And younger hearinges are quite rauished.
So sweete and voluble is his discourse.

PRINCESSE
God blesse my Ladyes, are they all in loue?
That euery one her owne hath garnished,
With such bedecking ornaments of praise.

A LORD
Heere comes *Boyet.*

    Enter Boyet

PRINCESSE   Now, What admittance Lord?

BOYET
Nauar had notice of your faire approch,
And he and his compettitours in oth,

Were all addrest to meete you gentle Lady
Before I came: Marrie thus much I haue learnt,
He rather meanes to lodge you in the feelde,
Like one that comes heere to besiedge his Court,
Then seeke a dispensation for his oth:
To let you enter his vnpeepled house.

    Enter Nauar, Longauill, Dumaine, & Berowne
Heere comes *Nauar.*

KING Faire Princesse, Welcome to the court of *Nauar.*

PRINCESSE Faire I giue you backe againe, and welcome I
haue not yet: the roofe of this Court is too high to be
yours, and welcome to the wide fieldes too base to be
mine.

KING
You shalbe welcome Madame to my Court.

PRINCESSE
I wilbe welcome then, Conduct me thither.

KING
Heare me deare Lady, I haue sworne an oth,

PRINCESSE
Our Lady helpe my Lord, he'le be forsworne.

KING
Not for the worlde faire Madame, by my will.

PRINCESSE
Why, will shall breake it, will, and nothing els.

KING
Your Ladishyp is ignoraunt what it is.

PRINCESSE
Were my Lord so, his ignoraunce were wise,
Where now his knowledge must proue ignorance.
I heare your grace hath sworne out Houskeeping:
Tis deadlie sinne to keepe that oath my Lord,
And sin to breake it:
But pardon me, I am too sodaine bold,
To teach a teacher ill beseemeth mee.
Vouchsafe to read the purpose of my comming,
And sodainelie resolue mee in my suite.

    She giues him a paper

KING
Madame I will, if sodainelie I may.

PRINCESSE
You will the sooner that I were awaie,
For youle proue periurde if you make me staie.

    Nauar reades the paper

BEROWNE (*to Rosaline*)
Did not I dance with you in *Brabant* once?

⌈ROSALINE⌉
Did not I dance with you in *Brabant* once?

BEROWNE
I know you did.

⌈ROSALINE⌉   How needles was it then
To aske the question?

BEROWNE   You must not be so quicke.

⌈ROSALINE⌉
Tis long of you that spur me with such questions.

BEROWNE
Your wit's too hot, it speedes too fast, twill tire.

⌈ROSALINE⌉
Not till it leaue the rider in the mire.

BEROWNE

What time a day?

⌈ROSALINE⌉

The houre that fooles should aske.

BEROWNE

600　Now faire befall your maske.

⌈ROSALINE⌉

Faire fall the face it couers.

BEROWNE

And send you manie louers.

⌈ROSALINE⌉

Amen, so you be none.

BEROWNE

Nay then will I be gon.

KING (to the Princesse)

Madame, your father heere doth intimate,

The payment of a hundred thousand Crownes,

Being but the one halfe of an intire summe,

Disbursed by my father in his warres.

But say that he, or we, as neither haue

610　Receiud that summe, yet there remaines vnpaide

A hundred thousand more, in suretie of the which,

One part of *Aquitaine* is bound to vs,

Although not valued to the monies worth.

If then the King your father will restore,

But that one halfe which is vnsatisfied,

We will giue vp our right in *Aquitaine*,

And holde faire friendship with his Maiestie,

But that it seemes he little purposeth:

For here he doth demaund to haue repaide,

620　A hundred thousand Crownes, and not demaunds

One paiment of a hundred thousand Crownes,

To haue his title liue in *Aquitaine*.

Which we much rather had depart withall,

And haue the money by our father lent,

Then *Aquitaine*, so guelded as it is.

Deare Princesse were not his requestes so farr

From reasons yeelding, your faire selfe should make

A yeelding gainst some reason in my brest,

And go well satisfied to France againe.

PRINCESSE

630　You do the King my father too much wrong,

And wrong the reputation of your name,

In so vnseeming to confesse receit,

Of that which hath so faithfully been paide.

KING

I do protest I neuer heard of it:

And if you proue it, Ile repay it backe,

Or yeelde vp *Aquitaine*.

PRINCESSE　　　　　　We arrest your worde.

Boyet you can produce acquittances,

For such a summe from speciall officers,

Of *Charles* his father.

KING　　　　　　Satisfie mee so.

BOYET

640　So please your Grace, the packet is not come,

Where that and other specialties are bound:

To morrow you shall haue a sight of them.

KING

It shall suffise me; at which enteruiew,

All liberall reason I will yeelde vnto.

Meane time receiue such welcome at my hand,

As honor (without breach of honor) may

Make tender of to thy true worthines.

You may not come (faire Princesse) within my gates,

But here without you shalbe so receiude,

As you shall deeme your selfe lodgd in my hart　　650

Though so denide faire harbour in my house,

Your owne good thoughtes excuse me, and farewell.

To morow shall we visite you againe.

PRINCESSE

Sweete health and faire desires consort your grace.

KING

Thy owne wish wish I thee in euery place.

　　　　　　　Exit with Longauill and Dumaine

BEROWNE (to Rosaline) Ladie I will commend you to my

　none hart.

ROSALINE Pray you, do my commendations, I would be

　glad to see it.

BEROWNE I would you heard it grone.　　660

ROSALINE Is the foole sicke.

BEROWNE Sicke at the hart.

ROSALINE

Alacke, let it blood.

BEROWNE

Would that do it good?

ROSALINE

My Phisicke saies I.

BEROWNE

Will you prickt with your eye.

ROSALINE

No poynt, with my knife.

BEROWNE

Now God saue thy life.

ROSALINE

And yours from long liuing.

BEROWNE

I cannot stay thankes-giuing.　　　　　*Exit*　670

　　　　　Enter Dumaine

DUMAINE (to Boyet)

Sir, I pray you a word, What Ladie is that same?

BOYET

The heire of *Alanson*, *Katherin* her name.

DUMAINE

A gallant Lady *Mounsir*, fare you wel.　　　*Exit*

　　　　　Enter Longauill

LONGAUILL (to Boyet)

I beseech you a word, What is she in the white?

BOYET

A woman sometimes, and you saw her in the light.

LONGAUILL

Perchance light in the light. I desire her name?

BOYET

She hath but one for her selfe, to desire that were a

　shame.

LONGAUILL

Pray you sir, Whose daughter?

BOYET

Her mothers, I haue heard.

LONGAUILL

680   Gods blessing on your beard.

BOYET

Good sir be not offended,

She is an heire of *Falconbridge*.

LONGAUILL

Nay my coller is ended.

She is a most sweet Ladie.

BOYET

Not vnlike sir, that may be.   *Exit Longauil*

     Enter Berowne

BEROWNE

Whats her name in the capp?

BOYET

Rosalin by good happ.

BEROWNE

Is she wedded or no?

BOYET

To her will sir, or so.

BEROWNE

690   O you are welcome sir, adew.

BOYET

Farewell to me sir, and welcome to you.

         Exit Berowne

MARIA

That last is *Berowne*, the merrie madcap L.

Not a word with him but a iest.

BOYET   And euery iest but a word.

PRINCESSE

It was well done of you to take him at his word.

BOYET

I was as willing to grapple as he was to boord.

⌈KATHERINE⌉

Two hot Sheepes marie.

BOYET   And wherefore not Shipps?

No Sheepe (sweete Lambe) vnlesse we feede on your

     lippes.

⌈KATHERINE⌉

You Sheepe and I pasture: shall that finish the iest?

BOYET

So you graunt pasture for me.

⌈KATHERINE⌉   Not so gentle Beast.

700   My lippes are no Common, though seuerall they be.

BOYET

Belonging to whom?

⌈KATHERINE⌉   To my fortunes and mee.

PRINCESSE

Good witts will be iangling, but gentles agree,

This ciuill warre of wittes were much better vsed

On *Nauar* and his Bookmen, for heere tis abused.

BOYET

If my obseruation (which very seldome lyes)

By the hartes still rethoricke, disclosed with eyes

Deceaue me not now, *Nauar* is infected.

PRINCESSE With what?

BOYET

With that which we Louers intitle Affected.

PRINCESSE Your reason.   710

BOYET

Why all his behauiours did make their retire,

To the court of his eye, peeping thorough desier.

His hart like an Agot with your print impressed,

Proud with his forme, in his eye pride expressed.

His tongue all impacient to speake and not see,

Did stumble with haste in his ey-sight to bee,

All sences to that sence did make their repaire,

To feele only looking on fairest of faire:

Mee thought all his senses were lokt in his eye,

As Iewels in Christall for some Prince to buy.   720

Who tendring their owne worth from where they

     were glast,

Did poynt you to buy them along as you past.

His faces owne margent did coate such amazes,

That all eyes saw his eyes inchaunted with gazes.

Ile giue you *Aquitaine*, and all that is his,

And you giue him for my sake but one louing kisse.

PRINCESSE

Come, to our Pauilion, *Boyet* is disposde.

BOYET

But to speak that in words, which his eie hath disclosd.

I onelie haue made a mouth of his eie,

By adding a tongue which I know will not lie.   730

⌈ROSALINE⌉

Thou art an old Loue-monger, & speakst skilfully.

⌈MARIA⌉

He is *Cupids* Graundfather, and learnes newes of him.

⌈KATHERINE⌉

Then was *Venus* like her mother, for her father is but

     grim.

BOYET

Do you heare my mad Wenches?

⌈MARIA⌉   No.

BOYET   What then, do you see?

⌈KATHERINE⌉

I, our way to be gone.

BOYET   You are too hard for mee.

         Exeunt omnes

     Enter Armado the Braggart and Moth his Boy   **Sc. 4**

ARMADO Warble child, make passionate my sense of   **(3.1)**

hearing.

BOY (*sings*) Concolinel.

ARMADO Sweete Ayer, go tendernes of yeeres, take this

Key, giue enlargement to the Swaine, bring him   740

festinatly hither, I must imploy him in a letter to my

loue.

BOY Maister, will you win your loue with a french braule?

ARMADO How meanest thou? brawling in French.

BOY No my complet Maister, but to Iigge off a tune at

the tongues ende, canarie to it with your feete, humour

it with turning vp your eylids, sigh a note and sing a

note somtime through the throate, as if you swallowed

loue with singing loue, sometime through the nose as

if you snufft vp loue by smelling loue with your hat   750

penthouse like ore the shop of your eyes, with your

armes crost on your thinbellie doblet like a Rabbet on

a spit, or your handes in your pocket like a man after the olde painting, and keepe not too long in one tune, but a snip and away: these are complementes, these are humours, these betraie nice wenches that would be betraied without these, and make them men of note: do you note? men, that most are affected to these.

ARMADO How hast thou purchased this experience?

760 BOY By my pennie of obseruation.

ARMADO But o but o.

BOY The Hobbie-horse is forgot.

ARMADO Calst thou my loue Hobbi-horse.

BOY No Maister, the Hobbi-horse is but a colt, and your loue perhaps, a hacknie: But haue you forgot your Loue?

ARMADO Almost I had.

BOY Necligent student, learne her by hart.

ARMADO By hart, and in hart boy.

770 BOY And out of hart Maister: all those three I will proue.

ARMADO What wilt thou proue?

BOY A man, if I liue (and this) by, in, and without, vpon the instant: by hart you loue her, because your hart cannot come by her: in hart you loue her, because your hart is in loue with her: and out of hart you loue her, being out of hart that you cannot enioy her.

ARMADO I am all these three.

BOY (aside) And three times as much more, and yet nothing at all.

780 ARMADO Fetch hither the Swaine, he must carrie me a letter.

BOY (aside) A message well simpathisd, a Horse to be embassadoure for an Asse.

ARMADO Ha ha, What saiest thou?

BOY Marrie sir, you must send the Asse vpon the Horse, for he is verie slow gated: but I go.

ARMADO The way is but short, away.

BOY As swift as Lead sir.

ARMADO The meaning prettie ingenius,
790   Is not Lead a mettal heauie, dull, and slow?

BOY
   Minnime honest Maister, or rather Maister no.

ARMADO
   I say Lead is slow.

BOY   You are too swift sir to say so.
   Is that Lead slow which is fierd from a Gunne?

ARMADO Sweete smoke of Rhetorike,
   He reputes me a Cannon, and the Bullet thats hee:
   I shoote thee at the Swaine.

BOY   Thump then, and I flee.
                                                 Exit

ARMADO
   A most acute Iuuenall, volable and free of grace,
   By thy fauour sweete Welkin, I must sigh in thy face:
   Most rude melancholie, Valour giues thee place.
800 My Herald is returnd.
          Enter Moth the Page and Costard the Clowne

BOY
   A wonder Maister, Heers a Costard broken in a shin.

ARMADO
   Some enigma, some riddle, come, thy Lenuoy begin.

CLOWNE No egma, no riddle, no lenuoy, no salue in the male sir. O sir, Plantan, a plaine Plantan: no lenuoy, no lenuoy, no Salue sir, but a Plantan.

ARMADO By vertue thou inforcest laughter, thy sillie thought, my spleene, the heauing of my lunges prouokes me to rediculous smyling: O pardone me my starres, doth the inconsiderate take salue for lenuoy, and the word lenuoy for a salue?   810

BOY
   Do the wise thinke them other, is not lenuoy a salue?

ARMADO
   No Page, it is an epilogue or discourse to make plaine,
   Some obscure presedence that hath tofore bin saine.
   I will example it.
          The Fox, the Ape, and the Humble-Bee,
          Were still at oddes being but three.
   Ther's the morrall: Now the lenuoy.

BOY I will adde the lenuoy, say the morrall againe.

ARMADO The Foxe, the Ape, and the Humble-Bee,
          Were still at oddes, being but three.   820

BOY   Vntill the Goose came out of doore,
          And staied the oddes by adding foure.
   Now will I begin your morrall, and do you follow with my lenuoy.
          The Foxe, the Ape, and the Humble-Bee,
          Were still at oddes, being but three.

ARMADO Vntill the Goose came out of doore,
          Staying the oddes by adding foure.

BOY A good Lenuoy, ending in the Goose: woulde you desire more?   830

CLOWNE
   The Boy hath sold him a bargaine, a Goose, that's flat.
   Sir, your penny-worth is good, and your Goose be fat.
   To sell a bargaine well is as cunning as fast and loose:
   Let me see a fat Lenuoy, I thats a fat Goose.

ARMADO
   Come hither, come hither: How did this argument begin?

BOY
   By saying that a Costard was broken in a shin.
   Then cald you for the Lenuoy.

CLOWNE True, and I for a Plantan, thus came your argument in, then the boyes fat Lenuoy, the Goose that you bought, and he ended the market.   840

ARMADO But tel me, How was there a Costard broken in a shin?

BOY I will tell you sencibly.

CLOWNE Thou hast no feeling of it Moth, I will speake that Lenuoy.
   I Costard running out, that was safely within,
   Fell ouer the threshold, and broke my shin.

ARMADO We will talke no more of this matter.

CLOWNE Till there be more matter in the shin.

ARMADO Sirra Costard, I will infranchise thee.   850

CLOWNE O marrie me to one Francis, I smell some Lenuoy, some Goose in this.

ARMADO By my sweete soule, I meane, setting thee at

libertie. Enfreedoming thy person: thou wert emured,
restrained, captiuated, bound.

CLOWNE True, true, and now you wilbe my purgation,
and let me loose.

ARMADO I giue thee thy libertie, set thee from durance,
and in lewe thereof, impose on thee nothing but this:
860 Beare this significant to the countrey Maide *Iaquenetta*:
(*giuing him a letter*) there is remuneration, (*giuing him
money*) for the best ward of mine honour, is rewarding
my dependants. *Moth*, follow.   *Exit*

BOY

Like the sequell I. Signeur *Costard* adew.   *Exit*

CLOWNE

My sweete oūce of mans flesh, my in-conie Iew:
Now will I looke to his remuneration. Remuneration,
O that's the latine word for three-farthings: Three-
farthings remuneration, What's the price of this yncle?
870 i.d. no, Ile giue you a remuneration: Why? it carries
it remuneration: Why? it is a fayrer name then French-
Crowne. I will neuer buy and sell out of this word.

        Enter Berowne

BEROWNE My good knaue *Costard*, exceedingly well met.

CLOWNE Pray you sir, How much Carnation Ribbon may
a man buy for a remuneration?

BEROWNE What is a remuneration?

CLOWNE Marie sir, halfepennie farthing.

BEROWNE Why then threefarthing worth of Silke.

CLOWNE I thanke your worship, God be wy you.

BEROWNE Stay slaue, I must employ thee.
880 As thou wilt win my fauour, good my knaue,
Do one thing for me that I shall intreate.

CLOWNE When would you haue it done sir?

BEROWNE This after-noone.

CLOWNE Well, I will do it sir: Fare you well.

BEROWNE Thou knowest not what it is.

CLOWNE I shall know sir when I haue done it.

BEROWNE Why villaine, thou must know first.

CLOWNE I will come to your worship to morrow morning.

BEROWNE

It must be done this after noone, harke slaue,
890 It is but this:
The Princesse comes to hunt here in the Parke,
And in her traine there is a gentle Ladie:
When tongues speake sweetely, then they name her
     name,
And *Rosaline* they call her, aske for her:
And to her white hand see thou do commend
This seald-vp counsaile. Ther's thy guerdon: (*giuing
him a letter and money*) goe.

CLOWNE Gardon, O sweete gardon, better then
remuneratiõ, a leuenpence-farthing better: most sweete
gardon. I will do it sir in print: gardon remuneration.
              Exit

BEROWNE
900 And I forsoth in loue, I that haue been loues whip?
A verie Bedell to a humerous sigh,
A Critick, nay a night-watch Constable,
A domineering pedant ore the Boy,

Then whom no mortall so magnificent.
This wimpled whyning purblind wayward Boy,
This signior *Iunior* gyant dwarffe, dan *Cupid*,
Regent of Loue-rimes, Lord of folded armes,
Th'annoynted soueraigne of sighes and groones:
Liedge of all loyterers and malecontents:
Dread Prince of Placcats, King of Codpeeces.   910
Sole Emperator and great generall
Of trotting Parrators (O my litle hart.)
And I to be a Corporall of his fielde,
And weare his coloures like a Tumblers hoope.
What? I loue, I sue, I seeke a wife,
A woman that is like a Iermane Clocke,
Still a repairing: euer out of frame,
And neuer going a right, being a Watch:
But being watcht, that it may still go right.
Nay to be periurde, which is worst of all: 920
And among three to loue the worst of all,
A whitly wanton, with a veluet brow,
With two pitch balles stucke in her face for eyes.
I and by heauen, one that will do the deede,
Though *Argus* were her eunuch and her garde.
And I to sigh for her, to watch for her,
To pray for her, go to: it is a plague
That *Cupid* will impose for my neglect,
Of his almightie dreadfull little might.
Well, I will loue, write, sigh, pray, shue, grone,   930
Some men must loue my Ladie, and some Ione.   *Exit*

        Enter the Princesse, a Forrester, her Ladyes   Sc. 5
        (*Rosaline, Maria, and Katherine*), *and her Lordes*,   (4.1)
        among them Boyet

PRINCESSE

Was that the king that spurd his horse so hard,
Against the steepe vp rising of the hill?

⌜BOYET⌝

I know not, but I thinke it was not he.

PRINCESSE

Who ere a was, a showd a mounting minde.
Well Lords, to day we shall haue our dispatch,
Ore Saterday we will returne to Fraunce.
Then Forrester my friend, Where is the Bush
That we must stand and play the murtherer in?

FORRESTER

Heereby vpon the edge of yonder Coppice,   940
A Stand where you may make the fairest shoote.

PRINCESSE

I thanke my Beautie, I am faire that shoote,
And thereupon thou speakst the fairest shoote.

FORRESTER

Pardon me Madam, for I meant not so.

PRINCESSE

What, what? First praise mee, and againe say no.
O short liu'd pride. Not faire? alacke for woe.

FORRESTER

Yes Madam faire.

PRINCESSE   Nay, neuer paint me now,
Where faire is not, praise cannot mend the brow.

Heere (good my glasse) take this for telling trew:
She giues him money

950 Faire payment for foule wordes, is more then dew.

FORRESTER
No thing but faire is that which you inherrit.

PRINCESSE
See see, my beautie wilbe sau'd by merrit.
O heresy in faire, fit for these dayes,
A giuing hand, though fowle, shall haue faire praise.
But come, the Bow: Now Mercie goes to kill,
And shooting well, is then accounted ill:
Thus will I saue my Credite in the shoote,
Not wounding, pittie would not let me doote.
If wounding then it was to shew my skill,

960 That more for praise, then purpose meant to kill.
And out of question so it is sometimes:
Glorie growes guyltie of detested crimes,
When for Fames sake, for praise an outward part,
We bend to that, the working of the hart.
As I for praise alone now seeke to spill
The poore Deares blood, that my hart meanes no ill.

BOYET
Do not curst wiues hold that selfe-soueraigntie
Onely for praise sake, when they striue to be
Lords ore their Lordes?

PRINCESSE
970 Onely for praise, and praise we may afford,
To any Lady that subdewes a Lord.
Enter Costard the Clowne

BOYET
Here comes a member of the common wealth.

CLOWNE God dig-you-den al, pray you which is the head
lady?

PRINCESSE Thou shalt know her fellow by the rest that
haue no heads.

CLOWNE Which is the greatest Ladie, the highest?

PRINCESSE The thickest, and the tallest.

CLOWNE
The thickest, and the tallest: it is so, trueth is trueth.
980 And your waste Mistres were as slender as my wit,
One a these Maides girdles for your waste should be
fit.
Are not you the chiefe woman? You are the thickest
heere.

PRINCESSE Whats your will sir? Whats your will?

CLOWNE
I haue a Letter from Monsier *Berowne*, to one Ladie
Rosaline.

PRINCESSE
O thy letter, thy letter: (*She takes it*) He's a good
friend of mine.
(*To Costard*) Stand a side good bearer. *Boyet* you can
carue,
Breake vp this Capon.
She giues the letter to Boyet

BOYET   I am bound to serue.
This letter is mistooke: it importeth none heere.
It is writ to *Iaquenetta*.

PRINCESSE   We will reade it, I sweare.

Breake the necke of the Waxe, and euery one giue
eare.   990

BOYET (*reedes*) By heauen, that thou art faire, is most
infallible: true that thou art beautious, trueth it selfe
that thou art louelie: more fairer then faire, beautifull
then beautious, truer then trueth it selfe: haue
comiseration on thy heroicall Vassall. The
magnanimous and most illustrate King *Cophetua* sets
eie vpon the penurious and indubitate Begger
Zenelophon: and he it was that might rightly say, *Veni,
vidi, vici*: Which to annothanize in the vulgar, O base
and obscure vulgar; *videliset*, He came, See, and   1000
ouercame: He came, one; see, two; ouercame, three.
Who came? the King. Why did he come? to see. Why
did he see? to ouercome. To whom came he? to the
Begger. What saw he? the Begger. Who ouercame he?
the Begger. The conclusion is victorie: On whose side?
the Kinges: the captiue is inricht, on whose side? the
Beggers. The catastrophe is a Nuptiall, on whose side?
the Kinges: no, on both in one, or one in both. I am
the King (for so standes the comparison) thou the
Begger, for so witnesseth thy lowlines. Shall I   1010
commande thy loue? I may. Shall I enforce thy loue?
I coulde. Shall I entreate thy loue? I will. What, shalt
thou exchange for raggs roabes, for tittles tytles, for
thy selfe, mee. Thus expecting thy replie, I prophane
my lippes on thy foote, my eyes on thy picture, and
my hart on thy euerie part.
             Thine in the dearest designe of industri,
                      Don Adriana de Armatho.
Thus dost thou heare the nemean Lion roare,
      Gainst thee thou Lambe, that standest as his pray: 1020
Submissiue fall his princely feete before,
      And he from forrage will incline to play.
But if thou striue (poore soule) what art thou then?
Foode for his rage, repasture for his den.

PRINCESSE
What plume of fethers is he that indited this letter?
What vaine? What Wethercock? Did you euer heare
better?

BOYET
I am much deceiued, but I remember the stile.

PRINCESSE
Els your memorie is bad, going ore it erewhile.

BOYET
This *Armado* is a *Spaniard* that keepes here in court,
A Phantasime a Monarcho, and one that makes sport   1030
To the Prince and his Booke-mates.

PRINCESSE (*to Costard*)   Thou fellow, a worde.
Who gaue thee this letter?

CLOWNE   I tolde you, my Lord.

PRINCESSE
To whom shouldst thou giue it?

CLOWNE   From my Lord to my Ladie.

PRINCESSE
From which Lord, to which Ladie?

CLOWNE
From my Lord *Berowne*, a good Maister of mine,
To a Ladie of France, that he calde *Rosaline*.

PRINCESSE

Thou hast mistaken his letter. Come Lords away.

(*To Rosaline, giuing her the letter*)

Here sweete, put vp this, twilbe thine annother day.

                             Exit, attended

BOYET

Who is the shooter? Who is the shooter?

ROSALINE   Shall I teach you to know.

BOYET

I my continent of beautie.

1040 ROSALINE   Why she that beares the Bow.

Finely put off.

BOYET

My Lady goes to kill hornes, but if thou marrie,

Hang me by the necke, if horns that yeere miscarrie.

Finely put on.

ROSALINE

Well then I am the shooter.

BOYET   And who is your Deare?

ROSALINE

If we choose by the hornes, your selfe come not neare.

Finely put on in deede.

MARIA

You still wrangle with her *Boyet*, and she strikes at

     the brow.

BOYET

But she her selfe is hit lower: Haue I hit her now?

1050 ROSALINE Shall I come vpon thee with an olde saying,

that was a man when King *Pippen* of Fraunce was a

litle boy, as touching the hit it.

BOYET So I may answere thee with one as olde that was

a woman when queene *Guinouer* of Brittaine was a litle

wench as toching the hit it.

ROSALINE (*sings*)

       Thou canst not hit it, hit it, hit it,

         Thou canst not hit it my good man.

BOYET (*sings*)

       And I cannot, cannot, cannot:

         And I cannot, an other can.   *Exit Rosaline*

CLOWNE

1060 By my troth most plesant, how both did fit it.

MARIA

A marke marueilous wel shot, for they both did hit it.

BOYET

A mark, O mark but that mark: a mark saies my Lady.

Let the mark haue a prick in't, to meate at, if it may

     be.

MARIA

Wide a'the bow hand, yfaith your hand is out.

CLOWNE

Indeed a'must shoot nearer, or hele neare hit the clout.

BOYET

And if my hand be out, then belike your hand is in.

CLOWNE

Then will she get the vpshoot by cleauing the pin.

MARIA

Come come, you talke greasely, your lips grow fowle.

CLOWNE

Shes to hard for you at pricks, sir challeng her to

     bowle.

BOYET

I feare too much rubbing: good night my good owle.   1070

           Exeunt Boyet, Maria, ⌐and Katherine⌐

CLOWNE

By my soule a Swaine, a most simple Clowne.

Lord, Lord, how the Ladies and I haue put him downe.

O my troth most sweete iestes, most inconie vulgar wit,

When it comes so smoothly off, so obscenly as it

     were, so fit.

Armatho ath toother side, o a most daintie man,

To see him walke before a Lady, and to beare her

     Fann.

To see him kisse his hand, & how most sweetly a wil

     sweare:

And his Page atother side, that handfull of wit,

Ah heauens, it is a most patheticall nit.

     Shoot within

Sowla, sowla.   *Exit*   1080

Enter Dull, Holofernes the Pedant and Nathaniel the   Sc. 6

Curate   (4.2)

NATHANIEL Very reuerent sport truly, and done in the

testimonie of a good conscience.

PEDANT The Deare was (as you know) *sanguis* in blood,

ripe as the Pomwater, who now hangeth like a Iewel

in the eare of *Celo* the skie, the welken the heauen, &

anon falleth like a Crab on the face of *Terra*, the soyle,

the land, the earth.

NATHANIEL Truely M. *Holofernes*, the epythithes are

sweetly varried like a scholler at the least: but sir I

assure ye it was a Bucke of the first head.   1090

PEDANT Sir *Nathaniel, haud credo*.

DULL Twas not a *haud credo*, twas a Pricket.

PEDANT Most barbarous intimation: yet a kind of

insinuation, as it were *in via*, in way of explication

facere: as it were replication, or rather *ostentare*, to

show as it were his inclination after his vndressed,

vnpolished, vneducated, vnpruned, vntrained, or rather

vnlettered, or ratherest vnconfirmed fashion, to insert

again my *haud credo* for a Deare.

DULL I said the Deare was not a *haud credo*, twas a Pricket.   1100

PEDANT Twice sodd simplicitie, *bis coctus*,

     O thou monster ignorance, How deformed doost thou

     looke.

NATHANIEL

Sir he hath neuer fed of the dainties that are bred in a

     booke.

He hath not eate paper as it were: he hath not drunke

inck. His intellect is not replenished, he is only an

annimall, only sensible in the duller partes:

And such barren plantes are set before vs, that we

     thankful should be:

Which we of taste, and feeling, are for those partes

     that doe fructifie in vs more then he.

For as it would ill become me to be vaine, indiscreet,
or a foole,
So were there a patch set on Learning, to see him in a
1110   schole.
But *omne bene* say I, being of an olde Fathers minde,
Many can brooke the weather, that loue not the
winde.

DULL
You two are book-men, Can you tel me by your wit,
What was a month old at *Cains* birth, that's not fiue
weeks old as yet?

PEDANT *Dictynna* goodman *Dull*, *Dictynna* goodman *Dull*.

DULL What is *dictima*?

NATHANIEL A title to *Phebe*, to *Luna*, to the *Moone*.

PEDANT
The Moone was a month old when *Adam* was no more.
And rought not to fiue-weeks when he came to
fiuescore.
1120   Th'allusion holdes in the Exchange.

DULL Tis true in deede, the Collusion holdes in the
Exchange.

PEDANT God comfort thy capacitie, I say th'allusion holdes
in the Exchange.

DULL And I say the polusion holdes in the Exchange: for
the Moone is neuer but a month olde: and I say beside
that, twas a Pricket that the Princesse kild.

PEDANT Sir *Nathaniel*, will you heare an extemporall
Epytaph on the death of the Deare, and to humour the
1130   ignoraunt call I the Deare the Princesse kild a Pricket.

NATHANIEL *Perge*, good M. *Holofernes perge*, so it shall
please you to abrogate squirilitie.

PEDANT I wil somthing affect the letter, for it argues
facilitie.
The prayfull Princesse pearst and prickt a prettie
pleasing Pricket,
Some say a Sore, but not a sore, till now made sore
with shooting.
The Dogges did yell, put ell to Sore, then Sorell iumps
from thicket:
Or Pricket-sore, or els Sorell, the people fall a
hooting.
If Sore be sore, then el to Sore, makes fiftie sores o
sore ell:
Of one sore I an hundred make by adding but one
1140   more l.

NATHANIEL A rare talent.

DULL If a talent be a claw, looke how he clawes him with
a talent.

PEDANT This is a gyft that I haue simple: simple, a foolish
extrauagant spirit, full of formes, figures, shapes,
obiectes, Ideas, aprehentions, motions, reuolutions.
These are begot in the ventricle of Memorie, nourisht
in the wombe of *pia mater*, and deliuered vpon the
mellowing of occasion: But the gyft is good in those in
1150   whom it is acute, and I am thankfull for it.

NATHANIEL Sir, I prayse the L. for you, and so may my
parishioners, for their Sonnes are well tuterd by you,
and their Daughters profite very greatly vnder you:
you are a good member of the common wealth.

PEDANT Me hercle, yf their Sonnes be ingenious, they shal
want no instruction: If their Daughters be capable, I
will put it to them. But *Vir sapit qui pauca loquitur*, a
soule Feminine saluteth vs.

Enter Iaquenetta and Costard the Clowne

IAQUENETTA God giue you good morrow M. Person.

PEDANT Maister Person, *quasi* Pers on? And if one shoulde   1160
be perst, Which is the one?

CLOWNE Marrie M. Scholemaster, he that is liklest to a
hoggshead.

PEDANT Of persing a Hogshead, a good luster of conceit
in a turph of Earth, Fier enough for a Flint, Pearle
enough for a Swine: tis prettie, it is well.

IAQUENETTA Good M. Parson be so good as read me this
letter, it was geuen me by *Costard*, and sent me from
Don Armatho: I beseech you read it.

She giues the letter to Nathaniel, who reades it

PEDANT (*to himselfe*) *Facile precor gellida, quando pecas omnia*   1170
sub vmbra ruminat, and so foorth. Ah good olde
Mantuan, I may speake of thee as the traueiler doth of
Venice,
Venichia, Venichia,
Que non te vide, que non te perrechia.
Olde *Mantuan*, olde *Mantuan*, Who vnderstandeth thee
not, loues thee not, (*he singes*) *vt re sol la mi fa*: (*To*
Nathaniel) Vnder pardon sir, What are the contentes?
or rather as *Horrace* sayes in his, What my soule verses.

NATHANIEL I sir, and very learned.   1180

PEDANT Let me heare a staffe, a stanze, a verse, *Lege*
domine.

NATHANIEL (*reades*)
If Loue make me forsworne, how shall I sweare to
loue?
Ah neuer fayth could hold, yf not to beautie vowed.
Though to my selfe forsworne, to thee Ile faythfull
proue.
Those thoughts to me were Okes, to thee like Osiers
bowed.
Studie his byas leaues, and makes his booke thine eyes
Where all those pleasures liue, that Art would
comprehend.
If knowledge be the marke, to know thee shall suffise.
Well learned is that tongue, that well can thee
commend.   1190
All ignorant that soule, that sees thee without wonder.
Which is to mee some prayse, that I thy partes
admire,
Thy eie *Ioues* lightning beares, thy voyce his dreadful
thũder
Which not to anger bent, is musique, and sweete
fier.
Celestiall as thou art, Oh pardon loue this wrong,
That singeth heauens prayse, with such an earthly
tong.

PEDANT You finde not the apostraphus, and so misse the

1200 accent. Let me superuise the canzonet. Here are onely numbers ratefied, but for the elegancie, facilitie, and golden cadence of poesie *caret*: *Ouiddius Naso* was the man. And why in deed *Naso*, but for smelling out the odoriferous flowers of fancie? the ierkes of inuention? *Imitarie* is nothing: So doth the Hound his maister, the Ape his keeper, the tyred Horse his rider: But *Damosella* virgin, Was this directed to you?

IAQUENETTA I sir.

PEDANT I will ouerglaunce the superscript.

> *To the snow-white hand of the most bewtious Lady* > *Rosaline.*

1210 I will looke againe on the intellect of the letter, for the nomination of the partie writing to the person written vnto.

> *Your Ladiships in all desired imployment*, Berowne.

Sir *Nathaniel*, this *Berowne* is one of the Votaries with the King, and here he hath framed a letter to a sequent of the stranger Queenes: which accidentally, or by the way of progression, hath miscarried. (*To Iaquenetta*) Trip and goe my sweete, deliuer this Paper into the royall hand of the King, it may concerne much: stay not thy complement, I forgiue thy dewtie, adue.

1220 IAQUENETTA Good *Costard* go with me: sir God saue your life.

CLOWNE Haue with thee my girle.   *Exit with Iaquenetta*

NATHANIEL Sir you haue done this in the feare of God verie religiously: and as a certaine Father saith

PEDANT Sir tell not mee of the Father, I do feare colourable coloures. But to returne to the Verses, Did they please you sir *Nathaniel*?

NATHANIEL Marueilous well for the pen.

PEDANT I do dine to day at the fathers of a certaine pupill
1230 of mine, where if (before repast) it shall please you to gratifie the table with a Grace, I will on my priuiledge I haue with the parentes of the foresaid childe or pupill, vndertake your *ben venuto*, where I will proue those Verses to be very vnlearned, neither sauouring of Poetrie, wit, nor inuention. I beseech your societie.

NATHANIEL And thanke you to: for societie (saith the text) is the happines of life.

PEDANT And certes the text most infallibly concludes it.
(*To Dull*) Sir I do inuite you too, you shall not say me
1240 nay: *pauca verba*. Away, the gentles are at their game, and we will to our recreation.   *Exeunt*

Sc. 7   *Enter Berowne with a paper in his hand, alone*
(4.3) BEROWNE The King he is hunting the Deare, I am coursing my selfe. They haue pitcht a Toyle, I am toyling in a pytch, pytch that defiles; defile, a foule worde: Well, set thee downe sorrow; for so they say the foole sayd, and so say I, and I the foole: Well proued wit. By the Lord this Loue is as madd as *Aiax*, it kills Sheepe, it kills mee, I a Sheepe well prooued againe a my side. I will not loue; if I do, hang mee: I'fayth I will not. O
1250 but her eye: by this light, but for her eye, I would not loue her; yes for her two eyes. Well, I do nothing in the world but lie, and lie in my throate. By heauen I doe loue, and it hath taught me to rime, and to be

mallicholie: and heere (*showing a paper*) is part of my Rime, and heare (*touching his brest*) my mallicholie. Well, she hath one a'my Sonnets already, the Clowne bore it, the Foole sent it, and the Lady hath it: sweete Clowne, sweeter Foole, sweetest Lady. By the worlde, I woulde not care a pin, if the other three were in. Heere comes one with a paper, God giue him grace to 1260 grone.

> *He standes a side. The King entreth with a paper*

KING Ay mee!

BEROWNE (*aside*) Shot by heauen, proceed sweet *Cupid*, thou hast thumpt him with thy Birdbolt vnder the left papp: in fayth secrets.

KING (*reades*)
> So sweete a kisse the golden Sunne giues not,
>   To those fresh morning dropps vpon the Rose,
> As thy eye beames, when their fresh rayse haue smot
>   The night of dew that on my cheekes downe
>   flowes.
> Nor shines the siluer Moone one halfe so bright,   1270
>   Through the transparent bosome of the deepe,
> As doth thy face through teares of mine giue light:
>   Thou shinst in euerie teare that I do weepe,
> No drop but as a Coach doth carrie thee:
>   So ridest thou triumphing in my wo.
> Do but beholde the teares that swell in me,
>   And they thy glorie through my griefe will show:
> But do not loue thy selfe, then thou wilt keepe
> My teares for glasses, and still make me weepe.
> O Queene of queenes, how farre doost thou excell,   1280
> No thought can thinke, nor tongue of mortall tell.

How shall she know my griefes? Ile drop the paper. Sweete leaues shade follie. Who is he comes heere?

> *Enter Longauill with papers. The King steps a side*

What *Longauill*, and reading: listen eare.

BEROWNE (*aside*)
Now in thy likenesse, one more foole appeare.

LONGAUILL Ay mee! I am forsworne.

BEROWNE (*aside*)
Why he comes in like a periure, wearing papers.

KING (*aside*)
In loue I hope, sweete fellowship in shame.

BEROWNE (*aside*)
One drunkard loues an other of the name.

LONGAUILL
Am I the first that haue been periurd so?   1290

BEROWNE (*aside*)
I could put thee in comfort, not by two that I know,
Thou makest the triumpherie, the corner cap of
    societie,
The shape of Loues Tiburne, that hanges vp Simplicitie.

LONGAUILL
I feare these stubborne lines lacke power to moue.
O sweete *Maria*, Empresse of my Loue,
These numbers will I teare, and write in prose.

BEROWNE (*aside*)
O Rimes are gardes on wanton *Cupids* hose,
Disfigure not his Slop.

LONGAUILL   This same shall go.

330

He reades the Sonnet
Did not the heauenly Rethorique of thine eye,
1300   Gainst whom the world cannot holde argument,
Perswade my hart to this false periurie?
     Vowes for thee broke deserue not punishment.
A Woman I forswore, but I will proue,
     Thou being a Goddesse, I forswore not thee.
My Vow was earthly, thou a heauenly Loue.
     Thy grace being gainde, cures all disgrace in mee.
Vowes are but breath, and breath a vapoure is.
     Then thou faire Sunne, which on my earth doost
          shine,
Exhalst this vapour-vow: in thee it is:
1310   If broken then, it is no fault of mine:
If by mee broke, What foole is not so wise,
     To loose an oth, to winn a Parradise?
BEROWNE (*aside*)
     This is the lyuer veine, which makes flesh a deitie,
     A greene Goose, a Goddesse, pure pure ydolatarie.
     God amende vs, God amende, we are much out a
          th'way.
          Enter Dumaine with a paper
LONGAUILL (*aside*)
     By whom shall I send this (companie?) Stay.
          He steps a side
BEROWNE (*aside*)
     All hid, all hid, an olde infant play,
     Like a demie God, here sit I in the skie,
     And wretched fooles secrets heedfully ore ey.
1320   More Sacks to the myll. O heauens I haue my wysh,
     Dumaine transformd, foure Woodcocks in a dysh.
DUMAINE O most deuine *Kate*.
BEROWNE (*aside*) O most prophane coxcombe.
DUMAINE
     By heauen the woonder in a mortall eye.
BEROWNE (*aside*)
     By earth she is not, corporall, there you ly.
DUMAINE
     Her Amber heires for foule hath amber coted.
BEROWNE (*aside*)
     An amber colourd Rauen was well noted.
DUMAINE
     As vpright as the Ceder.
BEROWNE (*aside*)   Stoope I say,
     Her shoulder is with child.
DUMAINE   As faire as day.
BEROWNE (*aside*)
1330   I as some dayes, but then no Sunne must shine.
DUMAINE O that I had my wish?
LONGAUILL (*aside*) And I had mine.
KING (*aside*) And I mine too good Lord.
BEROWNE (*aside*)
     Amen, so I had mine: Is not that a good word?
DUMAINE
     I would forget her, but a Feuer shee
     Raignes in my blood, and will remembred be.
BEROWNE (*aside*)
     A Feuer in your blood, why then incision
     Would let her out in Sawcers, sweete misprison.

DUMAINE
     Once more Ile reade the Ode that I haue writ.
BEROWNE (*aside*)
     Once more Ile marke how Loue can varrie Wit.   1340
          Dumaine reades his Sonnet
DUMAINE
     On a day, alacke the day:
     Loue, whose Month is euer May:
     Spied a blossome passing faire,
     Playing in the wanton aire:
     Through the Veluet leaues the wind,
     All vnseene, can passage finde:
     That the Louer sicke to death,
     Wisht himselfe the heauens breath.
     Ayre (quoth he) thy cheekes may blow,
     Ayre would I might triumph so.   1350
     But alacke my hand is sworne,
     Nere to plucke thee from thy thorne:
     Vow alacke for youth vnmeete,
     Youth so apt to pluck a sweete.
     Do not call it sinne in me,
     That I am forsworne for thee:
     Thou for whom great *Ioue* would sweare,
     Iuno but an Æthiop were,
     And denie himselfe for *Ioue*,
     Turning mortall for thy loue.   1360
This will I send, and something els more plaine
That shall expresse my true loues fasting paine.
O would the *King, Berowne,* and *Longauill,*
Were Louers too, ill to example ill,
Would from my forehead wipe a periurde note:
For none offende, where all alike do dote.
LONGAUILL (*comming forward*)
Dumaine thy Loue is farre from charitie,
That in loues griefe desirst societie:
You may looke pale, but I should blush I know,
To be ore-hard and taken napping so.   1370
KING (*comming forward*)
Come sir, you blush: as his, your case is such.
You chide at him, offending twice as much.
You do not loue *Maria?* Longauile,
Did neuer Sonnet for her sake compile,
Nor neuer lay his wreathed armes athwart
His louing bosome, to keepe downe his hart.
I haue been closely shrowded in this bush,
And markt you both, and for you both did blush.
I heard your guyltie Rimes, obserude your fashion:
Saw sighes reeke from you, noted well your pashion.   1380
Ay mee sayes one! O *Ioue* the other cryes!
One her haires were Golde, Christal the others eyes.
(*To Longauill*) You would for Parradise breake Fayth
     and troth,
(*To Dumaine*) And *Ioue* for your Loue would infringe
     an oth.
What will *Berowne* say when that he shall heare
Fayth so infringed, which such zeale did sweare.
How will he scorne, how will he spende his wit?
How will he triumph, leape, and laugh at it?

1390 For all the wealth that euer I did see,
I would not haue him know so much by mee.

BEROWNE (*comming forward*)

Now step I foorth to whip hipocrisie.
Ah good my Leidge, I pray thee pardon mee.
Good hart, What grace hast thou thus to reproue
These Wormes for louing, that art most in loue?
Your eyes do make no coaches. In your teares
There is no certaine Princesse that appeares.
Youle not be periurde, tis a hatefull thing:
Tush, none but Minstrels like of Sonnetting.
But are you not ashamd? nay, are you not
1400 All three of you, to be thus much ore'shot?
(*To Longauill*) You found his Moth, the King your
     Moth did see:
But I a Beame do finde in each of three.
O what a Scæne of foolrie haue I seene,
Of sighes, of grones, of sorrow, and of teene:
O mee, with what strickt patience haue I sat,
To see a King transformed to a Gnat.
To see great *Hercules* whipping a Gigge,
And profound *Sallomon* to tune a Iigge.
And *Nestor* play at push-pin with the boyes,
1410 And *Crittick Tymon* laugh at idle toyes.
Where lies thy griefe, o tell me good *Dumaine*?
And gentle *Longauill*, where lies thy paine?
And where my Liedges? all about the brest.
A Caudle hou!

KING   Too bitter is thy iest.
Are we betrayed thus to thy ouer-view?

BEROWNE

Not you to mee, but I betrayed by you.
I that am honest, I that holde it sinne
To breake the vow I am ingaged in.
I am betrayed by keeping companie
1420 With men like you, men of inconstancie.
When shall you see mee write a thing in rime?
Or grone for Ione? or spende a minutes time,
In pruning mee: when shall you heare that I
Will prayse a hand, a foote, a face, an eye:
A gate, a state, a brow, a brest, a wast,
A legge, a limme.

KING   Soft, Whither away so fast?
A true man, or a theefe, that gallops so.

BEROWNE

I post from Loue, good Louer let me go.

    Enter Iaquenetta, with a letter, and Costard the
    Clowne

IAQUENETTA

God blesse the King.

KING   What present hast thou there?

CLOWNE

Some certaine treason.

1430 KING   What makes treason heere?

CLOWNE

Nay it makes nothing sir.

KING   Yf it marr nothing neither,
The treason and you goe in peace away togeather.

IAQUENETTA

I beseech your Grace let this Letter be read,
Our person misdoubts it: twas treason he said.

KING *Berowne* reade it ouer.

    Berowne takes and reades the letter

(*To Iaquenetta*) Where hadst thou it?

IAQUENETTA Of *Costard*.

KING (*to Costard*) Where hadst thou it?

CLOWNE Of *Dun Adramadio, Dun Adramadio.*

    Berowne teares the letter

KING (*to Berowne*)

How now, What is in you? Why dost thou teare it?   1440

BEROWNE

A toy my Leedge, a toy: your grace needs not feare it.

LONGAUILL

It did moue him to passion, & therfore lets heare it.

DUMAINE (*taking vp a peece of the letter*)

It is *Berownes* writing, and heere is his name.

BEROWNE (*to Costard*)

Ah you whoreson loggerhead, you were borne to do
     me shame.
Guiltie my Lord, guiltie: I confesse, I confesse.

KING What?

BEROWNE

That you three fooles, lackt me foole, to make vp the
     messe.
Hee, hee, and you: ene you my Leege, and I,
Are pick-purses in Loue, and we deserue to die.
O dismisse this audience, and I shall tell you more.   1450

DUMAINE

Now the number is euen.

BEROWNE   True true, we are fower:
Will these turtles be gon?

KING   Hence sirs, away.

CLOWNE

Walke aside the true folke, and let the traytors stay.

    Exeunt Costard and Iaquenetta

BEROWNE

Sweete Lords, sweete Louers, O let vs imbrace,
     As true we are as flesh and blood can be,
The Sea will ebb and flow, heauen shew his face:
     Young blood doth not obay an olde decree.
We can not crosse the cause why we were borne:
Therefore of all handes must we be forsworne.

KING

What, did these rent lines shew some loue of thine?   1460

BEROWNE

Did they quoth you? Who sees the heauenly *Rosaline*,
That (like a rude and sauadge man of *Inde*)
     At the first opning of the gorgious East,
Bowes not his vassall head, and strooken blind
     Kisses the base ground with obedient breast.
What peromptorie Eagle-sighted eye
     Dares looke vpon the heauen of her brow,
That is not blinded by her maiestie?

KING

What zeale, what furie, hath inspirde thee now?
My Loue (her Mistres) is a gracious Moone,   1470
     Shee (an attending Starre) scarce seene a light.

BEROWNE

My eyes are then no eyes, nor I *Berowne*.
　O, but for my Loue, day would turne to night,
　Of all complexions the culd soueraigntie,
　　Do meete as at a faire in her faire cheeke,
　Where seuerall worthies make one dignitie,
　　Where nothing wantes, that want it selfe doth
　　　seeke.
　Lend me the florish of all gentle tongues,
　　Fie paynted Rethoricke, O shee needes it not,
1480　To thinges of sale, a sellers prayse belonges:
　　She passes prayse, then prayse too short doth blot.
　A witherd Hermight fiuescore winters worne,
　　Might shake off fiftie, looking in her eye:
　Beautie doth varnish Age, as if new borne,
　　And giues the Crutch the Cradles infancie.
　O tis the Sunne that maketh all thinges shine.

KING

　By heauen, thy Loue is blacke as Ebonie.

BEROWNE

　Is Ebonie like her? O word deuine!
　A wife of such wood were felicitie.
1490　O who can giue an oth? Where is a booke?
　　That I may sweare Beautie doth beautie lacke,
　If that she learne not of her eye to looke:
　　No face is fayre that is not full so blacke.

KING

　O paradox, Blacke is the badge of Hell,
　　The hue of dungions, and the Stile of night:
　And beauties crest becomes the heauens well.

BEROWNE

　Diuels soonest tempt resembling spirites of light.
　O if in blacke my Ladyes browes be deckt,
　　It mournes, that painting and vsurping haire
1500　Should rauish dooters with a false aspect:
　　And therefore is she borne to make blacke fayre.
　Her fauour turnes the fashion of the dayes,
　　For natiue blood is counted paynting now:
　And therefore redd that would auoyde disprayse,
　　Paintes it selfe blacke, to imitate her brow.

DUMAINE

　To looke like her are Chimnie-sweepers blake.

LONGAUILL

　And since her time are Colliers counted bright.

KING

　And *Æthiops* of their sweete complexion crake.

DUMAINE

　Darke needes no Candles now, for darke is light.

BEROWNE

1510　Your Mistresses dare neuer come in raine,
　　For feare their colours should be washt away.

KING

　Twere good yours did: for sir to tell you plaine,
　　Ile finde a fayrer face not washt to day.

BEROWNE

　Ile proue her faire, or talke till doomse-day heere.

KING

　No Diuel will fright thee then so much as shee.

DUMAINE

　I neuer knew man holde vile stuffe so deare.

LONGAUILL (*showing his foote*)

　Looke, heer's thy loue, my foote and her face see.

BEROWNE

　O if the streetes were paued with thine eyes,
　　Her feete were much too daintie for such tread.

DUMAINE

　O vile, then as she goes what vpward lyes　　　　　1520
　　The streete should see as she walkt ouer head.

KING

　But what of this, are we not all in loue?

BEROWNE

　Nothing so sure, and thereby all forsworne.

KING

　Then leaue this chat, and good *Berowne* now proue
　　Our louing lawfull, and our fayth not torne.

DUMAINE

　I marie there, some flatterie for this euyll.

LONGAUILL

　O some authoritie how to proceede,
　Some tricks, some quillets, how to cheate the diuell.

DUMAINE

　Some salue for periurie.

BEROWNE　　　　　　　　　　　　　O tis more then neede.
　Haue at you then affections men at armes,　　　　1530
　Consider what you first did sweare vnto:
　To fast, to study, and to see no woman:
　Flat treason gainst the kingly state of youth.
　Say, Can you fast? your stomacks are too young:
　And abstinence ingenders maladies.
　O we haue made a Vow to studie, Lordes,
　And in that Vow we haue forsworne our Bookes:
　For when would you (my Leedge) or you, or you?
　In leaden contemplation haue found out
　Such fierie Numbers as the prompting eyes,　　　　1540
　Of beautis tutors haue inritcht you with:
　Other slow Artes intirely keepe the braine:
　And therefore finding barraine practizers,
　Scarce shew a haruest of their heauie toyle.
　But Loue first learned in a Ladies eyes,
　Liues not alone emured in the braine:
　But with the motion of all elamentes,
　Courses as swift as thought in euery power,
　And giues to euery power a double power,
　Aboue their functions and their offices.　　　　　1550
　It adds a precious seeing to the eye:
　A Louers eyes will gaze an Eagle blinde.
　A Louers eare will heare the lowest sound
　When the suspitious head of theft is stopt.
　Loues feeling is more soft and sensible,
　Then are the tender hornes of Cockled Snayles.
　Loues tongue proues daintie *Bachus* grosse in taste,
　For Valoure, is not Loue a *Hercules?*
　Still clyming trees in the *Hesperides*.
　Subtil as *Sphinx*, as sweete and musicall,　　　　1560
　As bright *Appolos* Lute, strung with his haire.
　And when Loue speakes, the voyce of all the Goddes,

Make heauen drowsie with the harmonie.
Neuer durst Poet touch a pen to write,
Vntill his Incke were tempred with Loues sighes:
O then his lines would rauish sauage eares,
And plant in Tyrants milde humilitie.
From womens eyes this doctrine I deriue.
They sparcle still the right promethean fier,
1570 They are the Bookes, the Artes, the Achademes,
That shew, containe, and nourish all the worlde.
Els none at all in ought proues excellent.
Then fooles you were, these women to forsweare:
Or keeping what is sworne, you will proue fooles,
For Wisedomes sake, a worde that all men loue:
Or for Loues sake, a worde that loues all men.
Or for Mens sake, the authours of these Women:
Or Womens sake, by whom we Men are Men.
Let vs once loose our othes to finde our selues,
1580 Or els we loose our selues, to keepe our othes:
It is Religion to be thus forsworne.
For Charitie it selfe fulfilles the Law:
And who can seuer Loue from Charitie.

KING
Saint *Cupid* then and Souldiers to the fielde.

BEROWNE
Aduaunce your standards, and vpon them Lords.
Pell, mell, downe with them: but be first aduisd,
In conflict that you get the Sunne of them.

LONGAUILL
Now to plaine dealing, Lay these glozes by,
Shall we resolue to woe these gyrles of Fraunce?

KING
1590 And winn them too, therefore let vs deuise,
Some enterteinment for them in their Tentes.

BEROWNE
First from the Parke let vs conduct them thither,
Then homeward euery man attach the hand
Of his faire Mistres, in the after noone
We will with some strange pastime solace them:
Such as the shortnesse of the time can shape,
For Reuels, Daunces, Maskes, and merrie houres,
Forerunne faire Loue, strewing her way with flowers.

KING
Away, away, no time shalbe omitted,
1600 That will be time and may by vs be fitted.

BEROWNE
Alone alone sowed Cockell, reapt no Corne,
And Iustice alwayes whirles in equall measure:
Light Wenches may proue plagues to men forsworne,
If so our Copper byes no better treasure.   *Exeunt*

Sc. 8   *Enter Holofernes the Pedant, Nathaniel the Curat,*
(5.1)   *and Anthony Dull*

PEDANT *Satis quid sufficit.*

NATHANIEL I prayse God for you sir, your reasons at
Dinner haue been sharpe & sententious: pleasant
without scurillitie, wittie without affection, audatious
without impudencie, learned without opinion, and
1610 strange without heresie: I did conuerse this quondam

day with a companion of the kings, who is intituled,
nominated, or called, *Don Adriano de Armatho.*

PEDANT *Noui hominum tanquam te,* His humour is loftie,
his discourse peremptorie: his tongue fyled, his eye
ambitious, his gate maiesticall, and his generall
behauiour vaine, rediculous, & thrasonicall. He is too
picked, to spruce, too affected, to od as it were, too
peregrinat as I may call it.

NATHANIEL A most singuler and choyce Epithat,
Draw-out his Table-booke

PEDANT He draweth out the thred of his verbositie, finer   1620
then the staple of his argument. I abhorre such
phanatticall phantasims, such insociable and poynt
deuise companions, such rackers of ortagriphie, as to
speake dout *sine* b, when he should say doubt; det,
when he shold pronounce debt; d e b t, not d e t: he
clepeth a Calfe, Caufe: halfe, haufe: neighbour *vocatur*
nebour; neigh abreuiated ne: this is abhominable,
which he would call abbominable, it insinuateth me
of *insanire: ne intelligis domine,* to make frantique
lunatique?   1630

NATHANIEL *Laus deo, bone intelligo.*

PEDANT *Bone? Boon* for boon prescian, a litle scratcht, twil
serue.

*Enter Armado the Bragart, Moth his Boy, and
Costard the Clowne*

NATHANIEL *Videsne quis venit?*

PEDANT *Video, et gaudio.*

ARMADO (*to Moth*) Chirra.

PEDANT (*to Nathaniel*) *Quare* Chirra, not Sirra?

ARMADO Men of peace well incontred.

PEDANT Most millitarie sir salutation.

BOY (*aside to Costard*) They haue been at a great feast of   1640
Languages, and stolne the scraps.

CLOWNE (*aside to Moth*) O they haue lyud long on the
almsbasket of wordes. I maruaile thy M. hath not eaten
thee for a worde, for thou art not so long by the head
as *honorificabilitudinitatibus:* Thou art easier swallowed
then a flapdragon.

BOY (*aside to Costard*) Peace, the peale begins.

ARMADO (*to Holofernes*) Mounsier, are you not lettred?

BOY Yes yes, he teaches boyes the Horne-booke: What is
Ab speld backward with the horne on his head?   1650

PEDANT Ba, *puericia* with a horne added.

BOY Ba most seely Sheepe, with a horne: you heare his
learning.

PEDANT *Quis quis* thou Consonant?

BOY The last of the fiue Vowels if You repeate them, or
the fift if I.

PEDANT I will repeate them: a e I.

BOY The Sheepe, the other two concludes it o u.

ARMADO Now by the sault waue of the meditaranium, a
sweete tutch, a quicke venewe of wit, snip snap, quicke   1660
and home, it reioiceth my intellect, true wit.

BOY Offerd by a childe to an old man: which is wit-old.

PEDANT What is the figure? What is the figure?

BOY Hornes.

PEDANT Thou disputes like an Infant: goe whip thy Gigg.

BOY Lende me your Horne to make one, and I will whip about your Infamie *circum circa* a gigge of a Cuckolds horne.

CLOWNE And I had but one peny in the world thou 1670 shouldst haue it to buy Ginger bread: (*Giuing money*) Holde, there is the verie Remuneration I had of thy Maister, thou halfepennie purse of wit, thou Pidgin-egge of discretion. O and the heauens were so pleased, that thou wart but my Bastard; What a ioyfull father wouldest thou make me? Go to, thou hast it *ad dungil* at the fingers ends, as they say.

PEDANT Oh I smell false Latine, *dunghel* for *vnguem*.

ARMADO Arts-man *preambulat*, we will be singuled from the barbarous. Do you not educate youth at the Charg-1680 house on the top of the Mountaine?

PEDANT Or *Mons* the hill.

ARMADO At your sweete pleasure, for the Mountaine.

PEDANT I do *sans question*.

ARMADO Sir, it is the Kings most sweete pleasur & affection, to congratulate the Princesse at her Pauilion, in the *posteriors* of this day, which the rude multitude call the after-noone.

PEDANT The *posterior* of the day, most generous sir, is liable, congruent, and measurable for the after noone: 1690 the worde is well culd, choise, sweete, & apt I do assure you sir, I do assure.

ARMADO Sir, the King is a noble Gentleman, and my familier, I do assure ye very good friende: for what is inwarde betweene vs, let it passe. I do beseech thee remember thy curtesie. I beseech thee apparrell thy head: and among other important and most serious designes, and of great import in deede too: but let that passe, for I must tell thee it will please his Grace (by the worlde) sometime to leane vpon my poore shoulder, 1700 and with his royall finger thus dallie with my excrement, with my mustachio: but sweete hart let that passe. By the world I recount no fable, some certaine special honours it pleaseth his greatnes to impart to *Armado* a Souldier, a man of trauayle, that hath seene the worlde: but let that passe; the very all of all is: but sweet hart, I do implore secrecie, that the King would haue me present the Princesse (sweete chuck) with some delightfull ostentation, or show, or pageant, or antique, or fierworke: Now vnderstanding 1710 that the Curate and your sweete selfe, are good at such eruptions, and sodaine breaking out of myrth (as it were) I haue acquainted you withall, to the ende to craue your assistance.

PEDANT Sir, you shall present before her the Nine Worthies, Sir *Nathaniel*, as concerning some entertainment of time, some show in the posterior of this day, to be rendred by our assistance the Kinges commaund, and this most gallant illustrate and learned Gentleman, before the Princesse: I say none so fit as 1720 to present the nine Worthies.

NATHANIEL Where will you finde men worthie enough to present them?

PEDANT *Iosua*, your selfe, my selfe, *Iudas Machabeus*, and this gallant Gentleman, *Hector*; this Swaine (because of his great lim or ioynt) shall passe *Pompey* the great, the Page *Hercules*.

ARMADO Pardon sir, error: He is not quantitie enough for that worthies thumbe, he is not so big as the end of his Club.

PEDANT Shall I haue audience? He shall present *Hercules* 1730 in minoritie: his enter and exit shalbe strangling a Snake; and I will haue an Apologie for that purpose.

BOY An excellent deuice: so if any of the audience hisse, you may cry, Well done *Hercules*, now thou crusshest the Snake; that is the way to make an offence gracious, though few haue the grace to do it.

ARMADO For the rest of the Worthies?

PEDANT I will play three my selfe.

BOY Thrice worthie Gentleman.

ARMADO Shall I tell you a thing?   1740

PEDANT We attende.

ARMADO We will haue, if this fadge not, an Antique. I beseech you follow.

PEDANT *Via* good-man *Dull*, thou hast spoken no worde all this while.

DULL Nor vnderstoode none neither sir.

PEDANT Alone, we will employ thee.

DULL Ile make one in a daunce, or so: or I will play on the Taber to the worthies, and let them dance the hey.

PEDANT Most *Dull*, honest *Dull*, to our sport: away.   1750

Exeunt

Enter the Princesse and her Ladyes (Rosaline,   Sc. 9
Maria, and Katherine)   (5.2)

PRINCESSE
Sweete hartes we shalbe rich ere we depart,
Yf Fayrings come thus plentifully in.
A Ladie walde about with Diamondes:
Looke you, what I haue from the louing King.

ROSALINE
Madame, came nothing els along with that?

PRINCESSE
Nothing but this: yes as much loue in Rime,
As would be crambd vp in a sheete of paper
Writ a both sides the leafe, margent and all,
That he was faine to seale on *Cupids* name.

ROSALINE
That was the way to make his god-head Wax: 1760
For he hath been fiue thousand yeere a Boy.

KATHERINE
I and a shrowde vnhappie gallowes too.

ROSALINE
Youle neare be friendes with him, a kild your sister.

KATHERINE
He made her melancholie, sad, and heauie,
And so she died: had she bin Light like you,
Of such a mery nimble stiring spirit,
She might a bin a Grandam ere she died.
And so may you: For a light hart liues long.

ROSALINE
Whats your darke meaning mouce, of this light word?

KATHERINE

1770   A light condition in a beautie darke.

ROSALINE

   We neede more light to finde your meaning out.

KATHERINE

   Youle marre the light by taking it in snuffe:

   Therefore Ile darkly ende the argument.

ROSALINE

   Looke what you do, you do it still i'th darke.

KATHERINE

   So do not you, for you are a light Wench.

ROSALINE

   In deede I waigh not you, and therefore light.

KATHERINE

   You waigh me not, O thats you care not for me.

ROSALINE

   Great reason: for past care, is still past cure.

PRINCESSE

   Well bandied both, a set of Wit well played.

1780   But *Rosaline*, you haue a Fauour too?

   Who sent it? and what is it?

ROSALINE   I would you knew.

   And if my face were but as faire as yours,

   My Fauour were as great, be witnesse this,

   Nay I haue Vearses too, I thanke *Berowne*,

   The numbers true, and were the numbring too,

   I were the fayrest Goddesse on the ground.

   I am comparde to twentie thousand fairs.

   O he hath drawen my picture in his letter.

PRINCESSE Any thing like?

ROSALINE

1790   Much in the letters, nothing in the praise.

PRINCESSE

   Beautious as Incke: a good conclusion.

KATHERINE

   Faire as a text B in a Coppie booke.

ROSALINE

   Ware pensalls, How? Let me not die your debtor,

   My red Dominicall, my golden letter,

   O that your face were not so full of Oes.

PRINCESSE

   A Poxe of that iest, I beshrow all Shrowes,

   But *Katherine* what was sent to you from faire *Dumaine*?

KATHERINE

   Madame, this Gloue.

PRINCESSE   Did he not send you twaine?

KATHERINE Yes Madame: and moreouer,

1800   Some thousand Verses of a faithfull Louer.

   A hudge translation of hipocrisie,

   Vildly compyld, profound simplicitie.

MARIA

   This, and these Pearls, to me sent *Longauile*.

   The Letter is too long by halfe a mile.

PRINCESSE

   I thinke no lesse: Dost thou not wish in hart

   The Chaine were longer, and the Letter short.

MARIA

   I, or I would these handes might neuer part.

PRINCESSE

   We are wise girles to mocke our Louers so.

ROSALINE

   They are worse fooles to purchase mocking so.

   That same *Berowne* ile torture ere I go.   1810

   O that I knew he were but in by th'weeke,

   How I would make him fawne, and begge, and seeke,

   And wayte the season, and obserue the times,

   And spend his prodigall wittes in booteles rimes,

   And shape his seruice wholly to my hests,

   And make him proude to make me proude that iestes,

   So persuaunt like would I ore'sway his state,

   That he should be my foole, and I his fate.

PRINCESSE

   None are so surely caught, when they are catcht,

   As Wit turnde Foole, follie in Wisedome hatcht   1820

   Hath Wisedomes warrant, and the helpe of Schoole,

   And Wits owne grace to grace a learned Foole.

ROSALINE

   The blood of youth burnes not with such excesse,

   As grauities reuolt to wantonnesse.

MARIA

   Follie in Fooles beares not so strong a note,

   As foolrie in the Wise, when Wit doth dote:

   Since all the power thereof it doth apply,

   To proue by Wit, worth in simplicitie.

      Enter Boyet

PRINCESSE

   Heere comes *Boyet*, and myrth is in his face.

BOYET

   O I am stabde with laughter, Wher's her Grace?   1830

PRINCESSE

   Thy newes *Boyet*?

BOYET   Prepare Maddame, prepare.

   Arme Wenches arme, incounters mounted are,

   Against your Peace. Loue doth approch, disguysd:

   Armed in argumentes, you'll be surprisd.

   Muster your Wits, stande in your owne defence,

   Or hide your heades like Cowardes, and flie hence.

PRINCESSE

   Saint *Dennis* to S. *Cupid*: What are they,

   That charge their breath against vs? Say scout say.

BOYET

   Vnder the coole shade of a Siccamore,

   I thought to close mine eyes some halfe an houre: 1840

   When lo to interrupt my purposd rest,

   Toward that shade I might beholde addrest,

   The King and his companions, warely

   I stole into a neighbour thicket by,

   And ouer hard, what you shall ouer heare:

   That by and by disguysd they will be heere.

   Their Heralde is a prettie knauish Page:

   That well by hart hath cond his embassage.

   Action and accent did they teach him there.

   Thus must thou speake, and thus thy body beare.   1850

   And euer and anon they made a doubt,

   Presence maiesticall would put him out:

For quoth the King, an Angell shalt thou see:
Yet feare not thou but speake audaciously.
The Boy replyde, An Angell is not euill:
I should haue feard her had shee been a deuill.
With that all laught, and clapt him on the shoulder,
Making the bolde wagg by their prayses bolder.
One rubbd his elbow thus, and fleerd, and swore,
1860 A better speach was neuer spoke before.
Another with his fynger and his thume,
Cried *via* we will doo't come what wil come.
The thirde he caperd and cryed, All goes well.
The fourth turnd on the tooe, and downe he fell:
With that they all did tumble on the ground,
With such a zelous laughter so profound,
That in this spleene rediculous appeares,
To checke their follie pashions solembe teares.

PRINCESSE
But what, but what, come they to visite vs?

BOYET
1870 They do, they do; and are apparild thus,

⌈   ⌉

Like *Muscouites*, or *Russians*, as I gesse.
Their purpose is to parlee, to court, and daunce,
And euery one his Loue-suit will aduance,
Vnto his seuerall Mistres: which they'le know
By Fauours seuerall, which they did bestow.

PRINCESSE
And will they so? the Gallants shalbe taskt:
For Ladies, we will euery one be maskt,
And not a man of them shall haue the grace
1880 Despight of sute, to see a Ladies face.
(*To Rosaline*) Holde take thou this my sweete, and
    giue mee thine,
So shall *Berowne* take me for *Rosaline*.
    She changes Fauours with Rosaline
(*To Katherine and Maria*)
And change you Fauours too, so shall your Loues
Woo contrarie, deceyud by these remoues.
    Katherine and Maria change Fauours

ROSALINE
Come on then, weare the Fauours most in sight.

KATHERINE
But in this changing, What is your intent?

PRINCESSE
The effect of my intent is to crosse theirs:
They do it but in mockerie merement,
And mocke for mocke is onely my intent.
1890 Their seuerall counsailes they vnboosome shall,
To Loues mistooke, and so be mockt withall
Vpon the next occasion that we meete,
With Visages displayde to talke and greete.

ROSALINE
But shall we dance, if they desire vs toot?

PRINCESSE
No, to the death we will not moue a foot,
Nor to their pend speach render we no grace:
But while tis spoke each turne away hir face.

BOYET
Why that contempt will kill the speakers hart,
And quite diuorce his memorie from his part.

PRINCESSE
Therefore I do it, and I make no doubt,   1900
The rest will nere come in, if he be out.
Theres no such sport, as sport by sport orethrowne:
To make theirs ours, and ours none but our owne.
So shall we stay mocking entended game,
And they wel mockt depart away with shame.
    Sound Trom.

BOYET
The Trompet soundes, be maskt, the maskers come.
    The Ladies maske.
    Enter Black-moores with musicke, the Boy with a
    speach, the King and the rest of the Lordes disguysed
    as Russians

BOY
All haile, the richest Beauties on the earth.

BEROWNE (*aside*)
Beauties no richer then rich Taffata.

BOY
A holy parcell of the fayrest dames

    The Ladyes turne their backes to him

That euer turnd their backes to mortall viewes.   1910

BEROWNE Their eyes villaine, their eyes.

BOY
That euer turnde their eyes to mortall viewes.
Out

BOYET True, out in deede.

BOY
Out of your fauours heauenly spirites vouchsafe
Not to beholde.

BEROWNE Once to beholde, rogue.

BOY
Once to beholde with your Sunne beamed eyes,
With your Sunne beamed eyes.

BOYET
They will not answere to that Epythat.   1920
You were best call it Daughter beamed eyes.

BOY
They do not marke me, and that bringes me out.

BEROWNE
Is this your perfectnes? begon you rogue.   *Exit Moth*

ROSALINE (*as the Princesse*)
What would these strangers? Know their mindes *Boyet*.
If they do speake our language, tis our will
That some plaine man recount their purposes.
Know what they would?

BOYET   What would you with the Princes?

BEROWNE
Nothing but peace, and gentle visitation.

ROSALINE What would they, say they?

BOYET
Nothing but peace, and gentle visitation.   1930

ROSALINE
Why that they haue, and bid them so be gon.

BOYET

    She saies you haue it, and you may be gon.

KING

    Say to her we haue measurd many miles,

    To treade a Measure with her on this grasse.

BOYET

    They say that they haue measurd many a mile,

    To tread a Measure with you on this grasse.

ROSALINE

    It is not so. Aske them how manie inches

    Is in one mile? If they haue measurd manie,

    The measure then of one is easlie tolde.

BOYET

1940   If to come hither, you haue measurde miles,

    And manie miles: the Princesse bids you tell,

    How manie inches doth fill vp one mile?

BEROWNE

    Tell her we measure them by weerie steps.

BOYET

    She heares her selfe.

ROSALINE   How manie weerie steps,

    Of manie weerie miles you haue ore gone,

    Are numbred in the trauaile of one Mile?

BEROWNE

    We number nothing that we spend for you,

    Our duetie is so rich, so infinite,

    That we may do it still without accompt.

1950   Vouchsafe to shew the sunshine of your face,

    That we (like sauages) may worship it.

ROSALINE

    My face is but a Moone, and clouded too.

KING

    Blessed are cloudes, to do as such cloudes do.

    Vouchsafe bright Moone, and these thy Starrs to

        shine,

    (Those cloudes remooud) vpon our waterie eyne.

ROSALINE

    O vaine peticioner, begg a greater matter,

    Thou now requests but Mooneshine in the water.

KING

    Then in our measure, do but vouchsafe one change,

    Thou bidst me begge, this begging is not strange.

ROSALINE

    Play Musique then:

          ⌈*Musique playes*⌉

1960   nay you must do it soone.

    Not yet: no daunce: thus change I like the Moone.

KING

    Wil you not daunce? How come you thus estranged?

ROSALINE

    You tooke the moone at ful, but now shee's changed?

KING

    Yet still she is the Moone, and I the Man.

    ⌈   ⌉

    The musique playes, vouchsafe some motion to it.

ROSALINE

    Our eares vouchsafe it.

KING   But your legges should do it.

ROSALINE

    Since you are strangers, and come here by chance,

    Weele not be nice, take handes, we will not daunce.

KING

    Why take we handes then?

ROSALINE   Onely to part friendes.   1970

    Curtsie sweete hartes, and so the Measure endes.

KING

    More measure of this measure, be not nice.

ROSALINE

    We can affoord no more at such a price.

KING

    Prise you your selues: What buyes your company?

ROSALINE

    Your absence onely.

KING   That can neuer be.

ROSALINE

    Then cannot we be bought: and so adue,

    Twice to your Visore, and halfe once to you.

KING

    If you denie to daunce, lets holde more chat.

ROSALINE

    In priuat then.

KING   I am best pleasd with that.

        The King and Rosaline talke apart

BEROWNE (*to the Princesse, taking her for Rosaline*)

    White handed Mistres, one sweet word with thee.   1980

PRINCESSE

    Honie, and Milke, and Suger: there is three.

BEROWNE

    Nay then two treyes, an if you grow so nice,

    Methegline, Wort, and Malmsey; well runne dice:

    There's halfe a dosen sweetes.

PRINCESSE   Seuenth sweete adue,

    Since you can cogg, Ile play no more with you.

BEROWNE

    One word in secret.

PRINCESSE   Let it not be sweete.

BEROWNE

    Thou greeust my gall.

PRINCESSE   Gall, bitter,

BEROWNE   Therefore meete.

        Berowne and the Princesse talke apart

DUMAINE (*to Maria, taking her for Katherine*)

    Will you vouchsafe with me to change a word?

MARIA

    Name it.

DUMAINE   Faire Ladie.

MARIA   Say you so? Faire Lord,

    Take that for your faire Lady.

DUMAINE   Please it you,   1990

    As much in priuat, & ile bid adieu.

        Dumaine and Maria talke apart

KATHERINE

    What, was your vizard made without a tongue?

LONGAUILL (*taking Katherine for Maria*)

    I know the reason (Lady) why you aske.

KATHERINE

O for your reason, quickly sir, I long?

LONGAUILL

You haue a double tongue within your Maske,
And would afforde my speachles vizard halfe.

KATHERINE

Veale quoth the Dutch-man: is not veale a Calfe?

LONGAUILL

A Calfe faire Ladie.

KATHERINE   No, a faire Lorde Calfe.

LONGAUILL

Let's part the word?

KATHERINE   No, Ile not be your halfe:
2000 Take all and weane it, it may proue an Oxe.

LONGAUILL

Loke how you butt your selfe in these sharpe mocks,
Will you giue hornes chast Lady? do not so.

KATHERINE

Then die a Calfe, before your hornes do grow.

LONGAUILL

One word in priuate with you ere I die.

KATHERINE

Bleat softly then, the Butcher heares you crie.
    Longauill and Katherine talke apart

BOYET

The tongues of mocking Wenches are as keene
    As is the Rasors edge inuisible:
Cutting a smaller haire then may be seene,
    Aboue the sence of sence, so sensible
2010 Seemeth their conference, their conceites haue winges,
Fleeter then Arrowes, bullets wind thought swifter
    thinges.

ROSALINE

Not one word more my Maides, break off, break off.

BEROWNE

By heauen, all drie beaten with pure scoffe.

KING

Farewel mad Wenches, you haue simple wits.
    Exeunt the King, Lordes, and Black-moores
    ⌈*The Ladies vnmaske*⌉

PRINCESSE

Twentie adieus my frozen Muskouits.
Are these the breede of Wits so wonderd at?

BOYET

Tapers they are with your sweete breaths puft out.

ROSALINE

Wel-liking Wits they haue grosse grosse, fat fat.

PRINCESSE

O pouertie in wit, Kingly poore flout.
Will they not (thinke you) hange them selues to
2020   nyght?
Or euer but in vizards shew their faces.
This pert *Berowne* was out of countnance quite.

ROSALINE

Ah, they were all in lamentable cases,
The King was weeping ripe for a good word.

PRINCESSE

Berowne did sweare him selfe out of all suite.

MARIA

Dumaine was at my seruice, and his sword,
No poynt (quoth I) my seruant straight was mute.

KATHERINE

Lord *Longauill* said I came ore his hart:
And trow you what he calde me?

PRINCESSE   Qualme perhaps.

KATHERINE

Yes in good faith.

PRINCESSE   Goe sicknes as thou art.   2030

ROSALINE

Well, better wits haue worne plaine statute Caps.
But will you heare; the King is my Loue sworne.

PRINCESSE

And quicke *Berowne* hath plighted Fayth to me.

KATHERINE

And *Longauill* was for my seruice borne.

MARIA

Dumaine is mine as sure as barke on tree.

BOYET

Madame, and prettie mistresses giue eare.
Immediatly they will againe be heere,
In their owne shapes: for it can neuer be,
They will digest this harsh indignitie.

PRINCESSE

Will they returne?

BOYET   They will they will, God knowes,   2040
And leape for ioy, though they are lame with blowes:
Therefore change Fauours, and when they repaire,
Blow like sweete Roses, in this sommer aire.

PRINCESSE

How blow? how blow? Speake to be vnderstood.

BOYET

Faire Ladies maskt, are Roses in their bud:
Dismaskt, their dammaske sweete commixture
    showne,
Are Angels vailing cloudes, or Roses blowne.

PRINCESSE

Auaunt perplexitie, What shall we do,
If they returne in their owne shapes to woe?

ROSALINE

Good Madame, if by me youle be aduisde,   2050
Lets mocke them still as well knowne as disguysde:
Let vs complaine to them what fooles were heare,
Disguysd like *Muscouites* in shapeles geare:
And wonder what they were, and to what ende
Their shallow showes, and Prologue vildly pende,
And their rough carriage so rediculous,
Should be presented at our Tent to vs.

BOYET

Ladies, withdraw: the gallants are at hand.

PRINCESSE

Whip to our Tents as Roes run ouer land.
    Exeunt the Ladies
    Enter the King, Berowne, Dumaine, and Longauill
    as themselues

KING

Faire sir, God saue you: Wher's the Princesse?   2060

BOYET

    Gone to her Tent. Please it your Maiestie
    Commaunde me any seruice to her thither?

KING

    That she vouchsafe me audience for one word.

BOYET

    I will, and so will she, I know my Lord.   *Exit*

BEROWNE

    This fellow peckes vp Wit as Pidgions Pease,
    And vtters it againe when God dooth please.
    He is Witts Pedler, and retales his wares:
    At Wakes and Wassels, meetings, markets, Faires.
    And we that sell by grosse, the Lord doth know,
2070   Haue not the grace to grace it with such show.
    This Gallant pins the Wenches on his sleeue.
    Had he bin *Adam* he had tempted *Eue*.
    A can carue to, and lispe: Why this is hee
    That kist his hand, a way in courtisie.
    This is the Ape of Forme, Mounsier the nice,
    That when he playes at Tables chides the Dice
    In honorable tearmes; nay he can sing
    A meane most meanely, and in hushering,
    Mende him who can, the Ladies call him sweete.
2080   The staires as he treades on them kisse his feete.
    This is the floure that smyles on euery one,
    To shew his teeth as white as Whales bone.
    And consciences that will not die in debt,
    Pay him the due of honie-tongd *Boyet*.

KING

    A blister on his sweete tongue with my hart,
    That put *Armathoes* Page out of his part.
        Enter the Ladies and Boyet

BEROWNE

    See where it comes. Behauiour what wert thou
    Till this mad man shewed thee, and what art thou
        now?

KING

    All haile sweete Madame, and faire time of day.

PRINCESSE

2090   Faire in all Haile is foule, as I conceaue.

KING

    Consture my speaches better, if you may.

PRINCESSE

    Then wish me better, I will giue you leaue.

KING

    We came to visite you, and purpose now,
    To leade you to our Court, vouchsafe it then.

PRINCESSE

    This Feelde shall holde me, and so hold your vow:
    Nor God nor I delights in periurd men.

KING

    Rebuke me not for that which you prouoke:
    The vertue of your eie must breake my oth.

PRINCESSE

    You nickname vertue, vice you should haue spoke:
2100   For vertues office neuer breakes mens troth.
    Now by my maiden honour yet as pure,
    As the vnsallied Lilly I protest,

    A worlde of tormentes though I should endure,
    I would not yeelde to be your houses guest:
    So much I hate a breaking cause to be
    Of heauenly Othes vowed with integritie.

KING

    O you haue liu'd in desolation heere,
    Vnseene, vnuisited, much to our shame.

PRINCESSE

    Not so my Lord, it is not so I sweare,
    We haue had pastimes here and pleasant game,   2110
    A messe of *Russians* left vs but of late.

KING

    How Madame? *Russians?*

PRINCESSE   I in trueth My Lord.
    Trim gallants, full of Courtship and of state.

ROSALINE

    Madame speake true: It is not so my Lord:
    My Ladie (to the maner of the dayes)
    In curtesie giues vndeseruing praise.
    We foure in deede confronted were with foure,
    In *Russian* habite: heere they stayed an houre,
    And talkt apace: and in that houre (my Lord)
    They did not blesse vs with one happie word.   2120
    I dare not call them fooles; but this I thinke,
    When they are thirstie, fooles would faine haue
        drinke.

BEROWNE

    This iest is drie to me, gentle sweete,
    Your wits makes wise thinges foolish. When we greete
    With eies best seeing, heauens fierie eie:
    By light we loose light, your capacitie
    Is of that nature, that to your hudge stoore,
    Wise thinges seeme foolish, and rich thinges but poore.

ROSALINE

    This proues you wise and rich: for in my eie.

BEROWNE

    I am a foole, and full of pouertie.   2130

ROSALINE

    But that you take what doth to you belong,
    It were a fault to snatch wordes from my tongue.

BEROWNE

    O, I am yours and all that I possesse.

ROSALINE

    All the foole mine.

BEROWNE   I cannot giue you lesse.

ROSALINE

    Which of the Vizards was it that you wore?

BEROWNE

    Where, when, what Vizard? why demaund you this?

ROSALINE

    There, then, that Vizard, that superfluous case,
    That hid the worse, and shewed the better face.

KING (*aside to the Lordes*)

    We were descried, theyle mock vs now dounright.

DUMAINE (*aside to the King*)

    Let vs confesse and turne it to a iest.   2140

PRINCESSE

    Amazde my Lord? Why lookes your highnes sad?

ROSALINE
 Helpe holde his browes, heele sound: why looke you
   pale?
 Sea sicke I thinke comming from *Muscouie*.
BEROWNE
 Thus pooure the Starres downe plagues for periurie.
  Can anie face of brasse hold longer out?
 Heere stand I, Ladie dart thy skill at me,
  Bruse me with scorne, confound me with a flout.
 Thrust thy sharpe wit quite through my ignorance,
  Cut me to peeces with thy keene conceit.
2150 And I will wish thee neuer more to daunce,
  Nor neuer more in Russian habite waite.
 O neuer will I trust to speaches pend,
  Nor to the motion of a Schoole-boyes tongue:
 Nor neuer come in vizard to my friend,
  Nor woo in rime like a blind harpers songue.
 Taffata phrases, silken tearmes precise,
  Three pilde Hiperboles, spruce affectation:
 Figures pedanticall, these sommer flies,
  Haue blowne me full of maggot ostentation.
2160 I do forsweare them, and I here protest,
  By this white Gloue (how white the hand God
   knowes)
 Hencefoorth my wooing minde shalbe exprest
  In russet yeas, and honest kersie noes.
 And to begin: Wench, so God helpe me law,
  My loue to thee is sound, *sance* cracke or flaw.
ROSALINE
 Sans, sans, I pray you.
BEROWNE   Yet I haue a tricke,
 Of the olde rage: beare with me, I am sicke.
 Ile leaue it by degrees; soft, let vs see,
 Write *Lord haue mercie on vs*, on those three,
2170 They are infected, in their hartes it lyes:
 They haue the Plague, and caught it of your eyes,
 These Lordes are visited, you are not free,
 For the Lords tokens on you do I see.
PRINCESSE
 No, they are free that gaue these tokens to vs.
BEROWNE
 Our states are forfait, seeke not to vndoo vs.
ROSALINE
 It is not so, for how can this be true,
 That you stand forfait, being those that sue.
BEROWNE
 Peace, for I will not haue to doe with you.
ROSALINE
 Nor shall not, if I do as I intende.
BEROWNE (*to the Lordes*)
2180 Speake for your selues, my wit is at an ende.
KING
 Teach vs sweet Madame, for our rude transgression
 Some faire excuse.
PRINCESSE   The fairest is confession.
 Were not you here but euen now, disguysde?
KING
 Madame, I was.
PRINCESSE   And were you well aduisde?

KING
 I was faire Madame.
PRINCESSE   When you then were heere,
 What did you whisper in your Ladies eare?
KING
 That more then all the world, I did respect her.
PRINCESSE
 When she shall challenge this, you wil reiect her.
KING
 Vpon mine honour no.
PRINCESSE   Peace peace, forbeare:
 Your Oth once broke, you force not to forsweare. 2190
KING
 Despise me when I breake this oth of mine.
PRINCESSE
 I will, and therefore keepe it. *Rosaline*,
 What did the *Russian* whisper in your eare?
ROSALINE
 Madame, he swore that he did hold me deare,
 As precious ey-sight, and did value me
 Aboue this Worlde: adding thereto more ouer,
 That he would wed me, or els die my Louer.
PRINCESSE
 God giue thee ioy of him: the Noble Lord
 Most honourablie doth vphold his word.
KING
 What meane you Madame: by my life my troth, 2200
 I neuer swore this Lady such an oth.
ROSALINE
 By heauen you did; and to confirme it plaine,
 You gaue me this: but take it sir againe.
KING
 My faith and this, the Princesse I did giue,
 I knew her by this Iewell on her sleeue.
PRINCESSE
 Pardon me sir, this Iewell did she weare,
 And Lord *Berowne* (I thanke him) is my deare.
 (*To Berowne*) What? will you haue me, or your Pearle
   againe?
BEROWNE
 Neither of either: I remit both twaine.
 I see the tricke ant: here was a consent, 2210
 Knowing aforehand of our meriment,
 To dash it lik a Christmas Comedie:
 Some carry tale, some please-man, some sleight sanie:
 Some mumble newes, some trencher Knight, some Dick
 That smyles his cheeke in yeeres, and knowes the trick
 To make my Lady laugh, when shees disposd:
 Tolde our intentes before: which once disclosd,
 The Ladies did change Fauours; and then wee
 Folowing the signes, wood but the signe of shee.
 Now to our periurie, to add more terror, 2220
 We are againe forsworne in will and error.
 Much vpon this tis: (*to Boyet*) and might not you
 Forestall our sport, to make vs thus vntrue?
 Do not you know my Ladies foote by'th squier?
  And laugh vpon the apple of her eie?
 And stand betweene her backe sir and the fier,
  Holding a trencher, iesting merrilie?

You put our Page out: goe, you are aloude.
Die when you will, a Smocke shalbe your shroude.
2230   You leere vpon me, do you: ther's an eie
Woundes like a leaden sword.

BOYET   Full merely
Hath this braue manage, this carreere bin run.

BEROWNE
Loe, he is tilting straight. Peace, I haue don.

Enter Costard the Clowne

Welcome pure wit, thou partest a faire fray.

CLOWNE
O Lord sir, they would know,
Whether the three Worthis shall come in or no?

BEROWNE
What, are there but three?

CLOWNE   No sir, but it is vara fine,
For euerie one pursents three.

BEROWNE   And three times thrice is nine.

CLOWNE
Not so sir, vnder correction sir, I hope it is not so.
You cannot beg vs sir, I can assure you sir, we know
2240   what we know:
I hope sir three times thrice sir.

BEROWNE   Is not nine.

CLOWNE Vnder correction sir we know where-vntill it doth
amount.

BEROWNE By Ioue, I all wayes tooke three threes for nine.

CLOWNE O Lord sir, it were pittie you should get your
liuing by reckning sir.

BEROWNE How much is it?

CLOWNE O Lord sir, the parties themselues, the actors sir
will shew wher-vntill it doth amount: for mine owne
2250   part, I am (as they say, but to parfect one man in one
poore man) *Pompion* the great sir.

BEROWNE Art thou one of the Worthies?

CLOWNE It pleased them to thinke me worthie of *Pompey*
the great: for mine owne part I know not the degree
of the Worthy, but I am to stand for him.

BEROWNE Goe bid them prepare.

CLOWNE
We wil turne it finely off sir, we wil take some care.
                                                    Exit

KING
Berowne, they will shame vs: let them not approch.

BEROWNE
We are shame proofe my Lord: & tis some policie
To haue one show worse then the Kings and his
2260   company.

KING I say they shall not come.

PRINCESSE
Nay my good Lord let me ore'rule you now.
That sport best pleases, that doth least know how:
Where zeale striues to content, and the contentes
Dies in the zeale of that which it presentes:
Their forme confounded, makes most forme in myrth,
When great thinges labouring perish in their byrth.

BEROWNE
A right description of our sport my Lord.

Enter Armado the Bragart

ARMADO (*to the King*) Annoynted, I implore so much
expence of thy royal sweete breath, as will vtter a brace   2270
of wordes.

⌈*Armado and the King speake apart*⌉

PRINCESSE Doth this man serue God?

BEROWNE Why aske you?

PRINCESSE
A speakes not like a man of God his making.

ARMADO That is al one my faire sweete honie monarch,
For I protest, the Schoolemaister is exceeding
fantasticall, Too too vaine, too too vaine: but we will
put it (as they say) to *Fortuna delaguar*, I wish you the
peace of mind most royall cupplement.   *Exit*

KING Heere is like to be a good presence of Worthies: He   2280
presents *Hector* of *Troy*, the Swaine *Pompey* the great,
the parish Curate *Alexander*, *Armadoes* Page *Hercules*,
the Pedant *Iudas Machabeus*:
And if these foure Worthies in their first shew thriue,
These foure will change habites, and present the other
fiue.

BEROWNE
There is fiue in the first shew.

KING
You are deceiued, tis not so.

BEROWNE
The Pedant, the Bragart, the Hedge-Priest, the Foole,
and the Boy,
Abate throw at Nouum, and the whole world againe,
Cannot picke out fiue such, take each one in his vaine.   2290

KING
The Ship is vnder sayle, and heere she coms amaine.

Enter Costard the Clowne for Pompey

CLOWNE
I Pompey *am*.

BEROWNE   You lie, you are not he.

CLOWNE
I Pompey *am*,

BOYET   With Libbards head on knee.

BEROWNE
Well said old mocker, I must needes be friendes with
thee.

CLOWNE
I Pompey *am*, Pompey *surnamde the bigge*.

DUMAINE The great.

CLOWNE It is *great* sir,
Pompey *surnamd the great*,
*That oft in fielde with Targ and Shield did make my foe to
sweat*,
*And trauailing along this coast I heere am come by
chaunce*,   2300
*And lay my Armes before the Leggs of this sweete Lasse of
France*.
If your Ladishyp would say thankes *Pompey*, I had
done.

⌈PRINCESSE⌉ Great thankes great *Pompey*.

CLOWNE Tis not so much worth: but I hope I was perfect.
I made a litle fault in great.

BEROWNE My hat to a halfe-pennie, *Pompey* prooues the
best Worthie.

    Costard standes a side.

    Enter Nathaniel the Curate for Alexander

NATHANIEL

When in the world I liud, I was the worldes commander:

2310   *By East, West, North, and South, I spred my*
      conquering might:

My Scutchion plaine declares that I am Alisander.

BOYET

Your Nose saies no, you are not: for it stands too
    right.

BEROWNE (*to Boyet*)

Your nose smels no in this most tender smelling
    knight.

PRINCESSE

The conqueror is dismaid: proceed good *Alexander.*

NATHANIEL

When in the worlde I liud, I was the worldes commander.

BOYET

Most true, tis right: you were so *Alisander.*

BEROWNE (*to Costard*) *Pompey* the great.

CLOWNE Your seruant and *Costard.*

BEROWNE Take away the Conquerour, take away
2320 *Alisander.*

CLOWNE (*to Nathaniel*) O sir, you haue ouerthrowne
Alisander the Conquerour: you will be scrapt out of the
painted cloth for this. Your Lion that holdes his Polax
sitting on a close stoole, will be geuen to *Aiax.* He wilbe
the ninth Worthie: a Conquerour, and a feard to
speake? Run away for shame *Alisander.*

      ⌈*Exit Nathaniel the Curat*⌉

There ant shall please you a foolish mylde man, an
honest man; looke you, and soone dasht. He is a
marueylous good neighbour fayth, and a very good
2330 Bowler: but for *Alisander,* alas you see how tis a little
oreparted, but there are Worthies a comming will
speake their minde in some other sort.

PRINCESSE Stand aside good *Pompey.*

    Enter Holofernes the Pedant for Iudas, and the Boy
    Moth for Hercules

PEDANT

Great Hercules is presented by this Impe,

  Whose Clubb kilde Cerberus that three headed Canus,

And when he was a babe, a childe, a shrimpe,

  Thus did he strangle Serpents in his Manus,

Quoniam, *he seemeth in minoritie,*

Ergo, *I come with this Appologie.*

2340 (*To Moth*) Keepe some state in thy exit, and vanish.

                 Exit Moth

PEDANT

Iudas *I am.*

DUMAINE A Iudas.

PEDANT Not Iscariot sir.

Iudas *I am, ecliped* Machabeus.

DUMAINE *Iudas Machabeus* clipt, is plaine *Iudas.*

BEROWNE A kissing traytour. How art thou proud *Iudas?*

PEDANT

  Iudas *I am.*

DUMAINE The more shame for you *Iudas.*

PEDANT What meane you sir?

BOYET To make *Iudas* hang him selfe.   2350

PEDANT Begin sir, you are my elder.

BEROWNE Well folowed, *Iudas* was hanged on an Elder.

PEDANT I will not be put out of countenance.

BEROWNE Because thou hast no face.

PEDANT What is this?

BOYET A Cytterne head.

DUMAINE The head of a Bodkin.

BEROWNE A deaths face in a Ring.

LONGAUILL The face of an olde Roman coyne, scarce
    seene.   2360

BOYET The pummel of *Cæsars* Fauchion.

DUMAINE The carud-bone face on a Flaske.

BEROWNE Saint *Georges* halfe cheeke in a Brooch.

DUMAINE I and in a Brooch of Lead.

BEROWNE I and worne in the cappe of a Tooth-drawer:
  And now forward, for we haue put thee in countenance.

PEDANT You haue put me out of countenance.

BEROWNE False, we haue giuen thee faces.

PEDANT But you haue outfaste them all.

BEROWNE

And thou weart a Lyon, we would do so.   2370

BOYET

Therefore as he is, an Asse, let him go:

And so adue sweete *Iude.* Nay, Why dost thou stay?

DUMAINE For the latter ende of his name.

BEROWNE

For the *Asse* to the *Iude*: giue it him. *Iudas* away.

PEDANT

This is not generous, not gentle, not humble.

BOYET

A light for Mounsier *Iudas,* it growes darke, he may
    stumble.   *Exit Holofernes*

PRINCESSE Alas poore *Machabeus,* how hath he bin bayted.

    Enter Armado the Braggart, for Hector

BEROWNE Hide thy head *Achilles,* here comes *Hector* in
Armes.

DUMAINE Though my mockes come home by me, I will 2380
now be merrie.

KING *Hector* was but a *Troyan* in respect of this.

BOYET But is this *Hector?*

KING I thinke *Hector* was not so cleane timberd.

LONGAUILL His Legge is too bigge for *Hectors.*

DUMAINE More Calfe certaine.

BOYET No, he is best indued in the small.

BEROWNE This cannot be *Hector.*

DUMAINE Hee's a God or a Painter: for he makes faces.

ARMADO

The Armipotent Mars, *of Launces the almightie,*   2390

  Gaue Hector *a gift.*

DUMAINE A gilt Nutmegg.

BEROWNE A Lemmon.

LONGAUILL Stucke with Cloues.

DUMAINE No clouen.

ARMADO Peace.

> The Armipotent Mars, *of Launces the almighty,*
> Gaue Hector *a gift, the heir of Illion,*
> A man so breathed, that certaine he would fight; yea,
> From morne till night out of his Pauilion.
>
> I am that Flower.

DUMAINE   That Mint.

LONGAUILL   That Cullambine.

ARMADO Sweete Lord *Longauill* raine thy tongue.

LONGAUILL I must rather giue it the raine: for it runnes against *Hector.*

DUMAINE I and *Hector*'s a Greyhound.

ARMADO The sweete War-man is dead and rotten, Sweete chucks beat not the bones of the buried: When he breathed he was a man: But I will forward with my deuice; *(to the Princesse)* sweete royaltie bestow on me the sence of hearing.

> *Berowne steps foorth*

PRINCESSE
> Speake braue *Hector*, we are much delighted.

ARMADO I do adore thy sweete Graces Slipper.

BOYET Loues her by the foote.

DUMAINE He may not by the yarde.

ARMADO
> This Hector *far surmounted* Hanniball.

⌐   ¬

ARMADO The partie is gone.

CLOWNE Fellow *Hector*, she is gone; she is two months on her way.

ARMADO What meanest thou?

CLOWNE Faith vnlesse you play the honest *Troyan*, the poore wench is cast away: shee's quicke, the childe bragges in her bellie already: tis yours.

ARMADO Dost thou infamonize me among potentates: Thou shalt die.

CLOWNE Then shall *Hector* be whipt for *Iaquenetta* that is quicke by him, and hangd for *Pompey* that is dead by him.

DUMAINE Most rare *Pompey*.

BOYET Renowned *Pompey*.

BEROWNE Greater then great, great, great, great *Pompey*: *Pompey* the hudge.

DUMAINE *Hector* trembles.

BEROWNE *Pompey* is mooued more Ates more Atees stir them on stir them on.

DUMAINE *Hector* will challenge him.

BEROWNE I, if a'haue no more mans blood in his belly then wil suppe a Flea.

ARMADO By the North Pole I do challenge thee.

CLOWNE I will not fight with a Pole like a Northren man; Ile slash, Ile do it by the Sword: I bepray you let me borrow my Armes againe.

DUMAINE Roome for the incensed Worthies.

CLOWNE Ile do it in my shyrt.

DUMAINE Most resolute *Pompey*.

BOY *(aside to Armado)* Maister, let me take you a button hole lower. Do you not see, *Pompey* is vncasing for the Combat: What meane you? you will loose your reputation.

ARMADO Gentlemen and Souldiers, pardon me, I will not combat in my shyrt.

DUMAINE You may not deny it, *Pompey* hath made the challenge.

ARMADO Sweete bloodes, I both may and will.

BEROWNE What reason haue you fort.

ARMADO The naked trueth of it is, I haue no Shirt. I goe Woolward for pennance.

⌐BOY⌐ True, and it was inioyned him in *Rome* for want of Linnen: since when, Ile be sworne he wore none, but a dish-cloute of *Iaquenettaes*, and that a weares next his hart for a Fauour.

> *Enter a Messenger Mounsier Marcade*

MARCADE
> God saue you Madame.

PRINCESSE   Welcome *Marcade*,
> But that thou interrupptst our merriment.

MARCADE
> I am sorrie Madame for the newes I bring
> Is heauie in my tongue. The King your father

PRINCESSE
> Dead for my life.

MARCADE   Euen so: my tale is tolde.

BEROWNE
> Worthies away, the Scæne begins to cloude.

ARMADO For mine owne part I breath free breath: I haue seene the day of wrong through the litle hole of discretion, and I will right my selfe like a Souldier.

> *Exeunt Worthys*

KING How fares your Maiestie?

QUEENE
> *Boyet* prepare, I will away to nyght.

KING
> Madame Not so, I do beseech you stay.

QUEENE
> Prepare I say: I thanke you gracious Lords
> For all your faire endeuours and intreat
> Out of a new sad-soule, that you vouchsafe,
> In your rich wisedome to excuse, or hide,
> The liberall opposition of our spirites.
> If ouerboldly we haue borne our selues,
> In the conuerse of breath, your gentlenes
> Was guyltie of it. Farewell worthy Lord:
> A heauie hart beares not a nimble tongue.
> Excuse me so comming too short of thankes,
> For my great sute, so easely obtainde.

KING
> The extreame partes of time extreamly formes,
> All causes to the purpose of his speede:
> And often at his very loose decides
> That, which long processe could not arbitrate.
> And though the mourning brow of progenie
> Forbid the smyling courtecie of Loue
> The holy suite which faine it would conuince,
> Yet since Loues argument was first on foote,
> Let not the cloude of Sorrow iustle it

From what it purposd, since to wayle friendes lost,
Is not by much so holdsome profitable,
As to reioyce at friendes but newly found.

QUEENE
I vnderstand you not, my griefes are double.

BEROWNE
Honest plaine words, best pearce the eare of griefe,
And by these badges vnderstand the King,
2500 For your faire sakes, haue we neglected time,
Plaide fouleplay with our othes: your beautie Ladies
Hath much deformd vs, fashioning our humours
Euen to the opposed ende of our ententes.
And what in vs hath seemd rediculous:
As Loue is full of vnbefitting straines,
All wanton as a childe, skipping and vaine,
Formd by the eye, and therefore like the eye,
Full of straing shapes, of habites and of formes:
Varying in subiectes as the eye doth roule,
2510 To euery varied obiect in his glaunce:
Which partie coted presence of loose loue
Put on by vs, if in your heauenly eyes,
Haue misbecombd our othes and grauities,
Those heauenly eyes that looke into these faultes,
Suggested vs to make them, therefore Ladies
Our loue being yours, the errour that Loue makes
Is likewise yours: we to our selues proue false,
By being once falce, for euer to be true
To those that make vs both, faire Ladies you.
2520 And euen that falshood in it selfe a sinne,
Thus purifies it selfe and turns to grace.

QUEENE
We haue receiud your Letters, full of Loue:
Your Fauours, the embassadours of Loue.
And in our mayden counsaile rated them,
At courtshyp pleasant iest and courtecie,
As bombast and as lyning to the time:
But more deuout then this in our respectes,
Haue we not been, and therefore met your Loues,
In their owne fashyon like a merriment.

DUMAINE
2530 Our letters madame, shewed much more then iest.

LONGAUILL
So did our lookes.

ROSALINE   We did not cote them so.

KING
Now at the latest minute of the houre,
Graunt vs your loues.

QUEENE   A time me thinkes too short,
To make a world-without-end bargaine in:
No no my Lord, your Grace is periurde much,
Full of deare guiltines, and therefore this,
If for my Loue (as there is no such cause)
You will do ought, this shall you do for me:
Your oth I will not trust, but goe with speede
2540 To some forlorne and naked Hermytage,
Remote from all the pleasurs of the world:
There stay vntill the twelue Celestiall Signes
Haue brought about the annuall reckoning.

If this Austere insociable life,
Change not your offer made in heate of blood.
If frostes and fastes, hard lodging, and thin weedes,
Nip not the gaudie blossomes of your Loue:
But that it beare this tryall, and last Loue,
Then at the expiration of the yeere,
Come challenge me, challenge me by these desertes: 2550
And by this Virgin palme now kissing thine,
I wilbe thine: and till that instance shutt
My wofull selfe vp in a mourning house,
Rayning the teares of lamentation,
For the remembraunce of my Fathers death.
If this thou do deny, let our handes part,
Neither intitled in the others hart.

KING
If this, or more then this, I would denie,
    To flatter vp these powers of mine with rest,
The sodaine hand of death close vp mine eye.   2560
    Hence hermite then, my hart is in thy brest.
        They talke apart

DUMAINE (*to Katherine*)
But what to me my Loue? but what to me?
A wife?

KATHERINE A beard, faire health, and honestie,
With three folde loue I wish you all these three.

DUMAINE
O shall I say, I thanke you gentle Wife?

KATHERINE
Not so my Lord, a tweluemonth and a day,
Ile marke no wordes that smothfast wooers say,
Come when the King doth to my Lady come:
Then if I haue much loue, Ile giue you some.

DUMAINE
Ile serue thee true and faythfully till then.   2570

KATHERINE
Yet sweare not, least ye be forsworne agen.
        They talke apart

LONGAUILL
What saies *Maria*?

MARIA   At the tweluemonths ende,
Ile change my blacke Gowne for a faithfull frend.

LONGAUILL
Ile stay with patience, but the time is long.

MARIA
The liker you, few taller are so young.
        They talke apart

BEROWNE (*to Rosaline*)
Studdies my Ladie? Mistres looke on me,
Beholde the window of my hart, mine eye:
What humble suite attendes thy answere there,
Impose some seruice on me for thy Loue.

ROSALINE
Oft haue I heard of you my Lord *Berowne*,   2580
Before I saw you: and the worldes large tongue
Proclaymes you for a man repleat with mockes,
Full of comparisons and wounding floutes:
Which you on all estates will execute,
That lie within the mercie of your wit:

To weede this wormewood from your fructfull braine,
And therewithall to winne me, yf you please,
Without the which I am not to be won:
You shall this tweluemonth terme from day to day,
2590   Visite the speachlesse sicke, and still conuerse,
With groning wretches: and your taske shall be,
With all the fierce endeuour of your wit,
To enforce the pained impotent to smile.

BEROWNE

To moue wilde laughter in the throate of death?
It cannot be, it is impossible.
Mirth cannot moue a soule in agonie.

ROSALINE

Why thats the way to choake a gibing spirrit,
Whose influence is begot of that loose grace,
Which shallow laughing hearers giue to fooles,
2600   A iestes prosperitie lies in the eare,
Of him that heares it, neuer in the tongue
Of him that makes it: then if sickly eares
Deaft with the clamours of their owne deare grones,
Will heare your idle scornes; continue then,
And I will haue you, and that fault withall.
But if they will not, throw away that spirrit,
And I shall finde you emptie of that fault,
Right ioyfull of your reformation.

BEROWNE

A tweluemonth? well; befall what will befall,
2610   Ile iest a tweluemonth in an Hospitall.

QUEENE (to the King)

I sweete my Lord, and so I take my leaue.

KING

No Madame, we will bring you on your way.

BEROWNE

Our wooing doth not ende like an olde Play:
Iacke hath not Gill: these Ladies courtesie
Might well haue made our sport a Comedie.

KING

Come sir, it wants a tweluemonth an'aday,
And then twill ende.

BEROWNE   That's too long for a Play.

Enter Armado the Braggart

ARMADO (to the King) Sweete Maiestie vouchsafe me.

QUEENE Was not that *Hector*?

2620 DUMAINE The worthie Knight of *Troy*.

ARMADO

I will kisse thy royall finger, and take leaue.
I am a Votarie; I haue vowde to *Iaquenetta*
To holde the Plough for her sweete loue three yeere.
But most esteemed greatnes, will you heare the
Dialogue that the two Learned men haue compiled, in
prayse of the Owle and the Cuckow? it should haue
followed in the ende of our shew.

KING Call them foorth quickly, we will do so.

ARMADO

Holla, Approch.

*Enter Holofernes, Nathaniel, Costard, Moth, Dull,
Iaquenetta, and others*
          This side is *Hiems*, Winter.
This *Ver*, the Spring: The one maynteined by the
Owle,   2630
The other by the Cuckow. *Ver* begin.

The Song

SPRING

When Dasies pied, and Violets blew,
    And Ladi-smockes all siluer white,
And Cuckow-budds of yellow hew:
    Do paint the Meadowes with delight:
The Cuckow then on euerie tree,
Mocks married men; for thus singes hee,
    Cuckow.
Cuckow, Cuckow: O word of feare,
Vnpleasing to a married eare.   2640

When Shepheards pipe on Oten Strawes,
    And merrie Larkes are Ploughmens Clocks:
When Turtles tread and Rookes and Dawes,
    And Maidens bleach their summer smockes:
The Cuckow then on euerie tree,
Mockes married men, for thus singes he,
    Cuckow.
Cuckow, cuckow: O word of feare,
Vnpleasing to a married eare.

WINTER

When Isacles hang by the wall,   2650
    And Dicke the Sheepheard blowes his naile:
And Thom beares Logges into the hall,
    And Milke coms frozen home in paile:
When Blood is nipt, and wayes be foull,
Then nightly singes the staring Owle
Tu-whit to-who. A merrie note,
While greasie Ione doth keele the pot.

When all aloude the winde doth blow,
    And coffing drownes the Parsons saw;
And Birdes sit brooding in the Snow,   2660
    And Marrians nose lookes red and raw:
When roasted Crabbs hisse in the bowle,
Then nightly singes the staring Owle,
Tu-whit to-who. A merrie note,
While greasie Ione doth keele the pot.

⌈ARMADO⌉ The wordes of Mercurie, are harsh after the
songes of Apollo. You that way, we this way.
                       Exeunt omnes, seuerally

FINIS

ADDITIONAL PASSAGES

A. The following lines, found after line 1535 in the First Quarto, represent an unrevised version of parts of Berowne's long speech, 1529-83. The first six lines form the basis of 1536-41; the next three are revised at 1568-72; the next four at 1542-4; the last nine are less directly related to the revised version.

And where that you haue vowd to studie (Lordes)
In that each of you haue forsworne his Booke,
Can you still dreame and poare and thereon looke.
For when would you my Lord, or you, or you,
Haue found the ground of Studies excellence,
Without the beautie of a womans face?
From womens eyes this doctrine I deriue,
They are the Ground, the Bookes, the Achadems,
From whence doth spring the true *Promethean* fire.
10 Why vniuersall plodding poysons vp
The nimble spirites in the arteries,
As motion and long during action tyres
The sinnowy vigour of the trauayler.
Now for not looking on a womans face,
You haue in that forsworne the vse of eyes:
And studie too, the causer of your vow.
For where is any Authour in the worlde,
Teaches such beautie as a womãs eye:

Learning is but an adiunct to our selfe,
And where we are, our Learning likewise is.   20
Then when our selues we see in Ladies eyes,
With our selues.
Do we not likewise see our learning there?

B. The following two lines, spoken by the Princesse and found after 1880 in the First Quarto, seem to represent a first draft of 1881-2.

Holde *Rosaline*, this Fauour thou shalt weare,
And then the King will court thee for his Deare:

C. The following lines, found after 2561 in the First Quarto, represent a draft version of 2576-93.

BEROWNE
And what to me my Loue? and what to me?
ROSALINE
You must be purged to, your sinnes are ranke.
You are attaint with faultes and periurie:
Therefore if you my fauour meane to get,
A tweluemonth shall you spende and neuer rest,
But seeke the weery beddes of people sicke.

LOUES LABOURS WON
A BRIEF ACCOUNT

IN 1598, Francis Meres called as witnesses to Shakespeare's excellence in comedy 'his *Gĕtlemē of Verona*, his *Errors*, his *Loue labors lost*, his *Loue labours wonne*, his *Midsummers night dreame*, & his *Merchant of Venice*'. This was the only evidence that Shakespeare wrote a play called *Loues labours won* until the discovery in 1953 of a fragment of a bookseller's list that had been used in the binding of a volume published in 1637/8. The fragment itself appears to record items sold from 9 to 17 August 1603 by a book dealer in the south of England. Among items headed '[inte]rludes & tragedyes' are

> marchant of vennis
> taming of a shrew
> knak to know a knave
> knak to know an honest man
> loves labor lost
> loves labor won

No author is named for any of the items. All the plays named in the list except *Loves labor won* are known to have been printed by 1600; all were written by 1596-7. Taken together, Meres's reference in 1598 and the 1603 fragment appear to demonstrate that a play by Shakespeare called *Loues labours won* had been performed by the time Meres wrote and was in print by August 1603. Conceivably the phrase served as an alternative title for one of Shakespeare's other comedies, though the only one believed to have been written by 1598 but not listed by Meres is *The Taming of the Shrew*, which is named (as *taming of a shrew*) in the bookseller's fragment. Otherwise we must suppose that *Loues labours won* is the title of a lost play by Shakespeare, that no copy of the edition mentioned in the bookseller's list is extant, and that Heminges and Condell failed to include it in the 1623 Folio.

None of these suppositions is implausible. We know of at least one other lost play attributed to Shakespeare (see *Cardenio*, below), and of many lost works by contemporary playwrights. No copy of the first edition of *Titus Andronicus* was known until 1904; for *1 Henry IV* and *The Passionate Pilgrime* only a fragment of the first edition survives. And we now know that *Troylus and Cressida* was almost omitted from the 1623 Folio (probably for copyright reasons) despite its evident authenticity. It is also possible that, like most of the early editions of Shakespeare's plays, the lost edition of *Loues labours won* did not name him on the title-page, and this omission might go some way to explaining the failure of the edition to survive, or (if it does still survive) to be noticed. *Loues labours won* stands a much better chance of having survived, somewhere, than *Cardenio*: because it was printed, between 500 and 1,500 copies were once in circulation, whereas for *Cardenio* we know of only a single manuscript.

The evidence for the existence of the lost play (unlike that for *Cardenio*) gives us little indication of its content. Meres explicitly states, and the title implies, that it was a comedy. Its titular pairing with *loves labor lost* suggests that they may have been written at about the same time. Both Meres and the bookseller's catalogue place it after *Loues labors lost*; although neither list is necessarily chronological, Meres's does otherwise agree with our own view of the order of composition of Shakespeare's comedies.

A MIDSOMMER NIGHTS DREAME

FRANCIS MERES mentions *A Midsommer nights dreame* in his *Palladis Tamia*, of 1598, and it was first printed in 1600. It has often been thought that Shakespeare wrote the play for an aristocratic wedding, but there is no evidence to support this speculation, and the 1600 title-page states that it had been 'sundry times publickely acted' by the Lord Chamberlain's Men. In stylistic variation it resembles *Loues labors lost*: both plays employ a wide variety of verse measures and rhyme schemes, along with prose that is sometimes (as in Bottom's account of his dream, 1643–57) rhetorically patterned. Probably it was written in 1594 or 1595, either just before or just after *Romeo and Iuliet*.

Shakespeare built his own plot from diverse elements of literature, drama, legend, and folklore, supplemented by his imagination and observation. There are four main strands. One, which forms the basis of the action, shows the preparations for the marriage of Theseus, Duke of Athens, to Hyppolita, Queen of the Amazons, and (in the last act) its celebration. This is indebted to Chaucer's *Knight's Tale*, as is the play's second strand, the love story of Lysander and Hermia (who elope to escape her father's opposition) and of Demetrius. In Chaucer, two young men fall in love with the same girl and quarrel over her; Shakespeare adds the comic complication of another girl (Helena) jilted by, but still loving, one of the young men. A third strand shows the efforts of a group of Athenian workmen—the 'mechanicals'—led by Bottom the Weaver to prepare a play, *Pyramus and Thisbe* (based mainly on Arthur Golding's translation of Ovid's *Metamorphoses*) for performance at the Duke's wedding. The mechanicals themselves belong rather to Elizabethan England than to ancient Greece. Bottom's partial transformation into an ass has many literary precedents. Fourthly, Shakespeare depicts a quarrel between Oberon and Titania, King and Queen of the Fairies. Oberon's attendant, Robin Goodfellow, a puck (or pixie), interferes mischievously in the workmen's rehearsals and the affairs of the lovers. The fairy part of the play owes something to both folklore and literature; Robin Goodfellow was a well-known figure about whom Shakespeare could have read in Reginald Scot's *Discoverie of Witchcraft* (1586).

A Midsommer nights dreame offers a glorious celebration of the powers of the human imagination while also making comic capital out of its limitations. It is one of Shakespeare's most polished achievements, a poetic drama of exquisite grace, wit, and humanity. In performance, its imaginative unity has sometimes been violated, but it has become one of Shakespeare's most popular plays, with a special appeal for the young.

The first edition was apparently printed from Shakespeare's own papers.

THE NAMES OF THE ACTORS

THESEUS, Duke of Athens

HYPPOLITA, Queene of the Amasons, betrothed to Theseus

EGEUS, father of Hermia

HERMIA, daughter of Egeus, in loue with Lysander

LYSANDER, loued by Hermia

DEMETRIUS, suitor to Hermia

HELENA, in loue with Demetrius

OBERON, King of Fairies

TITANIA, Queene of Fairies

ROBIN goodfellow, a Pucke

PEASE-BLOSSOME
COBWEB
MOTH
MUSTARDSEEDE
} Fairies

Peter QUINCE, a Carpenter

Nick BOTTOM, a Weauer

Francis FLUTE, a Bellows mender

Tom SNOUT, a Tinker

SNUGGE, a Ioyner

Robin STARUELING, a Tayler

Attendant Lords and Fairies

A Midsommer nights dreame

Sc. 1
(1.1)

Enter Theseus, Hippolita, with others

THESEUS

Now faire *Hippolita*, our nuptiall hower
Draws on apase: fower happy daies bring in
An other Moone: but oh, me thinks, how slow
This old Moone wanes! She lingers my desires,
Like to a Stepdame, or a dowager,
Long withering out a yong mans reuenewe.

HYPPOLITA

Fower daies will quickly steepe themselues in night:
Fower nights will quickly dreame away the time:
And then the Moone, like to a siluer bowe,
10　New bent in heauen, shall beholde the night
Of our solemnities.

THESEUS　　　　　Goe *Philostrate*,
Stirre vp the *Athenian* youth to merriments,
Awake the peart and nimble spirit of mirth,
Turne melancholy foorth to funerals:
The pale companion is not for our pomp.　⌈*Exit one*⌉
Hyppolita, I woo'd thee with my sword,
And wonne thy loue, doing thee iniuries:
But I will wed thee in another key,
With pompe, with triumph, and with reueling.

Enter Egeus and his daughter Hermia, and Lysander
and Demetrius

EGEUS

20　Happy be *Theseus*, our renowned duke.

THESEUS

Thankes good *Egeus*. Whats the newes with thee?

EGEUS

Full of vexation, come I, with complaint
Against my childe, my daughter *Hermia*.
Stand forth *Demetrius*. My noble Lord,
This man hath my consent to marry her.
Stand forth *Lisander*. And my gratious Duke,
This hath bewitcht the bosome of my childe.
Thou, thou *Lysander*, thou hast giuen her rimes,
And interchang'd loue tokens with my childe:
30　Thou hast, by moone-light, at her windowe sung,
With faining voice, verses of faining loue,
And stolne the impression of her phantasie:
With bracelets of thy haire, rings, gawdes, conceites,
Knackes, trifles, nosegaies, sweete meates (messengers
Of strong preuailement in vnhardned youth)
With cunning hast thou filcht my daughters heart,
Turnd her obedience (which is due to mee)
To stubborne harshnesse. And, my gratious Duke,
Be it so, she will not here, before your Grace,
40　Consent to marry with *Demetrius*,
I beg the auncient priuiledge of *Athens*:
As she is mine, I may dispose of her:
Which shall be, either to this gentleman,
Or to her death; according to our lawe,
Immediatly prouided, in that case.

THESEUS

What say you, *Hermia*? Be aduis'd, faire maid.
To you, your father should be as a God:
One that compos'd your beauties: yea and one,
To whome you are but as a forme in wax,
By him imprinted, and within his power,　　　　50
To leaue the figure, or disfigure it:
Demetrius is a worthy gentleman.

HERMIA

So is *Lisander*.

THESEUS　　　　　In himselfe he is:
But in this kinde, wanting your fathers voice,
The other must be held the worthier.

HERMIA

I would my father lookt but with my eyes.

THESEUS

Rather your eyes must, with his iudgement, looke.

HERMIA

I doe intreat your grace, to pardon mee.
I know not by what power, I am made bould;
Nor how it may concerne my modesty,　　　　60
In such a presence, here to plead my thoughts:
But I beseech your Grace, that I may knowe
The worst that may befall mee in this case,
If I refuse to wed *Demetrius*.

THESEUS

Either to dy the death, or to abiure,
For euer, the society of men.
Therefore, faire *Hermia*, question your desires,
Knowe of your youth, examine well your blood,
Whether (if you yeelde not to your fathers choyce)
You can endure the liuery of a Nunne,　　　　70
For aye to be in shady cloyster, mew'd
To liue a barraine sister all your life,
Chaunting faint hymnes, to the colde fruitlesse Moone.
Thrise blessed they, that master so there bloode,
To vndergoe such maiden pilgrimage:
But earthlyer happy is the rose distild,
Then that, which, withering on the virgin thorne,
Growes, liues, and dies, in single blessednesse.

HERMIA

So will I growe, so liue, so die my Lord,
Ere I will yield my virgin Patent, vp　　　　80
Vnto his Lordshippe, whose vnwished yoake
My soule consents not to giue soueranity.

THESEUS

Take time to pawse, and by the next newe moone,
The sealing day, betwixt my loue and mee,
For euerlasting bond of fellowshippe,
Vpon that day either prepare to dye,
For disobedience to your fathers will,
Or else to wed *Demetrius*, as he would,
Or on *Dianaes* altar to protest,
For aye, austeritie and single life.　　　　90

DEMETRIUS

Relent, sweete *Hermia*, and, *Lysander*, yeeld
Thy crazed title to my certaine right.

LYSANDER

You haue her fathers loue, *Demetrius*:
Let me haue *Hermias*: doe you marry him.

EGEUS

Scornefull *Lysander*, true, he hath my loue:
And what is mine, my loue shall render him.
And she is mine, and all my right of her
I doe estate vnto *Demetrius*.

LYSANDER ⌈*to Theseus*⌉

I am my Lord, as well deriu'd as hee,
As well possest: my loue is more than his:
My fortunes euery way as fairely rankt
(If not with vantage) as *Demetrius*:
And (which is more then all these boastes can be)
I am belou'd of beautious *Hermia*.
Why should not I then prosecute my right?
Demetrius, Ile auouch it to his heade,
Made loue to *Nedars* daughter, *Helena*,
And won her soule: and she (sweete Ladie) dotes,
Deuoutly dotes, dotes in Idolatry,
Vpon this spotted and inconstant man.

THESEUS

I must confesse, that I haue heard so much;
And, with *Demetrius*, thought to haue spoke thereof:
But, being ouer full of selfe affaires,
My minde did loose it. But *Demetrius* come,
And come *Egeus*, you shall goe with mee:
I haue some priuate schooling for you both.
For you, faire *Hermia*, looke you arme your selfe,
To fit your fancies, to your fathers will;
Or else, the Law of *Athens* yeelds you vp
(Which by no meanes we may extenuate)
To death, or to a vowe of single life.
Come my *Hyppolita*: what cheare my loue?
Demetrius and *Egeus* goe along:
I must employ you in some businesse,
Against our nuptiall, and conferre with you
Of some thing, nerely that concernes your selues.

EGEUS

With duety and desire, we follow you.

Exeunt. Manet Lysander and Hermia

LYSANDER

How now my loue? Why is your cheeke so pale?
How chance the roses there doe fade so fast?

HERMIA

Belike, for want of raine: which I could well
Beteeme them, from the tempest of my eyes.

LYSANDER

Eigh me: for aught that I could euer reade,
Could euer here by tale or history,
The course of true loue neuer did runne smoothe:
But either it was different in bloud;

HERMIA

O crosse! too high to be inthrald to lowe.

LYSANDER

Or else misgraffed, in respect of yeares;

HERMIA

O spight! too olde to be ingag'd to young.

LYSANDER

Or merit stoode vpon the choyce of friends;

HERMIA

O hell, to choose loue by anothers eyes!

LYSANDER

Or, if there were a sympathy in choyce,
Warre, death or sicknesse, did lay siege to it;
Making it momentany, as a sound;
Swift, as a shadowe; short, as any dreame;
Briefe, as the lightning in the collied night,
That (in a spleene) vnfolds both heauen and earth;
And, ere a man hath power to say, beholde,
The iawes of darkenesse do deuoure it vp:
So quicke bright things come to confusion.

HERMIA

If then true louers haue bin euer crost,
It stands as an edict, in destiny:
Then let vs teach our triall patience:
Because it is a customary crosse,
As dewe to loue, as thoughts, and dreames, and sighes,
Wishes, and teares; poore Fancies followers.

LYSANDER

A good perswasion: therefore heare mee, *Hermia*:
I haue a widowe aunt, a dowager,
Of great reuenew, and she hath no childe:
And she respectes mee, as her only sonne:
From *Athens* is her house remote, seauen leagues:
There, gentle *Hermia*, may I marry thee:
And to that place, the sharpe *Athenian* law
Can not pursue vs. If thou lou'st mee, then
Steale forth thy fathers house, to morrow night:
And in the wood, a league without the towne
(Where I did meete thee once with *Helena*
To do obseruance to a morne of May)
There will I stay for thee.

HERMIA   My good *Lysander*,

I sweare to thee, by *Cupids* strongest bowe,
By his best arrowe, with the golden heade,
By the simplicitie of *Venus* doues,
By that which knitteth soules, and prospers loues,
And by that fire, which burnd the *Carthage* queene,
When the false *Troian* vnder saile was seene,
By all the vowes that euer men haue broke,
(In number more then euer women spoke)
In that same place thou hast appointed mee,
To morrow truely will I meete with thee.

LYSANDER

Keepe promise loue: looke, here comes *Helena*.

Enter Helena

HERMIA

God speede faire *Helena*: whither away?

HELENA

Call you mee faire? That faire againe vnsay.

Demetrius loues your faire: ô happy faire!
Your eyes are loadstarres, and your tongues sweete
    aire
More tunable then larke, to sheepeheards eare,
When wheat is greene, when hauthorne buddes
    appeare.
Sicknesse is catching: O, were fauour so,
Your words I catch, faire *Hermia*, ere I goe,
My eare should catch your voice, my eye, your eye,
My tongue should catch your tongues sweete melody.
190 Were the world mine, *Demetrius* being bated,
The rest ild giue to be to you translated.
O, teach mee how you looke, and with what Art,
You sway the motion of *Demetrius* heart.

HERMIA
I frowne vpon him; yet hee loues mee still.

HELENA
O that your frowns would teach my smiles such skil.

HERMIA
I giue him curses; yet he giues mee loue.

HELENA
O that my prayers could such affection mooue.

HERMIA
The more I hate, the more he followes mee.

HELENA
The more I loue, the more he hateth mee.

HERMIA
200 His folly, *Helen*, is no fault of mine.

HELENA
None but your beauty; would that fault were mine.

HERMIA
Take comfort: he no more shall see my face:
Lysander and my selfe will fly this place.
Before the time I did *Lisander* see,
Seem'd *Athens* as a Paradise to mee.
O then, what graces in my loue dooe dwell,
That hee hath turnd a heauen vnto a hell!

LYSANDER
Helen, to you our mindes wee will vnfould:
To morrow night, when *Phœbe* doth beholde
210 Her siluer visage, in the watry glasse,
Decking, with liquid pearle, the bladed grasse
(A time, that louers slights doth still conceale)
Through *Athens* gates, haue wee deuis'd to steale.

HERMIA
And in the wood, where often you and I,
Vpon faint Primrose beddes, were wont to lye,
Emptying our bosomes, of their counsell swete,
There my *Lysander*, and my selfe shall meete,
And thence, from *Athens*, turne away our eyes,
To seeke new friends and stranger companies.
220 Farewell, sweete playfellow: pray thou for vs:
And good lucke graunt thee thy *Demetrius*.
Keepe word *Lysander*: we must starue our sight,
From louers foode, till morrow deepe midnight.

LYSANDER
I will my *Hermia*.   *Exit Hermia*
    Helena adieu:
As you on him, *Demetrius* dote on you.   *Exit Lysander*

HELENA
How happie some, ore othersome, can be!
Through *Athens*, I am thought as faire as shee.
But what of that? *Demetrius* thinkes not so:
He will not knowe, what all, but hee doe know.
And as hee erres, doting on *Hermias* eyes: 230
So I, admiring of his qualities.
Things base and vile, holding no quantitie,
Loue can transpose to forme and dignitie.
Loue lookes not with the eyes, but with the minde:
And therefore is wingd *Cupid* painted blinde.
Nor hath loues minde of any iudgement taste:
Wings, and no eyes, figure, vnheedy haste.
And therefore is loue said to bee a childe:
Because, in choyce, he is so oft beguil'd.
As waggish boyes, in game, themselues forsweare: 240
So, the boy, Loue, is periur'd euery where.
For, ere *Demetrius* lookt on *Hermias* eyen,
Hee hayld downe othes, that he was onely mine.
And when this haile some heate, from *Hermia*, felt,
So he dissolu'd, and showrs of oathes did melt.
I will goe tell him of faire *Hermias* flight:
Then, to the wodde, will he, to morrow night,
Pursue her: and for this intelligence,
If I haue thankes, it is a deare expense:
But herein meane I to enrich my paine,   250
To haue his sight thither, and back againe.   *Exit*

   Enter Quince, the Carpenter; and Snugge, the   **Sc. 2**
   Ioyner; and Bottom, the Weauer; and Flute, the   **(1.2)**
   Bellowes mender; & Snout, the Tinker; and
   Starueling the Tayler

QUINCE Is all our company heere?

BOTTOM You were best to call them generally, man by
    man, according to the scrippe.

QUINCE Here is the scrowle of euery mans name, which
    is thought fit, through al *Athens*, to play in our
    Enterlude, before the Duke, & the Dutches, on his
    wedding day at night.

BOTTOM First good *Peeter Quince*, say what the Play treats
    on: then read the names of the Actors: & so grow to   260
    a point.

QUINCE Mary, our Play is the most lamentable comedy,
    and most cruell death of *Pyramus* and *Thisby*.

BOTTOM A very good peece of worke, I assure you, & a
    merry. Now good *Peeter Quince*, call forth your Actors,
    by the scrowle. Masters, spreade your selues.

QUINCE Answere, as I call you. *Nick Bottom*, the Weauer?

BOTTOM Readie: Name what part I am for, and proceede.

QUINCE You, *Nick Bottom* are set downe for *Pyramus*.

BOTTOM What is *Pyramus*? A louer, or a tyrant?   270

QUINCE A louer that kils himselfe, most gallant, for loue.

BOTTOM That will aske some teares in the true performing
    of it. If I doe it, let the Audience looke to their eyes: I
    wil mooue stones: I will condole, in some measure. To
    the rest, yet my chiefe humour is for a tyrant. I could
    play *Ercles* rarely, or a part to teare a Cat in, to make
    all split:

The raging rocks:
And shiuering shocks,
280   Shall breake the locks
      Of prison gates,
    And *Phibbus* carre
    Shall shine from farre,
    And make & marre
      The foolish Fates.
This was loftie. Now, name the rest of the Players. This
is *Ercles* vaine, a tyrants vaine: A louer is more
condoling.

QUINCE *Francis Flute*, the Bellowes mender?

290 FLUTE Here *Peeter Quince*.

QUINCE *Flute*, you must take *Thisby*, on you.

FLUTE What is *Thisby*? A wandring knight?

QUINCE It is the Lady, that *Pyramus* must loue.

FLUTE Nay faith: let not me play a womã: I haue a beard
cõming.

QUINCE Thats all one: you shall play it in a Maske: and
you may speake as small as you will.

BOTTOM And I may hide my face, let me play *Thisby* to:
Ile speake in a monstrous little voice; *Thisne, Thisne,*
300 ah *Pyramus*, my louer deare, thy *Thysby* deare, & Lady
deare.

QUINCE No, no: you must play *Pyramus*: & *Flute*, you
Thysby.

BOTTOM Well, proceede.

QUINCE *Robin Starueling*, the Tailer?

STARUELING Here *Peeter Quince*.

QUINCE *Robin Starueling*, you must play *Thysbyes* mother:
Tom Snowt, the Tinker.

SNOUT Here *Peter Quince*.

310 QUINCE You, *Pyramus* father; my selfe, *Thisbies* father;
Snugge, the Ioyner, you the Lyons part: And I hope
here is a Play fitted.

SNUGGE Haue you the Lyons part written? Pray you, if it
bee, giue it mee: for I am slowe of studie.

QUINCE You may doe it, *extempore*: for it is nothing but
roaring.

BOTTOM Let mee play the Lyon to. I will roare, that I will
doe any mans heart good to heare mee. I will roare,
that I will make the Duke say; Let him roare againe:
320 let him roare againe.

QUINCE And you should do it too terribly, you would
fright the Dutchesse, and the Ladies, that they would
shrike: and that were inough to hang vs all.

ALL THE REST That would hang vs, euery mothers sonne.

BOTTOM I grant you, friends, if you should fright the
Ladies out of their wits, they would haue no more
discretion, but to hang vs: but I will aggrauate my
voice so, that I wil roare you as gently, as any sucking
doue: I will roare you, and 'twere any Nightingale.

330 QUINCE You can play no part but *Piramus*: for *Piramus* is
a sweete fac't man; a proper man as one shall see in
a sommers day; a most louely gentlemanlike man:
therefore you must needes play *Piramus*.

BOTTOM Well: I will vndertake it. What beard were I best
to play it in?

QUINCE Why? what you will.

BOTTOM I wil discharge it, in either your straw colour
beard, your Orange tawnie bearde, your purple in
graine beard, or your french crowne colour beard, your
perfit yellow. 340

QUINCE Some of your french crownes haue no haire at
all; and then you will play bare fac't. But maisters here
are your parts, and I am to intreat you, request you,
and desire you, to con them by to morrow night: and
meete mee in the palace wood, a mile without the
towne, by Moonelight; there will wee rehearse: for if
wee meete in the city, wee shal be dogd with company,
and our deuises known. In the meane time, I will draw
a bill of properties, such as our play wants. I pray you
faile me not. 350

BOTTOM Wee will meete, & there we may rehearse most
obscenely, and coragiously. Take paines, bee perfit:
adieu.

QUINCE At the Dukes oke wee meete.

BOTTOM Enough: holde, or cut bowstrings.   *Exeunt*

Enter a Fairie at one doore, and Robin goodfellow   **Sc. 3**
at another   **(2.1)**

ROBIN
How now spirit, whither wander you?

FAIRY
    Ouer hill, ouer dale,
      Thorough bush, thorough brier,
    Ouer parke, ouer pale,
      Thorough flood, thorough fire: 360
I do wander euery where;
Swifter than the Moones sphere:
And I serue the Fairy Queene,
To dew her orbs vpon the greene.
The cowslippes tall her Pensioners bee,
In their gold coats, spottes you see:
Those be Rubies, Fairie fauours:
In those freckles, liue their sauours.
I must goe seeke some dew droppes here,
    And hang a pearle in euery couslippes eare.   370
Farewell thou Lobbe of spirits: Ile be gon.
Our Queene, and all her Elues come here anon.

ROBIN
The king doth keepe his Reuels here to night.
Take heede the Queene come not within his sight.
For *Oberon* is passing fell and wrath:
Because that she, as her attendant, hath
A louely boy stollen, from an Indian king:
She neuer had so sweete a changeling.
And iealous *Oberon* would haue the childe,
Knight of his traine, to trace the forrests wilde.   380
But shee, perforce, withhoulds the loued boy,
Crownes him with flowers, and makes him all her ioy.
And now, they neuer meete in groue, or greene,
By fountaine cleare, or spangled starlight sheene,
But they doe square, that all their Elues, for feare,
Creepe into acorne cups, and hide them there.

FAIRY

Either I mistake your shape, and making, quite,
Or els you are that shrewde and knauish sprite,
Call'd *Robin goodfellow*. Are not you hee,
390 That frights the maidens of the Villageree,
Skim milke, and sometimes labour in the querne,
And bootlesse make the breathlesse huswife cherne,
And sometime make the drinke to beare no barme,
Misselead nightwanderers, laughing at their harme?
Those, that Hobgoblin call you, and sweete Puck,
You doe their worke, and they shall haue good luck.
Are not you hee?

ROBIN   Thou speak'st aright;
I am that merry wanderer of the night.
I ieast to *Oberon*, and make him smile,
400 When I a fat and beane-fed horse beguile;
Neyghing, in likenesse of a filly fole,
And sometime lurke I in a gossippes bole,
In very likenesse of a rosted crabbe,
And when she drinkes, against her lips I bob,
And on her witherd dewlop, poure the ale.
The wisest Aunt, telling the saddest tale,
Sometime, for three foote stoole, mistaketh mee:
Then slippe I from her bumme, downe topples she,
And tailour cryes, and falles into a coffe;
And then the whole Quire hould their hippes, and
410   loffe,
And waxen in their myrth, and neeze, and sweare
A merrier hower was neuer wasted there.

*Enter Oberon the King of Fairies, at one doore, with
his traine; and Titania the Queene, at another,
with hers*

But make roome Faery: here comes *Oberon*.

FAIRY

And here, my mistresse. Would that he were gon.

OBERON

Ill met by moonelight, proud *Tytania*.

TITANIA

What, Iealous *Oberon*? Fairies skippe hence.
I haue forsworne his bedde, and company.

OBERON

Tarry, rash wanton. Am not I thy Lord?

TITANIA

Then I must be thy Lady: but I know
420 When thou hast stollen away from Fairy land,
And in the shape of *Corin*, sat all day,
Playing on pipes of corne, and versing loue,
To amorous *Phillida*. Why art thou here
Come from the farthest steppe of *India*?
But that, forsooth, the bounsing *Amason*,
Your buskind mistresse, and your warriour loue,
To *Theseus* must be wedded; and you come,
To giue their bedde, ioy and prosperitie.

OBERON

How canst thou thus, for shame, *Tytania*,
430 Glaunce at my credit, with *Hippolita*?
Knowing, I know thy loue to *Theseus*.

Didst not thou lead him through the glimmering
    night,
From *Perigouna*, whom he rauished?
And make him, with faire *Ægles*, breake his faith
With *Ariadne*, and *Antiopa*?

TITANIA

These are the forgeries of iealousie:
And neuer, since the middle Sommers spring,
Met we on hill, in dale, forrest, or meade,
By paued fountaine, or by rushie brooke,
Or in the beached margent of the Sea,   440
To daunce our ringlets to the whistling winde,
But with thy brawles thou hast disturbd our sport.
Therefore the windes, pyping to vs in vaine,
As in reuenge, haue suckt vp, from the Sea,
Contagious fogges: which, falling in the land,
Hath euery pelting riuer made so proude,
That they haue ouerborne their Continents.
The Oxe hath therefore stretcht his yoake in vaine,
The Ploughman lost his sweat, and the greene corne
Hath rotted, ere his youth attainde a bearde: 450
The fold stands empty, in the drowned field,
And crowes are fatted with the murrion flocke.
The nine mens Morris is fild vp with mudde:
And the queint Mazes, in the wanton greene,
For lacke of tread, are vndistinguishable.
The humane mortals want their winter cheere.
No night is now with hymne or carroll blest.
Therefore the Moone (the gouernesse of floods)
Pale in her anger, washes all the aire;
That Rheumaticke diseases doe abound.   460
And, thorough this distemperature, wee see
The seasons alter: hoary headed frosts
Fall in the fresh lappe of the Crymson rose,
And on old *Hyems* thinne and Icy crowne,
An odorous Chaplet of sweete Sommer buddes
Is, as in mockery, set. The Spring, the Sommer,
The childing Autumne, angry Winter change
Their wonted Liueries: and the mazed worlde,
By their increase, now knowes not which is which:
And this same progeny of euils, comes   470
From our debate, from our dissention:
We are their Parents and originall.

OBERON

Doe you amend it then: it lyes in you.
Why should *Titania* crosse her *Oberon*?
I doe but begge a little Changeling boy,
To be my Henchman.

TITANIA   Set your heart at rest.
The Faiery Land buies not the childe of mee.
His mother was a Votresse of my order:
And in the spiced *Indian* ayer, by night,
Full often hath she gossipt, by my side,   480
And sat, with me on *Neptunes* yellow sands
Marking th'embarked traders on the flood:
When we haue laught to see the sailes conceaue,
And grow bigge bellied, with the wanton winde:

Which she, with prettie, and with swimming gate,
Following (her wombe then rich with my young
    squire)
Would imitate, and saile vpon the land,
To fetch me trifles, and returne againe,
As from a voyage, rich with marchandise.

490 But she, being mortall, of that boy did dye,
And, for her sake, doe I reare vp her boy:
And, for her sake, I will not part with him.

OBERON

How long, within this wood, entend you stay?

TITANIA

Perchaunce, till after *Theseus* wedding day.
If you will patiently daunce in our Round,
And see our Moonelight Reuelles, goe with vs:
If not, shunne me, and I will spare your haunts.

OBERON

Giue mee that boy, and I will goe with thee.

TITANIA

Not for thy Fairy kingdome. Fairies away.
500 We shall chide downeright, if I longer stay.

                Exeunt Titania and her traine

OBERON

Well: goe thy way. Thou shalt not from this groue,
Till I torment thee, for this iniury.
My gentle *Pucke* come hither: thou remembrest,
Since once I sat vpon a promontory,
And heard a Mearemaide, on a Dolphins backe,
Vttering such dulcet and hermonious breath,
That the rude sea grewe ciuill at her song,
And certaine starres shot madly from their Spheares,
To heare the Sea-maids musicke.

ROBIN   I remember.

OBERON

510 That very time, I saw (but thou could'st not)
Flying betweene the colde Moone and the earth,
Cupid, all arm'd: a certaine aime he tooke
At a faire Vestall, throned by the west,
And loos'd his loue-shaft smartly, from his bowe,
As it should pearce a hundred thousand hearts:
But, I might see young *Cupids* fiery shaft
Quencht in the chast beames of the watry Moone:
And the imperiall Votresse passed on,
In maiden meditation, fancy free.

520 Yet markt I, where the bolt of *Cupid* fell.
It fell vpon a little westerne flower;
Before, milke white; now purple, with loues wound,
And maidens call it, Loue in idlenesse.
Fetch mee that flowre: the herbe I shewed thee once.
The iewce of it, on sleeping eyeliddes laide,
Will make or man or woman madly dote,
Vpon the next liue creature that it sees.
Fetch mee this herbe, and be thou here againe
Ere the *Leuiathan* can swimme a league.

ROBIN

530 Ile put a girdle, roũd about the earth,
In forty minutes.   *Exit*

OBERON   Hauing once this iuice,
Ile watch *Titania*, when she is a sleepe,

And droppe the liquor of it, in her eyes:
The next thing then she, waking, lookes vpon
(Be it on Lyon, Beare, or Wolfe, or Bull,
On medling Monky, or on busie Ape)
She shall pursue it, with the soule of Loue.
And ere I take this charme, from of her sight
(As I can take it with another herbe)
Ile make her render vp her Page, to mee.   540
But, who comes here? I am inuisible,
And I will ouerheare their conference.

    Enter Demetrius, Helena following him

DEMETRIUS

I loue thee not: therefore pursue me not,
Where is *Lysander*, and faire *Hermia*?
The one Ile slay: the other slayeth me.
Thou toldst me, they were stolne vnto this wood:
And here am I, and wodde, within this wood:
Because I cannot meete my *Hermia*.
Hence, get the gone, and follow mee no more.

HELENA

You draw mee, you hard hearted Adamant: 550
But yet you draw not Iron. For my heart
Is true as steele. Leaue you your power to draw,
And I shall haue no power to follow you.

DEMETRIUS

Doe I entise you? Doe I speake you faire?
Or rather doe I not in plainest truthe,
Tell you I doe not, nor I cannot loue you?

HELENA

And euen, for that, do I loue you, the more:
I am your Spaniell: and, *Demetrius*,
The more you beat mee, I will fawne on you.
Vse me but as your Spaniell: spurne me, strike mee,   560
Neglect mee, loose me: onely giue me leaue
(Vnworthie as I am) to follow you.
What worser place can I begge, in your loue
(And yet, a place of high respect with mee)
Then to be vsed as you vse your dogge.

DEMETRIUS

Tempt not, too much, the hatred of my spirit.
For I am sick, when I do looke on thee.

HELENA

And I am sick, when I looke not on you.

DEMETRIUS

You doe impeach your modestie too much,
To leaue the citie, and commit your selfe,   570
Into the hands of one that loues you not,
To trust the opportunitie of night,
And the ill counsell of a desert place,
With the rich worth of your virginitie.

HELENA

Your vertue is my priuiledge: For that
It is not night, when I doe see your face.
Therefore, I thinke, I am not in the night,
Nor doth this wood lacke worlds of company.
For you, in my respect, are all the world.
Then, how can it be saide, I am alone,   580
When all the world is here, to looke on mee?

DEMETRIUS

Ile runne from thee, and hide me in the brakes,
And leaue thee to the mercy of wilde beastes.

HELENA

The wildest hath not such a heart as you.
Runne when you will: The story shall be chaung'd:
Apollo flies and *Daphne* holds the chase:
The Doue pursues the Griffon: the milde Hinde
Makes speede to catch the Tigre. Bootelesse speede,
When cowardise pursues, and valour flies.

DEMETRIUS

590　　I will not stay thy questions. Let me goe:
Or if thou followe mee, do not beleeue,
But I shall doe thee mischiefe, in the wood.

HELENA

I, in the Temple, in the towne, the fielde,
You doe me mischiefe. Fy *Demetrius*.
Your wrongs doe set a scandall on my sex:
We cannot fight for loue, as men may doe:
We should be woo'd, and were not made to wooe.
Ile follow thee and make a heauen of hell,
To dy vpon the hand I loue so well.

⌐*Exit Demetrius, Helena following him*⌐

OBERON

600　　Fare thee well Nymph. Ere he do leaue this groue,
Thou shalt fly him, and he shall seeke thy loue.

Enter Robin the Pucke

Hast thou the flower there? Welcome wanderer.

ROBIN

I, there it is.

OBERON　　　　I pray thee giue it mee.

I know a banke where the wilde time blowes,
Where Oxlips, and the nodding Violet growes,
Quite ouercanopi'd with lushious woodbine,
With sweete muske roses, and with Eglantine:
There sleepes *Tytania*, sometime of the night,
Luld in these flowers, with daunces and delight:
610　　And there the snake throwes her enammeld skinne,
Weed wide enough to wrappe a Fairy in.
And, with the iuyce of this, Ile streake her eyes,
And make her full of hatefull phantasies.
Take thou some of it, and seeke through this groue:
A sweete *Athenian* Lady is in loue,
With a disdainefull youth: annoint his eyes.
But doe it, when the next thing he espies,
May be the Ladie. Thou shalt know the man,
By the *Athenian* garments he hath on.
620　　Effect it with some care; that he may prooue
More fond on her, then she vpon her loue:
And looke thou meete me ere the first Cocke crowe.

ROBIN

Feare not my Lord: your seruant shall do so.

Exeunt seuerally

Sc. 4　　　　*Enter Tytania Queene of Fairies, with her traine*
(2.2)　TITANIA

Come, now a Roundell, and a Fairy song:
Then, for the third part of a minute hence,
Some to kill cankers in the musk rose buds,

Some warre with Reremise, for their lethren wings,
To make my small Elues coates, and some keepe backe
The clamorous Owle, that nightly hootes and wonders
At our queint spirits: Sing me now a sleepe:　　　630
Then to your offices, and let mee rest.

She lyes downe. Fairies sing

⌐I. FAIRY⌐

You spotted Snakes, with double tongue,
Thorny Hedgehogges be not seene,
Newts and blindewormes do no wrong,
Come not neere our Fairy Queene.

⌐CHORUS⌐ ⌐*dauncing*⌐

Philomele, with melody,
Sing in our sweete Lullaby,
Lulla, lulla, lullaby, lulla, lulla, lullaby,
Neuer harme,
Nor spell, nor charme,　　　　640
Come our louely lady nigh.
So good night, with lullaby.

I. FAIRY　Weauing Spiders come not heere:
Hence you long legd Spinners, hence:
Beetles blacke approach not neere:
Worme nor snaile doe no offence.

⌐CHORUS⌐ ⌐*dauncing*⌐

Philomele with melody,
Sing in our sweete Lullaby,
Lulla, lulla, lullaby, lulla, lulla, lullaby,
Neuer harme,　　　　650
Nor spell, nor charme,
Come our louely lady nigh.
So good night, with lullaby.

Titania sleepes

2. FAIRY

Hence away: now all is well:
One aloofe, stand Centinell.

Exeunt. Manet Titania ⌐*and the Centinell*⌐
Enter Oberon. He droppes the iuice on Titanias
eyeliddes

OBERON

What thou seest, when thou doest wake,
Doe it for thy true loue take:
Loue and languish for his sake.
Be it Ounce, or Catte, or Beare,
Pard, or Boare with bristled haire,　　　660
In thy eye that shall appeare,
When thou wak'st, it is thy deare:
Wake, when some vile thing is neere.　　*Exit*

Enter Lysander: and Hermia

LYSANDER

Faire loue, you fainte, with wandring in the wood:
And to speake troth I haue forgot our way.
Weele rest vs *Hermia*, if you thinke it good,
And tarry for the comfort of the day.

HERMIA

Be it so *Lysander*: finde you out a bedde:
For I, vpon this banke, will rest my head.

⌐*She lyes down*⌐

LYSANDER

670 One turfe shall serue, as pillow, for vs both,
One heart, one bedde, two bosomes, and one troth.

HERMIA

Nay good *Lysander*: for my sake, my deere,
Ly further off, yet; doe not lye so neere.

LYSANDER

O take the sense, sweete, of my innocence.
Loue takes the meaning, in loues conference.
I meane that my heart vnto yours is knit;
So that but one heart wee can make of it:
Two bosomes interchained with an oath:
So then two bosomes, and a single troth.

680 Then, by your side, no bed-roome me deny:
For lying so, *Hermia*, I doe not lye.

HERMIA

Lysander riddles very prettily.
Now much beshrewe my manners, and my pride,
If *Hermia* meant to say, *Lysander* lyed.
But gentle friend, for loue and curtesie,
Ly further off, in humane modesty:
Such separation, as may well be said
Becomes a vertuous batcheler, and a maide,
So farre be distant, and good night sweete friend:

690 Thy loue nere alter till thy sweete life end.

LYSANDER

Amen, amen, to that faire prayer, say I,
And then end life, when I end loyalty.
Heere is my bed: sleepe giue thee all his rest.

He lyes down

HERMIA

With halfe that wish, the wishers eyes be prest.

They sleepe, apart.

Enter Robin the Pucke

ROBIN

Through the forrest haue I gone:
But *Athenian* found I none,
On whose eyes I might approue
This flowers force in stirring loue.
Night and silence. Who is heere?

700 Weedes of *Athens* he doth weare:
This is hee (my master saide)
Despised the *Athenian* maide:
And here the maiden, sleeping sound,
On the danke and dirty ground.
Pretty sowle, she durst not lye,
Neere this lack-loue, this kil-curtesie.
Churle, vpon thy eyes I throwe
All the power this charme doth owe:

He droppes the iuyce on Lysanders eyeliddes

When thou wak'st, let loue forbidde

710 Sleepe, his seat, on thy eye lidde.
So awake, when I am gon:
For I must now to *Oberon*.   *Exit*

Enter Demetrius and Helena running

HELENA

Stay; though thou kill mee, sweete *Demetrius*.

DEMETRIUS

I charge thee hence, and doe not haunt mee thus.

HELENA

O, wilt thou darkling leaue me? doe not so.

DEMETRIUS

Stay, on thy perill: I alone will goe.   *Exit Demetrius*

HELENA

O, I am out of breath, in this fond chase,
The more my prayer, the lesser is my grace.
Happie is *Hermia*, wheresoere she lies:
For she hath blessed, and attractiue eyes.   720
How came her eyes so bright? Not with salt teares.
If so, my eyes are oftner washt then hers.
No, no: I am as vgly as a Beare:
For beastes that meete mee, runne away, for feare.
Therefore, no maruaile, though *Demetrius*
Doe, as a monster, fly my presence, thus.
What wicked and dissembling glasse, of mine,
Made me compare with *Hermias* sphery eyen!
But, who is here? *Lysander*, on the ground?
Dead, or a sleepe? I see no blood, no wound.   730
Lysander, if you liue, good sir awake.

LYSANDER (*awaking*)

And runne through fire, I will for thy sweete sake.
Transparent *Helena*, nature shewes arte,
That through thy bosome, makes me see thy heart.
Where is *Demetrius*? Oh how fit a word
Is that vile name, to perish on my sworde!

HELENA

Do not say so, *Lysander*, say not so.
What though he loue your *Hermia*? Lord, what though?
Yet *Hermia* still loues you: then be content.

LYSANDER

Content with *Hermia*? No: I doe repent   740
The tedious minutes, I with her haue spent.
Not *Hermia*, but *Helena* I loue.
Who will not change a Rauen for a doue?
The will of man is by his reason swai'd:
And reason saies you are the worthier maide.
Things growing are not ripe, vntill their season:
So I, being young, till now ripe not to reason.
And touching now, the point of humane skill,
Reason becomes the Marshall to my will,
And leads mee to your eyes; where I orelooke   750
Loues stories, written in loues richest booke.

HELENA

Wherefore was I to this keene mockery borne?
When, at your hands, did I deserue this scorne?
Ist not enough, ist not enough, young man,
That I did neuer, no nor neuer can,
Deserue a sweete looke from *Demetrius* eye,
But you must flout my insufficiency?
Good troth you doe mee wrong (good sooth you doe)
In such disdainfull manner, mee to wooe.
But, fare you well: perforce, I must confesse,   760
I thought you Lord of more true gentlenesse.
O, that a Ladie, of one man refus'd,
Should, of another, therefore be abus'd!   *Exit*

LYSANDER

She sees not *Hermia*. *Hermia*, sleepe thou there,
And neuer maist thou come *Lysander* neere.

For, as a surfet of the sweetest things
The deepest loathing, to the stomacke bringes:
Or, as the heresies, that men doe leaue,
Are hated most of those they did deceiue:
770 So thou, my surfet, and my heresie,
Of all bee hated; but the most, of mee:
And all my powers addresse your loue and might,
To honour *Helen*, and to be her knight.   *Exit*

HERMIA (*awaking*)
Helpe mee *Lysander*, helpe mee: do thy best
To pluck this crawling serpent, from my brest.
Ay mee, for pittie. What a dreame was here?
Lysander looke, how I doe quake with feare.
Me thought, a serpent eate my heart away,
And you sate smiling at his cruell pray.
780 *Lysander* what, remou'd? *Lysander*, Lord,
What, out of hearing, gon? No sound, no word?
Alacke where are you? Speake, and if you heare:
Speake, of all loues. I swoune almost with feare.
No, then I well perceiue, you are not ny:
Either death, or you, Ile finde immediately.   *Exit*

(3.1)   *Enter the Clownes: Quince, Snug, Bottom, Flute,*
          Snout, and Starueling
BOTTOM Are wee all met?
QUINCE Pat, pat: and heres a maruailes conuenient place,
for our rehearsall. This greene plot shall be our stage,
this hauthorne brake our tyring house, and wee will
790 doe it in action, as wee will doe it before the Duke.
BOTTOM *Peeter Quince?*
QUINCE What saiest thou, bully *Bottom?*
BOTTOM There are things in this Comedy, of *Pyramus* and
Thisby, that will neuer please. First, *Pyramus* must draw
a sworde, to kill himselfe; which the Ladies cannot
abide. How answere you that?
SNOUT Berlakin, a parlous feare.
STARUELING I beleeue, we must leaue the killing, out,
when all is done.
800 BOTTOM Not a whit: I haue a deuise to make all well.
Write me a Prologue, and let the Prologue seeme to
say; we wil do no harme, with our swords, and that
Pyramus is not kild indeede: and for the more better
assurance, tel them, that I *Pyramus* am not *Pyramus*,
but *Bottom* the weauer: this will put them out of feare.
QUINCE Well: wee will haue such a Prologue, and it shall
be written in eight and six.
BOTTOM No: make it two more: let it be written in eight
& eight.
810 SNOUT Will not the ladies be afeard of the Lyon?
STARUELING I feare it, I promise you.
BOTTOM Masters, you ought to consider with your selfe,
to bring in (God shielde vs) a Lyon among Ladies, is a
most dreadfull thing. For there is not a more fearefull
wilde foule then your Lyon liuing: & we ought to looke
toote.
SNOUT Therfore, another Prologue must tel, he is not a
Lion.
BOTTOM Nay: you must name his name, and halfe his
820 face must be seene through the Lions necke, and he

himselfe must speake through, saying thus, or to the
same defect; Ladies, or faire Ladies, I would wish you,
or I would request you, or I wold intreat you, not to
feare, not to trēble: my life for yours. If you thinke I
come hither as a Lyon, it were pittie of my life. No: I
am no such thing: I am a man as other men are: &
there indeed, let him name his name, and tell them
plainely he is *Snugge*, the Ioyner.
QUINCE Well: it shall be so: but there is two hard things;
that is, to bring the Moone-light into a chamber: for   830
you know, *Pyramus* and *Thisby* meete by Moone-light.
⌈SNOUT⌉ Doth the Moone shine, that night, we play our
Play?
BOTTOM A Calender, a Calender: looke in the Almanack:
finde out Moone-shine, finde out Moone-shine.
     ⌈*Enter Robin the Pucke, inuisible*⌉
QUINCE ⌈*with a booke*⌉ Yes: it doth shine that night.
BOTTOM Why then, may you leaue a casement of the
great chamber window (where we play) open; and the
Moone may shine in at the casement.
QUINCE I: or els, one must come in, with a bush of thorns, 840
& a lātern, and say he comes to disfigure, or to present
the person of Moone-shine. Then, there is another
thing; we must haue a wal in the great chāber: for
Pyramus & *Thisby* (saies the story) did talke through
the chinke of a wall.
SNOUT You can neuer bring in a wal. What say you
Bottom?
BOTTOM Some man or other must present wall: and let
him haue some plaster, or som lome, or some rough
cast, about him, to signifie wall; and let him holde his   850
fingers thus: and through that crany, shall *Pyramus*
and *Thisby* whisper.
QUINCE If that may be, then all is well. Come, sit downe
euery mothers sonne, and reherse your parts. *Pyramus*,
you beginne: when you haue spoken your speech,
enter into that Brake, and so euery one according to
his cue.

ROBIN (*aside*)
What hempen homespunnes haue we swaggring here,
So neere the Cradle of the Fairy Queene?
What, a play toward? Ile be an Auditor,   860
An Actor to perhappes, If I see cause.
QUINCE Speake *Pyramus: Thysby* stand forth.
BOTTOM (*as Pyramus*)
Thisby the flowers of odious sauours sweete.
QUINCE Odours, odours.
BOTTOM (*as Pyramus*)   Odours sauours sweete.
So hath thy breath, my dearest *Thisby* deare.
But harke, a voice: stay thou but heere a while,
And by and by I will to thee appeare.   *Exit*
⌈ROBIN⌉ (*aside*)
A stranger *Pyramus*, then ere played heere.   *Exit*
FLUTE Must I speake now?   870
QUINCE I marry must you. For you must vnderstād, he
goes but to see a noyse, that he heard, and is to come
againe.

361

FLUTE (*as Thisby*)
Most radiant *Pyramus*, most lillie white of hewe,
    Of colour like the redrose, on triumphant bryer,
Most brisly *Iuuenall*, and eeke most louely *Iewe*,
    As true as truest horse, that yet would neuer tyre,
    Ile meete thee *Pyramus*, at *Ninnies* toumbe.

QUINCE *Ninus* toumbe, man. Why? you must not speake
880   that yet. That you answere to *Pyramus*. You speake al
your part at once, cues, and all. *Pyramus*, enter: your
cue is past: It is; neuer tire.

FLUTE O,
    (*As Thisby*) As true as truest horse, that yet would
        neuer tyre.
        Enter ⌜Robin, leading⌝ Bottom with the Asse head

BOTTOM (*as Pyramus*)
    If I were faire, *Thysby*, I were onely thine.

QUINCE O monstrous! O strange! We are haunted. Pray
    masters: fly masters: helpe.   ⌜*The Clownes all Exit*⌝

ROBIN
    Ile follow you: Ile leade you about a Round,
        Through bogge, through bush, through brake,
            through bryer:
890   Sometime a horse Ile be, sometime a hound,
        A hogge, a headelesse Beare, sometime a fier,
    And neigh, and barke, and grunt, and rore, and burne,
    Like horse, hound, hogge, beare, fire, at euery turne.
                                                            Exit
        ⌜*Enter Bottom againe with the Asse head*⌝

BOTTOM Why doe they runne away? This is a knauery of
    them to make mee afeard.
        Enter Snowte

SNOUT O *Bottom*, thou art chaung'd. What do I see on
    thee?

BOTTOM What doe you see? You see an Asse head of your
    owne. Do you?   ⌜*Exit Snout*⌝
        Enter Quince

900 QUINCE Blesse thee *Bottom*, blesse thee. Thou art trāslated.
                                                            Exit

BOTTOM I see their knauery. This is to make an asse of
    mee, to fright me, if they could: but I wil not stirre
    from this place, do what they can. I will walke vp and
    downe heere, and I will sing, that they shall heare I
    am not afraide.
        (*Sings*)
            The Woosell cock, so blacke of hewe,
                With Orange tawny bill,
            The Throstle, with his note so true,
                The Wren, with little quill.

TITANIA (*awaking*)
910   What Angell wakes me from my flowry bed?

BOTTOM (*sings*)
            The Fynch, the Sparrowe, and the Larke,
                The plainsong Cuckow gray:
            Whose note, full many a man doth marke,
                And dares not answere, nay.
    For indeede, who would set his wit to so foolish a
    birde? Who would giue a bird the ly, though hee cry
    Cuckow, neuer so?

TITANIA
    I pray thee, gentle mortall, sing againe.
    Myne eare is much enamourd of thy note:
    So is mine eye enthralled to thy shape,   920
    And thy faire vertues force (perforce) doth mooue mee,
    On the first viewe to say, to sweare, I loue thee.

BOTTOM Mee thinks mistresse, you should haue little
    reason for that. And yet, to say the truth, reason and
    loue keepe little company together, now a daies. The
    more the pitty, that some honest neighbours will not
    make them friends. Nay I can gleeke, vpon occasion.

TITANIA
    Thou art as wise, as thou art beautifull.

BOTTOM Not so neither: but if I had wit enough to get
    out of this wood, I haue enough to serue mine owne   930
    turne.

TITANIA
    Out of this wood, doe not desire to goe:
    Thou shalt remaine here, whether thou wilt or no.
    I am a spirit, of no common rate:
    The Sommer, still, doth tend vpon my state,
    And I doe loue thee: therefore goe with mee.
    Ile giue thee Fairies to attend on thee:
    And they shall fetch thee Iewels, from the deepe,
    And sing, while thou, on pressed flowers, dost sleepe:
    And I will purge thy mortall grossenesse so,   940
    That thou shalt, like an ayery spirit, goe.
    Pease-blossome, Cobweb, Moth, and Mustard-seede?
        Enter foure Fairyes: Pease-blossome, Cobweb,
        Moth, and Mustard-seede

A FAIRY
    Readie:

ANOTHER and I,

ANOTHER   and I,

ANOTHER   and I.

⌜ALL FOUR⌝   Where shall we goe?

TITANIA
·   Be kinde and curteous to this gentleman,
    Hop in his walkes, and gambole in his eyes,
    Feede him with Apricocks, and Dewberries,
    With purple Grapes, greene figges, and Mulberries,
    The hony bagges steale from the humble Bees,
    And for night tapers, croppe their waxen thighes,
    And light them at the fiery Glowe-wormes eyes,   950
    To haue my loue to bedde, and to arise,
    And pluck the wings, from painted Butterflies,
    To fanne the Moone-beames from his sleeping eyes,
    Nod to him Elues, and doe him curtesies.

A FAIRY Haile mortall.

⌜ANOTHER⌝ Haile.

ANOTHER Haile.

ANOTHER Haile.

BOTTOM I cry your worships mercy, hartily: I beseech
    your worshippes name.   960

COBWEB *Cobwebbe.*

BOTTOM I shall desire you of more acquaintance, good
    master *Cobweb*: if I cut my finger, I shall make bolde
    with you. Your name honest gentleman?

PEASE-BLOSSOME *Pease-blossome.*

BOTTOM I pray you commend mee to mistresse *Squash*,
your mother, and to master *Peascod*, your father. Good
master *Pease-blossome*, I shall desire you of more
acquaintance, to. Your name I beseech you sir?

970 MUSTARDSEEDE *Mustardseede*.

BOTTOM Good master *Mustardseede*, I know your patience
well. That same cowardly, gyantlike, Ox-beefe hath
deuourd many a gentleman of your house. I promise
you, your kindred hath made my eyes water, ere now.
I desire you of more acquaintance, good master
Mustardseede.

TITANIA (*to the Fairies*)

Come waite vpon him: leade him to my bower.
   The Moone, me thinkes, lookes with a watry eye:
And when shee weepes, weepes euery little flower,
980   Lamenting some enforced chastitie.
Ty vp my loue's tongue, bring him silently.   *Exeunt*

Sc. 5   *Enter Oberon King of Fairies, solus*
(3.2) OBERON

I wonder if *Titania* be awak't;
Then what it was, that next came in her eye,
Which she must dote on, in extreamitie.
   Enter Robin goodfellow the Pucke
Here comes my messenger. How now, mad spirit?
What nightrule now about this haunted groue?

ROBIN

My mistresse with a monster is in loue.
Neere to her close and consecrated bower,
While she was in her dull, and sleeping hower,
990 A crew of patches, rude Mechanicals,
That worke for bread, vpon *Athenian* stalles,
Were met together to rehearse a play,
Intended for great *Theseus* nuptiall day:
The shallowest thickskinne, of that barraine sort,
Who *Pyramus* presented, in their sport,
Forsooke his Scene, and entred in a brake:
When I did him at this aduantage take,
An Asses nole I fixed on his head.
Anon his *Thisbie* must be answered,
1000 And forth my Mimmick comes. When they him spy;
As wilde geese, that the creeping Fouler eye,
Or russet pated choughes, many in sort
(Rysing, and cawing, at the gunnes report)
Seuer themselues, and madly sweepe the sky:
So, at his sight, away his fellowes fly,
And at our stampe, here ore and ore, one falles:
He murther cryes, and helpe from *Athens* cals.
Their sense, thus weake, lost with their feares, thus
    strong,
Made senselesse things begin to doe them wrong.
1010 For, briers and thornes, at their apparell, snatch:
Some sleeues, some hats; from yeelders, all things
    catch.
I led them on, in this distracted feare,
And left sweete *Pyramus* translated there:
When in that moment (so it came to passe)
Tytania wak't, and straight way lou'd an Asse.

OBERON

This falles out better, then I could deuise.
But hast thou yet latcht the *Athenians* eyes,
With the loue iuice, as I did bid thee doe?

ROBIN

I tooke him sleeping (that is finisht to)
And the *Athenian* woman, by his side; 1020
That when he wak't, of force she must be ey'd.
   Enter Demetrius and Hermia

OBERON

Stand close: this is the same *Athenian*.

ROBIN

This is the woman: but not this the man.
   ⌐*They stand apart*⌐

DEMETRIUS

O, Why rebuke you him, that loues you so?
Lay breath so bitter, on your bitter foe.

HERMIA

Now I but chide: but I should vse thee worse.
For thou (I feare) hast giuen me cause to curse.
If thou hast slaine *Lysander*, in his sleepe;
Being ore shooes in blood, plunge in the deepe,
And kill mee to. 1030
The Sunne was not so true vnto the day,
As hee to mee. Would hee haue stollen away,
From sleeping *Hermia*? Ile beleeue, as soone,
This whole earth may be bor'd, and that the Moone
May through the Center creepe, and so displease
Her brothers noonetide, with th'*Antipodes*.
It cannot be, but thou hast murdred him.
So should a murtherer looke; so dead, so grimme.

DEMETRIUS

So should the murtherd looke, and so should I,
Pearst through the heart, with your sterne cruelty. 1040
Yet you, the murtherer, looke as bright, as cleere,
As yonder *Venus*, in her glimmering spheare.

HERMIA

Whats this to my *Lysander*? Where is hee?
Ah good *Demetrius*, wilt thou giue him mee?

DEMETRIUS

I had rather giue his carcasse to my hounds.

HERMIA

Out dog, out curre: thou driu'st me past the bounds
Of maidens patience. Hast thou slaine him then?
Henceforth be neuer numbred among men.
O, once tell true: tell true, euen for my sake:
Durst thou haue lookt vpon him, being awake? 1050
And hast thou kild him, sleeping? O braue tutch!
Could not a worme, an Adder do so much?
An Adder did it: For with doubler tongue
Then thyne (thou serpent) neuer Adder stung.

DEMETRIUS

You spende your passion, on a mispris'd mood:
I am not guilty of *Lysanders* bloode:
Nor is he deade, for ought that I can tell.

HERMIA

I pray thee, tell mee then, that he is well.

DEMETRIUS
And if I could, what should I get therefore?

HERMIA
1060 A priuiledge, neuer to see mee more:
And from thy hated presence part I so:
See me no more; whether he be dead or no.   *Exit*

DEMETRIUS
There is no following her in this fierce vaine.
Heere therefore, for a while, I will remaine.
So sorrowes heauinesse doth heauier growe,
For debt that bankrout sleepe doth sorrow owe:
Which now in some slight measure it will pay;
If for his tender here I make some stay.
          He lys doune and sleepes

OBERON (*to Robin*)
What hast thou done? Thou hast mistaken quite,
1070 And laid the loue iuice on some true loues sight.
Of thy misprision, must perforce ensue
Some true loue turnd, and not a false turnd true.

ROBIN
Then fate orerules, that one man holding troth,
A million faile, confounding oath on oath.

OBERON
About the wood, goe swifter then the winde,
And *Helena* of *Athens* looke thou finde.
All fancy sicke she is and pale of cheere,
With sighes of loue, that costs the fresh blood deare.
By some illusion see thou bring her here:
1080 Ile charme his eyes, against she doe appeare.

ROBIN
I goe, I goe, looke how I goe.
Swifter then arrow, from the *Tartars* bowe.   *Exit*

OBERON
Flower of this purple dy,
Hit with *Cupids* archery,
Sinke in apple of his eye,
          He droppes the iuyce on Demetrius eyeliddes
When his loue he doth espy,
Let her shine as gloriously
As the *Venus* of the sky.
When thou wak'st, if she be by,
1090 Begge of her, for remedy.
          Enter Robin the Puck

ROBIN
Captaine of our Fairy band,
Helena is heere at hande,
And the youth, mistooke by mee,
Pleading for a louers fee.
Shall wee their fond pageant see?
Lord, what fooles these mortals bee!

OBERON
Stand aside. The noyse, they make,
Will cause *Demetrius* to awake.

ROBIN
Then will two, at once, wooe one:
1100 That must needes be sport alone.
And those things do best please mee,
That befall prepost'rously.
          ⌈*They stand apart*⌉

          Enter Helena, Lysander ⌈*following her*⌉
LYSANDER
Why should you think, that I should wooe in scorne?
Scorne, and derision, neuer come in teares.
Looke when I vow, I weepe: and vowes so borne,
In their natiuitie all truth appeares.
How can these things, in mee, seeme scorne to you?
Bearing the badge of faith to prooue them true.

HELENA
You doe aduance your cunning, more, and more,
When trueth killes truth, ô diuelish holy fray!   1110
These vowes are *Hermias*. Will you giue her ore?
Weigh oath, with oath, and you will nothing waigh.
Your vowes to her, and mee (put in two scales)
Will euen weigh; and both as light as tales.

LYSANDER
I had no iudgement, when to her I swore.

HELENA
Nor none, in my minde, now you giue her ore.

LYSANDER
Demetrius loues her: and he loues not you.

⌈HELENA⌉
⌈   ⌉

DEMETRIUS (*awaking*)
O *Helen*, goddesse, nymph, perfect diuine,
To what, my loue, shall I compare thine eyne!   1120
Christall is muddy. O, how ripe, in showe,
Thy lippes, those kissing cherries, tempting growe!
That pure coniealed white, high *Taurus* snow,
Fand with the Easterne winde, turnes to a crowe,
When thou holdst vp thy hand. O, let me kisse
This Princesse of pure white, this seale of blisse.

HELENA
O spight! O hell! I see, you all are bent
To set against mee, for your merriment.
If you were ciuill, and knew curtesie,
You would not doe mee thus much iniury.   1130
Can you not hate mee, as I know you doe,
But you must ioyne, in soules, to mocke mee to?
If you were men, as men you are in showe,
You would not vse a gentle Lady so;
To vowe, and sweare, and superpraise my parts,
When I am sure, you hate mee with your hearts.
You both are Riuals, and loue *Hermia*:
And now both Riualles, to mock *Helena*.
A trim exploit, a manly enterprise,
To coniure teares vp, in a poore maides eyes,   1140
With your derision. None, of noble sort,
Would so offend a virgine, and extort
A poore soules patience, all to make you sport.

LYSANDER
You are vnkinde, *Demetrius*: be not so.
For you loue *Hermia*: this you know I know.
And heare, with all good will, with all my heart,
In *Hermias* loue I yeelde you vp my part:
And yours of *Helena*, to mee bequeath:
Whom I doe loue, and will do till my death.

HELENA
Neuer did mockers waste more idle breath.   1150

DEMETRIUS

    Lysander, keepe thy *Hermia*: I will none.

    If ere I lou'd her, all that loue is gone.

    My heart to her, but as guestwise, soiournd:

    And now to *Helen*, is it home returnd,

    There to remaine.

LYSANDER   *Helen*, it is not so.

DEMETRIUS

    Disparage not the faith, thou dost not know;

    Least to thy perill, thou aby it deare.

       Enter Hermia

    Looke where thy loue comes: yonder is thy deare.

HERMIA

    Darke night, that from the eye, his function takes,

1160   The eare more quicke of apprehension makes.

    Wherein it doth impaire the seeing sense,

    It payes the hearing double recompence.

    Thou art not, by myne eye, *Lysander*, found:

    Mine eare, I thanke it, brought me to thy sound.

    But why, vnkindly, didst thou leaue mee so?

LYSANDER

    Why should he stay, whom loue doth presse to go?

HERMIA

    What loue could presse *Lysander*, from my side?

LYSANDER

    Lysanders loue (that would not let him bide)

    Faire *Helena*: who more engilds the night

1170   Then all yon fiery oes, and eyes of light.

    Why seek'st thou me? Could not this make thee know,

    The hate I bare thee, made mee leaue thee so?

HERMIA

    You speake not as you thinke: It cannot bee.

HELENA ⌈*aside*⌉

    Lo: she is one of this confederacy.

    Now I perceiue, they haue conioynd all three,

    To fashion this false sport, in spight of mee.

    Iniurious *Hermia*, most vngratefull maide,

    Haue you conspir'd, haue you with these contriu'd

    To baite mee, with this foule derision?

1180   Is all the counsell that we two haue shar'd,

    The sisters vowes, the howers that we haue spent,

    When we haue chid the hastie footed time,

    For parting vs; O, is all quite forgot?

    All schooldaies friendshippe, childhood innocence?

    Wee, *Hermia*, like two artificiall gods,

    Haue with our needles, created both one flower,

    Both on one sampler, sitting on one cushion,

    Both warbling of one song, both in one key;

    As if our hands, our sides, voyces, and mindes

1190   Had bin incorporate. So wee grewe together,

    Like to a double cherry, seeming parted;

    But yet an vnion in partition,

    Two louely berries moulded on one stemme:

    So with two seeming bodies, but one heart,

    Two of the first like coats in heraldry,

    Due but to one, and crowned with one creast.

    And will you rent our auncient loue asunder,

    To ioyne with men, in scorning your poore friend?

    It is not friendly, tis not maidenly.

    Our sex, as well as I, may chide you for it;   1200

    Though I alone doe fele the iniury.

HERMIA

    I am amazed at your passionate words:

    I scorne you not. It seemes that you scorne mee.

HELENA

    Haue you not set *Lysander*, as in scorne,

    To follow mee, and praise my eyes and face?

    And made your other loue, *Demetrius*

    (Who euen but now did spurne mee with his foote)

    To call mee goddesse, nymph, diuine, and rare,

    Pretious celestiall? Wherefore speakes he this,

    To her he hates? And wherfore doth *Lysander*   1210

    Deny your loue (so rich within his soule)

    And tender mee (forsooth) affection,

    But by your setting on, by your consent?

    What, though I be not so in grace as you,

    So hung vpon with loue, so fortunate?

    (But miserable most, to loue vnlou'd)

    This you should pittie, rather then despise.

HERMIA

    I vnderstand not, what you meane by this.

HELENA

    I, doe. Perseuer, counterfait sad lookes:

    Make mouthes vpon mee, when I turne my back: 1220

    Winke each at other, holde the sweete ieast vp.

    This sport well carried, shall bee chronicled.

    If you haue any pitty, grace, or manners,

    You would not make mee such an argument.

    But fare ye well: tis partly my owne fault:

    Which death, or absence soone shall remedy.

LYSANDER

    Stay, gentle *Helena*: heare my excuse,

    My loue, my life, my soule, faire *Helena*.

HELENA

    O excellent!

HERMIA (*to Lysander*) Sweete, doe not scorne her so.

DEMETRIUS (*to Lysander*)

    If she cannot entreat, I can compell.   1230

LYSANDER

    Thou canst compell no more, then she intreat.

    Thy threats haue no more strength then her weake

        praiers.

    Helen, I loue thee, by my life I doe:

    I sweare by that which I will loose for thee;

    To prooue him false, that saies I loue thee not.

DEMETRIUS (*to Helena*)

    I say, I loue thee more then he can do.

LYSANDER

    If thou say so, withdrawe, and prooue it to.

DEMETRIUS

    Quick come.

HERMIA   *Lysander*, whereto tends all this?

       ⌈*She takes him by the arme*⌉

LYSANDER

    Away, you *Ethiop*.

DEMETRIUS   No, no, Sir: yeeld:

1240   Seeme to breake loose: take on as you would follow;
      But yet come not. You are a tame man, go.

LYSANDER (*to Hermia*)
      Hang of thou cat, thou bur: vile thing let loose;
      Or I will shake thee from mee, like a serpent.

HERMIA
      Why are you growne so rude? What change is this,
      Sweete loue?

LYSANDER   Thy loue? Out tawny *Tartar*, out:
      Out loathed medcine: ô hated potion hence.

HERMIA
      Doe you not ieast?

HELENA   Yes sooth: and so doe you.

LYSANDER
      Demetrius, I will keepe my word, with thee.

DEMETRIUS
      I would I had your bond. For I perceiue,
1250   A weake bond holds you. Ile not trust your word.

LYSANDER
      What? should I hurt her, strike her, kill her dead?
      Although I hate her, Ile not harme her so.

HERMIA
      What? Can you do me greater harme, then hate?
      Hate mee, wherefore? O me, what newes, my loue?
      Am not I *Hermia*? Are not you *Lysander*?
      I am as faire now, as I was ere while.
      Since night, you lou'd mee; yet since night, you left
          mee.
      Why then, you left mee (ô the gods forbid)
      In earnest, shall I say?

LYSANDER   I, by my life:
1260   And neuer did desire to see thee more.
      Therefore be out of hope, of question, doubt:
      Be certaine: nothing truer: tis no ieast,
      That I doe hate thee, and loue *Helena*.

HERMIA (*to Helena*)
      O mee, you iuggler, you canker blossome,
      You theefe of loue: what, haue you come by night,
      And stolne my loues heart, from him?

HELENA   Fine, Ifaith.
      Haue you no modesty, no maiden shame,
      No touch of bashfulnesse? What, will you teare
      Impatient answeres, from my gentle tongue?
1270   Fy, fy, you counterfait, you puppet, you.

HERMIA
      Puppet? Why so? I, that way goes the game.
      Now I perceiue that she hath made compare,
      Betweene our statures, she hath vrg'd her height,
      And with her personage, her tall personage,
      Her height (forsooth) she hath preuaild with him.
      And are you growne so high in his esteeme,
      Because I am so dwarfish and so lowe?
      How lowe am I, thou painted May-pole? Speake:
      How lowe am I? I am not yet so lowe,
1280   But that my nailes can reach vnto thine eyes.

HELENA (*to Demetrius and Lysander*)
      I pray you, though you mocke me, gentlemen,
      Let her not hurt me. I was neuer curst:

      I haue no gift at all in shrewishnesse:
      I am a right maid, for my cowardize:
      Let her not strike mee. You perhaps, may thinke,
      Because she is something lower then my selfe,
      That I can match her.

HERMIA   Lower? harke againe.

HELENA
      Good *Hermia*, do not be so bitter with mee,
      I euermore did loue you *Hermia*,
      Did euer keepe your counsels, neuer wrongd you;   1290
      Saue that in loue, vnto *Demetrius*,
      I tould him of your stealth vnto this wood.
      He followed you: for loue, I followed him.
      But he hath chid me hence, and threatned mee
      To strike mee, spurne mee; nay to kill mee to.
      And now, so you will let me quiet goe,
      To *Athens* will I beare my folly backe,
      And follow you no further. Let me goe.
      You see how simple, and how fond I am.

HERMIA
      Why? get you gon. Who ist that hinders you?   1300

HELENA
      A foolish heart, that I leaue here behind.

HERMIA
      What, with *Lysander*?

HELENA   With *Demetrius*.

LYSANDER
      Be not afraid: she shall not harme thee *Helena*.

DEMETRIUS
      No sir: she shall not, though you take her part.

HELENA
      O, when she is angry, she is keene and shrewd.
      She was a vixen, when she went to schoole:
      And though she be but little, she is fierce.

HERMIA
      Little againe? Nothing but low and little?
      Why will you suffer her to floute me thus?
      Let me come to her.

LYSANDER   Get you gon, you dwarfe;   1310
      You *minimus*, of hindring knot grasse, made;
      You bead, you acorne.

DEMETRIUS   You are too officious,
      In her behalfe, that scornes your seruices.
      Let her alone: speake not of *Helena*,
      Take not her part. For if thou dost intend
      Neuer so little shewe of loue to her,
      Thou shalt aby it.

LYSANDER   Now she holdes me not:
      Now follow, if thou dar'st, to try whose right,
      Of thine or mine, is most in *Helena*.

DEMETRIUS
      Follow? Nay: Ile go with thee, cheeke by iowle.   1320
           Exit Lysander and Demetrius

HERMIA
      You, mistresse, all this coyle is long of you.
      Nay: goe not backe.

HELENA   I will not trust you, I,
      Nor longer stay in your curst company.

Your hands, than mine, are quicker for a fray:
My legges are longer though, to runne away.   *Exit*

HERMIA

I am amaz'd, and know not what to say.   *Exit*
⌜*Oberon and Robin come forward*⌝

OBERON

This is thy negligence: still thou mistak'st,
Or else commitst thy knaueries wilfully.

ROBIN

Beleeue mee, king of shadowes, I mistooke.
1330   Did not you tell mee, I shoud know the man,
By the *Athenian* garments, he had on?
And, so farre blamelesse prooues my enterprise,
That I haue nointed an *Athenians* eyes:
And so farre am I glad, it so did sort,
As this their iangling I esteeme a sport.

OBERON

Thou seest, these louers seeke a place to fight:
Hy therefore *Robin*, ouercast the night,
The starry welkin couer thou anon,
With drooping fogge as blacke as *Acheron*,
1340   And lead these teasty Riuals so astray,
As one come not within anothers way.
Like to *Lysander*, sometime frame thy tongue:
Then stirre *Demetrius* vp, with bitter wrong:
And sometime raile thou like *Demetrius*:
And from each other, looke thou lead them thus;
Till ore their browes, death-counterfaiting, sleepe,
With leaden legs, and Batty wings doth creepe:
Then crush this hearbe into *Lysanders* eye;
Whose liquor hath this vertuous property,
1350   To take from thence all errour, with his might,
And make his eyebals roule with wonted sight.
When they next wake, all this derision
Shall seeme a dreame, and fruitelesse vision.
And backe to *Athens* shall the louers wend,
With league, whose date, till death shall neuer end.
Whiles I, in this affaire, doe thee imploy,
Ile to my Queene and beg her *Indian* boy:
And then I will her charmed eye release
From monsters viewe, and all things shall be peace.

ROBIN

1360   My Faiery Lord, this must be done with haste.
For nights swift Dragons cut the clouds full fast,
And yonder shines *Auroras* harbinger:
At whose approach, Ghosts, wandring here and there,
Troope home to Churchyards: damned spirits all,
That in crosse waies and floods haue buriall,
Already to their wormy beds are gone,
For feare least day should looke their shames vpon:
They wilfully themselues exild from light,
And must for aye consort with black browed night.

OBERON

1370   But we are spirits of another sort.
I, with the mornings loue, haue oft made sport,
And like a forrester, the groues may tread
Euen till the Easterne gate all fiery red,
Opening on *Neptune*, with faire blessed beames,
Turnes, into yellow golde, his salt greene streames.

But notwithstanding, haste, make no delay:
We may effect this businesse, yet ere day.   *Exit*

ROBIN

Vp & down, vp & down,
I will lead them vp & down:
I am feard in field & town.   1380
Goblin, lead them vp & downe.
Here comes one.
Enter Lysander

LYSANDER

Where art thou, proud *Demetrius*? Speak thou now.

ROBIN ⌜*shifting places*⌝

Here villaine, drawne & ready. Where art thou?

LYSANDER

I will be with thee straight.

ROBIN ⌜*shifting places*⌝   Follow me then
To plainer ground.   ⌜*Exit Lysander*⌝
Enter Demetrius

DEMETRIUS ⌜*shifting places*⌝ *Lysander*, speake againe.
Thou runaway, thou coward, art thou fled?
Speake: in some bush? Where doest thou hide thy
head?

ROBIN ⌜*shifting places*⌝

Thou coward art thou bragging, to the starres,
Telling the bushes that thou look'st for warres,   1390
And wilt not come? Come recreant, come thou childe,
Ile whippe thee with a rodde. He is defil'd,
That drawes a sword on thee.

DEMETRIUS ⌜*shifting places*⌝   Yea, art thou there?

ROBIN ⌜*shifting places*⌝

Follow my voice: weele try no manhood here.   *Exeūt*

⌜*Enter Lysander*⌝   Sc. 6
                       (3.3)

LYSANDER

He goes before me, and still dares me on:
When I come where he calles, then he is gon.
The villaine is much lighter heel'd then I;
I followed fast: but faster he did fly;
That fallen am I in darke vneauen way,
And here will rest me.
He lyes down
                Come thou gentle day.   1400
For if but once, thou shewe me thy gray light,
Ile finde *Demetrius*, and reuenge this spight.
                       He sleepes
Enter Robin, and Demetrius

ROBIN ⌜*shifting places*⌝

Ho, ho, ho: Coward, why comst thou not?

DEMETRIUS

Abide me, if thou dar'st. For well I wot,
Thou runst before mee, shifting euery place,
And dar'st not stand, nor looke me in the face.
Where art thou now?

ROBIN ⌜*shifting places*⌝   Come hither: I am here.

DEMETRIUS

Nay then thou mockst me. Thou shalt buy this dear,
If euer I thy face by day light see.
Now, goe thy way. Faintnesse constraineth mee,   1410

To measure, out my length, on this cold bed:
> *He lyes down*

By daies approach looke to be visited.   *He sleepes*
> *Enter Helena*

HELENA
O weary night, O long and tedious night,
   Abate thy houres, shine comforts, from the east;
That I may backe to *Athens*, by day light,
   From these that my poore company detest:
And sleepe, that sometimes shuts vp sorrowes eye,
Steale mee a while from mine owne companie.
> *She lyes down and sleepes*

ROBIN
   Yet but three? Come one more.
1420   Two of both kindes makes vp fower.
   > *⌈Enter Hermia⌉*

   Heare shee comes, curst and sadde.
   Cupid is a knauish ladde,
   Thus to make poore females madde.

HERMIA
Neuer so weary, neuer so in woe,
   Bedabbled with the deaw, and torne with briers:
I can no further crawle, no further goe:
   My legges can keepe no pase with my desires.
Here will I rest mee, till the breake of day:
> *She lyes down*

Heauens shielde *Lysander*, if they meane a fray.
> *She sleepes*

1430   ROBIN   On the ground, sleepe sound:
             Ile apply to your eye,
                Gentle louer, remedy.
   He droppes the iuyce on Lysanders eyeliddes
             When thou wak'st, thou tak'st
             True delight, in the sight,
                Of thy former ladies eye:
   And the country prouerbe knowne,
   That euery man should take his owne,
   In your waking shall be showen.
             Iacke shall haue *Iill*:
1440   Nought shall goe ill:
The man shall haue his mare again, & all shall be well.
> *Exit*

(4.1)   *Enter Titania Queene of Faieries, and Bottom the*
          Clowne with the Asse head, and Faieries: Pease-
          blossome, Cobweb, Moth, and Mustardseede

TITANIA *(to Bottom)*
Come sit thee downe vpon this flowry bed,
   While I thy amiable cheekes doe coy,
And stick musk roses in thy sleeke smooth head,
   And kisse thy faire large eares, my gentle ioy.
BOTTOM Where's *Pease-blossome?*
PEASE-BLOSSOME Ready.
BOTTOM Scratch my heade, *Pease-blossome*. Wher's Moun-
   sieur *Cobweb?*
1450 COBWEB Ready.
BOTTOM Mounsieur *Cobweb*, good Mounsieur, get you your
   weapons in your hand, and kill me a red hipt Humble
   Bee, on the toppe of a thistle: and good Mounsieur,

bring mee the hony bagge. Doe not fret your selfe too
much, in the action, Mounsieur: and good Mounsieur
haue a care, the honybagge breake not, I wold be loath
to haue you ouerflowen with a honibag *signior*.
> *⌈Exit Cobweb⌉*

Where's Mounsieur *Mustardseede?*
MUSTARDSEEDE Readie.
BOTTOM Giue me your neafe, Mounsieur *Mustardseede*.   1460
   Pray you, leaue your curtsie, good Mounsieur.
MUSTARDSEEDE What's your will?
BOTTOM Nothing good Mounsieur, but to helpe Caualery
   Pease-blossome, to scratch. I must to the Barbers,
   Mounsieur. For me thinkes I am maruailes hairy about
   the face. And I am such a tender Asse, if my haire doe
   but tickle mee, I must scratch.
TITANIA
What, wilt thou heare some musique, my sweete loue?
BOTTOM I haue a reasonable good eare in musique. Lets
   haue the tongs, and the bones.   1470
> *⌈Rurall Musicke⌉*

TITANIA
Or, say sweete loue, what thou desir'st to eate.
BOTTOM Truely a pecke of prouander. I could mounch
   your good dry Oates. Me thinkes, I haue a great desire
   to a bottle of hay. Good hay, sweete hay hath no fellow.
TITANIA
I haue a venturous Fairy, that shall seeke
   The Squirils hoord, and fetch thee of newe nuts.
BOTTOM I had rather haue a handfull, or two of dryed
   pease. But, I pray you: let none of your people stirre
   me: I haue an exposition of sleepe come vpon mee.
TITANIA
Sleepe thou, and I will winde thee in my armes.   1480
Faieries be gon, and be al waies away.   *Exeunt Fairies*
So doth the woodbine, the sweete Honisuckle,
Gently entwist: the female Iuy so
Enrings the barky fingers of the Elme.
O how I loue thee! How I dote on thee!
> *They sleepe.*
> *Enter Robin goodfellow ⌈and Oberon, meeting⌉*

OBERON
Welcome good *Robin*. Seest thou this sweete sight?
Her dotage now I doe beginne to pittie.
For meeting her of late, behinde the wood,
Seeking sweete fauours for this hatefull foole,
I did vpbraid her, and fall out with her.   1490
For she his hairy temples then had rounded,
With coronet of fresh and fragrant flowers.
And that same deawe which sometime on the buddes,
Was wont to swell, like round and orient pearles;
Stood now within the pretty flouriets eyes,
Like teares, that did their owne disgrace bewaile.
When I had, at my pleasure, taunted her,
And she, in milde tearmes, begd my patience,
I then did aske of her, her changeling childe:
Which straight she gaue mee, and her Fairy sent   1500
To beare him, to my bower, in Fairie land.
And now I haue the boy, I will vndoe

This hatefull imperfection of her eyes.
And, gentle *Puck*, take this transformed scalpe,
From of the heade of this *Athenian* swaine;
That hee, awaking when the other do,
May all to *Athens* backe againe repaire,
And thinke no more of this nights accidents,
But as the fearce vexation of a dreame.

1510 But first I will release the Fairy Queene.

He droppes the iuyce on Titanias eyeliddes

Be, as thou wast wont to bee:
See, as thou wast wont to see.
Dians budde, or *Cupids* flower,
Hath such force, and blessed power.
Now, my *Titania*, wake you, my sweete Queene.

TITANIA (*awaking*)
My *Oberon*, what visions haue I seene!
Me thought I was enamourd of an Asse.

OBERON
There lyes your loue.

TITANIA   How came these things to passe?
O, how mine eyes doe loath his visage now!

OBERON
1520 Silence a while. *Robin*, take off this head:
Titania, musicke call, and strike more dead
Then common sleepe: of all these fiue, the sense.

TITANIA
Musick, howe musick: such as charmeth sleepe.
⌈*Still Musick*⌉

ROBIN (*taking the Asse head off Bottom*)
Now, when thou wak'st, with thine own fools eyes
peepe.

OBERON
Sound Musick:
⌈*The Musick changes*⌉
      come, my queen, take hands with me,
And rocke the ground whereon these sleepers be.
Oberon and Titania daunce
Now, thou and I are new in amitie,
And will to morrow midnight, solemnely
Daunce, in Duke *Theseus* house triumphantly,
1530 And blesse it to all faire prosperitie.
There shall the paires of faithfull louers be
Wedded, with *Theseus*, all in iollitie.

ROBIN
Fairy King, attend, and marke:
I do heare the morning Larke.

OBERON
Then my Queene, in silence sad,
Trippe we after nightes shade:
We, the Globe, can compasse soone,
Swifter then the wandring Moone.

TITANIA
Come my Lord, and in our flight,
1540 Tell me how it came this night,
That I sleeping here was found,
With these mortals on the ground.

Exeunt Oberon, Titania, and
Robin. Sleepers Lye still

Winde hornes within. Enter Theseus, with Egeus,
Hippolita and all his traine

THESEUS
Goe one of you, finde out the forrester:
For now our obseruation is performde.
And since we haue the vaward of the day,
My loue shall heare the musicke of my hounds.
Vncouple, in the westerne vallie, let them goe:
Dispatch I say, and finde the forrester.   *Exit one*
Wee will, faire Queene, vp to the mountaines toppe,
And marke the musicall confusion   1550
Of hounds and Echo in coniunction.

HYPPOLITA
I was with *Hercules* and *Cadmus*, once,
When in a wood of *Creete* they bayed the Beare,
With hounds of *Sparta*: neuer did I heare
Such gallant chiding. For besides the groues,
The skyes, the fountaines, euery region neare
Seemd all one mutuall cry. I neuer heard
So musicall a discord, such sweete thunder.

THESEUS
My hounds are bred out of the *Spartane* kinde:
So flew'd, so sanded: and their heads are hung   1560
With eares, that sweepe away the morning deawe,
Crooke kneed, and deawlapt, like *Thessalian* Buls:
Slowe in pursuit; but matcht in mouth like bels,
Each vnder each. A cry more tunable
Was neuer hollowd to, nor cheerd with horne,
In *Creete*, in *Sparta*, nor in *Thessaly*.
Iudge when you heare. But soft. What nymphes are
these?

EGEUS
My Lord, this is my daughter heere a sleepe,
And this *Lysander*, this *Demetrius* is,
This *Helena*, old *Nedars Helena*.   1570
I wonder of their being here together.

THESEUS
No doubt, they rose vp earely, to obserue
The right of May: and hearing our intent,
Came heere, in grace of our solemnitie.
But speake, *Egeus*, is not this the day,
That *Hermia* should giue answer of her choyce?

EGEUS It is, my Lord.

THESEUS
Goe, bid the huntsmen wake them with their hornes.
⌈*Exit one*⌉
Shoute within: Winde hornes. The louers all start vp
Good morrow, friends. Saint *Valentine* is past.
Begin these wood birds but to couple, now?   1580

LYSANDER
Pardon, my Lord.
The louers kneel

THESEUS   I pray you all, stand vp.
The lovers stand
(*To Demetrius and Lysander*) I know, you two are
Riuall enemies.
How comes this gentle concord in the worlde,
That hatred is so farre from iealousie,
To sleepe by hate, and feare no enmitie.

LYSANDER

My Lord, I shal reply amazedly,
Halfe sleepe, halfe waking. But, as yet, I sweare,
I cannot truely say how I came here.
But as I thinke (for truely would I speake)
1590 And now I doe bethinke mee, so it is;
I came with *Hermia*, hither. Our intent
Was to be gon from *Athens*: where we might
Without the perill of the *Athenian* lawe,

EGEUS (*to Theseus*)

Enough, enough my Lord: you haue enough.
I begge the law, the law, vpon his head:
They would haue stolne away, they would, *Demetrius*,
Thereby to haue defeated you and me:
You of your wife, and mee, of my consent:
Of my consent, that she should be your wife.

DEMETRIUS (*to Theseus*)

1600 My Lord, faire *Helen* told me of their stealth,
Of this their purpose hither, to this wood,
And I in fury hither followed them;
Faire *Helena*, in fancy following mee.
But my good Lord, I wote not by what power
(But by some power it is) my loue to *Hermia*
(Melted as the snowe) seemes to me now
As the remembrance of an idle gaude,
Which in my childehoode I did dote vpon:
And all the faith, the vertue of my heart,
1610 The obiect and the pleasure of mine eye,
Is onely *Helena*. To her, my Lord,
Was I betroth'd, ere I see *Hermia*:
But like in sicknesse, did I loath this foode.
But, as in health, come to my naturall taste,
Now I doe wish it, loue it, long for it,
And will for euermore be true to it.

THESEUS

Faire louers, you are fortunately met.
Of this discourse, we more will here anon.
Egeus, I will ouerbeare your will:
1620 For in the Temple, by and by, with vs,
These couples shall eternally be knit.
And, for the morning now is somthing worne,
Our purpos'd hunting shall be set aside.
Away, with vs, to *Athens*. Three and three,
Weele holde a feast, in great solemnitie.
Come *Hyppolita*.

        Exit Duke Theseus, with Hippolita, Egeus, and
                            all his traine

DEMETRIUS

These things seeme small and vndistinguishable,
Like farre off mountaines turned into clouds.

HERMIA

Me thinks I see these things, with parted eye,
When euery thing seemes double.

1630 HELENA   So mee thinkes:

And I haue found *Demetrius*, like a iewell,
Mine owne, and not mine owne.

DEMETRIUS   It seemes to me,

That yet we sleepe, we dreame. Do not you thinke,
The Duke was here, and bid vs follow him?

HERMIA

Yea, and my father.

HELENA   And *Hyppolita*.

LYSANDER

And he did bid vs follow to the Temple.

DEMETRIUS

Why then, we are awake: lets follow him,
And by the way let vs recount our dreames.

                        Exeunt Louers

    Bottom wakes

BOTTOM When my cue comes, call mee, and I will answere.
My next is, most faire *Pyramus*. Hey ho. *Peeter Quince*?   1640
Flute, the bellowes mender? *Snout* the tinker?
Starueling? Gods my life! Stolne hence, and left mee a
sleepe? I haue had a most rare vision. I haue had a
dreame, past the wit of man, to say; what dreame it
was. Man is but an Asse, if hee goe about t'expound
this dreame. Me thought I was, there is no man can
tell what. Me thought I was, and me thought I had.
But man is but a patcht foole, If hee will offer to say,
what mee thought I had. The eye of man hath not
heard, the eare of man hath not seene, mans hand is   1650
not able to taste, his tongue to conceiue, nor his hearte
to report, what my dreame was. I will get *Peter Quince*
to write a Ballet of this dreame: it shall be call'd *Bottoms
Dreame*; because it hath no bottome: and I will sing it
in the latter end of a Play, before the Duke.
Peraduenture, to make it the more gratious, I shall
sing it at her death.   *Exit*

    Enter Quince, Flute, Snout, and Starueling   Sc. 7

QUINCE Haue you sent to *Bottoms* house? Is he come   (4.2)
home, yet?

STARUELING Hee cannot be heard of. Out of doubt he is   1660
transported.

FLUTE If hee come not, then the Play is mard. It goes not
forward. Doth it?

QUINCE It is not possible. You haue not a man, in all
Athens, able to discharge *Pyramus*, but he.

FLUTE No, hee hath simply the best wit of any handy-
craft man, in *Athens*.

QUINCE Yea, and the best person to, and hee is a very
Paramour, for a sweete voice.

FLUTE You must say, Paragon. A Paramour is (God blesse   1670
vs) a thing of nought.

    Enter Snug, the Ioyner

SNUGGE Masters, the Duke is comming from the Temple,
and there is two or three Lords and Ladies more
married. If our sport had gon forward, wee had all
beene made men.

FLUTE O sweete bully *Bottome*. Thus hath hee lost six
pence a day, during his life: hee coulde not haue scaped
sixe pence a day. And the Duke had not giuen him six
pence a day, for playing *Pyramus*, Ile be hanged. He
would haue deserued it. Six pence a day, in *Pyramus*,   1680
or nothing.

Enter Bottom

BOTTOM Where are these lads? Where are these harts?

QUINCE *Bottom*, ô most couragious day! O most happy
houre!

BOTTOM Masters, I am to discourse wonders: but aske me
not what. For if I tell you, I am no true *Athenian*. I will
tell you euery thing right as it fell out.

QUINCE Let vs heare, sweete *Bottom*.

1690 BOTTOM Not a word of mee. All that I will tell you, is,
that the Duke hath dined. Get your apparrell together,
good strings to your beardes, new ribands to your
pumpes, meete presently at the palace, euery man looke
ore his part. For, the short and the long is, our play is
preferd. In any case let *Thisby* haue cleane linnen: and
let not him, that plaies the Lyon, pare his nailes: for
they shall hang out for the Lyons clawes. And most
deare Actors, eate no Onions, nor garlicke: for we are
to vtter sweete breath: and I do not doubt but to hear
them say, it is a sweete Comedy. No more wordes.

1700 Away, go away.   *Exeunt*

Sc. 8   *Enter Theseus, Hyppolita, ⌈Egeus⌉, and his Lords*
(5.1) HYPPOLITA

Tis strange, my *Theseus*, that these louers speake of.

THESEUS

More straunge then true. I neuer may beleeue
These antique fables, nor these Fairy toyes.
Louers, and mad men haue such seething braines,
Such shaping phantasies, that apprehend
More, then coole reason euer comprehends.
The lunatick, the louer, and the Poet
Are of imagination all compact.
One sees more diuels, then vast hell can holde:

1710 That is the mad man. The louer, all as frantick,
Sees *Helens* beauty in a brow of *Ægypt*.
The Poets eye, in a fine frenzy, rolling,
Doth glance from heauen to earth, from earth to
heauen.
And as imagination bodies forth
The formes of things vnknowne: the Poets penne
Turnes them to shapes, and giues to ayery nothing,
A locall habitation, and a name.
Such trickes hath strong imagination,
That if it would but apprehend some ioy,

1720 It comprehends some bringer of that ioy.
Or in the night, imagining some feare,
How easie is a bush suppos'd a Beare?

HYPPOLITA

But, all the story of the night told ouer,
And all their minds transfigur'd so together,
More witnesseth than fancies images,
And growes to something of great constancy:
But howsoeuer, strange and admirable.

Enter Louers ; Lysander, Demetrius, Hermia and
Helena

THESEUS

Here come the louers, full of ioy and mirth.

Ioy, gentle friends, ioy and fresh daies of loue
Accompany your hearts.

LYSANDER   More then to vs,   1730
Waite in your royall walkes, your boorde, your bedde.

THESEUS

Come now: what maskes, what daunces shall wee
haue,
To weare away this long age of three hours,
Betweene oʳ after supper, & bed-time?
Where is our vsuall manager of mirth?
What Reuels are in hand? Is there no play,
To ease the anguish of a torturing hower?
Call *Egeus*.

⌈EGEUS⌉   Here mighty *Theseus*.

THESEUS

Say, what abridgement haue you for this euening?
What maske, what musicke? How shall we beguile   1740
The lazy tyme, if not with some delight?

⌈EGEUS⌉

There is a briefe, how many sports are ripe.
Make choyce, of which your Highnesse will see first.

⌈LYSANDER⌉ *(reads)*

The battell with the *Centaures* to be sung,
By an *Athenian* Eunuche, to the Harpe?

THESEUS

Weele none of that. That haue I tolde my loue,
In glory of my kinsman *Hercules*.

⌈LYSANDER⌉ *(reads)*

The ryot of the tipsie *Bachanals*,
Tearing the *Thracian* singer, in their rage?

THESEUS

That is an olde deuise: and it was plaid,   1750
When I from *Thebes* came last a conquerer.

⌈LYSANDER⌉ *(reads)*

The thrise three Muses, mourning for the death
Of learning, late deceast, in beggery?

THESEUS

That is some *Satire* keene and criticall,
Not sorting with a nuptiall ceremony.

⌈LYSANDER⌉ *(reads)*

A tedious briefe Scene of young *Pyramus*
And his loue *Thisby*; very tragicall mirth?

THESEUS

Merry, and tragicall? Tedious, and briefe?
That is hot Ise, and wõdrous strange blacke snow.
How shall we find the cõcord of this discord?   1760

⌈EGEUS⌉

A Play there is, my Lord, some ten words long;
Which is as briefe, as I haue knowne a play:
But, by ten words, my Lord it is too long:
Which makes it tedious. For in all the Play,
There is not one word apt, one player fitted.
And tragicall, my noble Lord, it is.
For *Pyramus*, therein, doth kill himselfe.
Which when I saw rehearst, I must confesse,
Made mine eyes water: but more merry teares
The passion of loud laughter neuer shed.   1770

THESEUS What are they, that doe play it?

⌈EGEUS⌉

Hard handed men, that worke in *Athens* here,
Which neuer labour'd in their minds till now:
And now haue toyld their vnbreathd memories,
With this same Play, against your nuptiall.

THESEUS

And wee will heare it.

⌈EGEUS⌉   No, my noble Lord,
It is not for you. I haue heard it ouer,
And it is nothing, nothing in the world;
Vnlesse you can finde sport in their entents,
1780   Extreamely stretcht, and cond with cruell paine,
To do you seruice.

THESEUS   I will heare that play.
For neuer any thing can be amisse,
When simplenesse and duety tender it.
Goe bring them in, and take your places, Ladies.
                                        Exit ⌈*Egeus*⌉

HYPPOLITA

I loue not to see wretchednesse orecharged;
And duety, in his seruice, perishing.

THESEUS

Why, gentle sweete, you shall see no such thing.

HYPPOLITA

He sayes, they can doe nothing in this kinde.

THESEUS

The kinder we, to giue them thanks, for nothing.
1790   Our sport shall be, to take what they mistake.
And what poore duty cannot doe,
Noble respect takes it in might, not merit.
Where I haue come, great Clerkes haue purposed
To greete me, with premeditated welcomes;
Where I haue seene them shiuer and looke pale,
Make periods in the midst of sentences,
Throttle their practiz'd accent in their feares,
And in conclusion dumbly haue broke off,
Not paying mee a welcome. Trust me, sweete,
1800   Out of this silence, yet, I pickt a welcome:
And in the modesty of fearefull duty,
I read as much, as from the rattling tongue
Of saucy and audacious eloquence.
Loue, therefore, and tong-tide simplicity,
In least, speake most, to my capacity.

          Enter ⌈*Egeus*⌉

⌈EGEUS⌉

So please your Grace, the Prologue is addrest.

THESEUS Let him approach.

          ⌈*Florish Trumpets.*⌉ *Enter* ⌈*Quince as*⌉ *the Prologue*

⌈QUINCE⌉ (*as prologue*)

If wee offend, it is with our good will.
    That you should thinke, we come not to offend,
1810   But with good will. To shew our simple skill,
    That is the true beginning of our end.
Consider then, we come but in despight.
    We doe not come, as minding to content you,
Our true intent is. All for your delight,
    Wee are not here. That you should here repent you,

The Actors are at hand: and, by their showe,
You shall know all, that you are like to knowe.

THESEUS This fellow doth not stand vpon points.

LYSANDER He hath rid his Prologue, like a rough Colte:
hee knowes not the stoppe. A good morall my Lord. It   1820
is not enough to speake; but to speake true.

HYPPOLITA Indeed he hath plaid on this Prologue, like a
child on a Recorder, a sound; but not in gouernement.

THESEUS His speach was like a tangled Chaine; nothing
impaired, but all disordered. Who is next?

          Enter ⌈*with a Trumpet before them*⌉ *Bottom as*
          Pyramus, and Flute as Thisby, and Snout as Wall,
          and Starueling as Moone-shine, and Snug as Lyon,
          for the Dumbe showe

⌈QUINCE⌉ (*as prologue*)

Gentles, perchance you wonder at this show.
    But, wonder on, till truthe make all things plaine.
This man is *Pyramus*, if you would knowe:
    This beautious Lady *Thisby* is certaine.
This man, with lyme and roughcast, doth present   1830
    Wall, that vile wall, which did these louers sunder:
And through wals chinke, poore soules, they are
          content
    To whisper. At the which, let no man wonder.
This man, with lanterne, dogge, and bush of thorne,
    Presenteth moone-shine. For if you will know,
By moone-shine did these louers thinke no scorne
    To meete at *Ninus* tombe, there, there to wooe:
This grizly beast (which Lyon hight by name)
    The trusty *Thysby*, comming first by night,
Did scarre away, or rather did affright: 1840
And as she fled, her mantle she did fall:
    Which Lyon vile with bloody mouth did staine.
Anon comes *Pyramus*, sweete youth, and tall,
    And findes his trusty *Thisbyes* mantle slaine:
Whereat, with blade, with bloody blamefull blade,
    He brauely broacht his boyling bloody breast.
And *Thisby*, tarying in Mulberry shade,
    His dagger drewe, and dyed. For all the rest,
Let *Lyon*, *Moone-shine*, *Wall*, and louers twaine,
At large discourse, while here they doe remaine.   1850
          ⌈*Exit all of the Clownes but Snout as Wall*⌉

THESEUS I wonder, if the Lyon be to speake.

DEMETRIUS No wonder, my Lord. One Lyon may, when
many Asses doe.

⌈SNOUT⌉ (*as Wall*)

In this same enterlude it doth befall,
That I, one *Snowt* (by name) present a wall:
And such a wall, as I would haue you thinke
That had in it a cranied hole or chinke:
Through which the louers, *Pyramus*, and *Thisby*,
Did whisper often, very secretly.
This lome, this roughcast, and this stone doth showe,   1860
That I am that same wall: the truth is so.
And this the cranie is, right and sinister,
Through which the fearefull louers are to whisper.

THESEUS Would you desire lime and haire to speake better?

DEMETRIUS It is the wittiest partition, that euer I heard
discourse, my Lord.

Enter Bottom as Pyramus

THESEUS *Pyramus* drawes neare the wall: silence.

BOTTOM (*as Pyramus*)

O grim lookt night, o night, with hue so blacke,
    O night, which euer art, when day is not:
1870   O night, O night, alacke, alacke, alacke,
    I feare my *Thisbyes* promise is forgot.
And thou ô wall, ô sweete, ô louely wall,
    That standst betweene her fathers ground and mine,
Thou wall, ô wall, O sweete and louely wall,
    Showe mee thy chinke, to blink through, with mine
      eyne.

Wall showes his chinke

Thankes curteous wall. *Ioue* shield thee well, for this.
    But what see I? No *Thisby* doe I see.
O wicked wall, through whome I see no blisse,
    Curst be thy stones, for thus deceiuing mee.

1880 THESEUS The wall mee thinkes, being sensible, should
    curse againe.

BOTTOM (*to Theseus*) No, in truth Sir, he should not.
Deceiuing mee is *Thisbyes* cue: she is to enter now, and
I am to spy her through the wall. You shall see it will
fall pat as I told you:

Enter Flute as Thisby

yonder she comes.

FLUTE (*as Thisby*)

O wall, full often hast thou heard my mones,
    For parting my faire *Pyramus*, and mee.
My cherry lips haue often kist thy stones;
1890   Thy stones, with lime and haire knit vp in thee.

BOTTOM (*as Pyramus*)

I see a voice: now will I to the chinke,
    To spy and I can heare my *Thisbyes* face.
Thysby?

FLUTE (*as Thisby*) My loue, thou art my loue I thinke.

BOTTOM (*as Pyramus*)

Thinke what thou wilt, I am thy louers Grace:
And, like *Limander*, am I trusty still.

FLUTE (*as Thisby*)

And I, like *Helen*, till the fates me kill.

BOTTOM (*as Pyramus*)

Not *Shafalus*, to *Procrus*, was so true.

FLUTE (*as Thisby*)

As *Shafalus* to *Procrus*, I to you.

BOTTOM (*as Pyramus*)

O kisse mee, through the hole of this vilde wall.

FLUTE (*as Thisby*)

1900 I kisse the walles hole; not your lips at all.

BOTTOM (*as Pyramus*)

Wilt thou, at *Ninnies* tombe, meete me straight way?

FLUTE (*as Thisby*)

Tide life, tyde death, I come without delay.

Exit Bottom and Flute, seuerally

SNOUT (*as Wall*)

Thus haue I, *Wall*, my part discharged so;
And, being done, thus wall away doth goe.   *Exit*

THESEUS Now is the wall downe between the two
neighbors.

DEMETRIUS No remedy, my Lord, when wals are so wilfull,
to heare without warning.

HYPPOLITA This is the silliest stuffe, that euer I heard.

THESEUS The best, in this kinde, are but shadowes: and   1910
the worst are no worse, if imagination amend them.

HYPPOLITA It must be your imagination, then; & not
theirs.

THESEUS If we imagine no worse of them, then they of
thēselues, they may passe for excellent men. Here come
two noble beasts in, a man and a Lyon.

Enter Snug as Lyon, and Starueling as Moone-
shine, with a lanthorne, thorne bush, and dogge

SNUG (*as Lyon*)

You Ladies, you (whose gentle hearts do feare
    The smallest monstrous mouse, that creepes on
      floore)
May now, perchance, both quake and tremble here,
    When Lyon rough, in wildest rage, doth roare.   1920
Then know that I, as *Snug* the Ioyner am
A Lyon fell, nor else no Lyons damme.
For, if I should, as Lyon, come in strife,
Into this place, 'twere pitty on my life.

THESEUS A very gentle beast, and of a good conscience.

DEMETRIUS The very best at a beast, my Lord, that ere I
saw.

LYSANDER This Lyon is a very fox, for his valour.

THESEUS True: and a goose for his discretion.

DEMETRIUS Not so my Lord. For his valour cannot carry   1930
his discretion: and the fox carries the goose.

THESEUS His discretion, I am sure, cannot carry his valour.
For the goose carries not the fox. It is well: leaue it to
his discretion, and let vs listen to the Moone.

STARUELING (*as Moone-shine*)

This lanthorne doth the horned moone present.

DEMETRIUS He should haue worne the hornes, on his
head.

THESEUS He is no crescent, and his hornes are inuisible,
within the circumference.

STARUELING (*as Moone-shine*)

This lanthorne doth the horned moone present,   1940
    My selfe, the man ith Moone, doe seeme to be.

THESEUS This is the greatest errour of all the rest; the
man should be put into the lanthorne. How is it else
the man ith Moone?

DEMETRIUS He dares not come there, for the candle. For,
you see, it is already in snuffe.

HYPPOLITA I am aweary of this Moone. Would hee woulde
change.

THESEUS It appeares, by his small light of discretion, that
hee is in the wane: but yet in curtesie, in all reason,   1950
wee must stay the time.

LYSANDER Proceede, Moone.

STARUELING All that I haue to say, is to tell you, that the
lanthorne is the Moone, I the man ith Moone, this
thorne bush my thorne bush, and this dogge my dogge.

DEMETRIUS Why? All these should be in the lanthorne:
for all these are in the Moone. But silence: here comes
Thisby.

Enter Flute as Thisby

FLUTE (*as Thisby*)

    This is ould *Ninies* tumbe. Where is my loue?

1960 SNUG (*as Lyon*) Oh.

    Lyon roares, Thisby droppes her mantle and runs off

DEMETRIUS Well roard, Lyon.

THESEUS Well runne, *Thisby*.

HYPPOLITA Well shone *Moone*. Truly, the Moone shines,
  with a good grace.

    Lyon worries Thisbyes mantle

THESEUS Well mouz'd, *Lyon*.

DEMETRIUS And then came *Pyramus*.

    ⌈*Enter Bottom as Pyramus*⌉

LYSANDER And so the Lyon vanisht.   ⌈*Exit Lyon*⌉

BOTTOM (*as Pyramus*)

    Sweete Moone, I thanke thee, for thy sunny beams.

    I thanke thee, Moone, for shining now so bright.

1970 For by thy gratious, golden, glittering gleames,

    I trust to take of truest *Thisby* sight.

        But stay: ô spight!

        But marke, poore knight,

    What dreadfull dole is here?

    Eyes do you see!

    How can it bee!

    O dainty duck, ô deare!

        Thy mantle good,

    What, staind with blood?

1980 Approach ye Furies fell,

        O fates come, come,

        Cut thread and thrumme,

    Quaile, crush, conclude, and quell.

THESEUS This passion, & the death of a deare friend would
  goe neere to make a man looke sad.

HYPPOLITA Beshrewe my heart, but I pitty the man.

BOTTOM (*as Pyramus*)

    O, wherefore, Nature, didst thou Lyons frame?

    Since Lyon vilde hath here deflour'd my deare.

    Which is, no, no: which was the fairest dame

        That liu'd, that lou'd, that lik't, that look't with

1990   cheere.

        Come teares, confound,

        Out sword, and wound

    The pappe of *Pyramus*:

        I, that left pappe,

    Where heart doth hoppe.

    Thus dy I, thus, thus, thus.

    He stabs himselfe

    Now am I dead,

    Now am I fled,

    My soule is in the sky.

2000   Tongue loose thy light,

        Moone take thy flight,   ⌈*Exit Moone-shine*⌉

    Now dy, dy, dy, dy, dy.   *He dies*

DEMETRIUS No Die, but an ace for him. For he is but one.

LYSANDER Lesse then an ace, man. For he is dead, he is
  nothing.

THESEUS With the helpe of a Surgeon, he might yet
  recouer, and prooue an Asse.

HYPPOLITA How chance Moone-shine is gone before *Thisby*
  comes backe, and findes her louer.

THESEUS Shee will finde him, by starre-light.   2010

    ⌈*Enter Flute as Thisby*⌉

  Here shee comes, and her passion ends the Play.

HYPPOLITA Me thinkes, she should not vse a long one, for
  such a *Pyramus*: I hope, she will be briefe.

DEMETRIUS A moth will turne the ballance; which
  Pyramus, which *Thisby* is the better: he for a man; God
  warnd vs: she, for a woman; God blesse vs.

LYSANDER She hath spied him already, with those sweete
  eyes.

DEMETRIUS And thus she meanes, *videlicet*;

FLUTE (*as Thisby*)

        A sleepe my loue?   2020

        What, dead my doue?

    O *Pyramus*, arise,

    Speake, speake. Quite dumbe?

    Dead, dead? A tumbe

    Must couer thy sweete eyes.

        These lilly lippes,

        This cherry nose,

    These yellow cowslippe cheekes

        Are gon, are gon:

        Louers make mone: 2030

    His eyes were greene, as leekes.

        O sisters three,

        Come, come, to mee,

    With hands as pale as milke,

        Lay them in gore,

    Since you haue shore

    With sheeres, his threede of silke.

        Tongue, not a word:

        Come trusty sword,

    Come blade, my breast imbrew: 2040

    She stabs herselfe

    And farewell friends:

    Thus *Thysby* ends:

    Adieu, adieu, adieu.   *She dies*

THESEUS *Moone-shine* and *Lyon* are left to bury the dead.

DEMETRIUS I, and *Wall* to.

⌈BOTTOM⌉ No, I assure you, the wall is downe, that parted
  their fathers. Will it please you, to see the Epilogue, or
  to heare a Bergomaske daunce, between two of our
  cõpany?

THESEUS No Epilogue, I pray you. For your Play needs no   2050
  excuse. Neuer excuse: For when the Players are all
  deade, there neede none to be blamed. Mary, if hee
  that writ it, had played *Pyramus*, and hangd himselfe
  in *Thisbies* garter, it would haue beene a fine Tragedy:
  and so it is truely, and very notably discharg'd. But
  come your Burgomaske: let your Epilogue alone.

    ⌈*Bottom and Flute*⌉ *daunce a Bergomaske, then*
    exeunt

  The iron tongue of midnight hath tolde twelue.

  Louers to bed, tis almost Fairy time.

  I feare we shall outsleepe the comming morne,

2060 As much as wee this night haue ouerwatcht.
This palpable grosse Play hath well beguil'd
The heauie gate of night. Sweete friends, to bed.
A fortnight holde we this solemnitie,
In nightly Reuels, and new iollity.   *Exeunt*

Sc. 9   *Enter Robin goodfellow with a broome*
(5.2)   ROBIN
     Now the hungry Lyon roares.
       And the wolfe behoules the Moone;
     Whilst the heauie ploughman snores,
       All with weary taske foredoone.
     Now the wasted brands doe glowe,
2070   Whilst the scriech-owle, scrieching lowd,
     Puts the wretch, that lyes in woe,
       In remembrance of a shrowde.
     Now it is the time of night,
       That the graues, all gaping wide,
     Euery one lets forth his spright,
       In the Churchway paths to glide.
     And wee Fairies, that doe runne,
       By the triple *Hecates* teame,
     From the presence of the Sunne,
2080   Following darkenesse like a dreame,
     Now are frollick: not a mouse
     Shall disturbe this hallowed house.
     I am sent, with broome, before,
     To sweepe the dust, behinde the dore.
     Enter Oberon and Titania, King and Queene of
     Fairies, with all their traine

     OBERON
     Through the house giue glimmering light,
       By the dead and drowsie fier,
     Euery Elfe and Fairy spright,
       Hop as light as birde from brier,
     And this dittie after mee,
2090   Sing, and daunce it trippingly.
     TITANIA
     First rehearse your song by rote,
     To each word a warbling note.
     Hand in hand, with Fairy grace,
     Will we sing and blesse this place.
     ⌈*The Song. The Fairies daunce*⌉

OBERON
Now, vntill the breake of day,
Through this house, each Fairy stray.
To the best bride bed will wee:
Which by vs shall blessed be:
And the issue, there create,
Euer shall be fortunate: 2100
So shall all the couples three
Euer true in louing be:
And the blots of natures hand
Shall not in their issue stand.
Neuer mole, hare-lippe, nor scarre,
Nor marke prodigious, such as are
Despised in natiuitie,
Shall vpon their children be.
With this field deaw consecrate,
Euery Fairy take his gate,   2110
And each seuerall chamber blesse,
Through this palace, with sweete peace,
And the owner of it blest,
Euer shall in safety rest.
Trippe away: make no stay:
Meete me all, by breake of day.
               Exeunt. Manet Robin

ROBIN
If we shadowes haue offended,
Thinke but this (and all is mended)
That you haue but slumbred here,
While these visions did appeare.   2120
And this weake and idle theame,
No more yielding but a dreame,
Gentles, doe not reprehend.
If you pardon, wee will mend.
And, as I am an honest *Puck,*
If we haue vnearned luck,
Now to scape the Serpents tongue,
We will make amends, ere long:
Else, the *Puck* a lyer call.
So, good night vnto you all.   2130
Giue me your hands, if we be friends:
And *Robin* shall restore amends.

               FINIS

ADDITIONAL PASSAGES

An unusual quantity and kind of mislineation in the first edition has persuaded most scholars that the text at the beginning of Sc. 8 was revised, with new material written in the margins. We here offer a reconstruction of the passage as originally drafted, which can be compared with 1700–86 of the edited text.

Sc. 8   *Enter Theseus, Hyppolita, and Philostrate*

(5.1) HYPPOLITA

    Tis strange, my *Theseus*, that these louers speake of.

THESEUS

    More straunge then true. I neuer may beleeue
    These antique fables, nor these Fairy toyes.
    Louers, and mad men haue such seething braines,
    One sees more diuels, then vast hell can holde:
    That is the mad man. The louer, all as frantick,
    Sees *Helens* beauty in a brow of *Ægypt*.
    Such trickes hath strong imagination,
    That if it would but apprehend some ioy,
10   It comprehends some bringer of that ioy.
    Or in the night, imagining some feare,
    How easie is a bush suppos'd a Beare?

HYPPOLITA

    But, all the story of the night told ouer,
    And all their minds transfigur'd so together,
    More witnesseth than fancies images,
    And growes to something of great constancy:
    But howsoeuer, strange and admirable.

       Enter Louers; Lysander, Demetrius, Hermia and
       Helena

THESEUS

    Here come the louers, full of ioy and mirth.
    Come now: what maskes, what daunces shall wee
      haue,
20   To ease the anguish of a torturing hower?
    Call *Philostrate*.

PHILOSTRATE   Here mighty *Theseus*.

THESEUS

    Say, what abridgement haue you for this euening?
    What maske, what musicke? How shall we beguile
    The lazy tyme, if not with some delight?

PHILOSTRATE

    There is a briefe, how many sports are ripe.
    Make choyce, of which your Highnesse will see first.

THESEUS

    The battell with the *Centaures* to be sung,
    By an *Athenian* Eunuche, to the Harpe?
    Weele none of that. That haue I tolde my loue,
    In glory of my kinsman *Hercules*.
30
    The ryot of the tipsie *Bachanals*,
    Tearing the *Thracian* singer, in their rage?
    That is an olde deuise: and it was plaid,
    When I from *Thebes* came last a conquerer.
    The thrise three Muses, mourning for the death
    Of learning, late deceast, in beggery?
    That is some *Satire* keene and criticall,
    Not sorting with a nuptiall ceremony.
    A tedious briefe Scene of young *Pyramus*
    And his loue *Thisby*; Tedious, and briefe?
40

PHILOSTRATE

    A Play there is, my Lord, some ten words long;
    Which is as briefe, as I haue knowne a play:
    But, by ten words, my Lord it is too long:
    Which makes it tedious. For in all the Play,
    There is not one word apt, one player fitted.

THESEUS What are they, that doe play it?

PHILOSTRATE

    Hard handed men, that worke in *Athens* here,
    Which neuer labour'd in their minds till now:
    And now haue toyled their vnbreathed memories,
    With this same Play, against your nuptiall.
50

THESEUS

    Goe bring them in, and take your places, Ladies.
          Exit Philostrate

HYPPOLITA

    I loue not to see wretchednesse orecharged;
    And duety, in his seruice, perishing.

ROMEO AND IULIET

ON its first appearance in print, in 1597, *Romeo and Iuliet* was described as 'An excellent conceited Tragedie' that had 'been often (with great applause) plaid publiquely'; its popularity is witnessed by the fact that this is a pirated version, put together from actors' memories as a way of cashing in on its success. A second printing, two years later, offered a greatly superior text apparently printed from Shakespeare's working papers. Probably he wrote it in 1594 or 1595.

The story was already well known, in Italian, French, and English. Shakespeare owes most to Arthur Brooke's long poem *The Tragicall Historye of Romeus and Juliet* (1562), which had already supplied hints for *The Two Gentlemen of Verona*; he may also have looked at some of the other versions. In his address 'To the Reader', Brooke says that he has seen 'the same argument lately set foorth on stage with more commendation, then I can looke for', but no earlier play survives.

Shakespeare's Prologue neatly sketches the plot of the two star-crossed lovers born of feuding families whose deaths 'burie their Parents strife'; and the formal verse structure of the Prologue—a sonnet—is matched by the carefully patterned layout of the action. At the climax of the first scene, Prince Escalus stills a brawl between representatives of the houses of Montague (Romeo's family) and Capulet (Iuliet's); at the end of Act 3, Scene 1 (Sc. 12), he passes judgement on another, more serious brawl, banishing Romeo for killing Iuliet's cousin Tibalt after Tibalt had killed Romeo's friend and the Prince's kinsman, Mercutio; and at the end of Act 5, the Prince presides over the reconciliation of Montagues and Capulets. Within this framework of public life Romeo and Iuliet act out their brief tragedy: in the first act they meet and declare their love—in another sonnet; in the second they arrange to marry in secret; in the third, after Romeo's banishment, they consummate their marriage and part; in the fourth, Iuliet drinks a sleeping draught prepared by Friar Lawrence so that she may escape marriage to Paris and, after waking in the family tomb, run off with Romeo; in the fifth, after Romeo, believing her to be dead, has taken poison, she stabs herself to death.

The play's structural formality is offset by an astonishing fertility of linguistic invention, showing itself no less in the comic bawdiness of the servants, the Nurse, and (on a more sophisticated level) Mercutio than in the rapt and impassioned poetry of the lovers. Shakespeare's mastery over a wide range of verbal styles combines with his psychological perceptiveness to create a richer gallery of memorable characters than in any of his earlier plays; and his theatrical imagination compresses Brooke's leisurely narrative into a dramatic masterpiece.

Our text is based on the second edition (1599), probably set from an autograph manuscript.

THE NAMES OF THE ACTORS

CHORUS

ROMEO
MOUNTAGUE, his father
MOUNTAGUES WIFE
BENUOLIO, Mountagues Nephew
ABRAM, Mountagues Seruingman
BALTHAZER, Romeos man

IULIET
CAPULET, her father
CAPULETS WIFE
TYBALT, her Nephew
His Page
PETRUCHIO
CAPULETS COZIN
Iuliets NURSE

PETER
SAMPSON } Seruingmen of the Capulets
GREGORY
Other SERUINGMEN
MUSITIONS

Escalus, PRINCE of Verona
MERCUTIO
Countie PARIS } his kinsmen
PAGE to Paris

FRIER LAWRENCE
FRIER IOHN
An APPOTHECARIE
CHIEFE WATCHMAN
Other CITIZENS OF THE WATCH

Masquers, Guests, Gentlewomen, followers of the Mountague and Capulet factions

The most excellent and lamentable
Tragedie, of Romeo and Iuliet

Prologue *Enter Corus*

CHORUS

Two housholds both alike in dignitie,
 (*In faire* Verona *where we lay our Scene*)
From auncient grudge, breake to new mutinie,
 Where ciuill bloud makes ciuill hands vncleane:
From forth the fatall loynes of these two foes,
 A paire of starre-crost louers, take their life:
Whose misaduentur'd pittious ouerthrowes,
 Doth with their death burie their Parents strife.
The fearfull passage of their death-markt loue,
10 *And the continuance of their Parents rage:*
Which but their childrens end nought could remoue:
 Is now the two houres trafficque of our Stage.
The which if you with patient eares attend,
What heare shall misse, our toyle shall striue to mend.

Exit

Sc. 1   *Enter Sampson and Gregorie, with Swords and*
(1.1)   *Bucklers, of the house of Capulet*

SAMPSON *Gregorie*, on my word weele not carrie Coles.

GREGORIE No, for then we should be Collyers.

SAMPSON I meane, and we be in choller, weele draw.

GREGORIE I while you liue, draw your necke out of choller.

SAMPSON I strike quickly being moued.

20 GREGORIE But thou art not quickly moued to strike.

SAMPSON A dog of the house of *Mountague* moues me.

GREGORIE To moue is to stirre, and to be valiant, is to
 stand: Therefore if thou art moued thou runst away.

SAMPSON A dog of that house shall moue me to stand: I
 will take the wall of any man or maide of *Mountagues*.

GREGORIE That shewes thee a weake slaue, for the weakest
 goes to the wall.

SAMPSON Tis true, & therfore women being the weaker
 vessels are euer thrust to the wall: therfore I wil push
30 *Mountagues* men from the wall, and thrust his maides
 to the wall.

GREGORIE The quarell is betweene our maisters, and vs
 their men.

SAMPSON Tis all one, I will shew my selfe a tyrant, when
 I haue fought with the men, I will be ciuil with the
 maides, I will cut off their heads.

GREGORIE The heads of the maids.

SAMPSON I the heads of the maides, or their maiden heads,
 take it in what sense thou wilt.

40 GREGORIE They must take it in sense that feele it.

SAMPSON Me they shall feele while I am able to stand,
 and tis knowne I am a pretie peece of flesh.

GREGORIE Tis well thou art not fish, if thou hadst, thou
 hadst bin poore Iohn:

Enter Abram and another seruing man of the
Mountagues

draw thy toole, here comes of the house of *Mountagues*.

SAMPSON My naked weapon is out, quarell, I will back
 thee.

GREGORIE How, turne thy backe and runne?

SAMPSON Feare me not.

GREGORIE No marrie, I feare thee.   50

SAMPSON Let vs take the law of our side, let them begin.

GREGORIE I will frown as I passe by, and let them take it
 as they list.

SAMPSON Nay as they dare, I wil bite my thumb at them,
 which is disgrace to them if they beare it.

He bites his thumbe

ABRAM Do you bite your thumbe at vs sir?

SAMPSON I do bite my thumbe sir.

ABRAM Do you bite your thumb at vs sir?

SAMPSON (*to Gregorie*) Is the law of our side if I say I?

GREGORIE No.   60

SAMPSON (*to Abram*) No sir, I do not bite my thumbe at
 you sir, but I bite my thumbe sir.

GREGORIE (*to Abram*) Do you quarell sir?

ABRAM Quarell sir, no sir.

SAMPSON But if you do sir, I am for you, I serue as good
 a mã as you.

ABRAM No better.

SAMPSON Well sir.

Enter Benuolio

GREGORIE Say better, here comes one of my maisters
 kinsmen.   70

SAMPSON (*to Abram*) Yes better sir.

ABRAM You lie.

SAMPSON Draw if you be men, *Gregorie*, remember thy
 washing blowe.

They draw and fight

BENUOLIO (*drawing*) Part fooles, put vp your swords, you
 know not what you do.

Enter Tibalt

TYBALT (*drawing*)

What art thou drawne among these hartlesse hindes?
Turne thee *Benuolio*, looke vpon thy death.

BENUOLIO

I do but keepe the peace, put vp thy sword,
Or manage it to part these men with me.   80

TYBALT

What drawne and talke of peace? I hate the word,
As I hate hell, all *Mountagues* and thee:
Haue at thee coward.

They fight. Enter three or foure Citizens ⌈of the
Watch⌉ with Clubs or partysons

379

⌈CITIZENS OF THE WATCH⌉
Clubs, Bils and Partisons, strike, beate them downe,
Downe with the Capulets, downe with the Mountagues.
Enter old Capulet in his gowne, and his wife
CAPULET
What noyse is this? giue me my long sword hoe.
CAPULETS WIFE
A crowch, a crowch, why call you for a sword?
Enter old Mountague, ⌈with his sword drawn,⌉ and his wife
CAPULET
My sword I say, old *Mountague* is come,
And florishes his blade in spight of me.
MOUNTAGUE
Thou villaine *Capulet*,
⌈*His wife holds him backe*⌉
90   hold me not, let me go.
MOUNTAGUES WIFE
Thou shalt not stir one foote to seeke a foe.
⌈*The Citizens of the Watch attempt to part the factions.*⌉
Enter Prince Eskales, with his traine
PRINCE
Rebellious subiects enemies to peace,
Prophaners of this neighbour-stayned steele,
Will they not heare? what ho, you men, you beasts:
That quench the fire of your pernicious rage,
With purple fountaines issuing from your veines:
On paine of torture from those bloudie hands
Throw your mistempred weapons to the ground,
And heare the sentence of your moued Prince.
⌈*Mountague, Capulet, and their followers throw downe their weapons*⌉
100 Three ciuill brawles bred of an ayrie word,
By thee old *Capulet* and *Mountague*,
Haue thrice disturbd the quiet of our streets,
And made *Veronas* auncient Citizens,
Cast by their graue beseeming ornaments,
To wield old partizans, in hands as old,
Cancred with peace, to part your cancred hate,
If euer you disturbe our streets againe,
Your liues shall pay the forfeit of the peace.
For this time all the rest depart away:
110 You *Capulet* shall go along with me,
And *Mountague* come you this afternoone,
To know our farther pleasure in this case:
To old Free-towne, our common iudgement place:
Once more on paine of death, all men depart.
Exeunt all but Mountague, his wife, and Benuolio
MOUNTAGUE
Who set this auncient quarell new abroach?
Speake Nephew, were you by when it began?
BENUOLIO
Here were the seruants of your aduersarie
And yours, close fighting ere I did approach,
I drew to part them, in the instant came
120 The fierie *Tybalt*, with his sword preparde,

Which as he breath'd defiance to my eares,
He swoong about his head and cut the windes,
Who nothing hurt withall, hist him in scorne:
While we were enterchaunging thrusts and blowes,
Came more and more, and fought on part and part,
Till the Prince came, who parted either part.
MOUNTAGUES WIFE
O where is *Romeo*, saw you him to day?
Right glad I am, he was not at this fray.
BENUOLIO
Madam, an houre before the worshipt Sun,
Peerde forth the golden window of the East,   130
A troubled minde driue me to walke abroad,
Where vnderneath the groue of Sycamour,
That Westward rooteth from this Citie side:
So early walking did I see your sonne,
Towards him I made, but he was ware of me,
And stole into the couert of the wood,
I measuring his affections by my owne,
Which then most sought, where most might not be found:
Being one too many by my wearie selfe,
Pursued my humor, not pursuing his,   140
And gladly shunnd, who gladly fled from me.
MOUNTAGUE
Many a morning hath he there bin seene,
With teares augmenting the fresh mornings deawe,
Adding to cloudes, more clowdes with his deepe sighes,
But all so soone, as the alcheering Sunne,
Should in the farthest East begin to draw,
The shadie curtaines from *Auroras* bed,
Away from light steales home my heauie sonne,
And priuate in his Chamber pennes himselfe,
Shuts vp his windowes, locks faire day-light out,   150
And makes himselfe an artificiall night:
Blacke and portendous must this humor proue,
Vnlesse good counsell may the cause remoue.
BENUOLIO
My Noble Vncle do you know the cause?
MOUNTAGUE
I neither know it, nor can learne of him.
BENUOLIO
Haue you importunde him by any meanes?
MOUNTAGUE
Both by my selfe and many other friends,
But he his owne affections counseller,
Is to himselfe (I will not say how true)
But to himselfe so secret and so close,   160
So farre from sounding and discouerie,
As is the bud bit with an enuious worme,
Ere he can spread his sweete leaues to the ayre,
Or dedicate his bewtie to the sunne.
Could we but learne from whence his sorrows grow,
We would as willingly giue cure as know.
Enter Romeo
BENUOLIO
See where he comes, so please you step aside,
Ile know his greeuance or be much denide.

MOUNTAGUE

I would thou wert so happie by thy stay,
170 To heare true shrift, come Madam lets away.

Exeunt Mountague and his wife

BENUOLIO

Good morrow Cousin.

ROMEO   Is the day so young?

BENUOLIO

But new strooke nine.

ROMEO   Ay me, sad houres seeme long:
Was that my father that went hence so fast?

BENUOLIO

It was: what sadnesse lengthens *Romeos* houres?

ROMEO

Not hauing that, which hauing, makes thē short.

BENUOLIO In loue.

ROMEO Out.

BENUOLIO Of loue.

ROMEO

Out of her fauour where I am in loue.

BENUOLIO

180 Alas that loue so gentle in his view,
Should be so tirannous and rough in proofe.

ROMEO

Alas that loue, whose view is muffled still,
Should without eyes, see pathwaies to his will:
Where shall we dine? ⌈seeing bloud⌉ ô me! what fray
    was here?
Yet tell me not, for I haue heard it all:
Heres much to do with hate, but more with loue:
Why then ô brawling loue, ô louing hate,
O any thing of nothing first create:
O heauie lightnesse, serious vanitie,
190 Mishapen Chaos of welseēing formes,
Feather of lead, bright smoke, cold fier, sicke health,
Still waking sleepe that is not what it is.
This loue feele I, that feele no loue in this,
Doest thou not laugh?

BENUOLIO   No Coze, I rather weepe.

ROMEO

Good hart at what?

BENUOLIO   At thy good harts oppression.

ROMEO Why such is loues transgression:
Griefes of mine owne lie heauie in my breast,
Which thou wilt propogate to haue it preast,
With more of thine, this loue that thou hast showne,
200 Doth ad more griefe, too too much of mine owne.
Loue is a smoke made with the fume of sighes,
Being purgd, a fire sparkling in louers eies,
Being vext, a sea nourisht with louers teares,
What is it else? a madnesse, most discreete,
A choking gall, and a preseruing sweete:
Farewell my Coze.

BENUOLIO   Soft I will go along:
And if you leaue me so, you do me wrong.

ROMEO

Tut I haue lost my selfe, I am not here,
This is not *Romeo*, hees some other where.

BENUOLIO

Tell me in sadnesse, who is that you loue?   210

ROMEO What shall I grone and tell thee?

BENUOLIO

Grone, why no: but sadly tell me who?

ROMEO

Bid a sicke man in sadnesse make his will:
A word ill vrgd to one that is so ill:
In sadnesse Cozin, I do loue a woman.

BENUOLIO

I aymde so neare, when I supposde you lou'd.

ROMEO

A right good mark man, and shees faire I loue.

BENUOLIO

A right faire marke faire Coze is soonest hit.

ROMEO

Well in that hit you misse, sheel not be hit
With *Cupids* arrow, she hath *Dians* wit: 220
And in strong proofe of chastitie well armd,
From loues weak childish bow she liues vnharmd.
Shee will not stay the siege of louing tearmes,
Nor bide th'incounter of assailing eies.
Nor ope her lap to sainct seducing gold,
O she is rich in bewtie, onely poore,
That when she dies, with bewtie dies her store.

BENUOLIO

Thē she hath sworn, that she wil stil liue chaste?

ROMEO

She hath, and in that sparing, makes huge waste:
For bewtie steru'd with her seueritie,   230
Cuts bewtie off from all posteritie.
She is too faire, too wise, wisely too faire,
To merit blisse by making me dispaire:
Shee hath forsworne to loue, and in that vow,
Do I liue dead, that liue to tell it now.

BENUOLIO

Be rulde by me, forget to thinke of her.

ROMEO

O teach me how I should forget to thinke.

BENUOLIO

By giuing libertie vnto thine eyes,
Examine other bewties.

ROMEO   Tis the way
To call hers (exquisit) in question more,   240
These happie maskes that kis faire Ladies browes,
Being black, puts vs in mind they hide the faire:
He that is strooken blind, cannot forget
The precious treasure of his eye-sight lost,
Shew me a mistresse that is passing faire,
What doth her bewtie serue but as a note,
Where I may reade who past that passing faire:
Farewel, thou canst not teach me to forget.

BENUOLIO

Ile pay that doctrine, or else die in debt.   *Exeunt*

Enter Capulet, Countie Paris, and ⌈*Peter,*⌉ *a*   Sc. 2
Seruingman   (1.2)

CAPULET

But *Mountague* is bound as well as I,   250

In penaltie alike, and tis not hard I thinke,
For men so old as we to keepe the peace.

PARIS

Of honourable reckoning are you both,
And pittie tis, you liu'd at ods so long:
But now my Lord, what say you to my sute?

CAPULET

But saying ore what I haue said before,
My child is yet a straunger in the world,
Shee hath not seene the chaunge of fourteene yeares,
Let two more Sommers wither in their pride,
260   Ere we may thinke her ripe to be a bride.

PARIS

Younger then she, are happie mothers made.

CAPULET

And too soone mard are those so early made:
But wooe her gentle *Paris*, get her hart,
My will to her consent, is but a part.
And shee agreed, within her scope of choise
Lyes my consent, and faire according voyce:
This night I hold, an old accustomd feast,
Whereto I haue inuited many a guest:
Such as I loue, and you among the store,
270   One more, most welcome makes my number more:
At my poore house, looke to behold this night,
Earthtreading starres, that make darke heauen light:
Such comfort as do lustie young men feele,
When well appareld Aprill on the heele,
Of limping winter treads, euen such delight
Among fresh femelle buds shall you this night
Inherit at my house, heare all, all see:
And like her most, whose merit most shall bee:
Which one more view, of many, mine being one,
280   May stand in number, though in reckning none.
Come go with me, (*giuing* ⌈*Peter*⌉ *a paper*) go sirrah
      trudge about,
Through faire *Verona*, find those persons out,
Whose names are written there, and to them say,
My house and welcome, on their pleasure stay.

Exit Capulet and Paris

⌈PETER⌉ Find them out whose names are written here: it
is written, that the shoo-maker should meddle with his
yard, and the tayler with his last, the fisher with his
pensill, & the painter with his nets. But I am sent to
find those persons whose names are here writ, and can
290   neuer find what names the writing person hath here
writ (I must to the learned)

Enter Benuolio, and Romeo

in good time.

BENUOLIO (*to Romeo*)

Tut man, one fire burnes out, an others burning,
   On paine is lesned by an others anguish,
Turne giddie, and be holpe by backward turning:
   One desperate greefe, cures with an others languish:
Take thou some new infection to thy eye,
And the rancke poyson of the old will dye.

ROMEO

Your Plantan leafe is excellent for that.

BENUOLIO For what I pray thee?   300
ROMEO For your broken shin.
BENUOLIO Why *Romeo* art thou mad?
ROMEO

Not mad, but bound more than a mad man is.
Shut vp in prison, kept without my foode,
Whipt and tormented, and (*to* ⌈*Peter*⌉) Godden good
      fellow.

⌈PETER⌉

Godgigoden, I pray sir can you read?

ROMEO

I mine owne fortune in my miserie.

⌈PETER⌉ Perhaps you haue learned it without booke: but
I pray can you read any thing you see?

ROMEO

I if I know the letters and the language.   310

⌈PETER⌉ Yee say honestly, rest you merrie.

ROMEO Stay fellow I can read.

      He reads the Letter

Seigneur Martino *and his wife and daughters,*
Countie Anselme *and his beauteous sisters,*
The Ladie widdow of Vitruuio,
Seigneur Placentio, *and his louelie Neeces,*
Mercutio *and his brother* Valentine,
Mine vncle Capulet *his wife and daughters,*
My faire Neece Rosaline *and* Liuia,
Seigneur Valentio *and his Cosen* Tibalt,   320
Lucio *and the liuelie* Hellena.
A faire assembly, whether should they come?

⌈PETER⌉ Vp.
ROMEO Whether?
⌈PETER⌉ To supper to our house.
ROMEO Whose house?
⌈PETER⌉ My Masters.
ROMEO

Indeed I should haue askt thee that before.

⌈PETER⌉ Now il'e tel you without asking. My Master is the
great rich *Capulet*, and if you be not of the house of   330
Mountagues, I pray come and crush a cup of wine. Rest
you merrie.   *Exit*

BENUOLIO

At this same auncient feast of *Capulets*,
Sups the faire *Rosaline* whom thou so loues:
With all the admired beauties of *Verona*,
Goe thither and with vnattainted eye,
Compare her face with some that I shall shew,
And I will make thee thinke thy swan a crow.

ROMEO

When the deuout religion of mine eye
   Maintaines such falshood, then turne teares to fires,   340
And these who often drownde could neuer die,
   Transparent Heretiques be burnt for liers.
One fairer than my loue, the all seeing sonne
Nere saw her match, since first the world begun.

BENUOLIO

Tut you saw her faire none els being by,
Her selfe poysd with her selfe in either eye:

But in that Cristall scales let there be waide,
Your Ladyes loue, against some other maide
That I will shew you shining at this feast,
350   And she shall scant shew well that now seemes best.

ROMEO
Ile goe along no such sight to be showne,
But to reioyce in splendor of mine owne.   *Exeunt*

Sc. 3   *Enter Capulets wife and Nurce*
(1.3)   CAPULETS WIFE
Nurce wher's my daughter: call her forth to mee.

NURSE
Now by my maiden head at twelue yeare old
I bad her come, what Lamb, what Ladie bird,
God forbid. Where is this girl? what *Iuliet.*
     Enter Iuliet

IULIET How now who calls?
NURSE Your Mother.

IULIET
Madame I am here, what is your will?

CAPULETS WIFE
360   This is the matter. Nurse giue leaue a while,
We must talke in secret. Nurse come back again,
I haue remembred me, thou'se heare our counsaile.
Thou knowest my daughters of a prettie age.

NURSE
Faith I can tell her age vnto an houre.

CAPULETS WIFE Shee's not fourteene.
NURSE Ile lay fourteene of my teeth, and yet to my teene
be it spoken, I haue but foure, shee's not fourteene.
How long is it now to *Lammas-tide?*

CAPULETS WIFE A fortnight and odde dayes.

NURSE
370   Euen or odde, of all dayes in the yeare
Come *Lammas* Eue at night shall she be fourteene.
Susan and she, God rest all Christian soules,
Were of an age. Well *Susan* is with God,
She was too good for me: But as I said,
On *Lammas* Eue at night shall she be fourteene,
That shall shee, marie I remember it well.
Tis since the Earth-quake nowe eleauen yeares,
And she was weand I neuer shall forget it,
Of all the daies of the yeare vpon that day:
380   For I had then laid wormewood to my dug,
Sitting in the sun vnder the Doue-house wall.
My Lord and you were then at *Mantua,*
Nay I do beare a braine: But as I said,
When it did tast the wormwood on the nipple
Of my dug, & felt it bitter, pretty foole
To see it teachie and fall out with Dugge.
Shake quoth the Doue-house, twas no need I trow
To bid me trudge,
And since that time it is a leuen yeares,
390   For then she could stand hylone, nay byth roode
She could haue run and wadled all about:
For euen the day before she broke her brow,
And then my husband, God be with his soule,
A was a merrie man, tooke vp the child,

Yea quoth he, doest thou fall vpon thy face?
Thou wilt fall backward when thou hast more wit,
Wilt thou not *Iule?* And by my holydam,
The pretie wretch left crying, and said I:
To see now how a ieast shall come about:
I warrant, and I should liue a thousand yeares,   400
I neuer should forget it: wilt thou not *Iule* quoth he?
And pretie foole it stinted, and said I.

CAPULETS WIFE
Inough of this, I pray thee hold thy peace.

NURSE
Yes Madam, yet I cannot chuse but laugh,
To thinke it should leaue crying, and say I:
And yet I warrant it had vpon it brow,
A bump as big as a young Cockrels stone:
A perillous knock, and it cryed bitterly.
Yea quoth my husband, fallst vpon thy face,
Thou wilt fall backward when thou commst to age: 410
Wilt thou not *Iule?* It stinted, and said I.

IULIET
And stint thou too, I pray thee Nurse, say I.

NURSE
Peace I haue done: God marke thee too his grace,
Thou wast the prettiest babe that ere I nurst,
And I might liue to see thee married once,
I haue my wish.

CAPULETS WIFE
Marrie, that marrie is the very theame
I came to talke of, tell me daughter *Iuliet,*
How stands your dispositions to be married?

IULIET
It is an honore that I dreame not of.   420

NURSE
An honore, were not I thine onely Nurse,
I would say thou hadst suckt wisedome from thy teate.

CAPULETS WIFE
Well thinke of marriage now, yonger then you
Here in *Verona,* Ladies of esteeme,
Are made alreadie mothers. By my count
I was your mother, much vpon these yeares
That you are now a maide, thus then in briefe:
The valiant *Paris* seekes you for his loue.

NURSE
A man young Lady, Lady, such a man
As all the world. Why hees a man of waxe.   430

CAPULETS WIFE
Veronas Sommer hath not such a flower.

NURSE
Nay hees a flower, in faith a very flower.

CAPULETS WIFE (*to Iuliet*)
What say you, can you loue the Gentleman?
This night you shall behold him at our feast,
Reade ore the volume of young *Paris* face,
And find delight, writ there with bewties pen,
Examine euery married liniament,
And see how one an other lends content:
And what obscurde in this faire volume lies,
Finde written in the margeant of his eyes.   440

This precious booke of loue, this vnbound louer,
To bewtifie him, onely lacks a Couer.
The fish liues in the sea, and tis much pride
For faire without the faire within to hide:
That booke in manies eyes doth share the glorie
That in gold claspes locks in the golden storie:
So shall you share all that he doth possesse,
By hauing him, making your selfe no lesse.

NURSE
No lesse, nay bigger: women grow by men.

CAPULETS WIFE (*to Iuliet*)
450   Speake briefly, can you like of *Paris* loue?

IULIET
Ile looke to like, if looking liking moue.
But no more deepe will I endart mine eye,
Then your consent giues strength to make it flie.
            Enter ⌜Peter⌝

⌜PETER⌝ Madam the guests are come, supper seru'd vp,
you cald, my young Lady askt for, the Nurse curst in
the Pantrie, and euerie thing in extremitie: I must
hence to wait, I beseech you follow straight.

CAPULETS WIFE
We follow thee,   *Exit ⌜Peter⌝*
            Iuliet the Countie staies.

NURSE
Go gyrle, seeke happie nights to happie dayes.   *Exeunt*

Sc. 4   *Enter Romeo, Mercutio, Benuolio, as Maskers, with*
(1.4)   *fiue or sixe other Maskers, ⌜bearing a drum and*
            torches⌝

ROMEO
460   What shall this speech be spoke for our excuse?
Or shall we on without appologie?

BENUOLIO
The date is out of such prolixitie,
Weele haue no *Cupid*, hudwinckt with a skarfe,
Bearing a Tartars painted bow of lath,
Skaring the Ladies like a Crowkeeper,
Nor no without booke Prologue faintly spoke
After the Prompter, for our entrance.
But let them measure vs by what they will,
Weele measure them a measure and be gone.

ROMEO
470   Giue me a torch, I am not for this ambling,
Being but heauie I will beare the light.

MERCUTIO
Nay gẽtle *Romeo*, we must haue you dance.

ROMEO
Not I beleeue me, you haue dancing shooes
With nimble soles, I haue a soule of Leade
So stakes me to the ground I cannot moue.

MERCUTIO
You are a Louer, borrow *Cupids* wings,
And sore with them aboue a common bound.

ROMEO
I am too sore enpearced with his shaft,
To sore with his light feathers, and so bound,
480   I cannot bound a pitch aboue dull woe,

Vnder loues heauie birthen do I sincke.

MERCUTIO
And to sink in it should you burthen loue,
Too great oppression for a tender thing.

ROMEO
Is loue a tender thing? it is too rough,
Too rude, too boystrous, and it pricks like thorne.

MERCUTIO
If loue be rough with you, be rough with loue:
Prick loue for pricking, and you beate loue downe,
Giue me a case to put my visage in,
A visor for a visor, what care I
What curious eye doth cote deformitie:
490   Here are the beetle browes shall blush for me.
            ⌜*They put on visors*⌝

BENUOLIO
Come knock and enter, and no sooner in,
But euery man betake him to his legs.

ROMEO
A torch for me, let wantons light of heart
Tickle the sencelesse rushes with their heeles:
For I am prouerbd with a graunsire phrase,
Ile be a candle-holder and looke on,
The game was nere so faire, and I am dun.
            ⌜*He takes a torch*⌝

MERCUTIO
Tut, duns the mouse, the Constables own word:
If thou art dun, weele draw thee from the mire   500
Of saue your reuerence loue, wherein thou stickest
Vp to the eares, come we burne daylight ho.

ROMEO
Nay thats not so.

MERCUTIO   I meane sir in delay
We waste our lights in vaine, like lights by day:
Take our good meaning, for our iudgement sits,
Fiue times in that, ere once in our fiue wits.

ROMEO
And we meane well in going to this Mask,
But tis no wit to go.

MERCUTIO   Why, may one aske?

ROMEO
I dreampt a dreame to night.

MERCUTIO   And so did I.

ROMEO
Well what was yours?

MERCUTIO   That dreamers often lie.   510

ROMEO
In bed asleep while they do dream things true.

MERCUTIO
O then I see Queene Mab hath bin with you.

BENUOLIO Queene Mab whats she?

MERCUTIO
She is the Fairies midwife, and she comes
In shape no bigger thẽ an Agot stone,
On the forefinger of an Alderman,
Drawne with a teeme of little ottamie,
Athwart mens noses as they lie asleep:
Her waggõ spokes made of lõg spinners legs:

520 The couer, of the wings of Grashoppers,
    Her traces of the moonshines watry beams,
    Her collors of the smallest spider web,
    Her whip of Crickets bone, the lash of Philome,
    Her waggoner, a small grey coated Gnat,
    Not half so big as a round litle worme,
    Prickt from the lazie finger of a maid.
    Her Charriot is an emptie Hasel nut,
    Made by the Ioyner squirrel or old Grub,
    Time out a mind, the Fairies Coatchmakers:
530 And in this state she gallops night by night,
    Throgh louers brains, and then they dreame of loue,
    Ore Courtiers knees, that dreame on Cursies strait,
    Ore Ladies lips who strait one kisses dream,
    Which oft the angrie Mab with blisters plagues,
    Because their breaths with sweete meates tainted are.
    Sometime she gallops ore a Lawyers lip,
    And then dreames he of smelling out a sute:
    And sometime comes she with a tithpigs tale,
    Tickling a Persons nose as a lies asleepe,
540 Then dreams he of an other Benefice.
    Sometime she driueth ore a souldiers neck,
    And then dreames he of cutting forrain throates,
    Of breaches, ambuscados, spanish blades:
    Of healths fiue fadome deepe, and then anon
    Drums in his eare, at which he starts and wakes,
    And being thus frighted, sweares a praier or two,
    And sleeps againe: this is that very Mab
    That plats the manes of horses in the night:
    And bakes the Elflocks in foule sluttish haires,
550 Which once vntangled, much misfortune bodes.
    This is the hag, when maides lie on their backs,
    That presses them and learnes them first to beare,
    Making them women of good carriage:
    This is she.
    ROMEO   Peace, peace, *Mercutio* peace,
    Thou talkst of nothing.
    MERCUTIO   True, I talke of dreames:
    Which are the children of an idle braine,
    Begot of nothing but vaine phantasie:
    Which is as thin of substance as the ayre,
    And more inconstant then the wind who wooes,
560 Euen now the frozen bosome of the North:
    And being angerd puffes away from thence,
    Turning his face to the dewe dropping South.
    BENUOLIO
    This wind you talk of, blows vs from our selues,
    Supper is done, and we shall come too late.
    ROMEO
    I feare too earlie, for my mind misgiues,
    Some consequence yet hanging in the starres,
    Shall bitterly begin his fearfull date,
    With this nights reuels, and expire the terme
    Of a despised life closde in my brest:
570 By some vile forfeit of vntimely death.
    But he that hath the stirrage of my course,
    Direct my saile, on lustie Gentlemen.
    BENUOLIO Strike drum.
        They march about the Stage, and ⌈*exeunt*⌉

⌈*Peter*⌉ *and other Seruingmen come forth with*   Sc. 5
Napkins   (1.5)
⌈PETER⌉ Wheres Potpan that he helpes not to take away?
    He shift a trencher, he scrape a trencher?
1. SERUINGMAN When good manners shall lie all in one
    or two mens hands and they vnwasht too, tis a foule
    thing.
⌈PETER⌉ Away with the ioynstooles, remoue the
    Courtcubbert, looke to the plate, good thou, saue me   580
    a peece of March-pane, and as thou loues me, let the
    porter let in *Susan Grindstone*, and *Nell, Anthonie* and
    Potpan.
2. SERUINGMAN I boy readie.
⌈PETER⌉ You are lookt for, and cald for, askt for, and
    sought for in the great chamber.
⌈1.⌉ SERUINGMAN We cannot be here and there too,
    chearely boyes, be brisk a while, and the longest liuer
    take all.
        ⌈*They come and go, setting forth tables and chaires.*⌉
        Enter ⌈*Musitions; then*⌉ *at one doore Capulet,* ⌈*his*
        wife,⌉ *his Cozin, Iuliet,* ⌈*Nurse,*⌉ *Tybalt, his Page,*
        Petruchio, and all the guests and gentlewomen; at
        another doore, the Maskers: ⌈*Romeo, Benuolio, and*
        Mercutio⌉
CAPULET (*to the Maskers*)
    Welcome gentlemen, Ladies that haue their toes   590
    Vnplagued with Cornes, will walke a bout with you:
    Ah ha my mistresses, which of you all
    Will now denie to daunce, she that makes daintie,
    She Ile swear hath Corns: am I come neare ye now?
    Welcome gentlemen, I haue seene the day
    That I haue worne a visor and could tell
    A whispering tale in a faire Ladies eare:
    Such as would please: tis gone, tis gone, tis gone,
    You are welcome, gentlemen: come, Musitions play.
        Musick plays and the Maskers, guests, and
        gentlewomen dance. ⌈*Romeo stands apart*⌉
    A hall, a hall, giue roome, and foote it gyrles,   600
    (*To Seruingmen*) More light you knaues, and turne the
        tables vp:
    And quench the fire, the roome is growne too hot.
    (*To his Cozin*) Ah sirrah, this vnlookt for sport comes
        well:
    Nay sit, nay sit, good Cozin *Capulet*,
    For you and I are past our dauncing dayes:
        ⌈*Capulet and his Cozin sit*⌉
    How long ist now since last your selfe and I
    Were in a maske?
CAPULETS COZIN   Berlady thirtie yeares.
CAPULET
    What man tis not so much, tis not so much,
    Tis since the nuptiall of *Lucientio*:
    Come Pentycost as quickly as it will,   610
    Some fiue and twentie yeares, and then we maskt.
CAPULETS COZIN
    Tis more, tis more, his sonne is elder sir:
    His sonne is thirtie.
CAPULET   Will you tell me that?
    His sonne was but a ward 2. yeares ago.

ROMEO (*to a Seruingman*)
　What Ladies that which doth enrich the hand
　Of yonder Knight?
SERUINGMAN　　　　　I know not sir.
ROMEO
　O she doth teach the torches to burn bright:
　It seemes she hangs vpon the cheeke of night:
　As a rich Iewel in an Ethiops eare,
620　Bewtie too rich for vse, for earth too deare:
　So showes a snowie Doue trooping with Crowes,
　As yonder Lady ore her fellowes showes:
　The measure done, Ile watch her place of stand,
　And touching hers, make blessed my rude hand.
　Did my hart loue till now, forsweare it sight,
　For I nere saw true bewtie till this night.
TYBALT
　This by his voyce, should be a *Mountague*.
　Fetch me my Rapier boy,　　　　　⌈*Exit Page*⌉
　　　　　　　　what dares the slaue
　Come hither couerd with an anticque face,
630　To fleere and scorne at our solemnitie?
　Now by the stocke and honor of my kin,
　To strike him dead, I hold it not a sin.
CAPULET ⌈*standing*⌉
　Why how now kinsman, wherefore storme you so?
TYBALT
　Vncle, this is a *Mountague* our foe:
　A villaine that is hither come in spight,
　To scorne at our solemnitie this night.
CAPULET
　Young *Romeo* is it.
TYBALT　　　　　Tis he, that villaine *Romeo*.
CAPULET
　Content thee gentle Coze, let him alone,
　A beares him like a portly Gentleman:
640　And to say truth, *Verona* brags of him,
　To be a vertuous and welgouernd youth,
　I would not for the wealth of all this Towne,
　Here in my house do him disparagement:
　Therefore be patient, take no note of him,
　It is my will, the which if thou respect,
　Shew a faire presence, and put off these frownes,
　An illbeseeming semblance for a feast.
TYBALT
　It fits when such a villaine is a guest,
　Ile not endure him.
CAPULET　　　　He shall be endured.
650　What goodman boy, I say he shall, go too,
　Am I the master here or you? go too,
　Youle not endure him, god shall mend my soule,
　Youle make a mutinie among my guests:
　You wil set cock a hoope, youle be the man.
TYBALT
　Why Vncle, tis a shame.
CAPULET　　　　　Go too, go too,
　You are a sawcie boy, ist so indeed?
　This trick may chance to scath you, I know what,
　You must contrarie me, marrie tis time,

⌈*A dance ends. Iuliet retires to her place of stand,*
　where Romeo awaits her⌉
(*To the guests*) Well said my hearts, (*to Tybalt*) you are
　a princox, go,
Be quiet, or (*to Seruingmen*) more light, more light (*to*　660
　Tybalt) for shame,
Ile make you quiet (*to the guests*) (what) chearely my
　hearts.
　　⌈*The Musicke playes againe, and the guests dance*⌉
TYBALT
　Patience perforce, with wilfull choller meeting,
　Makes my flesh tremble in their different greeting:
　I will withdraw, but this intrusion shall
　Now seeming sweet, conuert to bittrest gall.　　*Exit*
ROMEO (*to Iuliet, touching her hand*)
　If I prophane with my vnworthiest hand,
　　This holy shrine, the gentler sin is this,
　My lips two blushing Pylgrims readie stand,
　　To smoothe that rough touch with a tender kis.
IULIET
　Good Pilgrim you do wrõg your hãd too much　　　670
　　Which mannerly deuocion showes in this,
　For saints haue hands, that Pilgrims hands do tuch,
　　And palme to palme is holy Palmers kis.
ROMEO
　Haue not Saints lips and holy Palmers too?
IULIET
　I Pilgrim, lips that they must vse in praire.
ROMEO
　O then deare Saint, let lips do what hands do,
　　They pray (grant thou) least faith turne to dispaire.
IULIET
　Saints do not moue, thogh grant for praiers sake.
ROMEO
　Then moue not while my praiers effect I take,
　　He kisses her
　Thus from my lips, by thine my sin is purgd.　　680
IULIET
　Thẽ haue my lips the sin that they haue tooke.
ROMEO
　Sin from my lips, ô trespas sweetly vrgd:
　　Giue me my sin againe.
　　He kisses her
IULIET　　　　　Youe kisse bith booke.
NURSE
　Madam your mother craues a word with you.
　　⌈*Iuliet departs to her mother*⌉
ROMEO
　What is her mother?
NURSE　　　　　Marrie Batcheler,
　Her mother is the Lady of the house,
　And a good Ladie, and a wise and vertuous,
　I Nurst her daughter that you talkt withall:
　I tell you, he that can lay hold of her
　Shall haue the chincks.
ROMEO (*aside*)　　　　Is she a *Capulet*?　　690
　O deare account! my life is my foes debt.

BENUOLIO

Away begon, the sport is at the best.

ROMEO

I so I feare, the more is my vnrest.

CAPULET

Nay gentlemen prepare not to be gone,

We haue a trifling foolish banquet towards:

⌜*They whisper in his eare*⌝

Is it ene so? why then I thanke you all.

I thanke you honest gentlemen, good night:

More torches here, come on, then lets to bed.

(*To his Cozin*) Ah sirrah, by my faie it waxes late,

700 Ile to my rest.

Exeunt Capulet, ⌜his wife,⌝ and his Cozin. The
guests, gentlewomen, Maskers, Musitions, and
Seruingmen begin to leaue

IULIET

Come hither Nurse, what is yond gentleman?

NURSE

The sonne and heire of old *Tyberio*.

IULIET

Whats he that now is going out of doore?

NURSE

Marrie that I thinke be young *Petruchio*.

IULIET

Whats he that follows here that wold not dãce?

NURSE I know not.

IULIET

Go aske his name,

The Nurse goes

if he be married,

My graue is like to be my wedding bed.

NURSE (*returning*)

His name is *Romeo*, and a *Mountague*,

710 The onely sonne of your great enemie.

IULIET ⌜*aside*⌝

My onely loue sprung from my onely hate,

Too earlie seene, vnknowne, and knowne too late,

Prodigious birth of loue it is to mee,

That I must loue a loathed enemie.

NURSE

Whats tis? whats tis.

IULIET   A rime I learnt euen now

Of one I danct withall.

One cals within: Iuliet

NURSE   Anon, anon:

Come lets away, the strangers all are gone.   *Exeunt*

Sc. 6   *Enter Chorus*
(2.0) CHORUS

Now old desire doth in his deathbed lie,

And young affection gapes to be his heire,

720 That faire for which loue gronde for and would die,

With tender *Iuliet* matcht, is now not faire.

Now *Romeo* is belou'd, and loues againe,

Alike bewitched by the charme of lookes:

But to his foe supposd he must complaine,

And she steale loues sweete bait from fearful hookes:

Being held a foe, he may not haue accesse

To breathe such vowes as louers vse to sweare,

And she as much in loue, her meanes much lesse,

To meete her new beloued any where:

But passion lends them power, time meanes to meete,   730

Tempring extremities with extreme sweete.   *Exit*

Enter Romeo alone   Sc. 7
ROMEO   (2.1)

Can I go forward when my heart is here,

Turne backe dull earth and find thy Center out.

⌜*He turnes back and withdraws.*⌝

Enter Benuolio with Mercutio

BENUOLIO (*calling*)

Romeo, my Cosen *Romeo*, *Romeo*.

MERCUTIO

He is wise, and on my life hath stolne him home to
bed.

BENUOLIO

He ran this way and leapt this Orchard wall.

Call good *Mercutio*:

⌜MERCUTIO⌝   Nay Ile coniure too.

Romeo, humours, madman, passion, louer,

Appeare thou in the likenesse of a sigh,

Speake but on rime and I am satisfied: 740

Crie but ay me, pronounce but loue and doue,

Speake to my goship *Venus* one faire word,

One nickname for her purblind sonne and heir,

Young *Adam Cupid*: he that shot so trim,

When King *Cophetua* lou'd the begger mayd.

He heareth not, he stirreth not, he moueth not,

The Ape is dead, and I must coniure him.

I coniure thee by *Rosalines* bright eyes,

By her high forehead, and her Scarlet lip,

By her fine foot, straight leg, and quiuering thigh,   750

And the demeanes, that there adiacent lie,

That in thy likenesse thou appeare to vs.

BENUOLIO

And if he heare thee thou wilt anger him.

MERCUTIO

This cannot anger him, twould anger him

To raise a spirit in his mistresse circle,

Of some strange nature, letting it there stand

Till she had laid it, and coniurd it downe,

That were some spight. My inuocation

Is faire & honest, in his mistres name,

I coniure onely but to raise vp him.   760

BENUOLIO

Come, he hath hid himselfe among these trees

To be consorted with the humerous night:

Blind is his loue, and best befits the darke.

MERCUTIO

If loue be blind, loue cannot hit the marke,

Now will he sit vnder a Medler tree,

And wish his mistresse were that kind of fruite,

As maides call Medlers, when they laugh alone.

O *Romeo* that she were, ô that she were

An open ars and thou a Poprin Peare.

770 *Romeo* goodnight, ile to my truckle bed,
     This field-bed is too cold for me to sleepe,
     Come shall we go?

BENUOLIO   Go then, for tis in vaine
     To seeke him here that meanes not to be found.
                              Exit Benuolio and Mercutio

ROMEO ⌈*comming foward*⌉
     He ieasts at scarres that neuer felt a wound,
     But soft, what light through yonder window breaks?
     It is the East, and *Iuliet* is the Sun.
     Arise faire Sun and kill the enuious Moone,
     Who is alreadie sicke and pale with greefe,
     That thou her maide art far more faire then she:
780 Be not her maide since she is enuious,
     Her vestall liuery is but sicke and greene,
     And none but fooles do weare it, cast it off:
          ⌈*Enter Iuliet aloft*⌉
     It is my Lady, ô it is my loue,
     O that she knew she wer,
     She speakes, yet she saies nothing, what of that?
     Her eye discourses, I will answere it:
     I am too bold, tis not to me she speakes:
     Two of the fairest starres in all the heauen,
     Hauing some busines do entreate her eyes,
790 To twinckle in their spheres till they returne.
     What if her eyes were there, they in her head,
     The brightnesse of her cheek wold shame those stars,
     As day-light doth a lampe, her eye in heauen,
     Would through the ayrie region streame so bright,
     That birds would sing, and thinke it were not night:
     See how she leanes her cheeke vpon her hand.
     O that I were a gloue vpon that hand,
     That I might touch that cheeke.

IULIET   Ay me.

ROMEO (*aside*)   She speakes.
     Oh speake againe bright Angel, for thou art
800 As glorious to this night being ore my head,
     As is a winged messenger of heauen
     Vnto the white vpturned wondring eyes,
     Of mortalls that fall backe to gaze on him,
     When he bestrides the lazie passing Cloudes,
     And sayles vpon the bosome of the ayre.

IULIET
     O *Romeo, Romeo*, wherefore art thou *Romeo?*
     Denie thy father and refuse thy name:
     Or if thou wilt not, be but sworne my loue,
     And ile no longer be a *Capulet.*

ROMEO (*aside*)
810 Shall I heare more, or shall I speake at this?

IULIET
     Tis but thy name that is my enemie:
     Thou art thy selfe, though not a *Mountague,*
     Whats *Mountague?* it is nor hand nor foote,
     Nor arme nor face, nor any other parte
     Belonging to a man: ô be some other name.
     Whats in a name? that which we call a rose,
     By any other word would smell as sweete,
     So *Romeo* would were he not *Romeo* cald,

     Retaine that deare perfection which he owes,
     Without that tytle: *Romeo* doffe thy name,   820
     And for thy name which is no part of thee,
     Take all my selfe.

ROMEO (*to Iuliet*)   I take thee at thy word:
     Call me but loue, and Ile be new baptizde,
     Henceforth I neuer will be *Romeo.*

IULIET
     What man art thou, that thus beschreend in night
     So stumblest on my counsell?

ROMEO   By a name,
     I know not how to tell thee who I am:
     My name deare saint, is hatefull to my selfe,
     Because it is an enemie to thee,
     Had I it written, I would teare the word.   830

IULIET
     My eares haue yet not drunk a hundred words
     Of thy tongues vttering, yet I know the sound.
     Art thou not *Romeo*, and a *Mountague?*

ROMEO
     Neither faire maide, if either thee dislike.

IULIET
     How camst thou hither, tel me, and wherfore?
     The Orchard walls are high and hard to climbe,
     And the place death, considering who thou art,
     If any of my kĩsmen find thee here.

ROMEO
     With loues light wings did I orepearch these walls,
     For stonie limits cannot hold loue out,   840
     And what loue can do, that dares loue attempt:
     Therefore thy kinsmen are no stop to me.

IULIET
     If they do see thee, they will murther thee.

ROMEO
     Alack there lies more perill in thine eye,
     Then twentie of their swords, looke thou but sweete,
     And I am proofe against their enmitie.

IULIET
     I would not for the world they saw thee here.

ROMEO
     I haue nights cloake to hide me frõ their eies,
     And but thou loue me, let them finde me here,
     My life were better ended by their hate,   850
     Then death proroged wanting of thy loue.

IULIET
     By whose direction foundst thou out this place?

ROMEO
     By loue that first did promp me to enquire,
     He lent me counsell, and I lent him eyes:
     I am no Pylat, yet wert thou as farre
     As that vast shore washt with the farthest sea,
     I should aduenture for such marchandise.

IULIET
     Thou knowest the mask of night is on my face,
     Else would a maiden blush bepaint my cheeke,
     For that which thou hast heard me speake to night, 860
     Faine would I dwell on forme, faine, faine, denie
     What I haue spoke, but farwell complement.

Doest thou loue me? I know thou wilt say I:
And I will take thy word, yet if thou swearst,
Thou maiest proue false: at louers periuries
They say *Ioue* laughes, oh gentle *Romeo*,
If thou dost loue, pronounce it faithfully:
Or if thou thinkst I am too quickly wonne,
Ile frowne and be peruerse, and say thee nay,
870 So thou wilt wooe, but else not for the world,
In truth faire *Montague* I am too fond:
And therefore thou maiest think my hauior light,
But trust me gentleman, ile proue more true,
Then those that haue more conning to be strange,
I should haue bene more strange, I must confesse,
But that thou ouerheardst ere I was ware,
My trueloue passion, therefore pardon me,
And not impute this yeelding to light loue,
Which the darke night hath so discouered.

ROMEO
880 Lady, by yonder blessed Moone I vow,
That tips with siluer all these frute tree tops.

IULIET
O swear not by the moone th'inconstant moone,
That monethly changes in her circld orbe,
Least that thy loue proue likewise variable.

ROMEO
What shall I sweare by?

IULIET   Do not sweare at all:
Or if thou wilt, sweare by thy gracious selfe,
Which is the god of my Idolatrie,
And Ile beleeue thee.

ROMEO   If my hearts deare loue.

IULIET
Well do not sweare: although I ioy in thee,
890 I haue no ioy of this contract to night,
It is too rash, too vnaduisd, too sudden,
Too like the lightning which doth cease to bee,
Ere one can say, it lightens, sweete goodnight:
This bud of loue by Sommers ripening breath,
May proue a bewtious floure when next we meete,
Goodnight, goodnight, as sweete repose and rest,
Come to thy heart, as that within my brest.

ROMEO
O wilt thou leaue me so vnsatisfied?

IULIET
What satisfaction canst thou haue to night?

ROMEO
900 Th'exchange of thy loues faithful vow for mine.

IULIET
I gaue thee mine before thou didst request it:
And yet I would it were to giue againe.

ROMEO
Woldst thou withdraw it, for what purpose loue?

IULIET
But to be franke and giue it thee againe,
And yet I wish but for the thing I haue,
My bountie is as boundlesse as the sea,
My loue as deepe, the more I giue to thee

The more I haue, for both are infinite:
Nurse calls within
I heare some noyse within, deare loue adue:
Anon good nurse, sweete *Mountague* be true: 910
Stay but a little, I will come againe.   *Exit*

ROMEO
O blessed blessed night, I am afeard
Being in night, all this is but a dreame,
Too flattering sweete to be substantiall.
Enter Iuliet aloft

IULIET
Three words deare *Romeo*, & goodnight indeed,
If that thy bent of loue be honourable,
Thy purpose marriage, send me word to morrow,
By one that ile procure to come to thee,
Where and what time thou wilt performe the right,
And all my fortunes at thy foote ile lay,   920
And follow thee my L. throughout the world.

⌐NURSE⌐ (*within*) Madam.

IULIET
I come, anon: (*to Romeo*) but if thou meanst not well,
I do beseech thee

⌐NURSE⌐ (*within*) Madam.

IULIET (By and by I come)
To cease thy strife, and leaue me to my griefe.
To morrow will I send.

ROMEO So thriue my soule.

IULIET A thousand times goodnight.   *Exit* 930

ROMEO
A thousand times the worse to want thy light,
Loue goes toward loue as schooleboyes from their
          bookes,
But loue from loue, toward schoole with heauie lookes.
⌐*He is going.*⌐
Enter Iuliet aloft againe

IULIET
Hist *Romeo* hist, ô for a falkners voyce,
To lure this Tassel gentle back againe,
Bondage is hoarse, and may not speake aloude,
Else would I teare the Caue where Eccho lies,
And make her ayrie tongue more hoarse, then mine,
With repetition of my *Romeos* name. *Romeo?*

ROMEO
It is my soule that calls vpon my name.   940
How siluer sweete, sound louers tongues by night,
Like softest musicke to attending eares.

IULIET
Romeo.

ROMEO My Niesse.

IULIET   What a clocke to morrow
Shall I send to thee?

ROMEO   By the houre of nine.

IULIET
I will not faile, tis twentie yeare till then,
I haue forgot why I did call thee backe.

ROMEO
Let me stand here till thou remember it.

IULIET

I shall forget to haue thee still stand there,
Remembring how I loue thy companie.

ROMEO

950　And Ile still stay, to haue thee still forget,
Forgetting any other home but this.

IULIET

Tis almost morning, I would haue thee gone,
And yet no farther then a wantons bird,
That lets it hop a litle from his hand,
Like a poore prisoner in his twisted giues,
And with a silke threed, plucks it backe againe,
So louing Iealous of his libertie.

ROMEO

I would I were thy bird.

IULIET　　　　　　　Sweete so would I,

Yet I should kill thee with much cherishing:

960　Good night, good night. Parting is such sweete sorrow,
That I shall say good night, till it be morrow.

⌈ROMEO⌉

Sleep dwell vpon thine eyes, peace in thy breast.

　　　　　　　　　　　　　　　　Exit Iuliet

Would I were sleepe and peace so sweet to rest.
Hence will I to my ghostly siers close cell,
His helpe to craue, and my deare hap to tell.　　　Exit

Sc. 8　　　Enter Frier Lawrence with a basket, alone
(2.2)　FRIER LAWRENCE

The grey-eyed morne smiles on the frowning night,
Checkring the Easterne clowdes with streaks of light:
And fleckeld darknesse like a drunkard reeles,
From forth daies path, and Titans fierie wheeles:

970　Now ere the sun aduance his burning eie,
The day to cheere, and nights dancke dewe to drie,
I must vpfill this osier cage of ours,
With balefull weedes, and precious iuyced flowers,
The earth that's natures mother is her tombe,
What is her burying graue, that is her wombe:
And from her wombe children of diuers kinde,
We sucking on her naturall bosome finde:
Many for many vertues excellent:
None but for some, and yet all different.

980　O mickle is the powerfull grace that lies
In Plants, hearbes, stones, and their true quallities:
For nought so vile, that on the earth doth liue,
But to the earth some speciall good doth giue:
Nor ought so good but straind from that faire vse,
Reuolts from true birth, stumbling on abuse.
Vertue it selfe turnes vice being misapplied,
And vice sometimes by action dignified.

　　　Enter Romeo

Within the infant rinde of this weake flower
Poyson hath residence, and medicine power:

990　For this being smelt with that part, cheares each part,
Being tasted, slaies all sences with the hart.
Two such opposed Kings encamp them still,
In man as well as hearbes, grace and rude will:

And where the worser is predominant,
Full soone the Canker death eates vp that Plant.

ROMEO

Goodmorrow father.

FRIER LAWRENCE　　　　　Benedicitie.

What early tongue so sweete saluteth me?
Young sonne, it argues a distempred hed,
So soone to bid goodmorrow to thy bed:
Care keepes his watch in euery old mans eye,　　　1000
And where care lodges, sleepe will neuer lye:
But where vnbrused youth with vnstuft braine
Doth couch his lims, there golden sleepe doth raigne.
Therefore thy earlinesse doth me assure,
Thou art vprousd with some distemprature:
Or if not so, then here I hit it right,
Our Romeo hath not bene in bed to night.

ROMEO

That last is true, the sweeter rest was mine.

FRIER LAWRENCE

God pardon sin, wast thou with Rosaline?

ROMEO

With Rosaline, my ghostly father no,　　　1010
I haue forgot that name, and that names wo.

FRIER LAWRENCE

Thats my good son, but wher hast thou bin thē?

ROMEO

Ile tell thee ere thou aske it me agen:
I haue bene feasting with mine enemie,
Where on a sudden one hath wounded me:
Thats by me wounded, both our remedies
Within thy helpe and holy phisicke lies:
I beare no hatred blessed man: for loe
My intercession likewise steads my foe.

FRIER LAWRENCE

Be plaine good sonne and homely in thy drift,　　　1020
Ridling confession, findes but ridling shrift.

ROMEO

Then plainly know, my harts deare loue is set
On the faire daughter of rich Capulet:
As mine on hers, so hers is set on mine,
And all combind, saue what thou must combine
By holy marriage: when and where, and how,
We met, we wooed, and made exchange of vow,
Ile tell thee as we passe, but this I pray,
That thou consent to marrie vs to day.

FRIER LAWRENCE

Holy S. Frauncis what a change is here?　　　1030
Is Rosaline that thou didst loue so deare,
So soone forsaken? young mens loue then lies
Not truly in their hearts, but in their eies.
Iesu Maria, what a deale of brine
Hath washt thy sallow cheekes for Rosaline?
How much salt water throwne away in waste,
To season loue, that of it doth not taste.
The Sun not yet thy sighes from heauen cleares,
Thy old grones yet ring in mine auncient eares:
Lo here vpon thy cheeke the staine doth sit,　　　1040
Of an old teare that is not washt off yet.

If ere thou wast thy selfe, and these woes thine,
Thou and these woes were all for *Rosaline*.
And art thou chang'd, pronounce this sentence then,
Women may fall, when theres no strength in men.

ROMEO
Thou chidst me oft for louing *Rosaline*.

FRIER LAWRENCE
For doting, not for louing pupill mine.

ROMEO
And badst me burie loue.

FRIER LAWRENCE   Not in a graue,
To lay one in an other out to haue.

ROMEO
1050   I pray thee chide me not, her I loue now
Doth grace for grace, and loue for loue allow:
The other did not so.

FRIER LAWRENCE   O she knew well,
Thy loue did reade by rote, that could not spell:
But come young wauerer, come go with me,
In one respect ile thy assistant be:
For this alliance may so happie proue,
To turne your housholds rancor to pure loue.

ROMEO
O let vs hence, I stand on sudden hast.

FRIER LAWRENCE
Wisely and slow, they stumble that run fast.   *Exeunt*

Sc. 9   *Enter Benuolio and Mercutio*
(2.3)   MERCUTIO Where the deule should this *Romeo* be? came
1061   hee not home to night?

BENUOLIO
Not to his fathers, I spoke with his man.

MERCUTIO
Why that same pale hard hearted wench, that *Rosaline*,
Torments him so, that he will sure run mad.

BENUOLIO
Tibalt, the kĩsman to old *Capulet*,
Hath sent a leter to his fathers house.

MERCUTIO
A challenge on my life.

BENUOLIO   *Romeo* will answere it.

MERCUTIO Any man that can write may answere a letter.

BENUOLIO Nay, he wil answere the letters maister how he
1070   dares, being dared.

MERCUTIO Alas poore *Romeo*, he is alreadie dead, stabd
with a white wenches blacke eye, runne through the
eare with a loue song, the very pinne of his heart, cleft
with the blinde bowe-boyes but-shaft, and is hee a man
to encounter *Tybalt*?

⌈BENUOLIO⌉ Why what is *Tybalt*?

MERCUTIO More then Prince of Cats. Oh hees the
couragious captain of Complements: he fights as you
sing pricksong, keeps time, distance & proportion, he
1080   rests, his minum rests, one two, and the third in your
bosome: the very butcher of a silke button, a dualist a
dualist, a gentleman of the very first house of the first
and second cause, ah the immortall Passado, the Punto
reuerso, the Hay.

BENUOLIO The what?

MERCUTIO The Pox of such antique lisping affecting
phantacĩes, these new tuners of accent: by Iesu a very
good blade, a very tall man, a very good whore. Why
is not this a lamẽtable thing graundsir, that we should
be thus afflicted with these straunge flies: these fashion-   1090
mongers, these pardon mees, who stand so much on
the new forme, that they cannot sit at ease on the old
bench. O their bones, their bones.

Enter Romeo

BENUOLIO Here Comes *Romeo*, here comes *Romeo*.

MERCUTIO Without his Roe, like a dried Hering, O flesh,
flesh, how art thou fishified? now is he for the numbers
that Petrach flowed in: *Laura* to his Lady, was a kitchin
wench, marrie she had a better loue to berime her:
Dido a dowdie, *Cleopatra* a Gipsie, *Hellen* and *Hero*,
hildings and harlots: *Thisbie* a grey eye or so, but not   1100
to the purpose. Signior *Romeo*, *Bonieur*, theres a French
salutation to your French slop: you gaue vs the
counterfeit fairly last night.

ROMEO Goodmorrow to you both, what counterfeit did I
giue you?

MERCUTIO The slip sir, the slip, can you not conceiue?

ROMEO Pardon good *Mercutio*, my businesse was great,
and in such a case as mine, a man may straine curtesie.

MERCUTIO Thats as much as to say, such a case as yours,
constrains a man to bow in the hams.   1110

ROMEO Meaning to cursie.

MERCUTIO Thou hast most kindly hit it.

ROMEO A most curtuous exposition.

MERCUTIO Nay I am the very pinck of curtesie.

ROMEO Pinck for flower.

MERCUTIO Right.

ROMEO Why then is my pump well flowerd.

MERCUTIO Sure wit follow me this ieast, now till thou hast
worne out thy pump, that when the single sole of it is
worne, the ieast may remaine after the wearing, soly   1120
singular.

ROMEO O single solde ieast, solie singular for the
singlenesse.

MERCUTIO Come betweene vs good *Benuolio*, my wits
faints.

ROMEO Swits and spurs, swits and spurres, or ile crie a
match.

MERCUTIO Nay, if our wits run the wildgoose chase, I am
done: For thou hast more of the wildgoose in one of
thy wits, then I am sure I haue in my whole fiue. Was   1130
I with you there for the goose?

ROMEO Thou wast neuer with me for any thing, when
thou wast not there for the goose.

MERCUTIO I will bite thee by the eare for that ieast.

ROMEO Nay good goose bite not.

MERCUTIO Thy wit is very bitter sweeting, it is a most
sharp sawce.

ROMEO And is it not then well seru'd in to a sweete goose?

MERCUTIO Oh heres a wit of Cheuerell, that stretches from
an ynch narrow, to an ell broad.   1140

ROMEO I stretch it out for that word broad, which added
to the goose, proues thee farre and wide a broad goose.

MERCUTIO Why is not this better now then groning for
loue, now art thou sociable, now art thou *Romeo*: now
art thou what thou art, by art as well as by nature,
for this driueling loue is like a great naturall that runs
lolling vp and downe to hide his bable in a hole.

BENUOLIO Stop there, stop there.

MERCUTIO Thou desirest me to stop in my tale against the
1150 haire.

BENUOLIO Thou wouldst else haue made thy tale large.

MERCUTIO O thou art deceiu'd; I would haue made it
short, for I was come to the whole depth of my tale,
and meant indeed to occupie the argument no longer.

Enter Nurse and Peter her man

ROMEO Heeres goodly geare.

⌈BENUOLIO⌉ A sayle, a sayle.

MERCUTIO Two two, a shert and a smocke.

NURSE *Peter*.

PETER Anon.

1160 NURSE My fan *Peter*.

MERCUTIO Good *Peter* to hide her face, for her fans the
fairer face.

NURSE God ye goodmorrow Gentlemen.

MERCUTIO God ye goodden faire gentlewoman.

NURSE Is it good den?

MERCUTIO Tis no lesse I tell yee, for the bawdie hand of
the dyal, is now vpon the prick of noone.

NURSE Out vpon you, what a man are you?

ROMEO One gentlewoman, that God hath made, for
1170 himself to mar.

NURSE By my troth it is well said, for himselfe to mar
quoth a? Gĕtlemĕ cã any of you tel me wher I may
find the yong *Romeo*?

ROMEO I can tell you, but young *Romeo* will be older
when you haue found him, then he was when you
sought him: I am the youngest of that name, for fault
of a worse.

NURSE You say well.

MERCUTIO Yea is the worst wel, very wel took, ifaith,
1180 wisely, wisely.

NURSE *(to Romeo)* If you be he sir, I desire some confidence
with you.

BENUOLIO She will endite him to some supper.

MERCUTIO A baud, a baud, a baud. So ho.

ROMEO What hast thou found?

MERCUTIO No hare sir, vnlesse a hare sir in a lenten pie,
that is something stale and hoare ere it be spent.

⌈*He walks by them, and*⌉ *sings*

An old hare hoare,
And an old hare hoare
1190   Is very good meate in lent.
But a hare that is hore,
Is too much for a score,
When it hores ere it be spent.

Romeo, will you come to your fathers? weele to dinner
thither.

ROMEO I will follow you.

MERCUTIO Farewell auncient Lady, farewell ⌈*Sings*⌉ Lady,
Lady, Lady.   *Exeunt Mercutio and Benuolio*

NURSE I pray you sir, what sawcie merchant was this
that was so full of his roperie?   1200

ROMEO A gentleman Nurse, that loues to heare himselfe
talke, and will speake more in a minute, then hee will
stand too in a moneth.

NURSE And a speake any thing against me, Ile take him
downe, and a were lustier then he is, and twentie such
Iacks: and if I cannot, ile finde those that shall: scuruie
knaue, I am none of his flurt gills, I am none of his
skaines mates, *(to Peter)* and thou must stand by too
and suffer euery knaue to vse me at his pleasure.

PETER I saw no man vse you at his pleasure: if I had, my   1210
weapon shuld quickly haue bin out: I warrant you, I
dare draw assoone as an other man, if I see occasion
in a good quarel, & the law on my side.

NURSE Now afore God, I am so vext, that euery part about
me quiuers, skuruie knaue: *(to Romeo)* pray you sir a
word: and as I told you, my young Lady bid me enquire
you out, what she bid me say, I will keepe to my selfe:
but first let me tell ye, if ye should leade her in a fooles
paradise, as they say, it were a very grosse kind of
behauior as they say: for the Gentlewoman is yong: 1220
and therefore, if you should deale double with her,
truly it were an ill thing to be offred to any
Gentlewoman, and very weake dealing.

ROMEO Nurse, commend me to thy Lady and Mistresse, I
protest vnto thee.

NURSE Good heart, and yfaith I wil tel her as much: Lord,
Lord, she will be a ioyfull woman.

ROMEO What wilt thou tell her Nurse? thou dooest not
marke me?

NURSE I will tell her sir, that you do protest, which as I   1230
take it, is a gentlemanlike offer.

ROMEO Bid her deuise
Some means to come to shrift this afternoon,
And there she shall at Frier *Lawrence* Cell
Be shrieud and married: *(offering money)* here is for
thy paines.

NURSE No truly sir not a penny.

ROMEO Go too, I say you shall.

NURSE ⌈*taking the money*⌉
This afternoone sir, well she shall be there.

ROMEO
And stay good Nurse behinde the Abbey wall,
Within this houre my man shall be with thee,   1240
And bring thee cordes made like a tackled stayre,
Which to the high topgallant of my ioy,
Must be my conuoy in the secret night.
Farewell be trustie, and ile quit thy paines:
Farewel, commend me to thy Mistresse.

NURSE
Now God in heauen blesse thee, harke you sir.

ROMEO What saist thou my deare Nurse?

NURSE
Is your man secret, did you nere here say,
Two may keep counsell putting one away.

ROMEO
I warrant thee my mans as true as steele.   1250

NURSE
Well sir, my Mistresse is the sweetest Lady,
Lord, Lord, when twas a litle prating thing.
O there is a Noble man in town one *Paris*,
That would faine lay knife aboord: but she good soule
Had as leeue see a tode, a very tode
As see him: I anger her sometimes,
And tell her that *Paris* is the properer man,
But ile warrant you, when I say so, she lookes
As pale as any clout in the versall world,
1260 Doth not Rosemarie and *Romeo* begin
Both with a letter?

ROMEO
I Nurse, what of that? Both with an R.

NURSE A mocker thats the dogs name, *R.* is for the, no,
I know it begins with some other letter, and she hath
the pretiest sententious of it, of you and Rosemarie,
that it would do you good to heare it.

ROMEO Commend me to thy Lady.

NURSE I a thousand times. *Peter*.

PETER Anon.

1270 NURSE ⌈*giuing Peter her fan*⌉ Before and apace.
　　　　　　　　Exit ⌈*Peter and Nurse at one doore, Romeo at*
　　　　　　　　　　　　　　　　　　　　another doore⌉

Sc. 10　　　　*Enter Iuliet*
(2.4) IULIET
The clocke strooke nine when I did send the Nurse,
In halfe an houre she promisd to returne,
Perchance she cannot meete him, thats not so:
Oh she is lame, loues heraulds should be thoughts,
Which ten times faster glides then the Suns beames,
Driuing backe shadowes ouer lowring hills.
Therefore do nimble piniond doues draw loue,
And therefore hath the wind swift *Cupid* wings:
Now is the Sun vpon the highmost hill,
1280 Of this dayes iourney, and from nine till twelue,
Is three long houres, yet she is not come,
Had she affections and warme youthfull bloud,
She would be as swift in motion as a ball,
My words would bandie her to my sweete loue,
And his to me,
But old folks, many fain as they wer dead,
Vnwieldie, slowe, heauie, and pale as lead.
　　　　　Enter Nurse and Peter
O God she comes, ô hony Nurse what newes?
Hast thou met with him? send thy man away.

1290 NURSE *Peter* stay at the gate.　　　　*Exit Peter*

IULIET
Now good sweete *Nurse*, O Lord, why lookst thou sad?
Though newes be sad, yet tell them merily.
If good, thou shamst the musicke of sweete newes,
By playing it to me, with so sower a face.

NURSE
I am a wearie, giue me leaue a while,
Fie how my bones ake, what a iaunce haue I?

IULIET
I would thou hadst my bones, and I thy newes:
Nay come I pray thee speake, good good Nurse speake.

NURSE
Iesu what haste, can you not stay a while?
Do you not see that I am out of breath?　　　　1300

IULIET
How art thou out of breath, when thou hast breath
To say to me, that thou art out of breath?
The excuse that thou doest make in this delay,
Is longer then the tale thou doest excuse.
Is thy newes good or bad? answere to that,
Say either, and ile stay the circumstance:
Let me be satisfied, ist good or bad?

NURSE Well, you haue made a simple choyse, you know
not how to chuse a man: *Romeo*, no not he though his
face be better then any mans, yet his leg excels all　1310
mens, and for a hand and a foote and a body, though
they be not to be talkt on, yet they are past compare:
he is not the flower of curtesie, but ile warrant him,
as gentle as a lamme: go thy wayes wench, serue God.
What haue you dinde at home?

IULIET
No, no. But all this did I know before.
What sayes he of our marriage, what of that?

NURSE
Lord how my head akes, what a head haue I?
It beates as it would fall in twentie peeces.
My　back
　　⌈*Iuliet rubs her back*⌉
　　　　　a tother side, a my backe, my backe:　　1320
Beshrewe your heart for sending me about
To catch my death with iaunsing vp and downe.

IULIET
Ifaith I am sorrie that thou art not well.
Sweete, sweete, sweete Nurse, tell me what sayes my
　　loue?

NURSE Your loue sayes like an honest gentleman, an a
Courteous, and a kinde, and a handsome, and I warrant
a vertuous, where is your mother?

IULIET
Where is my mother, why she is within,
Wher shuld she be? How odly thou repliest:
Your loue sayes like an honest gentleman,　　　1330
Where is your mother?

NURSE　　　　　　　　　　O Gods lady deare,
Are you so hot, marrie come vp I trow,
Is this the poultis for my aking bones:
Henceforward do your messages your selfe.

IULIET
Heres such a coyle, come what saies *Romeo*?

NURSE
Haue you got leaue to go to shrift to day?

IULIET I haue.

NURSE
Then high you hence to Frier *Lawrence* Cell,
There stayes a husband to make you a wife:
Now comes the wanton bloud vp in your cheekes,　1340
Theile be in scarlet straight at any newes:
Hie you to Church, I must an other way,
To fetch a Ladder by the which your loue
Must climbe a birds neast soone when it is darke,

I am the drudge, and toyle in your delight:
But you shall beare the burthen soone at night.
Go, ile to dinner, hie you to the Cell.

IULIET
Hie to high fortune, honest Nurse farewell.

Exeunt ⌈seuerally⌉

Sc. 11   *Enter Frier Lawrence and Romeo*
(2.5)   FRIER LAWRENCE
So smile the heauens vpon this holy act,
1350   That after houres, with sorrow chide vs not.

ROMEO
Amen, amen, but come what sorrow can,
It cannot counteruaile the exchange of ioy
That one short minute giues me in her sight:
Do thou but close our hands with holy words,
Then loue-deuouring death do what he dare,
It is inough I may but call her mine.

FRIER LAWRENCE
These violent delights haue violent endes,
And in their triumph die like fier and powder:
Which as they kisse consume. The sweetest honey
1360   Is loathsome in his owne deliciousnesse,
And in the taste confoundes the appetite.
Therefore loue moderately, long loue doth so,
Too swift arriues, as tardie as too slowe.

Enter Iuliet ⌈somewhat fast, and embraceth Romeo⌉

Here comes the Lady, Oh so light a foote
Will nere weare out the euerlasting flint,
A louer may bestride the gossamours,
That ydeles in the wanton sommer ayre,
And yet not fall, so light is vanitie.

IULIET
Good euen to my ghostly confessor.

FRIER LAWRENCE
1370   *Romeo* shall thanke thee daughter for vs both.

IULIET
As much to him, else is his thankes too much.

ROMEO
Ah *Iuliet*, if the measure of thy ioy
Be heapt like mine, and that thy skill be more
To blason it, then sweeten with thy breath
This neighbour ayre and let rich musicks tongue,
Vnfold the imagind happines that both
Receiue in either, by this deare encounter.

IULIET
Conceit more rich in matter then in words,
Brags of his substance, not of ornament,
1380   They are but beggers that can count their worth,
But my true loue is growne to such excesse,
I cannot sum vp sum of halfe my wealth.

FRIER LAWRENCE
Come, come with me, and we will make short worke.
For by your leaues, you shall not stay alone,
Till holy Church incorporate two in one.   *Exeunt*

Sc. 12   *Enter Mercutio and his Page, Benuolio, and men*
(3.1)   BENUOLIO
I pray thee good *Mercutio* lets retire,

The day is hot, the *Capels* are abroad:
And if we meete we shall not scape a brawle,
For now these hot daies, is the mad blood stirring.

MERCUTIO Thou art like one of these fellowes, that when   1390
he enters the confines of a Tauerne, claps me his sword
vpon the table, and sayes, God send me no need of
thee: and by the operation of the second cup, draws
him on the drawer, when indeed there is no need.

BENUOLIO Am I like such a fellow?

MERCUTIO Come, come, thou art as hot a Iacke in thy
moode as any in *Italie*: and assoone moued to be
moodie, and assoone moodie to be moued.

BENUOLIO And what too?

MERCUTIO Nay and there were two such, we should haue   1400
none shortly, for one would kill the other: thou, why
thou wilt quarell with a man that hath a haire more,
or a haire lesse in his beard, then thou hast: thou wilt
quarell with a man for cracking Nuts, hauing no other
reason, but because thou hast hasel eyes: what eye,
but such an eye wold spie out such a quarrel? thy
head is as full of quarelles, as an egge is full of meate,
and yet thy head hath bene beaten as addle as an egge
for quarelling: thou hast quareld with a man for coffing
in the streete, because hee hath wakened thy dogge   1410
that hath laine asleep in the sun. Didst thou not fall
out with a taylor for wearing his new doublet before
Easter, with an other for tying his new shooes with
olde riband, and yet thou wilt tuter me from quarelling?

BENUOLIO And I were so apt to quarell as thou art, any
man should buy the fee-simple of my life for an houre
and a quarter.

MERCUTIO The fee-simple, ô simple.

Enter Tybalt, Petruchio, and others

BENUOLIO By my head here comes the *Capulets*.

MERCUTIO By my heele I care not.   1420

TYBALT (*to Petruchio and the others*)
Follow me close, for I will speake to them.
(*To the Mountagues*) Gentlemen, Good den, a word
with one of you.

MERCUTIO And but one word with one of vs, couple it
with something, make it a word and a blowe.

TYBALT You shall find me apt inough to that sir, and you
wil giue me occasion.

MERCUTIO Could you not take some occasion without
giuing?

TYBALT
Mercutio, thou consortst with *Romeo*.

MERCUTIO Consort, what doest thou make vs Minstrels?   1430
and thou make Minstrels of vs, looke to hear nothing
but discords: ⌈*touching his Rapier*⌉ heeres my fiddlesticke,
heeres that shall make you daunce: zounds consort.

BENUOLIO
We talke here in the publike haunt of men:
Either withdraw vnto some priuate place,
Or reason coldly of your greeuances:
Or else depart, here all eyes gaze on vs.

MERCUTIO
Mens eyes were made to looke, and let them gaze.
I will not budge for no mans pleasure I.

Enter Romeo

TYBALT

1440 Well peace be with you sir, here comes my man.

MERCUTIO

But ile be hangd sir if he weare your liuerie:
Marrie go before to field, heele be your follower,
Your worship in that sense may call him man.

TYBALT

Romeo, the loue I beare thee, can affoord
No better terme then this: thou art a villaine.

ROMEO

Tybalt, the reason that I haue to loue thee,
Doth much excuse the appertaining rage
To such a greeting: villaine am I none.
Therefore farewell, I see thou knowest me not.

TYBALT

1450 Boy, this shall not excuse the iniuries
That thou hast done me, therefore turne and draw.

ROMEO

I do protest I neuer iniurd thee,
But loue thee better then thou canst deuise,
Till thou shalt know the reason of my loue:
And so good *Capulet*, which name I tender
As dearely as mine owne, be satisfied.

MERCUTIO ⌈*drawing*⌉

O calme, dishonourable, vile submission:
Alla stucatho carries it away,
Tibalt, you ratcatcher, come, will you walke?

1460 TYBALT What wouldst thou haue with me?

MERCUTIO Good King of Cats, nothing but one of your
nine liues, that I meane to make bold withall, and as
you shall vse mee hereafter drie beate the rest of the
eight. Will you plucke your sword out of his pilcher by
the eares? make haste, least mine be about your eares
ere it be out.

TYBALT (*drawing*) I am for you.

ROMEO

Gentle *Mercutio*, put thy Rapier vp.

MERCUTIO (*to Tybalt*) Come sir, your Passado.
        They fight

ROMEO ⌈*drawing*⌉

1470 Draw *Benuolio*, beate downe their weapons,
Gentlemen, for shame forbeare this outrage,
Tibalt, *Mercutio*, the Prince expresly hath
Forbid this bandying in *Verona* streetes,
Hold *Tybalt*, good *Mercutio*.
    ⌈*Romeo beates downe their poynts and rushes
    betweene them. Tybalt vnder Romeos arme thrusts
    Mercutio in*⌉

⌈PETRUCHIO⌉ Away *Tybalt*.
        Exeunt Tybalt, Petruchio, and their followers

MERCUTIO I am hurt.
A plague a both your houses, I am sped,
Is he gone and hath nothing.

BENUOLIO   What art thou hurt?

MERCUTIO

I, I, a scratch, a scratch, marrie tis inough,
1480 Where is my Page? go villaine, fetch a Surgion.
                      Exit Page

ROMEO

Courage man, the hurt cannot be much.

MERCUTIO No tis not so deepe as a well, nor so wide as a
Church doore, but tis inough, twill serue: aske for me
to morrow, and you shall finde me a graue man. I am
peppered I warrant, for this world, a plague a both
your houses, sounds a dog, a rat, a mouse, a cat, to
scratch a man to death: a braggart, a rogue, a villaine,
that fights by the book of arithmatick, why the deule
came you betweene vs? I was hurt vnder your arme.

ROMEO I thought all for the best.   1490

MERCUTIO

Helpe me into some house *Benuolio*,
Or I shall faint, a plague a both your houses,
They haue made wormes meate of me,
I haue it, and soundly to, your houses.
              Exeunt: manet Romeo

ROMEO

This Gentleman the Princes neare alie,
My very friend hath got this mortall hurt
In my behalfe, my reputation staind
With *Tybalts* slaunder, *Tybalt* that an houre
Hath bene my Cozen, O sweete *Iuliet*,
Thy bewtie hath made me effeminate,   1500
And in my temper softned valours steele.
    Enter Benuolio

BENUOLIO

O *Romeo*, *Romeo*, braue *Mercutio* is dead,
That gallant spirit hath aspir'd the Clowdes,
Which too vntimely here did scorne the earth.

ROMEO

This dayes blacke fate, on mo daies doth depēd,
This but begins, the wo others must end.
    Enter Tybalt

BENUOLIO

Here comes the furious *Tybalt* backe againe.

ROMEO

He gad in triumph and *Mercutio* slaine,
Away to heauen, respectiue lenitie,
And fier eid furie, be my conduct now,   1510
Now *Tybalt* take the villaine backe againe,
That late thou gaust me, for *Mercutios* soule
Is but a little way aboue our heads,
Staying for thine to keepe him companie:
Either thou or I, or both, must go with him.

TYBALT

Thou wretched boy that didst cōsort him here,
Shalt with him hence.

ROMEO   This shall determine that.
    They Fight. Tibalt is wounded. He falles and dies

BENUOLIO *Romeo*, away be gone:
The Citizens are vp, and *Tybalt* slaine,
Stand not amazd, the Prince wil doome thee death, 1520
If thou art taken, hence be gone away.

ROMEO

O I am fortunes foole.

BENUOLIO   Why dost thou stay?
                      Exit Romeo

Enter Citizens ⌈of the Watch⌉

CITIZEN ⌈OF THE WATCH⌉

Which way ran he that kild *Mercutio*?

Tybalt that murtherer, which way ran he?

BENUOLIO

There lies that *Tybalt*.

CITIZEN ⌈OF THE WATCH⌉ (*to Tybalt*) Vp sir, go with me:

I charge thee in the Princes name obey.

*Enter Prince, olde Mountague, Capulet, their wiues
and all*

PRINCE

Where are the vile beginners of this fray?

BENUOLIO

O Noble Prince, I can discouer all

The vnluckie mannage of this fatall brall,

1530   There lies the man slaine by young *Romeo*,

That slew thy kīsman, braue *Mercutio*.

CAPULETS WIFE

Tybalt, my Cozin, O my brothers child,

O Prince, O Cozen, husband, O the bloud is spild

Of my deare kīsman, Prince as thou art true,

For bloud of ours, shead bloud of Mountague.

O Cozin, Cozin.

PRINCE   *Benuolio*, who began this fray?

BENUOLIO

Tybalt here slain, whom *Romeos* hand did slay,

Romeo that spoke him faire, bid him bethinke

How nice the quarell was, and vrgd withall

1540   Your high displeasure: all this vttered,

With gentle breath, calm look, knees humbly bowed

Could not take truce with the vnruly spleene

Of *Tybalt* deafe to peace, but that he tilts

With piercing steele at bold *Mercutios* breast,

Who all as hot, turnes deadly poynt to poynt,

And with a Martiall scorne, with one hand beates

Cold death aside, and with the other sends

It backe to *Tybalt*, whose dexteritie

Retorts it, *Romeo* he cries aloud,

1550   Hold friends, friends part, and swifter then his tongue,

His agent arme beates downe their fatall poynts,

And twixt them rushes, vnderneath whose arme,

An enuious thrust from *Tybalt*, hit the life

Of stout *Mercutio*, and then *Tybalt* fled,

But by and by comes backe to *Romeo*,

Who had but newly entertaind reuenge,

And toote they go like lightning, for ere I

Could draw to part them, was stout *Tybalt* slaine:

And as he fell, did *Romeo* turne and flie,

1560   This is the truth, or let *Benuolio* die.

CAPULETS WIFE

He is a kīsman to the *Mountague*,

Affection makes him false, he speakes not true:

Some twentie of them fought in this blacke strife,

And all those twentie could but kill one life.

I beg for Iustice which thou Prince must giue:

Romeo slew *Tybalt*, *Romeo* must not liue.

PRINCE

Romeo slew him, he slew *Mercutio*,

Who now the price of his deare bloud doth owe.

⌈MOUNTAGUE⌉

Not *Romeo* Prince, he was *Mercutios* friend,

His fault concludes, but what the law should end,   1570

The life of *Tybalt*.

PRINCE   And for that offence,

Immediately we do exile him hence:

I haue an interest in your hates proceeding:

My bloud for your rude brawles doth lie a bleeding.

But ile amerce you with so strong a fine,

That you shall all repent the losse of mine.

I will be deafe to pleading and excuses,

Nor teares, nor prayers shall purchase out abuses.

Therefore vse none, let *Romeo* hence in hast,

Else when he is found, that houre is his last.   1580

Beare hence this body, and attend our will,

Mercie but murders, pardoning those that kill.

Exeunt with the body

Enter Iuliet alone   Sc. 13

IULIET   (3.2)

Gallop apace, you fierie footed steedes,

Towards *Phœbus* lodging, such a wagoner

As *Phaetan* would whip you to the west,

And bring in clowdie night immediately.

Spread thy close curtaine loue-performing night,

That runnawayes eyes may wincke, and *Romeo*

Leape to these armes, vntalkt of and vnseene.

Louers can see to do their amorous rights,   1590

By their owne bewties, or if loue be blind,

It best agrees with night, come ciuill night,

Thou sober suted matron all in blacke,

And learne me how to loose a winning match,

Plaide for a paire of stainlesse maydenhoods.

Hood my vnmand bloud bayting in my cheekes,

With thy blacke mantle, till strange loue grown bold,

Thinke true loue acted simple modestie:

Come night, come *Romeo*, come thou day in night,

For thou wilt lie vpon the winges of night,   1600

Whiter then new snow on a Rauens backe:

Come gentle night, come louing black browd night,

Giue me my *Romeo*, and when I shall die,

Take him and cut him out in little starres,

And he will make the face of heauen so fine,

That all the world will be in loue with night,

And pay no worship to the garish Sun.

O I haue bought the mansion of a loue,

But not possest it, and though I am sold,

Not yet enioyd, so tedious is this day,   1610

As is the night before some festiuall,

To an impatient child that hath new robes

And may not weare them.

*Enter Nurse ⌈wringing her hands⌉, with the ladder
of cords ⌈in her lap⌉*

O here comes my Nurse:

And she brings newes, and euery tongue that speaks

But *Romeos* name, speakes heauenly eloquence:

Now Nurse, what newes? what hast thou there,

The cords that *Romeo* bid thee fetch?

NURSE ⌈*putting downe the cords*⌉   I, I, the cords.

IULIET

Ay me what news? why dost thou wring thy hãds?

NURSE

A weraday, hees dead, hees dead, hees dead,
1620   We are vndone Lady, we are vndone.
Alack the day, hees gone, hees kild, hees dead.

IULIET

Can heauen be so enuious?

NURSE   *Romeo* can,
Though heauen cannot. O *Romeo*, *Romeo*,
Who euer would haue thought it *Romeo*?

IULIET

What diuell art thou that dost torment me thus?
This torture should be rord in dismall hell,
Hath *Romeo* slaine himselfe? say thou but I,
And that bare vowell I shall poyson more
Then the death darting eye of Cockatrice,
1630   I am not I, if there be such an I.
Or those eyes shot, that makes thee answere I:
If he be slaine say I, or if not, no.
Briefe sounds determine of my weale or wo.

NURSE

I saw the wound, I saw it with mine eyes,
God saue the marke, here on his manly brest,
A piteous coarse, a bloudie piteous coarse,
Pale, pale as ashes, all bedawbde in bloud,
All in goare bloud, I sounded at the sight.

IULIET

O break my hart, poore banckrout break at once,
1640   To prison eyes, nere looke on libertie.
Vile earth too earth resigne, end motion here.
And thou and *Romeo* presse on heauie beare.

NURSE

O *Tybalt*, *Tybalt*, the best friend I had,
O curteous *Tybalt*, honest Gentleman,
That euer I should liue to see thee dead.

IULIET

What storme is this that blowes so contrarie?
Is *Romeo* slaughtred? and is *Tybalt* dead?
My dearest Cozen, and my dearer Lord,
Then dreadfull Trumpet sound the generall doome,
1650   For who is liuing, if those two are gone?

NURSE

Tybalt is gone and *Romeo* banished,
Romeo that kild him he is banished.

IULIET

O God, did *Romeos* hand shead *Tibalts* bloud?

⌈NURSE⌉

It did, it did, alas the day, it did.

⌈IULIET⌉

O serpent heart, hid with a flowring face.
Did euer draggon keepe so faire a Caue?
Bewtifull tirant, fiend angelicall:
Douefeatherd rauẽ, woluishrauening lamb,
Despised substance of diuinest showe:
1660   Iust opposite to what thou iustly seem'st,
A damned saint, an honourable villaine:
O nature what hadst thou to do in hell

When thou didst bower the spirit of a fiend,
In mortall paradise of such sweete flesh?
Was euer booke containing such vile matter
So fairely bound? ô that deceit should dwell
In such a gorgious Pallace.

NURSE

Theres no trust, no faith, no honestie in men,
All periurde, all forsworne, all naught, dissemblers all.
Ah wheres my man? giue me some Aqua-vitæ: 1670
These griefs, these woes, these sorrows make me old,
Shame come to *Romeo*.

IULIET   Blisterd be thy tongue
For such a wish, he was not borne to shame:
Vpon his brow shame is asham'd to sit:
For tis a throane where honour may be crownd
Sole Monarch of the vniuersal earth.
O what a beast was I to chide at him?

NURSE

Wil you speak wel of him that kild your cozin?

IULIET

Shall I speake ill of him that is my husband?
Ah poore my lord, what tongue shal smooth thy name,   1680
When I thy three houres wife haue mangled it?
But wherefore villaine didst thou kill my Cozin?
That villaine Cozin would haue kild my husband:
Backe foolish teares, backe to your natiue spring,
Your tributarie drops belong to woe,
Which you mistaking offer vp to ioy,
My husband liues that *Tybalt* would haue slaine,
And *Tybalts* dead that would haue slain my husband:
All this is comfort, wherefore weepe I then?
Some word there was, worser then *Tybalts* death   1690
That murdred me, I would forget it faine,
But oh it presses to my memorie,
Like damned guiltie deeds to sinners mindes,
Tybalt is dead and *Romeo* banished:
That banished, that one word banished,
Hath slaine ten thousand *Tybalts*: *Tybalts* death
Was woe inough if it had ended there:
Or if sower woe delights in fellowship,
And needly will be ranckt with other griefes,
Why followed not when she said *Tybalts* dead,   1700
Thy father or thy mother, nay or both,
Which moderne lamentation might haue moued,
But with a rereward following *Tybalts* death,
Romeo is banished: to speake that word,
Is father, mother, *Tybalt*, *Romeo*, *Iuliet*,
All slaine, all dead: *Romeo* is banished,
There is no end, no limit, measure bound,
In that words death, no words can that woe sound.
Where is my father and my mother Nurse?

NURSE

Weeping and wayling ouer *Tybalts* course,   1710
Will you go to them? I will bring you thither.

IULIET

Wash they his wounds with teares? mine shall be
        spent,
When theirs are drie, for *Romeos* banishment.

Take vp those cordes, poore ropes you are beguilde,
Both you and I for *Romeo* is exilde:
He made you for a highway to my bed,
But I a maide, die maiden widowed.
Come cordes, come Nurse, ile to my wedding bed,
And death not *Romeo*, take my maiden head.

NURSE (*taking vp the cords*)

1720   Hie to your chamber, Ile finde *Romeo*
To comfort you, I wot well where he is:
Harke ye, your *Romeo* will be here at night,
Ile to him, he is hid at *Lawrence* Cell.

IULIET (*giuing her a Ring*)

O find him, giue this ring to my true Knight,
And bid him come, to take his last farewell.

Exeunt ⌜*seuerally*⌝

Sc. 14   *Enter Frier Lawrence*
(3.3)   FRIER LAWRENCE

Romeo come forth, come forth thou fearefull man,
Affliction is enamourd of thy parts:
And thou art wedded to calamitie.

Enter Romeo

ROMEO

Father what newes? what is the Princes doome?

1730   What sorrow craues acquaintance at my hand,
That I yet know not?

FRIER LAWRENCE   Too familiar

Is my deare sonne with such sowre companie.
I bring thee tidings of the Princes doome.

ROMEO

What lesse then doomesday is the Princes doome?

FRIER LAWRENCE

A gentler iudgement vanisht from his lips,
Not bodies death, but bodies banishment.

ROMEO

Ha, banishment? be mercifull, say death:
For exile hath more terror in his looke,
Much more then death, do not say banishment.

FRIER LAWRENCE

1740   Hĕce from *Verona* art thou banished:
Be patient, for the world is broad and wide.

ROMEO

There is no world without *Verona* walls,
But purgatorie, torture, hell it selfe:
Hence banished, is banisht from the world.
And worlds exile is death. Then banished,
Is death, mistermd, calling death banished,
Thou cutst my head off with a golden axe,
And smilst vpon the stroke that murders me.

FRIER LAWRENCE

O deadly sin, ô rude vnthankfulnes,
1750   Thy fault our law calls death, but the kind Prince
Taking thy part, hath rusht aside the law,
And turnd that blacke word death to banishment.
This is deare mercie, and thou seest it not.

ROMEO

Tis torture and not mercie, heauen is here

Where *Iuliet* liues, and euery cat and dog,
And litle mouse, euery vnworthy thing
Liue here in heauen, and may looke on her,
But *Romeo* may not. More validitie,
More honourable state, more courtship liues
In carrion flies, then *Romeo*: they may seaze   1760
On the white wonder of deare *Iuliets* hand,
And steale immortall blessing from her lips,
Who euen in pure and vestall modestie
Still blush, as thinking their owne kisses sin.
But *Romeo* may not, he is banished.
Flies may do this, but I from this must flie:
They are freemen, but I am banished.
And sayest thou yet, that exile is not death?
Hadst thou no poyson mixt, no sharpe ground knife,
No sudden meane of death, though nere so meane,   1770
But banished to kill me: Banished?
O Frier, the damned vse that word in hell:
Howling attends it, how hast thou the heart
Being a Diuine, a ghostly Confessor,
A sin obsoluer, and my friend profest,
To mangle me with that word banished?

FRIER LAWRENCE

Thou fond mad man, heare me a little speake.

ROMEO

O thou wilt speake againe of banishment.

FRIER LAWRENCE

Ile giue thee armour to keepe off that word,
Aduersities sweete milke, Philosophie,   1780
To comfort thee though thou art banished.

ROMEO

Yet banished? hang vp philosophie,
Vnlesse Philosophie can make a *Iuliet*,
Displant a towne, reuerse a Princes doome,
It helpes not, it preuailes not, talke no more.

FRIER LAWRENCE

O then I see, that mad men haue no eares.

ROMEO

How should they when that wise men haue no eyes.

FRIER LAWRENCE

Let me dispute with thee of thy estate.

ROMEO

Thou canst not speak of that thou dost not feele,
Wert thou as young as I, *Iuliet* thy loue,   1790
An houre but married, *Tybalt* murdered,
Doting like me, and like me banished,
Then mightst thou speake, then mightst thou teare
thy hayre,
And fall vpon the ground as I do now,

He falls vpon the ground

Taking the measure of an vnmade graue.

Knocke within

FRIER LAWRENCE

Arise one knocks, good *Romeo* hide thy selfe.

ROMEO

Not I, vnlesse the breath of hartsicke grones,
Myst-like infold me from the search of eyes.

Knocking within

FRIER LAWRENCE

    Hark how they knock (whose there) *Romeo* arise,

1800   Thou wilt be taken, stay a while, stand vp.

      Still knocke within

    Run to my studie by and by, Gods will

    What simplenes is this?

      Knocke within

                  I come, I come.

    Who knocks so hard? whēce come you? whats your

    will?

NURSE (*within*)

    Let me come in, and you shal know my errant:

    I come from Lady *Iuliet*.

FRIER LAWRENCE ⌈*opening the door*⌉ Welcome then.

      Enter Nurse

NURSE

    O holy Frier, O tell me holy Frier,

    Where is my Ladyes Lord? wheres *Romeo*?

FRIER LAWRENCE

    There on the ground, with his owne teares made

    drunke.

NURSE

    O he is euen in my mistresse case,

1810   Iust in her case. O wofull simpathy:

    Pitious prediccament, euen so lies she,

    Blubbring and weeping, weeping and blubbring,

    (*To Romeo*) Stand vp, stand vp, stand and you be a

    man,

    For *Iuliets* sake, for her sake rise and stand:

    Why should you fall into so deepe an O?

ROMEO (*rising*)

    Nurse.

NURSE   Ah sir, ah sir, deaths the end of all.

ROMEO

    Spakst thou of *Iuliet*? how is it with her?

    Doth not she thinke me an old murtherer,

    Now I haue staind the childhood of our ioy,

1820   With bloud remoud, but little from her owne?

    Where is she? and how doth she? and what sayes

    My conceald Lady to our canceld loue?

NURSE

    Oh she sayes nothing sir, but weeps and weeps,

    And now falls on her bed, and then starts vp,

    And *Tybalt* calls, and then on *Romeo* cries,

    And then downe falls againe.

ROMEO   As if that name

    Shot from the deadly leuell of a gun,

    Did murther her, as that names cursed hand

    Murderd her kinsman. Oh tell me Frier, tell me,

1830   In what vile part of this Anatomie

    Doth my name lodge? Tell me that I may sacke

    The hatefull mansion.

      ⌈*He offers to stab himselfe, and Nurse snatches the*

      dagger away⌉

FRIER LAWRENCE   Hold thy desperate hand:

    Art thou a man? thy forme cries out thou art:

    Thy teares are womanish, thy wild acts denote

    The vnreasonable furie of a beast.

    Vnseemely woman in a seeming man,

    And ilbeseeming beast in seeming both,

    Thou hast amaz'd me. By my holy order,

    I thought thy disposition better temperd.

    Hast thou slaine *Tybalt*? wilt thou sley thy selfe?   1840

    And sley thy Lady, that in thy life liues,

    By doing damned hate vpon thy selfe?

    Why raylst thou on thy birth? the heauen and earth?

    Since birth, and heauen, and earth all three do meet,

    In thee at once, which thou at once wouldst loose.

    Fie, fie, thou shamst thy shape, thy loue, thy wit,

    Which like a Vsurer aboundst in all:

    And vsest none in that true vse indeed,

    Which should bedecke thy shape, thy loue, thy wit:

    Thy Noble shape is but a forme of waxe,   1850

    Digressing from the valour of a man,

    Thy deare loue sworne but hollow periurie,

    Killing that loue which thou hast vowd to cherish,

    Thy wit, that ornament, to shape and loue,

    Mishapen in the conduct of them both:

    Like powder in a skillesse souldiers flaske,

    Is set a fier by thine owne ignorance,

    And thou dismembred with thine owne defence.

    What rowse thee man, thy *Iuliet* is aliue,

    For whose deare sake thou wast but lately dead,   1860

    There art thou happie, *Tybalt* would kill thee,

    But thou slewest *Tibalt*, there art thou happie.

    The law that threatned death becomes thy friend,

    And turnes it to exile, there art thou happie.

    A packe of blessings light vpon thy backe,

    Happines courts thee in her best array,

    But like a mishaued and sullen wench,

    Thou pouts vpō thy fortune and thy loue:

    Take heede, take heede, for such die miserable.

    Go get thee to thy loue as was decreed,   1870

    Ascend her chamber, hence and comfort her:

    But looke thou stay not till the watch be set,

    For then thou canst not passe to *Mantua*,

    Where thou shalt liue till we can find a time

    To blaze your marriage, reconcile your friends,

    Beg pardon of the Prince and call thee backe,

    With twentie hundred thousand times more ioy

    Then thou wentst forth in lamentation.

    Go before Nurse, commend me to thy Lady,

    And bid her hasten all the house to bed,   1880

    Which heauie sorrow makes them apt vnto,

    Romeo is comming.

NURSE

    O Lord, I could haue staid here all the night,

    To heare good counsell, oh what learning is:

    My Lord, ile tell my Lady you will come.

ROMEO

    Do so, and bid my sweete prepare to chide.

      ⌈*Nurse offers to go in and turnes againe*⌉

NURSE (*giuing the Ring*)

    Here sir, a Ring she bid me giue you sir:

    Hie you, make hast, for it growes very late.

ROMEO

How well my comfort is reuiu'd by this.   *Exit Nurse*

FRIER LAWRENCE

1890 Go hẽce, goodnight, & here stands al your state:
Either be gone before the watch be set,
Or by the breake of day disguisd from hence,
Soiourne in *Mantua*, ile find out your man,
And he shall signifie from time to time,
Euery good hap to you, that chaunces here:
Giue me thy hand, tis late, farewell, goodnight.

ROMEO

But that a ioy past ioy calls out on me,
It were a griefe, so briefe to part with thee:
Farewell.   *Exeunt ⌐seuerally⌐*

Sc. 15   *Enter old Capulet, his wife and Paris*
(3.4)   CAPULET
1900 Things haue falne out sir so vnluckily,
That we haue had no time to moue our daughter,
Looke you, she lou'd her kinsman *Tybalt* dearely
And so did I. Well we were borne to die.
Tis very late, sheele not come downe to night:
I promise you, but for your companie,
I would haue bene a bed an houre ago.

PARIS

These times of wo affoord no times to wooe:
Madam goodnight, commend me to your daughter.

CAPULETS WIFE

I will, and know her mind early to morrow,
1910 To night shees mewed vp to her heauines.
⌐*Paris offers to go in, and Capulet calls him againe*⌐

CAPULET

Sir *Paris*, I will make a desperate tender
Of my childes loue: I thinke she will be rulde
In all respects by me: nay more, I doubt it not.
Wife go you to her ere you go to bed,
Acquaint her here, of my sonne *Paris* loue,
And bid her, marke you me? on wendsday next.
But soft, what day is this?

PARIS   Monday my Lord.

CAPULET

Monday, ha ha, well wendsday is too soone,
A thursday let it be, a thursday tell her
1920 She shall be married to this noble Earle:
Will you be ready? do you like this haste?
Weel keepe no great ado, a friend or two,
For harke you, *Tybalt* being slaine so late,
It may be thought we held him carelesly
Being our kinsman, if we reuell much:
Therefore weele haue some halfe a doozen friends,
And there an end, but what say you to Thursday?

PARIS

My Lord, I would that thursday were to morrow.

CAPULET

Well get you gone, a Thursday be it then:
1930 (*To his wife*) Go you to *Iuliet* ere you go to bed,
Prepare her wife, against this wedding day.
Farewell my Lord, light to my chamber ho,

Afore mee, it is so very late that wee
May call it early by and by, goodnight.
            *Exeunt ⌐Capulet and his wife at one
                doore, Paris at another doore⌐*

        *Enter Romeo and Iuliet aloft, ⌐with the ladder   Sc. 16
        of cords⌐*   (3.5)

IULIET

Wilt thou be gone? It is not yet neare day:
It was the Nightingale, and not the Larke,
That pierst the fearefull hollow of thine eare,
Nightly she sings on yond Pomgranet tree,
Beleeue me loue, it was the Nightingale.

ROMEO

It was the Larke the herauld of the morne,   1940
No Nightingale, looke loue what enuious streakes
Do lace the seuering cloudes in yonder East:
Nights candles are burnt out, and iocand day
Stands tiptoe on the mystie Mountaine tops,
I must be gone and liue, or stay and die.

IULIET

Yond light is not daylight, I know it I:
It is some Meteor that the Sun exhald,
To be to thee this night a Torch-bearer,
And light thee on thy way to *Mantua*.
Therefore stay yet, thou needst not to be gone.   1950

ROMEO

Let me be tane, let me be put to death,
I am content, so thou wilt haue it so.
Ile say yon gray is not the mornings eye,
Tis but the pale reflex of *Cinthias* brow.
Nor that is not the Larke whose noates do beate
The vaultie heauen so high aboue our heads,
I haue more care to stay then will to go:
Come death and welcome, *Iuliet* wills it so.
How ist my soule? lets talke, it is not day.

IULIET

It is, it is, hie hence be gone away: 1960
It is the Larke that sings so out of tune,
Straining harsh Discords, and vnpleasing Sharpes.
Some say, the Larke makes sweete Diuision:
This doth not so: for she diuideth vs.
Some say the Larke and loathed Toad changd eyes,
O now I would they had changd voyces too:
Since arme from arme that voyce doth vs affray,
Hunting thee hence, with Huntsup to the day.
O now be gone, more light and light it growes.

ROMEO

More light and light, more darke and darke our woes.   1970
        Enter Nurse ⌐hastily⌐

NURSE Madam.

IULIET Nurse.

NURSE

Your Lady Mother is cũming to your chãber,
The day is broke, be wary, looke about.   *Exit*

IULIET

Then window let day in, and let life out.

ROMEO
    Farewell, farewell, one kisse and Ile descend.
      ⌈*He lets downe the ladder of cords and goes downe*⌉
IULIET
    Art thou gone so? loue, Lord, my husband, friend,
    I must heare from thee euery day in the houre,
    For in a minute there are many dayes,
1980   O by this count I shall be much in yeares,
    Ere I againe behold my *Romeo*.
ROMEO Farewell:
    I will omit no opportunitie,
    That may conuey my greetings loue to thee.
IULIET
    O thinkst thou we shall euer meete againe?
ROMEO
    I doubt it not, and all these woes shall serue
    For sweete discourses in our times to come.
⌈IULIET⌉
    O God I haue an ill diuining soule,
    Me thinkes I see thee, now thou art so lowe,
1990   As one dead in the bottome of a tombe,
    Either my eye-sight failes, or thou lookst pale.
ROMEO
    And trust me loue, in my eye so do you:
    Drie sorrow drinkes our bloud. Adue, adue.   *Exit*
IULIET ⌈*pulling vp the ladder, and weeping*⌉
    O Fortune, Fortune, all men call thee fickle,
    If thou art fickle, what dost thou with him
    That is renowmd for faith? be fickle Fortune:
    For then I hope thou wilt not keepe him long,
    But send him backe.
      Enter her Mother (*Capulets wife*) ⌈*below*⌉
CAPULETS WIFE   Ho daughter, are you vp?
IULIET
    Who ist that calls? It is my Lady mother.
2000   Is she not downe so late or vp so early?
    What vnaccustomd cause procures her hither?
     ⌈*She goes downe, and enters below*⌉
CAPULETS WIFE
    Why how now *Iuliet*?
IULIET   Madam I am not well.
CAPULETS WIFE
    Euermore weeping for your Cozens death?
    What wilt thou wash him from his graue with teares?
    And if thou couldst, thou couldst not make him liue:
    Therfore haue done, some griefe shews much of loue,
    But much of greefe, shewes still some want of wit.
IULIET
    Yet let me weepe, for such a feeling losse.
CAPULETS WIFE
    So shall you feele the losse, but not the friend
    Which you so weepe for.
2010 IULIET   Feeling so the losse,
    I cannot chuse but euer weepe the friend.
CAPULETS WIFE
    Wel gyrle, thou weepst not so much for his death,
    As that the villaine liues which slaughterd him.

IULIET
    What villaine Madam?
CAPULETS WIFE   That same villaine *Romeo*.
IULIET (*aside*)
    Villaine and he be many miles a sunder:
    (*To her Mother*) God pardon him, I do with all my
      heart:
    And yet no man like he, doth greeue my heart.
CAPULETS WIFE
    That is because the Traytor murderer liues.
IULIET
    I Madam from the reach of these my hands:
    Would none but I might venge my Cozens death.   2020
CAPULETS WIFE
    We will haue vengeance for it, feare thou not.
    Then weepe no more, Ile send to one in *Mantua*,
    Where that same bannisht runnagate doth liue,
    Shall giue him such an vnaccustomd dram,
    That he shall soone keepe *Tybalt* companie:
    And then I hope thou wilt be satisfied.
IULIET
    Indeed I neuer shall be satisfied
    With *Romeo*, till I behold him. Dead
    Is my poore heart so for a kinsman vext:
    Madam if you could find out but a man   2030
    To beare a poyson, I would temper it:
    That *Romeo* should vpon receit thereof,
    Soone sleepe in quiet. O how my heart abhors
    To heare him namde and cannot come to him,
    To wreake the loue I bore my Cozen,
    Vpon his body that hath slaughterd him.
CAPULETS WIFE
    Find thou the means, and Ile find such a man,
    But now ile tell thee ioyfull tidings Gyrle.
IULIET
    And ioy comes well in such a needie time,
    What are they, I beseech your Ladyship?   2040
CAPULETS WIFE
    Well, well, thou hast a carefull father child,
    One who to put thee from thy heauines,
    Hath sorted out a sudden day of ioy,
    That thou expects not, nor I lookt not for.
IULIET
    Madam in happie time, what day is that?
CAPULETS WIFE
    Marrie my child, early next Thursday morne,
    The gallant, young, and Noble Gentleman,
    The Countie *Paris* at Saint *Peters* Church,
    Shall happily make thee there a ioyfull Bride.
IULIET
    Now by S. *Peters* Church, and *Peter* too,   2050
    He shall not make me there a ioyfull Bride.
    I wonder at this haste, that I must wed
    Ere he that should be husband comes to wooe:
    I pray you tell my Lord and father Madam,
    I will not marrie yet, and when I do, I sweare
    It shall be *Romeo*, whom you know I hate
    Rather then *Paris*, these are newes indeed.

Enter Iuliets father Capulet, and Nurse

CAPULETS WIFE

Here comes your father, tell him so your selfe:
And see how he will take it at your hands.

CAPULET

2060 When the Sun sets, the earth doth drisle deaw,
But for the Sunset of my brothers sonne,
It rains downright.
How now a Conduit girle, what still in tears
Euermore showring? in one litle body
Thou countefaits a Barke, a Sea, a Wind:
For still thy eyes, which I may call the sea,
Do ebbe and flowe with teares, the Barke thy body is:
Sayling in this salt floud, the windes thy sighes,
Who raging with thy teares and they with them,
2070 Without a sudden calme will ouerset
Thy tempest tossed body. How now wife,
Haue you deliured to her our decree?

CAPULETS WIFE

I sir, but she will none, she giues you thankes,
I would the foole were married to her graue.

CAPULET

Soft take me with you, take me with you wife,
How will she none? doth she not giue vs thanks?
Is she not proud? doth she not count her blest,
Vnworthy as she is, that we haue wrought
So worthy a Gentleman to be her Bride?

IULIET

2080 Not proud you haue, but thankful that you haue:
Proud can I neuer be of what I hate,
But thankfull euen for hate, that is meant loue.

CAPULET

How, how, how how, chopt lodgick, what is this?
Proud and I thanke you, and I thanke you not,
And yet not proud? mistresse minion you,
Thanke me no thankings, nor proud me no prouds,
But fettle your fine Ioynts gainst Thursday next,
To go with *Paris* to Saint *Peters* Church:
Or I will drag thee on a hurdle thither.
2090 Out you greene sicknesse carrion, out you baggage,
You tallow face.

CAPULETS WIFE   Fie, fie, what are you mad?

IULIET *(kneeling)*

Good Father, I beseech you on my knees,
Heare me with patience, but to speake a word.

CAPULET

Hang thee young baggage, disobedient wretch,
I tell thee what, get thee to Church a Thursday,
Or neuer after looke me in the face.
Speake not, replie not, do not answere me.
        ⌈*Iuliet rises*⌉
My fingers itch, wife, we scarce thought vs blest,
That God had lent vs but this onely childe,
2100 But now I see this one is one too much,
And that we haue a curse in hauing her:
Out on her hilding.

NURSE   God in heauen blesse her:
You are to blame my Lord to rate her so.

CAPULET

And why my Lady wisdome, hold your tongue,
Good Prudence, smatter with your gossips go.

NURSE

I speake no treason.

⌈CAPULET⌉   O Godigeden.

⌈NURSE⌉

May not one speake?

CAPULET   Peace you mumbling foole,
Vtter your grauitie ore a Goships bowle,
For here we need it not.

CAPULETS WIFE   You are too hot.

CAPULET

Gods bread, it makes me mad, day, night, worke, play,   2110
Alone in companie, still my care hath bene
To haue her matcht, and hauing now prouided
A Gentleman of noble parentage,
Of faire demeanes, youthfull and nobly lind,
Stuft as they say, with honourable parts,
Proportiond as ones thought would wish a man,
And then to haue a wretched puling foole,
A whining mammet, in her fortunes tender,
To answere, ile not wed, I cannot loue:
I am too young, I pray you pardon me.   2120
But and you will not wed, ile pardon you.
Graze where you will, you shall not house with me,
Looke too't, thinke on't, I do not vse to iest.
Thursday is neare, lay hand on hart, aduise,
And you be mine, ile giue you to my friend,
And you be not, hang, beg, starue, dye in the streets,
For by my soule ile nere acknowledge thee,
Nor what is mine shall neuer do thee good:
Trust too't, bethinke you, ile not be forsworne.   *Exit*

IULIET

Is there no pittie sitting in the cloudes   2130
That sees into the bottome of my greefe?
O sweet my Mother cast me not away,
Delay this marriage for a month, a weeke,
Or if you do not, make the Bridall bed
In that dim Monument where *Tibalt* lies.

CAPULETS WIFE

Talke not to me, for ile not speake a word,
Do as thou wilt, for I haue done with thee.   *Exit*

IULIET

O God, ô Nurse, how shall this be preuented?
My husband is on earth, my faith in heauen,
How shall that faith returne againe to earth,   2140
Vnlesse that husband send it me from heauen,
By leauing earth? comfort me, counsaile me:
Alack, alack, that heauen should practise stratagems
Vpon so soft a subiect as my selfe.
What sayst thou, hast thou not a word of ioy?
Some comfort Nurse.

NURSE   Faith here it is, *Romeo*
Is banished and all the world to nothing,
That he dares nere come back to challenge you:
Or if he do, it needs must be by stealth.
Then since the case so stands as now it doth,   2150

I thinke it best you married with the Countie,
O hees a louely Gentleman:
Romios a dishclout to him, an Eagle Madam
Hath not so greene, so quick, so faire an eye
As *Paris* hath, beshrow my very hart,
I thinke you are happie in this second match,
For it excels your first, or if it did not,
Your first is dead, or twere as good he were,
As liuing hēce, and you no vse of him.

2160   IULIET Speakst thou from thy heart?
NURSE
And from my soule too, else beshrew them both.
IULIET Amen.
NURSE What?
IULIET
Well thou hast comforted me maruellous much,
Go in, and tell my Lady I am gone,
Hauing displeas'd my father, to *Laurence* Cell,
To make confession, and to be obsolu'd.
NURSE
Marrie I will, and this is wisely done.   ⌈*Exit*⌉
IULIET (*watching her go*)
Auncient damnation, ô most wicked fiend,
2170   Is it more sin to wish me thus forsworne,
Or to dispraise my Lord with that same tongue,
Which she hath praisde him with aboue compare,
So many thousand times? Go Counsellor,
Thou and my bosome henceforth shall be twaine:
Ile to the Frier to know his remedie,
If all else faile, my selfe haue power to die.   *Exit*

Sc. 17   *Enter Frier Lawrence and Countie Paris*
(4.1)   FRIER LAWRENCE
On Thursday sir: the time is very short.
PARIS
My Father *Capulet* will haue it so,
And I am nothing slow to slacke his haste.
FRIER LAWRENCE
2180   You say you do not know the Ladies minde?
Vneuen is the course, I like it not.
PARIS
Immoderately she weepes for *Tybalts* death,
And therefore haue I little talkd of loue,
For *Venus* smiles not in a house of teares.
Now sir, her father counts it daungerous
That she do giue her sorrow so much sway:
And in his wisedome hastes our marriage,
To stop the inundation of her teares,
Which too much minded by her selfe alone
2190   May be put from her by societie.
Now do you know the reason of this haste.
FRIER LAWRENCE (*aside*)
I would I knew not why it should be slowed.
          Enter Iuliet
Looke sir, here comes the Lady toward my Cell.
PARIS
Happily met my Lady and my wife.
IULIET
That may be sir, when I may be a wife.

PARIS
That may be, must be loue, on Thursday next.
IULIET
What must be shall be.
FRIER LAWRENCE   Thats a certaine text.
PARIS
Come you to make confession to this Father?
IULIET
To aunswere that, I should confesse to you.
PARIS
Do not denie to him, that you loue me.   2200
IULIET
I will confesse to you that I loue him.
PARIS
So will ye, I am sure that you loue me.
IULIET
If I do so, it will be of more price,
Being spoke behind your backe, then to your face.
PARIS
Poore soule thy face is much abusde with tears.
IULIET
The teares haue got small victorie by that,
For it was bad inough before their spight.
PARIS
Thou wrongst it more then tears with that report.
IULIET
That is no slaunder sir, which is a truth,
And what I spake, I spake it to my face.   2210
PARIS
Thy face is mine, and thou hast slandred it.
IULIET
It may be so, for it is not mine owne.
Are you at leisure, holy Father now,
Or shall I come to you at euening Masse?
FRIER LAWRENCE
My leisure serues me pensiue daughter now,
My Lord we must entreate the time alone.
PARIS
Godshield, I should disturbe deuotion,
Iuliet, on Thursday early will I rowse yee,
(*Kissing her*) Till then adue, and keepe this holy kisse.
                                        Exit
IULIET
O shut the doore, and when thou hast done so,   2220
Come weepe with me, past hope, past cure, past help.
FRIER LAWRENCE
O *Iuliet* I already know thy greefe,
It straines me past the compasse of my wits,
I heare thou must, and nothing may prorogue it,
On Thursday next be married to this Countie.
IULIET
Tell me not Frier, that thou hearst of this,
Vnlesse thou tell me, how I may preuent it:
If in thy wisedome thou canst giue no helpe,
Do thou but call my resolution wise,
          She drawes a knife
And with this knife ile helpe it presently.   2230
God ioynd my heart and *Romeos*, thou our hands:
And ere this hand by thee to *Romeos* seald

Shall be the Labell to an other deed,
Or my true heart with trecherous reuolt,
Turne to an other, this shall sley them both:
Therefore out of thy long experienst time,
Giue me some present counsell, or behold
Twixt my extreames and me, this bloudie knife
Shall play the vmpeere, arbitrating that,
2240 Which the commission of thy yeares and art,
Could to no issue of true honour bring:
Be not so long to speake, I long to die,
If what thou speakst, speake not of remedie.

FRIER LAWRENCE
Hold daughter, I do spie a kind of hope,
Which craues as desperate an execution,
As that is desperate which we would preuent.
If rather then to marrie Countie *Paris*
Thou hast the strength of will to slay thy selfe,
Then is it likely thou wilt vndertake
2250 A thing like death to chide away this shame,
That coapst with death, himselfe to scape from it:
And if thou darst, Ile giue thee remedie.

IULIET
Oh bid me leape, rather then marrie *Paris*,
From of the battlements of any Tower,
Or walke in theeuish wayes, or bid me lurke
Where Serpents are: chaine me with roaring Beares,
Or hide me nightly in a Charnel house,
Orecouerd quite with dead mens ratling bones,
With reekie shanks and yealow chaples sculls:
2260 Or bid me go into a new made graue,
And hide me with a dead man in his Tombe,
Things that to heare them told, haue made me
        tremble,
And I will do it without feare or doubt,
To liue an vnstaind wife to my sweete loue.

FRIER LAWRENCE
Hold then, go home, be merrie, giue consent,
To marrie *Paris*: wendsday is to morrow,
To morrow night looke that thou lie alone,
Let not the Nurse lie with thee in thy Chamber:
Take thou this Violl being then in bed,
2270 And this distilling liquor drinke thou off,
When presently through all thy veines shall run,
A cold and drowzie humour: for no pulse
Shall keepe his natiue progresse but surcease,
No warmth, no breath shall testifie thou liuest,
The roses in thy lips and cheekes shall fade
Too wany ashes, thy eyes windowes fall:
Like death when he shuts vp the day of life.
Each part depriu'd of supple gouernment,
Shall stiffe and starke, and cold appeare like death,
2280 And in this borrowed likenesse of shrunke death
Thou shalt continue two and fortie houres,
And then awake as from a pleasant sleepe.
Now when the Bridegroome in the morning comes,
To rowse thee from thy bed, there art thou dead:
Then as the manner of our countrie is,

In thy best robes vncoured on the Beere,
Thou shalt be borne to that same auncient vault,
Where all the kindred of the *Capulets* lie,
In the meane time against thou shalt awake,
Shall *Romeo* by my Letters know our drift,   2290
And hither shall he come, an he and I
Will watch thy waking, and that very night
Shall *Romeo* beare thee hence to *Mantua*.
And this shall free thee from this present shame,
If no inconstant toy nor womanish feare,
Abate thy valour in the acting it.

IULIET
Giue me, giue me, O tell not me of feare.

FRIER LAWRENCE (*giuing her the Violl*)
Hold get you gone, be strong and prosperous
In this resolue, ile send a Frier with speed
To *Mantua*, with my Letters to thy Lord.   2300

IULIET
Loue giue me strength, and strength shall helpe afford:
Farewell deare father.   *Exeunt ⌐seuerally⌐*

Enter Father Capulet, his wife (Iuliets Mother),   Sc. 18
Nurse, and ⌐two⌐ Seruing men   (4.2)

CAPULET (*giuing a Seruingman a paper*)
So many guests inuite as here are writ,
                                  ⌐*Exit Seruingman*⌐
(*To the other Seruingman*) Sirrah, go hire me twentie
    cunning Cookes.

SERUINGMAN You shall haue none ill sir, for ile trie if they
    can lick their fingers.

CAPULET How canst thou trie them so?

SERUINGMAN Marrie sir, tis an ill Cooke that cannot lick
    his owne fingers: therefore hee that cannot lick his
    fingers goes not with me.   2310

CAPULET Go be gone,   ⌐*Exit Seruingman*⌐
    We shall be much vnfurnisht for this time:
    (*To Nurse*) What is my daughter gone to Frier
        Lawrence?

NURSE I forsooth.

CAPULET
    Well, he may chance to do some good on her,
    A peeuish selfewilld harlottry it is.
        Enter Iuliet

NURSE
See where she comes from shrift with merie looke.

CAPULET (*to Iuliet*)
How now my headstrong, where haue you bin
    gadding?

IULIET
Where I haue learnt me to repent the sin
Of disobedient opposition,   2320
To you and your behests, and am enioynd
By holy *Lawrence*, to fall prostrate here,
To beg your pardon, (*kneeling*) pardon I beseech you,
Henceforward I am euer rulde by you.

CAPULET ⌐*to Nurse*⌐
Send for the Countie, go tell him of this,
Ile haue this knot knit vp to morrow morning.

IULIET

I met the youthfull Lord at *Lawrence* Cell,
And gaue him what becoming loue I might,
Not stepping ore the bounds of modestie.

CAPULET

2330   Why I am glad ont, this is wel, stand vp,
            Iuliet rises
This is ast should be, let me see the Countie:
⌈*To Nurse*⌉ I marrie go I say and fetch him hither.
Now afore God, this reuerend holy Frier,
All our whole Citie is much bound to him.

IULIET

Nurse, will you go with me into my Closet,
To helpe me sort such needfull ornaments,
As you thinke fit to furnish me to morrow?

CAPULETS WIFE

No not till Thursday, there is time inough.

CAPULET

Go Nurse, go with her, weele to Church to morrow.
                    Exeunt Iuliet and Nurse

CAPULETS WIFE

2340   We shall be short in our prouision,
Tis now neare night.

CAPULET   Tush, I will stirre about,
And all things shall be well, I warrant thee wife:
Go thou to *Iuliet*, helpe to decke vp her,
Ile not to bed to night, let me alone:
Ile play the huswife for this once, what ho?
They are all forth, well I will walke my selfe
To Countie *Paris*, to prepare vp him
Against to morrow, my heart is wondrous light,
Since this same wayward Gyrle is so reclaymd.
                    Exeunt ⌈*seuerally*⌉

Sc. 19   *Enter Iuliet and Nurse* ⌈*with garments*⌉
(4.3)   IULIET

2350   I those attires are best, but gentle Nurse
I pray thee leaue me to my selfe to night:
For I haue need of many orysons,
To moue the heauens to smile vpon my state,
Which well thou knowest, is crosse and full of sin.
            Enter her Mother (*Capulets wife*)

CAPULETS WIFE

What are you busie ho? need you my helpe?

IULIET

No Madam, we haue culd such necessaries
As are behoofefull for our state to morrow:
So please you, let me now be left alone,
And let the Nurse this night sit vp with you,
2360   For I am sure you haue your hands full all,
In this so sudden businesse.

CAPULETS WIFE   Good night.
Get thee to bed and rest, for thou hast need.
                    Exeunt Capulets wife and Nurse

IULIET

Farewell, God knowes when we shall meete againe,
I haue a faint cold feare thrills through my veines,

That almost freezes vp the heate of life:
Ile call them backe againe to comfort me.
Nurse, what should she do here?
            ⌈*She opens curtaines, discouering her bed*⌉
My dismall sceane I needs must act alone.
Come Violl,
What if this mixture do not worke at all?   2370
Shall I be married then to morrow morning?
No, no, this shall forbid it, lie thou there,
            She laies downe a knife
What if it be a poyson which the Frier
Subtilly hath ministred to haue me dead,
Least in this marriage he should be dishonourd,
Because he married me before to *Romeo*?
I feare it is, and yet me thinks it should not,
For he hath still bene tried a holy man.
How if when I am laid into the Tombe,
I wake before the time that *Romeo*   2380
Come to redeeme me, theres a fearfull poynt:
Shall I not then be stiffled in the Vault?
To whose foule mouth no healthsome ayre breaths in,
And there die strangled ere my *Romeo* comes.
Or if I liue, is it not very like,
The horrible conceit of death and night,
Togither with the terror of the place,
As in a Vaulte, an auncient receptacle,
Where for this many hundred yeares the bones
Of all my buried auncestors are packt,   2390
Where bloudie *Tybalt* yet but greene in earth,
Lies festring in his shroude, where as they say,
At some houres in the night, spirits resort:
Alack, alack, is it not like that I
So early waking, what with loathsome smels,
And shrikes like mandrakes torne out of the earth,
That liuing mortalls hearing them run mad:
O if I wake, shall I not be distraught,
Inuironed with all these hidious feares,
And madly play with my forefathers ioynts?   2400
And pluck the mangled *Tybalt* from his shrowde,
And in this rage with some great kinsmans bone,
As with a club dash out my desprate braines.
O looke, me thinks I see my Cozins Ghost,
Seeking out *Romeo* that did spit his body
Vpon a Rapiers poynt: stay *Tybalt*, stay?
Romeo, *Romeo*, *Romeo*, heeres drinke, I drinke to thee.
            She drinkes from the Violl and falles vpon the bed,
            ⌈*pulling closed the curtaines*⌉

            Enter Lady of the house (*Capulets wife*) *and Nurse*   Sc. 20
            ⌈*with hearbes*⌉   (4.4)

CAPULETS WIFE

Hold take these keies & fetch more spices Nurse.

NURSE

They call for dates and quinces in the Pastrie.
            Enter old Capulet

CAPULET

Come, stir, stir, stir, the second Cock hath crowed.   2410

The Curphew bell hath roong, tis three a clock:
Looke to the bakte meates, good *Angelica*,
Spare not for cost.

NURSE   Go you cot-queane go,
Get you to bed, faith youle be sicke to morrow
For this nights watching.

CAPULET
No not a whit, what I haue watcht ere now,
All night for lesser cause, and nere bene sicke.

CAPULETS WIFE
I you haue bene a mouse-hunt in your time,
But I will watch you from such watching now.
            Exit Capulets wife and Nurse

CAPULET
A iealous hood, a iealous hood,
            Enter three or foure Seruingmen with spits and
            logs, and baskets
2420   now fellow, what is there?

I. SERUINGMAN
Things for the Cooke sir, but I know not what.

CAPULET
Make haste, make haste
            Exit I. Seruingman ⌈and one or two others⌉
                        sirra, fetch drier logs.
Call *Peter*, he will shew thee where they are.

2. SERUINGMAN
I haue a head sir, that will find out logs,
And neuer trouble *Peter* for the matter.

CAPULET
Masse and well said, a merrie horson, ha,
Thou shalt be loggerhead,   *Exit 2. Seruingman*
                        good faithe tis day.
The Countie will be here with musicke straight,
For so he said he would,
            Play Musicke within
                        I heare him neare.
2430   Nurse, wife, what ho, what Nurse I say?
            Enter Nurse
Go waken *Iuliet*, go and trim her vp,
Ile go and chat with *Paris*, hie, make haste,
Make hast, the bridgroome, he is come already,
Make hast I say.   *Exit*

NURSE
Mistris, what mistris, *Iuliet*, fast I warrant her she,
Why Lambe, why Lady, fie you sluggabed,
Why Loue I say, Madam, sweete heart, why Bride:
What not a word, you take your penniworths now,
Sleepe for a weeke, for the next night I warrant
2440   The Countie *Paris* hath set vp his rest,
That you shall rest but little, God forgiue me.
Marrie and Amen: how sound is she a sleepe:
I needs must wake her: Madam, Madam, Madam,
I, let the Countie take you in your bed,
Heele fright you vp yfaith, will it not be?
            ⌈*She drawes back the curtaines*⌉
What drest, and in your clothes, and downe againe?
I must needs wake you, Lady, Lady, Lady.
Alas, alas, helpe, helpe, my Ladyes dead.

Oh wereaday that euer I was borne,
Some Aqua-vitæ ho, my Lord my Lady.   2450
            Enter Capulets wife

CAPULETS WIFE
What noise is here?

NURSE   O lamentable day.

CAPULETS WIFE
What is the matter?

NURSE   Looke, looke, oh heauie day!

CAPULETS WIFE
O me, O me, my child, my onely life.
Reuiue, looke vp, or I will die with thee:
Helpe, helpe, call helpe.
            Enter Father Capulet

CAPULET
For shame bring *Iuliet* forth, her Lord is come.

NURSE
Shees dead: deceast, shees dead, alack the day.

CAPULETS WIFE
Alack the day, shees dead, shees dead, shees dead.

CAPULET
Hah let me see her, out alas shees cold,
Her bloud is setled, and her ioynts are stiffe: 2460
Life and these lips haue long bene separated,
Death lies on her like an vntimely frost,
Vpon the sweetest flower of all the field.

NURSE
O lamentable day!

CAPULETS WIFE   O wofull time!

CAPULET
Death that hath tane her hẽce to make me waile
Ties vp my tongue and will not let me speake.
            Enter Frier Lawrence and the Countie Paris,
            with Musitions

FRIER LAWRENCE
Come, is the Bride ready to go to Church?

CAPULET
Ready to go but neuer to returne.
(*To Paris*) O sonne, the night before thy wedding day
Hath death laine with thy wife, see there she lies,   2470
Flower as she was, deflowered by him,
Death is my sonne in law, death is my heire,
My daughter he hath wedded. I will die,
And leaue him all: life liuing, all is deaths.
            ⌈*Paris, Capulet and his wife, and the Nurse all at*
            once wring their hands and cry out together:⌉

PARIS
Haue I thought long to see this mornings face,
And doth it giue me such a sight as this?
Beguild, diuorced, wronged, spighted, slaine,
Most detestable death, by thee beguild,
By cruell, cruell, thee quite ouerthrowne,
O loue, O life, not life, but loue in death.   2480

CAPULETS WIFE
Accurst, vnhappie, wretched hatefull day,
Most miserable houre that ere time saw,
In lasting labour of his Pilgrimage,
But one poore one, one poore and louing child,

But one thing to reioyce and solace in,
And cruell death hath catcht it from my sight.

NURSE

O wo, O wofull, wofull, wofull day,
Most lamentable day, most wofull day
That euer, euer, I did yet behold.
2490   O day, O day, O day, O hatefull day,
Neuer was seene so blacke a day as this,
O wofull day, O wofull day.

CAPULET

Despisde, distressed, hated, martird, kild,
Vncomfortable time, why camst thou now,
To murther, murther, our solemnitie?
O childe, O childe, my soule and not my childe,
Dead art thou, alacke my child is dead,
And with my child my ioyes are buried.

FRIER LAWRENCE

Peace ho for shame, confusions cure liues not
2500   In these confusions, heauen and your selfe
Had part in this faire maide, now heauen hath all,
And all the better is it for the maid:
Your part in her, you could not keepe from death,
But heauen keepes his part in eternall life,
The most you sought was her promotion,
For twas your heauen she should be aduanst,
And weepe ye now, seeing she is aduanst
Aboue the Cloudes, as high as heauen it selfe.
O in this loue, you loue your child so ill,
2510   That you run mad, seeing that she is well:
Shees not well married, that liues married long,
But shees best married, that dies married young.
Drie vp your teares, and stick your Rosemarie
On this faire Coarse, and as the custome is,
All in her best array beare her to Church:
For though fond nature bids vs all lament,
Yet natures teares are reasons merriment.

CAPULET

All things that we ordained festiuall,
Turne from their office to black Funerall:
2520   Our instruments to melancholy bells,
Our wedding cheare to a sad buriall feast:
Our solemne himnes to sullen dyrges change:
Our Bridall flowers serue for a buried Coarse:
And all things change them to the contrarie.

FRIER LAWRENCE

Sir go you in, and Madam go with him,
And go sir *Paris*, euery one prepare
To follow this faire Coarse vnto her graue:
The heauens do lowre vpon you for some ill:
Moue them no more, by crossing their high wil.
      ⌜*They cast Rosemarie on Iuliet, and shut the*
      curtaines.⌝ *Exeunt: manet Nurse and Musitions*
2530   ⌜I.⌝ MUSITION Faith we may put vp our pipes and be gone.

NURSE

Honest good fellowes, ah put vp, put vp,
For well you know, this is a pitifull case.
⌜I.⌝ MUSITION
I by my troath, the case may be amended.   *Exit Nurse*

      Enter Peter
PETER Musitions, oh Musitions, harts ease, harts ease, O,
      and you will haue me liue, play harts ease.
⌜I.⌝ MUSITION Why harts ease?
PETER O Musitions, because my hart it selfe plaies my
      hart is full of woe: O play me some merie dump to
      comfort me.
⌜I. MUSITION⌝ Not a dump we, tis no time to play now.   2540
PETER You will not then?
I. MUSITION No.
PETER I will then giue it you soundly.
I. MUSITION What will you giue vs?
PETER No money on my faith, but the gleeke. I will giue
      you the Minstrell.
I. MUSITION Then will I giue you the Seruing-creature.
PETER (*drawing his dagger*) Then will I lay the seruing-
      creatures dagger on your pate. I will cary no Crochets,
      ile re you, Ile fa you, do you note me?   2550
I. MUSITION And you re vs, and fa vs, you note vs.
2. MUSITION Pray you put vp your dagger, and put out
      your wit.
⌜PETER⌝ Then haue at you with my wit. I will dry-beate
      you with an yron wit, and put vp my yron dagger.
      Answere me like men.
      ⌜*Sings*⌝
            When griping griefe the hart doth wound,
                  And dolefull dumps the minde oppresse,
            Then musique with her siluer sound.
Why siluer sound, why musique, with her siluer sound,   2560
what say you Mathew Minikine?
I. MUSITION Mary sir, because siluer hath a sweet sound.
PETER Prates, what say you Hugh Rebick?
2. MUSITION I say siluer sound, because Musitions sound
      for siluer.
PETER Prates to, what say you Simon sound post?
3. MUSITION Faith I know not what to say.
PETER O I cry you mercy, you are the singer. I will say
      for you, it is musique with her siluer sound, because
      Musitions haue no gold for sounding: 2570
      ⌜*Sings*⌝
            Then Musique with her siluer sound
                  With speedy help doth lend redresse.   *Exit*
I. MUSITION What a pestilent knaue is this same?
2. MUSITION Hang him Iack, come weele in here, tarrie
      for the mourners, and stay dinner.   *Exeunt*

      Enter Romeo   Sc. 21
ROMEO   (5.1)
If I may trust the flattering truth of sleepe,
My dreames presage some ioyfull newes at hand,
My bosomes L. sits lightly in his throne:
And all this day an vnaccustomd spirit,
Lifts me aboue the ground with chearfull thoughts,   2580
I dreamt my Lady came and found me dead,
Strange dreame that giues a deadman leaue to thinke,
And Breathd such life with kisses in my lips,
That I reuiude and was an Emperor.
Ah me, how sweete is loue it selfe possest

When but loues shadowes are so rich in ioy.
    Enter Balthazar, Romeos man, ⌐booted¬
Newes from *Verona,* how now *Balthazer,*
Dost thou not bring me Letters from the Frier?
How doth my Lady, is my Father well:
2590 How fares my *Iuliet?* that I aske againe,
For nothing can be ill if she be well.

BALTHAZER
Then she is well and nothing can be ill,
Her body sleepes in *Capels* monument,
And her immortall part with Angels liues.
I saw her laid lowe in her kindreds vault,
And presently tooke poste to tell it you:
O pardon me for bringing these ill newes,
Since you did leaue it for my office sir.

ROMEO
Is it in so? then I defie you starres.
2600 Thou knowest my lodging, get me inke and paper,
And hire post horses, I will hence to night.

BALTHAZER
I do beseech you sir, haue patience:
Your lookes are pale and wilde, and do import
Some misaduenture.

ROMEO   Tush thou art deceiu'd,
Leaue me, and do the thing I bid thee do.
Hast thou no Letters to me from the Frier?

BALTHAZER
No my good Lord.

ROMEO   No matter, get thee gone,
And hyre those horses, Ile be with thee straight.
                      Exit Balthazer
Well *Iuliet,* I will lie with thee to night:
2610 Lets see for meanes, O mischiefe thou art swift,
To enter in the thoughts of desperate men.
I do remember an Appothacarie,
And here abouts a dwells which late I noted,
In tattred weeds with ouerwhelming browes,
Culling of simples, meager were his lookes,
Sharpe miserie had worne him to the bones:
And in his needie shop a tortoyes hung,
An allegater stuft, and other skins
Of ill shapte fishes, and about his shelues,
2620 A beggerly account of emptie boxes,
Greene earthen pots, bladders and mustie seedes,
Remnants of packthred, and old cakes of Roses
Were thinly scattred, to make vp a shew.
Noting this penury, to my selfe I said,
An if a man did need a poyson now,
Whose sale is present death in *Mantua,*
Here liues a Catiffe wretch would sell it him.
O this same thought did but forerun my need,
And this same needie man must sell it me.
2630 As I remember this should be the house,
Being holy day, the beggers shop is shut.
What ho Appothecarie.
       Enter Apothecarie

APPOTHECARIE   Who calls so lowd?

ROMEO
Come hither man, I see that thou art poore,
    He offers money
Hold, there is fortie duckets, let me haue
A dram of poyson, such soone speeding geare,
As will dispearse it selfe through all the veines,
That the life-wearie-taker may fall dead,
And that the Trunke may be dischargd of breath,
As violently, as hastie powder fierd
Doth hurry from the fatall Canons wombe.   2640

APPOTHECARIE
Such mortall drugs I haue, but *Mantuas* lawe
Is death to any he that vtters them.

ROMEO
Art thou so bare and full of wretchednesse,
And fearst to die, famine is in thy cheekes,
Need and oppression starueth in thy eyes,
Contempt and beggerie hangs vpon thy backe:
The world is not thy friend, nor the worlds law,
The world affoords no law to make thee rich:
Then be not poore, but breake it and take this.

APPOTHECARIE
My pouertie, but not my will consents.   2650

ROMEO
I pay thy pouertie and not thy will.

APPOTHECARIE (*handing Romeo poyson*)
Put this in any liquid thing you will
And drinke it off, and if you had the strength
Of twentie men, it would dispatch you straight.

ROMEO (*giuing money*)
There is thy Gold, worse poyson to mens soules,
Doing more murther in this loathsome world,
Then these poore cõpounds that thou maiest not sell,
I sell thee poyson, thou hast sold me none,
Farewell, buy foode, and get thy selfe in flesh.
                 ⌐*Exit Apothecarie*¬
Come Cordiall and not poyson, go with me   2660
To *Iuliets* graue, for there must I vse thee.   *Exit*

    Enter Frier Iohn at one doore   Sc. 22
FRIER IOHN   (5.2)
Holy *Franciscan* Frier, brother, ho.
    Enter Lawrence at another doore

FRIER LAWRENCE
This same should be the voyce of Frier *Iohn,*
Welcome from *Mantua,* what sayes *Romeo?*
Or if his minde be writ, giue me his Letter.

FRIER IOHN
Going to find a barefoote brother out,
One of our order to assotiate me,
Here in this Citie visiting the sicke,
And finding him, the Searchers of the Towne
Suspecting that we both were in a house,   2670
Where the infectious pestilence did raigne,
Seald vp the doores, and would not let vs forth,
So that my speed to *Mantua* there was staid.

FRIER LAWRENCE
Who bare my Letter then to *Romeo?*

FRIER IOHN
  I could not send it, here it is againe,
  Nor get a messenger to bring it thee,
  So fearefull were they of infection.
FRIER LAWRENCE
  Vnhappie fortune, by my Brotherhood,
  The Letter was not nice but full of charge,
2680 Of deare import, and the neglecting it,
  May do much danger: Frier *Iohn* go hence,
  Get me an Iron Crow and bring it straight
  Vnto my Cell.
FRIER IOHN   Brother ile go and bring it thee.   *Exit*
FRIER LAWRENCE
  Now must I to the Monument alone,
  Within this three houres will faire *Iuliet* wake,
  Shee will beshrewe me much that *Romeo*
  Hath had no notice of these accidents:
  But I will write againe to *Mantua*,
  And keepe her at my Cell till *Romeo* come,
2690 Poore liuing Coarse, closde in a dead mans Tombe.
                                                    Exit

Sc. 23   *Enter Paris and his Page with flowers, sweete*
(5.3)   *water, and a torch*
PARIS
  Giue me thy Torch boy, hence and stand aloofe,
  Yet put it out, for I would not be seene:
        ⌜*His Page puts out the Torch*⌝
  Vnder yond yeug Trees lay thee all along,
  Holding thy eare close to the hollow ground,
  So shall no foote vpon the Church-yard tread,
  Being loose, vnfirme with digging vp of Graues,
  But thou shalt heare it, whistle then to me
  As signall that thou hearst some thing approach,
  Giue me those flowers, do as I bid thee, go.
PAGE ⌜*aside*⌝
2700 I am almost afraid to stand alone,
  Here in the Church-yard, yet I will aduenture.
        He hides himselfe at a distance from Paris
PARIS (*strewing flowers*)
  Sweet flower, with flowers thy Bridall bed I strew.
        He sprinkles water
    O woe, thy Canapie is dust and stones,
  Which with sweete water nightly I will dewe,
    Or wanting that, with teares distild by mones,
  The obsequies that I for thee will keepe:
  Nightly shall be, to strew thy graue and weepe.
        Whistle Page
  The Boy giues warning, something doth approach,
  What cursed foote wanders this way to night,
2710 To crosse my obsequies and true loues right?
        Enter Romeo and ⌜*Balthazer*⌝ *his man with a Torch,*
        a mattocke, and a Crow of Iron
  What with a Torch? muffle me night a while.
        He stands aside
ROMEO
  Giue me that mattocke and the wrenching Iron,

  Hold take this Letter, early in the morning
  See thou deliuer it to my Lord and Father,
  Giue me the light: vpon thy life I charge thee,
  What ere thou hearst or seest, stand all aloofe,
  And do not interrupt me in my course.
  Why I descend into this bed of death,
  Is partly to behold my Ladies face:
  But chiefly to take thence from her dead finger,   2720
  A precious Ring: a Ring that I must vse,
  In deare imployment, therefore hence be gone:
  But if thou iealous dost returne to prie
  In what I farther shall intend to doo,
  By heauen I will teare thee Ioynt by Ioynt,
  And strew this hungry Church-yard with thy lims:
  The time and my intents are sauage wilde,
  More fierce and more inexorable farre,
  Then emptie Tygers, or the roaring sea.
⌜BALTHAZER⌝
  I will be gone sir, and not trouble ye.   2730
ROMEO
  So shalt thou shew me friendship, take thou that,
        He giues money
  Liue and be prosperous, and farewell good fellow.
⌜BALTHAZER⌝ (*aside*)
  For all this same, ile hide me here about,
  His lookes I feare, and his intents I doubt.
        He hides himselfe at a distance from Romeo. ⌜*Romeo*
        begins to force open the Tombe⌝
ROMEO
  Thou detestable mawe, thou wombe of death,
  Gorg'd with the dearest morsell of the earth:
  Thus I enforce thy rotten Iawes to open,
  And in despight ile cram thee with more foode.
PARIS (*aside*)
  This is that banisht haughtie *Mountague*,
  That murdred my loues Cozin, with which greefe   2740
  It is supposed the faire creature died,
  And here is come to do some villainous shame
  To the dead bodies: I will apprehend him,
  ⌜*Drawing*⌝ Stop thy vnhallowed toyle vile *Mountague*:
  Can vengeance be pursued further then death?
  Condemned villaine, I do apprehend thee,
  Obey and go with me, for thou must die.
ROMEO
  I must indeed, and therefore came I hither,
  Good gentle youth tempt not a desprate man,
  Flie hence and leaue me, thinke vpon these gone,   2750
  Let them affright thee. I beseech thee youth,
  Put not an other sin vpon my head,
  By vrging me to furie, ô be gone,
  By heauen I loue thee better then my selfe,
  For I come hither armde against my selfe:
  Stay not, begone, liue, and hereafter say,
  A mad mans mercie bid thee run away.
PARIS
  I do defie thy conniuration,
  And apprehend thee for a Fellon here.

ROMEO (*drawing*)

2760   Wilt thou prouoke me? then haue at thee boy.
       They fight

⌈PAGE⌉

    O Lord they fight, I will go call the Watch.   *Exit*

PARIS

    O I am slaine, if thou be mercifull,
    Open the Tombe, lay me with *Iuliet*.

ROMEO

    In faith I will,   *Paris dies*
         let me peruse this face,
    Mercutios kinsman, Noble Countie *Paris*,
    What said my man, when my betossed soule
    Did not attend him as we rode? I thinke
    He told me *Paris* should haue married *Iuliet*,
    Said he not so? or did I dreame it so?

2770   Or am I mad, hearing him talke of *Iuliet*,
    To thinke it was so? O giue me thy hand,
    One writ with me in sowre misfortunes booke,
    Ile burie thee in a triumphant graue.
      ⌈*He opens the Tombe, discouering Iuliet*⌉
    A Graue, O no. A Lanthorne slaughtred youth:
    For here lies *Iuliet*, and her bewtie makes
    This Vault a feasting presence full of light.
      ⌈*He bears the body of Paris to the Tombe*⌉
    Death lie thou there by a dead man interd,
    How oft when men are at the point of death,
    Haue they bene merie? which their keepers call

2780   A lightning before death? Oh how may I
    Call this a lightning? O my Loue, my wife,
    Death that hath suckt the honey of thy breath,
    Hath had no power yet vpon thy bewtie:
    Thou art not conquerd, bewties ensigne yet
    Is crymson in thy lips and in thy cheeks,
    And deaths pale flag is not aduanced there.
    Tybalt lyest thou there in thy bloudie sheet?
    O what more fauour can I do to thee,
    Then with that hand that cut thy youth in twaine,

2790   To sunder his that was thine enemie?
    Forgiue me Couzen. Ah deare *Iuliet*
    Why art thou yet so faire? Shall I beleeue
    That vnsubstantiall death is amorous,
    And that the leane abhorred monster keepes
    Thee here in darke to be his parramour?
    For feare of that I still will staie with thee,
    And neuer from this pallat of dym night
    Depart againe, here, here, will I remaine,
    With wormes that are thy Chamber-maides: O here

2800   Will I set vp my euerlasting rest:
    And shake the yoke of inauspicious starres,
    From this world wearied flesh, eyes looke your last:
    Armes take your last embrace: And lips, O you
    The doores of breath, seale with a righteous kisse
    A datelesse bargaine to ingrossing death:
      ⌈*He kisses Iuliet, then pours poyson into a cup*⌉
    Come bitter conduct, come vnsauoury guide,
    Thou desperate Pilot, now at once run on
    The dashing Rocks, thy seasick weary barke:

    Heeres to my Loue.
      He drinkes the poyson
           O true Appothecary:
    Thy drugs are quicke. Thus with a kisse I die.   2810
      He kisses Iuliet, falles, and dies.
      Enter Frier Lawrence with Lanthorne, Crowe,
      and Spade

FRIER LAWRENCE

    S. Frances be my speede, how oft to night
    Haue my old feet stumbled at graues? Whoes there?

BALTHAZER

    Heeres one, a friend, and one that knowes you well.

FRIER LAWRENCE

    Blisse be vpon you. Tell me good my friend
    What torch is yond that vainly lends his light
    To grubs and eyelesse sculles: as I discerne,
    It burneth in the *Capels* monument.

BALTHAZER

    It doth so holy sir, and theres my maister,
    One that you loue.

FRIER LAWRENCE   Who is it?

BALTHAZER   *Romeo*.

FRIER LAWRENCE

    How long hath he bin there?

BALTHAZER   Full halfe an houre.   2820

FRIER LAWRENCE

    Go with me to the Vault.

BALTHAZER   I dare not sir.
    My Master knowes not but I am gone hence,
    And fearefully did menace me with death
    If I did stay to looke on his entents.

FRIER LAWRENCE

    Stay then ile go alone, feare comes vpon me.
    O much I feare some ill vnthriftie thing.

BALTHAZER

    As I did sleepe vnder this yeug tree heere,
    I dreampt my maister and another fought,
    And that my maister slew him.

FRIER LAWRENCE   *Romeo*.
      He ⌈*stoops and*⌉ *lookes on the blood and weapons*
    Alack alack, what bloud is this which staines   2830
    The stony entrance of this Sepulchre?
    What meane these maisterlesse and goarie swords
    To lie discolour'd by this place of peace?
    Romeo, oh pale! who else, what *Paris* too?
    And steept in bloud? ah what an vnkind hower
    Is guiltie of this lamentable chance?
      Iuliet awakes ⌈*and rises*⌉
    The Lady stirres.

IULIET

    O comfortable Frier, where is my Lord?
    I do remember well where I should be:
    And there I am, where is my *Romeo*?   2840

FRIER LAWRENCE

    I heare some noyse. Lady, come from that nest
    Of death, contagion, and vnnaturall sleepe,
    A greater power then we can contradict
    Hath thwarted our intents, come, come away,

Thy husband in thy bosome there lies dead:
And *Paris* too, come ile dispose of thee,
Among a Sisterhood of holy Nunnes:
Stay not to question, for the watch is comming,
Come go good *Iuliet*, I dare no longer stay.   *Exit*

IULIET

2850   Go get thee hence, for I will not away.
Whats heere? a cup closd in my true loues hand?
Poison I see hath bin his timelesse end:
O churle, drunke all, and left no friendly drop
To help me after, I will kisse thy lips,
Happlie some poyson yet doth hang on them,
To make me dye with a restoratiue.
        She kisses Romeos lips
Thy lips are warme.

CHIEF WATCHMAN ⌈*within*⌉ Leade boy, which way.

IULIET

Yea noise? then ile be briefe.
        She takes Romeos dagger
                        O happy dagger
This is thy sheath, there rust and let me dye.
        She stabs herselfe, falles, and dies.
        Enter Page and Watch

⌈PAGE⌉

2860   This is the place there where the torch doth burne.

CHIEF WATCHMAN

The ground is bloudie, search about the Churchyard.
Go some of you, who ere you find attach.
                        Exeunt some Watchmen
Pittifull sight, heere lies the Countie slaine,
And *Iuliet* bleeding, warme, and newlie dead:
Who heere hath laine this two daies buried.
Go tell the Prince, runne to the *Capulets*,
Raise vp the *Mountagues*, some others search,
                        Exeunt other Watchmen ⌈*seuerally*⌉
We see the ground whereon these woes do lye,
But the true ground of all these piteous woes

2870   We cannot without circumstance descry.
        Enter ⌈*Watchmen*⌉ *with Romeos man Balthazer*

⌈2.⌉ WATCHMAN

Heres *Romeos* man, we found him in the Churchyard.

CHIEF WATCHMAN

Hold him in safetie till the Prince come hither.
        Enter Frier Lawrence, and another Watchman

3. WATCHMAN

Here is a Frier that trembles, sighes, and weepes,
We tooke this Mattocke and this Spade from him,
As he was comming from this Church-yards side.

CHIEF WATCHMAN

A great suspition, stay the Frier too.
        Enter the Prince ⌈*with others*⌉

PRINCE

What misaduenture is so early vp,
That calls our person from our morning rest?
        Enter Capulet and his wife

CAPULET

What should it be that is so shrikd abroad?

CAPULETS WIFE

O the people in the street crie *Romeo*,   2880
Some *Iuliet*, and some *Paris*, and all runne
With open outcry toward our Monument.

PRINCE

What feare is this which startles in our eares?

CHIEF WATCHMAN

Soueraine, here lies the County *Paris* slain,
And *Romeo* dead, and *Iuliet* dead before,
Warme and new kild.

PRINCE

Search, seeke & know how this foule murder comes.

CHIEF WATCHMAN

Here is a Frier, and slaughterd *Romeos* man,
With Instruments vpon them, fit to open
These dead mens Tombes.   2890

CAPULET

O heauens! O wife looke how our daughter bleeds!
This dagger hath mistane, for loe his house
Is emptie on the back of *Mountague*,
And it missheathed in my daughters bosome.

CAPULETS WIFE

O me, this sight of death, is as a Bell
That warnes my old age to a sepulcher.
        Enter Mountague

PRINCE

Come *Mountague*, for thou art early vp
To see thy sonne and heire, more early downe.

MOUNTAGUE

Alas my liege, my wife is dead to night,
Griefe of my sonnes exile hath stopt her breath.   2900
What further woe conspires against mine age?

PRINCE Looke and thou shalt see.

MOUNTAGUE (*seeing Romeos body*)
O thou vntaught, what maners is in this,
To presse before thy father to a graue?

PRINCE

Seale vp the mouth of outrage for a while,
Till we can cleare these ambiguities,
And know their spring, their head, their true discent,
And then will I be generall of your woes,
And leade you euen to death, meane time forbeare,
And let mischance be slaue to patience,   2910
Bring foorth the parties of suspition.

FRIER LAWRENCE

I am the greatest able to do least,
Yet most suspected as the time and place
Doth make against me of this direfull murther:
And heere I stand both to impeach and purge
My selfe condemned, and my selfe excusde.

PRINCE

Then say at once what thou dost know in this?

FRIER LAWRENCE

I will be briefe, for my short date of breath
Is not so long as is a tedious tale.
Romeo there dead, was husband to that *Iuliet*,   2920
And she there dead, that *Romeos* faithfull wife:
I married them, and their stolne marriage day

411

Was *Tibalts* doomesday, whose vntimely death
Banisht the new-made Bridegroome from this Citie,
For whome, and not for *Tibalt, Iuliet* pinde.
You to remoue that siege of griefe from her
Betrothd and would haue married her perforce
To Countie *Paris*. Then comes she to me,
And with wild lookes bid me deuise some meane
2930   To rid her from this second mariage:
Or in my Cell there would she kill her selfe.
Then gaue I her (so tuterd by my art)
A sleeping potion, which so tooke effect
As I intended, for it wrought on her
The forme of death, meane time I writ to *Romeo*
That he should hither come as this dire night
To help to take her from her borrowed graue,
Being the time the potions force should cease.
But he which bore my letter, Frier *Iohn*,
2940   Was stayed by accident, and yesternight
Returnd my letter back, then all alone
At the prefixed hower of her waking,
Came I to take her from her kindreds Vault,
Meaning to keepe her closely at my Cell,
Till I conueniently could send to *Romeo*.
But when I came, some minute ere the time
Of her awakening, here vntimely lay,
The Noble *Paris*, and true *Romeo* dead.
She wakes, and I entreated her come forth
2950   And beare this worke of heauen with patience:
But then a noyse did scare me from the Tombe,
And she too desperate would not go with me:
But as it seemes, did violence on her selfe.
Al this I know, & to the marriage
Her Nurse is priuie: and if ought in this
Miscaried by my fault, let my old life
Be sacrific'd some houre before his time,
Vnto the rigour of seuerest law.

PRINCE

2960   We still haue knowne thee for a holy man,
Wheres *Romeos* man? what can he say to this?

BALTHAZER

I brought my maister newes of *Iuliets* death,
And then in poste he came from *Mantua*,
To this same place, to this same monument.
This Letter he early bid me giue his Father,

And threatned me with death, going in the Vault,
If I departed not, and left him there.

PRINCE

Giue me the Letter, I will looke on it.
He takes the Letter
Where is the Counties Page that raisd the Watch?
Sirrah, what made your maister in this place?

PAGE

He came with flowers to strew his Ladies graue,   2970
And bid me stand aloofe, and so I did,
Anon comes one with light to ope the Tombe,
And by and by my maister drew on him,
And then I ran away to call the Watch.

PRINCE

This Letter doth make good the Friers words,
Their course of Loue, the tidings of her death,
And here he writes, that he did buy a poyson
Of a poore Pothecarie, and therewithall,
Came to this Vault, to die and lye with *Iuliet*.
Where be these enemies? *Capulet, Mountague?*   2980
See what a scourge is laide vpon your hate?
That heauen finds means to kil your ioyes with loue,
And I for winking at your discords too,
Haue lost a brace of kinsmen, all are punisht.

CAPULET

O brother *Mountague*, giue me thy hand,
This is my daughters ioynture, for no more
Can I demaund.

MOUNTAGUE   But I can giue thee more,
For I will raise her statue in pure gold,
That whiles *Verona* by that name is knowne,
There shall no figure at such rate be set,   2990
As that of true and faithfull *Iuliet*.

CAPULET

As rich shall *Romeos* by his Ladies lie,
Poore sacrifices of our enmitie.

PRINCE

A glooming peace this morning with it brings,
The Sun for sorrow will not shew his head:
Go hence to haue more talke of these sad things,
Some shall be pardond, and some punished.
For neuer was a Storie of more wo,
Then this of *Iuliet* and her *Romeo*.
⌈*The Tombe is closed.*⌉ *Exeunt*

FINIS

RICHARD II

THE subject-matter of *Richard II* seemed inflammatorily topical to Shakespeare's contemporaries. Richard, who had notoriously indulged his favourites, had been compelled to yield his throne to Henry Bullingbrooke, Earl of Hereford: like Richard, the ageing Queen Elizabeth had no obvious successor, and she too encouraged favourites—such as the Earl of Essex—who might aspire to the throne. When Shakespeare's play first appeared in print (in 1597), and in the two succeeding editions printed during Elizabeth's life, the episode (1977-2140) showing Richard yielding the crown was omitted; and in 1601, on the day before Essex led his ill-fated rebellion against Elizabeth, his fellow conspirators commissioned a special performance in the hope of arousing popular support, even though the play was said to be 'long out of use'—surprisingly, since it was probably written no earlier than 1595.

But Shakespeare introduced no obvious topicality into his dramatization of Richard's reign, for which he read widely while using Raphael Holinshed's *Chronicles* (1577, revised and enlarged in 1587) as his main source of information. In choosing to write about Richard II (1367-1400) he was returning to the beginning of the story whose ending he had staged in *Richard III*; for Bullingbrooke's usurpation of the throne to which Richard's hereditary right was indisputable had set in train the series of events finally expiated only in the union of the houses of York and Lancaster celebrated in the last speech of *Richard III*. Like *Richard III*, this is a tragical history, focusing on a single character; but Richard II is a far more introverted and morally ambiguous figure than Richard III. In this play, written entirely in verse, Shakespeare forgoes stylistic variety in favour of an intense, plangent lyricism.

Our early impressions of Richard are unsympathetic. Having banished Mowbray and Bullingbrooke, he behaves callously to Bullingbrooke's father, Iohn of Gaunt, a stern upholder of the old order to whose warning against his irresponsible behaviour he pays no attention, and upon Gaunt's death confiscates his property with no regard for Bullingbrooke's rights. During Richard's absence on an Irish campaign, Bullingbrooke returns to England and gains support in his efforts to claim his inheritance. Gradually, as the balance of power shifts, Richard makes deeper claims on the audience's sympathy. When he confronts Bullingbrooke at Flint Castle (Sc. 9) he eloquently laments his imminent deposition even though Bullingbrooke insists that he comes only to claim what is his; soon afterwards (1930-5) the Duke of Yorke announces Richard's abdication. The transference of power is effected in a scene of lyrical expansiveness, and Richard becomes a pitiable figure as he is led to imprisonment in Pomfret (Pontefract) Castle while his former queen is banished to France. Richard's self-exploration reaches its climax in his soliloquy spoken shortly before his murder at the hands of Pierce Exton; at the end of the play, Henry, anxious and guilt-laden, denies responsibility for the murder and plans an expiatory pilgrimage to the Holy Land.

Our text is based upon the first edition (1597), probably printed from Shakespeare's papers; but we make use of the Folio (apparently prepared with access to a prompt-book) for the abdication episode (1977-2140) and occasional readings elsewhere.

THE NAMES OF THE ACTORS

KING RICHARD the second

The QUEENE, his wife

Iohn of GAUNT, Duke of Lancaster, Richards Vncle

Harry BULLINGBROOKE, Duke of Hereford, Iohn of Gauntes sonne,
  later KING HENRY the fourth

DUCHESSE OF GLOCESTER, wife of Gaunt and Yorkes brother

Duke of YORKE, King Richards Vncle

DUTCHESSE OF YORK

Duke of AUMERLE, their sonne

Thomas MOWBRAY, Duke of Norfolke

GREENE
BAGOT } followers of King Richard
BUSHIE

Percie, Earle of NORTHUMBERLAND
HARRY PERCIE, his sonne
Lord ROSSE } of Bullingbrookes partie
Lord WILLOUGHBY

Earle of SALISBURY
Bishop of CARLEIL } of King Richards partie
Sir Stephen SCROOPE

Lord BARKLY

Lord FITZWATERS

Duke of SURRIE

ABBOT of Westminster

Sir Pierce EXTON

LORD MARSHALL

HERALDS

CAPTAINE of the Welch Army

LADIES attending the Queene

GARDENER

Gardeners MEN

Extons MEN

KEEPER of the prison at Pomfret

GROOME of King Richards stable

Lords, Souldiers, Attendants

414

The Tragedie of King Richard the second

Enter King Richard, Iohn of Gaunt, with the Lord
Marshall, other Nobles and attendants

KING RICHARD

Ould Iohn of Gaunt time honourd Lancaster,
Hast thou according to thy oath and bande
Brought hither Henrie Herford thy bolde sonne,
Here to make good the boistrous late appeale,
Which then our leysure would not let vs heare
Against the Duke of Norfolke, Thomas Moubray?

GAUNT I haue my Leige.

KING RICHARD

Tell me moreouer hast thou sounded him,
If he appeale the Duke on ancient malice,
10   Or worthily as a good subiect should
On some knowne ground of treacherie in him.

GAUNT

As neere as I could sift him on that argument,
On some apparent daunger seene in him,
Aimde at your highnes, no inueterate malice.

KING RICHARD

Then call them to our presence,   ⌈*Exit one or more*⌉
                                    face to face,
And frowning brow to brow our selues will heare,
The accuser and the accused freely speake:
High stomackt are they both and full of ire,
In rage, deafe as the sea, hastie as fire.

Enter Bullingbrooke and Mowbray

BULLINGBROOKE

20   Manie yeares of happie daies befall,
My gratious soueraigne my most louing liege.

MOWBRAY

Each day still better others happines,
Vntill the heauens enuying earths good hap,
Adde an immortall title to your Crowne.

KING RICHARD

We thanke you both, yet one but flatters vs,
As well appeareth by the cause you come,
Namely to appeale each other of high treason:
Coosin of Herford, what dost thou obiect
Against the Duke of Norffolke Thomas Mowbray?

BULLINGBROOKE

30   First, heauen be the record to my speech,
In the deuotion of a subiects loue,
Tendring the pretious safetie of my Prince,
And free from other misbegotten hate,
Come I appellant to this princely presence.
Now Thomas Mowbray do I turne to thee,
And marke my greeting well: for what I speake
My body shall make good vpon this earth,
Or my diuine soule answer it in heauen:
Thou art a traitour and a miscreant,
40   Too good to be so, and too bad to liue,
Since the more faire and cristall is the skie,
The vglier seeme the cloudes that in it flie:

Once more, the more to aggrauate the note,
With a foule traitors name stuffe I thy throte,
And wish (so please my Soueraigne) ere I moue,
What my tong speaks, my right drawen sword may
     proue.

MOWBRAY

Let not my cold wordes here accuse my zeale,
Tis not the triall of a womans warre,
The bitter clamour of two eger tongues
Can arbitrate this cause betwixt vs twaine,   50
The bloud is hote that must be coold for this,
Yet can I not of such tame patience boast,
As to be huisht, and naught at all to say.
First the faire reuerence of your Highnesse curbs me,
From giuing reines and spurres to my free speech,
Which else would post vntill it had returnd
These termes of treason doubled downe his throat:
Setting aside his high blouds royaltie,
And let him be no kinsman to my Liege,
I do defie him, and I spit at him,   60
Call him a slaunderous coward, and a villaine,
Which to maintaine, I would allow him ods,
And meete him were I tied to runne afoote,
Euen to the frozen ridges of the Alpes,
Or any other ground inhabitable,
Where euer Englishman durst set his foote,
Meane time, let this defend my loyaltie,
By all my hopes most falsly doth he lie.

BULLINGBROOKE (*throwing downe his gage*)

Pale trembling coward there I throw my gage,
Disclaiming here the kinred of the King,   70
And lay aside my high bloudes royaltie,
Which Feare, not Reuerence makes thee to except.
If guilty dread haue left thee so much strength,
As to take vp mine honours pawne, then stowpe,
By that, and all the rites of Knighthoode else,
Will I make good against thee arme to arme,
What I haue spoke, or thou canst worse deuise.

MOWBRAY (*taking vp the gage*)

I take it vp, and by that sword I sweare,
Which gently laid my Knighthood on my shoulder,
Ile answer thee in any faire degree,   80
Or chiualrous designe of knightly triall:
And when I mount, aliue may I not light,
If I be traitor or vniustly fight.

KING RICHARD (*to Bullingbrooke*)

What doth our cousin lay to Mowbraies charge?
It must be great that can inherit vs,
So much as of a thought of ill in him.

BULLINGBROOKE

Looke what I speake, my life shall proue it true,
That Mowbray hath receiude eight thousand nobles
In name of Lendings for your Highnes souldiours,
The which he hath detaind for lewd imployments,   90

Like a false traitour, and iniurious villaine:
Besides I say, and will in battle proue,
Or here, or elsewhere to the furthest Verge
That euer was surueyed by English eye,
That all the treasons for these eighteene yeares,
Complotted and contriued in this land:
Fetch from false Mowbray their first head and spring.
Further I say and further will maintaine
Vpon his bad life to make all this good,
100   That he did plotte the Duke of Glocesters death,
Suggest his soone beleeuing aduersaries,
And consequently like a traitour coward,
Slucte out his innocent soule through streames of
    bloud,
Which bloud, like sacrificing Abels cries,
Euen from the tounglesse Cauernes of the earth,
To me for iustice and rough chastisement:
And by the glorious worth of my descent,
This arme shall do it, or this life be spent.
    KING RICHARD
How high a pitch his resolution soares,
110   Thomas of Norfolke what saist thou to this?
    MOWBRAY
Oh let my soueraigne turne awaie his face,
And bid his eares a little while be deafe,
Till I haue tolde this slaunder of his bloud,
How God and good men hate so foule a lier.
    KING RICHARD
Mowbray impartiall are our eies and eares,
Were he my brother, nay, my kingdomes heire,
As he is but my fathers brothers sonne,
Now by my scepters awe I make a vowe,
Such neighbour neerenes to our sacred bloud
120   Should nothing priuiledge him nor partialize
The vnstooping firmenesse of my vpright soule,
He is our subiect Mowbray so art thou,
Free speech and fearelesse I to thee allowe.
    MOWBRAY
Then Bullingbrooke as lowe as to thy heart
Through the false passage of thy throate thou liest.
Three partes of that receipte I had for Callice,
Disburst I duely to his highnesse souldiers,
The other part reserude I by consent,
For that my soueraigne liege was in my debt,
130   Vpon remainder of a deare account:
Since last I went to France to fetch his Queene:
Now swallow downe that lie. For Glocesters death,
I slewe him not but to my owne disgrace,
Neglected my sworne duety in that case:
For you my noble Lord of Lancaster,
The honourable father to my foe,
Once did I lay an ambushe for your life,
A trespasse that doth vex my grieued soule:
But ere I last receiude the Sacrament,
140   I did confesse it, and exactly begd
Your graces pardon, and I hope I had it.
This is my fault, as for the rest appeald
It issues from the rancour of a villaine,

A recreant and most degenerate traitour,
Which in my selfe I boldly will defende,
    He throwes downe his gage
And enterchangeably hurle downe my gage
Vpon this ouerweening traitors foote,
To proue my selfe a loyal Gentleman,
Euen in the best bloud chamberd in his bosome,
In haste wherof most hartily I pray   150
Your highnes to assigne our triall day.
    ⌜*Bullingbrooke takes vp the gage*⌝
    KING RICHARD
Wrath kindled gentlemen be ruld by me,
Lets purge this choler without letting bloud,
This we prescribe though no Phisition,
Deepe malice makes too deepe incision,
Forget, forgiue, conclude and be agreed,
Our doctors say, this is no time to bleede:
Good Vnckle let this ende where it begonne,
Weele calme the Duke of Norfolke, you your sonne.
    GAUNT
To be a make-peace shal become my age,   160
Throw downe (my sonne) the Duke of Norfolkes gage.
    KING RICHARD
And Norfolke throw downe his.
    GAUNT   When Harry, when?
Obedience bids I should not bid againe.
    KING RICHARD
Norfolke throw downe we bid, there is no boote.
    MOWBRAY (*kneeling*)
My selfe I throw dread soueraigne at thy foote,
My life thou shalt command, but not my shame,
The one my duety owes, but my faire name
Despight of death that liues vpon my graue,
To darke dishonours vse thou shalt not haue:
I am disgraste, impeacht, and baffuld heere,   170
Pierst to the soule with Slaunders venomd speare,
The which no balme can cure but his heart bloud
Which breathde this poyson.
    KING RICHARD   Rage must be withstoode,
Giue me his gage; Lions make Leopards tame.
    MOWBRAY ⌜*standing*⌝
Yea but not change his spots: take but my shame,
And I resigne my gage, my deare deare Lord,
The purest treasure mortall times afford,
Is spotlesse Reputation, that away
Men are but guilded loame, or painted clay,
A iewell in a ten times bard vp chest,   180
Is a bold spirit in a loyall breast:
Mine honour is my life, both grow in one,
Take honour from me, and my life is done:
Then (deare my Liege) mine honour let me trie,
In that I liue, and for that will I die.
    KING RICHARD
Coosin, throw downe your gage, do you beginne.
    BULLINGBROOKE
O God defend my soule from such deepe sinne,
Shall I seeme Crest-fallen in my fathers sight?
Or with pale beggar-feare impeach my height,

190 Before this out-darde Dastard? ere my tong
Shall wound my honour with such feeble wrong,
Or sound so base a parle, my teeth shall teare
The slauish motiue of recanting feare,
And spit it bleeding in his high disgrace,
Where Shame doth harbour euen in Mowbraies face.
                                        ⌈*Exit Gaunt*⌉
KING RICHARD
We were not borne to sue, but to commaund,
Which since we cannot do, to make you friends,
Be ready as your liues shall answere it,
At Couentry vpon saint Lamberts day,
200 There shall your swords and launces arbitrate
The swelling difference of your setled hate,
Since we cannot atone you, we shall see
Iustice designe the Victors chiualrie,
Lord Marshal, commaund our Officers at Armes,
Be ready to direct these home allarmes.   *Exeunt*

Sc. 2   *Enter Iohn of Gaunt with the Duchesse of Glocester*
(1.2) GAUNT
Alas, the part I had in Glocesters bloud,
Doth more sollicite me than your exclaimes,
To stirre against the butchers of his life,
But since correction lieth in those hands,
210 Which made the fault that we cannot correct:
Put we our quarrell to the will of heauen,
Who when they see the houres ripe on earth,
Will raine hot vengeance on offenders heads.
DUCHESSE OF GLOCESTER
Findes brotherhood in thee no sharper spurre?
Hath loue in thy old bloud no liuing fire?
Edwards seuen sonnes whereof thy selfe art one,
Were as seuen viols of his sacred bloud,
Or seuen faire branches springing from one roote:
Some of those seuen are dried by natures course,
220 Some of those branches by the Destinies cut:
But *Thomas* my deare Lord, my life, my Glocester,
One violl full of Edwards sacred bloud,
One flourishing branch of his most royall roote
Is crackt, and all the precious liquor spilt,
Is hackt downe, and his summer leaues all faded
By Enuies hand, and Murders bloudy axe.
Ah Gaunt, his bloud was thine, that bed, that womb,
That mettall, that selfe mould, that fashiond thee
Made him a man: and though thou liu'st and
          breathest,
230 Yet art thou slaine in him, thou doost consent
In some large measure to thy fathers death,
In that thou seest thy wretched brother die,
Who was the modell of thy fathers life:
Call it not patience Gaunt, it is dispaire,
In suffring thus thy brother to be slaughtred,
Thou shewest the naked pathway to thy life,
Teaching sterne Murder how to butcher thee:
That which in meane men we intitle Patience,
Is pale cold Cowardice in noble breasts.

What shall I saie? to safegard thine owne life,   240
The best way is to venge my Glocesters death.
GAUNT
Gods is the quarrell for Gods substitute,
His deputy annointed in his sight,
Hath causd his death, the which if wrongfully,
Let heauen reuenge, for I may neuer lift
An angry arme against his minister.
DUCHESSE OF GLOCESTER
Where then alas may I complaine my selfe?
GAUNT
To God the widdowes Champion and defence.
DUCHESSE OF GLOCESTER
Why then I will; farewell olde Gaunt,
Thou goest to Couentry, there to behold   250
Our Coosen Hereford and fell Mowbray fight.
O set my husbands wronges on Herefords speare,
That it may enter butcher Mowbraies brest:
Or if misfortune misse the first carier,
Be Mowbraies sinnes so heauy in his bosome
That they may breake his foming coursers backe,
And throw the rider headlong in the lists,
A caitiue recreant to my Coosen Hereford,
Farewell old Gaunt, thy sometimes brothers wife,
With her companion Griefe must end her life.   260
GAUNT
Sister farewell, I must to Couentry,
As much good stay with thee, as go with me.
DUCHESSE OF GLOCESTER
Yet one word more, griefe boundeth where it fals,
Not with the emptie hollownes, but weight:
I take my leaue before I haue begone,
For sorrow endes not when it seemeth done:
Commend me to thy brother Edmund Yorke,
Lo this is all: nay yet depart not so,
Though this be al, doe not so quickly go:
I shall remember more: Bid him, ah what?   270
With all good speede at Plashie visite me,
Alacke and what shall good olde Yorke there see,
But empty lodgings and vnfurnisht wals,
Vnpeopled offices, vntrodden stones,
And what heare there for welcome but my grones?
Therfore commend me, let him not come there,
To seeke out sorrow that dwels euery where,
Desolate desolate will I hence and die:
The last leaue of thee takes my weeping eie.
                              Exeunt ⌈*seuerally*⌉

             Enter Lord Marshall ⌈*with officers setting out*   Sc. 3
             chaires⌉, *and the Duke Aumerle*   (1.3)
LORD MARSHALL
My Lord Aumerle is Harry Herford armde?   280
AUMERLE
Yea at all points, and longs to enter in.
LORD MARSHALL
The Duke of Norfolke sprightfully and bold,
Staies but the summons of the appellants trumpet.

AUMERLE

  Why then the Champions are prepard and stay
  For nothing but his maiesties approach.
     The trumpets sound and the King enters with
     Gaunt, ⌈Bushie, Bagot, Greene,⌉ and other nobles;
     when they are set, enter Mowbray Duke of Norfolke
     in armes defendant, ⌈and Herald⌉

KING RICHARD (*to Mowbray*)

  Marshall demaunde of yonder Champion,
  The cause of his arriuall here in armes,
  Aske him his name, and orderly proceede
  To sweare him in the iustice of his cause.

LORD MARSHALL (*to Mowbray*)

290   In Gods name and the Kings say who thou art.
  And why thou comst thus knightly clad in armes,
  Against what man thou comst and what thy quarell.
  Speake truly on thy knighthoode, and thy oth,
  As so defend the heauen and thy valour.

MOWBRAY

  My name is Thomas Mowbray Duke of Norfolke,
  Who hither come ingaged by my oath,
  (Which God defende a Knight should violate)
  Both to defend my loyalty and truth,
  To God, my King, and my succeeding issue,
300   Against the Duke of Herford that appeales me,
  And by the grace of God, and this mine arme,
  To proue him in defending of my selfe,
  A traitour to my God, my King, and me,
  And as I truely fight, defend me heauen.
     ⌈*He sits.*⌉
     The trumpets sound. Enter Bullingbrooke Duke of
     Hereford appellant in armour, ⌈and Herald⌉

KING RICHARD

  Marshall aske yonder Knight in armes,
  Both who he is, and why he commeth hither,
  Thus plated in habiliments of warre,
  And formally according to our lawe,
  Depose him in the iustice of his cause.

LORD MARSHALL (*to Bullingbrooke*)

310   What is thy name? and wherfore comst thou hither,
  Before king Richard in his royall lists?
  Against whom comest thou? and whats thy quarrell?
  Speake like a true Knight, so defend thee heauen.

BULLINGBROOKE

  Harry of Herford, Lancaster and Darbie
  Am I, who ready here do stand in Armes
  To proue by Gods grace, and my bodies valour
  In lists, on *Thomas Mowbray* Duke of Norffolke,
  That he is a traitour foule and dangerous,
  To God of heauen, king Richard and to me:
320   And as I truely fight, defend me heauen.
     ⌈*He sits*⌉

LORD MARSHALL

  On paine of death, no person be so bold,
  Or daring, hardy, as to touch the listes,
  Except the Martiall and such officers
  Appoynted to direct these faire designes.

BULLINGBROOKE ⌈*standing*⌉

  Lord Martiall, let me kisse my Souereignes hand,
  And bow my knee before his Maiestie,
  For Mowbray and my selfe are like two men,
  That vow a long and wearie pilgrimage,
  Then let vs take a ceremonious leaue,
  And louing farewell of our seuerall friends.   330

LORD MARSHALL (*to King Richard*)

  The appellant in all duety greetes your Highnes,
  And craues to kisse your hand, and take his leaue.

KING RICHARD

  We will descend and fold him in our armes,
     He descends from his seat and embraces
     Bullingbrooke
  Coosin of Herford, as thy cause is iust,
  So be thy fortune in this royall fight:
  Farewell my bloud, which if to day thou shead,
  Lament we may, but not reuenge the dead.

BULLINGBROOKE

  O let no noble eie prophane a teare
  For me, if I be gorde with Mowbraies speare:
  As confident as is the Falcons flight   340
  Against a bird, do I with Mowbray fight.
  (*To the Lord Marshall*) My louing Lord, I take my
     leaue of you:
  (*To Aumerle*) Of you (my noble cousin) Lord Aumarle,
  Not sicke although I haue to do with death,
  But lusty, yong and cheerely drawing breth:
  Loe, as at English feasts so I regreet
  The daintiest last, to make the end most sweet.
  (*To Gaunt, ⌈kneeling⌉*) Oh thou the earthly Authour of
     my bloud,
  Whose youthfull spirite in me regenerate
  Doth with a two-fold vigour lift me vp,   350
  To reach at Victory aboue my head:
  Adde proofe vnto mine armour with thy prayers,
  And with thy blessings steele my launces point,
  That it may enter Mowbraies waxen cote.
  And furbish new the name of Iohn a Gaunt,
  Euen in the lustie hauiour of his sonne.

GAUNT

  God in thy good cause make thee prosperous,
  Be swift like lightning in the execution,
  And let thy blowes doubly redoubled,
  Fall like amazing thunder on the caske   360
  Of thy aduerse pernitious enemy,
  Rowze vp thy youthfull bloud, be valiant and liue.

BULLINGBROOKE ⌈*standing*⌉

  Mine innocence and saint George to thriue.

MOWBRAY ⌈*standing*⌉

  How euer God or Fortune cast my lot,
  There liues or dies true to King Richards throne,
  A loyall, iust, and vpright Gentleman:
  Neuer did captiue with a freer heart
  Cast off his chaines of bondage, and embrace
  His golden vncontrould enfranchisment,
  More than my dauncing soule doth celebrate   370
  This feast of battle with mine aduersarie,

Most mighty Liege, and my companion Peeres,
Take from my mouth the wish of happy yeeres,
As gentle, and as iocund as to iest
Go I to fight, truth hath a quiet brest.

KING RICHARD
Farewell (my Lord) securely I espie,
Vertue with Valour couched in thine eie,
Order the triall Martiall, and beginne.

LORD MARSHALL
Harry of Herford, Lancaster and Darby,
380 Receiue thy launce, and God defend the right.
         ⌈An officer beares a launce to Bullingbrooke⌉

BULLINGBROOKE
Strong as a tower in hope I cry, Amen.

LORD MARSHALL (to an officer)
Go beare this lance to Thomas Duke of Norfolke.
         ⌈An officer beares a launce to Mowbray⌉

HERALD I
Harry of Herford, Lancaster, and Darby
Stands here, for God, his soueraigne, and himselfe,
On paine to be found false and recreant,
To proue the Duke of Norfolke Thomas Mowbray
A traitor to his God, his king, and him,
And dares him to set forward to the fight.

HERALD 2
Here standeth Thomas Mowbray D. of Norfolk
390 On paine to be found false and recreant,
Both to defend himselfe, and to approue
Henry of Hereford, Lancaster, and Darby,
To God, his soueraigne, and to him disloyall,
Couragiously, and with a free desire,
Attending but the signall to beginne.

LORD MARSHALL
Sound trumpets, and set forward Combatants:
         ⌈A charge is sounded.⌉
         King Richard throws downe his warder
Stay, the king hath throwen his warder downe.

KING RICHARD
Let them lay by their helmets, and their speares,
And both returne backe to their chaires againe.
         ⌈Bullingbrooke and Mowbray disarme and sit⌉
(To the nobles) Withdraw with vs, and let the trumpets
400   sound,
While we returne these dukes what we decree.
         A long flourish, during which King Richard and his
         nobles withdraw and hold counsell, ⌈then come
         forward⌉. King Richard addresses Bullingbrooke and
         Mowbray
Draw neere and list what with our counsell we haue
         done:
For that our kingdomes earth should not be soild
With that deare bloud which it hath fostered:
And for our eies do hate the dire aspect
Of ciuill wounds plowd vp with neighbours swords,
Which so rouzde vp with boistrous vntunde drummes,
With harsh resounding trumpets dreadfull bray,
And grating shocke of wrathfull yron armes,
410 Might from our quiet confines fright faire Peace,

And make vs wade euen in our kinreds bloud;
Therefore we banish you our territories:
You cousin Hereford vpon paine of life,
Til twice fiue summers haue enricht our fields,
Shall not regreete our faire dominions,
But treade the stranger paths of banishment.

BULLINGBROOKE
Your will be done; this must my comfort be,
That Sunne that warmes you here, shall shine on me,
And those his golden beames to you heere lent,
Shall point on me, and guilde my banishment.   420

KING RICHARD
Norfolke, for thee remaines a heauier doome,
Which I with some vnwillingnesse pronounce,
The slie slow houres shall not determinate
The datelesse limite of thy deere exile,
The hoplesse word of neuer to returne,
Breathe I against thee, vpon paine of life.

MOWBRAY
A heauy sentence, my most soueraigne Liege,
And all vnlookt for from your Highnesse mouth,
A deerer merit not so deepe a maime,
As to be cast forth in the common ayre   430
Haue I deserued at your Highnesse hands:
The language I haue learnt these forty yeeres,
My natiue English now I must forgo,
And now my tongues vse is to me, no more
Than an vnstringed violl or a harpe,
Or like a cunning instrument casde vp,
Or being open, put into his hands
That knowes no touch to tune the harmonie:
Within my mouth you haue engaold my tongue,
Doubly portculist with my teeth and lippes,   440
And dull vnfeeling barren ignorance
Is made my Gaoler to attend on me:
I am too olde to fawne vpon a nurse,
Too far in yeeres to be a pupill now,
What is thy sentence then but speechlesse death?
Which robbes my tongue from breathing natiue breath.

KING RICHARD
It bootes thee not to be compassionate,
After our sentence playning comes too late.

MOWBRAY
Then thus I turne me from my countries light,
To dwel in solemne shades of endlesse night.   450

KING RICHARD
Returne againe, and take an othe with thee,
(To both) Lay on our royall sword your banist hands,
Sweare by the duty that you owe to God,
(Our part therein we banish with your selues,)
To keepe the oath that we administer:
You neuer shall, so helpe you truth and God,
Embrace each others loue in banishment,
Nor neuer looke vpon each others face,
Nor neuer write, regreete, nor reconcile
This lowring tempest of your home-bred hate,   460
Nor neuer by aduised purpose meete,
To plot, contriue, or complot any ill,
Gainst vs, our state, our subiects, or our land.

BULLINGBROOKE

I sweare.

MOWBRAY   And I, to keepe al this.

BULLINGBROOKE

Norffolke, so fare as to mine enemy:
By this time, had the King permitted vs,
One of our soules had wandred in the aire,
Banisht this fraile sepulchre of our flesh,
As now our flesh is banisht from this land,

470   Confesse thy treasons ere thou flie the realme,
Since thou hast far to go, beare not along
The clogging burthen of a guiltie soule.

MOWBRAY

No Bullingbrooke, if euer I were traitour,
My name be blotted from the booke of life,
And I from heauen banisht as from hence:
But what thou art, God, thou, and I, do know,
And al too soone (I feare) the King shall rew:
Farewell (my Liege) now no way can I stray,
Saue backe to England al the worlds my way.   *Exit*

KING RICHARD

480   Vncle, euen in the glasses of thine eyes,
I see thy grieued heart: thy sad aspect
Hath from the number of his banisht yeeres
Pluckt foure away, (*to Bullingbrooke*) six frozen
      winters spent,
Returne with welcome home from banishment.

BULLINGBROOKE

How long a time lies in one little word,
Foure lagging winters and foure wanton springes,
End in a word, such is the breath of Kinges.

GAUNT

I thanke my liege that in regard of me,
He shortens foure yeares of my sonnes exile,

490   But little vantage shall I reape thereby:
For eare the six yeares that he hath to spend
Can change their moones, and bring their times
      about,
My oile-dried lampe, and time bewasted light
Shall be extinct with age and endlesse night,
My inch of taper will be burnt and done,
And blindfold Death not let me see my sonne.

KING RICHARD

Why Vnckle thou hast many yeares to liue.

GAUNT

But not a minute King that thou canst giue,
Shorten my daies thou canst with sudden sorrowe,

500   And plucke nights from me, but not lend a morrow:
Thou canst helpe time to furrow me with age,
But stoppe no wrinckle in his pilgrimage:
Thy word is currant with him for my death,
But dead, thy kingdome cannot buy my breath.

KING RICHARD

Thy sonne is banisht vpon good aduise,
Whereto thy tong a party verdict gaue,
Why at our iustice seemst thou then to lowre?

GAUNT

Things sweet to taste, prooue in digestion sowre.

You vrgde me as a iudge, but I had rather,
You would haue bid me argue like a father: 510
Alas, I lookt when some of you should say,
I was too strict to make mine owne away:
But you gaue leaue to my vnwilling tongue,
Against my will to do my selfe this wrong.

KING RICHARD

Coosen farewel, and Vnckle, bid him so,
Six yeares we banish him and he shall go.
      ⌜*Flourish.*⌝ *Exeunt: Manet Aumerle, the Lord*
            Marshall, Gaunt, and Bullingbrooke

AUMERLE (*to Bullingbrooke*)

Cosin farewel, what presence must not know,
From where you doe remaine let paper shew.   ⌜*Exit*⌝

LORD MARSHALL (*to Bullingbrooke*)

My Lord, no leaue take I, for I will ride
As farre as land will let me by your side.   520

GAUNT (*to Bullingbrooke*)

Oh to what purpose doest thou hoard thy words,
That thou returnst no greeting to thy friends?

BULLINGBROOKE

I haue too few to take my leaue of you,
When the tongues office should be prodigall,
To breathe the aboundant dolor of the heart.

GAUNT

Thy griefe is but thy absence for a time.

BULLINGBROOKE

Ioy absent, griefe is present for that time.

GAUNT

What is six winters? they are quickly gone.

BULLINGBROOKE

To men in ioy, but griefe makes one hower ten.

GAUNT

Call it a trauaile that thou takst for pleasure.   530

BULLINGBROOKE

My heart will sigh when I miscall it so,
Which findes it an inforced pilgrimage.

GAUNT

The sullen passage of thy weary steps,
Esteeme as foyle wherein thou art to set,
The pretious Iewell of thy home returne.

BULLINGBROOKE

Oh who can hold a fier in his hand,
By thinking on the frosty Caucasus?
Or cloy the hungry edge of appetite,
By bare imagination of a feast?
Or wallow naked in December snow,   540
By thinking on fantasticke sommers heate?
Oh no, the apprehension of the good,
Giues but the greater feeling to the worse:
Fell sorrowes tooth doth neuer ranckle more,
Then when he bites, but launceth not the soare.

GAUNT

Come come my sonne Ile bring thee on thy way,
Had I thy youth and cause, I would not stay.

BULLINGBROOKE

Then Englands ground farewell, sweet soile adiew,
My mother and my nurse that beares me yet,

550 Where eare I wander boast of this I can,
Though banisht, yet a true borne English man.

Exeunt

Sc. 4
(1.4)

*Enter the King with ⌐Greene and Bagot¬ at one dore,
and the Lord Aumarle at another*

KING RICHARD
We did obserue. Coosen Aumarle,
How far brought you high Hereford on his way?

AUMERLE
I brought high Herford, if you call him so,
But to the next high way, and there I left him.

KING RICHARD
And say, what store of parting teares were shed?

AUMERLE
Faith none for me, except the Northeast winde,
Which then grew bitterly against our faces,
Awakt the sleeping rhewme, and so by chance
560 Did grace our hollow parting with a teare.

KING RICHARD
What said our cousin when you parted with him?

AUMERLE
Farewel, & for my hart disdained that my tongue
Should so prophane the word, that taught me craft
To counterfaite oppression of such griefe,
That words seemd buried in my sorrowes graue:
Marry would the word Farewel haue lengthned
     howers,
And added yeares to his short banishment,
He should haue had a volume of farewels:
But since it would not, he had none of me.

KING RICHARD
570 He is our Coosen, Coosin, but tis doubt,
When time shall call him home from banishment,
Whether our kinsman come to see his friends.
Our selfe and Bushie, Bagot heere and Greene,
Obserud his courtship to the common people,
How he did seeme to diue into their harts,
With humble and familiar courtesie,
What reuerence he did throw away on slaues,
Wooing poore craftsmen with the craft of smiles,
And patient vnder-bearing of his fortune,
580 As twere to banish their affects with him.
Off goes his bonnet to an oysterwench,
A brace of draimen bid God speed him well,
And had the tribute of his supple knee,
With thankes my countreymen my louing friendes,
As were our England in reuersion his,
And he our subiects next degree in hope.

GREENE
Wel, he is gone, and with him go these thoughts,
Now for the rebels which stand out in Ireland,
Expedient mannage must be made my liege,
590 Ere further leysure yeeld them further meanes,
For their aduantage and your highnes losse.

KING RICHARD
We will our selfe in person to this warre,
And for our coffers with too great a court,

And liberall larges are growen somewhat light,
We are inforst to farm our royall Realme,
The reuenew whereof shall furnish vs,
For our affaires in hand: if that come short,
Our substitutes at home shall haue blanke charters,
Whereto, when they shal know what men are rich,
They shal subscribe them for large summes of gold,   600
And send them after to supply our wants,
For we will make for Ireland presently.

Enter Bushie

Bushie, what newes?

BUSHIE
Olde Iohn of Gaunt is grieuous sicke my Lord,
Sodainely taken, and hath sent post haste,
To intreate your Maiestie to visite him.

KING RICHARD Where lies he?
BUSHIE At Ely house.
KING RICHARD
Now put it (God) in his Physitions mind,
To help him to his graue immediatly: 610
The lining of his coffers shall make coates
To decke our souldiers for these Irish warres.
Come gentlemen, lets all go visite him,
Pray God we may make haste and come too late.

Exeunt

*Enter Iohn of Gaunt sicke, ⌐carried in a chaire,¬
with the duke of Yorke*

Sc. 5
(2.1)

GAUNT
Wil the King come that I may breathe my last?
In holsome counsell to his vnstaied youth.

YORKE
Vex not your selfe, nor striue not with your breath,
For all in vaine comes counsell to his eare.

GAUNT
Oh but they say, the tongues of dying men,
Inforce attention like deepe harmony: 620
Where words are scarce they are seldome spent in
     vaine,
For they breathe truth that breathe their wordes in
     paine:
He that no more must say, is listned more
     Than they whom youth and ease haue taught to
     glose,
More are mens ends markt than their liues before:
     The setting Sunne, and Musike at the close,
As the last taste of sweetes is sweetest last,
Writ in remembrance more than things long past,
Though Richard my liues counsell would not heare,
My deaths sad tale may yet vndeafe his eare.   630

YORKE
No, it is stopt with other flattering soundes,
As praises of whose taste the wise are feard
Lasciuious meeters, to whose venome sound
The open eare of youth doth alwayes listen,
Report of fashions in proude Italie,
Whose maners still our tardy apish nation
Limps after in base imitation:

Where doth the world thrust forth a vanitie,
So it be new, theres no respect how vile,
640 That is not quickly buzde into his eares?
Then all too late comes Counsell to be heard,
Where will doth mutiny with wits regard:
Direct not him whose way himselfe wil chuse,
Tis breath thou lackst and that breath wilt thou loose.

GAUNT
Me thinkes I am a prophet new inspirde,
And thus expiring do foretell of him.
His rash fierce blaze of ryot cannot last:
For violent fires soone burne out themselues.
Small shoures last long, but sodaine stormes are
        short:
650 He tires betimes that spurs too fast betimes,
With eagre feeding foode doth choke the feeder,
Light vanitie insatiate cormorant,
Consuming meanes soone praies vpon it selfe:
This royall throne of Kings, this sceptred Ile,
This earth of maiestie, this seate of Mars,
This other Eden, demy Paradice,
This fortresse built by Nature for her selfe,
Against infection and the hand of warre,
This happy breede of men, this little world,
660 This precious stone set in the siluer sea,
Which serues it in the office of a wall,
Or as a moate defensiue to a house,
Against the enuie of lesse happier lands.
This blessed plot, this earth, this realme, this England,
This nurse, this teeming wombe of royall Kings,
Feard by their breed, and famous by theyr byrth,
Renowned for theyr deedes as far from home,
For christian seruice, and true chiualry,
As is the sepulchre in stubburne Iewry,
670 Of the worlds ransome blessed Maries sonne:
This land of such deare soules, this deere deere land,
Deare for her reputation through the world,
Is now leasde out; I dye pronouncing it,
Like to a tenement or pelting Farme.
England bound in with the triumphant sea,
Whose rockie shoare beates backe the enuious siege
Of watry Neptune, is now bound in with shame,
With inckie blots, and rotten parchment bonds:
That England that was wont to conquer others,
680 Hath made a shamefull conquest of it selfe:
Ah would the scandall vanish with my life,
How happy then were my ensuing death?

        Enter king and Queene, ⌜Aumerle,⌝ Bushie, ⌜Greene,
        Bagot,⌝ Rosse, and Willoughby

YORKE
The King is come, deale mildely with his youth,
For young hot colts being raignde, do rage the more.

QUEENE
How fares our noble vncle Lancaster?

KING RICHARD
What comfort man? how ist with aged Gaunt?

GAUNT
O how that name befits my composition!

Old Gaunt indeede, and gaunt in being olde:
Within me Griefe hath kept a tedious fast.
And who abstaines from meate that is not gaunt? 690
For sleeping England long time haue I watcht,
Watching breedes leanenesse, leanenesse is all gaunt:
The pleasure that some fathers feede vpon
Is my strict fast; I meane my childrens lookes,
And therein fasting hast thou made me gaunt:
Gaunt am I for the graue, gaunt as a graue,
Whose hollow wombe inherites naught but bones.

KING RICHARD
Can sicke men play so nicely with their names?

GAUNT
No, misery makes sport to mocke it selfe,
Since thou dost seeke to kill my name in me, 700
I mocke my name (great King) to flatter thee.

KING RICHARD
Should dying men flatter with those that liue?

GAUNT
No no, men liuing flatter those that die.

KING RICHARD
Thou now a dying sayest thou flattrest me.

GAUNT
Oh no, thou diest, though I the sicker be.

KING RICHARD
I am in health, I breathe, and see thee ill.

GAUNT
Now he that made me knowes I see thee ill,
Ill in my selfe to see, and in thee, seeing ill,
Thy death-bed is no lesser than thy land,
Wherein thou liest in reputation sicke, 710
And thou too carelesse pacient as thou art
Commitst thy annoynted body to the cure
Of those Physitions that first wounded thee,
A thousand flatterers sit within thy Crowne,
Whose compasse is no bigger than thy head,
And yet incaged in so small a verge,
The waste is no whit lesser than thy land:
Oh had thy grandsire with a Prophets eie,
Seene how his sonnes sonne should destroy his
        sonnes,
From forth thy reach he would haue laid thy shame, 720
Deposing thee before thou wert possest,
Which art possest now to depose thy selfe:
Why cousin wert thou regent of the world,
It were a shame to let this land by lease:
But for thy world enioying but this land,
Is it not more than shame to shame it so?
Landlord of England art thou now, not King,
Thy state of lawe is bondslaue to the lawe,
And

KING RICHARD
And thou a lunatike leane-witted foole, 730
Presuming on an agues priuiledge,
Darst with thy frozen admonition
Make pale our cheeke, chasing the royall bloud
With furie from his natiue residence.
Now by my seates right royall maiestie,

Wert thou not brother to great Edwards sonne,
This tong that runnes so roundly in thy head,
Should runne thy head from thy vnreuerent shoulders.

GAUNT

Oh spare me not my brother Edwards sonne,
740   For that I was his father Edwards sonne,
That bloud already like the Pellican,
Hast thou tapt out and drunkenly carowst,
My brother Glocester plaine well meaning soule,
Whom faire befall in heauen mongst happy soules,
Maie be a president and witnes good:
That thou respectst not spilling Edwards bloud:
Ioine with the present sicknes that I haue,
And thy vnkindnes be like crooked age,
To crop at once a too long withred flower,
750   Liue in thy shame, but die not shame with thee,
These words hereafter thy tormentors be,
(*To attendants*) Conuay me to my bed then to my
        graue,
Loue they to liue that loue and honour haue.

                          Exit ⌈carried in the chaire⌉

KING RICHARD

And let them die that age and sullens haue,
For both hast thou, and both become the graue.

YORKE

I doe beseech your Maiesty, impute his words
To waiward sicklines and age in him,
He loues you on my life, and holdes you deere,
As Harry Duke of Hereford were he here.

KING RICHARD

760   Right, you say true, as Herefords loue, so his,
As theirs, so mine, and all be as it is.

                          Enter Northumberland

NORTHUMBERLAND

My liege, old Gaunt commends him to your Maiestie.

KING RICHARD

What saies he?

NORTHUMBERLAND Nay nothing, all is said:

His tongue is now a stringlesse instrument,
Words, life, and al, old Lancaster hath spent.

YORKE

Be Yorke the next that must be bankrout so,
Though death be poore, it ends a mortall wo.

KING RICHARD

The ripest fruit first fals, and so doth he,
His time is spent, our pilgrimage must be;
770   So much for that. Now for our Irish wars,
We must supplant those rough rugheaded kernes,
Which liue like venome, where no venome else,
But onely they haue priuiledge to liue.
And for these great affaires do aske some charge,
Towards our assistance we doe seaze to vs:
The plate, coine, reuenewes, and moueables
Whereof our Vnckle Gaunt did stand possest.

YORKE

How long shal I be patient? ah how long
Shall tender duty make me suffer wrong?
780   Not Glocesters death, nor Herefords banishment,

Nor Gauntes rebukes, nor Englands priuate wrongs,
Nor the preuention of poore Bullingbrooke,
About his mariadge, nor my owne disgrace,
Haue euer made me sower my patient cheeke,
Or bende one wrinckle on my soueraignes face:
I am the last of noble Edwards sonnes,
Of whom thy father Prince of Wales was first.
In warre was neuer Lyon ragde more fierce,
In peace was neuer gentle lambe more milde,
Then was that young and princely Gentleman: 790
His face thou hast, for euen so lookt he,
Accomplisht with the number of thy howers;
But when he frownd it was against the french,
And not against his friends: his noble hand
Did win what he did spende, and spent not that
Which his triumphant fathers hand had wonne:
His hands were guilty of no kinred bloud,
But bloudie with the enemies of his kinne:
Oh Richard: Yorke is too far gone with griefe,
Or else he neuer would compare betweene.   800

KING RICHARD

Why Vnckle whats the matter?

YORKE   Oh my liege,

Pardone me if you please, if not I pleasd
Not to be pardond, am content with all,
Seeke you to seaze and gripe into your hands
The roialties and rights of banisht Hereford:
Is not Gaunt dead? and doth not Hereford liue?
Was not Gaunt iust? and is not Harrie true?
Did not the one deserue to haue an heire?
Is not his heire a well deseruing sonne?
Take Herefordes rightes away, and take from time   810
His charters, and his customarie rightes;
Let not to morrow then ensue to daie:
Be not thy selfe. For how art thou a King
But by faire sequence and succession?
Now afore God God forbidde I say true,
If you doe wrongfully seaze Herefords rightes,
Call in the letters patents that he hath
By his attourneies generall to sue
His liuery, and deny his offred homage,
You plucke a thousand dangers on your head,   820
You loose a thousand well disposed hearts,
And pricke my tender patience to those thoughts,
Which honour, and alleageance cannot thinke.

KING RICHARD

Thinke what you wil, we cease into our hands
His plate, his goods, his money and his landes.

YORKE

Ile not be by the while, my liege farewell,
What will ensue hereof thers none can tell:
But by bad courses may be vnderstood
That their euents can neuer fall out good.   *Exit*

KING RICHARD

Go Bushie to the Earle of Wiltshire straight,   830
Bid him repaire to vs to Ely house,
To see this busines: to morrow next
We will for Ireland, and tis time I trow,

And we create in absence of our selfe,
Our Vnckle Yorke Lord gouernour of England;
For he is iust, and alwaies lou'd vs well:
Come on our Queene, to morrow must we part,
Be merry, for our time of staie is short.

⌐Flourish.⌐ Exeunt ⌐Bushie at one doore, King,
Queene, Aumerle, Greene and Bagot at another
doore⌐: Manet Northumberland, Willoughby,
and Rosse

NORTHUMBERLAND
Well Lords, the Duke of Lancaster is dead.

ROSSE
840   And liuing to, for now his sonne is Duke.

WILLOUGHBY
Barely in title, not in reuenewes.

NORTHUMBERLAND
Richly in both if iustice had her right.

ROSSE
My heart is great, but it must breake with silence,
Eart be disburdned with a liberall tongue.

NORTHUMBERLAND
Nay speake thy mind, & let him nere speake more
That speakes thy words againe to doe thee harme.

WILLOUGHBY
Tends that that thou wouldst speake to the Duke of
     Herford?
If it be so, out with it boldly man,
Quicke is mine eare to heare of good towards him.

ROSSE
850   No good at all that I can doe for him,
Vnlesse you call it good to pitty him,
Bereft, and gelded of his patrimony.

NORTHUMBERLAND
Now afore God tis shame such wrongs are borne,
In him a royall Prince and many mo,
Of noble bloud in this declining land,
The King is not himselfe, but basely led
By flatterers, and what they will informe,
Meerely in hate gainst any of vs all,
That will the King seuerely prosecute,
860   Gainst vs, our liues, our children, and our heires.

ROSSE
The commons hath he pild with grieuous taxes,
And quite lost their hearts. The nobles hath he finde,
For ancient quarrels and quite lost their hearts.

WILLOUGHBY
And daily new exactions are deuisde,
As blanckes, beneuolences, and I wot not what:
But what a Gods name doth become of this?

NORTHUMBERLAND
Wars hath not wasted it, for warrde he hath not,
But basely yeelded vpon compromise,
That which his auncestors atchiude with blowes,
870   More hath he spent in peace then they in wars.

ROSSE
The Earle of Wiltshire hath the realme in farme.

WILLOUGHBY
The Kings growen banckrout like a broken man.

NORTHUMBERLAND
Reproch and dissolution hangeth ouer him.

ROSSE
He hath not money for these Irish wars,
His burthenous taxations notwithstanding,
But by the robbing of the banisht Duke.

NORTHUMBERLAND
His noble kinsman, most degenerate King,
But Lords we heare this fearefull tempest sing,
Yet seeke no shelter to auoid the storme:
We see the wind sit sore vpon our sailes,   880
And yet we strike not, but securely perish.

ROSSE
We see the very wracke that we must suffer,
And vnauoided is the danger now
For suffering so the causes of our wracke.

NORTHUMBERLAND
Not so, euen through the hollow eies of death,
I spie life peering but I dare not say,
How neere the tidings of our comfort is.

WILLOUGHBY
Nay let vs share thy thoughts as thou dost ours.

ROSSE
Be confident to speake Northumberland,
We three are but thy selfe, and speaking so   890
Thy words are but as thoughts, therefore be bold.

NORTHUMBERLAND
Then thus, I haue from Port le Blan
A Bay in Brittaine receiude intelligence,
That Harry duke of Herford, Rainold L. Cobham
Thomas sonne and heire to the Earle of Arundell,
That late broke from the Duke of Exeter,
His brother, archbishop late of Canterburie,
Sir Thomas Erpingham, sir Thomas Ramston,
Sir Iohn Norbery,
Sir Robert Waterton, and Francis Coint;   900
All these well furnisht by the Duke of Brittaine
With eight tall shippes, three thousand men of warre,
Are making hither with all due expedience,
And shortly meane to touch our Northerne shore:
Perhaps they had ere this but that they stay
The first departing of the King for Ireland.
If then we shall shake off our slauish yoke,
Impe out our drowping countries broken wing,
Redeeme from Broking pawne the blemisht Crowne,
Wipe off the dust that hides our Scepters guilt,   910
And make high Maiestie looke like it selfe,
Away with me in post to Rauenspurgh:
But if you faint, as fearing to do so,
Stay, and be secret, and my selfe will go.

ROSSE
To horse, to horse, vrge doubts to them that feare.

WILLOUGHBY
Holde out my horse, and I will first be there.   *Exeunt*

Enter the Queene, Bushie, Bagot   Sc. 6
                                     (2.2)

BUSHIE
Madam, your maiestie is too much sad,

You promist, when you parted with the King,
To lay aside life-harming heauines,
920   And entertaine a cheerefull disposition.

QUEENE
To please the king I did, to please my selfe
I cannot do it; yet I know no cause
Why I should welcome such a guest as Griefe,
Saue bidding farewell to so sweete a guest,
As my sweete Richard: yet agayne me thinkes
Some vnborne sorrow ripe in Fortunes wombe,
Is comming towardes me, and my inward soule
At nothing trembles, with something it grieues,
More then with parting from my Lord the King.

BUSHIE
930   Each substance of a griefe hath twenty shadowes,
Which shewes like griefe it selfe, but is not so:
For Sorrowes eye glazed with blinding teares,
Diuides one thing entire to many obiects,
Like perspectiues, which rightly gazde vpon
Shew nothing but confusion; eyde awry,
Distinguish forme: so your sweet maiestie,
Looking awry vpon your Lords departure,
Finde shapes of griefe more than himselfe to waile,
Which lookt on as it is, is naught but shadows
940   Of what it is not; then (thrice gracious Queene)
More then your Lords departure weep not, more is not
    seen
Or if it be, tis with false Sorrowes eye,
Which for things true, weepes things imaginarie.

QUEENE
It may be so; but yet my inward soule
Perswades me it is otherwise: how ere it be,
I cannot but be sad: so heauie sad,
As thought, on thinking on no thought I thinke,
Makes me with heauy nothing faint and shrinke.

BUSHIE
Tis nothing but conceit my gratious Lady.

QUEENE
950   Tis nothing lesse: conceit is still deriude,
From some forefather griefe, mine is not so,
For nothing hath begot my something griefe.
Or something hath the nothing that I grieue,
Tis in reuersion that I do possesse,
But what it is that is not yet knowen what,
I cannot name, tis namelesse woe I wot.

Enter Greene

GREENE
God saue your maiesty, and well met Gentlemen,
I hope the King is not yet shipt for Ireland.

QUEENE
Why hopst thou so? tis better hope he is,
960   For his designes craue haste, his haste good hope:
Then wherefore dost thou hope he is not shipt?

GREENE
That he our hope might haue retirde his power,
And driuen into despaire an enemies hope,
Who strongly hath set footing in this land,

The banisht Bullingbrooke repeales himselfe,
And with vplifted armes is safe ariude
At Rauenspurgh.

QUEENE   Now God in heauen forbid.

GREENE
Ah Madam! tis too true, and that is worse:
The lord Northumberland, his son yong H. Percie,
The lords of Rosse, Beaumond, and Willoughby,   970
With all their powerful friends are fled to him.

BUSHIE
Why haue you not proclaimd Northumberland
And al the rest reuolted faction, traitours?

GREENE
We haue, whereupon the earle of Worcester
Hath broke his Staffe, resignd his Stewardship,
And al the houshold seruants fled with him
To Bullingbrook.

QUEENE
So Greene, thou art the midwife to my woe,
And Bullingbrooke my sorowes dismall heire,
Now hath my soule brought forth her prodigie,   980
And I a gasping new deliuerd mother,
Haue woe to woe, sorow to sorrow ioynde.

BUSHIE
Dispaire not Madam.

QUEENE   Who shall hinder me?
I will dispaire and be at enmitie
With cousening Hope, he is a flatterer,
A parasite, a keeper backe of Death,
Who gently would dissolue the bands of life,
Which false Hope lingers in extremitie.

Enter Yorke ⌈wearing a gorget⌉

GREENE Here comes the Duke of Yorke.

QUEENE
With signes of war about his aged necke,   990
Oh ful of carefull busines are his lookes!
Vncle, for Gods sake speake comfortable wordes.

YORKE
Should I do so I should bely my thoughts,
Comfort's in heauen, and we are on the earth,
Where nothing liues but crosses, cares and griefe:
Your husband, he is gone to saue far off,
Whilst others come to make him loose at home:
Heere am I left to vnderprop his land,
Who weake with age cannot support my selfe,
Now comes the sicke houre that his surfet made,   1000
Now shall he trie his friends that flatterd him.

Enter a Seruingman

SERUINGMAN
My Lord, your son was gone before I came.

YORKE
He was; why so go all which way it will:
The nobles they are fled, the commons they are colde,
And will (I feare) reuolt on Herefords side.
Sirra, get thee to Plashie to my sister Glocester,
Bid her send me presently a thousand pound,
Hold take my ring.

SERUINGMAN

    My Lord, I had forgot to tel your Lordship:

1010   To day as I came by I called there,

    But I shall grieue you to report the rest.

YORKE   What ist knaue?

SERUINGMAN

    An houre before I came the Dutchesse died.

YORKE

    God for his mercy, what a tide of woes

    Comes rushing on this wofull land at once!

    I know not what to do: I would to God,

    (So my vntruth had not prouokt him to it)

    The King had cut off my head with my brothers.

    What are there no Posts dispatcht for Ireland?

1020   How shal we do for money for these wars?

    (*To the Queene*) Come sister, cousin I would say, pray

        pardon me:

    (*To the Seruingman*) Go fellow get thee home, prouide

        some cartes,

    And bring away the armour that is there.

                 ⌐*Exit Seruingman*⌐

    Gentlemen, will you go muster men?

    If I know how or which way to order these affayres

    Thus disorderly thrust into my hands,

    Neuer beleeue me: both are my kinsmen,

    Tone is my soueraigne, whom both my oath

    And duety bids defend; tother againe

1030   Is my kinsman, whom the King hath wrongd,

    Whom conscience, and my kinred bids to right.

    Wel somewhat we must do: (*To the Queene*) Come

        cousin,

    Ile dispose of you:

    Gentlemen, go muster vp your men,

    And meete me presently at Barkly Castle:

    I should to Plashie too, but time wil not permit:

    All is vneuen,

    And euery thing is left at sixe and seauen.

        Exeunt Duke of Yorke, Queene. Manet Bushie,

                            Bagot, Green

    BUSHIE

    The winde sits faire for newes to go for Ireland,

1040   But none returnes. For vs to leuie power

    Proportionable to the enemy

    Is all vnpossible.

GREENE

    Besides our neerenes to the King in loue,

    Is neare the hate of those loue not the King.

BAGOT

    And that is the wauering commons, for their loue

    Lies in their purses, and who so empties them,

    By so much fils their hearts with deadly hate.

BUSHIE

    Wherein the King stands generally condemnd.

BAGOT

    If iudgment lie in them, then so do we,

1050   Because we euer haue beene neere the King.

GREENE

    Well I will for refuge straight to Bristow Castle,

    The Earle of Wiltshire is already there.

BUSHIE

    Thither will I with you, for little office

    Will the hatefull commoners perfourme for vs,

    Except like curs to teare vs all to pieces:

    (*To Bagot*) Will you go along with vs?

BAGOT

    No, I will to Ireland to his Maiesty,

    Farewell if hearts presages be not vaine,

    We three here part that nere shall meete againe.

BUSHIE

    Thats as Yorke thriues to beat backe Bullingbrook.   1060

GREENE

    Alas poore Duke the taske he vndertakes,

    Is numbring sands, and drinking Oceans drie,

    Where one on his side fights, thousands will flie:

⌐BAGOT⌐

    Farewell at once, for once, for all, and euer.

BUSHIE

    Well, we may meete againe.

BAGOT   I feare me neuer.

        Exeunt ⌐*Bushie and Greene at one doore, Bagot*

                        at another doore⌐

    Enter Bullingbrooke Duke of Hereford,   **Sc. 7**

    Northumberland   **(2.3)**

BULLINGBROOKE

    How far is it my Lord to Barckly now?

NORTHUMBERLAND   Beleeue me noble Lord,

    I am a stranger here in Glocestershire,

    These high wild hils and rough vneuen waies,

    Drawes out our miles and makes them wearisome,   1070

    And yet your faire discourse hath beene as sugar,

    Making the hard way sweete and delectable,

    But I bethinke me what a weary way

    From Rauenspurgh to Cotshall will be found,

    In Rosse and Willoughby wanting your company,

    Which I protest hath very much beguild,

    The tediousnesse and processe of my trauell:

    But theirs is sweetned with the hope to haue

    The present benefit which I possesse,

    And hope to ioy is little lesse in ioye,   1080

    Then hope enioyed: by this the weary Lords

    Shall make their way seeme short as mine hath done,

    By sight of what I haue, your noble company.

BULLINGBROOKE

    Of much lesse value is my company,

    Then your good wordes.

        Enter Harry Persie

                      But who comes here?

NORTHUMBERLAND

    It is my sonne young Harry Persy,

    Sent from my brother Worcester whencesoeuer.

    Harry, how fares your Vnckle?

HARRY PERCIE

    I had thought my Lord to haue learnt his health of

    you.

NORTHUMBERLAND   Why is he not with the Queene?   1090

HARRY PERCIE

    No my good Lord, he hath forsooke the court,

Broken his staffe of office and disperst
The houshold of the King.

NORTHUMBERLAND   What was his reason,
He was not so resolude, when last we spake togither?

HARRY PERCIE
Because your Lo: was proclaimed traitor,
But he my Lo: is gone to Rauenspurgh,
To offer seruice to the Duke of Hereford,
And sent me ouer by Barckly to discouer,
What power the Duke of Yorke had leuied there,
1100   Then with directions to repaire to Rauenspurgh.

NORTHUMBERLAND
Haue you forgot the Duke of Hereford, boy?

HARRY PERCIE
No my good Lo: for that is not forgot,
Which nere I did remember, to my knowledge
I neuer in my life did looke on him.

NORTHUMBERLAND
Then learne to know him now, this is the Duke.

HARRY PERCIE
My gratious Lo: I tender you my seruice,
Such as it is, being tender, raw, and young,
Which elder daies shal ripen and confirme
To more approued seruice and desert.

BULLINGBROOKE
1110   I thanke thee gentle Persy, and be sure,
I count my selfe in nothing else so happy,
As in a soule remembring my good friends,
And as my fortune ripens with thy loue,
It shalbe still thy true loues recompence,
My heart this couenant makes, my hand thus seales it.
        He giues Percie his hand

NORTHUMBERLAND
How farre is it to Barckly, and what stur
Keepes good old Yorke there with his men of war?

HARRY PERCIE
There stands the Castle by yon tuft of trees,
Mand with 300. men as I haue heard,
1120   And in it are the Lords of Yorke Barkly and Seymer,
None else of name and noble estimate.
        Enter Rosse and Willoughby

NORTHUMBERLAND
Here come the Lords of Rosse and Willoughby,
Bloudy with spurring, fiery red with haste.

BULLINGBROOKE
Welcome my Lords, I wot your loue pursues,
A banisht traitor: all my treasury
Is yet but vnfelt thanks, which more inricht,
Shalbe your loue and labours recompence.

ROSSE
Your presence makes vs rich, most noble Lord.

WILLOUGHBY
And far surmounts our labour to attaine it.

BULLINGBROOKE
1130   Euermore thanke's the exchequer of the poore,
Which till my infant fortune comes to yeares,
Stands for my bounty:
        Enter Barkly
                but who comes here?

NORTHUMBERLAND
It is my Lord of Barkly as I guesse.

BARKLY
My Lord of Hereford my message is to you.

BULLINGBROOKE
My Lord my answere is to Lancaster,
And I am come to seeke that name in England,
And I must find that title in your tongue,
Before I make reply to ought you say.

BARKLY
Mistake me not my Lord, tis not my meaning,
To race one title of your honor out: 1140
To you my Lo: I come, what Lo: you will,
From the most gratious regent of this land
The Duke of Yorke: to know what prickes you on,
To take aduantage of the absent time,
And fright our natiue peace with selfeborne armes?
        Enter Yorke

BULLINGBROOKE
I shall not need transport my words by you,
Here comes his grace in person, my noble Vnckle.
        He kneeles

YORKE
Shew me thy humble heart, and not thy knee,
Whose duety is deceiueable and false.

BULLINGBROOKE My gratious Vnckle.   1150

YORKE
Tut tut, grace me no grace, nor vnckle me no vnckle,
I am no traitors Vnckle, and that word Grace
In an vngratious mouth is but prophane:
Why haue those banisht and forbidden legs,
Dard once to touch a dust of Englands ground:
But then more why? why haue they dard to march
So many miles vpon her peacefull bosome,
Frighting her pale fac't villadges with warre,
And ostentation of despised armes?
Comst thou because the annointed king is hence?   1160
Why foolish boy the King is left behinde,
And in my loiall bosome lies his power,
Were I but now the Lord of such hot youth,
As when braue Gaunt thy father and my selfe,
Rescued the blacke prince that young Mars of men,
From forth theranckes of many thousand french,
O then how quickly should this arme of mine,
Now prisoner to the Palsie chastise thee,
And minister correction to thy fault!

BULLINGBROOKE
My gratious Vnckle let me know my fault,   1170
On what condition stands it and wherein?

YORKE
Euen in condition of the worst degree,
In grosse rebellion and detested treason,
Thou art a banisht man and here art come,
Before the expiration of thy time,
In brauing armes against thy soueraigne.

BULLINGBROOKE ⌈standing⌉
As I was banisht, I was banisht Hereford,
But as I come, I come for Lancaster.
And noble Vnckle I beseech your grace,

1180 Looke on my wrongs with an indifferent eie:
You are my father, for me thinkes in you
I see old Gaunt aliue. Oh then my father,
Will you permit that I shall stand condemnd
A wandering vagabond, my rights and royalties
Pluckt from my armes perforce; and giuen away
To vpstart vnthrifts? wherefore was I borne?
If that my cousin King be King in England,
It must be granted I am duke of Lancaster:
You haue a sonne, Aumerle, my noble kinsman,
1190 Had you first died, and he bin thus trod downe,
He should haue found his vncle Gaunt a father,
To rowze his wrongs and chase them to the baie.
I am denyed to sue my Liuery here,
And yet my letters pattents giue me leaue.
My fathers goods are all distrainde and sold,
And these, and all, are all amisse employed.
What would you haue me do? I am a subiect;
And I challenge law, Atturnies are denied me,
And therefore personally I lay my claime
1200 To my inheritance of free descent.

NORTHUMBERLAND
The noble Duke hath bin too much abused.

ROSSE
It stands your Grace vpon to do him right.

WILLOUGHBY
Base men by his endowments are made great.

YORKE
My Lords of England, let me tell you this:
I haue had feeling of my cousins wrongs,
And labour all I could to do him right:
But in this kind to come, in brauing armes
Be his owne caruer, and cut out his way,
To finde out right wyth wrong, it may not be:
1210 And you that do abette him in this kinde,
Cherish rebellion, and are rebells all.

NORTHUMBERLAND
The noble Duke hath sworne his comming is,
But for his owne; and for the right of that,
We al haue strongly sworne to giue him ayde:
And let him neuer see ioy that breakes that oath.

YORKE
Wel wel, I see the issue of these armes,
I cannot mend it I must needes confesse,
Because my power is weake and all ill left:
But if I could, by him that gaue me life,
1220 I would attach you all, and make you stoope
Vnto the soueraigne mercie of the king;
But since I cannot, be it knowen to you,
I do remaine as newter, so fare you well,
Vnlesse you please to enter in the castle,
And there repose you for this night.

BULLINGBROOKE
An offer vncle that we will accept,
But we must winne your Grace to go with vs,
To Bristow castle, which they say is held
By Bushie, Bagot, and their complices,
1230 The caterpillers of the commonwealth,
Which I haue sworne to weede and plucke away.

YORKE
It may be I will go with you, but yet Ile pawse,
For I am loath to breake our countries lawes,
Nor friends, nor foes to me welcome you are:
Things past redresse, are now with me past care.
                                        Exeunt

Enter erle of Salisbury and a Welch captaine   Sc. 8
                                                   (2.4)
WELCH CAPTAINE
My lord of Salisbury, we haue stayed ten dayes,
And hardly kept our countrymen together,
And yet we heare no tidings from the King,
Therefore we will disperse our selues, farewell.

SALISBURY
Stay yet an other day, thou trustie Welchman.   1240
The King reposeth all his confidence in thee.

WELCH CAPTAINE
Tis thought the King is dead; we wil not stay,
The bay trees in our country are al witherd,
And Meteors fright the fixed starres of heauen,
The pale-facde moone lookes bloudie on the earth,
And leane-lookt prophets whisper fearefull change,
Rich men looke sad, and ruffians daunce and leape,
The one in feare to loose what they enioy,
The other to enioy by rage and warre:
These signes forerunne the death or fall of Kings. 1250
Farewell, our countrymen are gone and fled,
As well assurd Richard their King is dead.   *Exit*

SALISBURY
Ah Richard! with the eies of heauy mind
I see thy glory like a shooting starre
Fall to the base earth from the firmament,
Thy sunne sets weeping in the lowly west,
Witnessing stormes to come, wo, and vnrest,
Thy friends are fled to wait vpon thy foes,
And crosly to thy good all fortune goes.   *Exit*

Enter Bullingbrooke Duke of Hereford, Yorke,   Sc. 9
Northumberland, ⌈Rosse, Percie, Willoughby⌉   (3.1)
BULLINGBROOKE Bring forth these men.
    Enter Bushie and Greene, guarded as prisoners
Bushie and Greene, I will not vex your soules,   1261
Since presently your soules must part your bodies
With too much vrging your pernitious liues,
For twere no charitie; yet to wash your bloud
From off my hands, heere in the view of men
I will vnfold some causes of your deaths:
You haue misled a Prince, a royall King,
A happy Gentleman in bloud and lineaments,
By you vnhappied, and disfigurd cleane,
You haue in manner with your sinfull houres   1270
Made a diuorce betwixt his Queene and him,
Broke the possession of a royall bed,
And stainde the beutie of a faire Queenes cheekes
With teares, drawn from her eies by your fowle
    wrongs,
My selfe a Prince, by fortune of my birth,
Neere to the King in bloud, and neere in loue,

Till you did make him misinterpret me,
Haue stoopt my necke vnder your iniuries,
And sigh't my English breath in forren cloudes,
1280 Eating the bitter bread of banishment,
Whilst you haue fed vpon my segniories,
Disparkt my parkes, and felld my forrest woods,
From my owne windowes torne my houshold coate,
Rac't out my impreese, leauing me no signe,
Saue mens opinions, and my liuing bloud,
To shew the world I am a gentleman.
This and much more, much more then twice all this
Condemns you to the death: see them deliured ouer
To execution and the hand of death.

BUSHIE

1290 More welcome is the stroke of death to me,
Than Bullingbrooke to England.

GREENE

My comfort is, that heauen will take our soules,
And plague iniustice with the paines of hell.

BULLINGBROOKE

My Lord Northumberland, see them dispatcht:
          Exit Northumberland, with Bushie and Greene,
                                                    guarded

Vncle, you say the Queene is at your house,
For Gods sake fairely let her be intreated,
Tel her I send to her my kinde commends;
Take special care my greetings be deliuered.

YORKE

A gentleman of mine I haue dispatcht,
1300 With letters of your loue to her at large.

BULLINGBROOKE

Thankes (gentle vncle:) Come Lords, away,
To fight with Glendor and his complices,
A while to worke, and after holiday.   *Exeunt*

Sc. 10   ⌜*Flourish.*⌝ *Enter* ⌜*with drumme and colours*⌝ *the*
(3.2)   *King, Aumerle, Carleil, and* ⌜*souldiers*⌝

KING RICHARD

Hertloughly castle call they this at hand?

AUMERLE

Yea my Lord, How brookes your Grace the ayre
After your late tossing on the breaking seas?

KING RICHARD

Needes must I like it well, I weepe for ioy,
To stand vpon my kingdome once againe:
          He touches the ground
Deere earth I do salute thee with my hand,
1310 Though rebels wound thee with their horses hoofes:
As a long parted mother with her childe
Playes fondly with her teares and smiles in meeting;
So weeping, smiling greete I thee my earth,
And do thee fauours with my royall hands;
Feede not thy Soueraignes foe, my gentle earth,
Nor with thy sweetes comfort his rauenous sence,
But let thy Spiders that sucke vp thy venome,
And heauy-gated toades lie in theyr way,
Doing annoyance to the treacherous feete,

Which with vsurping steps do trample thee,   1320
Yeelde stinging nettles to mine enemies:
And when they from thy bosome plucke a flower,
Guard it I pray thee with a lurking Adder,
Whose double tongue may wyth a mortall touch,
Throwe death vpon thy soueraignes enemies,
Mocke not my senceles coniuration Lords,
This earth shall haue a feeling, and these stones,
Proue armed souldiers ere her natiue King,
Shall faulter vnder foule rebellions armes.

CARLEIL

Feare not my Lord, that power that made you king,   1330
Hath power to keepe you king in spight of all.

AUMERLE

He meanes my Lo: that we are too remisse,
Whilst Bullingbrooke through our security,
Growes strong and great in substance and in friends.

KING RICHARD

Discomfortable Coosen knowst thou not,
That when the searching eie of heauen is hid,
Behinde the globe that lights the lower world,
Then theeues and robbers range abroad vnseene,
In murthers and in outrage bloudy here,
But when from vnder this terrestriall ball,   1340
He fires the proud tops of the easterne pines,
And dartes his light through euery guilty hole,
Then murthers, treasons and detested sinnes,
The cloake of night being pluckt from off their backs,
Stand bare and naked trembling at themselues?
So when this thiefe, this traitor Bullingbrooke,
Who all this while hath reueld in the night,
Whilst we were wandring with the Antipodes,
Shall see vs rising in our throne the east,
His treasons will sit blushing in his face,   1350
Not able to endure the sight of day,
But selfe affrighted tremble at his sinne,
Not all the water in the rough rude sea,
Can wash the balme from an annointed King,
The breath of worldly men cannot depose,
The deputy elected by the Lord,
For euery man that Bullingbrooke hath prest,
To lifte shrewd steele against our golden crowne,
God for his Ric: hath in heauenly pay,
A glorious Angell; then if Angels fight,   1360
Weake men must fall, for heauen still gardes the right.
          Enter Salisbury
Welcome my Lo: how far off lies your power?

SALISBURY

Nor neare nor farther off my gratious Lo:
Than this weake arme; discomfort guides my tongue,
And bids me speake of nothing but Despaire,
One day too late I feare me noble Lo:
Hath clouded all thy happy daies on earth:
O call backe yesterday, bid Time returne,
And thou shalt haue twelue thousand fighting men,
To day to day vnhappie daie too late,   1370
Ouerthrowes thy ioies friends, fortune and thy state,

For all the Welshmen hearing thou wert dead,
Are gone to Bullingbrooke disperst and fled.

AUMERLE

Comfort my liege, why lookes your grace so pale.

KING RICHARD

But now the bloud of 20000. men,
    Did triumph in my face, and they are fled:
And till so much bloud thither come againe,
    Haue I not reason to looke pale and dead?
All soules that wilbe safe, flie from my side,
1380   For time hath set a blot vpon my pride.

AUMERLE

Comfort my liege remember who you are.

KING RICHARD

I had forgot my selfe, am I not King?
Awake thou sluggard Maiesty thou sleepest,
Is not the Kings name forty thousand names?
Arme arme, my name, a puny subiect strikes,
At thy great glorie, looke not to the ground,
Ye fauourites of a King, are we not high?
High be our thoughts, I know my Vnckle Yorke,
Hath power enough to serue our turne:
        Enter Scroope
                                but who comes here?

SCROOPE

1390   More health and happines betide my liege,
Then can my care tunde tongue deliuer him.

KING RICHARD

Mine eare is open, and my hart prepard,
The worst is worldly losse thou canst vnfold,
Say, is my kingdome lost? why twas my care,
And what losse is it to be rid of care?
Striues Bullingbrooke to be as great as we,
Greater he shall not be, if he serue God,
Weele serue him to, and be his fellow so?
Reuolt our subiects, that we cannot mende,
1400   They breake their faith to God as well as vs:
Crie woe, destruction, ruine, losse, decay,
The worst is death, and death will haue his day.

SCROOPE

Glad am I, that your highnes is so armde,
To beare the tidings of calamity,
Like an vnseasonable stormie day,
Which makes the siluer riuers drowne their shores,
As if the world were all dissolude to teares:
So high aboue his limits swels the rage
Of Bullingbrooke couering your fearefull land,
1410   With hard bright steele, and harts harder then steele,
White beards haue armd their thin and haireles
        scalpes
Against thy maiesty: boies with womens voices,
Striue to speake big and clap their femal ioints,
In stiffe vnweildy armes against thy crowne,
Thy very beadsmen learne to bend their bowes,
Of double fatall ewe against thy state.
Yea distaffe women mannage rustie bils
Against thy seate, both young and old rebell,
And all goes worse then I haue power to tell.

KING RICHARD

Too well too well thou telst a tale so ill,   1420
Where is the Earle of Wiltshire? where is Bagot?
What is become of Bushie? where is Greene?
That they haue let the dangerous enemy,
Measure our confines with such peacefull steps,
If we preuaile, their heads shall pay for it:
I warrant they haue made peace with Bullingbrooke.

SCROOPE

Peace haue they made with him indeed my Lord.

KING RICHARD

Oh villaines, vipers, damnd without redemption,
Dogs easily woon to fawne on any man.
Snakes in my hart bloud warmd, that sting my hart,   1430
Three Iudasses, each one thrise worse then Iudas,
Would they make peace? terrible hel, make war
Vpon their spotted soules for this offence.

SCROOPE

Sweet loue I see changing his property,
Turnes to the sowrest and most deadly hate,
Againe, vncurse their soules, their peace is made
With heads and not with hands, those whom you
        curse
Haue felt the worst of deathes destroying wound,
And lie full low grau'd in the hollow ground.

AUMERLE

Is Bushie, Greene, and the Earle of Wiltshire dead.   1440

SCROOPE

I all of them at Bristow lost their heads.

AUMERLE

Where is the Duke my father with his power?

KING RICHARD

No matter where, of comfort no man speake:
Lets talke of graues, of wormes, and Epitaphs,
Make dust our paper, and with rainy eies,
Write sorrow on the bosome of the earth.
Lets choose executors and talke of wils:
And yet not so, for what can we bequeath,
Saue our deposed bodies to the ground?
Our landes, our liues, and all are Bullingbrookes,   1450
And nothing can we call our owne, but death:
And that small modle of the barren earth,
Which serues as paste, and couer to our bones,
⌈*Sitting*⌉ For Gods sake let vs sit vpon the ground,
And tell sad stories of the death of Kings,
How some haue beene deposd, some slaine in warre,
Some haunted by the ghosts they haue deposed,
Some poisond by their wiues, some sleeping kild;
All murthred, for within the hollow crowne
That roundes the mortall temples of a king,   1460
Keepes death his court, and there the antique sits,
Scoffing his state and grinning at his pompe,
Allowing him a breath, a litle sceane,
To monarchise be feard, and kil with lookes,
Infusing him with selfe and vaine conceit,
As if this flesh which wals about our life,
Were brasse impregnable: and humord thus,
Comes at the last, and with a little pin

Boares thorough his Castle wall, and farewell King;
1470 Couer your heades, and mocke not flesh and bloud,
With solemne reuerence, throw a way respect,
Tradition, forme, and ceremonious duetie,
For you haue but mistooke me al this while:
I liue with bread like you, feele want,
Taste griefe, neede friends, subiected thus,
How can you say to me, I am a King?

CARLEIL
My lord, wisemen nere waile theyr present woes,
But presently preuent the wayes to waile,
To feare the foe, since feare oppresseth strength,
1480 Giues in your weakenes strength vnto your foe,
And so your follies fight against your selfe:
Feare and be slaine, no worse can come to fight,
And fight and die, is death destroying death,
Where fearing dying, paies death seruile breath.

AUMERLE
My father hath a power, inquire of him,
And learne to make a body of a limme.

KING RICHARD ⌜standing⌝
Thou chidst me well, prowd Bullingbrooke, I come
To change blowes with thee for our day of doome:
This agew fit of feare is ouerblowne,
1490 An easie taske it is to winne our owne.
Say Scroope, where lies our vncle with his power?
Speake sweetely man although thy lookes be sower.

SCROOPE
Men iudge by the complexion of the skie,
   The state and inclination of the day;
So may you by my dull and heauy eie:
   My tongue hath but a heauier tale to say,
I play the torturer by small and small
To lengthen out the worst that must be spoken:
Your vncle Yorke is ioynd with Bullingbrooke,
1500 And all your Northerne castles yeelded vp,
And all your Southerne Gentlemen in armes
Vpon his faction.

KING RICHARD   Thou hast said enough:
(To Aumerle) Beshrew thee cousin which didst leade
   me foorth
Of that sweete way I was in to dispaire.
What say you now? what comfort haue we now?
By heauen Ile hate him euerlastingly,
That bids me be of comfort any more.
Go to Flint Castle, there Ile pine away,
A King woes slaue shall kingly woe obey:
1510 That power I haue, discharge, and let them goe
To eare the land that hath some hope to grow,
For I haue none, let no man speake againe,
To alter this, for counsell is but vaine.

AUMERLE
My Liege, one word.

KING RICHARD   He does me double wrong,
That wounds me with the flatteries of his tong.
Discharge my followers, let them hence away,
From Richards night, to Bullingbrookes faire day.
                                             Exeunt

Enter ⌜with drumme and colours⌝ Bullingbrooke,   Sc. 11
Yorke, Northumberland, ⌜souldiers⌝   (3.3)

BULLINGBROOKE
So that by this intelligence we learne
The Welch men are disperst, and Salisburie
Is gone to meete the King, who lately landed   1520
With some few priuate friends vpon this coast.

NORTHUMBERLAND
The newes is very faire and good my lord,
Richard not farre from hence hath hid his head.

YORKE
It would beseeme the Lord Northumberland
To say King Richard; alacke the heauy day,
When such a sacred King should hide his head.

NORTHUMBERLAND
Your Grace mistakes; onely to be briefe
Left I his title out.

YORKE   The time hath bin,
Would you haue beene so briefe with him, he would
Haue bin so briefe with you to shorten you,   1530
For taking so the head, your whole heads length.

BULLINGBROOKE
Mistake not (vncle) further then you should.

YORKE
Take not (good cousin) further then you should,
Lest you mistake the heauens are ouer our heads.

BULLINGBROOKE
I know it vncle, and oppose not my selfe,
Against their will.
      Enter Percie ⌜and trumpeter⌝
                    But, who comes here?
Welcome Harry; what, will not this castle yeelde?

HARRY PERCIE
The Castle royally is mand my Lord
Against thy entrance.

BULLINGBROOKE   Royally,
Why it containes no King.

HARRY PERCIE   Yes (my good Lord,)   1540
It doth containe a King, King Richard lies
Within the limites of yon lime and stone,
And with him are the Lord Aumerle, Lord Salisbury,
Sir Stephen Scroope, besides a cleargie man
Of holy reuerence, who I cannot learne.

NORTHUMBERLAND
Oh belike it is the bishop of Carleil.

BULLINGBROOKE (*to Northumberland*) Noble Lord,
Go to the rude ribbes of that ancient Castle,
Through brazen trumpet send the breath of parlee
Into his ruinde eares, and thus deliuer.   1550
H. Bullingbrooke
Vpon his knees doth kisse king Richards hand,
And sends allegeance and true faith of heart
To his most royall person: hither come
Euen at his feete to lay my armes and power:
Prouided, that my banishment repeald,
And lands restord againe be freely granted;
If not, Ile vse the aduantage of my power,
And lay the summers dust with showres of bloud,
Rainde from the wounds of slaughtred English men, 1560

The which, how farre off from the minde of
    Bullingbrooke
It is, such crimson tempest should bedrench
The fresh greene lap of faire King Richards land:
My stooping duety tenderly shall shew:
Go signifie as much while here we march
Vpon the grassie carpet of this plaine;
Lets march without the noyse of threatning drumme,
That from this Castels tottred battlements
Our faire appointments may be well perusde.

1570 Me thinkes King Richard and my selfe should meete
With no lesse terrour than the elements
Of fire and water, when their thundring shocke
At meeting teares the cloudie cheekes of heauen.
Be he the fire, Ile be the yeelding water;
The rage be his, whilst on the earth I raigne
My waters on the earth, and not on him,
March on, and marke King Richard how he lookes.
    ⌜*They march about the stage, then Bullingbrooke,*
    Yorke, Percie, and souldiers stand at a distance
    from the walls; Northumberland and trumpeter
    aduance to the walls.⌝ *The trumpets sound* ⌜*a parlee*
    without, and an answer within; then a flourish
    within⌝; *Richard appeareth on the walls with*
    ⌜*Carleil,*⌝ *Aumerle,* ⌜*Scroope, and Salisbury*⌝
See see King Richard doth himselfe appeare,
As doth the blushing discontented Sunne,
1580 From out the fierie portall of the East,
When he perceiues the enuious cloudes are bent
To dimme his glorie, and to staine the tracke
Of his bright passage to the Occident.

YORKE
Yet lookes he like a King, beholde his eye,
As bright as is the Eagles, lightens forth
Controlling maiestie; alacke alacke for woe,
That any harme should staine so faire a shew.

KING RICHARD (*to Northumberland*)
We are amazde, and thus long haue we stoode,
To watch the feareful bending of thy knee,
1590 Because we thought our selfe thy lawful King:
And if wee be, howe dare thy ioynts forget
To pay their awefull duety to our presence?
If we be not, shew vs the hand of God
That hath dismist vs from our Stewardship;
For well we know no hand of bloud and bone
Can gripe the sacred handle of our Scepter,
Vnlesse he do prophane, steale, or vsurpe,
And though you thinke that all as you haue done
Haue torne their soules, by turning them from vs,
1600 And we are barren and bereft of friends:
Yet know, my maister God omnipotent,
Is mustering in his cloudes on our behalfe,
Armies of pestilence, and they shall strike
Your children yet vnborne, and vnbegot,
That lift your vassaile hands against my head,
And threat the glorie of my precious crowne.
Tell Bullingbrooke, for yon me thinkes he is,
That euery stride he makes vpon my land,
Is dangerous treason: he is come to open

The purple testament of bleeding warre: 1610
But ere the crowne he lookes for, liue in peace,
Ten thousand bloudy crownes of mothers sonnes,
Shall ill become the flower of Englands face,
Change the complexion of her maid-pale peace,
To scarlet indignation and bedew
Her pastors grasse with faithfull English bloud.

NORTHUMBERLAND ⌜*kneeling*⌝
The King of heauen forbid: our Lo: the king
Should so with ciuill and vnciuill armes,
Be rusht vpon. Thy thrise noble Cosen,
Harry Bullingbrooke doth humbly kisse thy hand,   1620
And by the honorable tombe he sweares,
That stands vpon your roiall grandsires bones,
And by the roialties of both your blouds,
Currents that spring from one most gratious head,
And by the buried hand of warlike Gaunt,
And by the worth and honor of himselfe,
Comprising all that may be sworne or said,
His comming hither hath no further scope,
Then for his lineall roialties, and to beg
Infranchisement immediate on his knees,   1630
Which on thy roiall partie granted once,
His glittering armes he will commend to rust,
His barbed steeds to stables, and his hart
To faithfull seruice of your Maiesty.
This sweares he, as he is a prince and iust,
And as I am a gentleman I credit him.

KING RICHARD
Northumberland, say thus, the King returnes,
His noble Cosen is right welcome hither,
And all the number of his faire demaunds,
Shall be accomplisht without contradiction,   1640
With all the gratious vtterance thou hast,
Speake to his gentle hearing kind commends.
    Northumberland and trumpeter returne to
    Bullingbrooke
(*To Aumerle*) We do debase our selfe, Cosen do we not,
To looke so poorely, and to speake so faire?
Shall we call backe Northumberland and send
Defiance to the traitor and so die?

AUMERLE
No good my Lo: lets fight with gentle words,
Till time lend friends, and friends their helpfull swords.

KING RICHARD
Oh God oh God that ere this tong of mine
That laid the sentence of dread banishment   1650
On yon prowde man should take it off againe
With words of sooth! Oh that I were as great
As is my griefe, or lesser than my name!
Or that I could forget what I haue beene!
Or not remember what I must be now!
Swellst thou (prowd heart) Ile giue thee scope to beate,
Since foes haue scope to beate both thee and me.
    Northumberland aduances to the walls

AUMERLE
Northumberland comes backe from Bullingbrooke.

KING RICHARD
What must the King do now? must he submit?

1660 The King shall do it: must he be deposde?
The king shall be contented: must he loose
The name of King? a Gods name let it go:
Ile giue my iewels for a set of Beades:
My gorgeous pallace for a hermitage:
My gay apparel for an almesmans gowne:
My figurde goblets for a dish of wood:
My scepter for a Palmers walking staffe:
My subiects for a paire of carued Saintes,
And my large kingdome for a little graue,
1670 A little little graue, an obscure graue,
Or Ile be buried in the Kings hie way,
Some way of common trade, where subiects feete
May hourely trample on their soueraignes head;
For on my heart they treade now whilst I liue:
And buried once, why not vpon my head?
Aumerle thou weepst (my tender-hearted coosin)
Weele make fowle weather with despised teares;
Our sighs and they shall lodge the summer corne,
And make a dearth in this reuolting land:
1680 Or shall we play the wantons with our woes,
And make some prety match with sheading teares,
As thus to drop them still vpon one place,
Till they haue fretted vs a paire of graues
Within the earth, and therein laide; there lies
Two kinsmen digd their graues with weeping eies:
Would not this ill do well? well well I see,
I talke but idlely, and you mocke at me.
Most mightie Prince my Lord Northumberland,
What saies king Bullingbroke, will his maiestie
1690 Giue Richard leaue to liue till Richard dye,
You make a leg and Bullingbroke saies I.

NORTHUMBERLAND
My Lord, in the base court he doth attend,
To speake with you, may it please you to come downe.

KING RICHARD
Downe, downe I come, like glistring Phaeton:
Wanting the manage of vnrulie Iades.
In the base court, base court where Kinges growe
    base,
To come at traitors calls, and do them grace,
In the base court come downe: downe court, downe
    King,
For nightowles shreeke where mounting larkes should
    sing.   *Exeunt King Richard and his partie.*
    Northumberland returnes to Bullingbrooke

BULLINGBROOKE
What saies his maiestie?

1700 NORTHUMBERLAND   Sorrowe and greife of hart,
Makes him speake fondly like a frantike man,
    Enter King Richard ⌜and his partie⌝, below
Yet he is come.

BULLINGBROOKE   Stand all apart,
And shew faire dutie to his Maiestie:
    He kneeles downe
My gratious Lord.

KING RICHARD
Faire coosen, you debase your princely knee,

To make the base earth proud with kissing it:
Me rather had my hart might feele your loue,
Then my vnpleasd eie see your curtesie:
Vp coosen vp, your hart is vp I knowe,
Thus high at least, although your knee be lowe.   1710

BULLINGBROOKE
My gratious Lord, I come but for mine owne.

KING RICHARD
Your owne is yours, and I am yours and all.

BULLINGBROOKE
So farre be mine my most redoubted Lord,
As my true seruice shall deserue your loue.

KING RICHARD
Well you deserue: they well deserue to haue,
That know the strong'st and surest way to get,
    ⌜*Bullingbrooke rises*⌝
(*To Yorke*) Vncle giue me your handes, nay drie your
    eies,
Teares shew their loue, but want their remedies.
(*To Bullingbrooke*) Coosen I am to yong to be your
    Father,
Though you are old enough to be my heire,   1720
What you will haue, Ile giue, and willing to,
For doe we must, what force will haue vs doe:
Set on towards London, Cosen is it so?

BULLINGBROOKE
Yea my good Lord.

KING RICHARD   Then I must not say no.
    ⌜*Flourish.*⌝ *Exeunt*

Enter the Queene with her two Ladies   Sc. 12
QUEENE   (3.4)
What sport shall we deuise here in this garden,
To driue away the heauy thought of care?

⌜1.⌝ LADY Madame weele play at bowles.

QUEENE
Twil make me thinke the world is full of rubs,
And that my fortune runs against the bias.

⌜2.⌝ LADY Madame weele daunce.   1730

QUEENE
My legs can keepe no measure in delight,
When my poore hart no measure keepes in griefe:
Therfore no dauncing girle, some other sport.

⌜1.⌝ LADY Madame weele tell tales.

QUEENE Of sorrow or of ioy.

⌜1.⌝ LADY Of either Madame.

QUEENE Of neither girle:
For if of ioy, being altogither wanting,
It doth remember me the more of sorrow:
Or if of griefe, being altogither had,   1740
It adds more sorrow to my want of ioy:
For what I haue I need not to repeate,
And what I want it bootes not to complaine.

⌜2.⌝ LADY
Madame Ile sing.

QUEENE   Tis well that thou hast cause,
But thou shouldst please me better, wouldst thou
    weepe.

⌈2.⌉ LADY
I could weepe, Madame would it doe you good.

QUEENE
And I could sing would weeping doe me good,
And neuer borrow any teare of thee.
   Enter a Gardener, and two men
But stay, here come the gardeners,
1750 Lets step into the shadow of these trees,
My wretchednes vnto a row of pines,
They will talke of state for euery one doth so,
Against a change: woe is fore-runne with woe.
   The Queene and her Ladies stand apart

GARDENER ⌈*to 1. Man*⌉
Go bind thou vp yong dangling Aphricokes,
Which like vnruly children make their sire,
Stoope with oppression of their prodigall weight,
Giue some supportance to the bending twigs,
⌈*To 2. Man*⌉ Go thou, and like an executioner
Cut off the heads of too fast growing spraies,
1760 That looke too loftie in our common-wealth,
All must be euen in our gouernement.
You thus employed, I will goe roote away
The noysome weedes which without profit sucke
The soiles fertilitie from wholsome flowers.

⌈1.⌉ MAN
Why should we in the compas of a pale,
Keepe law and forme, and due proportion,
Shewing as in a modle our firme estate,
When our sea-walled garden the whole land
Is full of weedes, her fairest flowers choakt vp,
1770 Her fruit trees all vnprunde, her hedges ruinde,
Her knots disordred, and her holsome hearbs
Swarming with caterpillers.

GARDENER   Hold thy peace,
He that hath suffred this disordred spring,
Hath now himselfe met with the fall of leafe:
The weedes which his broad spreading leaues did
   shelter,
That seemde in eating him to hold him vp,
Are pluckt vp roote and all by Bullingbrooke,
I meane the Earle of Wiltshire, Bushie, Greene.

⌈2.⌉ MAN
What are they dead?

GARDENER   They are. And Bullingbrooke
1780 Hath ceasde the wastefull king, Oh what pitie is it
That he had not so trimde, and drest his land
As we this garden. We at time of yeare
Do wound the barke, the skinne of our fruit trees,
Lest being ouer prowd in sap and bloud,
With too much riches it confound it selfe:
Had he done so to great and growing men,
They might haue liude to beare, and he to taste
Their fruits of duety: superfluous branches
We loppe away, that bearing boughes may liue:
1790 Had he done so, himselfe had borne the crowne,
Which waste of idle houres hath quite throwne
   downe.

⌈1.⌉ MAN
What, thinke you then the King shall be deposed?

GARDENER
Deprest he is already, and deposde
Tis doubt he will be. Letters came last night
To a deare friend of the good Duke of Yorkes,
That tell blacke tidings.

QUEENE
Oh I am prest to death through want of speaking:
   She comes forward
Thou old Adams likenesse set to dresse this garden,
How dares thy harsh rude tong sound this vnpleasing
   news?
What Eue? what serpent hath suggested thee   1800
To make a second fall of cursed man?
Why dost thou say king Richard is deposde?
Darst thou thou little better thing than earth
Diuine his downefall? say, where, when, and how,
Camst thou by this ill tidings speake thou wretch?

GARDENER
Pardon me Madam, little ioy haue I
To breathe this newes, yet what I say is true:
King Richard he is in the mightie hold
Of Bullingbrooke: their fortunes both are weyde.
In your Lo: scale is nothing but himselfe,   1810
And some few vanities that make him light:
But in the ballance of great Bullingbrooke,
Besides himselfe are all the English peeres,
And with that oddes he weighs King Richard downe;
Post you to London and you will find it so,
I speake no more than euery one doth know.

QUEENE
Nimble Mischance that arte so light of foote,
Doth not thy embassage belong to me,
And am I last that knowes it? Oh thou thinkest
To serue me last that I may longest keepe   1820
Thy sorrow in my breast: come Ladies go
To meete at London Londons king in wo.
What, was I borne to this that my sad looke
Should grace the triumph of great Bullingbrooke?
Gardner for telling me these newes of wo,
Pray God the plants thou graftst may neuer grow.
   Exit with Ladies

GARDENER
Poore Queene, so that thy state might be no worse,
I would my Skill were subiect to thy curse:
Here did she fall a teare, here in this place
Ile set a banke of Rew sowre hearb of grace,   1830
Rew euen for ruth heere shortly shall be seene,
In the remembrance of a weeping Queene.   *Exeunt*

Enter as to parliament, Bullingbrooke, Aumerle,   **Sc. 13**
Northumberland, Percie, Fitzwaters, Surry, Carleil,   **(4.1)**
and the Abbot of Westminster

BULLINGBROOKE
Call forth Bagot.
   Enter Bagot with officers
                Now Bagot, freely speake thy mind,

What thou doest know of noble Gloucesters death,
Who wrought it with the King, and who performde
The bloudy office of his timeles end.

BAGOT

Then set before my face the Lord Aumerle.

BULLINGBROOKE (*to Aumerle*)

Cousin, stand foorth, and looke vpon that man.
    Aumerle stands forth

BAGOT

My Lord Aumerle, I know your daring tong

1840   Scornes to vnsay what once it hath deliuered.
In that dead time when Glocesters death was plotted
I heard you say, Is not my arme of length,
That reacheth from the restful English court,
As farre as Callice to mine vncles head?
Amongst much other talke that very time
I heard you say, that you had rather refuse
The offer of an hundred thousand crownes,
Then Bullingbrookes returne to England
Adding withall, how blest this land would be
In this your cosins death.

1850 **AUMERLE**   Princes and noble Lords,
What answer shall I make to this base man?
Shall I so much dishonour my faire starres
On equall termes to giue him chasticement?
Either I must, or haue mine honour soild
With the attainder of his slaunderous lippes,
    He throwes downe his gage
There is my gage, the manual seale of death,
That markes thee out for hell, I say thou liest,
And wil maintaine what thou hast said is false
In thy heart bloud, though being all too base
1860   To staine the temper of my knightly sword.

BULLINGBROOKE

Bagot, forbeare, thou shalt not take it vp.

AUMERLE

Excepting one, I would he were the best
In all this presence that hath moude me so.

FITZWATERS

If that thy valure stand on simpathie,
There is my gage Aumerle, in gage to thine;
    He throwes downe his gage
By that faire Sunne which shews me where thou
    standst,
I heard thee say, and vauntingly thou spakst it,
That thou wert cause of noble Gloucesters death.
If thou deniest it twenty times, thou liest,
1870   And I will turne thy falshoode to thy heart,
Where it was forged with my rapiers point.

AUMERLE

Thou darst not (coward) liue to see that day.

FITZWATERS

Now by my soule, I would it were this houre.

AUMERLE

Fitzwaters, thou art damnd to hell for this.

HARRY PERCIE

Aumerle, thou liest, his honour is as true
In this appeale as thou art all vniust,

And that thou art so, there I throwe my gage,
    He throwes downe his gage
To prooue it on thee to the extreamest point
Of mortall breathing, ceaze it if thou darst.

AUMERLE

And if I do not, may my hands rot off,   1880
And neuer brandish more reuengefull steele
Ouer the glittering helmet of my foe.

SURRY

My lord Fitzwater, I do remember well
The very time Aumerle and you did talke.

FITZWATERS

Tis very true, you were in presence then,
And you can witnes with me this is true.

SURRY

As false, by heauen, as heauen it selfe is true.

FITZWATERS

Surrie thou liest.

SURRY   Dishonorable boy,
That lie shall lie so heauie on my sword,
That it shall render vengeance and reuenge,   1890
Till thou the lie-giuer, and that lie do lie,
In earth as quiet as thy fathers scull.
In proofe where of there is my honours pawne,
    He throwes downe his gage
Ingage it to the triall if thou darst.

FITZWATERS

How fondly doest thou spurre a forward horse!
If I dare eate, or drinke, or breathe, or liue,
I dare meet Surry in a wildernes,
And spit vpon him whilst I say, he lies,
And lies, and lies: there is my bond of faith,
To tie thee to my strong correction: 1900
As I intende to thriue in this new world,
Aumerle is guiltie of my true appeale.
Besides I heard the banisht Norffolke say,
That thou Aumerle didst send two of thy men,
To execute the noble Duke at Callice.

AUMERLE

Some honest Christian trust me with a gage,
    He takes anothers gage and throwes it downe
That Norffolke lies, heere do I throwe downe this,
If he may be repeald to trie his honour.

BULLINGBROOKE

These differences shall all rest vnder gage,
Till Norffolke be repeald, repeald he shallbe,   1910
And though mine enimie, restord againe
To all his landes and signiories: when he is returnd,
Against Aumerle we will inforce his triall.

CARLEIL

That honourable day shall neuer be seene,
Manie a time hath banisht Norffolke fought,
For Iesu Christ in glorious Christian feild,
Streaming the ensigne of the Christian Crosse,
Against blacke Pagans, Turkes, and Saracens,
And toild with workes of warre, retird him selfe
To Italie, and there at Venice gaue   1920
His bodie to that pleasant Countries earth,

And his pure soule vnto his Captaine Christ,
Vnder whose coulours he had fought so long.

BULLINGBROOKE

Why Bishop of Carleil is Norffolke dead?

CARLEIL

As surely as I liue my Lord.

BULLINGBROOKE

Sweet peace conduct his sweete soule to the bosome,
Of good olde Abraham: Lords Appellants,
Your differences shall all rest vnder gage,
Till we assigne you to your daies of triall.
          Enter Yorke

YORKE

1930 Great Duke of Lancaster I come to thee,
From plume-pluckt Richard, who with willing soule,
Adopts the heire, and his high scepter yeeldes,
To the possession of thy royall hand:
Ascend his throne, descending now from him,
And long liue Henry of that name the fourth.

BULLINGBROOKE

In Gods name Ile ascend the regall throne.

CARLEIL Mary God forbid.

Worst in this royall presence may I speake.
Yet best beseeming me to speake the truth,
1940 Would God that any in this noble presence,
Were enough noble to be vpright iudge
Of noble Richard. Then true noblesse would
Learne him forbearance from so foule a wrong,
What subiect can giue sentence on his King:
And who sits here that is not Richards subiect?
Theeues are not iudgd but they are by to heare,
Although apparant guilt be seene in them,
And shall the figure of Gods Maiesty,
His Captaine, steward, deputy, elect,
1950 Annointed, crowned, planted, many yeares
Be iudgd by subiect and inferiour breath,
And he himselfe not present? Oh forfend it God,
That in a Christian climate soules refinde,
Should shew so heinous blacke obsceene a deed.
I speake to subiects and a subiect speakes,
Stird vp by God thus boldly for his King,
My Lord of Hereford here whom you call King,
Is a foule traitour to proud Herefords King,
And if you crowne him let me prophesie,
1960 The bloud of English shall manure the ground,
And future ages groane for this foule act,
Peace shall go sleepe with turkes and infidels,
And in this seate of peace, tumultuous warres,
Shall kin with kin, and kinde with kind confound:
Disorder, horror, feare, and mutiny,
Shall heere inhabit, and this land be cald,
The field of Golgotha and dead mens sculs.
Oh if you reare this house against this house,
It will the wofullest diuision proue,
1970 That euer fell vpon this cursed earth:
Preuent, resist it, let it not be so,
Lest child, childs children, crie against you wo.

NORTHUMBERLAND

Well haue you argued sir, and for your paines,
Of Capitall treason, we arrest you heere:
My Lord of Westminster, be it your charge,
To keepe him safely till his day of triall.
May it please you, Lords, to grant the Commons Suit?

BULLINGBROOKE

Fetch hither *Richard*, that in common view
He may surrender: so we shall proceede
Without suspition.

YORKE   I will be his Conduct.   *Exit* 1980

BULLINGBROOKE

Lords, you that here are vnder our Arrest,
Procure your Sureties for your Dayes of Answer:
Little are we beholding to your Loue,
And little look'd for at your helping Hands.
          Enter Richard and Yorke ⌈with attendants bearing
          the Crowne and scepter⌉

RICHARD

Alack, why am I sent for to a King,
Before I haue shooke off the Regall thoughts
Wherewith I reign'd? I hardly yet haue learn'd
To insinuate, flatter, bowe, and bend my Knee.
Giue Sorrow leaue a while, to tuture me
To this submission. Yet I well remember   1990
The fauors of these men: were they not mine?
Did they not sometime cry, All hayle to me?
So *Iudas* did to Christ: but he in twelue,
Found truth in all, but one; I, in twelue thousand,
          none.
God saue the King: will no man say, Amen?
Am I both Priest, and Clarke? well then, Amen.
God saue the King, although I be not hee:
And yet Amen, if Heauen doe thinke him mee.
To doe what seruice, am I sent for hither?

YORKE

To doe that office of thine owne good will,   2000
Which tyred Maiestie did make thee offer:
The Resignation of thy State and Crowne
To *Henry Bullingbrooke.*

RICHARD (*to an attendant*)

Giue me the Crown. (*To Bullingbrooke*) Here Cousin,
          seize yᵉ Crown:
Here Cousin, on this side my Hand, on that side thine.
Now is this Golden Crowne like a deepe Well,
That owes two Buckets, filling one another,
The emptier euer dancing in the ayre,
The other downe, vnseene, and full of Water:
That Bucket downe, and full of Teares am I,   2010
Drinking my Griefes, whil'st you mount vp on high.

BULLINGBROOKE

I thought you had been willing to resigne.

RICHARD

My Crowne I am, but still my Griefes are mine:
You may my Glories and my State depose,
But not my Griefes; still am I King of those.

BULLINGBROOKE

Part of your Cares you giue me with your Crowne.

RICHARD

Your Cares set vp, do not pluck my Cares downe.
My Care, is losse of Care, by old Care done,
Your Care, is gaine of Care, by new Care wonne:
2020 The Cares I giue, I haue, though giuen away,
They 'tend the Crowne, yet still with me they stay.

BULLINGBROOKE

Are you contented to resigne the Crowne?

RICHARD

I, no; no, I: for I must nothing bee:
Therefore no, no, for I resigne to thee.
Now, marke me how I will vndoe my selfe.
I giue this heauie Weight from off my Head,
        ⌈*Bullingbrooke accepts the Crowne*⌉
And this vnwieldie Scepter from my Hand,
        ⌈*Bullingbrooke accepts the Scepter*⌉
The pride of Kingly sway from out my Heart.
With mine owne Teares I wash away my Balme,
2030 With mine owne Hands I giue away my Crowne,
With mine owne Tongue denie my Sacred State,
With mine owne Breath release all dutious Oathes;
All Pompe and Maiestie I doe forsweare:
My Manors, Rents, Reuenues, I forgoe;
My Acts, Decrees, and Statutes I denie:
God pardon all Oathes that are broke to mee,
God keepe all Vowes vnbroke are made to thee.
Make me, that nothing haue, with nothing grieu'd,
And thou with all pleas'd, that hast all atchieu'd.
2040 Long may'st thou liue in *Richards* Seat to sit,
And soone lye *Richard* in an Earthie Pit.
God saue King *Henry*, vn-King'd *Richard* sayes,
And send him many yeeres of Sunne-shine dayes.
What more remaines?

NORTHUMBERLAND (*giuing Richard papers*)

                    No more: but that you reade
These Accusations, and these grieuous Crymes,
Committed by your Person, and your followers,
Against the State, and Profit of this Land:
That by confessing them, the Soules of men
May deeme, that you are worthily depos'd.

RICHARD

2050 Must I doe so? and must I rauell out
My weau'd-vp follyes? Gentle *Northumberland*,
If thy Offences were vpon Record,
Would it not shame thee, in so faire a troupe,
To reade a Lecture of them? If thou would'st,
There should'st thou finde one heynous Article,
Contayning the deposing of a King,
And cracking the strong Warrant of an Oath,
Mark'd with a Blot, damn'd in the Booke of Heauen.
Nay, all of you, that stand and looke vpon,
2060 Whil'st that my wretchednesse doth bait my selfe,
Though some of you, with *Pilate*, wash your hands,
Shewing an outward pittie: yet you *Pilates*
Haue here deliuer'd me to my sowre Crosse,
And Water cannot wash away your sinne.

NORTHUMBERLAND

My Lord dispatch, reade o're these Articles.

RICHARD

Mine Eyes are full of Teares, I cannot see:
And yet salt-Water blindes them not so much,
But they can see a sort of Traytors here.
Nay, if I turne mine Eyes vpon my selfe,
I finde my selfe a Traytor with the rest: 2070
For I haue giuen here my Soules consent,
T'vndeck the pompous Body of a King;
Made Glory base; and Soueraigntie, a Slaue;
Prowd Maiestie, a Subiect; State, a Pesant.

NORTHUMBERLAND My Lord.

RICHARD

No Lord of thine, thou haught-insulting man;
Nor no mans Lord: I haue no Name, no Title;
No, not that Name was giuen me at the Font,
But 'tis vsurpt: alack the heauie day,
That I haue worne so many Winters out,   2080
And know not now, what Name to call my selfe.
Oh, that I were a Mockerie, King of Snow,
Standing before the Sunne of *Bullingbrooke*,
To melt my selfe away in Water-drops.
Good King, great King, and yet not greatly good,
And if my word be Sterling yet in England,
Let it command a Mirror hither straight,
That it may shew me what a Face I haue,
Since it is Bankrupt of his Maiestie.

BULLINGBROOKE

Goe some of you, and fetch a Looking-Glasse.   2090
                              Exit one or more

NORTHUMBERLAND

Read o're this Paper, while yᵉ Glasse doth come.

RICHARD

Fiend, thou torments me, ere I come to Hell.

BULLINGBROOKE

Vrge it no more, my Lord *Northumberland*.

NORTHUMBERLAND

The Commons will not then be satisfy'd.

RICHARD

They shall be satisfy'd: Ile reade enough,
When I doe see the very Booke indeede,
Where all my sinnes are writ, and that's my selfe.
        Enter one with a Glasse
Giue me that Glasse, and therein will I reade.
        Richard takes the Glasse, and lookes in it
No deeper wrinckles yet? hath Sorrow strucke
So many Blowes vpon this Face of mine,   2100
And made no deeper Wounds? Oh flatt'ring Glasse,
Like to my followers in prosperitie,
Thou do'st beguile me. Was this Face, the Face
That euery day, vnder his House-hold Roofe,
Did keepe ten thousand men? Was this the Face,
That like the Sunne, did make beholders winke?
Is this the Face, which fac'd so many follyes,
That was at last out-fac'd by *Bullingbrooke*?
A brittle Glory shineth in this Face,
As brittle as the Glory, is the Face,   2110
        He shatters the Glasse
For there it is, crackt in an hundred shiuers.

Marke silent King, the Morall of this sport,
How soone my Sorrow hath destroy'd my Face.

BULLINGBROOKE

The shadow of your Sorrow hath destroy'd
The shadow of your Face.

RICHARD　　　　　　　Say that againe.

The shadow of my Sorrow: ha, let's see,
'Tis very true, my Griefe lyes all within,
And these externall manner of Laments,
Are meerely shadowes, to the vnseene Griefe,
2120　That swells with silence in the tortur'd Soule.
There lyes the substance: and I thanke thee King
For thy great bountie, that not onely giu'st
Me cause to wayle, but teachest me the way
How to lament the cause. Ile begge one Boone,
And then be gone, and trouble you no more.
Shall I obtaine it?

BULLINGBROOKE　　　Name it, faire Cousin.

RICHARD

Faire Cousin? I am greater then a King:
For when I was a King, my flatterers
Were then but subiects; being now a subiect,
2130　I haue a King here to my flatterer:
Being so great, I haue no neede to begge.

BULLINGBROOKE　Yet aske.

RICHARD　And shall I haue?

BULLINGBROOKE　You shall.

RICHARD　Then giue me leaue to goe.

BULLINGBROOKE　Whither?

RICHARD

Whither you will, so I were from your sights.

BULLINGBROOKE

Goe some of you, conuey him to the Tower.

RICHARD

Oh good: conuey: Conueyers are you all,
2140　That rise thus nimbly by a true Kings fall.

⌐Exit guarded⌐

BULLINGBROOKE

On wednesday next, we solemnly set downe
Our Coronation, Lords prepare your selues.

Exeunt. Manent Westminster, Caleil, Aumerle

ABBOT

A wofull Pageant haue we heere beheld.

CARLEIL

The woe's to come, the children yet vnborne,
Shall feele this day as sharp to them as thorne.

AUMERLE

You holy Clergy men, is there no plot,
To ridde the realme of this pernitious blot?

ABBOT

My Lo. before I freely speake my mind heerein,
You shall not onely take the Sacrament,
2150　To burie mine intents, but also to effect,
What euer I shall happen to deuise:
I see your browes are full of discontent,
Your harts of sorrow, and your eies of teares:
Come home with me to supper, I will lay
A plot, shall shew vs all a merrie daie.　　　*Exeunt*

Enter the Queene with her Ladies　　Sc. 14
　　　　　　　　　　　　　　　　　　　　　(5.1)

QUEENE

This way the King will come, this is the way,
To Iulius Caesars ill erected Tower,
To whose flint bosome, my condemned Lord,
Is doomde a prisoner by proud Bullingbrooke.
Heere let vs rest, if this rebellious earth,　　2160
Haue any resting for her true Kings Queene.

Enter Richard ⌐and guard⌐

But soft, but see, or rather doe not see,
My faire Rose wither, yet looke vp, behold,
That you in pittie may dissolue to deaw,
And wash him fresh againe with true loue teares.
Ah thou the modle where olde Troy did stand!
Thou mappe of honour, thou King Richards tombe,
And not King Richard: thou most beauteous Inne,
Why should hard fauourd greife be lodgd in thee,
When triumph is become an alehouse guest?　　2170

RICHARD

Ioyne not with greife faire woman, doe not so,
To make my end too sudden, learne good soule,
To thinke our former state a happie dreame,
From which awakt the trueth of what we are
Shewes vs but this: I am sworne brother (sweet)
To grim necessitie, and he and I,
Will keepe a league till death. Hie thee to Fraunce,
And cloister thee in some religious house,
Our holy liues must win a new worlds crowne,
Which our prophane houres heere haue stricken
　　downe.　　2180

QUEENE

What is my Richard both in shape and minde
Transformd and weakened? hath Bullingbrooke,
Deposde thine intellect? hath he been in thy hart?
The Lyon dying thrusteth foorth his pawe,
And woundes the earth if nothing else with rage,
To be ore-powr'd, and wilt thou pupill-like
Take the correction, mildly kisse the rod,
And fawne on Rage with base humilitie,
Which art a Lion and the king of beasts.

RICHARD

A King of beasts indeed, if aught but beasts,　　2190
I had been still a happie King of men.
Good (sometimes Queene) prepare thee hence for
　　France,
Thinke I am dead, and that euen here thou takest
As from my death bed thy last liuing leaue;
In winters tedious nights sit by the fire,
With good old folkes, and let them tell the tales,
Of woefull ages long agoe betidde:
And ere thou bid good night to quite their griefes,
Tell thou the lamentable fall of me,
And send the hearers weeping to their beds:　　2200
For why, the senslesse brands will simpathize
The heauy accent of thy moouing tong,
And in compassion weepe the fire out,
And some wil mourne in ashes, some cole blacke,
For the deposing of a rightfull King.

Enter Northumberland

NORTHUMBERLAND

My Lord, the minde of Bullingbrooke is changde,
You must to Pomfret, not vnto the Tower.
And Madam, there is order tane for you,
With al swift speede you must away to France.

RICHARD

2210 Northumberland, thou ladder wherewithall
The mounting Bullingbrooke ascends my throne,
The time shall not be many houres of age
More than it is, ere foule sinne gathering head
Shall breake into corruption, thou shalt thinke,
Though he diuide the realme and giue thee halfe,
It is too little helping him to all.
He shall thinke that thou which knowst the way
To plant vnrightfull kings, wilt know againe,
Being nere so little vrgde another way,
2220 To plucke him headlong from the vsurped throne:
The loue of wicked friends conuerts to feare,
That feare to hate, and hate turnes one or both
To worthy daunger and deserued death.

NORTHUMBERLAND

My guilt be on my head, and there an end:
Take leaue and part, for you must part forthwith.

RICHARD

Doubly diuorst (bad men) you violate
A two-fold marriage twixt my crowne and me,
And then betwixt me and my married wife.
(*To the Queene*) Let me vnkisse the oathe twixt thee
          and me:
2230 And yet not so, for with a kisse twas made.
Part vs Northumberland, I towardes the north,
Where shiuering cold and sickenesse pines the clime:
My Queene to Fraunce, from whence set forth in pomp
She came adorned hither like sweete Maie,
Sent backe like Hollowmas or shortst of day.

QUEENE

And must we be diuided? must we part?

RICHARD

I hand from hand (my loue) and heart from heart.

QUEENE

Banish vs both, and send the King with me.

⌜NORTHUMBERLAND⌝

That were some loue, but little pollicie.

QUEENE

2240 Then whither he goes, thither let me go.

RICHARD

So two togither weeping make one woe,
Weepe thou for me in Fraunce, I for thee heere,
Better far off than neere be nere the neare,
Go count thy way with sighes, I mine with groanes.

QUEENE

So longest way shall haue the longest moanes.

RICHARD

Twise for one step Ile grone the way being short
And peece the way out with a heauy heart.
Come come in wooing sorrow lets be briefe,
Since wedding it, there is such length in griefe;

One kisse shall stop our mouthes, and dumbly part,   2250
Thus giue I mine, and thus take I thy heart.
          They kisse

QUEENE

Giue me mine owne againe, twere no good part
To take on me to keepe, and kill thy heart:
          They kisse
So now I haue mine owne againe, be gone,
That I may striue to kill it with a groane.

RICHARD

We make woe wanton with this fond delay,
Once more adue, the rest let sorrow say.
          *Exeunt ⌜Richard, guarded, and Northumberland
          at one doore, the Queene and her Ladies at
                              another doore⌝*

Enter Duke of Yorke and the Dutchesse   Sc. 15

DUTCHESSE OF YORKE   (5.2)

My Lord, you told me you would tell the rest,
When weeping made you breake the storie of
Of our two cousins comming into London.   2260

YORKE

Where did I leaue?

DUTCHESSE OF YORKE   At that sad stop my Lord,
Where rude misgouernd hands from windowes tops,
Threw dust and rubbish on king Richards head.

YORKE

Then (as I said) the Duke great Bullingbrooke
Mounted vpon a hote and fierie steede,
Which his aspiring rider seemd to know,
With slow, but stately pase kept on his course,
Whilst all tongues cried, God saue the Bullingbrooke,
You would haue thought the very windows spake:
So many greedy lookes of yong and old   2270
Through casements darted their desiring eies
Vpon his visage, and that all the walles
With painted imagery had said at once,
Iesu preserue the, welcome Bullingbrooke,
Whilst he from the one side to the other turning
Bare-headed, lower than his prowd steedes necke
Bespake them thus; I thanke you countrymen:
And thus still doing, thus he passt along.

DUTCHESSE OF YORKE

Alac poore Richard, where rode he the whilst?

YORKE

As in a Theater the eies of men,   2280
After a well-gract Actor leaues the stage,
Are ydly bent on him that enters next,
Thinking his prattle to be tedious;
Euen so, or with much more contempt mens eies
Did scowle on gentle Ric. no man cried, God saue
          him,
No ioyfull tongue gaue him his welcome home,
But dust was throwen vpon his sacred head:
Which with such gentle sorrow he shooke off,
His face still combating with teares and smiles,
The badges of his griefe and patience,   2290
That had not God for some strong purpose steeld

The hearts of men, they must perforce haue melted,
And Barbarisme it selfe haue pittied him:
But heauen hath a hand in these euents,
To whose high will we bound our calme contents.
To Bullingbrooke are we sworne subiects now,
Whose state and honour I for ay allow.

Enter Aumerle

DUTCHESSE OF YORKE

Here comes my sonne Aumerle.

YORKE　　　　　　　　　　　　　Aumerle that was,
But that is lost, for being Richards friend:
2300　And Madam, you must call him Rutland now:
I am in parleament pledge for his truth
And lasting fealtie to the new made king.

DUTCHESSE OF YORKE

Welcome my sonne, who are the violets now
That strew the greene lap of the new come spring.

AUMERLE

Madam, I know not, nor I greatly care not,
God knowes I had as leife be none as one.

YORKE

Well, beare you wel in this new spring of time,
Lest you be cropt before you come to prime.
What newes from Oxford, hold these iusts & triumphs?

AUMERLE

2310　For aught I know (my Lord) they do.

YORKE You will be there I know.

AUMERLE

If God preuent it not, I purpose so.

YORKE

What seale is that that hangs without thy bosome?
Yea, lookst thou pale? let me see the writing.

AUMERLE

My Lord, tis nothing.

YORKE　　　　　　　　No matter then who see it,
I will be satisfied, let me see the writing.

AUMERLE

I do beseech your grace to pardon me;
It is a matter of small consequence,
Which for some reasons I would not haue seene.

YORKE

2320　Which for some reasons sir I meane to see.
I feare I feare.

DUTCHESSE OF YORKE What should you feare?
Tis nothing but some band that he is entred into
For gay apparell gainst the triumph day.

YORKE

Bound to himselfe; what doth he with a bond
That he is bound to. Wife, thou art a foole:
Boy, let me see the writing.

AUMERLE

I do beseech you pardon me, I may not shew it.

YORKE

I will be satisfied, let me see it I say:

He pluckes it out of Aumerles bosome and reades it

Treason, foule treason, villaine, traitor, slaue.

2330　DUTCHESSE OF YORKE What is the matter my lord?

YORKE

Ho, who is within there? saddle my horse,
God for his mercy! what treachery is here?

DUTCHESSE OF YORKE Why what is it my Lord?

YORKE

Giue me my bootes I say, saddle my horse,
Now by mine honour, by my life, my troth
I will appeach the villaine.

DUTCHESSE OF YORKE What is the matter?

YORKE Peace foolish woman.

DUTCHESSE OF YORKE

I wil not peace, what is the matter sonne?

AUMERLE

Good mother be content, it is no more　　　2340
Then my poore life must answere.

DUTCHESSE OF YORKE　　　　　Thy life answere?

YORKE

Bring me my bootes, I will vnto the King.

His man enters with his bootes

DUTCHESSE OF YORKE

Strike him Aumerle, poore boy thou art amazd,
(*To Yorkes man*) Hence vilaine neuer more come in my
sight.

YORKE

Giue me my bootes I say.

DUTCHESSE OF YORKE　　　　Why Yorke what wilt thou doe?
Wilt thou not hide the trespasse of thine owne?
Haue we more sons? or are we like to haue?
Is not my teeming date drunke vp with time?
And wilt thou plucke my faire sonne from mine age?
And rob me of a happie mothers name,　　　2350
Is he not like the? is he not thine owne?

YORKE Thou fond mad woman,
Wilt thou conceale this darke conspiracie?
A doozen of them here haue tane the sacrament,
And interchaungeably set downe there hands,
To kill the king at Oxford.

DUTCHESSE OF YORKE　　　　He shal be none,
Weele keepe him heere, then what is that to him?

YORKE

Away fond woman, were he twentie times my sonne,
I would appeach him.

DUTCHESSE OF YORKE　　　Hadst thou groand for him
As I haue done, thou wouldst bee more pittifull.　　2360
But nowe I knowe thy minde, thou doest suspect
That I haue been disloiall to thy bed,
And that he is a bastard, not thy sonne:
Sweete Yorke, sweete husband, be not of that mind,
He is as like thee as a man may be,
Not like to me, or any of my kinne,
And yet I loue him.

YORKE　　　　　　Make way vnrulie woman.

Exit ⌈with his man⌉

DUTCHESSE OF YORKE

After Aumerle: mount thee vpon his horse,
Spur, post, and get before him to the King,
And beg thy pardon ere he do accuse thee,　　2370

Ile not be long behind, though I be old,
I doubt not but to ride as fast as Yorke.
An neuer will I rise vp from the ground,
Till Bullingbroke haue pardond thee: away, be gone.

       Exeunt ⌈seuerally⌉

Sc. 16   *Enter Bullingbrooke, crowned King Henry, with*
(5.3)   *Percie, and other nobles*

KING HENRY
Can no man tell of my vnthriftie sonne?
Tis full three moneths since I did see him last,
If any plague hang ouer vs tis he:
I would to God my Lordes he might be found:
Inquire at London, mongst the Tauernes there,
2380 For there (they say) he daylie doth frequent,
With vnrestrained loose companions,
Euen such (they say) as stand in narrow lanes,
And beate our watch, and rob our passengers,
Which he yong wanton and effeminate boy,
Takes on the point of honour to support
So dissolute a crew.

HARRY PERCIE
My Lord, some two dayes since I saw the prince,
And tould him of these triumphes helde at Oxford.

KING HENRY And what said the gallant?

HARRY PERCIE
2390 His answer was, he would vnto the stews,
And from the commonst creature plucke a gloue,
And weare it as a fauour, and with that,
He would vnhorse the lustiest Challenger.

KING HENRY
As dissolute as desperat, yet through both,
I see some sparkes of better hope, which elder dayes,
May happily bring foorth.

   Enter Aumerle amazed

      But who comes heere?

AUMERLE Where is the King?

KING HENRY
What meanes our cosen, that he stares and lookes so
  wildly.

AUMERLE *(kneeling)*
God saue your grace, I doe beseech your Maiestie,
2400 To haue some conference with your grace alone.

KING HENRY *(to Lords)*
Withdrawe your selues, and leaue vs here alone.

    Exeunt. Manet King Henry and Aumerle

What is the matter with our cosen nowe?

AUMERLE
For euer may my knees growe to the earth,
My tongue, cleaue to the rooffe within my mouth,
Vnlesse a pardon ere I rise or speake.

KING HENRY
Intended, or committed, was this fault?
If on the first, how heynous ere it be
To win thy after loue, I pardon thee.

AUMERLE *(rising)*
Then giue me leaue that I may turne the key,
2410 That no man enter till my tale be done.

KING HENRY
Haue thy desire.

  Aumerle lockes the dore.
  The Duke of Yorke knokes at the doore and crieth

YORKE *(within)* My leige beware, looke to thy selfe,
Thou hast a Traitor in thy presence there.

  King Henry drawes his sword

KING HENRY *(to Aumerle)* Vilain Ile make thee safe.

AUMERLE
Stay thy reuengefull hand, thou hast no cause to feare.

YORKE *(knoking within)*
Open the dore, secure foole, hardie King,
Shall I for loue speake treason to thy face,
Open the dore, or I will breake it open.

  ⌈King Henry⌉ opens the dore. Enter Yorke

KING HENRY
What is the matter vncle, speake,
Recouer breath, tell vs, how neare is daunger,
That wee may arme vs to encounter it?   2420

YORKE
Peruse this writing heere, and thou shalt know,
The treason that my haste forbids me shew.

  He giues King Henry the paper

AUMERLE
Remember as thou readst, thy promise past,
I do repent me, reade not my name there,
My hart is not confederate with my hand.

YORKE
It was (vilaine) ere thy hand did set it downe.
I tore it from the traitors bosome (King,)
Feare, and not loue, begets his penitence:
Forget to pittie him, lest pittie proue,
A Serpent that will sting thee to the hart.   2430

KING HENRY
O heynous, strong, and bould conspiracy;
O loyall Father, of a treacherous Sonne,
Thou sheere immaculate and siluer Fountaine,
From whence this streame, through muddy passages,
Hath held his current, and defild himselfe,
Thy ouerflow of good, conuerts to bad:
And thy aboundant goodnes, shall excuse,
This deadly blot in thy digressing sonne.

YORKE
So shall my vertue, be his vices baude,
An he shall spend mine honour, with his shame, 2440
As thriftles sonnes, their scraping Fathers gold:
Mine honour liues when his dishonour dies,
Or my shamde life in his dishonour lies,
Thou kilst me in his life, giuing him breath,
The traitor liues, the true man's put to death.

DUTCHESSE OF YORKE *(within)*
What ho, my Liege, for Gods sake let me in.

KING HENRY
What shril voicd suppliant makes this eger crie?

DUTCHESSE OF YORKE *(within)*
A woman, and thy aunt (great king) tis I,
Speake with me, pitie me, open the doore,
A beggar begs that neuer begd before.   2450

KING HENRY

    Our scene is altred from a serious thing,
    And now changde to the Beggar and the King:
    My dangerous cousin, let your mother in,
    I know she is come to pray for your foule sinne.
        Aumerle opens the dore. Enter Dutchesse of Yorke

YORKE

    If thou do pardon whosoeuer pray,
    More sinnes for this forgiuenes prosper may:
    This festred ioynt cut off, the rest rest sound,
    This let alone wil all the rest confound.

DUTCHESSE OF YORKE (*kneeling*)

    Oh king, beleeue not this hard-hearted man,
2460   Loue louing not it selfe, none other can.

YORKE

    Thou frantike woman, what dost thou make here?
    Shall thy old dugs once more a traitor reare?

DUTCHESSE OF YORKE

    Sweete Yorke be patient, heare me gentle Liege.

KING HENRY

    Rise vp good aunt.

DUTCHESSE OF YORKE Not yet I thee beseech,
    For euer wil I kneele vpon my knees,
    And neuer see day that the happy sees,
    Till thou giue ioy, vntil thou bid me ioy,
    By pardoning Rutland my transgressing boy.

AUMERLE (*kneeling*)

    Vnto my mothers prayers I bend my knee.

YORKE (*kneeling*)

2470   Against them both my true ioynts bended be,
    Ill maist thou thriue if thou graunt any grace.

DUTCHESSE OF YORKE

    Pleades he in earnest? looke vpon his face.
    His eies do drop no teares, his prayers are in iest,
    His words come from his mouth, ours from our breast,
    He prayes but faintly, and would be denied,
    We pray with heart and soule, and all beside,
    His weary ioynts would gladly rise I know,
    Our knees shall kneele till to the ground they grow,
    His prayers are full of false hypocrisie,
2480   Ours of true zeale and deepe integritie,
    Our prayers do outpray his, then let them haue
    That mercy which true prayer ought to haue.

⌈KING HENRY⌉

    Good aunt stand vp.

DUTCHESSE OF YORKE Nay, do not say, stand vp;
    Say Pardon first, and afterwards, stand vp,
    And if I were thy nurse thy tong to teach,
    Pardon should be the first word of thy speach:
    I neuer longd to heare a word till now,
    Say pardon King, let pitie teach thee how,
    The word is short, but not so short as sweete,
2490   No word like pardon for Kings mouthes so meete.

YORKE

    Speake it in French, King say, Pardonne moy.

DUTCHESSE OF YORKE

    Dost thou teach pardon pardon to destroy?
    Ah my sower husband, my hard-hearted Lord!
    That sets the word it selfe against the word:

    Speake pardon as tis currant in our land,
    The chopping French we do not vnderstand,
    Thine eie begins to speake, set thy tongue there:
    Or in thy piteous heart plant thou thine eare,
    That hearing how our plaints and prayers do pierce,
    Pitie may mooue thee pardon to rehearse.   2500

KING HENRY

    Good aunt stand vp.

DUTCHESSE OF YORKE I do not sue to stand.
    Pardon is all the sute I haue in hand.

KING HENRY

    I pardon him as God shall pardon me.
        ⌈*Yorke and Aumerle rise*⌉

DUTCHESSE OF YORKE

    Oh happy vantage of a kneeling knee,
    Yet am I sicke for feare, speake it againe,
    Twice saying pardon doth not pardon twaine,
    But makes one pardon strong.

KING HENRY   I pardon him
    With al my heart.

DUTCHESSE OF YORKE (*rising*) A god on earth thou art.

KING HENRY

    But for our trusty brother in law and the Abbot,
    With all the rest of that consorted crew,   2510
    Destruction strait shal dog them at the heeles,
    Good vncle, help to order seuerall powers,
    To Oxford, or where ere these traitors are,
    They shall not liue within this world I sweare,
    But I will haue them if I once know where.
    Vncle farewell, and cousin so adue,
    Your mother well hath prayed, and prooue you true.

DUTCHESSE OF YORKE

    Come my olde sonne, I pray God make thee new.
        Exeunt ⌈*King Henry at one doore; Yorke,*
        Dutchesse and Aumerle at another doore⌉

      Enter sir Pierce Exton, and his men   Sc. 17

EXTON   (5.4)

    Didst thou not marke the K. what words he spake?
    Haue I no friend will rid me of this liuing feare?   2520
    Was it not so?

⌈1.⌉ MAN   Those were his very words.

EXTON

    Haue I no friend quoth he? he spake it twice.
    And vrgde it twice togither, did he not?

⌈2.⌉ MAN He did.

EXTON

    And speaking it, he wishtly lookt on me,
    As who should say, I would thou wert the man,
    That would diuorce this terrour from my heart,
    Meaning the king at Pomfret. Come lets go,
    I am the kings friend, and will rid his foe.   *Exeunt*

           Enter Richard alone   Sc. 18

RICHARD   (5.5)

    I haue beene studying how I may compare   2530
    This prison where I liue, vnto the world:
    And forbecause the world is populous,
    And here is not a creature but my selfe,

I cannot do it: yet Ile hammer it out,
My braine Ile prooue, the female to my soule,
My soule the father, and these two beget
A generation of still-breeding thoughts:
And these same thoughts people this little world,
In humors like the people of this world:
2540 For no thought is contented: the better sort,
As thoughts of things diuine are intermixt
With scruples, and do set the faith it selfe
Against the faith, as thus: Come little ones,
And then againe
It is as hard to come, as for a Cammell
To threed the posterne of a small needles eie:
Thoughts tending to ambition they do plot,
Vnlikely wonders: how these vaine weake nailes
May teare a passage thorow the flinty ribs
2550 Of this hard world my ragged prison walles:
And for they cannot die in their owne pride.
Thoughts tending to content flatter themselues,
That they are not the first of fortunes slaues,
Nor shall not be the last, like seely beggars,
Who sitting in the stockes refuge their shame,
That many haue, and others must set there.
And in this thought they find a kind of ease,
Bearing their owne misfortunes on the backe
Of such as haue before indurde the like.
2560 Thus play I in one person many people,
And none contented; sometimes am I King,
Then treason makes me wish my selfe a beggar,
And so I am: then crushing penurie
Perswades me I was better when a king,
Then am I kingd againe, and by and by,
Thinke that I am vnkingd by Bullingbrooke,
And strait am nothing. But what ere I be,
Nor I, nor any man, that but man is,
With nothing shall be pleasde, till he be easde,
With being nothing.
          The musike plaies
2570   Musicke do I heare,
Ha ha keepe time, how sowre sweete Musicke is
When time is broke, and no proportion kept,
So is it in the musike of mens liues:
And here haue I the daintinesse of eare
To checke time broke in a disordred string:
But for the concord of my state and time,
Had not an eare to heare my true time broke,
I wasted time, and now doth time waste me:
For now hath time made me his numbring clocke;
2580 My thoughts are minutes, and with sighes they iarre
Their watches on vnto mine eyes the outward watch
Whereto my finger like a dialles poynt,
Is pointing still, in cleansing them from teares.
Now sir, the sounds that telle what houre it is,
Are clamorous groanes that strike vpon my hart,
Which is the bell, so sighs, and teares, and grones,
Shew minutes, houres, and times: but my time,
Runnes posting on in Bullingbrokes proud ioye,
While I stand fooling heere his iacke of the clocke.
2590 This musicke maddes me, let it sound no more,

For though it haue holp mad men to their witts,
In me it seemes it will make wise men mad:
          ⌈*The musicke ceases*⌉
Yet blessing on his hart that giues it me,
For tis a signe of loue: and loue to Richard,
Is a strange brooch in this al-hating world.
          Enter a groome of the stable
GROOME
Haile roiall Prince.
RICHARD   Thankes noble peare:
The cheapest of vs is ten grotes too deare.
What art thou, and how comst thou hither,
Where no man neuer comes, but that sad dog,
That brings me foode to make misfortune liue.   2600
GROOME
I was a poore groome of thy stable King,
When thou wert King: who trauailling towards Yorke,
With much adoe (at length) haue gotten leaue,
To looke vpon my sometimes roiall maisters face:
Oh how it ernd my hart when I beheld,
In London streetes, that Corronation day,
When Bullingbroke rode on Roane Barbarie,
That horse, that thou so often hast bestride,
That horse, that I so carefully haue drest.
RICHARD
Rode he on Barbarie, tell me gentle freind,   2610
How went he vnder him?
GROOME
So proudly as if he disdaind the ground.
RICHARD
So proud that Bullingbroke was on his backe:
That Iade hath eate bread from my royall hand,
This hand hath made him proud with clapping him:
Would he not stumble, would he not fall downe
Since pride must haue a fal; and breake the necke,
Of that proud man, that did vsurpe his backe?
Forgiuenes horse why do I raile on thee?
Since thou created to be awed by man,   2620
Wast borne to beare; I was not made a horse,
And yet I beare a burthen like an asse,
Spurre, galld, and tirde by iauncing Bullingbrooke.
          Enter keeper to Richard with meate
KEEPER (*to Groome*)
Fellow, giue place, heere is no longer stay.
RICHARD (*to Groome*)
If thou loue me, tis time thou wert away.
GROOME
What my tong dares not, that my heart shal say.   *Exit*
KEEPER
My Lord, wilt please you to fall to?
RICHARD
Taste of it first as thou art wont to do.
KEEPER
My Lord I dare not, sir Pierce of Exton,
Who lately came from the King commaunds the
          contrary.   2630
RICHARD (*striking the keeper*)
The diuell take Henry of Lancaster, and thee,
Patience is stale, and I am wearie of it.

KEEPER Help, help, help.

Exton and his men rush in

RICHARD

How now, what meanes Death in this rude assault?

He seazes a weapon from a man, and kils him

Villaine, thy owne hand yeelds thy deaths instrument,

He kils another

Go thou and fill another roome in hell.

Here Exton strikes him downe

RICHARD

That hand shall burne in neuer quenching fire,

That staggers thus my person: Exton, thy fierce hand

Hath with the kings bloud staind the kings owne land.

2640 Mount mount my soule, thy seate is vp on high,

Whilst my grosse flesh sinckes downeward here to die.

He dies

EXTON

As full of valure as of royall bloud:

Both haue I spilld, Oh would the deede were good!

For now the diuell that told me I did well,

Saies that this deede is chronicled in hell:

This dead king to the liuing king Ile beare.

Take hence the rest, and giue them buriall heere.

Exeunt ⌈Exton with Richards body at one doore,
and his men with the other bodies at another
doore⌉

Sc. 19   ⌈*Flourish.*⌉ *Enter King Henry and the duke of Yorke,*
(5.6)   ⌈*with other Lords and attendants*⌉

KING HENRY

Kind vncle Yorke, the latest newes we heare,

Is, that the rebels haue consumd with fire

2650 Our towne of Ciceter in Gloucestershire,

But whether they be tane or slaine we heare not.

Enter Northumberland

Welcome my Lord, what is the newes?

NORTHUMBERLAND

First to thy sacred state wish I all happinesse,

The next newes is, I haue to London sent

The heades of Salisbury, Spencer, Blunt and Kent,

The maner of their taking may appeare

At large discoursed in this paper heere.

He giues the paper to King Henry

KING HENRY

We thanke thee gentle Percie for thy paines,

And to thy woorth will adde right worthy gaines.

Enter Lord Fitzwaters

FITZWATERS

2660 My Lord, I haue from Oxford sent to London

The heads of Broccas, and sir Benet Seely,

Two of the daungerous consorted traitors,

That sought at Oxford thy dire ouerthrow.

KING HENRY

Thy paines Fitzwaters shall not be forgot,

Right noble is thy merit well I wot.

Enter Harry Percie, with Carleil, guarded

HARRY PERCIE

The grand conspirator Abbot of Westminster

With clog of conscience and sowre melancholy

Hath yeelded vp his body to the graue.

But here is Carleil liuing, to abide

Thy kingly doome, and sentence of his pride.   2670

KING HENRY Carleil, this is your doome;

Choose out some secret place, some reuerent roome

More than thou hast, and with it ioy thy life:

So as thou liu'st in peace, die free from strife,

For though mine enemy thou hast euer beene,

High sparkes of honour in thee haue I seene.

Enter Exton with ⌈his men bearing⌉ the coffin

EXTON

Great King, within this coffin I present

Thy buried feare: herein all breathlesse lies

The mightiest of thy greatest enemies,

Richard of Burdeaux, by me hither brought.   2680

KING HENRY

Exton, I thanke thee not, for thou hast wrought

A deed of slaunder with thy fatall hand,

Vpon my head and all this famous Land.

EXTON

From your owne mouth my Lo. did I this deed.

KING HENRY

They loue not poison that do poison neede,

Nor do I thee; though I did wish him dead,

I hate the murtherer, loue him murthered:

The guilt of conscience take thou for thy labor,

But neither my good word, nor Princely fauour;

With Cayne go wander through the shades of night,   2690

And neuer shew thy head by day nor light.

⌈Exeunt Exton and his men⌉

Lordes, I protest my soule is full of wo,

That bloud should sprincle me to make me grow:

Come mourne with me, for what I do lament,

And put on sulleyn blacke incontinent,

Ile make a voiage to the holly lande,

To wash this bloud off from my guiltie hand:

March sadly after, grace my mournings heere,

In weeping after this vntimely Beere.

Exeunt ⌈with the coffin⌉

FINIS

ADDITIONAL PASSAGES

The following passages of four lines or more appear in the 1597 Quarto but not the Folio; Shakespeare probably deleted them as part of his limited revisions to the text.

A. AFTER 406

> And for we thinke the Egle-winged pride
> Of skie-aspiring and ambitious thoughts,
> With riuall-hating enuy set on you
> To wake our peace, which in our Countries cradle
> Drawes the sweet infant breath of gentle sleepe,

B. AFTER 510

> Oh had't beene a stranger, not my child,
> To smooth his fault I should haue beene more milde:
> A partiall slaunder sought I to auoide,
> And in the sentence my owne life destroyed:

C. AFTER 535

BULLINGBROOKE

> Nay rather euery tedious stride I make,
> Will but remember what a deale of world:
> I wander from the Iewels that I loue.
> Must I not serue a long apprentishood,
> To forreine passages, and in the end,
> Hauing my freedome, boast of nothing else,
> But that I was a iourneyman to griefe.

GAUNT

> All places that the eie of heauen visits,
> Are to a wiseman portes and happie hauens:
> 10   Teach thy necessity to reason thus,
> There is no vertue like necessity,
> Thinke not the King did banish thee,

> But thou the King. Woe doth the heauier sit,
> Where it perceiues it is but faintly borne:
> Go, say I sent thee foorth to purchase honour,
> And not the King exilde thee; or suppose,
> Deuouring pestilence hangs in our aire,
> And thou art flying to a fresher clime:
> Looke what thy soule holds deare, imagine it
> To ly that way thou goest, not whence thou comst: 20
> Suppose the singing birds musitions,
> The grasse whereon thou treadst, the presence strowd,
> The flowers, faire Ladies, and thy steps, no more
> Then a delightfull measure or a dance,
> For gnarling sorrow hath lesse power to bite,
> The man that mocks at it, and sets it light.

D. AFTER 1331

> The meanes that heauens yeeld must be imbrac't
> And not neglected. Else heauen would,
> And we will not, heauens offer, we refuse,
> The profred meanes of succors and redresse.

E. AFTER 1882

ANOTHER LORD

> I taske the earth to the like (forsworne Aumerle)
> And spurre thee on with full as many lies
> As may be hollowed in thy treacherous eare
> From sunne to sunne: there is my honors pawne
> Ingage it to the triall if thou darest.
> *He throwes downe his gage*

AUMERLE

> Who sets me else? by heauen Ile throwe at all,
> I haue a thousand spirites in one breast,
> To answer twenty thousand such as you.

KING IOHN

A PLAY called *The Troublesome Raigne of Iohn, King of England*, published anonymously in 1591, has sometimes been thought to be a derivative version of Shakespeare's *King Iohn*, first published in the 1623 Folio; more probably Shakespeare wrote his play in 1595 or 1596, using *The Troublesome Raigne*—itself based on Holinshed's *Chronicles* and John Foxe's *Book of Martyrs* (1563)—as his principal source. Like *Richard II*, *King Iohn* is written entirely in verse.

King John (*c.*1167-1216) was famous as the opponent of papal tyranny, and *The Troublesome Raigne* is a violently anti-Catholic play; but Shakespeare is more moderate. He portrays selected events from John's reign—like *The Troublesome Raigne*, making no mention of Magna Carta—and ends with John's death, but John is not so dominant a figure in his play as Richard II or Richard III in theirs. Indeed, the longest—and liveliest—role is that of Richard Cordelion's illegitimate son, Philip Fauconbridge, the Bastard.

King John's reign was troublesome initially because of his weak claim to his brother Richard Cordelion's throne. Prince Arthur, son of Iohn's elder brother Geffrey, had no less strong a claim, which is upheld by his mother, Constance, and by King Philip of France. The waste and futility of the consequent war between power-hungry leaders is satirically demonstrated in the dispute over the French town of Angiers, which is resolved by a marriage between Iohn's niece, Lady Blanch of Spain, and Lewis, the French Dolphin. The moral is strikingly drawn by the Bastard—the man best fitted to be king, but debarred by accident of birth—in his speech (838-75) on 'commodity' (self-interest). King Philip breaks his treaty with England, and in the ensuing battle Prince Arthur is captured. He becomes the play's touchstone of humanity as he persuades Iohn's agent, Hubert, to disobey Iohn's orders to blind him, only to kill himself while trying to escape. Iohn's noblemen, thinking the King responsible for the boy's death, defect to the French, but return to their allegiance on learning that the Dolphin intends to kill them after conquering England. Iohn dies, poisoned by a monk; the play ends with the reunited noblemen swearing allegiance to Iohn's son, the young Henry III, and with the Bastard's boast that

> This England neuer did, nor neuer shall
> Lye at the proud foote of a Conqueror,
> But when it first did help to wound itself.

Twentieth-century revivals of *King Iohn* have been infrequent, but it was popular in the nineteenth century, when the roles of the King, the Bastard, and Constance all appealed to successful actors; a production of 1823 at Covent Garden inaugurated a trend for historically accurate settings and costumes which led to a number of spectacular revivals.

The Folio text (1623) is printed from a transcript apparently prepared by two scribes; the second seems to have taken over between lines 1792 and 1838.

THE NAMES OF THE ACTORS

KING IOHN of England

QUEENE ELINOR, his mother

LADY FAULCONBRIDGE

Philip the BASTARD, later knighted as Sir Richard Plantagenet,
    her illegittimate sonne by King Richard the first (Cordelion)

Robert FAULCONBRIDGE, her Legittimate sonne

Iames GURNEY, her attendant

Lady BLANCH of Spaine, Neece of King Iohn

PRINCE HENRY, sonne of King Iohn

HUBERT, a follower of King Iohn

Earle of SALISBURY

Earle of PEMBROKE

Earle of ESSEX

Lord BIGOT

KING PHILIP of France

LEWIS THE DOLPHIN, his sonne

ARTHUR Duke of Brittaine, Nephew of King Iohn

Lady CONSTANCE, his mother

Duke of AUSTRIA (Lymoges)

CHATTILION, Ambassador from France to England

Count MELOONE

A CITIZEN of Angiers

Cardinal PANDULPH, a Legate from the Pope

PETER OF POMFRET, a Prophet

HERALDS

EXECUTIONERS

MESSENGERS

SHERIFFE

Lords, Souldiers, Attendants

The life and death of King Iohn

⌜*Florish.*⌝ *Enter King Iohn, Queene Elinor,*
Pembroke, Essex, and Salisbury ; with them
Chattylion of France

KING IOHN

Now say *Chatillion*, what would *France* with vs?

CHATTILION

Thus (after greeting) speakes the King of France,
In my behauiour to the Maiesty,
The borrowed Maiesty of *England* heere.

QUEENE ELINOR

A strange beginning : borrowed Maiesty?

KING IOHN

Silence (good mother) heare the Embassie.

CHATTILION

Philip of *France*, in right and true behalfe
Of thy deceased brother, *Geffreyes* sonne,
Arthur Plantaginet, laies most lawfull claime

10 To this faire Iland, and the Territories :
To *Ireland, Poyctiers, Aniowe, Torayne, Maine*,
Desiring thee to lay aside the sword
Which swaies vsurpingly these seuerall titles,
And put the same into yong *Arthurs* hand,
Thy Nephew, and right royall Soueraigne.

KING IOHN

What followes if we disallow of this?

CHATTILION

The proud controle of fierce and bloudy warre,
To inforce these rights, so forcibly with-held,

KING IOHN

Heere haue we war for war, & bloud for bloud,

20 Controlement for controlement : so answer *France*.

CHATTILION

Then take my Kings defiance from my mouth,
The farthest limit of my Embassie.

KING IOHN

Beare mine to him, and so depart in peace,
Be thou as lightning in the eies of *France*;
For ere thou canst report, I will be there :
The thunder of my Cannon shall be heard.
So hence : be thou the trumpet of our wrath,
And sullen presage of your owne decay :
An honourable conduct let him haue,

30 *Pembroke* looke too't : farewell *Chattillion*.

Exit Chattilon and Pembroke

QUEENE ELINOR

What now my sonne, haue I not euer said
How that ambitious *Constance* would not cease
Till she had kindled *France* and all the world,
Vpon the right and party of her sonne.
This might haue beene preuented, and made whole
With very easie arguments of loue,
Which now the mannage of two kingdomes must
With fearefull bloudy issue arbitrate.

KING IOHN

Our strong possession, and our right for vs.

QUEENE ELINOR (*aside to King Iohn*)

Your strong possessiõ much more then your right, 40
Or else it must go wrong with you and me,
So much my conscience whispers in your eare,
Which none but heauen, and you, and I, shall heare.

Enter a Sheriffe ⌜*who whispers to Essex*⌝

ESSEX

My Liege, here is the strangest controuersie
Come from the Country to be iudg'd by you
That ere I heard : shall I produce the men?

KING IOHN Let them approach : ⌜*Exit Sheriffe*⌝
Our Abbies and our Priories shall pay
This expeditious charge :

Enter Robert Faulconbridge, and Philip the Bastard
⌜*with the Sheriffe*⌝

what men are you?

BASTARD

Your faithfull subiect, I a gentleman, 50
Borne in *Northamptonshire*, and eldest sonne
As I suppose, to *Robert Faulconbridge*,
A Souldier by the Honor-giuing-hand
Of *Cordelion*, Knighted in the field.

KING IOHN What art thou?

FAULCONBRIDGE

The son and heire to that same *Faulconbridge*.

KING IOHN

Is that the elder, and art thou the heyre?
You came not of one mother then it seemes.

BASTARD

Most certain of one mother, mighty King,
That is well knowne, and as I thinke one father : 60
But for the certaine knowledge of that truth,
I put you o're to heauen, and to my mother;
Of that I doubt, as all mens children may.

QUEENE ELINOR

Out on thee rude man, yᵘ dost shame thy mother,
And wound her honor with this diffidence.

BASTARD

I Madame? No, I haue no reason for it,
That is my brothers plea, and none of mine,
The which if he can proue, a pops me out,
At least from faire fiue hundred pound a yeere :
Heauen guard my mothers honor, and my Land. 70

KING IOHN

A good blunt fellow : why being yonger born
Doth he lay claime to thine inheritance?

BASTARD

I know not why, except to get the land :
But once he slanderd me with bastardy :
But where I be as true begot or no,
That still I lay vpon my mothers head,

But that I am as well begot my Liege
(Faire fall the bones that tooke the paines for me)
Compare our faces, and be Iudge your selfe.
80 If old Sir *Robert* did beget vs both,
And were our father, and this sonne like him:
O old sir *Robert* Father, on my knee
I giue heauen thankes I was not like to thee.

KING IOHN
Why what a mad-cap hath heauen lent vs here?

QUEENE ELINOR
He hath a tricke of *Cordelions* face,
The accent of his tongue affecteth him:
Doe you not read some tokens of my sonne
In the large composition of this man?

KING IOHN
Mine eye hath well examined his parts,
And findes them perfect *Richard*: (*to Robert*
90   *Faulconbridge*) sirra speake,
What doth moue you to claime your brothers land.

BASTARD
Because he hath a half-face like my father?
With halfe that face would he haue all my land,
A halfe-fac'd groat, fiue hundred pound a yeere?

FAULCONBRIDGE
My gracious Liege, when that my father liu'd,
Your brother did imploy my father much.

BASTARD
Well sir, by this you cannot get my land,
Your tale must be how he employ'd my mother.

FAULCONBRIDGE
And once dispatch'd him in an Embassie
100 To *Germany*, there with the Emperor
To treat of high affaires touching that time:
Th'aduantage of his absence tooke the King,
And in the meane time soiourn'd at my fathers;
Where how he did preuaile, I shame to speake:
But truth is truth, large lengths of seas and shores
Betweene my father, and my mother lay,
As I haue heard my father speake himselfe
When this same lusty gentleman was got:
Vpon his death-bed he by will bequeath'd
110 His lands to me, and tooke it on my death
That this my mothers sonne was none of his;
And if he were, he came into the world
Full fourteene weekes before the course of time:
Then good my Liedge let me haue what is mine,
My fathers land, as was my fathers will.

KING IOHN
Sirra, your brother is Legittimate,
Your fathers wife did after wedlocke beare him:
And if she did play false, the fault was hers,
Which fault lyes on the hazards of all husbands
120 That marry wiues: tell me, how if my brother
Who as you say, tooke paines to get this sonne,
Had of your father claim'd this sonne for his,
Insooth, good friend, your father might haue kept
This Calfe, bred from his Cow from all the world:
Insooth he might: then if he were my brothers,

My brother might not claime him, nor your father
Being none of his, refuse him: this concludes,
My mothers sonne did get your fathers heyre,
Your fathers heyre must haue your fathers land.

FAULCONBRIDGE
Shal then my fathers Will be of no force,   130
To dispossesse that childe which is not his.

BASTARD
Of no more force to dispossesse me sir,
Then was his will to get me, as I think.

QUEENE ELINOR
Whether hadst thou rather be: a *Faulconbridge*,
And like thy brother to enioy thy land:
Or the reputed sonne of *Cordelion*,
Lord of thy presence, and no land beside.

BASTARD
Madam, and if my brother had my shape
And I had his, sir *Roberts* his like him,
And if my legs were two such riding rods,   140
My armes, such eele-skins stuft, my face so thin,
That in mine eare I durst not sticke a rose,
Lest men should say, looke where three farthings
        goes,
And to his shape were heyre to all this land,
Would I might neuer stirre from off this place,
I would giue it euery foot to haue this face:
It would not be sir nobbe in any case.

QUEENE ELINOR
I like thee well: wilt thou forsake thy fortune,
Bequeath thy land to him, and follow me?
I am a Souldier, and now bound to *France*.   150

BASTARD
Brother, take you my land, Ile take my chance;
Your face hath got fiue hundred pound a yeere,
Yet sell your face for fiue pence and 'tis deere:
Madam, Ile follow you vnto the death.

QUEENE ELINOR
Nay, I would haue you go before me thither.

BASTARD
Our Country manners giue our betters way.

KING IOHN What is thy name?

BASTARD
Philip my Liege, so is my name begun,
Philip, good old Sir *Roberts* wiues eldest sonne.

KING IOHN
From henceforth beare his name whose forme thou
        bearest: 160
Kneele thou downe *Philip*, but arise more great,
        He knights the Bastard
Arise Sir *Richard*, and *Plantagenet*.

BASTARD
Brother by th'mothers side, giue me your hand,
My father gaue me honor, yours gaue land:
Now blessed be the houre by night or day
When I was got, Sir *Robert* was away.

QUEENE ELINOR
The very spirit of *Plantaginet*:
I am thy grandame *Richard*, call me so.

BASTARD

　170　Madam by chance, but not by truth, what tho;
　　　Something about a little from the right,
　　　　In at the window, or else ore the hatch:
　　　Who dares not stirre by day, must walke by night,
　　　　And haue is haue, how euer men doe catch:
　　　Neere or farre off, well wonne is still well shot,
　　　And I am I, how ere I was begot.

KING IOHN

　　　Goe, *Faulconbridge*, now hast thou thy desire,
　　　A landlesse Knight, makes thee a landed Squire:
　　　Come Madam, and come *Richard*, we must speed
　　　For *France*, for *France*, for it is more then need.

BASTARD

　180　Brother adieu, good fortune come to thee,
　　　For thou wast got i'th way of honesty.

　　　　　　　　　　　　　　Exeunt all but bastard

　　　A foot of Honor better then I was,
　　　But many a many foot of Land the worse.
　　　Well, now can I make any *Ioane* a Lady,
　　　Good den Sir *Richard*, Godamercy fellow,
　　　And if his name be *George*, Ile call him *Peter*;
　　　For new made honor doth forget mens names:
　　　'Tis too respectiue, and too sociable
　　　For your conuersion, now your traueller,
　190　Hee and his tooth-picke at my worships messe,
　　　And when my knightly stomacke is suffis'd,
　　　Why then I sucke my teeth, and catechize
　　　My picked man of Countries: my deare sir,
　　　Thus leaning on mine elbow I begin,
　　　I shall beseech you; that is question now,
　　　And then comes answer like an Absey booke:
　　　O sir, sayes answer, at your best command,
　　　At your employment, at your seruice sir:
　　　No sir, saies question, I sweet sir at yours,
　200　And so ere answer knowes what question would,
　　　Sauing in Dialogue of Complement,
　　　And talking of the Alpes and Appenines,
　　　The Perennean and the riuer *Poe*,
　　　It drawes toward supper in conclusion so.
　　　But this is worshipfull society,
　　　And fits the mounting spirit like my selfe;
　　　For he is but a bastard to the time
　　　That doth not smacke of obseruation,
　　　And so am I: whether I smacke or no,
　210　And not alone in habit and deuice,
　　　Exterior forme, outward accoutrement;
　　　But from the inward motion: to deliuer
　　　Sweet, sweet, sweet poyson for the ages tooth,
　　　Which though I will not practice to deceiue,
　　　Yet to auoid deceit I meane to learne;
　　　For it shall strew the footsteps of my rising:

　　　　　　Enter Lady Faulconbridge and Iames Gurney

　　　But who comes in such haste in riding robes?
　　　What woman post is this? hath she no husband
　　　That will take paines to blow a horne before her?
　220　O me, 'tis my mother: how now good Lady,
　　　What brings you heere to Court so hastily?

LADY FAULCONBRIDGE

　　　Where is that slaue thy brother? where is he?
　　　That holds in chase mine honour vp and downe.

BASTARD

　　　My brother *Robert*, old Sir *Roberts* sonne:
　　　Colbrand the Gyant, that same mighty man,
　　　Is it Sir *Roberts* sonne that you seeke so?

LADY FAULCONBRIDGE

　　　Sir *Roberts* sonne, I thou vnreuerend boy,
　　　Sir *Roberts* sonne? why scorn'st thou at sir *Robert*?
　　　He is Sir *Roberts* sonne, and so art thou.

BASTARD

　　　Iames Gournie, wilt thou giue vs leaue a while?　　230

GOURNIE

　　　Good leaue good *Philip*.

BASTARD　　　　　　　　　　*Philip*, sparrow, *Iames*,
　　　There's toyes abroad, anon Ile tell thee more.

　　　　　　　　　　　　　　　　　Exit Iames

　　　Madam, I was not old Sir *Roberts* sonne,
　　　Sir *Robert* might haue eat his part in me
　　　Vpon good Friday, and nere broke his fast:
　　　Sir *Robert* could doe well, marrie to confesse
　　　Could a get me, sir *Robert* could not doe it;
　　　We know his handy-worke, therefore good mother
　　　To whom am I beholding for these limmes?
　　　Sir *Robert* neuer holpe to make this legge.　　240

LADY FAULCONBRIDGE

　　　Hast thou conspired with thy brother too,
　　　That for thine owne gaine shouldst defend mine honor?
　　　What meanes this scorne, thou most vntoward knaue?

BASTARD

　　　Knight, knight good mother, Basilisco-like:
　　　What, I am dub'd, I haue it on my shoulder:
　　　But mother, I am not Sir *Roberts* sonne,
　　　I haue disclaim'd Sir *Robert* and my land,
　　　Legitimation, name, and all is gone;
　　　Then good my mother, let me know my father,
　　　Some proper man I hope, who was it mother?　　250

LADY FAULCONBRIDGE

　　　Hast thou denied thy selfe a *Faulconbridge*?

BASTARD

　　　As faithfully as I denie the deuill.

LADY FAULCONBRIDGE

　　　King Richard Cordelion was thy father,
　　　By long and vehement suit I was seduc'd
　　　To make roome for him in my husbands bed:
　　　Heauen lay not my transgression to my charge,
　　　Thou art the issue of my deere offence
　　　Which was so strongly vrg'd past my defence.

BASTARD

　　　Now by this light were I to get againe,
　　　Madam I would not wish a better father:　　260
　　　Some sinnes doe beare their priuiledge on earth,
　　　And so doth yours: your fault, was not your follie,
　　　Needs must you lay your heart at his dispose,
　　　Subiected tribute to commanding loue,
　　　Against whose furie and vnmatched force,
　　　The awlesse Lion could not wage the fight,

Nor keepe his Princely heart from *Richards* hand:
He that perforce robs Lions of their hearts,
May easily winne a womans: aye my mother,
270 With all my heart I thanke thee for my father:
Who liues and dares but say, thou didst not well
When I was got, Ile send his soule to hell.
Come Lady I will shew thee to my kinne,
   And they shall say, when *Richard* me begot,
If thou hadst sayd him nay, it had beene sinne;
   Who sayes it was, he lyes, I say twas not.   *Exeunt*

Sc. 2   ⌜*Florish.*⌝ *Enter before Angiers,* ⌜*at one doore*⌝ *Philip*
(2.1)   *King of France, Lewis Daulphin, Constance, Arthur,*
   with Souldiers; ⌜*at another doore*⌝ *Austria, wearing*
   a Lions hide, with Souldiers

⌜KING PHILIP⌝
Before *Angiers* well met braue *Austria*,
Arthur that great fore-runner of thy bloud,
Richard that rob'd the Lion of his heart,
280 And fought the holy Warres in *Palestine*,
By this braue Duke came early to his graue:
And for amends to his posteritie,
At our importance hether is he come,
To spread his colours boy, in thy behalfe,
And to rebuke the vsurpation
Of thy vnnaturall Vncle, English *Iohn*,
Embrace him, loue him, giue him welcome hether.

ARTHUR (*to Austria*)
God shall forgiue you *Cordelions* death
The rather, that you giue his off-spring life,
290 Shadowing their right vnder your wings of warre:
I giue you welcome with a powerlesse hand,
But with a heart full of vnstained loue,
Welcome before the gates of *Angiers* Duke.

⌜KING PHILIP⌝
A noble boy, who would not doe thee right?

AUSTRIA (*kissing Arthur*)
Vpon thy cheeke lay I this zelous kisse,
As seale to this indenture of my loue:
That to my home I will no more returne
Till *Angiers*, and the right thou hast in *France*,
Together with that pale, that white-fac'd shore,
300 Whose foot spurnes backe the Oceans roaring tides,
And coopes from other lands her Ilanders,
Euen till that *England* hedg'd in with the maine,
That Water-walled Bulwarke, still secure
And confident from forreine purposes,
Euen till that vtmost corner of the West
Salute thee for her King, till then faire boy
Will I not thinke of home, but follow Armes.

CONSTANCE
O take his mothers thanks, a widdows thanks,
Till your strong hand shall helpe to giue him
   strength,
310 To make a more requitall to your loue.

AUSTRIA
The peace of heauen is theirs yᵗ lift their swords
In such a iust and charitable warre.

KING PHILIP
Well, then to worke, our Cannon shall be bent
Against the browes of this resisting towne,
Call for our cheefest men of discipline,
To cull the plots of best aduantages:
Wee'll lay before this towne our Royal bones,
Wade to the market-place in *French*-mens bloud,
But we will make it subiect to this boy.

CONSTANCE
Stay for an answer to your Embassie,   320
Lest vnaduis'd you staine your swords with bloud,
My Lord *Chattilion* may from *England* bring
That right in peace which heere we vrge in warre,
And then we shall repent each drop of bloud,
That hot rash haste so indirectly shedde.
   Enter Chattilion

KING PHILIP
A wonder Lady: lo vpon thy wish
Our Messenger *Chattilion* is arriu'd,
What *England* saies, say breefely gentle Lord,
We coldly pause for thee, *Chatilion* speake.

CHATTILION
Then turne your forces from this paltry siege,   330
And stirre them vp against a mightier taske:
England impatient of your iust demands,
Hath put himselfe in Armes, the aduerse windes
Whose leisure I haue staid, haue giuen him time
To land his Legions all as soone as I:
His marches are expedient to this towne,
His forces strong, his Souldiers confident:
With him along is come the Mother Queene,
An Ate stirring him to bloud and strife,
With her her Neece, the Lady *Blanch of Spaine*,   340
With them a Bastard of the Kings deceast,
And all th'vnsetled humors of the Land,
Rash, inconsiderate, fiery voluntaries,
With Ladies faces, and fierce Dragons spleenes,
Haue sold their fortunes at their natiue homes,
Bearing their birth-rights proudly on their backs,
To make a hazard of new fortunes heere:
In briefe, a brauer choyse of dauntlesse spirits
Then now the *English* bottomes haue waft o're,
Did neuer flote vpon the swelling tide,   350
To doe offence and scathe in Christendome:
   Drum beats
The interruption of their churlish drums
Cuts off more circumstance, they are at hand,
To parlie or to fight, therefore prepare.

KING PHILIP
How much vnlook'd for, is this expedition.

AUSTRIA
By how much vnexpected, by so much
We must awake indeuor for defence,
For courage mounteth with occasion,
Let them be welcome then, we are prepar'd.
   Enter, ⌜*marching,*⌝ *King Iohn of England, Bastard,*
   Queene Mother, Blanch, Pembroke, and Souldiers

KING IOHN
Peace be to *France*: If France in peace permit   360

Our iust and lineall entrance to our owne;
If not, bleede *France*, and peace ascend to heauen,
Whiles we Gods wrathfull agent doe correct
Their proud contempt that beats his peace to heauen.

KING PHILIP

Peace be to *England*; if that warre returne
From *France* to *England*, there to liue in peace:
England we loue, and for that *Englands* sake,
With burden of our armor heere we sweat:
This toyle of ours should be a worke of thine;
370 But thou from louing *England* art so farre,
That thou hast vnder-wrought his lawfull King,
Cut off the sequence of posterity,
Out-faced Infant State, and done a rape
Vpon the maiden vertue of the Crowne:
(*Pointing to Arthur*)
Looke heere vpon thy brother *Geffreyes* face,
These eyes, these browes, were moulded out of his;
This little abstract doth containe that large,
Which died in *Geffrey*: and the hand of time,
Shall draw this breefe into as huge a volume:
380 That *Geffrey* was thy elder brother borne,
And this his sonne, *England* was *Geffreys* right,
And this is *Geffreyes*: in the name of God,
How comes it then that thou art call'd a King,
When liuing blood doth in these temples beat
Which owe the crowne, that thou ore-masterest?

KING IOHN

From whom hast thou this great commission *France*,
To draw my answer from thy Articles?

KING PHILIP

Frõ that supernal Iudge that stirs good thoughts
In any breast of strong authoritie,
390 To looke into the blots and staines of right,
That Iudge hath made me guardian to this boy,
Vnder whose warrant I impeach thy wrong,
And by whose helpe I meane to chastise it.

KING IOHN

Alack thou dost vsurpe authoritie.

KING PHILIP

Excuse it is to beat vsurping downe.

QUEENE ELINOR

Who is it thou dost call vsurper *France*?

CONSTANCE

Let me make answer: thy vsurping sonne.

QUEENE ELINOR

Out insolent, thy bastard shall be King,
That thou maist be a Queen, and checke the world.

CONSTANCE

400 My bed was euer to thy sonne as true
As thine was to thy husband, and this boy
Liker in feature to his father *Geffrey*
Then thou and *Iohn* in manners, being as like,
As raine to water, or deuill to his damme;
My boy a bastard? by my soule I thinke
His father neuer was so true begot,
It cannot be, and if thou wert his mother.

QUEENE ELINOR (*to Arthur*)

Theres a good mother boy, that blots thy father.

CONSTANCE (*to Arthur*)

There's a good grandame boy that would blot thee.

AUSTRIA

Peace.

BASTARD Heare the Cryer.

AUSTRIA   What the deuill art thou? 410

BASTARD

One that wil play the deuill sir with you,
And a may catch your hide and you alone:
You are the Hare of whom the Prouerb goes
Whose valour plucks dead Lyons by the beard;
Ile smoake your skin-coat and I catch you right,
Sirra looke too't, yfaith I will, yfaith.

BLANCH

O well did he become that Lyons robe,
That did disrobe the Lion of that robe.

BASTARD

It lies as sightly on the backe of him
As great *Alcides* shooes vpon an Asse: 420
But Asse, Ile take that burthen from your backe,
Or lay on that shall make your shoulders cracke.

AUSTRIA

What cracker is this same that deafes our eares
With this abundance of superfluous breath?
King *Philip*, determine what we shall doe strait.

⌈KING PHILIP⌉

Women & fooles, breake off your conference.
King *Iohn*, this is the very summe of all:
England and *Ireland*, *Aniowe*, *Toraine*, *Maine*,
In right of *Arthur* doe I claime of thee:
Wilt thou resigne them, and lay downe thy Armes? 430

KING IOHN

My life as soone: I doe defie thee *France*,
Arthur of *Britaine*, yeeld thee to my hand,
And out of my deere loue Ile giue thee more,
Then ere the coward hand of *France* can win;
Submit thee boy.

QUEENE ELINOR (*to Arthur*) Come to thy grandame child.

CONSTANCE (*to Arthur*)

Doe childe, goe to yt grandame childe,
Giue grandame kingdome, and it grandame will
Giue yt a plum, a cherry, and a figge,
There's a good grandame.

ARTHUR   Good my mother peace,
I would that I were low laid in my graue,
I am not worth this coyle that's made for me. 440

QUEENE ELINOR

His mother shames him so, poore boy hee weepes.

CONSTANCE

Now shame vpon you where she does or no,
His grandames wrongs, and not his mothers shames
Drawe those heauen-mouing pearles frõ his poor eies,
Which heauen shall take in nature of a fee:
I, with these Christall beads heauen shall be brib'd
To doe him Iustice, and reuenge on you.

QUEENE ELINOR

Thou monstrous slanderer of heauen and earth.

CONSTANCE

Thou monstrous Iniurer of heauen and earth, 450

Call not me slanderer, thou and thine vsurpe
The Dominations, Royalties, and rights
Of this oppressed boy; this is thy eld'st sonnes sonne,
Infortunate in nothing but in thee:
Thy sinnes are visited in this poore childe,
The Canon of the Law is laide on him,
Being but the second generation
Remoued from thy sinne-conceiuing wombe.

KING IOHN
Bedlam haue done.

CONSTANCE   I haue but this to say,
460 That he is not onely plagued for her sin,
But God hath made her sinne and her, the plague
On this remoued issue, plagued for her,
And with her plague: her sinne his iniury,
Her iniurie the Beadle to her sinne,
All punish'd in the person of this childe,
And all for her, a plague vpon her.

QUEENE ELINOR
Thou vnaduised scold, I can produce
A Will, that barres the title of thy sonne.

CONSTANCE
I who doubts that, a Will: a wicked will,
470 A womans will, a cankred Grandams will.

KING PHILIP
Peace Lady, pause, or be more temperate,
It ill beseemes this presence to cry ayme
To these ill-tuned repetitions:
Some Trumpet summon hither to the walles
These men of Angiers, let vs heare them speake,
Whose title they admit, *Arthurs* or *Iohns*.
          Trumpet sounds. Enter a Citizen vpon the walles

CITIZEN
Who is it that hath warn'd vs to the walles?

KING PHILIP
'Tis France, for England.

KING IOHN   England for it selfe:
You men of Angiers, and my louing subiects.

KING PHILIP
480 You louing men of Angiers, *Arthurs* subiects,
Our Trumpet call'd you to this gentle parle.

KING IOHN
For our aduantage, therefore heare vs first:
These flagges of France that are aduanced heere
Before the eye and prospect of your Towne,
Haue hither march'd to your endamagement.
The Canons haue their bowels full of wrath,
And ready mounted are they to spit forth
Their Iron indignation 'gainst your walles:
All preparation for a bloody siedge
490 And merciles proceeding, by these French,
Confront your Cities eies, your winking gates:
And but for our approch, those sleeping stones,
That as a waste doth girdle you about
By the compulsion of their Ordinance,
By this time from their fixed beds of lime
Had bin dishabited, and wide hauocke made
For bloody power to rush vppon your peace.

But on the sight of vs your lawfull King,
Who painefully with much expedient march
Haue brought a counter-checke before your gates,   500
To saue vnscratch'd your Cities threatned cheekes:
Behold the French amaz'd vouchsafe a parle,
And now insteed of bulletts wrapt in fire
To make a shaking feuer in your walles,
They shoote but calme words, folded vp in smoake,
To make a faithlesse errour in your eares,
Which trust accordingly kinde Cittizens,
And let vs in, your King, whose labour'd spirits
Fore-wearied in this action of swift speede,
Craues harbourage within your Citie walles.   510

KING PHILIP
When I haue saide, make answer to vs both.
          He takes Arthur's hand
Loe in this right hand, whose protection
Is most diuinely vow'd vpon the right
Of him it holds, stands yong *Plantagenet*,
Sonne to the elder brother of this man,
And King ore him, and all that he enioyes:
For this downe-troden equity, we tread
In warlike march, these greenes before your Towne,
Being no further enemy to you
Then the constraint of hospitable zeale,   520
In the releefe of this oppressed childe,
Religiously prouokes. Be pleased then
To pay that dutie which you truly owe,
To him that owes it, namely, this yong Prince,
And then our Armes, like to a muzled Beare,
Saue in aspect, hath all offence seal'd vp:
Our Cannons malice vainly shall be spent
Against th'inuolnerable clouds of heauen,
And with a blessed and vn-vext retyre,
With vnhack'd swords, and Helmets all vnbruis'd,   530
We will beare home that lustie blood againe,
Which heere we came to spout against your Towne,
And leaue your children, wiues, and you in peace.
But if you fondly passe our proffer'd offer,
'Tis not the rounder of your old-fac'd walles,
Can hide you from our messengers of Warre,
Though all these English, and their discipline
Were harbour'd in their rude circumference:
Then tell vs, Shall your Citie call vs Lord,
In that behalfe which we haue challeng'd it?   540
Or shall we giue the signall to our rage,
And stalke in blood to our possession?

CITIZEN
In breefe, we are the King of Englands subiects:
For him, and in his right, we hold this Towne.

KING IOHN
Acknowledge then the King, and let me in.

CITIZEN
That can we not: but he that proues the King
To him will we proue loyall, till that time
Haue we ramm'd vp our gates against the world.

KING IOHN
Doth not the Crowne of England, prooue the King?

550 And if not that, I bring you Witnesses
Twice fifteene thousand hearts of Englands breed.

BASTARD (*aside*) Bastards and else.

KING IOHN
To verifie our title with their liues.

KING PHILIP
As many and as well-borne bloods as those.

BASTARD (*aside*) Some Bastards too.

KING PHILIP
Stand in his face to contradict his claime.

CITIZEN
Till you compound whose right is worthiest,
We for the worthiest hold the right from both.

KING IOHN
Then God forgiue the sinne of all those soules,
560 That to their euerlasting residence,
Before the dew of euening fall, shall fleete
In dreadfull triall of our kingdomes King.

KING PHILIP
Amen, Amen, mount Cheualiers to Armes.

BASTARD
Saint *George* that swindg'd the Dragon, and ere since
Sit's on's horsebacke at mine Hostesse dore
Teach vs some fence. (*To Austria*) Sirrah, were I at
home
At your den sirrah, with your Lionnesse,
I would set an Oxe-head to your Lyons hide:
And make a monster of you.

AUSTRIA   Peace, no more.

BASTARD
570 O tremble: for you heare the Lyon rore.

KING IOHN
Vp higher to the plaine, where we'l set forth
In best appointment all our Regiments.

BASTARD
Speed then to take aduantage of the field.

KING PHILIP
It shall be so, and at the other hill
Command the rest to stand, God and our right.

*Exeunt ⌈seuerally⌉ King Iohn and King Philip
with their Powers. Manet Citizen
on the walles.*

⌈*Alarums.*⌉ *Heere after excursions, Enter ⌈at one
doore⌉ the Herald of France with ⌈Trumpet⌉ to
the gates*

FRENCH HERALD
You men of Angiers open wide your gates,
And let yong *Arthur* Duke of Britaine in,
Who by the hand of France, this day hath made
Much worke for teares in many an English mother,
580 Whose sonnes lye scattred on the bleeding ground:
Many a widdowes husband groueling lies,
Coldly embracing the discolourd earth,
And victorie with little losse doth play
Vpon the dancing banners of the French,
Who are at hand triumphantly displayed
To enter Conquerors, and to proclaime
Arthur of Britaine, Englands King, and yours.

*Enter ⌈at another doore⌉ English Herald with
Trumpet*

ENGLISH HERALD
Reioyce you men of Angiers, ring your bels,
King *Iohn*, your king and Englands, doth approach,
Commander of this hot malicious day,   590
Their Armours that march'd hence so siluer bright,
Hither returne all gilt with Frenchmens blood:
There stucke no plume in any English Crest,
That is remoued by a staffe of France.
Our colours do returne in those same hands
That did display them when we first marcht forth:
And like a iolly troope of Huntsmen come
Our lustie English, all with purpled hands,
Dide in the dying slaughter of their foes,
Open your gates, and giue the Victors way.   600

⌈CITIZEN⌉
Heralds, from off our towres we might behold
From first to last, the on-set and retyre,
Of both your Armies, whose equality
By our best eyes cannot be censured:
Blood hath bought blood, and blowes haue answerd
blowes:
Strength matcht with strength, and power confronted
power,
Both are alike, and both alike we like:
One must proue greatest. While they weigh so euen,
We hold our Towne for neither: yet for both.

*Enter at one doore King Iohn, Bastard, Elinor, and
Blanch, with Souldiers; at another doore King
Philip, Dolphin, and Austria, with Souldiers*

KING IOHN
France, hast thou yet more blood to cast away?   610
Say, shall the currant of our right ronne on,
Whose passage vext with thy impediment,
Shall leaue his natiue channell, and ore-swell
With course disturb'd euen thy confining shores,
Vnlesse thou let his siluer Water, keepe
A peacefull progresse to the Ocean.

KING PHILIP
England thou hast not sau'd one drop of blood
In this hot triall more then we of France,
Rather lost more. And by this hand I sweare
That swayes the earth this Climate ouer-lookes,   620
Before we will lay downe our iust-borne Armes,
Wee'l put thee downe, 'gainst whom these Armes wee
beare,
Or adde a royall number to the dead:
Gracing the scroule that tels of this warres losse,
With slaughter coupled to the name of kings.

BASTARD
Ha Maiesty: how high thy glory towres,
When the rich blood of kings is set on fire:
Oh now doth death line his dead chaps with steele,
The swords of souldiers are his teeth, his phangs,
And now he feasts, mousing the flesh of men   630
In vndetermin'd differences of kings.

Why stand these royall fronts amazed thus:
Cry hauocke kings, backe to the stained field
You equall Potents, fierie kindled spirits,
Then let confusion of one part confirm
The others peace: till then, blowes, blood, and death.

KING IOHN

Whose party do the Townesmen yet admit?

KING PHILIP

Speake Citizens for England, whose your king.

⌈CITIZEN⌉

The king of England, when we know the king.

KING PHILIP

640   Know him in vs, that heere hold vp his right.

KING IOHN

In Vs, that are our owne great Deputie,
And beare possession of our Person heere,
Lord of our presence Angiers, and of you.

⌈CITIZEN⌉

A greater powre then We denies all this,
And till it be vndoubted, we do locke
Our former scruple in our strong barr'd gates:
Kingd of our feare, vntill our feares resolu'd
Be by some certaine king, purg'd and depos'd.

BASTARD

By heauen, these scroyles of Angiers flout you kings,
650   And stand securely on their battlements,
As in a Theater, whence they gape and point
At your industrious Scenes and acts of death.
Your Royall presences be rul'd by mee,
Do like the Mutines of Ierusalem,
Be friends a-while, and both conioyntly bend
Your sharpest Deeds of malice on this Towne.
By East and West let France and England mount
Their battering Canon charged to the mouthes,
Till their soule-fearing clamours haue brau'ld downe
660   The flintie ribbes of this contemptuous Citie,
I'de play incessantly vpon these Iades,
Euen till vnfenced desolation
Leaue them as naked as the vulgar ayre:
That done, disseuer your vnited strengths,
And part your mingled colours once againe,
Turne face to face, and bloody point to point:
Then in a moment Fortune shall cull forth
Out of one side her happy Minion,
To whom in fauour she shall giue the day,
670   And kisse him with a glorious victory:
How like you this wilde counsell mighty States,
Smackes it not something of the policie.

KING IOHN

Now by the sky that hangs aboue our heads,
I like it well. France, shall we knit our powres,
And lay this Angiers euen with the ground,
Then after fight who shall be king of it?

BASTARD (to King Philip)

And if thou hast the mettle of a king,
Being wrong'd as we are by this peeuish Towne:
Turne thou the mouth of thy Artillerie,
680   As we will ours, against these sawcie walles,

And when that we haue dash'd them to the ground,
Why then defie each other, and pell-mell,
Make worke vpon our selues, for heauen or hell.

KING PHILIP

Let it be so: say, where will you assault?

KING IOHN

We from the West will send destruction
Into this Cities bosome.

AUSTRIA I from the North.

KING PHILIP Our Thunder from the South,
Shall raine their drift of bullets on this Towne.

BASTARD ⌈to King Iohn⌉

O prudent discipline! From North to South: 690
Austria and France shoot in each others mouth.
Ile stirre them to it: Come, away, away.

⌈CITIZEN⌉

Heare vs great kings, vouchsafe awhile to stay
And I shall shew you peace, and faire-fac'd league:
Win you this Citie without stroke, or wound,
Rescue those breathing liues to dye in beds,
That heere come sacrifices for the field.
Perseuer not, but heare me mighty kings.

KING IOHN

Speake on with fauour, we are bent to heare.

⌈CITIZEN⌉

That daughter there of Spaine, the Lady *Blanch*   700
Is neece to England, looke vpon the yeeres
Of *Lewes* the Dolphin, and that louely maid.
If lustie loue should go in quest of beautie,
Where should he finde it fairer, then in *Blanch*:
If zealous loue should go in search of vertue,
Where should he finde it purer then in *Blanch*?
If loue ambitious, sought a match of birth,
Whose veines bound richer blood then Lady *Blanch*?
Such as she is, in beautie, vertue, birth,
Is the yong Dolphin euery way compleat,   710
If not compleat o say he is not shee,
And she againe wants nothing, to name want,
If want it be not, that she is not hee:
He is the halfe part of a blessed man,
Left to be finished by such as shee,
And she a faire diuided excellence,
Whose fulnesse of perfection lyes in him.
O two such siluer currents when they ioyne
Do glorifie the bankes that bound them in:
And two such shores, to two such streames made
    one,   720
Two such controlling bounds shall you be, kings,
To these two Princes, if you marrie them:
This Vnion shall do more then batterie can
To our fast closed gates: for at this match,
With swifter spleene then powder can enforce
The mouth of passage shall we fling wide ope,
And giue you entrance: but without this match,
The sea enraged is not halfe so deafe,
Lyons more confident, Mountaines and rockes
More free from motion, no not death himselfe   730

In mortall furie halfe so peremptorie,
As we to keepe this Citie.

BASTARD ⌈aside⌉   Heeres a stay,
That shakes the rotten carkasse of old death
Out of his ragges. Here's a large mouth indeede,
That spits forth death, and mountaines, rockes, and
    seas,
Talkes as familiarly of roaring Lyons,
As maids of thirteene do of puppi-dogges.
What Cannoneere begot this lustie blood,
He speakes plaine Cannon, fire, and smoake, and
    bounce,
740   He giues the bastinado with his tongue:
Our eares are cudgel'd, not a word of his
But buffets better then a fist of France:
Zounds, I was neuer so bethumpt with words,
Since I first cal'd my brothers father Dad.

QUEENE ELINOR (aside to King Iohn)
Son, list to this coniunction, make this match,
Giue with our Neece a dowrie large enough,
For by this knot, thou shalt so surely tye
Thy now vnsur'd assurance to the Crowne,
That yon greene boy shall haue no Sunne to ripe
750   The bloome that promiseth a mightie fruite.
I see a yeelding in the lookes of France:
Marke how they whisper, vrge them while their
    soules
Are capeable of this ambition,
Least zeale now melted by the windie breath
Of soft petitions, pittie and remorse,
Coole and congeale againe to what it was.

⌈CITIZEN⌉
Why answer not the double Maiesties,
This friendly treatie of our threatned Towne.

KING PHILIP
Speake England first, that hath bin forward first
760   To speake vnto this Cittie: what say you?

KING IOHN
If that the Dolphin there thy Princely sonne,
Can in this booke of beautie read, I loue:
Her Dowrie shall weigh equall with a Queene:
For Aniow, and faire Toraine, Maine, Poyctiers,
And all that we vpon this side the Sea,
(Except this Cittie now by vs besiedg'd)
Finde liable to our Crowne and Dignitie,
Shall gild her bridall bed and make her rich
In titles, honors, and promotions,
770   As she in beautie, education, blood,
Holdes hand with any Princesse of the world.

KING PHILIP
What sai'st thou boy? looke in the Ladies face.

DOLPHIN
I do my Lord, and in her eie I find
A wonder, or a wondrous miracle,
The shadow of my selfe form'd in her eye,
Which being but the shadow of your sonne,
Becomes a sonne and makes your sonne a shadow:
I do protest I neuer lou'd my selfe

Till now, infixed I beheld my selfe,
Drawne in the flattering table of her eie.   780
    Whispers with Blanch

BASTARD (aside)
Drawne in the flattering table of her eie,
    Hang'd in the frowning wrinkle of her brow,
And quarter'd in her heart, hee doth espie
    Himselfe loues traytor, this is pittie now;
That hang'd, and drawne, and quarter'd there should
    be
In such a loue, so vile a Lout as he.

BLANCH (to the Dolphin)
My vnckles will in this respect is mine,
If he see ought in you that makes him like,
That any thing he see's which moues his liking,
I can with ease translate it to my will: 790
Or if you will, to speake more properly,
I will enforce it easlie to my loue.
Further I will not flatter you, my Lord,
That all I see in you is worthie loue,
Then this, that nothing do I see in you,
Though churlish thoughts themselues should bee your
    Iudge,
That I can finde, should merit any hate.

KING IOHN
What saie these yong-ones? What say you my Neece?

BLANCH
That she is bound in honor still to do
What you in wisedome shall vouchsafe to say.   800

KING IOHN
Speake then Prince Dolphin, can you loue this Ladie?

DOLPHIN
Nay aske me if I can refraine from loue,
For I doe loue her most vnfainedly.

KING IOHN
Then do I giue Volquessen, Toraine, Maine,
Poyctiers and Aniow, these fiue Prouinces
With her to thee, and this addition more,
Full thirty thousand Markes of English coyne:
Phillip of France, if thou be pleas'd withall,
Command thy sonne and daughter to ioyne hands.

KING PHILIP
It likes vs well young Princes: close your hands.   810

AUSTRIA
And your lippes too, for I am well assur'd,
That I did so when I was first assur'd.
    ⌈The Dolphin and Blanch ioyne hands and kisse⌉

KING PHILIP
Now Cittizens of Angires ope your gates,
Let in that amitie which you haue made,
For at Saint Maries Chappell presently,
The rights of marriage shallbe solemniz'd.
Is not the Ladie Constance in this troope?
(Aside) I know she is not for this match made vp,
Her presence would haue interrupted much.
(Aloud) Where is she and her sonne, tell me, who
    knowes?   820

DOLPHIN
She is sad and passionate at your highnes Tent.

KING PHILIP

And by my faith, this league that we haue made
Will giue her sadnesse very little cure:
Brother of England, how may we content
This widdow Lady? In her right we came,
Which we God knowes, haue turn'd another way,
To our owne vantage.

KING IOHN   We will heale vp all,
For wee'l create yong *Arthur* Duke of Britaine
And Earle of Richmond, and this rich faire Towne
830   We make him Lord of. Call the Lady *Constance*,
Some speedy Messenger bid her repaire
To our solemnity: I trust we shall,
(If not fill vp the measure of her will)
Yet in some measure satisfie her so,
That we shall stop her exclamation,
Go we as well as hast will suffer vs,
To this vnlook'd for vnprepared pompe.

⌈*Florish.*⌉ *Exeunt all but Bastard*

BASTARD

Mad world, mad kings, mad composition:
Iohn to stop *Arthurs* Title in the whole,
840   Hath willingly departed with a part,
And France, whose armour Conscience buckled on,
Whom zeale and charitie brought to the field,
As Gods owne souldier, rounded in the eare,
With that same purpose-changer, that slye diuel,
That Broker, that still breakes the pate of faith,
That dayly breake-vow, he that winnes of all,
Of kings, of beggers, old men, yong men, maids,
Who hauing no externall thing to loose,
But the word Maid, cheats the poore Maide of that.
850   That smooth-fac'd Gentleman, tickling commoditie,
Commoditie, the byas of the world,
The world, who of it selfe is peysed well,
Made to run euen, vpon euen ground;
Till this aduantage, this vile drawing byas,
This sway of motion, this commoditie,
Makes it take head from all indifferency,
From all direction, purpose, course, intent.
And this same byas, this Commoditie,
This Bawd, this Broker, this all-changing-word,
860   Clap'd on the outward eye of fickle France,
Hath drawne him from his owne determin'd ayd,
From a resolu'd and honourable warre,
To a most base and vile-concluded peace.
And why rayle I on this Commoditie?
But for because he hath not wooed me yet:
Not that I haue the power to clutch my hand,
When his faire Angels would salute my palme,
But for my hand, as vnattempted yet,
Like a poore begger, raileth on the rich.
870   Well, whiles I am a begger, I will raile,
And say there is no sin but to be rich:
And being rich, my vertue then shall be,
To say there is no vice, but beggerie:
Since Kings breake faith vpon commoditie,
Gaine be my Lord, for I will worship thee.   *Exit*

Enter Constance, Arthur, and Salisbury   Sc. 3
                                                           (2.2)
CONSTANCE (*to Salisbury*)

Gone to be married? Gone to sweare a peace?
False blood to false blood ioyn'd. Gone to be freinds?
Shall *Lewis* haue *Blaunch*, and *Blaunch* those
    Prouinces?
It is not so, thou hast mispoke, misheard,
Be well aduis'd, tell ore thy tale againe.   880
It cannot be, thou do'st but say 'tis so.
I trust I may not trust thee, for thy word
Is but the vaine breath of a common man:
Beleeue me, I doe not beleeue thee man,
I haue a Kings oath to the contrarie.
Thou shalt be punish'd for thus frighting me,
For I am sicke, and capeable of feares,
Opprest with wrongs, and therefore full of feares,
A widdow, husbandles, subiect to feares,
A woman naturally borne to feares;   890
And though thou now confesse thou didst but iest
With my vext spirits, I cannot take a Truce,
But they will quake and tremble all this day.
What dost thou meane by shaking of thy head?
Why dost thou looke so sadly on my sonne?
What meanes that hand vpon that breast of thine?
Why holdes thine eie that lamentable rhewme,
Like a proud riuer peering ore his bounds?
Be these sad signes confirmers of thy words?
Then speake againe, not all thy former tale,   900
But this one word, whether thy tale be true.

SALISBURY

As true as I beleeue you thinke them false,
That giue you cause to proue my saying true.

CONSTANCE

Oh if thou teach me to beleeue this sorrow,
Teach thou this sorrow, how to make me dye,
And let beleefe, and life encounter so,
As doth the furie of two desperate men,
Which in the very meeting fall, and dye.
Lewes marry *Blaunch*? (*To Arthur*) O boy, then where
    art thou?
France friend with *England*, what becomes of me?   910
(*To Salisbury*) Fellow be gone: I cannot brooke thy
    sight,
This newes hath made thee a most vgly man.

SALISBURY

What other harme haue I good Lady done,
But spoke the harme, that is by others done?

CONSTANCE

Which harme within it selfe so heynous is,
As it makes harmefull all that speake of it.

ARTHUR

I do beseech you Madam be content.

CONSTANCE

If thou that bidst me be content, wert grim
Vgly, and slandrous to thy Mothers wombe,
Full of vnpleasing blots, and sightlesse staines,
Lame, foolish, crooked, swart, prodigious,   920
Patch'd with foule Moles, and eye-offending markes,

I would not care, I then would be content,
For then I should not loue thee: no, nor thou
Become thy great birth, nor deserue a Crowne.
But thou art faire, and at thy birth (deere boy)
Nature and Fortune ioyn'd to make thee great.
Of Natures guifts, thou mayst with Lillies boast,
And with the halfe-blowne Rose. But Fortune, oh,
930　She is corrupted, chang'd, and wonne from thee,
Sh'adulterates hourely with thine Vnckle *Iohn*,
And with her golden hand hath pluckt on France
To tread downe faire respect of Soueraigntie,
And made his Maiestie the bawd to theirs.
France is a Bawd to Fortune, and king *Iohn*,
That strumpet Fortune, that vsurping *Iohn*:
(*To Salisbury*) Tell me thou fellow, is not France
　　forsworne?
Enuenom him with words, or get thee gone,
And leaue those woes alone, which I alone
Am bound to vnder-beare.

940　SALISBURY　　　　　　　　　　Pardon me Madam,
I may not goe without you to the kings.
CONSTANCE
Thou maist, thou shalt, I will not go with thee,
I will instruct my sorrowes to bee proud,
For greefe is proud, and makes his owner stoope,
　⌈*She sits vpon the ground*⌉
To me and to the state of my great greefe,
Let kings assemble: for my greefe's so great,
That no supporter but the huge firme earth
Can hold it vp: here I and sorrowes sit,
Heere is my Throne, bid kings come bow to it.
　　　　　　　　　　　　⌈*Exeunt Salisbury and Arthur*⌉
(3.1)　⌈*Florish.*⌉ *Enter King Iohn and King Philip* ⌈*hand in
　　　　hand*⌉; *Dolphin and Blanch,* ⌈*married,*⌉ *Elianor,
　　　　Philip the Bastard, and Austria*
　KING PHILIP (*to Blanch*)
950　'Tis true (faire daughter) and this blessed day,
Euer in *France* shall be kept festiuall:
To solemnize this day the glorious sunne
Stayes in his course, and playes the Alchymist,
Turning with splendor of his precious eye
The meager cloddy earth to glittering gold:
The yearely course that brings this day about,
Shall neuer see it, but a holy day.
CONSTANCE (*rising*)
A wicked day, and not a holy day.
What hath this day deseru'd? what hath it done,
960　That it in golden letters should be set
Among the high tides in the Kalender?
Nay, rather turne this day out of the weeke,
This day of shame, oppression, periury.
Or if it must stand still, let wiues with childe
Pray that their burthens may not fall this day,
Lest that their hopes prodigiously be crost:
But (on this day) let Sea-men feare no wracke,
No bargaines breake that are not this day made;
This day all things begun, come to ill end,
970　Yea, faith it selfe to hollow falshood change.

KING PHILIP
By heauen Lady, you shall haue no cause
To curse the faire proceedings of this day:
Haue I not pawn'd to you my Maiesty?
CONSTANCE
You haue beguil'd me with a counterfeit
Resembling Maiesty, which being touch'd and tride,
Proues valuelesse: you are forsworne, forsworne,
You came in Armes to spill mine enemies bloud,
But now in Armes, you strengthen it with yours.
The grapling vigor, and rough frowne of Warre
Is cold in amitie, and painted peace,　　　　　980
And our oppression hath made vp this league:
Arme, arme, you heauens, against these periur'd Kings,
A widdow cries, be husband to me (God)
Let not the howres of this vngodly day
Weare out the daie in Peace; but ere Sun-set,
Set armed discord 'twixt these periur'd Kings,
Heare me, Oh, heare me.
AUSTRIA　　　　　　　　　　Lady *Constance*, peace.
CONSTANCE
War, war, no peace, peace is to me a warre:
O *Lymoges*, O *Austria*, thou dost shame
That bloudy spoyle: thou slaue, thou wretch, y^u
　　coward,　　　　　　　　　　　　　　　990
Thou little valiant, great in villanie,
Thou euer strong vpon the stronger side;
Thou Fortunes Champion, that do'st neuer fight
But when her humourous Ladiship is by
To teach thee safety: thou art periur'd too,
And sooth'st vp greatnesse. What a foole art thou,
A ramping foole, to brag, and stamp, and sweare,
Vpon my partie: thou cold blooded slaue,
Hast thou not spoke like thunder on my side?
Beene sworne my Souldier, bidding me depend　1000
Vpon thy starres, thy fortune, and thy strength,
And dost thou now fall ouer to my foes?
Thou weare a Lyons hide, doff it for shame,
And hang a Calues skin on those recreant limbes.
AUSTRIA
O that a man should speake those words to me.
BASTARD
And hang a Calues-skin on those recreant limbs.
AUSTRIA
Thou dar'st not say so villaine for thy life.
BASTARD
And hang a Calues-skin on those recreant limbs.
KING IOHN (*to the Bastard*)
We like not this, thou dost forget thy selfe.
　　　Enter Pandulph
KING PHILIP
Heere comes the holy Legat of the Pope.　　　1010
PANDULPH
Haile you annointed deputies of God;
To thee King *Iohn* my holy errand is:
I *Pandulph*, of faire *Millane* Cardinall,
And from Pope *Innocent* the Legate heere,
Doe in his name religiously demand

Why thou against the Church, our holy Mother,
So wilfully dost spurne; and force perforce
Keepe *Stephen Langton* chosen Archbishop
Of *Canterbury* from that holy Sea:
1020 This in our foresaid holy Fathers name
Pope *Innocent*, I doe demand of thee.

KING IOHN
What earthie name to Interrogatories
Can task the free breath of a sacred King?
Thou canst not (Cardinall) deuise a name
So slight, vnworthy, and ridiculous
To charge me to an answere, as the Pope:
Tell him this tale, and from the mouth of *England*,
Adde thus much more, that no *Italian* Priest
Shall tythe or toll in our dominions:
1030 But as we, vnder God, are supreame head,
So vnder him that great supremacy
Where we doe reigne, we will alone vphold
Without th'assistance of a mortall hand:
So tell the Pope, all reuerence set apart
To him and his vsurp'd authoritie.

KING PHILIP
Brother of *England*, you blaspheme in this.

KING IOHN
Though you, and all the Kings of Christendom
Are led so grossely by this medling Priest,
Dreading the curse that money may buy out,
1040 And by the merit of vilde gold, drosse, dust,
Purchase corrupted pardon of a man,
Who in that sale sels pardon from himselfe:
Though you, and al the rest so grossely led,
This iugling witchcraft with reuennue cherish,
Yet I alone, alone doe me oppose
Against the Pope, and count his friends my foes.

PANDULPH
Then by the lawfull power that I haue,
Thou shalt stand curst, and excommunicate,
And blessed shall he be that doth reuolt
1050 From his Allegeance to an heretique,
And meritorious shall that hand be call'd,
Canonized and worship'd as a Saint,
That takes away by any secret course
Thy hatefull life.

CONSTANCE   O lawfull let it be
That I haue roome with *Rome* to curse a while,
Good Father Cardinall, cry thou Amen
To my keene curses; for without my wrong
There is no tongue hath power to curse him right.

PANDULPH
There's Law and Warrant (Lady) for my curse.

CONSTANCE
1060 And for mine too, when Law can do no right
Let it be lawfull, that Law barre no wrong:
Law cannot giue my childe his kingdome heere;
For he that holds his Kingdome, holds the Law:
Therefore since Law it selfe is perfect wrong,
How can the Law forbid my tongue to curse?

PANDULPH
Philip of *France*, on perill of a curse,

Let goe the hand of that Arch-heretique,
And raise the power of *France* vpon his head,
Vnlesse he doe submit himselfe to *Rome*.

QUEENE ELINOR
Look'st thou pale *France*? do not let go thy hand. 1070

CONSTANCE ⌈*to King Iohn*⌉
Looke to yt Deuill, lest that *France* repent,
And by disioyning hands hell lose a soule.

AUSTRIA
King *Philip*, listen to the Cardinall.

BASTARD
And hang a Calues-skin on his recreant limbs.

AUSTRIA
Well ruffian, I must pocket vp these wrongs,
Because,

BASTARD   Your breeches best may carry them.

KING IOHN
Philip, what saist thou to the Cardinall?

CONSTANCE
What should he say, but as the Cardinall?

DOLPHIN
Bethinke you father, for the difference
Is purchase of a heauy curse from *Rome*, 1080
Or the light losse of *England*, for a friend:
Forgoe the easier.

BLANCH   That's the curse of *Rome*.

CONSTANCE
O *Lewis*, stand fast, the deuill tempts thee heere
In likenesse of a new vntrimmed Bride.

BLANCH
The Lady *Constance* speakes not from her faith,
But from her need.

CONSTANCE ⌈*to King Philip*⌉ Oh, if thou grant my need,
Which onely liues but by the death of faith,
That need, must needs inferre this principle,
That faith would liue againe by death of need:
O then tread downe my need, and faith mounts vp, 1090
Keepe my need vp, and faith is trodden downe.

KING IOHN
The king is moud, and answers not to this.

CONSTANCE (*to King Philip*)
O be remou'd from him, and answere well.

AUSTRIA
Doe so king *Philip*, hang no more in doubt.

BASTARD
Hang nothing but a Calues skin most sweet lout.

KING PHILIP
I am perplext, and know not what to say.

PANDULPH
What canst thou say, but wil perplex thee more?
If thou stand excommunicate, and curst?

KING PHILIP
Good reuerend father, make my person yours,
And tell me how you would bestow your selfe? 1100
This royall hand and mine are newly knit,
And the coniunction of our inward soules
Married in league, coupled, and link'd together
With all religous strength of sacred vowes,

The latest breath that gaue the sound of words
Was deepe-sworne faith, peace, amity, true loue
Betweene our kingdomes and our royall selues,
And euen before this truce, but new before,
No longer then we well could wash our hands,
1110 To clap this royall bargaine vp of peace,
God knowes they were besmear'd and ouer-staind
With slaughters pencill; where reuenge did paint
The fearefull difference of incensed kings:
And shall these hands so lately purg'd of bloud?
So newly ioyn'd in loue? so strong in both,
Vnyoke this seysure, and this kinde regreete?
Play fast and loose with faith? so iest with heauen,
Make such vnconstant children of our selues
As now againe to snatch our palme from palme:
1120 Vn-sweare faith sworne, and on the marriage bed
Of smiling peace to march a bloody hoast,
And make a ryot on the gentle brow
Of true sincerity? O holy Sir
My reuerend father, let it not be so;
Out of your grace, deuise, ordaine, impose
Some gentle order, and then we shall be blest
To doe your pleasure, and continue friends.

PANDULPH
All forme is formelesse, Order orderlesse,
Saue what is opposite to *Englands* loue.
1130 Therefore to Armes, be Champion of our Church,
Or let the Church our mother breathe her curse,
A mothers curse, on her reuolting sonne:
France, thou maist hold a serpent by the tongue,
A crased Lion by the mortall paw,
A fasting Tyger safer by the tooth,
Then keepe in peace that hand which thou dost hold.

KING PHILIP
I may dis-ioyne my hand, but not my faith.

PANDULPH
So mak'st thou faith an enemy to faith,
And like a ciuill warre setst oath to oath,
1140 Thy tongue against thy tongue. O let thy vow
First made to heauen, first be to heauen perform'd,
That is, to be the Champion of our Church,
What since thou sworst, is sworne against thy selfe,
And may not be performed by thy selfe,
For that which thou hast sworne to doe amisse,
Is not amisse when it is truely done:
And being not done, where doing tends to ill,
The truth is then most done not doing it:
The better Act of purposes mistooke,
1150 Is to mistake again, though indirect,
Yet indirection thereby growes direct,
And falshood, falshood cures, as fire cooles fire
Within the scorched veines of one new burn'd:
It is religion that doth make vowes kept,
But thou hast sworne against religion:
By what thou swear'st against the thing thou swear'st,
And mak'st an oath the suretie for thy troth,
Against an oath the truth, thou art vnsure
To sweare, swearst onely not to be forsworne,

Else what a mockerie should it be to sweare?   1160
But thou dost sweare, onely to be forsworne,
And most forsworne, to keepe what thou dost sweare,
Therefore thy later vowes, against thy first,
Is in thy selfe rebellion to thy selfe:
And better conquest neuer canst thou make,
Then arme thy constant and thy nobler parts
Against these giddy loose suggestions:
Vpon which better part, our prayrs come in,
If thou vouchsafe them. But if not, then know
The perill of our curses light on thee   1170
So heauy, as thou shalt not shake them off
But in despaire, dye vnder their blacke weight.

AUSTRIA
Rebellion, flat rebellion.

BASTARD   Wilt not be?
Will not a Calues-skin stop that mouth of thine?

DOLPHIN
Father, to Armes.

BLANCH   Vpon thy wedding day?
Against the blood that thou hast married?
What, shall our feast be kept with slaughtred men?
Shall braying trumpets, and loud churlish drums
Clamors of hell, be measures to our pomp?
    She kneeles
O husband heare me: aye, alacke, how new   1180
Is husband in my mouth? euen for that name
Which till this time my tongue did nere pronounce;
Vpon my knee I beg, goe not to Armes
Against mine Vncle.

CONSTANCE (*kneeling*)   O, vpon my knee
Made hard with kneeling, I doe pray to thee,
Thou vertuous *Daulphin*, alter not the doome
Fore-thought by heauen.

BLANCH (*to the Dolphin*)
Now shall I see thy loue, what motiue may
Be stronger with thee, then the name of wife?

CONSTANCE
That which vpholdeth him, that thee vpholds,   1190
His Honor, Oh thine Honor, *Lewis* thine Honor.

DOLPHIN (*to King Philip*)
I muse your Maiesty doth seeme so cold,
When such profound respects doe pull you on?

PANDULPH
I will denounce a curse vpon his head.

KING PHILIP
Thou shalt not need. *England*, I will fall frõ thee.
    ⌈*He takes his hand from King Iohn's hand. Blanch
    and Constance rise*⌉

CONSTANCE
O faire returne of banish'd Maiestie.

QUEENE ELINOR
O foule reuolt of French inconstancy.

KING IOHN
France, yᵘ shalt rue this houre within this houre.

BASTARD
Old Time the clocke setter, yᵗ bald sexton Time:
Is it as he will? well then, *France* shall rue.   1200

BLANCH

The Sun's orecast with bloud: faire day adieu,
Which is the side that I must goe withall?
I am with both, each Army hath a hand,
And in their rage, I hauing hold of both,
They whurle a-sunder, and dismember mee.
Husband, I cannot pray that thou maist winne:
Vncle, I needs must pray that thou maist lose:
Father, I may not wish the fortune thine:
Grandam, I will not wish thy wishes thriue:
1210   Who-euer wins, on that side shall I lose:
Assured losse, before the match be plaid.

DOLPHIN

Lady, with me, with me thy fortune lies.

BLANCH

There where my fortune liues, there my life dies.

KING IOHN (*to the Bastard*)

Cosen, goe draw our puisance together, ⌈*Exit Bastard*⌉
France, I am burn'd vp with inflaming wrath,
A rage, whose heat hath this condition;
That nothing can allay, nothing but blood,
The blood and deerest valued bloud of *France*.

KING PHILIP

Thy rage shall burne thee vp, & thou shalt turne
1220   To ashes, ere our blood shall quench that fire:
Looke to thy selfe, thou art in ieopardie.

KING IOHN

No more then he that threats. To Arms le'ts hie.
                                    Exeunt ⌈*seuerally*⌉

Sc. 4   *Allarums, Excursions: Enter Bastard with Austria's*
(3.2)   *head*

BASTARD

Now by my life, this day grows wondrous hot,
Some ayery Deuill houers in the skie,
And pour's downe mischiefe. *Austrias* head lye there,
        Enter Iohn, Arthur, Hubert
While *Philip* breathes.

KING IOHN

Hubert, keepe this boy: *Philip* make vp,
My Mother is assayled in our Tent,
And tane I feare.

BASTARD   My Lord I rescued her,
1230   Her Highnesse is in safety, feare you not:
But on my Liege, for very little paines
Will bring this labor to an happy end.
                Exeunt ⌈*Iohn and the Bastard at one doore,*
                Hubert and Arthur at another doore⌉

Sc. 5   *Alarums, excursions, Retreat. Enter Iohn, Eleanor,*
(3.3)   *Arthur, Bastard, Hubert, Lords,* ⌈*with Souldiers*⌉

KING IOHN (*to Queene Elinor*)

So shall it be: your Grace shall stay behinde
So strongly guarded: (*To Arthur*) Cosen, looke not sad,
Thy Grandame loues thee, and thy Vnkle will
As deere be to thee, as thy father was.

ARTHUR

O this will make my mother die with griefe.

KING IOHN (*to the Bastard*)

Cosen away for *England*, haste before,
And ere our comming see thou shake the bags
Of hoording Abbots, the fat ribs of peace   1240
Must by the hungry now be fed vpon:
Imprison'd angells set at libertie:
Vse our Commission in his vtmost force.

BASTARD

Bell, Booke, & Candle, shall not driue me back,
When gold and siluer becks me to come on.
I leaue your highnesse: Grandame, I will pray
(If euer I remember to be holy)
For your faire safety: so I kisse your hand.

QUEENE ELINOR

Farewell gentle Cosen.

KING IOHN   Coz, farewell.   *Exit Bastard*

QUEENE ELINOR

Come hether little kinsman, harke, a worde.   1250
        She takes Arthur aside

KING IOHN

Come hether *Hubert*.
        He takes Hubert aside
                        O my gentle *Hubert*,
We owe thee much: within this wall of flesh
There is a soule counts thee her Creditor,
And with aduantage meanes to pay thy loue:
And my good friend, thy voluntary oath
Liues in this bosome, deerely cherished.
Giue me thy hand,
        He takes Huberts hand
                        I had a thing to say,
But I will fit it with some better tune.
By heauen *Hubert*, I am almost asham'd
To say what good respect I haue of thee.   1260

HUBERT

I am much bounden to your Maiesty.

KING IOHN

Good friend, thou hast no cause to say so yet,
But thou shalt haue: and creepe time nere so slow,
Yet it shall come, for me to doe thee good.
I had a thing to say, but let it goe:
The Sunne is in the heauen, and the proud day,
Attended with the pleasures of the world,
Is all too wanton, and too full of gawdes
To giue me audience: If the mid-night bell
Did with his yron tongue, and brazen mouth   1270
Sound on into the drowzie race of night:
If this same were a Church-yard where we stand,
And thou possessed with a thousand wrongs:
Or if that surly spirit melancholy
Had bak'd thy bloud, and made it heauy, thicke,
Which else runnes tickling vp and downe the veines,
Making that idiot laughter keepe mens eyes,
And straine their cheekes to idle merriment,
A passion hatefull to my purposes:
Or if that thou couldst see me without eyes,   1280
Heare me without thine eares, and make reply

Without a tongue, vsing conceit alone,
Without eyes, eares, and harmefull sound of words:
Then, in despight of broadeid watchfull day,
I would into thy bosome poure my thoughts:
But (ah) I will not, yet I loue thee well,
And by my troth I thinke thou lou'st me well.

HUBERT
So well, that what you bid me vndertake,
Though that my death were adiunct to my Act,
By heauen I would doe it.

1290 KING IOHN   Doe not I know thou wouldst?
Good *Hubert, Hubert, Hubert* throw thine eye
On yon young boy: Ile tell thee what my friend,
He is a very serpent in my way,
And wheresoere this foot of mine doth tread,
He lies before me: dost thou vnderstand me?
Thou art his keeper.

HUBERT   And Ile keepe him so,
That he shall not offend your Maiesty.

KING IOHN
Death.

HUBERT   My Lord.

KING IOHN   A Graue.

HUBERT   He shall not liue.

KING IOHN   Enough.
I could be merry now, *Hubert,* I loue thee.
1300 Well, Ile not say what I intend for thee:
Remember: (*To Queene Elinor*) Madam, Fare you well,
Ile send those powers o're to your Maiesty.

QUEENE ELINOR
My blessing goe with thee.

KING IOHN (*to Arthur*)   For *England* Cosen, goe.
Hubert shall be your man, attend on you
With al true duetie: On toward *Callice,* hoa.
          Exeunt ⌐Queene Elinor, attended, at one doore,
                              the rest at another doore⌐

Sc. 6   *Enter King Philip, Dolphin, Pandulph, Attendants*
(3.4) KING PHILIP
So by a roaring Tempest on the flood,
A whole Armado of conuicted saile
Is scattred and dis-ioyn'd from fellowship.

PANDULPH
Courage and comfort, all shall yet goe well.

KING PHILIP
1310 What can goe well, when we haue runne so ill?
Are we not beaten? Is not *Angiers* lost?
Arthur tane prisoner? diuers deere friends slaine?
And bloudy *England* into *England* gone,
Ore-bearing interruption spight of *France?*

DOLPHIN
What he hath won, that hath he fortified:
So hot a speed, with such aduice dispos'd,
Such temperate order in so fierce a cause,
Doth want example: who hath read, or heard
Of any kindred-action like to this?

KING PHILIP
1320 Well could I beare that *England* had this praise,
So we could finde some patterne of our shame:

*Enter Constance distracted, with her haire about
her eares*
Looke who comes heere? a graue vnto a soule,
Holding th'eternall spirit against her will,
In the vilde prison of afflicted breath:
I prethee Lady goe away with me.

CONSTANCE
Lo; now: now see the issue of your peace.

KING PHILIP
Patience good Lady, comfort gentle *Constance.*

CONSTANCE
No, I defie all Counsell, all redresse,
But that which ends all counsell, true Redresse:
Death, death, O amiable, louely death,   1330
Thou odoriferous stench: sound rottennesse,
Arise forth from the couch of lasting night,
Thou hate and terror to prosperitie,
And I will kisse thy detestable bones,
And put my eye-balls in thy vaultie browes,
And ring these fingers with thy houshold wormes,
And stop this gap of breath with fulsome dust,
And be a Carrion Monster like thy selfe;
Come, grin on me, and I will thinke thou smil'st,
And busse thee as thy wife: Miseries Loue,   1340
O come to me.

KING PHILIP   O faire affliction, peace.

CONSTANCE
No, no, I will not, hauing breath to cry:
O that my tongue were in the thunders mouth,
Then with a passion would I shake the world,
And rowze from sleepe that fell Anatomy
Which cannot heare a Ladies feeble voyce,
Which scornes a moderne Inuocation.

PANDULPH
Lady, you vtter madnesse, and not sorrow.

CONSTANCE
Thou art not holy to belye me so,
I am not mad: this haire I teare is mine,   1350
My name is *Constance,* I was *Geffreyes* wife,
Yong *Arthur* is my sonne, and he is lost:
I am not mad, I would to God I were,
For then 'tis like I should forget my selfe:
O, if I could, what griefe should I forget?
Preach some Philosophy to make me mad,
And thou shalt be Canoniz'd (Cardinall.)
For, being not mad, but sensible of greefe,
My reasonable part produces reason
How I may be deliuer'd of these woes,   1360
And teaches mee to kill or hang my selfe:
If I were mad, I should forget my sonne,
Or madly thinke a babe of clowts were he;
I am not mad: too well, too well I feele
The different plague of each calamitie.

KING PHILIP
Binde vp those tresses: O what loue I note
In the faire multitude of those her haires;
Where but by chance a siluer drop hath falne,
Euen to that drop ten thousand wiery friends

1370 Doe glew themselues in sociable griefe,
Like true, inseparable, faithfull loues,
Sticking together in calamitie.

CONSTANCE
To *England*, if you will.

KING PHILIP   Binde vp your haires.

CONSTANCE
Yes that I will: and wherefore will I do it?
I tore them from their bonds, and cride aloud,
O, that these hands could so redeeme my sonne,
As they haue giuen these hayres their libertie:
But now I enuie at their libertie,
And will againe commit them to their bonds,
1380 Because my poore childe is a prisoner.
        She bindes vp her haire
And Father Cardinall, I haue heard you say
That we shall see and know our friends in heauen:
If that be true, I shall see my boy againe;
For since the birth of *Caine*, the first male-childe
To him that did but yesterday suspire,
There was not such a gracious creature borne:
But now will Canker-sorrow eat my bud,
And chase the natiue beauty from his cheeke,
And he will looke as hollow as a Ghost,
1390 As dim and meager as an Agues fitte,
And so hee'll dye: and rising so againe,
When I shall meet him in the Court of heauen
I shall not know him: therefore neuer, neuer
Must I behold my pretty *Arthur* more.

PANDULPH
You hold too heynous a respect of greefe.

CONSTANCE
He talkes to me, that neuer had a sonne.

KING PHILIP
You are as fond of greefe, as of your childe.

CONSTANCE
Greefe fils the roome vp of my absent childe:
Lies in his bed, walkes vp and downe with me,
1400 Puts on his pretty lookes, repeats his words,
Remembers me of all his gracious parts,
Stuffes out his vacant garments with his forme;
Then, haue I reason to be fond of griefe?
Fareyouwell: had you such a losse as I,
I could giue better comfort then you doe.
        ⌈*She vnbindes her haire*⌉
I will not keepe this forme vpon my head,
When there is such disorder in my witte:
O Lord, my boy, my *Arthur*, my faire sonne,
My life, my ioy, my food, my all the world:
1410 My widow-comfort, and my sorrowes cure.   *Exit*

KING PHILIP
I feare some out-rage, and Ile follow her.
                              Exit ⌈*attended*⌉

DOLPHIN
There's nothing in this world can make me ioy,
Life is as tedious as a twice-told tale,
Vexing the dull eare of a drowsie man;

And bitter shame hath spoyl'd the sweet words taste,
That it yeelds nought but shame and bitternesse.

PANDULPH
Before the curing of a strong disease,
Euen in the instant of repaire and health,
The fit is strongest: Euils that take leaue
On their departure, most of all shew euill:
1420 What haue you lost by losing of this day?

DOLPHIN
All daies of glory, ioy, and happinesse.

PANDULPH
If you had won it, certainely you had.
No, no: when Fortune meanes to men most good,
Shee lookes vpon them with a threatning eye:
'Tis strange to thinke how much King *Iohn* hath lost
In this which he accounts so clearely wonne:
Are not you grieu'd that *Arthur* is his prisoner?

DOLPHIN
As heartily as he is glad he hath him.

PANDULPH
Your minde is all as youthfull as your blood.   1430
Now heare me speake with a propheticke spirit:
For euen the breath of what I meane to speake,
Shall blow each dust, each straw, each little rub
Out of the path which shall directly lead
Thy foote to Englands Throne. And therefore marke:
Iohn hath seiz'd *Arthur*, and it cannot be,
That whiles warme life playes in that infants veines,
The mis-plac'd-*Iohn* should entertaine an houre,
One minute, nay one quiet breath of rest.
A Scepter snatch'd with an vnruly hand,   1440
Must be as boysterously maintain'd as gain'd.
And he that stands vpon a slipp'ry place,
Makes nice of no vilde hold to stay him vp:
That *Iohn* may stand, then *Arthur* needs must fall,
So be it, for it cannot be but so.

DOLPHIN
But what shall I gaine by yong *Arthurs* fall?

PANDULPH
You, in the right of Lady *Blanch* your wife,
May then make all the claime that *Arthur* did.

DOLPHIN
And loose it, life and all, as *Arthur* did.

PANDULPH
How green you are, and fresh in this old world?   1450
Iohn layes you plots: the times conspire with you,
For he that steepes his safetie in true blood,
Shall finde but bloodie safety, and vntrue.
This Act soe vilely borne shall coole the hearts
Of all his people, and freeze vp their zeale,
That none so small aduantage shall step forth
To checke his reigne, but they will cherish it.
No naturall exhalation in the skie,
No scope of Nature, no distemper'd day,
No common winde, no customed euent,   1460
But they will plucke away his naturall cause,
And call them Meteors, prodigies, and signes,

Abbortiues, presages, and tongues of heauen,
Plainly denouncing vengeance vpon *Iohn*.

DOLPHIN
May be he will not touch yong *Arthurs* life,
But hold himselfe safe in his prisonment.

PANDULPH
O Sir, when he shall heare of your approach,
If that yong *Arthur* be not gone alreadie,
Euen at that newes he dies: and then the hearts
1470 Of all his people shall reuolt from him,
And kisse the lippes of vnacquainted change,
And picke strong matter of reuolt, and wrath
Out of the bloody fingers ends of *Iohn*.
Me thinkes I see this hurley all on foot;
And O, what better matter breeds for you,
Then I haue nam'd. The Bastard *Falconbridge*
Is now in England ransacking the Church,
Offending Charity: If but a dozen French
Were there in Armes, they would be as a Call
1480 To traine ten thousand English to their side;
Or, as a little snow, tumbled about,
Anon becomes a Mountaine. O noble Dolphine,
Go with me to the King, 'tis wonderfull,
What may be wrought out of their discontent,
Now that their soules are topfull of offence,
For England go; I will whet on the King.

DOLPHIN
Strong reasons make strange actions: let vs go,
If you say I, the King will not say no.   *Exeunt*

Sc. 7   *Enter Hubert and Executioners, with a rope and*
(4.1)   *Irons*

HUBERT
Heate me these Irons hot, and looke thou stand
1490 Within the Arras: when I strike my foot
Vpon the bosome of the ground, rush forth
And binde the boy, which you shall finde with me
Fast to the chaire: be heedfull: hence, and watch.

EXECUTIONER
I hope your warrant will beare out the deed.

HUBERT
Vncleanly scruples, feare not you: looke too't.
⌜*The Executioners withdraw behinde the Arras*⌝
Yong Lad come forth; I haue to say with you.
    Enter Arthur

ARTHUR
Good morrow *Hubert*.

HUBERT   Good morrow, little Prince.

ARTHUR
As little Prince, hauing so great a Title
To be more Prince, as may be: you are sad.

HUBERT
Indeed I haue beene merrier.

1500 ARTHUR   'Mercie on me:
Me thinkes no body should be sad but I:
Yet I remember, when I was in France,
Yong Gentlemen would be as sad as night
Onely for wantonnesse: by my Christendome,

So I were out of prison, and kept Sheepe
I should be as merry as the day is long:
And so I would be heere, but that I doubt
My Vnckle practises more harme to me:
He is affraid of me, and I of him:
Is it my fault, that I was *Geffreyes* sonne?   1510
No in deede is't not: and I would to God
I were your sonne, so you would loue me, Hubert.

HUBERT (*aside*)
If I talke to him, with his innocent prate
He will awake my mercie, which lies dead:
Therefore I will be sodaine, and dispatch.

ARTHUR
Are you sicke Hubert? you looke pale to day,
Insooth I would you were a little sicke,
That I might sit all night, and watch with you.
I warrant I loue you more then you do me.

HUBERT (*aside*)
His words do take possession of my bosome.   1520
    He shewes Arthur a Paper
Reade heere yong *Arthur*. (*Aside*) How now foolish
    rheume?
Turning dispitious torture out of doore?
I must be breefe, least resolution drop
Out at mine eyes, in tender womanish teares.
(*To Arthur*) Can you not reade it? Is it not faire writ?

ARTHUR
Too fairely *Hubert*, for so foule effect,
Must you with hot Irons, burne out both mine eyes?

HUBERT
Yong Boy, I must.

ARTHUR   And will you?

HUBERT   And I will.

ARTHUR
Haue you the heart? When your head did but ake,
I knit my hand-kercher about your browes   1530
(The best I had, a Princesse wrought it me)
And I did neuer aske it you againe:
And with my hand, at midnight held your head;
And like the watchfull minutes, to the houre,
Still and anon cheer'd vp the heauy time;
Saying, what lacke you? and where lies your greefe?
Or what good loue may I performe for you?
Many a poore mans sonne would haue lyen still,
And nere haue spoke a louing word to you:
But you, at your sicke seruice had a Prince: 1540
Nay, you may thinke my loue was craftie loue,
And call it cunning. Do, and if you will,
If heauen be pleas'd that you must vse me ill,
Why then you must. Will you put out mine eyes?
These eyes, that neuer did, nor neuer shall
So much as frowne on you.

HUBERT   I haue sworne to do it:
And with hot Irons must I burne them out.

ARTHUR
Ah, none but in this Iron Age, would do it:
The Iron of it selfe, though heate red hot,
Approaching neere these eyes, would drinke my teares,   1550

And quench his fierie indignation,
Euen in the matter of mine innocence:
Nay, after that, consume away in rust,
But for containing fire to harme mine eye:
Are you more stubborne hard, then hammer'd Iron?
And if an Angell should haue come to me,
And told me *Hubert* should put out mine eyes,
I would not haue beleeu'd him: no tongue but *Huberts*.

      Hubert stampes his foote

HUBERT

Come forth:

      The Executioners come forth
          Do as I bid you do.

ARTHUR

1560   O saue me *Hubert*, saue me: my eyes are out
Euen with the fierce lookes of these bloody men.

HUBERT (*to the Executioners*)

Giue me the Iron I say, and binde him heere.

      He takes the Iron

ARTHUR

Alas, what neede you be so boistrous rough?
I will not struggle, I will stand stone still:
For Gods sake *Hubert* let me not be bound:
Nay heare me *Hubert*, driue these men away,
And I will sit as quiet as a Lambe.
I will not stirre, nor winch, nor speake a word,
Nor looke vpon the Iron angerly:
1570   Thrust but these men away, and Ile forgiue you,
What euer torment you do put me too.

HUBERT (*to the Executioners*)

Go stand within: let me alone with him.

EXECUTIONER

I am best pleas'd to be from such a deede.

      Exeunt Executioners

ARTHUR

Alas, I then haue chid away my friend,
He hath a sterne looke, but a gentle heart:
Let him come backe, that his compassion may
Giue life to yours.

HUBERT   Come (Boy) prepare your selfe.

ARTHUR

Is there no remedie?

HUBERT   None, but to lose your eyes.

ARTHUR

O God: that there were but a moth in yours,
1580   A graine, a dust, a gnat, a wandering haire,
Any annoyance in that precious sense:
Then feeling what small things are boysterous there,
Your vilde intent must needs seeme horrible.

HUBERT

Is this your promise? Go too, hold your toong.

ARTHUR

Hubert, the vtterance of a brace of tongues,
Must needes want pleading for a paire of eyes:
Let me not hold my tongue: let me not *Hubert*,
Or *Hubert*, if you will cut out my tongue,
So I may keepe mine eyes. O spare mine eyes,
1590   Though to no vse, but still to looke on you.

Loe, by my troth, the Instrument is cold,
And would not harme me.

HUBERT   I can heate it, Boy.

ARTHUR

No, in good sooth: the fire is dead with griefe,
Being create for comfort, to be vs'd
In vndeserued extreames: See else your selfe,
There is no malice in this burning cole,
The breath of heauen, hath blowne his spirit out,
And strew'd repentant ashes on his head.

HUBERT

But with my breath I can reuiue it Boy.

ARTHUR

And if you do, you will but make it blush,   1600
And glow with shame of your proceedings, *Hubert*:
Nay, it perchance will sparkle in your eyes:
And, like a dogge that is compell'd to fight,
Snatch at his Master that doth tarre him on.
All things that you should vse to do me wrong
Deny their office: onely you do lacke
That mercie, which fierce fire, and Iron extends,
Creatures of note for mercy, lacking vses.

HUBERT

Well, see to liue: I will not touch thine eye,
For all the Treasure that thine Vnckle owes,   1610
Yet am I sworne, and I did purpose, Boy,
With this same very Iron, to burne them out.

ARTHUR

O now you looke like *Hubert*. All this while
You were disguis'd.

HUBERT   Peace: no more. Adieu,
Your Vnckle must not know but you are dead.
Ile fill these dogged Spies with false reports:
And, pretty childe, sleepe doubtlesse, and secure,
That *Hubert* for the wealth of all the world,
Will not offend thee.

ARTHUR   O God! I thanke you *Hubert*.

HUBERT

Silence, no more; go closely in with mee,   1620
Much danger do I vndergo for thee.   *Exeunt*

⌐*Florish.*⌐ *Enter Iohn, Pembroke, Salisbury, and*   Sc. 8
other Lordes. King Iohn ascends the Throne   (4.2)

KING IOHN

Heere once againe we sit: once againe crown'd
And look'd vpon, I hope, with chearefull eyes.

PEMBROKE

This once again (but that your Highnes pleas'd)
Was once superfluous: you were Crown'd before,
And that high Royalty was nere pluck'd off:
The faiths of men, nere stained with reuolt:
Fresh expectation troubled not the Land
With any long'd-for-change, or better State.

SALISBURY

Therefore, to be possess'd with double pompe,   1630
To guard a Title, that was rich before;
To gilde refined Gold, to paint the Lilly;
To throw a perfume on the Violet,

To smooth the yce, or adde another hew
Vnto the Raine-bow; or with Taper-light
To seeke the beauteous eye of heauen to garnish,
Is wastefull, and ridiculous excesse.

PEMBROKE
But that your Royall pleasure must be done,
This acte, is as an ancient tale new told,
1640 And, in the last repeating, troublesome,
Being vrged at a time vnseasonable.

SALISBURY
In this the Anticke, and well noted face
Of plaine old forme, is much disfigured,
And like a shifted winde vnto a saile,
It makes the course of thoughts to fetch about,
Startles, and frights consideration:
Makes sound opinion sicke, and truth suspected,
For putting on so new a fashion'd robe.

PEMBROKE
When Workemen striue to do better then wel,
1650 They do confound their skill in couetousnesse,
And oftentimes excusing of a fault,
Doth make the fault the worser by th'excuse:
As patches set vpon a little breach,
Discredite more in hiding of the fault,
Then did the fault before it was so patch'd.

SALISBURY
To this effect, before you were new crown'd
We breath'd our Councell: but it pleas'd your
    Highnes
To ouer-beare it, and we are all well pleas'd,
Since all, and euery part of what we would
1660 Doth make a stand, at what your Highnesse will.

KING IOHN
Some reasons of this double Corronation
I haue possest you with, and thinke them strong.
And more, more strong, when lesser is my feare
I shall indue you with: Meane time, but aske
What you would haue reform'd, that is not well,
And well shall you perceiue, how willingly
I will both heare, and grant you your requests.

PEMBROKE
Then I, as one that am the tongue of these
To sound the purposes of all their hearts,
1670 Both for my selfe, and them: but chiefe of all
Your safety: for the which, my selfe and them
Bend their best studies, heartily request
Th'infranchisement of *Arthur*, whose restraint
Doth moue the murmuring lips of discontent
To breake into this dangerous argument.
If what in rest you haue, in right you hold,
Why then your feares, which (as they say) attend
The steppes of wrong, should moue you to mew vp
Your tender kinsman, and to choake his dayes
1680 With barbarous ignorance, and deny his youth
The rich aduantage of good exercise?
That the times enemies may not haue this
To grace occasions: let it be our suite,
That you haue bid vs aske his libertie,

Which for our goods, we do no further aske,
Then, whereupon our weale on you depending,
Counts it your weale: he haue his liberty.
    Enter Hubert

KING IOHN
Let it be so: I do commit his youth
To your direction: *Hubert*, what newes with you?
    He takes Hubert aside

PEMBROKE
This is the man should do the bloody deed: 1690
He shew'd his warrant to a friend of mine,
The image of a wicked heynous fault
Liues in his eye: that close aspect of his,
Dos shew the mood of a much troubled brest,
And I do fearefully beleeue 'tis done,
What we so fear'd he had a charge to do.

SALISBURY
The colour of the King doth come, and go
Betweene his purpose and his conscience,
Like Heralds 'twixt two dreadfull battailes set:
His passion is so ripe, it needs must breake.   1700

PEMBROKE
And when it breakes, I feare will issue thence
The foule corruption of a sweet childes death.

KING IOHN (*comming forward*)
We cannot hold mortalities strong hand.
Good Lords, although my will to giue, is liuing,
The suite which you demand is gone, and dead.
He tels vs *Arthur* is deceas'd to night.

SALISBURY
Indeed we fear'd his sicknesse was past cure.

PEMBROKE
Indeed we heard how neere his death he was,
Before the childe himselfe felt he was sicke:
This must be answer'd either heere, or hence.   1710

KING IOHN
Why do you bend such solemne browes on me?
Thinke you I beare the Sheeres of destiny?
Haue I commandement on the pulse of life?

SALISBURY
It is apparant foule-play, and 'tis shame
That Greatnesse should so grossely offer it;
So thriue it in your game, and so farewell.

PEMBROKE
Stay yet (Lord Salisbury) Ile go with thee,
And finde th'inheritance of this poore childe,
His little kingdome of a forced graue.
That blood which ow'd the bredth of all this Ile,   1720
Three foot of it doth hold; bad world the while:
This must not be thus borne, this will breake out
To all our sorrowes, and ere long I doubt.
    Exeunt Pembroke, Salisbury, ⸢and other Lords⸣

KING IOHN
They burn in indignation: I repent:
There is no sure foundation set on blood:
No certaine life atchieu'd by others death:
    Enter Messenger
A fearefull eye thou hast. Where is that blood,

That I haue seene inhabite in those cheekes?
So foule a skie, cleeres not without a storme,
1730 Poure downe thy weather: how goes all in France?
MESSENGER
From France to England, neuer such a powre
For any forraigne preparation,
Was leuied in the body of a land.
The Copie of your speede is learn'd by them:
For when you should be told they do prepare,
The tydings comes, that they are all arriu'd.
KING IOHN
Oh where hath our Intelligence bin drunke?
Where hath it slept? Where is my Mothers eare?
That such an Army could be drawne in France,
And she not heare of it?
1740 **MESSENGER**   My Liege, her eare
Is stopt with dust: the first of Aprill di'de
Your noble mother; and as I heare, my Lord,
The Lady *Constance* in a frenzie di'de
Three dayes before: but this from Rumors tongue
I idely heard: if true, or false I know not.
KING IOHN
With-hold thy speed, dreadfull Occasion:
O make a league with me, 'till I haue pleas'd
My discontented Peeres. What? Mother dead?
How wildely then walkes my Estate in France?
1750 Vnder whose conduct came those powres of France,
That thou for truth giu'st out are landed heere?
MESSENGER
Vnder the Dolphin.
Enter Bastard and Peter of Pomfret
KING IOHN   Thou hast made me giddy
With these ill tydings: (*to the Bastard*) Now? What
    sayes the world
To your proceedings? Do not seeke to stuffe
My head with more ill newes: for it is full.
BASTARD
But if you be a-feard to heare the worst,
Then let the worst vn-heard, fall on your head.
KING IOHN
Beare with me Cosen, for I was amaz'd
Vnder the tide; but now I breath againe
1760 Aloft the flood, and can giue audience
To any tongue, speake it of what it will.
BASTARD
How I haue sped among the Clergy men,
The summes I haue collected shall expresse:
But as I trauail'd hither through the land,
I finde the people strangely fantasied,
Possest with rumors, full of idle dreames,
Not knowing what they feare, but full of feare.
And here's a Prophet that I brought with me
From forth the streets of Pomfret, whom I found
1770 With many hundreds treading on his heeles:
To whom he sung in rude harsh sounding rimes,
That ere the next Ascension day at noone,
Your Highnes should deliuer vp your Crowne.

KING IOHN
Thou idle Dreamer, wherefore didst thou so?
PETER OF POMFRET
Fore-knowing that the truth will fall out so.
KING IOHN
Hubert, away with him: imprison him,
And on that day at noone, whereon he sayes
I shall yeeld vp my Crowne, let him be hang'd.
Deliuer him to safety, and returne,
For I must vse thee.
                    Exeunt Hubert and Peter of Pomfret
            O my gentle Cosen,   1780
Hear'st thou the newes abroad, who are arriu'd?
BASTARD
The *French* (my Lord) mens mouths are ful of it:
Besides I met Lord *Bigot*, and Lord *Salisburie*
With eyes as red as new enkindled fire,
And others more, going to seeke the graue
Of *Arthur*, whom they say is kill'd to night,
On your suggestion.
KING IOHN   Gentle kinsman, go
And thrust thy selfe into their Companies,
I haue a way to winne their loues againe:
Bring them before me.
BASTARD   I will seeke them out.   1790
KING IOHN
Nay, but make haste: the better foote before.
O, let me haue no subiect enemies,
When aduerse Forreyners affright my Townes
With dreadfull pompe of stout inuasion.
Be Mercurie, set feathers to thy heeles,
And flye (like thought) from them, to me againe.
BASTARD
The spirit of the time shall teach me speed.   *Exit*
KING IOHN
Spoke like a sprightfull Noble Gentleman.
Go after him: for he perhaps shall neede
Some Messenger betwixt me, and the Peeres,   1800
And be thou hee.
MESSENGER With all my heart, my Liege.   *Exit*
KING IOHN My mother dead?
        Enter Hubert
HUBERT
My Lord, they say fiue Moones were seene to night:
Foure fixed, and the fift did whirle about
The other foure, in wondrous motion.
KING IOHN
Fiue Moones?
HUBERT   Old men, and Beldames, in the streets
Do prophesie vpon it dangerously:
Yong *Arthurs* death is common in their mouths,
And when they talke of him, they shake their heads,   1810
And whisper one another in the eare.
And he that speakes, doth gripe the hearers wrist,
Whilst he that heares, makes fearefull action
With wrinkled browes, with nods, with rolling eyes.
I saw a Smith stand with his hammer (thus)

The whilst his Iron did on the Anuile coole,
With open mouth swallowing a Taylors newes,
Who with his Sheeres, and Measure in his hand,
Standing on slippers, which his nimble haste
1820　Had falsely thrust vpon contrary feete,
Told of a many thousand warlike French,
That were embattailed, and rank'd in Kent.
Another leane, vnwash'd Artificer,
Cuts off his tale, and talkes of *Arthurs* death.

KING IOHN
Why seek'st thou to possesse me with these feares?
Why vrgest thou so oft yong *Arthurs* death?
Thy hand hath murdred him: I had a mighty cause
To wish him dead, but thou hadst none to kill him.

HUBERT
No had (my Lord?) why, did you not prouoke me?

KING IOHN
1830　It is the curse of Kings, to be attended
By slaues, that take their humors for a warrant,
To breake within the bloody house of life,
And on the winking of Authoritie
To vnderstand a Law; to know the meaning
Of dangerous Maiesty, when perchance it frownes
More vpon humor, then aduis'd respect.

HUBERT
Heere is your hand and Seale for what I did.
He shewes a Paper

KING IOHN
Oh, when the last accompt twixt heauen & earth
Is to be made, then shall this hand and Seale
1840　Witnesse against vs to damnation.
How oft the sight of meanes to do ill deeds,
Make deeds ill done? Had'st not thou beene by,
A fellow by the hand of Nature mark'd,
Quoted, and sign'd to do a deede of shame,
This murther had not come into my minde.
But taking note of thy abhorr'd Aspect,
Finding thee fit for bloody villanie:
Apt, liable to be employ'd in danger,
I faintly broke with thee of *Arthurs* death:
1850　And thou, to be endeered to a King,
Made it no conscience to destroy a Prince.

HUBERT My Lord.

KING IOHN
Had'st thou but shooke thy head, or made a pause
When I spake darkely, what I purposed:
Or turn'd an eye of doubt vpon my face;
As bid me tell my tale in expresse words:
Deepe shame had struck me dumbe, made me break
　　off,
And those thy feares, might haue wrought feares
　　in me.
But, thou didst vnderstand me by my signes,
1860　And didst in signes againe parley with sinne,
Yea, without stop, didst let thy heart consent,
And consequently, thy rude hand to acte
The deed, which both our tongues held vilde to name.
Out of my sight, and neuer see me more:

My Nobles leaue me, and my State is braued,
Euen at my gates, with rankes of forraigne powres;
Nay, in the body of this fleshly Land,
This kingdome, this Confine of blood, and breathe
Hostilitie, and ciuill tumult reignes
Betweene my conscience, and my Cosins death.　1870

HUBERT
Arme you against your other enemies:
Ile make a peace betweene your soule, and you.
Yong *Arthur* is aliue: This hand of mine
Is yet a maiden, and an innocent hand,
Not painted with the Crimson spots of blood,
Within this bosome, neuer entred yet
The dreadfull motion of a murderous thought,
And you haue slander'd Nature in my forme,
Which howsoeuer rude exteriorly,
Is yet the couer of a fayrer minde,　　　　　　1880
Then to be butcher of an innocent childe.

KING IOHN
Doth *Arthur* liue? O hast thee to the Peeres,
Throw this report on their incensed rage,
And make them tame to their obedience.
Forgiue the Comment that my passion made
Vpon thy feature, for my rage was blinde,
And foule immaginarie eyes of blood
Presented thee more hideous then thou art.
Oh, answer not; but to my Closset bring
The angry Lords, with all expedient hast,　　1890
I coniure thee but slowly: run more fast.
Exeunt ⌈seuerally⌉

Enter Arthur on the walles, like a Ship-boy　Sc. 9
ARTHUR　　　　　　　　　　　　　　　　　　　　(4.3)
The Wall is high, and yet will I leape downe.
Good ground be pittifull, and hurt me not:
There's few or none do know me, if they did,
This Ship-boyes semblance hath disguis'd me quite.
I am afraide, and yet Ile venture it.
If I get downe, and do not breake my limbes,
Ile finde a thousand shifts to get away;
As good to dye, and go; as dye, and stay.
He leapes downe
Oh me, my Vnckles spirit is in these stones,　1900
Heauen take my soule, and England keep my bones.
He dies

Enter Pembroke, Salisbury, & Bigot
SALISBURY
Lords, I will meet him at S. *Edmondsbury*,
It is our safetie, and we must embrace
This gentle offer of the perillous time.

PEMBROKE
Who brought that Letter from the Cardinall?

SALISBURY
The Count *Meloone*, a Noble Lord of France,
Whose priuate with me of the Dolphines loue,
Tis much more generall, then these lines import.

BIGOT
To morrow morning let vs meete him then.

SALISBURY

1910 Or rather then set forward, for 'twill be
 Two long dayes iourney (Lords) or ere we meete.
   Enter Bastard

BASTARD

 Once more to day well met, distemper'd Lords,
 The King by me requests your presence straight.

SALISBURY

 The king hath dispossest himselfe of vs,
 We will not lyne his thin-bestained cloake
 With our pure Honors: nor attend the foote
 That leaues the print of blood where ere it walkes.
 Returne, and tell him so: we know the worst.

BASTARD

 What ere you thinke, good words I thinke were best.

SALISBURY

1920 Our greefes, and not our manners reason now.

BASTARD

 But there is little reason in your greefe.
 Therefore 'twere reason you had manners now.

PEMBROKE

 Sir, sir, impatience hath his priuiledge.

BASTARD

 'Tis true, to hurt his master, no man else.

SALISBURY

 This is the prison:
   He sees Arthurs body
      What is he lyes heere?

PEMBROKE

 Oh death, made proud with pure & princely beuty,
 The earth had not a hole to hide this deede.

SALISBURY

 Murther, as hating what himselfe hath done,
 Doth lay it open to vrge on reuenge.

BIGOT

1930 Or when he doom'd this Beautie to a graue,
 Found it too precious Princely, for a graue.

SALISBURY (*to the Bastard*)

 Sir *Richard*, what thinke you? you haue beheld,
 Or haue you read, or heard, or could you thinke?
 Or do you almost thinke, although you see,
 That you do see? Could thought, without this obiect
 Forme such another? This is the very top,
 The heighth, the Crest: or Crest vnto the Crest
 Of murthers Armes: This is the bloodiest shame,
 The wildest Sauagery, the vildest stroke
1940 That euer wall-ey'd wrath, or staring rage
 Presented to the teares of soft remorse.

PEMBROKE

 All murthers past, do stand excus'd in this:
 And this so sole, and so vnmatcheable,
 Shall giue a holinesse, a puritie,
 To the yet vnbegotten sinne of times;
 And proue a deadly blood-shed, but a iest,
 Exampled by this heynous spectacle.

BASTARD

 It is a damned, and a bloody worke,

 The gracelesse action of a heauy hand,
 If that it be the worke of any hand.   1950

SALISBURY

 If that it be the worke of any hand?
 We had a kinde of light, what would ensue:
 It is the shamefull worke of *Huberts* hand,
 The practice, and the purpose of the king:
 From whose obedience I forbid my soule,
 Kneeling before this ruine of sweete life,
 And breathing to his breathlesse Excellence
 The Incense of a Vow, a holy Vow:
 Neuer to taste the pleasures of the world,
 Neuer to be infected with delight,   1960
 Nor conuersant with Ease, and Idlenesse,
 Till I haue set a glory to this hand,
 By giuing it the worship of Reuenge.

PEMBROKE *and* BIGOT

 Our soules religiously confirme thy words.
   Enter Hubert

HUBERT

 Lords, I am hot with haste, in seeking you,
 Arthur doth liue, the king hath sent for you.

SALISBURY

 Oh he is bold, and blushes not at death,
 Auant thou hatefull villain, get thee gone.

HUBERT

 I am no villaine.

SALISBURY   Must I rob the Law?
   He drawes his sword

BASTARD

 Your sword is bright sir, put it vp againe.   1970

SALISBURY

 Not till I sheath it in a murtherers skin.

HUBERT (*drawing his Sword*)

 Stand backe Lord Salsbury, stand backe I say:
 By heauen, I thinke my sword's as sharpe as yours.
 I would not haue you (Lord) forget your selfe,
 Nor tempt the danger of my true defence;
 Least I, by marking of your rage, forget
 Your Worth, your Greatnesse, and Nobility.

BIGOT

 Out dunghill: dar'st thou braue a Nobleman?

HUBERT

 Not for my life: But yet I dare defend
 My innocent life against an Emperor.   1980

SALISBURY

 Thou art a Murtherer.

HUBERT   Do not proue me so:
 Yet I am none. Whose tongue so ere speakes false,
 Not truely speakes: who speakes not truly, Lies.

PEMBROKE

 Cut him to peeces.

BASTARD (*drawing his Sword*) Keepe the peace, I say.

SALISBURY

 Stand by, or I shall gaul you *Faulconbridge*.

BASTARD

 Thou wer't better gaul the diuell Salsbury.

If thou but frowne on me, or stirre thy foote,
Or teach thy hastie spleene to do me shame,
Ile strike thee dead. Put vp thy sword betime,
1990 Or Ile so maule you, and your tosting-Iron,
That you shall thinke the diuell is come from hell.

BIGOT

What wilt thou do, renowned *Faulconbridge?*
Second a Villaine, and a Murtherer?

HUBERT

Lord *Bigot,* I am none.

BIGOT   Who kill'd this Prince?

HUBERT

'Tis not an houre since I left him well:
I honour'd him, I lou'd him, and will weepe
My date of life out, for his sweete liues losse.

SALISBURY

Trust not those cunning waters of his eyes,
For villanie is not without such rheume,
2000 And he, long traded in it, makes it seeme
Like Riuers of remorse and innocencie.
Away with me, all you whose soules abhorre
Th'uncleanly sauours of a Slaughter-house,
For I am stifled with this smell of sinne.

BIGOT

Away, toward *Burie,* to the Dolphin there.

PEMBROKE

There tel the king, he may inquire vs out.

                                        Exeunt Lords

BASTARD

Here's a good world: knew you of this faire work?
Beyond the infinite and boundlesse reach
Of mercie, (if thou didst this deed of death)
2010 Art yᵘ damn'd *Hubert.*

HUBERT Do but heare me sir.

BASTARD Ha? Ile tell thee what.
Thou'rt damn'd as blacke, nay nothing is so blacke,
Thou art more deepe damn'd then Prince Lucifer:
There is not yet so vgly a fiend of hell
As thou shalt be, if thou didst kill this childe.

HUBERT

Vpon my soule.

BASTARD   If thou didst but consent
To this most cruell Act: do but dispaire,
And if thou want'st a Cord, the smallest thred
2020 That euer Spider twisted from her wombe
Will serue to strangle thee: A rush will be a beame
To hang thee on. Or wouldst thou drowne thy selfe,
Put but a little water in a spoone,
And it shall be as all the Ocean,
Enough to stifle such a villaine vp.
I do suspect thee very greeuously.

HUBERT

If I in act, consent, or sinne of thought,
Be guiltie of the stealing that sweete breath
Which was embounded in this beauteous clay,
2030 Let hell want paines enough to torture me:
I left him well.

BASTARD   Go, beare him in thine armes:

I am amaz'd me thinkes, and loose my way
Among the thornes, and dangers of this world.

        Hubert takes vp Arthur in his armes

How easie dost thou take all *England* vp?
From forth this morcell of dead Royaltie,
The life, the right, and truth of all this Realme
Is fled to heauen: and *England* now is left
To tug and scamble, and to part by th'teeth
The vn-owed interest of proud swelling State:
Now for the bare-pickt bone of Maiesty,   2040
Doth dogged warre bristle his angry crest,
And snarleth in the gentle eyes of peace:
Now Powers from home, and discontents at home
Meet in one line: and vast confusion waites
As doth a Rauen on a sicke-falne beast,
The iminent decay of wrested pompe.
Now happy he, whose cloake and center can
Hold out this tempest. Beare away that childe,
And follow me with speed: Ile to the King:
A thousand businesses are briefe in hand,   2050
And heauen it selfe doth frowne vpon the Land.

                                Exeunt ⌈severally⌉

⌈*Florish.*⌉ *Enter King Iohn and Pandolph, attendants*   Sc. 10

KING IOHN ⌈*giuing Pandulph the crowne*⌉   (5.1)

Thus haue I yeelded vp into your hand
The Circle of my glory.

PANDULPH (*giuing backe the crowne*) Take againe
From this my hand, as holding of the Pope
Your Soueraigne greatnesse and authoritie.

KING IOHN

Now keep your holy word, go meet the *French,*
And from his holinesse vse all your power
To stop their marches 'fore we are enflam'd:
Our discontented Counties doe reuolt:
Our people quarrell with obedience,   2060
Swearing Allegiance, and the loue of soule
To stranger-bloud, to forren Royalty;
This inundation of mistempred humor,
Rests by you onely to be qualified.
Then pause not: for the present time's so sicke,
That present medcine must be ministred,
Or ouerthrow incureable ensues.

PANDULPH

It was my breath that blew this Tempest vp,
Vpon your stubborne vsage of the Pope:
But since you are a gentle conuertite,   2070
My tongue shall hush againe this storme of warre,
And make faire weather in your blustring land:
On this Ascension day, remember well,
Vpon your oath of seruice to the Pope,
Goe I to make the *French* lay downe their Armes.

                                ⌈*Exeunt: manet Iohn*⌉

KING IOHN

Is this Ascension day? did not the Prophet
Say, that before Ascension day at noone,
My Crowne I should giue off? euen so I haue:

I did suppose it should be on constraint,
2080 But (heau'n be thank'd) it is but voluntary.
     Enter Bastard

BASTARD
All Kent hath yeelded: nothing there holds out
But Douer Castle: London hath receiu'd
Like a kinde Host, the Dolphin and his powers.
Your Nobles will not heare you, but are gone
To offer seruice to your enemy:
And wilde amazement hurries vp and downe
The little number of your doubtfull friends.

KING IOHN
Would not my Lords returne to me againe
After they heard yong *Arthur* was aliue?

BASTARD
2090 They found him dead, and cast into the streets,
An empty Casket, where the Iewell of life
By some damn'd hand was rob'd, and tane away.

KING IOHN
That villaine *Hubert* told me he did liue.

BASTARD
So on my soule he did, for ought he knew:
But wherefore doe you droope? why looke you sad?
Be great in act, as you haue beene in thought:
Let not the world see feare and sad distrust
Gouerne the motion of a kinglye eye:
Be stirring as the time, be fire with fire,
2100 Threaten the threatner, and out-face the brow
Of bragging horror: So shall inferior eyes
That borrow their behauiours from the great,
Grow great by your example, and put on
The dauntlesse spirit of resolution.
Away, and glister like the god of warre
When he intendeth to become the field:
Shew boldnesse and aspiring confidence:
What, shall they seeke the Lion in his denne,
And fright him there? and make him tremble there?
2110 Oh let it not be said: forrage, and runne
To meet displeasure farther from the dores,
And grapple with him ere he come so nye.

KING IOHN
The Legat of the Pope hath beene with mee,
And I haue made a happy peace with him,
And he hath promis'd to dismisse the Powers
Led by the Dolphin.

BASTARD   Oh inglorious league:
Shall we vpon the footing of our land,
Send fayre-play-orders, and make comprimise,
Insinuation, parley, and base truce
2120 To Armes Inuasiue? Shall a beardlesse boy,
A cockred-silken wanton braue our fields,
And flesh his spirit in a warre-like soyle,
Mocking the ayre with colours idlely spred,
And finde no checke? Let vs my Liege to Armes:
Perchance the Cardinall cannot make your peace;
Or if he doe, let it at least be said
They saw we had a purpose of defence.

KING IOHN
Haue thou the ordering of this present time.

BASTARD
Away then with good courage: ⌜*aside*⌝ yet I know
Our Partie may well meet a prowder foe.   *Exeunt* 2130

     Enter ⌜*marching*⌝ *(in Armes) Dolphin, Salisbury,*   Sc. 11
     Meloone, Pembroke, Bigot, Souldiers   (5.2)

DOLPHIN
My Lord *Melloone*, let this be coppied out,
And keepe it safe for our remembrance:
     He giues Meloone a paper
Returne the president to these Lords againe,
That hauing our faire order written downe,
Both they and we, perusing ore these notes
May know wherefore we tooke the Sacrament,
And keepe our faithes firme and inuiolable.

SALISBURY
Vpon our sides it neuer shall be broken.
And Noble Dolphin, albeit we sweare
A voluntary zeale, and an vn-urged Faith   2140
To your proceedings: yet beleeue me Prince,
I am not glad that such a sore of Time
Should seeke a plaster by contemn'd reuolt,
And heale the inueterate Canker of one wound,
By making many: Oh it grieues my soule,
That I must draw this mettle from my side
To be a widdow-maker: oh, and there
Where honourable rescue, and defence
Cries out vpon the name of *Salisbury*.
But such is the infection of the time,   2150
That for the health and Physicke of our right,
We cannot deale but with the very hand
Of sterne Iniustice, and confused wrong:
And is't not pitty, (oh my grieued friends)
That we, the sonnes and children of this Isle,
Was borne to see so sad an houre as this,
Wherein we step after a stranger, march
Vpon her gentle bosom, and fill vp
Her Enemies rankes? I must withdraw, and weepe
Vpon the spot of this inforced cause,   2160
To grace the Gentry of a Land remote,
And follow vnacquainted colours heere:
     He weepes
What heere? O Nation that thou couldst remoue,
That *Neptunes* Armes who clippeth thee about,
Would beare thee from the knowledge of thy selfe,
And Gripple thee vnto a Pagan shore,
Where these two Christian Armies might combine
The bloud of malice, in a vaine of league,
And not to spend it so vn-neighbourly.

DOLPHIN
A noble temper dost thou shew in this,   2170
And great affections wrastling in thy bosome
Doth make an earth-quake of Nobility:
Oh, what a noble combat hast thou fought
Between compulsion, and a braue respect:
Let me wipe off this honourable dewe,

That siluerly doth progresse on thy cheekes:
My heart hath melted at a Ladies teares,
Being an ordinary Inundation:
But this effusion of such manly drops,
2180 This showre, blowne vp by tempest of the soule,
Startles mine eyes, and makes me more amaz'd
Then had I seene the vaultie top of heauen
Figur'd quite ore with burning Meteors.
Lift vp thy brow (renowned *Salisburie*)
And with a great heart heaue away this storme:
Commend these waters to those baby-eyes
That neuer saw the giant-world enrag'd,
Nor met with Fortune, other then at feasts,
Full warm of blood, of mirth, of gossipping:
2190 Come, come; for thou shalt thrust thy hand as deepe
Into the purse of rich prosperity
As *Lewis* himselfe: so (Nobles) shall you all,
That knit your sinewes to the strength of mine.
        ⌜*A trumpet sounds*⌝
And euen there, methinkes an Angell spake,
        Enter Pandulpho
Looke where the holy Legate comes apace,
To giue vs warrant from the hand of heauen,
And on our actions set the name of right
With holy breath.

PANDULPH   Haile noble Prince of *France*:
The next is this: King *Iohn* hath reconcil'd
2200 Himselfe to *Rome*, his spirit is come in,
That so stood out against the holy Church,
The great Metropolis and Sea of Rome:
Therefore thy threatning Colours now winde vp,
And tame the sauage spirit of wilde warre,
That like a Lion fostred vp at hand,
It may lie gently at the foot of peace,
And be no further harmefull then in shewe.

DOLPHIN
Your Grace shall pardon me, I will not backe:
I am too high-borne to be proportied
2210 To be a secondary at controll,
Or vsefull seruing-man, and Instrument
To any Soueraigne State throughout the world.
Your breath first kindled the dead coale of warres,
Betweene this chastiz'd kingdome and my selfe,
And brought in matter that should feed this fire;
And now 'tis farre too huge to be blowne out
With that same weake winde, which enkindled it:
You taught me how to know the face of right,
Acquainted me with interest to this Land,
2220 Yea, thrust this enterprize into my heart,
And come ye now to tell me *Iohn* hath made
His peace with *Rome*? what is that peace to me?
I (by the honour of my marriage bed)
After yong *Arthur*, claime this Land for mine,
And now it is halfe conquer'd, must I backe,
Because that *Iohn* hath made his peace with *Rome*?
Am I *Romes* slaue? What penny hath *Rome* borne?
What men prouided? What munition sent
To vnder-prop this Action? Is't not I

That vnder-goe this charge? Who else but I,   2230
And such as to my claime are liable,
Sweat in this businesse, and maintaine this warre?
Haue I not heard these Islanders shout out
Viue le Roy, as I haue bankd their Townes?
Haue I not heere the best Cards for the game
To winne this easie match, plaid for a Crowne?
And shall I now giue ore the yeelded Set?
No, no, on my soule it neuer shall be said.

PANDULPH
You looke but on the out-side of this worke.

DOLPHIN
Out-side or in-side, I will not returne   2240
Till my attempt so much be glorified,
As to my ample hope was promised,
Before I drew this gallant head of warre,
And cull'd these fiery spirits from the world
To out-looke Conquest, and to winne renowne
Euen in the iawes of danger, and of death:
        A trumpet sounds
What lusty Trumpet thus doth summon vs?
        Enter Bastard

BASTARD
According to the faire-play of the world,
Let me haue audience: I am sent to speake:
My holy Lord of Millane, from the King   2250
I come to learne how you haue dealt for him:
And, as you answer, I doe know the scope
And warrant limited vnto my tongue.

PANDULPH
The *Dolphin* is too wilfull opposite
And will not temporize with my intreaties:
He flatly saies, hee'll not lay downe his Armes.

BASTARD
By all the bloud that euer fury breath'd,
The youth saies well. Now heare our *English* King,
For thus his Royaltie doth speake in me:
He is prepar'd, and reason to he should,   2260
This apish and vnmannerly approach,
This harness'd Maske, and vnaduised Reuell,
This vn-heard sawcinesse and boyish Troopes,
The King doth smile at, and is well prepar'd
To whip this dwarfish warre, this Pigmy Armes
From out the circle of his Territories.
That hand which had the strength, euen at your
        dore,
To cudgell you, and make you take the hatch,
To diue like Buckets in concealed Welles,
To crowch in litter of your stable planckes,   2270
To lye like pawnes, lock'd vp in chests and truncks,
To hug with swine, to seeke sweet safety out
In vaults and prisons, and to thrill and shake,
Euen at the crying of your Nations crow,
Thinking his voyce an armed Englishman:
Shall that victorious hand be feebled heere,
That in your Chambers gaue you chasticement?
No: know the gallant Monarch is in Armes,
And like an Eagle, o're his ayerie towres,

2280   To sowsse annoyance that comes neere his Nest;
      (*To the English Lords*)
      And you degenerate, you ingrate Reuolts,
      You bloudy Nero's, ripping vp the wombe
      Of your deere Mother-England: blush for shame:
      For your owne Ladies, and pale-visag'd Maides,
      Like *Amazons*, come tripping after drummes:
      Their thimbles into armed Gantlets change,
      Their Needl's to Lances, and their gentle hearts
      To fierce and bloody inclination.

DOLPHIN
      There end thy braue, and turn thy face in peace,
2290   We grant thou canst out-scold vs: Far thee well,
      We hold our time too precious to be spent
      With such a brabler.

PANDULPH   Giue me leaue to speake.

BASTARD
      No, I will speake.

DOLPHIN   We will attend to neyther:
      Strike vp the drummes, and let the tongue of warre
      Pleade for our interest, and our being heere.

BASTARD
      Indeede your drums being beaten, wil cry out;
      And so shall you, being beaten: Do but start
      An eccho with the clamor of thy drumme,
      And euen at hand, a drumme is readie brac'd,
2300   That shall reuerberate all, as lowd as thine.
      Sound but another, and another shall
      (As lowd as thine) rattle the Welkins eare,
      And mocke the deepe mouth'd Thunder: for at hand
      (Not trusting to this halting Legate heere,
      Whom he hath vs'd rather for sport, then neede)
      Is warlike *Iohn*: and in his fore-head sits
      A bare-rib'd death, whose office is this day
      To feast vpon whole thousands of the French.

DOLPHIN
      Strike vp our drummes, to finde this danger out.

BASTARD
2310   And thou shalt finde it (Dolphin) do not doubt.
          ⌈*Drummes beate.*⌉ *Exeunt the Bastard*
          ⌈*at one doore*⌉, *all the rest* ⌈*marching,*
                   at another doore⌉

Sc. 12   *Alarums. Enter Iohn* ⌈*at one doore*⌉ *and Hubert* ⌈*at*
(5.3)   *another doore*⌉

KING IOHN
      How goes the day with vs? oh tell me *Hubert*.

HUBERT
      Badly I feare; how fares your Maiesty?

KING IOHN
      This Feauer that hath troubled me so long,
      Lyes heauie on me: oh, my heart is sicke.
          Enter a Messenger

MESSENGER
      My Lord: your valiant kinsman *Falconbridge*,
      Desires your Maiestie to leaue the field,
      And send him word by me, which way you go.

KING IOHN
      Tell him toward *Swinshed*, to the Abbey there.

MESSENGER
      Be of good comfort: for the great supply
      That was expected by the Dolphin heere,   2320
      Are wrack'd three nights ago on *Goodwin* sands.
      This newes was brought to *Richard* but euen now,
      The French fight coldly, and retyre themselues.

KING IOHN
      Aye me, this tyrant Feauer burnes mee vp,
      And will not let me welcome this good newes.
      Set on toward *Swinshed*: to my Litter straight,
      Weaknesse possesseth me, and I am faint.   *Exeunt*

       ⌈*Alarums.*⌉ *Enter Salisbury, Pembroke, and Bigot*   **Sc. 13**
SALISBURY   **(5.4)**
      I did not thinke the King so stor'd with friends.

PEMBROKE
      Vp once againe: put spirit in the French.
      If they miscarry: we miscarry too.   2330

SALISBURY
      That misbegotten diuell *Falconbridge*,
      In spight of spight, alone vpholds the day.

PEMBROKE
      They say King *Iohn* sore sick, hath left the field.
          Enter Meloone wounded, ⌈*led by a Souldier*⌉

MELOONE
      Lead me to the Reuolts of England heere.

SALISBURY
      When we were happie, we had other names.

PEMBROKE
      It is the Count *Meloone*.

SALISBURY   Wounded to death.

MELOONE
      Fly Noble English, you are bought and sold,
      Vnthred the rude eye of Rebellion,
      And welcome home againe discarded faith,
      Seeke out King *Iohn*, and fall before his feete: 2340
      For if the French be Lords of this loud day,
      He meanes to recompence the paines you take,
      By cutting off your heads: Thus hath he sworne,
      And I with him, and many moe with mee,
      Vpon the Altar at S. *Edmondsbury*,
      Euen on that Altar, where we swore to you
      Deere Amity, and euerlasting loue.

SALISBURY
      May this be possible? May this be true?

MELOONE
      Haue I not hideous death within my view,
      Retaining but a quantity of life,   2350
      Which bleeds away, euen as a forme of waxe
      Resolueth from his figure 'gainst the fire?
      What in the world should make me now deceiue,
      Since I must loose the vse of all deceite?
      Why should I then be false, since it is true
      That I must dye heere, and liue hence, by Truth?
      I say againe, if *Lewis* do win the day,
      He is forsworne, if ere those eyes of yours
      Behold another day breake in the East:
      But euen this night, whose blacke contagious breath   2360

Already smoakes about the burning Cresset
Of the old, feeble, and day-wearied Sunne,
Euen this ill night, your breathing shall expire,
Paying the fine of rated Treachery,
Euen with a treacherous fine of all your liues:
If *Lewis*, by your assistance win the day.
Commend me to one *Hubert*, with your King;
The loue of him, and this respect besides
(For that my Grandsire was an Englishman)
2370 Awakes my Conscience to confesse all this.
In lieu whereof, I pray you beare me hence
From forth the noise and rumour of the Field;
Where I may thinke the remnant of my thoughts
In peace: and part this bodie and my soule
With contemplation, and deuout desires.

SALISBURY
We do beleeue thee, and beshrew my soule,
But I do loue the fauour, and the forme
Of this most faire occasion, by the which
We will vntread the steps of damned flight,
2380 And like a bated and retired Flood,
Leauing our ranknesse and irregular course,
Stoope lowe within those bounds we haue ore-look'd,
And calmely run on in obedience
Euen to our Ocean, to our great King *Iohn*.
My arme shall giue thee helpe to beare thee hence,
For I do see the cruell pangs of death
Right in thine eye. Away, my friends, new flight,
And happie newnesse, that intends old right.   *Exeunt*

Sc. 14   ⌈*Alarums, Retreat.*⌉ *Enter Dolphin, and his Traine*
(5.5)
DOLPHIN
The Sun of heauen (me thought) was loth to set;
2390 But staid, and made the Westerne Welkin blush,
When English measurd backward their owne ground
In faint Retire: Oh brauely came we off,
When with a volley of our needlesse shot,
After such bloody toile, we bid good night,
And woon'd our tott'ring colours clearly vp,
Last in the field, and almost Lords of it.

Enter a Messenger

MESSENGER
Where is my Prince, the Dolphin?
DOLPHIN   Heere: what newes?
MESSENGER
The Count *Meloone* is slaine: The English Lords
By his perswasion, are againe falne off,
2400 And your supply, which you haue wish'd so long,
Are cast away, and sunke on *Goodwin* sands.
DOLPHIN
Ah fowle, shrew'd newes. Beshrew thy very hart:
I did not thinke to be so sad to night
As this hath made me. Who was he that said
King *Iohn* did flie an houre or two before
The stumbling night did part our wearie powres?
MESSENGER
Who euer spoke it, it is true my Lord.

DOLPHIN
Well: keepe good quarter, & good care to night,
The day shall not be vp so soone as I,
To try the faire aduenture of to morrow.   *Exeunt*   2410

Enter Bastard ⌈*with a Light*⌉ *and Hubert* ⌈*with a*   Sc. 15
Pistoll⌉, *seuerally*   (5.6)
HUBERT
Whose there? Speake hoa, speake quickely, or I
shoote.
BASTARD
A Friend. What art thou?
HUBERT   Of the part of England.
BASTARD
Whether doest thou go?
HUBERT   What's that to thee?
Why may not I demand of thine affaires,
As well as thou of mine?
BASTARD *Hubert*, I thinke.
HUBERT Thou hast a perfect thought:
I will vpon all hazards well beleeue
Thou art my friend, that know'st my tongue so well:
Who art thou?
BASTARD   Who thou wilt: and if thou please   2420
Thou maist be-friend me so much, as to thinke
I come one way of the *Plantagenets*.
HUBERT
Vnkinde remembrance: thou, & eieles night,
Haue done me shame: Braue Soldier, pardon me,
That any accent breaking from thy tongue,
Should scape the true acquaintance of mine eare.
BASTARD
Come, come: sans complement, What newes abroad?
HUBERT
Why heere walke I, in the black brow of night
To finde you out.
BASTARD   Breefe then: and what's the newes?
HUBERT
O my sweet sir, newes fitting to the night,   2430
Blacke, fearefull, comfortlesse, and horrible.
BASTARD
Shew me the very wound of this ill newes,
I am no woman, Ile not swound at it.
HUBERT
The King I feare is poyson'd by a Monke,
I left him almost speechlesse, and broke out
To acquaint you with this euill, that you might
The better arme you to the sodaine time,
Then if you had at leisure knowne of this.
BASTARD
How did he take it? Who did taste to him?
HUBERT
A Monke I tell you, a resolued villaine   2440
Whose Bowels sodainly burst out: The King
Yet speakes, and peraduenture may recouer.
BASTARD
Who didst thou leaue to tend his Maiesty?

HUBERT

    Why know you not? The Lords are all come backe,
    And brought Prince *Henry* in their companie,
    At whose request the king hath pardon'd them,
    And they are all about his Maiestie.

BASTARD

    With-hold thine indignation, mighty heauen,
    And tempt vs not to beare aboue our power.
2450   Ile tell thee *Hubert*, halfe my power this night
    Passing these Flats, are taken by the Tide,
    These Lincolne-Washes haue deuoured them,
    My selfe, well mounted, hardly haue escap'd.
    Away before: Conduct me to the king,
    I doubt he will be dead, or ere I come.   *Exeunt*

Sc. 16   *Enter Prince Henry, Salisburie, and Bigot*
(5.7) PRINCE HENRY
    It is too late, the life of all his blood
    Is touch'd, corruptibly: and his pure braine
    (Which some suppose the soules fraile dwelling house)
    Doth by the idle Comments that it makes,
2460   Fore-tell the ending of mortality.
      Enter Pembroke

PEMBROKE

    His Highnesse yet doth speak, & holds beleefe,
    That being brought into the open ayre,
    It would allay the burning qualitie
    Of that fell poison which assayleth him.

PRINCE HENRY

    Let him be brought into the Orchard heere:
      ⌈*Exit Bigot*⌉
    Doth he still rage?

PEMBROKE   He is more patient
    Then when you left him; euen now he sung.

PRINCE HENRY

    Oh vanity of sicknesse: fierce extreames
    In their continuance, will not feele themselues.
2470   Death hauing praide vpon the outward parts
    Leaues them inuinsible, and his seige is now
    Against the minde, the which he prickes and wounds
    With many legions of strange fantasies,
    Which in their throng, and presse to that last hold,
    Counfound themselues. 'Tis strange yᵗ death shold
        sing:
    I am the Signet to this pale faint Swan,
    Who chaunts a dolefull hymne to his owne death,
    And from the organ-pipe of frailety sings
    His soule and body to their lasting rest.

SALISBURY

2480   Be of good comfort (Prince) for you are borne
    To set a forme vpon that indigest
    Which he hath left so shapelesse, and so rude.
      Iohn brought in ⌈*with Bigot attending*⌉

KING IOHN

    I marrie, now my soule hath elbow roome,
    It would not out at windowes, nor at doores,
    There is so hot a summer in my bosome,
    That all my bowels crumble vp to dust:

    I am a scribled forme drawne with a pen
    Vpon a Parchment, and against this fire
    Do I shrinke vp.

PRINCE HENRY   How fares your Maiesty?

KING IOHN

    Poyson'd, ill fare: dead, forsooke, cast off,   2490
    And none of you will bid the winter come
    To thrust his ycie fingers in my maw;
    Nor let my kingdomes Riuers take their course
    Through my burn'd bosome: nor intreat the North
    To make his bleake windes kisse my parched lips,
    And comfort me with cold. I do not aske you much,
    I begge cold comfort: and you are so straight
    And so ingratefull, you deny me that.

PRINCE HENRY

    Oh that there were some vertue in my teares,
    That might releeue you.

KING IOHN   The salt in them is hot.   2500
    Within me is a hell, and there the poyson
    Is, as a fiend, confin'd to tyrannize,
    On vnrepreeuable condemned blood.
      Enter Bastard

BASTARD

    Oh, I am scalded with my violent motion
    And spleene of speede, to see your Maiesty.

KING IOHN

    Oh Cozen, thou art come to set mine eye:
    The tackle of my heart, is crack'd and burnt,
    And all the shrowds wherewith my life should saile,
    Are turned to one thred, one little haire:
    My heart hath one poore string to stay it by,   2510
    Which holds but till thy newes be vttered,
    And then all this thou seest, is but a clod,
    And module of confounded royalty.

BASTARD

    The Dolphin is preparing hither-ward,
    Where God he knowes how we shall answer him.
    For in a night the best part of my powre,
    As I vpon aduantage did remoue,
    Were in the *Washes* all vnwarily,
    Deuoured by the vnexpected flood.
      King Iohn dies

SALISBURY

    You breath these dead newes in as dead an eare.   2520
    (*To Iohn*) My Liege, my Lord: but now a King, now
        thus.

PRINCE HENRY

    Euen so must I run on, and euen so stop.
    What surety of the world, what hope, what stay,
    When this was now a King, and now is clay?

BASTARD (*to Iohn*)

    Art thou gone so? I do but stay behinde,
    To do the office for thee, of reuenge,
    And then my soule shall waite on thee to heauen,
    As it on earth hath bene thy seruant still.
    (*To the Lords*) Now, now you Starres, that moue in
        your right spheres,
    Where be your powres? Shew now your mended faiths, 2530

And instantly returne with me againe,
To push destruction, and perpetuall shame
Out of the weake doore of our fainting Land:
Straight let vs seeke, or straight we shall be sought,
The Dolphine rages at our verie heeles.

SALISBURY
It seemes you know not then so much as we,
The Cardinall *Pandulph* is within at rest,
Who halfe an houre since came from the Dolphin,
And brings from him such offers of our peace,
2540   As we with honor and respect may take,
With purpose presently to leaue this warre.

BASTARD
He will the rather do it, when he sees
Our selues well sinew'd to our own defence.

SALISBURY
Nay, 'tis in a manner done already,
For many carriages hee hath dispatch'd
To the sea side, and put his cause and quarrell
To the disposing of the Cardinall,
With whom your selfe, my selfe, and other Lords,
If you thinke meete, this afternoone will poast
2550   To consummate this businesse happily.

BASTARD
Let it be so, and you my noble Prince,
With other Princes that may best be spar'd,
Shall waite vpon your Fathers Funerall.

PRINCE HENRY
At Worster must his bodie be interr'd,
For so he will'd it.
BASTARD   Thither shall it then,
And happily may your sweet selfe put on
The lineall state, and glorie of the Land,
To whom with all submission on my knee,
I do bequeath my faithfull seruices
And true subiection euerlastingly.   2560
      He kneeles
SALISBURY
And the like tender of our loue wee make
To rest without a spot for euermore.
      Salisbury, Pembroke and Bigot kneele
PRINCE HENRY
I haue a kinde of soule, that would giue thankes,
And knowes not how to do it, but with teares.
      He weepes
BASTARD ⌈*rising*⌉
Oh let vs pay the time but needfull woe,
Since it hath beene before hand with our greefes.
This England neuer did, nor neuer shall
Lye at the proud foote of a Conqueror,
But when it first did helpe to wound it selfe.
Now, these her Princes are come home againe,   2570
Come the three corners of the world in Armes,
And we shall shocke them: Naught shall make vs rue,
If England to it selfe, do rest but true.
      ⌈*Florish.*⌉ *Exeunt* ⌈*with the body*⌉

THE MERCHANT OF VENICE

ENTRY of 'a booke of The Marchaunt of Venyce or otherwise called The Iewe of Venyce' in the Stationers' Register on 22 July 1598 probably represents an attempt by Shakespeare's company to prevent the unauthorized printing of a popular play: it eventually appeared in print as 'The comicall History of the Merchant of Venice' in 1600, when it was said to have 'beene diuers times acted by the Lord Chamberlaine his Seruants'; probably Shakespeare wrote it in 1596 or 1597. The alternative title—*The Iewe of Venyce*—probably reflects Shylocke's impact on the play's first audiences.

The play is constructed on the basis of two romantic tales using motifs well known to sixteenth-century readers. The story of Giannetto (Shakespeare's Bassanio) and the Lady (Portia) of Belmont comes from an Italian collection of fifty stories published under the title of *Il Pecorone* ('the big sheep', or 'dunce') and attributed to one Ser Giovanni of Florence. Written in the later part of the fourteenth century, the volume did not appear until 1558. No sixteenth-century translation is known, so (unless there was a lost intermediary) Shakespeare must have read it in Italian. It gave him the main outline of the plot involving Antonio (the merchant), Bassanio (the wooer), Portia, and the Jew (Shylocke). The pound of flesh motif was available also in other versions, one of which, in Alexander Silvayn's *The Orator* (translated 1596), influenced the climactic scene (Sc. 18) in which Shylocke attempts to exact the full penalty of his bond.

In the story from *Il Pecorone* the lady (a widow) challenges her suitors to seduce her, on pain of the forfeiture of their wealth, and thwarts them by drugging their wine. Shakespeare more romantically shows a maiden required by her father's will to accept only a wooer who will forswear marriage if he fails to make the right choice among caskets of gold, silver, and lead. The story of the caskets was readily available in versions by John Gower (in his *Confessio Amantis*) and Giovanni Boccaccio (in his *Decameron*), and in an anonymous anthology (the *Gesta Romanorum*). Shakespeare added the character of Iessica, Shylocke's daughter who elopes with the Christian Lorenzo—perhaps influenced by episodes in Christopher Marlowe's play *The Iew of Malta* (c.1589)—and made many adjustments to the stories from which he borrowed.

The Merchant of Venice is a natural development from Shakespeare's earlier comedies, especially *The Two Gentlemen of Verona*, with its heroine disguised as a boy and its portrayal of the competing demands of love and friendship. But Portia is the first of his great romantic heroines, and Shylocke his first great comic antagonist. Though the play grew out of fairy tales, its moral scheme is not entirely clear cut: the Christians are open to criticism, the Jew is true to his own code of conduct. The response of twentieth-century audiences has been complicated by racial issues; in any case, the role of Shylocke affords such strong opportunities for an actor capable of arousing an undercurrent of sympathy for a vindictive character that it has sometimes unbalanced the play in performance. But the so-called trial scene (Sc. 18) is unfailing in its impact on audiences, and the closing episodes modulate skilfully from romantic lyricism to high comedy, while sustaining the play's concern with true and false values.

Our text is based on the First Quarto (1600), probably printed from an authorial draft.

THE NAMES OF THE ACTORS

ANTHONIO, a Merchant of Venice

BASSANIO, his friend and Portias sutor

LEONARDO, Bassanios seruant

LORENZO
GRATIANO
SALERIO
SOLANIO
} friends of Anthonio and Bassanio

SHYLOCKE, a Iew

IESSICA, his daughter

TUBALL, a wealthy Hebrew of his Tribe

Launcelet, a CLOWNE, and seruant first to Shylocke and then to Bassanio

GOBBO, his father

PORTIA, a Lady in Belmont, richly left

NERRISSA, her wayting woman

BALTHAZER
Stephano, a MESSENGER
} Portias seruants

Prince of MOROCHO
Prince of ARRAGON
} Portias sutors

DUKE of Venice

Magnificoes of Venice

Iaylor, Attendants, Seruants

480

The comicall History of the Merchant of Venice, or otherwise called the Iewe of Venyce

Sc. 1   *Enter Anthonio, Salario, and Salanio*
(1.1) ANTHONIO
    In sooth I know not why I am so sad,
    It wearies me, you say it wearies you;
    But how I caught it, found it, or came by it,
    What stuffe tis made of, whereof it is borne,
    I am to learne:
    And such a want-wit sadnes makes of mee,
    That I haue much adoe to know my selfe.

SALERIO
    Your minde is tossing on the Ocean,
    There where your Argosies with portlie sayle
10   Like Signiors and rich Burgars on the flood,
    Or as it were the Pageants of the sea,
    Doe ouer-peere the petty traffiquers
    That cursie to them do them reuerence
    As they flie by them with theyr wouen wings.

SOLANIO (*to Anthonio*)
    Beleeue mee sir, had I such venture forth,
    The better part of my affections would
    Be with my hopes abroade. I should be still
    Plucking the grasse to know where sits the wind,
    Piring in Maps for ports, and peers and rodes:
20   And euery obiect that might make me feare
    Mis-fortune to my ventures, out of doubt
    Would make me sad.

SALERIO   My wind cooling my broth,
    Would blow me to an ague when I thought
    What harme a winde too great might doe at sea.
    I should not see the sandie howre-glasse runne
    But I should thinke of shallowes and of flatts,
    And see my wealthy *Andrew* decks in sand
    Vayling her high top lower then her ribs
    To kisse her buriall; should I goe to Church
30   And see the holy edifice of stone
    And not bethinke me straight of dangerous rocks,
    Which touching but my gentle vessels side
    Would scatter all her spices on the streame,
    Enrobe the roring waters with my silkes,
    And in a word, but euen now worth this,
    And now worth nothing. Shall I haue the thought
    To thinke on this, and shall I lack the thought
    That such a thing bechaunc'd would make me sad?
    But tell not me, I know *Anthonio*
40   Is sad to thinke vpon his merchandize.

ANTHONIO
    Beleeue me no, I thanke my fortune for it
    My ventures are not in one bottome trusted,
    Nor to one place; nor is my whole estate
    Vpon the fortune of this present yeere:
    Therefore my merchandize makes me not sad.

SOLANIO
    Why then you are in loue.

ANTHONIO   Fie, fie.

SOLANIO
    Not in loue neither: then let vs say you are sad
    Because you are not merry; and twere as easie
    For you to laugh and leape, and say you are merry
    Because you are not sad. Now by two-headed *Ianus*,   50
    Nature hath framd strange fellowes in her time:
    Some that will euermore peepe through their eyes,
    And laugh like Parrats at a bagpyper.
    And other of such vinigar aspect,
    That theyle not shew theyr teeth in way of smile
    Though *Nestor* sweare the iest be laughable.

       Enter Bassanio, Lorenso, and Gratiano
    Here comes *Bassanio* your most noble kinsman,
    Gratiano, and *Lorenso*. Faryewell,
    We leaue you now with better company.

SALERIO
    I would haue staid till I had made you merry,   60
    If worthier friends had not preuented me.

ANTHONIO
    Your worth is very deere in my regard.
    I take it your owne busines calls on you,
    And you embrace th'occasion to depart.

SALERIO Good morrow my good Lords.

BASSANIO
    Good signiors both when shal we laugh? say, when?
    You grow exceeding strange: must it be so?

SALERIO
    Weele make our leysures to attend on yours.
             Exeunt Salario, and Solanio

LORENZO
    My Lord *Bassanio*, since you haue found *Anthonio*
    We two will leaue you, but at dinner time   70
    I pray you haue in minde where we must meete.

BASSANIO I will not faile you.

GRATIANO
    You looke not well signior *Anthonio*,
    You haue too much respect vpon the world:
    They loose it that doe buy it with much care,
    Beleeue me you are meruailously changd.

ANTHONIO
    I hold the world but as the world *Gratiano*,
    A stage, where euery man must play a part,
    And mine a sad one.

GRATIANO   Let me play the foole,
    With mirth and laughter let old wrinckles come,   80
    And let my liuer rather heate with wine
    Then my hart coole with mortifying grones.
    Why should a man whose blood is warme within,

Sit like his grandsire, cut in Alablaster?
Sleepe when he wakes? and creepe into the Iaundies
By beeing peeuish? I tell thee what *Anthonio*,
I loue thee, and tis my loue that speakes:
There are a sort of men whose visages
Doe creame and mantle like a standing pond,
90 And doe a wilful stilnes entertaine,
With purpose to be drest in an opinion
Of wisedome, grauitie, profound conceit,
As who should say, I am sir Oracle,
And when I ope my lips, let no dogge barke.
O my *Anthonio* I doe know of these
That therefore onely are reputed wise
For saying nothing; when I am very sure
If they should speake, would almost dam those eares
Which hearing them would call their brothers fooles,
100 Ile tell thee more of this another time.
But fish not with this melancholy baite
For this foole gudgin, this opinion:
Come good *Lorenso*, faryewell a while,
Ile end my exhortation after dinner.

LORENZO (*to Anthonio and Bassanio*)
Well, we will leaue you then till dinner time.
I must be one of these same dumbe wise men,
For *Gratiano* neuer lets me speake.

GRATIANO
Well keepe me company but two yeeres moe
Thou shalt not know the sound of thine owne tongue.

ANTHONIO
110 Far you well, Ile grow a talker for this geare.

GRATIANO
Thanks yfaith, for silence is onely commendable
In a neates tõgue dried, and a mayde not vendable.
                    Exeunt Gratiano and Lorenzo

ANTHONIO Yet is that any thing now.

BASSANIO *Gratiano* speakes an infinite deale of nothing
more then any man in all Venice, his reasons are as
two graines of wheate hid in two bushels of chaffe:
you shall seeke all day ere you finde them, and when
you haue them, they are not worth the search.

ANTHONIO
Well, tell me now what Lady is the same
120 To whom you swore a secrete pilgrimage
That you to day promisd to tell me of.

BASSANIO
Tis not vnknowne to you *Anthonio*
How much I haue disabled mine estate,
By something showing a more swelling port
Then my faint meanes would graunt continuance:
Nor doe I now make mone to be abridg'd
From such a noble rate, but my cheefe care
Is to come fairely of from the great debts
Wherein my time something too prodigall
130 Hath left me gagd: to you *Anthonio*
I owe the most in money and in loue,
And from your loue I haue a warrantie
To vnburthen all my plots and purposes
How to get cleere of all the debts I owe.

ANTHONIO
I pray you good *Bassanio* let me know it,
And if it stand as you your selfe still doe,
Within the eye of honour, be assurd
My purse, my person, my extreamest meanes
Lie all vnlockt to your occasions.

BASSANIO
In my schoole dayes, when I had lost one shaft,   140
I shot his fellow of the selfe same flight
The selfe same way, with more aduised watch
To finde the other forth, and by aduenturing both,
I oft found both: I vrge this child-hood proofe
Because what followes is pure innocence.
I owe you much, and like a wilfull youth
That which I owe is lost, but if you please
To shoote another arrow that selfe way
Which you did shoote the first, I doe not doubt,
As I will watch the ayme or to find both,   150
Or bring your latter hazzard bake againe,
And thankfully rest debter for the first.

ANTHONIO
You know me well, and heerein spend but time
To wind about my loue with circumstance,
And out of doubt you doe me now more wrong
In making question of my vttermost
Then if you had made wast of all I haue:
Then doe but say to me what I should doe
That in your knowledge may by me be done,
And I am prest vnto it: therefore speake.   160

BASSANIO
In *Belmont* is a Lady richly left,
And she is faire, and fairer then that word,
Of wondrous vertues, sometimes from her eyes
I did receaue faire speechlesse messages:
Her name is *Portia*, nothing vndervallewd
To *Catos* daughter, *Brutus Portia*,
Nor is the wide world ignorant of her worth,
For the foure winds blow in from euery coast
Renowned sutors, and her sunny locks
Hang on her temples like a golden fleece,   170
Which makes her seat of *Belmont Cholchos* strond,
And many *Iasons* come in quest of her.
O my *Anthonio*, had I but the meanes
To hold a riuall place with one of them,
I haue a minde presages me such thrift
That I should questionlesse be fortunate.

ANTHONIO
Thou knowst that all my fortunes are at sea,
Neither haue I money, nor commoditie
To raise a present summe, therefore goe forth
Try what my credite can in Venice doe,   180
That shall be rackt euen to the vttermost
To furnish thee to *Belmont* to faire *Portia*.
Goe presently enquire and so will I
Where money is, and I no question make
To haue it of my trust, or for my sake.
                    Exeunt ⌈seuerally⌉

Enter Portia with her wayting woman Nerrissa

PORTIA By my troth *Nerrissa*, my little body is awearie of this great world.

NERRISSA You would be sweet Madam, if your miseries were in the same aboundance as your good fortunes are: and yet for ought I see, they are as sicke that surfeite with too much, as they that starue with nothing; it is no meane happines therfore to be seated in the meane, superfluitie comes sooner by white haires, but competencie liues longer.

PORTIA Good sentences, and well pronounc'd.

NERRISSA They would be better if well followed.

PORTIA If to do were as easie as to know what were good to do, Chappels had beene Churches, and poore mens cottages Princes Pallaces, it is a good diuine that followes his owne instructions, I can easier teach twentie what were good to be done, then to be one of the twentie to follow mine owne teaching: the braine may deuise lawes for the blood, but a hote temper leapes ore a colde decree, such a hare is madnes the youth, to skippe ore the meshes of good counsaile the cripple; but this reasoning is not in the fashion to choose mee a husband, ô mee the word choose, I may neyther choose who I would, nor refuse who I dislike, so is the will of a lyuing daughter curbd by the will of a deade father: is it not harde *Nerrissa*, that I cannot choose one, nor refuse none.

NERRISSA Your Father was euer vertuous, and holy men at theyr death haue good inspirations, therefore the lottrie that he hath deuised in these three chests of gold, siluer, and leade, whereof who chooses his meaning chooses you, will no doubt neuer be chosen by any rightlie, but one who you shall rightly loue: But what warmth is there in your affection towardes any of these Princelie suters that are already come?

PORTIA I pray thee ouer-name them, and as thou namest them, I will describe them, and according to my description leuell at my affection.

NERRISSA First there is the Neopolitane Prince.

PORTIA I thats a colt indeede, for he doth nothing but talke of his horse, & he makes it a great appropriation to his owne good parts that he can shoo him himselfe: I am much afeard my Ladie his mother plaid false with a Smyth.

NERRISSA Than is there the Countie Palentine.

PORTIA Hee doth nothing but frowne (as who should say, & you will not haue me, choose, he heares merry tales and smiles not, I feare hee will prooue the weeping Phylosopher when hee growes old, beeing so full of vnmannerly sadnes in his youth,) I had rather be married to a deaths head with a bone in his mouth, then to eyther of these: God defend me from these two.

NERRISSA How say you by the French Lord, Mounsier *Le Boune?*

PORTIA God made him, and therefore let him passe for a man, in truth I knowe it is a sinne to be a mocker, but hee, why hee hath a horse better then the Neopolitans, a better bad habite of frowning then the Count Palentine, he is euery man in no man, if a Trassell sing, he falls straght a capring, he will fence with his owne shadow. If I should marry him, I should marry twenty husbands: if hee would despise me, I would forgiue him, for if he loue me to madnes, I shall neuer requite him.

NERRISSA What say you then to Fauconbridge, the young Barron of England?

PORTIA You know I say nothing to him, for hee vnderstands not me, nor I him: he hath neither Latine, French, nor Italian, & you will come into the Court and sweare that I haue a poore pennieworth in the English: hee is a proper mans picture, but alas who can conuerse with a dumbe show? how odly hee is suted, I thinke he bought his doublet in Italie, his round hose in Fraunce, his bonnet in Germanie, and his behauiour euery where.

NERRISSA What thinke you of the Scottish Lorde his neighbour?

PORTIA That hee hath a neyghbourlie charitie in him, for hee borrowed a boxe of the eare of the Englishman, and swore hee would pay him againe when he was able: I think the Frenchman became his suretie, and seald vnder for another.

NERRISSA How like you the young Germaine, the Duke of Saxonies nephew?

PORTIA Very vildlie in the morning when hee is sober, and most vildly in the afternoone when he is drunke: when he is best, he is a little worse then a man, & when he is worst he is little better then a beast, and the worst fall that euer fell, I hope I shall make shift to goe without him.

NERRISSA Yf hee shoulde offer to choose, and choose the right Casket, you should refuse to performe your Fathers will, if you should refuse to accept him.

PORTIA Therefore for feare of the worst, I pray thee set a deepe glasse of Reynishe wine on the contrarie Casket, for if the deuill be within, and that temptation without, I knowe hee will choose it. I will doe any thing *Nerrissa* ere I will be married to a spunge.

NERRISSA You neede not feare Ladie the hauing anie of these Lords, they haue acquainted me with theyr determinations, which is indeede to returne to theyr home, and to trouble you with no more sute, vnlesse you may be wonne by some other sort thē your Fathers imposition, depending on the Caskets.

PORTIA Yf I liue to be as old as Sibilla, I will die as chast as Diana, vnlesse I be obtained by the maner of my Fathers will: I am glad this parcell of wooers are so reasonable, for there is not one among them but I doate on his very absence: & I pray God graunt them a faire departure.

NERRISSA Doe you not remember Lady in your Fathers time, a Venecian a Scholler & a Souldiour that came hether in companie of the Marquesse of Mountferrat?

PORTIA Yes, yes, it was *Bassanio*, as I thinke so was he calld.

NERRISSA True maddam, hee of all the men that euer my

foolish eyes look'd vpon, was the best deseruing a faire
Ladie.

PORTIA I remember him well, and I remember him worthie
of thy prayse.

    Enter a Seruingman

How nowe, what newes?

SERUANT The foure strangers seeke for you maddam to
take theyr leaue: and there is a fore-runner come from
a fift, the Prince of *Moroco*, who brings word the Prince
his Maister will be heere to night.

310 PORTIA Yf I could bid the fift welcome with so good hart
as I can bid the other foure farewell, I should bee glad
of his approch: if he haue the condition of a Saint, and
the complexion of a deuill, I had rather he should
shriue mee then wiue mee.

Come *Nerrissa*, (*to the Seruingman*) sirra goe before:
Whiles we shut the gate vpon one wooer,
Another knocks at the doore.   *Exeunt*

Sc. 3   *Enter Bassanio with Shylocke the Iew*
(1.3) SHYLOCKE Three thousand ducates, well.

BASSANIO I sir, for three months.

320 SHYLOCKE For three months, well.

BASSANIO For the which as I told you, *Anthonio* shalbe
bound.

SHYLOCKE *Anthonio* shall become bound, well.

BASSANIO May you sted me? Will you pleasure me? Shall
I know your aunswere.

SHYLOCKE Three thousand ducats for three months, and
Anthonio bound.

BASSANIO Your aunswere to that.

SHYLOCKE *Anthonio* is a good man.

330 BASSANIO Haue you heard any imputation to the contrary.

SHYLOCKE Ho no, no, no, no: my meaning in saying hee
is a good man, is to haue you vnderstand mee that
hee is sufficient, yet his meanes are in supposition: hee
hath an Argosie bound to Tripolis, another to the
Indies, I vnderstand moreouer vpon the Ryalta, hee
hath a third at Mexico, a fourth for England, and other
ventures he hath squandred abroad, but ships are but
boordes, Saylers but men, there be land rats, and water
rats, water theeues, and land theeues, I meane Pyrats,
340 and then there is the perrill of waters, windes, and
rockes: the man is notwithstanding sufficient, three
thousand ducats, I thinke I may take his bond.

BASSANIO Be assurd you may.

SHYLOCKE I will be assurd I may: and that I may bee
assured, I will bethinke mee, may I speake with
Anthonio?

BASSANIO Yf it please you to dine with vs.

SHYLOCKE ⌈*aside*⌉ Yes, to smell porke, to eate of the
habitation which your Prophet the Nazarit coniured
350 the deuill into: I wil buy with you, sell with you, talke
with you, walke with you, and so following: but I will
not eate with you, drinke with you, nor pray with you.

    Enter Anthonio

⌈*To Anthonio*⌉ What newes on the Ryalto, ⌈*to Bassanio*⌉
who is he comes heere?

BASSANIO This is signior *Anthonio*.

    ⌈*Bassanio and Anthonio speake apart*⌉

SHYLOCKE (*aside*)
How like a fawning publican he lookes.
I hate him for he is a Christian:
But more, for that in low simplicitie
He lends out money gratis, and brings downe
The rate of vsance heere with vs in Venice.   360
Yf I can catch him once vpon the hip,
I will feede fat the auncient grudge I beare him.
He hates our sacred Nation, and he rayles
Euen there where Merchants most doe congregate
On me, my bargaines, and my well-wone thrift,
Which hee calls interrest: Cursed be my Trybe
If I forgiue him.

BASSANIO   *Shyloch*, doe you heare.

SHYLOCKE
I am debating of my present store,
And by the neere gesse of my memorie
I cannot instantly raise vp the grosse   370
Of full three thousand ducats: what of that,
Tuball a wealthy Hebrew of my Tribe
Will furnish me; but soft, how many months
Doe you desire? ⌈*To Anthonio*⌉ Rest you faire good
    signior,
Your worship was the last man in our mouthes.

ANTHONIO
Shylocke, albeit I neither lend nor borrow
By taking nor by giuing of excesse,
Yet to supply the ripe wants of my friend,
Ile breake a custome: (*to Bassanio*) is hee yet possest
How much ye would?   380

SHYLOCKE I, I, three thousand ducats.

ANTHONIO And for three months.

SHYLOCKE
I had forgot, three months, (*to Bassanio*) you told me
    so.
Well then, your bond: and let me see, but heare you,
Me thoughts you said, you neither lend nor borrow
Vpon aduantage.

ANTHONIO   I doe neuer vse it.

SHYLOCKE
When *Iacob* grazd his Vncle *Labans* Sheepe,
This *Iacob* from our holy *Abram* was
(As his wise mother wrought in his behalfe)
The third possesser; I, he was the third.   390

ANTHONIO
And what of him, did he take interrest?

SHYLOCKE
No, not take interest, not as you would say
Directly intrest, marke what *Iacob* did,
When *Laban* and himselfe were compremyzd
That all the eanelings which were streakt and pied
Should fall as *Iacobs* hier, the Ewes being ranck
In end of Autume turned to the Rammes,
And when the worke of generation was
Betweene these wolly breeders in the act,
The skilful sheepheard pyld me certaine wands,   400

And in the dooing of the deede of kind
He stuck them vp before the fulsome Ewes,
Who then conceauing, did in eaning time
Fall party-colourd lambs, and those were *Iacobs*.
This was a way to thriue, and he was blest:
And thrift is blessing if men steale it not.

ANTHONIO
This was a venture sir that *Iacob* serud for,
A thing not in his power to bring to passe,
But swayd and fashiond by the hand of heauen.
410 Was this inserted to make interrest good?
Or is your gold and siluer ewes and rammes?

SHYLOCKE
I cannot tell, I make it breede as fast,
But note me signior.

ANTHONIO   Marke you this *Bassanio*,
The deuill can cite Scripture for his purpose,
An euill soule producing holy witnes
Is like a villaine with a smiling cheeke,
A goodly apple rotten at the hart.
O what a goodly out-side falshood hath.

SHYLOCKE
Three thousand ducats, tis a good round summe.
420 Three months from twelue, then let me see the rate.

ANTHONIO
Well *Shylocke*, shall we be beholding to you?

SHYLOCKE
Signior *Anthonio*, manie a time and oft
In the Ryalto you haue rated me
About my moneyes and my vsances:
Still haue I borne it with a patient shrug,
(For suffrance is the badge of all our Trybe)
You call me misbeleeuer, cut-throate dog,
And spet vpon my Iewish gaberdine,
And all for vse of that which is mine owne.
430 Well then, it now appeares you neede my helpe:
Goe to then, you come to me, and you say,
Shylocke, we would haue moneyes, you say so:
You that did voyde your rume vpon my beard,
And foote me as you spurne a stranger curre
Ouer your threshold, moneyes is your sute.
What should I say to you? Should I not say
Hath a dog money? is it possible
A curre can lend three thousand ducats? or
Shall I bend low, and in a bond-mans key
440 With bated breath, and whispring humblenes
Say this: Faire sir, you spet on me on Wednesday last,
You spurnd me such a day, another time
You calld me dogge: and for these curtesies
Ile lend you thus much moneyes.

ANTHONIO
I am as like to call thee so againe,
To spet on thee againe, to spurne thee to.
Yf thou wilt lend this money, lend it not
As to thy friends, for when did friendship take
A breede for barraine mettaile of his friend?
450 But lend it rather to thine enemie,

Who if he breake, thou maist with better face
Exact the penaltie.

SHYLOCKE   Why looke you how you storme,
I would be friends with you, and haue your loue,
Forget the shames that you haue staind me with,
Supply your present wants, and take no doyte
Of vsance for my moneyes, and youle not heare mee,
This is kinde I offer.

BASSANIO This were kindnesse.

SHYLOCKE This kindnesse will I showe,
Goe with me to a Notarie, seale me there   460
Your single bond, and in a merrie sport
If you repay me not on such a day
In such a place, such summe or summes as are
Exprest in the condition, let the forfaite
Be nominated for an equall pound
Of your faire flesh, to be cut off and taken
In what part of your bodie pleaseth me.

ANTHONIO
Content infaith, yle seale to such a bond,
And say there is much kindnes in the Iew.

BASSANIO
You shall not seale to such a bond for me,   470
Ile rather dwell in my necessitie.

ANTHONIO
Why feare not man, I will not forfaite it,
Within these two months, thats a month before
This bond expires, I doe expect returne
Of thrice three times the valew of this bond.

SHYLOCKE
O father Abram, what these Christians are,
Whose owne hard dealings teaches them suspect
The thoughts of others: (*To Bassanio*) Pray you tell me
    this,
If he should breake his day what should I gaine
By the exaction of the forfeyture?   480
A pound of mans flesh taken from a man,
Is not so estimable, profitable neither
As flesh of Muttons, Beefes, or Goates, I say
To buy his fauour, I extend this friendship,
Yf he wil take it, so, if not adiew,
And for my loue I pray you wrong me not.

ANTHONIO
Yes *Shylocke*, I will seale vnto this bond.

SHYLOCKE
Then meete me forthwith at the Noteries,
Giue him direction for this merry bond
And I will goe and purse the ducats straite,   490
See to my house left in the fearefull gard
Of an vnthriftie knaue: and presently
Ile be with you.

ANTHONIO   Hie thee gentle Iewe.   *Exit Shylocke*
The Hebrew will turne Christian, he growes kinde.

BASSANIO
I like not faire termes, and a villaines minde.

ANTHONIO
Come on, in this there can be no dismay,
My ships come home a month before the day.   *Exeunt*

*⌜Flourish Cornets.⌝ Enter Morochus a tawnie Moore
all in white, and three or foure followers
accordingly, with Portia, Nerrissa, and their traine*

MOROCHO (*to Portia*)

Mislike me not for my complexion,
The shadowed liuerie of the burnisht sunne,
500 To whom I am a neighbour, and neere bred.
Bring me the fayrest creature North-ward borne,
Where *Phœbus* fire scarce thawes the ysicles,
And let vs make incyzion for your loue,
To proue whose blood is reddest, his or mine.
I tell thee Lady this aspect of mine
Hath feard the valiant, (by my loue I sweare)
The best regarded Virgins of our Clyme
Haue lou'd it to: I would not change this hue,
Except to steale your thoughts my gentle Queene.

PORTIA

510 In termes of choyse I am not soly led
By nice direction of a maydens eyes:
Besides, the lottrie of my destenie
Barrs me the right of voluntary choosing:
But if my Father had not scanted me,
And hedgd me by his wit to yeeld my selfe
His wife, who winnes me by that meanes I told you,
Your selfe (renowned Prince) than stoode as faire
As any commer I haue look'd on yet
For my affection.

MOROCHO   Euen for that I thanke you,
520 Therefore I pray you leade me to the Caskets
To try my fortune: By this Symitare
That slewe the Sophy, and a Persian Prince
That wone three fields of Sultan Solyman,
I would ore-stare the sternest eyes that looke:
Out-braue the hart most daring on the earth:
Pluck the young sucking Cubs from the she Beare,
Yea, mock the Lyon when a rores for pray
To win the Lady. But alas, the while
If *Hercules* and *Lychas* play at dice
530 Which is the better man, the greater throw
May turne by fortune from the weaker hand:
So is *Alcides* beaten by his rage,
And so may I, blind Fortune leading me
Misse that which one vnworthier may attaine,
And die with greeuing.

PORTIA   You must take your chaunce,
And eyther not attempt to choose at all,
Or sweare before you choose, if you choose wrong
Neuer to speake to Lady afterward
In way of marriage, therefore be aduis'd.

MOROCHO

540 Nor will not, come bring me vnto my chaunce.

PORTIA

First forward to the temple, after dinner
Your hazard shall be made.

MOROCHO   Good fortune then,
To make me blest or cursed'st among men.

⌜Flourish Cornets.⌝ Exeunt

Enter the Clowne alone

CLOWNE Certainely, my conscience will serue me to runne
from this Iewe my Maister: the fiend is at mine elbow,
and tempts me, saying to me, *Iobbo, Launcelet Iobbo,*
good *Launcelet,* or good *Iobbo,* or good *Launcelet Iobbo,*
vse your legges, take the start, runne away, my
conscience sayes no; take heede honest *Launcelet,* take
heede honest *Iobbo,* or as afore-saide honest *Launcelet*
550 *Iobbo,* doe not runne, scorne running with thy heeles;
well, the most coragious fiend bids me packe, *fia* sayes
the fiend, away sayes the fiend, for the heauens rouse
vp a braue minde sayes the fiend, and runne; well, my
conscience hanging about the necke of my heart, sayes
very wisely to mee: my honest friend *Launcelet* beeing
an honest mans sonne, or rather an honest womans
sonne, for indeede my Father did something smacke,
something grow to; he had a kinde of tast; well, my
560 conscience sayes *Launcelet* bouge not, bouge sayes the
fiend, bouge not sayes my conscience, conscience say
I you counsaile wel, fiend say I you counsaile well, to
be ruld by my conscience, I should stay with the Iewe
my Maister, who (God blesse the marke) is a kinde of
deuill; and to runne away from the Iewe I should be
ruled by the fiend, who sauing your reuerence is the
deuill himselfe: certainely the Iewe is the very deuill
incarnation, and in my conscience, my conscience is
but a kinde of hard conscience, to offer to counsaile
570 mee to stay with the Iewe; the fiend giues the more
friendly counsaile: I will runne fiend, my heeles are at
your commaundement, I will runne.

Enter old Gobbo, ⌜blinde,⌝ with a basket

GOBBO Maister young-man, you I pray you, which is the
way to Maister Iewes?

CLOWNE (*aside*) O heauens, this is my true begotten Father,
who being more then sand blinde, high grauell blinde,
knowes me not, I will try confusions with him.

GOBBO Maister young Gentleman, I pray you which is the
way to Maister Iewes.

CLOWNE Turne vp on your right hand at the next turning,
580 but at the next turning of all on your left; marry at
the very next turning turne of no hand, but turne
downe indirectly to the Iewes house.

GOBBO Be Gods sonties twill be a hard way to hit, can
you tell mee whether one *Launcelet* that dwels with
him, dwell with him or no.

CLOWNE Talke you of young Maister *Launcelet,* (*aside*)
marke mee nowe, nowe will I raise the waters; (*to
Gobbo*) talke you of young Maister *Launcelet.*

GOBBO No Maister sir, but a poore mans Sonne, his Father
590 though I say't is an honest exceeding poore man, and
God bee thanked well to liue.

CLOWNE Well, let his Father be what a will, wee talke of
young Maister *Launcelet.*

GOBBO Your worships friend and *Launcelet* sir.

CLOWNE But I pray you *ergo* olde man, *ergo* I beseech you,
talke you of young Maister *Launcelet.*

GOBBO Of *Launcelet* ant please your maistership.

CLOWNE *Ergo* Maister *Launcelet*, talke not of maister
Launcelet Father, for the young Gentleman according
to fates and destenies, and such odd sayings, the sisters
three, and such braunches of learning, is indeede
deceased, or as you would say in plaine termes, gone
to heauen.

GOBBO Marry God forbid, the boy was the very staffe of
my age, my very prop.

CLOWNE ⌈*aside*⌉ Doe I looke like a cudgell or a houell post,
a staffe, or a prop: (*to Gobbo*) doe you know me Father.

GOBBO Alacke the day, I knowe you not young Gentleman,
but I pray you tell mee, is my boy GOD rest his soule
aliue or dead.

CLOWNE Doe you not know me Father.

GOBBO Alack sir I am sand blind, I know you not.

CLOWNE Nay, in deede if you had your eyes you might
fayle of the knowing mee: it is a wise Father that
knowes his owne childe. Well, olde man, I will tell you
newes of your sonne, (*kneeling*) giue mee your blessing,
trueth will come to light, murder cannot bee hidde
long, a mannes Sonne may, but in the ende trueth will
out.

GOBBO Pray you sir stand vp, I am sure you are not
Launcelet my boy.

CLOWNE Pray you let's haue no more fooling, about it,
but giue mee your blessing: I am *Launcelet* your boy
that was, your sonne that is, your child that shall be.

GOBBO I cannot thinke you are my sonne.

CLOWNE I know not what I shall think of that: but I am
Launcelet the Iewes man, and I am sure *Margerie* your
wife is my mother.

GOBBO Her name is *Margerie* in deede, ile be sworne if
thou bee *Launcelet*, thou art mine owne flesh and blood:

He feeles the Clownes head

Lord worshipt might he be, what a beard hast thou
got; thou hast got more haire on thy chinne, then
Dobbin my philhorse hase on his taile.

CLOWNE It should seeme then that Dobbins taile growes
backward. I am sure hee had more haire of his taile
then I haue of my face when I last saw him.

GOBBO Lord how art thou changd: how doost thou and
thy Master agree, I haue brought him a present; how
gree you now?

CLOWNE Well, well, but for mine owne part, as I haue set
vp my rest to runne away, so I will not rest till I haue
runne some ground; my Maister's a very Iewe, giue
him a present, giue him a halter, I am famisht in his
seruice. You may tell euery finger I haue with my ribs:
Father I am glad you are come, giue me your present
to one Maister *Bassanio*, who in deede giues rare newe
Lyuories, if I serue not him, I will runne as farre as
God has any ground.

Enter Bassanio with Leonardo and followers

O rare fortune, heere comes the man, to him Father,
for I am a Iewe if I serue the Iewe any longer.

BASSANIO (*to one of his men*) You may doe so, but let it be
so hasted that supper be ready at the farthest by fiue
of the clocke: see these Letters deliuered, put the
Lyueries to making, and desire *Gratiano* to come anone
to my lodging.   *Exit one*

CLOWNE (*to Gobbo*) To him Father.

GOBBO (*to Bassanio*) God blesse your worship.

BASSANIO Gramercie, wouldst thou ought with me.

GOBBO Heere's my sonne sir, a poore boy.

CLOWNE (*to Bassanio*) Not a poore boy sir, but the rich
Iewes man that would sir as my Father shall specifie.

GOBBO (*to Bassanio*) He hath a great infection sir, as one
would say to serue.

CLOWNE Indeede the short and the long is, I serue the
Iewe, & haue a desire as my Father shall specifie.

GOBBO (*to Bassanio*) His Maister and he (sauing your
worships reuerence) are scarce catercosins.

CLOWNE (*to Bassanio*) To be briefe, the very truth is, that
the Iewe hauing done me wrong, dooth cause me as
my Father being I hope an old man shall frutifie vnto
you.

GOBBO (*to Bassanio*) I haue heere a dish of Doues that I
would bestow vppon your worship, and my sute is.

CLOWNE (*to Bassanio*) In very briefe, the sute is impertinent
to my selfe, as your worship shall knowe by this honest
old man, and though I say it, though old man, yet
poore man my Father.

BASSANIO One speake for both, what would you?

CLOWNE Serue you sir.

GOBBO (*to Bassanio*) That is the very defect of the matter
sir.

BASSANIO (*to the Clowne*)
I know thee well, thou hast obtaind thy sute,
Shylocke thy Maister spoke with me this day,
And hath preferd thee, if it be preferment
To leaue a rich Iewes seruice, to become
The follower of so poore a Gentleman.

CLOWNE The old prouerb is very well parted betweene my
Maister *Shylocke* and you sir, you haue the grace of
God sir, and hee hath enough.

BASSANIO
Thou speakst it well; (*to Gobbo*) goe Father with thy
Sonne.
(*To the Clowne*)
Take leaue of thy old Maister, and enquire
My lodging out, (*to one of his Men*) giue him a Lyuerie
More garded then his fellowes: see it done.

CLOWNE (*to Gobbo*) Father in, I cannot get a seruice, no,
I haue nere a tong in my head, wel:

He lookes at his Palm

if any man in Italy haue a fayrer table which dooth
offer to sweare vpon a booke, I shall haue good fortune;
goe too, heere's a simple lyne of life, heeres a small
tryfle of wiues, alas, fifteene wiues is nothing, a leuen
widdowes and nine maydes is a simple comming in for
one man, and then to scape drowning thrice, and to
be in perrill of my life with the edge of a featherbed,
heere are simple scapes: well, if Fortune be a woman
she's a good wench for this gere: Father come, ile take
my leaue of the Iewe in the twinkling.

Exit Clowne with old Gobbo

BASSANIO

    I pray thee good *Leonardo* thinke on this,

    These things being bought and orderly bestowed

    Returne in hast, for I doe feast to night

710   My best esteemd acquaintance, hie thee goe.

LEONARDO

    My best endeuours shall be done heerein.

        He is going. Enter Gratiano

GRATIANO (*to Leonardo*)

    Where's your Maister.

LEONARDO   Yonder sir he walkes.

                        Exit Leonardo

GRATIANO

    Signior *Bassanio*.

BASSANIO   *Gratiano*.

GRATIANO

    I haue a sute to you.

BASSANIO   You haue obtaind it.

GRATIANO

    You must not deny me, I must goe with you to

      Belmont.

BASSANIO

    Why then you must but heare thee *Gratiano*,

    Thou art to wild, to rude, and bold of voyce,

    Parts that become thee happily enough,

    And in such eyes as ours appeare not faults

720   But where thou art not knowne; why there they show

    Somthing too liberall, pray thee take paine

    To allay with some cold drops of modestie

    Thy skipping spirit, least through thy wild behauiour

    I be misconstred in the place I goe to,

    And loose my hopes.

GRATIANO   Signor *Bassanio*, heare me,

    Yf I doe not put on a sober habite,

    Talke with respect, and sweare but now and than,

    Weare prayer bookes in my pocket, looke demurely,

    Nay more, while grace is saying hood mine eyes

730   Thus with my hat, and sigh and say amen:

    Vse all the obseruance of ciuillity

    Like one well studied in a sad ostent

    To please his Grandam, neuer trust me more.

BASSANIO Well, we shall see your bearing.

GRATIANO

    Nay but I barre to night, you shall not gage me

    By what we doe to night.

BASSANIO   No that were pitty,

    I would intreate you rather to put on

    Your boldest sute of mirth, for we haue friends

    That purpose merriment: but far you well,

740   I haue some busines.

GRATIANO

    And I must to *Lorenso* and the rest,

    But we will visite you at supper time.

                    Exeunt seuerally

Sc. 6   *Enter Iessica and the Clowne*

(2.3) IESSICA

    I am sorry thou wilt leaue my Father so,

    Our house is hell, and thou a merry deuill

    Didst rob it of some tast of tediousnes,

    But far thee well, there is a ducat for thee,

    And *Launcelet*, soone at supper shalt thou see

    Lorenso, who is thy new Maisters guest,

    Giue him this Letter, doe it secretly,

    And so farwell: I would not haue my Father   750

    See me in talke with thee.

CLOWNE Adiew, teares exhibit my tongue, most beautifull

    Pagan, most sweete Iewe, if a Christian doe not play

    the knaue and get thee, I am much deceaued; but

    adiew, these foolish drops doe somthing drowne my

    manly spirit: adiew.

IESSICA Farewell good *Launcelet*.   *Exit Clowne*

    Alack, what heynous sinne is it in me

    To be ashamde to be my Fathers child,

    But though I am a daughter to his blood   760

    I am not to his manners: ô *Lorenso*

    Yf thou keepe promise I shall end this strife,

    Become a Christian and thy louing wife.   *Exit*

       Enter Gratiano, Lorenso, Salario, and Salanio   Sc. 7

LORENZO   (2.4)

    Nay, we will slinke away in supper time,

    Disguise vs at my lodging, and returne

    All in an houre.

GRATIANO

    We haue not made good preparation.

SALERIO

    We haue not spoke as yet of Torch-bearers.

SOLANIO

    Tis vile vnlesse it may be quaintly ordered,

    And better in my minde not vndertooke.   770

LORENZO

    Tis now but foure of clocke, we haue two houres

    To furnish vs;

        Enter Launcelet the Clowne with a Letter

              friend *Launcelet* whats the newes.

CLOWNE (*presenting the Letter*) And it shal please you to

    breake vp this, it shal seeme to signifie.

LORENZO (*taking the Letter*)

    I know the hand, in faith tis a faire hand,

    And whiter then the paper it writ on

    Is the faire hand that writ.

GRATIANO   Loue, newes in faith.

CLOWNE ⌈*to Lorenzo*⌉ By your leaue sir.

LORENZO Whither goest thou.

CLOWNE Marry sir to bid my old Maister the Iewe to sup 780

    to night with my new Maister the Christian.

LORENZO

    Hold heere take this, (*giuing money*) tell gentle *Iessica*

    I will not faile her, speake it priuatly,

    Goe.   *Exit Clowne*

      Gentlemen,

    Will you prepare you for this maske to night,

    I am prouided of a Torch-bearer.

SALERIO

    I marry, ile be gone about it straite.

SOLANIO

And so will I.

LORENZO   Meete me and *Gratiano*

At *Gratianos* lodging some houre hence.

790 SALERIO Tis good we doe so.   *Exit with Solanio*

GRATIANO

Was not that Letter from faire *Iessica*.

LORENZO

I must needes tell thee all, she hath directed

How I shall take her from her Fathers house,

What gold and iewels she is furnisht with,

What Pages sute she hath in readines,

Yf ere the Iewe her Father come to heauen,

Yt will be for his gentle daughters sake,

And neuer dare misfortune crosse her foote,

Vnlesse she doe it vnder this excuse,

800 That she is issue to a faithlesse Iewe:

Come goe with me, peruse this as thou goest,

He giues Gratiano the Letter

Faire *Iessica* shall be my Torch-bearer.   *Exeunt*

Sc. 8   *Enter Shylocke the Iewe and his man that was, the*

(2.5)   *Clowne*

SHYLOCKE

Well, thou shalt see, thy eyes shall be thy iudge,

The difference of old *Shylocke* and *Bassanio*;

(*Calling*) What *Iessica*, (*to the Clowne*) thou shalt not

     gurmandize

As thou hast done with mee: (*calling*) what *Iessica*,

(*To the Clowne*) And sleepe, and snore, and rend

     apparraile out.

(*Calling*) Why *Iessica* I say.

CLOWNE (*calling*)   Why *Iessica*.

SHYLOCKE

Who bids thee call? I doe not bid thee call.

810 CLOWNE Your worship was wont to tell me, I could doe

     nothing without bidding.

     Enter Iessica

IESSICA (*to Shylocke*) Call you? what is your will?

SHYLOCKE

I am bid forth to supper *Iessica*,

There are my keyes: but wherefore should I goe?

I am not bid for loue, they flatter me,

But yet Ile goe in hate, to feede vpon

The prodigall Christian. *Iessica* my girle,

Looke to my house, I am right loth to goe,

There is some ill a bruing towards my rest,

820 For I did dreame of money baggs to night.

CLOWNE I beseech you sir goe, my young Maister doth

     expect your reproch.

SHYLOCKE So doe I his.

CLOWNE And they haue conspired together, I will not say

     you shall see a Maske, but if you doe, then it was not

     for nothing that my nose fell a bleeding on black

     monday last, at sixe a clocke ith morning, falling out

     that yeere on ashwensday was foure yeere in

     thafternoone.

SHYLOCKE

What are there maskes? heare you me *Iessica*,   830

Lock vp my doores, and when you heare the drumme

And the vile squealing of the wry-neckt Fiffe

Clamber not you vp to the casements then

Nor thrust your head into the publique streete

To gaze on Christian fooles with varnisht faces:

But stop my houses eares, I meane my casements,

Let not the sound of shallow fopprie enter

My sober house. By *Iacobs* staffe I sweare

I haue no minde of feasting forth to night:

But I will goe: (*to the Clowne*) goe you before me

     sirra,   840

Say I will come.

CLOWNE   I will goe before sir.

(*Aside to Iessica*)

Mistres looke out at window for all this,

     There will come a Christian by

     Will be worth a Iewes eye.   *Exit*

SHYLOCKE (*to Iessica*)

What sayes that foole of *Hagars* ofspring? ha.

IESSICA

His words were farewell mistris, nothing els.

SHYLOCKE

The patch is kinde enough, but a huge feeder,

Snaile slow in profit, and he sleepes by day

More then the wild-cat: drones hiue not with me,

Therefore I part with him, and part with him   850

To one that I would haue him helpe to wast

His borrowed purse. Well *Iessica* goe in,

Perhaps I will returne immediatlie,

Do as I bid you, shut dores after you,

Fast bind, fast find.

A prouerbe neuer stale in thriftie minde.

     Exit at one doore

IESSICA

Farewell, and if my fortune be not crost,

I haue a Father, you a daughter lost.

     Exit at another doore

     Enter the maskers, Gratiano and Salerio, ⌈with   Sc. 9

     Torch-bearers⌉   (2.6)

GRATIANO

This is the penthouse vnder which *Lorenzo*

Desird vs to make stand.

SALERIO   His howre is almost past.   860

GRATIANO

And it is meruaile he out-dwells his howre,

For louers euer runne before the clocke.

SALERIO

O tenne times faster *Venus* pidgions flie

To seale loues bonds new made, then they are wont

To keepe obliged faith vnforfaited.

GRATIANO

That euer holds: who riseth from a feast

With that keene appetite that he sits downe?

Where is the horse that doth vntread againe

His tedious measures with the vnbated fire
870 That he did pace them first: all things that are
Are with more spirit chased then enioyd.
How like a younker or a prodigall
The skarfed barke puts from her natiue bay
Hugd and embraced by the strumpet wind,
How like the prodigall doth she returne
With ouer-wetherd ribbs and ragged sailes
Leane, rent, and beggerd by the strumpet wind?
        Enter Lorenzo, ⌜with a torch⌝

SALERIO
Heere comes *Lorenzo*, more of this hereafter.

LORENZO
Sweet freends, your patience for my long abode
880 Not I but my affaires haue made you waite:
When you shall please to play the theeues for wiues
Ile watch as long for you therein: approch
Here dwels my father Iew. (*Calling*) Howe whose within?
        Enter Iessica aboue in boyes apparraile

IESSICA
Who are you? tell me for more certainty,
Albeit Ile sweare that I doe know your tongue.

LORENZO *Lorenzo* and thy loue.

IESSICA
Lorenzo certaine, and my loue indeed,
For who loue I so much? and now who knowes
But you *Lorenzo* whether I am yours?

LORENZO
890 Heauen & thy thoughts are witnes that thou art.

IESSICA
Heere catch this casket, it is worth the paines,
I am glad tis night you doe not looke on me,
For I am much ashamde of my exchange:
But loue is blinde, and louers cannot see
The pretty follies that themselues commit,
For if they could, *Cupid* himselfe would blush
To see me thus trans-formed to a boy.

LORENZO
Descend, for you must be my torch-bearer.

IESSICA
What, must I hold a candle to my shames,
900 They in themselues goodsooth are too too light.
Why, tis an office of discouery loue,
And I should be obscurd.

LORENZO   So are you sweet
Euen in the louely garnish of a boy,
But come at once,
For the close night doth play the runaway,
And we are staid for at *Bassanios* feast.

IESSICA
I will make fast the doores & guild my selfe
With some mo ducats, and be with you straight.
                    Exit aboue

GRATIANO
Now by my hoode a gentle, and no Iew.

LORENZO
910 Beshrow me but I loue her hartilie,
For she is wise, if I can iudge of her,

And faire she is, if that mine eyes be true,
And true she is, as she hath proou'd herselfe:
And therefore like herselfe, wise, faire, and true,
Shall she be placed in my constant soule.
        Enter Iessica below
What, art thou come, on gentlemen, away,
Our masking mates by this time for vs stay.
                    Exit with Iessica and Salerio
        Enter Anthonio

ANTHONIO
Whose there?

GRATIANO   Signior *Anthonio*?

ANTHONIO
Fie, fie Gratiano, where are all the rest?
Tis nine a clocke, our friends all stay for you, 920
No maske to night, the wind is come about
Bassanio presently will goe abord,
I haue sent twentie out to seeke for you.

GRATIANO
I am glad ont, I desire no more delight
Then to be vndersaile, and gone to night.   *Exeunt*

        ⌜*Flourish cornets.*⌝ *Enter Portia with Morrocho and*   Sc. 10
        both theyr traines   (2.7)

PORTIA
Goe, draw aside the curtaines and discouer
The seuerall caskets to this noble Prince:
        The curtaines are drawne aside discouering three
        caskets
(*To Morocho*) Now make your choyse.

MOROCHO
This first of gold, who this inscription beares,
(*Reades*) Who chooseth me, shall gaine what many
        men desire.   930
The second siluer, which this promise carries,
(*Reades*) Who chooseth me, shall get as much as he
        deserues.
This third, dull lead, with warning all as blunt,
(*Reades*) Who chooseth me, must giue and hazard all
        he hath.
How shall I know if I doe choose the right?

PORTIA
The one of them containes my picture Prince,
If you choose that, then I am yours withall.

MOROCHO
Some God direct my iudgement, let me see,
I will suruay th'inscriptions, back againe,
What saies this leaden casket?   940
(*Reades*) Who chooseth me, must giue and hazard all
        he hath,
Must giue, for what? for lead, hazard for lead?
This casket threatens, men that hazard all
Doe it in hope of faire aduantages:
A golden minde stoopes not to showes of drosse,
Ile then nor giue nor hazard ought for lead.
What sayes the siluer with her virgin hue?
(*Reades*) Who chooseth me, shal get as much as he
        deserues.

950 As much as he deserues, pause there *Morocho*,
And weigh thy valew with an euen hand,
If thou beest rated by thy estimation
Thou doost deserue enough, and yet enough
May not extend so farre as to the Ladie:
And yet to be afeard of my deseruing
Were but a weake disabling of my selfe.
As much as I deserue, why thats the Ladie.
I doe in birth deserue her, and in fortunes,
In graces, and in qualities of breeding:
But more then these, in loue I doe deserue,
960 What if I straid no farther, but chose heere?
Lets see once more this saying grau'd in gold:
(*Reades*) Who chooseth me shall gaine what many
    men desire:
Why thats the Ladie, all the world desires her.
From the foure corners of the earth they come
To kisse this shrine, this mortall breathing Saint.
The Hircanion deserts, and the vastie wildes
Of wide Arabia are as throughfares now
For Princes to come view faire *Portia*.
The waterie Kingdome, whose ambitious head
970 Spets in the face of heauen, is no barre
To stop the forraine spirits, but they come
As ore a brooke to see faire *Portia*.
One of these three containes her heauenly picture.
Ist like that leade containes her, twere damnation
To thinke so base a thought, it were too grosse
To ribb her serecloth in the obscure graue,
Or shall I thinke in siluer shees immurd
Beeing tenne times vnderualewed to tride gold,
O sinful thought, neuer so rich a Iem
980 Was set in worse then gold. They haue in England
A coyne that beares the figure of an Angell
Stampt in gold, but thats insculpt vpon:
But heere an Angell in a golden bed
Lies all within. Deliuer me the key:
Heere doe I choose, and thriue I as I may.
    He is giuen a key

  PORTIA
There take it Prince, and if my forme lie there
Then I am yours?
    Morocho opens the golden casket
MOROCHO   O hell! what haue wee heare,
A carrion death, within whose emptie eye
There is a written scroule, Ile reade the writing.
990   *All that glisters is not gold,*
   Often haue you heard that told,
   Many a man his life hath sold
   But my outside to behold,
   Guilded tombes doe wormes infold:
   Had you beene as wise as bold,
   Young in limbs, in iudgement old,
   Your aunswere had not beene inscrold,
   Fareyouwell, your sute is cold.
   Cold indeede and labour lost,
1000   Then farewell heate, and welcome frost:

Portia adiew, I haue too greeu'd a hart
To take a tedious leaue: thus loosers part.
    ⌈*Flourish Cornets.*⌉ *Exit with his Traine*
PORTIA
A gentle riddance, draw the curtaines, go,
Let all of his complexion choose me so.
    The curtaines are drawne. Exeunt

    Enter Salario and Solanio   Sc. 11
SALERIO   (2.8)
Why man I saw *Bassanio* vnder sayle,
With him is *Gratiano* gone along;
And in theyr ship I am sure *Lorenzo* is not.
SOLANIO
The villaine Iew with outcries raisd the Duke,
Who went with him to search *Bassanios* ship.
SALERIO
He came too late, the ship was vndersaile,   1010
But there the Duke was giuen to vnderstand
That in a Gondylo were seene together
Lorenzo and his amorous *Iessica*.
Besides, *Anthonio* certified the Duke
They were not with *Bassanio* in his ship.
SOLANIO
I neuer heard a passion so confusd,
So strange, outragious, and so variable
As the dogge Iew did vtter in the streets,
My daughter, ô my ducats, ô my daughter,
Fled with a Christian, ô my Christian ducats.   1020
Iustice, the law, my ducats, and my daughter,
A sealed bag, two sealed bags of ducats
Of double ducats, stolne from me by my daughter,
And Iewels, two stones, two rich and precious stones,
Stolne by my daughter: iustice, find the girle,
Shee hath the stones vpon her, and the ducats.
SALERIO
Why all the boyes in Venice follow him,
Crying his stones, his daughter, and his ducats.
SOLANIO
Let good *Anthonio* looke he keepe his day
Or he shall pay for this.
SALERIO   Marry well remembred.   1030
I reasond with a Frenchman yesterday,
Who told me, in the narrow seas that part
The French and English, there miscaried
A vessell of our country richly fraught:
I thought vpon *Anthonio* when he told me,
And wisht in silence that it were not his.
SOLANIO
You were best to tell *Anthonio* what you heare,
Yet doe not suddainely, for it may greeue him.
SALERIO
A kinder gentleman treades not the earth,
I saw *Bassanio* and *Anthonio* part,   1040
Bassanio told him he would make some speede
Of his returne: he aunswerd, doe not so,
Sluber not busines for my sake *Bassanio*,

But stay the very riping of the time,
And for the Iewes bond which he hath of me
Let it not enter in your minde of loue:
Be merry, and imploy your cheefest thoughts
To courtship, and such faire ostents of loue
As shall conueniently become you there,
1050   And euen there his eye being big with teares,
Turning his face, he put his hand behind him,
And with affection wondrous sencible
He wrung *Bassanios* hand, and so they parted.

SOLANIO
I thinke hee onely loues the world for him,
I pray thee let vs goe and finde him out
And quicken his embraced heauines
With some delight or other.

SALERIO   Doe we so.   *Exeunt*

Sc. 12   *Enter Nerrissa and a Seruiture*
(2.9)   NERRISSA
Quick, quick I pray thee, draw the curtain strait,
The Prince of Arragon hath tane his oath,
1060   And comes to his election presently.
        The Seruiture drawes aside the curtain discouering
        the three caskets. ⌈*Flourish Cornets.*⌉ *Enter*
        Arrogon, his trayne, and Portia

PORTIA
Behold, there stand the caskets noble Prince,
Yf you choose that wherein I am containd
Straight shall our nuptiall rights be solemniz'd:
But if you faile, without more speech my Lord
You must be gone from hence immediatly.

ARRAGON
I am enioynd by oath to obserue three things,
First, neuer to vnfold to any one
Which casket twas I chose; next, if I faile
Of the right casket, neuer in my life
1070   To wooe a maide in way of marriage:
Lastly, if I doe faile in fortune of my choyse,
Immediatly to leaue you, and be gone.

PORTIA
To these iniunctions euery one doth sweare
That comes to hazard for my worthlesse selfe.

ARRAGON
And so haue I addrest me, fortune now
To my harts hope: gold, siluer, and base lead.
        He reades the leaden casket
Who chooseth me, must giue and hazard all he hath.
You shall looke fairer ere I giue or hazard.
What saies the golden chest, ha, let me see,
(*Reades*) Who chooseth me, shall gaine what many
1080   men desire,
What many men desire, that many may be meant
By the foole multitude that choose by show,
Not learning more then the fond eye doth teach,
Which pries not to thinteriour, but like the Martlet
Builds in the weather on the outward wall,
Euen in the force and rode of casualty.
I will not choose what many men desire,

Because I will not iumpe with common spirits,
And ranke me with the barbarous multitudes.
Why then to thee thou siluer treasure house,   1090
Tell me once more what title thou doost beare;
(*Reades*) Who chooseth me shall get as much as he
        deserues,
And well sayde to; for who shall goe about
To cosen Fortune, and be honourable
Without the stampe of merrit, let none presume
To weare an vndeserued dignity:
O that estates, degrees, and offices,
Were not deriu'd corruptly, and that cleare honour
Were purchast by the merrit of the wearer,
How many then should couer that stand bare?   1100
How many be commaunded that commaund?
How much low peasantry would then be gleaned
From the true seede of honour? and how much honour
Pickt from the chaft and ruin of the times,
To be new varnist; well but to my choise.
(*Reades*) Who chooseth me shall get as much as he
        deserues,
I will assume desert; giue me a key for this,
And instantly vnlocke my fortunes heere.
        He is giuen a key. ⌈*He*⌉ *opens the siluer casket*

PORTIA
Too long a pause for that which you finde there.

ARRAGON
What's heere, the pourtrait of a blinking idiot   1110
Presenting me a shedule, I will reade it:
How much vnlike art thou to *Portia*?
How much vnlike my hopes and my deseruings.
Who chooseth me, shall haue as much as he deserues?
Did I deserue no more then a fooles head,
Is that my prize, are my deserts no better?

PORTIA
To offend and iudge are distinct offices,
And of opposed natures.

ARRAGON   What is heere?
        He reades the shedule
        The fier seauen times tried this,
        Seauen times tried that iudgement is,   1120
        That did neuer choose amis,
        Some there be that shadowes kis.
        Such haue but a shadowes blis:
        There be fooles aliue Iwis
        Siluerd o're, and so was this.
        Take what wife you will to bed,
        I will euer be your head:
        So be gone, you are sped.
        Still more foole I shall appeare
        By the time I linger heere,   1130
        With one fooles head I came to woo,
        But I goe away with two.
        Sweet adiew, ile keepe my oath,
        Paciently to beare my wroath.
        ⌈*Flourish Cornets.*⌉ *Exit with his Traine*

PORTIA
Thus hath the candle singd the moath:

O these deliberate fooles when they doe choose,
They haue the wisedome by their wit to loose.

NERRISSA
The auncient saying is no herisie,
Hanging and wiuing goes by destinie.

PORTIA
1140   Come draw the curtaine *Nerrissa*.
            Nerrissa drawes the curtaine.
            Enter Messenger

MESSENGER
Where is my Lady.

PORTIA   Heere, what would my Lord?

MESSENGER
Madame, there is a-lighted at your gate
A young Venetian, one that comes before
To signifie th'approching of his Lord,
From whom he bringeth sensible regreets;
To wit, (besides commends and curtious breath)
Gifts of rich valiew; yet I haue not seene
So likely an Embassador of loue.
A day in Aprill neuer came so sweete
1150   To show how costly Sommer was at hand,
As this fore-spurrer comes before his Lord.

PORTIA
No more I pray thee, I am halfe a-feard
Thou wilt say anone he is some kin to thee,
Thou spendst such high day wit in praysing him:
Come come *Nerryssa*, for I long to see
Quick *Cupids* Post that comes so mannerly.

NERRISSA
Bassanio, Lord loue if thy will it be.   *Exeunt*

Sc. 13   *Enter Solanio and Salario*
(3.1)   SOLANIO Now what newes on the Ryalto?

SALERIO Why yet it liues there vncheckt, that *Anthonio*
1160   hath a ship of rich lading wrackt on the narrow Seas;
the Goodwins I thinke they call the place, a very
dangerous flat, and fatall, where the carcasses of many
a tall ship lie buried, as they say, if my gossip report
be an honest woman of her word.

SOLANIO I would she were as lying a gossip in that, as
euer knapt Ginger, or made her neighbours beleeue she
wept for the death of a third husband: but it is true,
without any slips of prolixity, or crossing the plaine
high way of talke, that the good *Anthonio*, the honest
1170   *Anthonio*; ô that I had a tytle good enough to keepe
his name company.

SALERIO Come, the full stop.

SOLANIO Ha, what sayest thou, why the end is, he hath
lost a ship.

SALERIO I would it might proue the end of his losses.

SOLANIO Let me say amen betimes, least the deuil crosse
my praier,
            Enter Shylocke
for heere he comes in the likenes of a Iewe. How now
Shylocke, what newes among the Merchants?

1180   SHYLOCKE You knew, none so well, none so well as you,
of my daughters flight.

SALERIO Thats certaine, I for my part knew the Taylor
that made the wings she flew withall.

SOLANIO And *Shylocke* for his own part knew the bird was
flidge, and then it is the complexion of them all to
leaue the dam.

SHYLOCKE She is damnd for it.

SALERIO Thats certaine, if the deuill may be her Iudge.

SHYLOCKE My owne flesh and blood to rebell.

SOLANIO Out vpon it old carrion, rebels it at these yeeres.   1190

SHYLOCKE I say my daughter is my flesh and my blood.

SALERIO There is more difference betweene thy flesh and
hers, then betweene Iet and Iuorie, more betweene
your bloods, then there is betweene red wine and
rennish: but tell vs, doe you heare whether *Anthonio*
haue had any losse at sea or no?

SHYLOCKE There I haue another bad match, a bankrout,
a prodigall, who dare scarce shewe his head on the
Ryalto, a begger that was vsd to come so smug vpon
the Mart: let him looke to his bond, he was wont to   1200
call me vsurer, let him looke to his bond, hee was wont
to lende money for a Christian cursie, let him looke to
his bond.

SALERIO Why I am sure if he forfaite, thou wilt not take
his flesh, what's that good for?

SHYLOCKE To baite fish with all, if it will feede nothing
else, it will feede my reuenge; hee hath disgrac'd me,
and hindred me halfe a million, laught at my losses,
mockt at my gaines, scorned my Nation, thwarted my
bargaines, cooled my friends, heated mine enemies, and   1210
whats his reason, I am a Iewe: Hath not a Iewe eyes,
hath not a Iewe hands, organs, dementions, sences,
affections, passions, fed with the same foode, hurt with
the same weapons, subiect to the same diseases, healed
by the same meanes, warmed and cooled by the same
Winter and Sommer as a Christian is: if you pricke vs
doe we not bleede, if you tickle vs doe wee not laugh,
if you poyson vs doe wee not die, and if you wrong vs
shall wee not reuenge, if we are like you in the rest,
we will resemble you in that. If a Iewe wrong a   1220
Christian, what is his humillity, reuenge? If a Christian
wrong a Iewe, what should his sufferance be by
Christian example, why reuenge? The villanie you
teach me I will execute, and it shall goe hard but I will
better the instruction.
            Enter a man from Anthonio

MAN (*to Solanio and Salerio*) Gentlemen, my maister
Anthonio is at his house, and desires to speake with
you both.

SALERIO We haue beene vp and downe to seeke him.
            Enter Tuball

SOLANIO Heere comes another of the Tribe, a third cannot   1230
bee matcht, vnlesse the deuill himselfe turne Iewe.
            *Exeunt Gentlemen (Solanio and Salerio) with
                              Anthonios man*

SHYLOCKE How now *Tuball*, what newes from Genowa,
hast thou found my daughter?

TUBALL I often came where I did heare of her, but cannot
finde her.

SHYLOCKE Why there, there, there, there, a diamond gone
cost me two thousand ducats in Franckford, the curse
neuer fell vpon our Nation till now, I neuer felt it till
nowe, two thousand ducats in that, & other precious
1240 precious iewels; I would my daughter were dead at my
foote, and the iewels in her eare: would she were hearst
at my foote, and the ducats in her coffin: no newes of
them, why so? and I know not whats spent in the
search: why thou losse vpon losse, the theefe gone
with so much, and so much to finde the theefe, and
no satisfaction, no reuenge, nor no ill lucke stirring
but what lights a my shoulders, no sighs but a my
breathing, no teares but a my shedding.

TUBALL Yes, other men haue ill lucke to, *Anthonio* as I
1250 heard in Genowa?

SHYLOCKE What, what, what, ill lucke, ill lucke.

TUBALL Hath an Argosie cast away comming from
Tripolis.

SHYLOCKE I thank God, I thank God, is it true, is it true.

TUBALL I spoke with some of the Saylers that escaped the
wrack.

SHYLOCKE I thank thee good *Tuball*, good newes, good
newes: ha ha, heard in Genowa.

TUBALL Your daughter spent in Genowa, as I heard, one
1260 night fourescore ducats.

SHYLOCKE Thou stickst a dagger in me, I shall neuer see
my gold againe, foure score ducats at a sitting, foure
score ducats.

TUBALL There came diuers of *Anthonios* creditors in my
company to Venice, that sweare, he cannot choose but
breake.

SHYLOCKE I am very glad of it, ile plague him, ile torture
him, I am glad of it.

TUBALL One of them shewed mee a ring that hee had of
1270 your daughter for a Monky.

SHYLOCKE Out vpon her, thou torturest mee *Tuball*, it was
my Turkies, I had it of *Leah* when I was a Batcheler: I
would not haue giuen it for a Wildernes of Monkies.

TUBALL But *Anthonio* is certainly vndone.

SHYLOCKE Nay, that's true, that's very true, goe *Tuball* fee
me an Officer, bespeake him a fortnight before, I will
haue the hart of him if he forfeite, for were he out of
Venice I can make what merchandize I will: goe *Tuball*,
and meete me at our Sinagogue, goe good *Tuball*, at
1280 our Sinagogue *Tuball*.   *Exeunt seuerally*

Sc. 14 *Enter Bassanio, Portia, Nerrissa, Gratiano, and all*
(3.2) *their traynes.* ⌈*The curtaines are drawne aside*
discouering the three caskets⌉

PORTIA (*to Bassanio*)
I pray you tarry, pause a day or two
Before you hazard, for in choosing wrong
I loose your companie; therefore forbeare a while,
Theres something tells me (but it is not loue)
I would not loose you, and you know your selfe,
Hate counsailes not in such a quallity;
But least you should not vnderstand me well,
And yet a mayden hath no tongue, but thought,

I would detaine you heere some moneth or two
Before you venture for me. I could teach you   1290
How to choose right, but then I am forsworne,
So will I neuer be, so may you misse me,
But if you doe, youle make me wish a sinne,
That I had beene forsworne: Beshrow your eyes,
They haue ore-lookt me and deuided me,
One halfe of me is yours, the other halfe yours,
Mine owne I would say: but if mine then yours,
And so all yours; ô these naughty times
Puts barres betweene the owners and their rights,
And so though yours, not yours, (proue it so)   1300
Let Fortune goe to hell for it, not I.
I speake too long, but tis to peize the time.
To ech it, and to draw it out in length,
To stay you from election.

BASSANIO   Let me choose,
For as I am, I liue vpon the racke.

PORTIA
Vpon the racke *Bassanio*, then confesse
What treason there is mingled with your loue.

BASSANIO
None but that vgly treason of mistrust,
Which makes me feare th'inioying of my Loue,
There may as well be amity and life   1310
Tweene snow and fire, as treason and my loue.

PORTIA
I but I feare you speake vpon the racke
Where men enforced doe speake any thing.

BASSANIO
Promise me life, and ile confesse the truth.

PORTIA
Well then, confesse and liue.

BASSANIO   Confesse and loue
Had beene the very sum of my confession:
O happy torment, when my torturer
Doth teach me aunsweres for deliuerance:
But let me to my fortune and the caskets.

PORTIA
Away then, I am lockt in one of them,   1320
If you doe loue me, you will finde me out.
Nerryssa and the rest, stand all aloofe,
Let musique sound while he doth make his choyse,
Then if he loose he makes a Swan-like end,
Fading in musique. That the comparison
May stand more proper, my eye shall be the streame
And watry death-bed for him: he may win,
And what is musique than? Than musique is
Euen as the flourish, when true subiects bowe
To a new crowned Monarch: Such it is,   1330
As are those dulcet sounds in breake of day,
That creepe into the dreaming bride-groomes eare,
And summon him to marriage. Now he goes
With no lesse presence, but with much more loue
Then young Alcides, when he did redeeme
The virgine tribute, payed by howling Troy
To the Sea-monster: I stand for sacrifice,
The rest aloofe are the Dardanian wiues:

With bleared visages come forth to view
1340 The issue of th'exploit: Goe Hercules,
Liue thou, I liue. With much much more dismay,
I view the fight, then thou that mak'st the fray.
　⌈Here Musicke.⌉ A Song the whilst Bassanio
　comments on the caskets to himselfe

⌈ONE FROM PORTIAS TRAYNE⌉
　　　Tell me where is fancie bred,
　　　Or in the hart, or in the head,
　　　How begot, how nourished?
⌈ALL⌉　　　Replie, replie.

⌈ONE FROM PORTIAS TRAYNE⌉
　　　It is engendred in the eyes,
　　　With gazing fed, and Fancie dies
　　　In the cradle where it lies:
1350　　　Let vs all ring Fancies knell.
　　　Ile begin it. Ding, dong, bell.
ALL　　　Ding, dong, bell.

BASSANIO (aside)
So may the outward showes be least themselues,
The world is still deceau'd with ornament.
In Law, what plea so tainted and corrupt,
But being season'd with a gracious voyce,
Obscures the show of euill. In religion
What damned error but some sober brow
Will blesse it, and approue it with a text,
1360 Hiding the grosnes with faire ornament:
There is no voyce so simple, but assumes
Some marke of vertue on his outward parts;
How many cowards whose harts are all as false
As stayers of sand, weare yet vpon their chins
The beards of Hercules and frowning Mars,
Who inward searcht, haue lyuers white as milke,
And these assume but valours excrement
To render them redoubted. Looke on beauty,
And you shall see tis purchast by the weight,
1370 Which therein works a miracle in nature,
Making them lightest that weare most of it:
So are those crisped snaky golden locks
Which makes such wanton gambols with the wind
Vpon supposed fairenes, often knowne
To be the dowry of a second head,
The scull that bred them in the Sepulcher.
Thus ornament is but the guiled shore
To a most dangerous sea: the beautious scarfe
Vailing an Indian beauty; In a word,
1380 The seeming truth which cunning times put on
To intrap the wisest. (Aloud) Therefore thou gaudy
　gold,
Hard food for Midas, I will none of thee,
(To the siluer casket) Nor none of thee thou pale and
　common drudge
Tweene man and man: but thou, thou meager lead
Which rather threatenst then dost promise ought,
Thy palenes moues me more then eloquence,
And heere choose I, ioy be the consequence.

PORTIA (aside)
How all the other passions fleet to ayre,
As doubtfull thoughts, and rash imbrac'd despaire:
And shyddring feare, and greene-eyed iealousie.　1390
O loue be moderate, allay thy extasie,
In measure raine thy ioy, scant this excesse,
I feele too much thy blessing, make it lesse
For feare I surfeit.
　　Bassanio opens the leaden casket
BASSANIO　　　What finde I heere?
Faire Portias counterfeit. What demy God
Hath come so neere creation? moue these eyes?
Or whither riding on the balls of mine
Seeme they in motion? Heere are seuerd lips
Parted with suger breath, so sweet a barre
Should sunder such sweet friends: heere in her haires　1400
The Paynter playes the Spyder, and hath wouen
A golden mesh tyntrap the harts of men
Faster then gnats in cobwebs, but her eyes
How could he see to doe them? hauing made one,
Me thinkes it should haue power to steale both his
And leaue it selfe vnfurnisht: Yet looke how farre
The substance of my praise doth wrong this shadow
In vnderprysing it, so farre this shadow
Doth limpe behind the substance. Heeres the scroule,
The continent and summarie of my fortune.　1410
　He reades

　You that choose not by the view
　Chaunce as faire, and choose as true:
　Since this fortune falls to you,
　Be content, and seeke no new.
　If you be well pleasd with this,
　And hold your fortune for your blisse,
　Turne you where your Lady is,
　And claime her with a louing kis.
A gentle scroule: Faire Lady, by your leaue,
I come by note to giue, and to receaue,　1420
Like one of two contending in a prize
That thinks he hath done well in peoples eyes:
Hearing applause and vniuersall shoute,
Giddy in spirit, still gazing in a doubt
Whether those peales of praise be his or no,
So thrice faire Lady stand I euen so,
As doubtfull whether what I see be true,
Vntill confirmd, signd, ratified by you.
PORTIA
You see me Lord Bassanio where I stand,
Such as I am; though for my selfe alone　1430
I would not be ambitious in my wish
To wish my selfe much better, yet for you,
I would be trebled twentie times my selfe,
A thousand times more faire, tenne thousand times
　more rich,
That onely to stand high in your account,
I might in vertues, beauties, liuings, friends
Exceede account: but the full summe of me

Is sume of something: which to terme in grosse,
Is an vnlessond girle, vnschoold, vnpractized,
1440   Happy in this, she is not yet so old
But she may learne: happier then this,
Shee is not bred so dull but she can learne;
Happiest of all, is that her gentle spirit
Commits it selfe to yours to be directed,
As from her Lord, her gouernour, her King.
My selfe, and what is mine, to you and yours
Is now conuerted. But now I was the Lord
Of this faire mansion, maister of my seruants,
Queene ore my selfe: and euen now, but now,
1450   This house, these seruaunts, and this same my selfe
Are yours, my Lords, I giue them with this ring,
Which when you part from, loose, or giue away,
Let it presage the ruine of your loue,
And be my vantage to exclaime on you.

BASSANIO
Maddam, you haue bereft me of all words,
Onely my blood speakes to you in my vaines,
And there is such confusion in my powers,
As after some oration fairely spoke
By a beloued Prince, there doth appeare
1460   Among the buzzing pleased multitude,
Where euery somthing beeing blent together,
Turnes to a wild of nothing, saue of ioy
Exprest, and not exprest: but when this ring
Parts from this finger, then parts life from hence,
ô then be bold to say *Bassanios* dead.

NERRISSA
My Lord and Lady, it is now our time
That haue stoode by and seene our wishes prosper,
To cry good ioy, good ioy my Lord and Lady.

GRATIANO
My Lord *Bassanio*, and my gentle Lady,
1470   I wish you all the ioy that you can wish:
For I am sure you can wish none from me:
And when your honours meane to solemnize
The bargaine of your fayth: I doe beseech you
Euen at that time I may be married to.

BASSANIO
With all my hart, so thou canst get a wife.

GRATIANO
I thanke your Lordship, you haue got me one.
My eyes my Lord can looke as swift as yours:
You saw the mistres, I beheld the mayd:
You lou'd, I lou'd, for intermission
1480   No more pertaines to me my lord then you;
Your fortune stood vpon the caskets there,
And so did mine to as the matter falls:
For wooing heere vntill I swet againe,
And swearing till my very rough was dry
With oathes of loue, at last, if promise last
I got a promise of this faire one heere
To haue her loue: prouided that your fortune
Atchiu'd her mistres.

PORTIA   Is this true *Nerrissa*?

NERRISSA
Maddam it is, so you stand pleasd withall.

BASSANIO
And doe you *Gratiano* meane good fayth?   1490

GRATIANO Yes faith my Lord.

BASSANIO
Our feast shalbe much honord in your mariage.

GRATIANO (*to Nerrissa*)
Wele play with them the first boy for a thousand
    ducats.

NERRISSA What and stake downe?

GRATIANO
No, we shall nere win at that sport and stake downe.
     Enter Lorenzo, Iessica, and Salerio a messenger from
     Venice
But who comes heere? *Lorenzo* and his infidell?
What, and my old Venecian friend *Salerio*?

BASSANIO
Lorenzo and *Salerio*, welcome hether,
If that the youth of my newe intrest heere
Haue power to bid you welcome: (*to Portia*) by your
    leaue   1500
I bid my very friends and countrymen
Sweet *Portia* welcome.

PORTIA
So doe I my Lord, they are intirely welcome.

LORENZO
I thanke your honour, for my part my Lord
My purpose was not to haue seene you heere,
But meeting with *Salerio* by the way
He did intreate me past all saying nay
To come with him along.

SALERIO   I did my Lord,
And I haue reason for it, Signior *Anthonio*
Commends him to you.
     He giues Bassanio a letter

BASSANIO   Ere I ope his Letter   1510
I pray you tell me how my good friend doth.

SALERIO
Not sicke my Lord, vnlesse it be in mind,
Nor well, vnlesse in mind: his letter there
Will show you his estate.
     Bassanio: open the letter and reade

GRATIANO
Nerrissa, (*indicating Iessica*) cheere yond stranger, bid
    her welcom.
Your hand *Salerio*, what's the newes from Venice?
How doth that royall Merchant good *Anthonio*?
I know he will be glad of our successe,
We are the *Iasons*, we haue wone the fleece.

SALERIO
I would you had won the fleece that he hath lost.   1520

PORTIA
There are some shrowd contents in yond same paper
That steales the colour from *Bassanios* cheeke,
Some deere friend dead, else nothing in the world
Could turne so much the constitution
Of any constant man: what worse and worse?

With leaue *Bassanio* I am halfe your selfe,
And I must freely haue the halfe of any thing
That this same paper brings you.

BASSANIO   O sweete *Portia*,
Heere are a few of the vnpleasant'st words
1530   That euer blotted paper. Gentle Lady
When I did first impart my loue to you,
I freely told you all the wealth I had
Ranne in my vaines, I was a gentleman,
And then I told you true: and yet deere Lady
Rating my selfe at nothing, you shall see
How much I was a Braggart, when I told you
My state was nothing, I should then haue told you
That I was worse then nothing; for indeede
I haue ingag'd my selfe to a deere friend,
1540   Ingag'd my friend to his meere enemie
To feede my meanes. Heere is a letter Lady,
The paper as the body of my friend,
And euery word in it a gaping wound
Issuing life blood. But is it true *Salerio*
Hath all his ventures faild, what not one hit,
From Tripolis, from Mexico and England,
From Lisbon, Barbary, and India,
And not one vessell scape the dreadfull touch
Of Merchant-marring rocks?

SALERIO   Not one my Lord.
1550   Besides, it should appeare, that if he had
The present money to discharge the Iew,
Hee would not take it: neuer did I know
A creature that did beare the shape of man
So keene and greedie to confound a man.
He plyes the Duke at morning and at night,
And doth impeach the freedome of the state
If they deny him iustice. Twentie Merchants,
The Duke himselfe, and the Magnificoes
Of greatest port haue all perswaded with him,
1560   But none can driue him from the enuious plea
Of forfaiture, of iustice, and his bond.

IESSICA
When I was with him, I haue heard him sweare
To *Tuball* and to *Chus*, his country-men,
That he would rather haue *Anthonios* flesh
Then twentie times the value of the summe
That he did owe him: and I know my lord,
If law, authoritie, and power denie not,
It will goe hard with poore *Anthonio*.

PORTIA (*to Bassanio*)
Is it your deere friend that is thus in trouble?

BASSANIO
1570   The deerest friend to me, the kindest man,
The best conditiond and vnwearied spirit
In dooing curtesies: and one in whom
The auncient Romaine honour more appeares
Then any that drawes breath in Italie.

PORTIA What summe owes he the Iew?

BASSANIO
For me three thousand ducats.

PORTIA   What no more,

Pay him six thousand, & deface the bond:
Double sixe thousand, and then treble that,
Before a friend of this discription
Shall lose a haire thorough *Bassanios* fault.   1580
First goe with me to Church, and call me wife,
And then away to Venice to your friend:
For neuer shall you lie by *Portias* side
With an vnquiet soule. You shall haue gold
To pay the petty debt twenty times ouer.
When it is payd, bring your true friend along,
My mayd *Nerrissa*, and my selfe meane time
Will liue as maydes and widdowes; come away,
For you shall hence vpon your wedding day:
Bid your freends welcome, show a merry cheere,   1590
Since you are deere bought, I will loue you deere.
But let me heare the letter of your friend.

⌐BASSANIO⌐ (*reades*) *Sweet* Bassanio, *my ships haue all
miscaried, my Creditors growe cruell, my estate is very
low, my bond to the Iewe is forfaite, and since in paying
it, it is impossible I should liue, all debts are cleerd betweene
you and I if I might but see you at my death:
notwithstanding, vse your pleasure, if your loue do not
perswade you to come, let not my letter.*

PORTIA
O loue! dispatch all busines and be gone.   1600

BASSANIO
Since I haue your good leaue to goe away,
I will make hast; but till I come againe,
No bed shall ere be guiltie of my stay,
Nor rest be interposer twixt vs twaine.   *Exeunt*

Enter Shylocke the Iew, and Salanio, and Anthonio,   Sc. 15
and the Iaylor   (3.3)

SHYLOCKE
Iaylor, looke to him, tell not me of mercie,
This is the foole that lent out money gratis.
Iaylor, looke to him.

ANTHONIO   Heare me yet good *Shylock*.

SHYLOCKE
Ile haue my bond, speake not against my bond,
I haue sworne an oath, that I will haue my bond:
Thou call'dst me dogge before thou hadst a cause,   1610
But since I am a dog, beware my phanges,
The Duke shall graunt me iustice, I do wonder
Thou naughtie Iaylor that thou art so fond
To come abroade with him at his request.

ANTHONIO I pray thee heare me speake.

SHYLOCKE
Ile haue my bond. I will not heare thee speake,
Ile haue my bond, and therefore speake no more.
Ile not be made a soft and dull eyde foole,
To shake the head, relent, and sigh, and yeeld
To christian intercessers: follow not,   1620
Ile haue no speaking, I will haue my bond.   *Exit Iew*

SOLANIO
It is the most impenitrable curre
That euer kept with men.

ANTHONIO   Let him alone,

Ile follow him no more with bootlesse prayers,
Hee seekes my life, his reason well I know;
I oft deliuerd from his forfeytures
Many that haue at times made mone to me,
Therefore he hates me.

SOLANIO   I am sure the Duke
Will neuer grant this forfaiture to hold.

ANTHONIO

1630   The Duke cannot denie the course of law:
For the commoditie that strangers haue
With vs in Venice, if it be denyed,
Will much impeach the iustice of the state,
Since that the trade and profit of the citty
Consisteth of all Nations. Therefore goe,
These griefes and losses haue so bated me
That I shall hardly spare a pound of flesh
To morrow, to my bloody Creditor.
Well Iaylor on, pray God Bassanio come
1640   To see me pay his debt, and then I care not.   Exeunt

Sc. 16   Enter Portia, Nerrissa, Lorenzo, Iessica, and
(3.4)   Balthaser a man of Portias

LORENZO (to Portia)

Maddam, although I speake it in your presence,
You haue a noble and a true conceite
Of god-like amitie, which appeares most strongly
In bearing thus the absence of your Lord.
But if you knew to whom you show this honour,
How true a gentleman you send releefe,
How deere a louer of my Lord your husband,
I know you would be prouder of the worke
Then customarie bountie can enforce you.

PORTIA

1650   I neuer did repent for dooing good,
Nor shall not now: for in companions
That doe conuerse and wast the time together,
Whose soules doe beare an egall yoke of loue,
There must be needes a like proportion
Of lyniaments, of manners, and of spirit;
Which makes me thinke that this Anthonio
Beeing the bosome louer of my Lord,
Must needes be like my Lord. If it be so,
How little is the cost I haue bestowed
1660   In purchasing the semblance of my soule,
From out the state of hellish cruelty;
This comes too neere the praising of my selfe,
Therefore no more of it: heere other things.
Lorenso I commit into your hands,
The husbandry and mannage of my house,
Vntill my Lords returne: for mine owne part
I haue toward heauen breath'd a secret vowe,
To liue in prayer and contemplation,
Onely attended by Nerrissa heere,
1670   Vntill her husband and my Lords returne,
There is a Monastery two miles off,
And there we will abide. I doe desire you
Not to denie this imposition,

The which my loue and some necessity
Now layes vpon you.

LORENZO   Madame, with all my hart,
I shall obey you in all faire commaunds.

PORTIA

My people doe already know my mind,
And will acknowledge you and Iessica
In place of Lord Bassanio and my selfe.
So far you well till we shall meete againe.   1680

LORENZO

Faire thoughts and happy houres attend on you.

IESSICA

I wish your Ladiship all harts content.

PORTIA

I thank you for your wish, and am well pleasd
To wish it back on you: far you well Iessica.

                          Exeunt Lorenzo and Iessica

Now Balthaser,
As I haue euer found thee honest true,
So let me find thee still: take this same letter,
And vse thou all th'indeuour of a man,
In speede to Padua, see thou render this
Into my cosins hands Doctor Belario,   1690
And looke what notes and garments he doth giue thee,
Bring them I pray thee with imagin'd speede
Vnto the Traiect, to the common Ferrie
Which trades to Venice; wast no time in words
But get thee gone, I shall be there before thee.

BALTHASER

Madam, I goe with all conuenient speede.   Exit

PORTIA

Come on Nerrissa, I haue worke in hand
That you yet know not of; weele see our husbands
Before they thinke of vs?

NERRISSA   Shall they see vs?

PORTIA

They shall Nerrissa: but in such a habite,   1700
That they shall thinke we are accomplished
With that we lacke; Ile hold thee any wager
When we are both accoutered like young men,
Ile proue the prettier fellow of the two,
And weare my dagger with the brauer grace,
And speake betweene the change of man and boy,
With a reede voyce, and turne two minsing steps
Into a manly stride; and speake of frayes
Like a fine bragging youth: and tell quaint lyes
How honorable Ladies sought my loue,   1710
Which I denying, they fell sicke and dyed.
I could not doe withall: then ile repent,
And wish for all that, that I had not killd them;
And twenty of these punie lies ile tell,
That men shall sweare I haue discontinued schoole
Aboue a twelue-moneth: I haue within my minde
A thousand raw tricks of these bragging Iacks,
Which I will practise.

NERRISSA Why, shall we turne to men?

PORTIA Fie, what a question's that,   1720
If thou wert nere a lewd interpreter:

498

But come, ile tell thee all my whole deuice
When I am in my coach, which stayes for vs
At the Parke gate; and therefore hast away,
For we must measure twenty miles to day.   *Exeunt*

Sc. 17
(3.5)   *Enter Clowne and Iessica*

CLOWNE Yes truly, for looke you, the sinnes of the Father
are to be laid vpon the children, therefore I promise
you, I feare you, I was alwaies plaine with you, and
so now I speake my agitation of the matter: therefore
1730   be a good chere, for truly I thinke you are damnd,
there is but one hope in it that can doe you any good,
and that is but a kinde of bastard hope neither.

IESSICA And what hope is that I pray thee?

CLOWNE Marry you may partly hope that your Father got
you not, that you are not the Iewes daughter.

IESSICA That were a kind of bastard hope in deede, so the
sinnes of my mother should be visited vpon me.

CLOWNE Truly then I feare you are damnd both by father
and mother: thus when I shun *Scilla* your father, I fall
1740   into *Caribdis* your mother; well, you are gone both
wayes.

IESSICA I shall be sau'd by my husband, he hath made
me a Christian?

CLOWNE Truly the more to blame he, we were Christians
enow before, in as many as could well liue one by
another: this making of Christians will raise the price
of Hogs, if we grow all to be pork eaters, we shall not
shortly haue a rasher on the coles for mony.

          Enter Lorenzo

IESSICA Ile tell my husband *Launcelet* what you say, here
1750   he comes.

LORENZO I shall grow iealious of you shortly *Launcelet*, if
you thus get my wife into corners.

IESSICA Nay, you neede not feare vs *Lorenzo*, *Launcelet*
and I are out, he tells me flatly there's no mercy for
mee in heauen, because I am a Iewes daughter: and
he sayes you are no good member of the common-
wealth, for in conuerting Iewes to Christians, you raise
the price of porke.

LORENZO (*to the Clowne*) I shall aunswere that better to
1760   the common-wealth than you can the getting vp of the
Negroes belly: the Moore is with child by you *Launcelet*.

CLOWNE It is much that the Moore should be more then
reason: but if she be lesse then an honest woman, she
is indeede more then I tooke her for.

LORENZO How euery foole can play vpon the word, I
thinke the best grace of wit will shortly turne into
silence, and discourse grow commendable in none onely
but Parrats: goe in sirra, bid them prepare for dinner.

CLOWNE That is done sir, they haue all stomacks.

1770   LORENZO Goodly Lord what a wit snapper are you, than
bid them prepare dinner.

CLOWNE That is done to sir, onely couer is the word.

LORENZO Will you couer than sir?

CLOWNE Not so sir neither, I know my duty.

LORENZO Yet more quarrelling with occasion, wilt thou
shewe the whole wealth of thy wit in an instant; I
pray thee vnderstand a plaine man in his plaine
meaning: goe to thy fellowes, bid them couer the table,
serue in the meate, and we will come in to dinner.

CLOWNE For the table sir, it shall be seru'd in, for the   1780
meate sir, it shall be couerd, for your comming in to
dinner sir, why let it be as humors and conceites shall
gouerne.   *Exit Clowne*

LORENZO
O deare discretion, how his words are suted,
The foole hath planted in his memorie
An Armie of good words, and I doe know
A many fooles that stand in better place,
Garnisht like him, that for a tricksie word
Defie the matter: how cherst thou *Iessica*,
And now good sweet say thy opinion,   1790
How doost thou like the Lord *Bassanios* wife?

IESSICA
Past all expressing, it is very meete
The Lord *Bassanio* liue an vpright life
For hauing such a blessing in his Lady,
He findes the ioyes of heauen heere on earth,
And if on earth he doe not merrit it
In reason he should neuer come to heauen.
Why, if two Gods should play some heauenly match,
And on the wager lay two earthly women,
And *Portia* one: there must be somthing else   1800
Paund with the other, for the poore rude world
Hath not her fellow.

LORENZO   Euen such a husband
Hast thou of me, as she is for a wife.

IESSICA
Nay, but aske my opinion to of that.

LORENZO
I will anone, first let vs goe to dinner.

IESSICA
Nay, let me praise you while I haue a stomack.

LORENZO
No pray thee, let it serue for table talke,
Then how so mere thou speakst mong other things,
I shall disgest it.

IESSICA   Well, ile set you forth.   *Exeunt*

          Enter the Duke, the Magnificoes, Anthonio,   Sc. 18
          Bassanio, Gratiano, and Salerio   (4.1)

DUKE
What, is *Anthonio* heere?

ANTHONIO   Ready, so please your grace.   1810

DUKE
I am sorry for thee, thou art come to aunswere
A stonie aduersarie, an inhumaine wretch,
Vncapable of pitty, voyd, and empty
From any dram of mercie.

ANTHONIO   I haue heard
Your grace hath tane great paines to quallifie
His rigorous course; but since he stands obdurate,
And that no lawfull meanes can carry me
Out of his enuies reach, I doe oppose
My patience to his furie, and am armd

1820
To suffer with a quietnes of spirit,
The very tiranny and rage of his.

DUKE

Goe one and call the Iew into the Court.

SALERIO

He is ready at the dore, he comes my Lord.
Enter Shylocke

DUKE

Make roome, and let him stand before our face.
Shylocke the world thinks, and I thinke so to
That thou but leadst this fashion of thy mallice
To the last houre of act, and then tis thought
Thowlt shew thy mercy and remorse more strange,
Than is thy strange apparant cruelty;

1830
And where thou now exacts the penalty,
Which is a pound of this poore Merchants flesh,
Thou wilt not onely loose the forfaiture,
But toucht with humaine gentlenes and loue:
Forgiue a moytie of the principall,
Glauncing an eye of pitty on his losses
That haue of late so hudled on his backe,
Enow to presse a royall Merchant downe;
And pluck comiseration of his state
From brassie bosomes and rough harts of flint,

1840
From stubborne Turkes, and Tarters neuer traind
To offices of tender curtesie:
We all expect a gentle aunswere Iewe.

SHYLOCKE

I haue possest your grace of what I purpose,
And by our holy Sabaoth haue I sworne
To haue the due and forfet of my bond,
If you deny it, let the danger light
Vpon your charter and your Citties freedome.
Youle aske me why I rather choose to haue
A weight of carrion flesh, then to receaue

1850
Three thousand ducats: Ile not aunswer that.
But say it is my humour, is it aunswerd?
What if my house be troubled with a Rat,
And I be pleasd to giue ten thousand ducats
To haue it baind? what, are you aunswerd yet?
Some men there are loue not a gaping pigge.
Some that are mad if they behold a Cat.
And others when the bagpipe sings ith nose,
Cannot containe their vrine. For affection
M^{rs} of passion swayes it to the moode

1860
Of what it likes or loathes, now for your aunswer:
As there is no firme reason to be rendred
Why he cannot abide a gaping pigge,
Why he a harmelesse necessarie Cat,
Why he a woollen bagpipe: but of force
Must yeeld to such in euitable shame,
As to offend himselfe being offended:
So can I giue no reason, nor I will not,
More then a lodgd hate, and a certaine loathing
I beare *Anthonio*, that I follow thus

1870
A loosing sute against him. Are you aunswered?

BASSANIO

This is no aunswer thou vnfeeling man,
To excuse the currant of thy cruelty.

SHYLOCKE

I am not bound to please thee with my answers.

BASSANIO

Doe all men kill the things they doe not loue?

SHYLOCKE

Hates any man the thing he would not kill?

BASSANIO

Euery offence is not a hate at first.

SHYLOCKE

What wouldst thou haue a serpent sting thee twice?

ANTHONIO

I pray you think you question with the Iewe,
You may as well goe stand vpon the Beach
And bid the maine flood bate his vsuall height, 1880
You may as well vse question with the Woolfe,
Why he hath made the Ewe bleate for the Lambe:
You may as well forbid the mountaine Pines
To wag their high tops, and to make no noise
When they are fretten with the gusts of heauen:
You may as well doe any thing most hard
As seeke to soften that then which what's harder:
His Iewish hart. Therefore I doe beseech you
Make no moe offers, vse no farther meanes,
But with all briefe and plaine conueniencie 1890
Let me haue iudgement, and the Iewe his will.

BASSANIO (*to Shylocke*)

For thy three thousand ducats heere is sixe.

SHYLOCKE

If euery ducat in sixe thousand ducats
Were in sixe parts, and euery part a ducat,
I would not draw them, I would haue my bond.

DUKE

How shalt thou hope for mercy rendring none?

SHYLOCKE

What iudgment shall I dread doing no wrong?
You haue among you many a purchast slaue,
Which like your Asses, and your Dogs and Mules
You vse in abiect and in slauish parts, 1900
Because you bought them, shall I say to you,
Let them be free, marry them to your heires?
Why sweat they vnder burthens, let their beds
Be made as soft as yours, and let their pallats
Be seasond with such viands, you will aunswer
The slaues are ours, so doe I aunswer you:
The pound of flesh which I demaund of him
Is deerely bought, tis mine and I will haue it:
If you deny me, fie vpon your Law,
There is no force in the decrees of Venice: 1910
I stand for iudgement, aunswer, shall I haue it?

DUKE

Vpon my power I may dismisse this Court,
Vnlesse *Bellario* a learned Doctor,
Whom I haue sent for to determine this
Come heere to day.

SALERIO   My Lord, heere stayes without
A messenger with letters from the Doctor,
New come from Padua.

DUKE

Bring vs the letters. Call the Messenger.   ⌈*Exit Salerio*⌉

BASSANIO

Good cheere *Anthonio*. What man, courage yet:
1920   The Iew shall haue my flesh, blood, bones and all,
Ere thou shalt loose for me one drop of blood.

ANTHONIO

I am a tainted weather of the flocke,
Meetest for death, the weakest kind of fruite
Drops earliest to the ground, and so let me;
You cannot better be imployd *Bassanio*,
Then to liue still and write mine Epitaph.
    Enter ⌐Salerio, with⌐ Nerrissa apparrailed as a
    Iudges clarke

DUKE

Came you from Padua from *Bellario*?

NERRISSA

From both my L. *Bellario* greetes your grace.
    She giues a letter to the Duke.
    Shylocke whets his knife on his shoe

BASSANIO (to *Shylocke*)

Why doost thou whet thy knife so earnestly?

SHYLOCKE

1930   To cut the forfait from that bankrout there.

GRATIANO

Not on thy soule: but on thy soule harsh Iew
Thou makst thy knife keene: but no mettell can,
No, not the hangmans axe beare halfe the keenenesse
Of thy sharpe enuie: can no prayers pearce thee?

SHYLOCKE

No, none that thou hast wit enough to make.

GRATIANO

O be thou damnd, inexorable dogge,
And for thy life let iustice be accusd;
Thou almost mak'st me wauer in my faith,
To hold opinion with *Pythagoras*,
1940   That soules of Animalls infuse themselues
Into the trunks of men: Thy currish spirit
Gouernd a Woolfe, who hangd for humaine slaughter
Euen from the gallowes did his fell soule fleete,
And whilest thou layest in thy vnhallowed dam;
Infusd it selfe in thee: for thy desires
Are woluish, bloody, staru'd, and rauenous.

SHYLOCKE

Till thou canst raile the seale from off my bond,
Thou but offendst thy lungs to speake so loud:
Repaire thy wit good youth, or it will fall
1950   To curelesse ruine. I stand heere for law.

DUKE

This letter from *Bellario* doth commend
A young and learned Doctor to our Court:
Where is he?

NERRISSA   He attendeth here hard by
To know your aunswer whether youle admit him.

DUKE

With all my hart: some three or foure of you
Goe giue him curteous conduct to this place,
                  Exeunt three or foure
Meane time the Court shall heare *Bellarios* letter.
(*Reades*) Your Grace shall vnderstand, that at the receit
of your letter I am very sicke, but in the instant that

your messenger came, in louing visitation was with me   1960
a young Doctor of Rome, his name is *Balthazer*: I
acquainted him with the cause in cõtrouersie between
the Iew and *Anthonio* the Merchant, wee turnd ore
many bookes together, hee is furnished with my
opinion, which bettered with his owne learning, the
greatnes whereof I cannot enough commend, comes
with him at my importunitie, to fill vp your graces
request in my stead. I beseech you let his lacke of
yeeres be no impediment to let him lacke a reuerend
estimation, for I neuer knew so young a body with so   1970
olde a head: I leaue him to your gracious acceptance,
whose tryall shall better publish his commendation.
    Enter ⌐three or foure with⌐ Portia for Balthazer
You heare the learnd *Bellario* what he writes,
And heere I take it is the doctor come.
(*To Portia*) Giue me your hand, come you from old
    Bellario?

PORTIA

I did my Lord.

DUKE   You are welcome, take your place:
Are you acquainted with the difference
That holds this present question in the Court.

PORTIA

I am enformed throughly of the cause,
Which is the Merchant here? and which the Iew?   1980

DUKE

Anthonio and old *Shylocke*, both stand forth.
    Anthonio and Shylocke stand forth

PORTIA

Is your name *Shylocke*?

SHYLOCKE   *Shylocke* is my name.

PORTIA

Of a strange nature is the sute you follow,
Yet in such rule, that the Venetian law
Cannot impugne you as you doe proceed.
(*To Anthonio*) You stand within his danger, doe you
    not.

ANTHONIO

I, so he sayes.

PORTIA   Doe you confesse the bond?

ANTHONIO

I doe.

PORTIA Then must the Iew be mercifull.

SHYLOCKE

On what compulsion must I, tell me that.

PORTIA

The qualitie of mercie is not straind,   1990
It droppeth as the gentle raine from heauen
Vpon the place beneath: it is twise blest,
It blesseth him that giues, and him that takes,
Tis mightiest in the mightiest, it becomes
The throned Monarch better then his crowne.
His scepter showes the force of temporall power,
The attribut to awe and maiestie,
Wherein doth sit the dread and feare of Kings:
But mercie is aboue this sceptred sway,
It is enthroned in the harts of Kings,   2000
It is an attribut to God himselfe;

And earthly power doth then show likest gods
When mercie seasons iustice: therefore Iew,
Though iustice be thy plea, consider this,
That in the course of iustice, none of vs
Should see saluation: we doe pray for mercy,
And that same prayer, doth teach vs all to render
The deedes of mercie. I haue spoke thus much
To mittigate the iustice of thy plea,
2010 Which if thou follow, this strict Court of Venice
Must needes giue sentence gainst the Merchant there.

SHYLOCKE

My deeds vpon my head, I craue the law,
The penalty and forfaite of my bond.

PORTIA

Is he not able to discharge the money?

BASSANIO

Yes, heere I tender it for him in the Court,
Yea, twise the summe, if that will not suffise,
I will be bound to pay it ten times ore
On forfait of my hands, my head, my hart,
If this will not suffise, it must appeare
2020 That malice beares downe truth. And I beseech you
Wrest once the law to your authoritie,
To doe a great right, doe a little wrong,
And curbe this cruell deuill of his will.

PORTIA

It must not be, there is no power in Venice
Can altar a decree established:
Twill be recorded for a precedent,
And many an errour by the same example
Will rush into the state, it cannot be.

SHYLOCKE

A Daniell come to iudgement: yea a Daniell.
2030 O wise young Iudge how I doe honour thee.

PORTIA

I pray you let me looke vpon the bond.

SHYLOCKE

Heere tis most reuerend doctor, here it is.

PORTIA

Shylocke theres thrice thy money offred thee.

SHYLOCKE

An oath, an oath, I haue an oath in heauen,
Shall I lay periurie vpon my soule?
No not for Venice.

PORTIA   Why this bond is forfait,
And lawfully by this the Iew may claime
A pound of flesh, to be by him cut off
Neerest the Merchants hart: (*to Shylocke*) be mercifull,
2040 Take thrice thy money, bid me teare the bond.

SHYLOCKE

When it is payd, according to the tenure.
It doth appeare you are a worthy iudge,
You know the law, your exposition
Hath beene most sound: I charge you by the law,
Whereof you are a well deseruing piller,
Proceede to iudgement: by my soule I sweare,
There is no power in the tongue of man
To alter me, I stay here on my Bond.

ANTHONIO

Most hartelie I doe beseech the Court
To giue the iudgement.

PORTIA   Why than thus it is,   2050
You must prepare your bosome for his knife.

SHYLOCKE

O noble Iudge, ô excellent young man.

PORTIA

For the intent and purpose of the law
Hath full relation to the penaltie,
Which heere appeareth due vpon the bond.

SHYLOCKE

Tis very true: ô wise and vpright Iudge,
How much more elder art thou then thy lookes.

PORTIA (*to Anthonio*)

Therefore lay bare your bosome.

SHYLOCKE   I, his breast,
So sayes the bond, doth it not noble Iudge?
Neerest his hart, those are the very words.   2060

PORTIA

It is so, are there ballance here to weigh the flesh?

SHYLOCKE I haue them ready.

PORTIA

Haue by some Surgion *Shylocke* on your charge,
To stop his wounds, least he doe bleede to death.

SHYLOCKE

Is it so nominated in the bond?

PORTIA

It is not so exprest, but what of that?
Twere good you doe so much for charitie.

SHYLOCKE

I cannot finde it, tis not in the bond.

PORTIA (*to Anthonio*)

You Merchant, haue you any thing to say?

ANTHONIO

But little; I am armd and well prepard,   2070
Giue me your hand *Bassanio*, far you well,
Greeue not that I am falne to this for you:
For heerein Fortune showes her selfe more kind
Then is her custome: it is still her vse
To let the wretched man out-liue his wealth,
To view with hollow eye and wrinckled brow
An age of pouertie: from which lingring pennance
Of such misery doth she cut me of.
Commend me to your honourable wife,
Tell her the processe of *Anthonios* end,   2080
Say how I lou'd you, speake me faire in death:
And when the tale is told, bid her be iudge
Whether *Bassanio* had not once a loue:
Repent but you that you shall loose your friend
And he repents not that he payes your debt.
For if the Iew doe cut but deepe enough,
Ile pay it instantly with all my hart.

BASSANIO

Anthonio, I am married to a wife
Which is as deere to me as life it selfe,
But life it selfe, my wife, and all the world,   2090
Are not with me esteemd aboue thy life.

I would loose all, I sacrifize them all
Heere to this deuill, to deliuer you.

PORTIA ⌈aside⌉

Your wife would giue you little thankes for that
If she were by to heare you make the offer.

GRATIANO

I haue a wife who I protest I loue,
I would she were in heauen, so she could
Intreate some power to change this currish Iew.

NERRISSA ⌈aside⌉

Tis well you offer it behind her back,
2100   The wish would make else an vnquiet house.

SHYLOCKE ⌈aside⌉

These be the christian husbands, I haue a daughter
Would any of the stocke of Barrabas
Had beene her husband, rather then a Christian.
(Aloud) We trifle time, I pray thee pursue sentence.

PORTIA

A pound of that same Merchants flesh is thine,
The Court awards it, and the law doth giue it.

SHYLOCKE Most rightfull Iudge.

PORTIA

And you must cut this flesh from off his breast,
The law alowes it, and the court awards it.

SHYLOCKE

Most learned Iudge, a sentence, (to Anthonio) come
2110   prepare.

PORTIA

Tarry a little, there is some thing else,
This bond doth giue thee heere no iote of blood,
The words expresly are a pound of flesh:
Take then thy bond, take thou thy pound of flesh,
But in the cutting it, if thou doost shed
One drop of Christian blood, thy lands and goods
Are by the lawes of Venice confiscate
Vnto the state of Venice.

GRATIANO   O vpright Iudge,
Marke Iew, ô learned Iudge.

2120 SHYLOCKE Is that the law?

PORTIA Thy selfe shalt see the Act:
For as thou vrgest iustice, be assurd
Thou shalt haue iustice more then thou desirst.

GRATIANO

O learned iudge, mark Iew, a learned iudge.

SHYLOCKE

I take this offer then, pay the bond thrice
And let the Christian goe.

BASSANIO   Heere is the money.

PORTIA

Soft, the Iew shal haue all iustice, soft no hast,
He shall haue nothing but the penalty.

GRATIANO

O Iew, an vpright Iudge, a learned Iudge.

PORTIA (to Shylocke)

2130 Therefore prepare thee to cut of the flesh,
Shed thou no blood, nor cut thou lesse nor more
But iust a pound of flesh: if thou tak'st more
Or lesse then a iust pound, be it but so much

As makes it light or heauy in the substance,
Or the deuision of the twentith part
Of one poore scruple, nay if the scale doe turne
But in the estimation of a hayre,
Thou dyest, and all thy goods are confiscate.

GRATIANO

A second Daniell, a Daniell Iew,
Now infidell I haue you on the hip.   2140

PORTIA

Why doth the Iew pause, take thy forfaiture.

SHYLOCKE

Giue me my principall, and let me goe.

BASSANIO

I haue it ready for thee, here it is.

PORTIA

Hee hath refusd it in the open Court,
Hee shall haue meerely iustice and his bond.

GRATIANO

A Daniell still say I, a second Daniell,
I thanke thee Iew for teaching me that word.

SHYLOCKE

Shall I not haue barely my principall?

PORTIA

Thou shalt haue nothing but the forfaiture
To be so taken at thy perrill Iew.   2150

SHYLOCKE

Why then the deuill giue him good of it:
Ile stay no longer question.

PORTIA   Tarry Iew,
The law hath yet another hold on you.
It is enacted in the lawes of Venice,
If it be prou'd against an alien,
That by direct, or indirect attempts
He seeke the life of any Cittizen,
The party gainst the which he doth contriue,
Shall seaze one halfe his goods, the other halfe
Comes to the priuie coffer of the State,   2160
And the offenders life lies in the mercy
Of the Duke onely, gainst all other voyce.
In which predicament I say thou standst:
For it appeares by manifest proceeding,
That indirectly, and directly to
Thou hast contriud against the very life
Of the defendant: and thou hast incurd
The danger formorly by me rehearst.
Downe therefore, and beg mercie of the Duke.

GRATIANO (to Shylocke)

Beg that thou maist haue leaue to hang thy selfe,   2170
And yet thy wealth beeing forfait to the state,
Thou hast not left the value of a cord,
Therefore thou must be hangd at the states charge.

DUKE (to Shylocke)

That thou shalt see the difference of our spirit
I pardon thee thy life before thou aske it:
For halfe thy wealth, it is Anthonios,
The other halfe comes to the generall state,
Which humblenes may driue vnto a fine.

PORTIA
I for the state, not for *Anthonio*.

SHYLOCKE

2180   Nay, take my life and all, pardon not that,
You take my house, when you doe take the prop
That doth sustaine my house: you take my life
When you doe take the meanes whereby I liue.

PORTIA
What mercy can you render him *Anthonio*?

GRATIANO
A halter gratis, nothing else for Godsake.

ANTHONIO
So please my Lord the Duke, & all the Court
To quit the fine for one halfe of his goods,
I am content: so he will let me haue
The other halfe in vse, to render it

2190   Vpon his death vnto the Gentleman
That lately stole his daughter.
Two things prouided more, that for this fauour
He presently become a Christian:
The other, that he doe record a gift
Heere in the Court of all he dies possest
Vnto his sonne *Lorenzo* and his daughter.

DUKE
He shall doe this, or else I doe recant
The pardon that I late pronounced heere.

PORTIA
Art thou contented Iew? what dost thou say?

SHYLOCKE
I am content.

2200   PORTIA (*to Nerrissa*) Clarke, draw a deede of gift.

SHYLOCKE
I pray you giue me leaue to goe from hence,
I am not well, send the deede after me,
And I will signe it.

DUKE   Get thee gone, but doe it.

GRATIANO (*to Shylocke*)
In christning shalt thou haue two Godfathers,
Had I beene iudge, thou shouldst haue had ten more,
To bring thee to the gallowes, not the font.
                            Exit Shylocke

DUKE (*to Portia*)
Sir I entreate you home with me to dinner.

PORTIA
I humbly doe desire your Grace of pardon,
I must away this night toward Padua,

2210   And it is meete I presently set forth.

DUKE
I am sorry that your leysure serues you not.
Anthonio, gratifie this gentleman,
For in my mind you are much bound to him.
                            Exit Duke and his traine

BASSANIO (*to Portia*)
Most worthy gentleman, I and my friend
Haue by your wisedome been this day aquitted
Of greeuous penalties, in lewe whereof,
Three thousand ducats due vnto the Iew
Wee freely cope your curtious paines withall.

ANTHONIO
And stand indebted ouer and aboue
In loue and seruice to you euer-more.   2220

PORTIA
Hee is well payd that is well satisfied,
And I deliuering you, am satisfied,
And therein doe account my selfe well payd,
My minde was neuer yet more mercinarie.
I pray you know me when we meete againe,
I wish you well, and so I take my leaue.

BASSANIO
Deere sir, of force I must attempt you further,
Take some remembrance of vs as a tribute,
Not as fee: graunt me two things I pray you,
Not to deny me, and to pardon me.   2230

PORTIA
You presse me farre, and therefore I wil yeeld,
⌈*To Anthonio*⌉ Giue mee your gloues, Ile weare them
        for your sake,
(*To Bassanio*) And for your loue ile take this ring from
        you,
Doe not draw back your hand, ile take no more,
And you in loue shall not denie me this.

BASSANIO
This ring good sir, alas it is a trifle,
I will not shame my selfe to giue you this.

PORTIA
I will haue nothing else but onely this,
And now me thinks I haue a minde to it.

BASSANIO
There's more depends on this then on the valew,   2240
The dearest ring in Venice will I giue you,
And finde it out by proclamation,
Onely for this I pray you pardon me.

PORTIA
I see sir you are liberall in offers,
You taught me first to beg, and now me thinks
You teach me how a begger should be aunswerd.

BASSANIO
Good sir, this ring was giuen me by my wife,
And when she put it on, she made me vowe
That I should neither sell, nor giue, nor loose it.

PORTIA
That scuse serues many men to saue their gifts,   2250
And if your wife be not a mad woman,
And know how well I haue deseru'd this ring,
She would not hold out enemy for euer
For giuing it to me: well, peace be with you.
                            Exeunt Portia and Nerrissa

ANTHONIO
My L. *Bassanio*, let him haue the ring,
Let his deseruings and my loue withall
Be valued gainst your wiues commaundement.

BASSANIO
Goe *Gratiano*, runne and ouer-take him,
Giue him the ring, and bring him if thou canst
Vnto *Anthonios* house, away, make hast.   2260
                            Exit Gratiano

Come, you and I will thither presently,
And in the morning early will we both
Flie toward Belmont, come *Anthonio*.   *Exeunt*

Sc. 19   *Enter Portia and Nerrissa, disguisd*
(4.2) PORTIA
        Enquire the Iewes house out, giue him this deed,
        And let him signe it, weele away to night,
        And be a day before our husbands home:
        This deede will be well welcome to *Lorenzo*.
                Enter Gratiano
        GRATIANO Faire sir, you are well ore-tane:
        My L. *Bassanio* vpon more aduice,
2270   Hath sent you heere this ring, and doth intreate
        Your company at dinner.
        PORTIA   That cannot be;
        His ring I doe accept most thankfully,
        And so I pray you tell him: furthermore,
        I pray you shew my youth old *Shylockes* house.
        GRATIANO
        That will I doe.
        NERRISSA   Sir, I would speake with you:
        (*Aside to Portia*) Ile see if I can get my husbands ring
        Which I did make him sweare to keepe for euer.
        PORTIA (*aside to Nerrissa*)
        Thou maist I warrant, we shal haue old swearing
        That they did giue the rings away to men;
2280   But wele out-face them, and out-sweare them to:
        Away, make hast, thou knowst where I will tarry.
                        Exit ⌐at one doore⌐
        NERRISSA (*to Gratiano*)
        Come good sir, will you shew me to this house.
                        Exeunt ⌐at another doore⌐

Sc. 20   *Enter Lorenzo and Iessica*
(5.1) LORENZO
        The moone shines bright. In such a night as this,
        When the sweet winde did gently kisse the trees,
        And they did make no noyse, in such a night
        Troylus me thinks mounted the Troian walls,
        And sigh'd his soule toward the Grecian tents
        Where *Cressed* lay that night.
        IESSICA   In such a night
        Did *Thisbie* fearefully ore-trip the dewe,
2290   And saw the Lyons shadow ere him selfe,
        And ranne dismayed away.
        LORENZO   In such a night
        Stoode *Dido* with a willow in her hand
        Vpon the wilde sea banks, and waft her Loue
        To come againe to Carthage.
        IESSICA   In such a night
        Medea gathered the inchanted hearbs
        That did renew old *Eson*.
        LORENZO   In such a night
        Did *Iessica* steale from the wealthy Iewe,
        And with an vnthrift loue did runne from Venice,
        As farre as Belmont.
        IESSICA   In such a night

Did young *Lorenzo* sweare he lou'd her well,   2300
Stealing her soule with many vowes of faith,
And nere a true one.
LORENZO   In such a night
Did pretty *Iessica* (like a little shrow)
Slaunder her Loue, and he forgaue it her.
IESSICA
I would out-night you did no body come:
But harke, I heare the footing of a man.
        Enter a Messenger
LORENZO
Who comes so fast in silence of the night?
MESSENGER A friend.
LORENZO
A friend, what friend, your name I pray you friend?
MESSENGER
Stephano is my name, and I bring word   2310
My Mistres will before the breake of day
Be heere at Belmont, she doth stray about
By holy crosses where she kneeles and prayes
For happy wedlock houres.
LORENZO   Who comes with her?
MESSENGER
None but a holy Hermit and her mayd:
I pray you is my Maister yet returnd?
LORENZO
He is not, nor we haue not heard from him,
But goe we in I pray thee *Iessica*,
And ceremoniously let vs prepare
Some welcome for the Mistres of the house.   2320
        Enter Clowne, calling
CLOWNE Sola, sola: wo ha, ho sola, sola.
LORENZO Who calls?
CLOWNE Sola, did you see M. *Lorenzo*, M. *Lorenzo* sola,
sola.
LORENZO Leaue hollowing man, heere.
CLOWNE Sola, where, where?
LORENZO Heere?
CLOWNE Tell him there's a Post come from my Maister,
with his horne full of good newes, my Maister will be
heere ere morning.   *Exit*   2330
LORENZO (*to Iessica*)
Sweete soule, let's in, and there expect their
        comming.
And yet no matter: why should we goe in.
My friend *Stephano*, signifie I pray you
Within the house, your mistres is at hand,
And bring your musique foorth into the ayre.
                        Exit Messenger
How sweet the moone-light sleepes vpon this banke,
Heere will we sit, and let the sounds of musique
Creepe in our eares. Soft stilnes, and the night
Become the tutches of sweet harmonie:
Sit *Iessica*,
    ⌐They⌐ *sit*
            looke how the floore of heauen   2340
Is thick inlayed with pattens of bright gold,
There's not the smallest orbe which thou beholdst

But in his motion like an Angell sings,
Still quiring to the young eyde Cherubins;
Such harmonie is in immortall soules,
But whilst this muddy vesture of decay
Dooth grosly close it in, we cannot heare it:
⌐Enter Musicians⌐
(*To the Musicians*) Come hoe, and wake *Diana* with a
himne,
With sweetest tutches pearce your mistres eare,
2350   And draw her home with musique.
          play Musique
IESSICA
I am neuer merry when I heare sweet musique.
LORENZO
The reason is, your spirits are attentiue:
For doe but note a wild and wanton heard
Or race of youthfull and vnhandled colts
Fetching mad bounds, bellowing and neghing loude,
Which is the hote condition of their blood,
If they but heare perchance a trumpet sound,
Or any ayre of musique touch their eares,
You shall perceaue them make a mutuall stand,
2360   Their sauage eyes turn'd to a modest gaze,
By the sweet power of musique: therefore the Poet
Did faine that Orpheus drew trees, stones, and floods,
Since naught so stockish hard and full of rage,
But musique for the time doth change his nature.
The man that hath no musique in himselfe,
Nor is not moud with concord of sweet sounds,
Is fit for treasons, stratagems, and spoiles,
The motions of his spirit are dull as night,
And his affections darke as *Erebus*:
2370   Let no such man be trusted: marke the musique.
          Enter Portia and Nerrissa, as themselues
PORTIA
That light we see is burning in my hall:
How farre that little candell throwes his beames,
So shines a good deede in a naughty world.
NERRISSA
When the moone shone we did not see the candle.
PORTIA
So dooth the greater glory dim the lesse,
A substitute shines brightly as a King
Vntill a King be by, and then his state
Empties it selfe, as doth an inland brooke
Into the maine of waters: musique harke.
NERRISSA
2380   It is your musique Madame of the house.
PORTIA
Nothing is good I see without respect,
Me thinks it sounds much sweeter then by day.
NERRISSA
Silence bestowes that vertue on it Madam.
PORTIA
The Crow doth sing as sweetly as the Larke
When neither is attended: and I thinke
The Nightingale if she should sing by day
When euery Goose is cackling, would be thought

No better a Musition then the Renne.
How many things by season, seasond are
To their right prayse, and true perfection: 2390
          ⌐*She sees Lorenzo and Iessica*⌐
Peace, how
          ⌐*Musicke ceases*⌐
                    the moone sleepes with Endimion,
And would not be awak'd.
LORENZO ⌐*rising*⌐   That is the voyce,
Or I am much deceau'd of *Portia*.
PORTIA
He knowes me as the blind man knowes the Cuckoe
By the bad voyce.
LORENZO   Deere Lady welcome home.
PORTIA
We haue bin praying for our husbands welfare,
Which speed we hope the better for our words:
Are they return'd?
LORENZO   Madam, they are not yet:
But there is come a Messenger before
To signifie their comming.
PORTIA   Goe in *Nerrissa*.   2400
Giue order to my seruants, that they take
No note at all of our being absent hence,
Nor you *Lorenzo*, *Iessica* nor you.
          ⌐*A Tucket sounds*⌐
LORENZO
Your husband is at hand, I heare his trumpet,
We are no tell-tales Madame, feare you not.
PORTIA
This night me thinks is but the day light sicke,
It lookes a little paler, tis a day,
Such as the day is when the sunne is hid.
          Enter Bassanio, Anthonio, Gratiano, and their
          followers. Gratiano and Nerrissa speake apart
BASSANIO
We should hold day with the Antipodes,
If you would walke in absence of the sunne.   2410
PORTIA
Let me giue light, but let me not be light,
For a light wife doth make a heauie husband,
And neuer be *Bassanio* so for me,
But God sort all: you are welcome home my Lord.
BASSANIO
I thank you Madam, giue welcome to my friend,
This is the man, this is *Anthonio*,
To whom I am so infinitely bound.
PORTIA
You should in all sence be much bound to him,
For as I heare he was much bound for you.
ANTHONIO
No more then I am well acquitted of.   2420
PORTIA
Sir, you are very welcome to our house:
It must appeare in other wayes then words,
Therefore I scant this breathing curtesie.
GRATIANO (*to Nerrissa*)
By yonder moone I sweare you doe me wrong,

Infaith I gaue it to the Iudges Clarke,
Would he were gelt that had it for my part,
Since you doe take it Loue so much at hart.

PORTIA

A quarrell hoe already, what's the matter?

GRATIANO

About a hoope of gold, a paltry ring
2430 That she did giue me, whose posie was
For all the world like Cutlers poetry
Vpon a knife, *Loue me, and leaue me not.*

NERRISSA

What talke you of the posie or the valew:
You swore to me when I did giue it you,
That you would weare it till your houre of death,
And that it should lie with you in your graue,
Though not for me, yet for your vehement oathes,
You should haue beene respectiue and haue kept it.
Gaue it a Iudges Clarke: no Gods my Iudge
2440 The Clarke will nere weare haire ons face that had it.

GRATIANO

He will, and if he liue to be a man.

NERRISSA

I, if a woman liue to be a man.

GRATIANO

Now by this hand I gaue it to a youth,
A kind of boy, a little scrubbed boy,
No higher then thy selfe, the Iudges Clarke,
A prating boy that begd it as a fee,
I could not for my hart deny it him.

PORTIA

You were to blame, I must be plaine with you,
To part so slightly with your wiues first gift,
2450 A thing stuck on with oaths vpon your finger,
And so riueted with faith vnto your flesh.
I gaue my Loue a ring, and made him sweare
Neuer to part with it, and heere he stands:
I dare be sworne for him he would not leaue it,
Nor pluck it from his finger, for the wealth
That the world maisters. Now in faith *Gratiano*
You giue your wife too vnkind a cause of griefe,
And twere to me I should be mad at it.

BASSANIO (*aside*)

Why I were best to cut my left hand off,
2460 And sweare I lost the ring defending it.

GRATIANO ⌈*to Portia*⌉

My Lord *Bassanio* gaue his ring away
Vnto the Iudge that begd it, and indeede
Deseru'd it to: and then the boy his Clarke
That tooke some paines in writing, he begd mine,
And neither man nor maister would take ought
But the two rings.

PORTIA (*to Bassanio*) What ring gaue you my Lord?
Not that I hope which you receau'd of me.

BASSANIO

If I could add a lie vnto a fault,
I would deny it: but you see my finger
2470 Hath not the ring vpon it, it is gone.

PORTIA

Euen so voyd is your false hart of truth.
By heauen I will nere come in your bed
Vntill I see the ring.

NERRISSA (*to Gratiano*) Nor I in yours
Till I againe see mine.

BASSANIO   Sweet *Portia*,
If you did know to whom I gaue the ring,
If you did know for whom I gaue the ring,
And would conceaue for what I gaue the ring,
And how vnwillingly I left the ring,
When naught would be accepted but the ring,
You would abate the strength of your displeasure.   2480

PORTIA

If you had knowne the vertue of the ring,
Or halfe her worthines that gaue the ring,
Or your owne honour to containe the ring,
You would not then haue parted with the ring:
What man is there so much vnreasonable
If you had pleasd to haue defended it
With any termes of zeale: wanted the modesty
To vrge the thing held as a ceremonie:
Nerrissa teaches me what to beleeue,
Ile die for't, but some woman had the ring.   2490

BASSANIO

No by my honour Madam, by my soule
No woman had it, but a ciuill Doctor,
Which did refuse three thousand ducats of me,
And begd the ring, the which I did denie him,
And sufferd him to goe displeasd away,
Euen he that had held vp the very life
Of my deere friend. What should I say sweet Lady,
I was inforc'd to send it after him,
I was beset with shame and curtesie,
My honour would not let ingratitude   2500
So much besmere it: pardon me good Lady,
For by these blessed candels of the night,
Had you been there, I think you would haue begd
The ring of me to giue the worthy Doctor.

PORTIA

Let not that Doctor ere come neere my house
Since he hath got the iewell that I loued,
And that which you did sweare to keepe for me,
I will become as liberall as you,
Ile not deny him any thing I haue,
No, not my body, nor my husbands bed: 2510
Know him I shall, I am well sure of it.
Lie not a night from home. Watch me like Argos,
If you doe not, if I be left alone,
Now by mine honour which is yet mine owne,
Ile haue that Doctor for my bedfellow.

NERRISSA (*to Gratiano*)

And I his Clark: therefore be well aduisd
How you doe leaue me to mine owne protection.

GRATIANO

Well doe you so: let not me take him then,
For if I doe, ile mar the young Clarks pen.

ANTHONIO

2520　　I am th'vnhappy subiect of these quarrells.

PORTIA

Sir, greeue not you, you are welcome notwithstanding.

BASSANIO

Portia, forgiue me this enforced wrong,
And in the hearing of these many friends
I sweare to thee, euen by thine owne faire eyes
Wherein I see my selfe.

PORTIA　　　　　　　　　　Marke you but that?
In both my eyes he doubly sees himselfe:
In each eye one, sweare by your double selfe,
And there's an oath of credite.

BASSANIO　　　　　　　　　Nay, but heare me.
Pardon this fault, and by my soule I sweare

2530　　I neuer more will breake an oath with thee.

ANTHONIO (*to Portia*)

I once did lend my body for his wealth,
Which but for him that had your husbands ring
Had quite miscaried. I dare be bound againe,
My soule vpon the forfet, that your Lord
Will neuer more breake faith aduisedly.

PORTIA

Then you shall be his surety: giue him this,
And bid him keepe it better then the other.

ANTHONIO

Here Lord *Bassanio*, sweare to keepe this ring.

BASSANIO

By heauen it is the same I gaue the Doctor.

PORTIA

2540　　I had it of him: pardon me *Bassanio*,
For by this ring the Doctor lay with me.

NERRISSA

And pardon me my gentle *Gratiano*,
For that same scrubbed boy the Doctors Clarke
In liew of this, last night did lie with me.

GRATIANO

Why this is like the mending of high wayes
In Sommer where the wayes are faire enough?
What, are we cuckolds ere we haue deseru'd it.

PORTIA

Speake not so grosly, you are all amaz'd;
Heere is a letter, reade it at your leasure,

2550　　It comes from Padua from *Bellario*,
There you shall finde that *Portia* was the Doctor,
Nerrissa there her Clarke. *Lorenzo* heere
Shall witnes I set foorth as soone as you,

And euen but now returnd: I haue not yet
Enterd my house. *Anthonio* you are welcome,
And I haue better newes in store for you
Than you expect: vnseale this letter soone,
There you shall finde three of your Argosies
Are richly come to harbour sodainly.
You shall not know by what strange accident　　2560
I chaunced on this letter.

ANTHONIO　　　　　　　　I am dumb?

BASSANIO (*to Portia*)

Were you the Doctor, and I knew you not?

GRATIANO (*to Nerrissa*)

Were you the Clark that is to make me cuckold.

NERRISSA

I but the Clarke that neuer meanes to doe it,
Vnlesse he liue vntill he be a man.

BASSANIO (*to Portia*)

(Sweet Doctor) you shall be my bedfellow,
When I am absent then lie with my wife.

ANTHONIO (*to Portia*)

(Sweet Lady) you haue giuen me life and lyuing;
For heere I reade for certaine that my ships
Are safely come to Rode.

PORTIA　　　　　　　　How now *Lorenzo*?　　2570
My Clarke hath some good comforts to for you.

NERRISSA

I, and ile giue them him without a fee.
There doe I giue to you and *Iessica*
From the rich Iewe, a speciall deede of gift
After his death, of all he dies possest of.

LORENZO

Faire Ladies, you drop Manna in the way
Of starued people.

PORTIA　　　　　　　It is almost morning,
And yet I am sure you are not satisfied
Of these euents at full. Let vs goe in,
And charge vs there vpon intergotories,　　　　2580
And we will aunswer all things faithfully.

GRATIANO

Let it be so, the first intergotory
That my *Nerrissa* shall be sworne on, is,
Whether till the next night she had rather stay,
Or goe to bed now being two houres to day:
But were the day come, I should wish it darke
Till I were couching with the Doctors Clarke.
Well, while I liue, ile feare no other thing
So sore, as keeping safe *Nerrissas* ring.　　*Exeunt*

FINIS

1 HENRY IV

THE play described in the 1623 Folio as *The First Part of Henry the Fourth* had been entered on the Stationers' Register on 25 February 1598 as 'The historye of Henry the iiij^th', and that is the title of the first surviving edition, of the same year. An earlier edition, doubtless also printed in 1598, is known only from a single, eight-page fragment. Five more editions appeared before the Folio.

The printing of at least two editions within a few months, and the fact that one of them was read almost out of existence, reflect a matter of exceptional topical interest. The earliest title-page advertises the play's portrayal of '*the humorous conceits of Sir* Iohn Falstalffe'; but when it was first acted, probably in 1596, this character bore the name of his historical counterpart, the Protestant martyr Sir John Oldcastle. Shakespeare changed his surname as the result of protests from Oldcastle's descendants, the influential Cobham family, one of whom—William Brooke, 7th Lord Cobham—was Elizabeth I's Lord Chamberlain from August 1596 till he died on 5 March 1597. Our edition restores Sir Iohn's original surname for the first time in printed texts (though there is reason to believe that even after 1596 the name 'Olde-castle' was sometimes used on the stage).

Shakespeare had already shown Henry IV's rise to power, and his troubled state of mind on achieving power, in *Richard II*; that play also shows Henry's dissatisfaction with his wayward son, Prince Harry, later Henry V. *1 Henry IV* continues the story, but in a very different dramatic style. A play called *The Famous Victories of Henry the fifth*, entered in the Stationers' Register in 1594, was published anonymously, in a debased and shortened text, in 1598. This text—which also features Oldcastle as a reprobate—gives a sketchy version of the events portrayed in *1* and *2 Henry IV* and *Henry V*. Shakespeare must have known the original play, but in the absence of a full text we cannot tell how much he depended on it. The surviving version contains nothing about the rebellions against Henry IV, for which Shakespeare seems to have gone to Holinshed's, and perhaps other, *Chronicles*; he draws also on Samuel Daniel's poem *The First Fowre Bookes of the Ciuile Wars* (1595).

1 Henry IV is the first of Shakespeare's history plays to make extensive use of the techniques of comedy. On a national level, the play shows the continuing problems of Henry Bullingbrooke, insecure in his hold on the throne, and the victim of rebellions led by Worcester, Hotspur (Harry Percy), and Glendower. These scenes are counterpointed by others, written mainly in prose, which, in the manner of a comic sub-plot, provide humorous diversion while also reflecting and extending the concerns of the main plot. Henry suffers not only public insurrection but the personal rebellion of Prince Harry, in his unprincely exploits with the reprobate old knight, Olde-castle. Sir Iohn has become Shakespeare's most famous comic character, but Shakespeare shows that the Prince's treatment of him as a surrogate father who must eventually be abandoned has an intensely serious side.

The play seems to have been printed from a scribal transcript; for most of the text we are dependent on the 1598 reprint, which is even further from Shakespeare's own incidentals.

THE NAMES OF THE ACTORS

KING Henry the fourth

PRINCE HARRY, Prince of Wales,
   familiarly known as Hal

Lord Iohn of LANCASTER

Earle of WESTMERLAND

Sir Walter BLUNT

} King Henrys sonnes

Earle of WORCESTER

Percy, Earle of NORTHUMBERLAND, his brother

Henry Percy, knowne as HOTSPUR,
   Northumberlands sonne

Kate, LADY PERCY, Hotspurs wife

Lord Edmund MORTIMER, called Earle of March,
   Lady Percies brother

LADY MORTIMER, his wife

Owen GLENDOWER, Lady Mortimers father

Earle of DOUGLAS

Sir Richard VERNON

Scroope, ARCHBISHOP of Yorke

SIR MIGHELL, a member of the Archbishops
   houshould

} Rebels
against
King Henry

SIR IOHN Olde-castle

Yedward (Ned) POINES

ROSSILL

HARUEY

Mistris Quickly, HOSTESSE of a tauern in
   Eastcheape

FRANCES, a Drawer

VINTNER

} Associates
of Prince
Harry

GADSHILL

CARRIERS

CHAMBERLAINE

OSTLER

TRAUAILERS

SHERIFFE

MESSENGERS

SERUANT

Lords, Souldiors

510

The Hystorie of Henry the fourth

Sc. 1
(1.1)

Enter the King, Lord Iohn of Lancaster, Earle of
Westmerland, with other ⌐lords⌐

KING

So shaken as we are, so wan with care,
Find we a time for frighted peace to pant,
And breath short winded accents of new broiles
To be commencte in stronds a far remote:
No more the thirsty entrance of this soile
Shal dawbe her lips with her own childrens bloud,
No more shall trenching war channel her fields,
Nor bruise her flourets with the armed hoofes
Of hostile paces: those opposed eies,
10 Which like the meteors of a troubled heauen,
Al of one nature, of one substance bred,
Did lately meete in the intestine shocke
And furious close of ciuill butcherie,
Shall now in mutuall welbeseeming rankes,
March all one way, and be no more oppos'd
Against acquaintance, kindred and allyes.
The edge of war, like an ill sheathed knife,
No more shall cut his maister: therefore friends,
As far as to the sepulcher of Christ,
20 Whose soldiour now, vnder whose blessed crosse
We are impressed and ingag'd to fight,
Forthwith a power of English shall we leauy,
Whose armes were moulded in their mothers wombe,
To chase these pagans in those holy fields,
Ouer whose acres walkt those blessed feet,
Which 1400. yeares ago were naild,
For our aduantage on the bitter crosse.
But this our purpose now is twelue month old,
And bootelesse tis to tell you we wil go.
30 Therefore we meet not nowe: then let me heare
Of you my gentle Cosen Westmerland,
What yesternight our counsell did decree
In forwarding this deere expedience.

WESTMERLAND

My liege, this haste was hot in question,
And many limits of the charge set down
But yesternight, when all athwart there came
A post from Wales, loden with heauy newes,
Whose worst was that the noble Mortimer,
Leading the men of Herfordshire to fight
40 Against the irregular, and wild Glendower,
Was by the rude hands of that Welchman taken,
A thousand of his people butchered,
Vpon whose dead corpes there was such misuse,
Such beastly shamelesse transformation
By those Welch-women done, as may not be
Without much shame, retould, or spoken of.

KING

It seemes then that the tidings of this broile,
Brake off our businesse for the holy land.

WESTMERLAND

This matcht with other did, my gratious L.
50 For more vneuen and vnwelcome newes
Came from the North, and thus it did import,
On holly rode day, the gallant Hotspur there,
Yong Harry Percy, and braue Archibold,
That euer valiant and approued Scot,
At Holmedon met,
Where they did spend a sad and bloudy houre:
As by discharge of their artillery,
And shape of likelihood the newes was told:
For he that brought them in the very heat
60 And pride of their contention, did take horse
Vncertaine of the issue any way.

KING

Here is a deere, a true industrious friend,
Sir Walter Blunt new lighted from his horse,
Staind with the variation of each soile,
Betwixt that Holmedon and this seat of ours:
And he hath brought vs smothe and welcom newes,
The Earle of *Douglas* is discomfited,
Ten thousand bould Scots, two and twenty knights
Balkt in their own bloud did sir Walter see
70 On Holmedons plaines, of prisoners Hotspur tooke
Mordake the Earle of Fife, and eldest sonne
To beaten Douglas, and the Earle of Athol,
Of Murrey, Angus, and Menteith:
And is not this an honorable spoile?
A gallant prize? Ha coosen, is it not?

WESTMERLAND

In faith it is a conquest for a Prince to boast of.

KING

Yea, there thou makst me sad, and makst me sinne
In enuy, that my Lord Northumberland
Should be the father to so blest a sonne:
80 A sonne, who is the theame of honors tongue,
Amongst a groue, the very straightest plant,
Who is sweet fortunes minion and her pride,
Whilst I by looking on the praise of him
See ryot and dishonour staine the brow
Of my young Harry. O that it could be prou'd
That some night tripping fairy had exchang'd,
In cradle clothes our children where they lay,
And cald mine Percy, his Plantagenet,
Then would I haue his Harry, and he mine:
90 But let him from my thoughts. What think you coose
Of this young Percies pride? The prisoners
Which he in this aduenture hath surprizd
To his own vse he keepes, and sends me word
I shal haue none but Mordake Earle of Fife.

WESTMERLAND

This is his vncles teaching. This is Worcester,
Maleuolent to you in all aspects,

Which makes him prune himselfe, and bristle vp
The crest of youth against your dignity.

KING

But I haue sent for him to answere this:
100 And for this cause a while we must neglect
Our holy purpose to Ierusalem.
Coosen on wednesday next our councel we
Wil hold at Windsore, so informe the Lords:
But come your selfe with speed to vs againe,
For more is to be said and to be done,
Then out of anger can be vttered.

WESTMERLAND I will my liege.

Exeunt ⌈the King, Lancaster, and other lords at
one doore, Westmerland at another doore⌉

Sc. 2   *Enter prince of Wales, and Sir Iohn Olde-castle*
(1.2)   SIR IOHN Now *Hal,* what time of day is it lad?

PRINCE Thou art so fat-witted with drinking of olde sacke,
110   and vnbuttoning thee after supper, and sleeping vpon
benches after noone; that thou hast forgotten to
demaunde that truelie which thou wouldest trulie
knowe. What a diuell hast thou to do with the time of
the daie? vnles houres were cups of sacke, and minutes
capons, and clockes the tongues of Baudes, and Dialles
the signes of leaping houses, and the blessed sunne
himselfe a faire hot wench in flame-couloured taffata,
I see no reason why thou shouldst be so superfluous
to demaunde the time of the day.

120   SIR IOHN Indeede you come neere me nowe *Hal,* for wee
that take purses go by the moone and the seuen stars,
and not by *Phœbus,* he, that wandring knight so faire:
and I prethe sweet wag when thou art a king, as God
saue thy grace: maiestie I should say, for grace thou
wilt haue none.

PRINCE What none?

SIR IOHN No by my troth, not so much as will serue to
bee prologue to an egge and butter.

PRINCE Wel, how then? come roundly, roundly.

130   SIR IOHN Marry then sweet wag, when thou art king let
not vs that are squiers of the nights bodie, bee called
theeues of the daies beauty: let vs be *Dianaes* forresters,
gentlemen of the shade, minions of the moone, and let
men say wee be men of good gouernement, being
gouerned as the sea is, by our noble and chast mistresse
the moone, vnder whose countenaunce we steale.

PRINCE Thou saiest well, and it holds wel to, for the
fortune of vs that are the moones men, doth ebbe and
flow like the sea, being gouerned as the sea is by the
140   moone, as for proofe now. A purse of gold most
resolutely snatcht on Munday night and most
dissolutely spent on tuesday morning, got with
swearing, lay by, and spent with crying, bring in, now
in as low an ebbe as the foot of the ladder, and by and
by in as high a flow as the ridge of the gallowes.

SIR IOHN By the Lord thou saist true lad, and is not my
hostesse of the tauerne a most sweet wench?

PRINCE As the hony of *Hibla* my old lad of the castle, and
is not a buffe Ierkin a most sweet robe of durance?

SIR IOHN How now, how nowe mad wag, what in thy 150
quips and thy quiddities? what a plague haue I to doe
with a buffe Ierkin?

PRINCE Why what a poxe haue I to do with my hostesse
of the tauerne?

SIR IOHN Well, thou hast cald her to a reckoning many
a time and oft.

PRINCE Did I euer call for thee to pay thy part?

SIR IOHN No, ile giue thee thy due, thou hast paid all
there.

PRINCE Yea and else where, so far as my coine would 160
stretch, and where it would not, I haue vsed my credit.

SIR IOHN Yea, and so vs'd it that were it not here apparant
that thou art heire apparant. But I prethe sweet wag,
shall there be gallowes standing in England when thou
art king? and resolution thus fubd as it is with the
rusty curbe of olde father Anticke the law, do not thou
when thou art king hang a theefe.

PRINCE No, thou shalt.

SIR IOHN Shall I? O rare! by the Lord ile be a braue iudge.

PRINCE Thou iudgest false already, I meane thou shalt 170
haue the hanging of the theeues, and so become a rare
hangman.

SIR IOHN Well *Hall* well, and in some sort it iumpes with
my humour, as well as waighting in the Court I can
tell you.

PRINCE For obtaining of suites?

SIR IOHN Yea, for obtaining of suites, whereof the
hangman hath no leane wardrob. Zbloud I am as
melancholy as a gyb Cat, or a lugd beare.

PRINCE Or an old lyon, or a louers Lute. 180

SIR IOHN Yea, or the drone of a Lincolnshire bagpipe.

PRINCE What saiest thou to a Hare, or the malancholy of
Mooreditch?

SIR IOHN Thou hast the most vnsauory similes, and art
indeed the most comparatiue rascalliest sweet yong
Prince. But *Hal,* I prethe trouble me no more with
vanitie, I woulde to God thou and I knewe where a
commodity of good names were to be bought: an olde
Lorde of the councell rated me the other day in the
street about you sir, but I markt him not, and yet he 190
talkt very wisely, but I regarded him not, and yet hee
talkt wisely and in the street to.

PRINCE Thou didst well, for wisedome cries out in the
streets and no man regards it.

SIR IOHN O thou hast damnable iteration, and art indeed
able to corrupt a saint: thou hast done much harme
vpon me *Hal,* God forgiue thee for it: before I knewe
thee *Hal,* I knewe nothing, and now am I, if a man
should speake trulie, little better then one of the wicked:
I must giue ouer this life, and I will giue it ouer: by 200
the Lord and I doe not, I am a villaine, ile bee damnd
for neuer a kings sonne in Christendom.

PRINCE Where shal we take a purse to morrow Iacke?

SIR IOHN Zounds where thou wilt lad, ile make one, an I
do not call me villaine and baffell me.

PRINCE I see a good amendment of life in thee, from
praying to purse-taking.

SIR IOHN Why *Hall*, tis my vocation *Hall*, tis no sinne for
a man to labor in his vocation.

Enter Poines

210 Poynes: nowe shall we knowe if Gadshill haue set a
match. O if men were to be saued by merit, what hole
in hell were hot enough for him? this is the most
omnipotent villaine that euer cried, stand, to a true
man.

PRINCE Good morrow *Ned*.

POINES Good morrow sweete *Hal*. (*To sir Iohn*) What saies
Monsieur remorse? what saies sir Iohn, Sacke and
Sugar Iacke? howe agrees the Diuell and thee about
thy soule that thou souldest him on good friday last,
220 for a cup of Medera and a cold capons legge.

PRINCE Sir Iohn stands to his word, the diuell shall haue
his bargaine, for he was neuer yet a breaker of
prouerbes: he will giue the diuell his due.

POINES (*to sir Iohn*) Then art thou damnd for keeping thy
worde with the diuell.

PRINCE Else hee had bin damnd for coosening the diuell.

POINES But my lads, my lads, to morrow morning, by
foure a clocke early at Gadshill, there are pilgrims going
to Canturburie with rich offerings, and traders riding
230 to London with fat purses. I haue vizards for you al;
you haue horses for your selues, Gadshill lies to night
in Rochester, I haue bespoke supper to morrow night
in Eastcheape: we may do it as secure as sleepe, if you
will go I will stuffe your purses full of crownes: if you
will not, tarie at home and be hangd.

SIR IOHN Heare ye Yedward, if I tarry at home and go
not, ile hang you for going.

POINES You will chops.

SIR IOHN *Hal*, wilt thou make one?

240 PRINCE Who I rob, I a thiefe? not I by my faith.

SIR IOHN Theres neither honestie, manhood, nor good
fellowship in thee, nor thou camst not of the bloud
roiall, if thou darest not stand for ten shillings.

PRINCE Well then, once in my dayes ile be a madcap.

SIR IOHN Why thats well said.

PRINCE Well, come what wil, ile tarrie at home.

SIR IOHN By the lord, ile be a traitor then, when thou art
king.

PRINCE I care not.

250 POINES Sir Iohn, I preethe leaue the prince and mee alone,
I will lay him downe such reasons for this aduenture
that he shall go.

SIR IOHN Well God giue thee the spirit of perswasion, and
him the eares of profiting, that what thou speakest,
may moue, and what he heares, may be beleeued, that
the true prince may (for recreation sake) proue a false
thiefe, for the poore abuses of the time want
countenance: farewel, you shal find me in Eastcheap.

PRINCE Farewel the latter spring, farewel Alhallowne
260 summer.   *Exit sir Iohn*

POINES Now my good sweete hony Lord, ride with vs to
morrow. I haue a ieast to execute, that I cannot
mannage alone. Olde-castle, Haruey, Rossill, and
Gadshil, shal rob those men that we haue already way-
laid, your selfe and I will not bee there: and when they

haue the bootie, if you and I doe not rob them, cut
this head off from my shoulders.

PRINCE But how shall we part with them in setting forth?

POINES Why, we wil set forth before or after them, and
appoint them a place of meeting, wherein it is at our
270 pleasure to faile; and then wil they aduenture vpõ the
exploit themselues, which they shal haue no sooner
atchieued but weele set vpon them.

PRINCE I, but tis like that they wil know vs by our horses,
by our habits, and by euery other appointment to be
our selues.

POINES Tut, our horses they shal not see, ile tie them in
the wood, our vizards wee wil change after wee leaue
them: and sirrha, I haue cases of Buckrom for the
nonce, to immaske our noted outward garments.

280 PRINCE But I doubt they wil be too hard for vs.

POINES Wel, for two of them, I know them to bee as true
bred cowards as euer turnd backe: and for the third,
if he fight longer then he sees reason, ile forsweare
armes. The vertue of this ieast wil be the
incomprehensible lies, that this same fat rogue wil tel
vs when we meet at supper, how thirtie at least he
fought with, what wardes, what blowes, what
extremities he indured, and in the reproofe of this liues
the iest.

290 PRINCE Well, ile goe with thee, prouide vs all thinges
necessarie, and meete me to morrow night in
Eastcheape, there ile sup: farewell.

POINES Farewel my Lord.   *Exit*

PRINCE

I know you all, and wil a while vphold
The vnyokt humour of your idlenes,
Yet herein wil I imitate the sunne,
Who doth permit the base contagious clouds
To smother vp his beautie from the world,
That when he please againe to be himselfe,
300 Being wanted he may be more wondred at
By breaking through the foule and ougly mists
Of vapours, that did seeme to strangle him.
If all the yeere were playing holly-dayes,
To sport would be as tedious as to worke;
But when they seldome come, they wisht for come,
And nothing pleaseth but rare accidents:
So when this loose behauiour I throw off,
And pay the debt I neuer promised,
By how much better then my word I am,
310 By so much shall I falsifie mens hopes,
And like bright mettal on a sullein ground,
My reformation glittring ore my fault,
Shal shew more goodly, and attract more eyes
Then that which hath no foile to set it off.
Ile so offend, to make offence a skill,
Redeeming time when men thinke least I wil.   *Exit*

Enter the King, Northumberland, Worcester,   Sc. 3
Hotspur, sir Walter blunt, with other ⌈lords⌉   (1.3)

KING (*to Hotspur, Northumberland and Worcester*)
My blood hath bin too colde and temperate,
Vnapt to stir at these indignities,

320 And you haue found me, for accordingly
You tread vpon my patience, but be sure
I will from henceforth rather be my selfe
Mightie, and to be fearde, then my condition
Which hath bin smooth as oile, soft as yong downe,
And therefore lost that title of respect,
Which the proud soule neare payes but to the proud.

WORCESTER
Our house (my soueraigne liege) little deserues
The scourge of greatnes to be vsd on it,
And that same greatnesse to, which our owne hands
Haue holpe to make so portly.

330 NORTHUMBERLAND (*to the king*)   My Lord.

KING
Worcester get thee gone, for I do see
Danger, and disobedience in thine eie:
O sir, your presence is too bold and peremptorie,
And Maiestie might neuer yet endure
The moodie frontier of a seruant browe,
You haue good leaue to leaue vs, when we need
Your vse and counsel we shall send for you.

Exit Worcester

You were about to speake.

NORTHUMBERLAND   Yea my good Lord.
Those prisoners in your highnes name demanded,
340 Which Harry Percy here at Holmedon tooke,
Were as he saies, not with such strength denied
As was deliured to your maiestie.
Who either through enuie or misprision,
Was guiltie of this fault, and not my sonne.

HOTSPUR (*to the king*)
My liege, I did denie no prisoners,
But I remember when the fight was done,
When I was drie with rage, and extreame toile,
Breathles and faint, leaning vpon my sword,
Came there a certaine Lord, neat and trimly drest,
350 Fresh as a bridegroome, and his chin new rept,
Shewd like a stubble land at haruest home,
He was perfumed like a Milliner,
And twixt his finger and his thumbe he helde
A pouncet boxe, which euer and anon
He gaue his nose, and tookt away againe,
Who therewith angry, when it next came there
Tooke it in snuffe, and still hee smild and talkt:
And as the souldiours bore dead bodies by,
He cald them vntaught knaues, vnmanerlie,
360 To bring a slouenly vnhandsome coarse
Betwixt the winde and his nobilitie:
With many holly-day and ladie termes
He questiond me, amongst the rest demanded
My prisoners in your Maiesties behalfe.
I then, all smarting with my wounds being cold,
To be so pestred with a Popingay,
Out of my griefe and my impacience
Answerd neglectingly, I know not what
He should, or should not, for he made me mad
370 To see him shine so briske, and smell so sweet,
And talke so like a waiting gentlewoman,

Of guns, and drums, and wounds, God saue the mark:
And telling me the soueraignst thing on earth
Was Parmacitie, for an inward bruise,
And that it was great pitty, so it was,
This villanous saltpeeter, should be digd
Out of the bowels of the harmeles earth,
Which many a good tall fellow had destroyed
So cowardly, and but for these vile guns
He would himselfe haue beene a souldior.   380
This bald vnioynted chat of his (my Lord)
Made me to answere indirectly (as I said)
And I beseech you, let not his report
Come currant for an accusation
Betwixt my loue and your high maiestie.

BLUNT (*to the king*)
The circumstance considred, good my lord,
What ere Lord *Harry Percie* then had said
To such a person, and in such a place,
At such a time, with all the rest retold,
May reasonably die, and neuer rise   390
To do him wrong, or any way impeach
What then he said, so he vnsay it now.

KING
Why yet he doth denie his prisoners,
But with prouiso and exception,
That we at our owne charge shall ransome straight
His brother in law, the foolish Mortimer,
Who on my soule, hath wilfully betraid
The liues of those, that he did lead to fight
Against that great Magitian, damnd Glendower,
Whose daughter as we heare, the Earle of March   400
Hath lately married: shall our coffers then
Be emptied, to redeeme a traitor home?
Shall we buy treason? and indent with feares
When they haue lost and forfeited themselues?
No, on the barren mountaines let him starue:
For I shall neuer hold that man my friend,
Whose tongue shall aske me for one penny cost
To ransome home reuolted Mortimer,

HOTSPUR Reuolted Mortimer:
He neuer did fall off, my soueraigne liege   410
But by the chance of war, to proue that true
Needs no more but one tongue: for all those wounds,
Those mouthed wounds which valiantly he tooke,
When on the gentle Seuerns siedgie banke,
In single opposition hand to hand,
He did confound the best part of an houre,
In changing hardiment with great Glendower,
Three times they breathd, & three times did they drinke
Vpon agreement of swift Seuerns floud,
Who then affrighted with their bloudie lookes,   420
Ran fearefully among the trembling reedes,
And hid his crispe-head in the hollow banke,
Bloud-stained with these valiant combatants,
Neuer did bare and rotten pollicy
Colour her working with such deadly wounds,
Nor neuer could the noble Mortimer

Receiue so many, and all willingly,
Then let not him be slandred with reuolt.

KING

430 Thou dost bely him Percy, thou dost bely him,
He neuer did encounter with Glendower: I tel thee,
He durst as well haue met the diuell alone,
As Owen Glendower for an enemy.
Art thou not asham'd? but sirrha, henceforth
Let me not heare you speake of Mortimer:
Send me your prisoners with the speediest meanes,
Or you shal heare in such a kind from me
As will displease you. My Lord Northumberland:
We licence your departure with your sonne,
(*To Hotspur*) Send vs your prisoners, or youle heare of it.
    Exeunt King, Blunt and ⌈lords⌉: manent Hotspur
            and Northumberland

HOTSPUR

440 And if the diuel come and rore for them
I wil not send them: I will after straight
And tel him so, for I will ease my hart,
Although it be with hazard of my head.

NORTHUMBERLAND

What? dronk with choler, stay, & pause a while,
    Enter Worcester
Here comes your vncle.

HOTSPUR   Speake of Mortimer?
Zounds I will speake of him, and let my soule
Want mercy if I do not ioine with him:
In his behalfe, ile empty all these vaines,
And shed my deere bloud, drop by drop in the dust,
450 But I will lift the downfall Mortimer
As high in the aire as this vnthankefull king,
As this ingrate and cankred Bullingbrooke.

NORTHUMBERLAND (*to Worcester*)

Brother, the king hath made your nephew mad.

WORCESTER

Who strooke this heat vp after I was gone?

HOTSPUR

He wil forsooth haue all my prisoners,
And when I vrg'd the ransome once againe
Of my wiues brother, then his cheeke lookt pale,
And on my face he turn'd an eie of death,
Trembling euen at the name of Mortimer.

WORCESTER

460 I cannot blame him, was not he proclaim'd
By Richard that dead is, the next of bloud?

NORTHUMBERLAND

He was, I heard the proclamation:
And then it was, when the vnhappy king,
(Whose wrongs in vs God pardon) did set forth
Vpon his Irish expedition;
From whence he intercepted, did returne
To be depos'd, and shortly murdered.

WORCESTER

And for whose death, we in the worlds wide mouth
Liue scandaliz'd and fouly spoken of.

HOTSPUR

470 But soft, I pray you did king Richard then

Proclaime my brother Edmund Mortimer
Heire to the crowne?

NORTHUMBERLAND   He did, my selfe did heare it.

HOTSPUR

Nay then I cannot blame his coosen king,
That wisht him on the barren mountaines starue,
But shalit be that you that set the crowne
Vpon the head of this forgetful man,
And for his sake weare the detested blot
Of murtherous subornation? shal it be
That you a world of curses vndergo,
Being the agents, or base second meanes,   480
The cordes, the ladder, or the hangman rather,
O pardon me, that I descend so low,
To shew the line and the predicament,
Wherein you range vnder this subtil king!
Shall it for shame be spoken in these daies,
Or fil vp Chronicles in time to come,
That men of your nobility and power
Did gage them both in an vniust behalfe,
(As both of you God pardon it, haue done)
To put down Richard, that sweet louely Rose,   490
And plant this thorne, this canker Bullingbrooke?
And shal it in more shame be further spoken,
That you are foold, discarded, and shooke off
By him, for whom these shames ye vnderwent?
No, yet time serues, wherein you may redeeme
Your banisht honors, and restore your selues
Into the good thoughts of the world againe:
Reuenge the ieering and disdaind contempt
Of this proud king, who studies day and night
To answere all the debt he owes to you,   500
Euen with the bloudie paiment of your deaths:
Therefore I say.

WORCESTER   Peace coosen, say no more.
And now I will vnclaspe a secret booke,
And to your quicke conceiuing discontents
Ile reade you matter deepe and daungerous,
As full of perill and aduenterous spirit,
As to orewalke a Current roring lowd,
On the vnstedfast footing of a speare.

HOTSPUR

If he fall in, god-night, or sinke, or swim.
Send danger from the East vnto the West,   510
So honor crosse it, from the North to South,
And let them grapple: O the bloud more stirs
To rouse a lyon than to start a hare.

NORTHUMBERLAND (*to Worcester*)

Imagination of some great exploit
Driues him beyond the bounds of patience.

⌈**HOTSPUR**⌉

By heauen me thinkes it were an easie leape,
To plucke bright honor from the pale fac't moone,
Or diue into the bottome of the deepe,
Where fadome line could neuer touch the ground,
And plucke vp drowned honor by the locks,   520
So he that doth redeeme her thence might weare
Without corriuall all her dignities,
But out vpon this halfe fac't fellowship.

WORCESTER (*to Northumberland*)
> He apprehends a world of figures here,
> But not the forme of what he should attend,
> (*To Hotspur*) Good coosen giue me audience for a while,
> And list to me.

HOTSPUR
> I cry you mercy.

WORCESTER   Those same noble Scots
> That are your prisoners.

HOTSPUR   Ile keepe them all;
530 By God he shal not haue a Scot of them,
> No, if a Scot would saue his soule he shal not,
> Ile keepe them by this hand.

WORCESTER   You start away,
> And lend no eare vnto my purposes:
> Those prisoners you shal keepe.

HOTSPUR   Nay I wil, thats flat:
> He said he would not ransome Mortimer,
> Forbad my tongue to speake of Mortimer,
> But I wil find him when he lies asleepe,
> And in his eare ile hollow Mortimer:
> Nay, ile haue a starling shalbe taught to speake
540 Nothing but Mortimer, and giue it him
> To keepe his anger stil in motion.

WORCESTER Heare you cosen a word.

HOTSPUR
> All studies here I sollemnly defie,
> Saue how to gall and pinch this Bullingbrooke,
> And that same sword and buckler prince of Wales,
> But that I thinke his father loues him not,
> And would be glad he met with some mischance:
> I would haue him poisond with a pot of ale.

WORCESTER
> Farewel kinsman, ile talke to you
550 When you are better temperd to attend.

NORTHUMBERLAND (*to Hotspur*)
> Why what a waspe-stung and impatient foole
> Art thou, to breake into this womans moode,
> Tying thine eare to no tongue but thine owne.

HOTSPUR
> Why looke you? I am whipt and scourgd with rods,
> Netled, and stung with pismires, when I heare
> Of this vile polititian Bullingbrooke,
> In Richards time, what de'ye cal the place?
> A plague vpon't, it is in Glocestershire;
> Twas where the mad-cap duke his vnckle kept,
560 His vncle Yorke, where I first bowed my knee
> Vnto this king of smiles, this Bullingbrooke:
> Zbloud, when you and he came backe from
>   Rauenspurgh.

NORTHUMBERLAND
> At Barkly castle.

HOTSPUR   You say true.
> Why what a candy deale of curtesie,
> This fawning greyhound then did proffer me,
> Looke when his infant fortune came to age,
> And gentle Harry Percy, and kind coosen:

O the diuel take such coosoners, god forgiue me,
> Good vncle tel your tale, I haue done.

WORCESTER
> Nay, if you haue not, to't againe,   570
> Weele stay your leisure.

HOTSPUR   I haue done Ifaith.

WORCESTER
> Then once more to your Scottish prisoners,
> Deliuer them vp without their ransome straight,
> And make the Douglas sonne your onely meane
> For Powers in Scotland, which for diuers reasons
> Which I shal send you written, be assur'd
> Wil easely be granted. (*To Northumberland*) You my
>   Lord,
> Your sonne in Scotland being thus emploied,
> Shal secretly into the bosome creepe
> Of that same noble Prelat wel belou'd,   580
> The Archbishop.

HOTSPUR   Of Yorke, ist not?

WORCESTER   True, who beares hard
> His brothers death at Bristow the lord Scroop,
> I speake not this in estimation,
> As what I thinke might be, but what I know
> Is ruminated, plotted, and set downe,
> And onely stayes but to behold the face
> Of that occasion that shal bring it on.

HOTSPUR
> I smell it. Vpon my life it will do well.

NORTHUMBERLAND
> Before the game is afoote thou still letst slip.

HOTSPUR
> Why, it cannot chuse but be a noble plot,   590
> And then the power of Scotland, and of Yorke,
> To ioyne with Mortimer, ha.

WORCESTER   And so they shall,

HOTSPUR
> In faith it is exceedingly well, aimd.

WORCESTER
> And tis no little reason bids vs speed,
> To saue our heades by raising of a head,
> For beare our selues as euen as we can,
> The king will alwayes thinke him in our debt,
> And thinke we thinke our selues vnsatisfied,
> Till he hath found a time to pay vs home,
> And see alreadie how he doth begin   600
> To make vs strangers to his lookes of loue.

HOTSPUR
> He does, he does, weele be reuengd on him.

WORCESTER
> Coosen farewell. No further go in this,
> Then I by letters shall direct your course.
> When time is ripe, which will be suddenly,
> Ile steale to Glendower, and Lo: Mortimer,
> Where you and Douglas, and our powers at once,
> As I will fashion it shall happily meete,
> To beare our fortunes in our owne strong armes,
> Which now we hold at much vncertaintie.   610

NORTHUMBERLAND

    Farewell good brother, we shall thriue I trust.

HOTSPUR (*to Worcester*)

    Vncle adieu: O let the houres be short,

    Till fields, and blowes, and grones, applaud our sport.

                Exeunt ⌜Worcester at one doore,

      Northumberland and Hotspur at another doore⌝

Sc. 4   *Enter a Carrier with a lanterne in his hand*

(2.1) 1 CARRIER Heigh ho. Ant be not foure by the day ile be

    hangd, Charles-waine is ouer the new Chimney, and

    yet our horse not packt. What Ostler.

OSTLER (*within*) Anon, anon.

1 CARRIER I preethe Tom beat Cuts saddle, put a few

    flockes in the point, poore iade is wroong in the withers,

620   out of all cesse.

        Enter another Carier

2 CARRIER Pease and beanes are as danke here as a dog,

    and that is the next way to giue poore iades the bottes:

    this house is turned vpside downe since Robin Ostler

    died.

1 CARRIER Poore fellow neuer ioyed since the prise of

    Oates rose, it was the death of him.

2 CARRIER I thinke this bee the most villainous house in

    all London road for fleas, I am stung like a Tench.

1 CARRIER Like a Tench, by the Masse there is nere a

630   King christen could be better bit then I haue bin since

    the first cocke.

2 CARRIER Why, they will allowe vs nere a Iordan, and

    then we leake in your Chimney, and your chamber-lie

    breedes fleas like a loach.

1 CARRIER What Ostler, come away and be hangd, come

    away.

2 CARRIER I haue a gammon of bacon, and two razes of

    Ginger, to be deliuered as farre as Charing Crosse.

1 CARRIER Gods bodie, the Turkies in my Panier are quite

640   starued: what Ostler? a plague on thee, hast thou

    neuer an eie in thy heade? canst not heare, and twere

    not as good deed as drinke to break the pate on thee,

    I am a verie villain, come and be hangd, hast no faith

    in thee?

        Enter Gadshill

GADSHILL Good morrow Cariers, whats a clocke?

1 CARRIER I thinke it be two a clocke.

GADSHILL I preethe lend me thy lanterne, to see my

    gelding in the stable.

1 CARRIER Nay by God soft, I knowe a trike worth two

650   of that I fayth.

GADSHILL (*to 2 Carrier*) I pray thee lend me thine.

2 CARRIER I when canst tell? lend mee thy lanterne (quoth

    a) marry ile see thee hangd first.

GADSHILL Sirrha Carrier, what time do you meane to

    come to London?

2 CARRIER Time enough to go to bed with a candle, I

    warrant thee, come neighbour Mugs, weele call vp the

    Gentlemen, they will along with companie, for they

    haue great charge.   *Exeunt Carriers*

660 GADSHILL What ho: Chamberlaine.

        Enter Chamberlaine

CHAMBERLAINE At hand quoth pickepurse.

GADSHILL Thats euen as faire as at hand quoth the

    Chamberlaine: for thou variest no more from picking

    of purses, then giuing direction doth from labouring:

    thou layest the plot how.

CHAMBERLAINE Good morrow maister Gadshil, it holdes

    currant that I tolde you yesternight, ther's a Frankelin

    in the wild of Kent hath brought three hundred Markes

    with him in golde, I heard him tell it to one of his

    companie last night at supper, a kinde of Auditor, one 670

    that hath abundance of charge too, God knowes what,

    they are vp alreadie, and call for Egges and Butter,

    they will away presently.

GADSHILL Sirrha, if they meete not with Saint Nicholas

    clearkes, ile giue thee this necke.

CHAMBERLAINE No, ile none of it, I pray thee keepe that

    for the hangman, for I know thou worshippest Saine

    Nicholas, as trulie as a man of falshood may.

GADSHILL What talkest thou to me of the hãgman? if I

    hang, ile make a fat paire of Gallowes: for if I hang, 680

    olde sir Iohn hangs with me, and thou knowest hees

    no starueling: tut, there are other Troyans that thou

    dreamst not of, the which for sport sake are content to

    do the profession, some grace, that would (if matters

    should be lookt into) for their owne credit sake make

    all whole. I am ioyned with no foot landrakers, no

    long-staffe sixpennie strikers, none of these mad

    mustachio purplehewd maltworms, but with nobilitie,

    & tranquilitie, Burgomasters & great Oiezres, such as

    can hold in, such as wil strike sooner then speak, and 690

    speake sooner then drinke, and drinke sooner then

    pray, and yet (zoundes) I lie, for they pray continually

    to their Saint the Common-wealth, or rather not pray

    to her, but pray on her, for they ride vp and downe

    on her, and make her their bootes.

CHAMBERLAINE What, the Common-wealth their bootes?

    will shee hold out water in foule way?

GADSHILL She will, she will, Iustice hath liquord her: wee

    steale as in a Castell cocksure: we haue the receyte of

    Ferneseede, wee walke inuisible. 700

CHAMBERLAINE Nay by my faith, I thinke you are more

    beholding to the night then to Ferneseed, for your

    walking inuisible.

GADSHILL Giue me thy hand, thou shalt haue a share in

    our purchase, as I am a true man.

CHAMBERLAINE Nay rather let me haue it, as you are a

    false theefe.

GADSHILL Go to, *homo* is a common name to al men: bid

    the Ostler bring my gelding out of the stable, farewell

    you muddye knaue.   *Exeunt ⌜seuerally⌝* 710

    Enter Prince, Poynes, Haruey, ⌜Rossill⌝   **Sc. 5**

POINES Come shelter, shelter,   **(2.2)**

        ⌜Exeunt Haruey and Rossill at another doore⌝

    I haue remoude Olde-castles horse, and he frets like a

    gumd Veluet.

PRINCE Stand close.   ⌜*Exit Poynes*⌝

Enter sir Iohn Olde-castle

SIR IOHN Poynes, Poynes, and be hangd Poynes.

PRINCE Peace yee fat-kidneyd rascall, what a brawling dost thou keepe?

SIR IOHN Wheres Poynes, Hall?

PRINCE He is walkt vp to the top of the hill, Ile go seeke him.   ⌐Exit⌐

720

SIR IOHN I am accurst to rob in that theeues companie, the rascall hath remooued my horse, and tied him I know not where, if I trauell but foure foote by the squire further a foote, I shall breake my winde. Well, I doubt not but to die a faire death for all this, if I scape hanging for killing that rogue. I haue forsworne his companie hourly any time this xxii: yeares, and yet I am bewitcht with the rogues companie. If the rascall haue not giuen mee medicines to make me loue

730

him, ile be hangd. It could not be else, I haue drunke medicines. Poynes, Hall, a plague vpon you both. Rossill, Haruey, ile starue ere ile robbe a foote further, and twere not as good a deed as drinke to turne true-man, and to leaue these rogues, I am the veriest varlet that euer chewed with a tooth: Eight yeards of vneuen ground is threescore and ten myles a foote with mee, and the stonie hearted villiaines knowe it well enough, a plague vpon't when theeues cannot be true one to another.

They whistle. ⌐Enter Prince, Poynes, Haruey, Rossill⌐

740

Whew, a plague vpon you all, giue mee my horse you rogues, giue me my horse and be hangd.

PRINCE Peace yee fatte guts, lie downe, lay thine eare close to the grounde, and list if thou canst heare the treade of trauaylers.

SIR IOHN Haue you any leauers to lift me vp againe being down, zbloud ile not beare my owne flesh so farre a foote againe for all the coyne in thy fathers Exchequer: What a plague meane ye to colt me thus?

PRINCE Thou liest, thou art not colted, thou art vncolted.

750

SIR IOHN I preethe good prince, Hall, helpe me to my horse, good kings sonne.

PRINCE Out ye rogue, shall I be your Ostler?

SIR IOHN Hang thy selfe in thine owne heire apparant garters, if I be tane, ile peach for this: and I haue not Ballads made on you all, and sung to filthie tunes, let a cuppe of Sacke bee my poyson, when a ieast is so forward, and a foote too I hate it.

Enter Gadshill, ⌐vizarded⌐

GADSHILL Stand.

SIR IOHN So I do against my will.

760

POINES O tis our setter, I knowe his voice. Gadshill, what newes.

⌐GADSHILL⌐ Case ye, case yee on with your vizardes, theres mony of the kings comming downe the hill, tis going tothe kinges Exchequer.

SIR IOHN You lie, ye rogue, tis going to the kings tauerne.

GADSHILL Theres enough to make vs all.

SIR IOHN To be hangd.

⌐They put on vizardes⌐

PRINCE Sirs, you foure shall front them in the narrowe

lane: Ned Poynes and I will walke lower, if they scape from your encounter, then they light on vs.   770

HARUEY How many be there of them?

GADSHILL Some eight or ten.

SIR IOHN Zounds will they not rob vs?

PRINCE What, a coward sir Iohn paunch.

SIR IOHN In deed I am not Iohn of Gaunt your grandfather, but yet no coward, Hall.

PRINCE Well, we leaue that to the proofe.

POINES Sirrha Iacke, thy horse standes behinde the hedge, when thou needst him, there thou shalt find him: farewel & stand fast.   780

SIR IOHN Now can not I strike him if I should be hangd.

PRINCE *(aside to Poynes)* Ned, where are our disguises?

POINES *(aside to the Prince)* Here, hard by, stand close.

⌐Exeunt Prince and Poynes⌐

SIR IOHN Now my maisters, happieman be his dole, say I, euerie man to his businesse.

⌐They stand aside.⌐

Enter the trauailers, ⌐amongst them, the Carriers⌐

⌐I⌐ TRAUAILER Come neighbour, the boy shal lead our horses down the hill, weele walke a foote a while and ease their legs.

THEEUES ⌐comming forward⌐ Stand.

⌐2⌐ TRAUAILER Iesus blesse vs.   790

SIR IOHN Strike, downe with them, cut the villaines throates, a horesone Caterpillers, bacon-fed knaues, they hate vs youth, downe with them, fleece them.

⌐I⌐ TRAUAILER O we are vndone, both we and ours for euer.

SIR IOHN Hang ye gorbellied knaues, are yee vndone, no ye fatte chuffes I woulde your store were here: on bacons on, what yee knaues yong men must liue, you are grand iurers, are ye, weele iure ye faith.

Here they rob them and bind them. Exeunt the theeues with the trauailers

Enter the prince and Poynes disguised in Buckrom suites   Sc. 6 (2.3)

PRINCE The theeues haue bounde the true men, nowe 800 coulde thou and I rob the theeues, and go merrily to London, it woulde be argument for a weeke, laughter for a month, and a good ieast for euer.

POINES Stand close, I heare them comming.

They stand aside.

Enter sir Iohn Olde-castle, Rossill, Haruey, and Gadshill againe, with the trauailers money

SIR IOHN Come my maisters, let vs share and then to horse before day, and the prince and Poynes bee not two arrant cowardes theres no equitie stirring, theres no more valour in that Poynes, then in a wilde ducke.

As they are sharing the Prince & Poins set vpon them

PRINCE Your money.

POINES Villaines.   810

Gadshill, Rossill and Haruey runne away ⌐seuerally⌐, and Olde-castle after a blow or two ⌐roars and⌐ runs away too, leauing the bootie behind them

PRINCE

Got with much ease. Now merrily to horse:
The theeues are al scattred, and possest with feare
So strongly, that they dare not meete each other,
Each takes his fellowe for an officer,
Away good Ned, Olde-castle sweates to death,
And lards the leane earth as he walkes along,
Wert not for laughing I should pittie him.

POINES

How the fat rogue roard.   *Exeunt with the bootie*

Sc. 7   *Enter Hotspur solus reading a letter*
(2.4)
820 HOTSPUR *But for mine own part my Lord I could be well*
contented to bee there, in respect of the loue I beare your
house.
He could be contented, why is hee not then? in respect
of the loue he beares our house: he shewes in this, he
loues his own barne better then he loues our house.
Let me see some more.
The purpose you vndertake is dangerous,
Why thats certaine, tis daungerous to take a cold, to
sleepe, to drinke, but I tell you (my Lord foole) out of
this nettle danger, we plucke this flower safetie.
830 *The purpose you vndertake is dangerous, the friends you*
haue named vncertaine, the time it selfe vnsorted, and your
whole plot too light, for the counterpoyse of so great an
opposition.
Say you so, say you so, I say vnto you againe, you are
a shallow cowardly hind, and you lie: what a lacke
braine is this? by the Lord our plot is a good plot, as
euer was laid, our friends true and constant: a good
plot, good friends, and ful of expectation: an excellent
plot, verie good friends; what a frosty spirited rogue is
840 this? why my Lord of York commends the plot, and
the generall course of the Action. Zoundes and I were
nowe by this rascall I could braine him with his Ladies
fanne. Is there not my father, my vncle, and my selfe;
Lord Edmond Mortimer, my Lord of Yorke, and Owen
Glendower: is there not besides the Dowglas, haue I
not all their letters to meete me in armes by the ninth
of the next month, and are they not some of them set
forward alreadie? What a pagan rascall is this, an
infidell? Ha, you shall see now in very sinceritie of
850 feare and cold heart, will hee to the King, and lay open
all our proceedings? O I could deuide my selfe, and go
to buffets, for mouing such a dish of skim milke with
so honorable an action. Hang him, let him tell the
king, we are prepared: I will set forward to night.
          Enter his Lady
How now Kate, I must leaue you within these two
houres.

LADY PERCY

O my good Lord, why are you thus alone?
For what offence haue I this fortnight bin
A banisht woman from my Harries bed?
860 Tel me sweet Lord, what ist that takes from thee
Thy stomacke, pleasure, and thy goulden sleepe?
Why dost thou bend thine eies vpon the earth?

And start so often when thou sits alone?
Why hast thou lost the fresh bloud in thy cheekes?
And giuen my treasures and my rights of thee
To thicke eyde musing, and curst melancholy?
In thy faint slumbers I by thee haue watcht,
And heard the murmur tales of yron wars,
Speake tearmes of mannage to thy bounding steed,
Cry courage to the field. And thou hast talkt   870
Of sallies and retyres, of trenches tents,
Of pallizadoes, frontiers, parapets,
Of basilisks, of canon, culuerin,
Of prisoners ransomd, and of soldiors slaine,
And all the currents of a heddy fight.
Thy spirit within thee hath bin so at war,
And thus hath so bestird thee in thy sleepe,
That beads of sweat haue stood vpon thy brow
Like bubbles in a late disturbed streame
And in thy face strange motions haue appeard,   880
Such as we see when men restraine their breath,
On some great suddain hest. O what portents are
          these?
Some heauy businesse hath my Lord in hand,
And I must know it else he loues me not.

HOTSPUR

What ho,
          Enter Seruant
               is Gilliams with the packet gone?

SERUANT

He is my Lord, an houre ago.

HOTSPUR

Hath Butler brought those horses from the Sheriffe?

SERUANT

One horse my Lord he brought euen now.

HOTSPUR

What horse, a Roane? a cropeare is it not?

SERUANT

It is my Lord.

HOTSPUR   That roane shall be my throne.   890
Wel, I will backe him straight: O Esperance,
Bid Butler lead him forth into the parke.

LADY PERCY

But heare you my Lord.

HOTSPUR   What saist thou my Lady?

LADY PERCY

What is it carries you away?

HOTSPUR   Why, my horse
(My loue) my horse.

LADY PERCY   Out you madhedded ape,
A weazel hath not such a deale of spleene
As you are tost with.
In faith ile knowe your businesse Harry that I will,
I feare my brother Mortimer doth stir
About his title, and hath sent for you   900
To line his enterprise, but if you go.

HOTSPUR

So far a foot I shal be weary loue.

LADY PERCY

Come, come you Paraquito, answere me

Directly to this question that I aske,
In faith ile breake thy little finger Harry
And if thou wilt not tel me all things true.

HOTSPUR

Away, away you trifler, loue, I loue thee not,
I care not for thee Kate, this is no world
To play with mammets, and to tilt with lips,
910　We must haue bloudy noses, and crackt crownes,
And passe them currant too: gods me my horse:
What saist thou Kate? what wouldst thou haue
　　with me?

LADY PERCY

Do you not loue me? do you not indeed?
Wel, do not then, for since you loue me not
I will not loue my selfe. Do you not loue me?
Nay tel me if you speake in iest or no?

HOTSPUR Come, wilt thou see me ride?
And when I am a horsebacke I will sweare
I loue thee infinitely. But harke you Kate,
920　I must not haue you henceforth question me
Whither I go, nor reason where about,
Whither I must, I must, and to conclude
This euening must I leaue you gentle Kate,
I know you wise, but yet no farther wise
Then Harry Percies wife, constant you are,
But yet a woman, and for secrecy
No Lady closer, for I well beleeue
Thou wilt not vtter what thou dost not know,
And so far wil I trust thee gentle Kate.

930　LADY PERCY How, so far.

HOTSPUR

Not an inch further, but harke you Kate,
Whither I go, thither shal you go too:
To day will I set forth, to morrow you,
Will this content you Kate?

LADY PERCY　　　　　　　It must of force.　　　Exeunt

Sc. 8　　　Enter Prince
(2.5)　PRINCE Ned, preethe come out of that fat roome, and
lende me thy hand to laugh a little.
　　　Enter Poines ⌈at another doore⌉
POINES Where hast bin Hal?
PRINCE With three or foure loggerheades, amongest three
or fourescore hogsheades. I haue sounded the verie
940　base string of humilitie. Sirrha, I am sworne brother
to a leash of drawers, and can call them all by their
christen names, as Tom, Dicke, and Francis, they take
it already vpon their saluation, that though I be but
prince of Wales, yet I am the king of Curtesie, and tel
me flatly I am no proud Iacke like Olde-castle, but a
Corinthian, a lad of metall, a good boy (by the Lord so
they call me) and when I am king of England I shall
command all the good lads in Eastcheape. They call
drinking deepe, dying scarlet, and when you breath in
950　your watering they cry hem, and bid you play it off.
To conclude, I am so good a proficiēt in one quarter of
an houre that I can drinke with any Tinker in his owne
language, during my life. I tell thee Ned thou hast lost

much honour, that thou wert not with me in this
action; but sweete Ned, to sweeten which name of
Ned, I giue thee this peniworth of sugar, clapt euen
now into my hand by an vnderskinker, one that neuer
spake other English in his life then eight shillings and
sixe pence, and you are welcome, with this shrill
addition, anon, anon sir; skore a pint of bastard in the　960
halfe moone, or so. But Ned, to driue awaie the time
till Olde-castle come: I preethe doe thou stande in some
by-roome, while I question my puny drawer to what
end he gaue me the sugar, and do thou neuer leaue
calling Frances, that his tale to me may bee nothing
but anon, step aside and ile shew thee a president.
　　　　　　　　　　　Exit Poines

POINES (within) Frances.
PRINCE Thou art perfect.
POINES (within) Frances.
　　　Enter Frances, a Drawer
FRANCES Anon, anon sir. Looke downe into the　970
Pomgarnet, Ralphe.
PRINCE Come hether Frances.
FRANCES My Lord.
PRINCE How long hast thou to serue Frances?
FRANCES Forsooth fiue yeeres, and as much as to.
POINES (within) Frances.
FRANCES Anon, anon sir.
PRINCE Fiue yeare, berlady a long lease for the clinking
of pewter; but Frances, darest thou be so valiant, as
to play the cowarde with thy Indenture, and shewe it　980
a faire paire of heeles, and run from it?
FRANCES O Lord sir, ile be sworne vpon all the bookes in
England, I could find in my hart.
POINES (within) Frances.
FRANCES Anon sir.
PRINCE How old art thou Frances?
FRANCES Let me see, about Michelmas next I shalbe.
POINES (within) Frances.
FRANCES Anon sir, (to the Prince) pray stay a little my
Lord.　990
PRINCE Nay but harke you Frances, for the sugar thou
gauest me, twas a peniworth, wast not?
FRANCES O Lord, I would it had bin two.
PRINCE I will giue thee for it a thousand pound, aske me
when thou wilt, and thou shalt haue it,
POINES (within) Frances.
FRANCES Anon, anon.
PRINCE Anon Frances, no Frances, but to morrow
Frances: or Frances a Thursday; or indeede Fraunces
when thou wilt. But Fraunces.　1000
FRANCES My Lord.
PRINCE Wilt thou rob this leathern Ierkin, cristall button,
not-pated, agat ring, puke stocking, Caddice garter,
smothe tongue, spanish pouch?
FRANCES O Lord sir, who do you meane?
PRINCE Why then your brown bastard is your only drinke?
for looke you Fraunces, your white canuas doublet will
sulley. In Barbary sir, it cannot come to so much.
FRANCES What sir?

1010 POINES (*within*) Frances.

PRINCE Away you rogue, dost thou not heare them cal.
⌜*As he departs*⌝ *both cal him, the Drawer stands*
amazed not knowing which way to go.
Enter Vintner

VINTNER What standst thou stil and hearst such a calling?
looke to the guests within.   *Exit Frances*
My Lord, old sir Iohn with halfe a douzen more are at
the doore, shal I let them in?

PRINCE Let them alone awhile, and then open the doore:
Exit Vintner

Poines.

POINES ⌜*within*⌝ Anon, anon sir.

Enter Poines

PRINCE Sirrha, Olde-castle and the rest of the theeues are
1020 at the doore, shall we be merrie?

POINES As merry as Crickets my lad, but harke ye, what
cunning match haue you made with this iest of the
Drawer: come whats the issue?

PRINCE I am now of all humors, that haue shewed
themselues humors since the oulde dayes of good man
Adam, to the pupill age of this present twelue a clocke
at midnight.

⌜*Enter Frances*⌝

Whats a clocke Frances?

FRANCES Anon, anon sir.   ⌜*Exit at another doore*⌝

1030 PRINCE That euer this fellowe should haue fewer wordes
then a Parrat, and yet the sonne of a woman. His
industrie is vp staires and down staires, his eloquence
the parcel of a reckoning. I am not yet of Percyes
minde, the Hotspur of the North, he that kils mee some
sixe or seuen douzen of Scots at a breakefast: washes
his handes, and saies to his wife, fie vpon this quiet
life, I want worke. O my sweet Harry saies she! how
manie hast thou kild to day? Giue my roane horse a
drench (sayes hee) and aunsweres some foureteene, an
1040 houre after: a trifle, a trifle. I preethe call in Olde-
castle, ile play Percy, and that damnde brawne shall
play dame Mortimer his wife. *Riuo* saies the drunkarde:
call in Ribs, cal in Tallow.

Enter sir Iohn Olde-castle with sword and buckler,
Rossill, Haruey, Gadshill, ⌜*followed by*⌝ *Frances*
with wine

POINES Welcome Iacke, where hast thou bin?

SIR IOHN A plague of al cowards I say, and a vengeance
too, marry and Amen: giue me a cup of sacke boy.
Eare I lead this life long, ile sow neatherstocks and
mend them, and foote them too. A plague of all cowards.
Giue me a cup of sacke rogue, is there no vertue extant?

He drinketh

1050 PRINCE Didst thou neuer see Titan kisse a dish of butter,
pittifull harted Titan, that melted at the sweet tale of
the sonnes, if thou didst, then behold that compound.

SIR IOHN (*to Frances*) You rogue, heeres lime in this sacke
too: there is nothing but rogery to be found in villanous
man, yet a cowarde is worse then a cup of sacke with
lime in it.   ⌜*Exit Frances*⌝

A villanous cowarde. Go thy waies old Iacke, die when
thou wilt, if manhood, good manhood be not forgot

vpon the face of the earth, then am I a shotten herring:
there liues not three good men vnhangde in England, 1060
and one of them is fat, and growes old, God helpe the
while, a bad world I say, I would I were a weauer. I
could sing psalmes, or any thing. A plague of all
cowards I say still.

PRINCE How now Wolsacke, what mutter you?

SIR IOHN A kings sonne, if I do not beat thee out of thy
kingdom with a dagger of lath, and driue all thy
subiects afore thee like a flock of wild geese, ile neuer
weare haire on my face more, you prince of Wales.

PRINCE Why you horeson round-man, whats the matter? 1070

SIR IOHN Are not you a cowarde? aunswere mee to that,
and Poines there.

POINES Zoundes ye fat paunch, and ye call me cowarde
by the Lord ile stab thee.

SIR IOHN I call thee cowarde, ile see thee damnde ere I
call thee coward, but I woulde giue a thousand pound
I coulde runne as fast as thou canst. You are streight
enough in the shoulders, you care not who sees your
backe: call you that backing of your friends, a plague
vpon such backing, giue me them that will face me, 1080
giue me a cup of sacke. I am a rogue if I drunke to
day.

PRINCE O villain, thy lips are scarse wipt since thou
drunkst last.

SIR IOHN All is one for that.

He drinketh

A plague of all cowards still say I.

PRINCE Whats the matter?

SIR IOHN Whats the matter, there be foure of vs here
haue tane a thousand pound this day morning.

PRINCE Where is it Iacke, where is it?   1090

SIR IOHN Where is it? taken from vs it is: a hundred
vppon poore foure of vs.

PRINCE What, a hundred, man?

SIR IOHN I am a rogue if I were not at halfe sword with
a douzen of them two houres together. I haue scapt by
myracle. I am eight times thrust through the doublet,
foure through the hose, my buckler cut through and
through, my sworde hackt like a handsaw, *ecce signum.*

⌜*He shewes his sword*⌝

I neuer dealt better since I was a man, al would not
do. A plague of all cowards, (*pointing to Gadshill, Haruey,* 1100
Rossill) let them speake, if they speake more or lesse
then truth, they are villains, and the sonnes of
darknesse.

⌜PRINCE⌝ Speake sirs, how was it?

⌜GADSHILL⌝ We foure set vpon some douzen.

SIR IOHN (*to the Prince*) Sixteene at least my Lord.

⌜GADSHILL⌝ And bound them.

HARUEY No, no, they were not bound.

SIR IOHN You rogue they were bounde euerie man of
them, or I am a Iew else: an Ebrew Iew.   1110

⌜GADSHILL⌝ As we were sharing, some sixe or seuen fresh
men set vpon vs.

SIR IOHN And vnbound the rest, and then come in the
other.

PRINCE What, fought you with them all?

SIR IOHN Al, I know not what you cal al, but if I fought not with fiftie of them I am a bunch of radish: if there were not two or three and fiftie vpon poore olde Iacke, then am I no two legd Creature.

1120 PRINCE Pray God you haue not murdred some of them.

SIR IOHN Nay, thats past praying for, I haue pepperd two of them. Two I am sure I haue paied, two rogues in buckrom sutes: I tel thee what Hall, if I tell thee a lie, spit in my face; call me horse, thou knowest my olde warde:

⌜He stands as to fight⌝

here I lay, and thus I bore my poynt, foure rogues in Buckrom let driue at me.

PRINCE What foure? thou saidst but two euen now.

SIR IOHN Foure Hal, I told thee foure.

1130 POINES I, I, he said foure.

SIR IOHN These foure came all a front, and mainely thrust at me, I made me no more adoe, but tooke all their seuen points in my target, thus.

⌜He wardes himselfe with his buckler⌝

PRINCE Seuen, why there were but foure euen now.

SIR IOHN In Buckrom.

POINES I foure in Buckrom suites.

SIR IOHN Seuen by these hilts, or I am a villaine else.

PRINCE (aside to Poines) Preethe let him alone, we shall haue more anon.

1140 SIR IOHN Doest thou heare me Hal?

PRINCE I, and marke thee to Iacke.

SIR IOHN Do so, for it is worth the listning to, these nine in Buckrom that I told thee of.

PRINCE (aside to Poines) So, two more alreadie.

SIR IOHN Their points being broken.

POINES ⌜aside to the Prince⌝ Downe fell their hose.

SIR IOHN Began to giue me ground: but I followed me close, came in, foot, and hand, and with a thought, seuen of the eleuen I paid.

1150 PRINCE (aside to Poines) O monstrous! eleuen Buckrom men growne out of two.

SIR IOHN But as the diuell would haue it, three misbegotten knaues in Kendall greene came at my backe, and let driue at mee, for it was so darke Hal, that thou couldest not see thy hand.

PRINCE These lies are like their father that begets them, grosse as a mountaine, open, palpable. Why thou clay-braind guts, thou knotty-pated foole, thou horeson obscene greasie tallow-catch.

1160 SIR IOHN What art thou mad? art thou mad? is not the truth the truth?

PRINCE Why, how couldst thou know these men in Kendal greene when it was so darke thou couldst not see thy hand, come tell vs your reason. What sayest thou to this?

POINES Come your reason, Iacke, your reason.

SIR IOHN What, vppon compulsion: Zoundes, and I were at the strappado, or all the rackes in the worlde, I would not tell you on compulsion. Giue you a reason

1170 on compulsion? if reasons were as plentifull as blackberries, I would giue no man a reason vppon compulsion, I.

PRINCE Ile be no longer guiltie of this sinne. This sanguine coward, this bed-presser, this horse-backe-breaker, this huge hill of flesh.

SIR IOHN Zbloud you starueling, you elfskin, you dried neatstong, you bulspizzle, you stockfish: O for breath to vtter what is like thee, you tailers yard, you sheath, you bowcase, you vile standing tuck.

1180 PRINCE Wel, breath a while, and then to't againe, and when thou hast tired thy selfe in base comparisons heare mee speake but this.

POINES Marke Iacke.

PRINCE We two saw you foure set on foure, and bound them and were maisters of their wealth: marke now how a plaine tale shall put you downe, then did wee two set on you foure, and with a worde, outfac't you from your prize, & haue it, yea & can shew it you here in the house: and Olde-castle you carried your guts 1190 away as nimbly, with as quicke dexteritie, & roard for mercy, and stil run and roard, as euer I heard bul-calf. What a slaue art thou to hacke thy sworde as thou hast done? and then say it was in fight. What tricke? what deuice? what starting hole canst thou now find out, to hide thee from this open and apparant shame?

POINES Come, lets heare Iacke, what tricke hast thou now?

SIR IOHN By the Lord, I knew ye as wel as he that made ye. Why heare you my maisters, was it for me to kill the heire apparant? should I turne vpon the true 1200 prince? why thou knowest I am as valiant as Hercules: but beware instinct, the lion will not touch the true prince, instinct is a great matter. I was now a cowarde on instinct, I shall thinke the better of my selfe, and thee during my life; I for a valiant lion, and thou for a true prince: but by the Lord, lads, I am glad you haue the money, (calling) Hostesse clap to the doores, (to the others) watch to night, pray to morrowe, gallants, lads, boyes, hearts of golde, all the titles of good fellowship come to you. What shall wee bee merrie, 1210 shall wee haue a play extempore?

PRINCE Content, and the argument shall bee thy running away.

SIR IOHN A, no more of that Hal and thou louest me.

Enter hostesse

HOSTESSE O Iesu, my Lord the prince!

PRINCE How now my lady the hostesse, what saist thou to me?

HOSTESSE Marry my Lo. there is a noble man of the court at doore would speake with you: he saies he commes from your father.

1220 PRINCE Giue him as much as will make him a royall man, and send him backe againe to my mother.

SIR IOHN What maner of man is he?

HOSTESSE An olde man.

SIR IOHN What doth grauitie out of his bed at midnight? Shall I giue him his answere?

PRINCE Preethe do Iacke.

SIR IOHN Faith and ile send him packing.   *Exit*

PRINCE Now sirs, (to Gadshill) birlady you fought faire, so did you Haruey, so did you Rossill, you are lions to, 1230 you ran away vpon instinct, you will not touch the true prince, no fie.

ROSSILL Faith I ran when I saw others runne.

PRINCE Faith tell me now in earnest, how came Olde-castles sword so hackt?

HARUEY Why, he hackt it with his dagger, and said hee woulde sweare truth out of England, but hee would make you beleeue it was done in fight, and perswaded vs to do the like.

1240 ROSSILL Yea, and to tickle our noses with spearegrasse, to make them bleed, and then to beslubber our garments with it, and sweare it was the blood of true men. I did that I did not this seuen yeare before, I blusht to heare his monstrous deuices.

PRINCE O villaine, thou stolest a cup of Sacke eighteene yeares ago, and wert taken with the maner, and euer since thou hast blusht extempore, thou hadst fire and sword on thy side, and yet thou ranst away, what instinct hadst thou for it?

1250 ROSSILL (shewing his face) My Lord do you see these meteors? do you behold these exhalations?

PRINCE I do.

ROSSILL What thinke you they portend?

PRINCE Hot liuers, and cold purses.

ROSSILL Choler, my Lord, if rightly taken.   ⌈Exit⌉

PRINCE No if rightly taken halter.

        Enter sir Iohn Olde-castle

Here commes leane Iacke, here commes bare bone: how now my sweete creature of bumbast, how long ist ago Iacke since thou sawest thine owne knee?

1260 SIR IOHN My owne knee, when I was about thy yeares (Hall) I was not an Eagles talent in the waste, I could haue crept into anie Aldermans thumbe ring: a plague of sighing and grief, it blowes a man vp like a bladder. Thers villainous newes abroade, heere was sir Iohn Bracy, from your father: you must to the court in the morning. That same mad fellow of the North Percie, and he of Wales that gaue Amamon the bastinado, and made Lucifer cuckold, and swore the diuel his true liegeman vpõ the crosse of a Welsh hooke: what a
1270 plague call you him?

POINES O. Glendower.

SIR IOHN Owen, Owen, the same, and his sonne in lawe Mortimer, and olde Northumberland, and that sprightly Scot of Scottes, Dowglas, that runnes a horsebacke vp a hill perpendicular.

PRINCE He that rides at high speede, and with his pistoll killes a sparrow flying.

SIR IOHN You haue hit it.

PRINCE So did he neuer the sparrow.

1280 SIR IOHN Well, that rascall hath good mettall in him, hee will not runne.

PRINCE Why, what a rascall art thou then, to praise him so for running?

SIR IOHN A horsebacke (ye cuckoe) but a foote hee will not budge a foote.

PRINCE Yes Iacke, vpon instinct.

SIR IOHN I grant ye vpon instinct: well hee is there to,

and one Mordacke, and a thousand blew caps more. Worcester is stolne away to night, thy fathers beard is turnd white with the newes, you may buy land now 1290 as cheape as stinking Mackrel.

PRINCE Why then, it is like if there come a hote Iune, and this ciuill buffeting hold, we shall buy maidenheads as they buy hob nailes, by the hundreds.

SIR IOHN By the masse lad thou saiest true, it is like wee shall haue good trading that way: but tell mee Hall, art not thou horrible afearde? thou being heire apparant, could the world picke thee out three such enemies againe? as that fiend Dowglas, that spirit Percy, and that diuel Glendower, art thou not horribly 1300 afraid? doth not thy bloud thril at it?

PRINCE Not a whit ifaith, I lacke some of thy instinct.

SIR IOHN Well thou wilt bee horriblie chidde to morrowe when thou commest to thy father, if thou loue mee practise an aunswere.

PRINCE Do thou stand for my father and examine me vpon the particulars of my life.

SIR IOHN Shall I? content. This chaire shall be my state, this dagger my scepter, and this cushion my crowne.

        He sits

PRINCE Thy state is taken for a ioynd stoole, thy golden 1310 scepter for a leaden dagger, and thy precious rich crowne for a pittifull bald crowne.

SIR IOHN Well, and the fire of grace bee not quite out of thee nowe shalt thou be mooued. Giue me a cup of Sacke to make my eyes looke redde, that it maie be thought I haue wept, for I must speake in passion, and I will doe it in king Cambises vaine.

PRINCE (bowing) Well, here is my leg.

SIR IOHN And here is my speech; (to Haruey, Poines, and Gadshill) stand aside Nobilitie.   1320

HOSTESSE O Iesu, this is excellent sport ifaith.

SIR IOHN
Weepe not sweet Queene, for trickling teares are vain.

HOSTESSE O the father, how he holds his countenance?

SIR IOHN
For Gods sake Lords, conuay my tristfull Queene,
For teares do stop the floudgates of her eyes.

HOSTESSE O Iesu, he doth it as like one of these harlotrie plaiers as euer I see.

SIR IOHN
Peace good pint-pot, peace good tickle-braine.
Harrie, I doe not onelie maruaile where thou spendest thy time, but also how thou art accompanied. For 1330 though the cammomill, the more it is troden on, the faster it growes: yet youth the more it is wasted, the sooner it weares: that thou art my son I haue partly thy mothers worde, partlie my owne opinion, but chieflie a villainous tricke of thine eye, and a foolish hanging of thy neather lippe, that dooth warrant me. If then thou bee sonne to mee, heere lies the poynt, why beeing sonne to me, art thou so pointed at? shal the blessed sunne of heauen proue a micher, and eat black-berries? a question not to be askt. Shall the sonne 1340 of England proue a theefe, and take purses? a question

to be askt. There is a thing Harry, which thou hast often heard of, and it is knowne to many in our land by the name of pitch. This pitch (as ancient writers do report) doth defile, so doth the companie thou keepest: for Harrie, now I do not speake to thee in drinke, but in teares; not in pleasure but in passion: not in words onely, but in woes also: and yet there is a vertuous man, whom I haue often noted in thy companie, but I know not his name.

PRINCE What maner of man and it like your Maiestie?

SIR IOHN A goodly portly man ifayth, and a corpulent, of a cheerful looke, a pleasing eie, and a most noble cariage, and as I thinke his age some fiftie, or birladie inclining to threescore, and nowe I remember me, his name is *Olde-castle*, if that man shoulde bee lewdly giuen, hee deceiueth me. For Harry, I see vertue in his lookes: if then the tree may bee knowne by the fruit, as the fruit by the tree, then peremptorily I speake it, there is vertue in that *Olde-castle*, him keepe with, the rest banish, and tell me now thou naughtie varlet, tell me where hast thou beene this month?

PRINCE Dost thou speake like a king, do thou stand for me, and ile play my father.

SIR IOHN (*standing*) Depose me, if thou dost it halfe so grauely, so maiestically, both in word and matter, hang me vp by the heeles for a rabbet sucker, or a poulters Hare.

PRINCE (*sitting*) Well, here I am set.

SIR IOHN And here I stand, (*to the others*) iudge my maisters.

PRINCE Now Harry, whence come you?

SIR IOHN My noble Lord from Eastcheape.

PRINCE The complaints I heare of thee are greeuous.

SIR IOHN Zbloud my Lord they are false: ⌈*to the others*⌉ nay ile tickle ye for a yong prince I faith.

PRINCE Swearest thou vngratious boy, hence forth nere looke on me, thou art violently carried awaie from grace, there is a diuell haunts thee in the likenesse of an olde fat man, a tun of man is thy companion: why doest thou conuerse with that trunke of humours, that boultinghutch of beastlinesse, that swolne parcell of dropsies, that huge bombard of sacke, that stuft cloakebag of guts, that rosted Manningtre Oxe with the pudding in his belly, that reuerent vice, that gray iniquity, that father ruffian, that vanity in yeares, wherein is he good, but to tast sacke and drinke it? wherein neat and clenly, but to carue a capon and eat it? wherein cunning, but in craft? wherein crafty, but in villany? wherein villanous, but in al things? where in worthy, but in nothing?

SIR IOHN I would your grace would take me with you, whome meanes your grace?

PRINCE That villanous abhominable misleader of youth, Olde-castle, that olde white bearded Sathan.

SIR IOHN My Lord, the man I know.

PRINCE I know thou doest.

SIR IOHN But to say I knowe more harme in him then in my selfe, were to say more then I know: that he is

olde the more the pittie, his white haires doe witnesse it, but that he is sauing your reuerence, a whoremaster, that I vtterlie denie: if sacke and sugar be a fault, God helpe the wicked; if to be olde and merry be a sin, then many an old host that I know is damnd: if to be fat be to be hated, then Pharaos leane kine are to be loued. No my good lord banish Haruey, banish Rossill, banish Poines, but for sweet Iacke Olde-castle, kinde Iacke Olde-castle, true Iacke Olde-castle, valiant Iacke Olde-castle, & therfore more valiant being as he is old Iacke Olde-castle,
Banish not him thy Harries companie,
Banish not him thy Harries companie,
Banish plumpe Iacke, and banish all the world.

PRINCE I do, I will.

Knocking within. ⌈*Exit hostesse.*⌉
Enter Rossill running

ROSSILL O my Lord, my Lord, the Sheriffe with a most monstrous watch is at the doore.

SIR IOHN Out ye rogue, play out the play, I haue much to say in the behalfe of that Olde-castle.

Enter the hostesse

HOSTESSE O Iesu, my Lord, my Lord!

PRINCE Heigh, heigh, the Deuil rides vpon a fiddle sticke, whats the matter?

HOSTESSE The Sheriffe and al the watch are at the doore, they are come to search the house, shall I let them in?

SIR IOHN Doest thou heare Hal? neuer call a true piece of golde a counterfet, thou art essentially made without seeming so.

PRINCE And thou a naturall coward without instinct.

SIR IOHN I deny your Maior, if thou wil deny the Sheriffe so, if not, let him enter. If I become not a Cart as well as another man, a plague on my bringing vp, I hope I shall as soone bee strangled with a halter as another.

PRINCE Go hide thee behind the Arras, the rest walke vp aboue, now my masters for a true face, and good conscience.   *Exeunt Poines, Rossill, and Gadshill*

SIR IOHN Both which I haue had, but their date is out, and therefore ile hide me.

He withdrawes behind the Arras

PRINCE (*to hostesse*) Call in the Sheriffe.   *Exit hostesse*
Enter Sheriffe and a Carrier

Now master Sheriffe, what is your wil with me?

SHERIFFE
First pardon me my Lord. A hue and crie
Hath followed certaine men vnto this house.

PRINCE What men?

SHERIFFE
One of them is well known my gratious Lorde,
A grosse fat man.

CARRIER   As fat as butter.

PRINCE
The man I do assure you is not here,
For I my selfe at this time haue emploid him:
And Sheriffe, I will ingage my word to thee,
That I will by to morrow dinner time
Send him to answere thee or any man,

For any thing he shall be charg'd withal,
1450   And so let me intreat you leaue the house.
SHERIFFE
    I will my Lord: there are two gentlemen
    Haue in this robbery lost 300. markes.
PRINCE
    It may be so: if he haue robd these men
    He shal be answerable, and so farewell.
SHERIFFE God night my noble Lord.
PRINCE
    I thinke it is god morrow is it not?
SHERIFFE
    Indeed my Lord I thinke it be two a clocke.
                            Exeunt Sheriffe and Carrier
PRINCE
    This oylie rascall is knowne as well as Poules:
    Goe call him forth.
HARUEY   Olde-castle:
    ⌈*He drawes back the Arras, reuealing sir Iohn, a*
    sleepe⌉
                            fast a sleepe
1460   Behind the Arras, and snorting like a horse.
PRINCE
    Harke how hard he fetches breath, search his pockets.
    Haruey searcheth his pocket, and findeth certaine
    papers. He ⌈*closeth the Arras and*⌉ *cometh forward*
    What hast thou found?
HARUEY   Nothing but papers my Lord.
PRINCE Lets see what they be, read them.
⌈HARUEY⌉ (*reads*)
    Item a capon.   2.s, ii,d.
    Item sawce.   iiij,d.
    Item sacke two gallons.   v.s, viij,d.
    Item anchaues and sacke after supper. 2.s, vj,d.
    Item bread.   ob.
⌈PRINCE⌉ O monstrous! but one halfepeniworth of bread
1470   to this intollerable deale of sack? what there is else
    keepe close, weel read it at more aduantage; there let
    him sleepe till day, ile to the court in the morning. We
    must all to the wars, and thy place shal be honorable.
    Ile procure this fat rogue a charge of foot, and I know
    his death will bee a march of twelue skore, the money
    shall bee paid backe againe with aduantage; bee with
    me betimes in the morning, and so good morrow
    Haruey.
HARUEY Good morrow good my Lord.
                            Exeunt ⌈*seuerally*⌉

Sc. 9   *Enter Hotspur, Worcester, Lord Mortimer, Owen*
(3.1)   *Glendower, with a map*
MORTIMER
1480   These promises are faire, the parties sure,
    And our induction ful of prosperous hope.
HOTSPUR
    Lord Mortimer, and coosen Glendower
    Wil you sit down? and Vncle Worcester;
    ⌈*Mortimer, Glendower and Worcester sit*⌉
    A plague vpon it I haue forgot the map.

GLENDOWER
    No here it is; sit Coosen Percy, sit
    Good Coosen Hotspur,
    ⌈*Hotspur sits*⌉
                    for by that name
    As oft as Lancaster doth speake of you,
    His cheeke lookes pale, and with a rising sigh
    Hee wisheth you in heauen.
HOTSPUR   And you in hell,
    As oft as he heares Owen Glendower spoke of.   1490
GLENDOWER
    I cannot blame him; at my natiuity
    The front of heauen was full of fiery shapes
    Of burning cressets, and at my birth
    The frame and huge foundation of the earth
    Shakd like a coward.
HOTSPUR   Why so it woulde haue done
    At the same season if your mothers cat
    Had but kittend, though your selfe had neuer beene
    borne.
GLENDOWER
    I say the earth did shake when I was borne.
HOTSPUR
    And I say the earth was not of my mind,
    If you suppose as fearing you it shooke.   1500
GLENDOWER
    The heauens were all on fire, the earth did tremble,
HOTSPUR
    Oh then the earth shooke to see the heauens on fire,
    And not in feare of your natiuity,
    Diseased nature oftentimes breakes forth,
    In strange eruptions, oft the teeming earth
    Is with a kind of collicke pincht and vext,
    By the imprisoning of vnruly wind
    Within her wombe, which for enlargement striuing
    Shakes the old Beldame earth, and topples down
    Steeples and mossegrown towers. At your birth   1510
    Our Grandam earth, hauing this distemprature
    In passion shooke.
GLENDOWER   Coosen of many men
    I do not beare these crossings, giue me leaue
    To tell you once againe that at my birth
    The front of heauen was full of fiery shapes,
    The goates ran from the mountaines, and the heards
    Were strangely clamorous to the frighted fields.
    These signes haue markt me extraordinary,
    And all the courses of my life do shew
    I am not in the roule of commen men: 1520
    Where is he liuing clipt in with the sea,
    That chides the bancks of England, Scotland, Wales,
    Which cals me pupil or hath read to me?
    And bring him out that is but womans sonne,
    Can trace me in the tedious waies of Arte,
    And hold me pace in deepe experiments.
HOTSPUR ⌈*standing*⌉
    I thinke theres no man speaketh better Welsh:
    Ile to dinner.
MORTIMER
    Peace coosen Percy, you wil make him mad.

GLENDOWER

1530   I can cal spirits from the vasty deepe.

HOTSPUR

Why so can I, or so can any man,
But wil they come when you do cal for them?

GLENDOWER

Why I can teach you coosen to command the Deuil.

HOTSPUR

And I can teach thee coose to shame the deuil,
By telling truth. Tel truth and shame the deuil:
If thou haue power to raise him bring him hither,
And ile be sworne I haue power to shame him hence:
Oh while you liue tel truth and shame the deuil.

MORTIMER

Come, come, no more of this vnprofitable chat.

GLENDOWER

1540   Three times hath Henry Bullenbrooke made head
Against my power, thrice from the bankes of Wye,
And sandy bottomd Seuerne haue I sent him
Booteles home, and weather beaten backe.

HOTSPUR

Home without bootes, and in foule weather too,
How scapes he agues in the deuils name?

GLENDOWER

Come heres the map, shal we diuide our right?
According to our three fold order tane.

MORTIMER

The Archdeacon hath diuided it
Into three limits very equally:

1550   England from Trent, and Seuerne hitherto,
By South and East is to my part assignd:
Al westward, Wales beyond the Seuerne shore,
And al the fertile land within that bound
To Owen Glendower: (to Hotspur) and deare coose
        to you
The remnant Northward lying off from Trent,
And our indentures tripartite are drawn,
Which being sealed enterchangeably,
(A businesse that this night may execute:)
To morrow coosen Percy you and I

1560   And my good Lord of Worcester wil set forth
To meet your father and the Scottish power,
As is appointed vs at Shrewsbury.
My father Glendower is not ready yet,
Nor shal we need his helpe these fourteen daies,
Within that space you may haue drawne together
Your tenants, friends, and neighbouring gentlemen.

GLENDOWER

A shorter time shall send me to you Lords,
And in my conduct shall your Ladies come,
From whom you now must steale and take no leaue,

1570   For there wil be a world of water shed,
Vpon the parting of your wiues and you.

HOTSPUR

Me thinks my moity North from Burton here,
In quantity equals not one of yours,
See how this riuer comes me cranking in,
And cuts me from the best of all my land,

A huge halfe moone, a monstrous cantle out,
Ile haue the currant in this place damnd vp,
And here the smug and siluer Trent shall run
In a new channell faire and euenly,
It shall not wind with such a deepe indent,   1580
To rob me of so rich a bottome here.

GLENDOWER

Not wind? it shal, it must, you see it doth.

MORTIMER

Yea, but marke howe he beares his course, and runs
        mee vp
With like aduauntage on the other side,
Gelding the opposed continent as much
As on the other side it takes from you.

WORCESTER

Yea but a little charge wil trench him here,
And on this Northside win this cape of land,
And then he runs straight and euen.

HOTSPUR

Ile haue it so, a little charge will do it.   1590

GLENDOWER Ile not haue it altred.

HOTSPUR Will not you?

GLENDOWER No, nor you shall not.

HOTSPUR Who shall say me nay?

GLENDOWER Why that will I.

HOTSPUR

Let me not vnderstand you then, speake it in Welsh.

GLENDOWER

I can speake English Lord as well as you,
For I was traind vp in the English court,
Where being but yong I framed to the harpe
Many an English ditty louely well,   1600
And gaue the tongue a helpeful ornament,
A vertue that was neuer seene in you.

HOTSPUR

Marry and I am glad of it with all my hart,
I had rather be a kitten and cry mew,
Then one of these same miter ballet mongers,
I had rather heare a brazen cansticke turnd,
Or a drie wheele grate on the exle tree,
And that would set my teeth nothing an edge,
Nothing so much as minsing poetry,
Tis like the forc't gate of a shuffling nag.   1610

GLENDOWER Come, you shal haue Trent turnd.

HOTSPUR

I do not care, ile giue thrice so much land
To any well deseruing friend:
But in the way of bargaine marke ye me,
Ile cauill on the ninth part of a haire,
Are the Indentures drawn, shal we be gone?

GLENDOWER

The moon shines faire, you may away by night.
Ile haste the writer, and withal
Breake with your wiues of your departure hence,
I am afraid my daughter will run mad,   1620
So much she doteth on her Mortimer.   Exit

MORTIMER

Fie coosen Percy, how you crosse my father.

526

HOTSPUR

I cannot chuse, sometime he angers me
With telling me of the Moldwarp and the Ant,
Of the dreamer Merlin and his prophecies,
And of a Dragon and a finles fish,
A clipwingd Griffin and a molten rauen,
A couching Leon and a ramping Cat,
And such a deale of skimble scamble stuffe,
1630 As puts me from my faith. I tel you what,
He held me last night at the least nine houres
In reckoning vp the seueral Diuels names
That were his lackies, I cried hum, and wel go to,
But markt him not a word. O he is as tedious
As a tyred horse, a railing wife,
Worse then a smoky house. I had rather liue
With cheese and garlike in a Windmil far,
Then feed on cates and haue him talke to me,
In any summer house in Christendome.

MORTIMER

1640 In faith he is a worthy gentleman,
Exceedingly well read and profited
In strange concealements, valiant as a lion,
And wondrous affable; and as bountifull
As mines of India; shal I tell you coosen,
He holds your temper in a high respect
And curbs himselfe euen of his natural scope,
When you come crosse his humor, faith he does,
I warrant you that man is not aliue
Might so haue tempted him as you haue done,
1650 Without the tast of danger and reproofe,
But do not vse it oft, let me intreat you.

WORCESTER (to Hotspur)

In faith my Lord you are too wilfull blame,
And since your comming hither haue done enough
To put him quite besides his patience,
You must needes learne Lord to amend this fault,
Though sometimes it shew greatnes, courage, bloud,
And thats the dearest grace it renders you,
Yet oftentimes it doth present harsh rage,
Defect of maners, want of gouernment,
1660 Pride, hautinesse, opinion, and disdaine,
The least of which hanting a noble man,
Looseth mens harts and leaues behind a staine
Vpon the beauty of all parts besides,
Beguiling them of commendation.

HOTSPUR

Wel I am schoold, good maners be your speed,
    Enter Glendower with Lady Percy and Mortimers
    wife
Here come our wiues, and let vs take our leaue.
    ⌈*Mortimers wife weepes and speakes to him in*
    Welsh⌉

MORTIMER

This is the deadly spight that angers me,
My wife can speake no English, I no Welsh.

GLENDOWER

My daughter weepes, sheele not part with you,
1670 Sheele be a souldior to, sheele to the wars.

MORTIMER

Good father tell her, that she and my Aunt Percy
Shal follow in your conduct speedily.
    Glendower speakes to her in Welsh, and she
    answeres him in the same

GLENDOWER

She is desperate here, a peeuish selfe wild harlotrie,
One that no perswasion can doe good vpon.
    The Ladie speakes in Welsh

MORTIMER

I vnderstand thy lookes, that prettie Welsh,
Which thou downe powrest from these swelling
        heauens,
I am too perfect in, and but for shame
In such a parley should I answere thee.
    The Ladie kisses him, and speakes againe in welsh

MORTIMER

I vnderstand thy kisses, and thou mine,
And thats a feeling disputation,   1680
But I will neuer be a truant loue,
Till I haue learnt thy language, for thy tongue
Makes Welsh as sweet as ditties highly pend,
Sung by a faire Queene in a summers bowre,
With rauishing diuision to her Lute.

GLENDOWER

Nay, if you melt, then will she run mad.
    The Ladie ⌈*sits on the rushes and*⌉ *speakes againe in*
    Welsh

MORTIMER

O I am ignorance it selfe in this.

GLENDOWER

She bids you on the wanton rushes lay you downe,
And rest your gentle head vpon her lap,
And she will sing the song that pleaseth you,   1690
And on your eyelids crowne the God of sleepe,
Charming your bloud with pleasing heauinesse,
Making such difference twixt wake and sleepe,
As is the difference betwixt day and night,
The houre before the heauenly harnest teeme
Begins his golden progresse in the east.

MORTIMER

With all my heart ile sit and heare her sing,
By that time will our booke I thinke be drawne.
    He sits, ⌈*resting his head on the Welsh Ladies lap*⌉

GLENDOWER

Do so, & those musitions that shal play to you,
Hang in the aire a thousand leagues from hence,   1700
And straight they shalbe here, sit and attend.

HOTSPUR

Come Kate, thou art perfect in lying downe,
Come quick, quick, that I may lay my head in thy lap.

LADY PERCY (*sitting*) Go ye giddy goose.
    Hotspur sits, resting his head on his ladies lap.
    The musicke playes

HOTSPUR

Now I perceiue the diuell vnderstands Welsh,
And tis no maruaile he is so humorous,
Birlady hees a good musition.

LADY PERCY
　　Then should you be nothing but musicall,
　　For you are altogither gouernd by humors,
1710　Lie still ye thiefe, and heare the Lady sing in Welsh.
HOTSPUR I had rather heare lady my brache howle in
　　Irish.
LADY PERCY Wouldst thou haue thy head broken?
HOTSPUR No.
LADY PERCY Then be still.
HOTSPUR Neither, tis a womans fault.
LADY PERCY Nowe God helpe thee.
HOTSPUR To the Welsh Ladies bed.
LADY PERCY Whats that?
1720 HOTSPUR Peace, she sings.
　　　　　Here the Ladie sings a welsh song
HOTSPUR Come Kate, ile haue your song too.
LADY PERCY Not mine in good sooth.
HOTSPUR Not yours in good sooth. Hart, you sweare like
　　a comfit-makers wife, not you in good sooth, and as
　　true as I liue, and
　　As God shall mend me, and as sure as day:
　　And giu'st such sarcenet surety for thy oathes,
　　As if thou neuer walkst further then Finsbury.
　　Sweare me Kate like a ladie as thou art,
1730　A good mouthfilling oath, and leaue in sooth,
　　And such protest of pepper ginger bread
　　To veluet gards, and Sunday Citizens.
　　Come sing.
LADY PERCY I will not sing.
HOTSPUR Tis the next way to turne tayler, or be redbrest
　　teacher, (*rising*) and the indentures be drawn ile away
　　within these two houres, and so come in when ye will.
　　　　　　　　　　　　　　　　　　　　　Exit
GLENDOWER
　　Come, come, Lord Mortimer, you are as slow,
　　As hot Lord Percy is on fire to go:
1740　By this our booke is drawne, weele but seale,
　　And then to horse immediatlie.
MORTIMER (*rising*)　　　　　　With all my hart.
　　　　　　　The Ladies rise, and exeunt omnes

Sc. 10　　　*Enter the King, Prince of Wales, and Lords*
(3.2) KING
　　Lords giue vs leaue, the Prince of Wales and I,
　　Must haue some priuate conference, but be neare at
　　hand,
　　For we shall presently haue neede of you.
　　　　　　　　　　　　　　　　　　Exeunt Lords
　　I know not whether God will haue it so
　　For some displeasing seruice I haue done,
　　That in his secret doome out of my blood,
　　Heele breed reuengement and a scourge for me:
　　But thou dost in thy passages of life,
1750　Make me beleeue that thou art onely markt
　　For the hot vengeance, and the rod of heauen,
　　To punish my mistreadings. Tell me else
　　Could such inordinate and low desires,

Such poore, such bare, such lewd, such mean
　　attempts,
Such barren pleasures, rude societie
As thou art matcht withall, and grafted to,
Accompanie the greatnesse of thy blood,
And hold their leuell with thy princely heart?
PRINCE
　　So please your Maiestie, I would I could
　　Quit all offences with as cleare excuse,　　　　1760
　　As well as I am doubtlesse I can purge
　　My selfe of many I am chargd withall,
　　Yet such extenuation let me beg,
　　As in reproofe of many tales deuisde,
　　Which oft the eare of greatnes needs must heare
　　By smiling pickthanks, and base newes mongers,
　　I may for some things true, wherein my youth
　　Hath faulty wandred, and irregular,
　　Find pardon on my true submission.
KING
　　God pardon thee, yet let me wonder, Harry,　　1770
　　At thy affections, which do hold a wing
　　Quite from the flight of all thy auncestors,
　　Thy place in counsell thou hast rudely lost
　　Which by thy yonger brother is supplide,
　　And art almost an allien to the harts
　　Of all the Court and princes of my blood,
　　The hope and expectation of thy time
　　Is ruind, and the soule of euery man
　　Prophetically do forethinke thy fall:
　　Had I so lauish of my presence beene,　　　　　1780
　　So common hackneid in the eyes of men,
　　So stale and cheape to vulgar companie,
　　Opinion that did helpe me to the crowne,
　　Had still kept loyall to possession,
　　And left me in reputelesse banishment,
　　A fellow of no marke nor likelihoode.
　　By being seldome seene, I could not stirre
　　But like a Comet I was wondred at,
　　That men would tell their children this is he:
　　Others would say, where, which is Bullingbrooke?　1790
　　And then I stole all curtesie from heauen,
　　And drest my selfe in such humilitie
　　That I did plucke allegiance from mens hearts,
　　Loud shouts, and salutations from their mouths,
　　Euen in the presence of the crowned king.
　　Thus did I keepe my person fresh and new,
　　My presence like a roabe pontificall,
　　Nere seene but wondred at, and so my state
　　Seldome, but sumptuous shewd like a feast,
　　And wan by rarenesse such solemnitie.　　　　　1800
　　The skipping king, he ambled vp and downe,
　　With shallow iesters, and rash bauin wits,
　　Soone kindled, and soone burnt, carded his state,
　　Mingled his royaltie with capring fooles,
　　Had his great name prophaned with their scornes,
　　And gaue his countenance against his name
　　To laugh at gibing boyes, and stand the push

Of euery beardlesse vaine comparatiue,
Grew a companion to the common streetes,
1810   Enfeoft himselfe to popularitie,
That being dayly swallowed by mens eyes,
They surfetted with honie, and began
To loath the taste of sweetnesse, whereof a little
More then a little, is by much too much.
So when he had occasion to be seene,
He was but as the Cuckoe is in Iune,
Heard, not regarded: Seene, but with such eies
As sicke and blunted with communitie,
Affoord no extraordinary gaze,
1820   Such as is bent on sun-like maiestie,
When it shines seldome in admiring eies,
But rather drowzd, and hung their eie-lids down,
Slept in his face, and rendred such aspect
As cloudy men vse to their aduersaries,
Being with his presence glutted, gorgde, and full.
And in that very line Harry standest thou,
For thou hast lost thy princely priuiledge
With vile participation. Not an eye
But is a weary of thy common sight,
1830   Saue mine, which hath desird to see thee more,
Which now doth that I would not haue it do,
Make blind it selfe with foolish tendernesse.

He weeps

PRINCE
I shall hereafter my thrice gratious Lord,
Be more my selfe.

KING   For all the world,
As thou art to this houre was Richard then,
When I from France set foot at Rauenspurgh,
And euen as I was than, is Percy now,
Now by my scepter, and my soule to boote,
He hath more worthie interest to the state
1840   Then thou the shadow of succession.
For of no right, nor colour like to right,
He doth fill fields with harnesse in the realme,
Turnes head against the lions armed iawes,
And being no more in debt to yeares, then thou
Leads ancient Lords, and reuerend Bishops on
To bloudie battailes, and to bruising armes.
What neuer dying honour hath he got
Against renowmed Dowglas? Whose high deeds,
Whose hot incursions, and great name in armes,
1850   Holds from al souldiors chiefe maioritie
And militarie title capitall,
Through all the kingdoms that acknowledge Christ.
Thrice hath this Hotspur Mars in swathling cloaths,
This infant warrier in his enterprises,
Discomfited great Dowglas, tane him once,
Enlarged him, and made a friend of him,
To fill the mouth of deepe defiance vp,
And shake the peace and safety of our throne,
And what say you to this? Percy, Northumberland,
1860   The Archbishops grace of York, Dowglas, Mortimer,
Capitulate against vs, and are vp.

But wherefore do I tel these newes to thee?
Why Harry do I tell thee of my foes,
Which art my nearst and dearest enemy?
Thou that art like enough through vassall feare,
Base inclination, and the start of spleene,
To fight against me vnder Percies pay,
To dog his heeles, and curtsie at his frownes,
To shew how much thou art degenerate.

PRINCE
Do not thinke so, you shal not find it so,   1870
And God forgiue them that so much haue swaide
Your maiesties good thoughts away from me.
I will redeeme all this on Percies head,
And in the closing of some glorious day
Be bold to tell you that I am your sonne,
When I will weare a garment all of bloud,
And staine my fauors in a bloudy maske,
Which washt away shall scoure my shame with it,
And that shal be the day when ere it lights,
That this same child of honour and renowne,   1880
This gallant Hotspur, this all praised knight,
And your vnthought of Harry chance to meet,
For euery honor sitting on his helme
Would they were multitudes, and on my head
My shames redoubled. For the time will com
That I shal make this Northren youth exchange
His glorious deedes for my indignities.
Percy is but my factor, good my Lord,
To engrosse vp glorious deeds on my behalfe.
And I will call him to so strickt account,   1890
That he shall render euery glory vp,
Yea, euen the sleightest worship of his time,
Or I will teare the reckoning from his heart.
This in the name of God I promise heere,
The which if he be pleasd I shall performe:
I do beseech your maiesty may salue
The long grown wounds of my intemperature,
If not, the end of life cancels all bands,
And I will die a hundred thousand deaths
Ere breake the smallest parcell of this vow.   1900

KING
A hundred thousand rebels die in this,
Thou shalt haue charge and soueraine trust herein.

Enter Blunt

How now good blunt thy lookes are full of speed.

BLUNT
So hath the businesse that I come to speake of.
Lord Mortimer of Scotland hath sent word,
That Dowglas and the English Rebels met
The eleuenth of this month at Shrewsbury,
A mighty and a fearefull head they are,
If promises be kept on euery hand,
As euer offred foule play in a state.   1910

KING
The Earle of Westmerland set forth to day,
With him my sonne Lord Iohn of Lancaster,
For this aduertisement is fiue daies old.

529

On Wednesday next, Harry you shall set forward,
On thursday we our selues will march.
Our meeting is Bridgenorth, and Harry, you
Shall march through Glocestershire, by which account
Our businesse valued some twelue daies hence,
Our general forces at Bridgenorth shall meet:
1920 Our hands are full of businesse, lets away,
Aduantage feedes him fat while men delay.   *Exeunt*

Sc. 11
(3.3)   *Enter sir Iohn Olde-castle ⌈with a trunchion at his*
     waist⌉ and Rossill

SIR IOHN Rossill, am I not falne away vilely since this last
action? do I not bate? do I not dwindle? Why, my
skinne hangs about me like an old Ladies loose gowne.
I am withered like an oulde apple Iohn. Well, ile repent
and that suddainly, while I am in some liking, I shall
be out of heart shortly, and then I shall haue no
strength to repent. And I haue not forgotten what the
inside of a Church is made of, I am a Pepper corne, a
1930 brewers Horse, the inside of a Church. Company,
villainous company, hath been the spoile of me.

ROSSILL Sir Iohn, you are so fretfull you cannot liue long.

SIR IOHN Why, there is it; come sing me a bawdie song,
make me merry. I was as vertuously giuen as a
gentleman need to be, vertuous enough, swore little,
dic't not aboue seuen times a weeke, went to a baudy
house not aboue once in a quarter of an houre, paid
money that I borrowed three or foure times, liued wel,
and in good compasse, and nowe I liue out of all order,
1940 out of all compasse.

ROSSILL Why, you are so fat, sir Iohn, that you must
needes be out of all compasse: out of all reasonable
compasse, sir Iohn.

SIR IOHN Do thou amend thy face, and ile amend my life:
thou art our Admiral, thou bearest the lanterne in the
poope, but tis in the nose of thee: thou art the knight
of the burning lampe.

ROSSILL Why, sir Iohn, my face does you no harme.

SIR IOHN No ile be sworn, I make as good vse of it as
1950 many a man doth of a deaths head, or a *memento mori*.
I neuer see thy face, but I thinke vpon hell fire, and
Diues that liued in Purple: for there he is in his robes
burning, burning. If thou wert any waie giuen to
vertue, I would sweare by thy face: my oath should be
by this fire thats Gods Angell. But thou art altogether
giuen ouer: and wert indeede but for the light in thy
face, the sonne of vtter darkenesse. When thou ranst
vp Gadshill in the night to catch my horse, if I did not
thinke thou hadst beene an *ignis fatuus*, or a ball of
1960 wildfire, theres no purchase in money. O thou art a
perpetuall triumph, an euerlasting bonefire light, thou
hast saued me a thousand Markes in Linkes, and
Torches, walking with thee in the night betwixt tauerne
and tauerne: but the sacke that thou hast drunke me,
would haue bought me lights as good cheape, at the
dearest Chandlers in Europe. I haue maintained that
Sallamander of yours with fire any time this two and
thirty yeares, God reward me for it.

ROSSILL Zbloud, I would my face were in your belly.

SIR IOHN Godamercy, so should I be sure to be hartburnt. 1970
     Enter hostesse
How now dame Partlet the hen, haue you enquird yet
who pickt my pocket?

HOSTESSE Why sir Iohn, what do you thinke sir Iohn, doe
you thinke I keepe theeues in my house, I haue searcht,
I haue enquired, so has my husband, man by man,
boy by boy, seruant by seruant, the tith of a haire,
was neuer lost in my house before.

SIR IOHN Yee lie Hostesse, Rossill was shau'd, and lost
manie a haire, and ile be sworne my pocket was pickt:
go to, you are a woman, go. 1980

HOSTESSE Who I. No, I defie thee: Gods light I was neuer
cald so in mine owne house before.

SIR IOHN Go to. I know you well inough.

HOSTESSE No, sir Iohn, you do not know me, sir Iohn, I
knowe you sir Iohn, you owe me mony sir Iohn, and
now you picke a quarrell to beguile me of it, I bought
you a douzen of shirts to your backe.

SIR IOHN Doulas, filthie Doulas. I haue giuen them away
to Bakers wiues, they haue made boulters of them.

HOSTESSE Now as I am a true woman, holland of viii s. 1990
an ell, you owe mony here, besides sir Iohn, for your
diet, and bydrinkings, and money lent you xxiiii. pound.

SIR IOHN *(pointing at Rossill)* He had his part of it, let him
pay.

HOSTESSE He, alas he is poore, he hath nothing.

SIR IOHN How? poore? looke vpon his face. What call you
rich? let them coyne his nose, let them coyne his
cheekes, ile not pay a denyer: what will you make a
yonker of mee? shall I not take mine ease in mine Inne,
but I shall haue my pocket pickt? I haue lost a seale 2000
ring of my grandfathers worth fortie marke.

HOSTESSE O Iesu, *(to Rossill)* I haue heard the Prince tell
him I know not how oft, that that ring was copper.

SIR IOHN How? the prince is a iacke, a sneakeup, ⌈*raising*
his trunchion⌉ Zbloud and hee were here, I would cudgell
him like a dog if he would say so.
     Enter the prince and Haruey marching, and sir Iohn
     Olde-castle meetes them playing vpon his trunchion
     like a fife
How now lad, is the winde in that doore ifaith, must
we all march?

ROSSILL Yea, two, and two, Newgate fashion.

HOSTESSE My Lord, I pray you heare me. 2010

PRINCE
What saist thou mistris quickly, how doth thy
     husband?
I loue him well, he is an honest man.

HOSTESSE Good my Lord heare me?

SIR IOHN Preethe let her alone, and list to me.

PRINCE What saist thou Iacke.

SIR IOHN The other night I fel a sleepe here, behind the
Arras, and had my pocket pickt, this house is turn'd
baudy house, they pick pockets.

PRINCE What didst thou loose Iacke?

SIR IOHN Wilt thou beleeue me Hall, three or foure bonds 2020 of forty pound a peece, and a seale ring of my grandfathers.

PRINCE A trifle, some eight penie matter.

HOSTESSE So I told him my Lord, and I said I heard your grace say so: & my lord he speakes most vilely of you, like a foule mouthd man as he is, and said he would cudgel you.

PRINCE What he did not?

HOSTESSE Theres neither faith, truth, nor womanhood in 2030 me else.

SIR IOHN Theres no more faith in thee then in a stued prune, nor no more truth in thee then in a drawn fox, and for womanhood maid marion may be the deputies wife of the ward to thee. Go you thing, go.

HOSTESSE Say what thing, what thing?

SIR IOHN What thing? why a thing to thanke God on.

HOSTESSE I am nothing to thanke God on, I would thou shouldst know it, I am an honest mans wife, and setting thy knighthood aside, thou art a knaue to call me so.

2040 SIR IOHN Setting thy womanhood aside, thou art a beast to say otherwise.

HOSTESSE Say, what beast, thou knaue thou?

SIR IOHN What beast? why an Otter.

PRINCE An Otter sir Iohn, why an Otter?

SIR IOHN Why? shees neither fish nor flesh, a man knowes not where to haue her.

HOSTESSE Thou art an vniust man in saying so, thou or anie man knowes where to haue me, thou knaue thou.

PRINCE Thou saist true hostesse, and hee slaunders thee 2050 most grossely.

HOSTESSE So hee doth you my Lord, and saide this other day you ought him a thousand pound.

PRINCE (to sir Iohn) Sirrha, do I owe you a thousand pound?

SIR IOHN A thousand pound Hall? a million, thy loue is worth a million, thou owest me thy loue.

HOSTESSE Nay my Lord, he cald you iacke, and saide hee woulde cudgel you.

SIR IOHN Did I Rossill?

2060 ROSSILL Indeed sir Iohn you said so.

SIR IOHN Yea, if he said my ring was copper.

PRINCE I say tis copper, darest thou be as good as thy word now?

SIR IOHN Why Hall? Thou knowest as thou art but man I dare, but as thou art prince, I feare thee as I feare the roaring of the Lyons whelpe.

PRINCE And why not as the Lyon?

SIR IOHN The king himselfe is to be feared as the Lion, doest thou thinke ile feare thee as I feare thy father? 2070 nay and I doo, I pray God my girdle breake.

PRINCE O, if it should, howe woulde thy guts fall about thy knees? but sirrha, theres no roome for faith, trueth, nor honestie, in this bosome of thine. It is all fild vp with guttes, and midriffe. Charge an honest woman with picking thy pocket, why thou horeson impudent imbost rascall, if there were anie thing in thy pocket but tauerne reckonings, memorandums of baudie houses, and one poore peniworth of sugar-candie to

make thee long winded, if thy pocket were inricht with any other iniuries but these; I am a villain, and yet 2080 you will stand to it, you will not pocket vp wrong, art thou not ashamed?

SIR IOHN Doest thou heare Hall, thou knowest in the state of innocencie Adam fell, & what should poore Iacke Olde-castle do in the daies of villanie? thou seest I haue more flesh then another man, & therfore more frailty. You confesse then you pickt my pocket.

PRINCE It appeares so by the storie.

SIR IOHN Hostesse, I forgiue thee, go make ready breakfast, loue thy husband, looke to thy seruaunts, cherish thy 2090 ghesse, thou shalt find me tractable to any honest reason, thou seest I am pacified still, nay preethe be gone.   Exit Hostesse
Now Hal, to the newes at court, for the robbery lad, how is that answered?

PRINCE O my sweet beoffe, I must still bee good angel to thee, the mony is paid backe againe.

SIR IOHN O I do not like that paying backe, tis a double labor.

PRINCE I am good friends with my father and may do any 2100 thing.

SIR IOHN Rob me the exchequer the first thing thou doest, and doe it with vnwasht hands too.

ROSSILL Do my Lord.

PRINCE I haue procured thee Iacke a charge of foot.

SIR IOHN I would it had been of horse. Where shall I finde one that can steale well. O for a fine thiefe of the age of xxii. or thereabouts: I am hainously vnprouided. Well, God be thanked for these rebels, they offende none but the vertuous; I laude them, I praise them. 2110

PRINCE Rossill.

ROSSILL My Lord.

PRINCE (giuing letters)
Go beare this letter to Lord Iohn of Lancaster,
To my brother Iohn, this to my lord of Westmerland.
                                        Exit Rossill
Go Haruey to horse, to horse, for thou and I
Haue thirty miles to ride yet ere dinner time,
                                        Exit Haruey
Iacke, meete me to morrow in the temple haule
At two of clocke in the afternoone,
There shalt thou know thy charge, and there receiue
Money and order for their furniture,   2120
The land is burning, Percy stands on high,
And either we or they must lower lie.   Exit

SIR IOHN
Rare words, braue world, (calling) hostesse, my
    breakfast come,
Oh I could wish this tauerne were my drum.   Exit

Enter Hotspur, Worcester, Douglas   Sc. 12
HOTSPUR   (4.1)
Wel said my noble Scot, if speaking truth
In this fine age were not thought flattery,
Such attribution should the Douglas haue,
As not a souldior of this seasons stampe,

Should go so generall currant through the world.

2130 By God, I cannot flatter, I do defie
The tongues of soothers, but a brauer place
In my harts loue hath no man then your selfe,
Nay taske me to my word, approue me Lord.

DOUGLAS Thou art the King of honor,
No man so potent breaths vpon the ground,
But I will beard him.

HOTSPUR   Do so, and tis wel.
    Enter a Messenger with letters
What letters hast thou there? I can but thanke you.

MESSENGER These letters come from your father.

HOTSPUR
Letters from him, why comes he not himselfe?

MESSENGER
2140 He cannot come my lord, he is grieuous sicke.

HOTSPUR
Zounds, how has he the leisure to be sicke
In such a iustling time, who leads his power?
Vnder whose gouernment come they along?

MESSENGER
His letters beares his mind, not I my lord.
    Hotspur reads the letters

WORCESTER
I preethe tel me, doth he keepe his bed?

MESSENGER
He did my Lord, foure daies ere I set forth,
And at the time of my departure thence,
He was much fearde by his Phisitions.

WORCESTER
I would the state of time had first been whole,
2150 Eare he by sicknesse had bin visited,
His health was neuer better worth then now.

HOTSPUR
Sicke now, droupe now, this sicknes doth infect
The very life bloud of our enterprise,
Tis catching hither euen to our campe,
He writes me here that inward sicknesse staies him,
And that his friends by deputation
Could not so soone be drawn, nor did he thinke it meet
To lay so dangerous and deare a trust
On any soule remoou'd but on his own,
2160 Yet doth he giue vs bold aduertisement,
That with our small coniunction we should on,
To see how fortune is disposd to vs,
For as he writes there is no quailing now,
Because the king is certainly possest
Of al our purposes, what say you to it?

WORCESTER
Your fathers sicknesse is a maime to vs.

HOTSPUR
A perillous gash, a very limbe lopt off,
And yet in faith it is not, his present want
Seemes more then we shal find it: were it good
2170 To set the exact wealth of al our states
Al at one cast? to set so rich a maine
On the nice hazard of one doubtfull houre?

It were not good for therein should we read
The very bottome and the soule of hope,
The very list, the very vtmost bound
Of all our fortunes.

DOUGLAS
Faith, and so we should, where now remaines
A sweet reuersion, we may boldly spend
Vpon the hope of what is to come in,
A comfort of retirement liues in this.   2180

HOTSPUR
A randeuous, a home to flie vnto
If that the Diuel and mischance looke big
Vpon the maidenhead of our affaires.

WORCESTER
But yet I would your father had bin heere:
The quality and haire of our attempt
Brookes no deuision, it will be thought
By some that know not why he is away,
That wisedome, loialty, and meere dislike
Of our proceedings kept the Earle from hence,
And thinke how such an apprehension   2190
May turne the tide of fearefull faction,
And breed a kind of question in our cause:
For wel you know we of the offring side
Must keepe aloofe from strict arbitrement,
And stop al sight-holes euery loope from whence
The eie of reason may prie in vpon vs,
This absence of your fathers drawes a curtain
That shewes the ignorant a kind of feare
Before not dreamt of.

HOTSPUR   You straine too far.
I rather of his absence make this vse,   2200
It lends a lustre and more great opinion,
A larger dare to our great enterprise
Then if the Earle were here, for men must thinke
If we without his helpe can make a head
To push against a kingdome, with his helpe
We shal oreturne it topsie turuy down,
Yet all goes well yet all our ioints are whole.

DOUGLAS
As hart can thinke, there is not such a word
Spoke of in Scotland as this tearme of feare.
    Enter sir Ri: Vernon

HOTSPUR
My coosen Vernon, welcom by my soule.   2210

VERNON
Pray God my newes be worth a welcome lord,
The Earle of Westmerland seuen thousand strong
Is marching hetherwards, with him prince Iohn.

HOTSPUR
No harme, what more?

VERNON   And further I haue learnd,
The King himselfe in person is set forth,
Or hetherwards intended speedily
With strong and mighty preparation.

HOTSPUR
He shal be welcome too: where is his sonne?

The nimble footed madcap prince of Wales,
2220   And his Cumrades that daft the world aside
       And bid it passe?

VERNON   All furnisht al in Armes:
       All plumde like Estridges that with the wind
       ⌈   ⌉
       Baiting like Eagles hauing lately bathd,
       Glittering in golden coates like images,
       As ful of spirit as the month of May,
       And gorgeous as the sunne at Midsomer:
       Wanton as youthful goates, wild as young buls,
       I saw yong Harry with his beuer on,
2230   His cushes on his thighs gallantly armde,
       Rise from the ground like feathred Mercury,
       And vaulted with such ease into his seat,
       As if an Angel dropt down from the clouds,
       To turne and wind a fiery Pegasus,
       And witch the world with noble horsemanship.

HOTSPUR
       No more, no more, worse then the sun in March,
       This praise doth nourish agues, let them come,
       They come like sacrifices in their trim,
       And to the fire-eyd maide of smoky war,
2240   Al hot and bleeding will we offer them,
       The mailed Mars shal on his altar sit
       Vp to the eares in bloud. I am on fire
       To heare this rich reprizal is so nigh,
       And yet not ours: Come let me tast my horse,
       Who is to beare me like a thunderbolt,
       Against the bosome of the Prince of Wales,
       Harry to Harry shal hot horse to horse,
       Meete and neare part til one drop down a coarse,
       Oh that Glendower were come.

VERNON   There is more newes,
2250   I learnd in Worcester as I rode along,
       He cannot draw his power this fourteene daies.

DOUGLAS
       Thats the worst tidings that I heare of yet.

WORCESTER
       I by my faith, that beares a frosty sound.

HOTSPUR
       What may the kings whole battel reach vnto?

VERNON
       To thirty thousand.

HOTSPUR   Forty let it be,
       My father and Glendower being both away,
       The powers of vs may serue so great a day,
       Come let vs take a muster speedily,
       Doomes day is neare, die all, die merely.

DOUGLAS
2260   Talke not of dying, I am out of feare
       Of death or deaths hand for this one halfe yeare.

                                        Exeunt

Sc. 13   Enter sir Iohn Olde-castle, Rossill
(4.2)   SIR IOHN Rossill get thee before to Couentry, fill me a
       bottle of Sacke, our souldiors shall march through.
       Weele to Sutton cophill to night.

ROSSILL Will you giue me money captaine?

SIR IOHN Lay out, lay out.

ROSSILL This bottell makes an angel.

SIR IOHN ⌈giuing Rossill money⌉ And if it do, take it for thy
       labour, and if it make twenty take them all, ile answere
       the coynage, bid my Liuetenant Haruey meet me at   2270
       townes end.

ROSSILL I will captaine, farewell.   Exit

SIR IOHN If I be not ashamed of my soldiours, I am a
       souct gurnet, I haue misused the kinges presse
       damnablie. I haue got in exchange of 150. soldiours
       300. and odde poundes. I presse me none but good
       houshoulders, Yeomans sonnes, inquire me out
       contracted batchelers, such as had been askt twice on
       the banes, such a commodity of warme slaues, as had
       as lieue heare the Diuell as a drumme, such as feare   2280
       the report of a Caliuer, worse then a strucke foule, or
       a hurt wild ducke: I prest mee none but such tostes
       and butter with hearts in their bellies no bigger then
       pinnes heades, and they haue bought out their seruices,
       and now my whole charge consists of Ancients,
       Corporals, Lieutenants, gentlemen of companies: slaues
       as ragged as Lazarus in the painted cloth, where the
       gluttons dogs licked his sores, and such as indeed were
       neuer souldiours, but discarded, vniust seruingmen,
       yonger sonnes to yonger brothers, reuolted tapsters,   2290
       and Ostlers, tradefalne, the cankers of a calme world,
       and a long peace, ten times more dishonourable ragged
       then an olde fazd ancient, and such haue I to fill vp
       the roomes of them as haue bought out their seruices,
       that you woulde thinke that I had a hundred and fiftie
       tottered prodigals, iatelie come from swine keeping,
       from eating draffe and husks. A mad fellowe met mee
       on the way, and tolde mee I had vnloaded all the
       Gibbets, and prest the dead bodies. No eye hath seene
       such skarcrowes. Ile not march through Couentry with   2300
       them, thats flat: nay, and the villains march wide
       betwixt the legs as if they had giues on, for indeede I
       had the most of them out of prison, theres not a shert
       and a halfe in all my companie, and the halfe shert is
       two napkins tackt togither, and throwne ouer the
       shoulders like a Heralds coate without sleeues, and the
       shert to say the trueth stolne from my host at S.
       Albones, or the red-nose Inkeeper of Dauintry, but thats
       all one, theile find linnen inough on euerie hedge.

              Enter the Prince, Lord of Westmerland

PRINCE How now blowne Iacke? how now quilt?   2310

SIR IOHN What Hal, how now mad wag? what a diuel
       dost thou in Warwickshire? My good Lo. of
       Westmerland, I cry you mercy, I thought your honour
       had alreadie bin at shrewesburie.

WESTMERLAND Faith sir Iohn tis more then time that I
       were there, and you too, but my powers are there
       already, the king I can tel you lookes for vs all, we
       must away all night.

SIR IOHN Tut neuer feare mee, I am as vigilant as a Cat
       to steale Creame.   2320

PRINCE I thinke to steale Creame indeed, for thy theft

hath alreadie made thee butter, but tell me Iacke, whose fellowes are these that come after?

SIR IOHN Mine Hall, mine.

PRINCE I did neuer see such pitifull rascals.

SIR IOHN Tut, tut, good inough to tosse, foode for powder, foode for powder, theile fill a pit as well as better; tush man, mortall men, mortal men.

WESTMERLAND I but sir Iohn, me thinkes they are exceeding poore and bare, too beggerly.

SIR IOHN Faith for their pouerty I know not where they had that, and for their barenesse I am sure they neuer learnd that of me.

PRINCE No ile be sworne, vnlesse you call three fingers in the ribs bare, but sirrha make haste, Percy is already in the field.   *Exit*

SIR IOHN What is the king incampt?

WESTMERLAND He is sir Iohn I feare we shal stay too long.
⌈*Exit*⌉

SIR IOHN
    Wel, to the latter end of a fray,
    And the beginning of a feast
    Fits a dul fighter and a kene guest.   *Exit*

Sc. 14   *Enter Hotspur, Worcester, Douglas, Vernon*
(4.3)   HOTSPUR
    Weele fight with him to night.

WORCESTER   It may not be.

DOUGLAS
    You giue him then aduantage.

VERNON   Not a whit.

HOTSPUR
    Why say you so, lookes he not for supply?

VERNON
    So do we.

HOTSPUR   His is certaine, ours is doubtful.

WORCESTER
    Good coosen be aduisd, stir not to night.

VERNON (*to Hotspur*)
     Do not my Lord.

DOUGLAS   You do not counsel wel,
    You speake it out of feare, and cold hart.

VERNON
    Do me no slander Douglas, by my life,
    And I dare well maintaine it with my life,
    If well respected honor bid me on,
    I hould as little counsell with weake feare,
    As you my Lord, or any Scot that this day liues,
    Let it be seene to morrow in the battell
    Which of vs feares.

DOUGLAS Yea or to night.

VERNON Content.

HOTSPUR To night say I.

VERNON
    Come, come, it may not be. I wonder much
    Being men of such great leading as you are,
    That you foresee not what impediments
    Drag backe our expedition, certaine horse
    Of my coosen Vernons are not yet come vp,

Your Vncle Worcesters horse came but to day,
And now their pride and mettall is a sleepe,
Their courage with hard labour tame and dull,
That not a horse is halfe the halfe himselfe.

HOTSPUR
So are the horses of the enemie
In generall iourney bated and brought low,
The better part of ours are full of rest.

WORCESTER
The number of the King exceedeth our,
For Gods sake coosen stay till all come in.
        The trumpet sounds a parley ⌈*within*⌉. *Enter sir
        Walter Blunt*

BLUNT
I come with gracious offers from the king,
If you vouchsafe me hearing, and respect.

HOTSPUR
Welcome sir Walter Blunt: and would to God
You were of our determination,
Some of vs loue you well, and euen those some
Enuy your great deseruings and good name,
Because you are not of our qualitie,
But stand against vs like an enemie.

BLUNT
And God defend but still I should stand so,
So long as out of limit and true rule
You stand against annointed Maiestie.
But to my charge. The king hath sent to know
The nature of your griefes and whereupon
You coniure from the breast of ciuill peace
Such bold hostilitie: teaching his dutious land
Audacious crueltie. If that the king
Haue any way your good deserts forgot
Which he confesseth to be manifold,
He bids you name your griefes, and with all speede,
You shall haue your desires with interest
And pardon absolute for your selfe, and these
Herein misled by your suggestion.

HOTSPUR
The king is kind, and well we know the king
Knowes at what time to promise, when to pay:
My father, and my vncle, and my selfe,
Did giue him that same royaltie he weares,
And when he was not sixe and twentie strong,
Sicke in the worlds regard, wretched and low,
A poore vnminded outlaw sneaking home,
My father gaue him welcome to the shore:
And when he heard him sweare and vow to God,
He came but to be Duke of Lancaster,
To sue his liuery, and beg his peace
With teares of innocencie, and tearmes of zeale,
My father in kinde heart and pitie mou'd,
Swore him assistance, and performd it too.
Now when the Lords and Barons of the realme,
Perceiu'd Northumberland did leane to him,
The more and lesse came in with cap and knee,
Met him in Borroughs, Cities, Villages,
Attended him on bridges, stoode in lanes,

Laid gifts before him, profferd him their oathes,
Gaue him their heires as Pages, followed him,
Euen at the heeles, in golden multitudes,
He presently, as greatnesse knowes it selfe,
Steps me a little higher then his vow
Made to my father while his blood was poore
2420 Vpon the naked shore at Rauenspurgh,
And now forsooth takes on him to reforme
Some certaine edicts, and some streight decrees,
That lie too heauie on the Common-wealth,
Cries out vpon abuses, seemes to weepe
Ouer his Countreys wrongs, and by this face
This seeming brow of iustice did he winne
The hearts of all that he did angle for:
Proceeded further, cut me off the heads
Of all the fauourits that the absent king
2430 In deputation left behind him here,
When he was personall in the Irish warre.

BLUNT
  Tut, I came not to heare this.

HOTSPUR   Then to the poynt.
In short time after he deposd the king,
Soone after that depriu'd him of his life,
And in the necke of that taskt the whole state,
To make that woorse, suffred his kinsman March
(Who is if euerie owner were well plac'd
Indeed his king) to be ingagde in Wales,
There without raunsome to lie forfeited,
2440 Disgrac't me in my happy victories,
Sought to intrap me by intelligence,
Rated mine vnkle from the counsell boord,
In rage dismisd my father from the Court,
Broke oath on oath, committed wrong on wrong,
And in conclusion droue vs to seeke out
This head of safetie, and withall to prie
Into his title, the which we find
Too indirect for long continuance.

BLUNT
  Shall I returne this answere to the king?

HOTSPUR
2450 Not so sir Walter. Weele withdraw a while.
Go to the king, and let there be impawnde
Some surety for a safe returne againe,
And in the morning early shal mine vnkle
Bring him our purposes, and so farewell.

BLUNT
  I would you would accept of grace and loue.

HOTSPUR
  And may be so we shall.

BLUNT   Pray God you do.
  Exeunt ⌈Hotspur, Worcester, Douglas, Vernon
  at one doore, Blunt at another doore⌉

Sc. 15   *Enter Archbishop of Yorke, sir Mighell*
(4.4) ARCHBISHOP *(giuing letters)*
  Hie good sir Mighell, beare this sealed briefe
  With winged haste to the Lord Marshall,

This to my coosen Scroope, and all the rest
To whom they are directed. If you knew   2460
How much they do import you would make haste.

SIR MIGHELL My good Lord
  I gesse their tenor.

ARCHBISHOP   Like enough you do.
To morrow good sir Mighell is a day,
Wherein the fortune of ten thousand men
Must bide the touch. For sir at Shrewsbury
As I am truly giuen to vnderstand,
The king with mighty and quicke raised power
Meetes with Lord Harry. And I feare sir Mighell
What with the sicknesse of Northumberland,   2470
Whose power was in the first proportion,
And what with Owen Glendowers absence thence,
Who with them was a rated sinew too,
And comes not in ouerrulde by prophecies,
I feare the power of Percy is too weake
To wage an instant triall with the king.

SIR MIGHELL
  Why my good Lord, you need not feare, there is
      Douglas,
  And Lord Mortimer.

ARCHBISHOP   No, Mortimer is not there.

SIR MIGHELL
  But there is Mordake, Vernon, Lord Harry Percy.
  And there is my Lord of Worcester, and a head   2480
  Of gallant warriours, noble gentlemen.

ARCHBISHOP
  And so there is: but yet the king hath drawn
  The speciall head of all the land togither,
  The Prince of Wales, Lord Iohn of Lancaster,
  The noble Westmerland, and warlike Blunt,
  And many mo coriuals and deare men
  Of estimation and command in armes.

SIR MIGHELL
  Doubt not my Lo: they shalbe wel oppos'd.

ARCHBISHOP
  I hope no lesse, yet needfull tis to feare,
  And to preuent the worst, sir Mighell speed: 2490
  For if Lord Percy thriue not, ere the king
  Dismisse his power, he meanes to visit vs,
  For he hath heard of our confederacy,
  And tis but wisedome to make strong against him,
  Therefore make haste, I must go write againe
  To other friends, and so farewell sir Mighel.

                    Exeunt ⌈seuerally⌉

  Enter the King, Prince of Wales, Lord Iohn of   Sc. 16
  Lancaster, Earle of Westmerland, sir Walter Blunt,   (5.1)
  sir Iohn Olde-castle

KING
  How bloudily the sunne begins to peare
  Aboue yon bulky hill, the day lookes pale
  At his distemprature.

PRINCE   The Southren winde
  Doth play the trumpet to his purposes,   2500

And by his hollow whistling in the leaues
Foretels a tempest and a blustring day.

KING

Then with the loosers let it simpathize,
For nothing can seeme foule to those that winne.

The trumpet sounds ⌈a parley within⌉. Enter
Worcester ⌈and Vernon⌉

How now my Lord of Worcester, tis not wel,
That you and I should meet vpon such tearmes
As now we meete. You haue deceiu'd our trust,
And made vs doffe our easie roabes of peace,
To crush our old limbs in vngentle steele,
2510   This is not well my Lord, this is not well.
What say you to it? will you againe vnknit
This churlish knot of all abhorred war?
And moue in that obedient orbe againe,
Where you did giue a faire and naturall light,
And be no more an exhalde meteor,
A prodigie of feare, and a portent
Of broched mischiefe to the vnborne times.

WORCESTER Heare me my liege:
For mine own part I could be well content,
2520   To entertaine the lag end of my life
With quiet houres. For I protest
I haue not sought the day of this dislike.

KING

You haue not sought it, how comes it then?

SIR IOHN Rebellion lay in his way, and he found it.

PRINCE Peace chewet, peace.

WORCESTER (*to the king*)

It pleasd your maiesty to turne your lookes
Of fauor from my selfe, and all our house,
And yet I must remember you my Lord,
We were the first and dearest of your friends,
2530   For you my staffe of office did I breake
In Richards time, and posted day and night
To meet you on the way, and kisse your hand,
When yet you were in place, and in account
Nothing so strong and fortunate as I.
It was my selfe, my brother and his sonne,
That brought you home, and boldly did outdare
The dangers of the time. You swore to vs,
And you did sware that oath at Dancaster,
That you did nothing purpose gainst the state,
2540   Nor clame no further then your new falne right,
The seat of Gaunt, Dukedom of Lancaster:
To this we swore our aide: but in short space
It rainde downe fortune showring on your head,
And such a floud of greatnesse fell on you,
What with our helpe, what with the absent king,
What with the iniuries of a wanton time,
The seeming sufferances that you had borne,
And the contrarious winds that held the king
So long in his vnlucky Irish wars,
2550   That all in England did repute him dead:
And from this swarme of faire aduantages,
You tooke occasion to be quickly wooed
To gripe the general sway into your hand,

Forgot your oath to vs at Dancaster,
And being fed by vs, you vsd vs so
As that vngentle gull the Cuckoes bird
Vseth the sparrow, did oppresse our neast,
Grew by our feeding to so great a bulke,
That euen our loue durst not come neare your sight,
For feare of swallowing: but with nimble wing   2560
We were inforst for safety sake to flie
Out of your sight, and raise this present head,
Whereby we stand opposed by such meanes,
As you your selfe haue forgde against your selfe
By vnkind vsage, daungerous countenance,
And violation of all faith and troth,
Sworne to vs in your yonger enterprize.

KING

These things indeed you haue articulate,
Proclaimd at market Crosses, read in Churches,
To face the garment of rebellion   2570
With some fine colour that may please the eye
Of fickle changlings and poore discontents,
Which gape and rub the elbow at the newes
Of hurly burly innouation,
And neuer yet did insurrection want
Such water colors to impaint his cause
Nor moody beggars staruing for a time,
Of pell mell hauocke and confusion.

PRINCE

In both our armies there is many a soule,
Shall pay full dearely for this incounter   2580
If once they ioine in trial, tell your nephew
The prince of Wales doth ioine with all the world
In praise of Henrie Percy, by my hopes
This present enterprise set of his head,
I do not thinke a brauer Gentleman,
More actiue, valiant, or more valiant yong,
More daring, or more bold is now aliue
To grace this latter age with noble deedes,
For my part I may speake it to my shame,
I haue a truant beene to Chiualrie,   2590
And so I heare he doth account me too;
Yet this before my fathers maiestie,
I am content that he shall take the oddes
Of his great name and estimation,
And will to saue the blood on either side
Trie fortune with him in a single fight.

KING

And prince of Wales, so dare we venture thee,
Albeit, considerations infinite
Do make against it: no good Worcester no,
We loue our people well, euen those we loue   2600
That are misled vpon your coosens part,
And will they take the offer of our grace,
Both he, and they, and you, yea euery man
Shall be my friend againe, and ile be his,
So tell your coosen, and bring me word
What he will do. But if he will not yeeld,
Rebuke and dread correction waight on vs,
And they shall do their office. So be gone:

We will not now be troubled with replie,
2610 We offer faire, take it aduisedly.
                    Exeunt Worcester ⌈and Vernon⌉

PRINCE
It will not be accepted on my life,
The Dowglas and the Hotspur both togither,
Are confident against the world in armes.

KING
Hence therefore, euery leader to his charge,
For on their answere will we set on them,
And God befriend vs as our cause is iust.
                    Exeunt: manent Prince, Olde-castle

SIR IOHN Hal, if thou see me downe in the battel and
bestride me, so, tis a poynt of friendship.

PRINCE Nothing but a Colossus can do thee that friendship,
2620 say thy prayers, and farewell.

SIR IOHN I would twere bed time Hal, and all well.

PRINCE Why, thou owest God a death.   *Exit*

SIR IOHN Tis not due yet, I would be loath to pay him
before his day, what need I be so forwarde with him
that cals not on mee? Well, tis no matter, honor prickes
me on; yea, but how if honor pricke me off when I
come on? how then? can honor set to a leg? no, or
an arme? no, or take away the griefe of a wound? no,
honor hath no skil in surgerie then? no, what is honor?
2630 a word, what is in that word honor? what is that
honour? aire, a trim reckoning. Who hath it? he that
died a Wednesday, doth he feele it? no, doth he heare
it? no, tis insensible thẽ? yea, to the dead, but wil it
not liue with the liuing; no, why? detraction will not
suffer it, therefore ile none of it; honor is a meere
skutchion, and so ends my Catechisme.   *Exit*

Sc. 17   *Enter Worcester, sir Richard Vernon*
(5.2) WORCESTER
O no, my nephew must not know sir Richard,
The liberal and kind offer of the king.

VERNON
Twere best he did.

WORCESTER   Then are we all vndone.
2640 It is not possible, it cannot be
The king should keepe his word in louing vs,
He will suspect vs still, and find a time
To punish this offence in other faults,
Supposition, al our liues shall be stucke full of eyes,
For treason is but trusted like the Foxe,
Who nere so tame, so cherisht and lockt vp,
Will haue a wilde tricke of his ancesters,
Looke how we can, or sad or merely,
Interpretation will misquote our lookes,
2650 And we shall feed like oxen at a stall,
The better cherisht still the nearer death,
My nephewes trespasse may be well forgot,
It hath the excuse of youth and heat of blood,
And an adopted name of priueledge,
A hair-braind Hotspur gouernd by a spleene,
All his offences liue vpon my head
And on his fathers. We did traine him on,

And his corruption being tane from vs,
We as the spring of all shall pay for all:
Therefore good coosen; let not Harry know   2660
In any case the offer of the King.

VERNON
Deliuer what you will; ile say tis so.
                    Enter Hotspur and Douglas
Here coms your coosen.

HOTSPUR   My vncle is returnd,
Deliuer vp my Lord of Westmerland,
Vncle, what newes?

WORCESTER
The king will bid you battell presently.

DOUGLAS
Defie him by the Lord of Westmerland.

HOTSPUR
Lord Douglas go you and tell him so.

DOUGLAS
Marry and shal, and very willingly.   *Exit*

WORCESTER
There is no seeming mercie in the king.   2670

HOTSPUR
Did you beg any? God forbid.

WORCESTER
I tolde him gently of our greeuances,
Of his oath breaking, which he mended thus,
By now forswearing that he is forsworne,
He cals vs rebels, traitors, and will scourge
With haughtie armes this hatefull name in vs.
                    Enter Douglas

DOUGLAS
Arme gentlemen, to armes, for I haue throwne
A braue defiance in king Henries teeth,
And Westmerland that was ingag'd did beare it,
Which cannot chuse but bring him quickly on.   2680

WORCESTER (*to Hotspur*)
The Prince of Wales stept forth before the king,
And nephew, chalengd you to single fight.

HOTSPUR
O would the quarrel lay vpon our heads,
And that no man might draw short breath to day
But I and Harry Monmouth; tell me, tell me,
How shewed his tasking? seemd it in contempt?

VERNON
No, by my soule I neuer in my life
Did heare a chalenge vrgde more modestly,
Vnlesse a brother should a brother dare,
To gentle exercise and proofe of armes.   2690
He gaue you all the duties of a man,
Trimd vp your praises with a Princely tongue,
Spoke your deseruings like a Chronicle,
Making you euer better then his praise,
By still dispraising praise valued with you,
And which became him like a prince indeed,
He made a blushing citall of himselfe,
And chid his truant youth with such a grace
As if he mastred there a double spirit
Of teaching and of learning instantly,   2700

There did he pause, but let me tel the world
If he outliue the enuie of this day,
England did neuer owe so sweete a hope
So much misconstrued in his wantonnesse.

HOTSPUR
Coosen I thinke thou art enamored
On his follies, neuer did I heare
Of any prince so wilde a libertie,
But be he as he will, yet once ere night
I will imbrace him with a souldiours arme,
2710   That he shall shrinke vnder my curtesie,
Arme, arme with speed, and fellowes, soldiors, friends,
Better consider what you haue to do
Then I that haue not wel the gift of tongue
Can lift your blood vp with perswasion.
        Enter a Messenger

MESSENGER My Lord, here are letters for you.

HOTSPUR I cannot read them now,   ⌈*Exit Messenger*⌉
O Gentlemen the time of life is short,
To spend that shortnes basely were too long
If life did ride vpon a dials point,
2720   Still ending at the arriuall of an houre,
And if we liue we liue to tread on kings,
If die, braue death when princes die with vs,
Now for our consciences, the armes are faire
When the intent of bearing them is iust.
        Enter another Messenger

MESSENGER
My Lord, prepare the king comes on a pace.   ⌈*Exit*⌉

HOTSPUR
I thanke him that he cuts me from my tale,
For I professe not talking, onely this,
Let each man do his best, and here draw I
A sword, whose temper I intend to staine
2730   With the best bloud that I can meet withall,
In the aduenture of this perillous day.
Now esperance Percy and set on,
Sound all the loftie instruments of war,
And by that Musicke let vs all embrace,
For heauen to earth some of vs neuer shall
A second time do such a courtesie.
        The trumpets sound. Here they embrace. Exeunt

Sc. 18   *The king enters with his power, alarme and exeunt*
(5.3)   *to the battel, then enter Douglas, and sir Walter*
        Blunt disguised as the king

BLUNT
What is thy name that in the battell thus
Thou crossest me, what honour dost thou seeke
Vpon my head?

DOUGLAS   Know then my name is Douglas,
2740   And I do haunt thee in the battell thus
Because some tell me that thou art a king.

BLUNT They tell thee true.

DOUGLAS
The Lord of Stafford deare to day hath bought
Thy likenesse, for in steed of thee king Harry
This sword hath ended him, so shall it thee
Vnlesse thou yeeld thee as my prisoner.

BLUNT
I was not borne a yeelder thou proud Scot,
And thou shalt find a king that will reuenge
Lord Staffords death.
        They fight, Douglas kils Blunt, then enter Hotspur

HOTSPUR
O Douglas hadst thou fought at Holmedon thus   2750
I neuer had triumpht vpon a Scot.

DOUGLAS
Als done, als won, here breathles lies the king.

HOTSPUR Where?

DOUGLAS Here.

HOTSPUR
This Douglas? no, I know this face full well,
A gallant knight he was, his name was Blunt,
Semblably furnisht like the king himselfe.

DOUGLAS (*to Blunts body*)
A foole goe with thy soule whither it goes,
A borrowed title hast thou bought too deare.
Why didst thou tell me that thou wert a king?   2760

HOTSPUR
The king hath many marching in his coates.

DOUGLAS
Now by my sword I will kill al his coates.
Ile murder all his wardrop, peece by peece
Vntill I meete the king.

HOTSPUR   Vp and away,
Our souldiers stand full fairely for the day.
        Exeunt, leauing Blunts body
        Alarme, Enter sir Iohn Olde-castle solus

SIR IOHN Though I could scape shot-free at London, I
feare the shot here, heres no skoring but vpon the pate.
Soft, who are you? sir Walter Blunt, theres honour for
you, heres no vanitie, I am as hot as molten lead, &
as heauie too: God keepe leade out of me, I need no   2770
more weight then mine owne bowels. I haue led my
rag of Muffins where they are pepperd, theres not three
of my 150. left aliue, and they are for the townes ende,
to beg during life:
        Enter the Prince
but who comes here?

PRINCE
What, stands thou idle here? lend me thy sword,
Many a noble man lies starke and stiffe,
Vnder the hoofes of vaunting enemies,
Whose deaths as yet ar vnreuengd, I preethe
Lend mee thy sword.   2780

SIR IOHN
O Hal, I preethe giue me leaue to breath a while,
Turke Gregorie neuer did such deeds in armes
As I haue don this day, I haue paid Percy,
I haue made him sure.

PRINCE   He is indeed,
And liuing to kill thee: I preethe
Lend me thy sword.

SIR IOHN   Nay before God Hal,
If Percy be aliue thou gets not my sword,
But take my pistoll if thou wilt.

PRINCE
Giue it me, what? is it in the case?

SIR IOHN   I Hal,
2790   Tis hot, tis hot, theres that will sacke a Citie.
        The Prince drawes it out, and finds it to be a bottle
        of Sacke

PRINCE
What is it a time to iest and dally now?
        He throwes the bottle at him. Exit

SIR IOHN   Well if Percy be aliue, ile pierce him; if hee doe
come in my way so, if he doe not, if I come in his
willingly, let him make a Carbonado of me. I like not
such grinning honour as sir Walter hath, giue me life,
which if I can saue, so: if not, honor comes vnlookt
for, and theres an end.   *Exit ⌈with Blunts body⌉*

Sc. 19   *Alarme, excursions. Enter the King, the Prince,*
(5.4)   *wounded, Lord Iohn of Lancaster, Earle of*
        Westmerland

KING
I preethe Harry withdraw thy selfe, thou bleedst too
        much,
Lord Iohn of Lancaster go you with him.

LANCASTER
2800   Not I my Lord, vnlesse I did bleed too.

PRINCE (*to the king*)
I beseech your maiestie make vp,
Least your retirement do amaze your friends.

KING
I will do so. My Lord of Westmerland
Lead him to his tent.

WESTMERLAND (*to the Prince*)
Come my Lord, ile lead you to your tent.

PRINCE
Lead me my Lord? I do not need your helpe,
And God forbid a shallow scratch should driue
The Prince of Wales from such a field as this,
Where staind nobilitie lies troden on,
2810   And rebels armes triumphe in massacres.

LANCASTER
We breath too long, come coosen Westmerland
Our dutie this way lies: For Gods sake come.
        Exeunt Lancaster and Westmerland

PRINCE
By God thou hast deceiu'd me Lancaster,
I did not thinke thee Lord of such a spirit,
Before I lou'd thee as a brother Iohn,
But now I do respect thee as my soule.

KING
I saw him hold Lord Percy at the poynt,
With lustier maintenance then I did looke for
Of such an vngrowne warrior.

PRINCE
2820   O this boy lends mettall to vs all.   *Exit*
        Enter Douglas

DOUGLAS
Another king, they grow like Hydraes heads,
I am the Douglas fatall to all those

That weare those colours on them. What art thou
That counterfetst the person of a King?

KING
The king himself, who Douglas grieues at hart,
So many of his shadowes thou hast met
And not the verie king, I haue two boies
Seeke Percy and thy selfe about the field,
But seeing thou falst on me so luckily
I will assay thee and defend thy selfe.   2830

DOUGLAS
I feare thou art another counterfet,
And yet in faith thou bearst thee like a king,
But mine I am sure thou art who ere thou be,
And thus I winne thee.
        They fight, the king being in danger, Enter Prince of
        Wales

PRINCE
Hold vp thy head vile Scot, or thou art like
Neuer to hold it vp againe, the spirits
Of Valiant Sherly, Stafford, Blunt are in my armes,
It is the Prince of Wales that threatens thee,
Who neuer promiseth but he meanes to pay.
        They fight, Douglas flieth
Cheerly my Lord, how fares your grace?   2840
Sir Nicholas Gawsey hath for succour sent,
And so hath Clifton, ile to Clifton straight.

KING   Stay and breath a while,
Thou hast redeemd thy lost opinion,
And shewde thou makst some tender of my life,
In this faire rescue thou hast brought to me.

PRINCE
O God they did me too much iniury,
That euer said I harkned for your death,
If it were so, I might haue let alone
The insulting hand of Douglas ouer you,   2850
Which would haue been as speedy in your end
As al the poisonous potions in the world,
And sau'd the trecherous labour of your sonne.

KING
Make vp to Clifton, ile to S. Nicholas Gawsey.   *Exit*
        Enter Hotspur

HOTSPUR
If I mistake not, thou art Harry Monmouth.

PRINCE
Thou speakst as if I would deny my name.

HOTSPUR
My name is Harry Percy.

PRINCE   Why then I see
A very valiant rebel of the name;
I am the Prince of Wales, and thinke not Percy
To share with me in glory any more: 2860
Two stars keepe not their motion in one sphere,
Nor can one England brooke a double raigne
Of Harry Percy and the Prince of Wales.

HOTSPUR
Nor shal it Harry, for the houre is come
To end the one of vs, and would to God
Thy name in armes were now as great as mine.

PRINCE

Ile make it greater ere I part from thee,
And al the budding honors on thy crest
Ile crop to make a garland for my head.

HOTSPUR

2870 I can no longer brooke thy vanities.
They fight:
Enter sir Iohn Olde-castle

SIR IOHN Well said Hall, to it Hall. Nay you shall find no
boyes play here I can tel you.
Enter Douglas, he fighteth with sir Iohn, who fals
down as if he were dead, exit Douglas, the Prince
killeth Hotspur

HOTSPUR

Oh Harry thou hast robd me of my youth,
I better brooke the losse of brittle life
Then those proud titles thou hast won of me,
They wound my thoughts worse then thy sword my
flesh,
But thoughts the slaues of life, and life times foole,
And time that takes suruey of all the world
Must haue a stop. O I could prophecy,
2880 But that the earthy and cold hand of death
Lies on my tongue: no Percy thou art dust
And food for.   *He dies*

PRINCE

For wormes, braue Percy. Fare thee wel great hart,
Ill weaud ambition, how much art thou shrunke,
When that this body did containe a spirit,
A kingdom for it was too small a bound,
But now two paces of the vilest earth
Is roome inough, this earth that beares the dead
Beares not aliue so stout a gentleman,
2890 If thou wert sensible of curtesie
I should not make so deare a shew of zeale,
But let my fauors hide thy mangled face,
He couers Hotspurs face
And euen in thy behalfe ile thanke my selfe,
For doing these faire rights of tendernesse,
Adiew and take thy praise with thee to heauen,
Thy ignominy sleepe with thee in the graue,
But not remembred in thy Epitaph.
He spieth sir Iohn on the ground
What old acquaintance, could not all this flesh
Keepe in a little life? poore Iacke farewell,
2900 I could haue better sparde a better man:
O I should haue a heauy misse of thee,
If I were much in loue with vanitie:
Death hath not strooke so fat a Deere to day,
Though many dearer in this bloudy fray,
Inboweld will I see thee by and by,
Til then in bloud by noble Percy lie.   *Exit*
Sir Iohn riseth vp

SIR IOHN Inboweld, if thou inbowel me to day, ile giue
you leaue to powder me and eate me too to morrowe.
Zbloud twas time to counterfet, or that hot termagant
2910 Scot had paide me scot and lot too. Counterfet? I lie, I
am no counterfet, to die is to bee a counterfet, for he
is but the counterfet of a man, who hath not the life

of a mã: but to coũterfet dying when a man therby
liueth, is to be no counterfet, but the true & perfect
image of life indeed. The better parte of valour is
discretion, in the which better part I haue saued my
life. Zounds I am afraid of this gunpowder Percy, though
he be dead, how if he should counterfet too and rise?
by my faith I am afraid hee woulde proue the better
counterfet, therefore ile make him sure, yea, and ile   2920
sweare I kild him. Why may not he rise aswell as I?
nothing confutes me but eies, and no body sees me:
therefore sirrha, (*stabbing Hotspur*) with a new wound
in your thigh, come you along with me.
He takes vp Hotspur on his backe.
Enter Prince, Iohn of Lancaster

PRINCE

Come brother Iohn, full brauely hast thou flesht
Thy mayden sword.

LANCASTER   But soft, whom haue we heere?
Did you not tell me this fat man was dead?

PRINCE I did, I saw him dead,
Breathlesse and bleeding on the ground. (*To sir Iohn*)
Art thou aliue?
Or is it fantasie that playes vpon our eiesight?   2930
I preethe speake, we will not trust our eies
Without our eares, thou art not what thou seemst.

SIR IOHN No thats certaine, I am not a double man: but
if I bee not Iacke Olde-castle, then am I a Iacke: there
is Percy, if your father will doe me anie honour, so: if
not, let him kill the next Percie himselfe: I looke to bee
either Earle or Duke, I can assure you.

PRINCE

Why Percy, I kild my selfe, and saw thee dead.

SIR IOHN Didst thou? Lord, Lord, howe this world is giuen
to lying, I graunt you I was downe, and out of breath,   2940
and so was he, but we rose both at an instant, and
fought a long houre by Shrewesburie clocke, if I may
be beleeude so: if not, let them that should rewarde
valour, beare the sinne vppon their owne heads. Ile
take't on my death, I gaue him this wound in the
thigh, if the man were aliue, and would denie it, zounds
I would make him eate a peece of my sword.

LANCASTER

This is the strangest tale that ere I heard.

PRINCE

This is the strangest fellow, brother Iohn,
(*To sir Iohn*) Come bring your luggage nobly on your
backe.   2950
For my part, if a lie may do thee grace,
Ile guild it with the happiest termes I haue.
A retraite is sounded
The Trumpet sounds retrait, the day is our,
Come brother let vs to the highest of the field,
To see what friends are liuing, who are dead.
Exeunt Prince and Lancaster

SIR IOHN Ile follow as they say for reward. Hee that
rewardes mee God reward him. If I do growe great, ile
growe lesse, for ile purge and leaue Sacke, and liue
cleanlie as a noble man should do.

Exit bearing Hotspurs body

Sc. 20
(5.5)

The Trumpets sound. Enter the King, Prince of
Wales, Lord Iohn of Lancaster, Earle of
Westmerland, with Worcester, and Vernon
prisoners, ⌈and souldiours⌉

KING

2960
Thus euer did rebellion find rebuke,
Ill spirited Worcester, did not we send grace,
Pardon, and tearmes of loue to all of you?
And wouldst thou turne our offers contrary?
Misuse the tenor of thy kinsmans trust.
Three knights vpon our party slaine to day,
A noble Earle and many a creature else,
Had been aliue this houre,
If like a Christian thou hadst truly borne
Betwixt our armies true intelligence.

WORCESTER

2970
What I haue done my safety vrg'd me to:
And I embrace this fortune patiently,
Since not to be auoided it fals on me.

KING

Beare Worcester to the death and Vernon too:
Other Offendors we will pause vpon.

Exeunt Worcester and Vernon, garded

How goes the field?

PRINCE

The noble Scot Lord Dowglas, when he saw
The fortune of the day quite turnd from him,
The noble Percy slaine and all his men
Vpon the foot of feare, fled with the rest

2980
And falling from a hill, he was so bruisd,

That the pursuers tooke him. At my tent
The Douglas is: and I beseech your grace
I may dispose of him.

KING With all my hart.

PRINCE

Then brother Iohn of Lancaster,
To you this honorable bounty shal belong,
Go to the Douglas and deliuer him
Vp to his pleasure, ransomlesse and free,
His valours shewne vpon our Crests to daie
Haue taught vs how to cherish such high deeds,   2990
Euen in the bosome of our aduersaries.

LANCASTER

I thanke your grace for this high curtesie,
Which I shall giue away immediatly.

KING

Then this remaines that we deuide our power,
You sonne Iohn, and my coosen Westmerland
Towards York shal bend you with your deerest speed
To meet Northumberland and the Prelate Scroope,
Who as we heare are busily in armes:
My selfe and you sonne Harry will towards Wales,
To fight with Glendower and the Earle of March,   3000
Rebellion in this land shall loose his sway,
Meeting the checke of such another day,
And since this businesse so faire is done,
Let vs not leaue till all our owne be won.

Exeunt ⌈the king, the Prince, and their power at
one doore, Lancaster, Westmerland, and their
power at another doore⌉

FINIS

THE MERRY WIUES OF WINDSOR

A LEGEND dating from 1702 claims that Shakespeare wrote *The Merry Wiues of Windsor* in fourteen days and by command of Queen Elizabeth; in 1709 she was said to have wished particularly to see Falstaffe in love. Whether or not this is true, a passage towards the end of the play alluding directly to the ceremonies of the Order of the Garter, Britain's highest order of chivalry, encourages the belief that the play has a direct connection with a specific occasion. In 1597 George Carey, Lord Hunsdon, Lord Chamberlain and patron of Shakespeare's company, was installed at Windsor as a Knight of the Garter. The Queen was not present at the installation but had attended the Garter Feast at the Palace of Westminster on St George's Day (23 April). Shakespeare's play was probably performed in association with this occasion, and may have been written especially for it. It was first printed, in a corrupt text, in 1602; a better text appears in the 1623 Folio.

Some of the characters—Sir Iohn Falstaffe, Mistris Quickly, Pistoll, Nim, Iustice Shallow—appear also in *1* and *2 Henry IV* and *Henry V*, but in spite of a reference to 'the wilde Prince, and *Pointz*' at 1359-60, this is essentially an Elizabethan comedy, the only one that Shakespeare set firmly in England. The play is full of details that would have been familiar to Elizabethan Londoners, and the language is colloquial and up to date. The plot, however, is made up of conventional situations whose ancestry is literary rather than realistic. There are many analogues in medieval and other tales to Shakespeare's basic plot situations, some in books that he probably or certainly knew. The central story, of Sir Iohn's unsuccessful attempts to seduce Mistris Page and Mistris Ford, and of Master Ford's unfounded jealousy, is in the tradition of the Italian *novella*, and may have been suggested by Ser Giovanni Fiorentino's *Il Pecorone* (1558). Alongside it Shakespeare places the comical but finally romantic love story of Anne Page, wooed by the foolish but rich Abraham Slender and the irascible French Doctor Caius, but won by the young and handsome Fenton. The play contains a higher proportion of prose to verse than any other play by Shakespeare, and the action is often broadly comic; but it ends, after the midnight scene in Windsor Forest during which Sir Iohn is frightened out of his lechery, in forgiveness and love.

The play is known to have been acted for James I on 4 November 1604, and for Charles I in 1638. It was revived soon after the theatres reopened, in 1660; at first it was not particularly popular, but since 1720 it has consistently pleased audiences. Many artists have illustrated it, and it forms the basis for a number of operas, including Otto Nicolai's *Die lustigen Weiben von Windsor* (1848) and Giuseppe Verdi's comic masterpiece, *Falstaff* (1893).

The Folio was printed from a manuscript apparently prepared by the scribe Ralph Crane, who was himself probably copying a late prompt-book; so the incidentals are far removed from Shakespeare's own.

THE NAMES OF THE ACTORS

MISTRIS Margaret PAGE
Master George PAGE, her husband
ANNE Page, their daughter
WILLIAM Page, their sonne

MISTRIS Alice FORD
Master Frank FORD, her husband
IOHN
ROBERT } their Seruants

SIR IOHN Falstaffe
BARDOLFE
PISTOLL } Sir Iohns followers
NIM
ROBIN, Sir Iohns page

} Citizens of Windsor

The HOST of the Garter Inn

Sir Hugh EUANS, a Welch Parson

Doctor CAIUS, a French Physician
MISTRIS QUICKLY, his house-keeper
Iohn RUGBY, his Seruant

Master FENTON, a yong Gentleman, in loue with Anne Page

Master Abraham SLENDER
Robert SHALLOW, his vnckle, a Iustice
Peter SIMPLE, Slenders Seruant

Children of Windsor, appearing as Fairies

The Merry Wiues of Windsor

Enter Iustice Shallow, Slender, Sir Hugh Euans

SHALLOW Sir *Hugh*, perswade me not: I will make a Star-Chamber matter of it, if hee were twenty Sir *Iohn Falstoffs*, he shall not abuse *Robert Shallow* Esquire.

SLENDER In the County of *Glocester*, Iustice of Peace and Coram.

SHALLOW I (Cosen *Slender*) and *Cust-alorum*.

SLENDER I, and *Rato-lorum* too; and a Gentleman borne (Master Parson) who writes himselfe *Armigero*, in any Bill, Warrant, Quittance, or Obligation, *Armigero*.

10 SHALLOW I that I doe, and haue done any time these three hundred yeeres.

SLENDER All his successors (gone before him) hath don't: and all his Ancestors (that come after him) may: they may giue the dozen white Luces in their Coate.

SHALLOW It is an olde Coate.

EUANS The dozen white Lowses doe become an old Coad well: it agrees well passant: It is a familiar beast to man, and signifies Loue.

SHALLOW The Luse is the fresh-fish, the salt-fish, is an old
20 Code.

SLENDER I may quarter (Coz).

SHALLOW You may, by marrying.

EUANS It is marring indeed, if he quarter it.

SHALLOW Not a whit.

EUANS Yes per-lady: if he ha's a quarter of your coat, there is but three Skirts for your selfe, in my simple coniectures; but that is all one: if Sir *Iohn Falstaffe* haue committed disparagements vnto you, I am of the Church and will be glad to do my beneuolence, to make attonements and compremises betweene you.
30 SHALLOW The Councell shall heare it, it is a Riot.

EUANS It is not meet the Councell heare a Riot: there is no feare of Got in a Riot: The Councell (looke you) shall desire to heare the feare of Got, and not to heare a Riot: take your viza-ments in that.

SHALLOW Ha; o'my life, if I were yong againe, the sword should end it.

EUANS It is petter that friends is the sword, and end it: and there is also another deuice in my praine, which
40 peraduenture prings goot discretions with it. There is *Anne Page*, which is daughter to Master *Geo. Page*, which is pretty virginity.

SLENDER *Mistris Anne Page?* she has browne haire, and speakes small like a woman.

EUANS It is that ferry person for all the orld, as iust as you will desire, and seuen hundred pounds of Moneyes, and Gold, and Siluer, is her Grand-sire vpon his deaths-bed, (Got deliuer to a ioyfull resurrections) giue, when she is able to ouertake seuenteene yeeres old. It were
50 a goot motion, if we leaue our pribbles and prabbles, and desire a marriage betweene Master *Abraham*, and Mistris *Anne Page*.

SLENDER Did her Grand-sire leaue her seauen hundred pound?

EUANS I, and her father is make her a petter penny.

⌜SHALLOW⌝ I know the young Gentlewoman, she has good gifts.

EUANS Seuen hundred pounds, and possibilities, is goot gifts.

SHALLOW Wel, let vs see honest Mr *Page*: is *Falstaffe* there? 60

EUANS Shall I tell you a lye? I doe despise a lyer, as I doe despise one that is false, or as I despise one that is not true: the Knight Sir *Iohn* is there, and I beseech you be ruled by your well-willers: I will peat the doore for Mr. *Page*.

He knockes on the doore

What hoa? Got-plesse your house heere.

PAGE ⌜*within*⌝ Who's there?

EUANS Here is go't's plessing and your friend, and Iustice *Shallow*, and heere yong Master *Slender*: that perad-uentures shall tell you another tale, if matters grow to 70 your likings.

⌜*Enter Page*⌝

PAGE I am glad to see your Worships well: I thanke you for my Venison Master *Shallow*.

SHALLOW Master *Page*, I am glad to see you: much good doe it your good heart: I wish'd your Venison better, it was ill killd: how doth good Mistresse *Page?* and I thank you alwaies with my heart, la: with my heart.

PAGE Sir, I thanke you.

SHALLOW Sir, I thanke you: by yea, and no I doe.

PAGE I am glad to see you, good Master *Slender*. 80

SLENDER How do's your fallow Greyhound, Sir, I heard say he was out-run on *Cotsall*.

PAGE It could not be iudg'd, Sir.

SLENDER You'll not confesse: you'll not confesse.

SHALLOW That he will not, 'tis your fault, 'tis your fault: (*to Page*) 'tis a good dogge.

PAGE A Cur, Sir.

SHALLOW Sir: hee's a good dog, and a faire dog, can there be more said? he is good, and faire. Is Sir *Iohn Falstaffe* heere? 90

PAGE Sir, hee is within: and I would I could doe a good office betweene you.

EUANS It is spoke as a Christians ought to speake.

SHALLOW He hath wrong'd me (Master *Page*.)

PAGE Sir, he doth in some sort confesse it.

SHALLOW If it be confessed, it is not redressed; is not that so (M. *Page?*) he hath wrong'd me, indeed he hath, at a word he hath: beleeue me, *Robert Shallow* Esquire, saith he is wronged.

Enter Sir Iohn Falstoffe, Bardolph, Nym, Pistoll

PAGE Here comes Sir *Iohn*. 100

SIR IOHN Now, Master *Shallow*, you'll complaine of me to the King?

SHALLOW Knight, you haue beaten my men, kill'd my
deere, and broke open my Lodge.

SIR IOHN But not kiss'd your Keepers daughter?

SHALLOW Tut, a pin: this shall be answer'd.

SIR IOHN I will answere it strait, I haue done all this:
That is now answer'd.

SHALLOW The Councell shall know this.

110 SIR IOHN 'Twere better for you if it were known in
councell: you'll be laugh'd at.

EUANS *Pauca verba*; (Sir *Iohn*) good worts.

SIR IOHN Good worts? good Cabidge; *Slender*, I broke your
head: what matter haue you against me?

SLENDER Marry sir, I haue matter in my head against
you, and against your cony-catching Rascalls, *Bardolf*,
Nym, and *Pistoll*.

BARDOLFE You Banbery Cheese.

SLENDER I, it is no matter.

120 PISTOLL How now, *Mephostophilus*?

SLENDER I, it is no matter.

NYM Slice, I say; *pauca, pauca*: Slice, that's my humor.

SLENDER (*to Shallow*) Where's *Simple* my man? can you
tell, Cosen?

EUANS Peace, I pray you: now let vs vnderstand: there
is three Vmpires in this matter, as I vnderstand; that
is, Master *Page* (fidelicet Master *Page*,) & there is my
selfe, (fidelicet my selfe) and the three party is (lastly,
and finally) mine Host of the Garter.

130 PAGE We three to hear it, & end it between them.

EUANS Ferry goo't, I will make a priefe of it in my note-
booke, and we wil afterwards orke vpon the cause,
with as great discreetly as we can.

SIR IOHN *Pistoll*.

PISTOLL He heares with eares.

EUANS The Teuill and his Tam: what phrase is this? he
heares with eare? why, it is affectations.

SIR IOHN *Pistoll*, did you picke M. *Slenders* purse?

SLENDER I, by these gloues did hee, or I would I might
140 neuer come in mine owne great chamber againe else,
of seauen groates in mill-sixpences, and two *Edward*
Shouelboords, that cost me two shilling and two pence
a peece of *Yead Miller*: by these gloues.

SIR IOHN Is this true, *Pistoll*?

EUANS No, it is false, if it is a picke-purse.

PISTOLL

Ha, thou mountaine Forreyner: Sir *Iohn*, and Master
mine,

I combat challenge of this Latine Bilboe:

Word of deniall in thy *labras* here;

Word of denial; froth, and scum thou liest.

150 SLENDER (*pointing to Nim*) By these gloues, then 'twas he.

NYM Be auis'd sir, and passe good humours: I will say
marry trap with you, if you runne the nut-hooks humor
on me, that is the very note of it.

SLENDER By this hat, then he in the red face had it: for
though I cannot remember what I did when you made
me drunke, yet I am not altogether an asse.

SIR IOHN (*to Bardolfe*) What say you *Scarlet*, and *Iohn*?

BARDOLFE Why sir, (for my part) I say the Gentleman had
drunke himselfe out of his fiue sentences.

EUANS It is his fiue sences: fie, what the ignorance is.   160

BARDOLFE And being fap, sir, was (as they say) casheerd:
and so conclusions past the Car-eires.

SLENDER I, you spake in Latten then to: but 'tis no matter;
Ile nere be drunk whilst I liue againe, but in honest,
ciuill, godly company for this tricke: if I be drunke, Ile
be drunke with those that haue the feare of God, and
not with drunken knaues.

EUANS So got-udge me, that is a vertuous minde.

SIR IOHN You heare all these matters deni'd, Gentlemen;
you heare it.   170

Enter Anne Page (with wine)

PAGE Nay daughter, carry the wine in, wee'll drinke
within.   *Exit Anne*

SLENDER Oh heauen: This is Mistresse *Anne Page*.

⌐*Enter at another door Mistresse Ford and Mistresse
Page*⌐

PAGE How now Mistris *Ford*?

SIR IOHN *Mistris Ford*, by my troth you are very wel met:
by your leaue good Mistris.

⌐*He kisses her*⌐

PAGE Wife, bid these gentlemen welcome: come, we haue
a hot Venison pasty to dinner; Come gentlemen, I hope
we shall drinke downe all vnkindnesse.

Exeunt all but Slender

SLENDER I had rather then forty shillings I had my booke   180
of Songs and Sonnets heere:

Enter Simple

How now *Simple*, where haue you beene? I must wait
on my selfe, must I? you haue not the booke of Riddles
about you, haue you?

SIMPLE Booke of Riddles? why did you not lend it to *Alice
Short-cake* vpon Alhallowmas last, a fortnight afore
Michaelmas.

Enter Shallow and Euans

SHALLOW (*to Slender*) Come Coz, come Coz, we stay for
you: (*aside to him*) a word with you Coz:

He drawes Slender aside

marry this, Coz: there is as 'twere a tender, a kinde of   190
tender, made a farre-off by Sir *Hugh* here: doe you
vnderstand me?

SLENDER I Sir, you shall finde me reasonable; if it be so,
I shall doe that that is reason.

SHALLOW Nay, but vnderstand me.

SLENDER So I doe Sir.

EUANS Giue eare to his motions; (M^r. *Slender*) I will
description the matter to you, if you be capacity of it.

SLENDER Nay, I will doe as my Cozen *Shallow* saies: I pray
you pardon me, he's a Iustice of Peace in his Countrie,   200
simple though I stand here.

EUANS But that is not the question: the question is
concerning your marriage.

SHALLOW I, there's the point Sir.

EUANS Marry is it: the very point of it, to Mi. *An Page*.

SLENDER Why if it be so; I will marry her vpon any
reasonable demands.

EUANS But can you affection the 'o-man, let vs command
to know that of your mouth, or of your lips: for diuers
210 Philosophers hold, that the lips is parcell of the mouth:
therfore precisely, cã you carry your good wil to yᵉ
maid?

SHALLOW Cosen *Abraham Slender*, can you loue her?

SLENDER I hope sir, I will do as it shall become one that
would doe reason.

EUANS Nay, got's Lords, and his Ladies, you must speake
possitable, if you can carry-her your desires towards
her.

SHALLOW That you must: Will you, (vpon good dowry)
220 marry her?

SLENDER I will doe a greater thing then that, vpon your
request (Cosen) in any reason.

SHALLOW Nay conceiue me, conceiue mee, (sweet Coz):
what I doe is to pleasure you (Coz:) can you loue the
maid?

SLENDER I will marry her (Sir) at your request; but if
there bee no great loue in the beginning, yet Heauen
may decrease it vpon better acquaintance, when wee
are married, and haue more occasion to know one
230 another: I hope vpon familiarity will grow more
contempt: but if you say mary-her, I will mary-her,
that I am freely dissolued, and dissolutely.

EUANS It is a fery discretion-answere; saue the fall is in
the'ord, dissolutely: the ort is (according to our
meaning) resolutely: his meaning is good.

SHALLOW I: I thinke my Cosen meant well.

SLENDER I, or else I would I might be hang'd (la.)
Enter Anne Page

SHALLOW Here comes faire Mistris *Anne*; would I were
yong for your sake, Mistris *Anne*.

240 ANNE The dinner is on the Table, my Father desires your
worships company.

SHALLOW I will wait on him, (faire Mistris *Anne*.)

EUANS Od's plessed-wil: I wil not be absẽce at the grace.
Exeunt Shallow and Evans

ANNE (*to Slender*) Wil't please your worship to come in,
Sir?

SLENDER No, I thank you forsooth, hartely; I am very
well.

ANNE The dinner attends you, Sir.

SLENDER I am not a-hungry, I thanke you, forsooth: (*to
250 Simple*) goe, Sirha, for all you are my man, goe wait
vpon my Cosen *Shallow*:   *Exit Simple*
a Iustice of peace sometime may be beholding to his
friend, for a Man; I keepe but three Men, and a Boy
yet, till my Mother be dead: but what though, yet I
liue like a poore Gentleman borne.

ANNE I may not goe in without your worship: they will
not sit till you come.

SLENDER I'faith, ile eate nothing: I thanke you as much
as though I did.

260 ANNE I pray you Sir walke in.
⌜*Dogs barke within*⌝

SLENDER I had rather walke here (I thanke you) I bruiz'd
my shin th'other day, with playing at Sword and

Dagger with a Master of Fence (three veneys for a dish
of stew'd Prunes) and by my troth, I cannot abide the
smell of hot meate since. Why doe your dogs barke so?
be there Beares ith' Towne?

ANNE I thinke there are, Sir, I heard them talk'd of.

SLENDER I loue the sport well, but I shall as soone quarrell
at it, as any man in *England*: you are afraid if you see
the Beare loose, are you not?   270

ANNE I indeede Sir.

SLENDER That's meate and drinke to me now: I haue
seene *Sackerson* loose, twenty times, and haue taken
him by the Chaine: but (I warrant you) the women
haue so cride and shrekt at it, that it past: But women
indeede, cannot abide'em, they are very ill-fauour'd
rough things.
Enter Page

PAGE Come, gentle M. *Slender*, come; we stay for you.

SLENDER Ile eate nothing, I thanke you Sir.

PAGE By cocke and pie, you shall not choose, Sir: come,   280
come.

SLENDER Nay, pray you lead the way.

PAGE Come on, Sir.

SLENDER Mistris *Anne*: your selfe shall goe first.

ANNE Not I Sir, pray you keepe on.

SLENDER Truely I will not goe first: truely-la: I will not
doe you that wrong.

ANNE I pray you Sir.

SLENDER Ile rather be vnmannerly, then troublesome: you
doe your selfe wrong indeede-la.   290
Exeunt ⌜*Slender first, the others following*⌝

Enter Euans, and Simple, ⌜*from dinner*⌝   Sc. 2
EUANS Go your waies, and aske of Doctor *Caius* house,   (1.2)
which is the way; and there dwels one Mistris *Quickly*;
which is in the manner of his o'man; or his dry-Nurse;
or his Cooke; or his Laundry; his Washer, and his
Ringer.

SIMPLE Well Sir.

EUANS Nay, it is petter yet: giue her this letter; for it is
a'oman that altogeathers acquaintãce with Mistris *Anne
Page*; and the Letter is to desire, and require her to
solicite your Masters desires, to Mistris *Anne Page*: I   300
pray you be gon: ⌜*Exit Simple*⌝
I will make an end of my dinner; ther's Pippins and
Cheese to come.   *Exit*

Enter Sir Iohn Falstaffe, Bardolfe, Nym, Pistoll,   Sc. 3
Robin   (1.3)

SIR IOHN Mine *Host* of the *Garter*?
Enter Host

HOST What saies my Bully Rooke? speake schollerly, and
wisely.

SIR IOHN Truely mine *Host*; I must turne away some of
my followers.

HOST Discard, (bully *Hercules*) casheere; let them wag;
trot, trot.   310

SIR IOHN I sit at ten pounds a weeke.

HOST Thou'rt an Emperor (*Cesar*, *Keiser* and *Pheazar*) I

will entertaine *Bardolfe*: he shall draw; he shall tap; said I well (bully *Hector?*)

SIR IOHN Doe so (good mine *Host.*

HOST I haue spoke: let him follow: (*to Bardolfe*) let me see thee froth, and lime: I am at a word: follow.

                                      Exit

SIR IOHN *Bardolfe*, follow him: a *Tapster* is a good trade: an old Cloake, makes a new Ierkin: a wither'd Seruingman, a fresh Tapster: goe, adew.

320

BARDOLFE It is a life that I haue desir'd: I will thriue.

                                   ⌈*Exit*⌉

PISTOLL

O base hungarian wight: wilt yᵘ the spigot wield.

NIM He was gotten in drink: His minde is not heroick: is not the humor cõceited?

SIR IOHN I am glad I am so acquit of this Tinderbox: his Thefts were too open: his filching was like an vnskilfull Singer, he kept not time.

NIM The good humor is to steale at a minutes rest.

PISTOLL

    Conuay: the wise it call: Steale? foh: a fico for the phrase.

330 SIR IOHN Well sirs, I am almost out at heeles.

PISTOLL Why then let Kibes ensue.

SIR IOHN There is no remedy: I must conicatch, I must shift.

PISTOLL Yong Rauens must haue foode.

SIR IOHN Which of you know *Ford* of this Towne?

PISTOLL

I ken the wight: he is of substance good.

SIR IOHN My honest Lads, I will tell you what I am about.

PISTOLL Two yards, and more.

SIR IOHN No quips now *Pistoll*: (Indeede I am in the waste

340 two yards about: but I am now about no waste: I am about thrift) briefely: I doe meane to make loue to *Fords* wife: I spie entertainment in her: shee discourses: shee carues: she giues the leere of inuitation: I can construe the action of her familier stile, & the hardest voice of her behauior (to be english'd rightly) is, *I am Sir Iohn Falstafs.*

PISTOLL He hath studied her well; and translated her will: out of honesty, into English.

NIM The Anchor is deepe: will that humor passe?

350 SIR IOHN Now, the report goes, she has all the rule of her husbands Purse: he hath a legion of Angels.

PISTOLL

As many diuels entertaine: and to her Boy say I.

NIM The humor rises: it is good: humor me the angels.

SIR IOHN (*shewing Letters*) I haue writ me here a letter to her: & here another to *Pages* wife, who euen now gaue mee good eyes too; examind my parts with most iudicious illiads: sometimes the beame of her view, guilded my foote: sometimes my portly belly.

PISTOLL

Then did the Sun on dung-hill shine.

360 NIM I thanke thee for that humour.

SIR IOHN O she did so course o're my exteriors with such a greedy intention, that the appetite of her eye, did

seeme to scorch me vp like a burning-glasse: here's another letter to her: She beares the Purse too: She is a Region in *Guiana*: all gold, and bountie: I will be Cheaters to them both, and they shall be Exchequers to mee: they shall be my East and West Indies, and I will trade to them both: (*Giuing a letter to Pistoll*) Goe, beare thou this Letter to Mistris *Page*; (*giuing a letter to Nim*) and thou this to Mistris *Ford*: we will thriue (Lads) 370 we will thriue.

PISTOLL (*returning the Letter*)

Shall I Sir *Pandarus* of *Troy* become,
And by my side weare Steele? then Lucifer take all.

NIM (*returning the Letter*) I will run no base humor: here take the humor-Letter; I will keepe the hauior of reputation.

SIR IOHN (*to Robin*)

Hold Sirha, beare you these Letters tightly,
Saile like my Pinnasse to these golden shores.

    He giues Robin the Letters

Rogues, hence, auaunt, vanish like haile-stones; goe,
Trudge; plod away oth' hoofe: seeke shelter, packe: 380
Falstaffe will learne the humor of the age,
French-thrift, you Rogues, my selfe, and skirted *Page.*

                 Exeunt Sir Iohn and Robin

PISTOLL

Let Vultures gripe thy guts: for gourd, and Fullam
    holds:
And high and low beguiles the rich & poore,
Tester ile haue in pouch when thou shalt lacke,
Base *Phrygian* Turke.

NIM

I haue opperations, which be humors of reuenge.

PISTOLL

Wilt thou reuenge?

NIM   By Welkin, and her Stars.

PISTOLL

With wit, or Steele?

NIM   With both the humors, I:
I will discusse the humour of this Loue to *Ford*. 390

PISTOLL

And I to *Page* shall eke vnfold
    How *Falstaffe* (varlet vile)
His Doue will proue; his gold will hold,
    And his soft couch defile.

NIM My humour shall not coole: I will incense *Ford* to deale with poyson: I will possesse him with yallownesse, for this reuolt of mine is dangerous: that is my true humour.

PISTOLL

Thou art the *Mars* of *Malecontents*:
I second thee: troope on.   *Exeunt* 400

    Enter Mistris Quickly, and Simple   Sc. 4

MISTRIS QUICKLY What, *Iohn Rugby,*   (1.4)
    Enter Iohn Rugby

I pray thee goe to the Casement, and see if you can see my Master, Master Docter *Caius* comming: if he doe (I'faith) and finde any body in the house; here will be an old abusing of Gods patience, and the Kings English.

RUGBY Ile goe watch.

MISTRIS QUICKLY Goe, and we'll haue a posset for't soone at night, (in faith) at the latter end of a Sea-cole-fire:

Exit Rugby

An honest, willing, kinde fellow, as euer seruant shall
410 come in house withall: and I warrant you, no tel-tale, nor no breede-bate: his worst fault is, that he is giuen to prayer; hee is something peeuish that way: but no body but has his fault: but let that passe. *Peter Simple*, you say your name is?

SIMPLE I: for fault of a better.

MISTRIS QUICKLY And Master *Slender*'s your Master?

SIMPLE I forsooth.

MISTRIS QUICKLY Do's he not weare a great round Beard, like a Glouers pairing-knife?

420 SIMPLE No forsooth: he hath but a little wey-face; with a little yellow Beard: a Caine colourd Beard.

MISTRIS QUICKLY A softly-sprighted man, is he not?

SIMPLE I forsooth: but he is as tall a man of his hands, as any is betweene this and his head: he hath fought with a Warrener.

MISTRIS QUICKLY How say you: oh, I should remember him: do's he not hold vp his head (as it were?) and strut in his gate?

SIMPLE Yes indeede do's he.

430 MISTRIS QUICKLY Well, heauen send *Anne Page*, no worse fortune: Tell Master Parson *Euans*, I will doe what I can for your Master: *Anne* is a good girle, and I wish—

Enter Rugby

RUGBY Out alas: here comes my Master.   ⌈*Exit*⌉

MISTRIS QUICKLY We shall all be shent: Run in here, good young man: for Gods sake goe into this Closset: he will not stay long:

Simple steps into the Closset

what *Iohn Rugby? Iohn*: what *Iohn* I say?

⌈*Enter Rugby*⌉

⌈*speaking loudly*⌉ goe *Iohn*, goe enquire for my Master, I doubt he be not well, that hee comes not home:

⌈*Exit Rugby*⌉

440 (*Singing*) (*and downe, downe, adowne'a, &c.*

Enter Doctor Caius

CAIUS Vat is you sing? I doe not like des-toyes: pray you goe and vetch me in my Closset, *vn boyteere verd*; a Box, a greene-a-Box: do intend vat I speake? a greene-a-Box.

MISTRIS QUICKLY I forsooth ile fetch it you: (*aside*) I am glad hee went not in himselfe: if he had found the yong man he would haue bin horne-mad.

She goes to fetch the Box

CAIUS *Fe, ʃe, ʃe, ʃe, ma foy, il fait for chaude, Ie man vai a le Court, la grand affaire.*

450 MISTRIS QUICKLY Is it this Sir?

CAIUS *Ouy mette le a mon pochet, de-peech* quickly: Vere is dat knaue *Rugby*?

MISTRIS QUICKLY What *Iohn Rugby, Iohn*?

⌈*Enter Rugby*⌉

RUGBY Here Sir.

CAIUS You are *Iohn Rugby*, and you are *Iacke Rugby*: Come, take-a-your Rapier, and come after my heele to the Court.

RUGBY 'Tis ready Sir, here in the Porch.

He fetches the Rapier

CAIUS By my trot: I tarry too long: od's-me: *que ay ie*
460 *oublie*: dere is some Simples in my Closset, dat I vill not for the varld I shall leaue behinde.

MISTRIS QUICKLY (*aside*) Ay-me, he'll finde the yong man there, & be mad.

CAIUS (*discouering Simple*) O *Diable, Diable*: vat is in my Closset? Villanie, *La-roone*: *Rugby*, my Rapier.

He takes the Rapier

MISTRIS QUICKLY Good Master be content.

CAIUS Wherefore shall I be content-a?

MISTRIS QUICKLY The yong man is an honest man.

CAIUS What shall de honest man do in my Closset: dere
470 is no honest man dat shall come in my Closset.

MISTRIS QUICKLY I beseech you be not so flegmaticke: heare the truth of it. He came of an errand to mee, from Parson *Hugh*.

CAIUS Vell.

SIMPLE I forsooth: to desire her to—

MISTRIS QUICKLY Peace, I pray you.

CAIUS Peace-a-your tongue: (*to Simple*) speake-a-your Tale.

SIMPLE To desire this honest Gentlewoman (your Maid) to speake a good word to Mistris *Anne Page*, for my
480 Master in the way of Marriage.

MISTRIS QUICKLY This is all indeede-la: but ile nere put my finger in the fire, and neede not.

CAIUS Sir *Hugh* send-a you? *Rugby, ballee* mee some paper:

Rugby brings paper

(*to Simple*) tarry you a littell-a-while.

Caius writes

MISTRIS QUICKLY (*aside to Simple*) I am glad he is so quiet: if he had bin throughly moued, you should haue heard him so loud, and so melancholly: but notwithstanding man, Ile doe your Master what good I can: and the very yea, & the no is, yᵉ French Doctor my Master, (I
490 may call him my Master, looke you, for I keepe his house; and I wash, ring, brew, bake, scowre, dresse meat and drinke, make the beds, and doe all my selfe.)

SIMPLE (*aside to Mistris Quickly*) 'Tis a great charge to come vnder one bodies hand.

MISTRIS QUICKLY (*aside to Simple*) Are you a-uis'd o'that? you shall finde it a great charge: and to be vp early, and down late: but notwithstanding, (to tell you in your eare, I wold haue no words of it) my Master himselfe is in loue with Mistris *Anne Page*: but
500 notwithstanding that I know *Ans* mind, that's neither heere nor there.

CAIUS (*giuing the letter to Simple*) You, *Iack' Nape*: giue-'a this Letter to Sir *Hugh*, by gar it is a shallenge: I will cut his troat in de Parke, and I will teach a scuruy *Iack-a-nape* Priest to meddle, or make:—you may be gon: it is not good you tarry here: by gar I will cut all his two stones: by gar, he shall not haue a stone to throw at his dogge.   *Exit Simple*

510 MISTRIS QUICKLY Alas: he speakes but for his friend.

CAIUS It is no matter'a ver dat: do not you tell-a-me dat I shall haue *Anne Page* for my selfe? by gar, I vill kill de *Iack-Priest*: and I haue appointed mine Host of de Iarteer to measure our weapon: by gar, I wil my selfe haue *Anne Page*.

MISTRIS QUICKLY Sir, the maid loues you, and all shall bee well: We must giue folkes leaue to prate: what the good-ier.

CAIUS *Rugby*, come to the Court with me: (*to Mistris*
520 *Quickly*) by gar, if I haue not *Anne Page*, I shall turne your head out of my dore: follow my heeles, *Rugby*.

MISTRIS QUICKLY You shall haue *An—*

Exeunt Caius and Rugby

ass head of your owne: No, I know *Ans* mind for that: neuer a woman in *Windsor* knowes more of *Ans* minde then I doe, nor can doe more then I doe with her, I thanke heauen.

FENTON (*within*) Who's with in there, hoa?

MISTRIS QUICKLY Who's there, I troa? Come neere the house I pray you.

Enter Fenton

530 FENTON How now (good woman) how dost thou?

MISTRIS QUICKLY The better that it pleases your good Worship to aske?

FENTON What newes? how do's pretty Mistris *Anne*?

MISTRIS QUICKLY In truth Sir, and shee is pretty, and honest, and gentle, and one that is your friend, I can tell you that by the way, I praise heauen for it.

FENTON Shall I doe any good thinkst thou? shall I not loose my suit?

MISTRIS QUICKLY Troth Sir, all is in his hands aboue: but
540 notwithstanding (Master *Fenton*) Ile be sworne on a booke shee loues you: haue not your Worship a wart aboue your eye?

FENTON Yes marry haue I, what of that?

MISTRIS QUICKLY Wel, thereby hangs a tale: good faith, it is such another *Nan*; (but (I detest) an honest maid as euer broke bread: wee had an howres talke of that wart; I shall neuer laugh but in that maids company: but (indeed) shee is giuen too much to Allicholy and musing: but for you—well—goe too—
550 FENTON Well: I shall see her to day: hold, there's money for thee: Let mee haue thy voice in my behalfe: if thou seest her before me, commend me.—

MISTRIS QUICKLY Will I? I faith that I will: And I will tell your Worship more of the Wart, the next time we haue confidence, and of other wooers.

FENTON Well, fare-well, I am in great haste now.

MISTRIS QUICKLY Fare-well to your Worship:

Exit Fenton

truely an honest Gentleman: but *Anne* loues him not:
for I know *Ans* minde as well as another do's: out
560 vpon't: what haue I forgot?   *Exit*

Sc. 5   *Enter Mistris Page, with a letter*
(2.1) MISTRIS PAGE What, haue I scap'd Loue-letters in the holly-day-time of my beauty, and am I now a subiect for them? let me see?

She reades

Aske me no reason why I loue you, for though Loue vse Reason for his precisian, hee admits him not for his Counsailour: you are not yong, no more am I: goe to then, there's simpathie: you are merry, so am I: ha, ha, then there's more simpathie: you loue sacke, and so do I: would you desire better simpathie? Let it suffice thee (Mistris Page) at the least if the Loue of Souldier can suffice, that I
570 *loue thee: I will not say pitty mee, 'tis not a Souldier-like phrase; but I say, loue me:*

> *By me, thine owne true Knight,*
> *By day or night:*
> *Or any kinde of light,*
> *With all his might,*
> *For thee to fight.*

Iohn Falstaffe.

What a *Herod* of *Iurie* is this? O wicked, wicked world:
One that is well-nye worne to peeces with age to show
580 himselfe a yong Gallant? What an vnwaied behauiour hath this Flemish drunkard pickt (ith Deuills name) out of my conuersation, that he dares in this manner assay me? why, hee hath not beene thrice in my Company: what-should I say to him? I was then frugall of my mirth: (heauen forgiue mee:) why Ile exhibit a Bill in the Parliament for the putting downe of men: O God that I knew how to be reueng'd on him? for reueng'd I will be? as sure as his guts are made of puddings.

Enter Mistris Ford

MISTRIS FORD *Mistris Page*, by my faith, I was going to
590 your house.

MISTRIS PAGE And by my faith, I was comming to you: you looke very ill.

MISTRIS FORD Nay, Ile nere beleeue that; I haue to shew to the contrary.

MISTRIS PAGE 'Faith but you doe in my minde.

MISTRIS FORD Well: I doe then: yet I say, I could shew you to the contrary: O Mistris *Page*, giue mee some counsaile.

MISTRIS PAGE What's the matter, woman?   600

MISTRIS FORD O woman: if it were not for one trifling respect, I could come to such honour.

MISTRIS PAGE Hang the trifle (woman) take the honour: what is it? dispence with trifles: what is it?

MISTRIS FORD If I would but goe to hell, for an eternall moment, or so: I could be knighted.

MISTRIS PAGE What thou liest? Sir *Alice Ford*? these Knights will hacke, and so thou shouldst not alter the article of thy Gentry.

MISTRIS FORD Wee burne day-light: heere, read, read: 610

She giues Mistris Page a letter

perceiue how I might bee knighted,

Mistris Page reads

I shall thinke the worse of fat men, as long as I haue an eye to make difference of mens liking: and yet hee would not sweare: praisd womens modesty: and gaue such orderly and wel-behaued reproofe to al vncomelinesse, that I would haue sworne his disposition would haue gone to the truth of his words: but they doe no more adhere and keep place together, then the

150 Psalms to the tune of Greensleeues: What tempest
(I troa) threw this Whale, (with so many Tuns of oyle
in his belly) a'shoare at Windsor? How shall I bee
reuenged on him? I thinke the best way were, to
entertaine him with hope, till the wicked fire of lust
haue melted him in his owne greace: Did you euer
heare the like?

MISTRIS PAGE Letter for letter; but that the name of *Page*
and *Ford* differs:

She giues Mistris Ford her letter

to thy great comfort in this mystery of ill opinions,
heere's the twyn-brother of thy Letter: but let thine
inherit first, for I protest mine neuer shall: I warrant
he hath a thousand of these Letters, writ with blancke-
space for different names (sure more): and these are of
the second edition: hee will print them out of doubt:
for he cares not what hee puts into the presse, when
he would put vs two: I had rather be a Giantesse, and
lye vnder Mount *Pelion*: Well; I will find you twentie
lasciuiuous Turtles ere one chaste man.

MISTRIS FORD Why this is the very same: the very hand:
the very words: what doth he thinke of vs?

MISTRIS PAGE Nay I know not: it makes me almost readie
to wrangle with mine owne honesty: Ile entertaine my
selfe like one that I am not acquainted withall: for sure
vnlesse hee know some straine in mee, that I know
not my selfe, hee would neuer haue boorded me in this
furie.

MISTRIS FORD Boording, call you it? Ile bee sure to keepe
him aboue decke.

MISTRIS PAGE So will I: if hee come vnder my hatches, Ile
neuer to Sea againe: Let's bee reueng'd on him: let's
appoint him a meeting: giue him a show of comfort in
his Suit, and lead him on with a fine baited delay, till
hee hath pawn'd his horses to mine Host of the Garter.

MISTRIS FORD Nay, I wil consent to act any villany against
him, that may not sully the charinesse of our honesty:
oh that my husband saw this Letter: it would giue
eternall food to his iealousie.

*Enter Master Ford with Pistoll, Master Page with
Nim*

MISTRIS PAGE Why look where he comes; and my good
man too: hee's as farre from iealousie, as I am from
giuing him cause, and that (I hope) is an vnmeasurable
distance.

MISTRIS FORD You are the happier woman.

MISTRIS PAGE Let's consult together against this greasie
Knight: Come hither.

They withdraw

FORD (*to Pistoll*) Well: I hope, it be not so.

PISTOLL

Hope is a curtall-dog in some affaires:
Sir *Iohn* affects thy wife.

FORD Why sir, my wife is not young.

PISTOLL

He wooes both high and low, both rich & poor,
Both yong and old, one with another (*Ford*)
He loues the Gally-mawfry (*Ford*) perpend.

FORD Loue my wife?

PISTOLL

With liuer, burning hot: preuent:
Or goe thou like Sir *Acteon* he,
With Ring-wood at thy heeles:
O, odious is the name.

FORD What name Sir?

PISTOLL The horne I say: Farewell:
Take heed, haue open eye, for theeues doe foot by
night.
Take heed, ere sommer comes, or Cuckoo-birds do sing.
Away sir Corporall *Nim*: beleeue it (*Page*) he speakes
sence.   *Exit*

FORD (*aside*) I will be patient: I will find out this.

NIM (*to Page*) And this is true: I like not the humor of
lying: hee hath wronged mee in some humors: I should
haue borne the humour'd Letter to her: but I haue a
sword: and it shall bite vpon my necessitie: he loues
your wife; There's the short and the long:
My name is Corporall *Nim*: I speak, and I auouch; 'tis
true:
My name is *Nim*: and *Falstaffe* loues your wife: adieu,
I loue not the humour of bread and cheese: adieu.
                                              Exit

PAGE (*aside*) The humour of it (quoth'a?) heere's a fellow
frights English out of his wits.

FORD (*aside*) I will seeke out *Falstaffe*.

PAGE (*aside*) I neuer heard such a drawling-affecting rogue.

FORD (*aside*) If I doe finde it: well.

PAGE (*aside*) I will not beleeue such a *Cataian*, though the
Priest o' th'Towne commended him for a true man.

FORD (*aside*) 'Twas a good sensible fellow: well.

Mistris Page and Mistris Ford come forward

PAGE How now *Meg*?

MISTRIS PAGE Whether goe you (*George*?) harke you.

They talke apart

MISTRIS FORD How now (sweet *Frank*) why art thou
melancholy?

FORD I melancholy? I am not melancholy: Get you home:
goe.

MISTRIS FORD Faith, thou hast some crochets in thy head,
now: will you goe, *Mistris Page*?

MISTRIS PAGE Haue with you: you'll come to dinner
George?

Enter Quickly

(*Aside to Mistresse Ford*) Looke who comes yonder: shee
shall bee our Messenger to this paltrie Knight.

MISTRIS FORD (*aside to Mistresse Page*) Trust me, I thought
on her: shee'll fit it.

MISTRIS PAGE (*to Mistresse Quickly*) You are come to see
my daughter *Anne*?

MISTRIS QUICKLY I forsooth: and I pray how do's good
Mistresse *Anne*?

MISTRIS PAGE Go in with vs and see: we haue an houres
talke with you.

*Exeunt Mistresse Page, Mistresse Ford,
Mistresse Quickly*

PAGE How now Master Ford?

FORD You heard what this knaue told me, did you not?

720 PAGE Yes, and you heard what the other told me?

FORD Doe you thinke there is truth in them?

PAGE Hang 'em slaues: I doe not thinke the Knight would offer it: But these that accuse him in his intent towards our wiues, are a yoake of his discarded men: very rogues, now they be out of seruice.

FORD Were they his men?

PAGE Marry were they.

FORD I like it neuer the beter for that, do's he lye at the Garter?

730 PAGE I marry do's he: if hee should intend this voyage toward my wife, I would turne her loose to him; and what hee gets more of her, then sharpe words, let it lye on my head.

FORD I doe not misdoubt my wife: but I would bee loath to turne them together: a man may be too confident: I would haue nothing lye on my head: I cannot be thus satisfied.

Enter Host

PAGE Looke where my ranting-Host of the Garter comes: there is eyther liquor in his pate, or mony in his purse,

740 when hee lookes so merrily: How now mine Host?

HOST God blesse you Bully-Rooke, God blesse you: thou'rt a Gentleman.

Enter Shallow

Caueleiro Iustice, I say.

SHALLOW I follow, (mine Host) I follow: Good-euen, and twenty (good Master *Page*.) Master *Page*, wil you go with vs? we haue sport in hand.

HOST Tell him Caueleiro-Iustice: tell him Bully-Rooke.

SHALLOW Sir, there is a fray to be fought, betweene Sir *Hugh* the Welch Priest, and *Caius* the French Doctor.

750 FORD Good mine Host o'th'Garter: a word with you.

HOST What saist thou, my Bully-Rooke?

They talke apart

SHALLOW (*to Page*) Will you goe with vs to behold it? My merry Host hath had the measuring of their weapons; and (I thinke) hath appointed them contrary places: for (beleeue mee) I heare the Parson is no Iester: harke, I will tell you what our sport shall be.

They talke apart

HOST ⌐*to Ford*⌐ Hast thou no suit against my Knight? my guest-Caualeiro?

⌐FORD⌐ None, I protest: but Ile giue you a pottle of burn'd

760 sacke, to giue me recourse to him, and tell him my name is *Brooke*: onely for a iest.

HOST My hand, (Bully:) thou shalt haue egresse and regresse, (said I well?) and thy name shall be *Brooke*. It is a merry Knight: (*to Shallow and Page*) will you goe min-heires?

SHALLOW Haue with you mine Host.

PAGE I haue heard the French-man hath good skill in his Rapier.

SHALLOW Tut sir: I could haue told you more: In these

770 times you stand on distance: your Passes, Stoccado's, and I know not what: 'tis the heart (Master *Page*) ⌐*shewing his Rapier-passes*⌐ 'tis heere, 'tis heere: I haue

seene the time, with my long-sword, I would haue made you fowre tall fellowes skippe like Rattes.

HOST Heere boyes, heere, heere: shall we wag?

PAGE Haue with you: I had rather heare them scold, then fight. *Exeunt Host, Shallow, Page*

FORD Though *Page* be a secure foole, and stands so firmely on his wiues frailty; yet, I cannot put-off my opinion so easily: she was in his company at *Pages* house: and 780 what they made there, I know not. Well, I wil looke further into't, and I haue a disguise, to sound *Falstaffe*; if I finde her honest, I loose not my labor: if she be otherwise, 'tis labour well bestowed. *Exit*

Enter Sir Iohn Falstaffe, Pistoll   **Sc. 6**

SIR IOHN I will not lend thee a penny.   **(2.2)**

PISTOLL

I will retort the sum in equipage.

SIR IOHN Not a penny.

PISTOLL ⌐*drawing his sword*⌐ Why then the world's mine Oyster, which I, with sword will open.

SIR IOHN Not a penny: I haue beene content (Sir,) you 790 should lay my countenance to pawne: I haue grated vpon my good friends for three Repreeues for you, and your Coach-fellow *Nim*; or else you had look'd through the grate, like a Geminy of Baboones: I am damn'd in hell, for swearing to Gentlemen my friends, you were good Souldiers, and tall-fellowes. And when Mistresse *Briget* lost the handle of her Fan, I took't vpon mine honour thou hadst it not.

PISTOLL

Didst not thou share? hadst thou not fifteene pence?

SIR IOHN Reason, you roague, reason: thinkst thou Ile 800 endanger my soule, *gratis*? at a word, hang no more about mee, I am no gibbet for you: goe, a short knife, and a throng, to your Mannor of *Pickt-hatch*: goe, you'll not beare a Letter for mee you roague? you stand vpon your honor: why, (thou vnconfinable basenesse) it is as much as I can doe to keepe the termes of my honor precise: I, I, I my selfe sometimes, leauing the feare of God on the left hand, and hiding mine honor in my necessity, am faine to shuffle: to hedge, and to lurch, and yet you, you Rogue, will en-sconce your raggs; 810 your Cat-a-Mountaine-lookes, your red-lattice phrases, and your bold-beating-oathes, vnder the shelter of your honor? you will not doe it? you?

PISTOLL ⌐*sheathing his sword*⌐

I doe relent: what wouldst thou more of man?

Enter Robin

ROBIN Sir, here's a woman would speake with you.

SIR IOHN Let her approach.

Enter Mistresse Quickly

MISTRIS QUICKLY Giue your worship good morrow.

SIR IOHN Good-morrow, good-wife.

MISTRIS QUICKLY Not so, and't please your worship.

SIR IOHN Good maid then.   820

MISTRIS QUICKLY Ile be sworne, as my mother was the first houre I was borne.

SIR IOHN I doe beleeue the swearer; what with me?

MISTRIS QUICKLY Shall I vouch-safe your worship a word, or two?

SIR IOHN Two thousand (faire woman) and ile vouchsafe thee the hearing.

MISTRIS QUICKLY There is one Mistresse *Ford*, (Sir) I pray come a little neerer this waies:

She drawes Sir Iohn aside

830 I my selfe dwell with M. Doctor *Caius*:

SIR IOHN Well, on; Mistresse *Ford*, you say.

MISTRIS QUICKLY Your worship saies very true: I pray your worship come a little neerer this waies.

SIR IOHN I warrant thee, no-bodie heares: mine owne people, mine owne people.

MISTRIS QUICKLY Are they so? God-blesse them, and make them his Seruants.

SIR IOHN Well; Mistresse *Ford*, what of her?

MISTRIS QUICKLY Why, Sir; shee's a good-creature; Lord,
840 Lord, your Worship's a wanton: well: heauen forgiue you, and all of vs, I pray—.

SIR IOHN Mistresse *Ford*: come, Mistresse *Ford*.

MISTRIS QUICKLY Marry this is the short, and the long of it: you haue brought her into such a Canaries, as 'tis wonderfull: the best Courtier of them all (when the Court lay at *Windsor*) could neuer haue brought her to such a Canarie: yet there has beene Knights, and Lords, and Gentlemen, with their Coaches; I warrant you Coach after Coach, letter after letter, gift after gift,
850 smelling so sweetly; all Muske, and so rushling, I warrant you, in silke and golde, and in such alligant termes, and in such wine and suger of the best, and the fairest, that would haue wonne any womans heart: and I warrant you, they could neuer get an eye-winke of her: I had my selfe twentie Angels giuen me this morning, but I defie all Angels (in any such sort, as they say) but in the way of honesty: and I warrant you, they could neuer get her so much as sippe on a cup with the prowdest of them all, and yet there has
860 beene Earles: nay, (which is more) Pentioners, but I warrant you all is one with her.

SIR IOHN But what saies shee to mee? be briefe my good shee-*Mercurie*.

MISTRIS QUICKLY Marry, she hath receiu'd your Letter: for the which she thankes you a thousand times; and she giues you to notifie, that her husband will be absence from his house, betweene ten and eleuen.

SIR IOHN Ten, and eleuen.

MISTRIS QUICKLY I, forsooth: and then you may come and
870 see the picture (she sayes) that you wot of: Master *Ford* her husband will be from home: alas, the sweet woman leades an ill life with him: hee's a very iealousie-man; she leades a very frampold life with him, (good hart.)

SIR IOHN Ten, and eleuen. Woman, commend me to her, I will not faile her.

MISTRIS QUICKLY Why, you say well: But I haue another messenger to your worship: Mistresse *Page* hath her heartie commendations to you to: and let mee tell you in your eare, shee's as fartuous a ciuill modest wife,
880 and one (I tell you) that will not misse you morning nor euening prayer, as any is in *Windsor*, who ere bee the other: and shee bade me tell your worship, that her husband is seldome from home, but she hopes there will come a time. I neuer knew a woman so doate vpon a man; surely I thinke you haue charmes, la: yes in truth.

SIR IOHN Not I, I assure thee; setting the attraction of my good parts aside, I haue no other charmes.

MISTRIS QUICKLY Blessing on your heart for't.

SIR IOHN But I pray thee tell me this: has *Fords* wife, and 890 *Pages* wife acquainted each other, how they loue me?

MISTRIS QUICKLY O God no, sir; that were a iest indeed: they haue not so little grace I hope, that were a tricke indeed: But Mistris *Page* would desire you to send her your little Page of al loues: her husband has a maruellous infectiõ to the little Page: and truely Master *Page* is an honest man: neuer a wife in *Windsor* leades a better life then she do's: doe what shee will, say what she will, take all, pay all, goe to bed when she list, rise when she list, all is as she will: and truly she deserues 900 it; for if there be a kinde woman in *Windsor*, she is one: you must send her your Page, no remedie.

SIR IOHN Why, I will.

MISTRIS QUICKLY Nay, but doe so then, and looke you, hee may come and goe betweene you both: and in any case haue a nay-word, that you may know one anothers minde, and the Boy neuer neede to vnderstand any thing; for 'tis not good that children should know any wickednes: olde folkes you know, haue discretion, as they say, and know the world. 910

SIR IOHN Farethee-well, commend mee to them both: there's my purse, I am yet thy debter: Boy, goe along with this woman,   *Exeunt Mistris Quickly and Robin* (*aside*) this newes distracts me.

PISTOLL (*aside*)

This Puncke is one of *Cupids* Carriers,
Clap on more sailes, pursue: vp with your sights:
Giue fire: she is my prize, or Ocean whelme them all.

Exit

SIR IOHN Saist thou so (old *Iacke*) go thy waies: Ile make more of thy olde body then I haue done: will they yet looke after thee? wilt thou after the expence of so much 920 money, be now a gainer? good Body, I thanke thee: let them say 'tis grossely done, so it bee fairely done, no matter.

Enter Bardolffe ⌈with sacke⌉

BARDOLFE Sir *Iohn*, there's one Master *Brooke* below would faine speake with you, and be acquainted with you; and hath sent your worship a mornings draught of Sacke.

SIR IOHN *Brooke* is his name?

BARDOLFE I Sir.

SIR IOHN Call him in: ⌈*drinking Sacke*⌉ such *Brookes* are 930 welcome to mee, that ore'flowes such liquor:

Exit Bardolfe

Ah ha, Mistresse *Ford* and Mistresse *Page*, haue I encompass'd you? ⌈*drinking*⌉ goe to, *via*.

Enter Bardolfe, and Ford (disguis'd as Brooke)

FORD God blesse you sir.

SIR IOHN And you sir: would you speake with me?

FORD I make bold, to presse, with so little preparation vpon you.

SIR IOHN You'r welcome, what's your will? *(to Bardolfe)* giue vs leaue Drawer.   *Exit Bardolfe*

940 FORD Sir, I am a Gentleman that haue spent much, my name is *Brooke*.

SIR IOHN Good Master *Brooke*, I desire more acquaintance of you.

FORD Good Sir *Iohn*, I sue for yours: not to charge you, for I must let you vnderstand, I thinke my selfe in better plight for a Lender, then you are: the which hath something emboldned me to this vnseason'd intrusion: for they say, if money goe before, all waies doe lye open.

950 SIR IOHN Money is a good Souldier (Sir) and will on.

FORD Troth, and I haue a bag of money heere troubles me: if you will helpe to beare it (Sir *Iohn*) take halfe, or all, for easing me of the carriage.

SIR IOHN Sir, I know not how I may deserue to bee your Porter.

FORD I will tell you sir, if you will giue mee the hearing.

SIR IOHN Speake (good Master *Brooke*) I shall be glad to be your Seruant.

FORD Sir, I heare you are a Scholler: (I will be briefe with
960 you) and you haue been a man long knowne to me, though I had neuer so good means as desire, to make my selfe acquainted with you. I shall discouer a thing to you, wherein I must very much lay open mine owne imperfection: but (good Sir *Iohn*) as you haue one eye vpon my follies, as you heare them vnfolded, turne another into the Register of your owne, that I may passe with a reproofe the easier, sith you your selfe know how easie it is to be such an offender.

SIR IOHN Very well Sir, proceed.

970 FORD There is a Gentlewoman in this Towne, her husbands name is *Ford*.

SIR IOHN Well Sir.

FORD I haue long lou'd her, and I protest to you, bestowed much on her: followed her with a doating obseruance: Ingross'd opportunities to meete her: fee'd euery slight occasion that could but nigardly giue mee sight of her: not only bought many presents to giue her, but haue giuen largely to many, to know what shee would haue giuen: briefly, I haue pursu'd her, as Loue hath pursued
980 mee, which hath beene on the wing of all occasions: but whatsoeuer I haue merited, either in my minde, or in my meanes, meede I am sure I haue receiued none, vnlesse Experience be a Iewell. That I haue purchased at an infinite rate, and that hath taught mee to say this,

"*Loue like a shadow flies, when substance Loue pursues,*
"*Pursuing that that flies, and flying what pursues.*

SIR IOHN Haue you receiu'd no promise of satisfaction at her hands?

990 FORD Neuer.

SIR IOHN Haue you importun'd her to such a purpose?

FORD Neuer.

SIR IOHN Of what qualitie was your loue then?

FORD Like a fair house, built on another mans ground, so that I haue lost my edifice, by mistaking the place, where I erected it.

SIR IOHN To what purpose haue you vnfolded this to me?

FORD When I haue told you that, I haue told you all: Some say, that though she appeare honest to mee, yet in other places shee enlargeth her mirth so farre, that   1000 there is shrewd construction made of her. Now (Sir *Iohn*) here is the heart of my purpose: you are a gentleman of excellent breeding, admirable discourse, of great admittance, authenticke in your place and person, generally allow'd for your many war-like, court-like, and learned preparations.

SIR IOHN O Sir.

FORD Beleeue it, for you know it: there is money,
⌐*He offers money*⌐
spend it, spend it, spend more; spend all I haue, onely   1010 giue me so much of your time in exchange of it, as to lay an amiable siege to the honesty of this *Fords* wife: vse your Art of wooing; win her to consent to you: if any man may, you may as soone as any.

SIR IOHN Would it apply well to the vehemency of your affection that I should win what you would enioy? Methinkes you prescribe to your selfe very preposterously.

FORD O, vnderstand my drift: she dwells so securely on the excellency of her honor, that the folly of my soule dares not present it selfe: shee is too bright to be look'd   1020 against. Now, could I come to her with any detection in my hand; my desires had instance and argument to commend themselues, I could driue her then from the ward of her purity, her reputation, her marriage-vow, and a thousand other her defences, which now are too-too strongly embattaild against me: what say you too't, Sir *Iohn*?

SIR IOHN Master *Brooke*, I will first make bold with your money:
⌐*He takes the money*⌐
next, giue mee your hand: 1030
He takes his hand
and last, as I am a gentleman, you shall, if you will, enioy *Fords* wife.

FORD O good Sir.

SIR IOHN I say you shall.

FORD Want no money (Sir *Iohn*) you shall want none.

SIR IOHN Want no *Mistresse Ford* (Master *Brooke*) you shall want none: I shall be with her (I may tell you) by her owne appointment, euen as you came in to me, her spokes-mate, or goe-betweene, parted from me: I say I shall be with her betweene ten and eleuen: for   1040 at that time the iealious-rascally-knaue her husband will be forth: come you to me at night, you shall know how I speed.

FORD I am blest in your acquaintance: do you know *Ford* Sir?

SIR IOHN Hang him (poore Cuckoldly knaue) I know him

not: yet I wrong him to call him poore: They say the
iealous wittolly-knaue hath masses of money, for the
which his wife seemes to me well-fauourd: I will vse
1050 her as the key of the Cuckoldly-rogues Coffer, & ther's
my haruest-home.

FORD I would you knew *Ford*, sir, that you might auoid
him, if you saw him.

SIR IOHN Hang him, mechanicall-salt-butter rogue; I wil
stare him out of his wits: I will awe-him with my
cudgell: it shall hang like a Meteor ore the Cuckolds
horns: Master *Brooke*, thou shalt know, I will
predominate ouer the pezant, and thou shalt lye with
his wife. Come to me soone at night: *Ford*'s a knaue,
1060 and I will aggrauate his stile: thou (Master *Brooke*)
shalt know him for knaue, and Cuckold. Come to me
soone at night.   *Exit*

FORD What a damn'd Epicurian-Rascall is this? my heart
is ready to cracke with impatience: who saies this is
improuident iealousie? my wife hath sent to him, the
howre is fixt, the match is made: would any man haue
thought this? see the hell of hauing a false woman:
my bed shall be abus'd, my Coffers ransack'd, my
reputation gnawne at, and I shall not onely receiue
1070 this villanous wrong, but stand vnder the adoption of
abhominable termes, and by him that does mee this
wrong: Termes, names: *Amaimon* sounds well: *Lucifer*,
well: *Barbason*, well: yet they are Diuels additions, the
names of fiends: But Cuckold, Wittoll, Cuckold? the
Diuell himselfe hath not such a name. *Page* is an Asse,
a secure Asse; hee will trust his wife, hee will not be
iealous: I will rather trust a *Fleming* with my butter,
Parson *Hugh* the *Welsh-man* with my Cheese, an *Irishman* with my Aqua-vitæ-bottle, or a Theefe to walke
1080 my ambling gelding, then my wife with her selfe. Then
she plots, then shee ruminates, then shee deuises: and
what they thinke in their hearts they may effect; they
will breake their hearts but they will effect. God bee
prais'd for my iealousie: eleuen o' clocke the howre, I
will preuent this, detect my wife, bee reueng'd on
Falstaffe, and laugh at *Page*. I will about it, better three
houres too soone, then a mynute too late: Gods my
life: Cuckold, Cuckold, Cuckold.   *Exit*

Sc. 7   *Enter Caius, Rugby, with Rapiers*
(2.3) CAIUS *Iacke Rugby*.
1090 RUGBY Sir.
CAIUS Vat is the clocke, *Iack*.
RUGBY 'Tis past the howre (Sir) that Sir *Hugh* promis'd to
meet.
CAIUS By gar, he has saue his soule, dat he is no-come:
hee has pray his Pible well, dat he is no-come: by gar
(*Iack Rugby*) he is dead already, if he be come.
RUGBY Hee is wise Sir: hee knew your worship would kill
him if he came.
CAIUS ⌈*drawing his Rapier*⌉ By gar, de herring is no dead,
1100 so as I vill kill him: take your Rapier, (*Iacke*) I vill tell
you how I vill kill him.
RUGBY Alas sir, I cannot fence.

CAIUS Villanie, take your Rapier.
RUGBY Forbeare: heer's company.
          ⌈*Caius sheathes his Rapier.*⌉
          Enter Host, Shallow, Page, Slender
HOST God blesse thee, bully-Doctor.
SHALLOW God saue you Mr. Doctor *Caius*.
PAGE Now, good Mr. Doctor.
SLENDER 'Giue you good-morrow, sir.
CAIUS Vat be all you one, two, tree, fowre, come for?
HOST To see thee fight, to see thee foigne, to see thee   1110
trauerse, to see thee heere, to see thee there, to see
thee passe thy puncto, thy stock, thy reuerse, thy
distance, thy montant: Is he dead, my *Ethiopian*? Is
he dead, my *Francisco*? ha Bully? what saies my
Esculapius? my *Galien*? my heart of Elder? ha? is he
dead bully-Stale? is he dead?
CAIUS By gar, he is de Coward-Iack-Priest of de vorld: he
is not show his face.
HOST Thou art a Castalion-king-Vrinall: *Hector* of *Greece*
(my Boy.)   1120
CAIUS I pray you beare witnesse, that me haue stay, sixe
or seuen, two tree howres for him, and hee is no-come.
SHALLOW He is the wiser man (M. Doctor) he is a curer
of soules, and you a curer of bodies: if you should fight,
you goe against the haire of your professions: is it not
true, Master *Page*?
PAGE Master *Shallow*; you haue your selfe beene a great
fighter, though now a man of peace.
SHALLOW Body-kins M. *Page*, though I now be old, and
of the peace; if I see a sword out, my finger itches to   1130
make one: though wee are Iustices, and Doctors, and
Church-men (M. *Page*) wee haue some salt of our youth
in vs, we are the sons of women (M. *Page*.)
PAGE 'Tis true, Mr. *Shallow*.
SHALLOW It wil be found so, (M. *Page*:) M. Doctor *Caius*,
I am come to fetch you home: I am sworn of the peace:
you haue show'd your selfe a wise Physician, and Sir
Hugh hath showne himselfe a wise and patient Church-
man: you must goe with me, M. Doctor.
HOST Pardon, Guest-Iustice; (*to Caius*) a word Mounseur   1140
Mocke-water.
CAIUS Mock-vater? vat is dat?
HOST Mock-water, in our English tongue, is Valour
(Bully.)
CAIUS By gar, then I haue as much Mock-vater as de
Englishman: scuruy-Iack-dog-Priest: by gar, mee vill
cut his eares.
HOST He will Clapper-claw thee tightly (Bully.)
CAIUS Clapper-de-claw? vat is dat?
HOST That is, he will make thee amends.   1150
CAIUS By-gar, me doe looke hee shall clapper-de-claw me,
for by-gar, me vill haue it.
HOST And I will prouoke him to't, or let him wag.
CAIUS Me tanck you for dat.
HOST And moreouer, (Bully) (*aside to the others*) but first,
Mr. Ghuest, and M. *Page*, & eeke Caualeiro *Slender*, goe
you through the Towne to *Frogmore*.
PAGE Sir *Hugh* is there, is he?

HOST He is there, see what humor he is in: and I will
1160   bring the Doctor about by the Fields: will it doe well?
SHALLOW We will doe it.
⌈PAGE, SHALLOW, *and* SLENDER⌉ Adieu, good M. Doctor.
                              Exeunt Page, Shallow, Slender
CAIUS ⌈*drawing his Rapier*⌉ By-gar, me vill kill de Priest,
    for he speake for a Iack-an-Ape to *Anne Page*.
HOST Let him die: sheath thy impatience: throw cold
    water on thy Choller: goe about the fields with mee
    through *Frogmore*, I will bring thee where Mistris *Anne*
    Page is, at a Farm-house a Feasting: and thou shalt
    wooe her: Cride-game, said I well?
1170 CAIUS ⌈*sheathing his Rapier*⌉ By-gar, mee dancke you vor
    dat: by gar I loue you: and I shall procure'a you de
    good Guest: de Earle, de Knight, de Lords, de
    Gentlemen, my patiences.
HOST For the which, I will be thy aduersary toward *Anne*
    Page: said I well?
CAIUS By-gar, 'tis good: vell said.
HOST Let vs wag then.
CAIUS Come at my heeles, *Iack Rugby*.   *Exeunt*

Sc. 8   *Enter Euans, ⌈with a Rapier, and bearing a booke⌉*
(3.1)   *and Simple ⌈bearing Euans gowne⌉*
EUANS I pray you now, good Master *Slenders* seruingman,
1180   and friend *Simple* by your name; which way haue you
    look'd for Master *Caius*, that calls himselfe Doctor of
    Phisicke.
SIMPLE Marry Sir, the pittie-ward, the Parke-ward: euery
    way: olde *Windsor* way, and euery way but the Towne-
    way.
EUANS I most fehemently desire you, you will also looke
    that way.
SIMPLE I will sir.   ⌈*Exit*⌉
EUANS ⌈*opening the booke*⌉ Ieshu plesse me: how full of
1190   Chollors I am, and trempling of minde: I shall be glad
    if he haue deceiued me: how melancholies I am? I will
    knog his Vrinalls about his knaues costard, when I
    haue good oportunities for the orke: 'Plesse my soule:
    (*Singing*)
         To shallow Riuers to whose falls:
         Melodious Birds sings Madrigalls:
         There will we make our Peds of Roses:
         And a thousand fragrant posies.
         To shallow:

    'Mercie on mee, I haue a great dispositions to cry.
    (*Singing*)
1200   *Melodious birds sing Madrigalls:—*
         When as I sat in Pabilon:
         And a thousand vagram Posies.
         To shallow. &c.

         ⌈*Enter Simple*⌉
SIMPLE Yonder he is comming, this way, Sir *Hugh*.
EUANS Hee's welcome:
    (*Singing*) To shallow Riuers, to whose fals:
    God prosper the right: what weapons is he?
SIMPLE No weapons, Sir: there comes my Master, M^r.

Shallow, and another Gentleman; from *Frogmore*, ouer
the stile, this way.   1210
EUANS Pray you giue mee my gowne, or else keepe it in
    your armes.
         ⌈*He reades.*⌉
         Enter Shallow, Slender, Page
SHALLOW How now Master Parson? good morrow good
    Sir *Hugh*: keepe a Gamester from the dice, and a good
    Studient from his booke, and it is wonderfull.
SLENDER (*aside*) Ah sweet *Anne Page*.
PAGE God saue you, good Sir *Hugh*.
EUANS God plesse you from his mercy-sake, all of you.
SHALLOW What? the Sword, and the Word? Doe you
    study them both, M^r. Parson?   1220
PAGE And youthfull still, in your doublet and hose, this
    raw-rumaticke day?
EUANS There is reasons, and causes for it.
PAGE We are come to you, to doe a good office, M^r.
    Parson.
EUANS Fery-well: what is it?
PAGE Yonder is a most reuerend Gentleman; who (be-
    like) hauing receiued wrong by some person, is at most
    odds with his owne grauity and patience, that euer
    you saw.   1230
SHALLOW I haue liued foure-score yeeres, and vpward: I
    neuer heard a man of his place, grauity, and learning,
    so wide of his owne respect.
EUANS What is he?
PAGE I thinke you know him: M^r. Doctor *Caius* the
    renowned French Physician.
EUANS Got's-will, and his passion of my heart: I had as
    lief you would tell me of a messe of porredge.
PAGE Why?
EUANS He has no more knowledge in *Hibocrates* and *Galen*, 1240
    and hee is a knaue besides: a cowardly knaue, as you
    would desires to be acquainted withall.
PAGE ⌈*to Shallow*⌉ I warrant you, hee's the man should
    fight with him.
SLENDER (*aside*) O sweet *Anne Page*.
SHALLOW It appeares so by his weapons:
         Enter Host, Caius, Rugby
    keepe them asunder: here comes Doctor *Caius*.
         Euans and Caius draw and offer to fight
PAGE Nay good M^r. Parson, keepe in your weapon.
SHALLOW So doe you, good M^r. Doctor.
HOST Disarme them, and let them question: let them   1250
    keepe their limbs whole, and hack our English.
         Shallow and Page take Caius and Euans Rapiers
CAIUS (*to Euans*) I pray you let-a-mee speake a word with
    your eare: vherefore vill you not meet-a me?
EUANS ⌈*aside to Caius*⌉ Pray you vse your patience: ⌈*aloud*⌉
    in good time.
CAIUS By-gar, you are de Coward: de Iack dog: Iohn Ape.
EUANS (*aside to Caius*) Pray you let vs not be laughing-
    stocks to other mens humors: I desire you in friendship,
    and I will one way or other make you amends: (*Aloud*)
    By Ieshu I will knog your Vrinal about your knaues   1260
    Cogs-combe.

CAIUS *Diable*: *Iack Rugby*: mine *Host de Iarteer*: haue I not stay for him, to kill him? haue I not at de place I did appoint?

EUANS As I am a Christians-soule, now looke you: this is the place appointed, Ile bee iudgement by mine *Host of the Garter*.

HOST Peace, I say, *Gallia* and *Gaule*, French & *Welch*, Soule-Curer, and Body-Curer.

1270 CAIUS I, dat is very good, *excellant*.

HOST Peace, I say: heare mine Host of the Garter, am I politicke? Am I subtle? Am I a Machiuell? Shall I loose my Doctor? No, hee giues me the Potions and the Motions. Shall I loose my Parson? my Priest? my Sir *Hugh*? No, he giues me the Prouerbes, and the No-verbes. (*To Caius*) Giue me thy hand (Terestiall) so: (*To Euans*) Giue me thy hand (Celestiall) so: Boyes of Art, I haue deceiu'd you both: I haue directed you to wrong places: your hearts are mighty, your skinnes are whole,
1280 and let burn'd Sacke be the issue: (*To Shallow and Page*) Come, lay their swords to pawne: (*To Caius and Euans*) Follow me, Lads of peace, follow, follow, follow.   *Exit*

SHALLOW Afore God, a mad Host: follow Gentlemen, follow.   *Exeunt Shallow and Page*

SLENDER (*aside*) O sweet *Anne Page*.   *Exit*

CAIUS Ha'do I perceiue dat? Haue you make-a-de-sot of vs, ha, ha?

EUANS This is well, he has made vs his vlowting-stog: I desire you that we may be friends: and let vs knog our
1290 praines together to be reuenge on this same scall scuruy-cogging-companion the Host of the Garter.

CAIUS By gar, with all my heart: he promise to bring me where is *Anne Page*: by gar he deceiue me too.

EUANS Well, I will smite his noddles: pray you follow.
                                                Exeunt

Sc. 9   *Enter Robin, followed by Mist. Page*
(3.2) MISTRIS PAGE Nay keepe your way (little Gallant) you were wont to be a follower, but now you are a Leader: whether had you rather lead mine eyes, or eye your masters heeles?

ROBIN I had rather (forsooth) go before you like a man,
1300 then follow him like a dwarfe.

MISTRIS PAGE O you are a flattering boy, now I see you'l be a Courtier.

          Enter Ford

FORD
Well met mistris *Page*, whether go you.

MISTRIS PAGE Truly Sir, to see your wife, is she at home?

FORD I, and as idle as she may hang together for want of company: I thinke if your husbands were dead, you two would marry.

MISTRIS PAGE Be sure of that, two other husbands.

FORD Where had you this pretty weather-cocke?

1310 MISTRIS PAGE I cannot tell what (the dickens) his name is my husband had him of, what do you cal your Knights name sirrah?

ROBIN Sir *Iohn Falstaffe*.

FORD Sir *Iohn Falstaffe*.

MISTRIS PAGE He, he, I can neuer hit on's name; there is such a league betweene my goodman, and he: is your Wife at home indeed?

FORD Indeed she is.

MISTRIS PAGE By your leaue sir, I am sicke till I see her.
               Exeunt Robin and Mist. Page

FORD Has *Page* any braines? Hath he any eies? Hath he   1320 any thinking? Sure they sleepe, he hath no vse of them: why this boy will carrie a letter twentie mile as easie, as a Canon will shoot point-blanke twelue score: hee peeces out his wiues inclination: he giues her folly motion and aduantage: and now she's going to my wife, & *Falstaffes* boy with her: A man may heare this showre sing in the winde; and *Falstaffes* boy with her: good plots, they are laide, and our reuolted wiues share damnation together. Well, I will take him, then torture my wife, plucke the borrowed vaile of modestie from   1330 the so-seeming Mist. *Page*, divulge *Page* himselfe for a secure and wilfull *Acteon*, and to these violent proceedings all my neighbors shall cry aime.

     ⌈*Clocke strikes*⌉
The clocke giues me my Qu, and my assurance bids me search, there I shall finde *Falstaffe*: I shall be rather praisd for this, then mock'd, for it is as possitiue, as the earth is firme, that *Falstaffe* is there: I will go.

     Enter Page, Shallow, Slender, Host, Euans, Caius, Rugby

SHALLOW, PAGE, *&c*. Well met Mr *Ford*.

FORD (*aside*) By my faith, a good knotte; (*To them*) I haue good cheere at home, and I pray you all go with me.   1340

SHALLOW I must excuse my selfe Mr *Ford*.

SLENDER And so must I Sir, we haue appointed to dine with Mistris *Anne*, and I would not breake with her for more mony then Ile speake of.

SHALLOW We haue linger'd about a match betweene *An Page*, and my cozen *Slender*, and this day wee shall haue our answer.

SLENDER I hope I haue your good will Father *Page*.

PAGE You haue Mr *Slender*, I stand wholly for you, (*to Caius*) but my wife (Mr Doctor) is for you altogether.   1350

CAIUS I be-gar, and de Maid is loue-a-me: my nursh-a-Quickly tell me so mush.

HOST (*to Page*) What say you to yong Mr *Fenton*? He capers, he dances, he has eies of youth: he writes verses, hee speakes holliday, he smels April and May, he wil carry't, he will carry't, 'tis in his buttons, he will carry't.

PAGE Not by my consent I promise you. The Gentleman is of no hauing, hee kept companie with the wilde Prince, and *Pointz*: he is of too high a Region, he knows   1360 too much: no, hee shall not knit a knot in his fortunes, with the finger of my substance: if he take her, let him take her simply: the wealth I haue waits on my consent, and my consent goes not that way.

FORD I beseech you heartily, some of you goe home with me to dinner: besides your cheere you shall haue sport, I will shew you a monster: Mr Doctor, you shal go, so shall you Mr *Page*, and you Sir *Hugh*.

SHALLOW Well, God be with you: ⌈*Aside to Slender*⌉ We
1370   shall haue the freer woing at Mr *Pages*.
                          Exeunt Shallow and Slender

CAIUS Go home *Iohn Rugby*, I come anon.   *Exit Rugby*

HOST Farewell my hearts, I will to my honest Knight
    Falstaffe, and drinke Canarie with him.   *Exit*

FORD (*aside*) I thinke I shall drinke in Pipe-wine first with
    him, Ile make him dance. (*To Page, Caius, Euans*) Will
    you go, Gentles?

⌈PAGE, CAIUS, *and* EUANS⌉ Haue with you, to see this
    Monster.   *Exeunt*

Sc. 10   *Enter Mist. Ford, Mist. Page*
(3.3)
         MISTRIS FORD What *Iohn*, what *Robert*.

1380 MISTRIS PAGE Quickly, quickly: Is the Buck-basket—

MISTRIS FORD I warrant. What *Robert* I say.

MISTRIS PAGE Come, come, come.
      Enter Iohn and Robert with a Buck-basket

MISTRIS FORD Heere, set it downe.

MISTRIS PAGE Giue your men the charge, we must be
    briefe.

MISTRIS FORD Marrie, as I told you before (*Iohn & Robert*)
    be ready here hard-by in the Brew-house, & when I
    sodainly call you, come forth, and (without any pause,
    or staggering) take this basket on your shoulders: y^t
1390   done, trudge with it in all hast, and carry it among
    the Whitsters in *Dotchet* Mead, and there empty it in
    the muddie ditch, close by the Thames side.

MISTRIS PAGE (*to Iohn and Robert*) You will do it?

MISTRIS FORD I ha told them ouer and ouer, they lacke
    no direction. Be gone, and come when you are call'd.
                       Exeunt Iohn and Robert
       Enter Robin

MISTRIS PAGE Here comes little *Robin*.

MISTRIS FORD How now my Eyas-Musket, what newes
    with you?

ROBIN My M. Sir *Iohn* is come in at your backe doore
1400   (Mist. *Ford*, and requests your company.

MASTER PAGE You litle Iack-a-lent, haue you bin true to
    vs?

ROBIN I, Ile be sworne: my Master knowes not of your
    being heere: and hath threatnd to put me into
    euerlasting liberty, if I tell you of it: for he sweares
    he'll turne me away.

MISTRIS PAGE Thou'rt a good boy: this secrecy of thine
    shall be a Tailor to thee, and shal make thee a new
    doublet and hose. Ile go hide me.

1410 MISTRIS FORD Do so: (*to Robin*) go tell thy Master, I am
    alone: *Exit Robin*
    Mistris *Page*, remember you your *Qu*.

MISTRIS PAGE I warrant thee, if I do not act it, hisse me.

MISTRIS FORD Go-too then: ⌈*Exit Mistris Page*⌉
    we'l vse this vnwholsome humidity, this grosse-watry
    Pumpion; we'll teach him to know Turtles from Iayes.
       Enter Sir Iohn Falstaffe

SIR IOHN Haue I caught thee, my heauenly Iewell? Why
    now let me die, for I haue liu'd long enough: This is
    the period of my ambition: O this blessed houre.

MISTRIS FORD O sweet Sir *Iohn*.   1420

SIR IOHN Mistris *Ford*, I cannot cog, I cannot prate (Mist.
    Ford) now shall I sin in my wish; I would thy Husband
    were dead, Ile speake it before the best Lord, I would
    make thee my Lady.

MISTRIS FORD I your Lady Sir *Iohn*? Alas, I should bee a
    pittifull Lady.

SIR IOHN Let the Court of France shew me such another:
    I see how thine eye would emulate the Diamond: Thou
    hast the right arched-beauty of the brow, that becomes
    the Ship-tyre, the Tyre-valiant, or any Tire of Venetian   1430
    admittance.

MISTRIS FORD A plaine Kerchiefe, Sir *Iohn*: My browes
    become nothing else, nor that well neither.

SIR IOHN By the Lord, thou art a tyrant to say so: thou
    wouldst make an absolute Courtier, and the firme
    fixture of thy foote, would giue an excellent motion to
    thy gate, in a semicircled Farthingale. I see what thou
    wert if Fortune thy foe, were with Nature thy friend:
    Come, thou canst not hide it.

MISTRIS FORD Beleeue me, ther's no such thing in me.   1440

SIR IOHN What made me loue thee? Let that perswade
    thee ther's something extraordinary in thee: Come, I
    cannot cog, and say thou art this and that, like a-
    manie of these lisping-hauthorne buds, that come like
    women in mens apparrell, and smell like Bucklers-berry
    in simple time: I cannot, but I loue thee, none but
    thee; and thou deseru'st it.

MISTRIS FORD Do not betray me sir, I fear you loue M.
    Page.

SIR IOHN Thou mightst as well say, I loue to walke by   1450
    the Counter-gate, which is as hatefull to me, as the
    reeke of a Lime-kill.

MISTRIS FORD Well, heauen knowes how I loue you, and
    you shall one day finde it.

SIR IOHN Keepe in that minde, Ile deserue it.

MISTRIS FORD Nay, I must tell you, so you doe; Or else I
    could not be in that minde.
       Enter Robin

ROBIN Mistris *Ford*, Mistris *Ford*: heere's Mistris *Page* at
    the doore, sweating, and blowing, and looking wildely,
    and would needs speake with you presently.   1460

SIR IOHN She shall not see me, I will ensconce mee
    behinde the Arras.

MISTRIS FORD Pray you do so, she's a very tatling woman.
       Sir Iohn hides behind the Arras.
       Enter Mist. Page
    Whats the matter? How now?

MISTRIS PAGE O mistris *Ford* what haue you done? You'r
    sham'd, y'are ouerthrowne, y'are vndone for euer.

MISTRIS FORD What's the matter, good mistris *Page*?

MISTRIS PAGE O weladay, mist. *Ford*, hauing an honest
    man to your husband, to giue him such cause of
    suspition.   1470

MISTRIS FORD What cause of suspition?

MISTRIS PAGE What cause of suspition? Out vpon you:
    How am I mistooke in you?

MISTRIS FORD Why (alas) what's the matter?

MISTRIS PAGE Your husband's comming hether (Woman) with all the Officers in Windsor, to search for a Gentleman, that he sayes is heere now in the house; by your consent to take an ill aduantage of his absence: you are vndone.

1480 MISTRIS FORD 'Tis not so, I hope.

MISTRIS PAGE Pray heauen it be not so, that you haue such a man heere: but 'tis most certaine your husband's comming, with halfe Windsor at his heeles, to serch for such a one, I come before to tell you: If you know your selfe cleere, why I am glad of it: but if you haue a friend here, conuey, conuey him out. Be not amaz'd, call all your senses to you, defend your reputation, or bid farwell to your good life for euer.

MISTRIS FORD What shall I do? There is a Gentleman my
1490 deere friend: and I feare not mine owne shame so much, as his perill. I had rather then a thousand pound he were out of the house.

MISTRIS PAGE For shame, neuer stand (you had rather, and you had rather:) your husband's heere at hand, bethinke you of some conueyance: in the house you cannot hide him. Oh, how haue you deceiu'd me? Looke, heere is a basket, if he be of any reasonable stature, he may creepe in heere, and throw fowle linnen vpon him, as if it were going to bucking: Or it is
1500 whiting time, send him by your two men to *Datchet-Meade.*

MISTRIS FORD He's too big to go in there: what shall I do?

SIR IOHN (*comming forward*) Let me see't, let me see't, O let me see't: Ile in, Ile in: Follow your friends counsell, Ile in.

MISTRIS PAGE What Sir *Iohn Falstaffe*? (*Aside to him*) Are these your Letters, Knight?

SIR IOHN (*aside to Mist. Page*) I loue thee, helpe mee away:
1510 let me creepe in heere:

  He goes into the basket

ile neuer—

  *Mistris Page and Mistris Ford put foule cloathes
  ouer him*

MISTRIS PAGE (*to Robin*) Helpe to couer your master (Boy:) Call your men (Mist. *Ford.*) (*Aside to Sir Iohn*) You dissembling Knight.

MISTRIS FORD What *Iohn, Robert, Iohn;*

  Enter Iohn and Robert

Go, take vp these cloathes heere, quickly: Wher's the Cowle-staffe?

  Iohn and Robert fit the Cowle-staffe

Look how you drumble? Carry them to the Landresse in Datchet mead: quickly, come.

  They lift the basket and start to leaue.
  Enter Ford, Page, Caius, Euans

1520 FORD (*to Page, Caius and Euans*) 'Pray you come nere: if I suspect without cause, why then make sport at me, then let me be your iest, I deserue it: (*To Iohn and Robert*) How now? Whether beare you this?

⌈IOHN⌉ To the Landresse forsooth?

MISTRIS FORD Why, what haue you to doe whether they beare it? You were best meddle with buck-washing.

FORD Buck? I would I could wash my selfe of yᵉ Buck: Bucke, bucke, bucke, I bucke: I warrant you Bucke, and of the season too; it shall appeare.

  ⌈*Exeunt Iohn and Robert* (*with the basket*)⌉

Gentlemen, I haue dream'd to night, Ile tell you my 1530 dreame: heere, heere, heere bee my keyes, ascend my Chambers, search, seeke, finde out: Ile warrant wee'le vnkennell the Fox. Let me stop this way first:

  He locks the doore

so, now vncope.

PAGE Good master *Ford*, be contented: You wrong your selfe too much.

FORD True (master *Page*) vp Gentlemen, you shall see sport anon: Follow me Gentlemen.   *Exit*

EUANS This is fery fantasticall humors and iealousies.

CAIUS By gar, 'tis no-the fashion of France: It is not 1540 iealous in France.

PAGE Nay follow him (Gentlemen) see the yssue of his search.   *Exeunt Caius, Euans, Page*

MISTRIS PAGE Is there not a double excellency in this?

MISTRIS FORD I know not which pleases me better, that my husband is deceiued, or Sir *Iohn*.

MISTRIS PAGE What a taking was hee in, when your husband askt what was in the basket?

MISTRIS FORD I am halfe affraid he will haue neede of washing: so throwing him into the water, will doe him 1550 a benefit.

MISTRIS PAGE Hang him dishonest rascall: I would all of the same straine, were in the same distresse.

MISTRIS FORD I thinke my husband hath some speciall suspition of *Falstaffs* being heere: for I neuer saw him so grosse in his iealousie till now.

MISTRIS PAGE I will lay a plot to try that, and wee will yet haue more trickes with *Falstaffe*: his dissolute disease will scarse obey this medicine.

MISTRIS FORD Shall we send that foolish Carion, Mist. 1560 *Quickly* to him, and excuse his throwing into the water, and giue him another hope, to betray him to another punishment?

MISTRIS PAGE We will do it: let him be sent for to morrow eight a clocke to haue amends.

  Enter Ford, Page, Caius, Euans

FORD I cannot finde him: may be the knaue bragg'd of that he could not compasse.

MISTRIS PAGE (*to Mistris Ford*) Heard you that?

MISTRIS FORD You vse me well, M. *Ford*? Do you?

FORD I, I do so.   1570

MISTRIS FORD Heauen make me better then your thoghts.

FORD Amen.

MISTRIS PAGE You do your selfe mighty wrong (M. *Ford*)

FORD I, I: I must beare it.

EUANS If there be any pody in the house, & in the chambers, and in the coffers, and in the presses: heauen forgiue my sins at the day of iudgement.

CAIUS Be gar, nor I too: there is no-bodies.

PAGE Fy, fy, M. *Ford*, are you not asham'd? What spirit, what diuell suggests this imagination? I wold not ha 1580 your distemper in this kind, for yᵉ welth of *Windsor castle.*

FORD 'Tis my fault (M. *Page*) I suffer for it.

EUANS You suffer for a pad conscience: your wife is as honest a o'mans, as I will desires among fiue thousand, and fiue hundred too.

CAIUS By gar, I see 'tis an honest woman.

FORD Well, I promisd you a dinner: come, come, walk in the Parke, I pray you pardon me: I wil hereafter make 1590 knowne to you why I haue done this. Come wife, come Mi. *Page*, I pray you pardon me. Pray hartly pardon me.

PAGE (*to Caius and Euans*) Let's go in Gentlemen, (*aside to them*) but (trust me) we'l mock him: (*To Ford, Caius and Euans*) I doe inuite you to morrow morning to my house to breakfast: after we'll a Birding together, I haue a fine Hawke for the bush. Shall it be so?

FORD Any thing.

EUANS If there is one, I shall make two in the Companie.

1600 CAIUS If there be one, or two, I shall make-a-the-turd.

FORD Pray you go, M. *Page*.

                    Exeunt ⌈all but Euans and Caius⌉

EUANS I pray you now remembrance to morrow on the lowsie knaue, mine Host.

CAIUS Dat is good by gar, with all my heart.

EUANS A lowsie knaue, to haue his gibes, and his mockeries.   *Exeunt*

Sc. 11   *Enter Fenton, Anne Page*
(3.4)
FENTON
    I see I cannot get thy Fathers loue,
    Therefore no more turne me to him (sweet Nan.)
ANNE
    Alas, how then?
FENTON   Why thou must be thy selfe.
1610 He doth obiect, I am too great of birth,
    And that my state being gall'd with my expence,
    I seeke to heale it onely by his wealth.
    Besides these, other barres he layes before me,
    My Riots past, my wilde Societies,
    And tels me 'tis a thing impossible
    I should loue thee, but as a property.
ANNE May be he tels you true.
⌈FENTON⌉
    No, heauen so speed me in my time to come,
    Albeit I will confesse, thy Fathers wealth
1620 Was the first motiue that I woo'd thee (*Anne*:)
    Yet wooing thee, I found thee of more valew
    Then stampes in Gold, or summes in sealed bagges:
    And 'tis the very riches of thy selfe,
    That now I ayme at.
ANNE   Gentle M. *Fenton*,
    Yet seeke my Fathers loue, still seeke it sir,
    If opportunity and humblest suite
    Cannot attaine it, why then:
         Enter Shallow, Slender ⌈richly drest⌉ and Quickly
                         Harke you hither.
         They talke apart
SHALLOW Breake their talke Mistris *Quickly*, my Kinsman shall speake for himselfe.

SLENDER Ile make a shaft or a bolt on't, slid, tis but   1630 venturing.

SHALLOW
    Be not dismaid.

SLENDER   No, she shall not dismay me: I care not for that, but that I am affeard.

MISTRIS QUICKLY (*to Anne*) Hark ye, M. *Slender* would speak a word with you.

ANNE
    I come to him. (*To Fenton*) This is my Fathers choice: O what a world of vilde ill-fauour'd faults Lookes handsome in three hundred pounds a yeere?

MISTRIS QUICKLY And how do's good Master *Fenton*? Pray you a word with you.   1640
         She drawes Fenton aside

SHALLOW Shee's comming; to her Coz: O boy, thou hadst a father.

SLENDER I had a father (M. *An*) my vncle can tel you good iests of him: pray you Vncle, tel Mist. *Anne* the iest how my Father stole two Geese out of a Pen, good Vnckle.

SHALLOW Mistris *Anne*, my Cozen loues you.

SLENDER I that I do, as well as I loue any woman in Glocestershire.

SHALLOW He will maintaine you like a Gentlewoman.   1650

SLENDER I by God that I will, come cut and long-taile, vnder the degree of a Squire.

SHALLOW He will make you a hundred and fiftie pounds ioynture.

ANNE Good Maister *Shallow* let him woo for himselfe.

SHALLOW Marrie I thanke you for it: I thanke you for that good comfort: she cals you (Coz) Ile leaue you.
         He stands aside

ANNE Now Master *Slender*.

SLENDER Now good Mistris *Anne*.

ANNE What is your will?   1660

SLENDER My will? Odd's-hart-lings, that's a prettie iest indeede: I ne're made my Will yet (I thanke God:) I am not such a sickely creature, I giue God praise.

ANNE I meane (M. *Slender*) what wold you with me?

SLENDER Truely, for mine owne part, I would little or nothing with you: your father and my vncle hath made motions: if it be my lucke, so; if not, happy man bee his dole, they can tell you how things go, better then I can:
         Enter Page and Mistris Page
    you may aske your father, heere he comes.   1670

PAGE
    Now Mr *Slender*; Loue him daughter *Anne*.
    Why how now? What does Mr *Fenton* here?
    You wrong me Sir, thus still to haunt my house.
    I told you Sir, my daughter is disposd of.

FENTON
    Nay Mr *Page*, be not impatient.

MISTRIS PAGE
    Good M. *Fenton*, come not to my child.

PAGE She is no match for you.

FENTON Sir, will you heare me?

PAGE No, good M. *Fenton*.

1680 Come M. *Shallow*: Come sonne *Slender*, in;
Knowing my minde, you wrong me (M. *Fenton*.)
                    Exeunt Page, Shallow, Slender

MISTRIS QUICKLY (*to Fenton*) Speake to Mistris *Page*.

FENTON
Good Mist. *Page*, for that I loue your daughter
In such a righteous fashion as I do,
Perforce, against all checkes, rebukes, and manners,
I must aduance the colours of my loue,
And not retire. Let me haue your good will.

ANNE Good mother, do not marry me to yond foole.

MISTRIS PAGE I meane it not, I seeke you a better husband.

1690 MISTRIS QUICKLY ⌜*aside to Anne*⌝ That's my master, M.
Doctor.

ANNE
Alas I had rather be set quick i'th earth,
And bowl'd to death with Turnips.

MISTRIS PAGE
Come, trouble not your selfe good M. *Fenton*,
I will not be your friend, nor enemy:
My daughter will I question how she loues you,
And as I finde her, so am I affected:
Till then, farewell Sir, she must needs go in,
Her father will be angry.

FENTON
1700 Farewell gentle Mistris: farewell *Nan*.
                    Exeunt Mistris Page and Anne

MISTRIS QUICKLY This is my doing now: Nay, saide I, will
you cast away your childe on a Foole, and a Physitian:
Looke on M. *Fenton*, this is my doing.

FENTON
I thanke thee: (*giuing her a Ring*) and I pray thee once
    to night,
Giue my sweet *Nan* this Ring: (*giuing money*) there's
    for thy paines.

MISTRIS QUICKLY Now heauen send thee good fortune,
                    Exit Fenton
a kinde heart he hath: a woman would run through
fire & water for such a kinde heart. But yet, I would
my Maister had Mistris *Anne*, or I would M. *Slender* had
1710 her: or (in sooth) I would M. *Fenton* had her; I will do
what I can for them all three, for so I haue promisd,
and Ile bee as good as my word, but speciously for M.
Fenton. Well, I must of another errand to Sir *Iohn
Falstaffe* from my two Mistresses: what a beast am I to
slacke it.   *Exit*

Sc. 12   *Enter Sir Iohn Falstaffe*
(3.5) SIR IOHN *Bardolfe* I say.
            Enter Bardolfe

BARDOLFE Heere Sir.

SIR IOHN Go, fetch me a quart of Sacke, put a tost in't.
                    Exit Bardolfe
Haue I liu'd to be carried in a Basket like a barrow of
1720 butchers Offall? and to be throwne in the Thames?
Wel, if I be seru'd such another tricke, Ile haue my

braines 'tane out and butter'd, and giue them to a
dogge for a New-yeares gift. 'Sblood the rogues slighted
me into the riuer with as little remorse, as they would
haue drown'de a blinde bitches Puppies, fifteene i'th
litter: and you may know by my size, that I haue a
kinde of alacrity in sinking: if the bottome were as
deepe as hell, I shold down. I had beene drown'd, but
that the shore was sheluy and shallow: a death that I
abhorre: for the water swelles a man; and what a   1730
thing should I haue beene, when I had beene swel'd?
By the Lord a Mountaine of Mummie.

    Enter Bardolfe (with ⌜*two large cups of*⌝ *Sacke*)

BARDOLFE Here's M. *Quickly* Sir to speake with you.

SIR IOHN Come, let me poure in some Sack to the Thames
water: for my bellies as cold as if I had swallow'd
snowbals, for pilles to coole the reines.

    He drinkes
Call her in.

BARDOLFE Come in woman.

    Enter Mistris Quickly

MISTRIS QUICKLY (*to Sir Iohn*) By your leaue: I cry you
mercy? Giue your worship good morrow.   1740

SIR IOHN (⌜*drinking, then speaking*⌝ *to Bardolfe*) Take away
these Challices: Go, brew me a pottle of Sacke finely.

BARDOLFE With Egges, Sir?

SIR IOHN Simple of it selfe: Ile no Pullet-Spersme in my
brewage.   *Exit Bardolfe* ⌜*with cups*⌝
How now?

MISTRIS QUICKLY Marry Sir, I come to your worship from
M. *Ford*.

SIR IOHN *Mist. Ford*? I haue had Ford enough: I was
thrown into the Ford; I haue my belly full of Ford.   1750

MISTRIS QUICKLY Alas the day, (good-heart) that was not
her fault: she do's so take on with her men; they
mistooke their erection.

SIR IOHN So did I mine, to build vpon a foolish Womans
promise.

MISTRIS QUICKLY Well, she laments Sir for it, that it would
yern your heart to see it: her husband goes this
morning a birding; she desires you once more to come
to her, betweene eight and nine: I must carry her word
quickely, she'll make you amends I warrant you.   1760

SIR IOHN Well, I will visit her, tell her so: and bidde her
thinke what a-man is: Let her consider his frailety, and
then iudge of my merit.

MISTRIS QUICKLY I will tell her.

SIR IOHN Do so. Betweene nine and ten saist thou?

MISTRIS QUICKLY Eight and nine Sir.

SIR IOHN Well, be gone: I will not misse her.

MISTRIS QUICKLY Peace be with you Sir.   *Exit*

SIR IOHN I meruaile I heare not of Mr *Brooke*: he sent me
word to stay within: I like his money well.   1770

    Enter Ford (*disguis'd as Brooke*)
By the Masse, heere he comes.

FORD God blesse you Sir.

SIR IOHN Now M. *Brooke*, you come to know what hath
past betweene me, and *Fords* wife.

FORD That indeed (Sir *Iohn*) is my businesse.

SIR IOHN M. *Brooke* I will not lye to you, I was at her house the houre she appointed me.

FORD And sped you Sir?

SIR IOHN Very ill-fauouredly M. *Brooke*.

1780 FORD How so sir, did she change her determination?

SIR IOHN No (M. *Brooke*) but the peaking Cornuto her husband (M. *Brooke*) dwelling in a continual larum of ielousie, coms me in the instant of our encounter, after we had embrast, kist, protested, & (as it were) spoke the prologue of our Comedy: and at his heeles, a rabble of his companions, thither prouoked and instigated by his distemper, and (forsooth) to serch his house for his wiues Loue.

FORD What? While you were there?

1790 SIR IOHN While I was there.

FORD And did he search for you, & could not find you?

SIR IOHN You shall heare. As God would haue it, comes in one *Mist. Page*, giues intelligence of *Fords* approch: and by her inuention, and *Fords* wiues distraction, they conuey'd me into a bucke-basket.

FORD A Buck-basket?

SIR IOHN By the Lord: a Buck-basket: ram'd mee in with foule Shirts and Smockes, Socks, foule Stockings, greasie Napkins, that (Master *Brooke*) there was the rankest 1800 compound of villanous smell, that euer offended nostrill.

FORD And how long lay you there?

SIR IOHN Nay, you shall heare (Master *Brooke*) what I haue sufferd, to bring this woman to euill, for your good: Being thus cram'd in the Basket, a couple of *Fords* knaues, his Hindes, were cald forth by their Mistris, to carry mee in the name of foule Cloathes to *Datchet-lane*: they tooke me on their shoulders: met the iealous knaue their Master in the doore; who ask'd them once or twice what they had in their Basket? I 1810 quak'd for feare least the Lunatique Knaue would haue search'd it: but Fate (ordaining he should be a Cuckold) held his hand: well, on went hee, for a search, and away went I for foule Cloathes: But marke the sequell (Master *Brooke*) I suffered the pangs of three seuerall deaths: First, an intollerable fright, to be detected with a iealious rotten Bell-weather: Next to be compass'd like a good Bilbo in the circumference of a Pecke, hilt to point, heele to head. And then to be stopt in like a strong distillation with stinking Cloathes, that fretted 1820 in their owne grease: thinke of that, a man of my Kidney; thinke of that, that am as subiect to heate as butter; a man of continuall dissolution, and thaw: it was a miracle to scape suffocation. And in the height of this Bath (when I was more then halfe stew'd in grease (like a Dutch-dish) to be throwne into the Thames, and coold, glowing-hot, in that serge like a Horse-shoo; thinke of that; hissing hot: thinke of that (Master *Brooke*.)

FORD In good sadnesse Sir, I am sorry, that for my sake 1830 you haue sufferd all this. My suite then is desperate: You'll vndertake her no more?

SIR IOHN Master *Brooke*: I will be throwne into *Etna*, as I haue beene into Thames, ere I will leaue her thus; her Husband is this morning gone a Birding: I haue receiued from her another ambassie of meeting: 'twixt eight and nine is the houre (Master *Brooke*.)

FORD 'Tis past eight already Sir.

SIR IOHN Is it? I will then addresse mee to my appointment: Come to mee at your conuenient leisure, and you shall know how I speede: and the conclusion 1840 shall be crowned with your enioying her: adiew: you shall haue her (Master *Brooke*) Master *Brooke*, you shall cuckold *Ford*.   *Exit*

FORD Hum: ha? Is this a vision? Is this a dreame? doe I sleepe? Master *Ford* awake, awake Master *Ford*: ther's a hole made in your best coate (Master *Ford*:) this 'tis to be married; this 'tis to haue Lynnen, and Buck-baskets: Well, I will proclaime my selfe what I am: I will now take the Leacher: hee is at my house: hee cannot scape me: 'tis impossible hee should: hee cannot 1850 creepe into a halfe-penny purse, nor into a Pepper-Boxe: But least the Diuell that guides him, should aide him, I will search impossible places: though what I am, I cannot auoide; yet to be what I would not, shall not make me tame: If I haue hornes, to make one mad, let the prouerbe goe with me, Ile be horne-mad.   *Exit*

Enter Mistris Page, Quickly, William   Sc. 13

MISTRIS PAGE Is he at M. *Fords* already think'st thou?   (4.1)

MISTRIS QUICKLY Sure he is by this; or will be presently; but truely he is very couragious mad, about his throwing into the water. Mistris *Ford* desires you to 1860 come sodainely.

MISTRIS PAGE Ile be with her by and by: Ile but bring my yong-man here to Schoole:

Enter Euans

looke where his Master comes; 'tis a playing day I see: how now Sir *Hugh*, no Schoole to day?

EUANS No: Master *Slender* is let the Boyes leaue to play.

MISTRIS QUICKLY 'Blessing of his heart.

MISTRIS PAGE Sir *Hugh*, my husband saies my sonne profits nothing in the world at his Booke: I pray you aske him some questions in his Accidence.   1870

EUANS Come hither *William*; hold vp your head; come.

MISTRIS PAGE Come-on Sirha; hold vp your head; answere your Master, be not afraid.

EUANS *William*, how many Numbers is in Nownes?

WILLIAM Two.

MISTRIS QUICKLY Truely, I thought there had bin one Number more, because they say od's-Nownes.

EUANS Peace, your tatlings. What is (*Faire*) *William*?

WILLIAM *Pulcher*.

MISTRIS QUICKLY Powlcats? there are fairer things then   1880 Powlcats, sure.

EUANS You are a very simplicity o'man: I pray you peace. What is (*Lapis*) *William*?

WILLIAM A Stone.

EUANS And what is a Stone (*William?*)

WILLIAM A Peeble.

EUANS No; it is *Lapis*: I pray you remember in your praine.

WILLIAM *Lapis*.

1890 EUANS That is a good *William*: what is he (*William*) that do's lend Articles.

WILLIAM Articles are borrowed of the Pronoune; and be thus declined. *Singulariter nominatiuo hic, hæc, hoc.*

EUANS *Nominatiuo hig, hag, hog*: pray you marke: *genitiuo huius*: Well: what is your *Accusatiue-case?*

WILLIAM *Accusatiuo hinc.*

EUANS I pray you haue your remembrance (childe) *Accusatiuo hing, hang, hog.*

MISTRIS QUICKLY Hang-hog, is latten for Bacon, I warrant 1900 you.

EUANS Leaue your prables (o'man) What is the *Focatiue case* (*William?*)

WILLIAM O, *Vocatiuo*, O.

EUANS Remember *William, Focatiue*, is *caret*.

MISTRIS QUICKLY And that's a good roote.

EUANS O'man, forbeare.

MISTRIS PAGE (*to Mistris Quickly*) Peace.

EUANS What is your *Genitiue case plurall* (*William?*)

WILLIAM *Genitiue case?*

1910 EUANS I.

WILLIAM *Genitiuo horum, harum, horum.*

MISTRIS QUICKLY 'Vengeance of Ginyes case; fie on her; neuer name her (childe) if she be a whore.

EUANS For shame o'man.

MISTRIS QUICKLY You doe ill to teach the childe such words: hee teaches him to hic, and to hac; which they'll doe fast enough of themselues, and to call *horum*; fie vpon you.

EUANS O'man, art thou Lunatics? Hast thou no 1920 vnderstandings for thy Cases, & the numbers of the Genders? Thou art as foolish Christian creatures, as I would desires.

MISTRIS PAGE (*to Mistress Quickly*) Pre'thee hold thy peace.

EUANS Shew me now (*William*) some declensions of your Pronounes.

WILLIAM Forsooth, I haue forgot.

EUANS It is *Qui, que, quod*; if you forget your *Quies*, your *Ques*, and your *Quods*, you must be preeches: Goe your waies and play, go.

1930 MISTRIS PAGE He is a better scholler then I thought he was.

EUANS He is a good sprag-memory: Farewel *Mis. Page.*

MISTRIS PAGE Adieu good Sir *Hugh*:   *Exit Euans*
Get you home boy,   *Exit William*
(*to Mistris Quickly*) Come we stay too long.   *Exeunt*

Sc. 14   *Enter Sir Iohn Falstoffe and Mist. Ford*
(4.2) SIR IOHN *Mi. Ford*, Your sorrow hath eaten vp my sufferance; I see you are obsequious in your loue, and I professe requitall to a haires bredth, not onely Mist. *Ford*, in the simple office of loue, but in all the
1940 accustrement, complement, and ceremony of it: But are you sure of your husband now?

MISTRIS FORD Hee's a birding (sweet Sir *Iohn*.)

MISTRIS PAGE (*within*) What hoa, gossip *Ford*: what hoa.

MISTRIS FORD Step into th'chamber, Sir *Iohn*.
Sir Iohn steps into the Chamber.
Enter Mist. Page

MISTRIS PAGE How now (sweete heart) whose at home besides your selfe?

MISTRIS FORD Why none but mine owne people.

MISTRIS PAGE Indeed?

MISTRIS FORD No certainly: (*Aside to her*) Speake louder.

MISTRIS PAGE Truly, I am so glad you haue no body here.   1950

MISTRIS FORD Why?

MISTRIS PAGE Why woman, your husband is in his olde lines againe: he so takes on yonder with my husband, so railes against all married mankinde; so curses all *Eues* daughters, of what complexion soeuer; and so buffettes himselfe on the for-head: crying peere-out, peere-out, that any madnesse I euer yet beheld, seem'd but tamenesse, ciuility, and patience to this his distemper he is in now: I am glad the fat Knight is not heere.   1960

MISTRIS FORD Why, do's he talke of him?

MISTRIS PAGE Of none but him, and sweares he was caried out the last time hee search'd for him, in a Basket: Protests to my husband he is now heere, & hath drawne him and the rest of their company from their sport, to make another experiment of his suspition: But I am glad the Knight is not heere; now he shall see his owne foolerie.

MISTRIS FORD How neere is he Mistris *Page?*

MISTRIS PAGE Hard by, at street end; he wil be here anon.   1970

MISTRIS FORD I am vndone, the Knight is heere.

MISTRIS PAGE Why then you are vtterly sham'd, & hee's but a dead man. What a woman are you? Away with him, away with him: Better shame, then murther.

MISTRIS FORD Which way should he go? How should I bestow him? Shall I put him into the basket againe?
Sir Iohn comes forth from the Chamber

SIR IOHN No, Ile come no more i'th Basket: May I not go out ere he come?

MISTRIS PAGE Alas: three of M^r. *Fords* brothers watch the doore with Pistols, that none shall issue out: otherwise   1980 you might slip away ere hee came: But what make you heere?

SIR IOHN What shall I do? Ile creepe vp into the chimney.

MISTRIS FORD There they alwaies vse to discharge their Birding-peeces.

⌈MISTRIS PAGE⌉ Creepe into the Kill-hole.

SIR IOHN Where is it?

MISTRIS FORD He will seeke there on my word: Neyther Presse, Coffer, Chest, Trunke, Well, Vault, but he hath an abstract for the remembrance of such places, and   1990 goes to them by his Note: There is no hiding you in the house.

SIR IOHN Ile go out then.

MISTRIS ⌈PAGE⌉ If you goe out in your owne semblance, you die Sir *Iohn*, vnlesse you go out disguis'd.

MISTRIS FORD How might we disguise him?

MISTRIS PAGE Alas the day I know not, there is no womans gowne bigge enough for him: otherwise he might put on a hat, a muffler, and a kerchiefe, and so escape.

SIR IOHN Good hearts, deuise something: any extremitie, rather then a mischiefe.

MISTRIS FORD My Maids Aunt the fat woman of *Brainford*, has a gowne aboue.

MISTRIS PAGE On my word it will serue him: shee's as big as he is: and there's her thrum'd hat, and her muffler too: run vp Sir *Iohn*.

MISTRIS FORD Go, go, sweet Sir *Iohn*: *Mistris Page* and I will looke some linnen for your head.

MISTRIS PAGE Quicke, quicke, wee'le come dresse you straight: put on the gowne the while. *Exit Sir Iohn*

MISTRIS FORD I would my husband would meete him in this shape: he cannot abide the old woman of Brainford; he sweares she's a witch, forbad her my house, and hath threatned to beate her.

MISTRIS PAGE Heauen guide him to thy husbands cudgell: and the diuell guide his cudgell afterwards.

MISTRIS FORD But is my husband comming?

MISTRIS PAGE I in good sadnesse is he, and talkes of the basket too, howsoeuer he hath had intelligence.

MISTRIS FORD Wee'l try that: for Ile appoint my men to carry the basket againe, to meete him at the doore with it, as they did last time.

MISTRIS PAGE Nay, but hee'l be heere presently: let's go dresse him like the witch of *Brainford*.

MISTRIS FORD Ile first direct my men, what they shall doe with the basket: Goe vp, Ile bring linnen for him straight.

MISTRIS PAGE Hang him dishonest Varlet, we cannot misuse him enough: *⌈Exit Mistris Ford⌉*
We'll leaue a proofe by that which we will doo,
Wiues may be merry, and yet honest too:
We do not acte that often iest, and laugh,
'Tis old, but true, Still Swine eats all the draugh. *Exit*

Enter ⌈Mist. Ford, with⌉ Iohn and Robert

MISTRIS FORD Go Sirs, take the basket againe on your shoulders: your Master is hard at doore: if hee bid you set it downe, obey him: quickly, dispatch. *Exit*

⌈IOHN⌉ Come, come, take it vp.

⌈ROBERT⌉ Pray heauen it be not full of Knight againe.

⌈IOHN⌉ I hope not, I had as liefe beare so much lead.

They lift the basket.

Enter Ford, Page, Caius, Euans, Shallow

FORD I, but if it proue true (M^{r}. *Page*) haue you any way then to vnfoole me againe. (*To Iohn and Robert*) Set downe the basket villains:

Iohn and Robert set downe the basket

some body call my wife: Youth in a basket: Oh you Panderly Rascals, there's a knot: a ging, a packe, a conspiracie against me: Now shall the diuel be sham'd. What wife I say: Come, come forth: behold what honest cloathes you send forth to bleaching.

PAGE Why, this passes M. *Ford*: you are not to goe loose any longer, you must be pinnion'd.

EUANS Why, this is Lunaticks: this is madde, as a mad dogge.

SHALLOW Indeed *M. Ford*, this is not well indeed.

FORD So say I too Sir,

Enter Mist. Ford

come hither Mistress *Ford*, Mistris *Ford*, the honest woman, the modest wife, the vertuous creature, that hath the iealious foole to her husband: I suspect without cause (Mistris) do I?

MISTRIS FORD God be my witnesse you doe, if you suspect me in any dishonesty.

FORD Well said Brazon-face, hold it out:

He opens the basket, and starts to take out cloathes

Come forth sirrah.

PAGE This passes.

MISTRIS FORD (*to Ford*) Are you not asham'd, let the cloths alone.

FORD I shall finde you anon.

EUANS 'Tis vnreasonable; will you take vp your wiues cloathes? Come, away.

FORD ⌈*to Iohn and Robert*⌉ Empty the basket I say.

⌈PAGE⌉ Why man, why?

FORD Master *Page*, as I am a man, there was one conuay'd out of my house yesterday in this basket: why may not he be there againe, in my house I am sure he is: my Intelligence is true, my iealousie is reasonable, ⌈*to Iohn and Robert*⌉ pluck me out all the linnen.

He takes out cloathes

MISTRIS FORD If you find a man there, he shall dye a Fleas death.

PAGE Heer's no man.

SHALLOW By my fidelity this is not well M^{r}. *Ford*: This wrongs you.

EUANS Mr *Ford*, you must pray, and not follow the imaginations of your owne heart: this is iealousies.

FORD Well, hee's not heere I seeke for.

PAGE No, nor no where else but in your braine.

FORD Helpe to search my house this one time: if I find not what I seeke, shew no colour for my extremity: Let me for euer be your Table-sport: Let them say of me, as iealous as *Ford*, that search'd a hollow Wall-nut for his wiues Lemman. Satisfie me once more, once more serch with me.

⌈Exeunt Iohn and Robert with the basket⌉

MISTRIS FORD What hoa (Mistris *Page*,) come you and the old woman downe: my husband will come into the Chamber.

FORD Old woman? what old womans that?

MISTRIS FORD Why it is my maids Aunt of *Brainford*.

FORD A witch, a Queane, an olde couzening queane: Haue I not forbid her my house. She comes of errands do's she? We are simple men, wee doe not know what's brought to passe vnder the profession of Fortune-telling. She workes by Charmes, by Spels, by th'Figure, & such dawbry as this is, beyond our Element: wee know nothing. Come downe you Witch, you Hagge you, come downe I say.

⌜*Enter Mist. Page and Sir Iohn Falstaffe, disguis'd*
as an old woman.⌝
⌜*Ford makes towards them*⌝

MISTRIS FORD Nay, good sweet husband, good Gentlemen,
let him not strike the old woman.

MISTRIS PAGE (*to Sir Iohn*) Come mother *Prat*, Come giue
me your hand.

FORD Ile *Prat*-her:

He beates sir Iohn

Out of my doore, you Witch, you Ragge, you Baggage,
you Poulcat, you Runnion, out, out: Ile coniure you,
2110   Ile fortune-tell you.   *Exit Sir Iohn*

MISTRIS PAGE Are you not asham'd? I thinke you haue
kill'd the poore woman.

MISTRIS FORD Nay he will do it, 'tis a goodly credite for
you.

FORD Hang her witch.

EUANS By Ieshu, I thinke the o'man is a witch indeede:
I like not when a o'man has a great peard; I spie a
great peard vnder his muffler.

FORD Will you follow Gentlemen, I beseech you follow:
2120   see but the issue of my iealousie: If I cry out thus vpon
no traile, neuer trust me when I open againe.

PAGE Let's obey his humour a little further: Come
Gentlemen.   *Exeunt the men*

MISTRIS PAGE By my troth he beate him most pittifully.

MISTRIS FORD Nay by th'Masse that he did not: he beate
him most vnpittifully, me thought.

MISTRIS PAGE Ile haue the cudgell hallow'd, and hung ore
the Altar, it hath done meritorious seruice.

MISTRIS FORD What thinke you? May we with the warrant
2130   of woman-hood, and the witnesse of a good conscience,
pursue him with any further reuenge?

MISTRIS PAGE The spirit of wantonnesse is sure scar'd out
of him, if the diuell haue him not in fee-simple, with
fine and recouery, he will neuer (I thinke) in the way
of waste, attempt vs againe.

MISTRIS FORD Shall we tell our husbands how wee haue
seru'd him?

MISTRIS PAGE Yes, by all meanes: if it be but to scrape
the figures out of your husbands braines: if they can
2140   find in their hearts, the poore vnuertuous fat Knight
shall be any further afflicted, wee two will still bee the
ministers.

MISTRIS FORD Ile warrant, they'l haue him publiquely
sham'd, and me thinkes there would be no period to
the iest, should he not be publikely sham'd.

MISTRIS PAGE Come, to the Forge with it, then shape it:
I would not haue things coole.   *Exeunt*

Sc. 15
(4.3)   *Enter Host and Bardolfe*

BARDOLFE Sir, the Germanes desire to haue three of your
horses: the Duke himselfe will be to morrow at Court,
2150   and they are going to meet him.

HOST What Duke should that be comes so secretly? I
heare not of him in the Court: let mee speake with the
Gentlemen, they speake English?

BARDOLFE I Sir? Ile call them to you.

HOST They shall haue my horses, but Ile make them pay:
Ile sauce them, they haue had my house a week at
commaund: I haue turn'd away my other guests, they
must come off, Ile sawce them, come.   *Exeunt*

Enter Page, Ford, Mistris Page, Mistris Ford, and   Sc. 16
Euans   (4.4)

EUANS 'Tis one of the best discretions of a o'man as euer
I did looke vpon.   2160

PAGE And did he send you both these Letters at an
instant?

MISTRIS PAGE Within a quarter of an houre.

FORD
Pardon me (wife) henceforth do what yᵘ wilt:
I rather will suspect the Sunne with Cold,
Then thee with wantonnes: Now doth thy honor stand
(In him that was of late an Heretike)
As firme as faith.

PAGE   'Tis well, 'tis well, no more:
Be not as extreme in submission,
As in offence,   2170
But let our plot go forward: Let our wiues
Yet once againe (to make vs publike sport)
Appoint a meeting with this old fat-fellow,
Where we may take him, and disgrace him for it.

FORD
There is no better way then that they spoke of.

PAGE
How, to send him word they'll meete him in the Parke
At midnight? Fie, fie, he'll neuer come.

EUANS You say he has bin throwne in the Riuers: and
has bin greeuously peaten, as an old o'man: me-thinkes
there should be terrors in him, that he should not   2180
come: Me-thinkes his flesh is punish'd, hee shall haue
no desires.

PAGE So thinke I too.

⌜MISTRIS⌝ FORD
Deuise but how you'l vse him whẽ he comes,
And let vs two deuise to bring him thether.

MISTRIS PAGE
There is an old tale goes, that *Herne* the Hunter
(Sometime a keeper heere in Windsor Forrest)
Doth all the winter time, at still midnight
Walke round about an Oake, with great rag'd-hornes,
And there he blasts the trees, and takes the cattle,   2190
And makes milch-kine yeeld blood, and shakes a chaine
In a most hideous and dreadfull manner.
You haue heard of such a Spirit, and well you know
The superstitious idle-headed-Eld
Receiu'd, and did deliuer to our age
This tale of *Herne* the Hunter, for a truth.

PAGE
Why yet there want not many that do feare
In deepe of night to walke by this Hernes Oake:
But what of this?

MISTRIS FORD   Marry this is our deuise,

2200 That *Falstaffe* at that Oake shall meete with vs,
Disguis'd like *Herne*, with huge hornes on his head.

PAGE

Well, let it not be doubted but he'll come,
And in this shape. When you haue brought him
    thether,
What shall be done with him? What is your plot?

MISTRIS PAGE

That likewise haue we thoght vpon: & thus:
Nan Page (my daughter) and my little sonne,
And three or foure more of their growth, wee'l dresse
Like Vrchins, Ouphes, and Fairies, greene and white,
With rounds of waxen Tapers on their heads,
2210 And rattles in their hands; vpon a sodaine,
As *Falstaffe*, she, and I, are newly met,
Let them from forth a saw-pit rush at once
With some diffused song: Vpon their sight
We two, in great amazednesse will flye:
Then let them all encircle him about,
And Fairy-like to pinch the vncleane Knight;
And aske him why that houre of Fairy Reuell,
In their so sacred pathes, he dares to tread
In shape prophane.

⌜MISTRIS⌝ FORD   And till he tell the truth,
2220 Let the supposed Fairies pinch him, sound,
And burne him with their Tapers.

MISTRIS PAGE   The truth being knowne,
We'll all present our selues; dis-horne the spirit,
And mocke him home to Windsor.

FORD   The children must
Be practis'd well to this, or they'll neu'r doo't.

EUANS I will teach the children their behauiours: and I
will be like a Iacke-an-Apes also, to burne the Knight
with my Taber.

FORD

That will be excellent, Ile go buy them vizards.

MISTRIS PAGE

My *Nan* shall be the Queene of all the Fairies,
2230 Finely attired in a robe of white.

PAGE

That silke will I go buy, (*aside*) and in that tire
Shall M. *Slender* steale my *Nan* away,
And marry her at *Eaton*: (*to Mistris Page*) go, send to
    Falstaffe straight.

FORD

Nay, Ile to him againe in name of *Brooke*,
Hee'l tell me all his purpose: sure hee'l come.

MISTRIS PAGE

Feare not you that: (*To Page, Ford, and Euans*) Go get
    vs properties
And tricking for our Fayries.

EUANS Let vs about it, it is admirable pleasures, and ferry
honest knaueries.   *Exeunt Ford, Page, Euans*

MISTRIS PAGE   Go Mist. *Ford*,
2240 Send quickly to Sir *Iohn*, to know his minde:

                              Exit Mistris Ford
Ile to the Doctor, he hath my good will,

And none but he to marry with *Nan Page*:
That *Slender* (though well landed) is an Ideot:
And he, my husband best of all affects:
The Doctor is well monied, and his friends
Potent at Court: he, none but he shall haue her,
Though twenty thousand worthier come to craue her.

                              Exit

Enter Host and Simple   Sc. 17
                                            (4.5)
HOST What wouldst thou haue? (Boore) what? (thick
skin) speake, breathe, discusse: breefe, short, quicke,
snap.   2250

SIMPLE Marry Sir, I come to speake with Sir *Iohn Falstaffe*
from M. *Slender*.

HOST There's his Chamber, his House, his Castle, his
standing-bed and truckle-bed: 'tis painted about with
the story of the Prodigall, fresh and new: go, knock
and call: hee'l speake like an Anthropophaginian vnto
thee: Knocke I say.

SIMPLE There's an olde woman, a fat woman gone vp
into his chamber: Ile be so bold as stay Sir till she
come downe: I come to speake with her indeed.   2260

HOST Ha? A fat woman? The Knight may be robb'd: Ile
call. Bully-Knight, Bully Sir *Iohn*: speake from thy
Lungs Military: Art thou there? It is thine Host, thine
Ephesian cals.

SIR IOHN (*within*) How now, mine Host?

HOST Here's a Bohemian-Tartar taries the comming
downe of thy fat-woman: Let her descend (Bully) let
her descend: my Chambers are honourable: Fie,
priuacy? Fie.

                    Enter Sir Iohn Falstaffe

SIR IOHN There was (mine Host) an old-fat-woman euen   2270
now with me, but she's gone.

SIMPLE Pray you Sir, was't not the Wise-woman of
Brainford?

SIR IOHN I marry was it (Mussel-shell) what would you
with her?

SIMPLE My Master (Sir) my master *Slender*, sent to her
seeing her go thorough the streets, to know (Sir)
whether one *Nim* (Sir) that beguil'd him of a chaine,
had the chaine, or no.

SIR IOHN I spake with the old woman about it.   2280

SIMPLE And what sayes she, I pray Sir?

SIR IOHN Marry shee sayes, that the very same man that
beguil'd Master *Slender* of his Chaine, cozon'd him of
it.

SIMPLE I would I could haue spoken with the Woman
her selfe, I had other things to haue spoken with her
too, from him.

SIR IOHN What are they? let vs know.

HOST I: come: quicke.

SIMPLE I may not conceale them (Sir.)   2290

HOST Conceale them, or thou di'st.

SIMPLE Why sir, they were nothing but about Mistris
Anne Page, to know if it were my Masters fortune to
haue her, or no.

SIR IOHN 'Tis, 'tis his fortune.

SIMPLE What Sir?

SIR IOHN To haue her, or no: goe; say the woman told me so.

SIMPLE May I be bold to say so Sir?

2300 SIR IOHN I sir tike, who more bold.

SIMPLE I thanke your worship: I shall make my Master glad with these tydings.   *Exit*

HOST Thou art clearkly: thou art clearkly (Sir *Iohn*) was there a wise woman with thee?

SIR IOHN I that there was (mine *Host*) one that hath taught me more wit, then euer I learn'd before in my life: and I paid nothing for it neither, but was paid for my learning.

Enter Bardolfe, ⌈muddie⌉

BARDOLFE O Lord (Sir) cozonage: meere cozonage.

2310 HOST Where be my horses? speake well of them varletto.

BARDOLFE Run away with the cozoners: for so soone as I came beyond *Eaton*, they threw me off, from behinde one of them, in a slough of myre; and set spurres, and away; like three *Germane*-diuels; three *Doctor Faustasses*.

HOST They are gone but to meete the Duke (villaine) doe not say they be fled: *Germanes* are honest men.

Enter Euans

EUANS Where is mine *Host*?

HOST What is the matter Sir?

2320 EUANS Haue a care of your entertainments: there is a friend of mine come to Towne, tels mee there is three Cozen-Garmombles, that has cozend all the *Hosts of Readins*, of *Maidenhead*; of *Cole-brooke*, of horses and money: I tell you for good will (looke you) you are wise, and full of gibes, and vlouting-stocks: and 'tis not conuenient you should be cozoned. Fare you well.

Exit

Enter Caius

CAIUS Ver'is mine *Host de Iarteere*?

HOST Here (Master *Doctor*) in perplexitie, and doubtfull delemma.

2330 CAIUS I cannot tell vat is dat: but it is tell-a-me, dat you make grand preparation for a Duke *de Iamanie*: by my trot: der is no Duke that the Court is know, to come: I tell you for good will: adieu.   *Exit*

HOST (*to Bardolfe*) Huy and cry, (villaine) goe: (*to Sir Iohn*) assist me Knight, I am vndone: (*to Bardolfe*) fly, run: huy, and cry (villaine) I am vndone.

Exeunt Host and Bardolfe ⌈seuerally⌉

SIR IOHN I would all the world might be cozond, for I haue beene cozond and beaten too: if it should come to the eare of the Court, how I haue beene transformed;

2340 and how my transformation hath beene washd, and cudgeld, they would melt mee out of my fat drop by drop, and liquor Fishermens-boots with me: I warrant they would whip me with their fine wits, till I were as crest-falne as a dride-peare: I neuer prosper'd, since I forswore my selfe at *Primero*: well, if my winde were but long enough; I would repent:

Enter Quickly

Now? Whence come you?

MISTRIS QUICKLY From the two parties forsooth.

SIR IOHN The Diuell take one partie, and his Dam the other: and so they shall be both bestowed; I haue   2350 suffer'd more for their sakes; more then the villanous inconstancy of mans disposition is able to beare.

MISTRIS QUICKLY O Lord sir, and haue not they suffer'd? Yes, I warrant; speciously one of them; Mistris *Ford* (good heart) is beaten blacke and blew, that you cannot see a white spot about her.

SIR IOHN What tell'st thou mee of blacke, and blew? I was beaten my selfe into all the colours of the Rainebow: and I was like to be apprehended for the Witch of *Braineford*. But that my admirable dexteritie   2360 of wit, my counterfeiting the action of an old woman deliuer'd me, the knaue Constable had set me ith'Stocks, ith'common Stocks, for a Witch.

MISTRIS QUICKLY Sir: let me speake with you in your Chamber, you shall heare how things goe, and (I warrant) to your content: here is a Letter will say somewhat: (good-hearts) what a-doe here is to bring you together? Sure, one of you do's not serue heauen well, that you are so cross'd.

SIR IOHN Come vp into my Chamber.   *Exeunt* 2370

Enter Fenton, Host   Sc. 18
                                                 (4.6)
HOST Master *Fenton*, talke not to mee, my minde is heauy: I will giue ouer all.

FENTON

Yet heare me speake: assist me in my purpose,
And (as I am a gentleman) ile giue thee
A hundred pound in gold, more then your losse.

HOST I will heare you (Master *Fenton*) and I will (at the least) keepe your counsell.

FENTON

From time to time, I haue acquainted you
With the deare loue I beare to faire *Anne Page*,
Who, mutually, hath answer'd my affection,   2380
(So farre forth, as her selfe might be her chooser)
Euen to my wish; I haue a letter from her
Of such contents, as you will wonder at;
The mirth whereof, so larded with my matter,
That neither (singly) can be manifested
Without the shew of both: fat *Falstaffe*
Hath a great Scene; the image of the iest
Ile show you here at large (harke good mine *Host*:)
To night at *Hernes-Oke*, iust 'twixt twelue and one,
Must my sweet *Nan* present the *Faerie-Queene*:   2390
⌈*Shewing the Letter*⌉
The purpose why, is here: in which disguise
While other Iests are something ranke on foote,
Her father hath commanded her to slip
Away with *Slender*, and with him, at *Eaton*
Immediately to Marry: She hath consented:
Now Sir, her Mother, (euer strong against that match
And firme for Doctor *Caius*) hath appointed

That he shall likewise shuffle her away,
While other sports are tasking of their mindes,
2400 And at the *Deanry*, where a *Priest* attends
Strait marry her: to this her Mothers plot
She seemingly obedient) likewise hath
Made promise to the *Doctor*: Now, thus it rests,
Her Father meanes she shall be all in white;
And in that habit, when *Slender* sees his time
To take her by the hand, and bid her goe,
She shall goe with him: her Mother hath intended
(The better to denote her to the *Doctor*;
For they must all be mask'd, and vizarded)
2410 That quaint in greene, she shall be loose en-roab'd,
With Ribonds-pendant, flaring 'bout her head;
And when the Doctor spies his vantage ripe,
To pinch her by the hand, and on that token,
The maid hath giuen consent to go with him.

HOST
Which meanes she to deceiue? Father, or Mother.

FENTON
Both (my good Host) to go along with me:
And heere it rests, that you'l procure the Vicar
To stay for me at Church, 'twixt twelue, and one,
And in the lawfull name of marrying,
2420 To giue our hearts vnited ceremony.

HOST
Well, husband your deuice; Ile to the Vicar,
Bring you the Maid, you shall not lacke a Priest.

FENTON
So shall I euermore be bound to thee;
Besides, Ile make a present recompence.

Exeunt ⌈seuerally⌉

Sc. 19   *Enter Sir Iohn Falstoffe, and Quickly*
(5.1)
SIR IOHN Pre'thee no more pratling: go, Ile hold, this is
the third time: I hope good lucke lies in odde numbers:
Away, go, they say there is Diuinity in odde Numbers,
either in natiuity, chance, or death: away.

MISTRIS QUICKLY Ile prouide you a chaine, and Ile do what
2430 I can to get you a paire of hornes.

SIR IOHN Away I say, time weares, hold vp your head &
mince.   *Exit Mistris Quickly*

Enter Ford (disguis'd as Brooke)

How now M. *Brooke*? Master *Brooke*, the matter will
be knowne to night, or neuer. Bee you in the Parke
about midnight, at Hernes-Oake, and you shall see
wonders.

FORD Went you not to her yesterday (Sir) as you told me
you had appointed?

SIR IOHN I went to her (Master *Brooke*) as you see, like a
2440 poore-old-man, but I came from her (Master *Brooke*)
like a poore-old-woman; that same knaue (*Ford* hir
husband) hath the finest mad diuell of iealousie in him
(Master *Brooke*) that euer gouern'd Frensie. I will tell
you, he beate me greeuously, in the shape of a woman:
(for in the shape of Man (Master *Brooke*) I feare not
Goliah with a Weauers beame, because I know also,

life is a Shuttle) I am in hast, go along with mee, Ile
tell you all (Master *Brooke*:) since I pluckt Geese, plaide
Trewant, and whipt Top, I knew not what 'twas to be
beaten, till lately. Follow mee, Ile tell you strange things 2450
of this knaue *Ford*, on whom to night I will be reuenged,
and I will deliuer his wife into your hand. Follow,
straunge things in hand (M. *Brooke*) follow.   *Exeunt*

Enter Page, Shallow, Slender   Sc. 20
                                                  (5.2)
PAGE Come, come: wee'll couch i'th Castle-ditch, till we
see the light of our Fairies. Remember son *Slender*, my
daughter.

SLENDER I forsooth, I haue spoke with her, & we haue a
nay-word, how to know one another. I come to her in
white, and cry Mum; she cries Budget, and by that we
know one another.   2460

SHALLOW That's good too: But what needes either your
Mum, or her Budget? The white will decipher her well
enough. (*To Page*) It hath strooke ten a'clocke.

PAGE The night is darke, Lights and Spirits will become
it wel: God prosper our sport. No man means euill but
the deuill, and we shal know him by his hornes. Lets
away: follow me.   *Exeunt*

Enter Mist. Page, Mist. Ford, Caius   Sc. 21
                                                  (5.3)
MISTRIS PAGE Mʳ Doctor, my daughter is in green, when
you see your time, take her by the hand, away with
her to the Deanerie, and dispatch it quickly: go before 2470
into the Parke: we two must go together.

CAIUS I know vat I haue to do, adieu.

MISTRIS PAGE Fare you well (Sir:)   *Exit Caius*
my husband will not reioyce so much at the abuse of
Falstaffe, as he will chafe at the Doctors marrying my
daughter: But 'tis no matter; better a little chiding,
then a great deale of heart-breake.

MISTRIS FORD Where is *Nan* now? and her troop of Fairies?
and the Welch-deuill Hugh?

MISTRIS PAGE They are all couch'd in a pit hard by Hernes 2480
Oake, with obscur'd Lights; which at the very instant
of *Falstaffes* and our meeting, they will at once display
to the night.

MISTRIS FORD That cannot choose but amaze him.

MISTRIS PAGE If he be not amaz'd he will be mock'd: If
he be amaz'd, he will euery way be mock'd.

MISTRIS FORD Wee'll betray him finely.

MISTRIS PAGE
Against such Lewdsters, and their lechery,
Those that betray them, do no treachery.

MISTRIS FORD The houre drawes-on: to the Oake, to the 2490
Oake.   *Exeunt*

Enter Euans ⌈disguis'd as a Satyr⌉, and ⌈William   Sc. 22
and other⌉ children disguis'd as Fairies   (5.4)
EUANS Trib, trib Fairies: Come, and remember your parts:
be pold (I pray you) follow me into the pit, and when
I giue the watch'ords, do as I pid you: Come, come,
trib, trib.   *Exeunt*

Sc. 23
(5.5)

Enter Sir Iohn Falstaffe disguis'd as Herne, ⌜with
hornes on his head, and bearing a chaine⌝

SIR IOHN The Windsor-bell hath stroke twelue: the Minute
drawes-on: Now the hot-bloodied-Gods assist me:
Remember Ioue, thou was't a Bull for thy *Europa*, Loue
set on thy hornes. O powerfull Loue, that in some
2500   respects makes a Beast a Man: in som other, a Man a
beast. You were also (Iupiter) a Swan, for the loue of
Leda: O omnipotent Loue, how nere the God drew to
the complexion of a Goose: a fault done first in the
forme of a beast, (O Ioue, a beastly fault:) and then
another fault, in the semblance of a Fowle, thinke on't
(Ioue) a fowle-fault. When Gods haue hot backes, what
shall poore men do? For me, I am heere a Windsor
Stagge, and the fattest (I thinke) i'th Forrest. Send me
a coole rut-time (Ioue) or who can blame me to pisse
2510   my Tallow?

Enter Mistris Ford, ⌜followed by⌝ Mistris Page
Who comes heere? my Doe?

MISTRIS FORD Sir *Iohn*? Art thou there (my Deere?) My
male-Deere?

SIR IOHN My Doe, with the blacke Scut? Let the skie raine
Potatoes: let it thunder, to the tune of Greenesleeues,
haile-kissing Comfits, and snow Eringoes: Let there
come a tempest of prouocation, I will shelter mee heere.
⌜*He embraces her*⌝

MISTRIS FORD Mistris *Page* is come with me (sweet hart.)

SIR IOHN Diuide me like a brib'd-Bucke, each a Haunch:
2520   I will keepe my sides to my selfe, my shoulders for the
fellow of this walke; and my hornes I bequeath your
husbands. Am I a Woodman, ha? Speake I like *Herne*
the Hunter? Why, now is Cupid a child of conscience,
he makes restitution. As I am a true spirit, welcome.
⌜*A noise within*⌝

MISTRIS PAGE Alas, what noise?

MISTRIS FORD God forgiue our sinnes.

SIR IOHN What should this be?

MISTRIS FORD *and* MISTRIS PAGE Away, away.

Exeunt Mistris Ford and Mistris Page, ⌜running⌝

SIR IOHN I thinke the diuell wil not haue me damn'd,
2530   least the oyle that's in me should set hell on fire; He
would neuer else crosse me thus.

Enter Euans, ⌜William⌝ and children (disguis'd as
before, with tapers:) Quickly (disguis'd as the
Faerie-Queene:) Anne Page (disguis'd as a Fairy:)
and one disguis'd as Hob-goblyn

MISTRIS QUICKLY
Fairies blacke, gray, greene, and white,
You Moone-shine reuellers, and shades of night.
You Orphan heires of fixed destiny,
Attend your office, and your quality.
Crier Hob-goblyn, make the Fairy Oyes.

⌜HOB-GOBLYN⌝
Elues, list your names: Silence you aiery toyes.
Cricket, to Windsor-chimnies shalt thou leape;
Where fires thou find'st vnrak'd, and hearths vnswept,
2540   There pinch the Maids as blew as Bill-berry,
Our radiant Queene, hates Sluts, and Sluttery.

SIR IOHN *(aside)*
They are Fairies, he that speaks to them shall die,
Ile winke, and couch: No man their workes must eie.
He lies downe and hides his face

EUANS
Wher's *Bede*? Go you, and where you find a maid
That ere she sleepe has thrice her prayers said,
Raise vp the Organs of her fantasie,
Sleepe she as sound as carelesse infancie,
But those as sleepe, and thinke not on their sins,
Pinch them armes, legs, backes, shoulders, sides, &
shins.

MISTRIS QUICKLY About, about: 2550
Search Windsor Castle (Elues) within, and out.
Strew good lucke (Ouphes) on euery sacred roome,
That it may stand till the perpetuall doome,
In state as wholsome, as in state 'tis fit,
Worthy the Owner, and the Owner it.
The seuerall Chaires of Order, looke you scowre
With iuyce of Balme; and euery precious flowre,
Each faire Instalment, Coate, and seu'rall Crest,
With loyall Blazon, euermore be blest.
And Nightly-meadow-Fairies, looke you sing   2560
Like to the *Garters*-Compasse, in a ring,
Th'expressure that it beares: Greene let it be,
More fertile-fresh then all the Field to see:
And, *Hony Soit Qui Mal-y-Pence*, write
In Emrold-tuffes, Flowres purple, blew, and white,
Like Saphire-pearle, and rich embroiderie,
Buckled below faire Knight-hoods bending knee;
Fairies vse Flowres for their characterie.
Away, disperse: But till 'tis one a clocke,
Our Dance of Custome, round about the Oke   2570
Of *Herne* the Hunter, let vs not forget.

EUANS
Pray you lock hand in hand: your selues in order set:
And twenty glow-wormes shall our Lanthornes bee
To guide our Measure round about the Tree.
But stay, I smell a man of middle earth.

SIR IOHN *(aside)*
God defend me from that Welsh Fairy,
Least he transforme me to a peece of Cheese.

⌜HOB-GOBLYN⌝ *(to Sir Iohn)*
Vilde worme, thou wast ore-look'd euen in thy birth.

MISTRIS QUICKLY *(to Fairies)*
With Triall-fire touch me his finger end:
If he be chaste, the flame will backe descend   2580
And turne him to no paine: but if he start,
It is the flesh of a corrupted hart.

⌜HOB-GOBLYN⌝
A triall, come.

EUANS   Come: will this wood take fire?
They burne Sir Iohn with Tapers

SIR IOHN Oh, oh, oh.

MISTRIS QUICKLY
Corrupt, corrupt, and tainted in desire.
About him (Fairies) sing a scornfull rime,
And as you trip, still pinch him to your time.

They dance around Sir Iohn, pinching him, and
singing

FAIRIES   *Fie on sinnefull phantasie:*
        Fie on Lust, and Luxurie:
2590   *Lust is but a bloudy fire,*
        Kindled with vnchaste desire,
        Fed in heart whose flames aspire,
        As thoughts do blow them higher and higher.
        Pinch him (Fairies) mutually:
        Pinch him for his villanie.
     Pinch him, and burne him, and turne him about,
     Till Candles, & Star-light, & Moone-shine be out.

During the song: Enter Caius one way, and exit
stealing away a Fairy in greene; Enter Slender
another way, and exit taking a Fairy in white;
Enter Fenton, and exit stealing Anne Page.
After the song, a noise of hunting within. Exeunt
Mistris Quickly, Euans, Hobgoblyn, and Fairies,
running. Sir Iohn rises and starts to run away.
Enter Page, Ford, Mistris Page, Mistris Ford

PAGE
   Nay do not flye, I thinke we haue watcht you now:
   Will none but *Herne* the Hunter serue your turne?
MISTRIS PAGE
2600   I pray you come, hold vp the iest no higher.
   Now (good Sir *Iohn*) how like you *Windsor* wiues?
   (*Pointing to Falstaffes hornes*)
   See you these husband? Do not these faire yoakes
   Become the Forrest better then the Towne?
FORD (*to Sir Iohn*) Now Sir, whose a Cuckold now? M^r
   Brooke, *Falstaffes* a Knaue, a Cuckoldly knaue, heere
   are his hornes Master *Brooke*: And Master *Brooke*, he
   hath enioyed nothing of *Fords*, but his Buck-basket, his
   cudgell, and twenty pounds of money, which must be
   paid to Mr *Brooke*, his horses are arrested for it, M^r
2610   *Brooke*.
MISTRIS FORD Sir *Iohn*, we haue had ill lucke: wee could
   neuer meat: I will neuer take you for my Loue againe,
   but I will alwayes count you my Deere.
SIR IOHN I do begin to perceiue that I am made an Asse.
   ⌈*He takes off the hornes*⌉
FORD I, and an Oxe too: both the proofes are extant.
SIR IOHN And these are not Fairies: By the Lord I was
   three or foure times in the thought they were not
   Fairies, and yet the guiltinesse of my minde, the sodaine
   surprize of my powers, droue the grossenesse of the
2620   foppery into a receiu'd beleefe, in despight of the teeth
   of all rime and reason, that they were Fairies. See now
   how wit may be made a Iacke-a-Lent, when 'tis vpon
   ill imployment.
EUANS Sir *Iohn Falstaffe*, serue Got, and leaue your desires,
   and Fairies will not pinse you.
FORD Well said Fairy *Hugh*.
EUANS And leaue you your iealouzies too, I pray you.
FORD I will neuer mistrust my wife againe, till thou art
   able to woo her in good English.
2630 SIR IOHN Haue I laid my braine in the Sun, and dri'de it,
   that it wants matter to preuent so grosse ore-reaching

as this? Am I ridden with a Welch Goate too? Shal I
haue a Coxcombe of Frize? Tis time I were choak'd
with a peece of toasted Cheese.
EUANS Seese is not good to giue putter; your belly is al
putter.
SIR IOHN Seese, and Putter? Haue I liu'd to stand at the
taunt of one that makes Fritters of English? This is
enough to be the decay of lust and late-walking through
the Realme.   2640
MISTRIS PAGE Why Sir *Iohn*, do you thinke though wee
would haue thrust vertue out of our hearts by the head
and shoulders, and haue giuen our selues without
scruple to hell, that euer the deuill could haue made
you our delight?
FORD What, a hodge-pudding? A bag of flax?
MISTRIS PAGE A puft man?
PAGE Old, cold, wither'd, and of intollerable entrailes?
FORD And one that is as slanderous as Sathan?
PAGE And as poore as Iob?   2650
FORD And as wicked as his wife?
EUANS And giuen to Fornications, and to Tauernes, and
Sacke, and Wine, and Metheglins, and to drinkings and
swearings, and starings? Pribles and prables?
SIR IOHN Well, I am your Theame: you haue the start of
me, I am deiected: I am not able to answer the Welch
Flannell, Ignorance it selfe is a plummet ore me, vse
me as you will.
FORD Marry Sir, wee'l bring you to Windsor to one M^r
Brooke, that you haue cozon'd of money, to whom you   2660
should haue bin a Pander: ouer and aboue that you
haue suffer'd, I thinke, to repay that money will be a
biting affliction.
PAGE Yet be cheerefull Knight: thou shalt eat a posset to
night at my house, wher I will desire thee to laugh at
my wife, that now laughes at thee: Tell her Mr *Slender*
hath married her daughter.
MISTRIS PAGE (*aside*) Doctors doubt that; If *Anne Page* be
my daughter, she is (by this) Doctour *Caius* wife.
   Enter Slender
SLENDER Whoa hoe, hoe, Father *Page*.   2670
PAGE Sonne? How now? How now Sonne, Haue you
dispatch'd?
SLENDER Dispatch'd? Ile make the best in Glostershire
know on't: would I were hang'd la, else.
PAGE Of what sonne?
SLENDER I came yonder at *Eaton* to marry Mistris *Anne*
Page, and she's a great lubberly boy. If it had not bene
i'th Church, I would haue swing'd him, or hee should
haue swing'd me. If I did not thinke it had beene *Anne*
Page, would I might neuer stirre, and 'tis a Post-masters   2680
Boy.
PAGE Vpon my life then, you tooke the wrong.
SLENDER What neede you tell me that? I think so, when
I tooke a Boy for a Girle: If I had bene married to him,
(for all he was in womans apparrell) I would not haue
had him.
PAGE Why this is your owne folly, did not I tell you how
you should know my daughter, by her garments?

SLENDER I went to her in white, and cried Mum, and she
2690   cride budget, as *Anne* and I had appointed, and yet it
   was not *Anne*, but a Post-masters boy.

MISTRIS PAGE Good *George* be not angry, I knew of your
   purpose: turn'd my daughter into greene, and indeede
   she is now with the Doctor at the Deanrie, and there
   married.

     Enter Caius

CAIUS Ver is Mistris *Page*: by gar I am cozoned, I ha
   married *oon Garsoon*, a boy; *oon pesant*, by gar. A boy,
   it is not *An Page*, by gar, I am cozened.

PAGE Why? did you take her in greene?

2700 CAIUS I bee gar, and 'tis a boy: be gar, Ile raise all
   Windsor.

FORD This is strange: Who hath got the right *Anne*?
     Enter Fenton and Anne

PAGE
   My heart misgiues me, here comes Mr *Fenton*.
   How now Mr *Fenton*?

ANNE
   Pardon good father, good my mother pardon.

PAGE
   Now Mistris: How chance you went not with M^r
     Slender?

⌈MISTRIS⌉ PAGE
   Why went you not with Mr Doctor, maid?

FENTON
   You do amaze her: heare the truth of it,
   You would haue married her most shamefully,

Where there was no proportion held in loue: 2710
The truth is, she and I (long since contracted)
Are now so sure that nothing can dissolue vs:
Th'offence is holy, that she hath committed,
And this deceit looses the name of craft,
Of disobedience, or vnduteous title,
Since therein she doth euitate and shun
A thousand irreligious cursed houres
Which forced marriage would haue brought vpon her.

FORD (*to Page and Mistris Page*)
   Stand not amaz'd, here is no remedie:
   In Loue, the heauens themselues do guide the state, 2720
   Money buyes Lands, and wiues are sold by fate.

SIR IOHN I am glad, though you haue tane a special stand
   to strike at me, that your Arrow hath glanc'd.

PAGE
   Well, what remedy? *Fenton*, heauen giue thee ioy,
   What cannot be eschew'd, must be embrac'd.

SIR IOHN
   When night-dogges run, all sorts of Deere are chac'd.

MISTRIS PAGE
   Well, I will muse no further: Mr *Fenton*,
   Heauen giue you many, many merry dayes:
   Good husband, let vs euery one go home,
   And laugh this sport ore by a Countrie fire, 2730
   Sir *Iohn* and all.

FORD   Let it be so (Sir *Iohn*:)
   To Master *Brooke*, you yet shall hold your word,
   For he, to night, shall lye with Mistris *Ford*.   *Exeunt*

FINIS

2 HENRY IV

2 Henry IV, printed in 1600 as *The Second Part of Henrie the fourth*, was not reprinted until it was included in somewhat revised form in the 1623 Folio, with the same title. Shakespeare may have started to write it late in 1596, or in 1597, directly after *1 Henry IV*, but have laid it aside while he composed *The Merry Wiues of Windsor*. As in *1 Henry IV*, he drew on *The Famous Victories of Henry the Fifth*, Holinshed's *Chronicles*, and Samuel Daniel's *Fowre Bookes of the Ciuile Wars*, along with other, minor sources; but the play contains a greater proportion of non-historical material apparently invented by Shakespeare. In this play Shakespeare seems from the start to have accepted the change of Sir Iohn's surname to Falstaffe.

Like *1 Henry IV*, Part Two draws on the techniques of comedy, but its overall tone is more sombre. At its start, the Prince seems to have regressed from his reformed state at the end of Part One; his father still has many causes for anxiety, has not made his expiatory pilgrimage to the Holy Land, and is again the victim of rebellion, led this time by the Earle of Northumberland, the Archbishop of Yorke, and the Lords Hastings and Mowbray. Again Henry's public responsibilities are exacerbated by anxieties about Prince Harry's behaviour; the climax of their relationship comes after Harry, discovering his sick father asleep and thinking him dead, tries on his crown; after bitterly upbraiding him, Henry accepts his son's assertions of good faith, and, recalling the devious means by which he himself came to the throne, warns Harry that he may need to protect himself against civil strife by pursuing 'forraine quarrells'—the campaigning against France depicted in *Henry V*. The King dies in the Jerusalem Chamber of Westminster Abbey, the closest he will get to the Holy Land.

In this play the Prince spends less time than in Part One with Sir Iohn, who is shown much in the company of Mistris Quickly and Doll Tearesheete at the Boar's Head tavern in Eastcheap and later in Gloucestershire on his way to and from the place of battle. Shakespeare never excelled the bitter-sweet comedy of the passages involving Falstaffe and his old comrade Justice Shallow. The play ends in a counterpointing of major and minor keys as the newly crowned Henry V rejects Sir Iohn and all that he has stood for.

The Quarto is apparently printed from Shakespeare's foul papers. But certain passages were added in the Folio, printed from a heavily sophisticated scribal transcript.

THE NAMES OF THE ACTORS

RUMOUR, 'the Presenter'

EPILOGUE

KING Henry the Fourth

PRINCE HARRY, 'afterwards Crowned King
    Henrie the Fift'
PRINCE IOHN of Lancaster
Humphrey, Duke of GLOUCESTER
Thomas, Duke of CLARENCE

> 'Sonnes to
> Henry the
> Fourth'

Percy, Earle of NORTHUMBERLAND, of the Rebels Partie
NORTHUMBERLANDS WIFE
KATE, their sonne Hot-spurs 'widdow'
TRAUERS, Northumberlands seruant
MORTON, a bearer of newes from Shrewsbury

Scroope, ARCHBISHOP of York
LORD BARDOLPHE
Thomas Lord MOWBRAY, the Earle Marshall
Lord HASTINGS
Sir Iohn COLLEUILE

> 'Opposites
> against King
> Henrie the
> Fourth'

LORD CHIEFE IUSTICE
His SERUANT
GOWER, a Messenger

SIR IOHN Falstaffe
His PAGE
BARDOLPHE
POYNES
Ancient PISTOL
PETO

> 'Irregular Humorists'

Mistris 'Quickly', HOSTESSE of a tauern

DOLL TEARE-SHEETE, a whore

SNARE
PHANG

> '2. Seriants'

Neuel, Earle of WARWICKE
Earle of SURREY
Earle of WESTMERLAND
HARCOR
Sir Iohn Blunt

> 'Of the Kings Partie'

Robert SHALLOW
SCILENS

> 'Both Country Iustices'

DAUY, Seruant to Shallow

Rafe MOULDY
Simon SHADOW
Thomas WART
Francis FEEBLE
Peter BULL-CALFE

> 'Country Soldiers' leuied to fight for
> the King

PORTER of Northumberlands houshold

DRAWERS

BEADLES

GROOMES

MESSENGER

Sneak and other musitians

Lord chiefe Iustices men, Souldiers, Attendants

The second part of Henry the fourth

Induction *Enter Rumour ⌐in a robe⌐ painted full of Tongues*

RUMOUR

Open your eares; for which of you will stop
The vent of hearing, when lowd Rumor speaks?
I from the Orient to the drooping West,
(Making the wind my poste-horse) still vnfold
The acts commenced on this ball of earth,
Vpon my tongues continuall slanders ride,
The which in euery language I pronounce,
Stuffing the eares of men with false reports,
I speake of peace while couert enmity,
10   Vnder the smile of safety, woundes the world:
And who but Rumor, who but onely I,
Make fearefull musters, and prepar'd defence,
Whiles the bigge yeare, swolne with some other griefes,
Is thought with child by the sterne tyrant Warre?
And no such matter. Rumour is a pipe,
Blowne by surmizes, Iealousies coniectures,
And of so easie, and so plaine a stop,
That the blunt monster, with vncounted heads,
The still discordant wau'ring multitude,
20   Can play vpon it. But what need I thus
(My wel knowne body) to anothomize
Among my houshold? why is Rumor here?
I runne before King Harries victorie,
Who in a bloudy field by Shrewsbury,
Hath beaten downe yong Hot-spurre and his troopes,
Quenching the flame of bold rebellion,
Euen with the rebels bloud. But what meane I
To speake so true at first? my office is
To noyse abroad, that Harry Monmouth fell
30   Vnder the wrath of noble Hot-spurs sword,
And that the King before the Douglas rage,
Stoopt his annointed head as low as death.
This haue I rumour'd through the peasant townes,
Betweene that royall field of Shrewsbury,
And this worme-eaten hold of ragged stone,
Where Hot-spurs father old Northumberland
Lies crafty sicke, the postes come tyring on,
And not a man of them brings other newes,
Than they haue learnt of me, from Rumors tongues,
They bring smooth comforts false, worse then true
40   wrongs.   *exit*

Sc. 1   *Enter the Lord Bardolfe at one doore. ⌐He crosses*
(1.1)   *the stage to another doore⌐*

LORD BARDOLFE

Who keepes the gate here ho?
            Enter Porter ⌐aboue⌐
                              where is the Earle?

PORTER

What shall I say you are?

LORD BARDOLFE   Tell thou the Earle,
That the Lord Bardolfe doth attend him heere.

PORTER

His Lordship is walkt forth into the orchard,
Please it your honor knocke but at the gate,
And he himselfe will answer.
            Enter the Earle Northumberland ⌐at the other
            doore,⌐ as sicke, with a crutch and coife

LORD BARDOLFE   Here comes the Earle.
                              ⌐*exit Porter*⌐

NORTHUMBERLAND

What newes Lord Bardolfe? euery minute now
Should be the father of some Stratagem,
The times are wild, contention like a horse,
Full of high feeding, madly hath broke loose,   50
And beares downe all before him.

LORD BARDOLFE   Noble Earle,
I bring you certaine newes from Shrewsbury.

NORTHUMBERLAND

Good, and God will.

LORD BARDOLFE   As good as heart can wish:
The King is almost wounded to the death,
And in the fortune of my Lord your sonne,
Prince Harry slaine outright, and both the Blunts
Kild by the hand of Dowglas, yong prince Iohn,
And Westmerland and Stafford fled the field,
And Harry Monmouthes brawne, the hulke sir Iohn,
Is prisoner to your sonne: O such a day!   60
So fought, so followed, and so fairely wonne,
Came not till now to dignifie the times
Since Cæsars fortunes.

NORTHUMBERLAND   How is this deriu'd?
Saw you the field? came you from Shrewsbury?

LORD BARDOLFE

I spake with one, my lord, that came from thence,
A gentleman well bred, and of good name,
That freely rendred me these newes for true.
            Enter Trauers

NORTHUMBERLAND

Here comes my seruant Trauers who I sent
On tuesday last to listen after newes.

LORD BARDOLFE

My lord, I ouer-rode him on the way,   70
And he is furnisht with no certainties,
More then he haply may retale from me.

NORTHUMBERLAND

Now Trauers, what good tidings comes with you?

TRAUERS

My lord, Lord Bardolfe turnd me backe
With ioyfull tidings, and being better horst,
Out rode me, after him came spurring hard,
A gentleman almost forespent with specde,
That stopt by me to breathe his bloudied horse,
He askt the way to Chester, and of him
I did demand what newes from Shrewsbury,   80

He told me that rebellion had ill lucke,
And that yong Harrie Percies spur was cold:
With that he gaue his able horse the head,
And bending forward, strooke his armed heeles,
Against the panting sides of his poore iade,
Vp to the rowell head, and starting so,
He seem'd in running to deuoure the way,
Staying no longer question.

NORTHUMBERLAND   Ha? againe,
Said he, yong Harry Percies spur was cold,
90   Of Hot-spurre, Cold-spurre, that rebellion
Had met ill lucke?

LORD BARDOLFE   My lord, Ile tell you what,
If my yong Lord your sonne, haue not the day,
Vpon mine honor for a silken point,
Ile giue my Barony, neuer talke of it.

NORTHUMBERLAND
Why should the gentleman that rode by Trauers,
Giue then such instances of losse?

LORD BARDOLFE   Who he?
He was some hilding fellow that had stolne
The horse he rode on, and vpon my life
Spoke at a venter.

      Enter Morton
           Looke, here comes more news.

NORTHUMBERLAND
100   Yea this mans brow, like to a title leafe,
Foretells the nature of a tragicke volume,
So lookes the strond, whereon the imperious floud,
Hath left a witnest vsurpation.
Say Mourton, didst thou come from Shrewsbury?

MOURTON
I ranne from Shrewsbury my noble lord,
Where hatefull death put on his vgliest maske,
To fright our partie.

NORTHUMBERLAND   How doth my sonne and brother?
Thou tremblest, and the whitenes in thy cheeke,
Is apter then thy tongue to tell thy arrand,
110   Euen such a man, so faint, so spirritlesse,
So dull, so dead in looke, so woe begon,
Drew Priams curtaine in the dead of night,
And would haue told him, halfe his Troy was burnt:
But Priam found the fier, ere he, his tongue,
And I, my Percies death, ere thou reportst it.
This thou wouldst say, Your son did thus and thus,
Your brother thus: so fought the noble Dowglas,
Stopping my greedy eare with their bold deedes,
But in the end, to stop my eare indeed,
120   Thou hast a sigh to blow away this praise,
Ending with brother, sonne, and all are dead.

MOURTON
Douglas is liuing, and your brother yet,
But for my Lord your sonne:

NORTHUMBERLAND   Why he is dead.
See what a ready tongue Suspition hath!
He that but feares the thing hee would not know,
Hath by instinct, knowledge from others eies,
That what he feard is chanced: yet speake Mourton,

Tell thou an Earle, his diuination lies,
And I will take it as a sweete disgrace,
And make thee rich for doing me such wrong.   130

MOURTON
You are too great to be by me gainsaid,
Your spirite is too true, your feares too certaine.

NORTHUMBERLAND
Yet for all this, say not that Percie's dead,
I see a strange confession in thine eie,
Thou shakst thy head, and holdst it feare, or sinne,
To speake a truth: if he be slaine say so,
The tongue offends not that reports his death,
And he doth sinne that doth belie the dead,
Not he which saies the dead is not aliue,
Yet the first bringer of vnwelcome newes   140
Hath but a loosing office, and his tongue
Sounds euer after as a sullen bell,
Remembred knolling a departing friend.

LORD BARDOLFE
I cannot thinke, my Lord, your sonne is dead.

MOURTON (*to Northumberland*)
I am sory I should force you to beleeue,
That which I would to God I had not seene,
But these mine eies saw him in bloudy state,
Rendring faint quittance, wearied, and out-breathd,
To Harry Monmouth, whose swift wrath beat downe
The neuer daunted Percy to the earth,   150
From whence with life he neuer more sprung vp.
In few his death, whose spirite lent a fire,
Euen to the dullest peasant in his campe,
Being bruted once, tooke fire and heate away,
From the best temperd courage in his troopes,
For from his mettal was his party steeled,
Which once in him abated, al the rest
Turnd on themselues, like dull and heauy lead.
And as the thing thats heauy in it selfe,
Vpon enforcement flies with greatest speed: 160
So did our men, heauy in Hot-spurs losse,
Lend to this weight such lightnesse with their feare,
That arrowes fled not swifter toward their ayme,
Than did our souldiers aiming at their safetie,
Fly from the field: then was that noble Worcester,
To soone tane prisoner, and that furious Scot,
The bloudy Douglas whose well labouring sword,
Had three times slaine th'appearance of the King,
Gan vaile his stomacke, and did grace the shame
Of those that turnd their backes, and in his flight,   170
Stumbling in feare, was tooke: the summe of all
Is, that the King hath wonne, and hath sent out,
A speedy power to incounter you my lord,
Vnder the conduct of yong Lancaster,
And Westmerland: this is the news at ful.

NORTHUMBERLAND
For this I shal haue time enough to mourne,
In poison there is phisicke, and these newes,
Hauing beene wel, that would haue made me sicke:
Being sicke, haue (in some measure) made me wel:
And as the wretch whose feuer-weakned ioynts,   180

Like strengthlesse hinges buckle vnder life,
Impacient of his fit, breakes like a fire
Out of his keepers armes; euen so my limbes,
Weakned with griefe, being now enragde with griefe,
Are thrice themselues:

⌐He casts away his crutch⌐

　　　　　　　　hence therfore thou nice crutch,
A scaly gauntlet now with ioynts of steele
Must gloue this hand,

⌐He snatches off his coife⌐

　　　　　　　　and hence thou sickly coife,
Thou art a guard too wanton for the head,
Which princes, flesht with conquest, ayme to hit:
190　Now bind my browes with yron, and approach
The raggedst houre that Time and Spight dare bring,
To frowne vpon th'inragde Northumberland,
Let heauen kisse earth, now let not Natures hand
Keepe the wild floud confind, let Order die,
And let this world no longer be a stage,
To feed contention in a lingring act:
But let one spirite of the first borne Cain
Raigne in all bosomes, that ech heart being set
On bloudy courses, the rude sceane may end,
200　And darknesse be the burier of the dead.

LORD BARDOLFE
Sweet earle, diuorce not wisedom from your honor.

MOURTON
The liues of all your louing complices,
Leane on your health, the which if you giue ore
To stormy passion, must perforce decay.
You cast th'euent of Warre (my Noble Lord)
And summ'd the accompt of Chance, before you said
Let vs make head: It was your presurmize,
That in the dole of blowes, your Son might drop.
You knew he walk'd o're perils, on an edge
210　More likely to fall in, then to get o're:
You were aduis'd his flesh was capeable
Of Wounds, and Scarres; and that his forward Spirit
Would lift him, where most trade of danger rang'd,
Yet did you say go forth: and none of this
(Though strongly apprehended) could restraine
The stiffe-borne Action: What hath then befalne?
Or what doth this bold enterprize bring forth,
More then that Being, which was like to be?

LORD BARDOLFE
We all that are ingaged to this losse,
220　Knew that we venturd on such dangerous seas,
That if we wrought out life, was ten to one,
And yet we venturd for the gaine proposde,
Choakt the respect of likely perill fear'd,
And since we are oreset, venture againe:
Come, we will al put forth body and goods.

MOURTON
Tis more then time, and my most noble lord,
I heare for certaine, and dare speake the truth,
The gentle Arch-bishop of Yorke is vp
With well appointed Powres: he is a man
230　Who with a double Surety bindes his Followers.

My Lord (your Sonne) had onely but the Corpes,
But shadowes, and the shewes of men to fight.
For that same word (Rebellion) did diuide
The action of their bodies, from their soules,
And they did fight with queasinesse, constrain'd
As men drinke Potions; that their Weapons only
Seem'd on our side: but for their Spirits and Soules,
This word (Rebellion) it had froze them vp,
As Fish are in a Pond. But now the Bishop
Turnes Insurrection to Religion:　　　　　　　　240
Suppos'd sincere, and holy in his Thoughts,
He's follow'd both with Body, and with Minde:
And doth enlarge his Rising, with the blood
Of faire King *Richard*, scrap'd from Pomfret stones,
Deriues from heauen, his Quarrell, and his Cause:
Tels them, he doth bestride a bleeding Land,
Gasping for life, vnder great *Bullingbrooke*,
And more, and lesse, do flocke to follow him.

NORTHUMBERLAND
I knew of this before, but to speake truth,
This present griefe had wipte it from my mind,　　250
Go in with me and counsell euery man,
The aptest way for safety and reuenge,
Get postes and letters, and make friends with speed,
Neuer so few, and neuer yet more need.　　　　*exeunt*

Enter sir Iohn Falstaffe, ⌐followed by⌐ his page　Sc. 2
bearing his sword and buckler　　　　　　　　(1.2)

SIR IOHN Sirra, you giant, what saies the doctor to my
water?

PAGE He said sir, the water it self was a good healthy
water, but for the party that owed it, he might haue
moe diseases then he knew for.

SIR IOHN Men of al sorts take a pride to gird at me: the　260
braine of this foolish compoũded clay man is not able
to inuent any thing that tends to laughter, more then
I inuent, or is inuẽted on me, I am not only witty in
my selfe, but the cause that wit is in other men. I do
here walk before thee, like a sow that hath orewhelmd
al her litter but one, if the prince put thee into my
seruice for any other reason then to sett me off, why
then I haue no iudgement. Thou horeson mandrake,
thou art fitter to be worne in my cap, then to wait at
my heels. I was neuer manned with an agot till now,　270
but I wil set you, neither in golde nor siluer, but in
vile apparell, and send you backe againe to your master
for a iewell, the iuuenall the prince your master, whose
chin is not yet fledge, I will sooner haue a beard grow
in the palme of my hand, then he shal get one off his
cheek, & yet he will not sticke to say his face is a face
royal, God may finish it when he will, tis not a haire
amisse yet, he may keepe it still at a face royall, for a
barber shall neuer earne sixpence out of it, and yet
heele be crowing as if he had writte man euer since　280
his father was a batcheler, he may keepe his owne
grace, but hees almost out of mine I can assure him:
what said master Dommelton about the sattin for my
short cloake and sloppes?

PAGE He saide sir, you should procure him better assurance then Bardolfe, he would not take his band and yours, he liked not the securitie.

SIR IOHN Let him be damn'd like the glutton, pray God his tongue be hotter, a horeson Achitophel! a rascally
290 yea forsooth knaue, to beare a gentle man in hand, and then stand vpon security, the horson smooth-pates doe now weare nothing but hie shooes and bunches of keyes at their girdles, and if a man is through with them in honest taking vp, then they must stand vppon security, I had as liue they would put ratsbane in my mouth as offer to stop it with security, I lookt a should haue sent me two and twenty yards of sattin (as I am a true knight,) and he sends me security: well he may sleepe in security, for he hath the horne of aboundance,
300 and the lightnesse of his wife shines through it, & yet can not he see though he haue his owne lanthorne to light him: wheres Bardolf.

PAGE Hees gone in Smithfield to buy your worship a horse.

SIR IOHN I bought him in Paules, and heele buy me a horse in Smithfield, and I could get me but a wife in the stewes, I were man'd, horsde, and wiu'd.

Enter Lord chiefe Iustice and seruant

PAGE Sir, here comes the noble man that committed the prince for striking him about Bardolfe.
310 SIR IOHN ⌈*mouing away*⌉ Wait close, I will not see him.

IUSTICE (*to seruant*) Whats hee that goes there?

SERUANT Falstaffe, and't please your lordship.

IUSTICE He that was in question for the rob'ry?

SERUANT He my Lord, but he hath since done good seruice at Shrewsbury, & (as I heare,) is now going with some charge to the lord Iohn of Lancaster.

IUSTICE What to Yorke? call him backe againe.

SERUANT Sir Iohn Falstaffe.

SIR IOHN Boy, tell him I am deafe.
320 PAGE (*to seruant*) You must speake lowder, my master is deafe.

IUSTICE I am sure he is to the hearing of any thing good, (*to seruant*) goe plucke him by the elbow, I must speake with him.

SERUANT Sir Iohn?

SIR IOHN What? a yong knaue and begging? is there not wars? is there not employment? doth not the King lacke subiects? do not the rebels want souldiers, though it be a shame to be on any side but one, it is worse
330 shame to beg then to be on the worst side, were it worse then the name of Rebellion can tell how to make it.

SERUANT You mistake me sir.

SIR IOHN Why sir, did I say you were an honest man, setting my knighthood and my souldiership aside, I had lied in my throat if I had said so.

SERUANT I pray you sir then set your knighthood, and your soldiership aside, and giue me leaue to tell you, you lie in your throate, if you say I am any other then
340 an honest man.

SIR IOHN I giue thee leaue to tell me so, I lay aside that which growes to me, if thou getst any leaue of me, hang me, if thou takst leaue, thou wert better be hangd, you hunt coũter, hence, auaunt.

SERUANT Sir, my Lord would speake with you.

IUSTICE Sir Iohn Falstaffe, a word with you.

SIR IOHN My good Lord, God giue your lordship good time of day, I am glad to see your lordship abroade, I heard say your lordship was sicke, I hope your lordship goes abroade by aduise, your lordship, though not clean 350 past your youth, haue yet some smack of age in you, some relish of the saltnes of time in you, and I most humbly beseech your lordship to haue a reuerend care of your health.

IUSTICE Sir Iohn, I sent for you before your expedition to Shrewsbury.

SIR IOHN Andt please your lordship, I heare his maiesty is returnd with some discomfort from Wales.

IUSTICE I talke not of his maiesty, you would not come when I sent for you. 360

SIR IOHN And I heare moreouer, his highnes is falne into this same horson apoplexi.

IUSTICE Well, God mend him, I pray you let me speake with you.

SIR IOHN This appoplexi is as I take it, a kind of lethergie, and't please your lordship, a kind of sleeping in the bloud, a horson tingling.

IUSTICE What tell you me of it, be it as it is.

SIR IOHN It hath it originall from much griefe, from study, and perturbation of the braine, I haue read the cause 370 of his effects in Galen, it is a kind of deafenes.

IUSTICE I think you are falne into the disease, for you heare not what I say to you.

SIR IOHN Very wel my lord, very wel, rather and't please you it is the disease of not listning, the maladie of not marking that I am troubled withall.

IUSTICE To punish you by the heeles, would amend the attention of your eares, and I care not if I doe become your phisitian.

SIR IOHN I am as poore as Iob my lord, but not so pacient, 380 your Lordship may minister the potion of imprisonment to me, in respect of pouerty, but how I should be your pacient to follow your prescriptions, the wise may make som dramme of a scruple, or indeede a scruple it selfe.

IUSTICE I sent for you when there were matters against you for your life to come speake with me.

SIR IOHN As I was then aduisde by my learned counsail in the lawes of this land seruice, I did not come.

IUSTICE Wel, the truth is sir Iohn, you liue in great infamy. 390

SIR IOHN He that buckles himselfe in my belt cannot liue in lesse.

IUSTICE Your meanes are very slender, and your waste is great.

SIR IOHN I would it were otherwise, I would my meanes were greater and my waste slenderer.

IUSTICE You haue misled the youthfull prince.

SIR IOHN The yong prince hath misled me, I am the felow with the great belly, and he my dogge.

400 IUSTICE Wel, I am loth to gall a new heald wound, your daies seruice at Shrewsbury, hath a little guilded ouer your nights exploit on Gadshill, you may thanke th'vnquiet time, for your quiet oreposting that action.

SIR IOHN My lord.

IUSTICE But since all is well, keepe it so, wake not a sleeping wolfe.

SIR IOHN To wake a wolfe, is as bad as smell a fox.

IUSTICE What you are as a candle, the better part, burnt out.

410 SIR IOHN A wassel candle my lord, al tallow, if I did say of wax, my growth would approue the truth.

IUSTICE There is not a white haire in your face, but should haue his effect of grauity.

SIR IOHN His effect of grauy, grauie, grauie.

IUSTICE You follow the yong prince vp and downe, like his ill angell.

SIR IOHN Not so my lord, your ill angell is light, but I hope he that lookes vpon me will take me without weighing, and yet in some respects I grant I cannot

420 go. I cannot tell, vertue is of so little regard in these costar-mongers times, that true valour is turnd Berod, Pregnancie is made a Tapster, & his quick wit wasted in giuing reckonings, all the other giftes appertinent to man, as the malice of this age shapes thē are not worth a goosbery, you that are old consider not the capacities of vs that are yong, you doe measure the heate of our liuers with the bitternesse of your galles, and we that are in the vaward of our youth, I must confesse are wagges too.

430 IUSTICE Do you set downe your name in the scroule of youth, that are written downe, old with all the characters of age? haue you not a moist eie, a dry hand, a yelow cheeke, a white beard, a decreasing leg, an increasing belly? is not your voice broken, your winde short, your chinne double, your wit single, and euery part about you blasted with antiquitie, and will you yet call your selfe yong? fie, fie, fie, sir Iohn.

SIR IOHN My Lorde, I was borne about three of the clocke in the afternoone, with a white head, and something

440 a round bellie, for my voyce, I haue lost it with hallowing, and singing of Anthems: to approoue my youth further, I will not: the truth is, I am onely olde in iudgement and vnderstanding: and hee that wil caper with me for a thousand markes, let him lend me the money, and haue at him: for the boxe of th'yere that the Prince gaue you, he gaue it like a rude Prince, and you tooke it like a sensible Lord: I haue checkt him for it, and the yong lion repents, ⌈aside⌉ mary not in ashes and sackcloth, but in new silke, and olde

450 sacke.

IUSTICE Well, God send the prince a better companion.

SIR IOHN God send the companion a better prince, I cannot ridde my hands of him.

IUSTICE Well, the King hath seuerd you and prince Harry: I heare you are going with lord Iohn of Lancaster,

against the Archbishop and the Earle of Northumberland.

SIR IOHN Yea, I thanke your pretty sweet witte for it: but looke you pray, all you that kisse my lady Peace at home, that our armies ioyne not in a hote day, for, by 460 the Lord, I take but two shirts out with me, and I meane not to sweate extraordinarily: if it be a hot day, & I brandish any thing but my bottle, would I might neuer spit white again: there is not a dangerous action can peepe out his head but I am thrust vpon it. Wel, I cannot last euer, but it was alway yet the tricke of our English nation, if they haue a good thing, to make it too common. If yee will needs say I am an olde man, you should giue me rest: I would to God my name were not so terrible to the enemy as it is, I were better 470 to be eaten to death with a rust, than to be scoured to nothing with perpetuall motion.

IUSTICE Well, be honest, be honest, and God blesse your expedition.

SIR IOHN Will your lordship lend me a thousand pound to furnish me forth?

IUSTICE Not a penny, not a penny, you are too impatient to beare crosses: fare you well: commend mee to my coosine Westmerland.   exeunt Iustice and seruant

SIR IOHN If I do, fillip me with a three man beetle: A man 480 can no more separate age and couetousnesse, than a can part yong limbs and lechery, but the gowt galles the one, and the pox pinches the other, and so both the degrees preuent my curses, boy.

PAGE Sir.

SIR IOHN What money is in my purse?

PAGE Seuen groates and two pence.

SIR IOHN I can get no remedy against this consumption of the purse, borrowing onely lingers and lingers it out, but the disease is incurable: (Giuing letters) Go beare 490 this letter to my lord of Lancaster, this to the Prince, this to the Earle of Westmerland, and this to olde mistris Vrsula, whome I haue weekely sworne to marry since I perceiud the first white haire of my chin: about it, you know where to finde me: ⌈exit page⌉ a pox of this gowt, or a gowt of this pox, for the one or the other playes the rogue with my great toe. Tis no matter if I doe hault, I haue the warres for my color, and my pension shal seeme the more reasonable: a good wit will make vse of any thing; I will turne 500 diseases to commoditie.   exit

Enter th'Archbishop, Thomas Mowbray (Earle   Sc. 3
Marshall) the Lord Hastings, and Lord Bardolfe   (1.3)

ARCHBISHOP

Thus haue you heard our cause, and knowne our meanes,

And my most noble friends, I pray you al

Speake plainely your opinions of our hopes,

And first Lord Marshall, what say you to it?

MOWBRAY

I well allow the occasion of our armes,

But gladly would be better satisfied,

How in our meanes we should aduance our selues,
To looke with forehead, bold, and big enough,
510   Vpon the power and puissance of the King.

HASTINGS

Our present musters grow vpon the file,
To fiue and twenty thousand men of choise,
And our supplies liue largely in the hope
Of great Northumberland, whose bosome burnes
With an incensed fire of iniuries.

LORD BARDOLFE

The question then Lord Hastings standeth thus,
Whether our present fiue and twentie thousand,
May hold vp head without Northumberland.

HASTINGS

With him we may.

LORD BARDOLFE   Yea mary, theres the point,
520   But if without him we be thought too feeble,
My iudgement is we should not step too far,
Till we had his Assistance by the hand.
For in a Theame so bloody fac'd, as this,
Coniecture, Expectation, and Surmise
Of Aydes incertaine, should not be admitted.

ARCHBISHOP

Tis very true lord Bardolfe, for indeede
It was yong Hot-spurs case at Shrewsbury.

LORD BARDOLFE

It was my Lord, who lin'd himselfe with hope,
Eating the ayre, on promise of supplie,
530   Flattring himselfe with proiect of a power,
Much smaller then the smallest of his thoughts,
And so with great imagination,
Proper to mad-men, led his powers to death,
And winking, leapt into destruction.

HASTINGS

But by your leaue it neuer yet did hurt,
To lay downe likelihoods and formes of hope.

LORD BARDOLFE

Yes, if this present quality of warre,
Indeed the instant action: a cause on foot,
Liues so in hope: As in an early Spring,
540   We see th'appearing buds, which to proue fruite,
Hope giues not so much warrant, as Dispaire
That Frosts will bite them. When we meane to build,
We first suruey the Plot, then draw the Modell,
And when we see the figure of the house,
Then must we rate the cost of the Erection,
Which if we finde out-weighes Ability,
What do we then, but draw a-new the Modell
In fewer offices? Or at least, desist
To builde at all? Much more, in this great worke,
550   (Which is (almost) to plucke a Kingdome downe,
And set another vp) should we suruey
The plot of Situation, and the Modell;
Consent vpon a sure Foundation:
Question Surueyors, know our owne estate,
How able such a Worke to vndergo,
To weigh against his Opposite? Or else,

We fortifie in paper, and in figures,
Vsing the names of men in steed of men,
Like on that drawes the model of an house,
Beyond his power to build it, who (halfe thorough)   560
Giues o're, and leaues his part-created cost,
A naked subiect to the weeping clowdes,
And waste for churlish winters tyrannie.

HASTINGS

Grant that our hopes (yet likely of faire birth)
Should be stil-borne, and that we now possest
The vtmost man of expectation,
I thinke we are a body strong enough,
Euen as we are to equal with the King.

LORD BARDOLFE

What, is the King but fiue and twenty thousand?

HASTINGS

To vs no more, nay not so much, Lord Bardolfe,   570
For his diuisions, as the times do brawle,
Are in three heads, one power against the French,
And one against Glendower, perforce a third
Must take vp vs, so is the vnfirme King
In three diuided, and his coffers sound
With hollow pouertie and emptinesse.

ARCHBISHOP

That he should draw his seuerall strengths togither,
And come against vs in full puissance,
Need not be dreaded.

HASTINGS   If he should do so,
He leaues his back vnarmde, the French and Welch   580
Baying him at the heeles, neuer feare that.

LORD BARDOLFE

Who is it like should leade his forces hither?

HASTINGS

The Duke of Lancaster and Westmerland:
Against the Welsh, himself and Harry Monmouth:
But who is substituted gainst the French
I haue no certaine notice.

ARCHBISHOP   Let vs on:
And publish the occasion of our Armes.
The Common-wealth is sicke of their owne Choice,
Their ouer-greedy loue hath surfetted:
An habitation giddy, and vnsure   590
Hath he that buildeth on the vulgar heart.
O thou fond Many, with what loud applause
Did'st thou beate heauen with blessing *Bullingbrooke*,
Before he was, what thou would'st haue him be?
And being now trimm'd in thine owne desires,
Thou (beastly Feeder) art so full of him,
That thou prouok'st thy selfe to cast him vp.
So, so, (thou common Dogge) did'st thou disgorge
Thy glutton-bosome of the Royall *Richard*,
And now thou would'st eate thy dead vomit vp,   600
And howl'st to finde it. What trust is in these Times?
They, that when *Richard* liu'd, would haue him dye,
Are now become enamour'd on his graue.
Thou that threw'st dust vpon his goodly head
When through proud London he came sighing on,

After th'admired heeles of *Bullingbrooke*,
Cri'st now, O Earth, yeeld vs that King againe,
And take thou this (O thoughts of men accurs'd)
"*Past, and to Come, seemes best ; things Present, worst.*"
⌈MOWBRAY⌉
610 Shall we go draw our numbers, and set on?
HASTINGS
We are Times subiects, and Time bids be gone.

exeunt

Sc. 4   *Enter Hostesse of the Tauerne, and an Officer, Phang,*
(2.1)   ⌈*followed at a distance by*⌉ *another Officer, Snare*
HOSTESSE
Master Phang, haue you entred the action?
PHANG It is entred.
HOSTESSE Wheres your yeoman? ist a lusty yeoman? wil
a stand too't?
PHANG Sirra, wheres Snare?
HOSTESSE O Lord I, good master Snare.
SNARE ⌈*comming forward*⌉ Here, here.
PHANG Snare, we must arest sir Iohn Falstaffe.
620 HOSTESSE Yea good master Snare, I haue entred him and
all.
SNARE It may chaunce cost some of vs our liues, for he
will stabbe.
HOSTESSE Alas the day, take heed of him, he stabd me in
mine owne house, most beastly in good faith, a cares
not what mischiefe he does, if his weapon be out, he
will foyne like any diuell, he will spare neither man,
woman, nor child.
PHANG If I can close with him, I care not for his thrust.
630 HOSTESSE No nor I neither, Ile be at your elbow.
PHANG And I but fist him once, and a come but within
my vice.
HOSTESSE I am vndone by his going, I warrant you, hees
an infinitiue thing vppon my score, good maister Phang
holde him sure, good master Snare let him not scape,
a comes continuantly to Pie corner (sauing your
manhoods) to buy a saddle, and he is indited to dinner
to the Lubbers head in Lumbert streete to master
Smooths the silk man, I pray you since my exion is
640 entred, and my case so openly knowne to the worlde,
let him be brought in to his answer, a hundred marke
is a long one, for a poore lone woman to beare, and I
haue borne, and borne, and borne, and haue bin fubd
off, and fubd off, and fubd off, from this day to that
day, that it is a shame to be thought on, there is no
honesty in such dealing, vnlesse a woman should be
made an asse, and a beast, to beare euery knaues
wrong:
Enter sir Iohn Falstaffe, and Bardolfe, and the page
yonder he comes, and that arrant malmsie-nose knaue
650 Bardolfe with him, do your offices, do your offices
master Phãg, & master Snare, do me, do me, do me
your offices.
SIR IOHN How now, whose mare's dead? whats the
matter?

PHANG Sir Iohn, I arrest you at the sute of mistris quickly.
SIR IOHN ⌈*drawing*⌉ Away varlets, draw Bardolfe, cut me
off the villaines head, throw the queane in the channell.
⌈*Bardolfe drawes*⌉
HOSTESSE Throw me in the channell? Ile throw thee in
the channel,
A brawl
wilt thou, wilt thou, thou bastardly rogue, murder   660
murder, a thou honisuckle villaine, wilt thou kill Gods
officers and the Kings? a thou honiseed rogue, thou
art a honiseed, a man queller, and a woman queller.
SIR IOHN Keepe them off Bardolfe.
PHANG A reskew, a reskew.
HOSTESSE Good people bring a reskew or two, thou wot,
wot thou, thou wot, wot ta, do do thou rogue, do thou
hempseed.
PAGE Away you scullian, you rampallian, you fustilarian,
ile tickle your catastrophe.   670
Enter Lord chiefe iustice and his men
IUSTICE
What is the matter? keepe the peace here, ho.
Brawl ends. ⌈*Phang*⌉ *seizes sir Iohn*
HOSTESSE Good my lord be good to me, I beseech you
stand to me.
IUSTICE
How now sir Iohn, what are you brawling here?
Doth this become your place, your time, and businesse?
You should haue bin well on your way to Yorke:
⌈*To Phang*⌉ Stand from him fellow, wherefore hang'st
thou vpon him.
HOSTESSE O my most worshipful Lord, and't please your
grace I am a poore widdow of Eastcheape, and he is
arrested at my sute.   680
IUSTICE For what summe?
HOSTESSE It is more then for some my Lord, it is for al,
all I haue, he hath eaten me out of house and home,
he hath put all my substance into that fat belly of his,
(*to sir Iohn*) but I wil haue some of it out againe, or I
wil ride thee a nights like the mare.
SIR IOHN I think I am as like to ride the mare if I haue
any vantage of ground to get vp.
IUSTICE How comes this sir Iohn? fie, what man of good
temper would endure this tempest of exclamation, are   690
you not ashamed to inforce a poore widdow, to so
rough a course to come by her owne.
SIR IOHN (*to hostesse*) What is the grosse summe that I
owe thee?
HOSTESSE Mary if thou wert an honest man, thy selfe and
the mony too: thou didst sweare to me vpon a parcell
guilt goblet, sitting in my dolphin chamber, at the
round table by a sea cole fire, vpon wednesday in
Wheeson weeke, when the prince broke thy head, for
liking his father to a singing man of Winsor, thou didst   700
sweare to me thẽ, as I was washing thy wound, to
marry me, and make me my lady thy wife, canst thou
deny it, did not goodwife Keech the butchers wife come
in then and cal me gossip Quickly, comming in to

borow a messe of vinegar, telling vs she had a good
dish of prawnes, whereby thou didst desire to eate
some, whereby I told thee they were ill for a greene
wound, and didst thou not, when she was gone down
stayers, desire me, to be no more so familiarity, with
710 such poore people, saying that ere long they should cal
me madam, and didst thou not kisse me, and bid me
fetch thee thirtie shillings, I put thee now to thy booke
oath, denie it if thou canst.

⌈*She weepes*⌉

SIR IOHN My lord this is a poore made soule, and she
saies vp and downe the towne, that her eldest sonne
is like you, she hath bin in good case, and the trueth
is, pouerty hath distracted her, but for these foolish
officers, I beseech you I may haue redresse against
them.

720 IUSTICE Sir Iohn sir Iohn, I am wel acquainted with your
maner of wrenching the true cause, the false way: it
is not a confident brow, nor the throng of words that
come with such more then impudent sawcines from
you, can thrust me from a leuel consideration: you
haue as it appeares to me practisde vpon the easie
yeelding spirite of this woman, and made her serue
your vses both in purse and in person.

HOSTESSE Yea in truth my Lord.

IUSTICE Pray thee peace, pay her the debt you owe her,
730 and vnpay the villany you haue done with her, the
one you may doe with sterling mony, and the other
with currant repentance.

SIR IOHN My Lord I will not vndergoe this snepe without
reply, you cal honorable boldnes impudent sawcinesse,
if a man wil make curtsie and say nothing, he is
vertuous, no my Lord my humble duty remembred, I
will not bee your suter, I say to you I do desire
deliuerance from these officers, being vpon hasty
imployment in the Kings affayres.

740 IUSTICE You speake as hauing power to do wrong, but
answer in th'effect of your reputation, and satisfie the
poore woman.

SIR IOHN (*drawing apart*) Come hither hostesse.

She goes to him.
Enter master Gower, a messenger

IUSTICE Now master Gower, what newes.

GOWER
The King my Lord, and Harry prince of Wales,
Are neare at hand, the rest the paper tells.

⌈*Iustice reades the paper, and conuerses apart with*
Gower⌉

SIR IOHN As I am a gentleman!

HOSTESSE Faith you said so before.

SIR IOHN As I am a gentleman, come, no more words of
750 it.

HOSTESSE By this heauenly ground I tread on, I must be
faine to pawne both my plate, & the tapestry of my
dining chambers.

SIR IOHN Glasses glasses is the onely drinking, and for
thy wals a pretty sleight drollery, or the storie of the
prodigal, or the Iarman hunting in waterworke, is

worth a thousand of these bed-hangers, and these flie
bitten tapestries, let it be x. £ if thou canst: come, and
twere not for thy humors, theres not a better wench
in England, goe wash thy face and draw the action, 760
come thou must not be in this humor with me, dost
not know me, come, I know thou wast set on to this.

HOSTESSE Pray thee sir Iohn let it be but twentie nobles,
ifaith I am loath to pawne my plate so God saue me
law.

SIR IOHN Let it alone, ile make other shift, youle be a
foole stil.

HOSTESSE Well, you shall haue it, though I pawne my
gowne, I hope youle come to supper, youle pay me al
together. 770

SIR IOHN Wil I liue? ⌈*to Bardolfe and page*⌉ goe with her,
with her, hooke on, hooke on.

HOSTESSE Will you haue Doll Tere-sheet meete you at
supper.

SIR IOHN No more words, lets haue her.

exit hostesse, Bardolfe and page, Phang and Snare

IUSTICE (*to Gower*) I haue heard better newes.

SIR IOHN Whats the newes my good lord?

IUSTICE (*to Gower*) Where lay the King to night?

GOWER At Basingstoke my Lord.

SIR IOHN (*to Iustice*) I hope my Lord al's wel, what is the 780
newes my lord?

IUSTICE (*to Gower*) Come all his forces backe?

GOWER
No, fifteen hundred foot, fiue hundred horse
Are marcht vp to my lord of Lancaster,
Against Northumberland, and the Archbishop.

SIR IOHN (*to Iustice*)
Comes the King back from Wales, my noble lord?

IUSTICE (*to Gower*)
You shall haue letters of me presently,
Come, go along with me, good master Gower.

They are going

SIR IOHN My lord.

IUSTICE Whats the matter? 790

SIR IOHN Maister Gower, shall I intreate you with mee to
dinner?

GOWER I must waite vpon my good lord here, I thank
you good sir Iohn.

IUSTICE Sir Iohn, you loyter heere too long, being you are
to take souldiers vp in Counties as you go.

SIR IOHN Will you suppe with mee maister Gower?

IUSTICE What foolish maister taught you these manners,
sir Iohn?

SIR IOHN Maister Gower, if they become me not, hee was 800
a foole that taught them mee: (*to Iustice*) this is the
right fencing grace, my Lord, tap for tap, and so part
faire.

IUSTICE Now the Lord lighten thee, thou art a great foole.

exeunt ⌈*Iustice and Gower at one doore,*
sir Iohn at another doore⌉

Enter Prince Harry and Poynes   Sc. 5

PRINCE HARRY Before God, I am exceeding weary.   (2.2)

POYNES Ist come to that? I had thought wearines durst not haue attacht one of so hie bloud.

PRINCE HARRY Faith it does me, though it discolors the complexion of my greatnes to acknowledge it: doth it not shew vildly in me, to desire small beere?

810

POYNES Why a Prince should not be so loosely studied, as to remember so weake a composition.

PRINCE HARRY Belike then my appetite was not princely gote, for by my troth, I do now remember the poor creature smal beere. But indeed these humble considerations make me out of loue with my greatnesse. What a disgrace is it to mee to remember thy name? or to know thy face to morow? or to take note how many paire of silke stockings thou hast, viz these, and those that were thy peach coloured ones, or to beare the inuentorie of thy shirts, as one for superfluitie, and another for vse. But that the Tennis court keeper knows better than I, for it is a low eb of linnen with thee when thou keepest not racket there, as thou hast not done a great while, because the rest of thy low Countries haue made a shift to eate vp thy holland.

820

POYNES How ill it followes, after you haue labored so hard, you should talke so ydlely! tell me how many good yong princes woulde doe so, their fathers lying so sicke, as yours is.

830

PRINCE HARRY Shall I tel thee one thing Poynes?

POYNES Yes faith, and let it be an excellent good thing.

PRINCE HARRY It shall serue among wittes of no higher breeding then thine.

POYNES Go to, I stand the push of your one thing that youle tell.

PRINCE HARRY Mary I tell thee, it is not meete that I should bee sad now my father is sicke, albeit I could tell to thee, as to one it pleases me for fault of a better to call my friend, I could be sad, and sad indeede too.

840

POYNES Very hardly, vpon such a subiect.

PRINCE HARRY By this hand, thou thinkest me as farre in the diuels booke, as thou and Falstaffe, for obduracie and persistancie, let the end trie the man, but I tel thee, my heart bleeds inwardly that my father is so sick, and keeping such vile company as thou arte, hath in reason taken from me all ostentation of sorrowe.

POYNES The reason.

PRINCE HARRY What wouldst thou thinke of me if I should weep?

850

POYNES I woulde thincke thee a most princely hypocrite.

PRINCE HARRY It would bee euery mans thought, and thou arte a blessed felow, to thinke as euery man thinkes, neuer a mans thought in the world, keepes the rode way better then thine, euerie man would thinke me an hypocrite indeede, and what accites your most worshipfull thought to thinke so?

POYNES Why because you haue been so lewd and so much engraffed to Falstaffe.

860

PRINCE HARRY And to thee.

POYNES By this light I am well spoke on, I can heare it with mine owne eares, the worst that they can say of me is that I am a second brother, and that I am a proper fellow of my hands, and those two things I confesse I cannot helpe:

Enter Bardolfe ⌈followed by⌉ the page

by the masse here comes Bardolfe.

PRINCE HARRY And the boy that I gaue Falstaffe, a had him from me Christian, and looke if the fat villaine haue not transformd him Ape.

BARDOLFE God saue your grace.

870

PRINCE HARRY And yours most noble Bardolfe.

POYNES (*to Bardolfe*) Come you vertuous asse, you bashfull foole, must you be blushing, wherefore blush you now? what a maidenly man at armes are you become? ist such a matter to get a pottle-pots maidenhead?

PAGE A calls me enow my Lord, through a red lattice, and I could discerne no part of his face from the window, at last I spied his eies, and me thought he had made two holes in the ale wiues red peticote and so peept through.

880

PRINCE HARRY (*to Poynes*) Has not the boy profited?

BARDOLFE (*to page*) Away you horson vpright rabbet, away.

PAGE Away you rascally Altheas dreame, away.

PRINCE HARRY Instruct vs boy, what dreame boy?

PAGE Mary my lord, Althea dreampt she was deliuered of a firebrand, and therefore I call him her dreame.

PRINCE HARRY (*giuing him mony*) A crownes worth of good interpretation there tis boy.

POYNES O that this good blossome could be kept from cankers! (*giuing page mony*) well, there is sixpence to preserue thee.

890

BARDOLFE And you do not make him hangd among you, the gallowes shall be wrongd.

PRINCE HARRY And how doth thy master Bardolfe?

BARDOLFE Well my good Lord, he heard of your graces comming to towne, theres a letter for you.

POYNES Deliuerd with good respect, and how doth the martlemasse your master?

BARDOLFE In bodily health sir.

Prince Harry reades the letter

POYNES Mary the immortall part needes a phisitian, but that moues not him, though that be sicke, it dies not.

900

PRINCE HARRY I do allow this Wen to be as familiar with me, as my dogge, and he holds his place, for looke you how he writes.

⌈*He giues Poynes the letter*⌉

POYNES (*reads*) Iohn Falstaffe Knight, (*speaking to prince Harry*) euery man must know that as oft as he has occasion to name himselfe: euen like those that are kin to the King for they neuer pricke their finger, but they saye, theres some of the Kings bloud spilt: how comes that (*saies he*) that takes vppon him not to conceiue: the answer is as ready as a borowers cap: I am the Kings poore cosin, sir.

910

PRINCE HARRY Nay they will be kin to vs, or they will fetch it from Iaphet, (*taking the letter*) but the letter, (*reads*) Sir Iohn Falstaffe knight, to the sonne of the king, nearest his father, Harry prince of Wales, greeting.

POYNES Why this is a certificate.

PRINCE HARRY Peace. (*Reads*) I will imitate the honourable
     Romanes in breuitie.

920 POYNES ⌈*taking the letter*⌉ Sure he meanes breuity in breath,
     short winded, (*reads*) I commend mee to thee, I
     commend thee, and, I leaue thee, be not too familiar
     with Poynes, for he misuses thy fauours so much, that
     he sweares thou art to mary his sister Nel, repent at
     idle times as thou maist, and so farwel.

           Thine by yea, and no, which is as much as to say,
           as thou vsest him, Iacke Falstaffe with my
           familiars, Iohn with my brothers and sisters, and
           sir Iohn with all Europe.

930   My Lord, Ile steep this letter in sacke and make him
     eate it.

PRINCE HARRY Thats to make him eate twenty of his
     words, but do you vse me thus, Ned? must I marrie
     your sister?

POYNES God send the wench no worse fortune, but I neuer
     said so.

PRINCE HARRY Wel, thus we play the fooles with the time,
     and the spirits of the wise sit in the clowdes and mocke
     vs, (*to Bardolfe*) is your master here in London?

940 BARDOLFE Yea my Lord.

PRINCE HARRY Where sups he? doth the old boare feede
     in the old Franke?

BARDOLFE At the old place, my lord, in Eastcheape.

PRINCE HARRY What companie?

PAGE Ephesians, my lord, of the old church.

PRINCE HARRY Sup any women with him?

PAGE None my lord, but old mistris Quickly, and mistris
     Dol Tere-sheet.

PRINCE HARRY What Pagan may that be?

950 PAGE A proper gentlewoman sir, and a kinswoman of my
     masters.

PRINCE HARRY Euen such kinne as the parish Heicfors are
     to the towne bull, shall we steale vpon them Ned at
     supper?

POYNES I am your shadow my Lord, ile follow you.

PRINCE HARRY Sirra, you boy and Bardolfe, no worde to
     your master that I am yet come to towne; (*giuing
     money*) theres for your silence.

BARDOLFE I haue no tongue sir.

960 PAGE And for mine sir, I will gouerne it.

PRINCE HARRY Fare you well: go,

                              exeunt Bardolfe and page
     this Doll Tere-sheete should be some rode.

POYNS I warrant you, as common as the way between S.
     Albons and London.

PRINCE HARRY How might we see Falstaffe bestow himself
     to night in his true colours, and not our selues be
     seene?

POYNES Put on two letherne ierkins and aprons, and waite
     vpon him at his table like drawers.

970 PRINCE HARRY From a god to a bul, a heauy declension,
     it was Ioues case, from a prince to a prentise, a low
     transformation, that shal be mine, for in euery thing
     the purpose must weigh with the folly, follow me Ned.

                              exeunt

*Enter Northumberland, his wife, and Kate the
widow of Harry Percie*

NORTHUMBERLAND
     I pray thee louing wife and gentle daughter,
     Giue euen way vnto my rough affaires,
     Put not you on the visage of the times,
     And be like them to Percy troublesome.

WIFE
     I haue giuen ouer, I will speake no more,
     Do what you wil, your wisedome be your guide.

NORTHUMBERLAND
     Alas sweete wife, my honor is at pawne,   980
     And but my going, nothing can redeeme it.

KATE
     O yet for Gods sake, go not to these wars,
     The time was father, that you broke your word,
     When you were more endeerd to it then now,
     When your owne Percie, when my hearts deere Harry,
     Threw many a Northward looke, to see his father
     Bring vp his powers, but he did long in vaine.
     Who then perswaded you to stay at home?
     There were two honors lost, yours, and your sonnes,
     For yours, the God of heauen brighten it,   990
     For his, it stucke vpon him as the sunne
     In the grey vault of heauen, and by his light
     Did all the Cheualry of England moue
     To do braue acts, he was indeede the glasse
     Wherein the noble youth did dresse themselues.
     He had no Legges, that practic'd not his Gate:
     And speaking thicke (which Nature made his blemish)
     Became the Accents of the Valiant.
     For those that could speake low, and tardily,
     Would turne their owne Perfection, to Abuse,   1000
     To seeme like him. So that in Speech, in Gate,
     In Diet, in Affections of delight,
     In Militarie Rules, Humors of Blood,
     He was the Marke, and Glasse, Coppy, and Booke,
     That fashion'd others. And him, O wondrous him!
     O Miracle of Men! Him did you leaue
     (Second to none) vn-seconded by you,
     To looke vpon the hideous God of Warre,
     In dis-aduantage, to abide a field,
     Where nothing but the sound of *Hotspurs* Name   1010
     Did seeme defensible: so you left him.
     Neuer, O neuer doe his Ghost the wrong,
     To hold your Honor more precise and nice
     With others, then with him. Let them alone:
     The Marshall and the Arch-bishop are strong.
     Had my sweet *Harry* had but halfe their Numbers,
     To day might I (hanging on *Hotspurs* Necke)
     Haue talk'd of *Monmouth's* Graue.

NORTHUMBERLAND   Beshrew your heart,
     Faire daughter, you do draw my spirites from me,
     With new lamenting ancient ouersights,   1020
     But I must go and meete with danger there,
     Or it will seeke me in an other place,
     And find me worse prouided.

WIFE   O flie to Scotland,

Till that the nobles and the armed commons,
Haue of their puissance made a little taste.

KATE
If they get ground and vantage of the King,
Then ioyne you with them like a ribbe of steele,
To make strength stronger: but for al our loues,
First let them trie themselues, so did your sonne,
He was so suffred, so came I a widow,
And neuer shall haue length of life enough,
To raine vpon remembrance with mine eies,
That it may grow and sprout as high as heauen,
For recordation to my noble husband.

NORTHUMBERLAND
Come, come, go in with me, tis with my mind,
As with the tide, sweld vp vnto his height,
That makes a stil stand, running neither way,
Faine would I go to meete the Archbishop,
But many thousand reasons hold me backe,
I will resolue for Scotland, there am I,
Till time and vantage craue my company.   *exeunt*

Sc. 7   ⌈*A table and chaires set forth.*⌉ *Enter a Drawer*
(2.4)   ⌈*with wine*⌉ *and another Drawer* ⌈*with a dish of
apple Iohns*⌉
⌈I DRAWER⌉ What the diuel hast thou brought-there apple
Iohns? thou knowest sir Iohn cannot indure an apple
Iohn.
⌈2 DRAWER⌉ Mas thou saist true, the prince once set a
dish of apple Iohns before him, and tolde him there
were fiue more sir Iohns, and putting off his hat, said,
I will now take my leaue of these six drie, round, old,
withered Knights, it angred him to the heart, but he
hath forgot that.
⌈I DRAWER⌉ Why then couer and set them downe, and
see if thou canst find out Sneakes Noise, mistris Tere-
sheet would faine heare some musique.
                                      ⌈*exit 2 Drawer*⌉
⌈*I Drawer couers the table.*⌉
⌈*Enter 2 Drawer*⌉
⌈2 DRAWER⌉ Sirra, here wil be the prince and master
Poynes anon, and they will put on two of our ierkins
and aprons, and sir Iohn must not know of it, Bardolfe
hath brought word.
⌈I DRAWER⌉ By the mas here will be old vtis, it wil be an
excellent stratagem.
⌈2 DRAWER⌉ Ile see if I can find out Sneake.   *exeunt*
*Enter mistris Quickly the hostesse, and Doll Tere-
sheet, drunke*
HOSTESSE Yfaith sweet heart, me thinkes now you are in
an excellent good temperalitie. Your pulsidge beates as
extraordinarily as heart would desire, and your colour
I warrant you is as red as any rose, in good truth law:
but yfaith you haue drunke too much cannaries, and
thats a maruelous searching wine, and it perfumes the
bloud ere we can say, whats this, how do you now?
DOLL Better then I was: hem.
HOSTESSE Why thats well said, a good heart's worth gold:

Enter sir Iohn Falstaffe
loe here comes sir Iohn.   1070
SIR IOHN (*sings*) When Arthur first in court, ⌈*calls*⌉ empty
the iourdan (*sings*) and was a worthy King: (*speaks*)
how now mistris Doll?
HOSTESSE Sicke of a calme, yea good faith.
SIR IOHN So is all her sect, and they be once in a calme
they are sicke.
DOLL A pox damne you, you muddie rascall, is that all
the comfort you giue me?
SIR IOHN You make fat rascals mistris Dol.
DOLL I make them? gluttonie, and diseases make them, I   1080
make them not.
SIR IOHN If the cooke help to make the gluttonie, you
helpe to make the diseases Doll, we catch of you Doll,
we catch of you: graunt that my poore vertue, grant
that.
DOLL Yea Iesu, our chaines and our iewels.
SIR IOHN Your brooches, pearles, & ouches for to serue
brauely, is to come halting off, you know to come off
the breach, with his pike bent brauely, and to surgerie
brauely, to venture vpon the chargde chambers brauely. 1090
HOSTESSE By my troth this is the old fashion, you two
neuer meet but you fall to some discord, you are both
ygood truth as rewmatique as two dry tosts, you cannot
one beare with anothers cōfirmities, what the goodyere
one must beare, (*to Doll*) & that must be you, you are
the weaker vessell, as they say, the emptier vessel.
DOLL Can a weake empty vessell beare such a huge full
hogshead? theres a whole marchāts venture of Burdeux
stuffe in him, you haue not seene a hulke better stuft
in the hold. Come, ile be friends with thee iacke, thou   1100
art going to the wars, and whether I shall euer see
thee againe or no there is no body cares.
Enter drawer
DRAWER Sir, Antient pistol's belowe, and would speake
with you.
DOL TERE-SHEET Hang him swaggering rascal, let him not
come hither it is the foule-mouthd'st rogue in England.
HOSTESSE If he swagger, let him not come here, no by my
faith I must liue among my neighbours, Ile no
swaggerers, I am in good name, and fame with the
very best: shut the doore, there comes no swaggerers   1110
here, I haue not liu'd al this while to haue swaggering
now, shut the doore I pray you.
SIR IOHN Dost thou heare hostesse?
HOSTESSE Pray ye pacifie your selfe sir Iohn, there comes
no swaggerers here.
SIR IOHN Dost thou heare? it is mine Ancient.
HOSTESSE Tilly fally, sir Iohn, nere tel me: your ancient
swaggrer comes not in my doores: I was before maister
Tisicke the debuty tother day, & (as he said to me)
twas no longer ago than wedsday last, I good faith,   1120
neighbor Quickely, sayes he, maister Dumbe our
minister was by then, neighbor Quickely (saies he)
receiue those that are ciuil, for (saide he) you are in
an ill name: now a saide so, I can tell whereupon. For

(saies he) you are an honest woman, and well thought on, therefore take heede what ghests you receiue, receiue (saies he) no swaggering companions: there comes none here: you would blesse you to heare what he said: no, Ile no swaggrers.

1130 SIR IOHN Hees no swaggrer hostesse, a tame cheter yfaith, you may stroke him as gently as a puppy grey-hound, heele not swagger with a Barbary hen, if her feathers turne backe in any shew of resistance, call him vp Drawer.   ⌐exit Drawer⌐

HOSTESSE Cheter call you him? I will barre no honest man my house, nor no cheter, but I do not loue swagering by my troth, I am the worse when one saies swagger: feele maisters, how I shake, looke you, I warrant you.

DOL TERE-SHEET So you do hostesse.

1140 HOSTESSE Doe I? yea in very trueth doe I, and twere an aspen leafe, I cannot abide swaggrers.
    Enter antient Pistol, Bardolfe, page

PISTOL God saue you sir Iohn.

SIR IOHN Welcome ancient Pistoll, heere Pistoll, I charge you with a cuppe of sacke, do you discharge vpon mine hostesse.

PISTOL I will discharge vpon her sir Iohn, with two bullets.

SIR IOHN She is pistoll proofe, sir, you shall not hardely offend her.

HOSTESSE Come, Ile drink no proofes, nor no bullets, Ile
1150   drink no more than will do me good, for no mans pleasure, I.

PISTOL Then, to you mistris Dorothy, I will charge you.

DOLL Charge me? I scorne you, scuruy companion: what you poore base rascally cheting lacke-linnen mate? away you mouldie rogue, away, I am meate for your maister.

PISTOL I know you mistris Dorothy.

DOLL Away you cutpurse rascall, you filthy boung, away, by this wine Ile thrust my knife in your mouldie
1160   chappes, and you play the sawcie cuttle with me.
    ⌐She brandishes a knife⌐
    Away you bottle ale rascall, you basket hilt stale iuggler, you.
    ⌐Pistol drawes his sword⌐
    Since when, I pray you sir: Gods light, with two points on your shoulder? much.

PISTOL God let me not liue, but I will murther your ruffe for this.

HOSTESSE No, good captaine Pistoll, not here, sweete captaine.

DOLL Captain, thou abhominable damnd cheter, art thou
1170   not ashamed to be called Captaine? and Captaines were of my mind, they would trunchion you out, for taking their names vpon you, before you haue earnd them: you a captaine? you slaue, for what? for teareing a poore whoores ruffe in a bawdy house: hee a captaine! hang him rogue, he liues vpon mowldy stewd pruins, and dried cakes: a captaine? Gods light these villaines wil make the word captaine odious, therefore captains had neede look too't.

BARDOLFE Pray thee go downe good Ancient.

SIR IOHN Hearke thee hither mistris Dol.   1180
    He takes her aside

PISTOL Not I, I tell thee what corporall Bardolfe, I could teare her, Ile be reuengde of her.

PAGE Pray thee go downe.

PISTOL Ile see her damnd first,
    To Plutoes damnd lake by this hãd
    To th'infernal deep,
    Where erebus & tortures vile also:
    Holde hooke and line, say I:
    Downe, downe dogges, downe fates:
    Haue we not Hiren here?   1190

HOSTESSE Good captaine Peesell be quiet, tis very late yfaith, I beseeke you now aggrauate your choller.

PISTOL These be good humors indeede,
    Shal pack-horses,
    And hollow pamperd iades of Asia
    Which cannot goe but thirtie mile a day,
    Compare with Cæsars and with Canibals,
    And troiant Greekes?
    Nay rather damne them with King Cerberus,
    And let the Welkin roare, shall we fall foule for toies?   1200

HOSTESSE By my troth captane, these are very bitter words.

BARDOLFE Be gone good Ancient, this will grow to a brawle anon.

PISTOL
    Die men like dogges, giue crownes like pins,
    Haue we not Hiren here?

HOSTESSE A my word Captaine, theres none such here, what the goodyeare do you thinke I would denie her? for Gods sake be quiet.

PISTOL
    Then feed and be fat, my faire Calipolis,
    Come giues some sacke,
    Si fortune me tormente sperato me contento,   1210
    Feare we brode sides? no, let the fiend giue fire,
    Giue me some sacke, and sweet hart, lie thou there,
        ⌐He lays downe his sword⌐
    Come we to ful points here? and are & cæteraes, no things?
        ⌐He drinkes⌐

SIR IOHN Pistol, I would be quiet.

PISTOL Sweet Knight, I kisse thy neaffe, what, we haue seene the seuen starres.

DOLL For Gods sake thrust him down staires, I cannot indure such a fustian rascall.

PISTOL Thrust him downe staires, know we not Galloway   1220
    nagges?

SIR IOHN Quaite him downe Bardolfe like a shoue-groat shilling, nay, and a doe nothing but speake nothing, a shall be nothing here.

BARDOLFE (*to Pistol*) Come, get you downe staires.

PISTOL ⌐taking vp his sword⌐
    What shall we haue incision? shall we imbrew?
    Then death rocke me a sleepe, abridge my dolefull daies:
    Why then let grieuous gastly gaping wounds
    Vntwinde the sisters three, come Atropose I say.

1230 HOSTESSE Heres goodly stuffe toward.

SIR IOHN Giue me my rapier, boy.

DOLL I pray thee Iacke, I pray thee do not drawe.

SIR IOHN (*taking his rapier and speaking to Pistol*) Get you downe staires.

    Sir Iohn, Bardolfe, and Pistol brawl

HOSTESSE Heres a goodly tumult, ile forsweare keeping house afore ile be in these tirrits and frights,

    ⌐*Sir Iohn thrusts at Pistol*⌐

so,

    ⌐*Pistol thrusts at sir Iohn*⌐

murder I warant now, alas, alas, put vp your naked weapons, put vp your naked weapons.

    exit Pistol, pursued by Bardolfe

1240 DOLL I pray thee Iack be quiet, the rascal's gone, ah you horson little valiaunt villaine you.

HOSTESSE (*to sir Iohn*) Are you not hurte i'th groyne? me thought a made a shrewd thrust at your belly.

    Enter Bardolfe

SIR IOHN Haue you turnd him out a doores?

BARDOLFE Yea sir, the rascal's drunke, you haue hurt him sir i'th shoulder.

SIR IOHN A rascall to braue me?

DOLL A you sweet little rogue you, alas poore ape how thou sweatst, come let me wipe thy face, come on you

1250 horsone chops: a rogue, yfaith I loue thee, thou art as valorous as Hector of Troy, woorth fiue of Agamemnon, & ten times better then the nine Worthies, a villaine!

SIR IOHN A rascally slaue! I will tosse the rogue in a blanket.

DOLL Do and thou darst for thy heart, and thou dost, ile canuas thee betweene a payre of sheetes.

    Enter musicke

PAGE The musique is come sir.

SIR IOHN Let them play, play sirs,

    ⌐*Musicke plaies*⌐

sit on my knee Doll, a rascall bragging slaue! the rogue

1260 fled from me like quicksiluer.

DOLL Yfaith and thou followdst him like a church, thou horson little tydee Bartholemew borepigge, when wilt thou leaue fighting a daies and foyning a nights, and begin to patch vp thine old body for heauen.

    Enter Prince Harry and Poynes, disguisd as drawers

SIR IOHN Peace good Doll, do not speake like a deathes head, do not bid me remember mine end.

DOLL Sirra, what humour's the prince of?

SIR IOHN A good shallow yong fellow, a would haue made a good pantler, a would a chipt bread wel.

1270 DOLL They say Poines has a good wit.

SIR IOHN He a good wit? hang him baboon, his wit's as thicke as Tewksbury mustard, theres no more conceit in him then is in a mallet.

DOLL Why does the prince loue him so then?

SIR IOHN Because their legges are both of a bignesse, and a plaies at quoites well, and eates cunger and fennel, and drinkes off candles endes for flappe-dragons, and rides the wilde mare with the boyes, and iumpes vpon ioynd-stooles, and sweares with a good grace, and

weares his boote very smoothe like vnto the signe of 1280 the Legge, and breedes no bate with telling of discreet stories, and such other gambole faculties a has that show a weake minde, and an able bodie for the which the prince admits him: for the prince himself is such another, the weight of a haire wil turne the scales between their haber de poiz.

PRINCE HARRY (*aside to Poynes*) Would not this naue of a wheele haue his eares cut off?

POYNES Lets beate him before his whore.

PRINCE HARRY Looke where the witherd elder hath not 1290 his poule clawd like a parrot.

POYNES Is it not strange that desire should so many yeeres out liue performance.

SIR IOHN Kisse me Doll.

    They kisse

PRINCE HARRY (*aside to Poynes*) Saturne and Venus this yeere in coniunction? what saies th'Almanacke to that?

POYNS And look whether the fierie Trigon his man be not lisping to his masters old tables, his note booke, his counsel keeper?

SIR IOHN (*to Doll*) Thou dost giue me flattering busses. 1300

DOLL By my troth I kisse thee with a most constant heart.

SIR IOHN I am old, I am old.

DOLL I loue thee better then I loue, ere a scuruy yong boy of them all.

SIR IOHN What stuffe wilt haue a kirtle of? I shall receiue mony a thursday, shalt haue a cap to morrow: a merry song,

    ⌐*Musicke plaies againe*⌐

come it growes late, weele to bed, thou't forget me when I am gone.

DOLL By my troth thou't set me a weeping and thou saist 1310 so, proue that euer I dresse my selfe handsome til thy returne, wel hearken a'th end.

SIR IOHN Some sacke Francis.

PRINCE *and* POYNES (*comming forward*) Anon anon sir.

SIR IOHN Ha? a bastard sonne of the Kings? and arte not thou Poynes his brother?

PRINCE HARRY Why thou globe of sinfull continents, what a life dost thou leade?

SIR IOHN A better then thou, I am a gentleman, thou art a drawer. 1320

PRINCE HARRY Very true sir, and I come to drawe you out by the eares.

HOSTESSE O the Lord preserue thy grace: by my troth welcom to London, now the Lord blesse that sweete face of thine, O Iesu, are you come from Wales?

SIR IOHN (*to Prince Harry*) Thou horson madde compound of maiestie, by this light, flesh, and corrupt bloud, thou art welcome.

DOLL How? you fat foole I scorne you.

POYNES (*to prince Harry*) My lorde, he will driue you out 1330 of your reuenge, and turne all to a meriment if you take not the heate.

PRINCE HARRY (*to sir Iohn*) You horson candlemine you, how vildly did you speake of me now, before this honest, vertuous, ciuill gentlewoman?

HOSTESSE Gods blessing of your good heart, and so she is
  by my troth.

SIR IOHN (*to Prince Harry*) Didst thou heare me?

PRINCE HARRY Yea and you knew me as you did, when
1340 you ranne away by Gadshil, you knew I was at your
  backe, and spoke it, on purpose to trie my patience.

SIR IOHN No, no, no, not so, I did not thinke thou wast
  within hearing.

PRINCE HARRY I shall driue you then to confesse the wilfull
  abuse, and then I know how to handle you.

SIR IOHN No abuse Hall a mine honour, no abuse.

PRINCE HARRY Not to dispraise me, and cal me pantler
  and bread-chipper, and I know not what?

SIR IOHN No abuse Hall.

1350 POYNES No abuse?

SIR IOHN No abuse Ned i'th worlde, honest Ned, none, I
  dispraisde him before the wicked, that the wicked might
  not fall in loue with him: (*to prince Harry*) in which
  doing, I haue done the part of a carefull friend and a
  true subiect, and thy father is to giue me thankes for
  it, no abuse Hall, none Ned, none, no faith boyes none.

PRINCE HARRY See now whether pure feare and intire
  cowardize, doth not make thee wrong this virtuous
  gentlewoman to close with vs: is she of the wicked, is
1360 thine hostesse here of the wicked, or is thy boy of the
  wicked, or honest Bardolfe whose zeal burnes in his
  nose of the wicked?

POYNES (*to sir Iohn*) Answer thou dead elme, answer.

SIR IOHN The fiend hath prickt down Bardolfe
  irrecouerable, and his face is Lucifers priuy kitchin,
  where he doth nothing but rost mault-wormes, for the
  boy there is a good angel about him, but the diuel
  outbids him too.

PRINCE HARRY For the weomen.

1370 SIR IOHN For one of them shees in hell already, and
  burnes poore soules: for th'other I owe her mony, and
  whether she be damnd for that I know not.

HOSTESSE No I warrant you.

SIR IOHN No I thinke thou art not, I thinke thou art quit
  for that, mary there is another inditement vpon thee,
  for suffering flesh to be eaten in thy house contrary to
  the law, for the which I thinke thou wilt howle.

HOSTESSE Al vitlars do so, whats a ioynt of mutton or
  twoo in a whole Lent?

1380 PRINCE HARRY You gentlewoman.

DOLL What saies your grace?

SIR IOHN His grace saies that which his flesh rebels
  against.
    Peyto knockes at doore within

HOSTESSE Who knockes so lowd at doore? (*calls*) looke
  too'th doore there Francis.
    Enter Peyto

PRINCE HARRY Peyto, how now, what newes?

PEYTO
  The King your father is at Westminster,
  And there are twenty weake and wearied postes,
  Come from the North, and as I came along

I met and ouertooke a dozen captaines,   1390
  Bareheaded, sweating, knocking at the Tauernes,
  And asking euery one for sir Iohn Falstaffe.

PRINCE HARRY
  By heauen Poines, I feele me much too blame,
  So idely to prophane the precious time,
  When tempest of commotion like the south,
  Borne with blacke vapour doth begin to melt,
  And drop vpon our bare vnarmed heads,
  Giue me my sword and cloke: Falstaffe good night.
        exeunt Prince Harry and Poynes

SIR IOHN Now coms in the sweetest morsell of the night,
  & we must hence and leaue it vnpickt: 1400
        Knocking within. ⌈*Exit Bardolfe*⌉
  more knocking at the doore,
    Enter Bardolfe
  how now, whats the matter?

BARDOLFE
  You must away to court sir presently,
  A dozen captaines stay at doore for you.

SIR IOHN ⌈*to page*⌉ Pay the musitions sirra, farewel hostesse,
  farewel Dol, you see my good wenches how men of
  merrite are sought after, the vndeseruer may sleepe,
  when the man of action is cald on, farewell good
  wenches, if I be not sent away poste, I will see you
  againe ere I goe.   ⌈*exeunt musicke*⌉ 1410

DOLL ⌈*weeping*⌉ I cannot speake, if my hart be not ready
  to burst: wel sweete Iacke, haue a care of thy selfe.

SIR IOHN Farewell, farewell.
        exit ⌈*with Bardolfe, Peyto, and page Boy*⌉

HOSTESSE Wel, fare thee wel, I haue knowne thee these
  twentie nine yeeres, come pease-cod time, but an
  honester, and truer hearted man: wel, fare thee wel.
    ⌈*Enter Bardolfe*⌉

BARDOLFE Mistris Tere-sheete.

HOSTESSE Whats the matter?

BARDOLFE Bid mistris Tere-sheete come to my maister.
        ⌈*exit*⌉

HOSTESSE O runne Doll, runne, runne good Doll.   1420
        exeunt ⌈*Dol at one doore, hostesse at another*⌉

    Enter the King in his night-gowne, with a page   Sc. 8
KING (*giuing letters*)   (3.1)
  Go call the Earles of Surrey and of Warwicke.
  But ere they come, bid them o're-reade these letters,
  And well consider of them, make good speed.
        exit page
  How many thousand of my poorest subiects,
  Are at this howre asleepe? ô sleepe! ô gentle sleep!
  Natures soft nurse, how haue I frighted thee,
  That thou no more wilt weigh my eye-liddes downe,
  And steep my sences in forgetfulnesse,
  Why rather sleepe liest thou in smoaky cribbes,
  Vpon vneasie pallets stretching thee,
  And husht with buzzing night-flies to thy slumber,   1430
  Then in the perfumde chambers of the great,
  Vnder the canopies of costly state,
  And lulld with sound of sweetest melody?

O thou dull god, why li'ste thou with the vile
In lothsome beds, and leaust the kingly couch,
A watch-case, or a common larum bell?
Wilt thou vpon the high and giddy maste,
Seale vp the ship-boies eies, and rocke his braines,
1440 In cradle of the rude imperious surge,
And in the visitation of the winds,
Who take the ruffian billowes by the top,
Curling their monstrous heads, and hanging them
With deaffing clamour in the slippery clouds,
That with the hurly death it selfe awakes?
Canst thou, ô partiall sleepe, giue thy repose,
To the wet seaboy in an howre so rude,
And in the calmest, and most stillest night,
With al appliances and meanes to boote,
1450 Deny it to a King? then (happy) low lie downe,
Vneasie lies the head that weares a crowne.

Enter Warwike and Surry

WARWICKE
Many good morrowes to your maiestie.

KING
Is it good morrow lords?

WARWICKE   Tis one a clocke, and past.

KING
Why then good morrow to you all my lords.
Haue you read ore the letter that I sent you?

WARWICKE We haue my liege.

KING
Then you perceiue the body of our kingdome,
How foule it is, what rancke diseases grow,
And with what danger neare the heart of it.

WARWICKE
1460 It is but as a body yet distempered,
Which to his former strength may be restored,
With good aduise and little medicine,
My Lord Northumberland wil soone be coold.

KING
O God that one might reade the booke of fate,
And see the reuolution of the times,
Make mountaines leuell, and the continent
Weary of solide firmenesse melt it selfe
Into the sea, and other times to see,
The beachie girdle of the ocean,
1470 Too wide for Neptunes hips, how chances mockes,
And changes fill the cup of alteration,
With diuers liquors! Tis not ten yeeres gone,
Since Richard and Northumberland great friends,
Did feast togither, and in two yeare after,
Were they at warres: it is but eight yeares since,
This Percie was the man neerest my soule,
Who like a brother toyld in my affaires;
And laied his loue and life vnder my foote,
Yea for my sake, euen to the eyes of Richard,
1480 Gaue him defyance: but which of you was by?
(*To Warwicke*) You cousen Neuel, (as I may remember)
When Richard with his eye-brimme full of teares,
Then checkt and rated by Northumberland,

Did speake these wordes now proou'd a prophecie:
Northumberland, thou ladder by the which
My cousen Bolingbrooke ascends my throne,
(Though then (God knowes) I had no such intent,
But that necessitie so bowed the state,
That I and greatnesse were compeld to kisse.)
The time shall come, thus did he follow it,   1490
The time wil come, that foule sin gathering head,
Shall breake into corruption: so went on,
Foretelling this same times condition,
And the deuision of our amitie.

WARWICKE
There is a historie in all mens liues,
Figuring the natures of the times deceast:
The which obseru'd, a man may prophecie,
With a neere ayme of the maine chance of things,
As yet not come to life, who in their seedes,
And weake beginnings lie intreasured: 1500
Such thinges become the hatch and broode of time,
And by the necessary forme of this,
King Richard might create a perfect guesse,
That great Northumberland then false to him,
Would of that seede growe to a greater falsenesse,
Which should not find a ground to roote vpon
Vnlesse on you.

KING   Are these thinges then necessities,
Then let vs meet them like necessities,
And that same word euen now cries out on vs:
They say the Bishop and Northumberland,   1510
Are fiftie thousand strong.

WARWICKE   It cannot be my Lord,
Rumour doth double like the voice and eccho
The numbers of the feard, please it your grace,
To go to bedde: vpon my soule, my Lord,
The Powers that you alreadie haue sent foorth,
Shall bring this prise in very easily:
To comfort you the more, I haue receiued,
A certain instance that Glendour is dead:
Your Maiestie hath beene this fortnight ill,
And these vnseasond howers perforce must adde   1520
Vnto your sicknesse.

KING   I will take your counsaile,
And were these inward warres once out of hand,
We would (deare Lords) vnto the holy land.   *exeunt*

Enter Iustice Shallow, and Iustice Silens   Sc. 9
                                                   (3.2)
SHALLOW Come on, come on, come on, giue me your
     hand sir, giue me your hand sir, an early stirrer, by
     the Roode: and how doth my good coosin Silence?

SCILENS Good morrow good coosine Shallow.

SHALLOW And how doth my coosin your bedfellow? and
     your fairest daughter and mine, my god-daughter Ellen?

SCILENS Alas, a blacke woosel, coosin Shallow.   1530

SHALLOW By yea, and no, sir, I dare say my coosin
     William is become a good scholler, he is at Oxford stil,
     is he not?

SCILENS Indeede sir to my cost.

SHALLOW A must then to the Innes a court shortly: I was
once of Clements Inne, where I thinke they wil talke
of mad Shallow yet.

SCILENS You were calld Lusty Shallow then, coosin.

SHALLOW By the masse I was calld any thing, and I would
1540   haue done any thing indeede too, and roundly too:
there was I, and little Iohn Doyt of Staffordshire, and
blacke George Barnes, and Francis Pickebone, and Will
Squele a Cotsole man, you had not foure such swinge-
bucklers in all the Innes a court againe, and I may say
to you, wee knewe where the bona robas were, and
had the best of them all at commaundement: then was
Iacke Falstaffe, now sir Iohn, a boy, and page to
Thomas Mowbray duke of Norffolke.

SCILENS This sir Iohn, coosin, that comes hither anone
1550   about souldiers?

SHALLOW The same sir Iohn, the very same, I see him
breake Skoggins head at the Court gate, when a was
a Cracke, not thus high: and the very same day did I
fight with one Samson Stockefish a Fruiterer behinde
Greyes Inne: Iesu, Iesu, the mad dayes that I haue
spent! and to see how many of my olde acquaintance
are dead.

SCILENS We shal all follow, coosin.

SHALLOW Certaine, tis certaine, very sure, very sure, death
1560   (as the Psalmist saith) is certaine to all, all shall die.
How a good yoke of bullockes at Stamforth faire?

SCILENS By my troth I was not there.

SHALLOW Death is certaine: Is old Dooble of your towne
liuing yet?

SCILENS Dead sir.

SHALLOW Iesu, Iesu, dead! a drew a good bow, and dead?
a shot a fine shoote: Iohn a Gaunt loued him well, and
betted much money on his head. Dead? a woulde haue
clapt ith clowt at twelue score, and carried you a
1570   forehand shaft a fourteene and foureteene and a halfe,
that it would haue doone a mans heart good to see.
How a score of Ewes now?

SCILENS Thereafter as they bee, a score of good ewes may
bee worth ten pounds.

SHALLOW And is olde Dooble dead?

    Enter Bardolfe, and ⌈*page*⌉

SCILENS Here come two of sir Iohn Falstaffes men, as I
thinke.

⌈SHALLOW⌉ Good morrow honest gentlemen.

BARDOLFE I beseech you, which is iustice Shallow?

1580 SHALLOW I am Robart Shallowe, sir, a poore Esquier of
this Countie, and one of the Kings iustices of the peace:
what is your good pleasure with me?

BARDOLFE My Captaine, sir, commends him to you, my
Captain sir Iohn Falstaffe, a tall gentleman, by heauen,
and a most gallant Leader.

SHALLOW He greetes me wel, sir, I knew him a good
backsword man: how doth the good Knight? may I
aske how my Ladie his wife doth.

BARDOLFE Sir, pardon, a souldiour is better accommodated
1590   then with a wife.

SHALLOW It is well said infaith sir, and it is well said

indeed too, better accomodated, it is good, yea indeede
is it, good phrases are surely, and euer were, very
commendable, accommodated, it comes of *accommodo*,
very good, a good phrase.

BARDOLFE Pardon sir, I haue heard the word, Phrase call
you it? by this daye I knowe not the phrase, but I will
maintaine the word with my sword to be a souldierlike
word, and a word of exceeding good command by
heauen, accommodated, that is when a man is as they 1600
say, accommodated, or when a man is being whereby,
a may be thought to be accommodated, which is an
excellent thing.

    Enter sir Iohn Falstaffe

SHALLOW It is very iust, look, here comes good sir Iohn,
(*to sir Iohn*) giue me your hand, giue me your
worshippes good hand, by my troth you like well, and
beare your yeeres very well, welcome good sir Iohn.

SIR IOHN I am glad to see you well, good master Robert
Shallow, (*to Scilens*) master Surcard (as I thinke.)

SHALLOW No sir Iohn, it is my cosen Scilens, in 1610
commission with me.

SIR IOHN Good master Scilens, it well befits you should
be of the peace.

SCILENS Your good worship is welcome.

SIR IOHN Fie this is hot weather gentlemen, haue you
prouided me here halfe a dozen sufficient men?

SHALLOW Mary haue we sir, wil you sit?

SIR IOHN Let me see them I beseech you.

    ⌈*He sits*⌉

SHALLOW Wheres the roule? wheres the roule? wheres
the roule? let me see, let me see, let me see, so, so, so, 1620
so, so, yea mary sir, Rafe Mouldy, ⌈*to Scilens*⌉ let them
appeare as I cal, let them do so, let them do so, let me
see, (*calls*) where is Mouldy?

    ⌈*Enter Mouldy*⌉

MOULDY Here, and't please you.

SHALLOW What think you sir Iohn, a good limbde felow,
yong, strong, and of good friends.

SIR IOHN Is thy name Mouldie?

MOULDY Yea, and't please you.

SIR IOHN Tis the more time thou wert vsde.

SHALLOW Ha, ha, ha, most excellent yfaith, things that 1630
are mouldy lacke vse: very singular good, infaith well
said sir Iohn, very well said.

SIR IOHN Pricke him.

MOULDY I was prickt wel enough before, and you could
haue let me alone, my old dame will be vndone now
for one to doe her husbandrie, and her drudgery, you
need not to haue prickt me, there are other men fitter
to go out then I.

SIR IOHN Go to, peace Mouldy, you shall go, Mouldy it is
time you were spent. 1640

MOULDY Spent?

SHALLOW Peace fellow, peace, stand aside, know you
where you are?

    ⌈*Mouldy stands aside*⌉

for th'other sir Iohn: let me see, Simon Shadow.

SIR IOHN Yea mary, let me haue him to sit vnder, hees like to be a cold soldiour.

SHALLOW (calls) Wheres Shadow?

⌜Enter Shadow⌝

SHADOW Here sir.

1650 SIR IOHN Shadow, whose sonne art thou?

SHADOW My mothers sonne sir.

SIR IOHN Thy mothers sonne! like enough, and thy fathers shadow, so the sonne of the female is the shadow of the male: it is often so indeede, but not of the fathers substance.

SHALLOW Do you like him sir Iohn?

SIR IOHN Shadow wil serue for summer, pricke him, for we haue a number of shadowes, fill vp the muster booke.

⌜Shadow stands aside⌝

1660 SHALLOW (calls) Thomas Wart.

SIR IOHN Wheres he?

⌜Enter Wart⌝

WART Here sir.

SIR IOHN Is thy name Wart?

WART Yea sir.

SIR IOHN Thou art a very ragged wart.

SHALLOW Shall I pricke him sir Iohn?

SIR IOHN It were superfluous, for his apparell is built vpon his back, and the whole frame stands vpon pins, pricke him no more.

1670 SHALLOW Ha, ha, ha, you can do it sir, you can do it, I commend you well:

⌜Wart stands aside⌝

(Calls) Francis Feeble.

⌜Enter Feeble⌝

FEEBLE Here sir.

SHALLOW What trade art thou Feeble?

FEEBLE A womans tailer sir.

SHALLOW Shall I pricke him sir?

SIR IOHN You may, but if he had bin a mans tailer hee'd a prickt you: (to Feeble) wilt thou make as manie holes in an enemies battaile, as thou hast done in a womans peticoate.

1680 FEEBLE I will do my good will sir, you can haue no more.

SIR IOHN Well saide good womans tailer, well saide couragious Feeble, thou wilt be as valiant as the wrathfull doue, or most magnanimous mouse, pricke the womans tailer: wel M. Shallow, deepe M. Shallow.

FEEBLE I would Wart might haue gone sir.

SIR IOHN I would thou wert a mans tailer, that thou mightst mend him and make him fit to goe, I cannot put him to a priuate souldier, that is the leader of so many thousands, let that suffice most forcible Feeble.

1690 FEEBLE It shall suffice sir.

SIR IOHN I am bound to thee reuerend Feeble,

⌜Feeble stands aside⌝

who is next?

SHALLOW (calls) Peter Bul-calfe o'th greene.

SIR IOHN Yea mary, lets see Bul-calfe.

⌜Enter Bulcalfe⌝

BULCALFE Here sir.

SIR IOHN Fore God a likely fellow, come pricke Bul-calfe til hee roare againe.

BULCALFE O Lord, good my lord captaine.

SIR IOHN What, dost thou roare before th'art prickt? 1700

BULCALFE O Lord sir, I am a diseased man.

SIR IOHN What disease hast thou?

BULCALFE A horson cold sir, a cough sir, which I caught with ringing in the Kings affaires vpon his coronation day sir.

SIR IOHN Come thou shalt goe to the warres in a gowne, we wil haue away thy cold, and I wil take such order that thy friendes shal ring for thee.

⌜Bulcalfe stands aside⌝

Is here all?

SHALLOW There is two more cald then your number, you 1710 must haue but foure here sir, and so I pray you goe in with mee to dinner.

SIR IOHN Come, I wil go drink with you, but I cãnot tary dinner, I am glad to see you, by my troth master Shallow.

SHALLOW O sir Iohn, do you remember since we lay all night in the windmil in saint Georges field?

SIR IOHN No more of that good master Shallow, no more of that.

SHALLOW Ha, twas a merry night, and is Iane Night- 1720 worke aliue?

SIR IOHN She liues master Shallow.

SHALLOW She neuer could away with me.

SIR IOHN Neuer neuer, she wold alwaies say, she could not abide master Shallow.

SHALLOW By the masse I could anger her too'th heart, she was then a bona roba, doth she hold her owne wel?

SIR IOHN Old old master Shallow.

SHALLOW Nay she must be old, she cannot chuse but be old, certain shees old, & had Robin Night-work by old 1730 Night-work, before I came to Clem. inne.

SCILENS Thats fiftie fiue yeare ago.

SHALLOW Ha cousen Scilens that thou hadst seene that, that this Knight and I haue seene, ha sir Iohn said I well?

SIR IOHN We haue heard the chimes at midnight M. Shallow.

SHALLOW That we haue, that we haue, in faith sir Iohn we haue, our watch-worde was Hemboies, come lets to dinner, come lets to dinner, Iesus the daies that wee 1740 haue seene, come, come.

exeunt Shallow, Scilens, and sir Iohn

BULCALFE ⌜comming forward⌝ Good maister corporate Bardolfe, stand my friend, & heres foure Harry tenshillings in french crownes for you, in very truth sir, I had as liue be hangd sir as go, and yet for mine owne part sir I do not care, but rather because I am vnwilling, and for mine owne part haue a desire to stay with my friends, else sir I did not care for mine owne part so much.

BARDOLFE ⌜taking the mony⌝ Go to, stand aside. 1750

⌜Bulcalfe stands aside⌝

MOULDY ⌜comming forward⌝ And good master corporall

captaine, for my old dames sake stand my friend, she
has no body to doe any thing about her when I am
gone, and she is old and cannot helpe her selfe, you
shall haue forty sir.

BARDOLFE Go to, stand aside.

⌈*Mouldy stands aside*⌉

FEEBLE By my troth I care not, a man can die but once,
we owe God a death, ile nere beare a base mind, and't
bee my destiny: so, and't be not, so, no man's too good
to serue's prince, and let it go which way it will, he
1760 that dies this yeere is quit for the next.

BARDOLFE Well said, th'art a good fellow.

FEEBLE Faith ile beare no base mind.

Enter sir Iohn Falstaffe and the Iustices

SIR IOHN Come sir, which men shall I haue?

SHALLOW Foure of which you please.

BARDOLFE (*to sir Iohn*) Sir, a word with you, (*aside to him*)
I haue three pound to free Mouldy and Bulcalfe.

SIR IOHN Go to, well.

SHALLOW Come sir Iohn, which foure wil you haue?

SIR IOHN Do you chuse for me.

1770 SHALLOW Mary then, Mouldy, Bulcalfe, Feeble, and
Shadow.

SIR IOHN Mouldy and Bulcalfe, for you Mouldy stay at
home, til you are past seruice: and for your part
Bulcalfe, grow til you come vnto it, I will none of you.

⌈*exeunt Bulcalfe and Mouldy*⌉

SHALLOW Sir Iohn, sir Iohn, doe not your selfe wrong,
they are your likeliest men, and I would haue you
serude with the best.

SIR IOHN Wil you tel me (master Shallow) how to chuse
a man? care I for the limbe, the thewes, the stature,
1780 bulke and big assemblance of a man: giue me the spirit
M. Shalow: heres Wart, you see what a ragged
apparance it is, a shall charge you, and discharge you
with the motion of a pewterers hammer, come off and
on swifter then he that gibbets on the brewers bucket:
and this same halfe facde fellow Shadow, giue me this
man, he presents no marke to the enemy, the fo-man
may with as great aime leuel at the edge of a pen-
knife, and for a retraite how swiftly wil this Feeble the
womans Tailer runne off? O giue mee the spare men,
1790 and spare me the great ones, putte mee a caliuer into
Warts hand Bardolfe.

BARDOLFE (*giuing Wart a caliuer*) Hold Wart, trauers thas,
thas, thas.

⌈*Wart marches*⌉

SIR IOHN (*to Wart*) Come mannage me your caliuer: so,
very wel, go to, very good, exceeding good, O giue me
alwaies a little leane, olde chopt Ballde, shot: well said
yfaith Wart, th'art a good scab, hold, (*giuing a coin*)
theres a tester for thee.

SHALLOW He is not his crafts-master, he doth not do it
1800 right; I remember at Mile-end-greene, when I lay at
Clements Inne, I was then sir Dagonet in Arthurs show,
there was a little quiuer fellow, and a would mannage
you his peece thus, and a would about and about, and
come you in, and come you in, rah, tah, tah, would a

say, bounce would a say, and away again would a go,
and againe would a come: I shall nere see such a
fellow.

SIR IOHN These fellowes wooll doe well M. Shallow, God
keep you M. Scilens, I will not vse many words with
you, fare you wel gentlemen both, I thank you, I must   1810
a dosen mile to night: Bardolfe, giue the souldiers
coates.

SHALLOW Sir Iohn, the Lord blesse you, God prosper your
affaires, God send vs peace: as you returne, visit my
house, let our old acquaintance be renewed,
peraduenture I will with ye to the court.

SIR IOHN Fore God would you would.

SHALLOW Go to, I haue spoke at a word, God keep you.

SIR IOHN Fare you well gentle gentlemen.   *exit Iustices*
On Bardolfe, leade the men away,   1820

exeunt Bardolfe, Wart, Shadow, and Feeble

as I returne I will fetch off these iustices, I do see the
bottome of iustice Shallow, Lord, Lord, how subiect we
old men are to this vice of lying, this same staru'd
iustice hath done nothing but prate to me, of the
wildnesse of his youth, and the feates he hath done
about Turne-bull street, and euery third word a lie,
dewer paid to the hearer then the Turkes tribute, I doe
remember him at Clements Inne, like a man made after
supper of a cheese paring, when a was naked, he was
for all the worlde like a forkt reddish, with a head   1830
fantastically carued vpon it with a knife, a was so
forlorne, that his demensions to any thicke sight were
inuisible, a was the very genius of famine, and nowe
is this vices dagger become a squire, and talkes as
familiarly of Iohn a Gaunt, as if he had bin sworne
brother to him, and ile be sworn a nere saw him but
once in the tylt-yard, and then he burst his head for
crowding among the Marshalles men, I saw it, and told
Iohn a Gaunt he beate his owne name, for you might
haue trust him and all his aparell into an eele-skin,   1840
the case of a treble hoboy was a mansion for him a
Court, and now has he land and beefes. Well, ile be
acquainted with him if I returne, and t'shal go hard,
but ile make him a philosophers two stones to me, if
the yong Dase be a baite for the old Pike, I see no
reason in the law of nature but I may snap at him: let
Time shape, and there an end.   *exit*

Enter ⌈*in armes*⌉ *the Archbishop, Mowbray,*   Sc. 10
Hastings, ⌈*Colleuile,*⌉ *within the forrest of Gaultree*   (4.1)

ARCHBISHOP What is this forrest calld?

HASTINGS

Tis Gaultree forrest, and't shal please your grace.

ARCHBISHOP

Here stand, my lords, and send discouerers forth,   1850
To know the numbers of our enemies.

HASTINGS

We haue sent forth already.

ARCHBISHOP   Tis well done,
My friends and brethren (in these great affaires)
I must acquaint you, that I haue receiu'd

New dated letters from Northumberland,
Their cold intent, tenure, and substance thus:
Here doth he wish his person, with such powers,
As might hold sortance with his quallitie,
The which he could not leuy: whereupon
1860 He is retirde to ripe his growing fortunes,
To Scotland, and concludes in hearty prayers,
That your attempts may ouer-liue the hazard
And fearefull meeting of their opposite.

MOWBRAY
Thus do the hopes we haue in him touch ground,
And dash themselues to peeces.

    Enter messenger

HASTINGS   Now, what newes?
MESSENGER
West of this forrest, scarcely off a mile,
In goodly forme comes on the enemy,
And by the ground they hide, I iudge their number
Vpon, or neere the rate of thirty thousand.

MOWBRAY
1870 The iust proportion that we gaue them out,
Let vs sway on, and face them in the field.

    Enter Westmerland

ARCHBISHOP
What wel appointed Leader fronts vs heere?
MOWBRAY
I thinke it is my lord of Westmerland.
WESTMERLAND
Health and faire greeting from our Generall,
The prince lord Iohn and duke of Lancaster.
ARCHBISHOP
Say on my lord of Westmerland in peace,
What doth concerne your comming?
WESTMERLAND   Then my L.
Vnto your Grace doe I in chiefe addresse
The substance of my speech: if that rebellion
1880 Came like it selfe, in base and abiect rowtes,
Led on by bloody youth, guarded with rags,
And countenaunst by boyes and beggary.
I say, if damnd commotion so appeard,
In his true, natiue, and most proper shape,
You, reuerend father, and these noble Lordes,
Had not beene heere to dresse the owgly forme
Of base and bloody Insurrection
With your faire Honours. You (lord Archbishop)
Whose Sea is by a ciuile peace maintainde,
1890 Whose beard the siluer hand of Peace hath toucht,
Whose learning and good letters Peace hath tutord,
Whose white inuestments figure innocence,
The Doue, and very blessed spirite of peace:
Wherefore do you so ill translate your selfe
Out of the speech of peace that beares such grace,
Into the harsh and boystrous tongue of warre?
Turning your bookes to graues, your incke to bloud,
Your pennes to launces, and your tongue diuine,
To a lowd trumpet, and a point of warre?
ARCHBISHOP
1900 Wherefore do I this? so the question stands:

Briefly, to this end: we are all diseasde,
And with our surfetting, and wanton howres,
Haue brought our selues into a burning Feuer,
And wee must bleede for it: of which Disease,
Our late King *Richard* (being infected) dy'd.
But (my most Noble Lord of Westmerland)
I take not on me here as a Physician,
Nor doe I, as an Enemie to Peace,
Troope in the Throngs of Militarie men:
But rather shew a while like fearefull Warre,   1910
To dyet ranke Mindes, sicke of happinesse,
And purge th'obstructions, which begin to stop
Our very Veines of Life: heare me more plainely.
I haue in equall ballance iustly weigh'd,
What wrongs our Arms may do, what wrongs we
    suffer,
And finde our Griefes heauier then our Offences.
Wee see which way the streame of Time doth runne,
And are enforc'd from our most quiet shore,
By the rough Torrent of Occasion,
And haue the summarie of all our Griefes   1920
(When time shall serue) to shew in Articles;
Which long ere this, wee offer'd to the King,
And might, by no Suit, gayne our Audience:
When wee are wrong'd, and would vnfold our Griefes,
Wee are deny'd accesse vnto his Person,
Euen by those men, that most haue done vs wrong.
The dangers of the daies but newly gone,
Whose memorie is written on the earth,
With yet appearing blood, and the examples
Of euery minutes instance (present now,)   1930
Hath put vs in these ill-beseeming armes,
Not to breake peace, or any braunch of it,
But to establish heere a peace indeede,
Concurring both in name and quallitie.
WESTMERLAND
When euer yet was your appeale denied?
Wherein haue you beene galled by the King?
What peere hath beene subornde to grate on you?
That you should seale this lawlesse bloody booke
Of forgde rebellion with a seale diuine.
ARCHBISHOP
My brother Generall, the common wealth   1940
I make my quarrell in particular.
WESTMERLAND
There is no neede of any such redresse,
Or if there were, it not belongs to you.
MOWBRAY
Why not to him in part, and to vs all
That feele the bruises of the daies before?
And suffer the condition of these times,
To lay a heauy and vnequall hand
Vpon our honors.
WESTMERLAND   O my good Lord *Mowbray*,
Construe the Times to their Necessities,
And you shall say (indeede) it is the Time,   1950
And not the King, that doth you iniuries.
Yet for your part, it not appeares to me,

Either from the King, or in the present Time,
That you should haue an ynch of any ground
To build a Griefe on: were you not restor'd
To all the Duke of Norfolkes Seignories,
Your Noble, and right well-remembred Fathers?

MOWBRAY
1960   What thing, in Honor, had my Father lost,
That need to be reuiu'd, and breath'd in me?
The King that lou'd him, as the State stood then,
Was force, perforce compell'd to banish him:
And then, that *Henry Bullingbrooke* and hee
Being mounted, and both rowsed in their Seates,
Their neighing Coursers daring of the Spurre,
Their armed Staues in charge, their Beauers downe,
Their eyes of fire, sparkling through sights of Steele,
And the lowd Trumpet blowing them together:
Then, then, when there was nothing could haue stay'd
1970   My Father from the Breast of *Bullingbrooke*;
O, when the King did throw his Warder downe,
(His owne Life hung vpon the Staffe hee threw)
Then threw hee downe himselfe, and all their Liues,
That by Indictment, and by dint of Sword,
Haue since mis-carryed vnder *Bullingbrooke*.

WESTMERLAND
You speak (Lord *Mowbray*) now you know not what.
The Earle of Hereford was reputed then
In England the most valiant Gentleman.
Who knowes, on whom Fortune would then haue
     smil'd?
1980   But if your Father had beene Victor there,
Hee ne're had borne it out of Couentry.
For all the Countrey, in a generall voyce,
Cry'd hate vpon him: and all their prayers, and loue,
Were set on *Herford*, whom they doted on,
And bless'd, and grac'd, indeed more then the King.
But this is meere digression from my purpose.
Here come I from our princely generall,
To know your griefes, to tell you from his Grace,
That he will giue you audience, and wherein
1990   It shall appeere that your demaunds are iust,
You shall enioy them, euery thing set off
That might so much as thinke you enemies.

MOWBRAY
But he hath forcde vs to compel this offer,
And it proceedes from policie, not loue.

WESTMERLAND
Mowbray, you ouerweene to take it so:
This offer comes from mercy, not from feare:
For loe, within a ken our army lies:
Vpon mine honour, all too confident
To giue admittance to a thought of feare:
2000   Our battell is more full of names than yours,
Our men more perfect in the vse of armes,
Our armour all as strong, our cause the best:
Then Reason will our hearts should be as good:
Say you not then, our offer is compelld.

MOWBRAY
Well, by my will, we shall admit no parlee.

WESTMERLAND
That argues but the shame of your offence,
A rotten case abides no handling.

HASTINGS
Hath the prince Iohn a full commission,
In very ample vertue of his father,
To heare, and absolutely to determine   2010
Of what conditions we shall stand vpon?

WESTMERLAND
That is intended in the Generalles name,
I muse you make so slight a question.

ARCHBISHOP
Then take, my lord of Westmerland, this scedule,
For this containes our generall grieuances.
Each seuerall article herein redrest,
All members of our cause both here and hence,
That are ensinewed to this action,
Acquitted by a true substantiall forme,
And present execution of our willes,   2020
To vs and to our purposes consinde,
We come within our awefull bancks againe,
And knit our powers to the arme of peace.

WESTMERLAND (*taking the scedule*)
This will I shew the Generall, please you Lords,
In sight of both our battells we may meete,
And either end in peace, which God so frame,
Or to the place of diffrence call the swords,
Which must decide it.

ARCHBISHOP   My lord, we will doe so.
                   Exit Westmerland

MOWBRAY
There is a thing within my bosome tells me
That no conditions of our peace can stand.   2030

HASTINGS
Feare you not that, if we can make our peace,
Vpon such large termes, and so absolute,
As our conditions shall consist vpon,
Our peace shall stand as firme as rockie mountaines.

MOWBRAY
Yea but our valuation shal be such,
That euery slight, and false deriued cause,
Yea euery idle, nice, and wanton reason,
Shall to the King taste of this action,
That were our royal faiths martires in loue,
We shall be winow'd with so rough a wind,   2040
That euen our corne shal seeme as light as chaffe,
And good from bad find no partition.

ARCHBISHOP
No, no, my lord, note this, the King is weary
Of daintie and such picking greeuances,
For he hath found, to end one doubt by death,
Reuiues two greater in the heires of life:
And therefore will he wipe his tables cleane,
And keepe no tel-tale to his memorie,
That may repeate, and history his losse,
To new remembrance: for full wel he knowes,   2050
He cannot so precisely weed this land,
As his misdoubts present occasion,

His foes are so enrooted with his friends,
That plucking to vnfix an enemy,
He doth vnfasten so, and shake a friend,
So that this land, like an offensiue wife,
That hath enragde him on to offer strokes,
As he is striking, holdes his infant vp,
And hangs resolu'd correction in the arme,
2060   That was vpreard to execution.

HASTINGS
    Besides, the King hath wasted al his rods,
    On late offendors, that he now doth lacke
    The very instruments of chasticement,
    So that his power, like to a phanglesse lion,
    May offer, but not hold.

ARCHBISHOP   Tis very true,
    And therefore be assurde, my good Lord Marshall,
    If we do now make our attonement well,
    Our peace wil like a broken limbe vnited,
    Grow stronger for the breaking.

MOWBRAY   Be it so,
        Enter Westmerland
2070   Here is returnd my lord of Westmerland.

WESTMERLAND
    The prince is here at hand, pleaseth your Lordship
    To meet his grace iust distance tweene our armies.

MOWBRAY
    Your grace of York, in Gods name then set forward.

ARCHBISHOP
    Before, and greete his grace (my lord) we come.
        ⌈*They march ouer the stage.*⌉
        Enter Prince Iohn ⌈*with one or more souldiers*
        carrying wine⌉

PRINCE IOHN
    You are well incountred here, my cousen Mowbray,
    Good day to you, gentle Lord Archbishop,
    And so to you Lord Hastings, and to all.
    My Lord of Yorke, it better shewed with you,
    When that your flocke assembled by the bell,
2080   Encircled you, to heare with reuerence,
    Your exposition on the holy text,
    Than now to see you here, an yron man,
    Cheering a rowt of rebells with your drumme,
    Turning the word to sword, and life to death:
    That man that sits within a monarches heart,
    And ripens in the sun-shine of his fauor,
    Would he abuse the countenance of the King:
    Alacke what mischeefes might he set abroach,
    In shadow of such greatnesse? with you Lord bishop
2090   It is euen so, who hath not heard it spoken,
    How deepe you were within the bookes of God,
    To vs the speaker in his parliament,
    To vs th'imagind voice of God himselfe,
    The very opener and intelligencer,
    Betweene the grace, the sanctities of heauen,
    And our dull workings? O who shal beleeue,
    But you misuse the reuerence of your place,
    Imply the countenance and grace of heau'n,
    As a false fauorite doth his princes name,

In deedes dishonorable: you haue tane vp,   2100
Vnder the counterfeited zeale of God,
The subiects of his substitute my father,
And both against the peace of heauen and him,
Haue here vpswarmd them.

ARCHBISHOP   Good my Lord of Lancaster,
    I am not here against your fathers peace,
    But as I told my lord of Westmerland,
    The time misordred doth in common sense,
    Crowd vs and crush vs to this monstrous forme,
    To hold our safety vp: I sent your grace,
    The parcells and particulars of our griefe,   2110
    The which hath beene with scorne shoud from the
        court,
    Whereon this Hidra, sonne of warre is borne,
    Whose dangerous eies may well be charmd asleepe,
    With graunt of our most iust, and right desires,
    And true obedience of this madnes cured,
    Stoope tamely to the foote of maiestie.

MOWBRAY
    If not, we ready are to trie our fortunes,
    To the last man.

HASTINGS   And though we here fal downe,
    We haue supplies to second our attempt,
    If they miscarry, theirs shal second them,   2120
    And so successe of mischiefe shall be borne,
    And heire from heire shall hold this quarrell vp,
    Whiles England shall haue generation.

PRINCE IOHN
    You are too shallow Hastings, much too shallow,
    To sound the bottome of the after times.

WESTMERLAND
    Pleaseth your grace to answere them directly,
    How far forth you do like their articles.

PRINCE IOHN
    I like them all, and do allow them well,
    And sweare here by the honour of my bloud,
    My fathers purposes haue beene mistooke,   2130
    And some about him haue too lauishly,
    Wrested his meaning and authority.
        (*To the Archbishop*)
    My Lord, these griefes shall be with speed redrest,
    Vppon my soule they shal, if this may please you,
    Discharge your powers vnto their seuerall counties,
    As we will ours, and here betweene the armies,
    Lets drinke together friendly and embrace,
    That all their eies may beare those tokens home,
    Of our restored loue and amitie.

ARCHBISHOP
    I take your princely word for these redresses.   2140

⌈PRINCE IOHN⌉
    I giue it you, and will maintaine my word,
    And thereupon I drinke vnto your grace.
        He drinkes

⌈HASTINGS⌉ ⌈*to Colleuile*⌉
    Go Captaine, and deliuer to the armie
    This newes of peace, let them haue pay, and part.
    I know it will well please them, hie thee captaine.
        exit ⌈*Colleuile*⌉

ARCHBISHOP

    To you my noble lord of Westmerland.

        He drinkes

WESTMERLAND (*drinking*)

    I pledge your grace, and if you knew what paines,

    I haue bestowed to breed this present peace,

    You would drinke freely, but my loue to ye

2150   Shall shew it selfe more openly hereafter.

ARCHBISHOP

    I do not doubt you.

WESTMERLAND   I am glad of it,

    (*Drinking*) Health to my Lord, and gentle cosin

      Mowbray.

MOWBRAY

    You wish me health in very happy season,

    For I am on the sodaine something ill.

ARCHBISHOP

    Against ill chaunces men are euer mery,

    But heauinesse fore-runnes the good euent.

WESTMERLAND

    Therefore be mery coze, since sodaine sorrow

    Serues to say thus, some good thing comes to morow.

ARCHBISHOP

    Beleeue me I am passing light in spirit.

MOWBRAY

2160   So much the worse if your owne rule be true.

        shout within

PRINCE IOHN

    The word of peace is rendred, heark how they showt.

MOWBRAY

    This had bin cheerefull after victory.

ARCHBISHOP

    A peace is of the nature of a conquest,

    For then both parties nobly are subdued,

    And neither party looser.

PRINCE IOHN (*to Westmerland*) Go my lord,

    And let our army be discharged too,

        exit Westmerland

    (*To Archbishop*) And, good my lord, so please you, let

      our traines

    March by vs, that we may peruse the men,

    We should haue coap't withall.

ARCHBISHOP   Go, good Lord Hastings,

2170   And ere they be dismist, let them march by.

        exit Hastings

PRINCE IOHN

    I trust Lords we shal lie to night togither:

      Enter Westmerland ⌐with Captaines⌐

    Now coosin, wherefore stands our army stil?

WESTMERLAND

    The Leaders hauing charge from you to stand,

    Wil not goe off vntil they heare you speake.

PRINCE IOHN

    They know their dueties.

      Enter Hastings

HASTINGS ⌐*to Archbishop*⌐   Our army is disperst,

    Like youthfull steeres vnyoakt they take their courses,

East, weast, north, south, or like a schoole broke vp,

Each hurries toward his home, and sporting place.

WESTMERLAND

    Good tidings my lord Hastings, for the which

    I do arest thee traitor of high treason,   2180

    And you lord Archbishop, and you lord Mowbray,

    Of capitall treason I attach you both.

      Captaines guard Hastings, Archbishop, and Mowbray⌐

MOWBRAY

    Is this proceeding iust and honorable?

WESTMERLAND Is your assembly so?

ARCHBISHOP Will you thus breake your faith?

PRINCE IOHN I pawnde thee none,

    I promist you redresse of these same grieuances

    Whereof you did complaine, which by mine honour

    I will performe, with a most christian care.

    But for you rebels, looke to taste the due   2190

    Meete for rebellion and such acts as yours:

    Most shallowly did you these armes commence,

    Fondly brought heere, and foolishly sent hence.

    Strike vp our drummes, pursue the scattred stray:

    God, and not we, hath safely fought to day:

    Some guard this traitours to the blocke of death,

    Treasons true bed, and yeelder vp of breath.   *exeunt*

      Alarum. Excursions. Enter sir Iohn Falstaffe and   **Sc. 11**

      Colleuile   **(4.2)**

SIR IOHN Whats your name sir, of what condition are

    you, and of what place I pray?

COLLEUILE I am a Knight sir, and my name is Coleuile of   2200

    the Dale.

SIR IOHN Well then, Colleuile is your name, a Knight is

    your degree, and your place the dale: Coleuile shalbe

    still your name, a traitor your degree, & the dungeon

    your place, a place deep enough, so shall you be stil

    Colleuile of the Dale.

COLLEUILE Are not you sir Iohn Falstaffe?

SIR IOHN As good a man as he sir, who ere I am: doe ye

    yeelde sir, or shall I sweat for you? if I doe sweate,

    they are the drops of thy louers, and they weepe for   2210

    thy death, therefore rowze vp feare and trembling, and

    do obseruance to my mercie.

COLLEUILE (*kneeling*) I think you are sir Iohn Falstaffe, and

    in that thought yeelde me.

SIR IOHN (*aside*) I haue a whole schoole of tongs in this

    belly of mine, and not a tongue of them all speakes

    any other word but my name, and I had but a belly

    of any indifferencie, I were simply the most actiue

    fellow in Europe: my womb, my wombe, my womb

    vndoes me,   2220

      Enter Prince Iohn, Westmerland, Blunt, other lords,

      and souldiers

    heere comes our Generall.

PRINCE IOHN

    The heate is past, follow no further now,   *Retraite*

    Call in the powers good coosin Westmerland.

        exit Westmerland

Now Falstaffe, where haue you beene all this while?
When euery thing is ended, then you come:
These tardy trickes of yours wil on my life
One time or other breake some gallowes backe.

SIR IOHN I would bee sory my lord, but it shoulde bee
thus: I neuer knew yet but Rebuke and Checke, was
the rewarde of Valor: do you thinke me a swallow, an
2230   arrow, or a bullet? haue I in my poore and old motion
the expedition of thought? I haue speeded hither with
the very extreamest inch of possibility, I haue foundred
ninescore and od postes, and here trauell tainted as I
am, haue in my pure and immaculate valour, taken
sir Iohn Colleuile of the Dale, a most furious Knight
and valorous enemy: but what of that? he sawe me,
and yeelded, that I may iustly say with the hooke-
nosde fellow of Rome, I came, saw, and ouercame.

PRINCE IOHN It was more of his curtesie then your
2240   deseruing.

SIR IOHN I know not, here he is, and here I yeeld him,
and I beseech your grace let it be bookte with the rest
of this daies deedes, or by the Lord, I wil haue it in a
particular ballad else, with mine owne picture on the
top on't, (Coleuile kissing my foote) to the which course,
if I bee enforst, if you doe not all shew like guilt twoo
pences to mee, and I in the cleere skie of Fame, ore-
shine you as much as the full moone doth the cindars
of the element, (which shew like pinnes heads to her)
2250   beleeue not the worde of the noble: therefore let me
haue right, and let Desert mount.

PRINCE IOHN Thine's too heauy to mount.

SIR IOHN Let it shine then.

PRINCE IOHN Thines too thicke to shine.

SIR IOHN Let it do some thing, my good lord, that may
doe me good, and call it what you will.

PRINCE IOHN
Is thy name Colleuile?

COLLEUILE   It is my Lord.

PRINCE IOHN
A famous rebell art thou Colleuile.

SIR IOHN And a famous true subiect tooke him.

COLLEUILE
2260   I am my lord but as my betters are,
That led me hither, had they bin rulde by me,
You should haue wonne them deerer then you haue.

SIR IOHN
I know not how they sold themselues, but thou
Like a kind fellow gau'st thy selfe away
And I thanke thee for thee.

Enter Westmerland

PRINCE IOHN   Haue you left pursuit?

WESTMERLAND
Retraite is made, and execution stayd.

PRINCE IOHN
Send Colleuile with his confederates
To Yorke, to present execution,
Blunt leade him hence, and see you guard him sure.

exit Blunt with Colleuile

And now dispatch we toward the court my lordes,   2270
I heare the King my father is sore sick,
(*To Westmerland*) Our newes shall go before vs to his
maiestie,
Which cosin you shall beare to comfort him,
And we with sober speede will follow you.

SIR IOHN
My Lord, I beseech you giue me leaue to go
Through Glostershire, and when you come to court,
Stand my good lord pray in your good report.

PRINCE IOHN
Fare you wel Falstaffe, I, in my condition,
Shal better speake of you then you deserue.

exit all but sir Iohn

SIR IOHN I would you had but the wit, twere better than   2280
your dukedome, good faith this same yong sober
blouded boy doth not loue me, nor a mã cãnot make
him laugh, but thats no maruel, he drinkes no wine,
theres neuer none of these demure boyes come to any
proofe, for thin drinke doth so ouer-coole theyr blood,
and making many fish meales, that they fall into a
kind of male greene sicknes, and then when they marry,
they gette wenches, they are generally fooles and
cowards, which some of vs should be too, but for
inflammation: a good sherris sacke hath a two fold   2290
operation in it, it ascendes mee into the braine, dries
me there all the foolish, and dull, and crudy vapors
which enuirone it, makes it apprehensiue, quicke,
forgetiue, full of nimble, fiery, and delectable shapes,
which deliuered ore to the voyce, the tongue, which is
the birth, becomes excellent wit. The second property
of your excellent sherris, is the warming of the blood,
which before (cold & setled,) left the lyuer white & pale,
which is the badge of pusilanimitie and cowardize: but
the sherris warmes it, and makes it course from the   2300
inwards to the partes extreames, it illuminateth the
face, which as a beacon, giues warning to al the rest
of this little kingdom man to arme, and then the vitall
commoners, and inland petty spirits, muster me all to
their captaine, the heart: who great, and pufft vp with
his retinew, doth any deed of courage: and this valour
comes of sherris, so that skill in the weapon is nothing
without sacke (for that sets it aworke) and learning a
meere whoord of gold kept by a diuell, till sacke
commences it, and sets it in act and vse. Hereof comes   2310
it, that Prince Harry is valiant, for the cold blood he
did naturally inherite of his father, he hath like leane,
sterile, and bare land, manured, husbanded and tilld,
with excellent endeuour of drinking good and good
store of fertile sherris, that he is become very hote and
valiant. If I had a thousand sonnes, the first humane
principle I would teach them, should be, to forsweare
thin potations, and to addict themselues to sacke.

Enter Bardolfe

How now Bardolfe?

BARDOLFE
The army is discharged all, and gone.   2320

SIR IOHN Let them goe, ile through Glostershire, and there
will I visit M. Robert Shallow Esquire, I haue him
already tempring betweene my finger and my thumb,
and shortly will I seale with him, come away.

exeunt

Sc. 12
(4.3)
     Enter the King ⌈in his bed⌉, attended by Warwike,
Thomas duke of Clarence, Humphrey of Gloucester
⌈and others⌉

KING

Now lords, if God doth giue successefull end,
To this debate that bleedeth at our doores,
We will our youth leade on to higher fields,
And draw no swords but what are sanctified:
Our nauie is addrest, our power collected,

2330
Our substitutes in absence wel inuested,
And euery thing lies leuell to our wish,
Only we want a little personal strength:
And pawse vs til these rebels now afoote,
Come vnderneath the yoke of gouernment.

WARWICKE

Both which we doubt not, but your maiesty
Shal soone enioy.

KING   Humphrey my sonne of Gloster,
Where is the prince your brother?

GLOUCESTER

I thinke hees gone to hunt, my lord, at Winsor.

KING

And how accompanied?

GLOUCESTER   I do not know, my lord.

KING

2340
Is not his brother Thomas of Clarence with him?

GLOUCESTER

No, my good lord, he is in presence here.

CLARENCE What would my lord and father?

KING

Nothing but well to thee Thomas of Clarence,
How chance thou art not with the prince thy
     brother?
He loues thee, and thou dost neglect him, Thomas,
Thou hast a better place in his affection
Then all thy brothers, cherrish it my boy:
And noble offices thou maist effect
Of mediation after I am dead,

2350
Betweene his greatnesse and thy other brethren:
Therefore omit him not, blunt not his loue,
Nor loose the good aduantage of his grace,
By seeming cold, or carelesse of his will,
For he is gracious if he be obseru'de,
He hath a teare for pittie, and a hand,
Open as day for melting charitie,
Yet notwithstanding being incenst, he is flint,
As humorous as winter, and as sodaine
As flawes congealed in the spring of day:

2360
His temper therefore must be well obseru'd,
Chide him for faults, and do it reuerently,
When you perceiue his bloud inclind to mirth:
But being moody, giue him line and scope,

Till that his passions, like a whale on ground
Confound themselues with working, learne this
     Thomas,
And thou shalt proue a shelter to thy friends,
A hoope of gold to binde thy brothers in,
That the vnited vessell of their bloud,
(Mingled with venome of suggestion,
As force perforce, the age will powre it in,)
Shall neuer leake, though it doe worke as strong,
As Aconitum, or rash gunpowder.

2370

CLARENCE

I shall obserue him with all care and loue.

KING

Why art thou not at Winsore with him Thomas?

CLARENCE

He is not there to day, he dines in London.

KING

And how accompanied, canst thou tell that?

CLARENCE

With Poines, and other his continuall followers.

KING

Most subiect is the fattest soyle to weeds,
And he, the noble image of my youth,
Is ouerspread with them, therefore my griefe
Stretches it selfe beyond the howre of death:
The bloud weepes from my heart when I do shape,
In formes imaginary, th'unguyded daies,
And rotten times that you shall looke vpon,
When I am sleeping with my auncestors:
For when his head-strong riot hath no curbe,
When rage and hot bloud are his counsellors,
When meanes and lauish manners meete together,
Oh with what wings shal his affections flie,
Towards fronting peril and opposde decay?

2380

2390

WARWICKE

My gracious Lord, you looke beyond him quite,
The prince but studies his companions,
Like a strange tongue wherein to gaine the language:
Tis needfull that the most immodest word,
Be lookt vpon and learnt, which once attaind,
Your highnesse knowes comes to no further vse,
But to be knowne and hated: so, like grosse termes,
The prince will in the perfectnesse of time,
Cast off his followers, and their memory
Shall as a pattern, or a measure liue,
By which his grace must mete the liues of other,
Turning past-euils to aduantages.

2400

KING

Tis seldome, when the bee doth leaue her comb,
In the dead carion:

     Enter Westmerland

           who's here, Westmerland?

WESTMERLAND

Health to my soueraigne, and new happinesse
Added to that that I am to deliuer,
Prince Iohn your sonne doth kisse your graces hand.
Mowbray, the Bishop, Scroope, Hastings, and al,
Are brought to the correction of your law:

There is not now a rebels sword vnsheathd,
But Peace puts forth her oliue euery where,
The manner how this action hath bin borne,
Here at more leisure may your highnesse reade,
With euery course in his particular.
        He giues the King papers
KING
O Westmerland, thou art a summer bird,
Which euer in the haunch of winter sings
The lifting vp of day:
        Enter Harcor
                        looke heres more newes.
HARCOR
From enemies, heauen keep your maiesty,
2420   And when they stand against you, may they fall
As those that I am come to tell you of:
The Earle Northumberland, and the Lord Bardolfe,
With a great power of English, and of Scots,
Are by the shrieue of Yorkshire ouerthrowne,
The manner, and true order of the fight,
This packet, please it you, containes at large.
        He giues the King papers
KING
And wherfore should these good news make me sicke?
Will Fortune neuer come with both hands full,
But write her faire words stil in foulest letters?
2430   She either giues a stomach, and no foode,
Such are the poore in health: or else a feast,
And takes away the stomach, such are the rich
That haue aboundance, and enioy it not:
I should reioyce now at this happy newes,
And now my sight failes, and my braine is giddy,
O me, come neare me, now I am much ill.
        He swounds
GLOUCESTER
Comfort your maiesty.
CLARENCE   O my royall father!
WESTMERLAND
My soueraigne Lord, cheere vp your selfe, look vp.
WARWICKE
Be patient princes, you do know these fits
2440   Are with his highnesse very ordinary.
Stand from him, giue him ayre, heel straight be wel.
CLARENCE
No, no, he cannot long hold out these pangs,
Th'incessant care and labour of his mind,
Hath wrought the Mure that should confine it in,
So thin that life lookes through and will breake out.
GLOUCESTER
The people feare me, for they do obserue
Vnfather'd heires, and lothly births of nature,
The seasons change their manners, as the yeere
Had found some moneths a sleepe, and leapt them
        ouer.
CLARENCE
2450   The riuer hath thrice flowed, no ebbe between,
And the old folk, (Times doting chronicles,)
Say, it did so a little time before
That our great grandsire Edward, sickt and died.

WARWICKE
Speake lower, princes, for the King recouers.
GLOUCESTER
This apoplexi wil certaine be his end.
KING
I pray you take me vp, and beare me hence,
Into some other chamber: softly pray.
        ⌈The King is carried ouer the stage in his bed⌉
Let there be no noyse made, my gentle friends,
Vnlesse some dull and fauourable hand
Will whisper musique to my weary spirite.   2460
WARWICKE
Call for the musique in the other roome.
                ⌈exit one or more. Still musicke within⌉
KING
Set me the crowne vpon my pillow here.
        ⌈Clarence⌉ takes the crowne ⌈from the Kings head⌉,
        and sets it on his pillow
CLARENCE
His eie is hollow, and he changes much.
        ⌈A noyse within⌉
WARWICKE
Lesse noyse, lesse noyse.
        Enter Harry
PRINCE HARRY   Who saw the duke of Clarence?
CLARENCE
I am here brother, ful of heauinesse.
PRINCE HARRY
How now, raine within doores, and none abroad?
How doth the King?
GLOUCESTER   Exceeding ill.
PRINCE HARRY
Heard he the good newes yet? tell it him.
GLOUCESTER
He altred much vpon the hearing it.
PRINCE HARRY If he be sicke with ioy, heele recouer   2470
without phisicke.
WARWICKE
Not so much noyse my Lords, sweete prince, speake
        lowe,
The King your father is disposde to sleepe.
CLARENCE
Let vs withdraw into the other roome.
WARWICKE
Wilt please your Grace to go along with vs?
PRINCE HARRY
No, I wil sit and watch heere by the King.
                exeunt all but the King and prince Harry
Why doth the Crowne lie there vpon his pillow,
Being so troublesome a bedfellow?
O polisht perturbation! golden care!
That keepst the ports of Slumber open wide   2480
To many a watchfull night! Sleepe with it now,
Yet not so sound, and halfe so deeply sweete,
As he whose brow (with homely biggen bound)
Snores out the watch of night. O maiestie!
When thou dost pinch thy bearer, thou dost sit
Like a rich armour worne in heate of day,
That scaldst with safty (by his gates of breath)

There lies a dowlny feather which stirs not,
Did he suspire, that light and weightlesse dowlne
2490 Perforce must moue: my gracious lord my father:
This sleepe is sound indeede, this is a sleepe,
That from this golden Rigoll hath diuorst
So many English Kings, thy deaw from me,
Is teares and heauy sorowes of the blood,
Which nature, loue, and filiall tendernesse
Shall (O deare father) pay thee plenteously:
My due from thee is this imperiall Crowne,
Which as immediate from thy place and blood,
Deriues it selfe to me:

     He puts the crowne on his head
                 loe where it sits,
Which God shal guard, and put the worlds whole
2500   strength
Into one giant arme, it shal not force,
This lineal honor from me, this from thee
Will I to mine leaue, as tis left to me.   *exit*
    ⌈*Musicke ceases.*⌉ *The King awakes*

KING
Warwicke, Gloucester, Clarence.
    Enter Warwicke, Gloucester, Clarence

CLARENCE   Doth the King cal?

WARWICKE
What would your Maiestie? how fares your grace?

KING
Why did you leaue me here alone, my lords?

CLARENCE
We left the prince my brother here my liege,
Who vndertooke to sit and watch by you.

KING
The prince of Wales, where is he? let me see him.

WARWICKE
2510 This doore is open, he is gone this way.

GLOUCESTER
He came not through the chamber where we staide.

KING
Where is the Crowne? who took it from my pillow?

WARWICKE
When we withdrew, my liege, we left it here.

KING
The Prince hath tane it hence, go seeke him out:
Is he so hastie, that he doth suppose
My sleepe my death?
Finde him, my lord of Warwicke, chide him hither.
                     exit Warwicke
This part of his conioynes with my disease,
And helps to end me: see, sonnes, what things you
    are,
2520 How quickly nature falls into reuolt,
When gold becomes her obiect?
For this, the foolish ouer-carefull fathers
Haue broke their sleepe with thoughts, their braines
    with care,
Their bones with industry: For this they haue
Ingrossed and pilld vp, the cankred heapes
Of strange atcheeued gold: For this they haue

Beene thoughtfull to inuest their sonnes with arts
And martiall exercises, when like the bee
Culing from euery flower the vertuous sweetes,
Our thighs, packt with waxe, our mouthes with hony, 2530
We bring it to the hiue: and like the bees,
Are murdred for our paines, this bitter taste
Yeelds his engrossements to the ending father,
    Enter Warwicke
Now where is he that will not stay so long,
Till his friend sicknesse haue determind me.

WARWICKE
My Lord, I found the prince in the next roome,
Washing with kindly teares, his gentle cheekes,
With such a deepe demeanour in great sorrow,
That tyranny, which neuer quaft but bloud,
Would by beholding him, haue washt his knife,   2540
With gentle eie-drops, hee is comming hither.

KING
But wherefore did he take away the crowne?
    Enter Harry, with the crowne
Loe where he comes, come hither to me Harry,
(*To the others*) Depart the chamber, leaue vs here
    alone.   *exeunt all but the King and prince Harry*

PRINCE HARRY
I neuer thought to heare you speake againe.

KING
Thy wish was father (Harry,) to that thought:
I stay too long by thee, I weary thee,
Dost thou so hunger for mine emptie chaire,
That thou wilt needes inuest thee with my honors,
Before thy howre be ripe! O foolish youth,   2550
Thou seekst the greatnesse that will ouerwhelme thee,
Stay but a little, for my clowd of dignity
Is held from falling with so weake a wind,
That it will quickly drop: my day is dim,
Thou hast stolne that, which after some few houres,
Were thine, without offence, and at my death,
Thou hast seald vp my expectation,
Thy life did manifest thou lou'dst me not,
And thou wilt haue me die, assurde of it,
Thou hidst a thousand daggers in thy thoughts,   2560
Whom thou hast whetted on thy stony heart,
To stab at halfe an hower of my life.
What, canst thou not forbeare me halfe an hower?
Then get thee gone, and digge my graue thy selfe,
And bid the mery bells ring to thine eare,
That thou art crowned, not that I am dead:
Let all the teares that should bedew my hearse
Be drops of Balme, to sanctifie thy head,
Only compound me with forgotten dust.
Giue that which gaue thee life, vnto the wormes,   2570
Plucke downe my officers, breake my decrees,
For now a time is come to mocke at Forme:
Harry the fift is crownd, vp vanitie,
Downe royall state, all you sage counsailers, hence,
And to the English Court assemble now
From euery region, apes of idlenesse:
Now neighbour confines, purge you of your scumme:
Haue you a ruffin that will sweare, drinke, daunce,

Reuell the night, rob, murder, and commit
2580   The oldest sinnes, the newest kind of waies?
Be happy, he will trouble you no more.
England shal double gild his trebble gilt,
England shall giue him office, honour, might:
For the fift Harry, from curbd licence, plucks
The mussel of restraint, and the wild dogge
Shal flesh his tooth on euery innocent.
O my poore kingdome! sicke with ciuill blowes:
When that my care could not withhold thy riots,
What wilt thou do when riot is thy care?
2590   O thou wilt be a wildernesse againe,
Peopled with woolues, thy old inhabitants.
PRINCE HARRY
     O pardon me, my liege, but for my teares,
The moist impediments vnto my speech,
I had forestald this deere and deep rebuke,
Ere you with griefe had spoke, and I had heard
The course of it so far: there is your crowne:
     ⌈*He returnes the crowne and kneeles*⌉
And he that weares the crowne immortally,
Long gard it yours: if I affect it more,
Then as your honour, and as your renowne,
2600   Let me no more from this obedience rise,
Which my most true and inward duteous spirit,
Teacheth this prostrate and exterior bending.
God witnesse with me: When I here came in,
And found no course of breath within your maiesty,
How cold it strooke my heart! if I do faine,
O let me in my present wildnesse die,
And neuer liue to shew th'incredulous world,
The noble change that I haue purposed.
Comming to looke on you, thinking you dead,
2610   And dead almost, my liege, to thinke you were,
I spake vnto this crowne as hauing sence,
And thus vpbraided it: the care on thee depending,
Hath fed vpon the body of my father,
Therefore thou best of gold, art worst of gold,
Other lesse fine in karrat is more precious,
Preseruing life in medcine potable:
But thou, most fine, most honourd, most renown'd,
Hast eate thy bearer vp: thus my royall liege,
Accusing it, I put it on my head,
2620   To trie with it as with an enemy,
That had before my face murdred my father,
The quarrell of a true inheritour,
But if it did infect my bloud with ioy,
Or swell my thoughts to any straine of pride,
If any rebel or vaine spirit of mine,
Did with the least affection of a welcome,
Giue entertainment to the might of it,
Let God for euer keep it from my head,
And make me as the poorest vassaile is,
2630   That doth with aw and terror kneele to it.
KING   O my sonne,
     God put it in thy mind to take it hence,
That thou mightst win the more thy fathers loue,

Pleading so wisely in excuse of it:
Come hither Harry, sit thou by my bed,
And heare (I thinke) the very latest counsaile
That euer I shal breathe.
     Prince Harry ⌈*rises from kneeling, and*⌉ *sits
     by the bed*
                  God knowes (my sonne)
By what by-paths, and indirect crookt waies,
I met this crowne, and I my selfe know well,
How troublesome it sate vpon my head: 2640
To thee it shall descend with better quiet,
Better opinion, better confirmation,
For al the soyle of the atchieuement goes,
With me into the earth: it seemd in me,
But as an honor snatcht with boistrous hand,
And I had many liuing to vpbraide
My gaine of it, by their assistances,
Which daily grew to quarrell and to bloudshed,
Wounding supposed peace: all these bold feares
Thou seest with perill I haue answered: 2650
For all my raigne hath beene but as a Scene,
Acting that argument: and now my death
Changes the mood, for what in me was purchast,
Fals vpon thee in a more fairer sort.
So thou the garland wearst successiuely,
Yet though thou standst more sure then I could do,
Thou art not firme enough, since griefes are greene,
And all thy friends which thou must make thy friends,
Haue but their stings and teeth newly tane out:
By whose fell working I was first aduaunst,   2660
And by whose power I well might lodge a feare
To be againe displacde: which to auoyde,
I cut them off, and had a purpose, now
To leade out manie to the Holy Land,
Lest rest, and lying stil, might make them looke,
Too neare vnto my state: therefore, my Harry,
Be it thy course to busie giddie mindes
With forraine quarrells, that action hence borne out,
May waste the memory of the former dayes.
More would I, but my lungs are wasted so,   2670
That strength of speech is vtterly denied me:
How I came by the crowne, O God forgiue,
And grant it may with thee in true peace liue.
PRINCE HARRY   My gracious liege,
     You won it, wore it, kept it, gaue it me,
Then plaine and right must my possession be,
Which I with more then with a common paine,
Gainst all the world will rightfully maintaine.
     Enter Iohn of Lancaster ⌈*followed by*⌉ *Warwicke*
     ⌈*and others*⌉
KING
     Looke, looke, here comes my Iohn of Lancaster.
PRINCE IOHN
     Health, peace, and happinesse to my royall father.   2680
KING
     Thou bringst me happinesse and peace sonne Iohn,
But health (alacke) with youthfull wings is flowne

From this bare witherd trunke: vpon thy sight,
My worldly busines makes a period:
Where is my lord of Warwicke?

PRINCE HARRY   My Lord of Warwicke.
⌈*Warwicke comes forward to the King*⌉

KING
Doth any name perticular belong
Vnto the lodging where I first did swound?

WARWICKE
Tis cald Ierusalem, my noble Lord.

KING
Laud be to God, euen there my life must end.
It hath bin prophecide to me many yeares,
I should not die, but in Ierusalem,
2690   Which vainely I supposde the Holy Land:
But beare me to that chamber, there ile lie,
In that Ierusalem shall Harry die.

exeunt, bearing the King in his bed

Sc. 13   *Enter Shallow, ⌈Scilens,⌉ sir Iohn Falstaffe,*
(5.1)   *Bardolfe, and the page*

SHALLOW (*to sir Iohn*) By cock and pie, you shal not away
to night, what Dauy I say?

SIR IOHN You must excuse me master Robert Shallow.

SHALLOW I will not excuse you, you shall not be excusde,
excuses shall not be admitted, there is no excuse shall
serue, you shall not be excusde: why Dauy.

Enter Dauy

DAUY Here sir.

2700   SHALLOW Dauy, Dauy, Dauy, let me see Dauy, let me see,
William Cooke, bid him come hither, sir Iohn, you shal
not be excused.

DAUY Mary sir thus, those precepts can not be serued,
and againe sir, shal we sow the hade land with wheate?

SHALLOW With red wheat Dauy, but for William Cooke
are there no yong pigeons?

DAUY Yes sir, here is now the Smiths note for shooing
and plow-yrons.

SHALLOW Let it be cast and payed: sir Iohn, you shal not
2710   be excused.

DAUY Sir, a new lincke to the bucket must needes be had:
and sir, do you meane to stop any of Williams wages,
about the sacke he lost at Hinkly Faire?

SHALLOW A shall answer it: some pigeons Dauy, a couple
of short legg'd hens, a ioynt of mutton, and any pretty
little tinie Kick-shawes, tell william Cooke.

DAUY Doth the man of warre stay all night sir?

SHALLOW Yea Dauy, I will vse him well, a friend i'th court
is better then a penie in purse: vse his men wel Dauy,
2720   for they are arrant knaues, and will backbite.

DAUY No worse then they are back-bitten sir, for they
haue maruailes foule linnen.

SHALLOW Well conceited Dauy, about thy businesse Dauy.

DAUY I beseech you sir to countenance William Visor of
Woncote against Clement Perkes a'th hill.

SHALLOW There is many complaints Dauy against that
Visor, that Visor is an arrant knaue on my knowledge.

DAUY I graunt your worship that he is a knaue sir: but

yet God forbid sir, but a knaue should haue some
countenance at his friends request, an honest man sir   2730
is able to speake for himselfe, when a knaue is not: I
haue seru'de your worship truly sir this eight yeares,
and I cannot once, or twice in a quarter beare out a
knaue against an honest man, I haue litle credit with
your worship: the knaue is mine honest friend sir,
therfore I beseech you let him be countenaunst.

SHALLOW Go to, I say he shal haue no wrong, look about
Dauy: ⌈*exit Dauy*⌉
where are you sir Iohn? come, off with your boots,
giue me your hand master Bardolfe.   2740

BARDOLFE I am glad to see your worship.

SHALLOW I thank thee with all my heart kind master
Bardolfe, ⌈*to the page*⌉ and welcome my tall fellow, come
sir Iohn.

SIR IOHN Ile follow you good maister Robert Shallow:
exit Shallow ⌈and Scilens⌉
Bardolfe, looke to our horses:
exit Bardolfe ⌈and page⌉
if I were sawed into quantities, I should make foure
dozen of such berded hermites staues as maister
Shallow: it is a wonderfull thing to see the semblable
coherence of his mens spirits, and his, they, by   2750
obseruing him, do beare themselues like foolish Iustices:
hee, by conuersing with them, is turned into a Iustice-
like seruingman, their spirits are so married in
coniunction, with the participation of society, that they
flocke together in consent, like so many wild-geese. If
I had a suite to master Shallow, I would humour his
men with the imputation, of beeing neere their maister:
if to his men, I would curry with maister Shallow, that
no man could better commaund his seruants. It is
certaine, that eyther wise bearing, or ignorant cariage   2760
is caught, as men take diseases one of another: therefore
let men take heede of their company. I will deuise
matter enough out of this Shallow, to keepe prince
Harry in continuall laughter, the wearing out of sixe
fashions, which is foure termes, or two actions, and a
shal laugh without interuallums. O it is much that a
lie, with a slight oathe, and a iest, with a sad browe,
will doe with a fellow that neuer had the ach in his
shoulders: O you shall see him laugh til his face be like
a wet cloake ill laide vp.   2770

SHALLOW (*within*) Sir Iohn.

SIR IOHN I come maister Shallow, I come master Shallow.
exit

Enter Warwike ⌈at one doore,⌉ L. chiefe Iustice ⌈at   Sc. 14
another doore⌉   (5.2)

WARWICKE
How now, my lord chiefe Iustice, whither away?

IUSTICE How doth the King?

WARWICKE
Exceeding well, his cares are now all ended.

IUSTICE
I hope not dead.

WARWICKE   Hees walkt the way of nature,
And to our purposes he liues no more.

IUSTICE

2780 I would his Maiestie had calld me with him:
The seruice that I truely did his life,
Hath left me open to all iniuries.

WARWICKE

Indeede I thinke the yong King loues you not.

IUSTICE

I know he doth not, and do arme my selfe
To welcome the condition of the time,
Which cannot looke more hideously vpon me,
Than I haue drawne it in my fantasie.

Enter Prince Iohn, Thomas of Clarence, and
Humphrey of Gloucester

WARWICKE

Heere come the heauy issue of dead Harry:
O that the liuing Harry had the temper
2790 Of he, the worst of these three gentlemen!
How many Nobles then should holde their places,
That must strike saile to spirites of vile sort?

IUSTICE

O God, I feare all will be ouer-turnd.

PRINCE IOHN

Good morrow coosin Warwicke, good morrow.

GLOUCESTER *and* CLARENCE Good morrow coosin.

PRINCE IOHN

We meete like men that had forgot to speake.

WARWICKE

We do remember, but our argument
Is all too heauy to admit much talke.

PRINCE IOHN

Well, peace be with him that hath made vs heauy.

IUSTICE

2800 Peace be with vs, lest we be heauier.

GLOUCESTER

O good my lord, you haue lost a friend indeede,
And I dare sweare you borrow not that face
Of seeming sorrow, it is sure your owne.

PRINCE IOHN (*to Iustice*)

Though no man be assurde what grace to finde,
You stand in coldest expectation,
I am the sorier, would twere otherwise.

CLARENCE (*to Iustice*)

Well, you must now speake sir Iohn Falstaffe faire,
Which swimmes against your streame of quallitie.

IUSTICE

Sweet princes, what I did, I did in honor,
2810 Led by th'impartiall conduct of my soule.
And neuer shall you see that I will begge
A ragged and forestald remission.
If truth and vpright innocencie faile me,
Ile to the King my maister that is dead,
And tell him who hath sent me after him.

Enter Prince Harry, as King

WARWICKE Here comes the Prince.

IUSTICE

Good morrow, and God saue your maiesty.

PRINCE HARRY

This new and gorgeous garment Maiesty

Sits not so easie on me, as you thinke:
Brothers, you mixe your sadnesse with some feare,   2820
This is the English, not the Turkish court,
Not Amurath an Amurath succeedes,
But Harry Harry: yet be sad, good brothers,
For by my faith it very well becomes you:
Sorrow so royally in you appeares,
That I will deeply put the fashion on,
And weare it in my heart: why then be sad,
But entertaine no more of it, good brothers,
Then a ioynt burden layd vpon vs all,
For me, by heauen (I bid you be assurde)   2830
Ile be your father, and your brother too,
Let me but beare your loue, Ile beare your cares:
Yet weepe that Harries dead, and so will I,
But Harry liues, that shal conuert those teares
By number into howres of happinesse.

PRINCE IOHN, GLOUCESTER, *and* CLARENCE

We hope no other from your maiesty.

PRINCE HARRY

You al looke strangely on me, (*to Iustice*) and you most,
You are I thinke assurde I loue you not.

IUSTICE

I am assurde, if I be measurde rightly,
Your maiesty hath no iust cause to hate me.   2840

PRINCE HARRY

No? how might a prince of my great hopes forget,
So great indignities you laid vpon me?
What, rate, rebuke, and roughly send to prison,
Th'immediate heire of England? was this easie?
May this be washt in lethy and forgotten?

IUSTICE

I then did vse the person of your father,
The image of his power lay then in me,
And in th'administration of his law,
Whiles I was busie for the common wealth,
Your Highnesse pleased to forget my place,   2850
The maiestie and power of law and iustice,
The image of the King whom I presented,
And strooke me in my very seate of iudgement,
Whereon, (as an offendor to your father,)
I gaue bold way to my authority,
And did commit you: if the deed were ill,
Be you contented, wearing now the garland,
To haue a sonne set your decrees at naught?
To plucke downe Iustice from your awful bench?
To trip the course of law, and blunt the sword,   2860
That guards the peace and safetie of your person?
Nay more, to spurne at your most royall image,
And mocke your workings in a second body?
Question your royall thoughts, make the case yours,
Be now the father, and propose a sonne,
Heare your owne dignity so much prophan'd,
See your most dreadfull lawes so loosely slighted,
Behold your selfe so by a sonne disdained:
And then imagine me taking your part,
And in your power soft silencing your sonne,   2870
After this cold considerance sentence me,

And as you are a King, speake in your state,
What I haue done that misbecame my place,
My person, or my lieges soueraigntie.

PRINCE HARRY
You are right Iustice, and you weigh this well,
Therefore still beare the Ballance and the Sword,
And I do wish your honors may encrease,
Til you do liue to see a sonne of mine
Offend you, and obey you as I did:

2880　So shall I liue to speake my fathers words,
Happie am I that haue a man so bold,
That dares do iustice on my proper sonne:
And not lesse happie, hauing such a sonne,
That would deliuer vp his greatnesse so,
Into the hands of Iustice: you did commit me,
For which I do commit into your hand,
Th'vnstained sword that you haue vsde to beare,
With this remembrance, that you vse the same
With the like bold, iust, and impartial spirit,

2890　As you haue done gainst me: there is my hand,
You shall be as a father to my youth,
My voice shall sound as you do prompt mine eare,
And I wil stoope and humble my intents,
To your well practizde wise directions.
And princes all, beleeue me I beseech you,
My father is gone wild into his graue:
For in his toomb lie my affections,
And with his spirites sadly I suruiue,
To mocke the expectation of the world,

2900　To frustrate prophecies, and to race out,
Rotten opinion, who hath writ me downe
After my seeming, the tide of bloud in me
Hath prowdely flowd in vanitie till now:
Now doth it turne, and ebbe backe to the sea,
Where it shall mingle with the state of flouds,
And flow henceforth in formall maiestie.
Now call we our high court of parliament,
And let vs chuse such limbs of noble counsaile,
That the great bodie of our state may goe,

2910　In equall ranke with the best gouernd Nation,
That warre, or peace, or both at once, may be,
As things acquainted and familiar to vs,
(*To Iustice*) In which you father shall haue formost
　　hand:
(*To all*) Our coronation done, we wil accite,
(As I before remembred) all our state,
And (God consigning to my good intents,)
No prince nor peere shall haue iust cause to say,
God shorten Harries happy life one day.　　　　*exeunt*

Sc. 15
(5.3)　　⌜*A table and chaires set forth.*⌝ *Enter sir Iohn
Falstaffe, Shallow, Scilens, Dauy* ⌜*with vessels for
the table*⌝*, Bardolfe, page*

SHALLOW (*to sir Iohn*) Nay you shall see my orchard,

2920　where, in an arbour we will eate a last yeeres pippen
of mine owne graffing, with a dish of carrawaies and
so forth: come coosin Scilens, and then to bed.

SIR IOHN Fore God you haue here a goodly dwelling, and
a rich.

SHALLOW Barraine, barraine, barraine, beggars all,
beggars all sir Iohn, mary good ayre: spread Dauy,
spread Dauy,
　　⌜*Dauy begins to spread the table*⌝
well saide Dauy.

SIR IOHN This Dauy serues you for good vses, hee is your
seruing-man, and your husband.

SHALLOW A good varlet, a good varlet, a very good varlet　2930
sir Iohn: by the mas I haue drunke too much sacke at
supper: a good varlet: now sit downe, now sit downe,
(*to Scilens*) come cosin.

SCILENS A sirra quoth a, we shall
　　⌜*Sings*⌝
　　　Do nothing but eate and make good cheere,
　　　Do nothing but eate and make good cheere,
　　　And praise God for the merry yeere,
　　　When flesh is cheape and females deare,
　　　And lusty laddes roame here and there　　　2940
　　　So merely,
　　　And euer among so merily.

SIR IOHN Theres a merry heart, good M. Silens, ile giue
you a health for that anon.

SHALLOW Good master Bardolfe: some wine, Dauy.

DAUY ⌜*to sir Iohn*⌝ Sweet sir sit, ⌜*to Bardolfe*⌝ ile be with
you anon, ⌜*to sir Iohn*⌝ most sweet sir sit, master Page,
good master Page sit:
　　⌜*All but Dauy sit. Dauy pours wine*⌝
proface, what you want in meate, weele haue in drink,
but you must beare, the heart's al.　　　　　　　2950

SHALLOW Be mery master Bardolfe, and my litle souldier
there, be merry.

SCILENS (*sings*)
　　　Be merry, be mery, my wife has all,
　　　For women are shrowes both short and tall,
　　　Tis merry in hal when beards wags all,
　　　And welcome mery shrouetide,
be mery, be mery.

SIR IOHN I did not thinke master Scilens had bin a man
of this mettall.

SCILENS Who I? I haue beene mery twice and once ere　2960
now.
　　　Enter Dauy ⌜*with a dish of apples*⌝

DAUY Theres a dish of Lether-coates for you.

SHALLOW Dauy?

DAUY Your worship: Ile be with you straight, ⌜*to sir Iohn*⌝
a cup of wine sir.

SCILENS ⌜*sings*⌝
　　　A cup of wine
　　　Thats briske and fine,
　　　And drinke vnto the leman mine,
　　　And a mery heart liues long a.

SIR IOHN Well said master Scilens.　　　　　　　2970

SCILENS And we shall be mery, now comes in the sweete
a'th night.

SIR IOHN Health and long life to you master Scilens.
　　　He drinkes

SCILENS Fill the cuppe, and let it come, ile pledge you a
 mile too'th bottome.

SHALLOW Honest Bardolfe, welcome, if thou wantst any
 thing, and wilt not call, beshrew thy heart, (*to the page*)
 welcome my little tiny theefe, and welcome indeede
 too, Ile drink to master Bardolfe, and to all the cabileros
2980 about London.
  He drinkes

DAUY I hope to see London once ere I die.

BARDOLFE And I might see you there Dauy!

SHALLOW By the mas youle crack a quarte together, ha
 will you not master Bardolfe?

BARDOLFE Yea sir, in a pottle pot.

SHALLOW By Gods liggens I thanke thee, the knaue will
 sticke by thee, I can assure thee that, a wil not out,
 tis true bred!

BARDOLFE And ile stick by him sir.

2990 SHALLOW Why there spoke a King: lacke nothing, be
 mery,
  One knockes at doore within
 looke who's at doore there ho, who knockes?
        ⌜*exit Dauy*⌝
  ⌜*Scilens drinkes*⌝

SIR IOHN ⌜*to Scilens*⌝ Why now you haue done me right.

SCILENS ⌜*sings*⌝ Do me right,
       And dub me Knight,
       Samingo:
 ist not so?

SIR IOHN Tis so.

SCILENS Ist so, why then say an olde man can do
3000 somewhat.
  ⌜*Enter Dauy*⌝

DAUY And't please your worship, theres one Pistoll come
 from the court with newes.

SIR IOHN From the Court? let him come in,
  Enter Pistol
 how now Pistol?

PISTOL Sir Iohn, God saue you.

SIR IOHN What wind blew you hither Pistol?

PISTOL
 Not the ill winde which blowes no man to good:
 sweete Knight, thou art now one of the greatest men
 in this Realme.

3010 SCILENS Birlady I think a be, but goodman Puffe of Barson.

PISTOL Puffe?
 Puffe in thy teeth, most recreant coward, base,
 Sir Iohn, I am thy Pistol and thy frend,
 And helter skelter, haue I rode to thee,
 And tidings do I bring, and luckie ioyes,
 And golden times, and happy news of price.

SIR IOHN I pray thee now deliuer them like a man of this
 world.

PISTOL
 A footre for the world and worldlings base,
3020 I speake of Affrica and golden ioyes.

SIR IOHN
 O base Assirian Knight! what is thy newes?
 Let King Couetua know the truth thereof.

SCILENS ⌜*sings*⌝
 And Robin Hood, Scarlet, and Iohn.

PISTOL
 Shal dunghill curs confront the Helicons?
 And shall good newes be baffled?
 Then Pistoll lay thy head in Furies lap.

SHALLOW Honest gentleman, I know not your breeding.

PISTOL Why then lament therefore.

SHALLOW Giue me pardon sir, if sir you come with newes
 from the court, I take it theres but two waies, either 3030
 to vtter them, or conceale them, I am sir vnder the
 King in some authoritie.

PISTOL
 Vnder which King, Besonian? speake, or die.

SHALLOW
 Vnder King Harry.

PISTOL   Harry the fourth, or fift?

SHALLOW
 Harry the fourth.

PISTOL   A fowtre for thine office:
 Sir Iohn, thy tender lambkin now is King:
 Harry the fifts the man: I speake the truth:
 When Pistol lies, do this, (*making the fig*) and fig me,
 Like the bragging spaniard.

SIR IOHN   What is the old King dead?

PISTOL
 As nayle in doore, the things I speake are iust. 3040

SIR IOHN Away Bardolfe, saddle my horse, M. Robert
 Shallow, choose what office thou wilt in the land, tis
 thine: Pistol, I will double charge thee with dignities.

BARDOLFE O ioyful day!
 I would not take a Knighthood for my fortune.

PISTOL What? I do bring good newes.

SIR IOHN (*to Dauy*) Carry master Scilens to bed:
       ⌜*exit Dauy, with Scilens*⌝
 master Shallow, my lord Shalow, be what thou wilt, I
 am fortunes steward, get on thy boots, weel ride al
 night: ô sweet Pistol, away Bardolf, ⌜*exit Bardolfe*⌝ 3050
 com Pistol, vtter more to me, and withall, deuise
 something to doe thy selfe good, boote, boote master
 Shallow, I know the yong King is sicke for me: let vs
 take any mans horses, the lawes of England are at my
 commandement, blessed are they that haue bin my
 friends, and woe to my Lord chiefe Iustice.

PISTOL
 Let vultures vile seize on his lungs also:
 Where is the life that late I led, say they,
 Why here it is, welcome these plesant dayes. *exeunt*

  Enter Beadles, dragging in hostesse and the whoore Sc. 16
  Doll Tere-sheet   (5.4)

HOSTESSE No, thou arrant knaue, I would to God that I 3060
 might die, that I might haue thee hangd, thou hast
 drawn my shoulder out of ioynt.

I BEADLE The Constables haue deliuered her ouer to mee,
 and shee shal haue whipping cheere I warrant her,
 there hath beene a man or two kild about her.

DOLL Nut-hooke, Nut-hooke, you lie, come on, Ile tell

thee what, thou damnd tripe visagde rascall, and the
child I go with, do miscarry, thou wert better thou
hadst strook thy mother, thou paper-facde villaine.

HOSTESSE O the Lord, that sir Iohn were come! he would
3070 make this a bloody day to some body: but I pray God
the fruite of her wombe miscarry.

I BEADLE If it doe, you shall haue a dozzen of cushions
againe, you haue but eleuen nowe: come, I charge you
both goe with mee, for the man is dead that you and
Pistoll beat amongst you.

DOLL Ile tell you what, you thin man in a censor, I will
haue you as soundly swingde for this, you blewbottle
rogue, you filthy famisht correctioner, if you be not
swingde, Ile forsweare halfe kirtles.

3080 I BEADLE Come, come, you shee-Knight-arrant, come.

HOSTESSE O God, that right should thus orecom might!
wel, of sufferance comes ease.

DOLL Come you rogue, come bring me to a iustice.

HOSTESSE I come, you starude blood-hound.

DOLL Goodman death, goodman bones.

HOSTESSE Thou Atomy, thou.

DOLL Come you thinne thing, come you rascall.

I BEADLE Very well.   exeunt

Sc.17   Enter ⌈two⌉ groomes, strewing rushes
(5.5) I GROOME More rushes, more rushes.
3090 2 GROOME The trumpets haue sounded twice.
⌈I⌉ GROOME Twill be two a clocke ere they come from the
coronation.   exeunt

Enter sir Iohn Falstaffe, Shallow, Pistol, Bardolfe,
and the Page

SIR IOHN Stand heere by me maister Robert Shallow, I
will make the King doe you grace, I will leere vpon
him as a comes by, and do but marke the countenaunce
that he will giue me.

PISTOL God blesse thy lungs good Knight.

SIR IOHN Come heere Pistoll, stand behinde mee. (To
Shallow) O if I had had time to haue made new liueries:
3100 I woulde haue bestowed the thousand pound I borrowed
of you, but tis no matter, this poore shew doth better,
this doth inferre the zeale I had to see him.

⌈SHALLOW⌉ It doth so.

SIR IOHN It shewes my earnestnesse of affection.

PISTOL It doth so.

SIR IOHN My deuotion.

PISTOL It doth, it doth, it doth.

SIR IOHN As it were to ride day & night, and not to
deliberate, not to remember, not to haue pacience to
3110 shift me.

SHALLOW It is most certain.

⌈SIR IOHN⌉ But to stand stained with trauaile, and
sweating with desire to see him, thinking of nothing
els, putting all affaires in obliuion, as if there were
nothing els to bee done, but to see him.

PISTOL Tis *semper idem*, for, *absque hoc nihil est*, tis all in
euery part.

SHALLOW Tis so indeede.

PISTOL
My Knight, I will inflame thy noble liuer,
And make thee rage,   3120
Thy Dol, and Helen of thy noble thoughts,
Is in base durance, and contagious prison,
Halde thither
By most mechanical, and durtie hand:
Rowze vp reuenge from Ebon den, with fell Alectoes
snake,
For Doll is in: Pistoll speakes nought but truth.

SIR IOHN I will deliuer her.
    ⌈Shouts within.⌉ Trumpets sound

PISTOL
There roard the sea, and trumpet Clangor sounds.
    Enter King Harry the fift, prince Iohn, Clarence,
    Gloucester, Lord chiefe Iustice, ⌈and others⌉

SIR IOHN
God saue thy grace King Hall, my royall Hall.

PISTOL
The heauens thee gard and keep, most royal impe of
fame.   3130

SIR IOHN God saue thee, my sweet boy.

KING HARRY
My Lord chiefe iustice, speake to that vaine man.

IUSTICE (to sir Iohn)
Haue you your wits? know you what tis you speake?

SIR IOHN
My King, my Ioue, I speake to thee, my heart.

KING HARRY
I know thee not old man, fall to thy praiers,
How ill white heires becomes a fool and iester,
I haue long dreampt of such a kind of man,
So surfet-sweld, so old, and so prophane:
But being awake, I do despise my dreame,
Make lesse thy body (hence) and more thy grace,   3140
Leaue gourmandizing, know the graue doth gape
For thee, thrice wider then for other men,
Reply not to me with a foole-borne iest,
Presume not that I am the thing I was,
For God doth know, so shall the world perceiue,
That I haue turnd away my former selfe,
So will I those that kept me company:
When thou dost heare I am as I haue bin,
Approch me, and thou shalt be as thou wast,
The tutor and the feeder of my riots: 3150
Till then I banish thee, on paine of death,
As I haue done the rest of my misleaders,
Not to come neare our person by ten mile:
For competence of life, I wil allow you,
That lacke of meanes enforce you not to euills,
And as we heare you do reforme your selues,
We will according to your strengths and qualities,
Giue you aduauncement. (To Iustice) Be it your
charge, my lord,
To see performd the tenure of our word: (to his traine)
set on.   exit King, and his traine

SIR IOHN Master Shallow I ow you a thousand pound.   3160

SHALLOW Yea mary sir Iohn, which I beseech you to let me haue home with me.

SIR IOHN That can hardly be, master Shalow.: do not you grieue at this, I shall be sent for in priuate to him, looke you, hee must seeme thus to the world: feare not your aduauncements, I will be the man yet that shal make you great.

3170 SHALLOW I cannot perceiue how, vnlesse you giue me your dublet, and stuffe me out with straw: I beseech you good sir Iohn let me haue fiue hundred of my thousand.

SIR IOHN Sir I will be as good as my worde, this that you heard was but a collour.

SHALLOW A collor I feare that you will die in sir Iohn.

SIR IOHN Feare no colours, go with me to dinner: come lieftenant Pistol, come Bardolfe, I shall be sent for soone at night.

Enter Lord chiefe Iustice and prince Iohn, with officers

IUSTICE (*to officers*)
Go cary sir Iohn Falstaffe to the Fleet,
3180 Take all his company along with him.

SIR IOHN My lord, my lord.

IUSTICE
I cannot now speake, I will heare you soone,
Take them away.

PISTOL
Si fortuna me tormenta spero me contenta.
exeunt all but prince Iohn and Iustice

PRINCE IOHN
I like this faire proceeding of the Kings,
He hath intent his wonted followers
Shall all be very well prouided for,
But all are banisht till their conuersations
Appeare more wise and modest to the worlde.

3190 IUSTICE And so they are.

PRINCE IOHN
The King hath cald his parlament my lord.

IUSTICE He hath.

PRINCE IOHN
I wil lay ods, that ere this yeere expire,
We beare our ciuil swords and natiue fier,

As farre as France, I heard a bird so sing,
Whose musique, to my thinking, pleasde the King:
Come, will you hence? *exeunt*

Enter Epilogue **Epilogue**

EPILOGUE First my feare then my cursie, last my speech.
My feare, is your displeasure, my cursy, my duty, &
my speech, to beg your pardons: if you looke for a 3200
good speech now, you vndo me, for what I haue to
say is of mine owne making, and what indeed (I should
say) wil (I doubt) proue mine own marring: but to the
purpose, and so to the venture. Be it knowne to you,
as it is very well, I was lately here in the end of a
displeasing play, to pray your patience for it, and to
promise you a better: I did meane indeed to pay you
with this, which if like an il venture it come vnluckily
home, I breake, and you my gentle creditors loose, here
I promisde you I would be, and here I commit my body 3210
to your mercies, bate me some, and I will pay you
some, and (as most debtors do) promise you infinitely.

If my tongue cannot intreate you to acquit mee,
will you commaund me to vse my legges? And yet that
were but light payment, to daunce out of your debt,
but a good conscience will make any possible
satisfaction, and so woulde I: all the Gentlewomen
heere haue forgiuen me, if the Gentlemen will not, then
the Gentlemen doe not agree with the Gentlewomen,
which was neuer seene before in such an assemblie. 3220

One word more I beseech you, if you bee not too
much cloyd with fatte meate, our humble Author will
continue the storie, with sir Iohn in it, and make you
merry with faire Katharine of Fraunce, where (for any
thing I knowe) Falstaffe shall die of a sweat, vnlesse
already a be killd with your harde opinions; for Olde-
castle died a Martyre, and this is not the man: my
tongue is weary, when my legges are too, I wil bid
you, good night: and so kneele downe before you; but
indeed, to pray for the Queene. 3230

⌈*He daunces, then kneeles for applause.*⌉ *Exit*

FINIS

ADDITIONAL PASSAGES

Along with some substantial additions, Shakespeare probably made a number of short excisions when preparing the finished version of the play. The following, present in the Quarto but entirely or substantially omitted in the later Folio text, are the most significant:

A. AFTER 826

and God knows whether those that bal out the ruines of thy linnen shal inherite his kingdom: but the Midwiues say, the children are not in the fault, whereupon the world increases, and kinreds are mightily strengthened.

B. AFTER 'LIQUORS!', 1473

O if this were seene,
The happiest youth viewing his progresse through,
What perills past, what crosses to ensue?
Would shut the booke and sit him downe and die:

C. AFTER 'FAMINE', 1834

yet lecherous as a monkie, & the whores cald him mandrake, a came euer in the rereward of the fashion, and sung those tunes to the ouer-schutcht huswiues, that he heard the Car-men whistle, and sware they were his fancies or his good-nights,

MUCH ADOE ABOUT NOTHING

Much adoe about Nothing is not mentioned in the list of plays by Shakespeare given by Francis Meres in his *Palladis Tamia*, published in the autumn of 1598. Certain speech-prefixes of the first edition, published in 1600, suggest that as Shakespeare wrote he had in mind for the role of Dogbery the comic actor Will Kemp, who is believed to have left the Lord Chamberlain's Men during 1599. Probably Shakespeare wrote the play between summer 1598 and spring 1599.

The action is set in Sicily, where Don Pedro, Prince of Arragon, has recently defeated his half-brother, the bastard Don Iohn, in a military engagement. Apparently reconciled, they return to the capital, Messina, as guests of the Governor, Leonato. There Count Claudio, a young nobleman serving in Don Pedro's army, falls in love with Hero, Leonato's daughter, whom Don Pedro woos on his behalf. The play's central plot, written mainly in verse, shows how Don Iohn maliciously deceives Claudio into believing that Hero has taken a lover on the eve of her marriage, causing Claudio to repudiate her publicly, at the altar. This is a variation on an old tale that existed in many versions; it had been told in Italian verse by Ariosto, in his *Orlando Furioso* (1516, translated into English verse by Sir John Harington, 1591), in Italian prose by Matteo Bandello in his *Novelle* (1554, adapted into French by P. de Belleforest, 1569), in English prose by George Whetstone (*The Rocke of Regard*, 1576), in English verse by Edmund Spenser (*The Faerie Queene*, Book 2, canto 4, 1590), and in a number of plays including Luigi Pasqualigo's *Il Fedele* (1579), adapted into English—perhaps by Anthony Munday—as *Fedele and Fortunio* (published in 1583). Shakespeare, whose plot is an independent reworking of the traditional story, seems to owe most to Ariosto and Bandello, perhaps indirectly.

Don Iohn's deception, with its tragicomical resolution, is offset by a parallel plot written mainly in prose, portraying another, more light-hearted deception, by which Hero's cousin, Beatrice, and Benedicke—friend of Don Pedro and Claudio—are tricked into acknowledging, first to themselves and then to each other, that they are in love. This part of the play seems to be of Shakespeare's invention: the juxtaposition of this clever, sophisticated, apparently unillusioned pair with the more naïve Claudio and Hero recalls Shakespeare's earlier contrast of romantic and antiromantic attitudes to love and marriage in *The Taming of the Shrew*. The play's third main strand is provided by Constable Dogbery, his partner Verges, and the Watchmen, clearly English rather than Sicilian in origin. Although Benedicke and Beatrice are, technically, subordinate characters, they have dominated the imagination of both readers and playgoers.

The Quarto (upon which our text is based) was apparently printed from Shakespeare's own papers.

THE NAMES OF THE ACTORS

DON PEDRO, Prince of Arragon

BENEDICKE, of Padua
CLAUDIO, of Florence
} Lords, companions of Don Pedro

BALTHASAR, attendant on Don Pedro, a singer

DON IOHN, the bastard brother of Don Pedro

BORACHIO
CONRADE
} followers of Don Iohn

LEONATO, Gouernour of Messina

HERO, his daughter

BEATRICE, an orphan, his neece

ANTHONIO, an old man, brother of Leonato

MARGARET
VRSULA
} waiting gentlewomen attendant on Hero

FRIER Francis

DOGBERY, the Constable in charge of the watch
VERGES, the Headborough, Dogberys partner
A SEXTON
Men of the WATCH

A BOY, seruing Benedicke
Attendants and Messengers

610

Much adoe about Nothing

Sc. 1
(1.1)

Enter Leonato gouernour of Messina, Hero his
daughter, and Beatrice his neece, with a messenger

LEONATO I learne in this letter, that don Pedro of Arragon comes this night to Messina.

MESSENGER He is very neare by this, he was not three leagues off when I left him.

LEONATO How many gentlemen haue you lost in this action?

MESSENGER But few of any sort, and none of name.

LEONATO A victory is twice it selfe, when the atchiuer brings home ful numbers: I find here, that don Pedro
10 hath bestowed much honour on a yong Florentine called Claudio.

MESSENGER Much deseru'd on his part, and equally remembred by don Pedro, he hath borne himselfe beyond the promise of his age, doing in the figure of a lamb, the feats of a lion, he hath indeed better bettred expectation then you must expect of me to tell you how.

LEONATO He hath an vnckle here in Messina will be very much glad of it.

20 MESSENGER I haue already deliuered him letters, and there appeares much ioy in him, euen so much, that ioy could not shew it selfe modest enough, without a badge of bitternesse.

LEONATO Did he breake out into teares?

MESSENGER In great measure.

LEONATO A kind ouerflow of kindnesse, there are no faces truer then those that are so washt, how much better is it to weepe at ioy, then to ioy at weeping?

BEATRICE I pray you, is Signior Mountanto returnd from
30 the warres or no?

MESSENGER I know none of that name, ladie, there was none such in the army of any sort.

LEONATO What is he that you aske for neece?

HERO My cosen meanes Signior Benedicke of Padua.

MESSENGER O hee's returnd, and as pleasant as euer he was.

BEATRICE He set vp his bills here in Messina, and challengde Cupid at the Flight, and my vncles foole reading the chalenge subscribde for Cupid, and
40 challengde him at the Burbolt: I pray you, how many hath he kild and eaten in these warres? but how many hath he kild? for indeede I promised to eate all of his killing.

LEONATO Faith neece you taxe Signior Benedicke too much, but heele be meet with you, I doubt it not.

MESSENGER He hath done good seruice lady in these warres.

BEATRICE You had musty vittaile, and he hath holpe to eate it, he is a very valiaunt trencher man, he hath an
50 excellent stomacke.

MESSENGER And a good souldier too, lady.

BEATRICE And a good souldiour to a Lady, but what is he to a Lord?

MESSENGER A lord to a lord, a man to a man, stufft with al honorable vertues.

BEATRICE It is so indeed, he is no lesse then a stuft man, but for the stuffing wel, we are al mortall.

LEONATO You must not, sir, mistake my neece, there is a kind of mery warre betwixt Signior Benedicke and her, they neuer meet but there's a skirmish of wit betweene 60 them.

BEATRICE Alas he gets nothing by that, in our last conflict, 4 of his fiue wits went halting off, and now is the whole man gouernd with one, so that if he haue wit enough to keep himself warm, let him beare it for a difference between himself and his horse, for it is all the wealth that he hath left, to be known a reasonable creature, who is his companion now? he hath euery month a new sworne brother.

MESSENGER Ist possible? 70

BEATRICE Very easily possible, he weares his faith but as the fashion of his hat, it euer changes with the next blocke.

MESSENGER I see lady the gentleman is not in your bookes.

BEATRICE No, and he were, I would burne my study, but I pray you who is his companion? is there no yong squarer now that will make a voyage with him to the diuell?

MESSENGER He is most in the companie of the right noble Claudio. 80

BEATRICE O Lord, he will hang vpon him like a disease, hee is sooner caught than the pestilence, and the taker runs presently madde, God help the noble Claudio, if he haue caught the Benedict, it will cost him a thousand pound ere a be cured.

MESSENGER I will holde friends with you Ladie.

BEATRICE Do good friend.

LEONATO You will neuer runne madde niece.

BEATRICE No, not till a hote Ianuary.

MESSENGER Don Pedro is approacht. 90

Enter don Pedro, Claudio, Benedicke, Balthasar and
Iohn the bastard

DON PEDRO Good signior Leonato, are you come to meet your trouble: the fashion of the world is, to auoyd cost, and you incounter it.

LEONATO Neuer came trouble to my house, in the likenesse of your grace, for trouble being gone, comfort should remaine: but when you depart from mee, sorrow abides, and happines takes his leaue.

DON PEDRO You embrace your charge too willingly: I thincke this is your daughter.

LEONATO Her mother hath many times tolde me so. 100

BENEDICKE Were you in doubt sir that you askt her?

LEONATO Signior Benedicke, no, for then were you a child.

DON PEDRO You haue it full Benedicke, wee may ghesse by this, what you are, being a man, truely the Lady fathers her selfe: be happy Lady, for you are like an honourable father.

BENEDICKE If Signior Leonato be her father, she would not haue his head on her shoulders for all Messina as like him as she is.

110 BEATRICE I wonder that you will still be talking, signior Benedicke, no body markes you.

BENEDICKE What my deere lady Disdaine! are you yet liuing?

BEATRICE Is it possible Disdaine should die, while she hath such meete foode to feede it, as signior Benedicke? Curtesie it selfe must conuert to Disdaine, if you come in her presence.

BENEDICKE Then is curtesie a turne-coate, but it is certaine I am loued of all Ladies, onelie you excepted: and I 120 would I could finde in my heart that I had not a hard heart, for truely I loue none.

BEATRICE A deere happinesse to women, they would else haue beene troubled with a pernitious suter, I thanke God and my cold blood, I am of your humour for that, I had rather heare my dog barke at a crow, than a man sweare he loues me.

BENEDICKE God keepe your Ladiship stil in that mind, so some Gentleman or other shall scape a predestinate scratcht face.

130 BEATRICE Scratching could not make it worse, and twere such a face as yours were.

BENEDICKE Well, you are a rare parrat teacher.

BEATRICE A bird of my tongue, is better than a beast of yours.

BENEDICKE I would my horse had the speed of your tongue, and so good a continuer, but keep your way a Gods name, I haue done.

BEATRICE You always end with a iades tricke, I knowe you of olde.

140 DON PEDRO That is the summe of all, Leonato. Signior Claudio, and signior Benedicke, my deere friend Leonato, hath inuited you all, I tell him we shall stay here, at the least a moneth, and he heartily praies some occasion may detaine vs longer, I dare sweare he is no hypocrite, but praies from his heart.

LEONATO If you sweare, my lord, you shall not be forsworne, (to Don Iohn) let mee bidde you welcome, my lord, being reconciled to the Prince your brother, I owe you all duetie.

150 DON IOHN I thanke you, I am not of many wordes, but I thanke you.

LEONATO (to Don Pedro) Please it your grace leade on?

DON PEDRO Your hand Leonato, we wil go together.

Exeunt. Manent Benedicke & Claudio

CLAUDIO Benedicke, didst thou note the daughter of Signior Leonato?

BENEDICKE I noted her not, but I lookte on her.

CLAUDIO Is she not a modest yong ladie?

BENEDICKE Do you question me as an honest man should doe, for my simple true iudgement? or would you haue me speake after my custome, as being a professed tyrant 160 to their sex?

CLAUDIO No, I pray thee speake in sober iudgement.

BENEDICKE Why yfaith me thinks shees too low for a hie praise, too browne for a faire praise, and too litle for a great praise, onlie this commendation I can affoord her, that were shee other then she is, she were vnhansome, and being no other, but as she is, I do not like her.

CLAUDIO Thou thinkest I am in sport, I pray thee tell mee truelie how thou lik'st her.

BENEDICKE Would you buie her that you enquier after 170 her?

CLAUDIO Can the world buie such a iewel?

BENEDICKE Yea, and a case to putte it into, but speake you this with a sad brow? or doe you play the flowting iacke, to tell vs Cupid is a good Hare-finder, and Vulcan a rare Carpenter: Come, in what key shall a man take you to go in the song?

CLAUDIO In mine eie, shee is the sweetest Ladie that euer I lookt on.

BENEDICKE I can see yet without spectacles, and I see no 180 such matter: theres her cosin, and she were not possest with a fury, exceedes her as much in beautie, as the first of Maie dooth the last of December: but I hope you haue no intent to turne husband, haue you?

CLAUDIO I would scarce trust my selfe, though I had sworne the contrarie, if Hero would be my wife.

BENEDICKE Ist come to this? in faith hath not the worlde one man but he will weare his cappe with suspition? shall I neuer see a batcheller of three score againe? go to yfaith, and thou wilt needes thrust thy necke into a 190 yoke, weare the print of it, and sigh away sundaies: looke, don Pedro is returned to seeke you.

Enter don Pedro

DON PEDRO What secret hath held you here, that you followed not to Leonatoes?

BENEDICKE I would your Grace would constraine me to tell.

DON PEDRO I charge thee on thy allegeance.

BENEDICKE You heare, Count Claudio, I can be secret as a dumb man, I woulde haue you thinke so (but on my allegiance, marke you this, on my allegiance) he is in 200 loue, with who? now that is your Graces part: marke how short his answer is, with Hero Leonatoes short daughter.

CLAUDIO If this were so, so were it vttred.

BENEDICKE Like the olde tale, my Lord, it is not so, nor twas not so: but indeede, God forbid it should be so.

CLAUDIO If my passion change not shortly, God forbid it should be otherwise.

DON PEDRO Amen, if you loue her, for the Lady is very well worthy. 210

CLAUDIO You speake this to fetch me in, my Lord.

DON PEDRO By my troth I speake my thought.

CLAUDIO And in faith, my Lord, I spoke mine.

BENEDICKE And by my two faiths and troths, my Lorde, I spoke mine.

CLAUDIO That I loue her, I feele.

DON PEDRO That she is worthy, I know.

BENEDICKE That I neither feele how she should be loued, nor know how she should be worthie, is the opinion that fire can not melt out of me, I will die in it at the stake.

DON PEDRO Thou wast euer an obstinate heretique in the despight of Beauty.

CLAUDIO And neuer could maintaine his part, but in the force of his wil.

BENEDICKE That a woman conceiued me, I thanke her: that she brought me vp, I likewise giue her most humble thankes: but that I will haue a rechate winded in my forehead, or hang my bugle in an inuisible baldricke, all women shall pardon mee: because I will not doe them the wrong to mistrust any, I will doe my selfe the right to trust none: and the fine is, (for the which I may go the finer,) I will liue a bacheller.

DON PEDRO I shall see thee ere I die, looke pale with loue.

BENEDICKE With anger, with sickenesse, or with hunger, my Lord, not with loue: proue that euer I loose more blood with loue then I will get againe with drinking, picke out mine eies with a Ballad-makers penne, and hang me vp at the doore of a brothel house for the signe of blinde Cupid.

DON PEDRO Well, if euer thou dost fall from this faith, thou wilt prooue a notable argument.

BENEDICKE If I do, hang me in a bottle like a Cat, and shoote at me, and he that hits me, let him be clapt on the shoulder, and calld Adam.

DON PEDRO Well, as time shal trie: in time the sauage bull doth beare the yoake.

BENEDICKE The sauage bull may, but if euer the sensible Benedicke beare it, plucke off the bulls hornes, and set them in my forehead, and let me be vildly painted, and in such great letters as they write, here is good horse to hyre: let them signifie vnder my signe, here you may see Benedicke the married man.

CLAUDIO If this should euer happen, thou wouldst be horn madde.

DON PEDRO Nay, if Cupid haue not spent all his quiuer in Venice, thou wilt quake for this shortly.

BENEDICKE I looke for an earthquake too then.

DON PEDRO Well, you will temporize with the howres, in the meane time, good signior Benedicke, repaire to Leonatoes, commend me to him, and tell him I will not faile him at supper, for indeede he hath made great preparation.

BENEDICKE I haue almost matter enough in mee for suche an Embassage, and so I commit you.

CLAUDIO To the tuition of God: from my house if I had it.

DON PEDRO The sixt of Iuly: your louing friend Benedicke.

BENEDICKE Nay mocke not, mocke not, the body of your discourse is sometime guarded with fragments, and the guardes are but slightly basted on neither, ere you flowt old ends any further, examine your conscience, and so I leaue you.   *exit*

CLAUDIO

My liege, your Highnesse nowe may doe mee good.

DON PEDRO

My loue is thine to teach, teach it but how,
And thou shalt see how apt it is to learne
Any hard lesson that may do thee good.

CLAUDIO

Hath Leonato any sonne, my lord?

DON PEDRO

No childe but Hero, shees his onely heire:
Doost thou affect her Claudio?

CLAUDIO   O my lord,   290
When you went onward on this ended action,
I lookt vpon her with a souldiers eie,
That likt, but had a rougher taske in hand,
Than to driue liking to the name of loue:
But now I am returnde, and that warre-thoughts,
Haue left their places vacant: in their roomes,
Come thronging soft and delicate desires,
All prompting mee how faire yong Hero is,
Saying I likt her ere I went to warres.

DON PEDRO

Thou wilt be like a louer presently,   290
And tire the hearer with a booke of words,
If thou dost loue faire Hero, cherish it,
And I wil breake with hir, and with her father,
And thou shalt haue her: wast not to this end,
That thou beganst to twist so fine a storie?

CLAUDIO

How sweetly you do minister to loue,
That know loues griefe by his complexion!
But lest my liking might too sodaine seeme,
I would haue salude it with a longer treatise.

DON PEDRO

What need the bridge much broder then the flood?   300
The fairest graunt is the necessitie:
Looke what wil serue is fit: tis once, thou louest,
And I wil fit thee with the remedie,
I know we shall haue reuelling to night,
I wil assume thy part in some disguise,
And tell faire Hero I am Claudio,
And in her bosome ile vnclaspe my heart,
And take her hearing prisoner with the force
And strong incounter of my amorous tale:
Then after, to her father will I breake,   310
And the conclusion is, she shal be thine,
In practise let vs put it presently.   *exeunt*

Enter Leonato and Anthonio, an old man brother to   Sc. 2
Leonato, seuerally   (1.2)

LEONATO How now brother, where is my cosen your sonne, hath he prouided this musique?

ANTHONIO He is very busie about it, but brother, I can tell you strange newes that you yet dreampt not of.

LEONATO Are they good?

ANTHONIO As the euent stampes them, but they haue a good couer: they shew well outward, the prince and Count Claudio walking in a thicke pleached alley in   320
mine orchard, were thus much ouer-heard by a man of mine: the prince discouered to Claudio that he loued my niece your daughter, and meant to acknowledge it

this night in a daunce, and if he found her accordant, he meant to take the present time by the top, and instantly breake with you of it.

LEONATO Hath the fellow any wit that told you this?

ANTHONIO A good sharp fellow, I wil send for him, and question him your selfe.

330 LEONATO No, no, we wil hold it as a dreame til it appeare it self: but I will acquaint my daughter withall, that she may bee the better prepared for an answer, if peraduenture this be true: go you and tel hir of it:

⌈*Enter attendants*⌉

coosins, you know what you haue to doe, O I crie you mercie friend, go you with me and I wil vse your skill: good cosin haue a care this busie time.   *exeunt*

Sc. 3   *Enter sir Iohn the bastard, and Conrade his*
(1.3)   *companion*

CONRADE What the goodyeere my lord, why are you thus out of measure sad?

340 DON IOHN There is no measure in the occasion that breeds it, therfore the sadnesse is without limit.

CONRADE You should heare reason.

DON IOHN And when I haue heard it, what blessing brings it?

CONRADE If not a present remedy, at least a patient sufferance.

DON IOHN I wonder that thou (being as thou saist, thou art, borne vnder Saturne) goest about to apply a morall medicine, to a mortifying mischiefe: I cannot hide what I am: I must be sad when I haue cause, and smile at 350 no mans iests, eate when I haue stomack, and wait for no mans leisure: sleep when I am drowsie, and tend on no mans businesse, laugh when I am mery, and claw no man in his humor.

CONRADE Yea but you must not make the full show of this till you may do it without controllment, you haue of late stoode out against your brother, and he hath tane you newly into his grace, where it is impossible you should take true root, but by the faire weather that you make your self, it is needful that you frame 360 the season for your owne haruest.

DON IOHN I had rather be a canker in a hedge, then a rose in his grace, and it better fits my bloud to be disdain'd of all, then to fashion a cariage to rob loue from any: in this (thogh I cannot be said to be a flatering honest man) it must not be denied but I am a plain dealing villaine, I am trusted with a mussel, and enfraunchisde with a clogge, therfore I haue decreed, not to sing in my cage: if I had my mouth I would bite: if I had my liberty I would do my liking: 370 in the mean time, let me be that I am, and seeke not to alter me.

CONRADE Can you make no vse of your discontent?

DON IOHN I make all vse of it, for I vse it only. Who comes here?

Enter Borachio

what newes Borachio?

BORACHIO I came yonder from a great supper, the prince

your brother is royally entertain'd by Leonato, and I can giue you intelligence of an intended mariage.

DON IOHN Wil it serue for any model to build mischiefe on? what is he for a foole that betrothes himselfe to 380 vnquietnesse?

BORACHIO Mary it is your brothers right hand.

DON IOHN Who, the most exquisite Claudio?

BORACHIO Euen he.

DON IOHN A proper squier, and who, and who, which way looks he?

BORACHIO Mary one Hero the daughter and heire of Leonato.

DON IOHN A very forward March-chicke, how came you to this?   390

BORACHIO Being entertain'd for a perfumer, as I was smoaking a musty roome, comes me the prince and Claudio, hand in hand in sad conference: I whipt me behind the arras, and there heard it agreed vpon, that the prince should wooe Hero for himselfe, and hauing obtain'd her, giue her to Counte Claudio.

DON IOHN Come, come, let vs thither, this may proue food to my displeasure, that yong start-vp hath all the glory of my ouerthrow: if I can crosse him any way, I blesse my selfe euery way, you are both sure, and wil assist 400 me.

CONRADE To the death my Lord.

DON IOHN Let vs to the great supper, their cheere is the greater that I am subdued, would the cooke were a my mind, shall we go proue whats to be done?

BORACHIO Weele wait vpon your lordship.   *exeunt*

Enter Leonato, Anthonio his brother, Hero his   **Sc. 4**
daughter, Beatrice his neece, ⌈Margaret, and   **(2.1)**
Vrsula⌉

LEONATO Was not counte Iohn here at supper?

ANTHONIO I saw him not.

BEATRICE How tartely that gentleman lookes, I neuer can see him but I am heart-burn'd an hower after.   410

HERO He is of a very melancholy disposition.

BEATRICE He were an excellent man that were made iust in the mid-way between him and Benedick, the one is too like an image and saies nothing, and the other too like my ladies eldest sonne, euermore tatling.

LEONATO Then halfe signior Benedickes tongue in Counte Iohns mouth, and halfe Counte Iohns melancholy in Signior Benedickes face.

BEATRICE With a good legge and a good foote vnckle, and money inough in his purse, such a man would winne 420 any woman in the world if a could get her good will.

LEONATO By my troth neece thou wilt neuer get thee a husband, if thou be so shrewd of thy tongue.

ANTHONIO Infaith shees too curst.

BEATRICE Too curst is more then curst, I shall lessen Gods sending that way, for it is saide, God sends a curst cow short hornes, but to a cow too curst, he sends none.

LEONATO So, by being too curst, God will send you no hornes.

BEATRICE Iust, if he send me no husband, for the which 430

blessing, I am at him vpon my knees euery morning
and euening: Lord, I could not endure a husband with
a beard on his face, I had rather lie in the woollen!

LEONATO You may light on a husband that hath no beard.

BEATRICE What should I do with him, dresse him in my
apparell and make him my waiting gentlewoman? he
that hath a beard, is more then a youth: and he that
hath no beard, is lesse then a man: and he that is
more then a youth, is not for me, and he that is lesse
440 then a man, I am not for him, therefore I will euen
take sixpence in earnest of the Berrord, and leade his
apes into hell.

LEONATO Well then, go you into hell.

BEATRICE No but to the gate, and there will the diuell
meete me like an old cuckold with hornes on his head,
and say, get you to heauen Beatrice, get you to heauen,
heeres no place for you maids, so deliuer I vp my apes
and away to saint Peter for the heauens, he shewes
me where the Batchellers sit, and there liue we as mery
450 as the day is long.

ANTHONIO (to Hero) Well neece, I trust you will be rulde
by your father.

BEATRICE Yes faith, it is my cosens duetie to make cursie
and say, father, as it please you: but yet for all that
cosin, let him be a handsome fellow, or else make an
other cursie, and say, father, as it please me.

LEONATO Well neece, I hope to see you one day fitted
with a husband.

BEATRICE Not til God make men of some other mettal then
460 earth, would it not grieue a woman to be ouer-masterd
with a peece of valiant dust? to make an account of
her life to a clod of waiward marle? no vnckle, ile
none: Adams sonnes are my brethren, and truely I
holde it a sinne to match in my kinred.

LEONATO (to Hero) Daughter, remember what I told you,
if the prince do solicite you in that kind, you know
your answer.

BEATRICE The fault will be in the musique cosin, if you
be not wooed in good time: if the prince be too
470 important, tell him there is measure in euery thing,
and so daunce out the answer, for here me Hero,
wooing, wedding, and repenting, is as a Scotch ijgge,
a measure, and a cinquepace: the first suite is hot and
hasty like a Scotch ijgge (and ful as fantasticall) the
wedding manerly modest (as a measure) full of state
and aunchentry, and then comes Repentance, and with
his bad legs falls into the cinquepace faster and faster,
til he sincke into his graue.

LEONATO Cosin you apprehend passing shrewdly.

480 BEATRICE I haue a good eie vnckle, I can see a church by
day-light.

LEONATO The reuellers are entring brother, make good
roome.

*Enter prince Pedro, Claudio, Benedicke, and
Balthaser, all masked, Don Iohn, and Borachio,
⌈with a drummer⌉*

DON PEDRO (to Hero) Lady will you walke a bout with your
friend?

HERO So, you walke softly, and looke sweetly, and say
nothing, I am yours for the walke, and especially when
I walk away.

DON PEDRO With me in your company.

HERO I may say so when I please.   490

DON PEDRO And when please you to say so?

HERO When I like your fauour, for God defend the lute
should be like the case.

DON PEDRO
My visor is Philemons roofe, within the house is Ioue.

HERO
Why then your visor should be thatcht.

DON PEDRO   Speake low if you speake loue.
They moue aside

⌈BALTHASAR⌉ (to Margaret) Well, I would you did like me.

MARGARET So would not I for your owne sake, for I haue
many ill qualities.

⌈BALTHASAR⌉ Which is one?

MARGARET I say my praiers alowd.   500

⌈BALTHASAR⌉ I loue you the better, the hearers may cry
Amen.

MARGARET God match me with a good dauncer.

BALTHASAR Amen.

MARGARET And God keepe him out of my sight when the
daunce is done: answer Clarke.

BALTHASAR No more words, the Clarke is answered.
They moue aside

VRSULA (to Anthonio) I know you well enough, you are
signior Anthonio.

ANTHONIO At a word I am not.   510

VRSULA I knowe you by the wagling of your head.

ANTHONIO To tell you true, I counterfeit him.

VRSULA You coulde neuer doe him so ill well, vnlesse you
were the very man: heeres his drie hand vp and downe,
you are he, you are he.

ANTHONIO At a word, I am not.

VRSULA Come, come, do you thinke I do not know you
by your excellent wit? can vertue hide it selfe? go to,
mumme, you are he, graces will appeere, and theres
an end.   520
They moue aside

BEATRICE (to Benedicke) Will you not tell me who tolde
you so?

BENEDICKE No, you shall pardon me.

BEATRICE Nor will you not tell me who you are?

BENEDICKE Not now.

BEATRICE That I was disdainefull, and that I had my good
wit out of the hundred mery tales: wel, this was signior
Benedick that said so.

BENEDICKE Whats he?

BEATRICE I am sure you know him well enough.   530

BENEDICKE Not I, beleeue me.

BEATRICE Did he neuer make you laugh?

BENEDICKE I pray you what is he?

BEATRICE Why he is the princes ieaster, a very dul fool,
only his gift is, in deuising impossible slaunders, none
but Libertines delight in him, and the commendation
is not in his wit, but in his villanie, for he both pleases

men and angers them, and then they laugh at him, and beate him: I am sure he is in the Fleete, I would
540 he had boorded me.

BENEDICKE When I know the Gentleman, ile tell him what you say.

BEATRICE Do, do, heele but break a comparison or two on me, which peraduĕture, (not markt, or not laught at) strikes him into melancholy, and then theres a partrige wing saued, for the foole will eate no supper that night:
    ⌈*Musicke*⌉
wee must follow the leaders.

BENEDICKE In euery good thing.

550 BEATRICE Nay, if they leade to any ill, I will leaue them at the next turning.
    Dance. Exeunt all but Don Iohn, Borachio, and
    Claudio

DON IOHN (*aside to Borachio*) Sure my brother is amorous on Hero, and hath withdrawne her father to breake with him about it: the Ladies follow her, and but one visor remaines.

BORACHIO (*aside to Don Iohn*) And that is Claudio, I knowe him by his bearing.

DON IOHN Are not you signior Benedicke?

CLAUDIO You know me well, I am he.

560 DON IOHN Signior, you are very neere my brother in his loue, he is enamour'd on Hero, I pray you disswade him from her, she is no equall for his birth, you may doe the parte of an honest man in it.

CLAUDIO How know you he loues her?

DON IOHN I heard him sweare his affection.

BORACHIO So did I too, and he swore hee would marry her to night.

DON IOHN Come let vs to the banquet.
    exeunt: manet Claudio

CLAUDIO
Thus answer I in name of Benedicke,
570 But heare these ill newes with the eares of Claudio:
Tis certaine so, the Prince wooes for himselfe,
Friendship is constant in all other things,
Saue in the office and affaires of loue:
Therefore all hearts in loue vse their owne tongues.
Let euery eie negotiate for it selfe,
And trust no Agent: for Beauty is a witch,
Against whose charmes, faith melteth into blood:
This is an accident of hourely proofe,
Which I mistrusted not: farewel therefore Hero.
    Enter Benedicke
580 BENEDICKE Count Claudio.

CLAUDIO Yea, the same.

BENEDICKE Come, will you go with me?

CLAUDIO Whither?

BENEDICKE Euen to the next willow, about your owne busines, county: what fashion will you weare the garland of? about your necke, like an Vsurers chaine? or vnder your arme, like a Lieutenants scarffe? you must weare it one way, for the prince hath got your Hero.

CLAUDIO I wish him ioy of her.   590

BENEDICKE Why thats spoken like an honest Drouier, so they sell bullockes: but did you thinke the Prince would haue serued you thus?

CLAUDIO I pray you leaue me.

BENEDICKE Ho now you strike like the blindman, twas the boy that stole your meate, and youle beate the post.

CLAUDIO If it will not be, ile leaue you.   *exit*

BENEDICKE Alas poore hurt foule, now will hee creepe into sedges: but that my Ladie Beatrice should know me, and not know mee: the princes foole! hah, it may be   600 I goe vnder that title because I am merry: yea but so I am apte to doe my selfe wrong: I am not so reputed, it is the base (though bitter) disposition of Beatrice, that puts the world into her person, and so giues me out: well, ile be reuenged as I may.
    Enter Don Pedro the Prince

DON PEDRO Now signior, wheres the Counte, did you see him?

BENEDICKE Troth my lord, I haue played the part of Ladie Fame, I found him heere as melancholy as a Lodge in a Warren, I tolde him, and I thinke I tolde him true,   610 that your grace had got the goodwil of this yoong Lady, and I offred him my company to a willow tree, either to make him a garland, as being forsaken, or to binde him vp a rod, as being worthie to bee whipt.

DON PEDRO To be whipt, whats his fault?

BENEDICKE The flatte transgression of a Schoole-boy, who being ouer-ioyed with finding a birds nest, shewes it his companion, and he steales it.

DON PEDRO Wilt thou make a trust a transgression? the transgression is in the stealer.   620

BENEDICKE Yet it had not beene amisse the rodde had beene made, & the garland too, for the garland he might haue worn himselfe, and the rodde he might haue bestowed on you, who (as I take it) haue stolne his birds nest.

DON PEDRO I wil but teach them to sing, and restore them to the owner.

BENEDICKE If their singing answer your saying, by my faith you say honestly.

DON PEDRO The ladie Beatrice hath a quarrell to you, the   630 Gentleman that daunst with her, told her shee is much wrongd by you.

BENEDICKE O shee misusde me past the indurance of a blocke: an oake but with one greene leafe on it, would haue answered her: my very visor beganne to assume life, and scold with her: she tolde me, not thinking I had beene my selfe, that I was the Princes iester, that I was duller than a great thawe, huddleing iest vpon iest, with such impossible conueiance vpon me, that I stoode like a man at a marke, with a whole army   640 shooting at me: she speakes poynyards, and euery word stabbes: if her breath were as terrible as her terminations, there were no liuing neere her, shee would infect to the north starre: I woulde not marry her, though shee were indowed with al that Adam had left him before he transgrest, she would haue made

Hercules haue turnd spit, yea, and haue cleft his club
to make the fire too: come, talke not of her, you shall
find her the infernall Ate in good apparell, I would to
650 God some scholler woulde coniure her, for certainely,
while she is heere, a man may liue as quiet in hell, as
in a sanctuarie, and people sinne vpon purpose, because
they would goe thither, so indeede all disquiet, horrour,
and perturbation followes her.

*Enter Claudio and Beatrice, ⌜and Leonato with
Hero⌝*

DON PEDRO Looke heere she comes.

BENEDICKE Will your grace command me any seruice to
the worldes end? I will go on the slightest arrand now
to the Antypodes that you can deuise to send mee on:
I will fetch you a tooth-picker now from the furthest
660 inch of Asia: bring you the length of Prester Iohns
foot: fetch you a haire off the great Chams beard: doe
you any embassage to the Pigmies, rather than holde
three words conference, with this harpy, you haue no
imployment for me?

DON PEDRO None, but to desire your good company.

BENEDICKE O God sir, heeres a dish I loue not, I cannot
indure my Ladie Tongue. *exit*

DON PEDRO Come Lady, come, you haue lost the heart of
signior Benedicke.

670 BEATRICE Indeed my Lord, he lent it me awhile, and I
gaue him vse for it, a double heart for his single one,
mary once before he wonne it of me, with false dice,
therefore your grace may well say I haue lost it.

DON PEDRO You haue put him downe Lady, you haue put
him downe.

BEATRICE So I would not he should do me, my Lord, lest
I should prooue the mother of fooles: I haue brought
Counte Claudio, whom you sent me to seeke.

DON PEDRO Why how now Counte, wherefore are you
680 sad?

CLAUDIO Not sad my Lord.

DON PEDRO How then? sicke?

CLAUDIO Neither, my Lord.

BEATRICE The Counte is neither sad, nor sicke, nor merry,
nor well: but ciuill Counte, ciuil as an orange, and
something of that iealous complexion.

DON PEDRO Ifaith Lady, I think your blazon to be true,
though ile be sworne, if he be so, his conceit is false:
heere Claudio, I haue wooed in thy name, and faire
690 Hero is won, I haue broke with her father, and his
good will obtained, name the day of marriage, and God
giue thee ioy.

LEONATO Counte take of me my daughter, and with her
my fortunes: his grace hath made the match, and all
grace say Amen to it.

BEATRICE Speake Counte, tis your Qu.

CLAUDIO Silence is the perfectest Herault of ioy, I were
but little happy if I could say, how much? *(To Hero)*
Lady, as you are mine, I am yours, I giue away my
700 selfe for you, and doate vpon the exchange.

BEATRICE *(to Hero)* Speake cosin, or (if you cannot) stop
his mouth with a kisse, and let not him speake neither.

DON PEDRO Infaith lady you haue a merry heart.

BEATRICE Yea my lord I thanke it, poore foole it keepes
on the windy side of Care, my coosin tells him in his
eare that he is in her heart.

CLAUDIO And so she doth coosin.

BEATRICE Good Lord for aliance: thus goes euery one to
the world but I, and I am sun-burnt, I may sit in a
corner and crie, heigh ho for a husband. 710

DON PEDRO Lady Beatrice, I will get you one.

BEATRICE I would rather haue one of your fathers getting:
hath your grace ne're a brother like you? your father
got excellent husbands if a maide coulde come by them.

DON PEDRO Will you haue me? lady.

BEATRICE No my lord, vnles I might haue another for
working-daies, your grace is too costly to weare euery
day: but I beseech your grace pardon me, I was born
to speake all mirth, and no matter.

DON PEDRO Your silence most offends me, and to be merry, 720
best becomes you, for out a question, you were borne
in a merry hower.

BEATRICE No sure my lord, my mother cried, but then
there was a starre daunst, and vnder that was I borne,
(to Hero and Claudio) cosins God giue you ioy.

LEONATO Neece, will you looke to those things I tolde you
of?

BEATRICE I crie you mercy vncle, *(to Don Pedro)* by your
graces pardon. *exit Beatrice*

DON PEDRO By my troth a pleasant spirited lady. 730

LEONATO Theres little of the melancholy element in her
my lord, she is neuer sad, but when she sleeps, & not
euer sad then: for I haue heard my daughter say, she
hath often dreampt of vnhappines, and wakt her selfe
with laughing.

DON PEDRO She cannot indure to heare tell of a husband.

LEONATO O by no meanes, she mockes al her wooers out
of sute.

DON PEDRO She were an excellent wife for Benedick.

LEONATO O Lord, my lord, if they were but a weeke 740
married, they would talke themselues madde.

DON PEDRO Countie Claudio, when meane you to goe to
church?

CLAUDIO To morow my lord, Time goes on crutches, til
Loue haue all his rites.

LEONATO Not til monday, my deare sonne, which is hence
a iust seuennight, and a time too briefe too, to haue
al things answer my mind.

DON PEDRO Come, you shake the head at so long a
breathing, but I warrant thee Claudio, the time shall 750
not go dully by vs, I wil in the interim, vndertake one
of Hercules labors, which is, to bring Signior Benedick
and the lady Beatrice into a mountaine of affection,
th'one with th'other, I would faine haue it a match,
and I doubt not but to fashion it, if you three will but
minister such assistance as I shall giue you direction.

LEONATO My lord, I am for you, though it cost me ten
nights watchings.

CLAUDIO And I my Lord.

DON PEDRO And you too gentle Hero? 760

HERO I wil do any modest office, my lord, to help my
cosin to a good husband.

DON PEDRO And Benedicke is not the vnhopefullest
husband that I know: thus farre can I praise him, he
is of a noble strain, of approoued valour, and confirmde
honesty, I will teach you how to humour your cosin,
that she shall fal in loue with Benedicke, and I, with
your two helpes, wil so practise on Benedicke, that in
dispight of his quicke wit, and his queasie stomacke,
770 he shall fall in loue with Beatrice: if we can do this,
Cupid is no longer an Archer, his glory shall bee ours,
for we are the onely loue-gods, goe in with mee, and
I will tell you my drift.   *exeunt*

Sc. 5   *Enter Iohn and Borachio*
(2.2) DON IOHN It is so, the Counte Claudio shall marry the
daughter of Leonato.

BORACHIO Yea my lord, but I can crosse it.

DON IOHN Any barre, any crosse, any impediment, will
be medcinable to me, I am sicke in displeasure to him,
and whatsoeuer comes athwart his affection, ranges
780 euenly with mine, how canst thou crosse this marriage?

BORACHIO Not honestly my lord, but so couertly, that no
dishonesty shall appeare in me.

DON IOHN Shew me briefely how.

BORACHIO I thinke I told your lordship a yeere since, how
much I am in the fauour of Margaret, the waiting
gentlewoman to Hero.

DON IOHN I remember.

BORACHIO I can at any vnseasonable instant of the night,
appoint her to looke out at her ladies chamber window.

790 DON IOHN What life is in that to be the death of this
mariage?

BORACHIO The poison of that lies in you to temper, goe
you to the prince your brother, spare not to tell him,
that he hath wronged his honor in marrying the
renowned Claudio, whose estimation do you mightily
hold vp, to a contaminated stale, such a one as Hero.

DON IOHN What proofe shall I make of that?

BORACHIO Proofe enough, to misuse the prince, to vexe
Claudio, to vndoe Hero, and kill Leonato, looke you for
800 any other issue?

DON IOHN Onely to dispight them I will endeuour any
thing.

BORACHIO Go then, find me a meet houre, to draw don
Pedro and the Counte Claudio alone, tell them that you
know that Hero loues me, intend a kind of zeale both
to the prince & Claudio (as in loue of your brothers
honor who hath made this match) and his friends
reputation, who is thus like to bee cosen'd with the
semblance of a maid, that you haue discouer'd thus:
810 they wil scarcely beleeue this without triall: offer them
instances which shall beare no lesse likelihood, than to
see me at her chamber window, heare me call Margaret
Hero, heare Marg. terme me Claudio, & bring them to
see this the very night before the intended wedding,
for in the mean time, I wil so fashion the matter, that
Hero shal be absent and there shal appeere such

seeming truth of Heroes disloyaltie, that iealousie shal
be cald assurance, and al the preparation ouerthrowne.

DON IOHN Grow this to what aduerse issue it can, I will
put it in practise: be cunning in the working this, and   820
thy fee is a thousand ducates.

BORACHIO Be you constant in the accusation, and my
cunning shall not shame me.

DON IOHN I will presently go learne their day of marriage.
exeunt

Enter Benedicke alone   Sc. 6
BENEDICKE Boy.   (2.3)
⌐Enter Boy⌐

BOY Signior.

BENEDICKE In my chamber window lies a booke, bring it
hither to me in the orchard.

BOY I am here already sir.

BENEDICKE I know that, but I would haue thee hence and   830
here againe.   ⌐exit Boy⌐
I do much wonder, that one man seeing how much an
other man is a foole, when he dedicates his behauiours
to loue, wil after he hath laught at such shallow follies
in others, becom the argument of his owne scorne, by
falling in loue, and such a man is Claudio, I haue
knowne when there was no musique with him but the
drumme and the fife, and now had he rather heare the
taber and the pipe: I haue knowne when he would
haue walkt ten mile afoot, to see a good armour, and   840
now wil he lie ten nights awake caruing the fashion
of a new dublet: he was woont to speake plaine, and
to the purpose (like an honest man and a souldier) and
now is he turnd ortography, his words are a very
fantasticall banquet, iust so many strange dishes: may
I be so conuerted and see with these eies? I cannot tell,
I thinke not: I wil not be sworne but loue may
transforme me to an oyster, but ile take my oath on
it, till he haue made an oyster of me, he shall neuer
make me such a foole: one woman is faire, yet I am   850
well, an other is wise, yet I am well: an other vertuous,
yet I am wel: but till all graces be in one woman, one
womã shal not com in my grace: rich she shal be thats
certain, wise, or ile none, vertuous, or ile neuer cheapen
her: faire, or ile neuer looke on her, mild, or come not
neare me, noble, or not I for an angell, of good
discourse, an excellent musitian, and her haire shall
be of what colour it please God. hah! the prince and
monsieur Loue, I wil hide me in the arbor.

He hides.
Enter Don Pedro the prince, Leonato, Claudio

DON PEDRO Come shall we heare this musique?   860
CLAUDIO
Yea my good lord: how stil the euening is,
As husht on purpose to grace harmonie!

DON PEDRO (aside)
See you where Benedicke hath hid himselfe?

CLAUDIO (aside)
O very wel my lord: the musique ended,
Weele fit the hid-foxe with a penny worth.

Enter Balthaser with musicke

DON PEDRO

Come Balthaser, weele heare that song againe.

BALTHASAR

O good my lord, taxe not so bad a voice,
To slaunder musicke any more then once.

DON PEDRO

It is the witnesse still of excellencie,
870 To put a strange face on his owne perfection,
I pray thee sing, and let me wooe no more.

BALTHASAR

Because you talke of wooing I will sing,
Since many a wooer doth commence his sute,
To her he thinkes not worthy, yet he wooes,
Yet will he sweare he loues.

DON PEDRO   Nay pray thee come,
Or if thou wilt hold longer argument,
Do it in notes.

BALTHASAR   Note this before my notes,
Theres not a note of mine thats worth the noting.

DON PEDRO

Why these are very crotchets that he speakes,
880 Note notes forsooth, and nothing.

⌈*Musicke*⌉

BENEDICKE Now diuine aire, now is his soule rauisht, is
it not strange that sheepes guts should hale soules out
of mens bodies? well a horne for my mony when alls
done.

The Song

BALTHASAR

Sigh no more ladies, sigh no more,
   Men were deceiuers euer,
One foote in sea, and one on shore,
   To one thing constant neuer,
Then sigh not so, but let them go,
890 And be you blith and bonnie,
Conuerting all your soundes of woe,
   Into hey nony nony.

Sing no more ditties, sing no moe,
   Of dumps so dull and heauy,
The fraud of men was euer so,
   Since summer first was leauy,
Then sigh not so, but let them go,
   And be you blith and bonnie,
Conuerting all your soundes of woe,
900 Into hey nony nony.

DON PEDRO By my troth a good song.

BALTHASAR And an ill singer my lord.

DON PEDRO Ha, no no faith, thou singst wel enough for a
shift.

BENEDICKE (*aside*) And he had bin a dog that should haue
howld thus, they would haue hangd him, and I pray
God his bad voice bode no mischeefe, I had as liue
haue heard the night-rauen, come what plague could
haue come after it.

910 DON PEDRO Yea mary, doost thou heare Balthasar? I pray

thee get vs some excellent musique: for to morow night
we would haue it at the ladie Heroes chamber window.

BALTHASAR The best I can my lord.   *Exit Balthasar*

DON PEDRO Do so, farewell. Come hither Leonato, what
was it you told mee of to day, that your niece Beatrice
was in loue with signior Benedicke?

CLAUDIO (*aside*) O I, stalke on, stalk on, the foule sits.
(*Alowd*) I did neuer think that lady would haue loued
any man.

LEONATO No nor I neither, but most wonderful, that she   920
should so dote on signior Benedicke, whome she hath
in all outward behauiors seemd euer to abhorre.

BENEDICKE (*aside*) Ist possible? sits the wind in that corner?

LEONATO By my troth my Lord, I cannot tell what to
thinke of it, but that she loues him with an inraged
affection, it is past the infinite of thought.

DON PEDRO May be she doth but counterfeit.

CLAUDIO Faith like enough.

LEONATO O God! counterfeit? there was neuer counterfeit
of passion, came so neare the life of passion as she   930
discouers it.

DON PEDRO Why what effects of passion shewes she?

CLAUDIO (*aside*) Baite the hooke wel, this fish will bite.

LEONATO What effects my Lord? she wil sit you, you heard
my daughter tell you how.

CLAUDIO She did indeede.

DON PEDRO How, how I pray you! you amaze me, I would
haue thought her spirite had beene inuincible against
all assaults of affection.

LEONATO I would haue sworn it had, my lord, especially   940
against Benedicke.

BENEDICKE (*aside*) I should think this a gull, but that the
white bearded fellow speakes it: knauery cannot sure
hide himself in such reuerence.

CLAUDIO (*aside*) He hath tane th'infection, hold it vp.

DON PEDRO Hath shee made her affection knowne to
Benedicke?

LEONATO No, and sweares shee neuer will, thats her
torment.

CLAUDIO Tis true indeed, so your daughter saies: shall I,   950
saies she, that haue so oft encountred him with scorne,
write to him that I loue him?

LEONATO This saies she now when she is beginning to
write to him, for sheel be vp twenty times a night, and
there will she sit in her smocke, til she haue writ a
sheete of paper: my daughter tels vs all.

CLAUDIO Now you talk of a sheet of paper, I remember a
prety iest your daughter told vs of.

LEONATO O when she had writ it, and was reading it
ouer, she found Benedicke and Beatrice betweene the   960
sheete.

CLAUDIO That.

LEONATO O she tore the letter into a thousand halfpence,
raild at her self, that she should be so immodest to
write, to one that she knew would flout her, I measure
him, saies she, by my own spirit, for I should flout
him, if he writ to me, yea thogh I loue him I should.

619

CLAUDIO Then downe vpon her knees she falls, weepes, sobs, beates her heart, teares her haire, prayes, curses, O sweet Benedicke, God giue me patience.

LEONATO She doth indeed, my daughter saies so, and the extasie hath so much ouerborne her, that my daughter is sometime afeard shee will doe a desperate out-rage to her selfe, it is very true.

DON PEDRO It were good that Benedicke knew of it by some other, if she will not discouer it.

CLAUDIO To what end? he would make but a sport of it, and torment the poore Lady worse.

DON PEDRO And he should, it were an almes to hang him, shees an excellent sweete lady, and (out of all suspition,) she is vertuous.

CLAUDIO And she is exceeding wise.

DON PEDRO In euery thing but in louing Benedicke.

LEONATO O my Lord, wisedome and blood combating in so tender a body, we haue ten proofes to one, that bloud hath the victory, I am sory for her, as I haue iust cause, beeing her vncle, and her gardian.

DON PEDRO I would shee had bestowed this dotage on mee, I would haue daft all other respects, and made her halfe my self: I pray you tell Benedicke of it, and heare what a will say.

LEONATO Were it good thinke you?

CLAUDIO Hero thinks surely she will die, for she sayes shee will die, if he loue her not, and shee will die ere shee make her loue knowne, and she will die if he wooe her, rather than shee will bate one breath of her accustomed crosnesse.

DON PEDRO She doth well, if shee shoulde make tender of her loue, tis very possible heele scorne it, for the man (as you know all) hath a contemptible spirite.

CLAUDIO He is a very proper man.

DON PEDRO He hath indeede a good outward happines.

CLAUDIO Before God, and in my mind, very wise.

DON PEDRO Hee dooth indeede shew some sparkes that are like wit.

CLAUDIO And I take him to be valiant.

DON PEDRO As Hector, I assure you, and in the mannaging of quarrels you may say he is wise, for either hee auoydes them with great discretion, or vndertakes them with a most christianlike feare.

LEONATO If he do feare God, a must necessarily keep peace, if hee breake the peace, hee ought to enter into a quarrel with feare and trembling.

DON PEDRO And so will hee doe, for the man doth feare God, howsoeuer it seemes not in him, by some large iestes hee will make: well I am sory for your niece, shall we go seeke Benedicke, and tell him of her loue?

CLAUDIO Neuer tell him, my Lord, let her weare it out with good counsell.

LEONATO Nay thats impossible, shee may weare her heart out first.

DON PEDRO Well, we will heare further of it by your daughter, let it coole the while, I loue Benedicke wel, and I could wish he would modestly examine himselfe, to see how much he is vnworthy so good a lady.

LEONATO My lord, will you walke? dinner is ready.

CLAUDIO (aside) If he do not doate on her vppon this, I will neuer trust my expectation.

DON PEDRO (aside) Let there be the same nette spread for her, and that must your daughter and her gentlewomen carry: the sporte will be, when they holde one an opinion of an others dotage, and no such matter, thats the scene that I woulde see, which wil be meerely a dumbe shew: let vs send her to call him in to dinner.

exeunt Don Pedro, Claudio, and Leonato

BENEDICKE (*comming forward*) This can be no tricke, the conference was sadly borne, they haue the trueth of this from Hero, they seeme to pittie the Lady: it seemes her affections haue their full bent: loue me? why it must be requited: I heare how I am censurde, they say I will beare my selfe prowdly, if I perceiue the loue come from her: they say too, that she will rather die than giue anie signe of affection: I did neuer thinke to marry, I must not seeme prowd, happy are they that heare their detractions, and can put them to mending: they say the Lady is faire, tis a trueth, I can beare them witnesse: and vertuous, tis so, I cannot reprooue it, and wise, but for louing me, by my troth it is no addition to her wit, nor no great argument of her follie, for I will be horribly in loue with her, I may chaunce haue some odde quirkes and remnants of witte broken on me, because I haue railed so long against marriage: but doth not the appetite alter? a man loues the meate in his youth, that he cannot indure in his age. Shall quippes and sentences, and these paper bullets of the brain awe a man from the carreere of his humor? No, the world must be peopled. When I saide I woulde die a batcheller, I did not think I should liue til I were married, here comes Beatrice:

Enter Beatrice

by this day, shees a faire lady, I doe spie some markes of loue in her.

BEATRICE Against my will I am sent to bid you come in to dinner.

BENEDICKE
Faire Beatrice, I thanke you for your paines.

BEATRICE I tooke no more paines for those thankes, then you take paines to thanke me, if it had bin painful I would not haue come.

BENEDICKE You take pleasure then in the message.

BEATRICE Yea iust so much as you may take vppon a kniues point, and choake a daw withall: you haue no stomach signior, fare you well. *exit*

BENEDICKE Ha, against my will I am sent to bid you come in to dinner: theres a double meaning in that: I took no more paines for those thanks thẽ you took pains to thank me, thats as much as to say, any pains that I take for you is as easy as thanks: if I do not take pitty of her I am a villaine, if I do not loue her I am a Iew, I will go get her picture. *exit*

Enter Hero and two Gentlewomen, Margaret, and Vrsley   **Sc. 7 (3.1)**

HERO
Good Margaret runne thee to the parlour,

There shalt thou find my cosin Beatrice,
1080 Proposing with the prince and Claudio,
Whisper her eare and tell her I and Vrsley,
Walke in the orchard, and our whole discourse
Is all of her, say that thou ouer-heardst vs,
And bid her steale into the pleached bowere
Where hony-suckles ripend by the sunne,
Forbid the sunne to enter: like fauourites,
Made proud by princes, that aduaunce their pride,
Against that power that bred it, there will she hide
    her,
To listen our propose, this is thy office,
1090 Beare thee well in it, and leaue vs alone.

MARGARET
Ile make her come I warrant you presently.   *exit*

HERO
Now Vrsula, when Beatrice doth come,
As we do trace this alley vp and downe,
Our talke must onely be of Benedicke,
When I do name him let it be thy part,
To praise him more than euer man did merite,
My talke to thee must be how Benedicke,
Is sicke in loue with Beatrice: of this matter,
Is little Cupids crafty arrow made,
That onely wounds by heare-say:
    Enter Beatrice
1100   now begin,
For looke where Beatrice like a Lapwing runs
Close by the ground, to heare our conference.

VRSULA
The pleasantst angling is to see the fish
Cut with her golden ores the siluer streame,
And greedily deuoure the treacherous baite:
So angle we for Beatrice, who euen now,
Is couched in the wood-bine couerture,
Feare you not my part of the dialogue.

HERO
Then go we neare her that her eare loose nothing,
1110 Of the false sweete baite that we lay for it:
    They approach Beatrices hiding-place
No truly Vrsula, she is too disdainfull,
I know her spirits are as coy and wild,
As haggerds of the rocke.

VRSULA   But are you sure,
That Benedicke loues Beatrice so intirely?

HERO
So saies the prince, and my new trothed Lord.

VRSULA
And did they bid you tel her of it, madame?

HERO
They did intreate me to acquaint her of it,
But I perswaded them, if they lou'de Benedicke,
To wish him wrastle with affection,
1120 And neuer to let Beatrice know of it.

VRSULA
Why did you so, dooth not the gentleman
Deserue as full as fortunate a bed,
As euer Beatrice shall couch vpon?

HERO
O God of loue! I know he doth deserue,
As much as may be yeelded to a man:
But nature neuer framde a womans hart,
Of prowder stuffe then that of Beatrice:
Disdaine and Scorne ride sparkling in her eies,
Misprising what they looke on, and her wit
Valewes it selfe so highly, that to her   1130
All matter els seemes weake: she cannot loue,
Nor take no shape nor proiect of affection,
She is so selfe indeared.

VRSULA   Sure I thinke so,
And therefore certainely it were not good,
She knew his loue lest sheele make sport at it.

HERO
Why you speake truth, I neuer yet saw man,
How wise, how noble, yong, how rarely featured,
But she would spel him backward: if faire faced,
She would sweare the gentleman should be her sister:
If blacke, why Nature drawing of an antique,   1140
Made a foule blot: if tall, a launce ill headed:
If low, an agot very vildly cut:
If speaking, why a vane blowne with all winds:
If silent, why a blocke moued with none:
So turnes she euery man the wrong side out,
And neuer giues to Truth and Vertue, that
Which simplenesse and merite purchaseth.

VRSULA
Sure, sure, such carping is not commendable.

HERO
No not to be so odde, and from all fashions,
As Beatrice is, cannot be commendable,   1150
But who dare tell her so? if I should speake,
She would mocke me into ayre, O she would laugh me
Out of my selfe, presse me to death with wit,
Therefore let Benedicke like couerd fire,
Consume away in sighes, waste inwardly:
It were a better death, then die with mockes,
Which is as bad as die with tickling.

VRSULA
Yet tel her of it, heare what she wil say.

HERO
No rather I will go to Benedicke,
And counsaile him to fight against his passion,   1160
And truly ile deuise some honest slaunders,
To staine my cosin with, one doth not know,
How much an ill word may impoison liking.

VRSULA
O do not do your cosin such a wrong,
She cannot be so much without true iudgement,
Hauing so swift and excellent a wit,
As she is prisde to haue, as to refuse
So rare a gentleman as signior Benedicke.

HERO
He is the onely man of Italy,
Alwaies excepted my deare Claudio.   1170

VRSULA
I pray you be not angry with me, madame,

Speaking my fancy: signior Benedicke,
For shape, for bearing argument and valour,
Goes formost in report through Italy.

HERO
Indeed he hath an excellent good name.

VRSULA
His excellence did earne it, ere he had it:
When are you married madame?

HERO
Why euery day to morrow, come go in,
Ile shew thee some attyres, and haue thy counsaile,
1180   Which is the best to furnish me to morrow.

VRSULA (aside to Hero)
Shees limd I warrant you, we haue caught her
    madame.

HERO (aside to Vrsula)
If it proue so, then louing goes by haps,
Some Cupid kills with arrowes, some with traps.
                  Exeunt Hero and Vrsula

BEATRICE (comming forward)
What fire is in mine eares? can this be true?
    Stand I condemn'd for pride and scorne so much?
Contempt, farewel, and maiden pride, adew,
    No glory liues behind the backe of such.
And Benedicke, loue one I wil requite thee,
    Taming my wild heart to thy louing hand:
1190   If thou dost loue, my kindnesse shall incite thee
    To bind our loues vp in a holy band.
For others say thou dost deserue, and I
Beleeue it better then reportingly.   *exit*

Sc. 8   *Enter Don Pedro the Prince, Claudio, Benedicke, and*
(3.2)   *Leonato*

DON PEDRO I doe but stay til your mariage be consummate,
and then go I toward Arragon.

CLAUDIO Ile bring you thither my lord, if youle vouchsafe
me.

DON PEDRO Nay that would be as great a soyle in the new
glosse of your marriage, as to shew a child his new
1200   coate and forbid him to weare it, I wil only be bold
with Benedick for his company, for from the crowne of
his head, to the sole of his foot, he is al mirth, he hath
twice or thrice cut Cupides bow-string, and the little
hang-man dare not shoot at him, he hath a heart as
sound as a bell, and his tongue is the clapper, for what
his heart thinkes, his tongue speakes.

BENEDICKE Gallants, I am not as I haue bin.

LEONATO So say I, me thinkes you are sadder.

CLAUDIO I hope he be in loue.

1210   DON PEDRO Hang him truant, theres no true drop of bloud
in him to be truly toucht with loue, if he be sadde, he
wantes money.

BENEDICKE I haue the tooth-ach.

DON PEDRO Draw it.

BENEDICKE Hang it.

CLAUDIO You must hang it first, and draw it afterwards.

DON PEDRO What? sigh for the tooth-ach.

LEONATO Where is but a humour or a worme.

BENEDICKE Wel, euery one can master a griefe, but he
that has it.   1220

CLAUDIO Yet say I, he is in loue.

DON PEDRO There is no appeerance of fancie in him,
vnlesse it be a fancy that he hath to strange disguises,
as to be a Dutchman to day, a French-man to morrow,
or in the shape of two countries at once, as a Germaine
from the waste downward, all slops, and a Spaniard
from the hip vpward, no dublet: vnlesse he haue a
fancie to this foolery, as it appeares he hath, he is no
foole for fancy, as you would haue it appeare he is.

CLAUDIO If he be not in loue with some woman, there is   1230
no beleeuing old signes, a brushes his hat a mornings,
what should that bode?

DON PEDRO Hath any man seene him at the Barbers?

CLAUDIO No, but the barbers man hath bin seene with
him, and the olde ornament of his cheeke hath already
stufft tennis balls.

LEONATO Indeed he lookes yonger than he did, by the
losse of a beard.

DON PEDRO Nay a rubs himselfe with ciuit, can you smell
him out by that?   1240

CLAUDIO Thats as much as to say, the sweete youthe's in
loue.

DON PEDRO The greatest note of it is his melancholy.

CLAUDIO And when was he woont to wash his face?

DON PEDRO Yea or to paint himselfe? for the which I heare
what they say of him.

CLAUDIO Nay but his iesting spirit, which is now crept
into a lute-string, and now gouernd by stops.

DON PEDRO Indeed that tells a heauy tale for him:
conclude, conclude, he is in loue.   1250

CLAUDIO Nay but I know who loues him.

DON PEDRO That would I know too, I warrant one that
knows him not.

CLAUDIO Yes, and his ill conditions, and in dispight of al,
dies for him.

DON PEDRO She shall be buried with her face vpwards.

BENEDICKE Yet is this no charme for the tooth-ake, old
signior, walke aside with me, I haue studied eight or
nine wise wordes to speake to you, which these hobby-
horses must not heare.   1260
                      Exeunt Benedick and Leonato

DON PEDRO For my life to breake with him about Beatrice.

CLAUDIO Tis euen so, Hero and Margaret haue by this
played their parts with Beatrice, and then the two
beares will not bite one another when they meete.
    Enter Iohn the Bastard

DON IOHN My lord and brother, God saue you.

DON PEDRO Good den brother.

DON IOHN If your leisure seru'd, I would speake with you.

DON PEDRO In priuate?

DON IOHN If it please you, yet Count Claudio may heare,
for what I would speake of concernes him.   1270

DON PEDRO Whats the matter?

DON IOHN (to Claudio) Meanes your Lordship to be married
to morrow?

DON PEDRO You know he does.

DON IOHN I know not that, when he knowes what I know.

CLAUDIO If there be any impediment, I pray you discouer it.

DON IOHN You may think I loue you not, let that appeare hereafter, and ayme better at me by that I now will manifest, for my brother, I thinke, he holdes you well, and in dearenesse of heart, hath holpe to effect your ensuing mariage: surely sute ill spent, and labor ill bestowed.

DON PEDRO Why whats the matter?

DON IOHN I came hither to tel you, and circumstances shortned, for she has bin too long a talking of, the lady is disloyall.

CLAUDIO Who Hero?

DON IOHN Euen she, Leonatoes Hero, your Hero, euery mans Hero.

CLAUDIO Disloyall?

DON IOHN The word is too good to paint out her wickednesse, I could say she were worse, thinke you of a worse title, and I wil fit her to it: wonder not till further warrant: go but with me to night you shall see her chamber window entred, euen the night before her wedding day, if you loue her then, to morow wed her: But it would better fitte your honour to change your mind.

CLAUDIO May this be so?

DON PEDRO I wil not thinke it.

DON IOHN If you dare not trust that you see, confesse not that you knowe: if you will follow mee, I will shew you enough, and when you haue seene more, and heard more, proceede accordingly.

CLAUDIO If I see anie thing to night, why I should not marry her, to morrow, in the congregation where I should wed, there will I shame her.

DON PEDRO And as I wooed for thee to obtaine her, I wil ioyne with thee, to disgrace her.

DON IOHN I will disparage her no farther, till you are my witnesses, beare it coldely but till midnight, and let the issue shew it selfe.

DON PEDRO O day vntowardly turned!

CLAUDIO O mischiefe strangely thwarting!

DON IOHN O plague right well preuented! so will you say, when you haue seene the sequele.   *exeunt*

**Sc. 9
(3.3)**   *Enter Dogbery and his compartner Verges, with the Watch*

DOGBERY Are you good men and true?

VERGES Yea, or else it were pitty but they should suffer saluation body and soule.

DOGBERY Nay, that were a punishment too good for them, if they should haue any allegeance in them, being chosen for the Princes watch.

VERGES Well, giue them their charge, neighbour Dogbery.

DOGBERY First, who thinke you the most desartlesse man to be Constable?

WATCH 2 Hugh Ote-cake sir, or George Sea-cole, for they can write and reade.

DOGBERY Come hither neighbor Sea-cole, God hath blest you with a good name, to be a welfauoured man, is the gift of Fortune, but to write and reade, comes by nature.

WATCH 1 Both which maister Constable.

DOGBERY You haue: I knew it would be your answer: wel, for your fauour sir, why giue God thanks, and make no boast of it, and for your writing and reading, let that appeere when there is no neede of such vanity, you are thought heere to be the most senslesse and fit man for the Constable of the watch: therefore beare you the lanthorne: this is your charge, You shall comprehend all vagrom men, you are to bidde any man stand, in the Princes name.

WATCH 1 How if a will not stand?

DOGBERY Why then take no note of him, but let him goe, and presently call the rest of the watch together, and thanke god you are ridde of a knaue.

VERGES If he wil not stand when he is bidden, he is none of the Princes subiects.

DOGBERY True, and they are to meddle with none but the Princes subiects: you shall also make no noise in the streetes: for, for the watch to babble and to talke, is most tollerable, and not to be indured.

WATCH We will rather sleepe than talke, we know what belongs to a watch.

DOGBERY Why you speake like an antient and most quiet watchman, for I cannot see how sleeping should offend: onely haue a care that your billes bee not stolne: well, you are to cal at al the alehouses, and bid those that are drunke get them to bed.

WATCH How if they will not?

DOGBERY Why then let them alone til they are sober, if they make you not then the better answer, you may say, they are not the men you tooke them for.

WATCH Well sir.

DOGBERY If you meete a thiefe, you may suspect him, by vertue of your office, to be no true man: and for such kind of men, the lesse you meddle or make with them, why the more is for your honesty.

WATCH If we know him to be a thiefe, shal we not lay hands on him?

DOGBERY Truely by your office you may, but I thinke they that touch pitch will be defilde: the most peaceable way for you, if you doe take a thiefe, is, to let him shew himselfe what he is, and steale out of your companie.

VERGES You haue beene alwayes called a mercifull manne, partner.

DOGBERY Truely I would not hang a dogge by my will, much more a man who hath anie honestie in him.

VERGES (*to the Watch*) If you heare a child crie in the night you must call to the nurse and bid her stil it.

WATCH How if the nurse be asleepe and will not heare vs.

DOGBERY Why then depart in peace, and let the child wake her with crying, for the ewe that will not heare her lamb when it baes, will neuer answer a calfe when he bleates.

VERGES Tis very true.

DOGBERY This is the end of the charge: you constable are
1390 to present the princes owne person, if you meete the
prince in the night, you may stay him.

VERGES Nay birlady that I thinke a cannot.

DOGBERY Fiue shillings to one on't with any man that
knowes the statutes, he may stay him, mary not
without the prince be willing, for indeed the watch
ought to offend no man, and it is an offence to stay a
man against his will.

VERGES Birlady I thinke it be so.

DOGBERY Ha ah ha, wel masters good night, and there be
1400 any matter of weight chaunces, cal vp me, keepe your
fellowes counsailes, and your owne, and good night,
come neighbour.

WATCH ⌐1⌐ Well masters, we heare our charge, let vs goe
sitte here vppon the church bench till twoo, and then
all to bed.

DOGBERY One word more, honest neighbors, I pray you
watch about signior Leonatoes doore, for the wedding
being there to morrow, there is a great coyle to night,
adiew, be vigitant I beseech you.

           exeunt Dogbery and Verges. ⌐*The Watch sit*⌐
           Enter Borachio and Conrade

1410 BORACHIO What Conrade?

WATCH ⌐1⌐ (*aside*) Peace, stir not.

BORACHIO Conrade I say.

CONRADE Here man, I am at thy elbow.

BORACHIO Mas and my elbow itcht, I thought there would
a scabbe follow.

CONRADE I will owe thee an answer for that, and now
forward with thy tale.

BORACHIO Stand thee close then vnder this penthouse, for
it drissells raine, and I will, like a true drunckard, vtter
1420 all to thee.

WATCH (*aside*) Some treason masters, yet stand close.

BORACHIO Therefore know, I haue earned of Dun Iohn a
thousand ducates.

CONRADE Is it possible that any villanie should be so
deare?

BORACHIO Thou shouldst rather aske if it were possible
any villanie shuld be so rich? for when rich villains
haue need of poor ones, poore ones may make what
price they will.

1430 CONRADE I wonder at it.

BORACHIO That shewes thou art vnconfirm'd, thou
knowest that the fashion of a dublet, or a hat, or a
cloake, is nothing to a man.

CONRADE Yes it is apparell.

BORACHIO I meane the fashion.

CONRADE Yes the fashion is the fashion.

BORACHIO Tush, I may as well say the foole's the foole,
but seest thou not what a deformed theefe this fashion
is?

1440 WATCH (*aside*) I know that deformed, a has bin a vile
theefe, this vij. yeere a goes vp and down like a gentle
man: I remember his name.

BORACHIO Didst thou not heare some body?

CONRADE No, twas the vane on the house.

BORACHIO Seest thou not (I say) what a deformed thiefe
this fashion is, how giddily a turnes about all the Hot-
blouds, between foureteene and fiue and thirtie,
sometimes fashioning them like Pharaoes souldiours in
the rechie painting, sometime like god Bels priests in
the old church window, sometime like the shauen   1450
Hercules in the smircht worm-eaten tapestry, where
his cod-peece seemes as massie as his club.

CONRADE Al this I see, and I see that the fashion weares
out more apparrell then the man, but art not thou thy
selfe giddy with the fashion too, that thou hast shifted
out of thy tale into telling me of the fashion?

BORACHIO Not so neither, but know that I haue to night
wooed Margaret the Lady Heroes gentle-woman, by the
name of Hero, she leanes me out at her mistris chamber
window, bids me a thousand times good night: I tell   1460
this tale vildly. I should first tel thee how the prince
Claudio and my master planted, and placed, and
possessed, by my master Don Iohn, saw a farre off in
the orchard this amiable incounter.

CONRADE And thought they Margaret was Hero?

BORACHIO Two of them did, the prince and Claudio, but
the diuel my master knew she was Margaret, and partly
by his oths, which first possest them, partly by the
darke night which did deceiue them, but chiefely, by
my villany, which did confirme any slander that Don   1470
Iohn had made, away went Claudio enragde, swore he
would meet her as he was apointed next morning at
the Temple, and there, before the whole congregation
shame her, with what he saw o're night, and send her
home againe without a husband.

WATCH ⌐1⌐ (*comming forward*) We charge you in the
princes name stand.

⌐WATCH⌐ Call vppe the right maister Constable, wee haue
here recouerd the most dangerous peece of lechery,
that euer was knowne in the common wealth.   1480

WATCH ⌐1⌐ And one Deformed is one of them, I know
him, a weares a locke.

CONRADE Masters, masters.

⌐WATCH⌐ Youle be made bring deformed forth I warrant
you.

⌐CONRADE⌐ Masters,

⌐WATCH⌐ Neuer speake, we charge you, let vs obey you
to go with vs.

BORACHIO (*to Conrade*) We are like to proue a goodly
commoditie, being taken vp of these mens billes.   1490

CONRADE A commodity in question I warrant you, come
weele obey you.   *exeunt*

           Enter Hero, and Margaret, and Vrsula   Sc. 10

HERO Good Vrsula wake my cosin Beatrice, and desire   (3.4)
her to rise.

VRSULA I wil lady.

HERO And bid her come hither.

VRSULA Well.   *exit*

MARGARET Troth I thinke your other rebato were better.

HERO No pray thee good Meg, ile weare this.

MARGARET By my troth's not so good, and I warrant your cosin will say so.

HERO My cosin's a foole, and thou art another, ile weare none but this.

MARGARET I like the new tire within excelently, if the haire were a thought browner: and your gown's a most rare fashion yfaith, I saw the Dutchesse of Millaines gowne that they praise so.

HERO O that exceedes they say.

MARGARET By my troth's but a night-gown in respect of yours, cloth a gold and cuts, and lac'd with siluer, set with pearles, downe sleeues, side sleeues, and skirts, round vnderborne with a blewish tinsell, but for a fine queint gracefull and excelent fashion, yours is worth ten on't.

HERO God giue me ioy to weare it, for my heart is exceeding heauy.

MARGARET T'will be heauier soone by the weight of a man.

HERO Fie vpon thee, art not ashamed?

MARGARET Of what lady? of speaking honourably? is not marriage honourable in a beggar? is not your Lord honourable without mariage? I thinke you would haue me say, sauing your reuerence a husband: & bad thinking do not wrest true speaking, ile offend no body, is there any harm in the heauier, for a husband? none I thinke, and it be the right husband, and the right wife, otherwise tis light and not heauy, aske my lady Beatrice els, here she comes.

Enter Beatrice

HERO Good morrow coze.

BEATRICE Good morrow sweete Hero.

HERO Why how now? do you speake in the sicke tune?

BEATRICE I am out of all other tune, me thinkes.

MARGARET Clap's into Light a loue, (that goes without a burden,) do you sing it, and ile daunce it.

BEATRICE Ye Light aloue with your heels, then if your husband haue stables enough youle see he shall lacke no barnes.

MARGARET O illegitimate construction! I scorne that with my heeles.

BEATRICE (*to Hero*) Tis almost fiue a clocke cosin, tis time you were ready, by my troth I am exceeding ill, hey ho.

MARGARET For a hauke, a horse, or a husband?

BEATRICE For the letter that begins them al, H.

MARGARET Wel, and you be not turnde Turke, theres no more sayling by the starre.

BEATRICE What meanes the foole trow?

MARGARET Nothing I, but God send euery one their hearts desire.

HERO These gloues the Counte sent me, they are an excellent perfume.

BEATRICE I am stuft cosin, I cannot smell.

MARGARET A maide and stuft! theres goodly catching of colde.

BEATRICE O God help me, God help me, how long haue you profest apprehension?

MARGARET Euer since you left it, doth not my wit become me rarely?

BEATRICE It is not seene enough, you should weare it in your cap, by my troth I am sicke.

MARGARET Get you some of this distill'd *carduus benedictus*, and lay it to your heart, it is the onely thing for a qualme.

HERO There thou prickst her with a thissel.

BEATRICE *Benedictus*, why *benedictus*? you haue some moral in this *benedictus*.

MARGARET Morall? no by my troth I haue no morall meaning, I meant plaine holy thissel, you may thinke perchaunce that I think you are in loue, nay birlady I am not such a foole to think what I list, nor I list not to thinke what I can, nor indeed I can not think, if I would thinke my heart out of thinking, that you are in loue, or that you will be in loue, or that you can be in loue: yet Benedicke was such another, and now is he become a man, he swore he would neuer marry, and yet now in dispight of his heart he eates his meate without grudging, and how you may be conuerted I know not, but me thinkes you looke with your eies as other women do.

BEATRICE What pace is this that thy tongue keepes?

MARGARET Not a false gallop.

Enter Vrsula

VRSULA (*to Hero*) Madame withdraw, the prince, the Count, signior Benedicke, Don Iohn, and all the gallants of the towne are come to fetch you to church.

HERO Help to dresse me good coze, good Meg, good Vrsula.

exeunt

Enter Leonato, and Dogbery the Constable, and Verges the Headborough   Sc. 11 (3.5)

LEONATO What would you with me, honest neighbour?

DOGBERY Mary sir I would haue some confidence with you, that decernes you nearely.

LEONATO Briefe I pray you, for you see it is a busie time with me.

DOGBERY Mary this it is sir.

VERGES Yes in truth it is sir.

LEONATO What is it my good friends?

DOGBERY Goodman Verges sir speaks a little of the matter, an old man sir, and his wittes are not so blunt, as God helpe I would desire they were, but infaith honest, as the skin between his browes.

VERGES Yes I thank God, I am as honest as any man liuing, that is an old man, and no honester then I.

DOGBERY Comparisons are odorous, palabras, neighbour Verges.

LEONATO Neighbors, you are tedious.

DOGBERY It pleases your worship to say so, but we are the poore Dukes officers, but truly for mine owne part, if I were as tedious as a King I could find in my heart to bestow it all of your worship.

LEONATO Al thy tediousnesse on me, ah?

DOGBERY Yea, and 'twere a thousand pound more than tis, for I heare as good exclamation on your worshippe

1610　as of any man in the citie, and though I be but a poore
man, I am glad to heare it.

VERGES And so am I.

LEONATO I would faine know what you haue to say.

VERGES Mary sir our watch to night, excepting your
worships presence, ha tane a couple of as arrant knaues
as any in Messina.

DOGBERY A good old man sir, he will be talking. As they
say, when the age is in, the wit is out, God help vs, it
is a world to see, well said yfaith neighbour Verges,
1620　well, God's a good man, and two men ride of a horse,
one must ride behind, an honest soule yfaith sir, by
my troth he is, as euer broke bread, but God is to be
worshipt, all men are not alike, alas good neighbour.

LEONATO Indeed neighbour he comes too short of you.

DOGBERY Gifts that God giues.

LEONATO I must leaue you.

DOGBERY One word sir, our watch sir haue indeede
comprehended two aspitious persons, and wee woulde
haue them this morning examined before your worship.

1630　LEONATO Take their examination your selfe, and bring it
me, I am now in great haste, as it may appeare vnto
you.

DOGBERY It shall be suffigance.

LEONATO Drinke some wine ere you goe: fare you well.

　　　　　　　　Enter a Messenger

MESSENGER My lord, they stay for you, to giue your
daughter to her husband.

LEONATO Ile wait vpon them, I am ready.

　　　　　　　　Exeunt Leonato and Messenger

DOGBERY Go good partner, goe get you to Francis Sea-
cole, bid him bring his penne and inckehorne to the
1640　Gaole: we are now to examination these men.

VERGES And we must do it wisely.

DOGBERY We will spare for no witte I warrant you: heeres
that shall driue some of them to a noncome, only get
the learned writer to set downe our excommunication,
and meet me at the Iaile.　　　　　　　　*exeunt*

Sc. 12　　　*Enter Don Pedro the Prince, Iohn the Bastard,*
(4.1)　　　*Leonato, Frier, Claudio, Benedicke, Hero, and*
　　　　　Beatrice

LEONATO Come Frier Francis, be briefe, onely to the plaine
forme of marriage, and you shall recount their
particular dueties afterwards.

FRIAR (*to Claudio*) You come hither, my lord, to marry
1650　this lady.

CLAUDIO No.

LEONATO To bee married to her: Frier, you come to marry
her.

FRIER (*to Hero*) Lady, you come hither to be married to
this counte.

HERO I do.

FRIER If either of you know any inward impediment why
you should not be conioyned, I charge you on your
soules to vtter it.

1660　CLAUDIO Know you any, Hero?

HERO None my lord.

FRIER Know you any, Counte?

LEONATO I dare make his answer, None.

CLAUDIO O what men dare do! what men may do! what
men daily do, not knowing what they do!

BENEDICKE Howe nowe! interiections? why then, some be
of laughing, as, ah, ha, he.

CLAUDIO
Stand thee by Frier, father, by your leaue,
Will you with free and vnconstrained soule
Giue me this maide your daughter?　　　　　　　1670

LEONATO
As freely sonne as God did giue her mee.

CLAUDIO
And what haue I to giue you backe whose woorth
May counterpoise this rich and pretious gift?

DON PEDRO
Nothing, vnlesse you render her againe.

CLAUDIO
Sweete Prince, you learne me noble thankfulnes:
There Leonato, take her backe againe,
Giue not this rotten orenge to your friend,
Shee's but the signe and semblance of her honor:
Behold how like a maide she blushes heere!
O what authoritie and shew of truth　　　　　　　1680
Can cunning sinne couer it selfe withall!
Comes not that blood, as modest euidence,
To witnesse simple Vertue? would you not sweare
All you that see her, that she were a maide,
By these exterior shewes? But she is none:
She knowes the heate of a luxurious bed:
Her blush is guiltinesse, not modestie.

LEONATO
What do you meane, my lord?

CLAUDIO　　　　　　　　　　　　Not to be married,
Not to knit my soule to an approoued wanton.

LEONATO
Deere my lord, if you in your owne proofe,　　　　1690
Haue vanquisht the resistance of her youth,
And made defeate of her virginitie.

CLAUDIO
I know what you would say: if I haue knowne her,
You will say, she did imbrace me as a husband,
And so extenuate the forehand sinne:
No Leonato,
I neuer tempted her with word too large,
But as a brother to his sister, shewed
Bashfull sinceritie, and comelie loue.

HERO
And seemde I euer otherwise to you?　　　　　　　1700

CLAUDIO
Out on thee seeming, I wil write against it,
You seeme to me as Diane in her Orbe,
As chaste as is the budde ere it be blowne:
But you are more intemperate in your blood,
Than Venus, or those pampred animalls,
That rage in sauage sensualitie.

HERO
Is my Lord well that he doth speake so wide?

LEONATO
  Sweete prince, why speake not you?
DON PEDRO   What should I speake?
  I stand dishonourd that haue gone about,
1710   To lincke my deare friend to a common stale.
LEONATO
  Are these things spoken, or do I but dreame?
DON IOHN
  Sir, they are spoken, and these things are true.
BENEDICKE This lookes not like a nuptiall.
HERO True, O God!
CLAUDIO Leonato, stand I here?
  Is this the prince? is this the princes brother?
  Is this face Heroes? are our eies our owne?
LEONATO
  All this is so, but what of this my Lord?
CLAUDIO
  Let me but moue one question to your daughter,
1720   And by that fatherly and kindly power,
  That you haue in her, bid her answer truly.
LEONATO (to Hero)
  I charge thee do so, as thou art my child.
HERO
  O God defend me how am I beset,
  What kind of catechising call you this?
CLAUDIO
  To make you answer truly to your name.
HERO
  Is it not Hero, who can blot that name
  With any iust reproch?
CLAUDIO   Mary that can Hero,
  Hero it selfe can blot out Heroes vertue.
  What man was he talkt with you yesternight,
1730   Out at your window betwixt twelue and one?
  Now if you are a maide, answer to this.
HERO
  I talkt with no man at that hower my lord.
DON PEDRO
  Why then are you no maiden. Leonato,
  I am sory you must heare: vpon mine honor,
  My selfe, my brother, and this grieued Counte
  Did see her, heare her, at that howre last night,
  Talke with a ruffian at her chamber window,
  Who hath indeede most like a liberall villaine,
  Confest the vile encounters they haue had
  A thousand times in secret.
1740 DON IOHN   Fie, fie, they are
  Not to be namd my lord, not to be spoke of,
  There is not chastitie enough in language,
  Without offence to vtter them: thus pretty lady,
  I am sory for thy much misgouernement.
CLAUDIO
  O Hero! what a Hero hadst thou bin,
  If halfe thy outward graces had bin placed,
  About thy thoughts and counsailes of thy heart?
  But fare thee well, most foule, most faire, farewell
  Thou pure impietie, and impious puritie,

  For thee ile locke vp all the gates of Loue,   1750
  And on my eie-liddes shall Coniecture hang,
  To turne all beautie into thoughts of harme,
  And neuer shall it more be gracious.
LEONATO
  Hath no mans dagger here a point for me.
    Hero falls to the ground
BEATRICE
  Why how now cosin, wherfore sinke you down?
DON IOHN
  Come let vs go: these things come thus to light,
  Smother her spirits vp.
        Exeunt Don Pedro, Don Iohn, and Claudio
BENEDICKE
  How doth the Lady?
BEATRICE   Dead I thinke, help vncle,
  Hero, why Hero, vncle, signior Benedicke Frier.
LEONATO
  O Fate! take not away thy heauy hand,   1760
  Death is the fairest couer for her shame
  That may be wisht for.
BEATRICE   How now cosin Hero?
FRIER (to Hero) Haue comfort lady.
LEONATO (to Hero) Dost thou looke vp.
FRIER Yea, wherefore should she not?
LEONATO
  Wherfore? why doth not euery earthly thing,
  Cry shame vpon her? could she here deny
  The story that is printed in her bloud?
  Do not liue Hero, do not ope thine eies,
  For did I thinke thou wouldst not quickly die, 1770
  Thought I thy spirites were stronger than thy shames,
  My selfe would on the rereward of reproches
  Strike at thy life. Grieud I I had but one?
  Chid I for that at frugall Natures frame?
  O one too much by thee: why had I one?
  Why euer wast thou louely in my eies?
  Why had I not with charitable hand,
  Tooke vp a beggars issue at my gates,
  Who smirched thus, and mird with infamy,
  I might haue said, no part of it is mine,   1780
  This shame deriues it selfe from vnknowne loynes,
  But mine and mine I lou'd, and mine I praisde,
  And mine that I was prowd on mine so much,
  That I my selfe, was to my selfe not mine,
  Valewing of her: why she, O she is falne,
  Into a pit of incke, that the wide sea
  Hath drops too few to wash her cleane againe,
  And salt too little, which may season giue
  To her foule tainted flesh.
BENEDICKE   Sir, sir, be patient,
  For my part I am so attird in wonder,   1790
  I know not what to say.
BEATRICE
  O on my soule my cosin is belied.
BENEDICKE
  Lady were you her bedfellow last night.

BEATRICE

   No truly not, although vntill last night,
   I haue this tweluemonth bin her bedfellow.

LEONATO

   Confirmd, confirmd, O that is stronger made,
   Which was before bard vp with ribs of yron,
   Would the two princes lie, and Claudio lie,
   Who lou'd her so, that speaking of her foulenesse,
1800   Washt it with teares! hence from her, let her die.

FRIER Heare me a little,

   For I haue only bin silent so long,
   And giuen way vnto this course of fortune,
   ⌐   ¬
   By noting of the lady, I haue markt,
   A thousand blushing apparitions,
   To start into her face, a thousand innocent shames,
   In angel whitenesse beate away those blushes,
   And in her eie there hath appeard a fire,
1810   To burne the errors that these princes hold
   Against her maiden truth: call me a foole,
   Trust not my reading, nor my obseruations,
   Which with experimental seale doth warrant
   The tenure of my booke: trust not my age,
   My reuerence, calling, nor diuinitie,
   If this sweete ladie lie not guiltlesse here,
   Vnder some biting errour.

LEONATO   Frier, it cannot be,

   Thou seest that al the grace that she hath left,
   Is, that she will not adde to her damnation,
1820   A sinne of periury, she not denies it:
   Why seekst thou then to couer with excuse,
   That which appeares in proper nakednesse?

FRIER (to Hero)

   Lady, what man is he you are accusde of?

HERO

   They know that do accuse me, I know none,
   If I know more of any man aliue
   Then that which maiden modesty doth warrant,
   Let all my sinnes lacke mercie, O my father,
   Proue you that any man with me conuerst,
   At houres vnmeete, or that I yesternight
1830   Maintaind the change of words with any creature,
   Refuse me, hate me, torture me to death.

FRIER

   There is some strange misprision in the princes.

BENEDICKE

   Two of them haue the very bent of honour,
   And if their wisedomes be misled in this,
   The practise of it liues in Iohn the Bastard,
   Whose spirites toyle in frame of villanies.

LEONATO

   I know not, if they speake but truth of her,
   These hands shall teare her, if they wrong her
      honour,
   The prowdest of them shal wel heare of it.
1840   Time hath not yet so dried this bloud of mine,
   Nor age so eate vp my inuention,

   Nor Fortune made such hauocke of my meanes,
   Nor my bad life reft me so much of friends,
   But they shall find awakte in such a kind,
   Both strength of limbe, and policy of mind,
   Ability in meanes, and choise of friends,
   To quit me of them throughly.

FRIER   Pawse awhile,

   And let my counsell sway you in this case,
   Your daughter here the princes left for dead,
   Let her awhile be secretly kept in,   1850
   And publish it, that she is dead indeede,
   Maintaine a mourning ostentation,
   And on your families old monument,
   Hang mourneful epitaphes, and do all rites,
   That appertaine vnto a buriall.

LEONATO

   What shall become of this? what will this do?

FRIER

   Mary this well caried, shall on her behalfe,
   Change slaunder to remorse, that is some good,
   But not for that dreame I on this strange course,
   But on this trauaile looke for greater birth: 1860
   She dying, as it must be so maintaind,
   Vpon the instant that she was accusde,
   Shal be lamented, pittied, and excusde
   Of euery hearer: for it so falls out,
   That what we haue, we prize not to the worth,
   Whiles we enioy it, but being lackt and lost,
   Why then we racke the valew, then we find
   The vertue that possession would not shew vs
   Whiles it was ours, so will it fare with Claudio:
   When hee shall heare she died vpon his words, 1870
   Th'Idæa of her life shall sweetly creepe,
   Into his study of imagination,
   And euery louely Organ of her life,
   Shall come apparelld in more precious habite,
   More moouing delicate, and full of life,
   Into the eie and prospect of his soule
   Then when she liude indeed: then shall he mourne,
   If euer loue had interest in his liuer,
   And wish he had not so accused her:
   No, though he thought his accusation true: 1880
   Let this be so, and doubt not but successe
   Will fashion the euent in better shape,
   Then I can lay it downe in likelihood.
   But if all ayme but this be leuelld false,
   The supposition of the ladies death,
   Will quench the wonder of her infamie.
   And if it sort not wel, you may conceale her,
   As best befits her wounded reputation,
   In some reclusiue and religious life,
   Out of all eies, tongues, minds, and iniuries.   1890

BENEDICKE

   Signior Leonato, let the Frier aduise you,
   And though you know my inwardnesse and loue
   Is very much vnto the prince and Claudio,
   Yet, by mine honor, I will deale in this,

As secretly and iustly as your soule
Should with your body.

LEONATO Being that I flow in griefe,
The smallest twine may leade me.

FRIER

Tis wel consented, presently away,
1900 For to strange sores, strangely they straine the cure,
(*To Hero*) Come lady, die to liue, this wedding day
Perhaps is but prolong'd, haue patience and endure.

exit all but Beatrice and Benedicke

BENEDICKE Lady Beatrice, haue you wept al this while?

BEATRICE Yea, and I will weep a while longer.

BENEDICKE I will not desire that.

BEATRICE You haue no reason, I do it freely.

BENEDICKE Surely I do beleeue your faire cosin is wronged.

BEATRICE Ah, how much might the man deserue of me
that would right her!

1910 BENEDICKE Is there any way to shew such friendship?

BEATRICE A very euen way, but no such friend.

BENEDICKE May a man do it?

BEATRICE It is a mans office, but not yours.

BENEDICKE I doe loue nothing in the worlde so well as
you, is not that strange?

BEATRICE As strange as the thing I knowe not, it were as
possible for me to say, I loued nothing so wel as you,
but beleue me not, and yet I lie not, I confesse nothing,
nor I deny nothing, I am sory for my coosin.

1920 BENEDICKE By my sword Beatrice, thou louest me.

BEATRICE Do not sweare and eate it.

BENEDICKE I will sweare by it that you loue me, and I wil
make him eate it that sayes I loue not you.

BEATRICE Will you not eate your word?

BENEDICKE With no sawce that can be deuised to it, I
protest I loue thee.

BEATRICE Why then God forgiue me.

BENEDICKE What offence sweete Beatrice?

BEATRICE You haue stayed me in a happy houre, I was
1930 about to protest I loued you.

BENEDICKE And do it with all thy heart.

BEATRICE I loue you with so much of my heart, that none
is left to protest.

BENEDICKE Come bid me doe any thing for thee.

BEATRICE Kill Claudio.

BENEDICKE Ha, not for the wide world.

BEATRICE You kill me to deny it, farewell.

BENEDICKE Tarry sweete Beatrice.

BEATRICE I am gone, though I am here, there is no loue
1940 in you, nay I pray you let me go.

BENEDICKE Beatrice.

BEATRICE In faith I will go.

BENEDICKE Weele be friends first.

BEATRICE You dare easier be friends with mee, than fight
with mine enemy.

BENEDICKE Is Claudio thine enemy?

BEATRICE Is a not approoued in the height a villaine, that
hath slaundered, scorned, dishonored my kinswoman?
O that I were a man! what, beare her in hand, vntill
1950 they come to take handes, and then with publike

accusation vncouerd slander, vnmittigated rancour?
O God that I were a man! I woulde eate his heart in
the market place.

BENEDICKE Heare me Beatrice.

BEATRICE Talke with a man out at a window, a proper
saying.

BENEDICKE Nay but Beatrice.

BEATRICE Sweete Hero, she is wrongd, she is slaundred,
shee is vndone.

BENEDICKE Beat?   1960

BEATRICE Princes and Counties! surely a princely
testimonie, a goodly Counte, Counte Comfect, a sweete
Gallant surely, O that I were a man for his sake! or
that I had any friend woulde be a man for my sake!
But manhoode is melted into cursies, valour into
complement, and men are only turnd into tongue, and
trim ones too: he is now as valiant as Hercules, that
only tels a lie, and sweares it: I cannot be a man with
wishing, therfore I will die a woman with grieuing.

BENEDICKE Tarry good Beatrice, by this hand I loue thee.   1970

BEATRICE Vse it for my loue some other way than swearing
by it.

BENEDICKE Thinke you in your soule the Count Claudio
hath wrongd Hero?

BEATRICE Yea, as sure as I haue a thought, or a soule.

BENEDICKE Enough, I am engagde, I will challenge him,
I will kisse your hand, and so I leaue you: by this
hand, Claudio shal render me a deere account: as you
heare of me, so think of me: goe comforte your coosin,
I must say she is dead, and so farewell.   1980

Exeunt seuerally

Enter Dogbery and Verges the Constables, and the   Sc. 13
Sexton, in gownes and the Watch, Conrade and   (4.2)
Borachio

DOGBERY Is our whole dissembly appeard?

VERGES O a stoole and a cushion for the Sexton.

SEXTON ⌈*sits*⌉ Which be the malefactors?

DOGBERY Mary that am I, and my partner.

VERGES Nay thats certaine, we haue the exhibition to
examine.

SEXTON But which are the offenders? that are to be
examined, let them come before maister constable.

DOGBERY Yea mary, let them come before mee, what is
your name, friend?   1990

BORACHIO Borachio.

DOGBERY (*to the Sexton*) Pray write downe Borachio. (*To
Conrade*) Yours sirra.

CONRADE I am a gentleman sir, and my name is Conrade.

DOGBERY Write downe maister gentleman Conrade:
maisters, do you serue God?

CONRADE *and* BORACHIO Yea sir we hope.

DOGBERY Write downe, that they hope they serue God:
and write God first, for God defend but God shoulde
goe before such villaines: maisters, it is prooued alreadie   2000
that you are little better than false knaues, and it will
go neere to be thought so shortly, how answer you for
your selues?

CONRADE Mary sir we say, we are none.

DOGBERY A maruellous witty fellowe I assure you, but I
will go about with him: come you hither sirra, a word
in your eare sir, I say to you, it is thought you are
false knaues.

BORACHIO Sir, I say to you, we are none.

2010 DOGBERY Wel, stand aside, fore God they are both in a
tale: haue you writ downe, that they are none?

SEXTON Master constable, you go not the way to examine,
you must call foorth the watch that are their accusers.

DOGBERY Yea mary, thats the eftest way, let the watch
come forth: masters, I charge you in the Princes name
accuse these men.

WATCH 1 This man said sir, that don Iohn the Princes
brother was a villaine.

DOGBERY Write downe, prince Iohn a villaine: why this
2020 is flat periurie, to call a Princes brother villaine.

BORACHIO Maister Constable.

DOGBERY Pray thee fellowe peace, I doe not like thy looke
I promise thee.

SEXTON What heard you him say else?

WATCH 2 Mary that he had receiued a thousand duckats
of don Iohn, for accusing the Ladie Hero wrongfully.

DOGBERY Flat burglarie as euer was committed.

VERGES Yea by masse that it is.

SEXTON What else fellow?

2030 WATCH 1 And that Counte Claudio did meane vppon his
wordes, to disgrace Hero before the whole assemblie,
and not marrie her.

DOGBERY O villaine! thou wilt be condemnd into
euerlasting redemption for this.

SEXTON What else?

WATCH This is all.

SEXTON And this is more masters then you can deny,
prince Iohn is this morning secretlie stolne awaie: Hero
was in this manner accusde, in this verie manner
2040 refusde, and vppon the griefe of this, sodainlie died:
Maister Constable, let these men be bound, and brought
to Leonatoes, I will goe before and shew him their
examination.   exit

DOGBERY Come, let them be opiniond.

VERGES Let them be in the hands

⌜CONRADE⌝ Of Coxcombe.

DOGBERY Gods my life, wheres the Sexton? let him write
down the Princes officer Coxcombe: come, bind them.
Thou naughty varlet.

2050 CONRADE Away, you are an asse, you are an asse.

DOGBERY Doost thou not suspect my place? doost thou
not suspect my yeeres? O that he were here to write
me downe an asse! but maisters, remember that I am
an asse, though it bee not written downe, yet forget
not that I am an asse: No thou villaine, thou art full
of pietie as shal be prou'de vpon thee by good witnes,
I am a wise fellow, and which is more, an officer, and
which is more, a housholder, and which is more, as
pretty a peece of flesh as anie is in Messina, and one
2060 that knowes the Law, goe to, and a rich fellow enough,
go to, and a fellow that hath had losses, and one that

hath two gownes, and euery thing hansome about
him: bring him away: O that I had bin writ downe an
asse!   exeunt

Enter Leonato and Anthonio his brother   Sc. 14
ANTHONIO   (5.1)
If you go on thus, you will kill your selfe,
And tis not wisedome thus to second griefe,
Against your selfe.

LEONATO   I pray thee cease thy counsaile,
Which falles into mine eares as profitlesse,
As water in a syue: giue not me counsaile,
Nor let no comforter delight mine eare,   2070
But such a one whose wrongs doe sute with mine.
Bring me a father that so lou'd his child,
Whose ioy of her is ouer-whelmd like mine,
And bid him speake of patience,
Measure his woe the length and bredth of mine,
And let it answer euery straine for straine,
As thus for thus, and such a griefe for such,
In euery lineament, branch, shape, and forme:
If such a one will smile and stroke his beard,
Bid sorrow wagge, crie hem, when he should grone,   2080
Patch griefe with prouerbes, make misfortune drunke,
With candle-wasters: bring him yet to me,
And I of him will gather patience:
But there is no such man, for brother, men
Can counsaile, and speake comfort to that griefe,
Which they themselues not feele, but tasting it,
Their counsaile turnes to passion, which before,
Would giue preceptiall medcine to rage,
Fetter strong madnesse in a silken thred,
Charme ach with ayre, and agony with words,   2090
No, no, tis all mens office, to speake patience
To those that wring vnder the loade of sorrow
But no mans vertue nor sufficiencie
To be so morall, when he shall endure
The like himselfe: therefore giue me no counsaile,
My griefes crie lowder then aduertisement.

ANTHONIO
Therein do men from children nothing differ.

LEONATO
I pray thee peace, I wil be flesh and bloud,
For there was neuer yet Philosopher,
That could endure the tooth-ake patiently,   2100
How euer they haue writ the stile of gods,
And made a push at chance and sufferance.

ANTHONIO
Yet bend not all the harme vpon your selfe,
Make those that do offend you, suffer too.

LEONATO
There thou speakst reason, nay I will do so,
My soule doth tell me, Hero is belied,
And that shall Claudio know, so shall the prince,
And all of them that thus dishonour her.
Enter Don Pedro the Prince and Claudio

ANTHONIO
Here comes the Prince and Claudio hastily.

DON PEDRO
    Good den, good den.
2110 CLAUDIO   Good day to both of you.
LEONATO
    Heare you my Lords?
DON PEDRO   We haue some haste Leonato.
LEONATO
    Some haste my lord! well, fare you well my lord,
    Are you so hasty now? wel, all is one.
DON PEDRO
    Nay do not quarrel with vs, good old man.
ANTHONIO
    If he could right himselfe with quarrelling,
    Some of vs would lie low.
CLAUDIO   Who wrongs him?
LEONATO
    Mary thou dost wrong me, thou dissembler, thou:
    Nay, neuer lay thy hand vpon thy sword,
    I feare thee not.
CLAUDIO   Mary beshrew my hand,
2120 If it should giue your age such cause of feare,
    Infaith my hand meant nothing to my sword.
LEONATO
    Tush, tush man, neuer fleere and iest at me,
    I speake not like a dotard, nor a foole,
    As vnder priuiledge of age to bragge,
    What I haue done being yong, or what would doe,
    Were I not old, know Claudio to thy head,
    Thou hast so wrongd mine innocent child and me,
    That I am forst to lay my reuerence by,
    And with grey haires and bruise of many daies,
2130 Do challenge thee to triall of a man,
    I say thou hast belied mine innocent child.
    Thy slander hath gone through and through her heart,
    And she lies buried with her ancestors:
    O in a toomb where neuer scandal slept,
    Saue this of hers, framde by thy villanie.
CLAUDIO
    My villany?
LEONATO   Thine Claudio, thine I say.
DON PEDRO
    You say not right old man.
LEONATO   My Lord, my Lord,
    Ile prooue it on his body if he dare,
    Dispight his nice fence, and his actiue practise,
2140 His Maie of youth, and bloome of lustihood.
CLAUDIO
    Away, I will not haue to doe with you.
LEONATO
    Canst thou so daffe me? thou hast kild my child,
    If thou kilst me, boy, thou shalt kill a man.
ANTHONIO
    He shal kill two of vs, and men indeed,
    But thats no matter, let him kill one first:
    Win me and weare me, let him answer me,
    Come follow me boy, come sir boy, come follow me
    Sir boy, ile whip you from your foyning fence,
    Nay, as I am a gentleman, I will.
2150 LEONATO Brother.

ANTHONIO
    Content your self, God knowes, I lou'd my neece,
    And she is dead, slanderd to death by villaines,
    That dare as well answer a man indeed,
    As I dare take a serpent by the tongue,
    Boyes, apes, braggarts, Iackes, milke-sops.
LEONATO Brother Anthony.
ANTHONIO
    Hold you content, what man! I know them, yea
    And what they weigh, euen to the vtmost scruple,
    Scambling, out-facing, fashion-monging boies,
    That lie, and cogge, and flout, depraue, and slaunder,   2160
    Go antiquely, and shew an outward hidiousnesse,
    And speake of halfe a dozen dang'rous words,
    How they might hurt their enemies, if they durst,
    And this is all.
LEONATO But brother Anthonie.
ANTHONIO Come tis no matter,
    Do not you meddle, let me deale in this.
DON PEDRO
    Gentlemen both, we will not wake your patience,
    My heart is sory for your daughters death:
    But on my honour she was chargde with nothing   2170
    But what was true, and very full of proofe.
LEONATO
    My Lord, my Lord.
DON PEDRO   I will not heare you.
LEONATO
    No. Come brother, away, I wil be heard.
ANTHONIO
    And shal, or some of vs wil smart for it.
                                Exeunt ambo
        Enter Benedicke
DON PEDRO
    See see, heere comes the man we went to seeke.
CLAUDIO Now signior, what newes?
BENEDICKE (to Don Pedro) Good day my Lord.
DON PEDRO Welcome signior, you are almost come to
    parte almost a fray.
CLAUDIO Wee had likt to haue had our two noses snapt   2180
    off with two old men without teeth.
DON PEDRO Leonato and his brother what thinkst thou?
    had we fought, I doubt we should haue beene too yong
    for them.
BENEDICKE In a false quarrell there is no true valour, I
    came to seeke you both.
CLAUDIO We haue beene vp and downe to seeke thee, for
    we are high proofe melancholie, and would faine haue
    it beaten away, wilt thou vse thy wit?
BENEDICKE It is in my scabberd, shal I drawe it?   2190
DON PEDRO Doest thou weare thy wit by thy side?
CLAUDIO Neuer any did so, though very many haue been
    beside their wit, I will bid thee drawe, as wee doe the
    minstrels, draw to pleasure vs.
DON PEDRO As I am an honest man he lookes pale, art
    thou sicke, or angry?
CLAUDIO What, courage man: what though care kild a
    catte, thou hast mettle enough in thee to kill care.
BENEDICKE Sir, I shall meete your wit in the careere, and

2200 you charge it against me, I pray you chuse another
subiect.

CLAUDIO Nay then giue him another staffe, this last was
broke crosse.

DON PEDRO By this light, he chaunges more and more, I
thinke he be angry indeed.

CLAUDIO If he be, he knowes how to turne his girdle.

BENEDICKE (aside to Claudio) Shall I speake a word in your
eare?

CLAUDIO God blesse me from a challenge.

2210 BENEDICKE You are a villaine, I ieast not, I will make it
good howe you dare, with what you dare, and when
you dare: doe mee right, or I will protest your
cowardise: you haue killd a sweete Lady, and her death
shall fall heauie on you, let me heare from you.

CLAUDIO Well I wil meet you, so I may haue good cheare.

DON PEDRO What, a feast, a feast?

CLAUDIO I faith I thanke him he hath bid me to a calues
head & a capon, the which if I doe not carue most
curiously, say my kniffe's naught, shall I not find a
2220 woodcocke too?

BENEDICKE Sir your wit ambles well, it goes easily.

DON PEDRO Ile tell thee how Beatrice praisd thy witte the
other day: I said thou hadst a fine witte, true said she,
a fine little one: no said I, a great wit: right saies she,
a great grosse one: nay said I, a good wit, iust said
she, it hurts no body: nay said I, the gentleman is
wise: certaine said she, a wise gentleman: nay said I,
he hath the tongues: that I beleeue said shee, for he
swore a thing to mee on munday night, which hee
2230 forswore on tuesday morning, theres a double tongue
theirs two tongues, thus did shee an houre together
trans-shape thy particular vertues, yet at last she
cōcluded with a sigh, thou wast the properst man in
Italy.

CLAUDIO For the which shee wept heartily and saide she
cared not.

DON PEDRO Yea that she did, but yet for all that, and if
she did not hate him deadly, she would loue him
dearely, the old mans daughter told vs all.

2240 CLAUDIO All all, and moreouer, God sawe him when he
was hid in the garden.

DON PEDRO But when shall we set the sauage bulles hornes
one the sensible Benedicks head?

CLAUDIO Yea and text vnder-neath, here dwells Benedick
the married man.

BENEDICKE Fare you wel, boy, you know my minde, I wil
leaue you now to your gossep-like humor, you breake
iests as braggards do their blades, which God be thanked
hurt not: (to Don Pedro) my Lord, for your many
2250 courtisies I thanke you, I must discontinue your
company, your brother the bastard is fled from Messina:
you haue among you, kild a sweet and innocent lady:
for my Lord Lacke-beard there, hee and I shal meet,
and till then peace be with him.   exit

DON PEDRO He is in earnest.

CLAUDIO In most profound earnest, and ile warrant you,
for the loue of Beatrice.

DON PEDRO And hath challengde thee.

CLAUDIO Most sincerely.

DON PEDRO What a pretty thing man is, when he goes in   2260
his dublet and hose, and leaues off his wit!

*Enter Dogbery and Verges the Constables, the
Watch, Conrade, and Borachio*

CLAUDIO He is then a Giant to an Ape, but then is an
Ape a Doctor to such a man.

DON PEDRO But soft you, let me be, plucke vp my heart,
and be sad, did he not say my brother was fled?

DOGBERY Come you sir, if iustice cannot tame you, she
shall nere weigh more reasons in her ballance, nay,
and you be a cursing hypocrite once, you must be lookt
to.

DON PEDRO How now, two of my brothers men bound?   2270
Borachio one.

CLAUDIO Hearken after their offence my Lord.

DON PEDRO Officers, what offence haue these men done?

DOGBERY Mary sir, they haue committed false report,
moreouer they haue spoken vntruths, secondarily they
are slanders, sixt and lastly, they haue belyed a Lady,
thirdly they haue verefied vniust thinges, and to
conclude, they are lying knaues.

DON PEDRO First I aske thee what they haue done, thirdly
I ask thee whats their offence, sixt and lastly why they   2280
are committed, and to conclude, what you lay to their
charge.

CLAUDIO Rightly reasoned, and in his owne diuision, and
by my troth theres one meaning wel suted.

DON PEDRO (to Conrade and Borachio) Who haue you
offended maisters, that you are thus bound to your
answere? this learned Constable is too cunning to be
vnderstood, whats your offence?

BORACHIO Sweete prince, let me goe no farther to mine
answere: do you heare me, and let this Counte kill me: 2290
I haue deceiued euen your very eyes: what your
wisedoms could not discouer, these shallowe fooles
haue broght to light, who in the night ouerheard me
confessing to this man, how Don Iohn your brother
incensed me to slaunder the Lady Hero, howe you were
brought into the orchard, and saw me court Margaret
in Heroes garments, how you disgracde hir when you
should marry hir: my villany they haue vpon record,
which I had rather seale with my death, then repeate
ouer to my shame: the lady is dead vpon mine and my   2300
masters false accusation: and briefely, I desire nothing
but the reward of a villaine.

DON PEDRO (to Claudio)
Runnes not this speech like yron through your bloud?

CLAUDIO
I haue dronke poison whiles he vtterd it.

DON PEDRO (to Borachio)
But did my brother set thee on to this?

BORACHIO
Yea, and paid me richly for the practise of it.

DON PEDRO
He is composde and framde of treacherie,
And fled he is vpon this villanie.

CLAUDIO
Sweet Hero, now thy image doth appeare
In the rare semblance that I lou'd it first.

DOGBERY Come, bring away the plaintiffes, by this time
our sexton hath reformed Signior Leonato of the matter:
and masters, do not forget to specifie when time and
place shal serue, that I am an asse.

VERGES Here, here comes master Signior Leonato, and the
sexton too.

Enter Leonato, Anthonio his brother, and the Sexton

LEONATO
Which is the villaine? let me see his eies,
That when I note another man like him,
I may auoide him: which of these is he?

BORACHIO
If you would know your wronger, looke on me.

LEONATO
Art thou the slaue that with thy breath hast killd
Mine innocent child?

BORACHIO   Yea, euen I alone.

LEONATO
No, not so villaine, thou beliest thy selfe,
Here stand a paire of honourable men,
A third is fled that had a hand in it:
I thanke you Princes for my daughters death,
Record it with your high and worthy deeds,
Twas brauely done, if you bethinke you of it.

CLAUDIO
I know not how to pray your pacience,
Yet I must speake, choose your reuenge your selfe,
Impose me to what penance your inuention
Can lay vpon my sinne, yet sinnd I not,
But in mistaking.

DON PEDRO   By my soule nor I,
And yet to satisfie this good old man,
I would bend vnder any heauy waight,
That heele enioyne me to.

LEONATO
I cannot bid you bid my daughter liue,
That were impossible, but I pray you both,
Possesse the people in Messina here,
How innocent she died, and if your loue
Can labour aught in sad inuention,
Hang her an epitaph vpon her toomb,
And sing it to her bones, sing it to night:
To morrow morning come you to my house,
And since you could not be my son in law,
Be yet my nephew: my brother hath a daughter,
Almost the copie of my child thats dead,
And she alone is heyre to both of vs,
Giue her the right you should haue giu'n her cosin,
And so dies my reuenge.

CLAUDIO   O noble sir!
Your ouer kindnesse doth wring teares from me,
I do embrace your offer and dispose
For henceforth of poore Claudio.

LEONATO
To morrow then I wil expect your comming,
To night I take my leaue, this naughty man

Shal face to face be brought to Margaret,
Who I beleeue was packt in al this wrong,
Hyrd to it by your brother.

BORACHIO   No by my soule she was not,
Nor knew not what she did when she spoke to me,
But alwayes hath bin iust and vertuous,
In any thing that I do know by her.

DOGBERY (*to Leonato*) Moreouer sir, which indeede is not
vnder white and blacke, this plaintiffe heere, the
offendour, did call me asse, I beseech you let it be
remembred in his punishment, and also the watch
heard them talke of one Deformed, they say he weares
a key in his eare and a locke hanging by it, and borows
monie in Gods name, the which he hath vsde so long,
& neuer paied, that now men grow hard hearted and
wil lend nothing for Gods sake: praie you examine him
vpon that point.

LEONATO
I thanke thee for thy care and honest paines.

DOGBERY Your worship speakes like a most thankful and
reuerent youth, and I praise God for you.

LEONATO (*giuing him money*) Theres for thy paines.

DOGBERY God saue the foundation.

LEONATO Goe, I discharge thee of thy prisoner, and I
thanke thee.

DOGBERY I leaue an arrant knaue with your worship,
which I beseech your worship to correct your selfe, for
the example of others: God keepe your worship, I wish
your worship well, God restore you to health, I humblie
giue you leaue to depart and if a merie meeting may
be wisht, God prohibite it: come neighbour.

Exeunt Dogbery and Verges

LEONATO
Vntill to morrow morning, Lords, farewell.

ANTHONIO
Farewell my lords, we looke for you to morrow.

DON PEDRO
We will not faile.

CLAUDIO   To night ile mourne with Hero.

LEONATO (*to the Watch*)
Bring you these fellowes on, weel talke with Margaret,
How her acquaintance grew with this lewd felow.

exeunt

Enter Benedicke and Margaret   Sc. 15

BENEDICKE Praie thee sweete mistris Margaret, deserue
well at my hands, by helping me to the speech of
Beatrice.

MARGARET Wil you then write me a sonnet in praise of
my beautie?

BENEDICKE In so high a stile Margaret, that no man liuing
shall come ouer it, for in most comely truth thou
deseruest it.

MARGARET To haue no man come ouer me, why shal I
alwaies keep below staires.

BENEDICKE Thy wit is as quicke as the grey-hounds mouth,
it catches.

MARGARET And your's, as blunt as the Fencers foiles,
which hit, but hurt not.

BENEDICKE A most manly witte Margaret, it will not hurt a woman: and so I pray thee call Beatrice, I giue thee the bucklers.

MARGARET Giue vs the swordes, wee haue bucklers of our owne.

2410 BENEDICKE If you vse them Margaret, you must putte in the pikes with a vice, and they are daungerous weapons for maides.

MARGARET Well, I will call Beatrice to you, who I thinke hath legges.   *Exit Margarite*

BENEDICKE And therefore wil come.

(*He sings*)
> The God of loue
> That sits aboue,
> And knowes mee, and knowes me,
> How pittifull I deserue.

I meane in singing, but in louing, Leander the good
2420 swimmer, Troilus the first imploier of pandars, and a whole booke full of these quondam carpet-mongers, whose names yet runne smoothly in the euen rode of a blancke verse, why they were neuer so truly turnd ouer and ouer as my poore selfe in loue: mary I cannot shew it in rime, I haue tried, I can finde out no rime to Ladie but babie, an innocent rime: for scorne, horne, a hard rime: for schoole foole, a babling rime: very ominous endings, no, I was not borne vnder a riming plannet, nor I cannot wooe in festiuall termes:

       Enter Beatrice

2430 sweete Beatrice wouldst thou come when I cald thee?

BEATRICE Yea signior, and depart when you bid me.

BENEDICKE O stay but till then.

BEATRICE Then, is spoken: fare you wel now, and yet ere I goe, let me goe with that I came for, which is, with knowing what hath past betweene you and Claudio.

BENEDICKE Onely foule words, and therevpon I will kisse thee.

BEATRICE Foule words is but foule wind, and foule wind is but foule breath, and foule breath is noisome, therfore
2440 I wil depart vnkist.

BENEDICKE Thou hast frighted the word out of his right sence, so forcible is thy wit, but I must tel thee plainly, Claudio vndergoes my challenge, and either I must shortly heare from him, or I will subscribe him a coward, and I pray thee now tell me, for which of my bad parts didst thou first fal in loue with me?

BEATRICE For them all together, which maintaine so politique a state of euil, that they will not admitte any good part to intermingle with them: but for which of
2450 my good parts did you first suffer loue for me?

BENEDICKE Suffer loue! a good epithite, I do suffer loue indeed, for I loue thee against my will.

BEATRICE In spight of your heart I thinke, alas poore heart, if you spight it for my sake, I will spight it for yours, for I wil neuer loue that which my friend hates.

BENEDICKE Thou and I are too wise to wooe peaceably.

BEATRICE It appeares not in this confession, theres not one wise man among twentie that will praise himselfe.

BENEDICKE An old, an old instance Beatrice, that liu'd in
2460 the time of good neighbours, if a man do not erect in

this age his owne toomb ere he dies, he shall liue no longer in monument, then the bell rings, and the widow weepes.

BEATRICE And how long is that thinke you?

BENEDICKE Question, why an hower in clamour and a quarter in rhewme, therefore is it most expedient for the wise, if Don worme (his conscience) find no impediment to the contrary, to be the trumpet of his owne vertues, as I am to my self. So much for praising my selfe, who I my selfe will beare witnes is praise 2470 worthie, and now tell me, how doth your cosin?

BEATRICE Verie ill.

BENEDICKE And how do you?

BEATRICE Verie ill too.

BENEDICKE Serue God, loue me, and mend, there wil I leaue you too, for here comes one in haste.

       Enter Vrsula

VRSULA Madam, you must come to your vncle, yonders old coile at home, it is prooued my Lady Hero hath bin falsely accusde, the Prince and Claudio mightily abusde, and Don Iohn is the author of all, who is fled and 2480 gone: will you come presently?

BEATRICE Will you go heare this newes signior?

BENEDICKE I wil liue in thy heart, die in thy lap, and be buried in thy eies: and moreouer, I wil go with thee to thy vncles.   *exeunt*

       Enter Claudio, Don Pedro the Prince, and three or   Sc. 16
       foure with tapers, all in blacke   (5.3)

CLAUDIO
Is this the monument of Leonato?

A LORD
It is my Lord.

           Epitaph

⌈CLAUDIO (*reading from a scroll*)⌉
> Done to death by slanderous tongues,
>> Was the Hero that heere lies:
> Death in guerdon of her wronges,   2490
>> Giues her fame which neuer dies:
> So the life that dyed with shame,
> Liues in death with glorious fame.

He hangs the Epitaph on the toomb

> Hang thou there vpon the toomb,
> Praising hir when I am dumb.

Now musick sound & sing your solemne hymne.

          Song

> Pardon goddesse of the night,
> Those that slew thy virgin knight,
> For the which with songs of woe,
> Round about her tombe they goe: 2500
> Midnight assist our mone,
> Help vs to sigh & grone.
>> Heauily heauily.
> Graues yawne and yeeld your dead,
> Till death be vttered,
>> Heauily heauily.

⌈CLAUDIO⌉

Now vnto thy bones good night,
Yeerely will I do this right.

DON PEDRO

2510 Good morrow maisters, put your torches out,
    The wolues haue preied, and looke, the gentle day
Before the wheeles of Phoebus, round about
    Dapples the drowsie East with spots of grey:
Thanks to you al, and leaue vs, fare you well.

CLAUDIO

Good morrow masters, each his seuerall way.

DON PEDRO

Come let vs hence, and put on other weedes,
    And then to Leonatoes we will goe.

CLAUDIO

And Hymen now with luckier issue speeds,
    Then this for whom we rendred vp this woe.

                                        exeunt

Sc. 17   Enter Leonato, Anthonio, Benedick, Beatrice,
(5.4)   Margaret, Vrsula, Frier, Hero

FRIER

Did I not tell you shee was innocent?

LEONATO

2520 So are the Prince and Claudio who accusd her,
Vpon the errour that you heard debated:
But Margaret was in some fault for this,
Although against her will as it appeares,
In the true course of all the question.

ANTHONIO

Wel, I am glad that all things sorts so well.

BENEDICKE

And so am I, being else by faith enforst
To call young Claudio to a reckoning for it.

LEONATO

Well daughter, and you gentlewomen all,
Withdraw into a chamber by your selues,
2530 And when I send for you come hither masked:
        Exeunt Beatrice, Hero, Margaret, and Vrsula
The Prince and Claudio promisde by this howre
To visite me, you know your office brother,
You must be father to your brothers daughter,
And giue her to young Claudio.

ANTHONIO

Which I will doe with confirmd countenance.

BENEDICKE

Frier, I must intreate your paines, I thinke.

FRIER To doe what Signior?

BENEDICKE

To bind me, or vndo me, one of them:
Signior Leonato, truth it is good Signior,
2540 Your niece regards me with an eye of fauour.

LEONATO

That eye my daughter lent her, tis most true.

BENEDICKE

And I do with an eye of loue requite her.

LEONATO

The sight whereof I thinke you had from me,
From Claudio and the Prince, but whats your will?

BENEDICKE

Your answere sir is enigmaticall,
But for my wil, my will is, your good will
May stand with ours, this day to be conioynd,
In the state of honorable marriage,
In which (good Frier) I shal desire your help.

LEONATO

My heart is with your liking.

FRIER   And my helpe.   2550
Heere comes the Prince and Claudio.
        Enter Don Pedro the Prince, and Claudio, with
        attendants

DON PEDRO

Good morrow to this faire assembly.

LEONATO

Good morrow Prince, good morrow Claudio:
We heere attend you, are you yet determined,
To day to marry with my brothers daughter?

CLAUDIO

Ile hold my mind were she an Ethiope.

LEONATO

Call her foorth brother, heres the Frier ready.
                                Exit Anthonio

DON PEDRO

Good morrow Bened. why whats the matter?
That you haue such a Februarie face,
So full of frost, of storme, and clowdinesse.   2560

CLAUDIO

I thinke he thinkes vpon the sauage bull:
Tush feare not man, weele tip thy hornes with gold,
And all Europa shall reioyce at thee,
As once Europa did at lustie Ioue,
When he would play the noble beast in loue.

BENEDICKE

Bull Ioue sir had an amiable lowe,
And some such strange bull leapt your fathers cowe,
And got a calfe in that same noble feate,
Much like to you, for you haue iust his bleate.
        Enter Anthonio with Hero, Beatrice, Margaret, and
        Vrsula, masked

CLAUDIO

For this I owe you: here comes other recknings.   2570
Which is the Lady I must seize vpon?

⌈ANTHONIO⌉

This same is she, and I do giue you her.

CLAUDIO

Why then shees mine, sweet, let me see your face.

LEONATO

No that you shall not till you take her hand,
Before this Frier, and sweare to marry hir.

CLAUDIO (to Hero)

Giue me your hand before this holy Frier,
I am your husband if you like of me.

HERO (vnmasking)

And when I liu'd I was your other wife,
And when you lou'd, you were my other husband.

CLAUDIO

Another Hero.

HERO   Nothing certainer,   2580

635

One Hero died defilde, but I do liue,
And surely as I liue, I am a maide.

DON PEDRO

The former Hero, Hero that is dead.

LEONATO

She died my Lord, but whiles her slaunder liu'd.

FRIER

All this amazement can I qualifie,
When after that the holy rites are ended,
Ile tell you largely of faire Heroes death,
Meane time let wonder seeme familiar,
And to the chappell let vs presently.

BENEDICKE

2590   Soft and faire Frier, which is Beatrice?

BEATRICE (*vnmasking*)

I answer to that name, what is your will?

BENEDICKE

Do not you loue me?

BEATRICE   Why no, no more then reason.

BENEDICKE

Why then your vncle, and the prince, and Claudio,
Haue beene deceiu'd, they swore you did.

BEATRICE

Do not you loue me?

BENEDICKE   Troth no, no more then reason.

BEATRICE

Why then my cosin Margaret and Vrsula
Are much deceiu'd, for they did sweare you did.

BENEDICKE

They swore that you were almost sicke for me.

BEATRICE

They swore that you were welnigh dead for me.

BENEDICKE

2600   Tis no such matter, then you do not loue me.

BEATRICE

No truly, but in friendly recompence.

LEONATO

Come cosin, I am sure you loue the gentleman.

CLAUDIO

And ile be sworne vpon't, that he loues her,
For heres a paper written in his hand,
A halting sonnet of his owne pure braine,
Fashiond to Beatrice.

HERO   And heres another,

Writ in my cosins hand, stolne from her pocket,
Containing her affection vnto Benedicke.

BENEDICKE A miracle, heres our owne hands against our
hearts: come, I will haue thee, but by this light I take   2610
thee for pittie.

BEATRICE I would not denie you, but by this good day, I
yeeld vpon great perswasion, and partly to saue your
life, for I was told, you were in a consumption.

BENEDICKE (*kissing her*) Peace I will stop your mouth.

DON PEDRO

How dost thou Benedicke the married man?

BENEDICKE Ile tel thee what prince: a colledge of witte-
crackers cannot flout me out of my humour, dost thou
think I care for a Satyre or an Epigramme? no, if a
man will be beaten with braines, a shall weare nothing   2620
hansome about him: in briefe, since I doe purpose to
marrie, I will think nothing to anie purpose that the
world can saie against it, and therfore neuer flout at
me, for what I haue said against it: for man is a giddie
thing, and this is my conclusion: for thy part Claudio,
I did thinke to haue beaten thee, but in that thou art
like to be my kinsman, liue vnbruisde, and loue my
cousen.

CLAUDIO I had wel hopte thou wouldst haue denied
Beatrice, that I might haue cudgelld thee out of thy   2630
single life, to make thee a double dealer, which out of
question thou wilt be, if my coosin do not looke
exceeding narrowly to thee.

BENEDICKE Come, come, we are friends, lets haue a dance
ere we are maried, that we may lighten our own hearts,
and our wiues heeles.

LEONATO Weele haue dancing afterward.

BENEDICKE First, of my worde, therefore plaie musicke, (*to
Don Pedro*) Prince, thou art sad, get thee a wife, get
thee a wife, there is no staffe more reuerent then one   2640
tipt with horne.

     Enter Messenger

MESSENGER

My Lord, your brother Iohn is tane in flight,
And brought with armed men backe to Messina.

BENEDICKE Thinke not on him till to morrow, ile deuise
thee braue punishments for him: strike vp Pipers.
     dance, and exeunt

FINIS

HENRY V

THE Chorus to Act 5 of *Henry V* contains an uncharacteristic, direct topical reference:

> Were now the Generall of our gracious Empresse,
> As in good time he may, from Ireland comming,
> Bringing Rebellion broached on his Sword;
> How many would the peacefull Citie quit,
> To welcome him?

'The Generall' must be the Earl of Essex, whose 'Empresse'—Queen Elizabeth—had sent him on an Irish campaign on 27 March 1599; he returned, disgraced, on 28 September. Plans for his campaign had been known at least since the previous November; the idea that he might return in triumph would have been meaningless after September 1599, and it seems likely that Shakespeare wrote his play during 1599, probably in the spring. It appeared in print, in a debased text, in (probably) August 1600, when it was said to have 'bene sundry times playd by the Right honorable the Lord Chamberlaine his seruants'. Although this text seems to have been put together from memory by actors playing in an abbreviated adaptation, the Shakespearian text behind it appears to have been in a later state than the generally superior text printed from Shakespeare's own papers in the 1623 Folio. Our edition draws on the 1600 quarto in the attempt to represent the play as acted by Shakespeare's company. The principal difference is the reversion to historical authenticity in the substitution at Agincourt of the Duke of Burbon for the Dolphin.

As in the two plays about Henry IV, Shakespeare is indebted to *The Famous Victories of Henry the fifth* (printed 1598). Other Elizabethan plays about Henry V, now lost, may have influenced him; he certainly used the chronicle histories of Edward Hall (1542) and Holinshed (1577, revised and enlarged in 1587).

From the 'ciuil broils' of the earlier history plays, Shakespeare turns to portray a country united in war against France. Each act is prefaced by a Chorus, speaking some of the play's finest poetry, and giving it an epic quality. Henry V, 'Starre of England', is Shakespeare's most heroic warrior king, but (like his predecessors) has an introspective side, and is aware of the crime by which his father came to the throne. We are reminded of his 'wilder dayes', and see that the transition from 'madcap prince' to the 'Mirror of all Christian Kings' involves loss: although the epilogue to *2 Henry IV* had suggested that Sir Iohn would reappear, he is only, though poignantly, an off-stage presence. Yet Shakespeare's infusion of comic form into historical narrative reaches its natural conclusion in this play. Sir Iohn's cronies, Pistoll, Bardolfe, Nym, and Hostesse Quickly, reappear to provide a counterpart to the heroic action, and Shakespeare invents comic episodes involving an Englishman (Gower), a Welshman (Fluellen), an Irishman (Mackmorrice), and a Scot (Iamy). The play also has romance elements, in the almost incredible extent of the English victory over the French and in the disguised Henry's comradely mingling with his soldiers, as well as in his courtship of the French princess. The play's romantic and heroic aspects have made it popular especially in times of war and have aroused accusations of jingoism, but the horrors of war are vividly depicted, and the Chorus's closing speech reminds us that Henry died young, and that his son's protector 'lost France, and made his England bleed'.

THE NAMES OF THE ACTORS

CHORUS

KING HARRY the fift of England, claiming the French throne

Duke of GLOUCESTER ⎱
Duke of CLARENCE ⎰ his brothers

Duke of EXETER, his vnckle

Duke of YORKE

SALISBURY

WESTMERLAND

WARWICK

BISHOP OF CANTERBURY

BISHOP OF ELY

Richard, Earle of CAMBRIDGE ⎱
Henry, Lord SCROOPE of Masham ⎰ traytors
Sir Thomas GRAY

PISTOLL ⎱
NIM ⎰ former companions of Sir Iohn Falstaffe
BARDOLFE

BOY, former page of Sir Iohn Falstaffe

HOSTESSE, formerly Mistresse Quickly, now Pistolls wife

GOWER, an English Captaine

FLUELLEN, a Welch Captaine

MACKMORRICE, an Irish Captaine

IAMY, a Scots Captaine

Sir Thomas ERPINGHAM

Iohn BATES ⎱
Alexander COURT ⎰ English souldiers
Michael WILLIAMS

HERALD

FRENCH KING

QUEENE Isabel, his wife

The DOLPHIN, their sonne and Heire

KATHERINE, their daughter

ALICE, an old Gentlewoman

The CONSTABLE of France ⎱
Duke of BURBON
Duke of ORLEANCE
Duke of BERRY ⎰ French Nobles at Agincourt
Lord RAMBURES
Lord GRANDPREE

Duke of BURGONIE

MOUNTIOY, the French Herald

GOUERNOUR of Harflew

French AMBASSADORS to England

The Life of Henry the Fift

Prologue   *Enter Chorus as Prologue*

CHORUS

O for a Muse of Fire, that would ascend
The brightest Heauen of Inuention:
A Kingdome for a Stage, Princes to Act,
And Monarchs to behold the swelling Scene.
Then should the Warlike Harry, like himselfe,
Assume the Port of Mars, and at his heeles
(Leasht in, like Hounds) should Famine, Sword, and Fire
Crouch for employment. But pardon, Gentles all:
The flat vnraysed Spirits, that hath dar'd,
10 *On this vnworthy Scaffold, to bring forth*
So great an Obiect. Can this Cock-Pit hold
The vastie fields of France? Or may we cramme
Within this Woodden O, the very Caskes
That did affright the Ayre at Agincourt?
O pardon: since a crooked Figure may
Attest in little place a Million,
And let vs, Cyphers to this great Accompt,
On your imaginarie Forces worke.
Suppose within the Girdle of these Walls
20 *Are now confin'd two mightie Monarchies,*
Whose high, vp-reared, and abutting Fronts,
The perillous narrow Ocean parts asunder.
Peece out our imperfections with your thoughts:
Into a thousand parts diuide one Man,
And make imaginarie Puissance.
Thinke when we talke of Horses, that you see them
Printing their prowd Hoofes i'th' receiuing Earth:
For 'tis your thoughts that now must deck our Kings,
Carry them here and there: Iumping o're Times ;
30 *Turning th'accomplishment of many yeeres*
Into an Howre-glasse: for the which supplie,
Admit me Chorus to this Historie ;
Who Prologue-like, your humble patience pray,
Gently to heare, kindly to iudge our Play.   *Exit*

Sc. 1   *Enter the two Bishops of Canterbury and Ely*
(1.1) BISHOP OF CANTERBURY

My Lord, Ile tell you, that selfe Bill is vrg'd,
Which in th'eleuĕth yere of yᵉ last Kings reign
Was like, and had indeed against vs past,
But that the scambling and vnquiet time
Did push it out of farther question.

BISHOP OF ELY

40 But how my Lord shall we resist it now?

BISHOP OF CANTERBURY

It must be thought on: if it passe against vs,
We loose the better halfe of our Possession:
For all the Temporall Lands, which men deuout
By Testament haue giuen to the Church,
Would they strip from vs; being valu'd thus,
As much as would maintaine, to the Kings honor,

Full fifteene Earles, and fifteene hundred Knights,
Six thousand and two hundred good Esquires:
And to reliefe of Lazars, and weake age
Of indigent faint Soules, past corporall toyle,   50
A hundred Almes-houses, right well supply'd:
And to the Coffers of the King beside,
A thousand pounds by th'yeere. Thus runs the Bill.

BISHOP OF ELY This would drinke deepe.

BISHOP OF CANTERBURY 'Twould drinke the Cup and all.

BISHOP OF ELY But what preuention?

BISHOP OF CANTERBURY

The King is full of grace, and faire regard.

BISHOP OF ELY

And a true louer of the holy Church.

BISHOP OF CANTERBURY

The courses of his youth promis'd it not.
The breath no sooner left his Fathers body,   60
But that his wildnesse, mortify'd in him,
Seem'd to dye too: yea, at that very moment,
Consideration like an Angell came,
And whipt th'offending *Adam* out of him;
Leauing his body as a Paradise,
T'inuelop and containe Celestiall Spirits.
Neuer was such a sodaine Scholler made:
Neuer came Reformation in a Flood,
With such a heady currance scowring faults:
Nor neuer *Hidra*-headed Wilfulnesse   70
So soone did loose his Seat; and all at once;
As in this King.

BISHOP OF ELY   We are blessed in the Change.

BISHOP OF CANTERBURY

Heare him but reason in Diuinitie;
And all-admiring, with an inward wish
You would desire the King were made a Prelate:
Heare him debate of Common-wealth Affaires;
You would say, it hath been all in all his study:
List his discourse of Warre; and you shall heare
A fearefull Battaile rendred you in Musique.
Turne him to any Cause of Pollicy,   80
The Gordian Knot of it he will vnloose,
Familiar as his Garter: that when he speakes,
The Ayre, a Charter'd Libertine, is still,
And the mute Wonder lurketh in mens eares,
To steale his sweet and honyed Sentences:
So that the Art and Practique part of Life,
Must be the Mistresse to this Theorique.
Which is a wonder how his Grace should gleane it,
Since his addiction was to Courses vaine,
His Companies vnletter'd, rude, and shallow,   90
His Houres fill'd vp with Ryots, Banquets, Sports;
And neuer noted in him any studie,
Any retyrement, any sequestration,
From open Haunts and Popularitie.

BISHOP OF ELY

The Strawberry growes vnderneath the Nettle,
And holesome Berryes thriue and ripen best,
Neighbour'd by Fruit of baser qualitie:
And so the Prince obscur'd his Contemplation
Vnder the Veyle of Wildnesse, which (no doubt)
100   Grew like the Summer Grasse, fastest by Night,
Vnseene, yet cressiue in his facultie.

BISHOP OF CANTERBURY

It must be so; for Miracles are ceast:
And therefore we must needes admit the meanes,
How things are perfected.

BISHOP OF ELY   But my good Lord:

How now for mittigation of this Bill,
Vrg'd by the Commons? doth his Maiestie
Incline to it, or no?

BISHOP OF CANTERBURY He seemes indifferent:

Or rather swaying more vpon our part,
Then cherishing th'exhibiters against vs:
110   For I haue made an offer to his Maiestie,
Vpon our Spirituall Conuocation,
And in regard of Causes now in hand,
Which I haue open'd to his Grace at large,
As touching France, to giue a greater Summe,
Then euer at one time the Clergie yet
Did to his Predecessors part withall.

BISHOP OF ELY

How did this offer seeme receiu'd, my Lord?

BISHOP OF CANTERBURY

With good acceptance of his Maiestie:
Saue that there was not time enough to heare,
120   As I perceiu'd his Grace would faine haue done,
The seueralls and vnhidden passages
Of his true Titles to some certaine Dukedomes,
And generally, to the Crowne and Seat of France,
Deriu'd from *Edward*, his great Grandfather.

BISHOP OF ELY

What was th'impediment that broke this off?

BISHOP OF CANTERBURY

The French Embassador vpon that instant
Crau'd audience; and the howre I thinke is come,
To giue him hearing: Is it foure a Clock?

BISHOP OF ELY It is.

BISHOP OF CANTERBURY

130   Then goe we in, to know his Embassie:
Which I could with a ready guesse declare,
Before the Frenchman speake a word of it.

BISHOP OF ELY

Ile wait vpon you, and I long to heare it.   *Exeunt*

Sc. 2   *Enter King Harry, Gloucester, ⌈Clarence⌉, Warwick,*
(1.2)   *Westmerland, and Exeter*

KING HARRY

Where is my gracious Lord of Canterbury?

EXETER

Not here in presence.

KING HARRY   Send for him, good Vnckle.

WESTMERLAND

Shall we call in th'Ambassador, my Liege?

KING HARRY

Not yet, my Cousin: we would be resolu'd,
Before we heare him, of some things of weight,
That taske our thoughts, concerning vs and France.
            Enter the two Bishops of Canterbury and Ely

BISHOP OF CANTERBURY

God and his Angels guard your sacred Throne,   140
And make you long become it.

KING HARRY   Sure we thanke you.

My learned Lord, we pray you to proceed,
And iustly and religiously vnfold,
Why the Law *Salike*, that they haue in France,
Or should or should not barre vs in our Clayme:
And God forbid, my deare and faithfull Lord,
That you should fashion, wrest, or bow your reading,
Or nicely charge your vnderstanding Soule,
With opening Titles miscreate, whose right
Sutes not in natiue colours with the truth: 150
For God doth know, how many now in health,
Shall drop their blood, in approbation
Of what your reuerence shall incite vs to.
Therefore take heed how you impawne our Person,
How you awake our sleeping Sword of Warre;
We charge you in the Name of God take heed:
For neuer two such Kingdomes did contend,
Without much fall of blood, whose guiltlesse drops
Are euery one, a Woe, a sore Complaint,
'Gainst him, whose wrongs giues edge vnto the
      Swords,   160
That makes such waste in briefe mortalitie.
Vnder this Coniuration, speake my Lord:
For we will heare, note, and beleeue in heart,
That what you speake, is in your Conscience washt,
As pure as sinne with Baptisme.

BISHOP OF CANTERBURY

Then heare me gracious Soueraign, & you Peers,
That owe your selues, your liues, and seruices,
To this Imperiall Throne. There is no barre
To make against your Highnesse Clayme to France,
But this which they produce from *Pharamond*,   170
In terram Salicam Mulieres ne succedant,
No Woman shall succeed in *Salike* Land:
Which *Salike* Land, the French vniustly gloze
To be the Realme of France, and *Pharamond*
The founder of this Law, and Female Barre.
Yet their owne Authors faithfully affirme,
That the Land *Salike* is in Germanie,
Betweene the Flouds of Sala and of Elue:
Where *Charles* the Great hauing subdu'd the Saxons,
There left behind and settled certaine French: 180
Who holding in disdaine the German Women,
For some dishonest manners of their life,
Establisht ther this Law; to wit, No Female
Should be Inheritrix in *Salike* Land:
Which *Salike* (as I said) 'twixt Elue and Sala,

Is at this day in Germanie, call'd *Meisen*.
Then doth it well appeare, the *Salike* Law
Was not deuised for the Realme of France:
Nor did the French possesse the *Salike* Land,
190 Vntill foure hundred one and twentie yeeres
After defunction of King *Pharamond*,
Idly suppos'd the founder of this Law,
Who died within the yeere of our Redemption,
Foure hundred twentie six: and *Charles* the Great
Subdu'd the Saxons, and did seat the French
Beyond the Riuer *Sala*, in the yeere
Eight hundred fiue. Besides, their Writers say,
King *Pepin*, which deposed *Childerike*,
Did as Heire Generall, being descended
200 Of *Blithild*, which was Daughter to King *Clothair*,
Make Clayme and Title to the Crowne of France.
Hugh Capet also, who vsurpt the Crowne
Of *Charles* the Duke of Loraine, sole Heire male
Of the true Line and Stock of *Charles* the Great:
To fine his Title with some shewes of truth,
Though in pure truth it was corrupt and naught,
Conuey'd himselfe as Heire to th'Lady *Lingard*,
Daughter to *Charlemaine*, who was the Sonne
To *Lewes* the Emperour, and *Lewes* the Sonne
210 Of *Charles* the Great: also King *Lewes* the Ninth,
Who was sole Heire to the Vsurper *Capet*,
Could not keepe quiet in his conscience,
Wearing the Crowne of France, 'till satisfied,
That faire Queene *Isabel*, his Grandmother,
Was Lineall of the Lady *Ermengard*,
Daughter to *Charles* the foresaid Duke of Loraine:
By the which Marriage, the Lyne of *Charles* the Great
Was re-vnited to the Crowne of France.
So that, as cleare as is the Summers Sunne,
220 King *Pepins* Title, and *Hugh Capets* Clayme,
King *Lewes* his satisfaction, all appeare
To hold in Right and Title of the Female:
So doe the Kings of France vnto this day,
Howbeit they would hold vp this Salique Law,
To barre your Highnesse clayming from the Female,
And rather chuse to hide them in a Net,
Then amply to imbarre their crooked Titles,
Vsurpt from you and your Progenitors.

KING HARRY
May I with right and conscience make this claim?

BISHOP OF CANTERBURY
230 The sinne vpon my head, dread Soueraigne:
For in the Booke of *Numbers* is it writ,
When the sonne dyes, let the Inheritance
Descend vnto the Daughter. Gracious Lord,
Stand for your owne, vnwind your bloody Flagge,
Looke back into your mightie Ancestors:
Goe my dread Lord, to your great Grandsires Tombe,
From whom you clayme; inuoke his Warlike Spirit,
And your Great Vnckles, *Edward* the Black Prince,
Who on the French ground play'd a Tragedie,
240 Making defeat on the full Power of France:
Whiles his most mightie Father on a Hill

Stood smiling, to behold his Lyons Whelpe
Forrage in blood of French Nobilitie.
O Noble English, that could entertaine
With halfe their Forces, the full pride of France,
And let another halfe stand laughing by,
All out of worke, and cold for action.

BISHOP OF ELY
Awake remembrance of those valiant dead,
And with your puissant Arme renew their Feats;
You are their Heire, you sit vpon their Throne: 250
The Blood and Courage that renowned them,
Runs in your Veines: and my thrice-puissant Liege
Is in the very May-Morne of his Youth,
Ripe for Exploits and mightie Enterprises.

EXETER
Your Brother Kings and Monarchs of the Earth
Doe all expect, that you should rowse your selfe,
As did the former Lyons of your Blood.

WESTMERLAND
They know your Grace hath cause; and means, and
      might,
So hath your Highnesse: neuer King of England
Had Nobles richer, and more loyall Subiects,   260
Whose hearts haue left their bodyes here in England,
And lye pauillion'd in the fields of France.

BISHOP OF CANTERBURY
O let their bodyes follow my deare Liege
With Blood, and Sword and Fire, to win your Right:
In ayde whereof, we of the Spiritualtie
Will rayse your Highnesse such a mightie Summe,
As neuer did the Clergie at one time
Bring in to any of your Ancestors.

KING HARRY
We must not onely arme t'inuade the French,
But lay downe our proportions, to defend   270
Against the Scot, who will make roade vpon vs,
With all aduantages.

BISHOP OF CANTERBURY
They of those Marches, gracious Soueraign,
Shall be a Wall sufficient to defend
Our in-land from the pilfering Borderers.

KING HARRY
We do not meane the coursing snatchers onely,
But feare the maine intendment of the Scot,
Who hath been still a giddy neighbour to vs:
For you shall reade, that my great Grandfather
Neuer vnmaskt his power vnto France,   280
But that the Scot, on his vnfurnisht Kingdome,
Came pouring like the Tyde into a breach,
With ample and brim fulnesse of his force,
Galling the gleaned Land with hot Assayes,
Girding with grieuous siege, Castles and Townes:
That England being emptie of defence,
Hath shooke and trembled at the brute thereof.

BISHOP OF CANTERBURY
She hath bin thē more fear'd thē harm'd, my Liege:
For heare her but exampl'd by her selfe,
When all her Cheualrie hath been in France,   290

And shee a mourning Widow of her Nobles,
Shee hath her selfe not onely well defended,
But taken and impounded as a Stray,
The King of Scots: whom shee did send to France,
To fill King *Edwards* fame with prisoner Kings,
And make y^{or} Chronicle as rich with prayse,
As is the Owse and bottome of the Sea
With sunken Wrack, and sum-lesse Treasuries.

⌈A LORD⌉

But there's a saying very old and true,
300   *If that you will France win,*
      Then with Scotland first begin.
For once the Eagle (England) being in prey,
To her vnguarded Nest, the Weazell (Scot)
Comes sneaking, and so sucks her Princely Egges,
Playing the Mouse in absence of the Cat,
To tame and hauocke more then she can eate.

EXETER

It followes then, the Cat must stay at home,
Yet that is but a crush'd necessity,
Since we haue lockes to safegard necessaries,
310 And pretty traps to catch the petty theeues.
While that the Armed hand doth fight abroad,
Th'aduised head defends it selfe at home:
For Gouernment, though high, and low, and lower,
Put into parts, doth keepe in one consent,
Congreeing in a full and natural close,
Like Musicke.

BISHOP OF CANTERBURY

        True: Therefore doth heauen diuide
The state of man in diuers functions,
Setting endeuour in continual motion:
To which is fixed as an ayme or butt,
320 Obedience: for so worke the Hony Bees,
Creatures that by a rule in Nature teach
The Act of Order to a peopled Kingdome.
They haue a King, and Officers of sorts,
Where some like Magistrates correct at home:
Others, like Merchants venter Trade abroad:
Others, like Souldiers armed in their stings,
Make boote vpon the Summers Veluet buddes:
Which pillage, they with merry march bring home
To the Tent-royal of their Emperor:
330 Who busied in his Maiestie surueyes
The singing Masons building roofes of Gold,
The ciuil Citizens lading vp the hony;
The poore Mechanicke Porters, crowding in
Their heauy burthens at his narrow gate:
The sad-ey'd Iustice with his surly humme,
Deliuering ore to Executors pale
The lazie yawning Drone: I this inferre,
That many things hauing full reference
To one consent, may worke contrariously,
340 As many Arrowes loosed seuerall wayes
Flye to one marke: as many wayes meet in one
      towne,
As many fresh streames meet in one salt sea;
As many Lynes close in the Dials center:

So may a thousand actions once a foote,
End in one purpose, and be all well borne
Without defect. Therefore to France, my Liege,
Diuide your happy England into foure,
Whereof, take you one quarter into France,
And you withall shall make all Gallia shake.
If we with thrice such powers left at home, 350
Cannot defend our owne doores from the dogge,
Let vs be worried, and our Nation lose
The name of hardinesse and policie.

KING HARRY

Call in the Messengers sent from the Dolphin.

      Exit one or more

Now are we well resolu'd, and by Gods helpe
And yours, the noble sinewes of our power,
France being ours, wee'l bend it to our Awe,
Or breake it all to peeces. Or there wee'l sit,
(Ruling in large and ample Emperie,
Ore France, and all her (almost) Kingly Dukedomes) 360
Or lay these bones in an vnworthy Vrne,
Tomblesse, with no remembrance ouer them:
Either our History shall with full mouth
Speake freely of our Acts, or else our graue
Like Turkish mute, shall haue a tonguelesse mouth,
Not worshipt with a waxen Epitaph.

     Enter Ambassadors of France with a Tun

Now are we well prepar'd to know the pleasure
Of our faire Cosin Dolphin: for we heare,
Your greeting is from him, not from the King.

AMBASSADOR

May't please your Maiestie to giue vs leaue 370
Freely to render what we haue in charge:
Or shall we sparingly shew you farre off
The Dolphins meaning, and our Embassie.

KING HARRY

We are no Tyrant, but a Christian King,
Vnto whose grace our passion is as subiect
As is our wretches fettred in our prisons,
Therefore with franke and with vncurbed plainnesse,
Tell vs the *Dolphins* minde.

AMBASSADOR   Thus than in few:
Your Highnesse lately sending into France,
Did claime some certaine Dukedomes, in the right 380
Of your great Predecessor, King *Edward* the third.
In answer of which claime, the Prince our Master
Sayes, that you sauour too much of your youth,
And bids you be aduis'd: There's nought in France,
That can be with a nimble Galliard wonne:
You cannot reuell into Dukedomes there.
He therefore sends you meeter for your spirit
This Tun of Treasure; and in lieu of this,
Desires you let the dukedomes that you claime
Heare no more of you. This the *Dolphin* speakes. 390

KING HARRY

What Treasure Vncle?

EXETER (*opening the tun*) Tennis balles, my Liege.

KING HARRY

We are glad the *Dolphin* is so pleasant with vs,

His Present, and your paines we thanke you for:
When we haue matcht our Rackets to these Balles,
We will in France (by Gods grace) play a set,
Shall strike his fathers Crowne into the hazard.
Tell him, he hath made a match with such a
          Wrangler,
That all the Courts of France will be disturb'd
With Chaces. And we vnderstand him well,
How he comes o're vs with our wilder dayes, 400
Not measuring what vse we made of them.
We neuer valew'd this poore seate of England,
And therefore liuing hence, did giue our selfe
To barbarous license: As 'tis euer common,
That men are merriest, when they are from home.
But tell the *Dolphin*, I will keepe my State,
Be like a King, and shew my sayle of Greatnesse,
When I do rowse me in my Throne of France.
For that haue I layd by my Maiestie,
And plodded like a man for working dayes: 410
But I will rise there with so full a glorie,
That I will dazle all the eyes of France,
Yea strike the *Dolphin* blinde to looke on vs,
And tell the pleasant Prince, this Mocke of his
Hath turn'd his balles to Gun-stones, and his soule
Shall stand sore charged, for the wastefull vengeance
That shall flye from them: for many a thousand
          widows
Shall this his Mocke, mocke out of their deer husbands;
Mocke mothers from their sonnes, mock Castles
          downe:
I some are yet vngotten and vnborne, 420
That shal haue cause to curse the *Dolphins* scorne.
But this lyes all within the wil of God,
To whom I do appeale, and in whose name
Tel you the *Dolphin*, I am comming on,
To venge me as I may, and to put forth
My rightfull hand in a wel-hallow'd cause.
So get you hence in peace: And tell the *Dolphin*,
His Iest will sauour but of shallow wit,
When thousands weepe more then did laugh at it.
Conuey them with safe conduct. Fare you well. 430
                                   Exeunt Ambassadors
EXETER This was a merry Message.
KING HARRY
We hope to make the Sender blush at it:
Therefore, my Lords, omit no happy howre,
That may giue furth'rance to our Expedition:
For we haue now no thought in vs but France,
Saue those to God, that runne before our businesse.
Therefore let our proportions for these Warres
Be soone collected, and all things thought vpon,
That may with reasonable swiftnesse adde
More Feathers to our Wings: for God before, 440
Wee'le chide this *Dolphin* at his fathers doore.
Therefore let euery man now taske his thought,
That this faire Action may on foot be brought.
                                   ⌈*Flourish.*⌉ *Exeunt*

Enter Chorus
CHORUS
Now all the Youth of England are on fire,
And silken Dalliance in the Wardrobe lyes:
Now thriue the Armorers, and Honors thought
Reignes solely in the breast of euery man.
They sell the Pasture now, to buy the Horse;
Following the Mirror of all Christian Kings,
With winged heeles, as English *Mercuries*. 450
For now sits Expectation in the Ayre,
And hides a Sword, from Hilts vnto the Point,
With Crownes Imperiall, Crownes and Coronets,
Promis'd to *Harry*, and his followers.
The French aduis'd by good intelligence
Of this most dreadfull preparation,
Shake in their feare, and with pale Pollicy
Seeke to diuert the English purposes.
O England: Modell to thy inward Greatnesse,
Like little Body with a mightie Heart: 460
What mightst thou do, that honour would thee do,
Were all thy children kinde and naturall:
But see, thy fault France hath in thee found out,
A nest of hollow bosomes, which he filles
With treacherous Crownes, and three corrupted men:
One, *Richard* Earle of Cambridge, and the second
Henry Lord *Scroope* of *Masham*, and the third
Sir *Thomas Grey* Knight of Northumberland,
Haue for the Gilt of France (O guilt indeed)
Confirm'd Conspiracy with fearefull France, 470
And by their hands, this grace of Kings must dye,
If Hell and Treason hold their promises,
Ere he take ship for France; and in Southampton.
Linger your patience on, and wee'l digest
Th'abuse of distance; force perforce a play:
The summe is payde, the Traitors are agreed,
The King is set from London, and the Scene
Is now transported (Gentles) to Southampton,
There is the Play-house now, there must you sit,
And thence to France shall we conuey you safe, 480
And bring you backe: Charming the narrow seas
To giue you gentle Passe: for if we may,
Wee'l not offend one stomacke with our Play.
But till the King come forth, and not till then,
Vnto Southampton do we shift our Scene.   *Exit*

Enter Corporall Nym, and Lieutenant Bardolfe

BARDOLFE Well met Corporall *Nym*.
NYM Good morrow Lieutenant *Bardolfe*.
BARDOLFE What, are Ancient *Pistoll* and you friends yet?
NYM For my part, I care not: I say little: but when time
shall serue, there shall be smiles, but that shall be as 490
it may. I dare not fight, but I will winke and holde out
mine yron: it is a simple one, but what though? It will
toste Cheese, and it will endure cold, as another mans
sword will: and there's an end.
BARDOLFE I will bestow a breakfast to make you friendes,
and wee'l bee all three sworne brothers to France: Let't
be so good Corporall *Nym*.

NYM Faith, I will liue so long as I may, that's the certaine
  of it: and when I cannot liue any longer, I will doe as
500 I may: That is my rest, that is the rendeuous of it.

BARDOLFE It is certaine Corporall, that he is marryed to
  Nell Quickly, and certainly she did you wrong, for you
  were troth-plight to her.

NYM I cannot tell, Things must be as they may: men
  may sleepe, and they may haue their throats about
  them at that time, and some say, kniues haue edges:
  It must be as it may, though patience be a tyred mare,
  yet shee will plodde, there must be Conclusions, well,
  I cannot tell.

    Enter Pistoll, & Hostesse Quickly

510 BARDOLFE Godmorrow ancient *Pistoll*. (To Nym) Heere
  comes Ancient *Pistoll* and his wife: good Corporall be
  patient heere.

⌈NYM⌉ How now mine Hoaste *Pistoll?*

PISTOLL
  Base Tyke, cal'st thou mee Hoste, now by gads lugges
  I sweare I scorne the terme: nor shall my *Nel* keep
    Lodgers.

HOSTESSE No by my troth, not long: For we cannot lodge
  and board a dozen or fourteene Gentlewomen that liue
  honestly by the pricke of their Needles, but it will bee
  thought we keepe a Bawdy-house straight.

    ⌈*Nym drawes his sword*⌉

520 O welliday Lady, if he be not hewne now, we shall see
  wilful adultery and murther committed.

    ⌈*Pistoll drawes his sword*⌉

BARDOLFE Good Lieutenant, good Corporal offer nothing
  heere.

NYM Pish.

PISTOLL
  Pish for thee, Island dogge: thou prickeard cur of
    Island.

HOSTESSE Good Corporall *Nym* shew thy valor, and put
  vp your sword.

    They sheath their swords

NYM Will you shogge off? I would haue you solus.

PISTOLL
  Solus, egregious dog? O Viper vile;
530 The solus in thy most meruailous face,
  The solus in thy teeth, and in thy throate,
  And in thy hatefull Lungs, yea in thy Maw perdy;
  And which is worse, within thy nastie mouth.
  I do retort the solus in thy bowels,
  For I can take, and *Pistols* cocke is vp,
  And flashing fire will follow.

NYM I am not *Barbason*, you cannot coniure mee: I haue
  an humor to knocke you indifferently well: If you grow
  fowle with me Pistoll, I will scoure you with my Rapier,
540 as I may, in fayre tearmes. If you would walke off, I
  would pricke your guts a little in good tearmes, as I
  may, and that's the humor of it.

PISTOLL
  O Braggard vile, and damned furious wight,
  The Graue doth gape, and doting death is neere,
  Therefore exhale.

    Pistoll and Nym drawe

BARDOLFE Heare me, heare me what I say:
    ⌈*He drawes*⌉
  Hee that strikes the first stroake, Ile run him vp to the
  hilts, as I am a soldier.

PISTOLL
  An oath of mickle might, and fury shall abate.
    ⌈*They sheath their swords*⌉
  (To Nym) Giue me thy fist, thy fore-foote to me giue: 550
  Thy spirites are most tall.

NYM I will cut thy throate one time or other in faire
  termes, that is the humor of it.

PISTOLL *Couple a gorge,*
  That is the word. I thee defie againe.
  O hound of Creet, think'st thou my spouse to get?
  No, to the spittle goe,
  And from the Poudring tub of infamy,
  Fetch forth the Lazar Kite of *Cressids* kinde,
  Doll Teare-sheete, she by name, and her espouse. 560
  I haue, and I will hold the *Quondam Quickely*
  For the onely shee: and *Pauca*, there's enough, go to.
    Enter the Boy ⌈*running*⌉

BOY Mine Hoast *Pistoll*, you must come to my Mayster,
  and you Hostesse: He is very sicke, & would to bed.
  Good *Bardolfe*, put thy face betweene his sheets, and
  do the Office of a Warming-pan: Faith, he's very ill.

BARDOLFE Away you Rogue.

HOSTESSE By my troth he'l yeeld the Crow a pudding one
  of these dayes: the King has kild his heart. Good
  Husband come home presently.   *Exit* ⌈*with Boy*⌉ 570

BARDOLFE Come, shall I make you two friends. Wee must
  to France together: why the diuel should we keep
  kniues to cut one anothers throats?

PISTOLL
  Let floods ore-swell, and fiends for food howle on.

NYM You'l pay me the eight shillings I won of you at
  Betting?

PISTOLL Base is the Slaue that payes.

NYM That now I wil haue: that's the humor of it.

PISTOLL
  As manhood shal compound: push home.
    Pistoll and Nym draw

BARDOLFE ⌈*drawing his sword*⌉ By this sword, hee that 580
  makes the first thrust, Ile kill him: By this sword, I wil.

PISTOLL
  Sword is an Oath, & Oaths must haue their course.
    ⌈*He sheaths his sword*⌉

BARDOLFE Corporall *Nym*, & thou wilt be friends be frends,
  and thou wilt not, why then be enemies with me to:
  prethee put vp.

NYM I shall haue my eight shillings?

PISTOLL
  A Noble shalt thou haue, and present pay,
  And Liquor likewise will I giue to thee,
  And friendshippe shall combyne, and brotherhood.
  Ile liue by *Nymme*, & *Nymme* shall liue by me, 590
  Is not this iust? For I shal Sutler be
  Vnto the Campe, and profits will accrue.
  Giue mee thy hand.

NYM I shall haue my Noble?

PISTOLL In cash, most iustly payd.

NYM Well, then that's the humor of't.

⌈*Nym and Bardolfe sheath their swords.*⌉
Enter Hostesse Quickly

HOSTESSE As euer you come of women, come in quickly
to sir *Iohn*: A poore heart, hee is so shak'd of a burning
quotidian Tertian, that it is most lamentable to behold.
600 Sweet men, come to him.   ⌈*Exit*⌉

NYM The King hath run bad humors on the Knight, that's
the euen of it.

PISTOLL *Nym*, thou hast spoke the right,
His heart is fracted and corroborate.

NYM The King is a good King, but it must bee as it may:
he passes some humors, and carreeres.

PISTOLL
Let vs condole the Knight, for (Lambekins) we will liue.
Exeunt omnes

Sc. 5   *Enter Exeter*, ⌈*Gloucester*⌉, & *Westmerland*
(2.2) ⌈GLOUCESTER⌉
Fore God his Grace is bold to trust these traitors.

EXETER
They shall be apprehended by and by.

WESTMERLAND
610 How smooth and euen they do bear themselues,
As if allegeance in their bosomes sate
Crowned with faith, and constant loyalty.

⌈GLOUCESTER⌉
The King hath note of all that they intend,
By interception, which they dreame not of.

EXETER
Nay, but the man that was his bedfellow,
Whom he hath dull'd and cloy'd with gracious
fauours;
That he should for a forraigne purse, so sell
His Soueraignes life to death and treachery.

*Sound Trumpets. Enter King Harry, Scroope,
Cambridge, and Gray*

KING HARRY
Now sits the winde faire, and we will aboord.
620 My Lord of *Cambridge*, and my kinde Lord of *Masham*,
And you my gentle Knight, giue me your thoughts:
Thinke you not that the powres we beare with vs
Will cut their passage through the force of France?
Doing the execution, and the acte,
For which we haue in head assembled them.

SCROOPE
No doubt my Liege, if each man do his best.

KING HARRY
I doubt not that, since we are well perswaded
We carry not a heart with vs from hence,
That growes not in a faire consent with ours:
630 Nor leaue not one behinde, that doth not wish
Successe and Conquest to attend on vs.

CAMBRIDGE
Neuer was Monarch better fear'd and lou'd,
Then is your Maiesty; there's not I thinke a subiect
That sits in heart-greefe and vneasinesse
Vnder the sweet shade of your gouernment.

GRAY
True: those that were your Fathers enemies,
Haue steep'd their gauls in hony, and do serue you
With hearts create of duty, and of zeale.

KING HARRY
We therefore haue great cause of thankfulnes,
And shall forget the office of our hand   640
Sooner then quittance of desert and merit,
According to y^r weight and worthinesse.

SCROOPE
So seruice shall with steeled sinewes toyle,
And labour shall refresh it selfe with hope
To do your Grace incessant seruices.

KING HARRY
We Iudge no lesse. Vnkle of *Exeter*,
Inlarge the man committed yesterday,
That rayl'd against our person: We consider
It was excesse of Wine that set him on,
And on his more aduice, We pardon him.   650

SCROOPE
That's mercy, but too much security:
Let him be punish'd Soueraigne, least example
Breed (by his sufferance) more of such a kind.

KING HARRY
O let vs yet be mercifull.

CAMBRIDGE
So may your Highnesse, and yet punish too.

GRAY
Sir, you shew great mercy if you giue him life,
After the taste of much correction.

KING HARRY
Alas, your too much loue and care of me,
Are heauy Orisons 'gainst this poore wretch:
If little faults proceeding on distemper,   660
Shall not be wink'd at, how shall we stretch our eye
When capitall crimes, chew'd, swallow'd, and
digested,
Appeare before vs? Wee'l yet inlarge that man,
Though *Cambridge*, *Scroope*, and *Gray*, in their deere
care
And tender preseruation of our person
Wold haue him punish'd. And now to our French
causes,
Who are the late Commissioners?

CAMBRIDGE   I one my Lord,
Your Highnesse bad me aske for it to day.

SCROOPE
So did you me my Liege.

GRAY   And I my Royall Soueraigne.

KING HARRY
Then *Richard* Earle of *Cambridge*, there is yours: 670
There yours Lord *Scroope* of *Masham*, and Sir Knight,
Gray of *Northumberland*, this same is yours:
Reade them, and know I know your worthinesse.
My Lord of *Westmerland*, and Vnkle *Exeter*,
We will aboord to night. Why how now Gentlemen?
What see you in those papers, that you loose
So much complexion? Looke ye how they change:
Their cheekes are paper. Why, what read you there,

That haue so cowarded and chac'd your blood
Out of apparance.

680 CAMBRIDGE   I do confesse my fault,
And do submit me to your Highnesse mercy.

GRAY *and* SCROOPE To which we all appeale.

KING HARRY

The mercy that was quicke in vs but late,
By your owne counsaile is supprest and kill'd:
You must not dare (for shame) to talke of mercy,
For your owne reasons turne into your bosomes,
As dogs vpon their maisters, worrying you:
See you my Princes, and my Noble Peeres,
These English monsters: My Lord of *Cambridge* heere,

690 You know how apt our loue was, to accord
To furnish him with all appertiments
Belonging to his Honour; and this vilde man,
Hath for a few light Crownes, lightly conspir'd
And sworne vnto the practises of France
To kill vs heere in Hampton. To the which,
This Knight no lesse for bounty bound to Vs
Then Cambridge is, hath likewise sworne. But O,
What shall I say to thee Lord *Scroope*, thou cruell,
Ingratefull, sauage, and inhumane Creature?

700 Thou that didst beare the key of all my counsailes,
That knew'st the very bottome of my soule,
That (almost) might'st a coyn'd me into Golde,
Would'st thou a practis'd on me, for thy vse:
May it be possible, that forraigne hyer
Could out of thee extract one sparke of euill
That might annoy my finger? 'Tis so strange,
That though the truth of it stands off as grosse
As black one white, my eye will scarsely see it.
Treason, and murther, euer kept together,

710 As two yoake diuels sworne to eythers purpose,
Working so grossely in a naturall cause,
That admiration did not hoope at them.
But thou (gainst all proportion) didst bring in
Wonder to waite on treason, and on murther:
And whatsoeuer cunning fiend it was
That wrought vpon thee so preposterously,
Hath got the voyce in hell for excellence:
And other diuels that suggest by treasons,
Do botch and bungle vp damnation,

720 With patches, colours, and with formes being fetcht
From glist'ring semblances of piety:
But he that temper'd thee, bad thee stand vp,
Gaue thee no instance why thou shouldst do treason,
Vnlesse to dub thee with the name of Traitor.
If that same Dæmon that hath gull'd thee thus,
Should with his Lyon-gate walke the whole world,
He might returne to vastie Tartar backe,
And tell the Legions, I can neuer win
A soule so easie as that Englishmans.

730 Oh, how hast thou with iealousie infected
The sweetnesse of affiance? Shew men dutifull,
Why so didst thou: seeme they graue and learned?
Why so didst thou. Come they of Noble Family?
Why so didst thou. Seeme they religious?

Why so didst thou. Or are they spare in diet,
Free from grosse passion, or of mirth, or anger,
Constant in spirit, not sweruing with the blood,
Garnish'd and deck'd in modest complement,
Not working with the eye, without the eare,
And but in purged iudgement trusting neither,   740
Such and so finely boulted didst thou seeme:
And thus thy fall hath left a kinde of blot,
To marke the full fraught man, and best indued
With some suspition. I will weepe for thee,
For this reuolt of thine, me thinkes is like
Another fall of Man. Their faults are open,
Arrest them to the answer of the Law,
And God acquit them of their practises.

EXETER I arrest thee of High Treason, by the name of
Richard Earle of *Cambridge*. I arrest thee of High Treason,   750
by the name of *Henry* Lord *Scroope* of *Masham*. I arrest
thee of High Treason, by the name of *Thomas Grey*,
Knight of *Northumberland*.

SCROOPE

Our purposes, God iustly hath discouer'd,
And I repent my fault more then my death,
Which I beseech your Highnesse to forgiue,
Although my body pay the price of it.

CAMBRIDGE

For me, the Gold of France did not seduce,
Although I did admit it as a motiue,
The sooner to effect what I intended: 760
But God be thanked for preuention,
Which heartily in sufferance will reioyce,
Beseeching God, and you, to pardon mee.

GRAY

Neuer did faithfull subiect more reioyce
At the discouery of most dangerous Treason,
Then I do at this houre ioy ore my selfe,
Preuented from a damned enterprize;
My fault, but not my body, pardon Soueraigne.

KING HARRY

God quit you in his mercy: Hear your sentence.
You haue conspir'd against Our Royall person,   770
Ioyn'd with an enemy proclaim'd and fixt,
And from his Coffers,
Receyu'd the Golden Earnest of Our death:
Wherein you would haue sold your King to slaughter,
His Princes, and his Peeres to seruitude,
His Subiects to oppression, and contempt,
And his whole Kingdome into desolation:
Touching our person, seeke we no reuenge,
But we our Kingdomes safety must so tender,
Whose ruine you haue sought, that to her Lawes   780
We do deliuer you. Get ye therefore hence,
(Poore miserable wretches) to your death:
The taste whereof, God of his mercy giue
You patience to indure, and true Repentance
Of all your deare offences. Beare them hence.

                              Exit the Traitors, guarded
Now Lords for France: the enterprise whereof
Shall be to you as vs, like glorious.

We doubt not of a faire and luckie Warre,
Since God so graciously hath brought to light
790   This dangerous Treason, lurking in our way,
To hinder our beginnings. We doubt not now,
But euery Rubbe is smoothed on our way.
Then forth, deare Countreymen: Let vs deliuer
Our Puissance into the hand of God,
Putting it straight in expedition.
Chearely to Sea, the signes of Warre aduance,
No King of England, if not King of France.

Flourish. Exit omnes

Sc. 6   *Enter Pistoll, Nim, Bardolph, Boy, and Hostesse*
(2.3)   *Quickly*

HOSTESSE 'Prythee honey sweet Husband, let me bring
thee to Staines.

PISTOLL

800   No: for my manly heart doth erne. *Bardolph*,
Be blythe: *Nim*, rowse thy vaunting Veines: Boy,
     brissle
Thy Courage vp: for *Falstaffe* hee is dead,
And wee must erne therefore.

BARDOLFE Would I were with him, wheresomere hee is,
eyther in Heauen, or in Hell.

HOSTESSE Nay sure, hee's not in Hell: hee's in *Arthurs*
Bosome, if euer man went to *Arthurs* Bosome: a made
a finer end, and went away and it had beene any
Christome Childe: a parted eu'n iust betweene Twelue
810   and One, eu'n at the turning o'th'Tyde: for after I saw
him fumble with the Sheets, and play with Flowers,
and smile vpon his fingers end, I knew there was but
one way: for his Nose was as sharpe as a Pen, and a
babeld of greene fields. How now Sir *Iohn* (quoth I?)
what man? be a good cheare: so a cryed out, God,
God, God, three or foure times: now I, to comfort him,
bid him a should not thinke of God; I hop'd there was
no neede to trouble himselfe with any such thoughts
yet: so a bad me lay more Clothes on his feet: I put
820   my hand into the Bed, and felt them, and they were
as cold as any stone: then I felt to his knees, and so
vppard, and vpard, and all was as cold as any stone.

NYM They say he cryed out of Sack.

HOSTESSE I, that a did.

BARDOLFE And of Women.

HOSTESSE Nay, that a did not.

BOY Yes that a did, and said they were Deules incarnate.

HOSTESSE A could neuer abide Carnation, 'twas a Colour
he neuer lik'd.

830   BOY A said once, the Deule would haue him about
Women.

HOSTESSE A did in some sort (indeed) handle Women: but
then hee was rumatique, and talk'd of the Whore of
Babylon.

BOY Doe you not remember a saw a Flea sticke vpon
Bardolphs Nose, and a said it was a blacke Soule burning
in hellfire.

BARDOLFE Well, the fuell is gone that maintain'd that fire:
that's all the Riches I got in his seruice.

---

840   NYM Shall wee shogg? the King will be gone from
Southampton.

PISTOLL

Come, let's away. My Loue, giue me thy Lippes:
Looke to my Chattels, and my Moueables:
Let Sences rule: The word is, Pitch and pay:
Trust none: for Oathes are Strawes, mens Faiths are
     Wafer-Cakes,
And hold-fast is the onely Dogge, my Ducke:
Therefore *Caueto* bee thy Counsailor.
Goe, cleare thy Chrystalls. Yoke-fellowes in Armes,
Let vs to France, like Horse-leeches my Boyes,
850   To sucke, to sucke, the very blood to sucke.

BOY (*aside*) And that's but vnwholesome food, they say.

PISTOLL Touch her soft mouth, and march.

BARDOLFE Farwell Hostesse.

He kisses her

NYM I cannot kisse, that is the humor of it: but adieu.

PISTOLL (*to Hostesse*)

Let Huswiferie appeare: keepe close, I thee command.

HOSTESSE Farwell: adieu.   *Exeunt seuerally*

Flourish. Enter the French King, the Dolphin, the   **Sc. 7**
Constable, and the Dukes of Berry and ⌈Burbon⌉   **(2.4)**

FRENCH KING

Thus comes the English with full power vpon vs,
And more then carefully it vs concernes,
To answer Royally in our defences.
860   Therefore the Dukes of Berry and of Burbon,
Of Brabant and of Orleance, shall make forth,
And you Prince Dolphin, with all swift dispatch
To lyne and new repayre our Townes of Warre
With men of courage, and with meanes defendant:
For England his approaches makes as fierce,
As Waters to the sucking of a Gulfe.
It fits vs then to be as prouident,
As feare may teach vs, out of late examples
Left by the fatall and neglected English,
Vpon our fields.

DOLPHIN   My most redoubted Father,   870
It is most meet we arme vs 'gainst the Foe:
For Peace it selfe should not so dull a Kingdome,
(Though War nor no knowne Quarrel were in
     question)
But that Defences, Musters, Preparations,
Should be maintain'd, assembled, and collected,
As were a Warre in expectation.
Therefore I say, 'tis meet we all goe forth,
To view the sick and feeble parts of France:
And let vs doe it with no shew of feare,
No, with no more, then if we heard that England   880
Were busied with a Whitson Morris-dance:
For, my good Liege, shee is so idly King'd,
Her Scepter so phantastically borne,
By a vaine giddie shallow humorous Youth,
That feare attends her not.

CONSTABLE   O peace, Prince Dolphin,
You are too much mistaken in this King:

Question your Grace the late Embassadors,
With what great State he heard their Embassie,
How well supply'd with aged Councellors,
890 How modest in exception; and withall,
How terrible in constant resolution:
And you shall find, his Vanities fore-spent,
Were but the out-side of the Roman *Brutus*,
Couering Discretion with a Coat of Folly;
As Gardeners doe with Ordure hide those Roots
That shall first spring, and be most delicate.

DOLPHIN
Well, 'tis not so, my Lord High Constable.
But though we thinke it so, it is no matter:
In cases of defence, 'tis best to weigh
900 The Enemie more mightie then he seemes,
So the proportions of defence are fill'd:
Which of a weake and niggardly proiection,
Doth like a Miser spoyle his Coat, with scanting
A little Cloth.

FRENCH KING   Thinke we King *Harry* strong:
And Princes, looke you strongly arme to meet him.
The Kindred of him hath beene flesht vpon vs:
And he is bred out of that bloodie straine,
That haunted vs in our familiar Pathes:
Witnesse our too much memorable shame,
910 When Cressy Battell fatally was strucke,
And all our Princes captiu'd, by the hand
Of that black Name, *Edward*, black Prince of Wales:
Whiles that his Mountant Sire, on Mountaine
standing
Vp in the Ayre, crown'd with the Golden Sunne,
Saw his Heroicall Seed, and smil'd to see him
Mangle the Worke of Nature, and deface
The Patternes, that by God and by French Fathers
Had twentie yeeres been made. This is a Stem
Of that Victorious Stock: and let vs feare
920 The Natiue mightinesse and fate of him.
            Enter a Messenger

MESSENGER
Embassadors from *Harry* King of England,
Doe craue admittance to your Maiestie.

FRENCH KING
Weele giue them present audience. Goe, and bring
them.   *Exit Messenger*
You see this Chase is hotly followed, friends.

DOLPHIN
Turne head, and stop pursuit: for coward Dogs
Most spend their mouths, whē what they seem to
threaten
Runs farre before them. Good my Soueraigne
Take vp the English short, and let them know
Of what a Monarchie you are the Head:
930 Selfe-loue, my Liege, is not so vile a sinne,
As selfe-neglecting.
            Enter Exeter, ⌈attended⌉

FRENCH KING   From our Brother England?
EXETER
From him, and thus he greets your Maiestie:

He wills you in the Name of God Almightie,
That you deuest your selfe, and lay apart
The borrowed Glories, that by gift of Heauen,
By Law of Nature, and of Nations, longs
To him and to his Heires, namely, the Crowne,
And all wide-stretched Honors, that pertaine
By Custome, and the Ordinance of Times,
Vnto the Crowne of France: that you may know   940
'Tis no sinister, nor no awk-ward Clayme,
Pickt from the worme-holes of long-vanisht dayes,
Nor from the dust of old Obliuion rakt,
He sends you this most memorable Lyne,
In euery Branch truly demonstratiue;
Willing you ouer-looke this Pedigree:
And when you find him euenly deriu'd
From his most fam'd, of famous Ancestors,
Edward the third; he bids you then resigne
Your Crowne and Kingdome, indirectly held   950
From him, the Natiue and true Challenger.

FRENCH KING Or else what followes?

EXETER
Bloody constraint: for if you hide the Crowne
Euen in your hearts, there will he rake for it.
Therefore in fierce Tempest is he comming,
In Thunder and in Earth-quake, like a *Ioue*:
That if requiring faile, he will compell.
And bids you, in the Bowels of the Lord,
Deliuer vp the Crowne, and to take mercie
On the poore Soules, for whom this hungry Warre   960
Opens his vastie Iawes: and on your head
Turnes he the Widdowes Teares, the Orphans Cryes,
The dead-mens Blood, the pining Maidens Groanes,
For Husbands, Fathers, and betrothed Louers,
That shall be swallowed in this Controuersie.
This is his Clayme, his Threatning, and my Message:
Vnlesse the Dolphin be in presence here;
To whom expressely I bring greeting to.

FRENCH KING
For vs, we will consider of this further:
To morrow shall you beare our full intent   970
Back to our Brother England.

DOLPHIN   For the Dolphin,
I stand here for him: what to him from England?

EXETER
Scorne and defiance, sleight regard, contempt,
And any thing that may not mis-become
The mightie Sender, doth he prize you at.
Thus sayes my King: and if your Fathers Highnesse
Doe not, in graunt of all demands at large,
Sweeten the bitter Mock you sent his Maiestie;
Hee'le call you to so hot an Answer for it,
That Caues and Wombie Vaultages of France   980
Shall chide your Trespas, and returne your Mock
In second Accent of his Ordinance.

DOLPHIN
Say: if my Father render faire returne,
It is against my will: for I desire
Nothing but Oddes with England. To that end,

As matching to his Youth and Vanitie,
I did present him with the Paris-Balls.

EXETER

Hee'le make your Paris Louer shake for it,
Were it the Mistresse Court of mightie Europe:
990 And be assur'd, you'le find a diff'rence,
As we his Subiects haue in wonder found,
Betweene the promise of his greener dayes,
And these he masters now: now he weighes Time
Euen to the vtmost Graine: that you shall reade
In your owne Losses, if he stay in France.

FRENCH KING ⌐rising⌐

To morrow shall you know our mind at full.
        Flourish

EXETER

Dispatch vs with all speed, least that our King
Come here himselfe to question our delay;
For he is footed in this Land already.

FRENCH KING

1000 You shalbe soone dispatcht, with faire conditions.
A Night is but small breathe, and little pawse,
To answer matters of this consequence.
        ⌐Flourish.⌐ *Exeunt*

Sc. 8   *Enter Chorus*
(3.0) CHORUS

Thus with imagin'd wing our swift Scene flyes,
In motion of no lesse celeritie
Then that of Thought. Suppose, that you haue seene
The well-appointed King at Douer Peer,
Embarke his Royaltie: and his braue Fleet,
With silken Streamers, the young *Phebus* fanning;
Play with your Fancies: and in them behold,
1010 Vpon the Hempen Tackle, Ship-boyes climbing;
Heare the shrill Whistle, which doth order giue
To sounds confus'd: behold the threaden Sayles,
Borne with th'inuisible and creeping Wind,
Draw the huge Bottomes through the furrowed Sea,
Bresting the loftie Surge. O, doe but thinke
You stand vpon the Riuage, and behold
A Citie on th'inconstant Billowes dauncing:
For so appeares this Fleet Maiesticall,
Holding due course to Harflew. Follow, follow:
1020 Grapple your minds to sternage of this Nauie,
And leaue your England as dead Mid-night, still,
Guarded with Grandsires, Babyes, and old Women,
Eyther past, or not arriu'd to pyth and puissance:
For who is he, whose Chin is but enricht
With one appearing Hayre, that will not follow
These cull'd and choyse-drawne Caualiers to France?
Worke, worke your Thoughts, and therein see a
        Siege:
Behold the Ordenance on their Carriages,
With fatall mouthes gaping on girded Harflew.
1030 Suppose th'Embassador from the French comes back:
Tells *Harry*, That the King doth offer him
Katherine his Daughter, and with her to Dowrie,
Some petty and vnprofitable Dukedomes.

The offer likes not: and the nimble Gunner
With Lynstock now the diuellish Cannon touches,
        Alarum, and Chambers goe off
And downe goes all before them. Still be kind,
And eech out our performance with your mind.   *Exit*

        Alarum: Enter King Harry ⌐*and the English army,*   Sc. 9
        with⌐ *Scaling Ladders*   (3.1)

KING HARRY

Once more vnto the Breach, deare friends, once more;
Or close the Wall vp with our English dead:
In Peace, there's nothing so becomes a man,   1040
As modest stillnesse, and humilitie:
But when the blast of Warre blowes in our eares,
Then imitate the action of the Tyger:
Stiffen the sinewes, coniure vp the blood,
Disguise faire Nature with hard-fauour'd Rage:
Then lend the Eye a terrible aspect:
Let it pry through the portage of the Head,
Like the Brasse Cannon: let the Brow o'rewhelme it,
As fearefully, as doth a galled Rocke
O're-hang and iutty his confounded Base,   1050
Swill'd with the wild and wastfull Ocean.
Now set the Teeth, and stretch the Nosthrill wide,
Hold hard the Breath, and bend vp euery Spirit
To his full height. On, on, you Noblest English,
Whose blood is fet from Fathers of Warre-proofe:
Fathers, that like so many *Alexanders*,
Haue in these parts from Morne till Euen fought,
And sheath'd their Swords, for lack of argument.
Dishonour not your Mothers: now attest,
That those whom you call'd Fathers, did beget you.   1060
Be Coppy now to mē of grosser blood,
And teach them how to Warre. And you good
        Yeomen,
Whose Lyms were made in England; shew vs here
The mettell of your Pasture: let vs sweare,
That you are worth your breeding: which I doubt not:
For there is none of you so meane and base,
That hath not Noble luster in your eyes.
I see you stand like Grey-hounds in the slips,
Straÿing vpon the Start. The Game's afoot:
Follow your Spirit; and vpon this Charge,   1070
Cry, God for *Harry*, England, and S. *George*.
        Alarum, and Chambers goe off. Exeunt

        Enter Nim, Bardolph, Pistoll, and Boy   Sc. 10
BARDOLFE On, on, on, on, on, to the breach, to the breach.   (3.2)
NYM 'Pray thee Corporall stay, the Knocks are too hot:
and for mine owne part, I haue not a Case of Liues:
the humor of it is too hot, that is the very plaine-Song
of it.

PISTOLL

The plaine-Song is most iust: for humors doe abound:
Knocks goe and come: Gods Vassals drop and dye:
⌐*Sings*⌐ And Sword and Shield,
        In bloody Field,   1080
        Doth winne immortall fame.

BOY Would I were in a Ale-house in London, I would
giue all my fame for a Pot of Ale, and safetie.

PISTOLL ⌐sings⌐

> And I:
> If wishes would preuayle with me,
> My purpose should not fayle with me;
> But thither would I high.

BOY ⌐sings⌐

> As duly,
> But not as truly,
> As Bird doth sing on bough.

1090

Enter Fluellen and beates them in

FLUELLEN Godes plud vp to the breaches, you Dogges;
auaunt you Cullions.

PISTOLL

> Be mercifull great Duke to men of Mould:
> Abate thy Rage, abate thy manly Rage;
> Abate thy Rage, great Duke. Good Bawcock bate
> Thy Rage: vse lenitie sweet Chuck.

NYM These be good humors:

⌐*Fluellen begins to beate Nym*⌐
your Honor runs bad humors.   *Exit all but* ⌐*the Boy*⌐

BOY As young as I am, I haue obseru'd these three
1100   Swashers: I am Boy to them all three, but all they
three, though they would serue me, could not be Man
to me; for indeed three such Antiques doe not amount
to a man: for *Bardolph*, hee is white-liuer'd, and red-
fac'd; by the meanes whereof, a faces it out, but fights
not: for *Pistoll*, hee hath a killing Tongue, and a quiet
Sword; by the meanes whereof, a breakes Words, and
keepes whole Weapons: for *Nim*, hee hath heard, that
men of few Words are the best men, and therefore hee
scornes to say his Prayers, lest a should be thought a
1110   Coward: but his few bad Words are matcht with as
few good Deeds; for a neuer broke any mans Head but
his owne, and that was against a Post, when he was
drunke. They will steale any thing, and call it Purchase.
Bardolph stole a Lute-case, bore it twelue Leagues, and
sold it for three halfepence. *Nim* and *Bardolph* are
sworne Brothers in filching: and in Callice they stole a
fire-shouell. I knew by that peece of Seruice, the men
would carry Coales. They would haue me as familiar
with mens Pockets, as their Gloues or their Hand-
1120   kerchers: which makes much against my Manhood, if
I should take from anothers Pocket, to put into mine;
for it is plaine pocketting vp of Wrongs. I must leaue
them, and seeke some better Seruice: their Villany goes
against my weake stomacke, and therefore I must cast
it vp.   *Exit*

Sc. 11   *Enter Gower* ⌐*and Fluellen, meeting*⌐
(3.3) GOWER Captaine *Fluellen*, you must come presently to the
Mynes; the Duke of Gloucester would speake with you.

FLUELLEN To the Mynes? Tell you the Duke, it is not so
good to come to the Mynes: for looke you, the Mynes
1130   is not according to the disciplines of the Warre; the
concauities of it is not sufficient: for looke you,
th'athuersarie, you may discusse vnto the Duke, looke

you, is digt himselfe, foure yard vnder, the
Countermines: by *Cheshu*, I thinke a will plowe vp all,
if there is not better directions.

GOWER The Duke of Gloucester, to whom the Order of the
Siege is giuen, is altogether directed by an Irish man,
a very valiant Gentleman yfaith.

FLUELLEN It is Captaine *Makmorrice*, is it not?

GOWER I thinke it be.   1140

FLUELLEN By *Cheshu* he is an Asse, as in the World, I will
verifie as much in his Beard: he ha's no more directions
in the true disciplines of the Warres, looke you, of the
Roman disciplines, then is a Puppy-dog.

Enter Captaine Makmorrice, and Captaine Iamy

GOWER Here a comes, and the Scots Captaine, Captaine
Iamy, with him.

FLUELLEN Captaine *Iamy* is a maruellous falorous Gentleman, that is certain, and of great expedition and
knowledge in th'aunchiant Warres, vpon my particular
knowledge of his directions: by *Cheshu* he will maintaine   1150
his Argument as well as any Militarie man in the
World, in the disciplines of the Pristine Warres of the
Romans.

IAMY I say gudday, Captaine *Fluellen*.

FLUELLEN Godden to your Worship, good Captaine *Iames*.

GOWER How now Captaine *Mackmorrice*, haue you quit
the Mynes? haue the Pioners giuen o're?

MACKMORRICE By Chrish Law tish ill done: the Worke ish
giue ouer, the Trompet sound the Retreat. By my Hand
I sweare, and my fathers Soule, the Worke ish ill done: 1160
it ish giue ouer: I would haue blowed vp the Towne,
so Chrish saue me law, in an houre. O tish ill done,
tish ill done: by my Hand tish ill done.

FLUELLEN Captaine *Mackmorrice*, I beseech you now, will
you voutsafe me, looke you, a few disputations with
you, as partly touching or concerning the disciplines
of the Warre, the Roman Warres, in the way of
Argument, looke you, and friendly communication:
partly to satisfie my Opinion, and partly for the
satisfaction, looke you, of my Mind: as touching the   1170
direction of the Militarie discipline, that is the Point.

IAMY It sall be vary gud, gud feith, gud Captens bath,
and I sall quit you with gud leue, as I may pick
occasion: that sall I mary.

MACKMORRICE It is no time to discourse, so Chrish saue
me: the day is hot, and the Weather, and the Warres,
and the King, and the Dukes: it is no time to discourse,
the Town is beseech'd: and the Trumpet call vs to the
breech, and we talke, and be Chrish do nothing, tis
shame for vs all: so God sa'me tis shame to stand still,   1180
it is shame by my hand: and there is Throats to be
cut, and Workes to be done, and there ish nothing
done, so Christ sa'me law.

IAMY By the Mes, ere theise eyes of mine take themselues
to slomber, ayle de gud seruice, or Ile ligge i'th' grund
for it; ay ow got a death: and Ile pay't as valorously
as I may, that sal I suerly do, that is the breff and the
long: mary, I wad full faine heard some question tween
you tway.

1190 FLUELLEN Captaine *Mackmorrice*, I thinke, looke you, vnder your correction, there is not many of your Nation.

MACKMORRICE Of my Nation? What ish my Nation? Ish a Villaine, and a Basterd, and a Knaue, and a Rascall. What ish my Nation? Who talkes of my Nation?

FLUELLEN Looke you, if you take the matter otherwise then is meant, Captaine *Mackmorrice*, peraduenture I shall thinke you doe not vse me with that affabilitie, as in discretion you ought to vse me, looke you, being

1200 as good a man as your selfe, both in the disciplines of Warre, and in the deriuation of my Birth, and in other particularities.

MACKMORRICE I doe not know you so good a man as my selfe: so Chrish saue me, I will cut off your Head.

GOWER Gentlemen both, you will mistake each other.

IAMY A, that's a foule fault.

A Parley is sounded

GOWER The Towne sounds a Parley.

FLUELLEN Captaine *Mackmorrice*, when there is more better oportunitie to be required, looke you, I will be

1210 so bold as to tell you, I know the disciplines of Warre: and there is an end.   *Exit*

⌈*Flourish.*⌉ *Enter King Harry and all his Traine before the Gates*

KING HARRY

How yet resolues the Gouernour of the Towne?
This is the latest Parle we will admit:
Therefore to our best mercy giue your selues,
Or like to men prowd of destruction,
Defie vs to our worst: for as I am a Souldier,
A Name that in my thoughts becomes me best;
If I begin the batt'rie once againe,
I will not leaue the halfe-atchieued Harflew,

1220 Till in her ashes she lye buryed.
The Gates of Mercy shall be all shut vp,
And the flesh'd Souldier, rough and hard of heart,
In libertie of bloody hand, shall raunge
With Conscience wide as Hell, mowing like Grasse
Your fresh faire Virgins, and your flowring Infants.
What is it then to me, if impious Warre,
Arrayed in flames like to the Prince of Fiends,
Doe with his smyrcht complexion all fell feats,
Enlynckt to wast and desolation?

1230 What is't to me, when you your selues are cause,
If your pure Maydens fall into the hand
Of hot and forcing Violation?
What Reyne can hold licentious Wickednesse,
When downe the Hill he holds his fierce Carriere?
We may as bootlesse spend our vaine Command
Vpon th'enraged Souldiers in their spoyle,
As send Precepts to the *Leuiathan*,
To come ashore. Therefore, you men of Harflew,
Take pitty of your Towne and of your People,

1240 Whiles yet my Souldiers are in my Command,
Whiles yet the coole and temperate Wind of Grace
O're-blowes the filthy and contagious Clouds
Of headdy Murther, Spoyle, and Villany.

If not: why in a moment looke to see
The blind and bloody Souldier, with foule hand
Defile the Locks of your shrill-shriking Daughters:
Your Fathers taken by the siluer Beards,
And their most reuerend Heads dasht to the Walls:
Your naked Infants spitted vpon Pykes,
Whiles the mad Mothers, with their howles confus'd,   1250
Doe breake the Clouds; as did the Wiues of Iewry,
At *Herods* bloody-hunting slaughter-men.
What say you? Will you yeeld, and this auoyd?
Or guiltie in defence, be thus destroy'd.

Enter Gouernour ⌈*on the Wall*⌉

GOUERNOUR

Our expectation hath this day an end:
The Dolphin, whom of Succours we entreated,
Returnes vs, that his Powers are yet not ready,
To rayse so great a Siege: Therefore dread King,
We yeeld our Towne and Liues to thy soft Mercy:
Enter our Gates, dispose of vs and ours,   1260
For we no longer are defensible.

KING HARRY

Open your Gates: ⌈*Exit Gouernour*⌉
            Come Vnckle *Exeter*,
Goe you and enter Harflew; there remaine,
And fortifie it strongly 'gainst the French:
Vse mercy to them all. For vs, deare Vnckle,
The Winter comming on, and Sicknesse growing
Vpon our Souldiers, we will retyre to Calis.
To night in Harflew will we be your Guest,
To morrow for the March are we addrest.

⌈*The Gates are opened.*⌉ *Flourish, and enter the Towne*

Enter Princesse Katherine and Alice, an old   Sc. 12
Gentlewoman   (3.4)

KATHERINE *Alice, tu as este en Angleterre, & tu bien parlas* 1270
le Language.

ALICE *Vn peu Madame.*

KATHERINE *Ie te prie m'ensigniez, il faut que ie apprene a parler: Coment appelle vous le main en Anglois?*

ALICE *Le main il & appelle de Hand.*

KATHERINE *De Hand. E le doyts.*

ALICE *Le doyts, ma foy Ie oublie, le doyts, mays ie me souendray le doyts ie pense qu'ils sont appelle de fingres, oui de fingres.*

KATHERINE *Le main de Hand, le doyts de Fingres, ie pense* 1280
que ie suis le bon escholier. I'ay gaynie diux mots d'Anglois vistement, coment appelle vous le ongles?

ALICE *Le ongles, nous les appellons de Nayles.*

KATHERINE *De Nayles escoute: dites moy, si ie parle bien: de Hand, de Fingres, e de Nayles.*

ALICE *C'est bien dict Madame, il & fort bon Anglois.*

KATHERINE *Dites moy l'Anglois pour le bras.*

ALICE *De Arma, Madame.*

KATHERINE *E le coudee.*

ALICE *D'Elbow.*   1290

KATHERINE *D'Elbow: Ie men fay le repiticiõ de touts les mots que vous maues apprins des a present.*

ALICE *Il & trop difficile Madame, comme Ie pense.*

KATHERINE *Excuse moy Alice escoute, d'Hand, de Fingre, de Nayles, d'Arma, de Bilbow.*

ALICE *D'Elbow, Madame.*

KATHERINE *O Seigneur Dieu, ie men oublie d'Elbow, coment appelle vous le col.*

ALICE *De Nick, Madame.*

1300 KATHERINE *De Nick, e le menton.*

ALICE *De Chin.*

KATHERINE *De Sin: le col de Nick, le menton de Sin.*

ALICE *Ouy. Sauf vostre honneur en verite vous pronouncies les mots ausi droict, que le Natifs d'Angleterre.*

KATHERINE *Ie ne doute point d'apprendre par de grace de Dieu, & en peu de temps.*

ALICE *N'aue vos y desia oublie ce que ie vous a ensignie.*

KATHERINE *Non e ie recitera a vous promptement, d'Hand, de Fingre, de Maylees.*

1310 ALICE *De Nayles, Madame.*

KATHERINE *De Nayles, de Arma, de Ilbow.*

ALICE *Sauf vostre honeur d'Elbow.*

KATHERINE *Ainsi dy ie d'Elbow, de Nick, & de Sin: coment appelle vous les pieds & le robe.*

ALICE *De Foot Madame, & de Coune.*

KATHERINE *De Foot, & de Coune: O Seigneur Dieu, ils sont le mots de son mauuais corruptible grosse & impudique, & non pour le Dames de Honeur d'user: Ie ne voudray pronouncer ce mots deuant le Seigneurs de France, pour*
1320 *toute le monde, fo de Foot & de Coune, neant moÿs, Ie recitera vn autrefoys ma lecon ensembe, d'Hand, de Fingre, de Nayles, d'Arma, d'Elbow, de Nick, de Sin, de Foot, de Coune.*

ALICE *Excellent, Madame.*

KATHERINE *C'est asses pour vne foyes, alons nous a diner.*

Exeunt

Sc. 13   *Enter the King of France, the Dolphin, the*
(3.5)   *Constable of France, ⌈Burbon⌉, and others*

FRENCH KING
'Tis certaine he hath past the Riuer Some.

CONSTABLE
And if he be not fought withall, my Lord,
Let vs not liue in France: let vs quit all,
And giue our Vineyards to a barbarous People.

DOLPHIN
1330 O *Dieu viuant*: Shall a few Sprayes of vs,
The emptying of our Fathers Luxurie,
Our Syens, put in wilde and sauage Stock,
Spirt vp so suddenly into the Clouds,
And ouer-looke their Grafters?

⌈BURBON⌉
Normans, but bastard Normans, Norman bastards:
Mort de ma vie, if they march along
Vnfought withall, but I will sell my Dukedome,
To buy a slobbry and a durtie Farme
In that nooke-shotten Ile of Albion.

CONSTABLE
1340 *Dieu de Battailes*, where haue they this mettell?
Is not their Clymate foggy, raw, and dull?

On whom, as in despight, the Sunne lookes pale,
Killing their Fruit with frownes. Can sodden Water,
A Drench for sur-reyn'd Iades, their Barly broth,
Decoct their cold blood to such valiant heat?
And shall our quick blood, spirited with Wine,
Seeme frostie? O, for honor of our Land,
Let vs not hang like roping Isyckles
Vpon our Houses Thatch, whiles a more frostie People
Sweat drops of gallant Youth in our rich fields: 1350
Poore may we call them, in their Natiue Lords.

DOLPHIN By Faith and Honor,
Our Madames mock at vs, and plainely say,
Our Mettell is bred out, and they will giue
Their bodyes to the Lust of English Youth,
To new-store France with Bastard Warriors.

⌈BURBON⌉
They bid vs to the English Dancing-Schooles,
And teach *Lauolta's* high, and swift *Carranto's*,
Saying, our Grace is onely in our Heeles,
And that we are most loftie Run-awayes.   1360

FRENCH KING
Where is *Montioy* the Herald? speed him hence,
Let him greet England with our sharpe defiance.
Vp Princes, and with spirit of Honor edged,
More sharper then your Swords, high to the field:
Charles Delabreth, High Constable of France,
You Dukes of *Orleance, Burbon*, and of *Berry*,
Alanson, Brabant, Bar, and *Burgonie*,
Iaques Chattillion, Rambures, Vaudemont,
Beumont, Grand Pree, Roussi, and *Faulconbridge*,
Foys, Lestrake, Bouciqualt, and *Charolayes*,   1370
High Dukes, great Princes, Barons, Lords, and Knigts;
For your great Seats, now quit you of great shames:
Barre *Harry* England, that sweepes through our Land
With Penons painted in the blood of Harflew:
Rush on his Hoast, as doth the melted Snow
Vpon the Valleyes, whose low Vassall Seat,
The Alpes doth spit, and void his rhewme vpon.
Goe downe vpon him, you haue Power enough,
And in a Captiue Chariot, into Roan
Bring him our Prisoner.

CONSTABLE   This becomes the Great.   1380
Sorry am I his numbers are so few,
His Souldiers sick, and famisht in their March:
For I am sure, when he shall see our Army,
Hee'le drop his heart into the sinck of feare,
And for atchieuement, offer vs his Ransome.

FRENCH KING
Therefore Lord Constable, hast on *Montioy*,
And let him say to England, that we send,
To know what willing Ransome he will giue.
Prince *Dolphin*, you shall stay with vs in Roan.

DOLPHIN
Not so, I doe beseech your Maiestie.   1390

FRENCH KING
Be patient, for you shall remaine with vs.
Now forth Lord Constable, and Princes all,
And quickly bring vs word of Englands fall.

Exeunt seuerally

Sc. 14
(3.6)

Enter Captaines, English and Welch: Gower at one
doore and Fluellen at another

GOWER How now Captaine *Fluellen*, come you from the
Bridge?

FLUELLEN I assure you, there is very excellent Seruices
committed at the Bridge.

GOWER Is the Duke of Exeter safe?

FLUELLEN The Duke of Exeter is as magnanimous as
Agamemnon, and a man that I loue and honour with
my soule, and my heart, and my dutie, and my liue,
and my liuing, and my vttermost power. He is not, God
be praysed and blessed, any hurt in the World, but
keepes the Bridge most valiantly, with excellent
discipline. There is an aunchient Lieutenant there at
the Pridge, I thinke in my very conscience hee is as
valiant a man as *Marke Anthony*, and hee is a man of
no estimation in the World, but I did see him doe as
gallant seruice.

GOWER What doe you call him?

FLUELLEN Hee is call'd aunchient *Pistoll*.

GOWER I know him not.

Enter Pistoll

FLUELLEN Here is the man.

PISTOLL
Captaine, I thee beseech to doe me fauours:
The Duke of Exeter doth loue thee well.

FLUELLEN I, I prayse God, and I haue merited some loue
at his hands.

PISTOLL
Bardolph, a Souldier firme and sound of heart,
Of buxome valour, hath by cruell Fate,
And giddie Fortunes furious fickle Wheele,
That Goddesse blind, that stands vpon the rolling
restlesse Stone.

FLUELLEN By your patience, aunchient *Pistoll*: Fortune is
painted blinde, with a Muffler afore hir eyes, to signifie
to you, that Fortune is blinde; and shee is painted also
with a Wheele, to signifie to you, which is the Morall
of it, that shee is turning and inconstant, and
mutabilitie, and variation: and her foot, looke you, is
fixed vpon a Sphericall Stone, which rowles, and rowles,
and rowles: in good truth, the Poet makes a most
excellent description of it: Fortune is an excellent
Morall.

PISTOLL
Fortune is *Bardolphs* foe, and frownes on him:
For he hath stolne a Pax, and hanged must a be:
A damned death:
Let Gallowes gape for Dogge, let Man goe free,
And let not Hempe his Wind-pipe suffocate:
But *Exeter* hath giuen the doome of death,
For Pax of little price.
Therefore goe speake, the Duke will heare thy voyce;
And let not *Bardolphs* vitall thred bee cut
With edge of Penny-Cord, and vile reproach.
Speake Captaine for his Life, and I will thee requite.

FLUELLEN Aunchient *Pistoll*, I doe partly vnderstand your
meaning.

PISTOLL Why then reioyce therefore.

FLUELLEN Certainly Aunchient, it is not a thing to reioyce
at: for if, looke you, he were my Brother, I would desire
the Duke to vse his good pleasure, and put him to
executions; for discipline ought to be vsed.

PISTOLL
Dye, and be dam'd, and *Figo* for thy friendship.

FLUELLEN It is well.

PISTOLL The Figge of Spaine.

FLUELLEN Very good.

PISTOLL
I say the fig within thy bowels and thy durty maw.

Exit

FLUELLEN Captain *Gour*, cannot you hear it lighten &
thunder?

GOWER Why, is this the Ancient you told me of? I
remember him now: a Bawd, a Cut-purse.

FLUELLEN Ile assure you, a vtt'red as praue words at the
Pridge, as you shall see in a Summers day: but it is
very well: what he ha's spoke to me, that is well I
warrant you, when time is serue.

GOWER Why 'tis a Gull, a Foole, a Rogue, that now and
then goes to the Warres, to grace himselfe at his returne
into London, vnder the forme of a Souldier: and such
fellowes are perfit in the Great Commanders Names,
and they will learne you by rote where Seruices were
done; at such and such a Sconce, at such a Breach,
at such a Conuoy: who came off brauely, who was
shot, who disgrac'd, what termes the Enemy stood on:
and this they conne perfitly in the phrase of Warre;
which they tricke vp with new-tuned Oathes: and what
a Beard of the Generalls Cut, and a horride Sute of the
Campe, will doe among foming Bottles, and Ale-washt
Wits, is wonderfull to be thought on: but you must
learne to know such slanders of the age, or else you
may be maruellously mistooke.

FLUELLEN I tell you what, Captaine *Gower*: I doe perceiue
hee is not the man that hee would gladly make shew
to the World hee is: if I finde a hole in his Coat, I will
tell him my minde:

A Drum is heard

hearke you, the King is comming, and I must speake
with him from the Pridge.

Drum and Colours. Enter King Harry and his poore
Souldiers

God plesse your Maiestie.

KING HARRY
How now *Fluellen*, com'st thou from the Bridge?

FLUELLEN I, so please your Maiestie: The Duke of Exeter
ha's very gallantly maintain'd the Pridge; the French
is gone off, looke you, and there is gallant and most
praue passages: marry, th'athuersarie was haue
possession of the Pridge, but he is enforced to retyre,
and the Duke of Exeter is Master of the Pridge: I can
tell your Maiestie, the Duke is a praue man.

KING HARRY What men haue you lost, *Fluellen*?

FLUELLEN The perdition of th'athuersarie hath beene very
great, reasonnable great: marry for my part, I thinke

the Duke hath lost neuer a man, but one that is like
to be executed for robbing a Church, one *Bardolph*, if
your Maiestie know the man: his face is all bubukles
and whelkes, and knobs, and flames a fire, and his
1500   lippes blowes at his nose, and it is like a coale of fire,
sometimes plew, and sometimes red, but his nose is
executed, and his fire's out.

KING HARRY Wee would haue all such offendors so cut
off: and we here giue expresse charge, that in our
Marches through the Countrey, there be nothing
compell'd from the Villages; nothing taken, but pay'd
for: none of the French vpbrayded or abused in
disdainefull Language; for when Lenitie and Crueltie
play for a Kingdome, the gentler Gamester is the soonest
1510   winner.
          Tucket. Enter Mountioy

MOUNTIOY You know me by my habit.

KING HARRY
     Well then, I know thee: what shall I know of thee?

MOUNTIOY
     My Masters mind.

KING HARRY   Vnfold it.

MOUNTIOY   Thus sayes my King:
     Say thou to *Harry* of England, Though we seem'd dead,
we did but sleepe: Aduantage is a better Souldier then
rashnesse. Tell him, wee could haue rebuk'd him at
Harflewe, but that wee thought not good to bruise an
iniurie, till it were full ripe. Now wee speake vpon our
Q. and our voyce is imperiall: England shall repent his
1520   folly, see his weakenesse, and admire our sufferance.
Bid him therefore consider of his ransome, which must
proportion the losses we haue borne, the subiects we
haue lost, the disgrace we haue digested; which in
weight to re-answer, his pettinesse would bow vnder.
For our losses, his Exchequer is too poore; for th'effusion
of our bloud, the Muster of his Kingdome too faint a
number; and for our disgrace, his owne person kneeling
at our feet, but a weake and worthlesse satisfaction.
To this adde defiance: and tell him for conclusion, he
1530   hath betrayed his followers, whose condemnation is
pronounc't:
     So farre my King and Master; so much my Office.

KING HARRY
     What is thy name? I know thy qualitie.

MOUNTIOY *Mountioy.*

KING HARRY
     Thou doo'st thy Office fairely. Turne thee back,
     And tell thy King, I doe not seeke him now,
     But could be willing to march on to Callice,
     Without impeachment: for to say the sooth,
     Though 'tis no wisdome to confesse so much
1540   Vnto an enemie of Craft and Vantage,
     My people are with sicknesse much enfeebled,
     My numbers lessen'd: and those few I haue,
     Almost no better then so many French;
     Who when they were in health, I tell thee Herald,
     I thought, vpon one payre of English Legges
     Did march three Frenchmen. Yet forgiue me God,

That I doe bragge thus; this your ayre of France
Hath blowne that vice in me. I must repent:
Goe therefore tell thy Master, heere I am;
My Ransome, is this frayle and worthlesse Trunke;   1550
My Army, but a weake and sickly Guard:
Yet God before, tell him we will come on,
Though France himselfe, and such another Neighbor
Stand in our way. There's for thy labour *Mountioy*.
Goe bid thy Master well aduise himselfe.
If we may passe, we will: if we be hindred,
We shall your tawnie ground with your red blood
Discolour: and so *Mountioy*, fare you well.
The summe of all our Answer is but this:
We would not seeke a Battaile as we are,   1560
Nor as we are, we say we will not shun it:
So tell your Master.

MOUNTIOY
     I shall deliuer so: Thankes to your Highnesse.   *Exit*

GLOUCESTER
     I hope they will not come vpon vs now.

KING HARRY
     We are in Gods hand, Brother, not in theirs:
     March to the Bridge, it now drawes toward night,
     Beyond the Riuer wee'le encampe our selues,
     And on to morrow bid them march away.   *Exeunt*

     Enter the Constable of France, the Lord Ramburs,   Sc. 15
     Orleance, and ⌈*Burbon*⌉, *with others*   (3.7)

CONSTABLE Tut, I haue the best Armour of the World:
     would it were day.   1570

ORLEANCE You haue an excellent Armour: but let my
     Horse haue his due.

CONSTABLE It is the best Horse of Europe.

ORLEANCE Will it neuer be Morning?

⌈BURBON⌉ My Lord of Orleance, and my Lord High
     Constable, you talke of Horse and Armour?

ORLEANCE You are as well prouided of both, as any Prince
     in the World.

⌈BURBON⌉ What a long Night is this? I will not change
     my Horse with any that treades but on foure pasteres: 1580
     ah ha: he bounds from the Earth, as if his entrayles
     were hayres: *le Cheual volante*, the Pegasus, *che a les*
     narines de feu. When I bestryde him, I soare, I am a
     Hawke: he trots the ayre: the Earth sings, when he
     touches it: the basest horne of his hoofe, is more
     Musicall then the Pipe of *Hermes*.

ORLEANCE Hee's of the colour of the Nutmeg.

⌈BURBON⌉ And of the heat of the Ginger. It is a Beast for
     Perseus: hee is pure Ayre and Fire; and the dull
     Elements of Earth and Water neuer appeare in him,   1590
     but only in patient stillnesse while his Rider mounts
     him: hee is indeede a Horse, and all other Iades you
     may call Beasts.

CONSTABLE Indeed my Lord, it is a most absolute and
     excellent Horse.

⌈BURBON⌉ It is the Prince of Palfrayes, his Neigh is like
     the bidding of a Monarch, and his countenance enforces
     Homage.

ORLEANCE No more Cousin.

⌈BURBON⌉ Nay, the man hath no wit, that cannot from the rising of the Larke to the lodging of the Lambe, varie deserued prayse on my Palfray: it is a Theame as fluent as the Sea: Turne the Sands into eloquent tongues, and my Horse is argument for them all: 'tis a subiect for a Soueraigne to reason on, and for a Soueraignes Soueraigne to ride on: And for the World, familiar to vs, and vnknowne, to lay apart their particular Functions, and wonder at him, I once writ a Sonnet in his prayse, and began thus, *Wonder of Nature*.

ORLEANCE I haue heard a Sonnet begin so to ones Mistresse.

⌈BURBON⌉ Then did they imitate that which I compos'd to my Courser, for my Horse is my Mistresse.

ORLEANCE Your Mistresse beares well.

⌈BURBON⌉ Me well, which is the prescript prayse and perfection of a good and particular Mistresse.

CONSTABLE Nay, for me thought yesterday your Mistresse shrewdly shooke your back.

⌈BURBON⌉ So perhaps did yours.

CONSTABLE Mine was not bridled.

⌈BURBON⌉ O then belike she was old and gentle, and you rode like a Kerne of Ireland, your French Hose off, and in your strait Strossers.

CONSTABLE You haue good iudgement in Horsemanship.

⌈BURBON⌉ Be warn'd by me then: they that ride so, and ride not warily, fall into foule Boggs: I had rather haue my Horse to my Mistresse.

CONSTABLE I had as liue haue my Mistresse a Iade.

⌈BURBON⌉ I tell thee Constable, my Mistresse weares his owne hayre.

CONSTABLE I could make as true a boast as that, if I had a Sow to my Mistresse.

⌈BURBON⌉ *Le chien est retourne a son propre vomissement et la truye lauee au bourbier:* thou mak'st vse of any thing.

CONSTABLE Yet doe I not vse my Horse for my Mistresse, or any such Prouerbe, so little kin to the purpose.

RAMBURES My Lord Constable, the Armour that I saw in your Tent to night, are those Starres or Sunnes vpon it?

CONSTABLE Starres my Lord.

⌈BURBON⌉ Some of them will fall to morrow, I hope.

CONSTABLE And yet my Sky shall not want.

⌈BURBON⌉ That may be, for you beare a many superfluously, and 'twere more honor some were away.

CONSTABLE Eu'n as your Horse beares your prayses, who would trot as well, were some of your bragges dismounted.

⌈BURBON⌉ Would I were able to loade him with his desert. Will it neuer be day? I will trot to morrow a mile, and my way shall be paued with English Faces.

CONSTABLE I will not say so, for feare I should be fac't out of my way: but I would it were morning, for I would faine be about the eares of the English.

RAMBURES Who will goe to Hazard with me for twentie Prisoners?

CONSTABLE You must first goe your selfe to hazard, ere you haue them.

⌈BURBON⌉ 'Tis Mid-night, Ile goe arme my selfe.   *Exit*

ORLEANCE The Duke of *Burbon* longs for morning.

RAMBURES He longs to eate the English.

CONSTABLE I thinke he will eate all he kills.

ORLEANCE By the white Hand of my Lady, hee's a gallant Prince.

CONSTABLE Sweare by her Foot, that she may tread out the Oath.

ORLEANCE He is simply the most actiue Gentleman of France.

CONSTABLE Doing is actiuitie, and he will still be doing.

ORLEANCE He neuer did harme, that I heard of.

CONSTABLE Nor will doe none to morrow: hee will keepe that good name still.

ORLEANCE I know him to be valiant.

CONSTABLE I was told that, by one that knowes him better then you.

ORLEANCE What's hee?

CONSTABLE Marry hee told me so himselfe, and hee sayd hee car'd not who knew it.

ORLEANCE Hee needes not, it is no hidden vertue in him.

CONSTABLE By my faith Sir, but it is: neuer any body saw it, but his Lacquey: 'tis a hooded valour, and when it appeares, it will bate.

ORLEANCE Ill will neuer sayd well.

CONSTABLE I will cap that Prouerbe with, There is flatterie in friendship.

ORLEANCE And I will take vp that with, Giue the Deuill his due.

CONSTABLE Well plac't: there stands your friend for the Deuill: haue at the very eye of that Prouerbe with, A Pox of the Deuill.

ORLEANCE You are the better at Prouerbs, by how much a Fooles Bolt is soone shot.

CONSTABLE You haue shot ouer.

ORLEANCE 'Tis not the first time you were ouer-shot.

Enter a Messenger

MESSENGER My Lord high Constable, the English lye within fifteene hundred paces of your Tents.

CONSTABLE Who hath measur'd the ground?

MESSENGER The Lord *Grandpree*.

CONSTABLE A valiant and most expert Gentleman.

⌈*Exit Messenger*⌉

Would it were day? Alas poore *Harry* of England: hee longs not for the Dawning, as wee doe.

ORLEANCE What a wretched and peeuish fellow is this King of England, to mope with his fat-brain'd followers so farre out of his knowledge.

CONSTABLE If the English had any apprehension, they would runne away.

ORLEANCE That they lack: for if their heads had any intellectuall Armour, they could neuer weare such heauie Head-pieces.

RAMBURES That Iland of England breedes very valiant Creatures; their Mastiffes are of vnmatchable courage.

ORLEANCE Foolish Curres, that runne winking into the

mouth of a Russian Beare, and haue their heads crusht like rotten Apples: you may as well say, that's a valiant Flea, that dare eate his breakefast on the Lippe of a Lyon.

CONSTABLE Iust, iust: and the men doe sympathize with the Mastiffes, in robustious and rough comming on, leauing their Wits with their Wiues: and then giue 1720 them great Meales of Beefe, and Iron and Steele; they will eate like Wolues, and fight like Deuils.

ORLEANCE I, but these English are shrowdly out of Beefe.

CONSTABLE Then shall we finde to morrow, they haue only stomackes to eate, and none to fight. Now is it time to arme: come, shall we about it?

ORLEANCE

It is now two a Clock: but let me see, by ten
Wee shall haue each a hundred English men.   *Exeunt*

Sc. 16
(4.0)   *Enter Chorus*

CHORUS

Now entertaine coniecture of a time,
When creeping Murmure and the poring Darke
1730 Fills the wide Vessell of the Vniuerse.
From Camp to Camp, through the foule Womb of
      Night
The Humme of eyther Army stilly sounds;
That the fixt Centinels almost receiue
The secret Whispers of each others Watch.
Fire answers fire, and through their paly flames
Each Battaile sees the others vmber'd face.
Steed threatens Steed, in high and boastfull Neighs
Piercing the Nights dull Eare: and from the Tents,
The Armourers accomplishing the Knights,
1740 With busie Hammers closing Riuets vp,
Giue dreadfull note of preparation.
The Countrey Cocks doe crow, the Clocks doe towle:
And the third howre of drowsie Morning name.
Prowd of their Numbers, and secure in Soule,
The confident and ouer-lustie French,
Doe the low-rated English play at Dice;
And chide the creeple-tardy-gated Night,
Who like a foule and ougly Witch doth limpe
So tediously away. The poore condemned English,
1750 Like Sacrifices, by their watchfull Fires
Sit patiently, and inly ruminate
The Mornings danger: and their gesture sad,
Inuesting lanke-leane Cheekes, and Warre-worne
      Coats,
Presented them vnto the gazing Moone
So many horride Ghosts. O now, who will behold
The Royall Captaine of this ruin'd Band
Walking from Watch to Watch, from Tent to Tent;
Let him cry, Prayse and Glory on his head:
For forth he goes, and visits all his Hoast,
1760 Bids them good morrow with a modest Smyle,
And calls them Brothers, Friends, and Countreymen.
Vpon his Royall Face there is no note,
How dread an Army hath enrounded him;
Nor doth he dedicate one iot of Colour
Vnto the wearie and all-watched Night:

But freshly lookes, and ouer-beares Attaint,
With chearefull semblance, and sweet Maiestie:
That euery Wretch, pining and pale before,
Beholding him, plucks comfort from his Lookes.
A Largesse vniuersall, like the Sunne,   1770
His liberall Eye doth giue to euery one,
Thawing cold feare, that meane and gentle all
Behold, as may vnworthinesse define,
A little touch of *Harry* in the Night.
And so our Scene must to the Battaile flye:
Where, O for pitty, we shall much disgrace,
With foure or fiue most vile and ragged foyles,
(Right ill dispos'd, in brawle ridiculous)
The Name of Agincourt: Yet sit and see,
Minding true things, by what their Mock'ries bee.   1780

                                                    Exit

Sc. 17   *Enter King Harry and Gloucester, then ⌈Clarence⌉*
(4.1)
KING HARRY

Gloster, 'tis true that we are in great danger,
The greater therefore should our Courage be.
God morrow Brother *Clarence*: God Almightie,
There is some soule of goodnesse in things euill,
Would men obseruingly distill it out.
For our bad Neighbour makes vs early stirrers,
Which is both healthfull, and good husbandry.
Besides, they are our outward Consciences,
And Preachers to vs all; admonishing,
That we should dresse vs fairely for our end.   1790
Thus may we gather Honey from the Weed,
And make a Morall of the Diuell himselfe.

      Enter Erpingham

Good morrow old Sir *Thomas Erpingham*:
A good soft Pillow for that good white Head,
Were better then a churlish turfe of France.

ERPINGHAM

Not so my Liege, this Lodging likes me better,
Since I may say, now lye I like a King.

KING HARRY

'Tis good for men to loue their present paines,
Vpon example, so the Spirit is eased:
And when the Mind is quicknd, out of doubt   1800
The Organs, though defunct and dead before,
Breake vp their drowsie Graue, and newly moue
With casted slough, and fresh legeritie.
Lend me thy Cloake Sir *Thomas*:

      He puts on Erpinghams Cloake

                              Brothers both,
Commend me to the Princes in our Campe;
Doe my good morrow to them, and anon
Desire them all to my Pauillion.

GLOUCESTER We shall, my Liege.

ERPINGHAM Shall I attend your Grace?

KING HARRY No, my good Knight: 1810
Goe with my Brothers to my Lords of England:
I and my Bosome must debate a while,
And then I would no other company.

ERPINGHAM

The Lord in Heauen blesse thee, Noble *Harry*.

KING HARRY
  God a mercy old Heart, thou speak'st chearefully.
                Exeunt all but King Harry
    Enter Pistoll ⌈to him⌉

PISTOLL *Che vous la?*

KING HARRY A friend.

PISTOLL
  Discusse vnto me, art thou Officer,
  Or art thou base, common, and popular?

1820 KING HARRY I am a Gentleman of a Company.

PISTOLL Trayl'st thou the puissant Pyke?

KING HARRY Euen so: what are you?

PISTOLL
  As good a Gentleman as the Emperor.

KING HARRY Then you are a better then the King.

PISTOLL
  The King's a Bawcock, and a Heart of Gold,
  A Lad of Life, an Impe of Fame,
  Of Parents good, of Fist most valiant:
  I kisse his durtie shooe, and from heart-string
  I loue the louely Bully. What is thy Name?

1830 KING HARRY *Harry le Roy.*

PISTOLL
  Le Roy? a Cornish Name: art thou of Cornish Crew?

KING HARRY No, I am a Welchman.

PISTOLL Know'st thou *Fluellen?*

KING HARRY Yes.

PISTOLL
  Tell him Ile knock his Leeke about his Pate
  Vpon S. *Dauies* day.

KING HARRY Doe not you weare your Dagger in your
  Cappe that day, least he knock that about yours.

PISTOLL Art thou his friend?

1840 KING HARRY And his Kinsman too.

PISTOLL The *Figo* for thee then.

KING HARRY I thanke you: God be with you.

PISTOLL My name is *Pistol* call'd.

KING HARRY It sorts well with your fiercenesse.
                    Exit Pistoll
  Enter Fluellen and Gower ⌈seuerally⌉. The King
  stands apart

GOWER Captaine *Fluellen.*

FLUELLEN 'So, in the Name of Iesu Christ, speake fewer:
  it is the greatest admiration in the vniuersall World,
  when the true and aunchient Prerogatifes and Lawes
  of the Warres is not kept: if you would take the paines
1850   but to examine the Warres of *Pompey* the Great, you
  shall finde, I warrant you, that there is no tiddle tadle
  nor pibble bable in *Pompeyes* Campe: I warrant you,
  you shall finde the Ceremonies of the Warres, and the
  Cares of it, and the Formes of it, and the Sobrietie of
  it, and the Modestie of it, to be otherwise.

GOWER Why the Enemie is lowd, you heare him all Night.

FLUELLEN If the Enemie is an Asse and a Foole, and a
  prating Coxcombe; is it meet, thinke you, that wee
  should also, looke you, be an Asse and a Foole, and a
1860   prating Coxcombe, in your owne conscience now?

GOWER I will speake lower.

FLUELLEN I pray you, and beseech you, that you will.
               Exit Gower, and Fluellen

KING HARRY
  Though it appeare a little out of fashion,
  There is much care and valour in this Welchman.
    Enter three Souldiers: Iohn Bates, Alexander Court,
    and Michael Williams

COURT Brother *Iohn Bates,* is not that the Morning which
  breakes yonder?

BATES I thinke it be: but wee haue no great cause to
  desire the approach of day.

WILLIAMS Wee see yonder the beginning of the day, but
  I thinke wee shall neuer see the end of it. Who goes 1870
  there?

KING HARRY A Friend.

WILLIAMS Vnder what Captaine serue you?

KING HARRY Vnder Sir *Tho. Erpingham.*

WILLIAMS A good old Commander, and a most kinde
  Gentleman: I pray you, what thinkes he of our estate?

KING HARRY Euen as men wrackt vpon a Sand, that looke
  to be washt off the next Tyde.

BATES He hath not told his thought to the King?

KING HARRY No: nor it is not meet he should: for though 1880
  I speake it to you, I thinke the King is but a man, as I
  am: the Violet smells to him, as it doth to me; the
  Element shewes to him, as it doth to me; all his Sences
  haue but humane Conditions: his Ceremonies layd by,
  in his Nakednesse he appeares but a man; and though
  his affections are higher mounted then ours, yet when
  they stoupe, they stoupe with the like wing: therefore,
  when he sees reason of feares, as we doe; his feares,
  out of doubt, be of the same rellish as ours are: yet in
  reason, no man should possesse him with any 1890
  appearance of feare; least hee, by shewing it, should
  dis-hearten his Army.

BATES He may shew what outward courage he will: but
  I beleeue, as cold a Night as 'tis, hee could wish himselfe
  in Thames vp to the Neck; and so I would he were,
  and I by him, at all aduentures, so we were quit here.

KING HARRY By my troth, I will speake my conscience of
  the King: I thinke hee would not wish himselfe any
  where, but where hee is.

BATES Then I would he were here alone; so should he be 1900
  sure to be ransomed, and a many poore mens liues
  saued.

KING HARRY I dare say, you loue him not so ill, to wish
  him here alone, howsoeuer you speake this to feele
  other mens minds. Me thinks I could not dye any where
  so contented, as in the Kings company; his Cause being
  iust, and his Quarrell honorable.

WILLIAMS That's more then we know.

BATES I, or more then wee should seeke after; for wee
  know enough, if wee know wee are the Kings Subiects: 1910
  if his Cause be wrong, our obedience to the King wipes
  the Cryme of it out of vs.

WILLIAMS But if the Cause be not good, the King himselfe
  hath a heauie Reckoning to make, when all those
  Legges, and Armes, and Heads, chopt off in a Battaile,

shall ioyne together at the latter day, and cry all, Wee dyed at such a place, some swearing, some crying for a Surgean; some vpon their Wiues, left poore behind them; some vpon the Debts they owe, some vpon their
1920 Children rawly left: I am afear'd, there are few dye well, that dye in a Battaile: for how can they charitably dispose of any thing, when Blood is their argument? Now, if these men doe not dye well, it will be a black matter for the King, that led them to it; who to disobey, were against all proportion of subiection.

KING HARRY So, if a Sonne that is by his Father sent about Merchandize, doe sinfully miscarry vpon the Sea; the imputation of his wickednesse, by your rule, should be imposed vpon his Father that sent him: or if a
1930 Seruant, vnder his Masters command, transporting a summe of Money, be assayled by Robbers, and dye in many irreconcil'd Iniquities; you may call the businesse of the Master the author of the Seruants damnation: but this is not so: The King is not bound to answer the particular endings of his Souldiers, the Father of his Sonne, nor the Master of his Seruant; for they purpose not their deaths, when they propose their seruices. Besides, there is no King, be his Cause neuer so spotlesse, if it come to the arbitrement of Swords,
1940 can trye it out with all vnspotted Souldiers: some (peraduenture) haue on them the guilt of premeditated and contriued Murther; some, of beguiling Virgins with the broken Seales of Periurie; some, making the Warres their Bulwarke, that haue before gored the gentle Bosome of Peace with Pillage and Robberie. Now, if these men haue defeated the Law, and outrunne Natiue punishment; though they can out-strip men, they haue no wings to flye from God. Warre is his Beadle, Warre is his Vengeance: so that here men are punisht, for
1950 before breach of the Kings Lawes, in now the Kings Quarrell: where they feared the death, they haue borne life away; and where they would bee safe, they perish. Then if they dye vnprouided, no more is the King guiltie of their damnation, then hee was before guiltie of those Impieties, for the which they are now visited. Euery Subiects Dutie is the Kings, but euery Subiects Soule is his owne. Therefore should euery Souldier in the Warres doe as euery sicke man in his Bed, wash euery Moth out of his Conscience: and dying so, Death is to him
1960 aduantage; or not dying, the time was blessedly lost, wherein such preparation was gayned: and in him that escapes, it were not sinne to thinke, that making God so free an offer, he let him outliue that day, to see his Greatnesse, and to teach others how they should prepare.

⌈BATES⌉ 'Tis certaine, euery man that dyes ill, the ill vpon his owne head, the King is not to answer it. I doe not desire hee should answer for me, and yet I determine to fight lustily for him.

1970 KING HARRY I my selfe heard the King say he would not be ransom'd.

WILLIAMS I, hee said so, to make vs fight chearefully: but when our throats are cut, hee may be ransom'd, and wee ne're the wiser.

KING HARRY If I liue to see it, I will neuer trust his word after.

WILLIAMS You pay him then: that's a perillous shot out of an Elder Gunne, that a poore and a priuate displeasure can doe against a Monarch: you may as well goe about to turne the Sunne to yce, with fanning 1980 in his face with a Peacocks feather: You'le neuer trust his word after; come, 'tis a foolish saying.

KING HARRY Your reproofe is something too round, I should be angry with you, if the time were conuenient.

WILLIAMS Let it bee a Quarrell betweene vs, if you liue.

KING HARRY I embrace it.

WILLIAMS How shall I know thee againe?

KING HARRY Giue me any Gage of thine, and I will weare it in my Bonnet: Then if euer thou dar'st acknowledge it, I will make it my Quarrell.   1990

WILLIAMS Heere's my Gloue: Giue mee another of thine.

KING HARRY There.

They exchange Gloues

WILLIAMS This will I also weare in my Cap: if euer thou come to me, and say, after to morrow, This is my Gloue, by this Hand I will take thee a box on the eare.

KING HARRY If euer I liue to see it, I will challenge it.

WILLIAMS Thou dar'st as well be hang'd.

KING HARRY Well, I will doe it, though I take thee in the Kings companie.

WILLIAMS Keepe thy word: fare thee well.   2000

BATES Be friends you English fooles, be friends, wee haue French Quarrels enow, if you could tell how to reckon.

KING HARRY Indeede the French may lay twentie French Crownes to one, they will beat vs, for they beare them on their shoulders: but it is no English Treason to cut French Crownes, and to morrow the King himselfe will be a Clipper.   *Exit Souldiers*

Vpon the King,
Let vs our Liues, our Soules, our Debts, our carefull Wiues,
Our Children, and our Sinnes, lay on the King: 2010
We must beare all. O hard Condition,
Twin-borne with Greatnesse, subiect to the breath
Of euery foole, whose sence no more can feele,
But his owne wringing. What infinite hearts-ease
Must Kings neglect, that priuate men enioy?
And what haue Kings, that Priuates haue not too,
Saue Ceremonie, saue generall Ceremonie?
And what art thou, thou Idoll Ceremonie?
What kind of God art thou? that suffer'st more
Of mortall griefes, then doe thy worshippers.   2020
What are thy Rents? what are thy Commings in?
O Ceremonie, shew me but thy worth.
What is thy Soule of adoration?
Art thou ought else but Place, Degree, and Forme,
Creating awe and feare in other men?
Wherein thou art lesse happy, being fear'd,
Then they in fearing.

What drink'st thou oft, in stead of Homage sweet,
But poyson'd flatterie? O, be sick, great Greatnesse,
2030 And bid thy Ceremonie giue thee cure.
Thinks thou the fierie Feuer will goe out
With Titles blowne from Adulation?
Will it giue place to flexure and low bending?
Canst thou, when thou command'st the beggers knee,
Command the health of it? No, thou prowd Dreame,
That play'st so subtilly with a Kings Repose.
I am a King that find thee: and I know,
'Tis not the Balme, the Scepter, and the Ball,
The Sword, the Mase, the Crowne Imperiall,
2040 The enter-tissued Robe of Gold and Pearle,
The farsed Title running 'fore the King,
The Throne he sits on: nor the Tyde of Pompe,
That beates vpon the high shore of this World:
No, not all these, thrice-gorgeous Ceremonie;
Not all these, lay'd in Bed Maiesticall,
Can sleepe so soundly, as the wretched Slaue:
Who with a body fill'd, and vacant mind,
Gets him to rest, cram'd with distressefull bread,
Neuer sees horride Night, the Child of Hell:
2050 But like a Lacquey, from the Rise to Set,
Sweates in the eye of *Phebus*; and all Night
Sleepes in *Elizium*: next day after dawne,
Doth rise and helpe *Hiperiō* to his Horse,
And followes so the euer-running yeere
With profitable labour to his Graue:
And but for Ceremonie, such a Wretch,
Winding vp Dayes with toyle, and Nights with sleepe,
Had the fore-hand and vantage of a King.
The Slaue, a Member of the Countreyes peace,
2060 Enioyes it; but in grosse braine little wots,
What watch the King keepes, to maintaine the peace;
Whose howres, the Pesant best aduantages.

    Enter Erpingham

ERPINGHAM
My Lord, your Nobles iealous of your absence,
Seeke through your Campe to find you.
KING HARRY   Good old Knight,
Collect them all together at my Tent:
Ile be before thee.
ERPINGHAM   I shall doo't, my Lord.   *Exit*
KING HARRY
O God of Battailes, steele my Souldiers hearts,
Possesse them not with feare: Take from them now
The sence of reckning or th'opposed numbers
2070 Pluck their hearts from them. Not to day, O Lord,
O not to day, thinke not vpon the fault
My Father made, in compassing the Crowne.
I *Richards* body haue interred new,
And on it haue bestowed more contrite teares,
Then from it issued forced drops of blood.
Fiue hundred poore haue I in yeerely pay,
Who twice a day their wither'd hands hold vp
Toward Heauen, to pardon blood: and I haue built
Two Chauntries, where the sad and solemne Priests
2080 Sing still for *Richards* Soule. More will I doe:

Though all that I can doe, is nothing worth;
Since that my Penitence comes after ill,
Imploring pardon.
    Enter Gloucester
GLOUCESTER
My Liege.
KING HARRY My Brother *Gloucesters* voyce? I:
I know thy errand, I will goe with thee:
The day, my friends, and all things stay for me.
                      Exeunt

    Enter ⌐Burbon,⌐ Orleance, and Ramburs   Sc. 18
ORLEANCE   (4.2)
The Sunne doth gild our Armour, vp my Lords.
⌐BURBON⌐ *Monte Cheual*: My Horse, *Verlot Lacquay*: Ha.
ORLEANCE Oh braue Spirit.
⌐BURBON⌐ *Via les eaus & terre.*   2090
ORLEANCE *Rien plus? le air & feu.*
⌐BURBON⌐ *Cieu*, Cousin *Orleance.*
    Enter Constable
Now my Lord Constable?
CONSTABLE
Hearke how our Steedes, for present Seruice neigh.
⌐BURBON⌐
Mount them, and make incision in their Hides,
That their hot blood may spin in English eyes,
And doubt them with superfluous courage: ha.
RAMBURES
What, wil you haue them weep our Horses blood?
How shall we then behold their naturall teares?
    Enter Messenger
MESSENGER
The English are embattail'd, you French Peeres.   2100
CONSTABLE
To Horse you gallant Princes, straight to Horse.
Doe but behold yond poore and starued Band,
And your faire shew shall suck away their Soules,
Leauing them but the shales and huskes of men.
There is not worke enough for all our hands,
Scarce blood enough in all their sickly Veines,
To giue each naked Curtleax a stayne,
That our French Gallants shall to day draw out,
And sheath for lack of sport. Let vs but blow on
   them,
The vapour of our Valour will o're-turne them.   2110
'Tis positiue gainst all exceptions, Lords,
That our superfluous Lacquies, and our Pesants,
Who in vnnecessarie action swarme
About our Squares of Battaile, were enow
To purge this field of such a hilding Foe;
Though we vpon this Mountaines Basis by,
Tooke stand for idle speculation:
But that our Honours must not. What's to say?
A very little little let vs doe,
And all is done: then let the Trumpets sound   2120
The Tucket Sonnance, and the Note to mount:
For our approach shall so much dare the field,
That England shall couch downe in feare, and yeeld.

Enter Graundpree

GRANDPREE

Why do you stay so long, my Lords of France?
Yond Iland Carrions, desperate of their bones,
Ill-fauor'dly become the Morning field:
Their ragged Curtaines poorely are let loose,
And our Ayre shakes them passing scornefully.
Bigge *Mars* seemes banqu'rout in their begger'd Hoast,
2130   And faintly through a rustie Beuer peepes.
The Horsemen sit like fixed Candlesticks,
With Torch-staues in their hands: and their poore
          Iades
Lob downe their heads, drooping the hides and hips:
The gumme downe roping from their pale-dead eyes,
And in their pald dull mouthes the Iymold Bitt
Lyes foule with chaw'd-grasse, still and motionlesse.
And their executors, the knauish Crowes,
Flye o're them all impatient for their howre.
Description cannot sute it selfe in words,
2140   To demonstrate the Life of such a Battaile,
In life so liuelesse, as it shewes it selfe.

CONSTABLE

They haue said their prayers, and they stay for death.

⌈BURBON⌉

Shall we goe send them Dinners, and fresh Sutes,
And giue their fasting Horses Prouender,
And after fight with them?

CONSTABLE

I stay but for my Guidon. To the field,
I will the Banner from a Trumpet take,
And vse it for my haste. Come, come away,
The Sunne is high, and we out-weare the day.

                                          Exeunt

Sc. 19   *Enter Gloucester, ⌈Clarence⌉, Exeter, Erpingham*
(4.3)   *with all ⌈the⌉ Hoast: Salisbury, and ⌈Warwick⌉*

2150   GLOUCESTER Where is the King?

⌈CLARENCE⌉

The King himselfe is rode to view their Battaile.

⌈WARWICK⌉

Of fighting men they haue full threescore thousand.

EXETER

There's fiue to one, besides they all are fresh.

SALISBURY

Gods Arme strike with vs, 'tis a fearefull oddes.
God buy' you Princes all; Ile to my Charge:
If we no more meet, till we meet in Heauen;
Then ioyfully, my Noble Lord of Clarence,
My deare Lord Gloucester, and my good Lord Exeter,
And (*to Warwick*) my kind Kinsman, Warriors all,
          adieu.

⌈CLARENCE⌉

2160   Farwell good *Salisbury*, & good luck go with thee.

EXETER

Farwell kind Lord: fight valiantly to day:
And yet I doe thee wrong, to mind thee of it,
For thou art fram'd of the firme truth of valour.

                                      Exit Salisbury

⌈CLARENCE⌉

He is as full of Valour as of Kindnesse,
Princely in both.

          Enter King Harry behind

⌈WARWICK⌉   O that we now had here
But one ten thousand of those men in England,
That doe no worke to day.

KING HARRY   What's he that wishes so?
My Cousin *Warwick*. No, my faire Cousin:
If we are markt to dye, we are enow
To doe our Countrey losse: and if to liue,   2170
The fewer men, the greater share of honour.
Gods will, I pray thee wish not one man more.
By *Ioue*, I am not couetous for Gold,
Nor care I who doth feed vpon my cost:
It yernes me not, if men my Garments weare;
Such outward things dwell not in my desires.
But if it be a sinne to couet Honor,
I am the most offending Soule aliue.
No 'faith, my Couze, wish not a man from England:
Gods peace, I would not loose so great an Honor,   2180
As one man more me thinkes would share from me,
For the best hope I haue. O, doe not wish one more:
Rather proclaime it presently through my Hoast,
That he which hath no stomack to this fight,
Let him depart, his Pasport shall be made,
And Crownes for Conuoy put into his Purse:
We would not dye in that mans companie,
That feares his fellowship, to dye with vs.
This day is call'd the Feast of *Crispian*:
He that out-liues this day, and comes safe home,   2190
Will stand a tip-toe when this day is named,
And rowse him at the Name of *Crispian*.
He that shall see this day, and liue t'old age,
Will yeerely on the Vigil feast his neighbours,
And say, to morrow is Saint *Crispian*.
Then will he strip his sleeue, and shew his skarres:
And say, these wounds I had on *Crispines* day:
Old men forget; yet all shall be forgot:
But hee'le remember, with aduantages,
What feats he did that day. Then shall our Names,   2200
Familiar in his mouth as household words,
Harry the King, *Bedford* and *Exeter*,
Warwick and *Talbot*, *Salisbury* and *Gloucester*,
Be in their flowing Cups freshly remembred.
This story shall the good man teach his sonne:
And *Crispine Crispian* shall ne're goe by,
From this day to the ending of the World,
But we in it shall be remembred;
We few, we happy few, we band of brothers:
For he to day that sheds his blood with me,   2210
Shall be my brother: be he ne're so vile,
This day shall gentle his Condition.
And Gentlemen in England, now a bed,
Shall thinke themselues accurst they were not here;
And hold their Manhoods cheape, whiles any speakes,
That fought with vs vpon Saint *Crispines* day.

          Enter Salisbury

SALISBURY

My Soueraign Lord, bestow your selfe with speed:
The French are brauely in their battailes set,
And will with all expedience charge on vs.

KING HARRY

2220   All things are ready, if our minds be so.

⌈WARWICK⌉

Perish the man, whose mind is backward now.

KING HARRY

Thou do'st not wish more helpe from England, Couze?

⌈WARWICK⌉

Gods will, my Liege, would you and I alone,
Without more helpe, could fight this Royall battaile.

KING HARRY

Why now thou hast vnwisht fiue thousand men:
Which likes me better, then to wish vs one.
You know your places: God be with you all.
            Tucket. Enter Montioy

MOUNTIOY

Once more I come to know of thee King Harry,
If for thy Ransome thou wilt now compound,
2230   Before thy most assured Ouerthrow:
For certainly, thou art so neere the Gulfe,
Thou needs must be englutted. Besides, in mercy
The Constable desires thee, thou wilt mind
Thy followers of Repentance; that their Soules
May make a peacefull and a sweet retyre
From off these fields: where (wretches) their poore
            bodies
Must lye and fester.

KING HARRY Who hath sent thee now?

MOUNTIOY The Constable of France.

KING HARRY

2240   I pray thee beare my former Answer back:
Bid them atchieue me, and then sell my bones.
Good God, why should they mock poore fellowes
            thus?
The man that once did sell the Lyons skin
While the beast liu'd, was kill'd with hunting him.
A many of our bodyes shall no doubt
Find Natiue Graues: vpon the which, I trust
Shall witnesse liue in Brasse of this dayes worke.
And those that leaue their valiant bones in France,
Dying like men, though buryed in your Dunghills,
They shall be fam'd: for there the Sun shall greet
2250   them,
And draw their honors reeking vp to Heauen,
Leauing their earthly parts to choake your Clyme,
The smell whereof shall breed a Plague in France.
Marke then abounding valour in our English:
That being dead, like to the bullets grasing,
Breake out into a second course of mischiefe,
Killing in relapse of Mortalitie.
Let me speake prowdly: Tell the Constable,
We are but Warriors for the working day:
2260   Our Gaynesse and our Gilt are all besmyrcht
With raynie Marching in the painefull field.
There's not a piece of feather in our Hoast:

Good argument (I hope) we will not flye:
And time hath worne vs into slouenrie.
But by the Masse, our hearts are in the trim:
And my poore Souldiers tell me, yet ere Night,
They'le be in fresher Robes, as they will pluck
The gay new Coats o're yʳ French Souldiers heads,
And turne them out of seruice. If they doe this,
As if God please, they shall; my Ransome then   2270
Will soone be leuyed. Herauld, saue thou thy labour:
Come thou no more for Ransome, gentle Herauld,
They shall haue none, I sweare, but these my ioynts:
Which if they haue, as I will leaue 'em them,
Shall yeeld them little, tell the Constable.

MOUNTIOY

I shall, King Harry. And so fare thee well:
Thou neuer shalt heare Herauld any more.

KING HARRY

I feare thou wilt once more come for a Ransome.
                            Exit Mountioy
        Enter Yorke

YORKE

My Lord, most humbly on my knee I begge
The leading of the Vaward.   2280

KING HARRY

Take it, braue Yorke. Now Souldiers march away,
And how thou pleasest God, dispose the day.   Exeunt

    Alarum. Excursions. Enter Pistoll, French Souldier,   Sc. 20
    Boy   (4.4)

PISTOLL Yeeld Curre.

FRENCH SOULDIER Ie pense que vous estes le Gentilhome de
bon qualitee.

PISTOLL

Quallitie? calino custure me.
Art thou a Gentleman? What is thy Name? discusse.

FRENCH SOULDIER O Seigneur Dieu.

PISTOLL (aside)

O Signieur Dewe should be a Gentleman:
Perpend my words O Signieur Dewe, and marke: 2290
O Signieur Dewe, thou dyest on point of Fox,
Except O Signieur thou doe giue to me
Egregious Ransome.

FRENCH SOULDIER O prennes miserecorde aye pitiez de moy.

PISTOLL

Moy shall not serue, I will haue fortie Moyes:
Or I will fetch thy rymme out at thy Throat,
In droppes of Crimson blood.

FRENCH SOULDIER Est il impossible d'eschapper le force de ton
bras.

PISTOLL

Brasse, Curre? thou damned and luxurious Mountaine
            Goat,   2300
Offer'st me Brasse?

FRENCH SOULDIER O perdonne moy.

PISTOLL

Say'st thou me so? is that a Tonne of Moyes?
Come hither boy, aske me this slaue in French
What is his Name.

BOY *Escoute comment estes vous appelle?*

FRENCH SOULDIER *Mounsieur le Fer.*

BOY He sayes his Name is M. *Fer.*

PISTOLL M. *Fer*: Ile fer him, and firke him, and ferret him:
2310   Discusse the same in French vnto him.

BOY I doe not know the French for fer, and ferret, and
     firke.

PISTOLL
     Bid him prepare, for I will cut his throat.

FRENCH SOULDIER *Que dit il Mounsieur?*

BOY *Il me commande a vous dire que vous faite vous prest,
car ce soldat icy est disposee tout asture de couppes vostre
gorge.*

PISTOLL
     Owy, cuppele gorge permafoy
     Pesant, vnlesse thou giue me Crownes, braue
         Crownes;
2320   Or mangled shalt thou be by this my Sword.

FRENCH SOULDIER *O Ie vous supplie pour l'amour de Dieu:
ma pardonner, Ie suis le Gentilhome de bon maison, garde
ma vie, & Ie vous donneray deux cent escus.*

PISTOLL What are his words?

BOY He prayes you to saue his life, he is a Gentleman of
     a good house, and for his ransom he will giue you two
     hundred Crownes.

PISTOLL
     Tell him my fury shall abate, and I the Crownes will
         take.

FRENCH SOULDIER *Petit Monsieur que dit il?*

2330 BOY *Encore qu'il et contra son Iurement, de pardonner aucune
prisonier: neant-moins pour les escues que vous luy ci
promete, il est content a vous donnes le liberte le
franchisement.*

FRENCH SOULDIER (*kneeling to Pistoll*) *Sur mes genoux Ie
vous donnes milles remerciens, et Ie me estime heurex que
Ie ai tombe, entre les mains d'un Cheualier comme Ie pense
le plus braue valiant et tres distinie signieur d'Angleterre.*

PISTOLL Expound vnto me boy.

BOY He giues you vpon his knees a thousand thanks, and
2340   he esteemes himselfe happy, that he hath falne into
     the hands of one (as he thinkes) the most braue,
     valorous and thrice-worthy signeur of England.

PISTOLL
     As I sucke blood, I will some mercy shew.
     Follow mee.

BOY *Suiue vous le grand Capitaine?*

                   Exeunt Pistoll and French Souldier
I did neuer know so full a voyce issue from so emptie
a heart: but the saying is true, The empty vessel makes
the greatest sound, *Bardolfe* and *Nym* had tenne times
more valour, then this roaring diuell i'th olde play,
2350 that euerie one may payre his nayles with a woodden
dagger, and they are both hang'd, and so would this
be, if hee durst steale any thing aduenturously. I must
stay with the Lackies with the luggage of our camp,
the French might haue a good pray of vs, if he knew
of it, for there is none to guard it but boyes.   *Exit*

       Enter Constable, Orleance, ⌐Burbon,⌐ and Ramburs   Sc. 21
CONSTABLE *O Diable.*   (4.5)

ORLEANCE *O signeur le iour et perdu, toute et perdu.*

⌐BURBON⌐
     Mor du ma vie, all is confounded all,
     Reproach, and euerlasting shame
     Sits mocking in our Plumes.   2360
         A short Alarum
     O meschante Fortune, ⌐*to Rambures*⌐ do not runne
         away.

⌐ORLEANCE⌐
     We are enow yet liuing in the Field,
     To smother vp the English in our throngs,
     If any order might be thought vpon.

BURBON
     The diuell take Order, once more backe againe,
     And he that will not follow *Burbon* now,
     Let him go home, and with his cap in hand
     Like a base leno hold the Chamber doore,
     Whilst by a slaue, no gentler then my dogge,
     His fairest daughter is contaminated.   2370

CONSTABLE
     Disorder that hath spoyl'd vs, friend vs now,
     Let vs on heapes go offer vp our liues.

BURBON Ile to the throng;
     Let life be short, else shame will be too long.

                              Exit omnes

       Alarum. Enter King Harry and his trayne, with   Sc. 22
       Prisoners   (4.6)

KING HARRY
     Well haue we done, thrice-valiant Countrimen,
     But all's not done, yet keepe the French the field.
         ⌐*Enter Exeter*⌐

EXETER
     The D. of York commends him to your Maiesty.

KING HARRY
     Liues he good Vnckle: thrice within this houre
     I saw him downe; thrice vp againe, and fighting,
     From Helmet to the spurre, all blood he was.   2380

EXETER
     In which array (braue Soldier) doth he lye,
     Larding the plaine: and by his bloody side,
     (Yoake-fellow to his honour-owing-wounds)
     The Noble Earle of Suffolke also lyes.
     Suffolke first dyed, and Yorke all hagled ouer
     Comes to him, where in gore he lay insteeped,
     And takes him by the Beard, kisses the gashes
     That bloodily did yawne vpon his face,
     And cryes aloud; Tarry deare Cosin Suffolke,
     My soule shall thine keepe company to heauen: 2390
     Tarry (sweet soule) for mine, then flye a-brest:
     As in this glorious and well-foughten field
     We kept together in our Chiualrie.
     Vpon these words I came, and cheer'd him vp,
     He smil'd me in the face, raught me his hand,
     And with a feeble gripe, sayes: Deere my Lord,

Commend my seruice to my Soueraigne,
So did he turne, and ouer Suffolkes necke
He threw his wounded arme, and kist his lippes,
2400 And so espous'd to death, with blood he seal'd
A Testament of Noble-ending-loue:
The prettie and sweet manner of it forc'd
Those waters from me, which I would haue stop'd,
But I had not so much of man in mee,
And all my mother came into mine eyes,
And gaue me vp to teares.

KING HARRY   I blame you not,
For hearing this, I must perforce compound
With mistfull eyes, or they will issue to.

Alarum

But hearke, what new alarum is this same?
2410 The French haue re-enforc'd their scatter'd men:
Then euery souldiour kill his Prisoners,
⌈*The souldiours kill their Prisoners*⌉
Giue the word through.

⌈PISTOLL⌉ *Couple gorge.*   *Exit omnes*

Sc. 23   *Enter Fluellen and Gower*
(4.7)
FLUELLEN Kill the poyes and the luggage, 'Tis expressely
against the Law of Armes, tis as arrant a peece of
knauery marke you now, as can bee offert; in your
Conscience now, is it not?

GOWER Tis certaine, there's not a boy left aliue, and the
Cowardly Rascalls that ranne from the battaile ha'
2420 done this slaughter: besides they haue burned and
carried away all that was in the Kings Tent, wherefore
the King most worthily hath caus'd euery soldiour to
cut his prisoners throat. O 'tis a gallant King.

FLUELLEN I, hee was porne at *Monmouth*: Captaine *Gower*,
what call you the Townes name where *Alexander* the
pig was borne?

GOWER *Alexander* the Great.

FLUELLEN Why I pray you, is not pig, great? The pig, or
the great, or the mighty, or the huge, or the
2430 magnanimous, are all one reckonings, saue the phrase
is a litle variations.

GOWER I thinke *Alexander* the Great was borne in *Macedon*,
his Father was called *Phillip* of *Macedon*, as I take it.

FLUELLEN I thinke it is in *Macedon* where *Alexander* is
porne: I tell you Captaine, if you looke in the Maps of
the World, I warrant you sall finde in the comparisons
betweene *Macedon* & *Monmouth*, that the situations
looke you, is both alike. There is a Riuer in *Macedon*,
& there is also moreouer a Riuer at *Monmouth*, it is
2440 call'd Wye at *Monmouth*: but it is out of my praines,
what is the name of the other Riuer: but 'tis all one,
tis alike as my fingers is to my fingers, and there is
Salmons in both. If you marke *Alexanders* life well,
Harry of Monmouthes life is come after it indifferent
well, for there is figures in all things. *Alexander* God
knowes, and you know, in his rages, and his furies,
and his wraths, and his chollers, and his moodes, and
his displeasures, and his indignations, and also being

a little intoxicates in his praines, did in his Ales and
his angers (looke you) kill his best friend *Clytus*.   2450

GOWER Our King is not like him in that, he neuer kill'd
any of his friends.

FLUELLEN It is not well done (marke you now) to take the
tales out of my mouth, ere it is made an end and
finished. I speak but in the figures, and comparisons of
it: as *Alexander* kild his friend *Clytus*, being in his Ales
and his Cuppes; so also *Harry Monmouth* being in his
right wittes, and his good iudgements, turn'd away the
fat Knight with the great belly doublet: he was full of
iests, and gypes, and knaueries, and mockes, I haue   2460
forgot his name.

GOWER Sir *Iohn Falstaffe*.

FLUELLEN That is he: Ile tell you, there is good men porne
at *Monmouth*.

GOWER Heere comes his Maiesty.
        Alarum. Enter King Harry ⌈*and the English army*⌉
        with Burbon, ⌈*Orleance,*⌉ *and other prisoners.*
        Flourish

KING HARRY
I was not angry since I came to France,
Vntill this instant. Take a Trumpet Herald,
Ride thou vnto the Horsemen on yond hill:
If they will fight with vs, bid them come downe,
Or voyde the field: they do offend our sight.   2470
If they'l do neither, we will come to them,
And make them sker away, as swift as stones
Enforced from the old Assyrian slings:
Besides, wee'l cut the throats of those we haue,
And not a man of them that we shall take,
Shall taste our mercy. Go and tell them so.
        Enter Montioy

EXETER
Here comes the Herald of the French, my Liege.

GLOUCESTER
His eyes are humbler then they vs'd to be.

KING HARRY
How now, what meanes this Herald? Knowst thou
        not,
That I haue fin'd these bones of mine for ransome?   2480
Com'st thou againe for ransome?

MOUNTIOY   No great King:
I come to thee for charitable License,
That we may wander ore this bloody field,
To booke our dead, and then to bury them,
To sort our Nobles from our common men.
For many of our Princes (woe the while)
Lye drown'd and soak'd in mercenary blood:
So do our vulgar drench their peasant limbes
In blood of Princes, and our wounded steeds
Fret fet-locke deepe in gore, and with wilde rage   2490
Yerke out their armed heeles at their dead masters,
Killing them twice. O giue vs leaue great King,
To view the field in safety, and dispose
Of their dead bodies.

KING HARRY   I tell thee truly Herald,

I know not if the day be ours or no,
For yet a many of your horsemen peere,
And gallop ore the field.

MOUNTIOY   The day is yours.

KING HARRY
Praised be God, and not our strength for it:
What is this Castle call'd that stands hard by.

2500 MOUNTIOY They call it *Agincourt*.

KING HARRY
Then call we this the field of *Agincourt*,
Fought on the day of *Crispin Crispian*.

FLUELLEN Your Grandfather of famous memory (an't
please your Maiesty) and your great Vncle *Edward* the
Placke Prince of Wales, as I haue read in the Chronicles,
fought a most praue pattle here in France.

KING HARRY They did *Fluellen*.

FLUELLEN Your Maiesty sayes very true: If your Maiesties
is remembred of it, the Welchmen did good seruice in
2510 a Garden where Leekes did grow, wearing Leekes in
their *Monmouth* caps, which your Maiesty know to this
houre is an honourable badge of the seruice: And I do
beleeue your Maiesty takes no scorne to weare the
Leeke vppon S. Tauies day.

KING HARRY
I weare it for a memorable honor:
For I am Welch you know good Countriman.

FLUELLEN All the water in Wye, cannot wash your
Maiesties Welsh plood out of your pody, I can tell you
that: God plesse it, and preserue it, as long as it pleases
2520 his Grace, and his Maiesty too.

KING HARRY Thankes good my Countryman.

FLUELLEN By Ieshu, I am your Maiesties Countreyman, I
care not who know it: I will confesse it to all the
World, I need not to be ashamed of your Maiesty,
praised be God so long as your Maiesty is an honest
man.

KING HARRY
God keepe me so.

Enter Williams with a Gloue in his Cappe
          Our Heralds go with him,
Bring me iust notice of the numbers dead
On both our parts.

          Exit Mountioy, ⌜Gower,⌝ and an English herald
          Call yonder fellow hither.

2530 EXETER (*to Williams*) Souldier, you must come to the King.

KING HARRY Souldier, why wear'st thou that Gloue in thy
Cappe?

WILLIAMS And't please your Maiesty, tis the gage of one
that I should fight withall, if he be aliue.

KING HARRY An Englishman?

WILLIAMS And't please your Maiesty, a Rascall that
swagger'd with me last night: who if a liue, and euer
dare to challenge this Gloue, I haue sworne to take
him a boxe a'th ere: or if I can see my Gloue in his
2540 cappe, which he swore as he was a Souldier he would
weare (if a liud) I wil strike it out soundly.

KING HARRY What thinke you Captaine *Fluellen*, is it fit
this souldier keepe his oath.

FLUELLEN Hee is a Crauen and a Villaine else, and't please
your Maiesty in my conscience.

KING HARRY It may bee, his enemy is a Gentleman of
great sort quite from the answer of his degree.

FLUELLEN Though he be as good a Ientleman as the diuel
is, as Lucifer and Belzebub himselfe, it is necessary
(looke your Grace) that he keepe his vow and his oath: 2550
If hee bee periur'd (see you now) his reputation is as
arrant a villaine and a Iacke sawce, as euer his blacke
shoo trodd vpon Gods ground, and his earth, in my
conscience law.

KING HARRY Then keepe thy vow sirrah, when thou
meet'st the fellow.

WILLIAMS So I wil my Liege, as I liue.

KING HARRY Who seru'st thou vnder?

WILLIAMS Vnder Captaine *Gower*, my Liege.

FLUELLEN *Gower* is a good Captaine, and is good know-   2560
ledge and literatured in the Warres.

KING HARRY Call him hither to me, Souldier.

WILLIAMS I will my Liege.   *Exit*

KING HARRY (*giuing him Williams other Gloue*) Here *Fluellen*,
weare thou this fauour for me, and sticke it in thy
Cappe: when *Alanson* and my selfe were downe
together, I pluckt this Gloue from his Helme: If any
man challenge this, hee is a friend to *Alanson*, and an
enemy to our Person; if thou encounter any such,
apprehend him, and thou do'st me loue.   2570

FLUELLEN Your Grace doo's me as great Honors as can
be desir'd in the hearts of his Subiects: I would faine
see the man, that ha's but two legges, that shall find
himselfe agreefd at this Gloue; that is all: but I would
faine see it once, and please God of his grace that I
would see.

KING HARRY Know'st thou *Gower*?

FLUELLEN He is my deare friend, and please you.

KING HARRY Pray thee goe seeke him, and bring him to
my Tent.   2580

FLUELLEN I will fetch him.   *Exit*

KING HARRY
My Lord of *Warwick*, and my Brother *Gloster*,
Follow *Fluellen* closely at the heeles.
The Gloue which I haue giuen him for a fauour,
May haply purchase him a box a'th'eare.
It is the Souldiers: I by bargaine should
Weare it my selfe. Follow good Cousin *Warwick*:
If that the Souldier strike him, as I iudge
By his blunt bearing, he will keepe his word;
Some sodaine mischiefe may arise of it: 2590
For I doe know *Fluellen* valiant,
And toucht with Choler, hot as Gunpowder,
And quickly will returne an iniurie.
Follow, and see there be no harme betweene them.
Goe you with me, Vnckle of Exeter.   *Exeunt seuerally*

Enter Gower and Williams   Sc. 24

WILLIAMS I warrant it is to Knight you, Captaine.   (4.8)
          Enter Fluellen

FLUELLEN Gods will, and his pleasure, Captaine, I beseech

you now, come apace to the King: there is more good
toward you peraduenture, then is in your knowledge

2600 to dreame of.

WILLIAMS Sir, know you this Gloue?

FLUELLEN Know the Gloue? I know the Gloue is a Gloue.

WILLIAMS ⌈*plucking the Gloue from Fluellens Cappe*⌉ I know
this, and thus I challenge it.

     Strikes him

FLUELLEN Gods plud, and his, an arrant Traytor as anyes
in the Vniuersall World, or in France, or in England.

GOWER (*to Williams*) How now Sir? you Villaine.

WILLIAMS Doe you thinke Ile be forsworne?

FLUELLEN Stand away Captaine *Gower*, I will giue Treason

2610 his payment into plowes, I warrant you.

WILLIAMS I am no Traytor.

FLUELLEN That's a Lye in thy Throat. I charge you in his
Maiesties Name apprehend him, he's a friend of the
Duke *Alansons*.

     Enter Warwick and Gloucester

WARWICK How now, how now, what's the matter?

FLUELLEN My Lord of Warwick, heere is, praysed be God
for it, a most contagious Treason come to light, looke
you, as you shall desire in a Summers day.

     Enter King Harry and Exeter

Heere is his Maiestie.

2620 KING HARRY How now, what is the matter?

FLUELLEN My Liege, heere is a Villaine, and a Traytor,
that looke your Grace, ha's strooke the Gloue which
your Maiestie is take out of the Helmet of *Alanson*.

WILLIAMS My Liege, this was my Gloue, here is the fellow
of it: and he that I gaue it to in change, promis'd to
weare it in his Cappe: I promis'd to strike him, if he
did: I met this man with my Gloue in his Cappe, and
I haue been as good as my word.

FLUELLEN Your Maiestie heare now, sauing your Maiesties

2630 Manhood, what an arrant rascally, beggerly, lowsie
Knaue it is: I hope your Maiestie is peare me testimonie
and witnesse, and will auouchment, that this is the
Gloue of *Alanson*, that your Maiestie is giue me, in your
Conscience now.

KING HARRY Giue me thy Gloue Souldier; Looke, heere is
the fellow of it:

'Twas I indeed thou promised'st to strike,
And thou hast giuen me most bitter termes.

FLUELLEN And please your Maiestie, let his Neck answere

2640 for it, if there is any Marshall Law in the World.

KING HARRY
How canst thou make me satisfaction?

WILLIAMS All offences, my Lord, come from the heart:
neuer came any from mine, that might offend your
Maiestie.

KING HARRY
It was our selfe thou didst abuse.

WILLIAMS Your Maiestie came not like your selfe: you
appear'd to me but as a common man; witnesse the
Night, your Garments, your Lowlinesse: and what your
Highnesse suffer'd vnder that shape, I beseech you take

it for your owne fault, and not mine: for had you beene   2650
as I tooke you for, I made no offence; therefore I
beseech your Highnesse pardon me.

KING HARRY
Here Vnckle *Exeter*, fill this Gloue with Crownes,
And giue it to this fellow. Keepe it fellow,
And weare it for an Honor in thy Cappe,
Till I doe challenge it. Giue him the Crownes:
And Captaine, you must needs be friends with him.

FLUELLEN By this Day and this Light, the fellow ha's
mettell enough in his belly: Hold, there is twelue-pence
for you, and I pray you to serue God, and keepe you   2660
out of prawles and prabbles, and quarrels and
dissentions, and I warrant you it is the better for you.

WILLIAMS I will none of your Money.

FLUELLEN It is with a good will: I can tell you it will serue
you to mend your shooes: come, wherefore should you
be so pashfull, your shooes is not so good: 'tis a good
shilling I warrant you, or I will change it.

     Enter ⌈*an English*⌉ *Herauld*

KING HARRY Now Herauld, are the dead numbred?

HERALD
Heere is the number of the slaught'red French.

KING HARRY
What Prisoners of good sort are taken, Vnckle?   2670

EXETER
Charles Duke of Orleance, Nephew to the King,
Iohn Duke of Burbon, and Lord *Bouchiqualt*:
Of other Lords and Barons, Knights and Squires,
Full fifteene hundred, besides common men.

KING HARRY
This Note doth tell me of ten thousand French
That in the field lye slaine: of Princes in this number,
And Nobles bearing Banners, there lye dead
One hundred twentie six: added to these,
Of Knights, Esquires, and gallant Gentlemen,
Eight thousand and foure hundred: of the which,   2680
Fiue hundred were but yesterday dubb'd Knights.
So that in these ten thousand they haue lost,
There are but sixteene hundred Mercenaries:
The rest are Princes, Barons, Lords, Knights, Squires,
And Gentlemen of bloud and qualitie.
The Names of those their Nobles that lye dead:
Charles Delabreth, High Constable of France,
Iaques of Chatilion, Admirall of France,
The Master of the Crosse-bowes, Lord *Rambures*,
Great Master of France, the braue Sir *Guichard*
   Dolphin,   2690
Iohn Duke of Alanson, *Anthonie* Duke of Brabant,
The Brother to the Duke of Burgundie,
And *Edward* Duke of Barr: of lustie Earles,
Grandpree and *Roussie*, *Fauconbridge* and *Foyes*,
Beaumont and *Marle*, *Vaudemont* and *Lestrake*.
Here was a Royall fellowship of death.
Where is the number of our English dead?

     He is giuen another paper

Edward the Duke of Yorke, the Earle of Suffolke,

Sir *Richard Kyghley, Dauy Gam* Esquire;

2700 None else of name: and of all other men,
But fiue and twentie. O God, thy Arme was heere:
And not to vs, but to thy Arme alone,
Ascribe we all: when, without stratagem,
But in plaine shock, and euen play of Battaile,
Was euer knowne so great and little losse,
On one part and on th'other? take it God,
For it is none but thine.

EXETER   'Tis wonderfull.

KING HARRY
Come, goe we in procession to the Village:
And be it death proclaymed through our Hoast,

2710 To boast of this, or take that prayse from God,
Which is his onely.

FLUELLEN Is it not lawfull and please your Maiestie, to tell
how many is kill'd?

KING HARRY
Yes Captaine: but with this acknowledgement,
That God fought for vs.

FLUELLEN Yes, in my conscience, he did vs great good.

KING HARRY Doe we all holy Rights:
Let there be sung *Non nobis*, and *Te Deum*,
The dead with charitie enclos'd in Clay:

2720 And then to Callice, and to England then,
Where ne're from France arriu'd more happy men.

                                                   Exeunt

Sc. 25   *Enter Chorus*
(5.0) CHORUS
Vouchsafe to those that haue not read the Story,
That I may prompt them: and of such as haue,
I humbly pray them to admit th'excuse
Of time, of numbers, and due course of things,
Which cannot in their huge and proper life,
Be here presented. Now we beare the King
Toward Callice: Graunt him there; there seene,
Heaue him away vpon your winged thoughts,

2730 Athwart the Sea: Behold the English beach
Pales in the flood; with Men, Maids, Wiues, and
    Boyes,
Whose shouts & claps out-voyce the deep-mouth'd
    Sea,
Which like a mightie Whiffler 'fore the King,
Seemes to prepare his way: So let him land,
And solemnly see him set on to London.
So swift a pace hath Thought, that euen now
You may imagine him vpon Black-Heath:
Where that his Lords desire him, to haue borne
His bruised Helmet, and his bended Sword

2740 Before him, through the Citie: he forbids it,
Being free from vain-nesse, and selfe-glorious pride;
Giuing full Trophee, Signall, and Ostent,
Quite from himselfe, to God. But now behold,
In the quick Forge and working-house of Thought,
How London doth powre out her Citizens,
The Maior and all his Brethren in best sort,

Like to the Senatours of th'antique Rome,
With the Plebeians swarming at their heeles,
Goe forth and fetch their Conqu'ring *Cæsar* in:
As by a lower, but hy louing likelyhood,   2750
Were now the Generall of our gracious Empresse,
As in good time he may, from Ireland comming,
Bringing Rebellion broached on his Sword;
How many would the peacefull Citie quit,
To welcome him? much more, and much more cause,
Did they this *Harry*. Now in London place him.
As yet the lamentation of the French
Inuites the King of Englands stay at home:
The Emperour's comming in behalfe of France,
To order peace betweene them ⌈   2760
            ⌉: and omit
All the occurrences, what euer chanc't,
Till *Harryes* backe returne againe to France:
There must we bring him; and my selfe haue play'd
The *interim*, by remembring you 'tis past.
Then brooke abridgement, and your eyes aduance,
After your thoughts, straight backe againe to France.

                                                   Exit

*Enter Gower and Fluellen, with a Leeke in his   Sc. 26
Cappe, and a Cudgel*   (5.1)

GOWER Nay, that's right: but why weare you your Leeke
to day? S. *Dauies* day is past.

FLUELLEN There is occasions and causes why and   2770
wherefore in all things: I will tell you asse my friend,
Captaine *Gower*; the rascally, scauld, beggerly, lowsie,
pragging Knaue *Pistoll*, which you and your selfe, and
all the World, know to be no petter then a fellow, looke
you now, of no merits: hee is come to me, and prings
me pread and sault yesterday, looke you, and bid me
eate my Leeke: it was in a place where I could not
breed no contention with him; but I will be so bold as
to weare it in my Cap till I see him once againe, and
then I will tell him a little piece of my desires.   2780

        Enter Pistoll

GOWER Why heere a comes, swelling like a Turky-cock.

FLUELLEN 'Tis no matter for his swellings, nor his Turky-
cocks. God plesse you aunchient *Pistoll*: you scuruie
lowsie Knaue, God plesse you.

PISTOLL
Ha, art thou bedlam? doest thou thirst, base Troian,
To haue me fold vp *Parcas* fatall Web?
Hence; I am qualmish at the smell of Leeke.

FLUELLEN I peseech you heartily, scuruie lowsie Knaue,
at my desires, and my requests, and my petitions, to
eate, looke you, this Leeke; because, looke you, you   2790
doe not loue it, nor your affections, and your appetites
and your disgestions doo's not agree with it, I would
desire you to eate it.

PISTOLL
Not for *Cadwallader* and all his Goats.

FLUELLEN There is one Goat for you. (*Strikes him*) Will
you be so good, scauld Knaue, as eate it?

PISTOLL Base Troian, thou shalt dye.

FLUELLEN You say very true, scauld Knaue, when Gods will is: I will desire you to liue in the meane time, and
2800 eate your Victuals: come, there is sawce for it. (*Strikes him*) You call'd me yesterday Mountaine-Squier, but I will make you to day a squire of low degree. I pray you fall too, if you can mocke a Leeke, you can eate a Leeke.

⌐*Strikes him*⌐

GOWER Enough Captaine, you haue astonisht him.

FLUELLEN By Iesu, I will make him eate some part of my leeke, or I will peate his pate foure dayes and foure nights: bite I pray you, it is good for your greene wound, and your ploodie Coxecombe.

2810 PISTOLL Must I bite.

FLUELLEN Yes certainly, and out of doubt and out of question too, and ambiguities.

PISTOLL By this Leeke, I will most horribly reuenge

⌐*Fluellen threatens him*⌐

I eate and eate I sweare.

FLUELLEN Eate I pray you, will you haue some more sauce to your Leeke: there is not enough Leeke to sweare by.

PISTOLL

Quiet thy Cudgell, thou dost see I eate.

FLUELLEN Much good do you scald knaue, heartily. Nay, pray you throw none away, the skinne is good for your
2820 broken Coxcombe; when you take occasions to see Leekes heereafter, I pray you mocke at 'em, that is all.

PISTOLL Good.

FLUELLEN I, Leekes is good: hold you, there is a groat to heale your pate.

PISTOLL Me a groat?

FLUELLEN Yes verily, and in truth you shall take it, or I haue another Leeke in my pocket, which you shall eate.

PISTOLL

I take thy groat in earnest of reuenge.

2830 FLUELLEN If I owe you any thing, I will pay you in Cudgels, you shall be a Woodmonger, and buy nothing of me but cudgels: God bu'y you, and keepe you, & heale your pate.   *Exit*

PISTOLL All hell shall stirre for this.

GOWER Go, go, you are a counterfeit cowardly Knaue, will you mocke at an ancient Tradition began vppon an honourable respect, and worne as a memorable Trophee of predeceased valor, and dare not auouch in your deeds any of your words. I haue seene you
2840 gleeking & galling at this Gentleman twice or thrice. You thought, because he could not speake English in the natiue garb, he could not therefore handle an English Cudgell: you finde it otherwise, and henceforth let a Welsh correction, teach you a good English condition, fare ye well.   *Exit*

PISTOLL

Doeth fortune play the huswife with me now?
Newes haue I that my *Nell* is dead
I'th Spittle of a malady of France,

And there my rendeuous is quite cut off:
Old I do waxe, and from my wearie limbes   2850
Honour is Cudgeld. Well, Baud Ile turne,
And something leane to Cut-purse of quicke hand:
To England will I steale, and there Ile steale:
And patches will I get vnto these cudgeld scarres,
And swere I got them in the Gallia warres.   *Exit*

Enter at one doore, King Henry, Exeter, ⌐Clarence,⌐   Sc. 27
Warwicke, and other Lords. At another, Queene   (5.2)
Isabel, the King of France, the Duke of Bourgougne,
and other French, among them Katherine and Alice

KING HARRY

Peace to this meeting, wherefore we are met;
Vnto our brother France, and to our Sister
Health and faire time of day: Ioy and good wishes
To our most faire and Princely Cosine *Katherine*:
And as a branch and member of this Royalty,   2860
By whom this great assembly is contriu'd,
We do salute you Duke of *Burgogne*,
And Princes French and Peeres health to you all.

FRENCH KING

Right ioyous are we to behold your face,
Most worthy brother England, fairely met,
So are you Princes (English) euery one.

QUEENE

So happy be the Issue brother England
Of this good day, and of this gracious meeting,
As we are now glad to behold your eyes,
Your eyes which hitherto haue borne in them   2870
Against the French that met them in their bent,
The fatall Balls of murthering Basiliskes:
The venome of such Lookes we fairely hope
Haue lost their qualitie, and that this day
Shall change all griefes and quarrels into loue.

KING HARRY

To cry Amen to that, thus we appeare.

QUEENE

You English Princes all, I doe salute you.

BURGONIE

My dutie to you both, on equall loue.
Great Kings of France and England: that I haue
    labour'd
With all my wits, my paines, and strong endeuors,   2880
To bring your most Imperiall Maiesties
Vnto this Barre, and Royall enteruiew;
Your Mightinesse on both parts best can witnesse.
Since then my Office hath so farre preuayl'd,
That Face to Face, and Royall Eye to Eye,
You haue congreeted: let it not disgrace me,
If I demand before this Royall view,
What Rub, or what Impediment there is,
Why that the naked, poore, and mangled Peace,
Deare Nourse of Arts, Plentyes, and ioyfull Births,   2890
Should not in this best Garden of the World,
Our fertile France, put vp her louely Visage?
Alas, shee hath from France too long been chas'd,

And all her Husbandry doth lye on heapes,
Corrupting in it owne fertilitie.
Her Vine, the merry chearer of the heart,
Vnpruned, dyes: her Hedges euen pleach'd,
Like Prisoners wildly ouer-growne with hayre,
Put forth disorder'd Twigs: her fallow Leas,
2900 The Darnell, Hemlock, and ranke Femetary,
Doth root vpon; while that the Culter rusts,
That should deracinate such Sauagery:
The euen Meade, that erst brought sweetly forth
The freckled Cowslip, Burnet, and greene Clouer,
Wanting the Sythe, all vncorrected, ranke;
Conceiues by idlenesse, and nothing teemes,
But hatefull Docks, rough Thistles, Keksyes, Burres,
Loosing both beautie and vtilitie;
And all our Vineyards, Fallowes, Meades, and Hedges,
2910 Defectiue in their natures, grow to wildnesse,
Euen so our Houses, and our selues, and Children,
Haue lost, or doe not learne, for want of time,
The Sciences that should become our Countrey;
But grow like Sauages, as Souldiers will,
That nothing doe, but meditate on Blood,
To Swearing, and sterne Lookes, defus'd Attyre,
And euery thing that seemes vnnaturall.
Which to reduce into our former fauour,
You are assembled: and my speech entreats,
2920 That I may know the Let, why gentle Peace
Should not expell these inconueniences,
And blesse vs with her former qualities.

KING HARRY
If Duke of Burgonie, you would the Peace,
Whose want giues growth to th'imperfections
Which you haue cited; you must buy that Peace
With full accord to all our iust demands,
Whose Tenures and particular effects
You haue enschedul'd briefely in your hands.

BURGONIE
The King hath heard them: to the which, as yet
There is no Answer made.

2930 KING HARRY   Well then: the Peace
Which you before so vrg'd, lyes in his Answer.

FRENCH KING
I haue but with a cursetorie eye
O're-glanc't the Articles: Pleaseth your Grace
To appoint some of your Councell presently
To sit with vs once more, with better heed
To re-suruey them; we will suddenly
Passe our accept and peremptorie Answer.

KING HARRY
Brother we shall. Goe Vnckle Exeter,
And Brother Clarence, and you Brother Gloucester,
2940 Warwick, and Huntington, goe with the King,
And take with you free power, to ratifie,
Augment, or alter, as your Wisdomes best
Shall see aduantageable for our Dignitie,
Any thing in or out of our Demands,
And wee'le consigne thereto. Will you, faire Sister,
Goe with the Princes, or stay here with vs?

QUEENE
Our gracious Brother, I will goe with them:
Happily a Womans Voyce may doe some good,
When Articles too nicely vrg'd, be stood on.

KING HARRY
Yet leaue our Cousin Katherine here with vs,   2950
She is our capitall Demand, compris'd
Within the fore-ranke of our Articles.

QUEENE
She hath good leaue.   Exeunt omnes
        Manet King Harry, Katherine, and Alice

KING HARRY   Faire Katherine, and most faire,
Will you vouchsafe to teach a Souldier tearmes,
Such as will enter at a Ladyes eare,
And pleade his Loue-suit to her gentle heart.

KATHERINE Your Maiestie shall mock at me, I cannot
speake your England.

KING HARRY O faire Katherine, if you will loue me soundly
with your French heart, I will be glad to heare you   2960
confesse it brokenly with your English Tongue. Doe
you like me, Kate?

KATHERINE Pardonne moy, I cannot tell vat is like me.

KING HARRY An Angell is like you Kate, and you are like
an Angell.

KATHERINE (to Alice) Que dit il que Ie suis semblable a les
Anges?

ALICE Ouy verayment (sauf vostre Grace) ainsi dit il.

KING HARRY I said so, deare Katherine, and I must not
blush to affirme it.   2970

KATHERINE O bon Dieu, les langues des hommes sont plein
de tromperies.

KING HARRY (to Alice) What sayes she, faire one? that the
tongues of men are full of deceits?

ALICE Ouy, dat de tongeus of de mans is be full of deceits:
dat is de Princesse.

KING HARRY The Princesse is the better English-woman:
yfaith Kate, my wooing is fit for thy vnderstanding, I
am glad thou canst speake no better English, for if thou
could'st, thou would'st finde me such a plaine King,   2980
that thou wouldst thinke, I had sold my Farme to buy
my Crowne. I know no wayes to mince it in loue, but
directly to say, I loue you; then if you vrge me farther,
then to say, Doe you in faith? I weare out my suite:
Giue me your answer, yfaith doe, and so clap hands,
and a bargaine: how say you, Lady?

KATHERINE Sauf vostre honeur, me vnderstand well.

KING HARRY Marry, if you would put me to Verses, or to
Dance for your sake, Kate, why you vndid me: for the
one I haue neither words nor measure; and for the   2990
other, I haue no strength in measure, yet a reasonable
measure in strength. If I could winne a Lady at Leape-
frogge, or by vawting into my Saddle, with my Armour
on my backe; vnder the correction of bragging be it
spoken. I should quickly leape into a Wife: Or if I might
buffet for my Loue, or bound my Horse for her fauours,
I could lay on like a Butcher, and sit like a Iack an
Apes, neuer off. But before God Kate, I cannot looke
greenely, nor gaspe out my eloquence, nor I haue no

cunning in protestation; onely downe-right Oathes, which I neuer vse till vrg'd, nor neuer breake for vrging. If thou canst loue a fellow of this temper, *Kate*, whose face is not worth Sunne-burning? that neuer lookes in his Glasse, for loue of any thing he sees there? let thine Eye be thy Cooke. I speake to thee plaine Souldier: If thou canst loue me for this, take me? if not? to say to thee that I shall dye, is true; but for thy loue, by the L. No: yet I loue thee too. And while thou liu'st, deare *Kate*, take a fellow of plaine and vncoyned Constancie, for he perforce must do thee right, because he hath not the gift to wooe in other places: for these fellowes of infinit tongue, that can ryme themselues into Ladyes fauours, they doe always reason themselues out againe. What? a speaker is but a prater, a Ryme is but a Ballad; a good Legge will fall, a strait Backe will stoope, a blacke Beard will turne white, a curl'd Pate will grow bald, a faire Face will wither, a full Eye will wax hollow: but a good Heart, *Kate*, is the Sunne and the Moone, or rather the Sunne, and not the Moone; for it shines bright, and neuer changes, but keepes his course truly. If thou would haue such a one, take me? and take me; take a Souldier: take a Souldier; take a King. And what say'st thou then to my Loue? speake my faire, and fairely, I pray thee.

KATHERINE Is it possible dat I sould loue de ennemie of Fraunce?

KING HARRY No, it is not possible you should loue the Enemie of France, *Kate*; but in louing me, you should loue the Friend of France: for I loue France so well, that I will not part with a Village of it; I will haue it all mine: and *Kate*, when France is mine, and I am yours; then yours is France, and you are mine.

KATHERINE I cannot tell vat is dat.

KING HARRY No, *Kate*? I will tell thee in French, which I am sure will hang vpon my tongue, like a new-married Wife about her Husbands Necke, hardly to be shooke off; *Ie quand suis le possesseur de Fraunce, & quand vous aues le possession de moy.* (Let mee see, what then? Saint *Dennis* bee my speede) *Donc vostre est Fraunce, & vous estes mienne.* It is as easie for me, *Kate*, to conquer the Kingdome, as to speake so much more French: I shall neuer moue thee in French, vnlesse it be to laugh at me.

KATHERINE *Sauf vostre honeur, le Francois ques vous parleis, il & melieur que l'Anglois le quel Ie parle.*

KING HARRY No faith is't not, *Kate*: but thy speaking of my Tongue, and I thine, most truely falsely, must needes be graunted to be much at one. But *Kate*, doo'st thou vnderstand thus much English? Canst thou loue mee?

KATHERINE I cannot tell.

KING HARRY Can any of your Neighbours tell, *Kate*? Ile aske them. Come, I know thou louest me: and at night, when you come into your Closet, you'le question this Gentlewoman about me; and I know, *Kate*, you will to her disprayse those parts in me, that you loue with

your heart: but good *Kate*, mocke me mercifully, the rather gentle Princesse, because I loue thee cruelly. If euer thou beest mine, *Kate*, as I haue a sauing Faith within me tells me thou shalt; I get thee with skambling, and thou must therefore needes proue a good Souldier-breeder: Shall not thou and I, betweene Saint *Dennis* and Saint *George*, compound a Boy, halfe French halfe English, that shall goe to Constantinople, and take the Turke by the Beard. Shall wee not? what say'st thou, my faire Flower-de-Luce.

KATHERINE I doe not know dat.

KING HARRY No: 'tis hereafter to know, but now to promise: doe but now promise *Kate*, you will endeauour for your French part of such a Boy; and for my English moytie, take the Word of a King, and a Batcheler. How answer you. *La plus belle Katherine du monde mon trescher & deuin deesse.*

KATHERINE Your Maiestee aue fause Frenche enough to deceiue de most sage Damoiseil dat is en Fraunce.

KING HARRY Now fye vpon my false French: by mine Honor in true English, I loue thee *Kate*; by which Honor, I dare not sweare thou louest me, yet my blood begins to flatter me, that thou doo'st; notwithstanding the poore and vntempering effect of my Visage. Now beshrew my Fathers Ambition, hee was thinking of Ciuill Warres when hee got me, therefore was I created with a stubborne out-side, with an aspect of Iron, that when I come to wooe Ladyes, I fright them: but in faith *Kate*, the elder I wax, the better I shall appeare. My comfort is, that Old Age, that ill layer vp of Beautie, can doe no more spoyle vpon my Face. Thou hast me, if thou hast me, at the worst; and thou shalt weare me, if thou weare me, better and better: and therefore tell me, most faire *Katherine*, will you haue me? Put off your Maiden Blushes, auouch the Thoughts of your Heart with the Lookes of an Empresse, take me by the Hand, and say, *Harry* of England, I am thine: which Word thou shalt no sooner blesse mine Eare withall, but I will tell thee alowd, England is thine, Ireland is thine, France is thine, and *Henry Plantaginet* is thine; who, though I speake it before his Face, if he be not Fellow with the best King, thou shalt finde the best King of Good-fellowes. Come your Answer in broken Musick; for thy Voyce is Musick, and thy English broken: Therefore Queene of all, *Katherine*, breake thy minde to me in broken English; wilt thou haue me?

KATHERINE Dat is as it shall please de *Roy mon pere*.

KING HARRY Nay, it will please him well, *Kate*; it shall please him, *Kate*.

KATHERINE Den it sall also content me.

KING HARRY Vpon that I kisse your Hand, and I call you my Queene.

KATHERINE *Laisse mon Seigneur, laisse, laisse, may foy: Ie ne veus point que vous abbaisse vostre grandeur, en baisant le main d'une de vostre Seigneurie indigne seruiteur. Excuse moy Ie vous supplie mon tres-puissant Seigneur.*

KING HARRY Then I will kisse your Lippes, *Kate*.

KATHERINE *Les Dames & Damoisels pour estre baisee deuant leur nopcese il net pas le costume de Fraunce.*

KING HARRY *(to Alice)* Madame, my Interpreter, what sayes shee?

ALICE Dat it is not be de fashon pour le Ladies of Fraunce; I cannot tell vat is baisse en Anglish.

3120 KING HARRY To kisse.

ALICE Your Maiestee *entende bettre que moy.*

KING HARRY It is not a fashion for the Maids in Fraunce to kisse before they are marryed, would she say?

ALICE *Ouy verayment.*

KING HARRY O *Kate,* nice Customes cursie to great Kings. Deare *Kate,* you and I cannot bee confin'd within the weake Lyst of a Countreyes fashion: wee are the makers of Manners, *Kate;* and the libertie that followes our Places, stoppes the mouth of all finde-faults, as I will 3130 doe yours, for vpholding the nice fashion of your Countrey, in denying me a Kisse: therefore patiently, and yeelding. *(He kisses her)* You haue Witch-craft in your Lippes, *Kate:* there is more eloquence in a Sugar touch of them, then in the Tongues of the French Councell; and they should sooner perswade *Harry* of England, then a generall Petition of Monarchs. Heere comes your Father.

Enter the French King, Queene Isabel, Burgonie,
and the French and the English Lords

BURGONIE God saue your Maiestie, my Royall Cousin, teach you our Princesse English?

3140 KING HARRY I would haue her learne, my faire Cousin, how perfectly I loue her, and that is good English.

BURGONIE Is shee not apt?

KING HARRY Our Tongue is rough, Coze, and my Condition is not smooth: so that hauing neyther the Voyce nor the Heart of Flatterie about me, I cannot so coniure vp the Spirit of Loue in her, that hee will appeare in his true likenesse.

BURGONIE Pardon the franknesse of my mirth, if I answer you for that. If you would coniure in her, you must 3150 make a Circle: if coniure vp Loue in her in his true likenesse, hee must appeare naked, and blinde. Can you blame her then, being a Maid, yet ros'd ouer with the Virgin Crimson of Modestie, if shee deny the apparance of a naked blinde Boy in her naked seeing selfe? It were (my Lord) a hard Condition for a Maid to consigne to.

KING HARRY Yet they doe winke and yeeld, as Loue is blind and enforces.

BURGONIE They are then excus'd, my Lord, when they see 3160 not what they doe.

KING HARRY Then good my Lord, teach your Cousin to consent winking.

BURGONIE I will winke on her to consent, my Lord, if you will teach her to know my meaning: for Maides well Summer'd, and warme kept, are like Flyes at Bartholomew-tyde, blinde, though they haue their eyes, and then they will endure handling, which before would not abide looking on.

KING HARRY This Morall tyes me ouer to Time, and a hot Summer; and so I shall catch the Flye, your Cousin, 3170 in the latter end, and she must be blinde to.

BURGONIE As Loue is my Lord, before y^t it loues.

KING HARRY It is so: and you may, some of you, thanke Loue for my blindnesse, who cannot see many a faire French Citie for one faire French Maid that stands in my way.

FRENCH KING Yes my Lord, you see them perspectiuely: the Cities turn'd into a Maid; for they are all gyrdled with Maiden Walls, that Warre hath neuer entred.

KING HARRY Shall *Kate* be my Wife?   3180

FRENCH KING So please you.

KING HARRY I am content, so the Maiden Cities you talke of, may wait on her: so the Maid that stood in the way for my Wish, shall shew me the way to my Will.

FRENCH KING
Wee haue consented to all tearmes of reason.

KING HARRY Is't so, my Lords of England?

⌜WARWICK⌝
The King hath graunted euery Article:
His Daughter first; and so in sequele, all,
According to their firme proposed natures.

EXETER
Onely he hath not yet subscribed this: 3190
Where your Maiestie demands, ⌜*reads*⌝ That the King
of France hauing any occasion to write for matter of
Graunt, shall name your Highnesse in this forme, and
with this addition, in French: *Nostre trescher filz Henry*
Roy d'Angleterre Heretere de Fraunce: and thus in Latine;
Praeclarissimus Filius noster Henricus Rex Angliæ & Heres
Franciæ.

FRENCH KING
Nor this I haue not Brother so deny'd,
But your request shall make me let it passe.

KING HARRY
I pray you then, in loue and deare allyance,   3200
Let that one Article ranke with the rest,
And thereupon giue me your Daughter.

FRENCH KING
Take her faire Sonne, and from her blood rayse vp
Issue to me, that the contending Kingdomes
Of France and England, whose very shoares looke
    pale,
With enuy of each others happinesse,
May cease their hatred; and this deare Coniunction
Plant Neighbour-hood and Christian-like accord
In their sweet Bosomes: that neuer Warre aduance
His bleeding Sword 'twixt England and faire France.   3210

⌜ALL⌝ Amen.

KING HARRY
Now welcome *Kate*: and beare me witnesse all,
That here I kisse her as my Soueraigne Queene.
    Flourish

QUEENE
God, the best maker of all Marriages,
Combine your hearts in one, your Realmes in one:

As Man and Wife being two, are one in loue,
So be there 'twixt your Kingdomes such a Spousall,
That neuer may ill Office, or fell Iealousie,
Which troubles oft the Bed of blessed Marriage,
3220 Thrust in betweene the Paction of these Kingdomes,
To make diuorce of their incorporate League:
That English may as French, French Englishmen,
Receiue each other. God speake this Amen.

ALL Amen.

KING HARRY

Prepare we for our Marriage: on which day,
My Lord of Burgundy wee'le take your Oath
And all the Peeres, for suretie of our Leagues.
Then shall I sweare to *Kate*, and you to me,
And may our Oathes well kept and prosp'rous be.

Senet. Exeunt

Enter Chorus   Epilogue

CHORUS

Thus farre with rough, and all-vnable Pen,   3230
    Our bending Author hath pursu'd the Story,
In little roome confining mightie men,
    Mangling by starts the full course of their glory.
Small time: but in that small, most greatly liued
    This Starre of England. Fortune made his Sword;
By which, the Worlds best Garden he atchieued:
    And of it left his Sonne Imperiall Lord.
Henry the Sixt, in Infant Bands crown'd King
    Of France and England, did this King succeed:
Whose State so many had the managing,   3240
    That they lost France, and made his England bleed:
Which oft our Stage hath showne; and for their sake,
In your faire minds let this acceptance take.   *Exit*

FINIS

ADDITIONAL PASSAGES

The Dolphin/Burbon variant, which usually involves only
the alteration of speech-prefixes, has several consequences
for the dialogue and structure of Sc. 21. There follow edited
texts of the Folio and Quarto versions of this scene.

A. FOLIO

Enter Constable, Orleance, Burbon, Dolphin, and
Ramburs

CONSTABLE *O Diable.*

ORLEANCE *O signeur le iour et perdu, toute et perdu.*

DOLPHIN

Mor du ma vie, all is confounded all,
Reproach, and euerlasting shame
Sits mocking in our Plumes.
    A short Alarum
O meschante Fortune, do not runne away.

⌈*Exit Rambures*⌉

CONSTABLE Why all our rankes are broke.

DOLPHIN

O perdurable shame, let's stab our selues:
Be these the wretches that we plaid at dice for?

ORLEANCE

10 Is this the King we sent too, for his ransome?

BURBON

Shame, an eternall shame, nothing but shame,
Let vs dye in pride, in once more backe againe,
And he that will not follow *Burbon* now,
Let him go home, and with his cap in hand
Like a base leno hold the Chamber doore,
Whilst by a slaue, no gentler then my dogge,
His fairest daughter is contaminated.

CONSTABLE

Disorder that hath spoyl'd vs, friend vs now,
Let vs on heapes go offer vp our liues.

ORLEANCE

We are enow yet liuing in the Field,   20
To smother vp the English in our throngs,
If any order might be thought vpon.

BURBON

The diuell take Order now, Ile to the throng;
Let life be short, else shame will be too long. *Exeunt*

B. QUARTO

Enter the foure French Lords

GEBON O diabello.

CONSTABLE Mor du ma vie.

ORLEANCE O what a day is this!

BURBON

O Iour de honte all is gone, all is lost.

CONSTABLE We are inough yet liuing in the field,
To smother vp the English,
If any order might be thought vpon.

BURBON

A plague of order, once more to the field,
And he that will not follow *Burbon* now,
Let him go home, and with his cap in hand,   10
Like a bace leno hold the chamber doore,
Whylest by a slaue no gentler then my dog,
His fairest daughter is contaminated.

CONSTABLE

Disorder that hath spoyld vs, right vs now,
Come we in heapes, weele offer vp our liues
Vnto these English, or else die with fame.

⌈BURBON⌉ Come, come along,
Lets dye with honour, our shame doth last too long.

Exit omnes

IULIUS CÆSAR

ON 21 September 1599 a Swiss doctor, Thomas Platter, saw what can only have been Shakespeare's *Iulius Cæsar* 'very pleasingly performed' in the newly built Globe Theatre—'the straw-thatched house'—on the south side of the Thames. Francis Meres does not mention the play in *Palladis Tamia* of 1598, and minor resemblances with works printed in the early part of 1599 suggest that Shakespeare wrote it during that year. It was first printed in the 1623 Folio.

Iulius Cæsar shows Shakespeare turning from English to Roman history, which he had last used in *Titus Andronicus* and *The Rape of Lucrece*. Caesar was regarded as perhaps the greatest ruler in the history of the world, and his murder by Brutus as one of the foulest crimes: but it was also recognized that Caesar had faults and Brutus virtues. Other plays, some now lost, had been written about Caesar and may have influenced Shakespeare; but there is no question that he made extensive use (for the first time in this play) of Sir Thomas North's great translation (based on Jacques Amyot's French version and published in 1579) of *Liues of the noble Grecians and Romanes* by the Greek historian Plutarch, who lived from about AD 50 to 130.

Shakespeare was interested in the aftermath of Caesar's death as well as in the events leading up to it, and in the public and private motives of those responsible for it. So, although the Folio calls the play *The Tragedie of Iulius Cæsar*, Caesar is dead before the play is half over; Brutus, Cassius, and Antony have considerably longer roles, and Brutus is portrayed with a degree of introspection which links him more closely to Shakespeare's other tragic heroes. Shakespeare draws mainly on the last quarter of Plutarch's Life of Caesar, showing his fall; he also uses the Lives of Antony and Brutus for the play's first sweep of action, showing the rise of the conspiracy against Caesar, its leaders' efforts to persuade Brutus to join them, the assassination itself, and its immediate aftermath as Antony incites the citizens to revenge. The second part, showing the formation of the triumvirate of Antony, Lepidus, and Octauius Caesar, the uneasy alliance of Brutus and Cassius, and the battles in which Caesar's spirit revenges itself, depends mainly on the Life of Brutus. Facts are often altered and rearranged in the interests of dramatic economy and effectiveness.

Although Shakespeare wrote the play at a point in his career at which he was tending to use a high proportion of prose, *Iulius Cæsar* is written mainly in verse; as if to suit the subject matter, the style is classical in its lucidity and eloquence, reaching a climax of rhetorical effectiveness in the speeches over Caesar's body (Sc. 9). The play's stage-worthiness has been repeatedly demonstrated; it offers excellent opportunities in all its main roles, and the quarrel between Brutus and Cassius (Sc. 12) has been admired ever since Leonard Digges, a contemporary of Shakespeare, praised it at the expense of Ben Jonson:

> So have I seene, when Cesar would appeare,
> And on the Stage at half-sword parley were,
> *Brutus* and *Cassius*: oh how the Audience
> Were ravish'd, with what wonder they went thence,
> When some new day they would not brooke a line,
> Of tedious (though well laboured) *Catiline*.

The Folio text appears to have been set from a transcript.

THE NAMES OF THE ACTORS

Iulius CÆSAR

CALPHURNIA, his wife

Marcus BRUTUS, a noble Roman, opposed to Cæsar

PORTIA, his wife

LUCIUS, his seruant

Caius CASSIUS
CASKA
TREBONIUS
DECIUS Brutus } opposed to Cæsar
METELLUS Cymber
CINNA
Caius LIGARIUS

Mark ANTONY
OCTAUIUS Cæsar } rulers of Rome after Cæsars death
LEPIDUS

FLAUIUS
MURELLUS } Tribunes of the People

CICERO
PUBLIUS } Senators
POPILLIUS Lena

A SOOTHSAYER

ARTEMIDORUS
CINNA the Poet

PINDARUS, Cassius bondman
TITINIUS, an Officer in Cassius Army

LUCILLIUS
MESSALA
VARRUS
CLAUDIO
YONG CATO
STRATO } Officers and Souldiers in Brutus Army
VOLUMNIUS
FLAUIUS
DARDANIUS
CLITUS

A POET
GHOST of Cæsar

A COBBLER
A CARPENTER
Other PLEBEIANS
A MESSENGER
SERUANTS
Senators, Souldiers and Attendants

674

The Tragedie of Iulius Cæsar

Sc. 1
(1.1)

Enter Flauius, Murellus, and certaine Commoners
ouer the Stage

FLAUIUS

Hence: home you idle Creatures, get you home:
Is this a Holiday? What, know you not
(Being Mechanicall) you ought not walke
Vpon a labouring day, without the signe
Of your Profession? Speake, what Trade art thou?

CARPENTER Why Sir, a Carpenter.

MURELLUS

Where is thy Leather Apron, and thy Rule?
What dost thou with thy best Apparrell on?
You sir, what Trade are you?

10 COBLER Truely Sir, in respect of a fine Workman, I am
but as you would say, a Cobler.

MURELLUS

But what Trade art thou? Answer me directly.

COBLER A Trade Sir, that I hope I may vse, with a safe
Conscience, which is indeed Sir, a Mender of bad soules.

FLAUIUS

What Trade thou knaue? Thou naughty knaue, what
Trade?

COBLER Nay I beseech you Sir, be not out with me: yet if
you be out Sir, I can mend you.

MURELLUS

What mean'st thou by that? Mend mee, thou sawcy
Fellow?

COBLER Why sir, Cobble you.

20 FLAUIUS Thou art a Cobler, art thou?

COBLER Truly sir, all that I liue by, is with the Aule: I
meddle with no Tradesmans matters, nor womens
matters; but withal I am indeed Sir, a Surgeon to old
shooes: when they are in great danger, I recouer them.
As proper men as euer trod vpon Neats Leather, haue
gone vpon my handy-worke.

FLAUIUS

But wherefore art not in thy Shop to day?
Why do'st thou leade these men about the streets?

COBLER Truly sir, to weare out their shooes, to get my
30 selfe into more worke. But indeede sir, we make Holyday
to see *Cæsar*, and to reioyce in his Triumph.

MURELLUS

Wherefore reioyce? What Conquest brings he home?
What Tributaries follow him to Rome,
To grace in Captiue bonds his Chariot Wheeles?
You Blockes, you stones, you worse then senslesse
things:
O you hard hearts, you cruell men of Rome,
Knew you not *Pompey*? many a time and oft
Haue you climb'd vp to Walles and Battlements,
To Towres and Windowes? Yea, to Chimney tops,
40 Your Infants in your Armes, and there haue sate
The liue-long day, with patient expectation,

To see great *Pompey* passe the streets of Rome:
And when you saw his Chariot but appeare,
Haue you not made an Vniuersall shout,
That Tyber trembled vnderneath her bankes
To heare the replication of your sounds,
Made in her Concaue Shores?
And do you now put on your best attyre?
And do you now cull out a Holyday?
And do you now strew Flowers in his way, 50
That comes in Triumph ouer *Pompeyes* blood?
Be gone,
Runne to your houses, fall vpon your knees,
Pray to the Gods to intermit the plague
That needs must light on this Ingratitude.

FLAUIUS

Go, go, good Countrymen, and for this fault
Assemble all the poore men of your sort;
Draw them to Tyber bankes, and weepe your teares
Into the Channell, till the lowest streame
Do kisse the most exalted Shores of all. 60

Exeunt all the Commoners

See where their basest mettle be not mou'd,
They vanish tongue-tyed in their guiltinesse:
Go you downe that way towards the Capitoll,
This way will I: Disrobe the Images,
If you do finde them deckt with Ceremonies.

MURELLUS May we do so?
You know it is the Feast of Lupercall.

FLAUIUS

It is no matter, let no Images
Be hung with *Cæsars* Trophees: Ile about,
And driue away the Vulgar from the streets; 70
So do you too, where you perceiue them thicke.
These growing Feathers, pluckt from *Cæsars* wing,
Will make him flye an ordinary pitch,
Who else would soare aboue the view of men,
And keepe vs all in seruile fearefulnesse. *Exeunt*

⌈*Lowd Musicke.*⌉ *Enter Cæsar, Antony stript for the*   **Sc. 2**
Course, Calphurnia, Portia, Decius, Cicero, Brutus,   **(1.2)**
Cassius, Caska, a Soothsayer, ⌈a throng of Citizens⌉:
after them Murellus and Flauius

CÆSAR *Calphurnia.*

CASKA Peace ho, *Cæsar* speakes.
⌈*Musicke ceases*⌉

CÆSAR *Calphurnia.*

CALPHURNIA Heere my Lord.

CÆSAR

Stand you directly in *Antonio's* way, 80
When he doth run his course. *Antonio.*

ANTONY *Cæsar*, my Lord.

CÆSAR

Forget not in your speed *Antonio*,

To touch *Calphurnia*: for our Elders say,
The Barren touched in this holy chace,
Shake off their sterrile curse.
ANTONY   I shall remember;
When *Cæsar* sayes, Do this, it is perform'd.
CÆSAR
Set on, and leaue no Ceremony out.
⌈*Musicke*⌉
SOOTHSAYER *Cæsar*.
90 CÆSAR Ha? Who calles?
CASKA
Bid euery noyse be still: peace yet againe.
⌈*Musicke ceases*⌉
CÆSAR
Who is it in the presse, that calles on me?
I heare a Tongue shriller then all the Musicke
Cry, *Cæsar*: Speake, *Cæsar* is turn'd to heare.
SOOTHSAYER
Beware the Ides of March.
CÆSAR   What man is that?
BRUTUS
A Sooth-sayer bids you beware the Ides of March.
CÆSAR
Set him before me, let me see his face.
CASSIUS
Fellow, come from the throng, look vpon *Cæsar*.
The Soothsayer comes forward
CÆSAR
What sayst thou to me now? Speak once againe.
100 SOOTHSAYER Beware the Ides of March.
CÆSAR
He is a Dreamer, let vs leaue him: Passe.
Sennet. Exeunt. Manet Brutus & Cassius
CASSIUS
Will you go see the order of the course?
BRUTUS Not I.
CASSIUS I pray you do.
BRUTUS
I am not Gamesom: I do lacke some part
Of that quicke Spirit that is in *Antony*:
Let me not hinder *Cassius* your desires;
Ile leaue you.
CASSIUS
Brutus, I do obserue you now of late:
110 I haue not from your eyes, that gentlenesse
And shew of Loue, as I was wont to haue:
You beare too stubborne, and too strange a hand
Ouer your Friend, that loues you.
BRUTUS   *Cassius*,
Be not deceiu'd: If I haue veyl'd my looke,
I turne the trouble of my Countenance
Meerely vpon my selfe. Vexed I am
Of late, with passions of some difference,
Conceptions onely proper to my selfe,
Which giue some soyle (perhaps) to my Behauiours:
120 But let not therefore my good Friends be greeu'd
(Among which number *Cassius* be you one)
Nor construe any further my neglect,

Then that poore *Brutus* with himselfe at warre,
Forgets the shewes of Loue to other men.
CASSIUS
Then *Brutus*, I haue much mistook your passion,
By meanes whereof, this Brest of mine hath buried
Thoughts of great value, worthy Cogitations.
Tell me good *Brutus*, Can you see your face?
BRUTUS
No *Cassius*: For the eye sees not it selfe
But by reflection, by some other things.   130
CASSIUS 'Tis iust,
And it is very much lamented *Brutus*,
That you haue no such Mirrors, as will turne
Your hidden worthinesse into your eye,
That you might see your shadow: I haue heard,
Where many of the best respect in Rome,
(Except immortall *Cæsar*) speaking of *Brutus*,
And groaning vnderneath this Ages yoake,
Haue wish'd, that Noble *Brutus* had his eyes.
BRUTUS
Into what dangers, would you leade me *Cassius*?   140
That you would haue me seeke into my selfe,
For that which is not in me?
CASSIUS
Therefore good *Brutus*, be prepar'd to heare:
And since you know, you cannot see your selfe
So well as by Reflection; I your Glasse,
Will modestly discouer to your selfe
That of your selfe, which you yet know not of.
And be not iealous on me, gentle *Brutus*:
Were I a common Laughter, or did vse
To stale with ordinary Oathes my loue   150
To euery new Protester: if you know,
That I do fawne on men, and hugge them hard,
And after scandall them: Or if you know,
That I professe my selfe in Banquetting
To all the Rout, then hold me dangerous.
Flourish, and Shout within
BRUTUS
What meanes this Showting? I do feare, the People
Choose *Cæsar* for their King.
CASSIUS   I, do you feare it?
Then must I thinke you would not haue it so.
BRUTUS
I would not *Cassius*, yet I loue him well:
But wherefore do you hold me heere so long?   160
What is it, that you would impart to me?
If it be ought toward the generall good,
Set Honor in one eye, and Death i'th other,
And I will looke on both indifferently:
For let the Gods so speed mee, as I loue
The name of Honor, more then I feare death.
CASSIUS
I know that vertue to be in you *Brutus*,
As well as I do know your outward fauour.
Well, Honor is the subiect of my Story:
I cannot tell, what you and other men   170
Thinke of this life: But for my single selfe,

I had as liefe not be, as liue to be
In awe of such a Thing, as I my selfe.
I was borne free as *Cæsar*, so were you,
We both haue fed as well, and we can both
Endure the Winters cold, as well as hee.
For once, vpon a Rawe and Gustie day,
The troubled Tyber, chafing with her Shores,
Saide *Cæsar* to me, Dar'st thou *Cassius* now
180 Leape in with me into this angry Flood,
And swim to yonder Point? Vpon the word,
Accoutred as I was, I plunged in,
And bad him follow: so indeed he did.
The Torrent roar'd, and we did buffet it
With lusty Sinewes, throwing it aside,
And stemming it with hearts of Controuersie.
But ere we could arriue the Point propos'd,
Cæsar cride, Helpe me *Cassius*, or I sinke.
I (as *Æneas*, our great Ancestor,
190 Did from the Flames of Troy, vpon his shoulder
The old *Anchyses* beare) so, from the waues of Tyber
Did I the tyred *Cæsar*: And this Man,
Is now become a God, and *Cassius* is
A wretched Creature, and must bend his body,
If *Cæsar* carelesly but nod on him.
He had a Feauer when he was in Spaine,
And when the Fit was on him, I did marke
How he did shake: Tis true, this God did shake,
His Coward lippes did from their colour flye,
200 And that same Eye, whose bend doth awe the World,
Did loose his Lustre: I did heare him grone:
I, and that Tongue of his, that bad the Romans
Marke him, and write his Speeches in their Bookes,
Alas, it cried, Giue me some drinke *Titinius*,
As a sicke Girle: Ye Gods, it doth amaze me,
A man of such a feeble temper should
So get the start of the Maiesticke world,
And beare the Palme alone.
   ⌈*Flourish and Shout within*⌉

BRUTUS   Another generall shout?
I do beleeue, that these applauses are
210 For some new Honors, that are heap'd on *Cæsar*.

CASSIUS

Why man, he doth bestride the narrow world
Like a Colossus, and we petty men
Walke vnder his huge legges, and peepe about
To finde our selues dishonourable Graues.
Men at sometime, were Masters of their Fates.
The fault (deere *Brutus*) is not in our Starres,
But in our Selues, that we are vnderlings.
Brutus and *Cæsar*: What should be in that *Cæsar*?
Why should that name be sounded more then yours?
220 Write them together: Yours, is as faire a Name:
Sound them, it doth become the mouth aswell:
Weigh them, it is as heauy: Coniure with 'em,
Brutus will start a Spirit as soone as *Cæsar*.
Now in the names of all the Gods at once,
Vpon what meate doth this our *Cæsar* feede,

That he is growne so great? Age, thou art sham'd.
Rome, thou hast lost the breed of Noble Bloods.
When went there by an Age, since the great Flood,
But it was fam'd with more then with one man?
When could they say (till now) that talk'd of Rome, 230
That her wide Walles incompast but one man?
Now is it Rome indeed, and Roome enough
When there is in it but one onely man.
O! you and I, haue heard our Fathers say,
There was a *Brutus* once, that would haue brook'd
Th'eternall Diuell to keepe his State in Rome,
As easily as a King.

BRUTUS

That you do loue me, I am nothing iealous:
What you would worke me too, I haue some ayme:
How I haue thought of this, and of these times 240
I shall recount heereafter. For this present,
I would not (so with loue I might intreat you)
Be any further moou'd: What you haue said,
I will consider: what you haue to say
I will with patience heare, and finde a time
Both meete to heare, and answer such high things.
Till then, my Noble Friend, chew vpon this:
Brutus had rather be a Villager,
Then to repute himselfe a Sonne of Rome
Vnder these hard Conditions, as this time 250
Is like to lay vpon vs.

CASSIUS   I am glad
That my weake words haue strucke but thus much
  shew
Of fire from *Brutus*.
   ⌈*Musicke.*⌉ *Enter Cæsar and his Traine*

BRUTUS

The Games are done, and *Cæsar* is returning.

CASSIUS

As they passe by, plucke *Caska* by the Sleeue,
And he will (after his sowre fashion) tell you
What hath proceeded worthy note to day.

BRUTUS

I will do so: but looke you *Cassius*,
The angry spot doth glow on *Cæsars* brow,
And all the rest, looke like a chidden Traine; 260
Calphurnia's Cheeke is pale, and *Cicero*
Lookes with such Ferret, and such fiery eyes
As we haue seene him in the Capitoll
Being crost in Conference, by some Senators.

CASSIUS

Caska will tell vs what the matter is.

CÆSAR *Antonio*.

ANTONY *Cæsar*.

CÆSAR

Let me haue men about me, that are fat,
Sleeke-headed men, and such as sleepe a-nights:
Yond *Cassius* has a leane and hungry looke, 270
He thinkes too much: such men are dangerous.

ANTONY

Feare him not *Cæsar*, he's not dangerous,
He is a Noble Roman, and well giuen.

CÆSAR

Would he were fatter; But I feare him not:
Yet if my name were lyable to feare,
I do not know the man I should auoyd
So soone as that spare *Cassius*. He reades much,
He is a great Obseruer, and he lookes
Quite through the Deeds of men. He loues no Playes,
280 As thou dost *Antony*: he heares no Musicke;
Seldome he smiles, and smiles in such a sort
As if he mock'd himselfe, and scorn'd his spirit
That could be mou'd to smile at any thing.
Such men as he, be neuer at hearts ease,
Whiles they behold a greater then themselues,
And therefore are they very dangerous.
I rather tell thee what is to be fear'd,
Then what I feare: for alwayes I am *Cæsar*.
Come on my right hand, for this eare is deafe,
290 And tell me truely, what thou think'st of him.

Sennit. Exeunt Cæsar and his Traine. Manet
Brutus, Cassius and Caska

CASKA (*to Brutus*) You pul'd me by the cloake, would you
speake with me?

BRUTUS

I *Caska*, tell vs what hath chanc'd to day
That *Cæsar* lookes so sad.

CASKA Why you were with him, were you not?

BRUTUS

I should not then aske *Caska* what had chanc'd.

CASKA Why there was a Crowne offer'd him; & being
offer'd him, he put it by with the backe of his hand
thus, and then the people fell a shouting.

300 BRUTUS What was the second noyse for?

CASKA Why for that too.

CASSIUS

They shouted thrice: what was the last cry for?

CASKA Why for that too.

BRUTUS Was the Crowne offer'd him thrice?

CASKA I marry was't, and hee put it by thrice, euerie time
gentler then other; and at euery putting by, mine
honest Neighbors showted.

CASSIUS

Who offer'd him the Crowne?

CASKA   Why *Antony*.

BRUTUS

Tell vs the manner of it, gentle *Caska*.

310 CASKA I can as well bee hang'd as tell the manner of it:
It was meere Foolerie, I did not marke it. I sawe *Marke*
Antony offer him a Crowne, yet 'twas not a Crowne
neyther, 'twas one of these Coronets: and as I told you,
hee put it by once: but for all that, to my thinking, he
would faine haue had it. Then hee offered it to him
againe: then hee put it by againe: but to my thinking,
he was very loath to lay his fingers off it. And then he
offered it the third time; hee put it the third time by,
and still as hee refus'd it, the rabblement howted, and
320 clapp'd their chopt hands, and threw vppe their sweatie
Night-cappes, and vttered such a deale of stinking
breath, because *Cæsar* refus'd the Crowne, that it had

(almost) choaked *Cæsar*: for hee swoonded, and fell
downe at it: And for mine owne part, I durst not laugh,
for feare of opening my Lippes, and receyuing the bad
Ayre.

CASSIUS

But soft I pray you: what, did *Cæsar* swound?

CASKA He fell downe in the Market-place, and foam'd at
mouth, and was speechlesse.

BRUTUS

'Tis very like, he hath the Falling sicknesse.   330

CASSIUS

No, *Cæsar* hath it not: but you, and I,
And honest *Caska*, we haue the Falling sicknesse.

CASKA I know not what you meane by that, but I am
sure *Cæsar* fell downe. If the tag-ragge people did not
clap him, and hisse him, according as he pleas'd, and
displeas'd them, as they vse to doe the Players in the
Theatre, I am no true man.

BRUTUS

What said he, when he came vnto himselfe?

CASKA Marry, before he fell downe, when he perceiu'd
the common Heard was glad he refus'd the Crowne,   340
he pluckt me ope his Doublet, and offer'd them his
Throat to cut: and I had beene a man of any
Occupation, if I would not haue taken him at a word,
I would I might goe to Hell among the Rogues, and so
hee fell. When he came to himselfe againe, hee said, If
hee had done, or said any thing amisse, he desir'd their
Worships to thinke it was his infirmitie. Three or foure
Wenches where I stood, cryed, Alasse good Soule, and
forgaue him with all their hearts: But there's no heed
to be taken of them; if *Cæsar* had stab'd their Mothers,   350
they would haue done no lesse.

BRUTUS

And after that, he came thus sad away.

CASKA I.

CASSIUS Did *Cicero* say any thing?

CASKA I, he spoke Greeke.

CASSIUS To what effect?

CASKA Nay, and I tell you that, Ile ne're looke you i'th'
face againe. But those that vnderstood him, smil'd at
one another, and shooke their heads: but for mine
owne part, it was Greeke to me. I could tell you more   360
newes too: *Murrellus* and *Flauius*, for pulling Scarffes
off *Cæsars* Images, are put to silence. Fare you well.
There was more Foolerie yet, if I could remember it.

CASSIUS Will you suppe with me to Night, *Caska*?

CASKA No, I am promis'd forth.

CASSIUS Will you Dine with me to morrow?

CASKA I, if I be aliue, and your minde hold, and your
Dinner worth the eating.

CASSIUS Good, I will expect you.

CASKA Doe so: farewell both.   *Exit*   370

BRUTUS

What a blunt fellow is this growne to be?
He was quick Mettle, when he went to Schoole.

CASSIUS

So is he now, in execution

Of any bold, or Noble Enterprize,
How-euer he puts on this tardie forme:
This Rudenesse is a Sawce to his good Wit,
Which giues men stomacke to disgest his words
With better Appetite.

BRUTUS

And so it is: For this time I will leaue you:
380 To morrow, if you please to speake with me,
I will come home to you: or if you will,
Come home to me, and I will wait for you.

CASSIUS

I will doe so: till then, thinke of the World.

                                        Exit Brutus

Well *Brutus*, thou art Noble: yet I see,
Thy Honorable Mettle may be wrought
From that it is dispos'd: therefore it is meet,
That Noble mindes keepe euer with their likes:
For who so firme, that cannot be seduc'd?
Cæsar doth beare me hard, but he loues *Brutus*.
390 If I were *Brutus* now, and he were *Cassius*,
He should not humor me. I will this Night,
In seuerall Hands, in at his Windowes throw,
As if they came from seuerall Citizens,
Writings, all tending to the great opinion
That Rome holds of his Name: wherein obscurely
Cæsars Ambition shall be glanced at.
And after this, let *Cæsar* seat him sure,
For wee will shake him, or worse dayes endure.   *Exit*

Sc. 3   *Thunder, and Lightning. Enter Caska ⌈at one doore,*
(1.3)   *with his Sword drawne,⌉ and Cicero ⌈at another⌉*

CICERO

Good euen, *Caska*: brought you *Cæsar* home?
400 Why are you breathlesse, and why stare you so?

CASKA

Are not you mou'd, when all the sway of Earth
Shakes, like a thing vnfirme? O *Cicero*,
I haue seene Tempests, when the scolding Winds
Haue riu'd the knottie Oakes, and I haue seene
Th'ambitious Ocean swell, and rage, and foame,
To be exalted with the threatning Clouds:
But neuer till to Night, neuer till now,
Did I goe through a Tempest-dropping-fire.
Eyther there is a Ciuill strife in Heauen,
410 Or else the World, too sawcie with the Gods,
Incenses them to send destruction.

CICERO

Why, saw you any thing more wonderfull?

CASKA

A common slaue, you know him well by sight,
Held vp his left Hand, which did flame and burne
Like twentie Torches ioyn'd; and yet his Hand,
Not sensible of fire, remain'd vnscorch'd.
Besides, I ha'not since put vp my Sword,
Against the Capitoll I met a Lyon,
Who glaz'd vpon me, and went surly by,
420 Without annoying me. And there were drawne
Vpon a heape, a hundred gastly Women,

Transformed with their feare, who swore, they saw
Men, all in fire, walke vp and downe the streetes.
And yesterday, the Bird of Night did sit,
Euen at Noone-day, vpon the Market place,
Howting, and shreeking. When these Prodigies
Doe so conioyntly meet, let not men say,
These are their Reasons, they are Naturall:
For I beleeue, they are portentous things
Vnto the Clymate, that they point vpon.   430

CICERO

Indeed, it is a strange disposed time:
But men may construe things after their fashion,
Cleane from the purpose of the things themselues.
Comes *Cæsar* to the Capitoll to morrow?

CASKA

He doth: for he did bid *Antonio*
Send word to you, he would be there to morrow.

CICERO

Good-night then, *Caska*: This disturbed Skie
Is not to walke in.

CASKA   Farewell *Cicero*.   *Exit Cicero*
            Enter Cassius, ⌈vnbraced⌉

CASSIUS

Who's there?

CASKA   A Romane.

CASSIUS   *Caska*, by your Voyce.

CASKA

Your Eare is good. *Cassius*, what Night is this?   440

CASSIUS

A very pleasing Night to honest men.

CASKA

Who euer knew the Heauens menace so?

CASSIUS

Those that haue knowne the Earth so full of faults.
For my part, I haue walk'd about the streets,
Submitting me vnto the perillous Night;
And thus vnbraced, *Caska*, as you see,
Haue bar'd my Bosome to the Thunder-stone:
And when the crosse blew Lightning seem'd to open
The Brest of Heauen, I did present my selfe
Euen in the ayme, and very flash of it.   450

CASKA

But wherefore did you so much tempt the Heauens?
It is the part of men, to feare and tremble,
When the most mightie Gods, by tokens send
Such dreadfull Heraulds, to astonish vs.

CASSIUS

You are dull, *Caska*: And those sparkes of Life,
That should be in a Roman, you doe want,
Or else you vse not. You looke pale, and gaze,
And put on feare, and cast your selfe in wonder,
To see the strange impatience of the Heauens:
But if you would consider the true cause,   460
Why all these Fires, why all these gliding Ghosts,
Why Birds and Beasts, from qualitie and kinde,
Why Old men, Fooles, and Children calculate,
Why all these things change from their Ordinance,
Their Natures, and pre-formed Faculties,

To monstrous qualitie; why you shall finde,
That Heauen hath infus'd them with these Spirits,
To make them Instruments of feare, and warning,
Vnto some monstrous State. Now could I (*Caska*)
470   Name to thee a man, most like this dreadfull Night,
That Thunders, Lightens, opens Graues, and roares,
As doth the Lyon in the Capitoll:
A man no mightier then thy selfe, or me,
In personall action; yet prodigious growne,
And fearefull, as these strange eruptions are.

CASKA
'Tis *Cæsar* that you meane: Is it not, *Cassius*?

CASSIUS
Let it be who it is: for Romans now
Haue Thewes, and Limbes, like to their Ancestors;
But woe the while, our Fathers mindes are dead,
480   And we are gouern'd with our Mothers spirits,
Our yoake, and sufferance, shew vs Womanish.

CASKA
Indeed, they say, the Senators to morrow
Meane to establish *Cæsar* as a King:
And he shall weare his Crowne by Sea, and Land,
In euery place, saue here in Italy.

CASSIUS (*drawing his Dagger*)
I know where I will weare this Dagger then;
Cassius from Bondage will deliuer *Cassius*:
Therein, yee Gods, you make the weake most strong;
Therein, yee Gods, you Tyrants doe defeat.
490   Nor Stonie Tower, nor Walls of beaten Brasse,
Nor ayre-lesse Dungeon, nor strong Linkes of Iron,
Can be retentiue to the strength of spirit:
But Life being wearie of these worldly Barres,
Neuer lacks power to dismisse it selfe.
If I know this, know all the World besides,
That part of Tyrannie that I doe beare,
I can shake off at pleasure.
              Thunder still

CASKA   So can I:
So euery Bond-man in his owne hand beares
The power to cancell his Captiuitie.

CASSIUS
500   And why should *Cæsar* be a Tyrant then?
Poore man, I know he would not be a Wolfe,
But that he sees the Romans are but Sheepe:
He were no Lyon, were not Romans Hindes.
Those that with haste will make a mightie fire,
Begin it with weake Strawes. What trash is Rome?
What Rubbish, and what Offall? when it serues
For the base matter, to illuminate
So vile a thing as *Cæsar*. But oh Griefe,
Where hast thou led me? I (perhaps) speake this
510   Before a willing Bond-man: then I know
My answere must be made. But I am arm'd,
And dangers are to me indifferent.

CASKA
You speake to *Caska*, and to such a man,
That is no flearing Tell-tale. Hold, my Hand:
Be factious for redresse of all these Griefes,

And I will set this foot of mine as farre,
As who goes farthest.
              They ioyne hands

CASSIUS   There's a Bargaine made.
Now know you, *Caska*, I haue mou'd already
Some certaine of the Noblest minded Romans
To vnder-goe, with me, an Enterprize,   520
Of Honorable dangerous consequence;
And I doe know by this, they stay for me
In *Pompeyes* Porch: for now this fearefull Night,
There is no stirre, or walking in the streetes;
And the Complexion of the Element
In Fauors, like the Worke we haue in hand,
Most bloodie, fierie, and most terrible.
              Enter Cinna

CASKA
Stand close a while, for heere comes one in haste.

CASSIUS
'Tis *Cinna*, I doe know him by his Gate,
He is a friend. *Cinna*, where haste you so?   530

CINNA
To finde out you: Who's that, *Metellus Cymber*?

CASSIUS
No, it is *Caska*, one incorporate
To our Attempts. Am I not stay'd for, *Cinna*?

CINNA
I am glad on't. What a fearefull Night is this?
There's two or three of vs haue seene strange sights.

CASSIUS Am I not stay'd for? tell me.

CINNA Yes, you are.
O *Cassius*, if you could
But winne the Noble *Brutus* to our party—

CASSIUS
Be you content. Good *Cinna*, take this Paper,   540
              He giues Cinna Letters
And looke you lay it in the Pretors Chayre,
Where *Brutus* may but finde it: and throw this
In at his Window; set this vp with Waxe
Vpon old *Brutus* Statue: all this done,
Repaire to *Pompeyes* Porch, where you shall finde vs.
Is *Decius Brutus* and *Trebonius* there?

CINNA
All, but *Metellus Cymber*, and hee's gone
To seeke you at your house. Well, I will hie,
And so bestow these Papers as you bad me.

CASSIUS
That done, repayre to *Pompeyes* Theater.   *Exit Cinna* 550
Come *Caska*, you and I will yet, ere day,
See *Brutus* at his house: three parts of him
Is ours alreadie, and the man entire
Vpon the next encounter, yeelds him ours.

CASKA
O, he sits high in all the Peoples hearts:
And that which would appeare Offence in vs,
His Countenance, like richest Alchymie,
Will change to Vertue, and to Worthinesse.

CASSIUS
Him, and his worth, and our great need of him,

560 You haue right well conceited: let vs goe,
For it is after Mid-night, and ere day,
We will awake him, and be sure of him.   *Exeunt*

Sc. 4   *Enter Brutus in his Orchard*
(2.1) BRUTUS What *Lucius*, hoe?
I cannot, by the progresse of the Starres,
Giue guesse how neere to day—*Lucius*, I say?
I would it were my fault to sleepe so soundly.
When *Lucius*, when? awake, I say: what *Lucius*?
        Enter Lucius
LUCIUS Call'd you, my Lord?
BRUTUS
Get me a Tapor in my Study, *Lucius*:
570 When it is lighted, come and call me here.
LUCIUS I will, my Lord.   *Exit*
BRUTUS
It must be by his death: and for my part,
I know no personall cause, to spurne at him,
But for the generall. He would be crown'd:
How that might change his nature, there's the
        question?
It is the bright day, that brings forth the Adder,
And that craues warie walking: Crowne him, that,
And then I graunt we put a Sting in him,
That at his will he may doe danger with.
580 Th'abuse of Greatnesse, is, when it dis-ioynes
Remorse from Power: And to speake truth of *Cæsar*,
I haue not knowne, when his Affections sway'd
More then his Reason. But 'tis a common proofe,
That Lowlynesse is young Ambitions Ladder,
Whereto the Climber vpward turnes his Face:
But when he once attaines the vpmost Round,
He then vnto the Ladder turnes his Backe,
Lookes in the Clouds, scorning the base degrees
By which he did ascend: so *Cæsar* may;
590 Then least he may, preuent. And since the Quarrell
Will beare no colour, for the thing he is,
Fashion it thus; that what he is, augmented,
Would runne to these, and these extremities:
And therefore thinke him as a Serpents egge,
Which hatch'd, would as his kinde grow mischieuous;
And kill him in the shell.
        Enter Lucius, with a Letter
LUCIUS
The Taper burneth in your Closet, Sir:
Searching the Window for a Flint, I found
This Paper, thus seal'd vp, and I am sure
600 It did not lye there when I went to Bed.
        He giues him the Letter
BRUTUS
Get you to Bed againe, it is not day:
Is not to morrow (Boy) the Ides of March?
LUCIUS I know not, Sir.
BRUTUS
Looke in the Calender, and bring me word.
LUCIUS I will, Sir.   *Exit*

BRUTUS
The exhalations, whizzing in the ayre,
Giue so much light, that I may reade by them.
        He opens the Letter, and reades
Brutus thou sleep'st; awake, and see thy selfe:
Shall Rome, &c. Speake, strike, redresse.
Brutus, thou sleep'st: awake.   610
Such instigations haue beene often dropt,
Where I haue tooke them vp:
Shall Rome, &c. Thus must I piece it out:
Shall Rome stand vnder one mans awe? What Rome?
My Ancestors did from the streetes of Rome
The *Tarquin* driue, when he was call'd a King.
Speake, strike, redresse. Am I entreated
To speake, and strike? O Rome, I make thee promise,
If the redresse will follow, thou receiuest
Thy full Petition at the hand of *Brutus*.   620
        Enter Lucius
LUCIUS
Sir, March is wasted fifteene dayes.
        Knocke within
BRUTUS
'Tis good. Go to the Gate, some body knocks:
                                        Exit Lucius
Since *Cassius* first did whet me against *Cæsar*,
I haue not slept.
Betweene the acting of a dreadfull thing,
And the first motion, all the *Interim* is
Like a *Phantasma*, or a hideous Dreame:
The *Genius*, and the mortall Instruments
Are then in councell; and the state of man,
Like to a little Kingdome, suffers then   630
The nature of an Insurrection.
        Enter Lucius
LUCIUS
Sir, 'tis your Brother *Cassius* at the Doore,
Who doth desire to see you.
BRUTUS   Is he alone?
LUCIUS
No, Sir, there are moe with him.
BRUTUS   Doe you know them?
LUCIUS
No, Sir, their Hats are pluckt about their Eares,
And halfe their Faces buried in their Cloakes,
That by no meanes I may discouer them,
By any marke of fauour.
BRUTUS   Let 'em enter: *Exit Lucius*
They are the Faction. O Conspiracie,
Sham'st thou to shew thy dang'rous Brow by Night, 640
When euills are most free? O then, by day
Where wilt thou finde a Cauerne darke enough,
To maske thy monstrous Visage? Seek none
        Conspiracie,
Hide it in Smiles, and Affabilitie:
For if thou putte thy natiue semblance on,
Not *Erebus* it selfe were dimme enough,
To hide thee from preuention.

Enter the Conspirators, muffled: Cassius, Caska,
Decius, Cinna, Metellus, and Trebonius

CASSIUS

I thinke we are too bold vpon your Rest:
Good morrow *Brutus*, doe we trouble you?

BRUTUS

650   I haue beene vp this howre, awake all Night:
Know I these men, that come along with you?

CASSIUS

Yes, euery man of them; and no man here
But honors you: and euery one doth wish,
You had but that opinion of your selfe,
Which euery Noble Roman beares of you.
This is *Trebonius*.

BRUTUS   He is welcome hither.

CASSIUS

This, *Decius Brutus*.

BRUTUS   He is welcome too.

CASSIUS

This, *Caska*; *Cinna*, this; and this, *Metellus Cymber*.

BRUTUS They are all welcome.

660   What watchfull Cares doe interpose themselues
Betwixt your Eyes, and Night?

CASSIUS   Shall I entreat a word?

Cassius and Brutus ⌈stand aside and⌉ whisper

DECIUS

Here lyes the East: doth not the Day breake heere?

CASKA No.

CINNA

O pardon, Sir, it doth; and yon grey Lines,
That fret the Clouds, are Messengers of Day.

CASKA

You shall confesse, that you are both deceiu'd:
He points his Sword
Heere, as I point my Sword, the Sunne arises,
Which is a great way growing on the South,
Weighing the youthfull Season of the yeare.
Some two moneths hence, vp higher toward the
670   North
He first presents his fire, and the high East
Stands as the Capitoll, directly heere.
He points his Sword.
⌈Brutus and Cassius ioyne the other Conspirators⌉

BRUTUS

Giue me your hands all ouer, one by one.
He shakes their hands

CASSIUS

And let vs sweare our Resolution.

BRUTUS

No, not an Oath: if not the Face of men,
The sufferance of our Soules, the times Abuse;
If these be Motiues weake, breake off betimes,
And euery man hence, to his idle bed:
So let high-sighted-Tyranny range on,
680   Till each man drop by Lottery. But if these
(As I am sure they do) beare fire enough
To kindle Cowards, and to steele with valour
The melting Spirits of women. Then Countrymen,

What neede we any spurre, but our owne cause
To pricke vs to redresse? What other Bond,
Then secret Romans, that haue spoke the word,
And will not palter? And what other Oath,
Then Honesty to Honesty ingag'd,
That this shall be, or we will fall for it.
Sweare Priests and Cowards, and men Cautelous   690
Old feeble Carrions, and such suffering Soules
That welcome wrongs: Vnto bad causes, sweare
Such Creatures as men doubt; but do not staine
The euen vertue of our Enterprize,
Nor th'insuppressiue Mettle of our Spirits,
To thinke, that or our Cause, or our Performance
Did neede an Oath. When euery drop of blood
That euery Roman beares, and Nobly beares
Is guilty of a seuerall Bastardie,
If he do breake the smallest Particle   700
Of any promise that hath past from him.

CASSIUS

But what of *Cicero*? Shall we sound him?
I thinke he will stand very strong with vs.

CASKA

Let vs not leaue him out.

CINNA   No, by no meanes.

METELLUS

O let vs haue him, for his Siluer haires
Will purchase vs a good opinion:
And buy mens voyces, to commend our deeds:
It shall be sayd, his iudgement rul'd our hands,
Our youths, and wildenesse, shall no whit appeare,
But all be buried in his Grauity.   710

BRUTUS

O name him not; let vs not breake with him,
For he will neuer follow any thing
That other men begin.

CASSIUS Then leaue him out.

CASKA Indeed, he is not fit.

DECIUS

Shall no man else be toucht, but onely *Cæsar*?

CASSIUS

Decius well vrg'd: I thinke it is not meet,
Marke Antony, so well belou'd of *Cæsar*,
Should out-liue *Cæsar*, we shall finde of him
A shrew'd Contriuer. And you know, his meanes   720
If he improue them, may well stretch so farre
As to annoy vs all: which to preuent,
Let *Antony* and *Cæsar* fall together.

BRUTUS

Our course will seeme too bloody, *Caius Cassius*,
To cut the Head off, and then hacke the Limbes:
Like Wrath in death, and Enuy afterwards:
For *Antony*, is but a Limbe of *Cæsar*.
Let's be Sacrificers, but not Butchers *Caius*:
We all stand vp against the spirit of *Cæsar*,
And in the Spirit of men, there is no blood: 730
O that we then could come by *Cæsars* Spirit,
And not dismember *Cæsar*! But (alas)
Cæsar must bleed for it. And gentle Friends,

Let's kill him Boldly, but not Wrathfully:
Let's carue him, as a Dish fit for the Gods,
Not hew him as a Carkasse fit for Hounds:
And let our Hearts, as subtle Masters do,
Stirre vp their Seruants to an acte of Rage,
And after seeme to chide 'em. This shall make
740 Our purpose Necessary, and not Enuious.
Which so appearing to the common eyes,
We shall be call'd Purgers, not Murderers.
And for *Marke Antony*, thinke not of him:
For he can do no more then *Cæsars* Arme,
When *Cæsars* head is off.

CASSIUS   Yet I feare him,
For in the ingrafted loue he beares to *Cæsar*.

BRUTUS
Alas, good *Cassius*, do not thinke of him:
If he loue *Cæsar*, all that he can do
Is to himselfe; take thought, and dye for *Cæsar*,
750 And that were much he should: for he is giuen
To sports, to wildenesse, and much company.

TREBONIUS
There is no feare in him; let him not dye,
For he will liue, and laugh at this heereafter.
             Clocke strikes

BRUTUS
Peace, count the Clocke.

CASSIUS   The Clocke hath stricken three.

TREBONIUS
'Tis time to part.

CASSIUS   But it is doubtfull yet,
Whether *Cæsar* will come forth to day, or no:
For he is Superstitious growne of late,
Quite from the maine Opinion he held once,
Of Fantasie, of Dreames, and Ceremonies:
760 It may be, these apparant Prodigies,
The vnaccustom'd Terror of this night,
And the perswasion of his Augurers,
May hold him from the Capitoll to day.

DECIUS
Neuer feare that: If he be so resolu'd,
I can ore-sway him: For he loues to heare,
That Vnicornes may be betray'd with Trees,
And Beares with Glasses, Elephants with Holes,
Lyons with Toyles, and men with Flatterers.
But, when I tell him, he hates Flatterers,
He sayes, he does; being then most flattred. Let me
770   worke:
For I can giue his humour the true bent;
And I will bring him to the Capitoll.

CASSIUS
Nay, we will all of vs, be there to fetch him.

BRUTUS
By the eight houre, is that the vttermost?

CINNA
Be that the vttermost, and faile not then.

METELLUS
Caius Ligarius doth beare *Cæsar* hard,
Who rated him for speaking well of *Pompey*;
I wonder none of you haue thought of him.

BRUTUS
Now good *Metellus* go along by him:
He loues me well, and I haue giuen him Reasons,   780
Send him but hither, and Ile fashion him.

CASSIUS
The morning comes vpon's: Wee'l leaue you *Brutus*,
And Friends disperse your selues; but all remember
What you haue said, and shew your selues true
        Romans.

BRUTUS
Good Gentlemen, looke fresh and merrily,
Let not our lookes put on our purposes,
But beare it as our Roman Actors do,
With vntyr'd Spirits, and formall Constancie,
And so good morrow to you euery one.
                    Exeunt. Manet Brutus

Boy: *Lucius*: Fast asleepe? It is no matter,   790
Enioy the hony-heauy-Dew of Slumber:
Thou hast no Figures, nor no Fantasies,
Which busie care drawes, in the braines of men;
Therefore thou sleep'st so sound.
          Enter Portia

PORTIA   *Brutus*, my Lord.

BRUTUS
Portia: What meane you? wherfore rise you now?
It is not for your health, thus to commit
Your weake condition, to the raw cold morning.

PORTIA
Nor for yours neither. Y'haue vngently *Brutus*
Stole from my bed: and yesternight at Supper
You sodainly arose, and walk'd about,   800
Musing, and sighing, with your armes a-crosse:
And when I ask'd you what the matter was,
You star'd vpon me, with vngentle lookes.
I vrg'd you further, then you scratch'd your head,
And too impatiently stampt with your foote:
Yet I insisted, yet you answer'd not,
But with an angry wafter of your hand
Gaue signe for me to leaue you: So I did,
Fearing to strengthen that impatience
Which seem'd too much inkindled; and withall,   810
Hoping it was but an effect of Humor,
Which sometime hath his houre with euery man.
It will not let you eate, nor talke, nor sleepe;
And could it worke so much vpon your shape,
As it hath much preuayl'd on your Condition,
I should not know you *Brutus*. Deare my Lord,
Make me acquainted with your cause of greefe.

BRUTUS
I am not well in health, and that is all.

PORTIA
Brutus is wise, and were he not in health,
He would embrace the meanes to come by it.   820

BRUTUS
Why so I do: good *Portia* go to bed.

PORTIA
Is *Brutus* sicke? And is it Physicall
To walke vnbraced, and sucke vp the humours
Of the danke Morning? What, is *Brutus* sicke?

And will he steale out of his wholsome bed
To dare the vile contagion of the Night?
And tempt the Rhewmy, and vnpurged Ayre,
To adde vnto his sicknesse? No my *Brutus*,
You haue some sicke Offence within your minde,
830 Which by the Right and Vertue of my place
I ought to know of: (*Kneeling*) And vpon my knees,
I charme you, by my once commended Beauty,
By all your vowes of Loue, and that great Vow
Which did incorporate and make vs one,
That you vnfold to me, your selfe; your halfe
Why you are heauy: and what men to night
Haue had resort to you: for heere haue beene
Some sixe or seuen, who did hide their faces
Euen from darknesse.

BRUTUS   Kneele not gentle *Portia*.

PORTIA ⌈*rising*⌉
840 I should not neede, if you were gentle *Brutus*.
Within the Bond of Marriage, tell me *Brutus*,
Is it excepted, I should know no Secrets
That appertaine to you? Am I your Selfe,
But as it were in sort, or limitation?
To keepe with you at Meales, comfort your Bed,
And talke to you sometimes? Dwell I but in the
    Suburbs
Of your good pleasure? If it be no more,
Portia is *Brutus* Harlot, not his Wife.

BRUTUS
You are my true and honourable Wife,
850 As deere to me, as are the ruddy droppes
That visit my sad heart.

PORTIA
If this were true, then should I know this secret.
I graunt I am a Woman; but withall,
A Woman that Lord *Brutus* tooke to Wife:
I graunt I am a Woman; but withall,
A Woman well reputed: *Cato's* Daughter.
Thinke you, I am no stronger then my Sex
Being so Father'd, and so Husbanded?
Tell me your Counsels, I will not disclose 'em:
860 I haue made strong proofe of my Constancie,
Giuing my selfe a voluntary wound
Heere, in the Thigh: Can I beare that with patience,
And not my Husbands Secrets?

BRUTUS   O ye Gods!
Render me worthy of this Noble Wife.
    Knocke within
Harke, harke, one knockes: *Portia* go in a while,
And by and by thy bosome shall partake
The secrets of my Heart.
All my engagements, I will construe to thee,
All the Charractery of my sad browes:
Leaue me with hast.   *Exit Portia*
870   *Lucius*, who's that knockes.
    Enter Lucius and Ligarius with a Kerchiefe ⌈*round
    his head*⌉

LUCIUS
Heere is a sicke man that would speak with you.

BRUTUS
Caius Ligarius, that *Metellus* spake of.
Boy, stand aside.   ⌈*Exit*⌉ *Lucius*
                Caius Ligarius, how?

LIGARIUS
Vouchsafe good morrow from a feeble tongue.

BRUTUS
O what a time haue you chose out braue *Caius*
To weare a Kerchiefe? Would you were not sicke.

LIGARIUS
I am not sicke, if *Brutus* haue in hand
Any exploit worthy the name of Honor.

BRUTUS
Such an exploit haue I in hand *Ligarius*,
Had you a healthfull eare to heare of it.   880

LIGARIUS
By all the Gods that Romans bow before,
I heere discard my sicknesse.
    He pulls off his Kerchiefe
                        Soule of Rome,
Braue *Sonne*, deriu'd from Honourable Loines,
Thou like an Exorcist, hast coniur'd vp
My mortified Spirit. Now bid me runne,
And I will striue with things impossible,
Yea get the better of them. What's to do?

BRUTUS
A peece of worke, that will make sicke men whole.

LIGARIUS
But are not some whole, that we must make sicke?

BRUTUS
That must we also. What it is my *Caius*,   890
I shall vnfold to thee, as we are going,
To whom it must be done.

LIGARIUS   Set on your foote,
And with a heart new-fir'd, I follow you,
To do I know not what: but it sufficeth
That *Brutus* leads me on.

BRUTUS   Follow me then.   *Exeunt*

    Thunder & Lightning.   Sc. 5
    Enter Iulius Cæsar in his Night-gowne   (2.2)

CÆSAR
Nor Heauen, nor Earth, haue beene at peace to night:
Thrice hath *Calphurnia*, in her sleepe cryed out,
Helpe, ho: They murther *Cæsar*. Who's within?
    Enter a Seruant

SERUANT My Lord.

CÆSAR
Go bid the Priests do present Sacrifice,
And bring me their opinions of Successe.   900

SERUANT I will my Lord.   *Exit*
    Enter Calphurnia

CALPHURNIA
What mean you *Cæsar*? Think you to walk forth?
You shall not stirre out of your house to day.

CÆSAR
Cæsar shall forth; the things that threaten'd me,

Ne're look'd but on my backe: When they shall see
The face of *Cæsar*, they are vanished.

CALPHURNIA

Cæsar, I neuer stood on Ceremonies,
Yet now they fright me: There is one within,
910 Besides the things that we haue heard and seene,
Recounts most horrid sights seene by the Watch.
A Lionnesse hath whelped in the streets,
And Graues haue yawn'd, and yeelded vp their dead;
Fierce fiery Warriours fight vpon the Clouds
In Rankes and Squadrons, and right forme of Warre
Which drizel'd blood vpon the Capitoll:
The noise of Battell hurtled in the Ayre:
Horsses do neigh, and dying men did grone,
And Ghosts did shrieke and squeale about the streets.
920 O *Cæsar*, these things are beyond all vse,
And I do feare them.

CÆSAR   What can be auoyded
Whose end is purpos'd by the mighty Gods?
Yet *Cæsar* shall go forth: for these Predictions
Are to the world in generall, as to *Cæsar*.

CALPHURNIA

When Beggers dye, there are no Comets seen,
The Heauens themselues blaze forth the death of
Princes.

CÆSAR

Cowards dye many times before their deaths,
The valiant neuer taste of death but once:
Of all the Wonders that I yet haue heard,
930 It seemes to me most strange that men should feare,
Seeing that death, a necessary end
Will come, when it will come.

Enter a Seruant

What say the Augurers?

SERUANT

They would not haue you to stirre forth to day.
Plucking the intrailes of an Offering forth,
They could not finde a heart within the beast.

CÆSAR

The Gods do this in shame of Cowardice:
Cæsar should be a Beast without a heart
If he should stay at home to day for feare:
No *Cæsar* shall not; Danger knowes full well
940 That *Cæsar* is more dangerous then he.
We are two Lyons litter'd in one day,
And I the elder and more terrible,
And *Cæsar* shall go foorth.

CALPHURNIA   Alas my Lord,
Your wisedome is consum'd in confidence:
Do not go forth to day: Call it my feare,
That keepes you in the house, and not your owne.
Wee'l send *Mark Antony* to the Senate house,
And he shall say, you are not well to day:
Let me vpon my knee, preuaile in this.

She kneeles

CÆSAR

950 *Mark Antony* shall say I am not well,

And for thy humor, I will stay at home.

Enter Decius

Heere's *Decius Brutus*, he shall tell them so.
⌈*Calphurnia rises*⌉

DECIUS

Cæsar, all haile: Good morrow worthy *Cæsar*,
I come to fetch you to the Senate house.

CÆSAR

And you are come in very happy time,
To beare my greeting to the Senators,
And tell them that I will not come to day:
Cannot, is false: and that I dare not, falser:
I will not come to day, tell them so *Decius*.

CALPHURNIA

Say he is sicke.

CÆSAR   Shall *Cæsar* send a Lye?   960
Haue I in Conquest stretcht mine Arme so farre,
To be afear'd to tell Gray-beards the truth:
Decius, go tell them, *Cæsar* will not come.

DECIUS

Most mighty *Cæsar*, let me know some cause,
Lest I be laught at when I tell them so.

CÆSAR

The cause is in my Will, I will not come,
That is enough to satisfie the Senate.
But for your priuate satisfaction,
Because I loue you, I will let you know.
Calphurnia heere my wife, stayes me at home: 970
She dreampt to night, she saw my Statue,
Which like a Fountaine, with an hundred spouts
Did run pure blood: and many lusty Romans
Came smiling, & did bathe their hands in it:
And these does she apply, for warnings and portents,
Of euils imminent; and on her knee
Hath begg'd, that I will stay at home to day.

DECIUS

This Dreame is all amisse interpreted,
It was a vision, faire and fortunate:
Your Statue spouting blood in many pipes,   980
In which so many smiling Romans bath'd,
Signifies, that from you great Rome shall sucke
Reuiuing blood, and that great men shall presse
For Tinctures, Staines, Reliques, and Cognisance.
This by *Calphurnia's* Dreame is signified.

CÆSAR

And this way haue you well expounded it.

DECIUS

I haue, when you haue heard what I can say:
And know it now, the Senate haue concluded
To giue this day, a Crowne to mighty *Cæsar*.
If you shall send them word you will not come,   990
Their mindes may change. Besides, it were a mocke
Apt to be render'd, for some one to say,
Breake vp the Senate, till another time:
When *Cæsars* wife shall meete with better Dreames.
If *Cæsar* hide himselfe, shall they not whisper
Loe *Cæsar* is affraid?

Pardon me *Cæsar*, for my deere deere loue
To your proceeding, bids me tell you this:
And reason to my loue is liable.

CÆSAR

1000   How foolish do your fears seeme now *Calphurnia*?
I am ashamed I did yeeld to them.
Giue me my Robe, for I will go.

*Enter ⌈Cassius,⌉ Brutus, Ligarius, Metellus, Caska,
Trebonius, and Cynna*

And looke where *Cassius* is come to fetch me.

⌈**CASSIUS**⌉

Good morrow *Cæsar*.

CÆSAR   Welcome *Cassius*.

What *Brutus*, are you stirr'd so earely too?
Good morrow *Caska*: *Caius Ligarius*,
Cæsar was ne're so much your enemy,
As that same Ague which hath made you leane.
What is't a Clocke?

BRUTUS   *Cæsar*, 'tis strucken eight.

CÆSAR

1010   I thanke you for your paines and curtesie.

Enter Antony

See, *Antony* that Reuels long a-nights
Is notwithstanding vp. Good morrow *Antony*.

ANTONY

So to most Noble *Cæsar*.

CÆSAR ⌈*to Calphurnia*⌉   Bid them prepare within:
I am too blame to be thus waited for.

⌈*Exit Calphurnia*⌉

Now *Cynna*, now *Metellus*: what *Trebonius*,
I haue an houres talke in store for you:
Remember that you call on me to day:
Be neere me, that I may remember you.

TREBONIUS

Cæsar I will: ⌈*aside*⌉ and so neere will I be,
1020   That your best Friends shall wish I had beene further.

CÆSAR

Good Friends go in, and taste some wine with me
And we (like Friends) will straight way go together.

BRUTUS (*aside*)

That euery like is not the same, O *Cæsar*,
The heart of *Brutus* earnes to thinke vpon.   *Exeunt*

Sc. 6   *Enter Artemidorus, reading a Letter*
(2.3)   **ARTEMIDORUS** *Cæsar, beware of Brutus, take heede of
Cassius; come not neere Caska, haue an eye to Cynna,
trust not Trebonius, marke well Metellus Cymber, Decius
Brutus loues thee not: Thou hast wrong'd Caius Ligarius.
There is but one minde in all these men, and it is bent*
1030   *against Cæsar: If thou beest not Immortall, looke about
you: Security giues way to Conspiracie. The mighty Gods
defend thee.*

Thy Louer, Artemidorus.

Heere will I stand, till *Cæsar* passe along,
And as a Sutor will I giue him this:
My heart laments, that Vertue cannot liue
Out of the teeth of Emulation.

If thou reade this, O *Cæsar*, thou mayest liue;
If not, the Fates with Traitors do contriue.   *Exit*

Enter Portia and Lucius   Sc. 7
                                                        (2.4)

PORTIA

I prythee Boy, run to the Senate-house,   1040
Stay not to answer me, but get thee gone.
Why doest thou stay?

LUCIUS   To know my errand Madam.

PORTIA

I would haue had thee there and heere agen
Ere I can tell thee what thou should'st do there:
(*Aside*) O Constancie, be strong vpon my side,
Set a huge Mountaine 'tweene my Heart and Tongue:
I haue a mans minde, but a womans might:
How hard it is for women to keepe counsell.
(*To Lucius*) Art thou heere yet?

LUCIUS   Madam, what should I do?
Run to the Capitoll, and nothing else?   1050
And so returne to you, and nothing else?

PORTIA

Yes, bring me word Boy, if thy Lord look well,
For he went sickly forth: and take good note
What *Cæsar* doth, what Sutors presse to him.
Hearke Boy, what noyse is that?

LUCIUS I heare none Madam.

PORTIA Prythee listen well:
I heard a bussling Rumor like a Fray,
And the winde brings it from the Capitoll.

LUCIUS Sooth Madam, I heare nothing.   1060

Enter the Soothsayer

PORTIA

Come hither Fellow, which way hast thou bin?

SOOTHSAYER

At mine owne house, good Lady.

PORTIA What is't a clocke?

SOOTHSAYER About the ninth houre Lady.

PORTIA

Is *Cæsar* yet gone to the Capitoll?

SOOTHSAYER

Madam not yet, I go to take my stand,
To see him passe on to the Capitoll.

PORTIA

Thou hast some suite to *Cæsar*, hast thou not?

SOOTHSAYER

That I haue Lady, if it will please *Cæsar*
To be so good to *Cæsar*, as to heare me: 1070
I shall beseech him to befriend himselfe.

PORTIA

Why know'st thou any harmes intended towards him?

SOOTHSAYER

None that I know will be, much that I feare may
    chance:
Good morrow to you:
⌈*He moues away*⌉
                heere the street is narrow:
The throng that followes *Cæsar* at the heeles,
Of Senators, of Prætors, common Sutors,

Will crowd a feeble man (almost) to death:
Ile get me to a place more voyd, and there
Speake to great *Cæsar* as he comes along.   *Exit*

PORTIA (*aside*)
1080   I must go in: Aye me! How weake a thing
The heart of woman is? O *Brutus*,
The Heauens speede thee in thine enterprize.
Sure the Boy heard me: (*To Lucius*) *Brutus* hath a suite
That *Cæsar* will not grant. (*Aside*) O, I grow faint:
(*To Lucius*) Run *Lucius*, and commend me to my Lord,
Say I am merry; Come to me againe,
And bring me word what he doth say to thee.
                                          Exeunt ⌈*seuerally*⌉

Sc. 8   Enter ⌈*at one doore*⌉ *Artimedorus, the Soothsayer,*
(3.1)   *and Citizens. Flourish. Enter* ⌈*at another doore*⌉
          Cæsar, Brutus, Cassius, Caska, Decius, Metellus,
          Trebonius, Cynna, ⌈*Ligarius,*⌉ *Antony, Lepidus,*
          Publius, Popillius, ⌈*and other Senators*⌉
CÆSAR (*to the Soothsayer*) The Ides of March are come.
SOOTHSAYER I *Cæsar*, but not gone.
1090   ARTEMIDORUS Haile *Cæsar*: Read this Scedule.
DECIUS (*to Cæsar*)
    Trebonius doth desire you to ore-read
    (At your best leysure) this his humble suite.
ARTEMIDORUS
    O *Cæsar*, reade mine first: for mine's a suite
    That touches *Cæsar* neerer. Read it great *Cæsar*.
CÆSAR
    What touches vs our selfe, shall be last seru'd.
ARTEMIDORUS
    Delay not *Cæsar*, read it instantly.
CÆSAR
    What, is the fellow mad?
PUBLIUS (*to Artemidorus*)   Sirra, giue place.
CASSIUS (*to Artemidorus*)
    What, vrge you your Petitions in the street?
    Come to the Capitoll.
          ⌈*They walke about the Stage*⌉
POPILLIUS (*aside to Cassius*)
1100   I wish your enterprize to day may thriue.
CASSIUS
    What enterprize *Popillius*?
POPILLIUS   Fare you well.
      He leaues Cassius and makes to Cæsar
BRUTUS What said *Popillius Lena*?
CASSIUS
    He wisht to day our enterprize might thriue:
    I feare our purpose is discouered.
BRUTUS
    Looke how he makes to *Cæsar*: marke him.
CASSIUS
    Caska be sodaine, for we feare preuention.
    Brutus what shall be done? If this be knowne,
    Cassius or *Cæsar* neuer shall turne backe,
    For I will slay my selfe.
BRUTUS   *Cassius* be constant:
1110   *Popillius Lena* speakes not of our purposes,
    For looke he smiles, and *Cæsar* doth not change.

CASSIUS
    Trebonius knowes his time: for look you *Brutus*
    He drawes *Mark Antony* out of the way.
                    Exeunt Trebonius and Antony
DECIUS
    Where is *Metellus Cimber*, let him go,
    And presently preferre his suite to *Cæsar*.
          ⌈*Cæsar sits*⌉
BRUTUS
    He is addrest: presse neere, and second him.
CINNA
    Caska, you are the first that reares your hand.
          ⌈*The Conspirators and the other Senators take their*
          places⌉
CÆSAR
    Are we all ready? What is now amisse,
    That *Cæsar* and his Senate must redresse?
METELLUS (*comming forward and kneeling*)
    Most high, most mighty, and most puisant *Cæsar*   1120
    Metellus Cymber throwes before thy Seate
    An humble heart.
CÆSAR   I must preuent thee *Cymber*:
    These couchings, and these lowly courtesies
    Might fire the blood of ordinary men,
    And turne pre-Ordinance, and first Decree
    Into the lawe of Children. Be not fond,
    To thinke that *Cæsar* beares such Rebell blood
    That will be thaw'd from the true quality
    With that which melteth Fooles, I meane sweet words,
    Low-crooked-curtsies, and base Spaniell fawning: 1130
    Thy Brother by decree is banished:
    If thou doest bend, and pray, and fawne for him,
    I spurne thee like a Curre out of my way:
    Know, *Cæsar* doth not wrong, but with iust cause:
    Nor without cause will he be satisfied.
METELLUS
    Is there no voyce more worthy then my owne,
    To sound more sweetly in great *Cæsars* eare,
    For the repealing of my banish'd Brother?
BRUTUS (*comming forward and kneeling*)
    I kisse thy hand, but not in flattery *Cæsar*:
    Desiring thee, that *Publius Cymber* may   1140
    Haue an immediate freedome of repeale.
CÆSAR
    What *Brutus*?
CASSIUS (*comming forward and kneeling*)
                Pardon *Cæsar*: *Cæsar* pardon:
    As lowe as to thy foote doth *Cassius* fall,
    To begge infranchisement for *Publius Cymber*.
CÆSAR
    I could be well mou'd, if I were as you,
    If I could pray to mooue, Prayers would mooue me:
    But I am constant as the Northerne Starre,
    Of whose true fixt, and resting quality,
    There is no fellow in the Firmament.
    The Skies are painted with vnnumbred sparkes,   1150
    They are all Fire, and euery one doth shine:
    But, there's but one in all doth hold his place.
    So, in the World; 'Tis furnish'd well with Men,

And Men are Flesh and Blood, and apprehensiue;
Yet in the number, I do know but One
That vnassayleable holds on his Ranke,
Vnshak'd of Motion: and that I am he,
Let me a little shew it, euen in this:
That I was constant Cymber should be banish'd,
1160   And constant do remaine to keepe him so.
CINNA (comming forward and kneeling)
    O Cæsar.
CÆSAR   Hence: Wilt thou lift vp Olympus?
DECIUS (comming forward ⌈with Ligarius⌉ and kneeling)
    Great Cæsar.
CÆSAR   Doth not Brutus bootlesse kneele?
CASKA (comming forward ⌈and kneeling⌉)
    Speake hands for me.
        They stab Cæsar, ⌈Caska first, Brutus last⌉
CÆSAR   Et Tu Brutè?—Then fall Cæsar.
                                        Dyes
CINNA
    Liberty, Freedome; Tyranny is dead,
    Run hence, proclaime, cry it about the Streets.
CASSIUS
    Some to the common Pulpits, and cry out
    Liberty, Freedome, and Enfranchisement.
BRUTUS
    People and Senators, be not affrighted:
            ⌈Exeunt in a tumult Lepidus, Popillius, other
                Senators, Artemidorus, Soothsayer, and
                                        Citizens⌉
1170   Fly not, stand still: Ambitions debt is paid.
CASKA Go to the Pulpit Brutus.
DECIUS And Cassius too.
BRUTUS Where's Publius?
CINNA
    Heere, quite confounded with this mutiny.
METELLUS
    Stand fast together, least some Friend of Cæsars
    Should chance—
BRUTUS
    Talke not of standing. Publius good cheere,
    There is no harme intended to your person,
    Nor to no Roman else: so tell them Publius.
CASSIUS
1180   And leaue vs Publius, least that the people
    Rushing on vs, should do your Age some mischiefe.
BRUTUS
    Do so, and let no man abide this deede,
    But we the Doers.   ⌈Exit Publius⌉
        Enter Trebonius
CASSIUS Where is Antony?
TREBONIUS Fled to his House amaz'd:
    Men, Wiues, and Children, stare, cry out, and run,
    As it were Doomesday.
BRUTUS   Fates, we will know your pleasures:
    That we shall dye we know, 'tis but the time
    And drawing dayes out, that men stand vpon.
CASKA
1190   Why he that cuts off twenty yeares of life,
    Cuts off so many yeares of fearing death.

BRUTUS
    Grant that, and then is Death a Benefit:
    So are we Cæsars Friends, that haue abridg'd
    His time of fearing death. Stoope Romans, stoope,
    And let vs bathe our hands in Cæsars blood
    Vp to the Elbowes, and besmeare our Swords:
    Then walke we forth, euen to the Market place,
    And wauing our red Weapons o're our heads,
    Let's all cry Peace, Freedome, and Liberty.
CASSIUS
    Stoop then, and wash.
        They smear their hands with Caesars blood
                        How many Ages hence   1200
    Shall this our lofty Scene be acted ouer,
    In States vnborne, and Accents yet vnknowne?
BRUTUS
    How many times shall Cæsar bleed in sport,
    That now on Pompeyes Basis lye along,
    No worthier then the dust?
CASSIUS   So oft as that shall be,
    So often shall the knot of vs be call'd,
    The Men that gaue their Country liberty.
DECIUS
    What, shall we forth?
CASSIUS   I, euery man away.
    Brutus shall leade, and we will grace his heeles
    With the most boldest, and best hearts of Rome.   1210
        Enter Antonies Seruant
BRUTUS
    Soft, who comes heere? A friend of Antonies.
SERUANT (kneeling and falling prostrate)
    Thus Brutus did my Master bid me kneele;
    Thus did Mark Antony bid me fall downe,
    And being prostrate, thus he bad me say:
    Brutus is Noble, Wise, Valiant, and Honest;
    Cæsar was Mighty, Bold, Royall, and Louing:
    Say, I loue Brutus, and I honour him;
    Say, I fear'd Cæsar, honour'd him, and lou'd him.
    If Brutus will vouchsafe, that Antony
    May safely come to him, and be resolu'd   1220
    How Cæsar hath deseru'd to lye in death,
    Mark Antony, shall not loue Cæsar dead
    So well as Brutus liuing; but will follow
    The Fortunes and Affayres of Noble Brutus,
    Thorough the hazards of this vntrod State,
    With all true Faith. So sayes my Master Antony.
BRUTUS
    Thy Master is a Wise and Valiant Romane,
    I neuer thought him worse:
    Tell him, so please him come vnto this place
    He shall be satisfied: and by my Honor   1230
    Depart vntouch'd.
SERUANT ⌈rising⌉   Ile fetch him presently.   Exit
BRUTUS
    I know that we shall haue him well to Friend.
CASSIUS
    I wish we may: But yet haue I a minde
    That feares him much: and my misgiuing still
    Falles shrewdly to the purpose.

Enter Antony

BRUTUS

But heere comes *Antony*: Welcome *Mark Antony*.

ANTONY

O mighty *Cæsar*! Dost thou lye so lowe?
Are all thy Conquests, Glories, Triumphes, Spoiles,
Shrunke to this little Measure? Fare thee well.
1240   I know not Gentlemen what you intend,
Who else must be let blood, who else is ranke:
If I my selfe, there is no houre so fit
As *Cæsars* deaths houre; nor no Instrument
Of halfe that worth, as those your Swords; made rich
With the most Noble blood of all this World.
I do beseech yee, if you beare me hard,
Now, whil'st your purpled hands do reeke and
      smoake,
Fulfill your pleasure. Liue a thousand yeeres,
I shall not finde my selfe so apt to dye.
1250   No place will please me so, no meane of death,
As heere by *Cæsar*, and by you cut off,
The Choice and Master Spirits of this Age.

BRUTUS

O *Antony*! Begge not your death of vs:
Though now we must appeare bloody and cruell,
As by our hands, and this our present Acte
You see we do: Yet see you but our hands,
And this, the bleeding businesse they haue done:
Our hearts you see not, they are pittifull:
And pitty to the generall wrong of Rome,
1260   As fire driues out fire, so pitty, pitty
Hath done this deed on *Cæsar*. For your part,
To you, our Swords haue leaden points *Marke*
      Antony:
Our Armes unstrunge of malice, and our Hearts
Of Brothers temper, do receiue you in,
With all kinde loue, good thoughts, and reuerence.

CASSIUS

Your voyce shall be as strong as any mans,
In the disposing of new Dignities.

BRUTUS

Onely be patient, till we haue appeas'd
The Multitude, beside themselues with feare,
1270   And then, we will deliuer you the cause,
Why I, that did loue *Cæsar* when I strooke him,
Haue thus proceeded.

ANTONY   I doubt not of your Wisedome:
Let each man render me his bloody hand.
      He shakes hands with the Conspirators
First *Marcus Brutus* will I shake with you;
Next *Caius Cassius* do I take your hand;
Now *Decius Brutus* yours; now yours *Metellus*;
Yours *Cinna*; and my valiant *Caska*, yours;
Though last, not least in loue, yours good *Trebonius*.
Gentlemen all: Alas, what shall I say,
1280   My credit now stands on such slippery ground,
That one of two bad wayes you must conceit me,
Either a Coward, or a Flatterer.

That I did loue thee *Cæsar*, O 'tis true:
If then thy Spirit looke vpon vs now,
Shall it not greeue thee deerer then thy death,
To see thy *Antony* making his peace,
Shaking the bloody fingers of thy Foes?
Most Noble, in the presence of thy Coarse?
Had I as many eyes, as thou hast wounds,
Weeping as fast as they streame forth thy blood,   1290
It would become me better, then to close
In tearmes of Friendship with thine enemies.
Pardon me *Iulius*, heere was't thou bay'd braue Hart,
Heere did'st thou fall, and heere thy Hunters stand
Sign'd in thy Spoyle, and Crimson'd in thy Lethee.
O World! thou wast the Forrest to this Hart,
And this indeed, O World, the Hart of thee.
How like a Deere, stroken by many Princes,
Dost thou heere lye?

CASSIUS *Mark Antony*.   1300

ANTONY Pardon me *Caius Cassius*:
The Enemies of *Cæsar*, shall say this:
Then, in a Friend, it is cold Modestie.

CASSIUS

I blame you not for praising *Cæsar* so,
But what compact meane you to haue with vs?
Will you be prick'd in number of our Friends,
Or shall we on, and not depend on you?

ANTONY

Therefore I tooke your hands, but was indeed
Sway'd from the point, by looking downe on *Cæsar*.
Friends am I with you all, and loue you all,   1310
Vpon this hope, that you shall giue me Reasons,
Why, and wherein, *Cæsar* was dangerous.

BRUTUS

Or else were this a sauage Spectacle:
Our Reasons are so full of good regard,
That were you *Antony*, the Sonne of *Cæsar*,
You should be satisfied.

ANTONY   That's all I seeke,
And am moreouer sutor, that I may
Produce his body to the Market-place,
And in the Pulpit as becomes a Friend,
Speake in the Order of his Funerall.   1320

BRUTUS

You shall *Marke Antony*.

CASSIUS   *Brutus*, a word with you:
(*Aside to Brutus*) You know not what you do; Do not
      consent
That *Antony* speake in his Funerall:
Know you how much the people may be mou'd
By that which he will vtter.

BRUTUS (*aside to Cassius*)   By your pardon:
I will my selfe into the Pulpit first,
And shew the reason of our *Cæsars* death.
What *Antony* shall speake, I will protest
He speakes by leaue, and by permission:
And that we are contented *Cæsar* shall   1330
Haue all true Rites, and lawfull Ceremonies,
It shall aduantage more, then do vs wrong.

CASSIUS (*aside to Brutus*)
I know not what may fall, I like it not.

BRUTUS
Mark Antony, heere take you *Cæsars* body:
You shall not in your Funerall speech blame vs,
But speake all good you can deuise of *Cæsar*,
And say you doo't by our permission:
Else shall you not haue any hand at all
About his Funerall. And you shall speake
1340   In the same Pulpit whereto I am going,
After my speech is ended.

ANTONY Be it so:
I do desire no more.

BRUTUS
Prepare the body then, and follow vs.
    Exeunt. Manet Antony

ANTONY
O pardon me, thou bleeding peece of Earth:
That I am meeke and gentle with these Butchers.
Thou art the Ruines of the Noblest man
That euer liued in the Tide of Times.
Woe to the hand that shed this costly Blood.
Ouer thy wounds, now do I Prophesie,
1350   (Which like dumbe mouthes do ope their Ruby lips,
To begge the voyce and vtterance of my Tongue)
A Curse shall light vpon the limbes of men;
Domesticke Fury, and fierce Ciuill strife,
Shall cumber all the parts of Italy:
Blood and destruction shall be so in vse,
And dreadfull Obiects so familiar,
That Mothers shall but smile, when they behold
Their Infants quartred with the hands of Warre:
All pitty choak'd with custome of fell deeds,
1360   And *Cæsars* Spirit ranging for Reuenge,
With *Ate* by his side, come hot from Hell,
Shall in these Confines, with a Monarkes voyce,
Cry hauocke, and let slip the Dogges of Warre,
That this foule deede, shall smell aboue the earth
With Carrion men, groaning for Buriall.
    Enter Octauio's Seruant
You serue *Octauius Cæsar*, do you not?

SERUANT I do *Marke Antony*.

ANTONY
Cæsar did write for him to come to Rome.

SERUANT
He did receiue his Letters, and is comming,
1370   And bid me say to you by word of mouth—
    (*Seeing the body*) O *Cæsar*!

ANTONY
Thy heart is bigge: get thee a-part and weepe:
Passion I see is catching for mine eyes,
Seeing those Beads of sorrow stand in thine,
Began to water. Is thy Master comming?

SERUANT
He lies to night within seuen Leagues of Rome.

ANTONY
Post backe with speede, and tell him what hath
    chanc'd:
Heere is a mourning Rome, a dangerous Rome,

No Rome of safety for *Octauius* yet,
Hie hence, and tell him so. Yet stay a-while,   1380
Thou shalt not backe, till I haue borne this course
Into the Market place: There shall I try
In my Oration, how the People take
The cruell issue of these bloody men,
According to the which, thou shalt discourse
To yong *Octauius*, of the state of things.
Lend me your hand.   *Exeunt with Cæsars body*

    Enter Brutus and Cassius, with the Plebeians   Sc. 9

ALL THE PLEBEIANS   (3.2)
We will be satisfied: let vs be satisfied.

BRUTUS
Then follow me, and giue me Audience friends.
(*Aside to Cassius*) *Cassius* go you into the other streete,   1390
And part the Numbers:
(*To the Plebeians*) Those that will heare me speake, let
   'em stay here;
Those that will follow *Cassius*, go with him,
And publike Reasons shall be rendered
Of *Cæsars* death.
    Brutus ascends to the Pulpit

1. PLEBEIAN   I will heare *Brutus* speake.

2. PLEBEIAN
I will heare *Cassius*, and compare their Reasons,
When seuerally we heare them rendered.
    Exit Cassius, with some Plebeians
   ⌈*Enter*⌉ *Brutus* ⌈*aboue*⌉ *in the Pulpit*

3. PLEBEIAN
The Noble *Brutus* is ascended: Silence.

BRUTUS Be patient till the last.
Romans, Countrey-men, and Louers, heare mee for my   1400
cause, and be silent, that you may heare. Beleeue me
for mine Honor, and haue respect to mine Honor, that
you may beleeue. Censure me in your Wisedom, and
awake your Senses, that you may the better Iudge. If
there bee any in this Assembly, any deere Friend of
Cæsars, to him I say, that *Brutus* loue to *Cæsar*, was
no lesse then his. If then, that Friend demand, why
Brutus rose against *Cæsar*, this is my answer: Not that
I lou'd *Cæsar* lesse, but that I lou'd Rome more. Had
you rather *Cæsar* were liuing, and dye all Slaues; then   1410
that *Cæsar* were dead, to liue all Free-men? As *Cæsar*
lou'd mee, I weepe for him; as he was Fortunate, I
reioyce at it; as he was Valiant, I honour him: But, as
he was Ambitious, I slew him. There is Teares, for his
Loue: Ioy, for his Fortune: Honor, for his Valour: and
Death, for his Ambition. Who is heere so base, that
would be a Bondman? If any, speak, for him haue I
offended. Who is heere so rude, that would not be a
Roman? If any, speak, for him haue I offended. Who
is heere so vile, that will not loue his Countrey? If any,   1420
speake, for him haue I offended. I pause for a Reply.

ALL THE PLEBEIANS None *Brutus*, none.

BRUTUS Then none haue I offended. I haue done no more
to *Cæsar*, then you shall do to *Brutus*. The Question of
his death, is inroll'd in the Capitoll: his Glory not

extenuated, wherein he was worthy; nor his offences
enforc'd, for which he suffered death.

> *Enter Mark Antony, with ⌈others bearing⌉ Cæsars*
> *body ⌈in a Coffin⌉*

Heere comes his Body, mourn'd by *Marke Antony*, who
though he had no hand in his death, shall receiue the
1430   benefit of his dying, a place in the Cōmonwealth, as
which of you shall not. With this I depart, that as I
slewe my best Louer for the good of Rome, I haue the
same Dagger for my selfe, when it shall please my
Country to need my death.

ALL THE PLEBEIANS Liue *Brutus*, liue, liue.

I. PLEBEIAN
Bring him with Triumph home vnto his house.

⌈4.⌉ PLEBEIAN
Giue him a Statue with his Ancestors.

3. PLEBEIAN
Let him be *Cæsar*.

⌈5.⌉ PLEBEIAN   *Cæsars* better parts,
Shall be Crown'd in *Brutus*.

I. PLEBEIAN
Wee'l bring him to his House, with Showts and
1440   Clamors.

BRUTUS
My Country-men.

⌈4.⌉ PLEBEIAN   Peace, silence, *Brutus* speakes.

I. PLEBEIAN Peace ho.

BRUTUS
Good Countrymen, let me depart alone,
And (for my sake) stay heere with *Antony*:
Do grace to *Cæsars* Corpes, and grace his Speech
Tending to *Cæsars* Glories, which *Marke Antony*
(By our permission) is allow'd to make.
I do intreat you, not a man depart,
Saue I alone, till *Antony* haue spoke.   *Exit*

I. PLEBEIAN
Stay ho, and let vs heare *Mark Antony*.

3. PLEBEIAN
1450   Let him go vp into the publike Chaire,
Wee'l heare him: Noble *Antony* go vp.

ANTONY
For *Brutus* sake, I am beholding to you.

> *Antony ascends to the pulpit*

⌈5.⌉ PLEBEIAN
What does he say of *Brutus*?

3. PLEBEIAN   He sayes, for *Brutus* sake
He findes himselfe beholding to vs all.

⌈5.⌉ PLEBEIAN
'Twere best he speake no harme of *Brutus* heere?

I. PLEBEIAN
This *Cæsar* was a Tyrant.

3. PLEBEIAN   Nay that's certaine:
We are blest that Rome is rid of him.

> ⌈*Enter*⌉ *Antony in the Pulpit*

⌈4.⌉ PLEBEIAN
Peace, let vs heare what *Antony* can say.

ANTONY
You gentle Romans.

ALL THE PLEBEIANS   Peace hoe, let vs heare him.

ANTONY
Friends, Romans, Countrymen, lend me your ears: 1460
I come to bury *Cæsar*, not to praise him:
The euill that men do, liues after them,
The good is oft enterred with their bones,
So let it be with *Cæsar*. The Noble *Brutus*,
Hath told you *Cæsar* was Ambitious:
If it were so, it was a greeuous Fault,
And greeuously hath *Cæsar* answer'd it.
Heere, vnder leaue of *Brutus*, and the rest
(For *Brutus* is an Honourable man,
So are they all; all Honourable men)   1470
Come I to speake in *Cæsars* Funerall.
He was my Friend, faithfull, and iust to me;
But *Brutus* says, he was Ambitious,
And *Brutus* is an Honourable man.
He hath brought many Captiues home to Rome,
Whose Ransomes, did the generall Coffers fill:
Did this in *Cæsar* seeme Ambitious?
When that the poore haue cry'de, *Cæsar* hath wept:
Ambition should be made of sterner stuffe,
Yet *Brutus* says, he was Ambitious: 1480
And *Brutus* is an Honourable man.
You all did see, that on the *Lupercall*,
I thrice presented him a Kingly Crowne,
Which he did thrice refuse. Was this Ambition?
Yet *Brutus* says, he was Ambitious:
And sure he is an Honourable man.
I speake not to disprooue what *Brutus* spoke,
But heere I am, to speake what I do know;
You all did loue him once, not without cause,
What cause with-holds you then, to mourne for him?   1490
O Iudgement! thou art fled to brutish Beasts,
And Men haue lost their Reason.

> *He weepes*

                        Beare with me,
My heart is in the Coffin there with *Cæsar*,
And I must pawse, till it come backe to me.

I. PLEBEIAN
Me thinkes there is much reason in his sayings.

⌈4.⌉ PLEBEIAN
If thou consider rightly of the matter,
Cæsar ha's had great wrong.

3. PLEBEIAN   Ha's hee not Masters?
I feare there will a worse come in his place.

⌈5.⌉ PLEBEIAN
Mark'd ye his words? he would not take yᵉ Crown,
Therefore 'tis certaine, he was not Ambitious.   1500

I. PLEBEIAN
If it be found so, some will deere abide it.

⌈4.⌉ PLEBEIAN
Poore soule, his eyes are red as fire with weeping.

3. PLEBEIAN
There's not a Nobler man in Rome then *Antony*.

⌈5.⌉ PLEBEIAN
Now marke him, he begins againe to speake.

ANTONY
But yesterday, the word of *Cæsar* might
Haue stood against the World: Now lies he there,

And none so poore to do him reuerence.
O Maisters! If I were dispos'd to stirre
Your hearts and mindes to Mutiny and Rage,
1510 I should do *Brutus* wrong, and *Cassius* wrong:
Who (you all know) are Honourable men.
I will not do them wrong: I rather choose
To wrong the dead, to wrong my selfe and you,
Then I will wrong such Honourable men.
But heere's a Parchment, with the Seale of *Cæsar*,
I found it in his Closset, 'tis his Will:
Let but the Commons heare this Testament:
(Which pardon me) I do not meane to reade,
And they would go and kisse dead *Cæsars* wounds,
1520 And dip their Napkins in his Sacred Blood;
Yea, begge a haire of him for Memory,
And dying, mention it within their Willes,
Bequeathing it as a rich Legacie
Vnto their issue.

⌜5.⌝ PLEBEIAN
Wee'l heare the Will, reade it *Marke Antony*.

ALL THE PLEBEIANS
The Will, the Will; we will heare *Cæsars* Will.

ANTONY
Haue patience gentle Friends, I must not read it.
It is not meete you know how *Cæsar* lou'd you:
You are not Wood, you are not Stones, but men:
1530 And being men, hearing the Will of *Cæsar*,
It will inflame you, it will make you mad;
'Tis good you know not that you are his Heires,
For if you should, O what would come of it?

⌜5.⌝ PLEBEIAN
Read the Will, wee'l heare it *Antony*:
You shall reade vs the Will, *Cæsars* Will.

ANTONY
Will you be Patient? Will you stay a-while?
I haue o're-shot my selfe to tell you of it,
I feare I wrong the Honourable men,
Whose Daggers haue stabb'd *Cæsar*: I do feare it.

1540 ⌜5.⌝ PLEBEIAN They were Traitors: Honourable men?

ALL THE PLEBEIANS The Will, the Testament.

⌜4.⌝ PLEBEIAN They were Villaines, Murderers: the Will,
read the Will.

ANTONY
You will compell me then to read the Will:
Then make a Ring about the Corpes of *Cæsar*,
And let me shew you him that made the Will:
Shall I descend? And will you giue me leaue?

ALL THE PLEBEIANS
Come downe.

⌜4.⌝ PLEBEIAN   Descend.

3. PLEBEIAN   You shall haue leaue.

Antony descends from the Pulpit

⌜5.⌝ PLEBEIAN   A Ring,
Stand round.

I. PLEBEIAN
                  Stand from the Hearse, stand from the Body.

⌜4.⌝ PLEBEIAN
1550 Roome for *Antony*, most Noble *Antony*.

⌜Enter Antony below⌝

ANTONY
Nay presse not so vpon me, stand farre off.

ALL THE PLEBEIANS Stand backe: roome, beare backe.

ANTONY
If you haue teares, prepare to shed them now.
You all do know this Mantle, I remember
The first time euer *Cæsar* put it on,
'Twas on a Summers Euening in his Tent,
That day he ouercame the *Neruij*.
Looke, in this place ran *Cassius* Dagger through:
See what a rent the enuious *Caska* made:
Through this, the wel-beloued *Brutus* stabb'd,   1560
And as he pluck'd his cursed Steele away:
Marke how the blood of *Cæsar* followed it,
As rushing out of doores, to be resolu'd
If *Brutus* so vnkindely knock'd, or no:
For *Brutus*, as you know, was *Cæsars* Angel.
Iudge, O you Gods, how deerely *Cæsar* lou'd him:
This was the most vnkindest cut of all.
For when the Noble *Cæsar* saw him stab,
Ingratitude, more strong then Traitors armes,
Quite vanquish'd him: then burst his Mighty heart,   1570
And in his Mantle, muffling vp his face,
Euen at the Base of *Pompeyes* Statue
(Which all the while ran blood) great *Cæsar* fell.
O what a fall was there, my Countrymen?
Then I, and you, and all of vs fell downe,
Whil'st bloody Treason flourish'd ouer vs.
O now you weepe, and I perceiue you feele
The dint of pitty: These are gracious droppes.
Kinde Soules, what weepe you, when you but behold
Our *Cæsars* Vesture wounded? Looke you heere,   1580
Heere is Himselfe, marr'd as you see with Traitors.

He vncouers Cæsars body

I. PLEBEIAN
O pitteous spectacle!

⌜4.⌝ PLEBEIAN   O Noble *Cæsar*!

3. PLEBEIAN O wofull day!

⌜5.⌝ PLEBEIAN
O Traitors, Villaines!

I. PLEBEIAN   O most bloody sight!

⌜4.⌝ PLEBEIAN We will be reueng'd.

⌜ALL THE PLEBEIANS⌝
Reuenge, about, seeke, burne, fire, kill, slay,
Let not a Traitor liue.

ANTONY   Stay Country-men.

I. PLEBEIAN Peace there, heare the Noble *Antony*.

⌜4.⌝ PLEBEIAN Wee'l heare him, wee'l follow him, wee'l
dy with him.   1590

ANTONY
Good Friends, sweet Friends, let me not stirre you vp
To such a sodaine Flood of Mutiny:
They that haue done this Deede, are honourable.
What priuate greefes they haue, alas I know not,
That made them do it: They are Wise, and Honourable,
And will no doubt with Reasons answer you.
I come not (Friends) to steale away your hearts,

I am no Orator, as *Brutus* is;
But (as you know me all) a plaine blunt man
1600 That loue my Friend, and that they know full well,
That gaue me publike leaue to speake of him:
For I haue neyther wit nor words, nor worth,
Action, nor Vtterance, nor the power of Speech,
To stirre mens Blood. I onely speake right on:
I tell you that, which you your selues do know,
Shew you sweet *Cæsars* wounds, poor poor dum mouths
And bid them speake for me: But were I *Brutus*,
And *Brutus Antony*, there were an *Antony*
Would ruffle vp your Spirits, and put a Tongue
1610 In euery Wound of *Cæsar*, that should moue
The stones of Rome, to rise and Mutiny.

ALL THE PLEBEIANS
Wee'l Mutiny.

I. PLEBEIAN   Wee'l burne the house of *Brutus*.

3. PLEBEIAN
Away then, come, seeke the Conspirators.

ANTONY
Yet heare me Countrymen, yet heare me speake.

ALL THE PLEBEIANS
Peace hoe, heare *Antony*, most Noble *Antony*.

ANTONY
Why Friends, you go to do you know not what:
Wherein hath *Cæsar* thus deseru'd your loues?
Alas you know not, I must tell you then:
You haue forgot the Will I told you of.

ALL THE PLEBEIANS
1620 Most true, the Will, let's stay and heare the Wil.

ANTONY
Heere is the Will, and vnder *Cæsars* Seale:
To euery Roman Citizen he giues,
To euery seuerall man, seuenty fiue Drachmaes.

⌈4.⌉ PLEBEIAN
Most Noble *Cæsar*, wee'l reuenge his death.

3. PLEBEIAN
O Royall *Cæsar*.

ANTONY   Heare me with patience.

ALL THE PLEBEIANS   Peace hoe.

ANTONY
Moreouer, he hath left you all his Walkes,
His priuate Arbors, and new-planted Orchards,
On this side Tyber, he hath left them you,
And to your heyres for euer: common pleasures
1630 To walke abroad, and recreate your selues.
Heere was a *Cæsar*: when comes such another?

I. PLEBEIAN
Neuer, neuer: come, away, away:
Wee'l burne his body in the holy place,
And with the Brands fire the Traitors houses.
Take vp the body.

⌈4.⌉ PLEBEIAN Go fetch fire.

3. PLEBEIAN Plucke downe Benches.

⌈5.⌉ PLEBEIAN Plucke downe Formes, Windowes, any
        thing.   *Exeunt Plebeians ⌈with Cæsars body⌉*

ANTONY
Now let it worke: Mischeefe thou art a-foot,

Take thou what course thou wilt.
    Enter ⌈Octauio's⌉ Seruant
                        How now Fellow?   1640

SERUANT
Sir, *Octauius* is already come to Rome.

ANTONY Where is hee?

SERUANT
He and *Lepidus* are at *Cæsars* house.

ANTONY
And thither will I straight, to visit him:
He comes vpon a wish. Fortune is merry,
And in this mood will giue vs any thing.

SERUANT
I heard him say, *Brutus* and *Cassius*
Are rid like Madmen through the Gates of Rome.

ANTONY
Belike they had some notice of the people
How I had moud them. Bring me to *Octauius*.   *Exeunt* 1650

    Enter Cinna the Poet   Sc. 10

CINNA   (3.3)
I dreamt to night, that I did feast with *Cæsar*,
And things vnlucky charge my Fantasie:
I haue no will to wander foorth of doores,
Yet something leads me foorth.
    Enter the Plebeians

I. PLEBEIAN What is your name?

2. PLEBEIAN Whether are you going?

3. PLEBEIAN Where do you dwell?

4. PLEBEIAN Are you a married man, or a Batchellor?

2. PLEBEIAN Answer euery man directly.

I. PLEBEIAN I, and breefely.   1660

4. PLEBEIAN I, and wisely.

3. PLEBEIAN I, and truly, you were best.

CINNA What is my name? Whether am I going? Where
    do I dwell? Am I a married man, or a Batchellour?
    Then to answer euery man, directly and breefely, wisely
    and truly: wisely I say, I am a Batchellor.

2. PLEBEIAN That's as much as to say, they are fooles
    that marrie: you'l beare me a bang for that I feare:
    proceede directly.

CINNA Directly I am going to *Cæsars* Funerall.   1670

I. PLEBEIAN As a Friend, or an Enemy?

CINNA As a friend.

2. PLEBEIAN That matter is answered directly.

4. PLEBEIAN For your dwelling: breefely.

CINNA Breefely, I dwell by the Capitoll.

3. PLEBEIAN Your name sir, truly.

CINNA Truly, my name is *Cinna*.

I. PLEBEIAN Teare him to peeces, hee's a Conspirator.

CINNA I am *Cinna* the Poet, I am *Cinna* the Poet.

4. PLEBEIAN Teare him for his bad verses, teare him for 1680
    his bad Verses.

CINNA I am not *Cinna* the Conspirator.

4. PLEBEIAN It is no matter, his name's *Cinna*, plucke but
    his name out of his heart, and turne him going.

3. PLEBEIAN Teare him, tear him;
        ⌈They set vpon Cinna⌉

Come Brands hoe, Firebrands: to *Brutus*, to *Cassius*,
burne all. Some to *Decius* House, and some to *Caska's*;
some to *Ligarius*: Away, go.
> *Exeunt all the Plebeians with Cinna*

Sc. 11   *Enter Antony with Papers, Octauius, and Lepidus*
(4.1)
ANTONY
These many then shall die, their names are prickt.
OCTAUIUS (*to Lepidus*)
1690   Your Brother too must dye: consent you *Lepidus*?
LEPIDUS
I do consent.
OCTAUIUS   Pricke him downe *Antony*.
LEPIDUS
Vpon condition *Publius* shall not liue,
Who is your Sisters sonne, *Marke Antony*.
ANTONY
He shall not liue; looke, with a spot I dam him,
But *Lepidus*, go you to *Cæsars* house:
Fetch the Will hither, and we shall determine
How to cut off some charge in Legacies.
LEPIDUS What? shall I finde you heere?
OCTAUIUS Or heere, or at the Capitoll.   *Exit Lepidus*
ANTONY
1700   This is a slight vnmeritable man,
Meet to be sent on Errands: is it fit
The three-fold World diuided, he should stand
One of the three to share it?
OCTAUIUS   So you thought him,
And tooke his voyce who should be prickt to dye
In our blacke Sentence and Proscription.
ANTONY
Octauius, I haue seene more dayes then you,
And though we lay these Honours on this man,
To ease our selues of diuers sland'rous loads,
He shall but beare them, as the Asse beares Gold,
1710   To groane and swet vnder the Businesse,
Either led or driuen, as we point the way:
And hauing brought our Treasure, where we will,
Then take we downe his Load, and turne him off
(Like to the empty Asse) to shake his eares,
And graze in Commons.
OCTAUIUS   You may do your will:
But hee's a tried, and valiant Souldier.
ANTONY
So is my Horse *Octauius*, and for that
I do appoint him store of Prouender.
It is a Creature that I teach to fight,
1720   To winde, to stop, to run directly on:
His corporall Motion, gouern'd by my Spirit,
And in some taste, is *Lepidus* but so:
He must be taught, and train'd, and bid go forth:
A barren spirited Fellow; one that feeds
On Obiects, Arts, and Imitations.
Which out of vse, and stal'de by other men
Begin his fashion. Do not talke of him,
But as a property: and now *Octauius*,
Listen great things. *Brutus* and *Cassius*

Are leuying Powers; We must straight make head: 1730
Therefore let our Alliance be combin'd,
Our best Friends made, our meanies stretcht,
And let vs presently go sit in Councell,
How couert matters may be best disclos'd,
And open Perils surest answered.
OCTAUIUS
Let vs do so: for we are at the stake,
And bayed about with many Enemies,
And some that smile haue in their hearts I feare
Millions of Mischeefes.   *Exeunt*

Sc. 12   *Drum. Enter Brutus, Lucius, and the Army.*
(4.2)   ⌈*Lucillius,*⌉ *Titinius, and Pindarus meete them*
BRUTUS Stand ho.   1740
⌈SOULDIER⌉ Giue the word ho, and Stand.
BRUTUS
What now *Lucillius*, is *Cassius* neere?
LUCILLIUS
He is at hand, and *Pindarus* is come
To do you salutation from his Master.
BRUTUS
He greets me well. Your Master *Pindarus*
In his owne change, or by ill Officers,
Hath giuen me some worthy cause to wish
Things done, vndone: But if he be at hand
I shall be satisfied.
PINDARUS   I do not doubt
But that my Noble Master will appeare   1750
Such as he is, full of regard, and Honour.
BRUTUS
He is not doubted. A word *Lucillius*:
> *Brutus and Lucillius speake apart*
How he receiu'd you, let me be resolu'd.
LUCILLIUS
With courtesie, and with respect enough,
But not with such familiar instances,
Nor with such free and friendly Conference
As he hath vs'd of old.
BRUTUS   Thou hast describ'd
A hot Friend, cooling: Euer note *Lucillius*,
When Loue begins to sicken and decay
It vseth an enforced Ceremony.   1760
There are no trickes, in plaine and simple Faith:
But hollow men, like Horses hot at hand,
Make gallant shew, and promise of their Mettle:
> *Low March within*
But when they should endure the bloody Spurre,
They fall their Crests, and like deceitfull Iades
Sinke in the Triall. Comes his Army on?
LUCILLIUS
They meane this night in Sardis to be quarter'd:
The greater part, the Horse in generall
Are come with *Cassius*.
> *Enter Cassius and his Powers*
BRUTUS   Hearke, he is arriu'd:
March gently on to meete him.   1770
> *The Armies march*

CASSIUS Stand ho.

BRUTUS Stand ho, speake the word along.

⌈1.⌉ SOULDIER Stand.

⌈2.⌉ SOULDIER Stand.

⌈3.⌉ SOULDIER Stand.

CASSIUS

   Most Noble Brother, you haue done me wrong.

BRUTUS

   Iudge me you Gods; wrong I mine Enemies?

   And if not so, how should I wrong a Brother.

CASSIUS

   Brutus, this sober forme of yours, hides wrongs,

   And when you do them—

1780 BRUTUS   Cassius, be content,

   Speake your greefes softly, I do know you well.

   Before the eyes of both our Armies heere

   (Which should perceiue nothing but Loue from vs)

   Let vs not wrangle. Bid them moue away:

   Then in my Tent Cassius enlarge your Greefes,

   And I will giue you Audience.

CASSIUS   Pindarus,

   Bid our Commanders leade their Charges off

   A little from this ground.

BRUTUS

   Lucillius, do you the like, and let no man

1790   Come to our Tent, till we haue done our Conference.

   Let Lucius and Titinius guard our doore.

                       Exeunt the Armies

       Manet Brutus and Cassius, ⌈with Titinius and

       Lucius guarding the doore⌉

CASSIUS

   That you haue wrong'd me, doth appear in this:

   You haue condemn'd, and noted Lucius Pella

   For taking Bribes heere of the Sardians;

   Wherein my Letters, praying on his side,

   Because I knew the man was slighted off.

BRUTUS

   You wrong'd your selfe to write in such a case.

CASSIUS

   In such a time as this, it is not meet

   That euery nice offence should beare his Comment.

BRUTUS

1800   Let me tell you Cassius, you your selfe

   Are much condemn'd to haue an itching Palme,

   To sell, and Mart your Offices for Gold

   To Vndeseruers.

CASSIUS   I, an itching Palme?

   You know that you are Brutus that speakes this,

   Or, by the Gods, this speech were else your last.

BRUTUS

   The name of Cassius Honors this corruption,

   And Chasticement doth therefore hide his head.

CASSIUS Chasticement?

BRUTUS

   Remember March, the Ides of March remēber:

1810   Did not great Iulius bleede for Iustice sake?

   What Villaine touch'd his body, that did stab,

   And not for Iustice? What? Shall one of Vs,

That strucke the Formost man of all this World,

But for supporting Robbers: shall we now,

Contaminate our fingers, with base Bribes?

And sell the mighty space of our large Honors

For so much trash, as may be grasped thus?

I had rather be a Dogge, and bay the Moone,

Then such a Roman.

CASSIUS   Brutus, baye not me,

   Ile not indure it: you forget your selfe   1820

   To hedge me in. I am a Souldier, I,

   Older in practice, Abler then your selfe

   To make Conditions.

BRUTUS Go too: you are not Cassius.

CASSIUS I am.

BRUTUS I say, you are not.

CASSIUS

   Vrge me no more, I shall forget my selfe:

   Haue minde vpon your health: Tempt me no farther.

BRUTUS Away slight man.

CASSIUS Is't possible?   1830

BRUTUS Heare me, for I will speake.

   Must I giue way, and roome to your rash Choller?

   Shall I be frighted, when a Madman stares?

CASSIUS

   O ye Gods, ye Gods, Must I endure all this?

BRUTUS

   All this? I more: Fret till your proud hart break.

   Go shew your Slaues how Chollericke you are,

   And make your Bondmen tremble. Must I bouge?

   Must I obserue you? Must I stand and crouch

   Vnder your Testie Humour? By the Gods,

   You shall digest the Venom of your Spleene   1840

   Though it do Split you. For, from this day forth,

   Ile vse you for my Mirth, yea for my Laughter

   When you are Waspish.

CASSIUS   Is it come to this?

BRUTUS

   You say, you are a better Souldier:

   Let it appeare so; make your vaunting true,

   And it shall please me well. For mine owne part,

   I shall be glad to learne of Noble men.

CASSIUS

   You wrong me euery way: You wrong me Brutus:

   I saide, an Elder Souldier, not a Better.

   Did I say Better?

BRUTUS   If you did, I care not.   1850

CASSIUS

   When Cæsar liu'd, he durst not thus haue mou'd me.

BRUTUS

   Peace, peace, you durst not so haue tempted him.

CASSIUS I durst not.

BRUTUS No.

CASSIUS What? durst not tempt him?

BRUTUS For your life you durst not.

CASSIUS

   Do not presume too much vpon my Loue,

   I may do that I shall be sorry for.

BRUTUS

You haue done that you should be sorry for.

1860 There is no terror *Cassius* in your threats:
For I am Arm'd so strong in Honesty,
That they passe by me, as the idle winde,
Which I respect not. I did send to you
For certaine summes of Gold, which you deny'd me,
For I can raise no money by vile meanes:
By Heauen, I had rather Coine my Heart,
And drop my blood for Drachmaes, then to wring
From the hard hands of Peazants, their vile trash
By any indirection. I did send

1870 To you for Gold to pay my Legions,
Which you deny'd me: was that done like *Cassius*?
Should I haue answer'd *Caius Cassius* so?
When *Marcus Brutus* growes so Couetous,
To locke such Rascall Counters from his Friends,
Be ready Gods with all your Thunder-bolts,
Dash him to peeces.

CASSIUS   I deny'd you not.

BRUTUS

You did.

CASSIUS   I did not. He was but a Foole
That brought my answer back. *Brutus* hath riu'd my
        hart:
A Friend should beare his Friends infirmities;

1880 But *Brutus* makes mine greater then they are.

BRUTUS

I do not, till you practice them on me.

CASSIUS

You loue me not.

BRUTUS   I do not like your faults.

CASSIUS

A friendly eye could neuer see such faults.

BRUTUS

A Flatterers would not, though they do appeare
As huge as high Olympus.

CASSIUS

Come *Antony*, and yong *Octauius* come,
Reuenge your selues alone on *Cassius*,
For *Cassius* is a-weary of the World:
Hated by one he loues, brau'd by his Brother,

1890 Check'd like a bondman, all his faults obseru'd,
Set in a Note-booke, learn'd, and con'd by roate
To cast into my Teeth. O I could weepe
My Spirit from mine eyes. There is my Dagger,
And heere my naked Breast: Within, a Heart
Deerer then *Pluto*'s Mine, Richer then Gold:
If that thou bee'st a Roman, take it foorth.
I that deny'd thee Gold, will giue my Heart:
Strike as thou did'st at *Cæsar*: For I know,
When thou did'st hate him worst, yᵘ loud'st him better
Then euer thou loud'st *Cassius*.

1900 BRUTUS   Sheath your Dagger:
Be angry when you will, it shall haue scope:
Do what you will, Dishonor, shall be Humour.
O *Cassius*, you are yoaked with a Lambe
That carries Anger, as the Flint beares fire,

Who much inforced, shewes a hastie Sparke,
And straite is cold agen.

CASSIUS   Hath *Cassius* liu'd
To be but Mirth and Laughter to his *Brutus*,
When greefe and blood ill temper'd, vexeth him?

BRUTUS

When I spoke that, I was ill temper'd too.

CASSIUS

Do you confesse so much? Giue me your hand.   1910

BRUTUS

And my heart too.
        ⌜They embrace⌝

CASSIUS   O *Brutus*!

BRUTUS   What's the matter?

CASSIUS

Haue not you loue enough to beare with me,
When that rash humour which my Mother gaue me
Makes me forgetfull.

BRUTUS   Yes *Cassius*, and from henceforth
When you are ouer-earnest with your *Brutus*,
Hee'l thinke your Mother chides, and leaue you so.
        Enter ⌜*Lucillius and*⌝ *a Poet*

POET

Let me go in to see the Generals,
There is some grudge betweene 'em, 'tis not meete
They be alone.

LUCILLIUS   You shall not come to them.

POET

Nothing but death shall stay me.

CASSIUS   How now? What's the matter?   1920

POET

For shame you Generals; what do you meane?
Loue, and be Friends, as two such men should bee,
For I haue seene more yeeres I'me sure then yee.

CASSIUS

Ha, ha, how vildely doth this Cynicke rime?

BRUTUS (*to Poet*)

Get you hence sirra: Sawcy Fellow, hence.

CASSIUS

Beare with him *Brutus*, 'tis his fashion.

BRUTUS

Ile know his humor, when he knowes his time:
What should the Warres do with these Iigging Fooles?
(*To Poet*) Companion, hence.

CASSIUS (*to Poet*)   Away, away be gone.
                            Exit Poet

BRUTUS

Lucillius and *Titinius* bid the Commanders   1930
Prepare to lodge their Companies to night.

CASSIUS

And come your selues, & bring *Messala* with you
Immediately to vs.   *Exeunt Lucillius and Titinius*

BRUTUS   *Lucius*, a bowle of Wine.
                            Exit Lucius

CASSIUS

I did not thinke you could haue bin so angry.

BRUTUS

O *Cassius*, I am sicke of many greefes.

CASSIUS

    Of your Philosophy you make no vse,
    If you giue place to accidentall euils.

BRUTUS

    No man beares sorrow better. *Portia* is dead.

CASSIUS Ha? *Portia*?

1940 BRUTUS She is dead.

CASSIUS

    How scap'd I killing, when I crost you so?
    O insupportable, and touching losse!
    Vpon what sicknesse?

BRUTUS   Impatienc my absence,
    And greefe, that yong *Octauius* with *Mark Antony*
    Haue made themselues so strong: For with her death
    That tydings came. With this she fell distract,
    And (her Attendants absent) swallow'd fire.

CASSIUS

    And dy'd so?

BRUTUS   Euen so.

CASSIUS   O ye immortall Gods!

    Enter Lucius with Wine, and Tapers

BRUTUS

    Speak no more of her: (*To Lucius*) Giue me a bowl of
        wine,

1950   (*To Cassius*) In this I bury all vnkindnesse *Cassius*.

    He drinkes

CASSIUS

    My heart is thirsty for that Noble pledge.
    Fill *Lucius*, till the Wine ore-swell the Cup:
    I cannot drinke too much of *Brutus* loue.

    He drinkes.   ⌈*Exit Lucius*⌉
    Enter Titinius and Messala

BRUTUS

    Come in *Titinius*: Welcome good *Messala*:
    Now sit we close about this Taper heere,
    And call in question our necessities.

CASSIUS (*aside*)

    Portia, art thou gone?

BRUTUS   No more I pray you.

    ⌈*They sit*⌉
    Messala, I haue heere receiued Letters,
    That yong *Octauius*, and *Marke Antony*

1960   Come downe vpon vs with a mighty power,
    Bending their Expedition toward *Philippi*.

MESSALA

    My selfe haue Letters of the selfe-same Tenure.

BRUTUS With what Addition?

MESSALA

    That by proscription, and billes of Outlarie,
    Octauius, *Antony*, and *Lepidus*,
    Haue put to death, an hundred Senators.

BRUTUS

    Therein our Letters do not well agree:
    Mine speake of seuenty Senators, that dy'de
    By their proscriptions, *Cicero* being one.

CASSIUS

    Cicero one?

1970 MESSALA   I *Cicero* is dead,

    And by that order of proscription.
    (*To Brutus*)
    Had you your Letters from your wife, my Lord?

BRUTUS No *Messala*.

MESSALA

    Nor nothing in your Letters writ of her?

BRUTUS

    Nothing *Messala*.

MESSALA   That me thinkes is strange.

BRUTUS

    Why aske you? Heare you ought of her, in yours?

MESSALA No my Lord.

BRUTUS

    Now as you are a Roman tell me true.

MESSALA

    Then like a Roman, beare the truth I tell,
    For certaine she is dead, and by strange manner.   1980

BRUTUS

    Why farewell *Portia*: We must die *Messala*:
    With meditating that she must dye once,
    I haue the patience to endure it now.

MESSALA

    Euen so great men, great losses shold indure.

CASSIUS

    I haue as much of this in Art as you,
    But yet my Nature could not beare it so.

BRUTUS

    Well, to our worke aliue. What do you thinke
    Of marching to *Philippi* presently.

CASSIUS

    I do not thinke it good.

BRUTUS   Your reason?

CASSIUS   This it is:
    'Tis better that the Enemie seeke vs,   1990
    So shall he waste his meanes, weary his Souldiers,
    Doing himselfe offence, whil'st we lying still,
    Are full of rest, defence, and nimblenesse.

BRUTUS

    Good reasons must of force giue place to better:
    The people 'twixt *Philippi*, and this ground
    Do stand but in a forc'd affection:
    For they haue grug'd vs Contribution.
    The Enemy, marching along by them,
    By them shall make a fuller number vp,
    Come on refresht, new added, and encourag'd: 2000
    From which aduantage shall we cut him off.
    If at *Philippi* we do face him there,
    These people at our backe.

CASSIUS   Heare me good Brother.

BRUTUS

    Vnder your pardon. You must note beside,
    That we haue tride the vtmost of our Friends:
    Our Legions are brim full, our cause is ripe,
    The Enemy encreaseth euery day,
    We at the height, are readie to decline.
    There is a Tide in the affayres of men,
    Which taken at the Flood, leades on to Fortune: 2010
    Omitted, all the voyage of their life,

Is bound in Shallowes, and in Miseries.
On such a full Sea are we now a-float,
And we must take the current when it serues,
Or loose our Ventures.

CASSIUS   Then with your will go on:
Wee'l along our selues, and meet them at *Philippi*.

BRUTUS

The deepe of night is crept vpon our talke,
And Nature must obey Necessitie,
Which we will niggard with a little rest:
There is no more to say.

2020   CASSIUS   No more, good night,
Early to morrow will we rise, and hence.

BRUTUS

Lucius

    Enter Lucius
      my Gowne: *Exit Lucius*
        farewell good *Messala*,
Good night *Titinius*: Noble, Noble *Cassius*,
Good night, and good repose.

CASSIUS   O my deere Brother:
This was an ill beginning of the night:
Neuer come such diuision 'tweene our soules:
Let it not *Brutus*.

    Enter Lucius with the Gowne

BRUTUS   Euery thing is well.

CASSIUS

Good night my Lord.

BRUTUS   Good night good Brother.

TITINIUS *and* MESSALA

Good night Lord *Brutus*.

BRUTUS   Farwell euery one.

    Exeunt Cassius, Titinius and Messala

Giue me the Gowne.

    ⌈*He puts on the Gowne*⌉

2030   Where is thy Instrument?

LUCIUS

Heere in the Tent.

BRUTUS   What, thou speak'st drowsily?
Poore knaue I blame thee not, thou art ore-watch'd.
Call *Claudio*, and some other of my men,
Ile haue them sleepe on Cushions in my Tent.

LUCIUS

Varrus, and *Claudio*.

    Enter Varrus and Claudio

VARRUS   Cals my Lord?

BRUTUS

I pray you sirs, lye in my Tent and sleepe,
It may be I shall raise you by and by
On businesse to my Brother *Cassius*.

VARRUS

So please you, we will stand, and watch your
    pleasure.

BRUTUS

2040   I will not haue it so: Lye downe good sirs,
It may be I shall otherwise bethinke me.

    Varrus and Claudio lye downe to sleepe

Looke *Lucius*, heere's the booke I sought for so:
I put it in the pocket of my Gowne.

LUCIUS

I was sure your Lordship did not giue it me.

BRUTUS

Beare with me good Boy, I am much forgetfull.
Canst thou hold vp thy heauie eyes a-while,
And touch thy Instrument a straine or two.

LUCIUS

I my Lord, an't please you.

BRUTUS   It does my Boy:
I trouble thee too much, but thou art willing.

LUCIUS It is my duty Sir.   2050

BRUTUS

I should not vrge thy duty past thy might,
I know yong bloods looke for a time of rest.

LUCIUS I haue slept my Lord already.

BRUTUS

It was well done, and thou shalt sleepe againe:
I will not hold thee long. If I do liue,
I will be good to thee.

    Lucius plays Musicke and sings a Song, and so falls
    asleepe

This is a sleepy Tune: O Murd'rous slumber!
Layest thou thy Leaden Mace vpon my Boy,
That playes thee Musicke? Gentle knaue good night:
I will not do thee so much wrong to wake thee: 2060
If thou do'st nod, thou break'st thy Instrument,
Ile take it from thee, and (good Boy) good night.

    He takes away the Instrument, then opens the booke

Let me see, let me see; is not the Leafe turn'd downe
Where I left reading? Heere it is I thinke.

    Enter the Ghost of Cæsar

How ill this Taper burnes. Ha! Who comes heere?
I thinke it is the weakenesse of mine eyes
That shapes this monstrous Apparition.
It comes vpon me: Art thou any thing?
Art thou some God, some Angell, or some Diuell,
That mak'st my blood cold, and my haire to stare?   2070
Speake to me, what thou art.

GHOST Thy euill Spirit *Brutus*?

BRUTUS Why com'st thou?

GHOST

To tell thee thou shalt see me at *Philippi*.

BRUTUS

Well: then I shall see thee againe?

GHOST   I, at *Philippi*.

BRUTUS

Why I will see thee at *Philippi* then: *Exit Ghost*
Now I haue taken heart, thou vanishest.
Ill Spirit, I would hold more talke with thee.
Boy, *Lucius*, *Varrus*, *Claudio*, Sirs: Awake:
Claudio.

LUCIUS   The strings my Lord, are false.   2080

BRUTUS

He thinkes he still is at his Instrument.
Lucius, awake.

LUCIUS My Lord.

BRUTUS

Did'st thou dreame *Lucius*, that thou so cryedst out?

LUCIUS

My Lord, I do not know that I did cry.

BRUTUS

Yes that thou did'st: Did'st thou see any thing?

LUCIUS Nothing my Lord.

BRUTUS

Sleepe againe *Lucius*: Sirra *Claudio*,

(*To Varrus*)   Fellow,

Thou: Awake.

2090 VARRUS My Lord.

CLAUDIO My Lord.

BRUTUS

Why did you so cry out sirs, in your sleepe?

BOTH

Did we my Lord?

BRUTUS   I: saw you any thing?

VARRUS

No my Lord, I saw nothing.

CLAUDIO   Nor I my Lord.

BRUTUS

Go, and commend me to my Brother *Cassius*:

Bid him set on his Powres betimes before,

And we will follow.

BOTH   It shall be done my Lord.

              Exeunt ⌈Varrus and Claudio at one doore,

                 Brutus and Lucius at another doore⌉

Sc. 13   *Enter Octauius, Antony, and their Army*

(5.1) OCTAUIUS

Now *Antony*, our hopes are answered,

You said the Enemy would not come downe,

2100 But keepe the Hilles and vpper Regions:

It proues not so: their battailes are at hand,

They meane to warne vs at *Philippi* heere:

Answering before we do demand of them.

ANTONY

Tut I am in their bosomes, and I know

Wherefore they do it: They could be content

To visit other places, and come downe

With fearefull brauery: thinking by this face

To fasten in our thoughts that they haue Courage;

But 'tis not so.

              Enter a Messenger

MESSENGER   Prepare you Generals,

2110 The Enemy comes on in gallant shew:

Their bloody signe of Battell is hung out,

And something to be done immediately.

ANTONY

Octauius, leade your Battaile softly on

Vpon the left hand of the euen Field.

OCTAUIUS

Vpon the right hand I, keepe thou the left.

ANTONY

Why do you crosse me in this exigent.

OCTAUIUS

I do not crosse you: but I will do so.

⌈*Drum. Antony and Octauius march with their Army.*⌉

Drum within. Enter, marching, Brutus, Cassius, & their Army, amongst them Titinius, Lucillius, and Messala.

Octauius and Antonys army makes a stand

BRUTUS They stand, and would haue parley.

CASSIUS

Stand fast *Titinius*, we must out and talke.

Brutus and Cassius army makes a stand

OCTAUIUS

Mark Antony, shall we giue signe of Battaile?   2120

ANTONY

No *Cæsar*, we will answer on their Charge.

Make forth, the Generals would haue some words.

OCTAUIUS (*to his Army*)

Stirre not vntill the Signall.

Antony and Octauius meete Brutus and Cassius

BRUTUS

Words before blowes: is it so Countrymen?

OCTAUIUS

Not that we loue words better, as you do.

BRUTUS

Good words are better then bad strokes *Octauius*.

ANTONY

In your bad strokes *Brutus*, you giue good words:

Witnesse the hole you made in *Cæsars* heart,

Crying long liue, Haile *Cæsar*.

CASSIUS   *Antony*,

The posture of your blowes are yet vnknowne;   2130

But for your words, they rob the *Hibla* Bees,

And leaue them Hony-lesse.

ANTONY Not stinglesse too.

BRUTUS O yes, and soundlesse too:

For you haue stolne their buzzing *Antony*,

And very wisely threat before you sting.

ANTONY

Villains: you did not so, when your vile daggers

Hackt one another in the sides of *Cæsar*:

You shew'd your teethe like Apes, and fawn'd like

        Hounds,

And bow'd like Bondmen, kissing *Cæsars* feete;   2140

Whil'st damned *Caska*, like a Curre, behinde

Strooke *Cæsar* on the necke. O you Flatterers.

CASSIUS

Flatterers? Now *Brutus* thanke your selfe,

This tongue had not offended so to day,

If *Cassius* might haue rul'd.

OCTAUIUS

Come, come, the cause. If arguing make vs swet,

The proofe of it will turne to redder drops:

        He drawes

Looke, I draw a Sword against Conspirators,

When thinke you that the Sword goes vp againe?

Neuer till *Cæsars* three and thirtie wounds   2150

Be well aueng'd; or till another *Cæsar*

Haue added slaughter to the Swords of Traitors.

BRUTUS
  Cæsar, thou canst not dye by Traitors hands,
  Vnlesse thou bring'st them with thee.
OCTAUIUS   So I hope:
  I was not borne to dye on *Brutus* Sword.
BRUTUS
  O if thou wer't the Noblest of thy Straine,
  Yong-man, thou could'st not dye more honourable.
CASSIUS
  A peeuish School-boy, worthles of such Honor
  Ioyn'd with a Masker, and a Reueller.
ANTONY
  Old *Cassius* still.
2160 OCTAUIUS   Come *Antony*: away:
  Defiance Traitors, hurle we in your teeth.
  If you dare fight to day, come to the Field;
  If not, when you haue stomackes.
                    Exit Octauius, Antony, and Army
CASSIUS
  Why now blow winde, swell Billow, and swimme
      Barke:
  The Storme is vp, and all is on the hazard.
BRUTUS
  Ho *Lucillius*, hearke, a word with you.
LUCILLIUS   My Lord.
      He stands forth and speakes with Brutus
CASSIUS
  Messala.
MESSALS (*standing forth*) What sayes my Generall?
CASSIUS   *Messala*,
  This is my Birth-day: as this very day
  Was *Cassius* borne. Giue me thy hand *Messala*:
2170 Be thou my witnesse, that against my will
  (As *Pompey* was) am I compell'd to set
  Vpon one Battell all our Liberties.
  You know, that I held *Epicurus* strong,
  And his Opinion: Now I change my minde,
  And partly credit things that do presage.
  Comming from *Sardis*, on our former Ensigns
  Two mighty Eagles fell, and there they pearch'd,
  Gorging and feeding from our Soldiers hands,
  Who to *Philippi* heere consorted vs:
2180 This Morning are they fled away, and gone,
  And in their steeds, do Rauens, Crowes, and Kites
  Fly ore our heads, and downward looke on vs
  As we were sickely prey; their shadowes seeme
  A Canopy most fatall, vnder which
  Our Army lies, ready to giue the Ghost.
MESSALA
  Beleeue not so.
CASSIUS   I but beleeue it partly,
  For I am fresh of spirit, and resolu'd
  To meete all perils, very constantly.
BRUTUS
  Euen so *Lucillius*.
CASSIUS (*ioyning Brutus*) Now most Noble *Brutus*,
2190 The Gods to day stand friendly, that we may
  Louers in peace, leade on our dayes to age.

But since the affayres of men rest still incertaine,
Let's reason with the worst that may befall.
If we do lose this Battaile, then is this
The very last time we shall speake together:
What are you then determined to do?
BRUTUS
  Euen by the rule of that Philosophy,
  By which I did blame *Cato*, for the death
  Which he did giue himselfe, I know not how:
  But I do finde it Cowardly, and vile,   2200
  For feare of what might fall, so to preuent
  The time of life, arming my selfe with patience,
  To stay the prouidence of some high Powers,
  That gouerne vs below.
CASSIUS   Then, if we loose this Battaile,
  You are contented to be led in Triumph
  Thorow the streets of Rome.
BRUTUS No *Cassius*, no:
  Thinke not thou Noble Romane,
  That euer *Brutus* will go bound to Rome,
  He beares too great a minde. But this same day   2210
  Must end that worke, the Ides of March begun.
  And whether we shall meete againe, I know not:
  Therefore our euerlasting farewell take:
  For euer, and for euer, farewell *Cassius*,
  If we do meete againe, why we shall smile;
  If not, why then this parting was well made.
CASSIUS
  For euer, and for euer, farewell *Brutus*:
  If we do meete againe, wee'l smile indeede;
  If not, 'tis true, this parting was well made.
BRUTUS
  Why then leade on. O that a man might know   2220
  The end of this dayes businesse, ere it come:
  But it sufficeth, that the day will end,
  And then the end is knowne. Come ho, away.   *Exeunt*

          Alarum. Enter Brutus and Messala   Sc. 14
BRUTUS   (5.2)
  Ride, ride *Messala*, ride and giue these Billes
  Vnto the Legions, on the other side.
      Lowd Alarum
  Let them set on at once: for I perceiue
  But cold demeanor in *Octauio*'s wing:
  And sodaine push giues them the ouerthrow:
  Ride, ride *Messala*, let them all come downe.
                          Exeunt ⌐seuerally⌐

          Alarums. Enter Cassius ⌐with an Ensigne⌐ and   Sc. 15
          Titinius   (5.3)
CASSIUS
  O looke *Titinius*, looke, the Villaines flye: 2230
  My selfe haue to mine owne turn'd Enemy:
  This Ensigne heere of mine was turning backe,
  I slew the Coward, and did take it from him.
TITINIUS
  O *Cassius*, *Brutus* gaue the word too early,
  Who hauing some aduantage on *Octauius*,

Tooke it too eagerly: his Soldiers fell to spoyle,
Whilst we by *Antony* are all inclos'd.
    Enter Pindarus
PINDARUS
Fly further off my Lord: flye further off,
Mark Antony is in your Tents my Lord:
2240 Flye therefore Noble *Cassius*, flye farre off.
CASSIUS
This Hill is farre enough. Looke, look *Titinius*
Are those my Tents where I perceiue the fire?
TITINIUS
They are, my Lord.
CASSIUS   *Titinius*, if thou louest me,
Mount thou my horse, and hide thy spurres in him,
Till he haue brought thee vp to yonder Troopes
And heere againe, that I may rest assur'd
Whether yond Troopes, are Friend or Enemy.
TITINIUS
I will be heere againe, euen with a thought.   *Exit*
CASSIUS
Go *Pindarus*, get higher on that hill,
2250 My sight was euer thicke: regard *Titinius*,
And tell me what thou not'st about the Field.
                Exit Pindarus
This day I breathed first, Time is come round,
And where I did begin, there shall I end,
My life is run his compasse.
    Enter Pindarus aboue
              Sirra, what newes?
PINDARUS O my Lord.
CASSIUS What newes?
PINDARUS
Titinius is enclosed round about
With Horsemen, that make to him on the Spurre,
Yet he spurres on. Now they are almost on him:
2260 Now *Titinius*. Now some light: O he lights too.
Hee's tane.
    Showt within
And hearke, they shout for ioy.
CASSIUS   Come downe, behold no more:
             Exit Pindarus
O Coward that I am, to liue so long,
To see my best Friend tane before my face.
    Enter Pindarus below
Come hither sirrah: In Parthia did I take thee
    Prisoner,
And then I swore thee, sauing of thy life,
That whatsoeuer I did bid thee do,
Thou should'st attempt it. Come now, keepe thine oath,
Now be a Free-man, and with this good Sword
2270 That ran through *Cæsars* bowels, search this bosome.
Stand not to answer: Heere, take thou the Hilts,
    Pindarus takes the Sword
And when my face is couer'd, as 'tis now,
Guide thou the Sword—
    Pindarus stabs him
           Cæsar, thou art reueng'd,
Euen with the Sword that kill'd thee.   *He dyes*

PINDARUS
So, I am free, yet would not so haue beene
Durst I haue done my will. O *Cassius*,
Farre from this Country *Pindarus* shall run,
Where neuer Roman shall take note of him.   *Exit*
    Enter Titinius, wearing a wreath of Victorie, and
    Messala
MESSALA
It is but change, *Titinius*: for *Octauius*
Is ouerthrowne by Noble *Brutus* power,   2280
As *Cassius* Legions are by *Antony*.
TITINIUS
These tydings will well comfort *Cassius*.
MESSALA
Where did you leaue him.
TITINIUS   All disconsolate,
With *Pindarus* his Bondman, on this Hill.
MESSALA
Is not that he that lyes vpon the ground?
TITINIUS
He lies not like the Liuing. O my heart!
MESSALA
Is not that hee?
TITINIUS   No, this was he *Messala*,
But *Cassius* is no more. O setting Sunne:
As in thy red Rayes thou doest sinke to night;
So in his red blood *Cassius* day is set.   2290
The Sunne of Rome is set. Our day is gone,
Clowds, Dewes, and Dangers come; our deeds are done:
Mistrust of my successe hath done this deed.
MESSALA
Mistrust of good successe hath done this deed.
O hatefull Error, Melancholies Childe:
Why do'st thou shew to the apt thoughts of men
The things that are not? O Error soone conceyu'd,
Thou neuer com'st vnto a happy byrth,
But kil'st the Mother that engendred thee.
TITINIUS
What *Pindarus*? Where art thou *Pindarus*?   2300
MESSALA
Seeke him *Titinius*, whilst I go to meet
The Noble *Brutus*, thrusting this report
Into his eares; I may say thrusting it:
For piercing Steele, and Darts inuenomed,
Shall be as welcome to the eares of *Brutus*,
As tydings of this sight.
TITINIUS   Hye you *Messala*,
And I will seeke for *Pindarus* the while: *Exit Messala*
Why did'st thou send me forth braue *Cassius*?
Did I not meet thy Friends, and did not they
Put on my Browes this wreath of Victorie,   2310
And bid me giue it thee? Did'st thou not heare their
    showts?
Alas, thou hast misconstrued euery thing.
But hold thee, take this Garland on thy Brow,
Thy *Brutus* bid me giue it thee, and I
Will do his bidding. *Brutus*, come apace,
And see how I regarded *Caius Cassius*:

By your leaue Gods: This is a Romans part,
Come *Cassius* Sword, and finde *Titinius* hart.
　　　　He stabs himselfe, and dies.
　　　　Alarum. Enter Brutus, Messala, yong Cato, Strato,
　　　　Volumnius, Lucillius, ⌈Labio, and Flauio⌉
BRUTUS
Where, where *Messala*, doth his body lye?
MESSALA
2320　Loe yonder, and *Titinius* mourning it.
BRUTUS
Titinius face is vpward.
CATO　　　　　　　　　　　He is slaine.
BRUTUS
O *Iulius Cæsar*, thou art mighty yet,
Thy Spirit walkes abroad, and turnes our Swords
In our owne proper Entrailes.
　　　　Low Alarums
CATO　　　　　　　　　　　Braue *Titinius*,
Looke where he haue not crown'd dead *Cassius*.
BRUTUS
Are yet two Romans liuing such as these?
The last of all the Romans, far thee well:
It is impossible, that euer Rome
Should breed thy fellow. Friends I owe mo teares
2330　To this dead man, then you shall see me pay.
I shall finde time, *Cassius*: I shall finde time.
Come therefore, and to *Thasos* send his body,
His Funerals shall not be in our Campe,
Least it discomfort vs. *Lucillius* come,
And come yong *Cato*, let vs to the Field,
Labio and *Flauio* set our Battailes on:
'Tis three a clocke, and Romans yet ere night,
We shall try Fortune in a second fight.
　　　　　　　　Exeunt ⌈with the bodies⌉

Sc. 16　　　　　*Alarum. Enter Brutus, Messala, yong Cato,*
(5.4)　　　　　*Lucillius, and Flauius*
　BRUTUS
　Yet Country-men: O yet, hold vp your heads.
　　　　　　⌈*Exit with Messala and Flauius*⌉
CATO
2340　What Bastard doth not? Who will go with me?
I will proclaime my name about the Field.
I am the Sonne of *Marcus Cato*, hoe.
A Foe to Tyrants, and my Countries Friend.
I am the Sonne of *Marcus Cato*, hoe.
　　　　Enter Souldiers, and fight
⌈LUCILLIUS⌉
And I am *Brutus*, *Marcus Brutus*, I,
Brutus my Countries Friend: Know me for *Brutus*.
　　　　Souldiers kill Cato
O yong and Noble *Cato*, art thou downe?
Why now thou dyest, as brauely as *Titinius*,
And may'st be honour'd, being *Cato's* Sonne.
⌈1.⌉ SOULDIER
Yeeld, or thou dyest.
2350　LUCILLIUS　　　　　　Onely I yeeld to dye:
There is so much, that thou wilt kill me straight:
Kill *Brutus*, and be honour'd in his death.

⌈1.⌉ SOULDIER
We must not: a Noble Prisoner.
2. SOULDIER
Roome hoe: tell *Antony*, *Brutus* is tane.
　　　　Enter Antony
1. SOULDIER
Ile tell the newes. Heere comes the Generall,
(*To Antony*) *Brutus* is tane, *Brutus* is tane my Lord.
ANTONY Where is hee?
LUCILLIUS
Safe *Antony*, *Brutus* is safe enough:
I dare assure thee, that no Enemy
Shall euer take aliue the Noble *Brutus*:　　　　2360
The Gods defend him from so great a shame,
When you do finde him, or aliue, or dead,
He will be found like *Brutus*, like himselfe.
ANTONY (*to 1. Souldier*)
This is not *Brutus* friend, but I assure you,
A prize no lesse in worth; keepe this man safe,
Giue him all kindnesse. I had rather haue
Such men my Friends, then Enemies.
⌈*To another Souldier*⌉　　　　　　　Go on,
And see where *Brutus* be aliue or dead,
And bring vs word, vnto *Octauius* Tent:
How euery thing is chanc'd.　　　　　　2370
　　　　　Exeunt ⌈the Souldier at one doore, Antony,
　　　　　Lucillius and other Souldiers, some bearing
　　　　　Catos body, at another doore⌉

　　　　Enter Brutus, Dardanius, Clitus, Strato, and　　Sc. 17
　　　　Volumnius　　　　　　　　　　　　　　　　(5.5)
BRUTUS
Come poore remaines of friends, rest on this Rocke.
　　⌈*He sits. Strato rests and falles asleepe*⌉
CLITUS
Statillius shew'd the Torch-light, but my Lord
He came not backe: he is or tane, or slaine.
BRUTUS
Sit thee downe, *Clitus*: slaying is the word,
It is a deed in fashion. Hearke thee, *Clitus*.
　　　　He whispers
CLITUS
What I, my Lord? No, not for all the World.
BRUTUS
Peace then, no words.
CLITUS　　　　　　　　Ile rather kill my selfe.
　　　　He stands apart
BRUTUS
Hearke thee, *Dardanius*.
　　　　He whispers
DARDANIUS　　　　　　Shall I doe such a deed?
　　　　He ioynes Clitus
CLITUS O *Dardanius*.
DARDANIUS O *Clitus*.　　　　　　　　　　　　2380
CLITUS
What ill request did *Brutus* make to thee?
DARDANIUS
To kill him, *Clitus*: looke he meditates.

CLITUS

Now is that Noble Vessell full of griefe,
That it runnes ouer euen at his eyes.

BRUTUS

Come hither, good *Volumnius*, list a word.

VOLUMNIUS

What sayes my Lord?

BRUTUS   Why this, *Volumnius*:
The Ghost of *Cæsar* hath appear'd to me
Two seuerall times by Night: at Sardis, once;
And this last Night, here in Philippi fields:
I know my houre is come.

2390 VOLUMNIUS   Not so, my Lord.

BRUTUS

Nay, I am sure it is, *Volumnius*.
Thou seest the World, *Volumnius*, how it goes,
Our Enemies haue beat vs to the Pit:
    Low Alarums
It is more worthy, to leape in our selues,
Then tarry till they push vs. Good *Volumnius*,
Thou know'st, that we two went to Schoole together:
Euen for that our loue of old, I prethee
Hold thou my Sword Hilts, whilest I runne on it.

VOLUMNIUS

That's not an Office for a friend, my Lord.
    Alarum still

CLITUS

2400 Fly, flye my Lord, there is no tarrying heere.

BRUTUS

Farewell to you, and you, and you *Volumnius*.
Strato, thou hast bin all this while asleepe:
    ⌜*Strato wakes*⌝
Farewell to thee to, *Strato*. Countrymen:
My heart doth ioy, that yet in all my life,
I found no man, but he was true to me.
I shall haue glory by this loosing day
More then *Octauius*, and *Marke Antony*,
By this vile Conquest shall attaine vnto.
So fare you well at once, for *Brutus* tongue
2410 Hath almost ended his liues History:
Night hangs vpon mine eyes, my Bones would rest,
That haue but labour'd, to attaine this houre.
    Alarum. Cry within, Flye, flye, flye

CLITUS

Fly my Lord, flye.

BRUTUS   Hence: I will follow:
    Exeunt Clitus, Dardanius, and Volumnius
I prythee *Strato*, stay thou by thy Lord,
Thou art a Fellow of a good respect:
Thy life hath had some smatch of Honor in it,
Hold then my Sword, and turne away thy face,
While I do run vpon it. Wilt thou *Strato*?

STRATO

Giue me your hand first. Fare you wel my Lord.

BRUTUS

Farewell good *Strato*.—
    Strato holds the Sword, while Brutus runs on it
                    Cæsar, now be still,   2420
I kill'd not thee with halfe so good a will.   *He dyes*
    Alarum. Retreat. Enter Antony, Octauius, Messala,
    Lucillius, and the Army

OCTAUIUS What man is that?

MESSALA

My Masters man. *Strato*, where is thy Master?

STRATO

Free from the Bondage you are in *Messala*,
The Conquerors can but make a fire of him:
For *Brutus* onely ouercame himselfe,
And no man else hath Honor by his death.

LUCILLIUS

So *Brutus* should be found. I thank thee *Brutus*
That thou hast prou'd *Lucillius* saying true.

OCTAUIUS

All that seru'd *Brutus*, I will entertaine them.   2430
(*To Strato*)
Fellow, wilt thou bestow thy time with me?

STRATO

I, if *Messala* will preferre me to you.

OCTAUIUS

Do so, good *Messala*.

MESSALA   How dyed my Master *Strato*?

STRATO

I held the Sword, and he did run on it.

MESSALA

Octauius, then take him to follow thee,
That did the latest seruice to my Master.

ANTONY

This was the Noblest Roman of them all:
All the Conspirators saue onely hee,
Did that they did, in enuy of great *Cæsar*:
He, onely in a generall honest thought,   2440
And common good to all, made one of them.
His life was gentle, and the Elements
So mixt in him, that Nature might stand vp,
And say to all the world; This was a man.

OCTAUIUS

According to his Vertue, let vs vse him
With all Respect, and Rites of Buriall.
Within my Tent his bones to night shall ly,
Most like a Souldier ordred Honourably:
So call the Field to rest, and let's away,
To part the glories of this happy day.   2450
    Exeunt omnes, ⌜some bearing Brutus body⌝

FINIS

AS YOU LIKE IT

As you Like it is first heard of in the Stationers' Register on 4 August 1600, and was probably written not long before. In spite of its early entry for publication, it was not printed until 1623. This play, with its contrasts between court and country, its bucolic as well as its aristocratic characters, its inset songs and poems, its predominantly woodland setting, its conscious artifice and its romantic ending, is the one in which Shakespeare makes most use of the conventions of pastoral literature, though he does not wholly endorse them.

The story of the love between a high-born maiden—Rosalind—oppressed by the uncle—Duke Frederick—who has usurped his elder brother's dukedom, and Orlando, the third and youngest son of Duke Frederick's old enemy Sir Rowland de Boys, himself oppressed by his tyrannical eldest brother Oliuer, derives from Thomas Lodge's *Rosalynde*, a prose romance interspersed with verses, which first appeared in 1590 and was several times reprinted. There are many indications that Shakespeare thought of the action as taking place in the Ardenne area of France, as in *Rosalynde*, even though there was also a Forest of Arden in Warwickshire. Like Lodge, Shakespeare counterpoints the developing love between Rosalind—who for much of the action is disguised as a boy, Ganimed—with the idealized pastoral romance of Siluius and Phebe; he adds the down-to-earth, unromantic affair between the jester Touchstone and Audrey. Once Rosalind and her cousin Celia (also disguised) reach the forest, plot is virtually suspended in favour of a series of scintillating conversations making much use of prose. The sudden flowering of love between Celia and Orlando's brother Oliuer, newly converted to virtue, is based on *Rosalynde*, but Shakespeare alters the climax of the story, bringing Hymen, the god of marriage, on stage to resolve all complications. As well as Touchstone, Shakespeare added the melancholy courtier Iaques, both of whom act as commentators, though from very different standpoints.

The first performances of Shakespeare's text after his own time were given in 1740. It rapidly established itself in the theatrical repertoire, and has also been appreciated for its literary qualities. It has usually been played in picturesque settings, often since the late nineteenth century in the open air. Rosalind (written originally, of course, for a boy actor) is the dominant character, but other roles, especially Iaques, Touchstone, Audrey, Corin, and—in his single scene—William, have proved particularly effective when played by performers with a strong sense of their latent individuality.

Our text is based on the first surviving edition in the Folio of 1623, apparently printed from a scribal transcript.

THE NAMES OF THE ACTORS

DUKE SENIOR, liuing in banishment

ROSALIND, his daughter, later disguis'd as Ganimed

AMYENS
IAQUES } Lords attending on him

Two PAGES

DUKE FREDERICK, the Dukes brother and vsurper

CELIA, his daughter, later disguis'd as Aliena

LE BEU, a courtier attending on him

CHARLES, Duke Fredericks wrastler

CLOWNE, *alias* Touchstone

OLIUER, eldest sonne of Sir Rowland de Boys

IAQUES
ORLANDO } his yonger brothers

ADAM, a former seruant of Sir Rowland

DENNIS, Oliuers seruant

SIR OLIUER MAR-TEXT, a country Vicar

CORIN, an old shepheard

SILUIUS, a yong shepheard, in loue with Phebe

PHEBE, a shepheardesse

WILLIAM, a countryman, in loue with Audrey

AUDREY, a goatherd, betrothed to Touchstone

HYMEN, God of marriage

Lords, Pages, and other Attendants

As you Like it

Enter Orlando and Adam

ORLANDO As I remember *Adam*, it was vpon this fashion bequeathed me by will, but poore a thousand Crownes, and as thou saist, charged my brother on his blessing to breed mee well: and there begins my sadnesse: My brother *Iaques* he keepes at schoole, and report speakes goldenly of his profit: for my part, he keepes me rustically at home, or (to speak more properly) staies me heere at home vnkept: for call you that keeping for a gentleman of my birth, that differs not from the
10 stalling of an Oxe? his horses are bred better, for besides that they are faire with their feeding, they are taught their mannage, and to that end Riders deerely hir'd: but I (his brother) gaine nothing vnder him but growth, for the which his Animals on his dunghils are as much bound to him as I: besides this nothing that he so plentifully giues me, the something that nature gaue mee, his countenance seemes to take from me: hee lets mee feede with his Hindes, barres mee the place of a brother, and as much as in him lies, mines my gentility
20 with my education. This is it *Adam* that grieues me, and the spirit of my Father, which I thinke is within mee, begins to mutinie against this seruitude. I will no longer endure it, though yet I know no wise remedy how to auoid it.

Enter Oliuer

ADAM Yonder comes my Master, your brother.

ORLANDO Goe a-part *Adam*, and thou shalt heare how he will shake me vp.

Adam stands aside

OLIUER Now Sir, what make you heere?

ORLANDO Nothing: I am not taught to make any thing.

30 OLIUER What mar you then sir?

ORLANDO Marry sir, I am helping you to mar that which God made, a poore vnworthy brother of yours with idlenesse.

OLIUER Marry sir be better employed, and be naught a while.

ORLANDO Shall I keepe your hogs, and eat huskes with them? what prodigall portion haue I spent, that I should come to such penury?

OLIUER Know you where you are sir?

40 ORLANDO O sir, very well: heere in your Orchard.

OLIUER Know you before whom sir?

ORLANDO I, better then him I am before knowes mee: I know you are my eldest brother, and in the gentle condition of bloud you should so know me: the courtesie of nations allowes you my better, in that you are the first borne, but the same tradition takes not away my bloud, were there twenty brothers betwixt vs: I haue as much of my father in mee, as you, albeit I confesse your comming before me is neerer to his reuerence.

50 OLIUER (*assailing him*) What Boy.

ORLANDO (*seizing him by the throat*) Come, come elder brother, you are too yong in this.

OLIUER Wilt thou lay hands on me villaine?

ORLANDO I am no villaine: I am the yongest sonne of Sir *Rowland de Boys*, he was my father, and he is thrice a villaine that saies such a father begot villaines: wert thou not my brother, I would not take this hand from thy throat, till this other had puld out thy tongue for saying so, thou hast raild on thy selfe.

ADAM (*comming forward*) Sweet Masters bee patient, for 60 your Fathers remembrance, be at accord.

OLIUER (*to Orlando*) Let me goe I say.

ORLANDO I will not till I please: you shall heare mee: my father charg'd you in his will to giue me good education: you haue train'd me like a pezant, obscuring and hiding from me all gentleman-like qualities: the spirit of my father growes strong in mee, and I will no longer endure it: therefore allow me such exercises as may become a gentleman, or giue mee the poore allottery my father left me by testament, with that I 70 will goe buy my fortunes.

OLIUER And what wilt thou do? beg when that is spent? Well sir, get you in. I will not long be troubled with you: you shall haue some part of your will, I pray you leaue me.

ORLANDO I will no further offend you, then becomes mee for my good.

OLIUER (*to Adam*) Get you with him, you olde dogge.

ADAM Is old dogge my reward: most true, I haue lost my teeth in your seruice: God be with my olde master, he 80 would not haue spoke such a word.

Exeunt Orlando, Adam

OLIUER Is it euen so, begin you to grow vpon me? I will physicke your ranckenesse, and yet giue no thousand crownes neyther: holla *Dennis*.

Enter Dennis

DENNIS Calls your worship?

OLIUER Was not *Charles* the Dukes Wrastler heere to speake with me?

DENNIS So please you, he is heere at the doore, and importunes accesse to you.

OLIUER Call him in: *Exit Dennis* 90
'twill be a good way: and to morrow the wrastling is.

Enter Charles

CHARLES Good morrow to your worship.

OLIUER Good Mounsier *Charles*: what's the new newes at the new Court?

CHARLES There's no newes at the Court Sir, but the olde newes: that is, the old Duke is banished by his yonger brother the new Duke, and three or foure louing Lords haue put themselues into voluntary exile with him, whose lands and reuenues enrich the new Duke, therefore he giues them good leaue to wander. 100

OLIUER Can you tell if *Rosalind* the Dukes daughter bee banished with her Father?

CHARLES O no; for the Dukes daughter her Cosen so loues her, being euer from their Cradles bred together, that shee would haue followed her exile, or haue died to stay behind her; she is at the Court, and no lesse beloued of her Vncle, then his owne daughter, and neuer two Ladies loue̍d as they doe.

OLIUER Where will the old Duke liue?

110 CHARLES They say hee is already in the Forrest of *Arden*, and a many merry men with him; and there they liue like the old *Robin Hood* of *England*: they say many yong Gentlemen flocke to him euery day, and fleet the time carelesly as they did in the golden world.

OLIUER What, you wrastle to morrow before the new Duke.

CHARLES Marry doe I sir: and I came to acquaint you with a matter: I am giuen sir secretly to vnderstand, that your yonger brother *Orlando* hath a disposition to

120 come in disguis'd against mee to try a fall: to morrow sir I wrastle for my credit, and hee that escapes me without some broken limbe, shall acquit him well: your brother is but young and tender, and for your loue I would bee loth to foyle him, as I must for my owne honour if hee come in: therefore out of my loue to you, I came hither to acquaint you withall, that either you might stay him from his intendment, or brooke such disgrace well as he shall runne into, in that it is a thing of his owne search, and altogether against my

130 will.

OLIUER *Charles*, I thanke thee for thy loue to me, which thou shalt finde I will most kindly requite: I had my selfe notice of my Brothers purpose heerein, and haue by vnder-hand meanes laboured to disswade him from it; but he is resolute. Ile tell thee *Charles*, it is the stubbornest yong fellow of France, full of ambition, an enuious emulator of euery mans good parts, a secret & villanous contriuer against mee his naturall brother: therefore vse thy discretion, I had as liefe thou didst

140 breake his necke as his finger. And thou wert best looke to't; for if thou dost him any slight disgrace, or if hee doe not mightilie grace himselfe on thee, hee will practise against thee by poyson, entrap thee by some treacherous deuise, and neuer leaue thee till he hath tane thy life by some indirect meanes or other: for I assure thee, (and almost with teares I speake it) there is not one so young, and so villanous this day liuing. I speake but brotherly of him, but should I anathomize him to thee, as hee is, I must blush, and weepe, and

150 thou must looke pale and wonder.

CHARLES I am heartily glad I came hither to you: if hee come to morrow, Ile giue him his payment: if euer hee goe alone againe, Ile neuer wrastle for prize more: and so God keepe your worship.

OLIUER Farewell good *Charles*.   *Exit Charles*
Now will I stirre this Gamester: I hope I shall see an end of him; for my soule (yet I know not why) hates nothing more then he: yet hee's gentle, neuer school'd,

and yet learned, full of noble deuise, of all sorts enchantingly beloued, and indeed so much in the heart 160 of the world, and especially of my owne people, who best know him, that I am altogether misprised: but it shall not be so long, this wrastler shall cleare all: nothing remaines, but that I kindle the boy thither, which now Ile goe about.   *Exit*

Enter Rosalind, and Cellia   Sc. 2
                                                          (1.2)
CELIA I pray thee *Rosalind*, sweet my Coz, be merry.

ROSALIND Deere *Cellia*; I show more mirth then I am mistresse of, and would you yet I were merrier: vnlesse you could teach me to forget a banished father, you must not learne mee how to remember any 170 extraordinary pleasure.

CELIA Heerein I see thou lou'st mee not with the full waight that I loue thee; if my Vncle thy banished father had banished thy Vncle the Duke my Father, so thou hadst beene still with mee, I could haue taught my loue to take thy father for mine; so wouldst thou, if the truth of thy loue to me were so righteously temper'd, as mine is to thee.

ROSALIND Well, I will forget the condition of my estate, to reioyce in yours.   180

CELIA You know my Father hath no childe, but I, nor none is like to haue; and truely when he dies, thou shalt be his heire; for what hee hath taken away from thy father perforce, I will render thee againe in affection: by mine honor I will, and when I breake that oath, let mee turne monster: therefore my sweet *Rose*, my deare *Rose*, be merry.

ROSALIND From henceforth I will Coz, and deuise sports: let me see, what thinke you of falling in Loue?

CELIA Marry I prethee doe, to make sport withall: but 190 loue no man in good earnest, nor no further in sport neyther, then with safety of a pure blush, thou maist in honor come off againe.

ROSALIND What shall be our sport then?

CELIA Let vs sit and mocke the good houswife *Fortune* from her wheele, that her gifts may henceforth bee bestowed equally.

ROSALIND I would wee could doe so: for her benefits are mightily misplaced, and the bountifull blinde woman doth most mistake in her gifts to women.   200

CELIA 'Tis true, for those that she makes faire, she scarce makes honest, & those that she makes honest, she makes very illfauouredly.

ROSALIND Nay now thou goest from Fortunes office to Natures: Fortune reignes in gifts of the world, not in the lineaments of Nature.

Enter Touchstone the Clowne

CELIA No; when Nature hath made a faire creature, may she not by Fortune fall into the fire? though nature hath giuen us wit to flout at Fortune, hath not Fortune sent in this foole to cut off the argument?   210

ROSALIND Indeed there is fortune too hard for nature, when fortune makes natures naturall, the cutter off of natures witte.

CELIA Peraduenture this is not Fortunes work neither, but Natures, who perceiueth our naturall wits too dull to reason of such goddesses, and hath sent this Naturall for our whetstone: for alwaies the dulnesse of the foole, is the whetstone of the wits. How now Witte, whether wander you?

220 CLOWNE Mistresse, you must come away to your father.

CELIA Were you made the messenger?

CLOWNE No by mine honor, but I was bid to come for you.

ROSALIND Where learned you that oath foole?

CLOWNE Of a certaine Knight, that swore by his Honour they were good Pan-cakes, and swore by his Honor the Mustard was naught: Now Ile stand to it, the Pancakes were naught, and the Mustard was good, and yet was not the Knight forsworne.

230 CELIA How proue you that in the great heape of your knowledge?

ROSALIND I marry, now vnmuzzle your wisedome.

CLOWNE Stand you both forth now: stroke your chinnes, and sweare by your beards that I am a knaue.

CELIA By our beards (if we had them) thou art.

CLOWNE By my knauerie (if I had it) then I were: but if you sweare by that that is not, you are not forsworn: no more was this knight swearing by his Honor, for he neuer had anie; or if he had, he had sworne it away, before euer he saw those Pancakes, or that Mustard.

CELIA Prethee, who is't that thou means't?

CLOWNE One that old *Fredericke* your Father loues.

⌈CELIA⌉ My Fathers loue is enough to honor him. Enough, speake no more of him, you'l be whipt for taxation one of these daies.

CLOWNE The more pittie that fooles may not speak wisely, what Wisemen do foolishly.

CELIA By my troth thou saiest true: For, since the little
250 wit that fooles haue was silenced, the little foolerie that wise men haue makes a great shew; Heere comes Monsieur *le Beu*.

Enter le Beau

ROSALIND With his mouth full of newes.

CELIA Which he will put on vs, as Pigeons feed their young.

ROSALIND Then shal we be newes-cram'd.

CELIA All the better: we shalbe the more Marketable. *Boon-iour Monsieur le Beu*, what's the newes?

LE BEU Faire Princesse, you haue lost much good sport.

260 CELIA Sport: of what colour?

LE BEU What colour Madame? How shall I aunswer you?

ROSALIND As wit and fortune will.

CLOWNE Or as the destinies decrees.

CELIA Well said, that was laid on with a trowell.

CLOWNE Nay, if I keepe not my ranke.

ROSALIND Thou loosest thy old smell.

LE BEU You amaze me Ladies: I would haue told you of good wrastling, which you haue lost the sight of.

ROSALIND Yet tell vs the manner of the Wrastling.

LE BEU I wil tell you the beginning: and if it please your 270 Ladiships, you may see the end, for the best is yet to doe, and heere where you are, they are comming to performe it.

CELIA Well, the beginning that is dead and buried.

LE BEU There comes an old man, and his three sons.

CELIA I could match this beginning with an old tale.

LE BEU Three proper yong men, of excellent growth and presence.

ROSALIND With bils on their neckes: Be it knowne vnto all men by these presents. 280

LE BEU The eldest of the three, wrastled with *Charles* the Dukes Wrastler, which *Charles* in a moment threw him, and broke three of his ribbes, that there is little hope of life in him: So he seru'd the second, and so the third: yonder they lie, the poore old man their Father, making such pittiful dole ouer them, that all the beholders take his part with weeping.

ROSALIND Alas.

CLOWNE But what is the sport Monsieur, that the Ladies haue lost? 290

LE BEU Why this that I speake of.

CLOWNE Thus men may grow wiser euery day. It is the first time that euer I heard breaking of ribbes was sport for Ladies.

CELIA Or I, I promise thee.

ROSALIND But is there any else longs to see this broken Musicke in his sides? Is there yet another doates vpon rib-breaking? Shall we see this wrastling Cosin?

LE BEU You must if you stay heere, for heere is the place appointed for the wrastling, and they are ready to 300 performe it.

CELIA Yonder sure they are comming. Let vs now stay and see it.

Flourish. Enter Duke Frederick, Lords, Orlando,
Charles, and Attendants

DUKE FREDERICK Come on, since the youth will not be intreated his owne perill on his forwardnesse.

ROSALIND Is yonder the man?

LE BEU Euen he, Madam.

CELIA Alas, he is too yong: yet he looks successefully.

DUKE FREDERICK How now daughter, and Cousin: Are you crept hither to see the wrastling? 310

ROSALIND I my Liege, so please you giue vs leaue.

DUKE FREDERICK You wil take little delight in it, I can tell you there is such oddes in the man: In pitie of the challengers youth, I would faine disswade him, but he will not bee entreated. Speake to him Ladies, see if you can mooue him.

CELIA Call him hether good Monsieuer *Le Beu*.

DUKE FREDERICK Do so: Ile not be by.

He stands aside

LE BEU (*to Orlando*) Monsieur the Challenger, the Princesse cals for you. 320

ORLANDO I attend them with all respect and dutie.

ROSALIND Young man, haue you challeng'd *Charles* the Wrastler?

ORLANDO No faire Princesse: he is the generall challenger,
I come but in as others do, to try with him the strength
of my youth.

CELIA Yong Gentleman, your spirits are too bold for your
yeares: you haue seene cruell proofe of this mans
strength, if you saw your selfe with your eies, or knew
330 your selfe with your iudgment, the feare of your
aduenture would counsel you to a more equall
enterprise. We pray you for your owne sake to embrace
your own safetie, and giue ouer this attempt.

ROSALIND Do yong Sir, your reputation shall not therefore
be misprised: we wil make it our suite to the Duke,
that the wrastling might not go forward.

ORLANDO I beseech you, punish mee not with your harde
thoughts, wherein I confesse me much guiltie to denie
so faire and excellent Ladies anie thing. But let your
340 faire eies, and gentle wishes go with mee to my triall;
wherein if I bee foil'd, there is but one sham'd that
was neuer gracious: if kil'd, but one dead that is willing
to be so: I shall do my friends no wrong, for I haue
none to lament me: the world no iniurie, for in it I
haue nothing: onely in the world I fil vp a place, which
may bee better supplied, when I haue made it emptie.

ROSALIND The little strength that I haue, I would it were
with you.

CELIA And mine to eeke out hers.

350 ROSALIND Fare you well: praie heauen I be deceiu'd in
you.

CELIA Your hearts desires be with you.

CHARLES Come, where is this yong gallant, that is so
desirous to lie with his mother earth?

ORLANDO Readie Sir, but his will hath in it a more modest
working.

DUKE FREDERICK You shall trie but one fall.

CHARLES No, I warrant your Grace you shall not entreat
him to a second, that haue so mightilie perswaded him
360 from a first.

ORLANDO You meane to mocke me after: you should not
haue mockt me before: but come your waies.

ROSALIND (to Orlando) Now Hercules, be thy speede yong
man.

CELIA I would I were inuisible, to catch the strong fellow
by the legge.
Charles and Orlando wrastle

ROSALIND Oh excellent yong man.

CELIA If I had a thunderbolt in mine eie, I can tell who
should downe.
Orlando throws Charles. Shout

DUKE FREDERICK
No more, no more.

370 ORLANDO   Yes I beseech your Grace,
I am not yet well breath'd.

DUKE FREDERICK How do'st thou *Charles*?

LE BEU He cannot speake my Lord.

DUKE FREDERICK Beare him awaie:
Attendants carry Charles off
What is thy name yong man?

ORLANDO *Orlando* my Liege, the yongest sonne of Sir
Roland de Boys.

DUKE FREDERICK
I would thou hadst beene son to some man else,
The world esteem'd thy father honourable,
But I did finde him still mine enemie: 380
Thou should'st haue better pleas'd me with this
deede,
Hadst thou descended from another house:
But fare thee well, thou art a gallant youth,
I would thou had'st told me of another Father.
*Exeunt Duke Frederick, Le Beau, ⌈Touchstone,⌉
Lords, and Attendants*

CELIA (*to Rosalind*)
Were I my Father (Coze) would I do this?

ORLANDO
I am more proud to be Sir *Rolands* sonne,
His yongest sonne, and would not change that calling
To be adopted heire to *Fredricke*.

ROSALIND
My Father lou'd Sir *Roland* as his soule,
And all the world was of my Fathers minde,   390
Had I before knowne this yong man his sonne,
I should haue giuen him teares vnto entreaties,
Ere he should thus haue ventur'd.

CELIA   Gentle Cosen,
Let vs goe thanke him, and encourage him:
My Fathers rough and enuious disposition
Sticks me at heart: Sir, you haue well deseru'd,
If you doe keepe your promises in loue
But iustly as you haue exceeded all promise,
Your Mistris shall be happie.

ROSALIND (*giuing him a chain from her neck*) Gentleman,
Weare this for me: one out of suites with fortune   400
That could giue more, but that her hand lacks
meanes.
Shall we goe Coze?

CELIA   I: fare you well faire Gentleman.
Rosalind and Celia turn to go

ORLANDO (*aside*)
Can I not say, I thanke you? My better parts
Are all throwne downe, and that which here stands
vp
Is but a quintine, a meere liuelesse blocke.

ROSALIND (*to Celia*)
He cals vs back: my pride fell with my fortunes,
Ile aske him what he would: Did you call Sir?
Sir, you haue wrastled well, and ouerthrowne
More then your enemies.

CELIA Will you goe Coze?   410

ROSALIND Haue with you: (*to Orlando*) fare you well.
Exeunt Rosalind and Celia

ORLANDO
What passion hangs these waights vpõ my toong?
I cannot speake to her, yet she vrg'd conference.
Enter Le Beu
O poore *Orlando*! thou art ouerthrowne.
Or Charles, or something weaker masters thee.

LE BEU
Good Sir, I do in friendship counsaile you

To leaue this place; Albeit you haue deseru'd
High commendation, true applause, and loue;
420 Yet such is now the Dukes condition,
That he misconsters all that you haue done:
The Duke is humorous, what he is indeede
More suites you to conceiue, then I to speake of.
ORLANDO
I thanke you Sir; and pray you tell me this,
Which of the two was daughter of the Duke,
That here was at the Wrastling?
LE BEU
Neither his daughter, if we iudge by manners,
But yet indeede the shorter is his daughter,
The other is daughter to the banish'd Duke,
And here detain'd by her vsurping Vncle
430 To keepe his daughter companie, whose loues
Are deerer then the naturall bond of Sisters:
But I can tell you, that of late this Duke
Hath tane displeasure 'gainst his gentle Neece,
Grounded vpon no other argument,
But that the people praise her for her vertues,
And pittie her, for her good Fathers sake;
And on my life his malice 'gainst the Lady
Will sodainly breake forth: Sir, fare you well,
Hereafter in a better world then this,
440 I shall desire more loue and knowledge of you.
ORLANDO
I rest much bounden to you: fare you well.

Exit Le Beau

Thus must I from the smoake into the smother,
From tyrant Duke, vnto a tyrant Brother.
But heauenly *Rosalind*.   *Exit*

Sc. 3   *Enter Celia and Rosalind*
(1.3) CELIA Why Cosen, why *Rosalind*: *Cupid* haue mercie, not
a word?
ROSALIND Not one to throw at a dog.
CELIA No, thy words are too precious to be cast away
vpon curs, throw some of them at me; come lame mee
450 with reasons.
ROSALIND Then there were two Cosens laid vp, when the
one should be lam'd with reasons, and the other mad
without any.
CELIA But is all this for your Father?
ROSALIND No, some of it is for my childes Father: Oh how
full of briers is this working day world.
CELIA They are but burs, Cosen, throwne vpon thee in
holiday foolerie, if we walke not in the trodden paths
our very petty-coates will catch them.
460 ROSALIND I could shake them off my coate, these burs are
in my heart.
CELIA Hem them away.
ROSALIND I would try if I could cry hem, and haue him.
CELIA Come, come, wrastle with thy affections.
ROSALIND O they take the part of a better wrastler then
my selfe.
CELIA O, a good wish vpon you: you will trie in time in

dispight of a fall: but turning these iests out of seruice,
let vs talke in good earnest: Is it possible on such a
sodaine, you should fall into so strong a liking with   470
old Sir *Roulands* yongest sonne?
ROSALIND The Duke my Father lou'd his Father deerelie.
CELIA Doth it therefore ensue that you should loue his
Sonne deerelie? By this kinde of chase, I should hate
him, for my father hated his father deerely; yet I hate
not *Orlando*.
ROSALIND No faith, hate him not for my sake.
CELIA Why should I not? doth he not deserue well?
Enter Duke Frederick with Lords
ROSALIND Let me loue him for that, and do you loue him
because I doe. Looke, here comes the Duke.   480
CELIA With his eies full of anger.
DUKE FREDERICK (*to Rosalind*)
Mistris, dispatch you with your safest haste,
And get you from our Court.
ROSALIND Me Vncle.
DUKE FREDERICK You Cosen,
Within these ten daies if that thou beest found
So neere our publike Court as twentie miles,
Thou diest for it.
ROSALIND   I doe beseech your Grace
Let me the knowledge of my fault beare with me:
If with my selfe I hold intelligence,   490
Or haue acquaintance with mine owne desires,
If that I doe not dreame, or be not franticke,
(As I doe trust I am not) then deere Vncle,
Neuer so much as in a thought vnborne,
Did I offend your highnesse.
DUKE FREDERICK   Thus doe all Traitors,
If their purgation did consist in words,
They are as innocent as grace it selfe;
Let it suffice thee that I trust thee not.
ROSALIND
Yet your mistrust cannot make me a Traitor;
Tell me whereon the likelihood depends?   500
DUKE FREDERICK
Thou art thy Fathers daughter, there's enough.
ROSALIND
So was I when your highnes took his Dukdome,
So was I when your highnesse banisht him;
Treason is not inherited my Lord,
Or if we did deriue it from our friends,
What's that to me, my Father was no Traitor,
Then good my Leige, mistake me not so much,
To thinke my pouertie is treacherous.
CELIA Deere Soueraigne heare me speake.
DUKE FREDERICK
I *Celia*, we staid her for your sake,   510
Else had she with her Father rang'd along.
CELIA
I did not then intreat to haue her stay,
It was your pleasure, and your owne remorse,
I was too yong that time to value her,
But now I know her: if she be a Traitor,

Why so am I: we still haue slept together,
Rose at an instant, learn'd, plaid, eate together,
And wheresoere we went, like *Iunos* Swans,
Still we went coupled and inseperable.

DUKE FREDERICK

520 She is too subtile for thee, and her smoothnes;
Her verie silence, and her patience,
Speake to the people, and they pittie her:
Thou art a foole, she robs thee of thy name,
And thou wilt show more bright, & seem more
                              vertuous
When she is gone: then open not thy lips.
Firme, and irreuocable is my doombe,
Which I haue past vpon her, she is banish'd.

CELIA

Pronounce that sentence then on me my Leige,
I cannot liue out of her companie.

DUKE FREDERICK

530 You are a foole: you Neice prouide your selfe,
If you out-stay the time, vpon mine honor,
And in the greatnesse of my word you die.
                    Exit Duke Frederick, with Lords

CELIA

O my poore *Rosalind*, whether wilt thou goe?
Wilt thou change Fathers? I will giue thee mine:
I charge thee be not thou more grieu'd then I am.

ROSALIND

I haue more cause.

CELIA   Thou hast not Cosen,
Prethee be cheerefull; know'st thou not the Duke
Hath banish'd me his daughter?

ROSALIND   That he hath not.

CELIA

No, hath not? *Rosalind*, lacks thou then the loue
540 Which teacheth thee that thou and I am one,
Shall we be sundred? shall we part sweete girle?
No, let my Father seeke another heire:
Therefore deuise with me how we may flie
Whether to goe, and what to beare with vs,
And doe not seeke to take your change vpon you,
To beare your griefes your selfe, and leaue me out:
For by this heauen, now at our sorrowes pale;
Say what thou canst, Ile goe along with thee.

ROSALIND Why, whether shall we goe?

CELIA

550 To seeke my Vncle in the Forrest of *Arden*.

ROSALIND

Alas, what danger will it be to vs,
(Maides as we are) to trauell forth so farre?
Beautie prouoketh theeues sooner then gold.

CELIA

Ile put my selfe in poore and meane attire,
And with a kinde of vmber smirch my face,
The like doe you, so shall we passe along,
And neuer stir assailants.

ROSALIND   Were it not better,
Because that I am more then common tall,

That I did suite me all points like a man,
A gallant curtelax vpon my thigh,   560
A bore-speare in my hand, and in my heart
Lye there what hidden womans feare there will.
Weele haue a swashing and a marshall outside,
As manie other mannish cowards haue,
That doe outface it with their semblances.

CELIA

What shall I call thee when thou art a man?

ROSALIND

Ile haue no worse a name then *Ioues* owne Page,
And therefore looke you call me *Ganimed*.
But what will you be call'd?

CELIA

Something that hath a reference to my state: 570
No longer *Celia*, but *Aliena*.

ROSALIND

But Cosen, what if we assaid to steale
The clownish Foole out of your Fathers Court:
Would he not be a comfort to our trauaile?

CELIA

Heele goe along ore the wide world with me,
Leaue me alone to woe him; Let's away
And get our Iewels and our wealth together,
Deuise the fittest time, and safest way
To hide vs from pursuite that will be made
After my flight: now goe we in content   580
To libertie, and not to banishment.   *Exeunt*

Enter Duke Senior: Amyens, and two or three Lords   Sc. 4
like Forresters   (2.1)

DUKE SENIOR

Now my Coe-mates, and brothers in exile:
Hath not old custome made this life more sweete
Then that of painted pompe? Are not these woods
More free from perill then the enuious Court?
Heere feele we not the penaltie of *Adam*,
The seasons difference, as the Icie phange
And churlish chiding of the winters winde,
Which when it bites and blowes vpon my body
Euen till I shrinke with cold, I smile, and say   590
This is no flattery: these are counsellors
That feelingly perswade me what I am:
Sweet are the vses of aduersitie
Which like the toad, ougly and venemous,
Weares yet a precious Iewell in his head:
And this our life exempt from publike haunt,
Findes tongues in trees, bookes in the running
                              brookes,
Sermons in stones, and good in euery thing.

AMYENS

I would not change it, happy is your Grace
That can translate the stubbornnesse of fortune   600
Into so quiet and so sweet a stile.

DUKE SENIOR

Come, shall we goe and kill vs venison?
And yet it irkes me the poore dapled fooles
Being natiue Burgers of this desert City,

Should in their owne confines with forked heads
Haue their round hanches goard.

1. LORD   Indeed my Lord
The melancholy *Iaques* grieues at that,
And in that kinde sweares you doe more vsurpe
Then doth your brother that hath banish'd you:
610 To day my Lord of *Amiens*, and my selfe,
Did steale behinde him as he lay along
Vnder an oake, whose anticke roote peepes out
Vpon the brooke that brawles along this wood,
To the which place a poore sequestred Stag
That from the Hunters aime had tane a hurt,
Did come to languish; and indeed my Lord
The wretched annimall heau'd forth such groanes
That their discharge did stretch his leatherne coat
Almost to bursting, and the big round teares
620 Cours'd one another downe his innocent nose
In pitteous chase: and thus the hairie foole,
Much marked of the melancholie *Iaques*,
Stood on th'extremest verge of the swift brooke,
Augmenting it with teares.

DUKE SENIOR   But what said *Iaques*?
Did he not moralize this spectacle?

1. LORD
O yes, into a thousand similies.
First, for his weeping into the needlesse streame;
Poore Deere quoth he, thou mak'st a testament
As worldlings doe, giuing thy sum of more
630 To that which had too much: then being there alone,
Left and abandon'd of his veluet friend;
'Tis right quoth he, thus miserie doth part
The Fluxe of companie: anon a carelesse Heard
Full of the pasture, iumps along by him
And neuer staies to greet him: I quoth *Iaques*,
Sweepe on you fat and greazie Citizens,
'Tis iust the fashion; wherefore should you looke
Vpon that poore and broken bankrupt there?
Thus most inuectiuely he pierceth through
640 The body of the Countrie, Citie, Court,
Yea, and of this our life, swearing that we
Are meere vsurpers, tyrants, and whats worse
To fright the Annimals, and to kill them vp
In their assign'd and natiue dwelling place.

DUKE SENIOR
And did you leaue him in this contemplation?

2. LORD
We did my Lord, weeping and commenting
Vpon the sobbing Deere.

DUKE SENIOR   Show me the place,
I loue to cope him in these sullen fits,
For then he's full of matter.

1. LORD   Ile bring you to him strait.
Exeunt

Sc. 5   *Enter Duke Frederick, with Lords*
(2.2) **DUKE FREDERICK**
650   Can it be possible that no man saw them?
It cannot be, some villaines of my Court

Are of consent and sufferance in this.

1. LORD
I cannot heare of any that did see her,
The Ladies her attendants of her chamber
Saw her a bed, and in the morning early,
They found the bed vntreasur'd of their Mistris.

2. LORD
My Lord, the roynish Clown, at whom so oft,
Your Grace was wont to laugh is also missing,
Hisperia the Princesse Gentlewoman
Confesses that she secretly ore-heard   670 *(sic 660)*
Your daughter and her Cosen much commend
The parts and graces of the Wrastler
That did but lately foile the synowie *Charles*,
And she beleeues where euer they are gone
That youth is surely in their companie.

DUKE FREDERICK
Send to his brother, fetch that gallant hither,
If he be absent, bring his Brother to me,
Ile make him finde him: do this sodainly;
And let not search and inquisition quaile,
To bring againe these foolish runawaies.   670

Exeunt seuerally

Enter Orlando and Adam, meeting   Sc. 6
ORLANDO Who's there?   (2.3)
ADAM
What my yong Master, oh my gentle master,
Oh my sweet master, O you memorie
Of old Sir *Rowland*; why, what make you here?
Why are you vertuous? Why do people loue you?
And wherefore are you gentle, strong, and valiant?
Why would you be so fond to ouercome
The bonnie priser of the humorous Duke?
Your praise is come too swiftly home before you.
Know you not Master, to some kinde of men,   680
Their graces serue them but as enemies,
No more doe yours: your vertues gentle Master
Are sanctified and holy traitors to you:
Oh what a world is this, when what is comely
Enuenoms him that beares it?

ORLANDO Why, what's the matter?

ADAM O vnhappie youth,
Come not within these doores: within this roofe
The enemie of all your graces liues,
Your brother, no, no brother, yet the sonne   690
(Yet not the son, I will not call him son)
Of him I was about to call his Father,
Hath heard your praises, and this night he meanes,
To burne the lodging where you vse to lye,
And you within it: if he faile of that
He will haue other meanes to cut you off;
I ouerheard him: and his practises:
This is no place, this house is but a butcherie;
Abhorre it, feare it, doe not enter it.

ORLANDO
Why whether *Adam* would'st thou haue me go?   700

ADAM
No matter whether, so you come not here.

ORLANDO
    What, would'st thou haue me go & beg my food,
    Or with a base and boistrous Sword enforce
    A theeuish liuing on the common rode?
    This I must do, or know not what to do:
    Yet this I will not do, do how I can,
    I rather will subiect me to the malice
    Of a diuerted blood, and bloudie brother.

ADAM
    But do not so: I haue fiue hundred Crownes,
710   The thriftie hire I sau'd vnder your Father,
    Which I did store to be my foster Nurse,
    When seruice should in my old limbs lie lame,
    And vnregarded age in corners throwne,
    Take that, and he that doth the Rauens feede,
    Yea prouidently caters for the Sparrow,
    Be comfort to my age: here is the gold,
    All this I giue you, let me be your seruant,
    Though I looke old, yet I am strong and lustie;
    For in my youth I neuer did apply
720   Hot, and rebellious liquors in my bloud,
    Nor did not with vnbashfull forehead woe,
    The meanes of weaknesse and debilitie,
    Therefore my age is as a lustie winter,
    Frostie, but kindely; let me goe with you,
    Ile doe the seruice of a yonger man
    In all your businesse and necessities.

ORLANDO
    Oh good old man, how well in thee appeares
    The constant seruice of the antique world,
    When seruice sweate for dutie, not for meede:
730   Thou art not for the fashion of these times,
    Where none will sweate, but for promotion,
    And hauing that do choake their seruice vp,
    Euen with the hauing, it is not so with thee:
    But poore old man, thou prun'st a rotten tree,
    That cannot so much as a blossome yeelde,
    In lieu of all thy paines and husbandrie,
    But come thy waies, weele goe along together,
    And ere we haue thy youthfull wages spent,
    Weele light vpon some setled low content.

ADAM
740   Master goe on, and I will follow thee
    To the last gaspe with truth and loyaltie,
    From seauenteene yeeres, till now almost fourescore
    Here liued I, but now liue here no more.
    At seauenteene yeeres, many their fortunes seeke
    But at fourescore, it is too late a weeke,
    Yet fortune cannot recompence me better
    Then to die well, and not my Masters debter.   *Exeunt*

Sc. 7   *Enter Rosalind in mans clothes as Ganimed; Celia*
(2.4)   *as Aliena, a shepherdess; and Clowne, alias*
    Touchstone

ROSALIND O *Iupiter*, how wearie are my spirits?
CLOWNE I care not for my spirits, if my legges were not
750   wearie.
ROSALIND I could finde in my heart to disgrace my mans

apparell, and to cry like a woman: but I must comfort
the weaker vessell, as doublet and hose ought to show
it selfe coragious to petty-coate; therefore courage,
good *Aliena*.
CELIA I pray you beare with me, I cannot goe no further.
CLOWNE For my part, I had rather beare with you, then
beare you: yet I should beare no crosse if I did beare
you, for I thinke you haue no money in your purse.
ROSALIND Well, this is the Forrest of *Arden*.   760
CLOWNE I, now am I in *Arden*, the more foole I, when I
was at home I was in a better place, but Trauellers
must be content.
    Enter Corin and Siluius
ROSALIND I, be so good *Touchstone*: Look you, who comes
here, a yong man and an old in solemne talke.
CORIN (*to Siluius*)
    That is the way to make her scorne you still.
SILUIUS
    Oh *Corin*, that thou knew'st how I do loue her.
CORIN
    I partly guesse: for I haue lou'd ere now.
SILUIUS
    No *Corin*, being old, thou canst not guesse,
    Though in thy youth thou wast as true a louer   770
    As euer sigh'd vpon a midnight pillow:
    But if thy loue were euer like to mine,
    As sure I thinke did neuer man loue so:
    How many actions most ridiculous,
    Hast thou beene drawne to by thy fantasie?
CORIN
    Into a thousand that I haue forgotten.
SILUIUS
    Oh thou didst then neuer loue so hartily,
    If thou remembrest not the slightest folly,
    That euer loue did make thee run into,
    Thou hast not lou'd.   780
    Or if thou hast not sat as I doe now,
    Wearing thy hearer in thy Mistris praise,
    Thou hast not lou'd.
    Or if thou hast not broke from companie,
    Abruptly as my passion now makes me,
    Thou hast not lou'd.
    O *Phebe, Phebe, Phebe*.   *Exit*
ROSALIND
    Alas poore Shepheard searching of thy wound,
    I haue by hard aduenture found mine owne.
CLOWNE And I mine: I remember when I was in loue, I   790
broke my sword vpon a stone, and bid him take that
for comming a night to *Iane Smile*, and I remember the
kissing of her batlet, and the Cowes dugs that her
prettie chopt hands had milk'd; and I remember the
wooing of a peascod instead of her, from whom I tooke
two cods, and giuing her them againe, said with
weeping teares, weare these for my sake: wee that are
true Louers, runne into strange capers; but as all is
mortall in nature, so is all nature in loue, mortall in
folly.   800
ROSALIND Thou speak'st wiser then thou art ware of.

CLOWNE Nay, I shall nere be ware of mine owne wit, till
    I breake my shins against it.

ROSALIND
    Ioue, Ioue, this Shepherds passion,
    Is much vpon my fashion.

CLOWNE And mine, but it growes something stale with
    mee.

CELIA
    I pray you, one of you question yon'd man,
    If he for gold will giue vs any foode,
810   I faint almost to death.

CLOWNE (*to Corin*) Holla; you Clowne.

ROSALIND Peace foole, he's not thy kinsman.

CORIN Who cals?

CLOWNE Your betters Sir.

CORIN Else are they very wretched.

ROSALIND (*to Touchstone*)
    Peace I say; (*to Corin*) good euen to you friend.

CORIN
    And to you gentle Sir, and to you all.

ROSALIND
    I prethee Shepheard, if that loue or gold
    Can in this desert place buy entertainment,
820   Bring vs where we may rest our selues, and feed:
    Here's a yong maid with trauaile much oppressed,
    And faints for succour.

CORIN   Faire Sir, I pittie her,
    And wish for her sake more then for mine owne,
    My fortunes were more able to releeue her:
    But I am shepheard to another man,
    And do not sheere the Fleeces that I graze:
    My master is of churlish disposition,
    And little wreakes to finde the way to heauen
    By doing deeds of hospitalitie.
830   Besides his Coate, his Flockes, and bounds of feede
    Are now on sale, and at our sheep-coat now
    By reason of his absence there is nothing
    That you will feed on: but what is, come see,
    And in my voice most welcome shall you be.

ROSALIND
    What is he that shall buy his flocke and pasture?

CORIN
    That yong Swaine that you saw heere but erewhile,
    That little cares for buying any thing.

ROSALIND
    I pray thee, if it stand with honestie,
    Buy thou the Cottage, pasture, and the flocke,
840   And thou shalt haue to pay for it of vs.

CELIA
    And we will mend thy wages: I like this place,
    And willingly could waste my time in it.

CORIN
    Assuredly the thing is to be sold:
    Go with me, if you like vpon report,
    The soile, the profit, and this kinde of life,
    I will your very faithfull Feeder be,
    And buy it with your Gold right sodainly.   *Exeunt*

Enter Amyens, Iaques, & other Lords like   Sc. 8
Forresters   (2.5)

Song

⌜AMYENS⌝   *Vnder the greene wood tree,*
    Who loues to lye with mee,
    And turne his merrie Note,   850
    Vnto the sweet Birds throte:
  Come hither, come hither, come hither:
    Heere shall he see
    No enemie,
    But Winter and rough Weather.

IAQUES More, more, I pre'thee more.

AMYENS It will make you melancholly Monsieur *Iaques.*

IAQUES I thanke it: More, I prethee more, I can sucke
    melancholly out of a song, as a Weazel suckes egges:
    More, I pre'thee more.   860

AMYENS My voice is ragged, I know I cannot please you.

IAQUES I do not desire you to please me, I do desire you
    to sing: Come, more, another stanzo: Cal you 'em
    stanzo's?

AMYENS What you wil Monsieur *Iaques.*

IAQUES Nay, I care not for their names, they owe mee
    nothing. Wil you sing?

AMYENS More at your request, then to please my selfe.

IAQUES Well then, if euer I thanke any man, Ile thanke
    you: but that they cal complement is like th'encounter   870
    of two dog-Apes. And when a man thankes me hartily,
    me thinkes I haue giuen him a penie, and he renders
    me the beggerly thankes. Come sing; and you that wil
    not hold your tongues.

AMYENS Wel, Ile end the song. Sirs, couer the while,
    (*Lords prepare food and drink*)
    the Duke wil drinke vnder this tree; (*to Iaques*) he hath
    bin all this day to looke you.

IAQUES And I haue bin all this day to auoid him: He is
    too disputeable for my companie: I thinke of as many
    matters as he, but I giue Heauen thankes, and make   880
    no boast of them. Come, warble, come.

Song

ALL   *Who doth ambition shunne,*
    And loues to liue i'th Sunne:
    Seeking the food he eates,
    And pleas'd with what he gets:
  Come hither, come hither, come hither,
    Heere shall he see
    No enemie,
    But Winter and rough Weather.

IAQUES Ile giue you a verse to this note, that I made   890
    yesterday in despight of my Inuention.

AMYENS And Ile sing it.

IAQUES Thus it goes.

    If it do come to passe,
    That any man turne Asse:
    Leauing his wealth and ease,
    A stubborne will to please,

Ducdame, ducdame, ducdame:
Heere shall he see,
900   *Grosse fooles as he,*
And if he will come to me.

AMYENS What's that Ducdame?

IAQUES 'Tis a Greeke inuocation, to call fooles into a circle.
Ile go sleepe if I can: if I cannot, Ile raile against all
the first borne of Egypt.

AMYENS And Ile go seeke the Duke, his banket is prepar'd.

Exeunt

Sc. 9   *Enter Orlando, & Adam*
(2.6)   ADAM Deere Master, I can go no further: O I die for food.
Heere lie I downe, and measure out my graue. Farwel
kinde master.

910   ORLANDO Why how now *Adam?* No greater heart in thee:
Liue a little, comfort a little, cheere thy selfe a little. If
this vncouth Forrest yeeld any thing sauage, I wil
either be food for it, or bring it for foode to thee: Thy
conceite is neerer death, then thy powers. For my sake
be comfortable, hold death a while at the armes end:
I wil heere be with thee presently, and if I bring thee
not something to eate, I wil giue thee leaue to die: but
if thou diest before I come, thou art a mocker of my
labor. Wel said, thou look'st cheerely, and Ile be with
920   thee quickly: yet thou liest in the bleake aire. Come, I
wil beare thee to some shelter, and thou shalt not die
for lacke of a dinner, if there liue any thing in this
Desert. Cheerely good *Adam.*

Orlando carries Adam off

Sc. 10   *Enter Duke Senior & Lords, like Out-lawes*
(2.7)   DUKE SENIOR
I thinke he be transform'd into a beast,
For I can no where finde him, like a man.

I. LORD
My Lord, he is but euen now gone hence,
Heere was he merry, hearing of a Song.

DUKE SENIOR
If he compact of iarres, grow Musicall,
We shall haue shortly discord in the Spheares:
930   Go seeke him, tell him I would speake with him.

Enter Iaques

I. LORD
He saues my labor by his owne approach.

DUKE SENIOR
Why how now Monsieur, what a life is this
That your poore friends must woe your companie,
What, you looke merrily.

IAQUES
A Foole, a foole: I met a foole i'th Forrest,
A motley Foole (a miserable world:)
As I do liue by foode, I met a foole,
Who laid him downe, and bask'd him in the Sun,
And rail'd on Lady Fortune in good termes,
940   In good set termes, and yet a motley foole.
Good morrow foole (quoth I:) no Sir, quoth he,
Call me not foole, till heauen hath sent me fortune,

And then he drew a diall from his poake,
And looking on it, with lacke-lustre eye,
Sayes, very wisely, it is ten a clocke:
Thus we may see (quoth he) how the world wagges:
'Tis but an houre agoe, since it was nine,
And after one houre more, 'twill be eleuen,
And so from houre to houre, we ripe, and ripe,
And then from houre to houre, we rot, and rot,   950
And thereby hangs a tale. When I did heare
The motley Foole, thus morall on the time,
My Lungs began to crow like Chanticleere,
That Fooles should be so deepe contemplatiue:
And I did laugh, sans intermission
An houre by his diall. Oh noble foole,
A worthy foole: Motley's the onely weare.

DUKE SENIOR What foole is this?

IAQUES
O worthie Foole: One that hath bin a Courtier
And sayes, if Ladies be but yong, and faire,   960
They haue the gift to know it: and in his braine,
Which is as drie as the remainder bisket
After a voyage: He hath strange places cram'd
With obseruation, the which he vents
In mangled formes. O that I were a foole,
I am ambitious for a motley coat.

DUKE SENIOR
Thou shalt haue one.

IAQUES   It is my onely suite,
Prouided that you weed your better iudgements
Of all opinion that growes ranke in them,
That I am wise. I must haue liberty   970
Withall, as large a Charter as the winde,
To blow on whom I please, for so fooles haue:
And they that are most gauled with my folly,
They most must laugh: And why sir must they so?
The why is plaine, as way to Parish Church:
Hee, that a Foole doth very wisely hit,
Doth very foolishly, although he smart
Seeme aught but senselesse of the bob. If not,
The Wise-mans folly is anathomiz'd
Euen by the squandring glances of the foole.   980
Inuest me in my motley: Giue me leaue
To speake my minde, and I will through and through
Cleanse the foule bodie of th'infected world,
If they will patiently receiue my medicine.

DUKE SENIOR
Fie on thee. I can tell what thou wouldst do.

IAQUES
What, for a Counter, would I do, but good?

DUKE SENIOR
Most mischeeuous foule sin, in chiding sin:
For thou thy selfe hast bene a Libertine,
As sensuall as the brutish sting it selfe,
And all th'imbossed sores, and headed euils,   990
That thou with license of free foot hast caught,
Would'st thou disgorge into the generall world.

IAQUES Why who cries out on pride,
That can therein taxe any priuate party:

Doth it not flow as hugely as the Sea,
Till that the wearie verie meanes do ebbe.
What woman in the Citie do I name,
When that I say the City woman beares
The cost of Princes on vnworthy shoulders?
1000 Who can come in, and say that I meane her,
When such a one as shee, such is her neighbor?
Or what is he of basest function,
That sayes his brauerie is not on my cost,
Thinking that I meane him, but therein suites
His folly to the mettle of my speech,
There then, how then, what then, let me see wherein
My tongue hath wrong'd him: if it do him right,
Then he hath wrong'd himselfe: if he be free,
Why then my taxing like a wild-goose flies
1010 Vnclaim'd of any man. But who comes here?
      Enter Orlando with sword drawn

ORLANDO
   Forbeare, and eate no more.

IAQUES   Why I haue eate none yet.

ORLANDO
   Nor shalt not, till necessity be seru'd.

IAQUES Of what kinde should this Cocke come of?

DUKE SENIOR
   Art thou thus bolden'd man by thy distres?
   Or else a rude despiser of good manners,
   That in ciuility thou seem'st so emptie?

ORLANDO
   You touch'd my veine at first, the thorny point
   Of bare distresse, hath tane from me the shew
   Of smooth ciuility: yet am I in-land bred,
1020 And know some nourture: But forbeare, I say,
   He dies that touches any of this fruite,
   Till I, and my affaires are answered.

IAQUES And you will not be answer'd with reason, I must
   dye.

DUKE SENIOR
   What would you haue? Your gentlenesse shall force,
   More then your force moue vs to gentlenesse.

ORLANDO
   I almost die for food, and let me haue it.

DUKE SENIOR
   Sit downe and feed, & welcom to our table.

ORLANDO
   Speake you so gently? Pardon me I pray you,
1030 I thought that all things had bin sauage heere,
   And therefore put I on the countenance
   Of sterne command'ment. But what ere you are
   That in this desert inaccessible,
   Vnder the shade of melancholly boughes,
   Loose, and neglect the creeping houres of time:
   If euer you haue look'd on better dayes:
   If euer beene where bels haue knoll'd to Church:
   If euer sate at any good mans feast:
   If euer from your eye-lids wip'd a teare,
1040 And know what 'tis to pittie, and be pittied:
   Let gentlenesse my strong enforcement be,
   In the which hope, I blush, and hide my Sword.

DUKE SENIOR
   True is it, that we haue seene better dayes,
   And haue with holy bell bin knowld to Church,
   And sat at good mens feasts, and wip'd our eies
   Of drops, that sacred pity hath engendred:
   And therefore sit you downe in gentlenesse,
   And take vpon command, what helpe we haue
   That to your wanting may be ministred.

ORLANDO
   Then but forbeare your food a little while: 1050
   Whiles (like a Doe) I go to finde my Fawne,
   And giue it food. There is an old poore man,
   Who after me, hath many a weary steppe
   Limpt in pure loue: till he be first suffic'd,
   Opprest with two weake euils, age, and hunger,
   I will not touch a bit.

DUKE SENIOR   Go finde him out,
   And we will nothing waste till you returne.

ORLANDO
   I thanke ye, and be blest for your good comfort. *Exit*

DUKE SENIOR
   Thou seest, we are not all alone vnhappie:
   This wide and vniuersall Theater   1060
   Presents more wofull Pageants then the Sceane
   Wherein we play in.

IAQUES   All the world's a stage,
   And all the men and women, meerely Players;
   They haue their *Exits* and their *Entrances*,
   And one man in his time playes many parts,
   His Acts being seuen ages. At first the Infant,
   Mewling, and puking in the Nurses armes:
   Then, the whining Schoole-boy with his Satchell
   And shining morning face, creeping like snaile
   Vnwillingly to schoole. And then the Louer,   1070
   Sighing like Furnace, with a wofull ballad
   Made to his Mistresse eye-brow. Then, a Soldier,
   Full of strange oaths, and bearded like the Pard,
   Ielous in honor, sodaine, and quicke in quarrell,
   Seeking the bubble Reputation
   Euen in the Canons mouth: And then, the Iustice
   In faire round belly, with good Capon lin'd,
   With eyes seuere, and beard of formall cut,
   Full of wise sawes, and moderne instances,
   And so he playes his part. The sixt age shifts   1080
   Into the leane and slipper'd Pantaloone,
   With spectacles on nose, and pouch on side,
   His youthfull hose well sau'd, a world too wide,
   For his shrunke shanke, and his bigge manly voice,
   Turning againe toward childish trebble pipes,
   And whistles in his sound. Last Scene of all,
   That ends this strange euentfull historie,
   Is second childishnesse, and meere obliuion,
   Sans teeth, sans eyes, sans taste, sans euery thing.
         Enter Orlando bearing Adam

DUKE SENIOR
   Welcome: set downe your venerable burthen,   1090
   And let him feede.

ORLANDO I thanke you most for him.

ADAM So had you neede,
　　I scarce can speake to thanke you for my selfe.
DUKE SENIOR
　　Welcome, fall too: I wil not trouble you,
　　As yet to question you about your fortunes:
　　Giue vs some Musicke, and good Cozen, sing.

　　　　　　　　　Song
⌜AMYENS⌝
　　　　　Blow, blow, thou winter winde,
　　　　　Thou art not so vnkinde,
1100　　　　　　As mans ingratitude.
　　　　　Thy tooth is not so keene,
　　　　　Because thou art not seene,
　　　　　　Although thy breath be rude.
　　　　Heigh ho, sing heigh ho, vnto the greene holly,
　　　　Most frendship, is fayning; most Louing, meere folly:
　　　　　　Then heigh ho, the holly,
　　　　　　This Life is most iolly.

　　　　　Freize, freize, thou bitter skie
　　　　　That dost not bight so nigh
1110　　　　　　As benefitts forgot:
　　　　　Though thou the waters warpe,
　　　　　Thy sting is not so sharpe,
　　　　　　As freind remembred not.
　　　　Heigh ho, sing heigh ho, vnto the greene holly,
　　　　Most frendship, is fayning; most Louing, meere folly:
　　　　　　Then heigh ho, the holly,
　　　　　　This Life is most iolly.

　　DUKE SENIOR (to Orlando)
　　　If that you were the good Sir Rowlands son,
　　　As you haue whisper'd faithfully you were,
1120　　And as mine eye doth his effigies witnesse,
　　　Most truly limn'd, and liuing in your face,
　　　Be truly welcome hither: I am the Duke
　　　That lou'd your Father, the residue of your fortune,
　　　Go to my Caue, and tell mee. (To Adam) Good old
　　　　man,
　　　Thou art right welcome, as thy master is:
　　　(To Lords) Support him by the arme: (to Orlando) giue
　　　　me your hand,
　　　And let me all your fortunes vnderstand.   Exeunt

Sc. 11   Enter Duke Frederick, Lords, & Oliuer
(3.1) DUKE FREDERICK
　　Not see him since? Sir, sir, that cannot be:
　　But were I not the better part made mercie,
1130　I should not seeke an absent argument
　　Of my reuenge, thou present: but looke to it,
　　Finde out thy brother wheresoere he is,
　　Seeke him with Candle: bring him dead, or liuing
　　Within this tweluemonth, or turne thou no more
　　To seeke a liuing in our Territorie.
　　Thy Lands and all things that thou dost call thine,
　　Worth seizure, do we seize into our hands,
　　Till thou canst quit thee by thy brothers mouth,
　　Of what we thinke against thee.

OLIUER
　　Oh that your Highnesse knew my heart in this: 1140
　　I neuer lou'd my brother in my life.
DUKE FREDERICK
　　More villaine thou. (To Lords) Well push him out of
　　　dores
　　And let my officers of such a nature
　　Make an extent vpon his house and Lands:
　　Do this expediently, and turne him going.
　　　　　　　　　　　　　　Exeunt seuerally

　　　　Enter Orlando with a paper   Sc. 12
ORLANDO   (3.2)
　　Hang there my verse, in witnesse of my loue,
　　　And thou thrice crowned Queene of night suruey
　　With thy chaste eye, from thy pale spheare aboue
　　　Thy Huntresse name, that my full life doth sway.
　　O Rosalind, these Trees shall be my Bookes,   1150
　　　And in their barkes my thoughts Ile charracter,
　　That euerie eye, which in this Forrest lookes,
　　　Shall see thy vertue witnest euery where.
　　Run, run Orlando, carue on euery Tree,
　　The faire, the chaste, and vnexpressiue shee.   Exit
　　　Enter Corin & Touchstone the Clowne
CORIN And how like you this shepherds life Mr Touchstone?
CLOWNE Truely Shepheard, in respect of it selfe, it is a
　　good life; but in respect that it is a shepheards life, it
　　is naught. In respect that it is solitary, I like it verie
　　well: but in respect that it is priuate, it is a very vild   1160
　　life. Now in respect it is in the fields, it pleaseth mee
　　well: but in respect it is not in the Court, it is tedious.
　　As it is a spare life (looke you) it fits my humor well:
　　but as there is no more plentie in it, it goes much
　　against my stomacke. Has't any Philosophie in thee
　　shepheard?
CORIN No more, but that I know the more one sickens,
　　the worse at ease he is: and that hee that wants money,
　　meanes, and content, is without three good frends.
　　That the propertie of raine is to wet, and fire to burne: 1170
　　That good pasture makes fat sheepe: and that a great
　　cause of the night, is lacke of the Sunne: That hee that
　　hath learned no wit by Nature, nor Art, may complaine
　　of good breeding, or comes of a very dull kindred.
CLOWNE Such a one is a naturall Philosopher: Was't euer
　　in Court, Shepheard?
CORIN No truly.
CLOWNE Then thou art damn'd.
CORIN Nay, I hope.
CLOWNE Truly thou art damn'd, like an ill roasted Egge,   1180
　　all on one side.
CORIN For not being at Court? your reason.
CLOWNE Why, if thou neuer was't at Court, thou neuer
　　saw'st good manners: if thou neuer saw'st good
　　maners, then thy manners must be wicked, and
　　wickednes is sin, and sinne is damnation: Thou art in
　　a parlous state shepheard.
CORIN Not a whit Touchstone, those that are good maners
　　at the Court, are as ridiculous in the Countrey, as the
　　behauiour of the Countrie is most mockeable at the   1190

Court. You told me, you salute not at the Court, but you kisse your hands; that courtesie would be vncleanlie if Courtiers were shepheards.

CLOWNE Instance, briefly: come, instance.

CORIN Why we are still handling our Ewes, and their Fels you know are greasie.

CLOWNE Why do not your Courtiers hands sweate? and is not the grease of a Mutton, as wholesome as the sweat of a man? Shallow, shallow: A better instance I say: Come.

CORIN Besides, our hands are hard.

CLOWNE Your lips wil feele them the sooner. Shallow agen: a more sounder instance, come.

CORIN And they are often tarr'd ouer, with the surgery of our sheepe: and would you haue vs kisse Tarre? The Courtiers hands are perfum'd with Ciuet.

CLOWNE Most shallow man: Thou wormes meate in respect of a good peece of flesh indeed: learne of the wise and perpend: Ciuet is of a baser birth then Tarre, the verie vncleanly fluxe of a Cat. Mend the instance Shepheard.

CORIN You haue too Courtly a wit, for me, Ile rest.

CLOWNE Wilt thou rest damn'd? God helpe thee shallow man: God make incision in thee, thou art raw.

CORIN Sir, I am a true Labourer, I earne that I eate: get that I weare; owe no man hate, enuie no mans happinesse: glad of other mens good: content with my harme: and the greatest of my pride, is to see my Ewes graze, & my Lambes sucke.

CLOWNE That is another simple sinne in you, to bring the Ewes and the Rammes together, and to offer to get your liuing, by the copulation of Cattle, to be bawd to a Bel-weather, and to betray a shee-Lambe of a tweluemonth to a crooked-pated olde Cuckoldly Ramme, out of all reasonable match. If thou bee'st not damn'd for this, the diuell himselfe will haue no shepherds, I cannot see else how thou shouldst scape.

CORIN Heere comes yong Mr *Ganimed*, my new Mistrisses Brother.

Enter Rosalind as Ganimed

ROSALIND (*read*)

From the east to westerne Inde,
No iewel is like Rosalinde,
Hir worth being mounted on the winde,
Through all the world beares Rosalinde.
All the pictures fairest Linde,
Are but blacke to Rosalinde:
Let no face bee kept in mind,
But the faire of Rosalinde.

CLOWNE Ile rime you so, eight yeares together; dinners, and suppers, and sleeping hours excepted: it is the right Butter-womens ranke to Market.

ROSALIND Out Foole.

CLOWNE For a taste.

If a Hart doe lacke a Hinde,
Let him seeke out Rosalinde:
If the Cat will after kinde,
So be sure will Rosalinde:

Wintred garments must be linde,
So must slender Rosalinde:
They that reap must sheafe and binde,
Then to cart with Rosalinde.
Sweetest nut, hath sowrest rinde,
Such a nut is Rosalinde.
He that sweetest rose will finde,
Must finde Loues pricke, & Rosalinde.

This is the verie false gallop of Verses, why doe you infect your selfe with them?

ROSALIND
Peace you dull foole, I found them on a tree.

CLOWNE Truely the tree yeelds bad fruite.

ROSALIND Ile graffe it with you, and then I shall graffe it with a Medler: then it will be the earliest fruit i'th country: for you'l be rotten ere you bee halfe ripe, and that's the right vertue of the Medler.

CLOWNE You haue said: but whether wisely or no, let the Forrest iudge.

Enter Celia as Aliena, with a writing

ROSALIND
Peace, here comes my sister reading, stand aside.

CELIA (*read*)

Why should this a Desert bee?
For it is vnpeopled? Noe:
Tonges Ile hang on euerie tree,
That shall ciuill sayings shoe.
Some, how briefe the Life of man
Runs his erring pilgrimage,
That the stretching of a span,
Buckles in his summe of age.
Some of violated vowes,
Twixt the soules of friend, and friend:
But vpon the fairest bowes,
Or at euerie sentence end;
Will I Rosalinda write,
Teaching all that reade, to know
The quintessence of euerie sprite,
Heauen would in little show.
Therefore heauen Nature charg'd,
That one bodie should be fill'd
With all Graces wide enlarg'd,
Nature presently distill'd
Helens cheeke, but not hir heart,
Cleopatra's Maiestie:
Attalanta's *better* part,
Sad Lucrecia's Modestie.
Thus Rosalinde of manie parts,
By Heauenly Synode was deuis'd,
Of manie faces, eyes, and hearts,
To haue the touches deerest pris'd.
Heauen would that shee these gifts should haue,
And I to liue and die her slaue.

ROSALIND O most gentle Iupiter, what tedious homilie of Loue haue you wearied your parishioners withall, and neuer cri'de, haue patience good people.

CELIA How now backe friends: Shepheard, go off a little: go with him sirrah.

CLOWNE Come Shepheard, let vs make an honorable retreit, though not with bagge and baggage, yet with scrip and scrippage.   *Exit with Corin*

CELIA Didst thou heare these verses?

ROSALIND O yes, I heard them all, and more too, for some of them had in them more feete then the Verses would beare.

CELIA That's no matter: the feet might beare yᵉ verses.

ROSALIND I, but the feet were lame, and could not beare themselues without the verse, and therefore stood lamely in the verse.

CELIA But didst thou heare without wondering, how thy name should be hang'd and carued vpon these trees?

ROSALIND I was seuen of the nine daies out of the wonder, before you came: for looke heere what I found on a Palme tree; (*showing Celia the verses*) I was neuer so berim'd since *Pythagoras* time that I was an Irish Rat, which I can hardly remember.

CELIA Tro you, who hath done this?

ROSALIND Is it a man?

CELIA And a chaine that you once wore about his neck: change you colour?

ROSALIND I pre'thee who?

CELIA O Lord, Lord, it is a hard matter for friends to meete; but Mountaines may bee remoou'd with Earthquakes, and so encounter.

ROSALIND Nay, but who is it?

CELIA Is it possible?

ROSALIND Nay, I pre'thee now, with most petitionary vehemence, tell me who it is.

CELIA O wonderfull, wonderfull, and most wonderfull wonderfull, and yet againe wonderful, and after that out of all hooping.

ROSALIND Good my complection, dost thou think though I am caparison'd like a man, I haue a doublet and hose in my disposition? One inch of delay more, is a South-sea of discouerie. I pre'thee tell me, who is it quickely, and speake apace: I would thou couldst stammer, that thou might'st powre this conceal'd man out of thy mouth, as Wine comes out of a narrow-mouth'd bottle: either too much at once, or none at all. I pre'thee take the Corke out of thy mouth, that I may drinke thy tydings.

CELIA So you may put a man in your belly.

ROSALIND Is he of Gods making? What manner of man? Is his head worth a hat? Or his chin worth a beard?

CELIA Nay, he hath but a little beard.

ROSALIND Why God will send more, if the man will bee thankful: let me stay the growth of his beard, if thou delay me not the knowledge of his chin.

CELIA It is yong *Orlando*, that tript vp the Wrastlers heeles, and your heart, both in an instant.

ROSALIND Nay, but the diuell take mocking: speake sadde brow, and true maid.

CELIA I'faith (Coz) tis he.

ROSALIND *Orlando*?

CELIA *Orlando*.

ROSALIND Alas the day, what shall I do with my doublet & hose? What did he when thou saw'st him? What sayde he? How look'd he? Wherein went he? What makes hee heere? Did he aske for me? Where remaines he? How parted he with thee? And when shalt thou see him againe? Answer me in one word.

CELIA You must borrow me Gargantuas mouth first: 'tis a Word too great for any mouth of this Ages size, to say I and no, to these particulars, is more then to answer in a Catechisme.

ROSALIND But doth he know that I am in this Forrest, and in mans apparrell? Looks he as freshly, as he did the day he Wrastled?

CELIA It is as easie to count Atomies as to resolue the propositions of a Louer: but take a taste of my finding him, and rellish it with good obseruance. I found him vnder a tree like a drop'd Acorne.

ROSALIND It may wel be cal'd Ioues tree, when it droppes forth such fruite.

CELIA Giue me audience, good Madam.

ROSALIND Proceed.

CELIA There lay hee stretch'd along like a Wounded knight.

ROSALIND Though it be pittie to see such a sight, it well becomes the ground.

CELIA Cry holla, to thy tongue, I prethee: it curuettes vnseasonably. He was furnish'd like a Hunter.

ROSALIND O ominous, he comes to kill my Hart.

CELIA I would sing my song without a burthen, thou bring'st me out of tune.

ROSALIND Do you not know I am a woman, when I thinke, I must speake: sweet, say on.

Enter Orlando & Iaques

CELIA You bring me out. Soft, comes he not heere?

ROSALIND 'Tis he, slinke by, and note him.

Rosalind and Celia stand aside

IAQUES (*to Orlando*) I thanke you for your company, but good faith I had as liefe haue beene my selfe alone.

ORLANDO And so had I: but yet for fashion sake I thanke you too, for your societie.

IAQUES God buy you, let's meet as little as we can.

ORLANDO I do desire we may be better strangers.

IAQUES I pray you marre no more trees with Writing Loue-songs in their barkes.

ORLANDO I pray you marre no moe of my verses with reading them ill-fauouredly.

IAQUES *Rosalinde* is your loues name?

ORLANDO Yes, Iust.

IAQUES I do not like her name.

ORLANDO There was no thought of pleasing you when she was christen'd.

IAQUES What stature is she of?

ORLANDO Iust as high as my heart.

IAQUES You are ful of pretty answers: haue you not bin acquainted with goldsmiths wiues, & cond thē out of rings?

ORLANDO Not so: but I answer you right painted cloath, from whence you haue studied your questions.

IAQUES You haue a nimble wit; I thinke 'twas made of

Attalanta's heeles. Will you sitte downe with me, and wee two, will raile against our Mistris the world, and all our miserie.

ORLANDO I wil chide no breather in the world but my selfe against whom I know most faults.

1420 IAQUES The worst fault you haue, is to be in loue.

ORLANDO 'Tis a fault I will not change, for your best vertue: I am wearie of you.

IAQUES By my troth, I was seeking for a Foole, when I found you.

ORLANDO He is drown'd in the brooke, looke but in, and you shall see him.

IAQUES There I shal see mine owne figure.

ORLANDO Which I take to be either a foole, or a Cipher.

IAQUES Ile tarrie no longer with you, farewell good signior
1430   Loue.

ORLANDO I am glad of your departure: Adieu good Monsieur Melancholly.   *Exit Iaques*

ROSALIND (*to Celia*) I wil speake to him like a sawcie Lacky, and vnder that habit play the knaue with him, (*to Orlando*) do you hear Forrester.

ORLANDO Verie wel, what would you?

ROSALIND I pray you, what i'st a clocke?

ORLANDO You should aske me what time o'day: there's no clocke in the Forrest.

1440 ROSALIND Then there is no true Louer in the Forrest, else sighing euerie minute, and groaning euerie houre wold detect the lazie foot of time, as wel as a clocke.

ORLANDO And why not the swift foote of time? Had not that bin as proper?

ROSALIND By no meanes sir; Time trauels in diuers paces, with diuers persons: Ile tel you who Time ambles withall, who Time trots withal, who Time gallops withall, and who he stands stil withall.

ORLANDO I prethee, who doth he trot withal?

1450 ROSALIND Marry he trots hard with a yong maid, between the contract of her marriage, and the day it is solemnizd: if the interim be but a sennight, Times pace is so hard, that it seemes the length of seuen yeare.

ORLANDO Who ambles Time withal?

ROSALIND With a Priest that lacks Latine, and a rich man that hath not the Gowt: for the one sleepes easily because he cannot study, and the other liues merrily, because he feeles no paine: the one lacking the burthen of leane and wasteful Learning; the other knowing no
1460   burthen of heauie tedious penurie. These Time ambles withal.

ORLANDO Who doth he gallop withal?

ROSALIND With a theefe to the gallowes: for though hee go as softly as foot can fall, he thinkes himselfe too soon there.

ORLANDO Who staies it stil withal?

ROSALIND With Lawiers in the vacation: for they sleepe betweene Terme and Terme, and then they perceiue not how time moues.

1470 ORLANDO Where dwel you prettie youth?

ROSALIND With this Shepheardesse my sister: heere in the skirts of the Forrest, like fringe vpon a petticoat.

ORLANDO Are you natiue of this place?

ROSALIND As the Conie that you see dwell where shee is kindled.

ORLANDO Your accent is something finer, then you could purchase in so remoued a dwelling.

ROSALIND I haue bin told so of many: but indeed, an olde religious Vnckle of mine taught me to speake, who was in his youth an inland man, one that knew Courtship 1480 too well: for there he fel in loue. I haue heard him read many Lectors against it, and I thanke God, I am not a Woman to be touch'd with so many giddie offences as hee hath generally tax'd their whole sex withal.

ORLANDO Can you remember any of the principall euils, that he laid to the charge of women?

ROSALIND There were none principal, they were all like one another, as halfepence are, euerie one fault seeming monstrous, til his fellow-fault came to match it.   1490

ORLANDO I prethee recount some of them.

ROSALIND No: I wil not cast away my physick, but on those that are sicke. There is a man haunts the Forrest, that abuses our yong plants with caruing *Rosalinde* on their barkes; hangs Oades vpon Hauthornes, and Elegies on brambles; all (forsooth) deifying the name of *Rosalinde*. If I could meet that Fancie-monger, I would giue him some good counsel, for he seemes to haue the Quotidian of Loue vpon him.

ORLANDO I am he that is so Loue-shak'd, I pray you tel   1500 me your remedie.

ROSALIND There is none of my Vnckles markes vpon you: he taught me how to know a man in loue: in which cage of rushes, I am sure you are not prisoner.

ORLANDO What were his markes?

ROSALIND A leane cheeke, which you haue not: a blew eie and sunken, which you haue not: an vnquestionable spirit, which you haue not: a beard neglected, which you haue not: (but I pardon you for that, for simply your hauing in beard, is a yonger brothers reuennew)   1510 then your hose should be vngarter'd, your bonnet vnbanded, your sleeue vnbutton'd, your shoo vnti'de, and euerie thing about you, demonstrating a carelesse desolation: but you are no such man; you are rather point deuice in your accoustrements, as louing your selfe, then seeming the Louer of any other.

ORLANDO Faire youth, I would I could make thee beleeue I Loue.

ROSALIND Me beleeue it? You may assoone make her that you Loue beleeue it, which I warrant she is apter to   1520 do, then to confesse she do's: that is one of the points, in the which women stil giue the lie to their consciences. But in good sooth, are you he that hangs the verses on the Trees, wherein *Rosalind* is so admired?

ORLANDO I sweare to thee youth, by the white hand of *Rosalind*, I am that he, that vnfortunate he.

ROSALIND But are you so much in loue, as your rimes speak?

ORLANDO Neither rime nor reason can expresse how much.   1530

ROSALIND Loue is meerely a madnesse, and I tel you, deserues as wel a darke house, and a whip, as madmen do: and the reason why they are not so punish'd and cured, is that the Lunacie is so ordinarie, that the whippers are in loue too: yet I professe curing it by counsel.

ORLANDO Did you euer cure any so?

ROSALIND Yes one, and in this manner. Hee was to imagine me his Loue, his Mistris: and I set him euerie day to woe me. At which time would I, being but a moonish youth, greeue, be effeminate, changeable, longing, and liking, proud, fantastical, apish, shallow, inconstant, ful of teares, full of smiles; for euerie passion something, and for no passion truly any thing, as boyes and women are for the most part, cattle of this colour: would now like him, now loath him: then entertaine him, then forswear him: now weepe for him, then spit at him; that I draue my Sutor from his mad humor of loue, to a liuing humor of madnes, wᶜ was to forsweare the ful stream of yᵉ world, and to liue in a nooke meerly Monastick: and thus I cur'd him, and this way wil I take vpon mee to wash your Liuer as cleane as a sound sheepes heart, that there shal not be one spot of Loue in't.

ORLANDO I would not be cured, youth.

ROSALIND I would cure you, if you would but call me *Rosalind*, and come euerie day to my Coat, and woe me.

ORLANDO Now by the faith of my loue, I will; Tel me where it is.

ROSALIND Go with me to it, and Ile shew it you: and by the way, you shal tell me, where in the Forrest you liue: Wil you go?

ORLANDO With all my heart, good youth.

ROSALIND Nay, you must call mee *Rosalind*: Come sister, will you go?   *Exeunt*

Sc. 13
(3.3)   *Enter Touchstone the Clowne & Audrey, followed by Iaques*

CLOWNE Come apace good *Audrey*, I wil fetch vp your Goates, *Audrey*: and how *Audrey* am I the man yet? Doth my simple feature content you?

AUDREY Your features, Lord warrant vs: what features?

CLOWNE I am heere with thee, and thy Goats, as the most capricious Poet honest *Ouid* was among the Gothes.

IAQUES (*aside*) O knowledge ill inhabited, worse then Ioue in a thatch'd house.

CLOWNE When a mans verses cannot be vnderstood, nor a mans good wit seconded with the forward childe, vnderstanding: it strikes a man more dead then a great reckoning in a little roome: truly, I would the Gods hadde made thee poeticall.

AUDREY I do not know what Poetical is: is it honest in deed and word: is it a true thing?

CLOWNE No trulie: for the truest poetrie is the most faining, and Louers are giuen to Poetrie: and what they sweare in Poetrie, it may be said as Louers, they do feigne.

AUDREY Do you wish then that the Gods had made me Poeticall?

CLOWNE I do truly: for thou swear'st to me thou art honest: Now if thou wert a Poet, I might haue some hope thou didst feigne.

AUDREY Would you not haue me honest?

CLOWNE No truly, vnlesse thou wert hard fauour'd: for honestie coupled to beautie, is to haue Honie a sawce to Sugar.

IAQUES (*aside*) A materiall foole.

AUDREY Well, I am not faire, and therefore I pray the Gods make me honest.

CLOWNE Truly, and to cast away honestie vppon a foule slut, were to put good meate into an vncleane dish.

AUDREY I am not a slut, though I thanke the Goddes I am foule.

CLOWNE Well, praised be the Gods, for thy foulnesse; sluttishnesse may come heereafter. But be it, as it may bee, I wil marrie thee: and to that end, I haue bin with Sir *Oliuer Mar-text*, the Vicar of the next village, who hath promis'd to meete me in this place of the Forrest, and to couple vs.

IAQUES (*aside*) I would faine see this meeting.

AUDREY Wel, the Gods giue vs ioy.

CLOWNE Amen. A man may if he were of a fearful heart, stagger in this attempt: for heere wee haue no Temple but the wood, no assembly but horne-beasts. But what though? Courage. As hornes are odious, they are necessarie. It is said, many a man knowes no end of his goods; right: Many a man has good Hornes, and knows no end of them. Well, that is the dowrie of his wife, 'tis none of his owne getting; hornes, euen so. Poore men alone? No, no, the noblest Deere hath them as huge as the Rascall: Is the single man therefore blessed? No, as a wall'd Towne is more worthier then a village, so is the forehead of a married man, more honourable then the bare brow of a Batcheller: and by how much defence is better then no skill, by so much is a horne more precious then to want.

Enter Sir Oliuer Mar-text

Heere comes Sir *Oliuer*: Sir *Oliuer Mar-text* you are wel met. Will you dispatch vs heere vnder this tree, or shal we go with you to your Chappell?

SIR OLIUER MAR-TEXT Is there none heere to giue the woman?

CLOWNE I wil not take her on guift of any man.

SIR OLIUER MAR-TEXT Truly she must be giuen, or the marriage is not lawfull.

IAQUES (*comming forward*) Proceed, proceede: Ile giue her.

CLOWNE Good euen good Mʳ what ye cal't: how do you Sir, you are verie well met: goddild you for your last companie, I am verie glad to see you, euen a toy in hand heere Sir:

Iaques remoues his hat

Nay, pray be couer'd.

IAQUES Wil you be married, Motley?

CLOWNE As the Oxe hath his bow sir, the horse his curb, and the Falcon her bels, so man hath his desires, and as Pigeons bill, so wedlocke would be nibling.

IAQUES And wil you (being a man of your breeding) be married vnder a bush like a begger? Get you to church, and haue a good Priest that can tel you what marriage is, this fellow wil but ioyne you together, as they ioyne Wainscot, then one of you wil proue a shrunke pannell, and like greene timber, warpe, warpe.

1650 CLOWNE I am not in the minde, but I were better to bee married of him then of another, for he is not like to marrie me wel: and not being wel married, it wil be a good excuse for me heereafter, to leaue my wife.

IAQUES Goe thou with mee, and let me counsel thee.

CLOWNE

    Come sweete *Audrey,*
    We must be married, or we must liue in baudrey:
    Farewel good Mr *Oliuer:* Not
          O sweet *Oliuer,*
          O braue *Oliuer*
          Leaue me not behind thee:
1660 But
          Winde away,
          Bee gone I say,
          I wil not to wedding with thee.

SIR OLIUER MAR-TEXT *(aside)* 'Tis no matter; Ne're a fantastical knaue of them all shal flout me out of my calling.   *Exeunt*

Sc. 14   *Enter Rosalind as Ganimed & Celia as Aliena*
(3.4) ROSALIND Neuer talke to me, I wil weepe.

CELIA Do I prethee, but yet haue the grace to consider, that teares do not become a man.

1670 ROSALIND But haue I not cause to weepe?

CELIA As good cause as one would desire, therefore weepe.

ROSALIND His very haire is of the dissembling colour.

CELIA Something browner then Iudasses: Marrie his kisses are Iudasses owne children.

ROSALIND I'faith his haire is of a good colour.

CELIA An excellent colour. Your Chessenut was euer the onely colour.

ROSALIND And his kissing is as ful of sanctitie, as the touch of holy bread.

1680 CELIA Hee hath bought a paire of cast lips of *Diana*: a Nun of winters sisterhood kisses not more religiouslie, the very yce of chastity is in them.

ROSALIND But why did hee sweare hee would come this morning, and comes not?

CELIA Nay certainly there is no truth in him.

ROSALIND Doe you thinke so?

CELIA Yes, I thinke he is not a picke purse, nor a horse-stealer, but for his verity in loue, I doe thinke him as concaue as a couered goblet, or a Worme-eaten nut.

1690 ROSALIND Not true in loue?

CELIA Yes, when he is in, but I thinke he is not in.

ROSALIND You haue heard him sweare downright he was.

CELIA Was, is not is: besides, the oath of a Louer is no stronger then the word of a Tapster, they are both the confirmer of false reckonings, he attends here in the forrest on the Duke your father.

ROSALIND I met the Duke yesterday, and had much

question with him: he askt me of what parentage I was; I told him of as good as he, so he laugh'd and let mee goe. But what talke wee of Fathers, when there 1700 is such a man as *Orlando?*

CELIA O that's a braue man, hee writes braue verses, speakes braue words, sweares braue oathes, and breakes them brauely, quite trauers athwart the heart of his louer, as a puisny Tilter, y^t spurs his horse but on one side, breakes his staffe like a noble goose; but all's braue that youth mounts, and folly guides: who comes heere?

      Enter Corin

CORIN

Mistresse and Master, you haue oft enquired
After the Shepheard that complain'd of loue, 1710
Who you saw sitting by me on the Turph,
Praising the proud disdainfull Shepherdesse
That was his Mistresse.

CELIA   Well: and what of him?

CORIN

If you will see a pageant truely plaid
Betweene the pale complexion of true Loue,
And the red glowe of scorne and prowd disdaine,
Goe hence a little, and I shall conduct you
If you will marke it.

ROSALIND *(to Celia)*   O come, let vs remoue,
The sight of Louers feedeth those in loue:
(To Corin) Bring vs to this sight, and you shall say 1720
Ile proue a busie actor in their play.   *Exeunt*

      Enter Siluius and Phebe   **Sc. 15**
SILUIUS   **(3.5)**

Sweet *Phebe* doe not scorne me, do not *Phebe*.
Say that you loue me not, but say not so
In bitternesse; the common executioner
Whose heart th'accustom'd sight of death makes hard
Falls not the axe vpon the humbled neck,
But first begs pardon: will you sterner be
Then he that dies and liues by bloody drops?

      Enter Rosalind as Ganimed, Celia as Aliena, and
      Corin, and stand aside

PHEBE *(to Siluius)*

I would not be thy executioner,
I flye thee, for I would not iniure thee: 1730
Thou tellst me there is murder in mine eye,
'Tis pretty sure, and very probable,
That eyes that are the frailst, and softest things,
Who shut their coward gates on atomyes,
Should be called tyrants, butchers, murtherers.
Now I doe frowne on thee with all my heart,
And if mine eyes can wound, now let them kill thee:
Now counterfeit to swound, why now fall downe,
Or if thou canst not, oh for shame, for shame,
Lye not, to say mine eyes are murtherers: 1740
Now shew the wound mine eye hath made in thee,
Scratch thee but with a pin, and there remaines
Some scarre of it: Leane vpon a rush
The Cicatrice and capable impressure

Thy palme some moment keepes: but now mine eyes
Which I haue darted at thee, hurt thee not,
Nor I am sure there is no force in eyes
That can doe hurt.

SILUIUS O deere *Phebe*,
1750 If euer (as that euer may be neere)
You meet in some fresh cheeke the power of fancie,
Then shall you know the wounds inuisible
That Loues keene arrowes make.

PHEBE   But till that time
Come not thou neere me: and when that time comes,
Afflict me with thy mockes, pitty me not,
As till that time I shall not pitty thee.

ROSALIND (*comming forward*)
And why I pray you? who might be your mother
That you insult, exult, and all at once
Ouer the wretched? what though you haue no beauty
1760 As by my faith, I see no more in you
Then without Candle may goe darke to bed:
Must you be therefore prowd and pittilesse?
Why what meanes this? why do you looke on me?
I see no more in you then in the ordinary
Of Natures sale-worke? 'ods my little life,
I thinke she meanes to tangle my eies too:
No faith proud Mistresse, hope not after it,
'Tis not your inkie browes, your blacke silke haire,
Your bugle eye-balls, nor your cheeke of creame
1770 That can entame my spirits to your worship:
(*To Siluius*) You foolish Shepheard, wherefore do you
        follow her
Like foggy South, puffing with winde and raine,
You are a thousand times a properer man
Then she a woman. 'Tis such fooles as you
That makes the world full of ill-fauourd children:
'Tis not her glasse, but you that flatters her,
And out of you she sees her selfe more proper
Then any of her lineaments can show her:
(*To Phebe*) But Mistris, know your selfe, downe on
        your knees
1780 And thanke heauen, fasting, for a good mans loue;
For I must tell you friendly in your eare,
Sell when you can, you are not for all markets:
Cry the man mercy, loue him, take his offer,
Foule is most foule, being foule to be a scoffer.
So take her to thee Shepheard, fareyouwell.

PHEBE
Sweet youth, I pray you chide a yere together,
I had rather here you chide, then this man wooe.

ROSALIND (*to Phebe*) Hees falne in loue with your foulnesse,
(*to Siluius*) & shee'll fall in loue with my anger. If it be
1790 so, as fast as she answeres thee with frowning lookes,
ile sauce her with bitter words:
(*To Phebe*) Why looke you so vpon me?

PHEBE
For no ill will I beare you.

ROSALIND
I pray you do not fall in loue with mee,
For I am falser then vowes made in wine:

Besides, I like you not: if you will know my house,
'Tis at the tufft of Oliues, here hard by:
(*To Celia*) Will you goe Sister? (*To Siluius*) Shepheard
        ply her hard:
Come Sister: (*To Phebe*) Shepheardesse, looke on him
        better
And be not proud, though all the world could see,   1800
None could be so abus'd in sight as hee.
Come, to our flocke.

                    Exeunt Rosalind, Celia, and Corin
PHEBE (*aside*)
Dead Shepheard, now I find thy saw of might,
Who euer lou'd, that lou'd not at first sight?

SILUIUS
Sweet *Phebe*.

PHEBE   Hah: what saist thou *Siluius*?

SILUIUS Sweet *Phebe* pitty me.

PHEBE
Why I am sorry for thee gentle *Siluius*.

SILUIUS
Where euer sorrow is, reliefe would be:
If you doe sorrow at my griefe in loue,
By giuing loue your sorrow, and my griefe   1810
Were both extermin'd.

PHEBE
Thou hast my loue, is not that neighbourly?

SILUIUS
I would haue you.

PHEBE   Why that were couetousnesse:
Siluius; the time was, that I hated thee;
And yet it is not, that I beare thee loue,
But since that thou canst talke of loue so well,
Thy company, which erst was irkesome to me
I will endure; and Ile employ thee too:
But doe not looke for further recompence
Then thine owne gladnesse, that thou art employd.   1820

SILUIUS
So holy, and so perfect is my loue,
And I in such a pouerty of grace,
That I shall thinke it a most plenteous crop
To gleane the broken eares after the man
That the maine haruest reapes: loose now and then
A scattred smile, and that Ile liue vpon.

PHEBE
Knowst thou the youth that spoke to mee yerewhile?

SILUIUS
Not very well, but I haue met him oft,
And he hath bought the Cottage and the bounds
That the old *Carlot* once was Master of.   1830

PHEBE
Thinke not I loue him, though I ask for him,
'Tis but a peeuish boy, yet he talkes well,
But what care I for words? yet words do well
When he that speakes them pleases those that heare:
It is a pretty youth, not very prettie,
But sure hee's proud, and yet his pride becomes him;
Hee'll make a proper man: the best thing in him
Is his complexion: and faster then his tongue

Did make offence, his eye did heale it vp:
1840 He is not very tall, yet for his yeeres hee's tall:
His leg is but so so, and yet 'tis well:
There was a pretty rednesse in his lip,
A little riper, and more lustie red
Then that mixt in his cheeke: 'twas iust the difference
Betwixt the constant red, and mingled Damaske.
There be some women *Siluius*, had they markt him
In parcells as I did, would haue gone neere
To fall in loue with him: but for my part
I loue him not, nor hate him not: and yet
1850 Haue I more cause to hate him then to loue him,
For what had he to doe to chide at me?
He said mine eyes were black, and my haire blacke,
And now I am remembred, scorn'd at me:
I maruell why I answer'd not againe,
But that's all one: omittance is no quittance:
Ile write to him a very tanting Letter,
And thou shalt beare it, wilt thou *Siluius*?

SILUIUS
Phebe, with all my heart.

PHEBE   Ile write it strait:
The matter's in my head, and in my heart,
1860 I will be bitter with him, and passing short;
Goe with me *Siluius*.   *Exeunt*

Sc. 16   *Enter Rosalind as Ganimed, and Celia as Aliena, and*
(4.1)   *Iaques*

IAQUES I prethee, pretty youth, let me be better acquainted
with thee.

ROSALIND They say you are a melancholly fellow.

IAQUES I am so: I doe loue it better then laughing.

ROSALIND Those that are in extremity of either, are
abhominable fellowes, and betray themselues to euery
moderne censure, worse then drunkards.

IAQUES Why, 'tis good to be sad and say nothing.

1870 ROSALIND Why then 'tis good to be a poste.

IAQUES I haue neither the Schollers melancholy, which is
emulation: nor the Musitians, which is fantasticall;
nor the Courtiers, which is proud: nor the Souldiers,
which is ambitious: nor the Lawiers, which is politick:
nor the Ladies, which is nice: nor the Louers, which
is all these: but it is a melancholy of mine owne,
compounded of many simples, extracted from many
obiects, and indeed the sundrie contemplation of my
trauells, in which my often rumination, wraps me in
1880 a most humorous sadnesse.

ROSALIND A Traueller: by my faith you haue great reason
to be sad: I feare you haue sold your owne Lands, to
see other mens; then to haue seene much, and to haue
nothing, is to haue rich eyes and poore hands.

IAQUES Yes, I haue gain'd my experience.
        Enter Orlando

ROSALIND And your experience makes you sad: I had
rather haue a foole to make me merrie, then experience
to make me sad, and to trauaile for it too.

ORLANDO
Good day, and happinesse, deere *Rosalind*.

IAQUES Nay then God buy you, and you talke in blanke   1890
verse.

ROSALIND Farewell Mounsieur Trauellor: looke you lispe,
and weare strange suites; disable all the benefits of
your owne Countrie: be out of loue with your natiuitie,
and almost chide God for making you that countenance
you are; or I will scarce thinke you haue swam in a
Gundello.   ⌈*Exit Iaques*⌉
Why how now *Orlando*, where haue you bin all this
while? you a louer? and you serue me such another
tricke, neuer come in my sight more.   1900

ORLANDO My faire *Rosalind*, I come within an houre of
my promise.

ROSALIND Breake an houres promise in loue? hee that
will diuide a minute into a thousand parts, and breake
but a part of the thousand part of a minute in the
affaires of loue, it may be said of him that *Cupid* hath
clapt him oth' shoulder, but Ile warrant him heart
hole.

ORLANDO Pardon me deere *Rosalind*.

ROSALIND Nay, and you be so tardie, come no more in   1910
my sight, I had as liefe be woo'd of a Snaile.

ORLANDO Of a Snaile?

ROSALIND I, of a Snaile: for though he comes slowly, hee
carries his house on his head; a better ioyncture I
thinke then you make a woman: besides, he brings his
destinie with him.

ORLANDO What's that?

ROSALIND Why hornes: w^c such as you are faine to be
beholding to your wiues for: but he comes armed in
his fortune, and preuents the slander of his wife.   1920

ORLANDO Vertue is no horne-maker: and my *Rosalind* is
vertuous.

ROSALIND And I am your *Rosalind*.

CELIA It pleases him to call you so: but he hath a *Rosalind*
of a better leere then you.

ROSALIND Come, wooe me, wooe mee: for now I am in a
holy-day humor, and like enough to consent: What
would you say to me now, and I were your verie, verie
Rosalind?

ORLANDO I would kisse before I spoke.   1930

ROSALIND Nay, you were better speake first, and when
you were grauel'd, for lacke of matter, you might take
occasion to kisse: verie good Orators when they are
out, they will spit, and for louers, lacking (God warne
vs) matter, the cleanliest shift is to kisse.

ORLANDO How if the kisse be denide?

ROSALIND Then she puts you to entreatie, and there begins
new matter.

ORLANDO Who could be out, being before his beloued
Mistris?   1940

ROSALIND Marrie that should you if I were your Mistris,
or I should thinke my honestie ranker then my wit.

ORLANDO What, of my suite?

ROSALIND Not out of your apparrell, and yet out of your
suite: Am not I your *Rosalind*?

ORLANDO I take some ioy to say you are, because I would
be talking of her.

ROSALIND Well, in her person, I say I will not haue you.

ORLANDO Then in mine owne person, I die.

1950 ROSALIND No faith, die by Attorney: the poore world is almost six thousand yeeres old, and in all this time there was not anie man died in his owne person (videlicet) in a loue cause: Troilous had his braines dash'd out with a Grecian club, yet he did what hee could to die before, and he is one of the patternes of loue. Leander, he would haue liu'd manie a faire yeere though Hero had turn'd Nun; if it had not bin for a hot Midsomer-night, for (good youth) he went but forth to wash him in the Hellespont, and being taken with 1960 the crampe, was droun'd, and the foolish Chronoclers of that age, found it was Hero of Cestos. But these are all lies, men haue died from time to time, and wormes haue eaten them, but not for loue.

ORLANDO I would not haue my right Rosalind of this mind, for I protest her frowne might kill me.

ROSALIND By this hand, it will not kill a flie: but come, now I will be your Rosalind in a more comming-on disposition: and aske me what you will, I will grant it.

ORLANDO Then loue me Rosalind.

1970 ROSALIND Yes faith will I, fridaies and saterdaies, and all.

ORLANDO And wilt thou haue me?

ROSALIND I, and twentie such.

ORLANDO What saiest thou?

ROSALIND Are you not good?

ORLANDO I hope so.

ROSALIND Why then, can one desire too much of a good thing: (To Celia) Come sister, you shall be the Priest, and marrie vs: giue me your hand Orlando: What doe you say sister?

1980 ORLANDO (to Celia) Pray thee marrie vs.

CELIA I cannot say the words.

ROSALIND You must begin, will you Orlando.

CELIA Goe too: wil you Orlando, haue to wife this Rosalind?

ORLANDO I will.

ROSALIND I, but when?

ORLANDO Why now, as fast as she can marrie vs.

ROSALIND Then you must say, I take thee Rosalind for wife.

ORLANDO I take thee Rosalind for wife.

1990 ROSALIND I might aske you for your Commission, but I doe take thee Orlando for my husband: there's a girle goes before the Priest, and certainely a Womans thought runs before her actions.

ORLANDO So do all thoughts, they are wing'd.

ROSALIND Now tell me how long you would haue her, after you haue possest her?

ORLANDO For euer, and a day.

ROSALIND Say a day, without the euer: no, no Orlando, men are Aprill when they woe, December when they 2000 wed: Maides are May when they are maides, but the sky changes when they are wiues: I will bee more iealous of thee, then a Barbary cocke-pidgeon ouer his hen, more clamorous then a Parrat against raine, more new-fangled then an ape, more giddy in my desires, then a monkey: I will weepe for nothing, like Diana in the Fountaine, & I wil do that when you are dispos'd

to be merry: I will laugh like a Hyen, and that when thou art inclin'd to sleepe.

ORLANDO But will my Rosalind doe so?

ROSALIND By my life, she will doe as I doe.   2010

ORLANDO O but she is wise.

ROSALIND Or else shee could not haue the wit to doe this: the wiser, the waywarder: make the doores vpon a womans wit, and it will out at the casement: shut that, and 'twill out at the key-hole: stop that, 'twill flie with the smoake out at the chimney.

ORLANDO A man that had a wife with such a wit, he might say, wit whether wil't?

ROSALIND Nay, you might keepe that checke for it, till you met your wiues wit going to your neighbours bed.   2020

ORLANDO And what wit could wit haue, to excuse that?

ROSALIND Marry to say, she came to seeke you there: you shall neuer take her without her answer, vnlesse you take her without her tongue: ô that woman that cannot make her fault her husbands occasion, let her neuer nurse her childe her selfe, for she will breed it like a foole.

ORLANDO For these two houres Rosalinde, I wil leaue thee.

ROSALIND Alas, deere loue, I cannot lacke thee two houres.

ORLANDO I must attend the Duke at dinner, by two a   2030 clock I will be with thee againe.

ROSALIND I, goe your waies, goe your waies: I knew what you would proue, my friends told mee as much, and I thought no lesse: that flattering tongue of yours wonne me: 'tis but one cast away, and so come death: two o' clocke is your howre.

ORLANDO I, sweet Rosalind.

ROSALIND By my troth, and in good earnest, and so God mend mee, and by all pretty oathes that are not dangerous, if you breake one iot of your promise, or   2040 come one minute behinde your houre, I will thinke you the most patheticall breake-promise, and the most hollow louer, and the most vnworthy of her you call Rosalinde, that may bee chosen out of the grosse band of the vnfaithfull: therefore beware my censure, and keep your promise.

ORLANDO With no lesse religion, then if thou wert indeed my Rosalind: so adieu.

ROSALIND Well, Time is the olde Iustice that examines all such offenders, and let time try: adieu.   Exit Orlando   2050

CELIA You haue simply misus'd our sexe in your loue-prate: we must haue your doublet and hose pluckt ouer your head, and shew the world what the bird hath done to her owne neast.

ROSALIND O coz, coz, coz: my pretty little coz, that thou didst know how many fathome deepe I am in loue: but it cannot bee sounded: my affection hath an vnknowne bottome, like the Bay of Portugall.

CELIA Or rather bottomlesse, that as fast as you poure affection in, it runs out.   2060

ROSALIND No, that same wicked Bastard of Venus, that was begot of thought, conceiu'd of spleene, and borne of madnesse, that blinde rascally boy, that abuses euery ones eyes, because his owne are out, let him bee iudge, how deepe I am in loue: ile tell thee Aliena, I cannot

be out of the sight of *Orlando*: Ile goe finde a shadow,
and sigh till he come.

CELIA And Ile sleepe.   *Exeunt*

Sc. 17   *Enter Iaques and Lords, dressed as Forresters*
(4.2)   IAQUES Which is he that killed the Deare?

2070   A LORD Sir, it was I.

IAQUES (*to the others*) Let's present him to the Duke like
a Romane Conquerour, and it would doe well to set
the Deares horns vpon his head, for a branch of victory;
haue you no song Forrester for this purpose?

ANOTHER LORD Yes Sir.

IAQUES Sing it: 'tis no matter how it bee in tune, so it
make noyse enough.

Musicke, Song

⌜LORDS⌝   *What shall he haue that kild the Deare?*
              His Leather skin, and hornes to weare:
2080   *Then sing him home, the rest shall beare*
                This burthen;
              Take thou no scorne to weare the horne,
              It was a crest ere thou wast borne,
                Thy fathers father wore it,
                And thy father bore it,
              The horne, the horne, the lusty horne,
              Is not a thing to laugh to scorne.   *Exeunt*

Sc. 18   *Enter Rosalind as Ganimed and Celia as Aliena*
(4.3)   ROSALIND How say you now, is it not past two a clock?
And heere much *Orlando*.

2090   CELIA I warrant you, with pure loue, & troubled brain,
he hath t'ane his bow and arrowes, and is gone forth
to sleepe:

⌜*Enter Siluius*⌝

looke who comes heere.

SILUIUS (*to Rosalind*)
My errand is to you, faire youth,
My gentle *Phebe*, did bid me giue you this:

He offers Rosalind a letter, which she takes
and reads

I know not the contents, but as I guesse
By the sterne brow, and waspish action
Which she did vse, as she was writing of it,
It beares an angry tenure; pardon me,
2100   I am but as a guiltlesse messenger.

ROSALIND
Patience her selfe would startle at this letter,
And play the swaggerer, beare this, beare all:
Shee saies I am not faire, that I lacke manners,
She calls me proud, and that she could not loue me
Were man as rare as Phenix: 'od's my will,
Her loue is not the Hare that I doe hunt,
Why writes she so to me? well Shepheard, well,
This is a Letter of your owne deuice.

SILUIUS
No, I protest, I know not the contents,
Phebe did write it.

2110   ROSALIND   Come, come, you are a foole,

And turn'd into the extremity of loue.
I saw her hand, she has a leatherne hand,
A freestone colour'd hand: I verily did thinke
That her old gloues were on, but twas her hands:
She has a huswiues hand, but that's no matter:
I say she neuer did inuent this letter,
This is a mans inuention, and his hand.

SILUIUS Sure it is hers.

ROSALIND
Why, tis a boysterous and a cruell stile,
A stile for challengers: why, she defies me,   2120
Like Turke to Christian: womens gentle braine
Could not drop forth such giant rude inuention,
Such Ethiop words, blacker in their effect
Then in their countenance: will you heare the letter?

SILUIUS
So please you, for I neuer heard it yet:
Yet heard too much of *Phebes* crueltie.

ROSALIND
She *Phebes* me: marke how the tyrant writes.
(*Read*)   *Art thou god, to Shepherd turn'd?*
              That a maidens heart hath burn'd.
Can a woman raile thus?   2130

SILUIUS Call you this railing?

ROSALIND (*Read*)
                Why, thy godhead laid a part,
                War'st thou with a womans heart?
Did you euer heare such railing?
              Whiles the eye of man did wooe me,
              That could do no vengeance to me.
Meaning me a beast.
              If the scorne of your bright eine
              Haue power to raise such loue in mine,
              Alacke, in me, what strange effect   2140
              Would they worke in milde aspect?
              Whiles you chid me, I did loue,
              How then might your praiers moue?
              He that brings this loue to thee,
              Little knowes this Loue in me:
              And by him seale vp thy minde,
              Whether that thy youth and kinde
              Will the faithfull offer take
              Of me, and all that I can make,
              Or else by him my loue denie,   2150
              And then Ile studie how to die.

SILUIUS Call you this chiding?

CELIA Alas poore Shepheard.

ROSALIND Doe you pitty him? No, he deserues no pitty:
(*to Siluius*) wilt thou loue such a woman? what to
make thee an instrument, and play false straines vpon
thee? not to be endur'd. Well, goe your way to her;
(for I see Loue hath made thee a tame snake) and say
this to her; That if she loue me, I charge her to loue
thee: if she will not, I will neuer haue her, vnlesse   2160
thou intreat for her: if you bee a true louer hence, and
not a word; for here comes more company.

                                                  Exit Siluius

Enter Oliuer

OLIUER

Good morrow, faire ones: pray you, (if you know)
Where in the Purlews of this Forrest, stands
A sheep-coat, fenc'd about with Oliue-trees.

CELIA

West of this place, down in the neighbor bottom.
The ranke of Oziers, by the murmuring streame
Left on your right hand, brings you to the place:
But at this howre, the house doth keepe it selfe.
2170   There's none within.

OLIUER

If that an eye may profit by a tongue,
Then should I know you by description,
Such garments, and such yeeres: the boy is faire,
Of femall fauour, and bestowes himselfe
Like a ripe sister: the woman low
And browner then her brother: are not you
The owner of the house I did enquire for?

CELIA

It is no boast, being ask'd, to say we are.

OLIUER

Orlando doth commend him to you both,
2180   And to that youth hee calls his *Rosalind*,
He sends this bloudy napkin; are you he?

ROSALIND

I am: what must we vnderstand by this?

OLIUER

Some of my shame, if you will know of me
What man I am, and how, and why, and where
This handkercher was stain'd.

CELIA   I pray you tell it.

OLIUER

When last the yong *Orlando* parted from you,
He left a promise to returne againe
Within an houre, and pacing through the Forrest,
Chewing the food of sweet and bitter fancie,
2190   Loe what befell: he threw his eye aside,
And marke what obiect did present it selfe.
Vnder an old Oake, whose bows were moss'd with
    age
And high top, bald with drie antiquitie,
A wretched ragged man, ore-growne with haire
Lay sleeping on his back; about his necke
A greene and guilded snake had wreath'd it selfe,
Who with her head, nimble in threats approach'd
The opening of his mouth: but sodainly
Seeing *Orlando*, it vnlink'd it selfe,
2200   And with indented glides, did slip away
Into a bush, vnder which bushes shade
A Lyonnesse, with vdders all drawne drie,
Lay cowching head on ground, with catlike watch
When that the sleeping man should stirre; for 'tis
The royall disposition of that beast
To prey on nothing, that doth seeme as dead:
This seene, *Orlando* did approach the man,
And found it was his brother, his elder brother.

CELIA

O I haue heard him speake of that same brother,
And he did render him the most vnnaturall   2210
That liu'd amongst men.

OLIUER   And well he might so doe,
For well I know he was vnnaturall.

ROSALIND

But to *Orlando*: did he leaue him there
Food to the suck'd and hungry Lyonnesse?

OLIUER

Twice did he turne his backe, and purpos'd so:
But kindnesse, nobler euer then reuenge,
And Nature stronger then his iust occasion,
Made him giue battell to the Lyonnesse:
Who quickly fell before him, in which hurtling
From miserable slumber I awaked.   2220

CELIA

Are you his brother?

ROSALIND   Was't you he rescu'd?

CELIA

Was't you that did so oft contriue to kill him?

OLIUER

'Twas I: but 'tis not I: I doe not shame
To tell you what I was, since my conuersion
So sweetly tastes, being the thing I am.

ROSALIND

But for the bloody napkin?

OLIUER   By and by:
When from the first to last betwixt vs two,
Teares our recountments had most kindely bath'd,
As how I came into that Desert place,
I'briefe, he led me to the gentle Duke,   2230
Who gaue me fresh aray, and entertainment,
Committing me vnto my brothers loue,
Who led me instantly vnto his Caue,
There stript himselfe, and heere vpon his arme
The Lyonnesse had torne some flesh away,
Which all this while had bled; and now he fainted,
And cride in fainting vpon *Rosalinde*.
Briefe, I recouer'd him, bound vp his wound,
And after some small space, being strong at heart,
He sent me hither, stranger as I am   2240
To tell this story, that you might excuse
His broken promise, and to giue this napkin
Died in his bloud, vnto the Shepheard youth,
That he in sport doth call his *Rosalind*.

    Rosalind faints

CELIA

Why how now *Ganimed*, sweet *Ganimed*.

OLIUER

Many will swoon when they do look on bloud.

CELIA

There is more in it; Cosen *Ganimed*.

OLIUER Looke, he recouers.

ROSALIND I would I were at home.

CELIA Wee'll lead you thither: 2250
(*To Oliuer*) I pray you will you take him by the arme.

OLIUER Be of good cheere youth: you a man? You lacke a mans heart.

ROSALIND I doe so, I confesse it: Ah, sirra, a body would thinke this was well counterfeited, I pray you tell your brother how well I counterfeited: heigh-ho.

OLIUER This was not counterfeit, there is too great testimony in your complexion, that it was a passion of earnest.

2260 ROSALIND Counterfeit, I assure you.

OLIUER Well then, take a good heart, and counterfeit to be a man.

ROSALIND So I doe: but yfaith, I should haue beene a woman by right.

CELIA Come, you looke paler and paler: pray you draw homewards: good sir, goe with vs.

OLIUER
That will I: for I must beare answere backe
How you excuse my brother, *Rosalind*.

ROSALIND I shall deuise something: but I pray you
2270 commend my counterfeiting to him: will you goe?

Exeunt

Sc. 19   *Enter Touchstone the Clowne and Awdrie*
(5.1)
CLOWNE We shall finde a time *Awdrie*, patience gentle *Awdrie*.

AUDREY Faith the Priest was good enough, for all the olde gentlemans saying.

CLOWNE A most wicked Sir *Oliuer*, *Awdrie*, a most vile *Mar-text*. But *Awdrie*, there is a youth heere in the Forrest layes claime to you.

AUDREY I, I know who 'tis: he hath no interest in mee in the world: here comes the man you meane.

Enter William

2280 CLOWNE It is meat and drinke to me to see a Clowne, by my troth, we that haue good wits, haue much to answer for: we shall be flouting: we cannot hold.

WILLIAM Good eu'n *Audrey*.

AUDREY God ye good eu'n *William*.

WILLIAM (*to Touchstone*) And good eu'n to you Sir.

CLOWNE Good eu'n gentle friend. Couer thy head, couer thy head: Nay prethee bee couer'd. How olde are you Friend?

WILLIAM Fiue and twentie Sir.

2290 CLOWNE A ripe age: Is thy name *William*?

WILLIAM *William*, sir.

CLOWNE A faire name. Was't borne i'th Forrest heere?

WILLIAM I sir, I thanke God.

CLOWNE Thanke God: A good answer: Art rich?

WILLIAM 'Faith sir, so, so.

CLOWNE So, so, is good, very good, very excellent good: and yet it is not, it is but so, so: Art thou wise?

WILLIAM I sir, I haue a prettie wit.

CLOWNE Why, thou saist well. I do now remember a
2300 saying: The Foole doth thinke he is wise, but the wiseman knowes himselfe to be a Foole. The Heathen Philosopher, when he had a desire to eate a Grape, would open his lips when he put it into his mouth, meaning thereby, that Grapes were made to eate, and lippes to open. You do loue this maid?

WILLIAM I do sir.

CLOWNE Giue me your hand: Art thou Learned?

WILLIAM No sir.

CLOWNE Then learne this of me, To haue, is to haue. For
it is a figure in Rhetoricke, that drink being powr'd out   2310
of a cup into a glasse, by filling the one, doth empty
the other. For all your Writers do consent, that *ipse* is
hee: now you are not *ipse*, for I am he.

WILLIAM Which he sir?

CLOWNE He sir, that must marrie this woman: Therefore
you Clowne, abandon: which is in the vulgar, leaue
the societie: which in the boorish, is companie, of this
female: which in the common, is woman: which
together, is, abandon the society of this Female, or
Clowne thou perishest: or to thy better vnderstanding,   2320
dyest; or (to wit) I kill thee, make thee away, translate
thy life into death, thy libertie into bondage: I will
deale in poyson with thee, or in bastinado, or in steele:
I will bandy with thee in faction, I will ore-run thee
with policie: I will kill thee a hundred and fifty wayes,
therefore tremble and depart.

AUDREY Do good *William*.

WILLIAM God rest you merry sir.   *Exit*

Enter Corin

CORIN Our Master and Mistresse seekes you: come away,
away.   2330

CLOWNE Trip *Audry*, trip *Audry*, (*to Corin*) I attend, I
attend.   *Exeunt*

Enter Orlando & Oliuer   Sc. 20
                                                  (5.2)
ORLANDO Is't possible, that on so little acquaintance you
should like her? that, but seeing, you should loue her?
And louing woo? and wooing, she should graunt? And
will you perseuer to enioy her?

OLIUER Neither call the giddinesse of it in question; the
pouertie of her, the small acquaintance, my sodaine
woing, nor her sodaine consenting: but say with mee,
I loue *Aliena*: say with her, that she loues mee; consent   2340
with both, that we may enioy each other: it shall be
to your good: for my fathers house, and all the
reuennew, that was old Sir *Rowlands* will I estate vpon
you, and heere liue and die a Shepherd.

Enter Rosalind as Ganimed

ORLANDO You haue my consent. Let your Wedding be to
morrow: thither will I inuite the Duke, and all's
contented followers: Go you, and prepare *Aliena*; for
looke you, heere comes my *Rosalinde*.

ROSALIND God saue you brother.

OLIUER And you faire sister.   *Exit*   2350

ROSALIND Oh my deere *Orlando*, how it greeues me to see
thee weare thy heart in a scarfe.

ORLANDO It is my arme.

ROSALIND I thought thy heart had beene wounded with
the clawes of a Lion.

ORLANDO Wounded it is, but with the eyes of a Lady.

ROSALIND Did your brother tell you how I counterfeyted
to sound, when he shew'd me your handkercher?

ORLANDO I, and greater wonders then that.

ROSALIND O, I know where you are: nay, tis true: there   2360

was neuer any thing so sodaine, but the fight of two
Rammes, and *Cesars* Thrasonicall bragge of I came,
saw, and ouercame. For your brother, and my sister,
no sooner met, but they look'd: no sooner look'd, but
they lou'd; no sooner lou'd, but they sigh'd: no sooner
sigh'd but they ask'd one another the reason: no sooner
knew the reason, but they sought the remedie: and in
these degrees, haue they made a paire of staires to
marriage, which they will climbe incontinent, or else
2370 bee incontinent before marriage; they are in the verie
wrath of loue, and they will together. Clubbes cannot
part them.

ORLANDO They shall be married to morrow: and I will bid
the Duke to the Nuptiall. But O, how bitter a thing it
is, to looke into happines through another mans eies:
by so much the more shall I to morrow be at the height
of heart heauinesse, by how much I shal thinke my
brother happie, in hauing what he wishes for.

ROSALIND Why then to morrow, I cannot serue your
2380 turne for *Rosalind*?

ORLANDO I can liue no longer by thinking.

ROSALIND I will wearie you then no longer with idle
talking. Know of me then (for now I speake to some
purpose) that I know you are a Gentleman of good
conceit: I speake not this, that you should beare a good
opinion of my knowledge: insomuch (I say) I know
you are: neither do I labor for a greater esteeme then
may in some little measure draw a beleefe from you,
to do your selfe good, and not to grace me. Beleeue
2390 then, if you please, that I can do strange things: I haue
since I was three yeare old conuerst with a Magitian,
most profound in his Art, and yet not damnable. If you
do loue *Rosalinde* so neere the hart, as your gesture
cries it out: when your brother marries *Aliena*, shall
you marrie her. I know into what straights of Fortune
she is driuen, and it is not impossible to me, if it appeare
not inconuenient to you, to set her before your eyes to
morrow, humane as she is, and without any danger.

ORLANDO Speak'st thou in sober meanings?

2400 ROSALIND By my life I do, which I tender deerly, though
I say I am a Magitian: Therefore put you in your best
aray, bid your friends: for if you will be married to
morrow, you shall: and to *Rosalind* if you will.

Enter Siluius & Phebe

Looke, here comes a Louer of mine, and a louer of hers.

PHEBE (*to Rosalind*)
Youth, you haue done me much vngentlenesse,
To shew the letter that I writ to you.

ROSALIND
I care not if I haue: it is my studie
To seeme despightfull and vngentle to you:
You are there followed by a faithful shepheard,
2410 Looke vpon him, loue him: he worships you.

PHEBE (*to Siluius*)
Good shepheard, tell this youth what 'tis to loue.

SILUIUS
It is to be all made of sighes and teares,
And so am I for *Phebe*.

PHEBE And I for *Ganimed*.

ORLANDO And I for *Rosalind*.

ROSALIND And I for no woman.

SILUIUS
It is to be all made of faith and seruice,
And so am I for *Phebe*.

PHEBE And I for *Ganimed*.

ORLANDO And I for *Rosalind*.   2420

ROSALIND And I for no woman.

SILUIUS
It is to be all made of fantasie,
All made of passion, and all made of wishes,
All adoration, dutie, and obseruance,
All humblenesse, all patience, and impatience,
All puritie, all triall, all obedience:
And so am I for *Phebe*.

PHEBE And so am I for *Ganimed*.

ORLANDO And so am I for *Rosalind*.

ROSALIND And so am I for no woman.   2430

PHEBE (*to Rosalind*)
If this be so, why blame you me to loue you?

SILUIUS (*to Phebe*)
If this be so, why blame you me to loue you?

ORLANDO
If this be so, why blame you me to loue you?

ROSALIND Why do you speake too, Why blame you mee
to loue you.

ORLANDO
To her, that is not heere, nor doth not heare.

ROSALIND Pray you no more of this, 'tis like the howling
of Irish Wolues against the Moone: (*to Siluius*) I will
helpe you if I can: (*to Phebe*) I would loue you if I
could: To morrow meet me altogether: (*to Phebe*) I wil   2440
marrie you, if euer I marrie Woman, and Ile be married
to morrow: (*to Orlando*) I will satisfie you, if euer I
satisfie man, and you shall bee married to morrow. (*To
Siluius*) I wil content you, if what pleases you contents
you, and you shal be married to morrow: (*To Orlando*)
As you loue *Rosalind* meet, (*to Siluius*) as you loue
Phebe meet, and as I loue no woman, Ile meet: so fare
you wel: I haue left you commands.

SILUIUS Ile not faile, if I liue.

PHEBE Nor I.   2450

ORLANDO Nor I.   *Exeunt seuerally*

Enter Touchstone the Clowne and Audrey   Sc. 21
                                                  (5.3)
CLOWNE To morrow is the ioyfull day *Audrey*, to morow
will we be married.

AUDREY I do desire it with all my heart: and I hope it is
no dishonest desire, to desire to be a woman of ye
world? Heere come two of the banish'd Dukes Pages.

Enter two Pages

I. PAGE Wel met honest Gentleman.

CLOWNE By my troth well met: come, sit, sit, and a song.

2. PAGE We are for you, sit i'th middle.

I. PAGE Shal we clap into't roundly, without hauking, or   2460
spitting, or saying we are hoarse, which are the onely
prologues to a bad voice.

2. PAGE I faith, y'faith, and both in a tune like two gipsies on a horse.

Song

BOTH PAGES

> It was a Louer, and his lasse,
>   With a hey, and a ho, and a hey nonino,
> That o're the greene corne feild did passe,
>   In spring time, the onely pretty ring time.
> When Birds do sing, hey ding a ding, ding.
> Sweet Louers loue the spring.
>
> Betweene the acres of the Rie,
>   With a hey, and a ho, & a hey nonino:
> These prettie Country folks would lie.
>   In spring time, the onely pretty ring time.
> When Birds do sing, hey ding a ding, ding.
> Sweet Louers loue the spring.
>
> This Carroll they began that houre,
>   With a hey and a ho, & a hey nonino:
> How that a life was but a Flower,
>   In spring time, the onely pretty ring time.
> When Birds do sing, hey ding a ding, ding.
> Sweet Louers loue the spring.
>
> And therefore take the present time.
>   With a hey, & a ho, and a hey nonino,
> For loue is crowned with the prime.
>   In spring time, the onely pretty ring time.
> When Birds do sing, hey ding a ding, ding.
> Sweet Louers loue the spring.

CLOWNE Truly yong Gentlemen, though there was no great matter in the dittie, yet ye note was very vntunable.

I. PAGE You are deceiu'd Sir, we kept time, we lost not our time.

CLOWNE By my troth yes: I count it but time lost to heare such a foolish song. God buy you, and God mend your voices. Come *Audrie*.   *Exeunt seuerally*

Sc. 22
(5.4)

Enter Duke Senior, Amyens, Iaques, Orlando, Oliuer, Celia as Aliena

DUKE SENIOR

Dost thou beleeue *Orlando*, that the boy
Can do all this that he hath promised?

ORLANDO

I sometimes do beleeue, and somtimes do not,
As those that feare they hope, and know they feare.

Enter Rosalinde as Ganimed, Siluius, & Phebe

ROSALIND

Patience once more, whiles our cõpact is vrg'd:
(*To the Duke*) You say, if I bring in your *Rosalinde*,
You wil bestow her on *Orlando* heere?

DUKE SENIOR

That would I, had I kingdoms to giue with hir.

ROSALIND (*to Orlando*)

And you say you wil haue her, when I bring hir?

ORLANDO

That would I, were I of all kingdomes King.

ROSALIND (*to Phebe*)

You say, you'l marrie me, if I be willing.

PHEBE

That will I, should I die the houre after.

ROSALIND

But if you do refuse to marrie me,
You'l giue your selfe to this most faithfull Shepheard.

PHEBE So is the bargaine.

ROSALIND (*to Siluius*)

You say that you'l haue *Phebe* if she will.

SILUIUS

Though to haue her and death, were both one thing.

ROSALIND

I haue promis'd to make all this matter euen:
Keepe you your word, O Duke, to giue your daughter,
You yours *Orlando*, to receiue his daughter:
Keepe your word *Phebe*, that you'l marrie me,
Or else refusing me to wed this shepheard:
Keepe your word *Siluius*, that you'l marrie her
If she refuse me, and from hence I go
To make these doubts all euen.

Exit Rosalind and Celia

DUKE SENIOR

I do remember in this shepheard boy,
Some liuely touches of my daughters fauour.

ORLANDO

My Lord, the first time that I euer saw him,
Me thought he was a brother to your daughter:
But my good Lord, this Boy is Forrest borne,
And hath bin tutor'd in the rudiments
Of many desperate studies, by his vnckle,
Whom he reports to be a great Magitian,
Obscured in the circle of this Forrest.

⌈*Enter Touchstone the Clowne and Audrey*⌉

IAQUES There is sure another flood toward, and these couples are comming to the Arke. Here comes a payre of verie strange beasts, which in all tongues, are call'd Fooles.

CLOWNE Salutation and greeting to you all.

IAQUES (*to the Duke*) Good my Lord, bid him welcome: This is the Motley-minded Gentleman, that I haue so often met in the Forrest: he hath bin a Courtier he sweares.

CLOWNE If any man doubt that, let him put mee to my purgation, I haue trod a measure, I haue flattred a Lady, I haue bin politicke with my friend, smooth with mine enemie, I haue vndone three Tailors, I haue had foure quarrels, and like to haue fought one.

IAQUES And how was that tane vp?

CLOWNE 'Faith we met, and found the quarrel was vpon the seuenth cause.

IAQUES How seuenth cause? Good my Lord, like this fellow.

DUKE SENIOR I like him very well.

CLOWNE God'ild you sir, I desire you of the like: I presse in heere sir, amongst the rest of the Country copulatiues to sweare, and to forsweare, according as mariage binds and blood breakes: a poore virgin sir, an il-fauor'd thing sir, but mine owne, a poore humour of mine sir, to take that that no man else will: rich honestie dwels like a miser sir, in a poore house, as your Pearle in your foule oyster.

DUKE SENIOR By my faith, he is very swift, and sententious.

2560 CLOWNE According to the fooles bolt sir, and such dulcet diseases.

IAQUES But for the seuenth cause. How did you finde the quarrell on the seuenth cause?

CLOWNE Vpon a lye, seuen times remoued: (beare your bodie more seeming *Audry*) as thus sir: I did dislike the cut of a certaine Courtiers beard: he sent me word, if I said his beard was not cut well, hee was in the minde it was: this is call'd the retort courteous. If I sent him word againe, it was not well cut, he wold send me word he cut it to please himselfe: this is call'd the quip
2570 modest. If againe, it was not well cut, he disabled my iudgment: this is called, the reply churlish. If againe it was not well cut, he would answer I spake not true: this is call'd the reproofe valiant. If againe, it was not well cut, he wold say, I lie: this is call'd the counter-checke quarrelsome: and so to the lye circumstantiall, and the lye direct.

IAQUES And how oft did you say his beard was not well cut?

2580 CLOWNE I durst go no further then the lye circumstantial: nor he durst not giue me the lye direct: and so wee measur'd swords, and parted.

IAQUES Can you nominate in order now, the degrees of the lye.

CLOWNE O sir, we quarrel in print, by the booke: as you haue bookes for good manners: I will name you the degrees. The first, the Retort courteous: the second, the Quip-modest: the third, the reply Churlish: the fourth, the Reproofe valiant: the fift, the Counterchecke
2590 quarrelsome: the sixt, the Lye with circumstance: the seauenth, the Lye direct: all these you may auoyd, but the Lye direct: and you may auoide that too, with an If. I knew when seuen Iustices could not take vp a Quarrell, but when the parties were met themselues, one of them thought but of an If; as if you saide so, then I saide so: and they shooke hands, and swore brothers. Your If, is the onely peace-maker: much vertue in if.

IAQUES (*to the Duke*) Is not this a rare fellow my Lord?
2600 He's as good at any thing, and yet a foole.

DUKE SENIOR He vses his folly like a stalking-horse, and vnder the presentation of that he shoots his wit.
⌐*Still Musicke.*⌐ *Enter Hymen, with Rosalind and Celia as themselues*

HYMEN   *Then is there mirth in heauen,*
            When earthly things made eauen
                Attone together.
            Good Duke receiue thy daughter,
            Hymen from Heauen brought her,
                Yea brought her hether,
            That thou mightst ioyne hir hand with his,
2610   *Whose heart within his bosome is.*

ROSALIND (*to the Duke*)
    To you I giue my selfe, for I am yours.
    (*To Orlando*) To you I giue my selfe, for I am yours.

DUKE SENIOR
    If there be truth in sight, you are my daughter.

ORLANDO
    If there be truth in sight, you are my *Rosalind*.

PHEBE
    If sight & shape be true,
    Why then my loue adieu.

ROSALIND (*to the Duke*)
    Ile haue no Father, if you be not he:
    (*To Orlando*) Ile haue no Husband, if you be not he:
    (*To Phebe*) Nor ne're wed woman, if you be not shee.

HYMEN   Peace hoa: I barre confusion,   2620
            'Tis I must make conclusion
                Of these most strange euents:
            Here's eight that must take hands,
            To ioyne in *Hymens* bands,
                If truth holds true contents.
        (*To Orlando and Rosalind*)
            You and you, no crosse shall part;
        (*To Oliuer and Celia*)
            You and you, are hart in hart:
        (*To Phebe*)
            You, to his loue must accord,
            Or haue a Woman to your Lord.
        (*To Touchstone and Audrey*)
            You and you, are sure together,   2630
            As the Winter to fowle Weather:
        (*To All*)
            Whiles a Wedlocke Hymne we sing,
            Feede your selues with questioning:
            That reason, wonder may diminish
            How thus we met, and these things finish.

                        Song
        Wedding is great Iunos crowne,
            O blessed bond of boord and bed:
        'Tis Hymen peoples euerie towne,
            High wedlock then be honored:
        Honor, high honor and renowne   2640
        To Hymen, God of euerie Towne.

DUKE SENIOR (*to Celia*)
    O my deere Neece, welcome thou art to me,
    Euen daughter; welcome in no lesse degree.

PHEBE (*to Siluius*)
    I wil not eate my word, now thou art mine,
    Thy faith, my fancie to thee doth combine.
            Enter Iaques de Boys, the Second Brother

IAQUES DE BOYS
    Let me haue audience for a word or two:
    I am the second sonne of old *Sir Rowland*,
    That bring these tidings to this faire assembly.
    Duke Frederick hearing how that euerie day
    Men of great worth resorted to this forrest,   2650
    Addrest a mightie power, which were on foote
    In his owne conduct, purposely to take

His brother heere, and put him to the sword:
And to the skirts of this wilde Wood he came;
Where, meeting with an old Religious man,
After some question with him, was conuerted
Both from his enterprize, and from the world:
His crowne bequeathing to his banish'd Brother,
And all their Lands restor'd to them againe
2660   That were with him exil'd. This to be true,
I do engage my life.

DUKE SENIOR   Welcome yong man:
Thou offer'st fairely to thy brothers wedding:
To one his lands with-held, and to the other
A land it selfe at large, a potent Dukedome.
First, in this Forrest, let vs do those ends
That heere were well begun, and wel begot:
And after, euery of this happie number
That haue endur'd shrew'd daies, and nights with vs,
Shal share the good of our returned fortune,
2670   According to the measure of their states.
Meane time, forget this new-falne dignitie,
And fall into our Rusticke Reuelrie:
Play Musicke, and you Brides and Bride-groomes all,
With measure heap'd in ioy, to'th Measures fall.

IAQUES
Sir, by your patience: (*to Iaques de Boys*) if I heard
    you rightly,
The Duke hath put on a Religious life,
And throwne into neglect the pompous Court.

IAQUES DE BOYS He hath.

IAQUES
To him will I: out of these conuertites,
2680   There is much matter to be heard, and learn'd:
(*To the Duke*)
You to your former Honor, I bequeath:
Your patience, and your vertue, well deserues it.
(*To Orlando*)
You to a loue, that your true faith doth merit:
(*To Oliuer*)
You to your land, and loue, and great allies:

(*To Siluius*)
You to a long, and well-deserued bed:
(*To Touchstone*)
And you to wrangling, for thy louing voyage
Is but for two moneths victuall'd: (*To All*) So to your
    pleasures,
I am for other, then for dancing meazures.

DUKE SENIOR Stay, *Iaques*, stay.

IAQUES
To see no pastime, I: what you would haue,   2690
Ile stay to know, at your abandon'd caue.   *Exit*

DUKE SENIOR
Proceed, proceed: wee'l so begin these rights,
As we do trust they'l end, in true delights.
      ⌜*They dance; then*⌝ *exeunt all but Rosalind*

Epilogue

ROSALIND (*to the audience*) It is not the fashion to see the
Ladie the Epilogue: but it is no more vnhandsome, then
to see the Lord the Prologue. If it be true, that good
wine needs no bush, 'tis true, that a good play needes
no Epilogue. Yet to good wine they do vse good bushes:
and good playes proue the better by the helpe of good
Epilogues: What a case am I in then, that am neither   2700
a good Epilogue, nor cannot insinuate with you in the
behalfe of a good play? I am not furnish'd like a Begger,
therefore to begge will not become mee. My way is to
coniure you, and Ile begin with the Women. I charge
you (O women) for the loue you beare to men, to like
as much of this Play, as please you: And I charge you
(O men) for the loue you beare to women (as I perceiue
by your simpring, none of you hates them) that
betweene you, and the women, the play may please. If
I were a Woman, I would kisse as many of you as had   2710
beards that pleas'd me, complexions that lik'd me, and
breaths that I defi'de not: And I am sure, as many as
haue good beards, or good faces, or sweet breaths, will
for my kind offer, when I make curt'sie, bid me farewell.
                               Exit

FINIS

HAMLET

SEVERAL references from 1589 onwards witness the existence of a play about Hamlet, but Francis Meres did not attribute a play with this title to Shakespeare in 1598. The first clear reference to Shakespeare's play is its entry in the Stationers' Register on 26 July 1602 as *the Revenge of Hamlett Prince [of] Denmarke*, when it was said to have been 'latelie Acted by the Lo: Chamberleyn his servantes'. It survives in three versions; their relationship is a matter of dispute on which views about when Shakespeare wrote his play, and in what form, depend. In 1603 appeared an inferior text apparently assembled from actors' memories; it has only about 2,200 lines. In the following year, as if to put the record straight, James Roberts (to whom the play had been entered in 1602) published it as 'Newly imprinted and enlarged to almost as much againe as it was, according to the true and perfect Coppie'. At about 3,800 lines, this is the longest version. The 1623 Folio offers a still different text, some 230 lines shorter than the 1604 version, differing verbally from that at many points, and including about 70 additional lines. It is our belief that Shakespeare wrote *Hamlet* about 1600, and revised it later; that the 1604 edition was printed from his original papers; that the Folio represents the revised version; and that the 1603 edition represents a very imperfect report of an abridged version of the revision. So our text is based on the Folio; passages present in the 1604 quarto but absent from the Folio are printed as Additional Passages because we believe that, however fine they may be in themselves, Shakespeare decided that the play as a whole would be better without them.

The plot of *Hamlet* originates in a Scandinavian folk-tale told in the twelfth-century *Danish History* written in Latin by the Danish Saxo Grammaticus. François de Belleforest retold it in the fifth volume (1580) of his *Histoires Tragiques*, not translated into English until 1608. Saxo, through Belleforest, provided the basic story of a Prince of Denmark committed to revenge his father's murder by his own brother (Claudius) who has married the dead man's widow (Gertrard). As in Shakespeare, Hamlet pretends to be mad, kills his uncle's counsellor (Polonius) while he is eavesdropping, rebukes his mother, is sent to England under the escort of two retainers (Rosencrans and Guyldensterne) who bear orders that he be put to death on arrival, finds the letter containing the orders and alters it so that it is the retainers who are executed, returns to Denmark, and kills the King.

Belleforest's story differs at some points from Shakespeare's, and Shakespeare elaborates it, adding, for example, the Ghost of Hamlet's father, the coming of the actors to Elsinore, the performance of the play through which Hamlet tests his uncle's guilt, Ophelia's madness and death, Laertes' plot to revenge *his* father's death, the Clowne (a grave-digger), Ophelia's funeral, and the characters of Ostricke and Fortinbrasse. How much he owed to the lost Hamlet play we cannot tell; what is certain is that Shakespeare used his mastery of a wide range of diverse styles in both verse and prose, and his genius for dramatic effect, to create from these and other sources the most complex, varied, and exciting drama that had ever been seen on the English stage. Its popularity was instant and enduring. The play has had a profound influence on Western culture, and Shakespeare's Hamlet has himself entered the world of myth.

Our edition is based upon the 1604 Quarto (printed from Shakespeare's foul papers), with additions and alterations from the Folio (printed from a scribal transcript).

THE NAMES OF THE ACTORS

GHOST of Hamlet, the last King of Denmarke

Claudius, his brother, the new KING of Denmarke

Gertrard, QUEENE of Denmarke, widdow of King Hamlet, now wife
    of King Claudius

Prince HAMLET, sonne of King Hamlet and Queene Gertrard

POLONIUS, a Lord

LAERTES, sonne of Polonius

OPHELIA, daughter of Polonius

REYNALDO, seruant of Polonius

HORATIO
ROSENCRANS   } friends of Prince Hamlet
GUYLDENSTERNE

FRANCISCO
BARNARDO   } souldiers
MARCELLUS

VALTEMAND
CORNELIUS
OSTRICKE   } Courtiers
GENTLEMEN

A SAYLER

A CLOWNE, a Grauemaker

An OTHER Clowne

A PRIEST

FORTINBRASSE, Prince of Norway

A CAPTAINE in his Army

EMBASSADORS from England

PLAYERS, who play the parts of Prologue, Player King, Player
    Queene, and Lucianus, in the Mousetrap

Lords, messengers, attendants, guards, souldiers, followers of
    Laertes, Saylers

The Tragedie of Hamlet Prince of Denmarke

Sc. 1
(1.1)

Enter Barnardo, and Francisco, two Centinels, at
seuerall doores

BARNARDO Whose there?

FRANCISCO
Nay answere me. Stand and vnfolde your selfe.

BARNARDO
Long liue the King.

FRANCISCO   *Barnardo.*

BARNARDO   Hee.

FRANCISCO
You come most carefully vpon your houre.

BARNARDO
Tis now strooke twelfe, get thee to bed *Francisco.*

FRANCISCO
For this reliefe much thanks, tis bitter cold,
And I am sick at hart.

BARNARDO   Haue you had quiet guard?

FRANCISCO
Not a mouse stirring.

BARNARDO   Well, good night:
If you doe meete *Horatio* and *Marcellus,*
10   The riualls of my watch, bid them make hast.
Enter Horatio, and Marcellus

FRANCISCO
I thinke I heare them, stand, who's there?

HORATIO   Friends to this ground.

MARCELLUS
And Leedgemen to the Dane.

FRANCISCO   Giue you good night.

MARCELLUS
O, farwell honest souldier, who hath relieu'd you?

FRANCISCO
Barnardo ha's my place; giue you good night.
Exit Francisco

MARCELLUS Holla, *Barnardo.*

BARNARDO Say, what is *Horatio* there?

HORATIO A peece of him.

BARNARDO
Welcome *Horatio,* welcome good *Marcellus.*

MARCELLUS
What, ha's this thing appeard againe to night?

20 BARNARDO I haue seene nothing.

MARCELLUS
Horatio saies tis but our fantasie,
And will not let beliefe take holde of him,
Touching this dreaded sight twice seene of vs,
Therefore I haue intreated him along,
With vs to watch the minuts of this night,
That if againe this apparision come,
He may approoue our eyes and speake to it.

HORATIO
Tush, tush, twill not appeare.

BARNARDO   Sit downe a while,

And let vs once againe assaile your eares,
That are so fortified against our story,
What we two nights haue seene.   30

HORATIO   Well, sit we downe,
And let vs heare *Barnardo* speake of this.

BARNARDO Last night of all,
When yond same starre thats weastward from the
pole,
Had made his course t'illume that part of heauen
Where now it burnes, *Marcellus* and my selfe
The bell then beating one.
Enter Ghost in compleat Armor, holding a
tronchion, with his beauer vp

MARCELLUS
Peace, breake thee of, looke where it comes againe.

BARNARDO
In the same figure like the King thats dead.

MARCELLUS (*to Horatio*)
Thou art a scholler, speake to it *Horatio.*   40

BARNARDO
Lookes it not like the King? marke it *Horatio.*

HORATIO
Most like, it horrowes me with feare and wonder.

BARNARDO
It would be spoke to.

MARCELLUS   Question it *Horatio.*

HORATIO (*to the Ghost*)
What art thou that vsurpst this time of night,
Together with that faire and warlike forme,
In which the Maiestie of buried Denmarke
Did sometimes march, by heauen I charge thee
speake.

MARCELLUS
It is offended.

BARNARDO   See it staukes away.

HORATIO (*to the Ghost*)
Stay, speake, speake, I charge thee speake.   *Exit Ghost*

MARCELLUS Tis gone and will not answere.   50

BARNARDO
How now *Horatio,* you tremble and looke pale,
Is not this somthing more then phantasie?
What thinke you ont?

HORATIO
Before my God I might not this belieue,
Without the sencible and true auouch
Of mine owne eies.

MARCELLUS Is it not like the King?

HORATIO As thou art to thy selfe.
Such was the very Armor he had on,
When he th'ambitious *Norway* combated,   60
So frownd he once, when in an angry parle
He smot the sleaded pollax on the ice.
Tis strange.

MARCELLUS

    Thus twice before, and iust at this dead houre,

    With martiall stauke hath he gone by our watch.

HORATIO

    In what perticular thought, to worke I know not,

    But in the grosse and scope of my opinion,

    This bodes some strange eruption to our state.

MARCELLUS

    Good now sit downe, and tell me he that knowes,

70   Why this same strikt and most obseruant watch

    So nightly toiles the subiect of the land,

    And why such dayly cast of brazon Cannon

    And forraine marte, for implements of warre,

    Why such impresse of ship-writes, whose sore taske

    Does not deuide the Sunday from the weeke,

    What might be toward that this sweaty hast

    Doth make the night ioynt labourer with the day,

    Who ist that can informe mee?

HORATIO   That can I.

    At least the whisper goes so; our last King,

80   Whose image euen but now appear'd to vs,

    Was as you knowe by *Fortinbrasse* of *Norway*,

    Thereto prickt on by a most emulate pride

    Dar'd to the combat; in which our valiant *Hamlet*,

    (For so this side of our knowne world esteemd him)

    Did slay this *Fortinbrasse*, who by a seald compact

    Well ratified by lawe and heraldy

    Did forfait (with his life) all those his lands

    Which he stood seaz'd on, to the conquerour.

    Against the which a moitie competent

90   Was gaged by our King, which had returnd

    To the inheritance of *Fortinbrasse*,

    Had he bin vanquisher; as by the same cou'nant,

    And carriage of the article desseignd,

    His fell to Hamlet; now Sir, young *Fortinbrasse*

    Of vnimprooued mettle, hot and full,

    Hath in the skirts of *Norway* heere and there

    Sharkt vp a list of landlesse resolutes

    For foode and diet to some enterprise

    That hath a stomacke in't, which is no other

100   And it doth well appeare vnto our state

    But to recouer of vs by strong hand

    And tearmes compulsatiue, those foresaid lands

    So by his father lost; and this I take it,

    Is the maine motiue of our preparations

    The source of this our watch, and the chiefe head

    Of this post hast and Romeage in the land.

        Enter Ghost, as before

    But soft, behold, loe where it comes againe

    Ile crosse it though it blast mee: stay illusion,

        It spreads his armes

    If thou hast any sound or vse of voyce,

110   Speake to me,

    If there be any good thing to be done

    That may to thee doe ease, and grace to mee,

    Speake to me.

    If thou art priuie to thy countries fate

    Which happily foreknowing may auoyd

    O speake:

    Or if thou hast vphoorded in thy life

    Extorted treasure in the wombe of earth

    For which they say you spirits oft walke in death,

        The cocke crowes

    Speake of it, stay and speake, stop it *Marcellus*.   120

MARCELLUS

    Shall I strike at it with my partizan?

HORATIO

    Doe if it will not stand.

BARNARDO   Tis heere.

HORATIO   Tis heere.

                             Exit Ghost

MARCELLUS Tis gone.

    We doe it wrong being so Maiesticall

    To offer it the showe of violence,

    For it is as the ayre, invulnerable,

    And our vaine blowes malicious mockery.

BARNARDO

    It was about to speake when the cock crewe.

HORATIO

    And then it started like a guilty thing,

    Vpon a fearefull summons; I haue heard,   130

    The Cock that is the trumpet to the morne,

    Doth with his lofty and shrill sounding throat

    Awake the God of day, and at his warning

    Whether in sea or fire, in earth or ayre

    Th'extrauagant and erring spirit hies

    To his confine, and of the truth heerein

    This present obiect made probation.

MARCELLUS

    It faded on the crowing of the Cock.

    Some say that euer gainst that season comes

    Wherein our Sauiours birth is celebrated   140

    The bird of dawning singeth all night long,

    And then they say no spirit can walke abraode

    The nights are wholsome, then no plannets strike,

    No fairy takes, nor witch hath power to charme

    So hallowed, and so gratious is the time.

HORATIO

    So haue I heard and doe in part belieue it,

    But looke the morne in russet mantle clad

    Walkes ore the dewe of yon high Easterne hill

    Breake we our watch vp and by my aduise

    Let vs impart what we haue seene to night   150

    Vnto young *Hamlet*, for vppon my life

    This spirit dumb to vs, will speake to him:

    Doe you consent we shall acquaint him with it

    As needfull in our loues, fitting our duty.

MARCELLUS

    Lets doo't I pray, and I this morning knowe

    Where we shall find him most conueniently.   *Exeunt*

    Florish. Enter Claudius, King of Denmarke, Gertrad   Sc. 2

    the Queene, Counsaile: as Polonius, and his Sonne   (1.2)

    Laertes, and his Sister Ophelia, Hamlet dressed in

    black, Cum Alijs

KING

    Though yet of *Hamlet* our deare brothers death

    The memorie be greene, and that it vs befitted

To beare our harts in griefe, and our whole
    Kingdome,
160 To be contracted in one browe of woe
Yet so farre hath discretion fought with nature,
That we with wisest sorrowe thinke on him
Together with remembrance of our selues:
Therefore our sometime Sister, now our Queene
Th'imperiall ioyntresse of this warlike state
Haue we as twere with a defeated ioy
With one auspitious, and one dropping eye,
With mirth in funerall, and with dirdge in marriage,
In equall scale waighing delight and dole
170 Taken to wife: nor haue we heerein bard
Your better wisdomes, which haue freely gone
With this affaire along (for all our thankes)
Now followes that you knowe young *Fortinbrasse*,
Holding a weake supposall of our worth
Or thinking by our late deare brothers death
Our state to be disioynt, and out of frame
Coleagued with the dreame of his aduantage
He hath not faild to pestur vs with message
Importing the surrender of those lands
180 Lost by his father, with all bands of lawe
To our most valiant brother, so much for him:
    Enter Voltemand and Cornelius
Now for our selfe, and for this time of meeting,
Thus much the busines is, we haue heere writ
To *Norway* Vncle of young *Fortenbrasse*
Who impotent and bedred scarcely heares
Of this his Nephewes purpose; to suppresse
His further gate heerein, in that the leuies,
The lists, and full proportions are all made
Out of his subiect, and we heere dispatch
190 You good *Cornelius*, and you *Valtemand*,
For bearers of this greeting to old *Norway*,
Giuing to you no further personall power
To busines with the King, more then the scope
Of these delated articles allowe:
Farwell, and let your hast commend your dutie.

VALTEMAND

In that, and all things will we showe our dutie.

KING

We doubt it nothing, hartely farwell.
              Exit Voltemand and Cornelius
And now *Laertes* whats the newes with you?
You told vs of some sute, what ist *Laertes*?
200 You cannot speake of reason to the Dane
And lose your voyce; what wold'st thou begge *Laertes,*?
That shall not be my offer, not thy asking,
The head is not more natiue to the hart
The hand more instrumentall to the mouth
Then is the throne of Denmarke to thy father,
What would'st thou haue *Laertes*?

LAERTES   Dread my Lord,
Your leaue and fauour to returne to Fraunce,
From whence, though willingly I came to Denmarke,
To showe my dutie in your Coronation;
210 Yet now I must confesse, that duty done

My thoughts and wishes bend againe towards
    Fraunce
And bowe them to your gracious leaue and pardon.

KING

Haue you your fathers leaue, what saies *Polonius*?

POLONIUS

He hath my Lord wroung from me my slowe leaue
By laboursome petition, and at last
Vpon his will I seald my hard consent,
I doe beseech you giue him leaue to goe.

KING

Take thy faire houre *Laertes*, time be thine
And thy best graces spend it at thy will:
But now my Cosin *Hamlet*, and my sonne.   220

HAMLET

A little more then kin, and lesse then kind.

KING

How is it that the clowdes still hang on you.

HAMLET

Not so my Lord, I am too much i'th'sonne.

QUEENE

Good *Hamlet* cast thy nightly colour off
And let thine eye looke like a friend on *Denmarke*,
Doe not for euer with thy vailed lids
Seeke for thy noble Father in the dust,
Thou know'st tis common all that liues must die,
Passing through nature to eternitie.

HAMLET

I Maddam, it is common.

QUEENE   If it be   230
Why seemes it so perticuler with thee.

HAMLET

Seemes Maddam, nay it is, I know not seemes,
Tis not alone my incky cloake good mother
Nor customary suites of solembe blacke
Nor windie suspiration of forst breath
No, nor the fruitfull riuer in the eye,
Nor the deiected hauior of the visage
Together with all formes, moodes, shewes of griefe
That can denote me truely, these indeede seeme,
For they are actions that a man might play   240
But I haue that within which passeth showe
These but the trappings and the suites of woe.

KING

Tis sweete and commendable in your nature *Hamlet*,
To giue these mourning duties to your father
But you must knowe your father lost a father,
That father lost, lost his, and the suruiuer bound
In filliall obligation for some tearme
To doe obsequious sorrowe, but to perseuer
In obstinate condolement, is a course
Of impious stubbornes, tis vnmanly griefe,   250
It showes a will most incorrect to heauen
A hart vnfortified, a minde impatient
An vnderstanding simple and vnschoold
For what we knowe must be, and is as common
As any the most vulgar thing to sence,
Why should we in our peuish opposition

Take it to hart, fie, tis a fault to heauen,
A fault against the dead, a fault to nature,
To reason most absurd, whose common theame
260 Is death of fathers, and who still hath cryed
From the first course, till he that died to day
This must be so: we pray you throw to earth
This vnpreuailing woe, and thinke of vs
As of a father, for let the world take note
You are the most imediate to our throne,
And with no lesse nobilitie of loue
Then that which dearest father beares his sonne,
Doe I impart towards you: for your intent
In going back to schoole in *Wittenberg,*
270 It is most retrogard to our desire,
And we beseech you bend you to remaine
Heere in the cheare and comfort of our eye,
Our chiefest courtier, cosin, and our sonne.

QUEENE
Let not thy mother loose her prayers *Hamlet,*
I pray thee stay with vs, goe not to *Wittenberg.*

HAMLET
I shall in all my best obay you Madam.

KING
Why tis a louing and a faire reply,
Be as our selfe in Denmarke, (*to Queene*) Madam come,
This gentle and vnforc'd accord of *Hamlet*
280 Sits smiling to my hart, in grace whereof,
No iocond health that Denmarke drinkes to day,
But the great Cannon to the cloudes shall tell,
And the Kings rowse the heauens shall brute againe,
Respeaking earthly thunder; come away.
⌈*Florish.*⌉ *Exeunt all, but Hamlet*

HAMLET
O that this too too solid flesh would melt,
Thaw and resolue it selfe into a dewe,
Or that the euerlasting had not fixt
His cannon gainst sealfe slaughter, ô God, ô God,
How weary, stale, flat, and vnprofitable
290 Seeme to me all the vses of this world?
Fie on't, ah fie, fie, tis an vnweeded garden
That growes to seede, things rancke and grose in
      nature,
Possesse it meerely that it should come to this
But two months dead, nay not so much, not two,
So excellent a King, that was to this
Hiperion to a satire, so louing to my mother,
That he might not beteeme the winds of heauen
Visite her face too roughly, heauen and earth
Must I remember, why she would hang on him
300 As if increase of appetite had growne
By what it fed on, and yet within a month,
Let me not thinke on't; frailty thy name is woman
A little month or ere those shooes were old
With which she followed my poore fathers bodie
Like *Niobe* all teares, why she, euen she
O God, a beast that wants discourse of reason
Would haue mourn'd longer, married with mine Vncle,

My fathers brother, but no more like my father
Then I to *Hercules,* within a month,
Ere yet the salt of most vnrighteous teares,   310
Had left the flushing of her gauled eyes
She married, ô most wicked speede; to post
With such dexteritie to incestious sheets,
It is not, nor it cannot come to good,
But breake my hart, for I must hold my tongue.
Enter Horatio, Marcellus, and Bernardo

HORATIO
Haile to your Lordship.

HAMLET   I am glad to see you well;
Horatio, or I do forget my selfe.

HORATIO
The same my Lord, and your poore seruant euer.

HAMLET
Sir my good friend, Ile change that name with you,
And what make you from *Wittenberg Horatio?*   320
Marcellus.

MARCELLUS   My good Lord.

HAMLET
I am very glad to see you, (*to Barnardo*) (good euen sir)
(*To Horatio*) But what in faith make you from *Wittenberg?*

HORATIO
A truant disposition good my Lord.

HAMLET
I would not haue your enimie say so,
Nor shall you doe mine eare that violence
To make it truster of your owne report
Against your selfe, I knowe you are no truant,
But what is your affaire in *Elsonoure?*
Weele teach you to drinke deepe ere you depart.   330

HORATIO
My Lord, I came to see your fathers funerall.

HAMLET
I prethee doe not mocke me fellowe studient,
I thinke it was to see my mothers wedding.

HORATIO
Indeede my Lord it followed hard vppon.

HAMLET
Thrift, thrift, *Horatio,* the funerall bak't meates
Did coldly furnish forth the marriage tables,
Would I had met my dearest foe in heauen
Ere I had euer seene that day *Horatio,*
My father, me thinkes I see my father.

HORATIO
Oh where my Lord?

HAMLET   In my mindes eye *Horatio.*   340

HORATIO
I saw him once, a was a goodly King.

HAMLET
A was a man take him for all in all
I shall not looke vppon his like againe.

HORATIO
My Lord I thinke I saw him yesternight.

HAMLET   Saw, who?

HORATIO   My Lord the King your father.

HAMLET The King my father?

HORATIO
Season your admiration for a while
With an attent eare till I may deliuer
350 Vppon the witnes of these gentlemen
This maruile to you.

HAMLET   For Gods loue let me heare?

HORATIO
Two nights together had these gentlemen
Marcellus, and *Barnardo*, on their watch
In the dead wast and middle of the night
Beene thus incountred, a figure like your father
Arm'd at all poynts exactly, *Cap a Pe*
Appeares before them, and with solemne march,
Goes slowe and stately by them; thrice he walkt
By their opprest and feare surprised eyes
360 Within his tronchions length, whil'st they distil'd
Almost to gelly with the act of feare
Stand dumbe and speake not to him; this to me
In dreadfull secresie impart they did,
And I with them the third night kept the watch,
Where as they had deliuer'd both in time
Forme of the thing, each word made true and good,
The Apparision comes: I knewe your father,
These hands are not more like.

HAMLET   But where was this?

MARCELLUS
My Lord vppon the platforme where we watcht,

HAMLET
Did you not speake to it?

370 HORATIO   My Lord I did,
But answere made it none, yet once me thought
It lifted vp it head, and did addresse
It selfe to motion like as it would speake:
But euen then the morning Cock crewe loude,
And at the sound it shrunk in hast away
And vanisht from our sight.

HAMLET   Tis very strange.

HORATIO
As I doe liue my honor'd Lord tis true
And we did thinke it writ downe in our dutie
To let you knowe of it.

HAMLET
380 Indeede indeede Sirs but this troubles me,
Hold you the watch to night?

BOTH SOULDIERS   We doe my Lord.

HAMLET
Arm'd say you?

BOTH SOULDIERS   Arm'd my Lord.

HAMLET   From top to toe?

BOTH SOULDIERS
My Lord from head to foote.

HAMLET   Then sawe you not his face.

HORATIO
O yes my Lord, he wore his beauer vp.

HAMLET
What look't he frowningly?

HORATIO   A countenance more

In sorrow then in anger.

HAMLET   Pale, or red?

HORATIO
Nay very pale.

HAMLET   And fixt his eyes vpon you?

HORATIO Most constantly.

HAMLET I would I had beene there.

HORATIO It would haue much a maz'd you.   390

HAMLET
Very like, very like, stayd it long?

HORATIO
While one with moderate hast might tell a hundreth.

BOTH SOULDIERS Longer, longer.

HORATIO Not when I saw't.

HAMLET His beard was grisly, no.

HORATIO
It was as I haue seene it in his life
A sable siluer'd.

HAMLET   Ile watch to night; perchaunce
Twill walke againe.

HORATIO   I warrant you it will.

HAMLET
If it assume my noble fathers person,
Ile speake to it though hell it selfe should gape   400
And bid me hold my peace; I pray you all
If you haue hetherto conceald this sight
Let it be treble in your silence still,
And what soeuer els shall hap to night,
Giue it an vnderstanding but no tongue,
I will requite your loues, so farre ye well:
Vppon the platforme twixt a leauen and twelfe
Ile visite you.

ALL THREE   Our dutie to your honor.

HAMLET
Your loue, as mine to you, farwell.

                    Exeunt. Manet Hamlet
My fathers spirit (in armes) all is not well,   410
I doubt some foule play, would the night were come,
Till then sit still my soule, foule deedes will rise
Though all the earth ore-whelme them to mens eyes.

                                        Exit

Enter Laertes, and Ophelia his Sister   Sc. 3
                                             (1.3)
LAERTES
My necessaries are inbarckt, farwell,
And sister, as the winds giue benefit
And conuoy is assistant, doe not sleepe
But let me heere from you.

OPHELIA   Doe you doubt that?

LAERTES
For *Hamlet,* and the trifling of his fauour,
Hold it a fashion, and a toy in blood
A Violet in the youth of primy nature,   420
Forward, not permanent, sweete, not lasting,
The perfume and suppliance of a minute
No more.

OPHELIA   No more but so.

LAERTES   Thinke it no more.

For nature cressant does not growe alone
In thewes and bulke, but as his temple waxes
The inward seruice of the minde and soule
Growes wide withall, perhapes he loues you now,
And now no soyle nor cautell doth besmirch
The vertue of his will, but you must feare,
His greatnes wayd, his will is not his owne,
For hee himselfe is subiect to his Birth:
He may not as vnualewed persons doe,
Carue for himselfe, for on his choise depends
The sanity and health of the whole state,
And therefore must his choise be circumscribd
Vnto the voyce and yeelding of that body
Whereof he is the head, then if he saies he loues you,
It fits your wisdome so farre to belieue it
As he in his peculiar Sect and force
May giue his saying deede, which is no further
Then the maine voyce of Denmarke goes withall.
Then way what losse your honor may sustaine
If with too credent eare you list his songs
Or loose your hart, or your chast treasure open
To his vnmastred importunity.
Feare it *Ophelia*, feare it my deare sister,
And keepe within the reare of your affection
Out of the shot and danger of desire,
"The chariest maide is prodigall inough
If she vnmaske her butie to the Moone
"Vertue it selfe scapes not calumnious strokes
"The canker gaules the infants of the spring
Too oft before their buttons be disclos'd,
And in the morne and liquid dewe of youth
Contagious blastments are most iminent,
Be wary then, best safety lies in feare,
Youth to it selfe rebels, though non els neare.

OPHELIA

I shall th'effect of this good lesson keepe
As watchman to my hart, but good my brother
Doe not as some vngracious pastors doe,
Showe me the steepe and thorny way to heauen
Whilst like a puft, and reckles libertine
Himselfe the primrose path of dalience treads,
And reakes not his owne reed.

LAERTES   O feare me not,

Enter Polonius

I stay too long, but heere my father comes
A double blessing, is a double grace,
Occasion smiles vpon a second leaue.

POLONIUS

Yet heere *Laertes*? a bord, a bord for shame,
The wind sits in the shoulder of your saile,
And you are stayed for, there my blessing with thee,
And these fewe precepts in thy memory
See thou character, giue thy thoughts no tongue,
Nor any vnproportion'd thought his act,
Be thou familier, but by no meanes vulgar,
The friends thou hast, and their a doption tried,
Grapple them to thy soule with hoopes of steele,
But doe not dull thy palme with entertainment

Of each new hatcht vnfledgd comrade, beware
Of entrance to a quarrell, but being in,
Bear't that th'opposed may beware of thee,   480
Giue euery man thine eare, but fewe thy voyce,
Take each mans censure, but reserue thy iudgement,
Costly thy habite as thy purse can by,
But not exprest in fancy; rich not gaudy,
For the apparrell oft proclaimes the man
And they in Fraunce of the best ranck and station,
Ar of al most select and generous chiefe in that:
Neither a borrower nor a lender bee,
For lone oft looses both it selfe, and friend,
And borrowing duls the edge of husbandry;   490
This aboue all, to thine owne selfe be true
And it must followe as the night the day
Thou canst not then be false to any man:
Farwell, my blessing season this in thee.

LAERTES

Most humbly doe I take my leaue my Lord.

POLONIUS

The time inuites you goe, your seruants tend.

LAERTES

Farwell *Ophelia*, and remember well
What I haue sayd to you.

OPHELIA   Tis in my memory lockt
And you your selfe shall keepe the key of it.

LAERTES Farwell.   *Exit Laertes*   500

POLONIUS

What ist *Ophelia* he hath sayd to you?

OPHELIA

So please you, something touching the Lord *Hamlet*.

POLONIUS Marry well bethought
Tis tolde me he hath very oft of late
Giuen priuate time to you, and you your selfe
Haue of your audience beene most free and bountious,
If it be so, as so tis put on me,
And that in way of caution, I must tell you,
You doe not vnderstand your selfe so cleerely
As it behooues my daughter, and your honor,   510
What is betweene you giue me vp the truth.

OPHELIA

He hath my Lord of late made many tenders
Of his affection to me.

POLONIUS

Affection, puh, you speake like a greene girle
Vnsifted in such perrilous circumstance,
Doe you belieue his tenders as you call them?

OPHELIA

I doe not knowe my Lord what I should thinke.

POLONIUS

Marry Ile teach you, thinke your selfe a babie
That you haue tane his tenders for true pay
Which are not sterling, tender your selfe more dearely   520
Or (not to crack the winde of the poore phrase
Roning it thus) you'l tender me a foole.

OPHELIA

My Lord he hath importun'd me with loue
In honorable fashion.

POLONIUS

I, fashion you may call it, go to, go to.

OPHELIA

And hath giuen countenance to his speech my Lord,
With all the vowes of heauen.

POLONIUS

I, springes to catch wood-cockes, I doe knowe
When the blood burnes, how prodigall the soule
530 Lends the tongue vowes, these blazes daughter
Giuing more light then heate, extinct in both
Euen in their promise, as it is a making
You must not take for fire, from this time Daughter
Be somewhat scanter of your maiden presence
Set your intreatments at a higher rate
Then a commaund to parley; for Lord *Hamlet*,
Belieue so much in him that he is young,
And with a larger tider may he walke
Then may be giuen you: in fewe *Ophelia*,
540 Doe not belieue his vowes, for they are brokers
Not of the die which their inuestments showe
But meere imploratators of vnholy suites
Breathing like sanctified and pious bauds
The better to beguile: this is for all,
I would not in plaine tearmes from this time foorth
Haue you so slaunder any moment leasure
As to giue words or talke with the Lord *Hamlet*,
Looke too't I charge you, come your wayes.

OPHELIA I shall obey my Lord.   *Exeunt*

Sc. 4   *Enter Hamlet, Horatio and Marcellus*
(1.4) HAMLET
550 The ayre bites shroudly, it is very colde.

HORATIO

It is a nipping, and an eager ayre.

HAMLET What houre now?

HORATIO I thinke it lackes of twelfe.

MARCELLUS No, it is strooke.

HORATIO

Indeede; I heard it not, then it drawes neere the
      season,
Wherein the spirit held his wont to walke
      A florish of trumpets and 2. peeces goes of
What does this meane my Lord?

HAMLET

The King doth wake to night and takes his rowse,
Keepes wassell and the swaggring vp-spring reeles:
560 And as he draines his drafts of Rennish downe,
The kettle drumme, and trumpet, thus bray out
The triumph of his pledge.

HORATIO Is it a custome?

HAMLET I marry ist,
And to my minde, though I am natiue heere
And to the manner borne, it is a custome
More honourd in the breach, then the obseruance.
      Enter Ghost as before

HORATIO Looke my Lord it comes.

HAMLET

Angels and Ministers of grace defend vs:
570 Be thou a spirit of health, or goblin damn'd,

Bring with thee ayres from heauen, or blasts from hell,
Be thy intents wicked, or charitable,
Thou com'st in such a questionable shape,
That I will speake to thee, Ile call thee *Hamlet*,
King, father, royall Dane, ô answere mee,
Let me not burst in ignorance, but tell
Why thy canoniz'd bones hearsed in death
Haue burst their cerements? why the Sepulcher,
Wherein we saw thee quietly enurn'd
Hath op't his ponderous and marble iawes,   580
To cast thee vp againe? what may this meane
That thou dead corse, againe in compleat steele
Reuisites thus the glimses of the Moone,
Making night hideous, and we fooles of nature
So horridly to shake our disposition
With thoughts beyond the reaches of our soules,
Say why is this, wherefore, what should we doe?
      Ghost beckins Hamlet

HORATIO

It beckins you to goe away with it
As if it some impartment did desire
To you alone.

MARCELLUS (*to Hamlet*) Looke with what curteous action   590
It wafts you to a more remooued ground,
But doe not goe with it.

HORATIO (*to Hamlet*)   No, by no meanes.

HAMLET

It will not speake, then will I followe it.

HORATIO

Doe not my Lord.

HAMLET   Why what should be the feare,
I doe not set my life at a pinnes fee,
And for my soule, what can it doe to that
Being a thing immortall as it selfe;
      Ghost beckins Hamlet
It waues me forth againe, Ile followe it.

HORATIO

What if it tempt you toward the flood my Lord,
Or to the dreadfull somnet of the cleefe   600
That beetles ore his base into the sea,
And there assume some other horrable forme
Which might depriue your soueraigntie of reason,
And draw you into madnes, thinke of it?
      Ghost beckins Hamlet

HAMLET

It wafts me still, (*to Ghost*) goe on, Ile followe thee.

MARCELLUS

You shall not goe my Lord.

HAMLET   Hold of your hand.

HORATIO

Be rul'd, you shall not goe.

HAMLET   My fate cries out
And makes each petty arture in this body
As hardy as the Nemeon Lyons nerue;
      Ghost beckins Hamlet
Still am I cald, vnhand me Gentlemen   610
By heau'n Ile make a ghost of him that lets me,
I say away, (*to Ghost*) goe on, Ile followe thee.
      Exit Ghost and Hamlet

HORATIO

   He waxes desperate with imagination.

MARCELLUS

   Lets followe, tis not fit thus to obey him.

HORATIO

   Haue after, to what issue will this come?

MARCELLUS

   Something is rotten in the state of Denmarke.

HORATIO

   Heauen will direct it.

MARCELLUS   Nay lets follow him.   *Exeunt*

Sc. 5   *Enter Ghost, and Hamlet following*

(1.5) HAMLET

   Whether wilt thou leade me, speake, Ile goe no
      further.

GHOST

   Marke me.

HAMLET   I will.

GHOST   My houre is almost come

620   When I to sulphrus and tormenting flames
   Must render vp my selfe.

HAMLET   Alas poore Ghost.

GHOST

   Pitty me not, but lend thy serious hearing
   To what I shall vnfold.

HAMLET   Speake, I am bound to heare.

GHOST

   So art thou to reuenge, when thou shalt heare.

HAMLET What?

GHOST I am thy fathers spirit,

   Doomd for a certaine tearme to walke the night,
   And for the day confind to fast in fires,
   Till the foule crimes done in my dayes of nature

630   Are burnt and purg'd away: but that I am forbid
   To tell the secrets of my prison house,
   I could a tale vnfolde whose lightest word
   Would harrow vp thy soule, freeze thy young blood,
   Make thy two eyes like stars start from their spheres,
   Thy knotty and combined locks to part,
   And each particuler haire to stand an end,
   Like quils vpon the fretfull Porpentine,
   But this eternall blazon must not be
   To eares of flesh and blood, list *Hamlet* list, ô list:

640   If thou did'st euer thy deare father loue.

HAMLET O God.

GHOST

   Reuenge his foule, and most vnnaturall murther.

HAMLET Murther.

GHOST

   Murther most foule, as in the best it is,
   But this most foule, strange and vnnaturall.

HAMLET

   Hast, hast me to know it, that with wings as swift
   As meditation, or the thoughts of loue
   May sweepe to my reuenge.

GHOST   I find thee apt,

   And duller shouldst thou be then the fat weede

That rots it selfe in ease on *Lethe* wharffe,   650
Would'st thou not sturre in this; now *Hamlet* heare,
Tis giuen out, that sleeping in mine Orchard,
A Serpent stung me, so the whole eare of Denmarke
Is by a forged processe of my death
Ranckely abusde: but knowe thou noble Youth,
The Serpent that did sting thy fathers life
Now weares his Crowne.

HAMLET

   O my propheticke soule! mine Vncle?

GHOST

   I that incestuous, that adulterate beast,
   With witchcraft of his witt, with trayterous gifts, 660
   O wicked wit, and giftes that haue the power
   So to seduce; wonne to his shamefull lust
   The will of my most seeming vertuous Queene;
   O *Hamlet*, what a falling off was there
   From me whose loue was of that dignitie
   That it went hand in hand euen with the vowe
   I made to her in marriage, and to decline
   Vppon a wretch whose naturall gifts were poore,
   To those of mine;
   But vertue as it neuer will be mooued,   670
   Though lewdnesse court it in a shape of heauen
   So lust though to a radiant Angle linckt,
   Will sate it selfe in a celestiall bed
   And pray on garbage.
   But soft, me thinkes I sent the mornings ayre,
   Briefe let me be; sleeping within mine Orchard,
   My custome alwayes in the afternoone,
   Vpon my secure houre, thy Vncle stole
   With iuyce of cursed Hebonon in a viall,
   And in the porches of mine eares did poure 680
   The leaperous distilment, whose effect
   Holds such an enmitie with blood of man,
   That swift as quicksiluer it courses through
   The naturall gates and allies of the body,
   And with a sodaine vigour it doth posset
   And curde like eager droppings into milke,
   The thin and wholsome blood; so did it mine,
   And a most instant tetter barckt about
   Most Lazerlike with vile and lothsome crust
   All my smooth body.   690
   Thus was I sleeping by a brothers hand,
   Of life, of Crowne, of Queene at once dispatcht,
   Cut off euen in the blossomes of my sinne,
   Vnhuzled, disappointed, vnanneld,
   No reckning made, but sent to my account
   With all my imperfections on my head,
   O horrible, ô horrible, most horrible.
   If thou hast nature in thee beare it not,
   Let not the royall bed of Denmarke be
   A couch for luxury and damned incest.   700
   But howsoeuer thou pursuest this act,
   Tain't not thy minde, nor let thy soule contriue
   Against thy mother ought, leaue her to heauen,
   And to those thornes that in her bosome lodge
   To prick and sting her, fare thee well at once,

The Gloworme shewes the matine to be neere
And gins to pale his vneffectuall fire,
Adiew, adiew, *Hamlet*, remember me.   *Exit*
HAMLET
O all you host of heauen, ô earth, what els,
710 And shall I coupple hell, ô fie, hold, hold my hart,
And you my sinnowes, growe not instant old,
But beare me stiffely vp; remember thee,
I thou poore Ghost while memory holds a seate
In this distracted globe, remember thee,
Yea, from the table of my memory
Ile wipe away all triuiall fond records,
All sawes of bookes, all formes, all pressures past
That youth and obseruation coppied there,
And thy commandement all alone shall liue,
720 Within the booke and volume of my braine
Vnmixt with baser matter, yes, yes by heauen,
O most pernicious woman.
O villaine, villaine, smiling damned villaine,
My tables,
My tables, meet it is I set it downe
That one may smile, and smile, and be a villaine,
At least I'm sure it may be so in Denmarke.
          He writes
So Vncle, there you are, now to my word,
It is adew, adew, remember me.
730 I haue sworn't.
HORATIO & MARCELLUS (*within*) My Lord, my Lord.
          Enter Horatio, and Marcellus
MARCELLUS (*calling*) Lord *Hamlet*.
HORATIO Heauen secure him.
HAMLET So be it.
HORATIO (*calling*) Illo, ho, ho, my Lord.
HAMLET
Hillo, ho, ho, boy come, bird come.
MARCELLUS How i'st my noble Lord?
HORATIO (*to Hamlet*) What newes my Lord?
HAMLET O, wonderfull.
HORATIO
Good my Lord tell it.
740 HAMLET   No, you'l reueale it.
HORATIO
Not I my Lord by heauen.
MARCELLUS   Nor I my Lord.
HAMLET
How say you then, would hart of man once thinke it,
But you'le be secret.
BOOTH   I by heau'n, my Lord.
HAMLET
There's nere a villaine, dwelling in all Denmarke
But hee's an arrant knaue.
HORATIO
There needes no Ghost my Lord, come from the graue
To tell vs this.
HAMLET   Why right, you are i'th' right,
And so without more circumstance at all
I hold it fit that we shake hands and part,
750 You, as your busines and desires shall poynt you,

For euery man ha's busines and desire
Such as it is, and for mine owne poore part
Looke you, Ile goe pray.
HORATIO
These are but wilde and whurling words my Lord.
HAMLET
I'm sorry they offend you hartily,
Yes faith hartily.
HORATIO   There's no offence my Lord.
HAMLET
Yes by Saint *Patrick* but there is *Horatio*,
And much offence to, touching this vision heere,
It is an honest Ghost that let me tell you,
For your desire to knowe what is betweene vs   760
Oremastret as you may, and now good friends,
As you are friends, schollers, and souldiers,
Giue me one poore request.
HORATIO   What i'st my Lord, we will.
HAMLET
Neuer make knowne what you haue seene to night.
BOTH
My Lord we will not.
HAMLET   Nay but swear't.
HORATIO
In faith my Lord not I.
MARCELLUS   Nor I my Lord in faith.
HAMLET
Vppon my sword.
MARCELLUS   We haue sworne my Lord already.
HAMLET
Indeede vppon my sword, indeed.
          Ghost cries vnder the Stage
GHOST   Sweare.
HAMLET
Ah ha, boy, say'st thou so, art thou there trupenny?
Come on, you heare this fellowe in the Sellerige,   770
Consent to sweare.
HORATIO   Propose the oath my Lord.
HAMLET
Neuer to speake of this that you haue seene
Sweare by my sword.
GHOST (*vnder the Stage*) Sweare.
          ⌈*They sweare*⌉
HAMLET
Hic, & vbique, then weele shift our ground:
Come hether Gentlemen
And lay your hands againe vpon my sword,
Neuer to speake of this that you haue heard
Sweare by my sword.
GHOST (*vnder the Stage*) Sweare.   780
          ⌈*They sweare*⌉
HAMLET
Well sayd olde Mole, can'st worke it'h earth so fast,
A worthy Pioner, once more remooue good friends.
HORATIO
O day and night, but this is wondrous strange.
HAMLET
And therefore as a stranger giue it welcome,

There are more things in heauen and earth *Horatio*
Then are dream't of in our philosophie, but come
Heere as before, neuer so helpe you mercy,
(How strange or odde so ere I beare my selfe,
As I perchance heereafter shall thinke meet,
790   To put an Anticke disposition on
That you at such time seeing me, neuer shall
With armes incombred thus, or this head shake,
Or by pronouncing of some doubtfull phrase,
As well, we knowe, or we could and if we would,
Or if we list to speake, or there be and if they might,
Or such ambiguous giuing out) to note,
That you knowe ought of me, this not to doe,
So grace and mercy at your most neede helpe you:
          sweare.
GHOST (*vnder the Stage*) Sweare.
          ⌈*They sweare*⌉
HAMLET
800   Rest, rest, perturbed spirit: so Gentlemen,
With all my loue I doe commend me to you,
And what so poore a man as *Hamlet* is,
May doe t'expresse his loue and frending to you
God willing shall not lack, let vs goe in together,
And still your fingers on your lips I pray,
The time is out of ioynt, ô cursed spight
That euer I was borne to set it right.
Nay come, lets goe together.   *Exeunt*

Sc. 6   *Enter old Polonius, with his man Reynoldo*
(2.1) POLONIUS
Giue him this money, and these notes *Reynaldo*.
810   REYNALDO I will my Lord.
POLONIUS
You shall doe meruiles wisely good *Reynaldo*,
Before you visite him, to make inquire
Of his behauiour.
REYNALDO   My Lord, I did intend it.
POLONIUS
Mary well said, very well said; looke you sir,
Enquire me first what Danskers are in Parris,
And how, and who, what meanes, and where they
          keepe,
What companie, at what expence, and finding
By this encompasment, and drift of question
That they doe know my sonne, come you more neerer
820   Then your perticuler demaunds will tuch it,
Take you as t'were some distant knowledge of him,
As thus, I know his father, and his friends,
And in part him, doe you marke this *Reynaldo*?
REYNALDO I, very well my Lord.
POLONIUS
And in part him, but you may say, not well,
But y'ft be he I meane, hee's very wilde,
Adicted so and so, and there put on him
What forgeries you please, marry none so ranck
As may dishonour him, take heede of that,
830   But sir, such wanton, wild, and vsuall slips,
As are companions noted and most knowne
To youth and libertie.

REYNALDO As gaming my Lord.
POLONIUS I, or drinking, fencing, swearing,
Quarrelling, drabbing, you may goe so far.
REYNALDO
My Lord, that would dishonour him.
POLONIUS
Fayth no, as you may season it in the charge.
You must not put another scandell on him,
That he is open to incontinencie,
That's not my meaning, but breath his faults so quently   840
That they may seeme the taints of libertie,
The flash and out-breake of a fierie mind,
A sauagenes in vnreclamed blood,
Of generall assault.
REYNALDO   But my good Lord.
POLONIUS
Wherefore should you doe this?
REYNALDO   I my Lord,
I would know that.
POLONIUS   Marry sir, heer's my drift,
And I belieue it is a fetch of warrant,
You laying these slight sallies on my sonne
As t'were a thing a little soyld i'th' working,
Marke you, your partie in conuerse, him you would
          sound   850
Hauing euer seene in the prenominat crimes
The youth you breath of guiltie, be assur'd
He closes with you in this consequence,
Good sir, (or so,) or friend, or gentleman,
According to the phrase, and the addition
Of man and country.
REYNALDO   Very good my Lord.
POLONIUS
And then sir doos a this, a doos,
what was I about to say? By the masse I was about to
say something, where did I leaue?
REYNALDO
At closes in the consequence: at friend,   860
Or so, and Gentleman.
POLONIUS
At closes in the consequence, I marry,
He closes with you thus, I know the gentleman,
I saw him yesterday, or tother day,
Or then, or then, with such and such, and as you say,
There was a gaming, there ortooke in's rowse,
There falling out at Tennis, or perchance
I saw him enter such a house of sale,
Videlizet, a brothell, or so foorth, see you now,
Your bait of falshood takes this carpe of truth,   870
And thus doe we of wisedome, and of reach,
With windlesses, and with assaies of bias,
By indirections find directions out,
So by my former lecture and aduise
Shall you my sonne; you haue me, haue you not?
REYNALDO My Lord, I haue.
POLONIUS God buy ye, far ye well.
REYNALDO Good my Lord.
POLONIUS
Obserue his inclination in your selfe.

880 REYNALDO I shall my lord.

POLONIUS And let him ply his musique.

REYNALDO Well my Lord.

    Enter Ophelia

POLONIUS

  Farewell.   *Exit Reynaldo*

    How now *Ophelia*, whats the matter?

OPHELIA

  Alas my Lord, I haue beene so affrighted.

POLONIUS With what i'th name of God?

OPHELIA

  My Lord, as I was sowing in my Chamber,

  Lord *Hamlet* with his doublet all vnbrac'd,

  No hat vpon his head, his stockins fouled,

  Vngartred, and downe gyued to his ancle,

890   Pale as his shirt, his knees knocking each other,

  And with a looke so pittious in purport

  As if he had been loosed out of hell

  To speake of horrors, he comes before me.

POLONIUS

  Mad for thy loue?

OPHELIA   My lord I doe not know,

  But truly I doe feare it.

POLONIUS   What said he?

OPHELIA

  He tooke me by the wrist, and held me hard,

  Then goes he to the length of all his arme,

  And with his other hand thus ore his brow,

  He falls to such perusall of my face

900   As a would draw it, long stayd he so,

  At last, a little shaking of mine arme,

  And thrice his head thus wauing vp and downe,

  He raisd a sigh so pittious and profound

  That it did seeme to shatter all his bulke,

  And end his beeing; that done, he lets me goe,

  And with his head ouer his shoulder turn'd

  Hee seem'd to find his way without his eyes,

  For out adoores he went without theyr help,

  And to the last bended their light on me.

POLONIUS

910   Come, goe with mee, I will goe seeke the King,

  This is the very extacie of loue,

  Whose violent propertie fordoos it selfe,

  And leades the will to desperat vndertakings

  As oft as any passion vnder heauen

  That dooes afflict our natures: I am sorry,

  What, haue you giuen him any hard words of late?

OPHELIA

  No my good Lord, but as you did commaund

  I did repell his letters, and denied

  His accesse to me.

POLONIUS   That hath made him mad.

920   I am sorry, that with better speed and iudgement

  I had not coted him, I fear'd he did but trifle

  And meant to wrack thee, but beshrow my Ielousie:

  By heauen it is as proper to our age

  To cast beyond our selues in our opinions,

  As it is common for the younger sort

  To lack discretion; come, goe we to the King,

  This must be knowne, which beeing kept close, might moue

  More griefe to hide, then hate to vtter loue.   *Exeunt*

    ⌈*Florish.*⌉ *Enter King and Queene, Rosencrans and*   Sc. 7
    Guyldensterne Cum alijs   (2.2)

KING

  Welcome deere *Rosencrans*, and *Guyldensterne*,

  Moreouer, that we much did long to see you,   930

  The need we haue to vse you did prouoke

  Our hastie sending, something haue you heard

  Of *Hamlets* transformation, so I call it,

  Since not th'exterior, nor the inward man

  Resembles that it was, what it should be,

  More then his fathers death, that thus hath put him

  So much from th'vnderstanding of himselfe

  I cannot deeme of: I entreate you both

  That beeing of so young dayes brought vp with him,

  And since so nabor'd to his youth and humour,   940

  That you voutsafe your rest heere in our Court

  Some little time, so by your companies

  To draw him on to pleasures, and to gather

  So much as from occasions you may gleane,

  Whether ought to vs vnknowne afflicts him thus,

  That opend lyes within our remedie.

QUEENE

  Good gentlemen, he hath much talkt of you,

  And sure I am, two men there is not liuing

  To whom he more adheres, if it will please you

  To shew vs so much gentry and good will,   950

  As to expend your time with vs a while,

  For the supply and profit of our hope,

  Your visitation shall receiue such thanks

  As fits a Kings remembrance.

ROSENCRANS   Both your Maiesties

  Might by the soueraigne power you haue of vs,

  Put your dread pleasures more into commaund

  Then to entreatie.

GUYLDENSTERNE   But we both obey,

  And heere giue vp our selues in the full bent,

  To lay our seruice freely at your feete

  To be commaunded.   960

KING

  Thanks *Rosencrans*, and gentle *Guyldensterne*.

QUEENE

  Thanks *Guyldensterne*, and gentle *Rosencrans*.

  And I beseech you instantly to visite

  My too much changed sonne, goe some of ye

  And bring the gentlemen where *Hamlet* is.

GUYLDENSTERNE

  Heauens make our presence and our practices

  Pleasant and helpfull to him.

QUEENE   I Amen.

    Exeunt Rosencrans and Guyldensterne

    ⌈*Cum alijs*⌉

    Enter Polonius

POLONIUS

  Th'embassadors from *Norway* my good Lord,

  Are ioyfully returnd.

KING

970   Thou still hast been the father of good newes.

POLONIUS

Haue I my Lord? Assure you my good Liege
I hold my dutie as I hold my soule,
Both to my God, and to my gracious King;
And I doe thinke, or els this braine of mine
Hunts not the trayle of policie so sure
As it hath vsd to doe, that I haue found
The very cause of *Hamlets* lunacie.

KING

O speake of that, that I doe long to heare.

POLONIUS

Giue first admittance to th'embassadors,
980   My newes shall be the fruite to that great feast.

KING

Thy selfe doe grace to them, and bring them in.
                                        Exit Polonius
He tells me my sweet Queene, that he hath found
The head and source of all your sonnes distemper.

QUEENE

I doubt it is no other but the maine
His fathers death, and our o're-hastie marriage.

KING

Well, we shall sift him,
          Enter Polonius, Voltemand, and Cornelius
                    welcome my good friends,
Say *Voltemand*, what from our brother *Norway*?

VALTEMAND

Most faire returne of greetings and desires;
Vpon our first, he sent out to suppresse
990   His Nephews leuies, which to him appeard
To be a preparation gainst the *Pollacke*,
But better lookt into, he truly found
It was against your highnes, whereat greeu'd
That so his sicknes, age, and impotence
Was falsly borne in hand, sends out arrests
On *Fortenbrasse*, which he in breefe obeyes,
Receiues rebuke from *Norway*, and in fine,
Makes vow before his Vncle neuer more
To giue th'assay of Armes against your Maiestie:
1000   Whereon old *Norway* ouercome with ioy,
Giues him three thousand crownes in anuall fee,
And his commission to imploy those souldiers
So leuied (as before) against the *Pollacke*,
With an entreatie heerein further shone,
          He giues a Letter to Claudius
That it might please you to giue quiet passe
Through your dominions for his enterprise
On such regards of safety and allowance
As therein are set downe.

KING   It likes vs well,
And at our more consider'd time, wee'le read,
1010   Answer, and thinke vpon this busines:
Meane time, we thanke you for your well tooke labour,
Goe to your rest, at night weele feast together,
Most welcome home.
          Exeunt Embassadors Valtemand and Cornelius

POLONIUS

This busines is very well ended.
My Liege and Maddam, to expostulate
What maiestie should be, what dutie is,
Why day is day, night, night, and time is time,
Were nothing but to wast night, day, and time,
Therefore since breuitie is the soule of wit,
And tediousnes the lymmes and outward florishes,   1020
I will be briefe, your noble sonne is mad:
Mad call I it, for to define true madnes,
What ist but to be nothing els but mad,
But let that goe.

QUEENE   More matter with lesse art.

POLONIUS

Maddam, I sweare I vse no art at all,
That he is mad tis true, tis true, tis pitty,
And pitty tis tis true, a foolish figure,
But farewell it, for I will vse no art.
Mad let vs graunt him then, and now remaines
That we find out the cause of this effect,   1030
Or rather say, the cause of this defect,
For this effect defectiue comes by cause:
Thus it remaines, and the remainder thus.
Perpend,
I haue a daughter, haue whil'st she is mine,
Who in her dutie and obedience, marke,
Hath giuen me this, now gather and surmise,
          He reads the letter
To the Celestiall and my soules Idoll, the most beautified
Ophelia,
that's an ill phrase, a vile phrase, beautified is a vile   1040
phrase, but you shall heare:
these in her excellent white bosome, these.

QUEENE Came this from *Hamlet* to her?

POLONIUS

Good Maddam stay awhile, I will be faithfull,
          Doubt thou the starres are fire,
              Doubt that the Sunne doth moue,
          Doubt truth to be a lyer,
              But neuer doubt I loue.
O deere Ophelia, I am ill at these numbers, I haue not art
to recken my grones, but that I loue thee best, ô most best   1050
belieue it, adew. Thine euermore most deere Lady, whilst
this machine is to him.
                              Hamlet.
This in obedience hath my daughter shew'd me,
And more aboue hath his solicitings
As they fell out by time, by meanes, and place,
All giuen to mine eare.

KING   But how hath she
Receiu'd his loue?

POLONIUS   What doe you thinke of me?

KING

As of a man faithfull and honorable.

POLONIUS

I would faine proue so, but what might you thinke   1060
When I had seene this hote loue on the wing,
As I perceiu'd it (I must tell you that)

Before my daughter told me, what might you,
Or my deere Maiestie your Queene heere thinke,
If I had playd the Deske, or Table booke,
Or giuen my hart a winking mute and dumbe,
Or lookt vppon this loue with idle sight,
What might you thinke? no, I went round to worke,
And my young Mistris thus I did bespeake,
1070   Lord *Hamlet* is a Prince out of thy star,
This must not be: and then I precepts gaue her
That she should locke her selfe from his resort,
Admit no messengers, receiue no tokens,
Which done, she tooke the fruites of my aduise:
And he repulsed, a short tale to make,
Fell into a sadnes, then into a fast,
Thence to a watch, thence into a weakenes,
Thence to a lightnes, and by this declension,
Into the madnes wherein now he raues,
1080   And all we waile for.
KING (*to Queene*) Doe you thinke 'tis this?
QUEENE It may be very likely.
POLONIUS
Hath there been such a time, I'de faine know that,
That I haue positiuely said, tis so,
When it proou'd otherwise?
KING   Not that I know.
POLONIUS (*touching his head, then his shoulder*)
Take this, from this, if this be otherwise;
If circumstances leade me, I will finde
Where truth is hid, though it were hid indeede
Within the Center.
KING   How may we try it further?
POLONIUS
1090   You know sometimes he walkes foure houres together
Heere in the Lobby.
QUEENE   So he dooes indeede.
POLONIUS
At such a time, Ile loose my daughter to him,
(*To King*) Be you and I behind an Arras then,
Marke the encounter, if he loue her not,
And be not from his reason falne thereon
Let me be no assistant for a state
But keepe a farme and carters.
KING   We will try it.
        Enter Hamlet, madly attired, reading on a Booke
QUEENE
But looke where sadly the poore wretch comes reading.
POLONIUS
Away, I doe beseech you both away,
1100   Ile bord him presently, oh giue me leaue,
                                        Exit King and Queene
How dooes my good Lord *Hamlet*?
HAMLET Well, God a mercy.
POLONIUS Doe you knowe me my Lord?
HAMLET Excellent, excellent well, y'are a Fishmonger.
POLONIUS Not I my Lord.
HAMLET Then I would you were so honest a man.
POLONIUS Honest my Lord.

HAMLET I sir to be honest as this world goes, is to be one
man pickt out of tenne thousand.
POLONIUS That's very true my Lord.   1110
HAMLET For if the sunne breede maggots in a dead dogge,
being a good kissing carrion. Haue you a daughter?
POLONIUS I haue my Lord.
HAMLET Let her not walke i'th Sunne, conception is a
blessing, but not as your daughter may conceaue,
friend looke to't.
POLONIUS (*aside*) How say you by that, still harping on
my daughter, yet hee knewe me not at first, a sayd I
was a Fishmonger, a is farre gone, farre gone, and
truly in my youth, I suffred much extremity for loue,   1120
very neere this. Ile speake to him againe. (*To Hamlet*)
What doe you reade my Lord.
HAMLET Words, words, words.
POLONIUS What is the matter my Lord.
HAMLET Betweene who.
POLONIUS I meane the matter you reade my Lord.
HAMLET Slaunders sir; for the satericall slaue sayes heere,
that old men haue gray beards, that their faces are
wrinckled, their eyes purging thick Amber, or plumtree
gum, & that they haue a plentifull lacke of wit, together   1130
with most weake hams, all which sir though I most
powerfully and potentlie belieue, yet I hold it not
honesty to haue it thus set downe, for you your selfe
sir should be old as I am: if like a Crab you could goe
backward.
POLONIUS (*aside*) Though this be madnesse, yet there is
method in't, (*to Hamlet*) will you walke out of the ayre
my Lord?
HAMLET Into my graue.
POLONIUS Indeede that is out o'th'ayre; (*aside*) how   1140
pregnant sometimes his replies are, a happines that
often madnesse hits on, which reason and sanity could
not so prosperously be deliuered of. I will leaue him
and sodainely contriue the meanes of meeting betweene
him, and my daughter. (*To Hamlet*) My Lord, I will take
my leaue of you.
HAMLET You cannot Sir take from mee any thing that I
will more willingly part withall: except my life, my life,
my life.
POLONIUS (*going*) Fare you well my Lord.   1150
HAMLET These tedious old fooles.
        ⌜*Enter Guyldensterne, and Rosencrans*⌝
POLONIUS You goe to seeke the Lord *Hamlet*, there he is.
ROSENCRANS God saue you sir.
GUYLDENSTERNE ⌜*to Polonius*⌝ Mine honor'd Lord.
                                                ⌜*Exit Polonius*⌝
ROSENCRANS (*to Hamlet*) My most deere Lord.
HAMLET My exlent good friends, how doost thou
Guyldensterne? A *Rosencrans*, good lads how doe ye both?
ROSENCRANS
As the indifferent children of the earth.
GUYLDENSTERNE
Happy, in that we are not ouer happy
On Fortunes cap, we are not the very button.   1160

HAMLET Nor the soles of her shooe.

ROSENCRANS Neither my Lord.

HAMLET Then you liue about her wast, or in the middle of her fauor.

GUYLDENSTERNE Faith her priuates we.

HAMLET In the secret parts of Fortune, oh most true, she is a strumpet, what's the newes?

ROSENCRANS None my Lord, but that the worlds growne honest.

1170 HAMLET Then is Doomes day neere, but your newes is not true; Let me question more in particular: what haue you my good friends, deserued at the hands of Fortune, that she sends you to Prison hither?

GUYLDENSTERNE Prison, my Lord?

HAMLET Denmark's a Prison.

ROSENCRANS Then is the World one.

HAMLET A goodly one, in which there are many Confines, Wards, and Dungeons; *Denmarke* being one o'th' worst.

ROSENCRANS We thinke not so my Lord.

1180 HAMLET Why then 'tis none to you; for there is nothing either good or bad, but thinking makes it so: to me it is a prison.

ROSENCRANS Why then your Ambition makes it one: 'tis too narrow for your minde.

HAMLET O God, I could be bounded in a nutshell, and count my selfe a King of infinite space; were it not that I haue bad dreames.

GUYLDENSTERNE Which dreames indeed are Ambition: for the very substance of the Ambitious, is meerely the shadow of a Dreame.

1190 HAMLET A dreame it selfe is but a shadow.

ROSENCRANS Truely, and I hold Ambition of so ayry and light a quality, that it is but a shadowes shadow.

HAMLET Then are our Beggers bodies; and our Monarchs and out-stretcht Heroes the Beggers Shadowes: shall wee to th' Court: for, by my fey I cannot reason?

BOTH Wee'l wait vpon you.

HAMLET No such matter. I will not sort you with the rest of my seruants: for to speake to you like an honest man: I am most dreadfully attended; but in the beaten way of friendship, what make you at *Elsonoure*?

1200

ROSENCRANS To visit you my Lord, no other occasion.

HAMLET Begger that I am, I am euen poore in thankes, but I thanke you, and sure deare friends, my thankes are too deare a halfpeny: were you not sent for? is it your owne inclining? is it a free visitation? come, deale iustly with me, come, come, nay speake.

GUYLDENSTERNE What should we say my Lord?

HAMLET Why any thing but to'th purpose: you were sent for, and there is a kind of confession in your lookes, which your modesties haue not craft enough to cullour, I know the good King and Queene haue sent for you.

1210

ROSENCRANS To what end my Lord?

HAMLET That you must teach me: but let me coniure you, by the rights of our fellowship, by the consonancie of our youth, by the obligation of our euer preserued loue; and by what more deare a better proposer could

charge you withall, bee euen and direct with me whether you were sent for or no.

ROSENCRANS (*to Guyldensterne*) What say you.   1220

HAMLET Nay then I haue an eye of you? if you loue me hold not of.

GUYLDENSTERNE My Lord we were sent for.

HAMLET I will tell you why, so shall my anticipation preuent your discouery, and your secrecie to the King & Queene moult no feather, I haue of late, but wherefore I knowe not, lost all my mirth, forgon all custome of exercise: and indeede it goes so heauily with my disposition, that this goodly frame the earth, seemes to mee a sterill promontorie, this most excellent Canopie   1230 the ayre, looke you, this braue orehanging, this maiesticall roofe fretted with golden fire, why it appeares no other thing to me then a foule and pestilent congregation of vapoures. What a peece of worke is a man, how noble in reason, how infinit in faculty, in forme and moouing how expresse and admirable? in action, how like an Angell? in apprehension, how like a God: the beautie of the world; the paragon of Annimales; and yet to me, what is this Quintessence of dust: man delights not me, no, nor woman neither,   1240 though by your smilling, you seeme to say so.

ROSENCRANS My Lord, there was no such stuffe in my thoughts.

HAMLET Why did you laugh then, when I sayd man delights not me.

ROSENCRANS To thinke my Lord if you delight not in man, what Lenton entertainment the players shall receaue from you, we coted them on the way, and hether are they comming to offer you seruice.

HAMLET He that playes the King shal be welcome, his   1250 Maiestie shal haue tribute of me, the aduenterous Knight shall vse his foyle and target, the Louer shall not sigh gratis, the humorus Man shall end his part in peace, the Clowne shall make those laugh whose lungs are tickled a'th' sere, and the Lady shall say her minde freely: or the blank verse shall hault for't. What players are they?

ROSENCRANS Euen those you were wont to take delight in, the Tragedians of the Citty.

HAMLET How chances it they trauaile? their residence   1260 both in reputation, and profit was better both wayes.

ROSENCRANS I thinke their inhibition, comes by the meanes of the late innouasion.

HAMLET Doe they hold the same estimation they did when I was in the Citty; are they so followed.

ROSENCRANS No indeede they are not.

HAMLET How comes it? doe they grow rusty?

ROSENCRANS Nay, their indeauour keepes in the wonted pace; But there is Sir an ayrie of Children, little Yases, that crye out on the top of question; and are most   1270 tyrannically clap't for't: these are now the fashion, and so be-ratle the common Stages (so they call them) that many wearing Rapiers, are affraide of Goose-quils, and dare scarse come thither.

HAMLET What are they Children? Who maintains 'em? How are they escoted? Will they pursue the Quality no longer then they can sing? Will they not say afterwards if they should grow themselues to common Players (as it is like most will if their meanes are not better) their Writers do them wrong, to make them exclaim against their owne Succession.

ROSENCRANS Faith there ha's bene much to do on both sides: and the Nation holds it no sinne, to tarre them to Controuersie. There was for a while, no mony bid for argument, vnlesse the Poet and the Player went to Cuffes in the Question.

HAMLET Is't possible?

GUYLDENSTERNE Oh there ha's beene much throwing about of Braines.

HAMLET Do the Boyes carry it away?

ROSENCRANS I that they do my Lord, *Hercules* & his load too.

HAMLET It is not strange, for mine Vncle is King of Denmarke, and those that would make mowes at him while my father liued, giue twenty, fortie, an hundred duckets a peece, for his Picture in little, s'bloud there is somthing in this more then naturall, if Philosophie could find it out.

A Florish for the Players

GUYLDENSTERNE There are the players.

HAMLET Gentlemen you are welcome to *Elsonoure*, your hands come, th'appurtenance of welcome is fashion and ceremonie; let mee comply with you in the garb: lest my extent to the players, which I tell you must showe fairely outward, should more appeare like entertainment then yours?

⌈*He shakes hands with them*⌉

you are welcome: but my Vncle-father, and Aunt-mother, are deceaued.

GUYLDENSTERNE In what my deare Lord.

HAMLET I am but mad North North west; when the wind is Southerly, I knowe a Hauke, from a hand saw.

Enter Polonius

POLONIUS Well be with you Gentlemen.

HAMLET (*aside*) Harke you *Guyldensterne*, and you to, at each eare a hearer, that great baby you see there is not yet out of his swathing clouts.

ROSENCRANS (*aside*) Happily he's the second time come to them, for they say an old man is twice a child.

HAMLET (*aside*) I will prophecy, he comes to tell me of the players, mark it, ⌈*To Polonius*⌉ You say right sir, for a Monday morning, t'was so indeede.

POLONIUS My Lord I haue newes to tell you.

HAMLET My Lord I haue newes to tel you: when *Rossius* was an Actor in Rome.

POLONIUS The Actors are come hether my Lord.

HAMLET Buz, buz.

POLONIUS Vppon mine honor.

HAMLET Then came each Actor on his Asse.

POLONIUS The best actors in the world, either for Tragedie, Comedy, History, Pastorall, Pastoricall Comicall, Historicall Pastorall, Tragicall-Historicall: Tragicall-Comicall-Historicall-Pastorall: scene indeuidible, or Poem vnlimited. *Sceneca* cannot be too heauy, nor *Plautus* too light, for the lawe of writ, and the liberty these are the only men.

HAMLET O *Ieptha* Iudge of Israell, what a treasure had'st thou?

POLONIUS What a treasure had he my Lord?

HAMLET Why

One faire daughter and no more,
The which he loued passing well.

POLONIUS (*aside*) Still on my daughter.

HAMLET Am I not i'th right old *Ieptha*?

POLONIUS If you call me *Ieptha* my Lord, I haue a daughter that I loue passing well.

HAMLET Nay that followes not.

POLONIUS What followes then my Lord?

HAMLET Why

As by lot
God wot,

and then you knowe

It came to passe,
As most like it was;

the first rowe of the pious chanson will showe you more, for looke where my abridgments come.

Enter foure or fiue Players

Y'are welcome maisters, welcome all, I am glad to see thee well, welcome good friends, oh my old friend, thy face is valanct since I saw thee last, com'st thou to beard me in Denmark? what my young Lady and mistris, byr lady your Ladishippe is nerer heauen, then when I saw you last by the altitude of a chopine, pray God your voyce like a peece of vncurrant gold, bee not crackt within the ring: maisters you are all welcome, weele en to't like french Faukners, fly at any thing we see, weele haue a speech straite, come giue vs a tast of your quality, come a passionate speech.

1. PLAYER What speech my good Lord?

HAMLET I heard thee speake me a speech once, but it was neuer acted, or if it was, not aboue once, for the play I remember pleasd not the million, t'was cauiary to the generall, but it was as I receaued it & others, whose iudgements in such matters cried in the top of mine, an excellent play, well digested in the scenes, set downe with as much modestie as cunning. I remember one sayd there was no sallets in the lines, to make the matter sauory, nor no matter in the phrase that might indite the author of affectation, but cald it an honest method, as wholesome as sweete, & by very much, more handsome then fine: one speech in it I chiefely loued, t'was *Aeneas* tale to *Dido*, & there about of it especially where he speakes of *Priams* slaughter, if it liue in your memory begin at this line, let me see, let me see,

The rugged *Pirhus* like Th'ircanian beast,
tis not so, it beginnes with *Pirrhus*,
The rugged *Pirrhus*, he whose sable Armes,

Black as his purpose did the night resemble,
When he lay couched in the omynous horse,
Hath now this dread and black complection smeard,
With heraldy more dismall, head to foote
Now is he totall Gules horridly trickt
1390 With blood of fathers, mothers, daughters, sonnes,
Bak'd and empasted with the parching streetes
That lend a tirranus and damned light
To their vilde murthers, rosted in wrath and fire,
And thus ore-cised with coagulate gore,
With eyes like Carbunkles, the hellish *Phirrhus*
Old grandsire *Priam* seekes;
so proceede you.
POLONIUS Foregod my Lord well spoken, with good accent
and good discretion.
1400 I. PLAYER   Anon he finds him,
Striking too short at Greekes, his anticke sword
Rebellious to his arme, lies where it fals,
Repugnant to commaund; vnequall match,
Pirrhus at *Priam* driues, in rage strikes wide,
But with the whiffe and winde of his fell sword,
Th'vnnerued father fals: Then senselesse Illium,
Seeming to feele his blowe, with flaming top
Stoopes to his base; and with a hiddious crash
Takes prisoner *Pirrhus* eare, for loe his sword
1410 Which was declining on the milkie head
Of reuerent *Priam*, seem'd i'th ayre to stick,
So as a painted tirant *Pirrhus* stood
And like a newtrall to his will and matter,
Did nothing:
But as we often see against some storme,
A silence in the heauens, the racke stand still,
The bold winds speechlesse, and the orbe belowe
As hush as death, anon the dreadfull thunder
Doth rend the region, so after *Pirrhus* pause,
1420 A rowsed vengeance sets him new a worke,
And neuer did the Cyclops hammers fall,
On *Mars* his Armor forg'd for proofe eterne,
With lesse remorse then *Pirrhus* bleeding sword
Now falls on *Priam*.
Out, out, thou strumpet Fortune, all you gods,
In generall sinod take away her power,
Breake all the spokes, and fallies from her wheele,
And boule the round naue downe the hill of heauen
As lowe as to the fiends.
1430 POLONIUS This is too long.
HAMLET It shall to the barbers with your beard: (*To I.
Player*) prethee say on, he's for a ligge, or a tale of
bawdry, or he sleepes, say on, come to *Hecuba*.
I. PLAYER
But who, O who, had seene the mobled Queene,
HAMLET The mobled Queene.
POLONIUS Thats good: Mobled Queene is good.
I. PLAYER
Runne barefoote vp and downe, threatning the flames
With *Bison* rheume, a clout vppon that head
Where late the Diadem stood, and for a robe,
1440 About her lanck and all ore-teamed loynes,
A blancket in th'alarme of feare caught vp,

Who this had seene, with tongue in venom steept,
Gainst fortunes state would treason haue pronounst;
But if the gods themselues did see her then,
When she saw *Pirrhus* make malicious sport
In mincing with his sword her husbands limmes,
The instant burst of clamor that she made,
Vnlesse things mortall mooue them not at all,
Would haue made milch the burning eyes of heauen
And passion in the gods.   1450
POLONIUS Looke where he has not turnd his cullour, and
has teares in's eyes, (*to I. Player*) prethee no more.
HAMLET (*to I. Player*) Tis well, Ile haue thee speake out
the rest soone, (*To Polonius*) Good my Lord will you see
the players well bestowed; doe ye heare, let them be
well vsed, for they are the Abstracts and breefe
Chronicles of the time; after your death you were better
haue a bad Epitaph then their ill report while you liue.
POLONIUS My Lord, I will vse them according to their
desert.   1460
HAMLET Gods bodykins man, much better, vse euery man
after his desert, & who should scape whipping, vse
them after your owne honor and dignity, the lesse they
deserue the more merrit is in your bounty. Take them
in.
POLONIUS (*to Players*) Come sirs.   *Exit Polonius*
HAMLET (*to Players*) Follow him friends, weele heare a
play to morrowe, dost thou heare me old friend, can
you play the murther of *Gonzago*?
[PLAYERS] I my Lord.   1470
HAMLET Weele hate to morrowe night, you could for a
neede study a speech of some dosen or sixteene lines,
which I would set downe and insert in't, could ye not?
[PLAYERS] I my Lord.
HAMLET Very well, followe that Lord, & looke you mock
him not.   [*Exeunt Players*]
My good friends, Ile leaue you tell night, you are
welcome to *Elsonoure*.
ROSENCRANS Good my Lord.
HAMLET
I so God buy ye,   *Exeunt. Manet Hamlet*
      now I am alone,   1480
O what a rogue and pesant slaue am I.
Is it not monstrous that this player heere
But in a fixion, in a dreame of passion
Could force his soule so to his whole conceit
That from her working all his visage wand,
Teares in his eyes, distraction in's aspect,
A broken voyce, an his whole function suting
With formes to his conceit; and all for nothing,
For *Hecuba*.
What's *Hecuba* to him, or he to *Hecuba*,   1490
That he should weepe for her? what would he doe
Had he the motiue, and the Cue for passion
That I haue? he would drowne the stage with teares,
And cleaue the generall eare with horrid speech,
Make mad the guilty, and appale the free,
Confound the ignorant, and amaze indeede
The very faculty of eyes and eares; yet I,
A dull and muddy metteld raskall peake,

Like Iohn-a-dreames, vnpregnant of my cause,
1500 And can say nothing; no not for a King,
Vpon whose property and most deare life,
A damn'd defeate was made: am I a coward,
Who cals me villaine, breakes my pate a crosse,
Pluckes off my beard, and blowes it in my face,
Twekes me by'th'nose, giues me the lie i'th throate
As deepe as to the lunges, who does me this,
Hah, s'wounds I should take it: for it cannot be
But I am pidgion liuerd, and lack gall
To make oppression bitter, or ere this
1510 I should a fatted all the region kytes
With this slaues offall, bloody, baudy villaine,
Remorslesse, trecherous, lecherous, kindlesse villaine.
Oh Vengeance!
Why what an Asse am I, I sure, this is most braue,
That I the sonne of the deere murthered,
Prompted to my reuenge by heauen and hell,
Must like a whore vnpacke my hart with words,
And fall a cursing like a very drabbe;
A scullyon, fie vppont, foh. About my braine;
1520 I haue heard, that guilty creatures sitting at a play,
Haue by the very cunning of the scene,
Beene strooke so to the soule, that presently
They haue proclaim'd their malefactions:
For murther, though it haue no tongue will speake
With most miraculous organ: Ile haue these Players
Play something like the murther of my father
Before mine Vncle, Ile obserue his lookes,
Ile tent him to the quicke, if a but blench
I know my course. The spirit that I haue seene
1530 May be the deale, and the deale hath power
T'assume a pleasing shape, yea, and perhaps,
Out of my weakenes, and my melancholy,
As he is very potent with such spirits,
Abuses me to damne me; Ile haue grounds
More relatiue then this, the play's the thing
Wherein Ile catch the conscience of the King.   *Exit*

Sc. 8   *Enter King, Queene, Polonius, Ophelia, Rosencrans,*
(3.1)   *Guyldensterne, Lords*
KING (*to Rosencrans & Guyldensterne*)
An can you by no drift of circumstance
Get from him why he puts on this confusion,
Grating so harshly all his dayes of quiet
1540 With turbulent and dangerous lunacie?
ROSENCRANS
He dooes confesse he feeles himselfe distracted,
But from what cause, a will by no meanes speake.
GUYLDENSTERNE
Nor doe we find him forward to be sounded,
But with a craftie madnes keepes aloofe
When we would bring him on to some confession
Of his true state.
QUEENE Did he receiue you well?
ROSENCRANS Most like a gentleman.
GUYLDENSTERNE
But with much forcing of his disposition.

ROSENCRANS
Niggard of question, but of our demaunds   1550
Most free in his reply.
QUEENE   Did you assay him
To any pastime?
ROSENCRANS
Maddam, it so fell out that certaine Players
We ore-raught on the way, of these we told him,
And there did seeme in him a kind of ioy
To heare of it: they are about the Court,
And as I thinke, they haue already order
This night to play before him.
POLONIUS   Tis most true,
And he beseecht me to intreat your Maiesties
To heare and see the matter.
KING   1560
With all my hart, and it doth much content me
To heare him so inclin'd. Good gentlemen
Giue him a further edge, and driue his purpose on
To these delights.
ROSENCRANS We shall my Lord.
                Exeunt Rosencrans & Guyldensterne
KING Sweet *Gertrard*, leaue vs too,
For we haue closely sent for *Hamlet* hether,
That he as t'were by accedent, may heere
Affront *Ophelia*;
Her father and my selfe (lawful espials)   1570
Will so bestow our selues, that seeing vnseene,
We may of their encounter franckly iudge,
And gather by him as he is behau'd,
Ift be th'affliction of his loue or no
That thus he suffers for.
QUEENE   I shall obey you.
And for your part *Ophelia*, I doe wish
That your good beauties be the happy cause
Of *Hamlets* wildnes, so shall I hope your vertues,
Will bring him to his wonted way againe,
To both your honours.
OPHELIA   Maddam, I wish it may.   1580
                                    Exit Queene
POLONIUS
Ophelia walke you heere, gracious so please you,
We will bestow our selues; reade on this booke,
That show of such an exercise may cullour
Your lonelines; we are oft too blame in this,
Tis too much proou'd, that with deuotions visage
And pious action, we doe sugar ore
The deuill himselfe.
KING   O tis too true,
(*Aside*) How smart a lash that speech doth giue my
        conscience.
The harlots cheeke beautied with plastring art,
Is not more ougly to the thing that helps it,   1590
Then is my deede to my most painted word:
O heauy burthen.
POLONIUS
I heare him comming, let's with-draw my Lord.
                Exeunt King and Polonius

Enter Hamlet

HAMLET

To be, or not to be, that is the question,
Whether tis nobler in the minde to suffer
The slings and arrowes of outragious fortune,
Or to take Armes against a sea of troubles,
And by opposing, end them, to die to sleepe
No more, and by a sleepe, to say we end
1600   The hart-ake, and the thousand naturall shocks
That flesh is heire to; tis a consumation
Deuoutly to be wisht to die to sleepe,
To sleepe, perchance to dreame, I there's the rub,
For in that sleepe of death what dreames may come
When we haue shuffled off this mortall coyle
Must giue vs pause, there's the respect
That makes calamitie of so long life:
For who would beare the whips and scornes of time,
Th'oppressors wrong, the proude mans contumely,
1610   The pangs of despriz'd loue, the lawes delay,
The insolence of office, and the spurnes
That patient merrit of th'vnworthy takes,
When he himselfe might his quietas make
With a bare bodkin; who would these fardels beare,
To grunt and sweat vnder a wearie life,
But that the dread of something after death,
The vndiscouer'd country, from whose borne
No trauiler returnes, puzzels the will,
And makes vs rather beare those ills we haue,
1620   Then flie to others that we know not of.
Thus conscience dooes make cowards of vs all,
And thus the natiue hiew of resolution
Is sicklied ore with the pale cast of thought,
And enterprises of great pith and moment,
With this regard theyr currents turne awry,
And loose the name of action. Soft you now,
The faire *Ophelia*, Nimph in thy orizons
Be all my sinnes remembred.

OPHELIA   Good my Lord,
How dooes your honour for this many a day?

HAMLET

1630   I humbly thanke you well, well, well.

OPHELIA

My Lord, I haue remembrances of yours
That I haue longed long to redeliuer,
I pray you now receiue them.

HAMLET

No, no, I neuer gaue you ought.

OPHELIA

My honor'd Lord, you know right well you did,
And with them words of so sweet breath composd
As made the things more rich, their perfume lost
Take these againe, for to the noble mind
Rich gifts wax poore when giuers prooue vnkind,
1640   There my Lord.

HAMLET Ha, ha, are you honest.

OPHELIA My Lord.

HAMLET Are you faire?

OPHELIA What meanes your Lordship?

HAMLET That if you be honest & faire, your honestie
should admit no discourse to your beautie.

OPHELIA Could beauty my Lord haue better comerse then
with honestie?

HAMLET I truly, for the power of beautie will sooner
transforme honestie from what it is to a bawde, then   1650
the force of honestie can translate beautie into his
likenes, this was sometime a paradox, but now the
time giues it proofe, I did loue you once.

OPHELIA Indeed my Lord you made me belieue so.

HAMLET You should not haue beleeu'd me, for vertue
cannot so enoculat our old stock, but we shall relish
of it, I loued you not.

OPHELIA I was the more deceiued.

HAMLET Get thee to a Nunry, why would'st thou be a
breeder of sinners, I am my selfe indifferent honest, but   1660
yet I could accuse mee of such things, that it were
better my Mother had not borne mee: I am very proude,
reuengefull, ambitious, with more offences at my beck,
then I haue thoughts to put them in, imagination to
giue them shape, or time to act them in: what should
such fellowes as I do crauling betweene heauen and
earth, wee are arrant knaues all, beleeue none of vs,
goe thy waies to a Nunry. Where's your father?

OPHELIA At home my Lord.

HAMLET Let the doores be shut vpon him, that he may   1670
play the foole no where but in's owne house, farewell.

OPHELIA O helpe him you sweet heauens.

HAMLET If thou doost marry, Ile giue thee this plague for
thy dowrie, be thou as chast as yce, as pure as snow,
thou shalt not escape calumny; get thee to a Nunry,
go, farewell. Or if thou wilt needes marry, marry a
foole, for wise men knowe well enough what monsters
you make of them: to a Nunry goe, and quickly to,
farewell.

OPHELIA O heauenly powers restore him.   1680

HAMLET I haue heard of your paintings too well enough,
God hath giuen you one face, and you make your selfes
another, you gig, you amble, and you lispe, and
nickname Gods creatures, and make your wantonnes
your ignorance; goe to, Ile no more on't, it hath made
me madde, I say we will haue no more marriages,
those that are married alreadie, all but one shall liue,
the rest shall keep as they are: to a Nunry go.   *Exit*

OPHELIA

O what a noble mind is heere orethrowne!
The Courtiers, souldiers, schollers, eye, tongue,
          sword,   1690
Th'expectansie, and Rose of the faire state,
The glasse of fashion, and the mould of forme,
Th'obseru'd of all obseruers, quite quite downe,
And I of Ladies most deiect and wretched,
That suckt the honny of his musick vowes;
Now see that noble and most soueraigne reason
Like sweet bells iangled out of tune, and harsh,
That vnmatcht forme, and feature of blowne youth
Blasted with extacie, ô woe is mee
T'haue seene what I haue seene, see what I see.   1700

Enter King and Polonius

KING

Loue, his affections doe not that way tend,
Nor what he spake, though it lackt forme a little,
Was not like madnes, there's something in his soule
Ore which his melancholy sits on brood,
And I doe doubt, the hatch and the disclose
Will be some danger; which to preuent,
I haue in quick determination
Thus set it downe: he shall with speede to *England*,
For the demaund of our neglected tribute,
1710 Haply the seas, and countries different,
With variable obiects, shall expell
This something setled matter in his hart,
Whereon his braines still beating puts him thus
From fashion of himselfe. What thinke you on't?

POLONIUS

It shall doe well. But yet doe I belieue
The origin and comencement of this greefe,
Sprung from neglected loue: How now *Ophelia?*
You neede not tell vs what Lord *Hamlet* said,
We heard it all: my Lord, doe as you please,
1720 But if you hold it fit, after the play,
Let his Queene-mother all alone intreate him
To show his griefes, let her be round with him,
And Ile be plac'd (so please you) in the eare
Of all their conference, if she find him not,
To *England* send him: or confine him where
Your wisedome best shall thinke.

KING   It shall be so,
Madnes in great ones must not vnwatcht goe.   *Exeunt*

Sc. 9   *Enter Hamlet, and two or three of the Players*
(3.2) HAMLET Speake the speech I pray you as I pronounc'd it
to you, trippingly on the tongue, but if you mouth it
1730 as many of your Players do, I had as liue the towne
cryer had spoke my lines, nor doe not saw the ayre
too much with your hand thus, but vse all gently, for
in the very torrent tempest, and as I may say, the
whirlwind of your passion, you must acquire and beget
a temperance, that may giue it smoothnesse, ô it offends
mee to the soule, to heare a robustious perwig-pated
fellowe tere a passion to totters, to very rags, to spleet
the eares of the groundlings, who for the most part are
capable of nothing but inexplicable dumbe showes, and
1740 noyse: I would haue such a fellow whipt for ore-dooing
Termagant, it out Herods Herod, pray you auoyde it.

A PLAYER I warrant your honour.

HAMLET Be not too tame neither, but let your owne
discretion be your tutor, sute the action to the word,
the word to the action, with this speciall obseruance,
that you ore-steppe not the modestie of nature: For
any thing so ouer-doone, is from the purpose of playing,
whose end both at the first, and nowe, was and is, to
holde as twere the Mirrour vp to nature, to shew vertue
1750 her owne feature; scorne her own Image, and the very
age and body of the time his forme and pressure: Now
this ouer-done, or come tardie off, though it make the

vnskilfull laugh, cannot but make the iudicious greeue,
the censure of the which one, must in your allowance
ore-weigh a whole Theater of others. O there be Players
that I haue seene play, and heard others prayse, and
that highly, not to speake it prophanely, that neither
hauing the accent of Christians, nor the gate of
Christian, Pagan, nor no man, haue so strutted &
bellowed, that I haue thought some of Natures Iornimen 1760
had made men, and not made them well, they imitated
humanitie so abhominably.

A PLAYER I hope we haue reform'd that indifferently with
vs, Sir.

HAMLET O reforme it altogether, and let those that play
your clownes speake no more then is set downe for
them, for there be of them that wil themselues laugh,
to set on some quantitie of barraine spectators to laugh
to, though in the meane time, some necessary question
of the play be then to be considered, that's villanous, 1770
and shewes a most pittifull ambition in the foole that
vses it: goe make you readie.   *Exit Players*

Enter Polonius, Guyldensterne, & Rosencrans

(*To Polonius*) How now my Lord, will the King heare
this peece of worke?

POLONIUS And the Queene to, and that presently.

HAMLET Bid the Players make hast.   *Exit Polonius*
Will you two help to hasten thẽ.

ROSENCRANCE *and* GUILDENSTERNE   We will my Lord.

Exeunt they two

HAMLET

What howe, *Horatio*.

Enter Horatio

HORATIO   Heere sweet Lord, at your seruice.

HAMLET

Horatio, thou art een as iust a man
As ere my conuersation copt withall.   1780

HORATIO

O my deere Lord.

HAMLET   Nay, doe not thinke I flatter,
For what aduancement may I hope from thee
That no reuenew hast but thy good spirits
To feede and clothe thee, why should the poore be
        flatterd?
No, let the candied tongue licke absurd pompe,
And crooke the pregnant hindges of the knee
Where thrift may follow faining; doost thou heare,
Since my deare soule was mistris of her choice,
And could of men distinguish, her election
Hath seald thee for herselfe, for thou hast been   1790
As one in suffring all that suffers nothing,
A man that Fortunes buffets and rewards
Hath tane with equall thanks; and blest are those
Whose blood and iudgement are so well comingled,
That they are not a pype for Fortunes finger
To sound what stop she please: giue me that man
That is not passions slaue, and I will weare him
In my harts core, I in my hart of hart
As I doe thee. Something too much of this,
There is a play to night before the King,   1800

One scene of it comes neere the circumstance
Which I haue told thee of my fathers death,
I prethee when thou seest that act a foote,
Euen with the very comment of thy soule
Obserue mine Vncle, if his occulted guilt
Doe not it selfe vnkennill in one speech,
It is a damned ghost that we haue seene,
And my imaginations are as foule
As *Vulcans* stithy; giue him heedfull note,
1810 For I mine eyes will riuet to his face,
And after we will both our iudgements ioyne
To censure of his seeming.

HORATIO   Well my lord,
If a steale ought the whilst this play is playing
And scape detecting, I will pay the theft.
       ⌈*Sound a Flourish*⌉
HAMLET
They are comming to the play. I must be idle,
Get you a place.
       ⌈*Danish Marsh. Enter King, Queene, Polonius,*
       Ophelia, Rosencrans, Guyldensterne, and other
       Lords attendant with his Guard carrying Torches⌉
KING   How fares our cosin *Hamlet*?
HAMLET Excellent yfaith, of the Camelions dish, I eate the
       ayre, promiscram'd, you cannot feede Capons so.
KING I haue nothing with this aunswer *Hamlet*, these
1820 words are not mine.
HAMLET No, nor mine now, (*to Polonius*) my Lord you
       playd once i'th Vniuersitie you say.
POLONIUS That I did my Lord, and was accounted a good
       Actor.
HAMLET And what did you enact?
POLONIUS I did enact *Iulius Cæsar*, I was kild i'th Capitall,
       Brutus kild mee.
HAMLET It was a brute part of him to kill so capitall a
       calfe there, be the Players readie?
1830 ROSENCRANS I my Lord, they stay vpon your patience.
QUEENE
Come hether my good *Hamlet*, sit by me.
HAMLET No good mother, heere's mettle more attractiue.
       He sits by Ophelia
POLONIUS (*aside*) O ho, doe you marke that.
HAMLET (*to Ophelia*) Lady shall I lie in your lap?
OPHELIA No my Lord.
HAMLET I meane, my Head vpon your Lap?
OPHELIA I my Lord.
HAMLET Doe you thinke I meant country matters?
OPHELIA I thinke nothing my Lord.
1840 HAMLET That's a fayre thought to lye betweene maydes
       legs.
OPHELIA What is my Lord?
HAMLET Nothing.
OPHELIA You are merry my Lord.
HAMLET Who I?
OPHELIA I my Lord.
HAMLET O God your onely Iigge-maker, what should a
       man do but be merry, for looke you how cheerefully my
       mother lookes, and my father died within's two howres.

OPHELIA Nay, tis twice two months my Lord.   1850
HAMLET So long, nay then let the deule weare blacke, for
       Ile haue a sute of sables; ô heauens, die two months
       agoe, and not forgotten yet, then there's hope a great
       mans memorie may out-liue his life halfe a yeere, but
       ber Lady a must build Churches then, or els shall a
       suffer not thinking on, with the Hobby-horse, whose
       Epitaph is, for ô, for ô, the hobby-horse is forgot.
       Hoboyes play. The dumbe show enters.
       Enter a King and a Queene, very louingly; the
       Queene embracing him, she kneeles, and makes
       shew of Protestation vnto him, he takes her vp, and
       declines his head vpon her necke, he layes him
       downe vppon a bancke of flowers, she seeing him
       asleepe, leaues him: anon comes in a Fellow, takes
       off his crowne, kisses it, and pours poyson in the
       Kings eares, and Exits: the Queene returnes, finds
       the King dead, and makes passionate action, the
       poysner with some two or three Mutes comes in
       againe, seeming to lament with her, the dead body
       is carried away, the poysner wooes the Queene
       with gifts, shee seemes loath and vnwilling awhile,
       but in the end accepts his loue. Exeunt the Players
OPHELIA What meanes this my Lord?
HAMLET Marry this is miching *Mallico*, that meanes
       mischiefe.   1860
OPHELIA Belike this show imports the argument of the play.
       Enter Prologue
HAMLET We shall know by this fellow, the Players cannot
       keepe counsell, they'le tell all.
OPHELIA Will a tell vs what this show meant?
HAMLET I, or any show that you'l show him, be not you
       asham'd to show, heele not shame to tell you what it
       meanes.
OPHELIA You are naught, you are naught, Ile mark the
       play.
PROLOGUE
       For vs and for our Tragedie,   1870
       Heere stooping to your clemencie,
       We begge your hearing patiently.   *Exit*
HAMLET Is this a Prologue, or the posie of a ring?
OPHELIA Tis breefe my Lord.
HAMLET As womans loue.
       Enter Player King and his Queene
PLAYER KING
Full thirtie times hath *Phebus* cart gone round
Neptunes salt wash, and *Tellus* orbed ground,
And thirtie dosen Moones with borrowed sheene
About the world haue times twelue thirties beene
Since loue our harts, and *Hymen* did our hands   1880
Vnite comutuall in most sacred bands.
PLAYER QUEENE
So many iourneyes may the Sunne and Moone
Make vs againe count ore ere loue be doone,
But woe is me, you are so sicke of late,
So farre from cheere, and from your former state,
That I distrust you, yet though I distrust,
Discomfort you my Lord it nothing must.

For womens feare and loue holds quantitie,
In neither ought, or in extremitie,
1890 Now what my loue is proofe hath made you know,
And as my loue is ciz'd, my feare is so.

PLAYER KING
Faith I must leaue thee loue, and shortly to,
My operant powers their functions leaue to do,
And thou shalt liue in this faire world behind,
Honord, belou'd, and haply one as kind,
For husband shalt thou.

PLAYER QUEENE   O confound the rest,
Such loue must needes be treason in my brest,
In second husband let me be accurst,
None wed the second, but who kild the first.

1900 HAMLET Wormwood, wormwood.

PLAYER QUEENE
The instances that second marriage moue
Are base respects of thrift, but none of loue,
A second time I kill my husband dead,
When second husband kisses me in bed.

PLAYER KING
I doe belieue you thinke what now you speake,
But what we doe determine, oft we breake,
Purpose is but the slaue to memorie,
Of violent birth, but poore validitie,
Which now like fruite vnripe sticks on the tree,
1910 But fall vnshaken when they mellow bee.
Most necessary tis that we forget
To pay our selues what to our selues is debt,
What to our selues in passion we propose,
The passion ending, doth the purpose lose,
The violence of eyther, griefe, or ioy,
Their owne ennactures with themselues destroy,
Where ioy most reuels, griefe doth most lament,
Greefe ioyes, ioy griefes, on slender accedent,
This world is not for aye, nor tis not strange,
That euen our loues should with our fortunes
1920   change:
For tis a question left vs yet to proue,
Whether loue lead fortune, or els fortune loue.
The great man downe, you marke his fauourite flyes,
The poore aduaunc'd, makes friends of enemies,
And hetherto doth loue on fortune tend,
For who not needes, shall neuer lacke a friend,
And who in want a hollow friend doth try,
Directly seasons him his enemy.
But orderly to end where I begunne,
1930 Our wills and fates doe so contrary runne,
That our deuises still are ouerthrowne,
Our thoughts are ours, their ends none of our owne,
So thinke thou wilt no second husband wed,
But die thy thoughts when thy first Lord is dead.

PLAYER QUEENE
Nor earth to me giue foode, nor heauen light,
Sport and repose lock from me day and night,
Each opposite that blancks the face of ioy,
Meete what I would haue well, and it destroy,

Both heere and hence pursue me lasting strife,
If once a widdow, euer I be wife.   1940

HAMLET If she should breake it now.

PLAYER KING (to Player Queene)
Tis deeply sworne, sweet leaue me heere a while,
My spirits grow dull, and faine I would beguile
The tedious day with sleepe.

PLAYER QUEENE   Sleepe rock thy braine,
And neuer come mischance betweene vs twaine.
                    Player King sleepes. Exit Player Queene

HAMLET (to Queene) Madam, how like you this play?

QUEENE The Lady protests too much mee thinks.

HAMLET O but shee'le keepe her word.

KING Haue you heard the argument? is there no offence
in't?   1950

HAMLET No, no, they do but iest, poyson in iest, no
offence i'th world.

KING What doe you call the play?

HAMLET The Mousetrap, mary how? tropically, this play is
the Image of a murther doone in *Vienna, Gonzago* is the
Dukes name, his wife *Baptista*, you shall see anon, tis a
knauish peece of worke, but what o'that? your Maiestie,
and wee that haue free soules, it touches vs not, let the
gauled Iade winch, our withers are vnwrong.
     Enter Lucianus
This is one *Lucianus*, Nephew to the King.   1960

OPHELIA You are as good as a Chorus my Lord.

HAMLET I could interpret betweene you and your loue if
I could see the puppets dallying.

OPHELIA You are keene my lord, you are keene.

HAMLET It would cost you a groning to take off mine
edge.

OPHELIA Still better and worse.

HAMLET So you mistake your husbands. (*To Lucianus*)
Beginne murtherer, pox, leaue thy damnable faces and
begin, come, the croking Rauen doth bellow for   1970
reuenge.

PLAYER LUCIANUS
Thoughts black, hands apt, drugges fit, and time
     agreeing,
Confiderat season els no creature seeing,
Thou mixture ranck, of midnight weedes collected,
With *Hecats* ban thrice blasted, thrice infected,
Thy naturall magicke, and dire property,
On wholsome life vsurpe immediatly.
     He powres the poyson in the Player Kings eare

HAMLET A poysons him i'th Garden for's estate, his names
Gonzago, the story is extant, and writ in choice Italian,
you shall see anon how the murtherer gets the loue of   1980
Gonzagoes wife.

OPHELIA The King rises.

HAMLET What, frighted with false fire.

QUEENE (*to King*) How fares my Lord?

POLONIUS Giue ore the play.

KING Giue me some light, away.

⌜COURTIERS⌝ Lights, lights, lights.
                    Exeunt all but Hamlet & Horatio

HAMLET
 Why let the strooken Deere goe weepe,
  The Hart vngauled play,
1990 For some must watch while some must sleepe,
  So runnes the world away.
 Would not this sir & a forrest of feathers, if the rest of
my fortunes turne Turk with me, with two prouinciall
Roses on my raz'd shooes, get me a fellowship in a cry
of players sir?

HORATIO Halfe a share.

HAMLET A whole one I.
 For thou doost know oh *Damon* deere
  This Realme dismantled was
2000 Of *Ioue* himselfe, and now raignes heere
  A very very paiock.

HORATIO You might haue rym'd.

HAMLET O good *Horatio*, Ile take the Ghosts word for a
thousand pound. Did'st perceiue?

HORATIO Very well my Lord.

HAMLET Vpon the talke of the poysning.

HORATIO I did very well note him.

  Enter Rosencrans and Guyldensterne

HAMLET Ah ha, come some musique, come the Recorders,
 For if the King like not the Comedie,
2010 Why then belike he likes it not perdy.
 Come, some musique.

GUYLDENSTERNE Good my Lord, voutsafe me a word with
you.

HAMLET Sir a whole historie.

GUYLDENSTERNE The King sir.

HAMLET I sir, what of him?

GUYLDENSTERNE Is in his retirement meruilous distempred.

HAMLET With drinke sir?

GUYLDENSTERNE No my Lord, rather with choller.

2020 HAMLET Your wisedome should shewe it selfe more richer
to signifie this to his Doctor, for, for mee to put him to
his purgation, would perhaps plunge him into farre
more choller.

GUYLDENSTERNE Good my Lord put your discourse into
some frame, and start not so wildly from my affaire.

HAMLET I am tame sir, pronounce.

GUYLDENSTERNE The Queene your mother in most great
affliction of spirit, hath sent me to you.

HAMLET You are welcome.

2030 GUYLDENSTERNE Nay good my Lord, this curtesie is not
of the right breede, if it shall please you to make me
a wholsome aunswere, I will doe your mothers
commaundement, if not, your pardon and my returne,
shall be the end of my busines.

HAMLET Sir I cannot.

GUYLDENSTERNE What my Lord.

HAMLET Make you a wholsome answer, my wits diseasd,
but sir, such answers as I can make, you shall
commaund, or rather as you say, my mother, therefore
2040 no more, but to the matter, my mother you say.

ROSENCRANS Then thus she sayes, your behauiour hath
strooke her into amazement and admiration.

HAMLET O wonderful sonne that can so astonish a mother,
but is there no sequell at the heeles of this mothers
admiration.

ROSENCRANS She desires to speak with you in her closet
ere you go to bed.

HAMLET We shall obey, were she ten times our mother,
haue you any further trade with vs?

ROSENCRANS My Lord, you once did loue me. 2050

HAMLET So I doe still by these pickers and stealers.

ROSENCRANS Good my Lord, what is your cause of
distemper, you do freely barre the doore of your owne
liberty if you deny your griefes to your friend.

HAMLET Sir I lacke aduauncement.

ROSENCRANS How can that be, when you haue the voyce
of the King himselfe for your succession in Denmarke.

HAMLET I, but while the grasse growes, the prouerbe is
something musty,

  Enter one with a Recorder

ô the Recorder, let mee see, (*to Rosencrans and* 2060
Guyldensterne, drawing them aside) to withdraw with
you, why doe you goe about to recouer the wind of
mee, as if you would driue me into a toyle?

GUYLDENSTERNE O my lord, if my duty be too bold, my
loue is too vnmanerly.

HAMLET I do not wel vnderstand that, wil you play vpon
this pipe?

GUYLDENSTERNE My lord I cannot.

HAMLET I pray you.

GUYLDENSTERNE Beleeue me I cannot. 2070

HAMLET I doe beseech you.

GUYLDENSTERNE I know no touch of it my Lord.

HAMLET 'Tis as easie as lying; gouerne these ventages
with your fingers, & thumbe, giue it breath with your
mouth, & it wil discourse most excellent musique, looke
you, these are the stops.

GUYLDENSTERNE But these cannot I commaund to any
vttrance of harmonie, I haue not the skill.

HAMLET Why looke you now how vnwoorthy a thing you
make of me, you would play vpon mee, you would 2080
seeme to know my stops, you would plucke out the
hart of my mistery, you would sound mee from my
lowest note to the top of my compasse, and there is
much musique excellent voyce in this little organ, yet
cannot you make it speak, s'bloud do you think I am
easier to be plaid on then a pipe, call mee what
instrument you wil, though you can fret me, you
cannot play vpon me.

  Enter Polonius

God blesse you sir.

POLONIUS My Lord, the Queene would speake with you, 2090
& presently.

HAMLET Do you see yonder clowd that's almost in shape
of a Camel?

POLONIUS By'th masse and tis, like a Camell indeed.

HAMLET Mee thinks it is like a Wezell.

POLONIUS It is backt like a Wezell.

HAMLET Or like a Whale.

POLONIUS Very like a Whale.

HAMLET Then will I come to my mother by and by,

2100 (aside) they foole me to the top of my bent, (to Polonius)
     I will come by & by.
     POLONIUS I will say so.
     HAMLET By and by is easily said,   Exit Polonius
     leaue me friends.   Exit Rosencrans and Guydensterne
     Tis now the very witching time of night,
     When Churchyards yawne, and hell it selfe breaths out
     Contagion to this world: now could I drinke hote
          blood,
     And doe such bitter busines as the day
     Would quake to looke on: soft, now to my mother,
2110 O hart loose not thy nature, let not euer
     The soule of Nero enter this firme bosome,
     Let me be cruell, not vnnaturall,
     I will speake daggers to her, but vse none,
     My tongue and soule in this be hypocrites,
     How in my words someuer she be shent,
     To giue them seales neuer my soule consent.   Exit

Sc. 10   Enter King, Rosencrans, and Guyldensterne
(3.3) KING
     I like him not, nor stands it safe with vs
     To let his madnes range, therefore prepare you,
     I your commission will forth-with dispatch,
2120 And he to England shall along with you,
     The termes of our estate may not endure
     Hazerd so dangerous as doth hourely grow
     Out of his Lunacies.
     GUYLDENSTERNE   We will our selues prouide,
     Most holy and religious feare it is
     To keepe those many many bodies safe
     That liue and feede vpon your Maiestie.
     ROSENCRANS
     The single and peculier life is bound
     With all the strength and armour of the mind
     To keepe it selfe from noyance, but much more
2130 That spirit, vpon whose weale depends and rests
     The liues of many, the cesse of Maiestie
     Dies not alone; but like a gulfe doth draw
     What's neere it, with it, it is a massie wheele
     Fixt on the somnet of the highest mount,
     To whose hough spokes, tenne thousand lesser things
     Are morteist and adioynd, which when it falls,
     Each small annexment petty consequence
     Attends the boystrous ruine, neuer alone
     Did the King sigh, but with a generall grone.
     KING
2140 Arme you I pray you to this speedy viage,
     For we will fetters put vpon this feare
     Which now goes too free-footed.
     ROSENCRANS and GUYLDENSTERNE   We will hast vs.
                              Exeunt Gentlemen
          Enter Polonius
     POLONIUS
     My Lord, hee's going to his mothers closet,
     Behind the Arras I'le conuay my selfe
     To heare the processe, I'le warrant shee'le tax him
          home,

     And as you sayd, and wisely was it sayd,
     Tis meete that some more audience then a mother,
     Since nature makes them parciall, should ore-heare
     The speech of vantage; farre you well my Leige,
     I'le call vpon you ere you goe to bed,   2150
     And tell you what I knowe.
     KING   Thankes deere my Lord.
                              Exit Polonius
     O my offence is ranck, it smels to heauen,
     It hath the primall eldest curse vppont,
     A brothers murther, pray can I not,
     Though inclination be as sharp as will,
     My stronger guilt defeats my strong entent,
     And like a man to double bussines bound,
     I stand in pause where I shall first beginne,
     And both neglect, what if this cursed hand
     Were thicker then it selfe with brothers blood,   2160
     Is there not raine enough in the sweete Heauens
     To wash it white as snowe, whereto serues mercy
     But to confront the visage of offence?
     And what's in prayer but this two fold force,
     To be forestalled ere we come to fall,
     Or pardond being downe, then I'le looke vp.
     My fault is past, but oh what forme of prayer
     Can serue my turne, forgiue me my foule murther,
     That cannot be since I am still possest
     Of those effects for which I did the murther;   2170
     My Crowne, mine owne ambition, and my Queene;
     May one be pardond and retaine th'offence?
     In the corrupted currents of this world,
     Offences guilded hand may shoue by iustice,
     And oft tis seene the wicked prize it selfe
     Buyes out the lawe, but tis not so aboue,
     There is no shufling, there the action lies
     In his true nature, and we our selues compeld
     Euen to the teeth and forhead of our faults
     To giue in euidence, what then, what rests,   2180
     Try what repentance can, what can it not,
     Yet what can it, when one cannot repent?
     O wretched state, ô bosome blacke as death,
     O limed soule, that struggling to be free,
     Art more ingag'd; helpe Angels make assay,
     Bowe stubborne knees, and hart with strings of steale,
     Be soft as sinnewes of the new borne babe,
     All may be well.
          Hee kneeles.
          Enter Hamlet behind him
     HAMLET
     Now might I doe it pat, now a is praying,
     And now Ile doo't,
          ⌈He drawes his sword⌉
                    and so a goes to heauen,   2190
     And so am I reuendgd, that would be scand
     A villaine kills my father, and for that,
     I his sole sonne, doe this same villaine send
     To heauen.
     Oh, this is hyre and Sallery, not reuendge,
     A tooke my father grosly full of bread,

With all his crimes braod blowne, as flush as May,
And how his audit stands who knowes saue heauen,
But in our circumstance and course of thought,
2200 Tis heauy with him: and am I then reuendged
To take him in the purging of his soule,
When he is fit and seasond for his passage?
No.
     He sheathes his sword
Vp sword, and knowe thou a more horrid hent,
When he is drunke, a sleepe, or in his rage,
Or in th'incestious pleasure of his bed,
At gaming, swearing, or about some act
That has no relish of saluation in't,
Then trip him that his heels may kick at heauen,
2210 And that his soule may be as damnd and black
As hell whereto it goes; my mother staies,
This phisick but prolongs thy sickly daies.   *Exit*

KING
My words fly vp, my thoughts remaine belowe
Words without thoughts neuer to heauen goe.   *Exit*

Sc. 11   *Enter Gertrard and Polonius*
(3.4) POLONIUS
A will come strait, looke you lay home to him,
Tell him his prancks haue beene too braod to beare
    with,
And that your grace hath screend and stood betweene
Much heate and him, Ile silence me e'ene heere,
Pray you be round with him.
2220 HAMLET (*within*) Mother, mother, mother.
QUEENE
Ile warnt you, feare me not, with-drawe, I heare him
    comming.
    Polonius hides behinde the Arras.
    Enter Hamlet
HAMLET Now mother, what's the matter?
QUEENE
Hamlet, thou hast thy father much offended.
HAMLET
Mother, you haue my father much offended.
QUEENE
Come, come, you answere with an idle tongue.
HAMLET
Goe, goe, you question with a wicked tongue.
QUEENE
Why how now *Hamlet*?
HAMLET   What's the matter now?
QUEENE
Haue you forgot me?
HAMLET   No by the rood not so,
You are the Queene, your husbands brothers wife,
2230 But would you were not so you are my mother.
QUEENE
Nay, then Ile set those to you that can speake.
HAMLET
Come, come, and sit you downe, you shall not boudge,
You goe not till I set you vp a glasse
Where you may see the inmost part of you.

QUEENE
What wilt thou doe, thou wilt not murther me,
Helpe helpe how.
POLONIUS (*behind the Arras*)
    What how helpe, helpe, helpe.
HAMLET
How now, a Rat, dead for a Duckat, dead.
    He thrusts his sword through the Arras
POLONIUS
O I am slaine.
QUEENE (*to Hamlet*) O me, what hast thou done?
HAMLET
Nay I knowe not, is it the King?
QUEENE
O what a rash and bloody deede is this.   2240
HAMLET
A bloody deede, almost as bad, good mother
As kill a King, and marry with his brother.
QUEENE
As kill a King.
HAMLET   I Lady, 'twas my word.
(*To Polonius*) Thou wretched, rash, intruding foole
    farwell,
I tooke thee for thy better, take thy fortune,
Thou find'st to be too busie is some danger,
(*To Queene*) Leaue wringing of your hands, peace sit
    you downe,
And let me wring your hart, for so I shall
If it be made of penitrable stuffe,
If damned custome haue not brasd it so,   2250
That it is proofe and bulwark against sence.
QUEENE
What haue I done, that thou dar'st wagge thy tongue
In noise so rude against me?
HAMLET   Such an act
That blurres the grace and blush of modesty,
Cals vertue hippocrit, takes of the Rose
From the faire forhead of an innocent loue,
And sets a blister there, makes marriage vowes
As false as dicers oathes, ô such a deede,
As from the body of contraction plucks
The very soule, and sweet religion makes   2260
A rapsedy of words; heauens face doth glowe
Yea this solidity and compound masse
With tristfull visage, as against the doome
Is thought sick at the act.
QUEENE   Ay me, what act?
That roares so low'd, and thunders in the Index.
HAMLET
Looke heere vpon this Picture, and on this,
The counterfeit presentment of two brothers,
See what a grace was seated on this browe,
Hiperions curles, the front of *Ioue* himselfe,
An eye like *Mars*, to threaten or command,   2270
A station like the herald *Mercury*,
New lighted on a heauen-kissing hill,
A combination, and a forme indeede,
Where euery God did seeme to set his seale

To giue the world assurance of a man,
This was your husband, looke you now what followes,
Heere is your husband like a mildewed eare,
Blasting his wholsome brother, haue you eyes,
Could you on this faire mountaine leaue to feede,
2280 And batten on this Moore; ha, haue you eyes?
You cannot call it loue, for at your age
The heyday in the blood is tame, it's humble,
And waits vppon the iudgement, and what iudgement
Would step from this to this, what deuill wast
That thus hath cosund you at hodman blind;
O shame where is thy blush? Rebellious hell,
If thou canst mutine in a Matrons bones,
To flaming youth let vertue be as wax
And melt in her owne fire, proclaime no shame
2290 When the compulsiue ardure giues the charge,
Since frost it selfe as actiuely doth burne,
And reason panders will.
 QUEENE   O *Hamlet* speake no more,
Thou turnst mine eyes into my very soule,
And there I see such blacke and greined spots
As will not leaue their tin'ct.
 HAMLET   Nay but to liue
In the ranck sweat of an inseemed bed
Stewed in corruption, honying, and making loue
Ouer the nasty stie.
 QUEENE O speake to me no more,
These words like daggers enter in mine eares,
No more sweete *Hamlet*.
2300 HAMLET   A murtherer and a villaine,
A slaue that is not twentith part the tyth
Of your precedent Lord, a vice of Kings,
A cut-purse of the Empire and the rule,
That from a shelfe the precious Diadem stole
And put it in his pocket.
 QUEENE No more.
 HAMLET A King of shreds and patches,
  Enter Ghost in his night gowne
Saue me and houer ore me with your wings
You heauenly gards: (*to Ghost*) what would you
  gracious figure?
2310 QUEENE Alas hee's mad.
 HAMLET (*to Ghost*)
Doe you not come your tardy sonne to chide,
That lap'st in time and passion lets goe by
Th'important acting of your dread command,
O say.
 GHOST Doe not forget, this visitation
Is but to whet thy almost blunted purpose,
But looke, amazement on thy mother sits,
O step betweene her, and her fighting soule,
Conceit in weakest bodies strongest workes,
Speake to her *Hamlet*.
2320 HAMLET How is it with you Lady?
 QUEENE Alas how i'st with you?
That you doe bend your eye on vacancie,
And with th'incorporall ayre doe hold discourse,

Foorth at your eyes your spirits wildly peep,
And as the sleeping souldiers in th'alarme,
Your bedded haire like life in excrements
Start vp and stand an end, ô gentle sonne
Vpon the heat and flame of thy distemper
Sprinckle coole patience, whereon doe you looke?
 HAMLET
On him, on him, looke you how pale he glares, 2330
His forme and cause conioynd, preaching to stones
Would make them capable, (*to Ghost*) doe not looke
 vpon me,
Least with this pittious action you conuert
My stearne effects, then what I haue to doe
Will want true cullour, teares perchance for blood.
 QUEENE
To whom doe you speake this?
 HAMLET   Doe you see nothing there?
 QUEENE
Nothing at all, yet all that is I see.
 HAMLET
Nor did you nothing heare?
 QUEENE   No nothing but our selues.
 HAMLET
Why looke you there, looke how it steales away,
My father in his habit as he liued, 2340
Looke where he goes, euen now out at the portall.
         Exit Ghost
 QUEENE
This is the very coynage of your braine,
This bodilesse creation extacie
Is very cunning in.
 HAMLET   Extasie?
My pulse as yours doth temperatly keepe time,
And makes as healthfull musicke, it is not madnesse
That I haue vttred, bring me to the test,
And I the matter will reword, which madnesse
Would gambole from, mother for loue of grace,
Lay not a flattering vnction to your soule 2350
That not your trespasse but my madnesse speakes,
It will but skin and filme the vlcerous place
Whil'st ranck corruption mining all within
Infects vnseene, confesse your selfe to heauen,
Repent what's past, auoyd what is to come,
And doe not spread the compost or the weedes
To make them rancker, forgiue me this my vertue,
For in the fatnesse of these pursie times
Vertue it selfe of vice must pardon beg,
Yea curbe and wooe for leaue to doe him good. 2360
 QUEENE
O *Hamlet* thou hast cleft my hart in twaine.
 HAMLET
O throwe away the worser part of it,
And leue the purer with the other halfe,
Good night, but goe not to mine Vncles bed,
Assume a vertue if you haue it not,
Refraine to night,
And that shall lend a kind of easines

To the next abstinence, once more good night,
And when you are desirous to be blest,
2370 Ile blessing beg of you, for this same Lord
I doe repent; but heauen hath pleasd it so
To punish me with this, and this with me,
That I must be their scourge and minister,
I will bestowe him and will answere well
The death I gaue him; so againe good night
I must be cruell only to be kinde,
Thus bad beginnes, and worse remaines behind.

QUEENE What shall I doe?

HAMLET
Not this by no meanes that I bid you doe,
2380 Let the blowt King temp't you againe to bed,
Pinch wanton on your cheeke, call you his Mouse,
And let him for a paire of reechie kisses,
Or padling in your necke with his damn'd fingers,
Make you to rauell all this matter out
That I essentially am not in madnesse,
But mad in craft, t'were good you let him knowe,
For who that's but a Queene, faire, sober, wise,
Would from a paddack, from a bat, a gib,
Such deare concernings hide, who would doe so,
2390 No, in dispight of sence and secrecy,
Vnpeg the basket on the houses top,
Let the birds fly, and like the famous Ape,
To try conclusions in the basket creepe,
And breake your owne necke downe.

QUEENE
Be thou assur'd, if words be made of breath
And breath of life, I haue no life to breath
What thou hast sayd to me.

HAMLET   I must to *England*,
You knowe that.

QUEENE   Alack I had forgot.
Tis so concluded on.

HAMLET   This man shall set me packing,
2400 Ile lugge the guts into the neighbour roome;
Mother good night indeed, this Counsayler
Is now most still, most secret, and most graue,
Who was in life a foolish prating knaue.
Come sir, to draw toward an end with you.
Good night mother.   *Exit Hamlet tugging in Polonius*

(4.1)   *Enter King to Queene*

KING
There's matter in these sighes, these profound heaues,
You must translate, tis fit we vnderstand them,
Where is your sonne?

QUEENE
Ah my good Lord, what haue I seene to night?

2410 KING What *Gertrard*, how dooes *Hamlet*?

QUEENE
Mad as the sea and wind when both contend
Which is the mightier, in his lawlesse fit,
Behind the Arras hearing some thing stirre,
He whyps his Rapier out, and cryes a Rat, a Rat,
And in his brainish apprehension kills
The vnseene good old man.

KING   O heauy deede!

It had beene so with vs had wee been there,
His libertie is full of threates to all,
To you your selfe, to vs, to euery one,
Alas, how shall this bloody deede be answer'd?   2420
It will be layd to vs, whose prouidence
Should haue kept short, restraind, and out of haunt
This mad young man; but so much was our loue,
We would not vnderstand what was most fit,
But like the owner of a foule disease
To keepe it from divulging, let it feede
Euen on the pith of life: where is he gone?

QUEENE
To draw apart the body he hath kild,
Ore whom, his very madnes like some ore
Among a minerall of mettals base,   2430
Showes it selfe pure, a weepes for what is done.

KING O *Gertrard*, come away,
The sunne no sooner shall the mountaines touch,
But we will ship him hence, and this vile deede
We must with all our Maiestie and skill
Both countenaunce and excuse. Ho *Guyldensterne*,
        Enter Rosencrans & Guildensterne
Friends both, goe ioyne you with some further ayde,
Hamlet in madnes hath *Polonius* slaine,
And from his mothers closet hath he dreg'd him,
Goe seeke him out, speake fayre, and bring the body   2440
Into the Chappell; I pray you hast in this,
                              Exit Gentlemen
Come *Gertrard*, wee'le call vp our wisest friends,
To let them know both what we meane to doe
And whats vntimely doone, ô come away,
My soule is full of discord and dismay.   *Exeunt*

        Enter Hamlet   Sc. 12

HAMLET Safely stowd.   (4.2)

ROSENCRANS *and* GUYLDENSTERNE (*within*)
Hamlet, Lord *Hamlet*.

HAMLET
What noyse, who calls on *Hamlet*?
        Enter Rosencrans and Guyldensterne
                    O heere they come.

ROSENCRANS
What haue you doone my Lord with the dead body?

HAMLET
Compounded it with dust whereto tis kin.   2450

ROSENCRANS
Tell vs where tis that we may take it thence,
And beare it to the Chappell.

HAMLET Doe not beleeue it.

ROSENCRANS Beleeue what.

HAMLET That I can keepe your counsaile & not mine
owne, besides to be demaunded of a spunge, what
replycation should be made by the sonne of a King.

ROSENCRANS Take you me for a spunge my Lord?

HAMLET I sir, that sokes vp the Kings countenaunce, his
rewards, his authorities, but such Officers doe the King   2460
best seruice in the end, he keepes them like an ape an
apple in the corner of his iaw, first mouth'd to be last
swallowed, when hee needs what you haue gleand, it

is but squeesing you, and spunge you shall be dry
againe.

ROSENCRANS I vnderstand you not my Lord.

HAMLET I am glad of it, a knauish speech sleepes in a
foolish eare.

ROSENCRANS My Lord, you must tell vs where the body
2470   is, and goe with vs to the King.

HAMLET The body is with the King, but the King is not
with the body. The King is a thing.

GUYLDENSTERNE A thing my Lord.

HAMLET Of nothing, bring me to him, hide Fox, and all
after.   *Exit Hamlet running, pursu'd by the others*

Sc. 13   *Enter King*
(4.3) KING

I haue sent to seeke him, and to find the body,
How dangerous is it that this man goes loose,
Yet must not we put the strong Law on him,
Hee's lou'd of the distracted multitude,
2480 Who like not in their iudgement, but theyr eyes,
And where tis so, th'offenders scourge is wayed
But neuer the offence : to beare all smooth and euen,
This suddaine sending him away must seeme
Deliberate pause, diseases desperat growne,
By desperat applyance are relieu'd
Or not at all.
       Enter Rosencrans
          How now, what hath befalne ?

ROSENCRANS

Where the dead body is bestowd my Lord
We cannot get from him.

KING   But where is hee ?

ROSENCRANS

Without my lord, guarded to know your pleasure.

2490 KING Bring him before vs.

ROSENCRANS

How, *Guildensterne* ? bring in my Lord.
       Enter Hamlet and Guildensterne

KING

Now *Hamlet*, where's *Polonius* ?

HAMLET At supper.

KING At supper, where.

HAMLET Not where he eates, but where a is eaten, a
certaine conuacation of politique wormes are een at
him : your worme is your onely Emperour for dyet, we
fat all creatures els to fat vs, and wee fat our selues for
maggots, your fat King and your leane begger is but
2500 variable seruice, two dishes but to one table, that's the
end.

KING Alas, alas.

HAMLET A man may fish with the worme that hath eate
of a King, & eate of the fish that hath fedde of that
worme.

KING What doost thou meane by this ?

HAMLET Nothing but to shew you how a King may goe
a progresse through the guts of a begger.

KING Where is *Polonius* ?

2510 HAMLET In heauen, send thether to see, if your messenger
finde him not there, seeke him i'th other place your

selfe, but indeed if you find him not this month, you
shall nose him as you goe vp the stayres into the Lobby.

KING ⌈*to Rosencrans*⌉ Goe seeke him there.

HAMLET ⌈*to Rosencrans*⌉ A will stay till ye come.
                  Exit ⌈Rosencrans⌉

KING

Hamlet this deede of thine, for thine especiall safety
Which we do tender, as we deerely grieue
For that which thou hast done, must send thee hence
With fierie Quicknesse. Therefore prepare thy selfe,
The Barck is ready, and the wind at helpe,   2520
Th'associats tend, and euery thing is bent
For *England*.

HAMLET For *England*.

KING I *Hamlet*.

HAMLET Good.

KING

So is it if thou knew'st our purposes.

HAMLET I see a Cherub that sees thẽ, but come for *England*,
farewell deere Mother.

KING Thy louing Father *Hamlet*.

HAMLET My mother, Father and Mother is man and wife, 2530
man and wife is one flesh, and so my mother : come
for *England*.   *Exit*

KING ⌈*to Guyldensterne*⌉

Follow him at foote, tempt him with speede abord,
Delay it not, Ile haue him hence to night.
Away, for euery thing is seald and done
That els leanes on th'affayre, pray you make hast,
                  Exit ⌈Guyldensterne⌉
And *England*, if my loue thou hold'st at ought,
As my great power thereof may giue thee sence,
Since yet thy Cicatrice lookes raw and red,
After the Danish sword, and thy free awe   2540
Payes homage to vs, thou mayst not coldly set
Our soueraigne processe, which imports at full
By Letters coniuring to that effect
The present death of *Hamlet*, doe it *England*,
For like the Hectique in my blood he rages,
And thou must cure me ; till I know tis done,
How ere my haps, my ioyes were nere begun.   *Exit*

    Enter Fortinbrasse with an Army ouer the stage Sc. 14

FORTINBRASSE   (4.4)

Goe Captaine, from me greet the Danish King,
Tell him, that by his lycence *Fortinbrasse*
Claimes the conueyance of a promisd march   2550
Ouer his kingdome, you know the randeuous,
If that his Maiestie would ought with vs,
We shall expresse our dutie in his eye,
And let him know so.

CAPTAINE I will doo't my Lord.   ⌈*Exit*⌉

FORTINBRASSE Goe safely on.   *Exeunt marching*

    Enter Queene and Horatio   Sc. 15

QUEENE   (4.5)

I will not speake with her.

HORATIO   Shee is importunat,
Indeede distract, her moode will needes be pittied.

QUEENE What would she haue?

HORATIO

2560 She speakes much of her father, sayes she heares
There's tricks i'th world, and hems, and beates her hart,
Spurnes enuiously at strawes, speakes things in doubt
That carry but halfe sence, her speech is nothing,
Yet the vnshaped vse of it doth moue
The hearers to collection, they ayme at it,
And botch the words vp fit to theyr owne thoughts,
Which as her wincks, and nods, and gestures yeeld
     them,
Indeede would make one thinke there might be thought
Though nothing sure, yet much vnhappily.

QUEENE

2570 Twere good she were spoken with, for shee may strew
Dangerous coniectures in ill breeding mindes,
Let her come in.
          ⌈*Horatio withdraws, to admit Ophelia*⌉

QUEENE

'To my sicke soule, as sinnes true nature is,
'Each toy seemes prologue to some great amisse,
'So full of artlesse iealousie is guilt,
'It spills it selfe, in fearing to be spylt.
          Enter Ophelia distracted, ⌈*her haire downe, with a*
          Lute⌉

OPHELIA

Where is the beautious Maiestie of Denmarke?

QUEENE How now *Ophelia?*

OPHELIA (*sings*)
          How should I your true loue know
2580   From another one,
          By his cockle hat and staffe,
               And his Sendall shoone.

QUEENE

Alas sweet Lady, what imports this song?

OPHELIA Say you, nay pray you marke,
     (*Sings*)
          He is dead & gone Lady,
               He is dead and gone,
          At his head a grasgreene turph,
               At his heeles a stone.

QUEENE Nay but *Ophelia.*

2590 OPHELIA Pray you marke.
     (*Sings*)
          White his shrowd as the mountaine snow.
     Enter King

QUEENE Alas looke heere my Lord.

OPHELIA (*sings*)
          Larded with sweet flowers,
          Which beweept to the graue did not go
               With true loue showers.

KING How doe ye pretty Lady?

OPHELIA Well God dild you, they say the Owle was a
     Bakers daugter, Lord we know what we are, but know
     not what we may be. God be at your table.

2600 KING (*to Queene*) Conceit vpon her Father.

OPHELIA Pray you lets haue no words of this, but when
     they aske you what it meanes, say you this.

(*Sings*)
          To morrow is S. Valentines day,
               All in the morning betime,
          And I a mayde at your window
               To be your Valentine.

          Then vp he rose, and dond his close,
               And dupt the chamber doore,
          Let in the maide, that out a maide,
               Neuer departed more.   2610

KING Pretty *Ophelia.*

OPHELIA Indeede la? without an oath Ile make an end
     on't,
(*Sings*)
          By gis and by Saint Charitie,
               Alack and fie for shame,
          Young men will doo't if they come too't,
               By Cock they are too blame.

          Quoth she, Before you tumbled me,
               You promisd me to wed,
          So would I a done by yonder sunne   2620
               And thou hadst not come to my bed.

KING (*to Queene*) How long hath she beene thus?

OPHELIA I hope all will be well, we must be patient, but
     I cannot chuse but weepe to thinke they should lay
     him i'th cold ground, my brother shall know of it, and
     so I thanke you for your good counsaile. Come my
     Coach, God night Ladies, god night. Sweet Ladyes god
     night, god night.   *Exit*

KING (*to Horatio*)
Follow her close, giue her good watch I pray you.
                                      Exit Horatio
O this is the poyson of deepe griefe, it springs   2630
All from her Fathers death, ô *Gertrard, Gertrard,*
When sorrowes come, they come not single spyes,
But in battalians: first her Father slaine,
Next, your sonne gone, and he most violent Author
Of his owne iust remoue, the people muddied
Thick and vnwholsome in their thoughts, and whispers
For good *Polonius* death: and we haue done but
     greenly
In hugger mugger to inter him: poore *Ophelia*
Deuided from herselfe, and her faire iudgement,
Without the which we are pictures, or meere beasts,   2640
Last, and as much contayning as all these,
Her brother is in secret come from Fraunce,
Feeds on this wonder, keepes himselfe in clowdes,
And wants not buzzers to infect his eare
With pestilent speeches of his fathers death,
Wherein necessity of matter beggerd,
Will nothing stick our persons to arraigne
In eare and eare: ô my deare *Gertrard,* this
Like to a murdring peece in many places
Giues me superfluous death.
     A noise within

QUEENE   Alacke, what noyse is this? 2650

KING
Where is my Swissers, let them guard the doore,

Enter a Messenger
What is the matter?
MESSENGER   Saue your selfe my Lord.
The Ocean ouer-peering of his list
Eates not the flats with more impitious hast
Then young *Laertes* in a riotous head
Ore-beares your Officers: the rabble call him Lord,
And as the world were now but to beginne,
Antiquity forgot, custome not knowne,
The ratifiers and props of euery word,
2660   They cry choose we, *Laertes* shall be King,
Caps, hands, and tongues applau'd it to the clouds,
Laertes shall be King, *Laertes* King.
QUEENE
How cheerefully on the false traile they cry.
     A noise within
O this is counter you false Danish dogges.
KING The doores are broke.
     Enter Laertes ⌜*with his followers at the doore*⌝
LAERTES
Where is the King? sirs stand you all without.
ALL HIS FOLLOWERS No lets come in.
LAERTES I pray you giue me leaue.
ALL HIS FOLLOWERS We will, we will.
LAERTES
I thanke you, keepe the doore,   ⌜*Exeunt followers*⌝
2670   ô thou vile King,
Giue me my father.
QUEENE   Calmely good *Laertes.*
LAERTES
That drop of blood thats calme proclames me Bastard,
Cries cuckold to my father, brands the Harlot
Euen heere betweene the chast vnsmirched browe
Of my true mother.
KING   What is the cause *Laertes*
That thy rebellion lookes so gyant like?
Let him goe *Gertrard,* doe not feare our person,
There's such diuinitie doth hedge a King,
That treason can but peepe to what it would,
2680   Act's little of his will, tell me *Laertes*
Why thou art thus incenst, let him goe *Gertrard.*
Speake man.
LAERTES   Where is my father?
KING   Dead.
QUEENE (*to Laertes*)
But not by him.
KING   Let him demaund his fill.
LAERTES
How came he dead, I'le not be iugled with,
To hell allegiance, vowes to the blackest deuill,
Conscience and grace, to the profoundest pit
I dare damnation, to this poynt I stand,
That both the worlds I giue to negligence,
Let come what comes, onely I'le be reueng'd
2690   Most throughly for my father.
KING Who shall stay you?
LAERTES My will, not all the world:

And for my meanes I'le husband them so well,
They shall goe farre with little.
KING   Good *Laertes,*
If you desire to know the certainty
Of your deere Fathers death, i'st writ in your reuenge,
That soopstake, you will draw both friend and foe
Winner and looser.
LAERTES None but his enemies.
KING Will you know them then?   2700
LAERTES
To his good friends thus wide I'le ope my armes,
And like the kind life-rendring Pelican,
Repast them with my blood.
KING   Why now you speake
Like a good child, and a true Gentleman.
That I am guiltlesse of your fathers death,
And am most sencibly in griefe for it,
It shall as leuell to your iudgement pearce
As day dooes to your eye.
     A noyse within
VOYCES (*within*) Let her come in.
LAERTES How now, what noyse is that?   2710
     Enter Ophelia as before
O heate, dry vp my braines, teares seauen times salt
Burne out the sence and vertue of mine eye,
By heauen thy madnes shall be payd by weight
Tell our scale turnes the beame. O Rose of May,
Deere mayd, kind sister, sweet *Ophelia,*
O heauens, ist possible a young maids wits
Should be as mortall as an old mans life.
Nature is fine in Loue, and where 'tis fine,
It sends some precious instance of it selfe
After the thing it loues.   2720
OPHELIA (*sings*)
     They bore him bare-faste on the Beere,
       Hey non nony, nony, hey nony:
       And on his graue rain'd many a teare,
fare you well my Doue.
LAERTES
Hadst thou thy wits, and did'st perswade reuenge
It could not mooue thus.
OPHELIA You must sing downe a downe, and you call
him a downe a. O how the wheele becomes it, it is the
false Steward that stole his Maisters daughter.
LAERTES This nothing's more then matter.   2730
OPHELIA There's Rosemary, thats for remembrance, pray
loue remember, and there is Pancies, thats for thoughts.
LAERTES
A document in madnes, thoughts and remembrance
    fitted.
OPHELIA There's Fennill for you, and Colembines, there's
Rewe for you, & heere's some for me, we may call it
Herbe-Grace a Sondaies, Oh you must weare your Rewe
with a difference, there's a Dasie, I would giue you
some Violets, but they witherd all when my Father
dyed, they say a made a good end.
(*Sings*) For bonny sweet Robin is all my ioy.   2740

LAERTES

    Thought and affliction, passion, hell it selfe

    She turnes to fauour and to prettines.

OPHELIA (*sings*)

           And wil a not come againe,

           And wil a not come againe,

              No, no, he is dead,

              Goe to thy death bed,

           He neuer will come againe.

           His beard as white as snow,

           All Flaxen was his pole,

2750   He is gone, he is gone,

              And we cast away mone,

           God a mercy on his soule,

    and of all Christian soules, I pray God. God buy ye.

                ⌜*Exeunt Ophelia and Queene*⌝

LAERTES Doe you see this ô God.

KING

    Laertes, I must commune with your griefe,

    Or you deny me right, goe but apart,

    Make choice of whom your wisest friends you will,

    And they shall heare and iudge twixt you and me,

    If by direct, or by colaturall hand

2760   They find vs toucht, we will our kingdome giue,

    Our crowne, our life, and all that we call ours

    To you in satisfaction; but if not,

    Be you content to lend your patience to vs,

    And we shall ioyntly labour with your soule

    To giue it due content.

LAERTES   Let this be so.

    His meanes of death, his obscure buriall,

    No trophe sword, nor hatchment ore his bones,

    No noble right, nor formall ostentation,

    Cry to be heard as twere from heauen to earth,

    That I must call't in question.

2770 KING   So you shall,

    And where th'offence is, let the great axe fall.

    I pray you goe with me.   *Exeunt*

Sc. 16   *Enter Horatio, with a Seruant*

(4.6) HORATIO

    What are they that would speake with me?

SERUANT

    Saylors sir, they say they haue Letters for you.

HORATIO Let them come in.   *Exit Seruant*

    I doe not know from what part of the world

    I should be greeted, If not from Lord *Hamlet*.

        Enter ⌜*Saylers*⌝

SAYLER God blesse you sir.

HORATIO Let him blesse thee to.

2780 SAYLER A shall sir and please him, there's a Letter for

    you sir, it comes frõ th'Embassador that was bound for

    England, if your name be *Horatio*, as I am let to know

    it is.

HORATIO (*reads the Letter*) *Horatio, when thou shalt haue*

    ouer-lookt this, giue these fellowes some meanes to the

    King, they haue Letters for him: Ere wee were two

daies old at Sea, a Pyrat of very warlike appointment

gaue vs chase, finding our selues too slow of saile, wee

put on a compelled valour, and in the grapple I boorded

them, on the instant they got cleere of our shyp, so I 2790

alone became theyr prisoner, they haue dealt with me

like thieues of mercie, but they knew what they did, I

am to doe a good turne for them, let the King haue

the Letters I haue sent, and repayre thou to me with

as much hast as thou wouldest flie death, I haue wordes

to speake in thine eare will make thee dumbe, yet are

they much too light for the bore of the matter, these

good fellowes will bring thee where I am, Rosencrans

and Guyldensterne hold theyr course for England, of

them I haue much to tell thee, farewell. 2800

        He that thou knowest thine Hamlet.

    Come I will giue you way for these your letters,

    And doo't the speedier that you may direct me

    To him from whom you brought them.   *Exeunt*

       Enter King and Laertes   Sc. 17

KING   (4.7)

    Now must your conscience my acquittance seale,

    And you must put me in your hart for friend,

    Sith you haue heard and with a knowing eare,

    That he which hath your noble father slaine

    Pursued my life.

LAERTES   It well appeares: but tell mee

    Why you proceeded not against these feates   2810

    So crimefull and so capitall in nature,

    As by your safetie, wisdome, all things els

    You mainely were stirr'd vp.

KING   O for two speciall reasons

    Which may to you perhaps seeme much vnsinnow'd,

    And yet to mee tha'r strong, the Queene his mother

    Liues almost by his lookes, and for my selfe,

    My vertue or my plague, be it eyther which,

    She's so coniunctiue to my life and soule,

    That as the starre mooues not but in his sphere

    I could not but by her, the other motiue,   2820

    Why to a publique count I might not goe,

    Is the great loue the generall gender beare him,

    Who dipping all his faults in theyr affection,

    Would like the spring that turneth wood to stone,

    Conuert his Guilts to graces, so that my arrowes

    Too slightly tymberd for so loude a wind,

    Would haue reuerted to my bowe againe,

    And not where I had aym'd them.

LAERTES

    And so haue I a noble father lost,

    A sister driuen into desprat termes,   2830

    Who has, if prayses may goe backe againe

    Stood challenger on mount of all the age

    For her perfections, but my reuenge will come.

KING

    Breake not your sleepes for that, you must not thinke

    That we are made of stuffe so flat and dull,

    That we can let our beard be shooke with danger,

And thinke it pastime, you shortly shall heare more,
I lou'd your father, and we loue our selfe,
And that I hope will teach you to imagine.
     Enter a Messenger with Letters
How now? What Newes?

2840 MESSENGER   Letters my Lord from Hamlet.
This to your Maiestie, this to the Queene.
KING From *Hamlet*, who brought them?
MESSENGER
Saylers my Lord they say, I saw them not,
They were giuen me by *Claudio*, he receiu'd them.
KING
Laertes you shall heare them: leaue vs.
                   Exit Messenger
(*Reads*) High and mighty, you shall know I am set
naked on your kingdom, to morrow shall I begge leaue
to see your kingly eyes, when I shal first asking your
pardon, there-vnto recount th'occasions of my suddaine
2850 and more strange returne.
               Hamlet.
What should this meane, are all the rest come backe,
Or is it some abuse, and no such thing?
LAERTES
Know you the hand?
KING   Tis *Hamlets* caracter.
Naked, and in a postscript heere he sayes
Alone, can you aduise me?
LAERTES
I'm lost in it my Lord, but let him come,
It warmes the very sicknes in my hart
That I shall liue and tell him to his teeth
Thus diddest thou.
2860 KING   If it be so *Laertes*,
As how should it be so, how otherwise,
Will you be rul'd by me?
LAERTES
If so you'l not ore rule me to a peace.
KING
To thine owne peace, if he be now returned
As checking at his voyage, and that he meanes
No more to vndertake it, I will worke him
To an exployt, now ripe in my deuise,
Vnder the which he shall not choose but fall:
And for his death no wind of blame shall breathe,
2870 But euen his Mother shall vncharge the practise,
And call it accedent. Some two months since
Heere was a gentleman of *Normandy*,
I'ue seene my selfe, and seru'd against the French,
And they can well on horsebacke, but this gallant
Had witch-craft in't, he grew into his seate,
And to such wondrous dooing brought his horse,
As had he beene incorp'st, and demy natur'd
With the braue beast, so farre he past my thought,
That I in forgerie of shapes and tricks
Come short of what he did.
2880 LAERTES   A Norman wast?
KING A Norman.

LAERTES
Vppon my life *Lamord*.
KING   The very same.
LAERTES
I know him well, he is the brooch indeed
And Iem of all the Nation.
KING   He made confession of you,
And gaue you such a masterly report
For art and exercise in your defence,
And for your Rapier most especially,
That he cride out t'would be a sight indeed
If one could match you; sir this report of his
Did *Hamlet* so enuenom with his enuy,   2890
That he could nothing doe but wish and beg
Your sodaine comming ore to play with him.
Now out of this.
LAERTES   What out of this my Lord?
KING
Laertes was your father deare to you?
Or are you like the painting of a sorrowe,
A face without a hart?
LAERTES   Why aske you this?
KING
Not that I thinke you did not loue your father,
But that I knowe, loue is begunne by time,
And that I see in passages of proofe,
Time qualifies the sparke and fire of it,   2900
Hamlet comes back, what would you vndertake
To showe your selfe your fathers sonne in deede
More then in words?
LAERTES   To cut his thraot i'th Church.
KING
No place indeede should murther sanctuarise,
Reuendge should haue no bounds: but good *Laertes*
Will you doe this, keepe close within your chamber,
Hamlet return'd, shall knowe you are come home,
Weele put on those shall praise your excellence,
And set a double varnish on the fame
The french man gaue you, bring you in fine together   2910
And wager on your heads; he being remisse,
Most generous, and free from all contriuing,
Will not peruse the foyles, so that with ease,
Or with a little shuffling, you may choose
A sword vnbated, and in a passe of practise
Requite him for your Father.
LAERTES   I will doo't,
And for that purpose, Ile annoynt my sword.
I bought an vnction of a Mountibanck
So mortall, that but dippe a knife in it,
Where it drawes blood, no Cataplasme so rare,   2920
Collected from all simples that haue vertue
Vnder the Moone, can saue the thing from death
That is but scratcht withall, Ile tutch my point
With this contagion, that if I gall him slightly,
It may be death.
KING   Lets further thinke of this.
Wey what conuenience both of time and meanes

May fit vs to our shape, if this should fayle
And that our drift looke through our bad performance,
Twere better not assayd, therefore this proiect,
2930 Should haue a back or second that might hold
If this should blast in proofe; soft let me see,
Wee'le make a solemne wager on your cunnings,
I hate, when in your motion you are hote and dry,
As make your bouts more violent to that end,
And that he calls for drinke, Ile haue prepard him
A Challice for the nonce, whereon but sipping,
If he by chaunce escape your venom'd stuck,
Our purpose may hold there;

   Enter Queene

        how now sweet Queene.

QUEENE
One woe doth tread vpon anothers heele,
2940 So fast they follow; your Sisters drownd *Laertes*.

LAERTES Drown'd, ô where?

QUEENE
There is a Willow growes aslant a Brooke
That showes his hore leaues in the glassy streame,
Therewith fantastique garlands did she make
Of Crowflowers, Nettles, Daises, and long Purples
That liberall Shepheards giue a grosser name,
But our cold maydes doe dead mens fingers call them.
There on the pendant boughes her cronet weedes
Clambring to hang, an enuious sliuer broke,
2950 When downe the weedy trophies and her selfe
Fell in the weeping Brooke, her clothes spred wide,
And Marmaide like awhile they bore her vp,
Which time she chaunted snatches of old tunes,
As one incapable of her owne distresse,
Or like a creature natiue and indewed
Vnto that element, but long it could not be
Till that her garments heauy with theyr drinke,
Puld the poore wretch from her melodious lay
To muddy death.

2960 LAERTES Alas, then is she drownd.

QUEENE Drownd, drownd.

LAERTES
Too much of water hast thou poore *Ophelia*,
And therefore I forbid my teares; but yet
It is our tricke, nature her custome holds,
Let shame say what it will,

  He weepes

      when these are gone,
The woman will be out. Adiew my Lord,
I haue a speech of fire that faine would blase,
But that this folly doubts it.   *Exit*

KING   Let's follow *Gertrard*,
How much I had to doe to calme his rage,
2970 Now feare I this will giue it start againe,
Therefore lets follow.   *Exeunt*

Sc. 18   *Enter two Clownes ⌈carrying a spade and a pickax⌉*
(5.1) CLOWNE Is shee to be buried in Christian buriall, that
wilfully seekes her owne saluation?

OTHER I tell thee she is, and therfore make her graue
straight, the crowner hath sate on her, and finds it
Christian buriall.

CLOWNE How can that be, vnlesse she drown'd herselfe
in her owne defence.

OTHER Why tis found so.

CLOWNE It must be se offendēdo, it cannot be els, for heere   2980
lyes the poynt, if I drowne my selfe wittingly, it argues
an act, & an act hath three branches, it is to act, to
doe, and to performe; argall she drownd her selfe
wittingly.

OTHER Nay, but heare you good man deluer.

CLOWNE Giue mee leaue, here lyes the water, good, here
stands the man, good, if the man goe to this water &
drowne himselfe, it is will he, nill he, he goes, marke
you that, but if the water come to him, & drowne him,
he drownes not himselfe, argall, he that is not guilty   2990
of his owne death, shortens not his owne life.

OTHER But is this law?

CLOWNE I marry i'st, Crowners quest law.

OTHER Will you ha the truth an't, if this had not beene
a gentlewoman, she should haue been buried out a
christian buriall.

CLOWNE Why there thou sayst, and the more pitty that
great folke should haue countnaunce in this world to
drowne or hang thēselues, more then theyr euen
Christen: Come my spade, there is no auncient   3000
gentlemen but Gardners, Ditchers, and Grauemakers,
they hold vp Adams profession.

  ⌈*Clowne digges*⌉

OTHER Was he a gentleman?

CLOWNE A was the first that euer bore Armes.

OTHER Why he had none.

CLOWNE What, ar't a Heathen? how dost thou vnderstand
the Scripture? the Scripture sayes Adam dig'd; could
hee digge without Armes? Ile put another question to
thee, if thou answerest me not to the purpose, confesse
thy selfe.   3010

OTHER Goe to.

CLOWNE What is he that builds stronger then eyther the
Mason, the Shypwright, or the Carpenter.

OTHER The gallowes maker, for that Frame out-liues a
thousand tenants.

CLOWNE I like thy wit well in good fayth, the gallowes
dooes well, but howe dooes it well? It dooes well to
those that do ill, nowe thou doost ill to say the gallowes
is built stronger then the Church, argall, the gallowes
may doo well to thee. Too't againe, come.   3020

OTHER Who buildes stronger then a Mason, a Shipwright,
or a Carpenter.

CLOWNE I, tell me that and vnyoke.

OTHER Marry now I can tell.

CLOWNE Too't.

OTHER Masse I cannot tell.

  Enter Hamlet and Horatio a farre off

CLOWNE Cudgell thy braines no more about it, for your
dull asse wil not mend his pace with beating, and when
you are askt this question next, say a graue-maker,

3030 the houses that hee makes lasts till Doomesday. Goe
get thee to *Yaughan*, fetch mee a stoope of liquer.

Exit Other

(*Sings*)

> In youth when I did loue did loue,
>> Me thought it was very sweet
> To contract ô the time for a my behoue,
>> O me thought there a was nothing a meet.

HAMLET Has this fellowe no feeling of his busines, that a
sings at graue-making.

HORATIO Custome hath made it in him a propertie of
easines.

3040 HAMLET Tis een so, the hand of little imploiment hath the
daintier sence.

CLOWNE (*sings*)

> But age with his stealing steppes
>> Hath caught me in his clutch,
> And hath shipped me intill the land,
>> As if I had neuer been such.

⌈*He throwes vp a skull*⌉

HAMLET That skull had a tongue in it, and could sing
once, how the knaue iowles it to th' ground, as if twere
Caines iawbone, that did the first murder, this might
be the pate of a pollitician, which this asse ore-Offices;
3050 one that would circumuent God, might it not?

HORATIO It might my Lord.

HAMLET Or of a Courtier, which could say good morrow
sweet lord, how doost thou good lord? This might be
my Lord such a one, that praised my lord such a ones
horse when a ment to beg it, might it not?

HORATIO I my Lord.

HAMLET Why een so, & now my Lady wormes Choples,
& knockt about the masserd with a Sextens spade;
heere's fine reuolution and we had the tricke to see't,
3060 did these bones cost no more the breeding, but to play
at loggits with 'em: mine ake to thinke on't.

CLOWNE (*sings*)

> A pickax and a spade a spade,
>> For and a shrowding sheet,
> O a pit of Clay for to be made
>> For such a guest is meet.

⌈*He throwes vp another skull*⌉

HAMLET There's another, why might not that be the skull
of a Lawyer, where be his quiddits now, his quillets,
his cases, his tenurs, and his tricks? why dooes he
suffer this rude knaue now to knocke him about the
3070 sconce with a durtie shouell, and will not tell him of
his action of battery, hum, this fellowe might be in's
time a great buyer of Land, with his Statuts, his
recognisances, his fines, his double vouchers, his
recoueries, is this the fine of his Fines, and the recouery
of his recoueries, to haue his fine pate full of fine durt,
will his vouchers vouch him no more of his purchases
& double ones too then the length and breadth of a
payre of Indentures? The very conueyances of his Lands
will hardly lye in this box, & must th'inheritor himselfe
3080 haue no more, ha.

HORATIO Not a iot more my Lord.

HAMLET Is not Parchment made of sheepe-skinnes?

HORATIO I my Lord, and of Calues-skinnes to.

HAMLET They are Sheepe and Calues that seeke out
assurance in that, I wil speak to this fellow. (*To Clowne*)
Whose graue's this sirra?

CLOWNE Mine sir,

(*Sings*)   O a pit of clay for to be made,
>> For such a Guest is meete.

HAMLET I thinke it be thine indeede, for thou lyest in't.   3090

CLOWNE You lie out ont sir, and therefore it is not yours;
for my part I doe not lie in't, and yet it is mine.

HAMLET Thou doost lie in't to be in't & say 'tis thine, tis
for the dead, not for the quicke, therefore thou lyest.

CLOWNE Tis a quicke lye sir, twill away againe from me
to you.

HAMLET What man doost thou digge it for?

CLOWNE For no man sir.

HAMLET What woman then?

CLOWNE For none neither.   3100

HAMLET Who is to be buried in't?

CLOWNE One that was a woman sir, but rest her soule
shee's dead.

HAMLET How absolute the knaue is, we must speake by
the card, or equiuocation will vndoo vs. By the Lord
Horatio, this three yeeres I haue taken note of it, the
age is growne so picked, that the toe of the pesant
coms so neere the heele of the Courtier he galls his
kybe. (*To Clowne*) How long hast thou been a Graue-
maker?   3110

CLOWNE Of all the dayes i'th yere I came too't that day
that our last king *Hamlet* o'recame *Fortenbrasse*.

HAMLET How long is that since?

CLOWNE Cannot you tell that? euery foole can tell that,
it was the very day that young *Hamlet* was borne: hee
that was mad and sent into *England*.

HAMLET I marry, why was he sent into *England*?

CLOWNE Why because a was mad: a shall recouer his
wits there, or if a doo not, tis no great matter there.

HAMLET Why?   3120

CLOWNE Twill not be seene in him there, there the men
are as mad as hee.

HAMLET How came he mad?

CLOWNE Very strangely they say.

HAMLET How strangely?

CLOWNE Fayth eene with loosing his wits.

HAMLET Vpon what ground?

CLOWNE Why heere in Denmarke: I haue been Sexten
heere man and boy thirty yeeres.

HAMLET How long will a man lie i'th earth ere he rot?   3130

CLOWNE Ifayth if a be not rotten before a die, as we haue
many pockie corses now adaies, that will scarce hold
the laying in, a will last you som eyght yeere, or nine
yeere. A Tanner will last you nine yeere.

HAMLET Why he more then another?

CLOWNE Why sir, his hide is so tand with his trade, that
a will keepe out water a great while; & your water is
a sore decayer of your whorson dead body, heer's a
scull now: this Scul, has laine in the earth three &
twenty yeeres.   3140

HAMLET Whose was it?

CLOWNE A whorson mad fellowes it was, whose do you think it was?

HAMLET Nay I know not.

CLOWNE A pestilence on him for a madde rogue, a pourd a flagon of Renish on my head once; this same skull sir, was *Yoricks* skull, the Kings Iester.

HAMLET This?

CLOWNE Een that.

3150 HAMLET Let me see.

He takes the skull

Alas poore *Yoricke*, I knew him *Horatio*, a fellow of infinite iest, of most excellent fancie, hee hath borne me on his backe a thousand times, and now how abhorred my imagination is: my gorge rises at it. Heere hung those lyppes that I haue kist I know not howe oft, where be your gibes now? your gamboles, your songs, your flashes of merriment, that were wont to set the table on a roare, not one now to mocke your owne grinning, quite chopfalne. Now get you to my

3160 Ladies Chamber, & tell her, let her paint an inch thicke, to this fauour she must come, make her laugh at that. Prethee *Horatio* tell me one thing.

HORATIO What's that my Lord?

HAMLET Doost thou thinke *Alexander* lookt a this fashion i'th earth?

HORATIO Een so.

HAMLET And smelt so pah.

⌈*He throwes the skull downe*⌉

HORATIO Een so my Lord.

HAMLET To what base vses wee may returne *Horatio*?

3170 Why may not imagination trace the noble dust of *Alexander*, till a find it stopping a bunghole?

HORATIO Twere to consider too curiously to consider so.

HAMLET No faith, not a iot, but to follow him thether with modesty enough, and likelyhood to leade it; as thus. *Alexander* dyed, *Alexander* was buried, *Alexander* returneth into dust, the dust is earth, of earth wee make Lome, & why of that Lome whereto he was conuerted, might they not stoppe a Beare-barrell? Imperiall *Cæsar* dead, and turn'd to Clay,

3180 Might stoppe a hole, to keepe the wind away. O that that earth which kept the world in awe, Should patch a wall t'expell the winters flaw. But soft, but soft, aside,

Hamlet and Horatio stand aside. Enter King Queene Laertes and a Cooffin, with a Priest and Lords attendant

here comes the King, The Queene, the Courtiers, who is that they follow? And with such maimed rites? this doth betoken, The corse they follow, did with desprat hand Foredoo it owne life, twas of some estate, Couch we a while and marke.

LAERTES   What Ceremonie els?

HAMLET (*aside to Horatio*) That is *Laertes* a very noble youth, marke.

3190 LAERTES What Ceremonie els?

PRIEST

Her obsequies haue been as farre inlarg'd As we haue warrantis, her death was doubtfull, And but that great commaund ore-swayes the order, She should in ground vnsanctified haue lodg'd Till the last trumpet: for charitable prayers, Shardes, Flints and peebles should be throwne on her: Yet heere she is allow'd her virgin Rites, Her mayden strewments, and the bringing home Of bell and buriall.

LAERTES Must there no more be doone?   3200

PRIEST No more be doone. We should prophane the seruice of the dead, To sing sage Requiem and such rest to her As to peace-parted soules.

LAERTES   Lay her i'th earth, And from her faire and vnpolluted flesh May Violets spring: I tell thee churlish Priest, A ministring Angell shall my sister be When thou lyest howling.

HAMLET (*aside*) What, the faire *Ophelia*.

QUEENE (*scattering flowers*) Sweets to the sweet, farewell,   3210 I hop't thou should'st haue been my *Hamlets* wife, I thought thy bride-bed to haue deckt sweet maide, And not t'haue strew'd thy graue.

LAERTES   O treble woe Fall tenne times trebble on that cursed head, Whose wicked deede thy most ingenious sence Depriu'd thee of, hold off the earth a while, Till I haue caught her once more in mine armes;

Leaps in the graue

Now pile your dust vpon the quicke and dead, Till of this flat a mountaine you haue made To'retop old *Pelion*, or the skyesh head   3220 Of blew *Olympus*.

HAMLET (*comming forward*) What is he whose griefe Beares such an emphasis, whose phrase of sorrow Coniures the wandring starres, and makes them stand Like wonder wounded hearers: this is I *Hamlet* the Dane.

⌈*Hamlet leapes in after Laertes*⌉

LAERTES The deuill take thy soule.

HAMLET Thou pray'st not well, I prethee take thy fingers from my throat, For though I am not spleenatiue and rash, Yet haue I something in me dangerous,   3230 Which let thy wisenesse feare; away thy hand.

KING (*to Lords*) Pluck them a sunder.

QUEENE   *Hamlet, Hamlet.*

ALL ⌈THE LORDS⌉ Gentlemen.

HORATIO (*to Hamlet*) Good my Lord be quiet.

HAMLET Why, I will fight with him vpon this theame Vntil my eye-lids will no longer wagge.

QUEENE O my sonne, what theame?

HAMLET

   I lou'd *Ophelia*, forty thousand brothers

   Could not with all theyr quantitie of loue

   Make vp my summe. (*To Laertes*) What wilt thou doo

      for her.

3240 KING O he is mad *Laertes*.

   QUEENE (*to Laertes*) For loue of God forbeare him.

   HAMLET (*to Laertes*) S'wounds shew me what th'owt doe:

   Woo't weepe, woo't fight, woo't fast, woo't teare thy

      selfe,

   Woo't drinke vp Esill, eate a Crocadile?

   Ile doo't, doost thou come heere to whine?

   To out-face me with leaping in her graue?

   Be buried quicke with her, and so will I.

   And if thou prate of mountaines, let them throw

   Millions of Acres on vs, till our ground

3250 Sindging his pate against the burning Zone

   Make Ossa like a wart, nay and thou'lt mouthe,

   Ile rant as well as thou.

   KING ⌈*to Laertes*⌉   This is meere madnesse,

   And thus a while the fit will worke on him,

   Anon as patient as the female Doue

   When that her golden cuplets are disclosed

   His silence will sit drooping.

   HAMLET (*to Laertes*)   Heare you sir,

   What is the reason that you vse me thus?

   I lou'd you euer, but it is no matter,

   Let *Hercules* himselfe doe what he may

3260 The Cat will mew, and Dogge will haue his day.

                    Exit Hamlet

   KING

   I pray you good *Horatio* waite vpon him. *Exit Horatio*

   (*To Laertes*) Strengthen your patience in our last

      nights speech,

   Weele put the matter to the present push:

   Good *Gertrard* set some watch ouer your sonne,

   This graue shall haue a liuing monument,

   An houre of quiet shortly shall we see

   Tell then in patience our proceeding be.   *Exeunt*

Sc. 19   *Enter Hamlet and Horatio*

(5.2) HAMLET

   So much for this sir, now let me see the other,

   You doe remember all the circumstance.

3270 HORATIO Remember it my Lord.

   HAMLET

   Sir in my hart there was a kind of fighting

   That would not let me sleepe, me thought I lay

   Worse then the mutines in the bilbos, rashly,

   And praysd be rashnes for it: let vs knowe,

   Our indiscretion sometime serues vs well

   When our deare plots doe pall, & that should teach vs

   Ther's a diuinity that shapes our ends,

   Rough hew them how we will.

   HORATIO That is most certaine.

3280 HAMLET Vp from my Cabin,

   My sea-gowne scarft about me in the darke

   Gropt I to find out them, had my desire,

Fingard their packet, and in fine with-drew

To mine owne roome againe, making so bold

My feares forgetting manners to vnseale

Their graund commission; where I found *Horatio*

Oh royall knauery, an exact command

Larded with many seuerall sorts of reasons,

Importing Denmarkes health, and *Englands* to,

With hoe such bugges and goblines in my life,   3290

That on the superuise no leasure bated,

No not to stay the grinding of the Axe,

My head should be strooke off.

HORATIO   I'st possible?

HAMLET (*giuing it to him*)

   Heeres the commission, read it at more leasure,

   But wilt thou heare me how I did proceed.

HORATIO I beseech you.

HAMLET

   Being thus benetted round with villainies,

   Or I could make a prologue to my braines,

   They had begunne the play, I sat me downe,

   Deuisd a new commission, wrote it faire,   3300

   I once did hold it as our statists doe,

   A basenesse to write faire, and labourd much

   How to forget that learning, but sir now

   It did me yemans seruice, wilt thou know

   Th'effect of what I wrote?

HORATIO   I good my Lord.

HAMLET

   An earnest coniuration from the King,

   As *England* was his faithfull tributary,

   As loue betweene them like the palme should florish,

   As peace should still her wheaten garland weare

   And stand a Comma tweene their amities,   3310

   And many such like assis of great charge,

   That on the view, and know of these contents,

   Without debatement further more or lesse,

   He should the bearers put to suddaine death,

   Not shriuing time alow'd.

HORATIO   How was this seald?

HAMLET

   Why euen in that was heauen ordinant,

   I had my fathers signet in my purse

   Which was the modill of that Danish seale,

   Folded the writ vp in the forme of th'other,

   Subscribd it, gau't th'impression, plac'd it safely,   3320

   The changling neuer knowne: now the next day

   Was our Sea fight, and what to this was sequent

   Thou knowest already.

HORATIO

   So *Guyldensterne* and *Rosencrans* goe too't.

HAMLET

   Why man, they did make loue to this imployment.

   They are not neere my conscience, their defeat

   Doth by their owne insinnuation growe,

   Tis dangerous when the baser nature comes

   Betweene the passe and fell incenced points

   Of mighty opposits.

HORATIO   Why what a King is this!   3330

HAMLET
   Dooes it not thinkst thee stand me now vppon?
   He that hath kild my King, and whor'd my mother,
   Pop't in betweene th'election and my hopes,
   Throwne out his Angle for my proper life,
   And with such cusnage, i'st not perfect conscience,
   To quit him with this arme? And is't not to be damn'd
   To let this Canker of our nature come
   In further euill.
HORATIO
   It must be shortly knowne to him from England
3340   What is the issue of the businesse there.
HAMLET
   It will be short, the *interim's* mine,
   And a mans life's no more then to say one:
   But I am very sorry good *Horatio*,
   That to *Laertes* I forgot my selfe;
   For by the image of my Cause, I see
   The Portraiture of his; Ile court his fauours:
   But sure the brauery of his griefe did put me
   Into a Towring passion.
HORATIO   Peace, who comes heere?
     Enter young Osricke, a Courtier, ⌈taking off his hat⌉
OSTRICKE
   Your Lordship is right welcome backe to Denmarke.
3350 HAMLET I humbly thanke you sir. (*To Horatio*) Doost know
   this water fly?
HORATIO No my good Lord.
HAMLET Thy state is the more gracious, for tis a vice to
   know him, he hath much land and fertill: let a beast
   be Lord of beasts, and his crib shall stand at the Kings
   messe, tis a chough, but as I say, spacious in the
   possession of durt.
OSTRICKE Sweete Lord, if your friendshippe were at
   leasure, I should impart a thing to you from his
3360   Maiestie.
HAMLET I will receaue it sir with all dilligence of spirit,
   put your bonnet to his right vse, tis for the head.
OSTRICKE I thanke your Lordship, 'tis very hot.
HAMLET No belieue me, tis very cold, the wind is
   Northerly.
OSTRICKE It is indefferent cold my Lord indeed.
HAMLET Me thinkes it is very soultry and hot, for my
   complection.
OSTRICKE Exceedingly my Lord, it is very soultery, as
3370   t'were I cannot tell how: but my Lord his Maiestie bad
   me signifie to you, that a has layed a great wager on
   your head, sir this is the matter.
HAMLET I beseech you remember.
OSTRICKE Nay good my Lord for mine ease in good faith,
   sir you are not ignorant of what excellence *Laertes* is
   at his weapon.
HAMLET What's his weapon?
OSTRICKE Rapier and Dagger.
HAMLET That's two of his weapons, but well.
3380 OSTRICKE The King sir hath wagerd with him six Barbary
   horses, against the which hee impon'd as I take it six

French Rapiers and Poynards, with their assignes, as
girdle, hanger or so. Three of the carriages in faith, are
very deare to fancy, very responsiue to the hilts, most
delicate carriages, and of very liberall conceit.
HAMLET What call you the carriages?
OSTRICKE The carriages sir are the hangers.
HAMLET The phrase would bee more Ierman to the matter
   if wee could carry cannon by our sides, I would it
   might be hangers till then, but on, six Barbry horses   3390
   against six French swords their assignes, and three
   liberall conceited carriages, that's the French bet
   against the Danish, why is this impon'd as you call it?
OSTRICKE The King sir, hath layd sir, that in a dozen
   passes betweene you and him, hee shall not exceede
   you three hits, hee hath ont twelue for nine, and it
   would come to immediate triall, if your Lordshippe
   would vouchsafe the answere.
HAMLET How if I answere no?
OSTRICKE I meane my Lord the opposition of your person   3400
   in triall.
HAMLET Sir I will walke heere in the hall, if it please his
   Maiestie, 'tis the breathing time of day with me, let the
   foiles be brought, the Gentleman willing, and the King
   hold his purpose, I will winne for him and I can, if not,
   Ile gaine nothing but my shame, and the odde hits.
OSTRICKE Shall I redeliuer you e'en so?
HAMLET To this effect sir, after what florish your nature
   will.
OSTRICKE I commend my duty to your Lordshippe.   3410
HAMLET Yours, yours;   *Exit Ostricke*
   hee doo's well to commend it himselfe, there are no
   tongues els for's turne.
HORATIO This Lapwing runnes away with the shell on his
   head.
HAMLET A did Complie with his dugge before a suckt it,
   thus has he and many more of the same Beauy that I
   know the drossy age dotes on, only got the tune of the
   time, and outward habit of incounter, a kind of yisty
   colection, which carries them through and through the   3420
   most fand and wennowed opinions, and doe but blowe
   them to their triall, the bubbles are out.
HORATIO You will loose this wager my Lord.
HAMLET I doe not thinke so, since he went into France,
   I haue bene in continuall practise, I shall winne at the
   ods; but thou would'st not thinke how all heere about
   my hart, but it is no matter.
HORATIO Nay good my Lord.
HAMLET It is but foolery, but it is such a kinde of
   gaingiuing, as would perhapes trouble a woman.   3430
HORATIO If your minde dislike any thing, obay it. I will
   forstal their repaire hether, and say you are not fit.
HAMLET Not a whit, we defie augury, there's a speciall
   prouidence in the fall of a Sparrowe, if it be now, tis
   not to come, if it be not to come, it will be now, if it
   be not now, yet it well come, the readines is all, since
   no man ha's ought of what he leaues, what ist to leaue
   betimes.

Enter King, Queene, Laertes and Lords, with
Ostricke and other Attendants with ⌐Trumpets,
Drums, Cushions,⌐ Foiles, and Gauntlets, a table
and Flagons of Wine on it

KING
Come *Hamlet*, come and take this hand from me.

HAMLET (*to Laertes*)
3440   Giue me your pardon sir, I'ue done you wrong,
But pardon't as you are a gentleman,
This presence knowes,
And you must needs haue heard, how I am punnisht
With sore distraction, what I haue done
That might your nature, honor, and exception
Roughly awake, I heare proclame was madnesse,
Wast *Hamlet* wrong'd *Laertes*? neuer *Hamlet*.
If *Hamlet* from himselfe be tane away,
And when hee's not himselfe, dooes wrong *Laertes*,
3450   Then *Hamlet* dooes it not, *Hamlet* denies it,
Who dooes it then? his madnesse. Ift be so,
Hamlet is of the faction that is wronged,
His madnesse is poore *Hamlets* enimie,
Sir, in this Audience,
Let my disclaiming from a purpos'd euill,
Free me so farre in your most generous thoughts
That I haue shot mine arrowe ore the house
And hurt my brother.

LAERTES   I am satisfied in nature,
Whose motiue in this case should stirre me most
3460   To my reuendge, but in my tearmes of honor
I stand a loofe, and will no reconcilement,
Till by some elder Maisters of knowne honor
I haue a voyce and president of peace
To keepe my name vngord: but till that time
I doe receaue your offerd loue, like loue,
And will not wrong it.

HAMLET   I do embrace it freely,
And will this brothers wager franckly play.
(*To Attendants*) Giue vs the foiles: Come on.

LAERTES (*to Attendants*)   Come, one for me.

HAMLET
Ile be your foile *Laertes*, in mine ignorance
3470   Your skill shall like a starre i'th darkest night
Stick fiery of indeed.

LAERTES You mocke me sir.

HAMLET No by this hand.

KING
Giue them the foiles young *Ostricke*, cosin *Hamlet*,
You knowe the wager.

HAMLET   Very well my Lord.
Your grace hath layed the ods a'th weeker side.

KING
I doe not feare it, I haue seene you both,
But since he is better'd, we haue therefore ods.

LAERTES (*taking a foile*)
This is to heauy: let me see another.

HAMLET (*taking a foile*)
3480   This likes me well, these foiles haue all a length.

OSTRICKE I my good Lord.

Prepare to play

KING (*to Attendants*)
Set me the stoopes of wine vpon that table,
If *Hamlet* giue the first or second hit,
Or quit in answere of the third exchange,
Let all the battlements their ordnance fire.
The King shall drinke to *Hamlets* better breath,
And in the cup an Vniõ shall he throwe,
Richer then that which foure successiue Kings
In Denmarkes Crowne haue worne: giue me the cups,
And let the kettle to the trumpet speake,   3490
The trumpet to the Cannoneere without,
The Cannons to the heauens, the heauen to earth,
Now the King drinkes to *Hamlet*,
      Trumpets the while he drinkes
                              come beginne.
And you the Iudges beare a wary eye.

HAMLET (*to Laertes*) Come on sir.

LAERTES Come my Lord.
      They play

HAMLET One.

LAERTES No.

HAMLET (*to Ostricke*) Iudgement.

OSTRICKE A hit, a very palpable hit.   3500

LAERTES Well, againe.

KING
Stay, giue me drinke, *Hamlet* this pearle is thine.
Heeres to thy health:
      ⌐Drum,⌐ *Trumpets sound, and shot goes off*
                        giue him the cup.

HAMLET
Ile play this bout first, set it by a while
Come,
      They play againe
            another hit. What say you?

LAERTES
A touch, a touch, I doe confesse.

KING
Our sonne shall winne.

QUEENE   Hee's fat and scant of breath.
Heere *Hamlet* take my napkin rub thy browes,
The Queene carowses to thy fortune *Hamlet*.   3510

HAMLET
Good Madam.

KING   *Gertrard* doe not drinke.

QUEENE
I will my Lord, I pray you pardon me.
      Shee drinkes, then offers the cup to Hamlet

KING (*aside*)
It is the poysned cup, it is too late.

HAMLET
I dare not drinke yet Madam, by and by.

QUEENE (*to Hamlet*) Come, let me wipe thy face.

LAERTES (*aside to King*) My Lord, Ile hit him now.

KING (*aside to Laertes*) I doe not think't.

LAERTES (*aside*)
And yet 'tis almost 'gainst my conscience.

HAMLET

Come for the third *Laertes*, you but dally.

3520 I pray you passe with your best violence

I am affear'd you make a wanton of me.

LAERTES

Say you so, come on.

They play

OSTRICKE   Nothing neither way.

LAERTES (*to Hamlet*)

Haue at you now.

⌈*Laertes wounds Hamlet.*⌉ *In scuffling they change*

Rapiers, ⌈*and Hamlet wounds Laertes*⌉

KING (*to Attendants*) Part them, they are incenst.

HAMLET (*to Laertes*)

Nay come againe.

⌈*The Queene falles downe*⌉

OSTRICKE   Looke to the Queene there howe.

HORATIO

They bleed on both sides, (*to Hamlet*) how is't my

Lord?

OSTRICKE How ist *Laertes*?

LAERTES

Why as a woodcock to mine owne sprindge *Ostrick*,

I am iustly kild with mine owne treachery.

HAMLET

How dooes the Queene?

KING   Shee sounds to see them bleed.

QUEENE

3530 No, no, the drinke, the drinke, ô my deare *Hamlet*,

The drinke the drinke, I am poysned.   ⌈*She dies*⌉

HAMLET

O villanie, how let the doore be lock't,   ⌈*Exit Ostricke*⌉

Treachery, seeke it out.

LAERTES

It is heere *Hamlet*, *Hamlet* thou art slaine,

No medcin in the world can doe thee good,

In thee there is not halfe an houre of life,

The treacherous instrument is in thy hand

Vnbated and enuenom'd, the foule practise

Hath turn'd it selfe on me, loe heere I lie

3540 Neuer to rise againe, thy mother's poysned,

I can no more, the King, the Kings too blame.

HAMLET

The point inuenom'd to, then venome to thy worke.

Hurts the King

ALL THE COURTIERS Treason, treason.

KING

O yet defend me friends, I am but hurt.

HAMLET

Heare thou incestious murdrous damned Dane,

Drinke of this potion, is thy Vnion heere?

Follow my mother.   *King Dyes*

LAERTES   He is iustly serued,

It is a poyson temperd by himselfe,

Exchange forgiuenesse with me noble *Hamlet*,

3550 Mine and my fathers death come not vppon thee,

Nor thine on me.   *Dyes*

HAMLET

Heauen make thee free of it, I follow thee;

I am dead *Horatio*, wretched Queene adiew.

You that looke pale, and tremble at this chance,

That are but mutes, or audience to this act,

Had I but time, as this fell sergeant Death

Is strict in his arrest, ô I could tell you,

But let it be; *Horatio* I am dead,

Thou liu'st, report me and my cause a right

To the vnsatisfied.

HORATIO   Neuer belieue it;   3560

I am more an anticke Romaine then a Dane,

Heere's yet some liquer left.

HAMLET   As th'art a man

Giue me the cup, let goe, by heauen Ile hate,

O god *Horatio*, what a wounded name

Things standing thus vnknowne, shall liue behind me?

If thou did'st euer hold me in thy hart,

Absent thee from felicity a while,

And in this harsh world drawe thy breath in paine

To tell my story:

March a farre off, and shout within

what warlike noise is this?

Enter Osrick

OSTRICKE

Young *Fortenbrasse* with conquest come from Poland,   3570

To th'embassadors of *England* giues

This warlike volly.

HAMLET   O I die *Horatio*,

The potent poyson quite ore-crowes my spirit,

I cannot liue to heare the newes from *England*,

But I doe prophecie th'ellection lights

On *Fortinbrasse*, he has my dying voyce,

So tell him, with th'occurrants more and lesse

Which haue solicited, the rest is silence.

O, o, o, o.   *Dyes*

HORATIO

Now cracks a noble hart, good night sweete Prince,   3580

And flights of Angels sing thee to thy rest.

Why dooes the drum come hether?

Enter Fortenbrasse and English ⌈*Embassadors*⌉,

with Drumme, Colours, and Attendants

FORTINBRASSE Where is this sight?

HORATIO What is it ye would see.

If ought of woe, or wonder, cease your search.

FORTINBRASSE

This quarry cries on hauock, ô proud death

What feast is toward in thine eternall cell,

That thou so many Princes at a shot

So bloudily hast strook?

EMBASSADOR   The sight is dismall

And our affaires from *England* come too late,   3590

The eares are sencelesse that should giue vs hearing,

To tell him his commandment is fulfild,

That *Rosencrans* and *Guyldensterne* are dead,

Where should we haue our thankes?

HORATIO   Not from his mouth

Had it th'ability of life to thanke you;

He neuer gaue commandement for their death;
But since so iump vpon this bloody question
You from the *Pollack* warres, and you from *England*
Are heere arriu'd, giue order that these bodies
3600 High on a stage be placed to the view,
And let me speake, to th'yet vnknowing world
How these things came about; so shall you heare
Of carnall, bloody and vnnaturall acts,
Of accidentall iudgements, casuall slaughters,
Of deaths put on by cunning, and forc'd cause
And in this vpshot, purposes mistooke,
Falne on th'inuenters heads: all this can I
Truly deliuer.
FORTINBRASSE   Let vs hast to heare it,
And call the noblest to the audience,
3610 For me, with sorrowe I embrace my fortune,
I haue some rights, of memory in this kingdome,
Which now to clame my vantage doth inuite me.

HORATIO
Of that I shall haue also cause to speake,
And from his mouth, whose voyce will drawe on more,
But let this same be presently perform'd
Euen whiles mens mindes are wilde, least more
        mischance
On plots and errores happen.
FORTINBRASSE   Let foure Captaines
Beare *Hamlet* like a souldier to the stage,
For he was likely, had he beene put on,
To haue proou'd most royally; and for his passage,   3620
The souldiers musicke and the rights of warre
Speake loudly for him:
Take vp the body, such a sight as this,
Becomes the field, but heere showes much amisse.
Goe bid the souldiers shoote.
              Exeunt Marching, with the Bodies: after the
                  which, a Peale of Ordenance are shot off

FINIS

ADDITIONAL PASSAGES

A. Just before the second entrance of the Ghost in Scene
1 (l. 106.1), Q2 has these additional lines:

BARNARDO
  I thinke it be no other, but enso;
  Well may it sort that this portentous figure
  Comes armed through our watch so like the King
  That was and is the question of these warres.
HORATIO
  A moth it is to trouble the mindes eye:
  In the most high and palmy state of Rome,
  A little ere the mightiest *Iulius* fell
  The graues stood tenantlesse, and the sheeted dead
  Did squeake and gibber in the Roman streets
10 At starres with traines of fier, and dewes of blood
  Disasters in the sunne; and the moist starre,
  Vpon whose influence *Neptunes* Empier stands,
  Was sicke almost to doomesday with eclipse.
  And euen the like precurse of feard euents
  As harbindgers preceading still the fates
  And prologue to the *Omen* comming on
  Haue heauen and earth together demonstrated
  Vnto our Climature and countrymen.

B. Just before the entrance of the Ghost in Scene 4 (l.
567.1), Q2 has these additional lines, continuing Hamlet's
speech:

  This heauy headed reueale east and west
  Makes vs tradust, and taxde of other nations,
  They clip vs drunkards, and with Swinish phrase
  Soyle our addition, and indeede it takes

From our atchieuements, though perform'd at height
The pith and marrow of our attribute,
So oft it chaunces in particuler men,
That for some vicious mole of nature in them
As in their birth wherein they are not guilty,
(Since nature cannot choose his origin)   10
By the ore-grow'th of some complextion
Oft breaking downe the pales and forts of reason,
Or by some habit, that too much ore-leauens
The forme of plausiue manners, that these men
Carrying I say the stamp of one defect
Being Natures liuery, or Fortunes starre,
His vertues els be they as pure as grace,
As infinite as man may vndergoe,
Shall in the generall censure take corruption
From that particuler fault: the dram of euile   20
Doth all the noble substance ouer doube
To his owne scandle.

C. After 604, Q2 has these additional lines, continuing
Horatio's speech:

  The very place puts toyes of desperation
  Without more motiue, into euery braine
  That lookes so many fadoms to the sea
  And heares it rore beneath.

D. After 1891, Q2 has this additional couplet, concluding
the Player Queene's speech:

  Where loue is great, the litlest doubts are feare,
  Where little feares grow great, great loue growes there.

E. After 1936, Q2 has this additional couplet in the middle of the Player Queene's speech:

> To desperation turne my trust and hope,
> An Anchors cheere in prison be my scope,

F. After 'this' in 2284, Q2 has this more expansive version of Hamlet's lines (of which F retains only 'what deuill . . . blind'):

>   sence sure youe haue
> Els could you not haue motion, but sure that sence
> Is appoplext, for madnesse would not erre
> Nor sence to extacie was nere so thral'd
> But it reseru'd some quantity of choise
> To serue in such a difference, what deuill wast
> That thus hath cosund you at hodman blind;
> Eyes without feeling, feeling without sight,
> Eares without hands, or eyes, smelling sance all,
> Or but a sickly part of one true sence
> Could not so mope:

G. After 2365, Q2 has this more expansive version of Hamlet's lines (of which F retains only 'refraine . . . abstinence'):

> That monster custome, who all sence doth eate
> Of habits deuillish, is angell yet in this
> That to the vse of actions faire and good,
> He likewise giues a frock or Liuery
> That aptly is put on refraine to night,
> And that shall lend a kind of easines
> To the next abstinence, the next more easie:
> For vse almost can change the stamp of nature,
> And either in the deuill, or throwe him out
> With wonderous potency:

H. At 2399, Q2 has these additional lines before 'This man . . .':

HAMLET
> Ther's letters seald, and my two Schoolefellowes,
> Whom I will trust as I will Adders fang'd,
> They beare the mandat, they must sweep my way
> And marshall me to knauery: let it worke,
> For tis the sport to haue the enginer
> Hoist with his owne petar, an't shall goe hard
> But I will delue one yard belowe their mines,
> And blowe them at the Moone: ô tis most sweete
> When in one line two crafts directly meete,

I. After 'doone' in 2444, Q2 has these additional lines, continuing the King's speech (the first three words are an editorial conjecture):

>   so enuious slaunder,
> Whose whisper ore the worlds dyameter,
> As leuell as the Cannon to his blanck,
> Transports his poysned shot, may misse our Name,
> And hit the woundlesse ayre,

J. Q2 has this more expansive version of the ending of Scene 14:

CAPTAINE   I will doo't my Lord.
FORTINBRASSE
> Goe softly on.   *Exit with his Army*
>   *Enter Hamlet, Rosencrans, Guyldensterne, &c.*
HAMLET (*to the Captaine*) Good sir whose powers are these?
CAPTAINE
> They are of *Norway* sir.
HAMLET   How purposd sir I pray you?
CAPTAINE
> Against some part of *Poland.*
HAMLET   Who commaunds them sir?
CAPTAINE
> The Nephew to old *Norway, Fortenbrasse.*
HAMLET
> Goes it against the maine of *Poland* sir,
> Or for some frontire?
CAPTAINE
> Truly to speake, and with no addition,
> We goe to gaine a little patch of ground
> That hath in it no profit but the name
> To pay fiue duckets, fiue I would not farme it;
> Nor will it yeeld to *Norway* or the *Pole*
> A rancker rate, should it be sold in fee.
HAMLET
> Why then the *Pollacke* neuer will defend it.
CAPTAINE
> Yes, it is already garisond.
HAMLET
> Two thousand soules, & twenty thousand duckets
> Will now debate the question of this straw,
> This is th'Imposthume of much wealth and peace,
> That inward breakes, and showes no cause without
> Why the man dies. I humbly thanke you sir.
CAPTAINE
> God buy you sir.   *Exit*
ROSENCRANS   Wil't please you goe my Lord?
HAMLET
> Ile be with you straight, goe a little before.
>   *Exeunt all but Hamlet*
> How all occasions doe informe against me,
> And spur my dull reuenge. What is a man
> If his chiefe good and market of his time
> Be but to sleepe and feede, a beast, no more:
> Sure he that made vs with such large discourse
> Looking before and after, gaue vs not
> That capabilitie and god-like reason
> To fust in vs vnvsd, now whether it be

Bestiall obliuion, or some crauen scruple
Of thinking too precisely on th'euent,
A thought which quarterd hath but one part wisedom,
And euer three parts coward, I doe not know
Why yet I liue to say this thing's to doe,
Sith I haue cause, and will, and strength, and meanes
To doo't; examples grosse as earth exhort me,
Witnes this Army of such masse and charge,
Led by a delicate and tender Prince,
40 Whose spirit with diuine ambition puft,
Makes mouthes at the invisible euent,
Exposing what is mortall, and vnsure,
To all that fortune, death, and danger dare,
Euen for an Egge-shell. Rightly to be great,
Is not to stirre without great argument,
But greatly to find quarrell in a straw
When honour's at the stake, how stand I then
That haue a father kild, a mother staind,
Excytements of my reason, and my blood,
50 And let all sleepe, while to my shame I see
The iminent death of twenty thousand men,
That for a fantasie and tricke of fame
Goe to their graues like beds, fight for a plot
Whereon the numbers cannot try the cause,
Which is not tombe enough and continent
To hide the slaine, ô from this time forth,
My thoughts be bloody, or be nothing worth.　　*Exit*

K. After 'accedent' at 2871, Q2 has these additional lines:

LAERTES　　　My Lord I will be rul'd,
　　The rather if you could deuise it so
　　That I might be the organ.
KING　　　　　　　　It falls right,
　　You haue beene talkt of since your trauaile much,
　　And that in *Hamlets* hearing, for a qualitie
　　Wherein they say you shine, your summe of parts
　　Did not together plucke such enuie from him
　　As did that one, and that in my regard
　　Of the vnworthiest siedge.
LAERTES　　　　　　What part is that my Lord?
KING
10　A very riband in the cap of youth,
　　Yet needfull to, for youth no lesse becomes
　　The light and carelesse liuery that it weares
　　Then setled age, his sables, and his weedes
　　Importing health and grauenes;

L. After 'match you' at 2889, Q2 has these additional lines, continuing the King's speech:

　　　　　　　thescrimures of their nation
He swore had neither motion, guard, nor eye,
If you opposd them;

M. After 2900, Q2 has these additional lines, continuing the King's speech:

There liues within the very flame of loue
A kind of weeke or snufe that will abate it,
And nothing is at a like goodnes still,
For goodnes growing to a plurisie,
Dies in his owne too much, that we would doe
We should doe when we would: for this would changes,
And hath abatements and delayes as many,
As there are tongues, are hands, are accidents,
And then this should is like a spend thrifts sigh,
That hurts by easing; but to the quick of th'vlcer,　　10

N. After 'sir' at 3375, Q2 has these lines (in place of F's 'you are not ignorant of what excellence *Laertes* is at his weapon'):

here is newly com to Court *Laertes*, belieue me an absolute gentleman, ful of most excellent differences, of very soft society, and great showing: indeede to speake feelingly of him, hee is the card or kalender of gentry: for you shall find in him the continent of what part a Gentleman would see.

HAMLET Sir, his definement suffers no perdition in you, though I know to deuide him inuentorially, would dosie th'arithmaticke of memory, and yet but yaw neither, in respect of his quick saile, but in the veritie of　10 extolment, I take him to be a soule of great article, & his infusion of such dearth and rarenesse, as to make true dixion of him, his semblable is his mirrour, & who els would trace him, his vmbrage, nothing more.

OSTRICKE Your Lordship speakes most infallibly of him.

HAMLET The concernancy sir, why doe we wrap the gentleman in our more rawer breath?

OSTRICKE Sir.

HORATIO Ist not possible to vnderstand in another tongue, you will too't sir rarely.　20

HAMLET What imports the nomination of this gentleman.

OSTRICKE Of *Laertes*.

HORATIO (*aside to Hamlet*) His purse is empty already, all's golden words are spent.

HAMLET (*to Ostricke*) Of him sir.

OSTRICKE I know you are not ignorant.

HAMLET I would you did sir, yet in faith if you did, it would not much approoue me, well sir.

OSTRICKE You are not ignorant of what excellence *Laertes* is.　30

HAMLET I dare not confesse that, least I should compare with him in excellence, but to know a man wel, were to knowe himselfe.

OSTRICKE I meane sir for his weapon, but in the imputation laide on him, by them in his meed, hee's vnfellowed.

O. After 3386, Q2 has the following additional speech:

HORATIO (*aside to Hamlet*) I knew you must be edified by the margent ere you had done.

P. After 3422, Q2 has the following (in place of F's 'HORATIO You will lose this wager, my Lord'):

Enter a Lord

LORD (*to Hamlet*) My Lord, his Maiestie commended him to you by young *Ostricke*, who brings backe to him that you attend him in the hall, he sends to know if your pleasure hold to play with *Laertes*, or that you will take longer time?

HAMLET I am constant to my purposes, they followe the Kings pleasure, if his fitnes speakes, mine is ready: now or whensoeuer, prouided I be so able as now.
LORD The King, and Queene, and all are comming downe.
HAMLET In happy time. 10
LORD The Queene desires you to vse some gentle entertainment to *Laertes*, before you fall to play.
HAMLET Shee well instructs me. *Exit Lord*
HORATIO You will loose my Lord.

TWELFE NIGHT

TWELFTH NIGHT, the end of the Christmas season, was traditionally a time of revelry and topsy-turvydom; Shakespeare's title for a play in which a servant aspires to his mistress's hand has no more specific reference. It was thought appropriate to the festive occasion of Candlemas (2 February) 1602 when, in the first known allusion to it, John Manningham, a law student of the Middle Temple in London, noted 'At our feast wee had a play called "Twelue Night, or What You Will"'. References to 'the Sophy'— the Shah of Persia (1158, 1748)—probably post-date Sir Robert Shirley's return from Persia, in a ship named *The Sophy*, in 1599; and 'the new Mappe, with the augmentation of the Indies' (1423-4) appears to be one published in 1599 and reissued in 1600. Shakespeare may have picked up the name Orsino for his young duke from a Tuscan nobleman whom Queen Elizabeth entertained at Whitehall with a play performed by Shakespeare's company on Twelfth Night 1601. Probably he wrote *Twelfe Night* during that year.

Twelfe Night's romantic setting is Illyria, the Greek and Roman name for Adriatic territory roughly corresponding to modern Yugoslavia. Manningham had noted that the play was 'much like the Commedy of Errores, or Menechmi in Plautus', thinking no doubt of the confusions created by identical twins. Shakespeare may also have known an anonymous Italian comedy, *Gl'Ingannati* (*The Deceived Ones*), acted in 1531 and first printed in 1537, which influenced a number of other plays and prose tales including Barnaby Riche's story of Apolonius and Silla printed as part of *Riche his Farewell to Militarie profession* (1581). Riche gave Shakespeare his main plot of a shipwrecked girl (Viola) who, disguised as a boy (Cesario), serves a young Duke (Orsino) and undertakes love-errands on his behalf to a noble lady (Oliuia) who falls in love with her but mistakenly marries her twin brother (Sebastian). Shakespeare idealizes Riche's characters and purges the story of some its explicit sexuality: Riche's Oliuia, for example, is pregnant before marriage, and his Viola reveals her identity, in a manner impractical for a boy actor, by stripping to the waist. Shakespeare complicates the plot by giving Oliuia a reprobate uncle, Sir Toby Belch, and two additional suitors, the asinine Sir Andrew Ague-cheeke and her steward, Maluolio, tricked by members of her household into believing that she loves him. More important to the play than to the plot is the entirely Shakespearian Clowne (Feste), a wry and oblique commentator whose wit in folly is opposed to Maluolio's folly in wit.

Twelfe Night is the consummation of Shakespeare's romantic comedy, a play of wide emotional range, extending from the robust, brilliantly orchestrated humour of the scene of midnight revelry (Sc. 8) to the rapt wonder of the antiphon of recognition (2323-55) between the reunited twins. In performance the balance shifts, favouring sometimes the exposure and celebration of folly, at other times the poignancy of unattained love and of unheeded wisdom; but few other plays have so consistently provided theatrical pleasure of so high an order.

The Folio text was set from a scribal copy.

THE NAMES OF THE ACTORS

ORSINO, Duke of Illyria

VALENTINE

CURIO

} attending on Orsino

FIRST OFFICER

SECOND OFFICER

VIOLA, a lady, later disguised as Cesario

A CAPTAINE

SEBASTIAN, her twin Brother

ANTHONIO, another Sea-captaine

OLIUIA, a Countesse

MARIA, her Gentlewoman

SIR TOBY Belch, her Kinsman

SIR ANDREW Ague-cheeke, Companion of Sir Toby

MALUOLIO, Oliuias Steward

FABIAN, a member of Oliuias household

CLOWNE (Feste), Oliuias iester

A PRIEST

A SERUANT of Oliuia

Musitians, Saylors, Lords, Attendants

Twelfe Night, Or what you will

Musicke. Enter Orsino Duke of Illyria, Curio, and
other Lords

ORSINO

If Musicke be the food of Loue, play on,
Giue me excesse of it: that surfetting,
The appetite may sicken, and so dye.
That straine agen, it had a dying fall:
O, it came ore my eare, like the sweet sound
That breathes vpon a banke of Violets;
Stealing, and giuing Odour. Enough, no more,
'Tis not so sweet now, as it was before.
⌜Musicke ceases⌝
O spirit of Loue, how quicke and fresh art thou,
10 That notwithstanding thy capacitie
Receiueth as the Sea, nought enters there,
Of what validity, and pitch so ere,
But falles into abatement, and low price
Euen in a minute; so full of shapes is fancie,
That it alone, is high fantasticall.

CURIO

Will you go hunt my Lord?

ORSINO   What Curio?

CURIO   The Hart.

ORSINO

Why so I do, the Noblest that I haue:
O when mine eyes did see Oliuia first,
Me thought she purg'd the ayre of pestilence;
20 That instant was I turn'd into a Hart,
And my desires like fell and cruell hounds,
Ere since pursue me.
Enter Valentine
                    How now what newes from her?

VALENTINE

So please my Lord, I might not be admitted,
But from her handmaid do returne this answer:
The Element it selfe, till seuen yeares heate,
Shall not behold her face at ample view:
But like a Cloystresse she will vailed walke,
And water once a day her Chamber round
With eye-offending brine: all this to season
30 A brothers dead loue, which she would keepe fresh
And lasting, in her sad remembrance.

ORSINO

O she that hath a heart of that fine frame
To pay this debt of loue but to a brother,
How will she loue, when the rich golden shaft
Hath kill'd the flocke of all affections else
That liue in her. When Liuer, Braine, and Heart,
These soueraigne thrones, are all supply'd, and fill'd
Her sweete perfections with one selfe king:
Away before me, to sweet beds of Flowres,
40 Loue-thoughts lye rich, when canopy'd with bowres.
                                        Exeunt

Enter Viola, a Captaine, and Saylors

VIOLA

What Country (Friends) is this?

CAPTAINE   This is Illyria Ladie.

VIOLA

And what should I do in Illyria?
My brother he is in Elizium,
Perchance he is not drown'd: What thinke you
saylors?

CAPTAINE

It is perchance that you your selfe were saued.

VIOLA

O my poore brother, and so perchance may he be.

CAPTAINE

True Madam, and to comfort you with chance,
Assure your selfe, after our ship did split,
When you, and those poore number saued with you,
Hung on our driuing boate: I saw your brother   50
Most prouident in perill, binde himselfe,
(Courage and hope both teaching him the practise)
To a strong Maste, that liu'd vpon the sea:
Where like Arion on the Dolphines backe,
I saw him hold acquaintance with the waues,
So long as I could see.

VIOLA (giuing money)   For saying so, there's Gold:
Mine owne escape vnfoldeth to my hope,
Whereto thy speech serues for authoritie
The like of him. Know'st thou this Countrey?

CAPTAINE

I Madam well, for I was bred and borne   60
Not three houres trauaile from this very place.

VIOLA

Who gouernes heere?

CAPTAINE   A noble Duke in nature,
As in name.

VIOLA   What is his name?

CAPTAINE   Orsino.

VIOLA

Orsino: I haue heard my father name him.
He was a Batchellor then.

CAPTAINE

And so is now, or was so very late:
For but a month ago I went from hence,
And then 'twas fresh in murmure (as you know
What great ones do, the lesse will prattle of,)
That he did seeke the loue of faire Oliuia.   70

VIOLA What's shee?

CAPTAINE

A vertuous maid, the daughter of a Count
That dide some tweluemonth since, then leauing her
In the protection of his sonne, her brother,
Who shortly also dide: for whose deere loue

781

(They say) she hath abiur'd the sight
And company of men.

VIOLA   O that I seru'd that Lady,
And might not be deliuerd to the world
Till I had made mine owne occasion mellow
What my estate is.

80 CAPTAINE   That were hard to compasse,
Because she will admit no kinde of suite,
No, not the Dukes.

VIOLA
There is a faire behauiour in thee Captaine,
And though that nature, with a beauteous wall
Doth oft close in pollution: yet of thee
I will beleeue thou hast a minde that suites
With this thy faire and outward charracter.
I pray thee (and Ile pay thee bounteously)
Conceale me what I am, and be my ayde,
90 For such disguise as haply shall become
The forme of my intent. Ile serue this Duke,
Thou shalt present me as an Eunuch to him,
It may be worth thy paines: for I can sing,
And speake to him in many sorts of Musicke,
That will allow me very worth his seruice.
What else may hap, to time I will commit,
Onely shape thou thy silence to my wit.

CAPTAINE
Be you his Eunuch, and your Mute Ile bee,
When my tongue blabs, then let mine eyes not see.

VIOLA
100 I thanke thee: Lead me on.   Exeunt

Sc. 3   Enter Sir Toby, and Maria
(1.3) SIR TOBY What a plague meanes my Neece to take the
death of her brother thus? I am sure care's an enemie
to life.

MARIA By my troth sir Toby, you must come in earlyer
a nights: your Cosin, my Lady, takes great exceptions
to your ill houres.

SIR TOBY Why let her except, before excepted.

MARIA I, but you must confine your selfe within the
modest limits of order.

110 SIR TOBY Confine? Ile confine my selfe no finer then I am:
these cloathes are good enough to drinke in, and so
bee these boots too: and they be not, let them hang
themselues in their owne straps.

MARIA That quaffing and drinking will vndoe you: I
heard my Lady talke of it yesterday: and of a foolish
knight that you brought in one night here, to be hir
woer.

SIR TOBY Who, Sir Andrew Ague-cheeke?

MARIA I he.

120 SIR TOBY He's as tall a man as any's in Illyria.

MARIA What's that to th'purpose?

SIR TOBY Why he ha's three thousand ducates a yeare.

MARIA I, but hee'l haue but a yeare in all these ducates:
He's a very foole, and a prodigall.

SIR TOBY Fie, that you'l say so: he playes o'th Viol-de-
gamboys, and speaks three or four languages word for
word without booke, & hath all the good gifts of nature.

MARIA He hath indeed, almost naturall: for besides that
he's a foole, he's a great quarreller: and but that hee
hath the gift of a Coward, to allay the gust he hath in 130
quarrelling, 'tis thought among the prudent, he would
quickely haue the gift of a graue.

SIR TOBY By this hand they are scoundrels and substra-
ctors that say so of him. Who are they?

MARIA They that adde moreouer, hee's drunke nightly in
your company.

SIR TOBY With drinking healths to my Neece: Ile drinke
to her as long as there is a passage in my throat, &
drinke in Illyria: he's a Coward and a Coystrill that
will not drinke to my Neece, till his braines turne o'th 140
toe, like a parish top. What wench? Castiliano vulgo:
for here coms Sir Andrew Agueface.

Enter Sir Andrew

SIR ANDREW Sir Toby Belch. How now sir Toby Belch?

SIR TOBY Sweet sir Andrew.

SIR ANDREW (to Maria) Blesse you faire Shrew.

MARIA And you too sir.

SIR TOBY Accost Sir Andrew, accost.

SIR ANDREW What's that?

SIR TOBY My Neeces Chamber-maid.

SIR ANDREW Good Mistris accost, I desire better 150
acquaintance.

MARIA My name is Mary sir.

SIR ANDREW Good mistris Mary, accost.

SIR TOBY You mistake knight: Accost, is front her, boord
her, woe her, assayle her.

SIR ANDREW By my troth I would not vndertake her in
this company. Is that the meaning of Accost?

MARIA Far you well Gentlemen.

SIR TOBY And thou let part so Sir Andrew, would thou
mightst neuer draw sword agen. 160

SIR ANDREW And you part so mistris, I would I might
neuer draw sword agen: Faire Lady, doe you thinke
you haue fooles in hand?

MARIA Sir, I haue not you by'th hand.

SIR ANDREW Marry but you shall haue, and heeres my
hand.

MARIA (taking his hand) Now sir, thought is free: I pray
you bring your hand to'th Buttry barre, and let it
drinke.

SIR ANDREW Wherefore (sweet-heart?) What's your 170
Metaphor?

MARIA It's dry sir.

SIR ANDREW Why I thinke so: I am not such an asse, but
I can keepe my hand dry. But what's your iest?

MARIA A dry iest Sir.

SIR ANDREW Are you full of them?

MARIA I Sir, I haue them at my fingers ends: marry now
I let go your hand, I am barren.   Exit Maria

SIR TOBY O knight, thou lack'st a cup of Canarie: when
did I see thee so put downe? 180

SIR ANDREW Neuer in your life I thinke, vnlesse you see
Canarie put me downe: mee thinkes sometimes I haue
no more wit then a Christian, or an ordinary man
ha's: but I am a great eater of beefe, and I beleeue that
does harme to my wit.

SIR TOBY No question.

SIR ANDREW And I thought that, I'de forsweare it. Ile ride home to morrow sir *Toby*.

SIR TOBY *Pur-quoy* my deere knight?

190 SIR ANDREW What is *purquoy*? Do, or not do? I would I had bestowed that time in the tongues, that I haue in fencing, dancing, and beare-bayting: O had I but followed the Arts.

SIR TOBY Then hadst thou had an excellent head of haire.

SIR ANDREW Why, would that haue mended my haire?

SIR TOBY Past question, for thou seest it will not curle by nature.

SIR ANDREW But it becoms me wel enough, dost not?

SIR TOBY Excellent, it hangs like flax on a distaffe: & I
200 hope to see a huswife take thee between her legs, & spin it off.

SIR ANDREW Faith Ile home to morrow sir *Toby*, your niece wil not be seene, or if she be it's four to one, she'l none of me: the Count himselfe here hard by, wooes her.

SIR TOBY Shee'l none o'th Count, she'l not match aboue hir degree, neither in estate, yeares, nor wit: I haue heard her swear't. Tut there's life in't man.

SIR ANDREW Ile stay a moneth longer. I am a fellow o'th
210 strangest minde i'th world: I delight in Maskes and Reuels sometimes altogether.

SIR TOBY Art thou good at these kicke-chawses Knight?

SIR ANDREW As any man in Illyria, whatsoeuer he be, vnder the degree of my betters, & yet I will not compare with an old man.

SIR TOBY What is thy excellence in a galliard, knight?

SIR ANDREW Faith, I can cut a caper.

SIR TOBY And I can cut the Mutton too't.

SIR ANDREW And I thinke I haue the backe-tricke, simply
220 as strong as any man in Illyria.

SIR TOBY Wherefore are these things hid? Wherefore haue these gifts a Curtaine before 'em? Are they like to take dust, like mistris *Mals* picture? Why dost thou not goe to Church in a Galliard, and come home in a Carranto? My verie walke should be a Iigge: I would not so much as make water but in a Sinke-a-pace: What dooest thou meane? Is it a world to hide vertues in? I did thinke by the excellent constitution of thy legge, it was form'd vnder the starre of a Galliard.

230 SIR ANDREW I, 'tis strong, and it does indifferent well in a diuers colour'd stocke. Shall we sit about some Reuels?

SIR TOBY What shall we do else: were we not borne vnder Taurus?

SIR ANDREW Taurus? That's sides and heart.

SIR TOBY No sir, it is leggs and thighes: let me see thee caper.

⌈*Sir Andrew capers*⌉
Ha, higher: ha, ha, excellent.   *Exeunt*

Sc. 4   *Enter Valentine, and Viola (as Cesario) in mans*
(1.4)   *attire*

VALENTINE If the Duke continue these fauours towards
240 you *Cesario*, you are like to be much aduanc'd, he hath

known you but three dayes, and already you are no stranger.

VIOLA You either feare his humour, or my negligence, that you call in question the continuance of his loue. Is he inconstant sir, in his fauours.

VALENTINE No beleeue me.

Enter Duke, Curio, and Attendants

VIOLA I thanke you: heere comes the Count.

ORSINO Who saw *Cesario* hoa?

VIOLA On your attendance my Lord heere.

ORSINO (*to Curio and Attendants*)
Stand you a-while aloofe. (*To Viola*) Cesario,   250
Thou knowst no lesse, but all: I haue vnclasp'd
To thee the booke euen of my secret soule.
Therefore good youth, addresse thy gate vnto her,
Be not deni'de accesse, stand at her doores,
And tell them, there thy fixed foot shall grow
Till thou haue audience.

VIOLA   Sure my Noble Lord,
If she be so abandon'd to her sorrow
As it is spoke, she neuer will admit me.

ORSINO
Be clamorous, and leape all ciuill bounds,
Rather then make vnprofited returne.   260

VIOLA
Say I do speake with her (my Lord) what then?

ORSINO
O then, vnfold the passion of my loue,
Surprize her with discourse of my deere faith;
It shall become thee well to act my woes:
She will attend it better in thy youth,
Then in a Nuntio's of more graue aspect.

VIOLA
I thinke not so, my Lord.

ORSINO   Deere Lad, beleeue it;
For they shall yet belye thy happy yeeres,
That say thou art a man: *Dianas* lip
Is not more smooth, and rubious: thy small pipe   270
Is as the maidens organ, shrill, and sound,
And all is semblatiue a womans part.
I know thy constellation is right apt
For this affayre: (*to Curio and Attendants*) some foure
    or fiue attend him,
All if you will: for I my selfe am best
When least in companie: (*to Viola*) prosper well in
    this,
And thou shalt liue as freely as thy Lord,
To call his fortunes thine.

VIOLA   Ile do my best
To woe your Lady: ⌈*aside*⌉ yet a barrefull strife,
Who ere I woe, my selfe would be his wife. *Exeunt* 280

Enter Maria, and Clowne   Sc. 5
                                                   (1.5)
MARIA Nay, either tell me where thou hast bin, or I will
not open my lippes so wide as a brissle may enter, in
way of thy excuse: my Lady will hang thee for thy absence.

CLOWNE Let her hang me: hee that is well hang'de in this
world, needs to feare no colours.

MARIA Make that good.

CLOWNE He shall see none to feare.

MARIA A good lenton answer: I can tell thee where y^t saying was borne, of I feare no colours.

CLOWNE Where good mistris *Mary*?

MARIA In the warrs, & that may you be bolde to say in your foolerie.

CLOWNE Well, God giue them wisedome that haue it: & those that are fooles, let them vse their talents.

MARIA Yet you will be hang'd for being so long absent, or to be turn'd away: is not that as good as a hanging to you?

CLOWNE Many a good hanging, preuents a bad marriage: and for turning away, let summer beare it out.

MARIA You are resolute then?

CLOWNE Not so neyther, but I am resolu'd on two points.

MARIA That if one breake, the other will hold: or if both breake, your gaskins fall.

CLOWNE Apt in good faith, very apt: well go thy way, if sir *Toby* would leaue drinking, thou wert as witty a piece of *Eues* flesh, as any in Illyria.

MARIA Peace you rogue, no more o'that: here comes my Lady: make your excuse wisely, you were best.   *Exit*

Enter Lady Oliuia, with Maluolio and Attendants

CLOWNE ⌈*aside*⌉ Wit, and't be thy will, put me into good fooling: those wits that thinke they haue thee, doe very oft proue fooles: and I that am sure I lacke thee, may passe for a wise man. For what saies *Quinapalus*, Better a witty foole, then a foolish wit. (*To Oliuia*) God blesse thee Lady.

OLIUIA (*to Attendants*) Take the foole away.

CLOWNE Do you not heare fellowes, take away the Ladie.

OLIUIA Go too, y'are a dry foole: Ile no more of you: besides you grow dis-honest.

CLOWNE Two faults Madona, that drinke & good counsell wil amend: for giue the dry foole drink, then is the foole not dry: bid the dishonest man mend himself, if he mend, he is no longer dishonest; if hee cannot, let the Botcher mend him: any thing that's mended, is but patch'd: vertu that transgresses, is but patcht with sinne, and sin that amends, is but patcht with vertue. If that this simple Sillogisme will serue, so: if it will not, what remedy? As there is no true Cuckold but calamity, so beauties a flower; The Lady bad take away the foole, therefore I say againe, take her away.

OLIUIA Sir, I bad them take away you.

CLOWNE Misprision in the highest degree. Lady, *Cucullus non facit monachum*: that's as much to say, as I weare not motley in my braine: good *Madona*, giue mee leaue to proue you a foole.

OLIUIA Can you do it?

CLOWNE Dexteriously, good Madona.

OLIUIA Make your proofe.

CLOWNE I must catechize you for it Madona, Good my Mouse of vertue answer mee.

OLIUIA Well sir, for want of other idlenesse, Ile bide your proofe.

CLOWNE Good Madona, why mournst thou?

OLIUIA Good foole, for my brothers death.

CLOWNE I thinke his soule is in hell, Madona.

OLIUIA I know his soule is in heauen, foole.

CLOWNE The more foole (Madona) to mourne for your Brothers soule, being in heauen. Take away the Foole, Gentlemen.

OLIUIA What thinke you of this foole *Maluolio*, doth he not mend?

MALUOLIO Yes, and shall do, till the pangs of death shake him: Infirmity that decaies the wise, doth euer make the better foole.

CLOWNE God send you sir, a speedie Infirmity, for the better increasing your folly: Sir *Toby* will be sworn that I am no Fox, but he wil not passe his word for two pence that you are no Foole.

OLIUIA How say you to that *Maluolio*?

MALUOLIO I maruell your Ladyship takes delight in such a barren rascall: I saw him put down the other day, with an ordinary foole, that has no more braine then a stone. Looke you now, he's out of his gard already: vnles you laugh and minister occasion to him, he is gag'd. I protest I take these Wisemen, that crow so at these set kinde of fooles, no better then the fooles Zanies.

OLIUIA O you are sicke of selfe-loue *Maluolio*, and taste with a distemper'd appetite. To be generous, guiltlesse, and of free disposition, is to take those things for Birdbolts, that you deeme Cannon bullets: There is no slander in an allow'd foole, though he do nothing but rayle; nor no rayling, in a knowne discreet man, though hee do nothing but reproue.

CLOWNE Now Mercury indue thee with leasing, for thou speak'st well of fooles.

Enter Maria

MARIA Madam, there is at the gate, a young Gentleman, much desires to speake with you.

OLIUIA From the Count *Orsino*, is it?

MARIA I know not (Madam) 'tis a faire young man, and well attended.

OLIUIA Who of my people hold him in delay?

MARIA Sir *Toby* Madam, your kinsman.

OLIUIA Fetch him off I pray you, he speakes nothing but madman: Fie on him. Go you *Maluolio*; If it be a suit from the Count, I am sicke, or not at home. What you will, to dismisse it.   *Exit Maluolio*

Now you see sir, how your fooling growes old, & people dislike it.

CLOWNE Thou hast spoke for vs (Madona) as if thy eldest sonne should be a foole: whose scull, Ioue cramme with braines, for, heere he comes:

Enter Sir Toby

One of thy kin has a most weake *Pia-mater*.

OLIUIA By mine honor halfe drunke. What is he at the gate Cosin?

SIR TOBY A Gentleman.

OLIUIA A Gentleman? What Gentleman?

SIR TOBY 'Tis a Gentleman heere. (*He belches*) A plague o'these pickle herring: (*To the Clowne*) How now Sot.

400 CLOWNE Good Sir *Toby*.

OLIUIA Cosin, Cosin, how haue you come so earely by
this Lethargie?

SIR TOBY Letcherie, I defie Letchery: there's one at the
gate.

OLIUIA I marry, what is he?

SIR TOBY Let him be the diuell and he will, I care not:
giue me faith say I. Well, it's all one. *Exit*

OLIUIA What's a drunken man like, foole?

CLOWNE Like a drown'd man, a foole, and a madde man:
410   One draught aboue heate, makes him a foole, the
second maddes him, and a third drownes him.

OLIUIA Go thou and seeke the Crowner, and let him sitte
o'my Coz: for he's in the third degree of drinke: hee's
drown'd: go looke after him.

CLOWNE He is but mad yet Madona, and the foole shall
looke to the madman. *Exit*

Enter Maluolio

MALUOLIO Madam, yond young fellow sweares hee will
speake with you. I told him you were sicke, he takes
420   on him to vnderstand so much, and therefore comes
to speak with you. I told him you were asleepe, he
seems to haue a fore knowledge of that too, and
therefore comes to speake with you. What is to be said
to him Ladie, hee's fortified against any deniall.

OLIUIA Tell him, he shall not speake with me.

MALUOLIO Ha's beene told so: and hee sayes hee'l stand
at your doore like a Sheriffes post, and be the supporter
to a bench, but hee'l speake with you.

OLIUIA What kinde o'man is he?

MALUOLIO Why of mankinde.

430 OLIUIA What manner of man?

MALUOLIO Of verie ill manner: hee'l speake with you, will
you, or no.

OLIUIA Of what personage, and yeeres is he?

MALUOLIO Not yet old enough for a man, nor yong enough
for a boy: as a squash is before tis a pescod, or a
Codling when tis almost an Apple: Tis with him in
standing water, betweene boy and man. He is verie
well-fauour'd, and he speakes verie shrewishly: One
would thinke his mothers milke were scarse out of him.

OLIUIA
440   Let him approach: Call in my Gentlewoman.

MALUOLIO Gentlewoman, my Lady calles. *Exit*

Enter Maria

OLIUIA
Giue me my vaile: come throw it ore my face,
Wee'l once more heare *Orsinos* Embassie.

Enter Viola as Cesario

VIOLA The honorable Ladie of the house, which is she?

OLIUIA Speake to me, I shall answer for her: your will.

VIOLA Most radiant, exquisite, and vnmatchable beautie.
I pray you tell me if this bee the Lady of the house, for
I neuer saw her. I would bee loath to cast away my
speech: for besides that it is excellently well pend, I
450   haue taken great paines to con it. Good Beauties, let
mee sustaine no scorne; I am very comptible, euen to
the least sinister vsage.

OLIUIA Whence came you sir?

VIOLA I can say little more then I haue studied, & that
question's out of my part. Good gentle one, giue mee
modest assurance, if you be the Ladie of the house,
that I may proceede in my speech.

OLIUIA Are you a Comedian?

VIOLA No my profound heart: and yet (by the verie
phangs of malice, I sweare) I am not that I play. Are 460
you the Ladie of the house?

OLIUIA If I do not vsurpe my selfe, I am.

VIOLA Most certaine, if you are she, you do vsurp your
selfe: for what is yours to bestowe, is, not yours to
reserue. But this is from my Commission: I will on with
my speech in your praise, and then shew you the heart
of my message.

OLIUIA Come to what is important in't: I forgiue you the
praise.

VIOLA Alas, I tooke great paines to studie it, and 'tis 470
Poeticall.

OLIUIA It is the more like to be feigned, I pray you keep
it in. I heard you were sawcy at my gates, & allowd
your approach rather to wonder at you, then to heare
you. If you be not mad, be gone: if you haue reason,
be breefe: 'tis not that time of Moone with me, to make
one in so skipping a dialogue.

MARIA Will you hoyst sayle sir, here lies your way.

VIOLA No good swabber, I am to hull here a little longer.
(*To Oliuia*) Some mollification for your Giant, sweete 480
Ladie; tell me your minde, I am a messenger.

OLIUIA Sure you haue some hiddeous matter to deliuer,
when the curtesie of it is so fearefull. Speake your office.

VIOLA It alone concernes your eare: I bring no ouerture
of warre, no taxation of homage; I hold the Olyffe in
my hand: my words are as full of peace, as matter.

OLIUIA Yet you began rudely. What are you? What would
you?

VIOLA The rudenesse that hath appear'd in mee, haue I
learn'd from my entertainment. What I am, and what 490
I would, are as secret as maiden-head: to your eares,
Diuinity; to any others, prophanation.

OLIUIA (*to Maria ⌈and Attendants⌉*) Giue vs the place alone,
We will heare this diuinitie.

Exeunt Maria ⌈and Attendants⌉

Now sir, what is your text?

VIOLA Most sweet Ladie.

OLIUIA A comfortable doctrine, and much may bee saide
of it. Where lies your Text?

VIOLA In *Orsinoes* bosome.

OLIUIA In his bosome? In what chapter of his bosome? 500

VIOLA To answer by the method, in the first of his hart.

OLIUIA O, I haue read it: it is heresie. Haue you no more
to say?

VIOLA Good Madam, let me see your face.

OLIUIA Haue you any Commission from your Lord, to
negotiate with my face: you are now out of your Text:
but we will draw the Curtain, and shew you the picture.
She vnueils
Looke you sir, such a one I was this present: Ist not
well done?

VIOLA Excellently done, if God did all. 510

OLIUIA 'Tis in graine sir, 'twill endure winde and weather.

VIOLA

Tis beauty truly blent, whose red and white,
Natures owne sweet, and cunning hand laid on:
Lady, you are the cruell'st shee aliue,
If you will leade these graces to the graue,
And leaue the world no copie.

OLIUIA O sir, I will not be so hard-hearted: I will giue
out diuers scedules of my beautie. It shalbe Inuentoried
and euery particle and vtensile labell'd to my will: As,
520   Item two lippes indifferent redde, Item two grey eyes,
with lids to them: Item, one necke, one chin, & so
forth. Were you sent hither to praise me?

VIOLA

I see you what you are, you are too proud:
But if you were the diuell, you are faire:
My Lord, and master loues you: O such loue
Could be but recompenc'd, though you were crown'd
The non-pareil of beautie.

OLIUIA   How does he loue me?

VIOLA

With adorations, fertill teares,
With groanes that thunder loue, with sighes of fire.

OLIUIA

530   Your Lord does know my mind, I cannot loue him,
Yet I suppose him vertuous, know him noble,
Of great estate, of fresh and stainlesse youth;
In voyces well divulg'd, free, learn'd, and valiant,
And in dimension, and the shape of nature,
A gracious person; But yet I cannot loue him:
He might haue tooke his answer long ago.

VIOLA

If I did loue you in my masters flame,
With such a suffring, such a deadly life:
In your deniall, I would finde no sence,
I would not vnderstand it.

540   OLIUIA   Why, what would you?

VIOLA

Make me a willow Cabine at your gate,
And call vpon my soule within the house,
Write loyall Cantons of contemned loue,
And sing them lowd euen in the dead of night:
Hallow your name to the reuerberate hilles,
And make the babling Gossip of the aire,
Cry out Oliuia: O you should not rest
Betweene the elements of ayre, and earth,
But you should pittie me.

550   OLIUIA You might do much:
What is your Parentage?

VIOLA

Aboue my fortunes, yet my state is well:
I am a Gentleman.

OLIUIA   Get you to your Lord:
I cannot loue him: let him send no more,
Vnlesse (perchance) you come to me againe,
To tell me how he takes it: Fare you well:
I thanke you for your paines: (offering a purse) spend
this for mee.

VIOLA

I am no feede poast, Lady; keepe your purse,
My Master, not my selfe, lackes recompence.
Loue make his heart of flint, that you shal loue,   560
And let your feruour like my masters be,
Plac'd in contempt: Farwell fayre crueltie.   Exit

OLIUIA What is your Parentage?
Aboue my fortunes, yet my state is well;
I am a Gentleman. Ile be sworne thou art,
Thy tongue, thy face, thy limbes, actions, and spirit,
Do giue thee fiue-fold blazon: not too fast: soft, soft,
Vnlesse the Master were the man. How now?
Euen so quickly may one catch the plague?
Me thinkes I feele this youths perfections   570
With an inuisible, and subtle stealth
To creepe in at mine eyes. Well, let it be.
What hoa, Maluolio.

Enter Maluolio

MALUOLIO   Heere Madam, at your seruice.

OLIUIA

Run after that same peeuish Messenger
The Countes man: he left this Ring behinde him
Would I, or not: tell him, Ile none of it.
Desire him not to flatter with his Lord,
Nor hold him vp with hopes, I am not for him:
If that the youth will come this way to morrow,
Ile giue him reasons for't: hie thee Maluolio.   580

MALUOLIO Madam, I will.   Exit at one doore

OLIUIA

I do I know not what, and feare to finde
Mine eye too great a flatterer for my minde:
Fate, shew thy force, our selues we do not owe,
What is decreed, must be: and be this so.

Exit at another doore

Enter Antonio & Sebastian   Sc. 6
                                        (2.1)

ANTHONIO Will you stay no longer: nor will you not that
I go with you.

SEBASTIAN By your patience, no: my starres shine darkely
ouer me; the malignancie of my fate, might perhaps
distemper yours; therefore I shall craue of you your   590
leaue, that I may beare my euils alone. It were a bad
recompence for your loue, to lay any of them on you.

SIR ANDREW Let me yet know of you, whither you are
bound.

SEBASTIAN No sooth sir: my determinate voyage is meere
extrauagancie. But I perceiue in you so excellent a
touch of modestie, that you will not extort from me,
what I am willing to keepe in: therefore it charges me
in manners, the rather to expresse my selfe: you must
know of mee then Antonio, my name is Sebastian (which   600
I call'd Rodorigo) my father was that Sebastian of
Messaline, whom I know you haue heard of. He left
behinde him, my selfe, and a sister, both borne in an
houre: if the Heauens had beene pleas'd, would we
had so ended. But you sir, alter'd that, for some houre
before you tooke me from the breach of the sea, was
my sister drown'd.

ANTHONIO Alas the day.

SEBASTIAN A Lady sir, though it was said shee much
610 resembled me, was yet of many accounted beautiful:
but thogh I could not with such estimable wonder
ouer-farre beleeue that, yet thus farre I will boldly
publish her, shee bore a minde that enuy could not
but call faire: Shee is drown'd already sir with salt
water, though I seeme to drowne her remembrance
againe with more.

ANTHONIO Pardon me sir, your bad entertainment.

SEBASTIAN O good *Antonio*, forgiue me your trouble.

ANTHONIO If you will not murther me for my loue, let
620 mee be your seruant.

SEBASTIAN If you will not vndo what you haue done, that
is kill him, whom you haue recouer'd, desire it not.
Fare ye well at once, my bosome is full of kindnesse,
and I am yet so neere the manners of my mother, that
vpon the least occasion more, mine eyes will tell tales
of me: I am bound to the Count Orsino's Court, farewell.
⌈*Exit*⌉

ANTHONIO
The gentlenesse of all the gods go with thee:
I haue many enemies in Orsino's Court,
Else would I very shortly see thee there:
630 But come what may, I do adore thee so,
That danger shall seeme sport, and I will go.   *Exit*

Sc. 7   *Enter Viola as Cesario, and Maluolio, at seuerall*
(2.2)   *doores*

MALUOLIO Were not you eu'n now, with the Countesse
Oliuia?

VIOLA Euen now sir, on a moderate pace, I haue since
ariu'd but hither.

MALUOLIO (*offering a ring*) She returnes this Ring to you
(sir) you might haue saued mee my paines, to haue
taken it away your selfe. She adds moreouer, that you
should put your Lord into a desperate assurance, she
640 will none of him. And one thing more, that you be
neuer so hardie to come againe in his affaires, vnlesse
it bee to report your Lords taking of this: receiue it so.

VIOLA
She tooke the Ring of me, Ile none of it.

MALUOLIO Come sir, you peeuishly threw it to her: and
her will is, it should be so return'd:
He throws the ring downe
If it bee worth stooping for, there it lies, in your eye:
if not, bee it his that findes it.   *Exit*

VIOLA (*picking vp the ring*)
I left no Ring with her: what meanes this Lady?
Fortune forbid my out-side haue not charm'd her:
650 She made good view of me, indeed so much,
That straight me thought her eyes had lost her tongue,
For she did speake in starts distractedly.
She loues me sure, the cunning of her passion
Inuites me in this churlish messenger:
None of my Lords Ring? Why he sent her none;
I am the man, if it be so, as tis,

Poore Lady, she were better loue a dreame:
Disguise, I see thou art a wickednesse,
Wherein the pregnant enemie does much.
How easie is it, for the proper false   660
In womens waxen hearts to set their formes:
Alas, our frailtie is the cause, not wee,
For such as we are made of, such we bee:
How will this fadge? My master loues her deerely,
And I (poore monster) fond asmuch on him:
And she (mistaken) seemes to dote on me:
What will become of this? As I am man,
My state is desperate for my maisters loue:
As I am woman (now alas the day)
What thriftlesse sighes shall poore *Oliuia* breath?   670
O time, thou must vntangle this, not I,
It is too hard a knot for me t'vnty.   *Exit*

Enter Sir Toby, and Sir Andrew   Sc. 8
                                           (2.3)
SIR TOBY Approach Sir *Andrew*: not to bee a bedde after
midnight, is to be vp betimes, and *Deliculo surgere*, thou
know'st.

SIR ANDREW Nay by my troth I know not: but I know,
to be vp late, is to be vp late.

SIR TOBY A false conclusion: I hate it as an vnfill'd Canne.
To be vp after midnight, and to go to bed then is early:
so that to go to bed after midnight, is to goe to bed   680
betimes. Does not our liues consist of the foure
Elements?

SIR ANDREW Faith so they say, but I thinke it rather
consists of eating and drinking.

SIR TOBY Th'art a scholler; let vs therefore eate and
drinke. *Marian* I say, a stoope of wine.
Enter Clowne

SIR ANDREW Heere comes the foole yfaith.

CLOWNE How now my harts: Did you neuer see the
Picture of we three?

SIR TOBY Welcome asse, now let's haue a catch.   690

SIR ANDREW By my troth the foole has an excellent breast.
I had rather then forty shillings I had such a legge,
and so sweet a breath to sing, as the foole has. Insooth
thou wast in very gracious fooling last night, when
thou spok'st of *Pigrogromitus*, of the *Vapians* passing
the Equinoctial of *Queubus*: 'twas very good yfaith: I
sent thee sixe pence for thy Lemon, hadst it?

CLOWNE I did impeticos thy gratillity: for *Maluolios* nose
is no Whip-stocke. My Lady has a white hand, and the
Mermidons are no bottle-ale houses.   700

SIR ANDREW Excellent: Why this is the best fooling, when
all is done. Now a song.

SIR TOBY (*to Clowne*) Come on, there is sixe pence for you.
Let's haue a song.

SIR ANDREW (*to Clowne*) There's a testrill of me too: if one
knight giue a—

CLOWNE Would you haue a loue-song, or a song of good
life?

SIR TOBY A loue song, a loue song.

SIR ANDREW I, I. I care not for good life.   710

CLOWNE (*sings*)

> *O Mistris mine where are you roming?*
> *O stay and heare, your true loues coming,*
> > *That can sing both high and low.*
> *Trip no further prettie sweeting.*
> *Iourneys end in louers meeting,*
> > *Euery wise mans sonne doth know.*

SIR ANDREW Excellent good, ifaith.

SIR TOBY Good, good.

CLOWNE

> *What is loue, tis not heereafter,*
> *Present mirth, hath present laughter:*
> > *What's to come, is still vnsure.*
> *In delay there lies no plentie,*
> *Then come kisse me sweet and twentie:*
> > *Youths a stuffe will not endure.*

SIR ANDREW A mellifluous voyce, as I am true knight.

SIR TOBY A contagious breath.

SIR ANDREW Very sweet, and contagious ifaith.

SIR TOBY To heare by the nose, it is dulcet in contagion. But shall we make the Welkin dance indeed? Shall wee rowze the night-Owle in a Catch, that will drawe three soules out of one Weauer? Shall we do that?

SIR ANDREW And you loue me, let's doo't: I am dogge at a Catch.

CLOWNE Byrlady sir, and some dogs will catch well.

SIR ANDREW Most certaine: Let our Catch be, *Thou Knaue.*

CLOWNE *Hold thy peace, thou Knaue* knight. I shall be constrain'd in't, to call thee knaue, Knight.

SIR ANDREW 'Tis not the first time I haue constrained one to call me knaue. Begin foole: it begins, *Hold thy peace.*

CLOWNE I shall neuer begin if I hold my peace.

SIR ANDREW Good ifaith: Come begin.

> *Catch sung.*
> *Enter Maria*

MARIA What a catterwalling doe you keepe heere? If my Ladie haue not call'd vp her Steward *Maluolio*, and bid him turne you out of doores, neuer trust me.

SIR TOBY My Lady's a *Catayan*, we are politicians, *Maluolios* a Peg-a-ramsie, and *Three merry men be wee.* Am not I consanguinious? Am I not of her blood: tilly vally. Ladie, *There dwelt a man in Babylon, Lady, Lady.*

CLOWNE Beshrew me, the knights in admirable fooling.

SIR ANDREW I, he do's well enough if he be dispos'd, and so do I too: he does it with a better grace, but I do it more naturall.

SIR TOBY

> *O the twelfe day of December.*

MARIA For the loue o'God peace.

> *Enter Maluolio*

MALUOLIO My masters are you mad? Or what are you? Haue you no wit, manners, nor honestie, but to gabble like Tinkers at this time of night? Do yee make an Alehouse of my Ladies house, that ye squeak out your Coziers Catches without any mitigation or remorse of voice? Is there no respect of place, persons, nor time in you?

SIR TOBY We did keepe time sir in our Catches. Snecke vp.

MALUOLIO *Sir Toby*, I must be round with you. My Lady bad me tell you, that though she harbors you as her kinsman, she's nothing ally'd to your disorders. If you can separate your selfe and your misdemeanors, you are welcome to the house: if not, and it would please you to take leaue of her, she is very willing to bid you farewell.

SIR TOBY

> *Farewell deere heart, since I must needs be gone.*

MARIA Nay good Sir *Toby.*

CLOWNE

> *His eyes do shew his dayes are almost done.*

MALUOLIO Is't euen so?

SIR TOBY

> *But I will neuer dye.*

CLOWNE

> *Sir Toby there you lye.*

MALUOLIO This is much credit to you.

SIR TOBY

> *Shall I bid him go.*

CLOWNE

> *What and if you do?*

SIR TOBY

> *Shall I bid him go, and spare not?*

CLOWNE

> *O no, no, no, no, you dare not.*

SIR TOBY Out o'tune sir, ye lye: (*To Maluolio*) Art any more then a Steward? Dost thou thinke because thou art vertuous, there shall be no more Cakes and Ale?

CLOWNE Yes by *S.* Anne, and Ginger shall bee hotte y'th mouth too.

SIR TOBY Th'art i'th right. (*To Maluolio*) Goe sir, rub your Chaine with crums. (*To Maria*) A stope of Wine *Maria.*

MALUOLIO Mistris Mary, if you priz'd my Ladies fauour at any thing more then contempt, you would not giue meanes for this vnciuill rule; she shall know of it by this hand. *Exit*

MARIA Go shake your eares.

SIR ANDREW 'Twere as good a deede as to drink when a mans a hungrie, to challenge him the field, and then to breake promise with him, and make a foole of him.

SIR TOBY Doo't knight, Ile write thee a Challenge: or Ile deliuer thy indignation to him by word of mouth.

MARIA Sweet Sir Toby be patient for to night: Since the youth of the Counts was to day with my Lady, she is much out of quiet. For Monsieur Maluolio, let me alone with him: If I do not gull him into a nayword, and make him a common recreation, do not thinke I haue witte enough to lye straight in my bed: I know I can do it.

SIR TOBY Possesse vs, possesse vs, tell vs something of him.

MARIA Marrie sir, sometimes he is a kinde of Puritane.

SIR ANDREW O, if I thought that, Ide beate him like a dogge.

SIR TOBY What for being a Puritan, thy exquisite reason,
deere knight.

SIR ANDREW I haue no exquisite reason for't, but I haue
reason good enough.

MARIA The diu'll a Puritane that hee is, or any thing
constantly but a time-pleaser, an affection'd Asse, that
cons State without booke, and vtters it by great swarths.
The best perswaded of himselfe: so cram'd (as he
thinkes) with excellencies, that it is his grounds of faith,
820   that all that looke on him, loue him: and on that vice
in him, will my reuenge finde notable cause to worke.

SIR TOBY What wilt thou do?

MARIA I will drop in his way some obscure Epistles of
loue, wherein by the colour of his beard, the shape of
his legge, the manner of his gate, the expressure of his
eye, forehead, and complection, he shall finde himselfe
most feelingly personated. I can write very like my
Ladie your Neece, on a forgotten matter wee can hardly
make distinction of our hands.

830   SIR TOBY Excellent, I smell a deuice.

SIR ANDREW I hau't in my nose too.

SIR TOBY He shall thinke by the Letters that thou wilt
drop that they come from my Neece, and that shee's
in loue with him.

MARIA My purpose is indeed a horse of that colour.

SIR ANDREW And your horse now would make him an
Asse.

MARIA Asse, I doubt not.

SIR ANDREW O twill be admirable.

840   MARIA Sport royall I warrant you: I know my Physicke
will worke with him, I will plant you two, and let the
Foole make a third, where he shall finde the Letter:
obserue his construction of it: For this night to bed,
and dreame on the euent: Farewell.   Exit

SIR TOBY Good night Penthisilea.

SIR ANDREW Before me she's a good wench.

SIR TOBY She's a beagle true bred, and one that adores
me: what o'that?

SIR ANDREW I was ador'd once too.

850   SIR TOBY Let's to bed knight: Thou hadst neede send for
more money.

SIR ANDREW If I cannot recouer your Neece, I am a foule
way out.

SIR TOBY Send for money knight, if thou hast her not i'th
end, call me Cut.

SIR ANDREW If I do not, neuer trust me, take it how you
will.

SIR TOBY Come, come, Ile go burne some Sacke, tis too
late to go to bed now: Come knight, come knight.

                                          Exeunt

Sc. 9   Enter Duke, Viola as Cesario, Curio, and others
(2.4) ORSINO
860   Giue me some Musick; Now good morow frends.
Now good Cesario, but that peece of song,
That old and Anticke song we heard last night;
Me thought it did releeue my passion much,
More then light ayres, and recollected termes

Of these most briske and giddy-paced times.
Come, but one verse.

CURIO He is not heere (so please your Lordshippe) that
should sing it?

ORSINO Who was it?

CURIO Feste the Iester my Lord, a foole that the Ladie   870
Oliuiaes Father tooke much delight in. He is about the
house.

ORSINO
Seeke him out, and play the tune the while.

                                        Exit Curio

       Musicke playes

(To Viola) Come hither Boy, if euer thou shalt loue
In the sweet pangs of it, remember me:
For such as I am, all true Louers are,
Vnstaid and skittish in all motions else,
Saue in the constant image of the creature
That is belou'd. How dost thou like this tune?

VIOLA
It giues a verie eccho to the seate   880
Where loue is thron'd.

ORSINO   Thou dost speake masterly,
My life vpon't, yong though thou art, thine eye
Hath staid vpon some fauour that it loues:
Hath it not boy?

VIOLA   A little, by your fauour.

ORSINO
What kinde of woman ist?

VIOLA   Of your complection.

ORSINO
She is not worth thee then. What yeares ifaith?

VIOLA About your yeeres my Lord.

ORSINO
Too old by heauen: Let still the woman take
An elder then her selfe, so weares she to him;
So swayes she leuell in her husbands heart: 890
For boy, howeuer we do praise our selues,
Our fancies are more giddie and vnfirme,
More longing, wauering, sooner lost and worne,
Then womens are.

VIOLA   I thinke it well my Lord.

ORSINO
Then let thy Loue be yonger then thy selfe,
Or thy affection cannot hold the bent:
For women are as Roses, whose faire flowre
Being once displaid, doth fall that verie howre.

VIOLA
And so they are: alas, that they are so:
To die, euen when they to perfection grow.   900

       Enter Curio & Feste the Clowne

ORSINO (to Clowne)
O fellow come, the song we had last night:
Marke it Cesario, it is old and plaine;
The Spinsters and the Knitters in the Sun,
And the free maides that weaue their thred with bones,
Do vse to chaunt it: it is silly sooth,
And dallies with the innocence of loue,
Like the old age.

CLOWNE Are you ready Sir?

ORSINO I prethee sing.

    Musicke

        The Song

CLOWNE

910
  Come away, come away death,
    And in sad cypresse let me be laide.
  Fye away, fie away breath,
    I am slaine by a faire cruell maide:
  My shrowd of white, stuck all with Ew,
    O prepare it.
  My part of death no one so true
    Did share it.

  Not a flower, not a flower sweete
    On my blacke coffin, let there be strewne:
920
  Not a friend, not a friend greet
    My poore corpes, where my bones shall be throwne:
  A thousand thousand sighes to saue,
    Lay me ô where
  Sad true louer neuer find my graue,
    To weepe there.

DUKE (*giuing money*) There's for thy paines.

CLOWNE No paines sir, I take pleasure in singing sir.

ORSINO Ile pay thy pleasure then.

CLOWNE Truely sir, and pleasure will be paide one time,
930   or another.

ORSINO Giue me now leaue, to leaue thee.

CLOWNE Now the melancholly God protect thee, and the
  Tailor make thy doublet of changeable Taffata, for thy
  minde is a very Opall. I would haue men of such
  constancie put to Sea, that their businesse might be
  euery thing, and their intent euerie where, for that's
  it, that alwayes makes a good voyage of nothing.
  Farewell.   *Exit*

ORSINO
  Let all the rest giue place: *Exeunt Curio and others*
                    Once more *Cesario*,
940
  Get thee to yond same soueraigne crueltie:
  Tell her my loue, more noble then the world
  Prizes not quantitie of dirtie lands,
  The parts that fortune hath bestow'd vpon her
  Tell her I hold as giddily as Fortune:
  But 'tis that miracle, and Queene of Iems
  That nature prankes her in, attracts my soule.

VIOLA
  But if she cannot loue you sir.

ORSINO
  I cannot be so answer'd.

VIOLA   Sooth but you must.
  Say that some Lady, as perhappes there is,
950
  Hath for your loue as great a pang of heart
  As you haue for *Oliuia*: you cannot loue her:
  You tel her so: Must she not then be answer'd?

ORSINO There is no womans sides
  Can bide the beating of so strong a passion,
  As loue doth giue my heart: no womans heart

So bigge, to hold so much, they lacke retention.
Alas, their loue may be call'd appetite,
No motion of the Liuer, but the Pallat,
That suffer surfet, cloyment, and reuolt,
But mine is all as hungry as the Sea,   960
And can digest as much, make no compare
Betweene that loue a woman can beare me,
And that I owe *Oliuia*.

VIOLA I but I know.

ORSINO What dost thou knowe?

VIOLA
Too well what loue women to men may owe:
In faith they are as true of heart, as we.
My Father had a daughter lou'd a man
As it might be perhaps, were I a woman
I should your Lordship.

ORSINO   And what's her history?   970

VIOLA
A blanke my Lord: she neuer told her loue,
But let concealment like a worme i'th budde
Feede on her damaske cheeke: she pin'd in thought,
And with a greene and yellow melancholly,
She sate like Patience on a Monument,
Smiling at greefe. Was not this loue indeede?
We men may say more, sweare more, but indeed
Our shewes are more then will: for still we proue
Much in our vowes, but little in our loue.

ORSINO
But di'de thy sister of her loue my Boy?   980

VIOLA
I am all the daughters of my Fathers house,
And all the brothers too: and yet I know not.
Sir, shall I to this Lady?

ORSINO   I that's the Theame,
To her in haste: giue her this Iewell: say,
My loue can giue no place, bide no denay.

                      exeunt seuerally

      Enter Sir Toby, Sir Andrew, and Fabian   Sc. 10

SIR TOBY Come thy wayes Signior *Fabian*.   (2.5)

FABIAN Nay Ile come: if I loose a scruple of this sport, let
  me be boyl'd to death with Melancholly.

SIR TOBY Wouldst thou not be glad to haue the niggardly
  Rascally sheepe-biter, come by some notable shame?   990

FABIAN I would exult man: you know he brought me out
  o'fauour with my Lady, about a Beare-baiting heere.

SIR TOBY To anger him wee'l haue the Beare againe, and
  we will foole him blacke and blew, shall we not sir
  Andrew?

SIR ANDREW And we do not, it is pittie of our liues.

    Enter Maria with a Letter

SIR TOBY Heere comes the little villaine: How now my
  Mettle of India?

MARIA Get ye all three into the box tree: *Maluolio*'s
  comming downe this walke, he has beene yonder i'the   1000
  Sunne practising behauiour to his own shadow this
  halfe houre: obserue him for the loue of Mockerie: for

I know this Letter wil make a contemplatiue Ideot of him. Close in the name of ieasting,

The men hide. Maria places the Letter

lye thou there: for heere comes the Trowt, that must be caught with tickling. *Exit*

Enter Maluolio

MALUOLIO 'Tis but Fortune, all is fortune. *Maria* once told me she did affect me, and I haue heard her self come thus neere, that should shee fancie, it should bee one 1010 of my complection. Besides she vses me with a more exalted respect, then any one else that followes her. What should I thinke on't?

SIR TOBY Heere's an ouer-weening rogue.

FABIAN Oh peace: Contemplation makes a rare Turkey Cocke of him, how he iets vnder his aduanc'd plumes.

SIR ANDREW Slight I could so beate the Rogue.

SIR TOBY Peace I say.

MALUOLIO To be Count *Maluolio.*

SIR TOBY Ah Rogue.

1020 SIR ANDREW Pistoll him, pistoll him.

SIR TOBY Peace, peace.

MALUOLIO There is example for't: The Lady of the *Strachy,* married the yeoman of the wardrobe.

SIR ANDREW Fie on him Iezabel.

FABIAN O peace, now he's deepely in: looke how imagination blowes him.

MALUOLIO Hauing beene three moneths married to her, sitting in my state.

SIR TOBY O for a stone-bow to hit him in the eye.

1030 MALUOLIO Calling my Officers about me, in my branch'd Veluet gowne: hauing come from a day bedde, where I haue left *Oliuia* sleeping.

SIR TOBY Fire and Brimstone.

FABIAN O peace, peace.

MALUOLIO And then to haue the humor of state: and after a demure trauaile of regard: telling them I knowe my place, as I would they should doe theirs: to aske for my kinsman *Toby.*

SIR TOBY Boltes and shackles.

1040 FABIAN Oh peace, peace, peace, now, now.

MALUOLIO Seauen of my people with an obedient start, make out for him: I frowne the while, and perchance winde vp my watch, or play with my—(*touching his Chaine*) some rich Iewell: *Toby* approaches; curtsies there to me.

SIR TOBY Shall this fellow liue?

FABIAN Though our silence be drawne from vs with cars, yet peace.

MALUOLIO I extend my hand to him thus: quenching my 1050 familiar smile with an austere regard of controll.

SIR TOBY And do's not *Toby* take you a blow o'the lippes, then?

MALUOLIO Saying, Cosine *Toby,* my Fortunes hauing cast me on your Neece, giue me this prerogatiue of speech.

SIR TOBY What, what?

MALUOLIO You must amend your drunkennesse.

SIR TOBY Out scab.

FABIAN Nay patience, or we breake the sinewes of our plot?

MALUOLIO Besides you waste the treasure of your time, 1060 with a foolish knight.

SIR ANDREW That's mee I warrant you.

MALUOLIO One sir *Andrew.*

SIR ANDREW I knew 'twas I, for many do call mee foole.

MALUOLIO (*seeing the letter*) What employment haue we heere?

FABIAN Now is the Woodcocke neere the gin.

SIR TOBY Oh peace, and the spirit of humors intimate reading aloud to him.

MALUOLIO (*taking vp the letter*) By my life this is my Ladies 1070 hand: these bee her very *C's,* her *V's,* and her *T's,* and thus makes shee her great *P's.* It is in contempt of question her hand.

SIR ANDREW Her *C's,* her *V's,* and her *T's:* why that?

MALUOLIO (*reads*) *To the vnknowne belou'd, this, and my good Wishes:* Her very Phrases: (*opening the letter*) By your leaue wax. Soft, and the impressure her *Lucrece,* with which she vses to seale: tis my Lady: To whom should this be?

FABIAN This winnes him, Liuer and all. 1080

MALUOLIO *Ioue knowes I loue,*
    But who,
  Lips do not mooue,
    No man must know.

No man must know. What followes? The numbers alter'd: No man must know, If this should be thee *Maluolio?*

SIR TOBY Marrie hang thee brocke.

MALUOLIO
  I may command where I adore,
    But silence like a Lucresse knife: 1090
  With bloodlesse stroke my heart doth gore,
    M.O.A.I. doth sway my life.

FABIAN A fustian riddle.

SIR TOBY Excellent Wench, say I.

MALUOLIO *M.O.A.I.* doth sway my life. Nay but first let me see, let me see, let me see.

FABIAN What dish a poyson has she drest him?

SIR TOBY And with what wing the staniel checkes at it?

MALUOLIO *I may command, where I adore:* Why shee may command me: I serue her, she is my Ladie. Why this 1100 is euident to any formall capacitie. There is no obstruction in this, and the end: What should that Alphabeticall position portend, if I could make that resemble something in me? Softly, *M.O.A.I.*

SIR TOBY O I, make vp that, he is now at a cold sent.

FABIAN Sowter will cry vpon't for all this, though it bee as ranke as a Fox.

MALUOLIO *M. Maluolio, M.* why that begins my name.

FABIAN Did not I say he would worke it out, the Curre is excellent at faults. 1110

MALUOLIO *M.* But then there is no consonancy in the sequell. That suffers vnder probation: *A.* should follow, but *O.* does.

FABIAN And *O* shall end, I hope.

SIR TOBY I, or Ile cudgell him, and make him cry *O*.

MALUOLIO And then *I*. comes behind.

FABIAN I, and you had any eye behinde you, you might see more detraction at your heeles, then Fortunes before you.

1120 MALUOLIO *M,O,A,I*. This simulation is not as the former: and yet to crush this a little, it would bow to mee, for euery one of these Letters are in my name. Soft, here followes prose: *If this fall into thy hand, reuolue. In my stars I am aboue thee, but be not affraid of greatnesse: Some are borne great, some atcheeue greatnesse, and some haue greatnesse thrust vppon em. Thy fates open theyr hands, let thy blood and spirit embrace them, and to inure thy selfe to what thou art like to be: cast thy humble slough, and appeare fresh. Be opposite with a kinsman,*
1130 *surly with seruants: Let thy tongue tang arguments of state ; put thy selfe into the tricke of singularitie. Shee thus aduises thee, that sighes for thee. Remember who commended thy yellow stockings, and wish'd to see thee euer crosse garter'd: I say remember, goe too, thou art made if thou desir'st to be so: If not, let me see thee a steward still, the fellow of seruants, and not woorthie to touch Fortunes fingers. Farewell, Shee that would alter seruices with thee, the fortunate vnhappy.* Daylight and champian discouers not more: This is open, I will bee
1140 proud, I will reade pollticke Authours, I will baffle Sir *Toby*, I will wash off grosse acquaintance, I will be point deuise, the very man. I do not now foole my selfe, to let imagination iade mee; for euery reason excites to this, that my Lady loues me. She did commend my yellow stockings of late, shee did praise my legge being crossegarter'd, and in this she manifests her selfe to my loue, & with a kinde of iniunction driues mee to these habites of her liking. I thanke my starres, I am happy: I will bee strange, stout, in yellow stockings,
1150 and crosse Garter'd, euen with the swiftnesse of putting on. Ioue, and my starres be praised. Heere is yet a postscript. *Thou canst not choose but know who I am. If thou entertainst my loue, let it appeare in thy smiling, thy smiles become thee well. Therefore in my presence still smile, deere my sweete, I prethee.* Ioue I thanke thee, I will smile, I wil do euery thing that thou wilt haue me.

                                                        Exit

    Sir Toby, Sir Andrew, and Fabian come from hiding

FABIAN I will not giue my part of this sport for a pension of thousands to be paid from the Sophy.

SIR TOBY I could marry this wench for this deuice.

1160 SIR ANDREW So could I too.

SIR TOBY And aske no other dowry with her, but such another iest.

        Enter Maria

SIR ANDREW Nor I neither.

FABIAN Heere comes my noble gull catcher.

SIR TOBY (*to Maria*) Wilt thou set thy foote o'my necke.

SIR ANDREW (*to Maria*) Or o'mine either?

SIR TOBY (*to Maria*) Shall I play my freedome at tray-trip, and becom thy bondslaue?

SIR ANDREW (*to Maria*) Ifaith, or I either?

SIR TOBY (*to Maria*) Why, thou hast put him in such a 1170 dreame, that when the image of it leaues him, he must run mad.

MARIA Nay but say true, do's it worke vpon him?

SIR TOBY Like Aqua vite with a Midwife.

MARIA If you will then see the fruites of the sport, mark his first approach before my Lady: hee will come to her in yellow stockings, and 'tis a colour she abhorres, and crosse garter'd, a fashion shee detests: and hee will smile vpon her, which will now be so vnsuteable to her disposition, being addicted to a melancholly, as 1180 shee is, that it cannot but turn him into a notable contempt: if you wil see it follow me.

SIR TOBY To the gates of Tartar, thou most excellent diuell of wit.

SIR ANDREW Ile make one too.   *Exeunt*

    Enter Viola as Cesario, and Clowne, with ⌈pipe and⌉   Sc. 11
    tabor   (3.1)

VIOLA Saue thee Friend and thy Musick: dost thou liue by thy Tabor?

CLOWNE No sir, I liue by the Church.

VIOLA Art thou a Churchman?

CLOWNE No such matter sir, I do liue by the Church: For, 1190 I do liue at my house, and my house dooth stand by the Church.

VIOLA So thou maist say the King lyes by a begger, if a begger dwell neer him: or the Church stands by thy Tabor, if thy Tabor stand by the Church.

CLOWNE You haue said sir: To see this age: A sentence is but a cheu'rill gloue to a good witte, how quickely the wrong side may be turn'd outward.

VIOLA Nay that's certaine: they that dally nicely with words, may quickely make them wanton.   1200

CLOWNE I would therefore my sister had had no name Sir.

VIOLA Why man?

CLOWNE Why sir, her names a word, and to dallie with that word, might make my sister wanton: But indeede, words are very Rascals, since bonds disgrac'd them.

VIOLA Thy reason man?

CLOWNE Troth sir, I can yeeld you none without wordes, and wordes are growne so false, I am loath to proue reason with them.   1210

VIOLA I warrant thou art a merry fellow, and car'st for nothing.

CLOWNE Not so sir, I do care for something: but in my conscience sir, I do not care for you: if that be to care for nothing sir, I would it would make you inuisible.

VIOLA Art not thou the Lady *Oliuia's* foole?

CLOWNE No indeed sir, the Lady *Oliuia* has no folly, shee will keepe no foole sir, till she be married, and fooles are as like husbands, as Pilchers are to Herrings, the Husbands the bigger, I am indeede not her foole, but 1220 hir corrupter of words.

VIOLA I saw thee late at the Count *Orsino's*.

CLOWNE Foolery sir, does walke about the Orbe like the

Sun, it shines euery where. I would be sorry sir, but
the Foole should be as oft with your Master, as with
my Mistris: I thinke I saw your wisedome there.

VIOLA Nay, and thou passe vpon me, Ile no more with
thee. (*Giuing money*) Hold there's expences for thee.

CLOWNE Now Ioue in his next commodity of hayre, send
1230 thee a beard.

VIOLA By my troth Ile tell thee, I am almost sicke for one,
though I would not haue it grow on my chinne. Is thy
Lady within?

CLOWNE Would not a paire of these haue bred sir?

VIOLA Yes being kept together, and put to vse.

CLOWNE I would play Lord *Pandarus* of *Phrygia* sir, to
bring a *Cressida* to this *Troylus*.

VIOLA (*giuing money*) I vnderstand you sir, tis well begg'd.

CLOWNE The matter I hope is not great sir; begging, but
1240 a begger: *Cressida* was a begger. My Lady is within sir.
I will conster to them whence you come, who you are,
and what you would are out of my welkin, I might say
Element, but the word is ouer-worne.   *exit*

VIOLA
This fellow is wise enough to play the foole,
And to do that well, craues a kinde of wit:
He must obserue their mood on whom he iests,
The quality of persons, and the time:
And like the Haggard, checke at euery Feather
That comes before his eye. This is a practice,
1250 As full of labour as a Wise-mans Art:
For folly that he wisely shewes, is fit;
But wisemen folly falne, quite taint their wit.

Enter Sir Toby and Andrew

SIR TOBY Saue you Gentleman.

VIOLA And you sir.

SIR ANDREW *Dieu vou guard Monsieur.*

VIOLA *Et vouz ousie vostre seruiture.*

SIR ANDREW I hope sir, you are, and I am yours.

SIR TOBY Will you incounter the house, my Neece is
desirous you should enter, if your trade be to her.

1260 VIOLA I am bound to your Neece sir, I meane she is the
list of my voyage.

SIR TOBY Taste your legges sir, put them to motion.

VIOLA My legges do better vnderstand me sir, then I
vnderstand what you meane by bidding me taste my
legs.

SIR TOBY I meane to go sir, to enter.

VIOLA I will answer you with gate and entrance,

Enter Oliuia, and Maria, her Gentlewoman

but we are preuented. (*To Oliuia*) Most excellent
accomplish'd Lady, the heauens raine Odours on you.

1270 SIR ANDREW (*to Sir Toby*) That youth's a rare Courtier,
raine odours, wel.

VIOLA My matter hath no voice Lady, but to your owne
most pregnant and vouchsafed eare.

SIR ANDREW (*to Sir Toby*) Odours, pregnant, and
vouchsafed: Ile get 'em all three already.

OLIUIA Let the Garden doore be shut, and leaue mee to
my hearing.

Exeunt Sir Toby, Sir Andrew, and Maria

Giue me your hand sir.

VIOLA
My dutie Madam, and most humble seruice.

OLIUIA What is your name?   1280

VIOLA
Cesario is your seruants name, faire Princesse.

OLIUIA
My seruant sir? 'Twas neuer merry world,
Since lowly feigning was call'd complement:
Y'are seruant to the Count *Orsino* youth.

VIOLA
And he is yours, and his must needs be yours:
Your seruants seruant, is your seruant Madam.

OLIUIA
For him, I thinke not on him: for his thoughts,
Would they were blankes, rather then fill'd with me.

VIOLA
Madam, I come to whet your gentle thoughts
On his behalfe.

OLIUIA   O by your leaue I pray you.   1290
I bad you neuer speake againe of him;
But would you vndertake another suite
I had rather heare you, to solicit that,
Then Musicke from the spheares.

VIOLA   Deere Lady.

OLIUIA
Giue me leaue, beseech you: I did send,
After the last enchantment you did heare,
A Ring in chace of you. So did I abuse
My selfe, my seruant, and I feare me you:
Vnder your hard construction must I sit,
To force that on you in a shamefull cunning   1300
Which you knew none of yours. What might you
think?
Haue you not set mine Honor at the stake,
And baited it with all th'vnmuzled thoughts
That tyrannous heart can think? To one of your
receiuing
Enough is shewne, a Cipresse, not a bosome,
Hides my heart: so let me heare you speake.

VIOLA
I pittie you.

OLIUIA   That's a degree to loue.

VIOLA
No not a grize: for tis a vulgar proofe
That verie oft we pitty enemies.

OLIUIA
Why then me thinkes 'tis time to smile agen: 1310
O world, how apt the poore are to be proud?
If one should be a prey, how much the better
To fall before the Lion, then the Wolfe?

Clocke strikes

The clocke vpbraides me with the waste of time:
Be not affraid good youth, I will not haue you,
And yet when wit and youth is come to haruest,
Your wife is like to reape a proper man:
There lies your way, due West.

VIOLA   Then Westward hoe:
Grace and good disposition attend your Ladyship:
You'l nothing Madam to my Lord, by me?   1320

OLIUIA

Stay: I prethee tell me what thou thinkst of me?

VIOLA

That you do thinke you are not what you are.

OLIUIA

If I thinke so, I thinke the same of you.

VIOLA

Then thinke you right: I am not what I am.

OLIUIA

I would you were, as I would haue you be.

VIOLA

Would it be better Madam, then I am?

I wish it might, for now I am your foole.

OLIUIA (aside)

O what a deale of scorne, lookes beautifull

In the contempt and anger of his lip,

1330   A murdrous guilt shewes not it selfe more soone,

Then loue that would seeme hid: Loues night, is noone.

(To Viola) Cesario, by the Roses of the Spring,

By maid-hood, honor, truth, and euery thing,

I loue thee so, that maugre all thy pride,

Nor wit, nor reason, can my passion hide:

Do not extort thy reasons from this clause,

For that I woo, thou therefore hast no cause:

But rather reason thus, with reason fetter;

Loue sought, is good: but giuen vnsought, is better.

VIOLA

1340   By innocence I sweare, and by my youth,

I haue one heart, one bosome, and one truth,

And that no woman has, nor neuer none

Shall mistris be of it, saue I alone.

And so adieu good Madam, neuer more,

Will I my Masters teares to you deplore.

OLIUIA

Yet come againe: for thou perhaps mayst moue

That heart which now abhorres, to like his loue.

Exeunt ⌈seuerally⌉

Sc. 12   *Enter Sir Toby, Sir Andrew, and Fabian*

(3.2)   SIR ANDREW No faith, Ile not stay a iot longer.

SIR TOBY Thy reason deere venom, giue thy reason.

1350 FABIAN You must needes yeelde your reason, Sir *Andrew*?

SIR ANDREW Marry I saw your Neece do more fauours to the Counts Seruing-man, then euer she bestow'd vpon mee: I saw't i'th Orchard.

SIR TOBY Did she see thee the while, old boy, tell me that.

SIR ANDREW As plaine as I see you now.

FABIAN This was a great argument of loue in her toward you.

SIR ANDREW S'light; will you make an Asse o'me.

FABIAN I will proue it legitimate sir, vpon the Oathes of 1360 iudgement, and reason.

SIR TOBY And they haue beene grand Iurie men, since before *Noah* was a Saylor.

FABIAN Shee did shew fauour to the youth in your sight, onely to exasperate you, to awake your dormouse valour, to put fire in your Heart, and brimstone in your

Liuer: you should then haue accosted her, and with some excellent iests, fire-new from the mint, you should haue bangd the youth into dumbenesse: this was look'd for at your hand, and this was baulkt: the double gilt of this opportunitie you let time wash off, and you are 1370 now sayld into the North of my Ladies opinion, where you will hang like an ysickle on a Dutchmans beard, vnlesse you do redeeme it, by some laudable attempt, either of valour or policie.

SIR ANDREW And't be any way, it must be with Valour, for policie I hate: I had as liefe be a Brownist, as a Politician.

SIR TOBY Why then build me thy fortunes vpon the basis of valour. Challenge me the Counts youth to fight with him, hurt him in eleuen places, my Neece shall take 1380 note of it, and assure thy selfe, there is no loue-Broker in the world, can more preuaile in mans commendation with woman, then report of valour.

FABIAN There is no way but this sir *Andrew*.

SIR ANDREW Will either of you beare me a challenge to him?

SIR TOBY Go, write it in a martial hand, be curst and briefe: it is no matter how wittie, so it bee eloquent, and full of inuention: taunt him with the license of Inke: if thou thou'st him some thrice, it shall not be 1390 amisse, and as many Lyes, as will lye in thy sheete of paper, although the sheete were bigge enough for the bedde of *Ware* in England, set 'em downe, go about it. Let there bee gaulle enough in thy inke, though thou write with a Goose-pen, no matter: about it.

SIR ANDREW Where shall I finde you?

SIR TOBY Wee'l call thee at the Cubiculo: Go.

Exit Sir Andrew

FABIAN This is a deere Manakin to you Sir *Toby*.

SIR TOBY I haue beene deere to him lad, some two thousand strong, or so.   1400

FABIAN We shall haue a rare Letter from him; but you'le not deliuer't.

SIR TOBY Neuer trust me then: and by all meanes stirre on the youth to an answer. I thinke Oxen and waine-ropes cannot hale them together. For *Andrew*, if he were open'd and you finde so much blood in his Liuer, as will clog the foote of a flea, Ile eate the rest of th'anatomy.

FABIAN And his opposit the youth beares in his visage no great presage of cruelty.   1410

Enter Maria

SIR TOBY Looke where the youngest Wren of nine comes.

MARIA If you desire the spleene, and will laughe your selues into stitches, follow me; yond gull *Maluolio* is turned Heathen, a verie Renegatho; for there is no christian that meanes to be saued by beleeuing rightly, can euer beleeue such impossible passages of grossenesse. Hee's in yellow stockings.

SIR TOBY And crosse garter'd?

MARIA Most villanously: like a Pedant that keepes a Schoole i'th Church: I haue dogg'd him like his 1420 murtherer. He does obey euery point of the Letter that

I dropt, to betray him: He does smile his face into more
lynes, then is in the new Mappe, with the augmentation
of the Indies: you haue not seene such a thing as tis:
I can hardly forbeare hurling things at him, I know
my Ladie will strike him: if shee doe, hee'l smile, and
take't for a great fauour.

SIR TOBY Come bring vs, bring vs where he is.

Exeunt Omnes

Sc. 13   *Enter Sebastian and Anthonio*
(3.3)
SEBASTIAN
      I would not by my will haue troubled you,
1430   But since you make your pleasure of your paines,
      I will no further chide you.

ANTHONIO
      I could not stay behinde you: my desire
      (More sharpe then filed steele) did spurre me forth,
      And not all loue to see you (though so much
      As might haue drawne one to a longer voyage)
      But iealousie, what might befall your trauell,
      Being skillesse in these parts: which to a stranger,
      Vnguided, and vnfriended, often proue
      Rough, and vnhospitable. My willing loue,
1440   The rather by these arguments of feare
      Set forth in your pursuite.

SEBASTIAN   My kinde *Anthonio*,
      I can no other answer make, but thankes,
      And thankes: and euer oft good turnes,
      Are shuffel'd off with such vncurrant pay:
      But were my worth, as is my conscience firme,
      You should finde better dealing: what's to do?
      Shall we go see the reliques of this Towne?

ANTHONIO
      To morrow sir, best first go see your Lodging?

SEBASTIAN
      I am not weary, and 'tis long to night.
1450   I pray you let vs satisfie our eyes
      With the memorials, and the things of fame
      That do renowne this City.

ANTHONIO   Would you'l'd pardon me:
      I do not without danger walke these streetes.
      Once in a sea-fight 'gainst the Count his gallies,
      I did some seruice, of such note indeede,
      That were I tane heere, it would scarse be answer'd.

SEBASTIAN
      Belike you slew great number of his people.

ANTHONIO
      Th'offence is not of such a bloody nature,
      Albeit the quality of the time, and quarrell
1460   Might well haue giuen vs bloody argument:
      It might haue since bene answer'd in repaying
      What we tooke from them, which for Traffiques sake
      Most of our City did. Onely my selfe stood out,
      For which if I be latched in this place
      I shall pay deere.

SEBASTIAN   Do not then walke too open.

ANTHONIO
      It doth not fit me: hold sir, here's my purse,
      In the South Suburbes at the Elephant

Is best to lodge: I will bespeake our dyet,
Whiles you beguile the time, and feed your knowledge
With viewing of the Towne, there shall you haue me.   1470

SEBASTIAN Why I your purse?

ANTHONIO
      Haply your eye shall light vpon some toy
      You haue desire to purchase: and your store
      I thinke is not for idle Markets, sir.

SEBASTIAN
      Ile be your purse-bearer, and leaue you
      For an houre.

ANTHONIO   To th'Elephant.

SEBASTIAN   I do remember.

Exeunt seuerally

          Enter Oliuia and Maria   Sc. 14
OLIUIA (*aside*)   (3.4)
      I haue sent after him, he sayes hee'l come:
      How shall I feast him? What bestow of him?
      For youth is bought more oft, then begg'd, or borrow'd.
      I speake too loud: 1480
      (*To Maria*) Where's *Maluolio*, he is sad, and ciuill,
      And suites well for a seruant with my fortunes,
      Where is *Maluolio*?

MARIA He's comming Madame: But in very strange
      manner. He is sure possest Madam.

OLIUIA
      Why what's the matter, does he raue?

MARIA No Madam, he does nothing but smile: your
      Ladyship were best to haue some guard about you, if
      hee come, for sure the man is tainted in's wits.

OLIUIA
      Go call him hither.   *Exit Maria*
                  I am as madde as hee,   1490
      If sad and merry madnesse equall bee.
          *Enter Maluolio crosse garter'd and wearing yellow
          stockings, with Maria*
      How now *Maluolio*?

MALUOLIO Sweet Lady, ho, ho.

OLIUIA
      Smil'st thou? I sent for thee vpon a sad occasion.

MALUOLIO Sad Lady, I could be sad: This does make some
      obstruction in the blood: This crosse-gartering, but
      what of that? If it please the eye of one, it is with me
      as the very true Sonnet is: Please one, and please all.

⌐OLIUIA⌐
      Why how doest thou man? What is the matter with
          thee?

MALUOLIO Not blacke in my minde, though yellow in my   1500
      legges: It did come to his hands, and Commaunds shall
      be executed. I thinke we doe know the sweet Romane
      hand.

OLIUIA
      Wilt thou go to bed *Maluolio*?

MALUOLIO (*kissing his hand*) To bed? I sweet heart, and
      Ile come to thee.

OLIUIA God comfort thee: Why dost thou smile so, and
      kisse thy hand so oft?

MARIA How do you *Maluolio*?

1510 MALUOLIO At your request: Yes Nightingales answere Dawes.

MARIA Why appeare you with this ridiculous boldnesse before my Lady.

MALUOLIO Be not afraid of greatnesse: 'twas well writ.

OLIUIA What meanst thou by that *Maluolio?*

MALUOLIO Some are borne great.

OLIUIA Ha?

MALUOLIO Some atcheeue greatnesse.

OLIUIA What sayst thou?

1520 MALUOLIO And some haue greatnesse thrust vpon them.

OLIUIA Heauen restore thee.

MALUOLIO Remember who commended thy yellow stockings.

OLIUIA Thy yellow stockings?

MALUOLIO And wish'd to see thee crosse garter'd.

OLIUIA Crosse garter'd?

MALUOLIO Go too, thou art made, if thou desir'st to be so.

OLIUIA Am I made?

MALUOLIO If not, let me see thee a seruant still.

1530 OLIUIA Why this is verie Midsommer madnesse.

Enter Seruant

SERUANT Madame, the young Gentleman of the Count *Orsino's* is return'd, I could hardly entreate him backe: he attends your Ladyships pleasure.

OLIUIA Ile come to him.   *Exit Seruant*
Good *Maria*, let this fellow be look'd too. Where's my Cosine *Toby*, let some of my people haue a speciall care of him, I would not haue him miscarrie for the halfe of my Dowry.   *Exeunt Oliuia and Maria, seuerally*

MALUOLIO Oh ho, do you come neere me now: no worse
1540 man then sir *Toby* to looke to me. This concurres directly with the Letter, she sends him on purpose, that I may appeare stubborne to him: for she incites me to that in the Letter. Cast thy humble slough sayes she: be opposite with a Kinsman, surly with seruants, let thy tongue tang arguments of state, put thy selfe into the tricke of singularity: and consequently setts downe the manner how: as a sad face, a reuerend carriage, a slow tongue, in the habite of some Sir of note, and so foorth. I haue lymde her, but it is Ioues doing, and
1550 Ioue make me thankefull. And when she went away now, let this Fellow be look'd too: Fellow? not *Maluolio*, nor after my degree, but Fellow. Why euery thing adheres togither, that no dramme of a scruple, no scruple of a scruple, no obstacle, no incredulous or vnsafe circumstance: What can be saide? Nothing that can be, can come betweene me, and the full prospect of my hopes. Well Ioue, not I, is the doer of this, and he is to be thanked.

Enter Toby, Fabian, and Maria

SIR TOBY Which way is hee in the name of sanctity. If all
1560 the diuels of hell be drawne in little, and Legion himselfe possest him, yet Ile speake to him.

FABIAN Heere he is, heere he is: (*to Maluolio*) how ist with you sir? How ist with you man?

MALUOLIO Go off, I discard you: let me enioy my priuate: go off.

MARIA Lo, how hollow the fiend speakes within him; did

not I tell you? Sir *Toby*, my Lady prayes you to haue a care of him.

MALUOLIO Ah ha, does she so?

SIR TOBY Go too, go too: peace, peace, wee must deale 1570 gently with him: Let me alone. How do you *Maluolio?* How ist with you? What man, defie the diuell: consider, he's an enemy to mankinde.

MALUOLIO Do you know what you say?

MARIA La you, and you speake ill of the diuell, how he takes it at heart. Pray God he be not bewitch'd.

FABIAN Carry his water to th'wise woman.

MARIA Marry and it shall be done to morrow morning if I liue. My Lady would not loose him for more then ile say.   1580

MALUOLIO How now mistris?

MARIA Oh Lord.

SIR TOBY Prethee hold thy peace, this is not the way: Doe you not see you moue him? Let me alone with him.

FABIAN No way but gentlenesse, gently, gently: the Fiend is rough, and will not be roughly vs'd.

SIR TOBY Why how now my bawcock? how dost y^u chuck?

MALUOLIO Sir.

SIR TOBY I biddy, come with me. What man, tis not for 1590 grauity to play at cherrie-pit with sathan. Hang him foul Colliar.

MARIA Get him to say his prayers, good sir *Toby* gette him to pray.

MALUOLIO My prayers Minx.

MARIA No I warrant you, he will not heare of godlynesse.

MALUOLIO Go hang your selues all: you are ydle shallowe things, I am not of your element, you shall knowe more heereafter.   *Exit*

SIR TOBY Ist possible?   1600

FABIAN If this were plaid vpon a stage now, I could condemne it as an improbable fiction.

SIR TOBY His very genius hath taken the infection of the deuice man.

MARIA Nay pursue him now, least the deuice take ayre, and taint.

FABIAN Why we shall make him mad indeede.

MARIA The house will be the quieter.

SIR TOBY Come, wee'l haue him in a darke room & bound. My Neece is already in the beleefe that he's mad: we 1610 may carry it thus for our pleasure, and his pennance, til our very pastime tyred out of breath, prompt vs to haue mercy on him: at which time, we wil bring the deuice to the bar and crowne thee for a finder of madmen: but see, but see.

Enter Sir Andrew with a paper

FABIAN More matter for a May morning.

SIR ANDREW Heere's the Challenge, reade it: I warrant there's vinegar and pepper in't.

FABIAN Ist so sawcy?

SIR ANDREW I, ist? I warrant him: do but read.   1620

SIR TOBY Giue me.

(*Reads*) *Youth, whatsoeuer thou art, thou art but a scuruy fellow.*

FABIAN Good, and valiant.

SIR TOBY *Wonder not, nor admire not in thy minde why I doe call thee so, for I will shew thee no reason for't.*

FABIAN A good note, that keepes you from the blow of yͤ Law.

SIR TOBY *Thou comst to the Lady Oliuia, and in my sight she* 1630 *vses thee kindly: but thou lyest in thy throat, that is not the matter I challenge thee for.*

FABIAN Very breefe, and to exceeding good sence-lesse.

SIR TOBY *I will way-lay thee going home, where if it be thy chance to kill me.*

FABIAN Good.

SIR TOBY *Thou kilst me like a rogue and a villaine.*

FABIAN Still you keepe o'th windie side of the Law: good.

SIR TOBY *Fartheewell, and God haue mercie vpon one of our* 1640 *soules. He may haue mercie vpon mine, but my hope is better, and so looke to thy selfe. Thy friend as thou vsest him, & thy sworne enemie,*

                              Andrew Ague-cheeke.

If this Letter moue him not, his legges cannot: Ile giu't him.

MARIA You may haue verie fit occasion for't: he is now in some commerce with my Ladie, and will by and by depart.

SIR TOBY Go sir *Andrew*: scout mee for him at the corner of the Orchard like a bum-Baylie: so soone as euer 1650 thou seest him, draw, and as thou draw'st, sweare horrible: for it comes to passe oft, that a terrible oath, with a swaggering accent sharpely twang'd off, giues manhoode more approbation, then euer proofe it selfe would haue earn'd him. Away.

SIR ANDREW Nay let me alone for swearing.   *Exit*

SIR TOBY Now will not I deliuer his Letter: for the behauiour of the yong Gentleman, giues him out to be of good capacity, and breeding: his employment betweene his Lord and my Neece, confirmes no lesse. 1660 Therefore, this Letter being so excellently ignorant, will breed no terror in the youth: he will finde it comes from a Clodde-pole. But sir, I will deliuer his Challenge by word of mouth; set vpon *Ague-cheeke* a notable report of valor, and driue the Gentleman (as I know his youth will aptly receiue it) into a most hideous opinion of his rage, skill, furie, and impetuositie. This will so fright them both, that they wil kill one another by the looke, like Cockatrices.

          Enter Oliuia, and Viola as Cesario

FABIAN Heere he comes with your Neece, giue them way 1670 till he take leaue, and presently after him.

SIR TOBY I wil meditate the while vpon some horrid message for a Challenge.

          Exeunt Sir Toby, Fabian, and Maria

OLIUIA
I haue said too much vnto a hart of stone,
And laid mine honour too vnchary out:
There's something in me that reproues my fault:
But such a head-strong potent fault it is,
That it but mockes reproofe.

VIOLA   With the same hauiour
That your passion beares, goes on my Masters greefes.

OLIUIA (*giuing a Iewell*)
Heere, weare this Iewell for me, tis my picture:
Refuse it not, it hath no tongue, to vex you: 1680
And I beseech you come againe to morrow.
What shall you aske of me that Ile deny,
That honour (sau'd) may vpon asking giue.

VIOLA
Nothing but this, your true loue for my master.

OLIUIA
How with mine honor may I giue him that,
Which I haue giuen to you.

VIOLA   I will acquit you.

OLIUIA
Well, come againe to morrow: far-thee-well,
A Fiend like thee might beare my soule to hell.   *Exit*
          Enter Toby and Fabian

SIR TOBY Gentleman, God saue thee.

VIOLA And you sir.   1690

SIR TOBY That defence thou hast, betake the too't: of what nature the wrongs are thou hast done him, I knowe not: but thy intercepter full of despight, bloody as the Hunter, attends thee at the Orchard end: dismount thy tucke, be yare in thy preparation, for thy assaylant is quick, skilfull, and deadly.

VIOLA You mistake sir, I am sure no man hath any quarrell to me: my remembrance is very free and cleere from any image of offence done to any man.

SIR TOBY You'l finde it otherwise I assure you: therefore, 1700 if you hold your life at any price, betake you to your gard: for your opposite hath in him what youth, strength, skill, and wrath, can furnish man withall.

VIOLA I pray you sir what is he?

SIR TOBY He is knight dubb'd with vnhatch'd Rapier, and on carpet consideration, but he is a diuell in priuate brall, soules and bodies hath he diuorc'd three, and his incensement at this moment is so implacable, that satisfaction can be none, but by pangs of death and sepulcher: Hob, nob, is his word: giu't or take't.   1710

VIOLA I will returne againe into the house, and desire some conduct of the Lady. I am no fighter, I haue heard of some kinde of men, that put quarrells purposely on others, to taste their valour: belike this is a man of that quirke.

SIR TOBY Sir, no: his indignation deriues it selfe out of a very computent iniurie, therefore get you on, and giue him his desire. Backe you shall not to the house, vnlesse you vndertake that with me, which with as much safetie you might answer him: therefore on, or strippe   1720 your sword starke naked: for meddle you must that's certain, or forsweare to weare iron about you.

VIOLA This is as vnciuill as strange. I beseech you doe me this courteous office, as to know of the Knight what my offence to him is: it is something of my negligence, nothing of my purpose.

SIR TOBY I will doe so. Signiour *Fabian*, stay you by this Gentleman, till my returne.   *Exit Toby*

VIOLA Pray you sir, do you know of this matter?

FABIAN I know the knight is incenst against you, euen   1730 to a mortall arbitrement, but nothing of the circumstance more.

VIOLA I beseech you what manner of man is he?

FABIAN Nothing of that wonderfull promise to read him by his forme, as you are like to finde him in the proofe of his valour. He is indeede sir, the most skilfull, bloudy, & fatall opposite that you could possibly haue found in anie part of Illyria: will you walke towards him, I will make your peace with him, if I can.

1740 VIOLA I shall bee much bound to you for't: I am one, that had rather go with sir Priest, then sir knight: I care not who knowes so much of my mettle.

⌈*Exeunt*⌉

Enter Toby and Andrew

SIR TOBY Why man hee's a verie diuell, I haue not seen such a firago: I had a passe with him, rapier, scabberd, and all: and he giues me the stucke in with such a mortall motion that it is ineuitable: and on the answer, he payes you as surely, as your feete hits the ground they step on. They say, he has bin Fencer to the Sophy.

SIR ANDREW Pox on't, Ile not meddle with him.

1750 SIR TOBY I but he will not now be pacified, *Fabian* can scarse hold him yonder.

SIR ANDREW Plague on't, and I thought he had beene valiant, and so cunning in Fence, I'de haue seene him damn'd ere I'de haue challeng'd him. Let him let the matter slip, and Ile giue him my horse, gray Capilet.

SIR TOBY Ile make the motion: stand heere, make a good shew on't, this shall end without the perdition of soules, (*aside*) marry Ile ride your horse as well as I ride you.

Enter Fabian and Viola as Cesario

⌈*Aside to Fabian*⌉ I haue his horse to take vp the quarrell,
1760 I haue perswaded him the youths a diuell.

FABIAN (*aside to Sir Toby*) He is as horribly conceited of him: and pants, & lookes pale, as if a Beare were at his heeles.

SIR TOBY (*to Viola*) There's no remedie sir, he will fight with you for's oath sake: marrie hee hath better bethought him of his quarrell, and hee findes that now scarse to bee worth talking of: therefore draw for the supportance of his vowe, he protests he will not hurt you.

1770 VIOLA (*aside*) Pray God defend me: a little thing would make me tell them how much I lacke of a man.

FABIAN (*to Sir Andrew*) Giue ground if you see him furious.

SIR TOBY Come sir *Andrew*, there's no remedie, the Gentleman will for his honors sake haue one bowt with you: he cannot by the Duello auoide it: but hee has promised me, as he is a Gentleman and a Soldiour, he will not hurt you. Come on, too't.

SIR ANDREW Pray God he keepe his oath.

Enter Antonio

VIOLA
I do assure you tis against my will.

Sir Andrew and Viola draw their swords

ANTHONIO (*drawing his sword, to Sir Andrew*)
1780 Put vp your sword: if this yong Gentleman

Haue done offence, I take the fault on me:
If you offend him, I for him defie you.

SIR TOBY You sir? Why, what are you?

ANTHONIO
One sir, that for his loue dares yet do more
Then you haue heard him brag to you he will.

SIR TOBY (*drawing his sword*) Nay, if you be an vndertaker, I am for you.

Enter Officers

FABIAN O good sir *Toby* hold: heere come the Officers.

SIR TOBY (*to Anthonio*) Ile be with you anon.

VIOLA (*to Sir Andrew*) Pray sir, put your sword vp if you 1790 please.

SIR ANDREW Marry will I sir: and for that I promis'd you Ile be as good as my word. Hee will beare you easily, and raines well.

Sir Andrew and Viola put vp their swords

1. OFFICER This is the man, do thy Office.

2. OFFICER *Anthonio*, I arrest thee at the suit of Count *Orsino*.

ANTHONIO You do mistake me sir.

1. OFFICER
No sir, no iot: I know your fauour well:
Though now you haue no sea-cap on your head: 1800
(*To 2. Officer*) Take him away, he knowes I know him well.

ANTHONIO
I must obey. (*To Viola*) This comes with seeking you:
But there's no remedie, I shall answer it:
What will you do: now my necessitie
Makes me to aske you for my purse. It greeues mee
Much more, for what I cannot do for you,
Then what befals my selfe: you stand amaz'd,
But be of comfort.

2. OFFICER   Come sir away.

ANTHONIO (*to Viola*)
I must entreat of you some of that money.

VIOLA What money sir? 1810
For the fayre kindnesse you haue shew'd me heere,
And part being prompted by your present trouble,
Out of my leane and low ability
Ile lend you something: my hauing is not much,
Ile make diuision of my present with you:
Hold, (*offering money*) there's halfe my Coffer.

ANTHONIO   Will you deny me now,
Ist possible that my deserts to you
Can lacke perswasion. Do not tempt my misery,
Least that it make me so vnsound a man
As to vpbraid you with those kindnesses 1820
That I haue done for you.

VIOLA   I know of none,
Nor know I you by voyce, or any feature:
I hate ingratitude more in a man,
Then lying, vainnesse, babling drunkennesse,
Or any taint of vice, whose strong corruption
Inhabites our fraile blood.

ANTHONIO Oh heauens themselues.

2. OFFICER Come sir, I pray you go.

ANTHONIO

Let me speake a little. This youth that you see heere,
1830   I snatch'd one halfe out of the iawes of death,
Releeu'd him with such sanctitie of loue;
And to his image, which me thought did promise
Most venerable worth, did I deuotion.

I. OFFICER

What's that to vs, the time goes by: Away.

ANTHONIO

But oh, how vilde an idoll proues this God:
Thou hast *Sebastian* done good feature, shame.
In Nature, there's no blemish but the minde:
None can be call'd deform'd, but the vnkinde.
Vertue is beauty, but the beauteous euill
1840   Are empty trunkes, ore-flourish'd by the deuill.

I. OFFICER

The man growes mad, away with him: Come, come
    sir.

ANTHONIO Leade me on.   *Exit with Officers*

VIOLA (*aside*)

Me thinkes his words do from such passion flye
That he beleeues himselfe, so do not I:
Proue true imagination, oh proue true,
That I deere brother, be now tane for you.

SIR TOBY Come hither Knight, come hither *Fabian*: Weel
whisper ore a couplet or two of most sage sawes.

            They stand aside

VIOLA

He nam'd *Sebastian*: I my brother know
1850   Yet liuing in my glasse: euen such, and so
In fauour was my Brother, and he went
Still in this fashion, colour, ornament,
For him I imitate: Oh if it proue,
Tempests are kinde, and salt waues fresh in loue.

                                    Exit

SIR TOBY (*to Sir Andrew*) A very dishonest paltry boy, and
more a coward then a Hare, his dishonesty appeares,
in leauing his frend heere in necessity, and denying
him: and for his cowardship aske *Fabian*.

FABIAN A Coward, a most deuout Coward, religious in it.

1860   SIR ANDREW Slid Ile after him againe, and beate him.

SIR TOBY Do, cuffe him soundly, but neuer draw thy
sword.

SIR ANDREW And I do not.   *Exit*

FABIAN Come, let's see the euent.

SIR TOBY I dare lay any money, twill be nothing yet.

                                    Exeunt

Sc. 15
(4.1)
            Enter Sebastian and Clowne

CLOWNE Will you make me beleeue, that I am not sent
for you?

SEBASTIAN

Go too, go too, thou art a foolish fellow,
Let me be cleere of thee.

1870   CLOWNE Well held out yfaith: No, I do not know you,
nor I am not sent to you by my Lady, to bid you come
speake with her: nor your name is not Master *Cesario*,

nor this is not my nose neyther: Nothing that is so, is
so.

SEBASTIAN

I prethee vent thy folly some-where else,
Thou know'st not me.

CLOWNE Vent my folly: He has heard that word of some
great man, and now applyes it to a foole. Vent my
folly: I am affraid this great lubber the World will proue
a Cockney: I prethee now vngird thy strangenes, and   1880
tell me what I shall vent to my Lady? Shall I vent to
hir that thou art comming?

SEBASTIAN

I prethee foolish greeke depart from me,
There's money for thee, if you tarry longer,
I shall giue worse paiment.

CLOWNE By my troth thou hast an open hand: these
Wisemen that giue fooles money, get themselues a good
report, after foureteene yeares purchase.

            Enter Andrew, Toby, and Fabian

SIR ANDREW (*to Sebastian*) Now sir, haue I met you again:
(*striking him*) ther's for you.   1890

SEBASTIAN ⌜*striking Sir Andrew with his dagger*⌝

Why there's for thee, and there, and there,
Are all the people mad?

SIR TOBY (*to Sebastian, holding him back*) Hold sir, or Ile
throw your dagger ore the house.

CLOWNE This will I tell my Lady straight, I would not be
in some of your coats for two pence.   *Exit*

SIR TOBY Come on sir, hold.

SIR ANDREW Nay let him alone, Ile go another way to
worke with him: Ile haue an action of Battery against
him, if there be any law in Illyria: though I stroke him   1900
first, yet it's no matter for that.

SEBASTIAN Let go thy hand.

SIR TOBY Come sir, I will not let you go. Come my yong
souldier put vp your yron: you are well flesh'd: Come
on.

SEBASTIAN (*freeing him selfe*)

I will be free from thee. What wouldst y^u now?
If thou dar'st tempt me further, draw thy sword.

SIR TOBY What, what? Nay then I must haue an Ounce
or two of this malapert blood from you.

            Sir Toby and Sebastian draw their swords.
            Enter Oliuia

OLIUIA

Hold *Toby*, on thy life I charge thee hold.   1910

SIR TOBY Madam.

OLIUIA

Will it be euer thus? Vngracious wretch,
Fit for the Mountaines, and the barbarous Caues,
Where manners nere were preach'd: out of my sight.
Be not offended, deere *Cesario*:
(*To Sir Toby*) Rudesbey be gone.

            Exeunt Sir Toby, Sir Andrew, and Fabian
                        I prethee gentle friend,

Let thy fayre wisedome, not thy passion sway
In this vnciuill, and vniust extent
Against thy peace. Go with me to my house,

1920 And heare thou there how many fruitlesse prankes
This Ruffian hath botch'd vp, that thou thereby
Mayst smile at this: Thou shalt not choose but goe:
Do not denie, beshrew his soule for mee,
He started one poore heart of mine, in thee.

SEBASTIAN
What rellish is in this? How runs the streame?
Or I am mad, or else this is a dreame:
Let fancie still my sense in Lethe steepe,
If it be thus to dreame, still let me sleepe.

OLIUIA
Nay come I prethee, would thoud'st be rul'd by me.

SEBASTIAN
Madam, I will.

1930 OLIUIA   O say so, and so be.   *Exeunt*

Sc. 16   *Enter Maria carrying a gown and false beard, and*
(4.2)   *Clowne*

MARIA Nay, I prethee put on this gown, & this beard,
make him beleeue thou art sir *Topas* the Curate, doe it
quickly. Ile call sir *Toby* the whilst.   *Exit*

CLOWNE Well, Ile put it on, and I will dissemble my selfe
in't, and I would I were the first that euer dissembled
in such a gowne.
        He disguises him selfe
I am not tall enough to become the function well, nor
leane enough to bee thought a good Studient: but to
be said an honest man and a good houskeeper goes as
1940 fairely, as to say, a carefull man, & a great scholler.
The Competitors enter.
        Enter Toby and Maria

SIR TOBY Ioue blesse thee M. Parson.

CLOWNE *Bonos dies* sir *Toby*: for as the old hermit of *Prage*
that neuer saw pen and inke, very wittily sayd to a
Neece of King *Gorbodacke*, that that is, is: so I being M.
Parson, am M. Parson; for what is that, but that? and
is, but is?

SIR TOBY To him sir *Topas*.

CLOWNE What hoa, I say, Peace in this prison.

1950 SIR TOBY The knaue counterfets well: a good knaue.
        Maluolio within

MALUOLIO Who cals there?

CLOWNE Sir *Topas* the Curate, who comes to visit *Maluolio*
the Lunaticke.

MALUOLIO Sir *Topas*, sir *Topas*, good sir *Topas* goe to my
Ladie.

CLOWNE Out hyperbolicall fiend, how vexest thou this
man? Talkest thou nothing but of Ladies?

SIR TOBY Well said M. Parson.

MALUOLIO Sir *Topas*, neuer was man thus wronged, good
1960 sir *Topas* do not thinke I am mad: they haue layde mee
heere in hideous darknesse.

CLOWNE Fye, thou dishonest sathan: I call thee by the
most modest termes, for I am one of those gentle ones,
that will vse the diuell himselfe with curtesie: sayst
thou that house is darke?

MALUOLIO As hell sir *Topas*.

CLOWNE Why it hath bay Windowes transparant as
baricadoes, and the cleere stores toward the South

north, are as lustrous as Ebony: and yet complainest
thou of obstruction?   1970

MALUOLIO I am not mad sir *Topas*, I say to you this house
is darke.

CLOWNE Madman thou errest: I say there is no darknesse
but ignorance, in which thou art more puzel'd then
the Aegyptians in their fogge.

MALUOLIO I say this house is as darke as Ignorance, thogh
Ignorance were as darke as hell; and I say there was
neuer man thus abus'd, I am no more madde then you
are, make the triall of it in any constant question.

CLOWNE What is the opinion of *Pythagoras* concerning   1980
Wilde-fowle?

MALUOLIO That the soule of our grandam, might happily
inhabite a bird.

CLOWNE What thinkst thou of his opinion?

MALUOLIO I thinke nobly of the soule, and no way aproue
his opinion.

CLOWNE Fare thee well: remaine thou still in darkenesse,
thou shalt hold th'opinion of *Pythagoras*, ere I will
allow of thy wits, and feare to kill a Woodcocke, lest
thou dispossesse the soule of thy grandam. Fare thee   1990
well.

MALUOLIO Sir *Topas*, sir *Topas*.

SIR TOBY My most exquisite sir *Topas*.

CLOWNE Nay I am for all waters.

MARIA Thou mightst haue done this without thy berd
and gowne, he sees thee not.

SIR TOBY (*to Clowne*) To him in thine owne voyce, and
bring me word how thou findst him: I would we were
well ridde of this knauery. If he may bee conueniently
deliuer'd, I would he were, for I am now so farre in   2000
offence with my Niece, that I cannot pursue with any
safety this sport to the vppeshot. ⌜*To Maria*⌝ Come by
and by to my Chamber.   *Exit* ⌜*with Maria*⌝

CLOWNE (*sings*) Hey Robin, iolly Robin,
                Tell me how thy Lady does.

MALUOLIO Foole.

CLOWNE   My Lady is vnkind, *perdie*.

MALUOLIO Foole.

CLOWNE   Alas why is she so?

MALUOLIO Foole, I say.   2010

CLOWNE   She loues another.
        Who calles, ha?

MALUOLIO Good foole, as euer thou wilt deserue well at
my hand, helpe me to a Candle, and pen, inke, and
paper: as I am a Gentleman, I will liue to bee thankefull
to thee for't.

CLOWNE M. *Maluolio*?

MALUOLIO I good Foole.

CLOWNE Alas sir, how fell you besides your fiue witts?

MALUOLIO Foole, there was neuer man so notoriouslie   2020
abus'd: I am as well in my wits (foole) as thou art.

CLOWNE But as well: then you are mad indeede, if you
be no better in your wits then a foole.

MALUOLIO They haue heere propertied me: keepe mee in
darkenesse, send Ministers to me, Asses, and doe all
they can to face me out of my wits.

CLOWNE Aduise you what you say: the Minister is heere.

(*As Sir Topas*) Maluolio, Maluolio, thy wittes the heauens restore: endeauour thy selfe to sleepe, and leaue thy vaine bibble babble.

2030 MALUOLIO Sir *Topas*.

CLOWNE (*as Sir Topas*) Maintaine no words with him good fellow. (*As him selfe*) Who I sir, not I sir. God buy you good sir Topas: (*As Sir Topas*) Marry Amen. (*As him selfe*) I will sir, I will.

MALUOLIO Foole, foole, foole I say.

CLOWNE Alas sir be patient. What say you sir, I am shent for speaking to you.

MALUOLIO Good foole, helpe me to some light, and some
2040 paper, I tell thee I am as well in my wittes, as any man in Illyria.

CLOWNE Well-a-day, that you were sir.

MALUOLIO By this hand I am: good foole, some inke, paper, and light: and conuey what I will set downe to my Lady: it shall aduantage thee more, then euer the bearing of Letter did.

CLOWNE I will help you too't. But tel me true, are you not mad indeed, or do you but counterfeit.

MALUOLIO Beleeue me I am not, I tell thee true.

2050 CLOWNE Nay, Ile nere beleeue a madman till I see his brains. I will fetch you light, and paper, and inke.

MALUOLIO Foole, Ile requite it in the highest degree: I prethee be gone.

CLOWNE (*sings*) I am gone sir,
　　　　And anon sir,
　　　　　　Ile be with you againe:
　　　　In a trice,
　　　　Like to the old vice,
　　　　　　Your neede to sustaine.
2060 　　　　Who with dagger of lath,
　　　　In his rage and his wrath,
　　　　　　Cries ah ha, to the diuell:
　　　　Like a mad lad,
　　　　Paire thy nayles dad,
　　　　　　Adieu good man diuell.　　　　*Exit*

Sc. 17 　　　　*Enter Sebastian*
(4.3) SEBASTIAN

This is the ayre, that is the glorious Sunne,
This pearle she gaue me, I do feel't, and see't,
And though tis wonder that enwraps me thus,
Yet 'tis not madnesse. Where's *Anthonio* then,
2070 I could not finde him at the Elephant,
Yet there he was, and there I found this credite,
That he did range the towne to seeke me out,
His councell now might do me golden seruice,
For though my soule disputes well with my sence,
That this may be some error, but no madnesse,
Yet doth this accident and flood of Fortune,
So farre exceed all instance, all discourse,
That I am readie to distrust mine eyes,
And wrangle with my reason that perswades me
2080 To any other trust, but that I am mad,
Or else the Ladies mad; yet if 'twere so,
She could not sway her house, command her
　　followers,

Take, and giue backe affayres, and their dispatch,
With such a smooth, discreet, and stable bearing
As I perceiue she do's: there's something in't
That is deceiueable. But heere the Lady comes.
　　　　Enter Oliuia, and Priest

OLIUIA

Blame not this haste of mine: if you meane well
Now go with me, and with this holy man
Into the Chantry by: there before him,
And vnderneath that consecrated roofe,　　　　2090
Plight me the full assurance of your faith,
That my most iealious, and too doubtfull soule
May liue at peace. He shall conceale it,
Whiles you are willing it shall come to note,
What time we will our celebration keepe
According to my birth, what do you say?

SEBASTIAN

Ile follow this good man, and go with you,
And hauing sworne truth, euer will be true.

OLIUIA

Then lead the way good father, & heauens so shine,
That they may fairely note this acte of mine.　　*Exeunt*　2100

　　　　Enter Clowne and Fabian　　　　Sc. 18

FABIAN Now as thou lou'st me, let me see his Letter.　(5.1)

CLOWNE Good M. *Fabian*, grant me another request.

FABIAN Any thing.

CLOWNE Do not desire to see this Letter.

FABIAN This is to giue a dogge, and in recompence desire my dogge againe.

　　　　Enter Duke, Viola as Cesario, Curio, and Lords

ORSINO

Belong you to the Lady *Oliuia*, friends?

CLOWNE I sir, we are some of her trappings.

ORSINO

I know thee well: how doest thou my good Fellow?

CLOWNE Truely sir, the better for my foes, and the worse　2110
for my friends.

ORSINO

Iust the contrary: the better for thy friends.

CLOWNE No sir, the worse.

ORSINO How can that be?

CLOWNE Marry sir, they praise me, and make an asse of me, now my foes tell me plainly, I am an Asse: so that by my foes sir, I profit in the knowledge of my selfe, and by my friends I am abused: so that conclusions to be as kisses, if your foure negatiues make your two affirmatiues, why then the worse for my friends, and　2120
the better for my foes.

ORSINO Why this is excellent.

CLOWNE By my troth sir, no: though it please you to be one of my friends.

ORSINO (*giuing money*)

Thou shalt not be the worse for me, there's gold.

CLOWNE But that it would be double dealing sir, I would you could make it another.

ORSINO O you giue me ill counsell.

CLOWNE Put your grace in your pocket sir, for this once, and let your flesh and blood obey it.　　　　2130

ORSINO Well, I will be so much a sinner to be a double
    dealer: (*giuing money*) there's another.

CLOWNE *Primo, secundo, tertio,* is a good play, and the
    olde saying is, the third payes for all: the triplex sir, is
    a good tripping measure, or the belles of S. *Bennet* sir,
    may put you in minde, one, two, three.

ORSINO You can foole no more money out of mee at this
    throw: if you will let your Lady know I am here to
    speak with her, and bring her along with you, it may
2140   awake my bounty further.

CLOWNE Marry sir, lullaby to your bountie till I come
    agen. I go sir, but I would not haue you to thinke,
    that my desire of hauing is the sinne of couetousnesse:
    but as you say sir, let your bounty take a nappe, I will
    awake it anon.   *Exit*
        Enter Anthonio and Officers

VIOLA
    Here comes the man sir, that did rescue mee.

ORSINO
    That face of his I do remember well,
    Yet when I saw it last, it was besmear'd
    As blacke as Vulcan, in the smoake of warre:
2150   A bawbling Vessell was he Captaine of,
    For shallow draught and bulke vnprizable,
    With which such scathfull grapple did he make,
    With the most noble bottome of our Fleete,
    That very enuy, and the tongue of losse
    Cride fame and honor on him: What's the matter?

I. OFFICER
    Orsino, this is that *Anthonio*
    That tooke the *Phœnix,* and her fraught from *Candy,*
    And this is he that did the *Tiger* boord,
    When your yong Nephew *Titus* lost his legge;
2160   Heere in the streets, desperate of shame and state,
    In priuate brabble did we apprehend him.

VIOLA
    He did me kindnesse sir, drew on my side,
    But in conclusion put strange speech vpon me,
    I know not what 'twas, but distraction.

ORSINO (*to Anthonio*)
    Notable Pyrate, thou salt-water Theefe,
    What foolish boldnesse brought thee to their mercies,
    Whom thou in termes so bloudie, and so deere
    Hast made thine enemies?

ANTHONIO   *Orsino:* Noble sir,
    Be pleas'd that I shake off these names you giue mee:
2170   *Anthonio* neuer yet was Theefe, or Pyrate,
    Though I confesse, on base and ground enough
    Orsino's enemie. A witchcraft drew me hither:
    That most ingratefull boy there by your side,
    From the rude seas enrag'd and foamy mouth
    Did I redeeme: a wracke past hope he was:
    His life I gaue him, and did thereto adde
    My loue without retention, or restraint,
    All his in dedication. For his sake,
    Did I expose my selfe (pure for his loue)
2180   Into the danger of this aduerse Towne,
    Drew to defend him, when he was beset:
    Where being apprehended, his false cunning

(Not meaning to partake with me in danger)
Taught him to face me out of his acquaintance,
And grew a twentie yeeres remoued thing
While one would winke: denide me mine owne purse,
Which I had recommended to his vse,
Not halfe an houre before.

VIOLA How can this be?

ORSINO When came he to this Towne?   2190

ANTHONIO
    To day my Lord: and for three months before,
    No *intrim,* not a minutes vacancie,
    Both day and night did we keepe companie.
        Enter Oliuia and attendants

ORSINO
    Heere comes the Countesse, now heauen walkes on
        earth:
    But for thee fellow, fellow thy words are madnesse,
    Three monthes this youth hath tended vpon mee,
    But more of that anon. Take him aside.

OLIUIA
    What would my Lord, but that he may not haue,
    Wherein *Oliuia* may seeme seruiceable?
    Cesario, you do not keepe promise with me.   2200

VIOLA Madam:

ORSINO Gracious *Oliuia.*

OLIUIA
    What do you say *Cesario?* Good my Lord.

VIOLA
    My Lord would speake, my dutie hushes me.

OLIUIA
    If it be ought to the old tune my Lord,
    It is as fat and fulsome to mine eare
    As howling after Musicke.

ORSINO Still so cruell?

OLIUIA Still so constant Lord.

ORSINO
    What to peruersenesse? you vnciuill Ladie   2210
    To whose ingrate, and vnauspicious Altars
    My soule the faithfull'st offrings hath breath'd out
    That ere deuotion tender'd. What shall I do?

OLIUIA
    Euen what it please my Lord, that shal becom him.

ORSINO
    Why should I not, (had I the heart to do it)
    Like to th'Egyptian theefe, at point of death
    Kill what I loue: (a sauage iealousie,
    That sometime sauours nobly) but heare me this:
    Since you to non-regardance cast my faith,
    And that I partly know the instrument   2220
    That screwes me from my true place in your fauour:
    Liue you the Marble-brested Tirant still.
    But this your Minion, whom I know you loue,
    And whom, by heauen I sweare, I tender deerely,
    Him will I teare out of that cruell eye,
    Where he sits crowned in his masters spight.
    (*To Viola*) Come boy with me, my thoughts are ripe in
        mischiefe:
    Ile sacrifice the Lambe that I do loue,
    To spight a Rauens heart within a Doue.

VIOLA

2230 And I most iocund, apt, and willinglie,
To do you rest, a thousand deaths would dye.

OLIUIA

Where goes *Cesario*?

VIOLA   After him I loue,
More then I loue these eyes, more then my life,
More by all mores, then ere I shall loue wife.
If I do feigne, you witnesses aboue
Punish my life, for tainting of my loue.

OLIUIA

Aye me detested, how am I beguil'd?

VIOLA

Who does beguile you? who does do you wrong?

OLIUIA

Hast thou forgot thy selfe? Is it so long?
Call forth the holy Father.   *Exit an attendant*

2240 ORSINO (*to Viola*)   Come, away.

OLIUIA

Whether my Lord? *Cesario*, Husband, stay.

ORSINO

Husband?

OLIUIA   I Husband. Can he that deny?

ORSINO (*to Viola*)

Her husband, sirrah?

VIOLA   No my Lord, not I.

OLIUIA

Alas, it is the basenesse of thy feare,
That makes thee strangle thy propriety:
Feare not *Cesario*, take thy fortunes vp,
Be that thou know'st thou art, and then thou art
As great as that thou fear'st.
          Enter Priest
                    O welcome Father:
Father, I charge thee by thy reuerence
2250 Heere to vnfold, though lately we intended
To keepe in darkenesse, what occasion now
Reueales before 'tis ripe: what thou dost know
Hath newly past, betweene this youth, and me.

PRIEST

A Contract of eternall bond of loue,
Confirm'd by mutuall ioynder of your hands,
Attested by the holy close of lippes,
Strengthned by enterchangement of your rings,
And all the Ceremonie of this compact
Seal'd in my function, by my testimony:
2260 Since when, my watch hath told me, toward my graue
I haue trauail'd but two houres.

ORSINO (*to Viola*)

O thou dissembling Cub: what wilt thou be
When time hath sow'd a grizzle on thy case?
Or will not else thy craft so quickely grow,
That thine owne trip shall be thine ouerthrow:
Farewell, and take her, but direct thy feete,
Where thou, and I (henceforth) may neuer meet.

VIOLA

My Lord, I do protest.

OLIUIA   O do not sweare,
Hold little faith, though thou hast too much feare.

Enter Sir Andrew

SIR ANDREW For the loue of God a Surgeon, send one   2270
presently to sir *Toby*.

OLIUIA What's the matter?

SIR ANDREW H'as broke my head a-crosse, and has giuen
Sir *Toby* a bloody Coxcombe too: for the loue of God
your helpe, I had rather then forty pound I were at
home.

OLIUIA Who has done this sir *Andrew*?

SIR ANDREW The Counts Gentleman, one *Cesario*: we tooke
him for a Coward, but hee's the verie diuell, incardinate.

ORSINO My Gentleman *Cesario*?   2280

SIR ANDREW Odd's lifelings heere he is: (*to Viola*) you
broke my head for nothing, and that that I did, I was
set on to do't by sir *Toby*.

VIOLA

Why do you speake to me, I neuer hurt you:
You drew your sword vpon me without cause,
But I bespake you faire, and hurt you not.
          Enter Toby and Clowne

SIR ANDREW If a bloody coxcombe be a hurt, you haue
hurt me: I thinke you set nothing by a bloody
Coxecombe. Heere comes sir *Toby* halting, you shall
heare more: but if he had not beene in drinke, hee   2290
would haue tickel'd you other gates then he did.

ORSINO (*to Sir Toby*)

How now Gentleman? how ist with you?

SIR TOBY That's all one, has hurt me, and there's th'end
on't: (*To Clowne*) Sot, didst see Dicke Surgeon, sot?

CLOWNE O he's drunke sir *Toby* an houre agone: his eyes
were set at eight i'th morning.

SIR TOBY Then he's a Rogue, and a passy measures pauyn:
I hate a drunken rogue.

OLIUIA

Away with him? Who hath made this hauocke with
them?

SIR ANDREW Ile helpe you sir *Toby*, because we'll be drest   2300
together.

SIR TOBY Will you helpe, an Asse-head, and a coxcombe,
& a knaue: a thin fac'd knaue, a gull?

OLIUIA

Get him to bed, and let his hurt be look'd too.
          Exeunt Sir Toby, Sir Andrew, Clowne, and Fabian
          Enter Sebastian

SEBASTIAN (*to Oliuia*)

I am sorry Madam I haue hurt your kinsman:
But had it beene the brother of my blood,
I must haue done no lesse with wit and safety.
You throw a strange regard vpon me, and by that
I do perceiue it hath offended you:
Pardon me (sweet one) euen for the vowes   2310
We made each other, but so late ago.

ORSINO

One face, one voice, one habit, and two persons,
A naturall Perspectiue, that is, and is not.

SEBASTIAN

Anthonio: O my deere *Anthonio*,
How haue the houres rack'd, and tortur'd me,
Since I haue lost thee?

ANTHONIO *Sebastian* are you?

SEBASTIAN Fear'st thou that *Anthonio*?

ANTHONIO

    How haue you made diuision of your selfe,

2320   An apple cleft in two, is not more twin

    Then these two creatures. Which is *Sebastian*?

OLIUIA Most wonderfull.

SEBASTIAN *(seeing Viola)*

    Do I stand there? I neuer had a brother:

    Nor can there be that Deity in my nature

    Of heere, and euery where. I had a sister,

    Whom the blinde waues and surges haue deuour'd:

    Of charity, what kinne are you to me?

    What Countreyman? What name? What Parentage?

VIOLA

    Of *Messaline*: *Sebastian* was my Father,

2330   Such a *Sebastian* was my brother too:

    So went he suited to his watery tombe:

    If spirits can assume both forme and suite,

    You come to fright vs.

SEBASTIAN   A spirit I am indeed,

    But am in that dimension grossely clad,

    Which from the wombe I did participate.

    Were you a woman, as the rest goes euen,

    I should my teares let fall vpon your cheeke,

    And say, thrice welcome drowned *Viola*.

VIOLA

    My father had a moale vpon his brow.

2340 SEBASTIAN And so had mine.

VIOLA

    And dide that day when *Viola* from her birth

    Had numbred thirteene yeares.

SEBASTIAN

    O that record is liuely in my soule,

    He finished indeed his mortall acte

    That day that made my sister thirteene yeares.

VIOLA

    If nothing lets to make vs happie both,

    But this my masculine vsurp'd attyre:

    Do not embrace me, till each circumstance,

    Of place, time, fortune, do co-here and iumpe

2350   That I am *Viola*, which to confirme,

    Ile bring you to a Captaine in this Towne,

    Where lye my maiden weeds: by whose gentle helpe,

    I was preseru'd to serue this Noble Count:

    All the occurrence of my fortune since

    Hath beene betweene this Lady, and this Lord.

SEBASTIAN *(to Oliuia)*

    So comes it Lady, you haue beene mistooke:

    But Nature to her bias drew in that.

    You would haue bin contracted to a Maid,

    Nor are you therein (by my life) deceiu'd,

2360   You are betroth'd both to a maid and man.

ORSINO *(to Oliuia)*

    Be not amaz'd, right noble is his blood:

    If this be so, as yet the glasse seemes true,

    I shall haue share in this most happy wracke,

    (To Viola) Boy, thou hast saide to me a thousand times,

    Thou neuer should'st loue woman like to me.

VIOLA

    And all those sayings, will I ouer sweare,

    And all those swearings keepe as true in soule,

    As doth that Orbed Continent, the fire,

    That seuers day from night.

ORSINO   Giue me thy hand,

    And let me see thee in thy womans weedes.   2370

VIOLA

    The Captaine that did bring me first on shore

    Hath my Maides garments: he vpon some Action

    Is now in durance, at *Maluolio's* suite,

    A Gentleman, and follower of my Ladies.

OLIUIA

    He shall inlarge him: fetch *Maluolio* hither,

    And yet alas, now I remember me,

    They say poore Gentleman, he's much distract.

        Enter Clowne with a Letter, and Fabian

    A most extracting frensie of mine owne

    From my remembrance, clearly banisht his.

    How does he sirrah?   2380

CLOWNE Truely Madam, he holds *Belzebub* at the staues end as well as a man in his case may do: has heere writ a letter to you, I should haue giuen't you to day morning. But as a madmans Epistles are no Gospels, so it skilles not much when they are deliuer'd.

OLIUIA Open't, and read it.

CLOWNE Looke then to be well edified, when the Foole deliuers the Madman. *(Reads)* By the Lord Madam.

OLIUIA How now, art thou mad?

CLOWNE No Madam, I do but reade madnesse: and your   2390 Ladyship will haue it as it ought to bee, you must allow *Vox*.

OLIUIA Prethee reade i'thy right wits.

CLOWNE So I do Madona: but to reade his right wits, is to reade thus: therefore, perpend my Princesse, and giue eare.

OLIUIA *(to Fabian)* Read it you, sirrah.

        Clowne giues the Letter to Fabian

FABIAN *(Reads)* By the Lord Madam, you wrong me, and the world shall know it: Though you haue put mee into darkenesse, and giuen your drunken Cosine rule   2400 ouer me, yet haue I the benefit of my senses as well as your Ladieship. I haue your owne letter, that induced mee to the semblance I put on; with the which I doubt not, but to do my selfe much right, or you much shame: thinke of me as you please. I leaue my duty a little vnthought of, and speake out of my iniury. *The madly vs'd Maluolio.*

OLIUIA Did he write this?

CLOWNE I Madame.

ORSINO

    This sauours not much of distraction.   2410

OLIUIA

    See him deliuer'd *Fabian*, bring him hither:

    My Lord, so please you, these things further thought on,

    To thinke me as well a sister, as a wife,

    One day shall crowne th'alliance on't, so please you,

    Heere at my house, and at my proper cost.

ORSINO

Madam, I am most apt t'embrace your offer:

(*To Viola*) Your Master quits you: and for your seruice

done him,

So much against the mettle of your sex,

So farre beneath your soft and tender breeding,

2420 And since you call'd me Master, for so long:

Heere is my hand, you shall from this time bee

Your Masters Mistris.

OLIUIA (*to Viola*)   A sister, you are she.

Enter Maluolio

ORSINO

Is this the Madman?

OLIUIA   I my Lord, this same:

How now *Maluolio*?

MALUOLIO   Madam, you haue done me wrong,

Notorious wrong.

OLIUIA   Haue I *Maluolio*? No.

MALUOLIO (*shewing a Letter*)

Lady you haue, pray you peruse that Letter.

You must not now denie it is your hand,

Write from it if you can, in hand, or phrase,

Or say, tis not your seale, not your inuention:

2430 You can say none of this. Well, grant it then,

And tell me in the modestie of honor,

Why you haue giuen me such cleare lights of fauour,

Bad me come smiling, and crosse-garter'd to you,

To put on yellow stockings, and to frowne

Vpon sir *Toby*, and the lighter people:

And acting this in an obedient hope,

Why haue you suffer'd me to be imprison'd,

Kept in a darke house, visited by the Priest,

And made the most notorious gecke and gull,

2440 That ere inuention plaid on? Tell me why?

OLIUIA

Alas *Maluolio*, this is not my writing,

Though I confesse much like the Charracter:

But out of question, tis *Marias* hand.

And now I do bethinke me, it was shee

First told me thou wast mad; then cam'st in smiling,

And in such formes, which heere were presuppos'd

Vpon thee in the Letter: prethee be content,

This practice hath most shrewdly past vpon thee:

But when we know the grounds, and authors of it,

2450 Thou shalt be both the Plaintiffe and the Iudge

Of thine owne cause.

FABIAN   Good Madam heare me speake,

And let no quarrell, nor no braule to come,

Taint the condition of this present houre,

Which I haue wondred at. In hope it shall not,

Most freely I confesse my selfe, and *Toby*

Set this deuice against *Maluolio* heere,

Vpon some stubborne and vncourteous parts

We had conceiu'd against him. *Maria* writ

The Letter, at sir *Tobyes* great importance,

In recompence whereof, he hath married her: 2460

How with a sportfull malice it was follow'd,

May rather plucke on laughter then reuenge,

If that the iniuries be iustly weigh'd,

That haue on both sides past.

OLIUIA (*to Maluolio*)

Alas poore Foole, how haue they baffel'd thee?

CLOWNE Why some are borne great, some atchieue

greatnesse, and some haue greatnesse throwne vpon

them. I was one sir, in this Enterlude, one sir *Topas* sir,

but that's all one: By the Lord Foole, I am not mad:

but do you remember, Madam, why laugh you at such   2470

a barren rascall, and you smile not he's gag'd: and

thus the whirlegigge of time, brings in his reuenges.

MALUOLIO Ile be reueng'd on the whole packe of you?

Exit

OLIUIA

He hath bene most notoriously abus'd.

ORSINO

Pursue him, and entreate him to a peace:

He hath not told vs of the Captaine yet,

⌈*Exit one or more*⌉

When that is knowne, and golden time conuents

A solemne Combination shall be made

Of our deere soules. Meane time sweet sister,

We will not part from hence. *Cesario* come   2480

(For so you shall be while you are a man:)

But when in other habites you are seene,

Orsino's Mistris, and his fancies Queene.

Exeunt all but Clowne

Clowne sings

When that I was and a little tine boy,

  With hey, ho, the winde and the raine:

A foolish thing was but a toy,

  For the raine it raineth euery day.

But when I came to mans estate,

  With hey, ho, the winde and the raine:

Gainst Knaues and Theeues men shut their gate,   2490

  For the raine it raineth euery day.

But when I came alas to wiue,

  With hey, ho, the winde and the raine:

By swaggering could I neuer thriue,

  For the raine it raineth euery day.

But when I came vnto my beds,

  With hey, ho, the winde and the raine:

With tospottes still had drunken heades,

  For the raine it raineth euery day.

A great while ago the world begon,   2500

  With hey ho, the winde and the raine:

But that's all one, our Play is done,

  And wee'l striue to please you euery day.   *Exit*

FINIS

TROYLUS AND CRESSIDA

Troylus and Cressida, first heard of in a Stationers' Register entry of 7 February 1603, was probably written within the previous eighteen months. This entry did not result in publication; the play was re-entered on 28 January 1609, and a quarto appeared during that year. The version printed in the 1623 Folio adds a Prologue, and has many variations in dialogue. It includes the epilogue spoken by Pandarus (which we print as an Additional Passage), but certain features of the text suggest that it does so by accident, and that the epilogue had been marked for omission. Our text is based in substance on the Folio in the belief that this represents the play in its later, revised form.

The story of the siege of Troy was the main subject of one of the greatest surviving works of classical literature, Homer's *Iliad*; probably Shakespeare read George Chapman's 1598 translation of Books 1-2 and 7-11. It also figures prominently in Virgil's *Aeneid* and Ovid's *Metamorphoses*, both of which Shakespeare knew well. The war between Greece and Troy had been provoked by the abduction of the Grecian Helen (better, if confusingly, known as Helen of Troy) by the Trojan hero Paris, son of King Priam. Shakespeare's play opens when the Greek forces, led by Menelaus' brother Agamemnon, have already been besieging Troy for seven years. Shakespeare concentrates on the opposition between the Greek hero Achilles and the Trojan Hector. In the Folio, *Troylus and Cressida* is printed among the tragedies; if there is a tragic hero, it is Hector.

Shakespeare also shows how the war caused by one love affair destroys another. The stories of the love between the Trojan Troilus and the Grecian Cressida, encouraged by her uncle Pandarus, and of Cressida's desertion of Troilus for the Greek Diomedes, are medieval additions to the heroic narrative. Chaucer's long poem *Troilus and Criseyde* was already a classic, and Shakespeare would also have known Robert Henryson's continuation, *The Testament of Cresseid*, in which Cressida, deserted by Diomedes, dwindles into a leprous beggar.

Troylus and Cressida is a demanding play, Shakespeare's third longest, highly philosophical in tone and with an exceptionally learned vocabulary. Possibly (as has often been conjectured) he wrote it for private performance; the 1603 Stationers' Register entry says it had been acted by the King's Men, and the original title-page of the 1609 quarto repeats this claim, but while the edition was being printed this title-page was replaced by one that does not mention performance, and an epistle was added claiming that it was 'a new play, neuer stal'd with the Stage, neuer clapper-clawd with the palmes of the vulger'. An adaptation by John Dryden of 1679 was successfully acted from time to time for half a century, but the first verified performance of Shakespeare's play was in Germany in 1898, and that was heavily adapted. *Troylus and Cressida* has come into its own in the twentieth century, when its deflation of heroes, its radical questioning of human values (especially in relation to love and war), and its remorseless examination of the frailty of human aspirations in the face of the destructive powers of time have seemed particularly apposite to modern intellectual and ethical preoccupations.

Our edition preserves the incidental features of the 1609 quarto (printed from Shakespeare's foul papers) but accepts the Folio's substantive variants.

THE NAMES OF THE ACTORS

PROLOGUE

Troyans

PRIAM, King of Troy

HECTOR
DEIPHOBUS
HELENUS, a priest
PARIS   } his sonnes
TROYLUS
MARGARETON, a bastard

CASSANDRA, Priams daughter, a prophetesse

ANDROMACHE, wife of Hector

ÆNEAS   } Captaines
ANTENOR

PANDARUS, a Lord

CRESSID, his neece

CALCAS, her father, who has ioined the Greekes

HELLEN, wife of Menelaus, now liuing with Paris

Cressids MAN

Seruants of Troylus, Musicians, Souldiers, Attendants

Greekes

AGAMEMNON, Generall

MENELAUS, his brother

NESTOR

VLISSES

ACHILLES

PATROCLUS, his companion

DIOMED

AIAX

THERSITES

MYRMIDONS, souldiers of Achilles

Seruants of Diomed, Souldiers

808

Troylus and Cressida

Prologue   *Enter the Prologue arm'd*

PROLOGUE

In Troy there lyes the Scene: From Iles of Greece
The Princes Orgillous, their high blood chaf'd
Haue to the Port of Athens sent their shippes
Fraught with the ministers and instruments
Of cruell Warre: Sixty and nine that wore
Their Crownets Regall, from th'Athenian bay
Put forth toward Phrygia, and their vow is made
To ransacke Troy, within whose strong emures
The rauish'd Helen, Menelaus Queene,
10 *With wanton Paris sleepes, and that's the Quarrell.*
To Tenedos they come,
And the deepe-drawing Barkes do there disgorge
Their warlike frautage: now on Dardan Plaines
The fresh and yet vnbruised Greekes do pitch
Their braue Pauillions. Priams six-gated City,
Dardan and Timbria, Helias, Chetas, Troien,
And Antenorides with massie Staples
And corresponsiue and fulfilling Bolts
Sparre vp the Sonnes of Troy.
20 *Now Expectation tickling skittish spirits,*
On one and other side, Troian and Greeke,
Sets all on hazard. And hither am I come,
A Prologue arm'd, but not in confidence
Of Authors pen, or Actors voyce; but suited
In like conditions, as our Argument;
To tell you (faire Beholders) that our Play
Leapes ore the vaunt and firstlings of those broyles,
Beginning in the middle: starting thence away,
To what may be digested in a Play:
30 *Like, or finde fault, do as your pleasures are,*
Now good, or bad, 'tis but the chance of Warre.   *Exit*

Sc. 1   *Enter Pandarus, and Troylus arm'd*
(1.1)   TROYLUS

Call heere my varlet, Ile vnarme againe,
Why should I warre without the walls of Troy:
That finde such cruell battell here within,
Each Troyan that is maister of his heart,
Let him to field Troylus alas hath none.

PANDARUS   Will this geere nere be mended?

TROYLUS

The Greeks are strong and skilfull to their strength
Fierce to their skill, and to their fiercenesse valiant,
40 But I am weaker then a womans teare;
Tamer then sleepe; fonder then ignorance,
Lesse valiant then the Virgin in the night,
And skillesse as vnpractiz'd infancy.

PANDARUS   Well, I haue told you enough of this; for my
part ile not meddle nor make no farther; hee that will
haue a cake out of the wheate must tarry the grynding.

TROYLUS   Haue I not tarried?

PANDARUS   I the grinding; but you must tarry the boulting.

TROYLUS   Haue I not tarried?

PANDARUS   I the boulting; but you must tarry the   50
leauening.

TROYLUS   Still haue I tarried.

PANDARUS   I, to the leauening, but heares yet in the word
hereafter, the kneading, the making of the cake, the
heating the ouen, and the baking, nay you must stay
the cooling too, or yea may chance burne your lippes.

TROYLUS

Pacience her selfe, what Godesse ere she be,
Doth lesser blench at suffrance then I do:
At Priams royall table do I sit
And when faire Cressid comes into my thoughts,   60
So traitor when she comes: when is she thence.

PANDARUS   Well shee lookt yesternight fairer then euer I
saw her looke, or any woman els.

TROYLUS

I was about to tell thee when my heart,
As wedged with a sigh would riue in twaine,
Least Hector or my father should perceiue mee:
I haue (as when the Sunne doth light a sconce)
Buried this sigh in wrincle of a smyle,
But sorrow that is coucht in seeming gladnesse,
Is like that mirth fate turnes to suddaine sadnesse.   70

PANDARUS   And her haire were not some-what darker then
Hellens, well go to, there were no more comparison
betweene the women! but for my part she is my
kinswoman, I would not as they tearme it praise her,
but I would som-body had heard her talke yester-day
as I did, I will not dispraise your sister Cassandræs wit,
but—

TROYLUS

Oh Pandarus I tell thee Pandarus,
When I do tell thee there my hopes lie drown'd
Reply not in how many fadomes deepe,   80
They lie indrench'd, I tell thee I am madde
In Cressids loue: thou answerst she is faire,
Powrest in the open vlcer of my heart,
Her eyes, her haire her cheeke, her gate, her voice;
Handlest in thy discourse O that her hand
In whose comparison all whites are ynke
Writing their owne reproch; to whose soft seisure,
The cignets downe is harsh, and spirit of sence
Hard as the palme of plow-man; this thou telst me,
As true thou telst me, when I say I loue her,   90
But saying thus in steed of oyle and balme,
Thou layst in euery gash that loue hath giuen mee
The knife that made it.

PANDARUS   I speake no more then truth.

TROYLUS   Thou dost not speake so much.

PANDARUS   Faith Ile not meddle in it, let her bee as shee
is, if she bee faire tis the better for her, and shee bee
not, she has the mends in her owne hands.

TROYLUS   Good Pandarus, how now Pandarus?

100 PANDARUS I haue had my labour for my trauell, ill thought
on of her, and ill thought on of you, gon betweene and
betweene, but small thanks for my labour.

TROYLUS
What art thou angry *Pandarus*? what with me?

PANDARUS Because shee's kin to me therefore shee's not
so faire as *Hellen*, and she were not kin to me, she
would be as faire a Friday as *Hellen*, is on Sunday, but
what care I? I care not and shee were a blackeamore,
tis all one to mee.

TROYLUS Say I she is not faire?

110 PANDARUS I do not care whether you do or no, she's a
foole to stay behinde her father let her to the Greekes,
and so Ile tell her the next time I see her for my part
Ile meddle nor make no more ith'matter.

TROYLUS *Pandarus*.

PANDARUS Not I.

TROYLUS Sweete *Pandarus*.

PANDARUS Pray you speake no more to mee I will leaue
all as I found it and there an end.   *Exit*

Sound alarum

TROYLUS
Peace you vngracious clamors, peace rude sounds,
120 Fooles on both sides, *Hellen* must needes be faire,
When with your bloud you daylie paint her thus,
I cannot fight vpon this argument:
It is too staru'd a subiect for my sword,
But *Pandarus*: O gods! how do you plague me
I cannot come to *Cressid* but by *Pandar*,
And he's as teachy to be wood to woe,
As she is stubborne, chast, against all suite.
Tell me *Apollo* for thy *Daphnes* loue
What *Cressid* is, what *Pandar*, and what we:
130 Her bed is *India* there she lies, a pearle,
Betweene our Ilium, and where shee recides
Let it be cald the wild and wandring flood:
Our selfe the Marchant, and this sayling *Pandar*,
Our doubtfull hope, our conuoy and our barke.

Alarum   Enter Æneas

ÆNEAS
How now prince *Troylus*, wherefore not a field.

TROYLUS
Because not there; this womans answer sorts,
For womanish it is to be from thence.
What newes *Æneas* from the field to day?

ÆNEAS
That *Paris* is returned home and hurt.

TROYLUS
By whom *Æneas*?

140 ÆNEAS   *Troylus* by *Menelaus*.

TROYLUS
Let *Paris* bleed tis but a scar to scorne,
Paris is gor'd with *Menelaus* horne.

Alarum

ÆNEAS
Harke what good sport is out of towne to day.

TROYLUS
Better at home, if would I might were may:
But to the sport abrode are you bound thither?

ÆNEAS
In all swift hast.

TROYLUS   Come goe wee then togither.   *Exeunt*

Enter ⌐aboue⌐ Cressid and her man   Sc. 2
                                                              (1.2)
CRESSID
Who were those went by?

MAN   Queene *Hecuba*, and *Hellen*.

CRESSID
And whether goe they?

MAN   Vp to the Easterne tower,
Whose hight commands as subiect all the vaile,
To see the battell: *Hector* whose pacience,   150
Is as a vertue fixt, to day was mou'd:
Hee chid *Andromache* and strooke his armorer,
And like as there were husbandry in warre
Before the Sunne rose, hee was harnest lyte,
And to the field goes he; where euery flower
Did as a Prophet weepe what it foresawe,
In *Hectors* wrath.

CRESSID   What was his cause of anger.

MAN
The noise goes this, there is amonge the Greekes,
A Lord of Troian bloud, Nephew to *Hector*,
They call him *Aiax*.

CRESSID   Good; and what of him.   160

MAN
They say hee is a very man *per se*
And stands alone.

CRESSID   So do all men
Vnlesse they are dronke, sicke, or haue no legges.

MAN This man Lady, hath rob'd many beasts of their
particular additions, hee is as valiant as the Lyon,
churlish as the Beare, slowe as the Elephant: a man
into whome nature hath so crowded humors, that his
valour is crusht into folly, his folly farced with
discretion: there is no man hath a vertue, that he hath
not a glimpse of, nor any mã an attaint, but he carries   170
some staine of it. Hee is melancholy without cause and
merry against the haire, hee hath the ioynts of euery
thing, but euery thing so out of ioynt, that hee is a
gowtie *Briareus*, many hands, & no vse: or purblinde
Argus, al eyes, and no sight.

CRESSID But how should this man that makes me smile,
make *Hector* angry.

MAN They say hee yesterday cop't *Hector* in the battell
and stroke him downe, the disdaine and shame whereof
hath euer since kept *Hector* fasting and waking.   180

CRESSID Who comes here.

MAN Maddam your vncle *Pandarus*.

⌐*Enter Pandarus aboue*⌐

CRESSID *Hectors* a gallant man.

MAN As may be in the world Lady.

PANDARUS Whats that? whats that?

CRESSID Good morrow vncle *Pandarus*.

PANDARUS Good morrow cozen *Cressid*: what doe you
talke of? (*to her man*) good morrow *Alexander*: (*to
Cressid*) how doe you cozen? when were you at Illium?

190 CRESSID This morning vncle.

PANDARUS What were you talking of when I came? was *Hector* arm'd and gon ere yea came to Illium, *Hellen* was not vp was she?

CRESSID

Hector was gone but *Hellen* was not vp?

PANDARUS E'ene so, *Hector* was stirring early.

CRESSID

That were wee talking of, and of his anger.

PANDARUS Was he angry?

CRESSID So he saies here.

PANDARUS True hee was so; I know the cause to, heele 200 lay about him to day I can tel them that, & ther's *Troylus* wil not come farre behind him, let them take heede of *Troylus*; I can tell them that too.

CRESSID What is he angry too?

PANDARUS Who *Troylus*? *Troylus* is the better man of the two.

CRESSID

Oh *Iupiter* ther's no comparison.

PANDARUS What not betweene *Troylus* and *Hector*? do you know a man if you see him?

CRESSID

I, if I euer saw him before and knew him.

210 PANDARUS Well I say *Troylus* is *Troylus*.

CRESSID

Then you say as I say, for I am sure
Hee is not *Hector*.

PANDARUS No nor *Hector* is not *Troylus* in some degrees.

CRESSID

Tis iust to each of them he is himselfe.

PANDARUS Himselfe, alas poore *Troylus* I would he were.

CRESSID So he is.

PANDARUS Condition I had gone bare-foot to India.

CRESSID He is not *Hector*.

PANDARUS Himselfe? no? hee's not himselfe, would a were 220 himselfe, well the Gods are aboue, time must friend or end well *Troylus* well, I would my heart were in her body; no, *Hector* is not a better man then *Troylus*.

CRESSID Excuse me.

PANDARUS He is elder.

CRESSID Pardon me, pardon me.

PANDARUS Th'others not come too't, you shall tell me another tale when th'others come too't, *Hector* shall not haue his will this yeare.

CRESSID

He shall not neede it if he haue his owne.

230 PANDARUS Nor his qualities.

CRESSID No matter.

PANDARUS Nor his beautie.

CRESSID

Twould not become him, his own's better.

PANDARUS You haue no iudgement neece; *Hellen* her selfe swore th'other day that *Troylus* for a browne fauour (*for so tis I must confesse*) not browne neither.

CRESSID No, but browne.

PANDARUS Faith to say truth, browne and not browne.

CRESSID To say the truth, true and not true.

PANDARUS She praisd his complexion aboue *Paris*. 240

CRESSID Why *Paris* hath colour inough.

PANDARUS So he has.

CRESSID Then *Troylus* should haue too much, if shee praizd him aboue, his complexion is higher then his, hee hauing colour enough, and the other higher, is too flaming a praise for a good complexion, I had as lieue *Helens* golden tongue had commended *Troylus* for a copper nose.

PANDARUS I sweare to you I thinke *Helen* loues him better then *Paris*. 250

CRESSID Then shees a merry greeke indeed.

PANDARUS Nay I am sure she dooes, she came to him th'other day into the compast window, and you know hee has not past three or foure haires on his chinne.

CRESSID Indeed a Tapsters Arithmetique may soone bring his particulars therein to a totall.

PANDARUS Why he is very yong, and yet will he within three pound lifte as much as his brother *Hector*.

CRESSID Is he so yong a man, and so old a lifter.

PANDARUS But to prooue to you that *Hellen* loues him, 260 shee came and puts mee her white hand to his clouen chin.

CRESSID *Iuno* haue mercy, how came it clouen?

PANDARUS Why, you know tis dimpled, I thinke his smyling becomes him better then any man in all Phrigia.

CRESSID Oh he smiles valiantly.

PANDARUS Dooes hee not?

CRESSID Oh yes, and twere a clowd in *Autumne*.

PANDARUS Why go to then, but to proue to you that 270 *Hellen* loues *Troylus*.

CRESSID *Troylus* wil stand to the proofe if youle prooue it so.

PANDARUS *Troylus*, why hee esteemes her no more then I esteeme an addle egge.

CRESSID If you loue an addle egge as well as you loue an idle head you would eate chickens ith shell.

PANDARUS I cannot chuse but laugh to thinke how she ticled his chin, indeed shee has a maruel's white hand I must needs confesse. 280

CRESSID Without the rack.

PANDARUS And shee takes vpon her to spie a white heare on his chinne.

CRESSID Alas poore chin many a wart is ritcher.

PANDARUS But there was such laughing, Queene *Hecuba* laught that her eyes ran ore.

CRESSID With milstones.

PANDARUS And *Cassandra* laught.

CRESSID But there was a more temperate fire vnder the pot of her eyes: or did her eyes run ore to? 290

PANDARUS And *Hector* laught.

CRESSID At what was all this laughing.

PANDARUS Marry at the white heare that *Hellen* spied on *Troylus* chin.

CRESSID And t'had beene a greene heare I should haue laught too.

PANDARUS They laught not so much at the heare as at his pretty answere.

CRESSID What was his answere?

300 PANDARUS Quoth shee heere's but two and fifty heires on your chinne; and one of them is white.

CRESSID This is her question.

PANDARUS Thats true, make no question of that, two and fiftie heires quoth hee, and one white, that white heire is my father, and all the rest are his sonnes. *Iupiter* quoth shee, which of these heires is *Paris* my husband? the forked one quoth he, pluckt out and giue it him: but there was such laughing, and *Hellen* so blusht, and *Paris* so chaf't, and all the rest so laught that it past.

310 CRESSID So let it now for it has beene a great while going by.

PANDARUS Wel cozen I tould you a thing yesterday, think on't.

CRESSID So I doe.

PANDARUS Ile be sworne tis true, he will weepe you an'twere a man borne in Aprill.

CRESSID And Ile spring vp in his teares an'twere a nettle against May.

Sound a retreate

PANDARUS Harke they are comming from the field, shall 320 we stand vp here and see them as they passe toward Ilion, good Neece do, sweete Neece *Cresseida.*

CRESSID At your pleasure.

PANDARUS Heere, here, here's an excellent place, here wee may see most brauely, ile tell you them all by their names, as they passe by, but marke *Troylus* aboue the rest.

Enter Æneas passing by ⌈*below*⌉

CRESSID Speake not so lowde.

PANDARUS Thats *Æneas*, is not that a braue man, hees one of the flowers of Troy I can tell you, but marke 330 *Troylus*, you shal see anon.

Enter Antenor passing by ⌈*below*⌉

CRESSID Who's that?

PANDARUS Thats *Antenor*, he has a shrow'd wit I can tell you, and hee's a man good enough, hees one o'th soundest iudgements in Troy whosoeuer, and a proper man of person, when comes *Troylus*, ile shew you *Troylus* anon, if hee see me, you shall see him nod at mee.

CRESSID Will he giue you the nod?

PANDARUS You shall see.

340 CRESSID If he do the ritch shall haue more.

Enter Hector passing by ⌈*below*⌉

PANDARUS Thats *Hector*, that, that, looke you that, thers a fellow! goe thy way *Hector*, ther's a braueman Neece, O braue *Hector*, looke how hee lookes, theres a countenance, ist not a braue man?

CRESSID O a braue man.

PANDARUS Is a not? it dooes a mans heart good, looke you what hacks are on his helmet, looke you yonder, do you see, looke you there, thers no iesting, thers laying on, takt off who will as they say, there be hacks.

350 CRESSID Be those with swords?

Enter Paris passing by ⌈*below*⌉

PANDARUS Swords, any thing he cares not, and the diuell

come to him, its all one, by Gods lid it dooes ones heart good. Yonder comes *Paris*, yonder comes *Paris*, looke yee yonder Neece, ist not a gallant man to, ist not, why this is braue now, who said he came hurt home to day. Hee's not hurt, why this will do *Hellens* heart good now ha? would I could see *Troylus* now, you shall see *Troylus* anon.

Enter Helenus passing by ⌈*below*⌉

CRESSID Whose that?

PANDARUS Thats *Helenus*, I maruell where *Troylus* is, thats 360 *Helenus*, I thinke he went not forth to day, thats *Helenus*.

CRESSID Can *Helenus* fight vncle?

PANDARUS *Helenus* no: yes heele fight indifferent, well, I maruell where *Troylus* is;

⌈*A Shout*⌉

harke doe you not here the people crie *Troylus*? *Helenus* is a priest.

Enter Troylus passing by ⌈*below*⌉

CRESSID What sneaking fellow comes yonder?

PANDARUS Where? yonder? thats *Deiphobus*. Tis *Troylus*! theres a man Neece, hem? braue *Troylus* the Prince of chiualrie. 370

CRESSID Peace for shame peace.

PANDARUS Marke him, note him: O braue *Troylus*, looke well vpon him Neece, looke you how his sword is bloudied, and his helme more hackt then *Hectors*, and how hee lookes, and how hee goes? O admirable youth, hee ne're saw three and twenty, go thy way *Troylus*, go thy way, had I a sister were a grace, or a daughter a Goddesse, hee should take his choice, O admirable man! *Paris*? *Paris* is durt to him, and I warrant *Hellen* to change would giue an eye to boote. 380

Enter common Souldiers passing by ⌈*below*⌉

CRESSID Here comes more.

PANDARUS Asses, fooles, doults, chaff & bran, chaff & bran, porredge after meate, I could liue and die i'th'eyes of *Troylus*, nere looke, nere looke, the Eagles are gonne, crowes and dawes, crowes and dawes, I had rather bee such a man as *Troylus*, then *Agamemnon* and all Greece.

CRESSID There is among the Greekes *Achilles* a better man then *Troylus*.

PANDARUS *Achilles*, a dray-man, a porter, a very Cammell.

CRESSID Well, well. 390

PANDARUS Well, well, why haue you any discretion, haue you any eyes, doe you know what a man is? is not birth, beauty, good shape, discourse, man-hood, learning, gentlenesse, vertue youth, liberallity and so forth, the spice & salt that season a man.

CRESSID I a minst man, and then to bee bak't with no date in the pie, for then the mans date is out.

PANDARUS You are such another woman one knowes not at what ward you lie.

CRESSID Vpon my backe to defend my bellie, vpon my wit 400 to defend my wiles, vpon my secrecy to defend mine honesty, my maske to defend my beauty, and you to defend all these: and at al these wards I lie, at a thousand watches.

PANDARUS Say one of your watches.

CRESSID Nay Ile watch you for that; and thats one of the chiefest of them too: If I cannot ward what I would not haue hit: I can watch you for telling how I tooke the blowe vnlesse it swell past hiding, and then its past watching.

410

PANDARUS You are such another.

Enter Boy

BOY Sir my Lord would instantlie speake with you.

PANDARUS Where?

BOY At your owne house.

PANDARUS Good boy tell him I come,   *Exit Boy*
I doubt he be hurt, fare ye well good Neice.

CRESSID Adiew vncle.

PANDARUS Ile be with you Neice by and by.

CRESSID To bring vncle.

420

PANDARUS I a token from *Troylus.*

CRESSID By the same token you are a Bawde,
                    Exeunt Pandarus ⌜and Alexander⌝
Words, vowes, guifts, teares and loues full sacrifize:
He offers in anothers enterprize,
But more in *Troylus* thousand fould I see,
Then in the glasse of *Pandars* praise may bee:
Yet hold I off: women are angels woing,
"Things woone are done, ioyes soule lies in the dooing.
That shee belou'd, knows naught that knows not this,
"Men price the thing vngaind more then it is,

430

That she was neuer yet that euer knew
Loue got so sweet, as when desire did sue,
Therefore this *maxim* out of loue I teach,
"*Atchiuement is command; vngaind beseech*,
Then though my hearts contents firme loue doth beare,
Nothing of that shall from mine eyes appeare.   *Exit*

Sc. 3
(1.3)

Senet. Enter Agamemnon, Nestor, Vlisses,
Diomedes, Menelaus with others

AGAMEMNON

Princes: what griefe hath set the Iaundies on your cheekes?
The ample proposition that hope makes,
In all designes begun on earth below,
Failes in the promist largenesse, checks and disasters,

440

Grow in the vaines of actions highest reard,
As knots by the conflux of meeting sap,
Infects the sound Pine, and diuerts his graine,
Tortiue and errant from his course of growth.
Nor Princes is it matter new to vs,
That we come short of our suppose so farre,
That after seauen yeares siege, yet Troy walls stand,
Sith euery action that hath gone before,
Whereof we haue record, triall did draw,
Bias and thwart: not answering the ayme,

450

And that vnbodied figure of the thought,
That gau't surmised shape: why then you Princes,
Do you with cheekes abasht behold our workes,
And thinke them shames which are indeed naught else,
But the protractiue tryals of great *Ioue,*

To finde persistiue constancie in men.
The finenesse of which mettall is not found,
In fortunes loue: for then the bould and coward,
The wise and foole, the Artist and vnread,
The hard and soft seeme all affyn'd and kin,
But in the winde and tempest of her frowne,   460
Distinction with a lowd and powerfull fan,
Puffing at all, winnows the light away,
And what hath masse or matter by it selfe,
Lyes rich in vertue and vnmingled.

NESTOR

With due obseruance of thy godly seate,
Great *Agamemnon, Nestor* shall apply
Thy latest words. In the reproofe of chance,
Lies the true proofe of men: the sea being smooth,
How many shallow bauble boates dare saile,
Vpon her pacient brest, making their way   470
With those of nobler bulke?
But let the ruffian *Boreas* once enrage
The gentle *Thetis,* and anon, behold
The strong ribbd barke through liquid mountaines cut,
Bounding betweene the two moyst elements,
Like *Perseus* horse. Where's then the sawcie boate,
Whose weake vntymberd sides but euen now
Corriuald greatnesse? either to harbor fled,
Or made a toste for *Neptune*: euen so
Doth valours shew, and valours worth deuide   480
In stormes of fortune; for in her ray and brightnesse
The heard hath more annoyance by the Bryze
Then by the Tyger, but when the splitting winde,
Makes flexible the knees of knotted Okes,
And Flies flee vnder shade, why then the thing of courage,
As rouzd with rage, with rage doth simpathize,
And with an accent tun'd in selfe same key,
Retorts to chiding fortune.

VLISSES   *Agamemnon,*
Thou great Commander, nerue and bone of Greece,
Heart of our numbers, soule and onely spirit,   490
In whom the tempers and the minds of all
Should be shut vp: heere what *Vlisses* speakes,
Besides th'applause and approbation,
The which most mighty (for thy place and sway
(*To Nestor*) And thou most reuerend (for thy stretcht out life,
I giue to both your speeches; which were such
As *Agamemnon* euerye hand of Greece,
Should hold vp high in brasse, and such againe
(*To Nestor*) As venerable *Nestor* (hatcht in siluer)
Should with a bond of ayre strong as the Axel-tree,   500
(On which the heauens ride) knit all Greekes eares
To his experienc't tongue, yet let it please both
Thou (*to Agamemnon*) great and (*to Nestor*) wise, to heare *Vlisses* speake.

AGAMEMNON

Speak Prince of *Ithaca,* and be't of lesse expect:
That matter needlesse of importless burthen

Diuide thy lips; then we are confident
When ranke *Thersites* opes his Masticke iawes,
We shall heare Musicke, Wit, and Oracle.

VLISSES

Troy yet vpon his basis had beene downe
510 And the great *Hectors* sword had lackt a master
But for these instances.
The specialtie of rule hath beene neglected,
And looke how many Grecian tents do stand,
Hollow vpon this plaine, so many hollow factions,
When that the generall is not like the hiue,
To whom the forragers shall all repaire,
What honey is expected? Degree being visarded
Th'vnworthiest shewes as fairly in the maske
⌐   ⌐.
520 The heauens them-selues, the plannets and this center
Obserue degree, prioritie and place,
Infixture, course, proportion, season, forme,
Office and custome, in all line of order.
And therefore is the glorious planet Sol,
In noble eminence enthron'd and spherd,
Amidst the other; whose medcinable eye,
Corrects the ill Aspects of Planets euill,
And posts like the Commandment of a King,
Sans check to good and bad. But when the Planets,
530 In euill mixture to disorder wander,
What plagues, and what portents, what mutinie?
What raging of the sea, shaking of earth?
Commotion in the winds, frights, changes, horrors
Diuert and crack, rend and deracinate,
The vnitie and married calme of states
Quite from their fixure: O when degree is shakt,
Which is the ladder to all high designes,
The enterprise is sick. How could communities,
Degrees in schooles, and brother-hoods in Citties,
540 Peacefull commerce from deuidable shores,
The primogenitie and due of birth,
Prerogatiue of age, crownes, scepters, lawrels,
But by degree stand in authentique place:
Take but degree away, vntune that string,
And harke what discord followes, each thing meets
In meere oppugnancie: the bounded waters
Should lift their bosomes higher then the shores,
And make a sop of all this solid globe:
Strength should be Lord of imbecilitie,
550 And the rude sonne should strike his father dead.
Force should be right or rather right and wrong,
(*Betweene whose endlesse iarre Iustice recides*)
Should loose their names, and so should Iustice to?
Then euery thing includes it selfe in power,
Power into will, will into appetite,
And appetite an vniuersall Woolfe,
(So doubly seconded with will and power)
Must make perforce an vniuersall prey,
And last eate vp himselfe. Great *Agamemnon*,
560 This *chaos* when degree is suffocate,
Followes the choaking,
And this neglection of degree it is,

That by a pace goes backward in a purpose
It hath to clime. The generalls disdain,
By him one step below, he by the next,
That next by him beneath, so euery step,
Exampl'd by the first pace that is sick
Of his superior, growes to an enuious feauer
Of pale and bloudlesse emulation,
And 'tis this feauer that keepes Troy on foote,
Not her owne sinnews. To end a tale of length, 570
Troy in our weaknesse liues not in her strength.

NESTOR

Most wisely hath *Vlisses* here discouerd,
The feuer whereof all our power is sick.

AGAMEMNON

The nature of the sicknesse found, *Vlisses*
What is the remedie?

VLISSES

The great *Achilles* whom opinion crownes,
The sinnow and the fore-hand of our hoste,
Hauing his eare full of his ayrie fame,
Growes dainty of his worth, and in his Tent 580
Lies mocking our designes: with him *Patroclus*
Vpon a lazie bed the liue-long day,
Breakes scurrell iests,
And with ridiculous and aukward action,
Which (slanderer) he Imitation calls,
He pageants vs. Some-time great *Agamemnon*,
Thy toplesse deputation he puts on,
And like a strutting Player, whose conceit
Lyes in his ham-string, and doth thinke it rich
To heere the woodden dialogue and sound, 590
Twixt his stretcht footing and the scaffollage,
Such to be pitied and ore-rested seeming,
He acts thy greatnesse in. And when he speakes,
Tis like a chime a mending, with termes vnsquard,
Which from the tongue of roaring *Tiphon* dropt,
Would seeme hiperboles, at this fustie stuffe,
The large *Achilles* on his prest bed lolling,
From his deepe chest laughes out a lowd applause,
Cries excellent; 'tis *Agamemnon* iust,
Now play me *Nestor*, hem and stroake thy beard, 600
As he being drest to some Oration,
That's done, as neere as the extremest ends
Of paralells, as like as *Vulcan* and his wife:
Yet god *Achilles* still cries excellent,
Tis *Nestor* right: now play him me *Patroclus*,
Arming to answer in a night alarme,
And then forsooth the faint defects of age,
Must be the scæne of myrth, to coffe and spit,
And with a palsie fumbling on his gorget,
Shake in and out the riuet, and at this sport 610
Sir valour dyes, cryes O enough *Patroclus*,
Or giue me ribbs of steele, I shall split all
In pleasure of my spleene, and in this fashion,
All our abilities, guifts, natures shapes,
Seueralls and generalls of grace exact,
Atchiuements, plots, orders, preuentions,
Excitements to the field, or speech for truce,

Successe or losse, what is, or is not, serues
As stuffe for these two to make paradoxes.

NESTOR

620   And in the imitation of these twaine,
Who as *Vlisses* sayes opinion crownes,
With an imperiall voyce: many are infect,
Aiax is growne selfe-wild, and beares his head
In such a reyne, in full as proud a place
As broad *Achilles*: and keepes his Tent like him,
Makes factious feasts, railes on our state of warre,
Bould as an Oracle, and sets *Thersites*
A slaue, whose gall coynes slanders like a mint,
To match vs in comparisons with durt,
630   To weaken and discredit our exposure
How ranke so euer rounded in with danger.

VLISSES

They taxe our pollicie, and call it cowardice,
Count wisdome as no member of the warre,
Forstall prescience, and esteeme no act
But that of hand, the still and mentall parts,
That do contriue how many hands shall strike,
When fitnesse calls them on, and know by measure
Of their obseruant toyle the enemies waight,
Why this hath not a fingers dignitie,
640   They call this bed-worke, mappry, Closet warre,
So that the Ram that batters downe the wall,
For the great swinge and rudenesse of his poise,
They place before his hand that made the engine,
Or those that with the finesse of their soules,
By reason guide his execution.

NESTOR

Let this be granted, and *Achilles* horse
Makes many *Thetis* sonnes.
     Tucket

AGAMEMNON   What trumpet?
Looke *Menelaus*.

MENELAUS

From Troy.
     Enter Æneas ⌈and a trumpeter⌉

AGAMEMNON   What would you fore our tent.

ÆNEAS

650   Is this great *Agamemnons* tent I pray you?

AGAMEMNON   Euen this.

ÆNEAS

May one that is a Herrald and a Prince,
Do a faire message to his Kingly eares?

AGAMEMNON

With surety stronger then *Achilles* arme,
Fore all the Greekish heads, which with one voice,
Call *Agamemnon* heart and generall.

ÆNEAS

Faire leaue and large security, how may
A stranger to those most imperiall lookes,
Know them from eyes of other mortals?

AGAMEMNON   How?

ÆNEAS

660   I, I aske that I might waken reuerence,

And on the cheeke be ready with a blush,
Modest as morning, when shee coldly eyes
The youthfull *Phœbus*,
Which is that god in office guiding men,
Which is the high and mighty *Agamemnon*.

AGAMEMNON (*to the Greekes*)

This Troyan scornes vs, or the men of Troy,
Are ceremonious Courtiers.

ÆNEAS

Courtiers as free as debonaire, vnarm'd
As bending Angels, thats their fame in peace:
But when they would seeme soldiers, they haue galls,   670
Good armes, strong ioints, true swords, & great *Ioues*
     accorn
Nothing so full of heart: but peace *Æneas*,
Peace Troyan, lay thy finger on thy lips,
The worthinesse of praise distaines his worth,
If that the praisd him-selfe bring the praise forth.
But what repining the enemy commends,
That breath fame blowes, that praise sole pure
     transcends.

AGAMEMNON

Sir you of Troy, call you your selfe *Æneas*?

ÆNEAS

I Greeke, that is my name.

AGAMEMNON   Whats your affaire I pray you?

ÆNEAS

Sir pardon, 'tis for *Agamemnons* eares.   680

AGAMEMNON

He heeres naught priuately that comes from Troy.

ÆNEAS

Nor I from Troy come not to whisper him,
I bring a trumpet to awake his eare,
To set his sence on the attentiue bent,
And then to speake.

AGAMEMNON   Speake frankly as the winde,
It is not *Agamemnons* sleeping houre;
That thou shalt know Troyan he is awake,
Hee tels thee so himselfe.

ÆNEAS   Trumpet blowe lowd,
Send thy brasse voyce through all these lazie tents,
And euery Greeke of mettell let him know,   690
What Troy meanes fairely, shall be spoke alowd.
     Sound trumpet
We haue great *Agamemnon* heere in Troy,
A Prince calld *Hector*, *Priam* is his father,
Who in this dull and long continued truce,
Is restie growne: He bad me take a Trumpet,
And to this purpose speake. Kings, Princes, Lords,
If there be one among the fair'st of Greece,
That holds his honour higher then his ease,
That seeks his praise, more then he feares his perill,
That knowes his valour, and knowes not his feare,   700
That loues his Mistresse more then in confession,
(With truant vowes to her owne lips he loues)
And dare avowe her beautie, and her worth,
In other armes then hers: to him this challenge;

Hector in view of Troyans and of Greekes,
Shall make it good, or do his best to do it:
He hath a Lady, wiser, fairer, truer,
Then euer Greeke did compasse in his armes,
And will to morrow with his Trumpet call,
710 Mid-way betweene your tents and walls of Troy,
To rouze a Grecian that is true in loue:
If any come, *Hector* shall honor him:
If none, heele say in Troy when he retires,
The Grecian dames are sun-burnt, and not worth
The splinter of a Launce. Euen so much.
       AGAMEMNON
This shall be told our louers Lord *Æneas*,
If none of them haue soule in such a kinde,
We left them all at home, but we are souldiers,
And may that souldier a meere recreant prooue,
720 That meanes not, hath not, or is not in loue:
If then one is, or hath or meanes to be,
That one meetes *Hector*: if none else Ile be he.
       NESTOR (*to Æneas*)
Tell him of *Nestor*, one that was a man
When *Hectors* grand-sire suckt. He is old now,
But if there be not in our Grecian mould,
One noble man that hath on sparke of fire
To answer for his loue, tell him from me,
Ile hide my siluer beard in a gould beauer,
And in my vambrace put this wither'd braune
730 And meeting him wil tell him that my Lady,
Was fairer then his grandam, and as chast,
As may bee in the world, (his youth in flood)
Ile proue this troth with my three drops of bloud.
       ÆNEAS
Now heauens forbid such scarcity of youth.
       VLISSES Amen.
       AGAMEMNON
Faire Lord *Æneas* let me touch your hand,
To our pauilion shall I leade you first;
Achilles shall haue word of this intent,
So shall each Lord of Greece from tent to tent,
740 Your selfe shall feast with vs before you goe,
And finde the welcome of a noble foe.
                    Exeunt. Manet Vlysses, and Nestor
       VLISSES
Nestor.
       NESTOR   What saies *Vlisses*?
       VLISSES   I haue a yong
Conception in my braine, be you my time
To bring it to some shape.
       NESTOR   What ist?
       VLISSES   This 'tis:
Blunt wedges riue hard knots, the seeded pride,
That hath to this maturity blowne vp
In ranke *Achilles*, must or now be cropt,
Or shedding breede a noursery of like euill,
To ouer-bulk vs all.
       NESTOR   Well and how?
       VLISSES
750 This challeng that the gallant *Hector* sends,

How euer it is spread in generall name
Relates in purpose onely to *Achilles*.
       NESTOR
The purpose is perspicuous euen as substance,
Whose grosenesse little characters sum vp:
And in the publication make no straine,
But that *Achilles* weare his braine as barren,
As banks of libia (*though* Apollo *knowes*
Tis dry enough) will with great speed of iudgement,
I with celerity finde *Hectors* purpose,
Pointing on him.   760
       VLISSES
And wake him to the answere thinke you?
       NESTOR
Yes tis most meete; who may you elce oppose,
That can from *Hector* bring his honour off,
If not *Achilles*: though't be a sportfull combat,
Yet in this triall much opinion dwells:
For here the Troyans tast our deerst repute,
With their fin'st pallat, and trust to me *Vlisses*
Our imputation shalbe odly poizde
In this wilde action, for the successe,
Although perticuler shall giue a scantling   770
Of good or bad vnto the generall,
And in such *indexes* (although small pricks
To their subsequent volumes) there is seene,
The baby figure of the gyant masse,
Of things to come at large: It is suppos'd
He that meetes *Hector*, yssues from our choice,
And choice (being mutuall act of all our soules)
Makes merit her election, and doth boyle,
As twere, from forth vs all a man distill'd
Out of our vertues, who miscarrying,   780
What heart from hence receiues the conqu'ring part,
To steele a strong opinion to them selues,
Which entertain'd, Limbes are in his instruments,
In no lesse working, then are Swords and Bowes
Directiue by the Limbes.
       VLISSES   Giue pardon to my speech?
Therefore tis meete, *Achilles* meete not *Hector*,
Let vs like Marchants shew our foulest wares,
And thinke perchance theile sell; If not;
The luster of the better yet to shew,
Shall shew the better: do not consent,   790
That euer *Hector* and *Achilles* meet,
For both our honour and our shame in this,
Are dog'd with two strange followers.
       NESTOR
I see them not with my old eyes what are they?
       VLISSES
What glory our *Achilles* shares from *Hector*
Were he not proud, we all should weare with him:
But he already is too insolent.
And we were better partch in Afrique Sunne,
Then in the pride and sault scorne of his eyes
Should he scape *Hector* faire. If he were foild,   800
Why then we did our maine opinion crush
In taint of our best man. No, make a lottry

And by deuise let blockish *Aiax* draw
The sort to fight with *Hector*, among our selues,
Giue him allowance as the worthier man,
For that will phisick the great Myrmidon,
Who broyles in loud applause, and make him fall
His crest that prouder then blew Iris bends,
If the dull brainlesse *Aiax* come safe off

810 Weele dresse him vp in voices, if he faile
Yet go we vnder our opinion still,
That we haue better men, but hit or misse,
Our proiects life this shape of sence assumes
Aiax imploy'd plucks downe *Achilles* plumes.

NESTOR
Now *Vlisses* I begin to relish thy aduise,
And I will giue a taste of it forthwith,
To *Agamemnon*, go we to him straight
Two curres shall tame each other, pride alone
Must tarre the mastiffs on, as twere their bone.

Exeunt

Sc. 4   *Enter Aiax and Thersites*
(2.1)   AIAX *Thersites.*

821 THERSITES *Agamemnon*, how if he had biles, full, all ouer,
generally.

AIAX *Thersites.*

THERSITES And those byles did run (say so), did not the
generall run then, were not that a botchy core.

AIAX Dogge.

THERSITES Then there would come some matter from him,
I see none now.

AIAX Thou bitchwolfs son canst thou not heare, feele

830 then.

Strikes him

THERSITES The plague of Greece vpon thee thou mongrell
beefe witted Lord.

AIAX Speake then thou vnsifted leauen, speake, I will
beate thee into hansomnesse.

THERSITES I shall sooner raile thee into wit and holinesse,
but I thinke thy horse will sooner cunne an oration,
then thou learne a praier without booke, ⌈*Aiax strikes
him*⌉ thou canst strike canst thou? a red murrion a thy
Iades trickes.

840 AIAX Todes stoole? ⌈*He strikes him*⌉ learne me the
proclamation.

THERSITES Doost thou thinke I haue no sence thou strikest
mee thus?

AIAX The proclamation.

THERSITES Thou art proclaim'd a foole I thinke.

AIAX Do not Porpentin, do not, my fingers itch.

THERSITES I would thou didst itch from head to foote and
I had the scratching of the, I would make thee the
lothsomest scab in Greece.

850 AIAX I say the proclamation.

THERSITES Thou gromblest and raylest euery houre on
Achilles, and thou art as full of enuy at his greatnesse,
as *Cerberus* is at *Proserpinas* beauty, I that thou barkst
at him.

AIAX Mistres *Thersites.*

THERSITES Thou shouldst strike him.

AIAX *Coblofe.*

THERSITES Hee would punne thee into shiuers with his
fist, as a sayler breakes a bisket.

AIAX You horson curre.   860

⌈*Strikes him*⌉

THERSITES Do? do?

AIAX Thou stoole for a witch.

⌈*Strikes him*⌉

THERSITES I, Do? do? thou sodden witted Lord, thou hast
in thy skull no more braine then I haue in mine
elbowes, an *Asinico* may tutor thee, thou scuruy valiant
asse, thou art heere but to thrash Troyans, and thou
art bought and sould among those of any wit, like a
Barbarian slaue. If thou vse to beate mee I will beginne
at thy heele, and tell what thou art by ynches, thou
thing of no bowells thou.   870

AIAX You dog.

THERSITES You scuruy Lord.

AIAX You curre.

⌈*Strikes him*⌉

THERSITES *Mars* his Idiot, do rudenesse, do Camel, do, do.

Enter Achilles, and Patroclus

ACHILLES
Why how now *Aiax* wherefore do yee thus,
How now *Thersites* whats the matter man.

THERSITES You see him there? do you?

ACHILLES I whats the matter.

THERSITES Nay looke vpon him.

ACHILLES So I do, whats the matter?   880

THERSITES Nay but regard him well.

ACHILLES Well, why I do so.

THERSITES But yet you looke not well vpon him, for who
some euer you take him to be he is *Aiax.*

ACHILLES I know that foole.

THERSITES I but that foole knowes not himselfe.

AIAX Therefore I beate thee.

THERSITES Lo, lo, lo, lo, what *modicums* of wit he vtters,
his euasions haue eares thus long, I haue bobd his
braine more then he has beate my bones. I will buy   890
nine sparrowes for a penny, and his *pia mater* is not
worth the ninth part of a sparrow: this Lord (*Achilles*)
Aiax, who weares his wit in his belly, and his guts in
his head, Ile tell you what I say of him.

ACHILLES What.

THERSITES I say this *Aiax.*

⌈*Aiax threatens to strike him*⌉

ACHILLES Nay good *Aiax.*

THERSITES Has not so much wit.

⌈*Aiax threatens to strike him*⌉

ACHILLES (*to Aiax*) Nay I must hold you.

THERSITES As will stop the eye of *Hellens* needle, for whom 900
he comes to fight.

ACHILLES Peace foole?

THERSITES I would haue peace and quietnesse, but the
foole will not, he there, that he: looke you there?

AIAX Oh thou damned curre I shall—

ACHILLES (*to Aiax*) Will you set your wit to a fooles.

THERSITES No I warrant you, for a fooles will shame it.

PATROCLUS Good words *Thersites*.

ACHILLES (*to Aiax*) Whats the quarrell.

910 AIAX I bad the vile oule goe learne mee the tenor of the proclamation, and he railes vpon me.

THERSITES I serue thee not?

AIAX Well, go to, go to.

THERSITES I serue here voluntary.

ACHILLES Your last seruice was suffrance: twas not voluntary, no man is beaten voluntary, *Aiax* was here the voluntary, and you as vnder an Impresse.

THERSITES E'ene so, a great deale of your witte to, lies in your sinnewes, or els there bee liers, *Hector* shall haue

920 a great catch and a knocke out either of your brains, a were as good crack a fusty nut with no kernell.

ACHILLES What with me to *Thersites*.

THERSITES Thers *Vlisses* and old *Nestor*, whose wit was mouldy ere your grandsiers had nailes on their toes, yoke you like draught oxen, and make you plough vp the war.

ACHILLES What? what?

THERSITES Yes good sooth, to *Achilles*, to *Aiax*, to—

AIAX I shall cut out your tongue.

930 THERSITES Tis no matter, I shall speake as much wit as thou afterwards.

PATROCLUS No more words *Thersites* peace.

THERSITES I will hold my peace when *Achilles* brach bids me, shall I?

ACHILLES There's for you *Patroclus*.

THERSITES I will see you hang'd like *Clatpoles*, ere I come any more to your tents, I will keepe where there is wit stirring, and leaue the faction of fooles.   *Exit*

PATROCLUS A good riddance.

ACHILLES (*to Aiax*)

940 Marry this sir is proclaim'd through all our hoste,
That *Hector* by the fift houre of the Sunne:
Will with a trumpet twixt our Tents and Troy,
To morrow morning call some Knight to armes,
That hath a stomack, and such a one that dare,
Maintaine I know not what, (tis trash) farewell—

AIAX Farewell, who shall answer him.

ACHILLES

I know not, tis put to lottry, otherwise,
He knew his man.   ⌈*Exeunt Achilles and Patroclus*⌉

AIAX O meaning you? I will go learne more of it.

⌈*Exit*⌉

Sc. 5   ⌈*Senet.*⌉ *Enter Priam, Hector, Troylus, Paris and*
(2.2)   *Helenus*

PRIAM

950 After so many houres, liues, speeches spent,
Thus once againe saies *Nestor* from the Greekes:
Deliuer *Hellen*, and all domage els,
(As honour, losse of time, trauell, expence,
Wounds, friends and what els deere that is consum'd
In hot digestion of this cormorant warre)
Shalbe stroke off, *Hector* what say you to't?

HECTOR

Though no man lesser feares the Greekes then I
As farre as toucheth my particular: yet dread *Priam*
There is no Lady of more softer bowells,
More spungy to suck in the sence of feare: 960
More ready to cry out, who knowes what followes
Then *Hector* is: the wound of peace is surety
Surety secure, but modest doubt is calld
The beacon of the wise, the tent that serches,
Too'th bottome of the worst: let *Hellen* go,
Since the first sword was drawne about this question
Euery tith soule 'mongst many thousand dismes,
Hath beene as deere as *Hellen*. I meane of ours:
If we haue loste so many tenthes of ours,
To guard a thing not ours, nor worth to vs,   970
(Had it our name) the valew of one ten,
What merits in that reason which denies,
The yeelding of her vp?

TROYLUS   Fie, fie, my brother,
Way you the worth and honour of a King
So great as our dread father in a scale
Of common ounces? will you with *Compters* summe,
The past proportion of his infinite
And buckle in, a waste most fathomles,
With spanes and inches so dyminutiue:
As feares and reasons: Fie for Godly shame?   980

HELENUS

No maruell though you bite so sharpe at reasons,
You are so empty of them; should not our father
Beare the great sway of his affaires with reason,
Because your speech hath none that tells him so?

TROYLUS

You are for dreames and slumbers brother Priest,
You furre your gloues with reason, here are your
    reasons
You know an enemy intends you harme:
You know a sword imployde is perilous
And reason flies the obiect of all harme.
Who maruells then when *Helenus* beholds,   990
A Gretian and his sword, if he do set
The very wings of reason to his heeles,
And flie like chidden *Mercury* from *Ioue*
Or like a starre disorbd? nay if we talke of reason,
Lets shut our gates and sleepe: man-hood and honour,
Should haue hare hearts, would they but fat their
    thoughts
With this cram'd reason, reason and respect,
Make lyuers pale, and lustihood deiect.

HECTOR

Brother, shee is not worth, what shee doth cost
The holding.

TROYLUS   Whats aught but as tis valued.   1000

HECTOR

But valew dwells not in perticuler will,
It holds his estimate and dignity,
As well wherein tis precious of it selfe
As in the prizer, tis madde Idolatry

To make the seruice greater then the God,
And the will dotes that is inclineable
To what infectiously it selfe affects,
Without some image of th' affected merit.

TROYLUS
I take to day a wife, and my election:
1010   Is led on in the conduct of my will,
My will enkindled by mine eyes and eares,
Two traded pilots twixt the dangerous shores,
Of will and Iudgement: how may I auoyde?
(Although my will distast what it elected)
The wife I chose, there can be no euasion,
To blench from this and to stand firme by honor,
We turne not backe the silkes vpon the marchant
When we haue spoild them, nor the remainder viands,
We do not throw in vnrespectiue sure,
1020   Because we now are full, it was thought meete
Paris should do some vengeance on the Greekes.
Your breth of full consent bellied his sailes,
The seas and winds (old wranglers) tooke a truce:
And did him seruice, hee toucht the ports desir'd,
And for an old aunt whom the Greekes held Captiue,
He brought a Grecian Queene, whose youth and
     freshnesse,
Wrincles *Apolloes*, and makes stale the morning.
Why keepe we her? the Grecians keepe our Aunt,
Is she worth keeping? why shee is a pearle
1030   Whose price hath lansh't aboue a thousand ships:
And turn'd crown'd Kings to Marchants,
If youle auouch twas wisdome *Paris* went,
As you must needs, for you all cri'd go, go,
If youle confesse he brought home Noble prize:
As you must needs, for you all, clapt your hands,
And cry'd inestimable: why do you now
The yssue of your proper wisdomes rate,
And do a deed that neuer fortune did,
Begger the estimation, which you priz'd
1040   Ritcher then sea and land? O theft most base,
That wee haue stolne, what we do feare to keepe,
But theeues vnworthy of a thing so stolne:
That in their country did them that disgrace,
We feare to warrant in our natiue place.

CASSANDRA ⌜within⌝
Cry Troyans cry.

PRIAM   What noise? what shrike is this?

TROYLUS
Tis our madde sister I do know her voice.

CASSANDRA ⌜within⌝ Cry Troyans.

HECTOR It is *Cassandra*!
     ⌜*Enter Cassandra rauing with her haire about her*
     eares⌝

CASSANDRA
Cry Troyans cry, lend me ten thousand eyes,
1050   And I will fill them with prophetick teares.

HECTOR Peace sister peace.

CASSANDRA
Virgins, and boyes, mid-age, and wrinckled old,

Soft infancie, that nothing canst but crie,
Adde to my clamours: let vs pay be-times
A moytie of that masse of mone to come:
Crie *Troyans* crye, practise your eyes with teares,
Troy must not bee, nor goodly Illion stand.
Our fire-brand brother *Paris* burnes vs all,
Crie Troyans crie, a *Helen* and a woe,
Crie, crie, Troy burnes, or else let *Hellen* goe.   Exit   1060

HECTOR
Now youthfull *Troylus*, do not these high straines
Of diuination in our Sister, worke
Some touches of remorse? or is your bloud
So madly hott, that no discourse of reason,
Nor feare of bad successe in a bad cause,
Can qualifie the same?

TROYLUS   Why brother *Hector*,
We may not thinke the iustnesse of each act
Such, and no other then the euent doth forme it,
Nor once deiect the courage of our mindes,
Because *Cassandra's* madde, her brain-sick raptures   1070
Cannot distast the goodnesse of a quarrell,
Which hath our seuerall honors all engag'd,
To make it gratious. For my priuate part,
I am no more toucht then all *Priams* sonnes:
And *Ioue* forbid there should be done amongst vs,
Such things as might offend the weakest spleene,
To fight for and maintaine.

PARIS
Else might the world conuince of leuitie,
As well my vnder-takings as your counsells,
But I attest the gods, your full consent,   1080
Gaue wings to my propension, and cut off
All feares attending on so dire a proiect,
For what (alas) can these my single armes?
What propugnation is in one mans valour
To stand the push and enmitie of those
This quarrell would excite? Yet I protest
Were I alone to passe the difficulties,
And had as ample power, as I haue will,
Paris should nere retract, what he hath done,
Nor faint in the pursuite.

PRIAM   *Paris* you speake   1090
Like one be-sotted on your sweet delights,
You haue the hony still, but these the gall,
So to be valiant, is no praise at all.

PARIS
Sir, I propose not meerly to my selfe,
The pleasures such a beautie brings with it,
But I would haue the soile of her faire rape,
Wip't of in honorable keeping her,
What treason were it to the ransackt queene,
Disgrace to your great worths, and shame to me,
Now to deliuer her possession vp   1100
On tearmes of base compulsion? can it be,
That so degenerate a straine as this,
Should once set footing in your generous bosomes?
There's not the meanest spirit on our party,

Without a heart to dare, or sword to drawe,
When *Helen* is defended : nor none so noble,
Whose life were ill bestowd, or death vnfam'd,
Where *Helen* is the subiect. Then I say,
Well may we fight for her, whom we know well,
1110　The worlds large spaces cannot paralell.

HECTOR

Paris and *Troylus*, you haue both said well,
But on the cause and question now in hand,
Haue glozd, but superficially, not much
Vnlike young men, whom *Aristotle* thought
Vnfit to heere *Morrall Philosophie*;
The reasons you alleadge, do more conduce
To the hot passion of distempred blood,
Then to make vp a free determination
Twixt right and wrong : for pleasure and reuenge,
1120　Haue eares more deafe then Adders to the voyce
Of any true decision. Nature craues
All dues be rendred to their owners. Now
What neerer debt in all humanitie,
Then wife is to the husband ? if this lawe
Of nature be corrupted through affection
And that great mindes of partiall indulgence,
To their benummed wills resist the same,
There is a lawe in each well-orderd nation,
To curbe those raging appetites that are
1130　Most disobedient and refracturie;
If *Helen* then be wife to *Sparta's* King,
As it is knowne she is, these morrall lawes
Of nature and of nations, speake alowd
To haue her back returnd : thus to persist
In doing wrong, extenuates not wrong,
But makes it much more heauie. *Hectors* opinion
Is this in way of truth : yet nere the lesse,
My spritely brethren, I propend to you
In resolution to keepe *Helen* still,
1140　For 'tis a cause that hath no meane dependance,
Vpon our ioynt and seuerall dignities.

TROYLUS

Why there you toucht the life of our designe :
Were it not glory that we more affected,
Then the performance of our heauing spleenes,
I would not wish a drop of Troyan bloud,
Spent more in her defence. But worthy *Hector*,
She is a theame of honour and renowne,
A spurre to valiant and magnanimous deeds,
Whose present courage may beate downe our foes,
1150　And fame in time to come canonize vs,
For I presume braue *Hector* would not loose
So rich aduantage of a promisd glory,
As smiles vpon the fore-head of this action,
For the wide worlds reuenew.

HECTOR　　　　　　　　　　I am yours,
You valiant offspring of great *Priamus*,
I haue a roisting challenge sent amongst
The dull and factious nobles of the Greekes,
Will shrike amazement to their drowsie spirits,

I was aduertizd, their great generall slept,
Whilst emulation in the armie crept :　　　　1160
This I presume will wake him.　　⌈*Flowrish.*⌉ *Exeunt*

Enter Thersites solus　　　　Sc. 6
　　　　　　　　　　　　　　　　　　(2.3)
THERSITES How now *Thersites* ? what lost in the Labyrinth
of thy furie ? shall the Elephant *Aiax* carry it thus ? he
beates me, and I raile at him : O worthy satisfaction,
would it were otherwise : that I could beate him, whilst
hee raild at mee : Sfoote, Ile learne to coniure and raise
Diuels, but Ile see some issue of my spitefull execrations.
Then ther's *Achilles*, a rare inginer. If Troy bee not
taken till these two vndermine it, the walls will stand
till they fall of them-selues. O thou great thunder-darter　1170
of Olympus, forget that thou art *Ioue* the king of gods :
and *Mercury*, loose all the Serpentine craft of thy
Caduceus, if yee take not that little little lesse then little
witte from them that they haue : which short-armd
Ignorance it selfe knowes is so aboundant scarce, it
will not in circumuention deliuer a flie from a spider,
without drawing their massie Irons, and cutting the
web. After this the vengeance on the whole campe, or
rather the Neopolitan bone-ache : for that me thinkes
is the curse dependant on those that warre for a placket.　1180
I haue said my prayers, and diuell Enuie say *Amen*.
What ho my Lord *Achilles* ?

Enter Patroclus ⌈*at the doore to the Tent*⌉
PATROCLUS Whose there ? *Thersites* ? good *Thersites* come
in and raile.　　　　　　　　　　⌈*Exit*⌉
THERSITES If I could a remembred a guilt counterfeit, thou
wouldst not haue slipt out of my contemplation : but it
is no matter, thy selfe vpon thy selfe. The common
curse of mankinde, Folly and Ignorance, be thine in
great reuenew : Heauen blesse thee from a tutor, and
discipline come not neere thee. Let thy bloud be thy　　1190
direction till thy death : then if she that layes thee out
sayes thou art a faire course, Ile be sworne and sworne
vpon't, shee neuer shrowded any but lazars.

⌈*Enter Patroclus*⌉
Amen. Where's *Achilles* ?
PATROCLUS What art thou deuout ? wast thou in prayer ?
THERSITES I the heauens heare me.
PATROCLUS *Amen*.

Enter Achilles
ACHILLES Who's there ?
PATROCLUS *Thersites*, my Lord.
ACHILLES Where ? where ? O where ? (*to Thersites*) art thou　1200
come why my cheese, my digestion, why hast thou not
serued thy selfe into my table, so many meales, come
what's *Agamemnon* ?
THERSITES Thy commander *Achilles*, then tell me *Patroclus*,
whats *Achilles* ?
PATROCLUS Thy Lord *Thersites*. Then tell mee I pray thee,
what's *Thersites* ?
THERSITES Thy knower, *Patroclus* : then tell mee *Patroclus*,
what art thou ?
PATROCLUS Thou maist tell that knowest.　　　　　1210

ACHILLES O tell, tell.

THERSITES Ile decline the whole question. *Agamemnon* commands *Achilles*, *Achilles* is my Lord, I am *Patroclus* knower, and *Patroclus* is a foole.

PATROCLUS You rascall.

THERSITES Peace foole, I haue not done.

ACHILLES (*to Patroclus*) He is a priuileg'd man, proceede *Thersites*.

THERSITES *Agamemnon* is a foole, *Achilles* is a foole, 1220 *Thersites* is a foole, and as aforesaid, *Patroclus* is a foole.

ACHILLES Deriue this? come?

THERSITES *Agamemnon* is a foole to offer to command *Achilles*, *Achilles* is a foole to be commanded of *Agamemnon*. *Thersites* is a foole to serue such a foole, and *Patroclus* is a foole positiue.

PATROCLUS Why am I a foole?

THERSITES Make that demand to the Creator, it suffices mee thou art: looke you, who comes heere?

> *Enter Agamemnon, Vlisses, Nestor, Diomed, Aiax &*
> *Calcas*

ACHILLES *Patroclus*, Ile speake with no body: come in with 1230 me *Thersites*.   *Exit*

THERSITES Here is such patcherie, such iugling, and such knauery: all the argument is a whore, and a Cuckold, a good quarrell to draw emulous factions, & bleed to death vpon. Now the dry Suppeago on the Subiect, and Warre and Lecherie confound all.   *Exit*

AGAMEMNON (*to Patroclus*) Where is *Achilles*?

PATROCLUS

Within his tent, but ill disposd my Lord.

AGAMEMNON

Let it be knowne to him, that we are heere,
He facd our messengers and we lay by,
1240 Our appertainments, visiting of him
Let him be told so, least perchance he thinke,
We dare not moue the question of our place,
Or know not what we are.

PATROCLUS   I shall so say to him.
                                        ⌈*Exit*⌉

VLISSES

We saw him at the opening of his tent,
Hee is not sick.

AIAX Yes Lion sick, sick of proud heart, you may call it melancholy if you will fauour the man. But by my head 'tis pride: but why, why, let him shew vs the cause?
⌈*To Agamemnon*⌉ A word my Lord.

> ⌈*Aiax and Agamemnon talke apart*⌉

1250 NESTOR What mooues *Aiax* thus to bay at him?

VLYSSES *Achillis* hath inuegled his foole from him.

NESTOR Who *Thersites*?

VLISSES He.

NESTOR Thē wil *Aiax* lack matter, if he haue lost his argumēt.

VLISSES No, you see he is his argument, that has his argument *Achilles*.

NESTOR All the better, their fractiō is more our wish then their faction, but it was a strōg counsell that a foole 1260 could disunite.

VLISSES The amity, that wisdom knits not, folly may easily vnty,

> *Enter Patroclus*

heere comes *Patroclus*.

NESTOR No *Achilles* with him.

VLISSES The Elephant hath ioynts, but none for courtesie, his legs are legs for necessity, not for flexure.

PATROCLUS (*to Agamemnon*)

Achilles bids me say he is much sorry,
If any thing more then your sport and pleasure
Did mooue your greatnesse, and this noble state,
To call vpon him. He hopes it is no other   1270
But for your health, and your disgestion sake,
An after dinners breath.

AGAMEMNON   Heere you *Patroclus*:

We are too well acquainted with these answers,
But his euasion wingd thus swift with scorne,
Cannot out-flie our apprehensions,
Much attribute he hath, and much the reason
Why we ascribe it to him. Yet all his vertues,
Not vertuously on his owne part beheld,
Doe in our eyes begin to lose their glosse,
Yea and like faire fruite in an vnholsome dish,   1280
Are like to rott vntasted. Go and tell him,
We come to speake with him, and you shall not sinne,
If you do say, we thinke him ouer-proud
And vnder-honest: in selfe assumption greater
Then in the note of iudgement. And worthier then
        himselfe
Heere tend the sauage strangenesse he puts on
Disguise the holy strength of their commaund,
And vnder-write in an obseruing kinde,
His humorous predominance: yea watch
His pettish lunes, his ebbs, his flowes, as if   1290
The passage, and whole carriage of this action,
Rode on his tide. Goe tell him this, and adde,
That if he ouer-hold his price so much,
Weele none of him: But let him like an engine,
Not portable, lye vnder this report.
Bring action hither, this cannot go to warre,
A stirring dwarfe we doe allowance giue,
Before a sleeping gyant. Tell him so.

PATROCLUS

I shall, and bring his answer presently.

AGAMEMNON

In second voyce weele not be satisfied,   1300
We come to speake with him; *Vlisses* enter you.

> *Exit Vlisses* ⌈*with Patroclus*⌉

AIAX What is he more then another.

AGAMEMNON No more then what he thinkes he is.

AIAX Is he so much: doe you not thinke he thinkes himselfe a better man then I am?

AGAMEMNON No question.

AIAX Will you subscribe his thought, and say he is.

AGAMEMNON No noble *Aiax*, you are as strong, as valiant, as wise, no lesse noble, much more gentle, and altogether more tractable.   1310

AIAX Why should a man be proud? how doth pride grow?
I know not what it is.

AGAMEMNON Your minde is the cleerer *Aiax*, and your
vertues the fairer, hee that is proud eates vp him-selfe:
Pride is his owne glasse, his owne trumpet, his owne
chronicle, and what euer praises it selfe but in the
deed, deuoures the deed in the praise.

Enter Vlisses

AIAX I do hate a proud man, as I hate the ingendring of
Toades.

1320 NESTOR (*aside*) Yet he loues himselfe, ist not strange?

VLISSES
Achilles will not to the field to morrow.

AGAMEMNON
Whats his excuse?

VLISSES   He doth relye on none,
But carries on the streame of his dispose,
Without obseruance, or respect of any,
In will peculiar, and in selfe admission.

AGAMEMNON
Why will he not vpon our faire request,
Vntent his person, and share the ayre with vs.

VLISSES
Things small as nothing, for requests sake onely,
He makes important, possest he is with greatnesse,
1330 And speakes not to himselfe but with a pride,
That quarrels at selfe breath. Imagind worth,
Holds in his bloud such swolne and hott discourse,
That twixt his mentall and his actiue parts,
Kingdomd *Achilles* in commotion rages,
And batters gainst himselfe. What should I say,
He is so plaguie proud, that the death tokens of it,
Crie no recouerie.

AGAMEMNON   Let *Aiax* go to him,
(*To Aiax*) Deare Lord, go you, and greete him in his
tent,
'Tis said he holds you well, and will be lead,
1340 At your request a little from himselfe.

VLISSES
O *Agamemnon* let it not be so,
Weele consecrate the steps that *Aiax* makes,
When they go from *Achilles*: shall the proud Lord
That basts his arrogance with his owne seame,
And neuer suffers matter of the world
Enter his thoughts, saue such as do reuolue,
And ruminate him-selfe: shall he be worshipt,
Of that we hold an idoll more then hee,
No: this thrice worthy and right valiant Lord,
1350 Must not so staule his palme nobly acquird,
Nor by my will assubiugate his merit,
As amply titled as *Achilles* is,
By going to *Achilles*,
That were to enlard his fat already pride,
And adde more coles to *Cancer* when he burnes,
With entertaining great *Hiperion*,
This Lord go to him. *Iupiter* forbid,
And say in thunder *Achilles* go to him.

NESTOR (*aside to Diomed*)
O this is well, he rubs the vaine of him.

DIOMED (*aside to Nestor*)
And how his silence drinkes vp this applause.   1360

AIAX
If I go to him: with my armed fist
Ile pash him ore the face.

AGAMEMNON   O no, you shall not goe.

AIAX
And a be proud with me, Ile phese his pride,
Let me goe to him.

VLISSES
Not for the worth that hangs vpon our quarrell.

AIAX A paltry insolent fellow.

NESTOR (*aside*) How he describes him selfe.

AIAX Can he not be sociable.

VLISSES (*aside*) The Rauen chides blacknesse.

AIAX Ile let his humors bloud.   1370

AGAMEMNON (*aside*) Hee wilbe the phisition, that should
bee the pacient.

AIAX And all men were a my minde.

VLISSES (*aside*) Wit would bee out of fashion.

AIAX A should not beare it so, a should eate swords first?
shall pride carry it?

NESTOR (*aside*) And two'od yow'd carry halfe.

⌈AIAX⌉ A would haue ten shares.

⌈VLISSES⌉ (*aside*) I will kneade him, Ile make him supple,
he's not yet through warme?   1380

NESTOR (*aside*) Force him with praises poure in, poure in,
his ambition is drie.

VLISSES (*to Agamemnon*)
My Lord you feed to much on this dislike.

NESTOR (*to Agamemnon*)
Our noble generall do not do so?

DIOMED (*to Agamemnon*)
You must prepare to fight without *Achilles*.

VLISSES
Why tis this naming of him do's him harme,
Here is a man but tis before his face,
I wilbe silent.

NESTOR   Wherefore should you so?
He is not emulous as *Achilles* is.

VLISSES
Know the whole world hee is as valiant—   1390

AIAX A hoarson dog that shall palter thus with vs, would
he were a Troyan?

NESTOR
What a vice were it in *Aiax* now:

VLISSES
If hee were proude.

DIOMED   Or couetous of praise.

VLISSES
I or surly borne.

DIOMED   Or strange or selfe affected.

VLISSES (*to Aiax*)
Thank the heauens Lord, thou art of sweet composure
Praise him that gat thee, shee that gaue thee suck:

Fam'd be thy tutor, and thy parts of nature,
Thrice fam'd beyond, beyond all erudition:
1400   But hee that disciplind thine armes to fight,
Let *Mars* diuide eternity in twaine,
And giue him halfe, and for thy vigour:
Bull-bearing *Milo* his addition yeeld,
To sinowy *Aiax*, I will not praise thy wisdome,
Which like a boorn, a pale, a shore confines
Thy spacious and dilated parts, here's *Nestor*,
Instructed by the antiquary times:
He must, he is, he cannot but be wise,
But pardon father *Nestor* were your daies
1410   As greene as *Aiax*, and your braine so temper'd,
You should not haue the emynence of him,
But be as *Aiax*.

AIAX   Shall I call you father?

VLISSES
I my good Sonne.

DIOMED   Be ruld by him Lord *Aiax*.

VLISSES (*to Agamemnon*)
There is no tarrying here the Hart *Achilles*,
Keepes thicket, please it our great generall,
To call together all his state of warre,
Fresh Kings are come to day to Troy. To morrow
We must with all our maine of power stand fast,
And here's a Lord come Knights from East to West
1420   And cull their flower, *Aiax* shall cope the best.

AGAMEMNON
Go we to counsell, let *Achilles* sleepe,
Light boates saile swift, though greater hulkes draw
deepe.   *Exeunt*

Sc. 7   *Musicke sounds within. Enter Pandarus* ⌈*at one*
(3.1)   *doore*⌉ *and a Seruant* ⌈*at another doore*⌉

PANDARUS Friend you, pray you a word, doe not you
follow the yong Lord *Paris*.

SERUANT I sir when he goes before mee.

PANDARUS You depend vpon him I meane.

SERUANT Sir I do depend vpon the Lord.

PANDARUS You depend vpon a notable gentleman I must
needs praise him.

1430   SERUANT The Lord be praized?

PANDARUS You know me? doe you not?

SERUANT Faith sir superficially.

PANDARUS Friend know mee better, I am the Lord
Pandarus.

SERUANT I hope I shall know your honour better?

PANDARUS I do desire it.

SERUANT You are in the state of grace?

PANDARUS Grace? not so friend, honour and Lordship are
my titles, what musicke is this?

1440   SERUANT I do but partly know sir, it is musick in partes.

PANDARUS Know you the musicians?

SERUANT Wholy sir.

PANDARUS Who play they to?

SERUANT To the hearers sir.

PANDARUS At whose pleasure friend?

SERUANT At mine sir, and theirs that loue musicke.

PANDARUS Command I meane friend.

SERUANT Who shall I command sir?

PANDARUS Friend we vnderstand not one another, I am
to courtly and thou to cunning, at whose request do   1450
these men play?

SERUANT Thats to't indeed sir? marry sir, at the request
of *Paris* my Lord, who's there in person, with him the
mortall *Venus*, the heart bloud of beauty, loues visible
soule:

PANDARUS Who my cozen *Cressida*.

SERUANT No sir, *Hellen*, could not you finde out that by
her attributes.

PANDARUS It should seeme fellow that thou hast not seene
the Lady *Cressid* I come to speake with *Paris*, from the   1460
Prince *Troylus*. I will make a complementall assault
vpon him for my businesse seeth's.

SERUANT Sodden businesse, theirs a stew'd phrase indeed.
      Enter Paris and Hellen attended ⌈*by musicians*⌉

PANDARUS Faire be to you my Lord, and to al this faire
company, faire desires in all faire measure fairlie guide
them, especially to you faire Queene faire thoughts be
your faire pillow.

HELLEN Dere Lord you are full of faire words.

PANDARUS You speake your faire pleasure sweet Queene,
(*to Paris*) faire Prince here is good broken musicke.   1470

PARIS You haue broke it cozen: and by my life you shall
make it whole againe, you shall peece it out with a
peece of your performance. *Nel*, he is full of harmony.

PANDARUS Truely Lady no.

HELLEN O sir.
      ⌈*She ticles him*⌉

PANDARUS Rude in sooth, in good sooth very rude.

PARIS Well said my Lord, will you say so in fits.

PANDARUS I haue businesse to my Lord deere Queene?
my Lord will you vouchsafe me a word.

HELLEN Nay this shall not hedge vs out, weele here you   1480
sing certainely.

PANDARUS Well sweete Queene you are pleasant with
mee, but, mary thus my Lord my deere Lord, and most
esteemed friend your brother *Troylus*.

HELLEN My Lord *Pandarus*, hony sweet Lord.

PANDARUS Go too sweet Queene, go to? comends himselfe
most affectionatly to you.

HELLEN You shall not bob vs out of our melody, if you
do our melancholy vpon your head.

PANDARUS Sweet Queene, sweet Queene, thats a sweet   1490
Queene I faith—

HELLEN And to make a sweet Lady sad is a sower offence.

PANDARUS Nay that shall not serue your turne, that shall
it not in truth la? Nay I care not for such words, no,
no. (*To Paris*) And my Lord hee desires you that if the
King call for him at super, you will make his excuse.

HELLEN My Lord *Pandarus*.

PANDARUS What saies my sweete Queene, my very very
sweet Queene?

PARIS What exploit's in hand, where suppes he to night?   1500

HELLEN Nay but my Lord?

PANDARUS What saies my sweet Queene? my cozen will
fall out with you.

HELLEN (*to Paris*) You must not know where he sups.

PARIS Ile lay my life with my dispēser *Cresseida*.

PANDARUS No, no? no such matter you are wide, come
your dispēser is sicke.

PARIS Well ile makes excuse?

1510 PANDARUS I good my Lord, why should you say *Cresseida*,
no, your poore dispēsers sick.

PARIS I spie?

PANDARUS You spy? what doe you spie? ⌈*To a musician*⌉
come, giue mee an instrument, now sweete Queene.

HELLEN Why this is kindely done?

PANDARUS My Neece is horrible in loue with a thing you
haue sweete Queene.

HELLEN Shee shall haue it my Lord, if it bee not my Lord
Paris.

1520 PANDARUS Hee? no? sheele none of him, they two are
twaine.

HELLEN Falling in after falling out may make them three.

PANDARUS Come, come, Ile heare no more of this, Ile sing
you a song now.

HELLEN I, I, prethee, now: by my troth sweet lord thou
haste a fine fore-head.

⌈*She strokes his fore-head*⌉

PANDARUS I you may, you may.

HELLEN Let thy song be loue: this loue will vndoe vs all.
Oh *Cupid*, *Cupid*, *Cupid*.

PANDARUS Loue? I that it shall yfaith.

1530 PARIS I good now loue, loue, nothing but loue.

PANDARUS In good troth it begins so.

Song

Loue, loue, nothing but loue, still loue still more:
   For o loues bow,
   Shoots Bucke and Doe.
   The shaft confounds
   Not that it wounds
But ticles still the sore:

These louers cry, oh oh they dye,
   Yet that which seemes the wound to kill,
1540 *Doth turne oh oh, to ha ha he,*
   So dying loue liues still,
   Oh o a while, but ha ha ha,
   Oh o grones out for ha ha ha—

hey ho.

HELLEN In loue I faith to the very tip of the nose.

PARIS He eates nothing but doues loue, and that breeds
hot blood, and hot bloud begets hot thoughts, and hot
thoughts beget hot deedes, and hot deeds is loue.

1550 PANDARUS Is this the generation of loue: hot bloud hot
thoughts and hot deedes why they are vipers, is loue
a generation of vipers:

⌈*Alarum*⌉

Sweete Lord whose a field to day?

PARIS *Hector*, *Deiphobus*, *Helenus*, *Anthenor*, and all the

gallantry of *Troy*. I would faine haue arm'd to day, but
my *Nell* would not haue it so. How chance my brother
Troylus went not?

HELLEN He hangs the lippe at something, you know al
Lord *Pandarus*.

PANDARUS Not I hony sweete Queene, I long to heare how
they sped to day: Youle remember your brothers   1560
excuse?

PARIS To a hayre.

PANDARUS Farewell sweete Queene.

HELLEN Commend me to your neece.

PANDARUS I will sweet Queene.   *Exit*

   Sound a retreat

PARIS

  Their come from field: let vs to Priames Hall
  To greete the warriers. Sweet *Hellen* I must woe you,
  To helpe vn-arme our *Hector*: his stubborne bucles
  With this your white enchaunting fingers toucht;
  Shall more obey then to the edge of steele,   1570
  Or force of Greekish sinewes: you shall do more
  Then all the Iland Kinges, disarme great *Hector*.

HELLEN

  Twil make vs proud to be his seruant *Paris*?
  Yea what he shall receiue of vs in duty,
  Giues vs more palme in beauty then we haue.
  Yea ouershines our selfe.

PARIS   Sweet aboue thought I loue thee?

                          Exeunt

   Enter Pandarus ⌈*at one doore*⌉ *Troylus man* ⌈*at*   Sc. 8
   another doore⌉   (3.2)

PANDARUS How now wher's thy maister, at my Cousin
Cressidas?

MAN No sir he stayes for you to conduct him thether.

   Enter Troylus

PANDARUS O heere he comes? how now, how now?   1580

TROYLUS Sirra walke off.   *Exit Man*

PANDARUS Haue you seene my Cousine?

TROYLUS

  No *Pandarus*, I stalke about her dore
  Like a strange soule vpon the Stigian bankes
  Staying for waftage. O be thou my Charon.
  And giue me swift transportance to those fieldes,
  Where I may wallow in the lilly beds
  Propos'd for the deseruer. O gentle *Pandar*,
  From *Cupids* shoulder plucke his painted wings,
  And flye with me to *Cressid*.   1590

PANDARUS Walke heere ith'Orchard, Ile bring her straight.

                     Exit Pandarus

TROYLUS

  I am giddy; expectation whirles me round,
  Th'ymaginary relish is so sweete,
  That it inchaunts my sence: what will it be
  When that the watry pallats taste indeed
  Loues thrice repured Nectar? Death I feare me
  Sounding distruction, or some ioy to fyne,
  To subtill, potent, tun'd to sharp in sweetnesse
  For the capacity of my ruder powers;

1600 I feare it much, and I doe feare besides
That I shall loose distinction in my ioyes
As doth a battaile, when they charge on heapes
The enemy flying.

Enter Pandarus

PANDARUS Shees making her ready, sheele come straight,
you must be witty now, she does so blush, and fetches
her wind so short as if shee were fraid with a spirite:
Ile fetch her; it is the prettiest villaine, she fetches her
breath as short as a new tane sparrow.

Exit Pandarus

TROYLUS

Euen such a passion doth imbrace my bosome,
1610 My heart beats thicker then a feauorous pulse,
And all my powers do their bestowing loose
Like vassalage at vnawares encountring
The eye of maiesty.

Enter pandar and Cressid ⌈veiled⌉

PANDARUS (*to Cressid*) Come, come, what need you blush?
Shames a babie; (*to Troylus*) heere shee is now, sweare
the othes now to her that you haue sworne to me: (*to
Cressid*) what are you gone againe, you must be watcht
ere you be made tame, must you? come your waies
come your waies, and you draw backward weele put
1620 you ith filles: (*to Troylus*) why doe you not speake to
her. (*To Cressid*) Come draw this curtaine, and lets see
your picture; ⌈*He vnueils her*⌉ alasse the day? how loath
you are to offend day light; and twere darke youd close
sooner: so so, (*to Troylus*) rub on and kisse the
mistresse; (*They kisse*) how now a kisse in fee-farme:
build there Carpenter, the ayre is sweet. Nay, you shall
fight your hearts out ere I part you. The faulcon, as
the tercell: for all the ducks ith riuer: go too, go too.

TROYLUS You haue bereft me of all wordes Lady.

1630 PANDARUS Words pay no debts; giue her deeds: but sheele
bereaue you ath' deeds too if she call your actiuity in
question: (*They kisse*) what billing again: heeres in
witnesse whereof the parties interchangeably. Come in
come in Ile go get a fire?   *Exit*

CRESSID Will you walke in my Lord?

TROYLUS O *Cressida* how often haue I wisht me thus.

CRESSID Wisht my Lord? the gods graunt? O my Lord?

TROYLUS What should they graunt? what makes this
pretty abruption: what to curious dreg espies my sweete
1640 lady in the fountaine of our loue?

CRESSID More dregs then water if my feares haue eyes.

TROYLUS Feares make diuels of Cherubins, they neuer see
truly.

CRESSID Blinde feare that seeing reason leads, finds safer
footing, then blind reason, stumbling without feare: to
feare the worst oft cures the worse.

TROYLUS O let my Lady apprehend no feare, in all *Cupids*
pageant there is presented no monster.

CRESSID Nor nothing monstrous neither.

1650 TROYLUS Nothing but our vndertakings, when wee vow
to weepe seas, liue in fire, eate rockes, tame Tygers,
thinking it harder for our mistresse to deuise imposition
ynough then for vs to vndergoe any difficulty
imposed.—This is the monstruosity in loue Lady, that

the will is infinite and the execution confind, that the
desire is boundlesse, and the act a slaue to lymite.

CRESSID They say all louers sweare more performance
thene they are able, and yet reserue an ability that
they neuer performe: vowing more then the perfection
of ten: and discharging lesse then the tenth part of 1660
one. They that haue the voyce of Lyons, and the act
of Hares are they not monsters?

TROYLUS Are there such: such are not we; Praise vs as
wee are tasted, allow vs as we proue: our head shall
goe bare till merit crowne yt no perfection in reuersion
shall haue a praise in present: we will not name desert
before his birth, and being borne, his addition shall bee
humble: few wordes to faire faith. *Troylus* shall be such
to *Cressid*, as what enuy can say worst shall bee a
mocke for his truth, and what truth can speake truest 1670
not truer then *Troylus*.

CRESSID Will you walke in my Lord?

Enter Pandarus

PANDARUS What blushing still, haue you not done talking
yet?

CRESSID Well Vncle what folly I commit I dedicate to you.

PANDARUS I thanke you for that, if my Lord gette a boy
of you, youle giue him me: be true to my Lord, if he
flinch chide me for it.

TROYLUS (*to Cressid*) You know now your hostages, your
Vncles word and my firme faith.   1680

PANDARUS Nay Ile giue my word for her too: our kindred
though they be long ere they are woed, they are
constant being wonne, they are burres I can tell you,
theyle sticke where they are throwne.

CRESSID

Bouldnesse comes to me now and brings me heart:
Prince *Troylus* I haue loue'd you night and day,
For many weary moneths.

TROYLUS

Why was my *Cressid* then so hard to wyn?

CRESSID

Hard to seeme wonne: but I was wonne my Lord
With the first glance that euer: pardon me   1690
If I confesse much you will play the tyrant,
I loue you now, but till now not so much
But I might maister it; in faith I lye,
My thoughts were like vnbridled children grone
Too headstrong for their mother: see wee fooles,
Why haue I blab'd: who shall be true to vs
When we are so vnsecret to our selues.
But though I loue'd you well, I woed you not,
And yet good faith I wisht my selfe a man;
Or that we women had mens priuiledge   1700
Of speaking first. Sweete bid me hold my tongue,
For in this rapture I shall surely speake
The thing I shall repent: see see your scylence
Conning in dumbnesse, in my weaknesse drawes
My soule of councell from me. Stop my mouth.

TROYLUS

And shall, albeit sweet musique issues thence.

He kisses her

PANDARUS Pretty yfaith.

CRESSID (to Troylus)

My Lord I doe beseech you pardon me,
Twas not my purpose thus to begge a kisse:
1710   I am asham'd; O Heauens what haue I done!
For this time will I take my leaue my Lord.

TROYLUS Your leaue sweete Cressid.

PANDARUS Leaue: and you take leaue till to morrow
morning.

CRESSID

Pray you content you.

TROYLUS   What offends you Lady?

CRESSID Sir mine own company.

TROYLUS You cannot shun your selfe.

CRESSID Let me goe and try:
I haue a kind of selfe recids with you:
1720   But an vnkinde selfe, that it selfe will leaue,
To be anothers foole. Where is my wit?
I would be gone: I speake I know not what.

TROYLUS

Well know they what they speake, that speake so
    wisely.

CRESSID

Perchance my Lord I show more craft then loue,
And fell so roundly to a large confession,
To angle for your thoughts, but you are wise,
Or else you loue not: for to be wise and loue,
Exceeds mans might, that dwells with gods aboue.

TROYLUS

O that I thought it could be in a woman,
1730   As if it can I will presume in you,
To feed for aye her lampe and flames of loue,
To keepe her constancy in plight and youth,
Out-liuing beauties outward, with a mind,
That doth renew swifter then blood decays,
Or that persuasion could but thus conuince me,
That my integrity and truth to you,
Might be affronted with the match and waight,
Of such a winnowed purity in loue,
How were I then vp-lifted! but alasse,
1740   I am as true as truths simplicity,
And simpler then the infancy of truth.

CRESSID

In that ile war with you.

TROYLUS   O vertuous fight,
When right with right warres who shalbe most right,
True swains in loue shall in the world to come
Approue their trueth by Troylus, when their rimes,
Full of protest, of oath and big compare,
Wants simeles, truth tyrd with iteration:
As true as steele, as plantage to the moone:
As sunne to day: as turtle to her mate,
1750   As Iron to Adamant: as Earth to th' Center,
Yet after all comparisons of truth,
(As truths authentique author to be cited)
As true as Troylus, shall croune vp the verse,
And sanctifie the nombers.

CRESSID   Prophet may you bee,
If I bee falce or swarue a hayre from truth,

When time is ould and hath forgot it selfe,
When water drops haue worne the stones of Troy,
And blind obliuion swallowd Citties vp,
And mighty states character-les are grated,
To dusty nothing, yet let memory,   1760
From falce to falce among falce mayds in loue,
Vpbraid my falcehood, when th'haue said as falce,
As ayre, as water, wind or sandy earth,
As Fox to Lambe; or Wolfe to Heifers Calfe,
Pard to the Hind, or stepdame to her Sonne,
Yea let them say to sticke the heart of falsehood,
As false as Cressid.

PANDARUS Go to a bargaine made, seale it, seale it ile bee
the witnes here I hold your hand, here my Cozens, if
euer you proue false one, to another: since I haue   1770
taken such paine to bring you together let all pittifull
goers betweene be cald to the worlds end after my
name, call them all Panders, let all constant men be
Troylusses all false woemen Cressids, and all brokers
betweene panders; say Amen.

TROYLUS Amen.

CRESSID Amen.

PANDARUS Amen.
Whereupon I will shew you a Chamber, with a bed,
which bed because it shall not speake of your prety   1780
encounters presse it to death; away.

                 Exeunt Troylus and Cressid
And Cupid grant all tong-tide maydens here,
Bed, chamber, Pander to prouide this geere.   *Exit*

    Florish. Enter Vlisses, Diomed, Nestor,   Sc. 9
    Agamemnon, Menelaus, Aiax, Chalcas   (3.3)

CALCAS

Now Princes for the seruice I haue done you,
Th'aduantage of the time prompts me aloud,
To call for recompence: appere it to your mind,
That through the sight I beare in things to come,
I haue abandond Troy, left my profession,
Incurd a traytors name, exposd my selfe,
From certaine and possest conueniences,   1790
To doubtfull fortunes, sequestring from me all,
That time acquaintance, custome and condition,
Made tame, and most familiar to my nature:
And here to doe you seruice am become,
As new into the world, strange, vnacquainted,
I do beseech you as in way of tast,
To giue me now a little benefit,
Out of those many registred in promise,
Which you say liue to come in my behalfe.

AGAMEMNON

What wouldst thou of vs Troian? make demand?   1800

CALCAS

You haue a Troian prisoner cald Antenor,
Yesterday tooke, Troy holds him very deere.
Oft haue you (often haue you thankes therefore)
Desird my Cressed in right great exchange,
Whom Troy hath still deni'd but this Anthenor,
I know is such a wrest in their affaires:
That their negotiations all must slacke,

Wanting his mannage and they will almost,
Giue vs a Prince of blood a Sonne of *Pryam*,
1810 In change of him. Let him be sent great Princes,
And he shall buy my daughter: and her presence,
Shall quite strike of all seruice I haue done,
In most accepted paine.

AGAMEMNON   Let *Diomedes* beare him,
And bring vs *Cressid* hither, *Calcas* shall haue
What he requests of vs: good *Diomed*
Furnish you fairly for this enterchange,
Withall bring word If *Hector* will to morrow,
Bee answer'd in his challenge. *Aiax* is ready.

DIOMED
This shall I vndertake, and tis a burthen
1820 Which I am proud to beare.   *Exit, with Calcas*
          Enter Achilles and Patroclus in their tent

VLISSES
Achilles stands ith entrance of his tent,
Please it our generall passe strangely by him:
As if he were forgot, and princes all,
Lay negligent and loose regard vpon him,
I will come last, tis like heele question mee.
Why such vnplausiue eyes are bent? why turnd on him,
If so I haue derision medecinable,
To vse betweene your strangnes and his pride,
Which his owne will shall haue desire to drinke,
1830 It may doe good, pride hath no other glasse,
To show it selfe but pride for supple knees
Feed arrogance and are the proud mans fees.

AGAMEMNON
Weele execute your purpose and put on,
A forme of strangnesse as we pas along,
So do each Lord, and either greet him not
Or els disdaynfully, which shall shake him more:
Then if not lookt on. I will lead the way.
          They passe by the tent, in turne

ACHILLES
What comes the generall to speake with mee?
You know my minde Ile fight no more 'gainst Troy.

AGAMEMNON (*to Nestor*)
1840 What saies *Achilles* would he ought with vs?

NESTOR (*to Achilles*)
Would you my Lord ought with the generall.

ACHILLES   No.

NESTOR (*to Agamemnon*)
Nothing my Lord.

AGAMEMNON   The better.
          ⌜*Exeunt Agamemnon and Nestor*⌝

ACHILLES ⌜*to Menelaus*⌝   Good day, good day.

MENELAUS How do you? how do you?   ⌜*Exit*⌝

ACHILLES (*to Patroclus*)
What do's the Cuckould scorne me?

AIAX   How now *Patroclus*?

ACHILLES
Good morrow *Aiax*?

AIAX   Ha.

ACHILLES   Good morrow.

AIAX I and good next day too.   *Exit*

ACHILLES (*to Patroclus*)
What meane these fellowes know they not *Achilles*?

PATROCLUS
They passe by strangely: they were vs'd to bend,
To send their smiles before them to *Achilles*:
To come as humbly as they vse to creep,   1850
To holy aultars.

ACHILLES   What am I poore of late?
Tis certaine, greatnesse once falne out with fortune,
Must fall out with men to, what the declin'd is,
He shall as soone reade in the eyes of others
As feele in his owne fall: for men like butter-flies,
Shew not their mealy wings but to the Summer,
And not a man for being simply man,
Hath any honour, but honour for those honours
That are without him, as place, ritches, and fauour,
Prizes of accident as oft as merit   1860
Which when they fall as being slipery standers,
The loue that lean'd on them as slipery too,
Doth one pluck downe another, and to gether,
Die in the fall, but tis not so with mee,
Fortune and I are friends, I do enioy:
At ample point all that I did possesse,
Saue these mens lookes, who do me thinkes finde out:
Some thing not worth in me such ritch beholding,
As they haue often giuen. Here is *Vlisses*
Ile interrupt his reading, how now *Vlisses*?   1870

VLISSES Now great *Thetis* Sonne.

ACHILLES What are you reading?

VLISSES A strange fellow here,
Writes me that man, how derely euer parted:
How much in hauing or without or in
Cannot, make bost to haue that which he hath,
Nor feeles not what he owes but by reflection:
As when his vertues shining vpon others,
Heate them and they retort that heate againe
To the first giuers.

ACHILLES   This is not strange *Vlisses*,   1880
The beauty that is borne here in the face:
The bearer knowes not, but commends it selfe,
To others eyes, nor doth the eye it selfe
That most pure spirit of sence, behold it selfe
Not going from it selfe: but eye to eye opposed,
Sallutes each other, with each others forme.
For speculation turnes not to it selfe,
Till it hath trauel'd and is mirrord there?
Where it may see it selfe: this is not strange at all.

VLISSES
I do not straine at the position,   1890
It is familiar, but at the authors drift,
Who in his circumstance expressly prooues,
That no man is the Lord of any thing:
Though in and of him there be much consisting,
Till he communicate his parts to others,
Nor doth hee of himselfe know them for aught:
Till he behold them formed in th'applause,
Where th'are extended: who like an arch reuerb'rate

The voice againe or like a gate of steele:
1900   Fronting the Sunne, receiues and renders back
His figure and his heate. I was much rap't in this,
And apprehended here immediately,
The vnknowne *Aiax*,
Heauens what a man is there? A very horse,
That has he knowes not what. Nature what things
    there are.
Most abiect in regard, and deere in vse,
What things againe most deere in the esteeme:
And poore in worth, now shall we see to morrow,
An act that very chance doth throw vpon him
1910   *Aiax* renown'd? O heauens what some men doe,
While some men leaue to doe.
How some men creepe in skittish fortunes hall,
Whiles others play the Ideots in her eyes,
How one man eates into anothers pride,
While pride is fasting in his wantonesse.
To see these Grecian Lords, why euen already:
They clap the lubber *Aiax* on the shoulder
As if his foote were one braue *Hectors* brest,
And great *Troy* shrinking.

ACHILLES   I doe beleeue it,
1920   For they past by me as misers do by beggars,
Neither gaue to me good word nor looke:
What are my deeds forgot?

VLISSES   Time hath (my Lord)
A wallet at his back, wherein he puts
Almes for obliuion: a greatsiz'd monster
Of ingratitudes, those scraps are good deeds past,
Which are deuour'd as fast as they are made,
Forgot as soone as done, perseuerance deere my Lord:
Keepes honour bright, to haue done, is to hang,
Quite out of fashion like a rusty male,
1930   In monumentall mockry? take the instant way,
For honour trauells in a straight so narrow:
Where on but goes a brest, keepe then the path
For emulation hath a thousand Sonnes,
That one by one pursue, if you giue way,
Or hedge a side from the direct forth right:
Like to an entred tide they all rush by,
And leaue you hindmost,
Or like a gallant Horse falne in first ranke,
Lye there for pauement to the abiect reere
1940   Ore-run and trampled on: then what they do in present:
Though lesse then yours in paste, must ore top yours.
For time is like a fashionable hoast,
That slightly shakes his parting guest by th'hand,
And with his armes out-stretcht as he would flie,
Graspes in the commer: welcome euer smiles,
And farewell goes out sighing. O let not vertue seeke,
Remuneration for the thing it was.
For beauty, wit,
High birth, vigor of bone, desert in seruice,
1950   Loue, friendship, charity, are subiects all,
To enuious and calumniating time.
One touch of nature makes the whole world kin,
That all with one consent praise new-borne gaudes,

Though they are made and moulded of things past,
And giue to dust, that is a little guilt,
More laud then guilt ore-dusted.
The present eye praises the present obiect.
Then maruell not thou great and complet man,
That all the Greekes begin to worship *Aiax*;
Since things in motion sooner catch the eye,   1960
Than what not stirs. The crie went once on thee,
And still it might, and yet it may againe,
If thou wouldst not entombe thy selfe aliue,
And case thy reputation in thy tent,
Whose glorious deeds but in these fields of late,
Made emulous missions mongst the gods them-selues,
And draue great *Mars* to faction.

ACHILLES   Of this my priuacie,
I haue strong reasons.

VLISSES   But gainst your priuacie,
The reasons are more potent and heroycall:
Tis knowne *Achilles* that you are in loue   1970
With one of *Priams* daughters.

ACHILLES   Ha? knowne.

VLISSES   Is that a wonder:
The prouidence thats in a watchfull state,
Knowes almost euery graine of Plutoes gold,
Findes bottom in th'vncomprehensiue deepes,
Keepes place with ought and almost like the gods,
Do infant thoughts vnuaile in their dumbe cradles.
There is a mysterie (with whom relation
Durst neuer meddle) in the soule of state,
Which hath an operation more diuine,
Then breath or pen can giue expressure to: 1980
All the commerse that you haue had with Troy,
As perfectly is ours, as yours my Lord,
And better would it fitt *Achilles* much,
To throw downe *Hector* then *Polixena*.
But it must grieue young *Pirhus* now at home,
When fame shall in his Iland sound her trumpe,
And all the Greekish girles shall tripping sing,
Great *Hectors* sister did *Achilles* winne,
But our great *Aiax* brauely beate downe him:
Farewell my Lord: I as your louer speake,   1990
The foole slides ore the Ice that you should breake.
                         Exit

PATROCLUS
To this effect *Achilles* haue I moou'd you,
A woman impudent and mannish growne,
Is not more loth'd then an effeminate man
In time of action: I stand condemnd for this
They thinke my little stomack to the warre,
And your great loue to me, restraines you thus,
Sweete rouse your selfe, and the weake wanton *Cupid*,
Shall from your neck vnloose his amorous fould,
And like a dew drop from the Lions mane,   2000
Be shooke to ayre.

ACHILLES   Shall *Aiax* fight with *Hector*.

PATROCLUS
I and perhaps receiue much honor by him.

ACHILLES

   I see my reputation is at stake,

   My fame is shrowdly gor'd.

PATROCLUS   O then beware.

   Those wounds heale ill, that men do giue themselues,

   Omission to doe what is necessary,

   Seales a commission to a blanke of danger,

   And danger like an ague subtly taints

   Euen then when we sit idely in the sunne.

ACHILLES

2010   Go call *Thersites* hether sweet *Patroclus*,

   Ile send the foole to *Aiax*, and desire him

   T'inuite the Troyan lords after the combate,

   To see vs heere vnarmd. I haue a womans longing,

   An appetite that I am sick with-all,

   To see great *Hector* in his weeds of peace,

      Enter Thersites

   To talke with him, and to behold his visage,

   Euen to my full of view. A labour sau'd.

THERSITES A wonder.

ACHILLES What?

2020 THERSITES *Aiax* goes vp and downe the field as asking for

   himselfe.

ACHILLES How so?

THERSITES He must fight singly to morrow with *Hector*,

   and is so prophetically proud of an heroycall cudgeling,

   that he raues in saying nothing.

ACHILLES How can that be?

THERSITES Why a stalkes vp and downe like a peacock, a

   stride and a stand: ruminates like an hostisse, that

   hath no Arithmatique but her braine to set downe her

2030   reckoning: bites his lip with a politique regarde, as

   who should say there were witte in this head and

   twoo'd out: and so there is. But it lyes as coldly in

   him, as fire in a flint, which will not show without

   knocking, the mans vndone for euer, for if *Hector* breake

   not his neck ith' combate, hee'le breakt himselfe in

   vaine glory. Hee knowes not mee. I sayd good morrow

   Aiax: And hee replyes thankes *Agamemnon*. What

   thinke you of this man that takes mee for the Generall?

   Hees growne a very land-fish languagelesse, a monster,

2040   a plague of opinion, a man may weare it on both sides

   like a lether Ierkin.

ACHILLES Thou must be my Ambassador to him *Thersites*.

THERSITES Who I: why heele answer no body: hee

   professes not answering, speaking is for beggers: he

   weares his tongue in's armes. I will put on his presence,

   let *Patroclus* make demands to me. You shall see the

   pageant of *Aiax*.

ACHILLES To him *Patroclus*, tell him I humbly desire the

   valiant *Aiax*, to inuite the most valorous *Hector* to come

2050   vnarm'd to my tent, and to procure safe-conduct for

   his person, of the magnanimous and most illustrious,

   sixe or seauen times honour'd Captaine Generall of the

   Grecian armie, *Agamemnon*, &c. do this.

PATROCLUS (*to Thersites*) *Ioue* blesse great *Aiax*.

THERSITES Hum.

PATROCLUS I come from the worthy *Achilles*.

THERSITES Ha?

PATROCLUS Who most humbly desires you to inuite *Hector*

   to his tent.

THERSITES Hum?   2060

PATROCLUS And to procure safe conduct from *Agamemnon*.

THERSITES *Agamemnon*?

PATROCLUS I my Lord.

THERSITES Ha?

PATROCLUS What say you too't.

THERSITES God buy you with all my heart.

PATROCLUS Your answer sir.

THERSITES If to morrow be a faire day, by a leuen a clock

   it will goe one way or other, howsoeuer he shall pay

   for me ere hee ha's me.   2070

PATROCLUS Your answer sir.

THERSITES Fare yee well with all my heart.

ACHILLES Why, but he is not in this tune, is he?

THERSITES No: but he's out a tune thus. What musick

   will be in him, when *Hector* ha's knockt out his braines,

   I know not. But I am ferd none, vnlesse the fidler *Apollo*

   get his sinnews to make Catlings on.

ACHILLES

   Come, thou shalt beare a letter to him straight.

THERSITES Let mee carry another to his horse, for thats

   the more capable creature.   2080

ACHILLES

   My minde is troubled like a fountaine stird,

   And I my selfe see not the bottome of it.

                   Exit with Patroclus

THERSITES Would the fountaine of your minde were cleere

   againe, that I might water an Asse at it, I had rather

   be a tick in a sheepe, then such a valiant ignorance.

                         Exit

   Enter at one doore Æneas with a torch, at another   Sc. 10

   Paris, Deiphobus, Antenor, Diomed the Grecian with   (4.1)

   torches

PARIS See ho? who is that there?

DEIPHOBUS It is the Lord *Æneas*.

ÆNEAS Is the Prince there in person?

   Had I so good occasion to lye long

   As you prince *Paris*, nothing but heauenly businesse,   2090

   Should rob my bed mate of my company.

DIOMED

   That's my minde too? good morrow Lord *Æneas*.

PARIS

   A valiant Greeke *Æneas* take his hand.

   Witnesse the processe of your speech: wherein

   You told how *Dyomed* in a whole weeke by daies,

   Did haunt you in the field.

ÆNEAS (*to Diomed*)   Health to you valiant sir,

   During all question of the gentle truce:

   But when I meete you arm'd, as black defiance,

   As heart can thinke or courage execute.

DIOMED

   The one and other *Diomed* embraces,   2100

   Our blouds are now in calme, and so long helth:

   But when contention, and occasion meete,

By *Ioue* ile play the hunter for thy life,
With all my force, pursuite, and pollicy.

ÆNEAS

And thou shalt hunt a Lyon that will flie,
With his face back-ward: in humane gentlenesse,
Welcome to Troy, now by *Anchises* life,
Welcome indeed: by *Venus* hand I swere:
No man aliue can loue in such a sort,
2110 The thing he meanes to kill, more excellently.

DIOMED

We simpathize. *Ioue* let *Æneas* liue
(If to my sword his fate be not the glory)
A thousand compleate courses of the Sunne,
But in mine emulous honor let him die:
With euery ioynt a wound and that to morrow.

ÆNEAS We know each other well?

DIOMED

We do and long to know each other worse.

PARIS

This is the most despightfull'st gentle greeting,
The noblest hatefull loue that ere I heard of,
2120 What businesse Lord so earely?

ÆNEAS

I was sent for to the King? but why I know not.

PARIS

His purpose meetes you? twas to bring this Greeke,
To *Calcha's* house, and there to render him:
For the enfreed *Anthenor* the faire *Cressid*,
Lets haue your company, or if you please,
Hast there before vs. ⌈*Aside*⌉ I constantly doe thinke,
(Or rather call my thought a certaine knowledge)
My brother *Troylus* lodges there to night,
Rouse him and giue him note of our approch,
2130 With the whole quality wherefore: I feare
We shall be much vnwelcome.

ÆNEAS ⌈*aside*⌉   That I assure you:
Troylus had rather Troy were borne to Greece,
Then *Cresseid* borne from Troy.

PARIS ⌈*aside*⌉   There is no helpe.
The bitter disposition of the time
Will haue it so:
⌈*Aloud*⌉ On Lord, weele follow you.

ÆNEAS Good morrow all.   *Exit*

PARIS

And tell me noble *Diomed*, faith tell me true,
Euen in the soule of sound good fellowship,
2140 Who in your thoughts, merits faire *Helen* most,
My selfe, or *Menelaus*.

DIOMED   Both alike.
Hee merits well to haue her that doth seeke her,
Not making any scruple of her soylure,
With such a hell of paine, and world of charge.
And you as well to keepe her, that defend her,
Not pallating the taste of her dishonour
With such a costly losse of wealth and friends,
He like a puling Cuckold would drinke vp,
The lees and dregs of a flat tamed peece:
2150 You like a letcher out of whorish loynes,
Are pleasd to breed out your inheritors,

Both merits poyzd, each weighs nor lesse nor more,
But he as he, which heauier for a whore.

PARIS

You are too bitter to your country-woman.

DIOMED

Shees bitter to her country, heare me *Paris*,
For euery false drop in her bawdy veines,
A Grecians life hath sunke: for euery scruple
Of her contaminated carrion waight,
A Troyan hath beene slaine. Since she could speake,
Shee hath not giuen so many good words breath,   2160
As for her Greekes and Troyans suffred death.

PARIS

Faire *Diomed* you do as chapmen do,
Dispraise the thing that you desire to buy,
But we in silence hold this vertue well,
Weele but commend, what wee intend to sell.
Heere lyes our way.   *Exeunt*

Enter Troylus and Cresseida   Sc. 11
TROYLUS   (4.2)

Deere, trouble not your selfe, the morne is colde.

CRESSID

Then sweet my Lord ile call mine vnckle downe,
Hee shall vnbolt the gates.

TROYLUS   Trouble him not.
To bed to bed: sleepe lull those pritty eyes,   2170
And giue as soft attachment to thy sences,
As to infants empty of all thought.

CRESSID Good morrow then.

TROYLUS I prithee now to bed.

CRESSID Are you a weary of me?

TROYLUS

O *Cresseida*! but that the busie day,
Wak't by the Larke hath rouzd the ribald Crowes,
And dreaming night will hide our ioyes no longer,
I would not from thee.

CRESSID   Night hath beene too briefe.

TROYLUS

Beshrew the witch! with venemous wights she staies   2180
As hidiously as hell, But flies the graspes of loue,
With wings more momentary swift then thought,
You will catch colde and curse me.

CRESSID Prithee tarry, you men will neuer tarry,
O foolish *Cresseid*, I might haue still held of,
And then you would haue tarried. Harke ther's one vp.
⌈*She veils her selfe*⌉

PANDARUS (*within*) Whats all the doores open heere?

TROYLUS It is your Vncle.

CRESSID

A pestilence on him: now will he be mocking:
I shall haue such a life.   2190
⌈*Enter Pandarus*⌉

PANDARUS How now, how now, how go maiden-heads,
(*to Cressida*) heere you maide, where's my cozin
Cresseid?

CRESSID ⌈*vnueiling*⌉

Go hang your selfe, you naughty mocking vncle,
You bring me to doo—and then you floute me to.

PANDARUS To do what, to do what? let her say what, what haue I brought you to doe?

CRESSID

Come, come, beshrew your heart, youle nere be good, Nor suffer others.

2200 PANDARUS Ha, ha: alas poore wretch: a poore *chipochia*, hast not slept to night? would hee not (a naughty man) let it sleepe, a bug-beare take him.

CRESSID (*to Troylus*)

Did not I tell you? would he were knockt ith' head,

⌈*One knocks*⌉

Who's that at doore, good vnckle go and see. My Lord, come you againe into my chamber, You smile and mock me, as if I meant naughtily.

TROYLUS Ha, ha.

CRESSID

Come you are deceiu'd, I thinke of no such thing,

Knock

How earnestly they knock, pray you come in.

2210 I would not for halfe *Troy* haue you seene here.

Exeunt ⌈*Troylus and Cressida*⌉

PANDARUS Who's there? what's the matter? will you beate downe the doore?

He opens the doore. ⌈*Enter Æneas*⌉

How now, what's the matter?

ÆNEAS Good morrow Lord, good morrow.

PANDARUS

Who's there my Lord *Æneas*: by my troth I knew you not: what newes with you so early?

ÆNEAS

Is not Prince *Troylus* heere?

PANDARUS   Here, what should he do here?

ÆNEAS

Come he is here, my Lord, do not deny him, It doth import him much to speake with me.

2220 PANDARUS Is he here say you? its more then I know ile be sworne: For my owne part I came in late: what should hee doe here?

ÆNEAS

Who, nay then! Come, come, youle do him wrong, Ere you are ware, youle be so true to him, To be false to him: do not you know of him, But yet go fetch him hither, go.   ⌈*Exit Pandarus*⌉

Enter Troylus

TROYLUS How now, whats the matter?

ÆNEAS

My Lord, I scarce haue leisure to salute you, My matter is so rash: there is at hand,

2230 *Paris* your brother, and *Deiphobus*, The Grecian *Diomed*, and our *Anthenor* Deliuer'd to vs, and for him forth-with, Ere the first sacrifice, within this houre, We must giue vp to *Diomedes* hand The Lady *Cresseida*.

TROYLUS   Is it so concluded?

ÆNEAS

By *Priam* and the generall state of *Troy*, They are at hand, and ready to effect it.

TROYLUS How my atchiuements mock me, I will go meete them: and my Lord *Æneas*, We met by chance, you did not finde me here.   2240

ÆNEAS

Good, good, my lord, the secrecies of nature Haue not more guift in taciturnitie.   *Exeunt*

Enter Pandarus and Cressid   Sc. 12
(4.3)

PANDARUS Ist possible: no sooner got but lost, the diuell take *Anthenor*, the young Prince will go madde, a plague vpon *Anthenor*. I would they had brok's neck.

CRESSID How now? what's the matter? who was heere?

PANDARUS Ah, ah!

CRESSID Why sigh you so profoundly, wher's my Lord? gone? tell me sweete Vncle, whats the matter.

PANDARUS Would I were as deepe vnder the earth as I   2250
am aboue.

CRESSID O the Gods, whats the matter?

PANDARUS Pray thee get thee in: would thou hadst nere been borne, I knew thou wouldest be his death. O poore Gentleman, a plague vpon *Anthenor*.

CRESSID Good vnckle, I beseech you on my knees, I beseech you whats the matter?

PANDARUS Thou must be gone wench, thou must be gone: thou art chang'd for *Anthenor*. Thou must to thy father and bee gone from *Troylus*, twill be his death, twill bee   2260
his bane, hee cannot beare it.

CRESSID

O you immortall Gods, I will not go.

PANDARUS Thou must.

CRESSID

I will not Vncle. I haue forgot my father, I know no touch of consanguinitie, No kinne, no loue, no bloud, no soule so neere me As the sweete *Troylus*. O you gods diuine, Make *Cresseids* name the very crowne of falsehood, If euer she leaue *Troylus*. Time, force and death, Do to this body what extreamitie you can: 2270
But the strong base, and building of my loue, Is as the very center of the earth, Drawing all things to it. Ile go in and weepe.

PANDARUS Do, do.

CRESSID

Teare my bright haire, & scratch my praised cheekes, Crack my cleare voyce with sobs, and breake my heart, With sounding *Troylus*: I will not go from Troy.

Exeunt

Enter Paris, Troylus, Æneas, Deiphobus, Anthenor,   Sc. 13
Diomedes   (4.4)

PARIS

It is great morning, and the houre prefixt, Of her deliuery to this valiant Greeke, Comes fast vpon vs: good my brother *Troylus*   2280
Tell you the Lady what she is to doe, And hast her to the purpose.

TROYLUS   Walke into her house, Ile bring her to the Grecian presently: And to his hand when I deliuer her,

Thinke it an altar, and thy brother *Troylus*
A priest there offring to it his owne heart.
PARIS I know what tis to loue,
And would, as I shall pitty I could helpe:
Please you walke in my Lords?   ⌜*Exeunt*⌝

Sc. 14   *Enter Pandarus and Cresseida*
(4.5)   PANDARUS Be moderate, be moderate.
        CRESSID
2291   Why tell you me of moderation?
            The greife is fine, full, perfect that I taste,
            And violenteth in a sence as strong
            As that which causeth it, how can I moderate it?
            If I could temporize with my affection,
            Or brew it to a weake and coulder pallat,
            The like alayment could I giue my griefe:
            My loue admittes no qualifiing drosse,
            No more my griefe in such a precious losse.
                    Enter Troylus
2300   PANDARUS Here, here, here he comes, a sweete ducks.
        CRESSID (*embracing him*) Oh *Troylus*, *Troylus*.
        PANDARUS What a paire of spectacles is here, let me
            embrace you too, Oh heart, as the goodly saying is,
                Oh heart, heauy heart,
                    Why sighst thou without breaking:
            where hee answers againe,
                Because thou canst not ease thy smart
                    By friendshippe nor by speaking:
            there was neuer a truer rime. Let vs cast away nothing,
2310   for wee may liue to haue need of such a verse, We see
            it, we see it, how now lambs?
        TROYLUS
            Cressid I loue thee in so strain'd a purity,
            That the blest Gods as angry with my fancy:
            More bright in zeale then the deuotion, which
            Cold lippes blow to their dieties, take thee from me.
        CRESSID Haue the Gods enuy?
        PANDARUS I, I, I, I, tis to plaine a case.
        CRESSID
            And is it true that I must go from Troy?
        TROYLUS
            A hatefull truth.
        CRESSID   What and from *Troylus* to?
        TROYLUS
            From Troy, and *Troylus*.
2320   CRESSID   Is't possible?
        TROYLUS
            And suddenly, where iniury of chance
            Puts back, leaue taking: iussles roughly by,
            All time of pause: rudely beguiles our lippes
            Of all reioyndure: forcibly preuents
            Our lock't embrasures, strangles our dere vowes,
            Euen in the birth of our owne laboring breath:
            We two that with so many thousand sighes,
            Did buy each other, must poorely sell our selues,
            With the rude breuity, and discharge of one,
2330   Iniurious time now with a robbers hast,
            Cram's his ritch theeu'ry vp hee knowes not how.

As many farewells as be starres in heauen,
With distinct breath, and consignde kisses to them,
He fumbles vp into a loose adewe:
And skants vs with a single famisht kisse,
Distasted with the salt of broken teares.
        Enter Æneas
ÆNEAS My Lord is the Lady ready?
TROYLUS (*to Cressid*)
    Harke, you are call'd, some say the *Genius* so
    Cries, come to him that instantly must die,
    ⌜*To Pandarus*⌝ Bid them haue pacience she shall come
        anon.   2340
PANDARUS Where are my teares? raine to lay this winde,
    or my heart wilbe blowne vp by the root.
                    ⌜*Exit with Æneas*⌝
CRESSID
    I must then to the Grecians.
TROYLUS   No remedy?
CRESSID
    A wofull *Cressid* 'mongst the merry Greekes,
    When shall we see againe.
TROYLUS
    Here mee my loue? be thou but true of heart.
CRESSID
    I true? how now? what wicked deme is this?
TROYLUS
    Nay we must vse expostulation kindely,
    For it is parting from vs.
    I speake not be thou true as fearing thee.   2350
    For I will throw my gloue to death himselfe,
    That there's no maculation in thy heart:
    But bee thou true say I to fashion in,
    My sequent protestation, bee thou true,
    And I will see thee.
CRESSID
    Oh you shalbe expos'd my Lord to dangers,
    As infinite as imminent: but ile be true.
TROYLUS
    And ile grow friend with danger, were this sleeue.
CRESSID
    And you this gloue, when shall I see you?
TROYLUS
    I will corrupt the Grecian centinells,   2360
    To giue thee nightly visitation,
    But yet be true.
CRESSID Oh heauens be true againe?
TROYLUS Here why I speake it loue,
    The Grecian youths are full of quality,
    Their louing well compos'd, with guifts of nature
        flowing,
    And swelling ore with arts and excercise:
    How nouelty may moue, and parts with person,
    Alas a kinde of Godly iealousie,
    (Which I beseech you cal a vertuous sinne,)   2370
    Makes me a feard.
CRESSID Oh heauens you loue mee not!
TROYLUS Die I a villaine then,
    In this I do not call your faith in question:

So mainely as my merit. I cannot sing
Nor heele the high lauolt, nor sweeten talke,
Nor play at subtill games, faire vertues all:
To which the Grecians are most prompt and pregnant,
But I can tell that in each grace of these:
2380   There lurkes a still, and dumb-discoursiue diuell
That tempts most cunningly, but be not tempted.
CRESSID Do you thinke I will?
TROYLUS
No, but somthing may be done that we will not,
And sometimes we are diuells to our selues:
When we will tempt the frailty of our powers,
Presuming on their changefull potency.
ÆNEAS (within)
Nay good my Lord?
TROYLUS   Come kisse, and let vs part.
PARIS ⌈at the doore⌉
Brother Troylus?
TROYLUS   Good brother come you hither?
And bring Eneas and the Grecian with you.
                                  ⌈Exit Paris⌉
2390   CRESSID My Lord will you be true?
TROYLUS
Who I, alas it is my vice, my fault,
Whiles others fish with craft for great opinion,
I with great truth catch mere simplicity,
Whilst some with cunning guild their copper crownes,
With truth and plainesse I do were mine bare:
        Enter Paris, Æneas, Anthenor, Deiphobus, and
        Diomed
Feare not my truth, the morrall of my wit,
Is plaine and true? ther's all the reach of it,
Welcome sir Diomed, here is the Lady,
Which for Antenor we deliuer you.
2400   At the port (Lord) Ile giue her to thy hand,
And by the way possesse thee what she is
Entreate her faire, and by my soule faire Greeke,
If ere thou stand at mercy of my sword:
Name Cressid, and thy life shalbe as safe,
As Priam is in Illion?
DIOMED   Faire Ladie Cressid,
So please you saue the thankes this Prince expects:
The lustre in your eye, heauen in your cheeke,
Pleades your faire vsage, and to Diomed,
You shalbe mistres, and command him wholy.
TROYLUS
2410   Grecian thou do'st not vse me curteously,
To shame the zeale of my petition towards thee:
In praising her. I tell thee Lord of Greece,
She is as farre high soaring ore thy praises:
As thou vnworthy to be call'd her seruant,
I charge thee vse her well, euen for my charge:
For by the dreadfull Pluto, if thou dost not,
Though the great bulke Achilles be thy guard,
Ile cut thy throate.
DIOMED   Oh be not mou'd Prince Troylus,
Let me be priueledg'd by my place and message:
2420   To be a speaker free? when I am hence,

Ile answer to my lust, and know you Lord
Ile nothing do on charge, to her owne worth,
Shee shalbe priz'd: but that you say be't so,
Ile speake it in my spirit and honour no.
TROYLUS
Come to the port Ile tel thee Diomed,
This braue shall oft make thee to hide thy head,
Lady giue me your hand, and as we walke,
To our owne selues bend we our needfull talke.
                Exeunt Troylus, Cressid, and Diomed
        Sound Trumpet
PARIS
Harke Hectors trumpet?
ÆNEAS   How haue we spent this morning?
The Prince must thinke me tardy and remisse,   2430
That swore to ride before him in the field.
PARIS
Tis Troylus falte, come, come, to field with him.
DEIPHOBUS Let vs make ready straight.
ÆNEAS
Yea, with a Bridegroomes fresh alacritie
Let vs addresse to tend on Hectors heeles:
The glory of our Troy doth this day lye
On his faire worth, and single Chiualrie.   Exeunt

        Enter Aiax armed, Achilles, Patroclus, Agamemnon,   Sc. 15
        Menelaus, Vlisses, Nester, a trumpet, &c   (4.6)
AGAMEMNON
Here art thou in appointment fresh and faire,
Anticipating time, with starting courage.
Giue with thy trumpet a loude note to Troy   2440
Thou dreadfull Aiax that the appauled aire,
May pearce the head of the great Combatant,
And hale him hither.
AIAX   Thou, trumpet, ther's my purse,
        He giues him money
Now cracke thy lungs, and split thy brasen pipe:
Blow villaine, till thy sphered Bias cheeke,
Out-swell the collick of puft Aquilon,
Come stretch thy chest, and let thy eyes spout bloud:
Thou blowest for Hector.
        ⌈Trumpet sounds⌉
VLISSES No trumpet answers.
ACHILLES Tis but early daies.   2450
AGAMEMNON
Is not yond Diomed with Calcas daughter.
VLISSES
Tis he, I ken the manner of his gate,
He rises on the too: that spirit of his
In aspiration lifts him from the earth.
        Enter Diomed and Cressid
AGAMEMNON (to Diomed)
Is this the Lady Cressid?
DIOMED   Euen she.
AGAMEMNON
Most deerely welcome to the Greekes sweete Lady.
        He kisses her
NESTER (to Cressid)
Our generall doth salute you with a kisse.

VLISSES
    Yet is the kindnesse but perticular,
    Twere better shee were kist in general.

NESTOR
2460   And very courtly counsell. Ile beginne:
        He kisses her
    So much for *Nestor*.

ACHILLES
    Ile take that winter from your lips faire Lady,
        He kisses her
    Achilles bids you welcome.

MENELAUS (*to Cressid*)
    I had good argument for kissing once.

PATROCLUS
    But thats no argument for kissing now,
    For thus ⌜*stepping between them*⌝ pop't *Paris* in his
            hardiment,
    And parted thus, you and your argument.
        He kisses her

VLISSES ⌜*aside*⌝
    Oh deadly gall and theame of all our scornes,
    For which we loose our heads to guild his hornes.

PATROCLUS (*to Cressid*)
2470   The first was *Menelaus* kisse this mine,
    Patroclus kisses you.
        He kisses her againe

MENELAUS   Oh this is trim.

PATROCLUS (*to Cressid*)
    Paris and I kisse euermore for him.

MENELAUS
    Ile haue my kisse sir? Lady by your leaue.

CRESSID
    In kissing do you render or receiue.

⌜MENELAUS⌝
    Both take and giue.

CRESSID   Ile make my match to liue,
    The kisse you take is better then you giue:
    Therefore no kisse.

MENELAUS
    Ile giue you boote, ile giue you three for one.

CRESSID
    You are an od man giue euen or giue none.

MENELAUS
2480   An odde man Lady, euery man is odde.

CRESSID
    No *Paris* is not, for you know tis true,
    That you are odde and he is euen with you.

MENELAUS
    You fillip me a'th head.

CRESSID   No ile be sworne.

VLISSES
    It were no match, your naile against his horne,
    May I sweete Lady begge a kisse of you.

CRESSID
    You may.

VLISSES   I do desire it.

CRESSID   Why begge too.

VLISSES
    Why then for *Venus* sake giue me a kisse,
    When *Hellen* is a maide againe and his—

CRESSID
    I am your debtor, claime it when tis due.

VLISSES
    Neuers my day, and then a kisse of you.   2490

DIOMED
    Lady a word, ile bring you to your father.
        ⌜*They talke apart*⌝

NESTOR
    A woman of quick sence.

VLISSES   Fie, fie vpon her,
    Ther's language in her eye, her cheeke her lip,
    Nay her foote speakes, her wanton spirits looke out
    At euery ioynt and motiue of her body,
    Oh these encounterers so glib of tongue,
    That giue a coasting welcome ere it comes,
    And wide vnclaspe the tables of their thoughts,
    To euery ticklish reader, set them downe,
    For sluttish spoiles of opportunity: 2500
    And daughters of the game.
                ⌜*Exeunt Diomed and Cressid*⌝
        Flowrish

ALL The Troyans trumpet.
        Enter all of Troy: Hector ⌜*armed*⌝*, Paris, Æneas,*
        Helenus, and Attendants, among them Troylus

AGAMEMNON Yonder comes the troup.

ÆNEAS ⌜*comming forward*⌝
    Haile all you state of Greece: what shalbe done,
    To him that victory commands, or doe you purpose,
    A victor shalbe knowne, will you the knights
    Shall to the edge of all extremity
    Pursue each other, or shall they be diuided,
    By any voice or order of the field,
    Hector bad aske?

AGAMEMNON   Which way would *Hector* haue it?   2510

ÆNEAS
    He cares not, heele obay condicions.

⌜ACHILLES⌝
    Tis done like *Hector*, but securely done,
    A little proudly, and great deale disprising:
    The knight oppos'd.

ÆNEAS   If not *Achilles* sir,
    What is your name?

ACHILLES   If not *Achilles* nothing.

ÆNEAS
    Therefore *Achilles*, but what ere know this,
    In the extremity of great and little:
    Valour and pride excell themselues in *Hector*
    The one almost as infinite as all,
    The other blanke as nothing, way him well: 2520
    And that which lookes like pride is curtesie,
    This *Aiax* is halfe made of *Hectors* bloud,
    In loue whereof, halfe *Hector* staies at home,
    Halfe heart, halfe hand, halfe *Hector* comes to seeke:
    This blended knight halfe Troyan, and halfe Greeke.

ACHILLES
  A maiden battell then, Oh I perceiue you.
      Enter Diomed

AGAMEMNON
  Here is sir *Diomed*? go gentle knight,
  Stand by our *Aiax*. As you and Lord *Eneas*
  Consent vpon the order of their fight,
2530 So be it, either to the vttermost,
  Or els a breath,
          ⌐*Exeunt Aiax, Diomed, Hector, and Æneas*⌐
              the combatants being kin,
  Halfe stints their strife, before their strokes begin.

VLISSES They are oppos'd already.

AGAMEMNON
  What Troyan is that same that lookes so heauy?

VLISSES
  The yongest sonne of *Priam*, a true knight,
  They call him *Troylus*;
  Not yet mature, yet matchlesse firme of word,
  Speaking in deeds, and deedlesse in his tongue,
  Not soone prouok't nor beeing prouok't soone calm'd,
2540 His heart and hand both open and both free.
  For what he has he giues, what thinkes he shewes,
  Yet giues hee not till iudgement guide his bounty,
  Nor dignifies an impare thought with breath;
  Manly as *Hector*, but more dangerous,
  For *Hector* in his blaze of wrath subscribes
  To tender obiects, but he in heate of action,
  Is more vindicatiue then iealous loue.
  They call him *Troylus*, and on him erect,
  A second hope as fairely built as *Hector*:
2550 Thus saies *Æneas* one that knowes the youth,
  Euen to his ynches: and with priuate soule
  Did in great Illion thus translate him to me.
      Alarum

AGAMEMNON They are in action.

NESTOR Now *Aiax* hould thine owne.

TROYLUS *Hector* thou sleep'st awake thee.

AGAMEMNON
  His blowes are well dispos'd, there *Aiax*.   ⌐*Exeunt*⌐

Sc. 16   ⌐*Enter Hector and Aiax fighting, and Æneas and*
(4.7)   *Diomed interposing: trumpets cease*⌐

DIOMED
  You must no more.

ÆNEAS   Princes enough so please you.

AIAX
  I am not warme yet, let vs fight againe.

DIOMED
  As *Hector* pleases.

HECTOR   Why then will I no more,
2560 Thou art great Lord my fathers sisters Sonne,
  A couzen german to great *Priams* seede,
  The obligation of our bloud forbids,
  A gory emulation twixt vs twaine:
  Were thy commixtion Greeke and Troyan so,
  That thou couldst say this hand is Grecian all:
  And this is Troyan, the sinnewes of this legge

All Greeke, and this all Troy: my mothers bloud,
Runnes on the dexter cheeke, and this sinister
Bounds in my fathers. By *Ioue* multipotent
Thou shouldst not beare from mee a Greekish member,   2570
Wherein my sword had not impressure made
Of our ranke feud. But the iust Gods gainsay,
That any drop thou borrowd'st from thy mother,
My sacred Aunt, should by my mortal sword,
Be drain'd. Let me embrace thee *Aiax*:
By him that thunders thou hast lusty armes,
Hector would haue them fall vpon him thus.
Cozen all honor to thee.

AIAX   I thanke thee *Hector*,
Thou art to gentle, and too free a man,
I came to kill thee cozen, and beare hence,   2580
A great addition earned in thy death.

HECTOR
Not *Neoptolymus* so mirable,
On whose bright crest, fame with her lowdst (O yes)
Cries, this is he, could promise to himselfe,
A thought of added honor, torne from *Hector*.

ÆNEAS
There is expectance heere from both the sides,
What further you will do.

HECTOR   Weele answer it,
The issue is embracement, *Aiax* farewell.

AIAX
If I might in entreaties finde successe,
As seld I haue the chance, I would desire,   2590
My famous cosin to our Grecian tents.

DIOMED
Tis *Agamemnons* wish, and great *Achilles*
Doth long to see vnarm'd the valiant *Hector*.

HECTOR
Æneas call my brother *Troylus* to me.
And signifie this louing enterview
To the expectors of our Troyan part,
Desire them home.   ⌐*Exit Æneas*⌐
            Giue me thy hand my Cozen.
I will go eate with thee, and see your Knights.
    Enter Agamemnon and the rest: Æneas, Vlisses,
    Menelaus, Nestor, Achilles, Patroclus, Troylus, &c.

AIAX
Great *Agamemnon* comes to meete vs heere.

HECTOR (*to Æneas*)
The worthiest of them, tell me name by name: 2600
But for *Achilles* mine owne searching eyes,
Shall finde him by his large and portly size.

AGAMEMNON (*embracing him*)
Worthy of armes as welcome as to one
That would be rid of such an enemy.
But that's no welcome: vnderstand more cleere
What's past, and what's to come, is strew'd with huskes
And formelesse ruine of obliuion:
But in this extant moment, faith and troth,
Strain'd purely from all hollow bias drawing:
Bids thee with most diuine integritie,   2610
From heart of very heart, great *Hector* welcome.

HECTOR

I thanke thee most imperious *Agamemnon*.

AGAMEMNON ⌈*to Troylus*⌉

My well-fam'd Lord of Troy, no lesse to you.

MENELAUS

Let me confirme my princely brothers greeting:

You brace of warlike brothers: welcome hether.

⌈*He embraces Hector and Troylus*⌉

HECTOR (*to Æneas*)

Who must we answer?

ÆNEAS   The noble *Menelaus*.

HECTOR

O you my Lord, by *Mars* his gauntlet thankes,

(Mock not that I affect, th'vntraded oath)

Your *quondam* wife sweares still by *Venus* gloue,

2620   Shees well, but bad me not commend her to you.

MENELAUS

Name her not now sir, shee's a deadly theame.

HECTOR O pardon, I offend.

NESTOR

I haue thou gallant Troyan seene thee oft,

Laboring for destiny, make cruell way,

Through rankes of Greekish youth, and I haue seene
thee

As hot as *Perseus*, spurre thy Phrigian steed,

And seene thee scorning forfaits and subduments,

When thou hast hung th'aduanced sword ith'ayre,

Not letting it decline on the declined,

2630   That I haue said vnto my standers by,

Loe *Iupiter* is yonder dealing life.

And I haue seene thee pause, and take thy breath,

When that a ring of Greekes haue hem'd thee in,

Like an Olympian wrastling. This haue I seene,

But this thy countenance still lockt in steele,

I neuer saw till now: I knew thy grand-sire,

And once fought with him, he was a soldier good,

But by great *Mars* the Captaine of vs all,

Neuer like thee: let an old man embrace thee,

2640   And worthy warriour welcome to our tents.

He embraces Hector

ÆNEAS (*to Hector*) Tis the old *Nestor*.

HECTOR

Let me embrace thee good old Chronicle,

That hast so long walkt hand in hand with time,

Most reuerend *Nestor*, I am glad to claspe thee.

NESTOR

I would my armes could match thee in contention

As they contend with thee in courtesie.

HECTOR I would they could.

NESTOR

Ha? by this white beard Ide fight with thee to
morrow.

Well, welcome, welcome, I haue seene the time.

VLISSES

2650   I wonder now how yonder Citty stands,

When we haue here her base and piller by vs?

HECTOR

I know your fauour lord *Vlisses* well,

Ah sir, there's many a Greeke and Troyan dead,

Since first I saw your selfe and *Diomed*,

In Illion on your Greekish embassie.

VLISSES

Sir I foretold you then what would ensue,

My prophecie is but halfe his iourney yet,

For yonder walls that pertly front your towne,

Yon towers, whose wanton tops do busse the clouds,

Must kisse their owne feete.

HECTOR   I must not beleeue you.   2660

There they stand yet, and modestly I thinke,

The fall of euery Phrigian stone will cost,

A drop of Grecian bloud: the end crownes all,

And that old common arbitrator Time,

Will one day end it.

VLISSES   So to him we leaue it.

Most gentle and most valiant *Hector*, welcome:

⌈*He embraces him*⌉

After the Generall, I beseech you next

To feast with me, and see me at my tent.

ACHILLES

I shall forestall thee lord *Vlisses* ⌈*to Hector*⌉ thou:

Now *Hector* I haue fed mine eyes on thee,   2670

I haue with exact view perusde thee *Hector*,

And quoted ioynt by ioint.

HECTOR Is this *Achilles*?

ACHILLES I am *Achilles*.

HECTOR

Stand faire I pray thee, let me looke on thee.

ACHILLES

Behold thy fill.

HECTOR   Nay I haue done already.

ACHILLES

Thou art too briefe, I will the second time,

As I would buie thee, view thee lim by lim.

HECTOR

O like a booke of sport thou'lt read me ore:

But ther's more in me then thou vnderstandst,   2680

Why doost thou so oppresse me with thine eye.

ACHILLES

Tell me you heauens, in which part of his body

Shall I destroy him: whether there, or there, or there,

That I may giue the locall wound a name,

And make distinct the very breach, whereout

Hectors great spirit flew: answer me heauens.

HECTOR

It would discredit the blest gods, proud man,

To answer such a question: stand againe,

Thinkst thou to catch my life so pleasantly,

As to prenominate in nice coniecture,   2690

Where thou wilt hit me dead.

ACHILLES   I tell thee yea.

HECTOR

Wert thou the Oracle to tell me so,

Ide not beleeue thee. Hence-forth gard thee well,

For Ile not kill thee there, nor there, nor there,

But by the forge that stithied *Mars* his helme,

Ile kill thee euery where, yea ore and ore.

You wisest Grecians, pardon me this brag,
His insolence drawes folly from my lips,
But ile endeuour deeds to match these words,
Or may I neuer—

2700 AIAX   Do not chafe thee cozen.
And you *Achilles*, let these threats alone,
Till accident or purpose bring you too't,
You may haue euery day enough of *Hector*,
If you haue stomack. The generall state I feare,
Can scarce entreate you to be odde with him.

HECTOR (*to Achilles*)
I pray you let vs see you in the field,
We haue had pelting warres since you refusd,
The Grecians cause.

ACHILLES   Doost thou entreate me *Hector*?
To morow do I meet thee fell as death:
To night all friends.

2710 HECTOR   Thy hand vpon that match.

AGAMEMNON
First all you Peeres of Greece, go to my tent,
There in the full conuiue you: afterwards
As *Hectors* leisure, and your bounties shall
Concurre together, seuerally entreate him.
Beate lowd the Taborins, let the trumpets blowe,
That this great souldier may his welcome know.
Flowrish. Exeunt all but Troylus and Vlisses

TROYLUS
My Lord *Vlisses*, tell me I beseech you,
In what place of the field doth *Calcas* keepe.

VLISSES
At *Menelaus* tent, most princely *Troylus*:
2720 There *Diomed* doth feast with him to night,
Who neither lookes on heauen nor on earth,
But giues all gaze, and bent of amorous view,
On the faire *Cresseid*.

TROYLUS
Shall I sweete Lord be bound to you so much,
After we part from *Agamemnons* tent,
To bring me thether.

VLISSES   You shall command me sir.
As gentle tell me of what honor was
This *Cressida* in Troy? had she no louer there
That wailes her absence?

TROYLUS
2730 O sir to such as bosting shew their skarres,
A mocke is due; will you walke on my Lord,
Shee was belou'd, she lou'd, she is, and doth,
But still sweet loue is food for fortunes tooth.   *Exeunt*

Sc. 17   *Enter Achilles and Patroclus*
(5.1) ACHILLES
Ile heate his blood with greekish wine to night,
Which with my Cemitar ile cool to morrow,
Patroclus let vs feast him to the hight.

PATROCLUS
Here comes *Thersites*.
Enter Thersites

ACHILLES   How now thou core of enuy.

Thou crusty botch of nature whats the news?

THERSITES Why thou picture of what thou seemest, and
Idoll, of idiot worshippers, heers a letter for thee.   2740

ACHILLES From whence fragment.

THERSITES Why thou full dish of foole from Troy.
Achilles reads the letter

PATROCLUS Who keeps the tent now.

THERSITES The Surgeons box or the pacients wound.

PATROCLUS Well said aduersity, and what need this tricks.

THERSITES Prithee be silent boy I profit not by thy talke,
thou art thought to be *Achilles* male varlot.

PATROCLUS Male varlot you rogue whats that.

THERSITES Why his masculine whore, now the rotten
diseases of the south, guts griping ruptures: Catarres,   2750
loades a grauell i'th' back, lethergies, could palsies,
and the like, take and take againe such preposterous
discoueries.

PATROCLUS Why thou damnable box of enuy thou what
mean'st thou to curse thus.

THERSITES Do I curse thee.

PATROCLUS Why no you ruinous but, you horson
indistinguishable cur, no.

THERSITES No why art thou then exasperate, thou idle
immaterial skeine of sleide silke, thou greene sacenet   2760
flap for a sore eye, thou tossell of a prodigalls purse—
thou ah how the poore world is pestred with such
water flies, diminitiues of nature.

PATROCLUS Out gall.

THERSITES Finch egge.

ACHILLES
My sweet *Patroclus* I am thwarted quite,
From my great purpose in to morrowes battell,
Here is a letter from Queene *Hecuba*;
A token from her daughter my faire loue
Both taxing me, and gaging me to keepe: 2770
An oth that I haue sworne: I wil not breake it,
Fall Greekes, fayle fame, honour or go or stay,
My *maior* vow lies here; this ile obay,
Come, come, *Thersites* help to trim my tent?
This night in banquetting must al be spent,
Away *Patroclus*.   *Exeunt Achilles and Patroclus*

THERSITES With to much bloud, and to little braine, these
two may run mad, but if with to much braine and to
little bloud they do ile be a curer of mad-men, her's
Agamemnon, an honest fellow inough, and one that   2780
loues quailes, but hee has not so much braine as eare-
wax, and the goodly transformation of *Iupiter* there,
his br the Bull, the primitiue statue, and oblique
memorial of cuck-olds, a thrifty shooing-horne in a
chaine hanging at his brs legge, to what forme but
that hee is, should wit larded with malice, and malice
farced with witte, turne him to: to an Asse, were
nothing hee is both Asse and Oxe, to an Oxe were
nothing, he is both Oxe and Asse, to be a dog, a Moyle,
a Cat, a Fichooke, a Tode, a Lezard, an Oule, a Puttock,   2790
or a Herring without a rowe, I would not care, but to
bee *Menelaus*! I would conspire against desteny, aske

me not what I would be, if I were not *Thersites*, for I
care not to be the Louse of a Lazar, so I were not
Menelaus—hey-day sprites and fires.

      Enter Hector, Aiax, Agamemnon, Vlisses, Nestor,
      Menelaus, Troylus, and Diomed with lights

AGAMEMNON

We go wrong we goe wrong.

AIAX   No, yonder tis

There where we see the light.

HECTOR   I trouble you.

AIAX

No not a whit.

      Enter Achilles

VLISSES   Here comes himselfe to guide you.

ACHILLES

Welcome braue *Hector*, welcome Princes all.

AGAMEMNON (*to Hector*)

2800   So now faire Prince of Troy, I bid God night,
      Aiax commands the guard to tend on you.

HECTOR

Thanks and good night to the Greekes generall.

MENELAUS

Good night my Lord.

HECTOR   Good night sweet Lord *Menelaus*.

THERSITES (*aside*) Sweet draught, sweet quoth a, sweet
sinke, sweet sure.

ACHILLES

Good night and welcome both at once to those
That go or tarry.

AGAMEMNON Good night.

            Exeunt Agamemnon, Menelaus

ACHILLES

Old *Nestor* tarries, and you to *Diomed*.

2810   Keepe *Hector* company an houre or two.

DIOMED

I cannot Lord, I haue important businesse,
The tide whereof is now, good night great *Hector*.

HECTOR Giue me your hand.

VLISSES (*aside to Troylus*)

Follow his torch, he goes to *Calcas* tent,
Ile keepe you company.

TROYLUS (*aside*)   Sweet sir you honor me?

HECTOR (*to Diomedes*)

And so good night.

ACHILLES   Come, come, enter my tent.

      Exeunt Diomed, followed by Vlisses and
      Troylus, at one doore, and Achilles, Hector,
      Aiax, and Nestor at another doore

THERSITES That same *Diomeds* a false hearted roague, a
most vniust knaue, I will no more trust him when hee
leeres, then I will a serpent when hee hisses, hee will
2820   spend his mouth and promise like brabler the hound,
but when he performes, Astronomers foretell it, that is
prodigious, there will come some change, the Sonne
borrowes of the Moone when *Diomed* keepes his word,
I will rather leaue to see *Hector* then not to dog him,
they say hee keepes a Troyan drab, and vses the traytor

Calcas his tent. Ile after—nothing but letchery all
incontinent varlots.   *Exit*

      Enter Diomed   Sc. 18

DIOMED What are you vp here ho? speake?   (5.2)

CALCAS ⌈*at the doore*⌉ Who calls?

DIOMED *Diomed, Chalcas* I thinke wher's your daughter?   2830

CALCAS ⌈*at the doore*⌉ She comes to you.

      Enter Troylus and Vlisses, vnseene

VLISSES (*aside*)

Stand, where the torch may not discouer vs.

TROYLUS (*aside*)

Cressid comes forth to him.

      Enter Cressid

DIOMED   How now my charge.

CRESSID

Now my sweet gardian, harke a word with you.

      She whispers to him.

      ⌈*Enter Thersites, vnseene*⌉

TROYLUS (*aside*) Yea so familiar?

VLISSES (*aside*) Shee will sing any man at first sight.

THERSITES (*aside*) And any man may sing her, if hee can
take her Cliff, she's noted.

DIOMED Will you remember?

CRESSID Remember yes.   2840

DIOMED Nay but do then

And let your minde be coupled with your words.

TROYLUS (*aside*) What should she remember.

VLISSES (*aside*) List?

CRESSID

Sweet hony Greeke tempt me no more to folly.

THERSITES (*aside*) Roguery.

DIOMED Nay then.

CRESSID Ile tell you what.

DIOMED

Fo, fo, come tell a pin you are forsworne.

CRESSID

In faith I cannot, what would you haue me do?   2850

THERSITES (*aside*) A iugling tricke to be secretly open.

DIOMED

What did you sweare you would bestow on me?

CRESSID

I prethee do not hold me to mine oath,
Bid me do any thing but that sweete Greeke.

DIOMED Good night.

TROYLUS (*aside*)

Hold patience.

VLISSES (*aside*)   How now Troyan.

CRESSID   Diomed.

DIOMED

No, no, good night Ile be your foole no more.

TROYLUS (*aside*) Thy better must.

CRESSID Harke one word in your eare.

      She whispers to him

TROYLUS (*aside*) O plague and madnesse!   2860

VLISSES (*aside*)

You are moued Prince, let vs depart I pray you

Least your displeasure should inlarge it selfe
To wrathfull tearmes, this place is dangerous:
The time right deadly, I beseech you goe.

TROYLUS (*aside*)
Behold I pray you.

VLISSES (*aside*)   Nay good my Lord go off.
You flow to great distraction, come my Lord.

TROYLUS (*aside*)
I prethee stay.

VLISSES (*aside*)   You haue not patience, come.

TROYLUS (*aside*)
I pray you stay; by hell, and all hells torments,
I will not speake a word.

DIOMED   And so good night.

CRESSID
Nay but you part in anger.

2870 TROYLUS (*aside*)   Doth that grieue thee,
O wither'd truth.

VLISSES (*aside*)   Why how now Lord?

TROYLUS (*aside*)   By *Ioue*
I will be patient.
       ⌈*Diomed offers to go*⌉

CRESSID Gardian? why *Greeke*?

DIOMED Fo fo adew you palter.

CRESSID
In faith I doe not, come hether once again.

VLISSES (*aside*)
You shake my Lord at something, will you goe:
You wil break out.

TROYLUS (*aside*)   She stroakes his cheeke.

VLISSES (*aside*)   Come, come.

TROYLUS (*aside*)
Nay stay, by *Ioue* I will not speake a word.
There is betweene my will and all offences

2880 A guard of patience, stay a little while.

THERSITES (*aside*) How the diuell *Luxury* with his fat rumpe
and potato finger, tickles these together; frye lechery
frye.

DIOMED But will you then?

CRESSID
In faith I will la, neuer trust me else.

DIOMED
Giue me some token for the surety of it.

CRESSID Ile fetch you one.   *Exit*

VLISSES (*aside*) You haue sworne patience.

TROYLUS (*aside*) Feare me not sweete Lord.

2890 I will not be my selfe, nor haue cognition
Of what I feele, I am all patience.
       Enter Cressid with Troylus sleeue

THERSITES (*aside*) Now the pledge, now, now, now.

CRESSID Heere *Diomed* keepe this sleeue.

TROYLUS (*aside*) O beauty where is thy faith!

VLISSES (*aside*) My Lord.

TROYLUS (*aside*)
I will be patient, outwardly I will.

CRESSID
You looke vpon that sleeue behold it well,

Hee loue'd me (oh false wench) giu't me againe.
       She takes it back

DIOMED Whose wast?

CRESSID
It is no matter now I ha't againe.   2900
I will not meete with you to morrow night:
I prethee *Diomed* visite me no more.

THERSITES (*aside*) Now shee sharpens, well said *Whetstone*.

DIOMED I shall haue it.

CRESSID What this?

DIOMED I that.

CRESSID
O all you gods; O pretty pretty pledge!
Thy maister now lyes thinking on his bed
Of thee and mee, and sighes, and takes my gloue,
And giues memoriall dainty kisses to it,   2910

⌈DIOMED⌉
As I kisse thee.
       ⌈*He snatches the sleeue*⌉

⌈CRESSID⌉   Nay do not snatch it from me.
He that takes that doth take my heart withall.

DIOMED
I had your heart before, this followes it.

TROYLUS (*aside*) I did sweare patience.

CRESSID
You shall not haue it *Diomed*, faith you shall not,
Ile giue you something else.

DIOMED   I will haue this, whose was it?

CRESSID
It is no matter.

DIOMED   Come tell me whose it was?

CRESSID
Twas on's that lou'd me better then you will,
But now you haue it take it.

DIOMED   Whose was it?

CRESSID
By all *Dianas* wayting women yond   2920
And by her selfe I will not tell you whose.

DIOMED
To morrow will I weare it on my Helme,
And grieue his spirit that dares not challenge it.

TROYLUS (*aside*)
Wert thou the diuell, and wor'st it on thy horne,
It should be challengd.

CRESSID
Well, well, tis done, tis past: and yet it is not.
I will not keepe my word.

DIOMED   Why then farewell,
Thou neuer shalt mocke *Diomed* againe.

CRESSID
You shall not goe: one cannot speake a word
But it straight starts you.

DIOMED   I doe not like this fooling.   2930

⌈TROYLUS⌉ (*aside*)
Nor I by *Pluto*; but that that likes not you,
Pleases me best.

DIOMED   What shall I come? the houre—

839

CRESSID

    I come; *O Ioue*: do come, I shall be plagued.

DIOMED

    Farewell till then.

CRESSID   Good night, I prethee come:

                                   Exit Diomed

    Troylus farewell, one eye yet lookes on thee,

    But with my heart the other eye doth see,

    Ah poore our sex, this fault in vs I find,

    The error of our eye directs our mind,

    What error leads must erre: O then conclude,

2940   "Mindes swayd by eyes are full of turpitude.   *Exit*

THERSITES (*aside*)

    A proofe of strength, she could not publish more,

    Vnlesse shee said my mind is now turn'd whore.

VLISSES

    All's done my Lord.

TROYLUS   It is.

VLISSES   Why stay we then?

TROYLUS

    To make a recordation to my soule

    Of euery sillable that here was spoke:

    But if I tell how these two did Coact,

    Shall I not lye in publishing a truth,

    Sith yet there is a credence in my heart,

    An esperance so obstinatly strong,

2950   That doth inuert th'attest of eyes and eares,

    As if those organs had deceptious functions,

    Created onely to calumniate.

    Was *Cresseid* heere?

VLISSES   I cannot coniure Troyan.

TROYLUS

    Shee was not sure.

VLISSES   Most sure she was.

TROYLUS

    Why my negation hath no taste of madnesse.

VLISSES

    Nor mine my Lord: *Cresseid* was heere but now.

TROYLUS

    Let it not be beleeu'd for woman-hood.

    Thinke we had mothers, do not giue aduantage

    To stubborne Critiques apt without a theme

2960   For deprauation, to square the generall sex

    By *Cresseids* rule. Rather thinke this not *Cresseid*.

VLISSES

    What hath she done Prince that cã soile our mothers.

TROYLUS

    Nothing at all, vnlesse that this were she.

THERSITES (*aside*) Will a swagger himselfe out on's owne

    eyes.

TROYLUS

    This she, no this is *Diomeds Cresseida*,

    If beauty haue a soule this is not shee:

    If soules guide vowes, if vowes be sanctimonies,

    If sanctimony be the gods delight:

2970   If there be rule in vnitie it selfe,

    This is not shee: O madnesse of discourse,

    That cause sets vp with and against thy selfe,

By-fould authority: where reason can reuolt

Without perdition, and losse assume all reason,

Without reuolt. This is and is not *Cresseid*,

Within my soule there doth conduce a fight

Of this strange nature, that a thing inseparat,

Diuides more wider then the skie and earth:

And yet the spacious bredth of this diuision,

Admits no orifex for a point as subtle,   2980

As *Ariachne's* broken woofe to enter,

Instance, O instance strong as *Plutoes* gates,

Cresseid is mine, tied with the bonds of heauen,

Instance, O instance, strong as heauen it selfe,

The bonds of heauen are slipt, dissolu'd and loosd,

And with another knot fiue finger tied,

The fractions of her faith, orts of her loue,

The fragments, scraps, the bitts and greazie reliques,

Of her ore-eaten faith, are bound to *Diomed*.

VLISSES

May worthy *Troylus* in be halfe attached   2990

With that which heere his passion doth expresse?

TROYLUS

I Greeke, and that shall be divulged well

In Characters as red as *Mars* his heart

Inflam'd with *Venus*: neuer did young man fancy

With so eternall and so fixt a soule.

Harke Greeke, as much as I do *Cressid* loue,

So much by waight, hate I her *Diomed*:

That sleeue is mine, that heele beare in his Helme:

Were it a Caske compos'd by *Vulcans* skill

My sword should bite it: Not the dreadfull spout   3000

Which Shipmen do the hurricano call,

Constringd in Masse by the almighty sunne

Shal dizzy with more clamour Neptunes eare,

In his discent, then shall my prompted sword,

Falling on *Diomed*.

THERSITES (*aside*) Heele ticle it for his concupie.

TROYLUS

O *Cressid*, O false *Cressid*, false, false, false:

Let all vntruthes stand by thy stained name,

And theyle seeme glorious.

VLISSES   O containe your selfe;

Your passion drawes eares hether.   3010

    Enter Eneas

ÆNEAS (*to Troylus*)

I haue beene seeking you this houre my Lord:

Hector by this is arming him in Troy:

Aiax your guard stayes to conduct you home.

TROYLUS

Haue with you Prince: my curteous Lord adiew,

Farewell reuoulted faire: and *Diomed*

Stand fast, and weare a Castle on thy head.

VLISSES

Ile bring you to the gates.

TROYLUS   Accept distracted thankes.

    Exeunt Troylus, Eneas and Vlisses

THERSITES Would I could meete that roague *Diomed* I

would croke like a Rauen, I would bode, I would bode:

Patroclus will giue me any thing for the inteligence of   3020

this whore: the Parrot will not do more for an almond
then he for a commodious drab: Lechery, lechery, still
warres and lechery, nothing else holds fashion. A
burning diuell take them.   *Exit*

Sc. 19   *Enter Hector armed, and Andromache*
(5.3) ANDROMACHE
          When was my Lord so much vngently temperd,
          To stop his eares against admonishment:
          Vnarme, vnarme, and do not fight to day.
          HECTOR
          You traine me to offend you, get you in,
          By all the euerlasting gods Ile go.
          ANDROMACHE
3030   My dreames will sure prooue ominous to the day.
          HECTOR
          No more I say.
                 Enter Cassandra
          CASSANDRA   Where is my brother *Hector*?
          ANDROMACHE
          Here sister, arm'd and bloody in intent,
          Consort with me in lowd and deere petition,
          Pursue we him on knees: for I haue dreamt
          Of bloudy turbulence, and this whole night
          Hath nothing beene but shapes and formes of slaughter.
          CASSANDRA
          O tis true.
          HECTOR   Ho? bid my trumpet sound.
          CASSANDRA
          No notes of sallie for the heauens sweete brother.
          HECTOR
          Begon I say, the gods haue heard me sweare.
          CASSANDRA
3040   The gods are deafe to hotte and peeuish vowes,
          They are polluted offrings more abhord,
          Then spotted liuers in the sacrifice.
          ANDROMACHE (*to Hector*)
          O be perswaded, do not count it holy,
          To hurt by being iust; it is as lawfull,
          For we would giue much, to vse violent thefts,
          And rob in the behalfe of charitie.
          CASSANDRA
          It is the purpose that makes strong the vow,
          But vowes to euery purpose must not hold:
          Vnarme sweet *Hector*.
          HECTOR   Hold you still I say,
3050   Mine honor keepes the weather of my fate:
          Life euery man holds deere, but the deere man,
          Holds honor farre more precious deere then life,
                 Enter Troylus, armed
          How now yong man, mean'st thou to fight to day.
          ANDROMACHE ⌈*aside*⌉
          Cassandra call my father to perswade.   *Exit Cassandra*
          HECTOR
          No faith yong *Troylus*, doffe thy harnesse youth,
          I am to day ith' vaine of chiualrie,
          Let grow thy sinews till their knots be strong,

And tempt not yet the brushes of the warre.
Vnarme thee go, and doubt thou not braue boy,
Ile stand to day for thee and me and Troy.   3060
TROYLUS
Brother, you haue a vice of mercy in you,
Which better fits a Lion then a man.
HECTOR
What vice is that? good *Troylus* chide mee for it.
TROYLUS
When many times the captiue Grecian falls,
Euen in the fanne and winde of your faire sword,
You bid them rise and liue.
HECTOR O tis faire play.
TROYLUS Fooles play by heauen *Hector*.
HECTOR How now? how now?
TROYLUS For th'loue of all the gods   3070
Lets leaue the Hermit Pitty with our Mother,
And when we haue our armors buckled on,
The venomd vengeance ride vpon our swords,
Spur them to ruthfull worke, raine them from ruth.
HECTOR
Fie sauage, fie.
TROYLUS   *Hector* then 'tis warres.
HECTOR
Troylus I would not haue you fight to day.
TROYLUS Who should with-hold me?
Not fate, obedience, nor the hand of *Mars*,
Beckning with fierie trunchion my retire,
Not *Priamus* and *Hecuba* on knees,   3080
Their eyes ore-galled with recourse of teares,
Nor you my brother, with your true sword drawne,
Opposd to hinder me, should stop my way,
But by my ruine.
       Enter Priam and Cassandra
CASSANDRA
Lay hold vpon him, *Priam* hold him fast,
He is thy crutch: now if thou loose thy stay,
Thou on him leaning, and all Troy on thee,
Fall all together.
PRIAM   Come *Hector*, come, go back,
Thy wife hath dreamt, thy mother hath had visions,
Cassandra doth foresee, and I my selfe,   3090
Am like a prophet suddenly enrapt,
To tell thee that this day is ominous:
Therefore come back.
HECTOR   *Æneas* is a field,
And I do stand, engagd to many Greekes,
Euen in the faith of valour to appeare,
This morning to them.
PRIAM I but thou shalt not goe.
HECTOR ⌈*kneeling*⌉ I must not breake my faith,
You know me dutifull, therefore deere sir,
Let me not shame respect, but giue me leaue   3100
To take that course by your consent and voice,
Which you do here forbid me royall *Priam*.
CASSANDRA
O *Priam* yeeld not to him.
ANDROMACHE   Do not deere father.

HECTOR

    Andromache I am offended with you,

    Vpon the loue you beare me get you in.

                                 Exit Andromache

TROYLUS

    This foolish dreaming superstitious girle,

    Makes all these bodements.

CASSANDRA   O farewell deere *Hector*.

    Looke how thou dy'est, looke how thy eye turnes pale.

    Looke how thy wounds do bleed at many vents,

3110   Harke how Troy roares, how *Hecuba* cries out,

    How poore *Andromache* shrils her dolours foorth,

    Behold, distraction, frenzie, and amazement,

    Like witlesse antiques one another meete,

    And all crie *Hector*, *Hectors* dead, O *Hector*.

TROYLUS Away, away.

CASSANDRA

    Farewell, yet soft: *Hector* I take my leaue,

    Thou do'st thy selfe and all our Troy deceaue?   *Exit*

HECTOR (*to Priam*)

    You are amaz'd my liege, at her exclaime,

    Goe in and cheere the towne, weele forth and fight,

3120   Do deeds of praise, and tell you them at night.

PRIAM

    Farewell, the gods with safetie stand about thee.

            Exeunt Priam and Hector, seuerally. Alarum

TROYLUS

    They are at it harke, proud *Diomed* beleeue,

    I come to loose my arme, or winne my sleeue.

        Enter Pandar

PANDARUS Do you heere my Lord, do you heere.

TROYLUS What now?

PANDARUS Heer's a letter come from yond poore girle.

TROYLUS Let me read.

        Troylus reads the letter

PANDARUS A whorson tisick, a whorson rascally tisick, so

    troubles me, and the foolish fortune of this girle, and

3130   what one thing, what another, that I shall leaue you

    one athis dayes: and I haue a rheume in mine eyes

    too, and such an ache in my bones, that vnlesse a man

    were curst I cannot tell what to thinke on't. What

    sayes she there?

TROYLUS (*tearing the letter*)

    Words, words, meere words, no matter frõ the heart,

    Th'effect doth operate another way.

    Go winde to winde, there turne and change together:

    My loue with words and errors still she feedes,

    But edifies another with her deedes.

3140 PANDARUS Why, but heare you?

TROYLUS

    Hence broker, lacky, ignomie and shame

    Pursue thy life, and liue aye with thy name.

                        Exeunt seuerally

Sc. 20   *A Larum. Enter Thersites ⌈in⌉ excursions*

(5.4) THERSITES Now they are clapper-clawing one another: Ile

    go looke on, that dissembling abhominable varlet

Diomede, has got that same scuruie dooting foolish yong

knaues sleeue of Troy there in his helme. I would faine

see them meete, that that same young Troyan asse

that loues the whore there, might send that Greekish

whore-masterly villaine with the sleeue, back to the

dissembling luxurious drabbe of a sleeuelesse arrant. 3150

Ath' tother side, the pollicie of those craftie swearing

raskalls; that stale old Mouse-eaten drye cheese *Nestor*:

and that same dogge-foxe *Vlisses*, is proou'd not worth

a Black-berry. They set mee vp in pollicie, that mongrill

curre *Aiax*, against that dogge of as bad a kinde *Achilles*.

And now is the curre *Aiax*, prouder then the curre

Achilles, and will not arme to day. Where-vpon the

Grecians began to proclaime barbarisme, and pollicie

growes into an ill opinion.

    Enter Diomed followed by Troylus

Soft here comes sleeue & tother.   3160

TROYLUS (*to Diomed*)

    Flye not, for shouldst thou take the riuer Stix,

    I would swim after.

DIOMED   Thou doost miscall retire,

    I doe not flie, but aduantagious care,

    With-drew me from the ods of multitude, haue at thee?

        Fight

THERSITES Hold thy whore Grecian: now for thy whore

    Troian, now the sleeue, now the sleeue.

              Exit Diomed ⌈driuing in⌉ Troylus

    Enter Hector ⌈behind⌉

HECTOR

    What art thou Greeke, art thou for *Hectors* match.

    Art thou of bloud and honour.

THERSITES No, no, I am a rascall, a scuruy rayling knaue,

    a very filthy roague.   3170

HECTOR I do beleeue thee, liue.

THERSITES God a mercy, that thou wilt beleeue me,

                   ⌈*Exit Hector*⌉

but a plague breake thy neck—for frighting me: whats

become of the wenching roagues? I thinke they haue

swallowed one another. I would laugh at that miracle—

yet in a sort lechery eates it selfe, ile seeke them.

                                 Exit

    Enter Diomed and Seruants   Sc. 21

DIOMED   (5.5)

    Goe go, my seruant take thou *Troylus* horse,

    Present the faire steed to my Lady *Cressid*,

    Fellow commend my seruice to her beauty:

    Tell her I haue chastis'd the amorous Troyan,   3180

    And am her knight by proofe.

SERUANT   I goe my Lord.   *Exit*

    Enter Agamemnon

AGAMEMNON

    Renew, renew, the fierce *Polidamas*,

    Hath beate downe *Menon*: bastard *Margareton*,

    Hath *Doreus* prisoner,

    And stands *Colossus* wise wauing his beame,

    Vpon the pashed corses of the Kings:

Epistropus and *Cedius*, *Polixines* is slaine,
Amphimacus and *Thoas* deadly hurt,
Patroclus tane or slaine, and *Palamedes*
3190 Sore hurt and bruisd, the dreadfull Sagittary,
Appalls our numbers, hast we *Diomed*,
To re-enforcement or we perish all.
          Enter Nestor ⌈with Patroclus body⌉

NESTOR
Go beare *Patroclus* body to *Achilles*,
And bid the snail-pac't *Aiax* arme for shame,
                    ⌈Exit one or more with the body⌉
There is a thousand *Hectors* in the field:
Now here he fights on *Galathe* his horse,
And there lacks worke, anon he's there a foote
And there they flie or die, like scaled sculls,
Before the belching Whale, then is he yonder:
3200 And there the strawy Greekes ripe for his edge
Fall downe before him like the mowers swath,
Here, there and euery where, he leaues and takes,
Dexterity so obaying appetite,
That what he will he do's, and do's so much:
That proofe is call'd impossibility.
          Enter Vlisses

VLISSES
Oh courage, courage Princes, great *Achilles*,
Is arming, weeping, cursing, vowing vengeance,
Patroclus wounds haue rouz'd his drowzy bloud,
Together with his mangled *Myrmidons*
3210 That noselesse, handlesse, hackt and chipt come to
          him,
Crying on *Hector*, *Aiax* hath lost a friend,
And foames at mouth, and hee is armde and at it:
Roaring for *Troylus*, who hath done to day,
Madde and fantastique execution:
Engaging and redeeming of himselfe
With such a carelesse force, and forcelesse care,
As if that luck in very spight of cunning,
Bad him win all.
          Enter Aiax

AIAX *Troylus*, thou coward *Troylus*.   *Exit*
3220 DIOMED I there, there?   *⌈Exit⌉*
NESTOR So, so, we draw together.
          Enter Achilles
ACHILLES Where is this *Hector*?
Come, come, thou braue boy-queller shew thy face,
Know what it is to meete *Achilles* angry
Hector wher's *Hector*? I will none but *Hector*.
                              ⌈Exeunt⌉

Sc. 22   *Enter Aiax*
(5.6) AIAX
Troylus thou coward *Troylus* shew thy head.
          Enter Diomed
DIOMED
Troylus I say wher's *Troylus*?
AIAX   What wouldst thou.
DIOMED I would correct him.

AIAX
Were I the generall thou shouldst haue my office,
Ere that correction? *Troylus* I say what *Troylus*.   3230
          Enter Troylus
TROYLUS
Oh traytor *Diomed*, turne thy false face thou traytor,
And pay the life thou owest me for my horse.
DIOMED Ha art thou there?
AIAX
Ile fight with him alone stand *Diomed*.
DIOMED
He is my prize, I will not looke vpon.
TROYLUS
Come both you cogging Greekes haue at you both.
          Fight.
          Enter Hector
HECTOR
Yea *Troylus*, O well fought my yongest brother.
          Exit Troylus ⌈driuing Diomed and Aiax in⌉
          Enter Achilles ⌈behind⌉
ACHILLES
Now do I see thee ha, haue at thee *Hector*.
          Fight. ⌈Achilles is bested⌉
HECTOR Pause if thou wilt.
ACHILLES
I do disdaine thy curtesie proud Troyan,   3240
Be happy that my armes are out of vse:
My rest and negligence befriends thee now,
But thou anon shalt here of me againe:
Till when goe seeke thy fortune.   *Exit*
HECTOR   Fare thee well.
I would haue beene much more a fresher man,
Had I expected thee,
          Enter Troylus ⌈in haste⌉
                    how now my brother.
TROYLUS
Aiax hath tane *Æneas*, shall it be,
No by the flame of yonder glorious heauen
He shall not carry him ile be tane to,
Or bring him off, fate here me what I say: 3250
I wreake not though thou end my life to day.   *Exit*
          Enter one in sumptuous armour
HECTOR
Stand, stand thou Greeke, thou art a goodly marke,
No? wilt thou not. I like thy armor well,
Ile frush it and vnlock the riuets all:
But ile be maister of it,   *⌈Exit one in armour⌉*
                    wilt thou not beast abide,
Why then flie on, ile hunt thee for thy hide.   *Exit*

          Enter Achilles with Myrmidons   Sc. 23
ACHILLES   (5.7)
Come here about me you my *Myrmidons*,
Marke what I say, attend me where I wheele:
Strike not a stroke, but keepe your selues in breth,
And when I haue the bloudy *Hector* found: 3260
Empale him with your weapons round about,

In fellest manner execut your armes
Follow me sirs and my proceedings eye,
It is decreed *Hector* the great must die.   *Exeunt*

Sc. 24   *Enter Menelaus and Paris fighting, ⌈then⌉ Thersites*
(5.8)
THERSITES The cuck-old and the cuck-old-maker are at it,
now bull, now dogge lowe, *Paris* lowe, now my double
horn'd spartan, lowe *Paris*, lowe the bull has the game,
ware hornes ho?   *Exit Menelaus ⌈driuing in⌉ Paris*
Enter Bastard ⌈behind⌉

BASTARD Turne slaue and fight.

3270   THERSITES What art thou?

BASTARD A Bastard sonne of *Priams*.

THERSITES I am a bastard too, I loue bastards. I am bastard
begot, bastard instructed, bastard in minde, bastard in
valour, in euery thing illigitimate, one beare wil not
bite another, and wherefore should one bastard? take
heed, the quarrells most ominous to vs, if the sonne of
a whore fight for a whore, he tempts iudgement,
farewell bastard.   ⌈*Exit*⌉

BASTARD The diuell take thee coward.   *Exit*

Sc. 25   *Enter Hector ⌈dragging⌉ the one in sumptuous*
(5.9)   *armour*

HECTOR ⌈*taking off the helmet*⌉
3280   Most putrified core so faire without,
Thy goodly armor thus hath cost thy life;
Now is my daies worke done ile take good breth:
Rest sword thou hast thy fill of bloud and death.
Disarmes.
Enter Achilles and his Myrmidons enrounding
Hector

ACHILLES
Loke *Hector* how the Sunne begins to set,
How ougly night comes breathing at his heeles
Euen with the vaile and darkning of the Sunne,
To close the day vp, *Hectors* life is done.

HECTOR
I am vnarm'd forgoe this vantage Greeke.

ACHILLES
Strike fellowes strike, this is the man I seeke,
          ⌈*The Myrmidons*⌉ kill Hector
3290   So Illion fall thou, now Troy sinke downe,
Here lies thy heart, thy sinnewes and thy bone.
On *Myrmydons*, and cry you all amaine,
Achilles hath the mighty *Hector* slaine,
          Retreat
Harke a retire vpon our Grecian part.
          ⌈*Another Retreat*⌉

A MYRMIDON
The Troyan trumpets sound the like my Lord.

ACHILLES
The dragon wing of night orespreds the earth,
And stickler-like the armies separates.
My halfe supt sword that frankly would haue fedde,
Pleas'd with this dainty baite: thus goes to bed:
Sheathes his sword

Come tie his body to my horses taile,   3300
Along the field I will the Troyan traile.
          Exeunt, dragging the bodies

Sound Retreat. Enter Agamemnon, Aiax, Menelaus,   **Sc. 26**
Nestor, Diomedes, and the rest marching. ⌈Shout   **(5.10)**
within⌉

AGAMEMNON
Hark, harke, what shout is that?

NESTOR   Peace drums.

MYRMIDONS (*within*)   *Achilles,*
Achilles, Hectors slaine, *Achilles.*

DIOMED
The bruite is *Hectors* slaine and by *Achilles.*

AIAX
If it be so yet braglesse let it bee,
Great *Hector* was a man as good as he.

AGAMEMNON
March patiently along: let one bee sent,
To pray *Achilles* see vs at our tent:
If in his death the Gods haue vs befriended,
Great Troy is ours, and our sharpe wars are ended.   3310
          Exeunt ⌈marching⌉

Enter Æneas, Paris, Antenor, Diephobus   **Sc. 27**
ÆNEAS   **(5.11)**
Stand ho? yet are we masters of the field,
Neuer goe home, here starue we out the night.
          Enter Troylus

TROYLUS
Hector is slaine.

ALL THE OTHERS   *Hector!* the gods forbid.

TROYLUS
Hee's dead and at the murtherers horses taile,
In bestly sort dragd through the shamefull field:
Frowne on you heauens, effect your rage with speed,
Sit gods vpon your thrones, and smite at Troy.
I say at once, let your breefe plagues be mercy,
And linger not our sure destructions on.

ÆNEAS
My Lord you doe discomfort all the host.   3320

TROYLUS
You vnderstand me not that tell me so,
I do not speake of flight, of feare of death
But dare all immynence that gods and men
Addresse their daungers in. *Hector* is gone:
Who shall tell *Priam* so or *Hecuba*?
Let him that will a scrich-oule aye be call'd,
Goe into Troy and say their *Hectors* dead,
There is a word will *Priam* turne to stone,
Make wells and *Niobe's* of the maides and wiues:
Cool'd statues of the youth and in a word,   3330
Scarre Troy out of it selfe. But march away,
Hector is dead: there is no more to say,
Stay yet you vile abhominable tents:
Thus proudly pitcht vpon our Phrigian plaines,
Let *Tytan* rise as earely as he dare,

Ile through, and through you, and thou great siz'd
    coward,
No space of earth shall sunder our two hates:
Ile haunt thee like a wicked conscience still,

That mouldeth goblins swift as frienzes thoughts,
Strike a free march, to Troy with comfort goe   3340
Hope of reueng shall hide our inward woe.

                ⌈*Exeunt, marching*⌉

FINIS

ADDITIONAL PASSAGES

A. The Quarto (below) gives a more elaborate version of
Thersites' speech at 2750-4.

THERSITES Why his masculine whore, now the rotten
   diseases of the south, the guts griping ruptures: loades
   a grauell in the back, lethergies, could palsies, rawe
   eies, durtrottē liuers, whissing lungs, bladders full of
   impostume, Sciaticaes lime-kills ith' palme, incurable
   bone-ach, and the riueled fee simple of the tetter, take
   and take againe such preposterous discoueries.

B. The Quarto gives a different ending to the play (which
the Folio inadvertently repeats).

    Enter Pandarus
PANDARUS But here you, here you.
TROYLUS
   Hence broker, lacky, ⌈*Strikes him*⌉ ignomy, and shame,
   Pursue thy life, and liue aye with thy name.
                Exeunt all but Pandarus
PANDARUS A goodly medicine for my aking bones, Oh
   world, world, world—thus is the poore agent despis'd,

Oh traitors and bawds, how earnestly are you set a
worke, and how ill requited, why should our endeuour
bee so desir'd and the performance so loathed, what
verse for it? What instance for it? Let me see,
    Full merrily the humble Bee doth sing,   10
    Till he hath lost his hony and his sting.
    And being once subdude in armed taile,
    Sweet hony, and sweet notes together faile.
Good traiders in the flesh, set this in your painted
cloathes,
   As many as be here of *Pandars* hall,
   Your eyes halfe out weepe out at *Pandars* fall.
   Or if you cannot weepe yet giue some grones,
   Though not for me yet for your aking bones:
   Brethren and sisters of the hold-dore trade,   20
   Some two monthes hence my will shall here be made.
   It should be now, but that my feare is this,
   Some gauled goose of Winchester would hisse.
   Till then ile sweat and seeke about for eases,
   And at that time bequeath you my diseases.   *Exit*

SONNETS
AND 'A LOUERS COMPLAINT'

SHAKESPEARE'S Sonnets were published as a collection by Thomas Thorpe in 1609; the title-page declared that they were 'neuer before Imprinted'. Versions of two of them—138 and 144—had appeared in 1599, in *The Passionate Pilgrim*, a collection ascribed to Shakespeare but including some poems certainly written by other authors; and in the previous year Francis Meres, in *Palladis Tamia*, had alluded to Shakespeare's 'sugard Sonnets among his priuate friends'. The sonnet sequence had enjoyed a brief but intense vogue from the publication of Sir Philip Sidney's *Astrophel and Stella* in 1591 till about 1597. Some of Shakespeare's plays of this period reflect the fashion: in the comedy of *Loues labors lost* the writing of sonnets is seen as a laughable symptom of love, and in the tragedy of *Romeo and Iuliet* both speeches of the Chorus and the lovers' first conversation are in sonnet form. Later plays use it, too, but it seems likely that most, if not all, of Shakespeare's sonnets were first written during this period. But there are indications that some of them were revised; the two printed in *The Passionate Pilgrim* differ at certain points from Thorpe's version, and two other sonnets (2 and 106) exist in manuscript versions which also are not identical with those published in the sequence. We print these as 'Alternative Versions' of Sonnets 2, 106, 138, and 144.

The order in which Thorpe printed the Sonnets has often been questioned, but is not entirely haphazard: all the first seventeen, and no later ones, exhort a young man to marry; all those clearly addressed to a man are among the first 126, and all those clearly addressed to, or concerned with, a woman (the 'dark lady') follow. Some of the sonnets in the second group appear to refer to events that prompted sonnets in the first group; it seems likely that the poems were rearranged after composition. Moreover, the volume contains 'A Louers complaint', clearly ascribed to Shakespeare, which stylistic evidence suggests was written in the early seventeenth century and which may have been intended as a companion piece. So, printing the Sonnets in Thorpe's order, we place them according to the likely date of their revision.

Textual evidence suggests that Thorpe printed from a transcript by someone other than Shakespeare. His volume bears a dedication over his own initials to 'Mr W.H.'; we do not know whether this derives from the manuscript, and can only speculate about the dedicatee's identity. His initials are those of Shakespeare's only known dedicatee, Henry Wriothesley, Earl of Southampton, but in reverse order. We have even less clue as to the identity of the Sonnets' other personae, a rival poet and the dark woman.

Shakespeare's Sonnets may not be autobiographical, but they are certainly unconventional: the most idealistic poems celebrating love's mutuality are addressed by one man to another (Sonnet 20 implies that the relationship is not sexual), and the poems clearly addressed to a woman revile her morals, speak ill of her appearance, and explore the poet's self-disgust at his entanglement with her. The Sonnets include some of the finest love poems in the English language: the sequence itself presents an internal drama of great psychological complexity.

TO.THE.ONLIE.BEGETTER.OF.
THESE.INSVING.SONNETS.
M^r.W.H. ALL.HAPPINESSE.
AND.THAT.ETERNITIE.
PROMISED.
BY.
OVR.EVER-LIVING.POET.
WISHETH.
THE.WELL-WISHING.
ADVENTVRER.IN.
SETTING.
FORTH.

T.T.

Sonnets

1

From fairest creatures we desire increase,
That thereby beauties *Rose* might neuer die,
But as the riper should by time decease,
His tender heire might beare his memory:
But thou contracted to thine owne bright eyes,
Feed'st thy lights flame with selfe substantiall fewell,
Making a famine where aboundance lies,
Thy selfe thy foe, to thy sweet selfe too cruell:
Thou that art now the worlds fresh ornament,
And only herauld to the gaudy spring,
Within thine owne bud buriest thy content,
And tender chorle makst wast in niggarding:
  Pitty the world, or else this glutton be,
  To eate the worlds due, by the graue and thee.

2

When fortie Winters shall beseige thy brow,
And digge deep trenches in thy beauties field,
Thy youthes proud liuery so gaz'd on now,
Wil be a totter'd weed of smal worth held:
Then being askt, where all thy beautie lies,
Where all the treasure of thy lusty daies;
To say within thine owne deepe sunken eyes,
Were an all-eating shame, and thriftlesse praise.
How much more praise deseru'd thy beauties vse,
If thou couldst answere this faire child of mine
Shall sum my count, and make my old excuse,
Proouing his beautie by succession thine.
  This were to be new made when thou art ould,
  And see thy blood warme when thou feel'st it could.

3

Looke in thy glasse and tell the face thou vewest,
Now is the time that face should forme an other,
Whose fresh repaire if now thou not renewest,
Thou doo'st beguile the world, vnblesse some mother.
For where is she so faire whose vn-eard wombe
Disdaines the tillage of thy husbandry?
Or who is he so fond will be the tombe,
Of his selfe loue to stop posterity?
Thou art thy mothers glasse and she in thee
Calls backe the louely Aprill of her prime,
So thou through windowes of thine age shalt see,
Dispight of wrinkles this thy goulden time.
  But if thou liue remembred not to be,
  Die single and thine Image dies with thee.

4

Vnthrifty louelinesse why dost thou spend,
Vpon thy selfe thy beauties legacy?
Natures bequest giues nothing but doth lend,
And being franck she lends to those are free:
Then beautious nigard why doost thou abuse,
The bountious largesse giuen thee to giue?
Profitles vserer why doost thou vse
So great a summe of summes yet can'st not liue?
For hauing traffike with thy selfe alone,
Thou of thy selfe thy sweet selfe dost deceaue,
Then how when nature calls thee to be gone,
What acceptable *Audit* can'st thou leaue?
  Thy vnus'd beauty must be tomb'd with thee,
  Which vsed liues th'executor to be.

5

Those howers that with gentle worke did frame,
The louely gaze where euery eye doth dwell
Will play the tirants to the very same,
And that vnfaire which fairely doth excell:
For neuer resting time leads Summer on,
To hidious winter and confounds him there,
Sap checkt with frost and lustie leau's quite gon,
Beauty ore-snow'd and barenes euery where.
Then were not summers distillation left
A liquid prisoner pent in walls of glasse,
Beauties effect with beauty were bereft,
Nor it nor noe remembrance what it was.
  But flowers distil'd though they with winter meete,
  Leese but their show, their substance still liues sweet.

6

Then let not winters wragged hand deface,
In thee thy summer ere thou be distil'd:
Make sweet some viall; treasure thou some place,
With beauties treasure ere it be selfe kil'd:
That vse is not forbidden vsery,
Which happies those that pay the willing lone;
That's for thy selfe to breed an other thee,
Or ten times happier be it ten for one,
Ten times thy selfe were happier then thou art,
If ten of thine ten times refigur'd thee,
Then what could death doe if thou should'st depart,
Leauing thee liuing in posterity?
  Be not selfe-wild for thou art much too faire,
  To be deaths conquest and make wormes thine heire.

7

Loe in the Orient when the gracious light,
Lifts vp his burning head, each vnder eye
Doth homage to his new appearing sight,
Seruing with lookes his sacred maiesty,
And hauing climb'd the steepe vp heauenly hill,
Resembling strong youth in his middle age,
Yet mortall lookes adore his beauty still,
Attending on his goulden pilgrimage:
But when from high-most pich with wery car,
Like feeble age he reeleth from the day,
The eyes (fore dutious) now conuerted are
From his low tract and looke an other way:
　　So thou, thy selfe out-going in thy noon:
　　Vnlok'd on diest vnlesse thou get a sonne.

10

8

Musick to heare, why hear'st thou musick sadly,
Sweets with sweets warre not, ioy delights in ioy:
Why lou'st thou that which thou receaust not gladly,
Or else receau'st with pleasure thine annoy?
If the true concord of well tuned sounds,
By vnions married do offend thine eare,
They do but sweetly chide thee, who confounds
In singlenesse the parts that thou should'st beare:
Marke how one string sweet husband to an other,
Strikes each in each by mutuall ordering;
Resembling sier, and child, and happy mother,
Who all in one, one pleasing note do sing:
　　Whose speechlesse song being many, seeming one,
　　Sings this to thee, thou single wilt proue none.

10

9

Is it for feare to wet a widdowes eye,
That thou consum'st thy selfe in single life?
Ah; if thou issulesse shalt hap to die,
The world will waile thee like a makelesse wife,
The world wilbe thy widdow and still weepe,
That thou no forme of thee hast left behind,
When euery priuat widdow well may keepe,
By childrens eyes, her husbands shape in minde:
Looke what an vnthrift in the world doth spend
Shifts but his place, for still the world inioyes it.
But beauties waste hath in the world an end,
And kept vnvsde the vser so destroyes it:
　　No loue toward others in that bosome sits
　　That on himselfe such murdrous shame commits.

10

10

For shame deny that thou bear'st loue to any
Who for thy selfe art so vnprouident.
Graunt if thou wilt, thou art belou'd of many,
But that thou none lou'st is most euident:
For thou art so possest with murdrous hate,
That gainst thy selfe thou stickst not to conspire,
Seeking that beautious roofe to ruinate
Which to repaire should be thy chiefe desire:
O change thy thought, that I may change my minde,
Shall hate be fairer log'd then gentle loue?
Be as thy presence is gracious and kind,
Or to thy selfe at least kind harted proue,
　　Make thee an other selfe for loue of me,
　　That beauty still may liue in thine or thee.

10

11

As fast as thou shalt wane so fast thou grow'st,
In one of thine, from that which thou departest,
And that fresh bloud which yongly thou bestow'st,
Thou maist call thine, when thou from youth
　　conuertest,
Herein liues wisdome, beauty, and increase,
Without this follie, age, and could decay,
If all were minded so, the times should cease,
And threescoore yeare would make the world away:
Let those whom nature hath not made for store,
Harsh, featurelesse, and rude, barrenly perrish,
Looke whom she best indow'd, she gaue the more;
Which bountious guift thou shouldst in bounty
　　cherrish,
　　She caru'd thee for her seale, and ment therby,
　　Thou shouldst print more, not let that coppy die.

10

12

When I doe count the clock that tels the time,
And see the braue day sunck in hidious night,
When I behold the violet past prime,
And sable curls ensiluer'd ore with white:
When lofty trees I see barren of leaues,
Which erst from heat did canopie the herd
And Sommers greene all girded vp in sheaues
Borne on the beare with white and bristly beard:
Then of thy beauty do I question make
That thou among the wastes of time must goe,
Since sweets and beauties do them-selues forsake,
And die as fast as they see others grow,
　　And nothing gainst Times sieth can make defence
　　Saue breed to braue him, when he takes thee hence.

10

13

O that you were your selfe, but loue you are
No longer yours, then you your selfe here liue,
Against this cumming end you should prepare,
And your sweet semblance to some other giue.
So should that beauty which you hold in lease
Find no determination, then you were
Your selfe again after your selfes decease,
When your sweet issue your sweet forme should beare.
Who lets so faire a house fall to decay,
Which husbandry in honour might vphold,
Against the stormy gusts of winters day
And barren rage of deaths eternall cold?
    O none but vnthrifts, deare my loue you know,
    You had a Father, let your Son say so.

14

Not from the stars do I my iudgement plucke,
And yet me thinkes I haue Astronomy,
But not to tell of good, or euil lucke,
Of plagues, of dearths, or seasons quallity,
Nor can I fortune to breefe mynuits tell;
Pointing to each his thunder, raine and winde,
Or say with Princes if it shal go wel
By oft predict that I in heauen finde.
But from thine eies my knowledge I deriue,
And constant stars in them I read such art
As truth and beautie shal together thriue
If from thy selfe, to store thou wouldst conuert:
    Or else of thee this I prognosticate,
    Thy end is Truthes and Beauties doome and date.

15

When I consider euery thing that growes
Holds in perfection but a little moment.
That this huge stage presenteth nought but showes
Whereon the Stars in secret influence comment.
When I perceiue that men as plants increase,
Cheared and checkt euen by the selfe-same skie:
Vaunt in their youthfull sap, at height decrease,
And were their braue state out of memory.
Then the conceit of this inconstant stay,
Sets you most rich in youth before my sight,
Where wastfull time debateth with decay
To change your day of youth to sullied night,
    And all in war with Time for loue of you
    As he takes from you, I ingraft you new.

16

But wherefore do not you a mightier waie
Make warre vppon this bloudie tirant time?
And fortifie your selfe in your decay
With meanes more blessed then my barren rime?
Now stand you on the top of happie houres,
And many maiden gardens yet vnset,
With vertuous wish would beare your liuing flowers,
Much liker then your painted counterfeit:
So should the lines of life that life repaire
Which this (Times pensel or my pupill pen)
Neither in inward worth nor outward faire
Can make you liue your selfe in eies of men,
    To giue away your selfe, keeps your selfe still,
    And you must liue drawne by your owne sweet skill.

17

Who will beleeue my verse in time to come
If it were fild with your most high deserts?
Though yet heauen knowes it is but as a tombe
Which hides your life, and shewes not halfe your
    parts:
If I could write the beauty of your eyes,
And in fresh numbers number all your graces,
The age to come would say this Poet lies,
Such heauenly touches nere toucht earthly faces.
So should my papers (yellowed with their age)
Be scorn'd, like old men of lesse truth then tongue,
And your true rights be termd a Poets rage,
And stretched miter of an Antique song.
    But were some childe of yours aliue that time,
    You should liue twise, in it and in my rime.

18

Shall I compare thee to a Summers day?
Thou art more louely and more temperate:
Rough windes do shake the darling buds of Maie,
And Sommers lease hath all too short a date:
Sometime too hot the eye of heauen shines,
And often is his gold complexion dimm'd,
And euery faire from faire some-time declines,
By chance, or natures changing course vntrim'd:
But thy eternall Sommer shall not fade,
Nor loose possession of that faire thou ow'st,
Nor shall death brag thou wandr'st in his shade,
When in eternall lines to time thou grow'st,
    So long as men can breath or eyes can see,
    So long liues this, and this giues life to thee.

19

Deuouring time blunt thou the Lyons pawes,
And make the earth deuoure her owne sweet brood,
Plucke the keene teeth from the fierce Tygers iawes,
And burne the long liu'd Phænix in her blood,
Make glad and sorry seasons as thou fleet'st,
And do what ere thou wilt swift-footed time
To the wide world and all her fading sweets:
But I forbid thee one most hainous crime,
O carue not with thy howers my loues faire brow,
Nor draw noe lines there with thine antique pen,
Him in thy course vntainted doe allow,
For beauties patterne to succeding men.
    Yet doe thy worst ould Time, dispight thy wrong,
    My loue shall in my verse euer liue young.

20

A womans face with natures owne hand painted,
Haste thou the Master Mistris of my passion,
A womans gentle hart but not acquainted
With shifting change as is false womens fashion,
An eye more bright then theirs, lesse false in rowling:
Gilding the obiect where-vpon it gazeth,
A man in hew all *Hews* in his controwling,
Which steales mens eyes and womens soules amaseth.
And for a woman wert thou first created,
Till nature as she wrought thee fell a dotinge,
And by addition me of thee defeated,
By adding one thing to my purpose nothing.
    But since she prickt thee out for womens pleasure,
    Mine be thy loue and thy loues vse their treasure.

21

So is it not with me as with that Muse,
Stird by a painted beauty to his verse,
Who heauen it selfe for ornament doth vse,
And euery faire with his faire doth reherse,
Making a coopelment of proud compare
With Sunne and Moone, with earth and seas rich
        gems:
With Aprills first borne flowers and all things rare,
That heauens ayre in this huge rondure hems,
O let me true in loue but truly write,
And then beleeue me, my loue is as faire,
As any mothers childe, though not so bright
As those gould candells fixt in heauens ayer:
    Let them say more that like of heare-say well,
    I will not prayse that purpose not to sell.

22

My glasse shall not perswade me I am ould,
So long as youth and thou are of one date,
But when in thee times forrowes I behould,
Then look I death my daies should expiate.
For all that beauty that doth couer thee,
Is but the seemely rayment of my heart,
Which in thy brest doth liue, as thine in me,
How can I then be elder then thou art?
O therefore loue be of thy selfe so wary,
As I not for my selfe, but for thee will,
Bearing thy heart which I will keepe so chary
As tender nurse her babe from faring ill,
    Presume not on thy heart when mine is slaine,
    Thou gau'st me thine not to giue backe againe.

23

As an vnperfect actor on the stage,
Who with his feare is put besides his part,
Or some fierce thing repleat with too much rage,
Whose strengths abondance weakens his owne heart;
So I for feare of trust, forget to say,
The perfect ceremony of loues right,
And in mine owne loues strength seeme to decay,
Ore-charg'd with burthen of mine owne loues might:
O let my books be then the eloquence,
And domb presagers of my speaking brest,
Who pleade for loue, and look for recompence,
More then that tonge that more hath more exprest.
    O learne to read what silent loue hath writ,
    To heare with eies belongs to loues fine wit.

24

Mine eye hath play'd the painter and hath steeld,
Thy beauties forme in table of my heart,
My body is the frame wherein ti's held,
And perspectiue it is best Painters art.
For through the Painter must you see his skill,
To finde where your true Image pictur'd lies,
Which in my bosomes shop is hanging stil,
That hath his windowes glazed with thine eyes:
Now see what good-turnes eyes for eies haue done,
Mine eyes haue drawne thy shape, and thine for me
Are windowes to my brest, where-through the Sun
Delights to peepe, to gaze therein on thee.
    Yet eyes this cunning want to grace their art,
    They draw but what they see, know not the hart.

25

Let those who are in fauor with their stars,
Of publike honour and proud titles bost,
Whilst I whome fortune of such tryumph bars
Vnlookt for ioy in that I honour most;
Great Princes fauorites their faire leaues spread,
But as the Marygold at the suns eye,
And in them-selues their pride lies buried,
For at a frowne they in their glory die.
The painefull warrier famosed for might,
After a thousand victories once foild,
Is from the booke of honour rased quite,
And all the rest forgot for which he toild:
    Then happy I that loue and am beloued
    Where I may not remoue, nor be remoued.

26

Lord of my loue, to whome in vassalage
Thy merrit hath my dutie strongly knit;
To thee I send this written ambassage
To witnesse duty, not to shew my wit.
Duty so great, which wit so poore as mine
May make seeme bare, in wanting words to shew it;
But that I hope some good conceipt of thine
In thy soules thought (all naked) will bestow it:
Til whatsoeuer star that guides my mouing,
Points on me gratiously with faire aspect,
And puts apparrell on my totter'd louing,
To show me worthy of thy sweet respect,
    Then may I dare to boast how I doe loue thee,
    Til then, not show my head where thou maist
        proue me.

27

Weary with toyle, I hast me to my bed,
The deare repose for lims with trauaill tired,
But then begins a iourny in my head
To worke my mind, when boddies work's expired.
For then my thoughts (from far where I abide)
Intend a zelous pilgrimage to thee,
And keepe my drooping eye-lids open wide,
Looking on darknes which the blind doe see.
Saue that my soules imaginary sight
Presents thy shaddoe to my sightles view,
Which like a iewell (hunge in gastly night)
Makes blacke night beautious, and her old face new.
    Loe thus by day my lims, by night my mind,
    For thee, and for my selfe, noe quiet finde.

28

How can I then returne in happy plight
That am debard the benifit of rest?
When daies oppression is not eazd by night,
But day by night and night by day oprest.
And each (though enimies to ethers raigne)
Doe in consent shake hands to torture me,
The one by toyle, the other to complaine
How far I toyle, still farther off from thee.
I tell the Day to please him thou art bright,
And do'st him grace when clouds doe blot the heauen:
So flatter I the swart complexiond night,
When sparkling stars twire not thou guil'st the eauen.
    But day doth daily draw my sorrowes longer,
    And night doth nightly make greefes strength seeme
        stronger.

29

When in disgrace with Fortune and mens eyes,
I all alone beweepe my out-cast state,
And trouble deafe heauen with my bootlesse cries,
And looke vpon my selfe and curse my fate.
Wishing me like to one more rich in hope,
Featur'd like him, like him with friends possest,
Desiring this mans art, and that mans skope,
With what I most inioy contented least,
Yet in these thoughts my selfe almost despising,
Haplye I thinke on thee, and then my state,
(Like to the Larke at breake of daye arising)
From sullen earth sings himns at Heauens gate,
    For thy sweet loue remembred such welth brings,
    That then I skorne to change my state with Kings.

30

When to the Sessions of sweet silent thought,
I sommon vp remembrance of things past,
I sigh the lacke of many a thing I sought,
And with old woes new waile my deare times waste:
Then can I drowne an eye (vn-vs'd to flow)
For precious friends hid in deaths dateles night,
And weepe a fresh loues long since canceld woe,
And mone th'expence of many a vannisht sight.
Then can I greeue at greeuances fore-gon,
And heauily from woe to woe tell ore
The sad account of fore-bemoned mone,
Which I new pay as if not payd before.
    But if the while I thinke on thee (deare friend)
    All losses are restord, and sorrowes end.

31

Thy bosome is indeared with all hearts,
Which I by lacking haue supposed dead,
And there raignes Loue and all Loues louing parts,
And all those friends which I thought buried.
How many a holy and obsequious teare
Hath deare religious loue stolne from mine eye,
As interest of the dead, which now appeare,
But things remou'd that hidden in thee lie.
Thou art the graue where buried loue doth liue,
Hung with the trophies of my louers gon,
Who all their parts of me to thee did giue,
That due of many, now is thine alone.
　　Their images I lou'd, I view in thee,
　　And thou (all they) hast all the all of me.

32

If thou suruiue my well contented daie,
When that churle death my bones with dust shall
　　couer
And shalt by fortune once more re-suruay:
These poore rude lines of thy deceased Louer:
Compare them with the bett'ring of the time,
And though they be out-stript by euery pen,
Reserue them for my loue, not for their rime,
Exceeded by the hight of happier men.
Oh then voutsafe me but this louing thought,
Had my friends Muse growne with this growing age,
A dearer birth then this his loue had brought
To march in ranckes of better equipage:
　　But since he died and Poets better proue,
　　Theirs for their stile ile read, his for his loue.

33

Full many a glorious morning haue I seene,
Flatter the mountaine tops with soueraine eie,
Kissing with golden face the meddowes greene;
Guilding pale streames with heauenly alcumy:
Anon permit the basest cloudes to ride,
With ougly rack on his celestiall face,
And from the for-lorne world his visage hide
Stealing vnseene to west with this disgrace:
Euen so my Sunne one early morne did shine,
With all triumphant splendor on my brow,
But out alack, he was but one houre mine,
The region cloude hath mask'd him from me now.
　　Yet him for this, my loue no whit disdaineth,
　　Suns of the world may staine, whē heauens sun
　　　staineth.

34

Why didst thou promise such a beautious day,
And make me trauaile forth without my cloake,
To let bace cloudes ore-take me in my way,
Hiding thy brau'ry in their rotten smoke.
Tis not enough that through the cloude thou breake,
To dry the raine on my storme-beaten face,
For no man well of such a salue can speake,
That heales the wound, and cures not the disgrace:
Nor can thy shame giue phisicke to my griefe,
Though thou repent, yet I haue still the losse,
Th'offenders sorrow lends but weake reliefe
To him that beares the strong offenses crosse.
　　Ah but those teares are pearle which thy loue
　　　sheeds,
　　And they are ritch, and ransome all ill deeds.

35

No more bee greeu'd at that which thou hast done,
Roses haue thornes, and siluer fountaines mud,
Cloudes and eclipses staine both Moone and Sunne,
And loathsome canker liues in sweetest bud.
All men make faults, and euen I in this,
Authorizing thy trespas with compare,
My selfe corrupting saluing thy amisse,
Excusing thy sins more then thy sins are:
For to thy sensuall fault I bring in sence,
Thy aduerse party is thy Aduocate,
And gainst my selfe a lawfull plea commence,
Such ciuill war is in my loue and hate,
　　That I an accessary needs must be,
　　To that sweet theefe which sourely robs from me.

36

Let me confesse that we two must be twaine,
Although our vndeuided loues are one:
So shall those blots that do with me remaine,
Without thy helpe, by me be borne alone.
In our two loues there is but one respect,
Though in our liues a seperable spight,
Which though it alter not loues sole effect,
Yet doth it steale sweet houres from loues delight,
I may not euer-more acknowledge thee,
Least my bewailed guilt should do thee shame,
Nor thou with publike kindnesse honour me,
Vnlesse thou take that honour from thy name:
　　But doe not so, I loue thee in such sort,
　　As thou being mine, mine is thy good report.

37

As a decrepit father takes delight,
To see his actiue childe do deeds of youth,
So I, made lame by Fortunes dearest spight
Take all my comfort of thy worth and truth.
For whether beauty, birth, or wealth, or wit,
Or any of these all, or all, or more
Intitled in thy parts, do crowned sit,
I make my loue ingrafted to this store:
So then I am not lame, poore, nor dispis'd,
Whilst that this shadow doth such substance giue,
That I in thy abundance am suffic'd,
And by a part of all thy glory liue:
   Looke what is best, that best I wish in thee,
   This wish I haue, then ten times happy me.

38

How can my Muse want subiect to inuent
While thou dost breath that poor'st into my verse,
Thine owne sweet argument, to excellent,
For euery vulgar paper to rehearse:
Oh giue thy selfe the thankes if ought in me,
Worthy perusal stand against thy sight,
For who's so dumbe that cannot write to thee,
When thou thy selfe dost giue inuention light?
Be thou the tenth Muse, ten times more in worth
Then those old nine which rimers inuocate,
And he that calls on thee, let him bring forth
Eternal numbers to out-liue long date.
   If my slight Muse doe please these curious daies,
   The paine be mine, but thine shal be the praise.

39

Oh how thy worth with manners may I singe,
When thou art all the better part of me?
What can mine owne praise to mine owne selfe bring;
And what is't but mine owne when I praise thee,
Euen for this, let vs deuided liue,
And our deare loue loose name of single one,
That by this seperation I may giue
That due to thee which thou deseru'st alone:
Oh absence what a torment wouldst thou proue,
Were it not thy soure leisure gaue sweet leaue,
To entertaine the time with thoughts of loue,
Which time and thoughts so sweetly doth deceiue.
   And that thou teachest how to make one twaine,
   By praising him here who doth hence remaine.

40

Take all my loues, my loue, yea take them all,
What hast thou then more then thou hadst before?
No loue, my loue, that thou maist true loue call,
All mine was thine, before thou hadst this more:
Then if for my loue, thou my loue receiuest,
I cannot blame thee, for my loue thou vsest,
But yet be blam'd, if thou this selfe deceauest
By wilfull taste of what thy selfe refusest.
I doe forgiue thy robb'rie gentle theefe
Although thou steale thee all my pouerty:
And yet loue knowes it is a greater griefe
To beare loues wrong, then hates knowne iniury.
   Lasciuious grace, in whom all il wel showes,
   Kill me with spights yet we must not be foes.

41

Those pretty wrongs that liberty commits,
When I am some-time absent from thy heart,
Thy beautie, and thy yeares full well befits,
For still temptation followes where thou art.
Gentle thou art, and therefore to be wonne,
Beautious thou art, therefore to be assailed.
And when a woman woes, what womans sonne,
Will sourely leaue her till he haue preuailed.
Aye me, but yet thou mightst my seate forbeare,
And chide thy beauty, and thy straying youth,
Who lead thee in their ryot euen there
Where thou art forst to breake a two-fold truth:
   Hers by thy beauty tempting her to thee,
   Thine by thy beautie beeing false to me.

42

That thou hast her it is not all my griefe,
And yet it may be said I lou'd her deerely,
That she hath thee is of my wayling cheefe,
A losse in loue that touches me more neerely.
Louing offendors thus I will excuse yee,
Thou doost loue her, because thou knowst I loue her,
And for my sake euen so doth she abuse me,
Suffring my friend for my sake to approoue her,
If I loose thee, my losse is my loues gaine,
And loosing her, my friend hath found that losse,
Both finde each other, and I loose both twaine,
And both for my sake lay on me this crosse,
   But here's the ioy, my friend and I are one,
   Sweete flattery, then she loues but me alone.

43

When most I winke then doe mine eyes best see,
For all the day they view things vnrespected,
But when I sleepe, in dreames they looke on thee,
And darkely bright, are bright in darke directed.
Then thou whose shaddow shaddowes doth make
    bright,
How would thy shadowes forme, forme happy show,
To the cleere day with thy much cleerer light,
When to vn-seeing eyes thy shade shines so?
How would (I say) mine eyes be blessed made,
By looking on thee in the liuing day?
When in dead night thy faire imperfect shade,
Through heauy sleepe on sightlesse eyes doth stay?
    All dayes are nights to see till I see thee,
    And nights bright daies when dreams do shew thee
    me.

44

If the dull substance of my flesh were thought,
Iniurious distance should not stop my way,
For then dispight of space I would be brought,
From limits farre remote, where thou doost stay,
No matter then although my foote did stand
Vpon the farthest earth remoou'd from thee,
For nimble thought can iumpe both sea and land,
As soone as thinke the place where he would be.
But ah, thought kills me that I am not thought
To leape large lengths of miles when thou art gone,
But that so much of earth and water wrought,
I must attend times leasure with my mone.
    Receiuing naught by elements so sloe,
    But heauie teares, badges of eithers woe.

45

The other two, slight ayre, and purging fire,
Are both with thee, where euer I abide,
The first my thought, the other my desire,
These present absent with swift motion slide.
For when these quicker Elements are gone
In tender Embassie of loue to thee,
My life being made of foure, with two alone,
Sinkes downe to death, opprest with melancholie.
Vntill liues composition be recured,
By those swift messengers return'd from thee,
Who euen but now come back againe assured
Of thy faire health, recounting it to me.
    This told, I ioy, but then no longer glad,
    I send them back againe and straight grow sad.

46

Mine eye and heart are at a mortall warre,
How to deuide the conquest of thy sight,
Mine eye, my heart thy pictures sight would barre,
My heart, mine eye the freedome of that right,
My heart doth plead that thou in him doost lye,
(A closet neuer pearst with christall eyes)
But the defendant doth that plea deny,
And sayes in him thy faire appearance lyes.
To side this title is impannelled
A quest of thoughts, all tennants to the heart,
And by their verdict is determined
The cleere eyes moyitie, and the deare hearts part.
    As thus, mine eyes due is thy outward part,
    And my hearts right, thy inward loue of heart.

47

Betwixt mine eye and heart a league is tooke,
And each doth good turnes now vnto the other,
When that mine eye is famisht for a looke,
Or heart in loue with sighes himselfe doth smother;
With my loues picture then my eye doth feast,
And to the painted banquet bids my heart:
An other time mine eye is my hearts guest,
And in his thoughts of loue doth share a part.
So either by thy picture or my loue,
Thy selfe away, art present still with me,
For thou noe farther then my thoughts canst moue,
And I am still with them, and they with thee.
    Or if they sleepe, thy picture in my sight
    Awakes my heart, to hearts and eyes delight.

48

How carefull was I when I tooke my way,
Each trifle vnder truest barres to thrust,
That to my vse it might vn-vsed stay
From hands of falsehood, in sure wards of trust?
But thou, to whom my iewels trifles are,
Most worthy comfort, now my greatest griefe,
Thou best of deerest, and mine onely care,
Art left the prey of euery vulgar theefe.
Thee haue I not lockt vp in any chest,
Saue where thou art not, though I feele thou art,
Within the gentle closure of my brest,
From whence at pleasure thou maist come and part,
    And euen thence thou wilt be stolne I feare,
    For truth prooues theeuish for a prize so deare.

49

Against that time (if euer that time come)
When I shall see thee frowne on my defects,
When as thy loue hath cast his vtmost summe,
Cauld to that audite by aduis'd respects,
Against that time when thou shalt strangely passe,
And scarcely greete me with that sunne thine eye,
When loue conuerted from the thing it was
Shall reasons finde of setled grauitie.
Against that time do I insconce me here
Within the knowledge of mine owne desart,
And this my hand, against my selfe vpreare,
To guard the lawfull reasons on thy part,
    To leaue poore me, thou hast the strength of lawes,
    Since why to loue, I can alledge no cause.

50

How heauie doe I iourney on the way,
When what I seeke (my wearie trauels end)
Doth teach that ease and that repose to say
Thus farre the miles are measurde from thy friend.
The beast that beares me, tired with my woe,
Plods duly on, to beare that waight in me,
As if by some instinct the wretch did know
His rider lou'd not speed being made from thee:
The bloody spurre cannot prouoke him on,
That some-times anger thrusts into his hide,
Which heauily he answers with a grone,
More sharpe to me then spurring to his side,
    For that same grone doth put this in my mind,
    My greefe lies onward and my ioy behind.

51

Thus can my loue excuse the slow offence,
Of my dull bearer, when from thee I speed,
From where thou art, why should I hast me thence,
Till I returne of posting is noe need.
O what excuse will my poore beast then find,
When swift extremity can seeme but slow,
Then should I spurre though mounted on the wind,
In winged speed no motion shall I know,
Then can no horse with my desire keepe pace,
Therefore desire (of perfects loue being made)
Shall raign noe dull flesh in his fiery race,
But loue, for loue, thus shall excuse my iade,
    Since from thee going, he went wilfull slow,
    Towards thee ile run, and giue him leaue to goe.

52

So am I as the rich whose blessed key,
Can bring him to his sweet vp-locked treasure,
The which he will not eu'ry hower suruay,
For blunting the fine point of seldome pleasure.
Therefore are feasts so sollemne and so rare,
Since sildom comming in the long yeare set,
Like stones of worth they thinly placed are,
Or captaine Iewells in the carconet.
So is the time that keepes you as my chest,
Or as the ward-robe which the robe doth hide,
To make some speciall instant speciall blest,
By new vnfoulding his imprison'd pride.
    Blessed are you whose worthinesse giues skope,
    Being had to tryumph, being lackt to hope.

53

What is your substance, whereof are you made,
That millions of strange shaddowes on you tend?
Since euery one, hath euery one, one shade,
And you but one, can euery shaddow lend:
Describe *Adonis* and the counterfet,
Is poorely immitated after you,
On *Hellens* cheeke all art of beautie set,
And you in *Grecian* tires are painted new:
Speake of the spring, and foyzon of the yeare,
The one doth shaddow of your beautie show,
The other as your bountie doth appeare,
And you in euery blessed shape we know.
    In all externall grace you haue some part,
    But you like none, none you for constant heart.

54

Oh how much more doth beautie beautious seeme,
By that sweet ornament which truth doth giue,
The Rose lookes faire, but fairer we it deeme
For that sweet odor, which doth in it liue:
The Canker bloomes haue full as deepe a die,
As the perfumed tincture of the Roses,
Hang on such thornes, and play as wantonly,
When sommers breath their masked buds discloses:
But for their virtue only is their show,
They liue vnwoo'd, and vnrespected fade,
Die to themselues. Sweet Roses doe not so,
Of their sweet deathes, are sweetest odors made:
    And so of you, beautious and louely youth,
    When that shall vade, by verse distils your truth.

55

Not marble, nor the guilded monuments
Of Princes shall out-liue this powrefull rime,
But you shall shine more bright in these contents
Then vnswept stone, besmeer'd with sluttish time.
When wastefull warre shall *Statues* ouer-turne,
And broiles roote out the worke of masonry,
Nor *Mars* his sword, nor warres quick fire shall burne
The liuing record of your memory.
Gainst death, and all obliuious enmity
Shall you pace forth, your praise shall stil finde roome,
Euen in the eyes of all posterity
That weare this world out to the ending doome.
　　So til the iudgement that your selfe arise,
　　You liue in this, and dwell in louers eies.

56

Sweet loue renew thy force, be it not said
Thy edge should blunter be then apetite,
Which but too daie by feeding is alaied,
To morrow sharpned in his former might.
So loue be thou, although too daie thou fill
Thy hungrie eies, euen till they winck with fulnesse,
Too morrow see againe, and doe not kill
The spirit of Loue, with a perpetual dulnesse:
Let this sad *Intrim* like the Ocean be
Which parts the shore, where two contracted new,
Come daily to the banckes, that when they see
Returne of loue, more blest may be the view.
　　Or cal it Winter, which being ful of care,
　　Makes Sōmers welcome, thrice more wish'd, more
　　　　rare.

57

Being your slaue what should I doe but tend,
Vpon the houres, and times of your desire?
I haue no precious time at al to spend;
Nor seruices to doe til you require.
Nor dare I chide the world without end houre,
Whilst I (my soueraine) watch the clock for you,
Nor thinke the bitternesse of absence sowre,
When you haue bid your seruant once adieue.
Nor dare I question with my ieallous thought,
Where you may be, or your affaires suppose,
But like a sad slaue stay and thinke of nought
Saue where you are, how happy you make those.
　　So true a foole is loue, that in your Will,
　　(Though you doe any thing) he thinkes no ill.

58

That God forbid, that made me first your slaue,
I should in thought controule your times of pleasure,
Or at your hand th' account of houres to craue,
Being your vassail bound to staie your leisure.
Oh let me suffer (being at your beck)
Th' imprison'd absence of your libertie,
And patience, tame to sufferance bide each check,
Without accusing you of iniury.
Be where you list, your charter is so strong,
That you your selfe may priuiledge your time
To what you will, to you it doth belong,
Your selfe to pardon of selfe-doing crime.
　　I am to waite, though waiting so be hell,
　　Not blame your pleasure be it ill or well.

59

If their bee nothing new, but that which is,
Hath beene before, how are our braines beguild,
Which laboring for inuention beare amisse
The second burthen of a former child?
Oh that record could with a back-ward looke,
Euen of fiue hundreth courses of the Sunne,
Show me your image in some antique booke,
Since minde at first in carrecter was done.
That I might see what the old world could say,
To this composed wonder of your frame,
Whether we are mended, or where better they,
Or whether reuolution be the same.
　　Oh sure I am the wits of former daies,
　　To subiects worse haue giuen admiring praise.

60

Like as the waues make towards the pibled shore,
So do our minuites hasten to their end,
Each changing place with that which goes before,
In sequent toile all forwards do contend.
Natiuity once in the maine of light
Crawles to maturity, wherewith being crown'd,
Crooked eclipses gainst his glory fight,
And time that gaue, doth now his gift confound.
Time doth transfixe the florish set on youth,
And delues the paralels in beauties brow,
Feedes on the rarities of natures truth,
And nothing stands but for his sieth to mow.
　　And yet to times in hope, my verse shall stand
　　Praising thy worth, dispight his cruell hand.

61

Is it thy wil, thy Image should keepe open
My heauy eielids to the weary night?
Dost thou desire my slumbers should be broken,
While shadowes like to thee do mocke my sight?
Is it thy spirit that thou send'st from thee
So farre from home into my deeds to prye,
To find out shames and idle houres in me,
The skope and tenure of thy Ielousie?
O no, thy loue though much, is not so great,
It is my loue that keepes mine eie awake,
Mine owne true loue that doth my rest defeat,
To plaie the watch-man euer for thy sake.
　　For thee watch I, whilst thou dost wake elsewhere,
　　From me farre of, with others all to neere.

62

Sinne of selfe-loue possesseth al mine eie,
And all my soule, and al my euery part;
And for this sinne there is no remedie,
It is so grounded inward in my heart.
Me thinkes no face so gratious is as mine,
No shape so true, no truth of such account,
And for my selfe mine owne worth do define,
As I all other in all worths surmount.
But when my glasse shewes me my selfe indeed
Beated and chopt with tand antiquitie,
Mine owne selfe loue quite contrary I read.
Selfe, so selfe louing were iniquity,
　　T'is thee (my selfe) that for my selfe I praise,
　　Painting my age with beauty of thy daies.

63

Against my loue shall be as I am now
With times iniurious hand chrusht and ore-worne,
When houres haue dreind his blood and fild his brow
With lines and wrincles, when his youthfull morne
Hath trauaild on to Ages steepie night,
And all those beauties whereof now he's King
Are vanishing, or vanisht out of sight,
Stealing away the treasure of his Spring.
For such a time do I now fortifie
Against confounding Ages cruell knife,
That he shall neuer cut from memory
My sweet loues beauty, though my louers life.
　　His beautie shall in these blacke lines be seene,
　　And they shall liue, and he in them still greene.

64

When I haue seene by times fell hand defaced
The rich proud cost of outworne buried age,
When sometime loftie towers I see downe rased,
And brasse eternall slaue to mortall rage.
When I haue seene the hungry Ocean gaine
Aduantage on the Kingdome of the shoare,
And the firme soile win of the watry maine,
Increasing store with losse, and losse with store.
When I haue seene such interchange of state,
Or state it selfe confounded, to decay,
Ruine hath taught me thus to ruminate
That Time will come and take my loue away.
　　This thought is as a death which cannot choose
　　But weepe to haue, that which it feares to loose.

65

Since brasse, nor stone, nor earth, nor boundlesse sea,
But sad mortallity ore-swaies their power,
How with this rage shall beautie hold a plea,
Whose action is no stronger then a flower?
O how shall summers hunny breath hold out,
Against the wrackfull siedge of battring dayes,
When rocks impregnable are not so stoute,
Nor gates of steele so strong but time decayes?
O fearefull meditation, where alack,
Shall times best Iewell from times chest lie hid?
Or what strong hand can hold his swift foote back,
Or who his spoile of beautie can forbid?
　　O none, vnlesse this miracle haue might,
　　That in black inck my loue may still shine bright.

66

Tyr'd with all these for restfull death I cry,
As to behold desert a begger borne,
And needie Nothing trimd in iollitie,
And purest faith vnhappily forsworne,
And gilded honor shamefully misplast,
And maiden vertue rudely strumpeted,
And right perfection wrongfully disgrac'd,
And strength by limping sway disabled,
And arte made tung-tide by authoritie,
And Folly (Doctor-like) controuling skill,
And simple-Truth miscalde Simplicitie,
And captiue-good attending Captaine ill.
　　Tyr'd with all these, from these would I be gone,
　　Saue that to dye, I leaue my loue alone.

859

67

Ah wherefore with infection should he liue,
And with his presence grace impietie,
That sinne by him aduantage should atchiue,
And lace it selfe with his societie?
Why should false painting immitate his cheeke,
And steale dead seēing of his liuing hew?
Why should poore beautie indirectly seeke,
Roses of shaddow, since his Rose is true?
Why should he liue, now nature banckrout is,
Beggerd of blood to blush through liuely vaines,
For she hath no exchecker now but his,
And proud of many, liues vpon his gaines?
  O him she stores, to show what welth she had,
  In daies long since, before these last so bad.

68

Thus is his cheeke the map of daies out-worne,
When beauty liu'd and dy'ed as flowers do now,
Before these bastard signes of faire were borne,
Or durst inhabit on a liuing brow:
Before the goulden tresses of the dead,
The right of sepulchers, were shorne away,
To liue a second life on second head,
Ere beauties dead fleece made another gay:
In him those holy antique howers are seene,
Without all ornament, it selfe and true,
Making no summer of an others greene,
Robbing no ould to dresse his beauty new,
  And him as for a map doth Nature store,
  To shew faulse Art what beauty was of yore.

69

Those parts of thee that the worlds eye doth view,
Want nothing that the thought of hearts can mend:
All toungs (the voice of soules) giue thee that due,
Vttring bare truth, euen so as foes Commend.
Thy outward thus with outward praise is crownd,
But those same toungs that giue thee so thine owne,
In other accents doe this praise confound
By seeing farther then the eye hath showne.
They looke into the beauty of thy mind,
And that in guesse they measure by thy deeds,
Then churls their thoughts (although their eies were
    kind)
To thy faire flower ad the rancke smell of weeds,
  But why thy odor matcheth not thy show,
  The soyle is this, that thou doest common grow.

70

That thou are blam'd shall not be thy defect,
For slanders marke was euer yet the faire,
The ornament of beauty is suspect,
A Crow that flies in heauens sweetest ayre.
So thou be good, slander doth but approue,
Thy worth the greater beeing woo'd of time,
For Canker vice the sweetest buds doth loue,
And thou present'st a pure vnstained prime.
Thou hast past by the ambush of young daies,
Either not assayld, or victor beeing charg'd,
Yet this thy praise cannot be soe thy praise,
To tye vp enuy, euermore inlarg'd,
  If some suspect of ill maskt not thy show,
  Then thou alone kingdomes of hearts shouldst owe.

71

Noe Longer mourne for me when I am dead,
Then you shall heare the surly sullen bell
Giue warning to the world that I am fled
From this vile world with vildest wormes to dwell:
Nay if you read this line, remember not,
The hand that writ it, for I loue you so,
That I in your sweet thoughts would be forgot,
If thinking on me then should make you woe.
O if (I say) you looke vpon this verse,
When I (perhaps) compounded am with clay,
Do not so much as my poore name reherse;
But let your loue euen with my life decay.
  Least the wise world should looke into your mone,
  And mocke you with me after I am gon.

72

O least the world should taske you to recite,
What merit liu'd in me that you should loue
After my death (deare loue) forget me quite,
For you in me can nothing worthy proue.
Vnlesse you would deuise some vertuous lye,
To doe more for me then mine owne desert,
And hang more praise vpon deceased I,
Then nigard truth would willingly impart:
O least your true loue may seeme falce in this,
That you for loue speake well of me vntrue,
My name be buried where my body is,
And liue no more to shame nor me, nor you.
  For I am shamd by that which I bring forth,
  And so should you, to loue things nothing worth.

73

That time of yeare thou maist in me behold,
When yellow leaues, or none, or few doe hange
Vpon those boughes which shake against the could,
Bare ru'ind quiers, where late the sweet birds sang.
In me thou seest the twi-light of such day,
As after Sun-set fadeth in the West,
Which by and by blacke night doth take away,
Deaths second selfe that seals vp all in rest.
In me thou seest the glowing of such fire,
That on the ashes of his youth doth lye,
As the death bed, whereon it must expire,
Consum'd with that which it was nurrisht by.
 This thou perceu'st, which makes thy loue more
  strong,
 To loue that well, which thou must leaue ere long.

74

But be contented when that fell arest,
With out all bayle shall carry me away,
My life hath in this line some interest,
Which for memoriall still with thee shall stay.
When thou reuewest this, thou doest reuew,
The very part was consecrate to thee,
The earth can haue but earth, which is his due,
My spirit is thine the better part of me,
So then thou hast but lost the dregs of life,
The pray of wormes, my body being dead,
The coward conquest of a wretches knife,
To base of thee to be remembered,
 The worth of that, is that which it containes,
 And that is this, and this with thee remaines.

75

So are you to my thoughts as food to life,
Or as sweet season'd shewers are to the ground:
And for the peace of you I hold such strife,
As twixt a miser and his wealth is found.
Now proud as an inioyer, and anon
Doubting the filching age will steale his treasure,
Now counting best to be with you alone,
Then betterd that the world may see my pleasure,
Some-time all ful with feasting on your sight,
And by and by cleane starued for a looke,
Possessing or pursuing no delight
Saue what is had, or must from you be tooke.
 Thus do I pine and surfet day by day,
 Or gluttoning on all, or all away.

76

Why is my verse so barren of new pride?
So far from variation or quicke change?
Why with the time do I not glance aside
To new found methods, and to compounds strange?
Why write I still all one, euer the same,
And keepe inuention in a noted weed,
That euery word doth almost tel my name,
Shewing their birth, and where they did proceed?
O know sweet loue I alwaies write of you,
And you and loue are still my argument:
So all my best is dressing old words new,
Spending againe what is already spent:
 For as the Sun is daily new and old,
 So is my loue still telling what is told.

77

Thy glasse will shew thee how thy beauties were,
Thy dyall how thy pretious mynuits waste,
The vacant leaues thy mindes imprint will beare,
And of this booke, this learning maist thou taste.
The wrinckles which thy glasse will truly show,
Of mouthed graues will giue thee memorie,
Thou by thy dyals shady stealth maist know,
Times theeuish progresse to eternitie.
Looke what thy memorie cannot containe,
Commit to these waste blãcks, and thou shalt finde
Those children nurst, deliuerd from thy braine,
To take a new acquaintance of thy minde.
 These offices, so oft as thou wilt looke,
 Shall profit thee, and much inrich thy booke.

78

So oft haue I inuok'd thee for my Muse,
And found such faire assistance in my verse,
As euery *Alien* pen hath got my vse,
And vnder thee their poesie disperse.
Thine eyes, that taught the dumbe on high to sing,
And heauie ignorance aloft to flie,
Haue added fethers to the learneds wing,
And giuen grace a double Maiestie.
Yet be most proud of that which I compile,
Whose influence is thine, and borne of thee,
In others workes thou doost but mend the stile,
And Arts with thy sweete graces graced be.
 But thou art all my art, and doost aduance
 As high as learning, my rude ignorance.

79

Whilst I alone did call vpon thy ayde,
My verse alone had all thy gentle grace,
But now my gracious numbers are decayde,
And my sick Muse doth giue an other place.
I grant (sweet loue) thy louely argument
Deserues the trauaile of a worthier pen,
Yet what of thee thy Poet doth inuent,
He robs thee of, and payes it thee againe,
He lends thee vertue, and he stole that word,
From thy behauiour, beautie doth he giue
And found it in thy cheeke: he can affoord
No praise to thee, but what in thee doth liue.
   Then thanke him not for that which he doth say,
   Since what he owes thee, thou thy selfe doost pay.

80

O how I faint when I of you do write,
Knowing a better spirit doth vse your name,
And in the praise thereof spends all his might,
To make me toung-tide speaking of your fame.
But since your worth (wide as the Ocean is)
The humble as the proudest saile doth beare,
My sawsie barke (inferior farre to his)
On your broad maine doth wilfully appeare.
Your shallowest helpe will hold me vp a floate,
Whilst he vpon your soundlesse deepe doth ride,
Or (being wrackt) I am a worthlesse bote,
He of tall building, and of goodly pride.
   Then If he thriue and I be cast away,
   The worst was this, my loue was my decay.

81

Or I shall liue your Epitaph to make,
Or you suruiue when I in earth am rotten,
From hence your memory death cannot take,
Although in me each part will be forgotten.
Your name from hence immortall life shall haue,
Though I (once gone) to all the world must dye,
The earth can yeeld me but a common graue,
When you intombed in mens eyes shall lye,
Your monument shall be my gentle verse,
Which eyes not yet created shall ore-read,
And toungs to be, your beeing shall rehearse,
When all the breathers of this world are dead,
   You still shall liue (such vertue hath my Pen)
   Where breath most breaths, euen in the mouths of
      men.

82

I grant thou wert not married to my Muse,
And therefore maiest without attaint ore-looke
The dedicated words which writers vse
Of their faire subiect, blessing euery booke.
Thou art as faire in knowledge as in hew,
Finding thy worth a limmit past my praise,
And therefore art inforc'd to seeke anew,
Some fresher stampe of these time bettering dayes.
And do so loue, yet when they haue deuisde,
What strained touches Rhethorick can lend,
Thou truly faire, wert truly simpathizde,
In true plaine words, by thy true telling friend.
   And their grosse painting might be better vs'd,
   Where cheekes need blood, in thee it is abus'd.

83

I neuer saw that you did painting need,
And therefore to your faire no painting set,
I found (or thought I found) you did exceed,
The barren tender of a Poets debt:
And therefore haue I slept in your report,
That you your selfe being extant well might show,
How farre a moderne quill doth come to short,
Speaking of worth, what worth in you doth grow,
This silence for my sinne you did impute,
Which shall be most my glory being dombe,
For I impaire not beautie being mute,
When others would giue life, and bring a tombe.
   There liues more life in one of your faire eyes,
   Then both your Poets can in praise deuise.

84

Who is it that sayes most, which can say more,
Then this rich praise, that you alone, are you,
In whose confine immured is the store,
Which should example where your equall grew,
Leane penurie within that Pen doth dwell,
That to his subiect lends not some small glory,
But he that writes of you, if he can tell,
That you are you, so dignifies his story.
Let him but coppy what in you is writ,
Not making worse what nature made so cleere,
And such a counter-part shall fame his wit,
Making his stile admired euery where.
   You to your beautious blessings adde a curse,
   Being fond on praise, which makes your praises
      worse.

85

My toung-tide Muse in manners holds her still,
While comments of your praise richly compil'd,
Reserue thy Character with goulden quill,
And precious phrase by all the Muses fil'd.
I thinke good thoughts, whilst other write good
    wordes,
And like vnletter'd clarke still crie Amen,
To euery Himne that able spirit affords,
In polisht forme of well refined pen.
Hearing you praisd, I say 'tis so, 'tis true,
10 And to the most of praise adde some-thing more,
But that is in my thought, whose loue to you
(Though words come hind-most) holds his ranke
    before,
    Then others, for the breath of words respect,
    Me for my dombe thoughts, speaking in effect.

86

Was it the proud full saile of his great verse,
Bound for the prize of (all to precious) you,
That did my ripe thoughts in my braine inhearce,
Making their tombe the wombe wherein they grew?
Was it his spirit, by spirits taught to write,
Aboue a mortall pitch, that struck me dead?
No, neither he, nor his compiers by night
Giuing him ayde, my verse astonished.
He nor that affable familiar ghost
10 Which nightly gulls him with intelligence,
As victors of my silence cannot boast,
I was not sick of any feare from thence.
    But when your countinance fild vp his line,
    Then lackt I matter, that infeebled mine.

87

Farewell thou art too deare for my possessing,
And like enough thou knowst thy estimate,
The Charter of thy worth giues thee releasing:
My bonds in thee are all determinate.
For how do I hold thee but by thy granting,
And for that ritches where is my deseruing?
The cause of this faire guift in me is wanting,
And so my pattent back againe is sweruing.
Thy selfe thou gau'st, thy owne worth then not
    knowing,
10 Or mee to whom thou gau'st it, else mistaking,
So thy great guift vpon misprision growing,
Comes home againe, on better iudgement making.
    Thus haue I had thee as a dreame doth flatter,
    In sleepe a King, but waking no such matter.

88

When thou shalt be disposde to set me light,
And place my merrit in the eie of skorne,
Vpon thy side, against my selfe ile fight,
And proue thee virtuous, though thou art forsworne:
With mine owne weakenesse being best acquainted,
Vpon thy part I can set downe a story
Of faults conceald, wherein I am attainted:
That thou in loosing me, shall win much glory:
And I by this wil be a gainer too,
For bending all my louing thoughts on thee,   10
The iniuries that to my selfe I doe,
Doing thee vantage, duble vantage me.
    Such is my loue, to thee I so belong,
    That for thy right, my selfe will beare all wrong.

89

Say that thou didst forsake mee for some falt,
And I will comment vpon that offence,
Speake of my lamenesse, and I straight will halt:
Against thy reasons making no defence.
Thou canst not (loue) disgrace me halfe so ill,
To set a forme vpon desired change,
As ile my selfe disgrace, knowing thy wil,
I will acquaintance strangle and looke strange:
Be absent from thy walkes and in my tongue,
Thy sweet beloued name no more shall dwell,   10
Least I (too much profane) should do it wronge:
And haplie of our old acquaintance tell.
    For thee, against my selfe ile vow debate,
    For I must nere loue him whom thou dost hate.

90

Then hate me when thou wilt, if euer, now,
Now while the world is bent my deeds to crosse,
Ioyne with the spight of fortune, make me bow,
And doe not drop in for an after losse:
Ah doe not, when my heart hath scapte this sorrow,
Come in the rereward of a conquerd woe,
Giue not a windy night a rainie morrow,
To linger out a purposd ouer-throw.
If thou wilt leaue me, do not leaue me last,
When other pettie griefes haue done their spight,   10
But in the onset come, so shall I taste
At first the very worst of fortunes might.
    And other straines of woe, which now seeme woe,
    Compar'd with losse of thee, will not seeme so.

91

Some glory in their birth, some in their skill,
Some in their wealth, some in their bodies force,
Some in their garments though new-fangled ill:
Some in their Hawkes and Hounds, some in their
    Horse.
And euery humor hath his adiunct pleasure,
Wherein it findes a ioy aboue the rest,
But these perticulers are not my measure,
All these I better in one generall best.
Thy loue is better then high birth to me,
Richer then wealth, prouder then garments cost,
Of more delight then Hawkes or Horses bee:
And hauing thee, of all mens pride I boast.
    Wretched in this alone, that thou maist take
    All this away, and me most wretched make.

92

But doe thy worst to steale thy selfe away,
For tearme of life thou art assured mine,
And life no longer then thy loue will stay,
For it depends vpon that loue of thine.
Then need I not to feare the worst of wrongs,
When in the least of them my life hath end,
I see, a better state to me belongs
Then that, which on thy humor doth depend.
Thou canst not vex me with inconstant minde,
Since that my life on thy reuolt doth lie,
Oh what a happy title do I finde,
Happy to haue thy loue, happy to die!
    But whats so blessed faire that feares no blot,
    Thou maist be falce, and yet I know it not.

93

So shall I liue, supposing thou art true,
Like a deceiued husband, so loues face,
May still seeme loue to me, though alter'd new:
Thy lookes with me, thy heart in other place.
For their can liue no hatred in thine eye,
Therefore in that I cannot know thy change,
In manies lookes, the falce hearts history
Is writ in moods and frounes and wrinckles strange.
But heauen in thy creation did decree,
That in thy face sweet loue should euer dwell,
What ere thy thoughts, or thy hearts workings be,
Thy lookes should nothing thence, but sweetnesse tell.
    How like *Eaues* apple doth thy beauty grow,
    If thy sweet vertue answere not thy show.

94

They that haue powre to hurt, and will doe none,
That doe not do the thing, they most do showe,
Who mouing others, are themselues as stone,
Vnmooued, could, and to temptation slow:
They rightly do inherrit heauens graces,
And husband natures ritches from expence,
They are the Lords and owners of their faces,
Others, but stewards of their excellence:
The sommers flowre is to the sommer sweet,
Though to it selfe, it onely liue and die,
But if that flowre with base infection meete,
The basest weed out-braues his dignity:
    For sweetest things turne sowrest by their deedes,
    Lillies that fester, smell far worse then weeds.

95

How sweet and louely dost thou make the shame,
Which like a canker in the fragrant Rose,
Doth spot the beautie of thy budding name?
Oh in what sweets doest thou thy sinnes inclose!
That tongue that tells the story of thy daies,
(Making lasciuious comments on thy sport)
Cannot dispraise, but in a kinde of praise,
Naming thy name, blesses an ill report.
Oh what a mansion haue those vices got,
Which for their habitation chose out thee,
Where beauties vaile doth couer euery blot,
And all things turnes to faire, that eies can see!
    Take heed (deare heart) of this large priuiledge,
    The hardest knife ill vs'd doth loose his edge.

96

Some say thy fault is youth, some wantonesse,
Some say thy grace is youth and gentle sport,
Both grace and faults are lou'd of more and lesse:
Thou makst faults graces, that to thee resort:
As on the finger of a throned Queene,
The basest Iewell wil be well esteem'd:
So are those errors that in thee are seene,
To truths translated, and for true things deem'd.
How many Lambs might the sterne Wolfe betray,
If like a Lambe he could his lookes translate.
How many gazers mightst thou lead away,
If thou wouldst vse the strength of all thy state?
    But doe not so, I loue thee in such sort,
    As thou being mine, mine is thy good report.

97

How like a Winter hath my absence beene
From thee, the pleasure of the fleeting yeare?
What freezings haue I felt, what darke daies seene?
What old Decembers barenesse euery where?
And yet this time remou'd was sommers time,
The teeming Autumne big with ritch increase,
Bearing the wanton burthen of the prime,
Like widdowed wombes after their Lords decease:
Yet this aboundant issue seem'd to me,
But hope of Orphans, and vn-father'd fruite,
For Sommer and his pleasures waite on thee,
And thou away, the very birds are mute.
    Or if they sing, tis with so dull a cheere,
    That leaues looke pale, dreading the Winters neere.

98

From you haue I beene absent in the spring,
When proud pide Aprill (drest in all his trim)
Hath put a spirit of youth in euery thing:
That heauie *Saturne* laught and leapt with him.
Yet nor the laies of birds, nor the sweet smell
Of different flowers in odor and in hew,
Could make me any summers story tell:
Or from their proud lap pluck them where they grew:
Nor did I wonder at the Lillies white,
Nor praise the deepe vermillion in the Rose,
They weare but sweet, but figures of delight:
Drawne after you, you patterne of all those.
    Yet seem'd it Winter still, and you away,
    As with your shaddow I with these did play.

99

The forward violet thus did I chide,
Sweet theefe whence didst thou steale thy sweet that
    smels
If not from my loues breath, the purple pride,
Which on thy soft cheeke for complexion dwells,
In my loues veines thou hast too grosely died,
The Lillie I condemned for thy hand,
And buds of marierom had stolne thy haire,
The Roses fearefully on thornes did stand,
One blushing shame, an other white dispaire:
A third nor red, nor white, had stolne of both,
And to his robbry had annext thy breath,
But for his theft in pride of all his growth
A vengfull canker eate him vp to death.
    More flowers I noted, yet I none could see,
    But sweet, or culler it had stolne from thee.

100

Where art thou Muse that thou forgetst so long,
To speake of that which giues thee all thy might?
Spendst thou thy furie on some worthlesse songe,
Darkning thy powre to lend base subiects light.
Returne forgetfull Muse, and straight redeeme,
In gentle numbers time so idely spent,
Sing to the eare that doth thy laies esteeme,
And giues thy pen both skill and argument.
Rise resty Muse, my loues sweet face suruay,
If time haue any wrincle grauen there,
If any, be a *Satire* to decay,
And make times spoiles dispised euery where.
    Giue my loue fame faster then time wasts life,
    So thou preuenst his sieth, and crooked knife.

101

Oh truant Muse what shalbe thy amends,
For thy neglect of truth in beauty di'd?
Both truth and beauty on my loue depends:
So dost thou too, and therein dignifi'd:
Make answere Muse, wilt thou not haply saie,
Truth needs no collour with his collour fixt,
Beautie no pensell, beauties truth to lay:
But best is best, if neuer intermixt.
Because he needs no praise, wilt thou be dumb?
Excuse not silence so, for't lies in thee,
To make him much out-liue a gilded tombe:
And to be praisd of ages yet to be.
    Then do thy office Muse, I teach thee how,
    To make him seeme long hence, as he showes now.

102

My loue is strengthned though more weake in
    seeming,
I loue not lesse, thogh lesse the show appeare,
That loue is marchandiz'd, whose ritch esteeming,
The owners tongue doth publish euery where.
Our loue was new, and then but in the spring,
When I was wont to greet it with my laies,
As *Philomell* in summers front doth singe,
And stops hir pipe in growth of riper daies:
Not that the summer is lesse pleasant now
Then when her mournefull himns did hush the night,
But that wild musick burthens euery bow,
And sweets growne common loose their deare delight.
    Therefore like her, I some-time hold my tongue:
    Because I would not dull you with my songe.

103

Alack what pouerty my Muse brings forth,
That hauing such a skope to show her pride,
The argument all bare is of more worth
Then when it hath my added praise beside.
Oh blame me not if I no more can write!
Looke in your glasse and there appeares a face,
That ouer-goes my blunt inuention quite,
Dulling my lines, and doing me disgrace.
Were it not sinfull then striuing to mend,
To marre the subiect that before was well,
For to no other passe my verses tend,
Then of your graces and your gifts to tell.
  And more, much more then in my verse can sit,
  Your owne glasse showes you, when you looke in it.

104

To me faire friend you neuer can be old,
For as you were when first your eye I eyde,
Such seemes your beautie still: Three Winters colde,
Haue from the forrests shooke three summers pride,
Three beautious springs to yellow *Autumne* turn'd,
In processe of the seasons haue I seene,
Three Aprill perfumes in three hot Iunes burn'd,
Since first I saw you fresh which yet are greene.
Ah yet doth beauty like a Dyall hand,
Steale from his figure, and no pace perceiu'd,
So your sweete hew, which me thinkes still doth stand
Hath motion, and mine eye may be deceau'd.
  For feare of which, heare this thou age vnbred,
  Ere you were borne was beauties summer dead.

105

Let not my loue be cal'd Idolatrie,
Nor my beloued as an Idoll show,
Since all alike my songs and praises be
To one, of one, still such, and euer so.
Kinde is my loue to day, to morrow kinde,
Still constant in a wondrous excellence,
Therefore my verse to constancie confin'de,
One thing expressing, leaues out difference.
Faire, kinde, and true, is all my argument,
Faire, kinde and true, varrying to other words,
And in this change is my inuention spent,
Three theams in one, which wondrous scope affords.
  Faire, kinde, and true, haue often liu'd alone.
  Which three till now, neuer kept seate in one.

106

When in the Chronicle of wasted time,
I see discriptions of the fairest wights,
And beautie making beautifull old rime,
In praise of Ladies dead, and louely Knights,
Then in the blazon of sweet beauties best,
Of hand, of foote, of lip, of eye, of brow,
I see their antique Pen would haue exprest,
Eu'n such a beauty as you maister now.
So all their praises are but prophesies
Of this our time, all you prefiguring,
And for they look'd but with deuining eyes,
They had not skill enough your worth to sing:
  For we which now behold these present dayes,
  Haue eyes to wonder, but lack toungs to praise.

107

Not mine owne feares, nor the prophetick soule,
Of the wide world, dreaming on things to come,
Can yet the lease of my true loue controule,
Supposde as forfeit to a confin'd doome.
The mortall Moone hath her eclipse indur'de,
And the sad Augurs mock their owne presage,
Incertenties now crowne them-selues assur'de,
And peace proclaimes Oliues of endlesse age,
Now with the drops of this most balmie time,
My loue lookes fresh, and death to me subscribes,
Since spight of him Ile liue in this poore rime,
While he insults ore dull and speachlesse tribes.
  And thou in this shalt finde thy monument,
  When tyrants crests and tombs of brasse are spent.

108

What's in the braine that Inck may character,
Which hath not figur'd to thee my true spirit,
What's new to speake, what now to register,
That may expresse my loue, or thy deare merit?
Nothing sweet boy, but yet like prayers diuine,
I must each day say ore the very same,
Counting no old thing old, thou mine, I thine,
Euen as when first I hallowed thy faire name.
So that eternall loue in loues fresh case,
Waighes not the dust and iniury of age,
Nor giues to necessary wrinckles place,
But makes antiquitie for aye his page,
  Finding the first conceit of loue there bred,
  Where time and outward forme would shew it dead.

109

O neuer say that I was false of heart,
Though absence seem'd my flame to quallifie,
As easie might I from my selfe depart,
As from my soule which in thy brest doth lye:
That is my home of loue, if I haue rang'd,
Like him that trauels I returne againe,
Iust to the time, not with the time exchang'd,
So that my selfe bring water for my staine,
Neuer beleeue though in my nature raign'd,
All frailties that besiege all kindes of blood,
That it could so preposterouslie be stain'd,
To leaue for nothing all thy summe of good:
　　For nothing this wide Vniuerse I call,
　　Saue thou my Rose, in it thou art my all.

110

Alas 'tis true, I haue gone here and there,
And made my selfe a motley to the view,
Gor'd mine own thoughts, sold cheap what is most
　　deare,
Made old offences of affections new.
Most true it is, that I haue lookt on truth
Asconce and strangely: But by all aboue,
These blenches gaue my heart an other youth,
And worse essaies prou'd thee my best of loue,
Now all is done, haue what shall haue no end,
Mine appetite I neuer more will grin'de
On newer proofe, to trie an older friend,
A God in loue, to whom I am confin'd.
　　Then giue me welcome, next my heauen the best,
　　Euen to thy pure and most most louing brest.

111

O for my sake doe you with fortune chide,
The guiltie goddesse of my harmfull deeds,
That did not better for my life prouide,
Then publick meanes which publick manners breeds.
Thence comes it that my name receiues a brand,
And almost thence my nature is subdu'd
To what it workes in, like the Dyers hand,
Pitty me then, and wish I were renu'de,
Whilst like a willing pacient I will drinke,
Potions of Eysell gainst my strong infection,
No bitternesse that I will bitter thinke,
Nor double pennance to correct correction.
　　Pittie me then deare friend, and I assure yee,
　　Euen that your pittie is enough to cure mee.

112

Your loue and pittie doth th'impression fill,
Which vulgar scandall stampt vpon my brow,
For what care I who calles me well or ill,
So you ore-greene my bad, my good alow?
You are my All the world, and I must striue,
To know my shames and praises from your tounge,
None else to me, nor I to none aliue,
That my steel'd sence or changes right or wrong,
In so profound *Abisme* I throw all care
Of others voyces, that my Adders sence,
To cryttick and to flatterer stopped are:
Marke how with my neglect I doe dispence.
　　You are so strongly in my purpose bred,
　　That all the world besides me thinkes y'are dead.

113

Since I left you, mine eye is in my minde,
And that which gouernes me to goe about,
Doth part his function, and is partly blind,
Seemes seeing, but effectually is out:
For it no forme deliuers to the heart
Of bird, of flowre, or shape which it doth latch,
Of his quick obiects hath the minde no part,
Nor his owne vision houlds what it doth catch:
For if it see the rud'st or gentlest sight,
The most sweet-fauor or deformedst creature,
The mountaine, or the sea, the day, or night:
The Croe, or Doue, it shapes them to your feature.
　　Incapable of more, repleat with you,
　　My most true minde thus makes mine eye vntrue.

114

Or whether doth my minde being crown'd with you
Drinke vp the monarks plague this flattery?
Or whether shall I say mine eie saith true,
And that your loue taught it this *Alcumie*?
To make of monsters, and things indigest,
Such cherubines as your sweet selfe resemble,
Creating euery bad a perfect best
As fast as obiects to his beames assemble:
Oh tis the first, tis flatry in my seeing,
And my great minde most kingly drinkes it vp,
Mine eie well knowes what with his gust is greeing,
And to his pallat doth prepare the cup.
　　If it be poison'd, tis the lesser sinne,
　　That mine eye loues it and doth first beginne.

115

Those lines that I before haue writ doe lie,
Euen those that said I could not loue you deerer,
Yet then my iudgement knew no reason why,
My most full flame should afterwards burne cleerer.
But reckening time, whose milliond accidents
Creepe in twixt vowes, and change decrees of Kings,
Tan sacred beautie, blunt the sharp'st intents,
Diuert strong mindes to th' course of altring things:
Alas why fearing of times tiranie,
Might I not then say now I loue you best,
When I was certaine ore in-certainty,
Crowning the present, doubting of the rest:
    Loue is a Babe, then might I not say so
    To giue full growth to that which still doth grow.

116

Let me not to the marriage of true mindes
Admit impediments, loue is not loue
Which alters when it alteration findes,
Or bends with the remouer to remoue.
O no, it is an euer fixed marke
That lookes on tempests and is neuer shaken;
It is the star to euery wandring barke,
Whose worths vnknowne, although his higth be taken.
Lou's not Times foole, though rosie lips and cheeks
Within his bending sickles compasse come,
Loue alters not with his breefe houres and weekes,
But beares it out euen to the edge of doome:
    If this be error and vpon me proued,
    I neuer writ, nor no man euer loued.

117

Accuse me thus, that I haue scanted all,
Wherein I should your great deserts repay,
Forgot vpon your dearest loue to call,
Whereto al bonds do tie me day by day,
That I haue frequent binne with vnknown mindes,
And giuen to time your owne deare purchas'd right,
That I haue hoysted saile to al the windes
Which should transport me farthest from your sight.
Booke both my wilfulnesse and errors downe,
And on iust proofe surmise accumilate,
Bring me within the leuel of your frowne,
But shoote not at me in your waken'd hate:
    Since my appeale saies I did striue to prooue
    The constancy and virtue of your loue.

118

Like as to make our appetites more keene
With eager compounds we our pallat vrge,
As to preuent our malladies vnseene,
We sicken to shun sicknesse when we purge.
Euen so being full of your nere cloying sweetnesse,
To bitter sawces did I frame my feeding;
And sicke of wel-fare found a kind of meetnesse,
To be diseas'd ere that there was true needing.
Thus pollicie in loue t'anticipate
The ills that were not, grew to faults assured,
And brought to medicine a healthfull state
Which rancke of goodnesse would by ill be cured.
    But thence I learne and find the lesson true,
    Drugs poyson him that so fell sicke of you.

119

What potions haue I drunke of *Syren* teares
Distil'd from Lymbecks foule as hell within,
Applying feares to hopes, and hopes to feares,
Still loosing when I saw my selfe to win?
What wretched errors hath my heart committed,
Whilst it hath thought it selfe so blessed neuer?
How haue mine eies out of their Spheares bene fitted
In the distraction of this madding feuer?
O benefit of ill, now I finde true
That better is, by euil still made better.
And ruin'd loue when it is built anew
Growes fairer then at first, more strong, far greater.
    So I returne rebukt to my content,
    And gaine by ills thrise more then I haue spent.

120

That you were once vnkind be-friends mee now,
And for that sorrow, which I then didde feele,
Needes must I vnder my transgression bow,
Vnlesse my Nerues were brasse or hammer'd steele.
For if you were by my vnkindnesse shaken
As I by yours, y'haue past a hell of Time,
And I a tyrant haue no leasure taken
To waigh how once I suffer'd in your crime.
O that our night of wo might haue remembred
My deepest sence, how hard true sorrow hits,
And soone to you, as you to me then tendred
The humble salue, which wounded bosomes fits!
    But that your trespasse now becomes a fee,
    Mine ransoms yours, and yours must ransome mee.

121

Tis better to be vile then vile esteemed,
When not to be, receiues reproach of being,
And the iust pleasure lost, which is so deemed,
Not by our feeling, but by others seeing.
For why should others false adulterat eyes
Giue salutation to my sportiue blood?
Or on my frailties why are frailer spies;
Which in their wils count bad what I think good?
Noe, I am that I am, and they that leuell
At my abuses, reckon vp their owne,   10
I may be straight though they them-selues be beuel,
By their rancke thoughtes, my deedes must not be
            shown
    Vnlesse this generall euill they maintaine,
    All men are bad and in their badnesse raigne.

122

Thy guift, thy tables, are within my braine
Full characterd with lasting memory,
Which shall aboue that idle rancke remaine
Beyond all date euen to eternity.
Or at the least, so long as braine and heart
Haue facultie by nature to subsist,
Til each to raz'd obliuion yeeld his part
Of thee, thy record neuer can be mist:
That poore retention could not so much hold,
Nor need I tallies thy deare loue to skore,   10
Therefore to giue them from me was I bold,
To trust those tables that receaue thee more,
    To keepe an adiunckt to remember thee,
    Were to import forgetfulnesse in mee.

123

No! Time, thou shalt not bost that I doe change,
Thy pyramyds buylt vp with newer might
To me are nothing nouell, nothing strange,
They are but dressings of a former sight:
Our dates are breefe, and therefor we admire,
What thou dost foyst vpon vs that is ould,
And rather make them borne to our desire,
Then thinke that we before haue heard them tould:
Thy registers and thee I both defie,
Not wondring at the present, nor the past,   10
For thy records, and what we see doth lye,
Made more or les by thy continuall hast:
    This I doe vow and this shall euer be,
    I will be true dispight thy syeth and thee.

124

Yf my deare loue were but the childe of state,
It might for fortunes basterd be vnfather'd,
As subiect to times loue, or to times hate,
Weeds among weeds, or flowers with flowers gatherd.
No it was buylded far from accident,
It suffers not in smilinge pomp, nor falls
Vnder the blow of thralled discontent,
Whereto th'inuiting time our fashion calls:
It feares not policy that *Heriticke*,
Which workes on leases of short numbred howers,   10
But all alone stands hugely pollitick,
That it nor growes with heat, nor drownes with
            showres.
    To this I witnes call the foles of time,
    Which die for goodnes, who haue liu'd for crime.

125

Wer't ought to me I bore the canopy,
With my extern the outward honoring,
Or layd great bases for eternity,
Which proues more short then wast or ruining?
Haue I not seene dwellers on forme and fauor
Lose all, and more by paying too much rent,
For compound sweet, forgoing simple sauor,
Pittifull thriuors in their gazing spent.
Noe, let me be obsequious in thy heart,
And take thou my oblacion, poore but free,   10
Which is not mixt with seconds, knows no art,
But mutuall render, onely me for thee.
    Hence, thou subbornd *Informer*, a trew soule
    When most impeacht, stands least in thy controule.

126

O thou my louely Boy who in thy power,
Doest hould times fickle glasse, his sickle, hower:
Who hast by wayning growne, and therein shou'st,
Thy louers withering, as thy sweet selfe grow'st.
If Nature (soueraine misteres ouer wrack)
As thou goest onwards still will plucke thee backe,
She keepes thee to this purpose, that her skill,
May time disgrace, and wretched mynuits kill.
Yet feare her O thou minnion of her pleasure,
She may detaine, but not still keepe her tresure!   10
    Her *Audite* (though delayd) answer'd must be,
    And her *Quietus* is to render thee.

127

In the ould age blacke was not counted faire,
Or if it weare it bore not beauties name:
But now is blacke beauties successiue heire,
And Beautie slanderd with a bastard shame,
For since each hand hath put on Natures power,
Fairing the foule with Arts faulse borrow'd face,
Sweet beauty hath no name no holy boure,
But is prophan'd, if not liues in disgrace.
Therefore my Mistersse eyes are Rauen blacke,
Her brow so suted, and they mourners seeme,
At such who not borne faire no beauty lack,
Slandring Creation with a false esteeme,
    Yet so they mourne becomming of their woe,
    That euery toung saies beauty should looke so.

128

How oft when thou my musike musike playst,
Vpon that blessed wood whose motion sounds
With thy sweet fingers when thou gently swayst
The wiry concord that mine eare confounds,
Do I enuie those Iackes that nimble leape,
To kisse the tender inward of thy hand,
Whilst my poore lips which should that haruest reape,
At the woods bouldnes by thee blushing stand.
To be so tikled they would change their state,
And situation with those dancing chips,
Ore whome thy fingers walke with gentle gate,
Making dead wood more blest then liuing lips,
    Since sausie Iackes so happy are in this,
    Giue them thy fingers, me thy lips to kisse.

129

Th'expence of Spirit in a waste of shame
Is lust in action, and till action, lust
Is periurd, murdrous, blouddy full of blame,
Sauage, extreame, rude, cruell, not to trust,
Inioyd no sooner but dispised straight,
Past reason hunted, and no sooner had
Past reason hated as a swollowed bayt,
On purpose layd to make the taker mad.
Made in pursut and in possession so,
Had, hauing, and in quest to haue, extreame,
A blisse in proofe and proud a very wo,
Before a ioy proposd behind a dreame,
    All this the world well knowes yet none knowes
        well,
    To shun the heauen that leads men to this hell.

130

My Mistres eyes are nothing like the Sunne,
Currall is farre more red, then her lips red,
If snow be white, why then her brests are dun:
If haires be wiers, black wiers grow on her head:
I haue seene Roses damaskt, red and white,
But no such Roses see I in her cheekes,
And in some perfumes is there more delight,
Then in the breath that from my Mistres reekes.
I loue to heare her speake, yet well I know,
That Musicke hath a farre more pleasing sound:
I graunt I neuer saw a goddesse goe,
My Mistres when shee walkes treads on the ground.
    And yet by heauen I thinke my loue as rare,
    As any she beli'd with false compare.

131

Thou art as tiranous, so as thou art,
As those whose beauties proudly make them cruell;
For well thou know'st to my deare doting hart
Thou art the fairest and most precious Iewell.
Yet in good faith some say that thee behold,
Thy face hath not the power to make loue grone;
To say they erre, I dare not be so bold,
Although I sweare it to my selfe alone.
And to be sure that is not false I sweare,
A thousand grones but thinking on thy face,
One on anothers necke do witnesse beare
Thy blacke is fairest in my iudgements place.
    In nothing art thou blacke saue in thy deeds,
    And thence this slaunder as I thinke proceeds.

132

Thine eies I loue, and they as pittying me,
Knowing thy heart torment me with disdaine,
Haue put on black, and louing mourners bee,
Looking with pretty ruth vpon my paine.
And truly not the morning Sun of Heauen
Better becomes the gray cheeks of the East,
Nor that full Starre that vshers in the Eauen
Doth halfe that glory to the sober West
As those two morning eyes become thy face:
O let it then as well beseeme thy heart
To mourne for me since mourning doth thee grace,
And sute thy pitty like in euery part.
    Then will I sweare beauty her selfe is blacke,
    And all they foule that thy complexion lacke.

133

Beshrew that heart that makes my heart to groane
For that deepe wound it giues my friend and me;
I'st not ynough to torture me alone,
But slaue to slauery my sweet'st friend must be.
Me from my selfe thy cruell eye hath taken,
And my next selfe thou harder hast ingrossed,
Of him, my selfe, and thee I am forsaken,
A torment thrice three-fold thus to be crossed:
Prison my heart in thy steele bosomes warde,
But then my friends heart let my poore heart bale,
Who ere keepes me, let my heart be his garde,
Thou canst not then vse rigor in my Iaile.
   And yet thou wilt, for I being pent in thee,
   Perforce am thine and all that is in me.

134

So now I haue confest that he is thine,
And I my selfe am morgag'd to thy will,
My selfe Ile forfeit, so that other mine,
Thou wilt restore to be my comfort still:
But thou wilt not, nor he will not be free,
For thou art couetous, and he is kinde,
He learnd but suretie-like to write for me,
Vnder that bond that him as fast doth binde.
The statute of thy beauty thou wilt take,
Thou vsurer that put'st forth all to vse,
And sue a friend, came debter for my sake,
So him I loose through my vnkinde abuse.
   Him haue I lost, thou hast both him and me,
   He paies the whole, and yet am I not free.

135

Who euer hath her wish, thou hast thy *Will*,
And *Will* too boote, and *Will* in ouer-plus,
More then enough am I that vexe thee still,
To thy sweet will making addition thus.
Wilt thou whose will is large and spatious,
Not once vouchsafe to hide my will in thine,
Shall will in others seeme right gracious,
And in my will no faire acceptance shine:
The sea all water, yet receiues raine still,
And in aboundance addeth to his store,
So thou beeing rich in *Will* adde to thy *Will*,
One will of mine to make thy large *Will* more.
   Let no vnkinde, no faire beseechers kill,
   Thinke all but one, and me in that one *Will*.

136

If thy soule check thee that I come so neere,
Sweare to thy blind soule that I was thy *Will*,
And will thy soule knowes is admitted there,
Thus farre for loue, my loue-sute sweet fullfill.
Will, will fulfill the treasure of thy loue,
I fill it full with wils, and my will one,
In things of great receit with ease we prooue,
Among a number one is reckon'd none.
Then in the number let me passe vntold,
Though in thy stores account I one must be,
For nothing hold me, so it please thee hold,
That nothing me, a some-thing sweet to thee.
   Make but my name thy loue, and loue that still,
   And then thou lou'st me for my name is *Will*.

137

Thou blinde foole loue, what doost thou to mine eyes,
That they behold and see not what they see:
They know what beautie is, see where it lyes,
Yet what the best is, take the worst to be.
If eyes corrupt by ouer-partiall lookes,
Be anchord in the baye where all men ride,
Why of eyes falsehood hast thou forged hookes,
Whereto the iudgement of my heart is tide?
Why should my heart thinke that a seuerall plot,
Which my heart knowes the wide worlds common
     place?
Or mine eyes seeing this, say this is not,
To put faire truth vpon so foule a face,
   In things right true my heart and eyes haue erred,
   And to this false plague are they now transferred.

138

When my loue sweares that she is made of truth,
I do beleeue her though I know she lyes,
That she might thinke me some vntuterd youth,
Vnlearned in the worlds false subtilties.
Thus vainely thinking that she thinkes me young,
Although she knowes my dayes are past the best,
Simply I credit her false speaking tongue,
On both sides thus is simple truth supprest:
But wherefore sayes she not she is vniust?
And wherefore say not I that I am old?
O loues best habit is in seeming trust,
And age in loue, loues not to haue yeares told.
   Therefore I lye with her, and she with me,
   And in our faults by lyes we flatterd be.

139

O call not me to iustifie the wrong,
That thy vnkindnesse layes vpon my heart,
Wound me not with thine eye but with thy toung,
Vse power with power, and slay me not by Art,
Tell me thou lou'st else-where; but in my sight,
Deare heart forbeare to glance thine eye aside,
What needst thou wound with cunning when thy
    might
Is more then my ore-prest defence can bide?
Let me excuse thee, ah my loue well knowes,
Her prettie lookes haue beene mine enemies,
And therefore from my face she turnes my foes,
That they else-where might dart their iniuries:
    Yet do not so, but since I am neere slaine,
    Kill me out-right with lookes, and rid my paine.

140

Be wise as thou art cruell, do not presse
My toung-tide patience with too much disdaine:
Least sorrow lend me words and words expresse,
The manner of my pittie wanting paine.
If I might teach thee witte better it weare,
Though not to loue, yet loue to tell me so,
As testie sick-men when their deaths be neere,
No newes but health from their Phisitions know.
For if I should dispaire I should grow madde,
And in my madnesse might speake ill of thee,
Now this ill wresting world is growne so bad,
Madde slanderers by madde eares beleeued be.
    That I may not be so, nor thou belyde,
    Beare thine eyes straight, though thy proud heart
      goe wide.

141

In faith I doe not loue thee with mine eyes,
For they in thee a thousand errors note,
But 'tis my heart that loues what they dispise,
Who in dispight of view is pleasd to dote.
Nor are mine eares with thy toungs tune delighted,
Nor tender feeling to base touches prone,
Nor taste, nor smell, desire to be inuited
To any sensuall feast with thee alone:
But my fiue wits, nor my fiue sences can
Diswade one foolish heart from seruing thee,
Who leaues vnswai'd the likenesse of a man,
Thy proud hearts slaue and vassall wretch to be:
    Onely my plague thus farre I count my gaine,
    That she that makes me sinne, awards me paine.

142

Loue is my sinne, and thy deare vertue hate,
Hate of my sinne, grounded on sinfull louing,
O but with mine, compare thou thine owne state,
And thou shalt finde it merrits not reproouing,
Or if it do, not from those lips of thine,
That haue prophan'd their scarlet ornaments,
And seald false bonds of loue as oft as mine,
Robd others beds reuenues of their rents.
Be it lawfull I loue thee as thou lou'st those,
Whome thine eyes wooe as mine importune thee,
Roote pittie in thy heart that when it growes,
Thy pitty may deserue to pittied bee.
    If thou doost seeke to haue what thou doost hide,
    By selfe example mai'st thou be denide.

143

Loe as a carefull huswife runnes to catch,
One of her fether'd creatures broake away,
Sets downe her babe and makes all swift dispatch
In pursuit of the thing she would haue stay:
Whilst her neglected child holds her in chace,
Cries to catch her whose busie care is bent,
To follow that which flies before her face:
Not prizing her poore infants discontent;
So runst thou after that which flies from thee,
Whilst I thy babe chace thee a farre behind,
But if thou catch thy hope turne back to me:
And play the mothers part kisse me, be kind.
    So will I pray that thou maist haue thy *Will*,
    If thou turne back and my loude crying still.

144

Two loues I haue of comfort and dispaire,
Which like two spirits do sugiest me still,
The better angell is a man right faire:
The worser spirit a woman collour'd il.
To win me soone to hell my femall euill,
Tempteth my better angel from my side,
And would corrupt my saint to be a diuel:
Wooing his purity with her fowle pride.
And whether that my angel be turn'd finde,
Suspect I may, yet not directly tell,
But being both from me both to each friend,
I gesse one angel in an others hel.
    Yet this shal I nere know but liue in doubt,
    Till my bad angel fire my good one out.

145

Those lips that Loues owne hand did make,
Breath'd forth the sound that said I hate,
To me that languisht for her sake:
But when she saw my wofull state,
Straight in her heart did mercie come,
Chiding that tongue that euer sweet,
Was vsde in giuing gentle dome:
And tought it thus a new to greete:
I hate she alterd with an end,
That follow'd it as gentle day,
Doth follow night who like a fiend
From heauen to hell is flowne away.
 I hate, from hate away she threw,
 And sau'd my life saying not you.

146

Poore soule the center of my sinfull earth,
[   ] these rebbell powres that thee array,
Why dost thou pine within and suffer dearth
Painting thy outward walls so costlie gay?
Why so large cost hauing so short a lease,
Dost thou vpon thy fading mansion spend?
Shall wormes inheritors of this excesse
Eate vp thy charge? is this thy bodies end?
Then soule liue thou vpon thy seruants losse,
And let that pine to aggrauat thy store;
Buy tearmes diuine in selling houres of drosse:
Within be fed, without be rich no more,
 So shalt thou feed on death, that feeds on men,
 And death once dead, ther's no more dying then.

147

My loue is as a feauer longing still,
For that which longer nurseth the disease,
Feeding on that which doth preserue the ill,
Th'vncertaine sicklie appetite to please:
My reason the Phisition to my loue,
Angry that his prescriptions are not kept
Hath left me, and I desperate now approoue,
Desire is death, which Phisick did except.
Past cure I am, now Reason is past care,
And frantick madde with euer-more vnrest,
My thoughts and my discourse as mad mens are,
At randon from the truth vainely exprest.
 For I haue sworne thee faire, and thought thee
 bright,
 Who art as black as hell, as darke as night.

148

O me! what eyes hath loue put in my head,
Which haue no correspondence with true sight,
Or if they haue, where is my iudgment fled,
That censures falsely what they see aright?
If that be faire whereon my false eyes dote,
What meanes the world to say it is not so?
If it be not, then loue doth well denote,
Loues eye is not so true as all mens: no,
How can it? O how can loues eye be true,
That is so vext with watching and with teares?
No maruaile then though I mistake my view,
The sunne it selfe sees not, till heauen cleeres.
 O cunning loue, with teares thou keepst me blinde,
 Least eyes well seeing thy foule faults should finde.

149

Canst thou O cruell, say I loue thee not,
When I against my selfe with thee pertake:
Doe I not thinke on thee when I forgot
Am of my selfe, all tirant for thy sake?
Who hateth thee that I doe call my friend,
On whom froun'st thou that I doe faune vpon,
Nay if thou lowrst on me doe I not spend
Reuenge vpon my selfe with present mone?
What merrit do I in my selfe respect,
That is so proude thy seruice to dispise,
When all my best doth worship thy defect,
Commanded by the motion of thine eyes.
 But loue hate on for now I know thy minde,
 Those that can see thou lou'st, and I am blind.

150

Oh from what powre hast thou this powrefull might,
With insufficiency my heart to sway,
To make me giue the lie to my true sight,
And swere that brightnesse doth not grace the day?
Whence hast thou this becomming of things il,
That in the very refuse of thy deeds,
There is such strength and warrantise of skill,
That in my minde thy worst all best exceeds?
Who taught thee how to make me loue thee more,
The more I heare and see iust cause of hate,
Oh though I loue what others doe abhor,
With others thou shouldst not abhor my state.
 If thy vnworthinesse raisd loue in me,
 More worthy I to be belou'd of thee.

151

Loue is too young to know what conscience is,
Yet who knowes not conscience is borne of loue,
Then gentle cheater vrge not my amisse,
Least guilty of my faults thy sweet selfe proue.
For thou betraying me, I doe betray
My nobler part to my grose bodies treason,
My soule doth tell my body that he may
Triumph in loue, flesh staies no farther reason,
But rysing at thy name doth point out thee,
As his triumphant prize, proud of this pride,
He is contented thy poore drudge to be
To stand in thy affaires, fall by thy side.
   No want of conscience hold it that I call,
   Her loue, for whose deare loue I rise and fall.

152

In louing thee thou know'st I am forsworne,
But thou art twice forsworne to me loue swearing,
In act thy bed-vow broake and new faith torne,
In vowing new hate after new loue bearing:
But why of two othes breach doe I accuse thee,
When I breake twenty: I am periur'd most,
For all my vowes are othes but to misuse thee:
And all my honest faith in thee is lost.
For I haue sworne deepe othes of thy deepe kindnesse:
Othes of thy loue, thy truth, thy constancie,
And to inlighten thee gaue eyes to blindnesse,
Or made them swere against the thing they see.
   For I haue sworne thee faire: more periurde eye,
   To swere against the truth so foule a lie.

153

Cupid laid by his brand and fell a sleepe,
A maide of *Dyans* this aduantage found,
And his loue-kindling fire did quickly steepe
In a could vallie-fountaine of that ground:
Which borrowd from this holie fire of loue,
A datelesse liuely heat still to indure,
And grew a seething bath which yet men proue,
Against strang malladies a soueraigne cure:
But at my mistres eie loues brand new fired,
The boy for triall needes would touch my brest,
I sick withall the helpe of bath desired,
And thether hied a sad distemperd guest.
   But found no cure, the bath for my helpe lies,
   Where *Cupid* got new fire; my mistres eyes.

154

The little Loue-God lying once a sleepe,
Laid by his side his heart inflaming brand,
Whilst many Nymphes that vou'd chast life to keep,
Came tripping by, but in her maiden hand,
The fayrest votary tooke vp that fire,
Which many Legions of true hearts had warm'd,
And so the Generall of hot desire,
Was sleeping by a Virgin hand disarm'd.
This brand she quenched in a coole Well by,
Which from loues fire tooke heat perpetuall,
Growing a bath and healthfull remedy,
For men diseasd, but I my Mistrisse thrall,
   Came there for cure and this by that I proue,
   Loues fire heates water, water cooles not loue.

FINIS

A Louers complaint

From off a hill whose concaue wombe reworded,
A plaintfull story from a sistring vale
My spirrits t'attend this doble voyce accorded,
And downe I laid to list the sad tun'd tale,
Ere long espied a fickle maid full pale
Tearing of papers breaking rings a twaine,
Storming her world with sorrowes, wind and raine.

Vpon her head a plattid hiue of straw,
Which fortified her visage from the Sunne,
Whereon the thought might thinke sometime it saw
The carkas of a beauty spent and donne,
Time had not sithed all that youth begun,
Nor youth all quit, but spight of heauens fell rage,
Some beauty peept, through lettice of sear'd age.

Oft did she heaue her Napkin to her eyne,
Which on it had conceited charecters:
Laundring the silken figures in the brine,
That seasond woe had pelleted in teares,
And often reading what contents it beares:
As often shriking vndistinguisht wo,
In clamours of all size both high and low.

Some-times her leueld eyes their carriage ride,
As they did battry to the spheres intend:
Sometime diuerted their poore balls are tide,
To th'orbed earth; sometimes they do extend,
Their view right on, anon their gases lend,
To euery place at once and no where fixt,
The mind and sight distractedly commixt.

Her haire nor loose nor ti'd in formall plat,
Proclaimd in her a carelesse hand of pride;
For some vntuck'd descended her sheu'd hat,
Hanging her pale and pined cheeke beside,
Some in her threeden fillet still did bide,
And trew to bondage would not breake from thence,
Though slackly braided in loose negligence.

A thousand fauours from a maund she drew,
Of amber christall and of bedded Iet,
Which one by one she in a riuer threw,
Vpon whose weeping margent she was set,
Like vsery applying wet to wet,
Or Monarches hands that lets not bounty fall,
Where want cries some; but where excesse begs all.

Of folded schedulls had she many a one,
Which she perus'd, sighd, tore and gaue the flud,
Crackt many a ring of Posied gold and bone,
Bidding them find their Sepulchers in mud,

Found yet mo letters sadly pend in blood,
With sleided silke, feate and affectedly
Enswath'd and seald to curious secrecy.

These often bath'd she in her fluxiue eies,   50
And often kist, and often ganne to teare,
Cried O false blood thou register of lies,
What vnapproued witnes doost thou beare!
Inke would haue seem'd more blacke and damned
    heare!
This said in top of rage the lines she rents,
Big discontent, so breaking their contents.

A reuerend man that graz'd his cattell ny,
Sometime a blusterer that the ruffle knew
Of Court of Cittie, and had let go by
The swiftest houres obserued as they flew,   60
Towards this afflicted fancy fastly drew:
And priuiledg'd by age desires to know
In breefe the grounds and motiues of her wo.

So slides he downe vppon his greyned bat;
And comely distant sits he by her side,
When hee againe desires her, being satte,
Her greeuance with his hearing to deuide:
If that from him there may be ought applied
Which may her suffering extasie asswage
Tis promist in the charitie of age.   70

Father she saies, though in mee you behold
The iniury of many a blasting houre;
Let it not tell your Iudgement I am old,
Not age, but sorrow, ouer me hath power;
I might as yet haue bene a spreading flower
Fresh to my selfe, if I had selfe applyed
Loue to my selfe, and to no Loue beside.

But wo is mee, too early I attended
A youthfull suit it was to gaine my grace;
O one by natures outwards so commended,   80
That maidens eyes stucke ouer all his face,
Loue lackt a dwelling and made him her place.
And when in his faire parts shee didde abide,
Shee was new lodg'd and newly Deified.

His browny locks did hang in crooked curles,
And euery light occasion of the wind
Vpon his lippes their silken parcels hurles,
Whats sweet to do, to do wil aptly find,
Each eye that saw him did inchaunt the minde:
For on his visage was in little drawne,   90
What largenesse thinkes in parradise was sawne.

Smal shew of man was yet vpon his chinne,
His phenix downe began but to appeare
Like vnshorne veluet, on that termlesse skin
Whose bare out-brag'd the web it seem'd to were.
Yet shewed his visage by that cost more deare,
And nice affections wauering stood in doubt
If best were as it was, or best without.

His qualities were beautious as his forme,
100   For maiden tongu'd he was and thereof free;
Yet if men mou'd him, was he such a storme
As oft twixt May and Aprill is to see,
When windes breath sweet, vnruly though they bee.
His rudenesse so with his authoriz'd youth,
Did liuery falsenesse in a pride of truth.

Wel could hee ride, and often men would say
That horse his mettell from his rider takes
Proud of subiection, noble by the swaie,
What rounds, what bounds, what course what stop
    he makes
110   And controuersie hence a question takes,
Whether the horse by him became his deed,
Or he his mannad'g, by'th wel doing Steed.

But quickly on this side the verdict went,
His reall habitude gaue life and grace
To appertainings and to ornament,
Accomplisht in him-selfe not in his case:
All ayds them-selues made fairer by their place,
Came for addicions, yet their purpos'd trimme
Peec'd not his grace but were al grac'd by him.

120   So on the tip of his subduing tongue
All kinde of arguments and question deepe,
Al replication prompt, and reason strong
For his aduantage still did wake and sleep:
To make the weeper laugh, the laugher weepe,
He had the dialect and different skil,
Catching al passions in his craft of will.

That hee didde in the general bosome raigne
Of young, of old, and sexes both inchanted,
To dwel with him in thoughts, or to remaine
130   In personal duty, following where he haunted,
Consents bewitcht, ere he desire haue granted,
And dialogu'd for him what he would say,
Askt their own wils and made their wils obey.

Many there were that did his picture gette
To serue their eies, and in it put their mind,
Like fooles that in th' imagination set
The goodly obiects which abroad they find
Of lands and mansions, theirs in thought assign'd,
And labour in moe pleasures to bestow them,
140   Then the true gouty Land-lord which doth owe them.

So many haue that neuer toucht his hand
Sweetly suppos'd them mistresse of his heart:
My wofull selfe that did in freedome stand,
And was my owne fee simple (not in part)
What with his art in youth and youth in art
Threw my affections in his charmed power,
Reseru'd the stalke and gaue him al my flower.

Yet did I not as some my equals did
Demaund of him, nor being desired yeelded,
Finding my selfe in honour so forbidde,   150
With safest distance I mine honour sheelded,
Experience for me many bulwarkes builded
Of proofs new bleeding which remaind the foile
Of this false Iewell, and his amorous spoile.

But ah who euer shun'd by precedent,
The destin'd ill she must her selfe assay,
Or forc'd examples gainst her owne content
To put the by-past perrils in her way?
Counsaile may stop a while what will not stay:
For when we rage, aduise is often seene   160
By blunting vs to make our wils more keene.

Nor giues it satisfaction to our blood,
That wee must curbe it vppon others proofe,
To be forbod the sweets that seemes so good,
For feare of harmes that preach in our behoofe;
O appetite from iudgement stand aloofe!
The one a pallate hath that needs will taste,
Though reason weepe and cry it is thy last.

For further I could say this mans vntrue,
And knew the patternes of his foule beguiling,   170
Heard where his plants in others Orchards grew,
Saw how deceits were guilded in his smiling,
Knew vowes, were euer brokers to defiling,
Thought Characters and words meerly but art,
And bastards of his foule adulterat heart.

And long vpon these termes I held my Citty,
Till thus hee gan besiege me: Gentle maid
Haue of my suffering youth some feeling pitty
And be not of my holy vowes affraid,
Thats to ye sworne to none was euer said,   180
For feasts of loue I haue bene call'd vnto
Till now did nere inuite nor neuer woo.

All my offences that abroad you see
Are errors of the blood none of the mind:
Loue made them not, with acture they may be,
Where neither Party is nor trew nor kind,
They sought their shame that so their shame did find,
And so much lesse of shame in me remaines,
By how much of me their reproch containes,

190 Among the many that mine eyes haue seene,
Not one whose flame my hart so much as warmed,
Or my affection put to th' smallest teene,
Or any of my leisures euer Charmed,
Harme haue I done to them but nere was harmed,
Kept hearts in liueries, but mine owne was free,
And raignd commaunding in his monarchy.

Looke heare what tributes wounded fancies sent me,
Of palyd pearles and rubies red as blood:
Figuring that they their passions likewise lent me
200 Of greefe and blushes, aptly vnderstood
In bloodlesse white, and the encrimson'd mood,
Effects of terror and deare modesty,
Encampt in hearts but fighting outwardly.

And Lo behold these tallents of their heir,
With twisted mettle amorously empleacht
I haue receau'd from many a seuerall faire,
Their kind acceptance, wepingly beseecht,
With th'annexations of faire gems inricht,
And deepe brain'd sonnets that did amplifie
210 Each stones deare Nature, worth and quallity.

The Diamond? why twas beautifull and hard,
Whereto his inuis'd properties did tend,
The deepe greene Emrald in whose fresh regard,
Weake sights their sickly radience do amend.
The heauen hewd Saphir and the Opall blend
With obiects manyfold; each seuerall stone,
With wit well blazond smil'd or made some mone.

Lo all these trophies of affections hot,
Of pensiu'd and subdew'd desires the tender,
220 Nature hath chargd me that I hoord them not,
But yeeld them vp where I my selfe must render:
That is to you my origin and ender:
For these of force must your oblations be,
Since I their Aulter, you enpatrone me.

Oh then aduance (of yours) that phraseles hand,
Whose white weighes downe the airy scale of praise,
Take all these similies to your owne command,
Hollowed with sighes that burning lunges did raise:
What me your minister for you obaies
230 Workes vnder you, and to your audit comes
Their distract parcells, in combined summes.

Lo this deuice was sent me from a Nun,
A Sister sanctified of holiest note,
Which late her noble suit in court did shun,
Whose rarest hauings made the blossoms dote,
For she was sought by spirits of ritchest cote,
But kept cold distance, and did thence remoue,
To spend her liuing in eternall loue.

But oh my sweet what labour ist to leaue,
The thing we haue not, mastring what not striues, 240
Plaȳing the Place which did no forme receiue,
Playing patient sports in vnconstrained giues,
She that her fame so to her selfe contriues,
The scarres of battaile scapeth by the flight,
And makes her absence valiant, not her might.

Oh pardon me in that my boast is true,
The accident which brought me to her eie,
Vpon the moment did her force subdewe,
And now she would the caged cloister flie:
Religious loue put out religions eye: 250
Not to be tempted would she be emur'd,
And now to tempt all liberty procurd.

How mightie then you are, Oh heare me tell,
The broken bosoms that to me belong,
Haue emptied all their fountaines in my well:
And mine I powre your Ocean all amonge:
I strong ore them and you ore me being strong,
Must for your victorie vs all congest,
As compound loue to phisick your cold brest.

My parts had powre to charme a sacred Nunne, 260
Who disciplin'd I dieted in grace,
Beleeu'd her eies, when they t' assaile begun,
All vowes and consecrations giuing place:
O most potentiall loue, vowe, bond, nor space
In thee hath neither sting, knot, nor confine
For thou art all and all things els are thine.

When thou impressest what are precepts worth
Of stale example? when thou wilt inflame,
How coldly those impediments stand forth
Of wealth of filliall feare, lawe, kindred, fame, 270
Loues armes are peace, gainst rule, gainst sence,
        gainst shame
And sweetens in the suffring pangues it beares,
The *Alloes* of all forces, shockes and feares.

Now all these hearts that doe on mine depend,
Feeling it breake, with bleeding groanes they pine,
And supplicant their sighes to you extend
To leaue the battrie that you make gainst mine,
Lending soft audience, to my sweet designe,
And credent soule, to that strong bonded oth,
That shall preferre and vndertake my troth. 280

This said, his watrie eies he did dismount,
Whose sightes till then were leaueld on my face,
Each cheeke a riuer running from a fount,
With brynish currant downe-ward flowed a pace:
Oh how the channell to the streame gaue grace!
Who glaz'd with Christall gate the glowing Roses,
That flame through water which their hew incloses,

Oh father, what a hell of witch-craft lies,
In the small orb of one perticular teare?
290 But with the invndation of the eies:
What rocky heart to water will not weare?
What brest so cold that is not warmed heare,
O cleft effect, cold modesty hot wrath:
Both fire from hence, and chill extincture hath.

For loe his passion but an art of craft,
Euen there resolu'd my reason into teares,
There my white stole of chastity I daft,
Shooke off my sober gardes, and ciuill feares,
Appeare to him as he to me appeares:
300 All melting, though our drops this diffrence bore,
His poison'd me, and mine did him restore.

In him a plenitude of subtle matter,
Applied to Cautills, all straing formes receiues,
Of burning blushes, or of weeping water,
Or sounding palenesse: and he takes and leaues,
In eithers aptnesse as it best deceiues:
To blush at speeches ranck, to weepe at woes
Or to turne white and sound at tragick showes.

That not a heart which in his leuell came,
Could scape the haile of his all hurting ayme, 310
Shewing faire Nature is both kinde and tame:
And vaild in them did winne whom he would maime,
Against the thing he sought, he would exclaime,
When he most burnt in hart-wisht luxurie,
He preacht pure maide, and praisd cold chastitie.

Thus meerely with the garment of a grace,
The naked and concealed feind he couerd,
That th'vnexperient gaue the tempter place,
Which like a Cherubin aboue them houerd,
Who young and simple would not be so louerd. 320
Aye me I fell, and yet do question make,
What I should doe againe for such a sake.

O that infected moysture of his eye,
O that false fire which in his cheeke so glowd:
O that forc'd thunder from his heart did flye,
O that sad breath his spungie lungs bestowed,
O all that borrowed motion seeming owed,
Would yet againe betray the fore-betrayed,
And new peruert a reconciled Maide.

FINIS

ALTERNATIVE VERSIONS OF SONNETS 2, 106, 138, AND 144

Each of the four sonnets printed below exists in an alternative version. To the left, we give the text as it appeared in the volume of Shakespeare's sonnets printed in 1609. 'Spes Altera' and 'On His Mistris Beauty' derive from seventeenth-century manuscripts. The alternative versions of Sonnets 138 and 144 are from *The Passionate Pilgrime* (1599).

2

When fortie Winters shall beseige thy brow,
And digge deep trenches in thy beauties field,
Thy youthes proud liuery so gaz'd on now,
Wil be a totter'd weed of smal worth held:
Then being askt, where all thy beautie lies,
Where all the treasure of thy lusty daies;
To say within thine owne deepe sunken eyes,
Were an all-eating shame, and thriftlesse praise.
How much more praise deseru'd thy beauties vse,
10 If thou couldst answere this faire child of mine
Shall sum my count, and make my old excuse,
Proouing his beautie by succession thine.
  This were to be new made when thou art ould,
  And see thy blood warme when thou feel'st it could.

Spes Altera

When forty winters shall beseige thy brow
And trench deepe furrowes in y^t louely feild
Thy youthes faire Liu'rie so accounted now
Shall bee like rotten weeds of no worth held
Then beeing askt where all thy bewty lyes
Where all ye lustre of thy youthfull dayes
To say within these hollow suncken eyes
Were an all-eaten truth, & worthless prayse
O how much better were thy bewtyes vse
If thou coudst say this pretty child of mine   10
Saues my account & makes my old excuse
Making his bewty by succession thine
  This were to bee new borne when thou art old
  And see thy bloud warme when thou feelst it cold

106

When in the Chronicle of wasted time,
I see discriptions of the fairest wights,
And beautie making beautifull old rime,
In praise of Ladies dead, and louely Knights,
Then in the blazon of sweet beauties best,
Of hand, of foote, of lip, of eye, of brow,
I see their antique Pen would haue exprest,
Eu'n such a beauty as you maister now.
So all their praises are but prophesies
10 Of this our time, all you prefiguring,
And for they look'd but with deuining eyes,
They had not skill enough your worth to sing:
  For we which now behold these present dayes,
  Haue eyes to wonder, but lack toungs to praise.

On His Mistris Beauty

When in the Annalls of all wastinge Time
I see discriptions of the fairest wights
And beauty makeinge beautifull old rime
In praise of Ladyes dead and louely Knights
Then in the Blazon of sweet beauties best
Of face of hand, of lip, of eye, or brow
I see their antique pen would haue exprest
Ev'n such a beauty as you master now
Soe all their praises were but prophecies
Of these our dayes, all you prefiguringe   10
And for they saw but with diuininge eyes
they had not skill enough your worth to singe
  for wee which now behould these present dayes
  haue eyes to wonder, but no tongues to praise:

138

When my loue sweares that she is made of truth,
I do beleeue her though I know she lyes,
That she might thinke me some vntuterd youth,
Vnlearned in the worlds false subtilties.
Thus vainely thinking that she thinkes me young,
Although she knowes my dayes are past the best,
Simply I credit her false speaking tongue,
On both sides thus is simple truth supprest:
But wherefore sayes she not she is vniust?
10 And wherefore say not I that I am old?
O loues best habit is in seeming trust,
And age in loue, loues not to haue yeares told.
  Therefore I lye with her, and she with me,
  And in our faults by lyes we flatterd be.

When my Loue sweares that she is made of truth,
I do beleeue her (though I know she lies)
That she might thinke me some vntutor'd youth,
Vnskilful in the worlds false forgeries.
Thus vainly thinking that she thinkes me young,
Although I know my yeares be past the best:
I smiling, credite her false speaking toung,
Outfacing faults in loue, with loues ill rest.
But wherefore sayes my loue that she is young?
And wherefore say not I, that I am old: 10
O, Loues best habit's in a soothing toung,
And Age in loue, loues not to haue yeares told.
  Therefore I'le lye with Loue, and loue with me,
  Since that our faultes in loue thus smother'd be.

144

Two loues I haue of comfort and dispaire,
Which like two spirits do sugiest me still,
The better angell is a man right faire:
The worser spirit a woman collour'd il.
To win me soone to hell my femall euill,
Tempteth my better angel from my side,
And would corrupt my saint to be a diuel:
Wooing his purity with her fowle pride.
And whether that my angel be turn'd finde,
Suspect I may, yet not directly tell,
But being both from me both to each friend,
I gesse one angel in an others hel.
    Yet this shal I nere know but liue in doubt,
    Till my bad angel fire my good one out.

Two loues I haue, of Comfort and Despaire,
That like two Spirits, do suggest me still:
My better Angell, is a Man (right faire)
My worser spirite a Woman (colour'd ill.)
To win me soone to hell, my Female euill
Tempteth my better Angell from my side:
And would corrupt my Saint to be a Diuell,
Wooing his puritie with her faire pride.
And whether that my Angell be turnde feend,
Suspect I may (yet not directly tell:)
For being both to me; both, to each friend,
I ghesse one Angell in anothers hell:
    The truth I shall not know, but liue in dout,
    Till my bad Angell fire my good one out.

VARIOUS POEMS

A POET like Shakespeare may frequently have been asked to write verses for a variety of occasions, and it is entirely possible that he is the author of song lyrics and other short poems published without attribution or attributed only to 'W.S.' The poems in this section (arranged in an approximate chronological order) were all explicitly ascribed to him either in his lifetime or not long afterwards. Because they are short it is impossible to be sure, on stylistic grounds alone, of Shakespeare's authorship; but none of the poems is ever attributed to anyone else.

'Shall I die?' is transcribed, with Shakespeare's name appended, in a manuscript collection of poems, dating probably from the late 1630s, which is now in the Bodleian Library, Oxford; another, unascribed version is in the Beinecke Library, Yale University. The poem exhibits many parallels with plays and poems that Shakespeare wrote about 1593-5. Its stanza form has not been found elsewhere in the period, but most closely resembles Robin Goodfellow's lines spoken over the sleeping Lysander (*A Midsommer nights dreame*, 1430-40). Extended over nine stanzas it becomes a virtuoso exercise: every third word rhymes. The strain shows in a number of ellipses, but there is no strong reason to doubt the ascription: the Oxford manuscript is generally reliable, and if the poem is of no great consequence, that might explain why it did not reach print.

Perhaps the most trivial verse ever ascribed to a great poet is the 'posy' said to have accompanied a pair of gloves given by a Stratford schoolmaster, Alexander Aspinall, to his second wife, whom he married in 1594. The ascription is found in a manuscript compiled by Sir Francis Fane of Bulbeck (1611-80).

In 1599 William Jaggard published a collection of poems, which he ascribed to Shakespeare, under the title *The Passionate Pilgrime*. It includes versions of two of Shakespeare's Sonnets (which we print as Alternative Versions), three extracts from *Loues labors lost*, which had already appeared in print, several poems known to be by other poets, and eleven poems of unknown authorship. A reprint of 1612 added nine poems by Thomas Heywood, who promptly protested against the 'manifest iniury' done to him by printing his poems 'in a lesse volume, vnder the name of another, which may put the world in opinion I might steale them from him . . . but as I must acknowledge my lines not worthy his patronage, vnder whom he hath publisht them, so the Author I know much offended with M. *Iaggard* (that altogether vnknowne to him) presumed to make so bold with his name.' Probably as a result, the original title-page of the 1612 edition was replaced with one that did not mention Shakespeare's name. We print below the poems of unknown authorship since the attribution to Shakespeare has not been disproved.

The finest poem in this section, 'The Phœnix and Turtle', was ascribed to Shakespeare in 1601 when it appeared, without title, as one of the 'Poeticall Essaies' appended to Robert Chester's *Love's Martyr: Or Rosalins Complaint*, which is described as 'Allegorically shadowing the truth of Loue, in the constant Fate of the Phoenix and Turtle'. Chester's poem appears to have been composed as a compliment to Sir John and Lady Salusbury, his patron. We know of no link between Shakespeare and the Salusbury family; possibly his poem was not written specifically for the volume in which it appeared. Since the early nineteenth century it has been known as 'The Phoenix and the Turtle' or (following the title-page) 'The Phoenix and Turtle'. An incantatory elegy, it may well have irrecoverable allegorical significance.

It is not clear whether the two stanzas engraved at opposite ends of the Stanley tomb in the parish church of Tong, in Shropshire, constitute one epitaph or two, or which member (or members) of the family they commemorate. They are ascribed to Shakespeare in two manuscript miscellanies of the 1630s and by the antiquary Sir William Dugdale in a manuscript appended to his Visitation of Shropshire in 1664. Shakespeare had professional connections with the Stanleys early in his career: *Titus Andronicus* and *1 Henry VI* were performed by a theatrical company patronized by the family.

The satirical completion of an epitaph on Ben Jonson (written during his lifetime) is ascribed to Shakespeare in two different seventeenth-century manuscripts.

Shakespeare probably knew Elias James (*c*.1578–1620), who managed a brewery in the Blackfriars district of London. His epitaph is ascribed to Shakespeare in the same Oxford manuscript as 'Shall I die?'

The Combe family of Stratford-upon-Avon were friends of Shakespeare. He bequeathed his sword to one of them, and John Combe, who died in 1614, left Shakespeare £5. Several mock epitaphs similar to the first epitaph on John Combe have survived, one (on an unnamed usurer) printed as early as 1608; later versions mention three other men as the usurer. Shakespeare may have adapted some existing lines; or some existing lines may have been adapted anonymously in Stratford, and later attributed to Stratford's most famous poet. The ascription to him dates from 1634, and is supported by four other seventeenth-century manuscripts. The second Combe epitaph is found in only one manuscript; it seems entirely original, and alludes to a bequest to the poor made in Combe's will.

The lines on King James first appear, unattributed, beneath an engraving of the King printed as the frontispiece to the 1616 edition of his works. They are attributed to Shakespeare—the leading writer of the theatre company of which King James was patron—in at least two seventeenth-century manuscripts; the same attribution was recorded in a printed broadside now apparently lost.

Shakespeare's own epitaph is written in the first person; the tradition that he composed it himself is recorded in several manuscripts from the middle to the late seventeenth century.

Various Poems

A Song

1

Shall I dye, shall I flye
lovers baits, and deceipts
   sorrow breeding
Shall I tend shall I send
shall I shewe, and not rue
   my proceeding
In all duty her beawty
Binds me her servant for ever
  If she scorne I mourne
10 I retire, to despaire ioÿing never.

2

Yet I must, vent my lust
and explaine, inward paine
   by my loue conceaving
If she smiles, she exiles
all my moane, if she frowne
   all my hopes deceaving
Suspitious doubt, oh keepe out
For thou art my tormentor
  Fie away, pack away
20 I will loue for hope bids me venter

3

T'were abuse to accuse
my faire loue, ere I prove
   her affection
therefore try her reply
gives thee Ioy or annoy
   or affliction
Yet how ere, I will beare
Her pleasure with patience for beawty
  sure wil not seeme to blot
30 her deserts, wronging him, doth her duty.

4

In a dreame it did seeme
but alas, dreames doe passe
   as doe shaddowes
I did walke, I did talke
with my loue, with my dove
   through faire meadows
Still we past till at last
we sate to repose vs for pleasure
  being set lips mett
40 armes twin'd & did bind my hearts treasure

5

Gentle wind sport did find
wantonly to make fly
   her gold tresses

As they shooke, I did looke
but her faire, did impaire
   all my senses
As amaz'd I gaz'd
On more then a mortall complection
  You that loue, can prove
Such force in beawties inflection   50

6

Next her haire forehead faire
Smooth and high neat doth lye
   without wrinckle
Her faire browes vnder those
starlike eyes, win loues prize
   when they twinckle
In her cheekes, whoe seekes
Shall find there displaid beawties banner
  Oh admiring, desiring
breedes as I looke still vpon her   60

7

Thin lips red, fancies fed
with all sweets when he meetes
   and is granted
There to trade, and is made
happy sure, to endure
   still vndaunted
Pretty chinne, doth winne
Of all their culd comendations
  Fairest neck, noe speck
All her parts meritt high admiracions   70

8

Pretty bare, past compare
parts those plotts (which besots)
   still asunder
It is meet, nought but sweet
should come nere, that soe rare
   tis a wonder
Noe mishap, noe scape
Inferior to natures perfection
  noe blot, noe spot
Shees beawties queene in election   80

9

Whilst I dream't, I exempt
from all care seem'd to share
   pleasures plenty
but awake care take
for I find to my mind
   pleasures scanty
Therefore I will trie
To compasse my hearts cheife contenting
  to delay, some saye
In such a case causeth repenting   90

Vpon a peaire of gloues that master sent to his
mistris:

The gift is small:
The will is all:
A shey ander Asbenall:

Poems from *The Passionate Pilgrime*

4

Sweet Cytherea, sitting by a Brooke,
With young Adonis, louely, fresh, and greene,
Did court the Lad with many a louely looke,
Such lookes as none could looke but beauties queen.
She told him stories, to delight his eare;
She shew'd him fauors, to allure his eie,
To win his heart, she toucht him here and there,
Touches so soft, still conquer chastitie.
But whether vnripe yeares did want conceit,
Or he refusde to take her figur'd proffer,
The tender nibler would not touch the bait,
But smile, and ieast, at euery gentle offer:
　Then fel she on her back, faire queen, & toward,
　He rose and ran away, ah foole too froward.

6

Scarse had the Sunne dride vp the deawy morne,
And scarse the heard gone to the hedge for shade:
When Cytherea (all in Loue forlorne)
A longing tariance for Adonis made
Vnder an Osyer growing by a brooke,
A brooke, where Adon vsde to coole his spleene:
Hot was the day, she hotter that did looke
For his approch, that often there had beene.
Anon he comes, and throwes his Mantle by,
And stood starke naked on the brookes greene brim:
The Sunne look't on the world with glorious eie,
Yet not so wistly, as this Queene on him:
　He spying her, bounst in (whereas he stood)
　Oh Ioue (quoth she) why was not I a flood?

7

Faire is my loue, but not so faire as fickle.
Milde as a Doue, but neither true nor trustie,
Brighter then glasse, and yet as glasse is brittle,
Softer then waxe, and yet as Iron rusty:
　A lilly pale, with damaske die to grace her,
　None fairer, nor none falser to deface her.

Her lips to mine how often hath she ioyned,
Betweene each kisse her othes of true loue swearing:
How many tales to please me hath she coyned,
Dreading my loue, the losse whereof still fearing.
　Yet in the mids of all her pure protestings,
　Her faith, her othes, her teares, and all were ieastings.

She burnt with loue, as straw with fire flameth,
She burnt out loue, as soone as straw out burneth:
She fram'd the loue, and yet she foyld the framing,
She bad loue last, and yet she fell a turning.
　Was this a louer, or a Letcher whether?
　Bad in the best, though excellent in neither.

9

Faire was the morne, when the faire Queene of loue,
⌈　　　　　　　　　　　　　　　　　　　　　⌉
Paler for sorrow then her milke white Doue,
For Adons sake, a youngster proud and wilde,
Her stand she takes vpon a steepe vp hill.
Anon Adonis comes with horne and hounds,
She silly Queene, with more then loues good will,
Forbad the boy he should not passe those grounds,
Once (quoth she) did I see a faire sweet youth
Here in these brakes, deepe wounded with a Boare,
Deepe in the thigh a spectacle of ruth,
See in my thigh (quoth she) here was the sore,
　She shewed hers, he saw more wounds then one,
　And blushing fled, and left her all alone.

10

Sweet Rose, faire flower, vntimely pluckt, soon vaded,
Pluckt in the bud, and vaded in the spring:
Bright orient pearle, alacke too timely shaded,
Faire creature kilde too soon by Deaths sharpe sting:
　Like a greene plumbe that hangs vpon a tree:
　And fals (through winde) before the fall should be.

I weepe for thee, and yet no cause I haue,
For why: thou lefts me nothing in thy will:
And yet thou lefts me more then I did craue,
For why: I craued nothing of thee still:
　O yes (deare friend) I pardon craue of thee,
　Thy discontent thou didst bequeath to me.

12

Crabbed age and youth cannot liue together,
Youth is full of pleasance, Age is full of care,
Youth like summer morne, Age like winter weather,
Youth like summer braue, Age like winter bare.
Youth is full of sport, Ages breath is short,
Youth is nimble, Age is lame
Youth is hot and bold, Age is weake and cold,
Youth is wild, and Age is tame.
　Age I doe abhor thee, Youth I doe adore thee,
　　O my loue my loue is young:
　Age I doe defie thee. Oh sweet Shepheard hie thee:
　　For me thinks thou staies too long.

13

Beauty is but a vaine and doubtfull good,
A shining glosse, that vadeth sodainly,
A flower that dies, when first it gins to bud,
A brittle glasse, that's broken presently.
　A doubtfull good, a glosse, a glasse, a flower,
　Lost, vaded, broken, dead within an houre.

And as goods lost, are seld or neuer found,
As vaded glosse no rubbing will refresh:
As flowers dead, lie withered on the ground,
10 As broken glasse no symant can redresse.
   So beauty blemisht once, for euer lost,
   In spite of phisicke, painting, paine and cost.

14

Good night, good rest, ah neither be my share,
She bad good night, that kept my rest away,
And daft me to a cabben hangde with care:
To descant on the doubts of my decay.
   Farewell (quoth she) and come againe to morrow.
   Fare well I could not, for I supt with sorrow.

Yet at my parting sweetly did she smile,
In scorne or friendship, nill I conster whether:
'Tmay be she ioyd to ieast at my exile,
10 'Tmay be againe, to make me wander thither.
   Wander (a word) for shadowes like my selfe,
   As take the paine but cannot plucke the pelfe.

Lord how mine eies throw gazes to the East,
My hart doth charge the watch, the morning rise
Doth scite each mouing scence from idle rest,
Not daring trust the office of mine eies.
   While Philomela sings, I sit and mark,
   And wish her layes were tuned like the larke.

For she doth welcome daylight with her ditte,
20 And daylight driues away darke dreaming night:
The night so packt, I post vnto my pretty,
Hart hath his hope, and eies their wished sight,
   Sorrow changd to solace, and solace mixt with sorrow,
   For why, she sight, and bad me come to morrow.

Were I with her, the night would post too soone,
But now are minutes added to the houres:
To spite me now, ech minute seemes a moone,
Yet not for me, shine sun to succour flowers.
   Pack night, peep day, good day of night now borrow,
30   Short night to night, and length thy selfe to morrow.

SONNETS
To sundry notes of Musicke

15

It was a Lordings daughter, the fairest one of three
That liked of her maister, as well as well might be,
Till looking on an Englishman, the fairest that eie could
    see,
   Her fancie fell a turning.

Long was the combat doubtfull, that loue with loue did
    fight
To leaue the maister louelesse, or kill the gallant knight,
To put in practise either, alas it was a spite
   Vnto the silly damsell.

But one must be refused, more mickle was the paine,
That nothing could be vsed, to turne them both to gaine,   10
For of the two the trusty knight was wounded with
    disdaine,
   Alas she could not helpe it.

Thus art with armes contending, was victor of the day,
Which by a gift of learning, did beare the maid away,
Then lullaby the learned man hath got the Lady gay,
   For now my song is ended.

17

My flocks feede not, my Ewes breed not,
   My Rams speed not, all is amis:
Loue is dieng, Faithes defieng,
   Harts denieng, causer of this.
All my mery Iigges are quite forgot,
All my Ladyes loue is lost (god wot),
Where her faith was firmely fixt in loue:
There a nay is plac't without remoue,
   One silly crosse, wrought all my losse,
   Oh frowning fortune cursed fickle dame,   10
   For now I see, inconstancy,
   More in women then in men remaine.

In blacke morne I, all feares scorne I,
   Loue hath forlorne me, liuing in thrall:
Hart is bleeding, all helpe needing,
   O cruell speeding, fraughted with gall.
My shepherds pipe can sound no deale,
My wethers bell rings dolefull knell,
My curtaile dogge that wont to haue plaide,
Plaies not at all but seemes afraid,   20
   With sighs so deepe, procures to weepe
   In houling wise, to see my dolefull plight,
   How sighes resound through hartles ground
   Like a thousand vanquisht men in blodie fight.

Cleare wels spring not, sweet birdes sing not,
   Greene plants bring not forth their dye,
Heard stands weeping, flocks all sleeping,
   Nimphes backe peeping fearfully:
All our pleasure knowne to vs poore swaines:
All our merrie meetings on the plaines,   30
All our euening sport from vs is fled,
All our loue is lost, for loue is dead,
   Farewell sweete lasse thy like nere was,
   For a sweet content the cause of all my mone,
   Poore Coridon must liue alone,
   Other helpe for him, I see that there is none.

18

When as thine eye hath chose the Dame,
And stalde the deare that thou shouldst strike,
Let reason rule things worthy blame,
As wel as fancy (partyall might).
   Take counsell of some wiser head,
   Neither too young, nor yet vnwed,

And when thou comst thy tale to tell,
Smooth not thy toung with filed talke,
Least she some subtil practise smell,
10 A Cripple soone can finde a halt,
    But plainly saye thou loust her well,
    And set her person forth to sale.

And to her wil frame al thy waies,
Spare not to spend, and chiefly there,
Where thy desart may merit praise
By ringing in thy Ladies eare,
    The strongest castle, tower and towne,
    The golden bullet beats it downe.

Serue alwaies with assured trust,
20 And in thy sute be humble true,
Vnlesse thy Lady proue vniust,
Prease neuer thou to chuse anew:
    When time shal serue, be thou not slacke,
    To profer though she put thee backe.

What though her frowning browes be bent,
Her cloudy lookes wil calme yer night,
And then too late she wil repent,
That thus dissembled her delight.
    And twice desire yer it be day,
30   That which with scorne she put away.

What though she striue to try her strength,
And ban and braule, and say the nay:
Her feeble force wil yeeld at length,
When craft hath taught her thus to say:
    Had women been so strong as men,
    In faith you had not had it then.

The wiles and guiles that women worke,
Dissembled with an outward shew:
The trickes and toyes that in them lurke,
40 The Cocke that treades them shall not know:
    Haue you not heard it sayd full oft,
    A Womans nay doth stand for nought.

Thinke Women still to striue with men,
To sinne and neuer for to saint,
There is no heauen (be holy then)
When time with age shall them attaint,
    Were kisses all the ioyes in bed,
    One Woman would an other wed.

But soft enough, too much I feare,
50 Least that my mistresse heare my song,
She will not stick to rounde me on th'are,
To teach my toung to be so long:
    Yet wil she blush, here be it sayd,
    To heare her secrets so bewraide.

The Phœnix and Turtle

Let the bird of lowdest lay,
On the sole *Arabian* tree,
Herauld sad and trumpet be:
To whose sound chaste wings obay.

But thou shriking harbinger,
Foule precurrer of the fiend,
Augour of the fevers end,
To this troupe come thou not neere.

From this Session interdict
Every foule of tyrant wing,   10
Save the Eagle feath'red King,
Keepe the obsequie so strict.

Let the Priest in Surples white,
That defunctive Musicke can,
Be the death-devining Swan,
Lest the *Requiem* lacke his right.

And thou treble dated Crow,
That thy sable gender mak'st,
With the breath thou giv'st and tak'st,
Mongst our mourners shalt thou go.   20

Here the Antheme doth commence,
Love and Constancie is dead,
Phœnix and the *Turtle* fled,
In a mutuall flame from hence.

So they lov'd as love in twaine,
Had the essence but in one,
Two distincts, Division none,
Number there in love was slaine.

Hearts remote, yet not asunder;
Distance and no space was seene,   30
Twixt this *Turtle* and his Queene;
But in them it were a wonder.

So betweene them Love did shine,
That the *Turtle* saw his right,
Flaming in the *Phœnix* sight;
Either was the others mine.

Propertie was thus appalled,
That the selfe was not the same:
Single Natures double name,
Neither two nor one was called.   40

Reason in it selfe confounded,
Saw Division grow together,
To themselves yet either neither,
Simple were so well compounded,

That it cried, how true a twaine,
Seemeth this concordant one,
Love hath Reason, Reason none,
If what parts, can so remaine.

Whereupon it made this *Threne*,
To the *Phœnix* and the *Dove*,
Co-supremes and starres of Love,
As *Chorus* to their Tragique Scene.

Threnos

Beautie, Truth, and Raritie,
Grace in all simplicitie,
Here enclosde, in cinders lie.

Death is now the *Phœnix* nest,
And the *Turtles* loyall brest,
To eternitie doth rest.

Leaving no posteritie,
Twas not their infirmitie,
It was married Chastitie.

Truth may seeme, but cannot be,
Beautie bragge, but tis not she,
Truth and Beautie buried be.

To this urne let those repaire,
That are either true or faire,
For these dead Birds, sigh a prayer.

Verses on the Stanley Tombe at Tong

Written upon the East end of the Tombe

ASK WHO LYES HEARE, BUT DO NOT WEEP,
HE IS NOT DEAD, HE DOOTH BVT SLEEP
THIS STONY REGISTER, IS FOR HIS BONES
HIS FAME IS MORE PERPETVALL THĒ THEISE STONES
AND HIS OWNE GOODNES, Wᵗ HIM SELF BEING GON
SHALL LYVE WHEN EARTHLIE MONAMENT IS NONE

Written upon the West end thereof

NOT MONVMENTALL STONE PRESERVES OVR FAME
NOR SKY ASPYRING PIRAMIDS OVR NAME
THE MEMORY OF HIM FOR WHOM THIS STANDS
SHALL OVTLYVE MARBL AND DEFACERS HANDS
WHEN ALL TO TYMES CONSVMPTION SHALL BE GEAVEN
STANDLY FOR WHOM THIS STANDS SHALL STAND IN HEAVEN

On Ben Johnson

Mʳ Ben. Johnson and Mʳ Wᵐ. Shake-speare Being Merrye
att a Tavern, mʳ Jonson haueing begune this for his
Epitaph

Here lies Ben Johnson
That was once one

he giues it to mʳ Shakspear to make vpp who psently
wrightes

Who while hee liu'de was a sloo thing
And now being dead is Nothinge

An Epitaph on Elias Iames

When God was pleas'd, (the world unwilling yet)
Helias Iames, to Nature paid his debt,
And here reposeth: As he liv'd, he died,
The saying strongly in him verified,
Such life, such death: then a knowne truth to tell,
He liv'd a godly life, and died as well.

An extemporary Epitaph on John Combe, a noted usurer

Tenn in the hundred here lyes engraued
A hundred to tenn his soule is not saued
If anny one aske who lyes in this Tombe
Oh ho quoth the Diuell tis my John a Combe.

Another Epitaph on John Combe

hee being dead, and making the poore his heiers W. Shak.
after wrightes this for his Epitaph

How ere he liued Judge not
John Combe shall neuer be forgott
While poor, hath Memmorye for hee did gather
To make the poore his Issue; hee their father
As record of his tilth and seede
Did Crowne him In his Latter deede.

Upon the King

At the foot of the effigy of King James I, before his *Works*
(1616)

Crounes haue their compasse, length of dayes their date,
Triumphes their tombes, felicitie her fate:
Of more then earth, can earth make none partaker,
But knowledge makes the KING most like his maker.

Epitaph on Himselfe

GOOD FREND FOR IESUS SAKE FORBEARE
TO DIGG THE DUST ENCLOASED HEARE.
BLESTE BE Yᵉ MAN Yᵗ SPARES THES STONES,
AND CURST BE HE Yᵗ MOVES MY BONES.

SIR THOMAS MOORE

PASSAGES ATTRIBUTED TO SHAKESPEARE

IN the British Library is a manuscript play described on its first leaf as 'The Booke'—that is, the theatre manuscript—'of Sir Thomas Moore'. It is a heavily revised text with contributions in six different hands as well as annotations by the Master of the Revels. The basic manuscript appears to have been a fair copy by the dramatist Anthony Munday of a play that he wrote in collaboration with Henry Chettle and, perhaps, another writer. Alterations and additions were made by Chettle, Thomas Dekker, possibly Thomas Heywood, and the author of the pages in Addition II ascribed to 'Hand D', whom many scholars believe to be William Shakespeare.

The theory that Shakespeare was a contributor, first mooted in 1871, has led to intensive study of the manuscript. Our view is that the original play, dating from the early 1590s, was submitted in the normal way to the Master of the Revels, Sir Edmund Tilney, for a licence. But Tilney, disturbed by the play's political implications, called for substantial revisions which, if they had been carried out, would have required that about half the play be scrapped.

What happened next is not clear. The alterations and additions to the basic play do not meet Tilney's objections. Perhaps they had been made before the play was submitted for a licence. More probably (in our view) the original play was laid aside after Tilney had objected to it, and taken up again soon after Queen Elizabeth's death, in 1603, when the political objections would no longer be felt.

Sir Thomas Moore, based mainly on Holinshed's *Chronicles* and on William Roper's manuscript *Life of More*, is an episodic treatment of its hero's rise and fall, ending with his death on the scaffold. The principal episode attributed to Shakespeare comes towards the end of the scenes early in the play portraying events leading up to the riots of Londoners against resident foreigners on the 'ill May Day' of 1517. The leaders are John Lincoln, Williamson and his wife Doll, George and Ralph Betts, and Sherwin. Outraged by the illegal activities of foreign groups in London, they have planned that 'on May Day next in the morning weele go foorth a Maying, but make it the wurst May Day for the straungers'—i.e. foreigners—'that euer they sawe'. The authorities, dismayed by the violence, have sent Moore as a peacemaker. Shakespeare—if indeed he wrote the scene—seems not to have known the rest of the play; he was probably revising an original scene, now lost, with no other sources. The ascription of this scene to Shakespeare is based partly on comparison between the few surviving specimens of Shakespeare's handwriting (almost entirely in signatures) with that of Hand D; partly on spelling links with printed texts apparently deriving directly from Shakespeare's own papers; and partly on considerations of style and imagery.

Also attributed to Shakespeare is a soliloquy by Moore apparently intended to show his state of mind after having been appointed Lord Chancellor. It is written in the hand of a professional scribe (Addition III).

A diplomatic transcript of II.D—indicating deletions, scribal interventions, etc.—appears in the *Textual Companion*. We present here an edited text of the material as Shakespeare left it.

Sir Thomas Moore

Add.II.D *Lincoln. Doll. betts* ⌐Sherwin⌐ *and prentisses*
armed; ⌐Moor, the other sherif, Palmer,
Cholmeley, And A sergaunt at armes stand aloof⌐

LINCOLNE (*to the prentisses*) Peace heare me, he that will
not see a red hearing at a harry grote, butter at a
levenpence a pounde, meale at nyne shillinges a Bushell
and Beeff at fower nobles a stone, lyst to me.

OTHER Yt will Come to that passe yf straingers be sufferd
mark him.

LINCOLNE Our Countrie is a great eating Country, argo
they eate more in our Countrey then they do in their
owne.

10 OTHER By a half penny loff a day troy waight.

LINCOLNE They bring in straing rootes, which is meerly
to the vndoing of poor prentizes, for whates a sorry
psnyp to a good hart.

OTHER Trash trash,: they breed sore eyes and tis enough
to infect the Cytty w^t the palsey.

LINCOLNE Nay yt has infected yt w^t the palsey, for theise
basterdes of dung as you knowe they growe in Dvng
haue infected vs, and yt is our infeccion will make the
Cytty shake which ptly Coms through the eating of
20 psnyps.

OTHER Trewe and pumpions togeather.

SERIANT ⌐comming forward⌐
What say yo^u to the mercy of the king
Do yo^u refuse yt.

LINCOLNE Yo^u woold haue vs vppon thipp woold yo^u no
marry do we not, we accept of the kinges mercy but
wee will showe no mercy vppõ the straingers.

SERIANT   Yo^u ar the simplest thinges
That eu^{er} stood in such a question.

LINCOLNE How say yo^u now prentisses symple (*to the*
30 *prentisses*) downe wth him.

ALL Prentisses symple prentisses symple.
   Enter the L maier Surrey Shrewsbury

⌐SHERIFF⌐ (*to the prentisses*)
Hold in the kinges name hold.

SURREY (*to the prentisses*)   Frendes masters Countrymen.

MAYER (*to the prentisses*)
Peace how peace I Charg yo^u keep the peace.

SHREWSBURY (*to the prentisses*) My masters Countrymen.

⌐SHERWIN⌐ The noble Earle of Shrewsbury lettes hear him.

BETTES Weele heare the Earle of Surrey.

LINCOLNE The earle of Shrewsbury.

BETTES Weele heare both.

ALL Both both both both.

40 LINCOLNE Peace I say peace ar yo^u men of Wisdome or
what ar yo^u.

SURREY
What yo^u will haue them but not men of Wisdome.

⌐SOME⌐ Weele not heare my L of Surrey,

⌐OTHERS⌐ No no no no no Shrewsbury shr.

MOOR (*to the nobles and officers*)
Whiles they ar ore the banck of their obedyenc
Thus will they bere downe all thinges.

LINCOLNE (*to the prentisses*) Shreiff moor speakes shall we
heare shreef moor speake.

DOLL Lettes heare him a keepes a plentyfull shrevaltry,
and a made my Brother Arther watchins Seriant Safes   50
yeoman letes heare shreeve moore.

ALL Shreiue moor moor more Shreue moore.

MOOR
Even by the rule yo^u haue among yor sealues
Comand still audience.

SOME Surrey Sury.

OTHERS Moor moor.

LINCOLNE *and* BETTES Peace peace scilens peace.

MOOR
Yo^u that haue voyce and Credyt w^t the nvmber
Comaund them to a stilnes.

LINCOLNE A plaigue on them they will not hold their   60
peace the deule Cannot rule them.

MOOR
Then what a rough and ryotous charge haue yo^u
To Leade those that the deule Cannot rule
(*To the prentisses*) Good masters heare me speake.

DOLL I byth mas will we moor thart a good howskeeper
and I thanck thy good worship for my Brother Arthur
watchins.

ALL Peace peace.

MOOR
Look what yo^u do offend yo^u Cry vppõ
That is the peace; not on of yo^u heare present   70
Had there such fellowes lyvd when yo^u wer babes
That coold haue topt the peace, as nowe yo^u woold
The peace wherin yo^u haue till nowe growne vp
Had bin tane from yo^u, and the bloody tymes
Coold not haue brought yo^u to the state of men
Alas poor thinges what is yt yo^u haue gott
Although we graunt yo^u geat the thing yo^u seeke.

BETTES Marry the removing of the straingers wch cannot
choose but much advauntage the poor handycraftes of
the Cytty.   80

MOOR
Graunt them remoued and graunt that this yor noyce
Hath Chidd downe all the matie of Ingland
Ymagin that yo^u see the wretched straingers
Their babyes at their backes, w^t their poor lugage
Plodding tooth portes and costes for transportacion
And that yo^u sytt as kinges in your desyres
Aucthoryty quyte sylenct by yor braule
And yo^u in ruff of yor opynions clothd
What had yo^u gott; Ile tell yo^u, yo^u had taught
How insolenc and strong hand shoold prevayle   90

How ordere shoold be quelld, and by this patterne
Not on of yo^u shoold lyve an aged man
For other ruffians as their fancies wrought
Wth sealf same hand sealf reasons and sealf right
Woold shark on yo^u and men lyke ravenous fishes
Woold feed on on another.

DOLL Before god thates as trewe as the gospell.

BETTES Nay this a sound fellowe I tell yo^u lets mark him.

MOOR

Let me sett vp before yor thoughts good freindes
100 On supposytion, which if yo^u will marke
Yo^u shall pceaue howe horrible a shape
Your ynnovation beres, first tis a sinn
Which oft thappostle did forwarne vs of
Vrging obedienc to aucthoryty
And twere no error yf I told yo^u all
Yo^u wer in armes gainst god.

ALL Marry god forbid that.

MOOR Nay certainly yo^u ar
For to the king god hath his offyc lent
110 Of dread of Iustyce, power and Comaund
Hath bid him rule, and willd yo^u to obay
And to add ampler maĩie to this
He hath not only lent the king his figure
His throne & sword, but gyven him his owne name
Calls him a god on earth, what do yo^u then
Rysing gainst him that god himsealf enstalls
But ryse gainst god, what do yo^u to yor sowles
In doing this o desperat as you are
Wash your foule mynds w^t teares and those same
         handes
120 That yo^u lyke rebells lyft against the peace
Lift vp for peace, and your vnreuerent knees
Make them your feet to kneele to be forgyven
Is safer warrs, then euer yo^u can make
Whose discipline is ryot,
In in to yor obedienc· why euen yor hurly
Cannot pceed but by obedienc
What rebell captaine
As mutnyes ar incident, by his name
Can still the rout who will obay a traytor
130 Or howe can well that pclamation sounde
When ther is no adicion but a rebell
To quallyfy a rebell, youle put downe straingers
Kill them cutt their throts possesse their howses
And leade the matie of lawe in liom
To slipp him lyke a hound; alas alas
Say nowe the king
As he is clement,. yf thoffendor moorne
Shoold so much com to short of your great trespas
As but to banysh yo^u, whether woold yo^u go·

What Country by the nature of yor error   140
Shoold gyve you harber go yo^u to ffraunc or flanders
To any Iarman pvince, spane or portigall
Nay any where that not adheres to Ingland
Why yo^u must needes be straingers·, woold yo^u be
         pleasd
To find a nation of such barbarous temper
That breaking out in hiddious violence
Woold not afoord yo^u, an abode on earth
Whett their detested knyves against yor throtes
Spurne yo^u lyke dogges, and lyke as yf that god
Owed not nor made not yo^u, nor that the elamentes   150
Wer not all appropriat to yor Comfortes·
But Charterd vnto them, what woold yo^u thinck
To be thus vsd, this is the straingers case
And this your montanish inhumanyty.

⌈ONE⌉ (to the others) Fayth a saies trewe letts do as we
may be doon by.

⌈ANOTHER⌉ (to Moor) Weele be ruld by yo^u master moor
yf youle stand our freind to pcure our pdon.

MOOR

Submyt yo^u to theise noble gentlemen
Entreate their mediation to the kinge   160
Gyve vp yor sealf to forme obay the maiestrat
And thers no doubt, but mercy may be found
Yf yo^u so seek yt.

———

Enter moore   **Add.III**

MOOR

It is in heaven that I am thus and thus
And that wch we prophanlie terme o^r fortuns
Is the provision of the power aboue
Fitted and shapte Iust to that strength of nature
W^{ch} we are borne withal good god good god
That I from such an humble bench of birth
Should stepp as twere vp to my Countries head
And give the law out ther I in my fathers lif
To take prerogative and tyth of knees
From elder kinsmen and him bynd by my place   10
To give the smooth and dexter way to me
That owe it him by nature, sure thes things
Not phisickt by respecte might turne o^r bloud
To much Coruption· but moore the more thou hast
Ether of honor office wealth and calling
W^{ch} might accite thee to embrace and hugg them
The more doe thou in serpents natures thinke them
Feare ther gay skinns wth thought of ther sharpe stings
And lett this be thy maxime, to be greate
Is when the thred of hazard is once Spuñ   20
A bottom great woond vpp greatly vndonn.

MEASURE, FOR MEASURE

Measure, for Measure, first printed in the 1623 Folio, was performed at court on 26 December 1604. Plague had caused London's theatres to be closed from May 1603 to April 1604; the play was probably written and first acted during 1604. Dislocations and other features of the text as printed suggest that it may have undergone adaptation after Shakespeare's death. Someone—perhaps Thomas Middleton, to judge by the style—seems to have supplied a new, seedy opening to Act 1, Scene 2; and an adapter seems also to have altered 1625-1711 by transposing the Duke's two soliloquies, by introducing a stanza from a popular song, and by supplying dialogue to follow it. We print the text in what we believe to be its adapted form; a conjectured reconstruction' of Shakespeare's original version of the adapted sections is given in the Additional Passages.

The story of a woman who, in seeking to save the life of a male relative, arouses the lust of a man in authority was an ancient one that reached literary form in the mid sixteenth century. Shakespeare may have known the prose version in Giambattista Cinzio Giraldi's *Gli Ecatommiti* (1565, translated into French in 1583) and the same author's play *Epitia* (1573, published in 1583), but his main source was George Whetstone's unsuccessful, unperformed two-part tragicomedy *Promos and Cassandra*, published in 1578.

Shakespeare's title comes from Saint Matthew's account of Christ's Sermon on the Mount: 'with what measure yee mete, it shalbe measured to you againe'. The title is not expressive of the play's morality, but it alerts the spectator to Shakespeare's exploration of moral issues. His heroine, Isabella, is not merely, as in Whetstone, a virtuous young maiden: she is about to enter a nunnery. Her brother, Claudio, has not, as in Whetstone, been accused (however unjustly) of rape: his union with the girl (Iuliet) he has made pregnant has been ratified by a betrothal ceremony, and lacks only the church's formal blessing. So Angelo, deputizing for the absent Duke of Vienna, seems peculiarly harsh in attempting to enforce the city's laws against fornication by insisting on Claudio's execution; and Angelo's hypocrisy in demanding Isabella's chastity in return for her brother's life seems correspondingly greater. By adding the character of Mariana, to whom Angelo himself had once been betrothed, and by employing the traditional motif of the 'bed-trick', by which Mariana substitutes for Isabella in Angelo's bed, Shakespeare permits Isabella both to retain her virtue and to forgive Angelo without marrying him.

Although *Measure, for Measure*, like *The Merchant of Venice*, is much concerned with justice and mercy, its more explicit concern with sex and death along with the intense emotional reality, at least in the earlier part of the play, of its portrayal of Angelo, Isabella, and Claudio, creates a deeper seriousness of tone which takes it out of the world of romantic comedy into that of tragicomedy or, as the twentieth-century label has it, 'problem play'. Its low-life characters inhabit a diseased world of brothels and prisons, but there is a life-enhancing quality in their frank acknowledgement of sexuality; and the Duke's manipulation of events casts a tinge of romance over the play's later scenes.

Measure, for Measure's subtle and passionate exploration of issues of sexual morality, of the uses and abuses of power, has given it a special appeal in the later part of the twentieth century. Each of the 'good' characters fails in some respect; none of the 'bad' ones lacks some redeeming quality; all are, in the last analysis, 'desperately mortal' (1868-9).

The text was set from a transcript apparently prepared by the scrivener Ralph Crane.

THE NAMES OF THE ACTORS

'Vincentio', the DUKE of Vienna

ANGELO, appointed his 'Deputie'

ESCALUS, 'an ancient Lord', appointed Angelo's secondary

CLAUDIO, 'a yong Gentlman'

IULIET, 'beloued of Claudio'

ISABELLA, a Nouice of a Sisterhood and 'sister to Claudio'

LUCIO, 'a fantastique'

'2. Other like' GENTLEMEN

FROTH, 'a foolish Gentleman'

'Mistris Ouer-don', a BAWD

Pompey, a CLOWNE, in the seruice of Mistris Ouer-don

A PROUOST

ELBOW, 'a simple Constable'

A IUSTICE

ABHORSON, 'an Executioner'

BARNARDINE, 'a dissolute' condemned 'prisoner'

MARIANA, 'betrothed to Angelo'

A BOY, attendant on Mariana

FRIER PETER

'Francisca', a NUN

VARRIUS, a Lord, friend to the Duke

Lords, Officers, Citizens, and seruants

Measure, for Measure

1.1
(Sc. 1)

Enter Duke, Escalus, Lords

DUKE *Escalus*.

ESCALUS My Lord.

DUKE

Of Gouernment, the properties to vnfold,
Would seeme in me t'affect speech & discourse,
Since I am put to know, that your owne Science
Exceedes (in that) the lists of all aduice
My strength can giue you: Then no more remaines
But this, to your sufficiency, as your worth is able,
And let them worke: The nature of our People,
10   Our *Cities Institutions*, and the Termes
For Common Iustice, y'are as pregnant in
As Art, and practise, hath inriched any
That we remember:

He giues Escalus papers

There is our Commission,
From which, we would not haue you warpe; *(to a
Lord)* call hither,
I say, bid come before vs *Angelo*:   *Exit Lord*
(To Escalus) What figure of vs thinke you, he will beare.
For you must know, we haue with speciall soule
Elected him our absence to supply;
Lent him our terror, drest him with our loue,
20   And giuen his Deputation all the Organs
Of our owne powre: What thinke you of it?

ESCALUS

If any in *Vienna* be of worth
To vndergoe such ample grace, and honour,
It is Lord *Angelo*.

Enter Angelo

DUKE   Looke where he comes.

ANGELO

Always obedient to your Graces will,
I come to know your pleasure.

DUKE   *Angelo*:

There is a kinde of Character in thy life,
That to th'obseruer, doth thy history
Fully vnfold: Thy selfe, and thy belongings
30   Are not thine owne so proper, as to waste
Thy selfe vpon thy vertues; they on thee:
Heauen doth with vs, as we, with Torches doe,
Not light them for themselues: For if our vertues
Did not goe forth of vs, 'twere all alike
As if we had them not: Spirits are not finely touch'd,
But to fine issues: nor nature neuer lends
The smallest scruple of her excellence,
But like a thrifty goddesse, she determines
Her selfe the glory of a creditour,
40   Both thanks, and vse; but I do bend my speech
To one that can my part in him aduertise;
Hold therefore *Angelo*:
In our remoue, be thou at full, our selfe:
Mortallitie and Mercie in *Vienna*

Liue in thy tongue, and heart: Old *Escalus*
Though first in question, is thy secondary.
Take thy Commission.

ANGELO   Now good my Lord
Let there be some more test, made of my mettle,
Before so noble, and so great a figure
Be stamp't vpon it.

DUKE   No more euasion: 50
We haue with leauen'd, and prepared choice
Proceeded to you; therefore take your honors:
⌐Angelo takes his Commission⌐
Our haste from hence is of so quicke condition,
That it prefers it selfe, and leaues vnquestion'd
Matters of needfull value: We shall write to you
As time, and our concernings shall importune,
How it goes with vs, and doe looke to know
What doth befall you here. So fare you well:
To th' hopefull execution doe I leaue you,
Of your Commissions.

ANGELO   Yet giue leaue (my Lord,)   60
That we may bring you something on the way.

DUKE My haste may not admit it,
Nor neede you (on mine honor) haue to doe
With any scruple: your scope is as mine owne,
So to inforce, or qualifie the Lawes
As to your soule seemes good: Giue me your hand,
Ile priuily away: I loue the people,
But doe not like to stage me to their eyes:
Though it doe well, I doe not rellish well
Their lowd applause, and Aues vehement: 70
Nor doe I thinke the man of safe discretion
That do's affect it. Once more fare you well.

ANGELO
The heauens giue safety to your purposes.

ESCALUS
Lead forth, and bring you backe in happinesse.

DUKE I thanke you, fare you well.   *Exit*

ESCALUS
I shall desire you, Sir, to giue me leaue
To haue free speech with you; and it concernes me
To looke into the bottome of my place:
A powre I haue, but of what strength and nature,
I am not yet instructed.   80

ANGELO
'Tis so with me: Let vs with-draw together,
And we may soone our satisfaction haue
Touching that point.

ESCALUS   Ile wait vpon your honor.

Exeunt

Enter Lucio, and two other Gentlemen   **1.2**

LUCIO If the *Duke*, with the other Dukes, come not to   **(Sc. 2)**
composition with the King of *Hungary*, why then all
the Dukes fall vpon the King.

1. GENTLEMAN Heauen grant vs its peace, but not the King of *Hungaries*.

2. GENTLEMAN Amen.

90 LUCIO Thou conclud'st like the Sanctimonious Pirat, that went to sea with the ten Commandements, but scrap'd one out of the Table.

2. GENTLEMAN Thou shalt not Steale?

LUCIO I, that he raz'd.

1. GENTLEMAN Why? 'twas a commandement, to command the Captaine and all the rest from their functions: they put forth to steale: There's not a Souldier of vs all, that in the thanks-giuing before meate, do rallish the petition well, that praies for peace.

100 2. GENTLEMAN I neuer heard any Souldier dislike it.

LUCIO I beleeue thee: for I thinke thou neuer was't where Grace was said.

2. GENTLEMAN No? a dozen times at least.

1. GENTLEMAN What? In meeter?

LUCIO In any proportion, or in any language.

1. GENTLEMAN I thinke, or in any Religion.

LUCIO I, why not? Grace, is Grace, despight of all controuersie: as for example; Thou thy selfe art a wicked villaine, despight of all Grace.

110 1. GENTLEMAN Well: there went but a paire of sheeres betweene vs.

LUCIO I grant: as there may betweene the Lists, and the Veluet. Thou art the List.

1. GENTLEMAN And thou the Veluet; thou art good veluet; thou'rt a three pild-peece I warrant thee: I had as liefe be a Lyst of an English Kersey, as be pil'd, as thou art pil'd, for a French Veluet. Do I speake feelingly now?

LUCIO I thinke thou do'st: and indeed with most painfull feeling of thy speech: I will, out of thine owne con-

120 fession, learne to begin thy health; but, whilst I liue forget to drinke after thee.

1. GENTLEMAN I think I haue done my selfe wrong, haue I not?

2. GENTLEMAN Yes, that thou hast; whether thou art tainted, or free.

Enter Bawde

LUCIO Behold, behold, where Madam *Mitigation* comes. I haue purchas'd as many diseases vnder her Roofe, as come to

130 2. GENTLEMAN To what, I pray?

LUCIO Iudge.

2. GENTLEMAN To three thousand Dollours a yeare.

1. GENTLEMAN I, and more.

LUCIO A French crowne more.

1. GENTLEMAN Thou art alwayes figuring diseases in me; but thou art full of error, I am sound.

LUCIO Nay, not (as one would say) healthy: but so sound, as things that are hollow; thy bones are hollow; Impiety has made a feast of thee.

1. GENTLEMAN (*to Bawd*) How now, which of your hips

140 has the most profound Ciatica?

BAWD Well, well: there's one yonder arrested, and carried to prison, was worth fiue thousand of you all.

2. GENTLEMAN Who's that I pray'thee?

BAWD Marry Sir, that's *Claudio*, Signior *Claudio*.

1. GENTLEMAN *Claudio* to prison? 'tis not so.

BAWD Nay, but I know 'tis so: I saw him arrested: saw him carried away: and which is more, within these three daies his head to be chop'd off.

LUCIO But, after all this fooling, I would not haue it so: Art thou sure of this? 150

BAWD I am too sure of it: and it is for getting Madam *Iulietta* with childe.

LUCIO Beleeue me this may be: he promis'd to meete me two howres since, and he was euer precise in promise keeping.

2. GENTLEMAN Besides you know, it drawes somthing neere to the speech we had to such a purpose.

1. GENTLEMAN But most of all agreeing with the proclamatiõ.

LUCIO Away: let's goe learne the truth of it. 160

Exit Lucio and Gentlemen

BAWD Thus, what with the war; what with the sweat, what with the gallowes, and what with pouerty, I am Custom-shrunke.

Enter Clowne

How now? what's the newes with you.

CLOWNE You haue not heard of the proclamation, haue you?

BAWD What proclamation, man?

CLOWNE All howses in the Suburbs of *Vienna* must bee pluck'd downe.

BAWD And what shall become of those in the Citie? 170

CLOWNE They shall stand for seed: they had gon down to, but that a wise Burger put in for them.

BAWD But shall all our houses of resort in the Suburbs be puld downe?

CLOWNE To the ground, Mistris.

BAWD Why heere's a change indeed in the Commonwealth: what shall become of me?

CLOWNE Come: feare not you: good Counsellors lacke no Clients: though you change your place, you neede not change your Trade: Ile bee your Tapster still; courage, 180 there will bee pitty taken on you; you that haue worne your eyes almost out in the seruice, you will bee considered.

⌈*A noise within*⌉

BAWD What's to doe heere, *Thomas* Tapster? let's withdraw?

Enter Prouost, Claudio, Iuliet, Officers, Lucio, & 2. Gentlemen

CLOWNE Here comes Signior *Claudio*, led by the Prouost to prison: and there's Madam *Iuliet*.

Exeunt Bawd and Clowne

CLAUDIO (*to Prouost*)

Fellow, why do'st thou show me thus to th'world?

Beare me to prison, where I am committed.

PROUOST

I do it not in euill disposition, 190

But from Lord *Angelo* by speciall charge.

CLAUDIO

Thus can the demy-god (Authority)

896

Make vs pay downe, for our offence, by waight
The bonds of heauen; on whom it will, it will,
On whom it will not (soe) yet still 'tis iust.

LUCIO

Why how now *Claudio?* whence comes this restraint.

CLAUDIO

From too much liberty, (my *Lucio*) Liberty.
As surfet is the father of much fast,
So euery Scope by the immoderate vse
200   Turnes to restraint: Our Natures doe pursue
Like Rats that rauyn downe their proper Bane,
A thirsty euill, and when we drinke, we die.

LUCIO   If I could speake so wisely vnder an arrest, I would
send for certaine of my Creditors: and yet, to say the
truth, I had as lief haue the foppery of freedome, as
the morality of imprisonment: what's thy offence,
Claudio?

CLAUDIO

What (but to speake of) would offend againe.

LUCIO

What, is't murder?

CLAUDIO   No.

LUCIO   Lecherie?

CLAUDIO   Call it so.

210   PROUOST   Away, Sir, you must goe.

CLAUDIO

One word, good friend:
        ⌈*The Prouost showes assent*⌉
                    Lucio, a word with you.

LUCIO   A hundred: If they'll doe you any good:
        ⌈*Claudio and Lucio speake apart*⌉
Is *Lechery* so look'd after?

CLAUDIO

Thus stands it with me: vpon a true contract
I got possession of *Iulietas* bed,
You know the Lady, she is fast my wife,
Saue that we doe the denunciation lacke
Of outward Order. This we came not to,
Onely for propogation of a Dowre
220   Remaining in the Coffer of her friends,
From whom we thought it meet to hide our Loue
Till Time had made them for vs. But it chances
The stealth of our most mutuall entertainment
With Character too grosse, is writ on *Iuliet.*

LUCIO

With childe, perhaps?

CLAUDIO   Vnhappely, euen so.
And the new Deputie, now for the Duke,
Whether it be the fault and glimpse of newnes,
Or whether that the body publique, be
A horse whereon the Gouernor doth ride,
230   Who newly in the Seate, that it may know
He can command; lets it strait feele the spur:
Whether the Tirranny be in his place,
Or in his Eminence that fills it vp
I stagger in: But this new Gouernor
Awakes me all the inrolled penalties
Which haue (like vn-scowr'd Armor) hung by th'wall

So long, that foureteene Zodiacks haue gone round,
And none of them beene worne; and for a name
Now puts the drowsie and neglected Act
Freshly on me: 'tis surely for a name.   240

LUCIO   I warrant it is: And thy head stands so tickle on
thy shoulders, that a milke-maid, if she be in loue, may
sigh it off: Send after the Duke, and appeale to him.

CLAUDIO

I haue done so, but hee's not to be found.
I pre'thee (*Lucio*) doe me this kinde seruice:
This day, my sister should the Cloyster enter,
And there receiue her approbation.
Acquaint her with the danger of my state,
Implore her, in my voice, that she make friends
To the strict deputie: bid her selfe assay him,   250
I haue great hope in that: for in her youth
There is a prone and speechlesse dialect,
Such as moue men: beside, she hath prosperous Art
When she will play with reason, and discourse,
And well she can perswade.

LUCIO   I pray shee may; aswell for the encouragement of
thy like, which else would stand vnder greeuous
imposition: as for the enioying of thy life, who I would
be sorry should bee thus foolishly lost, at a game of
ticke-tacke: Ile to her.   260

CLAUDIO   I thanke you good friend *Lucio.*

LUCIO   Within two houres.

CLAUDIO   Come Officer, away.
            Exeunt ⌈*Lucio and Gentlemen at one doore;*
            Claudio, Iuliet, Prouost, and Officers at another⌉

            Enter Duke and Frier   **1.3**
DUKE   **(Sc. 3)**

No: holy Father, throw away that thought,
Beleeue not that the dribling dart of Loue
Can pierce a compleat bosome: why, I desire thee
To giue me secret harbour, hath a purpose
More graue, and wrinkled, then the aimes, and ends
Of burning youth.

FRIER   May your Grace speake of it?

DUKE

My holy Sir, none better knowes then you   270
How I haue euer lou'd the life remoued
And held in idle price, to haunt assemblies
Where youth, and cost, a witlesse brauery keepes.
I haue deliuerd to Lord *Angelo*
(A man of stricture and firme abstinence)
My absolute power, and place here in *Vienna,*
And he supposes me trauaild to *Poland,*
(For so I haue strewd it in the common eare)
And so it is receiu'd: Now (pious Sir)
You will demand of me, why I do this.   280

FRIER   Gladly, my Lord.

DUKE

We haue strict Statutes, and most biting Laws,
(The needfull bits and curbes to headstrong weedes,)
Which for this foureteene yeares, we haue let slip,
Euen like an ore-growne Lyon in a Caue

That goes not out to prey: Now, as fond Fathers,
Hauing bound vp the threatning twigs of birch,
Onely to sticke it in their childrens sight,
For terror, not to vse: in time the rod
290   More mock'd becomes, then fear'd: so our Decrees,
Dead to infliction, to themselues are dead,
And libertie, plucks Iustice by the nose;
The Baby beates the Nurse, and quite athwart
Goes all decorum.

FRIER   It rested in your Grace
To vnloose this tyde-vp Iustice, when you pleas'd:
And it in you more dreadfull would haue seem'd
Then in Lord *Angelo*.

DUKE   I doe feare: too dreadfull:
Sith 'twas my fault, to giue the people scope,
'T would be my tirrany to strike and gall them,
300   For what I bid them doe: For, we bid this be done
When euill deedes haue their permissiue passe,
And not the punishment: therefore indeede (my
        father)
I haue on *Angelo* impos'd the office,
Who may in th'ambush of my name, strike home,
And yet, my nature neuer in the fight
T'alow in slander: And to behold his sway
I will, as 'twere a brother of your Order,
Visit both Prince, and People: Therefore I pre'thee
Supply me with the habit, and instruct me
310   How I may formally in person beare
Like a true *Frier*: Moe reasons for this action
At our more leysure, shall I render you;
Onely, this one: Lord *Angelo* is precise,
Stands at a guard with Enuie: scarce confesses
That his blood flowes: or that his appetite
Is more to bread then stone: hence shall we see
If power change purpose: what our Seemers be.

                                        Exeunt

1.4   *Enter Isabell and Francisca a Nun*
(Sc. 4) ISABELLA
And haue you *Nuns* no farther priuiledges?
NUN Are not these large enough?
ISABELLA
320   Yes truely; I speake not as desiring more,
But rather wishing a more strict restraint
Vpon the Sisterhood, the Votarists of Saint *Clare*.
LUCIO (*within*)
Hoa? peace be in this place.
ISABELLA ⌈*to Nun*⌉   Who's that which cals?
NUN
It is a mans voice: gentle *Isabella*
Turne you the key, and know his businesse of him;
You may; I may not: you are yet vnsworne:
When you haue vowd, you must not speake with men,
But in the presence of the *Prioresse*;
Then if you speake, you must not show your face;
330   Or if you show your face, you must not speake.
            Lucio cals within
He cals againe: I pray you answere him.
            ⌈*She stands aside*⌉

ISABELLA
Peace and prosperitie: who is't that cals?
            She opens the doore.
            Enter Lucio
LUCIO
Haile Virgin, (if you be) as those cheeke-Roses
Proclaime you are no lesse: can you so steed me,
As bring me to the sight of *Isabella*,
A Nouice of this place, and the faire Sister
To her vnhappie brother *Claudio*?
ISABELLA
Why her vnhappy Brother? Let me aske,
The rather for I now must make you know
I am that *Isabella*, and his Sister.   340
LUCIO
Gentle & faire: your Brother kindly greets you;
Not to be weary with you; he's in prison.
ISABELLA Woe me; for what?
LUCIO
For that, which if my selfe might be his Iudge,
He should receiue his punishment, in thankes:
He hath got his friend with childe.
ISABELLA   Sir, make me not your storie.
LUCIO
'Tis true; I would not, though 'tis my familiar sin,
With Maids to seeme the Lapwing, and to iest
Tongue, far from heart: play with all Virgins so:
I hold you as a thing en-skied, and sainted,   350
By your renouncement, an imortall spirit
And to be talk'd with in sincerity,
As with a Saint.
ISABELLA
You doe blaspheme the good, in mocking me.
LUCIO
Doe not beleeue it: fewnes, and truth; tis thus,
Your brother, and his louer haue embrac'd;
As those that feed, grow full: as blossoming Time
That from the seednes, the bare fallow brings
To teeming foyson: euen so her plenteous wombe
Expresseth his full Tilth, and husbandry.   360
ISABELLA
Some one with childe by him? my cosen *Iuliet*?
LUCIO Is she your cosen?
ISABELLA
Adoptedly, as schoole-maids change their names
By vaine, though apt affection.
LUCIO   She it is.
ISABELLA
Oh, let him marry her.
LUCIO   This is the point.
The Duke is very strangely gone from hence;
Bore many gentlemen (my selfe being one)
In hand, and hope of action: but we doe learne,
By those that know the very Nerues of State,
His giuing-out, were of an infinite distance   370
From his true meant designe: vpon his place,
(And with full line of his authority)
Gouernes Lord *Angelo*; A man, whose blood
Is very snow-broth: one, who neuer feeles

The wanton stings, and motions of the sence;
But doth rebate, and blunt his naturall edge
With profits of the minde: Studie, and fast.
He (to giue feare to vse, and libertie,
Which haue, for long, run-by the hideous law,
380 As Myce, by Lyons) hath pickt out an act,
Vnder whose heauy sence, your brothers life
Fals into forfeit: he arrests him on it,
And followes close the rigor of the Statute
To make him an example: all hope is gone,
Vnlesse you haue the grace, by your faire praier
To soften *Angelo*: And that's my pith
Of businesse 'twixt you, and your poore brother.

ISABELLA
Doth he so, seeke his life?

LUCIO   Has censur'd him already,
And as I heare, the Prouost hath a warrant
For's execution.

390 ISABELLA   Alas: what poore
Abilitie's in me, to doe him good.

LUCIO Assay the powre you haue.

ISABELLA My power? alas, I doubt.

LUCIO Our doubts are traitors
And makes vs loose the good we oft might win,
By fearing to attempt: Goe to Lord *Angelo*
And let him learne to know, when Maidens sue
Men giue like gods: but when they weepe and kneele,
All their petitions, are as freely theirs
As they themselues would owe them.

400 ISABELLA   Ile see what I can doe.

LUCIO
But speedily.

ISABELLA   I will about it strait;
No longer staying, but to giue the Mother
Notice of my affaire: I humbly thanke you:
Commend me to my brother: soone at night
Ile send him certaine word of my successe.

LUCIO
I take my leaue of you.

ISABELLA   Good sir, adieu.
            Exeunt ⌈Isabella and Nun at one doore, Lucio at
                                        another doore⌉

❁

2.1   *Enter Angelo, Escalus, and seruants, Iustice*
(Sc. 5) ANGELO
We must not make a scar-crow of the Law,
Setting it vp to feare the Birds of prey,
And let it keepe one shape, till custome make it
Their pearch, and not their terror.

410 ESCALUS   I, but yet
Let vs be keene, and rather cut a little
Then fall, and bruise to death: alas, this gentleman
Whom I would saue, had a most noble father,
Let but your honour know
(Whom I beleeue to be most strait in vertue)
That in the working of your owne affections,
Had time coheard with Place, or place with wishing,

Or that the resolute acting of your blood
Could haue attaind th'effect of your owne purpose,
Whether you had not sometime in your life   420
Er'd in this point, which now you censure him,
And puld the Law vpon you.

ANGELO
'Tis one thing to be tempted (*Escalus*)
Another thing to fall: I not deny
The Iury passing on the Prisoners life
May in the sworne-twelue haue a thiefe, or two
Guiltier then him they try; What knowes the Lawe
That theeues do passe on theeues? what's open made
      to Iustice,
That Iustice ceizes; 'Tis very pregnant,
The Iewell that we finde, we stoope, and take't,   430
Because we see it; but what we doe not see,
We tread vpon, and neuer thinke of it.
You may not so extenuate his offence,
For I haue had such faults; but rather tell me
When I, that censure him, do so offend,
Let mine owne Iudgement patterne out my death,
And nothing come in partiall. Sir, he must dye.

ESCALUS
Be it as your wisedome will.

ANGELO   Where is the *Prouost*?
      Enter Prouost

PROUOST
Here if it like your honour.

ANGELO   See that *Claudio*
Be execute by nine to morrow morning,   440
Bring him his Confessor, let him be prepar'd,
For that's the vtmost of his pilgrimage.   *Exit Prouost*

ESCALUS
Well: heauen forgiue him; and forgiue vs all:
Some rise by sinne, and some by vertue fall:
Some run from brakes of vice, and answere none,
And some condemned for a fault alone.
      Enter Elbow, Froth, Clowne, Officers

ELBOW Come, bring them away: if these be good people
in a Common-weale, that doe nothing but vse their
abuses in common houses, I know no law: bring them
away.   450

ANGELO
How now Sir, what's your name? And what's the
      matter?

ELBOW If it please your honour, I am the poore Dukes
Constable, and my name is *Elbow*; I doe leane vpon
Iustice Sir, and doe bring in here before your good
honor, two notorious Benefactors.

ANGELO
Benefactors? Well: What Benefactors are they?
Are they not Malefactors?

ELBOW If it please your honour, I know not well what
they are: But precise villaines they are, that I am sure
of, and void of all prophanation in the world, that good   460
Christians ought to haue.

ESCALUS (*to Angelo*)
This comes off well: here's a wise Officer.

ANGELO Goe to: What quality are they of? *Elbow* is your name? Why do'st thou not speake *Elbow*?

CLOWNE He cannot Sir: he's out at Elbow.

ANGELO What are you Sir?

ELBOW He Sir: a Tapster Sir: parcell Baud: one that serues a bad woman: whose house Sir was (as they say) pluckt downe in the Suborbs: and now shee professes 470 a hot-house; which, I thinke is a very ill house too.

ESCALUS How know you that?

ELBOW My wife Sir: whom I detest before heauen, and your honour.

ESCALUS How? thy wife?

ELBOW I Sir: whom I thanke heauen is an honest woman.

ESCALUS Do'st thou detest her therefore?

ELBOW I say sir, I will detest my selfe also, as well as she, that this house, if it be not a Bauds house, it is pitty of her life, for it is a naughty house.

480 ESCALUS How do'st thou know that, Constable?

ELBOW Marry sir, by my wife, who, if she had bin a woman Cardinally giuen, might haue bin accus'd in fornication, adultery, and all vncleanlinesse there.

ESCALUS By the womans meanes?

ELBOW I sir, by Mistris *Ouer-dons* meanes: but as she spit in his face, so she defide him.

CLOWNE (*to Escalus*) Sir, if it please your honor, this is not so.

ELBOW Proue it before these varlets here, thou honorable 490 man, proue it.

ESCALUS (*to Angelo*) Doe you heare how he misplaces?

CLOWNE Sir, she came in great with childe: and longing (sauing your honors reuerence) for stewd prewyns; sir, we had but two in the house, which at that very distant time stood, as it were in a fruit dish (a dish of some three pence; your honours haue seene such dishes) they are not China-dishes, but very good dishes.

ESCALUS Go too: go too: no matter for the dish sir.

CLOWNE No indeede sir not of a pin; you are therein in 500 the right: but, to the point: As I say, this Mistris *Elbow*, being (as I say) with childe, and being great bellied, and longing (as I said) for prewyns: and hauing but two in the dish (as I said) Master *Froth* here, this very man, hauing eaten the rest (as I said) & (as I say) paying for them very honestly: for, as you know Master *Froth*, I could not giue you three pence againe.

FROTH No indeede.

CLOWNE Very well: you being then (if you be remembred) cracking the stones of the foresaid prewyns.

510 FROTH I, so I did indeede.

CLOWNE Why, very well: I telling you then (if you be remembred) that such a one, and such a one, were past cure of the thing you wot of, vnlesse they kept very good diet, as I told you.

FROTH All this is true.

CLOWNE Why very well then.

ESCALUS Come: you are a tedious foole: to the purpose: what was done to *Elbowes* wife, that hee hath cause to complaine of? Come me to what was done to her.

CLOWNE Sir, your honor cannot come to that yet. 520

ESCALUS No sir, nor I meane it not.

CLOWNE Sir, but you shall come to it, by your honours leaue: And I beseech you, looke into Master *Froth* here sir, a man of foure-score pound a yeare; whose father died at *Hallowmas*: Was't not at *Hallowmas* Master *Froth*?

FROTH Allhallond-Eue.

CLOWNE Why very well: I hope here be truthes: he Sir, sitting (as I say) in a lower chaire, Sir, 'twas in the bunch of Grapes, where indeede you haue a delight to 530 sit, haue you not?

FROTH I haue so, because it is an open roome, and good for winter.

CLOWNE Why very well then: I hope here be truthes.

ANGELO
This will last out a night in *Russia*
When nights are longest there: (*To Escalus*) Ile take my leaue,
And leaue you to the hearing of the cause;
Hoping youle finde good cause to whip them all.

ESCALUS
I thinke no lesse: good morrow to your Lordship.
                                        Exit Angelo
Now Sir, come on: What was done to *Elbowes* wife, 540 once more?

CLOWNE Once Sir? there was nothing done to her once.

ELBOW I beseech you Sir, aske him what this man did to my wife.

CLOWNE I beseech your honor, aske me.

ESCALUS Well sir, what did this Gentleman to her?

CLOWNE I beseech you sir, looke in this Gentlemans face: good Master *Froth* looke vpon his honor; 'tis for a good purpose: doth your honor marke his face?

ESCALUS I sir, very well. 550

CLOWNE Nay, I beseech you marke it well.

ESCALUS Well, I doe so.

CLOWNE Doth your honor see any harme in his face?

ESCALUS Why no.

CLOWNE Ile be supposd vpon a booke, his face is the worst thing about him: good then: if his face be the worst thing about him, how could Master *Froth* doe the Constables wife any harme? I would know that of your honour.

ESCALUS He's in the right (Constable) what say you to it? 560

ELBOW First, and it like you, the house is a respected house; next, this is a respected fellow; and his Mistris is a respected woman.

CLOWNE (*to Escalus*) By this hand Sir, his wife is a more respected person then any of vs all.

ELBOW Varlet, thou lyest; thou lyest wicked varlet: the time is yet to come that shee was euer respected with man, woman, or childe.

CLOWNE Sir, she was respected with him, before he married with her. 570

ESCALUS Which is the wiser here; *Iustice* or *Iniquitie*? (*To Elbow*) Is this true?

ELBOW (*to Clowne*) O thou caytiffe: O thou varlet: O thou
wicked *Hanniball*; I respected with her, before I was
married to her? (*To Escalus*) If euer I was respected
with her, or she with me, let not your worship thinke
mee the poore *Dukes* Officer: (*to Clowne*) proue this,
thou wicked *Hanniball*, or ile haue mine action of battry
on thee.

580 ESCALUS If he tooke you a box 'oth'eare, you might haue
your action of slander too.

ELBOW Marry I thanke your good worship for it: what
is't your Worships pleasure I shall doe with this wicked
Caitiffe?

ESCALUS Truly Officer, because he hath some offences in
him, that thou wouldst discouer, if thou couldst, let
him continue in his courses, till thou knowst what they
are.

ELBOW Marry I thanke your worship for it: Thou seest
590 thou wicked varlet now, what's come vpon thee. Thou
art to continue now thou Varlet, thou art to continue.

ESCALUS (*to Froth*) Where were you borne, friend?

FROTH Here in *Vienna*, Sir.

ESCALUS Are you of fourescore pounds a yeere?

FROTH Yes, and 't please you sir.

ESCALUS So: (*to Clowne*) what trade are you of, sir?

CLOWNE A Tapster, a poore widdowes Tapster.

ESCALUS Your Mistris name?

CLOWNE Mistris *Ouer-don*.

600 ESCALUS Hath she had any more then one husband?

CLOWNE Nine, sir: *Ouer-don* by the last.

ESCALUS Nine? come hether to me, Master *Froth*; Master
Froth, I would not haue you acquainted with Tapsters;
they will draw you Master *Froth*, and you wil hang
them: get you gon, and let me heare no more of you.

FROTH I thanke your worship: for mine owne part, I
neuer come into any roome in a Tap-house, but I am
drawne in.

ESCALUS Well: no more of it Master *Froth*: farewell:

Exit Froth

610 Come you hether to me, M^r. Tapster: what's your name
M^r. Tapster?

CLOWNE *Pompey*.

ESCALUS What else?

CLOWNE *Bum*, Sir.

ESCALUS Troth, and your bum is the greatest thing about
you, so that in the beastliest sence, you are *Pompey*
the great; *Pompey*, you are partly a bawd, *Pompey*;
howsoeuer you colour it in being a Tapster, are you
not? come, tell me true, it shall be the better for you.

620 CLOWNE Truly sir, I am a poore fellow that would liue.

ESCALUS How would you liue *Pompey*? by being a bawd?
what doe you thinke of the trade *Pompey*? is it a lawfull
trade?

CLOWNE If the Law would allow it, sir.

ESCALUS But the Law will not allow it *Pompey*; nor it shall
not be allowed in *Vienna*.

CLOWNE Do's your Worship meane to geld and splay all
the youth of the City?

ESCALUS No, *Pompey*.

CLOWNE Truely Sir, in my poore opinion they will too't   630
then: if your worship will take order for the drabs and
the knaues, you need not to feare the bawds.

ESCALUS There is pretty orders beginning I can tell you:
It is but heading, and hanging.

CLOWNE If you head, and hang all that offend that way
but for ten yeare together; you'll be glad to giue out
a Commission for more heads: if this law hold in *Vienna*
ten yeare, ile rent the fairest house in it after three
pence a Bay: if you liue to see this come to passe, say
Pompey told you so.   640

ESCALUS Thanke you good *Pompey*; and in requitall of
your prophesie, harke you: I aduise you let me not
finde you before me againe vpon any complaint
whatsoeuer; no, not for dwelling where you doe: if I
doe *Pompey*, I shall beat you to your Tent, and proue
a shrewd *Cæsar* to you: in plaine dealing *Pompey*, I
shall haue you whipt; so for this time, *Pompey*, fare
you well.

CLOWNE I thanke your Worship for your good counsell;
⌈*aside*⌉ but I shall follow it as the flesh and fortune shall   650
better determine.

Whip me? no, no, let Carman whip his Iade,
The valiant heart's not whipt out of his trade.   *Exit*

ESCALUS Come hether to me, Master *Elbow*: come hither
Master Constable: how long haue you bin in this place
of Constable?

ELBOW Seuen yeere, and a halfe sir.

ESCALUS I thought by the readinesse in the office, you had
continued in it some time: you say seauen yeares
together.   660

ELBOW And a halfe sir.

ESCALUS Alas, it hath beene great paines to you: they do
you wrong to put you so oft vpon't. Are there not men
in your Ward sufficient to serue it?

ELBOW 'Faith sir, few of any wit in such matters: as they
are chosen, they are glad to choose me for them; I do
it for some peece of money, and goe through with all.

ESCALUS Looke you bring mee in the names of some sixe
or seuen, the most sufficient of your parish.

ELBOW To your Worships house sir?   670

ESCALUS To my house: fare you well:

Exit Elbow with Officers

what's a clocke, thinke you?

IUSTICE Eleuen, Sir.

ESCALUS I pray you home to dinner with me.

IUSTICE I humbly thanke you.

ESCALUS
It grieues me for the death of *Claudio*
But there's no remedie.

IUSTICE Lord *Angelo* is seuere.

ESCALUS It is but needfull.
Mercy is not it selfe, that oft lookes so,   680
Pardon is still the nurse of second woe:
But yet, poore *Claudio*; there is no remedie.
Come Sir.   *Exeunt*

2.2   *Enter Prouost, Seruant*
(Sc. 6)   SERUANT
      Hee's hearing of a Cause; he will come straight,
      I'le tell him of you.
PROUOST   'Pray you doe;   *Exit Seruant*
                                      Ile know
      His pleasure, may be he will relent; alas
      He hath but as offended in a dreame,
      All Sects, all Ages smack of this vice, and he
      To die for't?
          Enter Angelo
ANGELO   Now, what's the matter *Prouost?*
PROUOST
690   Is it your will *Claudio* shall die to morrow?
ANGELO
      Did not I tell thee yea? hadst thou not order?
      Why do'st thou aske againe?
PROUOST   Lest I might be too rash:
      Vnder your good correction, I haue seene
      When after execution, Iudgement hath
      Repented ore his doome.
ANGELO   Goe to; let that be mine,
      Doe you your office, or giue vp your Place,
      And you shall well be spar'd.
PROUOST   I craue your Honours pardon:
      What shall be done Sir, with the groaning *Iuliet?*
      Shee's very neere her howre.
ANGELO   Dispose of her
700   To some more fitter place; and that with speed.
          Enter Seruant
SERUANT
      Here is the sister of the man condemn'd,
      Desires accesse to you.
ANGELO   Hath he a Sister?
PROUOST
      I my good Lord, a very vertuous maid,
      And to be shortlie of a Sister-hood,
      If not alreadie.
ANGELO   ·   Well: let her be admitted,
                            Exit Seruant
      See you the Fornicatresse be remou'd,
      Let her haue needfull, but not lauish meanes,
      There shall be order for't.
          Enter Lucio and Isabella
PROUOST   God saue your Honour.
ANGELO
      Stay a little while: (*to Isabella*) y'are welcome: what's
         your will?
ISABELLA
710   I am a wofull Sutor to your Honour,
      'Please but your Honor heare me.
ANGELO   Well: what's your suite.
ISABELLA
      There is a vice that most I doe abhorre,
      And most desire should meet the blow of Iustice;
      For which I would not plead, but that I must,
      For which I must not plead, but that I am
      At warre, twixt will, and will not.
ANGELO   Well: the matter?

ISABELLA
      I haue a brother is condemn'd to die,
      I doe beseech you let it be his fault,
      And not my brother.
PROUOST (*aside*)   Heauen giue thee mouing graces.
ANGELO
      Condemne the fault, and not the actor of it,   720
      Why euery fault's condemnd ere it be done:
      Mine were the verie Cipher of a Function
      To fine the faults, whose fine stands in record,
      And let goe by the Actor.
ISABELLA   Oh iust, but seuere Law:
      I had a brother then; heauen keepe your honour.
LUCIO (*aside to Isabella*)
      Giue 't not ore so: to him againe, entreat him,
      Kneele downe before him, hang vpon his gowne,
      You are too cold: if you should need a pin,
      You could not with more tame a tongue desire it:
      To him, I say.   730
ISABELLA (*to Angelo*) Must he needs die?
ANGELO Maiden, no remedie.
ISABELLA
      Yes: I doe thinke that you might pardon him,
      And neither heauen, nor man grieue at the mercy.
ANGELO
      I will not doe't.
ISABELLA   But can you if you would?
ANGELO
      Looke what I will not, that I cannot doe.
ISABELLA
      But might you doe't & do the world no wrong
      If so your heart were touch'd with that remorse,
      As mine is to him?
ANGELO Hee's sentenc'd, tis too late.   740
LUCIO (*aside to Isabella*) You are too cold.
ISABELLA
      Too late? why no: I that doe speak a word
      May call it againe: well, beleeue this,
      No ceremony that to great ones longs,
      Not the Kings Crowne; nor the deputed sword,
      The Marshalls Truncheon, nor the Iudges Robe
      Become them with one halfe so good a grace
      As mercie does:
      If he had bin as you, and you as he,
      You would haue slipt like him, but he like you   750
      Would not haue beene so sterne.
ANGELO   Pray you be gone.
ISABELLA
      I would to heauen I had your potencie,
      And you were *Isabell*: should it then be thus?
      No: I would tell what 'twere to be a Iudge,
      And what a prisoner.
LUCIO (*aside to Isabella*) I, touch him: there's the vaine.
ANGELO
      Your Brother is a forfeit of the Law,
      And you but waste your words.
ISABELLA   Alas, alas:
      Why all the soules that were, were forfeit once,
      And he that might the vantage best haue tooke,

760 Found out the remedie: how would you be,
If he, which is the top of Iudgement, should
But iudge you, as you are? Oh, thinke on that,
And mercie then will breathe within your lips
Like man new made.

ANGELO   Be you content, (faire Maid)
It is the Law, not I, condemne your brother,
Were he my kinsman, brother, or my sonne,
It should be thus with him: he must die to morrow.

ISABELLA

To morrow? oh, that's sodaine, spare him, spare him:
Hee's not prepar'd for death; euen for our kitchins
770 We kill the fowle of season: shall we serue heauen
With lesse respect then we doe minister
To our grosse-selues? good, good my Lord, bethink
    you;
Who is it that hath di'd for this offence?
There's many haue committed it.

LUCIO (aside)   I, well said.

ANGELO

The Law hath not bin dead, thogh it hath slept:
Those many had not dar'd to doe that euill
If the first, that did th' Edict infringe
Had answer'd for his deed. Now 'tis awake,
Takes note of what is done, and like a Prophet
780 Lookes in a glasse that shewes what future euils
Either raw, or by remissenesse, new conceiu'd,
And so in progresse to be hatch'd, and borne,
Are now to haue no successiue degrees,
But yeer they liue to end.

ISABELLA   Yet shew some pittie.

ANGELO

I shew it most of all, when I show Iustice;
For then I pittie those I doe not know,
Which a dismis'd offence, would after gaule
And doe him right, that answering one foule wrong
Liues not to act another. Be satisfied;
790 Your Brother dies to morrow; be content.

ISABELLA

So you must be ye first that giues this sentence,
And hee, that suffers: Oh, it is excellent
To haue a Giants strength: but it is tyrannous
To vse it like a Giant.

LUCIO (aside to Isabella) That's well said.

ISABELLA Could great men thunder
As Ioue himselfe do's, Ioue would neuer be quiet,
For euery pelting petty Officer
Would vse his heauen for thunder; Nothing but
    thunder:
800 Mercifull heauen,
Thou rather with thy sharpe and sulpherous bolt
Splits the vn-wedgable and gnarled Oke,
Then the soft Mertill: But man, proud man,
Drest in a little briefe authoritie,
Most ignorant of what he's most assur'd,
(His glassie Essence) like an angry Ape
Plaies such phantastique tricks before high heauen,
As makes the Angels weepe: who with our spleenes,
Would all themselues laugh mortall.

LUCIO (aside to Isabella)
Oh, to him, to him wench: he will relent,   810
Hee's comming: I perceiue't.

PROUOST (aside)   Pray heauen she win him.

ISABELLA

We cannot weigh our brother with our selfe,
Great men may iest with Saints: tis wit in them,
But in the lesse fowle prophanation.

LUCIO (aside to Isabella) Thou'rt i'th right (Girle) more
o'that.

ISABELLA

That in the Captaine 's but a chollericke word,
Which in the Souldier is flat blasphemie.

LUCIO (aside to Isabella) Art auis'd o'that? more on't.

ANGELO

Why doe you put these sayings vpon me?   820

ISABELLA

Because Authoritie, though it erre like others,
Hath yet a kinde of medicine in it selfe
That skins the vice o'th top; goe to your bosome,
Knock there, and aske your heart what it doth know
That's like my brothers fault: if it confesse
A naturall guiltinesse, such as is his,
Let it not sound a thought vpon your tongue
Against my brothers life.

ANGELO (aside)   Shee speakes, and 'tis such sence
That my Sence breeds with it; (to Isabella) fare you
well.

ISABELLA Gentle my Lord, turne backe.   830

ANGELO

I will bethinke me: come againe to morrow.

ISABELLA

Hark, how Ile bribe you: good my Lord turn back.

ANGELO How? bribe me?

ISABELLA

I, with such gifts that heauen shall share with you.

LUCIO (aside to Isabella) You had mar'd all else.

ISABELLA

Not with fond Sickles of the tested-gold,
Or Stones, whose rate are either rich, or poore
As fancie values them: but with true prayers,
That shall be vp at heauen, and enter there
Ere Sunne rise: prayers from preserued soules,   840
From fasting Maides, whose mindes are dedicate
To nothing temporall.

ANGELO Well: come to me to morrow.

LUCIO (aside to Isabella) Goe to: 'tis well; Away.

ISABELLA Heauen keepe your honour safe.

ANGELO (aside) Amen.
For I am that way going to temptation,
Where prayer is crossd.

ISABELLA   At what hower to morrow,
Shall I attend your Lordship?

ANGELO   At any time 'fore-noone.

ISABELLA

God saue your Honour.

ANGELO (aside)   From thee: euen from thy vertue. 850
                    Exeunt Isabella, Lucio and Prouost

What's this? what's this? is this her fault, or mine?
The Tempter, or the Tempted, who sins most? ha?
Not she: nor doth she tempt: but it is I,
That, lying by the Violet in the Sunne,
Doe as the Carrion do's, not as the flowre,
Corrupt with vertuous season: Can it be,
That Modesty may more betray our Sence
Then womans lightnesse? hauing waste ground
    enough,
Shall we desire to raze the Sanctuary
860 And pitch our euils there? oh fie, fie, fie:
What dost thou? or what art thou *Angelo*?
Dost thou desire her fowly, for those things
That make her good? oh, let her brother liue:
Theeues for their robbery haue authority,
When Iudges steale themselues: what, doe I loue her,
That I desire to heare her speake againe?
And feast vpon her eyes? what is't I dreame on?
Oh cunning enemy, that to catch a Saint,
With Saints dost bait thy hooke: most dangerous
870 Is that temptation, that doth goad vs on
To sinne, in louing vertue: neuer could the Strumpet
With all her double vigor, Art, and Nature
Once stir my temper: but this vertuous Maid
Subdues me quite: Euer till now
When men were fond, I smild, and wondred how.

                          Exit

2.3   *Enter ⌈at one doore⌉ the Duke (as a Frier) and ⌈at*
(Sc. 7)   *another doore⌉ the Prouost*
DUKE
    Haile to you, *Prouost*, so I thinke you are.
PROUOST
    I am the Prouost: whats your will, good Frier?
DUKE
    Bound by my charity, and my blest order,
    I come to visite the afflicted spirits
880 Here in the prison: doe me the common right
    To let me see them: and to make me know
    The nature of their crimes, that I may minister
    To them accordingly.
PROUOST
    I would do more then that, if more were needfull.
      Enter Iuliet
    Looke here comes one: a Gentlewoman of mine,
    Who falling in the flawes of her owne youth,
    Hath blisterd her report: She is with childe,
    And he that got it, sentenc'd: a yong man,
    More fit to doe another such offence,
890 Then dye for this.
DUKE When must he dye?
PROUOST As I do thinke to morrow.
    (*To Iuliet*) I haue prouided for you, stay a while
    And you shall be conducted.
DUKE
    Repent you (faire one) of the sin you carry?
IULIET
    I doe; and beare the shame most patiently.

DUKE
    Ile teach you how you shal araign your consciĕce
    And try your penitence, if it be sound,
    Or hollowly put on.
IULIET Ile gladly learne.   900
DUKE Loue you the man that wrong'd you?
IULIET
    Yes, as I loue the woman that wrong'd him.
DUKE
    So then it seemes your most offence full act
    Was mutually committed.
IULIET   Mutually.
DUKE
    Then was your sin of heauier kinde then his.
IULIET
    I doe confesse it, and repent it (Father.)
DUKE
    'Tis meet so (daughter) but least you do repent
    As that the sin hath brought you to this shame,
    Which sorrow is alwaies toward our selues, not
        heauen,
    Showing we would not spare heauen, as we loue it,   910
    But as we stand in feare.
IULIET
    I doe repent me, as it is an euill,
    And take the shame with ioy.
DUKE   There rest:
    Your partner (as I heare) must die to morrow,
    And I am going with instruction to him:
    Grace goe with you, *Benedicite*.   *Exit*
IULIET
    Must die to morrow? oh iniurious Lawe
    That respits me a life, whose very comfort
    Is still a dying horror.
PROUOST   'Tis pitty of him.   *Exeunt*

    Enter Angelo   **2.4**
ANGELO   **(Sc. 8)**
    When I would pray, & think, I thinke, and pray   920
    To seuerall subiects: heauen hath my empty words,
    Whilst my Inuention, hearing not my Tongue,
    Anchors on *Isabell*: God in my mouth,
    As if I did but onely chew his name,
    And in my heart the strong and swelling euill
    Of my conception: the state whereon I studied
    Is like a good thing, being often read
    Growne seard, and tedious: yea, my Grauitie
    Wherein (let no man heare me) I take pride,
    Could I, with boote, change for an idle plume   930
    Which the ayre beats in vaine: oh place, oh forme,
    How often dost thou with thy case, thy habit
    Wrench awe from fooles, and tye the wiser soules
    To thy false seeming? Blood, thou art blood,
    Let's write good Angell on the Deuills horne
    'Tis now the Deuills Crest:
      Enter Seruant
                         how now? who's there?
SERUANT One *Isabell*, a Sister, desires accesse to you.

ANGELO

  Teach her the way: *Exit Seruant*

            oh, heauens

  Why doe's my bloud thus muster to my heart,

940 Making both it vnable for it selfe,

  And dispossessing all my other parts

  Of necessary fitnesse?

  So play the foolish throngs with one that swounds,

  Come all to help him, and so stop the ayre

  By which hee should reuiue: and euen so

  The generall subiect to a wel-wisht King

  Quit their owne part, and in obsequious fondnesse

  Crowd to his presence, where their vn-taught loue

  Must needs appear offence:

      Enter Isabella

                      how now faire Maid.

950 ISABELLA I am come to know your pleasure.

ANGELO (*aside*)

  That you might know it, wold much better please me,

  Then to demand what 'tis: (*to Isabella*) your Brother

    cannot liue.

ISABELLA Euen so: heauen keepe your Honor.

ANGELO

  Yet may he liue a while: and it may be

  As long as you, or I: yet he must die.

ISABELLA Vnder your Sentence?

ANGELO Yea.

ISABELLA

  When, I beseech you: that in his Reprieue

  (Longer, or shorter) he may be so fitted

960 That his soule sicken not.

ANGELO

  Ha? fie, these filthy vices: It were as good

  To pardon him, that hath from nature stolne

  A man already made, as to remit

  Their sawcie sweetnes, that do coyne Gods Image

  In stamps that are forbid: 'tis all as easie,

  Falsely to take away a life true made,

  As to put mettle in restrained moalds

  To make a false one.

ISABELLA

  'Tis set downe so in heauen, but not in earth.

ANGELO

970 Say you so: then I shall poze you quickly.

  Which had you rather, that the most iust Law

  Now tooke your brothers life, or to redeeme him

  Giue vp your body to such sweet vncleannesse

  As she that he hath staind?

ISABELLA   Sir, beleeue this.

  I had rather giue my body, then my soule.

ANGELO

  I talke not of your soule: our compel'd sins

  Stand more for number, then for accompt.

ISABELLA   How say you?

ANGELO

  Nay Ile not warrant that: for I can speake

  Against the thing I say: Answere to this,

980 I (now the voyce of the recorded Law)

  Pronounce a sentence on your Brothers life,

  Might there not be a charitie in sinne,

  To saue this Brothers life?

ISABELLA   Please you to doo't,

  Ile take it as a perill to my soule,

  It is no sinne at all, but charitie.

ANGELO

  Pleas'd you to doo't, at perill of your soule

  Were equall poize of sinne, and charitie.

ISABELLA

  That I do beg his life, if it be sinne

  Heauen let me beare it: you granting of my suit,

  If that be sin, Ile make it my Morne-praier,   990

  To haue it added to the faults of mine,

  And nothing of your answere.

ANGELO   Nay, but heare me,

  Your sence pursues not mine: either you are ignorant,

  Or seeme so craftily; and that's not good.

ISABELLA

  Let me be ignorant, and in nothing good,

  But graciously to know I am no better.

ANGELO

  Thus wisdome wishes to appeare most bright,

  When it doth taxe it selfe: As these blacke Masques

  Proclaime an en-shield beauty ten times louder

  Then beauty could displaied: But marke me,   1000

  To be receiued plaine, Ile speake more grosse:

  Your Brother is to dye.

ISABELLA So.

ANGELO

  And his offence is so, as it appeares,

  Accountant to the Law, vpon that paine.

ISABELLA True.

ANGELO

  Admit no other way to saue his life

  (As I subscribe not that, nor any other)

  But in the losse of question, that you, his Sister,

  Finding your selfe desir'd of such a person,   1010

  Whose creadit with the Iudge, or owne great place,

  Could fetch your Brother from the Manacles

  Of the all-binding-Law: and that there were

  No earthly meane to saue him, but that either

  You must lay downe the treasures of your body,

  To this supposd, or else to let him suffer:

  What would you doe?

ISABELLA

  As much for my poore Brother, as my selfe;

  That is: were I vnder the tearmes of death,

  Th'impression of keene whips, I'ld weare as Rubies, 1020

  And strip my selfe to death, as to a bed,

  That longing haue bin sicke for, ere I'ld yeeld

  My body vp to shame.

ANGELO Then must your brother die.

ISABELLA And 'twer the cheaper way:

  Better it were a brother dide at once,

  Then that a sister, by redeeming him

  Should die for euer.

ANGELO

    Were not you then as cruell as the Sentence,
1030   That you haue slander'd so?

ISABELLA

    Ignominie in ransome, and free pardon
    Are of two houses: lawfull mercie,
    Is nothing kin to fowle redemption.

ANGELO

    You seem'd of late to make the Law a tirant,
    And rather prou'd the sliding of your brother
    A merriment, then a vice.

ISABELLA

    Oh pardon me my Lord, it oft fals out
    To haue, what we would haue, we speake not what
      we meane;
    I something do excuse the thing I hate,
1040   For his aduantage that I dearely loue.

ANGELO

    We are all fraile.

ISABELLA   Else let my brother die,
    If not a fedarie but onely he
    Owe, and succeed thy weaknesse.

ANGELO   Nay, women are fraile too.

ISABELLA

    I, as the glasses where they view themselues,
    Which are as easie broke as they make formes:
    Women? Helpe heauen; men their creation marre
    In profiting by them: Nay, call vs ten times fraile,
    For we are soft, as our complexions are,
    And credulous to false prints.

ANGELO   I thinke it well:
1050   And from this testimonie of your owne sex
    (Since I suppose we are made to be no stronger
    Then faults may shake our frames) let me be bold;
    I do arrest your words. Be that you are,
    That is a woman; if you be more, you'r none.
    If you be one (as you are well exprest
    By all externall warrants) shew it now,
    By putting on the destin'd Liuerie.

ISABELLA

    I haue no tongue but one; gentle my Lord,
    Let me entreate you speake the former language.

1060 ANGELO Plainlie conceiue I loue you.

ISABELLA

    My brother did loue *Iuliet*,
    And you tell me that he shall die for it.

ANGELO

    He shall not *Isabell* if you giue me loue.

ISABELLA

    I know your vertue hath a licence in't,
    Which seemes a little fouler then it is,
    To plucke on others.

ANGELO   Beleeue me on mine Honor,
    My words expresse my purpose.

ISABELLA

    Ha? Little honor, to be much beleeu'd,
    And most pernitious purpose: Seeming, seeming.

    I will proclaime thee *Angelo*, looke for't.   1070
    Signe me a present pardon for my brother,
    Or with an out-stretcht throate Ile tell the world aloud
    What man thou art.

ANGELO   Who will beleeue thee *Isabell*?
    My vnsoild name, th'austeerenesse of my life,
    My vouch against you, and my place i'th State,
    Will so your accusation ouer-weigh,
    That you shall stifle in your owne report,
    And smell of calumnie. I haue begun,
    And now I giue my sensuall race, the reine,
    Fit thy consent to my sharpe appetite,   1080
    Lay by all nicetie, and prolixious blushes
    That banish what they sue for: Redeeme thy brother,
    By yeelding vp thy bodie to my will,
    Or else he must not onelie die the death,
    But thy vnkindnesse shall his death draw out
    To lingring sufferance: Answer me to morrow,
    Or by the affection that now guides me most,
    Ile proue a Tirant to him. As for you,
    Say what you can; my false, ore-weighs your true.

                                     Exit

ISABELLA

    To whom should I complaine? Did I tell this,   1090
    Who would beleeue me? O perilous mouthes
    That beare in them, one and the selfesame tongue,
    Either of condemnation, or approofe,
    Bidding the Law make curtsie to their will,
    Hooking both right and wrong to th'appetite,
    To follow as it drawes. Ile to my brother,
    Though he hath falne by prompture of the blood,
    Yet hath he in him such a minde of Honor,
    That had he twentie heads to tender downe
    On twentie bloodie blockes, hee'ld yeeld them vp,   1100
    Before his sister should her bodie stoope
    To such abhord pollution.
    Then *Isabell* liue chaste, and brother die;
    "More then our Brother, is our Chastitie.
    Ile tell him yet of *Angelo*'s request,
    And fit his minde to death, for his soules rest.   *Exit*

                       ❂

      Enter Duke (as a Friar), Claudio, and Prouost   **3.1**

DUKE   (Sc. 9)

    So then you hope of pardon from Lord *Angelo*?

CLAUDIO

    The miserable haue no other medicine
    But onely hope:
    I'haue hope to liue, and am prepar'd to die.   1110

DUKE

    Be absolute for death: either death or life
    Shall thereby be the sweeter. Reason thus with life:
    If I do loose thee, I do loose a thing
    That none but fooles would keepe: a breath thou art,
    Seruile to all the skyie-influences,
    That dost this habitation where thou keepst
    Hourely afflict: Meerely, thou art deaths foole,

For him thou labourst by thy flight to shun,
And yet runst toward him still. Thou art not noble,
1120 For all th'accommodations that thou bearst,
Are nurst by basenesse: Thou'rt by no meanes valiant,
For thou dost feare the soft and tender forke
Of a poore worme: thy best of rest is sleepe,
And that thou oft prouoakst, yet grosselie fearst
Thy death, which is no more. Thou art not thy selfe,
For thou exists on manie a thousand graines
That issue out of dust. Happie thou art not,
For what thou hast not, still thou striu'st to get,
And what thou hast forgetst. Thou art not certaine,
1130 For thy complexion shifts to strange effects,
After the Moone: If thou art rich, thou'rt poore,
For like an Asse, whose backe with Ingots bowes;
Thou bearst thy heauie riches but a iournie,
And death vnloads thee; Friend hast thou none.
For thine owne bowels which do call thee, sire,
The meere effusion of thy proper loines
Do curse the Gowt, Sapego, and the Rheume
For ending thee no sooner. Thou hast nor youth, nor
    age
But as it were an after-dinners sleepe
1140 Dreaming on both, for all thy blessed youth
Becomes as aged, and doth begge the almes
Of palsied-Eld: and when thou art old, and rich
Thou hast neither heate, affection, limbe, nor beautie
To make thy riches pleasant: what's in this
That beares the name of life? Yet in this life
Lie hid moe thousand deaths; yet death we feare
That makes these oddes, all euen.

CLAUDIO   I humblie thanke you.
To sue to liue, I finde I seeke to die,
And seeking death, finde life: Let it come on.

ISABELLA (within)
1150 What hoa? Peace heere; Grace, and good companie.

PROUOST
Who's there? Come in, the wish deserues a welcome.

DUKE (to Claudio)
Deere sir, ere long Ile visit you againe.

CLAUDIO Most holie Sir, I thanke you.
    Enter Isabella

ISABELLA
My businesse is a word or two with Claudio.

PROUOST
And verie welcom: looke Signior, here's your sister.

DUKE
Prouost, a word with you.

PROUOST   As manie as you please.
    The Duke and Prouost draw aside

DUKE
Bring me to heare them speake, where I may be
    conceal'd.
    They conceale themselues

CLAUDIO Now sister, what's the comfort?

ISABELLA
Why, as all comforts are: most good, most good
    indeede,

Lord *Angelo* hauing affaires to heauen   1160
Intends you for his swift Ambassador,
Where you shall be an euerlasting Leiger;
Therefore your best appointment make with speed,
To Morrow you set on.

CLAUDIO   Is there no remedie?

ISABELLA
None, but such remedie, as to saue a head
To cleaue a heart in twaine.

CLAUDIO But is there anie?

ISABELLA Yes brother, you may liue;
There is a diuellish mercie in the Iudge,
If you'l implore it, that will free your life,   1170
But fetter you till death.

CLAUDIO   Perpetuall durance?

ISABELLA
I iust, perpetuall durance, a restraint
Though all the worlds vastiditie you had
To a determin'd scope.

CLAUDIO   But in what nature?

ISABELLA
In such a one, as you consenting too't,
Would barke your honor from that trunke you beare,
And leaue you naked.

CLAUDIO   Let me know the point.

ISABELLA
Oh, I do feare thee *Claudio*, and I quake,
Least thou a feauorous life shouldst entertaine,
And six or seuen winters more respect   1180
Then a perpetuall Honor. Dar'st thou die?
The sence of death is most in apprehension,
And the poore Beetle that we treade vpon
In corporall sufferance, finds a pang as great,
As when a Giant dies.

CLAUDIO   Why giue you me this shame?
Thinke you I can a resolution fetch
From flowrie tendernesse? If I must die,
I will encounter darknesse as a bride,
And hugge it in mine armes.

ISABELLA
There spake my brother: there my fathers graue   1190
Did vtter forth a voice. Yes, thou must die:
Thou art too noble, to conserue a life
In base appliances. This outward sainted Deputie,
Whose setled visage, and deliberate word
Nips youth i'th head, and follies doth ennew
As Falcon doth the Fowle, is yet a diuell:
His filth within being cast, he would appeare
A pond, as deepe as hell.

CLAUDIO   The precize *Angelo*?

ISABELLA
Oh 'tis the cunning Liuerie of hell,
The damnest bodie to inuest, and couer   1200
In precize gardes; dost thou thinke *Claudio*,
If I would yeeld him my virginitie
Thou might'st be freed?

CLAUDIO   Oh heauens, it cannot be.

ISABELLA
  Yes, he would giu't thee; from this rank offence
  So to offend him still. This night's the time
  That I should do what I abhorre to name,
  Or else thou diest to morrow.
CLAUDIO Thou shalt not do't.
ISABELLA O, were it but my life,
1210 I'de throw it downe for your deliuerance
  As frankely as a pin.
CLAUDIO   Thankes deere *Isabell*.
ISABELLA
  Be readie *Claudio*, for your death to morrow.
CLAUDIO
  Yes. Has he affections in him,
  That thus can make him bite the Law by th'nose,
  When he would force it? Sure it is no sinne,
  Or of the deadly seuen it is the least.
ISABELLA Which is the least?
CLAUDIO
  If it were damnable, he being so wise,
  Why would he for the momentarie tricke
1220 Be perdurablie fin'de? Oh *Isabell*.
ISABELLA What saies my brother?
CLAUDIO Death is a fearefull thing.
ISABELLA And shamed life, a hatefull.
CLAUDIO
  I, but to die, and go we know not where,
  To lie in cold obstruction, and to rot,
  This sensible warme motion, to become
  A kneaded clod; And the delated spirit
  To bath in fierie floods, or to recide
  In thrilling Region of thicke-ribbed Ice,
1230 To be imprison'd in the viewlesse windes
  And blowne with restlesse violence round about
  The pendant world: or to be worse then worst
  Of those, that lawlesse and incertaine thought
  Imagine howling, 'tis too horrible.
  The weariest, and most loathed worldly life
  That Age, Ache, penury, and imprisonment
  Can lay on nature, is a Paradise
  To what we feare of death.
ISABELLA Alas, alas.
1240 CLAUDIO Sweet Sister, let me liue.
  What sinne you do, to saue a brothers life,
  Nature dispenses with the deede so farre,
  That it becomes a vertue.
ISABELLA   Oh you beast,
  Oh faithlesse Coward, oh dishonest wretch,
  Wilt thou be made a man, out of my vice?
  Is't not a kinde of Incest, to take life
  From thine owne sisters shame? What should I thinke,
  Heauen shield my Mother plaid my Father faire:
  For such a warped slip of wildernesse
1250 Nere issu'd from his blood. Take my defiance,
  Die, perish: Might but my bending downe
  Repreeue thee from thy fate, it should proceede.
  Ile pray a thousand praiers for thy death,
  No word to saue thee.

CLAUDIO Nay heare me *Isabell*.
ISABELLA Oh fie, fie, fie:
  Thy sinn's not accidentall, but a Trade;
  Mercy to thee would proue it selfe a Bawd,
  'Tis best that thou diest quickly.
        ⌈*She parts from Claudio*⌉
CLAUDIO Oh heare me *Isabella*.   1260
DUKE (*comming forward to Isabella*)
  Vouchsafe a word, yong sister, but one word.
ISABELLA What is your Will.
DUKE Might you dispense with your leysure, I would by
  and by haue some speech with you: the satisfaction I
  would require, is likewise your owne benefit.
ISABELLA I haue no superfluous leysure, my stay must be
  stolen out of other affaires: but I will attend you a
  while.
DUKE ⌈*standing aside with Claudio*⌉ Son, I haue ouer-heard
  what hath past between you & your sister. *Angelo* had   1270
  neuer the purpose to corrupt her; onely he hath made
  an assay of her vertue, to practise his iudgement with
  the disposition of natures. She (hauing the truth of
  honour in her) hath made him that gracious deniall,
  which he is most glad to receiue: I am Confessor to
  Angelo, and I know this to be true, therfore prepare
  your selfe to death: do not falsifie your resolution with
  hopes that are fallible, to morrow you must die, goe to
  your knees, and make ready.
CLAUDIO Let me ask my sister pardon, I am so out of loue   1280
  with life, that I will sue to be rid of it.
DUKE Hold you there: farewell:
        ⌈*Claudio ioynes Isabella*⌉
  Prouost, a word with you.
PROUOST (*comming forward*) What's your will (father?)
DUKE That now you are come, you wil be gone: leaue
  me a while with the Maid, my minde promises with
  my habit, no losse shall touch her by my company.
PROUOST In good time.   *Exit* ⌈*with Claudio*⌉
DUKE The hand that hath made you faire, hath made you
  good: the goodnes that is cheape in beauty, makes   1290
  beauty briefe in goodnes; but grace being the soule of
  your complexion, shall keepe the body of it euer faire:
  the assault that *Angelo* hath made to you, Fortune hath
  conuaid to my vnderstanding; and but that frailty hath
  examples for his falling, I should wonder at *Angelo*:
  how will you doe to content this Substitute, and to
  saue your Brother?
ISABELLA I am now going to resolue him: I had rather
  my brother die by the Law, then my sonne should be
  vnlawfullie borne. But (oh) how much is the good Duke   1300
  deceiu'd in *Angelo*: if euer he returne, and I can speake
  to him, I will open my lips in vaine, or discouer his
  gouernment.
DUKE That shall not be much amisse: yet, as the matter
  now stands, he will auoid your accusation: he made
  triall of you onelie. Therefore fasten your eare on my
  aduisings; to the loue I haue in doing good, a remedie
  presents it selfe. I doe make my selfe beleeue that you
  may most vprighteously do a poor wronged Lady a

1310 merited benefit; redeem your brother from the angry
Law; doe no staine to your owne gracious person, and
much please the absent Duke, if peraduenture he shall
euer returne to haue hearing of this businesse.

ISABELLA Let me heare you speake farther; I haue spirit
to do any thing that appeares not fowle in the truth of
my spirit.

DUKE Vertue is bold, and goodnes neuer fearefull: Haue
you not heard speake of *Mariana* the sister of *Fredericke*
the great Souldier, who miscarried at Sea?

1320 ISABELLA I haue heard of the Lady, and good words went
with her name.

DUKE Shee should this *Angelo* haue married: was affianced
to her oath, and the nuptiall appointed: between which
time of the contract, and limit of the solemnitie, her
brother *Fredericke* was wrackt at Sea, hauing in that
perished vessell, the dowry of his sister: but marke how
heauily this befell to the poore Gentlewoman, there she
lost a noble and renowned brother, in his loue toward
her, euer most kinde and naturall: with him the portion
1330 and sinew of her fortune, her marriage dowry: with
both, her combynate-husband, this well-seeming
Angelo.

ISABELLA Can this be so? did *Angelo* so leaue her?

DUKE Left her in her teares, & dried not one of them with
his comfort: swallowed his vowes whole, pretending in
her, discoueries of dishonor: in few, bestow'd her on
her owne lamentation, which she yet weares for his
sake: and he, a marble to her teares, is washed with
them, but relents not.

1340 ISABELLA What a merit were it in death to take this poore
maid from the world? what corruption in this life, that
it will let this man liue? But how out of this can shee
auaile?

DUKE It is a rupture that you may easily heale: and the
cure of it not onely saues your brother, but keepes you
from dishonor in doing it.

ISABELLA Shew me how (good Father.)

DUKE This fore-named Maid hath yet in her the continuance of her first affection: his vniust vnkindenesse
1350 (that in all reason should haue quenched her loue)
hath (like an impediment in the Current) made it more
violent and vnruly: Goe you to *Angelo*, answere his
requiring with a plausible obedience, agree with his
demands to the point: onely referre your selfe to this
aduantage; first, that your stay with him may not be
long: that the time may haue all shadow, and silence
in it: and the place answere to conuenience: this being
granted in course, and now followes all: wee shall
aduise this wronged maid to steed vp your appointment,
1360 goe in your place: if the encounter acknowledge it selfe
heereafter, it may compell him to her recompence; and
heare, by this is your brother saued, your honor
vntainted, the poore *Mariana* aduantaged, and the
corrupt Deputy scaled. The Maid will I frame, and make
fit for his attempt: if you thinke well to carry this as
you may, the doublenes of the benefit defends the deceit
from reproofe. What thinke you of it?

ISABELLA The image of it giues me content already, and
I trust it will grow to a most prosperous perfection.

DUKE It lies much in your holding vp: haste you speedily   1370
to *Angelo*, if for this night he intreat you to his bed,
giue him promise of satisfaction: I will presently to S.
Lukes, there at the moated-Grange recides this deiected
Mariana; at that place call vpon me, and dispatch with
Angelo, that it may be quickly.

ISABELLA I thank you for this comfort: fare you well good
father.   *Exit*

Enter Elbow, Clowne, Officers

ELBOW Nay, if there be no remedy for it, but that you
will needes buy and sell men and women like beasts,
we shall haue all the world drinke browne & white   1380
bastard.

DUKE Oh heauens, what stuffe is heere.

CLOWNE Twas neuer merry world since of two vsuries the
merriest was put downe, and the worser allow'd by
order of Law; a fur'd gowne to keepe him warme; and
furd with Foxe one Lamb-skins too, to signifie, that
craft being richer then Innocency, stands for the facing.

ELBOW Come your way sir: 'blesse you good Father Frier.

DUKE And you good Brother Father; what offence hath
this man made you, Sir?   1390

ELBOW Marry Sir, he hath offended the Law; and Sir, we
take him to be a Theefe too Sir: for wee haue found
vpon him Sir, a strange Pick-lock, which we haue sent
to the Deputie.

DUKE (*to Clowne*)
Fie, sirrah, a Bawd, a wicked bawd,
The euill that thou causest to be done,
That is thy meanes to liue. Do thou but thinke
What 'tis to cram a maw, or cloath a backe
From such a filthie vice: say to thy selfe,
From their abhominable and beastly touches   1400
I drinke, I eate, array my selfe, and liue:
Canst thou beleeue thy liuing is a life,
So stinkingly depending? Go mend, go mend.

CLOWNE Indeed, it do's stinke in some sort, Sir: But yet
Sir I would proue.

DUKE
Nay, if the diuell haue giuen thee proofs for sin
Thou wilt proue his. Take him to prison Officer:
Correction, and Instruction must both worke
Ere this rude beast will profit.

ELBOW He must before the Deputy Sir, he ha's giuen him   1410
warning: the Deputy cannot abide a Whore-master: if
he be a Whore-monger, and comes before him, he were
as good go a mile on his errand.

DUKE
That we were all, as some would seeme to bee
Free from our faults, or faults from seeming free.

ELBOW His necke will come to your wast, a Cord sir.

Enter Lucio

CLOWNE I spy comfort, I cry baile: Here's a Gentleman,
and a friend of mine.

LUCIO How now noble *Pompey*? What, at the wheels of
Cæsar? Art thou led in triumph? What is there none   1420

909

of *Pigmalions* Images newly made woman to bee had now, for putting the hand in the pocket, and extracting clutch'd? What reply? Ha? What saist thou to this Tune, Matter, and Method? Is't not drown'd i'th last raine? Ha? What saist thou Trot? Is the world as it was Man? Which is the way? Is it sad, and few words? Or how? The tricke of it?

DUKE Still thus, and thus: still worse?

1430 LUCIO How doth my deere Morsell, thy Mistris? Procures she still? Ha?

CLOWNE Troth sir, shee hath eaten vp all her beefe, and she is her selfe in the tub.

LUCIO Why 'tis good: It is the right of it: it must be so. Euer your fresh Whore, and your pouder'd Baud, an vnshun'd consequence, it must be so. Art going to prison *Pompey*?

CLOWNE Yes faith sir.

LUCIO Why 'tis not amisse *Pompey*: farewell: goe, say I sent thee thether: for debt *Pompey*? Or how?

1440 ELBOW For being a baud, for being a baud.

LUCIO Well, then imprison him: If imprisonment be the due of a baud, why 'tis his right. Baud is he doubtlesse, and of antiquity too: Baud borne. Farwell good *Pompey*: Commend me to the prison *Pompey*, you will turne good husband now *Pompey*, you will keepe the house.

CLOWNE I hope Sir, your good Worship wil be my baile?

LUCIO No indeed wil I not *Pompey*, it is not the wear: I will pray (*Pompey*) to encrease your bondage: If you take it not patiently, why, your mettle is the more:

1450 Adieu trustie *Pompey*. Blesse you Friar.

DUKE And you.

LUCIO Do's *Bridget* paint still, *Pompey*? Ha?

ELBOW (*to Clowne*) Come your waies sir, come.

CLOWNE (*to Lucio*) You will not baile me then Sir?

LUCIO Then *Pompey*, nor now: what newes abroad *Frier*? What newes?

ELBOW (*to Clowne*) Come your waies sir, come.

LUCIO Goe to kennell (*Pompey*) goe:

Exeunt Elbow, Clowne, Officers

What newes *Frier* of the Duke?

1460 DUKE I know none: can you tell me of any?

LUCIO Some say he is with the Emperor of *Russia*: other some, he is in *Rome*: but where is he thinke you?

DUKE I know not where: but wheresoeuer, I wish him well.

LUCIO It was a mad fantasticall tricke of him to steale from the State, and vsurpe the beggerie hee was neuer borne to: Lord *Angelo* Dukes it well in his absence: he puts transgression too't.

DUKE He do's well in't.

1470 LUCIO A little more lenitie to Lecherie would doe no harme in him: Something too crabbed that way, *Frier*.

DUKE It is too general a vice, and seueritie must cure it.

LUCIO Yes in good sooth, the vice is of a great kindred; it is well allied, but it is impossible to extirpe it quite, Frier, till eating and drinking be put downe. They say this *Angelo* was not made by Man and Woman, after this downe-right way of Creation: is it true, thinke you?

DUKE How should he be made then?

LUCIO Some report, a Sea-maid spawn'd him. Some, that he was begot betweene two Stock-fishes. But it is 1480 certaine, that when he makes water, his Vrine is congeal'd ice, that I know to bee true: and he is a motion vngeneratiue, that's infallible.

DUKE You are pleasant sir, and speake apace.

LUCIO Why, what a ruthlesse thing is this in him, for the rebellion of a Cod-peece, to take away the life of a man? Would the Duke that is absent haue done this? Ere he would haue hang'd a man for the getting a hundred Bastards, he would haue paide for the Nursing a thousand. He had some feeling of the sport, hee knew 1490 the seruice, and that instructed him to mercie.

DUKE I neuer heard the absent Duke much detected for Women, he was not enclin'd that way.

LUCIO Oh Sir, you are deceiu'd.

DUKE 'Tis not possible.

LUCIO Who, not the Duke? Yes, your beggar of fifty: and his vse was, to put a ducket in her Clack-dish; the Duke had Crochets in him. Hee would be drunke too, that let me informe you.

DUKE You do him wrong, surely.   1500

LUCIO Sir, I was an inward of his: a shie fellow was the Duke, and I beleeue I know the cause of his with-drawing.

DUKE What (I prethee) might be the cause?

LUCIO No, pardon: 'Tis a secret must bee lockt within the teeth and the lippes: but this I can let you vnderstand, the greater file of the subiect held the Duke to be wise.

DUKE Wise? Why no question but he was.

LUCIO A very superficiall, ignorant, vnweighing fellow.

DUKE Either this is Enuie in you, Folly, or mistaking: The 1510 very streame of his life, and the businesse he hath helmed, must vppon a warranted neede, giue him a better proclamation. Let him be but testimonied in his owne bringings forth, and hee shall appeare to the enuious, a Scholler, a Statesman, and a Soldier: therefore you speake vnskilfully: or, if your knowledge bee more, it is much darkned in your malice.

LUCIO Sir, I know him, and I loue him.

DUKE Loue talkes with better knowledge, & knowledge with dearer loue.   1520

LUCIO Come Sir, I know what I know.

DUKE I can hardly beleeue that, since you know not what you speake. But if euer the Duke returne (as our praiers are he may) let mee desire you to make your answer before him: if it bee honest you haue spoke, you haue courage to maintaine it; I am bound to call vppon you, and I pray you your name?

LUCIO Sir my name is *Lucio*, wel known to the Duke.

DUKE He shall know you better Sir, if I may liue to report you.   1530

LUCIO I feare you not.

DUKE O, you hope the Duke will returne no more: or you imagine me to vnhurtfull an opposite: but indeed I can doe you little harme: You'll for-sweare this againe.

LUCIO Ile be hang'd first: Thou art deceiu'd in mee Friar.

But no more of this: Canst thou tell if *Claudio* die to morrow, or no?

DUKE Why should he die Sir?

1540 LUCIO Why? For filling a bottle with a Tunne-dish: I would the Duke we talke of were return'd againe: this vngenitur'd Agent will vn-people the Prouince with Continencie. Sparrowes must not build in his house-eeues, because they are lecherous: The Duke yet would haue darke deeds darkelie answered, hee would neuer bring them to light: would hee were return'd. Marrie this *Claudio* is condemned for vntrussing. Farwell good Friar, I prethee pray for me: The Duke (I say to thee againe) would eate Mutton on Fridaies. He's not past it, yet (and I say to thee) hee would mouth with a 1550 beggar, though she smelt browne-bread and Garlicke: say that I said so: Farewell.   *Exit*

DUKE

No might, nor greatnesse in mortality
Can censure scape: Back-wounding calumnie
The whitest vertue strikes. What King so strong,
Can tie the gall vp in the slanderous tong?

    Enter Escalus, Prouost, and Bawd

But who comes heere?

ESCALUS (*to Prouost*) Go, away with her to prison.

BAWD Good my Lord be good to mee, your Honor is accounted a mercifull man: good my Lord.

1560 ESCALUS Double, and trebble admonition, and still forfeite in the same kinde? This would make mercy sweare and play the Tirant.

PROUOST A Bawd of eleuen yeares continuance, may it please your Honor.

BAWD My Lord, this is one *Lucio's* information against me, Mistris *Kate Keepe-downe* was with childe by him in the Dukes time, he promis'd her marriage: his Childe is a yeere and a quarter olde come *Philip* and *Iacob*: I haue kept it my selfe; and see how hee goes about to 1570 abuse me.

ESCALUS That fellow is a fellow of much License: Let him be call'd before vs, Away with her to prison: Goe too, no more words. Prouost, my Brother *Angelo* will not be alter'd, *Claudio* must die to morrow: Let him be furnish'd with Diuines, and haue all charitable preparation. If my brother wrought by my pitie, it should not be so with him.

PROUOST So please you, this Friar hath beene with him, and aduis'd him for th'entertainment of death.

    ⌈*Exeunt Prouost and Bawd*⌉

1580 ESCALUS Good'euen, good Father.

DUKE Blisse, and goodnesse on you.

ESCALUS Of whence are you?

DUKE

Not of this Countrie, though my chance is now
To vse it for my time: I am a brother
Of gracious Order, late come from the Sea,
In speciall businesse from his Holinesse.

ESCALUS What newes abroad i'th World?

DUKE None, but that there is so great a Feauor on goodnesse, that the dissolution of it must cure it.

Noueltie is onely in request, and it is as dangerous to 1590 be aged in any kinde of course, as it is vertuous to be inconstant in any vndertaking. There is scarse truth enough aliue to make Societies secure, but Securitie enough to make Fellowships accurst: Much vpon this riddle runs the wisedome of the world: This newes is old enough, yet it is euerie daies newes. I pray you Sir, of what disposition was the Duke?

ESCALUS One, that aboue all other strifes, contended especially to know himselfe.

DUKE What pleasure was he giuen to?   1600

ESCALUS Rather reioycing to see another merry, then merrie at anie thing which profest to make him reioice. A Gentleman of all temperance. But leaue wee him to his euents, with a praier they may proue prosperous, & let me desire to know, how you finde *Claudio* prepar'd? I am made to vnderstand, that you haue lent him visitation.

DUKE He professes to haue receiued no sinister measure from his Iudge, but most willingly humbles himselfe to the determination of Iustice: yet had he framed to 1610 himselfe (by the instruction of his frailty) manie deceyuing promises of life, which I (by my good leisure) haue discredited to him, and now is he resolu'd to die.

ESCALUS You haue paid the heauens your Function, and the prisoner the verie debt of your Calling. I haue labour'd for the poore Gentleman, to the extremest shore of my modestie, but my brother-Iustice haue I found so seuere, that he hath forc'd me to tell him, hee is indeede Iustice.

DUKE If his owne life, answere the straitnesse of his 1620 proceeding, it shall become him well: wherein if he chance to faile he hath sentenc'd himselfe.

ESCALUS I am going to visit the prisoner, Fare you well.

DUKE Peace be with you.   *Exit Escalus*

He who the sword of Heauen will beare,
Should be as holy, as seueare:
Patterne in himselfe to know,
Grace to stand, and Vertue go:
More, nor lesse to others paying,
Then by selfe-offences weighing.   1630
Shame to him, whose cruell striking,
Kils for faults of his owne liking:
Twice trebble shame on *Angelo*,
To weede my vice, and let his grow.
Oh, what may Man within him hide,
Though Angel on the outward side?
How may likenesse made in crimes,
Make my practise on the Times,
To draw with ydle Spiders strings
Most ponderous and substantiall things?   1640
Craft against vice, I must applie.
With *Angelo* to night shall lye
His old betroathed (but despised:)
So disguise shall by th'disguised
Pay with falshood, false exacting,
And performe an olde contracting.   *Exit*

4.1
(Sc. 10)

Mariana ⌈discouer'd⌉ with a Boy singing

Song

BOY   *Take, oh take those lips away,*
     That so sweetly were forsworne,
     And those eyes: the breake of day
1650   *Lights that doe mislead the Morne;*
     But my kisses bring againe, bring againe,
     Seales of loue, though seal'd in vaine, seal'd in vaine.

Enter Duke (as a Frier)

MARIANA
Breake off thy song, and haste thee quick away,
Here comes a man of comfort, whose aduice
Hath often still'd my brawling discontent.   *Exit Boy*
I cry you mercie, Sir, and well could wish
You had not found me here so musicall.
Let me excuse me, and beleeue me so,
My mirth it much displeas'd, but pleas'd my woe.

DUKE
1660 'Tis good; though Musick oft hath such a charme
To make bad, good; and good prouoake to harme.
I pray you tell me, hath any body enquir'd for mee
here to day; much vpon this time haue I promis'd here
to meete.

MARIANA You haue not bin enquir'd after: I haue sat
here all day.

Enter Isabell

DUKE I doe constantly beleeue you: the time is come euen
now. I shall craue your forbearance alittle, may be I
will call vpon you anone for some aduantage to your
1670 selfe.

MARIANA I am always bound to you.   *Exit*
DUKE Very well met, and well come:
What is the newes from this good Deputie?

ISABELLA
He hath a Garden circummur'd with Bricke,
Whose westerne side is with a Vineyard back't;
And to that Vineyard is a planched gate,
That makes his opening with this bigger Key:
This other doth command a little doore,
Which from the Vineyard to the Garden leades,
1680 There haue I made my promise,
Vpon the heauy midle of the night,
To call vpon him.

DUKE
But shall you on your knowledge find this way?

ISABELLA
I haue t'ane a due, and wary note vpon't,
With whispering, and most guiltie diligence,
In action all of precept, he did show me
The way twice ore.

DUKE   Are there no other tokens
Betweene you 'greed, concerning her obseruance?

ISABELLA
No: none but onely a repaire ith' darke,
1690 And that I haue possest him, my most stay
Can be but briefe: for I haue made him know,

I haue a Seruant comes with me along
That staies vpon me; whose perswasion is,
I come about my Brother.

DUKE   'Tis well borne vp.
I haue not yet made knowne to *Mariana*
A word of this: what hoa, within; come forth,

Enter Mariana

(*To Mariana*) I pray you be acquainted with this Maid,
She comes to doe you good.

ISABELLA   I doe desire the like.

DUKE (*to Mariana*)
Do you perswade your selfe that I respect you?

MARIANA
Good Frier, I know you do, and so haue found it.   1700

DUKE
Take then this your companion by the hand
Who hath a storie readie for your eare:
I shall attend your leisure, but make haste,
The vaporous night approaches.

MARIANA (*to Isabella*)   Wilt please you walke aside.
⌈*Exit Mariana and Isabella*⌉

DUKE
Oh Place, and greatnes: millions of false eies
Are stucke vpon thee: volumes of report
Run with their false, and most contrarious Quest
Vpon thy doings: thousand escapes of wit
Make thee the father of their idle dreame,
And racke thee in their fancies.
⌈*Enter Mariana and Isabella*⌉

            Welcome, how agreed?   1710

ISABELLA
Shee'll take the enterprize vpon her father,
If you aduise it.

DUKE   It is not my consent,
But my entreaty too.

ISABELLA (*to Mariana*) Little haue you to say
When you depart from him, but soft and low,
Remember now my brother.

MARIANA   Feare me not.

DUKE
Nor gentle daughter, feare you not at all:
He is your husband on a pre-contract:
To bring you thus together 'tis no sinne,
Sith that the Iustice of your title to him
Doth flourish the deceit. Come, let vs goe,   1720
Our Corne's to reape, for yet our Tilthes to sow.

            Exeunt

Enter Prouost and Clowne   **4.2**
PROUOST Come hither sirha; can you cut off a mans head?   **(Sc. 11)**
CLOWNE If the man be a Bachelor Sir, I can: But if he be
a married man, he's his wiues head, and I can neuer
cut off a womans head.
PROUOST Come sir, leaue me your snatches, and yeeld
mee a direct answere. To morrow morning are to die
Claudio and *Barnardine*: heere is in our prison a common
executioner, who in his office lacks a helper, if you will

1730 take it on you to assist him, it shall redeeme you from
your Gyues: if not, you shall haue your full time of
imprisonment, and your deliuerance with an vnpittied
whipping; for you haue beene a notorious bawd.

CLOWNE Sir, I haue beene an vnlawfull bawd, time out
of minde, but yet I will bee content to be a lawfull
hangman: I would bee glad to receiue some instruction
from my fellow partner.

PROUOST What hoa, *Abhorson*: where's *Abhorson* there?
Enter Abhorson

ABHORSON Doe you call sir?

1740 PROUOST Sirha, here's a fellow will helpe you to morrow
in your execution: if you thinke it meet, compound
with him by the yeere, and let him abide here with
you, if not, vse him for the present, and dismisse him,
hee cannot plead his estimation with you: he hath
beene a Bawd.

ABHORSON A Bawd Sir? fie vpon him, he will discredit our
mysterie.

PROUOST Goe too Sir, you waigh equallie: a feather will
turne the Scale.   *Exit*

1750 CLOWNE Pray sir, by your good fauor: for surely sir, a
good fauor you haue, but that you haue a hanging
look: Doe you call sir, your occupation a Mysterie?

ABHORSON I, Sir, a Misterie.

CLOWNE Painting Sir, I haue heard say, is a Misterie; and
your Whores sir, being members of my occupation,
vsing painting, do proue my Occupation, a Misterie:
but what Misterie there should be in hanging, if I
should be hang'd, I cannot imagine.

ABHORSON Sir, it is a Misterie.

1760 CLOWNE Proofe.

ABHORSON Euerie true mans apparrell fits your Theefe.

CLOWNE If it be too little for your theefe, your true man
thinkes it bigge enough. If it bee too bigge for your
Theefe, your Theefe thinkes it little enough: So euerie
true mans apparrell fits your Theefe.
Enter Prouost

PROUOST Are you agreed?

CLOWNE Sir, I will serue him: For I do finde your Hangman
is a more penitent Trade then your Bawd: he doth
oftner aske forgiuenesse.

1770 PROUOST (*to Abhorson*) You sirrah, prouide your blocke
and your Axe to morrow, foure a clocke.

ABHORSON (*to Clowne*) Come on (Bawd) I will instruct thee
in my Trade: follow.

CLOWNE I do desire to learne sir: and I hope, if you haue
occasion to vse me for your owne turne, you shall finde
me y'are. For truly sir, for your kindnesse, I owe you
a good turne.

PROUOST
Call hether *Barnardine* and *Claudio*:
Exeunt Abhorson and Clowne
Th'one has my pitie; not a iot the other,

1780 Being a Murtherer, though he were my brother.
Enter Claudio
Looke, here's the Warrant *Claudio*, for thy death,

'Tis now dead midnight, and by eight to morrow
Thou must be made immortall. Where's *Barnardine*?

CLAUDIO
As fast lock'd vp in sleepe, as guiltlesse labour,
When it lies starkely in the Trauellers bones,
He will not wake.

PROUOST   Who can do good on him?
Well, go, prepare your selfe.
Knocking within
                                    But harke, what noise?
Heauen giue your spirits comfort: *Exit Claudio*
⌈*Knocking againe*⌉
                                    by, and by,
I hope it is some pardon, or repreeue
For the most gentle *Claudio*.
Enter Duke (as a Friar)
                            Welcome Father.   1790

DUKE
The best, and wholsomst spirits of the night,
Inuellop you, good Prouost: who call'd heere of late?

PROUOST None since the Curphew rung.

DUKE Not *Isabell*?

PROUOST No.

DUKE They will then er't be long.

PROUOST What comfort is for *Claudio*?

DUKE There's some in hope.

PROUOST It is a bitter Deputie.

DUKE
Not so, not so: his life is paralel'd   1800
Euen with the stroke and line of his great Iustice:
He doth with holie abstinence subdue
That in himselfe, which he spurres on his powre
To qualifie in others: were he meal'd with that
Which he corrects, then were he tirrannous,
But this being so, he's iust.
Knocking within
                            Now are they come.
⌈*Prouost goes to a doore*⌉
This is a gentle Prouost, sildome when
The steeled Gaoler is the friend of men:
Knocking within
(*To Prouost*) How now? what noise? That spirit's
possest with hast,
That wounds th'vnlisting Posterne with these strokes. 1810

PROUOST
There he must stay vntil the Officer
Arise to let him in: he is call'd vp.

DUKE
Haue you no countermand for *Claudio* yet?
But he must die to morrow?

PROUOST   None Sir, none.

DUKE
As neere the dawning Prouost, as it is,
You shall heare more ere Morning.

PROUOST   Happely
You something know: yet I beleeue there comes
No countermand: no such example haue we:

913

1820 Besides, vpon the verie siege of Iustice,
Lord *Angelo* hath to the publike eare
Profest the contrarie.
    Enter a Messenger
This is his Lords. man.
⌈DUKE⌉ And heere comes *Claudio*'s pardon.
MESSENGER (*giuing a paper to Prouost*) My Lord hath sent
you this note, and by mee this further charge; That
you swerue not from the smallest Article of it, neither
in time, matter, or other circumstance. Good morrow:
for as I take it, it is almost day.
PROUOST I shall obey him.   *Exit Messenger*
DUKE (*aside*)
1830 This is his Pardon purchas'd by such sin,
For which the Pardoner himselfe is in:
Hence hath offence his quicke celeritie,
When it is borne in high Authority.
When Vice makes Mercie; Mercie's so extended,
That for the faults loue, is th'offender friended.
Now Sir, what newes?
PROUOST I told you: Lord *Angelo* (be-like) thinking me
remisse in mine Office, awakens mee with this vnwonted
putting on, methinks strangely: For he hath not vs'd
1840 it before.
DUKE Pray you let's heare.
⌈PROUOST⌉ (*reading the Letter*) *Whatsoeuer you may heare to
the contrary, let Claudio be executed by foure of the clocke,
and in the afternoone Bernardine: For my better
satisfaction, let mee haue Claudios head sent me by fiue.
Let this be duely performed with a thought that more
depends on it, then we must yet deliuer. Thus faile not to
doe your Office, as you will answere it at your perill.*
What say you to this Sir?
1850 DUKE What is that *Barnardine*, who is to be executed in
th'afternoone?
PROUOST A Bohemian borne: But here nurst vp & bred,
one that is a prisoner nine yeeres old.
DUKE How came it, that the absent Duke had not either
deliuer'd him to his libertie, or executed him? I haue
heard it was euer his manner to do so.
PROUOST His friends still wrought Repreeues for him: And
indeed his fact till now in the gouernment of Lord
Angelo, came not to an vndoubtfull proofe.
1860 DUKE It is now apparant?
PROUOST Most manifest, and not denied by himselfe.
DUKE Hath he borne himselfe penitently in prison? How
seemes he to be touch'd?
PROUOST A man that apprehends death no more dreadfully, but as a drunken sleepe, carelesse, wreaklesse,
and fearelesse of what's past, present, or to come:
insensible of mortality, and desperately mortall.
DUKE He wants aduice.
PROUOST He wil heare none: he hath euermore had the
1870 liberty of the prison: giue him leaue to escape hence,
hee would not. Drunke many times a day, if not many
daies entirely drunke. We haue verie oft awak'd him,
as if to carrie him to execution, and shew'd him a
seeming warrant for it, it hath not moued him at all.
DUKE More of him anon: There is written in your brow

Prouost, honesty and constancie; if I reade it not truly,
my ancient skill beguiles me: but in the boldnes of my
cunning, I will lay my selfe in hazard: *Claudio*, whom
heere you haue warrant to execute, is no greater forfeit
to the Law, then *Angelo* who hath sentenc'd him. To 1880
make you vnderstand this in a manifested effect, I craue
but foure daies respit: for the which, you are to do me
both a present, and a dangerous courtesie.
PROUOST Pray Sir, in what?
DUKE In the delaying death.
PROUOST Alacke, how may I do it? Hauing the houre
limited, and an expresse command, vnder penaltie, to
deliuer his head in the view of *Angelo*? I may make my
case as *Claudio*'s, to crosse this in the smallest.
DUKE By the vow of mine Order, I warrant you, if my 1890
instructions may be your guide, let this *Barnardine* be
this morning executed, and his head borne to *Angelo*.
PROUOST *Angelo* hath seene them both, and will discouer
the fauour.
DUKE Oh, death's a great disguiser, and you may adde to
it; Shaue the head, and tie the beard, and say it was
the desire of the penitent to be so bar'de before his
death: you know the course is common. If any thing
fall to you vpon this, more then thankes and good
fortune, by the Saint whom I professe, I will plead 1900
against it with my life.
PROUOST Pardon me, good Father, it is against my oath.
DUKE Were you sworne to the Duke, or to the Deputie?
PROUOST To him, and to his Substitutes.
DUKE You will thinke you haue made no offence, if the
Duke auouch the iustice of your dealing?
PROUOST But what likelihood is in that?
DUKE Not a resemblance, but a certainty; yet since I see
you fearfull, that neither my coate, integrity, nor
perswasion, can with ease attempt you, I wil go further 1910
then I meant, to plucke all feares out of you. (*Shewing
a Letter*) Looke you Sir, heere is the hand and Seale of
the Duke: you know the Charracter I doubt not, and
the Signet is not strange to you?
PROUOST I know them both.
DUKE The Contents of this, is the returne of the Duke;
you shall anon ouer-reade it at your pleasure: where
you shall finde within these two daies, he wil be heere.
This is a thing that *Angelo* knowes not, for hee this
very day receiues letters of strange tenor, perchance of 1920
the Dukes death, perchance entering into some
Monasterie, but by chance nothing of what is writ.
Looke, th'vnfolding Starre calles vp the Shepheard; put
not your selfe into amazement, how these things should
be; all difficulties are but easie when they are knowne.
Call your executioner, and off with *Barnardines* head:
I will giue him a present shrift, and aduise him for a
better place. Yet you are amaz'd, but this shall
absolutely resolue you: Come away, it is almost cleere
dawne.   *Exeunt* 1930

Enter Clowne   **4.3**
CLOWNE I am as well acquainted heere, as I was in our (Sc. 12)
house of profession: one would thinke it were Mistris

Ouer-dons owne house, for heere be manie of her olde
Customers. First, here's yong Mr *Rash*, hee's in for a
commoditie of browne paper, and olde Ginger, nine
score and seuenteene pounds, of which hee made fiue
Markes readie money: marrie then, Ginger was not
much in request, for the olde Women were all dead.
Then is there heere one Mr *Caper*, at the suite of Master
1940 *Three-Pile* the Mercer, for some foure suites of Peach-
colour'd Satten, which now peaches him a beggar.
Then haue we heere, yong *Dizie*, and yong Mr *Deepe-
vow*, and Mr *Copperspurre*, and Mr *Starue-Lackey* the
Rapier and dagger man, and yong *Drop-heire* that kild
lustie *Pudding*, and Mr *Forthright* the Tilter, and braue
Mr *Shootie* the great Traueller, and wilde *Halfe-Canne*
that stabb'd Pots, and I thinke fortie more, all great
doers in our Trade, and are now for the Lords sake.

    Enter Abhorson

ABHORSON Sirrah, bring *Barnardine* hether.
1950 CLOWNE Mr *Barnardine*, you must rise and be hang'd, M^r
Barnardine.

ABHORSON What hoa *Barnardine*.

BARNARDINE (*within*) A pox o'your throats: who makes
that noyse there? What are you?

CLOWNE Your friends Sir, the Hangman: You must be so
good Sir to rise, and be put to death.

BARNARDINE Away you Rogue, away, I am sleepie.

ABHORSON Tell him he must awake, and that quickly too.

CLOWNE Pray Master *Barnardine*, awake till you are
1960 executed, and sleepe afterwards.

ABHORSON Go in to him, and fetch him out.

CLOWNE He is comming Sir, he is comming: I heare his
Straw russle.

ABHORSON Is the Axe vpon the blocke, sirrah?

CLOWNE Verie readie Sir.

    Enter Barnardine

BARNARDINE How now *Abhorson*? What's the newes with
you?

ABHORSON Truly Sir, I would desire you to clap into your
prayers: for looke you, the Warrants come.

1970 BARNARDINE You Rogue, I haue bin drinking all night, I
am not fitted for't.

CLOWNE Oh, the better Sir: for he that drinkes all night,
and is hanged betimes in the morning, may sleepe the
sounder all the next day.

    Enter Duke (as a Friar)

ABHORSON (*to Barnardine*) Looke you Sir, heere comes your
ghostly Father: do we iest now thinke you?

DUKE (*to Barnardine*) Sir, induced by my charitie, and
hearing how hastily you are to depart, I am come to
aduise you, comfort you, and pray with you.

1980 BARNARDINE Friar, not I: I haue bin drinking hard all
night, and I will haue more time to prepare mee, or
they shall beat out my braines with billets: I will not
consent to die this day, that's certaine.

DUKE
  Oh sir, you must: and therefore I beseech you
  Looke forward on the iournie you shall go.

BARNARDINE I sweare I will not die to day for anie mans
perswasion.

DUKE But heare you:

BARNARDINE Not a word: if you haue anie thing to say
to me, come to my Ward: for thence will not I to day. 1990
                              Exit

DUKE
  Vnfit to liue, or die: oh grauell heart.
  After him (Fellowes) bring him to the blocke.
           Exeunt Abhorson and Clowne

    Enter Prouost

PROUOST
  Now Sir, how do you finde the prisoner?

DUKE
  A creature vnpre-par'd, vnmeet for death,
  And to transport him in the minde he is,
  Were damnable.

PROUOST   Heere in the prison, Father,
  There died this morning of a cruell Feauor,
  One *Ragozine*, a most notorious Pirate,
  A man of *Claudio*'s yeares: his beard, and head
  Iust of his colour. What if we do omit   2000
  This Reprobate, til he were wel enclin'd,
  And satisfie the Deputie with the visage
  Of *Ragozine*, more like to *Claudio*?

DUKE
  Oh, 'tis an accident that heauen prouides:
  Dispatch it presently, the houre drawes on
  Prefixt by *Angelo*: See this be done,
  And sent according to command, whiles I
  Perswade this rude wretch willingly to die.

PROUOST
  This shall be done (good Father) presently:
  But *Barnardine* must die this afternoone,   2010
  And how shall we continue *Claudio*,
  To saue me from the danger that might come,
  If he were knowne aliue?

DUKE   Let this be done,
  Put them in secret holds, both *Barnardine* and *Claudio*,
  Ere twice the Sun hath made his iournall greeting
  To yonder generation, you shal finde
  Your safetie manifested.

PROUOST   I am your free dependant.

DUKE
  Quicke, dispatch, and send the head to *Angelo*.
                         Exit Prouost

  Now wil I write Letters to *Angelo*,
  (The Prouost he shal beare them) whose contents   2020
  Shal witnesse to him I am neere at home:
  And that by great Iniunctions I am bound
  To enter publikely: him Ile desire
  To meet me at the consecrated Fount,
  A League below the Citie: and from thence,
  By cold gradation, and weale-ballanc'd forme,
  We shal proceed with *Angelo*.

    Enter Prouost, with Ragozines head

PROUOST
  Heere is the head, Ile carrie it my selfe.

DUKE
  Conuenient is it: Make a swift returne,

2030 For I would commune with you of such things,
That want no eare but yours.

PROUOST Ile make all speede.   *Exit*

ISABELLA (*within*) Peace hoa, be heere.

DUKE
The tongue of *Isabell*. She's come to know,
If yet her brothers pardon be come hither:
But I will keepe her ignorant of her good,
To make her heauenly comforts of dispaire,
When it is least expected.

ISABELLA ⌈*within*⌉   Hoa, by your leaue.
⌈*Enter Isabella*⌉

DUKE
Good morning to you, faire, and gracious daughter.

ISABELLA
2040 The better giuen me by so holy a man,
Hath yet the Deputie sent my brothers pardon?

DUKE
He hath releasd him, *Isabell*, from the world,
His head is off, and sent to *Angelo*.

ISABELLA
Nay, but it is not so.

DUKE   It is no other,
Shew your wisedome daughter in your close patience.

ISABELLA
Oh, I wil to him, and plucke out his eies.

DUKE
You shal not be admitted to his sight.

ISABELLA (*weeping*)
Vnhappie *Claudio*, wretched *Isabell*,
Iniurious world, most damned *Angelo*.

DUKE
2050 This nor hurts him, nor profits you a iot,
Forbeare it therefore, giue your cause to heauen.
Marke what I say, which you shal finde
By euery sillable a faithful veritie.
The Duke comes home to morrow: nay drie your eyes,
One of our Couent, and his Confessor
Giues me this instance: Already he hath carried
Notice to *Escalus* and *Angelo*,
Who do prepare to meete him at the gates,
There to giue vp their powre: If you can pace your
        wisdome,
2060 In that good path that I would wish it go,
And you shal haue your bosome on this wretch,
Grace of the Duke, reuenges to your heart,
And general Honor.

ISABELLA   I am directed by you.

DUKE
This Letter then to Friar *Peter* giue,
'Tis that he sent me of the Dukes returne:
Say, by this token, I desire his companie
At *Mariana*'s house to night. Her cause, and yours
Ile perfect him withall, and he shal bring you
Before the Duke; and to the head of *Angelo*
2070 Accuse him home and home. For my poore selfe,
I am combined by a sacred Vow,
And shall be absent. (*Giuing the Letter*) Wend you
        with this Letter:

Command these fretting waters from your eies
With a light heart; trust not my holie Order
If I peruert your course:
    Enter Lucio
                        whose heere?

LUCIO   Good'euen;
Frier, where's the Prouost?

DUKE   Not within Sir.

LUCIO Oh prettie *Isabella*, I am pale at mine heart, to see
thine eyes so red: thou must be patient; I am faine to
dine and sup with water and bran: I dare not for my
head fill my belly. One fruitful Meale would set mee 2080
too't: but they say the Duke will be heere to Morrow.
By my troth *Isabell* I lou'd thy brother, if the olde
fantastical Duke of darke corners had bene at home,
he had liued.   ⌈*Exit Isabella*⌉

DUKE Sir, the Duke is marueilous little beholding to your
reports, but the best is, he liues not in them.

LUCIO Friar, thou knowest not the Duke so wel as I do:
he's a better woodman then thou tak'st him for.

DUKE Well: you'l answer this one day. Fare ye well.

LUCIO Nay tarrie, Ile go along with thee, I can tel thee 2090
pretty tales of the Duke.

DUKE You haue told me too many of him already sir if
they be true: if not true, none were enough.

LUCIO I was once before him for getting a Wench with
childe.

DUKE Did you such a thing?

LUCIO Yes marrie did I; but I was faine to forswear it,
They would else haue married me to the rotten Medler.

DUKE Sir your company is fairer then honest, rest you
well.   2100

LUCIO By my troth Ile go with thee to the lanes end: if
baudy talke offend you, we'el haue very litle of it: nay
Friar, I am a kind of Burre, I shal sticke.   *Exeunt*

Enter Angelo & Escalus   **4.4**

ESCALUS Euery Letter he hath writ, hath disuouch'd other. **(Sc. 13)**

ANGELO In most vneuen and distracted manner, his
actions show much like to madnesse, pray heauen his
wisedome bee not tainted: and why meet him at the
gates and redeliuer our authorities there?

ESCALUS I ghesse not.

ANGELO And why should wee proclaime it in an howre 2110
before his entring, that if any craue redresse of iniustice,
they should exhibit their petitions in the street?

ESCALUS He showes his reason for that: to haue a dispatch
of Complaints, and to deliuer vs from deuices heereafter,
which shall then haue no power to stand against vs.

ANGELO
Well: I beseech you let it bee proclaim'd:
Betimes i'th' morne, Ile call you at your house:
Giue notice to such men of sort and suite
As are to meete him.

ESCALUS I shall sir: fareyouwell.   2120

ANGELO Good night.   *Exit Escalus*
This deede vnshapes me quite, makes me vnpregnant
And dull to all proceedings. A deflowred maid,
And by an eminent body, that enforc'd

The Law against it? But that her tender shame
Will not proclaime against her maiden losse,
How might she tongue me? yet reason dares her no,
For my Authority beares of a credent bulke,
That no particular scandall once can touch
2130 But it confounds the breather. He should haue liu'd,
Saue that his riotous youth with dangerous sense
Might in the times to come haue ta'ne reuenge
By so receiuing a dishonor'd life
With ransome of such shame: would yet he had liued.
Alack, when once our grace we haue forgot,
Nothing goes right, we would, and we would not.
                                                Exit

4.5   *Enter Duke (in his owne habit) and Frier Peter*
(Sc. 14) DUKE
These Letters at fit time deliuer me.
The Prouost knowes our purpose and our plot,
The matter being a foote, keepe your instruction
2140 And hold you euer to our speciall drift,
Though sometimes you doe blench from this to that
As cause doth minister: Goe call at *Flauio*'s house,
And tell him where I stay: giue the like notice
To *Valentius*, *Rowland*, and to *Crassus*,
And bid them bring the Trumpets to the gate:
But send me *Flauius* first.
FRIER   It shall be speeded well.
                                                Exit

          Enter Varrius
DUKE
I thank thee *Varrius*, thou hast made good hast,
Come, we will walke: There's other of our friends
Will greet vs heere anon: my gentle *Varrius*.   *Exeunt*

4.6   *Enter Isabella and Mariana*
(Sc. 15) ISABELLA
2150 To speake so indirectly I am loath,
I would say the truth, but to accuse him so
That is your part, yet I am aduis'd to doe it,
He saies, to vaile full purpose.
MARIANA   Be rul'd by him.
ISABELLA
Besides he tells me, that if peraduenture
He speake against me on the aduerse side,
I should not thinke it strange, for 'tis a physicke
That's bitter, to sweet end.
          Enter Frier Peter
MARIANA I would *Frier Peter*
ISABELLA Oh peace, the *Frier* is come.
FRIER PETER
2160 Come I haue found you out a stand most fit,
Where you may haue such vantage on the *Duke*
He shall not passe you: Twice haue the Trumpets
          sounded.
The generous, and grauest Citizens
Haue hent the gates, and very neere vpon
The *Duke* is entring: Therefore hence away.   *Exeunt*

Enter ⌈at one doore⌉ Duke, Varrius, Lords; ⌈at   5.1
another doore⌉ Angelo, Esculus, Lucio, Citizens,   (Sc. 16)
⌈*Officers*⌉
DUKE (*to Angelo*)
My very worthy Cosen, fairely met,
(*To Escalus*) Our old, and faithfull friend, we are glad
     to see you.
ANGELO *and* ESCALUS
Happy returne be to your royall grace.
DUKE
Many and harty thankings to you both:
We haue made enquiry of you, and we heare   2170
Such goodnesse of your Iustice, that our soule
Cannot but yeeld you forth to publique thankes
Forerunning more requitall.
ANGELO   You make my bonds still greater.
DUKE
Oh your desert speaks loud, & I should wrong it
To locke it in the wards of couert bosome
When it deserues with characters of brasse
A forted residence 'gainst the tooth of time,
And razure of obliuion: Giue me your hand
And let the Subiect see, to make them know
That outward curtesies would faine proclaime   2180
Fauours that keepe within: Come *Escalus*,
You must walke by vs, on our other hand:
And good supporters are you.
          ⌈*They walke forward.*⌉
          Enter Frier Peter and Isabella
FRIER PETER
Now is your time. Speake loud, and kneele before him.
ISABELLA (*kneeling*)
Iustice, O royall *Duke*, vaile your regard
Vpon a wrong'd (I would faine haue said a Maid)
Oh worthy Prince, dishonor not your eye
By throwing it on any other obiect,
Till you haue heard me, in my true complaint,
And giuen me Iustice, Iustice, Iustice, Iustice.   2190
DUKE
Relate your wrongs; In what, by whom? be briefe:
Here is Lord *Angelo* shall giue you Iustice,
Reueale your selfe to him.
ISABELLA   Oh worthy *Duke*,
You bid me seeke redemption of the diuell,
Heare me your selfe: for that which I must speake
Must either punish me, not being beleeu'd,
Or wring redresse from you: Heare me: oh heare me,
          heare.
ANGELO
My Lord, her wits I feare me are not firme:
She hath bin a suitor to me, for her Brother
Cut off by course of Iustice.
ISABELLA ⌈*standing*⌉   By course of Iustice.   2200
ANGELO
And she will speake most bitterly, and strange.
ISABELLA
Most strange: but yet most truely wil I speake,
That *Angelo*'s forsworne, is it not strange?

That *Angelo's* a murtherer, is't not strange?
That *Angelo* is an adulterous thiefe,
An hypocrite, a virgin violator,
Is it not strange? and strange?

DUKE   Nay it is ten times strange?

ISABELLA
It is not truer he is *Angelo*,
Then this is all as true, as it is strange;
2210   Nay, it is ten times true, for truth is truth
To th'end of reckning.

DUKE   Away with her: poore soule
She speakes this, in th'infirmity of sence.

ISABELLA
Oh Prince, I coniure thee, as thou beleeu'st
There is another comfort, then this world,
That thou neglect me not, with that opinion
That I am touch'd with madnesse: make not
     impossible
That which but seemes vnlike, 'tis not impossible
But one, the wickedst caitiffe on the ground
May seeme as shie, as graue, as iust, as absolute:
2220   As *Angelo*, euen so may *Angelo*
In all his dressings, caracts, titles, formes,
Be an arch-villaine: Beleeue it, royall Prince
If he be lesse, he's nothing, but he's more,
Had I more name for badnesse.

DUKE   By mine honesty
If she be mad, as I beleeue no other,
Her madnesse hath the oddest frame of sense,
Such a dependancy of thing, on thing,
As ere I heard in madnesse.

ISABELLA   Oh gracious *Duke*
Harpe not on that; nor do not banish reason
2230   For inequality, but let your reason serue
To make the truth appeare, where it seemes hid,
And hide the false seemes true.

DUKE   Many that are not mad
Haue sure more lacke of reason: What would you
     say?

ISABELLA
I am the Sister of one *Claudio*,
Condemnd vpon the Act of Fornication
To loose his head, condemn'd by *Angelo*,
I, (in probation of a Sisterhood)
Was sent to by my Brother; one *Lucio*
As then the Messenger.

LUCIO   That's I, and't like your Grace:
2240   I came to her from *Claudio*, and desir'd her,
To try her gracious fortune with Lord *Angelo*,
For her poore Brothers pardon.

ISABELLA   That's he indeede.

DUKE (*to Lucio*)
You were not bid to speake.

LUCIO   No, my good Lord,
Nor wish'd to hold my peace.

DUKE
I wish you now then, pray you take note of it:

And when you haue a businesse for your selfe:
Pray heauen you then be perfect.

LUCIO   I warrant your honor.

DUKE
The warrant's for your selfe: take heede to't.

ISABELLA
This Gentleman told somewhat of my Tale.

LUCIO Right.   2250

DUKE
It may be right, but you are i'the wrong
To speake before your time: (*to Isabella*) proceed.

ISABELLA   I went
To this pernicious Caitiffe Deputie.

DUKE
That's somewhat madly spoken.

ISABELLA   Pardon it,
The phrase is to the matter.

DUKE   Mended againe:
The matter: proceed.

ISABELLA
In briefe, to set the needlesse processe by:
How I perswaded, how I praid, and kneel'd,
How he refeld me, and how I replide
(For this was of much length) the vild conclusion   2260
I now begin with griefe, and shame to vtter.
He would not, but by gift of my chaste body
To his concupiscible intemperate lust
Release my brother; and after much debatement,
My sisterly remorse, confutes mine honour,
And I did yeeld to him: But the next morne betimes,
His purpose surfetting, he sends a warrant
For my poore brothers head.

DUKE   This is most likely.

ISABELLA
Oh that it were as like as it is true.

DUKE
By heauen (fond wretch) y^u knowst not what thou
     speak'st,
Or else thou art suborn'd against his honor   2270
In hatefull practise: first his Integritie
Stands without blemish: next it imports no reason,
That with such vehemency he should pursue
Faults proper to himselfe: if he had so offended
He would haue waigh'd thy brother by himselfe,
And not haue cut him off: some one hath set you on:
Confesse the truth, and say by whose aduice
Thou cam'st heere to complaine.

ISABELLA   And is this all?
Then oh you blessed Ministers aboue   2280
Keepe me in patience, and with ripned time
Vnfold the euill, which is heere wrapt vp
In countenance: heauen shield your Grace from woe,
As I thus wrong'd, hence vnbeleeued goe.

DUKE
I know you'ld faine be gone: An Officer:
To prison with her:
     Officer guards Isabella
           Shall we thus permit

A blasting and a scandalous breath to fall,
On him so neere vs? This needs must be a practise;
Who knew of your intent and comming hither?

ISABELLA

2290   One that I would were heere, *Frier Lodowick*.
⌐*Exit guarded*⌐

DUKE

A ghostly Father, belike: Who knowes that *Lodowicke*?

LUCIO

My Lord, I know him, 'tis a medling Fryer,
I doe not like the man: had he been Lay my Lord,
For certaine words he spake against your Grace
In your retirment, I had swing'd him soundly.

DUKE

Words against mee? this' a good Fryer belike
And to set on this wretched woman here
Against our Substitute: Let this Fryer be found.
⌐*Exit one or more*⌐

LUCIO

But yesternight my Lord, she and that Fryer
2300   I saw them at the prison: a sawcy Fryar,
A very scuruy fellow.

FRIER PETER   Blessed be your Royall Grace:
I haue stood by my Lord, and I haue heard
Your royall eare abus'd: first hath this woman
Most wrongfully accus'd your Substitute,
Who is as free from touch, or soyle with her
As she from one vngot.

DUKE   We did beleeue no lesse.
Know you that Frier *Lodowick* that she speakes of?

FRIER PETER

I know him for a man diuine and holy,
Not scuruy, nor a temporary medler
2310   As he's reported by this Gentleman:
And on my trust, a man that neuer yet
Did (as he vouches) mis-report your Grace.

LUCIO My Lord, most villanously, beleeue it.

FRIER PETER

Well: he in time may come to cleere himselfe;
But at this instant he is sicke, my Lord:
Of a strange Feauor: vpon his meere request
Being come to knowledge, that there was complaint
Intended 'gainst Lord *Angelo*, came I hether
To speake as from his mouth, what he doth know
2320   Is true, and false: And what he with his oath
And all probation will make vp full cleare
Whensoeuer he's conuented: First for this woman,
To iustifie this worthy Noble man
So vulgarly and personally accus'd,
Her shall you heare disproued to her eyes,
Till she her selfe confesse it.

DUKE   Good Frier, let's heare it:
⌐*Exit Frier Peter*⌐
Doe you not smile at this, Lord *Angelo*?
Oh heauen, the vanity of wretched fooles.
Giue vs some seates,
⌐*Seates are brought in*⌐
Come cosen *Angelo*,

In this I'll be impartiall: be you Iudge   2330
Of your owne Cause:
    Duke and Angelo sit.
    Enter ⌐*Frier Peter, and*⌐ *Mariana, vailed*
                    Is this the Witnes Frier?
First, let her shew her face, and after, speake.

MARIANA

Pardon my Lord, I will not shew my face
Vntill my husband bid me.

DUKE What, are you married?

MARIANA No my Lord.

DUKE Are you a Maid?

MARIANA No my Lord.

DUKE A Widow then?

MARIANA Neither, my Lord.   2340

DUKE Why you are nothing then: neither Maid, Widow,
nor Wife?

LUCIO My Lord, she may be a Puncke: for many of them,
are neither Maid, Widow, nor Wife.

DUKE Silence that fellow: I would he had some cause to
prattle for himselfe.

LUCIO Well my Lord.

MARIANA

My Lord, I doe confesse I nere was married,
And I confesse besides, I am no Maid,
I haue known my husband, yet my husband   2350
Knowes not, that euer he knew me.

LUCIO He was drunk then, my Lord, it can be no better.

DUKE For the benefit of silence, would thou wert so to.

LUCIO Well, my Lord.

DUKE

This is no witnesse for Lord *Angelo*.

MARIANA Now I come to't, my Lord.
Shee that accuses him of Fornication,
In selfe-same manner, doth accuse my husband,
And charges him, my Lord, with such a time,
When I'le depose I had him in mine Armes   2360
With all th'effect of Loue.

ANGELO   Charges she moe then me?

MARIANA
Not that I know.

DUKE   No? you say your husband.

MARIANA
Why iust, my Lord, and that is *Angelo*,
Who thinkes he knowes, that he nere knew my body,
But knows, he thinkes, that he knowes *Isabels*.

ANGELO
This is a strange abuse: Let's see thy face.

MARIANA (*vnuailing*)
My husband bids me, now I will vnmaske.
This is that face, thou cruell *Angelo*
Which once thou sworst, was worth the looking on:
This is the hand, which with a vowd contract   2370
Was fast belockt in thine: This is the body
That tooke away the match from *Isabell*,
And did supply thee at thy garden-house
In her Imagin'd person.

DUKE (*to Angelo*) Know you this woman?

LUCIO Carnallie she saies.

DUKE Sirha, no more.

LUCIO Enough my Lord.

ANGELO

My Lord, I must confesse, I know this woman,

And fiue yeres since there was some speech of
          marriage

2380

Betwixt my selfe, and her: which was broke off,

Partly for that her promised proportions

Came short of Composition: But in chiefe

For that her reputation was dis-valued

In leuitie: Since which time of fiue yeres

I neuer spake with her, saw her, nor heard from her

Vpon my faith, and honor.

MARIANA ⌈*kneeling before the Duke*⌉ Noble Prince,

As there comes light from heauen, and words frõ
          breath,

As there is sence in truth, and truth in vertue,

2390

I am affiancd this mans wife, as strongly

As words could make vp vowes: And my good Lord,

But Tuesday night last gon, in's garden house,

He knew me as a wife. As this is true,

Let me in safety raise me from my knees,

Or else for euer be confixed here

A Marble Monument.

ANGELO   I did but smile till now,

Now, good my Lord, giue me the scope of Iustice,

My patience here is touch'd: I doe perceiue

These poore informall women, are no more

2400

But instruments of some more mightier member

That sets them on. Let me haue way, my Lord

To finde this practise out.

DUKE ⌈*standing*⌉   I, with my heart,

And punish them euen to your height of pleasure.

Thou foolish Frier, and thou pernicious woman

Compact with her that's gone: thinkst thou, thy
          oathes,

Though they would swear downe each particular
          Saint,

Were testimonies against his worth, and credit

That's seald in approbation? you, Lord *Escalus*

Sit with my Cozen, lend him your kinde paines

2410

To finde out this abuse, whence 'tis deriu'd.

There is another Frier that set them on,

Let him be sent for.

          Escalus sits

FRIER PETER

Would he were here, my Lord, for he indeed

Hath set the women on to this Complaint;

Your Prouost knowes the place where he abides,

And he may fetch him.

DUKE (*to one or more*)   Goe, doe it instantly:

                              Exit one or more

(*To Angelo*) And you, my noble and well-warranted
          Cosen

Whom it concernes to heare this matter forth,

Doe with your iniuries as seemes you best

2420

In any chastisement; I for a while will leaue you;

But stir not you till you haue well determin'd

Vpon these Slanderers.

ESCALUS   My Lord, wee'll doe it throughly:

                              Exit Duke

Signior *Lucio*, did not you say you knew that Frier

Lodowick to be a dishonest person?

LUCIO *Cucullus non facit Monachum*, honest in nothing but

in his Clothes, and one that hath spoke most villanous

speeches of the Duke.

ESCALUS We shall intreat you to abide heere till he come,

and inforce them against him: we shall finde this Frier

a notable fellow.   2430

LUCIO As any in *Vienna*, on my word.

ESCALUS Call that same *Isabell* here once againe, I would

speake with her: *Exit one or more*

(*to Angelo*) pray you, my Lord, giue mee leaue to

question, you shall see how Ile handle her.

LUCIO Not better then he, by her owne report.

ESCALUS Say you?

LUCIO Marry sir, I thinke, if you handled her priuately

shee would sooner confesse, perchance publikely she'll

be asham'd.   2440

ESCALUS I will goe darkely to worke with her.

LUCIO That's the way: for women are light at midnight.

          Enter Isabella, guarded

ESCALUS (*to Isabella*) Come on Mistris, here's a

Gentlewoman, denies all that you haue said.

          Enter Duke (as a Frier, hooded) and Prouost

LUCIO My Lord, here comes the rascall I spoke of, here,

with the *Prouost*.

ESCALUS In very good time: speake not you to him, till

we call vpon you.

LUCIO Mum.

ESCALUS (*to the Duke*) Come Sir, did you set these women 2450

on to slander Lord *Angelo*? they haue confes'd you did.

DUKE 'Tis false.

ESCALUS How? Know you where you are?

DUKE

Respect to your great place; and let the diuell

Be sometime honour'd, for his burning throne.

Where is the *Duke*? 'tis he should heare me speake.

ESCALUS

The *Duke's* in vs: and we will heare you speake,

Looke you speake iustly.

DUKE   Boldly, at least.

(*To Isabella and Mariana*)   But oh poore soules,

Come you to seeke the Lamb here of the Fox;

Good night to your redresse: Is the *Duke* gone?   2460

Then is your cause gone too: The *Duke's* vniust,

Thus to retort your manifest Appeale,

And put your triall in the villaines mouth,

Which here you come to accuse.

LUCIO

This is the rascall: this is he I spoke of.

ESCALUS

Why thou vnreuerend, and vnhallowed Fryer:

Is't not enough thou hast suborn'd these women,

To accuse this worthy man? but in foule mouth,

And in the witnesse of his proper eare,
2470 To call him villaine; and then to glance from him,
To th'*Duke* himselfe, to taxe him with Iniustice?
Take him hence; to th' racke with him: we'll towze
      you
Ioynt by ioynt, but we will know his purpose:
What? vniust?

DUKE   Be not so hot: the *Duke*
Dare no more stretch this finger of mine, then he
Dare racke his owne: his Subiect am I not,
Nor here Prouinciall: My businesse in this State
Made me a looker on here in *Vienna*,
Where I haue seene corruption boyle and bubble,
2480 Till it ore-run the Stew: Lawes, for all faults,
But faults so countenanc'd, that the strong Statutes
Stand like the forfeites in a Barbers shop,
As much in mocke, as marke.

ESCALUS Slander to th' State:
Away with him to prison.

ANGELO
What can you vouch against him Signior *Lucio*?
Is this the man that you did tell vs of?

LUCIO 'Tis he, my Lord: come hither goodman bald-pate,
doe you know me?

2490 DUKE I remember you Sir, by the sound of your voice, I
met you at the Prison, in the absence of the *Duke*.

LUCIO Oh, did you so? and do you remember what you
said of the *Duke*.

DUKE Most notedly Sir.

LUCIO Do you so Sir: And was the *Duke* a flesh-monger,
a foole, and a coward, as you then reported him to be?

DUKE You must (Sir) change persons with me, ere you
make that my report: you indeede spoke so of him,
and much more, much worse.

2500 LUCIO Oh thou damnable fellow: did not I plucke thee by
the nose, for thy speeches?

DUKE I protest, I loue the *Duke*, as I loue my selfe.

ANGELO Harke how the villaine would close now, after
his treasonable abuses.

ESCALUS Such a fellow is not to be talk'd withall: Away
with him to prison: Where is the *Prouost*? away with
him to prison: lay bolts enough vpon him: let him
speak no more: away with those Giglets too, and with
the other confederate companion.

⌈*Mariana is raised to her feete and is guarded.*⌉
Prouost makes to ceize Duke

2510 DUKE Stay Sir, stay a while.

ANGELO What, resists he? helpe him *Lucio*.

LUCIO (*to the Duke*) Come sir, come sir, come sir: foh sir,
why you bald-pated lying rascall: you must be hooded
must you? show your knaues visage with a poxe to
you: show your sheepe-biting face, and be hang'd an
houre: will't not off?

He pulls off the Friars hood and discouers the Duke.
⌈*Angelo and Escalus rise*⌉

DUKE
Thou art the first knaue, that ere mad'st a *Duke*.
First *Prouost*, let me bayle these gentle three:

(*To Lucio*) Sneake not away Sir, for the Fryer, and you,
Must haue a word anon: (*to one or more*) lay hold on
      him.   2520

LUCIO This may proue worse then hanging.

DUKE (*to Escalus*)
What you haue spoke, I pardon: sit you downe,
We'll borrow place of him;
      ⌈*Escalus sits*⌉
(*To Angelo*)   Sir, by your leaue:
      He takes Angelo's seate
Ha'st thou or word, or wit, or impudence,
That yet can doe thee office? If thou ha'st
Rely vpon it, till my tale be heard,
And hold no longer out.

ANGELO   Oh, my dread Lord,
I should be guiltier then my guiltinesse,
To thinke I can be vndiscerneable,
When I perceiue your grace, like powre diuine,   2530
Hath look'd vpon my passes. Then good Prince,
No longer Session hold vpon my shame,
But let my Triall, be mine owne Confession:
Immediate sentence then, and sequent death,
Is all the grace I beg.

DUKE   Come hither *Mariana*,
(*To Angelo*) Say: was't thou ere contracted to this
      woman?

ANGELO I was my Lord.

DUKE
Goe take her hence, and marry her instantly.
Doe you the office (*Fryer*) which consummate,
Returne him here againe: goe with him *Prouost*.   2540
      Exit Angelo, Mariana, Frier Peter, Prouost

ESCALUS
My Lord, I am more amaz'd at his dishonor,
Then at the strangenesse of it.

DUKE   Come hither *Isabell*,
Your *Frier* is now your Prince: As I was then
Aduertysing, and holy to your businesse,
(Not changing heart with habit) I am still,
Atturnied at your seruice.

ISABELLA   Oh giue me pardon
That I, your vassaile, haue imploid, and pain'd
Your vnknowne Soueraigntie.

DUKE   You are pardon'd *Isabell*:
And now, deere Maide, be you as free to vs.
Your Brothers death I know sits at your heart: 2550
And you may maruaile, why I obscur'd my selfe,
Labouring to saue his life: and would not rather
Make rash remonstrance of my hidden powre,
Then let him so be lost: oh most kinde Maid,
It was the swift celeritie of his death,
Which I did thinke, with slower foot came on,
That brain'd my purpose: but peace be with him,
That life is better life past fearing death,
Then that which liues to feare: make it your comfort,
So happy is your Brother.

ISABELLA   I doe my Lord.   2560

Enter Angelo, Mariana, Frier Peter, Prouost

DUKE

For this new-maried man, approaching here,
Whose salt imagination yet hath wrong'd
Your well defended honor: you must pardon
For *Mariana*'s sake: But as he adiudg'd your Brother,
Being criminall, in double violation
Of sacred Chastitie, and of promise-breach,
Thereon dependant for your Brothers life,
The very mercy of the Law cries out
Most audible, euen from his proper tongue:

2570 An *Angelo* for *Claudio*, death for death:
Haste still paies haste, and leasure, answers leasure;
Like doth quit like, and *Measure* still for *Measure*:
Then *Angelo*, thy fault's thus manifested;
Which though thou would'st deny, denies thee vantage.
We doe condemne thee to the very Blocke
Where *Claudio* stoop'd to death, and with like haste.
Away with him.

MARIANA   Oh my most gracious Lord,
I hope you will not mocke me with a husband?

DUKE

It is your husband mock't you with a husband,

2580 Consenting to the safe-guard of your honor,
I thought your marriage fit: else Imputation,
For that he knew you, might reproach your life,
And choake your good to come: For his Possessions,
Although by confiscation they are ours;
We doe en-state, and widow you with all,
To buy you a better husband.

MARIANA   Oh my deere Lord,
I craue no other, nor no better man.

DUKE

Neuer craue him, we are definitiue.

MARIANA

Gentle my Liege.

DUKE   You doe but loose your labour.

2590 Away with him to death: (*To Lucio*) Now Sir, to you.

MARIANA (*kneeling*)

Oh my good Lord, sweet *Isabell*, take my part,
Lend me your knees, and all my life to come,
I'll lend you all my life to doe you seruice.

DUKE

Against all sence you doe importune her,
Should she kneele downe, in mercie of this fact,
Her Brothers ghost, his paued bed would breake,
And take her hence in horror.

MARIANA   *Isabell*:
Sweet *Isabel*, doe yet but kneele by me,
Hold vp your hands, say nothing: I'll speake all.

2600 They say best men are moulded out of faults,
And for the most, become much more the better
For being a little bad: So may my husband.
Oh *Isabel*: will you not lend a knee?

DUKE

He dies for *Claudio*'s death.

ISABELLA (*kneeling*)   Most bounteous Sir.

Looke if it please you, on this man condemn'd,
As if my Brother liu'd: I partly thinke,
A due sinceritie gouernd his deedes,
Till he did looke on me: Since it is so,
Let him not die: my Brother had but Iustice,
In that he did the thing for which he dide.   2610
For *Angelo*,
His Act did not ore-take his bad intent,
And must be buried but as an intent
That perish'd by the way: thoughts are no subiects,
Intents, but meerely thoughts.

MARIANA   Meerely my Lord.

DUKE

Your suite's vnprofitable: stand vp I say:
⌈*Mariana and Isabella stand*⌉
I haue bethought me of another fault.
Prouost, how came it *Claudio* was beheaded
At an vnusuall howre?

PROUOST   It was commanded so.

DUKE

Had you a speciall warrant for the deed?   2620

PROUOST

No my good Lord: it was by priuate message.

DUKE

For which I doe discharge you of your office,
Giue vp your keyes.

PROUOST   Pardon me, noble Lord,
I thought it was a fault, but knew it not,
Yet did repent me after more aduice,
For testimony whereof, one in the prison
That should by priuate order else haue dide,
I haue reseru'd aliue.

DUKE What's he?

PROUOST His name is *Barnardine*.   2630

DUKE

I would thou hadst done so by *Claudio*:
Goe fetch him hither, let me looke vpon him.
                 Exit Prouost

ESCALUS

I am sorry, one so learned, and so wise
As you, Lord *Angelo*, haue stil appear'd,
Should slip so grosselie, both in the heat of bloud
And lacke of temper'd iudgement afterward.

ANGELO

I am sorrie, that such sorrow I procure,
And so deepe sticks it in my penitent heart,
That I craue death more willingly then mercy,
'Tis my deseruing, and I doe entreat it.   2640
     Enter Barnardine and Prouost, Claudio (*muffeld*)
     and Iulietta

DUKE

Which is that *Barnardine*?

PROUOST   This my Lord.

DUKE

There was a Friar told me of this man.
(*To Barnardine*) Sirha, thou art said to haue a
     stubborne soule
That apprehends no further then this world,

And squar'st thy life according: Thou'rt condemn'd,
But for those earthly faults, I quit them all,
And pray thee take this mercie to prouide
For better times to come: Frier aduise him,
I leaue him to your hand. (*To Prouost*) What muffeld
    fellow's that?

PROUOST
2650 This is another prisoner that I sau'd,
Who should haue di'd when *Claudio* lost his head,
As like almost to *Claudio*, as himselfe.
        He vnmuffels Claudio

DUKE (*to Isabella*)
If he be like your brother, for his sake
Is he pardon'd, and for your louelie sake
Giue me your hand, and say you will be mine,
He is my brother too: But fitter time for that:
By this Lord *Angelo* perceiues he's safe,
Methinkes I see a quickning in his eye:
Well *Angelo*, your euill quits you well.
Looke that you loue your wife: her worth, worth
2660   yours.
I finde an apt remission in my selfe:
And yet heere's one in place I cannot pardon,
(*To Lucio*) You sirha, that knew me for a foole, a
    Coward,
One all of Luxurie, an asse, a mad man:
Wherein haue I so deseru'd of you
That you extoll me thus?

LUCIO 'Faith my Lord, I spoke it but according to the
trick: if you will hang me for it you may: but I had
rather it would please you, I might be whipt.
2670 DUKE Whipt first, sir, and hang'd after.
Proclaime it Prouost round about the Citie,
If any woman wrong'd by this lewd fellow

(As I haue heard him sweare himselfe there's one
Whom he begot with childe) let her appeare,
And he shall marry her: the nuptiall finish'd,
Let him be whipt and hang'd.

LUCIO I beseech your Highnesse doe not marry me to a
Whore: your Highnesse said euen now I made you a
Duke, good my Lord do not recompence me, in making
me a Cuckold.   2680

DUKE
Vpon mine honor thou shalt marrie her.
Thy slanders I forgiue, and therewithall
Remit thy other forfeits: take him to prison,
And see our pleasure herein executed.

LUCIO Marrying a punke my Lord, is pressing to death,
whipping and hanging.

DUKE Slandering a Prince deserues it.
            ⌈*Exit Lucio, guarded*⌉
She *Claudio* that you wrong'd, looke you restore.
Ioy to you *Mariana*, loue her *Angelo*:
I haue confes'd her, and I know her vertue.   2690
Thanks good friend, *Escalus*, for thy much goodnesse,
There's more behinde that is more gratulate.
Thanks *Prouost* for thy care, and secrecie,
We shall imploy thee in a worthier place.
Forgiue him *Angelo*, that brought you home
The head of *Ragozine* for *Claudio's*,
Th'offence pardons it selfe. Deere *Isabell*,
I haue a motion much imports your good,
Whereto if you'll a willing eare incline;
What's mine is yours, and what is yours is mine.   2700
(*To all*) So bring vs to our Pallace, where wee'll show
What's yet behinde, thats meete you all should know.
                                                        Exeunt

FINIS

ADDITIONAL PASSAGES

The text of *Measure for Measure* given in this edition is
probably that of an adapted version made for
Shakespeare's company after his death. Adaptation seems
to have affected two passages, printed below as we believe
Shakespeare to have written them.

A. 83.1–196

The passage begins with seven lines which the adapter
(whom we believe to be Thomas Middleton) intended to
be replaced by 139–60 of the play as we print it. The
adapter must have contributed all of 83.1–163, which in
the earliest and subsequent printed texts precede the
discussion between the Clown (Pompey) and the Bawd
(Mistress Overdone) about Claudio's arrest. Lucio's entry
alone at l. 38.1 below, some eleven lines after his re-entry

with the two Gentlemen and the Provost's party in the
adapted text, probably represents Shakespeare's original
intention. In his version, Juliet, present but silent in the
adapted text both in Sc. 2 and Sc. 16, probably did not
appear in either scene; accordingly, the words 'and there's
Madam *Iuliet*' (187) must also be the reviser's work, and
do not appear below.

        Enter Clowne and Bawde, ⌈*meeting*⌉
BAWD How now? what's the newes with you.
CLOWNE Yonder man is carried to prison.
BAWD Well: what has he done?
CLOWNE A Woman.
BAWD But what's his offence?
CLOWNE Groping for Trowts, in a peculiar Riuer.
BAWD What? is there a maid with child by him?

CLOWNE No: but there's a woman with maid by him: you
haue not heard of the proclamation, haue you?

10 BAWD What proclamation, man?

CLOWNE All howses in the Suburbs of *Vienna* must bee
pluck'd downe.

BAWD And what shall become of those in the Citie?

CLOWNE They shall stand for seed: they had gon down
to, but that a wise Burger put in for them.

BAWD But shall all our houses of resort in the Suburbs
be puld downe?

CLOWNE To the ground, Mistris.

BAWD Why heere's a change indeed in the Common-
20 wealth: what shall become of me?

CLOWNE Come: feare not you: good Counsellors lacke no
Clients: though you change your place, you neede not
change your Trade: Ile bee your Tapster still; courage,
there will bee pitty taken on you; you that haue worne
your eyes almost out in the seruice, you will bee
considered.

⌜*A noise within*⌝

BAWD What's to doe heere, *Thomas* Tapster? let's
withdraw?

Enter Prouost, Claudio

CLOWNE Here comes Signior *Claudio*, led by the Prouost
30 to prison. *Exeunt Bawd and Clowne*

CLAUDIO

Fellow, why do'st thou show me thus to th'world?
Beare me to prison, where I am committed.

PROVOST

I do it not in euill disposition,
But from Lord *Angelo* by speciall charge.

CLAUDIO

Thus can the demy-god (Authority)
Make vs pay downe, for our offence, by waight
The bonds of heauen; on whom it will, it will,
On whom it will not (soe) yet still 'tis iust.

⌜*Enter Lucio*⌝

LUCIO

Why how now *Claudio*? whence comes this restraint.

B. 1623–1712

Before revision there would have been no act-break and
no song; the lines immediately following the song would
also have been absent. The Duke's soliloquies 'He who
the sword of Heauen will bear' and 'Oh Place, and
greatnes' have evidently been transposed in revision; in
the original, the end of Place, and greatnes' would have
led straight on to the Duke's meeting with Isabella and
then Mariana.

ESCALUS I am going to visit the prisoner, Fare you well.

DUKE Peace be with you. *Exit Escalus*

Oh Place, and greatnes: millions of false eies
Are stucke vpon thee: volumes of report
Run with their false, and most contrarious Quest
Vpon thy doings: thousand escapes of wit

Make thee the father of their idle dreame,
And racke thee in their fancies.

Enter Isabell

DUKE Very well met:
What is the newes from this good Deputie?

ISABELLA

He hath a Garden circummur'd with Bricke, 10
Whose westerne side is with a Vineyard back't;
And to that Vineyard is a planched gate,
That makes his opening with this bigger Key:
This other doth command a little doore,
Which from the Vineyard to the Garden leades,
There haue I made my promise,
Vpon the heauy midle of the night,
To call vpon him.

DUKE

But shall you on your knowledge find this way?

ISABELLA

I haue t'ane a due, and wary note vpon't, 20
With whispering, and most guiltie diligence,
In action all of precept, he did show me
The way twice ore.

DUKE Are there no other tokens
Betweene you 'greed, concerning her obseruance?

ISABELLA

No: none but onely a repaire ith' darke,
And that I haue possest him, my most stay
Can be but briefe: for I haue made him know,
I haue a Seruant comes with me along
That staies vpon me; whose perswasion is,
I come about my Brother.

DUKE 'Tis well borne vp. 30
I haue not yet made knowne to *Mariana*
A word of this: what hoa, within; come forth,

Enter Mariana

(*To Mariana*) I pray you be acquainted with this Maid,
She comes to doe you good.

ISABELLA I doe desire the like.

DUKE (*to Mariana*)

Do you perswade your selfe that I respect you?

MARIANA

Good Frier, I know you do, and so haue found it.

DUKE

Take then this your companion by the hand
Who hath a storie readie for your eare:
I shall attend your leisure, but make haste
The vaporous night approaches.

MARIANA (*to Isabella*) Wilt please you walke aside. 40

⌜*Exit Mariana and Isabella*⌝

DUKE

He who the sword of Heauen will beare,
Should be as holy, as seueare:
Patterne in himselfe to know,
Grace to stand, and Vertue go:
More, nor lesse to others paying,
Then by selfe-offences weighing.
Shame to him, whose cruell striking,
Kils for faults of his owne liking:

50 Twice trebble shame on *Angelo*,
To weede my vice, and let his grow.
Oh, what may Man within him hide,
Though Angel on the outward side?
How may likenesse made in crimes,
Make my practise on the Times,
To draw with ydle Spiders strings
Most ponderous and substantiall things?
Craft against vice, I must applie.
With *Angelo* to night shall lye

His old betroathed (but despised:) 60
So disguise shall by th'disguised
Pay with falshood, false exacting,
And performe an olde contracting.
⌈*Enter Mariana and Isabella*⌉
Welcome, how agreed?

ISABELLA
Shee'll take the enterprize vpon her father,
If you aduise it.

OTHELLO

Othello was given before James I in the Banqueting House at Whitehall on 1 November 1604. Information about the Turkish invasion of Cyprus appears to derive from Richard Knolles's *Historie of the Turkes*, published no earlier than 30 September 1603, so Shakespeare probably completed his play some time between that date and the summer of 1604. It first appeared in print in a quarto of 1622; the version printed in the 1623 Folio is about 160 lines longer, and has over a thousand differences in wording. It seems that Shakespeare partially revised his play, adding, for example, Desdemona's willow song (Sc. 13) and building up Emillia's role in the closing scenes. We base our text on the Folio as that seems to represent Shakespeare's second thoughts.

Shakespeare's decision to make a black man a tragic hero was bold and original: by an ancient tradition, blackness was associated with sin and death; and blackamoors in plays before Shakespeare are generally villainous (like Aron in *Titus Andronicus*). The story of a Moorish commander deluded by his ensign (standard-bearer) into believing that his young wife has been unfaithful to him with another soldier derives from a prose tale by the Italian Giambattista Cinzio Giraldi first published in 1565 in a collection of linked tales, *Gli Ecatommiti* (*The Hundred Tales*). Shakespeare must have read it either in Italian or in a French translation of 1584; he may have looked at both. Giraldi tells the tale in a few pages of compressed, matter-of-fact narrative interspersed with brief conversations. His main characters are a Moor of Venice (Othello), his Venetian wife (Desdemona), his ensign (Iago), his ensign's wife (Emillia), and a corporal (Cassio) 'who was very dear to the Moor'. Only Desdemona is named. Shakespeare's invented characters include Roderigo, a young, disappointed suitor of Desdemona, and Brabantio, Desdemona's father, who opposes her marriage to Othello. Bianca, Cassio's mistress, is developed from a few hints in the source. Shakespeare also introduces the military action between Turkey and Venice—infidels and Christians—which gives especial importance to Othello's posting to Cyprus, a Venetian protectorate which the Turks attacked in 1570 and conquered in the following year. In the source, Othello and Desdemona are already happily settled into married life when they go to Cyprus; Shakespeare compresses the time-scheme and makes many changes to the narrative.

Othello, a great success in Shakespeare's time, was one of the first plays to be acted after the reopening of the theatres in 1660, and since that time has remained one of the most popular plays on the English stage.

Our text adopts the spelling and punctuation of the Quarto text (1622), apparently printed from a scribal transcript, but incorporates passages and variant readings from the Folio (printed from a much more heavily sophisticated transcript).

THE NAMES OF THE ACTORS

OTHELLO, 'the Moore' of Venice

DESDEMONA, 'Wife to Othello'

Michael CASSIO, 'an honourable Lieutenant' to the Moore

BIANCA, 'a Curtezan', in loue with Cassio

IAGO, 'a Villaine', Ancient to the Moore

EMILLIA, 'Wife to Iago'

A CLOWNE, Seruant to Othello

The 'DUKE of Venice'

BRABANTIO, 'Father to Desdemona' and Senator of Venice

GRATIANO, brother to Brabantio ⎫ 'two Noble Venetians'
LODOUICO, kinsman of Brabantio ⎭

'SENATORS' of Venice

RODERIGO, 'a gull'd Gentleman' of Venice, in loue with Desdemona

MONTANO, 'Gouernour of Cyprus'

A HERALD

A MESSENGER

Attendants, Officers, 'Saylors', 'Gentlemen of Cyprus', Musitians

The Tragedy of Othello the Moore of Venice

Sc. 1   *Enter Iago and Roderigo*
(1.1)

RODERIGO

Tush, neuer tell me, I take it much vnkindly
That thou *Iago*, who hast had my purse,
As if the strings were thine, should'st know of this.

IAGO S'blood, but you'l not heare me,
If euer I did dreame of such a matter, abhorre me.

RODERIGO

Thou toldst me, thou didst hold him in thy hate.

IAGO Despise me
If I doe not: three great ones of the Citty
In personall suite to make me his Leiutenant,

10   Off-capt to him, and by the faith of man,
I know my price, I am worth no worse a place.
But he, as louing his owne pride and purposes,
Euades them, with a bumbast circumstance,
Horribly stuft with Epithites of warre:
Non-suits my mediators: for certes, sayes he,
I haue already chose my officer,
And what was he?
Forsooth, a great Arithmetition,
One *Michael Cassio*, a Florentine,

20   A fellow almost dambd in a faire wife,
That neuer set a squadron in the field,
Nor the deuision of a Battell knowes,
More then a Spinster, vnlesse the bookish Theorique,
Wherein the toged Consuls can propose
As masterly as he: meere prattle without practise,
Is all his souldier-shippe: but he sir had th'election,
And I, of whom his eyes had seene the proofe,
At *Rhodes*, at *Cipres*, and on other grounds,
Christen'd and Heathen, must be be-leed, and calm'd,

30   By Debitor and Creditor. This Counter-caster,
He in good time, must his Leiutenant be,
And I, God blesse the marke, his Morships Ancient.

RODERIGO

By heauen I rather would haue bin his hangman.

IAGO

Why there's no remedy, tis the curse of seruice,
Preferment goes by letter and affection,
And not by olde gradation, where each second
Stood heire to th' first: Now sir be iudge your selfe,
Whether I, in any iust tearme am affin'd
To loue the Moore.

40 **RODERIGO** I would not follow him then.

IAGO O sir, content you,
I follow him to serue my turne vpon him,
We cannot all be masters, nor all masters
Cannot be truely followed, you shall marke
Many a dutious and knee-crooking knaue,
That doting on his owne obsequious bondage,
Weares out his time much like his masters Asse,
For nought but prouender, and when hee's old
     cashierd,

Whip mee such honest knaues: Others there are,
Who trimd in formes, and vissages of duty,   50
Keepe yet their hearts, attending on themselues,
And throwing but shewes of seruice on their Lords,
Doe well thriue by 'em, and when they haue lin'd
     their coates,
Doe themselues homage, these fellowes haue some
     soule,
And such a one doe I professe my selfe,—for sir,
It is as sure as you are *Roderigo*,
Were I the Moore, I would not be *Iago*:
In following him, I follow but my selfe.
Heauen is my iudge, not I, for loue and duty,
But seeming so, for my peculiar end.   60
For when my outward action doth demonstrate
The natiue act, and figure of my heart,
In complement externe, tis not long after,
But I will weare my heart vpon my sleeue,
For Dawes to pecke at, I am not what I am.

RODERIGO

What a full fortune does the thicklips owe,
If he can carry't thus?

IAGO   Call vp her father,
Rowse him, make after him, poyson his delight,
Proclaime him in the streets, incense her Kinsmen,
And tho he in a fertile climate dwell,   70
Plague him with flyes: tho that his ioy be ioy,
Yet throw such chances of vexation on't,
As it may loose some colour.

RODERIGO

Here is her fathers house, Ile call aloud.

IAGO

Doe with like timerous accent, and dire yell,
As when by night and negligence, the fire
Is spied in populous Citties.

RODERIGO *(calling)*

What ho, *Brabantio*; Seignior *Brabantio*, ho.

IAGO *(calling)*

Awake, what ho, *Brabantio*, theeues, theeues, theeues:
Looke to your house, your Daughter, and your bags,   80
Theeues, theeues.

     Enter Brabantio in his night gowne at a window,
     aboue

BRABANTIO

What is the reason of this terrible summons?
What is the matter there?

RODERIGO

Seignior, is all your family within?

IAGO

Are your doores lockt?

BRABANTIO   Why, wherefore aske you this?

IAGO

Zounds sir y'are robd, for shame put on your gowne,
Your heart is burst, you haue lost halfe your soule;

Euen now, now, very now, an old blacke Ram
Is tupping your white Ewe; arise, arise,
90 Awake the snorting Citizens with the Bell,
Or else the Diuell will make a Grandsire of you,
Arise I say.

BRABANTIO What, haue you lost your wits?

RODERIGO
Most reuerend Seignior, doe you know my voyce?

BRABANTIO Not I, what are you?

RODERIGO My name is *Roderigo*.

BRABANTIO The worser welcome,
I haue charg'd thee, not to haunt about my dores,
In honest plainenesse, thou hast heard me say
My daughter is not for thee, and now in madnes,
100 Being full of supper, and distempering draughts,
Vpon malicious brauery, dost thou come
To start my quiet?

RODERIGO Sir, sir, sir.

BRABANTIO But thou must needes be sure
My spirits and my place haue in their power,
To make this bitter to thee.

RODERIGO Patience good sir.

BRABANTIO
What, tell'st thou me of robbing? this is *Venice*,
My house is not a graunge.

RODERIGO Most graue *Brabantio*,
In simple and pure soule I come to you.

110 IAGO (*to Brabantio*) Zouns Sir, you are one of those, that
will not serue God, if the Deuill bid you. Because we
come to doe you seruice, and you thinke we are
Ruffians, youle haue your daughter couered with a
Barbary horse; youle haue your Nephewes ney to you;
youle haue Coursers for Cousens, and Iennits for
Iermans.

BRABANTIO What prophane wretch art thou?

IAGO I am one sir, that comes to tell you, your daughter,
and the Moore, are now making the Beast with two
120 backes.

BRABANTIO
Thou art a villaine.

IAGO You are a Senator.

BRABANTIO
This thou shalt answer, I know thee *Roderigo*.

RODERIGO
Sir, I will answer any thing: But I beseech you,
If't be your pleasure, and most wise consent,
(As partly I find it is) that your faire Daughter,
At this odde Euen and dull watch o'th'night
Transported with no worse nor better guard,
But with a knaue of common hire, a Gundelier,
To the grosse claspes of a Lasciuious Moore:
130 If this be knowne to you, and your Allowance,
We then haue done you bold, and saucie wrongs.
But if you know not this, my Manners tell me,
We haue your wrong rebuke. Do not beleeue
That from the sence of all Ciuilitie,
I thus would play and trifle with your Reuerence.
Your Daughter (if you haue not giuen her leaue)

I say againe, hath made a grosse reuolt,
Tying her Dutie, Beautie, Wit, and Fortunes
In an extrauagant, and wheeling Stranger,
Of here, and euery where: straight satisfie your selfe. 140
If she be in her chamber, or your house,
Let loose on me the Iustice of the state,
For thus deluding you.

BRABANTIO (*calling*) Strike on the tinder, Ho:
Giue me a taper, call vp all my people:
This accident is not vnlike my dreame,
Beleefe of it oppresses me already:
Light I say, light. *Exit*

IAGO Farewell, for I must leaue you,
It seemes not meete, nor wholesome to my place,
To be producted, as if I stay I shall
Against the Moore, for I doe know the state, 150
How euer this may gaule him with some checke,
Cannot with safety cast him, for hee's imbark'd,
With such loud reason, to the Cipres warres,
Which euen now stands in act, that for their soules,
Another of his fathome, they haue none
To leade their businesse, in which regard,
Tho I doe hate him, as I doe hell paines,
Yet for necessity of present life,
I must shew out a flag, and signe of loue,
Which is indeed but signe, that you shall surely finde
    him 160
Lead to the Sagitary, the raised search,
And there will I be with him. So farewell. *Exit*
*Enter below Brabantio in his night gowne, and
seruants with Torches*

BRABANTIO
It is too true an euill, gone she is,
And what's to come, of my despised time,
Is nought but bitternesse: now *Roderigo*,
Where didst thou see her; O vnhappy girle,
With the Moore saist thou? who would be a father?
How didst thou know twas she? O she deceiues me
Past thought: what said she to you? (*to seruants*) get
    moe tapers,
Raise all my kindred, ⌜*Exit one or more*⌝
(*To Roderigo*) are they married thinke you? 170

RODERIGO Truely I thinke they are.

BRABANTIO
O heauen, how got she out? O treason of the blood;
Fathers, from hence trust not your Daughters mindes,
By what you see them act, is there not charmes,
By which the property of youth and maidhood
May be abus'd? haue you not read *Roderigo*,
Of some such thing.

RODERIGO Yes sir: I haue indeed.

BRABANTIO (*to seruants*)
Call vp my brother: (*to Roderigo*) O would you had
    had her,
(*To seruants*) Some one way, some another;
⌜*Exit one or more*⌝
(*To Roderigo*) doe you know
Where we may apprehend her, and the Moore? 180

RODERIGO

    I thinke I can discouer him, if you please
    To get good guard, and goe along with me.

BRABANTIO

    Pray you leade on, at euery house Ile call,
    I may command at most: (*calling*) get weapons ho,
    And raise some speciall Officers of night:
    On good *Roderigo*, I will deserue your paynes.   *Exeunt*

Sc. 2   *Enter Othello, Iago, and attendants with Torches*
(1.2)   IAGO

    Tho in the trade of warre, I haue slaine men,
    Yet doe I hold it very stuffe o'th' Conscience
    To doe no contriu'd murther; I lacke iniquity
190 Sometime to doe me seruice: nine or ten times,
    I had thought t'haue ierk'd him here, vnder the ribbes.

OTHELLO

    Tis better as it is.

IAGO   Nay, but he prated,

    And spoke such scuruy, and prouoking tearmes
    Against your Honor,
    That with the little godlinesse I haue,
    I did full hard forbeare him: but I pray you sir,
    Are you fast married? Be assur'd of this,
    That the Magnifico is much beloued,
    And hath in his effect, a voyce potentiall,
200 As double as the Dukes, he will diuorce you,
    Or put vpon you what restraint, or greeuance,
    The law with all his might to inforce it on,
    Will giue him cable.

OTHELLO   Let him doe his spite,

    My seruices which I haue done the Seigniorie,
    Shall out tongue his complaints, tis yet to know,
    Which when I know, that boasting is an honour,
    I shall promulgate, I fetch my life and being,
    From men of royall Seige, and my demerrits,
    May speake vnbonnited to as proud a fortune
210 As this that I haue reach'd; for know *Iago*,
    But that I loue the gentle *Desdemona*,
    I would not, my vnhoused free condition,
    Put into circumscription and confine
    For the seas worth,
        Enter Cassio and Officers with torches
                        but looke what lights come yond.

IAGO

    Those are the raised Father and his friends,
    You were best goe in.

OTHELLO   Not I, I must be found,

    My parts, my Title, and my perfect soule,
    Shall manifest me rightly: is it they?

IAGO By *Ianus* I thinke no.

OTHELLO

220 The seruants of the Duke, and my Leiutenant,
    The goodnesse of the night vpon you friends,
    What is the newes.

CASSIO   The Duke does greete you Generall,

    And he requires your hast, post hast appearance,
    Euen on the instant.

OTHELLO   What is the matter thinke you.

CASSIO

    Something from *Cipres*, as I may diuine,
    It is a businesse of some heate, the Galleyes
    Haue sent a dozen sequent messengers
    This very night, at one anothers heeles:
    And many of the Consuls rais'd, and met,
    Are at the Dukes already; you haue bin hotly cald for,   230
    When being not at your lodging to be found,
    The Senate sent about three seuerall quests
    To search you out.

OTHELLO   Tis well I am found by you,

    I will but spend a word here in the house,
    And goe with you.   *Exit*

CASSIO   Auncient, what makes he here?

IAGO

    Faith he to night, hath boorded a land Carrick:
    If it proue lawfull prize, hee's made for euer.

CASSIO

    I doe not vnderstand.

IAGO   Hee's married.

CASSIO   To who?

        *Enters Brabantio, Roderigo, and Officers with lights
        and weapons*

IAGO

    Marry to.—
        Enter Othello
    (*To Othello*) Come Captaine, will you goe?

OTHELLO   Haue with you.   240

CASSIO

    Here comes another troupe to seeke for you.

IAGO

    It is *Brabantio*, Generall be aduisde,
    He comes to bad intent.

OTHELLO   Holla, stand there.

RODERIGO (*to Brabantio*)

    Seignior, it is the Moore.

BRABANTIO   Downe with him theife.

IAGO (*drawing his sword*)

    You *Roderigo*, Come sir, I am for you.

OTHELLO

    Keepe vp your bright swords, for the dew will rust em,
    (*To Brabantio*) Good Seignior you shall more command
        with yeares
    Then with your weapons.

BRABANTIO

    O thou foule theefe, where hast thou stowed my
        daughter?
    Dambd as thou art, thou hast inchanted her,   250
    For ile referre me to all things of sense,
    (If she in Chaines of Magick were not bound)
    Whether a maide so tender, faire, and happy,
    So opposite to marriage, that she shund
    The wealthy curled darlings of our Nation,
    Would euer haue (t'incurre a general mocke)
    Runne from her gardage to the sooty bosome
    Of such a thing as thou? to feare, not to delight,
    Iudge me the world, if 'tis not grosse in sense,
    That thou hast practis'd on her with foule Charmes,   260
    Abus'd her delicate Youth, with Drugs or Minerals,

That weakens Motion. Ile haue't disputed on,
'Tis probable, and palpable to thinking;
I therefore apprehend and do attach thee,
For an abuser of the world, a practiser
Of Arts inhibited, and out of warrant;
(*To Officers*) Lay hold vpon him, if he doe resist,
Subdue him at his perill.

OTHELLO   Hold your hands:
Both you of my inclining and the rest,
270   Were it my Qu. to fight, I should haue knowne it,
Without a prompter, whether will you that I goe,
To answer this your charge?

BRABANTIO   To prison till fit time
Of Law, and course of direct Session,
Call thee to answer.

OTHELLO   What if I doe obey,
How may the Duke be therewith satisfied,
Whose Messengers are heere about my side,
Vpon some present businesse of the State,
To bring me to him.

OFFICER (*to Brabantio*) Tis true most worthy Seignior,
The Duke's in Councell, and your noble selfe,
I am sure is sent for.

280   BRABANTIO   How? the Duke in Councell?
In this time of the night? bring him away,
Mine's not an idle cause, the Duke himselfe,
Or any of my Brothers of the State,
Cannot but feele this wrong, as twere their owne.
For if such actions, may haue passage free,
Bondslaues, and Pagans, shal our Statesmen be.
                                        Exeunt

Sc. 3   *Enter Duke and Senators, set at a Table with lights*
(1.3)   *and Officers*

DUKE
There is no Composition in these newes,
That giues them credit.

I SENATOR   Indeede they are disproportioned,
My letters say, a hundred and seuen Gallies.

DUKE
And mine a hundred forty.

290   2 SENATOR   And mine two hundred:
But though they iumpe not on a iust account,
As in these cases, where the ayme reports,
Tis oft with difference, yet doe they all confirme
A *Turkish* fleete, and bearing vp to *Cipresse*.

DUKE
Nay, it is possible enough to iudgement:
I doe not so secure me in the error,
But the mayne Article I doe approue
In fearefull sense.

SAILOR (*within*)   What ho, what ho, what ho?
                Enter Sailor

OFFICER
A messenger from the Gallies.

DUKE   Now? What's the businesse?

SAILOR
300   The *Turkish* preparation makes for *Rhodes*,

So was I bid report here, to the state,
By Signior *Angelo*.

DUKE (*to Senators*) How say you by this change?

I SENATOR This cannot be
By no assay of reason—tis a Pageant,
To keepe vs in false gaze: when we consider
The importancy of *Cypresse* to the *Turke*:
And let our selues againe, but vnderstand,
That as it more concernes the *Turke* then *Rhodes*,
So may he with more facile question beare it,   310
For that it stands not in such Warrelike brace,
But altogether lackes th'abilities
That *Rhodes* is dress'd in. If we make thought of this,
We must not thinke the Turke is so vnskillfull,
To leaue that latest, which concernes him first,
Neglecting an attempt of ease, and gaine
To wake, and wage a danger profitlesse.

DUKE
Nay, in all confidence, hee's not for *Rhodes*.

OFFICER Here is more newes.
                Enter a Messenger

MESSENGER
The *Ottamites*, reuerend and gracious,   320
Steering with due course, toward the Isle of *Rhodes*,
Haue there inioynted them with an after fleete.

I SENATOR
I, so I thought: how many, as you guesse?

MESSENGER
Of 30. saile, and now they doe re-stem
Their backward course, bearing with franke appearance
Their purposes toward *Cypresse*: Seignior *Montano*,
Your trusty and most valiant seruitor,
With his free duty recommends you thus,
And prayes you to beleeue him.

DUKE   Tis certaine then for *Cypresse*,
Marcus Luccicos is not he in Towne.   330

I SENATOR Hee's now in *Florence*.

DUKE
Write from vs, to him post, post hast dispatch.
                Enter Brabantio, Othello, Roderigo, Iago, Cassio,
                and Officers

I SENATOR
Here comes *Brabantio* and the valiant *Moore*.

DUKE
Valiant *Othello*, we must straite imploy you,
Against the generall enemy *Ottaman*;
(*To Brabantio*) I did not see you, welcome gentle
    Seignior,
We lack't your counsell, and your helpe to night.

BRABANTIO
So did I yours, good your Grace pardon me,
Neither my place, nor ought I heard of businesse
Hath rais'd me from my bed, nor doth the generall care   340
Take hold on me, for my particular griefe,
Is of so floodgate and orebearing nature,
That it engluts and swallowes other sorrowes,
And it is still it selfe.

DUKE   Why, what's the matter?

BRABANTIO
My daughter, O my daughter.

⌈SENATORS⌉   Dead?

BRABANTIO   I to me:
She is abus'd, stolne from me and corrupted,
By spels and medicines, bought of mountebancks,
For nature so preposterously to erre,
(Being not deficient, blind, or lame of sense,)
350   Saunce witchcraft could not.

DUKE
Who ere he be, that in this foule proceeding
Hath thus beguild your daughter of her selfe,
And you of her, the bloody booke of Law,
You shall your selfe, read in the bitter letter,
After your owne sense, yea, tho our proper sonne
Stood in your action.

BRABANTIO   Humbly I thanke your Grace;
Here is the man, this Moore, whom now it seemes
Your speciall mandate, for the State affaires
Hath hither brought.

SENATORS   We are very sorry for't.

DUKE (to Othello)
360   What in your owne part can you say to this?

BRABANTIO Nothing, but this is so.

OTHELLO
Most potent, graue, and reuerend Seigniors,
My very noble and approou'd good maisters:
That I haue tane away this old mans daughter,
It is most true: true, I haue married her,
The very head and front of my offending,
Hath this extent no more. Rude am I in my speech,
And little blest with the soft phrase of peace,
For since these armes of mine had seuen yeares pith,
370   Till now some nine Moones wasted, they haue vs'd
Their dearest action in the tented field,
And little of this great world can I speake,
More then pertaines to feates of broyles, and battaile,
And therefore little shall I grace my cause,
In speaking for my selfe; yet by your gracious patience,
I will a round vnuarnish'd tale deliuer,
Of my whole course of loue, what drugs, what charmes,
What coniuration, and what mighty Magicke,
(For such proceeding I am charg'd withall:)
I wonne his daughter.

380   BRABANTIO   A maiden neuer bold:
Of spirit so still and quiet, that her motion
Blusht at her selfe: and she in spite of nature,
Of yeares, of Countrey, credit, euery thing,
To fall in loue with what she fear'd to looke on?
It is a iudgement maimd, and most imperfect,
That will confesse perfection, so could erre
Against all rules of Nature, and must be driuen,
To finde out practises of cunning hell,
Why this should be, I therefore vouch againe,
390   That with some mixtures powerfull ore the blood,
Or with some dram coniur'd to this effect,
He wrought vpon her.

DUKE   To vouch this is no proofe,
Without more wider and more ouert test,

Then these thin habits, and poore likelihoods,
Of moderne seeming, do preferre against him.

A SENATOR But Othello speake,
Did you by indirect and forced courses,
Subdue and poison this young maides affections?
Or came it by request, and such faire question,
As soule to soule affoordeth?

OTHELLO   I doe beseech you,   400
Send for the Lady to the Sagitary,
And let her speake of me before her father;
If you doe finde me foule in her report,
The Trust, the Office, I do hold of you,
Not onely take away, but let your sentence
Euen fall vpon my life.

DUKE (to Officers)   Fetch Desdemona hither.

OTHELLO
Ancient conduct them, you best know the place:

                    Exit Iago with two or three Officers

And till she come, as truely as to heauen,
I do confesse the vices of my blood,
So iustly to your graue eares I'le present,   410
How I did thriue in this faire Ladyes loue,
And she in mine.

DUKE   Say it Othello.

OTHELLO
Her Father lou'd me, oft inuited me,
Still question'd me the story of my life,
From yeare to yeare, the battailes, seiges, fortunes
That I haue past:
I ran it through, euen from my boyish dayes,
Toth' very moment that he bade me tell it.
Wherein I spoke of most disastrous chances,
Of moouing accidents by flood and field;   420
Of heire-breadth scapes ith imminent deadly breach;
Of being taken by the insolent foe:
And sold to slauery, of my redemption thence,
And portance in my trauellours Historie;
Wherein of Antrees vast, and Deserts idle,
Rough quarries, rocks and hils, whose heads touch
      heauen,
It was my hent to speake, such was my processe:
And of the Cannibals, that each other eate,
The Anthropophagie, and men whose heads
Doe grow beneath their shoulders: these things to
      heare,   430
Would Desdemona seriously incline;
But still the house affaires would draw her thence,
Which euer as she could with hast dispatch,
Shee'd come againe, and with a greedy eare
Deuoure vp my discourse; which I obseruing,
Tooke once a plyant houre, and found good meanes
To draw from her a prayer of earnest heart,
That I would all my pilgrimage dilate,
Whereof by parcells she had something heard,
But not intentiuely, I did consent,   440
And often did beguile her of her teares,
When I did speake of some distressefull stroake
That my youth suffer'd: my story being done,
She gaue me for my paines a world of kisses;

She swore in faith twas strange, twas passing strange;
Twas pittifull, twas wondrous pittifull;
She wisht she had not heard it, yet she wisht
That Heauen had made her such a man: she thanked
    me,
And bad me, if I had a friend that lou'd her,
450   I should but teach him how to tell my story,
And that would wooe her. Vpon this hent I spake:
She lou'd me for the dangers I had past,
And I lou'd her that she did pitty them.
This onely is the witchcraft I haue vs'd:
    Enter Desdemona, Iago, and Attendants
Here comes the Lady, let her witnesse it.
    DUKE
I thinke this tale would win my daughter to,—
Good *Brabantio*,
Take vp this mangled matter at the best,
Men doe their broken weapons rather vse,
Then their bare hands.
460 BRABANTIO   I pray you heare her speake.
If she confesse that she was halfe the wooer,
Destruction on my head, if my bad blame
Light on the man. Come hither gentle mistresse:
Doe you perceiue in all this noble company,
Where most you owe obedience?
    DESDEMONA   My noble father,
I doe perceiue here a deuided duty:
To you I am bound for life and education;
My life and education both doe learne me
How to respect you, you are the Lord of duty,
470   I am hitherto your daughter, But heere's my husband:
And so much duty as my mother shewed
To you, preferring you before her father,
So much I challenge, that I may professe,
Due to the Moore my Lord.
    BRABANTIO   God bu'y, I ha done:
Please it your Grace, on to the State affaires;
I had rather to adopt a child then get it;
Come hither Moore:
I here doe giue thee that, with all my heart
Which but thou hast already, with all my heart
I would keepe from thee: (*to Desdemona*) for your sake
480   Iewell,
I am glad at soule, I haue no other child,
For thy escape would teach me tyranny,
To hang clogs on em, I haue done my Lord.
    DUKE
Let me speake like your selfe, and lay a sentence
Which as a greese or step may helpe these louers
Into your fauour.
When remedies are past, the griefes are ended,
By seeing the worst, which late on hopes depended,
To mourne a mischeife that is past and gone,
490   Is the next way to draw new mischiefe on;
What cannot be preseru'd when fortune takes,
Patience her iniury a mockery makes.
The rob'd that smiles, steales something from the thiefe,
He robs himselfe, that spends a bootelesse griefe.

    BRABANTIO
So let the *Turke*, of *Cypres* vs beguile,
We lose it not so long as we can smile;
He beares the sentence well that nothing beares,
But the free comfort, which from thence he heares:
But he beares both the sentence and the sorrow,
That to pay griefe, must of poore patience borrow.   500
These sentences to sugar, or to gall,
Being strong on both sides, are equiuocall:
But words are words, I neuer yet did heare,
That the bruis'd heart was pierced through the eare:
I humbly beseech you proceed to th' affaires of state.
DUKE The *Turke* with a most mighty preparation makes
for *Cipres*: *Othello*, the fortitude of the place, is best
knowne to you, and tho we haue there a substitute
of most allowed sufficiency, yet opinion, a more
soueraigne mistresse of effects, throwes a more safer   510
voyce on you; you must therefore bee content to
slubber the glosse of your new fortunes, with this more
stubborne and boisterous expedition.
    OTHELLO
The tyrant custome most graue Senators,
Hath made the flinty and steele Cooch of warre,
My thrice driuen bed of downe: I doe agnize
A naturall and prompt alacrity,
I finde in hardnesse, and do vndertake
This present warres against the *Ottamites*,
Most humbly therefore, bending to your State,   520
I craue fit disposition for my wife,
Due reference of place and exhibition,
With such accomodation and besort
As leuels with her breeding.
DUKE Why at her Fathers?
BRABANTIO I will not haue it so.
OTHELLO Nor I.
DESDEMONA Nor would I there reside,
To put my father in impatient thoughts,
By being in his eye: most gracious Duke,   530
To my vnfolding lend your prosperous eare,
And let me finde a charter in your voyce,
T'assist my simplenesse.—
    DUKE   What would you *Desdemona*.
    DESDEMONA
That I did loue the Moore, to liue with him,
My downe right violence, and storme of Fortunes,
May trumpet to the world: my hearts subdued,
Euen to the very quality of my Lord:
I saw *Othelloes* vissage in his minde,
And to his Honors, and his valiant parts
Did I my soule and fortunes consecrate: 540
So that deere Lords, if I be left behinde,
A Mothe of peace, and he goe to the warre,
The rites for why I loue him, are bereft me,
And I a heauy interim shall support,
By his deare absence, let me goe with him.
OTHELLO (*to the Duke*) Let her haue your voyce.
Vouch with me Heauen, I therefore beg it not
To please the pallat of my appetite,

Nor to comply with heate, the young affects
550 In me defunct, and proper satisfaction,
But to be free and bounteous to her mind,
And heauen defend your good soules that you thinke
I will your serious and great businesse scant,
When she is with me;—no, when light-wingd toyes,
Of feather'd Cupid seele with wanton dulnesse,
My speculatiue and offic'd instruments,
That my disports, corrupt and taint my businesse,
Let huswiues make a skellet of my Helme,
And all indigne and base aduersities,
560 Make head against my Estimation.

DUKE
Be it, as you shall priuately determine,
Either for her stay or going, th'affaire cries hast,
And speede must answer it.

A SENATOR (*to Othello*)   You must away to night.

DESDEMONA
To night my Lord?

DUKE   This night.

OTHELLO   With all my heart.

DUKE
At nine i'th' morning here weel meete againe.
Othello, leaue some officer behind,
And he shall our Commission bring to you,
And such things else of quality and respect,
As doth import you.

OTHELLO   So please your Grace, my Ancient,
570 A man he is of honesty and trust,
To his conueyance I assigne my wife,
With what else needefull your good Grace shall
          thinke,
To be sent after me.

DUKE   Let it be so:
Good night to euery one, (*to Brabantio*) and noble
          Seignior,
If vertue no delighted beauty lacke,
Your son in law is farre more faire then blacke.

A SENATOR
Adue braue Moore, vse *Desdemona* well.

BRABANTIO
Looke to her Moore, if thou hast eyes to see,
She has deceiu'd her father, and may thee.

⌈*Exeunt Duke, Brabantio, Cassio, Senators,
and Officers*⌉

OTHELLO
580 My life vpon her faith: honest *Iago*,
My *Desdemona* must I leaue to thee,
I preethee let thy wife attend on her,
And bring them after in the best aduantage;
Come *Desdemona*, I haue but an houre
Of loue, of worldly matter, and direction,
To spend with thee, we must obey the time.

Exit Moore and Desdemona

RODERIGO *Iago*.

IAGO What saiest thou noble heart?

RODERIGO What will I doe think'st thou?

590 IAGO Why goe to bed and sleepe.

RODERIGO I will incontinently drowne my selfe.

IAGO If thou doest, I shall neuer loue thee after, why,
thou silly Gentleman.

RODERIGO It is sillinesse to liue, when to liue is torment,
and then haue we a prescription to dye, when death
is our Physition.

IAGO Oh villanous: I ha look'd vpon the world for foure
times seuen yeares, and since I could distinguish betwixt
a benefit, and an iniury, I neuer found man that knew
how to loue himselfe: ere I would say I would drowne 600
my selfe, for the loue of a Ginny Hen, I would change
my humanity with a Baboone.

RODERIGO What should I do? I confesse it is my shame to
be so fond, but it is not in my vertue to amend it.

IAGO Vertue? a fig, tis in our selues, that wee are thus,
or thus, our bodies are our gardens, to the which our
wills are Gardiners, so that if we will plant Nettles, or
sow Lettice, set Isop, and weed vp Time; supply it with
one gender of hearbes, or distract it with many; either
to haue it sterrill with Idlenesse, or manur'd with 610
Industry, why the power, and corrigible Authority of
this, lies in our wills. If the beame of our liues had not
one scale of reason, to poise another of sensuality; the
blood and basenesse of our natures, would conduct vs
to most preposterous conclusions. But wee haue reason
to coole our raging motions, our carnall stings, our
vnbitted lusts; whereof I take this, that you call loue
to be a sect, or syen.

RODERIGO It cannot be.

IAGO It is meerly a lust of the blood, and a permission of 620
the will: Come, be a man; drowne thy selfe? drowne
Cats and blinde Puppies: I haue profest me thy friend,
and I confesse me knit to thy deseruing, with cables of
perdurable toughnesse; I could neuer better steede thee
then now. Put money in thy purse; follow thou the
warres, defeate thy fauour with an vsurp'd beard; I
say, put money in thy purse. It cannot be long, that
Desdemona should continue her loue to the Moore,—
put money in thy purse,—nor he his to her; it was a
violent commencement in her, and thou shalt see an 630
answerable sequestration: put but money in thy
purse.—These Moores are changeable in their wills:—
fill thy purse with money. The food that to him now,
is as lushious as Locusts, shall be to him shortly as
bitter as Colloquintida. She must change for youth:
when shee is sated with his body, shee will finde the
error of her choyce. Therefore put money in thy purse:
if thou wilt needes damme thy selfe, doe it a more
delicate way then drowning; make all the money thou
canst. If sanctimony, and a fraile vow, betwixt an 640
erring *Barbarian*, and a super subtle *Venetian*, be not
too hard for my wits, and all the tribe of hell, thou
shalt enioy her; therefore make money,—a pox a
drowning thy selfe, it is cleane out of the way: seeke
thou rather to be hang'd in compassing thy ioy, then
to bee drowned, and goe without her.

RODERIGO Wilt thou be fast to my hopes, if I depend on
the issue?

IAGO Thou art sure of me—goe, make money—I haue
650   told thee often, and I re-tell thee againe, and againe, I
       hate the Moore, my cause is harted, thine hath no lesse
       reason, let vs be coniunctiue in our reuenge against
       him: If thou canst cuckold him, thou doest thy selfe a
       pleasure, me a sport. There are many euents in the
       womb of Time, which will be deliuered. Trauerce, go,
       prouide thy money, we will haue more of this to
       morrow, Adiue.

RODERIGO
       Where shall we meete i'th morning.

IAGO   At my lodging.

RODERIGO
       I'le be with thee betimes.

IAGO   Go to, farewell:—
       Doe you heare *Roderigo?*

660 RODERIGO   Ile sell all my Land.

                                              Exit Roderigo

IAGO
       Thus doe I euer make my foole my purse:
       For I mine owne gain'd knowledge should prophane,
       If I would time expend with such a snipe,
       But for my sport and profit: I hate the Moore,
       And it is thought abroad, that twixt my sheetes
       He ha's done my office; I know not, if't be true—
       But I, for meere suspition in that kind,
       Will doe, as if for surety: he holds me well,
       The better shall my purpose worke on him.
670   *Cassio's* a proper man, let me see now,
       To get his place, and to plume vp my will,
       In double knauery—how, how, let's see,
       After some time, to abuse *Othelloe's* eares,
       That he is too familiar with his wife:
       He hath a person and a smooth dispose,
       To be suspected, fram'd to make women false:
       The Moore is of a free and open nature,
       That thinkes men honest, that but seeme to be so:
       And will as tenderly be led bit'h nose—
680   As Asses are:
       I ha't, it is ingender'd: Hell and night
       Must bring this monstrous birth to the worlds light.

                                                              Exit

Sc. 4   *Enter below Montano, Gouernor of Cypres; two*
(2.1)   *other Gentlemen ⌈aboue⌉*

MONTANO
       What from the Cape can you discerne at Sea?

1 GENTLEMAN
       Nothing at all, it is a high wrought flood,
       I cannot twixt the heauen and the mayne
       Descry a saile.

MONTANO
       Me thinkes the wind hath spoke aloud at land,
       A fuller blast ne're shooke our Battlements:
       If it ha ruffiand so vpon the sea,
690   What ribbes of Oake, when mountaines melt on them,
       Can hold the morties,—What shall we heare of this?

2 GENTLEMAN
       A segregation of the *Turkish* Fleete:

For doe but stand vpon the foaming shore,
The chidden billow seemes to pelt the cloudes,
The winde shak'd surge, with high and monstrous
       mayne,
Seemes to cast water, on the burning Beare,
And quench the guards of th'euer fixed pole,
I neuer did, like molestation view,
On the inchafed flood.

MONTANO   If that the *Turkish* Fleete
Be not inshelter'd, and embayed, they are drown'd,   700
It is impossible to beare it out.
       Enter a third Gentleman

3 GENTLEMAN Newes Laddes: our warres are done:
The desperate Tempest hath so bang'd the *Turkes,*
That their designement halts: A noble shippe of *Venice*
Hath seene a greeuous wracke and sufferance
On most part of their Fleete.

MONTANO How, is this true?

3 GENTLEMAN The shippe is heere put in:
A Veronessa, *Michael Cassio,*
Leiutenant to the warlike Moore *Othello,*   710
Is come on Shore: the Moore himselfe at Sea,
And is in full Commission here for *Cypres.*

MONTANO
I am glad on't, tis a worthy Gouernour.

3 GENTLEMAN
But this same *Cassio,* tho he speake of comfort,
Touching the *Turkish* losse, yet he lookes sadly,
And prayes the Moore be safe, for they were parted,
With foule and violent Tempest.

MONTANO   Pray Heauens he be:
For I haue seru'd him, and the man commands
Like a full Souldier: Lets to the sea side, ho,
As well to see the vessell that's come in,   720
As to throw out our eyes for braue *Othello,*
Euen till we make the Maine, and th'Eriall blew,
An indistinct regard.

3 GENTLEMAN   Come, lets doe so,
For euery minute is expectancy
Of more arriuance.
       Enter Cassio

CASSIO
Thankes you, the valiant of this warlike Isle,
That so approue the Moore, Oh let the heauens
Giue him defence against the Elements,
For I haue lost him on a dangerous sea.

MONTANO Is he well shipt?   730

CASSIO
His Barke is stoutly timberd, and his Pilate
Of very expert and approu'd allowance,
Therefore my hope's not surfeited to death,
Stand in bold cure.

VOYCES (*within*)   A saile, a saile, a saile.

CASSIO What noyse?

A GENTLEMAN
The Towne is empty, on the brow o'th sea,
Stand ranckes of people, and they cry a sayle.

CASSIO
My hopes doe shape him for the gouernor.

A shot

A GENTLEMAN
They doe discharge their shot of courtesie,
Our friends at least.

740 CASSIO   I pray you sir goe forth,
And giue vs truth, who tis that is arriu'd.

A GENTLEMAN I shall.   *Exit*

MONTANO
But good Leiutenant, is your Generall wiu'd?

CASSIO
Most fortunately, he hath atchieu'd a maide,
That parragons description, and wild fame:
One that excells the quirkes of blasoning pens,
And in th'essentiall vesture of creation,
Does tyre the Ingeniuer.
          Enter Gentleman
                              How now, who has put in?

GENTLEMAN
Tis one *Iago*, ancient to the Generall.

CASSIO
750 Ha's had most fauourable and happy speede,
Tempests themselues, hy seas, and houling windes,
The gutter'd rocks, and congregated sands,
Traitors ensteep'd, to enclog the guiltlesse Keele,
As hauing sence of beauty, do omit
Their mortall natures, letting goe safely by
The diuine *Desdemona*.

MONTANO   What is she?

CASSIO
She that I spake of, our great Captains Captaine,
Left in the conduct of the bold *Iago*,
Whose footing here anticipates our thoughts
760 A sennights speede—great *Ioue Othello* guard,
And swell his saile with thine owne powerfull breath,
That he may blesse this Bay with his tall shippe,
Make loues quicke pants in *Desdemona's* armes,
Giue renewd fire, to our extincted spirits,
And bring all *Cypresse* comfort,—
          Enter Desdemona, Iago, Emillia, and Roderigo
                              O behold
The riches of the ship is come on shore.
You men of *Cypres*, let her haue your knees:
          Montano and Gentlemen make courtesie to
          Desdemona
Haile to thee Lady: and the grace of heauen,
Before, behinde thee, and on euery hand,
Enwheele thee round.

770 DESDEMONA   I thanke you valiant *Cassio*:
What tidings can you tell me of my Lord?

CASSIO
He is not yet arriu'd, nor know I ought,
But that hee's well, and will be shortly here.

DESDEMONA
O but I feare:—how lost you company?

CASSIO
The great contention of the sea and skies
Parted our fellowship:

VOYCES (*within*) A saile, a saile.

CASSIO But harke, A saile.
          A shot

A GENTLEMAN
They giue their greeting to the Cittadell,
This likewise is a friend.

CASSIO   See for the Newes: 780
                              Exit Gentleman
Good Ancient, you are welcome, (*kissing Emillia*)
          welcome Mistresse,
Let it not gall your patience, good *Iago*,
That I extend my manners, tis my breeding,
That giues me this bold shew of courtesie.

IAGO
Sir, would she giue you so much of her lips,
As of her tongue, she oft bestowes on me,
You would haue enough.

DESDEMONA Alas! shee has no speech.

IAGO Infaith too much.
I finde it still, when I ha leaue to sleepe,   790
Mary, before your Ladiship I grant,
She puts her tongue alittle in her heart,
And chides with thinking.

EMILLIA   You ha little cause to say so.

IAGO
Come on, Come on, you are Pictures out of doore:
Bells in your Parlors: Wildcats in your Kitchins:
Saints in your iniuries: Diuells being offended:
Players in your houswifery; and houswiues in your
          beds.

DESDEMONA
O fie vpon thee slanderer.

IAGO
Nay, it is true, or else I am a *Turke*,
You rise to play, and goe to bed to worke.   800

EMILLIA
You shall not write my praise.

IAGO   No, let me not.

DESDEMONA
What wouldst write of me, if thou shouldst praise me?

IAGO
O gentle Lady, doe not put me to't,
For I am nothing, if not Criticall.

DESDEMONA
Come on, assay—there's one gone to the Harbor?

IAGO I Madam.

DESDEMONA
I am not merry, but I doe beguile
The thing I am, by seeming otherwise:
Come, how wouldst thou praise me?

IAGO
I am about it, but indeed my inuention   810
Comes from my pate, as birdlime does from freeze,
It plucks out braines and all: but my Muse labors,
And thus she is deliuer'd:
If she be faire and wise, fairenesse and wit;
The one's for vse, the other vseth it.

DESDEMONA Well praisde: how if she be blacke and witty?

IAGO

If she be blacke, and thereto haue a wit,
Shee'le finde a white, that shall her blacknesse fit.

DESEMONA

Worse and worse.

EMILLIA   How if faire and foolish?

IAGO

820   She neuer yet was foolish, that was faire,
For euen her folly helpt her, to an haire.

DESEMONA These are old fond paradoxes, to make fooles
laugh i'th'Alehouse,
What miserable praise hast thou for her,
That's foule and foolish?

IAGO

There's none so foule, and foolish thereunto,
But does foule prankes, which faire and wise ones
doe.

DESEMONA O heauy ignorance, thou praisest the worst
best: but what praise couldst thou bestow on a
830   deseruing woman indeed? one, that in the authority of
her merrit, did iustly put on the vouch of very malice
it selfe?

IAGO

She that was euer faire, and neuer proud,
Had tongue at will, and yet was neuer lowd,
Neuer lackt gold, and yet went neuer gay,
Fled from her wish, and yet said, now I may:
She that being angred, her reuenge being nigh,
Bad her wrong stay, and her displeasure flye;
She that in wisedome, neuer was so fraile,
840   To change the Codshead for the Salmons taile.
She that could thinke, and ne're disclose her minde,
See Suitors following, and not looke behind:
She was a wight, if euer such wightes were.

DESEMONA To doe what?

IAGO

To suckle fooles, and chronicle small Beere.

DESEMONA O most lame and impotent conclusion: doe
not learne of him Emillia, tho he be thy husband; how
say you Cassio, is he not a most prophane and liberall
Counsellour?

850   CASSIO He speakes home Madam, you may rellish him
more in the Souldier then in the Scholler.

Cassio and Desdemona talke apart

IAGO (*aside*) He takes her by the palme; I well sed, whisper:
with as little a webbe as this will I ensnare as great a
Fly as Cassio. I smile vpon her, doe: I will giue thee in
thine owne courtship: you say true, tis so indeed. If
such trickes as these strip you out of your Leiutenantry,
it had beene better you had not kist your three fingers
so oft, which now againe, you are most apt to play the
sir in: very good, well kist, an excellent courtesie; tis
860   so indeed: yet againe, your fingers to your lips? Would
they were Clisterpipes for your sake.—

Trumpets within

(*Aloud*) The Moore, I know his Trumpet.

CASSIO   Tis truely so.

DESEMONA

Lets meete him, and receiue him.

CASSIO   Loe, where he comes.

Enter Othello, and Attendants

OTHELLO (*to Desdemona*)

O my faire Warriour.

DESEMONA   My deare *Othello*.

OTHELLO

It giues me wonder great as my content,
To see you here before me: O my soules ioy,
If after euery tempest, come such calmes,
May the winds blow, till they haue waken'd death,
And let the labouring Barke clime hills of seas,
Olympus high, and duck againe as low,   870
As hell's from Heauen: If it were now to dye,
T'were now to be most happy, for I feare
My soule hath her content so absolute,
That not another comfort, like to this
Succeeds in vnknowne Fate.

DESEMONA   The Heauens forbid,
But that our loues and comforts should increase,
Euen as our dayes doe growe.

OTHELLO   Amen to that sweete powers,
I cannot speake enough of this content,
It stops me heere, it is too much of ioy:
And this, (*they kisse*) and this, the greatest discords be,   880
That ere our hearts shall make.

IAGO (*aside*)   O, you are well tun'd now,
But I'le set downe the pegs, that make this musique,
As honest as I am.

OTHELLO   Come, let vs to the Castle:
Newes friends, our warres are done, the *Turks* are
drownd:
How does my old acquaintance of this Isle;
Honny, you shall be well desir'd in *Cypres*;
I haue found great loue amongst them: O my sweete,
I prattle out of fashion, and I dote,
In mine one comforts: I preethee good *Iago*,
Goe to the Bay, and disimbarke my Coffers;   890
Bring thou the Master to the Cittadell;
He is a good one, and his worthinesse,
Does challenge much respect: come *Desdemona*,
Once more well met at *Cypres*.

Exit Othello and Desdemona with all but Iago
and Roderigo

IAGO (*to an Attendant as he goes out*) Doe thou meete me
presently at the Harbour: (*to Roderigo*) come hither, If
thou beest valiant, as they say, base men being in loue,
haue then a Nobility in their natures, more then is
natiue to them—list me, the Leiutenant to night
watches on the Court of Guard: first I must tell thee   900
this: *Desdemona* is directly in loue with him.

RODERIGO With him? why tis not possible.

IAGO Lay thy finger thus, and let thy soule be instructed:
marke me, with what violence she first lou'd the Moore,
but for bragging, and telling her fantasticall lies; to
loue him still for prating? let not thy discreet heart

thinke it. Her eye must be fed, and what delight shall she haue to look on the Diuell? When the blood is made dull with the act of sport, there should be againe
910 to inflame it, and to giue saciety a fresh appetite, Louelines in fauour, sympathy in yeares, manners and beauties; all which the Moore is defectiue in: now for want of these requir'd conueniences, her delicate tendernesse will finde it selfe abus'd, beginne to heaue the gorge, disrellish and abhorre the Moore, very nature will instruct her in it, and compell her to some second choyce: now sir, this granted, as it is a most pregnant and vnforced position, who stands so eminent in the degree of this fortune, as *Cassio* does? a knaue very
920 voluble, no further conscionable, then in putting on the meere forme of ciuill and humaine seeming, for the better compasse of his salt and most hidden loose affection? Why none, why none: A slipper, and subtle knaue, a finder of occasion; that has an eye, can stampe and counterfeit aduantages, though true aduantage neuer present it selfe. A diuelish knaue. Besides, the knaue is handsome, yong, and hath all those requisites in him that folly and green mindes look after; a pestilent compleate knaue, and the woman
930 hath found him already.

RODERIGO I cannot beleeue that in her, shee's full of most blest condition.

IAGO Blest figs end: the wine shee drinkes is made of grapes: if she had beene blest, she would neuer haue lou'd the Moore. Blest pudding. Didst thou not see her paddle with the palme of his hand? Didst not marke that?

RODERIGO Yes, that I did: but that was but courtesie.

IAGO Lechery, by this hand: an Index and obscure
940 prologue to the history of lust and foule thoughts: they met so neere with their lips, that their breathes embrac'd together. Villanous thoughts *Roderigo*, when these mutualities so marshall the way, hard at hand, comes the Master, and maine exercise, th'incorporate conclusion. Pish. But sir, be you rul'd by mee, I haue brought you from *Venice*: watch you to night, for the command I'le lay't vpon you, *Cassio* knowes you not, I'le not be farre from you, do you finde some occasion to anger *Cassio*, either by speaking too loud, or tainting
950 his discipline, or from what other course you please; which the time shall more fauourably minister.

RODERIGO Well.

IAGO Sir he's rash, and very suddain in choler, and haply may strike at you; prouoke him that he may, for euen out of that, will I cause these of *Cypres* to mutiny, whose quallification shall come into no true taste againe, but by the displanting of *Cassio*: So shall you haue a shorter iourney to your desires by the meanes I shal then haue to prefer them, & the impediment,
960 most profitably remou'd, without the which there were no expectation of our prosperity.

RODERIGO I will doe this, if you can bring it to any opportunity.

IAGO I warrant thee, meete me by and by at the Cittadell; I must fetch his necessaries ashore.—Farewell.

RODERIGO Adue.   *Exit*

IAGO

That *Cassio* loues her, I doe well beleeue it;
That she loues him, tis apt and of great credit;
The Moore howbe't, that I indure him not,
Is of a constant, louing, noble nature;   970
And I dare thinke, hee'le proue to *Desdemona*,
A most deere husband: now I doe loue her too,
Not out of absolute lust, tho peraduenture
I stand accountant for as great a sin,
But partly lead to diet my reuenge,
For that I doe suspect the lustie Moore,
Hath leap'd into my seate, the thought whereof
Doth like a poisonous minerall gnaw my inwards,
And nothing can, or shall content my soule,
Till I am euen'd with him, wife, for wife: 980
Or failing so, yet that I put the Moore,
At least, into a Iealousie so strong,
That Iudgement cannot cure; which thing to doe,
If this poore trash of *Venice*, whom I trace,
For his quicke hunting, stand the putting on,
I'le haue our *Michael Cassio* on the hip,
Abuse him to the Moore, in the ranke garbe,
(For I feare *Cassio*, with my nightcap to)
Make the Moore thanke me, loue me, and reward me,
For making him egregiously an Asse,   990
And practising vpon his peace and quiet,
Euen to madnesse: tis here, but yet confus'd,
Knaueries plaine face is neuer seene, till vs'd.   *Exit*

Enter Othello's Herald reading a Proclamation   Sc. 5

HERALD It is *Othello's* pleasure; our noble and valiant   (2.2)
Generall, that vpon certaine tidings now arriued, importing the meere perdition of the *Turkish* Fleete; euery man put himselfe into triumph: Some to dance, some to make bonefires; each man to what sport and Reuels his addiction leades him; for besides these beneficiall newes, it is the celebration of his Nuptiall: 1000
So much was his pleasure should bee proclaimed. All Offices are open, and there is full liberty of Feasting, from this present houre of fiue, till the bell haue told eleuen. Heauen blesse the Isle of *Cypres*, and our noble Generall *Othello*.   *Exit*

Enter Othello, Desdemona, Cassio, and Attendants   Sc. 6

OTHELLO   (2.3)

Good *Michael*, looke you to the guard to night,
Lets teach our selues that honourable stoppe,
Not to out sport discretion.

CASSIO

Iago hath direction what to doe:
But notwithstanding with my personall eye   1010
Will I looke to't.

OTHELLO   *Iago* is most honest,
Michael good night, to morrow with your earliest,

Let me haue speech with you, (*to Desdemona*) come
  my deare loue,
The purchase made, the fruits are to ensue,
That profits yet to come 'tweene me and you,
(*To Cassio*) Good night.

          Exit Othello, Desdemona, and Attendants
    Enter Iago

CASSIO

Welcome *Iago*, we must to the watch.

IAGO Not this houre Leiutenant, tis not yet ten o'th'clock:
our Generall cast vs thus early for the loue of his
1020 *Desdemona*, who let vs not therefore blame, hee hath
not yet made wanton the night with her; and she is
sport for *Ioue*.

CASSIO She's a most exquisite Lady.

IAGO And I'le warrant her full of game.

CASSIO Indeede shes a most fresh and delicate creature.

IAGO What an eye she has? Me thinkes it sounds a parly
to prouocation.

CASSIO An inuiting eye, and yet me thinkes right moddest.

IAGO And when she speakes, is it not an alarme to loue?

1030 CASSIO She is indeede perfection.

IAGO Well, happinesse to their sheetes—come Leiutenant,
I haue a stope of Wine, and heere without are a brace
of *Cypres* Gallants, that would faine haue a measure to
the health of blacke *Othello*.

CASSIO Not to night, good *Iago*; I haue very poore and
vnhappy braines for drinking: I could well wish
courtesie would inuent some other custome of
entertainement.

IAGO O they are our friends,—but one cup: I'le drink for
1040 you.

CASSIO I ha drunke but one cup to night, and that was
craftily qualified to, and behold what innouation it
makes here: I am infortunate in the infirmity, and dare
not taske my weakenesse with any more.

IAGO What man, tis a night of Reuells, the Gallants desire
it.

CASSIO Where are they?

IAGO

Here at the dore, I pray you call them in.

CASSIO I'le do't, but it dislikes me.   *Exit*

IAGO

1050 If I can fasten but one cup vpon him,
With that which he hath drunke to night already,
Hee'll be as full of quarrell and offence,
As my young mistris dog:—Now my sicke foole
  Roderigo,
Whom loue hath turn'd almost the wrong side out,
To *Desdemona*, hath to night caroust
Potations pottle deepe, and hee's to watch.
Three else of *Cypres*, noble swelling spirits,
That hold their honours, in a wary distance,
The very Elements of this warlike Isle,
1060 Haue I to night flustred with flowing cups,
And they watch too: now mongst this flocke of
  drunkards,

Am I to put our *Cassio* in some action,
That may offend the Isle;

    Enter Montano, Cassio, Gentlemen ⌈and Seruants⌉
    with wine

             But here they come:
If consequence doe but approoue my dreame,
My boate sailes freely, both with winde and streame.

CASSIO

Fore God they haue giuen me a rouse already.

MONTANO

Good faith a little one, not past a pint,
As I am a souldier.

IAGO   Some wine ho:
(*Sings*) *And let me the Cannikin clinke, clinke,*
      And let me the Cannikin clinke: 1070
        A Souldier's a man,
        O, mans life's but a span,
        Why then let a souldier drinke.—
Some wine boyes.

CASSIO Fore God an excellent song.

IAGO I learn'd it in *England*, where indeed they are most
potent in potting: your *Dane*, your *Germaine*, and your
swag-bellied *Hollander*; drinke ho, are nothing to your
English.

CASSIO Is your *English* man so exquisite in his drinking? 1080

IAGO Why he drinkes you with facillity, your *Dane* dead
drunke: he sweats not to ouerthrow your *Almaine*; he
giues your *Hollander* a vomit, ere the next pottle can
be fild.

CASSIO To the health of our Generall.

MONTANO I am for it Leiutenant, and I'le doe you iustice.

IAGO O sweete *England*,—

(*Sings*) *King Stephen was and a worthy peere,*
      His breeches cost him but a crowne,
      He held them sixpence all too deere,   1090
      With that he cald the Taylor lowne,
      He was a wight of high renowne,
      And thou art but of low degree,
      Tis pride that puls the Countrey downe,
      Then take thy owd cloke about thee.—
Some wine ho.

CASSIO Fore God this is a more exquisite song then the
other.

IAGO Will you hear't agen?

CASSIO No, for I hold him to be vnworthy of his place, 1100
that does those things: well, God's aboue all, and there
bee soules must bee saued, and there be soules must
not be saued.

IAGO It's true good Leiutenant.

CASSIO For mine own part, no offence to the Generall,
nor any man of quality, I hope to be saued.

IAGO And so doe I too Leiutenant.

CASSIO I, but by your leaue, not before me; the Leiutenant
is to be saued before the Ancient. Let's ha no more of
this, let's to our affaires: God forgiue vs our sins: 1110
Gentlemen, let's looke to our businesse; Doe not thinke
Gentlemen I am drunke, this is my Ancient, this is my

right hand, and this is my left: I am not drunke now,
I can stand well enough, and I speake well enough.

GENTLEMEN Excellent well.

CASSIO Why very well then: you must not thinke then,
that I am drunke.   *Exit*

MONTANO
To th' plotforme maisters. Come, let's set the watch.
                                                    Exeunt Gentlemen

IAGO
You see this fellow that is gone before,
1120   He's a Souldier fit to stand by *Cæsar*,
And giue direction: and doe but see his vice,
Tis to his vertue, a iust equinox,
The one as long as th'other: tis pitty of him,
I feare the trust *Othello* puts him in,
On some odde time of his infirmity,
Will shake this Island.

MONTANO   But is he often thus.

IAGO
Tis euermore his Prologue to his sleepe:
Hee'le watch the horolodge a double set,
If drinke rocke not his cradle.

MONTANO   It were well
1130   The Generall were put in minde of it,
Perhaps he sees it not, or his good nature,
Prizes the vertue that appeares in *Cassio*,
And lookes not on his euills: is not this true?
                          Enter Roderigo

IAGO ⌈aside⌉ How now *Roderigo*,
I pray you after the Leiutenant, goe.   *Exit Roderigo*

MONTANO
And tis great pitty that the noble Moore
Should hazard such a place, as his owne second,
With one of an ingraft infirmity:
It were an honest action to say so
To the Moore.

1140   IAGO   Not I, for this faire Island:
I doe loue *Cassio* well, and would doe much,
To cure him of this euill:

VOYCES (*within*) Helpe, helpe.

IAGO   But harke, what noyse.
              Enter Cassio, driuing in Roderigo

CASSIO Zouns, you rogue, you rascall.

MONTANO What's the matter Leiutenant?

CASSIO A knaue, teach mee my duty: I'le beate the knaue
into a Twiggen-bottle.

RODERIGO Beate me?

1150   CASSIO Doest thou prate rogue?

MONTANO Nay, good Leiutenant; I pray you sir hold your
hand.

CASSIO Let me goe sir, or ile knocke you ore the mazzard.

MONTANO Come, come, you're drunke.

CASSIO Drunke?
              they fight

IAGO (*to Roderigo*)
Away I say, goe out and cry a muteny.   *Exit Roderigo*
Nay good Leiutenant: godswill Gentlemen,

Helpe ho, Leiutenant: Sir *Montano*, sir,
Helpe maisters, here's a goodly watch indeed,
      A bell rung
Who's that which rings the bell? Diablo—ho,   1160
The Towne will rise, godswill Leiutenant, hold,
You'le be asham'd for euer.
      Enter Othello, and Attendants with weapons

OTHELLO   What is the matter here?

MONTANO
Zouns, I bleed still, I am hurt, to th'death:
(*assailing Cassio*) He dies.

OTHELLO Hold, for your liues.

IAGO
Hold hoa: Leiutenant, sir *Montano*, Gentlemen,
Haue you forgot all place of sence, and duty:
Hold, the Generall speakes to you; hold, hold, for
      shame.

OTHELLO
Why how now ho, from whence ariseth this?
Are we turn'd *Turkes*, and to our selues doe that,
Which Heauen hath forbid the *Ottamites*:   1170
For Christian shame, put by this barbarous brawle;
He that stirres next, to carue for his owne rage,
Holds his soule light, he dies vpon his motion;
Silence that dreadfull bell, it frights the Isle
From her propriety:
      ⌈Bell stops⌉
                          what is the matter masters?
Honest *Iago*, that lookes dead with grieuing,
Speake, who began this, on thy loue I charge thee.

IAGO
I doe not know, friends all but now, euen now,
In quarter, and in termes, like bride and groome,
Deuesting them for bed, and then but now,   1180
As if some plannet had vnwitted men,
Swords out, and tilting one at others breastes,
In opposition bloody. I cannot speake
Any beginning to this peeuish odds;
And would in action glorious, I had lost
Those legges, that brought me to a part of it.

OTHELLO
How comes it *Michael*, you are thus forgot?

CASSIO
I pray you pardon me, I cannot speake.

OTHELLO
Worthy *Montano*, you were wont be ciuill,
The grauity and stilnesse of your youth,   1190
The world hath noted, and your name is great,
In mouthes of wisest censure: what's the matter
That you vnlace your reputation thus,
And spend your rich opinion, for the name
Of a night brawler? giue me answer to it?

MONTANO
Worthy *Othello*, I am hurt to danger,
Your Officer *Iago* can informe you,
While I spare speech, which something now offends
      me,

Of all that I doe know, nor know I ought
1200 By me, that's sed or done amisse this night,
Vnlesse selfe-charity be sometimes a vice,
And to defend our selues it be a sinne,
When violence assayles vs.

OTHELLO   Now by heauen
My blood begins my safer guides to rule,
And passion hauing my best iudgement collied,
Assayes to leade the way. Zouns, if I stirre,
Or doe but lift this arme, the best of you
Shall sinke in my rebuke: giue me to know
How this foule rout began, who set it on,
1210 And he that is approou'd in this offence,
Tho he had twin'd with me, both at a birth,
Shall loose me; what, in a Towne of warre,
Yet wild, the peoples hearts brim full of feare,
To mannage priuate and domesticke quarrel,
In night, and on the Court and guard of safety?
Tis monstrous. _Iago_, who began't?

MONTANO (_to Iago_)
If partially affin'd, or leagu'd in office,
Thou doest deliuer, more or lesse then truth,
Thou art no souldier.

IAGO   Touch me not so neere,
1220 I had rather ha this tongue cut from my mouth,
Then it should doe offence to _Michael Cassio_:
Yet I perswade my selfe to speake the truth,
Shall nothing wrong him. This it is Generall:
Montano and my selfe being in speech,
There comes a fellow, crying out for helpe,
And _Cassio_ following him with determin'd sword,
To execute vpon him: Sir this Gentleman
Steps in to _Cassio_, and intreates his pause;
My selfe the crying fellow did pursue,
1230 Lest by his clamour, as it so fell out,
The Towne might fall in fright: he swift of foote,
Out ran my purpose: and I returnd the rather,
For that I heard the clinke and fall of swords:
And _Cassio_ high in oath, which till to night,
I ne're might say before: when I came backe,
For this was briefe, I found them close together,
At blow and thrust, euen as agen they were,
When you your selfe did part them.
More of this matter cannot I report,
1240 But men are men, the best sometimes forget;
Tho _Cassio_ did some little wrong to him,
As men in rage strike those that wish them best,
Yet surely _Cassio_, I beleeue receiu'd
From him that fled, some strange indignity,
Which patience could not passe.

OTHELLO   I know _Iago_,
Thy honesty and loue doth mince this matter,
Making it light to _Cassio_: _Cassio_, I loue thee,
But neuer more be Officer of mine.
    Enter Desdemona, attended
Looke if my Gentle loue be not raisde vp:
1250 I'le make thee an example.

DESDEMONA What is the matter (Deere?)

OTHELLO All's well now sweeting:

Come away to bed: (_to Montano_) sir, for your hurts,
My selfe will be your surgeon; (_to Attendants_) leade
    him off;   _Exeunt Attendants with Montano_
Iago, looke with care about the Towne,
And silence those, whom this vile brawle distracted.
Come _Desdemona_: tis the Souldiers life,
To haue their balmy slumbers wak'd with strife.
                    Exit all but Iago and Cassio

IAGO What are you hurt Leiutenant?

CASSIO I, past all surgery.   1260

IAGO Mary God forbid.

CASSIO Reputation, reputation, reputation, Oh I ha lost
    my reputation: I ha lost the immortall part of my selfe,
    and what remaines is beastiall, my reputation, _Iago_,
    my reputation.

IAGO As I am an honest man, I thought you had receiu'd
    some bodily wound, there is more sence in that, then
    in Reputation: reputation is an idle and most false
    imposition, oft got without merit, and lost without
    deseruing, You haue lost no reputation at all, vnlesse   1270
    you repute your selfe such a loser; what man, there
    are more wayes to recouer the Generall agen: you are
    but now cast in his moode, a punishment more in
    pollicy, then in malice, euen so, as one would beate
    his offencelesse dog, to affright an imperious Lyon: sue
    to him againe, and hees yours.

CASSIO I will rather sue to be despis'd, then to deceiue so
    good a Commander, with so slight, so drunken, and so
    indiscreete an Officer: Drunke? And speake Parrat?
    And squabble? Swagger? Sweare? And discourse   1280
    Fustian with ones owne shadow? O thou inuisible spirit
    of wine, if thou hast no name to bee knowne by, let
    vs call thee Diuell.

IAGO What was he, that you followed with your sword?
    What had he done to you?

CASSIO I know not.

IAGO Ist possible?

CASSIO I remember a masse of things, but nothing
    distinctly; a quarrell, but nothing wherefore. O God,
    that men should put an enemy in there mouthes, to   1290
    steale away there braines; that wee should with ioy,
    pleasance, Reuell, and applause, transforme our selues
    into beasts.

IAGO Why, but you are now well enough: how came you
    thus recouered?

CASSIO It hath pleasde the Diuell drunkennesse, to giue
    place to the Diuell wrath; one vnperfectnesse, shewes
    me another, to make me frankely despise my selfe.

IAGO Come, you are too seuere a morraler; as the time,
    the place, & the condition of this Countrey stands, I   1300
    could heartily wish, this had not befalne; but since it
    is as it is, mend it, for your own good.

CASSIO I will aske him for my place againe, hee shall tell
    me I am a drunkard: had I as many mouthes as _Hydra_,
    such an answer would stop them all: to be now a
    sensible man, by and by a foole, and presently a beast.
    Oh strange! Euery inordinate cup is vnblest, and the
    ingredient is a diuell.

IAGO Come, come, good wine is a good familiar creature,

1310 if it be well vs'd; exclaime no more against it; and
good Leiutenant, I thinke you thinke I loue you.

CASSIO I haue well approou'd it sir,—I drunke?

IAGO You, or any man liuing may bee drunke at a time
man: I'le tell you what you shall do,—our Generals
wife is now the Generall; I may say so in this respect,
for that he hath deuoted and giuen vp himselfe to the
contemplation, marke and denotement of her parts and
graces. Confesse your selfe freely to her, importune her
helpe to put you in your place againe: she is of so free,
1320 so kind, so apt, so blessed a disposition, shee holds it
a vice in her goodnesse, not to doe more then shee is
requested. This broken ioynt betweene you and her
husband, intreate her to splinter, and my fortunes
against any lay, worth naming, this cracke of your
loue shall grow stronger then it was before.

CASSIO You aduise me well.

IAGO I protest in the sincerity of loue and honest
kindnesse.

CASSIO I thinke it freely, and betimes in the morning, I
1330 will beseech the vertuous *Desdemona*, to vndertake for
me; I am desperate of my fortunes, if they checke me
here.

IAGO You are in the right: Good night Leiutenant, I must
to the watch.

CASSIO Good night honest *Iago*.   *Exit*

IAGO
And what's he then, that sayes I play the villaine,
When this aduice is free I giue, and honest,
Proball to thinking, and indeed the course,
To win the Moore agen? For tis most easie
1340 Th'inclining *Desdemona* to subdue,
In any honest suite, she's fram'd as fruitfull,
As the free Elements: and then for her
To win the Moore, wer't to renounce his baptisme,
All seales and symbols of redeemed sin,
His soule is so infetter'd to her loue,
That she may make, vnmake, doe what she list,
Euen as her appetite shall play the god
With his weake function: how am I then a villaine?
To counsell *Cassio* to this parrallell course,
1350 Directly to his good: diuinity of hell,
When diuells will the blackest sins put on,
They doe suggest at first with heauenly shewes,
As I doe now: for whiles this honest foole
Plyes *Desdemona* to repaire his fortune,
And she for him, pleades strongly to the Moore:
I'le poure this pestilence into his eare,
That she repeales him for her bodyes lust;
And by how much she striues to doe him good,
She shall vndoe her credit with the Moore,
1360 So will I turne her vertue into pitch,
And out of her owne goodnesse make the net
That shall enmesh them all:
                    Enter Roderigo
                                        How now *Roderigo*?

RODERIGO I do follow here in the chase, not like a hound
that hunts, but one that filles vp the cry: my money

is almost spent, I ha bin to night exceedingly well
cudgeld: And I thinke the issue will be, I shall haue so
much experience for my paines, and so, with no money
at all, and a little more wit, returne againe to *Venice*.

IAGO
How poore are they, that ha not patience?
What wound did euer heale, but by degrees?   1370
Thou knowest we worke by wit, and not by
          wichcraft,
And wit depends on dilatory time.
Do'st not goe well? *Cassio* hath beaten thee,
And thou, by that small hurt, hast casheird *Cassio*,
Tho other things grow faire against the sun,
Yet fruites that blosome first, will first be ripe,
Content thy selfe awhile; bi'the masse tis morning;
Pleasure, and action, make the houres seeme short:
Retire thee, goe where thou art billited,
Away I say, thou shalt know more hereafter: 1380
Nay get thee gon.   *Exit Roderigo*
          Two things are to be done,
My wife must moue for *Cassio* to her mistris,
I'le set her on.
My selfe awhile, to draw the Moore apart,
And bring him iumpe, when he may *Cassio* finde,
Soliciting his wife: I, that's the way,
Dull not deuise by coldnesse and delay.   *Exit*

                    Enter Cassio, with Musitians   Sc. 7
CASSIO   (3.1)
Masters, play here, I will content your paines,
Something that's briefe, and bid good morrow
          Generall.
                    Musique. Enter Clowne

CLOWNE Why masters, ha your instruments bin in Naples, 1390
that they speake i'th'nose thus?

MUSITIAN How sir, how?

CLOWNE Are these I pray you, wind Instruments?

MUSITIAN I marry are they sir.

CLOWNE O, thereby hangs a tayle.

MUSITIAN Whereby hangs a tayle sir?

CLOWNE Marry sir, by many a winde Instrument that I
know: But maisters heere's money for you, and the
Generall so likes your musique, that hee desires you
for loues sake, to make no more noyse with it.   1400

MUSITIAN Well sir, we will not.

CLOWNE If you haue any musique that may not bee heard,
to't againe, but as they say, to heare musique, the
Generall does not greatly care.

MUSITIAN We ha none such sir.

CLOWNE Then put vp your pipes in your bag, for I'le
away; goe, vanish into ayre, away.   *Exit Musitians*

CASSIO Doest thou heare my honest friend?

CLOWNE No, I heare not your honest friend, I heare you.

CASSIO Preethee keepe vp thy quillets, there's a poore   1410
peece of gold for thee: if the Gentlewoman that attends
the Generals wife be stirring, tell her there's one *Cassio*,
entreates her alittle fauour of speech—wilt thou doe
this?

CLOWNE She is stirring sir, if she will stirre hither, I shall
　　　seeme to notifie vnto her.

CASSIO

　　Doe good my friend:　　　　　　　　　　　*Exit Clowne*
　　　　Enter Iago

　　　　　　　　　In happy time *Iago*.

IAGO

　　You ha not bin a bed then.

CASSIO　　　　　　　　　　Why no, the day had broke
　　Before we parted: I ha made bold *Iago*,
1420　To send in to your wife,—my suite to her,
　　Is, that she will to vertuous *Desdemona*,
　　Procure me some accesse.

IAGO

　　I'le send her to you presently,
　　And Ile deuise a meane to draw the Moore
　　Out of the way, that your conuerse and businesse,
　　May be more free.

CASSIO　　　　　　I humbly thanke you for't:
　　　　　　　　　　　　　　　　　　　Exit Iago
　　I neuer knew a Florentine more kinde and honest.
　　　　Enter Emillia

EMILLIA

　　Good morrow good Leiutenant, I am sorry
　　For your displeasure, but all will sure be well,
1430　The Generall and his wife are talking of it,
　　And she speakes for you stoutly: the Moore replies,
　　That he you hurt is of great fame in *Cypres*,
　　And great affinity, and that in wholesome wisedome,
　　He might not but refuse you: but he protests he loues
　　　　you,
　　And needes no other suitor but his likings,
　　To take the saf'st occasion by the front,
　　To bring you in againe.

CASSIO　　　　　　　Yet I beseech you,
　　If you thinke fit, or that it may be done,
　　Giue me aduantage of some briefe discourse
1440　With *Desdemon* alone.

EMILLIA　　　　　　　Pray you come in,
　　I will bestow you where you shall haue time,
　　To speake your bosome freely.

CASSIO　　　　　　　　　I am much bound to you.
　　　　　　　　　　　　　　　　　　　Exeunt

Sc. 8　　　*Enter Othello, Iago, and Gentlemen*
(3.2)　OTHELLO
　　These letters giue *Iago*, to the Pilate,
　　And by him, doe my duties to the Senate;
　　That done, I will be walking on the workes,
　　Repaire there to me.

IAGO　　　　　　　Well my good Lord, I'le do't.　　*Exit*

OTHELLO

　　This fortification Gentlemen, shall we see't?

A GENTLEMAN We'll waite vpon your Lordship.　　*Exeunt*

Sc. 9　　　*Enter Desdemona, Cassio and Emillia*
(3.3)　DESDEMONA
　　Be thou assur'd good *Cassio*, I will doe
1450　All my abilities in thy behalfe.

EMILLIA

　　Good Madam do, I warrant it grieues my husband,
　　As if the cause were his.

DESDEMONA

　　O that's an honest fellow:—do not doubt *Cassio*,
　　But I will haue my Lord and you againe,
　　As friendly as you were.

CASSIO　　　　　　　　　Bountious Madame,
　　What euer shall become of *Michael Cassio*,
　　Hee's neuer any thing but your true seruant.

DESDEMONA

　　I know't, I thanke you, you doe loue my Lord:
　　You haue knowne him long, and be you well assur'd,
　　He shall in strangenesse, stand no farther off,　　1460
　　Then in a politique distance.

CASSIO　　　　　　　　　I but Lady,
　　That pollicy may either last so long,
　　Or feede vpon such nice, and watrish diet,
　　Or breed it selfe, so out of circumstance,
　　That I being absent, and my place supplied,
　　My Generall will forget my loue and seruice.

DESDEMONA

　　Doe not doubt that, before *Emillia* here,
　　I giue thee warrant of thy place; assure thee
　　If I doe vow a friendship, I'le performe it
　　To the last Article; my Lord shall neuer rest,　　1470
　　I'le watch him tame, and talke him out of patience;
　　His bed shall seeme a schoole, his boord a shrift,
　　I'le intermingle euery thing he does,
　　With *Cassio's* suite; therefore be merry *Cassio*,
　　For thy solliciter shall rather die,
　　Then giue thy cause away.
　　　　Enter Othello and Iago

EMILLIA　　　　　　Madam, here comes my Lord.

CASSIO

　　Madam, I'le take my leaue.

DESDEMONA　　　　　Why stay and heare me speake.

CASSIO

　　Madam not now, I am very ill at ease,
　　Vnfit for mine owne purposes.

DESDEMONA Well, doe your discretion.　　*Exit Cassio*　1480

IAGO Ha, I like not that.

OTHELLO What doest thou say?

IAGO

　　Nothing my Lord, or if, I know not what.

OTHELLO

　　Was not that *Cassio* parted from my wife?

IAGO

　　Cassio my Lord?—no sure, I cannot thinke it,
　　That he would steale away so guilty-like,
　　Seeing your comming.

OTHELLO I doe beleeue twas he.

DESDEMONA How now my Lord,
　　I haue beene talking with a suiter here,　　　　1490
　　A man that languishes in your displeasure.

OTHELLO Who i'st you meane?

DESDEMONA

　　Why your Leiutenant *Cassio*, good my Lord,
　　If I haue any grace or power to moue you,

His present reconsiliation take:
For if he be not one that truely loues you,
That erres in ignorance, and not in cunning,
I haue no iudgement in an honest face,
I preethee call him backe.

1500 OTHELLO Went he hence now?

DESDEMONA Yes faith, so humbled,
That he hath left part of his griefe with me,
To suffer with him; good loue call him backe.

OTHELLO
Not now sweete *Desdemon* some other time.

DESDEMONA
But shal't be shortly?

OTHELLO   The sooner sweete for you.

DESDEMONA
Shal't be to night at supper?

OTHELLO   No, not to night.

DESDEMONA
To morrow dinner then?

OTHELLO   I shall not dine at home,
I meete the Captaines, at the Cittadell.

DESDEMONA
Why then to morrow night, or Tuesday morne,
1510 On Tuesday noone, or night, on Wensday morne,
I preethee name the time, but let it not
Exceed three dayes: Infaith hee's penitent,
And yet his trespasse, in our common reason,
(Saue that they say, the warres must make example,
Out of her best) is not almost a fault,
T'incurre a priuate checke: when shall he come?
Tell me *Othello*: I wonder in my soule,
What you would aske me, that I should deny?
Or stand so mam'ring on? What *Michael Cassio*?
1520 That came a wooing with you, and so many a time
When I haue spoke of you dispraisingly,
Hath tane your part, to haue so much to doe
To bring him in? Birlady I could doe much.

OTHELLO
Preethee no more, let him come when he will,
I will deny thee nothing.

DESDEMONA   Why this is not a boone,
Tis as I should intreate you weare your gloues:
Or feede on nourishing dishes, or keepe you warme,
Or sue to you, to doe a peculiar profit
To your owne person: nay, when I haue a suite,
1530 Wherein I meane to touch your loue indeed,
It shall be full of poise and difficult waight,
And fearefull to be granted.

OTHELLO   I will deny thee nothing,
Whereon I doe beseech thee grant me this,
To leaue me but a little to my selfe.

DESDEMONA
Shall I deny you? no, farewell my Lord.

OTHELLO
Farewell my *Desdomona*, I'le come to thee straight.

DESDEMONA
Emillia, come, (*to Othello*) be as your fancies teach you,
What ere you be I am obedient.

                    Exit Desdemona and Emillia

OTHELLO
Excellent wretch, perdition catch my soule,
But I doe loue thee, and when I loue thee not,   1540
Chaos is come againe.

IAGO My noble Lord.

OTHELLO What doest thou say *Iago*?

IAGO
Did *Michael Cassio* when you wooed my Lady,
Know of your loue?

OTHELLO
He did from first to last:—Why doest thou aske?

IAGO
But for a satisfaction of my thought.
No further harme.

OTHELLO   Why of thy thought *Iago*?

IAGO
I did not thinke he had beene acquainted with her.

OTHELLO
O yes, and went betweene vs very oft.   1550

IAGO Indeed?

OTHELLO
Indeed? I indeed, disern'st thou ought in that?
Is he not honest?

IAGO Honest my Lord?

OTHELLO Honest? I honest.

IAGO
My Lord, for ought I know.

OTHELLO   What doest thou thinke?

IAGO Thinke my Lord?

OTHELLO
Thinke my Lord? By heauen thou ecchos't me,
As if there were some monster in thy thought:
Too hideous to be shewne: thou dost meane
     something;   1560
I heard thee say euen now, thou lik'st not that,
When *Cassio* left my wife: what didst not like?
And when I told thee, he was of my counsell,
In my whole course of wooing, thou cridst indeed?
And didst contract, and purse thy brow together,
As if thou then hadst shut vp in thy braine,
Some horrible conceite: if thou doest loue me,
Shew me thy thought.

IAGO My Lord, you know I loue you.

OTHELLO I thinke thou doest,   1570
And for I know, thou'rt full of loue and honesty,
And weigh'st thy words, before thou giu'st them breath,
Therefore these stops of thine fright me the more:
For such things in a false disloyall knaue,
Are trickes of custome; but in a man that's iust,
They're close dilations working from the heart,
That passion cannot rule.

IAGO   For *Michael Cassio*,
I dare be sworne, I thinke that he is honest.

OTHELLO
I thinke so to.

IAGO   Men should be what they seeme,
Or those that be not, would they might seeme none.   1580

OTHELLO
Certaine, men should be what they seeme.

IAGO

Why then I thinke *Cassio's* an honest man.

OTHELLO Nay yet there's more in this,

I preethee speake to me as to thy thinkings:

As thou doest ruminate, and giue thy worst of thoughts,

The worst of words.

IAGO Good my Lord pardon me;

Though I am bound to euery act of duty,

I am not bound to that all slaues are free to,

Vtter my thoughts? Why, say they are vile and false:

1590 As where's that pallace, whereinto foule things

Sometimes intrude not? who has that breast so pure,

But some vncleanely apprehensions,

Keepe leetes and law-dayes, and in Sessions sit

With meditations lawfull?

OTHELLO

Thou doest conspire against thy friend *Iago*,

If thou but think'st him wrongd, and mak'st his eare

A stranger to thy thoughts.

IAGO I doe beseech you,

Though I perchance am vicious in my ghesse,

As I confesse it is my natures plague,

1600 To spy into abuses, and oft my iealousie

Shapes faults that are not, that your wisedome then,

From one that so imperfectly conceits,

Would take no notice, nor build your selfe a trouble,

Out of his scattering, and vnsure obseruance;

It were not for your quiet, nor your good,

Nor for my manhood, honesty, and wisedome,

To let you know my thoughts.

OTHELLO What dost thou meane?

IAGO

Good name in man and woman deere my Lord;

Is the immediate Iewell of their soules:

Who steales my purse, steals trash, tis something,

1610 nothing,

Twas mine, tis his, and has bin slaue to thousands:

But he that filches from me my good name,

Robs me of that, which not inriches him,

And makes me poore indeed.

OTHELLO By heauen I'le know thy thoughts.

IAGO

You cannot, if my heart were in your hand,

Nor shall not, whilst tis in my custody.

OTHELLO

Ha?

IAGO O beware my Lord, of iealousie.

It is the greene eyd monster, which doth mocke

The meate it feedes on. That Cuckold liues in blisse,

1620 Who certaine of his fate, loues not his wronger:

But oh, what damned minutes tells he ore,

Who dotes, yet doubts, suspects, yet fondly loues.

OTHELLO O misery.

IAGO

Poore and content, is rich, and rich enough,

But riches, finelesse, is as poore as winter,

To him that euer feares he shall be poore:

Good God, the soules of all my tribe defend

From iealousie.

OTHELLO Why, why is this?

Thinkst thou I'de make a life of iealousie?

To follow still the changes of the Moone 1630

With fresh suspitions? No, to be once in doubt,

Is once to be resolud: exchange me for a Goate,

When I shall turne the businesse of my soule

To such exufflicate, and blow'd surmises,

Matching thy inference: tis not to make me iealous,

To say my wife is faire, feedes well, loues company,

Is free of speech, sings, playes, and dances well;

Where vertue is, these are more vertuous:

Nor from mine owne weake merrits will I draw

The smallest feare, or doubt of her reuolt, 1640

For she had eies, and chose me: no *Iago*,

I'le see before I doubt, when I doubt, proue,

And on the proofe, there is no more but this:

Away at once with loue or iealousie.

IAGO

I am glad of this, for now I shall haue reason,

To shew the loue and duty that I beare you,

With franker spirit: therefore as I am bound

Receiue it from me: I speake not yet of proofe,

Looke to your wife, obserue her well with *Cassio*;

Weare your eies thus, not iealous, nor secure, 1650

I would not haue your free and noble nature,

Out of selfe-bounty be abus'd, looke to't:

I know our Countrey disposition well,

In *Venice* they doe let God see the prankes

They dare not shew their husbands: their best

conscience,

Is not to leaue't vndone, but keepe't vnknowne.

OTHELLO Doest thou say so.

IAGO

She did deceiue her father marrying you;

And when she seem'd to shake and feare your lookes,

She lou'd them most.

OTHELLO And so she did.

IAGO Why go too then, 1660

She that so young, could giue out such a seeming,

To seale her fathers eyes vp, close as Oake,

He thought twas witchcraft: but I am much too blame,

I humbly doe beseech you of your pardon,

For too much louing you.

OTHELLO I am bound to thee for euer.

IAGO

I see this hath a little dasht your spirits.

OTHELLO

Not a iot, not a iot.

IAGO Ifaith I feare it has.

I hope you will consider what is spoke,

Comes from my loue: But I doe see y'are moou'd,

I am to pray you, not to straine my speech, 1670

To groser issues, nor to larger reach,

Then to suspition.

OTHELLO I will not.

IAGO Should you doe so my Lord,
　　My speech should fall into such vile successe,
　　Which my thoughts aim'd not: *Cassio's* my worthy
　　　　friend:
　　My Lord, I see y'are moou'd.
OTHELLO　　　　　　　　　　　No, not much moou'd,
　　I doe not thinke but *Desdemona's* honest.
IAGO
　　Long liue she so, and long liue you to thinke so.
OTHELLO
1680　And yet how nature erring from it selfe.
IAGO
　　I, there's the point: as to be bold with you,
　　Not to affect many proposed matches,
　　Of her owne Clime, complexion, and degree,
　　Whereto we see in all things, nature tends;
　　Foh, one may smell in such, a will most ranke
　　Foule disproportions: thoughts vnnaturall.
　　But pardon me: I doe not in position,
　　Destinctly speake of her, tho I may feare
　　Her will recoyling to her better iudgement,
1690　May fall to match you with her countrey formes,
　　And happily repent.
OTHELLO　　　　　　　Farewell, farewell:
　　If more thou doest perceiue, let me know more,
　　Set on thy wife to obserue: leaue me *Iago*.
IAGO (*going*) My Lord I take my leaue.
OTHELLO
　　Why did I marry? This honest creature doubtlesse
　　Sees and knowes more, much more then he vnfoulds.
IAGO (*returning*)
　　My Lord, I would I might intreate your honour,
　　To scan this thing no farther, leaue it to time,
　　Although 'tis fit, that *Cassio* haue his place,
1700　For sure he fills it vp with great ability:
　　Yet if you please to hold him off awhile,
　　You shall by that perceiue him and his meanes;
　　Note if your Lady straine his entertainement,
　　With any strong or vehement importunity,
　　Much will be seene in that, in the meane time,
　　Let me be thought too busie in my feares,
　　As worthy cause I haue, to feare I am;
　　And hold her free, I doe beseech your honour.
OTHELLO
　　Feare not my gouernement.
IAGO　　　　　　　　I once more take my leaue.
　　　　　　　　　　　　　　　　　　　　　　Exit
OTHELLO
1710　This fellowe's of exceeding honesty,
　　And knowes all qualities, with a learn'd spirit
　　Of humaine dealings: if I doe prooue her haggard,
　　Tho that her Iesses were my deare heart strings,
　　I'de whistle her off, and let her downe the wind,
　　To prey at fortune. Happily, for I am blacke,
　　And haue not those soft parts of conuersation,
　　That Chamberers haue, or for I am declind
　　Into the vale of yeares; yet that's not much,

Shee's gone, I am abus'd, and my releife
Must be to lothe her: O curse of marriage,　　1720
That we can call these delicate creatures ours,
And not their appetites: I had rather be a Toade,
And liue vpon the vapor of a dungeon,
Then keepe a corner in the thing I loue,
For others vses: yet tis the plague of great ones,
Prerogatiu'd are they lesse then the base,
Tis desteny, vnshunnable, like death:
Euen then this forked plague is fated to vs,
When we doe quicken:
　　　　Enter Desdemona and Emillia
　　　　　　　　　　　Looke where she comes,
If she be false, O then heauen mocks it selfe,　　1730
I'le not beleeue't.
DESDEMONA　　　　How now my deare *Othello*?
　　Your dinner, and the generous Ilanders
　　By you inuited, doe attend your presence.
OTHELLO I am to blame.
DESDEMONA
　　Why do you speake so faintly? are you not well?
OTHELLO
　　I haue a paine vpon my forehead, here.
DESDEMONA
　　Faith that's with watching, t'will away againe;
　　Let me but bind it hard, within this houre
　　It will be well.
OTHELLO　　　　Your napkin is too little:
　　　　He puts the napkin from him. It drops
　　Let it alone, come I'le goe in with you.　　1740
DESDEMONA
　　I am very sorry that you are not well.
　　　　　　　　　Exit Othello and Desdemona
EMILLIA (*taking vp the napkin*)
　　I am glad I haue found this napkin,
　　This was her first remembrance from the Moore,
　　My wayward husband, hath a hundred times
　　Wooed me to steale it, but she so loues the token,
　　For he coniur'd her, she should euer keepe it,
　　That she reserues it euer more about her,
　　To kisse, and talke to; I'le ha the worke taine out,
　　And giu't *Iago*: what he will doe with it,
　　Heauen knowes, not I,　　1750
　　I nothing, but to please his fantasie.
　　　　Enter Iago
IAGO
　　How now, what doe you here alone?
EMILLIA
　　Doe not you chide, I haue a thing for you.
IAGO
　　You haue a thing for me, it is a common thing.
EMILLIA Ha?
IAGO To haue a foolish wife.
EMILLIA
　　O, is that all? what will you giue me now,
　　For that same handkercher?
IAGO What handkercher?

1760 EMILLIA What handkercher?
Why that the Moore first gaue to *Desdemona*,
That which so often you did bid me steale.
IAGO Ha'st stolne it from her?
EMILLIA
No faith, she let it drop by negligence,
And to th'aduantage, I being here, took't vp:
Looke here 'tis.
IAGO A good wench, giue it me.
EMILLIA
What will you doe with it, that you haue bin so
earnest
To haue me filch it?
IAGO Why, what is that to you?
He takes the napkin
EMILLIA
If it be not for some purpose of import,
1770 Giu't mee againe, poore Lady, shee'll run mad,
When she shall lacke it.
IAGO
Be not acknowne on't, I haue vse for it:—go leaue me;
Exit Emillia
I will in *Cassio's* Lodging lose this napkin,
And let him finde it: trifles light as ayre,
Are to the iealous, confirmations strong
As proofes of holy writ, this may doe something,
The Moore already changes with my poyson:
Dangerous conceits are in their natures poisons,
Which at the first are scarce found to distast,
1780 But with a little act vpon the blood,
Burne like the mines of sulphure:
Enter Othello
I did say so:
Looke where he comes, not Poppy, nor Mandragora,
Nor all the drousie sirrops of the world,
Shall euer medicine thee to that sweete sleepe,
Which thou owedst yesterday.
OTHELLO Ha, ha, false to me?
IAGO
Why how now Generall? no more of that.
OTHELLO
Auant, be gone, thou hast set me on the racke,
I sweare, tis better to be much abus'd,
Then but to know't a little.
IAGO How now my Lord?
OTHELLO
1790 What sense had I of her stolne houres of lust:
I saw't not, thought it not, it harm'd not me,
I slept the next night well, fed well, was free, and
merry;
I found not *Cassio's* kisses on her lips,
He that is rob'd, not wanting what is stolne,
Let him not know't, and hee's not rob'd at all.
IAGO I am sorry to heare this.
OTHELLO
I had bin happy if the generall Campe,
Pyoners, and all, had tasted her sweete body,
So I had nothing knowne: O now for euer
1800 Farewell the tranquile mind, farewell content:

Farewell the plumed troopes, and the big warres:
That makes ambition vertue: O farewell,
Farewell the neighing Steed, and the shrill Trumpe,
The spirit-stirring Drumme, th'eare-peircing Fife;
The royall Banner, and all quality,
Pride, pompe, and circumstance of glorious warre.
And O you mortall Engines, whose rude throates,
Th'immortall *Ioues* dread clamours counterfeit;
Farewell, *Othello's* Occupation's gone.
IAGO Ist possible my Lord? 1810
OTHELLO ⌈*taking Iago by the throat*⌉
Villaine, be sure thou proue my Loue a whore,
Be sure of it, giue me the oculer proofe,
Or by the worth of mine eternall soule,
Thou hadst bin better haue beene borne a dog,
Then answer my wak'd wrath.
IAGO Ist come to this?
OTHELLO
Make me to see't, or at the least so proue it,
That the probation, beare no hinge, nor loope,
To hang a doubt on: or woe vpon thy life.
IAGO My noble Lord.
OTHELLO
If thou doest slander her, and torture me, 1820
Neuer pray more, abandon all remorce.
On horrors head, horrors accumilate:
Do deeds, to make heauen weepe, all earth amaz'd,
For nothing canst thou to damnation ad
Greater then that.
IAGO O grace, O heauen forgiue me,
Are you a man, haue you a soule or sence?
God buy you, take mine office,—O wretched foole,
That lou'st to make thine honesty a vice,
O monstrous world, take note, take note, O world,
To be direct and honest, is not safe, 1830
I thanke you for this profit, and from hence,
I'le loue no friend, sith loue breedes such offence.
OTHELLO Nay stay, thou shouldst be honest.
IAGO
I should be wise, for honestie's a foole,
And looses that it workes for:
OTHELLO By the World,
I thinke my Wife be honest, and thinke she is not:
I thinke that thou art iust, and thinke thou art not:
Ile haue some proofe. My name that was as fresh
As *Dians* Visage, is now begrim'd and blacke
As mine own face. If there be Cords, or Kniues, 1840
Poyson, or Fire, or suffocating streames,
Ile not indure it. Would I were satisfied.
IAGO
I see sir, you are eaten vp with passion,
I doe repent me that I put it to you,
You would be satisfied.
OTHELLO Would, nay, and I will.
IAGO
And may, but how, how satisfied my Lord?
Would you, the superuisor grossely gape on,
Behold her topt?
OTHELLO Death and damnation—oh.

IAGO

    It were a tedious difficulty I thinke,

1850   To bring them to that prospect, dam them then,

    If euer mortall eyes do see them boulster

    More then their owne; what then, how then?

    What shall I say? where's satisfaction?

    It is impossible you should see this,

    Were they as prime as Goates, as hot as Monkies,

    As salt as Wolues, in pride; and fooles as grosse,

    As ignorance made drunke: But yet I say,

    If imputation and strong circumstances,

    Which leade directly to the doore of truth,

1860   Will giue you satisfaction, you might ha't.

OTHELLO

    Giue me a liuing reason, shee's disloyall.

IAGO I doe not like the office,

    But sith I am enter'd in this cause so farre,

    Prickt to't by foolish honesty and loue,

    I will goe on: I lay with *Cassio* lately,

    And being troubled with a raging tooth,

    I could not sleep. There are a kinde of men

    So loose of soule, that in their sleepes

    Will mutter their affaires, one of this kinde is *Cassio*:

1870   In sleepe I heard him say. Sweete *Desdemona*,

    Let vs be wary, let vs hide our loues;

    And then sir, would he gripe and wring my hand,

    Cry oh sweete creature, then kisse me hard,

    As if he pluckt vp kisses by the rootes,

    That grew vpon my lips, laie his leg ore my thigh,

    And sigh, and kisse, and then cry, cursed fate,

    That gaue thee to the Moore.

OTHELLO O Monstrous, monstrous.

IAGO Nay, this was but his dreame.

OTHELLO

1880   But this denoted a fore-gone conclusion.

IAGO

    Tis a shrewd doubt, tho it be but a dreame,

    And this may helpe to thicken other proofes,

    That doe demonstrate thinly.

OTHELLO   I'le teare her all to peeces.

IAGO

    Nay, yet be wise, yet we see nothing done,

    She may be honest yet, tell me but this,

    Haue you not sometimes seene a handkercher,

    Spotted with strawberries in your wiues hand.

OTHELLO

    I gaue her such a one, twas my first gift.

IAGO

    I know not that, but such a handkercher,

1890   I am sure it was your wiues, did I to day

    See *Cassio* wipe his beard with.

OTHELLO   If it be that.

IAGO

    If it be that, or any, y^t was hers,

    It speakes against her, with the other proofes.

OTHELLO

    O that the slaue had forty thousand liues,

    One is too poore, too weake for my reuenge:

    Now doe I see tis true, looke here *Iago*,

    All my fond loue, thus doe I blow to heauen,—tis gone.

    Arise blacke vengeance, from the hollow hell,

    Yeeld vp O loue thy crowne, and harted Throne,

    To tirranous hate, swell bosome with thy fraught,   1900

    For tis of Aspecks tongues.

IAGO   Yet be content.

OTHELLO

    O blood, blood, blood.

IAGO   Patience I say, your mind may change.

OTHELLO

    Neuer *Iago*. Like to the Ponticke Sea,

    Whose Icie Current, and compulsiue course,

    Neu'r knows retyring ebbe, but keepes due on

    To the Proponticke, and the Hellespont:

    Euen so my bloody thoughts, with violent pace

    Shall neu'r looke backe, neu'r ebbe to humble Loue,

    Till that a capeable, and wide Reuenge

    Swallow them vp.

    ⌈*he kneeles*⌉

              Now by yond Marble Heauen,   1910

    In the due reuerence of a sacred vow,

    I here ingage my words.

IAGO   Doe not rise yet:

    Iago kneeles

    Witnesse you euer-burning lights aboue,

    You Elements that clip vs round about,

    Witnesse that here, *Iago* doth giue vp

    The execution of his wit, hands, heart,

    To wrong'd *Othello's* seruice: let him command,

    And to obey, shall be in me remorce,

    What bloody businesse euer.

    ⌈*They rise*⌉

OTHELLO   I greete thy loue:

    Not with vaine thankes, but with acceptance

        bounteous,   1920

    And will vpon the instant put thee to't,

    Within these three dayes, let me heare thee say,

    That *Cassio's* not aliue.

IAGO   My friend is dead:

    Tis done at your request, but let her liue.

OTHELLO

    Dam her lewd minks: O dam her, dam her,

    Come, goe with me apart, I will withdraw

    To furnish me with some swift meanes of death,

    For the faire diuell: now art thou my Leiutenant.

IAGO I am your owne for euer.   *Exeunt*

    Enter Desdemonia Emilla and the Clowne   Sc. 10

DESDEMONA Do you know sirra, where Leiutenant *Cassio*   (3.4)

    lies?   1931

CLOWNE I dare not say he lies any where.

DESDEMONA Why man?

CLOWNE He's a Souldier, and for me to say a Souldier lies,

    'tis stabbing.

DESDEMONA Go to, where lodges he?

CLOWNE To tell you where he lodges, is to tel you where

    I lye.

DESDEMONA Can any thing be made of this?

CLOWNE I know not where he lodges, and for me to deuise   1940 a lodging, and say he lies here, or he lies there, were to lie in mine owne throate.

DESDEMONA Can you inquire him out, and be edified by report?

CLOWNE I will cathechize the world for him, that is, make questions and by them answer.

DESDEMONA Seeke him, bid him come hither, tell him I haue moued my Lord on his behalfe, and hope all will be well.

1950 CLOWNE To doe this is within the compasse of mans Wit, and therefore I will attempt the doing it.   *Exit*

DESDEMONA
Where should I loose the handkercher *Emillia*?

EMILLIA I know not Madam.

DESDEMONA
Beleeue me, I had rather haue lost my purse
Full of Crusadoes: and but my noble Moore
Is true of minde, and made of no such basenesse,
As iealous creatures are, it were enough,
To put him to ill thinking.

EMILLIA   Is he not iealous.

DESDEMONA
Who he? I thinke the Sun where he was borne,
Drew all such humors from him.
            Enter Othello

1960 EMILLIA   Looke were he comes.

DESDEMONA
I will not leaue him now, til *Cassio*
Be cald to him: how is't with you my Lord?

OTHELLO
Well my good Lady: (*aside*) O hardnesse to dissemble:
How doe you *Desdomona*?

DESDEMONA   Well, my good Lord.

OTHELLO
Giue me your hand, this hand is moist my Lady.

DESDEMONA
It hath felt no age, nor knowne no sorrow.

OTHELLO
This argues fruitfulnesse and liberall heart,
Hot, hot and moist, this hand of yours requires
A sequester from liberty: fasting and prayer,
1970 Much castigation, exercise deuout;
For heere's a young and swetting diuell here,
That commonly rebels: tis a good hand,
A franke one.

DESDEMONA   You may indeed say so,
For twas that hand that gaue away my heart.

OTHELLO
A liberall hand, the hearts of old gaue hands,
But our new herraldry is hands, not hearts.

DESDEMONA
I cannot speake of this, come, now your promise.

OTHELLO What promise chucke?

DESDEMONA
I haue sent to bid *Cassio* come speake with you.

OTHELLO
1980 I haue a salt and sorry rhume offends me,
Lend me thy handkercher.

DESDEMONA (*offering a handkercher*) Here my Lord.

OTHELLO
That which I gaue you.

DESDEMONA   I haue it not about me.

OTHELLO Not.

DESDEMONA
No faith my Lord.

OTHELLO   Thats a fault: that handkercher
Did an *Egyptian* to my mother giue,
She was a charmer, and could almost reade
The thoughts of people; she told her while she kept it,
Twould make her amiable, and subdue my father
Intirely to her loue: But if she lost it,
Or made a gift of it: my fathers eye   1990
Should hold her loathed, and his spirits should hunt
After new fancies: she dying, gaue it me,
And bid me when my fate would haue me wiu'd,
To giue it her; I did so, and take heede on't,
Make it a darling, like your pretious eye,
To loose't, or giue't away, were such perdition,
As nothing else could match.

DESDEMONA   I'st possible?

OTHELLO
Tis true, there's magicke in the web of it,
A Sybell that had numbred in the world,
The Sun to course two hundred compasses,   2000
In her prophetique fury, sowed the worke;
The wormes were hallowed that did breed the silke,
And it was died in Mummy, which the skilfull
Conseru'd of maidens hearts.

DESDEMONA   Ifaith i'st true?

OTHELLO
Most veritable, therefore looke to't well.

DESDEMONA
Then would to God, that I had neuer seene it.

OTHELLO Ha, wherefore?

DESDEMONA
Why doe you speake so startingly and rash.

OTHELLO
I'st lost? i'st gone? speake, is't out o'th'way?

DESDEMONA Heauen blesse vs.   2010

OTHELLO Say you?

DESDEMONA
It is not lost, but what and if it were?

OTHELLO How?

DESDEMONA
I say it is not lost.

OTHELLO   Fetch't, let me see't.

DESDEMONA
Why so I can sir, but I will not now,
This is a tricke, to put me from my suite,
Pray you let *Cassio*, be receiu'd againe.

OTHELLO
Fetch me the handkercher, my mind misgiues.

DESDEMONA
Come, come, you'll neuer meete a more sufficient
man.

OTHELLO
The handkercher.

DESDEMONA   I pray talke me of *Cassio*.   2020

OTHELLO
The handkercher.

DESDEMONA   A man that all his time,
Hath founded his good fortunes on your loue,
Shar'd dangers with you.

OTHELLO The handkercher.

DESDEMONA Ifaith you are too blame.

OTHELLO Zouns.   *Exit*

EMILLIA
Is not this man iealous?

DESDEMONA   I ne're saw this before:
Sure there's some wonder in this handkercher,
I am most vnhappy in the losse of it.

EMILLIA
2030   Tis not a yeere or two shewes vs a man,
They are all but stomacks, and we all but foode;
They eate vs hungerly, and when they are full,
They belch vs;
             Enter Iago and Cassio
                   looke you, *Cassio* and my husband.

IAGO (*to Cassio*)
There is no other way, tis she must doe't,
And loe the happinesse, goe, and importune her.

DESDEMONA
How now good *Cassio*, what's the news with you?

CASSIO
Madam, my former suite: I doe beseech you,
That by your vertuous meanes, I may againe
Exist, and be a member of his loue,
2040   Whom I, with all the Office of my heart,
Intirely honour, I would not be delayed:
If my offence be of such mortall kind,
That nor my seruice past, nor present sorrowes,
Nor purpos'd merrit, in futurity
Can ransome me, into his loue againe
But to know so, must be my benefit,
So shall I cloth me in a forc'd content,
And shut my selfe vp in some other course,
To fortunes almes.

DESDEMONA   Alas thrice gentle *Cassio*,
2050   My aduocation is not now in tune;
My Lord is not my Lord, nor should I know him,
Were he in fauour, as in humor altred.
So helpe me, euery spirit sanctified,
As I haue spoken for you, all my best,
And stood within the blanke of his displeasure,
For my free speech: you must a while be patient,
What I can doe I will, and more I will
Then for my selfe I dare, let that suffice you.

IAGO
Is my Lord angry?

EMILLIA   He went hence but now,
2060   And certainely in strange vnquietnesse.

IAGO
Can he be angry? I haue seene the Cannon,
When it hath blowne his rankes into the ayre;
And (like the Diuell) from his very arme,
Puft his owne brother, and is he angry?

Something of moment then: I will goe meete him,
There's matter in't indeed, if he be angry.

DESDEMONA
I preethee do so: *Exit Iago*
             something sure of State,
Either from *Venice*, or some vnhatcht practice,
Made demonstrable here in *Cipres* to him,
Hath pudled his cleere spirit, and in such cases   2070
Mens natures wrangle with inferior things,
Tho great ones are their obiect, tis euen so:
For let our finger ake, and it endues
Our other healthfull members, euen to a sence
Of paine; nay, we must thinke, men are not gods,
Nor of them looke for such obseruancie
As fits the Bridall: beshrew me much *Emillia*,
I was (vnhandsome warrior as I am)
Arraigning his vnkindnesse with my soule;
But now I finde, I had subbornd the witnesse,   2080
And hee's indited falsly.

EMILLIA   Pray heauen it be
State matters, as you thinke, and no conception,
Nor no iealous toy concerning you.

DESDEMONA
Alas the day, I neuer gaue him cause.

EMILLIA
But iealous soules will not be answer'd so,
They are not euer iealous for the cause,
But iealous for they're iealous: it is a monster,
Begot vpon it selfe, borne on it selfe.

DESDEMONA
Heauen keepe the monster from *Othello*'s mind.

EMILLIA Lady, Amen.   2090

DESDEMONA
I will goe seeke him, *Cassio*, walke here about,
If I doe finde him fit, I'le moue your suite,
And seeke to effect it to my vttermost.

CASSIO
I humbly thanke your Ladiship.
                   Exeunt Desdemona and Emillia
             Enter Bianca

BIANCA
Saue you friend *Cassio*.

CASSIO   What make you from home?
How is't with you my most faire *Bianca*?
Ifaith sweete loue I was comming to your house.

BIANCA
And I was going to your Lodging *Cassio*;
What, keepe a weeke away? seuen daies and nights,
Eightscore eight houres, and louers absent houres,   2100
More tedious then the diall, eightscore times,
Oh weary reckoning.

CASSIO   Pardon me *Bianca*,
I haue this while with leaden thoughts bin prest,
But I shall in a more continuate time,
Strike off this score of absence: sweete *Bianca*,
Take me this worke out.
             He giues her Desdemonas napkin

BIANCA   Oh *Cassio*, whence came this?

This is some token from a newer friend,
To the felt absence, now I feele a cause,
Ist come to this? Well, well.

CASSIO   Go to woman,

2110 Throw your vile ghesses in the diuells teeth,
From whence you haue them, you are iealous now,
That this is from some mistrisse, some remembrance,
No by my faith *Bianca*.

BIANCA   Why who's is it?

CASSIO

I know not neither, I found it in my chamber,
I like the worke well, ere it be demanded,
As like enough it will, I would haue it coppied,
Take it, and do't, and leaue me for this time.

BIANCA Leaue you, wherefore?

CASSIO

I doe attend here on the Generall,

2120 And thinke it no addition, nor my wish,
To haue him see me woman'd.

BIANCA   Why, I pray you?

CASSIO

Not that I loue you not.

BIANCA   But that you doe not loue me:
I pray you bring me on the way alittle,
And say, if I shall see you soone at night.

CASSIO

Tis but a little way, that I can bring you,
For I attend here, but I'le see you soone.

BIANCA

Tis very good, I must be circumstanc'd.   *Exeunt*

Sc. 11   *Enter Iago and Othello*
(4.1) IAGO
Will you thinke so?

OTHELLO   Thinke so *Iago*.

IAGO

What, to kisse in priuate?

OTHELLO   An vnauthoriz'd kisse.

IAGO

2130 Or to be naked with her friend in bed,
An houre, or more, not meaning any harme.

OTHELLO

Naked in bed *Iago*, and not meane harme?
It is hypocrisie against the diuell:
They that meane vertuously, and yet doe so,
The diuell their vertue tempts, and they tempt heauen:

IAGO

If they doe nothing, tis a veniall slip;
But if I giue my wife a handkercher.

OTHELLO What then?

IAGO

Why then tis hers my Lord, and being hers,

2140 She may, I thinke, bestow't on any man.

OTHELLO

She is protectres of her honour to,
May she giue that?

IAGO

Her honour is an essence that's not seene,

They haue it very oft, that haue it not:
But for the handkercher.

OTHELLO

By heauen, I would most gladly haue forgot it:
Thou saidst (O it comes o're my memory,
As doth the Rauen o're the infectious house,
Boding to all.) He had my handkercher.

IAGO

I, what of that?

OTHELLO   That's not so good now.   2150

IAGO

What if I had said I had seene him do you wrong?
Or heard him say, as knaues be such abroad,
Who hauing by their owne importunate suite,
Or voluntary dotage of some mistris,
Conuinced, or supplied them, cannot chuse,
But they must blab.

OTHELLO   Hath he said any thing?

IAGO

He hath my Lord, but be you well assur'd,
No more then hee'l vnsweare.

OTHELLO   What hath he sayd?

IAGO

Faith that he did—I know not what he did.

OTHELLO

What? What?

IAGO   Lye.

OTHELLO   With her?

IAGO   With her, on her, what you will.   2160

OTHELLO Lie with her, lie on her? We say lie on her,
when they bely her; lye with her, Zouns, that's fulsome,
handkercher, Confessions, hankercher. To confesse, and
be hang'd for his labour. First, to be hang'd, and then
to confesse: I tremble at it. Nature would not inuest
her selfe in such shadowing passion, without some
Instruction. It is not words that shakes me thus, (pish)
Noses, Eares, and Lippes: is't possible. Confesse?
Handkercher? O diuell.

          He fals downe in a traunce

IAGO

Worke on, my medicine workes: thus credulous fooles
          are caught,   2170
And many worthy and chaste dames, euen thus
All guiltlesse, meete reproach; What ho my Lord,
My Lord I say, *Othello*,—

          Enter Cassio

                              how now *Cassio*.

CASSIO What's the matter?

IAGO

My Lord is falne into an Epilepsy,
This is his second fit, he had one yesterday.

CASSIO

Rub him about the Temples.

IAGO   No, forbeare,
The Lethergie, must haue his quiet course,
If not he foames at mouth, and by and by
Breakes out to sauage madnesse: looke he stirres: 2180
Doe you withdraw your selfe a little while,

He will recouer straight, when he is gone,
I would on great occasion speake with you.

                              Exit Cassio

How is it Generall, haue you not hurt your head?

OTHELLO

O thou art wise, tis certaine.

Doest thou mocke me?

IAGO   I mocke you not, by Heauen,

Would you would beare your fortune like a man.

OTHELLO

A horned man's a monster, and a beast.

IAGO

There's many a beast then in a populous City,
And many a ciuill monster.

2190 OTHELLO Did he confesse it?

IAGO Good sir be a man,
Thinke euery bearded fellow, that's but yoak'd,
May draw with you, there's millions now aliue,
That nightly lye in those vnproper beds,
Which they dare sweare peculiar: your case is better:
O tis the spite of hell, the fiends arch mocke,
To lip a wanton in a secure Cowch,
And to suppose her chaste: No, let me know,
And knowing what I am, I know what she shall be.

OTHELLO

O thou art wise, tis certaine.

2200 IAGO   Stand you awhile apart,
Confine your selfe but in a patient list:
Whilst you were here, o're-whelmed with your griefe,
A passion most vnsuting such a man,
Cassio came hither, I shifted him away,
And layed good scuse, vpon your extacy,
Bad him anon returne, and here speake with me,
The which he promisde: Do but incaue your selfe,
And marke the Fleeres, the gibes, and notable scornes,
That dwell in euery region of his face;
2210 For I will make him tell the tale anew,
Where, how, how oft, how long agoe, and when,
He hath, and is againe to cope your wife:
I say, but marke his ieasture, mary patience,
Or I shall say, y'are all in all, in spleene,
And nothing of a man.

OTHELLO   Doest thou heare *Iago*,
I will be found most cunning in my patience;
But doest thou heare, most bloody.

IAGO   That's not amisse:
But yet keepe time in all; will you withdraw?

      Othello stands apart

Now will I question *Cassio* of *Bianca*;
2220 A huswife that by selling her desires,
Buys her selfe bread and cloath: it is a Creature,
That dotes on *Cassio*: as tis the strumpets plague
To beguile many, and be beguild by one,
He, when he heares of her, cannot restraine
From the excesse of laughter:

      Enter Cassio

                       here he comes:
As he shall smile, *Othello* shall goe mad,

And his vnbookish iealousie must conster
Poore *Cassio's* smiles, gestures, and light behauiours,
Quite in the wrong: How doe you now Leiutenant?

CASSIO

The worser, that you giue me the addition,   2230
Whose want euen kills me.

IAGO

Ply *Desdemona* well, and you are sure on't.
Now if this suite lay in *Bianca's* power,
How quickly should you speed.

CASSIO (*laughing*) Alas poore Catiue.

OTHELLO (*aside*) Looke how he laughes already.

IAGO

I neuer knew a woman loue man so.

CASSIO

Alas poore rogue, I thinke ifaith she loues me.

OTHELLO (*aside*)

Now he denyes it faintly, and laughes it out.

IAGO

Doe you heare *Cassio*?

OTHELLO (*aside*)   Now he importunes him   2240
To tell it or, goe to, well said, well said.

IAGO

She giues it out that you shall marry her,
Doe you intend it?

CASSIO   Ha, ha, ha.

OTHELLO (*aside*)

Doe ye triumph Roman, doe you triumph?

CASSIO I marry. What? A customer; prethee beare some
charity to my wit, doe not thinke it so vnwholesome:
ha, ha, ha.

OTHELLO (*aside*) So, so, so, so, they laugh that wins.

IAGO Faith the cry goes, that you marry her.

CASSIO Preethee say true.   2250

IAGO I am a very villaine else.

OTHELLO (*aside*) Ha you scor'd me? Well.

CASSIO This is the monkies own giuing out; she is
perswaded I wil marry her, out of her owne loue and
flattery, not out of my promise.

OTHELLO (*aside*) *Iago* beckons me, now he begins the story.

      Othello drawes closer

CASSIO She was heere euen now, shee haunts me in euery
place, I was the other day, talking on the sea banke,
with certaine *Venetians*, and thither comes the bauble,
and fals me thus about my neck.   2260

OTHELLO (*aside*) Crying, O deare *Cassio*, as it were: his
iesture imports it.

CASSIO So hangs, and lolls, and weepes vpon me; so
shakes, and puls me, ha, ha, ha.

OTHELLO (*aside*) Now he tells how she pluckt him to my
Chamber, oh, I see that nose of yours, but not that dog
I shall throw it to.

CASSIO Well, I must leaue her company.

      Enter Bianca

IAGO Before me, looke where she comes.

CASSIO Tis such another ficho; marry a perfum'd one, (*to* 2270
Bianca) what doe you meane by this hanting of me.

BIANCA Let the diuel and his dam haunt you, what did
you meane by that same handkercher, you gaue mee
euen now? I was a fine foole to take it; I must take
out the whole worke, a likely peece of worke, that you
should find it in your chamber, and know not who left
it there: this is some minxes token, and I must take
out the worke; there, giue it your hobby horse, (*giuing
Cassio the napkin*) wheresoeuer you had it, I'le take out
2280   no worke on't.
CASSIO How now my sweete *Bianca*, how now, how now?
OTHELLO (*aside*)
        By heauen that should be my handkercher.
BIANCA An you'll come to supper to night, you may, an you
will not, come when you are next prepar'd for.   *Exit*
IAGO After her, after her.
CASSIO Faith I must, shee'll raile in the streets else.
IAGO Will you sup there?
CASSIO Faith I intend so.
IAGO Well, I may chance to see you, for I would very
2290   faine speake with you.
CASSIO Preethee come, will you?
IAGO Goe to, say no more.   *Exit Cassio*
OTHELLO How shall I murder him *Iago*?
IAGO Did you perceiue, how he laughed at his vice?
OTHELLO O *Iago*.
IAGO And did you see the handkercher?
OTHELLO Was that mine?
IAGO Yours by this hand: and to see how he prizes the
foolish woman your wife: she gaue it him, and he hath
2300   giu'n it his whore.
OTHELLO I would haue him nine yeares a killing; a fine
woman, a faire woman, a sweete woman.
IAGO Nay you must forget that.
OTHELLO I, let her rot and perish, and be damb'd to night,
for she shall not liue: no, my heart is turn'd to stone;
I strike it, and it hurts my hand: O the world hath not
a sweeter creature, she might lie by an Emperours side,
and command him taskes.
IAGO Nay that's not your way.
2310   OTHELLO Hang her, I doe but say what she is: So delicate
with her needle, an admirable musition, O shee will
sing the sauagenesse out of a Beare; of so hye and
plentious wit and inuention.
IAGO Shee's the worse for all this.
OTHELLO Oh, a thousand, a thousand times: and then of
so gentle a condition.
IAGO I, too gentle.
OTHELLO Nay that's certaine, but yet the pitty of it *Iago*,
oh *Iago*, the pitty of it *Iago*.
2320   IAGO If you are so fond ouer her iniquity, giue her patent
to offend, for if it touch not you, it comes neere no
body.
OTHELLO I will chop her into messes—cuckold me!
IAGO O tis foule in her.
OTHELLO With mine Officer.
IAGO That's fouler.
OTHELLO Get me some poison *Iago*, this night. I'le not

expostulate with her, lest her body and beauty
vnprouide my minde agen, this night *Iago*.
IAGO Doe it not with poison, strangle her in her bed,   2330
euen the bed she hath contaminated.
OTHELLO Good, good, the iustice of it pleases very good.
IAGO And for *Cassio*, let me bee his vndertaker: you shall
heare more by midnight.
OTHELLO Excellent good:
        A Trumpet
What Trumpet is that same?
IAGO I warrant something from *Venice*,
        Enter Lodouico, Desdemona, and Attendants
tis *Lodouico*, this comes from the Duke, see your wife's
with him.
LODOUICO God saue the worthy Generall.   2340
OTHELLO With all my heart sir.
LODOUICO (*giuing Othello a letter*) The Duke and the
Senators of *Venice* greete you.
OTHELLO I kisse the instrument of their pleasures.
        He reades the letter
DESDEMONA
And what's the newes good cousen *Lodouico*?
IAGO (*to Lodouico*) I am very glad to see you Seignior:—
welcome to *Cypres*.
LODOUICO I thanke you, how does Leiutenant *Cassio*?
IAGO Liues sir.
DESDEMONA
Cousen, there's falne betweene him and my Lord,   2350
An vnkind breach, but you shall make all well.
OTHELLO Are you sure of that?
DESDEMONA My Lord.
OTHELLO (*reades*) This faile you not to doe, as you will.—
LODOUICO
He did not call, hee's busie in the paper:
Is there diuision 'twixt my Lord and *Cassio*?
DESDEMONA
A most vnhappy one, I would doe much
T'attone them, for the loue I beare to *Cassio*.
OTHELLO
Fire and Brimstone.
DESDEMONA   My Lord.
OTHELLO   Are you wise?
DESDEMONA
What, is he angry?
LODOUICO   May be the letter mou'd him;   2360
For as I thinke, they doe command him home,
Deputing *Cassio* in his gouernement.
DESDEMONA By my troth, I am glad on't.
OTHELLO Indeed.
DESDEMONA My Lord.
OTHELLO (*to Desdemona*) I am glad to see you mad.
DESDEMONA Why, sweete *Othello*?
OTHELLO Diuell.
        He strikes her
DESDEMONA I haue not deseru'd this.
LODOUICO
My Lord, this would not be beleeu'd in *Venice*,   2370

Tho I should sweare I saw't: tis very much,
Make her amends, she weepes.
OTHELLO   O Diuell, Diuell,
If that the earth could teeme with womans teares
Each drop she falls, would proue a Crocadile:
Out of my sight.
DESDEMONA (*going*) I will not stay to offend you.
LODOUICO
Truely an obedient Lady:
I doe beseech your Lordship, call her backe.
OTHELLO
Mistrisse.
DESDEMONA (*returning*) My Lord.
OTHELLO (*to Lodouico*) What would you with her sir?
2380 LODOUICO Who, I my Lord?
OTHELLO
I, you did wish that I would make her turne:
Sir she can turne, and turne, and yet go on,
And turne againe, and she can weepe sir, weepe;
And shee's obedient, as you say, obedient;
Very obedient, (*to Desdemona*) proceed you in your
    teares,
(*To Lodouico*) Concerning this sir: (*To Desdemona*) O
    well painted passion:
(*To Lodouico*) I am commanded home: (*to
    Desdemona*)—get you away,
I'le send for you anon: (*To Lodouico*)—Sir, I obey the
    mandat,
And will returne to *Venice*: (*to Desdemona*)—hence,
    auant,   *Exit Desdemona*
(*To Lodouico*) *Cassio* shall haue my place; and sir to
2390   night
I doe intreate that we may sup together,
You are welcome sir to *Cypres*,—goates and monkies.
                                              Exit
LODOUICO
Is this the noble Moore, whom our full Senate
Call all in all sufficient? Is this the nature,
Whom passion could not shake? Whose solid vertue,
The shot of accident, nor dart of chance
Could neither graze, nor peirce?
IAGO   He is much changed.
LODOUICO
Are his wits safe? is he not light of braine?
IAGO
He's that he is, I may not breathe my censure,
2400 What he might be, if what he might, he is not,
I would to heauen he were.
LODOUICO   What, strike his wife.
IAGO
Faith that was not so well; yet would I knew
That stroake would proue the worst.
LODOUICO   Is it his vse?
Or did the letters worke vpon his blood,
And new create his fault?
IAGO   Alas, alas.
It is not honesty in me to speake,
What I haue seene and knowne, you shall obserue him,

And his owne courses will denote him so,
That I may saue my speech: doe but goe after,
And marke how he continues.   2410
LODOUICO
I am sorry that I am deceiu'd in him.   *Exeunt*

    Enter Othello and Emillia   Sc. 12
OTHELLO You haue seene nothing then.   (4.2)
EMILLIA
Nor euer heard, nor euer did suspect.
OTHELLO
Yes, you haue seene *Cassio* and she together.
EMILLIA
But then I saw no harme, and then I heard
Each sillable that breath made vp betweene 'em.
OTHELLO What, did they neuer whisper?
EMILLIA Neuer, my Lord.
OTHELLO Nor send you out o'th'way?
EMILLIA Neuer.   2420
OTHELLO
To fetch her fan, her gloues, her mask, nor nothing?
EMILLIA Neuer, my Lord.
OTHELLO That's strange.
EMILLIA
I durst my Lord, to wager she is honest,
Lay downe my soule at stake: if you thinke other,
Remoue your thought, it doth abuse your bosome,
If any wretch ha put this in your head,
Let heauen requite it with the Serpents curse,
For if she be not honest, chaste, and true,
There's no man happy, the purest of their Wiues   2430
Is foule as slander.
OTHELLO   Bid her come hither, goe,
                                      Exit Emillia
She sayes enough, yet she's a simple bawde,
That cannot say as much: this is a subtle whore,
A closet, locke and key, of villainous secrets,
And yet shee'll kneele and pray, I ha seene her do't.
    Enter Desdemona and Emillia
DESDEMONA
My Lord, what is your will?
OTHELLO   Pray you chucke come hither.
DESDEMONA
What is your pleasure?
OTHELLO   Let me see your eyes—
Looke in my face.
DESDEMONA What horrible fancy's this?
OTHELLO (*to Emillia*) Some of your function mistrisse, 2440
Leaue procreants alone, and shut the dore,
Coffe, or cry hem, if any body come,
Your mistery, your mistery: nay dispatch. *Exit Emillia*
DESDEMONA
Vpon my knees, what doth your speech import?
I vnderstand a fury in your words,
But not the words.
OTHELLO   Why, what art thou?
DESDEMONA
Your wife my Lord, your true and loyall wife.

OTHELLO Come, sweare it, dam thy selfe,
   Least being like one of heauen, the diuells themselues
2450   Should feare to cease thee, therefore be double dambd,
   Sweare thou art honest.

DESDEMONA   Heauen doth truely know it.

OTHELLO
   Heauen truely knowes, that thou art false as hell.

DESDEMONA
   To whom, my Lord, with whom? how am I false?

OTHELLO (*weeping*)
   Ah *Desdemon*, away, away, away.

DESDEMONA
   Alas the heauy day, why do you weepe?
   Am I the motiue of these teares my Lord?
   If haply you my father doe suspect,
   An Instrument of this your calling backe,
   Lay not your blame on me; if you haue lost him,
   I haue lost him too.

2460 OTHELLO   Had it pleas'd God
   To try me with affliction, had he rain'd
   All kind of sores, and shames on my bare head,
   Steep'd me in pouerty, to the very lips,
   Giuen to captiuity, me and my vtmost hopes,
   I should haue found in some place of my soule
   A drop of patience; but alas, to make me
   The fixed figure, for the time of scorne,
   To point his slow and mouing finger at—
   Yet could I beare that too, well, very well.

2470   But there: where I haue garner'd vp my heart,
   Where either I must liue, or beare no life,
   The fountaine, from the which my currant runnes,
   Or else dryes vp, to be discarded thence,
   Or keepe it as a Cesterne, for foule Toades
   To knot and gender in: turne thy complexion there,
   Patience thou young and rose-lip'd Cherubin,
   I here looke grim as Hell.

DESDEMONA
   I hope my noble Lord esteemes me honest.

OTHELLO
   O I, as summer flies, are in the shambles,
2480   That quicken euen with blowing: O thou weede,
   Who art so louely faire, and smell'st so sweete,
   That the sence akes at thee, would thou hadst ne're
      bin borne.

DESDEMONA
   Alas, what ignorant sinne haue I committed?

OTHELLO
   Was this faire paper, this most goodly booke,
   Made to write whore vpon?—What, committed?
   Committed? Oh, thou publicke Commoner,
   I should make very Forges of my cheekes,
   That would to Cynders burne vp Modestie,
   Did I but speake thy deedes. What commited?
2490   Heauen stops the nose at it, and the Moone winkes,
   The bawdy wind, that kisses all it meetes,
   Is husht within the hollow mine of earth,
   And will not hear't:—what committed?

DESDEMONA By heauen you doe me wrong.

OTHELLO Are not you a strumpet?

DESDEMONA No, as I am a Christian:
   If to preserue this vessell for my Lord,
   From any other foule vnlawfull touch,
   Be not to be a strumpet, I am none.

OTHELLO
   What, not a whore?

DESDEMONA   No, as I shall be saued.   2500

OTHELLO Ist possible?

DESDEMONA O heauen forgiue vs.

OTHELLO I cry you mercy then,
   I tooke you for that cunning whore of *Venice*,
   That married with *Othello*: (*calling*) you mistrisse,
   That haue the office opposite to S. *Peter*,
   And keepes the gate of hell,
     Enter Emillia

                  you, you: I you;
   We ha done our course; (*giuing money*) there's money
    for your paines,
   I pray you turne the key, and keepe our counsell.

                            Exit

EMILLIA
   Alas, what does this Gentleman conceiue?   2510
   How doe you Madam, how doe you my good Lady?

DESDEMONA Faith halfe asleepe.

EMILLIA
   Good Madam, what's the matter with my Lord?

DESDEMONA
   With who?

EMILLIA   Why with my Lord Madam.

DESDEMONA
   Who is thy Lord?

EMILLIA   He that is yours, sweet Lady.

DESDEMONA
   I ha none, doe not talke to me *Emillia*,
   I cannot weepe, nor answeres haue I none,
   But what should goe by water: preethee to night
   Lay on my bed my wedding sheetes, remember,
   And call thy husband hither.

EMILLIA   Here's a change indeed.   2520
                           Exit

DESDEMONA
   Tis meete I should be vsde so, very meete;
   How haue I bin behau'd, that he might sticke
   The small'st opinion, on my least misvse.
     Enter Iago, and Emillia

IAGO
   What is your pleasure Madam, how ist with you?

DESDEMONA
   I cannot tell: those that doe teach young babes
   Doe it with gentle meanes, and easie taskes,
   He might ha chid me so, for in good faith,
   I am a child to chiding.

IAGO   What is the matter Lady?

EMILLIA
   Alas *Iago*, my Lord hath so bewhor'd her,
   Throwne such despite, and heauy termes vpon her,   2530
   That true hearts cannot beare it.

DESDEMONA Am I that name *Iago*?

IAGO What name faire Lady?

DESDEMONA

Such as she said my Lord did say I was?

EMILLIA

He call'd her whore: A begger in his drinke,
Could not haue layed such tearmes vpon his Callet.

IAGO Why did he so?

DESDEMONA

I doe not know, I am sure I am none such.

IAGO

Doe not weepe, doe not weepe: alas the day.

EMILLIA

2540 Hath she forsooke so many noble matches,
Her Father, and her Countrey, and her friends,
To be cald whore? would it not make one weepe?

DESDEMONA

It is my wretched fortune.

IAGO   Beshrew him for't;
How comes this tricke vpon him?

DESDEMONA   Nay, heauen doth know.

EMILLIA

I will be hang'd, if some eternall villaine,
Some busie and insinuating rogue,
Some cogging, cousening slaue, to get some office,
Haue not deuisde this slander, I will be hang'd else.

IAGO

Fie, there is no such man, it is impossible.

DESDEMONA

2550 If any such there be, heauen pardon him.

EMILLIA

A halter pardon him, and hell gnaw his bones:
Why should he call her whore? who keepes her
    company?
What place, what time, what forme, what likelihood?
The Moore's abus'd by some most villanous knaue:
Some base notorious knaue, some scuruy fellow,
O heauen, that such companions thoudst vnfold,
And put in euery honest hand a whip,
To lash the rascalls naked through the world,
Euen from the East to th'West.

IAGO   Speake within dore.

EMILLIA

2560 O fie vpon them; some such squire he was,
That turnd your wit, the seamy side without,
And made you to suspect me with the Moore.

IAGO

You are a foole, goe to.

DESDEMONA   O God *Iago*,
What shall I doe to win my Lord againe?
Good friend goe to him, for by this light of heauen,
I know not how I lost him.
      She kneeles
                              Here I kneele:
If ere my will did trespasse 'gainst his Loue,
Either in discourse of thought, or actuall deed,
Or that mine Eyes, mine Eares, or any Sence
2570 Delighted them in any other Forme,

Or that I do not yet, and euer did,
And euer will, (though he do shake me off
To beggerly diuorcement) Loue him deerely,
Comfort forsweare me. Vnkindnesse may do much,
And his vnkindnesse may defeat my life,
But neuer taynt my Loue.
      ⌈*She rises*⌉
                              I cannot say Whore,
It do's abhorre me now I speake the word,
To do the Act, that might the addition earne,
Not the worlds Masse of vanitie could make me.

IAGO

I pray you be content, tis but his humour,   2580
The businesse of the State does him offence,
And he does chide with you.

DESDEMONA If t'were no other.
      Flourish within

IAGO It is but so, I warrant,
Harke how these Instruments summon you to supper,
The Messengers of *Venice* staies the meate,
Goe in, and weepe not, all things shall be well.
                              Exit women

      Enter Roderigo
How now *Roderigo*?

RODERIGO

I doe not finde that thou dealst iustly with me.

IAGO What in the contrary?   2590

RODERIGO Euery day, thou dafts me, with some deuise
Iago; and rather, as it seemes to me now, keep'st from
me, all conueniency, then suppliest me, with the least
aduantage of hope: I will indeed no longer indure it,
nor am I yet perswaded to put vp in peace, what
already I haue foolishly sufferd.

IAGO Will you heare me *Roderigo*?

RODERIGO Faith I haue heard too much, for your words,
and performances are no kin together.

IAGO You charge me most vniustly.   2600

RODERIGO With naught but truth: I haue wasted my selfe
out of my meanes: the Iewels you haue had from me,
to deliuer *Desdemona*, would halfe haue corrupted a
Votarist: you haue told me she hath receiu'd em, and
return'd mee expectations, and comforts, of suddaine
respect, and acquaintance, but I finde none.

IAGO Well, goe to, very well.

RODERIGO Very well, goe to, I cannot goe to man, nor tis
not very well, nay I think it is scuruy, and begin to
finde my selfe fopt in it.   2610

IAGO Very well.

RODERIGO I tell you, 'tis not very well: I will make my
selfe knowne to *Desdemona*, if she will returne me my
Iewels, I will giue ouer my suite, and repent my
vnlawfull sollicitation, if not, assure your selfe I will
seeke satisfaction of you.

IAGO You haue said now.

RODERIGO I, and said nothing, but what I protest
endetment of doing.

IAGO Why now I see there's mettle in thee, and euen   2620
from this instant doe build on thee, a better opinion

then euer before, giue me thy hand *Roderigo*: Thou
hast taken against me a most iust exception, but yet I
protest, I haue delt most directly in thy affaire.

RODERIGO It hath not appeared.

IAGO I grant indeed it hath not appear'd, and your
suspition is not without wit and iudgement: But
Roderigo, if thou hast that in thee indeed, which I haue
greater reason to beleeue now, then euer, I meane
2630 purpose, courage, and valour, this night shew it, if
thou the next night following enioy not *Desdemona*,
take mee from this world with treachery, and deuise
engines for my life.

RODERIGO Well, what is it? Is it within reason and
compasse?

IAGO Sir, there is especiall commission come from *Venice*,
to depute *Cassio* in *Othello's* place.

RODERIGO Is that true? why then *Othello* and *Desdemona*
returne againe to *Venice*.

2640 IAGO O no, he goes into *Mauritania*, and takes away with
him the faire *Desdemona*, vnlesse his abode be linger'd
here by some accident, wherein none can be so
determinate, as the remouing of *Cassio*.

RODERIGO How doe you meane remouing of him?

IAGO Why, by making him vncapable of *Othello's* place,
knocking out his braines.

RODERIGO And that you would haue me to doe.

IAGO I: if you dare doe your selfe a profit, and a right,
hee sups to night with a harlotry, and thither will I
2650 goe to him;—he knowes not yet of his honourable
fortune: if you will watch his going thence, which I
will fashion to fall out betweene twelue and one, you
may take him at your pleasure: I will be neere to
second your attempt, and hee shall fall betweene vs:
come, stand not amaz'd at it, but goe along with mee,
I will shew you such a necessity in his death, that you
shall thinke your selfe bound to put it on him. It is
now high supper time, and the night growes to wast:
about it.

2660 RODERIGO I will heare further reason for this.

IAGO And you shall be satisfied.   *Exeunt*

Sc. 13   *Enter Othello, Desdemona, Lodouico, Emillia, and*
(4.3)   *Attendants*

LODOUICO
I do beseech you sir, trouble your selfe no further.

OTHELLO
O pardon me, 'twill doe me good to walke.

LODOUICO (*to Desdemona*)
Madame, good night, I humbly thanke your Ladiship.

DESDEMONA
Your honour is most welcome.

OTHELLO   Will you walke sir:—
O *Desdemona*.

DESDEMONA My Lord.

OTHELLO Get you to bed, on th'instant. I will be return'd
forthwith, dismisse your Attendant there,—looke't be
2670 done.

DESDEMONA I will my Lord.
                    Exeunt Othello, Lodouico, and Attendants

EMILLIA How goes it now? he lookes gentler then he did.

DESDEMONA
He saies he will returne incontinent:
He hath commanded me to goe to bed,
And bid me to dismisse you.

EMILLIA   Dismisse me?

DESDEMONA
It was his bidding, therefore good *Emillia*,
Giue me my nightly wearing, and adiue,
We must not now displease him.

EMILLIA I would you had neuer seene him.

DESDEMONA
So would not I, my loue doth so approue him,   2680
That euen his stubbornenesse, his checks, his
    frownes.
Prethee vnpin me; haue grace and fauour in them.
    Emillia helpes Desdemona to vndresse

EMILLIA
I haue laied those sheetes you bade me, on the bed.

DESDEMONA
All's one: good faith: how foolish are our minds?
If I doe die before thee, prethee shrowd me
In one of these same sheetes.

EMILLIA   Come, come, you talke.

DESDEMONA
My mother had a maid cald *Barbary*,
She was in loue, and he she lou'd, prou'd mad,
And did forsake her, she had a song of willow,
An old thing 'twas, but it exprest her fortune,   2690
And she died singing it, that Song to night,
Will not goe from my mind—I haue much to do,
But to go hang my head all at one side
And sing it like poore *Barbary*: prythee dispatch.

EMILLIA
Shall I go fetch your Night-gowne?

DESDEMONA   No, vn-pin me here,
This *Lodouico* is a proper man.

EMILLIA
A very handsome man.

DESDEMONA   He speakes well.

EMILLIA I know a Lady in Venice would haue walk'd
barefoot to Palestine for a touch of his nether lip.

DESDEMONA (*sings*)
The poore Soule sat sighing, by a Sicamour tree.   2700
    Sing all a greene Willough:
Her hand on her bosome her head on her knee,
    Sing Willough, Willough, Willough.
The fresh Streames ran by her, and murmur'd her moanes
    Sing Willough, Willough, Willough.
Her salt teares fell from her, and softned the stones,
    Sing Willough
(Lay by these)
                    Willough, Willough.
(Prythee high thee: he'le come anon)   2710
Sing all a greene Willough must be my Garland.
Let nobody blame him, his scorne I approue.
(Nay that's not next. Harke, who is't that knocks?)

EMILLIA It's the wind.

DESDEMONA

I call'd my Loue false Loue: but what said he then?
   Sing Willough, Willough, Willough.
If I court mo women, you'le couch with mo men.
So get thee gone, good night: Mine eyes doe itch,
Doth that bode weeping?

EMILLIA   Tis neither here nor there.

DESDEMONA

2720 I haue heard it said so. O these Men, these men!
Do'st thou in conscience thinke (tell me *Emillia*)
That there be women do abuse their husbands
In such grosse kinde?

EMILLIA   There be some such, no question.

DESDEMONA

Wouldst thou doe such a deed, for all the world?

EMILLIA

Why would not you.

DESDEMONA   No, by this heauenly light.

EMILLIA Nor I neither, by this heauenly light, I might
doe't as well i'th'darke.

DESDEMONA

Would'st thou doe such a deed for all the world?

EMILLIA The world's a huge thing, it is a great price, for
2730 a small vice.

DESDEMONA Introth I thinke thou wouldst not.

EMILLIA Introth I thinke I should, and vndo't when I had
done, mary I would not doe such a thing for a ioynt
ring; nor for measures of Lawne, nor for Gownes,
Petticotes, nor Caps, nor any petty exhibition; but for
all the whole world? vds pitty, who would not make
her husband a Cuckole, to make him a Monarch? I
should venture purgatory for't.

DESDEMONA

Beshrew me, if I would doe such a wrong,
2740 For the whole world.

EMILLIA Why, the wrong is but a wrong i'th'world; and
hauing the world for your labour, tis a wrong in your
owne world, and you might quickly make it right.

DESDEMONA

I doe not thinke there is any such woman.

EMILLIA

Yes, a dozen, and as many
To'th'vantage, as would store the world they played for.
But I do thinke it is their Husbands faults
If Wiues do fall: (Say, that they slacke their duties,
And powre our Treasures into forraigne laps;
2750 Or else breake out in peeuish Iealousies,
Throwing restraint vpon vs: Or say they strike vs,
Or scant our former hauing in despight)
Why we haue galles: and though we haue some Grace,
Yet haue we some Reuenge. Let Husbands know,
Their wiues haue sense like them: They see, and smell,
And haue their Palats both for sweet, and sowre,
As Husbands haue. What is it that they do,
When they change vs for others? Is it Sport?
I thinke it is: and doth Affection breed it?
2760 I thinke it doth. Is't Frailty that thus erres?
It is so too. And haue not we Affections?

Desires for Sport? and Frailty, as men haue?
Then let them vse vs well: else let them know,
The illes we do, their illes instruct vs so.

DESDEMONA

Good night, good night: God me such vses send,
Not to picke bad from bad, but by bad mend.   *Exeunt*

     Enter Iago and Roderigo   Sc. 14

IAGO   (5.1)

Here stand behind this Bulke, straite will he come,
Weare thy good Rapier bare, and put it home,
Quicke, quicke, feare nothing, I'le be at thy elboe;
It makes vs or it marres vs, thinke on that,   2770
And fixe most firme thy resolution.

RODERIGO

Be neere at hand, I may miscarry in't.

IAGO

Here at thy hand, be bold, and take thy stand.

RODERIGO *(aside)*

I haue no great deuotion to the deed;
And yet he hath giuen me satisfying reasons,
Tis but a man gone: forth my sword, he dies.

IAGO *(aside)*

I haue rubd this young quat almost to the sense,
And he growes angry: now whether he kill *Cassio*,
Or *Cassio* him, or each doe kill the other,
Euery way makes my gaine; liue *Roderigo*,   2780
He calls me to a restitution large,
Of Gold and Iewells, that I bobd from him,
As gifts to *Desdemona*:
It must not be, if *Cassio* doe remaine,
He hath a daily beauty in his life,
That makes me vgly: and besides, the Moore
May vnfould me to him; there stand I in much perrill:
No, he must die, but so, I heare him comming.
    Enter Cassio

RODERIGO

I know his gate, tis he, *(assailing Cassio)* villaine thou
   diest.

CASSIO

That thrust had bin mine enemy indeed,   2790
But that my coate is better then thou know'st,
I will make proofe of thine.
    He stabs Roderigo, who falls

RODERIGO   O I am slaine.
    Iago wounds Cassio in the leg from behind. Exit Iago

CASSIO *(falling)*

I am maimd for euer, helpe ho, murder, murder.
    Enter Othello ⌐aboue⌐

OTHELLO

The voice of *Cassio*, *Iago* keepes his word.

RODERIGO O villaine that I am.

OTHELLO It is euen so.

CASSIO O helpe ho, light, a Surgeon.

OTHELLO

Tis he, O braue *Iago*, honest and Iust,
That hast such noble sence of thy friends wrong,
Thou teachest me;—minion, your deare lies dead,   2800

And your vnblest fate hies; strumpet I come;
Forth of my heart, those charmes thine eyes are blotted,
Thy bed lust-staind, shall with lusts blood be spotted.

Exit

       Enter Lodouico and Gratiano

CASSIO

What ho, no watch, no passage, murder, murder.

GRATIANO

Tis some mischance, the voice is very direfull.

CASSIO O helpe.

LODOUICO Harke.

RODERIGO O wretched villaine.

LODOUICO

Two or three grone, 'tis heauy night,
2810   These may be counterfeits, let's think't vnsafe
To come into the cry without more helpe.

RODERIGO

No body come, then shall I bleed to death.

       Enter Iago with a light

LODOUICO Harke.

GRATIANO

Here's one comes in his shirt, with light and weapons.

IAGO

Who's there? whose noise is this, that cries on murder.

LODOUICO

We doe not know.

IAGO   Doe not you heare a cry?

CASSIO

Here, here, for heauen sake helpe me.

IAGO   What's the matter.

GRATIANO (*to Lodouico*)

This is *Othello's* Ancient, as I take it.

LODOUICO

The same indeed, a very valiant fellow.

IAGO (*to Cassio*)

2820   What are you here, that cry so greeuously?

CASSIO

Iago, O I am spoil'd, vndone by villaines,
Giue me some helpe.

IAGO

O me, Leiutenant: what villaines haue done this?

CASSIO

I thinke that one of them is heere about,
And cannot make away.

IAGO   O treacherous villaines:

(*To Lodouico and Gratiano*)

What are you there? come in and giue some helpe.

RODERIGO O helpe me there.

CASSIO That's one of em.

IAGO (*stabbing Roderigo*) O murderous slaue, O villaine.

RODERIGO

2830   O dambd *Iago*, O inhumaine dog.

IAGO

Kill men i'th'dark? where be these bloody theeues?
How silent is this Towne? Ho, murder, murder:

(*To Lodouico and Gratiano*)

What may you be, are you of good or euill?

LODOUICO

As you shall proue vs, praise vs.

IAGO   Seignior *Lodouico*.

LODOUICO He sir.

IAGO

I cry you mercy: here's *Cassio* hurt by villaines.

GRATIANO *Cassio*.

IAGO How is't brother?

CASSIO My leg is cut in two.

IAGO Mary heauen forbid: 2840
Light Gentlemen, I'le bind it with my shirt.

       Enter Bianca

BIANCA

What is the matter ho, who ist that cried?

IAGO

Who ist that cried.

BIANCA   O my deare *Cassio*,
My sweete *Cassio*, O *Cassio*, *Cassio*.

IAGO

O notable strumpet: *Cassio* may you suspect
Who they should be, that haue thus mangled you?

CASSIO No.

GRATIANO

I am sorry to find you thus, I haue bin to seeke you.

IAGO

Lend me a Garter. So:—Oh for a Chaire
To beare him easily hence.   2850

BIANCA

Alas he faints, O *Cassio*, *Cassio*, *Cassio*.

IAGO

Gentlemen all, I doe suspect this trash
To be a party in this Iniurie:
Patience a while good *Cassio*: Come, come;
Lend me a light; (*going to Roderigo*) know we this
    face, or no?
Alas my friend, and my deare countrey man:
Roderigo? no, yes sure: O heauen *Roderigo*.

GRATIANO What of *Venice*?

IAGO Euen he sir, did you know him?

GRATIANO Know him? I.   2860

IAGO

Seignior *Gratiano*, I cry your gentle pardon:
These bloody accidents must excuse my manners,
That so neglected you.

GRATIANO   I am glad to see you.

IAGO

How doe you *Cassio*? O a chaire, a chaire.

GRATIANO *Roderigo*.

IAGO

He, he tis he:

       Enter Attendants with a chaire

         O that's well said, the chaire:
Some good man beare him carefully from hence,
I'le fetch the Generalls Surgeon: (*to Bianca*) for you
    mistrisse,
Saue you your labour, he that lies slaine here *Cassio*,
Was my deare friend, what malice was between you? 2870

CASSIO

None in the world, nor doe I know the man.

IAGO (*to Bianca*)

What, looke you pale? (*To Attendants*) O beare him
     out o'th aire.
(*To Lodouico and Gratiano*)
Stay you good Gentlemen,
                    Exeunt Attendants with Cassio in the chaire,
                         ⌜*and with Roderigoes body*⌝
(*To Bianca*)   looke you pale mistrisse?
(*To Lodouico and Gratiano*)
Doe you perceiue the gastnesse of her eye,
(*To Bianca*) Nay, an you stare, we shall heare more
     anon:
(*To Lodouico and Gratiano*)
Behold her well I pray you, looke vpon her,
Doe you see Gentlemen? Nay guiltinesse
Will speake, though tongues were out of vse.
               Enter Emillia

EMILLIA

Alas what is the matter? What is the matter husband?

IAGO

2880   *Cassio* hath here bin set on in the darke,
By *Roderigo*, and fellowes that are scap't,
Hee's almost slaine, and *Roderigo* dead.

EMILLIA

Alas good gentleman, alas good *Cassio*.

IAGO

This is the fruites of whoring, prythe *Emillia*,
Goe know of *Cassio*, where he supt to night:
(*To Bianca*) What, doe you shake at that?

BIANCA

He supt at my house, but I therefore shake not.

IAGO

O did he so, I charge you goe with me.

EMILLIA (*to Bianca*) Oh fie vpon thee strumpet.

BIANCA

2890   I am no strumpet, but of life as honest,
As you, that thus abuse me.

EMILLIA   As I: fough, fie vpon thee.

IAGO

Kind Gentlemen, let's goe see poore *Cassio* drest,
(*To Bianca*) Come mistresse, you must tell's another
     tale.
Emillia, runne you to the Cittadell,
And tell my Lord and Lady what hath hapt:
Will you goe on afore,   *Exit Emillia*
(*Aside*)   this is the night,
That either makes me, or foredoes me quite.   *Exeunt*

Sc. 15   *Enter Othello with a light, Desdemona asleep in her*
(5.2)   *bed*

OTHELLO

It is the cause, it is the cause, my soule,
Let me not name it to you, you chaste starres:
2900   It is the cause, yet I'le not shed her blood,
Nor scarre that whiter skin of hers, then snow,

And smooth, as monumentall Alablaster;
Yet she must die, else shee'll betray more men,
Put out the light, and then put out the light:
If I quench thee, thou flaming minister,
I can againe, thy former light restore,
Should I repent me; but once put out thy light,
Thou cunning'st patterne of excelling nature,
I know not where is that promethian heate,
That can thy light re-Lume: when I haue pluckt thy
     rose,   2910
I cannot giue it vitall growth againe,
It needes must wither; I'le smell thee on the tree,
     ⌜*He kisses her*⌝
Oh balmy breath, that dost almost perswade
Iustice to breake her sword. One more, one more,
Be thus, when thou art dead, and I will kill thee,
And loue thee after: one more, and that's the last,
     He kisses her
So sweete was ne're so fatall: I must weepe,
But they are cruell teares; this sorrowes heauenly,
It strikes where it doth loue: she wakes.

DESDEMONA   Who's there, *Othello*?   2920

OTHELLO   I, *Desdemona*.

DESDEMONA   Will you come to bed my Lord?

OTHELLO   Haue you prayed to night, *Desdemon*?

DESDEMONA   I my Lord.

OTHELLO

If you bethinke your selfe of any crime,
Vnreconcil'd as yet to heauen and grace,
Sollicite for it straite.

DESDEMONA

Alacke my Lord, what may you meane by that?

OTHELLO

Well doe it, and be briefe, I will walke by,
I would not kill thy vnprepared spirit,   2930
No, heauens fore-fend, I would not kill thy soule.

DESDEMONA

Talke you of killing?

OTHELLO   I, I doe.

DESDEMONA   Then heauen
Haue mercy on me.

OTHELLO   Amen, with all my heart.

DESDEMONA

If you say so, I hope you will not kill me.

OTHELLO   Hum.

DESDEMONA

And yet I feare you, for you're fatall then,
When your eyes roule so: why I should feare, I know
     not,
Since guiltinesse I know not, but yet I feele I feare.

OTHELLO   Thinke on thy sinnes.

DESDEMONA   They are loues I beare to you.   2940

OTHELLO   I, and for that thou diest.

DESDEMONA

That death's vnnaturall, that kills for louing,
Alas, why gnaw you so your neather lip?
Some bloody passion shakes your very frame,

These are portents: but yet I hope, I hope,
They doe not point on me.

OTHELLO   Peace, and be still.

DESDEMONA
I will so, what's the matter?

OTHELLO   That handkercher
Which I so lou'd, and gaue thee, thou gau'st to *Cassio*.

DESDEMONA
No, by my life and soule, Send for the man
2950   And aske him.

OTHELLO
Sweete soule take heed, take heed of periury,
Thou art on thy death-bed.

DESDEMONA I, but not yet to die.

OTHELLO Presently:
Therefore confesse thee freely of thy sinne,
For to deny each article with oath,
Cannot remoue, nor choke the strong conception,
That I doe groane withall: thou art to die.

DESDEMONA
Then Lord haue mercy on me.

OTHELLO   I say Amen.

DESDEMONA
2960   And haue you mercy too: I neuer did
Offend you in my life,—neuer lou'd *Cassio*,
But with such generall warranty of heauen,
As I might loue: I neuer gaue him token.

OTHELLO
By heauen I saw my handkercher in's hand,
O periur'd woman, thou doest stone my heart,
And makes me call, what I intend to doe,
A murder, which I thought a sacrifice,
I saw the handkercher.

DESDEMONA   He found it then,
I neuer gaue it him, send for him hither,
Let him confesse a truth.

2970 OTHELLO   He hath confest.

DESDEMONA
What, my Lord?

OTHELLO   That he hath vsde the.

DESDEMONA How, vnlawfully?

OTHELLO I.

DESDEMONA He will not say so.

OTHELLO No, his mouth is stop'd,
Honest *Iago* hath tane order for't.

DESDEMONA
Oh, my feare interprets,—what is he dead?

OTHELLO
Had all his haires bin liues, my great reuenge
Had stomacke for 'em all.

DESDEMONA (*weeping*)
2980   Alas he is betraid, and I vndone.

OTHELLO
Out strumpet,—weep'st thou for him to my face?

DESDEMONA
O bannish me, my Lord, but kill me not.

OTHELLO (*assailing her*) Downe strumpet.

DESDEMONA
Kill me to morrow, let me liue to night.

OTHELLO Nay, an you striue.

DESDEMONA But halfe an houre.

OTHELLO Being done, there is no pawse.

DESDEMONA But while I say one prayer.

OTHELLO It is too late.

he smothers her

DESDEMONA O Lord, Lord, Lord.   2990

Emillia at the doore

EMILLIA (*within*)
My Lord, my Lord, what ho, my Lord, my Lord.

OTHELLO
What noise is this? not dead? not yet quite dead?
I that am cruell, am yet mercifull,
I would not haue thee linger in thy paine,—
So, so.

EMILLIA (*within*) What ho, my Lord, my Lord.

OTHELLO   Who's there?

EMILLIA (*within*)
O good my Lord, I would speake a word with you.

OTHELLO (*calling*)
Yes,—tis *Emillia*, (*calling*) by and by:—shee's dead:
Tis like she comes to speake of *Cassios* death;
The noyse was high; ha, no more mouing,
Still as the graue: shall she come in? were't good?   3000
I thinke she stirres againe; no, what's best to do?
If she come in, shee'll sure speake to my wife.
My wife, my wife: what wife? I ha no wife;
O insupportable: O heauy houre.
Me thinks it should be now a huge Ecclips
Of Sunne and Moone, and that th'affrighted Globe,
Should yawne at alteration.

EMILLIA (*within*)   I doe beseech you
That I may speake with you,—Oh good my Lord.

OTHELLO
I had forgot thee: O come in *Emillia*.
Soft, by and by; let me the Curtaines draw,   3010

He closes the bed Curtaines

Where art thou?

He opens the dore. Enter Emillia
             whats the matter with thee now?

EMILLIA
O my good Lord, yonder's foule murders done.

OTHELLO What, now?

EMILLIA But now my Lord.

OTHELLO
It is the very error of the Moone,
She comes more neerer earth, then she was wont,
And makes men mad.

EMILLIA
Cassio my Lord hath kil'd a yong *Venetian*,
Cal'd *Roderigo*.

OTHELLO   *Roderigo* kild,
And *Cassio* kild?

EMILLIA   No, *Cassio* is not kild.   3020

OTHELLO
Not *Cassio* kild, then murders out of tune,
And sweete reuenge growes harsh.

DESDEMONA O falsly, falsly murder'd.

EMILLIA O Lord, what cry is that?

OTHELLO That? what?

EMILLIA

   Out and alas, that was my Ladyes voyce,

     ⌈*She opens the bed Curtaines*⌉

   Helpe, helpe, ho helpe, O Lady speake againe,

   Sweete *Desdemona*, O sweete Mistresse speake.

DESDEMONA

   A guiltlesse death I die.

EMILLIA   O who hath done this deed?

DESDEMONA

3030   No body, I my selfe, farewell:

   Commend me to my kinde Lord, O farewell.   *she dies*

OTHELLO

   Why, how should she be murder'd?

EMILLIA   Alas, who knowes?

OTHELLO

   You heard her say, her selfe, it was not I.

EMILLIA

   She sayd so, I must needes report the truth.

OTHELLO

   She's like a lyer, gone to burning Hell,

   'Twas I that kild her.

EMILLIA

   O, the more Angell she, and you the blacker diuell.

OTHELLO

   She turn'd to folly, and she was a whore.

EMILLIA

   Thou doest bely her, and thou art a diuell.

OTHELLO

   She was false as water.

3040 EMILLIA   Thou art rash as fire,

   To say that she was false: O she was heauenly true.

OTHELLO

   Cassio did top her, aske thy husband else,

   O I were damn'd beneath all depth in hell,

   But that I did proceed, vpon iust grounds,

   To this extremity, thy husband knew it all.

EMILLIA

   My husband?

OTHELLO   Thy husband.

EMILLIA   That she was false to wedlocke?

OTHELLO

   I, with *Cassio*: had she bin true,

   If heauen would make me such another world,

   Of one intire and perfect Crisolite,

   I'de not haue sold her for it.

3050 EMILLIA   My husband?

OTHELLO

   I, twas he that told me on her first,

   An honest man he is, and hates the slime,

   That sticks on filthy deedes.

EMILLIA   My husband?

OTHELLO

   What needes this itterance, woman, I say thy husband.

EMILLIA

   Oh Mistris, villany hath made mockes with loue:

   My Husband say she was false?

OTHELLO   He, Woman;

I say thy Husband: Do'st vnderstand the word?

My Friend, thy Husband; honest, honest *Iago*.

EMILLIA

   If he say so, may his pernitious soule

   Rot halfe a graine a day: he lies to'th heart,   3060

   She was too fond of her most filthy bargaine.

OTHELLO Ha?

EMILLIA Doe thy worst,

   This deed of thine is no more worthy heauen,

   Then thou wast worthy her.

OTHELLO   Peace, you were best.

EMILLIA

   Thou hast not halfe that power to doe me harme,

   As I haue to be hurt: O gull, O dolt,

   As ignorant as dirtt; thou hast done a deed—

   I care not for thy sword, I'le make thee known,

   Tho I lost twenty liues : helpe, helpe, hoa, helpe;   3070

   The Moore hath kild my Mistresse, murder, murder.

     Enter Montano, Gratiano, and Iago

MONTANO

   What is the matter? how now Generall?

EMILLIA

   O, are you come *Iago*? you haue done well,

   That men must lay their murders on your neck.

GRATIANO What is the matter?

EMILLIA (*to Iago*)

   Disproue this villaine, if thou bee'st a man;

   He sayes thou toldst him that his wife was false,

   I know thou didst not, thou'rt not such a villaine:

   Speake, for my heart is full.

IAGO

   I told him what I thought, and told no more,   3080

   Then what he found himselfe was apt and true.

EMILLIA

   But did you euer tell him she was false?

IAGO I did.

EMILLIA

   You told a lie, an odious damned lie;

   Vpon my soule, a lie, a wicked lie:

   She false with *Cassio*; did you say with *Cassio*?

IAGO

   With *Cassio* mistresse; go to, charme your tongue.

EMILLIA

   I will not charme my tongue, I am bound to speake.

   My Mistris heere lyes murther'd in her bed.

⌈MONTANO *and* GRATIANO⌉ Oh Heauens, forefend.   3090

EMILLIA (*to Iago*)

   And your reports haue set the Murder on.

OTHELLO

   Nay stare not Masters, it is true indeede.

GRATIANO

   'Tis a strange Truth.

MONTANO   O monstrous Acte.

EMILLIA

   Villany, villany, villany:

   I thinke vpon't, I thinke: I smel't: O Villany:

   I thought so then: Ile kill my selfe for greefe.

   O villany! villany!

IAGO

    What are you mad, I charge you get you home.

EMILLIA

    Good Gentlemen let me haue leaue to speake,

3100   Tis proper I obey him, but not now:

    Perchance *Iago*, I will ne're goe home.

OTHELLO

    Oh, oh, oh.

        Othello fals on the bed

EMILLIA   Nay, lay thee downe, and rore,

    For thou hast kild the sweetest innocent,

    That ere did lift vp eye.

OTHELLO ⌈*rising*⌉   O she was foule:

    (*To Gratiano*) I scarce did know you Vncle, there lies

        your Niece,

    Whose breath indeed, these hands haue newly stopt,

    I know this act shewes horrible and grim.

GRATIANO

    Poore *Desdemon*, I am glad thy father's dead,

    Thy match was mortall to him, and pure griefe,

3110   Shore his old thread in twaine: did he liue now,

    This sight would make him doe a desperate turne,

    Yea curse his better Angell from his side,

    And fall to reprobance.

OTHELLO

    Tis pittifull, but yet *Iago* knowes,

    That she with *Cassio*, hath the act of shame

    A thousand times committed; *Cassio* confest it,

    And she did gratifie his amorous workes,

    With that recognisance and pledge of loue,

    Which I first gaue her; I saw it in his hand,

3120   It was a handkercher; an Antique token

    My father gaue my mother.

EMILLIA   O God, O heauenly God.

IAGO

    Zouns, hold your peace.

EMILLIA   'Twill out, 'twill out: I peace?

    No, I will speake as liberall as the North,

    Let heauen, and men, and diuells, let em all,

    All, all cry shame against me, yet I'le speake.

IAGO Be wise, and get you home.

EMILLIA I will not.

        Iago draws his sword

GRATIANO (*to Iago*) Fie, your sword vpon a woman?

EMILLIA

    O thou dull Moore, that handkercher thou speakst of,

3130   I found by fortune, and did giue my husband:

    For often with a solemne earnestnesse,

    More then indeed belong'd to such a trifle,

    He beg'd of me to steale't.

IAGO   Villainous whore.

EMILLIA

    She giue it *Cassio*? no alas I found it,

    And I did giu't my husband.

IAGO   Filth thou liest.

EMILLIA

    By heauen I doe not, I doe not Gentlemen,

O murderous Coxcombe! what should such a foole

Doe with so good a wife?

OTHELLO   Are there no stones in heauen,

    But what serues for the thunder? pretious villaine.

        The Moore runnes at Iago. Montano disarms

        Othello. Iago wounds his wife

GRATIANO

    The woman falls, sure he hath kild his wife.   3140

EMILLIA

    I, I, O lay me by my mistresse side.   *Exit Iago*

GRATIANO Hee's gone, but his wife's kild.

MONTANO

    Tis a notorious villaine, take you this weapon,

    Which I haue here recouer'd from the Moore:

    Come, guard the dore without, let him not passe,

    But kill him rather, I'le after that same villaine,

    For tis a damned slaue.   *Exit Montano and Gratiano*

OTHELLO   I am not valiant neither,

    But euery puny whipster gets my sword,

    But why should honour out liue honesty?

    Let it goe all.

EMILLIA   What did thy Song boad Lady?   3150

    Hearke, canst thou heare me? I will play the Swan,

    And dye in Musicke: (*Sings*) *Willough, Willough,*

       Willough.

    Moore, she was chast, she lou'd thee cruell Moore,

    So come my soule to blisse, as I speake true;

    So speaking as I thinke, alas, I die.   *she dies*

OTHELLO

    I haue another weapon in this chamber,

    It was a sword of Spaine, the Isebrookes temper;

    O here it is; (*calling*) Vncle I must come forth.

GRATIANO (*within*)

    If thou attempt it, it will cost thee deere,

    Thou hast no weapon, and perforce must suffer.   3160

OTHELLO

    Looke in vpon me then, and speake with me,

    Or naked as I am, I will assault thee.

        Enter Gratiano

GRATIANO

    What is the matter?

OTHELLO   Behold, I haue a weapon,

    A better neuer did it selfe sustaine

    Vpon a Souldiers thigh: I haue seene the day,

    That with this little arme, and this good sword,

    I haue made my way through more impediments,

    Then twenty times your stop: but O vaine boast,

    Who can controule his Fate? tis not so now,

    Be not affraid, though you do see me weapon'd: 3170

    Heere is my iournies end, heere is my butt

    And verie Sea-marke of my vtmost Saile.

    Do you go backe dismaid? 'Tis a lost feare:

    Man but a Rush against *Othello*'s brest,

    And he retires. Where should *Othello* go?

    (*To Desdemona*) Now: how dost thou looke now? Oh

       ill-Starr'd wench,

    Pale as thy smocke, when we shall meete at count,

This looke of thine, will hurle my soule from heauen,
And fiends will snatch at it:
　　　⌈*He touches her*⌉
　　　　　　　　　　　　cold, cold, my girle,
3180　Euen like thy chastity; O cursed, cursed slaue:
Whippe me ye Diuells,
From the possession of this heauenly sight,
Blow me about in winds, roast me in sulphure,
Wash me in steepe downe gulphes of liquid fire:
O *Desdemon*! dead *Desdemon*, dead, O, o.
　　　Enter Lodouico, Montano, Iago guarded by Officers,
　　　Cassio in a Chaire
LODOUICO
Where is this rash and most vnfortunate man.
OTHELLO
That's he that was *Othello*, here I am.
LODOUICO
Where is that Viper, bring the villaine forth.
OTHELLO
I looke downe towards his feet, but that's a fable,
3190　(*To Iago*) If that thou beest a diuell, I cannot kill thee.
　　　He wounds Iago
LODOUICO
Wrench his sword from him.
　　　Officers disarm Othello
IAGO　　　　　　　　　　　　　I bleed sir, but not kil'd.
OTHELLO
I am not sorry neither, I'de haue thee liue,
For in my sense tis happinesse to die.
LODOUICO
O thou *Othello*, that was once so good,
Falne in the practise of a cursed slaue,
What shall be said to thee?
OTHELLO　　　　　　　　　　Why any thing,
An honourable murderer if you will:
For nought I did in hate, but all in honour.
LODOUICO
This wretch hath part confest his villainy:
3200　Did you and he consent in *Cassio's* death?
OTHELLO I.
CASSIO
Deare Generall, I neuer gaue you cause.
OTHELLO
I doe beleeue it, and I aske your pardon,
Will you I pray, demand that demy diuell,
Why he hath thus insnar'd my soule and body?
IAGO
Demand me nothing, what you know you know,
From this time forth I neuer will speake word.
LODOUICO (*to Iago*) What not to pray?
GRATIANO (*to Iago*) Torments will op'e your lips.
3210　OTHELLO Well, thou doest best.
LODOUICO
Sir, you shall vnderstand what hath befalne,
Which, as I thinke you know not: here is a letter,
Found in the pocket of the slaine *Roderigo*;
And here another; the one of them imports

The death of *Cassio*; to be vndertooke—
By *Roderigo*.
OTHELLO O villaine.
CASSIO Most heathenish, and most grosse.
LODOUICO
Now heres another discontented paper,
Found in his pocket too, and this it seemes,　　　3220
Roderigo meant t'haue sent this damned villaine,
But that belike, *Iago*, in the interim
Came in, and satisfied him.
OTHELLO (*to Iago*) O thou pernitious catieffe!
How came you *Cassio* by that handkercher,
That was my wifes?
CASSIO　　　　　　　　I found it in my chamber,
And he himselfe confest it but euen now,
That there he dropt it, for a speciall purpose;
Which wrought to his desire.
OTHELLO　　　　　　　　　　O foole, foole, foole.
CASSIO
There is besides in *Roderigoes* letter　　　　3230
How he vpbraides *Iago*, that he made him,
Braue me vpon the watch, whereon it came,
That I was cast; and euen but now he spake,
After long seeming dead, *Iago* hurt him,
Iago set him on.
LODOUICO (*to Othello*)
You must forsake this roome, and goe with vs,
Your power and your command is taken off,
And *Cassio* rules in *Cypres*: for this slaue,
If there be any cunning cruelty,
That can torment him much, and hold him long,　　3240
It shall be his: you shall close prisoner rest,
Till that the nature of your fault be knowne
To the *Venetian* State; (*to Officers*) come, bring away.
OTHELLO
Soft you, a word or two before you goe,
I haue done the State some seruice, and they know't;
No more of that: I pray you in your letters,
When you shall these vnlucky deedes relate,
Speake of me, as I am; nothing extenuate,
Nor set downe ought in malice, then must you speake,
Of one that lou'd not wisely, but too well:　　　3250
Of one not easily iealous, but being wrought,
Perplext in the extreame; of one whose hand,
Like the base *Indian*, threw a pearle away,
Richer then all his Tribe: of one whose subdued eyes,
Albeit vnused to the melting moode,
Drops teares as fast as the *Arabian* trees,
Their medicinable gum; set you downe this,
And say besides, that in *Aleppo* once,
Where a *Malignant* and a *Turband Turke*,
Beate a *Venetian*, and traduc'd the State;　　　3260
I tooke bi'th throate the circumcised dog,
And smote him thus.
　　　He stabs himselfe
LODOUICO O bloody period.
GRATIANO All that is spoke is mard.

OTHELLO (*to Desdemona*)
　I kist thee ere I kild thee, no way but this,
　Killing my selfe, to die vpon a kisse.

　　　　　　　　　　　He kisses Desdemona, and dies

CASSIO
　This did I feare, but thought he had no weapon,
　For he was great of heart.

LODOUICO (*to Iago*)　　　　　O Spartane dog,
　More fell then anguish, hunger, or the Sea,
3270　Looke on the tragicke loading of this bed:
　This is thy worke, the obiect poisons sight,

Let it be hid:

　⌈*They close the bed Curtaines*⌉
　　　　　　Gratiano, keepe the house,
And ceaze vpon the fortunes of the Moore:
For they succeed on you, (*to Cassio*) to you Lord
　Gouernour,
Remaines the censure of this hellish villaine,
The time, the place, the torture: O inforce it,
My selfe will straite aboord, and to the State,
This heauy act with heauy heart relate.

　　　　　　　Exeunt omnes ⌈*with Emillias body*⌉

FINIS

ALL'S WELL THAT ENDS WELL

All's Well that Ends Well, first printed in the 1623 Folio, is often paired with *Measure, for Measure*. Though we lack external evidence as to its date of composition, internal evidence suggests that it, too, is an early Jacobean play. Like *Measure, for Measure*, it places its central characters in more painful situations than those in which the heroes and heroines of the earlier, more romantic comedies usually find themselves. The touching ardour with which Hellen, 'a poore Physitians daughter', pursues the young Bertram, son of her guardian the Countesse of Rossillion, creates embarrassments for both of them. When the King whose illness she cures by her semi-magical skills brings about their marriage as a reward, Bertram's flight to the wars seems to destroy all her chances of happiness. She achieves consummation of the marriage only by the ruse (resembling Isabella's 'bed-trick' in *Measure, for Measure*) of substituting herself for the Florentine maiden Diana whom Bertram believes himself to be seducing. The play's conclusion, in which the deception is exposed and Bertram is shamed into acknowledging Hellen as his wife, offers only a tentatively happy ending.

Shakespeare based the story of Bertram and Hellen on a tale from Boccaccio's *Decameron* either in the original or in the version included in William Painter's *Palace of Pleasure* (1566-7, revised 1575). But he created several important characters, including the Countesse and the old Lord, Lafew. He also invented the accompanying action exposing the roguery of Bertram's flashy friend Parolles, a man of words (as his name indicates) descending from the braggart soldier of Roman comedy.

Versions of the play performed in the eighteenth and nineteenth centuries, mostly emphasizing either the comedy of Parolles or the sentimental appeal of Hellen, had little success; but some twentieth-century productions have shown it in a more favourable light, demonstrating, for example, that the role of the Countesse is (in Bernard Shaw's words) 'the most beautiful old woman's part ever written', that the discomfiture of Parolles provides comedy that is subtle as well as highly laughable, and that the relationship of Bertram and Hellen is profoundly convincing in its emotional reality.

The only early text, in the 1623 Folio, shows every sign of having been printed from Shakespeare's foul papers.

THE NAME OF THE ACTORS

The COUNTESSE of Rossillion

BERTRAM, Count of Rossillion, her sonne

HELLEN, an orphan, attending on the Countesse

Lauatch, a CLOWNE, a seruant of the Countesse

Rynaldo, the STEWARD of the Countesse

PARROLLES, Bertrams Companion

The KING of France

LAFEW, an old Lord

I. LORD DUMAINE ⎱ brothers
2. LORD DUMAINE ⎰

INTERPRETER, a French souldier

An ASTRINGER

The DUKE of Florence

WIDDOW Capilet

DIANA, her daughter

MARIANA, a friend of the Widdow

Lords, attendants, souldiers, Citizens

All's Well that Ends Well

Enter yong Bertram Count of Rossillion, his Mother the Countesse, and Hellen, Lord Lafew, all in blacke

COUNTESSE In deliuering my sonne from me, I burie a second husband.

BERTRAM And I in going Madam, weep ore my fathers death anew; but I must attend his maiesties command, to whom I am now in Ward, euermore in subiection.

LAFEW You shall find of the King a husband Madame, you sir a father. He that so generally is at all times good, must of necessitie hold his vertue to you, whose worthinesse would stirre it vp where it wanted rather 10 then lack it where there is such abundance.

COUNTESSE What hope is there of his Maiesties amendment?

LAFEW He hath abandon'd his Phisitions Madam, vnder whose practises he hath persecuted time with hope, and finds no other aduantage in the processe, but onely the loosing of hope by time.

COUNTESSE This yong Gentlewoman had a father, O that had, how sad a passage tis, whose skill was almost as great as his honestie; had it stretch'd so far, would 20 haue made nature immortall, and death should haue play for lacke of worke. Would for the Kings sake hee were liuing, I thinke it would be the death of the Kings disease.

LAFEW How call'd you the man you speake of Madam?

COUNTESSE He was famous sir in his profession, and it was his great right to be so: *Gerard de Narbon.*

LAFEW He was excellent indeed Madam, the King very latelie spoke of him admiringly, and mourningly: hee was skilfull enough to haue liu'd stil, if knowledge 30 could be set vp against mortallitie.

BERTRAM What is it (my good Lord) the King languishes of?

LAFEW A Fistula my Lord.

BERTRAM I heard not of it before.

LAFEW I would it were not notorious. Was this Gentlewoman the Daughter of *Gerard de Narbon?*

COUNTESSE His sole childe my Lord, and bequeathed to my ouer looking. I haue those hopes of her good, that her education promises; her dispositions shee inherits, 40 which makes faire gifts fairer: for where an vncleane mind carries vertuous qualities, there commendations go with pitty, they are vertues and traitors too: in her they are the better for their simplenesse; she deriues her honestie, and atcheeues her goodnesse.

LAFEW Your commendations Madam get from her teares.

COUNTESSE 'Tis the best brine a Maiden can season her praise in. The remembrance of her father neuer approches her heart, but the tirrany of her sorrowes takes all liuelihood from her cheeke. No more of this 50 *Hellen,* go too, no more least it be rather thought you affect a sorrow, then to haue—

HELLEN I doe affect a sorrow indeed, but I haue it too.

LAFEW Moderate lamentation is the right of the dead, excessiue greefe the enemie to the liuing.

COUNTESSE If the liuing be not enemie to the greefe, the excesse makes it soone mortall.

BERTRAM (*kneeling*) Maddam I desire your holie wishes.

LAFEW How vnderstand we that?

COUNTESSE

Be thou blest *Bertrame,* and succeed thy father
In manners as in shape: thy blood and vertue   60
Contend for Empire in thee, and thy goodnesse
Share with thy birth-right. Loue all, trust a few,
Doe wrong to none: be able for thine enemie
Rather in power then vse: and keepe thy friend
Vnder thy owne lifes key. Be checkt for silence,
But neuer tax'd for speech. What heauen more wil,
That thee may furnish, and my prayers plucke
          downe,
Fall on thy head. Farwell. (*To Lafew*) My Lord,
'Tis an vnseason'd Courtier, good my Lord
Aduise him.

LAFEW   He cannot want the best   70
That shall attend his loue.

COUNTESSE Heauen blesse him: Farwell *Bertram.*

BERTRAM (*rising*) The best wishes that can be forg'd in your thoghts be seruants to you: ⌐*Exit Countesse*⌐
(*to Hellen*) be comfortable to my mother, your Mistris, and make much of her.

LAFEW Farewell prettie Lady, you must hold the credit of your father.   *Exeunt Bertram and Lafew*

HELLEN

O were that all, I thinke not on my father,
And these great teares grace his remembrance more   80
Then those I shed for him. What was he like?
I haue forgott him. My imagination
Carries no fauour in't but *Bertrams.*
I am vndone, there is no liuing, none,
If *Bertram* be away. 'Twere all one,
That I should loue a bright particuler starre,
And think to wed it, he is so aboue me.
In his bright radience and colaterall light,
Must I be comforted, not in his sphere;
Th'ambition in my loue thus plagues it selfe: 90
The hind that would be mated by the Lion
Must die for loue. 'Twas prettie, though a plague
To see him euerie houre to sit and draw
His arched browes, his hawking eie, his curles
In our hearts table: heart too capeable
Of euerie line and tricke of his sweet fauour.
But now he's gone, and my idolatrous fancie
Must sanctifie his Reliques. Who comes heere?

Enter Parrolles

One that goes with him: I loue him for his sake,

100   And yet I know him a notorious Liar,
Thinke him a great way foole, solie a coward,
Yet these fixt euils sit so fit in him,
That they take place, when Vertues steely bones
Lookes bleake i'th cold wind: withall, full ofte we see
Cold wisedome waighting on superfluous follie.

PARROLLES Saue you faire Queene.

HELLEN And you Monarch.

PARROLLES No.

HELLEN And no.

110   PARROLLES Are you meditating on virginitie?

HELLEN I: you haue some staine of souldier in you: Let mee aske you a question. Man is enemie to virginitie, how may we barracado it against him?

PARROLLES Keepe him out.

HELLEN But he assailes, and our virginitie though valiant in the defence, yet is weak: vnfold to vs some war-like resistance.

PARROLLES There is none: Man setting downe before you, will vndermine you, and blow you vp.

120   HELLEN Blesse our poore Virginity from vnderminers and blowers vp. Is there no Military policy how Virgins might blow vp men?

PARROLLES Virginity beeing blowne downe, Man will quicklier be blowne vp: marry in blowing him downe againe, with the breach your selues made, you lose your Citty. It is not politicke, in the Common-wealth of Nature, to preserue virginity. Losse of Virginitie, is rationall encrease, and there was neuer Virgin got, till virginitie was first lost. That you were made of, is

130   mettall to make Virgins. Virginitie, by beeing once lost, may be ten times found: by being euer kept, it is euer lost: 'tis too cold a companion: Away with't.

HELLEN I will stand for't a little, though therefore I die a Virgin.

PARROLLES There's little can bee saide in't, 'tis against the rule of Nature. To speake on the part of virginitie, is to accuse your Mothers; which is most infallible disobedience. He that hangs himselfe is a Virgin: Virginitie murthers it selfe, and should be buried in

140   highwayes out of all sanctified limit, as a desperate Offendresse against Nature. Virginitie breedes mites, much like a Cheese, consumes it selfe to the very payring, and so dies with feeding his owne stomacke. Besides, Virginitie is peeuish, proud, ydle, made of selfe-loue, which is the most inhibited sinne in the Cannon. Keepe it not, you cannot choose but loose by't. Out with't: within t'on yeare it will make it selfe two, which is a goodly increase, and the principall it selfe not much the worse. Away with't.

150   HELLEN How might one do sir, to loose it to her owne liking?

PARROLLES Let mee see. Marry ill, to like him that ne're it likes. 'Tis a commodity wil lose the glosse with lying: The longer kept, the lesse worth: Off with't while 'tis vendible. Answer the time of request, Virginitie like an olde Courtier, weares her cap out of fashion, richly suted, but vnsuteable, iust like the brooch & the tooth-pick, which were not now: your Date is better in your

Pye and your Porredge, then in your cheeke: and your virginity, your old virginity, is like one of our French 160 wither'd peares, it lookes ill, it eates drily, marry 'tis a wither'd peare: it was formerly better, marry yet 'tis a wither'd peare: Will you any thing with it?

HELLEN Not my virginity yet:
There shall your Master haue a thousand loues,
A Mother, and a Mistresse, and a friend,
A Phenix, Captaine, and an enemy,
A guide, a Goddesse, and a Soueraigne,
A Counsellor, a Traitoresse, and a Deare:
His humble ambition, proud humility: 170
His iarring, concord: and his discord, dulcet:
His faith, his sweet disaster: with a world
Of pretty fond adoptious christendomes
That blinking Cupid gossips. Now shall he:
I know not what he shall, God send him well,
The Courts a learning place, and he is one.

PARROLLES What one ifaith?

HELLEN That I wish well, 'tis pitty.

PARROLLES What's pitty?

HELLEN
That wishing well had not a body in't, 180
Which might be felt, that we the poorer borne,
Whose baser starres do shut vs vp in wishes,
Might with effects of them follow our friends,
And shew what we alone must thinke, which neuer
Returnes vs thankes.

Enter Page

PAGE
Monsieur *Parrolles*, my Lord cals for you.   ⌜*Exit*⌝

PARROLLES Little *Hellen* farewell, if I can remember thee, I will thinke of thee at Court.

HELLEN Monsieur *Parolles*, you were borne vnder a charitable starre. 190

PARROLLES Vnder *Mars* I.

HELLEN I especially thinke, vnder *Mars*.

PARROLLES Why vnder *Mars*?

HELLEN The warres hath so kept you vnder, that you must needes be borne vnder *Mars*.

PARROLLES When he was predominant.

HELLEN When he was retrograde I thinke rather.

PARROLLES Why thinke you so?

HELLEN You go so much backward when you fight.

PARROLLES That's for aduantage. 200

HELLEN So is running away, when feare proposes the safetie: But the composition that your valour and feare makes in you, is a vertue of a good wing, and I like the weare well.

PARROLLES I am so full of businesses, I cannot answere thee acutely: I will returne perfect Courtier, in the which my instruction shall serue to naturalize thee, so thou wilt be capeable of a Courtiers councell, and vnderstand what aduice shall thrust vppon thee, else thou diest in thine vnthankfulnes, and thine ignorance 210 makes thee away, farewell: When thou hast leysure, say thy praiers: when thou hast none, remember thy Friends: Get thee a good husband, and vse him as he vses thee: So farewell.   *Exit*

HELLEN
Our remedies oft in our selues do lye,
Which we ascribe to heauen: the fated skye
Giues vs free scope, onely doth backward pull
Our slow designes, when we our selues are dull.
What power is it, which mounts my loue so hye,
220   That makes me see, and cannot feede mine eye?
The mightiest space in fortune, Nature brings
To ioyne like, likes; and kisse like natiue things.
Impossible be strange attempts to those
That weigh their paines in sence, and do suppose
What hath beene, cannot be. Who euer stroue
To shew her merit, that did misse her loue?
(The Kings disease) my proiect may deceiue me,
But my intents are fixt, and will not leaue me.   *Exit*

Sc. 2   *Flourish Cornets. Enter the King of France with*
(1.2)   *Letters, the two Lords Dumaine, ⌜and diuers*
             Attendants⌝

KING
The *Florentines* and *Senoys* are by th'eares,
230   Haue fought with equall fortune, and continue
A brauing warre.
1. LORD DUMAINE   So tis reported sir.
KING
Nay tis most credible, we heere receiue it,
A certaintie vouch'd from our Cosin *Austria*,
With caution, that the *Florentine* will moue vs
For speedie ayde: wherein our deerest friend
Preiudicates the businesse, and would seeme
To haue vs make deniall.
1. LORD DUMAINE   His loue and wisedome
Approu'd so to your Maiesty, may pleade
For amplest credence.
KING   He hath arm'd our answer,
240   And *Florence* is deni'de before he comes:
Yet for our Gentlemen that meane to see
The *Tuscan* seruice, freely haue they leaue
To stand on either part.
2. LORD DUMAINE   It well may serue
A nursserie to our Gentrie, who are sicke
For breathing, and exploit.
KING   What's he comes heere.
     Enter Bertram, Lafew, and Parolles
1. LORD DUMAINE
It is the Count *Rosillion* my good Lord,
Yong *Bertram*.
KING (*to Bertram*) Youth, thou bear'st thy Fathers face,
Franke Nature rather curious then in hast
Hath well compos'd thee: Thy Fathers morall parts
250   Maist thou inherit too: Welcome to *Paris*.
BERTRAM
My thankes and dutie are your Maiesties.
KING
I would I had that corporall soundnesse now,
As when thy father, and my selfe, in friendship
First tride our souldiership: he did looke farre
Into the seruice of the time, and was

Discipled of the brauest. He lasted long,
But on vs both did haggish Age steale on,
And wore vs out of act: It much repaires me
To talke of your good father; in his youth
He had the wit, which I can well obserue   260
To day in our yong Lords: but they may iest
Till their owne scorne returne to them vnnoted
Ere they can hide their leuitie in honour:
So like a Courtier, contempt nor bitternesse
Were in his pride, or sharpnesse; if they were,
His equall had awak'd them, and his honour
Clocke to it selfe, knew the true minute when
Exception bid him speake: and at this time
His tongue obey'd his hand. Who were below him,
He vs'd as creatures of another place,   270
And bow'd his eminent top to their low rankes,
Making them proud of his humilitie,
In their poore praise he humbled: Such a man
Might be a copie to these yonger times;
Which followed well, would demonstrate them now
But goers backward.
BERTRAM   His good remembrance sir
Lies richer in your thoughts, then on his tombe:
So in approofe liues not his Epitaph,
As in your royall speech.
KING
Would I were with him: he would alwaies say,   280
(Me thinkes I heare him now) his plausiue words
He scatter'd not in eares, but grafted them
To grow there and to beare: Let me not liue,
This his good melancholly oft began
On the Catastrophe and heele of pastime
When it was out: Let me not liue (quoth hee)
After my flame lackes oyle, to be the snuffe
Of yonger spirits, whose apprehensiue senses
All but new things disdaine; whose iudgements are
Meere fathers of their garments: whose constancies 290
Expire before their fashions: this he wish'd.
I after him, do after him wish too:
Since I nor wax nor honie can bring home,
I quickly were dissolued from my hiue
To giue some Labourers roome.
2. LORD DUMAINE   You'r loued Sir,
They that least lend it you, shall lacke you first.
KING
I fill a place I know't: how long ist Count
Since the Physitian at your fathers died?
He was much fam'd.
BERTRAM   Some six moneths since my Lord.
KING
If he were liuing, I would try him yet.   300
Lend me an arme: the rest haue worne me out
With seuerall applications: Nature and sicknesse
Debate it at their leisure. Welcome Count,
My sonne's no deerer.
BERTRAM   Thanke your Maiesty.
                          ⌜*Flourish.*⌝ *Exeunt*

Sc. 3   *Enter Old Countesse, Steward, and ⌜behind⌝ Clowne*
(1.3)

COUNTESSE I will now heare, what say you of this
    gentlewoman.

STEWARD Maddam the care I haue had to euen your
    content, I wish might be found in the Kalender of my
    past endeuours, for then we wound our Modestie, and
310   make foule the clearnesse of our deseruings, when of
    our selues we publish them.

COUNTESSE What doe's this knaue heere? (*To Clowne*) Get
    you gone sirra: the complaints I haue heard of you I
    do not all beleeue, 'tis my slownesse that I doe not:
    For I know you lacke not folly to commit them, & haue
    abilitie enough to make such knaueries yours.

CLOWNE 'Tis not vnknown to you Madam, I am a poore
    fellow.

COUNTESSE Well sir.

320 CLOWNE No maddam, 'tis not so well that I am poore,
    though manie of the rich are damn'd, but if I may
    haue your Ladiships good will to goe to the world,
    Isbell the woman and I will doe as we may.

COUNTESSE Wilt thou needes be a begger?

CLOWNE I doe beg your good will in this case.

COUNTESSE In what case?

CLOWNE In *Isbels* case and mine owne: seruice is no
    heritage, and I thinke I shall neuer haue the blessing
    of God, till I haue issue a my bodie: for they say barnes
330 are blessings.

COUNTESSE Tell me thy reason why thou wilt marrie?

CLOWNE My poore bodie Madam requires it, I am driuen
    on by the flesh, and hee must needes goe that the diuell
    driues.

COUNTESSE Is this all your worships reason?

CLOWNE Faith Madam I haue other holie reasons, such
    as they are.

COUNTESSE May the world know them?

CLOWNE I haue beene Madam a wicked creature, as you
340 and all flesh and blood are, and indeede I doe marrie
    that I may repent.

COUNTESSE Thy marriage sooner then thy wickednesse.

CLOWNE I am out a friends Madam, and I hope to haue
    friends for my wiues sake.

COUNTESSE Such friends are thine enemies knaue.

CLOWNE Y'are shallow Madam—in great friends, for the
    knaues come to doe that for me which I am a wearie
    of: he that eres my Land, spares my teame, and giues
    mee leaue to Inne the crop: if I be his cuckold hee's
350 my drudge; he that comforts my wife, is the cherisher
    of my flesh and blood; hee that cherishes my flesh and
    blood, loues my flesh and blood; he that loues my flesh
    and blood is my friend: *ergo*, he that kisses my wife is
    my friend: if men could be contented to be what they
    are, there were no feare in marriage, for yong *Charbon*
    the Puritan, and old *Poyson* the Papist, how somere
    their hearts are seuer'd in Religion, their heads are
    both one, they may ioule horns together like any Deare
    i'th Herd.

360 COUNTESSE Wilt thou euer be a foule mouth'd and calum-
    nious knaue?

CLOWNE A Prophet? I Madam, and I speake the truth the
    next waie,
⌜*sings*⌝   For I the Ballad will repeate,
          Which men full true shall finde,
          Your marriage comes by destinie,
          Your Cuckow sings by kinde.

COUNTESSE Get you gone sir, Ile talke with you more anon.

STEWARD May it please you Madam, that hee bid *Hellen*
    come to you, of her I am to speake.   370

COUNTESSE (*to Clowne*) Sirra tell my gentlewoman I would
    speake with her, *Hellen* I meane.

CLOWNE ⌜*sings*⌝
    Was this faire face the cause, quoth she,
    Why the Grecians sacked *Troy*,
    Fond done, done fond, was this King *Priams* ioy,
    With that she sighed as she stood,
    With that she sighed as she stood,
      And gaue this sentence then,
    Among nine bad if one be good,
    Among nine bad if one be good,   380
      There's yet one good in ten.

COUNTESSE What, one good in tenne? you corrupt the
    song sirra.

CLOWNE One good woman in ten Madam, which is a
    purifying ath'song: would God would serue the world
    so all the yeere, weed finde no fault with the tithe
    woman if I were the Parson, one in ten quoth a? and
    wee might haue a good woman borne but ere euerie
    blazing starre, or at an earthquake, 'twould mend the
    Lotterie well, a man may draw his heart out ere a   390
    plucke one.

COUNTESSE Youle begone sir knaue, and doe as I command
    you?

CLOWNE That man should be at womans command, and
    yet no hurt done, though honestie be no Puritan, yet
    it will doe no hurt, it will weare the Surplis of humilitie
    ouer the blacke-Gowne of a bigge heart: I am going
    forsooth, the businesse is for *Helen* to come hither.

                                          Exit

COUNTESSE Well now.

STEWARD I know Madam you loue your Gentlewoman   400
    intirely.

COUNTESSE Faith I doe: her Father bequeath'd her to mee,
    and she her selfe without other aduantage, may
    lawfullie make title to as much loue as shee findes,
    there is more owing her then is paid, and more shall
    be paid her then sheele demand.

STEWARD Madam, I was verie late more neere her then I
    thinke shee wisht mee, alone shee was, and did
    communicate to her selfe her owne words to her owne
    eares, shee thought, I dare vowe for her, they toucht   410
    not anie stranger sence, her matter was, shee loued
    your Sonne; Fortune shee said was no goddesse, that
    had put such difference betwixt their two estates: Loue
    no god, that would not extend his might onelie, where
    qualities were leuell, *Dian* no Queene of Virgins, that
    would suffer her poore Knight surpris'd without rescue
    in the first assault or ransome afterward: This shee

deliuer'd in the most bitter touch of sorrow that ere I
heard Virgin exclaime in, which I held my dutie speedily
420 to acquaint you withall, sithence in the losse that may
happen, it concernes you something to know it.
COUNTESSE You haue discharg'd this honestlie, keepe it to
your selfe, manie likelihoods inform'd mee of this before,
which hung so tottring in the ballance, that I could
neither beleeue nor misdoubt: praie you leaue mee,
stall this in your bosome, and I thanke you for your
honest care: I will speake with you further anon.
                                              Exit Steward

       Enter Hellen
COUNTESSE (*aside*)
Euen so it was with me when I was yong:
     If euer we are natures, these are ours, this thorne
430 Doth to our Rose of youth rightlie belong:
     Our bloud to vs, this to our blood is borne,
It is the show, and seale of natures truth,
Where loues strong passion is imprest in youth,
By our remembrances of daies forgon,
Such were our faults, or then we thought them none,
Her eie is sicke on't, I obserue her now.
HELLEN
What is your pleasure Madam?
COUNTESSE   You know *Hellen*
I am a mother to you.
HELLEN
Mine honorable Mistris.
COUNTESSE   Nay a mother,
440 Why not a mother? when I sed a mother
Me thought you saw a serpent, what's in mother,
That you start at it? I say I am your mother,
And put you in the Catalogue of those
That were enwombed mine, 'tis often seene
Adoption striues with nature, and choise breedes
A natiue slip to vs from forraine seedes:
You nere opprest me with a mothers groane,
Yet I expresse to you a mothers care,
(Gods mercie maiden) dos it curd thy blood
450 To say I am thy mother? what's the matter,
That this distempred messenger of wet,
The manie colour'd Iris rounds thine eye?
—Why, that you are my daughter?
HELLEN   That I am not.
COUNTESSE
I say I am your Mother.
HELLEN   Pardon Madam.
The Count *Rosillion* cannot be my brother:
I am from humble, he from honord name:
No note vpon my Parents, his all noble,
My Master, my deere Lord he is, and I
His seruant liue, and will his vassall die:
He must not be my brother.
460 COUNTESSE   Nor I your Mother.
HELLEN
You are my mother Madam, would you were
So that my Lord your sonne were not my brother,
Indeede my mother, or were you both our mothers,

I care no more for, then I doe for heauen,
So I were not his sister, cant no other,
But I your daughter, he must be my brother.
COUNTESSE
Yes *Hellen*, you might be my daughter in law,
God shield you meane it not, daughter and mother
So striue vpon your pulse; what pale agen?
My feare hath catcht your fondnesse! now I see   470
The mistrie of your lonelinesse, and finde
Your salt teares head, now to all sence 'tis grosse:
You loue my sonne, inuention is asham'd
Against the proclamation of thy passion
To say thou doost not: therefore tell me true,
But tell me then 'tis so, for looke, thy cheekes
Confesse it 'ton tooth other, and thine eies
See it so grosely showne in thy behauiours,
That in their kinde they speake it, onely sinne
And hellish obstinacie tye thy tongue   480
That truth should be suspected, speake, ist so?
If it be so, you haue wound a goodly clewe:
If it be not, forsweare't: how ere I charge thee,
As heauen shall worke in me for thine auaile
To tell me truelie.
HELLEN   Good Madam pardon me.
COUNTESSE
Do you loue my Sonne?
HELLEN   Your pardon noble Mistris.
COUNTESSE
Loue you my Sonne?
HELLEN   Doe not you loue him Madam?
COUNTESSE
Goe not about; my loue hath in't a bond
Whereof the world takes note: Come, come, disclose
The state of your affection, for your passions   490
Haue to the full appeach'd.
HELLEN   Then I confesse
Here on my knee, before high heauen and you,
That before you, and next vnto high heauen,
I loue your Sonne:
My friends were poore but honest, so's my loue:
Be not offended, for it hurts not him
That he is lou'd of me; I follow him not
By any token of presumptuous suite,
Nor would I haue him, till I doe deserue him,
Yet neuer know how that desert should be: 500
I know I loue in vaine, striue against hope:
Yet in this captious, and intenable Siue,
I still poure in the waters of my loue
And lacke not to loose still; thus *Indian* like
Religious in mine error, I adore
The Sunne that lookes vpon his worshipper,
But knowes of him no more. My deerest Madam,
Let not your hate incounter with my loue,
For louing where you doe; but if your selfe,
Whose aged honor cites a vertuous youth,   510
Did euer, in so true a flame of liking,
Wish chastly, and loue dearely, that your *Dian*
Was both her selfe and loue, O then giue pittie

973

To her whose state is such, that cannot choose
But lend and giue where she is sure to loose;
That seekes to finde not that, her search implies,
But riddle like, liues sweetely where she dies.

COUNTESSE
Had you not lately an intent, speake truely,
To goe to *Paris*?

520 HELLEN Madam I had.

COUNTESSE Wherefore? tell true.

HELLEN
I will tell truth, by grace it selfe I sweare:
You know my Father left me some prescriptions
Of rare and prou'd effects, such as his reading
And manifest experience, had collected
For generall soueraigntie: and that he wil'd me
In heedefull'st reseruation to bestow them,
As notes, whose faculties inclusiue were,
More then they were in note: Amongst the rest,
530 There is a remedie, approu'd, set downe,
To cure the desperate languishings whereof
The King is render'd lost.

COUNTESSE   This was your motiue
For *Paris*, was it, speake?

HELLEN
My Lord, your sonne, made me to think of this;
Else *Paris*, and the medicine, and the King,
Had from the conuersation of my thoughts,
Happily beene absent then.

COUNTESSE   But thinke you *Hellen*,
If you should tender your supposed aide,
He would receiue it? He and his Phisitions
540 Are of a minde, he, that they cannot helpe him:
They, that they cannot helpe, how shall they credit
A poore vnlearned Virgin, when the Schooles
Embowel'd of their doctrine, haue left off
The danger to it selfe.

HELLEN   There's something in't
More then my Fathers skill, which was the great'st
Of his profession, that his good receipt,
Shall for my legacie be sanctified
Byth' luckiest stars in heauen, and would your honor
But giue me leaue to trie successe, I'de venture
550 The well lost life of mine, on his Graces cure,
By such a day, an houre.

COUNTESSE Doo'st thou beleeue't?

HELLEN I Madam knowingly.

COUNTESSE
Why *Hellen* thou shalt haue my leaue and loue,
Meanes and attendants, and my louing greetings
To those of mine in Court, Ile staie at home
And praie Gods blessing into thy attempt:
Begon to morrow, and be sure of this,
What I can helpe thee to, thou shalt not misse.

                                         Exeunt

Sc. 4   *Florish Cornets. Enter the King* ⌈*carried in a*
(2.1)   *chaire*⌉, *with the Lords Dumaine and diuers yong*
           Lords, taking leaue for the Florentine warre:
           Bertram Count Rosillion, and Parrolles

KING
Farewell yong Lords, these warlike principles   560
Doe not throw from you, and you my Lords farewell:
Share the aduice betwixt you, if both gaine all,
The guift doth stretch it selfe as 'tis receiu'd,
And is enough for both.

I. LORD DUMAINE   'Tis our hope sir,
After well entred souldiers, to returne
And finde your grace in health.

KING
No, no, it cannot be; and yet my heart
Will not confesse he owes the mallady
That doth my life besiege: farwell yong Lords,
Whether I liue or die, be you the sonnes   570
Of worthy French men: let higher Italy
(Those bated that inherit but the fall
Of the last Monarchy) see that you come
Not to wooe honour, but to wed it: when
The brauest questant shrinkes, finde what you seeke,
That fame may cry you loud: I say farewell.

I. LORD DUMAINE
Health at your bidding serue your Maiesty.

KING
Those girles of Italy, take heed of them,
They say our French, lacke language to deny
If they demand: beware of being Captiues   580
Before you serue.

BOTH LORDS DUMAINE Our hearts receiue your warnings.

KING Farewell, come hether to me.
           ⌈*Some Lords stand aside with the King*⌉

I. LORD DUMAINE (*to Bertram*)
Oh my sweet Lord yᵗ you wil stay behind vs.

PARROLLES
'Tis not his fault the spark.

2. LORD DUMAINE   Oh 'tis braue warres.

PARROLLES
Most admirable, I haue seene those warres.

BERTRAM
I am commanded here, and kept a coyle with,
Too young, and the next yeere, and 'tis too early.

PARROLLES
And thy minde stand too't boy, steale away brauely.

BERTRAM
I shal stay here the for-horse to a smocke,
Creeking my shooes on the plaine Masonry,   590
Till honour be bought vp, and no sword worne
But one to dance with: by heauen, Ile steale away.

I. LORD DUMAINE
There's honour in the theft.

PARROLLES   Commit it Count.

2. LORD DUMAINE
I am your accessary, and so farewell.

BERTRAM I grow to you,
And our parting is a tortur'd body.

I. LORD DUMAINE
Farwell Captaine.

2. LORD DUMAINE   Sweet Mounsier *Parolles*.

PARROLLES Noble *Heroes*; my sword and yours are kinne,

good sparkes and lustrous, a word good mettals. You
600 shall finde in the Regiment of the Spinij, one Captaine
Spurio with his sicatrice, an Embleme of warre heere
on his sinister cheeke; it was this very sword entrench'd
it: say to him I liue, and obserue his reports for me.

1. LORD DUMAINE We shall noble Captaine.

PARROLLES *Mars* doate on you for his nouices,
                                  Exeunt both Lords Dumaine
(*to Bertram*) what will ye doe?

BERTRAM Stay the King.

PARROLLES Vse a more spacious ceremonie to the Noble
Lords, you haue restrain'd your selfe within the List of
610 too cold an adieu: be more expressiue to them; for
they weare themselues in the cap of the time, there do
muster true gate; eat, speake, and moue vnder the
influence of the most receiu'd starre, and though the
deuill leade the measure, such are to be followed: after
them, and take a more dilated farewell.

BERTRAM And I will doe so.

PARROLLES Worthy fellowes, and like to prooue most
sinewie sword-men.   *Exeunt ⌈Bertram and Parrolles⌉*
        Enter Lafew to the King

LAFEW (*kneeling*)
Pardon my Lord for mee and for my tidings.

620 KING Ile fee thee to stand vp.

LAFEW (*rising*)
Then heres a man stands that has bought his pardon,
I would you had kneel'd my Lord to aske me mercy,
And that at my bidding you could so stand vp.

KING
I would I had, so I had broke thy pate
And askt thee mercy for't.

LAFEW   Goodfaith a-crosse,
But my good Lord 'tis thus, will you be cur'd
Of your infirmitie?

KING   No.

LAFEW   O will you eat
No grapes my royall foxe? Yes but you will,
My noble grapes, and if my royall foxe
630 Could reach them: I haue seen a medicine
That's able to breath life into a stone,
Quicken a rocke, and make you dance Canari
With sprightly fire and motion, whose simple touch
Is powerfull to arayse King *Pippen*, nay
To giue great *Charlemaine* a pen in's hand
And write to her a loue-line.

KING   What her is this?

LAFEW
Why doctor she: my Lord, there's one arriu'd,
If you will see her: now by my faith and honour,
If seriously I may conuay my thoughts
640 In this my light deliuerance, I haue spoke
With one, that in her sexe, her yeeres, profession,
Wisedome and constancy, hath amaz'd mee more
Then I dare blame my weakenesse: will you see her?
For that is her demand, and know her businesse?
That done, laugh well at me.

KING   Now good *Lafew*,

Bring in the admiration, that we with thee
May spend our wonder too, or take off thine
By wondring how thou tookst it.

LAFEW   Nay, Ile fit you,
And not be all day neither.
        ⌈*He goes to the doore*⌉

KING
Thus he his speciall nothing euer prologues.   650

LAFEW (*to Hellen, within*) Nay, come your waies.
        Enter Hellen ⌈disguised⌉

KING This haste hath wings indeed.

LAFEW (*to Hellen*) Nay, come your waies,
This is his Maiestie, say your minde to him,
A Traitor you doe looke like, but such traitors
His Maiesty seldome feares, I am *Cresseds* Vncle,
That dare leaue two together, far you well.
        Exit ⌈all but the King and Hellen⌉

KING
Now faire one, do's your busines follow vs?

HELLEN
I my good Lord, *Gerard de Narbon* was my father,
In what he did professe, well found.

KING   I knew him.   660

HELLEN
The rather will I spare my praises towards him,
Knowing him is enough: on's bed of death,
Many receits he gaue me, chieflie one,
Which as the dearest issue of his practice
And of his olde experience, th'onlie darling,
He bad me store vp, as a triple eye,
Safer then mine owne two, more deare: I haue so,
And hearing your high Maiestie is toucht
With that malignant cause, wherein the honour
Of my deare fathers gift, stands cheefe in power,   670
I come to tender it, and my appliance,
With all bound humblenesse.

KING   We thanke you maiden,
But may not be so credulous of cure,
When our most learned Doctors leaue vs, and
The congregated Colledge haue concluded,
That labouring Art can neuer ransome nature
From her inaydible estate: I say we must not
So staine our iudgement, or corrupt our hope,
To prostitute our past-cure malladie
To empericks, or to disseuer so   680
Our great selfe and our credit, to esteeme
A sencelesse helpe, when helpe past sence we deeme.

HELLEN
My dutie then shall pay me for my paines:
I will no more enforce mine office on you,
Humbly intreating from your royall thoughts,
A modest one to beare me backe againe.

KING
I cannot giue thee lesse to be cal'd gratefull:
Thou thoughtst to helpe me, and such thankes I giue,
As one neere death to those that wish him liue:
But what at full I know, thou knowst no part,   690
I knowing all my perill, thou no Art.

HELLEN
What I can doe, can doe no hurt to try,
Since you set vp your rest 'gainst remedie:
He that of greatest workes is finisher,
Oft does them by the weakest minister:
So holy Writ, in babes hath iudgement showne,
When Iudges haue bin babes; great flouds haue flowne
From simple sources: and great Seas haue dried.
When Miracles haue by th' great'st beene denied,
700   ⌈   ⌉
Oft expectation failes, and most oft there
Where most it promises: and oft it hits,
Where hope is coldest, and despaire most ffitts.

KING
I must not heare thee, fare thee wel kind maide,
Thy paines not vs'd, must by thy selfe be paid,
Proffers not tooke, reape thanks for their reward.

HELLEN
Inspired Merit so by breath is bard,
It is not so with him that all things knowes
As 'tis with vs, that square our guesse by showes:
710   But most it is presumption in vs, when
The help of heauen we count the act of men.
Deare sir, to my endeauors giue consent,
Of heauen, not me, make an experiment.
I am not an Imposture, that proclaime
My selfe against the leuill of mine aime,
But know I thinke, and thinke I know most sure,
My Art is not past power, nor you past cure.

KING
Art thou so confident? Within what space
Hop'st thou my cure?

HELLEN   The great'st grace lending grace,
720   Ere twice the horses of the sunne shall bring
Their fiery coacher his diurnall ring,
Ere twice in murke and occidentall dampe
Moist *Hesperus* hath quench'd her sleepy Lampe:
Or foure and twenty times the Pylots glasse
Hath told the theeuish minutes, how they passe:
What is infirme, from your sound parts shall flie,
Health shall liue free, and sickenesse freely dye.

KING
Vpon thy certainty and confidence,
What dar'st thou venter?

HELLEN   Taxe of impudence,
730   A strumpets boldnesse, a divulged shame;
Traduc'd by odious ballads, my maidens name
Seard otherwise, nay worse of worst extended
With vildest torture, let my life be ended.

KING
Methinks in thee some blessed spirit doth speak,
His powerfull sound, within an organ weake:
And what impossibility would slay
In common sence, sence saues another way:
Thy life is deere, for all that life can rate
Worth name of life, in thee hath estimate:
740   Youth, beauty, wisedome, courage, all
That happines and prime, can happy call:

Thou this to hazard, needs must intimate
Skill infinite, or monstrous desperate,
Sweet practiser, thy Physicke I will try,
That ministers thine owne death if I die.

HELLEN
If I breake time, or flinch in property
Of what I spoke, vnpittied let me die,
And well deseru'd: not helping, death's my fee,
But if I helpe, what doe you promise me.

KING
Make thy demand.

HELLEN   But will you make it euen?   750

KING
I by my Scepter, and my hopes of heauen.

HELLEN
Then shalt thou giue me with thy kingly hand
What husband in thy power I will command:
Exempted be from me the arrogance
To choose from forth the royall bloud of France,
My low and humble name to propagate
With any branch or image of thy state:
But such a one thy vassall, whom I know
Is free for me to aske, thee to bestow.

KING
Heere is my hand, the premises obseru'd,   760
Thy will by my performance shall be seru'd:
So make the choice of thy owne time, for I
Thy resolv'd Patient, on thee still relye:
More should I question thee, and more I must,
Though more to know, could not be more to trust:
From whence thou cam'st, how tended on, but rest
Vnquestion'd welcome, and vndoubted blest.
Giue me some helpe heere hoa, if thou proceed,
As high as word, my deed shall match thy deed.
Florish. Exit the King, ⌈carried⌉, and Hellen

Enter Lady Countesse and Clowne   Sc. 5
COUNTESSE Come on sir, I shall now put you to the height   (2.2)
of your breeding.   771

CLOWNE I will shew my selfe highly fed, and lowly taught,
I know my businesse is but to the Court.

COUNTESSE To the Court, why what place make you
speciall, when you put off that with such contempt,
but to the Court?

CLOWNE Truly Madam, if God haue lent a man any
manners, hee may easilie put it off at Court: hee that
cannot make a legge, put off's cap, kisse his hand, and
say nothing, has neither legge, hands, lippe, nor cap;   780
and indeed such a fellow, to say precisely, were not for
the Court, but for me, I haue an answere will serue all
men.

COUNTESSE Marry that's a bountifull answere that fits all
questions.

CLOWNE It is like a Barbers chaire that fits all buttockes,
the pin buttocke, the quatch-buttocke, the brawn
buttocke, or any buttocke.

COUNTESSE Will your answere serue fit to all questions?

CLOWNE As fit as ten groats is for the hand of an Atturney,   790

as your French Crowne for your taffety punke, as *Tibs*
rush for *Toms* fore-finger, as a pancake for Shroue-
tuesday, a Morris for May-day, as the naile to his hole,
the Cuckold to his horne, as a scolding queane to a
wrangling knaue, as the Nuns lip to the Friers mouth,
nay as the pudding to his skin.

COUNTESSE Haue you, I say, an answere of such fitnesse
for all questions?

CLOWNE From beyond your Duke, to beneath your
800   Constable, it will fit any question.

COUNTESSE It must be an answere of most monstrous size,
that must fit all demands.

CLOWNE But a triflle neither in good faith, if the learned
should speake truth of it: heere it is, and all that
belongs to't. Aske mee if I am a Courtier, it shall doe
you no harme to learne.

COUNTESSE To be young againe if we could: I will bee a
foole in question, hoping to bee the wiser by your
answer. I pray you sir, are you a Courtier?

810 CLOWNE O Lord sir theres a simple putting off: more,
more, a hundred of them.

COUNTESSE Sir I am a poore freind of yours, that loues
you.

CLOWNE O Lord sir, thicke, thicke, spare not me.

COUNTESSE I thinke sir, you can eate none of this homely
meate.

CLOWNE O Lord sir; nay put me too't, I warrant you.

COUNTESSE You were lately whipt sir as I thinke.

CLOWNE O Lord sir, spare not me.

820 COUNTESSE Doe you crie O Lord sir at your whipping, and
spare not me? Indeed your O Lord sir, is very sequent
to your whipping: you would answere very well to a
whipping if you were but bound too't.

CLOWNE I nere had worse lucke in my life in my O Lord
sir: I see things may serue long, but not serue euer.

COUNTESSE I play the noble huswife with the time, to
entertaine it so merrily with a foole.

CLOWNE O Lord sir, why there't serues well agen.

COUNTESSE
An end sir, to your businesse: giue *Hellen* this,
    She giues him a Letter
830 And vrge her to a present answer backe,
Commend me to my kinsmen, and my sonne,
This is not much.

CLOWNE Not much commendation to them.

COUNTESSE Not much imployement for you, you vnderstand me.

CLOWNE Most fruitfully, I am there, before my legges.

COUNTESSE Hast you agen.   *Exeunt seuerally*

Sc. 6   *Enter Count Bertram, Old Lafew ⌜with a ballad⌝,*
(2.3)   *and Parolles*

LAFEW They say miracles are past, and we haue our
Philosophicall persons, to make moderne and familiar
840 things supernaturall and causelesse. Hence is it, that
we make trifles of terrours, ensconcing our selues into
seeming knowledge, when we should submit our selues
to an vnknowne feare.

PARROLLES Why 'tis the rarest argument of wonder, that
hath shot out in our latter times.

BERTRAM And so 'tis.

LAFEW To be relinquisht of the Artists.

PARROLLES So I say both of *Galen* and *Paracelsus.*

LAFEW Of all the learned and authenticke fellowes.

PARROLLES Right so I say.   850

LAFEW That gaue him out incureable.

PARROLLES Why there 'tis, so say I too.

LAFEW Not to be help'd.

PARROLLES Right, as 'twere a man assur'd of a—

LAFEW Vncertaine life, and sure death.

PARROLLES Iust, you say well: so would I haue said.

LAFEW I may truly say, it is a noueltie to the world.

PARROLLES It is indeede; if you will haue it in shewing,
you shall reade it in ⌜*pointing to the ballad*⌝ what do ye
call there.   860

LAFEW ⌜*reads*⌝ A shewing of a heauenly effect in an earthly
Actor.

PARROLLES That's it, I would haue said, the verie same.

LAFEW Why your Dolphin is not lustier: fore mee I speake
in respect—

PARROLLES Nay 'tis strange, 'tis very straunge, that is the
breefe and the tedious of it, and he's of a most
facinerious spirit, that will not acknowledge it to be
the—

LAFEW Very hand of heauen.   870

PARROLLES I, so I say.

LAFEW In a most weake—

PARROLLES And debile minister great power, great
trancendence, which should indeede giue vs a further
vse to be made, then alone the recou'ry of the king,
as to bee

LAFEW Generally thankfull.
    Enter King, Hellen, and attendants

PARROLLES I would haue said it, you say well: heere
comes the King.

LAFEW Lustique, as the Dutchman saies: Ile like a maide   880
the Better whil'st I haue a tooth in my head:
    ⌜*The King and Hellen dance*⌝
why he's able to leade her a Carranto.

PARROLLES *Mor du vinager*, is not this *Helen?*

LAFEW Fore God I thinke so.

KING
Goe call before mee all the Lords in Court,
                Exit one or more
Sit my preseruer by thy patients side,
    ⌜*The King and Hellen sit*⌝
And with this healthfull hand whose banisht sence
Thou hast repeal'd, a second time receyue
The confirmation of my promis'd guift,
Which but attends thy naming.   890
    Enter 4 Lords
Faire Maide send forth thine eye, this youthfull parcell
Of Noble Batchellors, stand at my bestowing,
Ore whom both Soueraigne power, and fathers voice
I haue to vse; thy franke election make,
Thou hast power to choose, and they none to forsake.

HELLEN

    To each of you, one faire and vertuous Mistris
    Fall when loue please, marry to each but one.

LAFEW (*aside*)

    I'de giue bay curtall, and his furniture
    My mouth no more were broken then these boyes,
    And writ as little beard.

900 KING (*to Hellen*)   Peruse them well:
    Not one of these, but had a Noble father.

HELLEN Gentlemen,

    Heauen hath through me, restor'd the king to health.

⌈ALL BUT HELLEN⌉

    We vnderstand it, and thanke heauen for you.

HELLEN

    I am a simple Maide, and therein wealthiest
    That I protest, I simply am a Maide:
    Please it your Maiestie, I haue done already:
    The blushes in my cheekes thus whisper mee,
    We blush that thou shouldst choose; but be refused,
910   Let the white death sit on thy cheeke for euer,
    Wee'l nere come there againe.

KING   Make choise and see,
    Who shuns thy loue, shuns all his loue in mee.

HELLEN ⌈*rising*⌉

    Now *Dian* from thy Altar do I fly,
    And to imperiall loue, that God most high
    Do my sighes streame:

      ⌈*She addresses her to a Lord*⌉

                Sir, wil you heare my suite?

1. LORD

    And grant it.

HELLEN   Thankes sir, all the rest is mute.

LAFEW (*aside*) I had rather be in this choise, then throw
    Ames-ace for my life.

HELLEN (*to another Lord*)

    The honor sir that flames in your faire eyes,
920   Before I speake too threatningly replies:
    Loue make your fortunes twentie times aboue
    Her that so wishes, and her humble loue.

2. LORD

    No better if you please.

HELLEN   My wish receiue,
    Which great loue grant, and so I take my leaue.

LAFEW (*aside*) Do all they denie her? And they were sons
    of mine, I'de haue them whip'd, or I would send them
    to'th Turke to make Eunuches of.

HELLEN (*to another Lord*)

    Be not afraid that I your hand should take,
    Ile neuer do you wrong for your owne sake:
930   Blessing vpon your vowes, and in your bed
    Finde fairer fortune, if you euer wed.

LAFEW (*aside*) These boyes are boyes of Ice, they'le none
    haue her: sure they are bastards to the English, the
    French nere got em.

HELLEN (*to another Lord*)

    You are too young, too happie, and too good
    To make your selfe a sonne out of my blood.

4. LORD Faire one, I thinke not so.

LAFEW (*aside*) There's one grape yet, I am sure thy father
    drunke wine. But if thou be'st not an asse, I am a
    youth of fourteene: I haue knowne thee already.   940

HELLEN (*to Bertram*)

    I dare not say I take you, but I giue
    Me and my seruice, euer whilst I liue
    Into your guiding power: This is the man.

KING

    Why then young *Bertram* take her shee's thy wife.

BERTRAM

    My wife my Leige? I shal beseech your highnes
    In such a busines, giue me leaue to vse
    The helpe of mine owne eies.

KING   Know'st thou not *Bertram*
    What shee ha's done for mee?

BERTRAM   Yes my good Lord,
    But neuer hope to know why I should marrie her.

KING

    Thou know'st shee ha's rais'd me from my sickly bed.   950

BERTRAM

    But followes it my Lord, to bring me downe
    Must answer for your raising? I knowe her well:
    Shee had her breeding at my fathers charge:
    A poore Physitians daughter my wife? Disdaine
    Rather corrupt me euer.

KING

    Tis onely title thou disdainst in her, the which
    I can build vp: strange is it that our bloods
    Of colour, waight, and heat, pour'd all together,
    Would quite confound distinction: yet stands off
    In differences so mightie. If she bee   960
    All that is vertuous (saue what thou dislik'st,
    A poore Phisitians daughter) thou dislik'st
    Of vertue for the name: but doe not so:
    From lowest place, when vertuous things proceed,
    The place is dignified by th' doers deede.
    Where great additions swell's, and vertue none,
    It is a dropsied honour. Good alone,
    Is good without a name; Vilenesse is so:
    The propertie by what it is, should go,
    Not by the title. Shee is young, wise, faire,   970
    In these, to Nature shee's immediate heire:
    And these breed honour: that is honours scorne,
    Which challenges it selfe as honours borne,
    And is not like the sire: Honours thriue,
    When rather from our acts we them deriue
    Then our fore-goers: the meere words a slaue,
    Debosh'd on euerie tombe, on euerie graue
    A lying Trophee, and as oft is dumbe,
    Where dust, and damn'd obliuion is the Tombe
    Of honour'd bones indeed, what should be saide?   980
    If thou canst like this creature, as a maide,
    I can create the rest: Vertue, and shee
    Is her owne dower: Honour and wealth, from mee.

BERTRAM

    I cannot loue her, nor will striue to doo't.

KING

    Thou wrong'st thy selfe; if thou shold'st striue to
      choose—

HELLEN

    That you are well restor'd my Lord, I'me glad:
    Let the rest go.

KING

    My Honor's at the stake, which to defeate
    I must produce my power. Heere, take her hand,
990   Proud scornfull boy, vnworthie this good gift,
    That dost in vile misprision shackle vp
    My loue, and her desert: that canst not dreame,
    We poizing vs in her defectiue scale,
    Shall weigh thee to the beame: That wilt not know,
    It is in Vs to plant thine Honour, where
    We please to haue it grow. Checke thy contempt:
    Obey Our will, which trauailes in thy good:
    Beleeue not thy disdaine, but presentlie
    Do thine owne fortunes that obedient right
1000   Which both thy dutie owes, and Our power claimes,
    Or I will throw thee from my care for euer
    Into the staggers, and the carelesse lapse
    Of youth and ignorance: both my reuenge and hate
    Loosing vpon thee, in the name of iustice,
    Without all termes of pittie. Speake, thine answer.

BERTRAM (*kneeling*)

    Pardon my gracious Lord: for I submit
    My fancie to your eies: when I consider
    What great creation, and what dole of honour
    Flies where you bid it, I finde that she which late
1010   Was in my Nobler thoughts, most base: is now
    The praised of the King, who so ennobled,
    Is as 'twere borne so.

KING   Take her by the hand,

    And tell her she is thine: to whom I promise
    A counterpoize: If not to thy estate,
    A ballance more repleat.

BERTRAM (*rising*)   I take her hand.

KING

    Good fortune, and the fauour of the King
    Smile vpon this Contract: whose Ceremonie
    Shall seeme expedient on the now borne briefe,
    And be perform'd to night: the solemne Feast
1020   Shall more attend vpon the coming space,
    Expecting absent friends. As thou lou'st her,
    Thy loue's to me Religious: else, do's erre.

         ⌈*Flourish.*⌉ *Exeunt all but Parolles and Lafew*
         who stay behind, commenting of this wedding

LAFEW Do you heare Monsieur? A word with you.

PARROLLES Your pleasure sir.

LAFEW Your Lord and Master did well to make his
    recantation.

PARROLLES Recantation? My Lord? my Master?

LAFEW I: Is it not a Language I speake?

PARROLLES A most harsh one, and not to bee vnderstoode
1030   without bloudie succeeding. My Master?

LAFEW Are you Companion to the Count *Rosillion?*

PARROLLES To any Count, to all Counts: to what is man.

LAFEW To what is Counts man: Counts maister is of
    another stile.

PARROLLES You are too old sir: Let it satisfie you, you are
    too old.

LAFEW I must tell thee sirrah, I write Man: to which title
    age cannot bring thee.

PARROLLES What I dare too well do, I dare not do.

LAFEW I did thinke thee for two ordinaries: to bee a   1040
    prettie wise fellow, thou didst make tollerable vent of
    thy trauell, it might passe: yet the scarffes and the
    bannerets about thee, did manifoldlie disswade me from
    beleeuing thee a vessell of too great a burthen. I haue
    now found thee, when I loose thee againe, I care not:
    yet art thou good for nothing but taking vp, and that
    th'ourt scarce worth.

PARROLLES Hadst thou not the priuiledge of Antiquity
    vpon thee.

LAFEW Do not plundge thy selfe to farre in anger, least   1050
    thou hasten thy triall: which if, Lord haue mercie on
    thee for a hen, so my good window of Lettice fare thee
    well, thy casement I neede not open, for I look through
    thee. Giue me thy hand.

PARROLLES My Lord, you giue me most egregious
    indignity.

LAFEW I with all my heart, and thou art worthy of it.

PARROLLES I haue not my Lord deseru'd it.

LAFEW Yes good faith, eu'ry dramme of it, and I will not
    bate thee a scruple.   1060

PARROLLES Well, I shall be wiser.

LAFEW Eu'n as soone as thou can'st, for thou hast to pull
    at a smacke a'th contrarie. If euer thou bee'st bound
    in thy skarfe and beaten, thou shall finde what it is to
    be proud of thy bondage, I haue a desire to holde my
    acquaintance with thee, or rather my knowledge, that
    I may say in the default, he is a man I know.

PARROLLES My Lord you do me most insupportable
    vexation.

LAFEW I would it were hell paines for thy sake, and my   1070
    poore doing eternall: for doing I am past, as I will by
    thee, in what motion age will giue me leaue.   *Exit*

PARROLLES Well, thou hast a sonne shall take this disgrace
    off me; scuruy, old, filthy, scuruy Lord: Well, I must
    be patient, there is no fettering of authority. Ile beate
    him (by my life) if I can meete him with any
    conuenience, and he were double and double a Lord.
    Ile haue no more pittie of his age then I would haue
    of—Ile beate him, and if I could but meet him agen.

     Enter Lafew

LAFEW Sirra, your Lord and masters married, there's   1080
    newes for you: you haue a new Mistris.

PARROLLES I most vnfainedly beseech your Lordshippe to
    make some reseruation of your wrongs. He is my good
    Lord, whom I serue aboue is my master.

LAFEW Who? God.

PARROLLES I sir.

LAFEW The deuill it is, that's thy master. Why dooest
    thou garter vp thy armes a this fashion? Dost make
    hose of thy sleeues? Do other seruants so? Thou wert

1090 best set thy lower part where thy nose stands. By mine
Honor, if I were but two houres yonger, I'de beate
thee: meethink'st thou art a generall offence, and euery
man shold beate thee: I thinke thou wast created for
men to breath themselues vpon thee.

PARROLLES This is hard and vndeserued measure my Lord.

LAFEW Go too sir, you were beaten in *Italy* for picking a
kernell out of a Pomgranat, you are a vagabond, and
no true traueller: you are more sawcie with Lordes and
honourable personages, then the Commission of your
1100 birth and vertue giues you Heraldry. You are not worth
another word, else I'de call you knaue. I leaue you.

Exit

PARROLLES Good, very good, it is so then: good, very
good, let it be conceal'd awhile.

⌈*Enter Bertram Count Rossillion*⌉

BERTRAM
Vndone, and forfeited to cares for euer.

PARROLLES What's the matter sweet-heart?

BERTRAM
Although before the solemne Priest I haue sworne,
I will not bed her.

PARROLLES What? what sweet heart?

BERTRAM
O my *Parrolles*, they haue married me:
1110 Ile to the *Tuscan* warres, and neuer bed her.

PARROLLES
France is a dog-hole, and it no more merits,
The tread of a mans foot: too'th warres.

BERTRAM
There's letters from my mother: What th'import is,
I know not yet.

PARROLLES
I that would be knowne: too'th warrs my boy, too'th
    warres:
He weares his honor in a boxe vnseene,
That hugges his kickie wickie heare at home,
Spending his manlie marrow in her armes
Which should sustaine the bound and high curuet
1120 Of *Marses* fierie steed: to other Regions,
France is a stable, wee that dwell in't Iades,
Therefore too'th warre.

BERTRAM
It shall be so, Ile send her to my house,
Acquaint my mother with my hate to her,
And wherefore I am fled: Write to the King
That which I durst not speake. His present gift
Shall furnish me to those Italian fields
Where noble fellowes strike: Warres is no strife
To the darke house, and the detested wife.

PARROLLES
1130 Will this Caprichio hold in thee, art sure?

BERTRAM
Go with me to my chamber, and aduice me.
Ile send her straight away: To morrow,
Ile to the warres, she to her single sorrow.

PARROLLES
Why these bals bound, ther's noise in it. Tis hard:
A yong man maried, is a man that's mard:

Therefore away, and leaue her brauely: go,
The King ha's done you wrong: but hush 'tis so.

Exeunt

Enter Hellen, reading a letter, and Clowne   Sc. 7
                                                      (2.4)

HELLEN
My mother greets me kindly, is she well?

CLOWNE She is not well, but yet she has her health, she's
very merrie, but yet she is not well: but thankes be 1140
giuen she's very well, and wants nothing i'th world:
but yet she is not well.

HELLEN
If she be verie wel, what do's she ayle,
That she's not verie well?

CLOWNE Truly she's very well indeed, but for two things.

HELLEN What two things?

CLOWNE One, that she's not in heauen, whether God send
her quickly: the other, that she's in earth, from whence
God send her quickly.

Enter Parolles

PARROLLES Blesse you my fortunate Ladie.   1150

HELLEN
I hope sir I haue your good will to haue
Mine owne good fortunes.

PARROLLES You had my prayers to leade them on, and to
keepe them on, haue them still. O my knaue, how do's
my old Ladie?

CLOWNE So that you had her wrinkles, and I her money,
I would she did as you say.

PARROLLES Why I say nothing.

CLOWNE Marry you are the wiser man: for many a mans
tongue shakes out his masters vndoing: to say nothing, 1160
to do nothing, to know nothing, and to haue nothing,
is to be a great part of your title, which is within a
verie little of nothing.

PARROLLES Away, th'art a knaue.

CLOWNE You should haue said sir before a knaue, th'art
a knaue, that's before me th'art a knaue: this had
beene truth sir.

PARROLLES Go too, thou art a wittie foole, I haue found
thee.

CLOWNE Did you finde me in your selfe sir, or were you 1170
taught to finde me?

⌈PARROLLES⌉ In my selfe, knaue.

CLOWNE The search sir was profitable, and much Foole
may you find in you, euen to the worlds pleasure, and
the encrease of laughter.

PARROLLES (*to Hellen*) A good knaue ifaith, and well fed.
Madam, my Lord will go awaie to night,
A verie serrious businesse call's on him:
The great prerogatiue and rite of loue,
Which as your due time claimes, he do's
    acknowledge,   1180
But puts it off to a compell'd restraint:
Whose want, and whose delay, is strew'd with sweets
Which they distill now in the curbed time,
To make the comming houre oreflow with ioy,
And pleasure drowne the brim.

HELLEN   What's his will else?

PARROLLES

That you will take your instant leaue a'th king,
And make this hast as your owne good proceeding,
Strengthned with what Apologie you thinke
May make it probable neede.

HELLEN   What more commands hee?

PARROLLES

1190   That hauing this obtain'd, you presentlie
Attend his further pleasure.

HELLEN   In euery thing
I waite vpon his will.

PARROLLES   I shall report it so.

HELLEN I pray you,   ⌜Exit Parrolles at one doore⌝
come sirrah.   Exeunt ⌜at another doore⌝

Sc. 8   Enter Lafew and Bertram
(2.5) LAFEW But I hope your Lordshippe thinkes not him a
souldier.

BERTRAM Yes my Lord and of verie valiant approofe.

LAFEW You haue it from his owne deliuerance.

BERTRAM And by other warranted testimonie.

1200 LAFEW Then my Diall goes not true, I tooke this Larke
for a bunting.

BERTRAM I do assure you my Lord he is very great in
knowledge, and accordinglie valiant.

LAFEW I haue then sinn'd against his experience, and
transgrest against his valour, and my state that way
is dangerous, since I cannot yet find in my heart to
repent: Heere he comes, I pray you make vs freinds, I
will pursue the amitie.

        Enter Parrolles

PARROLLES (to Bertram) These things shall be done sir.

1210 LAFEW (to Bertram) Pray you sir whose his Tailor?

PARROLLES Sir?

LAFEW O I know him well, I sir, hee sirs a good workeman,
a verie good Tailor.

BERTRAM (aside to Parrolles) Is shee gone to the king?

PARROLLES Shee is.

BERTRAM Will shee away to night?

PARROLLES As you'le haue her.

BERTRAM

I haue writ my letters, casketted my treasure,
Giuen order for our horses, and to night,
1220   When I should take possession of the Bride,
End ere I doe begin.

LAFEW (aside) A good Trauailer is something at the latter
end of a dinner, but on that lies three thirds, and vses
a known truth to passe a thousand nothings with,
should bee once hard, and thrice beaten. (To Parrolles)
God saue you Captaine.

BERTRAM (to Parrolles) Is there any vnkindnes betweene
my Lord and you Monsieur?

PARROLLES I know not how I haue deserued to run into
1230   my Lords displeasure.

LAFEW You haue made shift to run into't, bootes and
spurres and all: like him that leapt into the Custard,
and out of it you'le runne againe, rather then suffer
question for your residence.

BERTRAM It may bee you haue mistaken him my Lord.

LAFEW And shall doe so euer, though I tooke him at's
prayers. Fare you well my Lord, and beleeue this of
me, there can be no kernell in this light Nut: the soule
of this man is his cloathes: Trust him not in matter of
heauie consequence: I haue kept of them tame, & know   1240
their natures. Farewell Monsieur, I haue spoken better
of you, then you haue wit or will to deserue at my
hand, but we must do good against euill.   Exit

PARROLLES An idle Lord, I sweare.

BERTRAM I thinke not so.

PARROLLES Why do you not know him?

BERTRAM

Yes, I do know him well, and common speech
Giues him a worthy passe. Heere comes my clog.
        Enter Hellen, ⌜attended⌝

HELLEN

I haue sir as I was commanded from you
Spoke with the King, and haue procur'd his leaue   1250
For present parting, onely he desires
Some priuate speech with you.

BERTRAM   I shall obey his will.
You must not meruaile Helen at my course,
Which holds not colour with the time, nor does
The ministration, and required office
On my particular. Prepar'd I was not
For such a businesse, therefore am I found
So much vnsetled: This driues me to intreate you,
That presently you take your way for home,
And rather muse then aske why I intreate you,   1260
For my respects are better then they seeme,
And my appointments haue in them a neede
Greater then shewes it selfe at the first view,
To you that know them not. This to my mother,
        He giues her a Letter
'Twill be two daies ere I shall see you, so
I leaue you to your wisedome.

HELLEN   Sir, I can nothing say,
But that I am your most obedient seruant.

BERTRAM

Come, come, no more of that.

HELLEN   And euer shall
With true obseruance seeke to eeke out that
Wherein toward me my homely starres haue faild   1270
To equall my great fortune.

BERTRAM   Let that goe:
My hast is verie great. Farwell: hie home.

HELLEN

Pray sir your pardon.

BERTRAM   Well, what would you say?

HELLEN

I am not worthie of the wealth I owe,
Nor dare I say 'tis mine: and yet it is,
But like a timorous theefe, most faine would steale
What law does vouch mine owne.

BERTRAM   What would you haue?

HELLEN

Something, and scarse so much: nothing indeed,
I would not tell you what I would my Lord: Faith yes,
Strangers and foes do sunder, and not kisse.   1280

BERTRAM

I pray you stay not, but in hast to horse.

HELLEN

I shall not breake your bidding, good my Lord:
Where are my other men? Monsieur, farwell.

Exit Hellen ⌜with attendants at one doore⌝

BERTRAM

Go thou toward home, where I wil neuer come,
Whilst I can shake my sword, or heare the drumme:
Away, and for our flight.

PARROLLES   Brauely, Coragio.

Exeunt ⌜at another doore⌝

Sc. 9
(3.1)

*Flourish. Enter the Duke of Florence, the two Lords
Dumaine, with a troope of Souldiers*

DUKE

So that from point to point, now haue you heard
The fundamentall reasons of this warre,
Whose great decision hath much blood let forth
And more thirsts after.

1290   1. LORD DUMAINE   Holy seemes the quarrell
Vpon your Graces part: blacke and fearefull
On the opposer.

DUKE

Therefore we meruaile much our Cosin France
Would in so iust a businesse, shut his bosome
Against our borrowing prayers.

2. LORD DUMAINE   Good my Lord,
The reasons of our state I cannot yeelde,
But like a common and an outward man,
That the great figure of a Counsaile frames,
By selfe vnable motion, therefore dare not
1300   Say what I thinke of it, since I haue found
My selfe in my incertaine grounds to faile
As often as I guest.

DUKE   Be it his pleasure.

1. LORD DUMAINE

But I am sure the yonger of our nation,
That surfet on their ease, will day by day
Come heere for Physicke.

DUKE   Welcome shall they bee:
And all the honors that can flye from vs,
Shall on them settle: you know your places well,
When better fall, for your auailes they fell,
To morrow to the field.   *Flourish. Exeunt*

Sc. 10
(3.2)

Enter Lady Countesse with a Letter, and Clowne

COUNTESSE It hath happen'd all, as I would haue had it,
1311   saue that he comes not along with her.

CLOWNE By my troth I take my young Lord to be a verie
melancholly man.

COUNTESSE By what obseruance I pray you.

CLOWNE Why he will looke vppon his boote, and sing:
mend the Ruffe and sing, aske questions and sing, picke
his teeth, and sing: I know a man that had this tricke
of melancholy sold a goodly Mannor for a song.

COUNTESSE Let me see what he writes, and when he
1320   meanes to come.

She opens a Letter and reads

CLOWNE *(aside)* I haue no minde to *Isbell* since I was at
Court. Our old Lings, and our *Isbels* a'th Country, are
nothing like your old Ling and your *Isbels* a'th Court:
the brains of my Cupid's knock'd out, and I beginne to
loue, as an old man loues money, with no stomacke.

COUNTESSE What haue we heere?

CLOWNE In that you haue there.   *exit*

COUNTESSE *(reads a Letter)* I haue sent you a daughter-in-
Law, shee hath recouered the King, and vndone me: I haue
wedded her, not bedded her, and sworne to make the not   1330
eternall. You shall heare I am runne away, know it before
the report come. If there bee bredth enough in the world, I
will hold a long distance. My duty to you.

Your vnfortunate sonne,
Bertram.

This is not well rash and vnbridled boy,
To flye the fauours of so good a King,
To plucke his indignation on thy head,
By the misprising of a Maide too vertuous
For the contempt of Empire.   1340

Enter Clowne

CLOWNE O Madam, yonder is heauie newes within
betweene two souldiers, and my yong Ladie.

COUNTESSE What is the matter.

CLOWNE Nay there is some comfort in the newes, some
comfort, your sonne will not be kild so soone as I
thoght he would.

COUNTESSE Why should he be kill'd?

CLOWNE So say I Madame, if he runne away, as I heare
he does, the danger is in standing too't, that's the losse
of men, though it be the getting of children. Heere they   1350
come will tell you more. For my part I onely heard
your sonne was run away.   ⌜*Exit*⌝

*Enter Hellen with a Letter, and the two Lords
Dumaine*

2. LORD DUMAINE *(to Countesse)* Saue you good Madam.

HELLEN

Madam, my Lord is gone, for euer gone.

1. LORD DUMAINE Do not say so.

COUNTESSE *(to Hellen)*

Thinke vpon patience, pray you Gentlemen,
I haue felt so many quirkes of ioy and greefe,
That the first face of neither on the start
Can woman me vntoo't. Where is my sonne I pray
you?

1. LORD DUMAINE

Madam he's gone to serue the Duke of Florence,   1360
We met him thitherward, for thence we came:
And after some dispatch in hand at Court,
Thither we bend againe.

HELLEN

Looke on his Letter Madam, here's my Pasport.

⌜*She*⌝ *reads alowd*

*When thou canst get the Ring vpon my finger, which neuer
shall come off, and shew mee a childe begotten of thy bodie,
that I am father too, then call me husband: but in such a
(then) I write a Neuer.*

This is a dreadfull sentence.

COUNTESSE

   Brought you this Letter Gentlemen?

1370   1. LORD DUMAINE   I Madam,

   And for the Contents sake are sorrie for our paines.

COUNTESSE

   I prethee Ladie haue a better cheere,

   If thou engrossest all the greefes are thine,

   Thou robst me of a moity: He was my sonne,

   But I do wash his name out of my blood,

   And thou art all my childe. Towards Florence is he?

  1. LORD DUMAINE

   I Madam.

COUNTESSE   And to be a souldier.

  1. LORD DUMAINE

   Such is his noble purpose, and beleeu't

   The Duke will lay vpon him all the honor

   That good conuenience claimes.

1380   COUNTESSE   Returne you thither.

  2. LORD DUMAINE

   I Madam, with the swiftest wing of speed.

HELLEN *Till I haue no wife, I haue nothing in France,*

   'Tis bitter.

COUNTESSE Finde you that there?

HELLEN I Madame.

  2. LORD DUMAINE

   'Tis but the boldnesse of his hand

   Haply, which his heart was not consenting too.

COUNTESSE

   Nothing in France, vntill he haue no wife:

   There's nothing heere that is too good for him

1390   But onely she, and she deserues a Lord

   That twenty such rude boyes might tend vpon,

   And call her hourely Mistris. Who was with him?

  2. LORD DUMAINE

   A seruant onely, and a Gentleman:

   Which I haue sometime knowne.

COUNTESSE *Parolles* was it not?

2. LORD DUMAINE I my good Ladie, hee.

COUNTESSE

   A verie tainted fellow, and full of wickednesse,

   My sonne corrupts a well deriued nature

   With his inducement.

  2. LORD DUMAINE   Indeed good Ladie

1400   The fellow has a deale of that, too much,

   Which holds him much to haue.

COUNTESSE   Y'are welcome Gentlemen,

   I will intreate you when you see my sonne,

   To tell him that his sword can neuer winne

   The honor that he looses: more Ile intreate you

   Written to beare along.

  1. LORD DUMAINE   We serue you Madam

   In that and all your worthiest affaires.

COUNTESSE

   Not so, but as we change our courtesies,

   Will you draw neere?   *Exit all but Hellen*

HELLEN *Till I haue no wife I haue nothing in France.*

1410   Nothing in France vntill he has no wife:

   Thou shalt haue none *Rossillion*, none in France,

Then hast thou all againe: poore Lord, is't I

That chase thee from thy Countrie, and expose

Those tender limbes of thine, to the euent

Of the none-sparing warre? And is it I,

That driue thee from the sportiue Court, where thou

Was't shot at with faire eyes, to be the marke

Of smoakie Muskets? O you leaden messengers,

That ride vpon the violent speede of fire,

Fly with false ayme, cleue the still-peecing aire   1420

That sings with piercing, do not touch my Lord:

Who euer shoots at him, I set him there.

Who euer charges on his forward brest

I am the Caitiffe that do hold him too't,

And though I kill him not, I am the cause

His death was so effected: Better 'twere

I met the rauine Lyon when he roar'd

With sharpe constraint of hunger: better 'twere,

That all the miseries which nature owes

Were mine at once. No come thou home *Rossillion*,   1430

Whence honor but of danger winnes a scarre,

As oft it looses all. I will be gone:

My being heere it is, that holds thee hence,

Shall I stay heere to doo't? No, no, although

The ayre of Paradise did fan the house,

And Angles offic'd all: I will be gone,

That pittifull rumour may report my flight

To consolate thine eare. Come night, end day,

For with the darke (poore theefe) Ile steale away.   *Exit*

     Flourish. Enter the Duke of Florence, Bertram   Sc. 11

     Count Rossillion, drum and trumpets, soldiers,   (3.3)

     Parrolles

DUKE (*to Bertram*)

   The Generall of our horse thou art, and we   1440

   Great in our hope, lay our best loue and credence

   Vpon thy promising fortune.

BERTRAM   Sir it is

   A charge too heauy for my strength, but yet

   Wee'l striue to beare it for your worthy sake,

   To th'extreme edge of hazard.

DUKE   Then go thou forth,

   And fortune play vpon thy prosperous helme

   As thy auspicious mistris.

BERTRAM   This very day

   Great Mars I put my selfe into thy file,

   Make me but like my thoughts, and I shall proue

   A louer of thy drumme, hater of loue.   *Exeunt omnes*   1450

     Enter Lady Countesse & Steward, with a Letter   Sc. 12

COUNTESSE   (3.4)

   Alas! and would you take the letter of her:

   Might you not know she would do, as she has done,

   By sending me a Letter. Reade it agen.

STEWARD (*reads the Letter*)

   I am S. Iaques Pilgrim, thither gone:

     Ambitious loue hath so in me offended,

   That bare-foot plod I the cold ground vpon

     With sainted vow my faults to haue amended.

Write, write, that from the bloodie course of warre,
 My deerest Master your deare sonne, may hie;
1460 *Blesse him at home in peace, whilst I from farre,*
 His name with zealous feruour sanctifie:
His taken labours bid him me forgiue:
 I his despightfull Iuno sent him forth,
From Courtly friends, with Camping foes to liue,
 Where death and danger dogges the heeles of worth.
He is too good and faire for death, and mee,
 Whom I my selfe embrace, to set him free.

COUNTESSE

Ah what sharpe stings are in her mildest words?
Rynaldo, you did neuer lacke aduice so much,
1470 As letting her passe so: had I spoke with her,
I could haue well diuerted her intents,
Which thus she hath preuented.

STEWARD   Pardon me Madam,
If I had giuen you this at ouer-night,
She might haue beene ore-tane: and yet she writes
Pursuite would be but vaine.

COUNTESSE   What Angell shall
Blesse this vnworthy husband, he cannot thriue,
Vnlesse her prayers, whom heauen delights to heare
And loues to grant, repreeue him from the wrath
Of greatest Iustice. Write, write *Rynaldo,*
1480 To this vnworthy husband of his wife,
Let euerie word waigh heauie of her worth,
That he does waigh too light: my greatest greefe,
Though little he do feele it, set downe sharpely.
Dispatch the most conuenient messenger,
When haply he shall heare that she is gone,
He will returne, and hope I may that shee
Hearing so much, will speede her foote againe,
Led hither by pure loue: which of them both
Is deerest to me, I haue no skill in sence
1490 To make distinction: prouide this Messenger:
My heart is heauie, and mine age is weake,
Greefe would haue teares, and sorrow bids me speake.

             Exeunt

Sc. 13   *A Tucket afarre off. Enter old Widdow of Florence,*
(3.5)   *her daughter Diana, and Mariana, with other*
     Citizens

WIDDOW Nay come, for if they do approach the Citty, we
shall loose all the sight.

DIANA They say, the French Count has done most
honourable seruice.

WIDDOW It is reported, that he has taken their greatest
Commander, and that with his owne hand he slew the
Dukes brother: (*Tucket*) we haue lost our labour, they
1500 are gone a contrarie way: harke, you may know by
their Trumpets.

MARIANA Come lets returne againe, and suffice our selues
with the report of it. Well *Diana,* take heed of this
French Earle, the honor of a Maide is her name, and
no Legacie is so rich as honestie.

WIDDOW (*to Diana*) I haue told my neighbour how you
haue beene solicited by a Gentleman his Companion.

MARIANA I know that knaue, hang him, one *Parolles,* a
filthy Officer he is in those suggestions for the young
Earle, beware of them *Diana;* their promises, 1510
entisements, oathes, tokens, and all their engines of
lust, are not the things they go vnder: many a maide
hath beene seduced by them, and the miserie is
example, that so terrible shewes in the wracke of
maiden-hood, cannot for all that disswade succession,
but that they are limed with the twigges that threatens
them. I hope I neede not to aduise you further, but I
hope your owne grace will keepe you where you are,
though there were no further danger knowne, but the
modestie which is so lost. 1520

DIANA You shall not neede to feare me.

    Enter Hellen as a Pilgrim

WIDDOW I hope so: looke here comes a pilgrim, I know
she will lye at my house, thither they send one another,
Ile question her.
God saue you pilgrim, whether are you bound?

HELLEN To S. *Iaques la grand.*
Where do the Palmers lodge, I do beseech you?

WIDDOW
At the S. *Francis* heere beside the Port.

HELLEN
Is this the way?

WIDDOW   I marrie ist.

    ⌈*A march afarre*⌉

Harke you, they come this way: if you will tarrie 1530
Holy Pilgrime but till the troopes come by,
I will conduct you where you shall be lodg'd,
The rather for I thinke I know your hostesse
As ample as my selfe.

HELLEN Is it your selfe?

WIDDOW If you shall please so Pilgrime.

HELLEN
I thanke you, and will stay vpon your leisure.

WIDDOW
You came I thinke from *France?*

HELLEN   I did so.

WIDDOW
Heere you shall see a Countriman of yours
That has done worthy seruice.

HELLEN   His name I pray you? 1540

DIANA
The Count *Rossillion:* know you such a one?

HELLEN
But by the eare that heares most nobly of him:
His face I know not.

DIANA   What somere he is
He's brauely taken heere. He stole from *France*
As 'tis reported: for the King had married him
Against his liking. Thinke you it is so?

HELLEN
I surely meere the truth, I know his Lady.

DIANA
There is a Gentleman that serues the Count,
Reports but coursely of her.

HELLEN   What's his name?

DIANA
  Monsieur *Parrolles*.

1550 HELLEN   Oh I beleeue with him,
  In argument of praise, or to the worth
  Of the great Count himselfe, she is too meane
  To haue her name repeated, all her deseruing
  Is a reserued honestie, and that
  I haue not heard examin'd.

DIANA   Alas poore Ladie,
  'Tis a hard bondage to become the wife
  Of a detesting Lord.

WIDDOW
  I war¹ good creature, wheresoere she is,
  Her hart waighes sadly: this yong maid might do her
  A shrewd turne if she pleas'd.

1560 HELLEN   How do you meane?
  May be the amorous Count solicites her
  In the vnlawfull purpose.

WIDDOW   He does indeede,
  And brokes with all that can in such a suite
  Corrupt the tender honour of a Maide:
  But she is arm'd for him, and keepes her guard
  In honestest defence.

MARIANA The goddes forbid else.
        ⌈*Drumme and Colours.*
        Enter Bertram Count Rossillion, Parrolles, and the
        whole Armie⌉

WIDDOW So, now they come:
  That is *Anthonio* the Dukes eldest sonne,
  That *Escalus.*

HELLEN   Which is the Frenchman?

1570 DIANA   Hee,
  That with the plume, 'tis a most gallant fellow,
  I would he lou'd his wife: if he were honester
  He were much goodlier. Is't not
  A handsom Gentleman?

HELLEN I like him well.

DIANA 'Tis pitty he is not honest:
  Yonds that same knaue that leades him to those places:
  Were I his Ladie, I would poison
  That vile Rascall.

HELLEN   Which is he?

DIANA   That Iacke-an-apes

1580 With scarfes. Why is hee melancholly?

HELLEN Perchance he's hurt i'th battaile.

PARROLLES (*aside*) Loose our drum? Well.

MARIANA He's shrewdly vext at something.
  Looke he has spyed vs.

WIDDOW (*to Parrolles*)   Marrie hang you.

MARIANA (*to Parrolles*)
  And your curtesie, for a ring-carrier.
        Exit Bertram, Parrolles, and the Armie

WIDDOW
  The troope is past: Come pilgrim, I wil bring you,
  Where you shall host: Of inioyn'd penitents
  There's foure or fiue, to great S. *Iaques* bound,
  Alreadie at my house.

HELLEN   I humbly thanke you:

Please it this Matron, and this gentle Maide   1590
To eate with vs to night, the charge and thanking
Shall be for me, and to requite you further,
I will bestow some precepts of this Virgin,
Worthy the note.

WIDDOW *and* MARIANA Wee'l take your offer kindly.

                    Exeunt

  Enter Bertram Count Rossillion and the two   Sc. 14
  Captaines Dumaine   (3.6)

2. LORD DUMAINE (*to Bertram*) Nay good my Lord put him
  too't: let him haue his way.

1. LORD DUMAINE (*to Bertram*) If your Lordshippe finde
  him not a Hilding, hold me no more in your respect.

2. LORD DUMAINE (*to Bertram*) On my life my Lord, a   1600
  bubble.

BERTRAM Do you thinke I am so farre deceiued in him.

2. LORD DUMAINE Beleeue it my Lord, in mine owne direct
  knowledge, without any malice, but to speake of him
  as my kinsman, hee's a most notable Coward, an
  infinite and endlesse Lyar, an hourely promise-breaker,
  the owner of no one good qualitie, worthy your
  Lordships entertainment.

1. LORD DUMAINE (*to Bertram*) It were fit you knew him,
  least reposing too farre in his vertue which he hath
  not, he might at some great and trustie businesse, in   1610
  a maine daunger, fayle you.

BERTRAM I would I knew in what particular action to try
  him.

1. LORD DUMAINE None better then to let him fetch off his
  drumme, which you heare him so confidently vndertake
  to do.

2. LORD DUMAINE (*to Bertram*) I with a troop of Florentines
  wil sodainly surprize him; such I will haue whom I am
  sure he knowes not from the enemie: wee will binde
  and hoodwinke him so, that he shall suppose no other   1620
  but that he is carried into the Leager of the aduersaries,
  when we bring him to our owne tents: be but your
  Lordship present at his examination, if he do not for
  the promise of his life, and in the highest compulsion
  of base feare, offer to betray you, and deliuer all the
  intelligence in his power against you, and that with
  the diuine forfeite of his soule vpon oath, neuer trust
  my iudgement in anie thing.

1. LORD DUMAINE (*to Bertram*) O for the loue of laughter,
  let him fetch his drumme, he says he has a stratagem   1630
  for't: when your Lordship sees the bottome of his
  successe in't, and to what mettle this counterfeyt lump
  of oure will be melted if you giue him not Iohn drummes
  entertainment, your inclining cannot be remoued.
  Heere he comes.

        Enter Parrolles

2. LORD DUMAINE O ⌈*aside*⌉ for the loue of laughter ⌈*alowd*⌉
  hinder not the honor of his designe, let him fetch off
  his drumme in any hand.

BERTRAM (*to Parrolles*) How now Monsieur? This drumme
  sticks sorely in your disposition.   1640

1. LORD DUMAINE A pox on't, let it go, 'tis but a drumme.

PARROLLES But a drumme: Ist but a drumme? A drum so
lost. There was excellent command, to charge in with
our horse vpon our owne wings, and to rend our owne
souldiers.

1. LORD DUMAINE That was not to be blam'd in the
command of the seruice: it was a disaster of warre that
Cæsar him selfe could not haue preuented, if he had
beene there to command.

1650 BERTRAM Well, wee cannot greatly condemne our
successe: some dishonor wee had in the losse of that
drum, but it is not to be recouered.

PARROLLES It might haue beene recouered.

BERTRAM It might, but it is not now.

PARROLLES It is to be recouered; but that the merit of
seruice is sildome attributed to the true and exact
performer, I would haue that drumme or another, or
hic iacet.

BERTRAM Why if you haue a stomacke, too't Monsieur:
1660 if you thinke your mysterie in stratagem, can bring
this instrument of honour againe into his natiue
quarter, be magnanimious in the enterprize and go on,
I wil grace the attempt for a worthy exploit: if you
speede well in it, the Duke shall both speake of it, and
extend to you what further becomes his greatnesse,
euen to the vtmost syllable of your worthinesse.

PARROLLES By the hand of a souldier I will vndertake it.

BERTRAM But you must not now slumber in it.

PARROLLES Ile about it this euening, and I will presently
1670 pen downe my dilemma's, encourage my selfe in my
certaintie, put my selfe into my mortall preparation:
and by midnight looke to heare further from me.

BERTRAM May I bee bold to acquaint his grace you are
gone about it.

PARROLLES I know not what the successe wil be my Lord,
but the attempt I vow.

BERTRAM I know th'art valiant, and to the possibility of
thy souldiership, will subscribe for thee: Farewell.

PARROLLES I loue not many words.   *Exit*

1680 2. LORD DUMAINE No more then a fish loues water. (*To
Bertram*) Is not this a strange fellow my Lord, that so
confidently seemes to vndertake this businesse, which
he knowes is not to be done, damnes himselfe to do,
& dares better be damnd then to doo't.

1. LORD DUMAINE (*to Bertram*) You do not know him my
Lord as we doe, certaine it is that he will steale himselfe
into a mans fauour, and for a weeke escape a great
deale of discoueries, but when you finde him out, you
haue him euer after.

1690 BERTRAM Why do you thinke he will make no deede at
all of this that so seriouslie hee dooes addresse himselfe
vnto?

2. LORD DUMAINE None in the world, but returne with an
inuention, and clap vpon you two or three probable
lies: but we haue almost imbost him, you shall see his
fall to night; for indeede he is not for your Lordshippes
respect.

1. LORD DUMAINE (*to Bertram*) Weele make you some sport
with the Foxe ere we case him. He was first smoak'd

by the old Lord *Lafew*, when his disguise and he is 1700
parted, tell me what a sprat you shall finde him, which
you shall see this verie night.

2. LORD DUMAINE
I must go looke my twigges, he shall be caught.

BERTRAM
Your brother he shall go along with me.

⌜2.⌝ LORD DUMAINE As't please your Lordship, Ile leaue
you.   *Exit*

BERTRAM
Now wil I lead you to the house, and shew you
The Lasse I spoke of.

⌜1.⌝ LORD DUMAINE   But you say she's honest.

BERTRAM
That's all the fault: I spoke with hir but once,
And found her wondrous cold, but I sent to her   1710
By this same Coxcombe that we haue i'th winde
Tokens and Letters, which she did resend,
And this is all I haue done: She's a faire creature,
Will you go see her?

⌜1.⌝ LORD DUMAINE   With all my heart my Lord.

Exeunt

Enter Hellen, and Widdow   Sc. 15
HELLEN   (3.7)
If you misdoubt me that I am not shee,
I know not how I shall assure you further,
But I shall loose the grounds I worke vpon.

WIDDOW
Though my estate be falne, I was well borne,
Nothing acquainted with these businesses,
And would not put my reputation now   1720
In any staining act.

HELLEN   Nor would I wish you.
First giue me trust, the Count he is my husband,
And what to your sworne counsaile I haue spoken,
Is so from word to word: and then you cannot
By the good ayde that I of you shall borrow,
Erre in bestowing it.

WIDDOW   I should beleeue you,
For you haue shew'd me that which well approues
Y'are great in fortune.

HELLEN   Take this purse of Gold,
And let me buy your friendly helpe thus farre,
Which I will ouer-pay, and pay againe   1730
When I haue found it. The Count he woes your
    daughter,
Layes downe his wanton siedge before her beautie,
Resolud to carrie her: let her in fine consent
As wee'l direct her how 'tis best to beare it:
Now his important blood will naught denie,
That shee'l demand: a ring the Countie weares,
That downward hath succeeded in his house
From sonne to sonne, some foure or fiue discents,
Since the first father wore it. This Ring he holds
In most rich choice: yet in his idle fire,   1740
To buy his will, it would not seeme too deere,
How ere repented after.

WIDDOW
Now I see the bottome of your purpose.

HELLEN
You see it lawfull then, it is no more,
But that your daughter ere she seemes as wonne,
Desires this Ring; appoints him an encounter;
In fine, deliuers me to fill the time,
Her selfe most chastly absent: after
To marry her, Ile adde three thousand Crownes
To what is past already.

1750 WIDDOW   I haue yeelded:
Instruct my daughter how she shall perseuer,
That time and place with this deceite so lawfull
May proue coherent. Euery night he comes
With Musickes of all sorts, and songs compos'd
To her vnworthinesse: It nothing steeds vs
To chide him from our eeues, for he persists
As if his life lay on't.

HELLEN   Why then to night
Let vs assay our plot, which if it speed,
Is wicked meaning in a lawfull deede;
1760 And lawfull meaning in a wicked act,
Where both not sinne, and yet a sinfull fact.
But let's about it.   *Exeunt*

Sc. 16   *Enter ⌐2. Lord Dumaine¬, with fiue or sixe other*
(4.1)   *souldiers in ambush*

⌐2.¬ LORD DUMAINE He can come no other way but by this
hedge corner: when you sallie vpon him, speake what
terrible Language you will: though you vnderstand it
not your selues, no matter: for we must not seeme to
vnderstand him, vnlesse some one among vs, whom
wee must produce for an Interpreter.

INTERPRETER Good Captaine, let me be th'Interpreter.

1770 ⌐2.¬ LORD DUMAINE Art not acquainted with him? knowes
he not thy voice?

INTERPRETER No sir I warrant you.

⌐2.¬ LORD DUMAINE But what linsie wolsy hast thou to
speake to vs againe.

INTERPRETER E'n such as you speake to me.

⌐2.¬ LORD DUMAINE He must thinke vs some band of
strangers, i'th aduersaries entertainment. Now he hath
a smacke of all neighbouring Languages: therefore we
must euery one be a man of his owne fancie: not to
1780 know what we speake one to another, so we seeme to
know, is to know straight our purpose: Choughs
language, gabble enough, and good enough. As for you
interpreter, you must seeme very politicke. But couch
hoa, heere hee comes, to beguile two houres in a sleepe,
and then to returne & swear the lies he forges.

They hide. Enter Parrolles. ⌐Clocke strikes¬

PARROLLES Ten a clocke: Within these three houres 'twill
be time enough to goe home. What shall I say I haue
done? It must bee a very plausiue inuention that carries
it. They beginne to smoake mee, and disgraces haue of
1790 late, knock'd too often at my doore: I finde my tongue
is too foole-hardie, but my heart hath the feare of Mars
before it, and of his creatures, not daring the reports
of my tongue.

⌐2.¬ LORD DUMAINE (*aside*) This is the first truth that ere
thine own tongue was guiltie of.

PARROLLES What the diuell should moue mee to vndertake
the recouerie of this drumme, being not ignorant of
the impossibility, and knowing I had no such purpose?
I must giue my selfe some hurts, and say I got them
in exploit: yet slight ones will not carrie it. They will   1800
say, came you off with so little? And great ones I dare
not giue, wherefore what's the instance. Tongue, I
must put you into a Butter-womans mouth, and buy
my selfe another of *Baiazeths* Mute, if you prattle mee
into these perilles.

⌐2.¬ LORD DUMAINE (*aside*) Is it possible he should know
what hee is, and be that he is.

PARROLLES I would the cutting of my garments wold serue
the turne, or the breaking of my Spanish sword.

⌐2.¬ LORD DUMAINE (*aside*) We cannot affoord you so.   1810

PARROLLES Or the baring of my beard, and to say it was
in stratagem.

⌐2.¬ LORD DUMAINE (*aside*) 'Twould not do.

PARROLLES Or to drowne my cloathes, and say I was
stript.

⌐2.¬ LORD DUMAINE (*aside*) Hardly serue.

PARROLLES Though I swore I leapt from the window of
the Citadell.

⌐2.¬ LORD DUMAINE (*aside*) How deepe?

PARROLLES Thirty fadome.   1820

⌐2.¬ LORD DUMAINE (*aside*) Three great oathes would scarse
make that be beleeued.

PARROLLES I would I had any drumme of the enemies, I
would sweare I recouer'd it.

⌐2.¬ LORD DUMAINE (*aside*) You shall heare one anon.

PARROLLES A drumme now of the enemies.

Alarum within. ⌐The Ambush rushes forth¬

⌐2.¬ LORD DUMAINE *Throca movousus, cargo, cargo, cargo.*

SOULDIERS (*seuerally*) *Cargo, cargo, cargo, villianda par corbo,
cargo.*

⌐They seize and muffle him¬

PARROLLES
O ransome, ransome, do not hide mine eyes.   1830

INTERPRETER *Boskos thromuldo boskos.*

PARROLLES
I know you are the *Muskos* Regiment,
And I shall loose my life for want of language.
If there be heere German or Dane, Low Dutch,
Italian, or French, let him speake to me,
Ile discouer that, which shal vndo the Florentine.

INTERPRETER *Boskos vauvado,*
I vnderstand thee, & can speake thy tongue:
(*To others*) *Kerelybonto* (*to Parrolles*) sir,
Betake thee to thy faith, for seuenteene ponyards   1840
Are at thy bosome.

PARROLLES   Oh.

INTERPRETER   Oh pray, pray, pray,
Manka reuania dulche.

⌐2.¬ LORD DUMAINE
Oscorbidulchos voliuorco.

INTERPRETER
The Generall is content to spare thee yet,

And hoodwinkt as thou art, will leade thee on
To gather from thee. Haply thou mayst informe
Something to saue thy life.

PARROLLES   O let me liue,
And all the secrets of our campe Ile shew,
Their force, their purposes: Nay, Ile speake that,
Which you will wonder at.

1850 INTERPRETER   But wilt thou faithfully?
PARROLLES
If I do not, damne me.

INTERPRETER (*to others*)   *Acordo linta.*
Come on, thou art granted space.

                    Exit all but ⌜2.⌝ *Lord Dumaine and a Soldier*
                    A short Alarum within

⌜2.⌝ LORD DUMAINE
Go tell the Count *Rossillion* and my brother,
We haue caught the woodcocke, and will keepe him
    mufled
Till we do heare from them.

SOLDIER   Captaine I will.

⌜2.⌝ LORD DUMAINE
A will betray vs all vnto our selues,
Informe on that.

SOLDIER   So I will sir.

⌜2.⌝ LORD DUMAINE
Till then Ile keepe him darke and safely lockt.

                    Exeunt seuerally

Sc. 17   *Enter Bertram, and the Maide called Diana*
(4.2) BERTRAM
1860
They told me that your name was *Fontybell.*

DIANA
No my good Lord, *Diana.*

BERTRAM   Titled Goddesse,
And worth it with addition: but faire soule,
In your fine frame hath loue no qualitie?
If the quicke fire of youth light not your minde,
You are no Maiden but a monument.
When you are dead you should be such a one
As you are now: for you are cold and sterne,
And now you should be as your mother was
When your sweet selfe was got.

1870 DIANA She then was honest.

BERTRAM So should you be.

DIANA   No:
My mother did but dutie, such (my Lord)
As you owe to your wife.

BERTRAM   No more a'that:
I prethee do not striue against my vowes:
I was compell'd to her, but I loue thee
By loues owne sweet constraint, and will for euer
Do thee all rights of seruice.

DIANA   I so you serue vs
Till we serue you: But when you haue our Roses,
1880 You barely leaue our thornes to pricke our selues,
And mocke vs with our barenesse.

BERTRAM   How haue I sworne.

DIANA
Tis not the many oathes that makes the truth,

But the plaine single vow, that is vow'd true:
What is not holie, that we sweare not by,
But take the high'st to witnesse: then pray you tell me,
If I should sweare by Ioues great attributes,
I lou'd you deerely, would you beleeue my oathes,
When I did loue you ill? This ha's no holding
To sweare by him whom I protest to loue
That I will worke against him. Therefore your oathes   1890
Are words and poore conditions, but vnseal'd
At lest in my opinion.

BERTRAM   Change it, change it:
Be not so holy cruell: Loue is holie,
And my integritie ne're knew the crafts
That you do charge men with: Stand no more off,
But giue thy selfe vnto my sicke desires,
Who then recouers. Say thou art mine, and euer
My loue as it beginnes, shall so perseuer.

DIANA
I see that men make toyes in such a surance,
That wee'l forsake our selues. Giue me that Ring.   1900

BERTRAM
Ile lend it thee my deere; but haue no power
To giue it from me.

DIANA   Will you not my Lord?

BERTRAM
It is an honour longing to our house,
Bequeathed downe from manie Ancestors,
Which were the greatest obloquie i'th world,
In me to loose.

DIANA   Mine Honors such a Ring,
My chastities the Iewell of our house,
Bequeathed downe from many Ancestors,
Which were the greatest obloquie i'th world,
In mee to loose. Thus your owne proper wisedome   1910
Brings in the Champion honor on my part,
Against your vaine assault.

BERTRAM   Heere, take my Ring,
My house, mine honor, yea my life be thine,
And Ile be bid by thee.

DIANA
When midnight comes, knocke at my chamber
    window:
Ile order take, my mother shall not heare.
Now will I charge you in the band of truth,
When you haue conquer'd my yet maiden-bed,
Remaine there but an houre, nor speake to mee:
My reasons are most strong, and you shall know
    them,
When backe againe this Ring shall be deliuer'd: 1920
And on your finger in the night, Ile put
Another Ring, that what in time proceeds,
May token to the future, our past deeds.
Adieu till then, then faile not: you haue wonne
A wife of me, though there my hope be done.

BERTRAM
A heauen on earth I haue won by wooing thee.

DIANA
For which, liue long to thank both heauen & me,
You may so in the end.   ⌜*Exit Bertram*⌝

1930 My mother told me iust how he would woo,
As if she sate in's heart. She sayes, all men
Haue the like oathes: He had sworne to marrie me
When his wife's dead: therfore Ile lye with him
When I am buried. Since Frenchmen are so braide,
Marry that will, I liue and die a Maid:
Onely in this disguise, I think't no sinne,
To cosen him that would vniustly winne.   *Exit*

Sc. 18   *Enter the two Captaines Dumaine, and some two or*
(4.3)   *three Souldiours*

1. LORD DUMAINE You haue not giuen him his mothers
letter.

1940 2. LORD DUMAINE I haue deliu'red it an houre since, there
is som thing in't that stings his nature: for on the
reading it, he chang'd almost into another man.

1. LORD DUMAINE He has much worthy blame laid vpon
him, for shaking off so good a wife, and so sweet a
Lady.

2. LORD DUMAINE Especially, hee hath incurred the
euerlasting displeasure of the King, who had euen tun'd
his bounty to sing happinesse to him. I will tell you a
thing, but you shall let it dwell darkly with you.

1950 1. LORD DUMAINE When you haue spoken it 'tis dead, and
I am the graue of it.

2. LORD DUMAINE Hee hath peruerted a young
Gentlewoman heere in *Florence*, of a most chaste
renown, & this night he fleshes his will in the spoyle
of her honour: hee hath giuen her his monumentall
Ring, and thinkes himselfe made in the vnchaste
composition.

1. LORD DUMAINE Now God delay our rebellion! as we are
our selues, what things are we.

1960 2. LORD DUMAINE Meerely our owne traitours. And as in
the common course of all treasons, we still see them
reueale themselues, till they attaine to their abhorr'd
ends: so he that in this action contriues against his
owne Nobility, in his proper streame ore-flowes
himselfe.

1. LORD DUMAINE Is it not meant damnable in vs, to be
Trumpeters of our vnlawfull intents? We shall not then
haue his company to night?

2. LORD DUMAINE Not till after midnight: for hee is dieted
1970 to his houre.

1. LORD DUMAINE That approaches apace: I would gladly
haue him see his company anathomiz'd, that hee might
take a measure of his owne iudgements, wherein so
curiously he had set this counterfeit.

2. LORD DUMAINE We will not meddle with him till he
come; for his presence must be the whip of the other.

1. LORD DUMAINE In the meane time, what heare you of
these Warres?

2. LORD DUMAINE I heare there is an ouerture of peace.

1980 1. LORD DUMAINE Nay, I assure you a peace concluded.

2. LORD DUMAINE What will Count *Rossillion* do then?
Will he trauaile higher, or returne againe into France?

1. LORD DUMAINE I perceiue by this demand, you are not
altogether of his councell.

2. LORD DUMAINE Let it be forbid sir, so should I bee a
great deale of his act.

1. LORD DUMAINE Sir, his wife some two months since
fledde from his house, her pretence is a pilgrimage to
Saint *Iaques le grand*; which holy vndertaking, with
most austere sanctimonie she accomplisht: and there   1990
residing, the tendernesse of her Nature, became as a
prey to her greefe: in fine, made a groane of her last
breath, & now she sings in heauen.

2. LORD DUMAINE How is this iustified?

1. LORD DUMAINE The stronger part of it by her owne
Letters, which makes her storie true, euen to the poynt
of her death: her death it selfe, which could not be her
office to say, is come: was faithfully confirm'd by the
Rector of the place.

2. LORD DUMAINE Hath the Count all this intelligence?   2000

1. LORD DUMAINE I, and the particular confirmations,
point from point, to the full arming of the veritie.

2. LORD DUMAINE I am heartily sorrie that hee'l bee gladde
of this.

1. LORD DUMAINE How mightily sometimes, we make vs
comforts of our losses.

2. LORD DUMAINE And how mightily some other times,
wee drowne our gaine in teares, the great dignitie that
his valour hath here acquir'd for him, shall at home
be encountred with a shame as ample.   2010

1. LORD DUMAINE The webbe of our life, is of a mingled
yarne, good and ill together: our vertues would bee
proud, if our faults whipt them not, and our crimes
would dispaire if they were not cherish'd by our vertues.

Enter a Seruant

How now? Where's your master?

SERUANT He met the Duke in the street sir, of whom hee
hath taken a solemne leaue: his Lordshippe will next
morning for France. The Duke hath offered him Letters
of commendations to the King.

2. LORD DUMAINE They shall bee no more then needfull   2020
there, if they were more then they can commend.

Enter Bertram Count Rossillion

⌈1. LORD DUMAINE⌉ They cannot be too sweete for the
Kings tartnesse, heere's his Lordship now. How now
my Lord, i'st not after midnight?

BERTRAM I haue to night dispatch'd sixteene businesses,
a moneths length a peece; by an abstract of successe:
I haue congied with the Duke, done my adieu with his
neerest; buried a wife, mourn'd for her, writ to my
Ladie mother, I am returning, entertain'd my Conuoy,
& betweene these maine parcels of dispatch, affected   2030
many nicer needs: the last was the greatest, but that
I haue not ended yet.

2. LORD DUMAINE If the businesse bee of any difficulty,
and this morning your departure hence, it requires hast
of your Lordship.

BERTRAM I meane the businesse is not ended, as fearing
to heare of it hereafter: but shall we haue this dialogue
betweene the Foole and the Soldiour. Come, bring forth
this counterfet module, ha's deceiu'd mee, like a double-
meaning Prophesier.   2040

2. LORD DUMAINE Bring him forth,   *Exit one or more*
ha's sate i'th stockes all night poore gallant knaue.

BERTRAM No matter, his heeles haue deseru'd it, in
vsurping his spurres so long. How does he carry
himselfe?

2. LORD DUMAINE I haue told your Lordship alreadie: The
stockes carrie him. But to answer you as you would
be vnderstood, hee weepes like a wench that had shed
her milke, he hath confest himselfe to *Morgan*, whom
2050   hee supposes to be a Friar, frõ the time of his
remembrance to this very instant disaster of his setting
i'th stockes: and what thinke you he hath confest?

BERTRAM Nothing of me, ha's a?

2. LORD DUMAINE His confession is taken, and it shall bee
read to his face, if your Lordshippe be in't, as I beleeue
you are, you must haue the patience to heare it.

     Enter Parolles ⌐guarded and¬ muffled, with the
     Interpreter

BERTRAM A plague vpon him, muffeld; he can say nothing
of me.

⌐I. LORD DUMAINE¬ (*aside to Bertram*) Hush, hush.

2060   ⌐2.¬ LORD DUMAINE (*aside to Bertram*) Hoodman comes:
(*aloud*) Porto tartarossa.

INTERPRETER (*to Parrolles*) He calles for the tortures, what
will you say without em.

PARROLLES I will confesse what I know without constraint,
If ye pinch me like a Pasty, I can say no more.

INTERPRETER *Bosko Chimurcho.*

⌐2.¬ LORD DUMAINE *Boblibindo chicurmurco.*

INTERPRETER You are a mercifull Generall: Our Generall
bids you answer to what I shall aske you out of a Note.

2070   PARROLLES And truly, as I hope to liue.

INTERPRETER ⌐*reads*¬ First demand of him, how many horse
the Duke is strong. What say you to that?

PARROLLES Fiue or sixe thousand, but very weake and
vnseruiceable: the troopes are all scattered, and the
Commanders verie poore rogues, vpon my reputation
and credit, and as I hope to liue.

INTERPRETER Shall I set downe your answer so?

PARROLLES Do, Ile take the Sacrament on't, how & which
way you will.

2080   ⌐I. LORD DUMAINE¬ (*aside*) All's one to him.

BERTRAM (*aside*) What a past-sauing slaue is this?

I. LORD DUMAINE (*aside*) Y'are deceiu'd my Lord, this is
Mounsieur *Parrolles* the gallant militarist, that was his
owne phrase that had the whole theoricke of warre in
the knot of his scarfe, and the practise in the chape of
his dagger.

2. LORD DUMAINE (*aside*) I will neuer trust a man againe,
for keeping his sword cleane, nor beleeue he can haue
euerie thing in him, by wearing his apparrell neatly.

2090   INTERPRETER (*to Parrolles*) Well, that's set downe.

PARROLLES Fiue or six thousand horse I sed, I will say
true, or thereabouts set downe, for Ile speake truth.

I. LORD DUMAINE (*aside*) He's very neere the truth in this.

BERTRAM (*aside*) But I con him no thankes for't in the
nature he deliuers it.

PARROLLES Poore rogues, I pray you say.

INTERPRETER Well, that's set downe.

PARROLLES I humbly thanke you sir, a truth's a truth,
the Rogues are maruailous poore.

INTERPRETER ⌐*reads*¬ Demaund of him of what strength   2100
they are a foot. What say you to that?

PARROLLES By my troth sir, if I were to dye this present
hour, I will tell true. Let me see, *Spurio* a hundred &
fiftie, *Sebastian* so many, *Corambus* so many, *Iaques* so
many: *Guilliam, Cosmo, Lodowicke*, and *Gratij*, two
hundred fiftie each: Mine owne Company, *Chitopher,
Vaumond, Bentij*, two hundred fiftie each: so that the
muster file, rotten and sound, vppon my life amounts
not to fifteene thousand pole, halfe of the which, dare
not shake the snow from off their Cassockes, least they   2110
shake themselues to peeces.

BERTRAM (*aside*) What shall be done to him?

I. LORD DUMAINE (*aside*) Nothing, but let him haue
thankes. (*To Interpreter*) Demand of him my condition:
and what credite I haue with the Duke.

INTERPRETER (*to Parrolles*) Well that's set downe: ⌐*reads*¬
you shall demaund of him, whether one Captaine
Dumaine bee i'th Campe, a Frenchman: what his
reputation is with the Duke, what his valour, honestie,
and expertnesse in warres: or whether he thinkes it   2120
were not possible with well-waighing summes of gold
to corrupt him to a reuolt. What say you to this? What
do you know of it?

PARROLLES I beseech you let me answer to the particular
of the intergatories. Demand them singly.

INTERPRETER Do you know this Captaine *Dumaine*?

PARROLLES I know him, a was a Botchers Prentize in
Paris, from whence he was whipt for getting the
Shrieues fool with childe, a dumbe innocent that could
not say him nay.   2130

BERTRAM (*aside to* I. *Lord Dumaine*) Nay, by your leaue
hold your hands, though I know his braines are forfeite
to the next tile that fals.

INTERPRETER Well, is this Captaine in the Duke of
Florences campe?

PARROLLES Vpon my knowledge he is, and lowsie.

I. LORD DUMAINE (*aside*) Nay looke not so vpon me: we
shall heare of your Lordship anon.

INTERPRETER What is his reputation with the Duke?

PARROLLES The Duke knowes him for no other, but a   2140
poore Officer of mine, and writ to mee this other day,
to turne him out a'th band. I thinke I haue his Letter
in my pocket.

INTERPRETER Marry we'll search.

PARROLLES In good sadnesse I do not know, either it is
there, or it is vpon a file with the Dukes other Letters,
in my Tent.

INTERPRETER Heere 'tis, heere's a paper, shall I reade it
to you?

PARROLLES I do not know if it be it or no.   2150

BERTRAM (*aside*) Our Interpreter do's it well.

I. LORD DUMAINE (*aside*) Excellently.

INTERPRETER (*reads the Letter*)
     Dian, the Counts a foole, and full of gold.

PARROLLES That is not the Dukes letter sir: that is an
aduertisement to a proper maide in Florence, one *Diana*,
to take heede of the allurement of one Count *Rossillion*,
a foolish idle boy: but for all that very ruttish. I pray
you sir put it vp againe.

2160 INTERPRETER Nay, Ile reade it first by your fauour.

PARROLLES My meaning in't I protest was very honest in
the behalfe of the maid: for I knew the young Count
to be a dangerous and lasciuious boy, who is a whale
to Virginity, and deuours vp all the fry it finds.

BERTRAM (*aside*) Damnable both-sides rogue.

INTERPRETER (*reads*)

When he sweares oathes, bid him drop gold, and take it:
    After he scores, he neuer payes the score:
Halfe won is match well made, match and well make it,
    He nere payes after-debts, take it before,
2170 And say a souldier (Dian) told thee this:
Men are to mell with, boyes are not to kis.
For count of this, the Counts a Foole I know it,
Who payes before, but not when he does owe it.
            Thine as he vow'd to thee in thine eare,
                    Parolles.

BERTRAM (*aside*) He shall be whipt through the Armie with
this rime in's forehead.

2. LORD DUMAINE (*aside*) This is your deuoted friend sir,
the manifold Linguist, and the army-potent souldier.

2180 BERTRAM (*aside*) I could endure any thing before but a
Cat, and now he's a Cat to me.

INTERPRETER I perceiue sir by yᵉ Generals lookes, wee
shall be faine to hang you.

PARROLLES My life sir in any case: Not that I am afraide
to dye, but that my offences beeing many, I would
repent out the remainder of Nature. Let me liue sir in
a dungeon, i'th stockes, or any where, so I may liue.

INTERPRETER Wee'le see what may bee done, so you
confesse freely: therefore once more to this Captaine
2190 *Dumaine*: you haue answer'd to his reputation with the
Duke, and to his valour. What is his honestie?

PARROLLES He will steale sir an Egge out of a Cloister: for
rapes and rauishments he paralels *Nessus*. Hee professes
not keeping of oaths, in breaking em he is stronger
then *Hercules*. He will lye sir, with such volubilitie, that
you would thinke truth were a foole: drunkennesse is
his best vertue, for he will be swine-drunke, and in his
sleepe he does little harme, saue to his bed-cloathes:
but they about him know his conditions, and lay him
2200 in straw. I haue but little more to say sir of his honesty,
he ha's euerie thing that an honest man should not
haue; what an honest man should haue, he has
nothing.

1. LORD DUMAINE (*aside*) I begin to loue him for this.

BERTRAM (*aside*) For this description of thine honestie? A
pox vpon him, for me he's more and more a Cat.

INTERPRETER What say you to his expertnesse in warre?

PARROLLES Faith sir, ha's led the drumme before the
English Tragedians: to belye him I will not, and more
2210 of his souldiership I know not, except in that Country,
he had the honour to be the Officer at a place there

called *Mile-end*, to instruct for the doubling of files. I
would doe the man what honour I can, but of this I
am not certaine.

1. LORD DUMAINE (*aside*) He hath out-villain'd villanie so
farre, that the raritie redeemes him.

BERTRAM (*aside*) A pox on him, he's a Cat still.

INTERPRETER His qualities being at this poore price, I neede
not to aske you, if Gold will corrupt him to reuolt.

PARROLLES Sir, for a Cardecue he will sell the fee-simple   2220
of his saluation, the inheritance of it, and cut th'intaile
from all remainders, and a perpetuall succession for it
perpetually.

INTERPRETER What's his Brother, the other Captaine
Dumain?

2. LORD DUMAINE (*aside*) Why do's he aske him of me?

INTERPRETER What's he?

PARROLLES E'ne a Crow a'th same nest: not altogether so
great as the first in goodnesse, but greater a great deale
in euill. He excels his Brother for a coward, yet his   2230
Brother is reputed one of the best that is. In a retreate
hee out-runnes any Lackey; marrie in comming on,
hee ha's the Crampe.

INTERPRETER If your life be saued, will you vndertake to
betray the Florentine.

PARROLLES I, and the Captaine of his horse, Count
Rossillion.

INTERPRETER Ile whisper with the Generall, and knowe
his pleasure.

PARROLLES Ile no more drumming, a plague of all   2240
drummes, onely to seeme to deserue well, and to beguile
the supposition of that lasciuious yong boy the Count,
haue I run into this danger: yet who would haue
suspected an ambush where I was taken?

INTERPRETER There is no remedy sir, but you must dye:
the Generall sayes, you that haue so traitorously
discouerd the secrets of your army, and made such
pestifferous reports of men very nobly held, can serue
the world for no honest vse: therefore you must dye.
Come headesman, off with his head.   2250

PARROLLES O Lord sir let me liue, or let me see my death.

INTERPRETER That shall you, and take your leaue of all
your friends:

            He vnmuffles Parrolles

So, looke about you, know you any heere?

BERTRAM Good morrow noble Captaine.

2. LORD DUMAINE God blesse you Captaine *Parolles*.

1. LORD DUMAINE God saue you noble Captaine.

2. LORD DUMAINE Captain, what greeting will you to my
Lord *Lafew*? I am for *France*.

1. LORD DUMAINE Good Captaine will you giue me a Copy   2260
of the sonnet you writ to *Diana* in behalfe of the Count
Rossillion, and I were not a verie Coward, I'de compell
it of you, but far you well.

            Exeunt all but Parrolles and Interpreter

INTERPRETER You are vndone Captaine all but your scarfe,
that has a knot on't yet.

PARROLLES Who cannot be crush'd with a plot?

INTERPRETER If you could finde out a Countrie where but

women were that had receiued so much shame, you
might begin an impudent Nation. Fare yee well sir, I
2270 am for *France* too, we shall speake of you there.   *Exit*

PARROLLES
Yet am I thankfull: if my heart were great
'Twould burst at this: Captaine Ile be no more,
But I will eate, and drinke, and sleepe as soft
As Captaine shall. Simply the thing I am
Shall make me liue: who knowes himselfe a braggart
Let him feare this; for it will come to passe,
That euery braggart shall be found an Asse.
Rust sword, coole blushes, and *Parrolles* liue
Safest in shame: being fool'd, by fool'rie thriue;
2280 There's place and meanes for euery man aliue.
Ile after them.   *Exit*

Sc. 19
(4.4)   *Enter Hellen, Widdow, and Diana*
       HELLEN
That you may well perceiue I haue not wrong'd you,
One of the greatest in the Christian world
Shall be my suretie: for whose throne 'tis needfull
Ere I can perfect mine intents, to kneele.
Time was, I did him a desired office
Deere almost as his life, which gratitude
Through flintie Tartars bosome would peepe forth,
And answer thankes. I duly am inform'd,
2290 His grace is at *Marcellæ*, to which place
We haue conuenient conuoy: you must know
I am supposed dead, the Army breaking,
My husband hies him home, where heauen ayding,
And by the leaue of my good Lord the King,
Wee'l be before our welcome.

WIDDOW   Gentle Madam,
You neuer had a seruant to whose trust
Your busines was more welcome.

HELLEN   Nor you Mistris
Euer a friend, whose thoughts more truly labour
To recompence your loue: Doubt not but heauen
2300 Hath brought me vp to be your daughters dower,
As it hath fated her to be my motiue
And helper to a husband. But O strange men,
That can such sweet vse make of what they hate,
When sawcie trusting of the cosin'd thoughts
Defiles the pitchy night, so lust doth play
With what it loathes, for that which is away,
But more of this heereafter: you *Diana*,
Vnder my poore instructions yet must suffer
Something in my behalfe.

DIANA   Let death and honestie
2310 Go with your impositions, I am yours
Vpon your will to suffer.

HELLEN   Yet I pray you:
But with yᵗ word the time will bring on summer,
When Briars shall haue leaues as well as thornes,
And be as sweet as sharpe: we must away,
Our Wagon is prepar'd, and time reuiues vs,
All's well that ends well, still the fines the Crowne;
What ere the course, the end is the renowne.   *Exeunt*

Enter Clowne, old Lady Countesse, and Lafew   Sc. 20
(4.5)
LAFEW No, no, no, your sonne was misled with a snipt
taffata fellow there, whose villanous saffron wold haue
made all the vnbak'd and dowy youth of a nation in   2320
his colour: else your daughter-in-law had beene aliue
at this houre, and your sonne heere at home, more
aduanc'd by the King, then by that red-tail'd humble
Bee I speak of.

COUNTESSE I would a had not knowne him, it was the
death of the most vertuous gentlewoman, that euer
Nature had praise for creating. If she had pertaken of
my flesh and cost mee the deerest groanes of a mother,
I could not haue owed her a more rooted loue.

LAFEW Twas a good Lady, 'twas a good Lady. Wee may   2330
picke a thousand sallets ere wee light on such another
hearbe.

CLOWNE Indeed sir she was the sweete Margerom of the
sallet, or rather the hearbe of grace.

LAFEW They are not grasse you knaue, they are nose-
hearbes.

CLOWNE I am no great *Nabuchadnezar* sir, I haue not much
skill in grace.

LAFEW Whether doest thou professe thy selfe, a knaue or
a foole?   2340

CLOWNE A foole sir at a womans seruice, and a knaue at
a mans.

LAFEW Your distinction.

CLOWNE I would cousen the man of his wife, and do his
seruice.

LAFEW So you were a knaue at his seruice indeed.

CLOWNE And I would giue his wife my bauble sir to doe
her seruice.

LAFEW I will subscribe for thee, thou art both knaue and
foole.   2350

CLOWNE At your seruice.

LAFEW No, no, no.

CLOWNE Why sir, if I cannot serue you, I can serue as
great a prince as you are.

LAFEW Whose that, a Frenchman?

CLOWNE Faith sir a has an English name, but his fisnamie
is more hotter in France then there.

LAFEW What prince is that?

CLOWNE The blacke prince sir, alias the prince of
darkenesse, alias the diuell.   2360

LAFEW Hold thee there's my purse, I giue thee not this
to suggest thee from thy master thou talk'st off, serue
him still.

CLOWNE I am a woodland fellow sir, that alwaies loued a
great fire, and the master I speak of euer keeps a good
fire, but since he is the Prince of the world, let the
Nobilitie remaine in's Court. I am for the house with
the narrow gate, which I take to be too little for pompe
to enter: some that humble themselues may, but the
manie will be too chill and tender, and theyle bee for   2370
the flowrie way that leads to the broad gate, and the
great fire.

LAFEW Go thy waies, I begin to bee a wearie of thee, and
I tell thee so before, because I would not fall out with

thee. Go thy wayes, let my horses be wel look'd too,
without any trickes.

CLOWNE If I put any trickes vpon em sir, they shall bee
Iades trickes, which are their owne right by the law of
Nature.   *exit*

2380 LAFEW A shrewd knaue and an vnhappie.

COUNTESSE So a is. My Lord that's gone made himselfe
much sport out of him, by his authoritie hee remaines
heere, which he thinkes is a pattent for his sawcinesse,
and indeede he has no pace, but runnes where he will.

LAFEW I like him well, 'tis not amisse: and I was about
to tell you, since I heard of the good Ladies death, and
that my Lord your sonne was vpon his returne home,
I moued the King my master to speake in the behalfe
of my daughter, which in the minoritie of them both,
2390 his Maiestie out of a selfe-gracious remembrance did
first propose, his Highnesse hath promis'd me to doe
it, and to stoppe vp the displeasure he hath conceiued
against your sonne, there is no fitter matter. How do's
your Ladyship like it?

COUNTESSE With verie much content my Lord, and I wish
it happily effected.

LAFEW His Highnesse comes post from *Marcellus*, of as
able bodie as when he number'd thirty, a will be heere
to morrow, or I am deceiu'd by him that in such
2400 intelligence hath seldome fail'd.

COUNTESSE It reioyces me, that I hope I shall see him ere
I die. I haue letters that my sonne will be heere to
night: I shall beseech your Lordship to remaine with
mee, till they meete together.

LAFEW Madam, I was thinking with what manners I
might safely be admitted.

COUNTESSE You neede but pleade your honourable
priuiledge.

LAFEW Ladie, of that I haue made a bold charter, but I
2410 thanke my God, it holds yet.

          Enter Clowne

CLOWNE O Madam, yonders my Lord your sonne with a
patch of veluet on's face, whether there bee a scar
vnder't or no, the Veluet knowes, but 'tis a goodly
patch of Veluet, his left cheeke is a cheeke of two pile
and a halfe, but his right cheeke is worne bare.

LAFEW A scarre nobly got, or a noble scarre, is a good
liu'rie of honor, so belike is that.

CLOWNE But it is your carbinado'd face.

LAFEW (*to Countesse*) Let vs go see your sonne I pray you,
2420 I long to talke with the yong noble souldier.

CLOWNE 'Faith there's a dozen of em, with delicate fine
hats, and most courteous feathers, which bow the head,
and nod at euerie man.   *Exeunt*

Sc. 21   *Enter Hellen, Widdow, and Diana, with two*
(5.1)   *Attendants*

HELLEN
But this exceeding posting day and night,
Must wear your spirits low, we cannot helpe it:
But since you haue made the daies and nights as one,
To weare your gentle limbes in my affayres,

Be bold you do so grow in my requitall,
As nothing can vnroote you.
          Enter a gentle Astringer
                              In happie time,
This man may helpe me to his Maiesties eare,   2430
If he would spend his power. God saue you sir.

GENTLEMAN And you.

HELLEN
Sir, I haue seene you in the Court of France.

GENTLEMAN I haue beene sometimes there.

HELLEN
I do presume sir, that you are not falne
From the report that goes vpon your goodnesse,
And therefore goaded with most sharpe occasions,
Which lay nice manners by, I put you to
The vse of your owne vertues, for the which
I shall continue thankefull.

GENTLEMAN   What's your will?   2440

HELLEN That it will please you
To giue this poore petition to the King,
And ayde me with that store of power you haue
To come into his presence.

GENTLEMAN The Kings not heere.

HELLEN Not heere sir?

GENTLEMAN   Not indeed,
He hence remou'd last night, and with more hast
Then is his vse.

WIDDOW Lord how we loose our paines.   2450

HELLEN All's well that ends well yet,
Though time seeme so aduerse, and meanes vnfit:
I do beseech you, whither is he gone?

GENTLEMAN
Marrie as I take it to *Rossillion*,
Whither I am going.

HELLEN   I do beseech you sir,
Since you are like to see the King before me,
Commend the paper to his gracious hand,
Which I presume shall render you no blame,
But rather make you thanke your paines for it,
I will come after you with what good speede   2460
Our meanes will make vs meanes.

GENTLEMAN (*taking the paper*)   This Ile do for you.

HELLEN
And you shall finde your selfe to be well thankt
What e're falles more. We must to horse againe,
Go, go, prouide.   *Exeunt seuerally*

          Enter Clowne and Parrolles, with a letter   Sc. 22

PARROLLES Good Mr *Lauatch* giue my Lord *Lafew* this letter,   (5.2)
I haue ere now sir beene better knowne to you, when
I haue held familiaritie with fresher cloathes: but I am
now sir muddied in fortunes mood, and smell somewhat
strong of her strong displeasure.

CLOWNE Truely, Fortunes displeasure is but sluttish if it   2470
smell so strongly as thou speak'st of: I will henceforth
eate no Fish of Fortunes butt'ring. Prethee alow the
winde.

PARROLLES Nay you neede not to stop your nose sir: I
spake but by a Metaphor.

CLOWNE Indeed sir, if your Metaphor stinke, I will stop
my nose, or against any mans Metaphor. Prethe get
thee further.

PARROLLES Pray you sir deliuer me this paper.

2480 CLOWNE Foh, prethee stand away: a paper from fortunes
close-stoole, to giue to a Nobleman. Looke heere he
comes himselfe.

      Enter Lafew

Heere is a purre of Fortunes sir, or of Fortunes Cat, but
not a Muscat, that ha's falne into the vncleane fish-
pond of her displeasure, and as he sayes is muddied
withall. Pray you sir, vse the Carpe as you may, for he
lookes like a poore decayed, ingenious, foolish, rascally
knaue. I doe pittie his distresse in my similes of comfort,
and leaue him to your Lordship.   *Exit*

2490 PARROLLES My Lord I am a man whom fortune hath
cruelly scratch'd.

LAFEW And what would you haue me to doe? 'Tis too
late to paire her nailes now. Wherein haue you played
the knaue with fortune that she should scratch you,
who of her selfe is a good Lady, and would not haue
knaues thriue long vnder her? There's a Cardecue for
you: Let the Iustices make you and fortune friends; I
am for other businesse.

PARROLLES I beseech your honour to heare mee one single
2500 word,

LAFEW You begge a single peny more: Come you shall
ha't, saue your word.

PARROLLES My name my good Lord is *Parrolles*.

LAFEW You begge more then one word then. Cox my
passion, giue me your hand: How does your drumme?

PARROLLES O my good Lord, you were the first that found
mee.

LAFEW Was I insooth? And I was the first that lost thee.

PARROLLES It lies in you my Lord to bring me in some
2510 grace for you did bring me out.

LAFEW Out vpon thee knaue, doest thou put vpon mee
at once both the office of God and the diuel: one brings
thee in grace, and the other brings thee out.

      Trumpets sound

The Kings comming, I know by his Trumpets. Sirrah,
inquire further after me, I had talke of you last night,
though you are a foole and a knaue, you shall eate,
go too, follow.

PARROLLES I praise God for you.   ⌈*Exeunt*⌉

Sc. 23   *Flourish. Enter King, old Lady Countesse, Lafew,*
(5.3)   *with attendants*

KING
      We lost a Iewell of her, and our esteeme
2520 Was made much poorer by it: but your sonne,
      As mad in folly, lack'd the sence to know
      Her estimation home.

COUNTESSE   'Tis past my Liege,
      And I beseech your Maiestie to make it
      Naturall rebellion, done i'th blade of youth,

When oyle and fire, too strong for reasons force,
Ore-beares it, and burnes on.

KING   My honour'd Lady,
      I haue forgiuen and forgotten all,
      Though my reuenges were high bent vpon him,
      And watch'd the time to shoote.

LAFEW   This I must say,
      But first I begge my pardon: the yong Lord   2530
      Did to his Maiesty, his Mother, and his Ladie,
      Offence of mighty note; but to himselfe
      The greatest wrong of all. He lost a wife,
      Whose beauty did astonish the suruey
      Of richest eies: whose words all eares tooke captiue,
      Whose deere perfection, hearts that scorn'd to serue,
      Humbly call'd Mistris.

KING   Praising what is lost,
      Makes the remembrance deere. Well, call him hither,
      We are reconcil'd, and the first view shall kill
      All repetition: Let him not aske our pardon,   2540
      The nature of his great offence is dead,
      And deeper then obliuion, we do burie
      Th'incensing reliques of it. Let him approach
      A stranger, no offender; and informe him
      So 'tis our will he should.

ATTENDANT   I shall my Liege.   *Exit*
KING (*to Lafew*)
      What sayes he to your daughter, haue you spoke?

LAFEW
      All that he is, hath reference to your Highnes.

KING
      Then shall we haue a match. I haue letters sent me,
      That sets him high in fame.

      Enter Count Bertram ⌈*with a patch of Veluet on his
      left cheeke, and kneeles*⌉

LAFEW He lookes well on't.   2550
KING (*to Bertram*) I am not a day of season,
      For thou maist see a sun-shine, and a haile
      In me at once: But to the brightest beames
      Distracted clouds giue way, so stand thou forth,
      The time is faire againe.

BERTRAM ⌈*rising*⌉   My high repented blames
      Deere Soueraigne pardon to me.

KING   All is whole,
      Not one word more of the consumed time,
      Let's take the instant by the forward top:
      For we are old, and on our quick'st decrees
      Th'inaudible, and noiselesse foot of time   2560
      Steales, ere we can effect them. You remember
      The daughter of this Lord?

BERTRAM
      Admiringly my Liege, at first
      I stucke my choice vpon her, ere my heart
      Durst make too bold a herauld of my tongue:
      Where the impression of mine eye enfixing,
      Contempt his scornfull Perspectiue did lend me,
      Which warpt the line, of euerie other fauour,
      Stain'd a faire colour, or exprest it stolne,
      Extended or contracted all proportions   2570

To a most hideous obiect. Thence it came,
That she whom all men prais'd, and whom my selfe,
Since I haue lost, haue lou'd; was in mine eye
The dust that did offend it.

KING   Well excus'd:
That thou didst loue her, strikes some scores away
From the great compt: but loue that comes too late,
Like a remorsefull pardon slowly carried,
To the grace sender turnes a sowre offence,
Crying, that's good that's gone: Our rash faults,
2580 Make triuiall price of serious things we haue,
Not knowing them, vntill we know their graue.
Oft our displeasures to our selues vniust,
Destroy our friends, and after weepe their dust:
Our owne loue waking, cries to see what's done,
While shamefull hate sleepes out the afternoone.
Be this sweet *Helens* knell, and now forget her.
Send forth your amorous token for faire *Maudlin*,
The maine consents are had, and heere wee'l stay
To see our widdowers second marriage day:

⌜COUNTESSE⌝
2590 Which better then the first, O deere heauen blesse,
Or, ere they meete, in me, O Nature cesse.

LAFEW (*to Bertram*)
Come on my sonne, in whom my houses name
Must be digested: giue a fauour from you
To sparkle in the spirits of my daughter,
That she may quickly come.
          Bertram giues Lafew a Ring
                    By my old beard,
And eu'rie haire that's on't, *Helen* that's dead
Was a sweet creature: such a ring as this,
The last that ere I tooke her leaue at Court,
I saw vpon her finger.

BERTRAM   Hers it was not.

KING
2600 Now pray you let me see it. For mine eye,
While I was speaking, oft was fasten'd too't:
          Lafew giues him the Ring
This Ring was mine, and when I gaue it *Hellen*,
I bad her if her fortunes euer stoode
Necessitied to helpe, that by this token
I would releeue her. Had you that craft to reaue her
Of what should stead her most?

BERTRAM   My gracious Soueraigne,
How ere it pleases you to take it so,
The ring was neuer hers.

COUNTESSE   Sonne, on my life
I haue seene her weare it, and she reckon'd it
At her liues rate.

2610 LAFEW   I am sure I saw her weare it.

BERTRAM
You are deceiu'd my Lord, she neuer saw it:
In Florence was it from a casement throwne mee,
Wrap'd in a paper, which contain'd the name
Of her that threw it: Noble she was, and thought
I stood ingag'd, but when I had subscrib'd
To mine owne fortune, and inform'd her fully,

I could not answer in that course of Honour
As she had made the ouerture, she ceast
In heauie satisfaction, and would neuer
Receiue the Ring againe.

KING   *Plutus* himselfe,   2620
That knowes the tinct and multiplying med'cine,
Hath not in natures mysterie more science,
Then I haue in this Ring. 'Twas mine, 'twas *Helens*,
Who euer gaue it you: then if you know
That you are well acquainted with your selfe,
Confesse 'twas hers, and by what rough enforcement
You got it from her. She call'd the Saints to suretie,
That she would neuer put it from her finger,
Vnlesse she gaue it to your selfe in bed,
Where you haue neuer come: or sent it vs   2630
Vpon her great disaster.

BERTRAM   She neuer saw it.

KING
Thou speak'st it falsely, as I loue mine Honor,
And mak'st coniecturall feares to come into me,
Which I would faine shut out; if it should proue
That thou art so inhumane, 'twill not proue so:
And yet I know not, thou didst hate her deadly,
And she is dead, which nothing but to close
Her eyes my selfe, could win me to beleeue,
More then to see this Ring. Take him away,
My fore-past proofes, how ere the matter fall   2640
Shall taxe my feares of little vanitie,
Hauing vainly fear'd too little. Away with him,
Wee'l sift this matter further.

BERTRAM   If you shall proue
This Ring was euer hers, you shall as easie
Proue that I husbanded her bed in Florence,
Where yet she neuer was.   *Exit, guarded*
          Enter the Gentleman Astringer with a paper

KING I am wrap'd in dismall thinkings.

GENTLEMAN Gracious Soueraigne.
Whether I haue beene too blame or no, I know not,
Here's a petition from a Florentine,   2650
Who hath for foure or fiue remoues come short,
To tender it her selfe. I vndertooke it,
Vanquish'd thereto by the faire grace and speech
Of the poore suppliant, who by this I know
Is heere attending: her businesse lookes in her
With an importing visage, and she told me
In a sweet verball breefe, it did concerne
Your Highnesse with her selfe.

⌜KING⌝ (*reads a Letter*) *Vpon his many protestations to marrie
mee when his wife was dead, I blush to say it, he wonne*   2660
*me. Now is the Count Rossillion a Widdower, his vowes
are forfeited to mee, and my honors payed to him. Hee
stole from Florence, taking no leaue, and I follow him to
his Countrey for Iustice: Grant it me, O King, in you it
best lies, otherwise a seducer flourishes, and a poore Maid
is vndone.*

          Diana Capilet.

LAFEW I will buy me a sonne in Law in a faire, and toule
for this. Ile none of him.

995

KING

2670   The heauens haue thought well on thee *Lafew*,
To bring forth this discou'rie; seeke these sutors:
Go speedily, and bring againe the Count.

Exit one or more

I am a-feard the life of *Hellen* (Ladie)
Was fowly snatcht.

⌈*Enter Bertram guarded*⌉

COUNTESSE   Now iustice on the doers.

KING (*to Bertram*)

I wonder sir, since wiues are monsters to you,
And that you flye them as you sweare them Lordship,
Yet you desire to marry.

Enter Widdow, and Diana

What woman's that?

DIANA

I am my Lord a wretched Florentine,
Deriued from the ancient Capilet,
2680   My suite as I do vnderstand you know,
And therefore know how farre I may be pittied.

WIDDOW (*to the King*)

I am her Mother sir, whose age and honour
Both suffer vnder this complaint we bring,
And both shall cease, without your remedie.

KING

Come hether Count, do you know these Women?

BERTRAM

My Lord, I neither can nor will denie,
But that I know them, do they charge me further?

DIANA

Why do you looke so strange vpon your wife?

BERTRAM (*to the King*)

She's none of mine my Lord.

DIANA   If you shall marrie
2690   You giue away this hand, and that is mine,
You giue away heauens vowes, and those are mine:
You giue away my selfe, which is knowne mine:
For I by vow am so embodied yours,
That she which marries you, must marrie me,
Either both or none.

LAFEW (*to Bertram*) Your reputation comes too short for
my daughter, you are no husband for her.

BERTRAM (*to the King*)

My Lord, this is a fond and desp'rate creature,
Whom sometime I haue laugh'd with: Let your
highnes
2700   Lay a more noble thought vpon mine honour,
Then for to thinke that I would sinke it heere.

KING

Sir for my thoughts, you haue them il to friend,
Till your deeds gaine them: fairer proue your honor,
Then in my thought it lies.

DIANA   Good my Lord,
Aske him vpon his oath, if hee do's thinke
He had not my virginity.

KING What saist thou to her?

BERTRAM She's impudent my Lord,
And was a common gamester to the Campe.

DIANA (*to the King*)

He do's me wrong my Lord: If I were so,   2710
He might haue bought me at a common price.
Do not beleeue him. O behold this Ring,
Whose high respect and rich validitie
Did lacke a Paralell: yet for all that
He gaue it to a Commoner a'th Campe
If I be one.

COUNTESSE   He blushes, and 'tis hit:
Of sixe preceding Ancestors, that Iemme;
Confer'd by testament to'th sequent issue
Hath it beene owed and worne. This is his wife,
That Ring's a thousand proofes.

KING (*to Diana*)   Me thought you saide   2720
You saw one heere in Court could witnesse it.

DIANA

I did my Lord, but loath am to produce
So bad an instrument, his names *Parrolles*.

LAFEW

I saw the man to day, if man he bee.

KING

Finde him, and bring him hether.   *Exit one*

BERTRAM   What of him:
He's quoted for a most perfidious slaue
With all the spots a'th world, taxt and debosh'd,
Whose nature sickens, but to speake a truth:
Am I, or that or this for what he'l vtter,
That will speake any thing.

KING   She hath that Ring of yours.   2730

BERTRAM

I thinke she has; certaine it is I lyk'd her,
And boorded her i'th wanton way of youth:
She knew her distance, and did angle for mee,
Madding my eagernesse with her restraint,
As all impediments in fancies course
Are motiues of more fancie, and in fine,
Her infinte conning with her moderne grace,
Subdu'd me to her rate, she got the Ring,
And I had that which my inferiour might
At Market price haue bought.

DIANA   I must be patient: 2740
You that haue turn'd off a first so noble wife,
May iustly dyet me. I pray you yet,
(Since you lacke vertue, I will loose a husband)
Send for your Ring, I will returne it home,
And giue me mine againe.

BERTRAM I haue it not.

KING (*to Diana*) What Ring was yours I pray you?

DIANA

Sir much like the same vpon your finger.

KING

Know you this Ring, this Ring was his of late.

DIANA

And this was it I gaue him being a bed.   2750

KING

The story then goes false, you threw it him
Out of a Casement.

DIANA   I haue spoke the truth.

Enter Parolles

BERTRAM (*to the King*)

  My Lord, I do confesse the ring was hers.

KING

  You boggle shrewdly, euery feather starts you:
  (*To Diana*) Is this the man you speake of?

DIANA   I, my Lord.

KING (*to Parrolles*)

  Tell me sirrah, but tell me true I charge you,
  Not fearing the displeasure of your master:
  Which on your iust proceeding, Ile keepe off,
  By him and by this woman heere, what know you?

2760 PARROLLES So please your Maiesty, my master hath bin
  an honourable Gentleman. Trickes hee hath had in
  him, which Gentlemen haue.

KING

  Come, come, to'th'purpose: Did hee loue this woman?

PARROLLES Faith sir he did loue her, but how.

KING How I pray you?

PARROLLES He did loue her sir, as a Gent. loues a Woman.

KING How is that?

PARROLLES He lou'd her sir, and lou'd her not.

KING As thou art a knaue and no knaue, what an
2770 equiuocall Companion is this?

PARROLLES I am a poore man, and at your Maiesties
  command.

LAFEW (*to the King*) Hee's a good drumme my Lord, but
  a naughtie Orator.

DIANA (*to Paroles*) Do you know he promist me marriage?

PARROLLES Faith I know more then Ile speake.

KING But wilt thou not speake all thou know'st?

PARROLLES Yes so please your Maiesty: I did goe betweene
  them as I said, but more then that he loued her, for
2780 indeede he was madde for her, and talkt of Sathan,
  and of Limbo, and of Furies, and I know not what: yet
  I was in that credit with them at that time, that I
  knewe of their going to bed, and of other motions, as
  promising her marriage, and things which would deriue
  mee ill will to speake of, therefore I will not speake
  what I know.

KING Thou hast spoken all alreadie, vnlesse thou canst
  say they are maried, but thou art too fine in thy
  euidence, therefore stand aside.
  This Ring you say was yours.

2790 DIANA   I my good Lord.

KING

  Where did you buy it? Or who gaue it you?

DIANA

  It was not giuen me, nor I did not buy it.

KING

  Who lent it you?

DIANA   It was not lent me neither.

KING

  Where did you finde it then?

DIANA   I found it not.

KING

  If it were yours by none of all these wayes,
  How could you giue it him?

DIANA   I neuer gaue it him.

LAFEW (*to the King*) This womans an easie gloue my Lord,
  she goes off and on at pleasure.

KING (*to Diana*)

  This Ring was mine, I gaue it his first wife.

DIANA

  It might be yours or hers for ought I know.   2800

KING (*to attendants*)

  Take her away, I do not like her now,
  To prison with her: and away with him.
  Vnlesse thou telst me where thou hadst this Ring,
  Thou diest within this houre.

DIANA   Ile neuer tell you.

KING (*to attendants*)

   Take her away.

DIANA   Ile put in baile my liedge.

KING

  I thinke thee now some common Customer.

DIANA

  By Ioue if euer I knew man 'twas you.

KING

  Wherefore hast thou accusde him al this while.

DIANA

  Because he's guiltie, and he is not guilty:
  He knowes I am no Maid, and hee'l sweare too't: 2810
  Ile sweare I am a Maid, and he knowes not.
  Great King I am no strumpet, by my life,
  I am either Maid, or else this old mans wife.

KING (*to attendants*)

  She does abuse our eares, to prison with her.

DIANA

  Good mother fetch my bayle.   *Exit Widdow*
                          Stay Royall sir,
  The Ieweller that owes the Ring is sent for,
  And he shall surety me. But for this Lord,
  Who hath abus'd me as he knowes himselfe,
  Though yet he neuer harm'd me, heere I quit him.
  He knowes himselfe my bed he hath defil'd,   2820
  And at that time he got his wife with childe:
  Dead though she be, she feeles her yong one kicke:
  So there's my riddle, one that's dead is quicke,
  And now behold the meaning.
              Enter Hellen and Widdow

KING   Is there no exorcist
  Beguiles the truer Office of mine eyes?
  Is't reall that I see?

HELLEN   No my good Lord,
  'Tis but the shadow of a wife you see,
  The name, and not the thing.

BERTRAM   Both, both, O pardon.

HELLEN

  Oh my good Lord, when I was like this Maid,
  I found you wondrous kinde, there is your Ring,   2830
  And looke you, heeres your letter: this it sayes,
  When from my finger you can get this Ring,
  And are by me with childe, &c. This is done,
  Will you be mine now you are doubly wonne?

BERTRAM (*to the King*)

  If she my Liege can make me know this clearly,
  Ile loue her dearely, euer, euer dearely.

HELLEN

If it appeare not plaine, and proue vntrue,
Deadly diuorce step betweene me and you.
O my deere mother do I see you liuing?

LAFEW

2840 Mine eyes smell Onions, I shall weepe anon:
(*To Parrolles*) Good Tom Drumme lend me a
handkercher. So I thanke thee, waite on me home, Ile
make sport with thee: Let thy curtsies alone, they are
scuruy ones.

KING (*to Hellen*)

Let vs from point to point this storie know,
To make the euen truth in pleasure flow:
(*To Diana*) If thou beest yet a fresh vncropped flower,
Choose thou thy husband, and Ile pay thy dower.

For I can guesse, that by thy honest ayde,
Thou keptst a wife her selfe, thy selfe a Maide.   2850
Of that and all the progresse more and lesse,
Resoluedly more leasure shall expresse:
All yet seemes well, and if it end so meete,
The bitter past, more welcome is the sweet.
    Flourish

Epilogue

The Kings a Begger, now the Play is done,
All is well ended, if this suite be wonne,
That you expresse Content: which we will pay,
With strift to please you, day exceeding day:
Ours be your patience then, and yours our parts,
Your gentle hands lend vs, and take our hearts.   2860
                                    Exeunt omnes

FINIS

TIMON OF ATHENS

BY WILLIAM SHAKESPEARE AND THOMAS MIDDLETON

WE know no more of *Timon of Athens* than we can deduce from the text printed in the 1623 Folio. Some episodes, such as the emblematic opening dialogue featuring a Poet and a Painter, are elegantly finished, but the play has more unpolished dialogue and loose ends of plot than usual: for example, the episode (Sc. 10) in which Alcibiades pleads for a soldier's life is only tenuously related to the main structure; and the final stretch of action seems imperfectly worked out. Various theories of collaboration and revision have been advanced to explain the play's peculiarities. During the 1970s and 1980s strong linguistic and other evidence has been adduced in support of the belief that it is a product of collaboration between Shakespeare and Thomas Middleton, a dramatist born in 1580 and educated at Queen's College, Oxford, who was writing for the stage by 1602 and was to develop into a great playwright. The major passages for which Middleton seems to have taken prime responsibility are Scenes 2, 3, 5 to 10, parts of Scene 11, and the closing episode (1888-1965) of Scene 14. The theory of collaboration explains some features of the text—Middleton's verse, for example, was less regular than Shakespeare's. There is no record of early performance; the play is conjecturally assigned to 1604.

The story of Timon was well known and had been told in an anonymous play which seems to have been acted at one of the Inns of Court in 1602 or 1603; Middleton has even been suggested as its author. The classical sources of Timon's story are a brief, anecdotal passage in Plutarch's Life of Mark Antony, and a Greek dialogue by Lucian, who wrote during the second century AD; the former was certainly known to the authors of *Timon of Athens*; the latter influences them directly or indirectly. Plutarch records two epitaphs, one written by Timon himself, which recur, conflated as one epitaph, almost word for word in the play. In Lucian, as in the play, Timon is a misanthrope because his friends flattered and sponged on him in prosperity but abandoned him in poverty. The first part of the play dramatizes this process; in the second part, as in Lucian, Timon finds gold and suddenly becomes attractive again to his old friends.

Timon of Athens is an exceptionally schematic play falling into two sharply contrasting parts, the second a kind of mirror image of the first. Many of the characters are presented two-dimensionally, as if the dramatists were more concerned with the play's pattern of ideas than with psychological realism. The overall tone is harsh and bitter; there are passages of magnificent invective along with some brilliant satire, but there is also tenderness in the portrayal of Timon's servants, especially his 'one honest man', Flauius. In the play's comparatively rare performances some adaptation has usually been found necessary; but the exceptionally long role of Timon offers great opportunities to an actor who can convey his vulnerability as well as his virulence, especially in the strange music of the closing scenes which suggests in him a vision beyond the ordinary.

The Folio text was apparently printed from the foul papers of the two collaborators, which had not been tidied up to remove loose ends or inconsistencies between them.

THE NAMES OF THE ACTORS

TIMON of Athens

A POET
A PAINTER
A IEWELLER
A MERCHANT
A Mercer
LUCILIUS, one of Timons Seruants
An OLD ATHENIAN

LORDS and SENATORS of Athens
VENTIDIUS, 'one of Tymons false Friends'
ALCIBIADES, 'an Athenian Captaine'
APEMANTUS, 'a Churlish Philosopher'

One dressed as CUPID in the Maske
LADIES dressed as Amazons in the Maske

Flauius, Timons STEWARD
FLAMINIUS, 'one of Tymons Seruants'
SERUILIUS, 'another'
Other SERUANTS of Timon

A FOOLE
A PAGE

CAPHIS
ISIDORES SERUANT   } 'Seuerall Seruants to Vsurers'
Two of VARROES SERUANTS

LUCULLUS }
LUCIUS   } 'two Flattering Lords'
Lucullus SERUANT
LUCIUS SERUANT
SEMPRONIUS, 'another flattering Lord'
Three STRANGERS, one call'd Hostilius

TITUS SERUANT   }
HORTENSIUS SERUANT   } 'Seuerall Seruants to Vsurers'
PHILOTUS SERUANT   }

PHRYNIA   }
           } Whores with Alcibiades
TIMANDRA   }
The Bandetti, THEEUES
SOULDIER of Alcibiades armie

Messengers, Attendants, Souldiers

The Life of Timon of Athens

*Enter Poet ⌈at one doore⌉, Painter carrying a
Picture ⌈at another doore⌉, ⌈followed by⌉ Ieweller,
Merchant, and Mercer, at seuerall doores*

POET
Good day Sir.

PAINTER   I am glad y'are well.

POET
I haue not seene you long, how goes the World?

PAINTER
It weares sir, as it growes.

POET   I that's well knowne:
But what particular Rarity? What strange,
Which manifold record not matches: see
Magicke of Bounty, all these spirits thy power
Hath coniur'd to attend.

⌈*Merchant and Ieweller meete. Mercer passes ouer
the Stage, and exits*⌉
                    I know the Merchant.

PAINTER
I know them both: th'others a Ieweller.

MERCHANT (*to Ieweller*)
O 'tis a worthy Lord.

IEWELLER   Nay that's most fixt.

MERCHANT
10 A most incomparable man, breath'd as it were,
To an vntyreable and continuate goodnesse:
He passes.

IEWELLER (*shewing a Iewell*) I haue a Iewell heere.

MERCHANT
O pray let's see't. For the Lord *Timon*, sir?

IEWELLER
If he will touch the estimate. But for that—

POET (*to himselfe*)
When we for recompence haue prais'd the vild,
It staines the glory in that happy Verse,
Which aptly sings the good.

MERCHANT (*to Ieweller*)   'Tis a good forme.

IEWELLER
And rich: heere is a Water looke ye.

PAINTER (*to Poet*)
You are rapt sir, in some worke, some Dedication
To the great Lord.

20 POET   A thing slipt idlely from me.
Our Poesie is as a Goume, which ouses
From whence 'tis nourisht: the fire i'th'Flint
Shewes not, till it be strooke: our gentle flame
Prouokes it selfe, and like the currant flyes
Each bound it chafes. What haue you there?

PAINTER
A Picture sir: when comes your Booke forth?

POET
Vpon the heeles of my presentment sir.
Let's see your peece.

PAINTER (*shewing the Picture*) 'Tis a good Peece.

POET
So 'tis, this comes off well, and excellent.

PAINTER
Indifferent.

POET   Admirable: How this grace   30
Speakes his owne standing: what a mentall power
This eye shootes forth? How bigge imagination
Moues in this Lip, to th'dumbnesse of the gesture,
One might interpret.

PAINTER
It is a pretty mocking of the life:
Heere is a touch: Is't good?

POET   I will say of it,
It Tutors Nature, Artificiall strife
Liues in these toutches, liuelier then life.

Enter certaine Senators

PAINTER How this Lord is followed.

POET
The Senators of Athens, happy man.   40

PAINTER Looke moe.

⌈*The Senators passe ouer the Stage, and exeunt*⌉

POET
You see this confluence, this great flood of visitors,
I haue in this rough worke, shap'd out a man
Whom this beneath world doth embrace and hugge
With amplest entertainment: My free drift
Halts not particularly, but moues it selfe
In a wide Sea of tax, no leuell'd malice
Infects one comma in the course I hold,
But flies an Eagle flight, bold, and forth on,
Leauing no Tract behinde.   50

PAINTER How shall I vnderstand you?

POET I will vnboult to you.
You see how all Conditions, how all Mindes,
As well of glib and slipp'ry Creatures, as
Of Graue and austere qualitie, tender downe
Their seruice to Lord *Timon*: his large Fortune,
Vpon his good and gracious Nature hanging,
Subdues and properties to his loue and tendance
All sorts of hearts; yea, from the glasse-fac'd Flatterer
To *Apemantus*, that few things loues better   60
Then to abhorre himselfe; euen hee drops downe
The knee before him, and returnes in peace
Most rich in *Timons* nod.

PAINTER   I saw them speake together.

POET
Sir, I haue vpon a high and pleasant hill
Feign'd Fortune to be thron'd. The Base o'th'Mount
Is rank'd with all deserts, all kinde of Natures
That labour on the bosome of this Sphere,
To propagate their states; among'st them all,
Whose eyes are on this Soueraigne Lady fixt,
One do I personate of Lord *Timons* frame,   70

Whom Fortune with her Iuory hand wafts to her,
Whose present grace, to present slaues and seruants
Translates his Riuals.

PAINTER   'Tis conceyu'd, to scope.
This Throne, this Fortune, and this Hill me thinkes
With one man becken'd from the rest below,
Bowing his head against the steepy Mount
To climbe his happinesse, would be well exprest
In our Condition.

POET   Nay Sir, but heare me on:
All those which were his Fellowes but of late,
80   Some better then his valew; on the moment
Follow his strides, his Lobbies fill with tendance,
Raine Sacrificiall whisperings in his eare,
Make Sacred euen his styrrop, and through him
Drinke the free Ayre.

PAINTER   I marry, what of these?

POET

When Fortune in her shift and change of mood
Spurnes downe her late beloued; all his Dependants
Which labour'd after him to the Mountaines top,
Euen on their knees and hands, let him fal downe,
Not one accompanying his declining foot.

90 PAINTER Tis common:
A thousand morall Paintings I can shew,
That shall demonstrate these quicke blowes of
     Fortunes,
More pregnantly then words. Yet you do well,
To shew Lord *Timon*, that meane eyes haue seene
The foot aboue the head.

         *Trumpets sound. Enter Lord Timon ⌈wearing a rich
         Iewell⌉, with a Messenger from Ventidius; Lucilius
         ⌈and other Seruants⌉ attending. Timon addresses
         himselfe curteously to euery Sutor, then speakes to
         the Messenger*

TIMON Imprison'd is he, say you?

MESSENGER
I my good Lord, fiue Talents is his debt,
His meanes most short, his Creditors most straite:
Your Honourable Letter he desires
100   To those haue shut him vp, which failing,
Periods his comfort.

TIMON   Noble *Ventidius*, well:
I am not of that Feather, to shake off
My Friend when he must neede me. I do know him
A Gentleman, that well deserues a helpe,
Which he shall haue. Ile pay the debt, and free him.

MESSENGER Your Lordship euer bindes him.

TIMON
Commend me to him, I will send his ransome,
And being enfranchizd bid him come to me;
'Tis not enough to helpe the Feeble vp,
110   But to support him after. Fare you well.

MESSENGER All happinesse to your Honor.   *Exit*
         Enter an old Athenian

OLDMAN
Lord *Timon*, heare me speake.

TIMON   Freely good Father.

OLDMAN
Thou hast a Seruant nam'd *Lucilius*.

TIMON I haue so: What of him?

OLDMAN
Most Noble *Timon*, call the man before thee.

TIMON
Attends he heere, or no? *Lucillius*.

LUCILIUS (*comming forward*)
Heere at your Lordships seruice.

OLDMAN
This Fellow heere, L. *Timon*, this thy Creature,
By night frequents my house. I am a man
That from my first haue beene inclin'd to thrift,   120
And my estate deserues an Heyre more rais'd,
Then one which holds a Trencher.

TIMON   Well: what further?

OLDMAN
One onely Daughter haue I, no Kin else,
On whom I may conferre what I haue got:
The Maid is faire, a'th'youngest for a Bride,
And I haue bred her at my deerest cost
In Qualities of the best. This man of thine
Attempts her loue: I prythee (Noble Lord)
Ioyne with me to forbid him her resort,
My selfe haue spoke in vaine.   130

TIMON The man is honest.

OLDMAN Therefore he will be *Timon*,
His honesty rewards him in it selfe,
It must not beare my Daughter.

TIMON Does she loue him?

OLDMAN She is yong and apt:
Our owne precedent passions do instruct vs
What leuities in youth.

TIMON (*to Lucilius*)   Loue you the Maid?

LUCILIUS
I my good Lord, and she accepts of it.

OLDMAN
If in her Marriage my consent be missing,   140
I call the Gods to witnesse, I will choose
Mine heyre from forth the Beggers of the world,
And dispossesse her all.

TIMON   How shall she be endowed,
If she be mated with an equall Husband?

OLDMAN
Three Talents on the present; in future, all.

TIMON
This Gentleman of mine hath seru'd me long:
To build his Fortune, I will straine a little,
For 'tis a Bond in men. Giue him thy Daughter,
What you bestow, in him Ile counterpoize,
And make him weigh with her.

OLDMAN   Most Noble Lord,   150
Pawne me to this your Honour, she is his.

TIMON
My hand to thee, mine Honour on my promise.

LUCILIUS
Humbly I thanke your Lordship, neuer may
That state or Fortune fall into my keeping,
Which is not owed to you.   *Exit Lucilius and Oldman*

POET (*presenting a Poem to Timon*)

Vouchsafe my Labour, and long liue your Lordship.

TIMON

I thanke you, you shall heare from me anon:
Go not away. (*To Painter*) What haue you there, my
    Friend?

PAINTER

A peece of Painting, which I do beseech
Your Lordship to accept.

160 TIMON   Painting is welcome.
The Painting is almost the Naturall man:
For since Dishonor Traffickes with mans Nature,
He is but out-side: These Pensil'd Figures are
Euen such as they giue out. I like your worke,
And you shall finde I like it; Waite attendance
Till you heare further from me.

PAINTER   The Gods preserue ye.

TIMON

Well fare you Gentleman: giue me your hand.
We must needs dine together:
(*To Ieweller*)   sir your Iewell
Hath suffred vnder praise.

IEWELLER   What my Lord, dispraise?

TIMON

170 A meere saciety of Commendations,
If I should pay you for't as 'tis extold,
It would vnclew me quite.

IEWELLER   My Lord, 'tis rated
As those which sell would giue: but you well know,
Things of like valew differing in the Owners,
Are prized by their Masters. Beleeu't deere Lord,
You mend the Iewell by the wearing it.

TIMON Well mock'd.

MERCHANT

No my good Lord, he speakes yᵉ common toong
Which all men speake with him.

        Enter Apermantus

TIMON   Looke who comes heere,
180 Will you be chid?

IEWELLER Wee will beare with your Lordship.

MERCHANT Hee'l spare none.

TIMON

Good morrow to thee, Gentle *Apermantus*.

APEMANTUS

Till I be gentle, stay thou for thy good morrow.
When thou art *Timons* dogge, and these Knaues honest.

TIMON

Why dost thou call them Knaues, thou know'st them
    not?

APEMANTUS Are they not Athenians?

TIMON Yes.

APEMANTUS Then I repent not.

190 IEWELLER You know me, Apemantus?

APEMANTUS

Thou know'st I do, I call'd thee by thy name.

TIMON Thou art proud *Apemantus*?

APEMANTUS Of nothing so much, as that I am not like
    Timon.

TIMON Whether art going?

APEMANTUS To knocke out an honest Athenians braines.

TIMON That's a deed thou't dye for.

APEMANTUS Right, if doing nothing be death by th'Law.

TIMON

How likest thou this picture *Apemantus*?

APEMANTUS The best, for the innocence.   200

TIMON

Wrought he not well that painted it.

APEMANTUS He wrought better that made the Painter,
    and yet he's but a filthy peece of worke.

PAINTER Y'are a Dogge.

APEMANTUS Thy Mothers of my generation: what's she,
    if I be a Dogge?

TIMON Wilt dine with me *Apemantus*?

APEMANTUS No: I eate not Lords.

TIMON And thou should'st, thoud'st anger Ladies.

APEMANTUS O they eate Lords; So they come by great 210
    bellies.

TIMON

That's a lasciuious apprehension.

APEMANTUS

So, thou apprehend'st it, take it for thy labour.

TIMON

How dost thou like this Iewell, *Apemantus*?

APEMANTUS Not so well as plain-dealing, which wil not
    cost a man a Doit.

TIMON

What dost thou thinke 'tis worth?

APEMANTUS   Not worth my thinking.
    How now Poet?

POET How now Philosopher?

APEMANTUS Thou lyest.   220

POET Art not one?

APEMANTUS Yes.

POET Then I lye not.

APEMANTUS Art not a Poet?

POET Yes.

APEMANTUS Then thou lyest: Looke in thy last worke,
    where thou hast feign'd him a worthy Fellow.

POET That's not feign'd, he is so.

APEMANTUS Yes he is worthy of thee, and to pay thee for
    thy labour. He that loues to be flattered, is worthy o'th 230
    flatterer. Heauens, that I were a Lord.

TIMON What wouldst do then *Apemantus*?

APEMANTUS E'ne as *Apemantus* does now, hate a Lord
    with my heart.

TIMON What thy selfe?

APEMANTUS I.

TIMON Wherefore?

APEMANTUS That I had no augury but to be a Lord. Art
    not thou a Merchant?

MERCHANT I *Apemantus*.   240

APEMANTUS

Traffick confound thee, if the Gods will not.

MERCHANT If Trafficke do it, the Gods do it.

APEMANTUS

Traffickes thy God, & thy God confound thee.
    Trumpet sounds. Enter a Messenger

TIMON What Trumpets that?

MESSENGER

'Tis *Alcibiades*, and some twenty Horse
All of Companionship.

TIMON (*to Seruants*)

Pray entertaine them, giue them guide to vs.

⌜*Exit one or more Seruants*⌝

⌜*To Ieweller*⌝ You must needs dine with me:
⌜*To Poet*⌝   go not you hence
Till I haue thankt you: ⌜*to Painter*⌝ when dinners done

250   Shew me this peece, ⌜*to all*⌝ I am ioyfull of your sights.

Enter Alcibiades with ⌜*his Horsemen*⌝

Most welcome Sir.

APEMANTUS ⌜*aside*⌝ So, so, their;

Aches contract, and sterue your supple ioynts:
That there should bee small loue mongst these sweet
    Knaues,
And all this Curtesie. The straine of mans bred out
Into Baboon and Monkey.

ALCIBIADES (*to Timon*)

Sir, you haue sau'd my longing, and I feed
Most hungerly on your sight.

TIMON   Right welcome Sir:

Ere we depart, wee'l share a bounteous time

260   In different pleasures. Pray you let vs in.

Exeunt all but Apemantus

Enter two Lords

1. LORD

What time a day is't *Apemantus*?

APEMANTUS

Time to be honest.

1. LORD   That time serues still.

APEMANTUS

The most accursed thou that still omitst it.

2. LORD

Thou art going to Lord *Timons* Feast.

APEMANTUS

I, to see meate fill Knaues, and Wine heat fooles.

2. LORD Farthee well, farthee well.

APEMANTUS

Thou art a Foole to bid me farewell twice.

2. LORD Why *Apemantus*?

APEMANTUS Should'st haue kept one to thy selfe, for I

270   meane to giue thee none.

1. LORD Hang thy selfe.

APEMANTUS No I will do nothing at thy bidding: Make
thy requests to thy Friend.

2. LORD Away vnpeaceable Dogge, or Ile spurne thee
hence.

APEMANTUS I will flye like a dogge, the heeles a'th'Asse.

Exit

1. LORD

Hee's opposite to humanity. Come shall we in,
And taste Lord *Timons* bountie: he out-goes
The verie heart of kindnesse.

2. LORD

280   He powres it out: *Plutus* the God of Gold
Is but his Steward: no meede but he repayes
Seuen-fold aboue it selfe: No guift to him,

But breeds the giuer a returne: exceeding
All vse of quittance.

1. LORD   The Noblest minde he carries,
That euer gouern'd man.

2. LORD

Long may he liue in Fortunes. Shall we in?

⌜1. LORD⌝ Ile keepe you Company.   *Exeunt*

Hoboyes Playing lowd Musicke. A great Banquet   Sc. 2
seru'd in, ⌜*Flauius Timons Steward and Seruants*   (1.2)
attending⌝: *and then, Enter Lord Timon, Alcibiades,*
the Senators, the Athenian Lords, Ventigius which
Timon redeem'd from prison. Then comes dropping
after all Apemantus discontentedly like himselfe

VENTIGIUS

Most honour'd *Timon*, it hath pleas'd the Gods to
    remember
My Fathers age, and call him to long peace:
He is gone happy, and has left me rich:
Then, as in gratefull Vertue I am bound   290
To your free heart, I do returne those Talents
Doubled with thankes and seruice, from whose helpe
I deriu'd libertie.

TIMON   O by no meanes,

Honest *Ventigius*: You mistake my loue,
I gaue it freely euer, and ther's none
Can truely say he giues, if he receiues:
If our betters play at that game, we must not dare
To imitate them: faults that are rich are faire.

VENTIGIUS

A Noble spirit.

⌜*The Lords stand with Ceremony*⌝

TIMON   Nay my Lords,   300
Ceremony was but deuis'd at first
To set a glosse on faint deeds, hollow welcomes,
Recanting goodnesse, sorry ere 'tis showne:
But where there is true friendship, there needs none.
Pray sit, more welcome are ye to my Fortunes,
Then my Fortunes to me.

⌜*They sit*⌝

1. LORD

My Lord, we alwaies haue confest it.

APEMANTUS

Ho ho, confest it? Hang'd it? Haue you not?

TIMON

O *Apermantus*, you are welcome.

APEMANTUS   No:
You shall not make me welcome: 310
I come to haue thee thrust me out of doores.

TIMON

Fie, th'art a churle, ye'haue got a humour there
Does not become a man, 'tis much too blame:
They say my Lords, *Ira furor breuis est*,
But yond man is euer angrie.
Go, let him haue a Table by himselfe:
For he does neither affect companie,
Nor is he fit for't indeed.

APEMANTUS

320 Let me stay at thine apperill *Timon*,
I come to obserue, I giue thee warning on't.

TIMON

I take no heede of thee: Th'art an *Athenian*,
Therefore welcome: I my selfe would haue no power,
Prythee let my meate make thee silent.

APEMANTUS I scorne thy meate, 'twould choake me: for
I should nere flatter thee. Oh you Gods! What a number
of men eats *Timon*, and he sees 'em not? It greeues me
to see so many dip there meate in one mans blood,
and all the madnesse is, he cheeres them vp too.
I wonder men dare trust themselues with men.
330 Me thinks they should enuite them without kniues,
Good for there meate, and safer for their liues.
There's much example for't, the fellow that sits next
him, now parts bread with him, pledges the breath of
him in a diuided draught: is the readiest man to kill
him. 'Tas beene proued. If I were a huge man I should
feare to drinke at meales,
Least they should spie my wind-pipes dangerous noates,
Great men should drinke with harnesse on their throates.

TIMON (*drinking to a Lord*)

My Lord in heart: and let the health go round.

2. LORD

340 Let it flow this way my good Lord.

APEMANTUS Flow this way? A braue fellow. He keepes his
tides well, those healths will make thee and thy state
looke ill, *Timon*.
Heere's that which is too weake to be a sinner,
Honest water, which nere left man i'th'mire:
This and my food are equals, there's no ods,
Feasts are to proud to giue thanks to the Gods.

> *Apermantus Grace*
> *Immortall Gods, I craue no pelfe,*
> *I pray for no man but my selfe,*
350 *Graunt I may neuer proue so fond,*
> *To trust man on his Oath or Bond.*
> *Or a Harlot for her weeping,*
> *Or a Dogge that seemes asleeping,*
> *Or a keeper with my freedome,*
> *Or my friends if I should need 'em.*
> *Amen. So fall too't:*
> *Richmen sin, and I eat root.*
> ⌐He eates⌐

Much good dich thy good heart, *Apermantus*.

TIMON Captaine *Alcibiades*, your hearts in the field now.

360 ALCIBIADES My heart is euer at your seruice, my Lord.

TIMON You had rather be at a breakefast of Enemies, then
a dinner of Friends.

ALCIBIADES So they were bleeding new my Lord, there's
no meat like 'em, I could wish my best friend at such
a Feast.

APEMANTUS

Would all those Flatterers were thine Enemies then,
That thou might'st kill 'em: & bid me to 'em.

I. LORD (*to Timon*) Might we but haue that happinesse

my Lord, that you would once vse our hearts, whereby
we might expresse some part of our zeales, we should 370
thinke our selues for euer perfect.

TIMON Oh no doubt my good Friends, but the Gods
themselues haue prouided that I shall haue much helpe
from you: how had you beene my Friends else. Why
haue you that charitable title from thousands, did not
you chiefely belong to my heart? I haue told more of
you to my selfe, then you can with modestie speake in
your owne behalfe. And thus farre I confirme you. Oh
you Gods (thinke I,) what need we haue any Friends; if
we should nere haue need of 'em? They were the most 380
needlesse Creatures liuing; should we nere haue vse for
'em; And would most resemble sweete Instruments hung
vp in Cases, that keepes there sounds to themselues.
Why I haue often wisht my selfe poorer, that I might
come neerer to you: we are borne to do benefits. And
what better or properer can we call our owne, then the
riches of our Friends? Oh what a pretious comfort 'tis, to
haue so many like Brothers commanding one anothers
Fortunes. Oh ioyes e'ne made away er't can be borne:
mine eies cannot hold out water me thinks: to forget 390
their Faults, I drinke to you.

APEMANTUS Thou weep'st to make them drinke, *Timon*.

2. LORD (*to Timon*)

Ioy had the like conception in our eies,
And at that instant, like a babe sprung vp.

APEMANTUS

Ho, ho: I laugh to thinke that babe a bastard.

3. LORD (*to Timon*)

I promise you my Lord you mou'd me much.

APEMANTUS Much.

> *Sound Tucket within*

TIMON What meanes that Trumpe?

> *Enter Seruant*

How now?

SERUANT Please you my Lord, there are certaine Ladies 400
most desirous of admittance.

TIMON Ladies? what are their wils?

SERUANT There comes with them a fore-runner my Lord,
which beares that office, to signifie their pleasures.

TIMON I pray let them be admitted.

> *Enter one as Cupid*

CUPID

Haile to thee worthy *Timon* and to all
That of his Bounties taste: the fiue best Sences
Acknowledge thee their Patron, and come freely
To gratulate thy plentious bosome. There
Tast, touch smell, all, pleas'd from thy Table rise: 410
They onely now come but to Feast thine eies.

TIMON

They'r welcome all, let 'em haue kind admittance.
Musicke make their welcome.   *Exit Cupid*

⌐I. LORD⌐

You see my Lord, how ample y'are belou'd.

> *Musicke. Enter a Maske of Ladies as Amazons, with*
> *Lutes in their hands, dauncing and playing*

APEMANTUS

    Hoyday, what a sweepe of vanitie comes this way.
    They daunce? They are madwomen,
    Like Madnesse is the glory of this life,
    As this pompe shewes to a little oyle and roote.
    We make our selues Fooles, to disport our selues,
420 And spend our Flatteries, to drinke those men,
    Vpon whose Age we voyde it vp agen
    With poysonous Spight and Enuy.
    Who liues, that's not depraued, or depraues;
    Who dyes, that beares not one spurne to their graues
    Of their Friends guift:
    I should feare, those that dance before me now,
    Would one day stampe vpon me: 'Tas bene done,
    Men shut their doores against a setting Sunne.

The Lords rise from Table, with much adoring of
Timon, and to shew their loues, each single out an
Amazon, and all Dance, men with women, a loftie
straine or two to the Hoboyes, and cease

TIMON

    You haue done our pleasures much grace (faire Ladies)
430 Set a faire fashion on our entertainment,
    Which was not halfe so beautifull, and kinde:
    You haue added worth vntoo't, and luster,
    And entertain'd me with mine owne deuice.
    I am to thanke you for't.

1. ⌈LADY⌉

    My Lord you take vs euen at the best.

APEMANTUS Faith for the worst is filthy, and would not
    hold taking, I doubt me.

TIMON

    Ladies, there is an idle banquet 'tends you,
    Please you to dispose your selues.

440 ALL LADIES Most thankfully, my Lord.   *Exeunt Ladies*

TIMON *Flauius.*

STEWARD My Lord.

TIMON The little Casket bring me hither.

STEWARD Yes, my Lord. (*Aside*) More Iewels yet?
    There is no crossing him in's humor,
    Else I should tell him well, yfaith I should;
    When all's spent, hee'ld be crost then, and he could:
    'Tis pitty Bounty had not eyes behinde,
    That man might ne're be wretched for his minde. *Exit*

450 1. LORD Where be our men?

SERUANT Heere my Lord, in readinesse.

2. LORD Our Horses.   ⌈*Exit Seruant*⌉

Enter Steward, with the Casket. He giues it to
Timon, ⌈and exits⌉

TIMON

    O my Friends: I haue one word to say to you:
    Looke you, my good L.
    I must intreat you honour me so much,
    As to aduance this Iewell, accept, and weare it,
    Kinde my Lord.

1. LORD

    I am so farre already in your guifts.

ALL LORDS So are we all.

    ⌈*Timon giues them Iewells.*⌉

Enter a Seruant

1. SERUANT My Lord, there are certaine Nobles of the 460
    Senate newly alighted, and come to visit you.

TIMON They are fairely welcome.   *Exit Seruant*

Enter Flauius, Timons Steward

STEWARD I beseech your Honor, vouchsafe me a word, it
    does concerne you neere.

TIMON

    Neere? why then another time Ile heare thee.
    I prythee let's be prouided to shew them entertainment.

STEWARD I scarse know how.

Enter another Seruant

2. SERUANT

    May it please your Honor, Lord *Lucius*
    (Out of his free loue) hath presented to you
    Foure Milke-white Horses, trapt in Siluer.   470

TIMON

    I shall accept them fairely: let the Presents
    Be worthily entertain'd.   *Exit Seruant*

Enter a third Seruant

             How now? What newes?

3. SERUANT Please you my Lord, that honourable
    Gentleman Lord *Lucullus*, entreats your companie to
    morrow, to hunt with him, and ha's sent your Honour
    two brace of Grey-hounds.

TIMON

    Ile hunt with him, and let them be receiu'd,
    Not without faire Reward.   *Exit Seruant*

STEWARD (*aside*)   What will this come to?
    He commands vs to prouide, and giue great guifts,
    And all out of an empty Coffer: 480
    Nor will he know his Purse, or yeeld me this,
    To shew him what a Begger his heart is,
    Being of no power to make his wishes good.
    His promises flye so beyond his state,
    That what he speaks is all in debt, he ows
    For eu'ry word: He is so kinde, that he now
    Payes interest for't; His Land's put to their Bookes.
    Well, would I were gently put out of Office,
    Before I were forc'd out:
    Happier is he that has no friend to feede,   490
    Then such that do e'ne Enemies exceede.
    I bleed inwardly for my Lord.   *Exit*

TIMON (*to the Lords*)   You do your selues
    Much wrong, you bate too much of your owne merits.
    (*To 2. Lord*) Heere my Lord, a trifle of our Loue.

2. LORD

    With more then common thankes I will receyue it.

3. LORD

    O he's the very soule of Bounty.

TIMON (*to 1. Lord*) And now I remember my Lord, you
    gaue good words the other day of a Bay Courser I rod
    on. Tis yours because you lik'd it.

1. LORD

    Oh, I beseech you pardon mee, my Lord, in that.   500

TIMON

    You may take my word my Lord: I know no man
    Can iustly praise, but what he does affect.

I weighe my Friends affection with mine owne:
Ile tell you true, Ile call to you.

ALL LORDS   O none so welcome.

TIMON
I take all, and your seuerall visitations
So kinde to heart, 'tis not enough to giue:
Me thinkes, I could deale Kingdomes to my Friends,
And nere be wearie. *Alcibiades*,
Thou art a Soldiour, therefore sildome rich,
⌈*Giuing a Present*⌉ It comes in Charitie to thee: for all
510   thy liuing
Is mong'st the dead: and all the Lands thou hast
Lye in a pitcht field.

ALCIBIADES   I, defil'd Land, my Lord.

1. LORD We are so vertuously bound.

TIMON And so am I to you.

2. LORD So infinitely endeer'd.

TIMON All to you. Lights, more Lights.

1. LORD
The best of Happines, Honor, and Fortunes
Keepe with you Lord *Timon*.

TIMON Ready for his Friends.

                    Exeunt all but Timon and Apermantus

520 APEMANTUS What a coiles heere,
Seruing of beckes, and iutting out of bummes.
I doubt whether their Legges be worth the summes
That are giuen for 'em. Friendships full of dregges,
Me thinkes false hearts, should neuer haue sound legges.
Thus honest Fooles lay out their wealth on Curtsies.

TIMON
Now *Apermantus* (if thou wert not sullen)
I would be good to thee.

APEMANTUS No, Ile nothing; for if I should be brib'd too,
there would be none left to raile vpon thee, and then
530   thou wouldst sinne the faster. Thou giu'st so long
Timon (I feare me) thou wilt giue away thy selfe in
paper shortly. What needs these Feasts, pompes, and
Vaine-glories?

TIMON Nay, and you begin to raile on Societie once, I am
sworne not to giue regard to you.
Farewell, & come with better Musicke.   *Exit*

APEMANTUS   So:
Thou wilt not heare mee now, thou shalt not then.
Ile locke thy heauen from thee: Oh that mens eares
     should be
To Counsell deafe, but not to Flatterie.   *Exit*

Sc. 3   *Enter a Senator* ⌈*with Bonds*⌉
(2.1) SENATOR
540 And late fiue thousand: to *Varro* and to *Isidore*
He owes nine thousand, besides my former summe,
Which makes it fiue and twenty. Still in motion
Of raging waste? It cannot hold, it will not.
If I want Gold, steale but a beggers Dogge,
And giue it *Timon*, why the Dogge coines Gold.
If I would sell my Horse, and buy twenty moe
Better then he; why giue my Horse to *Timon*.
Aske nothing, giue it him, it Foles me straight
And able Horses: No Porter at his gate,

But rather one that smiles, and still inuites   550
All that passe by. It cannot hold, no reason
Can sound his state in safety. *Caphis* hoa,
Caphis I say.
         Enter Caphis

CAPHIS   Heere sir, what is your pleasure.

SENATOR
Get on your cloake, & hast you to Lord *Timon*,
Importune him for my Moneyes, be not ceast
With slight deniall; nor then silenc'd, when
Commend me to your Master, and the Cap
Playes in the right hand, thus: but tell him,
My Vses cry to me; I must serue my turne
Out of mine owne, his dayes and times are past,   560
And my reliances on his fracted dates
Haue smit my credit. I loue, and honour him,
But must not breake my backe, to heale his finger.
Immediate are my needs, and my releefe
Must not be tost and turn'd to me in words,
But finde supply immediate. Get you gone,
Put on a most importunate aspect,
A visage of demand: for I do feare
When euery Feather stickes in his owne wing,
Lord *Timon* will be left a naked gull,   570
Which flashes now a Phœnix, get you gone.

CAPHIS
I go sir.

SENATOR ⌈*giuing him Bonds*⌉
         Take the Bonds along with you,
And haue the dates in Count.

CAPHIS   I will Sir.

SENATOR   Go.
                         Exeunt ⌈*seuerally*⌉

         Enter Steward, with many billes in his hand   Sc. 4
STEWARD   (2.2)
No care, no stop, so senselesse of expence,
That he will neither know how to maintaine it,
Nor cease his flow of Riot. Takes no accompt
How things go from him, nor resumes no care
Of what is to continue: neuer minde,
Was to be so vnwise, to be so kinde.
What shall be done, he will not heare, till feele: 580
     ⌈*A sound of Hornes within*⌉
I must be round with him, now he comes from
     hunting.
Fye, fie, fie, fie.
         Enter Caphis ⌈*at one doore*⌉, *and Seruants of Isidore*
         and Varro ⌈*at another doore*⌉

CAPHIS
Good euen *Varro*: what, you come for money?

VARROES SERUANT Is't not your businesse too?

CAPHIS
It is, and yours too, *Isidore*?

ISIDORES SERUANT   It is so.

CAPHIS
Would we were all discharg'd.

VARROES SERUANT   I feare it.

CAPHIS   Heere comes the Lord.

Enter Timon, and his Traine, amongst them
Alcibiades, ⌈as from hunting⌉

TIMON

So soone as dinners done, wee'l forth againe
My *Alcibiades*.

Caphis meetes Timon

With me, what is your will?

CAPHIS

My Lord, heere is a note of certaine dues.

590 TIMON Dues? whence are you?

CAPHIS Of Athens heere, my Lord.

TIMON Go to my Steward.

CAPHIS

Please it your Lordship, he hath put me off
To the succession of new dayes this moneth:
My Master is awak'd by great Occasion,
To call vpon his owne, and humbly prayes you,
That with your other Noble parts, you'l suite,
In giuing him his right.

TIMON   Mine honest Friend,
I prythee but repaire to me next morning.

CAPHIS

Nay, good my Lord.

600 TIMON   Containe thy selfe, good Friend.

VARROES SERUANT

One *Varroes* seruant, my good Lord.

ISIDORES SERUANT (*to Timon*)

From *Isidore*, he humbly prayes your speedy payment.

CAPHIS (*to Timon*)

If you did know my Lord, my Masters wants.

VARROES SERUANT (*to Timon*)

'Twas due on forfeyture my Lord, sixe weekes, and past.

ISIDORES SERUANT (*to Timon*)

Your Steward puts me off my Lord, and I
Am sent expressely to your Lordship.

TIMON   Giue me breath:
I do beseech you good my Lords keepe on,
Ile waite vpon you instantly.

Exeunt Alcibiades and Timons Traine

(*To Steward*)   Come hither: pray you
How goes the world, that I am thus encountred
610 With clamorous demands of broken Bonds,
And the detention of long since due debts
Against my Honor?

STEWARD (*to Seruants*) Please you Gentlemen,
The time is vnagreeable to this businesse:
Your importunacie cease, till after dinner,
That I may make his Lordship vnderstand
Wherefore you are not paid.

TIMON (*to Seruants*)   Do so my Friends,
(*To Steward*) See them well entertain'd.   *Exit*

STEWARD   Pray draw neere.
                                                Exit

Enter Apemantus and Foole

CAPHIS

Stay, stay, here comes the Foole with *Apemantus*,
Let's ha some sport with 'em.

620 VARROES SERUANT Hang him, hee'l abuse vs.

ISIDORES SERUANT A plague vpon him dogge.

VARROES SERUANT How dost Foole?

APEMANTUS Dost Dialogue with thy shadow?

VARROES SERUANT I speake not to thee.

APEMANTUS No 'tis to thy selfe. (*To Foole*) Come away.

ISIDORES SERUANT (*to Varroes Seruant*) There's the Foole
hangs on your backe already.

APEMANTUS No thou stand'st single, th'art not on him
yet.

CAPHIS (*to Isidores Seruant*) Where's the Foole now?   630

APEMANTUS He last ask'd the question. Poore Rogues, and
Vsurers men, Bauds betweene Gold and want.

ALL SERUANTS What are we *Apemantus*?

APEMANTUS Asses.

ALL SERUANTS Why?

APEMANTUS That you ask me what you are, and do not
know your selues. Speake to 'em Foole.

FOOLE How do you Gentlemen?

ALL SERUANTS Gramercies good Foole: How does your
Mistris?   640

FOOLE She's e'ne setting on water to scal'd such Chickens
as you are. Would we could see you at Corinth.

APEMANTUS Good, Gramercy.

Enter Page, with two Letters

FOOLE Looke you, heere comes my Mistris Page.

PAGE Why how now Captaine? what do you in this wise
Company. How dost thou *Apermantus*?

APEMANTUS Would I had a Rod in my mouth, that I might
answer thee profitably.

PAGE Prythee *Apemantus* reade me the superscription of
these Letters, I know not which is which.   650

APEMANTUS Canst not read?

PAGE No.

APEMANTUS There will litle Learning dye then that day
thou art hang'd. This is to Lord *Timon*, this to *Alcibiades*.
Go thou was't borne a Bastard, and thou'lt dye a Bawd.

PAGE Thou was't whelpt a Dogge, and thou shalt famish
a Dogges death. Answer not, I am gone.   *Exit*

APEMANTUS E'ne so thou out-runst Grace, Foole I will go
with you to Lord *Timons*.

FOOLE Will you leaue me there?   660

APEMANTUS If *Timon* stay at home. (*To Seruants*) You three
serue three Vsurers?

ALL SERUANTS I, would they seru'd vs.

APEMANTUS So would I: As good a tricke as euer Hangman
seru'd Theefe.

FOOLE Are you three Vsurers men?

ALL SERUANTS I Foole.

FOOLE I thinke no Vsurer, but ha's a Foole to his Seruant.
My Mistris is one, and I am her Foole: when men come
to borrow of your Masters, they approach sadly, and   670
go away merry: but they enter my Mistris house
merrily, and go away sadly. The reason of this?

VARROES SERUANT I could render one.

APEMANTUS Do it then, that we may account thee a
Whoremaster, and a Knaue, which notwithstanding
thou shalt be no lesse esteemed.

VARROES SERUANT What is a Whoremaster Foole?

FOOLE A Foole in good cloathes, and something like thee.
'Tis a spirit, sometime t'appeares like a Lord, somtime

680 like a Lawyer, sometime like a Philosopher, with two
stones moe then's artificiall one. Hee is verie often like
a Knight; and generally, in all shapes that man goes
vp and downe in, from fourescore to thirteen, this spirit
walkes in.

VARROES SERUANT Thou art not altogether a Foole.

FOOLE Nor thou altogether a Wise man, as much foolerie
as I haue, so much wit thou lack'st.

APEMANTUS That answer might haue become *Apemantus*.

        Enter Timon and Steward

ALL SERUANTS Aside, aside, heere comes Lord *Timon*.

690 APEMANTUS Come with me (Foole) come.

FOOLE I do not always follow Louer, elder Brother, and
Woman, sometime the Philosopher.

                          Exeunt Apemantus and Foole

STEWARD (*to Seruants*)
    Pray you walke neere, Ile speake with you anon.
                          Exeunt Seruants

TIMON
    You make me meruell wherefore ere this time
    Had you not fully laide my state before me,
    That I might so haue rated my expence
    As I had leaue of meanes.

STEWARD   You would not heare me:
    At many leysures I proposd.

TIMON   Go too:
    Perchance some single vantages you tooke,
700 When my indisposition put you backe,
    And that vnaptnesse made your minister
    Thus to excuse your selfe.

STEWARD   O my good Lord,
    At many times I brought in my accompts,
    Laid them before you, you would throw them off,
    And say you sumd them in mine honestie,
    When for some trifling present you haue bid me
    Returne so much, I haue shooke my head, and wept:
    Yea 'gainst th'Authoritie of manners, pray'd you
    To hold your hand more close: I did indure
710 Not sildome, nor no slight checkes, when I haue
    Prompted you in the ebbe of your estate,
    And your great flow of debts; my loued Lord,
    Though you heare now (too late) yet nowes a time,
    The greatest of your hauing, lackes a halfe,
    To pay your present debts.

TIMON   Let all my Land be sold.

STEWARD
    'Tis all engag'd, some forfeyted and gone,
    And what remaines will hardly stop the mouth
    Of present dues; the future comes apace:
    What shall defend the interim, and at length
720 How goes our reck'ning?

TIMON
    To Lacedemon did my Land extend.

STEWARD
    O my good Lord, the world is but a word,
    Were it all yours, to giue it in a breath,
    How quickely were it gone.

TIMON   You tell me true.

STEWARD
    If you suspect my Husbandry or Falshood,
    Call me before th'exactest Auditors,
    And set me on the proofe. So the Gods blesse me,
    When all our Offices haue beene opprest
    With riotous Feeders, when our Vaults haue wept
    With drunken spilth of Wine; when euery roome   730
    Hath blaz'd with Lights, and braid with Minstrelsie,
    I haue retyr'd me to a wastefull cocke,
    And set mine eyes at flow.

TIMON   Prythee no more.

STEWARD
    Heauens, haue I said, the bounty of this Lord:
    How many prodigall bits haue Slaues and Pezants
    This night englutted: who is not *Timons*,
    What heart, head, sword, force, meanes, but is L. *Timons*:
    Great *Timon*, Noble, Worthy, Royall *Timon*:
    Ah, when the meanes are gone, that buy this praise,
    The breath is gone, whereof this praise is made: 740
    Feast won, fast lost; one cloud of Winter showres,
    These flyes are coucht.

TIMON   Come sermon me no further.
    No villanous bounty yet hath past my heart;
    Vnwisely, not ignobly haue I giuen.
    Why dost thou weepe, canst thou the conscience lacke,
    To thinke I shall lacke friends: secure thy heart,
    If I would broach the vessels of my loue,
    And try the argument of hearts, by borrowing,
    Men, and mens fortunes could I frankely vse
    As I can bid thee speake.

STEWARD   Assurance blesse your thoughts.   750

TIMON
    And in some sort these wants of mine are crown'd,
    That I account them blessings. For by these
    Shall I trie Friends. You shall perceiue how you
    Mistake my Fortunes: I am wealthie in my Friends.
    Within there, *Flaminius*, *Seruilius*?
        Enter three Seruants: Flaminius, Seruilius, and another

ALL SERUANTS
    My Lord, my Lord.

TIMON   I will dispatch you seuerally.
    (*To Seruilius*) You to Lord *Lucius*, (*to Flaminius*) to
        Lord *Lucullus* you,
    I hunted with his Honor to day;
    (*To third Seruant*) You to *Sempronius*; commend me to
        their loues;
    And I am proud say, that my occasions haue   760
    Found time to vse 'em toward a supply of mony:
    Let the request be fifty Talents.

FLAMINIUS As you haue said, my Lord.   *Exeunt Seruants*

STEWARD
    Lord *Lucius* and *Lucullus*? Humh.

TIMON
    Go you sir to the Senators;
    Of whom, euen to the States best health, I haue
    Deseru'd this Hearing: bid 'em send o'th'instant
    A thousand Talents to me.

STEWARD   I haue beene bold

(For that I knew it the most generall way)
770 To them, to vse your Signet, and your Name,
But they do shake their heads, and I am heere
No richer in returne.

TIMON   Is't true? Can't be?

STEWARD
They answer in a ioynt and corporate voice,
That now they are at fall, want Treasure cannot
Do what they would, are sorrie: you are Honourable,
But yet they could haue wisht, they know not,
Something hath beene amisse; a Noble Nature
May catch a wrench; would all were well; tis pitty,
And so intending other serious matters,
780 After distastefull lookes; and these hard Fractions
With certaine halfe-caps, and cold mouing nods,
They froze me into Silence.

TIMON   You Gods reward them:
Prythee man looke cheerely. These old Fellowes
Haue their ingratitude in them Hereditary:
Their blood is cak'd, 'tis cold, it sildome flowes,
'Tis lacke of kindely warmth, they are not kinde;
And Nature, as it growes againe toward earth,
Is fashion'd for the iourney, dull and heauy.
Go to Ventiddius (prythee be not sad,
790 Thou art true, and honest; Ingeniously I speake,
No blame belongs to thee:) Ventiddius lately
Buried his Father, by whose death hee's stepp'd
Into a great estate: When he was poore,
Imprison'd, and in scarsitie of Friends,
I cleer'd him with fiue Talents: Greet him from me,
Bid him suppose, some good necessity
Touches his Friend, which craues to be remembred
With those fiue Talents; that had, giue't these Fellowes
To whom 'tis instant due. Neu'r speake, or thinke,
800 That Timons fortunes 'mong his Friends can sinke.

STEWARD
I would I could not thinke it: That thought is
    Bounties Foe;
Being free it selfe, it thinkes all others so.

                                    Exeunt ⌈seuerally⌉

Sc. 5   Flaminius, with a box vnder his Cloake, waiting to
(3.1)   speake with Lucullus, from his Master enters a
         seruant to him

SERUANT I haue told my Lord of you, he is comming down
    to you.

FLAMINIUS I thanke you Sir.
    Enter Lucullus

SERUANT Heere's my Lord.

LUCULLUS (aside) One of Lord Timons men? A Guift I
warrant. Why this hits right: I dreampt of a Siluer
Bason & Ewre to night. Flaminius, honest Flaminius,
810 you are verie respectiuely welcome sir. (To Seruant) Fill
me some Wine.   Exit Seruant
And how does that Honourable, Compleate, Free-
hearted Gentleman of Athens, thy very bountifull good
Lord and Mayster?

FLAMINIUS His health is well sir.

LUCULLUS I am right glad that his health is well sir: and
what hast thou there vnder thy Cloake, pretty
Flaminius?

FLAMINIUS Faith, nothing but an empty box Sir, which
in my Lords behalfe, I come to intreat your Honor to   820
supply: who hauing great and instant occasion to vse
fiftie Talents, hath sent to your Lordship to furnish
him: nothing doubting your present assistance therein.

LUCULLUS La, la, la, la: Nothing doubting sayes hee? Alas
good Lord, a Noble Gentleman 'tis, if he would not keep
so good a house. Many a time and often I ha din'd with
him, and told him on't, and come againe to supper to
him of purpose, to haue him spend lesse, and yet he
wold embrace no counsell, take no warning by my
comming, euery man has his fault, and honesty is his. I   830
ha told him on't, but I could nere get him from't.
    Enter Seruant with Wine

SERUANT Please your Lordship, heere is the Wine.

LUCULLUS Flaminius, I haue noted thee alwayes wise.
(Drinking) Heere's to thee.

FLAMINIUS Your Lordship speakes your pleasure.

LUCULLUS I haue obserued thee alwayes for a towardlie
prompt spirit, giue thee thy due, and one that knowes
what belongs to reason; and canst vse the time wel, if
the time vse thee well. (Drinking) Good parts in thee;
(to Seruant) get you gone sirrah.   Exit Seruant   840
Draw neerer honest Flaminius. Thy Lords a bountifull
Gentleman, but thou art wise, and thou know'st well
enough (although thou com'st to me) that this is no
time to lend money, especially vpon bare friendshippe
without securitie. (Giuing coines) Here's three Solidares
for thee, good Boy winke at me, and say thou saw'st
mee not. Fare thee well.

FLAMINIUS
Is't possible the world should so much differ,
And we aliue that liud?
    He throwes the coines at Lucullus
                    Fly damned basenesse
To him that worships thee.   850

LUCULLUS Ha? Now I see thou art a Foole, and fit for thy
Master.   Exit

FLAMINIUS
May these adde to the number yᵗ may scald thee:
Let moulten Coine be thy damnation,
Thou disease of a friend, and not himselfe:
Has friendship such a faint and milkie heart,
It turnes in lesse then two nights? O you Gods!
I feele my Masters passion. This Slaue
Vnto this Hower has my Lords meate in him:
Why should it thriue, and turne to Nutriment,   860
When he is turn'd to poyson?
O may Diseases onely worke vpon't:
And when he's sicke to death, let not that part of
    Nature
Which my Lord payd for, be of any power
To expell sicknesse, but prolong his hower.   Exit

Sc. 6
(3.2)

Enter Lucius, with three strangers

LUCIUS Who the Lord *Timon*? He is my very good friend
and an Honourable Gentleman.

1. STRANGER We know him for no lesse, thogh we are
but strangers to him. But I can tell you one thing my
870   Lord, and which I heare from common rumours, now
Lord *Timons* happie howres are done and past, and his
estate shrinkes from him.

LUCIUS Fye no, doe not beleeue it: hee cannot want for
money.

2. STRANGER But beleeue you this my Lord, that not long
agoe, one of his men was with the Lord *Lucullus*, to
borrow so many Talents, nay vrg'd extreamly for't,
and shewed what necessity belong'd too't, and yet was
deny'de.

880   LUCIUS How?

2. STRANGER I tell you, deny'de my Lord.

LUCIUS What a strange case was that? Now before the
Gods I am asham'd on't. Denied that honourable man?
There was verie little Honour shew'd in't. For my owne
part, I must needes confesse, I haue receyued some
small kindnesses from him, as Money, Plate, Iewels,
and such like Trifles; nothing comparing to his: yet
had hee not mistooke him, and sent to me, I should
ne're haue denied his Occasion so many Talents.

Enter Seruilius

890   SERUILIUS (*aside*) See, by good hap yonders my Lord, I
haue swet to see his Honor. (*To Lucius*) My Honor'd
Lord.

⌈LUCIUS⌉ *Seruilius*? You are kindely met sir. Farthewell,
commend me to thy Honourable vertuous Lord, my
very exquisite Friend.

SERUILIUS May it please your Honour, my Lord hath sent—

LUCIUS Ha? what ha's he sent? I am so much endeered
to that Lord; hee's euer sending: how shall I thank
him think'st thou? And what has he sent now?

900   SERUILIUS Has onely sent his present Occasion now my
Lord: requesting your Lordship to supply his instant
vse with so many Talents.

⌈LUCIUS⌉
I know his Lordship is but merry with me,
He cannot want fifty fiue hundred Talents.

SERUILIUS
But in the mean time he wants lesse my Lord.
If his occasion were not vertuous,
I should not vrge it halfe so faithfully.

LUCIUS
Dost thou speake seriously *Seruilius*?

SERUILIUS Vpon my soule 'tis true Sir.

910   LUCIUS What a wicked Beast was I to disfurnish my self
against such a good time, when I might ha shewn my
selfe Honourable? How vnluckily it hapned, that I shold
Purchase the day before a little part, and vndo a great
deale of Honour? *Seruilius*, now before the Gods I am
not able to do (the more beast I I say) I was sending to
vse Lord *Timon* my selfe, these Gentlemen can witnesse;
but I would not for the wealth of Athens I had done't
now. Commend me bountifully to his good Lordship,
and I hope his Honor will conceiue the fairest of mee,

because I haue no power to be kinde. And tell him this   920
from me, I count it one of my greatest afflictions say,
that I cannot pleasure such an Honourable Gentleman.
Good *Seruilius*, will you befriend mee so farre, as to vse
mine owne words to him?

SERUANT Yes sir, I shall.

⌈LUCIUS⌉
Ile looke you out a good turne *Seruilius*.   *Exit Seruilius*
True as you said, *Timon* is shrunke indeede,
And he that's once deny'de, will hardly speede.   *Exit*

1. STRANGER
Do you obserue this *Hostilius*?

2. STRANGER   I, to well.

1. STRANGER
Why this is the worlds soule, and iust of the same peece   930
Is euery Flatterers spirit: who can call him his Friend
That dips in the same dish? For in my knowing
Timon has bin this Lords Father,
And kept his credit with his purse:
Supported his estate, nay *Timons* money
Has paid his men their wages. He ne're drinkes,
But *Timons* Siluer treads vpon his Lip,
And yet, oh see the monstrousnesse of man,
When he lookes out in an vngratefull shape;
He does deny him (in respect of his)   940
What charitable men affoord to Beggers.

3. STRANGER
Religion grones at it.

1. STRANGER   For mine owne part,
I neuer tasted *Timon* in my life
Nor came any of his bounties ouer me,
To marke me for his Friend. Yet I protest,
For his right Noble minde, illustrious Vertue,
And Honourable Carriage,
Had his necessity made vse of me,
I would haue put my wealth into Donation,
And the best halfe should haue return'd to him,   950
So much I loue his heart: But I perceiue,
Men must learne now with pitty to dispence,
For Policy sits aboue Conscience.   *Exeunt*

Enter Timons third seruant with Sempronius,   Sc. 7
another of Timons Friends   (3.3)

SEMPRONIUS
Must he needs trouble me in't? Hum. 'Boue all others?
He might haue tried Lord *Lucius*, or *Lucullus*,
And now *Ventidgius* is wealthy too,
Whom he redeem'd from prison. All these
Owes their estates vnto him.

SERUANT   My Lord,
They haue all bin touch'd, and found Base-Mettle,
For they haue all denied him.

SEMPRONIUS   How? Haue they deny'de him?   960
Has *Ventidgius* and *Lucullus* deny'de him,
And does he send to me? Three? Humh?
It shewes but little loue, or iudgement in him.
Must I be his last Refuge? His Friends (like Physitians)
Thriue, giue him ouer: Must I take th'Cure vpon me?
Has much disgrac'd me in't, I'me angry at him,

That might haue knowne my place. I see no sense for't,
But his Occasions might haue wooed me first:
For in my conscience, I was the first man
970   That ere receiued guift from him.
And does he thinke so backwardly of me now,
That Ile requite it last? No:
So it may proue an Argument of Laughter
To th'rest, and I 'mong'st Lords be thought a Foole:
I'de rather then the worth of thrice the summe,
Had sent to me first, but for my mindes sake:
I'de such a courage to do him good. But now returne,
And with their faint reply, this answer ioyne;
Who bates mine Honor, shall not know my Coyne.

                                         Exit

980   SERUANT Excellent: Your Lordships a goodly Villain: the
diuell knew not what he did, when hee made man
Politicke; he crossed himselfe by't: and I cannot thinke,
but in the end, the Villanies of man will set him cleere.
How fairely this Lord striues to appeare foule? Takes
Vertuous Copies to be wicked: like those, that vnder
hotte ardent zeale, would set whole Realmes on fire, of
such a nature is his politike loue.
This was my Lords best hope, now all are fled
Saue onely the Gods. Now his Friends are dead,
990   Doores that were ne're acquainted with their Wards
Many a bounteous yeere, must be imploy'd
Now to guard sure their Master:
And this is all a liberall course allowes,
Who cannot keepe his wealth, must keep his house.

                                           Exit

Sc. 8
(3.4)   *Enter Varro's two men, meeting others, all Seruants of*
         Timons Creditors, to wait for his comming out. Then
         enter ⌜Seruants of⌝ Lucius, Titus, and Hortensius

⌜1.⌝ VARROES SERUANT
Well met, goodmorrow *Titus & Hortensius*.
TITUS SERUANT The like to you kinde *Varro*.
HORTENSIUS SERUANT
Lucius, what do we meet together?
LUCIUS SERUANT
I, and I think one businesse do's command vs all.
For mine is money.
TITUS SERUANT   So is theirs, and ours.
         Enter ⌜a Seruant of⌝ Philotus
LUCIUS SERUANT
And sir *Philotus* too.
1000 PHILOTUS SERUANT   Good day at once.
LUCIUS SERUANT
Welcome good Brother. What do you thinke the houre?
PHILOTUS SERUANT Labouring for Nine.
LUCIUS SERUANT So much?
PHILOTUS SERUANT Is not my Lord seene yet?
LUCIUS SERUANT Not yet.
PHILOTUS SERUANT
I wonder on't, he was wont to shine at seauen.
LUCIUS SERUANT
I, but the dayes are waxt shorter with him:
You must consider, that a Prodigall course
Is like the Sunnes,

But not like his recouerable: I feare,   1010
'Tis deepest Winter in Lord *Timons* purse, that is:
One may reach deepe enough, and yet finde little.
PHILOTUS SERUANT I am of your feare, for that.
TITUS SERUANT
Ile shew you how t'obserue a strange euent:
Your Lord sends now for Money?
HORTENSIUS SERUANT   Most true, he doe's.
TITUS SERUANT
And he weares Iewels now of *Timons* guift,
For which I waite for money.
HORTENSIUS SERUANT It is against my heart.
LUCIUS SERUANT Marke how strange it showes,
Timon in this, should pay more then he owes: 1020
And e'ne as if your Lord should weare rich Iewels,
And send for money for 'em.
HORTENSIUS SERUANT
I'me weary of this Charge, the Gods can witnesse:
I know my Lord hath spent of *Timons* wealth,
And now Ingratitude, makes it worse then stealth.
1. VARROES SERUANT
Yes, mine's three thousand Crownes: What's yours?
LUCIUS SERUANT   Fiue thousand mine.
1. VARROES SERUANT
'Tis much deepe, and it should seem by th'sum
Your Masters confidence was aboue mine,
Else surely his had equall'd.
       Enter Flaminius
TITUS SERUANT   One of Lord *Timons* men.
LUCIUS SERUANT
Flaminius? Sir, a word: Pray is my Lord   1030
Readie to come forth?
FLAMINIUS No, indeed he is not.
TITUS SERUANT We attend his Lordship:
Pray signifie so much.
FLAMINIUS   I need not tell
Him that, he knowes you are too diligent.
       Enter Steward in a Cloake, muffled
LUCIUS SERUANT
Ha: is not that his Steward muffled so?
He goes away in a Clowd: Call him, call him.
TITUS SERUANT (*to Steward*) Do you heare, sir?
2. VARROES SERUANT (*to Steward*) By your leaue, sir.
STEWARD What do ye aske of me, my Friend.   1040
TITUS SERUANT
We waite for certaine Money heere, sir.
STEWARD   I,
If Money were as certaine as your waiting,
'Twere sure enough.
Why then preferr'd you not your summes and Billes
When your false Masters eate of my Lords meat?
Then they could smile, and fawne vpon his debts,
And take downe th'Intrest into their glutt'nous Mawes.
You do your selues but wrong, to stirre me vp,
Let me passe quietly:
Beleeue't, my Lord and I haue made an end,   1050
I haue no more to reckon, he to spend.
LUCIUS SERUANT
I, but this answer will not serue.

STEWARD

    If 'twill not serue, 'tis not so base as you,

    For you serue Knaues.   *Exit*

1. VARROES SERUANT How? What does his casheer'd

    Worship mutter?

2. VARROES SERUANT No matter what, hee's poore, and

    that's reuenge enough. Who can speake broader, then

    hee that has no house to put his head in? Such may

1060   rayle against great buildings.

        Enter Seruilius

TITUS SERUANT Oh heere's *Seruilius*: now wee shall know

    some answere.

SERUILIUS If I might beseech you Gentlemen, to repayre

    some other houre, I should deriue much from't. For

    tak't of my soule, my Lord leanes wondrously to

    discontent: His comfortable temper has forsooke him,

    he's much out of health, and keepes his Chamber.

LUCIUS SERUANT

    Many do keepe their Chambers, are not sicke:

    And if it be so farre beyond his health,

1070   Me thinkes he should the sooner pay his debts,

    And make a cleere way to the Gods.

SERUILIUS   Good Gods.

TITUS SERUANT

    We cannot take this for an answer, sir.

FLAMINIUS (*within*)

    Seruilius helpe, my Lord, my Lord.

        Enter Timon in a rage

TIMON

    What, are my dores oppos'd against my passage?

    Haue I bin euer free, and must my house

    Be my retentiue Enemy? My Gaole?

    The place which I haue Feasted, does it now

    (Like all Mankinde) shew me an Iron heart?

LUCIUS SERUANT

    Put in now *Titus*.

TITUS SERUANT   My Lord, heere is my Bill.

LUCIUS SERUANT

    Here's mine.

⌈HORTENSIUS SERUANT⌉ And mine, my Lord.

1080 ⌈1. *and*⌉ 2. VARROES SERUANTS   And ours, my Lord.

PHILOTUS SERUANT All our Billes.

TIMON

    Knocke me downe with 'em, cleaue mee to the Girdle.

LUCIUS SERUANT Alas, my Lord.

TIMON Cut my heart in summes.

TITUS SERUANT Mine, fifty Talents.

TIMON

    Tell out my blood.

LUCIUS SERUANT   Fiue thousand Crownes, my Lord.

TIMON

    Fiue thousand drops payes that. What yours? and

      yours?

1. VARROES SERUANT My Lord.

2. VARROES SERUANT My Lord.

TIMON

1090   Teare me, take me, and the Gods fall vpon you.   *Exit*

HORTENSIUS SERUANT Faith I perceiue our Masters may

throwe their caps at their money, these debts may well

be call'd desperate ones, for a madman owes 'em.

                         Exeunt

    Enter Timon and Steward   Sc. 9

TIMON   (3.5)

    They haue e'ene put my breath from mee the slaues.

    Creditors? Diuels.

STEWARD My deere Lord.

TIMON What if it should be so?

STEWARD My Lord.

TIMON

    Ile haue it so. My Steward?

STEWARD   Heere my Lord.

TIMON

    So fitly? Go, bid all my Friends againe,   1100

    Lucius, Lucullus, and *Sempronius*: Al luxors, All,

    Ile once more feast the Rascals.

STEWARD   O my Lord,

    You onely speake from your distracted soule;

    There is not so much left to furnish out

    A moderate Table.

TIMON   Be it not in thy care:

    Go I charge thee, inuite them all, let in the tide

    Of Knaues once more: my Cooke and Ile prouide.

             Exeunt ⌈*seuerally*⌉

    Enter three Senators at one doore   Sc. 10

1. SENATOR   (3.6)

    My Lords, you haue my voyce too't, the faults Bloody:

    'Tis necessary he should dye:

    Nothing imboldens sinne so much, as Mercy.   1110

2. SENATOR Most true; the Law shall bruise'em.

    Enter Alcibiades at another doore, with Attendants

ALCIBIADES

    Honor, health, and compassion to the Senate.

1. SENATOR Now Captaine.

ALCIBIADES

    I am an humble Sutor to your Vertues;

    For pitty is the vertue of the Law,

    And none but Tyrants vse it cruelly.

    It pleases time and Fortune to lye heauie

    Vpon a Friend of mine, who in hot blood

    Hath stept into the Law: which is past depth

    To those that (without heede) do plundge intoo't.   1120

    He is a Man (setting his Fate aside)

    Of comely Vertues,

    Nor did he soyle the fact with Cowardice.

    (An Honour in him, which buyes out his fault)

    But with a Noble Fury, and faire spirit,

    Seeing his Reputation touch'd to death,

    He did oppose his Foe:

    And with such sober and vnnoted passion

    He did behaue his anger ere 'twas spent,

    As if he had but prou'd an Argument.   1130

1. SENATOR

    You vndergo too strict a Paradox,

    Striuing to make an vgly deed looke faire:

    Your words haue tooke such paines, as if they labour'd

To bring Man-slaughter into forme, and set Quarrelling
Vpon the head of Valour; which indeede
Is Valour mis-begot, and came into the world,
When Sects, and Factions were newly borne.
Hee's truly Valiant, that can wisely suffer
The worst that man can breath, and make his
    Wrongs, his Out-sides,
1140   To weare them like his Rayment, carelessely,
And ne're preferre his iniuries to his heart,
To bring it into danger.
If Wrongs be euilles, and inforce vs kill,
What Folly 'tis, to hazard life for Ill.
  ALCIBIADES
    My Lord.
  1. SENATOR You cannot make grosse sinnes looke cleare,
To reuenge is no Valour, but to beare.
  ALCIBIADES
    My Lords, then vnder fauour, pardon me,
If I speake like a Captaine.
Why do fond men expose themselues to Battell,
1150   And not endure all threats? Sleepe vpon't,
And let the Foes quietly cut their Throats
Without repugnancy? If there be
Such Valour in the bearing, what make wee
Abroad? Why then, Women are more valiant
That stay at home, if Bearing carry it:
And the Asse, more Captaine then the Lyon, the fellon
Loaden with Irons, wiser then the Iudge,
If Wisedome be in suffering, Oh my Lords,
As you are great, be pittifully Good,
1160   Who cannot condemne rashnesse in cold blood?
To kill, I grant, is sinnes extreamest Gust,
But in defence, by Mercy, 'tis most iust.
To be in Anger, is impietie:
But who is Man, that is not Angrie.
Weigh but the Crime with this.
  2. SENATOR   You breath in vaine.
  ALCIBIADES   In vaine?
    His seruice done at Lacedemon, and Bizantium,
Were a sufficient briber for his life.
  1. SENATOR
    What's that?
  ALCIBIADES   Why I say my Lords ha's done faire seruice,
And slaine in fight many of your enemies:
1170   How full of valour did he beare himselfe
In the last Conflict, and made plenteous wounds?
  2. SENATOR
    He has made too much plenty with em:
He's a sworne Riotor, he has a sinne
That often drownes him, and takes his valour prisoner.
If there were no Foes, that were enough
To ouercome him. In that Beastly furie,
He has bin knowne to commit outrages,
And cherrish Factions. 'Tis inferr'd to vs,
His dayes are foule, and his drinke dangerous.
  1. SENATOR
    He dyes.
1180   ALCIBIADES Hard fate: he might haue dyed in warre.
    My Lords, if not for any parts in him,

Though his right arme might purchase his owne time,
And be in debt to none: yet more to moue you,
Take my deserts to his, and ioyne 'em both.
And for I know,
Your reuerend Ages loue Security,
Ile pawne my Victories, all my Honour to you
Vpon his good returnes.
If by this Crime, he owes the Law his life,
Why let the Warre receiue't in valiant gore,   1190
For Law is strict, and Warre is nothing more.
  1. SENATOR
    We are for Law, he dyes, vrge it no more
On height of our displeasure: Friend, or Brother,
He forfeits his owne blood, that spilles another.
  ALCIBIADES
    Must it be so? It must not bee:
My Lords, I do beseech you know mee.
  2. SENATOR   How?
  ALCIBIADES
    Call me to your remembrances.
  3. SENATOR   What.
  ALCIBIADES
    I cannot thinke but your Age has forgot me,
It could not else be, I should proue so bace,
To sue and be deny'de such common Grace.   1200
My wounds ake at you.
  1. SENATOR   Do you dare our anger?
    'Tis in few words, but spacious in effect:
We banish thee for euer.
  ALCIBIADES   Banish me?
    Banish your dotage, banish vsurie,
That makes the Senate vgly.
  1. SENATOR   If after two dayes shine,
Athens containe thee, attend our waightier Iudgement.
And not to swell your Spirit, he shall be
Executed presently.   *Exeunt Senators ⌈and Attendants⌉*
  ALCIBIADES
    Now the Gods keepe you old enough, that you may liue
Onely in bone, that none may looke on you.   1210
I'm worse then mad: I haue kept backe their Foes
While they haue told their Money, and let out
Their Coine vpon large interest. I my selfe,
Rich onely in large hurts. All those, for this?
Is this the Balsome, that the vsuring Senat
Powres into Captaines wounds? Banishment.
It comes not ill: I hate not to be banisht,
It is a cause worthy my Spleene and Furie,
That I may strike at Athens. Ile cheere vp
My discontented Troopes, and lay for hearts;   1220
'Tis Honour with most Lands to be at ods,
Souldiers should brooke as little wrongs as Gods. *Exit*

  Enter diuers of Timons Friends, ⌈amongst them   **Sc. 11**
  Lucullus, Lucius, Sempronius, and other Lords and   **(3.7)**
  Senators,⌉ at seuerall doores
  1. LORD The good time of day to you, sir.
  2. LORD I also wish it to you: I thinke this Honorable
Lord did but try vs this other day.
  1. LORD Vpon that were my thoughts tyring when wee

encountred. I hope it is not so low with him as he
made it seeme in the triall of his seuerall Friends.

2. LORD It should not be, by the perswasion of his new
1230   Feasting.

1. LORD I should thinke so. He hath sent mee an earnest
inuiting, which many my neere occasions did vrge mee
to put off: but he hath coniur'd mee beyond them, and
I must needs appeare.

2. LORD In like manner was I in debt to my importunat
businesse, but he would not heare my excuse. I am
sorrie, when he sent to borrow of mee, that my
Prouision was out.

1. LORD I am sicke of that greefe too, as I vnderstand
1240   how all things go.

2. LORD Euery man heares so: what would hee haue
borrowed of you?

1. LORD A thousand Peeces.

2. LORD A thousand Peeces?

1. LORD What of you?

2. LORD He sent to me sir—
    ⌜Lowd Musicke.⌝ Enter Timon and Attendants
Heere he comes.

TIMON With all my heart Gentlemen both; and how fare
you?

1250 1. LORD Euer at the best, hearing well of your Lordship.

2. LORD The Swallow followes not Summer more willing,
then we your Lordship.

TIMON (aside) Nor more willingly leaues Winter, such
Summer Birds are men. (To them) Gentlemen, our
dinner will not recompence this long stay: Feast your
eares with the Musicke awhile: If they will fare so
harshly o'th'Trumpets sound: we shall too't presently.

1. LORD I hope it remaines not vnkindely with your
Lordship, that I return'd you an empty Messenger.

1260 TIMON O sir, let it not trouble you.

2. LORD My Noble Lord.

TIMON Ah my good Friend, what cheere?
    ⌜A Table and stooles⌝ brought in

2. LORD My most Honorable Lord, I am e'ne sick of shame,
that when your Lordship this other day sent to me, I
was so vnfortunate a Beggar.

TIMON Thinke not on't, sir.

2. LORD If you had sent but two houres before.

TIMON Let it not cumber your better remembrance. Come
bring in all together.
    ⌜Enter Seruants with couer'd Dishes⌝

1270 2. LORD All couer'd Dishes.

1. LORD Royall Cheare, I warrant you.

3. LORD Doubt not that, if money and the season can
yeild it.

1. LORD How do you? What's the newes?

3. LORD Alcibiades is banish'd: heare you of it?

1. and 2. LORDS Alcibiades banish'd?

3. LORD 'Tis so, be sure of it.

1. LORD How? How?

2. LORD I pray you vpon what?

1280 TIMON My worthy Friends, will you draw neere?

3. LORD Ile tell you more anon. Here's a Noble feast
toward.

2. LORD This is the old man still.

3. LORD Wilt hold? Wilt hold?

2. LORD It do's: but time will, and so.

3. LORD I do conceyue.

TIMON Each man to his stoole, with that spurre as hee
would to the lip of his Mistris: your dyet shall bee in
all places alike. Make not a Citie Feast of it, to let the
meat coole, ere we can agree vpon the first place. Sit,   1290
sit. The Gods require our Thankes.
    They sit
    You great Benefactors, sprinkle our Society with
    Thankefulnesse. For your owne guifts, make your selues
    prais'd: But reserue still to giue, least your Deities be
    despised. Lend to each man enough, that one neede not lend
    to another. For were your Godheads to borrow of men,
    men would forsake the Gods. Make the Meate be beloued,
    more then the Man that giues it. Let no Assembly of
    Twenty, be without a score of Villaines. If there sit twelue
    Women at the Table, let a dozen of them bee as they are.   1300
    The rest of your Foes, O Gods, the Senators of Athens,
    together with the common tagge of People, what is amisse
    in them, you Gods, make suteable for destruction. For these
    my present Friends, as they are to mee nothing, so in
    nothing blesse them, and to nothing are they welcome.
    Vncouer Dogges, and lap.
    The Dishes are vncouer'd, and seene to be full of
    smoking water ⌜and stones⌝

SOME LORDS What do's his Lordship meane?

OTHER LORDS I know not.

TIMON
May you a better Feast neuer behold
You knot of Mouth-Friends: Smoke, & lukewarm water   1310
Is your perfection. This is Timons last,
Who stucke and spangled with your Flatterie,
Washes it off, and sprinkles in your faces
Your reeking villany.
    ⌜He throwes water in their faces⌝
                Liue loath'd, and long
Most smiling, smooth, detested Parasites,
Curteous Destroyers, affable Wolues, meeke Beares:
You Fooles of Fortune, Trencher-friends, Times Flyes,
Cap and knee-Slaues, vapours, and Minute Iackes.
Of Man and Beast, the infinite Maladie
Crust you quite o're.
    ⌜A Lord is going⌝
               What do'st thou go?   1320
Soft, take thy Physicke first; thou too, and thou:
    ⌜He beates them⌝
Stay I will lend thee money, borrow none.
        Exeunt Lords, leauing Caps and Gownes
What? All in Motion? Henceforth be no Feast,
Whereat a Villaine's not a welcome Guest.
Burne house, sinke Athens, henceforth hated be
Of Timon Man, and all Humanity.   Exit
    Enter the Senators and other Lords

1. LORD How now, my Lords?

2. LORD
Know you the quality of Lord Timons fury?

3. LORD
Push, did you see my Cap?

4. LORD   I haue lost my Gowne.

1330 I. LORD He's but a mad Lord, & nought but humors
swaies him. He gaue me a Iewell th'other day, and
now hee has beate it out of my hat.
Did you see my Iewell?

⌜3.⌝ LORD   Did you see my Cap.

⌜2.⌝ LORD
Heere 'tis.

4. LORD   Heere lyes my Gowne.

I. LORD   Let's make no stay.

2. LORD
Lord *Timons* mad.

3. LORD   I feel't vpon my bones.

4. LORD
One day he giues vs Diamonds, next day stones.

                          Exeunt

Sc. 12   *Enter Timon*
(4.1)   TIMON
Let me looke backe vpon thee. O thou Wall
That girdles in those Wolues, diue in the earth,
And fence not Athens. Matrons, turne incontinent,
1340 Obedience fayle in Children: Slaues and Fooles
Plucke the graue wrinkled Senate from the Bench,
And minister in their steeds. To generall Filthes
Conuert o'th'Instant greene Virginity,
Doo't in your Parents eyes. Bankrupts, hold fast;
Rather then render backe, out with your Kniues,
And cut your Trusters throates. Bound Seruants, steale,
Large-handed Robbers your graue Masters are,
And pill by Law. Maide, to thy Masters bed,
Thy Mistris is o'th'Brothell. Sonne of sixteen,
1350 Plucke the lyn'd Crutch from thy old limping Sire,
With it, beate out his Braines. Piety, and Feare,
Religion to the Gods, Peace, Iustice, Truth,
Domesticke awe, Night-rest, and Neighbour-hood,
Instruction, Manners, Mysteries, and Trades,
Degrees, Obseruances, Customes, and Lawes,
Decline to your confounding contraries.
And let Confusion liue: Plagues incident to men,
Your potent and infectious Feauors, heape
On Athens ripe for stroke. Thou cold Sciatica,
1360 Cripple our Senators, that their limbes may halt
As lamely as their Manners. Lust, and Libertie
Creepe in the Mindes and Marrowes of our youth,
That 'gainst the streame of Vertue they may striue,
And drowne themselues in Riot. Itches, Blaines,
Sowe all th'Athenian bosomes, and their crop
Be generall Leprosie: Breath, infect breath,
That their Society (as their Friendship) may
Be meerely poyson.

    ⌜*He teares off his cloathes*⌝
                 Nothing Ile beare from thee
But nakednesse, thou detestable Towne,
1370 Take thou that too, with multiplying Bannes:
Timon will to the Woods, where he shall finde
Th'vnkindest Beast, more kinder then Mankinde.

The Gods confound (heare me you good Gods all)
Th'Athenians both within and out that Wall:
And graunt as *Timon* growes, his hate may grow
To the whole race of Mankinde, high and low.
Amen.   *Exit*

      Enter Steward with two or three Seruants   **Sc. 13**
                                               (4.2)
I. SERUANT
Heare you M. Steward, where's our Master?
Are we vndone, cast off, nothing remaining?

STEWARD
Alack my Fellowes, what should I say to you?   1380
Let me be recorded by the righteous Gods,
I am as poore as you.

I. SERUANT   Such a House broke?
So Noble a Master falne, all gone, and not
One Friend to take his Fortune by the arme,
And go along with him.

2. SERUANT   As we do turne our backes
From our Companion, throwne into his graue,
So his Familiars to his buried Fortunes
Slinke all away, leaue their false vowes with him
Like empty purses pickt; and his poore selfe
A dedicated Beggar to the Ayre,   1390
With his disease, of all shunn'd pouerty,
Walkes like contempt alone.

      Enter other Seruants
                       More of our Fellowes.

STEWARD
All broken Implements of a ruin'd house.

3. SERUANT
Yet do our hearts weare *Timons* Liuery,
That see I by our Faces: we are Fellowes still,
Seruing alike in sorrow: Leak'd is our Barke,
And we poore Mates, stand on the dying Decke,
Hearing the Surges threat: we must all part
Into this Sea of Ayre.

STEWARD   Good Fellowes all,
The latest of my wealth Ile share among'st you.   1400
Where euer we shall meete, for *Timons* sake,
Let's yet be Fellowes. Let's shake our heads, and say
As 'twere a Knell vnto our Masters Fortunes,
We haue seene better dayes.

      He giues them Money
                     Let each take some:
Nay put out all your hands: Not one word more,
Thus part we rich in sorrow, parting poore.

    Embrace and the Seruants part seuerall wayes
Oh the fierce wretchednesse that Glory brings vs!
Who would not wish to be from wealth exempt,
Since Riches point to Misery and Contempt?
Who would be so mock'd with Glory, or to liue   1410
But in a Dreame of Friendship,
To haue his pompe, and all what state compounds,
But onely painted like his varnisht Friends:
Poore honest Lord, brought lowe by his owne heart,
Vndone by Goodnesse: Strange vnvsuall blood,
When mans worst sinne is, He do's too much Good.

Who then dares to be halfe so kinde agen?
For Bounty that makes Gods, do's still marre Men.
My deerest Lord, blest to be most accurst,
1420   Rich onely to be wretched; thy great Fortunes
Are made thy cheefe Afflictions. Alas (kinde Lord)
Hee's flung in Rage from this ingratefull Seate
Of monstrous Friends:
Nor ha's he with him to supply his life,
Or that which can command it:
Ile follow and enquire him out.
Ile euer serue his minde, with my best will,
Whilst I haue Gold, Ile be his Steward still.   *Exit*

Sc. 14   *Enter Timon ⌈from his Caue⌉ in the woods, ⌈halfe*
(4.3)   *naked, and with a Spade⌉*

TIMON
O blessed breeding Sun, draw from the earth
1430   Rotten humidity: below thy Sisters Orbe
Infect the ayre. Twin'd Brothers of one wombe,
Whose procreation, residence, and birth,
Scarse is diuidant; touch them with seuerall fortunes,
The greater scornes the lesser. Not Nature
(To whom all sores lay siege) can beare great Fortune
But by contempt of Nature.
It is the Pastour Lards the Brothers sides,
The want that makes him leane:
Raise me this Begger, and demit that Lord,
1440   The Senator shall beare contempt Hereditary,
The Begger Natiue Honor. Who dares? who dares
In puritie of Manhood stand vpright
And say, this mans a Flatterer. If one be,
So are they all: for euerie grize of Fortune
Is smooth'd by that below. The Learned pate
Duckes to the Golden Foole. All's obliquie:
There's nothing leuell in our cursed Natures
But direct villanie. Therefore be abhorr'd,
All Feasts, Societies, and Throngs of men.
1450   His semblable, yea himselfe *Timon* disdaines,
Destruction phang mankinde; Earth yeeld me Rootes,
        He digs
Who seekes for better of thee, sawce his pallate
With thy most operant Poyson.
        He findes Gold
                        What is heere?
Gold? Yellow, glittering, precious Gold?
No Gods, I am no idle Votarist,
Roots you cleere Heauens. Thus much of this will make
Blacke, white; fowle, faire; wrong, right;
Base, Noble; Old, young; Coward, valiant.
Ha you Gods! why this? what this, you Gods? why this
1460   Will lugge your Priests and Seruants from your sides:
Plucke stout mens pillowes from below their heads.
This yellow Slaue,
Will knit and breake Religions, blesse th'accurst,
Make the hoare Leprosie ador'd, place Theeues,
And giue them Title, knee, and approbation
With Senators on the Bench: This is it
That makes the wapper'd Widdow wed againe;

Shee, whom the Spittle-house, and vlcerous sores,
Would cast the gorge at, this Embalmes and Spices
To'th'Aprill day againe. Come damned Earth,   1470
Thou common whore of Mankinde, that puttes oddes
Among the rout of Nations, I will make thee
Do thy right Nature.
        March afarre off
                        Ha? A Drumme? Th'art quicke,
But yet Ile bury thee:
        He buries Gold
                        Thou't go (strong Theefe)
When Gowty keepers of thee cannot stand:
        He keepes some Gold
Nay stay thou out for earnest.
        Enter Alcibiades with Drumme and Fife in warlike
        manner, and Phrynia and Timandra

ALCIBIADES   What art thou there? speake.
TIMON
A Beast as thou art. The Canker gnaw thy hart
For shewing me againe the eyes of Man.
ALCIBIADES
What is thy name? Is man so hatefull to thee,
That art thy selfe a Man?   1480
TIMON
I am *Misantropos*, and hate Mankinde.
For thy part, I do wish thou wert a dogge,
That I might loue thee something.
ALCIBIADES   I know thee well:
But in thy Fortunes am vnlearn'd, and strange.
TIMON
I know thee too, and more then that I know thee
I not desire to know. Follow thy Drumme,
With mans blood paint the ground Gules, Gules:
Religious Cannons, ciuill Lawes are cruell,
Then what should warre be? This fell whore of thine,
Hath in her more destruction then thy Sword,   1490
For all her Cherubin looke.
PHRYNIA   Thy lips rot off.
TIMON
I will not kisse thee, then the rot returnes
To thine owne lippes againe.
ALCIBIADES
How came the Noble *Timon* to this change?
TIMON
As the Moone do's, by wanting light to giue:
But then renew I could not like the Moone,
There were no Sunnes to borrow of.
ALCIBIADES
Noble *Timon*, what friendship may I do thee?
TIMON
None, but to maintaine my opinion.
ALCIBIADES What is it *Timon*?   1500
TIMON Promise me Friendship, but performe none. If thou
wilt promise, the Gods plague thee, for thou art a man:
if thou do'st not performe, confound thee, for thou art
a man.
ALCIBIADES
I haue heard in some sort of thy Miseries.

TIMON
Thou saw'st them when I had prosperitie.

ALCIBIADES
I see them now, then was a blessed time.

TIMON
As thine is now, held with a brace of Harlots.

TIMANDRA
Is this th'Athenian Minion, whom the world
Voic'd so regardfully?

1510   TIMON   Art thou *Timandra*?

TIMANDRA   Yes.

TIMON
Be a whore still, they loue thee not that vse thee,
Giue them diseases, leauing with thee their Lust.
Make vse of thy salt houres, season the slaues
For Tubbes and Bathes, bring downe Rose-cheekt youth
To the Tubfast, and the Diet.

TIMANDRA   Hang thee Monster.

ALCIBIADES
Pardon him sweet *Timandra*, for his wits
Are drown'd and lost in his Calamities.
I haue but little Gold of late, braue *Timon*,

1520   The want whereof, doth dayly make reuolt
In my penurious Band. I haue heard and greeu'd
How cursed Athens, mindelesse of thy worth,
Forgetting thy great deeds, when Neighbour states
But for thy Sword and Fortune trod vpon them.

TIMON
I prythee beate thy Drum, and get thee gone.

ALCIBIADES
I am thy Friend, and pitty thee deere *Timon*.

TIMON
How doest thou pitty him whom yᵘ dost troble,
I had rather be alone.

ALCIBIADES   Why fare thee well:
Heere is some Gold for thee.

TIMON   Keepe it, I cannot eate it.

ALCIBIADES
1530   When I haue laid proud Athens on a heape.

TIMON
Warr'st thou 'gainst Athens.

ALCIBIADES   I *Timon*, and haue cause.

TIMON
The Gods confound them all in thy Conquest,
And thee after, when thou hast Conquered.

ALCIBIADES
Why me, *Timon*?

TIMON   That by killing of Villaines
Thou was't borne to conquer my Country.
Put vp thy Gold.

      He giues Alcibiades Gold

                Go on, heeres Gold, go on;
Be as a Plannetary plague, when Ioue
Will o're some high-Vic'd City, hang his poyson
In the sicke ayre: let not thy sword skip one:

1540   Pitty not honour'd Age for his white Beard,
He is an Vsurer. Strike me the counterfet Matron,
It is her habite onely, that is honest,

Her selfe's a Bawd. Let not the Virgins cheeke
Make soft thy trenchant Sword: for those Milke pappes
That through the window Barres bore at mens eyes,
Are not within the Leafe of pitty writ,
But set them down horrible Traitors. Spare not the Babe
Whose dimpled smiles from Fooles exhaust their mercy;
Thinke it a Bastard, whom the Oracle

1550   Hath doubtfully pronounced, thy throat shall cut,
And mince it sans remorse. Sweare against Obiects,
Put Armour on thine eares, and on thine eyes,
Whose proofe, nor yels of Mothers, Maides, nor Babes,
Nor sight of Priests in holy Vestments bleeding,
Shall pierce a iot. There's Gold to pay thy Souldiers,
Make large confusion: and thy fury spent,
Confounded be thy selfe. Speake not, be gone.

ALCIBIADES
Hast thou Gold yet, Ile take the Gold thou giu'st me,
Not all thy Counsell.

TIMON
Dost thou or dost thou not, Heauens curse vpon thee.   1560

PHRYNIA and TIMANDRA
Giue vs some Gold good *Timon*, hast yᵘ more?

TIMON
Enough to make a Whore forsweare her Trade,
And to make Wholsōnes, a Bawd. Hold vp you Sluts
Your Aprons mountant;

      ⌐*He throwes Gold into their Aprons*⌐
                    you are not Othable,
Although I know you'l sweare, terribly sweare
Into strong shudders, and to heauenly Agues
Th'immortall Gods that heare you. Spare your Oathes:
Ile trust to your Conditions, be whores still.
And he whose pious breath seekes to conuert you,
Be strong in Whore, allure him, burne him vp,   1570
Let your close fire predominate his smoke,
And be no turne-coats: yet may your paine sick months
Be quite contrary, And Thatch your poore thin Roofes
With burthens of the dead, (some that were hang'd)
No matter: Weare them, betray with them; Whore still,
Paint till a horse may myre vpon your face:
A pox of wrinkles.

PHRYNIA and TIMANDRA   Well, more Gold, what then?
Beleeue't that wee'l do any thing for Gold.

TIMON   Consumptions sowe
In hollow bones of man, strike their sharpe shinnes,   1580
And marre mens spurring. Cracke the Lawyers voyce,
That he may neuer more false Title pleade,
Nor sound his Quillets shrilly: Hoare the Flamen,
That scolds against the quality of flesh,
And not beleeues himselfe. Downe with the Nose,
Downe with it flat, take the Bridge quite away
Of him, that his particular to foresee
Smels from the generall weale. Make curld'pate
      Ruffians bald
And let the vnscarr'd Braggerts of the Warre
Deriue some paine from you. Plague all,   1590
That your Actiuity may defeate and quell
The sourse of all Erection. There's more Gold.

Do you damne others, and let this damne you,
And ditches graue you all.

PHRYNIA *and* TIMANDRA

More counsell with more Money, bounteous *Timon*.

TIMON

More whore, more Mischeefe first, I haue giuen you
    earnest.

ALCIBIADES

Strike vp the Drum towardes Athens, farewell *Timon*:
If I thriue well, Ile visit thee againe.

TIMON

If I hope well, Ile neuer see thee more.

1600 ALCIBIADES I neuer did thee harme.

TIMON Yes, thou spok'st well of me.

ALCIBIADES Call'st thou that harme?

TIMON

Men dayly finde it. Get thee away,
And take thy Beagles with thee.

ALCIBIADES   We but offend him, strike.
        Exeunt ⌈to Drumme and Fife⌉ all but Timon

TIMON

That Nature being sicke of mans vnkindnesse
Should yet be hungry:
        He digs the earth
                    Common Mother, thou
Whose wombe vnmeasureable, and infinite brest
Teemes and feeds all: whose selfesame Mettle
Whereof thy proud Childe (arrogant man) is puft,
1610 Engenders the blacke Toad, and Adder blew,
The gilded Newt, and eyelesse venom'd Worme,
With all th'abhorred Births below Crispe Heauen,
Whereon *Hyperions* quickning fire doth shine:
Yeeld him, who all thy humane Sonnes do hate,
From foorth thy plenteous bosome, one poore roote:
Enseare thy Fertile and Conceptious wombe,
Let it no more bring out ingratefull man.
Goe great with Tygers, Dragons, Wolues, and Beares,
Teeme with new Monsters, whom thy vpward face
1620 Hath to the Marbled Mansion all aboue
Neuer presented.
        He findes a root
                    O, a Root, deare thankes:
Dry vp thy Marrowes, Vines, and Plough-torne Leas,
Whereof ingratefull man with Licourish draughts
And Morsels Vnctious, greases his pure minde,
That from it all Consideration slippes—
        Enter Apemantus
More man? Plague, plague.

APEMANTUS

I was directed hither. Men report,
Thou dost affect my Manners, and dost vse them.

TIMON

'Tis then, because thou dost not keepe a dogge
1630 Whom I would imitate. Consumption catch thee.

APEMANTUS

This is in thee a Nature but infected,
A poore vnmanly Melancholly sprung
From change of fortune. Why this Spade? this place?

This Slaue-like Habit, and these lookes of Care?
Thy Flatterers yet weare Silke, drinke Wine, lye soft,
Hugge their diseas'd Perfumes, and haue forgot
That euer *Timon* was. Shame not these Woods,
By putting on the cunning of a Carper.
Be thou a Flatterer now, and seeke to thriue
By that which ha's vndone thee; hindge thy knee,   1640
And let his very breath whom thou'lt obserue
Blow off thy Cap: praise his most vicious straine,
And call it excellent: thou wast told thus:
Thou gau'st thine eares (like Tapsters, that bad welcom)
To Knaues, and all approachers: 'Tis most iust
That thou turne Rascall, had'st thou wealth againe,
Rascals should haue't. Do not assume my likenesse.

TIMON

Were I like thee, I'de throw away my selfe.

APEMANTUS

Thou hast cast away thy selfe, being like thy self
A Madman so long, now a Foole: what think'st   1650
That the bleake ayre, thy boysterous Chamberlaine
Will put thy shirt on warme? Will these mosst Trees,
That haue out-liu'd the Eagle, page thy heeles
And skip when thou point'st out? Will the cold brooke
Candied with Ice, Cawdle thy Morning taste
To cure thy o're-nights surfet? Call the Creatures,
Whose naked Natures liue in all the spight
Of wrekefull Heauen, whose bare vnhoused Trunkes
To the conflicting Elements expos'd
Answer meere Nature: bid them flatter thee.   1660
O thou shalt finde.

TIMON   A Foole of thee: depart.

APEMANTUS

I loue thee better now, then ere I did.

TIMON

I hate thee worse.

APEMANTUS   Why?

TIMON   Thou flatter'st misery.

APEMANTUS

I flatter not, but say thou art a Caytiffe.

TIMON

Why do'st thou seeke me out?

APEMANTUS   To vex thee.

TIMON

Alwayes a Villaines Office, or a Fooles.
Dost please thy selfe in't?

APEMANTUS   I.

TIMON   What, a Knaue too?

APEMANTUS

If thou did'st put this sowre cold habit on
To castigate thy pride, 'twere well: but thou
Dost it enforcedly: Thou'dst Courtier be againe   1670
Wert thou not Beggar: willing misery
Out-liues incertaine pompe, is crown'd before:
The one is filling still, neuer compleat:
The other, at high wish: best state Contentlesse,
Hath a distracted and most wretched being,
Worse then the worst, Content.
Thou should'st desire to dye, being miserable.

TIMON

Not by his breath, that is more miserable.
Thou art a Slaue, whom Fortunes tender arme
1680   With fauour neuer claspt: but bred a Dogge.
Had'st thou like vs from our first swath proceeded,
The sweet degrees that this breefe world affords,
To such as may the passiue drugges of it
Freely command: thou would'st haue plung'd thy self
In generall Riot, melted downe thy youth
In different beds of Lust, and neuer learn'd
The Icie precepts of respect, but followed
The Sugred game before thee. But my selfe,
Who had the world as my Confectionarie,
1690   The mouthes, the tongues, the eyes, and hearts of men,
At duty more then I could frame employment;
That numberlesse vpon me stucke, as leaues
Do on the Oake, haue with one Winters brush
Fell from their boughes, and left me open, bare,
For euery storme that blowes. I to beare this,
That neuer knew but better, is some burthen:
Thy Nature, did commence in sufferance, Time
Hath made thee hard in't. Why should'st y^u hate Men?
They neuer flatter'd thee. What hast thou giuen?
1700   If thou wilt curse; thy Father (that poore ragge)
Must be thy subiect; who in spight put stuffe
To some shee-Begger, and compounded thee
Poore Rogue, hereditary. Hence, be gone,
If thou hadst not bene borne the worst of men,
Thou hadst bene a Knaue and Flatterer.

APEMANTUS Art thou proud yet?

TIMON I, that I am not thee.

APEMANTUS I, that I was
No Prodigall.

TIMON   I, that I am one now.
1710   Were all the wealth I haue shut vp in thee,
I'ld giue thee leaue to hang it. Get thee gone:
That the whole life of Athens were in this,
Thus would I eate it.

He bites the root

APEMANTUS ⌜*offering food*⌝ Heere, I will mend thy Feast.

TIMON

First mend my company, take away thy selfe.

APEMANTUS

So I shall mend mine owne, by'th'lacke of thine.

TIMON

'Tis not well mended so, it is but botcht;
If not, I would it were.

APEMANTUS   What would'st thou haue to Athens?

TIMON

Thee thither in a whirlewind: if thou wilt,
Tell them there I haue Gold, looke, so I haue.

APEMANTUS

Heere is no vse for Gold.

1720   **TIMON**   The best, and truest:
For heere it sleepes, and do's no hyred harme.

APEMANTUS Where lyest a nights *Timon*?

TIMON Vnder that's aboue me. Where feed'st thou a-dayes
Apemantus?

APEMANTUS Where my stomacke findes meate, or rather
where I eate it.

TIMON Would poyson were obedient, & knew my mind.

APEMANTUS Where would'st thou send it?

TIMON To sawce thy dishes.

APEMANTUS The middle of Humanity thou neuer knewest,   1730
but the extremitie of both ends. When thou wast in
thy Gilt, and thy Perfume, they mockt thee for too
much Curiositie: in thy Ragges thou know'st none, but
art despis'd for the contrary. There's a medler for thee,
eate it.

TIMON On what I hate, I feed not.

APEMANTUS Do'st hate a Medler?

TIMON I, though it looke like thee.

APEMANTUS And th'hadst hated Medlers sooner, y^u
should'st haue loued thy selfe better now. What man   1740
didd'st thou euer know vnthrift, that was beloued after
his meanes?

TIMON Who without those meanes thou talk'st of, didst
thou euer know belou'd?

APEMANTUS My selfe.

TIMON I vnderstand thee: thou had'st some meanes to
keepe a Dogge.

APEM What things in the world canst thou neerest
compare to thy Flatterers?

TIMON Women neerest, but men: men are the things   1750
themselues. What would'st thou do with the world
Apemantus, if it lay in thy power?

APEMANTUS Giue it the Beasts, to be rid of the men.

TIMON Would'st thou haue thy selfe fall in the confusion
of men, and remaine a Beast with the Beasts.

APEMANTUS I *Timon*.

TIMON A beastly Ambition, which the Goddes graunt thee
t'attaine to. If thou wert the Lyon, the Fox would
beguile thee: if thou wert the Lambe, the Foxe would
eate thee: if thou wert the Fox, the Lion would suspect   1760
thee, when peraduenture thou wert accus'd by the
Asse: If thou wert the Asse, thy dulnesse would torment
thee; and still thou liu'dst but as a Breakefast to the
Wolfe. If thou wert the Wolfe, thy greedinesse would
afflict thee, & oft thou should'st hazard thy life for thy
dinner. Wert thou the Vnicorne, pride and wrath would
confound thee, and make thine owne selfe the conquest
of thy fury. Wert thou a Beare, thou would'st be kill'd
by the Horse: wert thou a Horse, thou would'st be
seaz'd by the Leopard: wert thou a Leopard, thou wert   1770
Germane to the Lion, and the spottes of thy Kindred,
were Iurors on thy life. All thy safety were remotion,
and thy defence absence. What Beast could'st thou bee,
that were not subiect to a Beast: and what a Beast art
thou already, that seest not thy losse in transformation.

APEMANTUS If thou could'st please me with speaking to
me, thou might'st haue hit vpon it heere. The
Commonwealth of Athens, is become a Forrest of Beasts.

TIMON How ha's the Asse broke the wall, that thou art
out of the Citie.   1780

APEMANTUS Yonder comes a Poet and a Painter: The
plague of Company light vpon thee: I will feare to catch

it, and giue way. When I know not what else to do,
Ile see thee againe.

TIMON When there is nothing liuing but thee, thou shalt
be welcome. I had rather be a Beggers Dogge, then
Apemantus.

APEMANTUS
Thou art the Cap of all the Fooles aliue.

TIMON
Would thou wert cleane enough to spit vpon.

APEMANTUS
1790   A plague on thee, thou art too bad to curse.

TIMON
All Villaines that do stand by thee, are pure.

APEMANTUS
There is no Leprosie, but what thou speak'st.

TIMON If I name thee.
Ide beate thee, but I should infect my hands.

APEMANTUS
I would my tongue could rot them off.

TIMON
Away thou issue of a mangie dogge,
Choller does kill me, that thou art aliue,
I swoond to see thee.

APEMANTUS Would thou would'st burst.

1800 TIMON Away thou tedious Rogue,
        ⌈*He throwes a stone at Apemantus*⌉
I am sorry I shall lose a stone by thee.

APEMANTUS Beast.

TIMON Slaue.

APEMANTUS Toad.

TIMON Rogue, Rogue, Rogue.
I am sicke of this false world, and will loue nought
But euen the meere necessities vpon't:
Then *Timon* presently prepare thy graue:
Lye where the light Fome of the Sea may beate
1810   Thy graue stone dayly, make thine Epitaph,
That death in me, at others liues may laugh.
        He looks on the Gold
O thou sweete King-killer, and deare diuorce
Twixt naturall Sonne and sire: thou bright defiler
Of *Himens* purest bed, thou valiant Mars,
Thou euer, yong, fresh, lou'd, and delicate wooer,
Whose blush doth thawe the consecrated Snow
That lyes on Dians lap. Thou visible God,
That souldrest close Impossibilities,
And mak'st them kisse; that speak'st with euerie Tongue
1820   To euerie purpose: O thou touch of hearts,
Thinke thy slaue-man rebels, and by thy vertue
Set them into confounding oddes, that Beasts
May haue the world in Empire.

APEMANTUS   Would 'twere so,
But not till I am dead. Ile say th'hast Gold:
Thou wilt be throng'd too shortly.

TIMON   Throng'd too?

APEMANTUS   I.

TIMON
Thy backe I prythee.

APEMANTUS   Liue, and loue thy misery.

TIMON
Long liue so, and so dye. I am quit.
        Enter the Bandetti, theeues

APEMANTUS
Mo things like men, eate *Timon*, and abhorre them.
                                                    Exit

1. THEEFE Where should he haue this Gold? It is some
poore Fragment, some slender Ort of his remainder: 1830
the meere want of Gold, and the falling from of his
Friendes, droue him into this Melancholly.

2. THEEFE It is nois'd he hath a masse of Treasure.

3. THEEFE Let vs make the assay vpon him, if he care not
for't, he will supply vs easily: if he couetously reserue
it, how shall's get it?

2. THEEFE True: for he beares it not about him: 'Tis hid.

1. THEEFE Is not this hee?

OTHER THEEUES Where?

2. THEEFE 'Tis his description.   1840

3. THEEFE He? I know him.

ALL THEEUES (*comming forward*) Saue thee *Timon*.

TIMON Now Theeues.

ALL THEEUES
Soldiers, not Theeues.

TIMON   Both too, and womens Sonnes.

ALL THEEUES
We are not Theeues, but men that much do want.

TIMON
Your greatest want is, you want much of meat:
Why should you want? Behold, the Earth hath Rootes:
Within this Mile breake forth a hundred Springs:
The Oakes beare Mast, the Briars Scarlet Heps,
The bounteous Huswife Nature, on each bush,   1850
Layes her full Messe before you. Want? why Want?

1. THEEFE
We cannot liue on Grasse, on Berries, Water,
As Beasts, and Birds, and Fishes.

TIMON
Nor on the Beasts themselues, the Birds & Fishes,
You must eate men. Yet thankes I must you con,
That you are Theeues profest: that you worke not
In holier shapes: For there is boundlesse Theft
In limited Professions. (*Giuing Gold*) Rascall Theeues
Heere's Gold. Go, sucke the subtle blood o'th'Grape,
Till the high Feauor seeth your blood to froth,   1860
And so scape hanging. Trust not the Physitian,
His Antidotes are poyson, and he slayes
Moe then you Rob: Take wealth, and liues together,
Do Villanie do, since you protest to doo't,
Like Workemen. Ile example you with Theeuery:
The Sunnes a Theefe, and with his great attraction
Robbes the vaste Sea. The Moones an arrant Theefe,
And her pale fire, she snatches from the Sunne.
The Seas a Theefe, whose liquid Surge, resolues
The Moone into Salt teares. The Earth's a Theefe,   1870
That feeds and breeds by a composture stolne
From gen'rall excrement: each thing's a Theefe.
The Lawes, your curbe and whip, in their rough power
Ha's vncheck'd Theft. Loue not your selues, away,

Rob one another, there's more Gold, cut throates,
All that you meete are Theeues: to Athens go,
Breake open shoppes, nothing can you steale
But Theeues do loose it: steale no lesse, for this I giue
    you,
And Gold confound you howsoere: Amen.

1880 3. THEEFE Has almost charm'd me from my Profession,
by perswading me to it.

1. THEEFE 'Tis in the malice of mankinde, that he thus
aduises vs, not to haue vs thriue in our mystery.

2. THEEFE Ile beleeue him as an Enemy, and giue ouer
my Trade.

1. THEEFE Let vs first see peace in Athens, there is no time
so miserable, but a man may be true.   Exit Theeues

    Enter the Steward to Timon
STEWARD Oh you Gods!
Is yon'd despis'd and ruinous man my Lord?

1890 Full of decay and fayling? Oh Monument
And wonder of good deeds, euilly bestow'd!
What an alteration of Honor has desp'rate want made?
What vilder thing vpon the earth, then Friends,
Who can bring Noblest mindes, to basest ends.
How rarely does it meete with this times guise,
When man was wisht to loue his Enemies:
Grant I may euer loue, and rather woo
Those that would mischeefe me, then those that doo.
    Timon sees him
Has caught me in his eye, I will present

1900 My honest griefe vnto him; and as my Lord,
Still serue him with my life. My deerest Master.

TIMON
Away: what art thou?
STEWARD   Haue you forgot me, Sir?
TIMON
Why dost aske that? I haue forgot all men.
Then, if thou grant'st, th'art man, I haue forgot thee.
STEWARD An honest poore seruant of yours.
TIMON
Then I know thee not: I neuer had
Honest man about me, I all I kept were Knaues,
To serue in meate to Villaines.
STEWARD   The Gods are witnesse,
Neu'r did poore Steward weare a truer greefe

1910 For his vndone Lord, then mine eyes for you.
TIMON
What, dost thou weepe? Come neerer, then I loue thee
Because thou art a woman, and disclaim'st
Flinty mankinde: whose eyes do neuer giue,
But thorow Lust and Laughter: pittie's sleeping:
Strange times yᵗ weepe with laughing, not with weeping.
STEWARD
I begge of you to know me, good my Lord,
T'accept my greefe,
    ⌜He offers his money⌝
                and whil'st this poore wealth lasts,
To entertaine me as your Steward still.
TIMON Had I a Steward

1920 So true, so iust, and now so comfortable?

It almost turnes my dangerous Nature milde.
Let me behold thy face: Surely, this man
Was borne of woman.
Forgiue my generall, and exceptlesse rashnesse
You perpetuall sober Gods. I do proclaime
One honest man: Mistake me not, but one:
No more I pray, and hee's a Steward.
How faine would I haue hated all mankinde,
And thou redeem'st thy selfe. But all saue thee,
I fell with Curses.   1930
Me thinkes thou art more honest now, then wise:
For, by oppressing and betraying mee,
Thou might'st haue sooner got another Seruice:
For many so arriue at second Masters,
Vpon their first Lords necke. But tell me true,
(For I must euer doubt, though ne're so sure)
Is not thy kindnesse subtle, couetous,
A Vsuring kindnesse, and as rich men deale Guifts,
Expecting in returne twenty for one?

STEWARD
No my most worthy Master, in whose brest   1940
Doubt, and suspect (alas) are plac'd too late:
You should haue fear'd false times, when you did Feast.
Suspect still comes, where an estate is least.
That which I shew, Heauen knowes, is meerely Loue,
Dutie, and Zeale, to your vnmatched minde;
Care of your Food and Liuing, and beleeue it,
My most Honour'd Lord,
For any benefit that points to mee,
Either in hope, or present, I'de exchange
For this one wish, that you had power and wealth   1950
To requite me, by making rich your selfe.
TIMON
Looke thee, 'tis so: thou singly honest man,
    ⌜He giues his Steward Gold⌝
Heere take: the Gods out of my miserie
Ha's sent thee Treasure. Go, liue rich and happy,
But thus condition'd: Thou shalt build from men:
Hate all, curse all, shew Charity to none,
But let the famisht flesh slide from the Bone,
Ere thou releeue the Begger. Giue to dogges
What thou denyest to men. Let Prisons swallow 'em,
Debts wither 'em to nothing, be men like blasted woods 1960
And may Diseases licke vp their false bloods,
And so farewell, and thriue.
STEWARD   O let me stay,
And comfort you, my Master.
TIMON   If thou hat'st Curses
Stay not: flye, whil'st thou art blest and free:
Ne're see thou man, and let me ne're see thee.
                    Exit ⌜Timon into his Caue,
                        Steward another way⌝

    Enter Poet, and Painter   Sc. 15
PAINTER As I tooke note of the place, it cannot be farre (5.1)
where he abides.
POET What's to be thought of him? Does the Rumor hold
for true, that hee's so full of Gold?

1970 PAINTER Certaine. *Alcibiades* reports it: *Phrinia* and *Timandra* had Gold of him. He likewise enrich'd poore stragling Souldiers, with great quantity. 'Tis saide, he gaue vnto his Steward a mighty summe.

POET Then this breaking of his, ha's beene but a Try for his Friends?

PAINTER Nothing else: You shall see him a Palme in Athens againe, and flourish with the highest: Therefore, 'tis not amisse, we tender our loues to him, in this suppos'd distresse of his: It will shew honestly in vs, 1980 and is very likely, to loade our purposes with what they trauaile for, if it be a iust and true report, that goes of his hauing.

POET What haue you now to present vnto him?

PAINTER Nothing at this time but my Visitation: onely I will promise him an excellent Peece.

POET I must serue him so too; Tell him of an intent that's comming toward him.

PAINTER Good as the best.

⌈*Enter Timon from his Caue, vnobserued*⌉

Promising, is the verie Ayre o'th'Time; It opens the 1990 eyes of Expectation. Performance, is euer the duller for his acte, and but in the plainer and simpler kinde of people, the deede of Saying is quite out of vse. To Promise, is most Courtly and fashionable; Performance, is a kinde of Will or Testament which argues a great sicknesse in his iudgement that makes it.

TIMON (*aside*) Excellent Workeman, thou canst not paint a man so badde as is thy selfe.

POET (*to Painter*) I am thinking what I shall say I haue prouided for him: It must be a personating of himselfe: 2000 A Satyre against the softnesse of Prosperity, with a Discouerie of the infinite Flatteries that follow youth and opulencie.

TIMON (*aside*) Must thou needes stand for a Villaine in thine owne Worke? Wilt thou whip thine owne faults in other men? Do so, I haue Gold for thee.

POET (*to Painter*) Nay let's seeke him.
Then do we sinne against our owne estate,
When we may profit meete, and come too late.

PAINTER True:
2010 When the day serues before blacke-corner'd night;
Finde what thou want'st, by free and offer'd light.
Come.

TIMON (*aside*)
Ile meete you at the turne: What a Gods Gold,
That he is worshipt in a baser Temple,
Then where Swine feede?
'Tis thou that rigg'st the Barke, and plow'st the Fome,
Setlest admired reuerence in a Slaue,
To thee be worship, and thy Saints for aye
Be crown'd with Plagues, that thee alone obay.
2020 Fit I meet them.

He comes forward to them

POET
Haile worthy *Timon*.

PAINTER   Our late Noble Master.

TIMON
Haue I once liu'd to see two honest men?

POET
Sir: Hauing often of your open Bounty tasted,
Hearing you were retyr'd, your Friends falne off,
Whose thankelesse Natures (O abhorred Spirits)
Not all the Whippes of Heauen, are large enough.
What, to you,
Whose Starre-like Noblenesse gaue life and influence
To their whole being? I am rapt, and cannot couer
The monstrous bulke of this Ingratitude   2030
With any size of words.

TIMON
Let it go naked, men may see't the better:
You that are honest, by being what you are,
Make them best seene, and knowne.

PAINTER   He, and my selfe
Haue trauail'd in the great showre of your guifts,
And sweetly felt it.

TIMON   I, you are honest men.

PAINTER
We are hither come to offer you our seruice.

TIMON
Most honest men: Why how shall I requite you?
Can you eate Roots, and drinke cold water, no?

POET *and* PAINTER
What we can do, wee'l do to do you seruice.   2040

TIMON
Y'are honest men, y'haue heard that I haue Gold,
I am sure you haue, speake truth, y'are honest men.

PAINTER
So it is said my Noble Lord, but therefore
Came not my Friend, nor I.

TIMON
Good honest men: (*To Painter*) Thou draw'st a counterfet
Best in all Athens, th'art indeed the best,
Thou counterfet'st most liuely.

PAINTER   So, so, my Lord.

TIMON
E'ne so sir as I say. (*To Poet*) And for thy fiction,
Why thy Verse swels with stuffe so fine and smooth,
That thou art euen Naturall in thine Art.   2050
But for all this (my honest Natur'd friends)
I must needs say you haue a little fault,
Marry 'tis not monstrous in you, neither wish I
You take much paines to mend.

POET *and* PAINTER   Beseech your Honour
To make it knowne to vs.

TIMON   You'l take it ill.

POET *and* PAINTER Most thankefully, my Lord.

TIMON Will you indeed?

POET *and* PAINTER Doubt it not worthy Lord.

TIMON
There's neuer a one of you but trusts a Knaue,
That mightily deceiues you.

POET *and* PAINTER   Do we, my Lord?   2060

TIMON

I, and you heare him cogge, see him dissemble,
Know his grosse patchery, loue him, feede him,
Keepe in your bosome, yet remaine assur'd
That he's a made-vp-Villaine.

PAINTER I know none such, my Lord.

POET Nor I.

TIMON

Looke you, I loue you well, Ile giue you Gold
Rid me these Villaines from your companies;
Hang them, or stab them, drowne them in a draught,
2070 Confound them by some course, and come to me,
Ile giue you Gold enough.

POET and PAINTER Name them my Lord, let's know them.

TIMON

You that way, and you this: But two in Company:
Each man apart, all single, and alone,
Yet an arch Villaine keepes him company:
⌐To Painter¬ If where thou art, two Villaines shall not be,
Come not neere him. ⌐To Poet¬ If thou would'st not
        recide
But where one Villaine is, then him abandon.
Hence, packe, ⌐striking him¬ there's Gold, you came
        for Gold ye slaues:
⌐Striking Painter¬ You haue worke for me; there's
        payment, hence,
2080 ⌐Striking Poet¬ You are an Alcumist, make Gold of that:
Out Rascall dogges.

        Exeunt ⌐Poet and Painter one way,
                Timon into his Caue¬

Sc. 16   Enter Steward, and two Senators
(5.2) STEWARD

It is in vaine that you would speake with Timon:
For he is set so onely to himselfe,
That nothing but himselfe, which lookes like man,
Is friendly with him.

I. SENATOR   Bring vs to his Caue.
It is our part and promise to th'Athenians
To speake with Timon.

2. SENATOR   At all times alike
Men are not still the same: 'twas Time and Greefes
That fram'd him thus. Time with his fairer hand,
2090 Offering the Fortunes of his former dayes,
The former man may make him: bring vs to him
And chance it as it may.

STEWARD   Heere is his Caue:
(Calling) Peace and content be heere. Lord Timon, Timon,
Looke out, and speake to Friends: Th'Athenians
By two of their most reuerend Senate greet thee:
Speake to them Noble Timon.

        Enter Timon out of his Caue

TIMON

Thou Sunne that comforts burne, speake and be hang'd:
For each true word, a blister, and each false
Be as a Cantherizing to the root o'th'Tongue,
Consuming it with speaking.

2100 I. SENATOR   Worthy Timon.

TIMON

Of none but such as you, and you of Timon.

I. SENATOR

The Senators of Athens, greet thee Timon.

TIMON

I thanke them, and would send them backe the plague,
Could I but catch it for them.

I. SENATOR   O forget
What we are sorry for our selues in thee:
The Senators, with one consent of loue,
Intreate thee backe to Athens, who haue thought
On speciall Dignities, which vacant lye
For thy best vse and wearing.

2. SENATOR   They confesse
Toward thee, forgetfulnesse too generall grosse;   2110
Which now the publike Body, which doth sildome
Play the re-canter, feeling in it selfe
A lacke of Timons ayde, hath sence withall
Of it owne fail, restraining ayde to Timon,
And send forth vs, to make their sorrowed render,
Together, with a recompence more fruitfull
Then their offence can weigh downe by the Dramme,
I euen such heapes and summes of Loue and Wealth,
As shall to thee blot out, what wrongs were theirs,
And write in thee the figures of their loue,   2120
Euer to read them thine.

TIMON   You witch me in it;
Surprize me to the very brinke of teares;
Lend me a Fooles heart, and a womans eyes,
And Ile beweepe these comforts, worthy Senators.

I. SENATOR

Therefore so please thee to returne with vs,
And of our Athens, thine and ours to take
The Captainship, thou shalt be met with thankes,
Allowed with absolute power, and thy good name
Liue with Authoritie: so soone we shall driue backe
Of Alcibiades th'approaches wild,   2130
Who like a Bore too sauage, doth root vp
His Countries peace.

2. SENATOR   And shakes his threatning Sword
Against the walles of Athens.

I. SENATOR   Therefore Timon.

TIMON

Well sir, I will: therefore I will sir thus:
If Alcibiades kill my Countrymen,
Let Alcibiades know this of Timon,
That Timon cares not. But if he sacke faire Athens,
And take our goodly aged men by'th'Beards,
Giuing our holy Virgins to the staine
Of contumelious, beastly, mad-brain'd warre: 2140
Then let him know, and tell him Timon speakes it,
In pitty of our aged, and our youth,
I cannot choose but tell him that I care not,
And let him tak't at worst: For their Kniues care not,
While you haue throats to answer. For my selfe,
There's not a whittle, in th'vnruly Campe,
But I do prize it at my loue, before
The reuerends Throat in Athens. So I leaue you

To the protection of the prosperous Gods,
As Theeues to Keepers.

2150 STEWARD (*to Senators*)   Stay not, all's in vaine.

TIMON

Why I was writing of my Epitaph,
It will be seene to morrow. My long sicknesse
Of Health, and Liuing, now begins to mend,
And nothing brings me all things. Go, liue still,
Be *Alcibiades* your plague; you his,
And last so long enough.

I. SENATOR   We speake in vaine.

TIMON

But yet I loue my Country, and am not
One that reioyces in the common wracke,
As common bruite doth put it.

I. SENATOR   That's well spoke.

TIMON

2160 Commend me to my louing Countreymen.

I. SENATOR

These words become your lippes as they passe thorow
                            them.

2. SENATOR

And enter in our eares, like great Triumphers
In their applauding gates.

TIMON   Commend me to them,
And tell them, that to ease them of their greefes,
Their feares of Hostile strokes, their Aches losses,
Their pangs of Loue, with other incident throwes
That Natures fragile Vessell doth sustaine
In lifes vncertaine voyage, I will some kindnes do them,
Ile teach them to preuent wilde *Alcibiades* wrath.

I. SENATOR (*aside*)

2170 I like this well, he will returne againe.

TIMON

I haue a Tree which growes heere in my Close,
That mine owne vse inuites me to cut downe,
And shortly must I fell it. Tell my Friends,
Tell Athens, in the sequence of degree,
From high to low throughout, that who so please
To stop Affliction, let him take his haste;
Come hither ere my Tree hath felt the Axe,
And hang himselfe. I pray you do my greeting.

STEWARD (*to Senators*)

Trouble him no further, thus you still shall finde him.

TIMON

2180 Come not to me againe, but say to Athens,
Timon hath made his euerlasting Mansion
Vpon the Beached Verge of the salt Flood,
Who once a day with his embossed Froth
The turbulent Surge shall couer; thither come,
And let my graue-stone be your Oracle:
Lippes, let foure words go by, and Language end:
What is amisse, Plague and Infection mend.
Graues onely be mens workes, and Death their gaine;
Sunne, hide thy Beames, *Timon* hath done his Raigne.
                            Exit ⌈*into his Caue*⌉

I. SENATOR

2190 His discontents are vnremoueably
Coupled to Nature.

2. SENATOR

Our hope in him is dead: let vs returne,
And straine what other meanes is left vnto vs
In our deere perill.

I. SENATOR   It requires swift foot.   *Exeunt*

Enter two other Senators, with a Messenger   Sc. 17
                                                    (5.3)

⌈3.⌉ SENATOR

Thou hast painfully discouer'd: are his Files
As full as thy report?

MESSENGER   I haue spoke the least.
Besides his expedition promises
Present approach.

⌈4.⌉ SENATOR

We stand much hazard, if they bring not *Timon*.

MESSENGER

I met a Currier, one mine ancient Friend,   2200
Whom though in generall part we were oppos'd,
Yet our old loue made a particular force,
And made vs speake like Friends. This man was riding
From *Alcibiades* to *Timons* Caue,
With Letters of intreaty, which imported
His Fellowship i'th'cause against your City,
In part for his sake mou'd.

Enter the other Senators

⌈3.⌉ SENATOR   Heere come our Brothers.

⌈I.⌉ SENATOR

No talke of *Timon*, nothing of him expect,
The Enemies Drumme is heard, and fearefull scouring
Doth choake the ayre with dust: In, and prepare,   2210
Ours is the fall I feare, our Foes the Snare.   *Exeunt*

Enter a Souldier in the Woods, seeking Timon   Sc. 18
                                                      (5.4)

SOULDIER

By all description this should be the place.
Whose heere? Speake hoa. No answer?

⌈*He discouers a Grauestone*⌉

                            What is this?

Dead sure, and this his Graue, what's on this Tomb,
I cannot read: the Charracter Ile take with wax,
Our Captaine hath in euery Figure skill;
An ag'd Interpreter, though yong in dayes:
Before proud Athens hee's set downe by this,
Whose fall the marke of his Ambition is.   *Exit*

Trumpets sound. Enter Alcibiades with his Powers   Sc. 19
before Athens   (5.5)

ALCIBIADES

Sound to this Coward, and lasciuious Towne,   2220
Our terrible approach.

Sounds a Parly. The Senators appeare vpon the wals

Till now you haue gone on, and fill'd the time
With all Licentious measure, making your willes
The scope of Iustice. Till now, my selfe and such
As slept within the shadow of your power
Haue wander'd with our trauerst Armes, and breath'd
Our sufferance vainly: Now the time is flush,
When crouching Marrow in the bearer strong
Cries (of it selfe) no more: Now breathlesse wrong,

2230 Shall sit and pant in your great Chaires of ease,
And pursie Insolence shall breake his winde
With feare and horrid flight.

1. SENATOR   Noble, and young;
When thy first greefes were but a meere conceit,
Ere thou had'st power, or we had cause of feare,
We sent to thee, to giue thy rages Balme,
To wipe out our Ingratitude, with Loues
Aboue their quantitie.

2. SENATOR   So did we wooe
Transformed *Timon*, to our Cities loue
By humble Message, and by promist meanes:
2240 We were not all vnkinde, nor all deserue
The common stroke of warre.

1. SENATOR   These walles of ours,
Were not erected by their hands, from whom
You haue receyu'd your greefe: Nor are they such,
That these great Towres, Trophees, & Schools shold fall
For priuate faults in them.

2. SENATOR   Nor are they liuing
Who were the motiues that you first went out,
Shame (that they wanted cunning) in excesse
Hath broke their hearts. March, Noble Lord,
Into our City with thy Banners spred,
2250 By decimation and a tythed death
If thy Reuenges hunger for that Food
Which Nature loathes, take thou the destin'd tenth,
And by the hazard of the spotted dye,
Let dye the spotted.

1. SENATOR   All haue not offended:
For those that were, it is not square to take
On those that are, Reuenges: Crimes, like Lands
Are not inherited, then deere Countryman,
Bring in thy rankes, but leaue without thy rage,
Spare thy Athenian Cradle, and those Kin
2260 Which in the bluster of thy wrath must fall
With those that haue offended, like a Shepheard,
Approach the Fold, and cull th'infected forth,
But kill not altogether.

2. SENATOR   What thou wilt,
Thou rather shalt inforce it with thy smile,
Then hew too't, with thy Sword.

1. SENATOR   Set but thy foot
Against our rampyr'd gates, and they shall ope:
So thou wilt send thy gentle heart before,
To say thou't enter Friendly.

2. SENATOR   Throw thy Gloue,
Or any Token of thine Honour else,
2270 That thou wilt vse the warres as thy redresse,

And not as our Confusion: All thy Powers
Shall make their harbour in our Towne, till wee
Haue seal'd thy full desire.

ALCIBIADES ⌈*throwing vp a Gloue*⌉ Then there's my Gloue,
Desend and open your vncharged Ports,
Those Enemies of *Timons*, and mine owne
Whom you your selues shall set out for reproofe,
Fall and no more; and to attone your feares
With my more Noble meaning, not a man
Shall passe his quarter, or offend the streame
Of Regular Iustice in your Cities bounds,   2280
But shall be remedied to your publique Lawes
At heauiest answer.

BOTH SENATORS 'Tis most Nobly spoken.

ALCIBIADES Descend, and keepe your words.
        ⌈*Trumpets sound. Exeunt Senators from the walles.*⌉
        Enter Souldier, with a tablet of wax

SOULDIER
My Noble Generall, *Timon* is dead,
Entomb'd vpon the very hemme o'th'Sea,
And on his Grauestone, this Insculpture which
With wax I brought away: whose soft Impression
Interprets for my poore ignorance.
        Alcibiades reades the Epitaph

ALCIBIADES
    Heere lies a wretched Coarse,   2290
        Of wretched Soule bereft,
    Seek not my name: A Plague consume
        You wicked Caitifs left:
    Heere lye I Timon, who aliue,
        All liuing men did hate,
    Passe by, and curse thy fill, but passe
        And stay not here thy gate.
These well expresse in thee thy latter spirits:
Though thou abhorrd'st in vs our humane griefes,
Scornd'st our Braines flow, and those our droplets, which   2300
From niggard Nature fall; yet Rich Conceit
Taught thee to make vast Neptune weepe for aye
On thy low Graue, on faults forgiuen. Dead
Is Noble *Timon*, of whose Memorie
Heereafter more.
        ⌈*Enter Senators through the Gates*⌉
                        Bring me into your Citie,
And I will vse the Oliue, with my Sword:
Make war breed peace; make peace stint war, make
        each
Prescribe to other, as each others Leach.
Let our Drummes strike.
        ⌈*Drummes.*⌉ *Exeunt* ⌈*through the Gates*⌉

FINIS

THE HISTORIE OF KING LEAR
THE QUARTO TEXT

King Lear first appeared in print in a quarto of 1608. A substantially different text appeared in the 1623 Folio. Until now, editors, assuming that each of these early texts imperfectly represented a single play, have conflated them. But research conducted mainly during the 1970s and 1980s confirms an earlier view that the 1608 quarto represents the play as Shakespeare originally wrote it, and the 1623 Folio as he substantially revised it. He revised other plays, too, but usually by making many small changes in the dialogue and adding or omitting passages, as in *Hamlet*, *Troylus and Cressida*, and *Othello*. For these plays we print the revised text in so far as it can be ascertained. But in *King Lear* revisions are not simply local but structural, too; conflation, as Harley Granville-Barker wrote, 'may make for redundancy or confusion', so we print an edited version of each text. The first, printed in the following pages, represents the play as Shakespeare first conceived it, probably before it was performed.

The story of a king who, angry with the failure of his virtuous youngest daughter (Cordelia) to respond as he desires in a love-test, divides his kingdom between her two malevolent sisters (Gonorill and Regan), had been often told; Shakespeare would have come upon it in Holinshed's *Chronicles* and in *A Mirour for Magistrates* while reading for his plays on English history. It is told also (though briefly) in Edmund Spenser's *Faerie Queene* (Book 2, canto 10), and had been dramatized in a play of unknown authorship— *The True Chronicle History of King Leir, and his three daughters*—published in 1605, but probably written some fifteen years earlier. This play particularly gave Shakespeare much, including suggestions for the characters of Lear's loyal servant, Kent, and of Gonorill's husband, Albany, and her steward, Oswald; for the storm; for Lear's kneeling to Cordelia; and for many details of language. Nevertheless, his play is a highly original creation. Lear's madness and the harrowing series of disasters in *King Lear*'s final stages are of Shakespeare's invention, and he complicates the plot by adding the story (based on an episode of Sir Philip Sidney's *Arcadia*) of Gloster and his two sons, Edmund and Edgar. Edgar's love and loyalty to the father who, failing to see the truth, has rejected him in favour of the villainous Edmund makes him a counterpart to Cordelia; and the horrific blinding of Gloster brought about by Edmund creates a physical parallel to Lear's madness which reaches its consummation in the scene (Sc. 20) at Dover Cliff when the mad and the blind old men commune together.

The clear-eyed intensity of Shakespeare's tragic vision in *King Lear* has been too much for some audiences, and Nahum Tate's adaptation, which gave the play a happy ending, held the stage from 1681 to 1843; since then, increased understanding of Shakespeare's stagecraft along with a greater seriousness in theatre audiences has assisted in the rehabilitation of a play that is now recognized as one of the profoundest of all artistic explorations of the human condition.

The Quarto text was apparently printed from Shakespeare's foul papers.

THE NAMES OF THE ACTORS

LEAR, King of Britaine

GONERILL, Lears eldest Daughter

Duke of ALBANY, her husband

REGAN, Lears second Daughter

Duke of CORNWALL, her husband

CORDELIA, Lears youngest Daughter

King of FRANCE

Duke of BURGUNDY } suitors of Cordelia

Earle of KENT, later disguised as Caius

Earle of GLOUSTER

EDGAR, eldest sonne of Glouster, later disguised as Tom a Bedlam

EDMOND, Bastard sonne of Glouster

OLDMAN, a tenant of Glouster

CURAN, Glousters retainer

Lears FOOLE

Oswald, Gonerills STEWARD

A SERUANT of Cornwall

A KNIGHT

A HERALD

A CAPTAINE

Gentlemen, seruants, Souldiers, attendants, messengers

The Historie of King Lear

Sc. 1 *Enter Kent, Gloster, and Bastard*

KENT I thought the King had more affected the Duke of
Albany then *Cornwell*.

GLOSTER It did allwaies seeme so to vs, but now in the
diuision of the kingdomes, it appeares not which of the
Dukes he values most, for equalities are so weighed,
that curiositie in neither, can make choise of eithers
moytie.

KENT Is not this your sonne my Lord?

GLOSTER His breeding sir hath beene at my charge, I haue
10 so often blusht to acknowledge him, that now I am
braz'd to it.

KENT I cannot conceiue you.

GLOSTER Sir, this young fellowes mother Could, wheruppon
shee grew round wombed, and had indeed Sir a sonne
for her cradle, ere she had a husband for her bed, doe
you smell a fault?

KENT I cannot wish the fault vndone, the issue of it being
so proper.

GLOSTER But I haue sir a sonne by order of Law, some
20 yeare elder then this, who yet is no deerer in my
account, though this knaue came something sawcely
into the world before hee was sent for, yet was his
mother faire, there was good sport at his makeing, &
the whoreson must be acknowledged, (*to Bastard*) do
you know this noble gentleman *Edmund?*

BASTARD No my Lord.

GLOSTER (*to Bastard*) My Lord of Kent, remember him
hereafter as my honorable friend.

BASTARD (*to Kent*) My seruices to your Lordship.

30 KENT I must loue you, and sue to know you better.

BASTARD Sir I shall study deseruing.

GLOSTER (*to Kent*) Hee hath beene out nine yeares, and
away hee shall againe,

Sound a Sennet

the King is comming.

*Enter one bearing a Coronet, then Lear, then the
Dukes of Albany, and Cornwell, next Gonorill,
Regan, Cordelia, with followers*

LEAR

Attend my Lords of France and Burgundy, *Gloster*.

GLOSTER I shall my Leige.   ⌈*Exit*⌉

LEAR

Meane time we will expresse our darker purposes,
The map there; know we haue diuided
In three, our kingdome; and tis our first intent,
40 To shake all cares and busines of our state,
Confirming them on yonger yeares,
The two great Princes *France* and *Burgundy*,
Great ryuals in our youngest daughters loue,
Long in our Court haue made their amorous soiourne,
And here are to be answerd, tell me my daughters,
Which of you shall we say doth loue vs most,

That we our largest bountie may extend,
Where merit doth most challenge it,
Gonorill our eldest borne, speake first?

GONORILL

Sir I do loue you more then words can weild the
matter,   50
Dearer then eye-sight, space or libertie,
Beyond what can be valued rich or rare,
No lesse then life; with grace, health, beautie, honour,
As much as child ere loued, or father friend,
A loue that makes breath poore, and speech vnable,
Beyond all manner of so much I loue you.

CORDELIA (*aside*)

What shall *Cordelia* doe, loue and be silent.

LEAR (*to Gonorill*)

Of al these bounds, euen from this line to this,
With shady forrests, and wide skirted meades,
We make thee Lady, to thine and *Albanies* issue,   60
Be this perpetuall, what saies our second daughter?
Our deerest *Regan*, wife to *Cornwell*, speake?

REGAN Sir I am made
Of the selfe same mettall that my sister is,
And prize me at her worth in my true heart
I find she names my very deed of loue,
Onely she came short, that I professe
My selfe an enemie to all other ioyes,
Which the most precious square of sence possesses,
And find I am alone felicitate,   70
In your deere highnes loue.

CORDELIA (*aside*)   Then poore *Cord*.

And yet not so, since I am sure my loues
More richer then my tongue.

LEAR (*to Regan*)

To thee and thine hereditarie euer
Remaine this ample third of our faire kingdome,
No lesse in space, validity, and pleasure,
Then that confirm'd on *Gonorill*, (*to Cordelia*) but now
our ioy,
Although the last, not least in our deere loue,
What can you say to win a third, more opulent
Then your sisters.   80

CORDELIA Nothing my Lord.

LEAR

How, nothing can come of nothing, speake againe.

CORDELIA

Vnhappie that I am, I cannot heaue
My heart into my mouth, I loue your Maiestie
According to my bond, nor more nor lesse.

LEAR

Goe to, goe to, mend your speech a little,
Least it may mar your fortunes.

CORDELIA   Good my Lord,
You haue begot me, bred me, loued me,

I returne those duties backe as are right fit,
90 Obey you, loue you, and most honour you,
Why haue my sisters husbands if they say
They loue you all, happely when I shall wed,
That Lord whose hand must take my plight, shall cary
Halfe my loue with him, halfe my care and duty,
Sure I shall neuer mary like my sisters,
To loue my father all.
LEAR But goes this with thy heart?
CORDELIA I good my Lord.
LEAR So yong and so vntender.
100 CORDELIA So yong my Lord and true.
LEAR
Well let it be so, thy truth then be thy dower,
For by the sacred radience of the Sunne,
The misteries of *Heccat*, and the night,
By all the operation of the orbs,
From whome we doe exsist and cease to be
Heere I disclaime all my paternall care,
Propinquitie and property of blood,
And as a stranger to my heart and me
Hould thee from this for euer, the barbarous *Scythyan*,
110 Or he that makes his generation
Messes to gorge his appetite
Shall bee as well neighbour'd, pittyed and relieued
As thou my sometime daughter.
KENT   Good my Liege.
LEAR
Peace *Kent*, come not between the Dragon & his wrath,
I lou'd her most, and thought to set my rest
On her kind nurcery, ⌜*to Cordelia*⌝ hence and auoide
    my sight?
So be my graue my peace as here I giue,
Her fathers heart from her, call *France*, who stirres?
Call *Burgundy*,   ⌜*Exit one or more*⌝
              Cornwell, and *Albany*,
120 With my two daughters dowers digest this third,
Let pride, which she cals plainnes, marrie her:
I doe inuest you iointly in my powre,
Preheminence, and all the large effects
That troope with Maiestie, our selfe by monthly course
With reseruation of an hundred knights,
By you to be sustayn'd, shall our abode
Make with you by due turnes, onely we still retaine
The name and all the additions to a King,
The sway, reuenue, execution of the rest,
130 Beloued sonnes be yours, which to confirme,
This Coronet part betwixt you.
KENT   Royall *Lear*,
Whom I haue euer honor'd as my King,
Loued as my Father, as my maister followed,
As my great patron thought on in my prayers.
LEAR
The bow is bĕt & drawen make from the shaft.
KENT
Let it fall rather, though the forke inuade
The region of my heart, be *Kent* vnmannerly
When *Lear* is mad, what wilt thou doe ould man,

Think'st thou that dutie shall haue dread to speake,
When power to flatterie bowes, to plainnes honours
    bound   140
When Maiesty stoops to folly, reuerse thy doome,
And in thy best consideration checke
This hideous rashnes, answere my life my iudgement,
Thy yongest daughter does not loue thee least,
Nor are those empty harted whose low sound
Reuerbs no hollownes.
LEAR   ⌐Kent on thy life no more.
KENT
My life I neuer held but as a pawne
To wage against thy enemies, nor feare to lose it
Thy safty being the motiue.
LEAR   Out of my sight.
KENT
See better *Lear* and let me still remaine,   150
The true blanke of thine eye.
LEAR   Now by *Appollo*,
KENT
Now by *Appollo* King thou swearest thy Gods in vaine.
LEAR ⌜*making to strike him*⌝
Vassall, recreant.
KENT   Doe, kill thy Physicion,
And the fee bestow vpon the foule disease,
Reuoke thy doome, or whilst I can vent clamour
From my throat, ile tell thee thou dost euill.
LEAR
Heare me, on thy allegeance heare me?
Since thou hast sought to make vs breake our vow,
Which we durst neuer yet; and with straied pride,
To come betweene our sentence and our powre,   160
Which nor our nature nor our place can beare,
Our potency made good, take thy reward,
Foure dayes we doe allot thee for prouision,
To shield thee from diseases of the world,
And on the fift to turne thy hated backe
Vpon our kingdome, if on the next day following,
Thy banisht truncke be found in our dominions,
The moment is thy death, away, by *Iupiter*
This shall not be reuokt.
KENT
Why fare thee well king, since thus thou wilt appeare, 170
Friendship liues hence, and banishment is here,
(*To Cordelia*) The Gods to their protection take the
    maide,
That rightly thinks, and hast most iustly said,
(*To Gonorill and Regan*)
And your large speeches may your deedes approue,
That good effects may spring from wordes of loue:
Thus *Kent* O Princes, bids you all adew,
Heele shape his old course in a countrie new.   *Exit*
    Enter France and Burgundie with Gloster
GLOSTER
Heers *France* and *Burgundie* my noble Lord.
LEAR My L. of Burgũdie,
We first addres towards you, who with a King   180
Hath riuald for our daughter, what in the least

Will you require in present dower with her,
Or cease your quest of loue?
BURGUNDIE   Royall maiesty,
I craue no more then what your highnes offered,
Nor will you tender lesse?
LEAR   Right noble *Burgundie*,
When she was deere to vs we did hold her so,
But now her prise is fallen, sir there she stands,
If ought within that little seeming substāce,
Or al of it with our displeasure peec'st,
190   And nothing else may fitly like your grace,
Shees there, and she is yours.
BURGUNDIE   I know no answer.
LEAR
Sir will you with those infirmities she owes,
Vnfriended, new adopted to our hate,
Couered with our curse, and stranger'd with our oth,
Take her or leaue her.
BURGUNDIE   Pardon me royall sir,
Election makes not vp on such conditions.
LEAR
Then leaue her sir, for by the powre that made me
I tell you all her wealth, (*to France*) for you great
        King,
I would not from your loue make such a stray,
200   To match you where I hate, therefore beseech you,
To auert your liking a more worthier way,
Then on a wretch whome nature is ashamed
Almost to acknowledge hers.
FRANCE
This is most strange, that she, that euen but now
Was your best obiect, the argument of your praise,
Balme of your age, most best, most deerest,
Should in this trice of time commit a thing,
So monstrous to dismantell
So many foulds of fauour, sure her offence
210   Must be of such vnnaturall degree,
That monsters it, or your for voucht affections
Falne into taint, which to beleeue of her
Must be a faith that reason without miracle
Could neuer plant in me.
CORDELIA (*to Lear*)
I yet beseech your Maiestie,
If for I want that glib and oyly Art,
To speake and purpose not, since what I well entend
Ile do't before I speake, that you acknow
It is no vicious blot, murder or foulnes,
220   No vncleane action or dishonord step
That hath depriu'd me of your grace and fauour,
But euen the want of that, for which I am rich,
A still soliciting eye, and such a tongue,
As I am glad I haue not, though not to haue it,
Hath lost me in your liking.
LEAR   Goe to, goe to,
Better thou hadst not bin borne, then not to haue
        pleas'd me better.
FRANCE
Is it no more but this, a tardines in nature,
That often leaues the historie vnspoke

That it intends to do, my Lord of *Burgundie*,
What say you to the Lady? loue is not loue   230
When it is mingled with respects that stāds
Aloofe from the intire point wil you haue her?
She is her selfe a dowre.
BURGUNDIE   Royall *Leir*,
Giue but that portion which your selfe proposd,
And here I take *Cordelia* by the hand,
Dutches of *Burgundie*,
LEAR   Nothing, I haue sworne.
BURGUNDIE (*to Cordelia*)
I am sory then you haue so lost a father,
That you must loose a husband.
CORDELIA
Peace be with *Burgundie*, since that respects
Of fortune are his loue, I shall not be his wife.   240
FRANCE
Fairest *Cordelia* that art most rich being poore,
Most choise forsaken, and most loued despisd,
Thee and thy vertues here I ceaze vpon,
Be it lawfull I take vp whats cast away,
Gods, Gods! tis strāge, that from their couldst neglect,
My loue should kindle to inflam'd respect,
Thy dowreles daughter King throwne to my chance,
Is Queene of vs, of ours, and our faire *France*:
Not all the Dukes in watrish *Burgundie*,
Shall buy this vnprizd precious maide of me,   250
Bid them farewell *Cordelia*, though vnkind
Thou loosest here, a better where to find.
LEAR
Thou hast her *France*, let her be thine, for we
Haue no such daughter, nor shall euer see
That face of hers againe, therfore be gone,
Without our grace, our loue, our benizon?
Come noble *Burgūdy*.
            ⌈*Flourish.*⌉ *Exit Lear and Burgundie, then*
                Albany, Cornwell, Gloster, ⌈*Edmund,*⌉
                            and followers
FRANCE (*to Cordelia*)   Bid farewell to your sisters?
CORDELIA
Ye iewels of our father, with washt eyes
Cordelia leaues you, I know you what you are,
And like a sister am most loath to call   260
Your faults as they are named, vse well our Father,
To your professed bosoms I commit him,
But yet alas stood I within his grace,
I would preferre him to a better place:
So farewell to you both?
GONORILL Prescribe not vs our duties?
REGAN Let your study
Be to content your Lord, who hath receaued you
At Fortunes almes, you haue obedience scanted,
And well are worth the worst that you haue wanted.   270
CORDELIA
Time shal vnfould what pleated cūning hides,
Who couers faults, at last shame them derides:
Well may you prosper.
FRANCE   Come faire *Cordelia*?
                            Exit France & Cordelia

GONORILL Sister, it is not a little I haue to say, of what most neerely apperatines to vs both, I thinke our father will hence to night.

REGAN Thats most certaine, and with you, next moneth with vs.

280 GONORILL You see how full of changes his age is the obseruation we haue made of it hath not bin little; hee alwaies loued our sister most, and with what poore iudgement hee hath now cast her off, appeares too grosse.

REGAN Tis the infirmitie of his age, yet hee hath euer but slenderly knowne himselfe.

GONORILL The best and soundest of his time hath bin but rash, then must we looke to receiue from his age not alone the imperfection of long ingrafted condition, but therwithal vnruly waywardnes, that infirme and 290 cholericke yeares bring with them.

REGAN Such vnconstant starts are we like to haue from him, as this of *Kents* banishment.

GONORILL There is further complement of leaue taking betweene *France* and him, pray lets hit together, if our Father cary authority with such dispositions as he beares, this last surrender of his, will but offend vs.

REGAN We shall further thinke on't.

GONORILL We must doe something, and it'h heate.

Exeunt

Sc. 2   *Enter Bastard Solus*

BASTARD
Thou Nature art my Goddesse, to thy law
300 My seruices are bound, wherefore should I
Stand in the plague of custome, and permit
The curiositie of nations to depriue me,
For that I am some twelue or 14. mooneshines
Lag of a brother, why bastard? wherfore base,
When my dementions are as well compact,
My mind as generous, and my shape as true
As honest madams issue,
Why brand they vs with base, base bastardie?
Who in the lusty stealth of nature, take
310 More composition and feirce quality,
Then doth within a stale dull eyed bed, goe
To the creating a whole tribe of fops
Got tweene a sleepe and wake; well thē
Legitimate *Edgar*, I must haue your land,
Our Fathers loue is to the bastard *Edmund*,
As to the legitimate, well my legitimate, if
This letter speede, and my inuention thriue,
Edmund the base shall tooth'legitimate:
I grow, I prosper, now Gods stand vp for Bastards.

Enter Gloster. Bastard reads a letter

GLOSTER
320 *Kent* banisht thus, and *France* in choller parted,
And the King gone to night, subscribd his power,
Confined to exhibition, all this donne
Vpon the gadde; *Edmund* how now what newes?

BASTARD So please your Lordship, none.

GLOSTER Why so earnestly seeke you to put vp that letter?

BASTARD I know no newes my Lord.

GLOSTER What paper were you reading?

BASTARD Nothing my Lord.

GLOSTER No, what needes then that terrible dispatch of it into your pocket, the qualitie of nothing hath not such 330 need to hide it selfe, lets see, come if it bee nothing I shall not neede spectacles.

BASTARD I beseech you Sir pardon me, it is a letter from my brother, that I haue not all ore read, for so much as I haue perused, I find it not fit for your liking.

GLOSTER Giue me the letter sir.

BASTARD I shall offend either to detaine or giue it, the contents as in part I vnderstand them, are too blame.

GLOSTER Lets see, lets see?

BASTARD I hope for my brothers iustification, he wrot this 340 but as an essay, or tast of my vertue.

He giues Gloster a Letter

GLOSTER (*reads*) This policie of age makes the world bitter to the best of our times, keepes our fortunes from vs till our oldnes cannot relish them, I begin to find an idle and fond bondage in the oppression of aged tyranny, who swaies not as it hath power, but as it is suffered, come to me, that of this I may speake more, if our father would sleepe till I wakt him, you should inioy halfe his reuenew for euer, and liue the beloued of your brother *Edgar*.   350

Hum, conspiracie, slept till I wakt him, you should enioy halfe his reuenew, my sonne *Edgar*, had hee a hand to write this, a hart, and braine to breed it in, when came this to you, who brought it?

BASTARD It was not brought me my Lord, ther's the cunning of it, I found it throwne in at the casement of my closet.

GLOSTER You know the Caractar to be your brothers?

BASTARD If the matter were good, my Lord I durst sweare it were his but in respect of that I would faine thinke 360 it were not,

GLOSTER It is his?

BASTARD It is his hand my Lord, but I hope his heart is not in the contents.

GLOSTER Hath he neuer heretofore soūded you in this busines?

BASTARD Neuer my Lord, but I haue often heard him maintaine it to be fit, that sons at perfit age, & fathers declining, his father should be as ward to the sonne, and the sonne mannage the reuenew.   370

GLOSTER O villaine, villaine, his very opinion in the letter, abhorred villaine, vnnaturall detested brutish villaine, worse then brutish, go sir seeke him, I apprehend him, abhominable villaine where is he?

BASTARD I doe not well know my Lord, if it shall please you to suspend your indignation against my brother, til you can deriue from him better testimony of this intent: you should run a certaine course, where if you violently proceed against him, mistaking his purpose, it would make a great gap in your owne honour, &   380 shake in peeces the heart of his obediēce, I dare pawn downe my life for him, he hath wrote this to feele my affection to your honour, and to no further pretence of danger.

GLOSTER Thinke you so?

BASTARD If your honour iudge it meete, I will place you where you shall heare vs conferre of this, and by an aurigular assurance haue your satisfaction, and that without any further delay then this very euening.

390 GLOSTER He cannot be such a monster.

BASTARD Nor is not sure.

GLOSTER To his father, that so tenderly and intirely loues him, heauen and earth! *Edmund* seeke him out, wind mee into him, I pray you frame your busines after your owne wisedome, I would vnstate my selfe to be in a due resolution.

BASTARD I shall seeke him sir presently, conuey the businesse as I shall see meanes, and acquaint you withall.

400 GLOSTER These late eclipses in the Sunne and Moone portend no good to vs, though the wisedome of nature can reason thus and thus, yet nature finds it selfe scourg'd by the sequent effects, loue cooles, friendship fals off, brothers diuide, in Citties mutinies, in Countries discords, Pallaces treason, the bond crackt betweene sonne and father; find out this villaine *Edmund*, it shal loose thee nothing, doe it carefully, and the noble and true harted *Kent* banisht, his offence honesty, strange strange!   *Exit*

410 BASTARD This is the excellent foppery of the world, that when we are sicke in Fortune, often the surfeit of our owne behauiour, we make guiltie of our disasters, the Sunne, the Moone, and the Starres, as if we were Villaines by necessitie, Fooles by heauenly compulsion, Knaues, Theeues, and Trecherers by spiricall predominance, Drunkards, Lyars, and Adulterers by an enforst obedience of planitary influence, and all that wee are euill in, by a diuine thrusting on, an admirable euasion of whoremaster man, to lay his gotish 420 disposition to the charge of Starres: my Father compounded with my Mother vnder the Dragons taile, and my natiuitie was vnder *Vrsa maior*, so that it followes, I am rough and lecherous, Fut, I should haue beene that I am, had the maidenlest starre of the Firmament twinckled on my bastardy; *Edgar*;

          Enter Edgar

and ons Q out hee comes like the Catastrophe of the old Comedy, mine is villanous melancholy, with a sith like them of Bedlam; (*Aloud*) O these eclipses doe portend these diuisions.

430 EDGAR How now brother *Edmund*, what serious contemplation are you in?

BASTARD I am thinking brother of a prediction I read this other day, what should follow these Eclipses.

EDGAR Doe you busie your selfe about that?

BASTARD I promise you the effects he writ of, succeed vnhappily, as of vnnaturalnesse betweene the child and the parent, death, dearth, dissolutions of ancient amities, diuisions in state, menaces and maledictions against King and nobles, needles diffidences, banishment of friĕds, dissipation of Cohorts, nuptial 440 breaches, and I know not what.

EDGAR How long haue you beene a sectary Astronomicall?

BASTARD Come, come, when saw you my father last?

EDGAR Why, the night gon by.

BASTARD Spake you with him?

EDGAR Two houres together.

BASTARD Parted you in good tearmes? found you no displeasure in him by word or countenance?

EDGAR None at all.

BASTARD Bethinke your selfe wherein you may haue 450 offended him, and at my intreatie, forbeare his presence, till some little time hath qualified the heat of his displeasure, which at this instant so rageth in him, that with the mischiefe, of your parson it would scarce allay.

EDGAR Some villaine hath done me wrong.

BASTARD Thats my feare brother, I aduise you to the best, goe arm'd, I am no honest man if there bee any good meaning towards you, I haue told you what I haue seene & heard, but faintly, nothing like the image and 460 horror of it, pray you away?

EDGAR Shall I heare from you anon?

BASTARD I doe serue you in this busines: *Exit Edgar*
          A credulous Father, and a brother noble,
          Whose nature is so farre from doing harmes,
          That he suspects none, on whose foolish honesty
          My practises ride easie, I see the busines,
          Let me if not by birth, haue lands by wit,
          All with me's meete, that I can fashion fit.   *Exit*

Enter Gonorill and her Gentleman Steward   Sc. 3

GONORILL
          Did my Father strike my gentleman   470
          For chiding of his foole?

STEWARD   Yes Madam.

GONORILL
          By day and night he wrongs me, euery houre
          He flashes into one grosse crime or other
          That sets vs all at ods, ile not indure it,
          His Knights grow ryotous, and him selfe obrayds vs
          On euery trifell when he returnes from hunting
          I will not speake with him, say I am sicke,
          If you come slacke of former seruices,
          You shall doe well, the fault of it ile answere.
               ⌈*Hunting hornes within*⌉

STEWARD Hee's coming Madam, I heare him.   480

GONORILL
          Put on what wearie negligence you please,
          You and your fellow seruants, i'de haue it come in
               question,
          If he dislike it, let him to our sister,
          Whose mind and mine I know in that are one,
          Not to be ouerruld; idle old man
          That still would manage those authorities
          That hee hath giuen away, now by my life

Old fooles are babes again, & must be vs'd
With checkes as flatteries, when they are seene abusd,
Remember what I tell you.

490 STEWARD   Very well Madam.

GONORILL

And let his Knights haue colder looks among you,
What growes of it no matter, aduise your fellowes so,
I would breed from hence occasions, and I shall,
That I may speake, ile write straight to my sister
To hould my very course, goe prepare for dinner.

Exeunt seuerally

Sc. 4   *Enter Kent disguised*

KENT

If but as well I other accents borrow,
That can my speech defuse, my good intent
May carry through it selfe to that full issue
For which I raz'd my likenes, now banisht *Kent*,
500 If thou canst serue where thou dost stand condem'd,
Thy maister whom thou louest shall find the full of
labour.

Enter Lear and seruants, from hunting

LEAR Let me not stay a iot for dinner, goe get it readie,

⌈*Exit one*⌉

(*to Kent*) how now, what art thou?

KENT A man Sir.

LEAR What dost thou professe? what would'st thou with
vs?

KENT I doe professe to be no lesse then I seeme, to serue
him truly that will put me in trust, to loue him that is
honest, to conuerse with him that is wise, and sayes
510 little, to feare iudgement, to fight when I cannot chuse,
and to eate no fishe.

LEAR What art thou?

KENT A very honest harted fellow, and as poore as the
king.

LEAR If thou be as poore for a subiect, as he is for a King,
thar't poore enough, what would'st thou?

KENT Seruice.

LEAR Who would'st thou serue?

KENT You.

520 LEAR Do'st thou know me fellow?

KENT No sir, but you haue that in your countenance,
which I would faine call Maister.

LEAR Whats that?

KENT Authoritie.

LEAR What seruices canst doe?

KENT I can keepe honest counsaile, ride, run, mar a
curious tale in telling it, and deliuer a plaine message
bluntly, that which ordinarie men are fit for, I am
qualified in, and the best of me, is diligence.

530 LEAR How old art thou?

KENT Not so yong to loue a woman for singing, nor so
old to dote on her for any thing, I haue yeares on my
backe fortie eight.

LEAR Follow mee, thou shalt serue mee, if I like thee no
worse after dinner, I will not part from thee yet, dinner,

ho dinner, wher's my knaue, my foole, goe you and
call my foole hether,   ⌈*Exit one*⌉

Enter Steward

you sirra, whers my daughter?

STEWARD So please you,   *Exit*

LEAR What say's the fellow there, call the clat-pole backe, 540

Exeunt seruant ⌈*and Kent*⌉

whers my foole, ho I thinke the world's asleepe,

Enter Kent ⌈*and seruant*⌉

how now, wher's that mungrel?

KENT He say's my Lord, your daughter is not well.

LEAR Why came not the slaue backe to mee when I cal'd
him?

SERUANT Sir, hee answered mee in the roundest maner,
hee would not.

LEAR A would not?

SERUANT My Lord, I know not what the matter is, but to
my iudgemẽt, your highnes is not ẽtertained with that 550
ceremonious affection as you were wont, ther's a great
abatement, apeer's as well in the generall dependants,
as in the Duke himselfe also, and your daughter.

LEAR Ha, say'st thou so?

SERUANT I beseech you pardon mee my Lord, if I be
mistaken, for my dutie cannot bee silent, when I thinke
your highnesse wrong'd.

LEAR Thou but remember'st me of mine owne conception,
I haue perceiued a most faint neglect of late, which I
haue rather blamed as mine owne ielous curiositie, 560
then as a very pretence & purport of vnkindnesse, I
will looke further into't, but wher's this foole? I haue
not seene him this two dayes.

SERUANT Since my yong Ladies going into *France* sir, the
foole hath much pined away.

LEAR No more of that, I haue noted it, goe you and tell
my daughter, I would speake with her, ⌈*Exit one*⌉
goe you cal hither my foole,   ⌈*Exit one*⌉

Enter Steward ⌈*crossing the stage*⌉

O you sir, you sir, come you hither, who am I sir?

STEWARD My Ladies Father.   570

LEAR My Ladies father, my Lords knaue, you horeson
dog, you slaue, you cur.

STEWARD I am none of this my Lord, I beseech you pardon
me.

LEAR Doe you bandie lookes with me you rascall?

⌈*Lear strikes him*⌉

STEWARD Ile not be struck my Lord,

KENT (*tripping him*) Nor tript neither, you base football
player.

LEAR (*to Kent*) I thanke thee fellow, thou seru'st me, and
ile loue thee.   580

KENT (*to Steward*) Come sir ile teach you differences, away,
away, if you will measure your lubbers length againe,
tarry, but away, if you haue wisedome. *Exit Steward*

LEAR Now friendly knaue I thanke thee,

Enter Foole

their's earnest of thy seruice.

He giues Kent money

FOOLE Let me hire him too, (*to Kent*) heer's my coxcombe.

LEAR How now my pretty knaue, how do'st thou?

FOOLE (*to Kent*) Sirra, you were best take my coxcombe.

KENT Why Foole?

590 FOOLE Why for taking on's part, that's out of fauour, nay and thou can'st not smile as the wind sits, thou't catch cold shortly, there take my coxcombe; why this fellow hath banisht two on's daughters, and done the third a blessing against his will, if thou follow him, thou must needs weare my coxcombe, (*to Lear*) how now nuncle, would I had two coxcombes, and two daughters.

LEAR Why my boy?

FOOLE If I gaue them my liuing, id'e keepe my coxcombs my selfe, ther's mine, beg another of thy daughters.

600 LEAR Take heede sirra, the whip.

FOOLE Truth is a dog that must to kenell, hee must bee whipt out, when Ladie the brach may stand by the fire and stincke.

LEAR A pestilent gall to mee.

FOOLE ⌈*to Kent*⌉ Sirra ile teach thee a speech.

LEAR Doe.

FOOLE Marke it vncle,

    Haue more then thou shewest,

    Speake lesse then thou knowest,

610   Lend lesse then thou owest,

    Ride more then thou goest,

    Learne more then thou trowest,

    Set lesse then thou throwest,

    Leaue thy drinke and thy whore,

    And keepe in a doore,

    And thou shalt haue more,

    Then two tens to a score.

LEAR This is nothing foole.

FOOLE Then like the breath of an vnfeed Lawyer, you
620 gaue me nothing for't, can you make no vse of nothing vncle?

LEAR Why no boy, nothing can be made out of nothing.

FOOLE (*to Kent*) Preethe tell him so much the rent of his land comes to, he will not beleeue a foole.

LEAR A bitter foole.

FOOLE Doo'st know the difference my boy, betweene a bitter foole, and a sweete foole.

LEAR No lad, teach mee.

FOOLE ⌈*sings*⌉ That Lord that counsail'd thee
630   To giue away thy land,

    Come place him heere by mee,

    Doe thou for him stand,

    The sweet and bitter foole

    Will presently appeare,

    The one in motley here,

    The other found out there.

LEAR Do'st thou call mee foole boy?

FOOLE All thy other Titles thou hast giuen away, that thou wast borne with.

640 KENT (*to Lear*) This is not altogether foole my Lord.

FOOLE No faith, Lords and great men will not let me, if I had a monopolie out, they would haue part an't, and ladies too, they will not let me haue all the foole to my

selfe, they'l be snatching; giue me an egge Nuncle, and ile giue thee two crownes.

LEAR What two crownes shall they be?

FOOLE Why, after I haue cut the egge in the middle and eate vp the meate, the two crownes of the egge; when thou clouest thy crowne it'h middle, and gauest away
650 both parts, thou borest thy asse at'h backe or'e the durt, thou had'st little wit in thy bald crowne, when thou gauest thy golden one away, if I speake like my selfe in this, let him be whipt that first finds it so.

⌈*Sings*⌉

    Fooles had nere lesse wit in a yeare,

      For wise men are growne foppish,

    They know not how their wits doe weare,

      Their manners are so apish.

LEAR When were you wont to be so full of songs sirra?

FOOLE I haue vs'd it nuncle, euer since thou mad'st thy daughters thy mother, for when thou gauest them the
660 rod, and put'st downe thine own breeches,

⌈*sings*⌉ Then they for sudden ioy did weep,

    And I for sorrow sung,

    That such a King should play bo-peepe,

    And goe the fooles among:

prethe Nunckle keepe a schoolemaster that can teach thy foole to lye, I would faine learne to lye.

LEAR And you lye, weele haue you whipt.

FOOLE I maruell what kin thou and thy daughters are, they'l haue me whipt for speaking true, thou wilt haue
670 mee whipt for lying, and sometime I am whipt for holding my peace, I had rather be any kind of thing then a foole, and yet I would not bee thee Nuncle, thou hast pared thy wit a both sides, & left nothing in the middle,

    Enter Gonorill

here comes one of the parings.

LEAR

How now daughter, what makes that Frontlet on,

Me thinks you are too much alate it'h frowne.

FOOLE Thou wast a prettie fellow when thou had'st no need to care for her frowne, now thou art an O without
680 a figure, I am better then thou art now, I am a foole, thou art nothing, ⌈*to Gonorill*⌉ yes forsooth I will hould my tongue, so your face bids mee, though you say nothing.

⌈*Sings*⌉ Mum, mum,

    He that keepes neither crust nor crum,

    Wearie of all, shall want some.

That's a sheald pescod.

GONORILL (*to Lear*)

Not onely sir this, your all-licenc'd foole,

But other of your insolent retinue
690 Do hourely carpe and quarrell, breaking forth

In ranke & (not to be indured riots,)

Sir I had thought by making this well knowne vnto you,

To haue found a safe redres, but now grow fearefull

By what your selfe too late haue spoke and done,

That you protect this course, and put it on

By your allowance, which if you should, the fault
Would not scape censure, nor the redresse, sleepe,
Which in the tender of a wholsome weale,
700 Might in their working doe you that offence,
That else were shame, that then necessitie
Must call discreet proceedings.
FOOLE (*to Lear*) For you trow nuncle,
⌐*sings*⌐
      The hedge sparrow fed the Cookow so long,
      That it had it head bit off beit young,
so out went the candle, and we were left darkling.
LEAR (*to Gonorill*) Are you our daughter?
GONORILL
Come sir, I would you would make vse of that good
    wisedome
Whereof I know you are fraught, and put away
710 These dispositions, that of late transforme you
From what you rightly are.
FOOLE May not an Asse know when the cart drawes the
horse, ⌐*sings*⌐ Whoop *Iug* I loue thee.
LEAR
Doth any here know mee? why this is not *Lear*,
Doth *Lear* walke thus? speake thus? where are his eyes,
Either his notion weakens, or his discernings
Are lethergied, sleeping, or wakeing; ha!
Sure tis not so,
Who is it that can tell me who I am?
720 *Lears* shadow? I would learne that, for by the markes
Of soueraintie, knowledge, and reason,
I should bee false perswaded I had daughters.
FOOLE Which they, will make an obedient father.
LEAR (*to Gonorill*)
Your name faire gentlewoman?
GONORILL   Come sir,
This admiration is much of the sauour
Of other your new prankes, I doe beseech you
Vnderstand my purposes aright,
As you are old and reuerend, should be wise,
Here do you keepe a 100. Knights and Squires,
730 Men so disordred, so deboyst and bold,
That this our court infected with their manners,
Showes like a riotous Inne, epicurisme,
And lust make more like to a tauerne, or brothell,
Then a great pallace, the shame it selfe doth speake
For instant remedie, be thou desired
By her, that else will take the thing shee begs,
A little to disquantitie your traine,
And the remainder that shall still depend,
To bee such men as may besort your age,
That know themselues and you.
740 LEAR   Darkenes, and Deuils!
Saddle my horses, call my traine together,
               ⌐*Exit one or more*⌐
Degenerate bastard, ile not trouble thee,
Yet haue I left a daughter.
GONORILL
You strike my people, and your disordred rabble,
Make seruants of their betters.

Enter Duke of Albany
LEAR
We that too late repent's, O sir, are you come?
Is it your will that wee—prepare my horses,
               ⌐*Exit one or more*⌐
Ingratitude! thou marble harted fiend,
More hideous when thou shewest thee in a child,
Then the Sea-monster, (*to Gonorill*) detested kite, thou
list :   750
My traine, are men of choise and rarest parts,
That all particulars of dutie knowe,
And in the most exact regard, support
The worships of their name, O most small fault,
How vgly did'st thou in *Cordelia* shewe,
That like an engine wrencht my frame of nature
From the fixt place, drew from my heart all loue
And added to the gall, O *Lear*, *Lear*!
Beat at this gate that let thy folly in,
And thy deere iudgement out, goe goe, my people? 760
ALBANY
My Lord, I am giltles as I am ignorant.
LEAR
It may be so my Lord, harke *Nature*, heare
Deere Goddesse, suspend thy purpose, if
Thou did'st intend to make this creature fruitful
Into her wombe, conuey sterility,
Drie vp in hir the organs of increase,
And from her derogate body neuer spring
A babe to honour her, if shee must teeme,
Create her childe of spleene, that it may liue
And bee a thourt disnatur'd torment to her,   770
Let it stampe wrinckles in her brow of youth,
With cadent teares, fret channels in her cheeks,
Turne all her mothers paines and benefits
To laughter and contempt, that shee may feele,
That she may feele,
How sharper then a serpents tooth it is,
To haue a thanklesse child, goe, goe, my people?
        Exeunt Lear, ⌐*Kent, Foole, and seruants*⌐
ALBANY
Now Gods that we adore, whereof comes this!
GONORILL
Neuer afflict your selfe to know the cause,
But let his disposition haue that scope   780
That dotage giues it.
      Enter Lear ⌐*and Foole*⌐
LEAR
What, fiftie of my followers at a clap,
Within a fortnight?
ALBANY   What is the matter sir?
LEAR
Ile tell thee, life and death! (*To Gonorill*) I am asham'd
That thou hast power to shake my manhood thus,
That these hot teares that breake from me perforce,
And should make the, worst blasts and fogs vpon the,
Vntented woundings of a fathers cursse,
Pearce euery sence about the, old fond eyes,
Beweepe this cause againe, ile pluck you out,   790

And cast you with the waters that you make
To temper clay, yea,
I'st come to this? yet haue I left a daughter,
Whom I am sure is kind and comfortable,
When shee shall heare this of thee, with her nailes
Shee'l flea thy woluish visage, thou shalt find
That ile resume the shape, which thou dost thinke
I haue cast off for euer, thou shalt I warrant thee.
                                                                    Exit

GONORILL Doe you marke that my Lord?

ALBANY
800   I cannot bee so partiall *Gonorill*
      To the great loue I beare you,

GONORILL   Come sir no more,
      You, more knaue then foole, after your master?

FOOLE Nunckle *Lear*, Nunckle *Lear*, tary and take the foole
      with the:
                  A fox when one has caught her,
                  And such a daughter
                  Should sure to the slaughter,
                  If my cap would buy a halter,
                  So the foole followes after.   *Exit*

810   GONORILL What *Oswald*, ho.
            Enter Steward
      STEWARD Here Madam.
      GONORILL
      What haue you writ this letter to my sister?
      STEWARD Yes Madam.
      GONORILL
      Take you some company, and away to horse,
      Informe her full of my particular feares,
      And thereto add such reasons of your owne,
      As may compact it more, get you gon,
      And after your retinue   *Exit Steward*
                        now my Lord,
      This milkie gentlenes and course of yours
820   Though I dislike not, yet vnder pardon
      Y'are much more ataxt for want of wisedome,
      Then praisd for harmfull mildnes.

      ALBANY
      How farre your eyes may pearce I cannot tell,
      Striuing to better ought, we marre whats well.
      GONORILL Nay then.
      DUKE Well, well, the euent.   *Exeunt*

Sc. 5   *Enter Lear, Kent disguised, and Foole*
      LEAR ⌈*to Kent*⌉ Goe you before to *Gloster* with these letters,
            acquaint my daughter no further with any thing you
            know, then comes from her demand out of the letter,
830   if your diligence be not speedie, I shall be there before
            you.
      KENT I will not sleepe my Lord, till I haue deliuered your
            letter.   *Exit*
      FOOLE If a mans braines were in his heeles, wert not in
            danger of kibes?
      LEAR I boy.
      FOOLE Then I prethe be mery, thy wit shal nere goe
            slipshod.
      LEAR Ha ha ha.

FOOLE Shalt see thy other daughter will vse thee kindly,   840
      for though shees as like this, as a crab is like an apple,
      yet I con, what I can tel.
LEAR Why what canst thou tell my boy?
FOOLE Sheel tast as like this, as a crab doth to a crab,
      thou canst not tell why ones nose stands in the middle
      of his face?
LEAR No.
FOOLE Why, to keep his eyes on either side's nose, that
      what a man cannot smell out, a may spie into.
LEAR I did her wrong.   850
FOOLE Canst tell how an Oyster makes his shell.
LEAR No.
FOOLE Nor I neither, but I can tell why a snayle has a
      house.
LEAR Why?
FOOLE Why, to put his head in, not to giue it away to
      his daughter, and leaue his hornes without a case.
LEAR
      I will forget my nature, so kind a father;
      Be my horses readie?
FOOLE Thy Asses are gone about them, the reason why   860
      the seuen starres are no more then seuen, is a prettie
      reason.
LEAR Because they are not eight.
FOOLE Yes thou wouldst make a good foole.
LEAR
      To tak't againe perforce, Monster, ingratitude!
FOOL If thou wert my foole Nunckle, id'e haue thee beatē
      for being old before thy time.
LEAR Hows that?
FOOLE Thou shouldst not haue beene old, before thou
      hadst beene wise.   870
LEAR
      O let me not be mad sweet heauen!
      I would not be mad,
      Keepe me in temper, I would not be mad,
            Enter Seruant
      Are the horses readie?
SERUANT   Readie my Lord.
LEAR (*to Foole*) Come boy.   *Exeunt Lear and Seruant*
FOOLE
      Shee that is maide now, and laughs at my departure,
      Shall not be a maide long, except things be cut shorter.
                                                            Exit

            Enter Bastard and Curan meeting   Sc. 6
BASTARD Saue thee *Curan*.
CURAN And you Sir, I haue beene with your father, and
      giuen him notice, that the Duke of *Cornwall* and his   880
      Dutches will bee here with him to night.
BASTARD How comes that?
CURAN Nay, I know not, you haue heard of the newes
      abroad, I meane the whisperd ones, for there are yet
      but eare-bussing arguments.
BASTARD Not, I pray you what are they?
CURAN Haue you heard of no likely warres towards, twixt
      the two Dukes of *Cornwall* and *Albany*?
BASTARD Not a word.

890 CURAN You may then in time, fare you well sir.   *Exit*
BASTARD
The Duke be here to night! the better best,
This weaues it selfe perforce into my busines,
     ⌈*Enter Edgar at a window aboue*⌉
My father hath set gard to take my brother,
And I haue one thing of a quesie question,
Which must aske breefnes wit and fortune helpe;
Brother, a word, discend brother I say,
     ⌈*Edgar climbes downe*⌉
My father watches, O flie this place,
Intelligence is giuen where you are hid,
You haue now the good aduantage of the night,
Haue you not spoken gainst the Duke of *Cornwall*
900   ought,
Hee's coming hether now in the night, it'h hast,
And *Regan* with him, haue you nothing said
Vpon his partie against the Duke of *Albany*,
Aduise you—
EDGAR   I am sure on't not a word.
BASTARD
I heare my father coming, pardon me
In cunning, I must draw my sword vpon you,
Seeme to defend your selfe, now quit you well,
(*Calling*) Yeeld, come before my father, light here,
     here,
(*To Edgar*) Flie brother flie, (*calling*) torches, torches,
     (*to Edgar*) so farwell;   *Exit Edgar*
910 Some bloud drawne on mee would beget opinion
Of my more fierce indeuour,
     He wounds his arme
                         I haue seene
Drunckards doe more then this in sport, (*calling*) father,
     father,
Stop, stop, ho, helpe?
     Enter Gloster ⌈*and others*⌉
GLOSTER   Now *Edmund* where is the villaine?
BASTARD
Here stood he in the darke, his sharpe sword out,
Warbling of wicked charms, coniuring the Moone
To stand's auspicious Mistris.
GLOSTER   But where is he?
BASTARD
Looke sir, I bleed.
GLOSTER   Where is the villaine *Edmund*?
BASTARD
Fled this way sir, when by no meanes he could—
GLOSTER
Pursue him, go after,   *Exeunt others*
          by no meanes, what?
BASTARD
920 Perswade me to the murder of your Lordship,
But that I told him the reuengiue Gods,
Gainst Paracides did all their thunders bend,
Spoke with how many fould and strong a bond
The child was bound to the father, sir in fine,
Seeing how loathly opposite I stood,
To his vnnaturall purpose, with fell motion

With his prepared sword, hee charges home
My vnprouided body, lancht mine arme,
But when he saw my best alarumd spirits,
Bould in the quarrels rights, rousd to the encounter,   930
Or whether gasted by the noyse I made,
Or ⌈   ⌉ I know not,
But sodainly he fled.
GLOSTER   Let him flie farre,
Not in this land shall hee remaine vncaught
And found, dispatch, the noble Duke my maister,
My worthy Arch and Patron, comes to night,
By his authoritie I will proclaime it,
That he which finds him shall deserue our thankes,
Bringing the murderous caytife to the stake,
Hee that conceals him, death.   940
BASTARD
When I disswaded him from his intent,
And found him pight to doe it, with curst speech
I threatned to discouer him, he replyed,
Thou vnpossessing Bastard, dost thou thinke,
If I would stand against thee, could the reposure
Of any trust, vertue, or worth in thee
Make thy words fayth'd? no, what I should denie,
As this I would, I, though thou didst produce
My very character, id'e turne it all
To thy suggestion, plot, and damned pretence,   950
And thou must make a dullard of the world,
If they not thought the profits of my death,
Were very pregnant and potentiall spurres
To make thee seeke it.
GLOSTER   Strong and fastned villaine,
Would he denie his letter, I neuer got him,
     Trumpets within
Harke the Dukes trumpets, I know not why he comes,
All Ports ile barre, the villaine shall not scape,
The Duke must grant mee that, besides, his picture
I will send farre and neere, that all the kingdome
May haue note of him, and of my land   960
Loyall and naturall boy, ile worke the meanes
To make thee capable.
     Enter the Duke of Cornwall and Regan
CORNWALL
How now my noble friend, since I came hether,
Which I can call but now, I haue heard strange
     newes.
REGAN
If it be true, all vengeance comes too short
Which can pursue the offender, how dost my Lord?
GLOSTER
Madam my old heart is crackt, is crackt.
REGAN
What, did my fathers godson seeke your life?
He whom my father named your *Edgar*?
GLOSTER
I Ladie, Ladie, shame would haue it hid.   970
REGAN
Was he not companion with the ryotous knights,
That tende vpon my father?

GLOSTER
    I know not Madam, tis too bad, too bad.

BASTARD Yes Madam, he was.

REGAN
    No maruaile then though he were ill affected,
    Tis they haue put him on the old mans death,
    To haue the spoyle and wast of his reuenues:
    I haue this present euening from my sister,
    Beene well inform'd of them, and with such cautions,
980 That if they come to soiourne at my house,
    Ile not be there.

CORNWALL   Nor I, assure thee *Regan*;
    Edmund, I heard that you haue shewen your father
    A child-like office.

BASTARD   Twas my dutie Sir.

GLOSTER (*to Cornwall*)
    He did betray his practise, and receiued
    This hurt you see, striuing to apprehend him.

CORNWALL
    Is he pursued?

GLOSTER   I my good Lord.

CORNWALL
    If he be taken, he shall neuer more
    Be feard of doing harme, make your own purpose
    How in my strength you please, for you *Edmund*,
990 Whose vertue and obedience, doth this instant
    So much commend it selfe, you shall bee ours,
    Natures of such deepe trust, wee shall much need
    You we first seaze on.

BASTARD   I shall serue you truly,
    How euer else.

GLOSTER (*to Cornwall*) For him I thanke your grace.

CORNWALL
    You know not why we came to visit you?

REGAN
    This out of season, threatning darke ey'd night,
    Ocasions noble *Gloster* of some poyse,
    Wherein we must haue vse of your aduise,
    Our Father he hath writ, so hath our sister,
1000 Of deferences, which I lest thought it fit,
    To answer from our home, the seuerall messengers
    From hence attend dispatch, our good old friend,
    Lay comforts to your bosome, & bestow
    Your needfull councell to our busines,
    Which craues the instant vse.

GLOSTER I serue you Madam,
    Your Graces are right welcome.   *Exeunt*

Sc. 7   *Enter Kent disguised at one doore, and Steward at*
              another doore

STEWARD Good deuen to thee friend, art of the house?

KENT I.

1010 STEWARD Where may we set our horses?

KENT It'h mire.

STEWARD Prethee if thou loue me, tell me.

KENT I loue thee not.

STEWARD Why then I care not for thee.

KENT If I had thee in Lipsburie pinfold, I would make thee
    care for mee.

STEWARD Why dost thou vse me thus? I know thee not.

KENT Fellow I know thee.

STEWARD What dost thou know me for?

KENT A knaue, a rascall, an eater of broken meates, a   1020
    base, proud, shallow, beggerly, three suyted hundred
    pound, filthy wosted stocken knaue, a lilly lyuer'd
    action taking knaue, a whorson glassegazing
    superfinicall rogue, one truncke inheriting slaue, one
    that would'st bee a baud in way of good seruice, and
    art nothing but the composition of a knaue, begger,
    coward, pander, and the sonne and heire of a mungrell
    bitch, whom I will beat into clamarous whyning, if
    thou denie the least sillable of the addition.

STEWARD What a monstrous fellow art thou, thus to raile   1030
    on one, that's neither knowne of thee, nor knowes
    thee.

KENT What a brazen fac't varlet art thou, to deny thou
    knowest mee, is it two dayes agoe since I beat thee,
    and tript vp thy heeles before the King? draw you
    rogue, for though it be night the Moone shines,
        ⌈*He draws his sword*⌉
    ile make a sop of the moone-shine a'you, draw you
    whorson cullyonly barber-munger, draw?

STEWARD Away, I haue nothing to doe with thee.

KENT Draw you rascall, you bring letters against the King,   1040
    and take Vanitie the puppets part, against the royaltie
    of her father, draw you rogue or ile so carbonado your
    shankes, draw you rascall, come your wayes.

STEWARD Helpe, ho, murther, helpe.

KENT Strike you slaue, stand rogue, stand you neate
    slaue, strike.

STEWARD Helpe, ho, murther, helpe.
        Enter Edmund the Bastard with his rapier drawne,
        ⌈*then*⌉ *Gloster* ⌈*then*⌉ *the Duke of Cornwall and*
        Regan the Dutchesse

BASTARD ⌈*parting them*⌉ How now, whats the matter?

KENT With you goodman boy, and you please come, ile
    fleash you, come on yong maister.   1050

GLOSTER Weapons, armes, whats the matter here?

CORNWALL Keepe peace vpon your liues, hee dies that
    strikes againe, what's the matter?

REGAN The messengers from our sister, and the King.

CORNWALL (*to Kent and Steward*) Whats your difference,
    speake?

STEWARD I am scarse in breath my Lord.

KENT No maruaile you haue so bestir'd your valour, you
    cowardly rascall, nature disclaimes in thee, a Tayler
    made thee.   1060

CORNWALL Thou art a strange fellow, a Taylor make a
    man.

KENT I, a Tayler sir; a Stone-cutter, or a Painter could
    not haue made him so ill, though hee had beene but
    two houres at the trade.

GLOSTER Speake yet, how grew your quarrell?

STEWARD This ancient ruffen sir, whose life I haue spar'd
    at sute of his gray-beard.

KENT Thou whorson Zedd, thou vnnecessarie letter, (*to*
    Cornwall) my Lord if you'l giue mee leaue, I will tread   1070
    this vnboulted villaine into morter, and daube the

walles of a iaques with him, (*to Steward*) spare my gray
beard you wagtayle.

CORNWALL

Peace sir, you beastly Knaue haue you no reuerence.

KENT

Yes sir, but anger has a priuiledge.

CORNWALL Why art thou angry?

KENT

That such a slaue as this should weare a sword,
That weares no honesty, such smiling roges
As these, like Rats oft bite those cordes in twaine,
Which are to intrencht, to vnloose: smooth euery
1080   passion
That in the natures of their Lords rebell,
Bring oyle to fier, snow to their colder-moods,
Reneag, affirme, and turne their halcion beakes
With euery gale and varie of their maisters,
Knowing nought like doges but following,
(*To Steward*) A plague vpon your epeliptick visage,
Smoyle you my speeches, as I were a foole?
Goose and I had you vpon Sarum plaine,
Id'e send you cackling home to Camulot.

DUKE

What art thou mad old fellow?

1090 GLOSTER ⌈*to Kent*⌉   How fell you out, say that?

KENT

No contraries hold more antipathy,
Then I and such a knaue.

CORNWALL   Why dost thou call him knaue,
What's his offence.

KENT   His countenance likes me not.

CORNWALL

No more perchance does mine, or his, or hers.

KENT

Sir tis my occupation to be plaine,
I haue seene better faces in my time
Than stands on any shoulder that I see
Before me at this instant.

CORNWALL   This is a fellow
Who hauing beene praysd for bluntnes doth affect
1100 A sawcy ruffnes, and constraines the garb
Quite from his nature, he cannot flatter he,
He must be plaine, he must speake truth,
And they will tak't so, if not he's plaine,
These kind of knaues I know which in this plainnes
Harbour more craft, and more corrupter ends,
Then twentie silly ducking obseruants,
That stretch their duties nisely.

KENT

Sir in good sooth, or in sincere veritie,
Vnder the allowance of your graund aspect,
1110 Whose influence like the wreath of radient fire
In flickering *Phœbus* front.

CORNWALL   What mean'st thou by this?

KENT To goe out of my dialect which you discommend
so much, I know sir, I am no flatterer, he that beguild
you in a plain accent, was a plaine knaue, which for
my part I will not bee, though I should win your
displeasure, to intreat mee too't.

CORNWALL (*to Steward*)

What's the offence you gaue him?

STEWARD   I neuer gaue him any,
It pleas'd the King his maister very late
To strike at me vpon his misconstruction,
When he coniunct and flattering his displeasure   1120
Tript me behind, being downe, insulted, rayld,
And put vpon him such a deale of man, that,
That worthied him, got prayses of the King,
For him attempting who was selfe subdued,
And in the flechment of this dread exploit,
Drew on me here againe.

KENT   None of these roges & cowards
But *A'Iax* is their foole.

CORNWALL ⌈*calling*⌉   Bring forth the stockes ho?
(*To Kent*) You stubburne ansient knaue, you reuerent
          bragart,
Weele teach you.

KENT   I am too old to learne,
Call not your stockes for me, I serue the King,   1130
On whose imployments I was sent to you,
You should doe small respect, shew too bold malice
Against the Grace and person of my maister,
Stoking his messenger.

CORNWALL ⌈*calling*⌉   Fetch forth the stockes?
As I haue life and honour, there shall he set till noone.

REGAN

Till noone, till night my Lord, and all night too.

KENT

Why Madam, if I were your fathers dogge,
You could not vse me so.

REGAN   Sir being his knaue, I will.
⌈*Stockes brought out*⌉

CORNWALL

This is a fellow of the selfe same nature,
Our sister speakes of, come bring away the stockes?   1140

GLOSTER

Let me beseech your Grace not to doe so,
His fault is much, and the good King his maister
Will check him for't, your purpost low correction
Is such, as basest and contemned wretches
For pilfrings and most common trespasses
Are punisht with, the King must take it ill,
That hee's so slightly valued in his messenger,
Should haue him thus restrained.

CORNWALL   Ile answer that.

REGAN

My sister may receiue it much more worse,
To haue her Gentlemen abus'd, assalted   1150
For following her affaires, put in his legges,
They put Kent in the stockes
Come my good Lord away?

          Exeunt. Manet Gloster and Kent

GLOSTER

I am sory for thee friend, tis the Dukes pleasure,
Whose disposition all the world well knowes
Will not be rubd or stopt, ile intreat for thee.

KENT

Pray you doe not sir, I haue watcht and trauaild hard,

Sometime I shal sleepe out, the rest ile whistle,
A good mans fortune may grow out at heeles,
Giue you good morrow.

GLOSTER

1160   The Dukes to blame in this, twill be ill tooke.   *Exit*

KENT

Good King that must approue the cõmon say,
Thou out of heauens benediction comest
To the warme Sunne.
    ⌈*He takes out a letter*⌉
Approach thou beacon to this vnder gloabe,
That by thy comfortable beames I may
Peruse this letter, nothing almost sees myrackles
But miserie, I know tis from *Cordelia*,
Who hath now fortunately beene informed
Of my obscured course, and shall find time
1170   For this enormious state, seeking to giue
Losses yʳ remedies, all wearie and ouerwatcht
Take vantage heauie eyes not to behold
This shamefull lodging, Fortune goodnight,
Smile, once more turne thy wheele.   *He sleepes*
    Enter Edgar

EDGAR   I heard my selfe proclaim'd,
And by the happie hollow of a tree
Escapt the hunt, no Port is free, no place
That guard, and most vnusuall vigilence
Dos not attend my taking while I may scape
I will preserue my selfe, and am bethought
1180   To take the basest and most poorest shape,
That euer penury in contempt of man,
Brought neare to beast, my face ile grime with filth,
Blanket my loynes, elfe all my haire with knots,
And with presented nakednes outface,
The wind, and persecution of the skie,
The Countrie giues me proofe and president
Of Bedlam beggers, who with roring voyces,
Strike in their numb'd and mortified bare armes,
Pins, wodden prickes, nayles, sprigs of rosemary,
1190   And with this horrible obiect from low fermes,
Poore pelting villages, sheep-coates, and milles,
Sometime with lunaticke bans, sometime with prayers
Enforce their charitie, poore *Tuelygod*, poore *Tom*,
That's something yet, *Edgar* I nothing am.   *Exit*
    Enter King Lear, Foole, and Knight

LEAR

Tis strange that they should so depart from home,
And not send backe my messenger.

KNIGHT   As I learn'd,
The night before there was no purpose
Of his remoue.

KENT (*waking*)   Hayle to thee noble maister.

LEAR

How, mak'st thou this shame thy pastime?

1200 FOOLE Ha ha, looke he weares crewell garters, horses are
tide by the heedes, dogges and beares byt'h necke,
munkies bit'h loynes, and men byt'h legges, when a
mans ouer lusty at legs, then he weares wooden
neatherstockes.

LEAR (*to Kent*)
Whats he, that hath so much thy place mistooke
To set thee here?

KENT   It is both he and shee,
Your sonne & daughter.

LEAR   No.

KENT   Yes.

LEAR   No I say.

KENT

I say yea.

LEAR   No no, they would not.

KENT   Yes they haue.

LEAR

By *Iupiter* I sweare no, they durst not do't,
They would not, could not do't, tis worse then murder,   1210
To doe vpon respect such violent outrage,
Resolue me with all modest hast, which way
Thou may'st deserue, or they propose this vsage,
Coming from vs.

KENT   My Lord, when at their home
I did commend your highnes letters to them,
Ere I was risen from the place that shewed
My dutie kneeling, came there a reeking Post,
Stewd in his hast, halfe breathles, panting forth
From *Gonorill* his mistris, salutations,
Deliuered letters spite of intermission,   1220
Which presently they read, on whose contents
They summond vp their meinie, straight tooke horse,
Commanded me to follow, and attend
The leasure of their answere, gaue me cold lookes,
And meeting here the other messenger,
Whose welcome I perceau'd had poyson'd mine,
Being the very fellow that of late
Display'd so sawcily against your Highnes,
Hauing more man then wit about me drew,
He raised the house with loud and coward cries,   1230
Your sonne and daughter found this trespas worth
This shame which here it suffers.

LEAR

O how this mother swels vp toward my hart,
Histerica passio downe thou climing sorrow,
Thy element's below, where is this daughter?

KENT

With the Earle sir within.

LEAR   Follow me not, stay there?
                                  Exit

KNIGHT (*to Kent*)
Made you no more offẽce then what you speake of?

KENT

No, how chance the King comes with so small a traine?

FOOLE And thou hadst beene set in the stockes for that
question, thou ha'dst well deserued it.   1240

KENT Why foole?

FOOLE Weele set thee to schoole to an Ant, to teach thee
ther's no labouring in the winter, all that follow their
noses, are led by their eyes, but blind men, and ther's
not a nose among a 100. but can smell him thats
stincking, let goe thy hold when a great wheele runs

downe a hill, least it breake thy necke with following
it, but the great one that goes vp the hill, let him draw
thee after, when a wise man giues thee better councell,
1250   giue mee mine againe, I would haue none but knaues
follow it, since a foole giues it.
⌐Sings⌐ That Sir that serues for gaine,
    And followes but for forme:
    Will packe when it begin to raine,
    And leaue thee in the storme.

    But I will tarie, the foole will stay,
    And let the wise man flie:
    The knaue turnes foole that runs away,
    The foole no knaue perdy.
1260   KENT Where learnt you this foole?
FOOLE Not in the stockes.
    Enter Lear and Gloster
LEAR
Denie to speake with mee, th'are sicke, th'are weary,
They traueled hard to night, meare Insolêce,
I the Images of reuolt and flying off,
Fetch mee a better answere.
GLOSTER   My deere Lord,
You know the fierie qualitie of the Duke,
How vnremoueable and fixt he is
In his owne Course.
LEAR   Vengeance, death, plague, confusion,
What fierie quality, why *Gloster*, *Gloster*, id'e
1270   Speake with the Duke of *Cornwall*, and his wife.
GLOSTER I my good Lord.
LEAR
The King would speake with *Cornewal*, the deare fat'
Would with his daughter speake, commands tends
    seruise,
Fierie? the Duke, tell the hot Duke that *Lear*,
No but not yet may be he is not well,
Infirmitie doth still neglect all office,
Where to our health is boûd, we are not our selues,
When nature being oprest cõmands the mind
To suffer with the bodie, ile forbeare,
1280   And am fallen out with my more hedier will,
To take the indispos'd and sickly fit,
For the sound man, death on my state,
Wherfore should he sit here? This act perswades me,
That this remotion of the Duke & her
Is practise only giue me my seruant forth,
Tell the Duke and's wife, Ile speake with them
Now presently, bid them come forth and heare me,
Or at their chamber doore ile beat the drum,
Till it cry sleepe to death.
GLOSTER   I would haue all well
Betwixt you.   *Exit*
1290   LEAR   O my heart, my heart.
FOOLE Cry to it Nunckle, as the Coknay did to the eeles,
when she put vm it'h past aliue, she rapt vm ath
coxcombs with a stick, and cryed downe wantons
downe, twas her brother, that in pure kindnes to his
horse buttered his hay.

    Enter Duke of Cornwall and Regan, Gloster, and
    others
LEAR Good morrow to you both.
CORNWALL Hayle to your Grace.
    ⌐*Kent here set at liberty*⌐
REGAN I am glad to see your highnes.
LEAR
Regan I thinke you are, I know what reason
I haue to thinke so, if thou shouldst not be glad,   1300
I would deuorse me from thy mothers scrine,
Sepulchring an adultresse, (*to Kent*) yea are you free?
Some other time for that. Beloued *Regan*,
Thy sister is naught, oh *Regan* she hath tyed,
Sharpe tooth'd vnkindnes, like a vulture heare,
I can scarce speake to thee, thout not beleeue,
Of how deplored a qualitie, O *Regan*.
REGAN
I pray you sir take patience, I haue hope
You lesse know how to value her desert,
Then she to slacke her dutie.   1310
LEAR My cursses on her.
REGAN O Sir you are old,
Nature in you standes on the very verge
Of her confine, you should be rul'd and led
By some discretion, that discernes your state
Better thê you your selfe, therfore I pray
That to our sister, you do make returne,
Say you haue wrong'd her Sir?
LEAR   Aske her forgiuenes,
Doe you marke how this becomes the house,
⌐*Kneeling*⌐ Deare daughter, I confesse that I am old,   1320
Age is vnnecessarie, on my knees I beg,
That you'l vouchsafe me rayment, bed and food.
REGAN
Good sir no more, these are vnsightly tricks,
Returne you to my sister.
LEAR ⌐*rising*⌐   No *Regan*,
She hath abated me of halfe my traine,
Lookt blacke vpon me, strooke mee with her tongue
Most Serpent-like vpon the very heart,
All the stor'd vengeances of heauen fall
On her ingratful top, strike her yong bones,
You taking ayrs with lamenes.
CORNWALL   Fie fie sir.   1330
LEAR
You nimble lightnings dart your blinding flames,
Into her scornfull eyes, infect her beautie,
You Fen suckt fogs, drawne by the powrefull Sunne,
To fall and blast her pride.
REGAN   O the blest Gods,
So will you wish on me, when the rash mood—
LEAR
No *Regan*, thou shalt neuer haue my curse,
Thy têder hested nature shall not giue
The or'e to harshnes, her eies are fierce, but thine
Do cõfort & not burne tis not in thee
To grudge my pleasures, to cut off my traine,   1340
To bandy hasty words, to scant my sizes,

And in conclusion, to oppose the bolt
Against my coming in, thou better knowest,
The offices of nature, bond of child-hood,
Effects of curtesie, dues of gratitude,
Thy halfe of the kingdome, hast thou not forgot
Wherein I thee indow'd.

REGAN   Good sir too'th purpose.

LEAR
Who put my man i'th stockes?

  ⌈*Trumpets within*⌉

CORNWALL   What trumpets that?

  Enter Steward

REGAN
I know't my sisters, this approues her letters,
1350 That she would soone be here, is your Lady come?

LEAR
This is a slaue, whose easie borrowed pride
Dwels in the fickle grace of her a followes,

  ⌈*He strikes the Steward*⌉

Out varlot, from my sight.

CORNWALL   What meanes your Grace?

  Enter Gonorill

GONORILL
Who struck my seruant, *Regan* I haue good hope
Thou didst not know ant.

LEAR   Who comes here? O heauens!
If you doe loue old men, if your sweet sway
Alow obedience, if your selues are old,
Make it your cause, send downe and take my part,
(*To Gonorill*) Art not asham'd to looke vpon this beard?
1360 O *Regan* wilt thou take her by the hand?

GONORILL
Why not by the hand sir, how haue I offended?
Als not offence that indiscretion finds,
And dotage tearmes so.

LEAR   O sides you are too tough,
Will you yet hold? how came my man it'h stockes?

CORNWALL
I set him there sir, but his owne disorders
Deseru'd much lesse aduancement,

LEAR   You, did you?

REGAN
I pray you father being weake seeme so,
If till the expiration of your moneth,
You will returne and soiorne with my sister,
1370 Dismissing halfe your traine, come then to me,
I am now from home, and out of that prouision,
Which shall be needful for your entertainment.

LEAR
Returne to her, and fiftie men dismist,
No rather I abiure all roofes, and chuse
To be a Comrade with the Woolfe and owle,
To wage against the enmitie of the Ayre,
Necessities sharpe pinch, returne with her,
Why the hot bloud in *France*, that dowerles tooke
Our yongest borne, I could as well be brought
To knee his throne, and Squire-like pension beg,
1380 To keepe base life afoot, returne with her,

Perswade me rather to be slaue and sumter
To this detested groome.

GONORILL   At your choise sir.

LEAR
Now I prithee daughter do not make me mad,
I will not trouble thee my child, farewell,
Wee'le no more meete, no more see one another.
But yet thou art my flesh, my bloud, my daughter,
Or rather a disease that lies within my flesh,
Which I must needs call mine, thou art a bile,
A plague sore, an imbossed carbuncle   1390
In my corrupted bloud, but Ile not chide thee,
Let shame come when it will, I doe not call it,
I doe not bid the thunder bearer shoote,
Nor tell tales of thee to high Iudging *Ioue*,
Mend when thou canst, be better at thy leisure,
I can be patient, I can stay with *Regan*,
I and my hundred Knights.

REGAN   Not altogether so sir,
I looke not for you yet, nor am prouided
For your fit welcome, giue eare sir to my sister,
For those that mingle reason with your passion,   1400
Must be content to thinke you are old, and so,
But she knowes what shee does.

LEAR   Is this well spoken now?

REGAN
I dare auouch it sir, what fiftie followers,
Is it not well, what should you need of more,
Yea or so many, sith that both charge and danger
Speakes gainst so great a number, how in a house
Should many people vnder two commands
Hold amytie, tis hard, almost impossible.

GONORILL
Why might not you my Lord receiue attendãce
From those that she cals seruants, or from mine?   1410

REGAN
Why not my Lord? if then they chanc'st to slacke you,
We could controwle them, if you will come to me,
For now I spie a danger, I intreat you,
To bring but fiue and twentie, to no more
Will I giue place or notice.

LEAR I gaue you all.

REGAN And in good time you gaue it.

LEAR
Made you my guardians, my depositaries,
But kept a reseruation to be followed
With such a number, what, must I come to you   1420
With fiue and twentie, *Regan* said you so?

REGAN
And speak't againe my Lord, no more with me.

LEAR
Those wicked creatures yet do seem wel fauor'd
When others are more wicked, not being the worst
Stands in some ranke of prayse, (*to Gonorill*) Ile goe
 with thee,
Thy fifty yet doth double fiue and twentie,
And thou art twice her loue.

GONORILL   Heare me my Lord,

What need you fiue and twentie, tenne, or fiue,
To follow in a house, where twise so many
Haue a commaund to tend you.

1430 REGAN   What needes one?

LEAR
O reason not the need, our basest beggers,
Are in the poorest thing superfluous,
Allow not nature more then nature needes,
Mans life is cheape as beasts, thou art a Lady,
If onely to goe warme were gorgeous,
Why nature needes not, what thou gorgeous wearest
Which scarcely keepes thee warme, but for true need,
You heauens giue me that patience, patience I need,
You see me here (you Gods) a poore old fellow,
1440 As full of greefe as age, wretched in both,
If it be you that stirres these daughters hearts
Against their Father, foole me not so much,
To beare it tamely, touch me with noble anger,
O let not womens weapons, water drops
Stayne my mans cheekes, no you vnnaturall hags,
I will haue such reuenges on you both,
That all the world shall, I will doe such things,
What they are yet I know not, but they shalbe
The terrors of the earth, you thinke ile weepe,
1450 No ile not weepe,
        ⌜Storme within⌝
I haue full cause of weeping, but this heart
Shall breake, into a 100. thousand flawes
Or ere ile weepe, O foole I shall goe mad.
        Exeunt Lear, Gloster, Kent, ⌜Knight,⌝ and Foole

CORNWALL
Let vs withdraw, twill be a storme.

REGAN
This house is little the old man and his people,
Cannot be well bestowed.

GONORILL   Tis his own blame,
Hath put himselfe from rest, and must needs tast his
        folly.

REGAN
For his particuler, ile receiue him gladly,
But not one follower.

CORNWALL
1460 So am I purpos'd, where is my Lord of *Gloster?*

REGAN
Followed the old man forth,
        Enter Gloster
                        he is return'd.

GLOSTER
The King is in high rage, & wil I know not whether.

REGAN
Tis good to giue him way, he leads himselfe.

GONORILL *(to Gloster)*
My Lord, intreat him by no meanes to stay.

GLOSTER
Alack the night comes on, and the bleak winds
Do sorely russel, for many miles about
Ther's not a bush.

REGAN   O sir, to wilfull men

The iniuries that they themselues procure,
Must be their schoolemasters, shut vp your doores,
He is attended with a desperate traine,   1470
And what they may incense him to, being apt,
To haue his eare abusd, wisedome bids feare.

CORNWALL
Shut vp your doores my Lord, tis a wild night,
My *Reg.* counsails well, come out at'h storme.   *Exeūt*

        Storme. Enter Kent disguised and 1. Gentleman at   Sc. 8
        seuerall doores

KENT
Whats here beside foule weather?

1. GENTLEMAN   One minded like the weather
Most vnquietly.

KENT   I know you, whers the King?

1. GENTLEMAN
Contending with the fretfull element,
Bids the wind blow the earth into the sea,
Or swell the curled waters boue the maine
That things might change or cease, teares his white
        haire,   1480
Which the impetuous blasts with eyles rage
Catch in their furie, and make nothing of,
Striues in his little world of man to outstorme,
The too and fro conflicting wind and raine,
This night wherin the cub-drawne Beare would couch,
The Lyon, and the belly pinched Wolfe
Keepe their furre dry, vnbonneted he runnes,
And bids what will take all.

KENT   But who is with him?

1. GENTLEMAN
None but the foole, who labours to out-iest
His heart strooke iniuries.

KENT   Sir I doe know you,   1490
And dare vpon the warrant of my Arte,
Commend a deare thing to you, there is diuision,
Although as yet the face of it be couer'd,
With mutuall cunning, twixt *Albany* and *Cornwall*
But true it is, from *France* there comes a power
Into this scattered kingdome, who alreadie
Wise in our negligēce, haue secret feet
In some of our best Ports, and are at point
To shew their open banner, now to you,
If on my credit you dare build so farre,   1500
To make your speed to Douer, you shall find
Some that will thanke you, making iust report
Of how vnnaturall and bemadding sorrow
The King hath cause to plaine,
I am a Gentleman of blood and breeding,
And from some knowledge and assurance, offer
This office to you.

1. GENTLEMAN I will talke farther with you.

KENT No doe not,
For confirmation that I am much more   1510
Then my outwall, open this purse and take
What it containes, if you shall see *Cordelia,*
As feare not but you shall, shew her this ring,

And she will tell you who your fellow is,
That yet you doe not know, fie on this storme,
I will goe seeke the King.

1. GENTLEMAN   Giue me your hand,
Haue you no more to say?

KENT   Few words but to effect
More then all yet: that when we haue found the King,
In which indeuor Ile this way, you that,
1520   He that first lights on him, hollow the other.
                              Exeunt seuerally

Sc. 9   *Storme. Enter Lear and Foole*

LEAR
Blow wind & cracke your cheekes, rage, blow
You caterackes, & Hiricanos spout
Til you haue drencht the steeples drown'd the cockes,
You sulpherous and thought executing fires,
Vaunt-currers to oke-cleauing thunderboults,
Singe my white head, and thou all shaking thunder,
Smite flat the thicke Rotunditie of the world,
Cracke natures mold, all Germains spill at once
That make ingratefull man.

1530   FOOLE O Nunckle, Court holly water in a drie house is
better then this raine water out a doore, good Nunckle
in, and aske thy daughters blessing, heers a night pities
nether wise man nor foole.

LEAR
Rumble thy belly full, spit fire, spout raine,
Nor raine, wind, thunder, fire, are my daughters,
I taxe not you you elements with vnkindnes,
I neuer gaue you kingdome, cald you children,
You owe me no subscription, why then let fall
Your horrible plesure here I stãd your slaue,
1540   A poore infirme weak & despis'd ould man,
But yet I call you seruile ministers,
That haue with 2. pernitious daughters ioin'd
Your high engẽdred battel gainst a head
So old & white as this, O tis foule.

FOOLE Hee that has a house to put his head in, has a
good headpeece,
⌈*Sings*⌉   The Codpeece that will house
            Before the head, has any
            The head and hee shall lowse,
1550   So beggers mary many,

            The man that makes his toe,
            What hee his heart should make,
            Shall haue a corne cry woe,
            And turne his sleepe to wake,
for there was neuer yet faire woman but shee made
mouthes in a glasse.

LEAR
No I will be the patterne of all patience
   ⌈*He sits.*⌉ *Enter Kent disguised*
I will say nothing.

KENT Whose there?

1560   FOOLE Marry heers Grace, & a codpis, that's a wiseman
and a foole.

KENT (*to Lear*)
Alas sir, sit you here? Things that loue night,
Loue not such nights as these, the wrathfull Skies
Gallow the very wanderers of the darke,
And makes them keepe their caues, since I was man,
Such sheets of fire, such bursts of horred thunder,
Such grones of roaring winde, and rayne, I ne're
Remember to haue heard, mans nature cannot cary
The affliction, nor the force.

LEAR   Let the great Gods
That keepe this dreadful powther ore our heades,   1570
Find out their enemies now, tremble thou wretch
That hast within thee vndivulged crimes,
Vnwhipt of Iustice, hide thee thou bloudy hand,
Thou periur'd, and thou simular man of vertue
That art incestious, caytife in peeces shake,
That vnder couert and conuenient seeming,
Hast practised on mans life,
Close pent vp guilts, riue your concealed centers,
And cry these dreadfull summoners grace,
I am a man more sind against then sinning.   1580

KENT Alacke bare headed,
Gracious my Lord, hard by here is a houell,
Some friendship will it lend you gainst the tempest,
Repose you there, whilst I to this hard house,
More hard then is the stone whereof tis rais'd,
Which euen but now demaunding after you,
Denide me to come in, returne and force
Their scanted curtesie.

LEAR   My wit begins to turne,
(*To Foole*) Come on my boy, how dost my boy, art cold?
I am cold my selfe, (*to Kent*) where is this straw my
      fellow,   1590
The art of our necessities is strange
That can make vild things precious, come your houell
(*To Foole*) Poore foole and knaue, I haue one part of
      my heart
That sorrowes yet for thee.

FOOLE ⌈*sings*⌉
      Hee that has a little tine witte,
          With hey ho the wind and the raine,
      Must make content with his fortunes fit,
          For the raine, it raineth euery day.

LEAR
True my good boy, (*to Kent*) come bring vs to this
      houell?   *Exeunt*

            Enter Gloster and the Bastard with lights   Sc. 10

GLOSTER
Alacke alacke *Edmund* I like not this   1600
Vnnaturall dealing when I desir'd their leaue
That I might pitty him, they tooke from me
The vse of mine owne house, charg'd me on paine
Of their displeasure, neither to speake of him,
Intreat for him, nor any way sustaine him.

BASTARD Most sauage and vnnaturall.

GLOSTER Go toe say you nothing, ther's a diuisiõ betwixt
the Dukes, and a worse matter then that, I haue

1610 receiued a letter this night, tis dangerous to be spoken, I haue lockt the letter in my closet, these iniuries the King now beares, will be reuenged home, ther's part of a power already landed, we must incline to the King, I will seeke him, and priuily releeue him, goe you and maintaine talke with the Duke, that my charity be not of him perceiued, if hee aske for me, I am ill, and gon to bed, though I die for't, as no lesse is threatned me, the King my old master must be releeued, there is some stränge thing toward, *Edmund* pray you be carefull.   *Exit*

BASTARD
This curtesie forbid thee, shal the Duke
1620 Instätly know and of that letter to,
This seems a faire deseruing and must draw me
That which my father looses, no lesse then all,
The yonger rises when the old doe fall.   *Exit*

Sc. 11   *Storme. Enter Lear, Kent disguised, and foole*

KENT
Here is the place my Lord, good my Lord enter,
The tyrannie of the open nights too ruffe
For nature to indure.

LEAR   Let me alone.

KENT
Good my Lord enter here.

LEAR   Wilt breake my heart?

KENT
I had rather breake mine owne, good my Lord enter.

LEAR
Thou think'st tis much, that this contentious storme
1630 Inuades vs to the skin, so tis to thee,
But where the greater malady is fixt
The lesser is scarce felt, thoud'st shun a Beare,
But if thy flight lay toward the roring sea,
Thoud'st meet the beare it'h mouth, whē the mind's free
The bodies delicate, this tempest in my mind
Doth from my sences take all feeling else
Saue what beates their, filiall ingratitude,
Is it not as this mouth should teare this hand
For lifting food to't, but I will punish sure,
1640 No I will weepe no more,
In such a night as this! O *Regan, Gonorill,*
Your old kind father whose franke heart gaue you all,
O that way madnes lies, let me shun that,
No more of that.

KENT   Good my Lord enter.

LEAR
Prethe goe in thy selfe, seeke thy one ease
This tempest will not giue me leaue to ponder
On things would hurt me more, but ile goe in,
                    Exit Foole
Poore naked wretches, where so ere you are
That bide the pelting of this pittiles night,
1650 How shall your house-lesse heads, and vnfed sides,
Your loopt and windowed raggednes defend you
From seasons such as these, O I haue tane
Too little care of this, take physicke pompe,
Expose thy selfe to feele what wretches feele,

That thou mayst shake the superflux to them,
And shew the heauens more iust.
                    Enter Foole

FOOLE Come not in here Nunckle, her's a spirit, helpe me, helpe mee.

KENT Giue me thy hand, whose there.

FOOLE A spirit, he sayes, his nam's poore *Tom.*   1660

KENT
What art thou that dost grumble there in the straw,
Come forth?
                    Enter Edgar as a Bedlam begger

EDGAR Away, the fowle fiend followes me, thorough the sharpe hathorne blowes the cold wind, goe to thy cold bed and warme thee.

LEAR
Hast thou giuen all to thy two daughters,
And art thou come to this?

EDGAR Who giues any thing to poore *Tom,* whome the foule Fiende hath led, through fire, and through foord, and whirli-poole, ore bog and quagmire, that has layd   1670 kniues vnder his pillow, and halters in his pue, set ratsbane by his pottage, made him proud of heart, to ride on a bay trotting horse ouer foure incht bridges, to course his owne shadow for a traytor, blesse thy fiue wits, *Toms* a cold, blesse thee from whirle-winds, starre-blasting, and taking, doe poore *Tom* some charitie, whom the foule fiend vexes, there could I haue him now, and there, and there againe.

LEAR
What, has his daughters brought him to this passe,
(*To Edgar*) Couldst thou saue nothing, didst thou giue
them all?   1680

FOOLE Nay he reseru'd a blanket, else we had beene all sham'd.

LEAR (*to Edgar*)
Now all the plagues that in the pendulous ayre
Hang fated ore mens faults, fall on thy daughters.

KENT He hath no daughters sir.

LEAR
Death traytor, nothing could haue subdued nature
To such a lownes, but his vnkind daughters,
(*To Edgar*) Is it the fashion that discarded fathers,
Should haue thus little mercy on their flesh,
Iudicious punishment twas this flesh begot   1690
Those Pelicane daughters.

EDGAR Pilicock sate on pelicocks hill, a lo lo lo.

FOOLE This cold night will turne vs all to fooles & madmen.

EDGAR Take heede at'h foule fiend, obay thy parents, keep thy word iustly, sweare not, commit not with mans sworne spouse, set not thy sweet heart on proud array, *Toms* a cold.

LEAR What hast thou beene?

EDGAR A Seruingman, proud in heart and mind, that curld my haire, wore gloues in my cap, serued the lust   1700 of my mistris heart, and did the act of darkenes with her, swore as many oaths as I spake words, and broke them in the sweet face of heauen, one that slept in the contriuing of lust, and wakt to doe it, wine loued I deeply, dice deerely, and in woman out paramord the

Turke, false of heart, light of eare, bloudie of hand,
Hog in sloth, Fox in stealth, Woolfe in greedines, Dog
in madnes, Lyon in pray, let not the creeking of shooes,
nor the ruslings of silkes betray thy poore heart to
1710 women, keepe thy foote out of brothell, thy hand out
of placket, thy pen from lenders booke, and defie the
foule fiend, still through the hathorne blowes the cold
wind, hay no nonny, Dolphin my boy, my boy, cease,
let him trot by.

LEAR Why thou wert better in thy graue, then to answere
with thy vncouered bodie this extremitie of the skies,
is man no more but this cõsider him well, thou owest
the worme no silke, the beast no hide, the sheepe no
wooll, the cat no perfume, her's three ons are
1720 sophisticated, thou art the thing it selfe, vnaccomodated
man, is no more but such a poore bare forked Animall
as thou art, off off you lendings, come on bee true.

FOOLE Prithe Nunckle be content, this is a naughty night
to swim in, now a little fire in a wild field, were like
an old leachers heart, a small sparke, all the rest ons
bodie cold, looke here comes a walking fire.

Enter Gloster with a ⌈torch⌉

EDGAR This is the foule fiend *fliberdegibet*, hee begins at
curphew, and walks till the first cocke, he giues the
web, & the pin, squenies the eye, and makes the hare
1730 lip, mildewes the white wheate, and hurts the poore
creature of earth,

⌈*Sings*⌉ Swithune footed thrice the old

A mett the night mare and her nine fold
Bid her a light
And her troth plight
And arint thee, witch arint thee.

KENT (*to Lear*)
How fares your Grace?

LEAR   Whats hee?

KENT (*to Gloster*) Whose there, what i'st you seeke?

GLOSTER What are you there? your names?

1740 EDGAR Poore *Tom*, that eats the swimming frog, the tode,
the tode pole, the wall-neut, and the water, that in the
furie of his heart, when the foule fiend rages, eats cow-
dung for sallets, swallowes the old ratt, and the ditch
dogge, drinkes the greene mantle of the standing poole,
who is whipt from tithing to tithing, and stock-punisht
and imprisoned, who hath had three sutes to his backe,
six shirts to his bodie,

Horse to ride, and weapon to weare.
But mise and rats, and such small Deere,
1750 Hath beene *Toms* foode for seuen long yeare—
Beware my follower, peace smolking, peace thou fiend.

GLOSTER (*to Lear*)
What hath your Grace no better company?

EDGAR
The Prince of darkenes is a Gentleman,
Modo he's caled and mahu—

GLOSTER (*to Lear*)
Our flesh and bloud is growne so vild my Lord,
That it doth hate what gets it.

EDGAR   Poore *Toms* a cold.

GLOSTER (*to Lear*)
Go in with me, my dutie cãnot suffer
To obay in all your daughters hard commaunds,
Though their iniunction be to barre my doores,
And let this tyranous night take hold vpon you,   1760
Yet haue I venter'd to come seeke you out,
And bring you where both food and fire is readie.

LEAR
First let me talke with this Philosopher,
(*To Edgar*) What is the cause of thunder?

KENT   My good Lord
Take his offer, goe into the house.

LEAR
Ile talke a word with this most learned Theban,
(*To Edgar*) What is your studie?

EDGAR
How to preuent the fiend, and to kill vermine.

LEAR
Let me aske you one word in priuate.
They conuerse apart

KENT (*to Gloster*)
Importune him to goe my Lord,   1770
His wits begin to vnsettle.

GLOSTER   Canst thou blame him,
His daughters seeke his death, O that good *Kent*,
He said it would be thus, poore banisht man,
Thou sayest the King growes mad, ile tell thee friend
I am almost mad my selfe, I had a sonne
Now out-lawed from my bloud, a sought my life
But lately, very late, I lou'd him friend
No father his sonne deerer, true to tell thee,
The greefe hath craz'd my wits, what a nights this?
(*To Lear*) I doe beseech your Grace.

LEAR   O crie you mercie   1780
(*To Edgar*) Noble Philosopher, your company.

EDGAR   *Toms* a cold.

GLOSTER
In fellow there, in't houell keepe thee warme.

LEAR
Come lets in all.

KENT   This way my Lord.

LEAR   With him,
I wil keep stil with my Philosopher.

KENT (*to Gloster*)
Good my Lord sooth him, let him take the fellow.

GLOSTER Take him you on.

KENT ⌈*to Edgar*⌉
Sirah come on, goe along with vs?

LEAR (*to Edgar*)
Come good Athenian.

GLOSTER   No words, no words, hush.

EDGAR Child *Rowland*, to the darke towre come,
His word was still fy fo and fum,   1790
I smell the bloud of a British man.   *Exeunt*

Enter Cornewell and Bastard   Sc. 12

CORNWALL I will haue my reuenge ere I depart the house.

BASTARD How my Lord I may be censured, that nature

thus giues way to loyaltie, some thing feares me to thinke of.

CORNWALL I now perceiue it was not altogether your brothers euill disposition made him seeke his death, but a prouoking merit, set a worke by a reproueable badnes in himselfe.

1800 BASTARD How malicious is my fortune, that I must repent to bee iust? this is the letter he spoke of, which approues him an intelligent partie to the aduantages of *France*, O heauens that his treason were not, or not I the detecter.

CORNWALL Goe with me to the Dutches.

BASTARD If the matter of this paper be certaine, you haue mighty busines in hand.

CORNWALL True or false, it hath made thee Earle of *Gloster*, seeke out where thy father is, that hee may bee readie 1810 for our apprehension.

BASTARD ⌈*aside*⌉ If I find him comforting the King, it will stuffe his suspition more fully, (*to Cornwall*) I will perseuere in my course of loyaltie, though the conflict be sore betweene that and my bloud.

CORNWALL I will lay trust vpon thee, and thou shalt find a dearer father in my loue.   *Exeunt*

Sc. 13   *Enter Gloster and Lear, Kent disguised, Foole, and*
              Edgar as a Bedlam begger

GLOSTER Here is better then the open ayre, take it thankfully, I will peece out the comfort with what addition I can, I will not be long from you.

1820 KENT All the power of his wits haue giuen way to impatience, the Gods deserne your kindnes.

                              ⌈*Exit Gloster*⌉

EDGAR *Fratereto* cals me, and tels me *Nero* is an angler in the lake of darknes, pray innocent beware the foule fiend.

FOOLE (*to Lear*) Prithe Nunckle tell me, whether a mad man be a Gentleman or a Yeoman.

LEAR
A King, a King, to haue a thousand
With red burning spits come hiszing in vpon them.

EDGAR The foule fiend bites my backe.

1830 FOOLE (*to Lear*) He's mad, that trusts in the tamenes of a Wolfe, a horses health, a boyes loue, or a whores oath.

LEAR
It shalbe done, I wil arraigne them straight,
⌈*To Edgar*⌉ Come sit thou here most learned Iusticer
⌈*To Foole*⌉ Thou sapient sir sit here, no you shee
    Foxes—

EDGAR Looke where he stands and glars, wantst thou eyes, at trol madam
⌈*Sings*⌉ Come ore the boorne *Bessy* to mee.

FOOLE ⌈*sings*⌉
        Her boat hath a leake,
        And she must not speake,
1840   Why she dares not come, ouer to thee.

EDGAR The foule fiend haŭts poore *Tom* in the voyce of a nightingale, hoppedance cries in *Toms* belly for two white herring, croke not blacke Angell, I haue no foode for thee.

KENT (*to Lear*)
How doe you sir? stand you not so amazd,
Will you lie downe and rest vpon the cushings?

LEAR
Ile see their triall first, bring in the euidence,
⌈*To Edgar*⌉ Thou robbed man of Iustice take thy place,
⌈*To Foole*⌉ And thou his yokefellow of equity,
Bench by his side, ⌈*to Kent*⌉ you are ot'h commission, 1850
Sit you too.

EDGAR Let vs deale iustly
⌈*sings*⌉ Sleepest or wakest thou iolly shepheard,
        Thy sheepe bee in the corne,
        And for one blast of thy minikin mouth,
        Thy sheepe shall take no harme,
Pur the cat is gray.

LEAR Arraigne her first tis *Gonoril*, I here take my oath before this honorable assembly she kickt the poore king her father.   1860

FOOLE Come hither mistrisse is your name *Gonorill*.

LEAR She cannot deny it.

FOOLE Cry you mercy I tooke you for a ioyne stoole.

LEAR
And heres another whose warpt lookes proclaime,
What store her hart is made an, stop her there,
Armes, armes, sword, fire, corruption in the place,
False Iusticer why hast thou let her scape.

EDGAR Blesse thy fiue wits.

KENT (*to Lear*)
O pity sir, where is the patience now,
That you so oft haue boasted to retaine.   1870

EDGAR (*aside*)
My teares begin to take his part so much,
Theile marre my counterfeiting.

LEAR   The little dogs and all
Trey, Blanch, and Sweet hart, see they barke at me.

EDGAR *Tom* will throw his head at them, auant you curs,
    Be thy mouth, or blacke, or white,
    Tooth that poysons if it bite,
    Mastife, grayhoŭd, mungril grim,
    Hoŭd or spaniel, brach or him,
    Bobtaile tike, or trŭdletaile,
    Tom will make them weep & waile,   1880
    For with throwing thus my head,
    Dogs leape the hatch and all are fled,
Loudla doodla come march to wakes, and faires,
And market townes, poore *Tom* thy horne is dry.

LEAR Then let them anotomize *Regan*, see what breeds about her hart is there any cause in nature that makes this hardnes, (*to Edgar*) you sir, I entertaine you for one of my hundred, only I do not like the fashion of your garments, youle say, they are Persian attire, but let them be chang'd.   1890

KENT
Now good my Lord lie here awhile.

LEAR Make no noise, make no noise, draw the curtains, so, so, so, weele go to supper it'h morning, so, so, so.
        He sleepes. Enter Gloster

GLOSTER (*to Kent*)
Come hither friend, where is the King my maister.

KENT
  Here sir, but trouble him not his wits are gon.
GLOSTER
  Good friend I prithy take him in thy armes,
  I haue or'e heard a plot of death vpon him,
  Ther is a Litter ready lay him in't,
  And driue towards Douer frend, where thou shalt meet
1900 Both welcome & protection, take vp thy master,
  If thou should'st dally halfe an houre, his life
  With thine and all that offer to defend him
  Stand in assured losse, take vp take vp
  And followe me, that will to some prouision
  Giue thee quicke conduct.
  KENT (to Lear)   Oppressed nature sleepes,
  This rest might yet haue balmed thy broken sinewes,
  Which if conuenience will not alow
  Stand in hard cure, (to Foole) come helpe to beare thy
        maister,
  Thou must not stay behind.
  GLOSTER   Come, come away.
                              Exeunt. Manet Edgar
  EDGAR
1910 When we our betters see bearing our woes:
  We scarcely thinke, our miseries, our foes.
  Who alone suffers suffers most it'h mind,
  Leauing free things and happy showes behind,
  But then the mind much sufferance doth or'e scip,
  When griefe hath mates, and bearing fellowship:
  How light and portable my paine seemes now,
  When that which makes me bend, makes the King
        bow.
  He childed as I fathered, Tom away,
  Marke the high noyses and thy selfe bewray
1920 When false opinion whose wrong thoughts defile thee,
  In thy iust proofe repeals and reconciles thee,
  What will hap more to night, safe scape the King,
  Lurke, lurke.   Exit

Sc. 14   Enter Cornwall, and Regan, and Gonorill, and
          Bastard, and seruants
  CORNWALL (to Gonorill)
  Post speedily to my Lord your husband
  Shew him this letter, the army of France is landed,
  (To seruants) Seeke out the vilaine Gloster.
                                  Exeunt some
  REGAN   Hang him instantly.
  GONORILL
  Plucke out his eyes.
  CORNWALL   Leaue him to my displeasure,
  Edmūd keep you our sister company.
  The reuenges we are bound to take vpon your
1930 trayterous father, are not fit for your beholding, aduise
  the Duke where you are going to a most festinat
  preparatiō we are bound to the like, our posts shall be
  swift and intelligence betwixt vs,
  Farewell deere sister, farewell my Lord of Gloster,
      Enter Steward
  How now whers the King?

STEWARD
  My Lord of Gloster hath conueyd him hence,
  Some fiue or sixe and thirtie of his Knights
  Hot questants after him, met him at gate,
  Who with some other of the Lords dependants
  Are gone with him towards Douer, where they boast   1940
  To haue well armed friends.
CORNWALL Get horses for your mistris.   Exit Steward
GONORILL Farewell sweet Lord and sister.
CORNWALL
  Edmund farewell,   Exit Gonorill and Bastard
  (To seruants)   goe seeke the traytor Gloster.
  Pinion him like a theefe, bring him before vs,
                              Exeunt other seruants
  Though we may not passe vpon his life
  Without the forme of Iustice, yet our power
  Shall doe a curtesie to our wrath, which men
  May blame but not controule, whose there, the traytor?
      Enter Gloster brought in by two or three
REGAN
  Ingratfull Fox tis hee.
CORNWALL (to seruants) Bind fast his corkie armes.   1950
GLOSTER
  What meanes your Graces, good my friends consider,
  You are my gests, doe me no foule play friends.
CORNWALL (to seruants)
  Bind him I say,
REGAN   Hard hard, O filthie traytor!
GLOSTER
  Vnmercifull Lady as you are, I am true.
CORNWALL (to seruants)
  To this chaire bind him, (to Gloster) villaine thou shalt
      find—
      Regan plucks Glosters beard
GLOSTER
  By the kind Gods tis most ignobly done,
  To pluck me by the beard.
REGAN So white and such a Traytor.
GLOSTER Naughty Ladie,
  These haires which thou dost rauish from my chin   1960
  Will quicken and accuse thee, I am your host.
  With robbers hands my hospitable fauours
  You should not ruffell thus, what will you doe.
CORNWALL
  Come sir, what letters had you late from France?
REGAN
  Be simple answerer, for we know the truth.
CORNWALL
  And what confederacy haue you with the tratours
  Late footed in the kingdome?
REGAN   To whose hands
  You haue sent the lunatick King speake?
GLOSTER
  I haue a letter gessingly set downe
  Which came from one, that's of a neutrall heart,   1970
  And not from one oppos'd.
CORNWALL   Cunning.
REGAN   And false.

CORNWALL
    Where hast thou sent the King?
GLOSTER   To Douer.
REGAN
    Wherefore to Douer? wast thou not charg'd at perill—
CORNWALL
    Wherefore to Douer? let him first answere that.
GLOSTER
    I am tide tot'h stake, and I must stand the course.
REGAN Wherefore to Douer sir?
GLOSTER
    Because I would not see thy cruell nayles
    Pluck out his poore old eyes, nor thy fierce sister
    In his anoynted flesh rash borish phangs,
1980   The Sea with such a storme as his bowd head
    In hell blacke night indur'd, would haue boyd vp
    And quencht the stelled fires, yet poore old heart,
    Hee holpt the heauens to rage,
    If wolues had at thy gate hould that dearne time
    Thou shouldst haue said, good Porter turne the key,
    All cruels ile subscribe but I shall see
    The winged vengeance ouertake such children.
CORNWALL
    Seet shalt thou neuer, fellowes hold the chaire,
    Vpon those eyes of thine, Ile set my foote.
GLOSTER
1990   He that will thinke to liue till he be old
    Giue me some helpe, O cruell, O ye Gods!
        ⌈Cornwall pulls out one of Glosters eyes, and
        stampes on it⌉
REGAN (to Cornwall)
    One side will mocke another, tother to.
CORNWALL (to Gloster)
    If you see vengeance—
SERUANT   Hold your hand my Lord
    I haue seru'd you euer since I was a child
    But better seruice haue I neuer done you,
    Thẽ now to bid you hold.
REGAN   How now you dogge.
SERUANT
    If you did weare a beard vpon your chin
    I'de shake it on this quarrell, ⌈to Cornwall⌉ what doe
        you meane?
CORNWALL My villaine:
SERUANT
2000   Why then come on, and take the chance of anger.
        They draw and fight
REGAN ⌈to another seruant⌉
    Giue me thy sword, a pesant stand vp thus.
        Shee takes a sword and runs at him behind
SERUANT (to Gloster)
    Oh I am slaine my Lord, yet haue you one eye left
    To see some mischiefe on him,
        ⌈Regan stabs him again⌉
                    oh!   He dies
CORNWALL
    Least it see more preuent it, out vild Ielly
        He ⌈pulls out⌉ Glosters other eye
    Where is thy luster now?

GLOSTER
    All darke and comfortles, wher's my sonne Edmund?
    Edmund enkindle all the sparks of nature,
    To quit this horred act.
REGAN   Out villaine,
    Thou calst on him that hates thee, it was he
    That made the ouerture of thy treasons to vs,   2010
    Who is too good to pittie thee.
GLOSTER
    O my follies, then Edgar was abus'd,
    Kind Gods forgiue me that, and prosper him.
REGAN (to seruants)
    Goe thrust him out at gates, and let him smell
    His way to Douer, (to Cornwall) how ist my Lord?
        how looke you?
CORNWALL
    I haue receiu'd a hurt, follow me Ladie,
    (To seruants) Turne out that eyles villaine, throw this
        slaue
    Vpon the dungell
            Exit one or more with Gloster ⌈and the body⌉
                Regan, I bleed apace,
    Vntimely comes this hurt, giue me your arme.
                    Exeunt Cornwall and Regan
2 SERUANT
    Ile neuer care what wickednes I doe,   2020
    If this man come to good.
3 SERUANT   If she liue long,
    And in the end meet the old course of death,
    Women will all turne monsters.
2 SERUANT
    Lets follow the old Earle, and get the bedlom
    To lead him where he would, his rogish madnes
    Allows it selfe to any thing.
3 SERUANT
    Goe thou, ile fetch some flaxe and whites of egges
    To apply to his bleeding face, now heauen helpe him.
                    Exeunt seuerally

        Enter Edgar as a Bedlam begger   Sc. 15
EDGAR
    Yet better thus, and knowne to be contemnd,
    Then still contemn'd and flattered, to be worst   2030
    The lowest and most deiected thing of Fortune
    Stands still in esperance, liues not in feare,
    The lamentable change is from the best,
    The worst returnes to laughter,
        Enter Gloster led by an old man
    Who's here, my father partie,eyd, world, world, O
        world!
    But that thy strange mutations make vs hate thee,
    Life would not yeeld to age.
        ⌈Edgar stands aside⌉
OLD MAN (to Gloster)   O my good Lord,
    I haue beene your tenant, & your fathers tenant
    This forescore—
GLOSTER
    Away, get thee away, good friend be gon,   2040

Thy comforts can doe me no good at all,
Thee they may hurt.

OLD MAN
Alack sir, you cannot see your way.

GLOSTER
I haue no way, and therefore want no eyes,
I stumbled when I saw, full oft tis seene
Our meanes secure vs, and our meare defects
Proue our comodities, ah deere sonne *Edgar*,
The food of thy abused fathers wrath,
Might I but liue to see thee in my tuch,
I'de say I had eyes againe.

2050 OLD MAN   How now whose there?

EDGAR (*aside*)
O Gods, who ist can say I am at the worst,
I am worse then ere I was.

OLD MAN   Tis poore mad *Tom*.

EDGAR (*aside*)
And worse I may be yet, the worst is not,
As long as we can say, this is the worst.

OLD MAN (*to Edgar*) Fellow where goest?

GLOSTER Is it a begger man?

OLD MAN Mad man, and begger to.

GLOSTER
A has some reason, else he could not beg,
In the last nights storme I such a fellow saw,
Which made me thinke a man a worme, my sonne
Came then into my mind, and yet my mind
Was then scarce friendes with him, I haue heard
    more since,
As flies to wanton boyes, are we toth' Gods,
They kill vs for their sport.

EDGAR (*aside*)   How should this be,
Bad is the trade that must play foole to sorrow
Angring it selfe and others,
    ⌈*He comes forward*⌉
             blesse thee maister.

GLOSTER
Is that the naked fellow?

OLD MAN   I my Lord.

GLOSTER
Then prethee get thee gon, if for my sake
Thou wilt oretake vs hence a mile or twaine
2070 Ith' way toward Douer, doe it for ancient loue
And bring some couering for this naked soule
Who Ile intreate to leade me.

OLD MAN   Alack sir he is mad.

GLOSTER
Tis the times plague, when madmen lead the blind,
Doe as I bid thee, or rather doe thy pleasure,
Aboue the rest, be gon.

OLD MAN
Ile bring him the best parrell that I haue
Come on't what will.   *Exit*

GLOSTER   Sirrah naked fellow.

EDGAR
Poore *Tom*s a cold, I cannot dance it farther.

GLOSTER Come hither fellow.

EDGAR Blesse thy sweete eyes, they bleed.   2080

GLOSTER Knowst thou the way to Douer?

EDGAR Both stile and gate, horse-way, and foot-path,
poore *Tom* hath beene scard out of his good wits, blesse
the good man from the foule fiend, fiue fiends haue
beene in poore *Tom* at once, as *Obidicut*, of lust,
Hobbididence Prince of dumbnes, *mahu* of stealing, *Modo*
of murder, *fliberdigebit* of moking & mowing who since
possesses chambermaids and waiting women, so, blesse
thee maister.

GLOSTER
Here take this purse, thou whome the heauens plagues 2090
Haue humbled to all strokes, that I am wretched,
Makes thee the happier, heauens deale so still,
Let the superfluous and lust-dieted man
That stands your ordinance, that will not see
Because he does not feele, feele your power quickly,
So distribution should vndoe excesse,
And each man haue enough, dost thou know Douer?

EDGAR I master.

GLOSTER
There is a cliffe whose high & bending head
Lookes sawcely in the confined deepe,   2100
Bring me but to the very brimme of it
And ile repaire the misery thou dost beare
With something rich about me, from that place
I shal no leading need.

EDGAR Giue me thy arme,
Poore *Tom* shall lead thee.   *Exit Edgar guiding Gloster*

    Enter ⌈*at one doore*⌉ *Gonorill and Bastard*   Sc. 16

GONORILL
Welcome my Lord, I maruaile our mild husband
Not met vs on the way,
    Enter Steward ⌈*at another doore*⌉
            now wher's your maister?

STEWARD
Madame within, but neuer man so chang'd,
I told him of the army that was landed,   2110
He smild at it, I told him you were coming,
His answere was the worse, of *Glosters* treacherie,
And of the loyall seruice of his sonne
When I enform'd him, then hee cald me sott,
And told me I had turnd the wrong side out,
What hee should most defie seemes pleasant to him,
What like offensiue.

GONORILL (*to Bastard*) Then shall you goe no further,
It is the cowish terrer of his spirit
That dares not vndertake, hele not feele wrongs
Which tie him to an answere, our wishes on the way 2120
May proue effects, backe *Edmund* to my brother,
Hasten his musters, and conduct his powers
I must change armes at home, and giue the distaffe
Into my husbands hands, this trusty seruant
Shall passe betweene vs, ere long you are like to heare
If you dare venture in your owne behalfe

A mistresses comand, weare this, spare speech,
Decline your head: this kisse if it durst speake
Would stretch thy spirits vp into the ayre,
⌈*She kisses him*⌉
2130   Conceaue and far you well.
BASTARD Yours in the ranks of death.
GONORILL My most deere *Gloster*,   ⌈*Exit Bastard*⌉
To thee a womans seruices are dew
My foote vsurps my body.
STEWARD   Madam, here comes my Lord.
                     Exit Steward

    Enter Albany
GONORILL
I haue beene worth the whistling.
ALBANY   O *Gonoril*,
You are not worth the dust which the rude wind
Blowes in your face, I feare your disposition
That nature which contemnes it origin
Cannot be bordered certaine in it selfe,
2140   She that her selfe will sliuer and disbranch
From her materiall sap, perforce must wither,
And come to deadly vse.
GONORILL   No more, the text is foolish.
ALBANY
Wisedome and goodnes, to the vild seeme vild,
Filths sauor but themselues, what haue you done?
Tigers, not daughters, what haue you perform'd?
A father, and a gracious aged man
Whose reuerence euen the head-lugd beare would lick,
Most barbarous, most degenerate haue you madded,
Could my good brother suffer you to doe it?
2150   A man, a Prince, by him so benifacted,
If that the heauens doe not their visible spirits
Send quickly downe to tame this vild offences,
It will come
Humanity must perforce pray on it selfe
Like monsters of the deepe.
GONORILL   Milke liuerd man
That bearest a cheeke for bloes, a head for wrongs,
Who hast not in thy browes an eye deserning
Thine honour, from thy suffering, that not know'st,
Fools do those vilains pitty who are punisht
2160   Ere they haue done their mischiefe, wher's thy drum?
France spreds his banners in our noysles land,
With plumed helme, thy flaxen begin threats
Whil's thou a morall foole sits still and cries
Alack why does he so?
ALBANY   See thy selfe deuill,
Proper deformity shewes not in the fiend,
So horid as in woman.
GONORILL   O vaine foole!
ALBANY
Thou changed, and selfe-couerd thing for shame
Be-monster not thy feature, wer't my fitnes
To let these hands obay my bloud,
2170   They are apt enough to dislocate and teare
Thy flesh and bones, how ere thou art a fiend,
A womans shape doth shield thee.

GONORILL Marry your manhood mew—
    Enter ⌈*2.*⌉ *Gentleman*
ALBANY What newes.
⌈2.⌉ GENTLEMAN
O my good Lord the Duke of *Cornwals* dead,
Slaine by his seruant, going to put out
The other eye of *Gloster*.
ALBANY   *Glosters* eyes?
⌈2.⌉ GENTLEMAN
A seruant that he bred, thrald with remorse,
Oppos'd against the act, bending his sword
To his great maister, who thereat inraged   2180
Flew on him, and amongst them, feld him dead,
But not without that harmefull stroke, which since
Hath pluckt him after.
ALBANY   This shewes you are aboue
You Iustisers, that these our nether crimes
So speedely can venge. But O poore *Gloster*
Lost he his other eye.
⌈2.⌉ GENTLEMAN   Both, both my Lord,
(*To Gonorill*) This letter Madam craues a speedy
    answer,
Tis from your sister.
GONORILL (*aside*)   One way I like this well,
But being widow and my *Gloster* with her,
May all the building on my fancie plucke,   2190
Vpon my hatefull life, another way
The newes is not so tooke, Ile reade and answer.   *Exit*
ALBANY
Where was his sonne when they did take his eyes.
⌈2.⌉ GENTLEMAN
Come with my Lady hither.
ALBANY   He is not here.
⌈2.⌉ GENTLEMAN
No my good Lord I met him backe againe.
ALBANY Knowes he the wickednesse.
⌈2.⌉ GENTLEMAN
I my good Lord twas he informd against him,
And quit the house on purpose that there punishment
Might haue the freer course.
ALBANY   *Gloster* I liue
To thanke thee for the loue thou shewedst the King,   2200
And to reuenge thy eyes, come hither friend,
Tell me what more thou knowest.   *Exeunt*

    Enter Kent disguised and ⌈*1.*⌉ *Gentleman*   **Sc. 17**
KENT Why the King of *Fraunce* is so suddenly gone backe,
know you no reason.
1. GENTLEMAN
Something he left imperfect in the state,
Which since his comming forth is thought of, which
Imports to the Kingdome, so much feare and danger
That his personall returne was most required
And necessarie.
KENT
Who hath he left behind him, General.   2210
1. GENTLEMAN
The Marshall of *France* Monsier *la Far*.

KENT Did your letters pierce the queene to any
   demonstratiõ of griefe.
I. GENTLEMAN
   I sir she tooke them, read them in my presence,
   And now and then an ample teare trild downe
   Her delicate cheeke, it seemed she was a queene
   Ouer her passion, who most rebell-like,
   Sought to be King ore her.
KENT   O then it moued her.
I. GENTLEMAN
   Not to a rage, patience and sorow stroue,
2220 Who should expresse her goodliest, you haue seene
   Sun shine and raine at once, her smiles and teares
   Were like a better way, those happie smilets,
   That playd on her ripe lip seemd not to know
   What guests were in her eyes which parted thence
   As pearles from diamonds dropt, in briefe
   Sorow would be a raritie most beloued,
   If all could so become it.
KENT   Made she no verball question.
I. GENTLEMAN
   Faith once or twice she heau'd the name of father,
   Pantingly forth as if it prest her heart,
2230 Cried sisters, sisters, shame of Ladies sisters:
   Kent, father, sisters, what ith storme ith night,
   Let pietie not be beleeft there she shooke
   The holy water from her heauenly eyes,
   And clamour maystered, then away she started,
   To deale with griefe alone.
KENT   It is the stars,
   The stars aboue vs gouerne our conditions,
   Else one selfe mate and make could not beget
   Such different issues, you spoke not with her since.
I. GENTLEMAN No.
KENT
   Was this before the King returnd.
2240 I. GENTLEMAN   No, since.
KENT
   Well sir, the poore distressed Lear's ith towne,
   Who some time in his better tune remembers,
   What we are come about, and by no meanes
   Will yeeld to see his daughter.
I. GENTLEMAN   Why good sir?
KENT
   A soueraigne shame so elbows him his own vnkindnes
   That stript her from his benediction turnd her
   To forraine casualties gaue her deare rights
   To his dog-harted daughters, these things sting
   His mind so venomously that burning shame
   Detaines him from Cordelia.
2250 I. GENTLEMAN   Alack poore Gentleman.
KENT
   Of Albanies and Cornewals powers you heard not.
I. GENTLEMAN Tis so they are a foote.
KENT
   Well sir, ile bring you to our maister Lear,
   And leaue you to attend him some deere cause
   Will in concealement wrap me vp awhile,

When I am knowne aright you shall not greeue,
Lending me this acquaintance, I pray you go
Along with me.   Exeunt

Enter Cordelia, Doctor and others   Sc. 18
CORDELIA
   Alack tis he, why he was met euen now,
   As mad as the ract sea singing aloud,   2260
   Crownd with ranke femiter and furrow weedes,
   With bur-docks, hemlocke, netles, cookow flowers,
   Darnell and all the idle weedes that grow,
   In our sustayning corne, the centuries send forth,
   Search euery acre in the hie growne field,
   And bring him to our eye,   ⌈Exit one or more⌉
                         what can mans wisdome
   In the restoring his bereued sence,
   He that can helpe him
   Take all my outward worth.
DOCTOR There is meanes Madame.   2270
   Our foster nurse of nature is repose
   The which he lackes that to prouoke in him
   Are many simples operatiue whose power
   Will close the eye of anguish.
CORDELIA   All blest secrets
   All you vnpublisht vertues of the earth,
   Spring with my teares be aydant and remediat
   In the good mans distresse, seeke, seeke, for him,
   Lest his vngouernd rage dissolue the life
   That wants the meanes to lead it.
      Enter messenger
MESSENGER   News Madam,
   The Brittish powers are marching hitherward.   2280
CORDELIA
   Tis knowne before, our preparation stands,
   In expectation of them, ô deere father
   It is thy busines that I go about,
   Therfore great France
   My mourning and important teares hath pitied,
   No blowne ambition doth our armes insight
   But loue, deere loue, and our ag'd fathers right,
   Soone may I heare and see him.   Exeunt

      Enter Regan and Steward   Sc. 19
REGAN
   But are my brothers powers set forth?
STEWARD   I Madam.
REGAN
   Himselfe in person?
STEWARD   Madam with much ado,   2290
   Your sister is the better soldier.
REGAN
   Lord Edmund spake not with your L. at home.
STEWARD No Madam.
REGAN
   What might import my sisters letters to him?
STEWARD I know not Lady.
REGAN
   Faith he is posted hence on serious matter,

It was great ignorance, *Glosters* eyes being out
To let him liue, where he ariues he moues
All harts against vs, edmund I thinke is gone
2300 In pitie of his misery to dispatch
His nighted life, moreouer to discrie
The strength at'h army.

STEWARD
I must needs after with my letters Madam.

REGAN
Our troope sets forth to morrow stay with vs,
The wayes are dangerous.

STEWARD   I may not Madame,
My Lady charg'd my dutie in this busines.

REGAN
Why should she write to *Edmund*? might not you
Transport her purposes by word, belike
Some thing, I know not what, ile loue thee much,
Let me vnseale the letter.

2310 STEWARD   Madam I'de rather—

REGAN
I know your Lady does not loue her husband
I am sure of that, and at her late being here
Shee gaue strange aliads, and most speaking lookes
To noble *Edmund*, I know you are of her bosome.

STEWARD I Madam.

REGAN
I speake in vnderstanding, for I know't,
Therefore I doe aduise you take this note,
My Lord is dead, *Edmund* and I haue talkt,
And more conuenient is he for my hand
2320 Then for your Ladies, you may gather more,
If you doe find him, pray you giue him this,
And when your mistris heares thus much from you
I pray desire her call her wisedome to her,
So farewell,
If you doe chance to heare of that blind traytor,
Preferment fals on him that cuts him off.

STEWARD
Would I could meet him Madam, I would shew
What Lady I doe follow.

REGAN   Fare thee well.

                    Exeunt seuerally

Sc. 20   *Enter Edgar disguised as a pesant with a staff,*
              guiding blind Gloster

GLOSTER
When shall we come toth' top of that same hill?

EDGAR
2330 You do climbe vp it now, looke how we labour?

GLOSTER
Me thinks the ground is euen.

EDGAR   Horrible steepe,
Harke doe you heare the sea?

GLOSTER   No truly.

EDGAR
Why then your other sences grow imperfect
By your eyes anguish.

GLOSTER   So may it be indeed,

Me thinks thy voyce is altered, and thou speakest
With better phrase and matter then thou didst.

EDGAR
Y'ar much deceaued, in nothing am I chang'd
But in my garments.

GLOSTER   Me thinks y'ar better spoken.

EDGAR
Come on sir, her's the place, stand still, how feareful
And dizi tis to cast ones eyes so low   2340
The crowes and choghes that wing the midway ayre
Shew scarce so grosse as beetles, halfe way downe
Hangs one that gathers sampire, dreadfull trade,
Me thinkes he seemes no bigger then his head,
The fishermen that walke vpon the beach
Appeare like mise, and yon tall anchoring barke
Diminisht to her cock, her cock a boui
Almost too small for sight, the murmuring surge
That on the vnnumbred idle peeble chaffes
Cannot be heard, its so hie ile looke no more,   2350
Least my braine turne, and the deficient sight
Topple downe headlong.

GLOSTER   Set me where you stand?

EDGAR
Giue me your hand, you are now within a foot
Of th'extreame verge, for all beneath the Moone
Would I not leape vpright.

GLOSTER   Let goe my hand,
Here friend's another pursse, in it a iewell,
Well worth a poore mans taking, Fairies and Gods
Prosper it with thee, goe thou farther off,
Bid me farewell, and let me heare thee going.

EDGAR
Now fare you well good sir.

          He stands aside

GLOSTER   With all my heart.   2360

EDGAR (*aside*)
Why I do trifell thus with his dispaire
Is done to cure it.

GLOSTER   O you mightie Gods,

          He kneeles

This world I doe renounce, and in your sights
Shake patiently my great affliction off,
If I could beare it longer and not fall
To quarel with your great opposles wils
My snuff and loathed part of nature should
Burne it selfe out, if *Edgar* liue, O blesse him,
Now fellow fare thee well.

EDGAR   Gon sir, farewell,

          Gloster fals

(*Aside*) And yet I know not how conceit may robbe   2370
The treasurie of life, when life it selfe
Yealds to the theft, had he beene where he thought
By this had thought beene past, aliue or dead,
(*To Gloster*) Ho you sir, heare you sir, speak,
(*Aside*) Thus might he passe indeed, yet he reuiues,
(*To Gloster*) What are you sir?

GLOSTER   Away and let me die.

EDGAR

    Hadst thou beene ought but gosmore feathers ayre,

    So many fadome downe precipitating

    Thou hadst shiuerd like an egge, but thou dost breath

2380   Hast heauy substance, bleedst not, speakest, art sound,

    Ten masts alenth, make not the altitude,

    Which thou hast perpendicularly fell,

    Thy lifes a miracle, speake yet againe.

GLOSTER But haue I fallen or no?

EDGAR

    From the dread somnet of this chalkie borne,

    Looke vp a hight, the shrill gorg'd larke so farre

    Cannot bee seene or heard, doe but looke vp?

GLOSTER Alack I haue no eyes

    Is wretchednes depriu'd that benefit

2390   To end it selfe by death twas yet some comfort

    When misery could beguile the tyrants rage

    And frustrate his proud will.

EDGAR   Giue me your arme?

    Vp, so, how now feele you your legges, you stand.

GLOSTER

    Too well, too well.

EDGAR   This is aboue all strangenes

    Vpon the crowne of the cliffe what thing was that

    Which parted from you.

GLOSTER   A poore vnfortunate begger.

EDGAR

    As I stood here below me thoughts his eyes

    Were two full Moones, a had a thousand noses

    Hornes, welk't and waued like the enridged sea,

2400   It was some fiend, therefore thou happy father

    Thinke that the cleerest Gods, who made their honours

    Of mens impossibilities, haue preserued thee.

GLOSTER

    I doe remember now, henceforth ile beare

    Affliction till it doe crie out it selfe

    Enough, enough and die that thing you speake of,

    I tooke it for a man, often would it say

    The fiend the fiend, he led me to that place.

EDGAR

    Bare free & patient thoughts,

        Enter Lear mad ⌈crowned with weedes and flowers⌉

                  but who comes here

    The safer sence will neare accõmodate

2410   His maister thus.

LEAR No they cannot touch mee for coyning, I am the

    king himselfe.

EDGAR O thou side pearcing sight.

LEAR Nature is aboue Art in that respect, ther's your

    presse money, that fellow handles his bow like a crow-

    keeper, draw me a clothiers yard, looke, looke a mowse,

    peace, peace, this tosted cheese will do it, ther's my

    gauntlet, ile proue it on a gyant, bring vp the browne-

    billes, O well flowne bird in the ayre, hagh, giue the

2420   word?

EDGAR Sweet Margerum.

LEAR Passe.

GLOSTER I know that voyce.

LEAR Ha *Gonorill*, ha *Regan*, they flattered mee like a

    dogge, and tould me I had white haires in my beard,

    ere the black ones were there, to say I and no, to euery

    thing I saide I and no toe, was no good diuinitie, when

    the raine came to wet me once, and the winde to make

    mee chatter, when the thunder would not peace at my

    bidding, there I found them, there I smelt them out, 2430

    goe toe, they are not men of their words, they told mee

    I was euery thing, tis a lye, I am not ague-proofe.

GLOSTER

    The tricke of that voyce I doe well remember,

    Ist not the King?

LEAR   I euery inch a King

      ⌈*Gloster kneeles*⌉

    When I do stare, see how the subiect quakes,

    I pardon that mans life, what was thy cause,

    Adultery? thou shalt not die for adulterie,

    No the wren goes toot, and the smal guilded flie

    Dos letcher in my sight,

    Let copulation thriue, for *Glosters* bastard son 2440

    Was kinder to his father then my daughters

    Got tweene the lawfull sheets, toot luxurie, *pell*, *mell*,

    For I lacke souldiers, behold yon simpring dame

    Whose face between her forkes presageth snow,

    That minces vertue, and dos shake the head

    To heare of pleasures name

    The fichew nor the soyled horse goes toot

    With a more riotous appetite, down frõ the wast

    Tha're centaures, though women all aboue,

    But to the girdle doe the gods inherit, 2450

    Beneath is all the fiends, thers hell, thers darknesse,

    Ther's the sulphury pit, burning, scalding,

    Stench, consumation, fie, fie, fie, pah, pah,

    Giue mee an ounce of Ciuet, good Apothocarie,

    To sweeten my imagination,

    Ther's money for thee.

GLOSTER   O let me kisse that hand.

LEAR Here wipe it first, it smels of mortalitie.

GLOSTER

    O ruind peece of nature, this great world

    Shall so weare out to naught, do you know me?

LEAR I remember thy eyes well inough, dost thou squiny 2460

    on me,

    No do thy worst blind *Cupid*, ile not loue,

    Reade thou that challenge, marke the penning oft.

GLOSTER

    Were all the letters sunnes I could not see one.

EDGAR *(aside)*

    I would not take this from report, it is,

    And my heart breakes at it.

LEAR *(to Gloster)* Read.

GLOSTER What! with the case of eyes.

LEAR O ho, are you there with me, no eyes in your head,

    nor no mony in your purse, your eyes are in a heauie 2470

    case, your purse in a light, yet you see how this world

    goes.

GLOSTER I see it feelingly.

LEAR What art mad, a man may see how the world goes

with no eyes, looke with thy eares, see how yon Iustice
railes vpon yon simple theefe, harke in thy eare handy,
dandy, which is the theefe, which is the Iustice, thou
hast seene a farmers dogge barke at a begger.

GLOSTER I sir.

2480 LEAR And the creature runne from the cur, there thou
    mightst behold the great image of authoritie, a dogges
    obade in office,
    Thou rascall beadle hold thy bloudy hand,
    Why dost thou lash that whore, strip thine owne backe,
    Thy bloud as hotly lusts to vse her in that kind
    For which thou whipst her, the vsurer hangs the
            cosioner,
    Through tottered raggs, smal vices do appeare,
    Robes & furd-gownes hides all, get thee glasse eyes,
    And like a scuruy polititian seeme
2490   To see the things thou doest not, no teares now
    Pull off my bootes, harder, harder, so.

EDGAR (aside)
    O matter and impertinencie mixt
    Reason in madnesse.

LEAR
    If thou wilt weepe my fortune take my eyes,
    I knowe thee well inough thy name is *Gloster*,
    Thou must be patient, we came crying hither,
    Thou knowest the first time that we smell the aire,
    We wayl and cry, I will preach to thee marke me.

GLOSTER Alack alack the day.

LEAR ⌈*remouing his crowne of weedes*⌉
2500 When we are borne, we crie that wee are come
    To this great stage of fooles, this a good blocke.
    It were a delicate stratagem to shooe
    A troupe of horse with felt, & when I haue stole vpon
    These sonne in lawes, then kill, kill, kill, kill, kill, kill.
    Enter three Gentlemen

⌈I.⌉ GENTLEMAN
    O here he is, lay hands vpon him sirs,
    (*To Lear*) Your most deere

LEAR
    No reskue, what a prisoner, I am eene
    The naturall foole of Fortune, vse me well
    You shall haue ransome, let mee haue a churgion
2510 I am cut to the braines.

⌈I.⌉ GENTLEMAN You shall haue any thing.

LEAR No seconds, all my selfe,
    Why this would make a man a man of salt
    To vse his eyes for garden waterpots,
    I and laying Autums dust.

⌈I.⌉ GENTLEMAN   Good Sir.

LEAR
    I will die brauely like a bridegroome,
    What? I will be Iouiall, come, come,
    I am a King my maisters, know you that.

⌈I.⌉ GENTLEMAN
    You are a royall one, and we obey you.

2520 LEAR Then theres life int, nay and you get it you shall
    get it with running.
    Exit King running, pursued by two Gentlemen

⌈I.⌉ GENTLEMAN
    A sight most pitifull in the meanest wretch,
    Past speaking in a king: thou hast one daughter
    Who redeemes nature from the generall curse
    Which twaine hath brought her to.

EDGAR Haile gentle sir.

⌈I.⌉ GENTLEMAN Sir speed you, whats your will.

EDGAR
    Do you heare ought of a battell toward.

⌈I.⌉ GENTLEMAN
    Most sure and vulgar euery one here's that
    That can distinguish sence.

EDGAR   But by your fauour   2530
    How neers the other army.

⌈I.⌉ GENTLEMAN
    Neere and on speedy foot the maine, descryers
    Stands on the howerly thoughts.

EDGAR   I thanke you sir thats all.

⌈I.⌉ GENTLEMAN
    Though that the Queene on speciall cause is here,
    Hir army is moued on.

EDGAR   I thanke you sir.
            Exit Gentleman

GLOSTER
    You euer gentle gods take my breath from me,
    Let not my worser spirit tempt me againe,
    To dye before you please.

EDGAR Well pray you father.

GLOSTER Now good sir what are you.   2540

EDGAR
    A most poore man made lame by Fortunes blowes,
    Who by the Art of knowne and feeling sorrowes
    Am pregnant to good pitty, giue me your hand
    Ile leade you to some biding.

GLOSTER ⌈*rising*⌉   Hartie thankes,
    The bounty and the benizon of heauen
    To send thee boot, to boot.
    Enter Steward

STEWARD   A proclamed prize, most happy,
    That eyles head of thine was first framed flesh
    To rayse my fortunes, thou most vnhappy traytor,
    Briefly thy selfe remember, the sword is out
    That must destroy thee.

GLOSTER   Now let thy friendly hand   2550
    Put strength enough to't.

STEWARD (*to Edgar*)   Wherefore bould pesant
    Durst thou support a publisht traytor, hence
    Least the infection of his fortune take
    Like hold on thee, let goe his arme?

EDGAR Chill not let goe sir without cagion.

STEWARD Let goe slaue, or thou diest.

EDGAR Good Gentleman goe your gate, let poore voke
    passe, and chud haue beene swaggar'd out of my life,
    it would not haue beene so long by a vortnight, nay
    come not neare the old man, keepe out, cheuore ye,   2560
    or ile trie whether your costerd or my battone be the
    harder, ile be plaine with you.

STEWARD Out dunghill.

they fight

EDGAR Chill pick your teeth sir, come, no matter for your
foyns.

⌐*Edgar knockes him downe*⌐

STEWARD
Slaue thou hast slaine me, villaine take my pursse,
If euer thou wilt thriue, burie my bodie,
And giue the letters which thou find'st about me
To *Edmund* Earle of *Gloster*, seeke him out
2570   Vpon the *British* partie, ô vntimely death! death.

He dies

EDGAR
I know thee well, a seruiceable villaine,
As dutious to the vices of thy mistres,
As badnes would desire.

GLOSTER What is he dead?

EDGAR Sit you down father, rest you

Gloster sits

Lets see his pockets these letters that he speakes of
May be my friends, hee's dead, I am only sorrow
He had no other deathsmā let vs see,
Leaue gentle waxe, and manners blame vs not
2580   To know our enemies minds wee'd rip their hearts,
Their papers is more lawfull.

A letter

Let your reciprocall vowes bee remembred, you haue
many opportunities to cut him off, if your will want
not, time and place will be fruitfully offered, there is
nothing done, If he returne the conquerour, then am
I the prisoner, and his bed my gayle, from the lothed
warmth whereof deliuer me, and supply the place for
your labour, your wife (so I would say) your affectionate
seruant and for you her owne for venter, *Gonorill*.
2590   O Indistinguisht space of womans wit,
A plot vpon her vertuous husbands life,
And the exchange my brother (*to Stewards body*) heere
in the sands,
Thee ile rake vp, the post vnsanctified
Of murtherous leachers, and in the mature time,
With this vngratious paper strike the sight
Of the death practis'd Duke, for him tis well,
That of thy death and businesse I can tell.

⌐*Exit with body*⌐

GLOSTER
The King is mad, how stiffe is my vild sence,
That I stand vp and haue ingenious feeling
2600   Of my huge sorowes, better I were distract,
So should my thoughts be fenced from my griefes,
And woes by wrong imaginations loose
The knowledge of themselues.

A drum a farre off. ⌐*Enter Edgar*⌐

EDGAR   Giue me your hand
Far off me thinks I heare the beaten drum,
Come father ile bestow you with a friend.

Exit Edgar guiding Gloster

Sc. 21   ⌐*Soft musicke.*⌐ *Enter Cordelia, and Kent disguised*

CORDELIA O thou good *Kent*

How shall I liue and worke to match thy goodnes,
My life will be too short and euery measure faile me.

KENT
To be acknowlegd madame is ore payd,
All my reports go with the modest truth,   2610
Nor more, nor clipt, but so.

CORDELIA   Be better suited
These weeds are memories of those worser howers,
I prithe put them off.

KENT   Pardon me deere madame,
Yet to be knowne shortens my made intent,
My boone I make it that you know me not,
Till time and I thinke meete.

CORDELIA   Then beet so, my good Lord
⌐*Enter Doctor and* I. *Gentleman*⌐
How does the king.

DOCTOR   Madame sleepes still.

CORDELIA   O you kind Gods
Cure this great breach in his abused nature,
The vntund and hurrying sences, O wind vp
Of this child changed father.

DOCTOR   So please your Maiestie   2620
That we may wake the king, he hath slept long.

CORDELIA
Be gouernd by your knowledge and proceed
Ith sway of your owne will is he arayd?

⌐I. GENTLEMAN⌐
I madam, in the heauinesse of his sleepe,
We put fresh garments on him.

⌐DOCTOR⌐
Good madam be by, when we do awake him
I doubt not of his temperance.

CORDELIA   Very well.

DOCTOR
Please you draw neere, louder the musicke there.

Lear is ⌐*discouered*⌐ *asleepe*

CORDELIA
O my deer father restoratiõ hang
Thy medicin on my lips, and let this kis   2630
Repaire those violent harmes that my two sisters
Haue in thy reuerence made.

KENT   Kind and deere Princesse.

CORDELIA
Had you not bene their father these white flakes
Had challengd pitie of them, was this a face
To be exposd against the warring winds,
To stand against the deepe dread bolted thunder,
In the most terrible and nimble stroke
Of quick crosse lightning to watch poore *Perdu*
With this thin helme mine iniurors mean'st dogge,
Though he had bit me, should haue stood that night   2640
Against my fire, and wast thou faine poore father,
To houill thee with swine and rogues forlorne,
In short and mustie straw, alack, alack,
Tis wonder that thy life and wits at once
Had not concluded all, (*to the Doctor*) he wakes speake
to him.

DOCTOR Madam do you, tis fittest.

CORDELIA (to Lear)
How does my royall Lord, how fares your maiestie.

LEAR
You do me wrong to take me out ath graue,
Thou art a soule in blisse, but I am bound
2650 Vpon a wheele of fire, that mine owne teares
Do scald like molten lead.

CORDELIA   Sir know me.

LEAR
Yar a spirit I know, where did you dye.

CORDELIA (to the Doctor) Still, still, farre wide.

DOCTOR
Hees scarce awake, let him alone a while.

LEAR
Where haue I bene, where am I faire day light,
I am mightily abusd, I should ene dye with pitie,
To see another thus, I know not what to say,
I will not sweare these are my hands, lets see,
I feele this pin pricke, would I were assur'd
Of my condition.

2660 CORDELIA (kneeling) O looke vpon me sir,
And hold your hands in benediction or'e me,
No sir you must not kneele.

LEAR   Pray doe not mocke,
I am a very foolish fond old man,
Fourescore and vpward, and to deale plainly
I feare I am not in my perfect mind,
Mee thinks I should know you, and know this man;
Yet I am doubtfull, for I am mainly ignorant
What place this is, and all the skill I haue
Remembers not these garments, nor I know not
2670 Where I did lodge last night, doe not laugh at me,
For as I am a man, I thinke this Ladie
To be my child Cordelia.

CORDELIA   And so I am.

LEAR
Be your teares wet, yes faith, I pray weep not,
If you haue poyson for mee I will drinke it,
I know you doe not loue me, for your sisters
Haue as I doe remember, done me wrong,
You haue some cause, they haue not.

CORDELIA   No cause, no cause.

LEAR Am I in France?

KENT In your owne kingdome sir.

2680 LEAR Doe not abuse me?

DOCTOR
Be comforted good Madame, the great rage
You see is cured in him, and yet it is danger
To make him euen ore the time hee has lost,
Desire him to goe in, trouble him no more
Till further setling.

CORDELIA (to Lear) Wilt please your highnes walke?

LEAR You must beare with me,
Pray now forget and forgiue, I am old
And foolish.   Exeunt. Manet Kent and ⌈1.⌉ Gentleman

⌈1.⌉ GENTLEMAN Holds it true sir that the Duke
Of Cornwall was so slaine?

2690 KENT   Most certaine sir.

⌈1.⌉ GENTLEMAN
Who is conductor of his people?

KENT   As tis said,
The bastard sonne of Gloster.

⌈1.⌉ GENTLEMAN   They say Edgar
His banisht sonne is with the Earle of Kent
In Germanie.

KENT   Report is changeable,
Tis time to looke about, the powers of the kingdome
Approach apace.

⌈1.⌉ GENTLEMAN   The arbiterment is
Like to be bloudie, fare you well sir.   Exit

KENT
My poynt and period will be throughly wrought,
Or well, or ill, as this dayes battels fought.   Exit

        Enter Edmund the Bastard, Regan, and their powers   Sc. 22

BASTARD
Know of the Duke if his last purpose hold,   2700
Or whether since he is aduis'd by ought
To change the course, he's full of abdication
And selfe reprouing, bring his constant pleasure.

                              Exit one or more

REGAN
Our sisters man is certainly miscaried.

BASTARD
Tis to be doubted Madam.

REGAN   Now sweet Lord,
You know the goodnes I intend vpon you,
Tell me but truly, but then speak the truth,
Doe you not loue my sister?

BASTARD   I, honor'd loue.

REGAN
But haue you neuer found my brothers way,
To the forfended place?   2710

BASTARD That thought abuses you.

REGAN I am doubtfull
That you haue beene coniunct and bosom'd with hir,
As far as we call hirs.

BASTARD   No by mine honour Madam.

REGAN
I neuer shall indure hir, deere my Lord
Bee not familiar with her.

BASTARD Feare me not,
Shee and the Duke her husband.

        Enter Albany and Gonorill with troupes

GONORILL (aside)
I had rather loose the battaile, then that sister
Should loosen him and mee.   2720

ALBANY (to Regan)
Our very louing sister well be-met
For this I heare the King is come to his daughter
With others, whome the rigour of our state
Forst to crie out, where I could not be honest
I neuer yet was valiant, for this busines
It touches vs, as France inuades our land
Yet bolds the King, with others whome I feare,
Most iust and heauy causes make oppose.

BASTARD

Sir you speake nobly.

REGAN   Why is this reason'd?

GONORILL

2730   Combine togither gainst the enemy,

For these domestique pore particulars

Are not to question here.

ALBANY

Let vs then determine with the auntient of warre

On our proceedings.

BASTARD   I shall attend you

Presently at your tent.   ⌈Exit with his powers⌉

REGAN   Sister you'l goe with vs?

GONORILL No.

REGAN

Tis most conuenient, pray you goe with vs.

GONORILL ⌈aside⌉

O ho, I know the riddle, (to Regan) I will goe.

Enter Edgar disguised as a pesant

EDGAR (*to Albany*)

If ere your Grace had speech with man so poore,

Heare me one word.

ALBANY (*to the others*) Ile ouertake you,

Exeunt. Manet Albany and Edgar

2740   *speake.*

EDGAR

Before you fight the battell ope this letter,

If you haue victory let the trumpet sound

For him that brought it, wretched though I seeme,

I can produce a champion that will proue

What is auowched there, if you miscary,

Your busines of the world hath so an end,

Fortune loue you,

ALBANY Stay till I haue read the letter.

EDGAR I was forbid it,

2750   When time shall serue let but the Herald cry,

And ile appeare againe.

ALBANY Why fare thee well,

I will ore-looke the paper.   *Exit Edgar*

Enter Edmund the Bastard

BASTARD

The enemies in vew, draw vp your powers

He ⌈offers⌉ Albany a paper

Here is the guesse of their great strength and forces

By diligent discouery, but your hast

Is now vrg'd on you.

ALBANY   Wee will greet the time.   *Exit*

BASTARD

To both these sisters haue I sworne my loue,

Each iealous of the other as the stung

2760   Are of the Adder, which of them shall I take,

Both one or neither, neither can bee inioy'd

If both remaine aliue, to take the widdow

Exasperates, makes mad her sister *Gonorill*,

And hardly shall I cary out my side

Her husband being aliue, now then we'le vse

His countenance for the battaile, which being done

Let her that would be rid of him deuise

His speedie taking off, as for his mercy

Which he entends to *Lear* and to *Cordelia*:

The battaile done, and they within our power   2770

Shall neuer see his pardon, for my state

Stands on me to defend, not to debate.   *Exit*

Alarum. The powers of France passe ouer the stage,   Sc. 23

⌈*led by*⌉ *Cordelia with her father in her hand.*

Then enter Edgar disguised as a pesant, guiding

blind Gloster

EDGAR

Here father, take the shaddow of this bush

For your good hoast, pray that the right may thriue

If euer I returne to you againe

Ile bring you comfort.   *Exit*

GLOSTER   Grace goe with you sir.

Alarum and retreat. Enter Edgar

EDGAR

Away old man, giue me thy hand, away,

King *Lear* hath lost, he and his daughter taine,

Giue me thy hand, come on.

GLOSTER

No farther sir, a man may rot euen here.   2780

EDGAR

What in ill thoughts againe men must indure

Their going hence, euen as their coming hither,

Ripenes is all come on.   *Exit Edgar guiding Gloster*

Enter Edmund the Bastard, with Lear and Cordelia   Sc. 24

prisoners, a Captaine and souldiers

BASTARD

Some officers take them away, good guard

Vntill their greater pleasures best be knowne

That are to censure them.

CORDELIA (*to Lear*)   We are not the first

Who with best meaning haue incurd the worst,

For thee oppressed King am I cast downe,

My selfe could else outfrowne false Fortunes frowne,

Shall we not see these daughters, and these sisters?   2790

LEAR

No, no, come lets away to prison

We two alone will sing like birds it'h cage,

When thou dost aske me blessing, ile kneele downe

And aske of thee forgiuenes, so weele liue

And pray, and sing, and tell old tales and laugh

At guilded butterflies, and heare poore rogues

Talke of Court newes, and weele talke with them to,

Who looses, and who wins, whose in, whose out,

And take vpon's the mistery of things

As if we were Gods spies, and weele weare out   2800

In a wal'd prison, packs and sects of great ones

That ebbe and flow bith' Moone.

BASTARD (*to souldiers*)   Take them away.

LEAR (*to Cordelia*)

Vpon such sacrifices my *Cordelia*,

The Gods thēselues throw incense, haue I caught thee?

He that parts vs shall bring a brand from heauen,

And fire vs hence like Foxes, wipe thine eyes,

The goodier shall deuoure em, fleach and fell
Ere they shall make vs weepe? wele see vm starue
        first, come.   *Exeunt. Manet Edmund and Captaine*
BASTARD Come hither Captaine, harke.
2810 Take thou this note, goe follow them to prison,
One step, I haue aduanct thee, if thou dost
As this instructs thee, thou dost make thy way
To noble fortunes, know thou this that men
Are as the time is, to be tender minded
Does not become a sword, thy great imployment
Will not beare question, either say thout do't,
Or thriue by other meanes.

CAPTAINE   Ile do't my Lord.

BASTARD
About it, and write happy when thou hast don,
Marke I say instantly, and carie it so
As I haue set it downe.

2820 CAPTAINE   I cannot draw a cart,
Nor eate dride oats, if it bee mans worke ile do't. *Exit*
        Enter Duke of Albany, the two Ladies Gonorill and
        Regan, ⌈another Captaine,⌉ and others

ALBANY (*to Bastard*)
Sir you haue shewed to day your valiant strain,
And Fortune led you well you haue the captiues
That were the opposites of this dayes strife,
We doe require then of you, so to vse them,
As we shall find their merits, and our safty
May equally determine.

BASTARD   Sir I thought it fit,
To send the old and miserable King
To some retention, and appointed guard,
2830 Whose age has charmes in it, whose title more
To pluck the comen bossom on his side,
And turne our imprest launces in our eyes
Which doe commaund them, with him I sent the queen
My reason, all the same and they are readie
To morrow, or at further space, to appeare
Where you shall hold your session at this time
Wee sweat and bleed, the friend hath lost his friend
And the best quarrels in the heat are curst,
By those that feele their sharpnes,
2840 The question of *Cordelia* and her father
Requires a fitter place.

ALBANY   Sir by your patience,
I hold you but a subiect of this warre,
Not as a brother.

REGAN   That's as we list to grace him,
Me thinkes our pleasure should haue beene demanded
Ere you had spoke so farre, he led our powers,
Bore the commission of my place and person,
The which imediate may well stand vp,
And call it selfe your brother.

GONORILL   Not so hot,
In his owne grace hee doth exalt himselfe
More then in your aduancement.

2850 REGAN   In my right
By me inuested he com-peers the best.

GONORILL
That were the most, if hee should husband you.

REGAN
Iesters doe oft proue Prophets.

GONORILL   Hola, hola,
That eye that told you so, lookt but a squint.

REGAN
Lady I am not well, els I should answere
From a full flowing stomack, (*to Bastard*) Generall
Take thou my souldiers, prisoners, patrimonie,
Witnes the world that I create thee here
My Lord and maister.

GONORILL   Meane you to inioy him then?

ALBANY
The let alone lies not in your good will.   2860

BASTARD
Nor in thine Lord.

ALBANY   Halfe blouded fellow, yes.

BASTARD
Let the drum strike, and proue my title good.

ALBANY
Stay yet, heare reason, *Edmund* I arrest thee
On capitall treason, and in thine attaint,
This gilded Serpent, (*to Regan*) for your claime faire
        sister
I bare it in the interest of my wife.
Tis she is subcontracted to this Lord
And I her husband contradict the banes,
If you will mary, make your loue to me,
My Lady is bespoke, (*to Bastard*) thou art arm'd *Gloster*, 2870
If none appeare to proue vpon thy head,
Thy hainous, manifest, and many treasons,
        ⌈He throws downe a gloue⌉
There is my pledge, ile proue it on thy heart
Ere I tast bread, thou art in nothing lesse
Then I haue here proclaimd thee.

REGAN Sicke, ô sicke.

GONORILL (*aside*) If not, ile ne're trust poyson.

BASTARD (*to Albany, ⌈throwing downe a gloue⌉*)
Ther's my exchange, what in the world he is,
That names me traytor, villain-like he lies,
Call by thy trumpet, he that dares approach,   2880
On him, on you, who not, I will maintaine
My truth and honour firmely.

ALBANY A Herald ho.

BASTARD A Herald ho, a Herald.

ALBANY
Trust to thy single vertue, for thy souldiers
All leuied in my name, haue in my name
Tooke their discharge.

REGAN   This sicknes growes vpon me.

ALBANY
She is not well, conuey her to my tent,
                          Exit one or more with Regan
        ⌈Enter a Herald and a trumpet⌉
Come hether Herald, let the trumpet sound,
And read out this.   2890

2. CAPTAINE Sound trumpet?
        Trumpet sounds

HERALD (*reads*) If any man of qualitie or degree, in the
hoast of the army, will maintaine vpon *Edmund*

supposed Earle of *Gloster*, that he's a manifold traitour,
let him appeare at the third sound of the trumpet, he
is bold in his defence.

BASTARD Sound? (*Trumpet sounds*) Againe?

> *Enter Edgar armed at the third sound, a trumpet*
> *before him*

ALBANY (*to the Herald*)

Aske him his purposes why he appeares
Vpon this call oth' trumpet.

HERALD (*to Edgar*)   What are you?

2900 Your name and qualitie? And why you answere
This present summons.

EDGAR   O know my name is lost
By treasons tooth bare-gnawne and canker-bitte;
Yet are I mou't where is the aduersarie
I come to cope with all.

ALBANY   Which is that aduersarie?

EDGAR

What's he that speakes for *Edmund* Earle of *Gloster*.

BASTARD

Him selfe, what saiest thou to him?

EDGAR   Draw thy sword,
That if my speech offend a noble hart,
Thy arme may do thee Iustice, here is mine.

> *He drawes his sword*

Behold it is the priuiledge of my tongue,
2910 My oath and my profession, I protest,
Maugure thy strength, youth, place and eminence,
Despight thy victor, sword and fire new fortune,
Thy valor and thy heart thou art a traytor,
False to thy Gods thy brother and thy Father,
Conspirante gainst this high illustrious prince,
And from the'xtreamest vpward of thy head,
To the descent and dust beneath thy feet,
A most toad-spotted traytor say thou no
This sword, this arme, and my best spirits, ar bent
2920 To proue vpon thy heart whereto I speake
Thou liest.

BASTARD   In wisdome I should aske thy name,
But since thy outside lookes so faire and warlike,
And that thy tong some say of breeding breathes,
My right of knighthood, I disdaine and spurne
Heere do I tosse those treasons to thy head,
With the hell hated ly, oreturne thy heart,
Which for they yet glance by and scarcely bruse,
This sword of mine shall giue them instant way
Where they shall rest for euer, trumpets speake.

> ⌈*Flourish.*⌉ *They fight. Bastard is vanquisht*

⌈ALL⌉

Saue him, saue him.

2930 GONORILL   This is meere practise *Gloster*
By the law of armes thou art not bound to answere
An vnknowne opposite, thou art not vanquisht,
But cousned and beguild.

ALBANY   Stop your mouth dame,
Or with this paper shall I stople it,
Thou worse then any thing, reade thine owne euill,
Nay no tearing Lady, I perceiue you know't.

GONORILL

Say if I do, the lawes are mine not thine,
Who shal arraine me for't.

ALBANY   Most monstrous
Know'st thou this paper?

GONORILL   Aske me not what I know.

> *Exit Gonorill*

ALBANY

Go after her, shee's desperate, gouerne her.   2940

> *Exit one or more*

BASTARD

What you haue chargd me with, that haue I don
And more, much more, the time will bring it out.
Tis past, and so am I, (*to Edgar*) but what art thou
That hast this fortune on me? if thou bee'st noble
I do forgiue thee.

EDGAR   Let's exchange charity,
I am no lesse in bloud then thou art *Edmond*,
If more, the more ignobly thou hast wrongd me.

> ⌈*He takes off his helmet*⌉

My name is *Edgar*, and thy fathers sonne,
The Gods are iust, and of our pleasant vices
Make instruments to scourge vs   2950
The darke and vitious place where thee he gotte,
Cost him his eies.

BASTARD   Thou hast spoken truth,
The wheele is come full circled I am heere.

ALBANY (*to Edgar*)

Me thought thy very gate did prophecie
A royall noblenesse I must embrace thee.
Let sorow split my heart if I did euer hate
Thee or thy father.

EDGAR Worthy Prince I know't.

ALBANY Where haue you hid your selfe?
How haue you knowne the miseries of your father?   2960

EDGAR

By nursing them my Lord, list a briefe tale,
And when tis told O that my heart would burst
The bloudy proclamation to escape
That followed me so neere, O our liues sweetnes,
That with the paine of death, would hourly die,
Rather then die at once, taught me to shift
Into a mad-mans rags to assume a semblance
That very dogges disdain'd and in this habit
Met I my father with his bleeding rings
The precious stones new lost became his guide,   2970
Led him, beg'd for him, sau'd him from dispaire,
Neuer (O Father) reueald my selfe vnto him,
Vntill some halfe houre past, when I was armed,
Not sure, though hoping of this good successe,
I askt his blessing, and from first to last,
Told him my pilgrimage, but his flawd heart,
Alacke too weake, the conflict to support,
Twixt two extreames of passion, ioy and griefe,
Burst smillingly.

BASTARD   This speech of yours hath moued me,
And shall perchance do good, but speake you on,   2980
You looke as you had something more to say.

ALBANY

If there be more, more wofull, hold it in,
For I am almost ready to dissolue,
Hearing of this.

EDGAR   This would haue seemd a periode
To such as loue not sorow, but another
To amplifie, too much would make much more,
And top extreamitie
Whil'st I was big in clamor, came there in a man,
Who hauing seene me in my worst estate,
Shund my abhord society, but then finding
Who twas that so indur'd with his strong armes
He fastened on my necke and bellowed out,
As hee'd burst heauen, threw him on my father,
Told the most pitious tale of *Lear* and him,
That euer eare receiued, which in recounting
His griefe grew puissant and the strings of life
Began to cracke twice then the trumpets sounded,
And there I left him traunst.

ALBANY   But who was this.

EDGAR

Kent sir, the banisht *Kent*, who in disguise,
Followed his enemie king and did him seruice
Improper for a slaue.

Enter ⌈2.⌉ Gentleman with a bloudie knife

⌈2.⌉ GENTLEMAN   Helpe, helpe,

ALBANY   What kinde of helpe,
What meanes that bloudy knife?

⌈2.⌉ GENTLEMAN   Its hot it smokes,
It came euen from the heart of—

ALBANY   Who man, speake?

⌈2.⌉ GENTLEMAN

Your Lady sir, your Lady, and her sister
By her is poysoned, she hath confest it.

BASTARD

I was contracted to them both, all three
Now marie in an instant.

ALBANY

Produce their bodies, be they aliue or dead,
This Iustice of the heauens that makes vs tremble,
Touches vs not with pity.

Enter Kent as himselfe

EDGAR   Here comes *Kent* sir.

ALBANY

O tis he, the time will not allow
The complement that very manners vrges.

KENT I am come
To bid my King and maister ay good night,
Is he not here?

ALBANY   Great thing of vs forgot,
Speake *Edmund*, whers the king, and whers *Cordelia*
The bodies of Gonorill and Regan are brought in
Seest thou this obiect *Kent.*

KENT Alack why thus.

BASTARD Yet *Edmund* was beloued,
The one the other poysoned for my sake,
And after slue her selfe.

ALBANY   Euen so, couer their faces.

BASTARD

I pant for life, some good I meane to do,
Despight of my owne nature, quickly send,
Be briefe int toth' castle for my writ
Is on the life of *Lear* and on *Cordelia,*
Nay send in time.

ALBANY   Runne, runne, O runne.

EDGAR

To who my Lord, (*to Bastard*) who hath the office,
    send
Thy token of repreeue.

BASTARD

Well thought on, take my sword the Captaine,
Giue it the Captaine?

ALBANY   Hast thee for thy life.

Exit ⌈2. Captaine⌉

BASTARD

He hath Commission from thy wife and me,
To hang *Cordelia* in the prison, and
To lay the blame vpon her owne despaire,
That she fordid her selfe.

ALBANY

The Gods defend her, beare him hence a while.

Exeunt some with Bastard
Enter Lear with Cordelia in his armes, ⌈followed by
*   2. Captaine⌉*

LEAR

Howle, howle, howle, howle, O you are men of stones,
Had I your tongues and eyes, I would vse them so,
That heauens vault should cracke, shees gone for euer,
I know when one is dead, and when one liues,
Shees dead as earth,
    ⌈*He lays her downe*⌉
                    lend me a looking glasse,
If that her breath will mist or staine the stone,
Why then she liues.

KENT   Is this the promist end.

EDGAR

Or image of that horror.

ALBANY   Fall and cease.

LEAR

This feather stirs she liues, if it be so,
It is a chance which do's redeeme all sorowes
That euer I haue felt.

KENT ⌈*kneeling*⌉   A my good maister.

LEAR

Prethe away?

EDGAR   Tis noble *Kent* your friend.

LEAR

A plague vpon you murderous traytors all,
I might haue saued her, now shees gone for euer,
Cordelia, Cordelia, stay a little, ha,
What ist thou sayest, her voyce was euer soft,
Gentle and low, an excellent thing in women,
I kild the slaue that was a hanging thee.

⌈2.⌉ CAPTAINE

Tis true my Lords, he did.

LEAR   Did I not fellow?

2990

3000

3010

3020

3030

3040

3050

I haue seene the day, with my good biting Fauchon
I would haue made them skippe, I am old now,
And these same crosses spoyle me, (*to Kent*) who are
    you?
Mine eyes are not othe best, ile tell you straight.

KENT

If Fortune bragd of two she loued or hated,
One of them we behold.

3060 LEAR   Are not you *Kent*?

KENT

The same your seruant *Kent*, where is your seruant
    Caius.

LEAR

Hees a good fellow, I can tell you that,
Heele strike and quickly too, hees dead and rotten.

KENT

No my good Lord, I am the very man.

LEAR Ile see that straight.

KENT

That from your first of difference and decay,
Haue followed your sad steps.

LEAR   You'r welcome hither.

KENT

Nor no man else, als chearles, darke and deadly,
Your eldest daughters haue foredoone themselues,
And desperatly are dead.

3070 LEAR   So thinke I to.

ALBANY

He knowes not what he sees, and vaine it is,
That we present vs to him.

EDGAR   Very bootlesse.

    Enter another Captaine

⌐3.⌐ CAPTAINE (*to Albany*)
    Edmund is dead my Lord.

ALBANY   Thats but a trifle heere,
You Lords and noble friends, know our intent,
What comfort to this great decay may come,
Shall be applied: for vs we wil resigne
During the life of this old maiesty,

To him our absolute power, (*to Edgar and Kent*) you to
    your rights
With boote, and such addition as your honors
Haue more then merited, all friends shall tast   3080
The wages of their vertue, and al foes
The cup of their deseruings, O see, see.

LEAR

And my poore foole is hangd, no, no life,
Why should a dog, a horse, a rat haue life
And thou no breath at all, O thou wilt come no more,
Neuer, neuer, neuer, pray you vndo
This button, thanke you sir, O, o, o, o.

EDGAR He faints (*to Lear*) my Lord, my Lord.
LEAR Breake hart, I prethe breake.
EDGAR Look vp my Lord.   3090

KENT

Vex not his ghost, O let him passe, he hates him
That would vpon the wracke of this tough world
Stretch him out longer.
    ⌐*Lear dies*⌐
EDGAR   O he is gone indeed.

KENT

The wonder is, he hath endured so long,
He but vsurpt his life.

ALBANY (*to attendants*)
Beare them from hence, our present busines
Is to generall woe, (*to Kent and Edgar*) friends of my
    soule, you twaine
Rule in this kingdome, and the goard state sustaine.

KENT

I haue a iourney sir, shortly to go,
My maister cals, and I must not say no.   3100

ALBANY

The waight of this sad time we must obey,
Speake what we feele, not what we ought to say,
The oldest haue borne most, we that are yong,
Shall neuer see so much, nor liue so long.

                    Exeunt, carrying the bodies

                    FINIS

THE TRAGEDIE OF KING LEAR
THE FOLIO TEXT

THE text of *King Lear* given here represents the revision made probably two or three years after the first version had been written and performed; it is based on the text printed in the 1623 Folio. This is a more obviously theatrical text. It makes a number of significant cuts, amounting to some 300 lines. The most conspicuous ones are the dialogue in which Lear's Fool implicitly calls his master a fool (Quarto 629-44); Kent's account of the French invasion of England (Quarto 1495-1507); Lear's mock-trial, in his madness, of his daughters (Quarto 1829-67); Edgar's generalizing couplets at the end of that scene (Quarto 1910-23); the brief, compassionate dialogue of two of Gloucester's servants after his blinding (Quarto 2020-8); parts of Albany's protest to Goneril about the sisters' treatment of Lear (in Quarto Sc. 16); the entire scene (Quarto Sc. 17) in which a Gentleman tells Kent of Cordelia's grief on hearing of her father's condition; the presence of the Doctor and the musical accompaniment to the reunion of Lear and Cordelia; and Edgar's account of his meeting with Kent in which Kent's 'strings of life | Began to cracke' (Quarto 2983-3000). The Folio also adds about 100 lines that are not in the Quarto—mostly in short passages, including Kent's statement that Albany and Cornwall have servants who are in the pay of France (1508-15), Merlin's prophecy spoken by the Fool at the end of 3.2, and the last lines of both the Fool and Lear. In addition, several speeches are differently assigned, and there are many variations in wording.

The reasons for these variations, and their effect on the play, are to some extent matters of speculation and of individual interpretation. Certainly they streamline the play's action, removing some reflective passages, particularly at the ends of scenes. They affect the characterization of, especially, Edgar, Albany, and Kent, and there are significant differences in the play's closing passages. Structurally the principal differences lie in the presentation of the military actions in the later part of the play; in the Folio-based text Cordelia is more clearly in charge of the forces that come to Lear's assistance, and they are less clearly a French invasion force. The absence from this text of passages that appeared in the 1608 text implies no criticism of them in themselves. The play's revision may have been dictated in whole or in part by theatrical exigencies, or it may have emerged from Shakespeare's own dissatisfaction with what he had first written. Each version has its own integrity, which is distorted by the practice, traditional since the early eighteenth century, of conflation.

The Folio text has been heavily influenced, in its spelling and punctuation, by the Second Quarto (1619); the manuscript consulted was probably a scribal copy.

THE NAMES OF THE ACTORS

LEAR, King of Britaine

GONORILL, Lears eldest daughter

Duke of ALBANY, her husband

REGAN, Lears second daughter

Duke of CORNWALL, her husband

CORDELIA, Lears yongest daughter

King of FRANCE

Duke of BURGUNDIE } suitors of Cordelia

Earle of KENT, later disguised as Caius

Earle of GLOSTER

EDGAR, eldest sonne of Gloster, later disguised as Tom a Bedlam

Edmund, BASTARD sonne of Gloster

OLD MAN, a tenant of Gloster

CURAN, Glosters retainer

Lears FOOLE

Oswald, Gonorills STEWARD

3 SERUANTS of Cornwall

DOCTOR, attendant on Cordelia

3 CAPTAINES

A HERALD

A KNIGHT

A MESSENGER

Gentlemen, Seruants, Souldiers, followers, Trumpets, others

The Tragedie of King Lear

1.1   *Enter Kent, Gloucester, and Edmond*

KENT I thought the King had more affected the Duke of *Albany*, then *Cornwall*.

GLOUSTER It did always seeme so to vs: But now in the diuision of the Kingdome, it appeares not which of the Dukes hee valewes most, for qualities are so weigh'd, that curiosity in neither, can make choise of eithers moity.

KENT Is not this your Son, my Lord?

GLOUSTER His breeding Sir, hath bin at my charge. I haue
10 so often blush'd to acknowledge him, that now I am braz'd too't.

KENT I cannot conceiue you.

GLOUSTER Sir, this yong Fellowes mother could; where-vpon she grew round womb'd, and had indeede (Sir) a Sonne for her Cradle, ere she had a husband for her bed. Do you smell a fault?

KENT I cannot wish the fault vndone, the issue of it, being so proper.

GLOUSTER But I haue a Sonne, Sir, by order of Law, some
20 yeere elder then this; who, yet is no deerer in my account, though this Knaue came somthing sawcily to the world before he was sent for: yet was his Mother fayre, there was good sport at his making, and the horson must be acknowledged. (*To Edmond*) Doe you know this Noble Gentleman, *Edmond*?

EDMOND No, my Lord.

GLOUSTER (*to Edmond*) My Lord of Kent: remember him heereafter, as my Honourable Friend.

EDMOND (*to Kent*) My seruices to your Lordship.

30 KENT I must loue you, and sue to know you better.

EDMOND Sir, I shall study deseruing.

GLOUSTER (*to Kent*) My Lord of Kent: He hath bin out nine yeares, and away he shall againe.

    Sennet

The King is comming.

    Enter King Lear, Cornwall, Albany, Gonerill,
    Regan, Cordelia, and attendants

LEAR

Attend the Lords of France & Burgundy, Gloster.

GLOUSTER I shall, my Lord.   *Exit*

LEAR

Meane time we shal expresse our darker purpose.
Giue me the Map there. Know, that we haue diuided
In three our Kingdome: and 'tis our fast intent,
40 To shake all Cares and Businesse from our Age,
Conferring them on yonger strengths, while we
Vnburthen'd crawle toward death. Our son of *Cornwal*,
And you our no lesse louing Sonne of *Albany*,
We haue this houre a constant will to publish
Our daughters seuerall Dowers, that future strife
May be preuented now. The Princes, *France & Burgundy*,
Great Riuals in our yongest daughters loue,

Long in our Court, haue made their amorous soiourne,
And heere are to be answer'd. Tell me my daughters
(Since now we will diuest vs both of Rule,   50
Interest of Territory, Cares of State)
Which of you shall we say doth loue vs most,
That we, our largest bountie may extend
Where Nature doth with merit challenge. *Gonerill*,
Our eldest borne, speake first.

GONERILL

Sir, I loue you more then words can weild ye matter,
Deerer then eye-sight, space, and libertie,
Beyond what can be valewed, rich or rare,
No lesse then life, with grace, health, beauty, honor:
As much as Childe ere lou'd, or Father found.   60
A loue that makes breath poore, and speech vnable,
Beyond all manner of so much I loue you.

CORDELIA (*aside*)

What shall *Cordelia* speake? Loue, and be silent.

LEAR (*to Gonerill*)

Of all these bounds euen from this Line, to this,
With shadowie Forrests, and with Champains rich'd
With plenteous Riuers, and wide-skirted Meades
We make thee Lady. To thine and *Albanies* issues
Be this perpetuall. What sayes our second Daughter?
Our deerest *Regan*, wife of *Cornwall*?

REGAN

I am made of that selfe-mettle as my Sister,   70
And prize me at her worth. In my true heart,
I finde she names my very deede of loue:
Onely she comes too short, that I professe
My selfe an enemy to all other ioyes,
Which the most precious square of sense possesses,
And finde I am alone felicitate
In your deere Highnesse loue.

CORDELIA (*aside*)   Then poore *Cordelia*,

And yet not so, since I am sure my loue's
More ponderous then my tongue.

LEAR (*to Regan*)

To thee, and thine hereditarie euer,   80
Remaine this ample third of our faire Kingdome,
No lesse in space, validitie, and pleasure
Then that conferr'd on *Gonerill*. (*To Cordelia*) Now our Ioy,
Although our last and least; to whose yong loue,
The Vines of France, and Milke of Burgundie,
Striue to be interest. What can you say, to draw
A third, more opilent then your Sisters? speake.

CORDELIA Nothing my Lord.

LEAR Nothing?

CORDELIA Nothing.   90

LEAR

Nothing will come of nothing, speake againe.

CORDELIA

Vnhappie that I am, I cannot heaue
My heart into my mouth: I loue your Maiesty
According to my bond, no more nor lesse.

LEAR

How, how *Cordelia*? mend your speech a little,
Least you may marre your Fortunes.

CORDELIA　　　　　　　　　Good my Lord,

You haue begot me, bred me, lou'd me.
I returne those duties backe as are right fit,
Obey you, Loue you, and most Honour you.
100 Why haue my Sisters Husbands, if they say
They loue you all? Happily when I shall wed,
That Lord, whose hand must take my plight, shall
　　carry
Halfe my loue with him, halfe my Care, and Dutie,
Sure I shall neuer marry like my Sisters.

LEAR But goes thy heart with this?

CORDELIA I my good Lord.

LEAR So young, and so vntender?

CORDELIA So young my Lord, and true.

LEAR

Let it be so, thy truth then be thy dowre:
110 For by the sacred radience of the Sunne,
The misteries of *Heccat* and the night:
By all the operation of the Orbes,
From whom we do exist, and cease to be,
Heere I disclaime all my Paternall care,
Propinquity and property of blood,
And as a stranger to my heart and me,
Hold thee from this for euer. The barbarous *Scythian*,
Or he that makes his generation messes
To gorge his appetite, shall to my bosome
120 Be as well neighbour'd, pittied, and releeu'd,
As thou my sometime Daughter.

KENT　　　　　　　　　Good my Liege.

LEAR Peace *Kent*,

Come not betweene the Dragon and his wrath,
I lou'd her most, and thought to set my rest
On her kind nursery. ⌜*To Cordelia*⌝ Hence and auoid
　　my sight:
So be my graue my peace, as here I giue
Her Fathers heart from her; call *France*, who stirres?
Call *Burgundy*,　　　　　　　　⌜*Exit one or more*⌝
　　　　　Cornwall, and *Albanie*,
With my two Daughters Dowres, digest the third,
130 Let pride, which she cals plainnesse, marry her:
I doe inuest you ioyntly with my power,
Preheminence, and all the large effects
That troope with Maiesty. Our selfe by Monthly course,
With reseruation of an hundred Knights,
By you to be sustain'd, shall our abode
Make with you by due turne, onely we shall retaine
The name, and all th'addition to a King: the Sway,
Reuennew, Execution of the rest,
Beloued Sonnes be yours, which to confirme,
This Coronet part betweene you.

140 KENT　　　　　　　　　Royall *Lear*,

Whom I haue euer honor'd as my King,
Lou'd as my Father, as my Master follow'd,
As my great Patron thought on in my praiers.

LEAR

The bow is bent & drawne, make from the shaft.

KENT

Let it fall rather, though the forke inuade
The region of my heart, be *Kent* vnmannerly,
When *Lear* is mad, what wouldst thou do old man?
Think'st thou that dutie shall haue dread to speake,
When power to flattery bowes? To plainnesse
　　honour's bound,
When Maiesty falls to folly, reserue thy state,　　150
And in thy best consideration checke
This hideous rashnesse, answere my life, my iudgement:
Thy yongest Daughter do's not loue thee least,
Nor are those empty hearted, whose low sounds
Reuerbe no hollownesse.

LEAR　　　　　　　*Kent*, on thy life no more.

KENT

My life I neuer held but as a pawne
To wage against thine enemies, nere feard to loose it,
Thy safety being motiue.

LEAR　　　　　　　　Out of my sight.

KENT

See better *Lear*, and let me still remaine
The true blanke of thine eie.

LEAR　　　　　　　　　Now by *Apollo*,　　160

KENT

Now by *Apollo*, King thou swear'st thy Gods in vaine.

LEAR ⌜*making to strike him*⌝

O Vassall! Miscreant.

ALBANY and ⌜CORDELIA⌝ Deare Sir forbeare.

KENT (*to Lear*)

Kill thy Physition, and thy fee bestow
Vpon the foule disease, reuoke thy guift,
Or whil'st I can vent clamour from my throate,
Ile tell thee thou dost euill.

LEAR

Heare me recreant, on thine allegeance heare me;
That thou hast sought to make vs breake our vowes,
Which we durst neuer yet; and with strain'd pride,
To come betwixt our sentence, and our power,　　170
Which, nor our nature, nor our place can beare;
Our potencie made good, take thy reward.
Fiue dayes we do allot thee for prouision,
To shield thee from disasters of the world,
And on the sixt to turne thy hated backe
Vpon our kingdome; if on the seuenth day following,
Thy banisht trunke be found in our Dominions,
The moment is thy death, away. By *Iupiter*,
This shall not be reuok'd.

KENT

Fare thee well King, sith thus thou wilt appeare,　　180
Freedome liues hence, and banishment is here;
(*To Cordelia*) The Gods to their deere shelter take thee
　　Maid,
That iustly think'st, and hast most rightly said:

(*To Gonerill and Regan*) And your large speeches, may
    your deeds approue,
That good effects may spring from words of loue:
Thus *Kent*, O Princes, bids you all adew,
Hee'l shape his old course, in a Country new.   *Exit*
    Flourish. Enter Gloster with France, and Burgundy,
    Attendants
⌈CORDELIA⌉
    Heere's *France* and *Burgundy*, my Noble Lord.
LEAR My Lord of *Burgundie*,
190   We first addresse toward you, who with this King
    Hath riuald for our Daughter; what in the least
    Will you require in present Dower with her,
    Or cease your quest of Loue?
BURGUNDY   Most Royall Maiesty,
    I craue no more then hath your Highnesse offer'd,
    Nor will you tender lesse?
LEAR   Right Noble *Burgundy*,
    When she was deare to vs, we did hold her so,
    But now her price is fallen: Sir, there she stands,
    If ought within that little seeming substance,
    Or all of it with our displeasure piec'd,
200   And nothing more may fitly like your Grace,
    Shee's there, and she is yours.
BURGUNDY   I know no answer.
LEAR
    Will you with those infirmities she owes,
    Vnfriended, new adopted to our hate,
    Dow'rd with our curse, and stranger'd with our oath,
    Take her or, leaue her.
BURGUNDY   Pardon me Royall Sir,
    Election makes not vp in such conditions.
LEAR
    Then leaue her sir, for by the powre that made me,
    I tell you all her wealth. (*To France*) For you great King,
    I would not from your loue make such a stray,
210   To match you where I hate, therefore beseech you
    T'auert your liking a more worthier way,
    Then on a wretch whom Nature is asham'd
    Almost t'acknowledge hers.
FRANCE   This is most strange,
    That she whom euen but now, was your best obiect,
    The argument of your praise, balme of your age,
    The best, the deer'st, should in this trice of time
    Commit a thing so monstrous, to dismantle
    So many folds of fauour: sure her offence
    Must be of such vnnaturall degree,
220   That monsters it: Or your fore-voucht affection
    Fall into taint, which to beleeue of her
    Must be a faith that reason without miracle
    Should neuer plant in me.
CORDELIA (*to Lear*)
    I yet beseech your Maiesty,
    If for I want that glib and oylie Art,
    To speake and purpose not, since what I well intend,
    Ile do't before I speake, that you make knowne
    It is no vicious blot, murther, or foulenesse,
    No vnchaste action or dishonour'd step

That hath depriu'd me of your Grace and fauour,   230
But euen the want of that, for which I am richer,
A still soliciting eye, and such a tongue,
That I am glad I haue not, though not to haue it,
Hath lost me in your liking.
LEAR   Better thou
    Had'st not beene borne, then not t'haue pleas'd me
    better.
FRANCE
    Is it but this? A tardinesse in nature,
    Which often leaues the history vnspoke
    That it intends to do: my Lord of *Burgundy*,
    What say you to the Lady? Loue's not loue
    When it is mingled with regards, that stands   240
    Aloofe from th'intire point, will you haue her?
    She is herselfe a Dowrie.
BURGUNDY (*to Lear*)   Royall King,
    Giue but that portion which your selfe propos'd,
    And here I take *Cordelia* by the hand,
    Dutchesse of *Burgundie*.
LEAR Nothing, I haue sworne, I am firme.
BURGUNDY (*to Cordelia*)
    I am sorry then you haue so lost a Father,
    That you must loose a husband.
CORDELIA   Peace be with *Burgundie*,
    Since that respect and Fortunes are his loue,
    I shall not be his wife.   250
FRANCE
    Fairest *Cordelia*, that art most rich being poore,
    Most choise forsaken, and most lou'd despis'd,
    Thee and thy vertues here I seize vpon,
    Be it lawfull I take vp what's cast away.
    Gods, Gods! 'Tis strange, that from their cold'st neglect
    My Loue should kindle to enflam'd respect.
    Thy dowrelesse Daughter King, throwne to my chance,
    Is Queene of vs, of ours, and our faire *France*:
    Not all the Dukes of watrish *Burgundy*,
    Can buy this vnpriz'd precious Maid of me.   260
    Bid them farewell *Cordelia*, though vnkinde,
    Thou loosest here a better where to finde.
LEAR
    Thou hast her *France*, let her be thine, for we
    Haue no such Daughter, nor shall euer see
    That face of hers againe, therfore be gone,
    Without our Grace, our Loue, our Benizon:
    Come Noble *Burgundie*.
           Flourish. Exeunt. Manet France and the sisters
FRANCE   Bid farwell to your Sisters.
CORDELIA
    Ye Iewels of our Father, with wash'd eies
    Cordelia leaues you, I know you what you are,
    And like a Sister am most loth to call   270
    Your faults as they are nam'd. Loue well our Father:
    To your professed bosomes I commit him,
    But yet alas, stood I within his Grace,
    I would prefer him to a better place,
    So farewell to you both.
REGAN Prescribe not vs our dutie.

GONERILL Let your study
  Be to content your Lord, who hath receiu'd you
  At Fortunes almes, you haue obedience scanted,
280 And well are worth the want that you haue wanted.

CORDELIA
  Time shall vnfold what plighted cunning hides,
  Who couert faults, at last with shame derides:
  Well may you prosper.

FRANCE   Come my faire *Cordelia.*
                            Exit France and Cordelia

GONERILL Sister, it is not little I haue to say, of what most
  neerely appertaines to vs both, I thinke our Father will
  hence to night.

REGAN That's most certaine, and with you: next moneth
  with vs.

GONERILL You see how full of changes his age is, the
290 obseruation we haue made of it hath beene little; he
  alwaies lou'd our Sister most, and with what poore
  iudgement he hath now cast her off, appeares too
  grossely.

REGAN 'Tis the infirmity of his age, yet he hath euer but
  slenderly knowne himselfe.

GONERILL The best and soundest of his time hath bin but
  rash, then must we looke from his age, to receiue not
  alone the imperfections of long ingraffed condition, but
  therewithall the vnruly way-wardnesse, that infirme
300 and cholericke yeares bring with them.

REGAN Such vnconstant starts are we like to haue from
  him, as this of *Kents* banishment.

GONERILL There is further complement of leaue-taking
  betweene *France* and him, pray you let vs sit together,
  if our Father carry authority with such disposition as
  he beares, this last surrender of his will but offend vs.

REGAN We shall further thinke of it.

GONERILL We must do something, and i'th' heate.
                                   Exeunt

1.2   *Enter Edmond the Bastard*

EDMOND
  Thou Nature art my Goddesse, to thy Law
310 My seruices are bound, wherefore should I
  Stand in the plague of custome, and permit
  The curiosity of Nations, to depriue me?
  For that I am some twelue, or fourteene Moonshines
  Lag of a Brother? Why Bastard? Wherefore base?
  When my Dimensions are as well compact,
  My minde as generous, and my shape as true
  As honest Madams issue? Why brand they vs
  With Base? With basenes Bastardie? Base, Base?
  Who in the lustie stealth of Nature, take
320 More composition, and fierce qualitie,
  Then doth within a dull stale tyred bed
  Goe to th'creating a whole tribe of Fops
  Got 'tweene a sleepe, and wake? Well then,
  Legitimate *Edgar*, I must haue your land,
  Our Fathers loue, is to the Bastard *Edmond*,
  As to th'legitimate: fine word: Legitimate.

  Well, my Legittimate, if this Letter speed,
  And my inuention thriue, *Edmond* the base
  Shall to'th'Legitimate: I grow, I prosper:
  Now Gods, stand vp for Bastards.   330
     Enter Gloucester. Edmond reads a Letter

GLOUSTER
  Kent banish'd thus? and France in choller parted?
  And the King gone to night? Prescrib'd his powre,
  Confin'd to exhibition? All this done
  Vpon the gad? *Edmond*, how now? What newes?

EDMOND So please your Lordship, none.

GLOUSTER Why so earnestly seeke you to put vp y^t Letter?

EDMOND I know no newes, my Lord.

GLOUSTER What Paper were you reading?

EDMOND Nothing my Lord.

GLOUSTER No? what needed then that terrible dispatch of 340
  it into your Pocket? The quality of nothing, hath not
  such neede to hide it selfe. Let's see: come, if it bee
  nothing, I shall not neede Spectacles.

EDMOND I beseech you Sir, pardon mee; it is a Letter from
  my Brother, that I haue not all ore-read; and for so
  much as I haue perus'd, I finde it not fit for your ore-
  looking.

GLOUSTER Giue me the Letter, Sir.

EDMOND I shall offend, either to detaine, or giue it: the
  Contents, as in part I vnderstand them, are too blame. 350

GLOUSTER Let's see, let's see.

EDMOND I hope for my Brothers iustification, hee wrote
  this but as an essay, or taste of my Vertue.
     He giues Gloucester a Letter

GLOUSTER (*reads*) *This policie, and reuerence of Age, makes*
  the world bitter to the best of our times: keepes our
  Fortunes from vs, till our oldnesse cannot rellish them. I
  begin to finde an idle and fond bondage, in the oppression
  of aged tyranny, who swayes not as it hath power, but as
  it is suffer'd. Come to me, that of this I may speake more.
  If our Father would sleepe till I wak'd him, you should 360
  enioy halfe his Reuennew for euer, and liue the beloued of
  your Brother.   Edgar.
  Hum? Conspiracy? Sleepe till I wake him, you should
  enioy halfe his Reuennew: my Sonne *Edgar*, had hee
  a hand to write this? A heart and braine to breede it
  in? When came you to this? Who brought it?

EDMOND It was not brought mee, my Lord; there's the
  cunning of it. I found it throwne in at the Casement
  of my Closset.

GLOUSTER You know the character to be your Brothers? 370

EDMOND If the matter were good my Lord, I durst swear
  it were his: but in respect of that, I would faine thinke
  it were not.

GLOUSTER It is his.

EDMOND It is his hand, my Lord: but I hope his heart is
  not in the Contents.

GLOUSTER Has he neuer before sounded you in this
  busines?

EDMOND Neuer my Lord. But I haue heard him oft
  maintaine it to be fit, that Sonnes at perfect age, and 380

Fathers declin'd, the Father should bee as Ward to the Son, and the Sonne manage his Reuennew.

GLOUSTER O Villain, villain: his very opinion in the Letter. Abhorred Villaine, vnnaturall, detested, brutish Villaine; worse then brutish: Go sirrah, seeke him: Ile apprehend him. Abhominable Villaine, where is he?

EDMOND I do not well know my L. If it shall please you to suspend your indignation against my Brother, til you can deriue from him better testimony of his intent, you shold run a certaine course: where, if you violently proceed against him, mistaking his purpose, it would make a great gap in your owne Honor, and shake in peeces, the heart of his obedience. I dare pawne downe my life for him, that he hath writ this to feele my affection to your Honor, & to no other pretence of danger.

GLOUSTER Thinke you so?

EDMOND If your Honor iudge it meete, I will place you where you shall heare vs conferre of this, and by an Auricular assurance haue your satisfaction, and that without any further delay, then this very Euening.

GLOUSTER He cannot bee such a Monster. _Edmond_ seeke him out: winde me into him, I pray you: frame the Businesse after your owne wisedome. I would vnstate my selfe, to be in a due resolution.

EDMOND I will seeke him Sir, presently: conuey the businesse as I shall find meanes, and acquaint you withall.

GLOUSTER These late Eclipses in the Sun and Moone portend no good to vs: though the wisedome of Nature can reason it thus, and thus, yet Nature finds it selfe scourg'd by the sequent effects. Loue cooles, friendship falls off, Brothers diuide. In Cities, mutinies; in Countries, discord; in Pallaces, Treason; and the Bond crack'd, 'twixt Sonne and Father. This villaine of mine comes vnder the prediction; there's Son against Father, the King fals from byas of Nature, there's Father against Childe. We haue seene the best of our time. Machinations, hollownesse, treacherie, and all ruinous disorders follow vs disquietly to our Graues. Find out this Villain _Edmond_, it shall lose thee nothing, do it carefully: and the Noble & true-harted Kent banish'd; his offence, honesty. 'Tis strange.   _Exit_

EDMOND This is the excellent foppery of the world, that when we are sicke in fortune, often the surfets of our own behauiour, we make guilty of our disasters, the Sun, the Moone, and Starres, as if we were villaines on necessitie, Fooles by heauenly compulsion, Knaues, Theeues, and Treachers by Sphericall predominance, Drunkards, Lyars, and Adulterers by an inforc'd obedience of Planatary influence; and all that we are euill in, by a diuine thrusting on. An admirable euasion of Whore-master-man, to lay his Goatish disposition on the charge of a Starre. My father compounded with my mother vnder the Dragons taile, and my Natiuity was vnder _Vrsa Maior_, so that it followes, I am rough and Leacherous. Fut, I should haue bin that I am, had the

maidenlest Starre in the Firmament twinkled on my bastardizing.

Enter Edgar

Pat: he comes like the Catastrophe of the old Comedie: my Cue is villanous Melancholly, with a sith like _Tom_ o'Bedlam.

⌈_He reads a book_⌉

—O these Eclipses do portend these diuisions. Fa, Sol, La, Me.

EDGAR How now Brother _Edmond_, what serious contemplation are you in?

EDMOND I am thinking Brother of a prediction I read this other day, what should follow these Eclipses.

EDGAR Do you busie your selfe with that?

EDMOND I promise you, the effects he writes of, succeede vnhappily. When saw you my Father last?

EDGAR The night gone by.

EDMOND Spake you with him?

EDGAR I, two houres together.

EDMOND Parted you in good termes? Found you no displeasure in him, by word, nor countenance?

EDGAR None at all.

EDMOND Bethink your selfe wherein you may haue offended him: and at my entreaty forbeare his presence, vntill some little time hath qualified the heat of his displeasure, which at this instant so rageth in him, that with the mischiefe of your person, it would scarsely alay.

EDGAR Some Villaine hath done me wrong.

EDMOND That's my feare, I pray you haue a continent forbearance till the speed of his rage goes slower: and as I say, retire with me to my lodging, from whence I will fitly bring you to heare my Lord speake: pray ye goe, there's my key: if you do stirre abroad, goe arm'd.

EDGAR Arm'd, Brother?

EDMOND Brother, I aduise you to the best, I am no honest man, if ther be any good meaning toward you: I haue told you what I haue seene, and heard: But faintly. Nothing like the image, and horror of it, pray you away.

EDGAR Shall I heare from you anon?

EDMOND I do serue you in this businesse: _Exit Edgar_
A Credulous Father, and a Brother Noble,
Whose nature is so farre from doing harmes,
That he suspects none: on whose foolish honestie
My practises ride easie: I see the businesse.
Let me, if not by birth, haue lands by wit,
All with me's meete, that I can fashion fit.   _Exit_

Enter Gonerill, and Steward   **1.3**

GONERILL
Did my Father strike my Gentleman
For chiding of his Foole?

STEWARD   I Madam.

GONERILL
By day and night, he wrongs me, euery howre
He flashes into one grosse crime, or other,

That sets vs all at ods: Ile not endure it;
His Knights grow riotous, and himselfe vpbraides vs
490 On euery trifle. When he returnes from hunting,
I will not speake with him, say I am sicke,
If you come slacke of former seruices,
You shall do well, the fault of it Ile answer.
      ⌈Hornes within⌉
STEWARD He's comming Madam, I heare him.
GONERILL
Put on what weary negligence you please,
You and your Fellowes: I'de haue it come to question;
If he distaste it, let him to my Sister,
Whose mind and mine I know in that are one,
Remember what I haue said.
STEWARD   Well Madam.
GONERILL
500 And let his Knights haue colder lookes among you:
What growes of it no matter, aduise your fellowes so,
Ile write straight to my Sister to hold my course;
Prepare for dinner.   Exeunt seuerally

1.4   Enter Kent disguised
KENT
If but as well I other accents borrow,
That can my speech defuse, my good intent
May carry through it selfe to that full issue
For which I raiz'd my likenesse. Now banisht Kent,
If thou canst serue where thou dost stand condemn'd,
So may it come, thy Master whom thou lou'st,
510 Shall find thee full of labours.
      Hornes within. Enter Lear and Attendants from
      hunting
LEAR Let me not stay a iot for dinner, go get it ready:
                                    ⌈Exit one⌉
(To Kent) how now, what art thou?
KENT A man Sir.
LEAR What dost thou professe? What would'st thou with
vs?
KENT I do professe to be no lesse then I seeme; to serue
him truely that will put me in trust, to loue him that
is honest, to conuerse with him that is wise and saies
little, to feare iudgement, to fight when I cannot choose,
520 and to eate no fish.
LEAR What art thou?
KENT A very honest hearted Fellow, and as poore as the
King.
LEAR If thou be'st as poore for a subiect, as hee's for a
King, thar't poore enough. What wouldst thou?
KENT Seruice.
LEAR Who wouldst thou serue?
KENT You.
LEAR Do'st thou know me fellow?
530 KENT No Sir, but you haue that in your countenance,
which I would faine call Master.
LEAR What's that?
KENT Authority.
LEAR What seruices canst do?

KENT I can keepe honest counsaile, ride, run, marre a
curious tale in telling it, and deliuer a plaine message
bluntly: that which ordinary men are fit for, I am
quallified in, and the best of me, is Dilligence.
LEAR How old art thou?
KENT Not so young Sir to loue a woman for singing, nor 540
so old to dote on her for any thing. I haue yeares on
my backe forty eight.
LEAR Follow me, thou shalt serue me, if I like thee no
worse after dinner, I will not part from thee yet. Dinner
ho, dinner, where's my knaue? my Foole? Go you and
call my Foole hither.   ⌈Exit one⌉
      Enter Steward
You you Sirrah, where's my Daughter?
STEWARD So please you—   Exit
LEAR What saies the Fellow there? Call the Clot-pole
backe: Exit a Knight 550
wher's my Foole? Ho, I thinke the world's asleepe,
      Enter a Knight
how now? Where's that Mungrell?
KNIGHT He saies my Lord, your Daughter is not well.
LEAR Why came not the slaue backe to me when I call'd
him?
KNIGHT Sir, he answered me in the roundest manner, he
would not.
LEAR A would not?
KNIGHT My Lord, I know not what the matter is, but to
my iudgement your Highnesse is not entertain'd with 560
that Ceremonious affection as you were wont, theres a
great abatement of kindnesse appeares as well in the
generall dependants, as in the Duke himselfe also, and
your Daughter.
LEAR Ha? Saist thou so?
KNIGHT I beseech you pardon me my Lord, if I bee
mistaken, for my duty cannot be silent, when I thinke
your Highnesse wrong'd.
LEAR Thou but remembrest me of mine owne Conception,
I haue perceiued a most faint neglect of late, which I 570
haue rather blamed as mine owne iealous curiositie,
then as a very pretence and purpose of vnkindnesse; I
will looke further intoo't: but where's my Foole? I haue
not seene him this two daies.
KNIGHT Since my young Ladies going into France Sir, the
Foole hath much pined away.
LEAR No more of that, I haue noted it well, goe you and
tell my Daughter, I would speake with her.   ⌈Exit one⌉
Goe you call hither my Foole;   ⌈Exit one⌉
      Enter Steward ⌈crossing the stage⌉
Oh you Sir, you, come you hither Sir, who am I Sir? 580
STEWARD My Ladies Father.
LEAR My Ladies Father? my Lords knaue, you whorson
dog, you slaue, you curre.
STEWARD I am none of these my Lord, I beseech your
pardon.
LEAR Do you bandy lookes with me, you Rascall?
      ⌈Lear strikes him⌉
STEWARD Ile not be strucken my Lord.

KENT ⌜tripping him⌝ Nor tript neither, you base Foot-ball
    plaier.

590 LEAR (to Kent) I thanke thee fellow. Thou seru'st me, and
    Ile loue thee.

KENT (to Steward) Come sir, arise, away, Ile teach you
    differences: away, away, if you will measure your
    lubbers length againe, tarry, but away, goe too, haue
    you wisedome, so.   Exit Steward

LEAR Now my friendly knaue I thanke thee,

        Enter Foole

there's earnest of thy seruice.

        He giues Kent money

FOOLE Let me hire him too, (to Kent) here's my Coxcombe.

LEAR How now my pretty knaue, how dost thou?

600 FOOLE (to Kent) Sirrah, you were best take my Coxcombe.

LEAR Why my Boy?

FOOLE Why? for taking ones part that's out of fauour, (to
    Kent) nay, & thou canst not smile as the wind sits,
    thou'lt catch colde shortly, there take my Coxcombe;
    why this fellow ha's banish'd two on's Daughters, and
    did the third a blessing against his will, if thou follow
    him, thou must needs weare my Coxcombe. (To Lear)
    How now Nunckle? would I had two Coxcombes and
    two Daughters.

610 LEAR Why my Boy?

FOOL If I gaue them all my liuing, I'ld keepe my Cox-
    combes my selfe, there's mine, beg another of thy
    Daughters.

LEAR Take heed Sirrah, the whip.

FOOLE Truth's a dog must to kennell, hee must bee whipt
    out, when the Lady Brach may stand by'th'fire and
    stinke.

LEAR A pestilent gall to me.

FOOLE ⌜to Kent⌝ Sirha, Ile teach thee a speech.

620 LEAR Do.

FOOLE Marke it Nuncle;

      Haue more then thou showest,
      Speake lesse then thou knowest,
      Lend lesse then thou owest,
      Ride more then thou goest,
      Learne more then thou trowest,
      Set lesse then thou throwest;
      Leaue thy drinke and thy whore,
      And keepe in a dore,
630   And thou shalt haue more,
      Then two tens to a score.

KENT This is nothing Foole.

FOOLE Then 'tis like the breath of an vnfeed Lawyer, you
    gaue me nothing for't, (to Lear) can you make no vse
    of nothing Nuncle?

LEAR Why no Boy, nothing can be made out of nothing.

FOOLE (to Kent) Prythee tell him, so much the rent of his
    land comes to, he will not beleeue a Foole.

LEAR A bitter Foole.

640 FOOLE Do'st know the difference my Boy, betweene a
    bitter Foole, and a sweet one.

LEAR No Lad, teach me.

FOOLE Nunckle, giue me an egge, and Ile giue thee two
    Crownes.

LEAR What two Crownes shall they be?

FOOLE Why after I haue cut the egge i'th'middle and eate
    vp the meate, the two Crownes of the egge: when thou
    clouest thy Crowne i'th'middle, and gau'st away both
    parts, thou boar'st thine Asse at'h backe o're the durt,
    thou had'st little wit in thy bald crowne, when thou   650
    gau'st thy golden one away; if I speake like my selfe
    in this, let him be whipt that first findes it so.

⌜Sings⌝ Fooles had nere lesse grace in a yeere,
      For wisemen are growne foppish,
      And know not how their wits to weare,
      Their manners are so apish.

LEAR When were you wont to be so full of Songs sirrah?

FOOLE I haue vsed it Nunckle, ere since thou mad'st thy
    Daughters thy Mothers, for when thou gau'st them the
    rod, and put'st downe thine owne breeches,   660
    ⌜Sings⌝

      Then they for sodaine ioy did weepe,
        And I for sorrow sung,
      That such a King should play bo-peepe,
        And goe the Fooles among.

Pry'the Nunckle keepe a Schoolemaster that can teach
thy Foole to lie, I would faine learne to lie.

LEAR And you lie sirrah, wee'l haue you whipt.

FOOLE I maruell what kin thou and thy daughters are,
    they'l haue me whipt for speaking true: thou'lt haue
    me whipt for lying, and sometimes I am whipt for   670
    holding my peace. I had rather be any kind o'thing
    then a foole, and yet I would not be thee Nunckle,
    thou hast pared thy wit o'both sides, and left nothing
    i'th'middle;

        Enter Gonerill

heere comes one o'the parings.

LEAR

How now Daughter? what makes that Frontlet on?
You are too much of late i'th'frowne.

FOOLE Thou wast a pretty fellow when thou hadst no
    need to care for her frowning, now thou art an 0
    without a figure, I am better then thou art now, I am   680
    a Foole, thou art nothing. ⌜To Gonerill⌝ Yes forsooth I
    will hold my tongue, so your face bids me, though you
    say nothing.

⌜Sings⌝   Mum, mum,
      He that keepes nor crust, nor crum,
      Weary of all, shall want some.

That's a sheal'd Pescod.

GONERILL (to Lear)

Not only Sir this, your all-lycenc'd Foole,
But other of your insolent retinue
Do hourely Carpe and Quarrell, breaking forth   690
In ranke, and (not to be endured) riots. Sir,
I had thought by making this well knowne vnto you,
To haue found a safe redresse, but now grow fearefull
By what your selfe too late haue spoke and done,
That you protect this course, and put it on

By your allowance, which if you should, the fault
Would not scape censure, nor the redresses sleepe,
Which in the tender of a wholesome weale,
Might in their working do you that offence,
700   Which else were shame, that then necessitie
Will call discreet proceeding.

FOOLE (*to Lear*) For you know Nunckle,

⌈*Sings*⌉

     The Hedge-Sparrow fed the Cuckoo so long,
       That it's had it head bit off by it young,

so out went the Candle, and we were left darkling.

LEAR (*to Gonerill*) Are you our Daughter?

GONERILL

I would you would make vse of your good wisedome
(Whereof I know you are fraught), and put away
These dispositions, which of late transport you
710   From what you rightly are.

FOOLE May not an Asse know, when the Cart drawes the
Horse? ⌈*Sings*⌉ Whoop Iugge I loue thee.

LEAR

Do's any heere know me? This is not *Lear*:
Do's *Lear* walke thus? Speake thus? Where are his eies?
Either his Notion weakens, his Discernings
Are Lethargied. Ha! Waking? 'Tis not so?
Who is it that can tell me who I am?

FOOLE *Lears* shadow.

LEAR (*to Gonerill*) Your name, faire Gentlewoman?

GONERILL

720   This admiration Sir, is much o'th'sauour
Of other your new prankes. I do beseech you
To vnderstand my purposes aright:
As you are Old, and Reuerend, should be Wise.
Heere do you keepe a hundred Knights and Squires,
Men so disorder'd, so debosh'd, and bold,
That this our Court infected with their manners,
Shewes like a riotous Inne; Epicurisme and Lust
Makes it more like a Tauerne, or a Brothell,
Then a grac'd Pallace. The shame it selfe doth speake
730   For instant remedy. Be then desir'd
By her, that else will take the thing she begges,
A little to disquantity your Traine,
And the remainders that shall still depend,
To be such men as may besort your Age,
Which know themselues, and you.

LEAR   Darknesse, and Diuels.
Saddle my horses: call my Traine together.

⌈*Exit one or more*⌉

Degenerate Bastard, Ile not trouble thee;
Yet haue I left a daughter.

GONERILL

You strike my people, and your disorder'd rable,
Make Seruants of their Betters.

Enter Albany

740   LEAR   Woe, that too late repents:
Is it your will, speake Sir? Prepare my Horses.

⌈*Exit one or more*⌉

Ingratitude! thou Marble-hearted Fiend,
More hideous when thou shew'st thee in a Child,
Then the Sea-monster.

ALBANY Pray Sir be patient.

LEAR (*to Gonerill*) Detested Kite, thou lyest.
My Traine are men of choice, and rarest parts,
That all particulars of dutie know,
And in the most exact regard, support
The worships of their name. O most small fault,   750
How vgly did'st thou in *Cordelia* shew?
Which like an Engine, wrencht my frame of Nature
From the fixt place: drew from my heart all loue,
And added to the gall. O *Lear, Lear, Lear*!
Beate at this gate that let thy Folly in,
And thy deere Iudgement out. Go, go, my people.

ALBANY

My Lord, I am guiltlesse, as I am ignorant
Of what hath mou'd you.

LEAR   It may be so, my Lord.
Heare Nature, heare deere Goddesse, heare:
Suspend thy purpose, if thou did'st intend   760
To make this Creature fruitfull:
Into her Wombe conuey stirrility,
Drie vp in her the Organs of increase,
And from her derogate body, neuer spring
A Babe to honor her. If she must teeme,
Create her childe of Spleene, that it may liue
And be a thwart disnatur'd torment to her.
Let it stampe wrinkles in her brow of youth,
With cadent Teares fret Channels in her cheekes,
Turne all her Mothers paines, and benefits   770
To laughter, and contempt: That she may feele,
That she may feele,
How sharper then a Serpents tooth it is,
To haue a thanklesse Childe. Away, away.

Exit Lear, ⌈Kent, and Attendants⌉

ALBANY

Now Gods that we adore, whereof comes this?

GONERILL

Neuer afflict your selfe to know more of it:
But let his disposition haue that scope
As dotage giues it.

Enter Lear

LEAR

What fiftie of my Followers at a clap?
Within a fortnight?

ALBANY   What's the matter, Sir?   780

LEAR

Ile tell thee: (*to Gonerill*) life and death, I am asham'd
That thou hast power to shake my manhood thus,
That these hot teares, which breake from me perforce
Should make thee worth them. Blastes and Fogges
   vpon thee:
Th'vntented woundings of a Fathers curse
Pierce euerie sense about thee. Old fond eyes,
Beweepe this cause againe, Ile plucke ye out,
And cast you with the waters that you loose
To temper Clay. Ha? Let it be so.
I haue another daughter,   790
Who I am sure is kinde and comfortable:
When she shall heare this of thee, with her nailes
Shee'l flea thy Woluish visage. Thou shalt finde,

That Ile resume the shape which thou dost thinke
I haue cast off for euer.   *Exit*

GONERILL   Do you marke that?

ALBANY
I cannot be so partiall *Gonerill*,
To the great loue I beare you.

GONERILL
Pray you content. What *Oswald*, hoa?
You Sir, more Knaue then Foole, after your Master.

FOOLE
800   Nunkle *Lear*, Nunkle *Lear*,
       Tarry, take the Foole with thee:
       A Fox, when one has caught her,
       And such a Daughter,
       Should sure to the Slaughter,
       If my Cap would buy a Halter,
       So the Foole followes after.   *Exit*

GONERILL
This man hath had good Counsell, a hundred Knights?
'Tis politike, and safe to let him keepe
At point a hundred Knights: yes, that on euerie dreame,
810   Each buz, each fancie, each complaint, dislike,
He may enguard his dotage with their powres,
And hold our liues in mercy. *Oswald*, I say.

ALBANY
Well, you may feare too farre.

GONERILL   Safer then trust too farre;
Let me still take away the harmes I feare,
Not feare still to be taken. I know his heart,
What he hath vtter'd I haue writ my Sister:
If she sustaine him, and his hundred Knights
When I haue shew'd th'vnfitnesse.
              Enter Steward

                         How now *Oswald?*
What haue you writ that Letter to my Sister?

820   STEWARD I Madam.

GONERILL
Take you some company, and away to horse,
Informe her full of my particular feare,
And thereto adde such reasons of your owne,
As may compact it more. Get you gone,
And hasten your returne;   *Exit Steward*
                         no, no, my Lord,
This milky gentlenesse, and course of yours
Though I condemne not, yet vnder pardon
You are much more attaskt for want of wisedome,
Then prais'd for harmefull mildnesse.

ALBANY
830   How farre your eies may pierce I cannot tell;
Striuing to better, oft we marre what's well.

GONERILL Nay then—

ALBANY Well, well, the'uent.   *Exeunt*

1.5   *Enter Lear, Kent disguised, First Gentleman, and Foole*
LEAR ⌜*to Gentleman, giuing him a Letter*⌝ Go you before to
Gloster with these Letters;   ⌜*Exit Gentleman*⌝
⌜*to Kent, giuing him a Letter*⌝ acquaint my Daughter no
further with any thing you know, then comes from

her demand out of the Letter, if your Dilligence be not
speedy, I shall be there afore you.

KENT I will not sleepe my Lord, till I haue deliuered your   840
Letter.   *Exit*

FOOLE If a mans braines were in's heeles, wert not in
danger of kybes?

LEAR I Boy.

FOOLE Then I prythee be merry, thy wit shall not go slipshod.

LEAR Ha, ha, ha.

FOOL Shalt see thy other Daughter will vse thee kindly,
for though she's as like this, as a Crabbe's like an
Apple, yet I can tell what I can tell.   850

LEAR What can'st tell Boy?

FOOLE She will taste as like this as, a Crabbe do's to a
Crab: thou canst tell why ones nose stands i'th'middle
on's face?

LEAR No.

FOOLE Why to keepe ones eyes of either side 's nose, that
what a man cannot smell out, a may spy into.

LEAR I did her wrong.

FOOLE Can'st tell how an Oyster makes his shell?

LEAR No.   860

FOOLE Nor I neither; but I can tell why a Snaile ha's a
house.

LEAR Why?

FOOLE Why to put's head in, not to giue it away to his
daughters, and leaue his hornes without a case.

LEAR
I will forget my Nature, so kind a Father?
Be my Horsses ready?

FOOLE Thy Asses are gone about 'em; the reason why
the seuen Starres are no mo then seuen, is a pretty
reason.   870

LEAR Because they are not eight.

FOOLE Yes indeed, thou would'st make a good Foole.

LEAR
To tak't againe perforce; Monster Ingratitude!

FOOLE If thou wert my Foole Nunckle, Il'd haue thee
beaten for being old before thy time.

LEAR How's that?

FOOLE Thou shouldst not haue bin old, till thou hadst bin
wise.

LEAR
O let me not be mad, not mad sweet Heauen:
Keepe me in temper, I would not be mad.   880
              ⌜*Enter First Gentleman*⌝
How now are the Horses ready?

⌜1⌝ GENTLEMAN   Ready my Lord.

LEAR (*to Foole*) Come Boy.
                         ⌜*Exeunt Lear and Gentleman*⌝

FOOLE
She that's a Maid now, & laughs at my departure,
Shall not be a Maid long, vnlesse things be cut
shorter.   ⌜*Exit*⌝

              Enter Edmond the Bastard, and Curan, seuerally   2.1

EDMOND Saue thee *Curan*.

CURAN And you Sir, I haue bin with your Father, and
giuen him notice that the Duke of *Cornwall*, and *Regan*
his Duchesse will be here with him this night.

EDMOND How comes that?

890　CURAN Nay I know not, you haue heard of the newes
abroad, I meane the whisper'd ones, for they are yet
but eare-kissing arguments.

EDMOND Not I: pray you what are they?

CURAN Haue you heard of no likely Warres toward, 'twixt
the Dukes of *Cornwall*, and *Albany*?

EDMOND Not a word.

CURAN You may do then in time, fare you well Sir.
　　　　　　　　　　　　　　　　　　　　　Exit

EDMOND

The Duke be here to night? The better best,
　　⌈*Enter Edgar at a window aboue*⌉
This weaues it selfe perforce into my businesse,

900　My Father hath set guard to take my Brother,
And I haue one thing of a queazie question
Which I must act, Briefenesse, and Fortune worke.
Brother, a word, discend; Brother I say,
　　⌈*Edgar climbes downe*⌉
My Father watches: O Sir, fly this place,
Intelligence is giuen where you are hid;
You haue now the good aduantage of the night,
Haue you not spoken 'gainst the Duke of *Cornewall*?
Hee's comming hither, now i'th' night, i'th' haste,
And *Regan* with him, haue you nothing said

910　Vpon his partie 'gainst the Duke of *Albany*?
Aduise your selfe.

EDGAR　　　　　　I am sure on't, not a word.

EDMOND

I heare my Father comming, pardon me:
In cunning, I must draw my Sword vpon you:
Draw, seeme to defend your selfe, now quit you well.
(*Calling*) Yeeld, come before my Father, light hoa,
　　here,
(*To Edgar*) Fly Brother, (*Calling*) Torches, Torches, (*to
　　Edgar*) so farewell.　　　　　　　*Exit Edgar*
Some blood drawne on me, would beget opinion
Of my more fierce endeauour.
　　　　　He wounds his arme
　　　　　　　　　　　　　I haue seene drunkards
Do more then this in sport; (*Calling*) Father, Father,
Stop, stop, ho, helpe?
　　　　Enter Gloster, and Seruants with Torches

920　GLOUSTER　　　　　Now *Edmund*, where's the villaine?

EDMOND

Here stood he in the dark, his sharpe Sword out,
Mumbling of wicked charmes, coniuring the Moone
To stand's auspicious Mistris.

GLOUSTER　　　　　　But where is he?

EDMOND

Looke Sir, I bleed.

GLOUSTER　　　　Where is the villaine, *Edmund*?

EDMOND

Fled this way Sir, when by no meanes he could.

GLOUSTER

Pursue him, ho: go after.　　　*Exeunt Seruants*
　　　　　　　　By no meanes, what?

EDMOND

Perswade me to the murther of your Lordship,
But that I told him the reuenging Gods,
'Gainst Paricides did all the thunder bend,
Spoke with how manifold, and strong a Bond　　　930
The Child was bound to'th' Father; Sir in fine,
Seeing how lothly opposite I stood
To his vnnaturall purpose, in fell motion
With his prepared Sword, he charges home
My vnprouided body, latch'd mine arme;
And when he saw my best alarum'd spirits
Bold in the quarrels right, rouz'd to th'encounter,
Or whether gasted by the noyse I made,
Full sodainely he fled.

GLOUSTER　　　　　　Let him fly farre:
Not in this Land shall he remaine vncaught　　　940
And found, dispatch, the Noble Duke my Master,
My worthy Arch and Patron comes to night,
By his authoritie I will proclaime it,
That he which finds him shall deserue our thankes,
Bringing the murderous Coward to the stake:
He that conceales him death.

EDMOND

When I disswaded him from his intent,
And found him pight to doe it, with curst speech
I threaten'd to discouer him; he replied,
Thou vnpossessing Bastard, dost thou thinke,　　950
If I would stand against thee, would the reposall
Of any trust, vertue, or worth in thee
Make thy words faith'd? No, what I should denie,
(As this I would, I, though thou didst produce
My very Character) I'ld turne it all
To thy suggestion, plot, and damned practise:
And thou must make a dullard of the world,
If they not thought the profits of my death
Were very pregnant and potentiall spirits
To make thee seeke it.

GLOUSTER　　　　　O strange and fastned Villaine,　960
Would he deny his Letter, said he?
　　　Tucket within
Harke, the Dukes Trumpets, I know not why he comes;
All Ports Ile barre, the villaine shall not scape,
The Duke must grant me that: besides, his picture
I will send farre and neere, that all the kingdome
May haue due note of him, and of my land,
(Loyall and naturall Boy) Ile worke the meanes
To make thee capable.
　　　Enter Cornwall, Regan, and Attendants

CORNWALL

How now my Noble friend, since I came hither
(Which I can call but now,) I haue heard strange newes.　970

REGAN

If it be true, all vengeance comes too short
Which can pursue th'offender; how dost my Lord?

GLOUSTER

  O Madam, my old heart is crack'd, it's crack'd.

REGAN

  What, did my Fathers Godsonne seeke your life?
  He whom my Father nam'd, your *Edgar*?

GLOUSTER

  O Lady, Lady, shame would haue it hid.

REGAN

  Was he not companion with the riotous Knights
  That tend vpon my Father?

GLOUSTER

  I know not Madam, 'tis too bad, too bad.

EDMOND

980 Yes Madam, he was of that consort.

REGAN

  No maruaile then, though he were ill affected,
  'Tis they haue put him on the old mans death,
  To haue th'expence and spoyle of his Reuenues:
  I haue this present euening from my Sister
  Beene well inform'd of them, and with such cautions,
  That if they come to soiourne at my house,
  Ile not be there.

CORNWALL   Nor I, assure thee *Regan*;
  Edmund, I heare that you haue shewne your Father
  A Child-like Office.

EDMOND   It was my duty Sir.

GLOUSTER (*to Cornwall*)

990 He did bewray his practise, and receiu'd
  This hurt you see, striuing to apprehend him.

CORNWALL

  Is he pursued?

GLOUSTER   I my good Lord.

CORNWALL

  If he be taken, he shall neuer more
  Be fear'd of doing harme, make your owne purpose,
  How in my strength you please: for you *Edmund*,
  Whose vertue and obedience doth this instant
  So much commend it selfe, you shall be ours,
  Nature's of such deepe trust, we shall much need:
  You we first seize on.

EDMOND   I shall serue you Sir,
  Truely, how euer else.

1000 GLOUSTER (*to Cornwall*)   For him I thanke your Grace.

CORNWALL

  You know not why we came to visit you?

REGAN

  Thus out of season, thredding darke ey'd night,
  Occasions Noble *Gloster* of some poyse,
  Wherein we must haue vse of your aduise.
  Our Father he hath writ, so hath our Sister,
  Of differences, which I lest thought it fit
  To answere from our home: the seuerall Messengers
  From hence attend dispatch, our good old Friend,
  Lay comforts to your bosome, and bestow
1010 Your needfull counsaile to our businesses,
  Which craues the instant vse.

GLOUSTER I serue you Madam,
  Your Graces are right welcome.   *Flourish. Exeunt*

Enter Kent disguised, and Steward seuerally   2.2

STEWARD Good dawning to thee Friend, art of this house?

KENT I.

STEWARD Where may we set our horses?

KENT I'th'myre.

STEWARD Prythee, if thou lou'st me, tell me.

KENT I loue thee not.

STEWARD Why then I care not for thee.   1020

KENT If I had thee in *Lipsbury* Pinfold, I would make thee
  care for me.

STEWARD Why do'st thou vse me thus? I know thee not.

KENT Fellow I know thee.

STEWARD What do'st thou know me for?

KENT A Knaue, a Rascall, an eater of broken meates, a
  base, proud, shallow, beggerly, three-suited, hundred
  pound, filthy woosted-stocking knaue, a Lilly-liuered,
  action-taking, whoreson glasse-gazing super-seruiceable
  finicall Rogue, one Trunke-inheriting slaue, one that   1030
  would'st be a Baud in way of good seruice, and art
  nothing but the composition of a Knaue, Begger, Coward,
  Pandar, and the Sonne and Heire of a Mungrill Bitch,
  one whom I will beate into clamourous whining, if thou
  deny'st the least sillable of thy addition.

STEWARD Why, what a monstrous Fellow art thou, thus
  to raile on one, that is neither knowne of thee, nor
  knowes thee?

KENT What a brazen-fac'd Varlet art thou, to deny thou
  knowest me? Is it two dayes since I tript vp thy heeles,   1040
  and beate thee before the King? Draw you rogue, for
  though it be night, yet the Moone shines,
    ⌈*He draws his Sword*⌉
  Ile make a sop oth' Moonshine of you, you whoreson
  Cullyenly Barber-monger, draw.

STEWARD Away, I haue nothing to do with thee.

KENT Draw you Rascall, you come with Letters against
  the King, and take Vanitie the puppets part, against
  the Royaltie of her Father: draw you Rogue, or Ile so
  carbonado your shanks, draw you Rascall, come your
  waies.   1050

STEWARD Helpe, ho, murther, helpe.

KENT Strike you slaue: stand rogue, stand you neat slaue,
  strike.

STEWARD Helpe hoa, murther, murther.
    Enter Edmond the Bastard, ⌈then⌉ Cornwall,
    Regan, Gloster, Seruants

EDMOND How now, what's the matter? Part.

KENT With you goodman Boy, if you please, come, Ile
  flesh ye, come on yong Master.

GLOUSTER Weapons? Armes? what's the matter here?

CORNWALL

  Keepe peace vpon your liues, he dies that strikes againe,
  What is the matter?   1060

REGAN The Messengers from our Sister, and the King?

CORNWALL (*to Kent and Steward*) What is your difference,
  speake?

STEWARD I am scarce in breath my Lord.

KENT No Maruell, you haue so bestir'd your valour, you

cowardly Rascall, nature disclaimes in thee: a Taylor
made thee.

CORNWALL Thou art a strange fellow, a Taylor make a
man?

1070 KENT A Taylor Sir, a Stone-cutter, or a Painter, could not
haue made him so ill, though they had bin but two
yeares oth'trade.

CORNWALL Speake yet, how grew your quarrell?

STEWARD This ancient Ruffian Sir, whose life I haue spar'd
at sute of his gray-beard.

KENT Thou whoreson Zed, thou vnnecessary letter: (to
Cornwall) my Lord, if you'l giue me leaue, I will tread
this vnboulted villaine into morter, and daube the wall
of a Iakes with him. (To Steward) Spare my gray-beard,
1080 you wagtaile?

CORNWALL Peace sirrah,
You beastly knaue, know you no reuerence?

KENT
Yes Sir, but anger hath a priuiledge.

CORNWALL Why art thou angrie?

KENT
That such a slaue as this should weare a Sword,
Who weares no honesty: such smiling rogues as these,
Like Rats oft bite the holly cords a twaine,
Which are to intrince, t'vnloose: smooth euery passion
That in the natures of their Lords rebell,
1090 Being oile to fire, snow to the colder moodes,
Reneag, affirme, and turne their Halcion beakes
With euery gall, and varry of their Masters,
Knowing naught (like dogges) but following:
⌈To Steward⌉ A plague vpon your Epilepticke visage,
Smoile you my speeches, as I were a Foole?
Goose, and I had you vpon Sarum Plaine,
I'ld driue ye cackling home to Camelot.

CORNWALL
What art thou mad old Fellow?

GLOUSTER ⌈to Kent⌉　　　　　　How fell you out, say that?

KENT
No contraries hold more antipathy,
Then I, and such a knaue.

1100 CORNWALL　　　　　　Why do'st thou call him Knaue?
What is his fault?

KENT　　　　　　His countenance likes me not.

CORNWALL
No more perchance do's mine, nor his, nor hers.

KENT
Sir, 'tis my occupation to be plaine,
I haue seene better faces in my time,
Then stands on any shoulder that I see
Before me, at this instant.

CORNWALL　　　　　　This is some Fellow,
Who hauing beene prais'd for bluntnesse, doth affect
A saucy roughnes, and constraines the garb
Quite from his Nature. He cannot flatter he,
1110 An honest mind and plaine, he must speake truth,
And they will tak't so, if not, hee's plaine.
These kind of Knaues I know, which in this plainnesse
Harbour more craft, and more corrupter ends,

Then twenty silly-ducking obseruants,
That stretch their duties nicely.

KENT
Sir, in good faith, in sincere verity,
Vnder th'allowance of your great aspect,
Whose influence like the wreath of radient fire
On flickring Phœbus front.

CORNWALL　　　　　　What mean'st by this?

KENT To go out of my dialect, which you discommend so　1120
much; I know Sir, I am no flatterer, he that beguild
you in a plaine accent, was a plaine Knaue, which for
my part I will not be, though I should win your
displeasure to entreat me too't.

CORNWALL (to Steward)
What was th'offence you gaue him?

STEWARD　　　　　　I neuer gaue him any:
It pleas'd the King his Master very late
To strike at me vpon his misconstruction,
When he compact, and flattering his displeasure
Tript me behind: being downe, insulted, rail'd,
And put vpon him such a deale of Man,　　　　　　1130
That worthied him, got praises of the King,
For him attempting, who was selfe-subdued,
And in the fleshment of this dread exploit,
Drew on me here againe.

KENT　　　　　　None of these Rogues, and Cowards
But Aiax is there Foole.

CORNWALL　　　　　　Fetch forth the Stocks?
　　　　　　　　　⌈Exeunt some seruants⌉
You stubborne ancient Knaue, you reuerent Bragart,
Wee'l teach you.

KENT　　　　　　Sir, I am too old to learne:
Call not your Stocks for me, I serue the King,
On whose imployment I was sent to you,
You shall doe small respect, show too bold malice　　1140
Against the Grace, and Person of my Master,
Stocking his Messenger.

CORNWALL ⌈calling⌉　　　　　　Fetch forth the Stocks;
As I haue life and Honour, there shall he sit till Noone.

REGAN
Till noone? till night my Lord, and all night too.

KENT
Why Madam, if I were your Fathers dog,
You should not vse me so.

REGAN　　　　　　Sir, being his Knaue, I will.
　　　　　　Stocks brought out

CORNWALL
This is a Fellow of the selfe same colour,
Our Sister speakes of. Come, bring away the Stocks.

GLOUSTER
Let me beseech your Grace, not to do so,
The King his Master, needs must take it ill　　　　　1150
That he so slightly valued in his Messenger,
Should haue him thus restrain'd.

CORNWALL　　　　　　Ile answere that.
　　　⌈They put Kent in the Stocks⌉

REGAN
My Sister may recieue it much more worsse,
To haue her Gentlemen abus'd, assaulted.

CORNWALL Come my good Lord, away.

Exeunt. Manet Glouster and Kent

GLOUSTER

I am sorry for thee friend, 'tis the Dukes pleasure,
Whose disposition all the world well knowes
Will not be rub'd nor stopt, Ile entreat for thee.

KENT

Pray do not Sir, I haue watch'd and trauail'd hard,
1160 Some time I shall sleepe out, the rest Ile whistle:
A good mans fortune may grow out at heeles:
Giue you good morrow.

GLOUSTER

The Duke's to blame in this, 'twill be ill taken.   *Exit*

KENT

Good King, that must approue the common say,
Thou out of Heauens benediction com'st
To the warme Sun.
      ⌈*He takes out a Letter*⌉
Approach thou Beacon to this vnder Globe,
That by thy comfortable Beames I may
Peruse this Letter. Nothing almost sees miracles
1170 But miserie. I know 'tis from *Cordelia*,
Who hath now fortunately beene inform'd
Of my obscured course. And shall finde time
For this enormous State, seeking to giue
Losses their remedies. All weary and o're-watch'd,
Take vantage heauie eyes, not to behold
This shamefull lodging. Fortune goodnight,
Smile once more, turne thy wheele.   *He sleepes*
      Enter Edgar

EDGAR   I heard my selfe proclaim'd,
And by the happy hollow of a Tree,
Escap'd the hunt. No Port is free, no place
1180 That guard, and most vnusuall vigilance
Do's not attend my taking. Whiles I may scape
I will preserue myselfe: and am bethought
To take the basest, and most poorest shape
That euer penury in contempt of man,
Brought neere to beast; my face Ile grime with filth,
Blanket my loines, elfe all my haires in knots,
And with presented nakednesse out-face
The Windes, and persecutions of the skie;
The Country giues me proofe, and president
1190 Of Bedlam beggers, who with roaring voices,
Strike in their num'd and mortified Armes,
Pins, Wodden-prickes, Nayles, Sprigs of Rosemarie:
And with this horrible obiect, from low Farmes,
Poore pelting Villages, Sheep-Coates, and Milles,
Sometime with Lunaticke bans, sometime with Praiers
Inforce their charitie: poore *Tuelygod*, poore *Tom*,
That's something yet: *Edgar* I nothing am.   *Exit*
      Enter Lear, Foole, and ⌈*First*⌉ *Gentleman*

LEAR

'Tis strange that they should so depart from home,
And not send backe my Messenger.

⌈I⌉ GENTLEMAN   As I learn'd,
1200 The night before, there was no purpose in them
Of this remoue.

KENT (*waking*)   Haile to thee Noble Master.

LEAR

Ha? Mak'st thou this shame thy pastime?

KENT   No my Lord.

FOOLE Hah, ha, he weares Cruell Garters, Horses are tide
by the heads, Dogges and Beares by'th'necke, Monkies
by'th'loynes, and Men by'th' legs: when a mans
ouerlustie at legs, then he weares wodden nether-
stocks.

LEAR (*to Kent*)

What's he, that hath so much thy place mistooke
To set thee heere?

KENT   It is both he and she,
Your Son, and Daughter.

LEAR   No.

KENT   Yes.

LEAR   No I say.   1210

KENT

I say yea.

LEAR   By *Iupiter* I sweare no.

KENT

By *Iuno*, I sweare I.

LEAR   They durst not do't:
They could not, would not do't: 'tis worse then murther,
To do vpon respect such violent outrage:
Resolue me with all modest haste, which way
Thou might'st deserue, or they impose this vsage,
Comming from vs.

KENT   My Lord, when at their home
I did commend your Highnesse Letters to them,
Ere I was risen from the place, that shewed
My dutie kneeling, came there a reeking Poste,   1220
Stew'd in his haste, halfe breathlesse, painting forth
From *Gonerill* his Mistris, salutations;
Deliuer'd Letters spight of intermission,
Which presently they read; on whose contents
They summon'd vp their meiney, straight tooke Horse,
Commanded me to follow, and attend
The leisure of their answer, gaue me cold lookes,
And meeting heere the other Messenger,
Whose welcome I perceiu'd had poison'd mine,
Being the very fellow which of late   1230
Displaid so sawcily against your Highnesse,
Hauing more man then wit about me, drew;
He rais'd the house, with loud and coward cries,
Your Sonne and Daughter found this trespasse worth
The shame which heere it suffers.

FOOLE Winters not gon yet, if the wild Geese fly that way,
⌈*Sings*⌉   Fathers that weare rags,
      Do make their Children blind,
      But Fathers that beare bags,
      Shall see their children kind.   1240
      Fortune that arrant whore,
      Nere turns the key toth' poore.
But for all this thou shalt haue as many Dolors for thy
Daughters, as thou canst tell in a yeare.

LEAR

Oh how this Mother swels vp toward my heart!
Histerica passio, downe thou climing sorrow,
Thy Elements below, where is this Daughter?

KENT

With the Earle Sir, here within.

LEAR　　　　　　　　　　　　Follow me not, stay here.

Exit

⌈1⌉ GENTLEMAN (*to Kent*)

Made you no more offence, but what you speake of?

1250　KENT None:

How chance the King comes with so small a number?

FOOLE And thou hadst beene set i'th' Stockes for that
question, thoud'st well deseru'd it.

KENT Why Foole?

FOOLE Wee'l set thee to schoole to an Ant, to teach thee
ther's no labouring i'th' winter. All that follow their
noses, are led by their eyes, but blinde men, and there's
not a nose among twenty, but can smell him that's
stinking; let go thy hold, when a great wheele runs
1260　downe a hill, least it breake thy necke with following.
But the great one that goes vpward, let him draw thee
after: when a wiseman giues thee better counsell, giue
me mine againe, I would haue none but knaues follow
it, since a Foole giues it.

⌈*Sings*⌉

That Sir, which serues and seekes for gaine,
　And followes but for forme;
Will packe, when it begin to raine,
　And leaue thee in the storme,

But I will tarry, the Foole will stay,
1270　　And let the wiseman flie:
The knaue turnes Foole that runnes away,
　The Foole no knaue perdie.

KENT Where learn'd you this Foole?

FOOLE Not i'th' Stockes Foole.

Enter Lear, and Gloster

LEAR

Deny to speake with me? They are sicke, they are
　weary,
They haue trauail'd all the night? meere fetches,
The images of reuolt and flying off.
Fetch me a better answer.

GLOUSTER　　　　　　　　　My deere Lord,
You know the fiery quality of the Duke,
1280　How vnremoueable and fixt he is
In his owne course.

LEAR　　　　　　　　Vengeance, Plague, Death, Confusion:
Fiery? What quality? Why *Gloster*, *Gloster*,
I'ld speake with the Duke of *Cornewall*, and his wife.

GLOUSTER

Well my good Lord, I haue inform'd them so.

LEAR

Inform'd them? Do'st thou vnderstand me man.

GLOUSTER I my good Lord.

LEAR

The King would speake with *Cornwall*, the deere Father
Would with his Daughter speake, commands, tends,
　seruice,
Are they inform'd of this? My breath and blood:

Fiery? The fiery Duke, tell the hot Duke that—　　1290
No, but not yet, may be he is not well,
Infirmity doth still neglect all office,
Whereto our health is bound, we are not our selues,
When Nature being opprest, commands the mind
To suffer with the body; Ile forbeare,
And am fallen out with my more headier will,
To take the indispos'd and sickly fit,
For the sound man. Death on my state: wherefore
Should he sit heere? This act perswades me,
That this remotion of the Duke and her　　　　　1300
Is practise only. Giue me my Seruant forth;
Goe tell the Duke, and's wife, Il'd speake with them:
Now, presently: bid them come forth and heare me,
Or at their Chamber doore Ile beate the Drum,
Till it crie sleepe to death.

GLOUSTER　　　　　　I would haue all well betwixt you.

Exit

LEAR

Oh me my heart! My rising heart! But downe.

FOOLE Cry to it Nunckle, as the Cockney did to the Eeles,
when she put 'em i'th' Paste aliue, she knapt 'em o'th'
coxcombs with a sticke, and cryed downe wantons,
downe; 'twas her Brother, that in pure kindnesse to　1310
his Horse buttered his Hay.

Enter Cornewall, Regan, Gloster, Seruants

LEAR Good morrow to you both.

CORNWALL Haile to your Grace.

Kent here set at liberty

REGAN I am glad to see your Highnesse.

LEAR

Regan, I thinke you are. I know what reason
I haue to thinke so, if thou should'st not be glad,
I would diuorce me from thy Mothers scrine,
Sepulchring an Adultresse. (*To Kent*) O are you free?
Some other time for that.　　　　⌈*Exit Kent*⌉
　　　　　　　　Beloued *Regan*,
Thy Sisters naught: oh *Regan*, she hath tied　　　1320
Sharpe-tooth'd vnkindnesse, like a vulture heere,
I can scarce speake to thee, thou'lt not beleeue
With how deprau'd a quality. Oh *Regan*.

REGAN

I pray you Sir, take patience, I haue hope
You lesse know how to value her desert,
Then she to scant her dutie.

LEAR　　　　　　　　Say? How is that?

REGAN

I cannot thinke my Sister in the least
Would faile her Obligation. If Sir perchance
She haue restrain'd the Riots of your Followres,
'Tis on such ground, and to such wholesome end,　1330
As cleeres her from all blame.

LEAR My curses on her.

REGAN O Sir, you are old,
Nature in you stands on the very Verge
Of his confine: you should be rul'd, and led
By some discretion, that discernes your state

Better then you your selfe: therefore I pray you,
That to our Sister, you do make returne,
Say you haue wrong'd her.

LEAR   Aske her forgiuenesse?

1340 Do you but marke how this becomes the house?
⌈Kneeling⌉ Deere daughter, I confesse that I am old;
Age is vnnecessary: on my knees I begge,
That you'l vouchsafe me Rayment, Bed, and Food.

REGAN
Good Sir, no more: these are vnsightly trickes:
Returne you to my Sister.

LEAR ⌈rising⌉   Neuer Regan:
She hath abated me of halfe my Traine;
Look'd blacke vpon me, strooke me with her Tongue
Most Serpent-like, vpon the very Heart.
All the stor'd Vengeances of Heauen, fall

1350 On her ingratefull top: strike her yong bones
You taking Ayres, with Lamenesse.

CORNWALL   Fye sir, fie.

LEAR
You nimble Lightnings, dart your blinding flames
Into her scornfull eyes: Infect her Beauty,
You Fen-suck'd Fogges, drawne by the powrfull Sunne,
To fall, and blister.

REGAN   O the blest Gods!
So will you wish on me, when the rash moode is on.

LEAR
No Regan, thou shalt neuer haue my curse:
Thy tender-hefted Nature shall not giue
Thee o're to harshnesse: Her eyes are fierce, but thine

1360 Do comfort, and not burne. 'Tis not in thee
To grudge my pleasures, to cut off my Traine,
To bandy hasty words, to scant my sizes,
And in conclusion, to oppose the bolt
Against my comming in. Thou better know'st
The Offices of Nature, bond of Childhood,
Effects of Curtesie, dues of Gratitude:
Thy halfe o'th'Kingdome hast thou not forgot,
Wherein I thee endow'd.

REGAN   Good Sir, to'th'purpose.

LEAR
Who put my man i'th'Stockes?
        Tucket within

CORNWALL   What Trumpet's that?
        Enter Steward

REGAN
1370 I know't, my Sisters: this approues her Letter,
That she would soone be heere. (To Steward) Is your
        Lady come?

LEAR
This is a Slaue, whose easie borrowed pride
Dwels in the sickly grace of her a followes.
(To Steward) Out Varlet, from my sight.

CORNWALL   What meanes your Grace?
        Enter Gonerill

LEAR
Who stockt my Seruant? Regan, I haue good hope
Thou did'st not know on't. Who comes here? O Heauens!

If you do loue old men; if your sweet sway
Allow Obedience; if you your selues are old,
Make it your cause: Send downe, and take my part.
(To Gonerill) Art not asham'd to looke vpon this Beard? 1380
O Regan, will you take her by the hand?

GONERILL
Why not by'th'hand Sir? How haue I offended?
All's not offence that indiscretion findes,
And dotage termes so.

LEAR   O sides, you are too tough!
Will you yet hold? How came my man i'th'Stockes?

CORNWALL
I set him there, Sir: but his owne Disorders
Deseru'd much lesse aduancement.

LEAR   You? Did you?

REGAN
I pray you Father being weake, seeme so.
If till the expiration of your Moneth
You will returne and soiourne with my Sister,   1390
Dismissing halfe your traine, come then to me,
I am now from home, and out of that prouision
Which shall be needfull for your entertainement.

LEAR
Returne to her? and fifty men dismiss'd?
No, rather I abiure all roofes, and chuse
To be a Comrade with the Wolfe, and Owle,
To wage against the enmity oth'ayre,
Necessities sharpe pinch. Returne with her?
Why the hot-bloodied France, that dowerlesse tooke
Our yongest borne, I could as well be brought   1400
To knee his Throne, and Squire-like pension beg,
To keepe base life a foote; returne with her?
Perswade me rather to be slaue and sumpter
To this detested groome.

GONERILL   At your choice Sir.

LEAR
I prythee Daughter do not make me mad,
I will not trouble thee my Child: farewell:
Wee'l no more meete, no more see one another.
But yet thou art my flesh, my blood, my Daughter,
Or rather a disease that's in my flesh,
Which I must needs call mine. Thou art a Byle,   1410
A plague sore, or imbossed Carbuncle
In my corrupted blood. But Ile not chide thee,
Let shame come when it will, I do not call it,
I do not bid the Thunder-bearer shoote,
Nor tell tales of thee to high-iudging Ioue,
Mend when thou can'st, be better at thy leisure,
I can be patient, I can stay with Regan,
I and my hundred Knights.

REGAN   Not altogether so,
I look'd not for you yet, nor am prouided
For your fit welcome, giue eare Sir to my Sister,   1420
For those that mingle reason with your passion,
Must be content to thinke you old, and so,
But she knowes what she doe's.

LEAR   Is this well spoken?

REGAN

I dare auouch it Sir, what fifty Followers?
Is it not well? What should you need of more?
Yea, or so many? Sith that both charge and danger,
Speake 'gainst so great a number? How in one house
Should many people, vnder two commands
Hold amity? 'Tis hard, almost impossible.

GONERILL

1430   Why might not you my Lord, receiue attendance
From those that she cals Seruants, or from mine?

REGAN

Why not my Lord? If then they chanc'd to slacke ye,
We could comptroll them; if you will come to me,
(For now I spie a danger) I entreate you
To bring but fiue and twentie, to no more
Will I giue place or notice.

LEAR   I gaue you all.

REGAN   And in good time you gaue it.

LEAR

Made you my Guardians, my Depositaries,
1440   But kept a reseruation to be followed
With such a number? What, must I come to you
With fiue and twenty? *Regan*, said you so?

REGAN

And speak't againe my Lord, no more with me.

LEAR

Those wicked Creatures yet do look wel fauor'd
When others are more wicked, not being the worst
Stands in some ranke of praise, (*To Gonerill*) Ile go
        with thee,
Thy fifty yet doth double fiue and twenty,
And thou art twice her Loue.

GONERILL   Heare me my Lord;
What need you fiue and twenty? Ten? Or fiue?
1450   To follow in a house, where twice so many
Haue a command to tend you?

REGAN   What need one?

LEAR

O reason not the need: our basest Beggers
Are in the poorest thing superfluous.
Allow not Nature, more then Nature needs:
Mans life is cheape as Beastes. Thou art a Lady;
If onely to go warme were gorgeous,
Why Nature needs not what thou gorgeous wear'st,
Which scarcely keepes thee warme, but for true need:
You Heauens, giue me that patience, patience I need,
1460   You see me heere (you Gods) a poore old man,
As full of griefe as age, wretched in both,
If it be you that stirres these Daughters hearts
Against their Father, foole me not so much,
To beare it tamely: touch me with Noble anger,
And let not womens weapons, water drops,
Staine my mans cheekes. No you vnnaturall Hags,
I will haue such reuenges on you both,
That all the world shall—I will do such things,
What they are yet, I know not, but they shalbe
1470   The terrors of the earth? you thinke Ile weepe,
No, Ile not weepe, I haue full cause of weeping,

Storme and Tempest

But this heart shal break into a hundred thousand flawes
Or ere Ile weepe; O Foole, I shall go mad.

        Exeunt Lear, Foole, Gentleman, and Glouster

CORNWALL

Let vs withdraw, 'twill be a Storme.

REGAN

This house is little, the old man and's people,
Cannot be well bestow'd.

GONERILL   'Tis his owne blame,
Hath put himselfe from rest, and must needs taste his
        folly.

REGAN

For his particular, Ile receiue him gladly,
But not one follower.

GONERILL   So am I purpos'd,
Where is my Lord of *Gloster*?   1480

CORNWALL

Followed the old man forth,
        ⌜*Enter Gloster*⌝
                                    he is return'd.

GLOUSTER

The King is in high rage.

CORNWALL   Whether is he going?

GLOUSTER

He cals to Horse, but will I know not whether.

CORNWALL

'Tis best to giue him way, he leads himselfe.

GONERILL (*to Glouster*)

My Lord, entreate him by no meanes to stay.

GLOUSTER

Alacke the night comes on, and the high windes
Do sorely ruffle, for many Miles about
There's scarce a Bush.

REGAN   O Sir, to wilfull men,
The iniuries that they themselues procure,
Must be their Schoole-Masters: shut vp your doores,   1490
He is attended with a desperate traine,
And what they may incense him to, being apt,
To haue his eare abus'd, wisedome bids feare.

CORNWALL

Shut vp your doores my Lord, 'tis a wild night,
My *Regan* counsels well: come out oth'storme.

                                    Exeunt

Storme still. Enter Kent disguised, and ⌜First⌝   **3.1**
Gentleman, seuerally

KENT

Who's there besides foule weather?

⌜I⌝ GENTLEMAN   One minded like the weather,
Most vnquietly.

KENT   I know you: Where's the King?

⌜I⌝ GENTLEMAN

Contending with the fretfull Elements;
Bids the winde blow the Earth into the Sea,
Or swell the curled Waters 'boue the Maine,   1500
That things might change, or cease.

KENT   But who is with him?

⌈I⌉ GENTLEMAN
  None but the Foole, who labours to out-iest
  His heart-strooke iniuries.
KENT   Sir, I do know you,
  And dare vpon the warrant of my note
  Commend a deere thing to you. There is diuision
  (Although as yet the face of it is couer'd
  With mutuall cunning) 'twixt Albany, and Cornwall:
  Who haue, as who haue not, that their great Starres
  Thron'd and set high; Seruants, who seeme no lesse,
1510 Which are to France the Spies and Speculations
  Intelligent of our State. What hath bin seene,
  Either in snuffes, and packings of the Dukes,
  Or the hard Reine which both of them hath borne
  Against the old kinde King; or something deeper,
  Whereof (perchance) these are but furnishings.
⌈I⌉ GENTLEMAN
  I will talke further with you.
KENT   No, do not:
  For confirmation that I am much more
  Then my out-wall; open this Purse, and take
  What it containes. If you shall see *Cordelia*,
1520 (As feare not but you shall) shew her this Ring,
  And she will tell you who that Fellow is
  That yet you do not know. Fye on this Storme,
  I will go seeke the King.
⌈I⌉ GENTLEMAN
  Giue me your hand, haue you no more to say?
KENT
  Few words, but to effect more then all yet;
  That when we haue found the King, in which your
    pain
  That way, Ile this: He that first lights on him,
  Holla the other.   *Exeunt seuerally*

3.2   *Storme still. Enter Lear, and Foole*
LEAR
  Blow windes, & crack your cheeks; Rage, blow
1530 You Cataracts, and Hyrricano's spout,
  Till you haue drench'd our Steeples, drownd the
    Cockes.
  You Sulph'rous and Thought-executing Fires,
  Vaunt-curriors of Oake-cleauing Thunder-bolts,
  Sindge my white head. And thou all-shaking Thunder,
  Strike flat the thicke Rotundity o'th'world,
  Cracke Natures moulds, all germaines spill at once
  That makes ingratefull Man.
FOOLE O Nunkle, Court holy-water in a dry house, is
  better then this Rain-water out o'doore. Good Nunkle,
1540 in, aske thy Daughters blessing, heere's a night pitties
  neither Wisemen, nor Fooles.
LEAR
  Rumble thy belly full: spit Fire, spowt Raine:
  Nor Raine, Winde, Thunder, Fire are my Daughters;
  I taxe not you, you Elements with vnkindnesse.
  I neuer gaue you Kingdome, call'd you Children;
  You owe me no subscription. Then let fall
  Your horrible pleasure. Heere I stand your Slaue,
  A poore, infirme, weake, and dispis'd old man:

  But yet I call you Seruile Ministers,
  That will with two pernicious Daughters ioyne   1550
  Your high-engender'd Battailes, 'gainst a head
  So old, and white as this. O, ho! 'tis foule.
FOOLE He that has a house to put's head in, has a good
  Head-peece:
⌈*Sings*⌉   The Codpiece that will house,
                Before the head has any;
             The Head, and he shall Lowse:
                So Beggers marry many.
             The man yᵗ makes his Toe,
                What he his Hart shold make,   1560
             Shall of a Corne cry woe,
                And turne his sleepe to wake.
  For there was neuer yet faire woman, but shee made
  mouthes in a glasse.
    Enter Kent disguised
LEAR
  No, I will be the patterne of all patience,
  I will say nothing.
KENT Who's there?
FOOLE Marry here's Grace, and a Codpiece, that's a
  Wiseman, and a Foole.
KENT (*to Lear*)
  Alas Sir are you here? Things that loue night,   1570
  Loue not such nights as these: The wrathfull Skies
  Gallow the very wanderers of the darke
  And make them keepe their Caues: Since I was man,
  Such sheets of Fire, such bursts of horrid Thunder,
  Such groanes of roaring Winde, and Raine, I neuer
  Remember to haue heard. Mans Nature cannot carry
  Th'affliction, nor the feare.
LEAR   Let the great Goddes
  That keepe this dreadfull pudder o're our heads,
  Finde out their enemies now. Tremble thou Wretch,
  That hast within thee vndivulged Crimes   1580
  Vnwhipt of Iustice. Hide thee, thou Bloudy hand;
  Thou Periur'd, and thou Simular of Vertue
  That art Incestuous. Caytiffe, to peeces shake
  That vnder couert, and conuenient seeming
  Ha's practis'd on mans life. Close pent-vp guilts,
  Riue your concealing Continents, and cry
  These dreadfull Summoners grace. I am a man,
  More sinn'd against, then sinning.
KENT   Alacke, bare-headed?
  Gracious my Lord, hard by heere is a Houell,
  Some friendship will it lend you 'gainst the Tempest: 1590
  Repose you there, while I to this hard house,
  (More harder then the stones whereof 'tis rais'd,
  Which euen but now, demanding after you,
  Deny'd me to come in) returne, and force
  Their scanted curtesie.
LEAR   My wits begin to turne.
  (*To Foole*) Come on my boy. How dost my boy? Art
    cold?
  I am cold my selfe. (*To Kent*) Where is this straw, my
    Fellow?
  The Art of our Necessities is strange,

And can make vilde things precious. Come, your Houel;
(*To Foole*) Poore Foole, and Knaue, I haue one part in
1600   my heart
That's sorry yet for thee.
FOOLE ⌈*Sings*⌉
He that has and a little-tyne wit,
    With heigh-ho, the Winde and the Raine,
Must make content with his Fortunes fit,
    Though the Raine it raineth euery day.
LEAR
True Boy: (*To Kent*) Come bring vs to this Houell.
                                        Exeunt Lear and Kent
FOOLE This is a braue night to coole a Curtizan: Ile speake
a Prophesie ere I go:
1610   When Priests are more in word, then matter;
When Brewers marre their Malt with water;
When Nobles are their Taylors Tutors,
No Heretiques burn'd, but wenches Sutors;
Then shal the Realme of *Albion*,
Come to great confusion:

When euery Case in Law, is right;
No Squire in debt, nor no poore Knight;
When Slanders do not liue in Tongues;
Nor Cut-purses come not to throngs;
When Vsurers tell their Gold i'th'Field,
1620   And Baudes, and whores, do Churches build,
Then comes the time, who liues to see't,
That going shalbe vs'd with feet.
This prophecie *Merlin* shall make, for I liue before his
time.   *Exit*

3.3   *Enter Gloster, and Edmund*
GLOUSTER Alacke, alacke *Edmund*, I like not this vnnaturall
dealing; when I desired their leaue that I might pity
him, they tooke from me the vse of mine owne house,
charg'd me on paine of perpetuall displeasure, neither
to speake of him, entreat for him, or any way sustaine
1630   him.
EDMOND Most sauage and vnnaturall.
GLOUSTER Go too; say you nothing. There is diuision betweene the Dukes, and a worsse matter then that: I haue
receiued a Letter this night, 'tis dangerous to be spoken,
I haue lock'd the Letter in my Closset, these iniuries the
King now beares, will be reuenged home; ther is part of
a Power already footed, we must incline to the King, I
will looke him, and priuily relieue him; goe you and
maintaine talke with the Duke, that my charity be not of
1640   him perceiued; If he aske for me, I am ill, and gone to
bed, if I die for't, (as no lesse is threatned me) the King
my old Master must be relieued. There is strange things
toward *Edmund*, pray you be carefull.   *Exit*
EDMOND
This Curtesie forbid thee, shall the Duke
Instantly know, and of that Letter too;
This seemes a faire deseruing, and must draw me
That which my Father looses: no lesse then all,
The yonger rises, when the old doth fall.   *Exit*

Enter Lear, Kent disguised, and Foole   3.4
KENT
Here is the place my Lord, good my Lord enter,
The tirrany of the open night's too rough   1650
For Nature to endure.
    Storme still
LEAR   Let me alone.
KENT
Good my Lord enter heere.
LEAR   Wilt breake my heart?
KENT
I had rather breake mine owne, good my Lord enter.
LEAR
Thou think'st 'tis much that this contentious storme
Inuades vs to the skin: so 'tis to thee,
But where the greater malady is fixt,
The lesser is scarce felt. Thou'dst shun a Beare,
But if thy flight lay toward the roaring Sea,
Thou'dst meete the Beare i'th' mouth, when the
    mind's free,
The bodies delicate: this tempest in my mind,   1660
Doth from my sences take all feeling else,
Saue what beates there, Filliall ingratitude,
Is it not as this mouth should teare this hand
For lifting food too't? But I will punish home;
No, I will weepe no more; in such a night,
To shut me out? Poure on, I will endure:
In such a night as this? O *Regan*, *Gonerill*,
Your old kind Father, whose franke heart gaue all,
O that way madnesse lies, let me shun that:
No more of that.
KENT   Good my Lord enter here.   1670
LEAR
Prythee go in thy selfe, seeke thine owne ease,
This tempest will not giue me leaue to ponder
On things would hurt me more, but Ile goe in,
(*To Foole*) In Boy, go first. ⌈*Kneeling*⌉ You houselesse
    pouertie,
Nay get thee in; Ile pray, and then Ile sleepe.
                                        Exit Foole
Poore naked wretches, where so ere you are
That bide the pelting of this pittilesse storme,
How shall your House-lesse heads, and vnfed sides,
Your lop'd, and window'd raggednesse defend you
From seasons such as these? O I haue tane   1680
Too little care of this: Take Physicke, Pompe,
Expose thy selfe to feele what wretches feele,
That thou maist shake the superflux to them,
And shew the Heauens more iust.
    *Enter Foole ⌈and Edgar as a Bedlam Beggar in the
    Houell⌉*
EDGAR
Fathom, and halfe, Fathom and halfe; poore *Tom*.
FOOLE Come not in heere Nuncle, here's a spirit, helpe
me, helpe me.
KENT Giue my thy hand, who's there?
FOOLE A spirite, a spirite, he sayes his name's poore *Tom*.

KENT

1690 What art thou that dost grumble there i'th' straw?
Come forth.

⌈*Edgar comes forth*⌉

EDGAR   Away, the foule Fiend followes me,
thorough the sharpe Hauthorne blow the windes.
Humh, goe to thy cold bed and warme thee.

LEAR

Did'st thou giue all to thy two Daughters?
And art thou come to this?

EDGAR Who giues any thing to poore *Tom*? Whom the
foule fiend hath led through Fire, and through Flame,
through Foord, and Whirle-Poole, o're Bog, and
Quagmire, that hath laid Kniues vnder his Pillow, and
1700 Halters in his Pue, set Rats-bane by his Porredge, made
him Proud of heart, to ride on a Bay trotting Horse,
ouer foure incht Bridges, to course his owne shadow
for a Traitor. Blisse thy fiue Wits, *Toms* a cold. O do,
de, do, de, do de, blisse thee from Whirle-Windes,
Starre-blasting, and taking, do poore *Tom* some charitie,
whom the foule Fiend vexes. There could I haue him
now, and there, and there againe, and there.

Storme still

LEAR

Ha's his Daughters brought him to this passe?
(*To Edgar*) Could'st thou saue nothing? Would'st thou
giue 'em all?

1710 FOOLE Nay, he reseru'd a Blanket, else we had bin all
sham'd.

LEAR (*to Edgar*)

Now all the plagues that in the pendulous ayre
Hang fated o're mens faults, light on thy Daughters.

KENT He hath no Daughters Sir.

LEAR

Death Traitor, nothing could haue subdu'd Nature
To such a lownesse, but his vnkind Daughters.
(*To Edgar*) Is it the fashion, that discarded Fathers,
Should haue thus little mercy on their flesh:
Iudicious punishment, 'twas this flesh begot
1720 Those Pelicane Daughters.

EDGAR Pillicock sat on Pillicock hill, alow: alow, loo, loo.

FOOLE This cold night will turne vs all to Fooles, and
Madmen.

EDGAR Take heed o'th'foule Fiend, obey thy Parents,
keepe thy words Iustice, sweare not, commit not with
mans sworne Spouse; set not thy Sweet-heart on proud
array. *Tom's* a cold.

LEAR What hast thou bin?

EDGAR A Seruingman? Proud in heart, and minde; that
1730 curl'd my haire, wore Gloues in my cap; seru'd the
Lust of my Mistris heart, and did the acte of darkenesse
with her. Swore as many Oathes, as I spake words, &
broke them in the sweet face of Heauen. One, that slept
in the contriuing of Lust, and wak'd to doe it. Wine
lou'd I deeply, Dice deerely; and in Woman, out-
Paramour'd the Turke. False of heart, light of eare,
bloody of hand; Hog in sloth, Foxe in stealth, Wolfe in
greedinesse, Dog in madnes, Lyon in prey. Let not the
creaking of shooes, nor the rustling of Silkes, betray

thy poore heart to woman. Keepe thy foote out of   1740
Brothels, thy hand out of Plackets, thy pen from Lenders
Bookes, and defye the foule Fiend. Still through the
Hauthorne blowes the cold winde: Sayes suum, mun,
nonny, Dolphin my Boy, Boy *sesey*: let him trot by.

Storme still

LEAR Thou wert better in a Graue, then to answere with
thy vncouer'd body, this extremitie of the Skies. Is man
no more then this? Consider him well. Thou ow'st the
Worme no Silke; the Beast, no Hide; the Sheepe, no
Wooll; the Cat, no perfume. Ha? Here's three on's are
sophisticated. Thou art the thing it selfe; vnaccommo-   1750
dated man, is no more but such a poore, bare, forked
Animall as thou art. Off, off you Lendings: Come,
vnbutton heere.

Enter Gloucester, with a Torch

FOOLE Prythee Nunckle be contented, 'tis a naughtie night
to swimme in. Now a little fire in a wilde Field, were
like an old Letchers heart, a small spark, all the rest
on's body, cold: Looke, heere comes a walking fire.

EDGAR This is the foule fiend Flibbertigibbet; hee begins
at Curfew, and walkes till the first Cocke: Hee giues
the Web and the Pin, squints the eye, and makes the   1760
Hare-lippe; Mildewes the white Wheate, and hurts the
poore Creature of earth.

⌈*Sings*⌉

Swithune footed thrice the old,
A met the Night-Mare, and her nine fold;
Bid her a-light,
And her troth plight,
And aroynt thee Witch, aroynt thee.

KENT (*to Lear*)

How fares your Grace?

LEAR   What's he?

KENT (*to Glouster*) Who's there? What is't you seeke?

GLOUSTER What are you there? Your Names?   1770

EDGAR Poore Tom, that eates the swimming Frog, the
Toad, the Tod-pole, the wall-Neut, and the water: that
in the furie of his heart, when the foule Fiend rages,
eats Cow-dung for Sallets; swallowes the old Rat, and
the ditch-Dogge; drinkes the green Mantle of the
standing Poole: who is whipt from Tything to Tything,
and stockt, punish'd, and imprison'd: who hath had
three Suites to his backe, six shirts to his body:

Horse to ride, and weapon to weare:
But Mice, and Rats, and such small Deare,   1780
Haue bin Toms food, for seuen long yeare:

Beware my Follower. Peace Smulkin, peace thou Fiend.

GLOUSTER (*to Lear*)

What, hath your Grace no better company?

EDGAR

The Prince of Darkenesse is a Gentleman.
Modo he's call'd, and *Mahu*.

GLOUSTER (*to Lear*)

Our flesh and blood, my Lord, is growne so vilde,
That it doth hate what gets it.

EDGAR   Poore Tom's a cold.

GLOUSTER (*to Lear*)

Go in with me; my duty cannot suffer

T'obey in all your daughters hard commands:
1790 Though their Iniunction be to barre my doores,
And let this Tyrannous night take hold vpon you,
Yet haue I ventur'd to come seeke you out,
And bring you where both fire, and food is ready.

LEAR
First let me talke with this Philosopher,
(*To Edgar*) What is the cause of Thunder?

KENT
Good my Lord take his offer, go into th'house.

LEAR
Ile talke a word with this same lerned Theban:
(*To Edgar*) What is your study?

EDGAR
How to preuent the Fiend, and to kill Vermine.

LEAR
1800 Let me aske you one word in priuate.
They conuerse apart

KENT (*to Glouster*)
Importune him once more to go my Lord,
His wits begin t'vnsettle.

GLOUSTER   Canst thou blame him?
Storm still
His Daughters seeke his death: Ah, that good Kent,
He said it would be thus: poore banish'd man:
Thou sayest the King growes mad, Ile tell thee Friend
I am almost mad my selfe. I had a Sonne,
Now out-law'd from my blood: a sought my life
But lately: very late: I lou'd him (Friend)
No Father his Sonne deerer: true to tell thee,
1810 The greefe hath craz'd my wits. What a night's this?
(*To Lear*) I do beseech your grace.

LEAR   O cry you mercy, Sir:
(*To Edgar*) Noble Philosopher, your company.

EDGAR   Tom's a cold.

GLOUSTER
In fellow there, in't Houel; keep thee warm.

LEAR
Come, let's in all.

KENT   This way, my Lord.

LEAR   With him;
I will keepe still with my Philosopher.

KENT (*to Glouster*)
Good my Lord, sooth him: let him take the Fellow.

GLOUSTER Take him you on.

KENT ⌈*to Edgar*⌉
Sirra, come on: go along with vs.

LEAR (*to Edgar*)
Come, good Athenian.

GLOUSTER   No words, no words, hush.

EDGAR
1820 Childe *Rowland* to the darke Tower came,
His word was still, fie, foh, and fumme,
I smell the blood of a Brittish man.   *Exeunt*

3.5   *Enter Cornwall, and Edmund*
CORNWALL I will haue my reuenge, ere I depart his house.
EDMOND How my Lord, I may be censured, that Nature

thus giues way to Loyaltie, something feares mee to
thinke of.

CORNWALL I now perceiue, it was not altogether your
Brothers euill disposition made him seeke his death:
but a prouoking merit set a-worke by a reprouable
badnesse in himselfe.   1830

EDMOND How malicious is my fortune, that I must repent
to be iust? This is the Letter which hee spoake of;
which approues him an intelligent partie to the
aduantages of France. O Heauens! that this Treason
were not; or not I the detector.

CORNWALL Go with me to the Dutchesse.

EDMOND If the matter of this Paper be certain, you haue
mighty businesse in hand.

CORNWALL True or false, it hath made thee Earle of
Gloucester: seeke out where thy Father is, that hee   1840
may bee ready for our apprehension.

EDMOND ⌈*aside*⌉ If I finde him comforting the King, it will
stuffe his suspition more fully. (*To Cornwall*) I will
perseuer in my course of Loyalty, though the conflict
be sore betweene that, and my blood.

CORNWALL I will lay trust vpon thee: and thou shalt finde
a deerer Father in my loue.   *Exeunt*

       Enter Kent disguised, and Gloucester   3.6
GLOUSTER Heere is better then the open ayre, take it
thankfully: I will peece out the comfort with what
addition I can: I will not be long from you.   1850

KENT All the powre of his wits, haue giuen way to his
impatience: the Gods reward your kindnesse.
                                          Exit Glouster
       Enter Lear, Edgar as a Bedlam Beggar, and Foole
EDGAR *Fraterretto* cals me, and tells me *Nero* is an Angler
in the Lake of Darknesse: pray Innocent, and beware
the foule Fiend.

FOOLE Prythee Nunkle tell me, whether a madman be a
Gentleman, or a Yeoman.

LEAR A King, a King.

FOOLE No, he's a Yeoman, that ha's a Gentleman to his
Sonne: for hee's a mad Yeoman that sees his Sonne a   1860
Gentleman before him.

LEAR
To haue a thousand with red burning spits
Come hizzing in vpon 'em.

EDGAR   Blesse thy fiue wits.

KENT (*to Lear*)
O pitty: Sir, where is the patience now
That you so oft haue boasted to retaine?

EDGAR (*aside*)
My teares begin to take his part so much,
They marre my counterfetting.

LEAR   The little dogges, and all;
Trey, Blanch, and Sweet-heart: see, they barke at me.

EDGAR Tom, will throw his head at them: Auaunt you
Curres,   1870
Be thy mouth or blacke or white:
Tooth that poysons if it bite:

Mastiffe, Grey-hound, Mongrill Grim,
Hound or Spaniell, Brache, or Hym:
Bobtaile tike, or Trondle taile,
Tom will make him weepe and waile,
For with throwing thus my head;
Dogs leapt the hatch, and all are fled.
Do, de, de, de: sese: Come, march to Wakes and Fayres,
1880 And Market Townes: poore Tom thy horne is dry.

LEAR Then let them Anatomize *Regan*: See what breeds
about her heart. Is there any cause in Nature that
makes these hard-hearts. (*To Edgar*) You sir, I entertaine
for one of my hundred; only, I do not like the fashion
of your garments. You will say they are Persian; but
let them bee chang'd.

KENT
Now good my Lord, lye heere, and rest awhile.

LEAR Make no noise, make no noise, draw the Curtaines:
so, so, wee'l go to Supper i'th'morning.
⌈*He sleepes*⌉

1890 FOOLE And Ile go to bed at noone.
Enter Gloster

GLOUSTER (*to Kent*)
Come hither Friend: where is the King my Master?

KENT
Here Sir, but trouble him not, his wits are gon.

GLOUSTER
Good friend, I prythee take him in thy armes;
I haue ore-heard a plot of death vpon him:
There is a Litter ready, lay him in't,
And driue toward Douer friend, where thou shalt meete
Both welcome, and protection. Take vp thy Master,
If thou should'st dally halfe an houre, his life
With thine, and all that offer to defend him,
1900 Stand in assured losse. Take vp, take vp,
And follow me, that will to some prouision
Giue thee quicke conduct. Come, come, away.
Exeunt, ⌈*Kent carrying Lear in his armes*⌉

3.7   *Enter Cornwall, Regan, Gonerill, Edmund the
           Bastard, and Seruants*

CORNWALL (*to Gonerill*)
Poste speedily to my Lord your husband,
Shew him this Letter, the Army of France is landed:
(*To Seruants*) Seeke out the Traitor Glouster.
Exeunt some

REGAN   Hang him instantly.

GONERILL
Plucke out his eyes.

CORNWALL   Leaue him to my displeasure.
Edmond, keepe you our Sister company:
the reuenges wee are bound to take vppon your
Traitorous Father, are not fit for your beholding. Aduice
1910 the Duke where you are going, to a most festinate
preparation: we are bound to the like. Our Postes shall
be swift, and intelligent betwixt vs. (*To Gonerill*)
Farewell deere Sister, (*to Edmond*) farewell my Lord of
Glouster.

Enter Steward
How now? Where's the King?

STEWARD
My Lord of Glouster hath conuey'd him hence.
Some fiue or six and thirty of his Knights
Hot Questrists after him, met him at gate,
Who, with some other of the Lords dependants,
Are gone with him toward Douer; where they boast   1920
To haue well armed Friends.

CORNWALL Get horses for your Mistris.   *Exit Steward*

GONERILL Farewell sweet Lord, and Sister.

CORNWALL
Edmund farewell: *Exeunt Gonerill and Edmond*
              (*to Seruants*) go seek the Traitor Gloster,
Pinnion him like a Theefe, bring him before vs:
                        Exeunt other seruants
Though well we may not passe vpon his life
Without the forme of Iustice: yet our power
Shall do a curt'sie to our wrath, which men
May blame, but not comptroll.
Enter Gloucester, and Seruants
                        Who's there? the Traitor?

REGAN
Ingratefull Fox, 'tis he.

CORNWALL (*to Seruants*) Binde fast his corky armes.   1930

GLOUSTER
What meanes your Graces? Good my Friends consider
You are my Ghests: do me no foule play, Friends.

CORNWALL (*to Seruants*)
Binde him I say.

REGAN   Hard, hard: O filthy Traitor.

GLOUSTER
Vnmercifull Lady, as you are, I'me none.

CORNWALL (*to Seruants*)
To this Chaire binde him, (*to Glouster*) villaine, thou
shalt finde.
Regan pluckes Glouster's Beard

GLOUSTER
By the kinde Gods, 'tis most ignobly done
To plucke me by the Beard.

REGAN So white, and such a Traitor?

GLOUSTER Naughty Ladie,
These haires which thou dost rauish from my chin   1940
Will quicken and accuse thee. I am your Host,
With Robbers hands, my hospitable fauours
You should not ruffle thus. What will you do?

CORNWALL
Come Sir. What Letters had you late from France?

REGAN
Be simple answer'd, for we know the truth.

CORNWALL
And what confederacie haue you with the Traitors,
Late footed in the Kingdome?

REGAN   To whose hands
You haue sent the Lunaticke King: Speake.

GLOUSTER
I haue a Letter guessingly set downe

1950 Which came from one that's of a newtrall heart,
And not from one oppos'd.

CORNWALL   Cunning.

REGAN   And false.

CORNWALL

Where hast thou sent the King?

GLOUSTER   To Douer.

REGAN

Wherefore to Douer? Was't thou not charg'd at perill.

CORNWALL

Wherefore to Douer? Let him answer that.

GLOUSTER

I am tyed to'th'Stake, and I must stand the Course.

REGAN Wherefore to Douer?

GLOUSTER

Because I would not see thy cruell Nailes
Plucke out his poore old eyes: nor thy fierce Sister,
In his Annointed flesh, sticke boarish phangs.
1960 The Sea, with such a storme as his bare head,
In Hell-blacke-night indur'd, would haue buoy'd vp
And quench'd the Stelled fires:
Yet poore old heart, he holpe the Heauens to raine.
If Wolues had at thy Gate howl'd that sterne time,
Thou should'st haue said, good Porter turne the Key:
All Cruels ile subscribe: but I shall see
The winged Vengeance ouertake such Children.

CORNWALL

See't shalt thou neuer. Fellowes hold yᵉ Chaire,
Vpon these eyes of thine, Ile set my foote.

GLOUSTER

1970 He that will thinke to liue, till he be old,
Giue me some helpe.—O cruell! O you Gods.
    ⌜Cornwall pulls out one of Glousters eyes and
    stampes on it⌝

REGAN (to Cornwall)

One side will mocke another: Th'other too.

CORNWALL (to Glouster)

If you see vengeance.

SERUANT   Hold your hand, my Lord:
I haue seru'd you euer since I was a Childe:
But better seruice haue I neuer done you,
Then now to bid you hold.

REGAN   How now, you dogge?

SERUANT

If you did weare a beard vpon your chin,
I'ld shake it on this quarrell. ⌜To Cornwall⌝ What do
    you meane?

CORNWALL My Villaine?

SERUANT

1980 Nay then come on, and take the chance of anger.
    They draw and fight

REGAN (to another Seruant)

Giue me thy Sword. A pezant stand vp thus?
    ⌜She takes a Sword and runs at him behind⌝

SERUANT (to Glouster)

Oh I am slaine: my Lord, you haue one eye left
To see some mischefe on him.
    ⌜Regan stabs him againe⌝
                Oh.   He dies

CORNWALL

Lest it see more, preuent it; Out vilde gelly:
    He ⌜pulls out⌝ Glousters other eye
Where is thy luster now?

GLOUSTER

All darke and comfortlesse? Where's my Sonne Edmund?
Edmund, enkindle all the sparkes of Nature
To quit this horrid acte.

REGAN   Out treacherous Villaine,
Thou call'st on him, that hates thee. It was he
That made the ouerture of thy Treasons to vs: 1990
Who is too good to pitty thee.

GLOUSTER

O my Follies! then Edgar was abus'd,
Kinde Gods, forgiue me that, and prosper him.

REGAN (to Seruants)

Go thrust him out at gates, and let him smell
His way to Douer.   Exit one or more with Glouster
                How is't my Lord? How looke you?

CORNWALL

I haue receiu'd a hurt: Follow me Lady;
(To Seruants) Turne out that eyelesse Villaine: throw
    this Slaue
Vpon the Dunghill: Regan, I bleed apace,
Vntimely comes this hurt. Giue me your arme.
                Exeunt ⌜with the body⌝

    Enter Edgar as a Bedlam Beggar   4.1

EDGAR

Yet better thus, and knowne to be contemn'd,   2000
Then still contemn'd and flatter'd: to be worst,
The lowest, and most deiected thing of Fortune,
Stands still in esperance, liues not in feare:
The lamentable change is from the best,
The worst returnes to laughter. Welcome then,
Thou vnsubstantiall ayre that I embrace:
The Wretch that thou hast blowne vnto the worst,
Owes nothing to thy blasts.
    Enter Glouster, led by an Oldman
                But who comes heere?
My Father partie-eyd? World, World, O world!
But that thy strange mutations make vs hate thee,   2010
Life would not yeelde to age.
    ⌜Edgar stands aside⌝

OLDMAN (to Glouster)   O my good Lord,
I haue bene your Tenant, and your Fathers Tenant,
These fourescore yeares.

GLOUSTER

Away, get thee away: good Friend be gone,
Thy comforts can do me no good at all,
Thee, they may hurt.

OLDMAN   You cannot see your way.

GLOUSTER

I haue no way, and therefore want no eyes:
I stumbled when I saw. Full oft 'tis seene,
Our meanes secure vs, and our meere defects
Proue our Commodities. Oh deere Sonne Edgar,   2020
The food of thy abused Fathers wrath:

Might I but liue to see thee in my touch,
I'ld say I had eyes againe.

OLDMAN   How now? who's there?

EDGAR *(aside)*
O Gods! Who is't can say I am at the worst?
I am worse then ere I was.

OLDMAN *(to Glouster)*   'Tis poore mad Tom.

EDGAR *(aside)*
And worse I may be yet: the worst is not,
So long as we can say this is the worst.

OLDMAN *(to Edgar)* Fellow, where goest?

GLOUSTER Is it a Beggar-man?

2030 OLDMAN Madman, and beggar too.

GLOUSTER
A has some reason, else he could not beg.
I'th'last nights storme, I such a fellow saw;
Which made me thinke a Man, a Worme. My Sonne
Came then into my minde, and yet my minde
Was then scarse Friends with him. I haue heard more
    since:
As Flies to wanton Boyes, are we to th'Gods,
They kill vs for their sport.

EDGAR *(aside)*   How should this be?
Bad is the Trade that must play Foole to sorrow,
Ang'ring it selfe, and others.
    ⌈*He comes forward*⌉
                    Blesse thee Master.

GLOUSTER
Is that the naked Fellow?

2040 OLDMAN   I, my Lord.

GLOUSTER
Get thee away: If for my sake
Thou wilt ore-take vs hence a mile or twaine
I'th'way toward Douer, do it for ancient loue,
And bring some couering for this naked Soule,
Which Ile intreate to leade me.

OLDMAN   Alacke sir, he is mad.

GLOUSTER
'Tis the times plague, when Madmen leade the blinde:
Do as I bid thee, or rather do thy pleasure:
Aboue the rest, be gone.

OLDMAN
Ile bring him the best Parrell that I haue
Come on't, what will.   *Exit*

2050 GLOUSTER   Sirrah, naked fellow.

EDGAR
Poore Tom's a cold. *(Aside)* I cannot daub it further.

GLOUSTER
Come hither fellow.

EDGAR *(aside)*   And yet I must:
(To Glouster) Blesse thy sweete eyes, they bleede.

GLOUSTER   Know'st thou the way to Douer?

EDGAR Both style, and gate; Horseway, and foot-path:
poore Tom hath bin scarr'd out of his good wits. Blesse
thee good mans sonne, from the foule Fiend.

GLOUSTER
Here take this purse, yᵘ whom the heauens plagues
Haue humbled to all strokes: that I am wretched

Makes thee the happier: Heauens deale so still:
Let the superfluous, and Lust-dieted man,   2060
That slaues your ordinance, that will not see
Because he do's not feele, feele your powre quickly:
So distribution should vndoo excesse,
And each man haue enough. Dost thou know Douer?

EDGAR I Master.

GLOUSTER
There is a Cliffe, whose high and bending head
Lookes fearfully in the confined Deepe:
Bring me but to the very brimme of it,
And Ile repayre the misery thou do'st beare
With something rich about me: from that place,   2070
I shall no leading neede.

EDGAR Giue me thy arme;
Poore Tom shall leade thee.

                    Exit Edgar guiding Glouster

Enter Gonerill, and Edmond the Bastard ⌈at one   **4.2**
    doore⌉, and Steward ⌈at another⌉

GONERILL
Welcome my Lord. I meruell our mild husband
Not met vs on the way. *(To Steward)* Now, where's
    your Master?

STEWARD
Madam within, but neuer man so chang'd:
I told him of the Army that was Landed:
He smil'd at it. I told him you were comming,
His answer was, the worse. Of Glosters Treachery,
And of the loyall Seruice of his Sonne   2080
When I inform'd him, then he call'd me Sot,
And told me I had turn'd the wrong side out:
What most he should dislike, seemes pleasant to him;
What like, offensiue.

GONERILL *(to Edmond)* Then shall you go no further.
It is the Cowish terror of his spirit
That dares not vndertake: Hee'l not feele wrongs
Which tye him to an answer: our wishes on the way
May proue effects. Backe *Edmond* to my Brother,
Hasten his Musters, and conduct his powres.
I must change names at home, and giue the Distaffe   2090
Into my Husbands hands. This trustie Seruant
Shall passe betweene vs: ere long you are like to heare
(If you dare venture in your owne behalfe)
A Mistresses command. Weare this; spare speech,
Decline your head. This kisse, if it durst speake
Would stretch thy Spirits vp into the ayre:
    ⌈*She kisses him*⌉
Conceiue, and fare thee well.

EDMOND Yours, in the rankes of death.

GONERILL My most deere Gloster.   *Exit Edmond*
Oh, the difference of man, and man,   2100
To thee a Womans seruices are due,
My Foole vsurpes my body.

STEWARD   Madam, here come's my Lord.
    Enter Albany

GONERILL
I haue beene worth the whistling.

ALBANY   Oh *Gonerill*,

You are not worth the dust which the rude winde
Blowes in your face.

GONERILL   Milke-Liuer'd man,
That bear'st a cheeke for blowes, a head for wrongs,
Who hast not in thy browes an eye discerning
Thine Honor, from thy suffering.

ALBANY   See thy selfe diuell:
Proper deformitie shewes not in the Fiend
So horrid as in woman.

2110   GONERILL   Oh vaine Foole.

    Enter a Messenger

MESSENGER
Oh my good Lord, the Duke of *Cornwals* dead,
Slaine by his Seruant, going to put out
The other eye of Glouster.

ALBANY   Glousters eyes.

MESSENGER
A Seruant that he bred, thrill'd with remorse,
Oppos'd against the act: bending his Sword
To his great Master, who, thereat-enrag'd
Flew on him, and among'st them fell'd him dead,
But not without that harmefull stroke, which since
Hath pluckt him after.

ALBANY   This shewes you are aboue
2120   You Iusticers, that these our neather crimes
So speedily can venge. But (O poore Glouster)
Lost he his other eye?

MESSENGER   Both, both, my Lord.—
This Leter Madam, craues a speedy answer:
'Tis from your Sister.

GONERILL (*aside*)   One way I like this well.
But being widdow, and my Glouster with her,
May all the building in my fancie plucke
Vpon my hatefull life. Another way
The Newes is not so tart. Ile read, and answer.

                           ⌐*Exit with Oswald*⌐

ALBANY
Where was his Sonne, when they did take his eyes?

MESSENGER
Come with my Lady hither.

2130   ALBANY   He is not heere.

MESSENGER
No my good Lord, I met him backe againe.

ALBANY Knowes he the wickednesse?

MESSENGER
I my good Lord: 'twas he inform'd against him
And quit the house on purpose, that their punishment
Might haue the freer course.

ALBANY   Glouster, I liue
To thanke thee for the loue thou shew'dst the King,
And to reuenge thine eyes. Come hither Friend,
Tell me what more thou know'st.   *Exeunt*

4.3   *Enter with Drum and Colours, Cordelia, Gentlemen,*
      and Souldiours

CORDELIA
Alacke, 'tis he: why he was met euen now
2140   As mad as the vext Sea, singing alowd,

Crown'd with ranke Femitar, and furrow weeds,
With Burdockes, Hemlocke, Nettles, Cuckoo flowres,
Darnell and all the idle weedes that grow
In our sustaining Corne. A Centery send forth;
Search euery Acre in the high-growne field,
And bring him to our eye.   ⌐*Exit one or more*⌐
           What can mans wisedome
In the restoring his bereaued Sense;
He that helpes him, take all my outward worth.

⌐I⌐ GENTLEMAN There is meanes Madam:
Our foster Nurse of Nature, is repose,   2150
The which he lackes: that to prouoke in him
Are many Simples operatiue, whose power
Will close the eye of Anguish.

CORDELIA   All blest Secrets,
All you vnpublish'd Vertues of the earth
Spring with my teares; be aydant, and remediate
In the Good mans distres: seeke, seeke for him,
Least his vngouern'd rage, dissolue the life
That wants the meanes to leade it.

    Enter a Messenger

MESSENGER   Newes Madam,
The Brittish Powres are marching hitherward.

CORDELIA
'Tis knowne before. Our preparation stands   2160
In expectation of them. O deere Father,
It is thy businesse that I go about:
Therfore great France
My mourning, and importun'd teares hath pittied:
No blowne Ambition doth our Armes incite,
But loue, deere loue, and our ag'd Fathers Rite:
Soone may I heare, and see him.   *Exeunt*

    Enter Regan, and Steward   **4.4**

REGAN
But are my Brothers Powres set forth?

STEWARD   I Madam.

REGAN
Himselfe in person there?

STEWARD   Madam with much ado:
Your Sister is the better Souldier.   2170

REGAN
Lord *Edmund* spake not with your Lord at home?

STEWARD No Madam.

REGAN
What might import my Sisters Letters to him?

STEWARD I know not, Lady.

REGAN
Faith he is poasted hence on serious matter:
It was great ignorance, Glousters eyes being out
To let him liue. Where he arriues, he moues
All hearts against vs: *Edmnd*, I thinke is gone
In pitty of his misery, to dispatch
His nighted life: Moreouer to descry   2180
The strength o'th'Enemy.

STEWARD
I must needs after, Madam, with my Letter.

REGAN

Our troopes set forth to morrow, stay with vs:
The wayes are dangerous.

STEWARD   I may not Madam:
My Lady charg'd my dutie in this busines.

REGAN

Why should she write to *Edmund*? Might not you
Transport her purposes by word? Belike,
Some things, I know not what. Ile loue thee much,
Let me vnseale the Letter.

STEWARD   Madam, I had rather—

REGAN

2190   I know your Lady do's not loue her Husband,
I am sure of that: and at her late being heere,
She gaue strange Eliads, and most speaking lookes
To Noble *Edmund*. I know you are of her bosome.

STEWARD   I, Madam?

REGAN

I speake in vnderstanding: Y'are: I know't,
Therefore I do aduise you take this note:
My Lord is dead: *Edmond*, and I haue talk'd,
And more conuenient is he for my hand
Then for your Ladies: You may gather more:

2200   If you do finde him, pray you giue him this;
And when your Mistris heares thus much from you,
I pray desire her call her wisedome to her.
So fare you well:
If you do chance to heare of that blinde Traitor,
Preferment fals on him, that cuts him off.

STEWARD

Would I could meet him Madam, I should shew
What party I do follow.

REGAN   Fare thee well.

Exeunt seuerally

4.5   *Enter Edgar disguised as a pezant with a staff,*
           guiding blind Gloucester

GLOUSTER

When shall I come to th'top of that same hill?

EDGAR

You do climbe vp it now. Look how we labor.

GLOUSTER

Me thinkes the ground is eeuen.

2210   EDGAR   Horrible steepe.
Hearke, do you heare the Sea?

GLOUSTER   No truly.

EDGAR

Why then your other Senses grow imperfect
By your eyes anguish.

GLOUSTER   So may it be indeed.
Me thinkes thy voyce is alter'd, and thou speak'st
In better phrase, and matter then thou did'st.

EDGAR

Y'are much deceiu'd: In nothing am I chang'd
But in my Garments.

GLOUSTER   Me thinkes y'are better spoken.

EDGAR

Come on Sir, heere's the place: stand still: how fearefull

And dizie 'tis, to cast ones eyes so low,
The Crowes and Choughes, that wing the midway ayre   2220
Shew scarse so grosse as Beetles. Halfe way downe
Hangs one that gathers Sampire: dreadfull Trade:
Me thinkes he seemes no bigger then his head.
The Fishermen, that walke vpon the beach
Appeare like Mice: and yond tall Anchoring Barke,
Diminish'd to her Cocke: her Cocke, a Buoy
Almost too small for sight. The murmuring Surge,
That on th'vnnumbred idle Pebble chafes
Cannot be heard so high. Ile looke no more,
Least my braine turne, and the deficient sight   2230
Topple downe headlong.

GLOUSTER   Set me where you stand.

EDGAR

Giue me your hand: you are now within a foote
Of th'extreme Verge: for all beneath the Moone
Would I not leape vpright.

GLOUSTER   Let go my hand:
Heere Friend's another purse: in it, a Iewell
Well worth a poore mans taking. Fayries, and Gods
Prosper it with thee. Go thou further off,
Bid me farewell, and let me heare thee going.

EDGAR

Now fare ye well, good Sir.

He stands aside

GLOUSTER   With all my heart.

EDGAR (*aside*)

Why I do trifle thus with his dispaire,   2240
Is done to cure it.

GLOUSTER (*kneeling*) O you mighty Gods!
This world I do renounce, and in your sights
Shake patiently my great affliction off:
If I could beare it longer, and not fall
To quarrell with your great opposelesse willes,
My snuffe, and loathed part of Nature should
Burne it selfe out. If *Edgar* liue, O blesse him:
Now Fellow, fare thee well.

EDGAR   Gone Sir, farewell:

Glouster falls forward

(*Aside*) And yet I know not how conceit may rob
The Treasury of life, when life it selfe   2250
Yeelds to the Theft. Had he bin where he thought,
By this had thought bin past. Aliue, or dead?
(*To Glouster*) Hoa, you Sir: Friend, heare you Sir,
    speake:
(*Aside*) Thus might he passe indeed: yet he reuiues.
(*To Glouster*) What are you Sir?

GLOUSTER   Away, and let me dye.

EDGAR

Had'st thou beene ought but Gozemore, Feathers,
    Ayre,
(So many fathome downe precipitating)
Thou'dst shiuer'd like an Egge: but thou do'st breath:
Hast heauy substance, bleed'st not, speak'st, art sound,
Ten Masts alenth, make not the altitude   2260
Which thou hast perpendicularly fell,
Thy life's a Myracle. Speake yet againe.

GLOUSTER But haue I falne, or no?

EDGAR
From the dread Somnet of this Chalkie Bourne,
Looke vp a height, the shrill-gorg'd Larke so farre
Cannot be seene, or heard: Do but looke vp.

GLOUSTER Alacke, I haue no eyes:
Is wretchednesse depriu'd that benefit
To end it selfe by death? 'Twas yet some comfort,
2270 When misery could beguile the Tyrants rage,
And frustrate his proud will.

EDGAR   Giue me your arme.
Vp, so: How is't? Feele you your Legges? You stand.

GLOUSTER
Too well, too well.

EDGAR   This is aboue all strangenesse.
Vpon the crowne o'th'Cliffe, what thing was that
Which parted from you?

GLOUSTER   A poore vnfortunate Beggar.

EDGAR
As I stood heere below, me thoughts his eyes
Were two full Moones: he had a thousand Noses,
Hornes wealk'd, and waued like the enraged Sea:
It was some Fiend: Therefore thou happy Father,
Thinke that the cleerest Gods, who make them
2280   Honors
Of mens Impossibilities, haue preseru'd thee.

GLOUSTER
I do remember now: henceforth Ile beare
Affliction, till it do cry out it selfe
Enough, enough, and dye. That thing you speake of,
I tooke it for a man: often 'twould say
The Fiend, the Fiend, he led me to that place.

EDGAR
Beare free and patient thoughts.

Enter Lear mad ⌈crowned with weedes and flowres⌉
                 But who comes heere?
The safer sense will ne're accommodate
His Master thus.

2290 LEAR No, they cannot touch me for crying. I am the King
himselfe.

EDGAR O thou side-piercing sight!

LEAR Nature's aboue Art, in that respect. Ther's your
Presse-money. That fellow handles his bow, like a
Crow-keeper: draw mee a Cloathiers yard. Looke, looke,
a Mouse: peace, peace, this peece of toasted Cheese will
doo't. There's my Gauntlet, Ile proue it on a Gyant.
Bring vp the browne Billes. O well flowne Bird: i'th'
clout, i'th'clout: Hewgh. Giue the word.

2300 EDGAR Sweet Mariorum.

LEAR Passe.

GLOUSTER I know that voice.

LEAR Ha! *Gonerill* with a white beard? They flatter'd me
like a Dogge, and told mee I had the white hayres in
my Beard, ere the blacke ones were there. To say I,
and no, to euery thing that I said I, and no too, was
no good Diuinity. When the raine came to wet me
once, and the winde to make me chatter: when the
Thunder would not peace at my bidding, there I found
2310 'em, there I smelt 'em out. Go too, they are not men

o'their words; they told me, I was euery thing: 'Tis a
Lye, I am not Agu-proofe.

GLOUSTER
The tricke of that voyce, I do well remember:
Is't not the King?

LEAR   I, euery inch a King.
⌈*Glouster kneeles*⌉
When I do stare, see how the Subiect quakes.
I pardon that mans life. What was thy cause?
Adultery? thou shalt not dye: dye for Adultery?
No, the Wren goes too't, and the small gilded Fly
Do's letcher in my sight. Let Copulation thriue:
For Glousters bastard Son   2320
Was kinder to his Father, then my Daughters
Got 'tweene the lawfull sheets. Too't Luxury pell-mell,
For I lacke Souldiers. Behold yond simpring Dame,
Whose face betweene her Forkes presages Snow;
That minces Vertue, & do's shake the head
To heare of pleasures name.
The Fitchew, nor the soyled Horse goes too't
With a more riotous appetite: Downe from the waste
Tha're Centaures, though Women all aboue:
But to the Girdle do the Gods inherit,   2330
Beneath is all the Fiends. There's hell, there's darkenes,
there is the sulphurous pit; burning, scalding, stench,
consumption: Fye, fie, fie; pah, pah: Giue me an Ounce
of Ciuet; good Apothecary sweeten my immagination:
There's money for thee.

GLOUSTER   O let me kisse that hand.

LEAR Let me wipe it first, it smelles of Mortality.

GLOUSTER
O ruin'd peece of Nature, this great world
Shall so weare out to naught. Do'st thou know me?

LEAR I remember thine eyes well enough: dost thou
squiny at me?   2340
No, doe thy worst blinde Cupid, Ile not loue.
Reade thou this challenge, marke but the penning of it.

GLOUSTER
Were all thy Letters Sunnes, I could not see.

EDGAR (*aside*)
I would not take this from report, it is,
And my heart breakes at it.

LEAR (*to Glouster*) Read.

GLOUSTER What with the Case of eyes?

LEAR Oh ho, are you there with me? No eies in your
head, nor no mony in your purse? Your eyes are in a
heauy case, your purse in a light, yet you see how this   2350
world goes.

GLOUSTER I see it feelingly.

LEAR What, art mad? A man may see how this world
goes, with no eyes. Looke with thine eares: See how
yond Iustice railes vpon yond simple theefe. Hearke in
thine eare: Change places, and handy-dandy, which is
the Iustice, which is the theefe: Thou hast seene a
Farmers dogge barke at a Beggar?

GLOUSTER I Sir.

LEAR And the Creature run from the Cur: there thou   2360
might'st behold the great image of Authoritie, a Dogg's
obey'd in Office.

Thou, Rascall Beadle, hold thy bloody hand:
Why dost thou lash that Whore? Strip thy owne backe,
Thou hotly lusts to vse her in that kind,
For which thou whip'st her. The Vsurer hangs the
    Cozener.
Through tatter'd cloathes great Vices do appeare:
Robes, and Furr'd gownes hide all. Plate sinne with
    Gold,
And the strong Lance of Iustice, hurtlesse breakes:
2370 Arme it in ragges, a Pigmies straw do's pierce it.
None do's offend, none, I say none, Ile able 'em;
Take that of me my Friend, who haue the power
To seale th'accusers lips. Get thee glasse-eyes,
And like a scuruy Politician, seeme
To see the things thou dost not. Now, now, now, now.
Pull off my Bootes: harder, harder, so.

EDGAR (aside)
O matter, and impertinency mixt,
Reason in Madnesse.

LEAR
If thou wilt weepe my Fortunes, take my eyes.
2380 I know thee well enough, thy name is Glouster:
Thou must be patient; we came crying hither:
Thou know'st, the first time that we smell the Ayre
We wawle, and cry. I will preach to thee: Marke.

GLOUSTER Alacke, alacke the day.

LEAR ⌜remouing his crowne of weedes⌝
When we are borne, we cry that we are come
To this great stage of Fooles. This a good blocke:
It were a delicate stratagem to shoo
A Troope of Horse with Felt: Ile put't in proofe,
And when I haue stolne vpon these Son in Lawes,
2390 Then kill, kill, kill, kill, kill, kill.
    Enter ⌜2⌝ Gentlemen

⌜1⌝ GENTLEMAN
Oh heere he is: lay hand vpon him. ⌜To Lear⌝ Sir,
Your most deere Daughter—

LEAR
No rescue? What, a Prisoner? I am euen
The Naturall Foole of Fortune. Vse me well,
You shall haue ransome. Let me haue Surgeons,
I am cut to'th'Braines.

⌜1⌝ GENTLEMAN You shall haue any thing.

LEAR No Seconds? All my selfe?
Why, this would make a man, a man of Salt
2400 To vse his eyes for Garden water-pots.
I wil die brauely, like a smugge Bridegroome. What?
I will be Iouiall: Come, come, I am a King,
Masters, know you that?

⌜1⌝ GENTLEMAN
You are a Royall one, and we obey you.

LEAR Then there's life in't. Come, and you get it, you
shall get it by running: Sa, sa, sa, sa.
    Exit running ⌜pursued by a Gentleman⌝

⌜1⌝ GENTLEMAN
A sight most pittifull in the meanest wretch,
Past speaking in a King. Thou hast a Daughter
Who redeemes Nature from the generall curse
2410 Which twaine haue brought her to.

EDGAR Haile gentle Sir.

⌜1⌝ GENTLEMAN Sir, speed you: what's your will?

EDGAR
Do you heare ought (Sir) of a Battell toward.

⌜1⌝ GENTLEMAN
Most sure, and vulgar: euery one heares that,
That can distinguish sound.

EDGAR But by your fauour:
How neere's the other Army?

⌜1⌝ GENTLEMAN
Neere, and on speedy foot: the maine descry
Stands in the hourely thought.

EDGAR   I thanke you Sir, that's all.

⌜1⌝ GENTLEMAN
Though that the Queen on special cause is here   2420
Her Army is mou'd on.

EDGAR   I thanke you Sir.
    Exit Gentleman

GLOUSTER
You euer gentle Gods, take my breath from me,
Let not my worser Spirit tempt me againe
To dye before you please.

EDGAR Well pray you Father.

GLOUSTER Now good sir, what are you?

EDGAR
A most poore man, made tame to Fortunes blows
Who, by the Art of knowne, and feeling sorrowes,
Am pregnant to good pitty. Giue me your hand,
Ile leade you to some biding.

GLOUSTER ⌜rising⌝   Heartie thankes: 2430
The bountie, and the benizon of Heauen
To boot, and boot.
    Enter Steward

STEWARD   A proclaim'd prize: most happie;
That eyelesse head of thine, was first fram'd flesh
To raise my fortunes. Thou old, vnhappy Traitor,
Breefely thy selfe remember: the Sword is out
That must destroy thee.

GLOUSTER   Now let thy friendly hand
Put strength enough too't.

STEWARD (to Edgar)   Wherefore, bold Pezant,
Durst thou support a publish'd Traitor? Hence,
Least that th'infection of his fortune take
Like hold on thee. Let go his arme.   2440

EDGAR Chill not let go Zir, without vurther 'cagion.

STEWARD Let go Slaue, or thou dy'st.

EDGAR Good Gentleman goe your gate, and let poore voke
passe: and 'chud ha' bin swaggerd out of my life,
'twould not ha' bin so long as 'tis, by a vortnight. Nay,
come not neere th'old man: keepe out che vor'ye, or
ice try whither your Costard, or my Batton be the
harder; ile be plaine with you.

STEWARD Out Dunghill.

EDGAR Chill picke your teeth Sir: come, no matter vor   2450
your foynes.
    ⌜Edgar knockes him downe⌝

STEWARD
Slaue thou hast slaine me: Villain, take my purse;
If euer thou wilt thriue, bury my bodie,

And giue the Letters which thou find'st about me,
To *Edmund* Earle of Glouster: seeke him out
Vpon the English party. Oh vntimely death, death.

He dies

EDGAR
I know thee well. A seruiceable Villaine,
As duteous to the vices of thy Mistris,
As badnesse would desire.

2460 GLOUSTER What, is he dead?

EDGAR Sit you downe Father: rest you.

Glouster sits

Let's see these Pockets; the Letters that he speakes of
May be my Friends: hee's dead; I am onely sorrow
He had no other Deathsman. Let vs see:
Leaue gentle waxe, and manners: blame vs not.
To know our enemies mindes, we rip their hearts,
Their Papers is more lawfull.

He reads the Letter

Let our reciprocall vowes be remembred. You haue manie
opportunities to cut him off: if your will want not, time
2470 *and place will be fruitfully offer'd. There is nothing done,*
If hee returne the Conqueror, then am I the Prisoner, and
his bed, my Gaole, from the loathed warmth whereof,
deliuer me, and supply the place for your Labour.

Your (Wife, so I would say) affectionate
Seruant, and for you her owne for venter.

Gonerill.

Oh indistinguish'd space of Womans will,
A plot vpon her vertuous Husbands life,
And the exchange my Brother: heere, in the sands
2480 Thee Ile rake vp, the poste vnsanctified
Of murtherous Letchers: and in the mature time,
With this vngracious paper strike the sight
Of the death-practis'd Duke: for him 'tis well,
That of thy death, and businesse, I can tell.

⌈*Exit with body*⌉

GLOUSTER
The King is mad: how stiffe is my vilde sense
That I stand vp, and haue ingenious feeling
Of my huge Sorrowes? Better I were distract,
So should my thoughts be seuer'd from my greefes,

Drum afarre off

And woes, by wrong imaginations loose
The knowledge of themselues.

⌈*Enter Edgar*⌉

2490 EDGAR   Giue me your hand:
Farre off methinkes I heare the beaten Drumme.
Come Father, Ile bestow you with a Friend.

Exit Edgar guiding Gloster

4.6   *Enter Cordelia, Kent disguised, and* ⌈*First*⌉
           Gentleman

CORDELIA
O thou good *Kent*, how shall I liue and worke
To match thy goodnesse? My life will be too short,
And euery measure faile me.

KENT
To be acknowledg'd Madam is ore-pai'd,

All my reports go with the modest truth,
Nor more, nor clipt, but so.

CORDELIA   Be better suited,
These weedes are memories of those worser houres:
I prythee put them off.

KENT   Pardon deere Madam,   2500
Yet to be knowne shortens my made intent,
My boone I make it, that you know me not,
Till time, and I, thinke meet.

CORDELIA   Then be't so my good Lord:
How do's the King?

⌈I⌉ GENTLEMAN   Madam sleepes still.

CORDELIA   O you kind Gods!
Cure this great breach in his abused Nature,
Th'vntun'd and iarring senses, O winde vp,
Of this childe-changed Father.

⌈I⌉ GENTLEMAN   So please your Maiesty,
That we may wake the King, he hath slept long?

CORDELIA
Be gouern'd by your knowledge, and proceede
I'th'sway of your owne will: is he array'd?   2510

⌈I⌉ GENTLEMAN
I Madam: in the heauinesse of sleepe,
We put fresh garments on him.

Enter Lear asleepe in a chaire carried by Seruants

Be by good Madam when we do awake him,
I doubt not of his Temperance.

CORDELIA
O my deere Father, restauratian hang
Thy medicine on my lippes, and let this kisse
Repaire those violent harmes, that my two Sisters
Haue in thy Reuerence made.

KENT   Kind and deere Princesse.

CORDELIA
Had you not bin their Father, these white flakes
Did challenge pitty of them. Was this a face   2520
To be oppos'd against the warring windes?
Mine Enemies dogge, though he had bit me, should
     haue stood
That night against my fire, and was't thou faine
     (poore Father)
To houell thee with Swine and Rogues forlorne,
In short, and musty straw? Alacke, alacke,
'Tis wonder that thy life and wits, at once
Had not concluded all. (*To Gentleman*) He wakes,
     speake to him.

⌈I⌉ GENTLEMAN Madam do you, 'tis fittest.

CORDELIA (*to Lear*)
How does my Royall Lord? How fares your Maiesty?

LEAR
You do me wrong to take me out o'th'graue,   2530
Thou art a Soule in blisse, but I am bound
Vpon a wheele of fire, that mine owne teares
Do scal'd, like molten Lead.

CORDELIA   Sir, do you know me?

LEAR
You are a spirit I know, where did you dye?

CORDELIA (*to Gentleman*) Still, still, farre wide.

⌐1⌐ GENTLEMAN

He's scarse awake, let him alone a while.

LEAR

Where haue I bin? Where am I? Faire day light?

I am mightily abus'd; I should eu'n dye with pitty

To see another thus. I know not what to say:

2540   I will not sweare these are my hands: let's see,

I feele this pin pricke, would I were assur'd

Of my condition.

CORDELIA (kneeling)   O looke vpon me Sir,

And hold your hands in benediction o're me,

You must not kneele.

LEAR   Pray do not mocke:

I am a very foolish fond old man,

Fourescore and vpward,

Not an houre more, nor lesse: and to deale plainely,

I feare I am not in my perfect mind.

Me thinkes I should know you, and know this man,

2550   Yet I am doubtfull: For I am mainely ignorant

What place this is: and all the skill I haue

Remembers not these garments: nor I know not

Where I did lodge last night. Do not laugh at me,

For (as I am a man) I thinke this Lady

To be my childe Cordelia.

CORDELIA   And so I am: I am.

LEAR

Be your teares wet? Yes faith: I pray weepe not,

If you haue poyson for me, I will drinke it:

I know you do not loue me, for your Sisters

Haue (as I do remember) done me wrong.

You haue some cause, they haue not.

2560   CORDELIA   No cause, no cause.

LEAR Am I in France?

KENT In your owne kingdome Sir.

LEAR Do not abuse me.

⌐1⌐ GENTLEMAN

Be comforted good Madam, the great rage

You see is kill'd in him: desire him to go in,

Trouble him no more till further setling.

CORDELIA (to Lear) Wilt please your Highnesse walke?

LEAR

You must beare with me: pray you now forget,

And forgiue, I am old and foolish.   Exeunt

5.1   Enter with Drumme and Colours, Edmund, Regan,
              Gentlemen, and Souldiers

EDMOND

2570   Know of the Duke if his last purpose hold,

Or whether since he is aduis'd by ought

To change the course, he's full of abdication,

And selfe-reprouing, bring his constant pleasure.

                              Exit one or more

REGAN

Our Sisters man is certainely miscarried.

EDMOND

'Tis to be doubted Madam.

REGAN   Now sweet Lord,

You know the goodnesse I intend vpon you:

Tell me but truly, but then speake the truth,

Do you not loue my Sister?

EDMOND   In honour'd Loue.

REGAN

But haue you neuer found my Brothers way,

To the fore-fended place?

EDMOND   No by mine honour, Madam.   2580

REGAN

I neuer shall endure her, deere my Lord

Be not familiar with her.

EDMOND Feare me not,

She and the Duke her husband.

              Enter with Drum and Colours, Albany, Gonerill,
              Soldiers

ALBANY (to Regan)

Our very louing Sister, well be-met:

(To Edmond) Sir, this I heard, the King is come to his
              Daughter

With others, whom the rigour of our State

Forc'd to cry out.

REGAN   Why is this reasond?

GONERILL

Combine together 'gainst the Enemie:

For these domesticke and particular broiles,   2590

Are not the question heere.

ALBANY

Let's then determine with th'ancient of warre

On our proceeding.

REGAN   Sister you'le go with vs?

GONERILL No.

REGAN

'Tis most conuenient, pray go with vs.

GONERILL (aside)

Oh ho, I know the Riddle, (to Regan) I will goe.

              Enter Edgar disguised as a Pezant

EDGAR (to Albany)

If ere your Grace had speech with man so poore,

Heare me one word.

ALBANY (to the others) Ile ouertake you,

                              Exeunt both the Armies
                                      speake.

EDGAR

Before you fight the Battaile, ope this Letter:

If you haue victory, let the Trumpet sound   2600

For him that brought it: wretched though I seeme,

I can produce a Champion, that will proue

What is auouched there. If you miscarry,

Your businesse of the world hath so an end,

And machination ceases. Fortune loue you.

ALBANY

Stay till I haue read the Letter.

EDGAR   I was forbid it:

When time shall serue, let but the Herald cry,

And Ile appeare againe.

ALBANY Why fare thee well,

I will o're-looke thy paper.   Exit Edgar   2610

Enter Edmund

EDMOND

The Enemy's in view, draw vp your powers,
He ⌈offers⌉ Albany a paper
Heere is the guesse of their true strength and Forces,
By dilligent discouerie, but your hast
Is now vrg'd on you.

ALBANY   We will greet the time.   *Exit*

EDMOND

To both these Sisters haue I sworne my loue:
Each iealous of the other, as the stung
Are of the Adder. Which of them shall I take?
Both? One? Or neither? Neither can be enioy'd
If both remaine aliue: To take the Widdow,
2620   Exasperates, makes mad her Sister *Gonerill*,
And hardly shall I carry out my side,
Her husband being aliue. Now then, wee'l vse
His countenance for the Battaile, which being done,
Let her who would be rid of him, deuise
His speedy taking off. As for the mercie
Which he intends to *Lear* and to *Cordelia*,
The Battaile done, and they within our power,
Shall neuer see his pardon: for my state,
Stands on me to defend, not to debate.   *Exit*

5.2   *Alarum within. Enter with Drumme and Colours,
Lear, Cordelia, and Souldiers, ouer the Stage, and
Exeunt. Enter Edgar disguised as a Pezant, guiding
blind Gloster*

EDGAR

2630   Heere Father, take the shadow of this Tree
For your good hoast: pray that the right may thriue:
If euer I returne to you againe,
Ile bring you comfort.

GLOUSTER   Grace go with you Sir.
                                        Exit Edgar
        Alarum and Retreat within. Enter Edgar

EDGAR

Away old man, giue me thy hand, away:
King *Lear* hath lost, he and his Daughter tane,
Giue me thy hand: Come on.

GLOUSTER

No further Sir, a man may rot euen heere.

EDGAR

What in ill thoughts againe? Men must endure
Their going hence, euen as their comming hither,
Ripenesse is all come on.

2640   GLOUSTER   And that's true too.
                        Exit Edgar, guiding Glouster

5.3   *Enter in conquest with Drum and Colours, Edmund,
Lear, and Cordelia, as prisoners, Souldiers, Captaine*

EDMOND

Some Officers take them away: good guard,
Vntill their greater pleasures first be knowne
That are to censure them.

CORDELIA (*to Lear*)   We are not the first,
Who with best meaning haue incurr'd the worst:

For thee oppressed King I am cast downe,
My selfe could else out-frowne false Fortunes frowne.
Shall we not see these Daughters, and these Sisters?

LEAR

No, no, no, no: come let's away to prison,
We two alone will sing like Birds i'th'Cage:
When thou dost aske me blessing, Ile kneele downe   2650
And aske of thee forgiuenesse: So wee'l liue,
And pray, and sing, and tell old tales, and laugh
At gilded Butterflies: and heere poore Rogues
Talke of Court newes, and wee'l talke with them too,
Who looses, and who wins; who's in, who's out;
And take vpon's the mystery of things,
As if we were Gods spies: And wee'l weare out
In a wall'd prison, packs and sects of great ones,
That ebbe and flow by th'Moone.

EDMOND (*to Souldiers*)   Take them away.

LEAR

Vpon such sacrifices my *Cordelia*,   2660
The Gods themselues throw Incense. Haue I caught
        thee?
He that parts vs, shall bring a Brand from Heauen,
And fire vs hence, like Foxes: wipe thine eyes,
The goodyeare shall deuoure them, flesh and fell,
Ere they shall make vs weepe? Weele see 'em staru'd
        first: come.
                Exeunt. Manet Edmond and the Captaine

EDMOND Come hither Captaine, hearke.
Take thou this note, go follow them to prison,
One step I haue aduanc'd thee, if thou do'st
As this instructs thee, thou dost make thy way
To Noble Fortunes: know thou this, that men   2670
Are as the time is; to be tender minded
Do's not become a Sword, thy great imployment
Will not beare question: either say thou'lt do't,
Or thriue by other meanes.

CAPTAINE   Ile do't my Lord.

EDMOND

About it, and write happy, when th'hast done,
Marke I say instantly, and carry it so
As I haue set it downe.   *Exit Captaine*
        *Flourish. Enter Albany, Gonerill, Regan ⌈with
        Drumme and Trumpet⌉, Soldiers*

ALBANY

Sir, you haue shew'd to day your valiant straine,
And Fortune led you well: you haue the Captiues
Who were the opposites of this dayes strife: 2680
I do require them of you so to vse them,
As we shall find their merites, and our safety
May equally determine.

EDMOND   Sir, I thought it fit,
To send the old and miserable King
To some retention, and appointed guard,
Whose age had Charmes in it, whose Title more,
To plucke the common bosome on his side,
And turne our imprest Launces in our eies
Which do command them. With him I sent the Queen:
My reason all the same, and they are ready   2690

To morrow, or at further space, t'appeare
Where you shall hold your Session.

ALBANY   Sir, by your patience,
I hold you but a subiect of this Warre,
Not as a Brother.

REGAN   That's as we list to grace him.
Methinkes our pleasure might haue bin demanded
Ere you had spoke so farre. He led our Powers,
Bore the Commission of my place and person,
The which immediacie may well stand vp,
And call it selfe your Brother.

GONERILL   Not so hot:

2700   In his owne grace he doth exalt himselfe,
More then in your addition.

REGAN   In my rights,
By me inuested, he compeeres the best.

ALBANY
That were the most, if he should husband you.

REGAN
Iesters do oft proue Prophets.

GONERILL   Hola, hola,
That eye that told you so, look'd but a squint.

REGAN
Lady I am not well, else I should answere
From a full flowing stomack. (To Edmond) Generall,
Take thou my Souldiers, prisoners, patrimony,
Dispose of them, of me, the walls is thine:

2710   Witnesse the world, that I create thee heere
My Lord, and Master.

GONERILL   Meane you to enioy him?

ALBANY
The let alone lies not in your good will.

EDMOND
Nor in thine Lord.

ALBANY   Halfe-blooded fellow, yes.

REGAN (to Edmond)
Let the Drum strike, and proue my title thine.

ALBANY
Stay yet, heare reason: Edmund, I arrest thee
On capitall Treason; and in thy attaint,
This guilded Serpent: (to Regan) for your claime faire
    Sister,
I bare it in the interest of my wife,
'Tis she is sub-contracted to this Lord,

2720   And I her husband contradict your Banes.
If you will marry, make your loues to me,
My Lady is bespoke.

GONERILL   An enterlude.

ALBANY
Thou art arm'd Gloster, let the Trumpet sound:
If none appeare to proue vpon thy person,
Thy heynous, manifest, and many Treasons,
There is my pledge:
     ⌈He throws downe a gloue⌉
           Ile make it on thy heart
Ere I taste bread, thou art in nothing lesse
Then I haue heere proclaim'd thee.

REGAN Sicke, O sicke.

GONERILL (aside) If not, Ile nere trust medicine.   2730

EDMOND (to Albany, ⌈throwing downe a gloue⌉)
There's my exchange, what in the world he is
That names me Traitor, villain-like he lies,
Call by the Trumpet: he that dares approach;
On him, on you, who not, I will maintaine
My truth and honor firmely.

ALBANY   A Herald, ho.
    Enter a Herald
(To Edmond) Trust to thy single vertue, for thy Souldiers
All leuied in my name, haue in my name
Tooke their discharge.

REGAN   My sicknesse growes vpon me.

ALBANY
She is not well, conuey her to my Tent.
              Exit one or more with Regan
Come hither Herald, let the Trumpet sound,   2740
And read out this.
    A Trumpet sounds

HERALD (reads) If any man of qualitie or degree, within the
   lists of the Army, will maintaine vpon Edmund, supposed
   Earle of Gloster, that he is a manifold Traitor, let him
   appeare by the third sound of the Trumpet: he is bold in
   his defence.
    1 Trumpet
Againe.
    2 Trumpet
Againe.
    3 Trumpet.
    Trumpet answers within. Enter Edgar armed

ALBANY (to Herald)
Aske him his purposes, why he appeares
Vpon this Call o'th'Trumpet.

HERALD (to Edgar)   What are you?   2750
Your name, your quality, and why you answer
This present Summons?

EDGAR   Know my name is lost:
By Treasons tooth bare-gnawne, and Canker-bit,
Yet am I Noble as the Aduersary
I come to cope.

ALBANY   Which is that Aduersary?

EDGAR
What's he that speakes for Edmund Earle of Gloster?

EDMOND
Himselfe, what saist thou to him?

EDGAR   Draw thy Sword,
That if my speech offend a Noble heart,
Thy arme may do thee Iustice, heere is mine:
    He drawes his Sword
Behold it is the priuiledge of mine Honour,   2760
My oath, and my profession. I protest,
Maugre thy strength, place, youth, and eminence,
Despight thy victor-Sword, and fire new Fortune,
Thy valor, and thy heart, thou art a Traitor:
False to thy Gods, thy Brother, and thy Father,
Conspirant 'gainst this high illustrious Prince,
And from th'extremest vpward of thy head,
To the discent and dust below thy foote,

A most Toad-spotted Traitor. Say thou no,
2770 This Sword, this arme, and my best spirits are bent
To proue vpon thy heart, whereto I speake,
Thou lyest.

EDMOND   In wisedome I should aske thy name,
But since thy out-side lookes so faire and Warlike,
And that thy tongue some say of breeding breathes,
What safe, and nicely I might well demand,
By rule of Knight-hood, I disdaine and spurne:
Backe do I tosse those Treasons to thy head,
With the hell-hated Lye, ore-whelme thy heart,
Which for they yet glance by, and scarsely bruise,
2780 This Sword of mine shall giue them instant way,
Where they shall rest for euer. Trumpets speake.
Alarums. Fight. Edmond is vanquished

⌈ALL⌉
Saue him, saue him.

GONERILL   This is practise *Gloster*,
By th'law of Armes, thou wast not bound to answer
An vnknowne opposite: thou art not vanquish'd,
But cozend, and beguild.

ALBANY   Shut your mouth Dame,
Or with this paper shall I stople it:
⌈*To Edmond*⌉ Hold Sir, thou worse then any name,
    reade thine owne euill:
(*To Gonerill*) No tearing Lady, I perceiue you know it.

GONERILL
Say if I do, the Lawes are mine not thine,
Who can araigne me for't?   *Exit*

2790 ALBANY   Most monstrous!
(*To Edmond*) O, know'st thou this paper?

EDMOND   Aske me not what I know.

ALBANY
Go after her, she's desperate, gouerne her.
          Exit one or more

EDMOND
What you haue charg'd me with, that haue I done,
And more, much more, the time will bring it out.
'Tis past, and so am I: (*To Edgar*) But what art thou
That hast this Fortune on me? If thou'rt Noble,
I do forgiue thee.

EDGAR   Let's exchange charity:
I am no lesse in blood then thou art *Edmond*,
If more, the more th'hast wrong'd me.
    ⌈*He takes off his helmet*⌉
2800 My name is *Edgar*, and thy Fathers Sonne,
The Gods are iust, and of our pleasant vices
Make instruments to plague vs:
The darke and vitious place where thee he got,
Cost him his eyes.

EDMOND   Th'hast spoken right, 'tis true,
The Wheele is come full circle, I am heere.

ALBANY (*to Edgar*)
Me thought thy very gate did prophesie
A Royall Noblenesse: I must embrace thee,
Let sorrow split my heart, if euer I
Did hate thee, or thy Father.

2810 EDGAR Worthy Prince I know't.

ALBANY Where haue you hid your selfe?
How haue you knowne the miseries of your Father?

EDGAR
By nursing them my Lord. List a breefe tale,
And when 'tis told, O that my heart would burst.
The bloody proclamation to escape
That follow'd me so neere, (O our liues sweetnesse,
That we the paine of death would hourely dye,
Rather then die at once) taught me to shift
Into a mad-mans rags, t'assume a semblance
That very Dogges disdain'd: and in this habit   2820
Met I my Father with his bleeding Rings,
Their precious Stones new lost: became his guide,
Led him, begg'd for him, sau'd him from dispaire.
Neuer (O fault) reueal'd my selfe vnto him,
Vntill some halfe houre past when I was arm'd,
Not sure, though hoping of this good successe,
I ask'd his blessing, and from first to last
Told him our pilgrimage. But his flaw'd heart
(Alacke too weake the conflict to support)
Twixt two extremes of passion, ioy and greefe,   2830
Burst smilingly.

EDMOND   This speech of yours hath mou'd me,
And shall perchance do good, but speake you on,
You looke as you had something more to say.

ALBANY
If there be more, more wofull, hold it in,
For I am almost ready to dissolue,
Hearing of this.
    Enter a Gentleman with a bloody Knife

GENTLEMAN
Helpe, helpe: O helpe.

EDGAR   What kinde of helpe?

ALBANY   Speake man.

EDGAR
What meanes this bloody Knife?

GENTLEMAN   'Tis hot, it smoakes,
It came euen from the heart of—O she's dead.

ALBANY Who dead? Speake man.   2840

GENTLEMAN
Your Lady Sir, your Lady; and her Sister
By her is poyson'd: she confesses it.

EDMOND
I was contracted to them both, all three
Now marry in an instant.

EDGAR   Here comes *Kent*.
    Enter Kent as himselfe

ALBANY
Produce the bodies, be they aliue or dead;
    Gonerill and Regans bodies brought out
This iudgement of the Heauens that makes vs tremble,
Touches vs not with pitty: O, is this he?
(*To Kent*) The time will not allow the complement
Which very manners vrges.

KENT   I am come
To bid my King and Master aye good night.   2850
Is he not here?

ALBANY   Great thing of vs forgot,

Speake *Edmund*, where's the King? and where's
   Cordelia?
Seest thou this obiect *Kent*?
KENT Alacke, why thus?
EDMOND Yet *Edmund* was belou'd:
The one the other poison'd for my sake,
And after slew herselfe.
ALBANY   Euen so: couer their faces.
EDMOND
I pant for life: some good I meane to do
Despight of mine owne Nature. Quickly send,
2860 (Be briefe in it) to'th'Castle, for my Writ
Is on the life of *Lear*, and on *Cordelia*:
Nay, send in time.
ALBANY   Run, run, O run.
EDGAR
To who my Lord? Who ha's the Office? Send
Thy token of repreeue.
EDMOND
Well thought on, take my Sword, the Captaine,
Giue it the Captaine.
EDGAR   Hast thee for thy life.
                     Exit ⌈*Gentleman*⌉
EDMOND (*to Albany*)
He hath Commission from thy Wife and me,
To hang *Cordelia* in the prison, and
To lay the blame vpon her owne dispaire,
2870 That she for-did her selfe.
ALBANY
The Gods defend her, beare him hence awhile.
                 Exeunt some with Edmond
Enter Lear with Cordelia in his armes, ⌈*followed by*
the Gentleman⌉
LEAR
Howle, howle, howle, howle: O you are men of stones,
Had I your tongues and eyes, Il'd vse them so,
That Heauens vault should crack: she's gone for euer.
I know when one is dead, and when one liues,
She's dead as earth:
   ⌈*He lays her downe*⌉
              Lend me a Looking-glasse,
If that her breath will mist or staine the stone,
Why then she liues.
KENT   Is this the promis'd end?
EDGAR
Or image of that horror.
ALBANY   Fall and cease.
LEAR
2880 This feather stirs, she liues: if it be so,
It is a chance which do's redeeme all sorrowes
That euer I haue felt.
KENT ⌈*kneeling*⌉   O my good Master.
LEAR
Prythee away.
EDGAR   'Tis Noble *Kent* your Friend.
LEAR
A plague vpon you Murderors, Traitors all,
I might haue sau'd her, now she's gone for euer:

Cordelia, Cordelia, stay a little. Ha:
What is't thou saist? Her voice was euer soft,
Gentle, and low, an excellent thing in woman.
I kill'd the Slaue that was a hanging thee.
GENTLEMAN
'Tis true (my Lords) he did.
LEAR   Did I not fellow?   2890
I haue seene the day, with my good biting Faulchion
I would haue made them skip: I am old now,
And these same crosses spoile me. (*To Kent*) Who are
   you?
Mine eyes are not o'th'best, Ile tell you straight.
KENT
If Fortune brag of two, she lou'd and hated,
One of them we behold.
LEAR   This a dull sight,
Are you not *Kent*?
KENT The same: your Seruant *Kent*,
Where is your Seruant *Caius*?
LEAR
He's a good fellow, I can tell you that,   2900
He'le strike and quickly too, he's dead and rotten.
KENT
No my good Lord, I am the very man.
LEAR Ile see that straight.
KENT
That from your first of difference and decay,
Haue follow'd your sad steps.
LEAR   You'r welcome hither.
KENT
Nor no man else: all's cheerlesse, darke, and deadly,
Your eldest Daughters haue fore-done themselues,
And desperately are dead.
LEAR   I so thinke I.
ALBANY
He knowes not what he saies, and vaine is it
That we present vs to him.
   Enter a Messenger
EDGAR   Very bootlesse.   2910
MESSENGER (*to Albany*)
Edmund is dead my Lord.
ALBANY   That's but a trifle heere:
You Lords and Noble Friends, know our intent,
What comfort to this great decay may come,
Shall be appli'd. For vs we will resigne,
During the life of this old Maiesty
To him our absolute power, (*to Edgar and Kent*) you to
   your rights,
With boote, and such addition as your Honours
Haue more then merited. All Friends shall taste
The wages of their vertue, and all Foes
The cup of their deseruings: O see, see.   2920
LEAR
And my poore Foole is hang'd: no, no, no life?
Why should a Dog, a Horse, a Rat haue life,
And thou no breath at all? Thou'lt come no more,
Neuer, neuer, neuer, neuer, neuer.
⌈*To Kent*⌉ Pray you vndo this Button. Thanke you Sir,

Do you see this? Looke on her? Looke her lips,
Looke there, looke there.   *He dies*
EDGAR   He faints, (*to Lear*) my Lord, my Lord.
KENT ⌈*to Lear*⌉
Breake heart, I prythee breake.
EDGAR (*to Lear*)   Looke vp my Lord.
KENT
Vex not his ghost, O let him passe, he hates him,
2930   That would vpon the wracke of this tough world
Stretch him out longer.
EDGAR   He is gon indeed.
KENT
The wonder is, he hath endur'd so long,
He but vsurpt his life.

ALBANY
Beare them from hence, our present businesse
Is generall woe: (*To Edgar and Kent*) Friends of my
       soule, you twaine,
Rule in this Realme, and the gor'd state sustaine.
KENT
I haue a iourney Sir, shortly to go,
My Master calls me, I must not say no.
EDGAR
The waight of this sad time we must obey,
Speake what we feele, not what we ought to say: 2940
The oldest hath borne most, we that are yong,
Shall neuer see so much, nor liue so long.
         Exeunt with a dead March, carrying the bodies

FINIS

MACBETH

BY WILLIAM SHAKESPEARE
(ADAPTED BY THOMAS MIDDLETON)

SHORTLY after James VI of Scotland succeeded to the English throne, in 1603, he gave his patronage to Shakespeare's company; the Lord Chamberlain's Men became the King's Men, entering into a special relationship with their sovereign. *Macbeth* is the play of Shakespeare's that most clearly reflects this relationship. James regarded the virtuous and noble Banquo, Macbeth's comrade at the start of the action, as his direct ancestor; eight Stuart kings were said to have preceded James, just as, in the play, Banquo points to 'a shew of eight Kings' as his descendants (1418.1–1431); and in the play the English king (historically Edward the Confessor) is praised for the capacity, on which James also prided himself, to cure 'the king's evil' (scrofula). *Macbeth* is obviously a Jacobean play, composed probably in 1606.

But the first printed text, in the 1623 Folio, shows signs of having been adapted at a later date. It is exceptionally short by comparison with Shakespeare's other tragedies; and it includes episodes which there is good reason to believe are not by Shakespeare. These are Act 3, Scene 5 and parts of Act 4, Scene 1: 1329.1–1351 and 1432–9.1. These episodes feature Hecat, who does not appear elsewhere in the play; they are composed largely in octosyllabic couplets in a style conspicuously different from the rest of the play; and they call for the performance of two songs that are found in *The Witch*, a play of uncertain date by Thomas Middleton. Probably Middleton himself adapted Shakespeare's play some years after its first performance. We do not attempt to excise passages probably not written by Shakespeare, because the adapter's hand may have affected the text at other, indeterminable points. The Folio text of *Macbeth* cites only the opening words of the songs; drawing on *The Witch*, we attempt a reconstruction of their staging in *Macbeth*.

Shakespeare took materials for his story from the account in Raphael Holinshed's *Chronicle* of the reigns of Duncan and Macbeth (AD 1034–57). Occasionally (especially in the English episodes of Act 4, Scene 2) he closely followed Holinshed's wording; but essentially the play's structure is his own. He invented the framework of the three witches who tempted both Macbeth and Banquo with prophecies of greatness. His Macbeth is both more introspective and more intensely evil than the competent warrior-king portrayed by Holinshed; conversely, Shakespeare made Duncan, the king whom Macbeth murders, far more venerable and saintly. Some of the play's features, notably the character of Macbeth's Lady, originate in Holinshed's account of the murder of an earlier Scottish king, Duff; he was killed in his castle at Forres by Donwald, who had been 'set on' by his wife.

Macbeth can be enjoyed at many levels. It is an exciting story of witchcraft, murder, and retribution that can also be seen as a study in the philosophy and psychology of evil. The witches are not easily made credible in modern performances, and Shakespeare seems deliberately to have drained colour away from some parts of his composition in order to concentrate attention on Macbeth and his Lady. It is Macbeth's neurotic self-absorption, his fear, his anger, and his despair, along with his wife's steely determination, her invoking of the powers of evil, and her eventual revelation in sleep of her repressed humanity, that have given the play its long-proven power to fascinate readers and to challenge performers.

The Folio text was set from a scribal transcript.

THE NAMES OF THE ACTORS

Duncan, KING of Scotland

MALCOLME
DONALBAINE } his Sonnes

A CAPTAINE in Duncans Army

MACBETH, Thane of Glamis, later Thane of Cawdor, then King of Scotland

A PORTER at Macbeths Castle

3 MURTHERERS attending on Macbeth

SEYTON, seruant of Macbeth

Macbeths LADY

A DOCTOR of Physicke
A Wayting GENTLEWOMAN } attending on Macbeths Lady

BANQUO, a Scottish Thane

FLEANCE, his Sonne

MACDUFFE, Thane of Fife

Macduffes WIFE

Macduffes SON

LENOX
ROSSE
ANGUS } Scottish Thanes
CATHNES
MENTETH

SEYWARD, Earle of Northumberland

YOUNG SEYWARD, his Sonne

An English DOCTOR

HECAT, Queene of the Witches

Six WITCHES

3 APPARITIONS, one an Armed Head, one a Bloody Childe, one a Childe Crowned

A SPIRIT LIKE A CAT

Other SPIRITS

An OLD MAN

A MESSENGER

MURTHERERS

SERUANTS

A shew of eight Kings; Lords and Thanes, Attendants, Soldiers, Drummers

1102

The Tragedie of Macbeth

1.1
(Sc. 1)

Thunder and Lightning. Enter three Witches

1. WITCH
When shall we three meet againe?
In Thunder, Lightning, or in Raine?

2. WITCH
When the Hurley-burley's done,
When the Battaile's lost, and wonne.

3. WITCH
That will be ere the set of Sunne.

1. WITCH
Where the place?

2. WITCH   Vpon the Heath.

3. WITCH
There to meet with *Macbeth*.

1. WITCH
I come, *Gray-Malkin*.

2. WITCH
Padock calls.

3. WITCH   Anon.

ALL
10   Faire is foule, and foule is faire,
Houer through the fogge and filthie ayre.   *Exeunt*

1.2
(Sc. 2)

Alarum within. Enter King, Malcome, Donalbaine,
Lenox, with attendants, meeting a bleeding Captaine

KING
What bloody man is that? he can report,
As seemeth by his plight, of the Reuolt
The newest state.

MALCOLME   This is the Serieant,
Who like a good and hardie Souldier fought
'Gainst my Captiuitie: Haile braue friend;
Say to the King, the knowledge of the Broyle,
As thou didst leaue it.

CAPTAINE   Doubtfull it stood,
20   As two spent Swimmers, that doe cling together,
And choake their Art: The mercilesse *Macdonwald*
(Worthie to be a Rebell, for to that
The multiplying Villanies of Nature
Doe swarme vpon him) from the Westerne Isles
Of Kernes and Gallowglasses is supply'd,
And Fortune on his damned Quarry smiling,
Shew'd like a Rebells Whore: but all's too weake:
For braue *Macbeth* (well hee deserues that Name)
Disdayning Fortune, with his brandisht Steele,
Which smoak'd with bloody execution
30   (Like Valours Minion)
Caru'd out his passage, till hee fac'd the Slaue:
Which neu'r shooke hands, nor bad farwell to him,
Till he vnseam'd him from the Naue toth' Chops,
And fix'd his Head vpon our Battlements.

KING
O valiant Cousin, worthy Gentleman.

CAPTAINE
As whence the Sunne 'gins his reflection,
Shipwracking Stormes, and direfull Thunders breake:
So from that Spring, whence comfort seem'd to come,
Discomfort swells: Marke King of Scotland, marke,
No sooner Iustice had, with Valour arm'd,   40
Compell'd these skipping Kernes to trust their heeles,
But the Norweyan Lord, surueying vantage,
With furbusht Armes, and new supplyes of men,
Began a fresh assault.

KING
Dismay'd not this our Captaines, *Macbeth* and
Banquoh?

CAPTAINE
Yes, as Sparrowes, Eagles; or the Hare, the Lyon:
If I say sooth, I must report they were
As Cannons ouer-charg'd with double Cracks,
So they doubly redoubled stroakes vpon the Foe:
Except they meant to bathe in reeking Wounds,   50
Or memorize another *Golgotha*,
I cannot tell:
But I am faint, my Gashes cry for helpe.

KING
So well thy words become thee, as thy wounds,
They smack of Honor both: Goe get him Surgeons.
                              Exit Captaine with attendants

Enter Rosse and Angus
Who comes here?

MALCOLME   The worthy *Thane* of Rosse.

LENOX
What haste lookes through his eyes? So should he
looke,
That seemes to speake things strange.

ROSSE   God saue the King.

KING
Whence cam'st thou, worthy *Thane*?

ROSSE   From Fiffe, great King,
Where the Norweyan Banners flowt the Skie,   60
And fanne our people cold.
Norway himselfe, with terrible numbers,
Assisted by that most disloyall Traytor,
The *Thane* of Cawdor, began a dismall Conflict,
Till that *Bellona's* Bridegroome, lapt in proofe,
Confronted him with selfe-comparisons,
Point against Point, rebellious Arme 'gainst Arme,
Curbing his lauish spirit: and to conclude,
The Victorie fell on vs.

KING   Great happinesse.

ROSSE   That now
Sweno, the Norwayes King, craues composition: 70
Nor would we deigne him buriall of his men,
Till he disbursed, at Saint *Colmes* ynch,
Ten thousand Dollars, to our generall vse.

KING

No more that *Thane* of Cawdor shall deceiue
Our Bosome interest: Goe pronounce his present
    death,
And with his former Title greet *Macbeth*.

ROSSE Ile see it done.

KING

What he hath lost, Noble *Macbeth* hath wonne.

                                Exeunt seuerally

1.3   *Thunder. Enter the three Witches*
(Sc. 3) 1. WITCH
                Where hast thou beene, Sister?

2. WITCH
                Killing Swine.

80 3. WITCH   Sister, where thou?

1. WITCH

A Saylors Wife had Chestnuts in her Lappe,
And mouncht, & mouncht, and mouncht: Giue me,
    quoth I.
Aroynt thee, Witch, the rumpe-fed Ronyon cryes.
Her Husband's to Aleppo gone, Master o'th' *Tiger*:
    But in a Syue Ile thither sayle,
    And like a Rat without a tayle,
    Ile doe, Ile doe, and Ile doe.

2. WITCH
                Ile giue thee a Winde.

1. WITCH
                Th'art kinde.

3. WITCH

90 And I another.

1. WITCH

I my selfe haue all the other,
And the very Ports they blow,
All the Quarters that they know,
I'th' Ship-mans Card.
Ile dreyne him drie as Hay:
Sleepe shall neyther Night nor Day
Hang vpon his Pent-house Lid:
He shall liue a man forbid:
Wearie Seu'nights, nine times nine,
100 Shall he dwindle, peake, and pine:
Though his Barke cannot be lost,
Yet it shall be Tempest-tost.
Looke what I haue.

2. WITCH   Shew me, shew me.

1. WITCH

Here I haue a Pilots Thumbe,
Wrackt, as homeward he did come.
                Drum within

3. WITCH

A Drumme, a Drumme:
Macbeth doth come.

ALL (*dancing in a ring*)

The weyward Sisters, hand in hand,
Posters of the Sea and Land,
110 Thus doe goe, about, about,

Thrice to thine, and thrice to mine,
And thrice againe, to make vp nine.
Peace, the Charme's wound vp.
                Enter Macbeth and Banquo

MACBETH

So foule and faire a day I haue not seene.

BANQUO

How farre is't call'd to Foris? What are these,
So wither'd, and so wilde in their attyre,
That looke not like th'Inhabitants o'th'Earth,
And yet are on't? Liue you, or are you aught
That man may question? you seeme to vnderstand me,
By each at once her choppie finger laying   120
Vpon her skinnie Lips: you should be Women,
And yet your Beards forbid me to interprete
That you are so.

MACBETH (*to the Witches*)

                Speake if you can: what are you?

1. WITCH

All haile *Macbeth*, haile to thee *Thane* of Glamis.

2. WITCH

All haile *Macbeth*, haile to thee *Thane* of Cawdor.

3. WITCH

All haile *Macbeth*, that shalt be King hereafter.

BANQUO

Good Sir, why doe you start, and seeme to feare
Things that doe sound so faire? (*to the Witches*) i'th'
    name of truth
Are ye fantasticall, or that indeed
Which outwardly ye shew? My Noble Partner   130
You greet with present Grace, and great prediction
Of Noble hauing, and of Royall hope,
That he seemes wrapt withall: to me you speake not.
If you can looke into the Seedes of Time,
And say, which Graine will grow, and which will not,
Speake then to me, who neyther begge, nor feare
Your fauors, nor your hate.

1. WITCH Hayle.

2. WITCH Hayle.

3. WITCH Hayle.   140

1. WITCH

Lesser then *Macbeth*, and greater.

2. WITCH

Not so happy, yet much happyer.

3. WITCH

Thou shalt get Kings, though thou be none:
So all haile *Macbeth*, and *Banquo*.

1. WITCH

Banquo, and *Macbeth*, all haile.

MACBETH

Stay you imperfect Speakers, tell me more:
By *Sinells* death, I know I am *Thane* of Glamis,
But how, of Cawdor? the *Thane* of Cawdor liues
A prosperous Gentleman: And to be King,
Stands not within the prospect of beleefe,   150
No more then to be Cawdor. Say from whence
You owe this strange Intelligence, or why

Vpon this blasted Heath you stop our way
With such Prophetique greeting? Speake, I charge you.
    Witches vanish

BANQUO
The Earth hath bubbles, as the Water ha's,
And these are of them: whither are they vanish'd?

MACBETH
Into the Ayre: and what seem'd corporall,
Melted, as breath into the Winde. Would they had
    stay'd.

BANQUO
Were such things here, as we doe speake about?
160 Or haue we eaten on the insane Root,
That takes the Reason Prisoner?

MACBETH
Your Children shall be Kings.

BANQUO   You shall be King.

MACBETH
And *Thane* of Cawdor too: went it not so?

BANQUO
Toth' selfe-same tune, and words: who's here?
    Enter Rosse and Angus

ROSSE
The King hath happily receiu'd, *Macbeth*,
The newes of thy successe: and when he reades
Thy personall Venture in the Rebels sight,
His Wonders and his Prayses doe contend,
Which should be thine, or his: silenc'd with that,
170 In viewing o're the rest o'th'selfe-same day,
He findes thee in the stout Norweyan Rankes,
Nothing afeard of what thy selfe didst make,
Strange Images of death, as thick as haile
Came post with post, and euery one did beare
Thy prayses in his Kingdomes great defence,
And powr'd them downe before him.

ANGUS (*to Macbeth*)   Wee are sent,
To giue thee from our Royall Master thanks,
Onely to harrold thee into his sight,
Not pay thee.

ROSSE
180 And for an earnest of a greater Honor,
He bad me, from him, call thee *Thane* of Cawdor:
In which addition, haile most worthy *Thane*,
For it is thine.

BANQUO   What, can the Deuill speake true?

MACBETH
The *Thane* of Cawdor liues: why doe you dresse me
In borrowed Robes?

ANGUS   Who was the *Thane*, liues yet,
But vnder heauie Iudgement beares that Life,
Which he deserues to loose. Whether he was
    combin'd
With those of Norway, or did lyne the Rebell
With hidden helpe, and vantage; or that with both
190 He labour'd in his Countreyes wracke, I know not:
But Treasons Capitall, confess'd, and prou'd,
Haue ouerthrowne him.

MACBETH (*aside*)   Glamys, and *Thane* of Cawdor:

The greatest is behinde. (*To Rosse and Angus*) Thankes
    for your paines.
(*To Banquo*) Doe you not hope your Children shall be
    Kings,
When those that gaue the *Thane* of Cawdor to me,
Promis'd no lesse to them.

BANQUO   That trusted home,
Might yet enkindle you vnto the Crowne,
Besides the *Thane* of Cawdor. But 'tis strange:
And oftentimes, to winne vs to our harme,
The Instruments of Darknesse tell vs Truths,   200
Winne vs with honest Trifles, to betray's
In deepest consequence.
(*To Rosse and Angus*) Cousins, a word, I pray you.

MACBETH (*aside*) Two Truths are told,
As happy Prologues to the swelling Act
Of the Imperiall Theame. (*To Rosse and Angus*) I
    thanke you Gentlemen:
(*Aside*) This supernaturall solliciting
Cannot be ill; cannot be good. If ill?
Why hath it giuen me earnest of successe,
Commencing in a Truth? I am *Thane* of Cawdor.   210
If good? why doe I yeeld to that suggestion,
Whose horrid Image doth vnfixe my Heire,
And make my seated Heart knock at my Ribbes,
Against the vse of Nature? Present Feares
Are lesse then horrible Imaginings:
My Thought, whose Murther yet is but fantasticall,
Shakes so my single state of Man, that Function
Is smother'd in surmise, and nothing is,
But what is not.

BANQUO (*to Rosse and Angus*)
          Looke how our Partner's rapt.

MACBETH (*aside*)
If Chance will haue me King, why Chance may
    Crowne me,   220
Without my stirre.

BANQUO (*to Rosse and Angus*)
          New Honors come vpon him
Like our strange Garments, cleaue not to their mould,
But with the aid of vse.

MACBETH (*aside*)   Come what come may,
Time, and the Houre, runs through the roughest Day.

BANQUO
Worthy *Macbeth*, wee stay vpon your leysure.

MACBETH
Giue me your fauour: my dull Braine was wrought
With things forgotten. (*To Rosse and Angus*) Kinde
    Gentlemen, your paines
Are registred, where euery day I turne
The Leafe, to reade them. Let vs toward the King:
(*Aside to Banquo*) Thinke vpon what hath chanc'd:
    and at more time,   230
The *Interim* hauing weigh'd it, let vs speake
Our free Hearts each to other.

BANQUO Very gladly.

MACBETH Till then enough: (*to Rosse and Angus*) come
    friends.   *Exeunt*

1.4
(Sc. 4)   *Flourish. Enter King, Lenox, Malcolme, Donalbaine,*
              and Attendants

KING
    Is execution done on *Cawdor*? Are not
    Those in Commission yet return'd?

MALCOLME   My Liege,
    They are not yet come back. But I haue spoke
    With one that saw him die: who did report,
    That very frankly hee confess'd his Treasons,
240 Implor'd your Highnesse Pardon, and set forth
    A deepe Repentance: nothing in his Life
    Became him, like the leauing it. Hee dy'de,
    As one that had beene studied in his death,
    To throw away the dearest thing he ow'd,
    As 'twere a carelesse Trifle.

KING   There's no Art,
    To finde the Mindes construction in the Face:
    He was a Gentleman, on whom I built
    An absolute Trust.

         Enter Macbeth, Banquo, Rosse, and Angus
    (*To Macbeth*)   O worthyest Cousin,
    The sinne of my Ingratitude euen now
250 Was heauie on me. Thou art so farre before,
    That swiftest Wing of Recompence is slow,
    To ouertake thee. Would thou hadst lesse deseru'd,
    That the proportion both of thanks, and payment,
    Might haue beene mine: onely I haue left to say,
    More is thy due, then more then all can pay.

MACBETH
    The seruice, and the loyaltie I owe,
    In doing it, payes it selfe. Your Highnesse part,
    Is to receiue our Duties: and our Duties
    Are to your Throne, and State, children, and Seruants;
260 Which doe but what they should, by doing euery thing
    Safe toward your Loue and Honor.

KING   Welcome hither:
    I haue begun to plant thee, and will labour
    To make thee full of growing. Noble *Banquo*,
    That hast no lesse deseru'd, nor must be knowne
    No lesse to haue done so: Let me enfold thee,
    And hold thee to my Heart.

BANQUO   There if I grow,
    The Haruest is your owne.

KING   My plenteous Ioyes,
    Wanton in fulnesse, seeke to hide themselues
270 In drops of sorrow. Sonnes, Kinsmen, *Thanes*,
    And you whose places are the nearest, know,
    We will establish our Estate vpon
    Our eldest, *Malcolme*, whom we name hereafter,
    The Prince of Cumberland: which Honor must
    Not vnaccompanied, inuest him onely,
    But signes of Noblenesse, like Starres, shall shine
    On all deseruers. (*To Macbeth*) From hence to Envernes,
    And binde vs further to you.

MACBETH
    The Rest is Labor, which is not vs'd for you:
280 Ile be my selfe the Herbenger, and make ioyfull

The hearing of my Wife, with your approach:
So humbly take my leaue.

KING   My worthy *Cawdor*.

MACBETH (*aside*)
    The Prince of Cumberland: that is a step,
    On which I must fall downe, or else o're-leape,
    For in my way it lyes. Starres hide your fires,
    Let not Light see my black and deepe desires:
    The Eye winke at the Hand; yet let that bee,
    Which the Eye feares, when it is done to see.   *Exit*

KING
    True, worthy *Banquo*: he is full so valiant,
    And in his commendations, I am fed: 290
    It is a Banquet to me. Let's after him,
    Whose care is gone before, to bid vs welcome:
    It is a peerelesse Kinsman.   *Flourish. Exeunt*

         Enter Macbeths Wife alone with a Letter   **1.5**
LADY *They met me in the day of successe: and I haue learn'd* **(Sc. 5)**
    by the perfect'st report, they haue more in them, then
    mortall knowledge. When I burnt in desire to question them
    further, they made themselues Ayre, into which they
    vanish'd. Whiles I stood rapt in the wonder of it, came
    Missiues from the King, who all-hail'd me Thane of
    Cawdor, by which Title before, these weyward Sisters   300
    saluted me, and referr'd me to the comming on of time,
    with haile King that shalt be. This haue I thought good to
    deliuer thee (my dearest Partner of Greatnesse) that thou
    might'st not loose the dues of reioycing by being ignorant
    of what Greatnesse is promis'd thee. Lay it to thy heart,
    and farewell.
    Glamys thou art, and Cawdor, and shalt be
    What thou art promis'd: yet doe I feare thy Nature,
    It is too full o'th' Milke of humane kindnesse,
    To catch the neerest way. Thou would'st be great,   310
    Art not without Ambition, but without
    The illnesse should attend it. What thou would'st highly,
    That would'st thou holily: would'st not play false,
    And yet would'st wrongly winne. Thould'st haue,
         great Glamys,
    That which cryes, thus thou must doe, if thou haue it;
    And that which rather thou do'st feare to doe,
    Then wishest should be vndone. High thee hither,
    That I may powre my Spirits in thine Eare,
    And chastise with the valour of my Tongue
    All that impeides thee from the Golden Round,   320
    Which Fate and Metaphysicall ayde doth seeme
    To haue thee crown'd withall.

         Enter Seruant

                              What is your tidings?
SERUANT
    The King comes here to Night.
LADY   Thou'rt mad to say it.
    Is not thy Master with him? who, wer't so,
    Would haue inform'd for preparation.
SERUANT
    So please you, it is true: our *Thane* is comming:

One of my fellowes had the speed of him;
Who almost dead for breath, had scarcely more
Then would make vp his Message.

LADY   Giue him tending,
He brings great newes.   Exit Seruant
330   The Rauen himselfe is hoarse,
That croakes the fatall entrance of *Duncan*
Vnder my Battlements. Come you Spirits,
That tend on mortall thoughts, vnsex me here,
And fill me from the Crowne to the Toe, top-full
Of direst Crueltie: make thick my blood,
Stop vp th'accesse, and passage to Remorse,
That no compunctious visitings of Nature
Shake my fell purpose, nor keepe peace betweene
Th'effect, and hit. Come to my Womans Brests,
340 And take my Milke for Gall, you murth'ring Ministers,
Where-euer, in your sightlesse substances,
You wait on Natures Mischiefe. Come thick Night,
And pall thee in the dunnest smoake of Hell,
That my keene Knife see not the Wound it makes,
Nor Heauen peepe through the Blanket of the darke,
To cry, hold, hold.
          Enter Macbeth
               Great Glamys, worthy Cawdor,
Greater then both, by the all-haile hereafter,
Thy Letters haue transported me beyond
This ignorant present, and I feele now
The future in the instant.

350 MACBETH   My dearest Loue,
Duncan comes here to Night.

LADY   And when goes hence?

MACBETH
To morrow, as he purposes.

LADY   O neuer,
Shall Sunne that Morrow see.
Your Face, my *Thane*, is as a Booke, where men
May reade strange matters, to beguile the time,
Looke like the time, beare welcome in your Eye,
Your Hand, your Tongue: looke like the innocent flower,
But be the Serpent vnder't. He that's comming,
Must be prouided for: and you shall put
360 This Nights great Businesse into my dispatch,
Which shall to all our Nights, and Dayes to come,
Giue solely soueraigne sway, and Masterdome.

MACBETH
We will speake further.

LADY   Onely looke vp cleare:
To alter fauor, euer is to feare:
Leaue all the rest to me.   *Exeunt*

1.6   ⌜*Hoboyes, and Torches.*⌝ *Enter King, Malcolme,*
(Sc. 6)   *Donalbaine, Banquo, Lenox, Macduff, Rosse,*
          Angus, and Attendants

KING
This Castle hath a pleasant seat, the ayre
Nimbly and sweetly recommends it selfe
Vnto our gentle sences.

BANQUO   This Guest of Summer,

The Temple-haunting Marlet does approue,
By his lou'd Mansonry, that the Heauens breath   370
Smells wooingly here: no Iutty, frieze,
Buttrice, nor Coigne of Vantage, but this Bird
Hath made his pendant Bed, and procreant Cradle,
Where they most breed, and haunt: I haue obseru'd
The ayre is delicate.
          Enter Lady

KING   See, see, our honor'd Hostesse:
The Loue that followes vs, sometime is our trouble,
Which still we thanke as Loue. Herein I teach you,
How you shall bid God-eyld vs for your paines,
And thanke vs for your trouble.

LADY   All our seruice,
In euery point twice done, and then done double,   380
Were poore, and single Businesse, to contend
Against those Honors deepe, and broad, wherewith
Your Maiestie loades our House: for those of old,
And the late Dignities, heap'd vp to them,
We rest your Ermites.

KING   Where's the Thane of Cawdor?
We courst him at the heeles, and had a purpose
To be his Purueyor: But he rides well,
And his great Loue (sharpe as his Spurre) hath holp
     him
To his home before vs: Faire and Noble Hostesse
We are your guest to night.

LADY   Your Seruants euer,   390
Haue theirs, themselues, and what is theirs in compt,
To make their Audit at your Highnesse pleasure,
Still to returne your owne.

KING   Giue me your hand:
Conduct me to mine Host we loue him highly,
And shall continue, our Graces towards him.
By your leaue Hostesse.   *Exeunt*

          Ho-boyes. Torches. Enter a Sewer, and diuers   1.7
          Seruants with Dishes and Seruice ouer the Stage.   (Sc. 7)
          Then enter Macbeth

MACBETH
If it were done, when 'tis done, then 'twer well,
It were done quickly: If th'Assassination
Could trammell vp the Consequence, and catch
With his surcease, Successe: that but this blow   400
Might be the be all, and the end all, heere,
But heere, vpon this Banke and Schoole of time,
Wee'ld iumpe the life to come. But in these Cases,
We still haue iudgement heere, that we but teach
Bloody Instructions, which being taught, returne
To plague th'Inuenter. This euen-handed Iustice
Commends th'Ingredience of our poyson'd Challice
To our owne lips. Hee's heere in double trust;
First, as I am his Kinsman, and his Subiect,
Strong both against the Deed: Then, as his Host,   410
Who should against his Murtherer shut the doore,
Not beare the knife my selfe. Besides, this *Duncane*
Hath borne his Faculties so meeke; hath bin
So cleere in his great Office, that his Vertues

Will pleade like Angels, Trumpet-tongu'd against
The deepe damnation of his taking off:
And Pitty, like a naked New-borne-Babe,
Striding the blast, or Heauens Cherubin, hors'd
Vpon the sightlesse Curriors of the Ayre,
420 Shall blow the horrid deed in euery eye,
That teares shall drowne the winde. I haue no Spurre
To pricke the sides of my intent, but onely
Vaulting Ambition, which ore-leapes it selfe,
And falles on th'other.
      Enter Lady
                   How now? What Newes?
LADY
    He has almost supt: why haue you left the chamber?
MACBETH
    Hath he ask'd for me?
LADY
                Know you not, he ha's?
MACBETH
    We will proceed no further in this Businesse:
He hath Honour'd me of late, and I haue bought
Golden Opinions from all sorts of people,
430 Which would be worne now in their newest glosse,
Not cast aside so soone.
LADY
                 Was the hope drunke,
Wherein you drest your selfe? Hath it slept since?
And wakes it now to looke so greene, and pale,
At what it did so freely? From this time,
Such I account thy loue. Art thou affear'd
To be the same in thine owne Act, and Valour,
As thou art in desire? Would'st thou haue that
Which thou esteem'st the Ornament of Life,
And liue a Coward in thine owne Esteeme?
440 Letting I dare not, wait vpon I would,
Like the poore Cat i'th'Addage.
MACBETH
              Prythee peace:
I dare do all that may become a man,
Who dares do more, is none.
LADY
             What Beast was't then
That made you breake this enterprize to me?
When you durst do it, then you were a man:
And to be more then what you were, you would
Be so much more the man. Nor time, nor place
Did then adhere, and yet you would make both:
They haue made themselues, and that their fitnesse now
450 Do's vnmake you. I haue giuen Sucke, and know
How tender 'tis to loue the Babe that milkes me,
I would, while it was smyling in my Face,
Haue pluckt my Nipple from his Bonelesse Gummes,
And dasht the Braines out, had I so sworne
As you haue done to this.
MACBETH
           If we should faile?
LADY
                   We faile?
But screw your courage to the sticking place,
And wee'le not fayle: when *Duncan* is asleepe,
(Whereto the rather shall his dayes hard Iourney
Soundly inuite him) his two Chamberlaines
460 Will I with Wine, and Wassell, so conuince,
That Memorie, the Warder of the Braine,

Shall be a Fume, and the Receit of Reason
A Lymbeck onely: when in Swinish sleepe,
Their drenched Natures lyes as in a Death,
What cannot you and I performe vpon
Th'vnguarded *Duncan*? What not put vpon
His spungie Officers? who shall beare the guilt
Of our great quell.
MACBETH
             Bring forth Men-Children onely:
For thy vndaunted Mettle should compose
Nothing but Males. Will it not be receiu'd,   470
When we haue mark'd with blood those sleepie two
Of his owne Chamber, and vs'd their very Daggers,
That they haue don't?
LADY
                Who dares receiue it other,
As we shall make our Griefes and Clamor rore,
Vpon his Death?
MACBETH
           I am settled, and bend vp
Each corporall Agent to this terrible Feat.
Away, and mock the time with fairest show,
False Face must hide what the false Heart doth know.
                            Exeunt

                        ✹

  Enter Banquo, and Fleance, with a Torch before him   **2.1**
BANQUO How goes the Night, Boy?   **(Sc. 8)**
FLEANCE
    The Moone is downe: I haue not heard the Clock.   480
BANQUO
    And she goes downe at Twelue.
FLEANCE
                 I take't, 'tis later, Sir.
BANQUO (*giuing Fleance his Sword*)
    Hold, take my Sword: there's Husbandry in Heauen,
Their Candles are all out: take thee that too.
A heauie Summons lyes like Lead vpon me,
And yet I would not sleepe: mercifull Powers,
Restraine in me the cursed thoughts that Nature
Giues way to in repose.
      Enter Macbeth, and a Seruant with a Torch
               Giue me my Sword: who's there?
MACBETH A Friend.
BANQUO
    What Sir, not yet at rest? the King's a bed.
He hath beene in vnusuall Pleasure, and   490
Sent forth great Largesse to your Offices.
This Diamond he greetes your Wife withall,
By the name of most kind Hostesse, and shut vp
In measurelesse content.
MACBETH
              Being vnprepar'd,
Our will became the seruant to defect,
Which else should free haue wrought.
BANQUO
                 All's well.
I dreamt last Night of the three weyward Sisters:
To you they haue shew'd some truth.
MACBETH
              I thinke not of them:
Yet when we can entreat an houre to serue,
We would spend it in some words vpon that Businesse,   500
If you would graunt the time.
BANQUO
             At your kind'st leysure.

MACBETH
  If you shall cleaue to my consent, when 'tis,
  It shall make Honor for you.

BANQUO   So I lose none,
  In seeking to augment it, but still keepe
  My Bosome franchis'd, and Allegeance cleare,
  I shall be counsail'd.

MACBETH Good repose the while.

BANQUO Thankes Sir: the like to you.
                              Exeunt Banquo and Fleance

MACBETH (*to Seruant*)
  Goe bid thy Mistresse, when my drinke is ready,
510 She strike vpon the Bell. Get thee to bed.   *Exit Seruant*
  Is this a Dagger, which I see before me,
  The Handle toward my Hand? Come, let me clutch thee:
  I haue thee not, and yet I see thee still.
  Art thou not fatall Vision, sensible
  To feeling, as to sight? or art thou but
  A Dagger of the Minde, a false Creation,
  Proceeding from the heat-oppressed Braine?
  I see thee yet, in forme as palpable,
  As this which now I draw.
520 Thou marshall'st me the way that I was going,
  And such an Instrument I was to vse.
  Mine Eyes are made the fooles o'th'other Sences,
  Or else worth all the rest: I see thee still;
  And on thy Blade, and Dudgeon, Gouts of Blood,
  Which was not so before. There's no such thing:
  It is the bloody Businesse, which informes
  Thus to mine Eyes. Now o're the one halfe World
  Nature seemes dead, and wicked Dreames abuse
  The Curtain'd sleepe: Witchcraft celebrates
530 Pale *Heccats* Offerings: and wither'd Murther,
  Alarum'd by his Centinell, the Wolfe,
  Whose howle's his Watch, thus with his stealthy pace,
  With *Tarquins* rauishing strides, towards his designe
  Moues like a Ghost. Thou sure and firme-set Earth
  Heare not my steps, which way they walke, for feare
  Thy very stones prate of my where-about,
  And take the present horror from the time,
  Which now sutes with it. Whiles I threat, he liues:
  Words to the heat of deedes too cold breath giues.
                              A Bell rings
540 I goe, and it is done: the Bell inuites me.
  Heare it not, *Duncan*, for it is a Knell,
  That summons thee to Heauen, or to Hell.   *Exit*

2.2   *Enter Lady*
(Sc. 9) LADY
  That which hath made thẽ drunk, hath made me bold:
  What hath quench'd them, hath giuen me fire.
      Hearke, peace:
  It was the Owle that shriek'd, the fatall Bell-man,
  Which giues the stern'st good-night. He is about it,
  The Doores are open: And the surfeted Groomes
  Doe mock their charge with Snores. I haue drugg'd
      their Possets,

That Death and Nature doe contend about them,
Whether they liue, or dye.
    Enter Macbeth ⌈aboue⌉
MACBETH   Who's there? what hoa?   550
                                                Exit

LADY
  Alack, I am afraid they haue awak'd,
  And 'tis not done: th'attempt, and not the deed,
  Confounds vs: hearke: I lay'd their Daggers ready,
  He could not misse 'em. Had he not resembled
  My Father as he slept, I had don't.
    ⌈*Enter Macbeth below*⌉
                              My Husband?

MACBETH
  I haue done the deed: Didst thou not heare a noyse?

LADY
  I heard the Owle schreame, and the Crickets cry.
  Did not you speake?

MACBETH   When?

LADY   Now.

MACBETH   As I descended?

LADY
  I.

MACBETH Hearke, who lyes i'th' second Chamber?

LADY
  Donalbaine.

MACBETH (*looking at his hands*) This is a sorry sight.   560

LADY
  A foolish thought, to say a sorry sight.

MACBETH
  There's one did laugh in's sleepe, and one cry'd
      Murther,
  That they did wake each other: I stood, and heard them:
  But they did say their Prayers, and addrest them
  Againe to sleepe.

LADY   There are two lodg'd together.

MACBETH
  One cry'd God blesse vs, and Amen the other,
  As they had seene me with these Hangmans hands:
  Listning their feare, I could not say Amen,
  When they did say God blesse vs.

LADY
  Consider it not so deepely.   570

MACBETH
  But wherefore could not I pronounce Amen?
  I had most need of Blessing, and Amen
  Stuck in my throat.

LADY   These deeds must not be thought
  After these wayes: so, it will make vs mad.

MACBETH
  Me thought I heard a voyce cry, Sleep no more:
  Macbeth does murther Sleepe, the innocent Sleepe,
  Sleepe that knits vp the rauel'd Sleeue of Care,
  The death of each dayes Life, sore Labors Bath,
  Balme of hurt Mindes, great Natures second Course,
  Chiefe nourisher in Life's Feast.

LADY   What doe you meane?   580

MACBETH

Still it cry'd, Sleepe no more to all the House:
Glamis hath murther'd Sleepe, and therefore *Cawdor*
Shall sleepe no more: *Macbeth* shall sleepe no more.

LADY

Who was it, that thus cry'd? why worthy *Thane*,
You doe vnbend your Noble strength, to thinke
So braine-sickly of things: Goe get some Water,
And wash this filthie Witnesse from your Hand.
Why did you bring these Daggers from the place?
They must lye there: goe carry them, and smeare
The sleepie Groomes with blood.

590 MACBETH   Ile goe no more:

I am afraid, to thinke what I haue done:
Looke on't againe, I dare not.

LADY   Infirme of purpose:

Giue me the Daggers: the sleeping, and the dead,
Are but as Pictures: 'tis the Eye of Child-hood,
That feares a painted Deuill. If he doe bleed,
Ile guild the Faces of the Groomes withall,
For it must seeme their Guilt.   *Exit*

Knocke within

MACBETH   Whence is that knocking?

How is't with me, when euery noyse appalls me?
What Hands are here? hah: they pluck out mine Eyes.
600 Will all great *Neptunes* Ocean wash this blood
Cleane from my Hand? no: this my Hand will rather
The multitudinous Seas incarnardine,
Making the Greene one, Red.

Enter Lady

LADY

My Hands are of your colour: but I shame
To weare a Heart so white.

Knocke

                                I heare a knocking

At the South entry: retyre we to our Chamber:
A little Water cleares vs of this deed.
How easie is it then? your Constancie
Hath left you vnattended.

Knocke

                                Hearke, more knocking.

610 Get on your Night-Gowne, least occasion call vs,
And shew vs to be Watchers: be not lost
So poorely in your thoughts.

MACBETH

To know my deed, 'twere best not know my selfe.

Knocke

Wake *Duncan* with thy knocking: I would thou
could'st.   *Exeunt*

2.3   *Enter a Porter. Knocking within*
(Sc. 10) PORTER Here's a knocking indeede: if a man were Porter
        of Hell Gate, hee should haue old turning the Key.

Knock

Knock, Knock, Knock. Who's there i'th' name of
Belzebub? Here's a Farmer, that hang'd himselfe on
th'expectation of Plentie: Come in time, haue Napkins
620 enow about you, here you'le sweat for't.

Knock

Knock, knock. Who's there in th'other Deuils Name?
Faith here's an Equiuocator, that could sweare in both
the Scales against eyther Scale, who committed Treason
enough for Gods sake, yet could not equiuocate to
Heauen: oh come in, Equiuocator.

Knock

Knock, Knock, Knock. Who's there? 'Faith here's an
English Taylor come hither, for stealing out of a French
Hose: Come in Taylor, here you may rost your Goose.

Knock

Knock, Knock. Neuer at quiet: What are you? but this
place is too cold for Hell. Ile Deuill-Porter it no further: 630
I had thought to haue let in some of all Professions,
that goe the Primrose way to th'euerlasting Bonfire.

Knock

Anon, anon,

He opens the gate

I pray you remember the Porter.

Enter Macduff, and Lenox

MACDUFFE

Was it so late, friend, ere you went to Bed,
That you doe lye so late?

PORTER Faith Sir, we were carowsing till the second Cock:
And Drinke, Sir, is a great prouoker of three things.

MACDUFFE What three things does Drinke especially
prouoke?   640

PORTER Marry, Sir, Nose-painting, Sleepe, and Vrine.
Lecherie, Sir, it prouokes, and vnprouokes: it prouokes
the desire, but it takes away the performance. Therefore
much Drinke may be said to be an Equiuocator with
Lecherie: it makes him, and it marres him; it sets him
on, and it takes him off; it perswades him, and dis-
heartens him; makes him stand too, and not stand too:
in conclusion, equiuocates him in a sleepe, and giuing
him the Lye, leaues him.

MACDUFFE I beleeue, Drinke gaue thee the Lye last Night. 650

PORTER That it did, Sir, i'the very Throat on me: but I
requited him for his Lye, and (I thinke) being too strong
for him, though he tooke vp my Legges sometime, yet
I made a Shift to cast him.

MACDUFFE Is thy Master stirring?

Enter Macbeth

Our knocking ha's awak'd him: here he comes.

⌈Exit Porter⌉

LENOX (*to Macbeth*)
Good morrow, Noble Sir.

MACBETH   Good morrow both.

MACDUFFE

Is the King stirring, worthy *Thane*?

MACBETH   Not yet.

MACDUFFE

He did command me to call timely on him,
I haue almost slipt the houre.

MACBETH   Ile bring you to him. 660

MACDUFFE

I know this is a ioyfull trouble to you:
But yet 'tis one.

MACBETH

   The labour we delight in, Physicks paine:
   This is the Doore.

MACDUFFE   Ile make so bold to call,
   For 'tis my limitted seruice.   *Exit Macduffe*

LENOX

   Goes the King hence to day?

MACBETH   He does: he did appoint so.

LENOX

   The Night ha's been vnruly: where we lay,
   Our Chimneys were blowne downe, and (as they say)
   Lamentings heard i'th'Ayre; strange Schreemes of Death,
670   And Prophecying, with Accents terrible,
   Of dyre Combustion, and confus'd Euents,
   New hatch'd toth' wofull time. The obscure Bird
   Clamor'd the liue-long Night. Some say, the Earth
   Was Feuorous, and did shake.

MACBETH   'Twas a rough Night.

LENOX

   My young remembrance cannot paralell
   A fellow to it.

      Enter Macduff

MACDUFFE   O horror, horror, horror,
   Tongue nor Heart cannot conceiue, nor name thee.

MACBETH *and* LENOX What's the matter?

MACDUFFE

   Confusion now hath made his Master-peece:
680   Most sacrilegious Murther hath broke ope
   The Lords anoynted Temple, and stole thence
   The Life o'th' Building.

MACBETH What is't you say, the Life?

LENOX Meane you his Maiestie?

MACDUFFE

   Approch the Chamber, and destroy your sight
   With a new *Gorgon*. Doe not bid me speake:
   See, and then speake your selues:

                 Exeunt Macbeth and Lenox
                 awake, awake,
   Ring the Alarum Bell: Murther, and Treason,
   Banquo, and *Donalbaine*: *Malcolme* awake,
690   Shake off this Downey sleepe, Deaths counterfeit,
   And looke on Death it selfe: vp, vp, and see
   The great Doomes Image: *Malcolme, Banquo*,
   As from your Graues rise vp, and walke like Sprights,
   To countenance this horror.

      Bell rings. Enter Lady

LADY   What's the Businesse?
   That such a hideous Trumpet calls to parley
   The sleepers of the House? speake, speake.

MACDUFFE   O gentle Lady,
   'Tis not for you to heare what I can speake:
   The repetition in a Womans eare,
   Would murther as it fell.

      Enter Banquo

          O *Banquo, Banquo*,
   Our Royall Master's murther'd.

700 LADY   Woe, alas:
   What, in our House?

BANQUO   Too cruell, any where.

Deare *Duff*, I prythee contradict thy selfe,
And say, it is not so.

      Enter Macbeth, Lenox, ⌈and Rosse⌉

MACBETH

   Had I but dy'd an houre before this chance,
   I had liu'd a blessed time: for from this instant,
   There's nothing serious in Mortalitie:
   All is but Toyes: Renowne and Grace is dead,
   The Wine of Life is drawne, and the meere Lees
   Is left this Vault, to brag of.

      Enter Malcolme and Donalbaine

DONALBAINE What is amisse?   710

MACBETH You are, and doe not know't:
   The Spring, the Head, the Fountaine of your Blood
   Is stopt, the very Source of it is stopt.

MACDUFFE

   Your Royall Father's murther'd.

MALCOLME   Oh, by whom?

LENOX

   Those of his Chamber, as it seem'd, had don't:
   Their Hands and Faces were all badg'd with blood,
   So were their Daggers, which vnwip'd, we found
   Vpon their Pillowes: they star'd, and were distracted,
   No mans Life was to be trusted with them.

MACBETH

   O, yet I doe repent me of my furie,   720
   That I did kill them.

MACDUFFE   Wherefore did you so?

MACBETH

   Who can be wise, amaz'd, temp'rate, & furious,
   Loyall, and Neutrall, in a moment? No man:
   Th'expedition of my violent Loue
   Out-ran the pawser, Reason. Here lay *Duncan*,
   His Siluer skinne, lac'd with his Golden Blood,
   And his gash'd Stabs, look'd like a Breach in Nature,
   For Ruines wastfull entrance: there the Murtherers,
   Steep'd in the Colours of their Trade; their Daggers
   Vnmannerly breech'd with gore: who could refraine, 730
   That had a heart to loue; and in that heart,
   Courage, to make's loue knowne?

LADY   Helpe me hence, hoa.

MACDUFFE

   Looke to the Lady.

MALCOLME *(aside to Donalbaine)*
         Why doe we hold our tongues,
   That most may clayme this argument for ours?

DONALBAINE *(aside to Malcolme)*
   What should be spoken here, where our Fate
   Hid in an augure hole, may rush, and seize vs?
   Let's away, our Teares are not yet brew'd.

MALCOLME *(aside to Donalbaine)*   Nor our strong Sorrow
   Vpon the foot of Motion.

BANQUO   Looke to the Lady:
               Exit Lady, attended
   And when we haue our naked Frailties hid,
   That suffer in exposure; let vs meet,   740
   And question this most bloody piece of worke,
   To know it further. Feares and scruples shake vs:
   In the great Hand of God I stand, and thence,

Against the vndivulg'd pretence, I fight
Of Treasonous Mallice.

MACDUFFE   And so doe I.

ALL   So all.

MACBETH
Let's briefely put on manly readinesse,
And meet i'th' Hall together.

ALL   Well contented.

Exeunt all but Malcolme and Donalbaine

MALCOLME
What will you doe? Let's not consort with them:
To shew an vnfelt Sorrow, is an Office
750 Which the false man do's easie. Ile to England.

DONALBAINE
To Ireland, I: our seperated fortune
Shall keepe vs both the safer: where we are,
There's Daggers in mens Smiles; the neere in blood,
The neerer bloody.

MALCOLME   This murtherous Shaft that's shot,
Hath not yet lighted: and our safest way,
Is to auoid the ayme. Therefore to Horse,
And let vs not be daintie of leaue-taking,
But shift away: there's warrant in that Theft,
Which steales it selfe, when there's no mercie left.

Exeunt

2.4   *Enter Rosse, with an Old man*
(Sc. 11) OLD MAN
760 Threescore and ten I can remember well,
Within the Volume of which Time, I haue seene
Houres dreadfull, and things strange: but this sore Night
Hath trifled former knowings.

ROSSE   Ha, good Father,
Thou seest the Heauens, as troubled with mans Act,
Threatens his bloody Stage: byth' Clock 'tis Day,
And yet darke Night strangles the trauailing Lampe:
Is't Nights predominance, or the Dayes shame,
That Darknesse does the face of Earth intombe,
When liuing Light should kisse it?

OLD MAN   'Tis vnnaturall,
770 Euen like the deed that's done: On Tuesday last,
A Faulcon towring in her pride of place,
Was by a Mowsing Owle hawkt at, and kill'd.

ROSSE
And *Duncans* Horses, (a thing most strange, and
      certaine)
Beauteous, and swift, the Minions of their Race,
Turn'd wilde in nature, broke their stalls, flong out,
Contending 'gainst Obedience, as they would
Make Warre with Mankinde.

OLD MAN   'Tis said, they eate each other.

ROSSE
They did so: to th'amazement of mine eyes
That look'd vpon't.

Enter Macduffe

                Heere comes the good *Macduffe*.
How goes the world Sir, now?

780 MACDUFFE   Why see you not?

ROSSE
Is't known who did this more then bloody deed?

MACDUFFE
Those that *Macbeth* hath slaine.

ROSSE   Alas the day,
What good could they pretend?

MACDUFFE   They were subborned,
Malcolme, and *Donalbaine* the Kings two Sonnes
Are stolne away and fled, which puts vpon them
Suspition of the deed.

ROSSE   'Gainst Nature still,
Thriftlesse Ambition, that will rauen vp
Thine owne liues meanes: Then 'tis most like,
The Soueraignty will fall vpon *Macbeth*.

MACDUFFE
He is already nam'd, and gone to Scone   790
To be inuested.

ROSSE Where is *Duncans* body?

MACDUFFE Carried to Colmekill,
The Sacred Store-house of his Predecessors,
And Guardian of their Bones.

ROSSE   Will you to Scone?

MACDUFFE
No Cosin, Ile to Fife.

ROSSE   Well, I will thither.

MACDUFFE
Well, may you see things wel done there: Adieu
Least our old Robes sit easier then our new.

ROSSE Farewell, Father.

OLD MAN
Gods benyson go with you, and with those   800
That would make good of bad, and Friends of Foes.

Exeunt omnes, seuerally

◈

Enter Banquo   **3.1**
BANQUO   (Sc. 12)
Thou hast it now, King, Cawdor, Glamis, all,
As the weyard Women promis'd, and I feare
Thou playd'st most fowly for't: yet it was saide
It should not stand in thy Posterity,
But that my selfe should be the Roote, and Father
Of many Kings. If there come truth from them,
As vpon thee *Macbeth*, their Speeches shine,
Why by the verities on thee made good,
May they not be my Oracles as well,   810
And set me vp in hope. But hush, no more.

Senit sounded. Enter Macbeth as King, Lady as
Queene, Lenox, Rosse, Lords, and Attendants

MACBETH
Heere's our chiefe Guest.

LADY   If he had beene forgotten,
It had bene as a gap in our great Feast,
And all-thing vnbecomming.

MACBETH
To night we hold a solemne Supper sir,
And Ile request your presence.

BANQUO   Let your Highnesse

Command vpon me, to the which my duties
Are with a most indissoluble tye
For euer knit.

820 MACBETH Ride you this afternoone?

BANQUO I, my good Lord.

MACBETH

We should haue else desir'd your good aduice
(Which still hath been both graue, and prosperous)
In this dayes Councell: but wee'le talke to morrow.
Is't farre you ride?

BANQUO

As farre, my Lord, as will fill vp the time
'Twixt this, and Supper. Goe not my Horse the better,
I must become a borrower of the Night,
For a darke houre, or twaine.

830 MACBETH Faile not our Feast.

BANQUO My Lord, I will not.

MACBETH

We heare our bloody Cozens are bestow'd
In England, and in Ireland, not confessing
Their cruell Parricide, filling their hearers
With strange inuention. But of that to morrow,
When therewithall, we shall haue cause of State,
Crauing vs ioyntly. Hye you to Horse: adieu,
Till you returne at Night. Goes *Fleance* with you?

BANQUO

I, my good Lord: our time does call vpon's.

MACBETH

840 I wish your Horses swift, and sure of foot:
And so I doe commend you to their backs.
Farwell.   *Exit Banquo*
Let euery man be master of his time,
Till seuen at Night, to make societie
The sweeter welcome: we will keepe our selfe
Till Supper time alone: while then, God be with you.
            Exeunt all but Macbeth and a Seruant
Sirrha, a word with you: Attend those men
Our pleasure?

SERUANT

They are, my Lord, without the Pallace Gate.

MACBETH

Bring them before vs.   *Exit Seruant*
850   To be thus, is nothing,
But to be safely thus: our feares in *Banquo*
Sticke deepe, and in his Royaltie of Nature
Reignes that which would be fear'd. 'Tis much he dares,
And to that dauntlesse temper of his Minde,
He hath a Wisdome, that doth guide his Valour,
To act in safetie. There is none but he,
Whose being I doe feare: and vnder him,
My *Genius* is rebuk'd, as it is said
Mark Anthonies was by *Cæsar*. He chid the Sisters,
860 When first they put the Name of King vpon me,
And bad them speake to him. Then Prophet-like,
They hayl'd him Father to a Line of Kings.
Vpon my Head they plac'd a fruitlesse Crowne,
And put a barren Scepter in my Gripe,

Thence to be wrencht with an vnlineall Hand,
No Sonne of mine succeeding: if't be so,
For *Banquo's* Issue haue I fil'd my Minde,
For them, the gracious *Duncan* haue I murther'd,
Put Rancours in the Vessell of my Peace
Onely for them, and mine eternall Iewell   870
Giuen to the common Enemie of Man,
To make them Kings, the Seedes of *Banquo* Kings.
Rather then so, come Fate into the Lyst,
And champion me to th'vtterance. Who's there?
        Enter Seruant, and two Murtherers
(*To Seruant*) Now goe to the Doore, and stay there till
        we call.   *Exit Seruant*
Was it not yesterday we spoke together?

MURTHERERS

It was, so please your Highnesse.

MACBETH   Well then, now
Haue you consider'd of my speeches: know,
That it was he, in the times past, which held you
So vnder fortune, which you thought had been   880
Our innocent selfe. This I made good to you,
In our last conference, past in probation with you:
How you were borne in hand, how crost: the
        Instruments:
Who wrought with them: and all things else, that might
To halfe a Soule, and to a Notion craz'd,
Say, Thus did *Banquo*.

I. MURTHERER   You made it knowne to vs.

MACBETH

I did so: and went further, which is now
Our point of second meeting. Doe you finde
Your patience so predominant, in your nature,
That you can let this goe? Are you so Gospell'd,   890
To pray for this good man, and for his Issue,
Whose heauie hand hath bow'd you to the Graue,
And begger'd yours for euer?

I. MURTHERER   We are men, my Liege.

MACBETH

I, in the Catalogue ye goe for men,
As Hounds, and Greyhounds, Mungrels, Spaniels,
        Curres,
Showghes, Water-Rugs, and Demy-Wolues are clipt
All by the Name of Dogges: the valued file
Distinguishes the swift, the slow, the subtle,
The House-keeper, the Hunter, euery one
According to the gift, which bounteous Nature   900
Hath in him clos'd: whereby he does receiue
Particular addition, from the Bill,
That writes them all alike: and so of men.
Now, if you haue a station in the file,
Not i'th' worst ranke of Manhood, say't,
And I will put that Businesse in your Bosomes,
Whose execution takes your Enemie off,
Grapples you to the heart and loue of vs,
Who weare our Health but sickly in his Life,
Which in his Death were perfect.

2. MURTHERER   I am one, my Liege,   910

Whom the vile Blowes and Buffets of the World
Hath so incens'd, that I am recklesse what
I doe, to spight the World.

1. MURTHERER   And I another,
So wearie with Disasters, tugg'd with Fortune,
That I would set my Life on any Chance,
To mend it, or be rid on't.

MACBETH   Both of you
Know *Banquo* was your Enemie.

MURTHERERS   True, my Lord.

MACBETH

So is he mine: and in such bloody distance,
That euery minute of his being, thrusts
920   Against my neer'st of Life: and though I could
With bare-fac'd power sweepe him from my sight,
And bid my will auouch it; yet I must not,
For certaine friends that are both his, and mine,
Whose loues I may not drop, but wayle his fall,
Who I my selfe struck downe: and thence it is,
That I to your assistance doe make loue,
Masking the Businesse from the common Eye,
For sundry weightie Reasons.

2. MURTHERER   We shall, my Lord,
Performe what you command vs.

1. MURTHERER   Though our Liues—

MACBETH

Your Spirits shine through you. Within this houre, at
930   most,
I will aduise you where to plant your selues,
Acquaint you with the perfect Spy o'th' time,
The moment on't, for't must be done to Night,
And something from the Pallace: always thought,
That I require a clearenesse; and with him,
To leaue no Rubs nor Botches in the Worke:
Fleans, his Sonne, that keepes him companie,
Whose absence is no lesse materiall to me,
Then is his Fathers, must embrace the fate
940   Of that darke houre: resolue your selues apart,
Ile come to you anon.

MURTHERERS   We are resolu'd, my Lord.

MACBETH

Ile call vpon you straight: abide within,
                                        Exeunt Murtherers
It is concluded: *Banquo*, thy Soules flight,
If it finde Heauen, must finde it out to Night.   *Exit*

3.2   *Enter Macbeths Lady, and a Seruant*
(Sc. 13) LADY Is *Banquo* gone from Court?

SERUANT

I, Madame, but returnes againe to Night.

LADY

Say to the King, I would attend his leysure,
For a few words.

SERUANT Madame, I will.   *Exit*

950   LADY Nought's had, all's spent,
Where our desire is got without content:
'Tis safer, to be that which we destroy,
Then by destruction dwell in doubtfull ioy.

Enter Macbeth

How now, my Lord, why doe you keepe alone?
Of sorryest Fancies your Companions making,
Vsing those Thoughts, which should indeed haue dy'd
With them they thinke on: things without all remedie
Should be without regard: what's done, is done.

MACBETH

We haue scorch'd the Snake, not kill'd it:
Shee'le close, and be her selfe, whilest our poore
        Mallice   960
Remaines in danger of her former Tooth.
But let the frame of things dis-ioynt, both the Worlds
        suffer,
Ere we will eate our Meale in feare, and sleepe
In the affliction of these terrible Dreames,
That shake vs Nightly: Better be with the dead,
Whom we, to gayne our peace, haue sent to peace,
Then on the torture of the Minde to lye
In restlesse extasie. *Duncane* is in his Graue:
After Lifes fitfull Feuer, he sleepes well,
Treason ha's done his worst: nor Steele, nor Poyson,   970
Mallice domestique, forraine Leuie, nothing,
Can touch him further.

LADY   Come on: Gentle my Lord,
Sleeke o're your rugged Lookes, be bright and Iouiall
Among your Guests to Night.

MACBETH   So shall I Loue,
And so I pray be you: Let your remembrance
Apply to *Banquo*, present him Eminence,
Both with Eye and Tongue: vnsafe the while, that wee
Must laue our Honors in these flattering streames,
And make our Faces Vizards to our Hearts,
Disguising what they are.

LADY   You must leaue this.   980

MACBETH

O, full of Scorpions is my Minde, deare Wife:
Thou know'st, that *Banquo* and his *Fleans* liues.

LADY

But in them, Natures Coppie's not eterne.

MACBETH

There's comfort yet, they are assaileable,
Then be thou iocund: ere the Bat hath flowne
His Cloyster'd flight, ere to black *Heccats* summons
The shard-borne Beetle, with his drowsie hums,
Hath rung Nights yawning Peale, there shall be done
A deed of dreadfull note.

LADY   What's to be done?

MACBETH

Be innocent of the knowledge, dearest Chuck,   990
Till thou applaud the deed: Come, seeling Night,
Skarfe vp the tender Eye of pittifull Day,
And with thy bloodie and inuisible Hand
Cancell and teare to pieces that great Bond,
Which keepes me pale. Light thickens, and the Crow
Makes Wing toth'Rookie Wood:
Good things of Day begin to droope, and drowse,
Whiles Nights black Agents to their Prey's doe rowse.

1000 Thou maruell'st at my words: but hold thee still,
Things bad begun, make strong themselues by ill:
So prythee goe with me.   *Exeunt*

3.3   *Enter three Murtherers*
Sc. 14)   1. MURTHERER (*to* 3. *Murtherer*)
              But who did bid thee ioyne with vs?
              3. MURTHERER   *Macbeth.*
              2. MURTHERER (*to* 1. *Murtherer*)
              He needes not our mistrust, since he deliuers
              Our Offices, and what we haue to doe,
              To the direction iust.
              1. MURTHERER (*to* 3. *Murtherer*) Then stand with vs:
              The West yet glimmers with some streakes of Day.
              Now spurres the lated Traueller apace,
              To gayne the timely Inne, and neere approches
              The subiect of our Watch.
              3. MURTHERER   Hearke, I heare Horses.
              BANQUO (*within*)
              Giue vs a Light there, hoa.
1010   2. MURTHERER   Then 'tis hee: the rest,
              That are within the note of expectation,
              Alreadie are i'th'Court.
              1. MURTHERER   His Horses goe about.
              3. MURTHERER
              Almost a mile: but he does vsually,
              So all men doe, from hence toth' Pallace Gate
              Make it their Walke.
                    Enter Banquo and Fleans, with a Torch
              2. MURTHERER (*aside*)   A Light, a Light.
              3. MURTHERER (*aside*)   'Tis hee.
              1. MURTHERER (*aside*) Stand too't.
              BANQUO
              It will be Rayne to Night.
              1. MURTHERER   Let it come downe.
                    1. Murtherer strikes out the torch. The others attack
                    Banquo
              BANQUO
              O, Trecherie! Flye good *Fleans,* flye, flye, flye,
1020   Thou may'st reuenge. O Slaue!   *He dies. Exit Fleans*
              3. MURTHERER Who did strike out the Light?
              1. MURTHERER Was't not the way?
              3. MURTHERER
              There's but one downe: the Sonne is fled.
              2. MURTHERER
              We haue lost best halfe of our Affaire.
              1. MURTHERER
              Well, let's away, and say how much is done.
                                     Exeunt with Banquos Body

3.4   *Banquet prepar'd. Enter Macbeth as King, Lady*
(Sc. 15) *as Queene, Rosse, Lenox, Lords, and Attendants.*
                    ⌈Lady sits⌉
              MACBETH
              You know your owne degrees, sit downe: at first and
                    last,
              The hearty welcome.
              LORDS   Thankes to your Maiesty.

              They sit
MACBETH
Our selfe will mingle with Society,
And play the humble Host: our Hostesse keepes her
      State,
But in best time we will require her welcome.
LADY
Pronounce it for me Sir, to all our Friends,   1030
For my heart speakes, they are welcome.
      Enter first Murtherer ⌈to the doore⌉
MACBETH
See they encounter thee with their harts thanks.
Both sides are euen: heere Ile sit i'th'mid'st,
Be large in mirth, anon wee'l drinke a Measure
The Table round. (*To* 1. *Murtherer*) There's blood
      vpon thy face.
1. MURTHERER (*aside to Macbeth*) 'Tis *Banquo's* then.
MACBETH
'Tis better thee without, then he within.
Is he dispatch'd?
1. MURTHERER
My Lord his throat is cut, that I did for him.
MACBETH
Thou art the best o'th'Cut-throats, yet hee's good   1040
That did the like for *Fleans*: if thou did'st it,
Thou art the Non-pareill.
1. MURTHERER   Most Royall Sir
Fleans is scap'd.
MACBETH
Then comes my Fit againe: I had else beene perfect;
Whole as the Marble, founded as the Rocke,
As broad, and generall, as the casing Ayre:
But now I am cabin'd, crib'd, confin'd, bound in
To sawcy doubts, and feares. But *Banquo's* safe?
1. MURTHERER
I, my good Lord: safe in a ditch he bides,
With twenty trenched gashes on his head;   1050
The least a Death to Nature.
MACBETH   Thankes for that:
There the growne Serpent lyes, the worme that's fled
Hath Nature that in time will Venom breed,
No teeth for th'present. Get thee gone, to morrow
Wee'l heare our selues againe.   *Exit* 1. *Murderer*
LADY   My Royall Lord,
You do not giue the Cheere, the Feast is sold
That is not often vouch'd, while 'tis a making:
'Tis giuen, with welcome: to feede were best at home:
From thence, the sawce to meate is Ceremony,
Meeting were bare without it.
      Enter the Ghost of Banquo, and sits in Macbeths
      place
MACBETH   Sweet Remembrancer: 1060
Now good digestion waite on Appetite,
And health on both.
LENOX   May't please your Highnesse sit.
MACBETH
Here had we now our Countries Honor, roof'd,
Were the grac'd person of our *Banquo* present:

Who, may I rather challenge for vnkindnesse,
Then pitty for Mischance.

ROSSE   His absence (Sir)
Layes blame vpon his promise. Pleas't your Highnesse
To grace vs with your Royall Company?

MACBETH
The Table's full.

LENOX   Heere is a place reseru'd Sir.

1070 MACBETH Where?

LENOX
Heere my good Lord. What is't that moues your
      Highnesse?

MACBETH
Which of you haue done this?

LORDS   What, my good Lord?

MACBETH (to the Ghost)
Thou canst not say I did it: neuer shake
Thy goary lockes at me.

ROSSE (rising)
Gentlemen rise, his Highnesse is not well.

LADY (rising)
Sit worthy Friends: my Lord is often thus,
And hath beene from his youth. Pray you keepe Seat,
The fit is momentary, vpon a thought
He will againe be well. If much you note him
1080 You shall offend him, and extend his Passion,
Feed, and regard him not.
            She speakes apart with Macbeth
                  Are you a man?

MACBETH
I, and a bold one, that dare looke on that
Which might appall the Diuell.

LADY   O proper stuffe:
This is the very painting of your feare:
This is the Ayre-drawne-Dagger which you said
Led you to Duncan. O, these flawes and starts
(Impostors to true feare) would well become
A womans story, at a Winters fire
Authoriz'd by her Grandam: shame it selfe,
1090 Why do you make such faces? When all's done
You looke but on a stoole.

MACBETH
Prythee see there: behold, looke, loe, how say you:
Why what care I, if thou canst nod, speake too.
If Charnell houses, and our Graues must send
Those that we bury, backe; our Monuments
Shall be the Mawes of Kytes.   Exit Ghost

LADY   What? quite vnmann'd in folly.

MACBETH
If I stand heere, I saw him.

LADY   Fie for shame.

MACBETH
Blood hath bene shed ere now, i'th'olden time
Ere humane Statute purg'd the gentle Weale:
1100 I, and since too, Murthers haue bene perform'd
Too terrible for the eare. The time has bene,
That when the Braines were out, the man would dye,
And there an end: But now they rise againe

With twenty mortall murthers on their crownes,
And push vs from our stooles. This is more strange
Then such a murther is.

LADY (aloud)   My worthy Lord
Your Noble Friends do lacke you.

MACBETH   I do forget:
Do not muse at me my most worthy Friends,
I haue a strange infirmity, which is nothing
To those that know me. Come, loue and health to all,   1110
Then Ile sit downe:
(To an Attendant)   Giue me some Wine, fill full:
      Enter Ghost
I drinke to th'generall ioy of th'whole Table,
And to our deere Friend Banquo, whom we misse:
Would he were heere: to all, and him we thirst,
And all to all.

LORDS   Our duties, and the pledge.
      They drinke

MACBETH (seeing the Ghost)
Auant, & quit my sight, let the earth hide thee:
Thy bones are marrowlesse, thy blood is cold:
Thou hast no speculation in those eyes
Which thou dost glare with.

LADY   Thinke of this good Peeres
But as a thing of Custome: 'Tis no other,   1120
Onely it spoyles the pleasure of the time.

MACBETH What man dare, I dare:
Approach thou like the rugged Russian Beare,
The arm'd Rhinoceros, or th'Hircan Tiger,
Take any shape but that, and my firme Nerues
Shall neuer tremble. Or be aliue againe,
And dare me to the Desart with thy Sword:
If trembling I inhabit then, protest mee
The Baby of a Girle. Hence horrible shadow,
Vnreall mock'ry hence.   Exit Ghost
                  Why so, being gone   1130
I am a man againe: pray you sit still.

LADY
You haue displac'd the mirth, broke the good
      meeting,
With most admir'd disorder.

MACBETH   Can such things be,
And ouercome vs like a Summers Clowd,
Without our speciall wonder? You make me strange
Euen to the disposition that I owe,
When now I thinke you can behold such sights,
And keepe the naturall Rubie of your Cheekes,
When mine is blanch'd with feare.

ROSSE   What sights, my Lord?

LADY
I pray you speake not: he growes worse & worse.   1140
Question enrages him: at once, goodnight.
Stand not vpon the order of your going,
But go at once.

LENOX   Good night, and better health
Attend his Maiesty.

LADY   A kinde goodnight to all.
                              Exit Lords

MACBETH

It will haue blood they say: Blood will haue Blood:
Stones haue beene knowne to moue, & Trees to speake:
Augures, and vnderstood Relations, haue
By Maggot Pyes, & Choughes, & Rookes brought forth
The secret'st man of Blood. What is the night?

LADY

1150   Almost at oddes with morning, which is which.

MACBETH

How say'st thou that *Macduff* denies his person
At our great bidding.

LADY   Did you send to him Sir?

MACBETH

I heare it by the way: But I will send:
There's not a one of them but in his house
I keepe a Seruant Feed. I will to morrow
(And betimes I will) to the weyard Sisters.
More shall they speake: for now I am bent to know
By the worst meanes, the worst: for mine owne good,
All causes shall giue way. I am in blood
1160   Stept in so farre, that should I wade no more,
Returning were as tedious as go ore:
Strange things I haue in head, that will to hand,
Which must be acted, ere they may be scand.

LADY

You lacke the season of all Natures, sleepe.

MACBETH

Come, wee'l to sleepe: My strange & self-abuse
Is the initiate feare, that wants hard vse:
We are yet but yong in deed.   *Exeunt*

3.5   *Thunder. Enter the three Witches, meeting Hecat*
Sc. 16)   I. WITCH

Why how now *Hecat*, you looke angerly?

HECAT

Haue I not reason (Beldams) as you are?
1170   Sawcy, and ouer-bold, how did you dare
To Trade, and Trafficke with *Macbeth*,
In Riddles, and Affaires of death;
And I the Mistris of your Charmes,
The close contriuer of all harmes,
Was neuer call'd to beare my part,
Or shew the glory of our Art?
And which is worse, all you haue done
Hath bene but for a wayward Sonne,
Spightfull, and wrathfull, who (as others do)
1180   Loues for his owne ends, not for you.
But make amends now: Get you gon,
And at the pit of Acheron
Meete me i'th'Morning: thither he
Will come, to know his Destinie.
Your Vessels, and your Spels prouide,
Your Charmes, and euery thing beside;
I am for th'Ayre: This night Ile spend
Vnto a dismall, and a Fatall end.
Great businesse must be wrought ere Noone.
1190   Vpon the Corner of the Moone

There hangs a vap'rous drop, profound,
Ile catch it ere it come to ground;
And that distill'd by Magicke slights,
Shall raise such Artificiall Sprights,
As by the strength of their illusion,
Shall draw him on to his Confusion.
He shall spurne Fate, scorne Death, and beare
His hopes 'boue Wisedome, Grace, and Feare:
And you all know, Security
Is Mortals cheefest Enemie.   1200

SPIRITS (*singing dispersedly within*)

Come away: Come away:
Heccat: Heccat, Come away.

HECAT

Hearke, I am call'd: my little Spirit see
Sits in a Foggy cloud, and stayes for me.

The Song

SPIRITS ⌈*within*⌉

Come away: Come away:
Heccat: Heccat, Come away.

HECAT   *I come, I come, I come, I come,*
With all the speed I may,
With all the speed I may.
Wher's Stadlin?

SPIRIT ⌈*within*⌉   *Heere.*

HECAT   *Wher's Puckle?*

ANOTHER SPIRIT ⌈*within*⌉   *Heere.*   1210

OTHER SPIRITS ⌈*within*⌉

And Hoppo too, and Hellwaine too
We lack but you; we lack but you,
Come away, make vp the count.

HECAT   *I will but noynt, and then I mount.*

⌈*Spirits appear aboue.*⌉ *A Spirit like a Cat descends*

SPIRITS ⌈*aboue*⌉

Ther's one comes downe to fetch his dues
A kisse, a Coll, a Sip of Blood
And why thou staist so long I muse, I muse,
Since the Air's so sweet, and good.

HECAT   *Oh art thou come? what newes: what newes?*

SPIRIT LIKE A CAT

All goes still to our delight,   1220
Either come, or els Refuse: Refuse.

HECAT   *Now I am furnishd for the Flight.*

She ascends with the spirit and sings

Now I goe, now I flie,
Malkin my sweete Spirit, and I.

⌈SPIRITS *and* HECAT⌉

Oh what a daintie pleasure 'tis
To ride in the Aire
When the Moone shines faire
And sing, and daunce, and toy, and kiss;
Ouer Woods, high Rocks, and Mountaines,
Ouer Seas, and misty Fountaines,   1230
Ouer Steeples Towres, and Turretts,
We fly by night, 'mongst troopes of Spiritts,

No Ring of Bells, to our Eares sounds,
No howles of Woolues, no yelps of Hounds.
No, not the noyse of waters-breache
Or Cannons throat, our height can reache.

SPIRITS ⌈*aboue*⌉

No Ring of Bells, to our Eares sounds,
No howles of Woolues, no yelps of Hounds.
No, not the noyse of waters-breache
1240   *Or Cannons throat, our height can reache.*

Exeunt into the Heauens
Spirit like a Cat and Hecat

1. WITCH

Come, let's make hast, shee'l soone be backe againe.
Exeunt

3.6   *Enter Lenox, and another Lord*
(Sc. 17) LENOX

My former Speeches, haue but hit your Thoughts
Which can interpret farther: Onely I say
Things haue bin strangely borne. The gracious *Duncan*
Was pittied of *Macbeth*: marry he was dead:
And the right valiant *Banquo* walk'd too late,
Whom you may say (if't please you) *Fleans* kill'd,
For *Fleans* fled: Men must not walke too late.
Who cannot want the thought, how monstrous
1250   It was for *Malcolme*, and for *Donalbane*
To kill their gracious Father? Damned Fact,
How it did greeue *Macbeth*? Did he not straight
In pious rage, the two delinquents teare,
That were the Slaues of drinke, and thralles of sleepe?
Was not that Nobly done? I, and wisely too:
For 'twould haue anger'd any heart aliue
To heare the men deny't. So that I say,
He ha's borne all things well, and I do thinke,
That had he *Duncans* Sonnes vnder his Key,
1260   (As, and't please Heauen he shall not) they should finde
What 'twere to kill a Father: So should *Fleans*.
But peace; for from broad words, and cause he fayl'd
His presence at the Tyrants Feast, I heare
Macduffe liues in disgrace. Sir, can you tell
Where he bestowes himselfe?

LORD   The Sonne of *Duncane*
(From whom this Tyrant holds the due of Birth)
Liues in the English Court, and is receyu'd
Of the most Pious *Edward*, with such grace,
That the maleuolence of Fortune, nothing
1270   Takes from his high respect. Thither *Macduffe*
Is gone, to pray the Holy King, vpon his ayd
To wake Northumberland, and warlike *Seyward*,
That by the helpe of these (with him aboue
To ratifie the Worke) we may againe
Giue to our Tables meate, sleepe to our Nights:
Free from our Feasts, and Banquets bloody kniues;
Do faithfull Homage, and receiue free Honors,
All which we pine for now. And this report
Hath so exasperate their King, that hee
1280   Prepares for some attempt of Warre.

LENOX Sent he to *Macduffe?*
LORD

He did: and with an absolute Sir, not I
The clowdy Messenger turnes me his backe,
And hums; as who should say, you'l rue the time
That clogges me with this Answer.

LENOX   And that well might
Aduise him to a Caution, t'hold what distance
His wisedome can prouide. Some holy Angell
Flye to the Court of England, and vnfold
His Message ere he come, that a swift blessing
May soone returne to this our suffering Country,   1290
Vnder a hand accurs'd.

LORD   Ile send my Prayers with him.
Exeunt

✦

A Cauldron. Thunder. Enter the three Witches   **4.1**
                                                        (Sc. 18
1. WITCH

Thrice the brinded Cat hath mew'd.

2. WITCH

Thrice, and once the Hedge-Pigge whin'd.

3. WITCH

Harpier cries, 'tis time, 'tis time.

1. WITCH

Round about the Caldron go:
In the poysond Entrailes throw.
Toad, that vnder cold stone,
Dayes and Nights, ha's thirty one:
Sweltred Venom sleeping got,
Boyle thou first i'th'charmed pot.   1300

ALL

Double, double, toile and trouble;
Fire burne, and Cauldron bubble.

2. WITCH

Fillet of a Fenny Snake,
In the Cauldron boyle and bake:
Eye of Newt, and Toe of Frogge,
Wooll of Bat, and Tongue of Dogge:
Adders Forke, and Blinde-wormes Sting,
Lizards legge, and Howlets wing:
For a Charme of powrefull trouble,
Like a Hell-broth, boyle and bubble.   1310

ALL

Double, double, toyle and trouble,
Fire burne, and Cauldron bubble.

3. WITCH

Scale of Dragon, Tooth of Wolfe,
Witches Mummey, Maw, and Gulfe
Of the rauin'd salt Sea sharke,
Roote of Hemlocke, digg'd i'th'darke:
Liuer of Blaspheming Iew,
Gall of Goate, and Slippes of Yew,
Sliuer'd in the Moones Ecclipse:
Nose of Turke, and Tartars lips: 1320
Finger of Birth-strangled Babe,
Ditch-deliuer'd by a Drab,
Make the Grewell thicke, and slab.

Adde thereto a Tigers Chawdron,
For th'Ingredience of our Cawdron.

ALL

Double, double, toyle and trouble,
Fire burne, and Cauldron bubble.

2. WITCH

Coole it with a Baboones blood,
Then the Charme is firme and good.

Enter Hecat, and the other three Witches

HECAT

1330   O well done: I commend your paines,
And euery one shall share i'th'gaines:
And now about the Cauldron sing
Like Elues and Fairies in a Ring,
Inchanting all that you put in.

The Song

HECAT

Black Spiritts, and white: Red Spiritts, and Gray,
Mingle, Mingle, Mingle, you that mingle may.

4. WITCH

Titty, Tiffin: keepe it stiff in.
Fire-drake, Puckey, Make it Luckey.
Liard, Robin, you must bob in.

1340   ALL   *Round, a-round, a-round, about, about*
All ill come runing-in, all Good keepe-out.

4. WITCH

Heeres the Blood of a Bat.

HECAT

Put in that: oh put in that.

5. WITCH

Heer's Libbards Bane.

HECAT

Put-in a graine.

4. WITCH

The Iuice of Toad: the Oile of Adder.

5. WITCH

Those will make the yonker madder.

HECAT

Put in: ther's all, and rid the Stench.

A WITCH

Nay heeres three ounces of a red-haird wench.

1350   ALL   *Round: around: around, about, about*
All ill come runing-in, all Good keepe-out.

2. WITCH

By the pricking of my Thumbes,
Something wicked this way comes:
⌈*Knocke*⌉
Open Lockes, who euer knockes.

Enter Macbeth

MACBETH

How now you secret, black, & midnight Hags?
What is't you do?

ALL   A deed without a name.

MACBETH

I coniure you, by that which you Professe,
(How ere you come to know it) answer me:

Though you vntye the Windes, and let them fight
Against the Churches: Though the yesty Waues   1360
Confound and swallow Nauigation vp:
Though bladed Corne be lodg'd, & Trees blown downe,
Though Castles topple on their Warders heads:
Though Pallaces, and Pyramids do slope
Their heads to their Foundations: Though the treasure
Of Natures Germaines, tumble altogether,
Euen till destruction sicken: Answer me
To what I aske you.

1. WITCH   Speake.

2. WITCH   Demand.

3. WITCH   Wee'l answer.

1. WITCH

Say, if th'hadst rather heare it from our mouthes,
Or from our Masters.

MACBETH   Call 'em: let me see 'em.   1370

1. WITCH

Powre in Sowes blood, that hath eaten
Her nine Farrow: Greaze that's sweaten
From the Murderers Gibbet, throw
Into the Flame.

ALL   Come high or low:
Thy Selfe and Office deaftly show.

Thunder. 1. Apparition, an Armed Head

MACBETH

Tell me, thou vnknowne power.

1. WITCH   He knowes thy thought:
Heare his speech, but say thou nought.

1. APPARITION

Macbeth, Macbeth, Macbeth: Beware Macduffe,
Beware the Thane of Fife: dismisse me. Enough.

He Descends

MACBETH

What ere thou art, for thy good caution, thanks,   1380
Thou hast harp'd my feare aright. But one word more.

1. WITCH

He will not be commanded: heere's another
More potent then the first.

Thunder. 2 Apparition, a Bloody Childe

2. APPARITION *Macbeth, Macbeth, Macbeth.*

MACBETH Had I three eares, Il'd heare thee.

2. APPARITION

Be bloody, bold, & resolute: Laugh to scorne
The powre of man: For none of woman borne
Shall harme *Macbeth.*

Descends

MACBETH

Then liue *Macduffe*: what need I feare of thee?
But yet Ile make assurance double sure,   1390
And take a Bond of Fate: thou shalt not liue,
That I may tell pale-hearted Feare, it lies;
And sleepe in spight of Thunder.

Thunder. 3 Apparition, a Childe Crowned,
with a Tree in his hand

What is this,
That rises like the issue of a King,

And weares vpon his Baby-brow, the round
And top of Soueraignty?

ALL   Listen, but speake not too't.

3. APPARITION
Be Lyon metled, proud, and take no care:
Who chafes, who frets, or where Conspirers are:
Macbeth shall neuer vanquish'd be, vntill
1400 Great Byrnam Wood, to high Dunsinane Hill
Shall come against him.
                    Descend

MACBETH   That will neuer bee:
Who can impresse the Forrest, bid the Tree
Vnfixe his earth-bound Root? Sweet boadments, good:
Rebellious dead, rise neuer till the Wood
Of Byrnan rise, and on's high place *Macbeth*
Shall liue the Lease of Nature, pay his breath
To time, and mortall Custome. Yet my Hart
Throbs to know one thing: Tell me, if your Art
Can tell so much: Shall *Banquo's* issue euer
Reigne in this Kingdome?

1410 ALL   Seeke to know no more.

MACBETH
I will be satisfied. Deny me this,
And an eternall Curse fall on you: Let me know.
        The Caldron sinkes. Hoboyes
Why sinkes that Caldron? & what noise is this?

1. WITCH Shew.
2. WITCH Shew.
3. WITCH Shew.

ALL
Shew his Eyes, and greeue his Hart,
Come like shadowes, so depart.
        A shew of eight Kings, the last with a glasse in his
        hand, and Banquo

MACBETH
Thou art too like the Spirit of *Banquo*: Down:
1420 Thy Crowne do's seare mine Eye-bals. And thy haire
Thou other Gold-bound-brow, is like the first:
A third, is like the former. Filthy Hagges,
Why do you shew me this?—A fourth? Start eyes!
What will the Line stretch out to'th'cracke of Doome?
Another yet? A seauenth? Ile see no more:
And yet the eight appeares, who beares a glasse,
Which shewes me many more: and some I see,
That two-fold Balles, and trebble Scepters carry.
Horrible sight: Now I see 'tis true,
1430 For the Blood-bolter'd *Banquo* smiles vpon me,
And points at them for his.
                Exeunt Kings and Banquo
                What? is this so?

⌈HECAT⌉
I Sir, all this is so. But why
Stands *Macbeth* thus amazedly?
Come Sisters, cheere we vp his sprights,
And shew the best of our delights.
Ile Charme the Ayre to giue a sound,
While you performe your Antique round:
That this great King may kindly say,
Our duties, did his welcome pay.

        Musicke. The Witches Dance, and vanish

MACBETH
Where are they? Gone? Let this pernitious houre,   1440
Stand aye accursed in the Kalender.
Come in, without there.
        Enter Lenox

LENOX   What's your Graces will.

MACBETH
Saw you the Weyard Sisters?

LENOX   No my Lord.

MACBETH
Came they not by you?

LENOX   No indeed my Lord.

MACBETH
Infected be the Ayre whereon they ride,
And damn'd all those that trust them. I did heare
The gallopping of Horse. Who was't came by?

LENOX
'Tis two or three my Lord, that bring you word:
Macduff is fled to England.

MACBETH   Fled to England?

LENOX I, my good Lord.   1450

MACBETH (*aside*)
Time, thou anticipat'st my dread exploits:
The flighty purpose neuer is o're-tooke
Vnlesse the deed go with it. From this moment,
The very firstlings of my heart shall be
The firstlings of my hand. And euen now
To Crown my thoughts with Acts: be it thoght & done:
The Castle of *Macduff*, I will surprize.
Seize vpon Fife; giue to th'edge o'th'Sword
His Wife, his Babes, and all vnfortunate Soules
That trace him in his Line. No boasting like a Foole, 1460
This deed Ile do, before this purpose coole,
But no more sights. (*To Lenox*) Where are these
        Gentlemen?
Come bring me where they are.   *Exeunt*

        Enter Macduffes Wife, her Son, and Rosse   **4.2**
                                                    (Sc.19)
WIFE
What had he done, to make him fly the Land?

ROSSE
You must haue patience Madam.

WIFE   He had none:
His flight was madnesse: when our Actions do not,
Our feares do make vs Traitors.

ROSSE   You know not
Whether it was his wisedome, or his feare.

WIFE
Wisedom? to leaue his wife, to leaue his Babes,
His Mansion, and his Titles, in a place
From whence himselfe do's flye? He loues vs not,   1470
He wants the naturall touch. For the poore Wren
(The most diminitiue of Birds) will fight,
Her yong ones in her Nest, against the Owle:
All is the Feare, and nothing is the Loue;
As little is the Wisedome, where the flight
So runnes against all reason.

ROSSE   My deerest Cooz,

I pray you schoole your selfe. But for your Husband,
He is Noble, Wise, Iudicious, and best knowes
1480 The fits o'th'Season. I dare not speake much further,
But cruell are the times, when we are Traitors
And do not know our selues: when we hold Rumor
From what we feare, yet know not what we feare,
But floate vpon a wilde and violent Sea
Each way, and none. I take my leaue of you:
Shall not be long but Ile be heere againe:
Things at the worst will cease, or else climbe vpward,
To what they were before. My pretty Cosine,
Blessing vpon you.

WIFE
1490 Father'd he is, and yet hee's Father-lesse.

ROSSE
I am so much a Foole, should I stay longer
It would be my disgrace, and your discomfort.
I take my leaue at once.   *Exit Rosse*

WIFE   Sirra, your Fathers dead,
And what will you do now? How will you liue?

SON
As Birds do Mother.

WIFE   What with Wormes, and Flyes?

SON
With what I get I meane, and so do they.

WIFE
Poore Bird, thou'dst neuer Feare the Net, nor Lime,
The Pitfall, nor the Gin.

SON
Why should I Mother? Poore Birds they are not set
    for:
1500 My Father is not dead for all your saying.

WIFE Yes, he is dead: how wilt thou do for a Father?

SON Nay how will you do for a Husband?

WIFE Why I can buy me twenty at any Market.

SON Then you'l by 'em to sell againe.

WIFE Thou speak'st with all thy wit, and yet I'faith with
    wit enough for thee.

SON Was my Father a Traitor, Mother?

WIFE I, that he was.

SON What is a Traitor?

1510 WIFE Why one that sweares, and lyes.

SON And be all Traitors, that do so.

WIFE Euery one that do's so, is a Traitor, and must be
    hang'd.

SON And must they all be hang'd, that swear and lye?

WIFE Euery one.

SON Who must hang them?

WIFE Why, the honest men.

SON Then the Liars and Swearers are Fools: for there are
    Lyars and Swearers enow, to beate the honest men,
1520   and hang vp them.

WIFE Now God helpe thee, poore Monkie: But how wilt
    thou do for a Father?

SON If he were dead, youl'd weepe for him: if you would
    not, it were a good signe, that I should quickely haue
    a new Father.

WIFE Poore pratler, how thou talk'st?

Enter a Messenger

MESSENGER
Blesse you faire Dame: I am not to you known,
Though in your state of Honor I am perfect;
I doubt some danger do's approach you neerely.
If you will take a homely mans aduice,   1530
Be not found heere: Hence with your little ones.
To fright you thus me thinkes I am too sauage:
To do worse to you, were fell Cruelty,
Which is too nie your person. Heauen preserue you,
I dare abide no longer.   *Exit Messenger*

WIFE   Whether should I flye?
I haue done no harme. But I remember now
I am in this earthly world: where to do harme
Is often laudable, to do good sometime
Accounted dangerous folly. Why then (alas)
Do I put vp that womanly defence,   1540
To say I haue done no harme?

Enter Murtherers

                              What are these faces?

A MURTHERER Where is your Husband?

WIFE
I hope in no place so vnsanctified,
Where such as thou may'st finde him.

A MURTHERER   He's a Traitor.

SON
Thou ly'st thou shagge-hear'd Villaine.

A MURTHERER (*stabbing him*)   What you Egge?
Yong fry of Treachery?

SON   He ha's kill'd me Mother,
Run away I pray you.

    ⌜*He dies.*⌝ *Exit Macduffes Wife, crying Murther,*
    followed by Murtherers ⌜*with the Sonnes body*⌝

Enter Malcolme and Macduffe   **4.3**

MALCOLME   **(Sc. 20)**
Let vs seeke out some desolate shade, & there
Weepe our sad bosomes empty.

MACDUFFE   Let vs rather
Hold fast the mortall Sword: and like good men,   1550
Bestride our downfall Birthdome: each new Morne,
New Widdowes howle, new Orphans cry, new sorowes
Strike heauen on the face, that it resounds
As if it felt with Scotland, and yell'd out
Like Syllable of Dolour.

MALCOLME   What I beleeue, Ile waile;
What know, beleeue; and what I can redresse,
As I shall finde the time to friend: I wil.
What you haue spoke, it may be so perchance.
This Tyrant, whose sole name blisters our tongues,
Was once thought honest: you haue lou'd him well,   1560
He hath not touch'd you yet. I am yong, but something
You may discerne of him through me, and wisedome
To offer vp a weake, poore innocent Lambe
T'appease an angry God.

MACDUFFE I am not treacherous.

MALCOLME But *Macbeth* is.
A good and vertuous Nature may recoyle

In an Imperiall charge. But I shall craue your pardon:
That which you are, my thoughts cannot transpose;
1570 Angels are bright still, though the brightest fell.
Though all things foule, would wear the brows of grace
Yet Grace must still looke so.

MACDUFFE   I haue lost my Hopes.

MALCOLME
Perchance euen there where I did finde my doubts.
Why in that rawnesse left you Wife, and Childe?
Those precious Motiues, those strong knots of Loue,
Without leaue-taking. I pray you,
Let not my Iealousies, be your Dishonors,
But mine owne Safeties: you may be rightly iust,
What euer I shall thinke.

MACDUFFE   Bleed, bleed poore Country,
1580 Great Tyrrany, lay thou thy basis sure,
For goodnesse dare not check thee: wear y^u thy wrongs,
The Title, is affear'd. Far thee well Lord,
I would not be the Villaine that thou think'st,
For the whole Space that's in the Tyrants Graspe,
And the rich East to boot.

MALCOLME   Be not offended:
I speake not as in absolute feare of you:
I thinke our Country sinkes beneath the yoake,
It weepes, it bleeds, and each new day a gash
Is added to her wounds. I thinke withall,
1590 There would be hands vplifted in my right:
And heere from gracious England haue I offer
Of goodly thousands. But for all this,
When I shall treade vpon the Tyrants head,
Or weare it on my Sword; yet my poore Country
Shall haue more vices then it had before,
More suffer, and more sundry wayes then euer,
By him that shall succeede.

MACDUFFE   What should he be?

MALCOLME
It is my selfe I meane: in whom I know
All the particulars of Vice so grafted,
1600 That when they shall be open'd, blacke *Macbeth*
Will seeme as pure as Snow, and the poore State
Esteeme him as a Lambe, being compar'd
With my confinelesse harmes.

MACDUFFE   Not in the Legions
Of horrid Hell, can come a Diuell more damn'd
In euils, to top *Macbeth*.

MALCOLME   I grant him Bloody,
Luxurious, Auaricious, False, Deceitfull,
Sodaine, Malicious, smacking of euery sinne
That ha's a name. But there's no bottome, none
In my Voluptuousnesse: Your Wiues, your Daughters,
1610 Your Matrons, and your Maides, could not fill vp
The Cesterne of my Lust, and my Desire
All continent Impediments would ore-beare
That did oppose my will. Better *Macbeth*,
Then such an one to reigne.

MACDUFFE   Boundlesse intemperance
In Nature is a Tyranny: It hath beene

Th'vntimely emptying of the happy Throne,
And fall of many Kings. But feare not yet
To take vpon you what is yours: you may
Conuey your pleasures in a spacious plenty,
And yet seeme cold. The time you may so hoodwinke: 1620
We haue willing Dames enough: there cannot be
That Vulture in you, to deuoure so many
As will to Greatnesse dedicate themselues,
Finding it so inclinde.

MALCOLME   With this, there growes
In my most ill-compos'd Affection, such
A stanchlesse Auarice, that were I King,
I should cut off the Nobles for their Lands,
Desire his Iewels, and this others House,
And my more-hauing, would be as a Sawce
To make me hunger more, that I should forge   1630
Quarrels vniust against the Good and Loyall,
Destroying them for wealth.

MACDUFFE   This Auarice
Stickes deeper: growes with more pernicious roote
Then Summer-seeming Lust: and it hath bin
The Sword of our slaine Kings: yet do not feare,
Scotland hath Foysons, to fill vp your will
Of your meere Owne. All these are portable,
With other Graces weigh'd.

MALCOLME
But I haue none. The King-becoming Graces,
As Iustice, Verity, Temp'rance, Stablenesse,   1640
Bounty, Perseuerance, Mercy, Lowlinesse,
Deuotion, Patience, Courage, Fortitude,
I haue no rellish of them, but abound
In the diuision of each seuerall Crime,
Acting it many wayes. Nay, had I powre, I should
Poure the sweet Milke of Concord, into Hell,
Vprore the vniuersall peace, confound
All vnity on earth.

MACDUFFE   O Scotland, Scotland.

MALCOLME
If such a one be fit to gouerne, speake:
I am as I haue spoken.

MACDUFFE   Fit to gouern?   1650
No not to liue. O Natiõ miserable!
With an vntitled Tyrant, bloody Sceptred,
When shalt thou see thy wholsome dayes againe?
Since that the truest Issue of thy Throne
By his owne Interdiction stands accust,
And do's blaspheme his breed? Thy Royall Father
Was a most Sainted-King: the Queene that bore thee,
Oftner vpon her knees, then on her feet,
Dy'de euery day she liu'd. Fare thee well,
These Euils thou repeat'st vpon thy selfe,   1660
Hath banish'd me from Scotland. O my Brest,
Thy hope ends heere.

MALCOLME   *Macduff*, this Noble passion
Childe of integrity, hath from my soule
Wip'd the blacke Scruples, reconcil'd my thoughts
To thy good Truth, and Honor. Diuellish *Macbeth*,

By many of these traines, hath sought to win me
Into his power: and modest Wisedome pluckes me
From ouer-credulous hast: but God aboue
Deale betweene thee and me; For euen now
1670   I put my selfe to thy Direction, and
Vnspeake mine owne detraction. Heere abiure
The taints, and blames I laide vpon my selfe,
For strangers to my Nature. I am yet
Vnknowne to Woman, neuer was forsworne,
Scarsely haue coueted what was mine owne.
At no time broke my Faith, would not betray
The Deuill to his Fellow, and delight
No lesse in truth then life. My first false speaking
Was this vpon my selfe. What I am truly
1680   Is thine, and my poore Countries to command:
Whither indeed, before thy heere approach
Old *Seyward* with ten thousand warlike men
Already at a point, was setting foorth:
Now wee'l together, and the chance of goodnesse
Be like our warranted Quarrell. Why are you silent?

MACDUFFE

Such welcome, and vnwelcom things at once
'Tis hard to reconcile.

Enter a Doctor

MALCOLME

Well, more anon. (*To the Doctor*) Comes the King forth
  I pray you?

DOCTOR

I Sir: there are a crew of wretched Soules
1690   That stay his Cure: their malady conuinces
The great assay of Art. But at his touch,
Such sanctity hath Heauen giuen his hand,
They presently amend.

MALCOLME   I thanke you Doctor.

Exit Doctor

MACDUFFE

What's the Disease he meanes?

MALCOLME   Tis call'd the Euill.
A most myraculous worke in this good King,
Which often since my heere remaine in England,
I haue seene him do: How he solicites heauen
Himselfe best knowes: but strangely visited people
All swolne and Vlcerous, pittifull to the eye,
1700   The meere dispaire of Surgery, he cures,
Hanging a golden stampe about their neckes,
Put on with holy Prayers, and 'tis spoken
To the succeeding Royalty he leaues
The healing Benediction. With this strange vertue,
He hath a heauenly guift of Prophesie,
And sundry Blessings hang about his Throne,
That speake him full of Grace.

Enter Rosse

MACDUFFE   See who comes heere.

MALCOLME

My Countryman: but yet I know him not.

MACDUFFE

My euer gentle Cozen, welcome hither.

MALCOLME

I know him now. Good God betimes remoue   1710
The meanes that makes vs Strangers.

ROSSE   Sir, Amen.

MACDUFFE

Stands Scotland where it did?

ROSSE   Alas poore Countrey,
Almost affraid to know it selfe. It cannot
Be call'd our Mother, but our Graue; where nothing
But who knowes nothing, is once seene to smile:
Where sighes, and groanes, and shrieks that rent the
    ayre
Are made, not mark'd: Where violent sorrow seemes
A Moderne extasie: The Deadmans knell,
Is there scarse ask'd for who, and good mens liues
Expire before the Flowers in their Caps,   1720
Dying, or ere they sicken.

MACDUFFE   Oh Relation
Too nice, and yet too true.

MALCOLME   What's the newest griefe?

ROSSE

That of an houres age, doth hisse the speaker,
Each minute teemes a new one.

MACDUFFE   How do's my Wife?

ROSSE

Why well.

MACDUFFE   And all my Children?

ROSSE   Well too.

MACDUFFE

The Tyrant ha's not batter'd at their peace?

ROSSE

No, they were wel at peace, when I did leaue 'em.

MACDUFFE

Be not a niggard of your speech: How gos't?

ROSSE

When I came hither to transport the Tydings
Which I haue heauily borne, there ran a Rumour   1730
Of many worthy Fellowes, that were out,
Which was to my beleefe witnest the rather,
For that I saw the Tyrants Power a-foot.
Now is the time of helpe: (*to Malcolme*) your eye in
    Scotland
Would create Soldiours, make our women fight,
To doffe their dire distresses.

MALCOLME   Bee't their comfort
We are comming thither: Gracious England hath
Lent vs good *Seyward*, and ten thousand men,
An older, and a better Souldier, none
That Christendome giues out.

ROSSE   Would I could answer   1740
This comfort with the like. But I haue words
That would be howl'd out in the desert ayre,
Where hearing should not latch them.

MACDUFFE   What concerne they,
The generall cause, or is it a Fee-griefe
Due to some single brest?

ROSSE   No minde that's honest

But in it shares some woe, though the maine part
Pertaines to you alone.

MACDUFFE   If it be mine
Keepe it not from me, quickly let me haue it.

ROSSE
Let not your eares dispise my tongue for euer,
1750 Which shall possesse them with the heauiest sound
That euer yet they heard.

MACDUFFE   Humh: I guesse at it.

ROSSE
Your Castle is surpriz'd: your Wife, and Babes
Sauagely slaughter'd: To relate the manner
Were on the Quarry of these murther'd Deere
To adde the death of you.

MALCOLME   Mercifull Heauen:
(To Macduffe) What man, ne're pull your hat vpon
    your browes:
Giue sorrow words; the griefe that do's not speake,
Whispers the o're-fraught heart, and bids it breake.

MACDUFFE
My Children too?

ROSSE   Wife, Children, Seruants, all
That could be found.

1760 MACDUFFE   And I must be from thence?
My wife kil'd too?

ROSSE   I haue said.

MALCOLME   Be comforted.
Let's make vs Med'cines of our great Reuenge,
To cure this deadly greefe.

MACDUFFE
He ha's no Children. All my pretty ones?
Did you say All? Oh Hell-Kite! All?
What, All my pretty Chickens, and their Damme
At one fell swoope?

MALCOLME Dispute it like a man.

MACDUFFE I shall do so:
1770 But I must also feele it as a man;
I cannot but remember such things were
That were most precious to me: Did heauen looke on,
And would not take their part? Sinfull Macduff,
They were all strooke for thee: Naught that I am,
Not for their owne demerits, but for mine
Fell slaughter on their soules: Heauen rest them now.

MALCOLME
Be this the Whetstone of your sword, let griefe
Conuert to anger: blunt not the heart, enrage it.

MACDUFFE
O I could play the woman with mine eyes,
1780 And Braggart with my tongue. But gentle Heauens,
Cut short all intermission: Front to Front,
Bring thou this Fiend of Scotland, and my selfe,
Within my Swords length set him, if he scape
Heauen forgiue him too.

MALCOLME   This tune goes manly:
Come go we to the King, our Power is ready,
Our lacke is nothing but our leaue. Macbeth
Is ripe for shaking, and the Powres aboue

Put on their Instruments: Receiue what cheere you may,
The Night is long, that neuer findes the Day.   Exeunt

Enter a Doctor of Physicke, and a Wayting
Gentlewoman

DOCTOR I haue too Nights watch'd with you, but can
perceiue no truth in your report. When was it shee last 1791
walk'd?

GENTLEWOMAN Since his Maiesty went into the Field, I
haue seene her rise from her bed, throw her Night-
Gown vppon her, vnlocke her Closset, take foorth paper,
folde it, write vpon't, read it, afterwards Seale it, and
againe returne to bed; yet all this while in a most fast
sleepe.

DOCTOR A great perturbation in Nature, to receyue at
once the benefit of sleep, and do the effects of watching. 1800
In this slumbry agitation, besides her walking, and
other actuall performances, what (at any time) haue
you heard her say?

GENTLEWOMAN That Sir, which I will not report after her.

DOCTOR You may to me, and 'tis most meet you should.

GENTLEWOMAN Neither to you, nor any one, hauing no
witnesse to confirme my speech.

Enter Lady, with a Taper

Lo you, heere she comes: This is her very guise, and
vpon my life fast asleepe: obserue her, stand close.

DOCTOR How came she by that light?   1810

GENTLEWOMAN Why it stood by her: she ha's light by her
continually, 'tis her command.

DOCTOR You see her eyes are open.

GENTLEWOMAN I but their sense are shut.

DOCTOR What is it she do's now? Looke how she rubbes
her hands.

GENTLEWOMAN It is an accustom'd action with her, to
seeme thus washing her hands: I haue knowne her
continue in this a quarter of an houre.

LADY Yet heere's a spot.   1820

DOCTOR Heark, she speaks, I will set downe what comes
from her, to satisfie my remembrance the more strongly.

LADY Out damned spot: out I say. One: Two: Why then
'tis time to doo't: Hell is murky. Fye, my Lord, fie, a
Souldier, and affear'd? what need we feare who knowes
it, when none can call our powre to accompt: yet who
would haue thought the olde man to haue had so
much blood in him.

DOCTOR Do you marke that?

LADY The Thane of Fife, had a wife: where is she now? 1830
What will these hands ne're be cleane? No more o'that
my Lord, no more o'that: you marre all with this
starting.

DOCTOR Go too, go too: you haue knowne what you
should not.

GENTLEWOMAN She ha's spoke what shee should not, I
am sure of that: Heauen knowes what she ha's knowne.

LADY Heere's the smell of the blood still: all the perfumes
of Arabia will not sweeten this little hand. Oh, oh, oh.

1840 DOCTOR What a sigh is there? The hart is sorely charg'd.

GENTLEWOMAN I would not haue such a heart in my bosome, for the dignity of the whole body.

DOCTOR Well, well, well.

GENTLEWOMAN Pray God it be sir.

DOCTOR This disease is beyond my practise: yet I haue knowne those which haue walkt in their sleep, who haue dyed holily in their beds.

LADY Wash your hands, put on your Night-Gowne, looke not so pale: I tell you yet againe *Banquo*'s buried; he 1850 cannot come out on's graue.

DOCTOR Euen so?

LADY To bed, to bed: there's knocking at the gate: Come, come, come, come, giue me your hand: What's done, cannot be vndone. To bed, to bed, to bed.   *Exit Lady*

DOCTOR Will she go now to bed?

GENTLEWOMAN Directly.

DOCTOR

Foule whisp'rings are abroad: vnnaturall deeds
Do breed vnnaturall troubles: infected mindes
To their deafe pillowes will discharge their Secrets:
1860 More needs she the Diuine, then the Physitian:
God, God forgiue vs all. Looke after her,
Remoue from her the meanes of all annoyance,
And still keepe eyes vpon her: So goodnight,
My minde she ha's mated, and amaz'd my sight.
I thinke, but dare not speake.

GENTLEWOMAN   Good night good Doctor.

                                                    Exeunt

5.2   *Drum and Colours. Enter Menteth, Cathnes, Angus,*
(Sc. 22)   *Lenox, Soldiers*

MENTETH

The English powre is neere, led on by *Malcolm*,
His Vnkle *Seyward*, and the good *Macduff*.
Reuenges burne in them: for their deere causes
Would to the bleeding, and the grim Alarme
Excite the mortified man.

1870 ANGUS   Neere Byrnan wood
Shall we well meet them, that way are they comming.

CATHNES

Who knowes if *Donalbane* be with his brother?

LENOX

For certaine Sir, he is not: I haue a File
Of all the Gentry; there is *Seywards* Sonne,
And many vnruffe youths, that euen now
Protest their first of Manhood.

MENTETH   What do's the Tyrant.

CATHNES

Great Dunsinane he strongly Fortifies:
Some say hee's mad: Others, that lesser hate him,
Do call it valiant Fury, but for certaine
1880 He cannot buckle his distemper'd cause
Within the belt of Rule.

ANGUS   Now do's he feele
His secret Murthers sticking on his hands,
Now minutely Reuolts vpbraid his Faith-breach:
Those he commands, moue onely in command,

Nothing in loue: Now do's he feele his Title
Hang loose about him, like a Giants Robe
Vpon a dwarfish Theefe.

MENTETH   Who then shall blame
His pester'd Senses to recoyle, and start,
When all that is within him, do's condemne
It selfe, for being there.

CATHNES   Well, march we on,   1890
To giue Obedience, where 'tis truly ow'd:
Meet we the Med'cine of the sickly Weale,
And with him poure we in our Countries purge,
Each drop of vs.

LENOX   Or so much as it needes,
To dew the Soueraigne Flower, and drowne the Weeds:
Make we our March towards Birnan.

                                        Exeunt marching

                Enter Macbeth, the Doctor of Physicke, and   **5.3**
                Attendants   (Sc. 23)

MACBETH

Bring me no more Reports, let them flye all:
Till Byrnane wood remoue to Dunsinane,
I cannot taint with Feare. What's the Boy *Malcolme*?
Was he not borne of woman? The Spirits that know   1900
All mortall Consequences, haue pronounc'd me thus:
Feare not *Macbeth*, no man that's borne of woman
Shall ere haue power vpon thee. Then fly false Thanes,
And mingle with the English Epicures,
The minde I sway by, and the heart I beare,
Shall neuer sagge with doubt, nor shake with feare.
                Enter Seruant
The diuell damne thee blacke, thou cream-fac'd Loone:
Where got'st thou that Goose-looke.

SERUANT There is ten thousand.

MACBETH Geese Villaine?   1910

SERUANT   Souldiers Sir.

MACBETH

Go pricke thy face, and ouer-red thy feare
Thou Lilly-liuer'd Boy. What Soldiers, Patch?
Death of thy Soule, those Linnen cheekes of thine
Are Counsailers to feare. What Soldiers Whay-face?

SERUANT The English Force, so please you.

MACBETH

Take thy face hence.   *Exit Seruant*
                Seyton, I am sick at hart,
When I behold: *Seyton*, I say, this push
Will cheere me euer, or dis-eate me now.
I haue liu'd long enough: my way of life   1920
Is falne into the Seare, the yellow Leafe,
And that which should accompany Old-Age,
As Honor, Loue, Obedience, Troopes of Friends,
I must not looke to haue: but in their steed,
Curses, not lowd but deepe, Mouth-honor, breath
Which the poore heart would faine deny, and dare not.
Seyton?
                Enter Seyton

SEYTON What's your gracious pleasure?

MACBETH   What Newes more?

SEYTON

All is confirm'd my Lord, which was reported.

MACBETH
Ile fight, till from my bones, my flesh be hackt.
1930   Giue me my Armor.
SEYTON 'Tis not needed yet.
MACBETH Ile put it on:
Send out moe Horses, skirre the Country round,
Hang those that talke of Feare. Giue me mine Armor:
How do's your Patient, Doctor?
DOCTOR   Not so sicke my Lord,
As she is troubled with thicke-comming Fancies
That keepe her from her rest.
MACBETH   Cure her of that:
Can'st thou not Minister to a minde diseas'd,
Plucke from the Memory a rooted Sorrow,
1940   Raze out the written troubles of the Braine,
And with some sweet Obliuious Antidote
Cleanse the fraught bosome, of that perillous stuffe
Which weighes vpon the heart?
DOCTOR   Therein the Patient
Must minister to himselfe.
MACBETH
Throw Physicke to the Dogs, Ile none of it.
(*To an Attendant*) Come, put mine Armour on: giue
     me my Staffe:
Seyton, send out: Doctor, the Thanes flye from me:
(*To an Attendant*) Come sir, dispatch. (*To the Doctor*) If
     thou could'st Doctor, cast
The Water of my Land, finde her Disease,
1950   And purge it to a sound and pristine Health,
I would applaud thee to the very Eccho,
That should applaud againe. (*To an Attendant*) Pull't
     off I say,
(*To the Doctor*) What Rubarb, Cyme, or what
     Purgatiue drugge
Would scowre these English hence: hear'st y^u of them?
DOCTOR
I my good Lord: your Royall Preparation
Makes vs heare something.
MACBETH (*to an Attendant*)   Bring it after me:
I will not be affraid of Death and Bane,
Till Birnane Forrest come to Dunsinane.
DOCTOR (*aside*)
Were I from Dunsinane away, and cleere,
1960   Profit againe should hardly draw me heere.   *Exeunt*

5.4
(Sc. 24)   *Drum and Colours. Enter Malcolme, Seyward,*
     Macduffe, Seywards Sonne, Menteth, Cathnes,
     Angus, and Soldiers Marching
MALCOLME
Cosins, I hope the dayes are neere at hand
That Chambers will be safe.
MENTETH   We doubt it nothing.
SEYWARD
What wood is this before vs?
MENTETH   The wood of Birnane.
MALCOLME
Let euery Souldier hew him downe a Bough,

And bear't before him, thereby shall we shadow
The numbers of our Hoast, and make discouery
Erre in report of vs.
A SOLDIER   It shall be done.
SEYWARD
We learne no other, but the confident Tyrant
Keepes still in Dunsinane, and will indure
Our setting downe befor't.
MALCOLME   'Tis his maine hope: 1970
For where there is aduantage to be gone,
Both more and lesse haue giuen him the Reuolt,
And none serue with him, but constrained things,
Whose hearts are absent too.
MACDUFFE   Let our iust Censures
Attend the true euent, and put we on
Industrious Souldiership.
SEYWARD   The time approaches,
That will with due decision make vs know
What we shall say we haue, and what we owe:
Thoughts speculatiue, their vnsure hopes relate,
But certaine issue, stroakes must arbitrate,   1980
Towards which, aduance the warre.
                   Exeunt marching

    Enter Macbeth, Seyton, & Souldiers, with Drum   **5.5**
    and Colours   **(Sc. 25)**
MACBETH
Hang out our Banners on the outward walls,
The Cry is still, they come: our Castles strength
Will laugh a Siedge to scorne: Heere let them lye,
Till Famine and the Ague eate them vp:
Were they not forc'd with those that should be ours,
We might haue met them darefull, beard to beard,
And beate them backward home.
    A Cry within of Women
                     What is that noyse?
SEYTON
It is the cry of women, my good Lord.   ⌈*Exit*⌉
MACBETH
I haue almost forgot the taste of Feares: 1990
The time ha's beene, my sences would haue cool'd
To heare a Night-shrieke, and my Fell of haire
Would at a dismall Treatise rowze, and stirre
As life were in't. I haue supt full with horrors,
Direnesse familiar to my slaughterous thoughts
Cannot once start me.
    ⌈*Enter Seyton*⌉
                 Wherefore was that cry?
SEYTON
The Queene (my Lord) is dead.
MACBETH   She should haue dy'de heereafter;
There would haue beene a time for such a word:
To morrow, and to morrow, and to morrow,
Creepes in this petty pace from day to day,
To the last Syllable of Recorded time: 2000
And all our yesterdayes, haue lighted Fooles
The way to dusty death. Out, out, breefe Candle,

Life's but a walking Shadow, a poore Player,
That struts and frets his houre vpon the Stage,
And then is heard no more. It is a Tale
Told by an Ideot, full of sound and fury
Signifying nothing.
    Enter a Messenger
       Thou com'st to vse
Thy Tongue: thy Story quickly.
MESSENGER   Gracious my Lord,

2010 I should report that which I say I saw,
But know not how to doo't.
MACBETH   Well, say sir.
MESSENGER
As I did stand my watch vpon the Hill
I look'd toward Byrnane, and anon me thought
The Wood began to moue.
MACBETH   Lyar, and Slaue.
MESSENGER
Let me endure your wrath, if't be not so:
Within this three Mile may you see it comming.
I say, a mouing Groue.
MACBETH   If thou speak'st false,
Vpon the next Tree shall thou hang aliue
Till Famine cling thee: If thy speech be sooth,

2020 I care not if thou dost for me as much.
I pall in Resolution, and begin
To doubt th'Equiuocation of the Fiend,
That lies like truth. Feare not, till Byrnane Wood
Do come to Dunsinane, and now a Wood
Comes toward Dunsinane. Arme, Arme, and out,
If this which he auouches, do's appeare,
There is nor flying hence, nor tarrying here.
I 'ginne to be a-weary of the Sun,
And wish th'estate o'th'world were now vndon.
Ring the Alarum Bell, ⌈*Alarums*⌉ blow Winde, come

2030 wracke,
At least wee'l dye with Harnesse on our backe.
           Exeunt

5.6
(Sc. 26) *Drumme and Colours. Enter Malcolme, Seyward,*
  Macduffe, and their Army, with Boughes
MALCOLME
Now neere enough: your leauy Skreenes throw
  downe,
And shew like those you are:
  ⌈*They throw downe the Boughes*⌉
      You (worthy Vnkle)
Shall with my Cosin your right Noble Sonne
Leade our first Battell. Worthy *Macduffe*, and wee
Shall take vpon's what else remaines to do,
According to our order.
SEYWARD   Fare you well:
Do we but finde the Tyrants power to night,
Let vs be beaten, if we cannot fight.
MACDUFFE
2040 Make all our Trumpets speak, giue thē all breath
Those clamorous Harbingers of Blood, & Death.
     Exeunt. Alarums continued

    Enter Macbeth   **5.7**
MACBETH   **(Sc. 27)**
They haue tied me to a stake, I cannot flye,
But Beare-like I must fight the course. What's he
That was not borne of Woman? Such a one
Am I to feare, or none.
   Enter young Seyward
YOUNG SEYWARD What is thy name?
MACBETH Thou'lt be affraid to heare it.
YOUNG SEYWARD
No: though thou call'st thy selfe a hoter name
Then any is in hell.
MACBETH   My name's *Macbeth*.
YOUNG SEYWARD
The diuell himselfe could not pronounce a Title 2050
More hatefull to mine eare.
MACBETH   No: nor more fearefull.
YOUNG SEYWARD
Thou lyest abhorred Tyrant, with my Sword
Ile proue the lye thou speak'st.
  Fight, and young Seyward slaine
MACBETH   Thou was't borne of woman;
But Swords I smile at, Weapons laugh to scorne,
Brandish'd by man that's of a Woman borne.
      Exit ⌈*with the Body*⌉

   Alarums. Enter Macduffe   **5.8**
MACDUFFE   **(Sc. 28)**
That way the noise is: Tyrant shew thy face,
If thou beest slaine, and with no stroake of mine,
My Wife and Childrens Ghosts will haunt me still:
I cannot strike at wretched Kernes, whose armes
Are hyr'd to beare their Staues; either thou *Macbeth*, 2060
Or else my Sword with an vnbattred edge
I sheath againe vndeeded. There thou should'st be,
By this great clatter, one of greatest note
Seemes bruited. Let me finde him Fortune,
And more I begge not.   *Exit. Alarums*

   Enter Malcolme and Seyward   **5.9**
SEYWARD   **(Sc. 29)**
This way my Lord, the Castles gently rendred:
The Tyrants people, on both sides do fight,
The Noble Thanes do brauely in the Warre,
The day almost it selfe professes yours,
And little is to do.
MALCOLME   We haue met with Foes 2070
That strike beside vs.
SEYWARD   Enter Sir, the Castle.
       Exeunt. Alarum

    Enter Macbeth   **5.10**
MACBETH   **(Sc. 30)**
Why should I play the Roman Foole, and dye
On mine owne sword? whiles I see liues, the gashes
Do better vpon them.
   Enter Macduffe
MACDUFFE   Turne Hell-hound, turne.

MACBETH

Of all men else I haue auoyded thee:
But get thee backe, my soule is too much charg'd
With blood of thine already.

MACDUFFE   I haue no words,
My voice is in my Sword, thou bloodier Villaine
Then tearmes can giue thee out.

Fight: Alarum

MACBETH   Thou loosest labour.

2080   As easie may'st thou the intrenchant Ayre
With thy keene Sword impresse, as make me bleed:
Let fall thy blade on vulnerable Crests,
I beare a charmed Life, which must not yeeld
To one of woman borne.

MACDUFFE   Dispaire thy Charme,
And let the Angell whom thou still hast seru'd
Tell thee, *Macduffe* was from his Mothers womb
Vntimely ript.

MACBETH

Accursed be that tongue that tels mee so;
For it hath Cow'd my better part of man:

2090   And be these Iugling Fiends no more beleeu'd,
That palter with vs in a double sence,
That keepe the word of promise to our eare,
And breake it to our hope. Ile not fight with thee.

MACDUFFE Then yeeld thee Coward,
And liue to be the shew, and gaze o'th'time.
Wee'l haue thee, as our rarer Monsters are
Painted vpon a pole, and vnder-writ,
Heere may you see the Tyrant.

MACBETH   I will not yeeld
To kisse the ground before young *Malcolmes* feet,

2100   And to be baited with the Rabbles curse.
Though Byrnane wood be come to Dunsinane,
And thou oppos'd, being of no woman borne,
Yet I will try the last. Before my body,
I throw my warlike Shield: Lay on *Macduffe*,
And damn'd be him, that first cries hold, enough.

Exeunt fighting. Alarums

Enter Fighting, and Macbeth slaine. ⌜*Exit Macduffe
with Macbeths body*⌝

5.11   *Retreat, and Flourish. Enter with Drumme and*
(Sc. 31)   *Colours, Malcolm, Seyward, Rosse, Thanes, &
Soldiers*

MALCOLME

I would the Friends we misse, were safe arriu'd.

SEYWARD

Some must go off: and yet by these I see,
So great a day as this is cheapely bought.

MALCOLME

Macduffe is missing, and your Noble Sonne.

ROSSE

Your son my Lord, ha's paid a souldiers debt,   2110
He onely liu'd but till he was a man,
The which no sooner had his Prowesse confirm'd
In the vnshrinking station where he fought,
But like a man he dy'de.

SEYWARD   Then he is dead?

ROSSE

I, and brought off the field: your cause of sorrow
Must not be measur'd by his worth, for then
It hath no end.

SEYWARD   Had he his hurts before?

ROSSE

I, on the Front.

SEYWARD   Why then, Gods Soldier be he:
Had I as many Sonnes, as I haue haires,
I would not wish them to a fairer death: 2120
And so his Knell is knoll'd.

MALCOLME   Hee's worth more sorrow,
And that Ile spend for him.

SEYWARD   He's worth no more,
They say he parted well, and paid his score,
And so God be with him. Here comes newer comfort.

Enter Macduffe, with Macbeths head

MACDUFFE (*to Malcolme*)

Haile King, for so thou art. Behold where stands
Th'Vsurpers cursed head: the time is free:
I see thee compast with thy Kingdomes Pearle,
That speake my salutation in their minds:
Whose voyces I desire alowd with mine.
Haile King of Scotland.

ALL BUT MALCOLME   Haile King of Scotland.   2130

Flourish

MALCOLME

We shall not spend a large expence of time,
Before we reckon with your seuerall loues,
And make vs euen with you. My Thanes and
    Kinsmen
Henceforth be Earles, the first that euer Scotland
In such an Honor nam'd: What's more to do,
Which would be planted newly with the time,
As calling home our exil'd Friends abroad,
That fled the Snares of watchfull Tyranny,
Producing forth the cruell Ministers
Of this dead Butcher, and his Fiend-like Queene;   2140
Who (as 'tis thought) by selfe and violent hands,
Tooke off her life. This, and what needfull else
That call's vpon vs, by the Grace of Grace,
We will performe in measure, time, and place:
So thankes to all at once, and to each one,
Whom we inuite, to see vs Crown'd at Scone.

Flourish. Exeunt Omnes

FINIS

ANTHONIE, AND CLEOPATRA

FIRST printed in the 1623 Folio, *Anthonie, and Cleopatra* had been entered on the Stationers'
Register on 20 May 1608. Echoes of it in Barnabe Barnes's tragedy *The Divils Charter*,
acted by Shakespeare's company in February 1607, suggest that Shakespeare wrote his
play no later than 1606, and stylistic evidence supports that date.

The Life of Marcus Antonius in Sir Thomas North's translation of Plutarch's *Liues of the
noble Grecians and Romanes* (1579) was one of the sources for *Iulius Cæsar*; it also provided
Shakespeare with most of his material for *Anthonie, and Cleopatra*, in which he draws upon
its language to a remarkable extent even in some of the play's most poetic passages. For
example, Enobarbus' famous description of Cleopatra in her barge (772-99) incorporates
phrase after phrase of North's prose. And the play's action stays close to North's account,
though with significant adjustments, particularly compressions of the time-scheme. It
opens in 40 BC, two years after the end of *Iulius Cæsar*, and portrays events that took place
over a period of ten years. Mark Anthony has become an older man, though Octauius is
still 'scarse-bearded'. Plutarch, who was a connoisseur of human behaviour, also afforded
many hints for the characterization; but some characters, particularly Anthony's comrade
Domitius Enobarbus and Cleopatra's women, Charmian and Iras, are largely created by
Shakespeare.

In the earlier play, Mark Anthony had formed a triumvirate with Octauius Cæsar and
Lepidus. In *Anthonie, and Cleopatra* the triumvirate is in a state of disintegration, partly
because Mark Anthony—married at the play's opening to Fuluia, who is rebelling against
Octauius Cæsar—is infatuated with Cleopatra, Queen of Egypt (and the former mistress of
Iulius Cæsar). The play's action swings between Rome and Alexandria as Anthony is torn
between the claims of Rome—strengthened for a while by his marriage, after Fuluia's
death, to Octauius Cæsar's sister Octauia—and the temptations of Egypt. Gradually opposition between Anthony and Octauius increases, until they engage in a sea-fight near
Actium (in Greece), in which Anthony follows Cleopatra's navy in ignominious retreat.
The closing stages of the double tragedy portray Anthony's shame, humiliation, and suicide
after Cleopatra falsely causes him to believe that she has killed herself; faced with the
threat that Cæsar will take her captive to Rome, Cleopatra too commits suicide. According
to Plutarch, she was thirty-eight years old; as for Anthony, 'some say that he liued three
and fiftie yeares: and others say, six and fiftie'.

In *Anthonie, and Cleopatra* the classical restraint of *Iulius Cæsar* gives way to a fine excess
of language, of dramatic action, and of individual behaviour. The style is hyperbolical,
overflowing the measure of the iambic pentameter. The action is amazingly fluid, shifting
with an ease and rapidity that caused bewilderment to ages unfamiliar with the conventions of Shakespeare's theatre. And the characterization is correspondingly extravagant, delighting in the quirks of individual behaviour, above all in the paradoxes and
inconsistencies of the Egyptian queen who contains within herself the capacity for every
extreme of feminine behaviour, from vanity, meanness, and frivolity to the sublime self-
transcendence with which she faces and embraces death.

The copy for the Folio text, often thought to be authorial, may in fact be scribal.

THE NAMES OF THE ACTORS

Mark ANTHONY (Marcus Antonius), Triumuir of Rome

DEMETRIUS
PHILO
Domitius ENOBARBUS
VENTIDIUS
SILLIUS   } friends and followers of Anthony
EROS
CAMIDIUS
SCARRUS
DECRETAS

Octauius CÆSAR, Triumuir of Rome

OCTAUIA, his sister

MECENAS
AGRIPPA
TOWRUS
DOLABELLA   } friends and followers of Cæsar
THIDIAS
GALLUS
PROCULEIUS

LEPIDUS, Triumuir of Rome

Sextus POMPEY (Pompeius)

MENECRATES
MENAS   } friends of Pompey
VARRIUS

CLEOPATRA, Queene of Egypt

CHARMIAN
IRAS
ALEXAS
MARDIAN, an eunuch   } attendants on Cleopatra
DIOMED
SELEUCUS

A SOOTHSAYER

An AMBASSADOR

MESSENGERS

A BOY who sings

A CENTERIE and men of his WATCH

Men of the GUARD

An ÆGYPTIAN

A CLOWNE

SERUANTS

SOULDIERS

Eunuchs, Attendants, Captaines, Souldiers, Seruants

The Tragedie of Anthonie, and Cleopatra

Sc. 1   *Enter Demetrius and Philo*
(1.1)   PHILO

Nay, but this dotage of our Generals
Ore-flowes the measure: those his goodly eyes
That o're the Files and Musters of the Warre,
Haue glow'd like plated Mars: Now bend, now turne
The Office and Deuotion of their view
Vpon a Tawny Front. His Captaines heart,
Which in the scuffles of great Fights hath burst
The Buckles on his brest, reneages all temper,
And is become the Bellowes and the Fan
To coole a Gypsies Lust.

> *Flourish. Enter Anthony, Cleopatra, her Ladies, the*
> *Traine, with Eunuchs fanning her*

10   Looke where they come:
Take but good note, and you shall see in him
(The triple Pillar of the world) transform'd
Into a Strumpets Foole. Behold and see.

CLEOPATRA *(to Anthony)*

If it be Loue indeed, tell me how much.

ANTHONY

There's beggery in the loue that can be reckon'd.

CLEOPATRA

Ile set a bourne how farre to be belou'd.

ANTHONY

Then must thou needes finde out new Heauen, new
    Earth.

> *Enter a Messenger*

MESSENGER Newes (my good Lord) from Rome.

ANTHONY Grates me, the summe.

20 CLEOPATRA Nay heare them *Anthony*.

Fuluia perchance is angry: Or who knowes,
If the scarse-bearded *Cæsar* haue not sent
His powrefull Mandate to you. Do this, or this;
Take in that Kingdome, and Infranchise that:
Perform't, or else we damne thee.

ANTHONY How, my Loue?

CLEOPATRA Perchance? Nay, and most like:

You must not stay heere longer, your dismission
Is come from *Cæsar*, therefore heare it *Anthony*,
30 Where's *Fuluias* Processe? (*Cæsars* I would say) both?
Call in the Messengers: As I am Egypts Queene,
Thou blushest *Anthony*, and that blood of thine
Is *Cæsars* homager: else so thy cheeke payes shame,
When shrill-tongu'd *Fuluia* scolds. The Messengers.

ANTHONY

Let Rome in Tyber melt, and the wide Arch
Of the raing'd Empire fall: Heere is my space,
Kingdomes are clay: Our dungie earth alike
Feeds Beast as Man; the Noblenesse of life
Is to do thus: when such a mutuall paire,
40 And such a twaine can doo't, in which I binde

One paine of punishment, the world to weete
We stand vp Peerelesse.

CLEOPATRA ⌜*aside*⌝   Excellent falshood:

Why did he marry *Fuluia*, and not loue her?
Ile seeme the Foole I am not. (*To Anthony*) *Anthony*
Will be himselfe.

ANTHONY   But stirr'd by *Cleopatra*.

Now for the loue of Loue, and her soft houres,
Let's not confound the time with Conference harsh;
There's not a minute of our liues should stretch
Without some pleasure now. What sport to night?

CLEOPATRA

Heare the Ambassadors.

ANTHONY   Fye wrangling Queene: 50

Whom euery thing becomes, to chide, to laugh,
To weepe: how euery passion fully striues
To make it selfe (in Thee) faire, and admir'd.
No Messenger but thine, and all alone,
To night wee'l wander through the streets, and note
The qualities of people. Come my Queene,
Last night you did desire it. (*To the Messenger*) Speake
    not to vs.

> *Exeunt Anthony and Cleopatra with the Traine*
> ⌜*and, by another doore, the Messenger*⌝

DEMETRIUS

Is *Cæsar* with *Anthonius* priz'd so slight?

PHILO

Sir sometimes when he is not *Anthony*,
He comes too short of that great Property   60
Which still should go with *Anthony*.

DEMETRIUS   I am full sorry,

That hee approues the common Lyar, who
Thus speakes of him at Rome; but I will hope
Of better deeds to morrow. Rest you happy.   *Exeunt*

> *Enter Enobarbus, a Southsayer, Charmian, Iras,*   **Sc. 2**
> *Mardian the Eunuch, Alexas, ⌜and attendants⌝*   **(1.2)**

CHARMIAN L. *Alexas*, sweet *Alexas*, most any thing *Alexas*,
    almost most absolute *Alexas*, where's the Soothsayer
    that you prais'd so to'th'Queene?
Oh that I knewe this Husband, which you say,
Must charge his Hornes with Garlands.

ALEXAS   Soothsayer.

SOOTHSAYER Your will?   70

CHARMIAN

Is this the Man? Is't you sir that know things?

SOOTHSAYER

In Natures infinite booke of Secrecie,
A little I can read.

ALEXAS *(to Charmian)* Shew him your hand.

ENOBARBUS *(calling)* Bring in the Banket quickly:
Wine enough, *Cleopatra's* health to drinke.

> ⌜*Enter seruants with food and wine, and exeunt*⌝

CHARMIAN (*to Soothsayer*) Good sir, giue me good Fortune.

SOOTHSAYER I make not, but foresee.

CHARMIAN
Pray then, foresee me one.

SOOTHSAYER   You shall be yet
Farre fairer then you are.

80 CHARMIAN   He meanes in flesh.

IRAS
No, you shall paint when you are old.

CHARMIAN   Wrinkles forbid.

ALEXAS
Vex not his prescience, be attentiue.

CHARMIAN   Hush.

SOOTHSAYER
You shall be more belouing, then beloued.

CHARMIAN I had rather heate my Liuer with drinking.

ALEXAS Nay, heare him.

CHARMIAN Good now some excellent Fortune: Let mee be married to three Kings in a forenoone, and Widdow them all: Let me haue a Childe at fifty, to whom *Herode* of Iewry may do Homage. Finde me to marrie me with
90 *Octauius Cæsar*, and companion me with my Mistris.

SOOTHSAYER
You shall out-liue the Lady whom you serue.

CHARMIAN Oh excellent, I loue long life better then Figs.

SOOTHSAYER
You haue seene and prou'd a fairer former fortune,
Then that which is to approach.

CHARMIAN Then belike my Children shall haue no names: Prythee how many Boyes and Wenches must I haue.

SOOTHSAYER
If euery of your wishes had a wombe,
And fertill euery wish, a Million.

CHARMIAN Out Foole, I forgiue thee for a Witch.

100 ALEXAS You thinke none but your sheets are priuie to your wishes.

CHARMIAN (*to the Soothsayer*) Nay come, tell *Iras* hers.

ALEXAS Wee'l know all our Fortunes.

ENOBARBUS Mine, and most of our Fortunes to night, shall be drunke to bed.

IRAS (*showing her hand to the Soothsayer*) There's a Palme presages Chastity, if nothing els.

CHARMIAN E'ne as the o're-flowing Nylus presageth Famine.

110 IRAS Go you wilde Bedfellow, you cannot Soothsay.

CHARMIAN Nay, if an oyly Palme bee not a fruitfull Prognostication, I cannot scratch mine eare. (*To the Soothsayer*) Prythee tel her but a worky day Fortune.

SOOTHSAYER Your Fortunes are alike.

IRAS
But how, but how, giue me particulars.

SOOTHSAYER I haue said.

IRAS Am I not an inch of Fortune better then she?

CHARMIAN Well, if you were but an inch of fortune better then I: where would you choose it.

120 IRAS Not in my Husbands nose.

CHARMIAN Our worser thoughts Heauens mend. *Alexas,*

come, his Fortune, his Fortune. Oh let him mary a woman that cannot go, sweet *Isis*, I beseech thee, and let her dye too, and giue him a worse, and let worse follow worse, till the worst of all follow him laughing to his graue, fifty-fold a Cuckold. Good *Isis* heare me this Prayer, though thou denie me a matter of more waight: good *Isis* I beseech thee.

IRAS Amen, deere Goddesse, heare that prayer of the people. For, as it is a heart-breaking to see a handsome 130 man loose-Wiu'd, so it is a deadly sorrow, to beholde a foule Knaue vncuckolded: Therefore deere *Isis* keep *decorum*, and Fortune him accordingly.

CHARMIAN Amen.

ALEXAS Lo now, if it lay in their hands to make mee a Cuckold, they would make themselues Whores, but they'ld doo't.

    Enter Cleopatra

ENOBARBUS
Hush, heere comes *Anthony.*

CHARMIAN   Not he, the Queene.

CLEOPATRA
Saw you my Lord.

ENOBARBUS   No Lady.

CLEOPATRA   Was he not heere?

CHARMIAN No Madam.   140

CLEOPATRA
He was dispos'd to mirth, but on the sodaine
A Romane thought hath strooke him. *Enobarbus?*

ENOBARBUS Madam.

CLEOPATRA
Seeke him, and bring him hither: wher's *Alexas?*

ALEXAS
Heere at your seruice. My Lord approaches.

    Enter Anthony, with a Messenger

CLEOPATRA
We will not looke vpon him: Go with vs.

        Exeunt all but Anthony and the Messenger

MESSENGER
Fuluia thy Wife, first came into the Field.

ANTHONY Against my Brother *Lucius?*

MESSENGER
I: but soone that Warre had end, and the times state
Made friends of them, ioynting their force 'gainst *Cæsar,* 150
Whose better issue in the warre, from Italy
Vpon the first encounter draue them.

ANTHONY   Well, what worst.

MESSENGER
The Nature of bad newes infects the Teller.

ANTHONY
When it concernes the Foole or Coward: On.
Things that are past, are done. With me 'tis thus,
Who tels me true, though in his Tale lye death,
I heare him as he flatter'd.

MESSENGER   *Labienus*
(This is stiffe-newes) hath with his Parthian Force
Extended Asia: from Euphrates   160
His conquering banner shooke, from Syria

To Lydia, and to Ionia,
Whil'st—

ANTHONY   *Anthony thou would'st say.*

MESSENGER   Oh my Lord.

ANTHONY
Speake to me home, mince not the generall tongue,
Name *Cleopatra* as she is call'd in Rome:
Raile thou in *Fuluia's* phrase, and taunt my faults
With such full License, as both Truth and Malice
Haue power to vtter. Oh then we bring forth weeds,
When our quicke windes lye still, and our illes told vs
170   Is as our earing: fare thee well awhile.

MESSENGER   At your Noble pleasure.   *Exit Messenger*

          Enter another Messenger

ANTHONY
From *Scicion* how the newes? Speake there.

⌈2. MESSENGER⌉
The man from *Scicion*,

⌈ANTHONY⌉   Is there such an one?

⌈2. MESSENGER⌉
He stayes vpon your will.

ANTHONY   Let him appeare:
                              Exit 2. Messenger
These strong Egyptian Fetters I must breake,
Or loose my selfe in dotage.

          Enter another Messenger with a Letter
                              What are you?

⌈3. MESSENGER⌉
Fuluia thy wife is dead.

ANTHONY   Where dyed she.

3. MESSENGER   In *Scicion*,
Her length of sicknesse, with what else more serious,
Importeth thee to know, this beares.
          He giues Anthony the Letter

180   ANTHONY   Forbeare me.
                              ⌈*Exit 3. Messenger*⌉
There's a great Spirit gone, thus did I desire it:
What our contempts doth often hurle from vs,
We wish it ours againe. The present pleasure,
By reuolution lowring, does become
The opposite of it selfe: she's good being gon,
The hand could plucke her backe, that shou'd her on.
I must from this enchanting Queene breake off,
Ten thousand harmes, more then the illes I know
My idlenesse doth hatch. How now *Enobarbus*.
          ⌈*Enter Enobarbus*⌉

ENOBARBUS
What's your pleasure, Sir?

190   ANTHONY   I must with haste from hence.

ENOBARBUS   Why then we kill all our Women. We see how
mortall an vnkindnesse is to them, if they suffer our
departure death's the word.

ANTHONY   I must be gone.

ENOBARBUS   Vnder a compelling occasion, let women die.
It were pitty to cast them away for nothing, though
betweene them and a great cause, they should be
esteemed nothing. *Cleopatra* catching but the least noyse
of this, dies instantly: I haue seene her dye twenty

times vppon farre poorer moment: I do think there is   200
mettle in death, which commits some louing acte vpon
her, she hath such a celerity in dying.

ANTHONY   She is cunning past mans thought.

ENOBARBUS   Alacke Sir no, her passions are made of
nothing but the finest part of pure Loue. We cannot
cal her winds and waters, sighes and teares: They are
greater stormes and Tempests then Almanackes can
report. This cannot be cunning in her; if it be, she
makes a showre of Raine as well as Ioue.

ANTHONY   Would I had neuer seene her.   210

ENOBARBUS   Oh sir, you had then left vnseene a wonderfull
peece of worke, which not to haue beene blest withall,
would haue discredited your Trauaile.

ANTHONY   *Fuluia* is dead.

ENOBARBUS   Sir.

ANTHONY   *Fuluia* is dead.

ENOBARBUS   *Fuluia?*

ANTHONY   Dead.

ENOBARBUS   Why sir, giue the Gods a thankefull Sacrifice:
when it pleaseth their Deities to take the wife of a man   220
from him, it shewes to man the Tailors of the earth:
comforting therein, that when olde Robes are worne
out, there are members to make new. If there were no
more Women but *Fuluia*, then had you indeede a cut,
and the case to be lamented: This greefe is crown'd
with Consolation, your old Smocke brings foorth a new
Petticoate, and indeed the teares liue in an Onion, that
should water this sorrow.

ANTHONY
The businesse she hath broached in the State,
Cannot endure my absence.   230

ENOBARBUS   And the businesse you haue broach'd heere
cannot be without you, especially that of *Cleopatra's*,
which wholly depends on your abode.

ANTHONY
No more light Answeres: Let our Officers
Haue notice what we purpose. I shall breake
The cause of our Expedience to the Queene,
And get her leue to part. For not alone
The death of *Fuluia*, with more vrgent touches
Do strongly speake to vs: but the Letters too
Of many our contriuing Friends in Rome,   240
Petition vs at home. *Sextus Pompeius*
Hath giuen the dare to *Cæsar*, and commands
The Empire of the Sea. Our slippery people,
Whose Loue is neuer link'd to the deseruer,
Till his deserts are past, begin to throw
Pompey the great, and all his Dignities
Vpon his Sonne, who high in Name and Power,
Higher then both in Blood and Life, stands vp
For the maine Souldier. Whose quality going on,
The sides o'th'world may danger. Much is breeding,   250
Which like the Coursers heire, hath yet but life,
And not a Serpents poyson. Say our pleasure,
To such whose place is vnder vs, requires
Our quicke remoue from hence.

ENOBARBUS   I shall doo't.
                              Exeunt seuerally

Sc. 3
(1.3)
            Enter Cleopatra, Charmian, Alexas, and Iras

CLEOPATRA
    Where is he?

CHARMIAN   I did not see him since.

CLEOPATRA ⌈*to Alexas*⌉
    See where he is, whose with him, what he does:
    I did not send you. If you finde him sad,
    Say I am dauncing: if in Myrth, report
    That I am sodaine sicke. Quicke, and returne.

                                Exit ⌈*Alexas*⌉

CHARMIAN
260   Madam, me thinkes if you did loue him deerly,
    You do not hold the method, to enforce
    The like from him.

CLEOPATRA   What should I do, I do not?

CHARMIAN
    In each thing giue him way, crosse him in nothing.

CLEOPATRA
    Thou teachest like a foole: the way to lose him.

CHARMIAN
    Tempt him not so too farre. Iwis forbeare,
    In time we hate that which we often feare.

      Enter Anthony

    But heere comes *Anthony.*

CLEOPATRA   I am sicke, and sullen.

ANTHONY
    I am sorry to giue breathing to my purpose.

CLEOPATRA
    Helpe me away deere *Charmian,* I shall fall,
270   It cannot be thus long, the sides of Nature
    Will not sustaine it.

ANTHONY   Now my deerest Queene.

CLEOPATRA
    Pray you stand farther from mee.

ANTHONY   What's the matter?

CLEOPATRA
    I know by that same eye ther's some good news.
    What sayes the married woman you may goe?
    Would she had neuer giuen you leaue to come.
    Let her not say 'tis I that keepe you heere,
    I haue no power vpon you: Hers you are.

ANTHONY
    The Gods best know.

CLEOPATRA   Oh neuer was there Queene
    So mightily betrayed: yet at the first
    I saw the Treasons planted.

280 ANTHONY   *Cleopatra.*

CLEOPATRA
    Why should I thinke you can be mine, & true,
    (Though you in swearing shake the Throaned Gods)
    Who haue beene false to *Fuluia?* Riotous madnesse,
    To be entangled with those mouth-made vowes,
    Which breake themselues in swearing.

ANTHONY   Most sweet Queene.

CLEOPATRA
    Nay pray you seeke no colour for your going,
    But bid farewell, and goe: When you sued staying,
    Then was the time for words: No going then,

Eternity was in our Lippes, and Eyes,
Blisse in our browes bent: none our parts so poore,   290
But was a race of Heauen. They are so still,
Or thou the greatest Souldier of the world,
Art turn'd the greatest Lyar.

ANTHONY   How now Lady?

CLEOPATRA
I would I had thy inches, thou should'st know
There were a heart in Egypt.

ANTHONY   Heare me Queene:
The strong necessity of Time, commands
Our Seruicies a-while: but my full heart
Remaines in vse with you. Our Italy,
Shines o're with ciuill Swords; *Sextus Pompeius*
Makes his approaches to the Port of Rome,   300
Equality of two Domesticke powers,
Breed scrupulous faction: The hated growne to
    strength
Are newly growne to Loue: The condemn'd *Pompey,*
Rich in his Fathers Honor, creepes apace
Into the hearts of such, as haue not thriued
Vpon the present state, whose Numbers threaten,
And quietnesse growne sicke of rest, would purge
By any desperate change: My more particular,
And that which most with you should safe my going,
Is *Fuluias* death.   310

CLEOPATRA
Though age from folly could not giue me freedom
It does from childishnesse. Can *Fuluia* dye?

ANTHONY She's dead my Queene.

    He offers Letters

Looke heere, and at thy Soueraigne leysure read
The Garboyles she awak'd: at the last, best,
See when, and where shee died.

CLEOPATRA   O most false Loue!
Where be the Sacred Violles thou should'st fill
With sorrowfull water? Now I see, I see,
In *Fuluias* death, how mine receiu'd shall be.

ANTHONY
Quarrell no more, but bee prepar'd to know   320
The purposes I beare: which are, or cease,
As you shall giue th'aduice. By the fire
That quickens Nylus slime, I go from hence
Thy Souldier, Seruant, making Peace or Warre,
As thou affects.

CLEOPATRA   Cut my Lace, *Charmian* come,
But let it be, I am quickly ill, and well,
So *Anthony* loues.

ANTHONY   My precious Queene forbeare,
And giue true euidence to his Loue, which stands
An honourable Triall.

CLEOPATRA   So *Fuluia* told me.
I prythee turne aside, and weepe for her,   330
Then bid adiew to me, and say the teares
Belong to Egypt. Good now, play one Scene
Of excellent dissembling, and let it looke
Like perfect Honor.

ANTHONY   You'l heat my blood: no more?

CLEOPATRA
You can do better yet: but this is meetly.

ANTHONY
Now by my Sword.

CLEOPATRA   And Target. Still he mends.
But this is not the best. Looke prythee *Charmian*,
How this Herculean Roman do's become
The carriage of his chafe.

340 ANTHONY Ile leaue you Lady.

CLEOPATRA Courteous Lord, one word:
Sir, you and I must part, but that's not it:
Sir, you and I haue lou'd, but there's not it:
That you know well, something it is I would:
Oh, my Obliuion is a very *Anthony*,
And I am all forgotten.

ANTHONY   But that your Royalty
Holds Idlenesse your subiect, I should take you
For Idlenesse it selfe.

CLEOPATRA   'Tis sweating Labour,
To beare such Idlenesse so neere the heart
350 As *Cleopatra* this. But Sir, forgiue me,
Since my becommings kill me, when they do not
Eye well to you. Your Honor calles you hence,
Therefore be deafe to my vnpittied Folly,
And all the Gods go with you. Vpon your Sword
Sit Lawrell victory, and smooth successe
Be strew'd before your feete.

ANTHONY   Let vs go.
Come: Our separation so abides and flies,
That thou reciding heere, goes yet with mee;
And I hence fleeting, heere remaine with thee.
360 Away.   *Exeunt seuerally*

Sc. 4   *Enter Octauius reading a Letter, Lepidus, and their*
(1.4)   *Traine*

CÆSAR
You may see *Lepidus*, and henceforth know,
It is not *Cæsars* Naturall vice, to hate
Our great Competitor. From Alexandria
This is the newes: He fishes, drinkes, and wastes
The Lampes of night in reuell: Is not more manlike
Then *Cleopatra*: nor the Queene of *Ptolomy*
More Womanly then he. Hardly gaue audience
Or vouchsafd to thinke he had Partners. You shall
        finde there
A man, who is the abstracte of all faults,
That all men follow.

370 LEPIDUS   I must not thinke there are,
Euils enow to darken all his goodnesse:
His faults in him, seeme as the Spots of Heauen,
More fierie by nights Blacknesse; Hereditarie,
Rather then purchaste: what he cannot change,
Then what he chooses.

CÆSAR
You are too indulgent. Let's graunt it is not
Amisse to tumble on the bed of *Ptolomy*,
To giue a Kingdome for a Mirth, to sit
And keepe the turne of Tipling with a Slaue,

To reele the streets at noone, and stand the Buffet   380
With knaues that smels of sweate: Say this becoms him
(As his composure must be rare indeed,
Whom these things cannot blemish) yet must *Anthony*
No way excuse his foyles, when we do beare
So great waight in his lightnesse. If he fill'd
His vacancie with his Voluptuousnesse,
Full surfets, and the drinesse of his bones,
Call on him for't. But to confound such time,
That drummes him from his sport, and speakes as lowd
As his owne State, and ours, 'tis to be chid: 390
As we rate Boyes, who being mature in knowledge,
Pawne their experience to their present pleasure,
And so rebell to iudgement.

        Enter a Messenger

LEPIDUS   Heere's more newes.

MESSENGER
Thy biddings haue beene done, & euerie houre
Most Noble *Cæsar*, shalt thou haue report
How 'tis abroad. *Pompey* is strong at Sea,
And it appeares, he is belou'd of those
That only haue feard *Cæsar*: to the Ports
The discontents repaire, and mens reports
Giue him much wrong'd.   *Exit*

CÆSAR   I should haue knowne no lesse, 400
It hath bin taught vs from the primall state
That he which is was wisht, vntill he were:
And the ebb'd man, ne're lou'd, till ne're worth loue,
Comes dear'd, by being lack'd. This common bodie,
Like to a Vagabond Flagge vpon the Streame,
Goes too, and backe, lackying the varrying tyde
To rot it selfe with motion.

        Enter a Second Messenger

2. MESSENGER   *Cæsar* I bring thee word,
Menecrates and *Menas* famous Pyrates
Makes the Sea serue them, which they eare and
        wound
With keeles of euery kinde. Many hot inrodes   410
They make in Italy, the Borders Maritime
Lacke blood to thinke on't, and flush youth reuolt,
No Vessell can peepe forth: but 'tis as soone
Taken as seene: for *Pompeyes* name strikes more
Then could his Warre resisted.   *Exit*

CÆSAR   *Anthony*,
Leaue thy lasciuious Wassailes. When thou once
Was beaten from *Modena*, where thou slew'st
Hirsius, and *Pansa* Consuls, at thy heele
Did Famine follow, whom thou fought'st against,
(Though daintily brought vp) with patience more   420
Then Sauages could suffer. Thou did'st drinke
The stale of Horses, and the gilded Puddle
Which Beasts would cough at. Thy pallat thē did daine
The roughest Berry, on the rudest Hedge.
Yea, like the Stagge, when Snow the Pasture sheets,
The barkes of Trees thou brows'd. On the Alpes,
It is reported thou did'st eate strange flesh,
Which some did dye to looke on: And all this
(It wounds thine Honor that I speake it now)

430 Was borne so like a Soldiour, that thy cheeke
So much as lank'd not.

LEPIDUS 'Tis pitty of him.

CÆSAR Let his shames quickely
Driue him to Rome, 'tis time we twaine
Did shew our selues i'th'Field, and to that end
Assemble we immediate counsell, *Pompey*
Thriues in our Idlenesse.

LEPIDUS   To morrow *Cæsar*,
I shall be furnisht to informe you rightly
Both what by Sea and Land I can be able
To front this present time.

440 CÆSAR   Til which encounter,
It is my busines too. Farwell.

LEPIDUS
Farwell my Lord, what you shal know mean time
Of stirres abroad, I shall beseech you Sir
To let me be partaker.

CÆSAR
Doubt not sir, I knew it for my Bond.   *Exeunt*

Sc. 5   *Enter Cleopatra, Charmian, Iras, & Mardian*
(1.5) CLEOPATRA *Charmian.*

CHARMIAN Madam.

CLEOPATRA (*yawning*)
Ha, ha, giue me to drinke *Mandragora.*

CHARMIAN Why Madam?

CLEOPATRA
450 That I might sleepe out this great gap of time
My *Anthony* is away.

CHARMIAN   You thinke of him too much.

CLEOPATRA
O 'tis Treason.

CHARMIAN   Madam, I trust not so.

CLEOPATRA
Thou, Eunuch *Mardian?*

MARDIAN   What's your Highnesse pleasure?

CLEOPATRA
Not now to heare thee sing. I take no pleasure
In ought an Eunuch ha's: Tis well for thee,
That being vnseminar'd, thy freer thoughts
May not flye forth of Egypt. Hast thou Affections?

MARDIAN Yes gracious Madam.

CLEOPATRA Indeed?

MARDIAN
460 Not in deed Madam, for I can do nothing
But what in deede is honest to be done:
Yet haue I fierce Affections, and thinke
What Venus did with Mars.

CLEOPATRA   Oh *Charmion:*
Where think'st thou he is now? Stands he, or sits he?
Or does he walke? Or is he on his Horse?
Oh happy horse to beare the weight of *Anthony!*
Do brauely Horse, for wot'st thou whom thou moou'st,
The demy *Atlas* of this Earth, the Arme
And Burganet of men. Hee's speaking now,
470 Or murmuring, where's my Serpent of old Nyle,
(For so he cals me:) Now I feede my selfe

With most delicious poyson. Thinke on me
That am with *Phœbus* amorous pinches blacke,
And wrinkled deepe in time. Broad-fronted *Cæsar*,
When thou was't heere aboue the ground, I was
A morsell for a Monarke: and great *Pompey*
Would stand and make his eyes grow in my brow,
There would he anchor his Aspect, and dye
With looking on his life.

          Enter Alexas

ALEXAS   Soueraigne of Egypt, haile.

CLEOPATRA
How much vnlike art thou *Marke Anthony?*   480
Yet comming from him, that great Med'cine hath
With his Tinct gilded thee. How goes it
With my braue *Marke Anthonie?*

ALEXAS   Last thing he did (deere Queene)
He kist the last of many doubled kisses
This Orient Pearle. His speech stickes in my heart.

CLEOPATRA
Mine eare must plucke it thence.

ALEXAS   Good Friend, quoth he:
Say the firme Roman to great Egypt sends
This treasure of an Oyster: at whose foote
To mend the petty present, I will peece
Her opulent Throne, with Kingdomes. All the East,   490
(Say thou) shall call her Mistris. So he nodded,
And soberly did mount an Arme-iaunct Steede,
Who neigh'd so hye, that what I would haue spoke,
Was beastly dumbd by him.

CLEOPATRA   What was he sad, or merry?

ALEXAS
Like to the time o'th'yeare, between yᵉ extremes
Of hot and cold, he was nor sad nor merrie.

CLEOPATRA
Oh well diuided disposition: Note him,
Note him good *Charmian*, 'tis the man; but note him.
He was not sad, for he would shine on those
That make their lookes by his. He was not merrie,   500
Which seem'd to tell them, his remembrance lay
In Egypt with his ioy, but betweene both.
Oh heauenly mingle! Bee'st thou sad, or merrie,
The violence of either thee becomes,
So do's it no man else. Met'st thou my Posts?

ALEXAS
I Madam, twenty seuerall Messengers.
Why do you send so thicke?

CLEOPATRA   Who's borne that day,
When I forget to send to *Anthonie*,
Shall dye a Begger. Inke and paper *Charmian*.
Welcome my good *Alexas*. Did I *Charmian*,   510
Euer loue *Cæsar* so?

CHARMIAN   Oh that braue *Cæsar!*

CLEOPATRA
Be choak'd with such another Emphasis,
Say the braue *Anthony*.

CHARMIAN   The valiant *Cæsar.*

CLEOPATRA
By *Isis*, I will giue thee bloody teeth,

If thou with *Cæsar* Paragon againe
My man of men.
CHARMIAN   By your most gracious pardon,
I sing but after you.
CLEOPATRA   My Sallad dayes,
When I was greene in iudgement, cold in blood,
To say, as I saide then. But come, away,
520   Get me Inke and Paper,
Hee shall haue euery day a seuerall greeting,
Or Ile vnpeople Egypt.   *Exeunt*

Sc. 6   *Enter Pompey, Menecrates, and Menas, in warlike*
(2.1)   *manner*
POMPEY
If the great Gods be iust, they shall assist
The deeds of iustest men.
⌐MENECRATES⌐   Know worthy *Pompey*,
That what they do delay, they not deny.
POMPEY
Whiles we are sutors to their Throne, decayes
The thing we sue for.
⌐MENECRATES⌐   We ignorant of our selues,
Begge often our owne harmes, which the wise Powres
Deny vs for our good: so finde we profit
By loosing of our Prayers.
530   POMPEY   I shall do well:
The people loue me, and the Sea is mine;
My powers are Cressent, and my Auguring hope
Sayes it will come to'th'full. *Marke Anthony*
In Egypt sits at dinner, and will make
No warres without doores. *Cæsar* gets money where
He looses hearts: *Lepidus* flatters both,
Of both is flatter'd: but he neither loues,
Nor either cares for him.
⌐MENAS⌐   *Cæsar* and *Lepidus*
Are in the field, a mighty strength they carry.
POMPEY
Where haue you this? 'Tis false.
540   ⌐MENAS⌐   From *Siluius*, Sir.
POMPEY
He dreames: I know they are in Rome together
Looking for *Anthony*: but all the charmes of Loue,
Salt *Cleopatra* soften thy wand lip,
Let Witchcraft ioyne with Beauty, Lust with both,
Tye vp the Libertine, in a field of Feasts
Keepe his Braine fuming. Epicurean Cookes,
Sharpen with cloylesse sawce his Appetite,
That sleepe and feeding may prorogue his Honour,
Euen till a Lethied dulnesse—
            Enter Varrius
                              How now *Varrius?*
VARRIUS
550   This is most certaine, that I shall deliuer:
Marke Anthony is euery houre in Rome
Expected. Since he went from Egypt, 'tis
A space for farther Trauaile.
POMPEY   I could haue giuen lesse matter
A better eare. *Menas*, I did not thinke

This amorous Surfetter would haue donn'd his Helme
For such a petty Warre: His Souldiership
Is twice the other twaine: But let vs reare
The higher our Opinion, that our stirring
Can from the lap of Egypts Widdow, plucke
The neere Lust-wearied *Anthony.*
MENAS   I cannot hope,   560
Cæsar and *Anthony* shall well greet together;
His Wife that's dead, did trespasses to *Cæsar*,
His Brother war'd vpon him, although I thinke
Not mou'd by *Anthony.*
POMPEY   I know not *Menas*,
How lesser Enmities may giue way to greater,
Were't not that we stand vp against them all
'Twer pregnant they should square between
            themselues,
For they haue entertained cause enough
To draw their swords: but how the feare of vs
May Ciment their diuisions, and binde vp   570
The petty difference, we yet not know:
Bee't as our Gods will haue't; it onely stands
Our liues vpon, to vse our strongest hands.
Come *Menas.*   *Exeunt*

            Enter Enobarbus and Lepidus   Sc. 7
LEPIDUS   (2.2)
Good *Enobarbus*, 'tis a worthy deed,
And shall become you well, to intreat your Captaine
To soft and gentle speech.
ENOBARBUS   I shall intreat him
To answer like himselfe: if *Cæsar* moue him,
Let *Anthony* looke ouer *Cæsars* head,
And speake as lowd as Mars. By Iupiter,   580
Were I the wearer of *Anthonio's* Beard,
I would not shaue't to day.
LEPIDUS   'Tis not a time
For priuate stomacking.
ENOBARBUS   Euery time
Serues for the matter that is then borne in't.
LEPIDUS
But small to greater matters must giue way.
ENOBARBUS
Not if the small come first.
LEPIDUS   Your speech is passion:
But pray you stirre no Embers vp. Heere comes
The Noble *Anthony.*
            Enter at one doore Anthony and Ventidius
ENOBARBUS   And yonder *Cæsar.*
            Enter at another doore Cæsar, Mecenas, and
            Agrippa
ANTHONY (*to Ventidius*)
If we compose well heere, to Parthia:
Hearke *Ventidius.*
CÆSAR   I do not know   590
Mecenas, aske *Agrippa.*
LEPIDUS (*to Cæsar and Anthony*) Noble Friends:
That which combin'd vs was most great, and let not
A leaner action rend vs. What's amisse,

May it be gently heard. When we debate
Our triuiall difference loud, we do commit
Murther in healing wounds. Then Noble Partners,
The rather for I earnestly beseech,
Touch you the sowrest points with sweetest tearmes,
Nor curstnesse grow to'th'matter.

ANTHONY   'Tis spoken well:
600   Were we before our Armies, and to fight,
I should do thus.

    ⌈*Anthony and Cæsar embrace.*⌉ *Flourish*

CÆSAR Welcome to Rome.

ANTHONY Thanke you.

CÆSAR Sit.

ANTHONY Sit sir.

CÆSAR Nay then.

    They sit

ANTHONY
I learne, you take things ill, which are not so:
Or being, concerne you not.

CÆSAR   I must be laught at,
If or for nothing, or a little, I
610   Should say my selfe offended, and with you
Chiefely i'th'world. More laught at, that I should
Once name you derogately: when to sound your name
It not concern'd me.

ANTHONY
My being in Egypt *Cæsar*, what was't to you?

CÆSAR
No more then my reciding heere at Rome
Might be to you in Egypt: yet if you there
Did practise on my State, your being in Egypt
Might be my question.

ANTHONY   How intend you, practis'd?

CÆSAR
You may be pleas'd to catch at mine intent,
620   By what did heere befall me. Your Wife and Brother
Made warres vpon me, and their contestation
Was Theame for you, you were the word of warre.

ANTHONY
You do mistake yᵉ busines, my Brother neuer
Did vrge me in his Act: I did inquire it,
And haue my Learning from some true reports
That drew their swords with you, did he not rather
Discredit my authority with yours,
And make the warres alike against my stomacke,
Hauing alike your cause. Of this, my Letters
630   Before did satisfie you. If you'l patch a quarrell,
As matter whole you haue to make it with,
It must not be with this.

CÆSAR   You praise your selfe,
By laying defects of iudgement to me: but
You patcht vp your excuses.

ANTHONY   Not so, not so:
I know you could not lacke, I am certaine on't,
Very necessity of this thought, that I
Your Partner in the cause 'gainst which he fought,
Could not with gracefull eyes attend those Warres
Which fronted mine owne peace. As for my wife,

I would you had her spirit, in such another,   640
The third oth'world is yours, which with a Snaffle,
You may pace easie, but not such a wife.

ENOBARBUS Would we had all such wiues, that the men
might go to Warres with the women.

ANTHONY
So much vncurbable, her Garboiles (*Cæsar*)
Made out of her impatience: which not wanted
Shrodenesse of policie to: I greeuing grant,
Did you too much disquiet, for that you must
But say I could not helpe it.

CÆSAR   I wrote to you,
When rioting in Alexandria you   650
Did pocket vp my Letters: and with taunts
Did gibe my Misiue out of audience.

ANTHONY
Sir, he fell vpon me, ere admitted, then:
Three Kings I had newly feasted, and did want
Of what I was i'th'morning: but next day
I told him of my selfe, which was as much
As to haue askt him pardon. Let this Fellow
Be nothing of our strife: if we contend
Out of our question wipe him.

CÆSAR   You haue broken
The Article of your oath, which you shall neuer   660
Haue tongue to charge me with.

LEPIDUS Soft *Cæsar*.

ANTHONY No *Lepidus*, let him speake,
The Honour is Sacred which he talks on now,
Supposing that I lackt it: but on *Cæsar*,
The Article of my oath.

CÆSAR
To lend me Armes, and aide when I requir'd them,
The which you both denied.

ANTHONY   Neglected rather:
And then when poyson'd houres had bound me vp
From mine owne knowledge: as neerely as I may,   670
Ile play the penitent to you. But mine honesty,
Shall not make poore my greatnesse, nor my power
Worke without it. Truth is, that *Fuluia*,
To haue me out of Egypt, made Warres heere,
For which my selfe, the ignorant motiue, do
So farre aske pardon, as befits mine Honour
To stoope in such a case.

LEPIDUS   'Tis Noble spoken.

MECENAS
If it might please you, to enforce no further
The griefes betweene ye: to forget them quite,
Were to remember: that the present neede,   680
Speakes to attone you.

LEPIDUS   Worthily spoken *Mecenas*.

ENOBARBUS Or if you borrow one anothers Loue for the
instant, you may when you heare no more words of
Pompey returne it againe: you shall haue time to
wrangle in, when you haue nothing else to do.

ANTHONY
Thou art a Souldier onely, speake no more.

ENOBARBUS That trueth should be silent, I had almost
    forgot.
ANTHONY
    You wrong this presence, therefore speake no more.
690 ENOBARBUS Go too then: your Considerate stone.
CÆSAR
    I do not much dislike the matter, but
    The manner of his speech: for't cannot be,
    We shall remaine in friendship, our conditions
    So diffring in their acts. Yet if I knew,
    What Hoope should hold vs staunch, from edge to edge
    Ath'world I would persue it.
AGRIPPA Giue me leaue Cæsar.
CÆSAR Speake Agrippa.
AGRIPPA
    Thou hast a Sister by the Mothers side,
700   Admir'd Octauia: Great Mark Anthony
    Is now a widdower.
CÆSAR   Say not so Agrippa;
    If Cleopater heard you, your reproofe
    Were well deseru'd of rashnesse.
ANTHONY
    I am not married Cæsar: let me heere
    Agrippa further speake.
AGRIPPA
    To hold you in perpetuall amitie,
    To make you Brothers, and to knit your hearts
    With an vn-slipping knot, take Anthony,
    Octauia to his wife: whose beauty claimes
710   No worse a husband then the best of men:
    Whose Vertue, and whose generall graces, speake
    That which none else can vtter. By this marriage,
    All little Ielousies which now seeme great,
    And all great feares, which now import their dangers,
    Would then be nothing. Truth's would be tales,
    Where now halfe tales be truth's: her loue to both,
    Would each to other, and all loues to both
    Draw after her. Pardon what I haue spoke,
    For 'tis a studied not a present thought,
    By duty ruminated.
720 ANTHONY   Will Cæsar speake?
CÆSAR
    Not till he heares how Anthony is toucht,
    With what is spoke already.
ANTHONY What power is in Agrippa,
    If I would say Agrippa, be it so,
    To make this good?
CÆSAR   The power of Cæsar,
    And his power, vnto Octauia.
ANTHONY   May I neuer
    (To this good purpose, that so fairely shewes)
    Dreame of impediment: let me haue thy hand.
    Further this act of Grace: and from this houre,
730   The heart of Brothers gouerne in our Loues,
    And sway our great Designes.
CÆSAR   There's my hand:
        Anthony and Cæsar shake hands

A Sister I bequeath you, whom no Brother
    Did euer loue so deerely. Let her liue
    To ioyne our kingdomes, and our hearts, and neuer
    Flie off our Loues againe.
LEPIDUS   Happily, Amen.
ANTHONY
    I did not think to draw my Sword 'gainst Pompey,
    For he hath laid strange courtesies, and great
    Of late vpon me. I must thanke him onely,
    Least my remembrance, suffer ill report:
    At heele of that, defie him.
LEPIDUS   Time cals vpon's,   740
    Of vs must Pompey presently be sought,
    Or else he seekes out vs.
ANTHONY   Where lies he?
CÆSAR
    About the Mount-Mesena.
ANTHONY   What is his strength
    By land?
CÆSAR   Great, and encreasing: But by Sea
    He is an absolute Master.
ANTHONY   So is the Fame,
    Would we had spoke together. Hast we for it,
    Yet ere we put our selues in Armes, dispatch we
    The businesse we haue talkt of.
CÆSAR   With most gladnesse,
    And do inuite you to my Sisters view,
    Whether straight Ile lead you.
ANTHONY   Let vs Lepidus   750
    Not lacke your companie.
LEPIDUS   Noble Anthony,
    Not sickenesse should detaine me.
                Flourish. Exit omnes. Manet Enobarbus,
                                Agrippa, Mecenas
MECENAS (to Enobarbus) Welcome from Ægypt Sir.
ENOBARBUS Halfe the heart of Cæsar, worthy Mecenas. My
    honourable Friend Agrippa.
AGRIPPA Good Enobarbus.
MECENAS We haue cause to be glad, that matters are so
    well disgested: you staid well by't in Egypt.
ENOBARBUS I Sir, we did sleepe day out of countenaunce:
    and made the night light with drinking.   760
MECENAS Eight Wilde-Boares rosted whole at a breakfast:
    and but twelue persons there. Is this true?
ENOBARBUS This was but as a Flye by an Eagle: we had
    much more monstrous matter of Feast, which worthily
    deserued noting.
MECENAS She's a most triumphant Lady, if report be
    square to her.
ENOBARBUS When she first met Marke Anthony, she purst
    vp his heart vpon the Riuer of Sidnis.
AGRIPPA There she appear'd indeed: or my reporter   770
    deuis'd well for her.
ENOBARBUS I will tell you,
    The Barge she sat in, like a burnisht Throne
    Burnt on the water: the Poope was beaten Gold,
    Purple the Sailes: and so perfumed that

The Windes were Loue-sicke with them. The Owers
    were Siluer,
Which to the tune of Flutes kept stroke, and made
The water which they beate, to follow faster;
As amorous of their strokes. For her owne person,
780 It beggerd all discription, she did lye
In her Pauillion, cloth of Gold, of Tissue,
O're-picturing that Venus, where we see
The fancie out-worke Nature. On each side her,
Stood pretty Dimpled Boyes, like smiling Cupids,
With diuers coulour'd Fannes whose winde did seeme,
To gloue the delicate cheekes which they did coole,
And what they vndid did.

AGRIPPA   Oh rare for *Anthony*.

ENOBARBUS
Her Gentlewomen, like the Nereides,
So many Mer-maides tended her i'th'eyes,
790 And made their bends adornings. At the Helme,
A seeming Mer-maide steeres: The Silken Tackle,
Swell with the touches of those Flower-soft hands,
That yarely frame the office. From the Barge
A strange inuisible perfume hits the sense
Of the adiacent Wharfes. The Citty cast
Her people out vpon her: and *Anthony*
Enthron'd i'th'Market-place, did sit alone,
Whisling to'th'ayre: which but for vacancie,
Had gone to gaze on *Cleopater* too,
And made a gap in Nature.

800 AGRIPPA   Rare Egiptian.

ENOBARBUS
Vpon her landing, *Anthony* sent to her,
Inuited her to Supper: she replyed,
It should be better, he became her guest:
Which she entreated, our Courteous *Anthony*,
Whom nere the word of no woman hard speake,
Being barber'd ten times o're, goes to the Feast;
And for his ordinary, paies his heart,
For what his eyes eate onely.

AGRIPPA   Royall Wench:
She made great *Cæsar* lay his Sword to bed,
He ploughed her, and she cropt.

810 ENOBARBUS   I saw her once
Hop forty Paces through the publicke streete,
And hauing lost her breath, she spoke, and panted,
That she did make defect, perfection,
And breathlesse powre breath forth.

MECENAS   Now *Anthony*,
Must leaue her vtterly.

ENOBARBUS   Neuer he will not:
Age cannot wither her, nor custome stale
Her infinite variety: other women cloy
The appetites they feede, but she makes hungry,
Where most she satisfies. For vildest things
820 Become themselues in her, that the holy Priests
Blesse her, when she is Riggish.

MECENAS
If Beauty, Wisedome, Modesty, can settle

The heart of *Anthony*: *Octauia* is
A blessed Lottery to him.

AGRIPPA   Let vs go.
Good *Enobarbus*, make your selfe my guest,
Whilst you abide heere.

ENOBARBUS   Humbly Sir I thanke you.
                                 Exeunt

    Enter Anthony, Cæsar, Octauia betweene them   Sc. 8

ANTHONY   (2.3)
The world, and my great office, will sometimes
Deuide me from your bosome.

OCTAUIA   All which time,
Before the Gods my knee shall bowe my prayers
To them for you.

ANTHONY   Goodnight Sir. My *Octauia*   830
Read not my blemishes in the worlds report:
I haue not kept my square, but that to come
Shall all be done byth'Rule: good night deere Lady:
Good night Sir.

CÆSAR Goodnight.   *Exeunt Cæsar and Octauia*
    Enter Soothsaier

ANTHONY
Now sirrah: you do wish your selfe in Egypt?

SOOTHSAYER
Would I had neuer come from thence, nor you
Gone thither.

ANTHONY   If you can, your reason?

SOOTHSAYER
I see it in my motion: haue it not in my tongue,
But yet hie you to Egypt againe.

ANTHONY   Say to me,   840
Whose Fortunes shall rise higher *Cæsars* or mine?

SOOTHSAYER
Cæsars. Therefore (oh *Anthony*) stay not by his side.
Thy Dæmon that thy spirit which keepes thee, is
Noble, Couragious, high vnmatchable,
Where *Cæsars* is not. But neere him, thy Angell
Becomes a feard, as being o're-powr'd: therefore
Make space enough betweene you.

ANTHONY   Speake this no more.

SOOTHSAYER
To none but thee: no more but when to thee,
If thou dost play with him at any game,
Thou art sure to loose: And of that Naturall lucke,   850
He beats thee 'gainst the oddes. Thy Luster thickens,
When he shines by: I say againe, thy spirit
Is all affraid to gouerne thee neere him:
But he away 'tis Noble.

ANTHONY   Get thee gone:
Say to *Ventigius* I would speake with him.
                             Exit Soothsaier
He shall to Parthia, be it Art or hap,
He hath spoken true. The very Dice obey him,
And in our sports my better cunning faints,
Vnder his chance, if we draw lots he speeds,
His Cocks do winne the Battaile, still of mine,   860
When it is all to naught: and his Quailes euer

Beate mine (in hoopt) at odd's. I will to Egypte:
And though I make this marriage for my peace,
I'th'East my pleasure lies.
   Enter Ventigius
      Oh come *Ventigius.*
You must to Parthia, your Commissions ready:
Follow me, and reciue't.   *Exeunt*

Sc. 9   *Enter Lepidus, Mecenas and Agrippa*
(2.4) LEPIDUS
  Trouble your selues no further: pray you hasten
  Your Generals after.
  AGRIPPA   Sir, *Marke Anthony,*
  Will e'ne but kisse *Octauia,* and weele follow.
  LEPIDUS
870 Till I shall see you in your Souldiers dresse,
  Which will become you both: Farewell.
  MECENAS   We shall:
  As I conceiue the iourney, be at the Mount
  Before you *Lepidus.*
  LEPIDUS   Your way is shorter,
  My purposes do draw me much about,
  You'le win two dayes vpon me.
  MECENAS *and* AGRIPPA   Sir good successe.
  LEPIDUS Farewell.
    Exeunt Mecenas and Agrippa at one doore,
      Lepidus at another

Sc. 10 *Enter Cleopater, Charmian, Iras, and Alexas*
(2.5) CLEOPATRA
  Giue me some Musicke: Musicke, moody foode
  Of vs that trade in Loue.
  CHARMIAN, IRAS *and* ALEXAS The Musicke, hoa.
    Enter Mardian the Eunuch
  CLEOPATRA
  Let it alone, let's to Billards: come *Charmian.*
  CHARMIAN
880 My arme is sore, best play with *Mardian.*
  CLEOPATRA
  As well a woman with an Eunuch plaide,
  As with a woman. Come you'le play with me Sir?
  MARDIAN As well as I can Madam.
  CLEOPATRA
  And when good will is shewed, though't come to
    short
  The Actor may pleade pardon. Ile none now,
  Giue me mine Angle, weele to'th'Riuer. There
  My Musicke playing farre off I will betray
  Tawny find fishes, my bended hooke shall pierce
  Their slimy iawes: and as I draw them vp,
890 Ile thinke them euery one an *Anthony,*
  And say, ah ha; y'are caught.
  CHARMIAN   'Twas merry when
  You wager'd on your Angling, when your diuer
  Did hang a salt fish on his hooke which he
  With feruencie drew vp.
  CLEOPATRA   That time? Oh times:
  I laught him out of patience: and that night
  I laught him into patience, and next morne,

Ere the ninth houre, I drunke him to his bed:
Then put my Tires and Mantles on him, whilst
I wore his Sword Phillippan.
  Enter a Messenger
      Oh from Italie,
Ramme thou thy fruitefull tidings in mine eares, 900
That long time haue bin barren.
MESSENGER   Madam, Madam.
CLEOPATRA
Anthonyo's dead. If thou say so Villaine,
Thou kil'st thy Mistris: But well and free,
If thou so yeild him, there is Gold, and heere
My blewest vaines to kisse: a hand that Kings
Haue lipt, and trembled kissing.
MESSENGER   First Madam, he is well.
CLEOPATRA
Why there's more Gold. But sirrah marke, we vse
To say, the dead are well: bring it to that,
The Gold I giue thee, will I melt and powr
Downe thy ill vttering throate.   910
MESSENGER Good Madam heare me.
CLEOPATRA Well, go too I will:
But there's no goodnesse in thy face. If *Anthony*
Be free and healthfull; so tart a fauour
To trumpet such good tidings. If not well,
Thou shouldst come like a Furie crown'd with Snakes,
Not like a formall man.
MESSENGER   Wilt please you heare me?
CLEOPATRA
I haue a mind to strike thee ere thou speak'st:
Yet if thou say *Anthony* liues, is well,
Or friends with *Cæsar,* or not Captiue to him, 920
Ile set thee in a shower of Gold, and haile
Rich Pearles vpon thee.
MESSENGER   Madam, he's well.
CLEOPATRA   Well said.
MESSENGER
And Friends with *Cæsar.*
CLEOPATRA   Th'art an honest man.
MESSENGER
Cæsar, and he, are greater Friends then euer.
CLEOPATRA
Make thee a Fortune from me.
MESSENGER   But yet Madam.
CLEOPATRA
I do not like but yet, it does alay
The good precedence, fie vpon but yet,
But yet is as a Iaylor to bring foorth
Some monstrous Malefactor. Prythee Friend,
Powre out the packe of matter to mine eare, 930
The good and bad together: he's friends with *Cæsar,*
In state of health thou saist, and thou saist, free.
MESSENGER
Free Madam, no: I made no such report,
He's bound vnto *Octauia.*
CLEOPATRA   For what good turne?
MESSENGER
For the best turne i'th'bed.
CLEOPATRA   I am pale *Charmian.*

MESSENGER
Madam, he's married to *Octauia*.
CLEOPATRA
The most infectious Pestilence vpon thee.
            Strikes him downe
MESSENGER
Good Madam patience.
CLEOPATRA   What say you?
            Strikes him
Hence horrible Villaine, or Ile spurne thine eyes
940 Like balls before me: Ile vnhaire thy head,
            She hales him vp and downe
Thou shalt be whipt with Wyer, and stew'd in brine,
Smarting in lingring pickle.
MESSENGER   Gratious Madam,
I that do bring the newes, made not the match.
CLEOPATRA
Say 'tis not so, a Prouince I will giue thee,
And make thy Fortunes proud: the blow thou had'st
Shall make thy peace, for mouing me to rage,
And I will boot thee with what guift beside
Thy modestie can begge.
MESSENGER   He's married Madam.
CLEOPATRA
Rogue, thou hast liu'd too long.
            Draw a knife
MESSENGER   Nay then Ile runne:
950 What meane you Madam, I haue made no fault.   *Exit*
CHARMIAN
Good Madam keepe your selfe within your selfe,
The man is innocent.
CLEOPATRA
Some Innocents scape not the thunderbolt:
Melt Egypt into Nyle: and kindly creatures
Turne all to Serpents. Call the slaue againe,
Though I am mad, I will not byte him: Call?
CHARMIAN
He is afeard to come.
CLEOPATRA   I will not hurt him,
                    ⌈*Exit Charmian*⌉
These hands do lacke Nobility, that they strike
A meaner then my selfe: since I my selfe
Haue giuen my selfe the cause.
            Enter the Messenger againe, ⌈*with Charmian*⌉
960   Come hither Sir.
Though it be honest, it is neuer good
To bring bad newes: giue to a gratious Message
An host of tongues, but let ill tydings tell
Themselues, when they be felt.
MESSENGER I haue done my duty.
CLEOPATRA Is he married?
I cannot hate thee worser then I do,
If thou againe say yes.
MESSENGER   He's married Madam.
CLEOPATRA
The Gods confound thee, dost thou hold there still?
MESSENGER
Should I lye Madame?
970 CLEOPATRA   Oh, I would thou didst:

So halfe my Egypt were submerg'd and made
A Cesterne for scal'd Snakes. Go get thee hence,
Had'st thou *Narcissus* in thy face to me,
Thou would'st appeere most vgly: He is married?
MESSENGER
I craue your Highnesse pardon.
CLEOPATRA   He is married?
MESSENGER
Take no offence, that I would not offend you,
To punnish me for what you make me do
Seemes much vnequall, he's married to *Octauia*.
CLEOPATRA
Oh that his fault should make a knaue of thee,
That act not what th'art sure of. Get thee hence, 980
The Marchandize which thou hast brought from Rome
Are all too deere for me: Lye they vpon thy hand,
And be vndone by em.   *Exit Messenger*
CHARMIAN   Good your Highnesse patience.
CLEOPATRA
In praysing *Anthony*, I haue disprais'd *Cæsar*.
CHARMIAN Many times Madam.
CLEOPATRA
I am paid for't now: lead me from hence,
I faint, oh *Iras*, *Charmian*: 'tis no matter.
Go to the Fellow, good *Alexas* bid him
Report the feature of *Octauia*: her yeares,
Her inclination, let him not leaue out 990
The colour of her haire. Bring me word quickly,
                    Exit Alexas
Let him for euer go, let him not *Charmian*,
Though he be painted one way like a Gorgon,
The other wayes a Mars. ⌈*To Mardian*⌉ Bid you *Alexas*
Bring me word, how tall she is: pitty me *Charmian*,
But do not speake to me. Lead me to my Chamber.
                    Exeunt

Flourish. Enter Pompey and Menas, at one doore   Sc. 11
with Drum and Trumpet: at another Cæsar,   (2.6)
Lepidus, Anthony, Enobarbus, Mecenas, Agrippa,
with Souldiers Marching
POMPEY
Your Hostages I haue, so haue you mine:
And we shall talke before we fight.
CÆSAR   Most meete
That first we come to words, and therefore haue we
Our written purposes before vs sent, 1000
Which if thou hast consider'd, let vs know,
If 'twill tye vp thy discontented Sword,
And carry backe to Cicelie much tall youth,
That else must perish heere.
POMPEY   To you all three,
The Senators alone of this great world,
Chiefe Factors for the Gods. I do not know,
Wherefore my Father should reuengers want,
Hauing a Sonne and Friends, since *Iulius Cæsar*,
Who at Phillippi the good *Brutus* ghosted,
There saw you labouring for him. What was't 1010
That mou'd pale *Cassius* to conspire? And what
Made the all-honor'd, honest, Romaine *Brutus*,

With the arm'd rest, Courtiers of beautious freedome,
To drench the Capitoll, but that they would
Haue one man but a man, and that is it
Hath made me rigge my Nauie. At whose burthen,
The anger'd Ocean fomes, with which I meant
To scourge th'ingratitude, that despightfull Rome
Cast on my Noble Father.

CÆSAR   Take your time.

ANTHONY
1020   Thou can'st not feare vs *Pompey* with thy sailes.
Weele speake with thee at Sea. At land thou know'st
How much we do o're-count thee.

POMPEY   At Land indeed
Thou dost orecount me of my Fathers house:
But since the Cuckoo buildes not for himselfe,
Remaine in't as thou maist.

LEPIDUS   Be pleas'd to tell vs,
(For this is from the present) how you take
The offers we haue sent you.

CÆSAR   There's the point.

ANTHONY
Which do not be entreated too, but waigh
What it is worth imbrac'd.

CÆSAR   And what may follow
To try a larger Fortune.

1030 POMPEY   You haue made me offer
Of Cicelie, Sardinia : and I must
Rid all the Sea of Pirats. Then, to send
Measures of Wheate to Rome : this greed vpon,
To part with vnhackt edges, and beare backe
Our Targes vndinted.

CÆSAR, ANTHONY *and* LEPIDUS That's our offer.

POMPEY   Know then
I came before you heere, a man prepar'd
To take this offer. But *Marke Anthony*,
Put me to some impatience : though I loose
The praise of it by telling, you must know
1040   When *Cæsar* and your Brother were at blowes,
Your Mother came to Cicelie, and did finde
Her welcome Friendly.

ANTHONY   I haue heard it *Pompey*,
And am well studied for a liberall thanks,
Which I do owe you.

POMPEY   Let me haue your hand :
   Pompey and Anthony shake hands
I did not thinke Sir, to haue met you heere.

ANTHONY
The beds i'th'East are soft, and thanks to you,
That cal'd me timelier then my purpose hither :
For I haue gain'd by't.

CÆSAR (*to Pompey*)   Since I saw you last,
Ther is a change vpon you.

POMPEY   Well, I know not,
1050   What counts harsh Fortune cast's vpon my face,
But in my bosome shall she neuer come,
To make my heart her vassaile.

LEPIDUS   Well met heere.

POMPEY
I hope so *Lepidus*, thus we are agreed :

I craue our composition may be written
And seal'd betweene vs.

CÆSAR   That's the next to do.

POMPEY
Weele feast each other, ere we part, and lett's
Draw lots who shall begin.

ANTHONY That will I *Pompey*.

POMPEY No *Anthony* take the lot :
But first or last, your fine Egyptian cookerie   1060
Shall haue the fame, I haue heard that *Iulius Cæsar*,
Grew fat with feasting there.

ANTHONY   You haue heard much.

POMPEY I haue faire meanings Sir.

ANTHONY And faire words to them.

POMPEY Then so much haue I heard,
And I haue heard *Appolodorus* carried—

ENOBARBUS
No more o'that : he did so.

POMPEY   What I pray you ?

ENOBARBUS
A certaine Queene to *Cæsar* in a Matris.

POMPEY
I know thee now, how far'st thou Souldier ?

ENOBARBUS
Well, and well am like to do, for I perceiue   1070
Foure Feasts are toward.

POMPEY   Let me shake thy hand,
   Pompey and Enobarbus shake hands
I neuer hated thee : I haue seene thee fight,
When I haue enuied thy behauiour.

ENOBARBUS
Sir, I neuer lou'd you much, but I ha'prais'd ye,
When you haue well deseru'd ten times as much,
As I haue said you did.

POMPEY
Inioy thy plainnesse, it nothing ill becomes thee :
Aboord my Gally, I inuite you all.
Will you leade Lords ?

CÆSAR, ANTHONY *and* LEPIDUS Shew's the way, sir :

POMPEY   Come.
           Exeunt. Manet Enobarbus & Menas

MENAS (*aside*)
Thy Father *Pompey* would ne're haue made this
      Treaty.   1080
(*To Enobarbus*) You, and I haue knowne sir.

ENOBARBUS At Sea, I thinke.

MENAS We haue Sir.

ENOBARBUS You haue done well by water.

MENAS And you by Land.

ENOBARBUS I will praise any man that will praise me,
   thogh it cannot be denied what I haue done by Land.

MENAS Nor what I haue done by water.

ENOBARBUS Yes some-thing you can deny for your owne
   safety : you haue bin a great Theefe by Sea.   1090

MENAS And you by Land.

ENOBARBUS There I deny my Land seruice : but giue mee
   your hand *Menas*, if our eyes had authority, heere they
   might take two Theeues kissing.

They shake hands

MENAS All mens faces are true, whatsomere their hands
are.

ENOBARBUS But there is neuer a fayre Woman, ha's a true
Face.

MENAS No slander, they steale hearts.

1100 ENOBARBUS We came hither to fight with you.

MENAS For my part, I am sorry it is turn'd to a Drinking.
Pompey doth this day laugh away his Fortune.

ENOBARBUS If he do, sure he cannot weep't backe againe.

MENAS Y'haue said Sir, we look'd not for *Marke Anthony*
heere, pray you, is he married to *Cleopatra?*

ENOBARBUS *Cæsars* Sister is call'd *Octauia.*

MENAS True Sir, she was the wife of *Caius Marcellus.*

ENOBARBUS But she is now the wife of *Marcus Anthonius.*

MENAS Pray'ye sir.

1110 ENOBARBUS 'Tis true.

MENAS Then is *Cæsar* and he, for euer knit together.

ENOBARBUS If I were bound to Diuine of this vnity, I wold
not Prophesie so.

MENAS I thinke the policy of that purpose, made more in
the Marriage, then the loue of the parties.

ENOBARBUS I thinke so too. But you shall finde the band
that seemes to tye their friendship together, will bee
the very strangler of their Amity: *Octauia* is of a holy,
cold, and still conuersation.

1120 MENAS Who would not haue his wife so?

ENOBARBUS Not he that himselfe is not so: which is *Marke
Anthony*: he will to his Egyptian dish againe: then shall
the sighes of *Octauia* blow the fire vp in *Cæsar*, and (as
I said before) that which is the strength of their Amity,
shall proue the immediate Author of their variance.
Anthony will vse his affection where it is. Hee married
but his occasion heere.

MENAS And thus it may be. Come Sir, will you aboord?
I haue a health for you.

1130 ENOBARBUS I shall take it sir: we haue vs'd our Throats
in Egypt.

MENAS Come, let's away.   *Exeunt*

Sc. 12   *Musicke playes. Enter two or three Seruants with a*
(2.7)   *Banket*

1. SERUANT Heere they'l be man: some o'their Plants are
ill rooted already, the least winde i'th'world wil blow
them downe.

2. SERUANT *Lepidus* is high Coulord.

1. SERUANT They haue made him drinke Almes drinke.

2. SERUANT As they pinch one another by the disposition,
hee cries out, no more; reconciles them to his entreatie,
1140   and himselfe to'th'drinke.

1. SERUANT But it raises the greater warre betweene him
& his discretion.

2. SERUANT Why this it is to haue a name in great mens
Fellowship: I had as liue haue a Reede that will doe
me no seruice, as a Partizan I could not heaue.

1. SERUANT To be call'd into a huge Sphere, and not to
be seene to moue in't, are the holes where eyes should
bee, which pittifully disaster the cheekes.

*A Sennet sounded. Enter Cæsar, Anthony, Pompey,
Lepidus, Agrippa, Mecenas, Enobarbus, Menas,
with other Captaines ⌈and a Boy⌉*

ANTHONY (*to Cæsar*)
Thus do they Sir: they take the flow o'th'Nyle
By certaine scales i'th'Pyramid: they know   1150
By'th'height, the lownesse, or the meane: If dearth
Or Foizon follow. The higher Nilus swels,
The more it promises: as it ebbes, the Seedsman
Vpon the slime and Ooze scatters his graine,
And shortly comes to Haruest.

LEPIDUS Y'haue strange Serpents there?

ANTHONY I *Lepidus.*

LEPIDUS Your Serpent of Egypt, is bred now of your mud
by the operation of your Sun: so is your Crocodile.

ANTHONY They are so.   1160

POMPEY
Sit, and some Wine: A health to *Lepidus.*
⌈*Anthony, Pompey and Lepidus sit*⌉

LEPIDUS I am not so well as I should be: But Ile ne're
out.

ENOBARBUS Not till you haue slept: I feare me you'l bee
in till then.

LEPIDUS Nay certainly, I haue heard the *Ptolomies*
Pyramisis are very goodly things: without contradiction
I haue heard that.

MENAS (*aside to Pompey*)
Pompey, a word.

POMPEY (*aside to Menas*) Say in mine eare, what is't.

MENAS (*aside to Pompey*)
Forsake thy seate I do beseech thee Captaine,
And heare me speake a word.   1170

POMPEY (*aside to Menas*)   Forbeare me till anon.
(*Aloud*) This Wine for *Lepidus.*
Menas whispers in Pompey's Eare

LEPIDUS What manner o'thing is your Crocodile?

ANTHONY It is shap'd sir like it selfe, and it is as broad as
it hath bredth; It is iust so high as it is, and mooues
with it owne organs. It liues by that which nourisheth
it, and the Elements once out of it, it Transmigrates.

LEPIDUS What colour is it of?

ANTHONY Of it owne colour too.

LEPIDUS 'Tis a strange Serpent.   1180

ANTHONY 'Tis so, and the teares of it are wet.

CÆSAR (*to Anthony*)
Will this description satisfie him?

ANTHONY With the Health that *Pompey* giues him, else he
is a very Epicure.

POMPEY (*aside to Menas*)
Go hang sir, hang: tell me of that? Away:
Do as I bid you. (*Aloud*) Where's this Cup I call'd for?

MENAS (*aside to Pompey*)
If for the sake of Merit thou wilt heare mee,
Rise from thy stoole.

POMPEY ⌈*rising*⌉   I thinke th'art mad: the matter?
⌈*Menas and Pompey stande apart*⌉

MENAS
I haue euer held my cap off to thy Fortunes.

POMPEY

1190   Thou hast seru'd me with much faith: what's else to
       say?
       Be iolly Lords.

ANTHONY   These Quicke-sands Lepidus,
       Keepe off them, for you sinke.

MENAS
       Wilt thou be Lord of all the world?

POMPEY   What saist thou?

MENAS
       Wilt thou be Lord of the whole world? That's twice.

POMPEY
       How should that be?

MENAS   But entertaine it,
       And though thou thinke me poore, I am the man
       Will giue thee all the world.

POMPEY   Hast thou drunke well.

MENAS
       No Pompey, I haue kept me from the cup,
       Thou art if thou dar'st be, the earthly Ioue:
1200   What ere the Ocean pales, or skie inclippes,
       Is thine, if thou wilt ha't.

POMPEY   Shew me which way?

MENAS
       These three World-sharers, these Competitors
       Are in thy vessell. Let me cut the Cable,
       And when we are put off, fall to their throates:
       All there is thine.

POMPEY   Ah, this thou shouldst haue done,
       And not haue spoke on't. In me 'tis villanie,
       In thee, 't had bin good seruice: thou must know,
       'Tis not my profit that does lead mine Honour:
       Mine Honour it, Repent that ere thy tongue,
1210   Hath so betraide thine acte. Being done vnknowne,
       I should haue found it afterwards well done,
       But must condemne it now: desist, and drinke.
             He returnes to the others

MENAS (aside)
       For this, Ile neuer follow thy paul'd Fortunes more,
       Who seekes and will not take, when once 'tis offer'd,
       Shall neuer finde it more.

POMPEY   This health to Lepidus.

ANTHONY
       Beare him ashore, Ile pledge it for him Pompey.

ENOBARBUS
       Heere's to thee Menas.

MENAS   Enobarbus, welcome.

POMPEY
       Fill till the cup be hid.
             One liftes Lepidus, drunk, and carries him off

ENOBARBUS   There's a strong Fellow Menas.

MENAS Why?

ENOBARBUS
1220   A beares the third part of the world man: seest not?

MENAS
       The third part then is drunk: would it were all,
       That it might go on wheeles.

ENOBARBUS   Drinke thou: encrease the Reeles.

MENAS Come.

POMPEY
       This is not yet an Alexandrian Feast.

ANTHONY
       It ripen's towards it: strike the Vessells hoa.
       Heere's to Cæsar.

CÆSAR   I could well forbear't,
       It's monstrous labour when I wash my braine,
       And it grow fouler.

ANTHONY Be a Child o'th'time.

CÆSAR Possesse it, Ile make answer: 1230
       But I had rather fast from all, foure dayes,
       Then drinke so much in one.

ENOBARBUS (to Anthony)   Ha my braue Emperour,
       Shall we daunce now the Egyptian Backenals,
       And celebrate our drinke?

POMPEY Let's ha't good Souldier.

ANTHONY Come, let's all take hands,
       Till that the conquering Wine hath steep't our sense,
       In soft and delicate Lethe.

ENOBARBUS   All take hands:
       Make battery to our eares with the loud Musicke,
       The while, Ile place you, then the Boy shall sing.   1240
       The holding euery man shall beate as loud,
       As his strong sides can volly.
             Musicke Playes. Enobarbus places them hand in
             hand
                    The Song

⌈BOY⌉   Come thou Monarch of the Vine,
        Plumpie Bacchus, with pinke eyne:
        In thy Fattes our Cares be drown'd,
        With thy Grapes our haires be Crown'd.
        Cup vs till the world go round,
        Cup vs till the world go round.

CÆSAR
       What would you more? Pompey goodnight.
       (To Anthony)   Good Brother
       Let me request you of: our grauer businesse   1250
       Frownes at this leuitie. Gentle Lords let's part,
       You see we haue burnt our cheekes. Strong Enobarbe
       Is weaker then the Wine, and mine owne tongue
       Spleet's what it speakes: the wilde disguise hath almost
       Antickt vs all. What needs more words? goodnight.
       Good Anthony your hand.

POMPEY   Ile try you on the shore.

ANTHONY
       And shall Sir, giues your hand.

POMPEY   Oh Anthony,
       You haue my Fathers house. But what, we are Friends?
       Come downe into the Boate.
             Exeunt all but Enobarbus and Menas

ENOBARBUS
       Take heed you fall not Menas.

MENAS   Ile not on shore,   1260
       No to my Cabin: these Drummes, these Trumpets,
       Flutes: what
       Let Neptune heare, we bid a loud farewell
       To these great Fellowes. Sound and be hang'd, sound
       out.

Sound a Flourish with Drummes
ENOBARBUS (*throwing his Cap in the Ayre*)
　Hoo saies a there's my Cap.
MENAS   Hoa Noble Captaine, come.
　　　　　　　　　　　　　　　　　　　　Exeunt

Sc. 13　　　*Enter Ventidius with Sillius and other Roman*
(3.1)　　　*Soldiours as it were in triumph, the dead body of*
　　　　　　Pacorus borne before him
　　VENTIDIUS
　　　Now darting Parthya art thou stroke, and now
　　　Pleas'd Fortune does of *Marcus Crassus* death
　　　Make me reuenger. Beare the Kings Sonnes body,
　　　Before our Army, thy *Pacorus Orades*,
　　　Paies this for *Marcus Crassus*.
　　SILLIUS   Noble *Ventidius*,
1270　　Whil'st yet with Parthian blood thy Sword is warme,
　　　The Fugitiue Parthians follow. Spurre through Media,
　　　Mesapotamia, and the shelters, whether
　　　The routed flie. So thy grand Captaine *Anthony*
　　　Shall set thee on triumphant Chariots, and
　　　Put Garlands on thy head.
　　VENTIDIUS   Oh *Sillius, Sillius*,
　　　I haue done enough. A lower place note well
　　　May make to great an act. For learne this *Sillius*,
　　　Better to leaue vndone, then by our deed
　　　Acquire too high a Fame, when him we serues away.
1280　　*Cæsar* and *Anthony*, haue euer wonne
　　　More in their officer, then person. *Sossius*
　　　One of my place in Syria, his Lieutenant,
　　　For quicke accumulation of renowne,
　　　Which he atchiu'd by'th'minute, lost his fauour.
　　　Who does i'th'Warres more then his Captaine can,
　　　Becomes his Captaines Captaine: and Ambition
　　　(The Souldiers vertue) rather makes choise of losse
　　　Then gaine, which darkens him.
　　　I could do more to do *Anthonius* good,
1290　　But 'twould offend him. And in his offence,
　　　Should my performance perish.
　　SILLIUS   Thou hast *Ventidius* that,
　　　Without the which a Souldier and his Sword
　　　Graunts scarce distinction: thou wilt write to *Anthony*.
　　VENTIDIUS
　　　Ile humbly signifie what in his name,
　　　That magicall word of Warre we haue effected,
　　　How with his Banners, and his well paid ranks,
　　　The nere-yet beaten Horse of Parthia,
　　　We haue iaded out o'th'Field.
　　SILLIUS   Where is he now?
　　VENTIDIUS
　　　He purposeth to Athens, whither with what hast
1300　　The waight we must conuay with's, will permit:
　　　We shall appeare before him. On there, passe along.
　　　　　　　　　　　　　　　　　　　　Exeunt

Sc. 14　　　*Enter Agrippa at one doore, Enobarbus at another*
(3.2)　AGRIPPA　What are the Brothers parted?
　　ENOBARBUS
　　　They haue dispatcht with *Pompey*, he is gone,

The other three are Sealing. *Octauia* weepes
To part from Rome: *Cæsar* is sad, and *Lepidus*
Since *Pompey's* feast, as *Menas* saies, is troubled
With the Greene-Sicknesse.
AGRIPPA   'Tis a Noble *Lepidus*.
ENOBARBUS
　A very fine one: oh, how he loues *Cæsar*.
AGRIPPA
　Nay but how deerely he adores *Mark Anthony*.
ENOBARBUS
　Cæsar? why he's the Iupiter of men.   1310
AGRIPPA
　What's *Anthony*, the God of Iupiter?
ENOBARBUS
　Spake you of *Cæsar*? How, the non-pareill?
AGRIPPA
　Oh *Anthony*, oh thou Arabian Bird!
ENOBARBUS
　Would you praise *Cæsar*, say *Cæsar* go no further.
AGRIPPA
　Indeed he plied them both with excellent praises.
ENOBARBUS
　But he loues *Cæsar* best, yet he loues *Anthony*:
　Hoo, Hearts, Tongues, Figures, Scribes, Bards, Poets,
　　cannot
　Thinke speake, cast, write, sing, number: hoo,
　His loue to *Anthony*. But as for *Cæsar*,
　Kneele downe, kneele downe, and wonder.
AGRIPPA   Both he loues.   1320
ENOBARBUS
　They are his Shards, and he their Beetle,
　　⌈*Trumpet within*⌉   so:
　This is to horse: Adieu, Noble *Agrippa*.
AGRIPPA
　Good Fortune worthy Souldier, and farewell.
　　　Enter Cæsar, Anthony, Lepidus, and Octauia
ANTHONY (*to Cæsar*) No further Sir.
CÆSAR
　You take from me a great part of my selfe:
　Vse me well in't. Sister, proue such a wife
　As my thoughts make thee, and as my farthest Band
　Shall passe on thy approofe: most Noble *Anthony*,
　Let not the peece of Vertue which is set
　Betwixt vs, as the Cyment of our loue   1330
　To keepe it builded, be the Ramme to batter
　The Fortresse of it: for better might we
　Haue lou'd without this meane, if on both parts
　This be not cherisht.
ANTHONY   Make me not offended,
　In your distrust.
CÆSAR   I haue said.
ANTHONY   You shall not finde,
　Though you be therein curious, the lest cause
　For what you seeme to feare, so the Gods keepe you,
　And make the hearts of Romaines serue your ends:
　We will heere part.
CÆSAR
　Farewell my deerest Sister, fare thee well,   1340

The Elements be kind to thee, and make
Thy spirits all of comfort: farethee well.

OCTAUIA (*weeping*) My Noble Brother.

ANTHONY
The Aprill's in her eyes, it is Loues spring,
And these the showers to bring it on: be cheerfull.

OCTAUIA
Sir, looke well to my Husbands house: and—

CÆSAR
What *Octauia*?

OCTAUIA   Ile tell you in your eare.

    She whispers to Cæsar

ANTHONY
Her tongue will not obey her heart, nor can
Her heart informe her tongue. The Swannes downe
    feather
1350 That stands vpon the Swell at full of Tide:
And neither way inclines.

ENOBARBUS (*aside to Agrippa*) Will *Cæsar* weepe?

AGRIPPA (*aside to Enobarbus*) He ha's a cloud in's face.

ENOBARBUS (*aside to Agrippa*)
He were the worse for that, were he a Horse
So is he being a man.

AGRIPPA (*aside to Enobarbus*) Why *Enobarbus*:
When *Anthony* found *Iulius Cæsar* dead,
He cried almost to roaring: And he wept,
When at Phillippi he found *Brutus* slaine.

ENOBARBUS (*aside to Agrippa*)
That yeare indeed, he was troubled with a rume,
1360 What willingly he did confound, he wail'd,
Beleeu't till I weept too.

CÆSAR   No sweet *Octauia*,
You shall heare from me still: the time shall not
Out-go my thinking on you.

ANTHONY   Come Sir, come,
Ile wrastle with you in my strength of loue,
Looke heere I haue you, (*embracing Cæsar*) thus I let
    you go,
And giue you to the Gods.

CÆSAR   Adieu, be happy.

LEPIDUS
Let all the number of the Starres giue light
To thy faire way.

CÆSAR   Farewell, farewell.

    Kisses Octauia

ANTHONY   Farewell.

    *Trumpets sound. Exeunt Anthony, Octauia, and
    Enobarbus at one doore, Cæsar, Lepidus, and
    Agrippa at another*

Sc. 15   *Enter Cleopatra, Charmian, Iras, and Alexas*
(3.3) CLEOPATRA
Where is the Fellow?

ALEXAS   Halfe afeard to come.

CLEOPATRA
Go too, go too:

    Enter the Messenger as before
    Come hither Sir.

1370 ALEXAS   Good Maiestie:

Herod of Iury dare not looke vpon you,
But when you are well pleas'd.

CLEOPATRA   That *Herods* head,
Ile haue: but how? When *Anthony* is gone,
Through whom I might commaund it:
(*To the Messenger*)   Come thou neere.

MESSENGER
Most gratious Maiestie.

CLEOPATRA   Did'st thou behold
Octauia?

MESSENGER I dread Queene.

CLEOPATRA   Where?

MESSENGER   Madam in Rome,
I lookt her in the face: and saw her led
Betweene her Brother, and *Marke Anthony*.

CLEOPATRA
Is she as tall as me?

MESSENGER   She is not Madam.

CLEOPATRA
Didst heare her speake? Is she shrill tongu'd or low? 1380

MESSENGER
Madam, I heard her speake, she is low voic'd.

CLEOPATRA
That's not so good: he cannot like her long.

CHARMIAN
Like her? Oh *Isis*: 'tis impossible.

CLEOPATRA
I thinke so *Charmian*: dull of tongue, & dwarfish,
What Maiestie is in her gate, remember
If ere thou look'st on Maiestie.

MESSENGER   She creepes:
Her motion, & her station are as one.
She shewes a body, rather then a life,
A Statue, then a Breather.

CLEOPATRA   Is this certaine?

MESSENGER
Or I haue no obseruance.

CHARMIAN   Three in Egypt 1390
Cannot make better note.

CLEOPATRA   He's very knowing,
I do perceiu't, there's nothing in her yet.
The Fellow ha's good iudgement.

CHARMIAN   Excellent.

CLEOPATRA (*to the Messenger*)
Guesse at her yeares, I prythee.

MESSENGER   Madam,
She was a widdow.

CLEOPATRA   Widdow? *Charmian*, hearke.

MESSENGER And I do thinke she's thirtie.

CLEOPATRA
Bear'st thou her face in mind? is't long or round?

MESSENGER Round, euen to faultinesse.

CLEOPATRA
For the most part too, they are foolish that are so.
Her haire what colour?

MESSENGER   Browne Madam: and her forehead 1400
As low as she would wish it.

CLEOPATRA (*giuing money*)   There's Gold for thee,
Thou must not take my former sharpenesse ill,

I will employ thee backe againe: I finde thee
Most fit for businesse. Go, make thee ready,
Our Letters are prepar'd.   *Exit Messenger*

CHARMIAN   A proper man.

CLEOPATRA

Indeed he is so: I repent me much
That so I harried him. Why me think's by him,
This Creature's no such thing.

CHARMIAN   Nothing Madam.

CLEOPATRA

The man hath seene some Maiesty, and should know.

CHARMIAN

1410   Hath he seene Maiestie? *Isis* else defend:
And seruing you so long.

CLEOPATRA

I haue one thing more to aske him yet good *Charmian*:
But 'tis no matter, thou shalt bring him to me
Where I will write; all may be well enough.

CHARMIAN I warrant you Madam.   *Exeunt*

Sc. 16   *Enter Anthony and Octauia*
(3.4)   ANTHONY

Nay, nay *Octauia*, not onely that,
That were excusable, that and thousands more
Of semblable import, but he hath wag'd
New Warres 'gainst *Pompey*. Made his will, and read it,
1420   To publicke eare, spoke scantly of me;
When perforce he could not
But pay me tearmes of Honour: cold and sickly
He vented them, most narrow measure lent me.
When the best hint was giuen him: he not took't,
Or did it from his teeth.

OCTAUIA   Oh my good Lord,
Beleeue not all, or if you must beleeue,
Stomacke not all. A more vnhappie Lady,
If this deuision chance, ne're stood betweene
Praying for both parts:
1430   The good Gods wil mocke me presently,
When I shall pray: Oh blesse my Lord, and Husband,
Vndo that prayer, by crying out as loud,
Oh blesse my Brother. Husband winne, winne Brother,
Prayes, and distroyes the prayer, no midway
'Twixt these extreames at all.

ANTHONY   Gentle *Octauia*,
Let your best loue draw to that point which seeks
Best to preserue it: if I loose mine Honour,
I loose my selfe: better I were not yours
Then yours so branchlesse. But as you requested,
1440   Your selfe shall go between's, the meane time Lady,
Ile raise the preparation of a Warre
Shall staine your Brother, make your soonest hast,
So your desires are yours.

OCTAUIA   Thanks to my Lord,
The Ioue of power make me most weake, most weake,
Your reconciler: Warres 'twixt you twaine would be,
As if the world should cleaue, and that slaine men
Should soader vp the Rift.

ANTHONY

When it appeeres to you where this begins,
Turne your displeasure that way, for our faults
Can neuer be so equall, that your loue   1450
Can equally moue with them. Prouide your going,
Choose your owne company, and command what cost
Your heart ha's mind too.   *Exeunt*

Enter Enobarbus at one doore and Eros at another   Sc. 17
    doore   (3.5)

ENOBARBUS How now Friend *Eros*?

EROS Ther's strange Newes come Sir.

ENOBARBUS What man?

EROS *Cæsar* & *Lepidus* haue made warres vpon *Pompey*.

ENOBARBUS This is old, what is the successe?

EROS *Cæsar* hauing made vse of him in the warres 'gainst
Pompey: presently denied him riuality, would not let   1460
him partake in the glory of the action, and not resting
here, accuses him of Letters he had formerly wrote to
Pompey. Vpon his owne appeale seizes him, so the poore
third is vp, till death enlarge his Confine.

ENOBARBUS

Then world thou hast a paire of chaps, no more,
And throw betweene them all the food thou hast,
They'le grinde the one the other. Where's *Anthony*?

EROS

He's walking in the garden thus, and spurnes
The rush that lies before him. Cries Foole *Lepidus*,
And threats the throate of that his Officer,   1470
That murdred *Pompey*.

ENOBARBUS   Our great Nauies rig'd.

EROS

For Italy and *Cæsar*, more *Domitius*,
My Lord desires you presently: my Newes
I might haue told heareafter.

ENOBARBUS   'Twillbe naught,
But let it be: bring me to *Anthony*.

EROS   Come Sir.   *Exeunt*

Enter Agrippa, Mecenas, and Cæsar   Sc. 18
CÆSAR   (3.6)

Contemning Rome he ha's done all this, & more
In Alexandria: heere's the manner of't:
I'th'Market-place on a Tribunall siluer'd,
Cleopatra and himselfe in Chaires of Gold
Were publikely enthron'd: at the feet, sat   1480
Cæsarion whom they call my Fathers Sonne,
And all the vnlawfull issue, that their Lust
Since then hath made betweene them. Vnto her,
He gaue the stablishment of Egypt, made her
Of lower Syria, Cyprus, Lydia,
Absolute Queene.

MECENAS   This in the publike eye?

CÆSAR

I'th'common shew place, where they exercise,
His Sonnes he ther proclaim'd the Kings of Kings,
Great Media, Parthia, and Armenia

1490 He gaue to *Alexander*. To *Ptolomy* he assign'd,
Syria, Silicia, and Phœnetia : she
In th'abiliments of the Goddesse *Isis*
That day appeer'd, and oft before gaue audience,
As 'tis reported, so.
MECENAS   Let Rome be thus inform'd.
AGRIPPA
Who queazie with his insolence already,
Will their good thoughts call from him.
CÆSAR   The people knowes it,
And haue now receiu'd his accusations.
AGRIPPA Who does he accuse?
CÆSAR
Cæsar, and that hauing in Cicilie
1500 *Sextus Pompeius* spoil'd, we had not rated him
His part o'th'Isle. Then does he say, he lent me
Some shipping vnrestor'd. Lastly, he frets
That *Lepidus* of the Triumpherate,
Should be depos'd, and being, that we detaine
All his Reuenue.
AGRIPPA   Sir, this should be answer'd.
CÆSAR
'Tis done already, and the Messenger gone:
I haue told him *Lepidus* was growne too cruell,
That he his high Authority abus'd,
And did deserue his change: for what I haue
     conquer'd,
1510 I grant him part: but then in his Armenia,
And other of his conquer'd Kingdoms,
I demand the like.
MECENAS   Hee'l neuer yeeld to that.
CÆSAR
Nor must not then be yeelded to in this.
     Enter Octauia with her Traine
OCTAUIA
Haile *Cæsar*, and my L. haile most deere *Cæsar*.
CÆSAR
That euer I should call thee Cast-away.
OCTAUIA
You haue not call'd me so, nor haue you cause.
CÆSAR
Why haue you stoln vpon vs thus? you come not
Like *Cæsars* Sister, The wife of *Anthony*
Should haue an Army for an Vsher, and
1520 The neighes of Horse to tell of her approach,
Long ere she did appeare. The trees by'th'way
Should haue borne men, and expectation fainted,
Longing for what it had not. Nay, the dust
Should haue ascended to the Roofe of Heauen,
Rais'd by your populous Troopes: But you are come
A Market-maid to Rome, and haue preuented
The ostentation of our loue; which left vnshewne,
Is often left vnlou'd: we should haue met you
By Sea, and Land, supplying euery Stage
With an augmented greeting.
1530 OCTAUIA   Good my Lord,
To come thus was I not constrain'd, but did it

On my free-will. My Lord *Marke Anthony*,
Hearing that you prepar'd for Warre, acquainted
My greeued eare withall: whereon I begg'd
His pardon for returne.
CÆSAR   Which soone he granted,
Being an obstruct 'tweene his Lust, and him.
OCTAUIA
Do not say so, my Lord.
CÆSAR   I haue eyes vpon him,
And his affaires come to me on the wind:
Wher is he now?
OCTAUIA   My Lord, in Athens.
CÆSAR
No my most wronged Sister, *Cleopatra*   1540
Hath nodded him to her. He hath giuen his Empire
Vp to a Whore, who now are leuying
The Kings o'th'earth for Warre. He hath assembled,
Bochus the King of Lybia, *Archilaus*
Of Cappadocia, *Philadelphos* King
Of Paphlagonia: the Thracian King *Adullas*,
King *Mauchus* of Arabia, King of Pont,
Herod of Iewry, *Mithridates* King
Of Comagene, *Polemon* and *Amintas*,
The Kings of Mede, and Licaonia,   1550
With a more larger List of Scepters.
OCTAUIA   Aye me most wretched,
That haue my heart parted betwixt two Friends,
That does afflict each other.
CÆSAR   Welcom hither:
Your Letters did with-holde our breaking forth
Till we perceiu'd both how you were wrong led,
And we in negligent danger: cheere your heart,
Be you not troubled with the time, which driues
O're your content, these strong necessities,
But let determin'd things to destinie
Hold vnbewayl'd their way. Welcome to Rome,   1560
Nothing more deere to me: You are abus'd
Beyond the marke of thought: and the high Gods
To do you Iustice, makes their Ministers
Of vs, and those that loue you. Best of comfort,
And euer welcom to vs.
AGRIPPA   Welcome Lady.
MECENAS Welcome deere Madam,
Each heart in Rome does loue and pitty you,
Onely th'adulterous *Anthony*, most large
In his abhominations, turnes you off,
And giues his potent Regiment to a Trull   1570
That noyses it against vs.
OCTAUIA   Is it so sir?
CÆSAR
Most certaine: Sister welcome: pray you
Be euer knowne to patience. My deer'st Sister.
                              Exeunt

     Enter Cleopatra, and Enobarbus   Sc. 19
CLEOPATRA   (3.7)
I will be euen with thee, doubt it not.
ENOBARBUS But why, why, why?

CLEOPATRA
Thou hast forespoke my being in these warres,
And say'st it is not fit.

ENOBARBUS   Well: is it, is it.

CLEOPATRA
Is't not denounc'd against vs, why should not we
Be there in person.

ENOBARBUS ⌈aside⌉   Well, I could reply:
1580   If wee should serue with Horse and Mares together,
The Horse were meerly lost: the Mares would beare
A Soldiour and his Horse.

CLEOPATRA   What is't you say?

ENOBARBUS
Your presence needs must puzle *Anthony*,
Take from his heart, take from his Braine, from's time,
What should not then be spar'd. He is already
Traduc'd for Leuity, and 'tis said in Rome,
That *Photinus* an Eunuch, and your Maides
Mannage this warre.

CLEOPATRA   Sinke Rome, and their tongues rot
That speake against vs. A Charge we beare i'th'Warre,
1590   And as the president of my Kingdome will
Appeare there for a man. Speake not against it,
I will not stay behinde.

Enter Anthony and Camidias

ENOBARBUS   Nay I haue done,
Here comes the Emperor.

ANTHONY   Is it not strange *Camidius*,
That from Tarrentum, and Brundisium,
He could so quickly cut the Ionian Sea,
And take in Torine. You haue heard on't (Sweet?)

CLEOPATRA
Celerity is neuer more admir'd,
Then by the negligent.

ANTHONY   A good rebuke,
Which might haue well becom'd the best of men
1600   To taunt at slacknesse. *Camidius*, wee
Will fight with him by Sea.

CLEOPATRA   By Sea, what else?

CAMIDIUS
Why will my Lord, do so?

ANTHONY   For that he dares vs too't.

ENOBARBUS
So hath my Lord, dar'd him to single fight.

CAMIDIUS
I, and to wage this Battell at Pharsalia,
Where *Cæsar* fought with *Pompey*. But these offers
Which serue not for his vantage, he shakes off,
And so should you.

ENOBARBUS   Your Shippes are not well mann'd,
Your Marriners are Muliters, Reapers, people
Ingrost by swift Impresse. In *Cæsars* Fleete,
1610   Are those, that often haue 'gainst *Pompey* fought,
Their shippes are yare, yours heauy: no disgrace
Shall fall you for refusing him at Sea,
Being prepar'd for Land.

ANTHONY   By Sea, by Sea.

ENOBARBUS
Most worthy Sir, you therein throw away
The absolute Soldiership you haue by Land,
Distract your Armie, which doth most consist
Of Warre-markt-footmen, leaue vnexecuted
Your owne renowned knowledge, quite forgoe
The way which promises assurance, and
Giue vp your selfe meerly to chance and hazard,   1620
From firme Securitie.

ANTHONY   Ile fight at Sea.

CLEOPATRA
I haue sixty Sailes, *Cæsar* none better.

ANTHONY
Our ouer-plus of shipping will we burne,
And with the rest full mann'd, from th'head of
    Actium
Beate th'approaching *Cæsar*. But if we faile,
We then can doo't at Land.

Enter a Messenger

                    Thy Businesse?

MESSENGER
The Newes is true, my Lord, he is descried,
Cæsar ha's taken Toryne.

ANTHONY
Can he be there in person? 'Tis impossible;
Strange, that his power should be. *Camidius*,   1630
Our nineteene Legions thou shalt hold by Land,
And our twelue thousand Horse. Wee'l to our Ship,
Away my *Thetis*.

Enter a Soldiour

                    How now worthy Souldier?

SOULDIER
Oh Noble Emperor, do not fight by Sea,
Trust not to rotten plankes: Do you misdoubt
This Sword, and these my Wounds; let th'Egyptians
And the Phœnicians go a ducking: wee
Haue vs'd to conquer standing on the earth,
And fighting foot to foot.

ANTHONY   Well, well, away.

exit Anthony, Cleopatra & Enobarbus

SOULDIER
By *Hercules* I thinke I am i'th'right.   1640

CAMIDIUS
Souldier thou art: but his whole action growes
Not in the power on't: so our Leaders leade,
And we are Womens men.

SOULDIER   You keepe by Land
The Legions and the Horse whole, do you not?

CAMIDIUS
Marcus Octauius, Marcus Iusteus,
Publicola, and *Celius*, are for Sea:
But we keepe whole by Land. This speede of *Cæsars*
Carries beyond beleefe.

SOULDIER   While he was yet in Rome,
His power went out in such distractions,
As beguilde all Spies.

CAMIDIUS   Who's his Lieutenant, heare you?   1650

SOULDIER
They say, one *Towrus*.

CAMIDIUS   Well I know the man.

Enter a Messenger

MESSENGER
The Emperor cals *Camidius*.

CAMIDIUS
With Newes the times in Labour, and throwes forth
Each minute, some.   *exeunt*

Sc. 20   *Enter Cæsar with his Army, marching, and Towrus*
(3.8)   CÆSAR *Towrus?*

TOWRUS My Lord.

CÆSAR
Strike not by Land, keepe whole, prouoke not Battaile
Till we haue done at Sea. (*Giuing a Scroule*) Do not
    exceede
The Prescript of this Scroule: Our fortune lyes
1660   Vpon this iumpe.
            *exit Cæsar and his Army at one doore, Towrus
                                        at another*

Sc. 21   *Enter Anthony, and Enobarbus*
(3.9)   ANTHONY
Set we our Squadrons on yond side o'th'Hill,
In eye of *Cæsars* battaile, from which place
We may the number of the Ships behold,
And so proceed accordingly.   *exeunt*

Sc. 22   *Camidius Marcheth with his Land Army one way
(3.10)   ouer the stage, and Towrus the Lieutenant of Cæsar
                with his Army the other way: After their going in,
                is heard the noise of a Sea-fight. Alarum. Enter
                Enobarbus*

ENOBARBUS
Naught, naught, al naught, I can behold no longer:
Thantoniad, the Egyptian Admirall,
With all their sixty flye, and turne the Rudder:
To see't, mine eyes are blasted.

Enter Scarrus

SCARRUS   Gods, & Goddesses,
All the whol synod of them!

ENOBARBUS   What's thy passion.

SCARRUS
1670   The greater Cantle of the world, is lost
With very ignorance, we haue kist away
Kingdomes, and Prouinces.

ENOBARBUS   How appeares the Fight?

SCARRUS
On our side, like the Token'd Pestilence,
Where death is sure. Yon riband red Nagge of Egypt,
(Whom Leprosie o're-take) i'th'midst o'th'fight,
When vantage like a payre of Twinnes appear'd
Both as the same, or rather ours the elder;
(The Breeze vpon her) like a Cow in Iune,
Hoists Sailes, and flyes.

ENOBARBUS   That I beheld:

Mine eyes did sicken at the sight, and could not   1680
Indure a further view.

SCARRUS   She once being looft,
The Noble ruine of her Magicke, *Anthony*,
Claps on his Sea-wing, and (like a doting Mallard)
Leauing the Fight in heighth, flyes after her:
I neuer saw an Action of such shame;
Experience, Man-hood, Honor, ne're before,
Did violate so it selfe.

ENOBARBUS   Alacke, alacke.

Enter Camidius

CAMIDIUS
Our Fortune on the Sea is out of breath,
And sinkes most lamentably. Had our Generall
Bin what he knew himselfe, it had gone well: 1690
Oh he ha's giuen example for our flight,
Most grossely by his owne.

ENOBARBUS
I, are you thereabouts? Why then goodnight indeede.

CAMIDIUS
Toward Peloponnesus are they fled.

SCARRUS
'Tis easie toot, and there I will attend
What further comes.

CAMIDIUS   To *Cæsar* will I render
My Legions and my Horse, sixe Kings alreadie
Shew me the way of yeelding.

ENOBARBUS   Ile yet follow
The wounded chance of *Anthony*, though my reason
Sits in the winde against me.   ⌈*Exeunt seuerally*⌉   1700

          Enter Anthony with Attendants   Sc. 23
ANTHONY   (3.11)
Hearke, the Land bids me tread no more vpon't,
It is asham'd to beare me. Friends, come hither,
I am so lated in the world, that I
Haue lost my way for euer. I haue a shippe,
Laden with Gold, take that, diuide it: flye,
And make your peace with *Cæsar*.

ATTENDANTS   Fly? Not wee.

ANTHONY
I haue fled my selfe, and haue instructed cowards
To runne, and shew their shoulders. Friends be gone,
I haue my selfe resolu'd vpon a course,
Which has no neede of you. Be gone,   1710
My Treasure's in the Harbour. Take it: Oh,
I follow'd that I blush to looke vpon,
My very haires do mutiny: for the white
Reproue the browne for rashnesse, and they them
For feare, and doting. Friends be gone, you shall
Haue Letters from me to some Friends, that will
Sweepe your way for you. Pray you looke not sad,
Nor make replyes of loathnesse, take the hint
Which my dispaire proclaimes. Let that be left
Which leaues it selfe, to the Sea-side straight way;   1720
I will possesse you of that ship and Treasure.
Leaue me, I pray a little: pray you now,

Nay do so: for indeede I haue lost command,
Therefore I pray you, Ile see you by and by.
                                    Exeunt attendants
    Sits downe.
    Enter Cleopatra led by Charmian, Iras, and Eros

EROS
    Nay gentle Madam, to him, comfort him.

IRAS Do most deere Queene.

CHARMIAN Do, why, what else?

CLEOPATRA Let me sit downe: Oh *Iuno*.
    Sits downe

ANTHONY No, no, no, no, no.

1730 EROS (*to Anthony*) See you heere, Sir?

ANTHONY Oh fie, fie, fie.

CHARMIAN Madam.

IRAS Madam, oh good Empresse.

EROS Sir, sir.

ANTHONY
    Yes my Lord, yes; he at Philippi kept
    His sword e'ne like a dancer, while I strooke
    The leane and wrinkled *Cassius*, and 'twas I
    That the mad *Brutus* ended: he alone
    Dealt on Lieutenantry, and no practise had
1740   In the braue squares of Warre: yet now: no matter.

CLEOPATRA (⌈*rising;*⌉ *to Charmian and Iras*) Ah stand by.

EROS The Queene my Lord, the Queene.

IRAS Go to him, Madam,
    Speake to him, hee's vnqualited
    With very shame.

CLEOPATRA   Well then, sustaine me: Oh.

EROS
    Most Noble Sir arise, the Queene approaches,
    Her head's declin'd, and death will cease her, but
    Your comfort makes the rescue.

ANTHONY
    I haue offended Reputation,
    A most vnnoble sweruing.

1750 EROS   Sir, the Queene.

ANTHONY ⌈*rising*⌉
    Oh whether hast thou lead me Egypt, see
    How I conuey my shame, out of thine eyes,
    By looking backe what I haue left behinde
    Stroy'd in dishonor.

CLEOPATRA   Oh my Lord, my Lord,
    Forgiue my fearfull sayles, I little thought
    You would haue followed.

ANTHONY   Egypt, thou knew'st too well,
    My heart was to thy Rudder tyed by'th'strings,
    And thou should'st towe me after. O're my spirit
    Thy full supremacie thou knew'st, and that
1760   Thy becke, might from the bidding of the Gods
    Command mee.

CLEOPATRA   Oh my pardon.

ANTHONY   Now I must
    To the young man send humble Treaties, dodge
    And palter in the shifts of lownes, who
    With halfe the bulke o'th'world plaid as I pleas'd,
    Making, and marring Fortunes. You did know

How much you were my Conqueror, and that
My Sword, made weake by my affection, would
Obey it on all cause.

CLEOPATRA   Pardon, pardon.

ANTHONY
    Fall not a teare I say, one of them rates
    All that is wonne and lost: Giue me a kisse,   1770
    He kisses her
    Euen this repayes me. (*To an Attendant*) We sent our
        Schoolemaster,
    Is a come backe? (*To Cleopatra*) Loue I am full of
        Lead: (*calling*) some Wine
    Within there, and our Viands: Fortune knowes,
    We scorne her most, when most she offers blowes.
                                            Exeunt

    Enter Cæsar, ⌈Agrippa,⌉ Thidias, and Dollabella,   Sc. 24
        with others   (3.12)

CÆSAR
    Let him appeare that's come from *Anthony*.
    Know you him.

DOLABELLA   *Cæsar*, 'tis his Schoolemaster,
    An argument that he is pluckt, when hither
    He sends so poore a Pinnion of his Wing,
    Which had superfluous Kings for Messengers,
    Not many Moones gone by.
        Enter Ambassador from Anthony

CÆSAR   Approach, and speake.   1780

AMBASSADOR
    Such as I am, I come from *Anthony*:
    I was of late as petty to his ends,
    As is the Morne-dew on the Mertle leafe
    To his grand Sea.

CÆSAR   Bee't so, declare thine office.

AMBASSADOR
    Lord of his Fortunes he salutes thee, and
    Requires to liue in Egypt, which not granted
    He Lessens his Requests, and to thee sues
    To let him breath betweene the Heauens and Earth
    A priuate man in Athens: this for him.
    Next, *Cleopatra* does confesse thy Greatnesse,   1790
    Submits her to thy might, and of thee craues
    The Circle of the *Ptolomies* for her heyres,
    Now hazarded to thy Grace.

CÆSAR   For *Anthony*,
    I haue no eares to his request. The Queene,
    Of Audience, nor Desire shall faile, so shee
    From Egypt driue her all-disgraced Friend,
    Or take his life there. This if shee performe,
    She shall not sue vnheard. So to them both.

AMBASSADOR
    Fortune pursue thee.

CÆSAR   Bring him through the Bands:
                        Exit Ambassador, attended
    (*To Thidias*) To try thy Eloquence, now 'tis time,
        dispatch,   1800
    From *Anthony* winne *Cleopatra*, promise
    And in our Name, what she requires, adde more

As thine inuention offers. Women are not
In their best Fortunes strong; but want will periure
The ne're touch'd Vestall. Try thy cunning *Thidias*,
Make thine owne Edict for thy paines, which we
Will answer as a Law.

THIDIAS   *Cæsar*, I go.

CÆSAR

Obserue how *Anthony* becomes his flaw,
And what thou think'st his very action speakes
In euery power that mooues.

1810   THIDIAS   *Cæsar*, I shall.

> *exeunt Cæsar and his train at one doore, and*
> *Thidias at another*

Sc. 25   *Enter Cleopatra, Enobarbus, Charmian, & Iras*
(3.13)   CLEOPATRA

What shall we do, *Enobarbus*?

ENOBARBUS   Thinke, and dye.

CLEOPATRA

Is *Anthony*, or we in fault for this?

ENOBARBUS

Anthony onely, that would make his will
Lord of his Reason. What though you fled,
From that great face of Warre, whose seuerall ranges
Frighted each other? Why should he follow?
The itch of his Affection should not then
Haue nickt his Captain-ship, at such a point,
When halfe to halfe the world oppos'd, he being
1820   The mooted question? 'Twas a shame no lesse
Then was his losse, to course your flying Flagges,
And leaue his Nauy gazing.

CLEOPATRA   Prythee peace.

> *Enter the Ambassador, with Anthony*

ANTHONY

Is that his answer?

AMBASSADOR   I my Lord.

ANTHONY

The Queene shall then haue courtesie, so she
Will yeeld vs vp.

AMBASSADOR   He sayes so.

ANTHONY   Let her know't.
(*To Cleopatra*) To the Boy *Cæsar* send this grizled head,
And he will fill thy wishes to the brimme,
With Principalities.

CLEOPATRA   That head my Lord?

ANTHONY (*to the Ambassador*)

To him againe, tell him he weares the Rose
Of youth vpon him: from which, the world should
1830   note
Something particular: His Coine, Ships, Legions,
May be a Cowards, whose Ministers would preuaile
Vnder the seruice of a Childe, as soone
As i'th'Command of *Cæsar*. I dare him therefore
To lay his gay Caparisons a-part,
And answer me declin'd, Sword against Sword,
Our selues alone: Ile write it: Follow me.

> *Exeunt Anthony and Ambassador*

ENOBARBUS (*aside*)

Yes like enough: hye battel'd *Cæsar* will
Vnstate his happinesse, and be Stag'd to'th'shew
Against a Sworder. I see mens Iudgements are   1840
A parcell of their Fortunes, and things outward
Do draw the inward quality after them
To suffer all alike. That he should dreame,
Knowing all measures, the full *Cæsar* will
Answer his emptinesse; *Cæsar* thou hast subdu'de
His iudgement too.

> *Enter a Seruant*

SERUANT   A Messenger from *Cæsar*.

CLEOPATRA

What no more Ceremony? See my Women,
Against the blowne Rose may they stop their nose,
That kneel'd vnto the Buds. Admit him sir.

> *Exit Seruant*

ENOBARBUS (*aside*)

Mine honesty, and I, beginne to square,   1850
The Loyalty well held to Fooles, does make
Our Faith meere folly: yet he that can endure
To follow with Allegeance a falne Lord,
Does conquer him that did his Master conquer,
And earnes a place i'th'Story.

> *Enter Thidias*

CLEOPATRA   *Cæsars* will.

THIDIAS

Heare it apart.

CLEOPATRA   None but Friends: say boldly.

THIDIAS

So haply are they Friends to *Anthony*.

ENOBARBUS

He needs as many (Sir) as *Cæsar* ha's,
Or needs not vs. If *Cæsar* please, our Master
Will leape to be his Friend: For vs you know,   1860
Whose he is, we are, and that is *Cæsars*.

THIDIAS

So. (*To Cleopatra*) Thus then thou most renown'd,
      Cæsar intreats,
Not to consider in what case thou stand'st
Further then he is *Cæsar*.

CLEOPATRA   Go on, right Royall.

THIDIAS

He knowes that you embracd not *Anthony*
As you did loue, but as you feared him.

CLEOPATRA Oh.

THIDIAS

The scarre's vpon your Honor, therefore he
Does pitty, as constrained blemishes,
Not as deserud.

CLEOPATRA   He is a God, and knowes   1870
What is most right. Mine Honour was not yeelded,
But conquer'd meerely.

ENOBARBUS (*aside*)   To be sure of that,
I will aske *Anthony*. Sir, sir, thou art so leakie
That we must leaue thee to thy sinking, for
Thy deerest quit thee.   *Exit Enobarbus*

THIDIAS   Shall I say to *Cæsar*,

What you require of him: for he partly begges
To be desir'd to giue. It much would please him,
That of his Fortunes you should make a staffe
To leane vpon. But it would warme his spirits

1880 To heare from me you had left *Anthony*,
And put your selfe vnder his shrowd,
The vniuersal Landlord.

CLEOPATRA   What's your name?

THIDIAS
My name is *Thidias*.

CLEOPATRA   Most kinde Messenger,
Say to great *Cæsar* this in deputation,
I kisse his conqu'ring hand: Tell him, I am prompt
To lay my Crowne at's feete, and there to kneele
Till from his all-obeying breath, I heare
The doome of Egypt.

THIDIAS   'Tis your Noblest course:
Wisedome and Fortune combatting together,

1890 If that the former dare but what it can,
No chance may shake it. Giue me grace to lay
My dutie on your hand.

He kisses Cleopatras hand

CLEOPATRA   Your *Cæsars* Father oft,
(When he hath mus'd of taking kingdomes in)
Bestow'd his lips on that vnworthy place,
As it rain'd kisses.

Enter Anthony and Enobarbus

ANTHONY   Fauours? By Ioue that thunders.
What art thou Fellow?

THIDIAS   One that but performes
The bidding of the fullest man, and worthiest
To haue command obey'd.

ENOBARBUS   You will be whipt.

ANTHONY (*calling*)
Approch there: ah you Kite. Now Gods & diuels

1900 Authority melts from me of late. When I cried hoa,
Like Boyes vnto a musse, Kings would start forth,
And cry, your will. Haue you no eares? I am
Anthony yet.

Enter Seruants
Take hence this Iack, and whip him.

ENOBARBUS ⌜*aside, to Thidias*⌝
'Tis better playing with a Lions whelpe,
Then with an old one dying.

ANTHONY   Moone and Starres,
Whip him: wer't twenty of the greatest Tributaries
That do acknowledge *Cæsar*, should I finde them
So sawcy with the hand of she heere, what's her
    name
Since she was *Cleopatra*? Whip him Fellowes,

1910 Till like a Boy you see him crindge his face,
And whine aloud for mercy. Take him hence.

THIDIAS
Marke Anthony.

ANTHONY   Tugge him away: being whipt
Bring him againe, this Iacke of *Cæsars* shall
Beare vs an arrant to him.

Exeunt Seruants with Thidius

You were halfe blasted ere I knew you: Ha?
Haue I my pillow left vnprest in Rome,
Forborne the getting of a lawfull Race,
And by a Iem of women, to be abus'd
By one that lookes on Feeders?

CLEOPATRA Good my Lord.   1920

ANTHONY You haue beene a boggeler euer,
But when we in our viciousnesse grow hard
(Oh misery on't) the wise Gods seele our eyes:
In our owne filth, drop our cleare iudgements, make vs
Adore our errors, laugh at's while we strut
To our confusion.

CLEOPATRA   Oh, is't come to this?

ANTHONY
I found you as a Morsell, cold vpon
Dead *Cæsars* Trencher: Nay, you were a Fragment
Of *Gneius Pompeyes*, besides what hotter houres
Vnregistred in vulgar Fame, you haue   1930
Luxuriously pickt out. For I am sure,
Though you can guesse what Temperance should be,
You know not what it is.

CLEOPATRA   Wherefore is this?

ANTHONY
To let a Fellow that will take rewards,
And say, God quit you, be familiar with
My play-fellow, your hand; this Kingly Seale,
And plighter of high hearts. O that I were
Vpon the hill of Basan, to out-roare
The horned Heard, for I haue sauage cause,
And to proclaime it ciuilly, were like   1940
A halter'd necke, which do's the Hangman thanke,
For being yare about him.

Enter a Seruant with Thidias
Is he whipt?

SERUANT Soundly, my Lord.

ANTHONY Cried he? and begg'd a Pardon?

SERUANT He did aske fauour.

ANTHONY (*to Thidias*)
If that thy Father liue, let him repent
Thou was't not made his daughter, and be thou sorrie
To follow *Cæsar* in his Triumph, since
Thou hast bin whipt for following him, henceforth
The white hand of a Lady Feauer thee,   1950
Shake thou to looke on't. Get thee backe to *Cæsar*,
Tell him thy entertainment: looke thou say
He makes me angry with him. For he seemes
Proud and disdainfull, harping on what I am,
Not what he knew I was. He makes me angry,
And at this time most easie 'tis to doo't:
When my good Starres, that were my former guides
Haue empty left their Orbes, and shot their Fires
Into th'Abisme of hell. If he mislike,
My speech, and what is done, tell him he has   1960
Hiparchus, my enfranched Bondman, whom
He may at pleasure whip, or hang, or torture,
As he shall like to quit me. Vrge it thou:
Hence with thy stripes, be gone.

Exit ⌜Seruant with⌝ Thidias

CLEOPATRA Haue you done yet?

ANTHONY Alacke our Terrene Moone
 Is now Eclipst, and it portends alone
 The fall of *Anthony*.

CLEOPATRA *(aside)*   I must stay his time?

ANTHONY
 To flatter *Cæsar*, would you mingle eyes
 With one that tyes his points.

1970 CLEOPATRA   Not know me yet?

ANTHONY
 Cold-hearted toward me?

CLEOPATRA   Ah (Deere) if I be so,
 From my cold heart let Heauen ingender haile,
 And poyson it in the sourse, and the first stone
 Drop in my necke: as it determines so
 Dissolue my life, the next Cæsarian smite,
 Till by degrees the memory of my wombe,
 Together with my braue Egyptians all,
 By the discandying of this pelleted storme,
 Lye grauelesse, till the Flies and Gnats of Nyle
 Haue buried them for prey.

1980 ANTHONY   I am satisfied:
 Cæsar sets downe in Alexandria, where
 I will oppose his Fate. Our force by Land,
 Hath Nobly held, our seuer'd Nauie too
 Haue knit againe, and Fleete, threatning most Sea-
  like.
 Where hast thou bin my heart? Dost thou heare
  Lady?
 If from the Field I shall returne once more
 To kisse these Lips, I will appeare in Blood,
 I, and my Sword, will earne our Chronicle,
 There's hope in't yet.

CLEOPATRA   That's my braue Lord.

ANTHONY
1990 I will be trebble-sinewed, hearted, breath'd,
 And fight maliciously: for when mine houres
 Were nice and lucky, men did ransome liues
 Of me for iests: But now, Ile set my teeth,
 And send to darkenesse all that stop me. Come,
 Let's haue one other gawdy night: Call to me
 All my sad Captaines, fill our Bowles once more:
 Let's mocke the midnight Bell.

CLEOPATRA   It is my Birth-day,
 I had thought t'haue held it poore. But since my Lord
 Is *Anthony* againe, I will be *Cleopatra*.

2000 ANTHONY We will yet do well.

CLEOPATRA
 Call all his Noble Captaines to my Lord.

ANTHONY
 Do so, wee'l speake to them, and to night Ile force
 The Wine peepe through their scarres. Come on (my
  Queene)
 There's sap in't yet. The next time I do fight
 Ile make death loue me: for I will contend
 Euen with his pestilent Sythe.

        Exeunt all but Enobarbus

ENOBARBUS
 Now hee'l out-stare the Lightning, to be furious
 Is to be frighted out of feare, and in that moode
 The Doue will pecke the Estridge; and I see still
 A diminution in our Captaines braine,   2010
 Restores his heart; when valour prayes on reason,
 It eates the Sword it fights with: I will seeke
 Some way to leaue him.   *Exit*

  Enter Cæsar, Agrippa, & Mecenas with his Army, Sc. 26
  Cæsar reading a Letter   (4.1)

CÆSAR
 He calles me Boy, and chides as he had power
 To beate me out of Egypt. My Messenger
 He hath whipt with Rods, dares me to personal
  Combat,
 Cæsar to *Anthony*: let the old Ruffian know,
 I haue many other wayes to dye: meane time
 Laugh at his Challenge.

MECENAS   *Cæsar* must thinke,
 When one so great begins to rage, hee's hunted 2020
 Euen to falling. Giue him no breath, but now
 Make boote of his distraction: Neuer anger
 Made good guard for it selfe.

CÆSAR   Let our best heads
 Know, that to morrow, the last of many Battailes
 We meane to fight. Within our Files there are,
 Of those that seru'd *Marke Anthony* but late,
 Enough to fetch him in. See it done,
 And Feast the Army, we haue store to doo't,
 And they haue earn'd the waste. Poore *Anthony*.

             Exeunt

  Enter Anthony, Cleopatra, Enobarbus, Charmian, Sc. 27
  Iras, Alexas, with others   (4.2)

ANTHONY
 He will not fight with me, *Domitius*?

ENOBARBUS   No?   2030

ANTHONY Why should he not?

ENOBARBUS
 He thinks, being twenty times of better fortune,
 He is twenty men to one.

ANTHONY   To morrow Soldier,
 By Sea and Land Ile fight: or I will liue,
 Or bathe my dying Honor in the blood
 Shall make it liue againe. Woo't thou fight well.

ENOBARBUS
 Ile strike, and cry, Take all.

ANTHONY   Well said, come on:
 Call forth my Houshold Seruants, lets to night
 Be bounteous at our Meale.

  Enter Seruitors

        Giue me thy hand,
 Thou hast bin rightly honest, so hast thou,   2040
 Thou, and thou, and thou: you haue seru'd me well,
 And Kings haue beene your fellowes.

CLEOPATRA *(to Enobarbus)*   What meanes this?

ENOBARBUS (*to Cleopatra*)
   'Tis one of those odde tricks which sorow shoots
   Out of the minde.
ANTHONY (*to a Seruitor*) And thou art honest too:
   I wish I could be made so many men,
   And all of you clapt vp together, in
   An *Anthony*: that I might do you seruice,
   So good as you haue done.
SERUITORS   The Gods forbid.
ANTHONY
   Well, my good Fellowes, wait on me to night:
2050   Scant not my Cups, and make as much of me,
   As when mine Empire was your Fellow too,
   And suffer'd my command.
CLEOPATRA (*aside to Enobarbus*) What does he meane?
ENOBARBUS (*aside to Cleopatra*)
   To make his Followers weepe.
ANTHONY   Tend me to night;
   May be, it is the period of your duty,
   Haply you shall not see me more, or if,
   A mangled shadow. Perchance to morrow,
   You'l serue another Master. I looke on you,
   As one that takes his leaue. Mine honest Friends,
   I turne you not away, but like a Master
2060   Married to your good seruice, stay till death:
   Tend me to night two houres, I aske no more,
   And the Gods yeeld you for't.
ENOBARBUS   What meane you (Sir)
   To giue them this discomfort? Looke they weepe,
   And I an Asse, am Onyon-ey'd; for shame,
   Transforme vs not to women.
ANTHONY   Ho, ho, ho:
   Now the Witch take me, if I meant it thus.
   Grace grow where those drops fall (my hearty Friends)
   You take me in too dolorous a sense,
   For I spake to you for your comfort, did desire you
2070   To burne this night with Torches: Know (my hearts)
   I hope well of to morrow, and will leade you,
   Where rather Ile expect victorious life,
   Then death, and Honor. Let's to Supper, come,
   And drowne consideration.   *Exeunt*

Sc. 28   *Enter a Company of Soldiours*
(4.3) 1. SOLDIOUR
   Brother, goodnight: to morrow is the day.
   2. SOLDIOUR
   It will determine one way: Fare you well.
   Heard you of nothing strange about the streets.
   1. SOLDIOUR Nothing: what newes?
   2. SOLDIOUR
   Belike 'tis but a Rumour, good night to you.
   1. SOLDIOUR
   Well sir, good night.
     Enter other Soldiers, meeting them
2080 2. SOLDIOUR   Souldiers, haue carefull Watch.
   3. SOLDIOUR
   And you: Goodnight, goodnight.
     They place themselues in euery corner of the Stage
   2. SOLDIOUR   Heere we: and if to morrow

Our Nauie thriue, I haue an absolute hope
Our Landmen will stand vp.
1. SOLDIOUR   'Tis a braue Army,
   And full of purpose.
     Musicke of the Hoboyes is vnder the Stage
2. SOLDIOUR   Peace, what noise?
1. SOLDIOUR   List, list.
2. SOLDIOUR
   Hearke.
1. SOLDIOUR Musicke i'th'Ayre.
3. SOLDIOUR   Vnder the earth.
4. SOLDIOUR
   It signes well, do's it not?
3. SOLDIOUR   No.
1. SOLDIOUR   Peace I say:
   What should this meane?
2. SOLDIOUR
   'Tis the God *Hercules*, whom *Anthony* loued,
   Now leaues him.
1. SOLDIOUR   Walke, let's see if other Watchmen
   Do heare what we do?
2. SOLDIOUR   How now Maisters?
OMNES (*speaking together*)   How now?   2090
   How now? do you heare this?
1. SOLDIOUR   I, is't not strange?
3. SOLDIOUR
   Do you heare Masters? Do you heare?
1. SOLDIOUR
   Follow the noyse so farre as we haue quarter.
   Let's see how it will giue off.
OMNES   Content: 'Tis strange.
      Exeunt

   Enter Anthony and Cleopatra, with Charmian and   Sc. 29
   others   (4.4)
ANTHONY (*calling*)
   Eros, mine Armour *Eros*.
CLEOPATRA   Sleepe a little.
ANTHONY
   No my Chucke. *Eros*, come mine Armor *Eros*.
     Enter Eros with Armour
   Come good Fellow, put thine Iron on,
   If Fortune be not ours to day, it is
   Because we braue her. Come.
CLEOPATRA   Nay, Ile helpe too,
   What's this for?
ANTHONY   Ah let be, let be, thou art   2100
   The Armourer of my heart: False, false: This, this.
CLEOPATRA
   Sooth-law Ile helpe: Thus it must bee.
     She helpes Anthony to arme
ANTHONY   Well, well,
   We shall thriue now. Seest thou my good Fellow.
   Go, put on thy defences.
EROS   Briefely Sir.
CLEOPATRA
   Is not this buckled well?
ANTHONY   Rarely, rarely:

He that vnbuckles this, till we do please
To daft for our Repose, shall heare a storme.
Thou fumblest Eros, and my Queenes a Squire
More tight at this, then thou: Dispatch. O Loue,
2110   That thou couldst see my Warres to day, and knew'st
The Royall Occupation, thou should'st see
A Workeman in't.

    Enter an Armed Soldier

               Good morrow to thee, welcome,
Thou look'st like him that knowes a warlike Charge:
To businesse that we loue, we rise betime,
And go too't with delight.

SOULDIER   A thousand Sir,
Early though't be, haue on their riueted trim,
And at the Port expect you.

    Showt within. Trumpets Flourish. Enter
    ⌈*Captaines,*⌉ *and Souldiers*

CAPTAINE
The Morne is faire: Good morrow Generall.

SOULDIERS
Good morrow Generall.

ANTHONY   'Tis well blowne Lads.
2120   This Morning, like the spirit of a youth
That meanes to be of note, begins betimes.
So, so: Come giue me that, this way, well-sed.
Fare thee well Dame, what ere becomes of me,
This is a Soldiers kisse:

    He kisses Cleopatra

             rebukeable,
And worthy shamefull checke it were, to stand
On more Mechanicke Complement, Ile leaue thee
Now like a man of Steele, you that will fight,
Follow me close, Ile bring you too't: Adieu.

    Exeunt Anthony, Eros, Captaines, and Souldiers

CHARMIAN
Please you retyre to your Chamber?

CLEOPATRA   Lead me:
2130   He goes forth gallantly: That he and Cæsar might
Determine this great Warre in single fight;
Then Anthony; but now. Well on.   *Exeunt*

Sc. 30   *Trumpets sound. Enter Anthony, and Eros, meeting*
(4.5)   *a Souldier*

SOULDIER
The Gods make this a happy day to Anthony.

ANTHONY
Would thou, & those thy scars had once preuaild
To make me fight at Land.

SOULDIER   Had'st thou done so,
The Kings that haue reuolted, and the Soldier
That has this morning left thee, would haue still
Followed thy heeles.

ANTHONY   Whose gone this morning?

SOULDIER
Who? one euer neere thee, call for Enobarbus,
2140   Hee shall not heare thee, or from Cæsars Campe,
Say I am none of thine.

ANTHONY   What sayest thou?

SOULDIER
Sir he is with Cæsar.

EROS (*to Anthony*)   Sir, his Chests and Treasure
He has not with him.

ANTHONY   Is he gone?

SOULDIER   Most certaine.

ANTHONY
Go Eros, send his Treasure after, do it,
Detaine no iot I charge thee: write to him,
(I will subscribe) gentle adieu's, and greetings;
Say, that I wish he neuer finde more cause
To change a Master. Oh my Fortunes haue
Corrupted honest men. Dispatch. Enobarbus.   *Exeunt*

    Flourish. Enter Agrippa, Cæsar, with Enobarbus,   Sc. 31
    and Dollabella   (4.6)

CÆSAR
Go forth Agrippa, and begin the fight: 2150
Our will is Anthony be tooke aliue:
Make it so knowne.

AGRIPPA   Cæsar, I shall.   *Exit*

CÆSAR
The time of vniuersall peace is neere:
Proue this a prosp'rous day, the three nook'd world
Shall beare the Oliue freely.

    Enter a Messenger

MESSENGER   Anthony
Is come into the Field.

CÆSAR   Go charge Agrippa,
Plant those that haue reuolted in the Vant,
That Anthony may seeme to spend his Fury
Vpon himselfe.

    Exeunt Messenger ⌈*at one doore*⌉, *Cæsar and*
                     Dolabella ⌈*at another*⌉

ENOBARBUS
Alexas did reuolt, and went to Iewry on   2160
Affaires of Anthony, there did disswade
Great Herod to incline himselfe to Cæsar,
And leaue his Master Anthony. For this paines,
Cæsar hath hang'd him: Camidius and the rest
That fell away, haue entertainment, but
No honourable trust: I haue done ill,
Of which I do accuse my selfe so sorely,
That I will ioy no more.

    Enter a Soldier of Cæsars

SOLDIER   Enobarbus, Anthony
Hath after thee sent all thy Treasure, with
His Bounty ouer-plus. The Messenger   2170
Came on my guard, and at thy Tent is now
Vnloading of his Mules.

ENOBARBUS I giue it you.

SOLDIER Mocke not Enobarbus,
I tell you true: Best you saf't the bringer
Out of the hoast, I must attend mine Office,
Or would haue done't my selfe. Your Emperor
Continues still a Ioue.   *Exit*

ENOBARBUS
I am alone the Villaine of the earth,

2180   And feele I am so most. Oh *Anthony*,
Thou Mine of Bounty, how would'st thou haue payed
My better seruice, when my turpitude
Thou dost so Crowne with Gold. This blowes my hart,
If swift thought breake it not: a swifter meane
Shall out-strike thought, but thought will doo't, I
   feele.
I fight against thee: No I will go seeke
Some Ditch, wherein to dye: the foul'st best fits
My latter part of life.   *Exit*

Sc. 32
(4.7)
   Alarum. Enter Agrippa ⌜*with Drummes and*
   Trumpets⌝
AGRIPPA
2190   Retire, we haue engag'd our selues too farre:
Cæsar himselfe ha's worke, and our oppression
Exceeds what we expected.   *Exeunt*

Sc. 33
(4.8)
   Alarums. Enter Anthony, and Scarrus wounded
SCARRUS
O my braue Emperor, this is fought indeed,
Had we done so at first, we had drouen them home
With clowts about their heads.
ANTHONY   Thou bleed'st apace.
SCARRUS
I had a wound heere that was like a T,
But now 'tis made an H.
   Retreat sounded far off
ANTHONY   They do retyre.
SCARRUS
Wee'l beat 'em into Bench-holes, I haue yet
Roome for six scotches more.
   Enter Eros
EROS
They are beaten Sir, and our aduantage serues
For a faire victory.
2200 SCARRUS   Let vs score their backes,
And snatch 'em vp, as we take Hares behinde,
'Tis sport to maul a Runner.
ANTHONY (*to Eros*)   I will reward thee
Once for thy sprightly comfort, and ten-fold
For thy good valour. Come thee on.
SCARRUS   Ile halt after.
   Exeunt

Sc. 34
(4.9)
   Alarum. Enter Anthony againe in a March.
   Drummes and trumpets, Scarrus, with others
ANTHONY
We haue beate him to his Campe: Runne one before,
And let the Queen know of our gests: ⌜*Exit a Soldier*⌝
                  to morrow
Before the Sun shall see's, wee'l spill the blood
That ha's to day escap'd. I thanke you all,
For doughty handed are you, and haue fought
2210 Not as you seru'd the Cause, but as't had beene
Each mans like mine: you haue shewne all *Hectors*.
Enter the Citty, clip your Wiues, your Friends,
Tell them your feats, whil'st they with ioyfull teares

Wash the congealement from your wounds, and kisse
The Honour'd-gashes whole.
   Enter Cleopatra
(*To Scarrus*)   Giue me thy hand,
To this great Faiery, Ile commend thy acts,
Make her thankes blesse thee.
(*To Cleopatra, embracing her*)   Oh thou day o'th'world,
Chaine mine arm'd necke, leape thou, Attyre and all
Through proofe of Harnesse to my heart, and there
Ride on the pants triumphing.
CLEOPATRA   Lord of Lords.   2220
Oh infinite Vertue, comm'st thou smiling from
The worlds great snare vncaught.
ANTHONY   My Nightingale,
We haue beate them to their Beds. What Gyrle,
   though gray
Do somthing mingle with our yonger brown, yet ha we
A Braine that nourishes our Nerues, and can
Get gole for gole of youth. Behold this man,
Commend vnto his Lippes thy fauouring hand,
Kisse it my Warriour:
   Scarrus kisses Cleopatras hand
            He hath fought to day,
As if a God in hate of Mankinde, had
Destroyed in such a shape.
CLEOPATRA   Ile giue thee Friend   2230
An Armour all of Gold: it was a Kings.
ANTHONY
He has deseru'd it, were it Carbunkled
Like holy Phœbus Carre. Giue me thy hand,
Through Alexandria make a iolly March,
Beare our hackt Targets, like the men that owe them.
Had our great Pallace the capacity
To Campe this hoast, we all would sup together,
And drinke Carowses to the next dayes Fate
Which promises Royall perill, Trumpetters
With brazen dinne blast you the Citties eare,   2240
Make mingle with our ratling Tabourines,
That heauen and earth may strike their sounds
   together,
Applauding our approach.   *Trumpets sound. Exeunt*

   Enter a Centerie, and his Company, Enobarbus   **Sc. 35**
   followes   **(4.10)**
CENTERIE
If we be not releeu'd within this houre,
We must returne to'th'Court of Guard: the night
Is shiny, and they say, we shall embattaile
By'th'second houre i'th'Morne.
I. WATCH   This last day was
A shrew'd one too's.
ENOBARBUS   Oh beare me witnesse night.
2. WATCH
What man is this?
I. WATCH   Stand close, and list him.
ENOBARBUS
Be witnesse to me (O thou blessed Moone)   2250
When men reuolted shall vpon Record

Beare hatefull memory: poore *Enobarbus* did
Before thy face repent.

CENTERIE   *Enobarbus?*

2. WATCH   Peace: Hearke further.

ENOBARBUS

Oh Soueraigne Mistris of true Melancholly,
The poysonous dampe of night dispunge vpon me,
That Life, a very Rebell to my will,
May hang no longer on me. Throw my heart
Against the flint and hardnesse of my fault,
Which being dried with greefe, will breake to powder,
2260 And finish all foule thoughts. Oh *Anthony*,
Nobler then my reuolt is Infamous,
Forgiue me in thine owne particular,
But let the world ranke me in Register
A Master leauer, and a fugitiue:
Oh *Anthony*! Oh *Anthony*!   *He dies*

1. WATCH Let's speake to him.

CENTERIE

Let's heare him, for the things he speakes
May concerne *Cæsar*.

2. WATCH   Let's do so, but he sleepes.

CENTERIE

Swoonds rather, for so bad a Prayer as his
Was neuer yet for sleepe.

2270 1. WATCH   Go we to him.

2. WATCH

Awake sir, awake, speake to vs.

1. WATCH   Heare you sir?

CENTERIE

The hand of death hath raught him.
         Drummes afarre off
                    Hearke the Drummes
Demurely wake the sleepers: Let vs beare him
To'th'Court of Guard: he is of note: Our houre
Is fully out.

2. WATCH

Come on then, he may recouer yet.
                    Exeunt with the body

Sc. 36   *Enter Anthony and Scarrus, with their Army*
(4.11) ANTHONY

Their preparation is to day by Sea,
We please them not by Land.

SCARRUS   For both, my Lord.

ANTHONY

I would they'ld fight i'th'Fire, or i'th' Ayre,
2280 Wee'ld fight there too. But this it is, our Foote
Vpon the hilles adioyning to the Citty
Shall stay with vs. Order for Sea is giuen,
They haue put forth the Hauen:
Where their appointment we may best discouer,
And looke on their endeuour.   *exeunt*

Sc. 37   *Enter Cæsar, and his Army*
(4.12) CÆSAR

But being charg'd, we will be still by Land,
Which as I tak't we shall, for his best force
Is forth to Man his Gallies. To the Vales,
And hold our best aduantage.   *exeunt*

⌐Alarum afarre off, as at a Sea-fight.⌐   Sc. 38
Enter Anthony, and Scarrus   (4.13)

ANTHONY

Yet they are not ioyn'd: Where yon'd Pine does stand,   2290
I shall discouer all. Ile bring thee word
Straight, how 'tis like to go.   *exit*

SCARRUS   Swallowes haue built

In *Cleopatra's* Sailes their nests. The Augures
Say, they know not, they cannot tell, looke grimly,
And dare not speake their knowledge. *Anthony*,
Is valiant, and deiected, and by starts
His fretted Fortunes giue him hope and feare
Of what he has, and has not.
         Enter Anthony

ANTHONY   All is lost:

This fowle Egyptian hath betrayed me:
My Fleete hath yeelded to the Foe, and yonder   2300
They cast their Caps vp, and Carowse together
Like Friends long lost. Triple-turn'd Whore, 'tis thou
Hast sold me to this Nouice, and my heart
Makes onely Warres on thee. Bid them all flye:
For when I am reueng'd vpon my Charme,
I haue done all. Bid them all flye, be gone.
                    ⌐*Exit Scarrus*⌐
Oh Sunne, thy vprise shall I see no more,
Fortune, and *Anthony* part heere, euen heere
Do we shake hands? All come to this? The hearts
That spannell'd me at heeles, to whom I gaue   2310
Their wishes, do dis-Candie, melt their sweets
On blossoming *Cæsar*: And this Pine is barkt,
That ouer-top'd them all. Betray'd I am.
Oh this false Soule of Egypt! this graue Charme,
Whose eye beck'd forth my Wars, & cal'd them home:
Whose Bosome was my Crownet, my chiefe end,
Like a right Gypsie, hath at fast and loose
Beguil'd me, to the very heart of losse.
What *Eros*, *Eros*?
         Enter Cleopatra
                    Ah, thou Spell! Auaunt.

CLEOPATRA

Why is my Lord enrag'd against his Loue?   2320

ANTHONY

Vanish, or I shall giue thee thy deseruing,
And blemish *Cæsars* Triumph. Let him take thee,
And hoist thee vp to the shouting Plebeians,
Follow his Chariot, like the greatest spot
Of all thy Sex. Most Monster-like be shewne
For poor'st Diminitiues, for Dolts, and let
Patient *Octauia*, plough thy visage vp
With her prepared nailes.   *exit Cleopatra*
                    'Tis well th'art gone,
If it be well to liue. But better 'twere
Thou fell'st into my furie, for one death   2330
Might haue preuented many. *Eros*, hoa?
The shirt of *Nessus* is vpon me, teach me
Alcides, thou mine Ancestor, thy rage.
Let me lodge *Licas* on the hornes o'th'Moone,
And with those hands that graspt the heauiest Club,
Subdue my worthiest selfe: The Witch shall die,

To the young Roman Boy she hath sold me, and I fall
Vnder this plot: She dyes for't. *Eros* hoa?   *exit*

Sc. 39   *Enter Cleopatra, Charmian, Iras, Mardian*
(4.14) CLEOPATRA

Helpe me my women: Oh hee's more mad
2340   Then *Telamon* for his Shield, the Boare of Thessaly
Was neuer so imbost.

CHARMIAN   To'th'Monument,
There locke your selfe, and send him word you are
          dead:
The Soule and Body riue not more in parting,
Then greatnesse going off.

CLEOPATRA   To'th'Monument:
Mardian, go tell him I haue slaine my selfe:
Say, that the last I spoke was *Anthony*,
And word it (prythee) pitteously. Hence *Mardian*,
And bring me how he takes my death. To'th'Monument.
                                   Exeunt

Sc. 40   *Enter Anthony, and Eros*
(4.15) ANTHONY

Eros, thou yet behold'st me?

EROS   I Noble Lord.

ANTHONY
2350   Sometime we see a clowd that's Dragonish,
A vapour sometime, like a Beare, or Lyon,
A towerd Cittadell, a pendant Rocke,
A forked Mountaine, or blew Promontorie
With Trees vpon't, that nodde vnto the world,
And mocke our eyes with Ayre. Thou hast seene these
          Signes,
They are blacke Vespers Pageants.

EROS   I my Lord.

ANTHONY
That which is now a Horse, euen with a thoght
The Racke distaines, and makes it indistinct
As water is in water.

EROS   It does my Lord.

ANTHONY
2360   My good Knaue *Eros*, now thy Captaine is
Euen such a body: Heere I am *Anthony*,
Yet cannot hold this visible shape (my Knaue)
I made these warres for Egypt, and the Queene,
Whose heart I thought I had, for she had mine:
Which whil'st it was mine, had annext vntoo't
A Million moe, (now lost:) shee *Eros* has
Packt Cards with *Cæsar*, and false plaid my Glory
Vnto an Enemies triumph.
Nay, weepe not gentle *Eros*, there is left vs
Our selues to end our selues.
          Enter Mardian
2370   Oh thy vilde Lady,
She has rob'd me of my Sword.

MARDIAN   No *Anthony*,
My Mistris lou'd thee, and her Fortunes mingled
With thine intirely.

ANTHONY   Hence sawcy Eunuch peace,
She hath betraid me, and shall dye the death.

MARDIAN
Death of one person, can be paide but once,
And that she ha's discharg'd. What thou would'st do
Is done vnto thy hand: the last she spake
Was *Anthony*, most Noble *Anthony*.
Then in the midd'st a tearing grone did breake
The name of *Anthony*: it was diuided   2380
Betweene her heart, and lips: she rendred life
Thy name so buried in her.

ANTHONY   Dead then?

MARDIAN   Dead.

ANTHONY
Vnarme *Eros*, the long dayes taske is done,
And we must sleepe: (*to Mardian*) That thou depart'st
          hence safe
Does pay thy labour richly: Go.   *exit Mardian*
                    Off, plucke off,
          Eros helpes Anthony to vnarme
The seuen-fold shield of *Aiax* cannot keepe
The battery from my heart. Oh cleaue my sides.
Heart, once be stronger then thy Continent,
Cracke thy fraile Case. Apace *Eros*, apace;
No more a Soldier: bruised peeces go,   2390
You haue bin Nobly borne. From me awhile.
                                   exit Eros
I will o're-take thee *Cleopatra*, and
Weepe for my pardon. So it must be, for now
All length is Torture: since the Torch is out,
Lye downe and stray no farther. Now all labour
Marres what it does: yea, very force entangles
It selfe with strength: Seale then, and all is done.
Eros? I come my Queene. *Eros?* Stay for me,
Where Soules do couch on Flowers, wee'l hand in
          hand,
And with our sprightly Port make the Ghostes gaze: 2400
Dido, and her *Æneas* shall want Troopes,
And all the haunt be ours. Come *Eros*, *Eros*.
          Enter Eros
EROS
What would my Lord?

ANTHONY   Since *Cleopatra* dyed,
I haue liu'd in such dishonour, that the Gods
Detest my basenesse. I, that with my Sword,
Quarter'd the World, and o're greene Neptunes backe
With Ships, made Cities; condemne my selfe, to lacke
The Courage of a Woman, lesse Noble minde
Then she which by her death, our *Cæsar* telles
I am Conqueror of my selfe. Thou art sworne *Eros*, 2410
That when the exigent should come, which now
Is come indeed: When I should see behinde me
Th'ineuitable prosecution of
Disgrace and horror, that on my command,
Thou then would'st kill me. Doo't, the time is come:
Thou strik'st not me, 'tis *Cæsar* thou defeat'st.
Put colour in thy Cheeke.

EROS   The Gods with-hold me,
Shall I do that which all the Parthian Darts,
(Though Enemy) lost ayme, and could not.

ANTHONY   *Eros*,

2420 Would'st thou be window'd in great Rome, and see
Thy Master thus with pleacht Armes, bending downe
His corrigible necke, his face subdu'de
To penetratiue shame; whil'st the wheel'd seate
Of Fortunate *Cæsar* drawne before him, branded
His Basenesse that ensued.

EROS   I would not see't.

ANTHONY
Come then: for with a wound I must be cur'd.
Draw that thy honest Sword, which thou hast worne
Most vsefull for thy Country.

EROS   Oh sir, pardon me.

ANTHONY
When I did make thee free, swor'st yᵘ not then
2430 To do this when I bad thee? Do it at once,
Or thy precedent Seruices are all
But accidents vnpurpos'd. Draw, and come.

EROS
Turne from me then that Noble countenance,
Wherein the worship of the whole world lyes.

ANTHONY (*turning away*) Loe thee.

EROS
My sword is drawne.

ANTHONY   Then let it do at once
The thing why thou hast drawne it.

EROS   My deere Master,
My Captaine, and my Emperor. Let me say
Before I strike this bloody stroke, Farewell.

2440 ANTHONY 'Tis said man, and farewell.

EROS
Farewell great Chiefe. Shall I strike now?

ANTHONY   Now *Eros*.

⌈*Eros stabs himselfe*⌉

EROS
Why there then: Thus I do escape the sorrow
Of *Anthonies* death.   *Dies*

ANTHONY   Thrice-Nobler then my selfe,
Thou teachest me: Oh valiant *Eros*, what
I should, and thou could'st not, my Queene and *Eros*
Haue by their braue instruction got vpon me
A Noblenesse in Record. But I will bee
A Bride-groome in my death, and run intoo't
As to a Louers bed. Come then, and *Eros*,
2450 Thy Master dies thy Scholler; to do thus
I learnt of thee.

Stabs himselfe

                    How, not dead? Not dead?
The Guard, how? Oh dispatch me.

Enter a Guard ⌈and Decretas⌉

1. GUARD   What's the noise?

ANTHONY
I haue done my worke ill Friends: Oh make an end
Of what I haue begun.

2. GUARD   The Starre is falne.

1. GUARD
And time is at his Period.

ALL THE GUARDS   Alas,
And woe.

ANTHONY   Let him that loues me, strike me dead.

1. GUARD
Not I.

2. GUARD Nor I.

3. GUARD   Nor any one.   *exeunt the Guard*

DECRETAS
Thy death and fortunes bid thy folowers fly.
He takes Anthonies Sword
This sword but shewne to *Cæsar* with this tydings,
Shall enter me with him.

Enter Diomedes

DIOMEDES   Where's *Anthony?*   2460

DECRETAS
There *Diomed* there.

DIOMEDES   Liues he: wilt thou not answer man?
                                Exit Decretas

ANTHONY
Art thou there *Diomed?* Draw thy sword, and giue mee,
Suffising strokes for death.

DIOMEDES   Most absolute Lord:
My Mistris *Cleopatra* sent me to thee.

ANTHONY
When did shee send thee?

DIOMEDES   Now my Lord.

ANTHONY   Where is she?

DIOMEDES
Lockt in her Monument: she had a Prophesying feare
Of what hath come to passe: for when she saw
(Which neuer shall be found) you did suspect
She had dispos'd with *Cæsar*, and that your rage
Would not be purg'd, she sent word she was dead: 2470
But fearing since how it might worke, hath sent
Me to proclaime the truth, and I am come
I dread, too late.

ANTHONY
Too late good *Diomed*: call my Guard I prythee.

DIOMEDES
What hoa: the Emperors Guard, the Guard, what hoa?
Come, your Lord calles.

Enter 4. or 5. of the Guard of Anthony

ANTHONY
Beare me good Friends where *Cleopatra* bides,
'Tis the last seruice that I shall command you.

1. GUARD
Woe, woe are we sir, you may not liue to weare
All your true Followers out.

ALL THE GUARDS   Most heauy day.   2480

ANTHONY
Nay good my Fellowes, do not please sharp fate
To grace it with your sorrowes. Bid that welcome
Which comes to punish vs, and we punish it
Seeming to beare it lightly. Take me vp,
I haue led you oft, carry me now good Friends,
And haue my thankes for all.

                    Exeunt bearing Anthony ⌈and Eros⌉

Enter Cleopatra, ⌈and her Maides aloft,⌉ with   Sc. 41
Charmian & Iras   (4.16)

CLEOPATRA
Oh *Charmian*, I will neuer go from hence.

CHARMIAN
    Be comforted deere Madam.
CLEOPATRA   No, I will not:
    All strange and terrible euents are welcome,
2490   But comforts we dispise; our size of sorrow
    Proportion'd to our cause, must be as great
    As that which makes it.
        Enter Diomed, ⌈below⌉
                 How now? is he dead?
DIOMEDES
    His death's vpon him, but not dead.
    Looke out o'th other side your Monument,
    His Guard haue brought him thither.
        Enter below Anthony, borne by the Guard
CLEOPATRA   Oh Sunne,
    Burne the great Sphere thou mou'st in, darkling stand
    The varrying shore o'th'world. O *Antony*,
    Antony, Antony. Helpe *Charmian*,
    Helpe *Iras* helpe: helpe Friends below,
    Let's draw him hither.
2500 ANTHONY   Peace, not *Cæsars* Valour
    Hath o'rethrowne *Anthony*, but *Anthonie's*
    Hath Triumpht on it selfe.
CLEOPATRA   So it should be,
    That none but *Anthony* should conquer *Anthony*,
    But woe 'tis so.
ANTHONY
    I am dying Egypt, dying; onely
    I heere importune death a-while, vntill
    Of many thousand kisses, the poore last
    I lay vpon thy lippes.
CLEOPATRA   I dare not Deere,
    Deere my Lord pardon: I dare not,
2510   Least I be taken: nor th'Imperious shew
    Of the full-Fortun'd *Cæsar*, euer shall
    Be brooch'd with me, if Knife, Drugges, Serpents haue
    Edge, sting, or operation. I am safe:
    Your Wife *Octauia*, with her modest eyes,
    And still Conclusion, shall acquire no Honour
    Demuring vpon me: but come, come *Anthony*,
    Helpe me my women, we must draw thee vp:
    Assist good Friends.
ANTHONY   Oh quicke, or I am gone.
CLEOPATRA
    Heere's sport indeede: How heauy weighes my Lord?
2520   Our strength is all gone into heauinesse,
    That makes the waight. Had I great *Iuno's* power,
    The strong wing'd Mercury should fetch thee vp,
    And set thee by Ioues side. Yet come a little,
    Wishers were euer Fooles. Oh come, come, come,
        They heaue Anthony aloft to Cleopatra
    And welcome, welcome. Dye when thou hast liu'd,
    Quicken with kissing: had my lippes that power,
    Thus would I weare them out.
        They kisse
ALL THE LOOKERS-ON   A heauy sight.
ANTHONY I am dying Egypt, dying.
2530   Giue me some Wine, and let me speake a little.

CLEOPATRA
    No, let me speake, and let me rayle so hye,
    That the false Huswife Fortune, breake her Wheele,
    Prouok'd by my offence.
ANTHONY   One word (sweet Queene)
    Of *Cæsar* seeke your Honour, with your safety. Oh.
CLEOPATRA
    They do not go together.
ANTHONY   Gentle heare me,
    None about *Cæsar* trust, but *Proculeius*.
CLEOPATRA
    My Resolution, and my hands, Ile trust,
    None about *Cæsar*.
ANTHONY
    The miserable change now at my end,
    Lament nor sorrow at: but please your thoughts   2540
    In feeding them with those my former Fortunes
    Wherein I liud the greatest Prince o'th'world,
    The Noblest: and do now not basely dye,
    Not Cowardly put off my Helmet to
    My Countreyman. A Roman, by a Roman
    Valiantly vanquish'd. Now my Spirit is going,
    I can no more.
CLEOPATRA   Noblest of men, woo't dye?
    Hast thou no care of me, shall I abide
    In this dull world, which in thy absence is
    No better then a Stye?
        Anthony dies
                Oh see my women: 2550
    The Crowne o'th'earth doth melt. My Lord?
    Oh wither'd is the Garland of the Warre,
    The Souldiers pole is falne: young Boyes and Gyrles
    Are leuell now with men: The oddes is gone,
    And there is nothing left remarkeable
    Beneath the visiting Moone.
        She falls
CHARMIAN Oh quietnesse, Lady.
IRAS She's dead too, our Soueraigne.
CHARMIAN
    Lady.
IRAS   Madam.
CHARMIAN   Oh Madam, Madam, Madam.
IRAS
    Royall Egypt: Empresse.
CHARMIAN   Peace, peace, *Iras*.   2560
CLEOPATRA *(recouering)*
    No more but in a Woman, and commanded
    By such poore passion, as the Maid that Milkes,
    And doe's the meanest chares. It were for me,
    To throw my Scepter at the iniurious Gods,
    To tell them that this World did equall theyrs,
    Till they had stolne our Iewell. All's but naught:
    Patience is sottish, and impatience does
    Become a Dogge that's mad: Then is it sinne,
    To rush into the secret house of death,
    Ere death dare come to vs. How do you Women?   2570
    What, what good cheere? Why how now *Charmian*?
    My Noble Gyrles? Ah Women, women! Looke

Our Lampe is spent, it's out. Good sirs, take heart,
Wee'l bury him: And then, what's braue, what's
    Noble,
Let's do it after the high Roman fashion,
And make death proud to take vs. Come, away,
This case of that huge Spirit now is cold.
Ah Women, Women! Come, we haue no Friend
But Resolution, and the breefest end.
            Exeunt, those aboue bearing of Anthonies body

Sc. 42   *Enter Cæsar with his Counsell of Warre, Agrippa,*
(5.1)   *Dollabella, Mecenas, Gallus, Proculeius*
    CÆSAR
2580   Go to him *Dollabella*, bid him yeeld,
        Being so frustrate, tell him, he but mockes
        The pawses that he makes.
    DOLABELLA   *Cæsar*, I shall.
                        Exit Dolabella
        Enter Decretas with the sword of Anthony
    CÆSAR
        Wherefore is that? And what art thou that dar'st
        Appeare thus to vs?
    DECRETAS   I am call'd *Decretas*,
        Marke Anthony I seru'd, who best was worthie
        Best to be seru'd: whil'st he stood vp, and spoke
        He was my Master, and I wore my life
        To spend vpon his haters. If thou please
        To take me to thee, as I was to him,
2590   Ile be to *Cæsar*: if y^u pleasest not,
        I yeild thee vp my life.
    CÆSAR   What is't thou say'st?
    DECRETAS
        I say (Oh *Cæsar*) *Anthony* is dead.
    CÆSAR
        The breaking of so great a thing, should make
        A greater cracke. The reaued World
        Should haue shooke Lyons into ciuill streets,
        And Cittizens to their dennes. The death of *Anthony*
        Is not a single doome, in y^t name lay
        A moity of the world.
    DECRETAS   He is dead *Cæsar*,
        Not by a publike minister of Iustice,
2600   Nor by a hyred Knife, but that selfe-hand
        Which writ his Honor in the Acts it did,
        Hath with the Courage which the heart did lend it,
        Splitted the heart. This is his Sword,
        I robb'd his wound of it: behold it stain'd
        With his most Noble blood.
    CÆSAR (*weeping*)   Looke you sad Friends,
        The Gods rebuke me, but it is a Tydings
        To wash the eyes of Kings.
    ⌈AGRIPPA⌉   And strange it is,
        That Nature must compell vs to lament
        Our most persisted deeds.
    MECENAS   His taints and Honours,
        Wag'd equal with him.
2610   ⌈AGRIPPA⌉   A Rarer spirit neuer

Did steere humanity: but you Gods will giue vs
Some faults to make vs men. *Cæsar* is touch'd.
    MECENAS
        When such a spacious Mirror's set before him,
        He needes must see him selfe.
    CÆSAR   Oh *Anthony*,
        I haue followed thee to this, but we do launch
        Diseases in our Bodies. I must perforce
        Haue shewne to thee such a declining day,
        Or looke on thine: we could not stall together,
        In the whole world. But yet let me lament
        With teares as Soueraigne as the blood of hearts,   2620
        That thou my Brother, my Competitor,
        In top of all designe; my Mate in Empire,
        Friend and Companion in the front of Warre,
        The Arme of mine owne Body, and the Heart
        Where mine his thoughts did kindle; that our Starres
        Vnreconciliable, should diuide
        Our equalnesse to this. Heare me good Friends,
                Enter an Ægyptian
        But I will tell you at some meeter Season,
        The businesse of this man lookes out of him,
        Wee'l heare him what he sayes. Whence are you?   2630
    ÆGYPTIAN
        A poore Egyptian, yet the Queen my mistris
        Confin'd in all she has, her Monument
        Of thy intents, desires instruction,
        That she preparedly may frame her selfe
        To'th'way shee's forc'd too.
    CÆSAR   Bid her haue good heart,
        She soone shall know of vs, by some of ours,
        How honourable, and how kindely Wee
        Determine for her. For *Cæsar* cannot liue
        To be vngentle.
    ÆGYPTIAN   So the Gods preserue thee.   *Exit*
    CÆSAR
        Come hither *Proculeius*. Go and say   2640
        We purpose her no shame: giue her what comforts
        The quality of her passion shall require;
        Least in her greatnesse, by some mortall stroke
        She do defeate vs. For her life in Rome,
        Would be eternall in our Triumph: Go,
        And with your speediest bring vs what she sayes,
        And how you finde of her.
    PROCULEIUS   *Cæsar* I shall.
                        Exit Proculeius
    CÆSAR
        Gallus, go you along: *Exit Gallus*
                where's *Dolabella*,
        To second *Proculeius*?
    ALL BUT CÆSAR   *Dolabella*.
    CÆSAR
        Let him alone: for I remember now   2650
        How hee's imployd: he shall in time be ready.
        Go with me to my Tent, where you shall see
        How hardly I was drawne into this Warre,
        How calme and gentle I proceeded still

In all my Writings. Go with me, and see
What I can shew in this.   *Exeunt*

Sc. 43   *Enter Cleopatra, Charmian, Iras, and Mardian*
(5.2)   CLEOPATRA
         My desolation does begin to make
         A better life: Tis paltry to be *Cæsar*:
         Not being Fortune, hee's but Fortunes knaue,
2660   A minister of her will: and it is great
         To do that thing that ends all other deeds,
         Which shackles accedents, and bolts vp change;
         Which sleepes, and neuer pallates more the dung,
         The beggers Nurse, and *Cæsars*.
              Enter Proculeius
         PROCULEIUS
         Cæsar sends greeting to the Queene of Egypt,
         And bids thee study on what faire demands
         Thou mean'st to haue him grant thee.
         CLEOPATRA   What's thy name?
         PROCULEIUS
         My name is *Proculeius*.
         CLEOPATRA   *Anthony*
         Did tell me of you, bad me trust you, but
2670   I do not greatly care to be deceiu'd
         That haue no vse for trusting. If your Master
         Would haue a Queene his begger, you must tell him,
         That Maiesty to keepe *decorum*, must
         No lesse begge then a Kingdome: If he please
         To giue me conquer'd Egypt for my Sonne,
         He giues me so much of mine owne, as I
         Will kneele to him with thankes.
         PROCULEIUS   Be of good cheere:
         Y'are falne into a Princely hand, feare nothing,
         Make your full reference freely to my Lord,
2680   Who is so full of Grace, that it flowes ouer
         On all that neede. Let me report to him
         Your sweet dependācie, and you shall finde
         A Conqueror that will pray in ayde for kindnesse,
         Where he for grace is kneel'd too.
         CLEOPATRA   Pray you tell him,
         I am his Fortunes Vassall, and I send him
         The Greatnesse he has got. I hourely learne
         A Doctrine of Obedience, and would gladly
         Looke him i'th'Face.
         PROCULEIUS   This Ile report (deere Lady)
         Haue comfort, for I know your plight is pittied
2690   Of him that caus'd it.
              ⌈*Enter Roman soldiers from behind*⌉
         PROCULEIUS (*to the soldiers*)
         You see how easily she may be surpriz'd:
         Guard her till *Cæsar* come.
         IRAS   Royall Queene.
         CHARMIAN
         Oh *Cleopatra*, thou art taken Queene.
         CLEOPATRA (*drawing a dagger*)
         Quicke, quicke, good hands.
         PROCULEIUS (*disarming Cleopatra*)
                             Hold worthy Lady, hold:

Doe not your selfe such wrong, who are in this
Releeu'd, but not betraid.
CLEOPATRA   What of death too
That rids our dogs of languish?
PROCULEIUS   *Cleopatra*,
Do not abuse my Masters bounty, by
Th'vndoing of your selfe: Let the World see
His Noblenesse well acted, which your death   2700
Will neuer let come forth.
CLEOPATRA   Where art thou Death?
Come hither come; Come, come, and take a Queene
Worth many Babes and Beggers.
PROCULEIUS   Oh temperance Lady.
CLEOPATRA
Sir, I will eate no meate, Ile not drinke sir,
If idle talke will once be necessary
Ile not sleepe neither. This mortall house Ile ruine,
Do *Cæsar* what he can. Know sir, that I
Will not waite pinnion'd at your Masters Court,
Nor once be chastic'd with the sober eye
Of dull *Octauia*. Shall they hoyst me vp,   2710
And shew me to the showting Varlotarie
Of censuring Rome? Rather a ditch in Egypt
Be gentle graue vnto me, rather on *Nylus* mudde
Lay me starke-nak'd, and let the water-Flies
Blow me into abhorring; rather make
My Countries high pyramides my Gibbet,
And hang me vp in Chaines.
PROCULEIUS   You do extend
These thoughts of horror further then you shall
Finde cause in *Cæsar*.
     Enter Dolabella
DOLABELLA   *Proculeius*,
What thou hast done, thy Master *Cæsar* knowes,   2720
And he hath sent for thee: for the Queene,
Ile take her to my Guard.
PROCULEIUS   So *Dolabella*,
It shall content me best: Be gentle to her,
(*To Cleopatra*) To *Cæsar* I will speake, what you shall
     please,
If you'l imploy me to him.
CLEOPATRA   Say, I would dye.
                             Exit Proculeius
DOLABELLA
Most Noble Empresse, you haue heard of me.
CLEOPATRA
I cannot tell.
DOLABELLA   Assuredly you know me.
CLEOPATRA
No matter sir, what I haue heard or knowne:
You laugh when Boyes or Women tell their Dreames,
Is't not your tricke?
DOLABELLA   I vnderstand not, Madam.   2730
CLEOPATRA
I dreampt there was an Emperor *Anthony*.
Oh such another sleepe, that I might see
But such another man.
DOLABELLA   If it might please ye.

CLEOPATRA
His face was as the Heau'ns, and therein stucke
A Sunne and Moone, which kept their course, &
    lighted
The little O o'th'earth.
DOLABELLA   Most Soueraigne Creature.
CLEOPATRA
His legges bestrid the Ocean, his rear'd arme
Crested the world: His voyce was propertied
As all the tuned Spheres, and that to Friends:
2740   But when he meant to quaile, and shake the Orbe,
He was as ratling Thunder. For his Bounty,
There was no winter in't. An *Automne* 'twas,
That grew the more by reaping: His delights
Were Dolphin-like, they shew'd his backe aboue
The Element they liu'd in: In his Liuery
Walk'd Crownes and Crownets: Realms & Islands were
As plates dropt from his pocket.
DOLABELLA   *Cleopatra.*
CLEOPATRA
Thinke you there was, or might be such a man
As this I dreampt of?
DOLABELLA   Gentle Madam, no.
CLEOPATRA
2750   You Lye vp to the hearing of the Gods:
But if there be, or euer were one such
It's past the size of dreaming: Nature wants stuffe
To vie strange formes with fancie, yet t'imagine
An *Anthony* were Natures peece, 'gainst Fancie,
Condemning shadowes quite.
DOLABELLA   Heare me, good Madam:
Your losse is as your selfe, great; and you beare it
As answering to the waight, would I might neuer
Ore-take pursu'de successe: But I do feele
By the rebound of yours, a greefe that smites
My very heart at roote.
2760   CLEOPATRA   I thanke you sir:
Know you what *Cæsar* meanes to do with me?
DOLABELLA
I am loath to tell you what, I would you knew.
CLEOPATRA
Nay pray you sir.
DOLABELLA   Though he be Honourable.
CLEOPATRA
Hee'l leade me then in Triumph.
DOLABELLA   Madam he will, I know't.
   Flourish. Enter Cæsar, Proculeius, Gallus, Mecenas,
   and others of his Traine
ALL
Make way there *Cæsar.*
CÆSAR   Which is the Queene of Egypt.
DOLABELLA *(to Cleopatra)*
It is the Emperor Madam.
   Cleopatra kneeles
CÆSAR   Arise, you shall not kneele:
I pray you rise, rise Egypt.
CLEOPATRA *(rising)*   Sir, the Gods

Will haue it thus, my Master and my Lord
I must obey.
CÆSAR   Take to you no hard thoughts,
The Record of what iniuries you did vs,   2770
Though written in our flesh, we shall remember
As things but done by chance.
CLEOPATRA   Sole Sir o'th'World,
I cannot proiect mine owne cause so well
To make it cleare, but do confesse I haue
Bene laden with like frailties, which before
Haue often sham'd our Sex.
CÆSAR   *Cleopatra* know,
We will extenuate rather then inforce:
If you apply your selfe to our intents,
Which towards you are most gentle, you shall finde
A benefit in this change: but if you seeke   2780
To lay on me a Cruelty, by taking
Anthonies course, you shall bereaue your selfe
Of my good purposes, and put your children
To that destruction which Ile guard them from,
If thereon you relye. Ile take my leaue.
CLEOPATRA
And may through all the world: tis yours, & we
Your Scutcheons, and your signes of Conquest shall
Hang in what place you please. (*Giuing a paper*) Here
     my good Lord.
CÆSAR
You shall aduise me in all for *Cleopatra.*
CLEOPATRA
This is the breefe: of Money, Plate, & Iewels   2790
I am possest of, 'tis exactly valewed,
Not petty things admitted. Where's *Seleucus?*
   ⌈*Enter Seleucus*⌉
SELEUCUS Heere Madam.
CLEOPATRA *(to Cæsar)*
This is my Treasurer, let him speake (my Lord)
Vpon his perill, that I haue reseru'd
To my selfe nothing. Speake the truth *Seleucus.*
SELEUCUS
Madam, I had rather seele my lippes,
Then to my perill speake that which is not.
CLEOPATRA What haue I kept backe.
SELEUCUS
Enough to purchase what you haue made known.   2800
CÆSAR
Nay blush not *Cleopatra*, I approue
Your Wisedome in the deede.
CLEOPATRA   See *Cæsar*: Oh behold,
How pompe is followed: Mine will now be yours,
And should we shift estates, yours would be mine.
The ingratitude of this *Seleucus*, does
Euen make me wilde. Oh Slaue, of no more trust
Then loue that's hyr'd? What goest thou backe, y^u
    shalt
Go backe I warrant thee: but Ile catch thine eyes
Though they had wings. Slaue, Soule-lesse Villain, Dog.
O rarely base!
CÆSAR   Good Queene, let vs intreat you.   2810

CLEOPATRA

O *Cæsar*, what a wounding shame is this,
That thou vouchsafing heere to visit me,
Doing the Honour of thy Lordlinesse
To one so meeke, that mine owne Seruant should
Parcell the summe of my disgraces, by
Addition of his Enuy. Say (good *Cæsar*)
That I some Lady trifles haue reseru'd,
Immoment toyes, things of such Dignitie
As we greet moderne Friends withall, and say
2820 Some Nobler token I haue kept apart
For *Liuia* and *Octauia*, to induce
Their mediation, must I be vnfolded
With one that I haue bred: The Gods! it smites me
Beneath the fall I haue. (*To Seleucus*) Prythee go
        hence,
Or I shall shew the Cynders of my spirits
Through th'Ashes of my chance: Wer't thou a man,
Thou would'st haue mercy on me.

CÆSAR   Forbeare *Seleucus*.
                                    Exit Seleucus

CLEOPATRA

Be it known, that we the greatest are mis-thoght
For things that others do: and when we fall,
2830 We answer others merits in our name,
Are therefore to be pittied.

CÆSAR   *Cleopatra*,
Not what you haue reseru'd, nor what acknowledg'd
Put we i'th'Roll of Conquest: still bee't yours,
Bestow it at your pleasure, and beleeue
Cæsars no Merchant, to make prize with you
Of things that Merchants sold. Therefore be cheer'd,
Make not your thoughts your prisons: No deere
        Queen,
For we intend so to dispose you, as
Your selfe shall giue vs counsell: Feede, and sleepe:
2840 Our care and pitty is so much vpon you,
That we remaine your Friend, and so adieu.

CLEOPATRA

My Master, and my Lord.

CÆSAR   Not so: Adieu.
                        Flourish. Exeunt Cæsar, and his Traine

CLEOPATRA

He words me Gyrles, he words me, that I should not
Be Noble to my selfe. But hearke thee *Charmian*.
        She whispers to Charmian

IRAS

Finish good Lady, the bright day is done,
And we are for the darke.

CLEOPATRA (*to Charmian*)   Hye thee againe,
I haue spoke already, and it is prouided,
Go put it to the haste.

CHARMIAN   Madam, I will.
        Enter Dolabella

DOLABELLA

Where's the Queene?

CHARMIAN   Behold sir.   *Exit*

CLEOPATRA   *Dolabella*.

DOLABELLA

Madam, as thereto sworne, by your command   2850
(Which my loue makes Religion to obey)
I tell you this: *Cæsar* through Syria
Intends his iourney, and within three dayes,
You with your Children will he send before,
Make your best vse of this. I haue perform'd
Your pleasure, and my promise.

CLEOPATRA   *Dolabella*,
I shall remaine your debter.

DOLABELLA   I your Seruant:
Adieu good Queene, I must attend on *Cæsar*.

CLEOPATRA

Farewell, and thankes.   *Exit Dolabella*
                        Now *Iras*, what think'st thou?
Thou, an Egyptian Puppet shall be shewne   2860
In Rome aswell as I: Mechanicke Slaues
With greazie Aprons, Rules, and Hammers shall
Vplift vs to the view. In their thicke breathes,
Ranke of grosse dyet, shall we be enclowded,
And forc'd to drinke their vapour.

IRAS   The Gods forbid.

CLEOPATRA

Nay, 'tis most certaine *Iras*: sawcie Lictors
Will catch at vs like Strumpets, and scald Rimers
Ballad vs out a Tune. The quicke Comedians
Extemporally will stage vs, and present
Our Alexandrian Reuels: *Anthony*   2870
Shall be brought drunken forth, and I shall see
Some squeaking *Cleopatra* Boy my greatnesse
I'th'posture of a Whore.

IRAS   O the good Gods!

CLEOPATRA Nay that's certaine.

IRAS

Ile neuer see't? for I am sure my Nailes
Are stronger then mine eyes.

CLEOPATRA   Why that's the way
To foole their preparation, and to conquer
Their most absurd intents.
        Enter Charmian
                                    Now *Charmian*.
Shew me my Women like a Queene: Go fetch
My best Attyres. I am againe for *Cidnus*,   2880
To meete *Marke Anthony*. Sirra *Iras*, go
(Now Noble *Charmian*, wee'l dispatch indeede,)
And when thou hast done this chare, Ile giue thee
        leaue
To play till Doomesday: bring our Crowne, and all.
                                    ⌈*Exit Iras*⌉
        A noise within
Wherefore's this noise?
        Enter a Guardsman

GUARDSMAN   Heere is a rurall Fellow,
That will not be deny'de your Highnesse presence,
He brings you Figges.

CLEOPATRA

Let him come in.   *Exit Guardsman*
        What poore an Instrument

2890 May do a Noble deede: he brings me liberty:
My Resolution's plac'd, and I haue nothing
Of woman in me: Now from head to foote
I am Marble constant: now the fleeting Moone
No Planet is of mine.

Enter Guardsman, and Clowne with a basket

GUARDSMAN   This is the man.

CLEOPATRA
Auoid, and leaue him.   *Exit Guardsman*
                    Hast thou the pretty worme
Of Nylus there, that killes and paines not?

CLOWNE Truly I haue him: but I would not be the partie
that should desire you to touch him, for his byting is
immortall: those that doe dye of it, doe seldome or
neuer recouer.

2900 CLEOPATRA Remember'st thou any that haue dyed on't?

CLOWNE Very many, men and women too. I heard of one
of them no longer then yesterday, a very honest
woman, but something giuen to lye, as a woman
should not do, but in the way of honesty, how she
dyed of the byting of it, what paine she felt: Truely,
she makes a verie good report o'th'worme: but he that
wil beleeue all that they say, shall neuer be saued by
halfe that they do: but this is most falliable, the
Worme's an odde Worme.

2910 CLEOPATRA Get thee hence, farewell.

CLOWNE I wish you all ioy of the Worme.

CLEOPATRA Farewell.

CLOWNE You must thinke this (looke you,) that the Worme
will do his kinde.

CLEOPATRA I, I, farewell.

CLOWNE Looke you, the Worme is not to bee trusted, but
in the keeping of wise people: for indeede, there is no
goodnesse in the Worme.

CLEOPATRA Take thou no care, it shall be heeded.

2920 CLOWNE Very good: giue it nothing I pray you, for it is
not worth the feeding.

CLEOPATRA Will it eate me?

CLOWNE You must not think I am so simple, but I know
the diuell himselfe will not eate a woman: I know, that
a woman is a dish for the Gods, if the diuell dresse her
not. But truly, these same whorson diuels doe the Gods
great harme in their women: for in euery tenne that
they make, the diuels marre fiue.

CLEOPATRA Well, get thee gone, farewell.

2930 CLOWNE Yes forsooth: I wish you ioy o'th'worm.
                    Exit leauing the basket
Enter ⌈Iras⌉ with a Robe, Crowne, and other Iewels

CLEOPATRA
Giue me my Robe, put on my Crowne, I haue
Immortall longings in me. Now no more
The iuyce of Egypts Grape shall moyst this lip.
    Charmian and Iras helpe her to dresse
Yare, yare, good *Iras*; quicke: Me thinkes I heare
Anthony call: I see him rowse himselfe
To praise my Noble Act. I heare him mock
The lucke of *Cæsar*, which the Gods giue men
To excuse their after wrath. Husband, I come:

Now to that name, my Courage proue my Title.
I am Fire, and Ayre; my other Elements   2940
I giue to baser life. So, haue you done?
Come then, and take the last warmth of my Lippes.
    She kisses them
Farewell kinde *Charmian, Iras*, long farewell.
    Iras falls and dies
Haue I the Aspicke in my lippes? Dost fall?
If thou, and Nature can so gently part,
The stroke of death is as a Louers pinch,
Which hurts, and is desir'd. Dost thou lye still?
If thus thou vanishest, thou tell'st the world,
It is not worth leaue-taking.

CHARMIAN
Dissolue thicke clowd, & Raine, that I may say   2950
The Gods themselues do weepe.

CLEOPATRA   This proues me base:
If she first meete the Curled *Anthony*,
Hee'l make demand of her, and spend that kisse
Which is my heauen to haue.
    *She takes an Aspicke from the basket and puts it to
    her Breast*
                    Come thou mortal wretch,
With thy sharpe teeth this knot intrinsicate,
Of life at once vntye: Poore venomous Foole,
Be angry, and dispatch. Oh could'st thou speake,
That I might heare thee call great *Cæsar* Asse,
Vnpolicied.

CHARMIAN   Oh Easterne Starre.

CLEOPATRA   Peace, peace:
Dost thou not see my Baby at my breast,   2960
That suckes the Nurse asleepe.

CHARMIAN   O breake! O breake!

CLEOPATRA
As sweet as Balme, as soft as Ayre, as gentle.
O *Anthony*!
    She puts another Aspicke to her Arme
                    Nay I will take thee too.
What should I stay—   *Dyes*

CHARMIAN   In this vilde World? So fare thee well:
Now boast thee Death, in thy possession lyes
A Lasse vnparalell'd. Downie Windowes cloze,
And golden Phœbus, neuer be beheld
Of eyes againe so Royall: your Crownes awry,
Ile mend it, and then play—
    Enter the Guard rustling in

I. GUARD Where's the Queene?   2970

CHARMIAN Speake softly, wake her not.

I. GUARD
Cæsar hath sent—

CHARMIAN   Too slow a Messenger.
    She applies an Aspicke
Oh come apace, dispatch, I partly feele thee.

I. GUARD
Approach hoa, all's not well: *Cæsar's* beguild.

2. GUARD
There's *Dolabella* sent from *Cæsar*: call him.
                    ⌈*Exit a Guardsman*⌉

1. GUARD

What worke is heere *Charmian*? Is this well done?

CHARMIAN

It is well done, and fitting for a Princesse
Descended of so many Royall Kings.
Ah Souldier.   *Charmian dyes*
   Enter Dolabella

DOLABELLA

How goes it heere?

2. GUARD   All dead.

2980 DOLABELLA   *Cæsar*, thy thoughts
Touch their effects in this: Thy selfe art comming
To see perform'd the dreaded Act which thou
So sought'st to hinder.

ALL   A way there, a way for *Cæsar*.
   Enter Cæsar and all his Traine, marching

DOLABELLA (*to Cæsar*)

Oh sir, you are too sure an Augurer:
That you did feare, is done.

CÆSAR   Brauest at the last,
She leuell'd at our purposes, and being Royall
Tooke her owne way: the manner of their deaths,
I do not see them bleede.

DOLABELLA (*to a Guardsman*) Who was last with them?

1. GUARD

A simple Countryman, that broght hir Figs:
This was his Basket.

CÆSAR   Poyson'd then.

2990 1. GUARD   Oh *Cæsar*:
This *Charmian* liu'd but now, she stood and spake:

I found her trimming vp the Diadem
On her dead Mistris; tremblingly she stood,
And on the sodaine dropt.

CÆSAR   Oh Noble weakenesse:
If they had swallow'd poyson, 'twould appeare
By externall swelling: but she lookes like sleepe,
As she would catch another *Anthony*
In her strong toyle of Grace.

DOLABELLA   Heere on her brest,
There is a vent of Bloud, and something blowne,
The like is on her Arme.

1. GUARD   This is an Aspickes traile,   3000
And these Figge-leaues haue slime vpon them, such
As th'Aspicke leaues vpon the Caues of Nyle.

CÆSAR Most probable
That so she dyed: for her Physitian tels mee
She hath pursu'de Conclusions infinite
Of easie wayes to dye. Take vp her bed,
And beare her Women from the Monument,
She shall be buried by her *Anthony*.
No Graue vpon the earth shall clip in it
A payre so famous: high euents as these   3010
Strike those that make them: and their Story is
No lesse in pitty, then his Glory which
Brought them to be lamented. Our Army shall
In solemne shew, attend this Funerall,
And then to Rome. Come *Dolabella*, see
High Order, in this great Solemnity.
              Exeunt omnes, Soldiers bearing Cleopatra ⌈on
                 her bed⌉, Charmian, and Iras

FINIS

PERICLES

BY WILLIAM SHAKESPEARE AND GEORGE WILKINS
A RECONSTRUCTED TEXT

ON 20 May 1608 *Pericles* was entered on the Stationers' Register to Edward Blount; but he did not publish it. Probably the players allowed him to license it in the hope of preventing its publication by anyone else, for it was one of the most popular plays of the period. Its success was exploited, also in 1608, by the publication of a novel, by George Wilkins, 'The Painfull Aduentures of *Pericles* Prince of Tyre, *Being* The True History of the Play of *Pericles*, as it was lately presented by the worthy and ancient Poet *Iohn Gower*'. The play itself appeared in print in the following year, with an ascription to Shakespeare, but in a manifestly corrupt text that gives every sign of having been put together from memory. This quarto was several times reprinted; but the play was not included in the 1623 Folio (perhaps because Heminges and Condell knew that Shakespeare was responsible for only part of it).

In putting together *The Painfull Aduentures*, Wilkins drew on an earlier version of the tale, *The Patterne of Paynfull Aduentures*, by Laurence Twine, written in the mid-1570s and reprinted in 1607. Twine's book is also a source of the play, which draws too on the story of Apollonius of Tyre as told by John Gower in his *Confessio Amantis*, and, to a lesser extent, on Sir Philip Sidney's *Arcadia*. Wilkins not only incorporated verbatim passages from Twine's book, he also drew heavily on *Pericles* itself. Since the play text is so corrupt, it is quite likely that Wilkins reports parts of it both more accurately and more fully than the quarto. And he may have had special qualifications for doing so. He was a dramatist whose popular play *The Miseries of Inforst Mariage* had been performed by Shakespeare's company. *Pericles* has usually been regarded as either a collaborative play or one in which Shakespeare revised a pre-existing script. Our edition is based on the hypothesis (not new) that Wilkins was its joint author. Our attempt to reconstruct the play draws more heavily than is usual on Wilkins's novel, especially in the first two acts (which he probably wrote); in general, because of its obvious corruption, the original text is more freely emended than usual. So that readers may experience the play as originally printed, an unemended reprint of the 1609 quarto follows our edited text. The deficiences of the text are in part compensated for by the survival of an unusual amount of relevant visual material, reproduced overleaf.

The complex textual background of *Pericles* should not be allowed to draw attention away from the merits of this dramatic romance, which we hope will be more apparent as the result of our treatment of the text. If the original play had survived, it might well have been as highly valued as *The Winters Tale* or *The Tempest*; as it is, it contains some hauntingly beautiful episodes, above all that in Scene 21 in which Marina, Pericles' long-lost daughter, draws him out of the comatose state to which his sufferings have reduced him.

The true History of the Play of *Pericles*, as it was lately presented by the worthy and ancient Poet *Iohn Gower*.

Iohn   Gower.

The Description of Iohn Gower

Large he was, his height was long,
Broad of brest, his lims were strong,
But couller pale, and wan his looke,
Such have they that plyen their booke,
His head was gray and quaintly shorne,
Neatley was his beard worne.
His visage graue, sterne and grim,
Cato was most like to him.
His Bonnet was a Hat of blew,
His sleeues straight of that same hew,
A surcoate of a tawnie die,
Hung in pleights ouer his thigh,
A breech close vnto his dock,
Handsomd with a long stock,
Pricked before were his shoone,
He wore such as others doone,
A bag of red by his side,
And by that his napkin tide,
Thus Iohn Gower did appeare,
Quaint attired as you heere.

11. From the title-page of *The Painfull Aduentures of Pericles Prince of Tyre* (1608), by George Wilkins; artist unknown. Since Gower is not a character in Wilkins's novel, the choice of woodcut undoubtedly reflects both the play's popularity and Gower's own impact in early performances, and it is as likely to reflect the visual detail of performance as any early title-page. The sprig of laurel (or posy) in Gower's left hand is symbolic of his poetic status.

12. From *Greenes Vision* (1592), sig. C1ʳ–C1ᵛ; probably by Robert Greene. The description here fits reasonably well the *Painfull Aduentures* title-page, though the woodcut does not contain the 'bag of red', 'napkin', or tight-fitting 'breech'.

Bridge Gate

13. Severed heads displayed on the gate of London Bridge, from an etching by Claes Jan Visscher (1616). In the play's sources, and *Painfull Aduentures*, the heads of previous suitors (Sc. 1) are placed on the 'gate' of Antioch. In performance they could have been thrust out on poles from the upper stage; but the timing and method of their display is not clear.

Me pompæ prouexit apex.
The desire of renowne hath promoted me, or set me forward.

14. From *The Heroicall Deuises of M. Claudius Paradin*, translated by P.S. (1591), sig. V3. This is the source for the impresa of the Third Knight, in Sc. 6.

Qui me alit, me extinguit.
He that nourisheth me, killeth me.

15. From *The Heroicall Deuises of M. Claudius Paradin*, translated by P.S. (1591), sig. Z3. This is the source for the impresa of the Fourth Knight, in Sc. 6.

17. A miniature of Diana by Isaac Oliver (1615): the dress is yellow, the scarf a gauzy pink-white, the cloak over her right shoulder blue; the leaf-shaped brooch topped by the crescent moon, gold. In Samuel Daniel's masque *The Vision of the Twelve Goddesses* (1604), 'Diana, in a greene Mantle, imbrodered with siluer halfe moones, and a croissant of pearle on her head: presents a Bow and a Quiuer' (sig. A5). The 'crescent of pearl'—an ornamental crescent moon, also detectable in Jones's sketch—can be seen in many emblematic representations of the goddess.

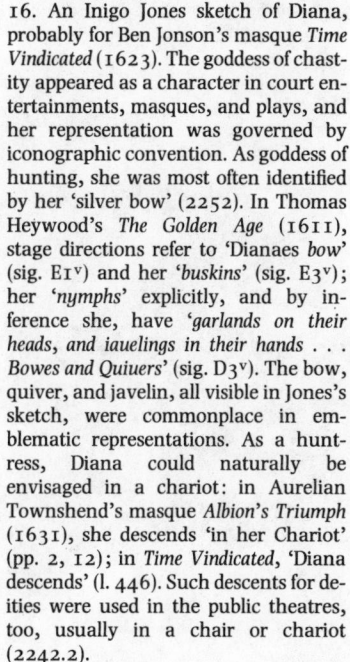

16. An Inigo Jones sketch of Diana, probably for Ben Jonson's masque *Time Vindicated* (1623). The goddess of chastity appeared as a character in court entertainments, masques, and plays, and her representation was governed by iconographic convention. As goddess of hunting, she was most often identified by her 'silver bow' (2252). In Thomas Heywood's *The Golden Age* (1611), stage directions refer to 'Dianaes *bow*' (sig. E1ᵛ) and her '*buskins*' (sig. E3ᵛ); her '*nymphs*' explicitly, and by inference she, have '*garlands on their heads, and iauelings in their hands . . . Bowes and Quiuers*' (sig. D3ᵛ). The bow, quiver, and javelin, all visible in Jones's sketch, were commonplace in emblematic representations. As a huntress, Diana could naturally be envisaged in a chariot: in Aurelian Townshend's masque *Albion's Triumph* (1631), she descends 'in her Chariot' (pp. 2, 12); in *Time Vindicated*, 'Diana descends' (l. 446). Such descents for deities were used in the public theatres, too, usually in a chair or chariot (2242.2).

18. For the pastoral *Florimène* (1635), Inigo Jones designed two scenic views of 'The Temple of Diana' (see l. 2283.1). Though such scenes were not used in the public theatres in Shakespeare's time, the columns supporting the overhanging roof of the public stage (see General Introduction, pp. xxv–xxvii) could have created a scenic effect roughly similar to Jones's recessed classical temple. Statues were also available as props in the public theatre; in *Pericles*, as in *The Winters Tale*, the statue could have been impersonated by an actor on a pedestal. Whether or not a statue was visible, the temple could be identified by an altar (as in *The Two Noble Kinsmen*).

THE NAMES OF THE PERSONAGES IN THIS HISTORIE

Iohn Gower the Presenter

Antiochus that built Antioch

His daughter

Pericles Prince of *Tyre*

Thalyart a villaine

Helycanus
Eschines } Twoo graue Counsellors

Cleon Gouernor of *Tharsus*

Dyonysa his wife

Three Fishermen

Symonides king of *Pentapolis*

Thaysa his daughter

Fiue Princes

A Marshall

Lichorida a Nurse

Cerimon a Phisition

Phylemon his seruant

Marina, Pericles daughter

Leonine a Murtherer

Pirates

A Bawde

Boult, a *Leno*

A Pander

Lysimachus Gouernour of *Meteline*

Diana Goddesse of chastitie

Lords, Ladies, Pages, Messengers, Saylers, and Gentlemen

A Reconstructed Text of
Pericles Prynce of Tyre

Enter Gower as Prologue

GOWER

To sing a Song that old was sung,
From ashes, auntient *Gower* is come,
Assuming mans infirmities,
To glad your eare, and please your eyes:
It hath been sung at Feastiuals,
On Ember eues, and Holyales:
And Lords and Ladyes in their liues,
Haue red it for restoratiues:
The purchase is to make men glorious,
Et bonum quo Antiquius eo melius:

10 If you, borne in these latter times,
When Witts more ripe, accept my rimes;
And that to heare an old man sing,
May to your Wishes pleasure bring:
I life would wish, and that I might
Waste it for you, like Taper light.
This *Antioch*, then; *Antiochus* the great,
Buylt vp this Citie, for his chiefest Seat;
The fayrest in all *Syria*.

20 I tell you what mine Authors saye:
This King vnto him tooke a Pheere,
Who dyed, and left a female heyre,
So bucksome, blith, and full of face,
As heau'n had lent her all his grace:
With whom the Father liking tooke,
And her to Incest did prouoke:
Bad child, worse father, to intice his owne
To euill, should be done by none:
By custome what they did begin,

30 Was with long vse, account'd no sinne;
The beautie of this sinfull Dame,
Made many Princes thither frame,
To seeke her as a bedfellow,
In maryage pleasures, playfellow:
Which to preuent, he made a Law,
To keepe her still, and men in awe:
That who so askt her for his wife,
His Riddle tould not, lost his life:
So for her many a wight did die,
⌐A row of heads is reuealed⌐

40 As yon grimme lookes do testifie.
What now ensues, to th' iudgement of your eye
I giue, my cause who best can iustifie.   *Exit*
⌐*Sennet.*⌐ *Enter Antiochus, Prince Pericles, and*
⌐*Lords and Peeres in their richest ornaments*⌐

ANTIOCHUS

Young Prince of *Tyre*, you haue at large receiued
The danger of the taske you vndertake.

PERICLES

I haue (*Antiochus*) and with a soule
Emboldned with the glory of her prayse,
Thinke death no hazard, in this enterprise.

ANTIOCHUS Musicke!

   Musicke sounds

Bring in our daughter, clothed like a bride,
Fit for th'embracements eu'n of *Ioue* himselfe;   50
At whose conception, till *Lucina* rained,
Nature this dowry gaue, to glad her presence;
The Seanate house of Planets all did sit,
In her, their best perfections to knit.
   Enter Antiochus daughter

PERICLES

See where she comes, apparel'd like the Spring,
Graces her subiects, and her thoughts the King,
Of eu'ry Vertue giues renowne to men:
Her face the booke of prayses, where is read,
Nothing but curious pleasures, as from thence,
Sorrow were euer racte, and teastie wrath   60
Could neuer be her milde companion.
You Gods that made me man, and sway in loue;
That haue enflamde desire in my breast,
To taste the fruite of yon celestiall tree,
(Or die in the aduenture) be my helpes,
As I am sonne and seruant to your will,
To compasse such a boundlesse happinesse.

ANTIOCHUS Prince *Pericles*.

PERICLES

That would be sonne to great *Antiochus*.

ANTIOCHUS

Before thee standes this faire *Hesperides*,   70
With golden fruite, but dang'rous to be toucht:
⌐*He gestures towards the heads*⌐
For Death like Dragons heere affright thee hard:
⌐*He gestures towards his daughter*⌐
Her Heau'n like face, inticeth thee to view
Her countlesse glory; which desert must gaine:
And which without desert, because thine eye
Presumes to reach, all the whole heape must die:
Yon sometimes famous Princes, like thy selfe,
Drawne by report, aduentrous by desire,
Tell thee with speachlesse tongues, and semblants
   bloodlesse,
That without couering, saue yon field of Starres,   80
Heere they stand Martyrs slaine in *Cupids* Warres:
And with dead cheekes, aduise thee to desist,
From going on deaths net, whom none resist.

PERICLES

Antiochus, I thanke thee, who hath taught,

My frayle mortalitie to know it selfe;
And by those fearefull obiectes, to prepare
This body, like to them, to what I must:
For Death remembred should be like a myrrour,
Who tels vs, life's but breath, to trust it errour:
90   Ile make my Will then, and as sickemen doe,
Who know the World, see Heau'n, but feeling woe,
Gripe not at earthly ioyes as earst they did;
So I bequeath a happy peace to you,
And all good men, as eu'ry Prince should doe;
My ritches to the earth, from whence they came;
(To the daughter) But my vnspotted fire of Loue, to you:
(To Antiochus) Thus ready for the way of life or death,
I wayte the sharpest blow *(Antiochus)*
ANTIOCHUS
    Scorning aduice; read the conclusion then:
        ⌈*He angrily throwes downe the Riddle*⌉
100   Which read and not expounded, tis decreed,
As these before thee, thou thy selfe shalt bleed.
DAUGHTER *(to Pericles)*
    Of all sayd yet, mayst thou prooue prosperous,
Of all sayd yet, I wish thee happinesse.
PERICLES
    Like a bold Champion I assume the Listes,
Nor aske aduise of any other thought,
But faythfulnesse and courage.
        ⌈*He takes vp and*⌉ *reads aloude*
                The Riddle
    I am no Viper, yet I feed
    On mothers flesh which did me breed:
    I sought a Husband, in which labour,
110   *I found that kindnesse in a Father;*
    Hee's Father, Sonne, and Husband milde;
    I, Mother, Wife; and yet his Child:
    How this may be, and yet in two,
    As you will liue resolue it you.
Sharpe Phisicke is the last: ⌈*Aside*⌉ But ô you powers!
That giues heau'n countlesse eyes to view mens actes,
Why cloude they not their sights perpetually,
If this be true, which makes me pale to read it?
        ⌈*He gazes on the daughter*⌉
Faire Glasse of light, I lou'd you, and could still,
120   Were not this glorious Casket stor'd with ill:
But I must tell you, now my thoughts reuolt,
For hee's no man on whom perfections waite,
That knowing sinne within, will touch the gate.
Y'are a faire Violl, and your sense, the stringes;
Who finger'd to make man his lawfull musicke,
Would draw Heau'n downe, and all the Gods to
        harken:
But being playd vpon before your time,
Hell onely daunceth at so harsh a chime:
Good sooth, I care not for you.
ANTIOCHUS
130   Prince *Pericles*, touch not, vpon thy life;
For that's an Article within our Law,
As dang'rous as the rest: your time's expir'd,
Either expound now, or receiue your sentence.

PERICLES Great King,
Few loue to heare the sinnes they loue to act,
T'would brayde your selfe too neare for me to tell it:
Who has a booke of all that Monarches doe,
Hee's more secure to keepe it shut, then showne.
For Vice repeated, like the wandring Wind,
Blowes dust in others eyes to spread it selfe;   140
And yet the end of all is bought thus deare,
The breath is gone, and the sore eyes see cleare,
To stop the Ayre would hurt them; the blind Mole
        castes
Copt hilles towards heau'n, to tell the earth is throng'd
By mans oppression, and the poore Worme doth die
        for't:
Kinges are earths Gods; in vice, their law's their will:
And if *Ioue* stray, who dares say, *Ioue* doth ill:
It is enough you know, and it is fit;
What being more knowne, growes worse, to smother it.
All loue the Wombe that their first beeing bred,   150
Then giue my tongue like leaue, to loue my head.
ANTIOCHUS *(aside)*
    Heau'n, that I had thy head; ha's found the meaning:
But I will gloze with him. *(To Pericles)* Young Prince of
        Tyre,
Though by the tenour of our strict edict,
Your exposition misinterpreting,
We might proceed to cansell of your dayes;
Yet hope, succeeding from so faire a tree
As your faire selfe, doth tune vs otherwise;
Fourtie dayes longer we doe respite you,
If by which time, our secret be vndone,   160
This mercy shewes, wee'le ioy in such a Sonne:
And vntill then, your entertaine shall bee
As doth befit your worth and our degree.
        ⌈*Flourish.*⌉ *Exeunt. Manet Pericles solus*
PERICLES
    How courtesie would seeme to couer sinne,
When what is done, is like an hipocrite,
The which is good in nothing but in sight.
If it be true that I interpret false,
Then were it certaine you were not so bad,
As with foule Incest to abuse your soule:
Where now you'r both a Father and a Sonne,   170
By your vncomely claspings with your Child,
(Which pleasures fittes a husband, not a father)
And shee an eater of her Mothers flesh,
By the defiling of her Parents bed,
And both like Serpents are; who though they feed
On sweetest Flowers, yet they Poyson breed.
Antioch farewell, for Wisedome sees those men,
Blush not in actions blacker then the night,
Will shew no course to keepe them from the light:
One sinne (I know) another doth prouoke;   180
Murther's as neere to Lust, as Flame to Smoake:
Poyson and Treason are the hands of Sinne,
I, and the targets to put off the shame,
Then least my life be cropt, to keepe you cleare,
By flight, Ile shun the danger which I feare.   *Exit*

Enter Antiochus

ANTIOCHUS

    He hath found the meaning. For the which we meane

    To haue his head: he must not liue

    To trumpet foorth my infamie, nor tell the world

    Antiochus doth sinne in such a loathed manner:

190   And therefore instantly this Prince must die,

    For by his fall, my honour must keepe hie.

    Who attends vs there?

        Enter Thaliart

THALYART   Doth your highnes call?

ANTIOCHUS

    Thaliart, you are of our Chamber, *Thaliart*,

    And to your secrecie our minde pertakes

    Her priuat actions; for your faythfulnes,

    We will aduaunce you, *Thaliart*: Behold,

    Heere's Poyson, and heere's Gold:

    Wee hate the Prince of *Tyre*, and thou must kill him;

    It fittes thee not to aske the reason why?

200   Because we bid it: say, is it done?

THALYART My Lord, tis done.

ANTIOCHUS Enough.

        Enter a Messenger hastily

    Let your breath coole your selfe, telling your haste.

MESSENGER

    Your Maiestie, Prince *Pericles* is fled.   ⌈*Exit*⌉

ANTIOCHUS (*to Thalyart*)

    As thou wilt liue flie after; like an arrow

    Shot from a well experienst Archer hits

    The marke his eye doth leuell at: so thou

    Neuer returne vnlesse it be to say

    Your Maiestie, Prince *Pericles* is dead.

THALYART

210   If I can get him in my Pistols length,

    Ile make him sure enough, farewell your highnesse.

ANTIOCHUS

    Thaliart adieu,   ⌈*Exit Thalyart*⌉

        till *Pericles* be dead,

    My heart can lend no succour to my head.

        Exit. ⌈*The heads are concealed*⌉

Sc. 2   *Enter Pericles distempered with his Lords*

PERICLES

    Let none disturb vs,   *Exeunt Lords*

        why shold this chãge of thoughts

    The sad companion dull eyde melancholie,

    Be my so vsde a guest, as not an houre

    In the dayes glorious walke or peacefull night,

    The tombe where griefe should sleepe can breed me

        quiet,

    Here pleasures court mine eies, and mine eies shun

        them,

220   And daunger which I fearde's at *Antioch*,

    Whose arme seemes farre too short to hit me here,

    Yet neither pleasures Art can ioy my spirits,

    Nor yet cares authors distance comfort me,

    Then it is thus, the passions of the mind,

    That haue their first conception by misdread,

    Haue after nourishment and life, by care

    And what was first but feare, what might be done,

    Growes elder now, and cares it be not done.

    And so with me; the great *Antiochus*,

    Gainst whom I am too little to contend,   230

    Since hee's so great, can make his will his act,

    Will thinke me speaking, though I sweare to silence,

    Nor bootes it me to say, I honour him,

    If he suspect I may dishonour him.

    And what may make him blush in being knowne,

    Heele stop the course by which it might be knowne,

    With hostile forces heele ore-spread the land,

    And with thostint of warre will looke so huge,

    Amazement shall driue courage from the state,

    Our men be vanquisht ere they doe resist,   240

    And subiects punisht that nere thought offence,

    Which care of them, not pittie of my selfe,

    Who am no more but as the tops of trees,

    Which fence the rootes they grow by and defend them,

    Makes both my bodie pine, and soule to languish,

    And punish that before that he would punish.

        Enter all the Lords (among them olde Helicanus) to

        Pericles

1. LORD

    Ioy and all comfort in your sacred brest.

2. LORD

    And keepe your mind peacefull and comfortable.

HELICANUS

    Peace, peace, and giue experience tongue,

    (*To Pericles*) You do not wel so to abuse yourselfe,   250

    To waste your body here with pyning sorrow,

    Vpon whose safety doth depend the liues

    And the prosperity of a whole kingdome,

    Tis ill in you to doe it, and no lesse

    Ill in your counsell, not to contradict it.

    They doe abuse the King that flatter him,

    For flattrie is the bellowes blowes vp sinne,

    The thing the which is flattred, but a sparke,

    To which that winde giues heate, and stronger

        glowing,

    Whereas reproofe obedient and in order,   260

    Fits kings as they are men, for they may erre,

    When *signior* sooth here does proclaime a peace,

    He flatters you, makes warre vpon your life.

        ⌈*He kneeles*⌉

    Prince pardon me, or strike me if you please,

    I cannot be much lower then my knees.

PERICLES

    All leaue vs else: but let your cares ore-looke,

    What shipping, and what ladings in our hauen,

    And then returne to vs,   *Exeunt Lords*

        Hellicane thou

    Hast mooued vs, what seest thou in our lookes?

HELICANUS An angrie brow, dread Lord.   270

PERICLES

    If there be such a dart in Princes frownes,

    How durst thy tongue moue anger to our browes?

HELICANUS

    How dares the plants looke vp to heau'n, from whence

    They haue their nourishment?

PERICLES
Thou knowest I haue pow'r to take thy life from thee.
HELICANUS
I haue ground the Axe my selfe, doe you but strike
    the blowe.
PERICLES ⌈*lifting him vp*⌉
Rise, prethee rise, sit downe, thou art no flatterer,
I thanke thee for it, and the heau'ns forbid
That kings should let their eares heare their faults hid.
280 Fit Counsellor, and seruant for a Prince,
Who by thy wisdome makst a Prince thy seruant,
What wouldst thou haue me doe?
HELICANUS   To beare with patience
Such griefes as you doe lay vpon your selfe.
PERICLES
Thou speakst like a Physition *Hellicanus*,
That ministers a potion vnto me:
That thou wouldst tremble to receiue thy selfe,
Attend me then, I went to *Antioch*,
Where as thou knowst against the face of death,
I sought the purchase of a glorious beautie,
290 From whence an issue I might propogate,
As children are heau'ns blessings, to parents obiects,
Are armes to Princes, and bring ioies to subiects,
Her face was to mine eye beyond all wonder,
The rest harke in thine eare, as blacke as incest,
Which by my knowledge found, the sinful father
Seemde not to strike, but smooth, but thou knowst
    this,
Tis time to feare when tyrants seemes to kisse.
Which feare so grew in me I hither fled,
Vnder the couering of carefull night,
300 Who seemd my good protector, and being here,
Bethought me what was past, what might succeed,
I knew him tyrannous, and tyrants feares
Decrease not, but grow faster then the yeares,
And should he dout, as doubt no doubt he doth,
That I should open to the listning ayre,
How many worthie Princes blouds were shed,
To keepe his bed of blacknesse vnlayde ope,
To lop that doubt, hee'le fill this land with armes,
And make pretence of wrong that I haue done him,
310 When all for mine, if I may call offence,
Must feel wars blow, who spares not innocence,
Which loue to all of which thy selfe art one,
Who now reprou'dst me fort.
HELICANUS   Alas sir.
PERICLES
Drew sleep out of mine eies, blood frõ my cheekes,
Musings into my mind, with thousand doubts
How I might stop this tempest ere it came,
And finding little comfort to relieue them,
I thought it princely charity to griue them.
HELICANUS
Well my Lord, since you haue giu'n mee leaue to
    speake,
320 Freely will I speake, *Antiochus* you feare,

And iustly too, I thinke you feare the tyrant,
Who either by publike warre, or priuat treason,
Will take away your life:
Therfore my Lord, go trauell for a while,
Till that his rage and anger be forgot,
Or Destinies doe cut his threed of life:
Your rule direct to anie, if to me,
Day serues not light more faithfull then Ile be.
PERICLES I doe not doubt thy faith.
But should he in my absence wrong thy liberties?   330
HELICANUS
Weele mingle our bloods togither in the earth,
From whence we had our being, and our birth.
PERICLES
Tyre I now looke from thee then, and to *Tharsus*
Intend my trauaile, where Ile heare from thee,
And by whose Letters Ile dispose my selfe.
The care I had and haue of subiects good,
On thee I lay, whose wisdomes strength can beare it,
Ile take thy word, for faith not aske thine oath,
Who shuns not to breake one, will sure cracke both.
But in our orbs we'll liue so round, and safe,   340
That time of both this truth shall nere conuince,
Thou shewdst a subiects shine, I a true Prince.
                                    Exeunt

Enter Thaliart solus   **Sc. 3**
THALYART So this is *Tyre*, and this the Court, heere must
I kill King *Pericles*, and if I doe it and am caught I am
like to be hang'd abroad, but if I doe it not, I am sure
to be hang'd at home: t'is daungerous. Well, I perceiue
he was a wise fellowe, and had good discretion, that
beeing bid to aske what hee would of the King, desired
he might knowe none of his secrets. Now doe I see hee
had some reason for't: for if a king bidde a man bee a   350
villaine, hee's bound by the indenture of his oath to
bee one. Husht, heere comes the Lords of *Tyre*.
    Enter Hellicanus, Escanes, with other Lords
HELICANUS
You shall not neede my fellow-Peers of *Tyre*,
Further to question of your kings departure:
His seald Commission left in trust with mee,
Does speake sufficiently hee's gone to trauaile.
THALYART (*aside*) How? the King gone?
HELICANUS
If further yet you will be satisfied,
Why (as it were vnlicensde of your loues)
He would depart? Ile giue some light vnto you,   360
Beeing at *Antioch*,
THALYART (*aside*)   What from *Antioch*?
HELICANUS
Royall *Antiochus* on what cause I knowe not,
Tooke some displeasure at him, at least hee iudg'de so:
And doubting lest that hee had err'de or sinn'de,
To shewe his sorrow, hee'de correct himselfe;
So puts himselfe vnto the Ship-mans toyle,
With whome each minute threatens life or death.

THALYART (*aside*)

Well, I perceiue I shall not be hang'd now,
Although I would,
370   But since hee's gone, the Kings ears it must please:
Hee scap'te the Land to perish on the Seas,
I'le present my selfe. (*Comming forward*) Peace to the
        Lords of *Tyre*.
Lord *Thaliart* am I, of *Antioch*.

⌈HELICANUS⌉

Lord *Thaliart* of *Antioch* is welcome.

THALYART

From King *Antiochus* I come
With message vnto princely *Pericles*,
But since my landing, I haue vnderstood
Your Lord's betoke himselfe to vnknowne trauailes,
Now my message must returne from whence it came.

HELICANUS

380   Wee haue no reason to enquire it,
Commended to our maister not to vs,
Yet ere you shall depart, this wee desire
As friends to *Antioch* wee may feast in *Tyre*.   *Exeunt*

Sc. 4   *Enter Cleon the Gouernour of Tharsus, with*
              Dyonysa his wife and others

CLEON

My *Dyonysa* shall wee rest vs heere,
And by relating tales of others griefes,
See if t'will teach vs to forget our owne?

DYONYSA

That were to blow at fire in hope to quench it,
For who digs hills because they doe aspire,
Throwes downe one mountaine to cast vp a higher:
390   O my distressed Lord, ene such our griefes are,
Heere they're but felt, and seene with midges eyes,
But like to Groues, being topt, they higher rise.

CLEON   O *Dyonysa*.

Who wanteth food, and will not say hee wants it,
Or can conceale his hunger till hee famish?
Our toungs our sorrowes dictate to sound deepe
Our woes into the aire, our eyes to weepe,
Till loungs fetch breath that may proclaime them
        louder,
That if heau'n slumber, while their creatures want,
400   They may awake their helpes, to comfort them.
Ile then discourse our woes felt seu'rall yeares,
And wanting breath to speake, helpe mee with teares.

DYONYSA   As you thinke best Syr.

CLEON

This *Tharsus* ore which I haue the gouernment,
A Cittie or whom plentie held full hand:
For riches strew'de her selfe eu'n in the streetes,
Whose tow'rs bore heads so high they kist the clowds,
And strangers nere beheld, but wondred at,
Whose men and dames so ietted and adorn'de,
410   Like one anothers glasse to trim them by,
Their tables were stor'de full to glad the sight,
And not so much to feede on as delight,

All pouertie was scor'nde, and pride so great,
The name of helpe grewe odious to repeat.

DYONYSA   O t'is too true.

CLEON

But see what heau'n can doe by this our change,
Those mouthes who but of late, earth, sea, and ayre,
Were all too little to content and please,
Although they gaue their creatures in abundance,
As houses are defil'de for want of vse,   420
They are now staru'de for want of exercise,
Those pallats who not yet two sumers younger,
Must haue inuentions to delight the tast,
Would now be glad of bread and beg for it,
Those mothers who to nouzell vp their babes,
Thought nought too curious, are readie now
To eat those little darlings whom they lou'de,
So sharpe are hungers teeth, that man and wife,
Drawe lots who first shall die, to lengthen life.
Heere weeping stands a Lord, there lies a Ladie dying: 430
Heere manie sincke, yet those which see them fall,
Haue scarce strength left to giue them buryall.
Is not this true?

DYONYSA

Our cheekes and hollow eyes doe witnesse it.

CLEON

O let those Cities that of plenties cup,
And her prosperities so largely taste,
With their superfluous riots heede these teares,
The miserie of *Tharsus* may be theirs.
        Enter a ⌈*fainting*⌉ *Lord of Tharsus* ⌈*slowely*⌉

LORD   Wheres the Lord Gouernour?

CLEON

Here, speake out thy sorrowes, which thou bringst, in
        hast,   440
For comfort is too farre for vs t'expect.

LORD

Wee haue descryed vpon our neighbouring shore,
A portlie saile of ships make hitherward.

CLEON   I thought as much.

One sorrowe neuer comes but brings an heire,
That may succeede as his inheritor:
And so in ours, some neighbour nation,
Taking aduantage of our miserie,
Hath stuff't these hollow vessels with their power,
To beat vs downe, the which are downe alreadie,   450
And make a conquest of vnhappie mē,
Whereas no glories got to ouercome.

LORD

That's the least feare. For by the semblance
Of their white flagges displayde, they bring vs peace,
And come to vs as fauourers, not foes.

CLEON

Thou speak'st like hims vntuterd to repeat,
Who makes the fairest showe, meanes most deceipt.
But bring they what they will, and what they can,
What need wee feare?
Our graues the lowest, and wee are halfe way there: 460

Goe tell their Gen'rall wee attend him heere,
To know for what he comes, and whence he comes?
LORD I goe my Lord.   *Exit*
CLEON
    Welcome is peace, if he on peace consist,
    If warres, wee are vnable to resist.
            Enter ⌈*the Lord again, conducting*⌉ *Pericles with*
            attendants
    PERICLES (*to Cleon*)
        Lord Gouernour, for so wee heare you are,
        Let not our Ships and number of our men,
        Be like a beacon fier'de, t'amaze your eyes,
        Wee haue heard your miseries as farre as *Tyre*,
470   Since entering your vnshut gates haue witness'd
        The widow'd desolation of your streets,
        Nor come we to adde sorrow to your hearts,
        But to relieue them of their heauy loade,
        And these our Ships you happily may thinke,
        Are like the Troian Horse, was fraught within
        With bloody veines importing ouerthrow,
        Are stor'd with Corne, to make your needie bread,
        And giue them life, whom hunger staru'd halfe dead.
    OMNES ⌈*falling on their knees and weeping*⌉
        The Gods of *Greece* protect you, and wee'le pray for
            you.
480 PERICLES Arise I pray you, rise;
        We do not looke for reuerence, but for loue,
        And harborage for me, my ships, & men.
    CLEON
        The which when any shall not gratifie,
        Or pay you with vnthankfulnesse in thought,
        Be it our Wiues, our Children, or our selues,
        The Curse of heau'n and men succeed their euils:
        Till when the which (I hope) shall neare be seene:
        Your Grace is welcome to our Towne and vs.
    PERICLES
        Which welcome wee'le accept, feast here awhile,
490   Vntill our Starres that frowne, lend vs a smile.
                                                Exeunt

Sc. 5   *Enter Gower*
    GOWER
        Heere haue you seene a mightie King,
        His child I'wis to incest bring:
        A better Prince, and benigne Lord,
        Proue awfull both in deed and word:
        Be quiet then, as men should bee,
        Till he hath past necessitie:
        I'le shew you those in troubles raigne;
        Loosing a Mite, a Mountaine gaine:
        The good in conuersation,
500   To whom I giue my benizon:
        Is still at *Tharsis*, where each man,
        Thinkes all is writ, he speken can:
        And to remember what he does,
        His Statue build to make him glorious:
        But tidinges to the contrarie,
        Are brought your eyes, what need speake I.

            Dombe shew.
        Enter at one dore Pericles talking with Cleon, all the
        traine with them: Enter at an other dore, a
        Gentleman with a Letter to Pericles, Pericles shewes
        the Letter to Cleon; Pericles giues the Messenger a
        reward, and Knights him: Exit with their traines
        Pericles at one dore, and Cleon at an other
        Good *Helican* that stayde at home,
        Not to eate Hony like a Drone,
        From others labours; for that he striue
        To killen bad, keepe good aliue: 510
        And to fulfill his prince desire,
        Sent word of all that haps in *Tyre*:
        How *Thaliart* came full bent with sinne,
        And hid intent to murdren him;
        And that in *Tharsis* was not best,
        Longer for him to make his rest:
        He dēing so, put foorth to Seas;
        Where when men been there's seldome ease,
        For now the Wind begins to blow,
        Thunder aboue, and deepes below,   520
        Makes such vnquiet, that the Shippe,
        Should house him safe; is wrackt and split,
        And he (good Prince) hauing all lost,
        By Waues, from coast to coast is tost:
        All perishen of man of pelfe,
        Ne ought escapend but himselfe;
        Till Fortune tir'd with doing bad,
        Threw him a shore, to giue him glad:
            ⌈*Enter Pericles wette and halfe naked*⌉
        And heere he comes: what shall be next,
        Pardon old *Gower*, this long's the text.   *Exit* 530
            ⌈*Thunder and lightning*⌉
    PERICLES
        Yet cease your ire you angry Starres of heauen,
        Wind, Raine, and Thunder, remember earthly man
        Is but a substaunce that must yeeld to you:
        And I (as fits my nature) do obey you.
        Alasse, the Seas hath cast me on the Rocks,
        Washt me from shore to shore, and left my breath
        Nothing to thinke on, but ensuing death:
        Let it suffize the greatnesse of your powers,
        To haue bereft a Prince of all his fortunes;
        And hauing throwne him from your watry graue,   540
        Heere to haue death in peace, is all hee'le craue.
            ⌈*He sits.*⌉
            Enter two poore Fisher-men
    MAISTER ⌈*calling*⌉ What ho, pelch?
    2. FISHER-MAN ⌈*calling*⌉ Ha, come and bring away the
        Nets.
    MAISTER ⌈*calling*⌉ What Patch-breech, I say.
            ⌈*Enter a third rough Fisher-man, with an hoode*
            vpon his head, and a filthie leatherne pelt vpon his
            backe, vnseemely clad, and homely to beholde; he
            brings Nets to dry and repaire⌉
    3. FISHER-MAN What say you Maister?
    MAISTER Looke how thou stirr'st now: come away, or Ile
        fetch'th with a wanion.

3. FISHER-MAN Fayth Maister, I am thinking of the poore
550 men, that were cast away before vs euen now.

MAISTER Alasse poore soules, it grieued my heart to heare,
what pittifull cryes they made to vs, to helpe them,
when (welladay) we could scarce helpe our selues.

3. FISHER-MAN Nay Maister, sayd not I as much, when I
saw the Porpas how he bounst and tumbled? They say
they're halfe fish, halfe flesh: a plague on them, they
nere come but I looke to be washt. Maister, I maruell
how the Fishes liue in the Sea?

MAISTER Why, as Men doe a-land; the great ones eate vp
560 the little ones: I can compare our rich Misers to nothing
so fitly, as to a Whale; a playes and tumbles, dryuing
the poore Fry before him, and at last, deuowres them
all at a mouthfull: such Whales haue I heard on, a'th
land, who neuer leaue gaping, till they swallow'd the
whole Parish, Church, Steeple, Belles and all.

PERICLES (aside) A prettie morall.

3. FISHER-MAN But Maister, if I had been the Sexton, I
would haue been that day in the belfrie.

2. FISHER-MAN Why, Man?

570 3. FISHER-MAN Because he should haue swallowed mee
too, and when I had been in his belly, I would haue
kept such a iangling of the Belles, that he should neuer
haue left, till he cast Belles, Steeple, Church and Parish
vp againe: but if the good King *Simonides* were of my
minde,

PERICLES (aside) *Simonides*?

3. FISHER-MAN We would purge the land of these Drones,
that robbe the Bee of her Hony.

PERICLES (aside)
580 How from the fenny subiect of the Sea,
These Fishers tell th'infirmities of men,
And from their watry empire recollect,
All that may men approue, or men detect.
⌈Comming foward⌉ Peace be at your labour, honest
Fisher-men.

2. FISHER-MAN Honest, good fellow what's that, if it be a
day fits you scracht out of the Kalender, and no body
looke after it?

PERICLES
May see the Sea hath cast vpon your coast:

2. FISHER-MAN What a drunken Knaue was the Sea, to
cast thee in our way?

PERICLES
590 A man whom both the Waters and the Winde,
In that vast Tennis-court, hath made the Ball
For them to play vpon, intreates you pittie him:
Hee askes of you, that neuer vs'd to begge.

MAISTER No friend, cannot you begge? Heer's them in
our countrey of *Greece*, gets more with begging, then
we can doe with working.

2. FISHER-MAN Canst thou catch any Fishes then?

PERICLES I neuer practizde it.

2. FISHER-MAN Nay then thou wilt starue sure: for heer's
600 nothing to be got now-adayes, vnlesse thou canst fish
for't.

PERICLES
What I haue been, I haue forgot to know;
But what I am, want teaches me to thinke on:
A man throng'd vp with cold, my Veines are chill,
And haue no more of life then may suffize,
To giue my tongue that heat to craue your helpe:
Which if you shall refuse, when I am dead,
For that I am a man, pray see me buried.
⌈He fals downe⌉

MAISTER Die, ke-tha; now Gods forbid't, and I haue a
Gowne heere, ⌈to Pericles, lifting him vp from the ground⌉ 610
come put it on, keepe thee warme: now afore mee a
handsome fellow: Come, thou shalt goe home, and
wee'le haue Flesh for halidays, Fish for fasting-dayes
and more or Puddinges and Flap-iackes, and thou shalt
be welcome.

PERICLES I thanke you sir.

2. FISHER-MAN Harke you my friend: You sayd you could
not beg?

PERICLES I did but craue.

2. FISHER-MAN But craue? Then Ile turne Crauer too, and 620
so I shall scape whipping.

PERICLES Why, are all your Beggers whipt then?

2. FISHER-MAN Oh not all, my friend, not all: for if all
your Beggers were whipt, I would wish no better office,
then to be Beadle.

MAISTER Thine office knaue,

2. FISHER-MAN Is to draw vp the other Nets, Ile goe.
                              Exit with 3. Fisherman

PERICLES (aside)
How well this honest mirth becomes their labour?

MAISTER ⌈seating himselfe by Pericles⌉ Harke you sir; doe
you know where yee are?   630

PERICLES Not well.

MAISTER Why Ile tell you, this is cald *Pantapoles*, and our
King, the good *Symonides*.

PERICLES
The good *Symonides*, doe you call him?

MAISTER I sir, and he deserues so to be cal'd, for his
peaceable raigne, and good gouernement.

PERICLES
He is a happy King, since from his subiects
He gaines the name of good, by his gouernment.
How farre is his Court distant from this shore?

MAISTER Mary sir, some halfe a dayes iourney: And Ile 640
tell you, he hath a faire Daughter, and to morrow is
her birth-day, and there are Princes and Knights come
from all partes of the World, to Iust and Turney for
her loue.

PERICLES
Were but my fortunes aunswerable
To my desires, I could wish to make one there.

MAISTER O sir, things must be as they may: and what a
man can not get himselfe, he may lawfully deale for
with his Wiues soule.
                    Enter the two Fisher-men, drawing vp a Net

2. FISHER-MAN Helpe Maister helpe; heere's a Fish hanges 650

in the Net, like a poore mans right in the law: t'will
hardly come out.

⌜*Before helpe comes, vp comes their prize*⌝

Ha bots on't, tis come at last; & tis turnd to a rusty
Armour.

PERICLES

An Armour friends; I pray you let me see it.

(*Aside*) Thankes Fortune, yeat that after all thy
    crosses,

Thou giu'st me somewhat to repaire my losses:

And though it was mine owne, part of my heritage,

Which my dead Father did bequeath to me,

660 With this strict charge eu'n as he left his life,

Keepe it my *Perycles*, it hath been a Shield

Twixt me and death, and poynted to this brayse,

For that it sau'd me, keepe it: in like necessitie,

The which the Gods forfend, the same may defend
    thee:

It kept where I kept, I so dearely lou'd it,

Till the rough Seas, that spares not any man,

Tooke it in rage, though calm'd, haue giu'n't againe:

I thanke thee for't, my shipwracke now's no ill,

Since I haue heere my Father gaue in's Will.

670 MAISTER What meane you sir?

PERICLES

To begge of you (kind friends) this Coate of worth,

For it was sometime Target to a King;

I know it by this marke: he lou'd me dearely,

And for his sake, I wish the hauing of it;

And that you'd guide me to your Sou'raignes Court,

Where with't, I may appeare a Gentleman:

And if that euer my low fortunes better,

Ile pay your bounties; till then, rest your debter.

MAISTER Why wilt thou turney for the Lady?

PERICLES

680 Ile shew the vertue I haue lernd in Armes.

MAISTER Why di'e take it: and the Gods giue thee good
an't.

2. FISHER-MAN I but harke you my friend, t'was wee that
made vp this Garment through the rough seames of
the Waters: there are certaine Condolements, certaine
Vailes: I hope sir, if you thriue, you'le remember from
whence you had this.

PERICLES Beleeue't, I will:

By your furtherance I'm cloth'd in Steele,

690 And spight of all the rapture of the Sea,

This Iewell holdes his buylding on my arme:

Vnto thy value I will mount my selfe

Vpon a Courser, whose delightsome steps,

Shall make the gazer ioy to see him tread;

Onely (my friends) I yet am vnprouided

Of a paire of Bases.

2. FISHER-MAN Wee'le sure prouide, thou shalt haue my
best Gowne to make thee a paire; and Ile bring thee
to the Court my selfe.

PERICLES

700 Then Honour be but equale to my Will,

This day Ile rise, or else adde ill to ill.

Exeunt with Nets and Armour

⌜*Sennet.*⌝ *Enter King Simonydes and Thaisa, with
Lords in attendaunce,* ⌜*and sit on 2. thrones*⌝   Sc. 6

KING

Are the Knights ready to begin the Tryumph?

1. LORD They are my Leidge,

And stay your comming, to present them selues.

KING

Returne them, We are ready, & our daughter,

In honour of whose Birth, these Triumphs are,

Sits heere like Beauties child, whom Nature gat,

For men to see; and seeing, woonder at.   ⌜*Exit one*⌝

THAYSA

It pleaseth you (my Father) to expresse

My Commendations great, whose merit's lesse.   710

KING

It's fit it should be so, for Princes are

A modell which Heau'n makes like to it selfe:

As Iewels loose their glory, if neglected,

So Princes their Renowne, if not respected:

T'is now your office (Daughter) to entertaine

The labour of each Knight, in his deuice.

THAYSA

Which to preserue mine honour, I'le performe.

⌜*Flourish.*⌝ *The first Knight passes by* ⌜*richly armed,
and his Page before him bearing his Deuice on his
shield deliuers it to the Lady Thaysa*⌝

KING

Who is the first, that doth preferre himselfe?

THAYSA

A Knight of *Sparta* (my renowned father)

And the deuice he beares vpon his Shield,   720

Is a blacke Ethyope reaching at the Sunne:

The word: *Lux tua vita mihi.*

⌜*She presents it to the King*⌝

KING

He loues you well, that holdes his life of you.

⌜*He returnes it to the Page, who exits with the first
Knight.*⌝

⌜*Flourish.*⌝ *The second Knight passes by* ⌜*richly
armed, and his Page before him bearing his Deuice
on his shield deliuers it to the Lady Thaysa*⌝

Who is the second, that presents himselfe?

THAYSA

A Prince of *Macedon* (my royall father)

And the deuice he beares vpon his Shield,

An Armed Knight, that's conquer'd by a Lady:

The motto thus. *Pue Per dolceza kee per forsa.*

⌜*She presents it to the King*⌝

KING

You winne him, more by lenitie than force.

⌜*He returnes it to the Page, who exits with the
second Knight.*⌝

⌜*Flourish.*⌝ *3. Knight passes by* ⌜*richly armed, and
his Page before him bearing his Deuice on his shield
deliuers it to the Lady Thaysa*⌝

And what's the third?

THAYSA   The third, of *Antioch*;   730

And his deuice, a wreath of Chiualry:

The word: *Me pompae prouexit apex.*

⌜*She presents it to the King*⌝

KING

Desire of renowne he doth deuise,

The which hath drawn him to this enterprise.

⌜*He returnes it to the Page, who exits with 3.
Knight.*⌝

⌜*Flourish.*⌝ *4. Knight passes by* ⌜*richly armed, and
his Page before him bearing his Deuice on his shield
deliuers it to the Lady Thaysa*⌝

What is the fourth.

THAYSA   A Knight of *Athens*, bearing

A burning Torch that's turned vpside downe;

The word: *Qui me alit me extinguit.*

⌜*She presents it to the King*⌝

KING

Which shewes that Beautie hath this power & will,

Which can as well enflame, as it can kill.

⌜*He returnes it to the Page, who exits with 4.
Knight.*⌝

⌜*Flourish.*⌝ *5. Knight passes by* ⌜*richly armed, and
his Page before him bearing his Deuice on his shield
deliuers it to the Lady Thaysa*⌝

And who the fift?

740 THAYSA   The fift, a Prince of *Corinth*,

Presents an Hand enuironed with Clouds,

Holding out Gold, that's by the Touch-stone tride:

The motto thus: *Sic spectanda fides.*

⌜*She presents it to the King*⌝

KING

So faith is to be look'd into.

⌜*He returnes it to the Page, who exits with 5.
Knight.*⌝

⌜*Flourish.*⌝ *6. knight, Pericles, in a rusty Armour,
who hauing neither Page to deliuer his shield, nor
shield to deliuer, presents his Deuice vnto the Lady
Thaysa*

And what's the sixt, and last; the which, the knight
himself

With such a graceful courtesie deliuereth?

THAYSA

Hee seemes to be a Stranger: but his Present is

A wither'd Branch, that's onely greene at top,

The motto: *In hac spe viuo.*

KING

750 Frõ the deiected state wherein he is,

He hopes by you, his fortunes yet may flourish.

1. LORD

He had need meane better, then his outward shew

Can any way speake in his iust commend:

For by his rustie outside, he appeares,

T'haue practis'd more the Whipstocke, then the
Launce.

2. LORD

He well may be a Stranger, for he comes

Vnto an honour'd tryumph, strangly furnisht.

3. LORD

And on set purpose let his Armour rust

Vntill this day, to scowre it in the dust.

KING

Opinion's but a foole, that makes vs scan   760

The outward habit, for the inward man.

⌜*Cornets*⌝

But stay, the Knights are comming, we will with-draw

Into the Gallerie.   ⌜*Exeunt*⌝

⌜*Cornets and*⌝ *great shoutes* ⌜*within*⌝, *and all cry,
the meane Knight*

⌜*A stately banquet is brought in.*⌝ *Enter the King,*   Sc. 7
Thaysa, ⌜*and their traine at one doore,*⌝ *and* ⌜*at
another doore*⌝ *a Marshall* ⌜*conducting*⌝ *Pericles and
the other Knights from Tilting*

KING (*to the Knights*)

To say you're welcome, were superfluous.

To place vpon the volume of your deedes,

As in a Title page, your worth in armes,

Were more then you expect, or more then's fit,

Since euery worth in shew commends it selfe:

Prepare for mirth, for mirth becomes a Feast.

You're Princes, and my guestes.

THAYSA (*to Pericles*)   But you my Knight and guest,   770

To whom this Wreath of victorie I giue,

And crowne you King of this dayes happinesse.

PERICLES

Tis more by Fortune (Lady) then my Merit.

KING

Call it by what you will, the day is yours,

And here (I hope) is none that enuies it:

In framing Artists, art hath thus decreed,

To make some good, but others to exceed,

You are her labourd scholler: (*to Thaysa*) come
Queene a th'feast,

For (Daughter) so you are; heere take your place:

(*To Marshall*) Martiall the rest, as they deserue their
grace.   780

KNIGHTS

We are honour'd much by good *Symonides.*

KING

Your presence glads our dayes, honour we loue,

For who hates honour, hates the Gods aboue.

MARSHAL (*to Pericles*)

Sir, yonder is your place.

PERICLES   Some other is more fit.

1. KNIGHT

Contend not sir, for we are Gentlemen,

Haue neither in our hearts, nor outward eyes,

Enuied the great, nor shall the low despise.

PERICLES

You are right courtious Knights.

KING   Sit sir, sit.

⌜*Pericles sits, directly ouer-against the King and
Thaysa. The guests feed apace; Pericles sits still
and eates nothing*⌝

⌜*Aside*⌝ By *Ioue* (I wonder) that is King of thoughts,

These Cates distast mee, hee but thought vpon.   790

THAYSA ⌜*aside*⌝

By *Iuno* (that is Queene of mariage)

(I am amaz'd) all Viands that I eate
Do seeme vnsauery, wishing him my meat:
⌐To the King⌐ Sure hee's a gallant Gentleman.

KING
Hee's but a countrie Gentleman:
Ha's done no more then other Knights haue done,
Ha's broke a Staffe, or so; so let it passe.

THAYSA ⌐aside⌐
To mee he seemes like Diamond, to Glasse.

PERICLES ⌐aside⌐
Yon Kings to mee, like to my fathers picture,
800   Which tels me in what glory once he was,
Had Princes sit like Starres about his Throane,
And hee the Sunne for them to reuerence;
None that beheld him, but like lesser lights,
Did vaile their Crownes to his supremacie;
Where now his sonnes a Gloworme in the night,
The which hath Fire in darknesse, none in light:
Whereby I see that Time's the King of men,
Hee's both their Parent, and he is their Graue,
And giues them what he will, not what they craue.

810   KING What, are you merry, Knights?

⌐THE OTHER KNIGHTS⌐
Who can be other, in this royall presence.

KING
Heere, with a Cup that's stor'd vnto the brim,
As you do loue, full to your Mistris lippes,
Wee drinke this health to you.

⌐THE OTHER KNIGHTS⌐   We thanke your Grace.

KING
Yet pause awhile, yon Knight doth sit too melancholy,
As if the entertainement in our Court,
Had not a shew might counteruaile his worth:
Note it not you, *Thaisa*.

THAYSA   What is't to me, my father?

KING
O attend my Daughter, princes in this,
820   Should liue like Gods aboue, who freely giue
To eu'ry one that come to honour them:
And Princes not so doing, are like Gnats,
Which make a sound, but kild, are wondred at:
Therefore to make his entertaine more sweet,
Heere, beare this standing boule of wine to him.

THAYSA
Alas my Father, it befits not mee,
Vnto a stranger Knight to be so bold,
He may my profer take for an offence,
Since men take womens giftes for impudence.

KING
830   How? doe as I bid you, or you'le mooue me else.

THAYSA (aside)
Now by the Gods, he could not please me better.

KING
Furthermore tell him, we desire to know
Of whence he is, his name, and Parentage?
⌐Thaysa beares the cup to Pericles⌐

THAYSA
The King my father (sir) has drunke to you,
Wishing it so much blood vnto your life.

PERICLES
I thanke both him and you, and pledge him freely.
He pledges the King

THAYSA
And further, he desires to know of you,
Of whence you are, your name and parentage?

PERICLES
A Gentleman of *Tyre*, my name *Pericles*,
My education beene in Artes and Armes: 840
Who looking for aduentures in the world,
Was by the rough vnconstant Seas bereft
Vnfortunately both of Ships and men,
And after shipwracke, driuen vpon this shore.
⌐Thaysa returnes to the King⌐

THAYSA
He thankes your Grace; names himselfe *Pericles*,
A Gentleman of *Tyre*: who (seeking aduentures)
Was solely by misfortune of the seas,
Bereft of Shippes and Men, cast on this shore.

KING
Now by the Gods, I pitty his mis-haps,
And will awake him from his melancholy.   850
⌐The King, rising from his state, goes foorthwith
and imbraces Pericles⌐
Be cheer'd, for what misfortune hath impayr'd you of,
Fortune, by my helpe, can repayre to you,
My selfe and Countrey both shall be your friends.
And presently a goodly milke white Steede,
And golden spurres, I first bestowe vppon you,
The prises due your merite, and ordain'd
For this dayes enterprise.

PERICLES
Your kingly curtesie I thankefully accept.

KING
Come Gentlemen, we sit too long on trifles,
And waste the time which lookes for other reuels: 860
Eu'n in your Armours as you are addrest,
Your limbs will well become a Souldiers daunce:
I will not haue excuse with saying this,
Lowd Musicke is too harsh for Ladyes heads,
Since they loue men in armes, as well as beds.
The Knights daunce
So, this was well askt, t'was so well perform'd.
Come, heer's a Lady that wants breathing too,
(*To Pericles*) And I haue heard, sir, that yᵉ Knights of
Tyre,
Are excellent in making Ladyes trippe;
And that their Measures are as excellent.   870

PERICLES
In those that practize them, they are (my Lord.)

KING
Oh that's as much, as you would be denyed
Of your faire courtesie: vnclaspe, vnclaspe.
They daunce
Thankes Gentlemen to all, all haue done well;
(*To Pericles*) But you the best: (*Calling*) Lights, pages,
to conduct
These Knights vnto their seu'rall Lodgings: Yours sir,
We haue giu'n order should be next our owne.

PERICLES I am at your Graces pleasure.

KING

880   Princes, it is too late to talke of Loue,
And that's the marke I know, you leuell at:
Therefore each one betake him to his rest,
To morrow all for speeding do their best.

            Exeunt ⌈seuerally⌉

Sc. 8   *Enter Hellicanus and Escanes*

HELICANUS

No *Escanes*, know this of mee,
Antiochus from incest liu'd not free:
For which the most high Gods not minding longer
To hold the vengeance that they had in store,
Due to this heynous capitall offence,
Euen in the height and pride of all his glory,
When he was seated in a Chariot
890   Of an inestimable value, and
His daughter with him, both apparrell'd all in Iewells;
A fire from heauen came and shriueld vp
Their bodyes ene to lothing, for they so stounke,
That all those eyes ador'd them, ere their fall,
Scorne now their hands should giue them buriall.

ESCHINES

T'was very strange.

HELICANUS   And yet but iustice; for though
This King were great, his greatnesse was no gard
To barre heau'ns shaft, but sinne had his reward.

ESCHINES Tis very true.

        Enter three Lords and stand aside

I. LORD

900   See, not a man in priuate conference,
Or counsaile, ha's respect with him but hee.

2. LORD

It shall no longer grieue, without reprofe.

3. LORD

And curst be he that will not second it.

I. LORD

Follow me then: Lord *Hellicane*, a word.

HELICANUS

With mee? and welcome, happy day, my Lords.

I. LORD

Know, that our griefes are risen to the top,
And now at length they ouer-flow their bankes.

HELICANUS

Your griefes, for what? Wrong not your Prince, you
    loue.

I. LORD

Wrong not your selfe then, noble *Hellican*,
910   But if the Prince do liue, let vs salute him,
Or know what ground's made happy by his step:
And be resolude he liues to gouerne vs:
Or dead, giue's cause to mourne his funerall,
And leaue vs to our free election.

2. LORD

Whose death in deeds the strongest in our sensure,
And knowing this: Kingdomes without a head,
Like goodly Buyldings left without a Roofe,
Soone fall to vtter ruine: your noble selfe,

That best know how to rule, and how to raigne,
Wee thus submit vnto as Soueraigne.   920

OMNES ⌈*kneeling*⌉ Liue noble *Hellicane*.

HELICANUS

By honours cause, forbeare your suffrages:
If that you loue Prince *Pericles*, forbeare,
    ⌈*The Lords rise*⌉
(Take I your wish, I leape into the seas,
Where's howerly trouble, for a minuts ease)
But if I cannot winne you to this loue,
A twelue-month longer then, let me intreat you
Further to beare the absence of your King;
If in which time expir'd, he not returne,
I shall with aged patience beare your yoake: 930
Goe seeke your noble Prince, like noble subiects,
And in your search, spend your aduenturous worth,
Whom if you find, and winne vnto returne,
You shall like Diamonds sit about his Crowne.

I. LORD

To wisedome, hee's a foole, that will not yeeld:
And since Lord *Hellicane* enioyneth vs,
We with our trauels will endeauour vs.
If in the world he liue, wee'le seeke him out:
If in his Graue he rest, wee'le find him there.

HELICANUS

Then you loue vs, we you, & wee'le claspe hands: 940
When Peeres thus knit, a Kingdome euer stands.

            Exeunt

        Enter Pericles, with Gentlemen with lights   Sc. 8a

I. GENTLEMAN

Here is your lodging, sir.

PERICLES   Pray leaue me priuate:
Only for instant solace, pleasure me
With some delightfull Instrument, with which,
And with my former practise I intend
To passe away the tediousnesse of night,
Though slumbers were more fitting.

I. GENTLEMAN   Presently.

            Exit I. Gentleman

2. GENTLEMAN

Your wil's obeyed in all things; for our master
Commaunded you be disobeyed in nothing.

        Enter I. Gentleman with a stringed Instrument

PERICLES

I thanke you. Now, betake you to your pillowes,   950
And to the nourishment of quiet sleepe.

            Exeunt Gentlemen

        Pericles playes, and singes

Day, that hath still that soueraigntie to drawe backe
The empire of the night, though for a while
In darkenesse shee vsurpe, brings morning on.
I will go giue his Grace that salutation
Morning requires of me.   *Exit with Instrument*

        Enter the King reading of a letter at one doore, the   Sc. 9
        Knightes ⌈entering at another doore⌉ meete him

I. KNIGHT

Good morrow to the good *Simonides*.

1183

KING

    Knights, from my daughter this I let you know,
    That for this twelue-month, shee'le not vndertake
960   A maried life: her reason to her selfe
    Is onely knowne, which from her, none can get.

2. KNIGHT

    May we not haue accesse to her (my Lord?)

KING

    Fayth, by no meanes, it is impossible,
    She hath so strictly tyed her to her Chamber:
    One twelue Moones more shee'le weare *Dianas* liu'rie:
    This by the eye of *Cinthya* hath she vowed,
    And on her Virgin honour, will not breake it.

3. KNIGHT

    Loth to bid farewell, we take our leaues.

                          Exeunt Knightes

KING

    So, they are well dispatcht: now to my daughters
        Letter;
970   She telles me heere, shee'le wedde the stranger Knight,
    Or neuer more to view nor day nor light.
    I like that well: nay how absolute she's in't,
    Not minding whether I dislike or no.
    Mistris t'is well, I do commend your choyce,
    And will no longer haue it be delayed:
        Enter Pericles
    Soft, heere he comes, I must dissemble that
    In shew, I haue determin'd on in heart.

PERICLES

    All fortune to the good *Symonides.*

KING

    To you as much, Sir, I am behoulding to you
980   For your sweete Musicke this last night: my eares,
    I do protest, were neuer better fedde
    With such delightfull pleasing harmonie.

PERICLES

    It is your Graces pleasure to commend,
    Not my desert.

KING   Sir, you are Musickes maister.

PERICLES

    The worst of all her schollers (my good Lord.)

KING

    Let me aske you one thing: what thinke you of my
        Daughter?

PERICLES

    A most vertuous Princesse.

KING   And faire too, is she not?

PERICLES

    As a faire day in Sommer: woondrous faire.

KING

    My Daughter sir, thinkes very well of you,
990   So well indeed, that you must be her Maister,
    And she will be your Scholler; therefore looke to it.

PERICLES

    I am vnworthy for her Scholemaister.

KING

    She thinkes not so: peruse this writing else.
        He giues the letter to Pericles, who reads

PERICLES (*aside*)

    What's here, a letter that she loues the knight of *Tyre?*
    T'is the Kings subtiltie to haue my life:
       ⌈*He prostrates himselfe at the kings feete*⌉
    Oh seeke not to intrappe me, gracious Lord,
    A Stranger, and distressed Gentleman,
    That neuer aymde so hie, to loue your Daughter,
    But bent all offices to honour her.
    Neuer did thought of mine leuie offence;   1000
    Nor neuer did my actions yet commence
    A deed might gaine her loue, or your displeasure.

KING

    Thou lyest like a Traytor.

PERICLES   Traytor?

KING   I, traytor,
    That thus disguis'd, art stolne into my Court,
    With witchcraft of thy actions to bewitch,
    The yeelding spirit of my tender Childe.

PERICLES ⌈*rising*⌉

    Who cals me Traytor, vnlesse it be the King,
    Eu'n in his bosome, I will write the lye.

KING (*aside*)

    Now by the Gods, I do applaude his courage.

PERICLES

    My actions are as noble as my bloud,   1010
    That neuer relisht of a base discent:
    I came vnto your Court in search of Honour,
    And not to be a Rebell to your state:
    And he that otherwise accountes of mee,
    This Sword shall prooue, hee's Honours enemie.

KING

    I shall prooue otherwise, since both your practise
    And her consent therin, is euident,
    There by my daughters hand, as she can witnesse.
        Enter Thaisa

PERICLES (*to Thaysa*)

    Then as you are as vertuous, as faire,
    By what you hope of heauen, or desire   1020
    By your best wishes heere i'th' worlde fulfill'd,
    Resolue your angry Father, if my tongue
    Did ere solicite, or my hand subscribe
    To any sillable made loue to you?

THAYSA Why sir, say if you had,
    Who takes offence? at that, would make me glad?

KING

    How minion, are you so peremptorie?
    (*Aside*) I am glad on't, (*to Thaysa*) is this a fit match
        for you?
    A stragling *Theseus* borne we knowe not where,
    One that hath neither bloud nor merite   1030
    For thee to hope for, or himselfe to challenge
    Of thy perfections ene the least allowaunce.

THAYSA (*kneeling*)

    Suppose his birth were base (when that his life
    Shewes that hee is not so) yet hee hath vertue,
    The very ground of all nobilitie,
    Enough to make him noble: I intreat you
    To remember that I am in loue,

The power of which loue cannot be confin'd
By th' power of your will. Most royall Father,
1040   What with my penne I haue in secret written,
With my tongue now I openly confirme,
Which is, I haue no life but in his loue,
Nor any being but in ioying of his worth.

KING

Equalles to equalls, good to good is ioyned,
This not being so, the bauine of your minde
In rashnesse kindled, must againe be quenched,
Or purchase our displeasure. (*To Pericles*) And for you
    sir,
First learne to know, I banish you my Court,
And yet I scorne our rage should stoope so lowe,
1050   For your ambition sir, Ile haue your life.

THAYSA (*to Pericles*)

For euerie droppe of blood hee sheades of yours,
Heele draw an other from his onely childe.

KING

Ile tame you; yea Ile bring you in subiection.
Will you not hauing my consent,
Bestow your loue and your affections,
Vpon a Stranger? (*aside*) who for ought I know,
May be (nor can I thinke the contrary)
As great in blood as I my selfe:
    ⌈*He catches Thaysa rashly by the hand*⌉
Therefore, heare you Mistris, either frame your will to
    mine:
    ⌈*He catches Pericles rashly by the hand*⌉
1060   And you sir, heare you; either be rul'd by mee,
Or I shall make you,
    ⌈*He claps their handes together*⌉
              man and wife:
Nay come, your hands, and lippes must seale it too:
    Pericles and Thaysa kisse
And being ioynd, Ile thus your hopes destroy,
    ⌈*He parts them*⌉
And for your further griefe: God giue you ioy;
What are you pleas'd?

THAYSA   Yes, (*to Pericles*) if you loue me sir?

PERICLES

Eu'n as my life, my blood that fosters it.

KING

What are you both agreed?

AMBO   Yes, if't please your Maiestie.

KING

It pleaseth me so well, that I will see you wed,
Then with what haste you can, get you to bed.

                           Exeunt

Sc. 10   *Enter Gower*

GOWER

1070   Now sleepe yslacked hath the rout,
No din but snores the house about,
Made louder by the orefed breast,
Of this most pompous maryage Feast:
The Catte with eyne of burning cole,
Now coutches fore the Mouses hole;

And Crickets sing at th' Ouens mouth,
As the blyther for their drouth:
Hymen hath brought the Bride to bed,
Where by the losse of maydenhead,
A Babe is moulded: be attent,   1080
And Time that is so briefly spent,
With your fine fancies quaintly each,
What's dumbe in shew, I'le plaine with speach.
            Dumbe shew.
Enter Pericles and Symonides at one dore with
attendantes, a Messenger comes ⌈hastily⌉ in to them,
kneeles and giues Pericles a letter, Pericles shewes it
Symonides, the Lords kneele to him; then enter
Thaysa with child, with Lichorida a nurse, the King
shewes her the letter, she reioyces: she and Pericles
take leaue of her father, and depart with Lichorida
at one dore; Symonides ⌈and attendantes⌉ depart at
an other
By many a dearne and painefull pearch
Of *Perycles* the carefull search,
By the fower opposing Coignes,
Which the world togeather ioynes,
Is made with all due diligence,
That horse and sayle and hie expence,
Can steed the quest: at last from *Tyre*   1090
Fame answering the most strange enquire,
To'th Court of King *Symonides*,
Are Letters brought, the tenour these:
Antiochus and his daughter dead,
The men of *Tyrus*, on the head
Of *Helycanus* would set on
The Crowne of *Tyre*, but he will none:
The mutanie there, hee hastes t'appease,
Sayes to'em, if King *Pericles*
Come not home in twise six Moones,   1100
He obedient to their doomes,
Will take the Crowne: the summe of this,
Brought hither to *Pentapolis*,
Irauyshed the regions round,
And euery one with claps can sound,
Our heyre apparant is a King:
Who dreampt? who thought of such a thing?
Briefe he must hence depart to *Tyre*,
His Queene with child, makes her desire,
Which who shall crosse? along to goe,   1110
Omit we all their dole and woe:
Lichorida her Nurse she takes,
And so to Sea; their vessell shakes,
On *Neptunes* billow, halfe the flood,
Hath their Keele cut: but fortunes mood
Varies againe, the grisled North
Disgorges such a tempest forth,
That as a Ducke for life that diues,
So vp and downe the poore Ship driues:
The Lady shreekes, and wel-a-neare,   1120
Do's fall in trauayle with her feare:
And what ensues in this fell storme,
Shall for it selfe, it selfe performe:

I nill relate, action may
Conueniently the rest conuay,
Which might not what by me is told;
In your imagination hold
This Stage, the Ship, vpon whose Decke
The sea tost *Pericles* appeares to specke.   *Exit*

Sc. 11   ⌐*Thunder and Lightning.*¬ *Enter Pericles a Shipboard*

PERICLES

1130   The God of this great Vast, rebuke these surges,
Which wash both heau'n and hell, and thou that hast
Vpon the Windes commaund, bind them in Brasse,
Hauing call'd them from the deepe; ô still
Thy deafning dreadfull thunders, gently quench
Thy nimble sulph'rous flashes: ô How *Lychorida*!
How does my Queene? thou stormest venomously,
Wilt thou speat all thy selfe? the sea-mans Whistle
Is as a whisper in the eares of death,
Vnheard. *Lychorida*? *Lucina*, oh!

1140   Diuinest patrionesse, and mydwife gentle
To those that cry by night, conuey thy deitie
Aboard our dauncing Boat, make swift the pangues
Of my Queenes trauayles? now *Lychorida*.
     Enter Lychorida with an Infant

LICHORIDA

Heere is a thing too young for such a place,
Who if it had conceit, would die, as I
Am like to doe: take in your armes this peece
Of your dead Queene.

PERICLES   How? how *Lychorida*?

LICHORIDA

Patience (good sir) do not assist the storme,
Heer's all that is left liuing of your Queene;

1150   A litle Daughter: for the sake of it,
Be manly, and take comfort.

PERICLES   O you Gods!
Why do you make vs loue your goodly gyfts,
And snatch them straight away? we heere below,
Recall not what we giue, and therein may
Vse honour with you.

LICHORIDA   Patience (good sir)
Ene for this charge.
     She giues him the Infant. ⌐*Pericles looking*
     mournfully vpon it, shakes his head, and weepes¬

PERICLES   Now mylde may be thy life,
For a more blust'rous birth had neuer Babe:
Quiet and gentle thy conditions; for
Thou art the rudelyest welcome to this world,

1160   That e'er was Princes Child: happy what followes,
Thou hast as chiding a natiuitie,
As Fire, Ayre, Water, Earth, and Heau'n can make,
To harould thee from th' wombe: Poore inch of Nature,
Eu'n at the first, thy losse is more then can
Thy partage quit, with all thou canst find heere:
Now the good Gods throw their best eyes vpon't.
     Enter ⌐*the Maister*¬ *and a Sayler*

⌐MAISTER¬ What courage sir? God saue you.

PERICLES

Courage enough, I do not feare the flaw,
It hath done to me its worst: yet for the loue
Of this poore Infant, this fresh new sea-farer,   1170
I would it would be quiet.

⌐MAISTER¬ (*calling*) Slake the bolins there; thou wilt not
wilt thou: blow and split thy selfe.

SAYLER But Sea-roome, and the brine and cloudy billow
kisse the Moone, I care not.

⌐MAISTER¬ (*to Pericles*) Sir your Queene must ouer board,
the sea workes hie, the Wind is lowd, and will not lie
till the Ship be cleard of the dead.

PERICLES

That's but your superstition.

⌐MAISTER¬ Pardon vs, sir; with vs at Sea it hath bin still   1180
obserued, and we are strong in custome, therefore
briefly yeeld'er, for she must ouer board straight.

PERICLES

As you thinke meet; most wretched Queene.

LICHORIDA   Heere she lyes sir.
     She ⌐*drawes the curtains and discouers*¬ *the body of*
     Thaysa in a ⌐*bed. Pericles giues Lichorida the Infant*¬

PERICLES (*to Thaysa*)

A terrible Child-bed hast thou had (my deare,
No light, no fire, th'vnfriendly elements,
Forgot thee vtterly, nor haue I time
To giue thee hallowd to thy graue, but straight,
Must cast thee scarcly Coffind, in the oaze,
Where for a monument vpon thy bones,
And aye remayning lampes, the belching Whale,   1190
And humming Water must orewelme thy corpes,
Lying with simple shels: ô *Lychorida*,
Bid *Nestor* bring me Spices, Incke, and Paper,
My Casket, and my Iewels; and bid *Nicander*
Bring me the Sattin Coffer: lay the Babe
Vpon the Pillow; hie thee whiles I say
A priestly farewell to her: sodainely, woman.
     Exit Lichorida

⌐SAYLER¬ Sir, we haue a Chist beneath the hatches, caulkt
and bittumed ready.

PERICLES

I thanke thee: ⌐*To the Maister*¬ Mariner say, what
   Coast is this?   1200

⌐MAISTER¬

Wee are neere *Tharsus*.

PERICLES   Thither gentle Mariner,
Alter thy course from *Tyre*: When canst thou reach it?

⌐MAISTER¬

By breake of day, if the Wind cease.

PERICLES   Make for *Tharsus*,
There will I visit *Cleon*, for the Babe
Cannot hold out to *Tyrus*; there Ile leaue it
At carefull nursing: goe thy wayes good Mariner,
Ile bring the body presently.
     ⌐*Exit Maister at one dore, and Sayler beneath*
     the hatches; exit Pericles to Thaysa,
     closing the curtaines¬

Sc. 12   *Enter Lord Cerymon with a ⌐poore man and a¬*
            seruant

CERIMON

    Phylemon, hoe.
            Enter Phylemon

PHYLEMON   Doth my Lord call?

CERIMON

    Get Fire and meat for those poore men,
                                          ⌐*Exit Phylemon*¬

1210   T'as been a turbulent and stormie night.

SERUANT

    I haue seen many; but such a night as this,
    Till now, I neare endured.

CERIMON

    Your Maister will be dead ere you returne,
    There's nothing can be ministred in Nature,
    That can recouer him: ⌐*to poore man*¬ giue this to th'
       Pothecary,
    And tell me how it workes.
                      ⌐*Exeunt poore man and seruant*¬
            Enter two Gentlemen

1. GENTLEMAN   Good morrow.

2. GENTLEMAN

    Good morrow to your Lordship.

CERIMON   Gentlemen,

    Why doe you stirre so early?

1. GENTLEMAN   Sir,

    Our lodgings standing bleake vpon the sea,

1220   Shooke as the earth did quake:
    The very principals did seeme to rend
    And all to topple: pure surprize and feare,
    Made me to quite the house.

2. GENTLEMAN

    That is the cause we trouble you so early,
    T'is not our husbandry.

CERIMON   O you say well.

1. GENTLEMAN

    But I much maruaile that your Lordship should,
    Hauing rich tire about you, at this hower,
    Shake off the golden slumber of repose; tis most
      strange
    Nature to be so conuersant with Paine,
    Being thereto not compell'd.

1230   CERIMON   I held it euer
    Vertue and Cunning, were endowments greater,
    Then Noblenesse & Riches; carelesse Heyres,
    May the two latter darken and dispend;
    But Immortalitie attendes the former,
    Making a man a god: t'is knowne, I euer
    Haue studied Physicke: through which secret Art,
    By turning ore Authorities, I haue
    Togeather with my practize, made famyliar,
    To me and to my ayde, the blest infusions

1240   That dwels in Vegetiues, in Mettals, Stones:
    And so can speake of the disturbances
    That Nature works, and of her cures; which doth
      giue me
    A more content and cause of true delight

    Then to be thirsty after tott'ring honour,
    Or tie my pleasure vp in silken Bagges,
    To glad the Foole and Death.

2. GENTLEMAN   Your honour has

    Through *Ephesus*, pour'd foorth your charitie,
    And hundreds call themselues, your Creatures; who
      by you,
    Haue been restor'd; and not alone your knowledge,
    Your personall payne, but ene your Purse still open,   1250
    Hath built Lord *Cerimon*, such strong renowne,
    As time shall neuer—
            Enter ⌐Phylemon and one or¬ two with a Chist

⌐PHYLEMON¬ So, lift there.

CERIMON What's that?

⌐PHYLEMON¬ Sir, euen now

    The sea tost vp vpon our shore this Chist;
    Tis of some wracke.

CERIMON   Set't downe, let's looke vpon't.

2. GENTLEMAN

    T'is like a Coffin, sir.

CERIMON   What ere it be,

    T'is woondrous heauie; did the sea cast it vp?

⌐PHYLEMON¬

    I neuer saw so huge a billow sir,   1260
    Or a more eager.

CERIMON   Wrench it open straight:
    The others start to worke
    If the Seas stomacke be orecharg'd with Gold,
    T'is by a good constraint of queasy Fortune
    It belches vpon vs.

2. GENTLEMAN   T'is so, my Lord.

CERIMON

    How close tis caulkt & bittum'd,
    ⌐*They force the lid*¬
                                          soft; it smels
    Most sweetly in my sense.

2. GENTLEMAN   A delicate Odour.

CERIMON

    As euer hit my nostrill: so, vp with it.
    They take the lid off
    Oh you most potent Gods! what's here, a Corse?

2. GENTLEMAN

    Most strange.

CERIMON   Shrowded in Cloth of state, and crownd,
    Balm'd and entreasur'd with full bagges of Spices,   1270
    A Pasport to!
    He takes a paper from the Chist
    Apollo, perfect mee i'th' the Characters:
    Heere I giue to vnderstand,
    If ere this Coffin driues aland;
    I King Pericles *haue lost*
    This Queene, worth all our mundaine cost:
    Who finds her, giue her burying,
    She was the Daughter of a King:
    Besides this Treasure for a fee,
    The Gods requit his charitie.   1280
    If thou liu'st *Pericles*, thou hast a heart,
    That euen cracks for woe, this chaunc'd to night.

2. GENTLEMAN
  Most likely sir.
CERIMON   Nay certainely to night,
  For looke how fresh she looks. They were too rash,
  That threw her in the sea. Make a Fire within;
  Fetch hither all my Boxes in my Closet,

                              ⌈*Exit Phylemon*⌉

  Death may vsurpe on Nature many howers,
  And yet the fire of life kindle againe
  The oreprest spirits: I haue heard
1290 Of an *Egiptian* 9. howers dead,
  Who was by good applyaunces recouer'd.

        Enter ⌈*Phylemon*⌉ *with Napkins and Fire*

  Well sayd, well sayd; the fire and clothes:
  The still and wofull Musick that we haue,
  Cause it to sound beseech you:

        Musick

                          the Violl once more;
  How thou stirr'st thou blocke? The Musicke there:
  I pray you giue her ayre: Gentlemen,
  This Queene will liue, Nature awakes; a warmth
  Breaths out of her; she hath not been entranc'st
  Aboue fiue howers: see how she ginnes to blow
  Into lifes flow'r againe.
1300 I. GENTLEMAN   The Heauens,
  Through you, encrease our wonder, and set vp
  Your fame for euer.
CERIMON   She is aliue, behold
  Her ey-lids, cases to those heau'nly iewels
  Which *Pericles* hath lost,
  Begin to part their fringes of bright gold,
  The Diamonds of a most praysed water
  Doth appeare, to make the world twise rich, liue,
  And make vs weepe, to heare your fate, faire creature,
  Rare as you seeme to bee.

        Shee moues

THAYSA   O deare *Diana*,
1310 Where am I? where's my Lord? what world is this?
2. GENTLEMAN
  Is not this strange?
I. GENTLEMAN   Most rare.
CERIMON   Hush (gentle neighbours)
  Lend me your hands, to the next Chamber beare her:
  Get linnen: now this matter must be lookt to
  For her relapse is mortall: come, come;
  And *Escelapius* guide vs.

        They carry her away. Exeunt omnes

Sc. 13   *Enter Pericles, at Tharsus, with Cleon and Dionisa,*
          and Lichorida with a Babe

PERICLES
  Most honor'd *Cleon*, I must needs be gone,
  My twelue months are expir'd, and *Tyrus* standes
  In a litigious peace: you and your Lady
  Take from my heart all thankfulnesse, the Gods
  Make vp the rest vpon you.
1320 CLEON   Your strokes of fortune,

Though they hurt you mortally yet glaunce
  Full woundingly on vs.
DYONYSA   O your sweet Queene!
  That the strict fates had pleas'd, you'd brought her
    hither
  T'haue blest mine eies with her.
PERICLES   We cannot but obey
  The pow'rs aboue vs; should I rage and rore
  As doth the sea she lies in, yet the end
  Must be as tis: my gentle babe *Marina*,
  Whom, for she was borne at sea, I haue nam'd so,
  Here I charge your charitie withall; and leaue her
  The infant of your care, beseeching you   1330
  To giue her princely training, that she may be
  Manere'd as she is borne.
CLEON   Feare not (my Lord) but thinke
  Your Grace, that fed my Countrie with your Corne;
  For which, the peoples pray'rs still fall vpon you,
  Must in your child be thought on, if neglection
  Should therein make me vile, the common body
  By you relieu'd, would force me to my duety:
  But if to that, my nature neede a spurre,
  The Gods reuenge it vpon me and mine,
  To th' end of generation.
PERICLES   I beleeue you,   1340
  Your honour and your goodnes, teach me too't
  Without your vowes, till she be maried, Madame,
  By bright *Diana*, whom we honour all
  Vnsisserd shall this heyre of mine remayne,
  Though I shew ill in't; so I take my leaue:
  Good Madame, make me blessed in your care
  In bringing vp my Child.
DYONYSA   I haue one my selfe,
  Who shall not be more deere to my respect
  Then yours, my Lord.
PERICLES   Madam, my thanks and prayers.
CLEON
  Weel bring your Grace ene to the edge ath shore,   1350
  Then giue you vp to th' masted *Neptune*, and
  The gentlest winds of heauen.
PERICLES
  I will imbrace your offer, come deer'st Madame,
  O no teares *Licherida*, no teares,
  Looke to your litle Mistris, on whose grace
  You may depend hereafter: come my Lord.   *Exeunt*

        Enter Cerimon, and Thaisa   Sc. 14

CERIMON
  Madam, this Letter, and some certaine Iewels,
  Lay with you in your Coffer, which are al
  At your command: know you the Charecter?
THAYSA
  It is my Lords, that I was shipt at sea   1360
  I well remember, eu'n on my eaning time,
  But whether there deliuerd, by th' holie gods
  I cannot rightly say: but since King *Pericles*
  My wedded Lord, I nere shall see againe,

A vastall liu'rie will I take me to,
And neuer more haue ioy.

CLEON

Madam, if this you purpose as ye speake,
Dianaes Temple is not distant farre,
Where till your date expire you may abide,
1370   Moreouer if you please a Neece of mine,
Shall there attend you.

THAYSA

My recompence is thanks, thats all,
Yet my good will is great, though the gift small.

                                        Exeunt

Sc. 15   *Enter Gower*

GOWER

Imagine *Pericles* arriude at *Tyre*,
Welcomd and setled to his owne desire:
His wofull Queene we leaue at *Ephesus*,
Vnto *Diana* ther's a Votarisse.
      Now to *Marina* bend your mind,
      Whom our fast growing scene must finde
1380   At *Tharsus*, and by *Cleon* traind
      In Musick, letters, who hath gaind
      Of education all the grace,
      Which makes hir both the hart and place
      Of gen'rall wonder: but alacke
      That monster Enuie oft the wracke
      Of earned praise, *Marinas* life
      Seeks to take off by treasons knife,
      And in this kind: our *Cleon* has
      One daughter and a full growne lasse,
1390   Ene ripe for marriage right: this Maid
      Hight *Philoten*: and it is said
      For certaine in our storie, shee
      Would euer with *Marina* bee.
      Beet when they weaude the sleded silke,
      With fingers long, small, white as milke,
      Or when she would with sharpe neele wound,
      The Cambricke which she made more sound
      By hurting it, or when too'th Lute
      She sung, and made the night bird mute,
1400   That still records with mone, or when
      She would with rich and constant pen,
      Vaile to her Mistresse *Dian*, still
      This *Phyloten* contends in skill
      With absolute *Marina*: so
      With Doue of *Paphos* might the crow
      Vie feathers white, *Marina* gets
      All prayses, which are paid as debts,
      And not as giuen, this so darkes
      In *Phyloten* all gracefull markes,
1410   That *Cleons* wife with Enuie rare,
      A present murder does prepare
      For good *Marina*, that her daughter
      Might stand peerlesse by this slaughter.
      The sooner her vile thoughts to stead,
      Lichorida our nurse is dead,
            ⌈*A tombe is reuealed*⌉

And cursed *Dioniza* hath
The pregnant instrument of wrath
Prest for this blow, th'vnborne euent,
I doe commend to your content,
Onely I carrie winged Time,   1420
Post one the lame feete of my rime,
Which neuer could I so conuey,
Vnlesse your thoughts went on my way,
      ⌈*Enter Dioniza, with Leonine*⌉
Dioniza does appeare,
With *Leonine* a murtherer.   *Exit*

DYONYSA

Thy oath remember, thou hast sworne to doo't,
Tis but a blowe which neuer shall bee knowne,
Thou canst not doe a thing i'th' worlde so soone
To yeelde thee so much profite: let not conscience
Which is but cold, or fanning loue thy bosome   1430
Vnflame too nicelie, nor let pittie which
Ene women haue cast off, melt thee, but be
A souldier to thy purpose.

LEONINE   I will doo't,
But yet she is a goodly creature.

DYONYSA

The fitter then the Gods should haue her.
      Enter Marina ⌈*to the tombe*⌉ *with a Basket of*
      flowers
Here she comes weeping her onely nurses death,
Thou art resolude.

LEONINE   I am resolude.

MARINA

No: I will rob *Tellus* of her weede
To strowe thy graue with Flow'rs, the yellowes, blewes,
The purple Violets, and Marigolds,   1440
Shall as a Carpet hang vpon thy tombe,
While Sommer dayes doth last: Aye me poore maid,
Borne in a tempest, when my mother dide,
This world to me is but a ceaselesse storme,
Whirring me from my friends.

DYONYSA

How now *Marina*, why doe yow keep alone?
How chaunce my daughter is not with you?
Doe not consume your bloud with sorrowing,
Haue you a nurse of me? Lord how your fauour
Is changd with this vnprofitable woe: 1450
Giue me your flowers come, ore the sea margent,
Walke with *Leonine*, the ayre is percing there,
And quicke, it sharpes the stomacke, come *Leonine*
Take her by th' arme, walke with her.

MARINA   No I pray you,
Ile not bereaue you of your seruãt.

DYONYSA   Come, come,
I loue the king your father, and your selfe,
With more then forraine heart, wee eu'ry day
Expect him here, when he shall come and find
Our Paragon to all reports thus blasted,
He will repent the breadth of his great voyage,   1460
Blame both my Lord and me, that we haue taken
No care to your best courses, go I pray you,

Walke and be chearfull once againe, resume
That excellent complexion, which did steale
The eyes of yong and old. Care not for me,
I can goe home alone.
MARINA   Well, I will goe,
But truly I haue no desire too it.
DYONYSA
Nay, I know tis good for you, walke halfe an houre
Leonine, at the least, remember
What I haue sed.
1470 LEONINE   I warnt you Madam.
DYONYSA (*to Marina*)
Ile leaue you my sweete Ladie, for a while,
Pray you walke softly, doe not heate your bloud,
What, I must haue care of you.
MARINA   My thanks sweete Madame,
                              Exit Dioniza
Is this wind Westerlie that blowes?
LEONINE   Southwest.
MARINA
When I was borne the wind was North.
LEONINE   Wast so?
MARINA
My father, as nurse ses, did neuer feare,
But cryed good sea-men to the Mariners,
Galling his kingly hands with haling ropes,
And clasping to the Mast, endur'd a sea
1480 That almost burst the decke.
LEONINE When was this?
MARINA When I was borne,
Neuer was waues nor winde more violent,
Once from the ladder tackle, washes off
A canuas clymer, ha ses one, wolt out?
And with a dropping industrie they skip
From stemme to sterne, the Boatswaine whistles, and
The Maister calles and trebles their confusion.
LEONINE Come say your prayers.
1490 MARINA What meane you?
LEONINE
If you require a little space for praier,
I graunt it, pray, but bee not tedious,
The Gods are quicke of eare, and I am sworne
To do my worke with haste.
MARINA   Why would you kill me?
LEONINE
To satisfie my Ladie.
MARINA   Why would shee haue mee kild?
Now as I can remember by my troth,
I neuer did her hurt in all my life,
I neuer spake bad worde, nor did ill turne
To anie liuing creature: Beleeue me law,
1500 I neuer killd a Mouse, nor hurt a Fly:
I trode once on a worme against my will,
But I wept for it. How haue I offended,
Wherein my death might yeeld her anie profit,
Or my life imply her danger?
LEONINE   My Commission
Is not to reason of the deed, but doo't.

MARINA
You will not doo't for all the world I hope:
You are well fauour'd, and your lookes foreshew
You haue a gentle heart, I saw you latelie
When you caught hurt in parting two that fought:
Good sooth it shewde well in you, do so now,   1510
Your Ladie seekes my life, Come you betweene,
And saue poore mee the weaker.
LEONINE ⌈*drawing out his sword*⌉   I am sworne
And will dispatch.
          Enter Pirats ⌈*running*⌉
PIRAT 1. Hold villaine.
          Leonine runs away ⌈*and hides behind the tombe*⌉
PIRAT 2. A prize, a prize.
PIRAT 3. Halfe part mates, halfe part. Come lets haue her
aboord sodainly.   *Exit Pirats,* ⌈*carrying*⌉ *Marina*
          Leonine ⌈*steales backe*⌉
LEONINE
These rogueing theeues serue the great Pyrate *Valdes*,
And they haue seizd *Marina*, let her goe,
Ther's no hope shee'le returne, Ile sweare shees dead, 1520
And throwne into the Sea, but ile see further:
Perhappes they will but please themselues vpon her,
Not carrie her aboord, if shee remaine
Whome they haue rauisht, must by mee be slaine.
          Exit. ⌈*The tombe is concealed*⌉

⌈*A brothel signe.*⌉ *Enter the Pander, his wife the*   Sc. 16
Bawd, and their man Boult
PANDER *Boult.*
BOULT Sir.
PANDER Searche the market narrowely, *Mettelyne* is full
of gallants, wee lose too much money this mart by
beeing wenchlesse.
BAWD Wee were neuer so much out of Creatures, we   1530
haue but poore three, and they can doe no more then
they can doe, and they with continuall action, are euen
as good as rotten.
PANDER Therefore lets haue fresh ones what ere wee pay
for them, if there bee not a conscience to be vsde in
euerie trade, wee shall neuer prosper.
BAWD Thou sayst true, tis not our bringing vp of poore
bastards, as I thinke, I haue brought vp some eleuen.
BOULT I to eleuen, and brought them downe againe, but
shall I searche the market?   1540
BAWD What else man? the stuffe we haue, a strong winde
will blowe it to peeces, they are so pittifully sodden.
PANDER Thou sayest true, they're too vnwholesome a
conscience, the poore *Transiluanian* is dead that laye
with the little baggadge.
BOULT I, shee quickly poupt him, she made him roast-
meate for wormes, but Ile goe searche the market.
                              Exit
PANDER Three or foure thousande Checkins were as prettie
a proportion to liue quietly, and so giue ouer.
BAWD Why, to giue ouer I pray you? Is it a shame to get 1550
when wee are olde?
PANDER Oh our credite comes not in like the commoditie,

nor the commoditie wages not with the daunger: therefore if in our youthes we could picke vp some prettie estate, t'were not amisse to keepe our doore hatch't, besides the sore tearmes we stand vpon with the gods, wilbe strong with vs for giuing ore.

BAWD Come other sorts offend as well as wee.

PANDER As well as wee, I, and better too, wee offende
1560   worse, neither is our profession any mystery, It's no calling, but heere comes *Boult*.

     Enter Boult with the Pirates and Marina

BOULT ⌈*to the Pirats*⌉ Come your wayes my maisters, you say shee's a virgin.

A PIRAT O Sir, wee doubt it not.

BOULT (*to Pander*) Master, I haue gone through for this peece you see, if you like her so, if not I haue lost my earnest.

BAWD *Boult*, has shee anie qualities?

BOULT Shee has a good face, speakes well, and has
1570   excellent good cloathes: theres no farther necessitie of qualities can make her be refuz'd.

BAWD What's her price *Boult*?

BOULT I cannot be bated one doit of a hundred Sestercies.

PANDER (*to Pirats*) Well, follow me my maisters, you shall haue your money presently, (*to Bawd*) wife take her in, instruct her what she has to doe, that she may not be rawe in her entertainment.

     Exeunt Pander and Pirats

BAWD *Boult*, take you the markes of her, the colour of her haire, complexion, height, her age, with warrant
1580   of her virginitie, and crie; He that wil giue most shal haue her first, such a maydenhead were no cheape thing, if men were as they haue beene: get this done as I command you.

BOULT Performance shall follow.   *Exit*

MARINA
  Alacke that *Leonine* was so slacke, so slow,
  He should haue strooke, not spoke, or that these
    Pirates,
  Not enough barbarous, had but oreboord throwne me,
  To seeke my mother.

BAWD Why lament you prettie one?

1590 MARINA That I am prettie.

BAWD Come, the Gods haue done their part in you.

MARINA I accuse them not.

BAWD You are light into my hands, where you are like to liue.

MARINA The more my fault,
  To scape his handes, where I was like to die.

BAWD I, and you shall liue in pleasure.

MARINA No.

BAWD Yes indeed shall you, and taste Gentlemen of all
1600   fashions, you shall fare well, you shall haue the difference of all complexions, what doe you stop your eares?

MARINA Are you a woman?

BAWD What would you haue mee be, and I bee not a woman?

MARINA
  An honest woman, or not a woman.

BAWD Marie whip the Gosseling, I thinke I shall haue something to doe with you, come you'r a young foolish sapling, and must be bowed as I would haue you.

MARINA The Gods defend me.   1610

BAWD If it please the Gods to defend you by men, then men must comfort you, men must feed you, men must stir you vp:

     Enter Boult

Now sir, hast thou cride her through the Market?

BOULT I haue cryde her almost to the number of her haires, I haue drawne her picture with my voice.

BAWD And I prethee tell me, how dost thou find the inclination of the people, especially of the yonger sort?

BOULT Faith they listened to mee, as they would haue harkened to their fathers testament, there was a 1620 Spaniards mouth watred, as he went to bed to her verie description.

BAWD We shall haue him here to morrow with his best ruffe on.

BOULT To night, to night, but Mistresse doe you knowe the French knight, that cowres ethe hams?

BAWD Who, *Mounsieur Verolles*?

BOULT I, he, he offered to cut a caper at the proclamation, but he made a groane at it, and swore he would see her to morrow.   1630

BAWD Well, well, as for him, hee brought his disease hither, here he does but repaire it, I knowe hee will come in our shadow, to scatter his crownes of the Sunne.

BOULT Well, if we had of euerie Nation a traueller, wee should lodge them all with this signe.

BAWD (*to Marina*) Pray you come hither a while, you haue Fortunes comming vppon you, marke mee, you must seeme to doe that fearefully, which you commit willingly, to despise profite, where you haue most gaine, 1640 to weepe that you liue as yee doe, makes pittie in your Louers, seldome but that pittie begets you a good opinion, and that opinion a meere profite.

MARINA I vnderstand you not.

BOULT (*to Baud*) O take her home Mistresse, take her home, these blushes of hers must bee quencht with some present practise.

BAWD Thou sayest true yfaith, so they must, for your Bride goes to that with shame, which is her way to goe with warrant.   1650

BOULT Faith some doe, and some doe not, but Mistresse if I haue bargaind for the ioynt.

BAWD Thou maist cut a morsell off the spit.

BOULT I may so.

BAWD Who should denie it? (*To Marina*) Come young one, I like the manner of your garments well.

BOULT I by my faith, they shall not be changd yet.

BAWD (*giuing him money*) *Boult*, spend thou that in the towne: report what a soiourner we haue, youle loose nothing by custome. When Nature framde this peece, 1660 shee meant thee a good turne, therefore say what a parragon she is, and thou reapst the haruest out of thine owne setting forth.

BOULT I warrant you Mistresse, thunder shall not so

awake the beds of Eeles, as my giuing out her beautie
stirs vp the lewdly enclined, Ile bring home some to
night.　　　　　　　　　　　　　　　　　⌈*Exit*⌉

BAWD Come your wayes, follow me.

MARINA

　If fires be hote, kniues sharpe, or waters deepe,
1670　Vntide I still my virgin knot will keepe.
　Diana ayde my purpose.

BAWD What haue we to doe with *Diana*, pray you will
　you goe with me?　　　　*Exeunt.* ⌈*The signe is remoued*⌉

Sc. 17　　　　*Enter* ⌈*in mourning garments*⌉ *Cleon, and Dioniza*

DYONYSA

　Why are you foolish, can it be vndone?

CLEON

　O *Dioniza*, such a peece of slaughter,
　The Sunne and Moone nere lookt vpon.

DYONYSA

　I thinke youle turne a childe agen.

CLEON

　Were I chiefe Lord of all this spacious world,
　Ide giue it to vndo the deede, a Ladie
1680　Much lesse in bloud then vertue, yet a Princes
　To equall any single Crowne ath earth
　Ith Iustice of compare, O villaine, *Leonine*
　Whom thou hast poisned too,
　If thou hadst drunke to him tad beene a kindnesse
　Becomming well thy fact, what canst thou say
　When noble *Pericles* demaunds his child?

DYONYSA

　That shee is dead. Nurses are not the fates
　To foster is not euer to preserue,
　She dide at night, Ile say so, who can crosse it
1690　Vnlesse you play the pious Innocent,
　And for an honest attribute, crie out
　Shee dyde by foule play.

CLEON　　　　　　　O goe too, well, well,
　Of all the faults beneath the heau'ns, the Gods
　Doe like this worst.

DYONYSA　　　　　Be one of those that thinkes
　The pettie wrens of *Tharsus* will flie hence,
　And open this to *Pericles*, I do shame
　To thinke of what a noble straine you are,
　And of how cow'd a spirit.

CLEON　　　　　　　　To such proceeding
1700　Who euer but his approbation added,
　Though not his prime consent, he did not flow
　From honourable sourses.

DYONYSA　　　　　Be it so then,
　Yet none does knowe but you how shee came dead,
　Nor none can knowe *Leonine* being gone.
　Shee did distaine my childe, and stoode betweene
　Her and her fortunes: none woulde looke on her,
　But cast their gazes on *Marinas* face,
　Whilst ours was blurted at, and helde a Mawkin
　Not worth the time of day. It pierst me thorow,
　And though you call my course vnnaturall,
1710　You not your childe well louing, yet I finde

It greets mee as an enterprize of kindnesse
Performd to your sole daughter.

CLEON Heauens forgiue it.

DYONYSA And as for *Pericles*,
　What should hee say, we wept after her hearse,
　And yet we mourne, her monument
　Is almost finish'd, & her epitaphs
　In glittring goldē characters expres
　A gen'rrall prayse to her, and care in vs
　At whose expence tis done.

CLEON　　　　　　　Thou art like the Harpie,　1720
　Which to betray, doest with thine Angell face
　Ceaze in thine Eagle talents.

DYONYSA

　Yere like one that supersticiously,
　Doe sweare too'th Gods, that Winter kills the Flies,
　But yet I know, youle doe as I aduise.　　　*Exeunt*

　　　　Enter Gower　　　　　　　　　　Sc. 18

GOWER

　Thus time we waste, & long leagues make we short,
　Saile seas in Cockles, haue and wish but fort,
　Making to take imagination,
　From bourne to bourne, region to region,
　By you being pard'ned we commit no crime,　1730
　To vse one language, in each seu'rall clime,
　Where our sceane seemes to liue, I doe beseech you
　To learne of me who stand ith gappes to teach you
　The stages of our storie, *Pericles*
　Is now againe thwarting the wayward seas,
　Attended on by many a Lord and Knight,
　To see his daughter all his liues delight.
　Old *Helicanus* goes along, behind
　Is left to gouerne, if you beare in mind,
　Old *Escenes*, whom *Hellicanus* late　　　　1740
　Aduancde in Tyre to great and hie estate.
　Well sayling ships, and bounteous winds haue brought
　This king to *Tharsus*, thinke his Pilat thought,
　So with his sterage, shall your thoughts go one
　To fetch his daughter home, who first is gone;
　Like moats and shadowes, see them moue a while,
　Your eares vnto your eyes Ile reconcile.

　　　　Dombe shew.

　　Enter Pericles at one doore, with all his trayne,
　　Cleon and Dioniza ⌈*in mourning garments*⌉ *at the*
　　other. Cleon ⌈*drawes the curtaine and*⌉ *shewes*
　　Pericles the tombe, whereat Pericles makes
　　lamentation, puts on sacke-cloth, and in a mighty
　　passion departs followed by his trayne; Cleon and
　　Dioniza depart at the other doore

See how beleefe may suffer by fowle showe,
This borrowed passion stands for true owde woe:
And *Pericles* in sorrowe all deuour'd,　　　　1750
With sighes shot through, and biggest teares ore-
　showr'd,
Leaues *Tharsus*, and againe imbarques, hee sweares
Neuer to wash his face, nor cut his hayres:

Hee puts on sack-cloth, and to Sea, he beares
A Tempest which his mortall vessell teares,
And yet hee rydes it out. Nowe please you wit
The Epitaph is for *Marina* writ,
By wicked *Dioniza*.

    He reads Marinaes Epitaph on the tombe

    The fairest, sweetest, best lyes heere,
1760   *Who withred in her spring of yeare:*
    In Natures garden, though by growth a Bud,
    Shee was the chiefest flower, she was good.

No vizor does become blacke villanie,
So well as soft and tender flatterie:
Let *Pericles* beleeue his daughter's dead,
And beare his courses to be ordered
By Lady *Fortune*, while our Sceane must play,
His daughters woe and heauie welladay,
In her vnholie seruice: Patience then,
1770 And thinke you now are all in *Mittelin*.   *Exit*

Sc. 19   ⌈*A brothel signe.*⌉ *Enter two Gentlemen*

1. GENTLEMAN Did you euer heare the like?

2. GENTLEMAN No, nor neuer shall doe in such a place as
this, shee beeing once gone.

1. GENTLEMAN But to haue diuinitie preach't there, did
you euer dreame of such a thing?

2. GENTLEMAN No, no, come, I am for no more bawdie
houses, shall's goe heare the Vestalls sing?

1. GENTLEMAN Ile doe any thing now that is vertuous,
but I am out of the road of rutting for euer.   *Exeunt*

    Enter Bawdes 3: Pander, Bawd, and Boult

1780 PANDER Well, I had rather then twice the worth of her
shee had nere come heere.

BAWD Fye, fye, vpon her, shee's able to freze the god
Priapus, and vndoe the whole of generation, we must
either get her rauished, or be rid of her, when she
should doe for Clyents her fitment, and doe mee the
kindenesse of our profession, shee has me her quirks,
her reasons, her master reasons, her prayers, her knees,
that shee would make a *Puritaine* of the diuell, if hee
should cheapen a kisse of her.

1790 BOULT Faith I must rauish her, or shee'le disfurnish vs of
all our Caualereea, and make our swearers priests.

PANDER Now the poxe vpon her greene sicknes for mee.

BAWD Faith ther's no way to be ridde on't but by the
way to the pox.

    Enter Lysimachus disguised

Here comes the Lord *Lysimachus* disguised.

BOULT Wee should haue both Lorde and Lowne, if the
peeuish baggadge would but giue way to custome.

LYSIMACHUS How now, how a douzen of virginities?

BAWD Now the Gods to blesse your Honour.

1800 BOULT I am glad to see your Honour in good health.

LYSIMACHUS You may so, t'is the better for you that your
resorters stand vpon sound legges, how now? wholsome
iniquitie haue you, that a man may deale withall, and
defie the Surgion?

BAWD Wee haue heere one Sir, if shee would, but there
neuer came her like in *Meteline*.

LYSIMACHUS If shee'd doe the deede of darknes thou
wouldst say.

BAWD Your Honor knows what t'is to say wel enough.

LYSIMACHUS Well, call forth, call forth.   ⌈*Exit Pander*⌉ 1810

BOULT For flesh and bloud Sir, white and red, you shall
see a rose, and she were a rose indeed, if shee had but.

LYSIMACHUS What prithi?

BOULT O Sir, I can be modest.

LYSIMACHUS That dignifies the renowne of a Bawde, no
lesse then it giues a good report to a noble to be chaste.

    ⌈*Enter Pander with Marina*⌉

BAWD Heere comes that which growes to the stalke, neuer
pluckt yet I can assure you. Is shee not a faire creature?

LYSIMACHUS Faith shee would serue after a long voyage
at Sea, well theres for you, leaue vs.   1820

    ⌈*He pays the Bawd*⌉

BAWD I beseeche your Honor giue me leaue: a word, and
Ile haue done presently.

LYSIMACHUS I beseech you doe.

BAWD (*aside to Marina*) First, I would haue you note, this
is an Honorable man.

MARINA I desire to finde him so, that I may honorably
know him.

BAWD Next hees the Gouernor of this countrey, and a
man whom I am bound too.

MARINA If he gouerne the countrey you are bound to 1830
him indeed, but how honorable hee is in that, I knowe
not.

BAWD Pray you without anie more virginall fencing, will
you vse him kindly? he will lyne your apron with gold.

MARINA What hee will doe gratiously, I will thankfully
receiue.

LYSIMACHUS (*to Bawd*) Ha you done?

BAWD My Lord shees not pac'ste yet, you must take some
paines to worke her to your mannage, (*to Boult and
Pander*) come wee will leaue his Honor, and hers 1840
together, goe thy wayes.   *Exit 3. Bawds*

LYSIMACHUS
Faire one, how long haue you beene at this trade?

MARINA What trade Sir?

LYSIMACHUS
I cannot name it but I shall offend.

MARINA
I cannot be offended with my trade,
Please you to name it.

LYSIMACHUS   How long haue you bene
Of this profession?

MARINA   Ere since I can remember.

LYSIMACHUS
Did you goe too't so young, were you a gamester
At fiue, or seuen?

MARINA   Earlyer too Sir,
If now I bee one.

LYSIMACHUS   Why? the house you dwell in 1850
Proclaimeth you a Creature of sale.

MARINA
And doe you knowe this house to be a place
Of such resort, and will come intoo it?

I heare say you're of honourable bloud,
And are the Gouernour of this whole Prouince.

LYSIMACHUS
What, hath your principall inform'd you who I am?

MARINA
Who is my principall?

LYSIMACHUS   Why, your hearbe-woman,
She that sets seeds of shame, rootes of iniquitie.
       ⌜She weepes⌝
O y'haue heard something of my pow'r, and so
1860   Stand off alofe for a more serious wooing,
But I protest to thee
Prettie one, my authoritie can wincke
At blemishes, or can on faults looke friendly,
Or my displeasure punish at my pleasure,
From which displeasure, not thy beauty shall
Priuiledge thee, nor my affection, which
Hath drawn me here abate, with further ling'ring.
Come bring me to some priuate place: Come, come.

       MARINA
Let not authoritie, which teaches you
1870   To gouerne others, be the meanes to make you
Mis-gouerne much your selfe:
If you were borne to honour, shew it now,
If put vpon you, make the iudgement good,
That thought you worthie of it. What reason's in
Your Iustice, who hath power ouer all,
To vndoe any? If you take from mee
Mine honour, y'are like him, that makes a gappe
Into forbidden ground, whome after
Too many enter, and of all their euilles
1880   Your selfe are guiltie: my life is yet vnspotted,
My chastitie vnstained eu'n in thought.
Then if your violence deface this building,
The workemanship of heau'n, you do kill your
       honour,
Abuse your iustice, and impouerish me.
(My yet good Lord) if there be fire before me,
Must I strait flie and burne my selfe? Suppose this
       house
(Which too too many feele such houses are)
Should be the Doctors patrimony, and
The Surgeons feeding; folowes it, that I
1890   Must needs infect my self to giue them maint'nance?

LYSIMACHUS
How's this? how's this? some more, be sage.

MARINA ⌜kneeling⌝   For me
That am a maide, though most vngentle Fortune
Haue frãc't mee in this Stie, where since I came,
Diseases haue beene solde deerer then Phisicke,
That the gods would set me free from this vnhalowed
       place,
Though they did chaunge mee to the meanest byrd
That flyes i'th purer ayre.

LYSIMACHUS ⌜mooued⌝   I did not thinke
Thou couldst haue spoke so well, nere dremp't thou
       could'st,
       ⌜Hee lifts her vp with his hands⌝

Though I brought hither a corrupted minde,
Thy speeche hath alter'd it,
       ⌜He wipes the wet from her eyes⌝
                              and my foule thoughtes,   1900
Thy teares so well hath lau'd, that they're now white,
I came heere meaning but to pay the price,
A peece of golde for thy virginitie,
Heeres twenty to releeue thine honesty.
Perseuer still in that cleare way thou goest
And the gods strengthen thee.

MARINA   The good Gods preserue you.

LYSIMACHUS
The very dores and windows sauor vilely,
Fare thee well, thou art a peece of vertue,
The best wrought vppe, that euer Nature made,
And I doubt not thy training hath bene noble,   1910
A curse vpon him, die he like a theefe
That robs thee of thy honour, hold, heeres more golde,
If thou doest heare from me it shalbe for thy good.
       ⌜Enter Boult, standing ready at the doore, making
       his obeysaunce vnto him as Lysimachus should goe
       out⌝

BOULT I beseeche your Honor one peece for me.

LYSIMACHUS
Auaunt thou damned dore-keeper,
Your house but for this virgin that doeth prop it,
Would sincke and ouer-whelme you. Away.   Exit

BOULT How's this? wee must take another course with
you? if your peeuish chastitie, which is not worth a
breakefast in the cheapest countrey vnder the coap,   1920
shall vndoe a whole houshold, let me be gelded like a
spaniel, come your wayes.

MARINA Whither would you haue mee?

BOULT I must haue your mayden-head taken off, or the
cõmon executioner shal doe it, weele haue no more
Gentlemen driuen away, come your wayes I say.
       Enter Bawd and Pander

BAWD How now, whats the matter?

BOULT Worse and worse mistris, shee has heere spoken
holie words to the Lord Lisimachus.

BAWD O abhominable.   1930

BOULT She makes our profession as it were to stincke
afore the face of the gods.

BAWD Marie hang her vp for euer.

BOULT The Noble man would haue dealt with her like a
Noble man, and shee sent him away as colde as a
Snoweball, saying his prayers too.

⌜PANDER⌝ Boult take her away, vse her at thy pleasure,
crack the ice of her virginitie, and make the rest
maliable.

BOULT And if shee were a thornyer peece of ground then   1940
shee is, shee shall be plowed.

MARINA Harke, harke you Gods.

BAWD She coniures, away with her, would she had neuer
come within my doores, Marrie hang you: shees borne
to vndoe vs, (to Marina) will you not goe the way of
wemen-kinde? Marry come vp my dish of chastitie with
rosemary & baies.   Exeunt Bawd and Pander

BOULT ⌈*catching her rashly by the hand*⌉ Come mistris, come
  your way with mee.
1950 MARINA Whither wilt thou haue mee?
BOULT To take from you the Iewell you hold so deere.
MARINA Prithee tell mee one thing first.
BOULT Come now your one thing.
MARINA
  What canst thou wish thine enemie to be.
BOULT Why, I could wish him to bee my master, or rather
  my mistris.
MARINA
  Neither of these can be so bad as thou art,
  Since they doe better thee in their command,
  Thou hold'st a place the painedst feende of hell
1960 Would not in reputation change with thee:
  Thou damned doore-keeper to eu'ry custrell
  That comes enquiring for his Tib.
  To th' cholerike fisting of eu'ry rogue,
  Thy eare is lyable, thy foode is such
  As hath beene belch't on by infected lungs.
BOULT What wold you haue me do? go to the wars, wold
  you? wher a man may serue 7. yeers for the losse of
  a leg, & haue not money enough in the end to buy
  him a woodden one?
MARINA
1970 Doe any thing but this thou doest, emptie
  Olde receptacles, or common-shores of filthe,
  Serue by indenture, to the publike hang-man,
  Anie of these are yet better then this:
  For what thou professest, a Baboone could he speak,
  Would owne a name too deere, heers gold for thee,
  If that thy master would make gaine by me,
  Proclaime that I can sing, weaue, sow, & dance,
  With other vertues, which Ile keep from boast,
  And I will vndertake all these to teache.
1980 I doubt not but this populous Cittie will
  Yeelde manie schollers.
BOULT But can you teache all this you speake of?
MARINA
  Prooue that I cannot, take mee home againe,
  And prostitute mee to the basest groome
  That doeth frequent your house.
BOULT Well I will see what I can doe for thee: if I can
  place thee I will.
MARINA But amongst honest women.
BOULT Faith my acquaintance lies little amongst them,
1990 but since my master and mistris hath bought you,
  theres no going but by their consent: therefore I will
  make them acquainted with your purpose, and I doubt
  not but I shall finde them tractable enough. Come, Ile
  doe for thee what I can, come your wayes.
                     Exeunt. ⌈*The signe is remoued*⌉

Sc. 20   *Enter Gower*
GOWER
  Marina thus the Brothell scapes, and chaunces
    Into an *Honest-house* our Storie sayes:
  Shee sings like one immortall, and shee daunces
    As Goddesse-like to her admired layes.

Deepe clearks she dumb's, and with her neele composes,
  Natures owne shape, of budde, bird, branche, or
    berry,   2000
That ene her art sisters the naturall Roses;
  Her Inckle, Silke, Twine with the rubied Cherrie,
That puples lackes she none of noble race,
  Who powre their bountie on her: and her gaine
She giues the cursed Bawd, here wee her place,
  And to hir Father turne our thoughts againe,
Wee left him on the Sea, waues there him tost,
  Whence driuen tofore the windes, hee is arriu'de
Heere where his daughter dwels, and on this coast,
  Suppose him now at Anchor: the Citie striu'de 2010
God *Neptunes Annuall* feast to keepe, from whence
  Lysimachus our *Tyrian* Shippe espies,
His banners Sable, trim'd with rich expence,
  And to him in his Barge with feruer hyes,
In your supposing once more put your sight,
  Of heauy *Pericles* thinke this the Barke:
Where what is done in action, more if might
  Shalbe discouerd, please you sit and harke.   *Exit*

    Enter Helicanus ⌈*aboue; below, at the first doore* Sc. 21
    enter⌉ *to him* 2. *Saylers* ⌈*one of Tyre, the other of*
    Metaline⌉
SAYLER OF TYRE (*to Sayler of Metaline*)
  Lord *Helicanus* can resolue you, Sir,
  (*To Helicanus*) There is a barge put off from *Metaline*, 2020
  In it *Lysimachus* the Gouernour,
  Who craues to come aboord, what is your will?
HELICANUS
  That hee haue his,
          ⌈*Exit Sayler of Metaline at first doore*⌉
          call vp some Gentlemen.
                ⌈*Exit Helicanus aboue*⌉
⌈SAYLER OF TYRE⌉
  Ho, my Lord calls.
    Enter ⌈*from below the stage*⌉ *two or three*
    Gentlemen; ⌈*to them enter Helicanus*⌉
I. GENTLEMAN   What is your Lordships pleasure?
HELICANUS
  Gentlemen some of worth would come aboord,
  I pray you greet him fairely.
    Enter Lysimachus ⌈*at first doore, with the Sayler*
    and Lords of Metaline⌉
⌈SAYLER OF METALINE⌉ (*to Lysimachus*)
  This is the man that can in ought resolue you.
LYSIMACHUS (*to Helicanus*)
  Hayle reuerent Syr, the Gods preserue you.
HELICANUS
  And you Syr to out-liue the age I am,
  And die as I would doe.
LYSIMACHUS   You wish mee well, 2030
  I am the Gouernour of *Metaline*,
  Beeing on shore, honoring of *Neptunes* triumphs,
  Seeing this goodly vessell ride before vs,
  I made to it, to knowe of whence you are.
HELICANUS
  Our vessell is of *Tyre*, in it our King,

A man, who for this three moneths hath not spoken
To anie one, nor taken sustenance,
But to prorogue his griefe.

LYSIMACHUS
Vpon what ground grew his distemp'rature?

HELICANUS
2040   Twould be too tedious to tell it ouer,
But the mayne griefe springs frõ the precious losse
Of a beloued daughter & a wife.

LYSIMACHUS
May wee not see him?

HELICANUS   See him Sir you may,
But bootlesse is your sight, hee will not speake
To any.

LYSIMACHUS Let me yet obtaine my wish.

HELICANUS
Behold him,
    ⌈*Helicanus draws a curtain, reuealing Pericles lying*
    vppon a cowch, with a long ouer-growne beard,
    diffused hayre, vndecent nayles on his fingers, and
    attired in sacke-cloth⌉
          this was a goodly person,
Till the disaster of one mortall night
Droue him to this.

LYSIMACHUS (*to Pericles*)
Sir King all haile, haile royall sir.
    ⌈*Pericles shrinckes himselfe downe vppon his pillow*⌉

HELICANUS
2050   It is in vaine, he will not speake to you.

LORD
Sir we haue a maid in *Metiline*, I durst wager
Would win some words of him.

LYSIMACHUS   Tis well bethought,
She questionlesse with her sweet harmonie,
And other choise attractions, would allarum
And make a battrie through his defend ports,
Which now are midway stopt, shee in all happie
As the fair'st of all, among her fellow maides,
Dwells now i'th' leauie shelter that abutts
Against the Islands side. Goe fetch her hither.
                  ⌈*Exit Lord*⌉

HELICANUS
2060   Sure all effectlesse, yet nothing weele omit
That beares recou'ries name. But since your kindnesse
Wee haue stretcht thus farre, let vs beseech you,
That for our golde we may prouision haue,
Wherein we are not destitute for want,
But wearie for the stalenesse.

LYSIMACHUS   O sir, a curtesie,
Which if we should denie, the most iust Gods
For euery graffe would send a Caterpillar,
And so inflict our Prouince: yet once more
Let mee intreate to knowe at large the cause
Of your kings sorrow.

2070 HELICANUS   Sit sir, I will recount it,
    ⌈*Enter Lord, with Marina and another maid*⌉
But see I am preuented.

LYSIMACHUS
O heer's the Ladie that I sent for,
Welcome faire one, ist not a goodly presenc?

HELICANUS Shee's a gallant Ladie.

LYSIMACHUS
Shee's such a one, that were I well assurde
Came of gentle kinde, or noble stocke, Ide wish
No better choise, to thinke me rarely wed,
Faire on, all goodnesse that consists in bountie
Expect ene here, where is a kingly patient,
If that thy prosperous and artificiall fate,   2080
Can draw him but to answere thee in ought,
Thy sacred Physicke shall receiue such pay,
As thy desires can wish.

MARINA   Sir I will vse
My vtmost skill in his recure, prouided
That none but I and my companion maid
Be suffer'd to come neere him.

LYSIMACHUS (*to the others*)   Let vs leaue her,
And the Gods prosper her.   ⌈*The men withdraw*⌉
    The Song

LYSIMACHUS ⌈*comming forward*⌉ Markt he your Musicke?

⌈MAID⌉
No nor lookt on vs.

LYSIMACHUS (*to the others*) See she will speake to him.

MARINA (*to Pericles*)
Haile sir, my Lord lend eare.

PERICLES Hum, ha.   2090
    ⌈*He roughly repulses her*⌉

MARINA   I am a maid,
My Lorde, that nere before inuited eyes,
But haue beene gaz'd on like a Comet: She speaks
My Lord, that may be, hath endur'd a griefe
Might equall yours, if both were iustly wayde,
Though wayward fortune did maligne my state,
My deriuation was from ancestors,
Who stood equiuolent with mightie Kings,
But time hath rooted out my parentage,
And to the world, and augward casualties,   2100
Bound me in seruitude, (*aside*) I will desist,
But there is something glowes vpon my cheeke,
And whispers in mine eare, stay till he speake.

PERICLES
My fortunes, parentage, good parentage,
To equall mine, was it not thus, what say you?

MARINA
I sed, if you did know my parentage,
My Lord, you would not do me violence.

PERICLES
I do thinke so, pray you turne your eyes vpon me,
Your like something that, what Countrey woman?
Heere of these shores?

MARINA   No, nor of any shores,   2110
Yet I was mortally brought forth, and am
No other then I seeme.

PERICLES ⌈*aside*⌉
I am great with woe, and shall deliuer weeping:

My dearest wife was like this maid, and such
My daughter might haue beene: My Queenes square
    browes,
Her stature to an inch, as wandlike-straight,
As siluer voyst, her eyes as Iewell-like,
And caste as richly, in pace an other *Iuno*,
Who starues the eares shee feedes, and makes them
    hungrie,
2120 The more she giues them speech, Where doe you liue?
MARINA
Where I am but a straunger, from the decke
You may discerne the place.
PERICLES   Where were you bred?
And how atchieu'd you these indowments which
You make more rich to owe?
MARINA   If I should tell
My Hystorie, it would seeme like lies
Disdaind in the reporting.
PERICLES   Prethee speake,
Falsnesse cannot come from thee, for thou look'st
Modest as iustice, & thou seem'st a Pallas
For the crownd truth to dwell in, I wil beleeue thee
2130 And make my senses credit thy relation,
To points that seeme impossible, thou show'st
Like one I lou'd indeede: what were thy friends?
Didst thou not say when I did push thee backe,
Which was when I perceiu'd thee that thou camst
From good discending.
MARINA   So indeed I did.
PERICLES
Report thy parentage, I think thou saidst
Thou hadst beene tost from wrong to iniurie,
And that thou thoughts thy griefs might equall mine,
If both were open'd.
MARINA   Some such thing I sed,
2140 And sed no more, but what my circumstance
Did warrant me was likely.
PERICLES   Tell thy storie,
If thine consider'd proue the thousand part
Of my enduraunce, thou art a man, and I
Haue suffer'd like a girle, yet thou doest looke
Like patience, gazing on Kings graues, and smiling
Extremitie out of act, what were thy friends?
Howe lost thou them? thy name, my most kinde
    Virgin?
Recount I doe beseech thee, Come sit by mee.
    She sits
MARINA
My name sir, is *Marina*.
PERICLES   Oh I am mockt,
2150 And thou by some insenced God sent hither
To make the world to laugh at me.
MARINA   Patience good sir:
Or here Ile cease.
PERICLES   Nay Ile be patient:
Thou little knowst howe thou doest startle me
To call thy selfe *Marina*.
MARINA   The name

Was giuen mee by one that had some power,
My father, and a King.
PERICLES   How, a Kings daughter,
And cald *Marina*?
MARINA   You sed you would beleeue me,
But not to bee a troubler of your peace,
I will end here.
PERICLES   But are you flesh and bloud?
Haue you a working pulse, and are no Fairie? 2160
Motion as well? speake on, where were you borne?
And wherefore calld *Marina*?
MARINA   Calld *Marina*,
For I was borne at sea.
PERICLES   At sea, what mother?
MARINA
My mother was the daughter of a King,
Who died when I was borne, as my good Nurse
Licherida hath oft recounted weeping.
PERICLES
O stop there a little, ⌜*aside*⌝ this is the rarest dreame
That ere duld sleepe did mocke sad fooles withall,
This cannot be my daughter, buried, well,
(*To Marina*) Where were you bred? Ile heare you
    more too'th bottome   2170
Of your storie, and neuer interrupt you.
MARINA
You will scarce beleeue me, twere best I did giue ore.
PERICLES
I will beleeue you by the syllable
Of what you shall deliuer, yet giue me leaue,
How came you in these parts? where were you bred?
MARINA
The King my father did in *Tharsus* leaue me,
Till cruel *Cleon* with his wicked wife,
Did seeke to murther me: and wooed a villaine,
To attempt the deed, who hauing drawne to doo't,
A crew of Pirats came and rescued me,   2180
To *Metaline* they brought me, but good sir
What wil you of me? why doe you weep? It may be
You thinke mee an imposture, no good fayth:
I am the daughter to King *Pericles*,
If good king *Pericles* be.
PERICLES ⌜*rising*⌝ Hoe, *Hellicanus*?
HELICANUS (*comming forward*) Calls my Lord.
PERICLES
Thou art a graue and noble Counseller,
Most wise in gen'rall, tell me if thou canst,
What this mayde is, or what is like to bee,   2190
That thus hath made mee weepe.
HELICANUS   I know not,
But heres the Regent sir of *Metaline*,
Speakes nobly of her.
LYSIMACHUS   She would neuer tell
Her parentage, being demaunded that,
She would sit still and weepe.
PERICLES
Oh *Hellicanus*, strike me honor'd sir,

Giue mee a gash, put me to present paine,
Least this great sea of ioyes rushing vpon me,
Ore-beare the shores of my mortalitie,
And drowne me with their sweetnesse: (*To Marina*) Oh
2200   come hither,
⌈*Marina stands*⌉
Thou that begetst him that did thee beget,
Thou that wast borne at sea, buried at *Tharsus*,
And found at sea agen, O *Hellicanus*,
Downe on thy knees, thanke the holie Gods as loud
As thunder threatens vs this is *Marina*.
(*To Marina*) What was thy mothers name? tell me, but
that
For truth can neuer be confirm'd inough,
Though doubts did euer sleepe.
MARINA   First sir, I pray
What is your title?
PERICLES   I am *Pericles*
2210   Of *Tyre*, but tell mee now my drownd Queenes name,
As in the rest, thou hast beene God-like perfit,
So proue but true in that, thou art my daughter,
The heir of kingdomes, and an other life
To *Pericles* thy father.
MARINA ⌈*kneeling*⌉   Is it no more
To be your daughter, then to say, my mothers name,
Thaisa was my mother, who did end
The minute I began.
PERICLES
Now blessing on thee, rise thou art my child.
⌈*Marina stands. He kisses her*⌉
⌈*To attendants*⌉ Giue me fresh garments, mine owne
Hellicanus,
2220   Not dead at *Tharsus* as shee should haue beene
By sauage *Cleon*, she shall tell thee all,
When thou shalt kneele, and iustifie in knowledge,
She is thy verie Princes; who is this?
HELICANUS
Sir, tis the gouernor of *Metaline*,
Who hearing of your melancholie state,
Did come to see you.
PERICLES (*to Lysimachus*) I embrace you sir,
Giue me my robes.
⌈*He is attired in fresh robes*⌉
I am wilde in my beholding,
O heauens blesse my girle,
⌈*Celestiall Musicke*⌉
but harke what Musicke,
Tell *Hellicanus* my *Marina*, tell him
2230   Ore point by point, for yet he seemes to dout,
How sure you are my daughter, but what musicke?
HELICANUS My Lord I heare none.
PERICLES
None, the Musicke of the *Spheres*, list my *Marina*.
LYSIMACHUS (*aside to the others*)
It is not good to crosse him, giue him way.
PERICLES Rar'st sounds, do ye not heare?
LYSIMACHUS Musicke my Lord?
PERICLES I heare most heau'nly Musicke.

It raps me vnto listning, and thicke slumber
Hangs vpon mine eyelids, let me rest.
He sleeps
LYSIMACHUS
A Pillow for his head.
⌈*To Marina & others*⌉ Companion friends,   2240
If this but answere to my iust beliefe,
Ile well remember you. So leaue him all.
Exeunt all but Pericles
Diana ⌈*discends from the heauens*⌉
DIANA
My Temple stands in *Ephesus*, hie thee thither,
And doe vppon mine Altar sacrifice,
There when my maiden priests are met together
At large discourse thy fortunes, in this wise:
With a full voyce before the people all,
Reueale how thou at sea didst loose thy wife,
To mourne thy crosses with thy daughters, call,
And giue them repetition to the life,   2250
Performe my bidding, or thou liu'st in woe:
Doo't, and rest happie, by my siluer bow,
Awake and tell thy dreame.
⌈*Diana ascends into the heauens*⌉
PERICLES
Celestiall *Dian*, Goddesse *Argentine*,
I will obey thee (*calling*) *Hellicanus*.
Enter Helicanus, Lysimachus, and Marina
HELICANUS   Sir.
PERICLES
My purpose was for *Tharsus*, there to strike,
Th'inhospitable *Cleon*, but I am
For other seruice first, toward *Ephesus*
Turne our blowne sayles, eftsoones Ile tell thee why,
⌈*Exit Helicanus*⌉
Shall we refresh vs sir vpon your shore,   2260
And giue you golde for such prouision
As our intents will neede.
LYSIMACHUS   With all my heart, sir,
And when you come a shore, I haue a shuit.
PERICLES
You shall preuaile were it to wooe my daughter,
For it seemes you haue beene noble towards her.
LYSIMACHUS
Sir, lend me your arme.
PERICLES   Come my *Marina*.
⌈*Exit Pericles, with Lysimachus at one arme,*
Marina at the other⌉

Enter Gower   Sc. 22
GOWER
Now our sands are almost run,
More a little, and then dum.
This my last boone giue mee,
For such kindnesse must relieue mee: 2270
That you aptly will suppose,
What pageantry, what feats, what showes,
What minstrelsie, and prettie din,
The Regent made in *Metalin*,

To greet the King, so well he thriued,
That he is promisde to be wiued
To faire *Marina*, but in no wise,
Till he had done his sacrifice,
As *Dian* bad, whereto being bound,
2280   The *Int'rim* pray you, all confound.
In fetherd briefenes sayles are fild,
And wishes fall out as they'r wild,
At *Ephesus* the Temple see,
      ⌜*An alter, Thaysa, and other Vestalls are reuealed*⌝
Our King and all his companie.
      ⌜*Enter Pericles, Marina, Lysimachus, Helicanus,*
      Cerimon, with attendantes⌝
That he can hither come so soone,
Is by your fancies thankfull doome.
      ⌜*Gower stands aside*⌝
PERICLES
   Haile *Dian*, to performe thy iust commaund,
   I here confesse my selfe the King of *Tyre*,
   Who frighted from my countrey did espouse
   The faire *Thaysa*,
      ⌜*Thaysa startes*⌝
2290   at *Pentapolis*,
   At Sea in childbed died she, but brought forth
   A Mayd child called *Marina* who O Goddesse
   Wears yet thy siluer liurey, shee at *Tharsus*
   Was nurst with *Cleon*, whom at fourteene yeares
   He sought to murder, but her better stars
   Bore her to *Meteline*, gainst whose shore ryding,
   Her Fortunes brought the mayde aboord our Barke,
   Where by her owne most cleere remembrance, shee
   Made knowne her selfe my Daughter.
THAYSA   Voyce and fauour,
2300   You are, you are, O royall *Pericles*.
      She falls
PERICLES
   What meanes the nun? shee die's, helpe Gentlemen.
CERIMON Noble Sir,
   If you haue tolde *Dianaes* Altar true,
   This is your wife?
PERICLES   Reuerent appearer no,
   I threwe her ouer-boord with these same armes.
CERIMON
   Vpon this coast, I warnt you.
PERICLES   T'is most certaine.
CERIMON
   Looke to the Ladie, O shee's but oer-joyde,
   Earlie on blustering morne this Ladie
   Was throwne vpon this shore. I op't the coffin,
   Found there rich Iewells, recouer'd her, and plac'ste
2310   her
   Heere in *Dianaes* temple.
PERICLES   May we see them?
CERIMON
   Great Sir, they shalbe brought you to my house,
   Whither I inuite you, looke *Thaysa* is
   Recouered.
THAYSA   O let me looke vpon him!
   If hee be none of mine, my sanctitie

Will to my sense bende no licentious eare,
But curbe it spight of seeing: O my Lord
Are you not *Pericles*? like him you spake,
Like him you are, did you not name a tempest,
A birth, and death?   2320
PERICLES The voyce of dead *Thaisa*.
THAYSA That *Thaisa*
   Am I, supposed dead and drownd.
PERICLES ⌜*taking Thaysas hand*⌝ Imortall *Dian*.
THAYSA Now I knowe you better,
   When wee with teares parted *Pentapolis*,
   The king my father gaue you such a ring.
PERICLES
   This, this, no more, you gods, your present kindenes
   Makes my past miseries sports, you shall doe well
   That on the touching of her lips I may   2330
   Melt, and no more be seene, O come, be buried
   A second time within these armes.
      ⌜*They embrace, and kisse*⌝
MARINA (*kneeling to Thaisa*)   My heart
   Leaps to be gone into my mothers bosome.
PERICLES
   Looke who kneeles here, flesh of thy flesh *Thaisa*,
   Thy burden at the Sea, and call'd *Marina*,
   For she was yeelded there.
THAYSA ⌜*embracing Marina*⌝ Blest, and mine owne.
HELICANUS ⌜*kneeling to Thaysa*⌝
   Hayle Madame, and my Queene.
THAYSA   I knowe you not.
PERICLES
   You haue heard mee say when I did flie from *Tyre*,
   I left behind an ancient substitute,
   Can you remember what I call'd the man,   2340
   I haue nam'de him oft.
THAYSA T'was *Hellicanus* then.
PERICLES Still confirmation,
   Imbrace him deere *Thaisa*, this is hee,
   Now doe I long to heare how you were found?
   How possiblie preseru'd? and who to thanke
   (Besides the gods) for this great miracle?
THAYSA
   Lord *Cerimon*, my Lord, this is the man
   Through whom the Gods haue showne their pow'r,
      that can
   From first to last resolue you.
PERICLES (*to Cerimon*)   Reuerent Syr,   2350
   The gods can haue no mortall officer
   More like a god then you, will you deliuer
   How this dead Queene reliues?
CERIMON   I will my Lord,
   Beseech you first, goe with mee to my house,
   Where shall be showne you all was found with her,
   And tolde how in this Temple shee came plac'ste,
   No needfull thing omitted.
PERICLES   Pure *Diana*
   I blesse thee for thy vision, and will offer
   Nightly oblations to thee; belou'd *Thaisa*,
   This Prince, the faire betrothed of your daughter,   2360
   At *Pentapolis* shall marrie her,

(*To Marina*) And now this ornament
Makes mee looke dismall, will I clip to forme,
And what this fourteene yeeres no razer touch't,
To grace thy marridge-day, Ile beautifie.

THAYSA

Lord *Cerimon* hath letters of good credit,
Sir, from Pentapolis; my father's dead.

PERICLES

Heau'n make a Starre of him, yet there my Queene,
Wee'le celebrate their Nuptialls, and our selues
2370   Will in that kingdome spend our following daies,
Our sonne and daughter shall in *Tyrus* raigne.
Lord *Cerimon* wee doe our longing stay,
To heare the rest vntolde, Sir lead's the way.

                            Exeunt ⌈all but Gower⌉

GOWER

In *Antiochus* and his daughter you haue heard
Of monstrous lust, the due and iust reward:

In *Pericles*, his Queene and Daughter seene,
Although assayl'de with *Fortune* fierce and keene,
Vertue preserud from fell destructions blast,
Led on by heau'n, and crown'd with ioy at last.
In *Helycanus* may you well descrie,   2380
A figure of trueth, of faith, of loyaltie:
In reuerend *Cerimon* there well appeares,
The worth that learned charitie aye weares.
For wicked *Cleon* and his wife, when Fame
Had spred thir cursed deede to th' honor'd name
Of *Pericles*, to rage the Cittie turne,
That him and his they in his Pallace burne:
The gods for murder seemed so content,
To punish them, although not done, but meant.
So on your Patience euermore attending,   2390
New ioy wayte on you, heere our play has ending.

                                            Exit

FINIS

ADDITIONAL PASSAGE

Q gives this more expansive version of Marina's Epitaph
(1761–4):

The fairest, sweetest, best lyes heere,
Who withred in her spring of yeare:
She was of Tyrus the Kings daughter,

On whom fowle death hath made this slaughter.
Marina was shee call'd, and at her byrth,
Thetis being prowd, swallowed some part ath'earth:
Therefore the earth fearing to be ore-flowed,
Hath Thetis byrth-childe on the heau'ns bestowed.
Wherefore she does and sweares sheele neuer stint,
Make raging Batt'ry vpon shores of flint.   10

A DIPLOMATIC REPRINT OF 'PERICLES' (1609)

THE text which follows reproduces as exactly as possible the uncorrected state of the first edition of *Pericles*. It preserves the spelling, punctuation, italicization, and capitalization of that edition; it also reproduces ligatures and the use of 'vv' for 'w'.

For ease of reference, each page is identified by a signature; as is normal in quartos of the period, the original does not mark versos at all, or the final recto of each sheet; nor does it provide a signature for the title-page ('A1'). Blank pages are not reproduced. Beneath each signature reference we identify the compositor believed to have set the page: X worked in the shop of William White; Y and Z in the shop of Thomas Creede. For two pages (F3, F4ᵛ) the compositor is uncertain: it was either Y or a fourth workman. In addition to this signature information, each type line is numbered consecutively.

We do not reproduce the catchwords, which merely duplicate at the bottom right of each page the first words on the next, except in the following cases: *king.* (D3), *1.Sayl.* Sir (E2), *Cler.* I (E4ᵛ), *Bawd.* (F4ᵛ), *Cle.* (G1ᵛ), *Gower.* (G3, uncorrected state), golde, (G4ᵛ), Hoe (H4ᵛ).

We do not preserve differences in type size, or in the exact face of different types. We have placed a space after all punctuation marks: the practice of the original is erratic. We have tried to reproduce anomalies of spacing (or the lack of it) between words and letters; but sometimes the original is ambiguous. We have not attempted to indicate spacing around stage directions, such as the use of blank lines above or below directions, or the exact indentation of stage directions on the page. Nor do we preserve the ornaments on the title-page and A2, or the ornamental letter which begins the first word of Gower's first speech.

The reprint is based upon collation of the Bodleian copy, supplemented by consultation of a facsimile of the Huntington copy, and of the published record of press variants in all nine known copies.

A Diplomatic Reprint of
Pericles (1609)

THE LATE,
And much admired Play,
Called
Pericles, Prince
of Tyre.
With the true Relation of the whole Hiſtorie,
aduentures, and fortunes of the ſaid Prince:
As alſo,
The no leſſe ſtrange, and worthy accidents,
in the Birth and Life, of his Daughter
MARIANA.
As it hath been diuers and ſundry times acted by
his Maieſties Seruants, at the Globe on
the Banck-ſide.
By William Shakeſpeare.
Imprinted at London for *Henry Goſſon*, and are
to be ſold at the ſigne of the Sunne in
Pater-noſter row, &c.
1609.

The Play of Pericles
Prince of Tyre. &c.
Enter Gower.
To ſing a Song that old was ſung,
From aſhes, auntient *Gower* is come,
Aſſuming mans infirmities,
To glad your eare, and pleaſe your eyes:
It hath been ſung at Feaſtiuals,
On Ember eues, and Holydayes:
And Lords and Ladyes in their liues,
Haue red it for reſtoratiues:
The purchaſe is to make men glorious,
Et bonum quo Antiquius eo melius:
If you, borne in thoſe latter times,
When Witts more ripe, accept my rimes;
And that to heare an old man ſing,
May to your Wiſhes pleaſure bring:
I life would wiſh, and that I might
Waſte it for you, like Taper light.
This *Antioch*, then *Antiochus* the great,
Buylt vp this Citie, for his chiefeſt Seat;
The fayreſt in all *Syria*.
I tell you what mine Authors ſaye:
This King vnto him tooke a Peere,
Who dyed, and left a female heyre,
So buckſome, blith, and full of face,
As heauen had lent her all his grace:
With whom the Father liking tooke,
And her to Inceſt did prouoke:
Bad child, worſe father, to intice his owne

To euill, ſhould be done by none:
But cuſtome what they did begin,
Was with long vſe, account'd no ſinne;
The beautie of this ſinfull Dame,
Made many Princes thither frame,
To ſeeke her as a bedfellow,
In maryage pleaſures, playfellow:

Which to preuent, he made a Law,
To keepe her ſtill, and men in awe:
That who ſo askt her for his wife,
His Riddle tould, not loſt his life:
So for her many of wight did die,
As yon grimme lookes do teſtifie.
What now enſues, to the iudgement of your eye,
I giue my cauſe, who beſt can iuſtifie. *Exit.*
Enter Antiochus, Prince Pericles, and followers.
Anti. Young Prince of *Tyre*, you haue at large receiued
The danger of the taske you vndertake.
Peri. I haue (*Antiochus*) and with a ſoule emboldned
With the glory of her prayſe, thinke death no hazard,
In this enterprise.
Ant. Muſicke bring in our daughter, clothed like a bride,
For embracements euen of *Ioue* himſelfe;
At whoſe conception, till *Lucina* rained,
Nature this dowry gaue; to glad her preſence,
The Seanate houſe of Planets all did ſit,
To knit in her, their beſt perfections.
Enter Antiochus daughter.
Per. See where ſhe comes, appareled like the Spring,
Graces her ſubiects, and her thoughts the King,
Of euery Vertue giues renowne to men:
Her face the booke of prayſes, where is read,
Nothing but curious pleaſures, as from thence,
Sorrow were euer racte, and teaſtie wrath
Could neuer be her milde companion.

You Gods that made me man, and ſway in loue;
That haue enflamde deſire in my breaſt,
To taſte the fruite of yon celeſtiall tree,
(Or die in th'aduenture) be my helpes,
As I am ſonne and ſeruant to your will,
To compaſſe ſuch a bondleſſe happineſſe.
Anti. Prince *Pericles*.
Peri. That would be ſonne to great *Antiochus*.
Ant. Before thee ſtandes this faire *Heſperides*,
With golden fruite, but dangerous to be toucht:
For Death like Dragons heere affright thee hard:
Her fa ce like Heauen, inticeth thee to view
Her countleſſe glory; which deſert muſt gaine:
And which without deſert, becauſe thine eye
Preſumes to reach, all the whole heape muſt die:
Yon ſometimes famous Princes, like thy ſelfe,
Drawne by report, aduentrous by deſire,
Tell thee with ſpeachleſſe tongues, and ſemblance pale,
That without couering, ſaue yon field of Starres,
Heere they ſtand Martyrs ſlaine in *Cupids* Warres:
And with dead cheekes, aduiſe thee to deſiſt,
For going on deaths net, whom none reſiſt.
Per. Antiochus, I thanke thee, who hath taught,
My frayle mortalitie to know it ſelfe;
And by thoſe fearefull obiectes, to prepare
This body, like to them, to what I muſt:
For Death remembered ſhould be like a myrrour,
Who tels vs, life's but breath, to truſt it errour:
Ile make my Will then, and as ſickemen doe,
Who know the World, ſee Heauen, but feeling woe,
Gripe not at earthly ioyes as earſt they did;

So I bequeath a happy peace to you,
And all good men, as euery Prince fhould doe;
My ritches to the earth, from whence they came;
But my vnfpotted fire of Loue, to you:
120 Thus ready for the way of life or death,
I wayte the fharpeft blow (*Antiochus*)

A3v
(X)
Scorning aduice; read the conclufion then:
Which read and not expounded, tis decreed,
As thefe before thee, thou thy felfe fhalt bleed.
   Daugh. Of all fayd yet, mayft thou prooue profperous,
Of all fayd yet, I wifh thee happineffe.
   Peri. Like a bold Champion I affume the Liftes,
Nor aske aduife of any other thought,
But faythfulneffe and courage.

130   *The Riddle.*
   I am no Viper, yet I feed
   On mothers flefh which did me breed:
   I fought a Hufband, in which labour,
   I found that kindneffe in a Father;
   Hee's Father, Sonne, and Hufband milde;
   I, Mother, Wife; and yet his child:
   How they may be, and yet in two,
   As you will liue refolue it you.
Sharpe Phificke is the laft: But ô you powers!
140 That giues heauen countleffe eyes to view mens actes,
Why cloude they not their fights perpetually,
If this be true, which makes me pale to read it?
Faire Glaffe of light, I lou'd you, and could ftill,
Were not this glorious Casket ftor'd with ill:
But I muft tell you, now my thoughts reuolt,
For hee's no man on whom perfections waite,
That knowing finne within, will touch the gate.
You are a faire Violl, and your fenfe, the ftringes;
Who finger'd to make man his lawfull muficke,
150 Would draw Heauen downe, and all the Gods to harken:
But being playd vpon before your time,
Hell onely daunceth at fo harfh a chime:
Good footh, I care not for you.
   Ant. Prince *Pericles*, touch not, vpon thy life;
For that's an Article within our Law,
As dangerous as the reft: your time's expir'd,
Either expound now, or receiue your fentence.

A4
(X)
   Peri. Great King,
Few loue to heare the finnes they loue to act,
160 T'would brayde your felfe too neare for me to tell it:
Who has a booke of all that Monarches doe,
Hee's more fecure to keepe it fhut, then fhowne.
For Vice repeated, is like the wandring Wind,
Blowes duft in others eyes to fpread it felfe;
And yet the end of all is bought thus deare,
The breath is gone, and the fore eyes fee cleare:
To ftop the Ayre would hurt them, the blind Mole caftes
Copt hilles towards heauen, to tell the earth is throng'd
By mans oppreffion, and the poore Worme doth die for't:
170 Kinges are earths Gods; in vice, their law's their will:
And if *Ioue* ftray, who dares fay, *Ioue* doth ill:
It is enough you know, and it is fit;
What being more knowne, growes worfe, to fmother it.
All loue the Wombe that their firft beeing bred,
Then giue my tongue like leaue, to loue my head. (ning:
   Ant. Heauen, that I had thy head; he ha's found the mea-
But I will gloze with him. Young Prince of *Tyre,*
Though by the tenour of your ftrict edict,
Your expofition mifinterpreting,
180 We might proceed to counfell of your dayes;
Yet hope, fucceeding from fo faire a tree

As your faire felfe, doth tune vs otherwife;
Fourtie dayes longer we doe refpite you,
If by which time, our fecret be vndone,
This mercy fhewes, wee'le ioy in fuch a Sonne:
And vntill then, your entertaine fhall bee
As doth befit our honour and your worth.
           Manet Pericles folus.
   Peri. How courtefie would feeme to couer finne,
When what is done, is like an hipocrite, 190
The which is good in nothing but in fight.
If it be true that I interpret falfe,
Then were it certaine you were not fo bad,
As with foule Inceft to abufe your foule:

A4v
(X)
Where now you both a Father and a Sonne,
By your vntimely clafpings with your Child,
(Which pleafures fittes a husband, not a father)
And fhee an eater of her Mothers flefh,
By the defiling of her Parents bed,
And both like Serpents are; who though they feed 200
On fweeteft Flowers, yet they Poyfon breed.
Antioch farewell, for Wifedome fees thofe men,
Blufh not in actions blacker then the night,
Will fhew no courfe to keepe them from the light:
One finne (I know) another doth prouoke;
Murther's as neere to Luft, as Flame to Smoake:
Poyfon and Treafon are the hands of Sinne,
I, and the targets to put off the fhame,
Then leaft my life be cropt, to keepe you cleare,
By flight, Ile fhun the danger which I feare.   *Exit.* 210
          Enter Antiochus.
   Anti. He hath found the meaning.
For which we meane to haue his head:
He muft not liue to trumpet foorth my infamie,
Nor tell the world *Antiochus* doth finne
In fuch a loathed manner:
And therefore inftantly this Prince muft die,
For by his fall, my honour muft keepe hie.
Who attends vs there?
          Enter Thaliard. 220
   Thali. Doth your highnes call?
   Antio. Thaliard, you are of our Chamber, *Thaliard,*
And our minde pertakes her priuat actions,
To your fecrecie; and for your faythfulnes,
We will aduaunce you, *Thaliard:*
Behold, heere's Poyfon, and heere's Gold:
Wee hate the Prince of *Tyre,* and thou muft kill him;
It fittes thee not to aske the reafon why?
Becaufe we bid it: fay, is it done?
   Thali. My Lord, tis done. 230

B1
(Y)
         Enter a Meffenger.
   Anti. Enough. Let your breath coole your felfe, telling
your hafte.
   Meff. My Lord, Prince *Pericles* is fled.
   Antin. As thou wilt liue flie after, and like an arrow fhot
from a well experienft Archer hits the marke his eye doth
leuell at: fo thou neuer returne vnleffe thou fay Prince *Pe-*
ricles is dead.
   Thal. My Lord, if I can get him within my Piftols
length, Ile make him fure enough, fo farewell to your 240
highneffe.
Thaliard adieu, till *Pericles* be dead,
My heart can lend no fuccour to my head.
        Enter Pericles with his Lords.
   Pe. Let none difturb vs, why fhold this chãge of thoughts
The fad companion dull eyde melancholie,
By me fo vfde a gueft, as not an houre

In the dayes glorious walke or peacefull night,
The tombe where griefe ſtould ſleepe can breed me quiet,
250 Here pleaſures court mine eies, and mine eies ſhun them,
And daunger which I fearde is at *Antioch*,
Whoſe arme ſeemes farre too ſhort to hit me here,
Yet neither pleaſures Art can ioy my ſpirits,
Nor yet the others diſtance comfort me,
Then it is thus, the paſſions of the mind,
That haue their firſt conception by miſdread,
Haue after nouriſhment and life, by care
And what was firſt but feare, what might be done,
Growes elder now, and cares it be not done.
260 And ſo with me the great *Antiochus*,
Gainſt whom I am too little to contend,
Since hee's ſo great, can make his will his act,
Will thinke me ſpeaking, though I ſweare to ſilence,
Nor bootes it me to ſay, I honour,
If he ſuſpect I may diſhonour him.

B1v
(Y)
And what may make him bluſh in being knowne,
Heele ſtop the courſe by which it might be knowne,
With hoſtile forces heele ore-ſpread the land,
And with the ſtint of warre will looke ſo huge,
270 Amazement ſhall driue courage from the ſtate,
Our men be vanquiſht ere they doe reſiſt,
And ſubiects puniſht that nere thought offence,
Which care of them, not pittie of my ſelfe,
Who once no more but as the tops of trees,
Which fence the rootes they grow by and defend them,
Makes both my bodie pine, and ſoule to languiſh,
And puniſh that before that he would puniſh.
                Enter all the Lords to Pericles.
      1. *Lord.* Ioy and all comfort in your ſacred breſt.
280 2. *Lord.* And keepe your mind till you returne to vs
peacefull and comfortable.
      Hel. Peace, peace, and giue experience tongue,
They doe abuſe the King that flatter him,
For flatterie is the bellowes blowes vp ſinne,
The thing the which is flattered, but a ſparke,
To which that ſparke giues heate, and ſtronger
Glowing, whereas reproofe obedient and in order,
Fits kings as they are men, for they may erre,
When *ſignior* ſooth here does proclaime peace,
290 He flatters you, makes warre vpon your life.
Prince paadon me, or ſtrike me if you pleaſe,
I cannot be much lower then my knees.
      Per. All leaue vs elſe: but let your cares ore-looke,
What ſhipping, and what ladings in our hauen,
And then returne to vs, *Hellicans* thou haſt
Mooude vs, what ſeeſt thou in our lookes?
      Hel. An angrie brow, dread Lord.
      Per. If there be ſuch a dart in Princes frownes,
How durſt thy tongue moue anger to our face?
300 *Hel.* How dares the plants looke vp to heauen,

B2
(Y)
From whence they haue their nouriſhment?
      Per. Thou knoweſt I haue power to take thy life from
      Hel. I haue ground the Axe my ſelfe,   (thee.
Doe but you ſtrike the blowe.
      Per. Riſe, prethee riſe, ſit downe, thou art no flatterer,
I thanke thee fort, and heaue forbid
That kings ſhould let their eares heare their faults hid.
Fit Counſellor, and ſeruant for a Prince,
Who by thy wiſdome makes a Prince thy ſeruant,
310 What wouldſt thou haue me doe?
      Hel. To beare with patience ſuch griefes as you your
ſelfe doe lay vpon your ſelfe.

      Per. Thou ſpeakſt like a Phyſition *Hellicanus*,
That miniſters a potion vnto me:
That thou wouldſt tremble to receiue thy ſelfe,
Attend me then, I went to *Antioch*,
Whereas thou knowſt againſt the face of death,
I ſought the purchaſe of a glorious beautie,
From whence an iſſue I might propogate,
Are armes to Princes, and bring ioies to ſubiects,   320
Her face was to mine eye beyond all wonder,
The reſt harke in thine eare, as blacke as inceſt,
Which by my knowledge found, the ſinful father
Seemde not to ſtrike, but ſmooth, but thou knowſt this,
Tis time to feare when tyrants ſeemes to kiſſe.
Which feare ſo grew in me I hither fled,
Vnder the couering of a carefull night,
Who ſeemd my good protector, and being here,
Bethought what was paſt, what might ſucceed,
I knew him tyrannous, and tyrants feare   330
Decreaſe not, but grow faſter then the yeares,
And ſhould he doo't, as no doubt he doth,
That I ſhould open to the liſtning ayre,
How many worthie Princes blouds were ſhed,
To keepe his bed of blackneſſe vnlayde ope,

B2v
(Y)
To lop that doubt, hee'le fill this land with armes,
And make pretence of wrong that I haue done him,
When all for mine, if I may call offence,
Muſt feel wars blow, who ſpares not innocence,   340
Which loue to all of which thy ſelfe art one,
Who now reprou'dſt me fort.
      Hell. Alas ſir.
      Per. Drew ſleep out of mine eies, blood frõ my cheekes,
Muſings into my mind, with thouſand doubts
How I might ſtop this tempeſt ere it came,
And finding little comfort to relieue them,
I thought it princely charity to griue for them.
      Hell. Well my Lord, ſince you haue giuen mee leaue to
Freely will I ſpeake, *Antiochus* you feare,   (ſpeake,
And iuſtly too, I thinke you feare the tyrant,   350
Who either by publike warre, or priuat treaſon,
Will take away your life: therfore my Lord, go trauell for
a while, till that his rage and anger be forgot, or till the De-
ſtinies doe cut his threed of life: your rule direct to anie,
if to me, day ſerues not light more faithfull then Ile be.
      Per. I doe not doubt thy faith.
But ſhould he wrong my liberties in my abſence?
      Hel. Weele mingle our bloods togither in the earth,
From whence we had our being, and our birth.
      Per. *Tyre* I now looke from thee then, and to *Tharſus*   360
Intend my trauaile, where Ile heare from thee,
And by whoſe Letters Ile diſpoſe my ſelfe.
The care I had and haue of ſubiects good,
On thee I lay, whoſe wiſdomes ſtrength can beare it,
Ile take thy word, for faith not aske thine oath,
Who ſhuns not to breake one, will cracke both.
But in our orbs will liue ſo round, and ſafe,
That time of both this truth ſhall nere conuince,
Thou ſhewdſt a ſubiects ſhine, I a true Prince.   *Exit.*

B3
(Z)
            Enter Thaliard ſolus.
      So this is *Tyre*, and this the Court, heere muſt I kill   371
King *Pericles*, and if I doe it not, I am ſure to be hang'd at
home: t'is daungerous.
      Well, I perceiue he was a wiſe fellowe, and had good
diſcretion, that beeing bid to aske what hee would of the
King, deſired he might knowe none of his ſecrets.
      Now doe I ſee hee had ſome reaſon for't: for if a

king bidde a man bee a villaine, hee's bound by the indenture of his oath to bee one.
380   Huſht, heere comes the Lords of *Tyre*.
*Enter Hellicanus, Eſcanes, with
other Lords.*
Helli. You ſhall not neede my fellow-Peers of *Tyre*,
further to queſtion mee of your kings departure: his ſea-
led Commiſſion left in truſt with mee, does ſpeake ſuffici-
ently hee's gone to trauaile.
Thaliard. How? the King gone?
Hell. If further yet you will be ſatisfied, (why as it
were vnlicenſed of your loues) he would depart? Ile giue
390   ſome light vnto you, beeing at *Antioch*.
Thal. What from *Antioch*?
Hell. Royall *Antiochus* on what cauſe I knowe not,
tooke ſome diſpleaſure at him, at leaſt hee iudg'de ſo: and
doubting leſt hee had err'de or ſinn'de, to ſhewe his ſorrow,
hee'de correct himſelfe; ſo puts himſelfe vnto the Ship-
mans toyle, with whome each minute threatens life or
death.
Thaliard. Well, I perceiue I ſhall not be hang'd now,
although I would, but ſince hee's gone, the Kings ſeas
400   muſt pleaſe: hee ſcap'te the Land to periſh at the Sea, I'le
preſent my ſelfe. Peace to the Lords of *Tyre*.

B3v
(Z)   Lord *Thaliard* from *Antiochus* is welcome.
Thal. From him I come with meſſage vnto princely
Pericles, but ſince my landing, I haue vnderſtood your Lord
has betake himſelfe to vnknowne trauailes, now meſſage
muſt returne from whence it came.
Hell. Wee haue no reaſon to deſire it, commended
to our maiſter not to vs, yet ere you ſhall depart, this wee
deſire as friends to *Antioch* wee may feaſt in *Tyre*.   Exit.
410   *Enter Cleon the Gouernour of Tharſus, with
his wife and others.*
Cleon. My *Dyoniza* ſhall wee reſt vs heere,
And by relating tales of others griefes,
See if t'will teach vs to forget our owne?
Dion. That were to blow at fire in hope to quench it,
For who digs hills becauſe they doe aſpire?
Throwes downe one mountaine to caſt vp a higher:
O my diſtreſſed Lord, euen ſuch our griefes are,
Heere they are but felt, and ſeene with miſchiefs eyes,
420   But like to Groues, being topt, they higher riſe.
Cleon. O *Dioniza*.
Who wanteth food, and will not ſay hee wants it,
Or can conceale his hunger till hee famiſh?
Our toungs and ſorrowes to ſound deepe:
Our woes into the aire, our eyes to weepe.
Till toungs feteh breath that may proclaime
Them louder, that if heauen ſlumber, while
Their creatures want, they may awake
Their helpers, to comfort them.
430   Ile then diſcourſe our woes felt ſeuerall yeares,
And wanting breath to ſpeake, helpe mee with teares.
Dyoniza. Ile doe my beſt Syr.   (ment,
Cleon. This *Tharſus* ore which I haue the gouerne-
A Cittie on whom plentie held full hand:
For riches ſtrew'de her ſelfe euen in her ſtreetes,

B4
(Z)   Whoſe towers bore heads ſo high they kiſt the clowds,
And ſtrangers nere beheld, but wondred at,
Whoſe men and dames ſo jetted and adorn'de,
Like one anothers glaſſe to trim them by,
440   Their tables were ſtor'de full to glad the ſight,
And not ſo much to feede on as delight,
All pouertie was ſcor'nde, and pride ſo great,
The name of helpe grewe odious to repeat.

Dion. O t'is too true.
Cle. But ſee what heauen can doe by this our change,
Theſe mouthes who but of late, earth, ſea, and ayre,
Were all too little to content and pleaſe,
Although thy gaue their creatures in abundance,
As houſes are defil'de for want of vſe,
450   They are now ſtaru'de for want of exerciſe,
Thoſe pallats who not yet too ſauers younger,
Muſt haue inuentions to delight the taſt,
Would now be glad of bread and beg for it,
Thoſe mothers who to nouzell vp their babes,
Thought nought too curious, are readie now
To eat thoſe little darlings whom they lou'de,
So ſharpe are hungers teeth, that man and wife,
Drawe lots who firſt ſhall die, to lengthen life.
Heere ſtands a Lord, and there a Ladie weeping:
460   Heere manie ſincke, yet thoſe which ſee them fall,
Haue ſcarce ſtrength left to giue them buryall.
Is not this true?
Dion. Our cheekes and hollow eyes doe witneſſe it.
Cle. O let thoſe Cities that of plenties cup,
And her proſperities ſo largely taſte,
With their ſuperfluous riots heare theſe teares,
The miſerie of *Tharſus* may be theirs.
Enter a Lord.
Lord. Wheres the Lord Gouernour?
Cle. Here, ſpeake out thy ſorrowes, which thee bringſt 470

B4v
(Z)
in haſt, for comfort is too farre for vs to expect.
Lord. Wee haue deſcryed vpon our neighbouring
ſhore, a portlie ſaile of ſhips make hitherward.
Cleon. I thought as much.
One ſorrowe neuer comes but brings an heire,
That may ſuccede as his inheritor:
And ſo in ours, ſome neighbouring nation,
Taking aduantage of our miſerie,
That ſtuff't the hollow veſſels with their power,
480   To beat vs downe, the which are downe alreadie,
And make a conqueſt of vnhappie mee,
Whereas no glories got to ouercome.
Lord. That's the leaſt feare.
For by the ſemblance of their white flagges diſplayde, they
bring vs peace, and come to vs as fauourers, not as foes.
Cleon. Thou ſpeak'ſt like himnes vntuterd to repeat,
Who makes the faireſt ſhowe, meanes moſt deceipt.
But bring they what they will, and what they can,
What need wee leaue our grounds the loweſt?
And wee are halfe way there: Goe tell their Generall wee 490
attend him heere, to know for what he comes, and whence
he comes, and what he craues?
Lord. I goe my Lord.
Cleon. Welcome is peace, if he on peace conſiſt,
If warres, wee are vnable to reſiſt.
Enter Pericles with attendants.
Per. Lord Gouernour, for ſo wee heare you are,
Let not our Ships and number of our men,
Be like a beacon fier'de, t'amaze your eyes,
Wee haue heard your miſeries as farre as *Tyre*,   500
And ſeene the deſolation of your ſtreets,
Nor come we to adde ſorrow to your teares,
But to relieue them of their heauy loade,
And theſe our Ships you happily may thinke,

C1
(X)
Are like the Troian Horſe, was ſtuft within
With bloody veines expecting ouerthrow,
Are ſtor'd with Corne, to make your needie bread,
And giue them life, whom hunger-ſtaru'd halfe dead.
Omnes. The Gods of *Greece* protect you,
And wee'le pray for you.   510

Per. Arife I pray you, rife; we do not looke for reuerence,
But for loue, and harborage for our felfe, our fhips, & men.
  Cleon. The which when any fhall not gratifie,
Or pay you with vnthankfulneffe in thought,
Be it our Wiues, our Children, or our felues,
The Curfe of heauen and men fucceed their euils:
Till when the which (I hope) fhall neare be feene:
Your Grace is welcome to our Towne and vs.
  Peri. Which welcome wee'le accept, feaft here awhile,
520 Vntill our Starres that frowne, lend vs a fmile.   *Exeunt.*

──────────────────────

Enter Gower.
Heere haue you feene a mightie King,
His child I'wis to inceft bring:
A better Prince, and benigne Lord,
That Will proue awfull both in deed and word:
Be quiet then, as men fhould bee,
Till he hath paft necefsitie:
I'le fhew you thofe in troubles raigne;
Loofing a Mite, a Mountaine gaine:
530 The good in conuerfation,
To whom I giue my benizon:
Is ftill at *Tharftill*, where each man,
Thinkes all is writ, he fpoken can:
And to remember what he does,
Build his Statue to make him glorious:
But tidinges to the contrarie,
Are brought your eyes, what need fpeake I.

Dombe fhew.
  Enter at one dore Pericles *talking with* Cleon, *all the traine*
540   *with them: Enter at an other dore, a Gentleman with a*
      Letter to Pericles, Pericles *fhewes the Letter to* Cleon;
      Pericles *giues the Meffenger a reward, and Knights him:*
      Exit Pericles *at one dore, and* Cleon *at an other.*
Good *Helicon* that ftayde at home,
Not to eate Hony like a Drone,
From others labours; for though he ftriue
To killen bad, keepe good aliue:
And to fulfill his prince defire,
Sau'd one of all that haps in *Tyre*:
550 How *Thaliart* came full bent with finne,
And hid in Tent to murdred him;
And that in *Tharfis* was not beft,
Longer for him to make his reft:
He doing fo, put foorth to Seas;
Where when men been there's feldome eafe,
For now the Wind begins to blow,
Thunder aboue, and deepes below,
Makes fuch vnquiet, that the Shippe,
Should houfe him fafe; is wrackt and fplit,
560 And he (good Prince) hauing all loft,
By Waues, from coaft to coaft is toft:
All perifhen of man of pelfe,
Ne ought efcapend but himfelfe;
Till Fortune tir'd with doing bad,
Threw him a fhore, to giue him glad:
And heere he comes: what fhall be next,
Pardon old *Gower*, this long's the text.
        Enter Pericles wette.
  Peri. Yet ceafe your ire you angry Starres of heauen,
570 Wind, Raine, and Thunder, remember earthly man
Is but a fubftaunce that muft yeeld to you:
And I (as fits my nature) do obey you.

Alaffe, the Seas hath caft me on the Rocks,
Wafht me from fhore to fhore, and left my breath
Nothing to thinke on, but enfuing death:

Let it fuffize the greatneffe of your powers,
To haue bereft a Prince of all his fortunes;
And hauing throwne him from your watry graue,
Heere to haue death in peace, is all hee'le craue.
        Enter three Fifher-men.   580
  1. What, to pelch?
  2. Ha, come and bring away theNets.
  1. What Patch-breech, I fay.
  3. What fay you Maifter?
  1. Looke how thou ftirr'ft now:
Come away, or Ile fetch'th with a wanion.
  3. Fayth Maifter, I am thinking of the poore men,
That were caft away before vs euen now.
  1. Alaffe poore foules, it grieued my heart to heare,
What pittifull cryes they made to vs, to helpe them,   590
When (welladay) we could fcarce helpe our felues.
  3. Nay Maifter, fayd not I as much,
When I faw the Porpas how he bounft and tumbled?
They fay they're halfe fifh, halfe flefh:
A plague on them, they nere come but I looke to be wafht.
Maifter, I maruell how the Fifhes liue in the Sea?
  1. Why, as Men doe a-land;
The great ones eate vp the little ones:
I can compare our rich Mifers to nothing fo fitly,
As to a Whale; a playes and tumbles,   600
Dryuing the poore Fry before him,
And at laft, deuowre them all at a mouthfull:
Such Whales haue I heard on, a'th land,
Who neuer leaue gaping, till they fwallow'd
The whole Parifh, Church, Steeple, Belles and all.
  Peri. A prettie morall.
  3. But Maifter, if I had been the Sexton,
I would haue been that day in the belfrie.
  2. Why, Man?

  1. Becaufe he fhould haue fwallowed mee too,
And when I had been in his belly,
I would haue kept fuch a iangling of the Belles,
That he fhould neuer haue left,
Till he caft Belles, Steeple, Church and Parifh vp againe:
But if the good King *Simonides* were of my minde.
  Per. *Simonides*?
  3. We would purge the land of thefe Drones,
That robbe the Bee of her Hony.
  Per. How from the fenny fubiect of the Sea,
Thefe Fifhers tell the infirmities of men,   620
And from their watry empire recollect,
All that may men approue, or men detect.
Peace be at your labour, honeft Fifher-men.
  2. Honeft good fellow what's that, if it be a day fits you
Search out of the Kalender, and no body looke after it?
  Peri. May fee the Sea hath caft vpon your coaft:
  2. What a drunken Knaue was the Sea,
To caft thee in our way?
  Per. A man whom both the Waters and the Winde,
In that vaft Tennis-court, hath made the Ball   630
For them to play vpon, intreates you pittie him:
Hee askes of you, that neuer vs'd to begge.
  1. No friend, cannot you begge?
Heer's them in our countrey of *Greece*,
Gets more with begging, then we can doe with working.
  2. Canft thou catch any Fifhes then?
  Peri. I neuer practizde it.
  2. Nay then thou wilt ftarue fure: for heer's nothing to
be got now-adayes, vnleffe thou canft fifh for't.
  Per. What I haue been, I haue forgot to know;   640
But what I am, want teaches me to thinke on:
A man throng'd vp with cold, my Veines are chill,
And haue no more of life then may fuffize,

To giue my tongue that heat to aske your helpe:
Which if you ſhall refuſe, when I am dead,
For that I am a man, pray you ſee me buried.

C3
(X)

   1. Die, ke-tha; now Gods forbid't, and I haue a Gowne
heere, come put it on, keepe thee warme: now afore mee a
handſome fellow: Come, thou ſhalt goe home, and wee'le
650 haue Fleſh for all day, Fiſh for faſting-dayes and more; or
Puddinges and Flap-iackes, and thou ſhalt be welcome.
   Per. I thanke you ſir.
   2. Harke you my friend: You ſayd you could not beg?
   Per. I did but craue.
   2. But craue?
Then Ile turne Crauer too, and ſo I ſhall ſcape whipping.
   Per. Why, are you Beggers whipt then?
   2. Oh not all, my friend, not all: for if all your Beggers
were whipt, I would wiſh no better office, then to be Beadle:
660 But Maiſter, Ile goe draw vp the Net.
   Per. How well this honeſt mirth becomes their labour?
   1. Harke you ſir; doe you know vvhere yee are?
   Per. Not well.
   1. Why Ile tell you, this I cald *Pantapoles,*
And our King, the good *Symonides.*
   Per. The good *Symonides,* doe you call him?
   1. I ſir, and he deſerues ſo to be cal'd,
For his peaceable raigne, and good gouernement.
   Per. He is a happy King, ſince he gaines from
670 His ſubiects the name of good, by his gouernment.
How farre is his Court diſtant from this ſhore?
   1. Mary ſir, halfe a dayes iourney: And Ile tell you,
He hath a faire Daughter, and to morrow is her birth-day,
And there are Princes and Knights come from all partes of
the World, to Iuſt and Turney for her loue.
   Per. Were my fortunes equall to my deſires,
I could wiſh to make one there.
   1. O ſir, things muſt be as they may: and what a man can
not get, he may lawfully deale for his Wiues ſoule.
680   *Enter the two Fiſher-men, drawing vp a Net.*
   2. Helpe Maiſter helpe; heere's a Fiſh hanges in the Net,
Like a poore mans right in the law: t'will hardly come out.
Ha bots on't, tis come at laſt; & tis turnd to a ruſty Armour.

C3v
(X)

   Per. An Armour friends; I pary you let me ſee it.
Thankes Fortune, yeat that after all croſſes,
Thou giueſt me ſomewhat to repaire my ſelfe:
And though it was mine owne part of my heritage,
Which my dead Father did bequeath to me,
With this ſtrict charge euen as he left his life,
690 Keepe it my *Perycles,* it hath been a Shield
Twixt me and death, and poynted to this brayſe,
For that it ſaued me, keepe it in like neceſsitie:
The which the Gods protect then, Fame may defend thee:
It kept where I kept, I ſo dearely lou'd it,
Till the rough Seas, that ſpares not any man,
Tooke it in rage, though calm'd, haue giuen't againe:
I thanke thee for't, my ſhipwracke now's no ill,
Since I haue heere my Father gaue in his Will.
   1. What meane you ſir?
700   *Peri.* To begge of you (kind friends) this Coate of worth,
For it was ſometime Target to a King;
I know it by this marke: he loued me dearely,
And for his ſake, I wiſh the hauing of it;
And that you'd guide me to your Soueraignes Court,
Where with it, I may appeare a Gentleman:
And if that euer my low fortune's better,
Ile pay your bounties; till then, reſt your debter.
   1. Why wilt thou turney for the Lady?
   Peri. Ile ſhew the vertue I haue borne in Armes.

   1. Why di'e take it: and the Gods giue thee good an't.   710
   2. I but harke you my friend, t'was wee that made vp
this Garment through the rough ſeames of the Waters:
there are certaine Condolements, certaine Vailes: I hope
ſir, if you thriue, you'le remember from whence you had
them.
   Peri. Beleeue't, I will:
By your furtherance I am cloth'd in Steele,
And ſpight of all the rupture of the Sea,
This Iewell holdes his buylding on my arme:
Vnto thy value I will mount my ſelfe   720

C4
(X)

Vpon a Courſer, whoſe delight ſteps,
Shall make the gazer ioy to ſee him tread;
Onely (my friend) I yet am vnprouided of a paire of Baſes.
   2. Wee'le ſure prouide, thou ſhalt haue
My beſt Gowne to make thee a paire;
And Ile bring thee to the Court my ſelfe.
   Peri. Then Honour be but a Goale to my Will,
This day Ile riſe, or elſe adde ill to ill.
       Enter Simonydes, with attendaunce, and Thaiſa.
   King. Are the Knights ready to begin the Tryumph?   730
   1. *Lord.* They are my Leidge, and ſtay your comming,
To preſent them ſelues.
   King. Returne them, We are ready, & our daughter heere,
In honour of whoſe Birth, theſe Triumphs are,
Sits heere like Beauties child, whom Nature gat,
For men to ſee; and ſeeing, woonder at.
   Thai. It pleaſeth you (my royall Father) to expreſſe
My Commendations great, whoſe merit's leſſe.
   King. It's fit it ſhould be ſo, for Princes are
A modell which Heauen makes like to it ſelfe: 740
As Iewels looſe their glory, if neglected,
So Princes their Renownes, if not reſpected:
T'is now your honour (Daughter) to entertaine
The labour of each Knight, in his deuice.
   Thai. Which to preſerue mine honour, I'le performe.
       The firſt Knight paſſes by.
   King. Who is the firſt, that doth preferre himſelfe?
   Thai. A Knight of *Sparta* (my renowned father)
And the deuice he beares vpon his Shield,
Is a blacke Ethyope reaching at the Sunne: 750
The word: *Lux tua vita mihi.*
   King. He loues you well, that holdes his life of you.
       The ſecond Knight.
Who is the ſecond, that preſents himſelfe?

C4v
(X)

   Tha. A Prince of *Macedon* (my royall father)
And the deuice he beares vpon his Shield,
Is an Armed Knight, that's conquered by a Lady:
The motto thus in Spaniſh. *Pue Per doleera kee per forſa.*
   3. *Knight. Kin.* And with the third?
   Thai. The third, of *Antioch;* and his deuice,   760
A wreath of Chiually: the word: *Me Pompey prouexit apex.*
   4. *Knight. Kin.* What is the fourth.
   Thai. A burning Torch that's turned vpſide downe;
The word: *Qui me alit me extinguit.*
   Kin. Which ſhewes that Beautie hath his power & will,
Which can as well enflame, as it can kill.
   5. *Knight. Thai.* The fift, an Hand enuironed with Clouds,
Holding out Gold, that's by the Touch-ſtone tride:
The motto thus: *Sic ſpectanda fides.*
   6. *Knight. Kin.* And what's the ſixt, and laſt; the which,   770
The knight himſelf with ſuch a graceful courteſie deliuered?
   Thai. Hee ſeemes to be a Stranger: but his Preſent is
A withered Branch, that's onely greene at top,
The motto: *In hac ſpe viuo.*

Kin. A pretty morrall frō the deiected ſtate wherein he is,
He hopes by you, his fortunes yet may flouriſh.

   1. Lord. He had need meane better, then his outward ſhew
Can any way ſpeake in his iuſt commend:
For by his ruſtie outſide, he appeares,
780   To haue practis'd more the Whipſtocke, then the Launce.

   2. Lord. He well may be a Stranger, for he comes
To an honour'd tryumph, ſtrangly furniſht.

   3. Lord. And on ſet purpoſe let his Armour ruſt
Vntill this day, to ſcowre it in the duſt.

   Kin. Opinion's but a foole, that makes vs ſcan
The outward habit, by the inward man.
But ſtay, the Knights are comming,
We will with-draw into the Gallerie.

       Great ſhoutes, and all cry, the meane Knight.

D1
(X)
       Enter the King and Knights from Tilting.
791   *King.* Knights, to ſay you're welcome, were ſuperfluous.
I place vpon the volume of your deedes,
As in a Title page, your worth in armes,
Were more then you expect, or more then's fit,
Since euery worth in ſhew commends it ſelfe:
Prepare for mirth, for mirth becomes a Feaſt.
You are Princes, and my gueſtes.

   Thai. But you my Knight and gueſt,
800 To whom this Wreath of victorie I giue,
And crowne you King of this dayes happineſſe.

   Peri. Tis more by Fortune (Lady) then my Merit.

   King. Call it by what you will, the day is your,
And here (I hope) is none that enuies it:
In framing an Artiſt, art hath thus decreed,
To make ſome good, but others to exceed,
And you are her labour'd ſcholler: come Queene a th'feaſt,
For (Daughter) ſo you are; heere take your place:
Martiall the reſt, as they deſerue their grace.

   Knights. We are honour'd much by good *Symonides.*

810   *King.* Your preſence glads our dayes, honour we loue,
For who hates honour, hates the Gods aboue.

   Marſhal. Sir, yonder is your place.

   Peri. Some other is more fit.

   1. Knight. Contend not ſir, for we are Gentlemen,
Haue neither in our hearts, nor outward eyes,
Enuies the great, nor ſhall the low deſpiſe.

   Peri. You are right courtious Knights.

   King. Sit ſir, ſit.
By *Ioue* (I wonder) that is King of thoughts,
820 Theſe Cates reſiſt mee, hee not thought vpon.

   Tha. By *Iuno* (that is Queene of mariage)
All Viands that I eate do ſeeme vnſauery,
Wiſhing him my meat: ſure hee's a gallant Gentleman.

   Kin. Hee's but a countrie Gentleman: ha's done no more
Then other Knights haue done, ha's broken a Staffe,

D1v
(X)
Or ſo; ſo let it paſſe.

   Tha. To mee he ſeemes like Diamond, to Glaſſe.

   Peri. You Kings to mee, like to my fathers picture,
Which tels in that glory once he was,
830 Had Princes ſit like Starres about his Throane,
And hee the Sunne for them to reuerence;
None that beheld him, but like leſſer lights,
Did vaile their Crownes to his ſupremacie;
Where now his ſonne like a Gloworme in the night,
The which hath Fire in darkneſſe, none in light:
Whereby I ſee that Time's the King of men,
Hee's both their Parent, and he is their Graue,
And giues them what he will, not what they craue.

   King. What, are you merry, Knights?

840   *Knights.* Who can be other, in this royall preſence.

   King. Heere, with a Cup that's ſtur'd vnto the brim,
As do you loue, fill to your Miſtris lippes,
Wee drinke this health to you.

   Knights. We thanke your Grace.

   King. Yet pauſe awhile, yon Knight doth ſit too melan-
As if the entertainement in our Court,   (choly,
Had not a ſhew might counteruaile his worth:
Note it not you, *Thaiſa.*

   Tha. What is't to me, my father?

   king. O attend my Daughter,   850
Princes in this, ſhould liue like Gods aboue,
Who freely giue to euery one that come to honour them:
And Princes not doing ſo, are like to Gnats,
Which make a ſound, but kild, are wondred at:
Therefore to make his entraunce more ſweet,
Heere, ſay wee drinke this ſtanding boule of wine to him.

   Tha. Alas my Father, it befits not mee,
Vnto a ſtranger Knight to be ſo bold,
He may my profer take for an offence,
Since men take womens giftes for impudence.   860

   king. How? doe as I bid you, or you'le mooue me elſe.

   Tha. Now by the Gods, he could not pleaſe me better.

D2
(X)
   king. And furthermore tell him, we deſire to know of him
Of whence he is, his name, and Parentage?

   Tha. The King my father (ſir) has drunke to you.

   Peri. I thanke him.

   Tha. Wiſhing it ſo much blood vnto your life.

   Peri. I thanke both him and you, and pledge him freely.

   Tha. And further, he deſires to know of you,
Of whence you are, your name and parentage?   870

   Peri. A Gentleman of *Tyre*, my name *Pericles*,
My education beene in Artes and Armes:
Who looking for aduentures in the world,
Was by the rough Seas reft of Ships and men,
and after ſhipwracke, driuen vpon this ſhore.

   Tha. He thankes your Grace; names himſelfe *Pericles*,
A Gentleman of *Tyre*: who onely by misfortune of the ſeas,
Bereft of Shippes and Men, caſt on this ſhore.

   king. Now by the Gods, I pitty his misfortune,
And will awake him from his melancholy.   880
Come Gentlemen, we ſit too long on trifles,
And waſte the time which lookes for other reuels:
Euen in your Armours as you are addreſt,
Will well become a Souldiers daunce:
I will not haue excuſe with ſaying this,
Lowd Muſicke is too harſh for Ladyes heads,
Since they loue men in armes, as well as beds.

        They daunce.
So, this was well askt, t'was ſo well perform'd.
Come ſir, heer's a Lady that wants breathing too,   890
And I haue heard, you Knights of *Tyre*,
Are excellent in making Ladyes trippe;
And that their Meaſures are as excellent.

   Peri. In thoſe that practize them, they are (my Lord.)

   king. Oh that's as much, as you would be denyed
Of your faire courteſie: vnclaſpe, vnclaſpe.

        They daunce.
Thankes Gentlemen to all, all haue done well;
But you the beſt: Pages and lights, to conduct

D2v
(X)
Theſe Knights vnto their ſeuerall Lodgings:
Yours ſir, we haue giuen order be next our owne.   901

   Peri. I am at your Graces pleaſure.

   Princes, it is too late to talke of Loue,
And that's the marke I know, you leuell at:
Therefore each one betake him to his reſt,
To morrow all for ſpeeding do their beſt:

Enter Hellicanus and Efcanes.

Hell. No *Efcanes*, know this of mee,

Antiochus from inceſt liued not free:

910　For which the moſt high Gods not minding,

Longer to with-hold the vengeance that

They had in ſtore, due to this heynous

Capitall offence, euen in the height and pride

Of all his glory, when he was ſeated in

A Chariot of an ineſtimable value, and his daughter

With him; a fire from heauen came and ſhriueld

Vp thoſe bodyes euen to lothing, for they ſo ſtounke,

That all thoſe eyes ador'd them, ere their fall,

Scorne now their hand ſhould giue them buriall.

920　*Efcanes.* T'was very ſtrange.

Hell. And yet but iuſtice; for though this King were great,

His greatneſſe was no gard to barre heauens ſhaft,

But ſinne had his reward.

Efcan. Tis very true.

Enter two or three Lords.

1. Lord. See, not a man in priuate conference,

Or counſaile, ha's reſpect with him but hee.

2. Lord. It ſhall no longer grieue, without reprofe.

3. Lord. And curſt be he that will not ſecond it.

930　*1. Lord.* Follow me then: Lord *Hellicane*, a word.

Hell. With mee? and welcome happy day, my Lords.

1. Lord. Know, that our griefes are riſen to the top,

And now at length they ouer-flow their bankes.

Hell. Your griefes, for what?

Wrong not your Prince, you loue.

1. Lord. Wrong not your ſelfe then, noble *Hellican*,

But if the Prince do liue, let vs ſalute him,

Or know what ground's made happy by his breath:

If in the world he liue, wee'le ſeeke him out:

940　If in his Graue he reſt, wee'le find him there,

And be reſolued he liues to gouerne vs:

Or dead, giue's cauſe to mourne his funerall,

And leaue vs to our free election.

2. Lord. Whoſe death in deed, the ſtrongeſt in our ſenſure,

And knowing this Kingdome is without a head,

Like goodly Buyldings left without a Roofe,

Soone fall to ruine: your noble ſelfe,

That beſt know how to rule, and how to raigne,

Wee thus ſubmit vnto our Soueraigne.

950　*Omnes.* Liue noble *Hellicane.*

Hell. Try honours cauſe; forbeare your ſuffrages:

If that you loue Prince *Pericles*, forbeare,

(Take I your wiſh, I leape into the ſeas,

Where's howerly trouble, for a minuts eaſe)

A twelue-month longer, let me intreat you

To forbeare the abſence of your King;

If in which time expir'd, he not returne,

I ſhall with aged patience beare your yoake:

But if I cannot winne you to this loue,

960　Goe ſearch like nobles, like noble ſubiects,

And in your ſearch, ſpend your aduenturous worth,

Whom if you find, and winne vnto returne,

You ſhall like Diamonds ſit about his Crowne.

1. Lord. To wiſedome, hee's a foole, that will not yeeld:

And ſince Lord *Hellicane* enioyneth vs,

We with our trauels will endeauour.

Hell. Then you loue vs, we you, & wee'le claſpe hands:

When Peeres thus knit, a Kingdome euer ſtands.

Enter the King reading of a letter at one doore,

the Knightes meete him.

970　*1. Knight.* Good morrow to the good *Simonides.*

King. Knights, from my daughter this I let you know,

That for this twelue-month, ſhee'le not vndertake

A maried life: her reaſon to her ſelfe is onely knowne,

Which from her, by no meanes can I get.

2. Knight. May we not get acceſſe to her (my Lord?)

king. Fayth, by no meanes, ſhe hath ſo ſtrictly

Tyed her to her Chamber, that t'is impoſſible:

One twelue Moones more ſhee'le weare *Dianas* liuerie:

This by the eye of *Cinthya* hath ſhe vowed,

980　And on her Virgin honour, will not breake it.

3. knight. Loth to bid farewell, we take our leaues.

king. So, they are well diſpatcht:

Now to my daughters Letter; ſhe telles me heere,

Shee'le wedde the ſtranger Knight,

Or neuer more to view nor day nor light.

T'is well Miſtris, your choyce agrees with mine:

I like that well: nay how abſolute ſhe's in't,

Not minding whether I diſlike or no.

Well, I do commend her choyce, and will no longer

990　Haue it be delayed: Soft, heere he comes,

I muſt diſſemble it.

Enter Pericles.

Peri. All fortune to the good *Symonides.*

King. To you as much: Sir, I am behoulding to you

For your ſweete Muſicke this laſt night:

I do proteſt, my eares were neuer better ſedde

With ſuch delightfull pleaſing harmonie.

Peri. It is your Graces pleaſure to commend,

Not my deſert.

1000　*king.* Sir, you are Muſickes maiſter.

Peri. The worſt of all her ſchollers (my good Lord.)

king. Let me aſke you one thing:

What do you thinke of my Daughter, ſir?

Peri. A moſt vertuous Princeſſe.

king. And ſhe is faire too, is ſhe not?

Peri. As a faire day in Sommer: woondrous faire.

king. Sir, my Daughter thinkes very well of you,

I ſo well, that you muſt be her Maiſter,

And ſhe will be your Scholler; therefore looke to it.

1010　*Peri.* I am vnworthy for her Scholemaiſter.

king. She thinkes not ſo: peruſe this writing elſe.

Per. What's here, a letter that ſhe loues the knight of *Tyre*?

T'is the Kings ſubtiltie to haue my life:

Oh ſeeke not to intrappe me, gracious Lord,

A Stranger, and diſtreſſed Gentleman,

That neuer aymed ſo hie, to loue your Daughter,

But bent all offices to honour her.

king. Thou haſt bewitcht my daughter,

And thou art a villaine.

1020　*Peri.* By the Gods I haue not; neuer did thought

Of mine leuie offence; nor neuer did my actions

Yet commence a deed might gaine her loue,

Or your diſpleaſure.

king. Traytor, thou lyeſt.

Peri. Traytor?

king. I, traytor.

Peri. Euen in his throat, vnleſſe it be the King,

That cals me Traytor, I returne the lye.

king. Now by the Gods, I do applaude his courage.

1030　*Peri.* My actions are as noble as my thoughts,

That neuer reliſht of a baſe diſcent:

I came vnto your Court for Honours cauſe,

And not to be a Rebell to her ſtate:

And he that otherwiſe accountes of mee,

This Sword ſhall prooue, hee's Honours enemie.

king. No? heere comes my Daughter, ſhe can witneſſe it.

Enter Thaiſa.

Peri. Then as you are as vertuous, as faire,

Reſolue your angry Father, if my tongue　1040

Did ere folicite, or my hand fubfcribe
To any fillable that made loue to you?
   Thai. Why fir, fay if you had, who takes offence?

D4v
(X)
At that, would make me glad?
   King. Yea Miftris, are you fo peremptorie?
I am glad on't with all my heart,
Ile tame you; Ile bring you in fubieftion.   *Afide.*
Will you not, hauing my confent,
Beftow your loue and your affeftions,
1050 Vpon a Stranger? who for ought I know,
May be (nor can I thinke the contrary)   *Afide.*
As great in blood as I my felfe:
Therefore, heare you Miftris, either frame
Your will to mine: and you fir, heare you;
Either be rul'd by mee, or Ile make you,
Man and wife: nay come, your hands,
And lippes muft feale it too: and being ioynd,
Ile thus your hopes deftroy, and for further griefe:
God giue you ioy; what are you both pleafed?
1060 *Tha.* Yes, if you loue me fir?
   Peri. Euen as my life, my blood that fofters it.
   King. What are you both agreed?
   Ambo. Yes, if't pleafe your Maieftie.
   King. It pleafeth me fo well, that I will fee you wed,
And then with what hafte you can, get you to bed.   *Exeunt.*

              Enter Gower.
Now fleepe yflacked hath the rout,
No din but fnores about the houfe,
Made louder by the orefed breaft,
1070 Of this moft pompous maryage Feaft:
The Catte with eyne of burning cole,
Now coutches from the Moufes hole;
And Cricket fing at the Ouens mouth,
Are the blyther for their drouth:
Hymen hath brought the Bride to bed,
Whereby the loffe of maydenhead,
A Babe is moulded: be attent,

E1
(X)
And Time that is fo briefly fpent,
With your fine fancies quaintly each,
1080 What's dumbe in fhew, I'le plaine with fpeach.
   Enter Pericles *and* Symonides *at one dore with attendantes,*
     a Meffenger meetes them, kneeles and giues Pericles *a letter,*
     Pericles *fhewes it* Symonides, *the Lords kneele to him;*
     then enter Thayfa *with child, with* Lichorida *a nurfe,*
     the King fhewes her the letter, fhe reioyces: fhe and Pericles
     take leaue of her father, and depart.
By many a dearne and painefull pearch
Of *Perycles* the carefull fearch,
By the fower oppofing Crignes,
1090 Which the world togeather ioynes,
Is made with all due diligence,
That horfe and fayle and hie expence,
Can fteed the queft at laft from *Tyre*:
Fame anfwering the moft ftrange enquire,
To'th Court of King *Symonides,*
Are Letters brought, the tenour thefe:
Antiochus and his daughter dead,
The men of *Tyrus,* on the head
Of *Helycanus* would fet on
1100 The Crowne of *Tyre,* but he will none:
The mutanie, hee there haftes t'oppreffe,
Sayes to'em, if King *Pericles*
Come not home in twife fixe Moones,
He obedient to their doomes,

Will take the Crowne: the fumme of this,
Brought hither to *Penlapolis,*
Iranyfhed the regions round,
And euery one with claps can found,
Our heyre apparant is a King:
Who dreampt? who thought of fuch a thing?   1110
Briefe he muft hence depart to *Tyre,*
His Queene with child, makes her defire,

E1v
(X)
Which who fhall croffe along to goe,
Omit we all their dole and woe:
Lichorida her Nurfe fhe takes,
And fo to Sea; their veffell fhakes,
On *Neptunes* billow, halfe the flood,
Hath their Keele cut: but fortune mou'd,
Varies againe, the grifled North
Difgorges fuch a tempeft forth,   1120
That as a Ducke for life that diues,
So vp and downe the poore Ship driues:
The Lady fhreekes, and wel-a-neare,
Do's fall in trauayle with her feare:
And what enfues in this fell ftorme,
Shall for it felfe, it felfe performe:
I nill relate, aftion may
Conueniently the reft conuay;
Which might not? what by me is told,
In your imagination hold: 1130
This Stage, the Ship, vpon whofe Decke
The feas toft *Pericles* appeares to fpeake.
       Enter Pericles a Shipboard.
   Peri. The God of this great Vaft, rebuke thefe furges,
Which wafh both heauen and hell, and thou that haft
Vpon the Windes commaund, bind them in Braffe;
Hauing call'd them from the deepe, ô ftill
Thy deafning dreadfull thunders, gently quench
Thy nimble fulphirous flafhes: ô How *Lychorida!*
How does my Queene? then ftorme venomoufly,   1140
Wilt thou fpeat all thy felfe? the fea-mans Whiftle
Is as a whifper in the eares of death,
Vnheard *Lychorida? Lucina,* oh!
Diuineft patrioneffe, and my wife gentle
To thofe that cry by night, conuey thy deitie
Aboard our dauncing Boat, make fwift the pangues
Of my Queenes trauayles? now *Lychorida.*

E2
(X)
        Enter Lychorida.
   Lychor. Heere is a thing too young for fuch a place,
Who if it had conceit, would die, as I am like to doe: 1150
Take in your armes this peece of your dead Queene.
   Peri. How? how *Lychorida?*
   Lycho. Patience (good fir) do not afsift the ftorme,
Heer's all that is left liuing of your Queene;
A litle Daughter: for the fake of it,
Be manly, and take comfort.
   Per. O you Gods!
Why do you make vs loue your goodly gyfts,
And fnatch them ftraight away? we heere below,
Recall not what we giue, and therein may   1160
Vfe honour with you.
   Lycho. Patience (good fir) euen for this charge.
   Per. Now mylde may be thy life,
For a more blufterous birth had neuer Babe:
Quiet and gentle thy conditions; for
Thou art the rudelyeft welcome to this world,
That euer was Princes Child: happy what followes,
Thou haft as chiding a natiuitie,
As Fire, Ayre, Water, Earth, and Heauen can make,
To harould thee from the wombe: 1170

Euen at the firſt, thy loſſe is more then can
Thy portage quit, with all thou canſt find heere:
Now the good Gods throw their beſt eyes vpon't.
     Enter two Saylers.
 1. Sayl. What courage ſir? God ſaue you.
 Per. Courage enough, I do not feare the flaw,
It hath done to me me the worſt: yet ſor the loue
Of this poore Infant, this freſh new ſea-farer,
I would it would be quiet.
 1. Sayl. Slake the bolins there; thou wilt not wilt thou:
Blow and ſplit thy ſelſe.
 2. Sayl. But Sea-roome, and the brine and cloudy billow
Kiſſe the Moone, I care not.

 1. Sir your Queene muſt ouer board, the ſea workes hie,
The Wind is lowd, and will not lie till the Ship
Be cleard of the dead.
 Per. That's your ſuperſtition.
 1. Pardon vs, ſir; with vs at Sea it hath bin ſtill obſerued.
And we are ſtrong in eaſterne, therefore briefly yeeld'er,
 Per. As you thinke meet; for ſhe muſt ouer board ſtraight:
Moſt wretched Queene
 Lychor. Heere ſhe lyes ſir.
 Peri. A terrible Child-bed haſt thou had (my deare,
No light, no fire, th'vnfriendly elements,
Forgot thee vtterly, nor haue I time
To giue thee hallowd to thy graue, but ſtraight,
Muſt caſt thee ſcarcly Coffind, in oare,
Where for a monument vpon thy bones,
The ayre remayning lampes, the belching Whale,
And humming Water muſt orewelme thy corpes,
Lying with ſimple ſhels: ô *Lychorida,*
Bid *Neſtor* bring me Spices, Incke, and Taper,
My Casket, and my Iewels; and bid *Nicander*
Bring me the Sattin Coffin: lay the Babe
Vpon the Pillow; hie thee whiles I ſay
A prieſtly farewell to her: ſodainely, woman.
 2. Sir, we haue a Chiſt beneath the hatches,
Caulkt and bittumed ready.
 Peri. I thanke thee: Mariner ſay, what Coaſt is this?
 2. Wee are neere *Tharſus.*
 Peri. Thither gentle Mariner,
Alter thy courſe for *Tyre:* When canſt thou reach it?
 2. By breake of day, if the Wind ceaſe.
 Peri. O make for *Tharſus,*
There will I viſit *Cleon,* for the Babe
Cannot hold out to *Tyrus*; there Ile leaue it
At careſull nurſing: goe thy wayes good Mariner,
Ile bring the body preſently.   *Exit.*

    Enter Lord Cerymon with a ſeruant.
 Cery. *Phylemon,* hoe.
     Enter Phylemon.
 Phyl. Doth my Lord call?
 Cery. Get Fire and meat for theſe poore men,
T'as been a turbulent and ſtormie night.
 Seru. I haue been in many; but ſuch a night as this,
Till now, I neare endured.
 Cery. Your Maiſter will be dead ere you returne,
There's nothing can be miniſtred to Nature,
That can recouer him: giue this to the Pothecary,
And tell me how it workes.
     Enter two Gentlemen.
 1. Gent. Good morrow.
 2. Gent. Good morrow to your Lordſhip,
 Cery. Gentlemen, why doe you ſtirre ſo early?
 1. Gent. Sir, our lodgings ſtanding bleake vpon the ſea,
Shooke as the earth did quake:

The very principals did ſeeme to rend and all to topple:
Pure ſurprize and feare, made me to quite the houſe.
 2. Gent. That is the cauſe we trouble you ſo early,
T'is not our husbandry.
 Cery. O you ſay well.
 1. Gent. But I much maruaile that your Lordſhip,
Hauing rich tire about you, ſhould at theſe early howers,
Shake off the golden ſlumber of repoſe; tis moſt ſtrange
Nature ſhould be ſo conuerſant with Paine,
Being thereto not compelled.
 Cery. I hold it euer Vertue and Cunning,
Were endowments greater, then Nobleneſſe & Riches;
Careleſſe Heyres, may the two latter darken and expend;
But Immortalitie attendes the former,
Making a man a god:
T'is knowne, I euer haue ſtudied Phyſicke:
Through which ſecret Art, by turning ore Authorities,

I haue togeather with my practize, made famyliar,
To me and to my ayde, the bleſt infuſions that dwels
In Vegetiues, in Mettals, Stones: and can ſpeake of the
Diſturbances that Nature works, and of her cures;
which doth giue me a more content in courſe of true delight
Then to be thirſty after tottering honour, or
Tie my pleaſure vp in ſilken Bagges,
To pleaſe the Foole and Death.
 2. Gent. Your honour has through *Epheſus,*
Poured foorth your charitie, and hundreds call themſelues,
Your Creatures; who by you, haue been reſtored;
And not your knowledge, your perſonall payne,
But euen your Purſe ſtill open, hath built Lord *Cerimon,*
Such ſtrong renowne, as time ſhall neuer.
    Enter two or three with a Chiſt.
 Seru. So, lift there.
 Cer. What's that?
 Ser. Sir, euen now did the ſea toſſe vp vpon our ſhore
This Chiſt; tis of ſome wracke.
 Cer. Set't downe, let's looke vpon't.
 2. Gent. T'is like a Coffin, ſir.
 Cer. What ere it be, t'is woondrous heauie;
Wrench it open ſtraight:
If the Seas ſtomacke be orecharg'd with Gold,
T'is a good conſtraint of Fortune it belches vpon vs.
 2. Gent. T'is ſo, my Lord.
 Cer. How cloſe tis caulkt & bottomed, did the ſea caſt it vp?
 Ser. I neuer ſaw ſo huge a billow ſir, as toſt it vpon ſhore.
 Cer. Wrench it open ſoft; it ſmels moſt ſweetly in my ſenſe.
 2. Gent. A delicate Odour.
 Cer. As euer hit my noſtrill: ſo, vp with it.
Oh you moſt potent Gods! what's here, a Corſe?
 2. Gent. Moſt ſtrange.
 Cer. Shrowded in Cloth of ſtate, balmed and entreaſured
with full bagges of Spices, a Paſport to *Apollo,* perfect mee
in the Characters:

Heere I giue to vnderſtand,
If ere this Coffin driues aland;
I King Pericles haue loſt
This Queene, worth all our mundaine coſt:
Who finds her, giue her burying,
She was the Daughter of a King:
Beſides, this Treaſure for a fee,
The Gods requit his charitie.
If thou liueſt *Pericles,* thou haſt a heart,
That euer cracks for woe, this chaunc'd to night.
 2. Gent. Moſt likely ſir.
 Cer. Nay certainely to night, for looke how freſh ſhe looks

    1180

    E2v
    (X)

    1190

    1200

    1210

    E3
    (X)
    1220

    1230

    1240

    1250

    E3v
    (X)

    1260

    1270

    1280

    E4
    (X)
    1291

    1300

They were too rough, that threw her in the sea.
Make a Fire within; fetch hither all my Boxes in my Closet,
Death may vsurpe on Nature many howers, and yet
The fire of life kindle againe the ore-prest spirits:
I heard of an *Egiptian* that had 9. howers lien dead,
Who was by good applyaunce recouered.

        Enter one with Napkins and Fire.

1310   Well sayd, well sayd; the fire and clothes: the rough and
Wofull Musick that we haue, cause it to sound beseech you:
The Violl once more; how thou stirr'st thou blocke?
The Musicke there: I pray you giue her ayre:
Gentlemen, this Queene will liue,
Nature awakes a warmth breath out of her;
She hath not been entranc'st aboue fiue howers:
See how she ginnes to blow into lifes flower againe.

    1. Gent. The Heauens, through you, encrease our wonder,
And sets vp your fame for euer.

    Cer. She is aliue, behold her ey-lids,
1320   Cases to those heauenly iewels which *Pericles* hath lost,
Begin to part their fringes of bright gold,
The Diamonds of a most praysed water doth appeare,
To make the world twise rich, liue, and make vs weepe.
To heare your fate, faire creature, rare as you seeme to bee.

        Shee moues.

    Thai. O deare *Diana*, where am I? where's my Lord?

E4v
(X)   What world is this?

    2. Gent. Is not this strange?   *1. Gent.* Most rare.

    Ceri. Hush (my gentle neighbours) lend me your hands,
1330   To the next Chamber beare her: get linnen:
Now this matter must be lookt to for her relapse
Is mortall: come, come; and *Escelapius* guide vs.

        They carry her away. Exeunt omnes.
    Enter Pericles, Atharsus, with Cleon and Dionisa.

    Per. Most honor'd *Cleon*, I must needs be gone, my twelue
months are expir'd, and *Tyrus* standes in a litigious peace:
You and your Lady take from my heart all thankfulnesse,
The Gods make vp the rest vpon you.

    Cle. Your shakes of fortune, though they hant you mor-
1340   Yet glaunce full wondringly on vs.   (tally

    Di. O your sweet Queene! that the strict fates had pleas'd,
you had brought her hither to haue blest mine eies with her.

    Per. We cannot but obey the powers aboue vs;
Could I rage and rore as doth the sea she lies in,
Yet the end must be as tis: my gentle babe *Marina*,
Whom, for she was borne at sea, I haue named so,
Here I charge your charitie withall; leauing her
The infant of your care, beseeching you to giue her
Princely training, that she may be manere'd as she is borne.

1350   *Cle.* Feare not (my Lord) but thinke your Grace,
That fed my Countrie with your Corne; for which,
The peoples prayers still fall vpon you, must in your child
Be thought on, if neglection should therein make me vile,
The common body by you relieu'd,
Would force me to my duety: but if to that,
My nature neede a spurre, the Gods reuenge it
Vpon me and mine, to the end of generation.

    Per. I beleeue you, your honour and your goodnes,
Teach me too't without your vowes, till she be maried,
1360   Madame, by bright *Diana*, whom we honour,
All vnsisterd shall this heyre of mine remayne,
Though I shew will in't; so I take my leaue:
Good Madame, make me blessed in your care
In bringing vp my Child.

F1
(Y)   *Dion.* I haue one my selfe, who shall not be more deere
to my respect then yours, my Lord.

    Peri. Madam, my thanks and prayers.

    Cler. Weel bring your Grace ene to the edge ath shore,
then giue you vp to the mask'd *Neptune*, and the gentlest
winds of heauen.   1370

    Peri. I will imbrace your offer, come deerest Madame,
O no teares *Licherida*, no teares, looke to your litle Mistris,
on whose grace you may depend hereafter: come my
Lord.

    Enter Cerimon, and Tharsa.

    Cer. Madam, this Letter, and some certaine Iewels,
Lay with you in your Coffer, which are at your command:
Know you the Charecter?

    Thar. It is my Lords, that I was shipt at sea I well remem-
ber, euen on my learning time, but whether there deliue- 1380
red, by the holie gods I cannot rightly say: but since King
Pericles my wedded Lord, I nere shall see againe, a vastall
liuerie will I take me to, and neuer more haue ioy.

    Cler. Madam, if this you purpose as ye speake,
Dianaes Temple is not distant farre,
Where you may abide till your date expire,
Moreouer if you please a Neece of mine,
Shall there attend you.

    Thin. My recompence is thanks, thats all,
Yet my good will is great, though the gift small.   *Exit.* 1390

    Enter Gower.

Imagine *Pericles* arriude at *Tyre*,
Welcomd and setled to his owne desire:
His wofull Queene we leaue at *Ephesus*,
Vnto *Diana* ther's a Votarisse.

F1v
(Y)

Now to *Marina* bend your mind,
Whom our fast growing scene must finde
At *Tharsus*, and by *Cleon* traind
In Musicks letters, who hath gaind
Of education all the grace,   1400
Which makes hie both the art and place
Of generall wonder: but alacke
That monster Enuie oft the wracke
Of earned praise, *Marinas* life
Seeke to take off by treasons knife,
And in this kinde, our *Cleon* hath
One daughter and a full growne wench,
Euen right for marriage light: this Maid
Hight *Philoten*: and it is said
For certaine in our storie, shee   1410
Would euer with *Marina* bee.
Beet when they weaude the sleded silke,
With fingers long, small, white as milke,
Or when she would with sharpe needle wound,
The Cambricke which she made more sound
By hurting it or when too'th Lute
She sung, and made the night bed mute,
That still records with mone, or when
She would with rich and constant pen,
Vaile to her Mistresse *Dian* still,   1420
This *Phyloten* contends in skill
With absolute *Marina*: so
The Doue of *Paphos* might with the crow
Vie feathers white, *Marina* gets
All prayses, which are paid as debts,
And not as giuen, this so darkes
In *Phyloten* all gracefull markes,
That *Cleons* wife with Enuie rare,
A present murderer does prepare
For good *Marina*, that her daughter   1430

F2
(Y)

Might stand peerlesse by this slaughter.
The sooner her vile thoughts to stead,
Lichorida our nurse is dead,

And curfed *Dioniza* hath
The pregnant inftrument of wrath.
Preft for this blow, the vnborne euent,
I doe commend to your content,
Onely I carried winged Time,
Poft one the lame feete of my rime,
1440   Which neuer could I fo conuey,
Vnleffe your thoughts went on my way,
Dioniza does appeare,
With *Leonine* a murtherer.   *Exit.*
            Enter Dioniza, with Leonine.
    Dion. Thy oath remember, thou haft fworne to doo't,
tis but a blowe which neuer fhall bee knowne, thou
canft not doe a thing in the worlde fo foone to yeelde
thee fo much profite: let not confcience which is but
cold, in flaming, thy loue bofome, enflame too nicelie,
1450   nor let pittie which euen women haue caft off, melt thee,
but be a fouldier to thy purpofe.
    Leon. I will doo't, but yet fhe is a goodly creature.
    Dion. The fitter then the Gods fhould haue her.
Here fhe comes weeping for her onely Miftreffe death,
Thou art refolu'de.
    Leon. I am refolude.
            Enter Marina with a Basket of flowers.
    Mari. No: I will rob *Tellus* of her weede to ftrowe
thy greene with Flowers, the yellowes, blewes, the purple
1460   Violets, and Marigolds, fhall as a Carpet hang vpon thy
graue, while Sommer dayes doth laft: Aye me poore maid,

borne in a tempeft, when my mother dide, this world to me
is a lafting ftorme, whirring me from my friends.
    Dion. How now *Marina*, why doe yow keep alone?
How chaunce my daughter is not with you?
Doe not confume your bloud with forrowing,
Haue you a nurfe of me? Lord how your fauours
Changd with this vnprofitable woe:
Come giue me your flowers, ere the fea marre it,
1470   Walke with *Leonine*, the ayre is quicke there,
And it perces and fharpens the ftomacke,
Come *Leonine* take her by the arme, walke with her.
    Mari. No I pray you, Ile not bereaue you of your feruãt.
    Dion. Come, come, I loue the king your father, and your
felfe, with more then forraine heart, wee euery day expect
him here, when he fhall come and find our Paragon to all
reports thus blafted,
He will repent the breadth of his great voyage, blame both
my Lord and me, that we haue taken no care to your beft
1480   courfes, go I pray you, walke and be chearfull once againe,
referue that excellent complexion, which did fteale the
eyes of yong and old. Care not for me, I can goe home a-
lone.
    Mari. Well, I will goe, but yet I haue no defire too it.
    Dion. Come, come, I know tis good for you, walke halfe
an houre *Leonine*, at the leaft, remember what I haue fed.
    Leon. I warrant you Madam.
    Dion. Ile leaue you my fweete Ladie, for a while, pray
walke foftly, doe not heate your bloud, what, I muft haue
1490   care of you.
    Mari. My thanks fweete Madame, Is this wind Wefterlie
that blowes?
    Leon. Southweft.
    Mari. When I was borne the wind was North.
    Leon. Waft fo?
    Mari. My father, as nutfe fes, did neuer feare, but cryed

good fea-men to the Saylers, galling his kingly hands haling ropes, and clafping to the Maft, endured a fea that almoft burft the decke.
1500   *Leon.* When was this?

    Mari. When I was borne, neuer was waues nor winde
more violent, and from the ladder tackle, wafhes off a canuas clymer, ha fes one, wolt out? and with a dropping in-
duftrie they skip from fterne to fterne, the Boatfwaine
whiftles, and the Maifter calles and trebles their confufion.
    Leon. Come fay your prayers.
    Mari. What meane you?
    Leon. If you require a little fpace for praier, I graunt it,
pray, but bee not tedious, for the Gods are quicke of eare,
and I am fworne to do my worke with hafte.   1510
    Mari. Why will you kill me?
    Leon. To fatisfie my Ladie.
    Mari. Why would fhee haue mee kild now? as I can re-
member by my troth, I neuer did her hurt in all my life, I
neuer fpake bad worde, nor did ill turne to anie liuing creature: Beleeue me law, I neuer killd a Moufe, nor hurt a Fly:
I trode vpon a worme againft my will, but I wept fort. How
haue I offended, wherein my death might yeeld her anie
profit, or my life imply her any danger?
    Leon. My Commiffion is not to reafon of the deed, but   1520
doo't.
    Mari. You will not doo't for all the world I hope: you
are well fauoured, and your lookes forefhew you haue a
gentle heart, I faw you latelie when you caught hurt in parting two that fought: good footh it fhewde well in you, do
fo now, your Ladie feekes my lifeCome, you betweene, and
faue poore mee the weaker.
    Leon. I am fworne and will difpatch.   *Enter Pirats.*
    Pirat. 1. Hold villaine.
    Pira. 2. A prize, a prize.   1530
    Pirat. 3. Halfe part mates, halfe part. Come lets haue

her aboord fodainly.
                                            Exit.
            Enter Leonine.
    Leon. Thefe rogueing theeues ferue the great Pyrate
Valdes, and they haue feizd *Marina*, let her goe, ther's no
hope fhee will returne, Ile fweare fhees dead, and throwne
into the Sea, but ile fee further: perhappes they will but
pleafe themfelues vpon her, not carrie her aboord, if fhee
remaine   1540
Whome they haue rauifht, muft by mee be flaine.
                                            Exit.
            Enter the three Bawdes.
    Pander. Boult.
    Boult. Sir.
    Pander. Searche the market narrowely, *Mettelyne* is
full of gallants, wee loft too much much money this mart
by beeing too wenchleffe.
    Bawd. Wee were neuer fo much out of Creatures, we
haue but poore three, and they can doe no more then they   1550
can doe, and they with continuall action, are euen as good
as rotten.
    Pander. Therefore lets haue frefh ones what ere wee pay
for them, if there bee not a confcience to be vfde in euerie
trade, wee fhall neuer profper.
    Bawd. Thou fayft true, tis not our bringing vp of poore
baftards, as I thinke, I haue brought vp fome eleuen.
    Boult. I to eleuen, and brought them downe againe,
but fhall I fearche the market?
    Bawde. What elfe man? the ftuffe we haue, a ftrong   1560
winde will blowe it to peeces, they are fo pittifully fodden.

    Pandor. Thou fayeft true, ther's two vnwholefome a
confcience, the poore *Tranfiluanian* is dead that laye with
the little baggadge.
    Boult. I, fhee quickly poupt him, fhe made him roaft-
meate for wormes, but Ile goe fearche the market.
                                            Exit.

Pand. Three or foure thoufande Checkins were as prettie a proportion to liue quietly, and fo giue ouer.

1570 *Bawd.* Why, to giue ouer I pray you? Is it a fhame to get when wee are olde?

Pand. Oh our credite comes not in like the commoditie, nor the commoditie wages not with the daunger: therefore if in our youthes we could picke vp fome prettie eftate, t'were not amiffe to keepe our doore hatch't, befides the fore tearmes we ftand vpon with the gods, wilbe ftrong with vs for giuing ore.

Bawd. Come other forts offend as well as wee.

1580 *Pand.* As well as wee, I, and better too, wee offende worfe, neither is our profeffion any trade, It's no calling, but heere comes *Boult.*

>   *Enter Boult with the Pirates and Marina.*

Boult. Come your wayes my maifters, you fay fhee's a virgin.

Sayler. O Sir, wee doubt it not.

Boult. Mafter, I haue gone through for this peece you fee, if you like her fo, if not I haue loft my earneft.

Bawd. *Boult,* has fhee anie qualities?

1590 *Boult.* Shee has a good face, fpeakes well, and has excellent good cloathes: theres no farther neceffitie of qualities can make her be refuz'd.

Bawd. What's her price *Boult?*

F4v
(Y?)

Boult. I cannot be bated one doit of a thoufand peeces.

Pand. Well, follow me my maifters, you fhall haue your money prefenly, wife take her in, inftruct her what fhe has to doe, that fhe may not be rawe in her entertainment.

Bawd. *Boult,* take you the markes of her, the colour of her haire, complexion, height, her age, with warrantof her virginitie, and crie; He that wil giue moft fhal haue her firft,

1600 fuch a maydenhead were no cheape thing, if men were as they haue beene: get this done as I command you.

Boult. Performance fhall follow.   *Exit.*

Mar. Alacke that *Leonine* was fo flacke, fo flow, he fhould haue ftrooke, not fpoke, or that thefe Pirates, not enough barbarous, had not oreboord throwne me, for to feeke my mother.

Bawd. Why lament you prettie one?

Mar. That I am prettie.

1610 *Bawd.* Come, the Gods haue done their part in you.

Mar. I accufe them not.

Bawd. You are light into my hands, where you are like to liue.

Mar. The more my fault, to fcape his handes, where I was to die.

Bawd. I, and you fhall liue in peafure.

Mar. No.

Bawd. Yes indeed fhall you, and tafte Gentlemen of all fafhions, you fhall fare well, you fhall haue the difference of all complexions, what doe you ftop your eares?

1620 *Mar.* Are you a woman?

Bawd. What would you haue mee be, and I bee not a woman?

Mar. An honeft woman, or not a woman.

Bawd. Marie whip the Goffeling, I thinke I fhall haue fomething to doe with you, come you'r a young foolifh fapling, and muft be bowed as I would haue you.

Mar. The Gods defend me.

G1
(Y)

1630 *Baud.* If it pleafe the Gods to defend you by men, then men muft comfort you, men muft feed you, men ftir you vp: *Boults* returnd. Now fir, haft thou cride her through the Market?

Boult. I haue cryde her almoft to the number of her haires, I haue drawne her picture with my voice.

Baud. And I prethee tell me, how doft thou find the inclination of the people, efpecially of the yonger fort?

Boult. Faith they liftened to mee, as they would haue harkened to their fathers teftament, there was a Spaniards mouth watred, and he went to bed to her verie defcription.

Baud. We fhall haue him here to morrow with his beft ruffe on.   1640

Boult. To night, to night, but Miftreffe doe you knowe the French knight, that cowres ethe hams?

Baud. Who, *Mounfieur Verollus?*

Boult. I, he, he offered to cut a caper at the proclamation, but he made a groane at it, and fwore he would fee her to morrow.

Baud. Well, well, as for him, hee brought his difeafe hither, here he does but repaire it, I knowe hee will come in our fhadow, to fcatter his crownes in the Sunne.

Boult. Well, if we had of euerie Nation a traueller, wee   1650 fhould lodge them with this figne.

Baud. Pray you come hither a while, you haue Fortunes comming vppon you, marke mee, you muft feeme to doe that fearefully, which you commit willingly, defpife profite, where you haue moft gaine, to weepe that you liue as yee doe, makes pittie in your Louers feldome, but that pittie begets you a good opinion, and that opinion a meere profite.

Mari. I vnderftand you not.

Boult. O take her home Miftreffe, take her home, thefe   1660 blufhes of hers muft bee quencht with fome prefent practife.

G1v
(Y)

Mari. Thou fayeft true yfaith, fo they muft, for your Bride goes to that with fhame, which is her way to goe with warrant.

Boult. Faith fome doe, and fome doe not, but Miftreffe if I haue bargaind for the ioynt.

Baud. Thou maift cut a morfell off the fpit.

Boult. I may fo.

Baud. Who fhould denie it?   1670
Come young one, I like the manner of your garments well.

Boult. I by my faith, they fhall not be changd yet.

Baud. *Boult,* fpend thou that in the towne: report what a foiourner we haue, youle loofe nothing by cuftome. When Nature framde this peece, fhee meant thee a good turne, therefore fay what a parragon fhe is, and thou haft the harueft out of thine owne report.

Boult. I warrant you Miftreffe, thunder fhall not fo a-   1680 wake the beds of Eeles, as my giuing out her beautie ftirs vp the lewdly enclined, Ile bring home fome to night.

Baud. Come your wayes, follow me.

Mari. If fires be hote, kniues fharpe, or waters deepe,
Vntide I ftill my virgin knot will keepe.
Diana ayde my purpofe.

Baud. What haue we to doe with *Diana,* pray you will you goe with vs?

>   *Exit.*
>   *Enter Cleon, and Dioniza.*

Dion. Why ere you foolifh, can it be vndone?   1690

Cleon. O *Dioniza,* fuch a peece of flaughter,
The Sunne and Moone nere lookt vpon.

Dion. I thinke youle turne a chidle agen.

G2
(Y)

Cleon. Were I chiefe Lord of all this fpacious world, Ide giue it to vndo the deede. O Ladie much leffe in bloud then vertue, yet a Princes to equall any fingle Crowne ath earthith Iuftice of compare, O villaine, *Leonine* whom thou haft poifned too, if thou hadft drunke to him tad beene a kindneffe becomming well thy face, what canft thou fay when noble *Pericles* fhall demaund his child?   1700

Dion. That fhee is dead. Nurfes are not the fates to fo-
fter it, not euer to preferue, fhe dide at night, Ile fay fo, who
can croffe it vnleffe you play the impious Innocent, and
for an honeft attribute, crie out fhee dyde by foule
play.

Cle. O goe too, well, well, of all the faults beneath the
heauens, the Gods doe like this worft.

Dion. Be one of thofe that thinkes the pettie wrens of
Tharfus will flie hence, and open this to *Pericles,* I do fhame
1710 to thinke of what a noble ftraine you are, and of how coward a fpirit.

Cle. To fuch proceeding who euer but his approbation added, though not his prince confent, he did not flow
from honourable courfes.

Dion. Be it fo then, yet none does knowe but you
how fhee came dead, nor none can knowe *Leonine* being
gone. Shee did difdaine my childe, and ftoode betweene
her and her fortunes: none woulde looke on her, but
1720 caft their gazes on *Marianas* face, whileft ours was blurted at, and helde a Mawkin not worth the time of day.
It pierft me thorow, and though you call my courfe vnnaturall, you not your childe well louing, yet I finde it
greets mee as an enterprize of kindneffe performd to your
fole daughter.

Cle. Heauens forgiue it.

Dion. And as for *Pericles,* what fhould hee fay, we wept
after her hearfe, & yet we mourne, her monument is almoft
finifhed, & her epitaphs in glittring goldĕcharaċters expres

1730 a generrall prayfe to her, and care in vs at whofe expence
tis done.

Cle. Thou art like the Harpie,
Which to betray, doeft with thine Angells face ceaze with
thine Eagles talents.

Dion. Yere like one that fuperfticioufly,
Doe fweare too'th Gods, that Winter kills
The Fliies, but yet I know, youle
doe as I aduife.

Gower. Thus time we wafte, & long leagues make fhort,
1740 Saile feas in Cockles, haue and wifh but fort,
Making to take our imagination,
From bourne to bourne, region to region,
By you being pardoned we commit no crime,
To vfe one language, in each feuerall clime,
Where our fceanes feemes to liue,
I doe befeech you
To learne of me who ftand with gappes
To teach you.
The ftages of our ftorie *Pericles*
Is now againe thwarting thy wayward feas,
1750 Attended on by many a Lord and Knight,
To fee his daughter all his liues delight.
Old *Helicanus* goes along behind,
Is left to gouerne it, you beare in mind.
Old *Efcenes,* whom *Hellicanus* late
Aduancde in time to great and hie eftate.
Well fayling fhips, and bounteous winds
Haue brought
This king to *Tharfus,* thinke this Pilat thought
So with his fterage, fhall your thoughts grone
1760 To fetch his daughter home, who firft is gone
Like moats and fhadowes, fee them
Moue a while,
Your eares vnto your eyes Ile reconcile.

*Enter Pericles at one doore, with all his trayne, Cleon and Dio-
niza at the other. Cleon fhewes Pericles the tombe, whereat Pericles makes lamentation, puts on facke-cloth, and in a mighty
paffion departs.*

Gowr. See how beleefe may fuffer by fowle fhowe,
This borrowed paffion ftands for true olde woe:
And *Pericles* in forrowe all deuour'd,
With fighes fhot through, and biggeft teares ore-fhowr'd.   1770
Leaues *Tharfus,* and againe imbarques, hee fweares
Neuer to wafh his face, nor cut his hayres:
Hee put on fack-cloth, and to Sea he beares,
A Tempeft which his mortall veffell teares.
And yet hee rydes it out, Nowe pleafe you wit:
The Epitaph is for *Marina* writ, by wicked *Dioniza.*

 The faireft, fweeteft, and beft lyes heere,
 Who withered in her fpring of yeare:
 She was of Tyrus the Kings daughter,
 On whom fowle death hath made this flaughter.   1780
 Marina was fhee call'd, and at her byrth,
 Thetis being prowd, fwallowed fome part ath'earth:
 Therefore the earth fearing to be ore-flowed,
 Hath Thetis byrth-childe on the heauens beftowed.
 Wherefore fhe does and fweares fheele neuer ftint,
 Make raging Battery vpon fhores of flint.

No vizor does become blacke villanie,
So well as foft and tender flatterie:
Let *Pericles* beleeue his daughter's dead,   1790
And beare his courfes to be ordered;
By Lady *Fortune,* while our Steare muft play,
His daughters woe and heauie welladay.
In her vnholie feruice: Patience then,
And thinke you now are all in *Mittelin.*

                                        Exit.

Enter two Gentlemen.
 1. *Gent.* Did you euer heare the like?

 2. *Gent.* No, nor neuer fhall doe in fuch a place as this,   1800
fhee beeing once gone.
 1. But to haue diuinitie preach't there, did you euer
dreame of fuch a thing?
 2. No, no, come, I am for no more bawdie houfes, fhall's
goe heare the Veftalls fing?
 1. Ile doe any thing now that is vertuous, but I am out
of the road of rutting for euer.   *Exit.*

Enter Bawdes 3.
Pand. Well, I had rather then twice the worth of her
fhee had nere come heere.

Bawd. Fye, fye, vpon her, fhee's able to freze the god   1810
Priapus, and vndoe a whole generation, we muft either get
her rauifhed, or be rid of her, when fhe fhould doe for Clyents her fitment, and doe mee the kindeneffe of our profeffion, fhee has me her quirks, her reafons, her mafter reafons, her prayers, her knees, that fhee would make a *Puritaine* of the diuell, if hee fhould cheapen a kiffe of her.

Boult. Faith I muft rauifh her, or fhee'le disfurnifh vs
of all our Caualereea, and make our fwearers priefts.

Pand. Now the poxe vpon her greene ficknes for mee.

Bawd. Faith ther's no way to be ridde on't but by the   1820
way to the pox. Here comes the Lord *Lyfimachus* difguifed.

Boult. Wee fhould haue both Lorde and Lowne, if the
peeuifh baggadge would but giue way to cuftomers.

Enter Lyfimachus.
Lyfim. How now, how a douzen of virginities?
Bawd. Now the Gods to bleffe your Honour.
Boult. I am glad to fee your Honour in good health.
Li. You may, fo t'is the better for you that your re-
forters ftand vpon found legges, how now? wholfome ini-
quitie haue you, that a man may deale withall, and defie   1830
the Surgion?

Bawd. Wee haue heere one Sir, if fhee would, but

there neuer came her like in *Meteline.*   (fay.
Li. If fhee'd doe the deedes of darknes thou wouldft

Bawd. Your Honor knows what t'is to say wel enough.

Li. Well, call forth, call forth.

Boult. For flesh and bloud Sir, white and red, you shall see a rose, and she were a rose indeed, if shee had but.

Li. What prithi?

1840   *Boult.* O Sir, I can be modest.

Li. That dignities the renowne of a Bawde, no lesse then it giues a good report to a number to be chaste.

Bawd. Heere comes that which growes to the stalke, Neuer pluckt yet I can assure you.

Is shee not a faire creature?

Ly. Faith shee would serue after a long voyage at Sea, Well theres for you, leaue vs.

Bawd. I beseeche your Honor giue me leaue a word, And Ile haue done presently.

1850   *Li.* I beseech you doe.

Bawd. First, I would haue you note, this is an Honorrable man.   (note him.

Mar. I desire to finde him so, that I may worthilie

Bawd. Next hees the Gouernor of this countrey, and a man whom I am bound too.

Ma. If he gouerne the countrey you are bound to him indeed, but how honorable hee is in that, I knowe not.

Bawd. Pray you without anie more virginall fencing, will you vse him kindly? he will lyne your apron with gold.

1860   *Ma.* What hee will doe gratiously, I will thankfully receiue.

Li. Ha you done?

Bawd. My Lord shees not pac'ste yet, you must take some paines to worke her to your mannage, come wee will leaue his Honor, and her together, goe thy wayes.   (trade?

Li. Now prittie one, how long haue you beene at this

Ma. What trade Sir?

Li. Why, I cannot name but I shall offend.   (name it.

Ma. I cannot be offended with my trade, please you to

1870   *Li.* How long haue you bene of this profession?

Ma. Ere since I can remember.

Li. Did you goe too't so young, were you a gamester at fiue, or at seuen?

Ma. Earlyer too Sir, if now I bee one.

Ly. Why? the house you dwell in proclaimes you to be a Creature of sale.

Ma. Doe you knowe this house to be a place of such resort, and will come intoo't? I heare say you're of honourable parts, and are the Gouernour of this place.

1880   *Li.* Why, hath your principall made knowne vnto you who I am?

Ma. Who is my principall?

Li. Why, your hearbe-woman, she that sets seeds and rootes of shame and iniquitie.

O you haue heard something of my power, and so stand aloft for more serious wooing, but I protest to thee prettie one, my authoritie shall not see thee, or else looke friendly vpon thee, come bring me to some priuate place: Come, come.

1890   *Ma.* If you were borne to honour, shew it now, if put vpon you, make the iudgement good, that thought you worthie of it.

Li. How's this? how's this? some more, be sage.

Mar. For me that am a maide, though most vngentle Fortune haue plac't mee in this Stie, where since I came, diseases haue beene solde deerer then Phisicke, that the gods would set me free from this vnhalowed place, though they did chaunge mee to the meanest byrd that flyes i'th purer ayre.

1900   *Li.* I did not thinke thou couldst haue spoke so well, nere dremp't thou could'st, had I brought hither a corrupted minde, thy speeche had altered it, holde, heeres

golde for thee, perseuer in that cleare way thou goest and the gods strengthen thee.   (H1 (Z)

Ma. The good Gods preserue you.

Li. For me be you thoughten, that I came with no ill intent, for to me the very dores and windows sauor vilely, fare thee well, thou art a peece of vertue, & I doubt not but thy training hath bene noble, hold, heeres more golde for thee, a curse vpon him, die he like a theefe that robs thee of 1910 thy goodnes, if thou doest heare from me it shalbe for thy good.

Boult. I beseeche your Honor one peece for me.

Li. Auaunt thou damned dore-keeper, your house but for this virgin that doeth prop it, would sincke and ouerwhelme you. Away.

Boult. How's this? wee must take another course with you? if your peeuish chastitie, which is not worth a breakefast in the cheapest countrey vnder the coap, shall vndoe a whole houshold, let me be gelded like a spaniel, come your 1920 way.

Ma. Whither would you haue mee?   (wayes.

Boult. I must haue your mayden-head taken off, or the cõmon hãg-man shal execute it, come your way, weele haue no more Gentlemen driuen away, come your wayes I say.

                 Enter Bawdes.

Bawd. How now, whats the matter?

Boult. Worse and worse mistris, shee has heere spoken holie words to the Lord *Lisimachus.*

Bawd. O abhominable.

Boult. He makes our profession as it were to stincke a- 1930 fore the face of the gods.

Bawd. *Marie* hang her vp for euer.

Boult. The Noble man would haue dealt with her like a Noble man, and shee sent him away as colde as a Snoweball, saying his prayers too.

Bawd. *Boult* take her away, vse her at thy pleasure, crack the glasse of her virginitie, and make the rest maliable.

Boult. And if shee were a thornyer peece of ground then shee is, shee shall be plowed.

Ma. Harke, harke you Gods.   1940

Bawd. She coniures, away with her, would she had neuer come within my doores, Marrie hang you: shees borne to vndoe vs, will you not goe the way of wemen-kinde? Marry come vp my dish of chastitie with rosemary & baies.

Boult. Come mistris, come your way with mee.

Ma. Whither wilt thou haue mee?

Boult. To take from you the Iewell you hold so deere.

Ma. Prithee tell mee one thing first.

Boult. Come now your one thing.

Ma. What canst thou wish thine enemie to be.   1950

Boult. Why, I could wish him to bee my master, or rather my mistris.

Ma. Neither of these are so bad as thou art, since they doe better thee in their command, thou hold'st a place for which the painedst feende of hell would not in reputation change: Thou art the damned doore-keeper to euery custerell that comes enquiring for his Tib. To the cholerike fisting of euery rogue, thy eare is lyable, thy foode is such as hath beene belch't on by infected lungs.

Bo. What wold you haue me do? go to the wars, wold you? 1960 wher a man may serue 7. yeers for the losse of a leg, & haue not money enough in the end to buy him a woodden one?

Ma. Doe any thing but this thou doest, emptie olde receptacles, or common-shores of filthe, serue by indenture, to the common hang-man, anie of these wayes are yet better then this: for what thou professest, a Baboone could he speak, would owne a name too deere, that the gods wold safely deliuer me from this place: here, heers gold for thee, if that thy master would gaine by me, proclaime that I can

1970   fing, weaue, fow, & dance, with other vertues, which Ile keep
from boaft, and will vndertake all thefe to teache. I doubt
not but this populous Cittie will yeelde manie fchollers.

H2
(Z)

     Boult. But can you teache all this you fpeake of?

     Ma. Prooue that I cannot, take mee home againe,
And proftitute mee to the bafeft groome that doeth frequent your houfe.

     Boult. Well I will fee what I can doe for thee: if I can
place thee I will.

     Ma. But amongft honeft woman.

1980   *Boult.* Faith my acquaintance lies little amongft them,
But fince my mafter and miftris hath bought you, theres
no going but by their confent: therefore I will make them
acquainted with your purpofe, and I doubt not but I fhall
finde them tractable enough. Come, Ile doe for thee what
I can, come your wayes.   *Exeunt.*

            Enter Gower.

   Marina thus the Brothell fcapes, and chaunces
Into an *Honeft-houfe* our Storie fayes:
Shee fings like one immortall, and fhee daunces

1990   As Goddeffe-like to her admired layes.   (fes,
Deepe clearks fhe dumb's, and with her neele compo-
Natures owne fhape, of budde, bird, branche, or berry.
That euen her art fifters the naturall Rofes
Her Inckle, Silke Twine, with the rubied Cherrie,
That puples lackes fhe none of noble race,
Who powre their bountie on her: and her gaine
She giues the curfed Bawd, here wee her place,
And to hir Father turne our thoughts againe,
Where wee left him on the Sea, wee there him left,

2000   Where driuen before the windes, hee is arriu'de
Heere where his daughter dwels, and on this coaft,
Suppofe him now at *Anchor:* the Citie ftriu'de
God *Neptunes Annuall* feaft to keepe, from whence
Lyfimachus our *Tyrian* Shippe efpies,
His banners Sable, trim'd with rich expence,

H2v
(Z)

And to him in his Barge with former hyes,
In your fuppofing once more put your fight,
Of heauy *Pericles,* thinke this his Barke:
Where what is done in action, more if might

2010   Shalbe difcouerd, pleafe you fit and harke.   *Exit.*

     Enter Helicanus, to him 2. Saylers.

     1. *Say.* Where is Lord *Helicanus?* hee can refolue you,
O here he is Sir, there is a barge put off from *Metaline,* and
in it is *Lyfimachus* the Gouernour, who craues to come a-
boord, what is your will?

     Helly. That hee haue his, call vp fome Gentlemen.

     2. *Say.* Ho Gentlemen, my Lord calls.

        Enter two or three Gentlemen.

     1. *Gent.* Doeth your Lordfhip call?

2020   *Helli.* Gentlemen there is fome of worth would come
aboord, I pray greet him fairely.

        Enter Lyfimachus.

     Hell. Sir, this is the man that can in ought you would
refolue you.

     Lyf. Hayle reuerent Syr, the Gods preferue you.

     Hell. And you to out-liue the age I am, and die as I
would doe.

     Li. You wifh mee well, beeing on fhore, honoring of
Neptunes triumphs, feeing this goodly veffell ride before

2030   vs, I made to it, to knowe of whence you are.

     Hell. Firft what is your place?

     Ly. I am the Gouernour of this place you lie before.

     Hell. Syr our veffell is of *Tyre,* in it the King, a man,
who for this three moneths hath not fpoken to anie one,
nor taken fuftenance, but to prorogue his griefe.

     Li. Vpon what ground is his diftemperature?

     Hell Twould be too tedious to repeat, but the mayne
griefe fprings frõ the loffe of a beloued daughter & a wife.

     Li. May wee not fee him?

H3
(Y)

     Hell. You may, but bootleffe. Is your fight, fee will not
fpeake to any, yet let me obtaine my wifh.   2041

     Lyf. Behold him, this was a goodly perfon.

     Hell. Till the difafter that one mortall wight droue him
to this.

     Lyf. Sir King all haile, the Gods preferue you, haile
royall fir.

     Hell. It is in vaine, he will not fpeake to you.

     Lord. Sir we haue a maid in *Metiliue,* I durft wager would
win fome words of him.

     Lyf. Tis well bethought, fhe queftionleffe with her fweet   2050
harmonie, and other chofen attractions, would allure and
make a battrie through his defend parts, which now are
midway ftopt, fhee is all happie as the faireft of all, and her
fellow maides, now vpon the leauie fhelter that abutts a-
gainft the Iflands fide.

     Hell. Sure all effectleffe, yet nothing weele omit that
beares recoueries name. But fince your kindneffe wee haue
ftretcht thus farre, let vs befeech you, that for our golde
we may prouifion haue, wherein we are not deftitute for
want, but wearie for the ftaleneffe.   2060

     Lyf. O fir, a curtefie, which if we fhould denie, the moft
iuft God for euery graffe would fend a Caterpillar, and fo
inflict our Prouince: yet once more let mee intreate to
knowe at large the caufe of your kings forrow.

     Holl. Sit fir, I will recount it to you, but fee I am pre-
uented.

     Lyf. O hee'rs the Ladie that I fent for,
Welcome faire one, ift not a goodly prefent?

     Hell. Shee's a gallant Ladie.

     Lyf. Shee's fuch a one, that were I well affurde   2070
Came of a gentle kinde, and noble ftocke, I do wifh
No better choife, and thinke me rarely to wed,
Faire on all goodneffe that confifts in beautie,
Expect euen here, where is a kingly patient,

H3v
(Y)

If that thy profperous and artificiall fate,
Can draw him but to anfwere thee in ought,
Thy facred Phyficke fhall receiue fuch pay,
As thy defires can wifh.

     Mar. Sir I willvfe my vtmoft skill in his recouerie, pro-
uided that none but I and my companion maid be fuffered   2080
to come neere him.

     Lyf. Come, let vs leaue her, and the Gods make her pro-
fperous.   *The Song.*

     Lyf. Marke he your Muficke?

     Mar. No nor lookt on vs.

     Lyf. See fhe will fpeake to him.

     Mar. Haile fir, my Lord lend eare.

     Per. Hum, ha.

     Mar. I am a maid, my Lorde, that nere before inuited
eyes, but haue beene gazed on like a Comet: She fpeaks   2090
my Lord, that may be, hath endured a griefe might equall
yours, if both were iuftly wayde, though wayward fortune
did maligne my ftate, my deriuation was from anceftors,
who ftood equiuolent with mightie Kings, but time hath
rooted out my parentage, and to the world, and augward
cafualties, bound me in feruitude, I will defift, but there is
fomething glowes vpon my cheek, and whifpers in mine
eare, go not till he fpeake.

     Per. My fortunes, parentage, good parentage, to equall
mine, was it not thus, what fay you?   2100

Mari. I fed my Lord, if you did know my parentage, you would not do me violence.

Per. I do thinke fo, pray you turne your eyes vpon me, your like fomething that, what Countrey women heare of thefe fhewes?

Mar. No, nor of any fhewes, yet I was mortally brought forth, and am no other then I appeare.

Per. I am great with woe, and fhall deliuer weeping: my deareft wife was like this maid, and fucha one my daugh-

H4
(Y)
2111

ter might haue beene: My Queenes fquare browes, her ftature to an inch, as wandlike-ftraight, as filuer voyft, her eyes as Iewell-like, and cafte as richly, in pace an o-ther *Iuno*. Who ftarues the eares fhee feedes, and makes them hungrie, the more fhe giues them fpeech, Where doe you liue?

Mar. Where I am but a ftraunger from the decke, you may difcerne the place.

Per. Where were you bred? and how atchieu'd you thefe indowments which you make more rich to owe?

2120

Mar. If I fhould tell my hyftorie, it would feeme like lies difdaind in the reporting.

Per. Prethee fpeake, falfneffe cannot come from thee, for thou lookeft modeft as iuftice, & thou feemeft a *Pallas* for the crownd truth to dwell in, I wil beleeue thee & make fenfes credit thy relation, to points that feeme impoffible, for thou lookeft like one I loued indeede: what were thy friends? didft thou not ftay when I did pufh thee backe, which was when I perceiu'd thee that thou camft from good difcending.   *Mar.* So indeed I did.

2130

Per. Report thy parentage, I think thou faidft thou hadft beene toft from wrong to iniurie, and that thou thoughts thy griefs might equall mine, if both were opened.

Mar. Some fuch thing I fed, and fed no more, but what my thoughts did warrant me was likely.

Per. Tell thy ftorie, if thine confidered proue the thou-fand part of my enduraunce, thou art a man, and I haue fuffered like a girle, yet thou doeft looke like patience, gazing on Kings graues, and fmiling extremitie out of act, what were thy friends? howe loft thou thy name, my moft kinde Virgin? recount I doe befeech thee, Come fit by mee.

2140

Mar. My name is *Marina*.

Per. Oh I am mockt, and thou by fome infenced God fent hither to make the world to laugh at me.

H4v
(Y)

Mar. Patience good fir: or here Ile ceafe.

Per. Nay Ile be patient: thou little knowft howe thou doeft ftartle me to call thy felfe *Marina*.

Mar. The name was giuen mee by one that had fome power, my father, and a King.

2150

Per. How, a Kings daughter, and cald *Marina*?

Mar. You fed you would beleeue me, but not to bee a troubler of your peace, I will end here.

Per. But are you flefh and bloud?
Haue you a working pulfe, and are no Fairie?
Motion well, fpeake on, where were you borne?
And wherefore calld *Marina*?

Mar. Calld *Marina*, for I was borne at fea.

Plr. At fea, what mother?

2160

Mar. My mother was the daughter of a King, who died the minute I was borne, as my good Nurfe *Licherida* hath oft deliuered weeping.

Per. O ftop there a little, this is the rareft dreame
That ere duld fleepe did mocke fad fooles withall,
This cannot be my daughter, buried, well, where were you bred? Ile heare you more too'th bottome of your ftorie, and neuer interrupt you.

Mar. You fcorne, beleeue me twere beft I did giue ore.

Per. I will beleeue you by the fyllable of what you fhall deliuer, yet giue me leaue, how came you in thefe parts? where were you bred?   2170

Mar. The King my father did in *Tharfus* leaue me,
Till cruel *Cleon* with his wicked wife,
Did feeke to murther me: and hauing wooed a villaine,
To attempt it, who hauing drawne to doo't,
A crew of Pirats came and refcued me,
Brought me to *Metaline*,
But good fir whither wil you haue me? why doe you weep?
It may be you thinke mee an impofture, no good fayth: I
am the dsughter to King *Pericles*, if good king *Pericles* be.

I1
(Y)
2181

Hell. Hoe, *Hellicanus*?

Hel. Calls my Lord.

Per. Thou art a graue and noble Counfeller,
Moft wife in generall, tell me if thou canft, what this mayde
is, or what is like to bee, that thus hath made mee weepe.

Hel. I know not, but heres the Regent fir of *Metaline*,
fpeakes nobly of her.

Lyf. She neuer would tell her parentage,
Being demaunded, that fhe would fit ftill and weepe.

Per. Oh *Hellicanus*, ftrike me honored fir, giue mee a   2190
gafh, put me to prefent paine, leaft this great fea of ioyes ru-fhing vpon me, ore-beare the fhores of my mortalitie, and
drowne me with their fweetneffe: Oh come hither,
thou that begetft him that did thee beget,
Thou that waft borne at fea, buried at *Tharfus*,
And found at fea agen, O *Hellicanus*,
Downe on thy knees, thanke the holie Gods as loud
As thunder threatens vs, this is *Marina*.
What was thy mothers name? tell me, but that
for truth can neuer be confirm'd inough,   2200
Though doubts did euer fleepe.

Mar. Frift fir, I pray what is your title?

Per. I am *Pericles* of *Tyre*, but tell mee now my
Drownd Queenes name, as in the reft you fayd,
Thou haft beene God-like perfit, the heir of kingdomes,
And an other like to *Pericles* thy father.

Ma. Is it no more to be your daughter, then to fay, my
mothers name was *Thaifa*, *Thaifa* was my mother, who did
end the minute I began.

Pe. Now bleffing on thee, rife th'art my child.   2210
Giue me frefh garments, mine owne *Hellicanus*, fhee is not
dead at *Tharfus* as fhee fhould haue beene by fauage *Cleon*,
fhe fhall tell thee all, when thou fhalt kneele, and iuftifie in
knowledge, fhe is thy verie Princes, who is this?

I1v
(Y)

Hel. Sir, tis the gouernor of *Metaline*, who hearing of
your melancholie ftate, did come to fee you.

Per. I embrace you, giue me my robes.
I am wilde in my beholding, O heauens bleffe my girle,
But harke what Muficke tell, *Hellicanus* my *Marina*,
Tell him ore point by point, for yet he feemes to doat.   2220
How fure you are my daughter, but what muficke?

Hel My Lord I heare none.

Per. None, the Muficke of the *Spheres*, lift my *Marina*.

Lyf. It is not good to croffe him, giue him way.

Per. Rareft founds, do ye not heare?

Lyf. Muficke my Lord? I heare.

Per. Moft heauenly Muficke.
It nips me vnto liftning, and thicke flumber
Hangs vpon mine eyes, let me reft.

Lyf. A Pillow for his head, fo leaue him all.   2230
Well my companion friends, if this but anfwere to my iuft
beliefe, Ile well remember you.

Diana.

Dia. My Temple ſtands in *Epheſus,*
Hie thee thither, and doe vppon mine Altar ſacrifice,
There when my maiden prieſts are met together before the
people all, reueale how thou at ſea didſt looſe thy wife, to
mourne thy croſſes with thy daughters, call, & giue them
repetition to the like, or performe my bidding, or thou li-
2240 ueſt in woe: doo't, and happie, by my ſiluer bow, awake and
tell thy dreame.

Per. Celeſtiall *Dian,* Goddeſſe *Argentine.*
I will obey thee *Hellicanus.*   *Hell.* Sir.

Per. My purpoſe was for *Tharſus,* there to ſtrike,
The inhoſpitable *Cleon,* but I am for other ſeruice firſt,
Toward *Epheſus* turne our blowne ſayles,
Eftſoones Ile tell thee why, ſhall we refreſh vs ſir vpon your
ſhore, and giue you golde for ſuch prouiſion as our in-
tents will neede.

I2
(Y)
2251   *Lyſ* Sir, with all my heart, and when you come a ſhore,
I haue another ſleight.

Per. You ſhall preuaile were it to wooe my daughter, for
it ſeemes you haue beene noble towards her.

Lyſ. Sir, lend me your arme.

Per. Come my *Marina.*

Exeunt.

Gower. Now our ſands are almoſt run,
More a little, and then dum.
This my laſt boone giue mee,
2260 For ſuch kindneſſe muſt relieue mee:
That you aptly will ſuppoſe,
What pageantry, what feats, what ſhowes,
What minſtrelſie, and prettie din,
The Regent made in *Metalin.*
To greet the King, ſo he thriued,
That he is promiſde to be wiued
To faire *Marina,* but in no wiſe,
Till he had done his ſacrifice.
As *Dian* bad, whereto being bound,
2270 The *Interim* pray, you all confound.
In fetherd briefeneſſe ſayles are fild,
And wiſhes fall out as they'r wild,
At *Epheſus* the Temple ſee,
Our King and all his companie.
That he can hither come ſo ſoone,
Is by your fancies thankfull doome.

Per. Haile *Dian,* to performe thy iuſt commaund,
I here confeſſe my ſelfe the King of *Tyre,*
Who frighted from my countrey did wed at *Pentapolis,* the
faire *Thaiſa,* at Sea in childbed died ſhe, but brought forth a
2280 Mayd child calld *Marina* whom O Goddeſſe wears yet thy
ſiluer liuerey, ſhee at *Tharſus* was nurſt with *Cleon,* who at
fourteene yeares he ſought to murder, but her better ſtars

I2v
(Z)
brought her to *Meteline,* gainſt whoſe ſhore ryding, her
Fortunes brought the mayde aboord vs, where by her
owne moſt cleere remembrance, ſhee made knowne her
ſelfe my Daughter.

Th. Voyce and fauour, you are, you are, O royall
Pericles.

2290   *Per.* What meanes the mum? ſhee die's, helpe Gentlemen.

Ceri. Noble Sir, if you haue tolde *Dianaes* Altar
true, this is your wife?

Per. Reuerent appearer no, I threwe her ouer-boord
with theſe verie armes.

Ce. Vpon this coaſt, I warrant you.

Pe. T'is moſt certaine.

Cer. Looke to the Ladie, O ſhee's but ouer-joyde,

Earlie in bluſtering morne this Ladie was throwne vpon
this ſhore.   2300
I op't the coffin, found there rich Iewells, recouered her, and plac'ſte her heere in *Dianaes* temple.

Per. May we ſee them?

Cer. Great Sir, they ſhalbe brought you to my houſe,
whither I inuite you, looke *Thaiſa* is recouered.

Th. O let me looke if hee be none of mine, my ſan-
ctitie will to my ſenſe bende no licentious eare, but curbe
it ſpight of ſeeing: O my Lord are you not *Pericles?* like
him you ſpake, like him you are, did you not name a tempeſt, a birth, and death?   2310

Per. The voyce of dead *Thaiſa.*

Th. That *Thaiſa* am I, ſuppoſed dead and drownd.

Per. I mortall *Dian.*

Th. Now I knowe you better, when wee with teares
parted *Pentapolis,* the king my father gaue you ſuch a ring.

Per. This, this, no more, you gods, your preſent kindenes makes my paſt miſeries ſports, you ſhall doe well that
on the touching of her lips I may melt, and no more be

I3
(Z)
ſeene, O come, be buried a ſecond time within theſe armes.

Ma. My heart leaps to be gone into my mothers bo-   2320
ſome.

Per. Looke who kneeles here, fleſh of thy fleſh *Thaiſa,*
thy burden at the Sea, and call'd *Marina,* for ſhe was yeelded there.

Th. Bleſt, and mine owne.

Hell. Hayle Madame, and my Queene.

Th. I knowe you not.

Hell. You haue heard mee ſay when I did flie from
Tyre, I left behind an ancient ſubſtitute, can you remember what I call'd the man, I haue nam'de him oft.   2330

Th. T'was *Hellicanus* then.

Per. Still confirmation, imbrace him deere *Thaiſa,* this
is hee, now doe I long to heare how you were found? how
poſſiblie preſerued? and who to thanke (beſides the gods)
for this great miracle?

Th. Lord *Cerimon,* my Lord, this man through whom
the Gods haue ſhowne their power, that can from firſt to
laſt reſolue you.

Per. Reuerent Syr, the gods can haue no mortall officer
more like a god then you, will you deliuer how this dead   2340
Queene reliues?

Cer. I will my Lord, beſeech you firſt, goe with mee
to my houſe, where ſhall be ſhowne you all was found with
her. How ſhee came plac'ſte heere in the Temple, no
needfulll thing omitted.

Per. Pure *Dian* bleſſe thee for thy viſion, and will offer
night oblations to thee *Thaiſa,* this Prince, the faire betrothed of your daughter, ſhall marrie her at *Pentapolis,* and
now this ornament makes mee looke diſmall, will I clip to
forme, and what this fourteene yeeres no razer touch't, to   2350
grace thy marridge-day, Ile beautifie.

Th. Lord *Cerimon* hath letters of good credit. Sir,
my father's dead.

I3v
(Z)
Per. Heauens make a Starre of him, yet there my
Queene, wee'le celebrate their Nuptialls, and our ſelues
will in that kingdome ſpend our following daies, our ſonne
and daughter ſhall in *Tyrus* raigne.
Lord *Cerimon* wee doe our longing ſtay,
To heare the reſt vntolde, Sir lead's the way.

FINIS.   2360

Gower.

In *Antiochus* and his daughter you haue heard
Of monſtrous luſt, the due and iuſt reward:
In *Pericles* his Queene and Daughter ſeene,
Although aſſayl'de with *Fortune* fierce and keene.

Vertue preferd from fell deſtructions blaſt,
  Lead on by heauen, and crown'd with ioy at laſt.
In *Helycanus* may you well deſcrie,
  A figure of trueth, of faith, of loyaltie:
2370 In reuerend *Cerimon* there well appeares,
  The worth that learned charitie aye weares.
      For wicked *Cleon* and his wife, when Fame
      Had ſpred his curſed deede, the honor'd name

Of *Pericles*, to rage the Cittie turne,
That him and his they in his Pallace burne:
The gods for murder ſeemde ſo content,
To puniſh, although not done, but meant.
    So on your Patience euermore attending,
    New ioy wayte on you, heere our play has ending.
                    FINIS.   2380

CORIOLANUS

FOR *Coriolanus*, Shakespeare turned once more to Roman history as told by Plutarch and translated by Sir Thomas North in the *Liues of the noble Grecians and Romanes* published in 1579. This time he dramatized early events, not much subsequent to those he had written about many years previously in *The Rape of Lucrece*. Plutarch gave him most of his material, but he also drew on other writings, including William Camden's *Remaines of a Greater Worke concerning Britaine*, published in 1605, for Menenius' fable of the belly (Sc. 1). Though he needed no source other than Plutarch for the insurrections and corn riots of ancient Rome, similar happenings in England during 1607 and 1608 may have stimulated his interest in the story. The cumulative evidence suggests that *Coriolanus*, first printed in the 1623 Folio, is Shakespeare's last Roman play, written around 1608.

In the fifth century BC, following the expulsion of the Tarquins, Rome was an aristocratically controlled republic in which power was invested primarily in two annually elected magistrates, or consuls. For many years the main issues confronting the republic were the internal class struggle between patricians and plebeians, and the external struggle for domination over neighbouring peoples. Among the republic's early enemies were the Volsci (or Volscians), who inhabited an area to the south and south-east of Rome; their towns included Antium and Corioli. According to ancient historians, Rome's greatest leader in campaigns against the Volsci was the patrician Gnaeus (or Caius) Marcius, who, at a time of famine which caused the plebeians to rebel against the patricians, led an army against the Volsci and captured Corioli; as a reward he was granted the cognomen, or surname, of Coriolanus. After this he is said to have been charged with behaving tyrannically in opposing the distribution of corn to starving plebeians, and as a result to have abandoned Rome, joined the Volsci, and led a Volscian army against his native city.

This is the story of conflict between public and private issues that Shakespeare dramatizes, concentrating on the later part of Plutarch's Life and speeding up its time-scheme, while also alluding retrospectively to earlier incidents. He increases the responsibility of the Tribunes, Scicinius Velutus and Iunius Brutus, for Coriolanus' banishment, and greatly develops certain characters, such as the Volscian leader Tullus Auffidius and the patrician Menenius Agrippa. The roles of the womenfolk are almost entirely of Shakespeare's devising up to the scene (Sc. 26) of their embassy; here, as in certain other set speeches, Shakespeare draws heavily on the language of North's translation.

Coriolanus is an austere play, gritty in style, deeply serious in its concern with the relationship between personal characteristics and national destiny, but relieved by flashes of comedy (especially in the scenes in which Coriolanus begs for the plebeians' votes in his election campaign for the consulship) which are more apparent on the stage than on the page. Though Coriolanus is arrogant, choleric, and self-centered, he is also a blazingly successful warrior, conspicuous for integrity, who ultimately yields to a tenderness which, he knows, will destroy him. *Coriolanus* is a deeply human as well as a profoundly political play.

The copy for the Folio text was probably a scribal transcript.

THE NAMES OF THE ACTORS

Caius MARTIUS, later surnam'd CORIOLANUS

MENENIUS Agrippa

Titus LARTIUS } Generalls

COMINIUS

Patricians of Rome

VOLUMNIA, Coriolanus Mother

VIRGILIA, his Wife

YONG MARTIUS, his Sonne

VALERIA, a chaste Ladie of Rome

SCICINIUS Velutus } Tribunes of the Roman People

Iunius BRUTUS

CITIZENS of Rome

SOULDIERS in the Roman Army

Tullus AUFFIDIUS, Generall of the Volcean Army

His LIEUTENANT

His SERUINGMEN

CONSPIRATORS with Auffidius

Volcean LORDS

Volcean CITIZENS

SOULDIERS in the Volcean Army

ADRIAN, a Roman

NICANOR, a Volcean

A Roman HERALD

MESSENGERS

ÆDILES

A Gentlewoman, an Vsher, Roman and Volcean Senators and Nobles, Captaines in the Roman Army, Officers, Lictors

The Tragedy of Coriolanus

1.1
(Sc. 1)

Enter a Company of Mutinous Citizens, with
Staues, Clubs, and other weapons

1 CITIZEN Before we proceed any further, heare me speake.

ALL Speake, speake.

1 CITIZEN You are all resolu'd rather to dy then to famish?

ALL Resolu'd, resolu'd.

1 CITIZEN First you know, *Caius Martius* is chiefe enemy
to the people.

ALL We know't, we know't.

1 CITIZEN Let vs kill him, and wee'l haue Corne at our
own price. Is't a Verdict?

10 ALL No more talking on't; Let it be done, away, away.

2 CITIZEN One word, good Citizens.

1 CITIZEN We are accounted poore Citizens, the Patricians
good: what Authority surfets one, would releeue vs. If
they would yeelde vs but the superfluitie while it were
wholsome, wee might guesse they releeued vs
humanely: But they thinke we are too deere, the
leannesse that afflicts vs, the obiect of our misery, is
as an inuentory to particularize their abundance, our
sufferance is a gaine to them. Let vs reuenge this with
20 our Pikes, ere we become Rakes. For the Gods know, I
speake this in hunger for Bread, not in thirst for
Reuenge.

2 CITIZEN Would you proceede especially against *Caius*
Martius.

⌈3 CITIZEN⌉ Against him first.

⌈4 CITIZEN⌉ He's a very dog to the Commonalty.

2 CITIZEN Consider you what Seruices he ha's done for
his Country?

1 CITIZEN Very well, and could bee content to giue him
30 good report for't, but that hee payes himselfe with
beeing proud.

⌈5 CITIZEN⌉ Nay, but speak not maliciously.

1 CITIZEN I say vnto you, what he hath done Famouslie,
he did it to that end: though soft conscienc'd men can
be content to say it was for his Countrey, he did it to
please his Mother, and to be partly proud, which he
is, euen to the altitude of his vertue.

2 CITIZEN What he cannot helpe in his Nature, you
account a Vice in him: You must in no way say he is
40 couetous.

1 CITIZEN If I must not, I neede not be barren of
Accusations. He hath faults (with surplus) to tyre in
repetition.

Showts within

What showts are these? The other side a'th City is
risen: why stay we prating heere? To th'Capitoll.

ALL Come, come.

Enter Menenius Agrippa

1 CITIZEN Soft, who comes heere?

2 CITIZEN Worthy *Menenius Agrippa*, one that hath
alwayes lou'd the people.

1 CITIZEN He's one honest enough, wold al the rest wer so. 50

MENENIUS
What work's my Countrimen in hand? Where go you
With Bats and Clubs? The matter, speake I pray you.

⌈1⌉ CITIZEN Our busines is not vnknowne to th'Senat,
they haue had inkling this fortnight what we intend
to do, wᶜ now wee'l shew em in deeds: they say poore
Suters haue strong breaths, they shal know we haue
strong arms too.

MENENIUS
Why Masters, my good Friends, mine honest Neighbours,
Will you vndo your selues?

⌈1⌉ CITIZEN
We cannot Sir, we are vndone already. 60

MENENIUS
I tell you Friends, most charitable care
Haue the Patricians of you. For your wants,
Your suffering in this dearth, you may as well
Strike at the Heauen with your staues, as lift them
Against the Roman State, whose course will on
The way it takes: cracking ten thousand Curbes
Of more strong linke assunder, then can euer
Appeare in your impediment. For the Dearth,
The Gods, not the Patricians make it, and
Your knees to them (not armes) must helpe. Alacke, 70
You are transported by Calamity
Thether, where more attends you, and you slander
The Helmes o'th State; who care for you like Fathers,
When you curse them, as Enemies.

⌈1⌉ CITIZEN Care for vs? True indeed, they nere car'd for
vs yet. Suffer vs to famish, and their Store-houses
cramm'd with Graine: Make Edicts for Vsurie, to
support Vsurers; repeale daily any wholsome Act
established against the rich, and prouide more piercing
Statutes daily, to chaine vp and restraine the poore. If 80
the Warres eate vs not vppe, they will; and there's all
the loue they beare vs.

MENENIUS Either you must
Confesse your selues wondrous Malicious,
Or be accus'd of Folly. I shall tell you
A pretty Tale, it may be you haue heard it,
But since it serues my purpose, I will venture
To stale't a little more.

⌈1⌉ CITIZEN Well, Ile heare it Sir: yet you must not thinke
to fobbe off our disgrace with a tale: But and't please 90
you deliuer.

MENENIUS
There was a time, when all the bodies members
Rebell'd against the Belly; thus accus'd it:
That onely like a Gulfe it did remaine
I'th midd'st a th'body, idle and vnactiue,
Still cubbording the Viand, neuer bearing
Like labour with the rest, where th'other Instruments

Did see, and heare, deuise, instruct, walke, feele,
And mutually participate, did minister
100 Vnto the appetite; and affection common
Of the whole body. The Belly answer'd.
⌜1⌝ CITIZEN
Well sir, what answer made the Belly.
MENENIUS
Sir, I shall tell you: with a kinde of Smile,
Which ne're came from the Lungs, but euen thus:
For looke you I may make the belly Smile,
As well as speake, it tantingly replyed
To'th'discontented Members, the mutinous parts
That enuied his receite: euen so most fitly,
As you maligne our Senators, for that
They are not such as you.
110 ⌜1⌝ CITIZEN   Your Bellies answer: What:
The Kingly crowned head, the vigilant eye,
The Counsailor Heart, the Arme our Souldier,
Our Steed the Legge, the Tongue our Trumpeter,
With other Muniments and petty helpes
In this our Fabricke, if that they—
MENENIUS   What then?
Foreme, this Fellow speakes. What then? What then?
⌜1⌝ CITIZEN
Should by the Cormorant belly be restrain'd,
Who is the sinke a th'body.
MENENIUS   Well, what then?
⌜1⌝ CITIZEN
The former Agents, if they did complaine,
What could the Belly answer?
120 MENENIUS   I will tell you,
If you'l bestow a small (of what you haue little)
Patience awhile; you'st heare the Bellies answer.
⌜1⌝ CITIZEN
Y'are long about it.
MENENIUS   Note me this good Friend;
Your most graue Belly was deliberate,
Not rash like his Accusers, and thus answered.
True is it my Incorporate Friends (quoth he)
That I receiue the generall Food at first
Which you do liue vpon: and fit it is,
Because I am the Store-house, and the Shop
130 Of the whole Body. But, if you do remember,
I send it through the Riuers of your blood
Euen to the Court, the Heart, to th'seate o'th'Braine,
And through the Crankes and Offices of man,
The strongest Nerues, and small inferiour Veines
From me receiue that naturall competencie
Whereby they liue. And though that all at once
(You my good Friends, this sayes the Belly) marke me.
⌜1⌝ CITIZEN
I sir, well, well.
MENENIUS   Though all at once, cannot
See what I do deliuer out to each,
140 Yet I can make my Awdit vp, that all
From me do backe receiue the Flowre of all,
And leaue me but the Bran. What say you too't?

⌜1⌝ CITIZEN
It was an answer, how apply you this?
MENENIUS
The Senators of Rome, are this good Belly,
And you the mutinous Members: For examine
Their Counsailes, and their Cares; disgest things rightly,
Touching the Weale a'th Common, you shall finde
No publique benefit which you receiue
But it proceeds, or comes from them to you,
And no way from your selues. What do you thinke? 150
You, the great Toe of this Assembly?
⌜1⌝ CITIZEN
I the great Toe? Why the great Toe?
MENENIUS
For that being one o'th lowest, basest, poorest
Of this most wise Rebellion, thou goest formost:
Thou Rascall, that art worst in blood to run,
Lead'st first to win some vantage.
But make you ready your stiffe bats and clubs,
Rome, and her Rats, are at the point of battell,
The one side must haue baile.
    Enter Caius Martius
                    Hayle, Noble *Martius*.
MARTIUS
Thanks. What's the matter you dissentious rogues 160
That rubbing the poore Itch of your Opinion,
Make your selues Scabs.
⌜1⌝ CITIZEN   We haue euer your good word.
MARTIUS
He that will giue good words to thee, wil flatter
Beneath abhorring. What would you haue, you Curres,
That like nor Peace, nor Warre? The one affrights you,
The other makes you proud. He that trusts to you,
Where he should finde you Lyons, findes you Hares:
Where Foxes, Geese: you are no surer, no,
Then is the coale of fire vpon the Ice,
Or Hailstone in the Sun. Your Vertue is, 170
To make him worthy, whose offence subdues him,
And curse that Iustice did it. Who deserues Greatnes,
Deserues your Hate: and your Affections are
A sickmans Appetite; who desires most that
Which would encrease his euill. He that depends
Vpon your fauours, swimmes with finnes of Leade,
And hewes downe Oakes, with rushes. Hang ye: trust
    ye?
With euery Minute you do change a Minde,
And call him Noble, that was now your Hate:
Him vilde, that was your Garland. What's the matter, 180
That in these seuerall places of the Citie,
You cry against the Noble Senate, who
(Vnder the Gods) keepe you in awe, which else
Would feede on one another?
(*To Menenius*)   What's their seeking?
MENENIUS
For Corne at their owne rates, wherof they say
The Citie is well stor'd.
MARTIUS   Hang 'em: They say?

They'l sit by th'fire, and presume to know
What's done i'th Capitoll: Who's like to rise,
Who thriues, & who declines: Side factions, & giue out
190 Coniecturall Marriages, making parties strong,
And feebling such as stand not in their liking,
Below their cobled Shooes. They say ther's grain
      enough?
Would the Nobility lay aside their ruth,
And let me vse my Sword, I'de make a Quarrie
With thousands of these quarter'd slaues, as high
As I could picke my Lance.

MENENIUS
Nay these are al most thoroughly perswaded:
For though abundantly they lacke discretion
Yet are they passing Cowardly. But I beseech you,
What sayes the other Troope?

200 MARTIUS   They are dissolu'd: Hang em;
They said they were an hungry, sigh'd forth
      Prouerbes
That Hunger broke stone wals: that dogges must eate
That meate was made for mouths. That the gods sent
      not
Corne for the Richmen onely: With these shreds
They vented their Complainings, which being
      answer'd
And a petition granted them, a strange one,
To breake the heart of generosity,
And make bold power looke pale, they threw their caps
As they would hang them on the hornes a'th Moone,
Shooting their Emulation.

210 MENENIUS   What is graunted them?

MARTIUS
Fiue Tribunes to defend their vulgar wisdoms
Of their owne choice. One's *Iunius Brutus*,
Sicinius Velutus, and I know not. Sdeath,
The rabble should haue first vnroo'ft the City
Ere so preuayl'd with me; it will in time
Win vpon power, and throw forth greater Theames
For Insurrections arguing.

MENENIUS This is strange.

MARTIUS (*to the Citizens*) Go get you home you Fragments.
      Enter a Messenger hastily
220 MESSENGER Where's *Caius Martius*?

MARTIUS Heere: what's the matter?

MESSENGER
The newes is sir, the Volcies are in Armes.

MARTIUS
I am glad on't, then we shall ha meanes to vent
Our mustie superfluity.
      Enter Sicinius Velutus, Iunius Brutus, Cominius,
      Titus Lartius, with other Senatours
                        See our best Elders.

I SENATOR
Martius 'tis true, that you haue lately told vs,
The Volces are in Armes.

MARTIUS   They haue a Leader,
Tullus Auffidius that will put you too't:
I sinne in enuying his Nobility:

And were I any thing but what I am,
I would wish me onely he.

COMINIUS   You haue fought together? 230

MARTIUS
Were halfe to halfe the world by th'eares, & he
Vpon my partie, I'de reuolt to make
Onely my warres with him. He is a Lion
That I am proud to hunt.

I SENATOR   Then worthy *Martius*,
Attend vpon *Cominius* to these Warres.

COMINIUS (*to Martius*)
It is your former promise.

MARTIUS   Sir it is,
And I am constant: *Titus Latius*, thou
Shalt see me once more strike at *Tullus* face.
What art thou stiffe? Stand'st out?

LARTIUS   No *Caius Martius*,
Ile leane vpon one Crutch, and fight with tother, 240
Ere stay behinde this Businesse.

MENENIUS   Oh true-bred.

⌈I⌉ SENATOR
Your Company to'th'Capitoll, where I know
Our greatest Friends attend vs.

LARTIUS (*to Cominius*)   Lead you on:
(*To Martius*) Follow *Cominius*, we must followe you,
Right worthy your Priority.

COMINIUS   Noble *Martius*.

⌈I⌉ SENATOR (*to the Citizens*)
Hence to your homes, be gone.

MARTIUS   Nay let them follow,
The Volces haue much Corne: take these Rats thither,
To gnaw their Garners.   *Citizens steale away*
                        Worshipfull Mutiners,
Your valour puts well forth: (*To the Nobles*) Pray
      follow.   *Exeunt. Manet Sicinius & Brutus*

SCICINIUS
Was euer man so proud as is this *Martius*? 250

BRUTUS He has no equall.

SCICINIUS
When we were chosen Tribunes for the people.

BRUTUS
Mark'd you his lip and eyes.

SCICINIUS   Nay, but his taunts.

BRUTUS
Being mou'd, he will not spare to gird the Gods.

SCICINIUS Bemocke the modest Moone.

BRUTUS
The present Warres deuoure him, he is growne
Too proud to be so valiant.

SCICINIUS   Such a Nature,
Tickled with good successe, disdaines the shadow
Which he treads on at noone, but I do wonder,
His insolence can brooke to be commanded 260
Vnder *Cominius*?

BRUTUS   Fame, at the which he aymes,
In whom already he's well grac'd, cannot
Better be held, nor more attain'd then by
A place below the first: for what miscarries

Shall be the Generals fault, though he performe
To th'vtmost of a man, and giddy censure
Will then cry out of *Martius*: Oh, if he
Had borne the businesse.

SCICINIUS   Besides, if things go well,
Opinion that so stickes on *Martius*, shall
Of his demerits rob *Cominius*.

270 BRUTUS   Come:
Halfe all *Cominius* Honors are to *Martius*
Though *Martius* earn'd them not: and all his faults
To *Martius* shall be Honors, though indeed
In ought he merit not.

SCICINIUS   Let's hence, and heare
How the dispatch is made, and in what fashion
More then his singularity, he goes
Vpon this present Action.

BRUTUS   Let's along.   *Exeunt*

1.2   *Enter Tullus Auffidius with Senators of Coriolus*
(Sc. 2) 1 SENATOR
So, your opinion is *Auffidius*,
That they of Rome are entred in our Counsailes,
And know how we proceede.

280 AUFFIDIUS   Is it not yours?
What euer haue bin thought one in this State
That could be brought to bodily act, ere Rome
Had circumuention: 'tis not foure dayes gone
Since I heard thence, these are the words, I thinke
I haue the Letter heere: yes, heere it is;
        ⌜*He reads the Letter*⌝
They haue prest a Power, but it is not knowne
Whether for East or West: the Dearth is great,
The people Mutinous: And it is rumour'd,
Cominius, *Martius* your old Enemy
290 (Who is of Rome worse hated then of you)
And *Titus Lartius*, a most valiant Roman,
These three leade on this Preparation
Whether 'tis bent: most likely, 'tis for you:
Consider of it.

1 SENATOR   Our Armie's in the Field:
We neuer yet made doubt but Rome was ready
To answer vs.

AUFFIDIUS   Nor did you thinke it folly,
To keepe your great pretences vayl'd, till when
They needs must shew themselues, which in the
            hatching
It seem'd appear'd to Rome. By the discouery,
300 We shalbe shortned in our ayme, which was
To take in many Townes, ere (almost) Rome
Should know we were a-foot.

2 SENATOR   Noble *Auffidius*,
Take your Commission, hye you to your Bands,
Let vs alone to guard *Corioles*.
If they set downe before's: for the remoue
Bring vp your Army: but (I thinke) you'l finde
Th'haue not prepar'd for vs.

AUFFIDIUS   O doubt not that,
I speake from Certainties. Nay more,

Some parcels of their Power are forth already,
And onely hitherward. I leaue your Honors.   310
If we, and *Caius Martius* chance to meete,
'Tis sworne betweenĕ vs, we shall euer strike
Till one can do no more.

ALL THE SENATORS   The Gods assist you.
AUFFIDIUS
And keepe your Honors safe.

1 SENATOR   Farewell.
2 SENATOR   Farewell.
ALL   Farewell.
        Exeunt omnes, ⌜Auffidius at one doore, Senators
                            at another doore⌝

Enter Volumnia and Virgilia, mother and wife to   1.3
Martius: They set them downe on two lowe stooles   (Sc. 3)
and sowe

VOLUMNIA I pray you daughter sing, or expresse your
selfe in a more comfortable sort: If my Sonne were my
Husband, I should freelier reioyce in that absence
wherein he wonne Honor, then in the embracements
of his Bed, where he would shew most loue. When yet
hee was but tender-bodied, and the onely Sonne of my   320
womb; when youth with comelinesse pluck'd all gaze
his way; when for a day of Kings entreaties, a Mother
should not sel him an houre from her beholding; I
considering how Honour would become such a person,
that it was no better then Picture-like to hang by
th'wall, if renowne made it not stirre, was pleas'd to
let him seeke danger, where he was like to finde fame:
To a cruell Warre I sent him, from whence he return'd,
his browes bound with Oake. I tell thee Daughter, I
sprang not more in ioy at first hearing he was a Man-   330
child, then now in first seeing he had proued himselfe
a man.

VIRGILIA But had he died in the Businesse Madame, how
then?

VOLUMNIA Then his good report should haue beene my
Sonne, I therein would haue found issue. Heare me
professe sincerely, had I a dozen sons each in my loue
alike, and none lesse deere then thine, and my good
Martius, I had rather had eleuen dye Nobly for their
Countrey, then one voluptuously surfet out of Action. 340
        Enter a Gentlewoman

GENTLEWOMAN Madam, the lady *Valeria* is come to visit
you.

VIRGILIA (*to Volumnia*) Beseech you giue me leaue to retire
my selfe.

VOLUMNIA Indeed you shall not:
Me thinkes, I heare hither your Husbands Drumme:
See him plucke *Auffidius* downe by th'haire:
(As children from a Beare) the *Volces* shunning him:
Me thinkes I see him stampe thus, and call thus,
Come on you Cowards, you were got in feare   350
Though you were borne in Rome; his bloody brow
With his mail'd hand then wiping, forth he goes
Like to a Haruest man, thats task'd to mowe
Or all, or loose his hyre.

VIRGILIA

His bloody Brow? Oh Iupiter, no blood.

VOLUMNIA

Away you Foole; it more becomes a man
Then gilt his Trophe. The brests of *Hecuba*
When she did suckle *Hector*, look'd not louelier
Then *Hectors* forhead, when it spit forth blood
At *Grecian* sword Contemning.

360 (*To the Gentlewoman*)   Tell *Valeria*
We are fit to bid her welcome.   *Exit Gentlewoman*

VIRGILIA

Heauens blesse my Lord from fell *Auffidius*.

VOLUMNIA

Hee'l beat *Auffidius* head below his knee,
And treade vpon his necke.

           Enter Valeria with an Vsher, and a Gentlewoman

VALERIA My Ladies both good day to you.

VOLUMNIA Sweet Madam.

VIRGILIA I am glad to see your Ladyship.

VALERIA How do you both? You are manifest house-
370 keepers. What are you sowing heere? A fine spotte in
good faith. How does your little Sonne?

VIRGILIA I thanke your Lady-ship: Well good Madam.

VOLUMNIA He had rather see the swords, and heare a
Drum, then looke vpon his Schoolmaster.

VALERIA A my word the Fathers Sonne: Ile sweare 'tis a
very pretty boy. A my troth, I look'd vpon him a
Wensday halfe an houre together: ha's such a confirm'd
countenance. I saw him run after a gilded Butterfly, &
when he caught it, he let it go againe, and after it
againe, and ouer and ouer he comes, and vp againe:
380 catcht it again: or whether his fall enrag'd him, or
how 'twas, hee did so set his teeth, and teare it. Oh, I
warrant how he mammockt it.

VOLUMNIA One on's Fathers moods.

VALERIA Indeed la, tis a Noble childe.

VIRGILIA A Cracke Madam.

VALERIA Come, lay aside your stitchery, I must haue you
play the idle Huswife with me this afternoone.

VIRGILIA No (good Madam) I will not out of doores.

VALERIA Not out of doores?

390 VOLUMNIA She shall, she shall.

VIRGILIA Indeed no, by your patience; Ile not ouer the
threshold, till my Lord returne from the Warres.

VALERIA Fye, you confine your selfe most vnreasonably:
Come, you must go visit the good Lady that lies in.

VIRGILIA I will wish her speedy strength, and visite her
with my prayers: but I cannot go thither.

VOLUMNIA Why I pray you.

VIRGILIA 'Tis not to saue labour, nor that I want loue.

VALERIA You would be another *Penelope*: yet they say,
400 all the yearne she spun in *Vlisses* absence, did but fill
Ithaca full of Mothes. Come, I would your Cambrick
were sensible as your finger, that you might leaue
pricking it for pitie. Come you shall go with vs.

VIRGILIA No good Madam, pardon me, indeed I will not
foorth.

VALERIA In truth la go with me, and Ile tell you excellent
newes of your Husband.

VIRGILIA Oh good Madam, there can be none yet.

VALERIA Verily I do not iest with you: there came newes
from him last night.   410

VIRGILIA Indeed Madam.

VALERIA In earnest it's true; I heard a Senatour speake
it. Thus it is: the Volcies haue an Army forth, against
whõ *Cominius* the Generall is gone, with one part of
our Romane power. Your Lord, and *Titus Lartius*, are
set down before their Citie *Carioles*, they nothing doubt
preuailing, and to make it breefe Warres. This is true
on mine Honor, and so I pray go with vs.

VIRGILIA Giue me excuse good Madame, I will obey you
in euery thing heereafter.   420

VOLUMNIA (*to Valeria*) Let her alone Ladie: as she is now,
she will but disease our better mirth.

VALERIA In troth I thinke she would: Fare you well then.
Come good sweet Ladie. Prythee *Virgilia* turne thy
solemnesse out a doore, and go along with vs.

VIRGILIA No at a word Madam; Indeed I must not, I wish
you much mirth.

VALERIA Well, then farewell.

           Exeunt ⌈Valeria, Volumnia, and
           Vsher at one doore, Virgilia and
           Gentlewoman at another⌉

Enter Martius, Titus Lartius, with Drumme,   1.4
⌈Trumpet,⌉ Colours, with Captaines and Souldiers   (Sc. 4)
⌈carrying Scaling Ladders⌉, as before the City
Corialus: to them a Messenger

MARTIUS

Yonder comes Newes: A Wager they haue met.

LARTIUS

My horse to yours, no.

MARTIUS   Tis done.

LARTIUS   Agreed.   430

MARTIUS (*to the Messenger*)

Say, ha's our Generall met the Enemy?

MESSENGER

They lye in view, but haue not spoke as yet.

LARTIUS

So, the good Horse is mine.

MARTIUS   Ile buy him of you.

LARTIUS

No, Ile nor sel, nor giue him: Lend you him I will
For halfe a hundred yeares:
(*To Trumpeter*)   Summon the Towne.

MARTIUS (*to the Messenger*)

How farre off lie these Armies?

MESSENGER   Within this mile and halfe.

MARTIUS

Then shall we heare their Larum, & they Ours.
Now Mars, I prythee make vs quicke in worke,
That we with smoaking swords may march from hence
To helpe our fielded Friends.
(*To Trumpeter*)   Come, blow thy blast.   440

They Sound a Parley: Enter two Senators with
others on the Walles of Corialus

(*To the Senators*) Tullus Auffidious, is he within your
    Walles?

1 SENATOR

No, nor a man that feares you lesse then he,
That's lesser then a little:
        Drum a farre off
⌐To the Volceans⌐   Hearke, our Drummes
Are bringing forth our youth: Wee'l breake our Walles
Rather then they shall pound vs vp: our Gates,
Which yet seeme shut, we haue but pin'd with Rushes,
They'le open of themselues.
        Alarum farre off
(*To the Romans*)   Harke you, farre off.
There is Auffidious. List what worke he makes
Among'st your clouen Army.
                    ⌐*Exeunt Volceans from the Walles*⌐
MARTIUS   Oh they are at it.
LARTIUS
450 Their noise be our instruction. Ladders hoa.
        ⌐*They prepare to assault the Walles.*⌐
        Enter the Army of the Volces from the Gates
MARTIUS
They feare vs not, but issue forth their Citie.
Now put your Shields before your hearts, and fight
With hearts more proofe then Shields. Aduance braue
    Titus,
They do disdaine vs much beyond our Thoughts,
Which makes me sweat with wrath. Come on my
    fellowes.
He that retires, Ile take him for a Volce,
And he shall feele mine edge.
        Alarum, the Romans are beat back ⌐*and exeunt*⌐
            to their Trenches, ⌐*the Volces following*⌐

1.5   *Enter* ⌐*Roman Souldiers, in Retreat, followed by*⌐
(Sc. 5) *Martius Cursing*
MARTIUS
All the contagion of the South, light on you,
You Shames of Rome: you Heard of—Byles and Plagues
460 Plaister you o're, that you may be abhorr'd
Farther then seene, and one infect another
Against the Winde a mile: you soules of Geese,
That beare the shapes of men, how haue you run
From Slaues, that Apes would beate; Pluto and Hell,
All hurt behinde, backes red, and faces pale
With flight and agued feare, mend and charge home,
Or by the fires of heauen, Ile leaue the Foe,
And make my Warres on you: Looke too't: Come on,
If you'l stand fast, wee'l beate them to their Wiues,
470 As they vs to our Trenches. Followe.
        ⌐*The Romans come forward towards the Walles.*⌐
        Another Alarum, and ⌐*enter the Army of the*
        Volces.⌐ *Martius beates them back* ⌐*through*⌐ *the*
        gates
So, now the gates are ope: now proue good Seconds,
'Tis for the followers Fortune widens them,
Not for the flyers: Marke me, and do the like.

        He enters the Gates
1 SOULDIER
Foole-hardinesse, not I.
2 SOULDIER   Nor I.
        Alarum continues. The Gates close, and Martius is
        shut in
1 SOULDIER
See they haue shut him in.
⌐3 SOULDIER⌐   To th'pot I warrant him.
        Enter Titus Lartius
LARTIUS
What is become of Martius?
⌐4 SOULDIER⌐   Slaine (Sir) doubtlesse.
1 SOULDIER
Following the Flyers at the very heeles,
With them he enters: who vpon the sodaine
Clapt to their Gates, he is himselfe alone,
To answer all the City.
LARTIUS   Oh Noble Fellow!   480
Who sensibly out-dares his sencelesse Sword,
And when it bowes, stand'st vp: Thou art lost Martius,
A Carbuncle intire: as big as thou art
Weare not so rich a Iewell. Thou was't a Souldier
Euen to Catoes wish, not fierce and terrible
Onely in strokes, but with thy grim lookes, and
The Thunder-like percussion of thy sounds
Thou mad'st thine enemies shake, as if the World
Were Feauorous, and did tremble.
        Enter Martius bleeding, assaulted by the Enemy
1 SOULDIER   Looke Sir.
LARTIUS   O 'tis Martius.
Let's fetch him off, or make remaine alike.   490
        They fight, and all exeunt into the City

        Enter certaine Romanes with spoiles   1.6
1 ROMAN This will I carry to Rome.   (Sc. 6)
2 ROMAN And I this.
3 ROMAN A Murrain on't, I tooke this for Siluer.
        ⌐*He throwes it away.*⌐ *Alarum continues still a-farre*
        off. Enter Martius, bleeding, and Titus Lartius with
        a Trumpet. Exeunt Romans with spoiles
MARTIUS
See heere these mouers, that do prize their honors
At a crack'd Drachme: Cushions, Leaden Spoones,
Irons of a Doit, Dublets that Hangmen would
Bury with those that wore them, these base slaues,
Ere yet the fight be done, packe vp, downe with them.
And harke, what noyse the Generall makes: To him.
There is the man of my soules hate, Auffidious,   500
Piercing our Romanes: Then Valiant Titus take
Conuenient Numbers to make good the City,
Whil'st I with those that haue the spirit, wil haste
To helpe Cominius.
LARTIUS   Worthy Sir, thou bleed'st,
Thy exercise hath bin too violent,
For a second course of Fight.
MARTIUS   Sir, praise me not:
My worke hath yet not warm'd me. Fare you well:
The blood I drop, is rather Physicall

Then dangerous to me: To *Auffidious* thus,
I will appear and fight.

510 LARTIUS   Now the faire Goddesse Fortune,
Fall deepe in loue with thee, and her great charmes
Misguide thy Opposers swords, Bold Gentleman:
Prosperity be thy Page.

MARTIUS   Thy Friend no lesse,
Then those she placeth highest: So farewell.

LARTIUS Thou worthiest *Martius*.   *Exit Martius*
Go sound thy Trumpet in the Market place,
Call thither all the Officers a'th'Towne,
Where they shall know our minde. Away.

                              Exeunt ⌜*seuerally*⌝

1.7   *Enter Cominius as it were in retire, with soldiers*
(Sc. 7) COMINIUS
Breath you my friends, wel fought, we are come off,
520 Like Romans, neither foolish in our stands,
Nor Cowardly in retyre: Beleeue me Sirs,
We shall be charg'd againe. Whiles we haue strooke
By Interims and conueying gusts, we haue heard
The Charges of our Friends. The Roman Gods,
Leade their successes, as we wish our owne,
That both our powers, with smiling Fronts
     encountring,
May giue you thankfull Sacrifice.

          Enter a Messenger

                              Thy Newes?

MESSENGER
The Cittizens of *Corioles* haue yssued,
And giuen to *Lartius* and to *Martius* Battaile:
530 I saw our party to their Trenches driuen,
And then I came away.

COMINIUS   Though thou speak'st truth,
Me thinkes thou speak'st not well. How long is't since?

MESSENGER Aboue an houre, my Lord.

COMINIUS
'Tis not a mile: briefely we heard their drummes.
How could'st thou in a mile confound an houre,
And bring thy Newes so late?

MESSENGER   Spies of the *Volces*
Held me in chace, that I was forc'd to wheele
Three or foure miles about, else had I sir
Halfe an houre since brought my report.   ⌜*Exit*⌝

          Enter Martius, bloody

COMINIUS   Whose yonder,
540 That doe's appeare as he were Flead? O Gods,
He has the stampe of *Martius*, and I haue
Before time seene him thus.

MARTIUS   Come I too late?

COMINIUS
The Shepherd knowes not Thunder frō a Taber,
More then I know the sound of *Martius* Tongue
From euery meaner man.

MARTIUS   Come I too late?

COMINIUS
I, if you come not in the blood of others,
But mantled in your owne.

MARTIUS   Oh! let me clip ye

In Armes as sound, as when I woo'd, in heart
As merry, as when our Nuptiall day was done,
And Tapers burnt to Bedward.   550
          ⌜*They embrace*⌝

COMINIUS
Flower of Warriors, how is't with *Titus Lartius*?

MARTIUS
As with a man busied about Decrees:
Condemning some to death, and some to exile,
Ransoming him, or pittying, threatning th'other;
Holding *Corioles* in the name of Rome,
Euen like a fawning Grey-hound in the Leash,
To let him slip at will.

COMINIUS   Where is that Slaue
Which told me they had beate you to your Trenches?
Where is he? Call him hither.

MARTIUS   Let him alone,
He did informe the truth: but for our Gentlemen,   560
The common file, (a plague—Tribunes for them)
The Mouse ne're shunn'd the Cat, as they did budge
From Rascals worse then they.

COMINIUS   But how preuail'd you?

MARTIUS
Will the time serue to tell, I do not thinke:
Where is the enemy? Are you Lords a'th Field?
If not, why cease you till you are so?

COMINIUS
Martius, we haue at disaduantage fought,
And did retyre to win our purpose.

MARTIUS
How lies their Battell? Know you on wᶜ side
They haue plac'd their men of trust?

COMINIUS   As I guesse *Martius*,   570
Their Bands i'th Vaward are the Antiats
Of their best trust: O're them *Auffidious*,
Their very heart of Hope.

MARTIUS   I do beseech you,
By all the Battailes wherein we haue fought,
By th'Blood we haue shed together, by th'Vowes we
     haue made
To endure Friends, that you directly set me
Against *Affidious*, and his *Antiats*,
And that you not delay the present (but
Filling the aire with Swords aduanc'd) and Darts,
We proue this very houre.

COMINIUS   Though I could wish,   580
You were conducted to a gentle Bath,
And Balmes applyed to you, yet dare I neuer
Deny your asking, take your choice of those
That best can ayde your action.

MARTIUS   Those are they
That most are willing; if any such be heere,
(As it were sinne to doubt) that loue this painting
Wherein you see me smear'd, if any feare
Lesser his person, then an ill report:
If any thinke, braue death out-weighes bad life,
And that his Countries deerer then himselfe,   590
Let him alone: Or so many so minded,

He waues his Sword
Waue thus to expresse his disposition,
And follow *Martius*.
    They all shout and waue their swords, ⌈then some⌉
    take him vp in their Armes, and they cast vp their
    Caps
O' me alone, make you a sword of me:
If these shewes be not outward, which of you
But is foure *Volces*? None of you, but is
Able to beare against the great *Auffidious*
A Shield, as hard as his. A certaine number
600   The rest shall beare the businesse in some other fight
(As cause will be obey'd:) please you to March,
And I shall quickly draw out my Command,
Which men are best inclin'd.
COMINIUS   March on my Fellowes:
Make good this ostentation, and you shall
Diuide in all, with vs.   *Exeunt marching*

1.8   *Enter Titus Lartius ⌈through the Gates of Corioles⌉,*
(Sc. 8)   *with Drum and Trumpet, a Lieutenant, other*
            Souldiours, and a Scout
LARTIUS (*to the Lieutenant*)
So, let the Ports be guarded; keepe your Duties
As I haue set them downe. If I do send, dispatch
Those Centuries to our ayd, the rest will serue
For a short holding, if we loose the Field,
610   We cannot keepe the Towne.
LIEUTENANT Feare not our care Sir.
LARTIUS Hence; and shut your gates vpon's:
                                ⌈*Exit Lieutenant*⌉
(*To the Scout*) Our Guider come, to th'Roman Campe
    conduct vs.
            Exeunt towards Cominius, and Caius Martius

1.9   *Alarum, as in Battaile. Enter Martius, bloody, and*
(Sc. 9)   *Auffidius at seuerall doores*
MARTIUS
Ile fight with none but thee, for I do hate thee
Worse then a Promise-breaker.
AUFFIDIUS   We hate alike:
Not Affricke ownes a Serpent I abhorre
More then thy Fame and Enuy: Fix thy foot.
MARTIUS
Let the first Budger dye the others Slaue,
And the Gods doome him after.
AUFFIDIUS   If I flye *Martius*,
Hollow me like a Hare.
620 MARTIUS   Within these three houres *Tullus*
Alone I fought in your *Corioles* walles,
And made what worke I pleas'd: 'Tis not my blood,
Wherein thou seest me maskt, for thy Reuenge
Wrench vp thy power to th'highest.
AUFFIDIUS   Wer't thou the *Hector*,
That was the whip of your bragg'd Progeny,
Thou should'st not scape me heere.

Heere they fight, and certaine Volces come in the
ayde of Auffidius. Martius fights til the Volces be
driuen in breathles, ⌈Martius following⌉
Officious and not valiant, you haue sham'd me
In your condemned Seconds.   *Exit*

    Alarum. A Retreat is sounded. Flourish. Enter at   **1.10**
    one Doore Cominius, with the Romanes: At   **(Sc. 10)**
    another Doore Martius, with his Arme in a Scarfe
COMINIUS (*to Martius*)
If I should tell thee o're this thy dayes Worke,
Thou't not beleeue thy deeds: but Ile report it,   630
Where Senators shall mingle teares with smiles,
Where great Patricians shall attend, and shrug,
I'th'end admire: where Ladies shall be frighted,
And gladly quak'd, heare more: where the dull
    Tribunes,
That with the fustie Plebeans, hate thine Honors,
Shall say against their hearts, We thanke the Gods
Our Rome hath such a Souldier.
Yet cam'st thou to a Morsell of this Feast,
Hauing fully din'd before.
    Enter Titus Lartius with his Power, from the
    Pursuit
LARTIUS   Oh Generall:
Here is the Steed, wee the Caparison: 640
Hadst thou beheld—
MARTIUS   Pray now, no more: My Mother,
Who ha's a Charter to extoll her Bloud,
When she do's prayse me, grieues me: I haue done
As you haue done, that's what I can, induc'd
As you haue beene, that's for my Countrey:
He that ha's but effected his good will,
Hath ouerta'ne mine Act.
COMINIUS   You shall not be
The Graue of your deseruing, Rome must know
The value of her owne: 'Twere a Concealement
Worse then a Theft, no lesse then a Traducement,   650
To hide your doings, and to silence that,
Which to the spire, and top of prayses vouch'd,
Would seeme but modest: therefore I beseech you,
In signe of what you are, not to reward
What you haue done, before our Armie heare me.
MARTIUS
I haue some Wounds vpon me, and they smart
To heare themselues remembred.
COMINIUS   Should they not:
Well might they fester 'gainst Ingratitude,
And tent themselues with death: of all the Horses,
Whereof we haue ta'ne good, and good store, of all   660
The Treasure in this field atchieud, and Citie,
We render you the Tenth, to be ta'ne forth,
Before the common distribution,
At your onely choyse.
MARTIUS   I thanke you Generall:
But cannot make my heart consent to take
A Bribe, to pay my Sword: I doe refuse it,

And stand vpon my common part with those,
That haue vpheld the doing.

> *A long flourish. They all cry, Martius, Martius,*
> *cast vp their Caps and Launces: Cominius and*
> *Lartius stand bare*

670 May these same Instruments, which you prophane,
Neuer sound more: when Drums and Trumpets shall
I'th'field proue flatterers, let Courts and Cities be
Made all of false-fac'd soothing: When Steele growes
Soft, as the Parasites Silke, let him be made
An Ouerture for th' Warres: No more I say,
For that I haue not wash'd my Nose that bled,
Or foyl'd some debile Wretch, which without note,
Here's many else haue done, you shoot me forth
In acclamations hyperbolicall,
As if I lou'd my little should be dieted
In prayses, sawc'st with Lyes.

680 COMINIUS   Too modest are you:
More cruell to your good report, then gratefull
To vs, that giue you truly: by your patience,
If 'gainst your selfe you be incens'd, wee'le put you
(Like one that meanes his proper harme) in Manacles,
Then reason safely with you: Therefore be it knowne,
As to vs, to all the World, That *Caius Martius*
Weares this Warres Garland: in token of the which,
My Noble Steed, knowne to the Campe, I giue him,
With all his trim belonging; and from this time,
690 For what he did before *Corioles*, call him,
With all th'applause and Clamor of the Hoast,
Marcus Caius Coriolanus. Beare th'addition
Nobly euer?

> *Flourish. Trumpets sound, and Drums*

OMNES *Marcus Caius Coriolanus.*

CORIOLANUS (*to Cominius*) I will goe wash:
And when my Face is faire, you shall perceiue
Whether I blush, or no: howbeit, I thanke you,
I meane to stride your Steed, and at all times
To vnder-crest your good Addition,
To th'fairenesse of my power.

700 COMINIUS   So, to our Tent:
Where ere we doe repose vs, we will write
To Rome of our successe: you *Titus Lartius*
Must to *Corioles* backe, send vs to Rome
The best, with whom we may articulate,
For their owne good, and ours.

LARTIUS   I shall, my Lord.

CORIOLANUS The Gods begin to mocke me: I that now
Refus'd most Princely gifts, am bound to begge
Of my Lord Generall.

COMINIUS   Tak't, 'tis yours: what is't?

CORIOLANUS
I sometime lay here in *Corioles*,
710 And at a poore mans house: he vs'd me kindly,
He cry'd to me: I saw him Prisoner:
But then *Auffidius* was within my view,
And Wrath o're-whelm'd my pittie: I request you
To giue my poore Host freedome.

COMINIUS   Oh well begg'd:

Were he the Butcher of my Sonne, he should
Be free, as is the Winde: deliuer him, *Titus.*

LARTIUS
Martius, his Name.

CORIOLANUS   By *Iupiter* forgot:
I am wearie, yea, my memorie is tyr'd:
Haue we no Wine here?

COMINIUS   Goe we to our Tent:
The bloud vpon your Visage dryes, 'tis time   720
It should be lookt too: come.

> *A flourish. Cornets. Exeunt*

> *Enter Tullus Auffidius bloudie, with two or three*   1.11
> *Souldiors*   (Sc. 11)

AUFFIDIUS The Towne is ta'ne.

A SOULDIER
'Twill be deliuer'd backe on good Condition.

AUFFIDIUS Condition?
I would I were a Roman, for I cannot,
Being a *Volce*, be that I am. Condition?
What good Condition can a Treatie finde
I'th'part that is at mercy? fiue times, *Martius*,
I haue fought with thee; so often hast thou beat me:
And would'st doe so, I thinke, should we encounter   730
As often as we eate. By th'Elements,
If ere againe I meet him beard to beard,
He's mine, or I am his: Mine Emulation
Hath not that Honor in't it had: For where
I thought to crush him in an equall Force,
True Sword to Sword: Ile potche at him some way,
Or Wrath, or Craft may get him.

A SOULDIER   He's the diuell.

AUFFIDIUS
Bolder, though not so subtle: my valor, poison'd
With onely suff'ring staine by him, for him
Shall flye out of it selfe, nor sleepe, nor sanctuary,   740
Being naked, sicke; nor Phane, nor Capitoll,
The Prayers of Priests, nor times of Sacrifice:
Embarquements all of Fury, shall lift vp
Their rotten Priuiledge, and Custome 'gainst
My hate to *Martius*. Where I finde him, were it
At home, vpon my Brothers Guard, euen there
Against the hospitable Canon, would I
Wash my fierce hand in's heart. Go you to th'Citie,
Learne how 'tis held, and what they are that must
Be Hostages for Rome.

A SOULDIER   Will not you go?   750

AUFFIDIUS
I am attended at the Cyprus groue. I pray you
('Tis South the City Mils) bring me word thither
How the world goes: that to the pace of it
I may spurre on my iourney.

A SOULDIER   I shall sir.

> *Exeunt ⌈Auffidius at one doore,*
> *Souldiers at another doore⌉*

2.1   *Enter Menenius with the two Tribunes of the people,*
(Sc. 12)   *Sicinius & Brutus*

MENENIUS The Agurer tels me, wee shall haue Newes to
  night.

BRUTUS Good or bad?

MENENIUS Not according to the prayer of the people, for
  they loue not *Martius*.

760 SCICINIUS Nature teaches Beasts to know their Friends.

MENENIUS Pray you, who does the Wolfe loue?

SCICINIUS The Lambe.

MENENIUS I, to deuour him, as the hungry Plebeians
  would the Noble *Martius*.

BRUTUS He's a Lambe indeed, that baes like a Beare.

MENENIUS Hee's a Beare indeede, that liues like a Lambe.
  You two are old men, tell me one thing that I shall
  aske you.

BOTH TRIBUNES Well sir.

770 MENENIUS In what enormity is *Martius* poore in, that you
  two haue not in abundance?

BRUTUS He's poore in no one fault, but stor'd with all.

SCICINIUS Especially in Pride.

BRUTUS And topping all others in boasting.

MENENIUS This is strange now: Do you two know, how
  you are censured heere in the City, I mean of vs
  a'th'right hand File, do you?

BOTH TRIBUNES Why? how are we censur'd?

MENENIUS Because you talke of Pride now, will you not
780 be angry.

BOTH TRIBUNES Well, well sir, well.

MENENIUS Why 'tis no great matter: for a very little theefe
  of Occasion, will rob you of a great deale of Patience:
  Giue your dispositions the reines, and bee angry at
  your pleasures (at the least) if you take it as a pleasure
  to you, in being so: you blame *Martius* for being proud.

BRUTUS We do it not alone, sir.

MENENIUS I know you can doe very little alone, for your
  helpes are many, or else your actions would growe
790 wondrous single: your abilities are to Infant-like, for
  dooing much alone. You talke of Pride: Oh, that you
  could turn your eyes toward the Napes of your neckes,
  and make but an Interiour suruey of your good selues.
  Oh that you could.

BOTH TRIBUNES What then sir?

MENENIUS Why then you should discouer a brace of
  vnmeriting, proud, violent, testie Magistrates (alias
  Fooles) as any in Rome.

SCICINIUS *Menenius*, you are knowne well enough too.

800 MENENIUS I am knowne to be a humorous *Patritian*, and
  one that loues a cup of hot Wine, with not a drop of
  alaying Tiber in't: Said, to be something imperfect in
  fauouring the first complaint, hasty and Tinder-like
  vppon to triuiall motion: One, that conuerses more
  with the Buttocke of the night, then with the forhead
  of the morning. What I think, I vtter, and spend my
  malice in my breath. Meeting two such Weales men as
  you are (I cannot call you *Licurgusses*,) if the drinke
  you giue me, touch my Palat aduersly, I make a crooked
810 face at it, I can not say, your Worshippes haue deliuer'd
  the matter well, when I finde the Asse in compound,

with the Maior part of your syllables. And though I
must be content to beare with those, that say you are
reuerend graue men, yet they lye deadly, that tell you
haue good faces, if you see this in the Map of my
Microcosme, followes it that I am knowne well enough
too? What harme can your beesome Conspectuities
gleane out of this Charracter, if I be knowne well
enough too.

BRUTUS Come sir come, we know you well enough.   820

MENENIUS You know neither mee, your selues, nor any
  thing: you are ambitious, for poore knaues cappes and
  legges: you weare out a good wholesome Forenoone,
  in hearing a cause betweene an Orendge wife, and a
  Forset-seller, and then reiourne the Controuersie of
  three-pence to a second day of Audience. When you
  are hearing a matter betweene party and party, if you
  chaunce to bee pinch'd with the Collike, you make
  faces like Mummers, set vp the bloodie Flagge against
  all Patience, and in roaring for a Chamber-pot, dismisse   830
  the Controuersie bleeding, the more intangled by your
  hearing: All the peace you make in their Cause, is
  calling both the parties Knaues. You are a payre of
  strange ones.

BRUTUS Come, come, you are well vnderstood to bee a
  perfecter gyber for the Table, then a necessary Bencher
  in the Capitoll.

MENENIUS Our very Priests must become Mockers, if they
  shall encounter such ridiculous Subiects as you are.
  When you speake best vnto the purpose, it is not   840
  woorth the wagging of your Beards, and your Beards
  deserue not so honourable a graue, as to stuffe a
  Botchers Cushion, or to be intomb'd in an Asses Packe-
  saddle; yet you must bee saying, *Martius* is proud: who
  in a cheape estimation, is worth all your predecessors,
  since *Deucalion*, though peraduenture some of the best
  of 'em were hereditarie hangmen. Godden to your
  Worships, more of your conuersation would infect my
  Braine, being the Heardsmen of the Beastly Plebeans.
  I will be bold to take my leaue of you.   850

  He leaues Brutus and Scicinius, who stand aside.
  Enter in haste Volumnia, Virgilia, and Valeria

How now (my as faire as Noble) Ladyes, and the Moone
were shee Earthly, no Nobler; whither doe you follow
your Eyes so fast?

VOLUMNIA Honorable *Menenius*, my Boy *Martius* approches: for the loue of *Iuno* let's goe.

MENENIUS Ha? *Martius* comming home?

VOLUMNIA I, worthy *Menenius*, and with most prosperous
  approbation.

MENENIUS ⌈*throwing vp his Cappe*⌉ Take my Cappe *Iupiter*,
  and I thanke thee: hoo, *Martius* comming home?   860

VIRGILIA *and* VALERIA Nay, 'tis true.

VOLUMNIA Looke, here's a Letter from him, the State hath
  another, his Wife another, and (I thinke) there's one
  at home for you.

MENENIUS I will make my very house reele to night: A
  Letter for me?

VIRGILIA Yes certaine, there's a Letter for you, I saw't.

MENENIUS A Letter for me? it giues me an Estate of seuen

yeeres health; in which time, I will make a Lippe at
the Physician: The most soueraigne Prescription in
Galen, is but Emperickqutique; and to this Preseruatiue,
of no better report then a Horse-drench. Is he not
wounded? he was wont to come home wounded?

VIRGILIA Oh no, no, no.

VOLUMNIA Oh, he is wounded, I thanke the Gods for't.

MENENIUS So doe I too, if it be not too much: brings a
Victorie in his Pocket? the wounds become him.

VOLUMNIA On's Browes, *Menenius*, hee comes the third
time home with the Oaken Garland.

MENENIUS Ha's he disciplin'd *Auffidius* soundly?

VOLUMNIA *Titus Lartius* writes, they fought together, but
Auffidius got off.

MENENIUS And 'twas time for him too, Ile warrant him
that: and he had stay'd by him, I would not haue been
so fiddious'd, for all the Chests in Carioles, and the
Gold that's in them. Is the Senate possest of this?

VOLUMNIA Good Ladies let's goe. Yes, yes, yes: The Senate
ha's Letters from the Generall, wherein hee giues my
Sonne the whole Name of the Warre: he hath in this
action out-done his former deeds doubly.

VALERIA In troth, there's wondrous things spoke of him.

MENENIUS Wondrous: I, I warrant you, and not without
his true purchasing.

VIRGILIA The Gods graunt them true.

VOLUMNIA True? pow waw.

MENENIUS True? Ile be sworne they are true: where is
hee wounded, (*to the Tribunes*) God saue your good
Worships? *Martius* is comming home: hee ha's more
cause to be prowd: (*to Volumnia*) where is he wounded?

VOLUMNIA Ith' Shoulder, and ith' left Arme: there will be
large Cicatrices to shew the People, when hee shall
stand for his place: he receiued in the repulse of *Tarquin*
seuen hurts ith' Body.

MENENIUS One ith' Neck, and two ith'Thigh, there's nine
that I know.

VOLUMNIA Hee had, before this last Expedition, twentie
fiue Wounds vpon him.

MENENIUS Now it's twentie seuen; euery gash was an
Enemies Graue.
        A showt, and flourish
Hearke, the Trumpets.

VOLUMNIA These are the Vshers of *Martius*: Before him,
hee carryes Noyse; And behinde him, hee leaues Teares:
Death, that darke Spirit, in's neruie Arme doth lye,
Which being aduanc'd, declines, and then men dye.
        A Sennet. Trumpets sound. Enter ⌈in State⌉
        Cominius the Generall, and Titus Latius: betweene
        them Coriolanus, crown'd with an Oaken Garland,
        with Captaines and Souldiers, and a Herauld

HERAULD
Know Rome, that all alone *Martius* did fight
Within Corioles Gates: where he hath wonne,
With Fame, a Name to *Martius Caius*: These
In honor followes *Coriolanus*.
Welcome to Rome, renowned *Coriolanus*.
        Sound Flourish

ALL
Welcome to Rome, renowned *Coriolanus*.

CORIOLANUS
No more of this, it does offend my heart:
Pray now no more.

COMINIUS   Looke, Sir, your Mother.

CORIOLANUS (*to Volumnia*)   Oh!
You haue, I know, petition'd all the Gods
For my prosperitie.
        He kneeles

VOLUMNIA   Nay, my good Souldier, vp:
My gentle *Martius*, worthy *Caius*,
        ⌈*He rises*⌉
And by deed-atchieuing Honor newly nam'd,
What is it (*Coriolanus*) must I call thee?
But oh, thy Wife.

CORIOLANUS (*to Virgilia*) My gracious silence, hayle:
Would'st thou haue laugh'd, had I come Coffin'd home,
That weep'st to see me triumph? Ah my deare,
Such eyes the Widowes in Carioles were,
And Mothers that lacke Sonnes.

MENENIUS   Now the Gods Crowne thee.

⌈CORIOLANUS⌉ (*to Valeria*)
And liue you yet? Oh my sweet Lady, pardon.

VOLUMNIA
I know not where to turne. Oh welcome home:
And welcome Generall, and y'are welcome all.

MENENIUS
A hundred thousand Welcomes: I could weepe,
And I could laugh, I am light, and heauie; welcome:
A Curse begnaw at very root on's heart,
That is not glad to see thee. You are three,
That Rome should dote on: Yet by the faith of men,
We haue some old Crab-trees here at home, that will not
Be grafted to your Rallish. Yet welcome Warriors:
Wee call a Nettle, but a Nettle; And
The faults of fooles, but folly.

COMINIUS Euer right.

CORIOLANUS *Menenius*, euer, euer.

HERAULD
Giue way there, and goe on.

CORIOLANUS ⌈*to Volumnia and Virgilia*⌉
                    Your Hand, and yours?
Ere in our owne house I doe shade my Head,
The good Patricians must be visited,
From whom I haue receiu'd not onely greetings,
But with them, change of Honors.

VOLUMNIA   I haue liued,
To see inherited my very Wishes,
And the Buildings of my Fancie: Onely
There's one thing wanting, which (I doubt not) but
Our Rome will cast vpon thee.

CORIOLANUS   Know, good Mother,
I had rather be their seruant in my way,
Then sway with them in theirs.

COMINIUS   On, to the Capitall.
        Flourish Cornets. Exeunt in State, as before, all
        but Brutus and Scicinius, who come forward

BRUTUS

All tongues speake of him, and the bleared sights
Are spectacled to see him. Your pratling Nurse
960   Into a rapture lets her Baby crie,
While she chats him: the Kitchin *Malkin* pinnes
Her richest Lockram 'bout her reechie necke,
Clambring the Walls to eye him: Stalls, Bulkes,
    Windowes,
Are smother'd vp, leades fill'd, and Ridges hors'd
With variable Complexions; all agreeing
In earnestnesse to see him: seld-showne Flamins
Doe presse among the popular Throngs, and puffe
To winne a vulgar station: our veyl'd Dames
Commit the Warre of White and Damaske in
970   Their nicely garded Cheekes, toth' wanton spoyle
Of *Phœbus* burning Kisses: such a poother,
As if that whatsoeuer God, who leades him,
Were slyly crept into his humane powers,
And gaue him gracefull posture.

SCICINIUS   On the suddaine,
I warrant him Consull.

BRUTUS   Then our Office may,
During his power, goe sleepe.

SCICINIUS

He cannot temp'rately transport his Honors,
From where he should begin, and end, but will
Lose those he hath wonne.

BRUTUS   In that there's comfort.

SCICINIUS   Doubt not,
980   The Commoners, for whom we stand, but they
Vpon their ancient mallice, will forget
With the least cause, these his new Honors, which
That he will giue them, make I as little question,
As he is prowd to doo't.

BRUTUS   I heard him sweare,
Were he to stand for Consull, neuer would he
Appeare i'th'Market place, nor on him put
The Naples Vesture of Humilitie,
Nor shewing (as the manner is) his Wounds
Toth' People, begge their stinking Breaths.

SCICINIUS   'Tis right.

BRUTUS

990   It was his word: Oh he would misse it, rather
Then carry it, but by the suite of the Gentry to him,
And the desire of the Nobles.

SCICINIUS   I wish no better,
Then haue him hold that purpose, and to put it
In execution.

BRUTUS   'Tis most like he will.

SCICINIUS

It shall be to him then, as our good wills;
A sure destruction.

BRUTUS   So it must fall out
To him, or our Authorities for an end.
We must suggest the People, in what hatred
He still hath held them: that to's power he would
1000   Haue made them Mules, silenc'd their Pleaders,

And dispropertied their Freedomes; holding them,
In humane Action, and Capacitie,
Of no more Soule, nor fitnesse for the World,
Then Cammels in their Warre, who haue their Prouand
Onely for bearing Burthens, and sore blowes
For sinking vnder them.

SCICINIUS   This (as you say) suggested,
At some time, when his soaring Insolence
Shall touch the People, which time shall not want,
If he be put vpon't, and that's as easie,
As to set Dogges on Sheepe, will be his fire   1010
To kindle their dry Stubble: and their Blaze
Shall darken him for euer.

    Enter a Messenger

BRUTUS   What's the matter?

MESSENGER

You are sent for to the Capitoll: 'Tis thought,
That *Martius* shall be Consull: I haue seene
The dumbe men throng to see him, and the blind
To heare him speak: Matrons flong Gloues,
Ladies and Maids their Scarffes, and Handkerchers,
Vpon him as he pass'd: the Nobles bended
As to *Ioues* Statue, and the Commons made
A Shower, and Thunder, with their Caps, and Showts: 1020
I neuer saw the like.

BRUTUS   Let's to the Capitoll,
And carry with vs Eares and Eyes for th' time,
But Hearts for the euent.

SCICINIUS   Haue with you.   *Exeunt*

    Enter two Officers, to lay Cushions, as it were, in   2.2
    the Capitoll   (Sc. 13

1 OFFICER Come, come, they are almost here: how many
stand for Consulships?

2 OFFICER Three, they say: but 'tis thought of euery one,
Coriolanus will carry it.

1 OFFICER That's a braue fellow: but hee's vengeance
prowd, and loues not the common people.

2 OFFICER 'Faith, there hath beene many great men that   1030
haue flatter'd the people, who ne're loued them; and
there be many that they haue loued, they know not
wherefore: so that if they loue they know not why,
they hate vpon no better a ground. Therefore, for
Coriolanus neyther to care whether they loue, or hate
him, manifests the true knowledge he ha's in their
disposition, and out of his Noble carelesnesse lets them
plainely see't.

1 OFFICER If he did not care whether he had their loue,
or no, hee waued indifferently, 'twixt doing them   1040
neyther good, nor harme: but hee seekes their hate
with greater deuotion, then they can render it him;
and leaues nothing vndone, that may fully discouer
him their opposite. Now to seeme to affect the mallice
and displeasure of the People, is as bad, as that which
he dislikes, to flatter them for their loue.

2 OFFICER Hee hath deserued worthily of his Countrey,
and his assent is not by such easie degrees as those,

who hauing beene supple and courteous to the People,
Bonnetted, without any further deed, to haue them at
all into their estimation, and report: but hee hath so
planted his Honors in their Eyes, and his actions in
their Hearts, that for their Tongues to be silent, and
not confesse so much, were a kinde of ingratefull
Iniurie: to report otherwise, were a Mallice, that giuing
it selfe the Lye, would plucke reproofe and rebuke from
euery Eare that heard it.

1 OFFICER No more of him, hee's a worthy man: make
way, they are comming.

> *A Sennet. Enter the Patricians, and the Tribunes of*
> *the People, Lictors before them: Coriolanus,*
> *Menenius, Cominius the Consul: ⌈The Patricians*
> *take their places and sit:⌉ Scicinius and Brutus*
> *take their places by themselues: Coriolanus stands*

MENENIUS
Hauing determin'd of the Volces, and
To send for *Titus Lartius*: it remaines,
As the maine Point of this our after-meeting,
To gratifie his Noble seruice, that
Hath thus stood for his Countrey. Therefore please you,
Most reuerend and graue Elders, to desire
The present Consull, and last Generall,
In our well-found Successes, to report
A little of that worthy Worke, perform'd
By *Martius Caius Coriolanus*: whom
We met here, both to thanke, and to remember,
With Honors like himselfe.

> ⌈*Coriolanus sits*⌉

1 SENATOR   Speake, good *Cominius*:
Leaue nothing out for length, and make vs thinke
Rather our states defectiue for requitall,
Then we to stretch it out. (*To the Tribunes*) Masters
    a'th' People,
We doe request your kindest eares: and after
Your louing motion toward the common Body,
To yeeld what passes here.

SCICINIUS   We are conuented
Vpon a pleasing Treatie, and haue hearts
Inclinable to honor and aduance
The Theame of our Assembly.

BRUTUS   Which the rather
Wee shall be blest to doe, if he remember
A kinder value of the People, then
He hath hereto priz'd them at.

MENENIUS   That's off, that's off:
I would you rather had been silent: Please you
To heare *Cominius* speake?

BRUTUS   Most willingly:
But yet my Caution was more pertinent
Then the rebuke you giue it.

MENENIUS   He loues your People,
But tye him not to be their Bed-fellow:
Worthie *Cominius* speake.

> *Coriolanus rises, and offers to goe away*

(*To Coriolanus*)   Nay, keepe your place.

⌈1⌉ SENATOR Sit *Coriolanus*: neuer shame to heare
What you haue Nobly done.

CORIOLANUS   Your Honors pardon:
I had rather haue my Wounds to heale againe,
Then heare say how I got them.

BRUTUS   Sir, I hope
My words dis-bench'd you not?

CORIOLANUS   No Sir: yet oft,
When blowes haue made me stay, I fled from words.
You sooth'd not, therefore hurt not: but your People,
I loue them as they weigh—

MENENIUS   Pray now sit downe.

CORIOLANUS
I had rather haue one scratch my Head i'th' Sun,
When the Alarum were strucke, then idly sit
To heare my Nothings monster'd.   *Exit*

MENENIUS   Masters of the People,
Your multiplying Spawne, how can he flatter?
That's thousand to one good one, when you now see
He had rather venture all his Limbes for Honor,
Then on ones Eares to heare it. Proceed *Cominius*.

COMINIUS
I shall lacke voyce: the deeds of *Coriolanus*
Should not be vtter'd feebly: it is held,
That Valour is the chiefest Vertue, and
Most dignifies the hauer: if it be,
The man I speake of, cannot in the World
Be singly counter-poys'd. At sixteene yeeres,
When *Tarquin* made a Head for Rome, he fought
Beyond the marke of others: our then Dictator,
Whom with all prayse I point at, saw him fight,
When with his Amazonian Shinne he droue
The brizled Lippes before him: he bestrid
An o're-prest Roman, and i'th' Consuls view
Slew three Opposers: *Tarquins* selfe he met,
And strucke him on his Knee: in that dayes feates,
When he might act the Woman in the Scene,
He prou'd best man i'th' field, and for his meed
Was Brow-bound with the Oake. His Pupill age
Man-entred thus, he waxed like a Sea,
And in the brunt of seuenteene Battailes since,
He lurcht all Swords of the Garland: for this last,
Before, and in Corioles, let me say
I cannot speake him home: he stopt the flyers,
And by his rare example made the Coward
Turne terror into sport: as Weeds before
A Vessell vnder sayle, so men obey'd,
And fell below his Stem: his Sword, Deaths stampe,
Where it did marke, it tooke: from face to foot
He was a thing of Blood, whose euery motion
Was tim'd with dying Cryes: alone he entred
The mortall Gate of th' Citie, which he, painted
With shunlesse destinie: aydelesse came off,
And with a sudden re-inforcement strucke
Carioles like a Planet: now all's his,
When by and by the dinne of Warre gan pierce
His readie sence: then straight his doubled spirit

1050
1060
1070
1080

1090
1100
1110
1120
1130

1140 Requickned what in flesh was fatigate,
And to the Battaile came he, where he did
Runne reeking o're the liues of men, as if
'Twere a perpetuall spoyle: and till we call'd
Both Field and Citie ours, he neuer stood
To ease his Brest with panting.

MENENIUS   Worthy man.

⌈1⌉ SENATOR
He cannot but with measure fit the Honors
Which we deuise him.

COMINIUS   Our spoyles he kickt at,
And look'd vpon things precious, as they were
The common Muck of the World: he couets lesse
1150 Then Miserie it selfe would giue, rewards
His deeds with doing them, and is content
To spend the time, to end it.

MENENIUS   Hee's right Noble,
Let him be call'd for.

⌈1⌉ SENATOR Call *Coriolanus*.

OFFICER He doth appeare.

            Enter Coriolanus

MENENIUS
The Senate, *Coriolanus*, are well pleas'd
To make thee Consull.

CORIOLANUS   I doe owe them still
My Life, and Seruices.

MENENIUS   It then remaines,
That you doe speake to the People.

CORIOLANUS   I doe beseech you,
1160 Let me o're-leape that custome: for I cannot
Put on the Gowne, stand naked, and entreat them
For my Wounds sake, to giue their sufferage:
Please you that I may passe this doing.

SCICINIUS   Sir, the People
Must haue their Voyces, neyther will they bate
One iot of Ceremonie.

MENENIUS (*to Coriolanus*) Put them not too't:
Pray you goe fit you to the Custome, and
Take to you, as your Predecessors haue,
Your Honor with your forme.

CORIOLANUS   It is a part
That I shall blush in acting, and might well
Be taken from the People.

1170 BRUTUS (*to Sicinius*)   Marke you that.

CORIOLANUS
To brag vnto them, thus I did, and thus,
Shew them th'vnaking Skarres, which I should hide,
As if I had receiu'd them for the hyre
Of their breath onely.

MENENIUS   Doe not stand vpon't:
We recommend to you Tribunes of the People
Our purpose to them, and to our Noble Consull
Wish we all Ioy, and Honor.

SENATORS
To *Coriolanus* come all ioy and Honor.

                Flourish Cornets. Then Exeunt.
                Manet Sicinius and Brutus

BRUTUS
You see how he intends to vse the people.

SCICINIUS
May they perceiue's intent: he wil require them   1180
As if he did contemne what he requested,
Should be in them to giue.

BRUTUS   Come, wee'l informe them
Of our proceedings heere: on th'Market place,
I know they do attend vs.   *Exeunt*

            Enter seuen or eight Citizens   2.3
                                                          (Sc. 14
1 CITIZEN Once if he do require our voyces, wee ought
not to deny him.

2 CITIZEN We may Sir if we will.

3 CITIZEN We haue power in our selues to do it, but it is
a power that we haue no power to do: For, if hee shew
vs his wounds, and tell vs his deeds, we are to put our   1190
tongues into those wounds, and speake for them: So if
he tel vs his Noble deeds, we must also tell him our
Noble acceptance of them. Ingratitude is monstrous,
and for the multitude to be ingratefull, were to make
a Monster of the multitude; of the which, we being
members, should bring our selues to be monstrous
members.

1 CITIZEN And to make vs no better thought of a little
helpe will serue: for once we stood vp about the Corne,
he himselfe stucke not to call vs the many-headed   1200
Multitude.

3 CITIZEN We haue beene call'd so of many, not that our
heads are some browne, some blacke, some Abram,
some bald; but that our wits are so diuersly Coulord;
and truely I thinke, if all our wittes were to issue out
of one Scull, they would flye East, West, North, South,
and their consent of one direct way, should be at once
to all the points a'th Compasse.

2 CITIZEN Thinke you so? Which way do you iudge my
wit would flye.   1210

3 CITIZEN Nay your wit will not so soone out as another
mans will, 'tis strongly wadg'd vp in a blocke-head:
but if it were at liberty, 'twould sure Southward.

2 CITIZEN Why that way?

3 CITIZEN To loose it selfe in a Fogge, where being three
parts melted away with rotten Dewes, the fourth would
returne for Conscience sake, to helpe to get thee a Wife.

2 CITIZEN You are neuer without your trickes, you may,
you may.

3 CITIZEN Are you all resolu'd to giue your voyces? But   1220
that's no matter, the greater part carries it. I say: If
hee would incline to the people, there was neuer a
worthier man.

            Enter Coriolanus in a gowne of Humility, with
            Menenius

Heere he comes, and in the Gowne of humility, marke
his behauiour: we are not to stay altogether, but to
come by him where he stands, by ones, by twoes, &
by threes. He's to make his requests by particulars,
wherein euerie one of vs ha's a single Honor, in giuing

1230 him our own voices with our owne tongues, therefore
follow me, and Ile direct you how you shall go by him.

ALL THE CITIZENS Content, content.   *Exeunt Citizens*

MENENIUS

Oh Sir, you are not right: haue you not knowne
The worthiest men haue done't?

CORIOLANUS   What must I say,
I pray Sir? Plague vpon't, I cannot bring
My tongue to such a pace. Looke Sir, my wounds,
I got them in my Countries Seruice, when
Some certaine of your Brethren roar'd, and ranne
From th'noise of our owne Drummes.

MENENIUS   Oh me the Gods,
You must not speak of that, you must desire them
To thinke vpon you.

1240 CORIOLANUS   Thinke vpon me? Hang 'em,
I would they would forget me, like the Vertues
Which our Diuines lose by em.

MENENIUS   You'l marre all,
Ile leaue you: Pray you speake to em, I pray you
In wholsome manner.

CORIOLANUS   Bid them wash their Faces,
And keepe their teeth cleane: *Exit Menenius*
     Enter three of the Citizens
                         So, heere comes a brace,
You know the cause (Sir) of my standing heere.

3 CITIZEN
We do Sir, tell vs what hath brought you too't.

CORIOLANUS Mine owne desert.

2 CITIZEN Your owne desert.

1250 CORIOLANUS I, but not mine owne desire.

3 CITIZEN How not your owne desire?

CORIOLANUS No Sir, 'twas neuer my desire yet to trouble
the poore with begging.

3 CITIZEN You must thinke if we giue you any thing, we
hope to gaine by you.

CORIOLANUS Well then I pray, your price a'th'Consulship.

1 CITIZEN The price is, to aske it kindly.

CORIOLANUS Kindly sir, I pray let me ha't: I haue wounds
to shew you, which shall bee yours in priuate: (*to 2*
1260 *Citizen*) your good voice Sir, what say you?

2 CITIZEN You shall ha't worthy Sir.

CORIOLANUS A match Sir, there's in all two worthie voyces
begg'd: I haue your Almes, Adieu.

3 CITIZEN (*to the other Citizens*) But this is something odde.

2 CITIZEN And 'twere to giue againe: but 'tis no matter.
                                   Exeunt Citizens
     Enter two other Citizens

CORIOLANUS Pray you now, if it may stand with the tune
of your voices, that I may bee Consull, I haue heere
the Customarie Gowne.

⌐4⌐ CITIZEN You haue deserued Nobly of your Countrey,
1270 and you haue not deserued Nobly.

CORIOLANUS Your Ænigma.

⌐4⌐ CITIZEN You haue bin a scourge to her enemies, you
haue bin a Rod to her Friends, you haue not indeede
loued the Common people.

CORIOLANUS You should account mee the more Vertuous,
that I haue not bin common in my Loue, I will sir
flatter my sworne Brother the people to earne a deerer
estimation of them, 'tis a condition they account gentle:
& since the wisedome of their choice, is rather to haue
my Hat, then my Heart, I will practice the insinuating 1280
nod, and be off to them most counterfetly, that is sir,
I will counterfet the bewitchment of some popular man,
and giue it bountifull to the desirers: Therefore beseech
you, I may be Consull.

⌐5⌐ CITIZEN Wee hope to finde you our friend: and
therefore giue you our voices heartily.

⌐4⌐ CITIZEN You haue receyued many wounds for your
Countrey.

CORIOLANUS I wil not Seale your knowledge with shewing
them. I will make much of your voyces, and so trouble 1290
you no farther.

BOTH CITIZENS The Gods giue you ioy Sir heartily.

CORIOLANUS Most sweet Voyces: *Exeunt Citizens*
Better it is to dye, better to sterue,
Then craue the hier, which first we do deserue.
Why in this Womanish togue should I stand heere,
To begge of Hob and Dicke, that does appeere
Their needlesse Vouches: Custome calls me too't.
What Custome wills in all things should we doo't,
The Dust on antique Time would lye vnswept,   1300
And mountainous Error be too highly heapt,
For Truth to o're-peere. Rather then foole it so,
Let the high Office and the Honor go
To one that would doe thus. I am halfe through,
The one part suffred, the other will I doe.
     Enter three Citizens more
Here come moe Voyces.
Your Voyces? for your Voyces I haue fought,
Watcht for your Voyces: for your Voyces, beare
Of Wounds, two dozen odde: Battailes thrice six
I haue seene, and heard of: for your Voyces, haue   1310
Done many things, some lesse, some more: Your Voyces?
Indeed I would be Consull.

⌐6⌐ CITIZEN Hee ha's done Nobly, and cannot goe without
any honest mans Voyce.

⌐7⌐ CITIZEN Therefore let him be Consull: the Gods giue
him ioy, and make him good friend to the People.

ALL THE CITIZENS Amen, Amen. God saue thee, Noble
Consull.

CORIOLANUS Worthy Voyces.   *Exeunt Citizens*
     Enter Menenius, with Brutus and Scicinius

MENENIUS
You haue stood your Limitation: And the Tribunes   1320
Endue you with the Peoples Voyce, remaines,
That in th'Officiall Markes inuested, you
Anon doe meet the Senate.

CORIOLANUS   Is this done?

SCICINIUS
The Custome of Request you haue discharg'd:
The People doe admit you, and are summon'd
To meet anon, vpon your approbation.

CORIOLANUS
    Where? at the Senate-house?
SCICINIUS   There, *Coriolanus.*
CORIOLANUS
    May I change these Garments?
SCICINIUS   You may, Sir.
CORIOLANUS
    That Ile straight do: and knowing my selfe again,
1330   Repayre toth' Senatehouse.
MENENIUS
    Ile keepe you company. (*To the Tribunes*) Will you along?
BRUTUS
    We stay here for the People.
SCICINIUS   Fare you well.
            Exeunt Coriolanus and Menenius
    He ha's it now: and by his Lookes, me thinkes,
    'Tis warme at's heart.
BRUTUS   With a prowd heart he wore
    His humble Weeds: Will you dismisse the People?
            Enter the Plebeians
SCICINIUS
    How now, my Masters, haue you chose this man?
1 CITIZEN He ha's our Voyces, Sir.
BRUTUS
    We pray the Gods, he may deserue your loues.
2 CITIZEN
    Amen, Sir: to my poore vnworthy notice,
1340   He mock'd vs, when he begg'd our Voyces.
3 CITIZEN
    Certainely, he flowted vs downe-right.
1 CITIZEN
    No, 'tis his kind of speech, he did not mock vs.
2 CITIZEN
    Not one amongst vs, saue your selfe, but sayes
    He vs'd vs scornefully: he should haue shew'd vs
    His Marks of Merit, Wounds receiu'd for's Countrey.
SCICINIUS
    Why so he did, I am sure.
ALL THE CITIZENS   No, no: no man saw 'em.
3 CITIZEN
    Hee said hee had Wounds, which he could shew in
            priuate:
    And with his Hat, thus wauing it in scorne,
    I would be Consull, sayes he: aged Custome,
1350   But by your Voyces, will not so permit me.
    Your Voyces therefore: when we graunted that,
    Here was, I thanke you for your Voyces, thanke you
    Your most sweet Voyces: now you haue left your
            Voyces,
    I haue no further with you. Was not this mockerie?
SCICINIUS
    Why eyther were you ignorant to see't?
    Or seeing it, of such Childish friendlinesse,
    To yeeld your Voyces?
BRUTUS (*to the Citizens*)   Could you not haue told him,
    As you were lesson'd: When he had no Power,
    But was a pettie seruant to the State,

He was your Enemie, euer spake against   1360
Your Liberties, and the Charters that you beare
I'th' Body of the Weale: and now arriuing
A place of Potencie, and sway o'th' State,
If he should still malignantly remaine
Fast Foe toth' *Plebeij*, your Voyces might
Be Curses to your selues. You should haue said,
That as his worthy deeds did clayme no lesse
Then what he stood for: so his gracious nature
Would thinke vpon you, for your Voyces, and
Translate his Mallice towards you, into Loue,   1370
Standing your friendly Lord.
SCICINIUS (*to the Citizens*)   Thus to haue said,
As you were fore-aduis'd, had toucht his Spirit,
And try'd his Inclination: from him pluckt
Eyther his gracious Promise, which you might
As cause had call'd you vp, haue held him to;
Or else it would haue gall'd his surly nature,
Which easily endures not Article,
Tying him to ought, so putting him to Rage,
You should haue ta'ne th'aduantage of his Choller,
And pass'd him vnelected.
BRUTUS (*to the Citizens*)   Did you perceiue,   1380
He did sollicite you in free Contempt,
When he did need your Loues: and doe you thinke,
That his Contempt shall not be brusing to you,
When he hath power to crush? Why, had your Bodyes
No Heart among you? Or had you Tongues, to cry
Against the Rectorship of Iudgement?
SCICINIUS (*to the Citizens*)   Haue you,
Ere now, deny'd the asker: And now againe,
Of him that did not aske, but mock, bestow
Your su'd-for Tongues?
3 CITIZEN
    Hee's not confirm'd, we may deny him yet.   1390
2 CITIZEN And will deny him:
    Ile haue fiue hundred Voyces of that sound.
1 CITIZEN
    I twice fiue hundred, & their friends, to piece 'em.
BRUTUS
    Get you hence instantly, and tell those friends,
    They haue chose a Consull, that will from them take
    Their Liberties, make them of no more Voyce
    Then Dogges, that are as often beat for barking,
    As therefore kept to doe so.
SCICINIUS (*to the Citizens*)   Let them assemble:
    And on a safer Iudgement, all reuoke
    Your ignorant election: Enforce his Pride,   1400
    And his old Hate vnto you: besides, forget not
    With what Contempt he wore the humble Weed,
    How in his Suit he scorn'd you: but your Loues,
    Thinking vpon his Seruices, tooke from you
    Th'apprehension of his present portance,
    Which most gibingly, vngrauely, he did fashion
    After the inueterate Hate he beares you.
BRUTUS (*to the Citizens*)   Lay
    A fault on vs, your Tribunes, that we labour'd

(No impediment betweene) but that you must
Cast your Election on him.

1410   SCICINIUS (*to the Citizens*)   Say you chose him,
More after our commandment, then as guided
By your owne true affections, and that your Minds
Pre-occupy'd with what you rather must do,
Then what you should, made you against the graine
To Voyce him Consull. Lay the fault on vs.

    BRUTUS (*to the Citizens*)
I, spare vs not: Say, we read Lectures to you,
How youngly he began to serue his Countrey,
How long continued, and what stock he springs of,
The Noble House o'th'*Martians*: from whence came
1420   That *Ancus Martius, Numaes* Daughters Sonne:
Who after great *Hostilius* here was King,
Of the same House *Publius* and *Quintus* were,
That our best Water, brought by Conduits hither,
And *Censorinus* that was so surnam'd,
And Nobly named so, twice being Censor,
Was his great Ancestor.

    SCICINIUS (*to the Citizens*)   One thus descended,
That hath beside well in his person wrought,
To be set high in place, we did commend
To your remembrances: but you haue found,
1430   Skaling his present bearing with his past,
That hee's your fixed enemie; and reuoke
Your suddaine approbation.

    BRUTUS (*to the Citizens*)   Say you ne're had don't,
(Harpe on that still) but by our putting on:
And presently, when you haue drawne your number,
Repaire toth' Capitoll.

⌈A CITIZEN⌉   We will so.
⌈ANOTHER CITIZEN⌉   Almost all
Repent in their election.   *Exeunt Plebeians*

    BRUTUS   Let them goe on:
This Mutinie were better put in hazard,
Then stay past doubt, for greater:
1440   If, as his nature is, he fall in rage
With their refusall, both obserue and answer
The vantage of his anger.

    SCICINIUS   Toth' Capitoll, come:
We will be there before the streame o'th' People:
And this shall seeme, as partly 'tis, their owne,
Which we haue goaded on-ward.   *Exeunt*

⬡

3.1   *Cornets. Enter Coriolanus, Menenius, all the Gentry,*
(Sc. 15)   *Cominius, Titus Latius, and other Senators*

    CORIOLANUS
Tullus Auffidius then had made new head.

    LARTIUS
He had, my Lord, and that it was which caus'd
Our swifter Composition.

    CORIOLANUS
So then the Volces stand but as at first,
1450   Readie when time shall prompt them, to make roade
Vpon's againe.

    COMINIUS   They are worne (Lord Consull) so,

That we shall hardly in our ages see
Their Banners waue againe.

    CORIOLANUS (*to Lartius*)   Saw you *Auffidius*?

    LARTIUS
On safegard he came to me, and did curse
Against the Volces, for they had so vildly
Yeelded the Towne: he is retyrd to Antium.

    CORIOLANUS
Spoke he of me?

    LARTIUS   He did, my Lord.

    CORIOLANUS   How? what?

    LARTIUS
How often he had met you Sword to Sword:
That of all things vpon the Earth, he hated
Your person most: That he would pawne his fortunes   1460
To hopelesse restitution, so he might
Be call'd your Vanquisher.

    CORIOLANUS At Antium liues he?

    LARTIUS At Antium.

    CORIOLANUS
I wish I had a cause to seeke him there,
To oppose his hatred fully. Welcome home.
          Enter Scicinius and Brutus
Behold, these are the Tribunes of the People,
The Tongues o'th' Common Mouth. I do despise them:
For they doe pranke them in Authoritie,
Against all Noble sufferance.   1470

    SCICINIUS Passe no further.

    CORIOLANUS Hah? what is that?

    BRUTUS
It will be dangerous to goe on—No further.

    CORIOLANUS What makes this change?

    MENENIUS The matter?

    COMINIUS
Hath he not pass'd the Noble, and the Common?

    BRUTUS
Cominius, no.

    CORIOLANUS   Haue I had Childrens Voyces?

    ⌈1⌉ SENATOR
Tribunes giue way, he shall toth' Market place.

    BRUTUS
The People are incens'd against him.

    SCICINIUS   Stop,
Or all will fall in broyle.

    CORIOLANUS   Are these your Heard?   1480
Must these haue Voyces, that can yeeld them now,
And straight disclaim their toungs? what are your
    Offices?
You being their Mouthes, why rule you not their Teeth?
Haue you not set them on?

    MENENIUS   Be calme, be calme.

    CORIOLANUS
It is a purpos'd thing, and growes by Plot,
To curbe the will of the Nobilitie:
Suffer't, and liue with such as cannot rule,
Nor euer will be ruld.

    BRUTUS   Call't not a Plot:
The People cry you mockt them: and of late,

1490 When Corne was giuen them *gratis*, you repin'd,
Scandal'd the Suppliants for the People, call'd them
Time-pleasers, flatterers, foes to Noblenesse.

CORIOLANUS
Why this was knowne before.

BRUTUS   Not to them all.

CORIOLANUS
Haue you inform'd them sithence?

BRUTUS   How? I informe them?

⌈CORIOLANUS⌉
You are like to doe such businesse.

BRUTUS Not vnlike
Each way to better yours.

CORIOLANUS
Why then should I be Consull? by yond Clouds
Let me deserue so ill as you, and make me
Your fellow Tribune.

1500 SCICINIUS   You shew too much of that,
For which the People stirre: if you will passe
To where you are bound, you must enquire your
            way,
Which you are out of, with a gentler spirit,
Or neuer be so Noble as a Consull,
Nor yoake with him for Tribune.

MENENIUS   Let's be calme.

COMINIUS
The People are abus'd, set on: this paltring
Becomes not Rome: nor ha's *Coriolanus*
Deseru'd this so dishonor'd Rub, layd falsely
I'th' plaine Way of his Merit.

CORIOLANUS   Tell me of Corne:
1510 This was my speech, and I will speak't againe.

MENENIUS Not now, not now.

⌈1⌉ SENATOR Not in this heat, Sir, now.

CORIOLANUS Now as I liue,
I will. My Nobler friends, I craue their pardons:
For the mutable ranke-sented Meynie,
Let them regard me, as I doe not flatter,
And therein behold themselues: I say againe,
In soothing them, we nourish 'gainst our Senate
The Cockle of Rebellion, Insolence, Sedition,
Which we our selues haue plowed for, sow'd, &
1520   scatter'd,
By mingling them with vs, the honor'd Number,
Who lack not Vertue, no, nor Power, but that
Which they haue giuen to Beggers.

MENENIUS   Well, no more.

⌈1⌉ SENATOR
No more words, we beseech you.

CORIOLANUS   How? no more?
As for my Country, I haue shed my blood,
Not fearing outward force: So shall my Lungs
Coine words till their decay, against those Meazels
Which we disdaine should Tetter vs, yet sought
The very way to catch them.

BRUTUS
1530 You speake a'th'people, as if you were a God,
To punish; Not a man, of their Infirmity.

SCICINIUS
'Twere well we let the people know't.

MENENIUS   What, what? His Choller?

CORIOLANUS
Choller? Were I as patient as the midnight sleep,
By Ioue, 'twould be my minde.

SCICINIUS   It is a minde
That shall remain a poison where it is:
Not poyson any further.

CORIOLANUS   Shall remaine?
Heare you this Triton of the *Minnoues*? Marke you
His absolute Shall?

COMINIUS   'Twas from the Cannon.

CORIOLANUS   Shall?
O good, but most vnwise Patricians: why
You graue, but wreaklesse Senators, haue you thus   1540
Giuen Hidra heere to choose an Officer,
That with his peremptory Shall, being but
The horne, and noise o'th'Monsters, wants not spirit
To say, hee'l turne your Current in a ditch,
And make your Channell his? If he haue power,
Then vale your ipotance: If none, awake
Your dangerous Lenity: If you are Learn'd,
Be not as common Fooles; if you are not,
Let them haue Cushions by you. You are Plebeians,
If they be Senators: and they are no lesse,   1550
When both your voices blended, the great'st taste
Most pallates theirs. They choose their Magistrate,
And such a one as he, who puts his Shall,
His popular Shall, against a grauer Bench
Then euer frown'd in Greece. By Ioue himselfe,
It makes the Consuls base; and my Soule akes
To know, when two Authorities are vp,
Neither Supreame; How soone Confusion
May enter 'twixt the gap of Both, and take
The one by th'other.

COMINIUS   Well, on to'th'Market place.   1560

CORIOLANUS
Who euer gaue that Counsell, to giue forth
The Corne a'th'Store-house gratis, as 'twas vs'd
Sometime in Greece.

MENENIUS   Well, well, no more of that.

CORIOLANUS
Thogh there the people had more absolute powre
I say they norisht disobedience: fed,
The ruin of the State.

BRUTUS   Why shall the people giue
One that speakes thus, their voyce?

CORIOLANUS   Ile giue my Reasons,
More worthier then their Voyces. They know the Corne
Was not our recompence, resting well assur'd
They ne're did seruice for't; being prest to'th'Warre,   1570
Euen when the Nauell of the State was touch'd,
They would not thred the Gates: This kinde of Seruice
Did not deserue Corne gratis. Being i'th'Warre,
There Mutinies and Reuolts, wherein they shew'd
Most Valour, spoke not for them. Th'Accusation
Which they haue often made against the Senate,

All cause vnborne, could neuer be the Natiue
Of our so franke Donation. Well, what then?
How shall this Bosome-multiplied, digest
1580   The Senates Courtesie? Let deeds expresse
What's like to be their words, We did request it,
We are the greater pole, and in true feare
They gaue vs our demands. Thus we debase
The Nature of our Seats, and make the Rabble
Call our Cares, Feares; which will in time
Breake ope the Lockes a'th'Senate, and bring in
The Crowes to pecke the Eagles.

MENENIUS   Come enough.

BRUTUS
Enough, with ouer measure.

CORIOLANUS   No, take more.
What may be sworne by, both Diuine and Humane,
1590   Seale what I end withall. This double worship,
Where on part do's disdaine with cause, the other
Insult without all reason: where Gentry, Title, wisedom
Cannot conclude, but by the yea and no
Of generall Ignorance, it must omit
Reall Necessities, and giue way the while
To vnstable Slightnesse. Purpose so barr'd, it followes,
Nothing is done to purpose. Therefore beseech you,
You that will be lesse fearefull, then discreet,
That loue the Fundamentall part of State
1600   More then you doubt the change on't: That preferre
A Noble life, before a Long, and Wish,
To iumpe a Body with a dangerous Physicke,
That's sure of death without it: at once plucke out
The Multitudinous Tongue, let them not licke
The sweet which is their poyson. Your dishonor
Mangles true iudgement, and bereaues the State
Of that Integrity which should becom't:
Not hauing the power to do the good it would
For th'ill which doth controul't.

BRUTUS   Has said enough.

SCICINIUS
1610   Ha's spoken like a Traitor, and shall answer
As Traitors do.

CORIOLANUS   Thou wretch, despight ore-whelme thee:
What should the people do with these bald Tribunes?
On whom depending, their obedience failes
To'th'greater Bench: in a Rebellion,
When what's not meet, but what must be, was Law,
Then were they chosen: in a better houre,
Let what is meet, be saide it must be meet,
And throw their power i'th'dust.

BRUTUS
Manifest Treason.

SCICINIUS   This a Consull? No.

BRUTUS
The Ediles hoe:
        Enter an Ædile
1620   Let him be apprehended.

SCICINIUS
Go call the people,   ⌐*Exit Ædile*⌐
(*To Coriolanus*)   in whose name my Selfe

Attach thee as a Traitorous Innouator:
A Foe to'th'publike Weale. Obey I charge thee,
And follow to thine answer.

CORIOLANUS   Hence old Goat.

ALL ⌐THE PATRICIANS⌐
Wee'l Surety him.

COMINIUS (*to Scicinius*)   Ag'd sir, hands off.

CORIOLANUS (*to Scicinius*)
Hence rotten thing, or I shall shake thy bones
Out of thy Garments.

SCICINIUS   Helpe ye Citizens.
     Enter a rabble of Plebeians with the Ædiles

MENENIUS
On both sides more respect.

SCICINIUS   Heere's hee,
That would take from you all your power.

BRUTUS   Seize him Ædiles.

ALL ⌐THE CITIZENS⌐
Downe with him, downe with him.

2 SENATOR   Weapons, weapons, weapons.   1630
     They all bustle about Coriolanus

⌐CITIZENS *and* PATRICIANS⌐ ⌐*in dispersed cries*⌐
Tribunes, Patricians, Citizens: what ho:
Sicinius, Brutus, Coriolanus, Citizens.

⌐SOME CITIZENS *and* PATRICIANS⌐
Peace, peace, peace, stay, hold, peace.

MENENIUS
What is about to be? I am out of Breath,
Confusions neere, I cannot speake. You, Tribunes
To'th'people: *Coriolanus*, patience:
Speak good *Sicinius*.

SCICINIUS   Heare me, People peace.

ALL ⌐THE CITIZENS⌐
Let's here our Tribune: peace, speake, speake, speake.

SCICINIUS
You are at point to lose your Liberties:
Martius would haue all from you; *Martius*,   1640
Whom late you haue nam'd for Consull.

MENENIUS   Fie, fie, fie,
This is the way to kindle, not to quench.

⌐1⌐ SENATOR
To vnbuild the Citie, and to lay all flat.

SCICINIUS
What is the Citie, but the People?

ALL ⌐THE CITIZENS⌐   True,
The People are the Citie.

BRUTUS   By the consent of all,
We were establish'd the Peoples Magistrates.

ALL ⌐THE CITIZENS⌐
You so remaine.

MENENIUS   And so are like to doe.

⌐CORIOLANUS⌐
That is the way to lay the Citie flat,
To bring the Roofe to the Foundation,
And burie all, which yet distinctly raunges   1650
In heapes, and piles of Ruine.

SCICINIUS   This deserues Death.

BRUTUS
　Or let vs stand to our Authoritie,
　Or let vs lose it: we doe here pronounce,
　Vpon the part o'th' People, in whose power
　We were elected theirs, *Martius* is worthy
　Of present Death.
SCICINIUS　　　　　Therefore lay hold of him:
　Beare him toth' Rock Tarpeian, and from thence
　Into destruction cast him.
BRUTUS　　　　　Ædiles seize him.
ALL THE CITIZENS
　Yeeld *Martius*, yeeld.
MENENIUS　　　　　Heare me one word,
1660　'Beseech you Tribunes, heare me but a word.
EDILES Peace, peace.
MENENIUS (*to the Tribunes*)
　Be that you seeme, truly your Countries friend,
　And temp'rately proceed to what you would
　Thus violently redresse.
BRUTUS　　　　　Sir, those cold wayes,
　That seeme like prudent helpes, are very poysones,
　Where the Disease is violent. Lay hands vpon him,
　And beare him to the Rock.
　　　Coriolanus drawes his Sword
CORIOLANUS　　　　　No, Ile die here:
　There's some among you haue beheld me fighting,
　Come trie vpon your selues, what you haue seene me.
MENENIUS
1670　Downe with that Sword, Tribunes withdraw a while.
BRUTUS
　Lay hands vpon him.
MENENIUS　　　　　Helpe *Martius*, helpe:
　You that be noble, helpe him young and old.
ALL ⌈THE CITIZENS⌉ Downe with him, downe with him.
　　　In this Mutinie, the Tribunes, the Aediles, and the
　　　People are beat in
MENENIUS (*to Coriolanus*)
　Goe, get you to your House: be gone, away.
　All will be naught else.
2 SENATOR (*to Coriolanus*) Get you gone.
⌈CORIOLANUS⌉
　Stand fast, we haue as many friends as enemies.
MENENIUS
　Shall it be put to that?
⌈1⌉ SENATOR　　　　　The Gods forbid:
　(*To Coriolanus*) I prythee noble friend, home to thy
　　　House,
　Leaue vs to cure this Cause.
MENENIUS　　　　　For 'tis a Sore vpon vs,
1680　You cannot Tent your selfe: be gone, 'beseech you.
⌈COMINIUS⌉ Come Sir, along with vs.
⌈CORIOLANUS⌉
　I would they were Barbarians, as they are,
　Though in Rome litter'd: not Romans, as they are
　　　not,
　Though calued i'th' Porch o'th' Capitoll.
⌈MENENIUS⌉　　　　　Be gone,

Put not your worthy Rage into your Tongue,
　One time will owe ancther.
CORIOLANUS　　　　　On faire ground,
　I could beat fortie of them.
MENENIUS　　　　　I could my selfe
　Take vp a Brace o'th' best of them, yea, the two
　　　Tribunes.
COMINIUS
　But now 'tis oddes beyond Arithmetick,
　And Manhood is call'd Foolerie, when it stands　　1690
　Against a falling Fabrick. (*To Coriolanus*) Will you hence,
　Before the Tagge returne? whose Rage doth rend
　Like interrupted Waters, and o're-beare
　What they are vs'd to beare.
MENENIUS (*to Coriolanus*)　　　　　Pray you be gone:
　Ile trie whether my old Wit be in request
　With those that haue but little: this must be patcht
　With Cloth of any Colour.
COMINIUS Nay, come away.
　　　　　　　Exeunt Coriolanus and Cominius
A PATRICIAN This man ha's marr'd his fortune.
MENENIUS
　His nature is too noble for the World:　　　　　1700
　He would not flatter *Neptune* for his Trident,
　Or *Ioue*, for's power to Thunder: his Heart's his Mouth:
　What his Brest forges, that his Tongue must vent,
　And being angry, does forget that euer
　He heard the Name of Death.
　　　A Noise within
　　　　　　　Here's goodly worke.
A PATRICIAN
　I would they were a bed.
MENENIUS　　　　　I would they were in Tyber.
　What the vengeance, could he not speake'em faire?
　　　Enter Brutus and Sicinius with the rabble againe
SCICINIUS Where is this Viper,
　That would depopulate the city, and
　Be euery man himself.
MENENIUS　　　　　You worthy Tribunes.　　1710
SCICINIUS
　He shall be throwne downe the Tarpeian rock
　With rigorous hands: he hath resisted Law,
　And therefore Law shall scorne him further Triall
　Then the seuerity of the publike Power,
　Which he so sets at naught.
1 CITIZEN　　　　　He shall well know
　The Noble Tribunes are the peoples mouths,
　And we their hands.
ALL ⌈THE CITIZENS⌉　　　　　He shall sure ont.
MENENIUS　　　　　Sir, sir.
SCICINIUS Peace.
MENENIUS
　Do not cry hauocke, where you shold but hunt
　With modest warrant.
SCICINIUS　　　　　Sir, how com'st that you　　1720
　Haue holpe to make this rescue?
MENENIUS　　　　　Heere me speake?

As I do know the Consuls worthinesse,
So can I name his Faults.

SCICINIUS Consull? what Consull?

MENENIUS The Consull *Coriolanus.*

BRUTUS He Consull.

ALL ⌜THE CITIZENS⌝ No, no, no, no, no.

MENENIUS
If by the Tribunes leaue, and yours good people,
I may be heard, I would craue a word or two,
1730   The which shall turne you to no further harme,
Then so much losse of time.

SCICINIUS   Speake breefely then,
For we are peremptory to dispatch
This Viporous Traitor: to eiect him hence
Were but our danger, and to keepe him heere
Our certaine death: therefore it is decreed,
He dyes to night.

MENENIUS   Now the good Gods forbid,
That our renowned Rome, whose gratitude
Towards her deserued Children, is enroll'd
In Ioues owne Booke, like an vnnaturall Dam
1740   Should now eate vp her owne.

SCICINIUS
He's a Disease that must be cut away.

MENENIUS
Oh he's a Limbe, that ha's but a Disease:
Mortall, to cut it off: to cure it, easie.
What ha's he done to Rome, that's worthy death?
Killing our Enemies, the blood he hath lost
(Which I dare vouch, is more then that he hath
By many an Ounce) he dropp'd it for his Country:
And what is left, to loose it by his Countrey,
Were to vs all that doo't, and suffer it
A brand to th'end a'th World.

1750   SCICINIUS   This is cleane kamme.

BRUTUS
Meerely awry: When he did loue his Country,
It honour'd him.

⌜SCICINIUS⌝   The seruice of the foote
Being once gangren'd, is not then respected
For what before it was.

BRUTUS   Wee'l heare no more:
Pursue him to his house, and plucke him thence,
Least his infection being of catching nature,
Spred further.

MENENIUS   One word more, one word:
This Tiger-footed-rage, when it shall find
The harme of vnskan'd swiftnesse, will (too late)
1760   Tye Leaden pounds too's heeles. Proceed by Processe,
Least parties (as he is belou'd) breake out,
And sacke great Rome with Romanes.

BRUTUS If it were so?

SCICINIUS (*to Menenius*) What do ye talke?
Haue we not had a taste of his Obedience?
Our Ediles smot: our selues resisted: come.

MENENIUS
Consider this: He ha's bin bred i'th'Warres
Since a could draw a Sword, and is ill-school'd

In boulted Language: Meale and Bran together
He throwes without distinction. Giue me leaue,   1770
Ile go to him, and vndertake to bring him,
Where he shall answer by a lawfull Forme
(In peace) to his vtmost perill.

I SENATOR   Noble Tribunes,
It is the humane way: the other course
Will proue to bloody: and the end of it,
Vnknowne to the Beginning.

SCICINIUS   Noble *Menenius,*
Be you then as the peoples officer:
(*To the Citizens*) Masters, lay downe your Weapons.

BRUTUS   Go not home.

SCICINIUS
Meet on the Market place: (*to Menenius*) wee'l attend
    you there:
Where if you bring not *Martius,* wee'l proceede   1780
In our first way.

MENENIUS   Ile bring him to you.
(*To the Senators*) Let me desire your company: he must
    come,
Or what is worst will follow.

⌜I⌝ SENATOR   Pray you let's to him.
        Exeunt Omnes: ⌜*Tribunes and Citizens at one*
            doore, Patricians at another doore⌝

        Enter Coriolanus with Nobles   3.2
CORIOLANUS   Sc. 16
Let them pull all about mine eares, present me
Death on the Wheele, or at wilde Horses heeles,
Or pile ten hilles on the Tarpeian Rocke,
That the precipitation might downe stretch
Below the beame of sight; yet will I still
Be thus to them.
        Enter Volumnia

A PATRICIAN   You do the Nobler.

CORIOLANUS   I muse my Mother
Do's not approue me further, who was wont   1790
To call them Wollen Vassailes, things created
To buy and sell with Groats, to shew bare heads
In Congregations, to yawne, be still, and wonder,
When one but of my ordinance stood vp
To speake of Peace, or Warre. (*To Volumnia*) I talke of
    you,
Why did you wish me milder? Would you haue me
False to my Nature? Rather say, I play
The man I am.

VOLUMNIA   Oh sir, sir, sir,
I would haue had you put your power well on
Before you had worne it out.

CORIOLANUS   Let go.   1800

VOLUMNIA
You might haue beene enough the man you are,
With striuing lesse to be so: Lesser had bin
The taxings of your dispositions, if
You had not shew'd them how ye were dispos'd
Ere they lack'd power to crosse you.

CORIOLANUS   Let them hang.

VOLUMNIA I, and burne too.
    Enter Menenius with the Senators
MENENIUS (*to Coriolanus*)
    Come, come, you haue bin too rough, somthing too
        rough:
    You must returne, and mend it.
⌈1⌉ SENATOR   There's no remedy,
    Vnlesse by not so doing, our good Citie
    Cleaue in the midd'st, and perish.

1810 VOLUMNIA (*to Coriolanus*)   Pray be counsail'd;
    I haue a heart as little apt as yours,
    But yet a braine, that leades my vse of Anger
    To better vantage.
MENENIUS   Well said, Noble woman:
    Before he should thus stoope to'th'heard, but that
    The violent fit a'th'time craues it as Physicke
    For the whole State; I would put mine Armour on,
    Which I can scarsely beare.
CORIOLANUS What must I do?
MENENIUS Returne to th'Tribunes.

1820 CORIOLANUS Well, what then? what then?
MENENIUS Repent, what you haue spoke.
CORIOLANUS
    For them, I cannot do it to the Gods,
    Must I then doo't to them?
VOLUMNIA   You are too absolute,
    Though therein you can neuer be too Noble,
    But when extremities speake. I haue heard you say,
    Honor and Policy, like vnseuer'd Friends,
    I'th'Warre do grow together: Grant that, and tell me
    In Peace, what each of them by th'other loose,
    That they combine not there?
CORIOLANUS   Tush, tush.
MENENIUS   A good demand.
VOLUMNIA
1830 If it be Honor in your Warres, to seeme
    The same you are not, which for your best ends
    You adopt your policy: How is it lesse or worse
    That it shall hold Companionship in Peace
    With Honour, as in Warre; since that to both
    It stands in like request.
CORIOLANUS   Why force you this?
VOLUMNIA
    Because, that now it lyes you on to speake to
        th'people:
    Not by your owne instruction, nor by'th'matter
    Which your heart prompts you, but with such words
    That are but roated in your Tongue; Though but
1840 Bastards, and Syllables of no allowance,
    To your bosomes truth. Now, this no more
    Dishonors you at all, then to take in
    A Towne with gentle words, which else would put you
    To your fortune, and the hazard of much blood.
    I would dissemble with my Nature, where
    My Fortunes and my Friends at stake, requir'd
    I should do so in Honor. I am in this
    Your Wife, your Sonne, these Senators, the Nobles,
    And you will rather shew our generall Lowts,
1850 How you can frowne, then spend a fawne vpon'em,

For the inheritance of their loues, and safegard
Of what that want might ruine.
MENENIUS   Noble Lady,
(*To Coriolanus*) Come goe with vs, speake faire: you
    may salue so,
Not what is dangerous present, but the losse
Of what is past.
VOLUMNIA   I prythee now, my Sonne,
    ⌈*She takes his Bonnet*⌉
Goe to them, with this Bonnet in thy hand,
And thus farre hauing stretcht it (here be with them)
Thy Knee bussing the stones: for in such businesse
Action is eloquence, and the eyes of th'ignorant
More learned then the eares, wauing thy head,   1860
W^{th} often thus correcting thy stout heart,
Now humble as the ripest Mulberry,
That will not hold the handling: or say to them,
Thou art their Souldier, and being bred in broyles,
Hast not the soft way, which thou do'st confesse
Were fit for thee to vse, as they to clayme,
In asking their good loues, but thou wilt frame
Thy selfe (forsooth) hereafter theirs so farre,
As thou hast power and person.
MENENIUS (*to Coriolanus*)   This but done,
Euen as she speakes, why their hearts were yours: 1870
For they haue Pardons, being ask'd, as free,
As words to little purpose.
VOLUMNIA (*to Coriolanus*)   Prythee now,
Goe, and be rul'd: although I know thou hadst rather
Follow thine Enemie in a fierie Gulfe,
Then flatter him in a Bower.
    Enter Cominius
                Here is *Cominius.*
COMINIUS
I haue beene i'th' Market place: and Sir 'tis fit
You make strong partie, or defend your selfe
By calmenesse, or by absence: all's in anger.
MENENIUS
Onely faire speech.
COMINIUS   I thinke 'twill serue, if he
Can thereto frame his spirit.
VOLUMNIA   He must, and will: 1880
Prythee now say you will, and goe about it.
CORIOLANUS
Must I goe shew them my vnbarbed Sconce?
Must I with my base Tongue giue to my Noble Heart
A Lye, that it must beare? well, I will doo't:
Yet were there but this single Plot to loose,
This Mould of *Martius*, they to dust should grinde it,
And throw't against the Winde. Toth' Market place:
You haue put me now to such a part, which neuer
I shall discharge toth' Life.
COMINIUS   Come, come, wee'le prompt you.
VOLUMNIA
I prythee now sweet Son, as thou hast said   1890
My praises made thee first a Souldier; so
To haue my praise for this, performe a part
Thou hast not done before.
CORIOLANUS   Well, I must doo't:

Away my disposition, and possesse me
Some Harlots spirit: My throat of Warre be turn'd,
Which quier'd with my Drumme into a Pipe,
Small as an Eunuch, or the Virgin voyce
That Babies lull a-sleepe: The smiles of Knaues
1900 The Glasses of my sight: A Beggars Tongue
Make motion through my Lips, and my Arm'd knees
Who bow'd but in my Stirrop, bend like his
That hath receiu'd an Almes. I will not doo't,
Least I surcease to honor mine owne truth,
And by my Bodies action, teach my Minde
A most inherent Basenesse.

VOLUMNIA   At thy choice then:
To begge of thee, it is my more dis-honor,
Then thou of them. Come all to ruine, let
Thy Mother rather feele thy Pride, then feare
1910 Thy dangerous Stoutnesse: for I mocke at death
With as bigge heart as thou. Do as thou list,
Thy Valiantnesse was mine, thou suck'st it from me:
But owe thy Pride thy selfe.

CORIOLANUS   Pray be content:
Mother, I am going to the Market place:
Chide me no more. Ile Mountebanke their Loues,
Cogge their Hearts from them, and come home belou'd
Of all the Trades in Rome. Looke, I am going:
Commend me to my Wife, Ile returne Consull,
Or neuer trust to what my Tongue can do
I'th way of Flattery further.

1920 VOLUMNIA   Do your will.
                                    Exit Volumnia

COMINIUS
Away, the Tribunes do attend you: arm your self
To answer mildely: for they are prepar'd
With Accusations, as I heare more strong
Then are vpon you yet.

CORIOLANUS
The word is, Mildely. Pray you let vs go,
Let them accuse me by inuention: I
Will answer in mine Honor.

MENENIUS I, but mildely.

CORIOLANUS Well mildely be it then, Mildely.   *Exeunt*

3.3   *Enter Sicinius and Brutus*
Sc. 17) BRUTUS
1930 In this point charge him home, that he affects
Tyrannicall power: If he euade vs there,
Inforce him with his enuy to the people,
And that the Spoile got on the *Antiats*
Was ne're distributed.
              Enter an Edile
                        What, will he come?

EDILE
Hee's comming.

BRUTUS   How accompanied?

EDILE
With old *Menenius*, and those Senators
That alwayes fauour'd him.

SCICINIUS   Haue you a Catalogue

Of all the Voices that we haue procur'd,
Set downe by'th Pole?

EDILE   I haue: 'tis ready.

SCICINIUS
Haue you collected them by Tribes?

EDILE   I haue.   1940

SCICINIUS
Assemble presently the people hither:
And when they heare me say, it shall be so,
I'th'right and strength a'th'Commons: be it either
For death, for fine, or Banishment, then let them
If I say Fine, cry Fine; if Death, cry Death,
Insisting on the olde prerogatiue
And power i'th Truth a'th Cause.

EDILE   I shall informe them.

BRUTUS
And when such time they haue begun to cry,
Let them not cease, but with a dinne confus'd
Inforce the present Execution   1950
Of what we chance to Sentence.

EDILE   Very well.

SCICINIUS
Make them be strong, and ready for this hint
When we shall hap to giu't them.

BRUTUS ⌜*to the Edile*⌝   Go about it,
                              ⌜*Exit Edile*⌝
Put him to Choller straite, he hath bene vs'd
Euer to conquer, and to haue his worth
Of contradiction. Being once chaft, he cannot
Be rein'd againe to Temperance, then he speakes
What's in his heart, and that is there which lookes
With vs to breake his necke.
            *Enter Coriolanus, Menenius, and Cominius, with
            other ⌜Senators and Patricians⌝*

SCICINIUS Well, heere he comes.   1960

MENENIUS (*to Coriolanus*) Calmely, I do beseech you.

CORIOLANUS
I, as an Hostler, that forth poorest peece
Will beare the Knaue by'th Volume: Th'honor'd
   Goddes
Keepe Rome in safety, and the Chaires of Iustice
Supplied with worthy men, plant loue amongs
Throng our large Temples with yᵉ shewes of peace
And not our streets with Warre.

I SENATOR Amen, Amen.

MENENIUS A Noble wish.
            Enter the Edile with the Plebeians

SCICINIUS
Draw neere ye people.

EDILE   List to your Tribunes. Audience: 1970
Peace I say.

CORIOLANUS First heare me speake.

BOTH TRIBUNES   Well, say: Peace hoe.

CORIOLANUS
Shall I be charg'd no further then this present?
Must all determine heere?

SCICINIUS   I do demand,
If you submit you to the peoples voices,
Allow their Officers, and are content

To suffer lawfull Censure for such faults
As shall be prou'd vpon you.
CORIOLANUS   I am Content.
MENENIUS
Lo Citizens, he sayes he is Content.
The warlike Seruice he ha's done, consider: Thinke
1980   Vpon the wounds his body beares, which shew
Like Graues i'th holy Church-yard.
CORIOLANUS   Scratches with Briars,
Scarres to moue Laughter onely.
MENENIUS   Consider further:
That when he speakes not like a Citizen,
You finde him like a Soldier: do not take
His rougher Accents for malicious sounds:
But as I say, such as become a Soldier,
Rather then enuy you.
COMINIUS Well, well, no more.
CORIOLANUS What is the matter,
1990   That being past for Consull with full voyce:
I am so dishonour'd, that the very houre
You take it off againe.
SCICINIUS Answer to vs.
CORIOLANUS Say then: 'tis true, I ought so.
SCICINIUS
We charge you, that you haue contriu'd to take
From Rome all season'd Office, and to winde
Your selfe into a power tyrannicall,
For which you are a Traitor to the people.
CORIOLANUS
How? Traytor?
MENENIUS   Nay temperately: your promise.
CORIOLANUS
2000   The fires i'th'lowest hell fould in the people:
Call me their Traitor, thou iniurious Tribune.
Within thine eyes sate twenty thousand deaths:
In thy hands clutcht as many Millions, in
Thy lying tongue, both numbers: I would say
Thou lyest vnto thee, with a voice as free,
As I do pray the Gods.
SCICINIUS Marke you this people?
ALL ⌈THE CITIZENS⌉ To'th'Rocke, to'th'Rocke with him.
SCICINIUS Peace:
2010   We neede not put new matter to his charge:
What you haue seene him do, and heard him speake:
Beating your Officers, cursing your selues,
Opposing Lawes with stroakes, and heere defying
Those whose great power must try him.
Euen this so criminall, and in such capitall kinde
Deserues th'extreamest death.
BRUTUS   But since he hath
Seru'd well for Rome.
CORIOLANUS   What do you prate of Seruice.
BRUTUS
I talke of that, that know it.
CORIOLANUS   You?
MENENIUS
Is this the promise that you made your mother.

COMINIUS
Know, I pray you.
CORIOLANUS   Ile know no further: 2020
Let them pronounce the steepe Tarpeian death,
Vagabond exile, Fleaing, pent to linger
But with a graine a day, I would not buy
Their mercie, at the price of one faire word,
Nor checke my Courage for what they can giue,
To haue't with saying, Good morrow.
SCICINIUS   For that he ha's
(As much as in him lies) from time to time
Enuei'd against the people; seeking meanes
To plucke away their power: as now at last,
Giuen Hostile strokes, and that not in the presence   2030
Of dreaded Iustice, but on the Ministers
That doth distribute it: In the name a'th'people,
And in the power of vs the Tribunes, wee
(Eu'n from this instant) banish him our Citie
In perill of precipitation
From off the Rocke Tarpeian, neuer more
To enter our Rome gates. I'th'Peoples name,
I say it shall bee so.
ALL ⌈THE CITIZENS⌉   It shall be so,
It shall be so: let him away: Hee's banish'd,
And it shall be so.   2040
COMINIUS
Heare me my Masters, and my common friends.
SCICINIUS
He's sentenc'd: No more hearing.
COMINIUS   Let me speake:
I haue bene Consull, and can shew for Rome
Her Enemies markes vpon me. I do loue
My Countries good, with a respect more tender,
More holy, and profound, then mine owne life,
My deere Wiues estimate, her wombes encrease,
And treasure of my Loynes: then if I would
Speake that.
SCICINIUS   We know your drift. Speake what?
BRUTUS
There's no more to be said, but he is banish'd   2050
As Enemy to the people, and his Countrey.
It shall bee so.
ALL ⌈THE CITIZENS⌉ It shall be so, it shall be so.
CORIOLANUS
You common cry of Curs, whose breath I hate,
As reeke a'th'rotten Fennes: whose Loues I prize,
As the dead Carkasses of vnburied men,
That do corrupt my Ayre: I banish you,
And heere remaine with your vncertaintie.
Let euery feeble Rumor shake your hearts:
Your Enemies, with nodding of their Plumes
Fan you into dispaire: Haue the power still   2060
To banish your Defenders, till at length
Your ignorance (which findes not till it feeles,
Making but reseruation of your selues,
Still your owne Foes) deliuer you
As most abated Captiues, to some Nation

That wonne you without blowes. Despising
For you the City, thus I turne my backe;
There is a world elsewhere.

Exeunt Coriolanus, Cominius, Menenius,
Cum alijs. The Citizens all shout, and
throw vp their Caps

EDILE
The peoples Enemy is gone, is gone.

ALL THE CITIZENS
2070   Our enemy is banish'd, he is gone: Hoo, oo.

SCICINIUS
Go see him out at Gates, and follow him
As he hath follow'd you, with all despight.
Giue him deseru'd vexation. Let a guard
Attend vs through the City.

ALL THE CITIZENS
Come, come, lets see him out at gates, come:
The Gods preserue our Noble Tribunes, come.   *Exeunt*

4.1   *Enter Coriolanus, Volumnia, Virgilia, Menenius,*
(Sc. 18)   *Cominius, with the yong Nobility of Rome*

CORIOLANUS
Come leaue your teares: a brief farwel: the beast
With many heads butts me away. Nay Mother,
Where is your ancient Courage? You were vs'd
2080   To say, Extreamities was the trier of spirits,
That common chances Common men could beare,
That when the Sea was calme, all Boats alike
Shew'd Mastership in floating. Fortunes blowes,
When most strooke home, being gentle wounded,
craues
A Noble cunning. You were vs'd to load me
With Precepts that would make inuincible
The heart that conn'd them.

VIRGILIA   Oh heauens! O heauens!

CORIOLANUS   Nay, I prythee woman.

VOLUMNIA
2090   Now the Red Pestilence strike al Trades in Rome,
And Occupations perish.

CORIOLANUS   What, what, what:
I shall be lou'd when I am lack'd. Nay Mother,
Resume that Spirit, when you were wont to say,
If you had beene the Wife of *Hercules,*
Six of his Labours youl'd haue done, and sau'd
Your Husband so much swet. *Cominius,*
Droope not, Adieu: Farewell my Wife, my Mother,
Ile do well yet. Thou old and true *Menenius,*
Thy teares are salter then a yonger mans,
2100   And venomous to thine eyes. My (sometime) Generall,
I haue seene the Sterne, and thou hast oft beheld
Heart-hardning spectacles. Tell these sad women,
'Tis fond to waile ineuitable strokes,
As 'tis to laugh at 'em. My Mother, you wot well
My hazards still haue beene your solace, and
Beleeu't not lightly, though I go alone
Like to a lonely Dragon, that his Fenne

Makes fear'd, and talk'd of more then seene: your
Sonne
Will or exceed the Common, or be caught
With cautelous baits and practice.

VOLUMNIA   My first sonne,   2110
Whether will thou go? Take good *Cominius*
With thee awhile: Determine on some course
More then a wilde expouture, to each chance
That start's i'th'way before thee.

⌜VIRGILIA⌝   O the Gods!

COMINIUS
Ile follow thee a Moneth, deuise with thee
Where thou shalt rest, that thou may'st heare of vs,
And we of thee. So if the time thrust forth
A cause for thy Repeale, we shall not send
O're the vast world, to seeke a single man,
And loose aduantage, which doth euer coole   2120
Ith'absence of the needer.

CORIOLANUS   Fare ye well:
Thou hast yeares vpon thee, and thou art too full
Of the warres surfets, to go roue with one
That's yet vnbruis'd: bring me but out at gate.
Come my sweet wife, my deerest Mother, and
My Friends of Noble touch: when I am forth,
Bid me farewell, and smile. I pray you come:
While I remaine aboue the ground, you shall
Heare from me still, and neuer of me ought
But what is like me formerly.

MENENIUS   That's worthily   2130
As any eare can heare. Come, let's not weepe,
If I could shake off but one seuen yeeres
From these old armes and legges, by the good Gods
I'ld with thee, euery foot.

CORIOLANUS   Giue me thy hand, come.

Exeunt

Enter the two Tribunes, Sicinius, and Brutus, with   **4.2**
the Edile   **(Sc. 19)**

SCICINIUS (*to the Edile*)
Bid them all home, he's gone: & wee'l no further,
The Nobility are vexd, whom we see haue sided
In his behalfe.

BRUTUS   Now we haue shewne our power,
Let vs seeme humbler after it is done,
Then when it was a dooing.

SCICINIUS (*to the Edile*)   Bid them home:
Say their great enemy is gone, and they,   2140
Stand in their ancient strength.

BRUTUS   Dismisse them home.

Exit Edile

Enter Volumnia, Virgilia, ⌜weeping,⌝ and Menenius
Here comes his Mother.

SCICINIUS   Let's not meet her.

BRUTUS   Why?

SCICINIUS   They say she's mad.

BRUTUS
They haue tane note of vs: keepe on your way.

VOLUMNIA

  Oh y'are well met: Th'hoorded plague a'th'Gods
  Requit your loue.

MENENIUS   Peace, peace, be not so loud.

VOLUMNIA (*to the Tribunes*)

  If that I could for weeping, you should heare,
2150 Nay, and you shall heare some. Will you be gone?

VIRGILIA (*to the Tribunes*)

  You shall stay too: I would I had the power
  To say so to my Husband.

SCICINIUS (*to Volumnia*)   Are you mankinde?

VOLUMNIA

  I foole, is that a shame. Note but this Foole,
  Was not a man my Father? Had'st thou Foxship
  To banish him that strooke more blowes for Rome
  Then thou hast spoken words.

SCICINIUS   Oh blessed Heauens!

VOLUMNIA

  Moe Noble blowes, then euer yᵘ wise words,
  And for Romes good. Ile tell thee what: yet goe:
  Nay but thou shalt stay too: I would my Sonne
2160 Were in Arabia, and thy Tribe before him,
  His good Sword in his hand.

SCICINIUS   What then?

VIRGILIA   What then?

  Hee'ld make an end of thy posterity.

VOLUMNIA Bastards, and all.

  Good man, the Wounds that he does beare for Rome!

MENENIUS Come, come, peace.

SCICINIUS

  I would he had continued to his Country
  As he began, and not vnknit himselfe
  The Noble knot he made.

BRUTUS   I would he had.

VOLUMNIA

  I would he had? 'Twas thou incenst the rable.
2170 Cats, that can iudge as fitly of his worth,
  As I can of those Mysteries which heauen
  Will not haue earth to know.

BRUTUS (*to Scicinius*) Pray let's go.

VOLUMNIA Now pray sir get you gone.

  You haue done a braue deede: Ere you go, heare this:
  As farre as doth the Capitoll exceede
  The meanest house in Rome; so farre my Sonne
  This Ladies Husband heere; this (do you see)
  Whom you haue banish'd, does exceed you all.

BRUTUS

  Well, well, wee'l leaue you.

2180 SCICINIUS   Why stay we to be baited
  With one that wants her Wits.   *Exit Tribunes*

VOLUMNIA   Take my Prayers with you.

  I would the Gods had nothing else to do,
  But to confirme my Cursses. Could I meete 'em
  But once a day, it would vnclogge my heart
  Of what lyes heauy too't.

MENENIUS   You haue told them home,
  And by my troth you haue cause: you'l Sup with me.

VOLUMNIA

  Angers my Meate: I suppe vpon my selfe,
  And so shall sterue with Feeding:
  (*To Virgilia*)   Come, let's go,
  Leaue this faint-puling, and lament as I do,
  In Anger, *Iuno*-like: Come, come, come.

                Exeunt Volumnia and Virgilia

MENENIUS   Fie, fie, fie.   2190

                                Exit

        Enter a Roman, and a Volce   4.3

ROMAN I know you well sir, and you know mee: your   (Sc. 2
  name I thinke is *Adrian*.

VOLCEAN It is so sir, truly I haue forgot you.

ROMAN I am a Roman, and my Seruices are as you are,
  against 'em. Know you me yet.

VOLCEAN *Nicanor*: no.

ROMAN The same sir.

VOLCEAN You had more Beard when I last saw you, but
  your Fauour is well approu'd by your Tongue. What's
  the Newes in Rome: I haue a Note from the Volcean   2200
  state to finde you out there. You haue well saued mee
  a dayes iourney.

ROMAN There hath beene in Rome straunge Insurrections:
  The people, against the Senatours, Patricians, and Nobles.

VOLCEAN Hath bin; is it ended then? Our State thinks not
  so, they are in a most warlike preparation, & hope to
  com vpon them, in the heate of their diuision.

ROMAN The maine blaze of it is past, but a small thing
  would make it flame againe. For the Nobles receyue so
  to heart, the Banishment of that worthy *Coriolanus*,   2210
  that they are in a ripe aptnesse, to take al power from
  the people, and to plucke from them their Tribunes for
  euer. This lyes glowing I can tell you, and is almost
  mature for the violent breaking out.

VOLCEAN *Coriolanus* Banisht?

ROMAN Banish'd sir.

VOLCEAN You will be welcome with this intelligence
  Nicanor.

ROMAN The day serues well for them now. I haue heard
  it saide, the fittest time to corrupt a mans Wife, is when   2220
  shee's falne out with her Husband. Your Noble *Tullus
  Auffidius* will appeare well in these Warres, his great
  Opposer *Coriolanus* being now in no request of his
  countrey.

VOLCEAN He cannot choose: I am most fortunate, thus
  accidentally to encounter you. You haue ended my
  Businesse, and I will merrily accompany you home.

ROMAN I shall betweene this and Supper, tell you most
  strange things from Rome: all tending to the good of
  their Aduersaries. Haue you an Army ready say you?   2230

VOLCEAN A most Royall one: The Centurions, and their
  charges distinctly billetted already in th'entertainment,
  and to be on foot at an houres warning.

ROMAN I am ioyfull to heare of their readinesse, and am
  the man I thinke, that shall set them in present Action.
  So sir, heartily well met, and most glad of your Company.

VOLCEAN You take my part from me sir, I haue the most
cause to be glad of yours.

ROMAN Well, let vs go together.   *Exeunt*

4.4   *Enter Coriolanus in meane Apparrell, Disguisd, and*
(c. 21)   *muffled*

CORIOLANUS

2240   A goodly City is this *Antium*. Citty,
’Tis I that made thy Widdowes: Many an heyre
Of these faire Edifices fore my Warres
Haue I heard groane, and drop: Then know me not,
Least that thy Wiues with Spits, and Boyes with stones
In puny Battell slay me.

        Enter a Citizen

                              Saue you sir.

CITIZEN

And you.

CORIOLANUS Direct me, if it be your will,
Where great *Auffidius* lies: Is he in *Antium*?

CITIZEN

He is, and Feasts the Nobles of the State,
At his house this night.

CORIOLANUS   Which is his house, beseech you?

CITIZEN

This heere before you.

2250   CORIOLANUS   Thanke you sir, farewell.

                                        Exit Citizen

Oh World, thy slippery turnes! Friends now fast
    sworn,
Whose double bosomes seeme to weare one heart,
Whose Houres, whose Bed, whose Meale and Exercise
Are still together: who Twin (as ’twere) in Loue,
Vnseparable, shall within this houre,
On a dissention of a Doit, breake out
To bitterest Enmity: So fellest Foes,
Whose Passions, and whose Plots haue broke their sleep
To take the one the other, by some chance,
Some tricke not worth an Egge, shall grow deere

2260   friends
And inter-ioyne their yssues. So with me,
My Birth-place hate I, and my loues vpon
This Enemie Towne: Ile enter, if he slay me
He does faire Iustice: if he giue me way,
Ile do his Country Seruice.   *Exit*

4.5   *Musicke playes. Enter a Seruingman*
(c. 22) I SERUINGMAN Wine, Wine, Wine: What seruice is heere?
I thinke our Fellowes are asleepe.   ⌈*Exit*⌉

        Enter another Seruingman

2 SERUINGMAN Where’s *Cotus*: my M. cals for him: *Cotus*.

                                              Exit

        Enter Coriolanus, as before

CORIOLANUS A goodly House: The Feast

2270   Smels well: but I appeare not like a Guest.

        Enter the first Seruingman

I SERUINGMAN What would you haue Friend? whence
are you? Here’s no place for you: Pray go to the doore?

                                              Exit

CORIOLANUS

I haue deseru’d no better entertainment,
In being *Coriolanus*.

        Enter second Seruant

2 SERUINGMAN Whence are you sir? Ha’s the Porter his
eyes in his head, that he giues entrance to such
Companions? Pray get you out.

CORIOLANUS Away.

2 SERUINGMAN Away? Get you away.

CORIOLANUS Now th’art troublesome.   2280

2 SERUINGMAN Are you so braue: Ile haue you talkt with
anon.

        Enter 3 Seruingman, the 1 meets him

3 SERUINGMAN What Fellowes this?

I SERUINGMAN A strange one as euer I look’d on: I cannot
get him out o’th’house: Prythee call my Master to him.

3 SERUINGMAN (*to Coriolanus*) What haue you to do here
fellow? Pray you auoid the house.

CORIOLANUS

Let me but stand, I will not hurt your Harth.

3 SERUINGMAN What are you?

CORIOLANUS A Gentleman.   2290

3 SERUINGMAN A maru’llous poore one.

CORIOLANUS True, so I am.

3 SERUINGMAN Pray you poore Gentleman, take vp some
other station: Heere’s no place for you, pray you auoid:
Come.

CORIOLANUS

Follow your Function, go, and batten on colde bits.

        He pushes him away from him

3 SERUINGMAN What you will not? Prythee tell my Maister
what a strange Guest he ha’s heere.

2 SERUINGMAN And I shall.   *Exit second Seruingman*

3 SERUINGMAN Where dwel’st thou?   2300

CORIOLANUS Vnder the Canopy.

3 SERUINGMAN Vnder the Canopy?

CORIOLANUS I.

3 SERUINGMAN Where’s that?

CORIOLANUS I’th City of Kites and Crowes.

3 SERUINGMAN I’th City of Kites and Crowes? What an
Asse it is, then thou dwel’st with Dawes too?

CORIOLANUS No, I serue not thy Master.

3 SERUINGMAN How sir? Do you meddle with my Master?

CORIOLANUS I, tis an honester seruice, then to meddle   2310
with thy Mistris: Thou prat’st, and prat’st, serue with
thy trencher: Hence.

        He beats him away.

        Enter Auffidius with the second Seruingman

AUFFIDIUS Where is this Fellow?

2 SERUINGMAN Here sir, I’de haue beaten him like a
dogge, but for disturbing the Lords within.

        ⌈*The Seruingmen stand aside*⌉

AUFFIDIUS

Whence com’st thou? What wouldst yᵘ? Thy name?
Why speak’st not? Speake man: What’s thy name?

CORIOLANUS ⌈*vnmuffling his head*⌉   If *Tullus*
Not yet thou know’st me, and seeing me, dost not

Thinke me for the man I am, necessitie
Commands me name my selfe.

2320 AUFFIDIUS   What is thy name?
CORIOLANUS
A name vnmusicall to the Volcians eares,
And harsh in sound to thine.
AUFFIDIUS   Say, what's thy name?
Thou hast a Grim apparance, and thy Face
Beares a Command in't: Though thy Tackles torne,
Thou shew'st a Noble Vessell: What's thy name?
CORIOLANUS
Prepare thy brow to frowne: knowst yᵘ me yet?
AUFFIDIUS I know thee not? Thy Name?
CORIOLANUS
My name is *Caius Martius*, who hath done
To thee particularly, and to all the Volces
2330 Great hurt and Mischiefe: thereto witnesse may
My Surname *Coriolanus*. The painfull Seruice,
The extreme Dangers, and the droppes of Blood
Shed for my thanklesse Country, are requitted:
But with that Surname, a good memorie
And witnesse of the Malice and Displeasure
Which thou should'st beare me, only that name
      remains.
The Cruelty and Enuy of the people,
Permitted by our dastard Nobles, who
Haue all forsooke me, hath deuour'd the rest:
2340 And suffer'd me by th'voyce of Slaues to be
Hoop'd out of Rome. Now this extremity,
Hath brought me to thy Harth, not out of Hope
(Mistake me not) to saue my life: for if
I had fear'd death, of all the Men i'th'World
I would haue voided thee. But in meere spight
To be full quit of those my Banishers,
Stand I before thee heere: Then if thou hast
A heart of wreake in thee, that wilt reuenge
Thine owne particular wrongs, and stop those maimes
2350 Of shame seene through thy Country, speed thee straight
And make my misery serue thy turne: So vse it,
That my reuengefull Seruices may proue
As Benefits to thee. For I will fight
Against my Cankred Countrey, with the Spleene
Of all the vnder Fiends. But if so be,
Thou dar'st not this, and that to proue more Fortunes
Th'art tyr'd, then in a word, I also am
Longer to liue most wearie: and present
My throat to thee, and to thy Ancient Malice:
2360 Which not to cut, would shew thee but a Foole,
Since I haue euer followed thee with hate,
Drawne Tunnes of Blood out of thy Countries brest,
And cannot liue but to thy shame, vnlesse
It be to do thee seruice.
AUFFIDIUS   Oh *Martius*, *Martius*;
Each word thou hast spoke, hath weeded from my heart
A roote of Ancient Enuy. If Iupiter
Should from yond clowd speake diuine things,
And say 'tis true; I'de not beleeue them more
Then thee all-Noble *Martius*. Let me twine

Mine armes about that body, where against   2370
My grained Ash an hundred times hath broke,
And scarr'd the Moone with splinters:
    He embraces Coriolanus
                              heere I cleep
The Anuile of my Sword, and do contest
As hotly, and as Nobly with thy Loue,
As euer in Ambitious strength, I did
Contend against thy Valour. Know thou first,
I lou'd the Maid I married: neuer man
Sigh'd truer breath. But that I see thee heere
Thou Noble thing, more dances my rapt heart,
Then when I first my wedded Mistris saw   2380
Bestride my Threshold. Why, thou Mars I tell thee,
We haue a Power on foote: and I had purpose
Once more to hew thy Target from thy Brawne,
Or loose mine Arme for't: Thou hast beate mee out
Twelue seuerall times, and I haue nightly since
Dreamt of encounters 'twixt thy selfe and me:
We haue beene downe together in my sleepe,
Vnbuckling Helmes, fisting each others Throat,
And wak'd halfe dead with nothing. Worthy *Martius*,
Had we no other quarrell else to Rome, but that   2390
Thou art thence Banish'd, we would muster all
From twelue, to seuentie: and powring Warre
Into the bowels of vngratefull Rome,
Like a bold Flood o're-beart. Oh come, go in,
And take our Friendly Senators by'th'hands
Who now are heere, taking their leaues of mee,
Who am prepar'd against your Territories,
Though not for Rome it selfe.
CORIOLANUS   You blesse me Gods.
AUFFIDIUS
Therefore most absolute Sir, if thou wilt haue
The leading of thine owne Reuenges, take   2400
Th'one halfe of my Commission, and set downe
As best thou art experienc'd, since thou know'st
Thy Countries strength and weaknesse, thine own waies:
Whether to knocke against the Gates of Rome,
Or rudely visit them in parts remote,
To fright them, ere destroy. But come in,
Let me commend thee first, to those that shall
Say yea to thy desires. A thousand welcomes,
And more a Friend, then ere an Enemie,
Yet *Martius* that was much. Your hand: most welcome.   2410
                              Exeunt
⌈*The two Seruingmen come forward*⌉
1 SERUINGMAN Heere's a strange alteration?
2 SERUINGMAN By my hand, I had thoght to haue stroken
him with a Cudgell, and yet my minde gaue me, his
cloathes made a false report of him.
1 SERUINGMAN What an Arme he has, he turn'd me about
with his finger and his thumbe, as one would set vp a
Top.
2 SERUINGMAN Nay, I knew by his face that there was
some-thing in him. He had sir, a kinde of face me
thought, I cannot tell how to tearme it.   2420
1 SERUINGMAN He had so, looking as it were, would I

were hang'd but I thought there was more in him, then I could think.

2 SERUINGMAN So did I, Ile be sworne: He is simply the rarest man i'th'world.

1 SERUINGMAN I thinke he is yet a greater soldier then he you wot one.

2 SERUINGMAN Who my Master?

1 SERUINGMAN Nay, it's no matter for that.

2430 2 SERUINGMAN Worth six on him.

1 SERUINGMAN Nay not so neither: but I take him to be the greater Souldiour.

2 SERUINGMAN Faith looke you, one cannot tell how to say that: for the Defence of a Towne, our Generall is excellent.

1 SERUINGMAN I, and for an assault too.

Enter the third Seruingman

3 SERUINGMAN Oh Slaues, I can tell you Newes, News you Rascals.

1 *and* 2 SERUINGMEN What, what, what? Let's partake.

2440 3 SERUINGMAN I would not be a Roman of all Nations; I had as liue be a condemn'd man.

1 *and* 2 SERUINGMEN Wherefore? Wherefore?

3 SERUINGMAN Why here's he that was wont to thwacke our Generall, *Caius Martius.*

1 SERUINGMAN Why do you say, thwacke our Generall?

3 SERUINGMAN I do not say thwacke our Generall, but he was alwayes good enough for him.

2 SERUINGMAN Come we are fellowes and friends: he was euer too hard for him, I haue heard him say so himselfe.

2450 1 SERUINGMAN He was too hard for him directly, to say the Troth on't before *Corioles*, he scotcht him, and notcht him like a Carbinado.

2 SERUINGMAN And hee had bin Cannibally giuen, hee might haue broyld and eaten him too.

1 SERUINGMAN But more of thy Newes.

3 SERUINGMAN Why he is so made on heere within, as if hee were Son and Heire to Mars, set at vpper end o'th'Table: No question askt him by any of the Senators, but they stand bald before him. Our Generall himselfe

2460 makes a Mistris of him, Sanctifies himselfe with's hand, and turnes vp the white o'th'eye to his Discourse. But the bottome of the Newes is, our Generall is cut i'th'middle, & but one halfe of what he was yesterday. For the other ha's halfe, by the intreaty and graunt of the whole Table. Hee'l go he sayes, and sole the Porter of Rome Gates by th'eares. He will mowe all downe before him, and leaue his passage poul'd.

2 SERUINGMAN And he's as like to do't, as any man I can imagine.

2470 3 SERUINGMAN Doo't? he will doo't: for look you sir, he has as many Friends as Enemies: which Friends sir as it were, durst not (looke you sir) shew themselues (as we terme it) his Friends, whilest he's in Deiectitude.

1 SERUINGMAN Deiectitude? What's that?

3 SERUINGMAN But when they shall see sir, his Crest vp againe, and the man in blood, they will out of their Burroughes (like Conies after Raine) and reuell all with him.

1 SERUINGMAN But when goes this forward?

3 SERUINGMAN To morrow, to day, presently, you shall 2480 haue the Drum strooke vp this afternoone: 'Tis as it were a parcel of their Feast, and to be executed ere they wipe their lips.

2 SERUINGMAN Why then wee shall haue a stirring World againe: This peace is nothing, but to rust Iron, encrease Taylors, and breed Ballad-makers.

1 SERUINGMAN Let me haue Warre say I, it exceeds peace as farre as day do's night: It's sprightly walking, audible, and full of Vent. Peace, is a very Apoplexy, Lethargie, mull'd, deafe, sleepie, insensible, a getter of 2490 more bastard Children, then warres a destroyer of men.

2 SERUINGMAN 'Tis so, and as warre in some sort may be saide to be a Rauisher, so it cannot be denied, but peace is a great maker of Cuckolds.

1 SERUINGMAN I, and it makes men hate one another.

3 SERUINGMAN Reason, because they then lesse neede one another: The Warres for my money. I hope to see Romanes as cheape as Volcians.

⌈*A sound within*⌉

They are rising, they are rising.

1 *and* 2 SERUINGMEN In, in, in, in.   *Exeunt* 2500

Enter the two Tribunes, Sicinius, and Brutus   **4.6**

SCICINIUS   **(Sc. 23)**
We heare not of him, neither need we fear him,
His remedies are tame, the present peace,
And quietnesse of the people, which before
Were in wilde hurry. Heere do we make his Friends
Blush, that the world goes well: who rather had,
Though they themselues did suffer by't, behold
Dissentious numbers pestring streets, then see
Our Tradesmen singing in their shops, and going
About their Functions friendly.

Enter Menenius

BRUTUS
We stood too't in good time. Is this *Menenius*?   2510

SCICINIUS
'Tis he, 'tis he: O he is grown most kind of late:
Haile Sir.

MENENIUS Haile to you both.

SCICINIUS
Your *Coriolanus* is not much mist,
But with his Friends: the Commonwealth doth stand,
And so would do, were he more angry at it.

MENENIUS
All's well, and might haue bene much better, if
He could haue temporiz'd.

SCICINIUS Where is he, heare you?

MENENIUS Nay I heare nothing: 2520
His Mother and his wife, heare nothing from him.

Enter three or foure Citizens

ALL THE CITIZENS (*to the Tribunes*)
The Gods preserue you both.

SCICINIUS   Gooden our Neighbours.

BRUTUS
Gooden to you all, gooden to you all.

1 CITIZEN
  Our selues, our wiues, and children, on our knees,
  Are bound to pray for you both.
SCICINIUS   Liue, and thriue.
BRUTUS Farewell kinde Neighbours:
  We wisht *Coriolanus* had lou'd you as we did.
ALL THE CITIZENS
  Now the Gods keepe you.
BOTH TRIBUNES   Farewell, farewell.
                              Exeunt Citizens
SCICINIUS
  This is a happier and more comely time,
2530 Then when these Fellowes ran about the streets,
  Crying Confusion.
BRUTUS   *Caius Martius* was
  A worthy Officer i'th'Warre, but Insolent,
  O'recome with Pride, Ambitious, past all thinking,
  Selfe-louing.
SCICINIUS   And affecting one sole Throne,
  Without assistãce.
MENENIUS   I thinke not so.
SCICINIUS
  We should by this, to all our Lamentation,
  If he had gone forth Consull, found it so.
BRUTUS
  The Gods haue well preuented it, and Rome
  Sits safe and still, without him.
                    Enter an Ædile
EDILE   Worthy Tribunes,
2540 There is a Slaue whom we haue put in prison,
  Reports the Volces with two seuerall Powers
  Are entred in the Roman Territories,
  And with the deepest malice of the Warre,
  Destroy, what lies before 'em.
MENENIUS   'Tis *Auffidius*,
  Who hearing of our *Martius* Banishment,
  Thrusts forth his hornes againe into the world
  Which were In-shell'd, when *Martius* stood for Rome,
  And durst not once peepe out.
SCICINIUS   Come, what talke you of *Martius*.
BRUTUS (*to the Edile*)
  Go see this Rumorer whipt, it cannot be,
  The Volces dare breake with vs.
2550 MENENIUS   Cannot be?
  We haue Record, that very well it can,
  And three examples of the like, hath beene
  Within my Age. But reason with the fellow
  Before you punish him, where he heard this,
  Least you shall chance to whip your Information,
  And beate the Messenger, who bids beware
  Of what is to be dreaded.
SCICINIUS   Tell not me:
  I know this cannot be.
BRUTUS   Not possible.
        Enter a Messenger
MESSENGER
  The Nobles in great earnestnesse are going

  All to the Senate-house: some newes is come   2560
  That turnes their Countenances.
SCICINIUS   'Tis this Slaue:
  (*To the Edile*) Go whip him fore the peoples eyes: His
     raising,
  Nothing but his report.   ⌜*Exit Edile*⌝
MESSENGER   Yes worthy Sir,
  The Slaues report is seconded, and more
  More fearfull is deliuer'd.
SCICINIUS   What more fearefull?
MESSENGER
  It is spoke freely out of many mouths,
  How probable I do not know, that *Martius*
  Ioyn'd with *Auffidius*, leads a power 'gainst Rome,
  And vowes Reuenge as spacious, as betweene
  The yong'st and oldest thing.
SCICINIUS   This is most likely.   2570
BRUTUS
  Rais'd onely, that the weaker sort may wish
  Good *Martius* home againe.
SCICINIUS The very tricke on't.
MENENIUS This is vnlikely,
  He, and *Auffidius* can no more attone
  Then violent'st Contrariety.
      Enter another Messenger
2 MESSENGER
  You are sent for to the Senate:
  A fearefull Army, led by *Caius Martius*,
  Associated with *Auffidius*, Rages
  Vpon our Territories, and haue already   2580
  O're-borne their way, consum'd with fire, and tooke
  What lay before them.
      Enter Cominius
COMINIUS Oh you haue made good worke.
MENENIUS What newes? What newes?
COMINIUS
  You haue holp to rauish your owne daughters, &
  To melt the Citty Leades vpon your pates,
  To see your Wiues dishonour'd to your Noses.
MENENIUS What's the newes? What's the newes?
COMINIUS
  Your Temples burned in their Ciment, and
  Your Franchises, whereon you stood, confin'd   2590
  Into an Augors boare.
MENENIUS   Pray now, your Newes:
  (*To the Tribunes*) You haue made faire worke I feare
     me: (*to Cominius*) pray your newes,
  If *Martius* should be ioyn'd with Volceans.
COMINIUS
  If? He is their God, he leads them like a thing
  Made by some other Deity then Nature,
  That shapes man Better: and they follow him
  Against vs Brats, with no lesse Confidence,
  Then Boyes pursuing Summer Butter-flies,
  Or Butchers killing Flyes.
MENENIUS (*to the Tribunes*) You haue made good worke,
  You and your Apron men: you, that stood so much   2600

Vpon the voyce of occupation, and
The breath of Garlicke-eaters.

COMINIUS *(to the Tribunes)*
Hee'l shake your Rome about your eares.

MENENIUS
As *Hercules* did shake downe Mellow Fruite:
(To the Tribunes) You haue made faire worke.

BRUTUS But is this true sir?

COMINIUS I, and you'l looke pale
Before you finde it other. All the Regions
Do smilingly Reuolt, and who resists

2610   Are mock'd for valiant Ignorance,
And perish constant Fooles: who is't can blame him?
Your Enemies and his, finde something in him.

MENENIUS We are all vndone, vnlesse
The Noble man haue mercy.

COMINIUS   Who shall aske it?
The Tribunes cannot doo't for shame; the people
Deserue such pitty of him, as the Wolfe
Doe's of the Shepheards: For his best Friends, if they
Should say be good to Rome, they charg'd him, euen
As those should do that had deseru'd his hate,
And therein shew'd like Enemies.

2620   MENENIUS   'Tis true,
If he were putting to my house, the brand
That should consume it, I haue not the face
To say, beseech you cease.
(To the Tribunes)   You haue made faire hands,
You and your Crafts, you haue crafted faire.

COMINIUS *(to the Tribunes)*   You haue brought
A Trembling vpon Rome, such as was neuer
S'incapeable of helpe.

BOTH TRIBUNES Say not, we brought it.

MENENIUS How? Was't we?
We lou'd him, but like Beasts, and Cowardly Nobles,

2630   Gaue way vnto your Clusters, who did hoote
Him out o'th'Citty.

COMINIUS   But I feare
They'l roare him in againe. *Tullus Affidius*,
The second name of men, obeyes his points
As if he were his Officer: Desperation,
Is all the Policy, Strength, and Defence
That Rome can make against them.

Enter a Troope of Citizens

MENENIUS   Heere come the Clusters.
(To the Citizens) And is *Auffidius* with him? You are
    they
That made the Ayre vnwholsome, when you cast
Your stinking, greasie Caps, in hooting at

2640   *Coriolanus* Exile. Now he's comming,
And not a haire vpon a Souldiers head
Which will not proue a whip: As many Coxcombes
As you threw Caps vp, will he tumble downe,
And pay you for your voyces. 'Tis no matter,
If he could burne vs all into one coale,
We haue deseru'd it.

ALL THE CITIZENS Faith, we heare fearfull Newes.

1 CITIZEN For mine owne part,
When I said banish him, I said 'twas pitty.

2 CITIZEN And so did I.   2650

3 CITIZEN And so did I: and to say the truth, so did very
many of vs, that we did we did for the best, and though
wee willingly consented to his Banishment, yet it was
against our will.

COMINIUS
Y'are goodly things, you Voyces.

MENENIUS   You haue made good worke
You and your cry. Shal's to the Capitoll?

COMINIUS Oh I, what else?   *Exeunt both*

SCICINIUS
Go Masters get you home, be not dismaid,
These are a Side, that would be glad to haue
This true, which they so seeme to feare. Go home,   2660
And shew no signe of Feare.

1 CITIZEN The Gods bee good to vs: Come Masters let's
home, I euer said we were i'th wrong, when we
banish'd him.

2 CITIZEN So did we all. But come, let's home.

Exit Citizens

BRUTUS
I do not like this Newes.

SCICINIUS   Nor I.

BRUTUS
Let's to the Capitoll: would halfe my wealth
Would buy this for a lye.

SCICINIUS   Pray let's go.   *Exeunt*

Enter Auffidius with his Lieutenant   **4.7**

AUFFIDIUS Do they still flye to'th'Roman?   (Sc. 24)

LIEUTENANT
I do not know what Witchcraft's in him: but   2670
Your Soldiers vse him as the Grace 'fore meate,
Their talke at Table, and their Thankes at end,
And you are darkned in this action Sir,
Euen by your owne.

AUFFIDIUS   I cannot helpe it now,
Vnlesse by vsing meanes I lame the foote
Of our designe. He beares himselfe more proudlier,
Euen to my person, then I thought he would
When first I did embrace him. Yet his Nature
In that's no Changeling, and I must excuse
What cannot be amended.

LIEUTENANT   Yet I wish Sir,   2680
(I meane for your particular) you had not
Ioyn'd in Commission with him: but either
Haue borne the action of your selfe, or else
To him, had left it soly.

AUFFIDIUS
I vnderstand thee well, and be thou sure
When he shall come to his account, he knowes not
What I can vrge against him. Although it seemes
And so he thinkes, and is no lesse apparant
To th'vulgar eye, that he beares all things fairely:
And shewes good Husbandry for the Volcian State,   2690

Fights Dragon-like, and does atcheeue as soone
As draw his Sword: yet he hath left vndone
That which shall breake his necke, or hazard mine,
When ere we come to our account.

LIEUTENANT
Sir, I beseech you, think you he'l carry Rome?

AUFFIDIUS
All places yeelds to him ere he sits downe,
And the Nobility of Rome are his:
The Senators and Patricians loue him too:
The Tribunes are no Soldiers: and their people
2700 Will be as rash in the repeale, as hasty
To expell him thence. I thinke hee'l be to Rome
As is the Aspray to the Fish, who takes it
By Soueraignty of Nature. First, he was
A Noble seruant to them, but he could not
Carry his Honors eeuen: whether 'twas Pride
Which out of dayly Fortune euer taints
The happy man; whether defect of iudgement,
To faile in the disposing of those chances
Which he was Lord of: or whether Nature,
2710 Not to be other then one thing, not moouing
From th'Caske to th'Cushion: but commanding peace
Euen with the same austerity and garbe,
As he controll'd the warre. But one of these
(As he hath spices of them all) not all,
For I dare so farre free him, made him fear'd,
So hated, and so banish'd: but he ha's a Merit
To choake it in the vtt'rance: So our Vertues
Lie in th'interpretation of the time,
And power vnto it selfe most commendable,
2720 Hath not a Tombe so euident as a Chaire
T'extoll what it hath done.
One fire driues out one fire; one Naile, one Naile;
Rights by rights foulter, strengths by strengths do faile.
Come let's away: when *Caius* Rome is thine,
Thou art poor'st of all; then shortly art thou mine.

exeunt

⬡

5.1   *Enter Menenius, Cominius, Sicinius and Brutus, the*
(Sc. 25)   *two Tribunes, with others*
MENENIUS
No, ile not go: you heare what he hath said
Which was sometime his Generall: who lou'd him
In a most deere particular. He call'd me Father:
But what o'that? (*To the Tribunes*) Go you that
        banish'd him
2730 A Mile before his Tent, fall downe, and knee
The way into his mercy: Nay, if he coy'd
To heare *Cominius* speake, Ile keepe at home.

COMINIUS
He would not seeme to know me.

MENENIUS (*to the Tribunes*)   Do you heare?

COMINIUS
Yet one time he did call me by my name:
I vrg'd our old acquaintance, and the drops
That we haue bled together. *Coriolanus*

He would not answer too: Forbad all Names,
He was a kinde of Nothing, Titlelesse,
Till he had forg'd himselfe a name a'th'fire
Of burning Rome.

MENENIUS (*to the Tribunes*)
              Why so: you haue made good worke: 2740
A paire of Tribunes, that haue wrack'd fair Rome,
To make Coales cheape: A Noble memory.

COMINIUS
I minded him, how Royall 'twas to pardon
When it was lesse expected. He replyed
It was a bare petition of a State
To one whom they had punish'd.

MENENIUS   Very well,
Could he say lesse.

COMINIUS
I offred to awaken his regard
For's priuate Friends. His answer to me was
He could not stay to picke them, in a pile   2750
Of noysome musty Chaffe. He said, 'twas folly
For one poore graine or two, to leaue vnburnt
And still to nose th'offence.

MENENIUS   For one poore graine or two?
I am one of those: his Mother, Wife, his Childe,
And this braue Fellow too: we are the Graines,
(*To the Tribunes*) You are the musty Chaffe, and you
        are smelt
Aboue the Moone. We must be burnt for you.

SCICINIUS
Nay, pray be patient: If you refuse your ayde
In this so neuer-needed helpe, yet do not
Vpbraid's with our distresse. But sure if you   2760
Would be your Countries Pleader, your good tongue
More then the instant Armie we can make
Might stop our Countryman.

MENENIUS   No: Ile not meddle.

SCICINIUS
Pray you go to him.

MENENIUS   What should I do?

BRUTUS
Onely make triall what your Loue can do,
For Rome, towards *Martius*.

MENENIUS
Well, and say that *Martius* returne mee,
As *Cominius* is return'd, vnheard: what then?
But as a discontented Friend, greefe-shot
With his vnkindnesse. Say't be so?

SCICINIUS   Yet your good will   2770
Must haue that thankes from Rome, after the
        measure
As you intended well.

MENENIUS   Ile vndertak't:
I thinke hee'l heare me. Yet to bite his lip,
And humme at good *Cominius*, much vnhearts mee.
He was not taken well, he had not din'd,
The Veines vnfill'd, our blood is cold, and then
We powt vpon the Morning, are vnapt
To giue or to forgiue; but when we haue stufft

These Pipes, and these Conueyances of our blood
2780 With Wine and Feeding, we haue suppler Soules
Then in our Priest-like Fasts: therefore Ile watch him
Till he be dieted to my request,
And then Ile set vpon him.

BRUTUS
You know the very rode into his kindnesse,
And cannot lose your way.

MENENIUS   Good faith Ile proue him.
Speed how it will, I shall ere long, haue knowledge
Of my successe.   *Exit*

COMINIUS   Hee'l neuer heare him.

SCICINIUS   Not.

COMINIUS
I tell you, he doe's sit in Gold, his eye
Red as 'twould burne Rome: and his Iniury
2790 The Gaoler to his pitty. I kneel'd before him,
'Twas very faintly he said Rise: dismist me
Thus with his speechlesse hand. What he would do
He sent in writing after me: what he would not,
Bound with an Oath to hold to his conditions:
So that all hope is vaine, vnlesse his Noble Mother,
And his Wife, who (as I heare) meane to solicite him
For mercy to his Countrey: therefore let's hence,
And with our faire intreaties hast them on.   *Exeunt*

5.2   *Enter Menenius to the Watch or Guard*
(Sc. 26)
      1 WATCHMAN Stay: whence are you.
2800 2 WATCHMAN Stand, and go backe.
MENENIUS You guard like men, 'tis well.
But by your leaue, I am an Officer
Of State, & come to speak with *Coriolanus*.

1 WATCHMAN From whence?

MENENIUS
From Rome.

1 WATCHMAN You may not passe, you must returne:
Our Generall will no more heare from thence.

2 WATCHMAN
You'l see your Rome embrac'd with fire, before
You'l speake with *Coriolanus*.

MENENIUS   Good my Friends,
If you haue heard your Generall talke of Rome,
2810 And of his Friends there, it is Lots to Blankes,
My name hath touch't your eares: it is *Menenius*.

1 WATCHMAN
Be it so, go back: the vertue of your name,
Is not heere passable.

MENENIUS   I tell thee Fellow,
Thy Generall is my Louer: I haue beene
The booke of his good Acts, whence men haue read
His Fame vnparalell'd, happely amplified:
For I haue euer verified my Friends,
(Of whom hee's cheefe) with all the size that verity
Would without lapsing suffer: Nay, sometimes,
2820 Like to a Bowle vpon a subtle ground
I haue tumbled past the throw: and in his praise
Haue (almost) stampt the Leasing. Therefore Fellow,
I must haue leaue to passe.

1 WATCHMAN Faith Sir, if you had told as many lies in

his behalfe, as you haue vttered words in your owne,
you should not passe heere: no, though it were as
vertuous to lye, as to liue chastly. Therefore go backe.

MENENIUS Prythee fellow, remember my name is
Menenius, always factionary on the party of your
Generall.   2830

2 WATCHMAN Howsoeuer you haue bin his Lier, as you
say you haue, I am one that telling true vnder him,
must say you cannot passe. Therefore go backe.

MENENIUS Ha's he din'd can'st thou tell? For I would not
speake with him, till after dinner.

1 WATCHMAN You are a Roman, are you?

MENENIUS I am as thy Generall is.

1 WATCHMAN Then you should hate Rome, as he do's.
Can you, when you haue pusht out your gates, the
very Defender of them, and in a violent popular   2840
ignorance, giuen your enemy your shield, thinke to
front his reuenges with the easie groanes of old women,
the Virginall Palms of your daughters, or with the
palsied intercession of such a decay'd Dotant as you
seeme to be? Can you think to blow out the intended
fire, your City is ready to flame in, with such weake
breath as this? No, you are deceiu'd, therfore backe to
Rome, and prepare for your execution: you are
condemn'd, our Generall has sworne you out of
repreeue and pardon.   2850

MENENIUS Sirra, if thy Captaine knew I were heere, he
would vse me with estimation.

1 WATCHMAN Come, my Captaine knowes you not.

MENENIUS I meane thy Generall.

1 WATCHMAN My Generall cares not for you. Back I say,
go: least I let forth your halfe pinte of blood. Backe,
that's the vtmost of your hauing, backe.

MENENIUS Nay but Fellow, Fellow.
          Enter Coriolanus with Auffidius

CORIOLANUS What's the matter?

MENENIUS (*to 1 Watchman*) Now you Companion: Ile say   2860
an arrant for you: you shall know now that I am in
estimation: you shall perceiue, that a Iacke gardant
cannot office me from my Son *Coriolanus*: guesse but by
my entertainment with him, if thou stand'st not i'th
state of hanging, or of some death more long in
Spectatorship, and crueller in suffering: behold now
presently, and swoond for what's to come vpon thee. (*To
Coriolanus*) The glorious Gods sit in hourely Synod about
thy particular prosperity, and loue thee no worse then
thy old Father *Menenius* do's. (*Weeping*) O my Son, my   2870
Son! thou art preparing fire for vs: looke thee, heere's
water to quench it. I was hardly moued to come to thee:
but beeing assured none but my selfe could moue thee, I
haue bene blowne out of our Gates with sighes: and
coniure thee to pardon Rome, and thy petitionary
Countrimen. The good Gods asswage thy wrath, and
turne the dregs of it, vpon this Varlet heere: This, who
like a blocke hath denyed my accesse to thee.

CORIOLANUS Away.

MENENIUS How? Away?   2880

CORIOLANUS
Wife, Mother, Child, I know not. My affaires

Are Seruanted to others: Though I owe
My Reuenge properly, my remission lies
In Volcean brests. That we haue beene familiar,
Ingrate forgetfulnesse shall poison rather
Then pitty note how much, therefore be gone.
Mine eares against your suites, are stronger then
Your gates against my force. Yet for I lou'd thee,
 He giues him a Letter
Take this along, I writ it for thy sake,

2890 And would haue sent it. Another word *Menenius*,
I will not heare thee speake. This man *Auffidius*
Was my belou'd in Rome: yet thou behold'st.

AUFFIDIUS You keepe a constant temper.
     Exeunt. Manet the Guard and Menenius

1 WATCHMAN Now sir, is your name *Menenius*?

2 WATCHMAN 'Tis a spell you see of much power: You
know the way home againe.

1 WATCHMAN Do you heare how wee are shent for keeping
your greatnesse backe?

2 WATCHMAN What cause do you thinke I haue to
2900 swoond?

MENENIUS I neither care for th'world, nor your General:
for such things as you, I can scarse thinke ther's any,
y'are so slight. He that hath a will to die by himselfe,
feares it not from another: Let your Generall do his
worst. For you, bee that you are, long; and your misery
encrease with your age. I say to you, as I was said to,
Away.   *Exit*

1 WATCHMAN A Noble Fellow I warrant him.

2 WATCHMAN The worthy Fellow is our General. He's the
2910 Rock, the Oake not to be winde-shaken. *Exit Watch*

5.3
(Sc. 27)   *Enter Coriolanus and Auffidius, with Volcean*
   Souldiers. ⌈*Coriolanus and Auffidius sit*⌉

CORIOLANUS
We will before the walls of Rome to morrow
Set downe our Hoast. My partner in this Action,
You must report to th'Volcian Lords, how plainly
I haue borne this Businesse.

AUFFIDIUS   Onely their ends
You haue respected, stopt your eares against
The generall suite of Rome: Neuer admitted
A priuat whisper, no not with such frends
That thought them sure of you.

CORIOLANUS   This last old man,
Whom with a crack'd heart I haue sent to Rome,
2920 Lou'd me, aboue the measure of a Father,
Nay godded me indeed. Their latest refuge
Was to send him: for whose old Loue I haue
(Though I shew'd sowrely to him) once more offer'd
The first Conditions which they did refuse,
And cannot now accept: to grace him onely,
That thought he could do more, a very little
I haue yeelded too. Fresh Embasses, and Suites,
Nor from the State, nor priuate friends heereafter
Will I lend eare to.
  Shout within
     Ha? what shout is this?

Shall I be tempted to infringe my vow   2930
In the same time 'tis made? I will not.
  Enter Virgilia, Volumnia, Valeria, yong Martius,
   with Attendants
My wife comes formost, then the honour'd mould
Wherein this Trunke was fram'd, and in her hand
The Grandchilde to her blood. But out affection,
All bond and priuiledge of Nature breake;
Let it be Vertuous to be Obstinate.
  ⌈*Virgilia*⌉ *curtsies*
What is that Curt'sie worth? Or those Doues eyes,
Which can make Gods forsworne? I melt, and am not
Of stronger earth then others:
  Volumnia bowes
        my Mother bowes,
As if Olympus to a Mole-hill should   2940
In supplication Nod: and my yong Boy
Hath an Aspect of intercession, which
Great Nature cries, Deny not. Let the Volces
Plough Rome, and harrow Italy, Ile neuer
Be such a Gosling to obey instinct; but stand
As if a man were Author of himself,
And knew no other kin.

VIRGILIA   My Lord and Husband.

CORIOLANUS
These eyes are not the same I wore in Rome.

VIRGILIA
The sorrow that deliuers vs thus chang'd,
Makes you thinke so.

CORIOLANUS   Like a dull Actor now, 2950
I haue forgot my part, and I am out,
Euen to a full Disgrace. ⌈*Rising*⌉ Best of my Flesh,
Forgiue my Tyranny: but do not say,
For that forgiue our Romanes.
  ⌈*Virgilia kisses him*⌉
        O a kisse
Long as my Exile, sweet as my Reuenge!
Now by the iealous Queene of Heauen, that kisse
I carried from thee deare; and my true Lippe
Hath Virgin'd it ere since. You Gods, I prayte,
And the most noble Mother of the world
Leaue vnsaluted: Sinke my knee i'th'earth,   2960
  He kneeles
Of thy deepe duty, more impression shew
Then that of common Sonnes.

VOLUMNIA   Oh stand vp blest!
  ⌈*Coriolanus rises*⌉
Whil'st with no softer Cushion then the Flint
I kneele before thee, and vnproperly
Shew duty as mistaken, all this while,
Betweene the Childe, and Parent.
  She kneeles

CORIOLANUS   What's this?
Your knees to me? To your Corrected Sonne?
  ⌈*He raises her*⌉
Then let the Pibbles on the hungry beach
Fillop the Starres: Then, let the mutinous windes
Strike the proud Cedars 'gainst the fiery Sun: 2970

Murd'ring Impossibility, to make
What cannot be, slight worke.

VOLUMNIA   Thou art my Warriour,
I holpe to frame thee. Do you know this Lady?

CORIOLANUS
The Noble Sister of *Publicola*;
The Moone of Rome: Chaste as the Isicle
That's candied by the Frost, from purest Snow,
And hangs on *Dians* Temple: Deere *Valeria*.

VOLUMNIA (*shewing Coriolanus his Sonne*)
This is a poore Epitome of yours,
Which by th'interpretation of full time,
May shew like all your selfe.

2980   **CORIOLANUS** (*to yong Martius*)   The God of Souldiers:
With the consent of supreame Ioue, informe
Thy thoughts with Noblenesse, that thou mayst proue
To shame vnvulnerable, and sticke i'th Warres
Like a great Sea-marke standing euery flaw,
And sauing those that eye thee.

VOLUMNIA (*to yong Martius*) Your knee, Sirrah.
⌈*Yong Martius kneeles*⌉

CORIOLANUS That's my braue Boy.

VOLUMNIA
Euen he, your wife, this Ladie, and my selfe,
Are Sutors to you.

CORIOLANUS   I beseech you peace:
2990   Or if you'ld aske, remember this before;
The things I haue forsworne to graunt, may neuer
Be held by you denials. Do not bid me
Dismisse my Soldiers, or capitulate
Againe, with Romes Mechanickes. Tell me not
Wherein I seeme vnnaturall: Desire not t'allay
My Rages and Reuenges, with your colder reasons.

VOLUMNIA Oh no more, no more:
You haue said you will not grant vs any thing:
For we haue nothing else to aske, but that
3000   Which you deny already: yet we will aske,
That if you faile in our request, the blame
May hang vpon your hardnesse, therefore heare vs.

CORIOLANUS
Auffidius, and you Volces marke, for wee'l
Heare nought from Rome in priuate.
⌈*He sits*⌉
                                             Your request?

VOLUMNIA
Should we be silent & not speak, our Raiment
And state of Bodies would bewray what life
We haue led since thy Exile. Thinke with thy selfe,
How more vnfortunate then all liuing women
Are we come hither; since that thy sight, which should
Make our eies flow with ioy, harts dance with
3010   comforts,
Constraines them weepe, and shake with feare &
          sorow,
Making the Mother, wife, and Childe to see,
The Sonne, the Husband, and the Father tearing
His Countries Bowels out; and to poore we
Thine enmities most capitall: Thou barr'st vs

Our prayers to the Gods, which is a comfort
That all but we enioy. For how can we?
Alas! how can we, for our Country pray?
Whereto we are bound, together with thy victory:
Whereto we are bound: Alacke, or we must loose   3020
The Countrie our deere Nurse, or else thy person
Our comfort in the Country. We must finde
An euident Calamity, though we had
Our wish, which side should win. For either thou
Must as a Forraine Recreant be led
With Manacles thorough our streets, or else
Triumphantly treade on thy Countries ruine,
And beare the Palme, for hauing brauely shed
Thy Wife and Childrens blood: For my selfe, Sonne,
I purpose not to waite on Fortune, till   3030
These warres determine: If I cannot perswade thee,
Rather to shew a Noble grace to both parts,
Then seeke the end of one; thou shalt no sooner
March to assault thy Country, then to treade
(Trust too't, thou shalt not) on thy Mothers wombe
That brought thee to this world.

VIRGILIA   I, and mine,
That brought you forth this boy, to keepe your name
Liuing to time.

YONG MARTIUS   A shall not tread on me:
Ile run away till I am bigger, but then Ile fight.

CORIOLANUS
Not of a womans tendernesse to be,   3040
Requires nor Childe, nor womans face to see:
I haue sate too long.
⌈*He rises and turnes away*⌉

VOLUMNIA   Nay, go not from vs thus:
If it were so, that our request did tend
To saue the Romanes, thereby to destroy
The Volces whom you serue, you might condemne vs
As poysonous of your Honour. No, our suite
Is that you reconcile them: While the Volces
May say, this mercy we haue shew'd: the Romanes,
This we receiu'd, and each in either side
Giue the All-haile to thee, and cry be Blest   3050
For making vp this peace. Thou know'st (great Sonne)
The end of Warres vncertaine: but this certaine,
That if thou conquer Rome, the benefit
Which thou shalt thereby reape, is such a name
Whose repetition will be dogg'd with Curses:
Whose Chronicle thus writ, The man was Noble,
But with his last Attempt, he wip'd it out:
Destroy'd his Country, and his name remaines
To th'insuing Age, abhorr'd. Speake to me Son:
Thou hast affected the fine straines of Honor,   3060
To imitate the graces of the Gods,
To teare with Thunder the wide Cheekes a'th'Ayre,
And yet to charge thy Sulphure with a Boult
That should but riue an Oake. Why do'st not speake?
Think'st thou it Honourable for a Nobleman
Still to remember wrongs? Daughter, speake you:
He cares not for your weeping. Speake thou Boy,
Perhaps thy childishnesse will moue him more

3070 Then can our Reasons. There's no man in the world
More bound to's Mother, yet heere he let's me prate
Like one i'th'Stockes. Thou hast neuer in thy life,
Shew'd thy deere Mother any curtesie,
When she (poore Hen) fond of no second brood,
Ha's clock'd thee to the Warres: and safelie home
Loden with Honor. Say my Request's vniust,
And spurne me backe: But, if it be not so
Thou art not honest, and the Gods will plague thee
That thou restrain'st from me the Duty, which
To a Mothers part belongs. He turnes away:
3080 Down Ladies: let vs shame him with our knees.
To his sur-name *Coriolanus* longs more pride
Then pitty to our Prayers. Downe: an end,
This is the last.
          The Ladies and yong Martius kneele
                    So, we will home to Rome,
And dye among our Neighbours: Nay, behold's,
This Boy that cannot tell what he would haue,
But kneeles, and holds vp hands for fellowship,
Doe's reason our Petition with more strength
Then thou hast to deny't. Come, let vs go:
This Fellow had a Volcean to his Mother:
3090 His Wife is in *Corioles*, and this Childe
Like him by chance: yet giue vs our dispatch:
I am husht vntill our City be afire,
And then Ile speak a litle.
          He holds her by the hand silent
CORIOLANUS   O Mother, Mother!
What haue you done? Behold, the Heauens do ope,
The Gods looke downe, and this vnnaturall Scene
They laugh at. Oh my Mother, Mother: Oh!
You haue wonne a happy Victory to Rome.
But for your Sonne, beleeue it: Oh beleeue it,
Most dangerously you haue with him preuail'd,
3100 If not most mortall to him. But let it come:
          ⌜*The Ladies and yong Martius rise*⌝
Auffidius, though I cannot make true Warres,
Ile frame conuenient peace. Now good *Auffidius*,
Were you in my steed, would you haue heard
A Mother lesse? or granted lesse *Auffidius*?
AUFFIDIUS
I was mou'd withall.
CORIOLANUS   I dare be sworne you were:
And sir, it is no little thing to make
Mine eyes to sweat compassion. But (good sir)
What peace you'l make, aduise me: For my part,
Ile not to Rome, Ile backe with you, and pray you
3110 Stand to me in this cause. Oh Mother! Wife!
AUFFIDIUS (*aside*)
I am glad thou hast set thy mercy, & thy Honor
At difference in thee: Out of that Ile worke
My selfe a former Fortune.
CORIOLANUS (*to Volumnia and Virgilia*) I by and by;
But we will drinke together: And you shall beare
A better witnesse backe then words, which we
On like conditions, will haue Counter-seal'd.
Come enter with vs: Ladies you deserue

To haue a Temple built you: All the Swords
In Italy, and her Confederate Armes
Could not haue made this peace.   *Exeunt* 3120

          Enter Menenius and Sicinius   5.4
MENENIUS See you yon'd Coin a'th Capitol, yon'd corner (Sc. 2)
stone?
SICINIUS Why what of that?
MENENIUS If it be possible for you to displace it with your
little finger, there is some hope the Ladies of Rome,
especially his Mother, may preuaile with him. But I
say, there is no hope in't, our throats are sentenc'd,
and stay vppon execution.
SICINIUS Is't possible, that so short a time can alter the
condition of a man.   3130
MENENIUS There is difference between a Grub & a Butterfly, yet your Butterfly was a Grub: this *Martius*, is
growne from Man to Dragon: He has wings, hee's more
then a creeping thing.
SICINIUS He lou'd his Mother deerely.
MENENIUS So did he mee: and he no more remembers his
Mother now, then an eight yeare old horse. The
tartnesse of his face, sowres ripe Grapes. When he
walks, he moues like an Engine, and the ground
shrinkes before his Treading. He is able to pierce a 3140
Corslet with his eye: Talkes like a knell, and his hum
is a Battery. He sits in his State, as a thing made for
Alexander. What he bids bee done, is finisht with his
bidding. He wants nothing of a God but Eternity, and
a Heauen to Throne in.
SICINIUS Yes, mercy, if you report him truly.
MENENIUS I paint him in the Character. Mark what mercy
his Mother shall bring from him: There is no more
mercy in him, then there is milke in a male-Tyger, that
shall our poore City finde: and all this is long of you. 3150
SICINIUS The Gods be good vnto vs.
MENENIUS No, in such a case the Gods will not bee good
vnto vs. When we banish'd him, we respected not
them: and he returning to breake our necks, they
respect not vs.
          Enter a Messenger
MESSENGER (*to Sicinius*)
Sir, if you'ld saue your life, flye to your House,
The Plebeians haue got your Fellow Tribune,
And hale him vp and downe; all swearing, if
The Romane Ladies bring not comfort home
They'l giue him death by Inches.
          Enter another Messenger
SICINIUS   What's the Newes? 3160
2 MESSENGER
Good Newes, good newes, the Ladies haue preuayl'd,
The Volcians are dislodg'd, and *Martius* gone:
A merrier day did neuer yet greet Rome,
No, not th'expulsion of the *Tarquins*.
SICINIUS   Friend,
Art thou certaine this is true? Is't most certaine.
2 MESSENGER
As certaine as I know the Sun is fire:

Where haue you lurk'd that you make doubt of it:
Ne're through an Arch so hurried the blowne Tide,
As the recomforted through th'gates.
Trumpets, Hoboyes, Drums beate, altogether
                                Why harke you:
3170   The Trumpets, Sack-buts, Psalteries, and Fifes,
Tabors, and Symboles, and the showting Romans
Make the Sunne dance.
            A shout within
                        Hearke you.
MENENIUS   This is good Newes:
I will go meete the Ladies. This *Volumnia*,
Is worth of Consuls, Senators, Patricians,
A City full: Of Tribunes such as you,
A Sea and Land full: you haue pray'd well to day:
This Morning, for ten thousand of your throates,
I'de not haue giuen a doit.
            Sound Musicke still with the Shouts
                        Harke, how they ioy.
SCICINIUS (*to the Messenger*)
First, the Gods blesse you for your tydings: Next,
3180   ⌈*Giuing money*⌉ Accept my thankefulnesse.
2 MESSENGER
Sir, we haue all great cause to giue great thanks.
SCICINIUS
They are neere the City.
2 MESSENGER   Almost at point to enter.
SCICINIUS Wee'l meet them, and helpe the ioy.   *Exeunt*

5.5   *Enter ⌈at one doore⌉ Lords ⌈and Citizens⌉, ⌈at another*
(Sc. 29)   *doore⌉ two Senators, with the Ladies Volumnia,*
            Virgilia, and Valeria, passing ouer the Stage
A SENATOR
Behold our Patronnesse, the life of Rome:
Call all your Tribes together, praise the Gods,
And make triumphant fires, strew Flowers before them:
Vnshoot the noise that Banish'd *Martius*;
Repeale him, with the welcome of his Mother:
Cry welcome Ladies, welcome.
ALL   Welcome Ladies, welcome.
            A Flourish with Drummes & Trumpets. Exeunt

5.6   *Enter Tullus Auffidius, with Attendants*
(Sc. 30) AUFFIDIUS
3190   Go tell the Lords a'th'City, I am heere:
Deliuer them this Paper: hauing read it,
Bid them repayre to th'Market place, where I
Euen in theirs, and in the Commons eares
Will vouch the truth of it. Him I accuse:
The City Ports by this hath enter'd, and
Intends t'appeare before the People, hoping
To purge himselfe with words. Dispatch.
                        Exeunt Attendants
            Enter 3 or 4 Conspirators of Auffidius Faction
                                Most Welcome.
1 CONSPIRATOR
How is it with our Generall?
AUFFIDIUS   Euen so,

As with a man by his owne Almes impoyson'd,
And with his Charity slaine.
2 CONSPIRATOR   Most Noble Sir,   3200
If you do hold the same intent wherein
You wisht vs parties: Wee'l deliuer you
Of your great danger.
AUFFIDIUS   Sir, I cannot tell,
We must proceed as we do finde the People.
3 CONSPIRATOR
The People will remaine vncertaine, whil'st
'Twixt you there's difference: but the fall of either
Makes the Suruiuor heyre of all.
AUFFIDIUS   I know it:
And my pretext to strike at him, admits
A good construction. I rais'd him, and I pawn'd
Mine Honor for his truth: who being so heighten'd,   3210
He watred his new Plants with dewes of Flattery,
Seducing so my Friends: and to this end,
He bow'd his Nature, neuer knowne before,
But to be rough, vnswayable, and free.
3 CONSPIRATOR Sir, his stoutnesse
When he did stand for Consull, which he lost
By lacke of stooping.
AUFFIDIUS   That I would haue spoke of:
Being banish'd for't, he came vnto my Harth,
Presented to my knife his Throat: I tooke him,
Made him ioynt-seruant with me: Gaue him way   3220
In all his owne desires: Nay, let him choose
Out of my Files, his proiects to accomplish,
My best and freshest men, seru'd his designements
In mine owne person: holpe to reape the Fame
Which he did end all his; and tooke some pride
To do my selfe this wrong: Till at the last
I seem'd his Follower, not Partner; and
He wadg'd me with his Countenance, as if
I had bin Mercenary.
1 CONSPIRATOR   So he did my Lord:
The Army marueyl'd at it, and in the last,   3230
When he had carried Rome, and that we look'd
For no lesse Spoile, then Glory.
AUFFIDIUS   There was it:
For which my sinewes shall be stretcht vpon him.
At a few drops of Womens rhewme, which are
As cheape as Lies, he sold the Blood and Labour
Of our great Action; therefore shall he dye,
And Ile renew me in his fall.
            Drummes and Trumpets sounds, with great showts
                of the people
                        But hearke.
1 CONSPIRATOR
Your Natiue Towne you enter'd like a Poste,
And had no welcomes home, but he returnes
Splitting the Ayre with noyse.
2 CONSPIRATOR   And patient Fooles,   3240
Whose children he hath slaine, their base throats teare
With giuing him glory.
3 CONSPIRATOR   Therefore at your vantage,
Ere he expresse himselfe, or moue the people

With what he would say, let him feele your Sword:
Which we will second: when he lies along
After your way, his Tale pronounc'd, shall bury
His Reasons, with his Body.

Enter the Lords of the City

AUFFIDIUS   Say no more.
Heere come the Lords.

ALL THE LORDS You are most welcome home.

3250 AUFFIDIUS I haue not deseru'd it.
But worthy Lords, haue you with heede perused
What I haue written to you?

ALL THE LORDS   We haue.

1 LORD   And greeue to heare't:
What faults he made before the last, I thinke
Might haue found easie Fines: But there to end
Where he was to begin, and giue away
The benefit of our Leuies, answering vs
With our owne charge: making a Treatie, where
There was a yeelding; this admits no excuse.

AUFFIDIUS He approaches, you shall heare him.

Enter Coriolanus marching with Drumme, and
Colours. The Commoners being with him

CORIOLANUS

3260 Haile Lords, I am return'd your Souldier:
No more infected with my Countries loue
Then when I parted hence: but still subsisting
Vnder your great Command. You are to know,
That prosperously I haue attempted, and
With bloody passage led your Warres, euen to
The gates of Rome: Our spoiles we haue brought home
Doth more then counterpoize a full third part
The charges of the Action. We haue made peace
With no lesse Honor to the *Antiates*

3270 Then shame to th'Romaines. And we heere deliuer
Subscrib'd by'th'Consuls, and Patricians,
Together with the Seale a'th Senat, what
We haue compounded on.

He giues the Lords a Paper

AUFFIDIUS   Read it not Noble Lords,
But tell the Traitor in the highest degree
He hath abus'd your Powers.

CORIOLANUS Traitor? How now?

AUFFIDIUS I Traitor, *Martius*.

CORIOLANUS *Martius?*

AUFFIDIUS

I *Martius, Caius Martius:* Do'st thou thinke
3280 Ile grace thee with that Robbery, thy stolne name
Coriolanus in *Corioles?*
You Lords and Heads a'th'State, perfidiously
He ha's betray'd your businesse, and giuen vp
For certaine drops of Salt, your City Rome:
I say your City to his Wife and Mother,
Breaking his Oath and Resolution, like
A twist of rotten Silke, neuer admitting
Counsaile a'th'warre: But at his Nurses teares
He whin'd and roar'd away your Victory,
3290 That Pages blush'd at him, and men of heart
Look'd wond'ring each at others.

CORIOLANUS   Hear'st thou Mars?

AUFFIDIUS
Name not the God, thou boy of Teares.

CORIOLANUS   Ha?

AUFFIDIUS   No more.

CORIOLANUS
Measurelesse Lyar, thou hast made my heart
Too great for what containes it. Boy? Oh Slaue,
Pardon me Lords, 'tis the first time that euer
I was forc'd to scoul'd. Your iudgments my graue Lords
Must giue this Curre the Lye: and his owne Notion,
Who weares my stripes imprest vpon him, that
Must beare my beating to his Graue, shall ioyne
To thrust the Lye vnto him.

1 LORD   Peace both, and heare me speake.   3300

CORIOLANUS
Cut me to peeces Volces men and Lads,
Staine all your edges on me. Boy, false Hound:
If you haue writ your Annales true, 'tis there,
That like an Eagle in a Doue-coat, I
Flutter'd your Volcians in *Corioles*.
Alone I did it, Boy.

AUFFIDIUS   Why Noble Lords,
Will you be put in minde of his blinde Fortune,
Which was your shame, by this vnholy Braggart?
'Fore your owne eyes, and eares?

ALL THE CONSPIRATORS   Let him dye for't.

ALL THE PEOPLE ⌈*shouting dispersedly*⌉
Teare him to peeces, do it presently: 3310
He kill'd my Sonne, my daughter, he kill'd my Cosine
Marcus, he kill'd my Father.

2 LORD   Peace hoe: no outrage, peace:
The man is Noble, and his Fame folds in
This Orbe o'th'earth: His last offences to vs
Shall haue Iudicious hearing. Stand *Auffidius*,
And trouble not the peace.

CORIOLANUS ⌈*drawing his Sword*⌉
O that I had him, with six *Auffidiusses*,
Or more: His Tribe, to vse my lawfull Sword.

AUFFIDIUS ⌈*drawing his Sword*⌉
Insolent Villaine.

ALL THE CONSPIRATORS Kill, kill, kill, kill, kill him.

Draw two Conspirators, and kils Martius, who
falles, Auffidius ⌈and Conspirators⌉ stands on him

LORDS
Hold, hold, hold, hold.

AUFFIDIUS   My Noble Masters, heare me speake.   3320

1 LORD
O *Tullus*.

2 LORD (*to Auffidius*) Thou hast done a deed, whereat
Valour will weepe.

3 LORD ⌈*to Auffidius and the Conspirators*⌉
                  Tread not vpon him Masters,
All be quiet, put vp your Swords.

AUFFIDIUS My Lords,
When you shall know (as in this Rage
Prouok'd by him, you cannot) the great danger
Which this mans life did owe you, you'l reioyce
That he is thus cut off. Please it your Honours
To call me to your Senate, Ile deliuer

3330 My selfe your loyall Seruant, or endure
Your heauiest Censure.
1 LORD   Beare from hence his body,
And mourne you for him. Let him be regarded
As the most Noble Coarse, that euer Herald
Did follow to his Vrne.
2 LORD   His owne impatience,
Takes from *Auffidius* a great part of blame:
Let's make the Best of it.
AUFFIDIUS   My Rage is gone,

And I am strucke with sorrow. Take him vp:
Helpe three a'th'cheefest Souldiers, Ile be one.
Beate thou the Drumme that it speake mournfully:
Traile your steele Pikes. Though in this City hee   3340
Hath widdowed and vnchilded many a one,
Which to this houre bewaile the Iniury,
Yet he shall haue a Noble Memory. Assist.
                    Exeunt bearing the Body of Martius. A dead
                    March Sounded

FINIS

THE WINTERS TALE

THE astrologer Simon Forman saw *The Winters Tale* at the Globe on 15 May 1611. Just how much earlier the play was written is not certainly known. During the sheep-shearing feast in Act 4, twelve countrymen perform a satyrs' dance that three of them are said to have already 'danc'd before the King'. This is not necessarily a topical reference, but satyrs danced in Ben Jonson's *Masque of Oberon*, performed before King James on 1 January 1611. It seems likely that this dance was incorporated in *The Winters Tale* (just as, later, another masque dance seems to have been transferred to *The Two Noble Kinsmen*). But it occurs in a self-contained passage that may well have been added after Shakespeare wrote the play itself. *The Winters Tale*, first printed in the 1623 Folio, is usually thought to have been written after *Cymbeline*, but stylistic evidence places it before that play, perhaps in 1609-10.

A mid sixteenth-century book classes 'winter tales' along with 'old wiues tales'; Shakespeare's title prepared his audiences for a tale of romantic improbability, one to be wondered at rather than believed; and within the play itself characters compare its events to 'an old tale' (2716; 2982). The comparison is just: Shakespeare is dramatizing a story by his old rival Robert Greene, published as *Pandosto: The Triumph of Time* in or before 1588. This gave Shakespeare his plot outline, of a king (Leontes) who believes his wife (Hermione) to have committed adultery with another king (Polixenes), his boyhood friend, and who casts off his new-born daughter (Perdita—the lost one) in the belief that she is his friend's bastard. In both versions the baby is brought up as a shepherdess, falls in love with her supposed father's son (Florizell in the play), and returns to her real father's court where she is at last recognized as his daughter. In both versions, too, the wife's innocence is demonstrated by the pronouncement of the Delphic oracle, and her husband passes the period of his daughter's absence in penitence; but Shakespeare alters the ending of his source story, bringing it into line with the conventions of romance. He adopts Greene's tripartite structure, but greatly develops it, adding for instance Leontes' steward Antigonus and his redoubtable wife Paulina, along with the comic rogue Autolicus, 'snapper-vp of vnconsidered trifles'.

The intensity of poetic suffering with which Leontes expresses his irrational jealousy is matched by the lyrical rapture of the love episodes between Florizell and Perdita. In both verse and prose *The Winters Tale* shows Shakespeare's verbal powers at their greatest, and his theatrical mastery is apparent in, for example, Hermione's trial (3.1) and the daring final scene in which time brings about its triumph.

The Folio text was set from a transcript apparently prepared by the scrivener Ralph Crane.

THE NAMES OF THE ACTORS

LEONTES, King of Sicillia

HERMIONE, his wife

MAMILLIUS, his sonne

PERDITA, his daughter

CAMILLO

ANTIGONUS

CLEOMINES

DION

} Lords at Leontes court

PAULINA, wife of Antigonus

EMILIA, a lady attending on Hermione

A GAOLER

A MARRINER

Other Lords and Gentlemen, Ladies, Officers and Seruants at Leontes court

POLIXENES, King of Bohemia

FLORIZELL, his sonne, in loue with Perdita; known as Doricles

ARCHIDAMUS, a Bohemian lord

AUTOLICUS, a rogue, once in the seruice of Florizell

OLD SHEPHEARD, supposed father of Perdita

CLOWNE, his sonne

MOPSA

DORCAS

} shepherdesses

SERUANT of the Old Shepheard

Other Shepheards and Shepherdesses

Twelue countreymen disguised as satyres

TIME, as Chorus

The Winters Tale

1.1
(Sc. 1)

Enter Camillo and Archidamus

ARCHIDAMUS If you shall chance (*Camillo*) to visit *Bohemia*,
on the like occasion whereon my seruices are now on-
foot, you shall see (as I haue said) great difference
betwixt our *Bohemia*, and your *Sicilia*.

CAMILLO I thinke, this comming Summer, the King of
Sicilia meanes to pay *Bohemia* the Visitation, which hee
iustly owes him.

ARCHIDAMUS Wherein our Entertainment shall shame vs,
we will be iustified in our Loues: for indeed—

10 CAMILLO 'Beseech you—

ARCHIDAMUS Verely I speake it in the freedome of my
knowledge: we cannot with such magnificence—in so
rare—I know not what to say—Wee will giue you
sleepie Drinkes, that your Sences (vn-intelligent of our
insufficience) may, though they cannot prayse vs, as
little accuse vs.

CAMILLO You pay a great deale to deare, for what's giuen
freely.

ARCHIDAMUS 'Beleeue me, I speake as my vnderstanding
20 instructs me, and as mine honestie puts it to vtterance.

CAMILLO *Sicilia* cannot shew himselfe ouer-kind to
Bohemia: They were trayn'd together in their Child-
hoods; and there rooted betwixt them then such an
affection, which cannot chuse but braunch now. Since
their more mature Dignities, and Royall Necessities,
made seperation of their Societie, their Encounters
(though not Personall) hath been Royally attornyed
with enter-change of Gifts, Letters, louing Embassies,
that they haue seem'd to be together, though absent:
30 shooke hands, as ouer a Vast; and embrac'd as it were
from the ends of opposed Winds. The Heauens continue
their Loues.

ARCHIDAMUS I thinke there is not in the World, either
Malice or Matter, to alter it. You haue an vnspeakable
comfort of your young Prince *Mamillius*: it is a
Gentleman of the greatest Promise, that euer came into
my Note.

CAMILLO I very well agree with you, in the hopes of him:
it is a gallant Child; one, that (indeed) Physicks the
40 Subiect, makes old hearts fresh: they that went on
Crutches ere he was borne, desire yet their life, to see
him a Man.

ARCHIDAMUS Would they else be content to die?

CAMILLO Yes; if there were no other excuse, why they
should desire to liue.

ARCHIDAMUS If the King had no Sonne, they would desire
to liue on Crutches till he had one.   *Exeunt*

1.2
(Sc. 2)

Enter Leontes, Hermione, Mamillius, Polixenes,
⌈*Camillo*⌉

POLIXENES
Nine Changes of the Watry-Starre hath been

The Shepheards Note, since we haue left our Throne
Without a Burthen: Time as long againe   50
Would be fill'd vp (my Brother) with our Thanks,
And yet we should, for perpetuitie,
Goe hence in debt: And therefore, like a Cypher
(Yet standing in rich place) I multiply
With one we thanke you, many thousands moe,
That goe before it.

LEONTES   Stay your Thanks a while,
And pay them when you part.

POLIXENES   Sir, that's to morrow:
I am question'd by my feares, of what may chance,
Or breed vpon our absence, that may blow
No sneaping Winds at home, to make vs say,   60
This is put forth too truly: besides, I haue stay'd
To tyre your Royaltie.

LEONTES   We are tougher (Brother)
Then you can put vs to't.

POLIXENES   No longer stay.

LEONTES
One Seue'night longer.

POLIXENES   Very sooth, to morrow.

LEONTES
Wee'le part the time betweene's then: and in that
Ile no gaine-saying.

POLIXENES   Presse me not ('beseech you) so:
There is no Tongue that moues; none, none i'th'World
So soone as yours, could win me: so it should now,
Were there necessitie in your request, although
'Twere needfull I deny'd it. My Affaires   70
Doe euen drag me home-ward: which to hinder,
Were (in your Loue) a Whip to me; my stay,
To you a Charge, and Trouble: to saue both,
Farewell (our Brother.)

LEONTES   Tongue-ty'd our Queene? speake you.

HERMIONE
I had thought (Sir) to haue held my peace, vntill
You had drawne Oathes from him, not to stay: you
    (Sir)
Charge him too coldly. Tell him, you are sure
All in *Bohemia*'s well: this satisfaction,
The by-gone-day proclaym'd, say this to him,
He's beat from his best ward.

LEONTES   Well said, *Hermione*.   80

HERMIONE
To tell, he longs to see his Sonne, were strong:
But let him say so then, and let him goe;
But let him sweare so, and he shall not stay,
Wee'l thwack him hence with Distaffes.
    (*To Polixenes*) Yet of your Royall presence, Ile aduenture
The borrow of a Weeke. When at *Bohemia*
You take my Lord, Ile giue him my Commission,
To let him there a Moneth, behind the Gest

90 Prefix'd for's parting: yet (good-deed) *Leontes*,
I loue thee not a Iarre o'th'Clock, behind
What Lady she her Lord. You'le stay?

POLIXENES   No, Madame.

HERMIONE Nay, but you will?

POLIXENES I may not verely.

HERMIONE Verely?
You put me off with limber Vowes: but I,
Though you would seek t'vnsphere the Stars with
          Oaths,
Should yet say, Sir, no going: Verely
You shall not goe; a Ladyes Verely'is
As potent as a Lords. Will you goe yet?
100 Force me to keepe you as a Prisoner,
Not like a Guest: so you shall pay your Fees
When you depart, and saue your Thanks. How say
          you?
My Prisoner? or my Guest? by your dread Verely,
One of them you shall be.

POLIXENES   Your Guest then, Madame:
To be your Prisoner, should import offending;
Which is for me, lesse easie to commit,
Then you to punish.

HERMIONE   Not your Gaoler then,
But your kind Hostesse. Come, Ile question you
Of my Lords Tricks, and yours, when you were Boyes:
You were pretty Lordings then?

110 POLIXENES   We were (faire Queene)
Two Lads, that thought there was no more behind,
But such a day to morrow, as to day,
And to be Boy eternall.

HERMIONE Was not my Lord
The veryer Wag o'th'two?

POLIXENES
We were as twyn'd Lambs, that did frisk i'th'Sun,
And bleat the one at th'other: what we chang'd,
Was Innocence, for Innocence: we knew not
The Doctrine of ill-doing, nor dream'd
120 That any did: Had we pursu'd that life,
And our weake Spirits ne're been higher rear'd
With stronger blood, we should haue answer'd Heauen
Boldly, not guilty; the Imposition clear'd,
Hereditarie ours.

HERMIONE   By this we gather
You haue tript since.

POLIXENES   O my most sacred Lady,
Temptations haue since then been borne to's: for
In those vnfledg'd dayes, was my Wife a Girle;
Your precious selfe had then not cross'd the eyes
Of my young Play-fellow.

HERMIONE   Grace to boot:
130 Of this make no conclusion, least you say
Your Queene and I are Deuils: yet goe on,
Th'offences we haue made you doe, wee'le answere,
If you first sinn'd with vs: and that with vs
You did continue fault; and that you slipt not
With any, but with vs.

LEONTES   Is he woon yet?

HERMIONE
Hee'le stay (my Lord.)

LEONTES   At my request, he would not:
Hermione (my dearest) thou neuer spoak'st
To better purpose.

HERMIONE   Neuer?

LEONTES   Neuer, but once.

HERMIONE
What? haue I twice said well? when was't before?
I prethee tell me: cram's with prayse, and make's   140
As fat as tame things: One good deed, dying
          tonguelesse,
Slaughters a thousand, wayting vpon that.
Our prayses are our Wages. You may ride's
With one soft Kisse a thousand Furlongs, ere
With Spur we heat an Acre. But to th' Goale:
My last good deed, was to entreat his stay.
What was my first? it ha's an elder Sister,
Or I mistake you: O, would her Name were *Grace*.
But once before I spoke to th'purpose? when?
Nay, let me haue't: I long.

LEONTES   Why, that was when   150
Three crabbed Moneths had sowr'd themselues to
          death,
Ere I could make thee open thy white Hand:
And clap thy selfe, my Loue; then didst thou vtter,
I am yours for euer.

HERMIONE   'Tis Grace indeed.
Why lo-you now; I haue spoke to th' purpose twice:
The one, for euer earn'd a Royall Husband;
Th'other, for some while a Friend.

⌜*She giues her hand to Polixenes. They stand aside*⌝

LEONTES (*aside*)   Too hot, too hot:
To mingle friendship farre, is mingling bloods.
I haue *Tremor Cordis* on me: my heart daunces,
But not for ioy; not ioy. This Entertainment   160
May a free face put on: deriue a Libertie
From Heartinesse, from Bountie, fertile Bosome,
And well become the Agent: 't may; I graunt:
But to be padling Palmes, and pinching Fingers,
As now they are, and making practis'd Smiles
As in a Looking-Glasse; and then to sigh, as 'twere
The Mort o'th'Deere: oh, that is entertainment
My Bosome likes not, nor my Browes. *Mamillius*,
Art thou my Boy?

MAMILLIUS   I, my good Lord.

LEONTES   I'fecks:
Why that's my Bawcock: what? has't smutch'd thy
          Nose?   170
They say it is a Coppy out of mine. Come Captaine,
We must be neat; not neat, but cleanly, Captaine:
And yet the Steere, the Heycfer, and the Calfe,
Are all call'd Neat. Still Virginalling
Vpon his Palme? How now (you wanton Calfe)
Art thou my Calfe?

MAMILLIUS   Yes, if you will (my Lord.)

LEONTES
Thou want'st a rough pash, & the shoots that I haue
To be full, like me: yet they say we are

180 Almost as like as Egges; Women say so,
(That will say any thing.) But were they false
As o're-dy'd Blacks, as Wind, as Waters; false
As Dice are to be wish'd, by one that fixes
No borne 'twixt his and mine; yet were it true,
To say this Boy were like me. Come (Sir Page)
Looke on me with your Welkin eye: sweet Villaine,
Most dear'st, my Collop: Can thy Dam, may't be—
Affection? thy Intention stabs the Center.
Thou do'st make possible things not so held,
Communicat'st with Dreames (how can this be?)
190 With what's vnreall thou coactiue art,
And fellow'st nothing. Then 'tis very credent,
Thou may'st co-ioyne with something, and thou do'st,
(And that beyond Commission) and I find it,
(And that to the infection of my Braines,
And hardning of my Browes.)

POLIXENES   What meanes *Sicilia?*
HERMIONE
He something seemes vnsetled.
POLIXENES   How? my Lord?
LEONTES
What cheere? how is't with you, best Brother?
HERMIONE   You look
As if you held a Brow of much distraction:
Are you mou'd (my Lord?)
LEONTES   No, in good earnest.
200 How sometimes Nature will betray it's folly?
It's tendernesse? and make it selfe a Pastime
To harder bosomes? Looking on the Lynes
Of my Boyes face, me thoughts I did requoyle
Twentie three yeeres, and saw my selfe vn-breech'd,
In my greene Veluet Coat; my Dagger muzzel'd,
Least it should bite it's Master, and so proue
(As Ornament oft do's) too dangerous:
How like (me thought) I then was to this Kernell,
This Squash, this Gentleman. Mine honest Friend,
Will you take Egges for Money?
210 MAMILLIUS   No (my Lord) Ile fight.
LEONTES
You will: why happy man be's dole. My Brother
Are you so fond of your young Prince, as we
Doe seeme to be of ours?
POLIXENES   If at home (Sir)
He's all my Exercise, my Mirth, my Matter;
Now my sworne Friend, and then mine Enemy;
My Parasite, my Souldier: States-man; all:
He makes a Iulyes day, short as December,
And with his varying child-nesse, cures in me
Thoughts, that would thick my blood.
LEONTES   So stands this Squire
220 Offic'd with me: We two will walke (my Lord)
And leaue you to your grauer steps. *Hermione,*
How thou lou'st vs, shew in our Brothers welcome;
Let what is deare in Sicily, be cheape:
Next to thy selfe, and my young Rouer, he's
Apparant to my heart.
HERMIONE   If you would seeke vs,
We are yours i'th'Garden: shall's attend you there?

LEONTES
To your owne bents dispose you: you'le be found,
Be you beneath the Sky: (*Aside*) I am angling now,
(Though you perceiue me not how I giue Lyne)
Goe too, goe too.   230
How she holds vp the Neb? the Byll to him?
And armes her with the boldnesse of a Wife
To her allowing Husband.
                    Exeunt Polixenes and Hermione
                    Gone already,
Ynch-thick, knee-deepe; ore head and eares a fork'd
     one.
Goe play (Boy) play: thy Mother playes, and I
Play too; but so disgrac'd a part, whose issue
Will hisse me to my Graue: Contempt and Clamor
Will be my Knell. Goe play (Boy) play, there haue been
(Or I am much deceiu'd) Cuckolds ere now,
And many a man there is (euen at this present,   240
Now, while I speake this) holds his Wife by th'Arme,
That little thinkes she ha's been sluyc'd in's absence,
And his Pond fish'd by his next Neighbor (by
Sir *Smile,* his Neighbor:) nay, there's comfort in't,
Whiles other men haue Gates, and those Gates open'd
(As mine) against their will. Should all despaire
That haue reuolted Wiues, the tenth of Mankind
Would hang themselues. Physick for't, there's none:
It is a bawdy Planet, that will strike
Where 'tis predominant; and 'tis powrefull: thinke it: 250
From East, West, North, and South, be it concluded,
No Barricado for a Belly. Know't,
It will let in and out the Enemy,
With bag and baggage: many thousand on's
Haue the Disease, and feele't not. How now Boy?
MAMILLIUS
I am like you they say.
LEONTES   Why, that's some comfort.
What? *Camillo* there?
CAMILLO ⌈*comming forward*⌉ I, my good Lord.
LEONTES
Goe play (*Mamillius*) thou'rt an honest man:
                              Exit Mamillius
Camillo, this great Sir will yet stay longer.
CAMILLO
You had much adoe to make his Anchor hold,   260
When you cast out, it still came home.
LEONTES   Didst note it?
CAMILLO
He would not stay at your Petitions, made
His Businesse more materiall.
LEONTES   Didst perceiue it?
(*Aside*) They're here with me already; whisp'ring,
     rounding:
Sicilia is a so-forth: 'tis farre gone,
When I shall gust it last. How cam't (*Camillo*)
That he did stay?
CAMILLO   At the good Queenes entreatie.
LEONTES
At the Queenes be't: Good should be pertinent,
But so it is, it is not. Was this taken

270 By any vnderstanding Pate but thine?
    For thy Conceit is soaking, will draw in
    More then the common Blocks. Not noted, is't,
    But of the finer Natures? by some Seueralls
    Of Head-peece extraordinarie? Lower Messes
    Perchance are to this Businesse purblind? say.
    CAMILLO
    Businesse, my Lord? I thinke most vnderstand
    Bohemia stayes here longer.
    LEONTES Ha?
    CAMILLO Stayes here longer.
280 LEONTES I, but why?
    CAMILLO
    To satisfie your Highnesse, and the Entreaties
    Of our most gracious Mistresse.
    LEONTES   Satisfie?
    Th'entreaties of your Mistresse? Satisfie?
    Let that suffice. I haue trusted thee (*Camillo*)
    With all the neer'st things to my heart, as well
    My Chamber-Councels, wherein (Priest-like) thou
    Hast cleans'd my Bosome: I, from thee departed
    Thy Penitent reform'd: but we haue been
    Deceiu'd in thy Integritie, deceiu'd
    In that which seemes so.
290 CAMILLO   Be it forbid (my Lord.)
    LEONTES
    To bide vpon't: thou art not honest: or
    If thou inclin'st that way, thou art a Coward,
    Which hoxes honestie behind, restrayning
    From Course requir'd: or else thou must be counted
    A Seruant, grafted in my serious Trust,
    And therein negligent: or else a Foole,
    That seest a Game play'd home, the rich Stake drawne,
    And tak'st it all for ieast.
    CAMILLO   My gracious Lord,
    I may be negligent, foolish, and fearefull,
300 In euery one of these, no man is free,
    But that his negligence, his folly, feare,
    Among the infinite doings of the World,
    Sometime puts forth. In your affaires (my Lord)
    If euer I were wilfull-negligent,
    It was my folly: if industriously
    I play'd the Foole, it was my negligence,
    Not weighing well the end: if euer fearefull
    To doe a thing, where I the issue doubted,
    Whereof the execution did cry out
310 Against the non-performance, 'twas a feare
    Which oft infects the wisest: these (my Lord)
    Are such allow'd Infirmities, that honestie
    Is neuer free of. But beseech your Grace
    Be plainer with me, let me know my Trespas
    By it's owne visage; if I then deny it,
    'Tis none of mine.
    LEONTES   Ha' not you seene *Camillo*?
    (But that's past doubt: you haue, or your eye-glasse
    Is thicker then a Cuckolds Horne) or heard?
    (For to a Vision so apparant, Rumor
320 Cannot be mute) or thought? (for Cogitation

    Resides not in that man, that do's not thinke)
    My Wife is slipperie? If thou wilt confesse,
    Or else be impudently negatiue,
    To haue nor Eyes, nor Eares, nor Thought, then say
    My Wife's a Hoby-Horse, deserues a Name
    As ranke as any Flax-Wench, that puts to
    Before her troth-plight: say't, and iustify't.
    CAMILLO
    I would not be a stander-by, to heare
    My Soueraigne Mistresse clouded so, without
330 My present vengeance taken: 'shrew my heart,
    You neuer spoke what did become you lesse
    Then this; which to reiterate, were sin
    As deepe as that, though true.
    LEONTES   Is whispering nothing?
    Is leaning Cheeke to Cheeke? is meating Noses?
    Kissing with in-side Lip? stopping the Cariere
    Of Laughter, with a sigh? (a Note infallible
    Of breaking Honestie) horsing foot on foot?
    Skulking in corners? wishing Clocks more swift?
    Houres, Minutes? Noone, Mid-night? and all Eyes
340 Blind with the Pin and Web, but theirs; theirs onely,
    That would vnseene be wicked? Is this nothing?
    Why then the World, and all that's in't, is nothing,
    The couering Skie is nothing, *Bohemia* nothing,
    My Wife is nothing, nor Nothing haue these
         Nothings,
    If this be nothing.
    CAMILLO   Good my Lord, be cur'd
    Of this diseas'd Opinion, and betimes,
    For 'tis most dangerous.
    LEONTES   Say it be, 'tis true.
    CAMILLO
    No, no, my Lord.
    LEONTES   It is: you lye, you lye:
    I say thou lyest *Camillo*, and I hate thee,
350 Pronounce thee a grosse Lowt, a mindlesse Slaue,
    Or else a houering Temporizer, that
    Canst with thine eyes at once see good and euill,
    Inclining to them both: were my Wiues Liuer
    Infected (as her life) she would not liue
    The running of one Glasse.
    CAMILLO   Who do's infect her?
    LEONTES
    Why he that weares her like her Medull, hanging
    About his neck (*Bohemia*) who, if I
    Had Seruants true about me, that bare eyes
    To see alike mine Honor, as their Profits,
360 (Their owne particular Thrifts) they would doe that
    Which should vndoe more doing: I, and thou
    His Cup-bearer, whom I from meaner forme
    Haue Bench'd, and rear'd to Worship, who may'st see
    Plainely, as Heauen sees Earth, and Earth sees
         Heauen,
    How I am gall'd, might'st be-spice a Cup,
    To giue mine Enemy a lasting Winke:
    Which Draught to me, were cordiall.
    CAMILLO   Sir (my Lord)

I could doe this, and that with no rash Potion,
But with a lingring Dram, that should not worke
370 Maliciously, like Poyson: But I cannot
Beleeue this Crack to be in my dread Mistresse
(So soueraignely being Honorable.)
I haue lou'd thee,

LEONTES   Make that thy question, and goe rot:
Do'st thinke I am so muddy, so vnsetled,
To appoint my selfe in this vexation?
Sully the puritie and whitenesse of my Sheetes
(Which to preserue, is Sleepe; which being spotted,
Is Goades, Thornes, Nettles, Tayles of Waspes)
Giue scandall to the blood o'th' Prince, my Sonne,
380 (Who I doe thinke is mine, and loue as mine)
Without ripe mouing to't? Would I doe this?
Could man so blench?

CAMILLO   I must beleeue you (Sir.)
I doe, and will fetch off Bohemia for't:
Prouided, that when hee's remou'd, your Highnesse
Will take againe your Queene, as yours at first,
Euen for your Sonnes sake, and thereby for sealing
The Iniurie of Tongues, in Courts and Kingdomes
Knowne, and ally'd to yours.

LEONTES   Thou do'st aduise me,
Euen so as I mine owne course haue set downe:
390 Ile giue no blemish to her Honor, none.

CAMILLO
My Lord, goe then; and with a countenance as cleare
As Friendship weares at Feasts, keepe with Bohemia,
And with your Queene: I am his Cup-bearer,
If from me he haue wholesome Beueridge,
Account me not your Seruant.

LEONTES   This is all:
Do't, and thou hast the one halfe of my heart;
Do't not, thou splitt'st thine owne.

CAMILLO   Ile do't, my Lord.

LEONTES
I wil seeme friendly, as thou hast aduis'd me.   Exit

CAMILLO
O miserable Lady. But for me,
400 What case stand I in? I must be the poysoner
Of good Polixenes, and my ground to do't,
Is the obedience to a Master; one,
Who in Rebellion with himselfe, will haue
All that are his, so too. To doe this deed,
Promotion followes: If I could find example
Of thousand's that had struck anoynted Kings,
And flourish'd after, Il'd not do't: But since
Nor Brasse, nor Stone, nor Parchment beares not one,
Let Villanie it selfe forswear't. I must
410 Forsake the Court: to do't, or no, is certaine
To me a breake-neck.

          Enter Polixenes
                    Happy Starre raigne now,
Here comes Bohemia.

POLIXENES (aside)   This is strange: Me thinkes
My fauor here begins to warpe. Not speake?
Good day Camillo.

CAMILLO   Hayle most Royall Sir.

POLIXENES
What is the Newes i'th' Court?

CAMILLO   None rare (my Lord.)

POLIXENES
The King hath on him such a countenance,
As he had lost some Prouince, and a Region
Lou'd, as he loues himselfe: euen now I met him
With customarie complement, when hee
Wafting his eyes to th' contrary, and falling   420
A Lippe of much contempt, speedes from me, and
So leaues me, to consider what is breeding,
That changes thus his Manners.

CAMILLO   I dare not know (my Lord.)

POLIXENES
How, dare not? doe not? doe you know, and dare
   not?
Be intelligent to me, 'tis thereabouts:
For to your selfe, what you doe know, you must,
And cannot say, you dare not. Good Camillo,
Your chang'd complexions are to me a Mirror,
Which shewes me mine chang'd too: for I must be
A partie in this alteration, finding   430
My selfe thus alter'd with't.

CAMILLO   There is a sicknesse
Which puts some of vs in distemper, but
I cannot name th'Disease, and it is caught
Of you, that yet are well.

POLIXENES   How caught of me?
Make me not sighted like the Basilisque.
I haue look'd on thousands, who haue sped the better
By my regard, but kill'd none so: Camillo,
As you are certainely a Gentleman, thereto
Clerke-like experienc'd, which no lesse adornes
Our Gentry, then our Parents Noble Names,   440
In whose successe we are gentle: I beseech you,
If you know ought which do's behoue my knowledge,
Thereof to be inform'd, imprison't not
In ignorant concealement.

CAMILLO   I may not answere.

POLIXENES
A Sicknesse caught of me, and yet I well?
I must be answer'd. Do'st thou heare Camillo,
I coniure thee, by all the parts of man,
Which Honor do's acknowledge, whereof the least
Is not this Suit of mine, that thou declare
What incidencie thou do'st ghesse of harme   450
Is creeping toward me; how farre off, how neere,
Which way to be preuented, if to be:
If not, how best to beare it.

CAMILLO   Sir, I will tell you,
Since I am charg'd in Honor, and by him
That I thinke Honorable: therefore marke my
          counsaile,
Which must be eu'n as swiftly followed, as
I meane to vtter it; or both your selfe, and me,
Cry lost, and so good night.

POLIXENES   On, good Camillo.

CAMILLO
I am appointed him to murther you.

POLIXENES

By whom, *Camillo*?

CAMILLO By the King.

460 POLIXENES For what?

CAMILLO

He thinkes, nay with all confidence he sweares,
As he had seen't, or beene an Instrument
To vice you to't, that you haue toucht his Queene
Forbiddenly.

POLIXENES Oh then, my best blood turne
To an infected Gelly, and my Name
Be yoak'd with his, that did betray the Best:
Turne then my freshest Reputation to
A sauour, that may strike the dullest Nosthrill
Where I arriue, and my approch be shun'd,
470 Nay hated too, worse then the great'st Infection
That ere was heard, or read.

CAMILLO Sweare his thought ouer
By each particular Starre in Heauen, and
By all their Influences; you may as well
Forbid the Sea for to obey the Moone,
As (or by Oath) remoue, or (Counsaile) shake
The Fabrick of his Folly, whose foundation
Is pyl'd vpon his Faith, and will continue
The standing of his Body.

POLIXENES How should this grow?

CAMILLO

I know not: but I am sure 'tis safer to
480 Auoid what's growne, then question how 'tis borne.
If therefore you dare trust my honestie,
That lyes enclosed in this Trunke, which you
Shall beare along impawnd, away to Night,
Your Followers I will whisper to the Businesse,
And will by twoes, and threes, at seuerall Posternes,
Cleare them o'th' Citie: For my selfe, Ile put
My fortunes to your seruice (which are here
By this discouerie lost.) Be not vncertaine,
For by the honor of my Parents, I
490 Haue vttred Truth: which if you seeke to proue,
I dare not stand by; nor shall you be safer,
Then one condemned by the Kings owne mouth:
Thereon his Execution sworne.

POLIXENES I doe beleeue thee:
I saw his heart in's face. Giue me thy hand,
Be Pilot to me, and thy places shall
Still neighbour mine. My Ships are ready, and
My people did expect my hence departure
Two dayes agoe. This Iealousie
Is for a precious Creature: as shee's rare,
500 Must it be great; and, as his Person's mightie,
Must it be violent: and, as he do's conceiue,
He is dishonor'd by a man, which euer
Profess'd to him: why his Reuenges must
In that be made more bitter. Feare ore-shades me:
Good Expedition be my friend, and comfort
The gracious Queene, part of his Theame; but nothing
Of his ill-ta'ne suspition. Come *Camillo*,
I will respect thee as a Father, if
Thou bear'st my life off hence: Let vs auoid.

CAMILLO

It is in mine authoritie to command   510
The Keyes of all the Posternes: Please your Highnesse
To take the vrgent houre. Come Sir, away.   *Exeunt*

❦

Enter Hermione, Mamillius, Ladies   2.1
(Sc. 3)
HERMIONE

Take the Boy to you: he so troubles me,
'Tis past enduring.

1. LADY Come (my gracious Lord)
Shall I be your play-fellow?

MAMILLIUS No, Ile none of you.

1. LADY Why (my sweet Lord?)

MAMILLIUS

You'le kisse me hard, and speake to me, as if
I were a Baby still. (*To 2. Lady*) I loue you better.

2. LADY

And why so (my Lord?)

MAMILLIUS Not for because   520
Your Browes are blacker (yet black-browes they say
Become some Women best, so that there be not
Too much haire there, but in a Cemicircle,
Or a halfe-Moone, made with a Pen.)

2. LADY Who taught 'this?

MAMILLIUS

I learn'd it out of Womens faces: pray now,
What colour are your eye-browes?

1. LADY Blew (my Lord.)

MAMILLIUS

Nay, that's a mock: I haue seene a Ladies Nose
That ha's beene blew, but not her eye-browes.

1. LADY Harke ye,
The Queene (your Mother) rounds apace: we shall
Present our seruices to a fine new Prince   530
One of these dayes, and then youl'd wanton with vs,
If we would haue you.

2. LADY She is spread of late
Into a goodly Bulke (good time encounter her.)

HERMIONE

What wisdome stirs amongst you? Come Sir, now
I am for you againe: 'Pray you sit by vs,
And tell's a Tale.

MAMILLIUS Merry, or sad, shal't be?

HERMIONE As merry as you will.

MAMILLIUS

A sad Tale's best for Winter: I haue one
Of Sprights, and Goblins.

HERMIONE Let's haue that (good Sir.)   540
Come-on, sit downe, come-on, and doe your best,
To fright me with your Sprights: you're powrefull at it.

MAMILLIUS

There was a man.

HERMIONE Nay, come sit downe: then on.

MAMILLIUS (*sitting*)

Dwelt by a Church-yard: I will tell it softly,
Yond Crickets shall not heare it.

HERMIONE

Come on then, and giu't me in mine eare.

Enter apart Leontes, Antigonus, and Lords

LEONTES

Was hee met there? his Traine? *Camillo* with him?

A LORD

Behind the tuft of Pines I met them, neuer
Saw I men scowre so on their way: I eyed them
Euen to their Ships.

550 LEONTES   How blest am I
In my iust Censure? in my true Opinion?
Alack, for lesser knowledge, how accurs'd,
In being so blest? There may be in the Cup
A Spider steep'd, and one may drinke; depart,
And yet partake no venome: (for his knowledge
Is not infected) but if one present
Th'abhor'd Ingredient to his eye, make knowne
How he hath drunke, he cracks his gorge, his sides
With violent Hefts: I haue drunke, and seene the Spider.

560 *Camillo* was his helpe in this, his Pandar:
There is a Plot against my Life, my Crowne;
All's true that is mistrusted: that false Villaine,
Whom I employ'd, was pre-employ'd by him:
He ha's discouer'd my Designe, and I
Remaine a pinch'd Thing; yea, a very Trick
For them to play at will: how came the Posternes
So easily open?

A LORD   By his great authority,
Which often hath no lesse preuail'd, then so,
On your command.

LEONTES   I know't too well.
(*To Hermione*) Giue me the Boy, I am glad you did not
570   nurse him:
Though he do's beare some signes of me, yet you
Haue too much blood in him.

HERMIONE   What is this? Sport?

LEONTES (*to a Lord*)

Beare the Boy hence, he shall not come about her,
Away with him, and let her sport her selfe
With that shee's big-with, (*to Hermione*) for 'tis
      Polixenes
Ha's made thee swell thus.   *Exit one with Mamillius*

HERMIONE   But Il'd say he had not;
And Ile be sworne you would beleeue my saying,
How e're you leane to th'Nay-ward.

LEONTES   You (my Lords)
Looke on her, marke her well: be but about
580 To say she is a goodly Lady, and
The iustice of your hearts will thereto adde
'Tis pitty shee's not honest: Honorable;
Prayse her but for this her without-dore-Forme,
(Which on my faith deserues high speech) and straight
The Shrug, the Hum, or Ha, (these Petty-brands
That Calumnie doth vse; Oh, I am out,
That Mercy do's, for Calumnie will seare
Vertue it selfe) these Shrugs, these Hum's, and Ha's,
When you haue said shee's goodly, come betweene,
590 Ere you can say shee's honest: But be't knowne
(From him that ha's most cause to grieue it should be)
Shee's an Adultresse.

HERMIONE   Should a Villaine say so,

(The most replenish'd Villaine in the World)
He were as much more Villaine: you (my Lord)
Doe but mistake.

LEONTES   You haue mistooke (my Lady)
Polixenes for *Leontes*: O thou Thing,
(Which Ile not call a Creature of thy place,
Least Barbarisme (making me the precedent)
Should a like Language vse to all degrees,
And mannerly distinguishment leaue out,   600
Betwixt the Prince and Begger:) I haue said
Shee's an Adultresse, I haue said with whom:
More; shee's a Traytor, and *Camillo* is
A Federarie with her, and one that knowes
What she should shame to know her selfe,
But with her most vild Principall: that shee's
A Bed-swaruer, euen as bad as those
That Vulgars giue bold'st Titles; I, and priuy
To this their late escape.

HERMIONE   No (by my life)
Priuy to none of this: how will this grieue you,   610
When you shall come to clearer knowledge, that
You thus haue publish'd me? Gentle my Lord,
You scarce can right me throughly, then, to say
You did mistake.

LEONTES   No: if I mistake
In those Foundations which I build vpon,
The Centre is not bigge enough to beare
A Schoole-Boyes Top. Away with her, to Prison:
He who shall speake for her, is a farre-off guiltie,
But that he speakes.

HERMIONE   There's some ill Planet raignes:
I must be patient, till the Heauens looke   620
With an aspect more fauorable. Good my Lords,
I am not prone to weeping (as our Sex
Commonly are) the want of which vaine dew
Perchance shall dry your pitties: but I haue
That honorable Griefe lodg'd here, which burnes
Worse then Teares drowne: 'beseech you all (my
      Lords)
With thoughts so qualified, as your Charities
Shall best instruct you, measure me; and so
The Kings will be perform'd.

LEONTES   Shall I be heard?

HERMIONE

Who is't that goes with me? 'beseech your Highnes   630
My Women may be with me, for you see
My plight requires it. Doe not weepe (good Fooles)
There is no cause: When you shall know your Mistris
Ha's deseru'd Prison, then abound in Teares,
As I come out; this Action I now goe on,
Is for my better grace. Adieu (my Lord)
I neuer wish'd to see you sorry, now
I trust I shall: my Women come, you haue leaue.

LEONTES Goe, doe our bidding: hence.

      Exit Hermione, guarded, with Ladies

A LORD

Beseech your Highnesse call the Queene againe.   640

ANTIGONUS (*to Leontes*)

Be certaine what you do (Sir) least your Iustice

Proue violence, in the which three great ones suffer,
Your Selfe, your Queene, your Sonne.

A LORD (*to Leontes*)   For her (my Lord)
I dare my life lay downe, and will do't (Sir)
Please you t'accept it, that the Queene is spotlesse
I'th'eyes of Heauen, and to you (I meane
In this, which you accuse her.)

ANTIGONUS (*to Leontes*)   If it proue
Shee's otherwise, Ile keepe my Stables where
I lodge my Wife, Ile goe in couples with her:
650   Then when I feele, and see her, no farther trust her:
For euery ynch of Woman in the World,
I, euery dram of Womans flesh is false,
If she be.

LEONTES   Hold your peaces.
A LORD   Good my Lord.
ANTIGONUS (*to Leontes*)
It is for you we speake, not for our selues:
You are abus'd, and by some putter on,
That will be damn'd for't: would I knew the Villaine,
I would Land-damne him: be she honor-flaw'd,
I haue three daughters: the eldest is eleuen;
The second, and the third, nine: and some fiue:
660   If this proue true, they'l pay for't. By mine Honor
Ile gell'd em all: fourteene they shall not see
To bring false generations: they are co-heyres,
And I had rather glib my selfe, then they
Should not produce faire issue.

LEONTES   Cease, no more:
You smell this businesse with a sence as cold
As is a dead-mans nose: but I do see't, and feel't,
As you feele doing thus: and see withall
The Instruments that feele.

ANTIGONUS   If it be so,
We neede no graue to burie honesty,
670   There's not a graine of it, the face to sweeten
Of the whole dungy-earth.

LEONTES   What? lacke I credit?
A LORD
I had rather you did lacke then I (my Lord)
Vpon this ground: and more it would content me
To haue her Honor true, then your suspition
Be blam'd for't how you might.

LEONTES   Why what neede we
Commune with you of this? but rather follow
Our forcefull instigation? Our prerogatiue
Cals not your Counsailes, but our naturall goodnesse
Imparts this: which, if you, or stupified,
680   Or seeming so, in skill, cannot, or will not
Rellish a truth, like vs: informe your selues,
We neede no more of your aduice: the matter,
The losse, the gaine, the ord'ring on't, is all
Properly ours.

ANTIGONUS   And I wish (my Liege)
You had onely in your silent iudgement tride it,
Without more ouerture.

LEONTES   How could that be?
Either thou art most ignorant by age,

Or thou wer't borne a foole: *Camillo's* flight
Added to their Familiarity
(Which was as grosse, as euer touch'd coniecture,   690
That lack'd sight onely, nought for approbation
But onely seeing, all other circumstances
Made vp to'th deed) doth push-on this proceeding.
Yet, for a greater confirmation
(For in an Acte of this importance, 'twere
Most pitteous to be wilde) I haue dispatch'd in post,
To sacred *Delphos*, to *Appollo's* Temple,
Cleomines and *Dion*, whom you know
Of stuff'd-sufficiency: Now, from the Oracle
They will bring all, whose spirituall counsaile had   700
Shall stop, or spurre me. Haue I done well?

A LORD Well done (my Lord.)
LEONTES
Though I am satisfide, and neede no more
Then what I know, yet shall the Oracle
Giue rest to th'mindes of others; such as he
Whose ignorant credulitie, will not
Come vp to th'truth. So haue we thought it good
From our free person, she should be confinde,
Least that the treachery of the two, fled hence,
Be left her to performe. Come follow vs,   710
We are to speake in publique: for this businesse
Will raise vs all.

ANTIGONUS (*aside*) To laughter, as I take it,
If the good truth, were knowne.   *Exeunt*

Enter Paulina, a Gentleman, and Attendants   2.2
PAULINA   (Sc. 4)
The Keeper of the prison, call to him:
Let him haue knowledge who I am.   *Exit Gentleman*
                                  Good Lady,
No Court in Europe is too good for thee,
What dost thou then in prison?
    Enter Gaoler and Gentleman
                                  Now good Sir,
You know me, do you not?
GAOLER   For a worthy Lady,
And one, who much I honour.
PAULINA Pray you then,   720
Conduct me to the Queene.
GAOLER
I may not (Madam) to the contrary
I haue expresse commandment.
PAULINA   Here's a-do,
To locke vp honesty & honour from
Th'accesse of gentle visitors. Is't lawfull pray you
To see her Women? Any of them? *Emilia*?
GAOLER So please you (Madam)
To put a-part these your attendants, I
Shall bring *Emilia* forth.
PAULINA I pray now call her: 730
With-draw your selues.
                    Exeunt Gentleman and Attendants
GAOLER And Madam,
I must be present at your Conference.

PAULINA Well: be't so: prethee.   *Exit Gaoler*
  Heere's such a-doe, to make no staine, a staine,
  As passes colouring.
      Enter Gaoler and Emilia
             Deare Gentlewoman,
  How fares our gracious Lady?
EMILIA
  As well as one so great, and so forlorne
  May hold together: On her frights, and greefes
740 (Which neuer tender Lady hath borne greater)
  She is, something before her time, deliuer'd.
PAULINA
  A boy?
EMILIA   A daughter, and a goodly babe,
  Lusty, and like to liue: the Queene receiues
  Much comfort in't: Sayes, my poore prisoner,
  I am innocent as you.
PAULINA   I dare be sworne:
  These dangerous, vnsafe Lunes i'th'King, beshrew
    them:
  He must be told on't, and he shall: the office
  Becomes a woman best. Ile take't vpon me,
  If I proue hony-mouth'd, let my tongue blister,
750 And neuer to my red-look'd Anger bee
  The Trumpet any more: pray you (*Emilia*)
  Commend my best obedience to the Queene,
  If she dares trust me with her little babe,
  I'le shew't the King, and vndertake to bee
  Her Aduocate to th'lowd'st. We do not know
  How he may soften at the sight o'th'Childe:
  The silence often of pure innocence
  Perswades, when speaking failes.
EMILIA   Most worthy Madam,
  Your honor, and your goodnesse is so euident,
760 That your free vndertaking cannot misse
  A thriuing yssue: there is no Lady liuing
  So meete for this great errand; please your Ladiship
  To visit the next roome, Ile presently
  Acquaint the Queene of your most noble offer,
  Who, but to day hammerd of this designe,
  But durst not tempt a minister of honour
  Least she should be deny'd.
PAULINA   Tell her (*Emilia*)
  Ile vse that tongue I haue: If wit flow from't
  As boldnesse from my bosome, le't not be doubted
  I shall do good.
770 EMILIA   Now be you blest for it.
  Ile to the Queene: please you come something neerer.
GAOLER
  Madam, if't please the Queene to send the babe,
  I know not what I shall incurre, to passe it,
  Hauing no warrant.
PAULINA   You neede not feare it (sir.)
  This Childe was prisoner to the wombe, and is
  By Law and processe of great Nature, thence
  Free'd, and enfranchis'd, not a partie to
  The anger of the King, nor guilty of
  (If any be) the trespasse of the Queene.

GAOLER I do beleeue it.   780
PAULINA
  Do not you feare: vpon mine honor,
  I will stand twixt you, and danger.   *Exeunt*

      Enter Leontes   **2.3**
LEONTES   **(Sc. 5)**
  Nor night, nor day, no rest: It is but weaknesse
  To beare the matter thus: meere weaknesse; if
  The cause were not in being: part o'th cause,
  She, th'Adultresse: for the harlot-King
  Is quite beyond mine Arme, out of the blanke
  And leuell of my braine: plot-proofe: but shee,
  I can hooke to me: say that she were gone,
  Giuen to the fire, a moity of my rest   790
  Might come to me againe. Whose there?
      Enter a Seruant
SERUANT   My Lord.
LEONTES
  How do's the boy?
SERUANT   He tooke good rest to night:
  'Tis hop'd his sicknesse is discharg'd.
LEONTES To see his Noblenesse,
  Conceyuing the dishonour of his Mother,
  He straight declin'd, droop'd, tooke it deeply,
  Fasten'd, and fix'd the shame on't in himselfe:
  Threw-off his Spirit, his Appetite, his Sleepe,
  And down-right languish'd. Leaue me solely: goe,
  See how he fares: *Exit Seruant*
          Fie, fie, no thought of him,   800
  The very thought of my Reuenges that way
  Recoyle vpon me: in himselfe too mightie,
  And in his parties, his Alliance; Let him be,
  Vntill a time may serue. For present vengeance
  Take it on her: *Camillo*, and *Polixenes*
  Laugh at me: make their pastime at my sorrow:
  They should not laugh, if I could reach them, nor
  Shall she, within my powre.
      Enter Paulina, carrying a babe, with Antigonus,
      Lords, and the Seruant, trying to restrayne her
A LORD   You must not enter.
PAULINA
  Nay rather (good my Lords) be second to me:
  Feare you his tyrannous passion more (alas)   810
  Then the Queenes life? A gracious innocent soule,
  More free, then he is iealous.
ANTIGONUS   That's enough.
SERUANT
  Madam; he hath not slept to night, commanded
  None should come at him.
PAULINA   Not so hot (good Sir)
  I come to bring him sleepe. 'Tis such as you
  That creepe like shadowes by him, and do sighe
  At each his needlesse heauings: such as you
  Nourish the cause of his awaking. I
  Do come with words, as medicinall, as true;
  (Honest, as either;) to purge him of that humor,   820
  That presses him from sleepe.
LEONTES   What noyse there, hoe?

PAULINA
No noyse (my Lord) but needfull conference,
About some Gossips for your Highnesse.

LEONTES   How?
Away with that audacious Lady. *Antigonus*,
I charg'd thee that she should not come about me,
I knew she would.

ANTIGONUS   I told her so (my Lord)
On your displeasures perill, and on mine,
She should not visit you.

LEONTES   What? canst not rule her?

PAULINA
From all dishonestie he can: in this
830   (Vnlesse he take the course that you haue done,
Commit me, for committing honor) trust it,
He shall not rule me.

ANTIGONUS   La-you now, you heare,
When she will take the raine, I let her run,
But shee'l not stumble.

PAULINA (*to Leontes*)   Good my Liege, I come:
And I beseech you heare me, who professes
My selfe your loyall Seruant, your Physitian,
Your most obedient Counsailor: yet that dares
Lesse appeare so, in comforting your Euilles,
Then such as most seeme yours. I say, I come
840   From your good Queene.

LEONTES Good Queene?

PAULINA
Good Queene (my Lord) good Queene, I say good
        Queene,
And would by combate, make her good, so were I
A man, the worst about you.

LEONTES (*to Lords*)   Force her hence.

PAULINA
Let him that makes but trifles of his eyes
First hand me: on mine owne accord, Ile off,
But first, Ile do my errand. The good Queene
(For she is good) hath brought you forth a daughter,
Heere 'tis. Commends it to your blessing.
        She layes downe the babe

LEONTES   Out:
850   A mankinde Witch? Hence with her, out o'dore:
A most intelligencing bawd.

PAULINA   Not so:
I am as ignorant in that, as you,
In so entit'ling me: and no lesse honest
Then you are mad: which is enough, Ile warrant
(As this world goes) to passe for honest.

LEONTES (*to Lords*)   Traitors;
Will you not push her out?
(*To Antigonus*)   Giue her the Bastard,
Thou dotard, thou art woman-tyr'd: vnroosted
By thy dame *Partlet* heere. Take vp the Bastard,
Take't vp, I say: giue't to thy Croane.

PAULINA (*to Antigonus*)   For euer
860   Vnvenerable be thy hands, if thou
Tak'st vp the Princesse, by that forced basenesse
Which he ha's put vpon't.

LEONTES   He dreads his Wife.

PAULINA
So I would you did: then 'twere past all doubt
Youl'd call your children, yours.

LEONTES   A nest of Traitors.

ANTIGONUS
I am none, by this good light.

PAULINA   Nor I: nor any
But one that's heere: and that's himselfe: for he,
The sacred Honor of himselfe, his Queenes,
His hopefull Sonnes, his Babes, betrayes to Slander,
Whose sting is sharper then the Swords; and will not
(For as the case now stands, it is a Curse   870
He cannot be compell'd too't) once remoue
The Root of his Opinion, which is rotten,
As euer Oake, or Stone was sound.

LEONTES (*to Lords*)   A Callat
Of boundlesse tongue, who late hath beat her Husband,
And now bayts me: This Brat is none of mine,
It is the Issue of *Polixenes*.
Hence with it, and together with the Dam,
Commit them to the fire.

PAULINA   It is yours:
And might we lay th'old Prouerb to your charge,
So like you, 'tis the worse. Behold (my Lords)   880
Although the Print be little, the whole Matter
And Coppy of the Father: (Eye, Nose, Lippe,
The trick of's Frowne, his Fore-head, nay, the Valley,
The pretty dimples of his Chin, and Cheeke; his Smiles:
The very Mold, and frame of Hand, Nayle, Finger.)
And thou good Goddesse *Nature*, which hast made it
So like to him that got it, if thou hast
The ordering of the Mind too, 'mongst all Colours
No Yellow in't, least she suspect, as he do's,
Her Children, not her Husbands.

LEONTES (*to Antigonus*)   A grosse Hagge: 890
And Lozell, thou art worthy to be hang'd,
That wilt not stay her Tongue.

ANTIGONUS   Hang all the Husbands
That cannot doe that Feat, you'le leaue your selfe
Hardly one Subiect.

LEONTES   Once more take her hence.

PAULINA
A most vnworthy, and vnnaturall Lord
Can doe no more.

LEONTES   Ile ha' thee burnt.

PAULINA   I care not:
It is an Heretique that makes the fire,
Not she which burnes in't. Ile not call you Tyrant:
But this most cruell vsage of your Queene
(Not able to produce more accusation   900
Then your owne weake-hindg'd Fancy) somthing
        sauors
Of Tyrannie, and will ignoble make you,
Yea, scandalous to the World.

LEONTES (*to Antigonus*)   On your Allegeance,
Out of the Chamber with her. Were I a Tyrant,
Where were her life? she durst not call me so,
If she did know me one. Away with her.

PAULINA

I pray you doe not push me, Ile be gone.
Looke to your Babe (my Lord) 'tis yours: *Ioue* send her
A better guiding Spirit. What needs these hands?
910 You that are thus so tender o're his Follyes,
Will neuer doe him good, not one of you.
So, so: Farewell, we are gone.   *Exit*

LEONTES (*to Antigonus*)

Thou (Traytor) hast set on thy Wife to this.
My Child? away with't? euen thou, that hast
A heart so tender o're it, take it hence,
And see it instantly consum'd with fire.
Euen thou, and none but thou. Take it vp straight:
Within this houre bring me word 'tis done,
(And by good testimonie) or Ile seize thy life,
920 With what thou else call'st thine: if thou refuse,
And wilt encounter with my Wrath, say so;
The Bastard-braynes with these my proper hands
Shall I dash out. Goe, take it to the fire,
For thou sett'st on thy Wife.

ANTIGONUS   I did not, Sir:

These Lords, my Noble Fellowes, if they please,
Can cleare me in't.

LORDS   We can: my Royall Liege,

He is not guiltie of her comming hither.

LEONTES You're lyers all.

A LORD

Beseech your Highnesse, giue vs better credit:
930 We haue alwayes truly seru'd you, and beseech'
So to esteeme of vs: and on our knees we begge,
(As recompence of our deare seruices
Past, and to come) that you doe change this purpose,
Which being so horrible, so bloody, must
Lead on to some foule Issue. We all kneele.

LEONTES

I am a Feather for each Wind that blows:
Shall I liue on, to see this Bastard kneele,
And call me Father? better burne it now,
Then curse it then. But be it: let it liue.
It shall not neyther. (*To Antigonus*) You Sir, come you
940   hither:
You that haue beene so tenderly officious
With Lady *Margerie*, your Mid-wife there,
To saue this Bastards life; for 'tis a Bastard,
So sure as this Beard's gray. What will you aduenture,
To saue this Brats life?

ANTIGONUS   Any thing (my Lord)

That my abilitie may vndergoe,
And Noblenesse impose: at least thus much;
Ile pawne the little blood which I haue left,
To saue the Innocent: any thing possible.

LEONTES

950 It shall be possible: Sweare by this Sword
Thou wilt performe my bidding.

ANTIGONUS   I will (my Lord.)

LEONTES

Marke, and performe it: seest thou? for the faile
Of any point in't, shall not onely be
Death to thy selfe, but to thy lewd-tongu'd Wife,

(Whom for this time we pardon) We enioyne thee,
As thou art Liege-man to vs, that thou carry
This female Bastard hence, and that thou beare it
To some remote and desart place, quite out
Of our Dominions; and that there thou leaue it
(Without more mercy) to it owne protection,   960
And fauour of the Climate: as by strange fortune
It came to vs, I doe in Iustice charge thee,
On thy Soules perill, and thy Bodyes torture,
That thou commend it strangely to some place,
Where Chance may nurse, or end it: take it vp.

ANTIGONUS

I sweare to doe this: though a present death
Had beene more mercifull. Come on (poore Babe)
Some powerfull Spirit instruct the Kytes and Rauens
To be thy Nurses. Wolues and Beares, they say,
(Casting their sauagenesse aside) haue done   970
Like offices of Pitty. Sir, be prosperous
In more then this deed do's require; (*to the babe*) and
    Blessing
Against this Crueltie, fight on thy side
(Poore Thing, condemn'd to losse.)
                              Exit with the babe

LEONTES   No: Ile not reare

Anothers Issue.
        Enter a Seruant

SERUANT   Please' your Highnesse, Posts

From those you sent to th'Oracle, are come
An houre since: *Cleomines* and *Dion*,
Being well arriu'd from Delphos, are both landed,
Hasting to th' Court.

A LORD (*to Leontes*)   So please you (Sir) their speed

Hath beene beyond accompt.

LEONTES   Twentie three dayes   980

They haue beene absent: 'tis good speed: fore-tells
The great *Apollo* suddenly will haue
The truth of this appeare: Prepare you Lords,
Summon a Session, that we may arraigne
Our most disloyall Lady: for as she hath
Been publikely accus'd, so shall she haue
A iust and open Triall. While she liues,
My heart will be a burthen to me. Leaue me,
And thinke vpon my bidding.   *Exeunt seuerally*

Enter Cleomines and Dion   3.1

CLEOMINES   (Sc. 6)

The Clymat's delicate, the Ayre most sweet,   990
Fertile the Isle, the Temple much surpassing
The common prayse it beares.

DION   I shall report,

For most it caught me, the Celestiall Habits,
(Me thinkes I so should terme them) and the
    reuerence
Of the graue Wearers. O, the Sacrifice,
How ceremonious, solemne, and vn-earthly
It was i'th'Offring?

CLEOMINES   But of all, the burst

And the eare-deaff'ning Voyce o'th'Oracle,

Kin to *Ioues* Thunder, so surpriz'd my Sence,
That I was nothing.

DION   If th'euent o'th'Iourney
1000   Proue as successefull to the Queene (O be't so)
As it hath beene to vs, rare, pleasant, speedie,
The time is worth the vse on't.

CLEOMINES   Great *Apollo*
Turne all to th'best: these Proclamations,
So forcing faults vpon *Hermione*,
I little like.

DION   The violent carriage of it
Will cleare, or end the Businesse, when the Oracle
(Thus by *Apollo's* great Diuine seal'd vp)
Shall the Contents discouer: something rare
1010   Euen then will rush to knowledge. Goe: fresh Horses,
And gracious be the issue.   *Exeunt*

3.2   *Enter Leontes, Lords, Officers*
(Sc. 7)   **LEONTES**
This Sessions (to our great griefe we pronounce)
Euen pushes 'gainst our heart. The partie try'd,
The Daughter of a King, our Wife, and one
Of vs too much belou'd. Let vs be clear'd
Of being tyrannous, since we so openly
Proceed in Iustice, which shall haue due course,
Euen to the Guilt, or the Purgation:
Produce the Prisoner.

OFFICER   It is his Highnesse pleasure,
1020   That the Queene appeare in person, here in Court.
      Enter Hermione (as to her Triall), with Paulina and
      Ladies
Silence.

LEONTES Reade the Indictment.

OFFICER (*reading*) Hermione, *Queene to the worthy* Leontes,
King of Sicilia, thou art here accused and arraigned of High
Treason, in committing Adultery with Polixenes *King of*
Bohemia, and conspiring with Camillo *to take away the*
Life of our Soueraigne Lord the King, thy Royall Husband:
the pretence whereof being by circumstances partly layd
open, thou (Hermione) contrary to the Faith and Allegeance
1030   *of a true Subiect, didst counsaile and ayde them, for their*
better safetie, to flye away by Night.

HERMIONE
Since what I am to say, must be but that
Which contradicts my Accusation, and
The testimonie on my part, no other
But what comes from my selfe, it shall scarce boot me
To say, Not guiltie: mine Integritie
Being counted Falsehood, shall (as I expresse it)
Be so receiu'd. But thus, if Powres Diuine
Behold our humane Actions (as they doe)
1040   I doubt not then, but Innocence shall make
False Accusation blush, and Tyrannie
Tremble at Patience. You (my Lord) best know
(Who least will seeme to doe so) my past life
Hath beene as continent, as chaste, as true,
As I am now vnhappy; which is more
Then Historie can patterne, though deuis'd,

And play'd, to take Spectators. For behold me,
A Fellow of the Royall Bed, which owe
A Moitie of the Throne: a great Kings Daughter,
The Mother to a hopefull Prince, here standing   1050
To prate and talke for Life, and Honor, fore
Who please to come, and heare. For Life, I prize it
As I weigh Griefe (which I would spare:) For Honor,
'Tis a deriuatiue from me to mine,
And onely that I stand for. I appeale
To your owne Conscience (Sir) before *Polixenes*
Came to your Court, how I was in your grace,
How merited to be so: Since he came,
With what encounter so vncurrant, I
Haue strayn'd t'appeare thus; if one iot beyond   1060
The bound of Honor, or in act, or will
That way enclining, hardned be the hearts
Of all that heare me, and my neer'st of Kin
Cry fie vpon my Graue.

LEONTES   I ne're heard yet,
That any of these bolder Vices wanted
Lesse Impudence to gaine-say what they did,
Then to performe it first.

HERMIONE   That's true enough,
Though 'tis a saying (Sir) not due to me.

LEONTES
You will not owne it.

HERMIONE   More then Mistresse of,
Which comes to me in name of Fault, I must not   1070
At all acknowledge. For *Polixenes*
(With whom I am accus'd) I doe confesse
I lou'd him, as in Honor he requir'd:
With such a kind of Loue, as might become
A Lady like me; with a Loue, euen such,
So, and no other, as your selfe commanded:
Which, not to haue done, I thinke had been in me
Both Disobedience, and Ingratitude
To you, and toward your Friend, whose Loue had
      spoke,
Euen since it could speake, from an Infant, freely,   1080
That it was yours. Now for Conspiracie,
I know not how it tastes, though it be dish'd
For me to try how: All I know of it,
Is, that *Camillo* was an honest man;
And why he left your Court, the Gods themselues
(Wotting no more then I) are ignorant.

LEONTES
You knew of his departure, as you know
What you haue vnderta'ne to doe in's absence.

HERMIONE Sir,
You speake a Language that I vnderstand not: 1090
My Life stands in the leuell of your Dreames,
Which Ile lay downe.

LEONTES   Your Actions are my Dreames.
You had a Bastard by *Polixenes*,
And I but dream'd it: As you were past all shame,
(Those of your Fact are so) so past all truth;
Which to deny, concernes more then auailes: for as
Thy Brat hath been cast out, like to it selfe,

No Father owning it (which is indeed
More criminall in thee, then it) so thou
1100 Shalt feele our Iustice; in whose easiest passage,
Looke for no lesse then death.

HERMIONE   Sir, spare your Threats:
The Bugge which you would fright me with, I seeke:
To me can Life be no commoditie;
The crowne and comfort of my Life (your Fauor)
I doe giue lost, for I doe feele it gone,
But know not how it went. My second Ioy,
And first Fruits of my body, from his presence
I am bar'd, like one infectious. My third comfort
(Star'd most vnluckily) is from my breast
1110 (The innocent milke in it most innocent mouth)
Hal'd out to murther. My selfe on euery Post
Proclaym'd a Strumpet: With immodest hatred
The Child-bed priuiledge deny'd, which longs
To Women of all fashion. Lastly, hurried
Here, to this place, i'th' open ayre, before
I haue got strength of limit. Now (my Liege)
Tell me what blessings I haue here aliue,
That I should feare to die? Therefore proceed:
But yet heare this: mistake me not: no Life,
1120 (I prize it not a straw) but for mine Honor,
Which I would free: if I shall be condemn'd
Vpon surmizes (all proofes sleeping else,
But what your Iealousies awake) I tell you
'Tis Rigor, and not Law. Your Honors all,
I doe referre me to the Oracle:
Apollo be my Iudge.

A LORD   This your request
Is altogether iust: therefore bring forth
(And in Apollo's Name) his Oracle.
                          ⌈Exeunt certaine Officers⌉

HERMIONE
The Emperor of Russia was my Father.
1130 Oh that he were aliue, and here beholding
His Daughters Tryall: that he did but see
The flatnesse of my miserie; yet with eyes
Of Pitty, not Reuenge.
          ⌈Enter Officers with Cleomines and Dion⌉

OFFICER
You here shal sweare vpon this Sword of Iustice,
That you (Cleomines and Dion) haue
Been both at Delphos, and from thence haue brought
This seal'd-vp Oracle, by the Hand deliuer'd
Of great Apollo's Priest; and that since then,
You haue not dar'd to breake the holy Seale,
1140 Nor read the Secrets in't.

CLEOMINES and DION All this we sweare.

LEONTES Breake vp the Seales, and read.

OFFICER (reading) Hermione is chast, Polixenes blamelesse,
Camillo a true Subiect, Leontes a iealous Tyrant, his
innocent Babe truly begotten, and the King shall liue
without an Heire, if that which is lost, be not found.

LORDS
Now blessed be the great Apollo.

HERMIONE   Praysed.

LEONTES Hast thou read truth?

OFFICER
I (my Lord) euen so as it is here set downe.

LEONTES
There is no truth at all i'th'Oracle: 1150
The Sessions shall proceed: this is meere falsehood.
          Enter a Seruant

SERUANT
My Lord the King: the King?

LEONTES   What is the businesse?

SERUANT
O Sir, I shall be hated to report it.
The Prince your Sonne, with meere conceit, and feare
Of the Queenes speed, is gone.

LEONTES   How? gone?

SERUANT   Is dead.

LEONTES
Apollo's angry, and the Heauens themselues
Doe strike at my Iniustice.
          Hermione falls to the ground
                    How now there?

PAULINA
This newes is mortall to the Queene: Look downe
And see what Death is doing.

LEONTES   Take her hence:
Her heart is but o're-charg'd: she will recouer.   1160
I haue too much beleeu'd mine owne suspition:
'Beseech you tenderly apply to her
Some remedies for life.
          Exeunt Paulina and Ladies, carrying Hermione
                    Apollo pardon
My great prophanenesse 'gainst thine Oracle.
Ile reconcile me to Polixenes,
New woe my Queene, recall the good Camillo
(Whom I proclaime a man of Truth, of Mercy:)
For being transported by my Iealousies
To bloody thoughts, and to reuenge, I chose
Camillo for the minister, to poyson   1170
My friend Polixenes: which had been done,
But that the good mind of Camillo tardied
My swift command: though I with Death, and with
Reward, did threaten and encourage him,
Not doing it, and being done: he (most humane,
And fill'd with Honor) to my Kingly Guest
Vnclasp'd my practise, quit his fortunes here
(Which you knew great) and to the certaine hazard
Of all Incertainties, himselfe commended,
No richer then his Honor: How he glisters   1180
Through my Rust? and how his Pietie
Do's my deeds make the blacker?
          Enter Paulina

PAULINA   Woe the while:
O cut my Lace, least my heart (cracking it)
Breake too.

A LORD   What fit is this? good Lady?

PAULINA (to Leontes)
What studied torments (Tyrant) hast for me?
What Wheeles? Racks? Fires? What flaying? boyling?

In Leads, or Oyles? What old, or newer Torture
Must I receiue? whose euery word deserues
To taste of thy most worst. Thy Tyranny
1190 (Together working with thy Iealousies,
Fancies too weake for Boyes, too greene and idle
For Girles of Nine) O thinke what they haue done,
And then run mad indeed: starke-mad: for all
Thy by-gone fooleries were but spices of it.
That thou betrayed'st *Polixenes*, 'twas nothing,
(That did but shew thee, of a Foole, inconstant,
And damnable ingratefull:) Nor was't much,
Thou would'st haue poyson'd good *Camillo's* Honor,
To haue him kill a King: poore Trespasses,
1200 More monstrous standing by: whereof I reckon
The casting forth to Crowes, thy Baby-daughter,
To be or none, or little; though a Deuill
Would haue shed water out of fire, ere don't;
Nor is't directly layd to thee, the death
Of the young Prince, whose honorable thoughts
(Thoughts high for one so tender) cleft the heart
That could conceiue a grosse and foolish Sire
Blemish'd his gracious Dam: this is not, no,
Layd to thy answere: but the last: O Lords,
1210 When I haue said, cry woe: the Queene, the Queene,
The sweet'st, deer'st creature's dead: & vengeance for't
Not drop'd downe yet.

A LORD   The higher powres forbid.

PAULINA
I say she's dead: Ile swear't. If word, nor oath
Preuaile not, go and see: if you can bring
Tincture, or lustre in her lip, her eye,
Heate outwardly, or breath within, Ile serue you
As I would do the Gods. But, O thou Tyrant,
Do not repent these things, for they are heauier
Then all thy woes can stirre: therefore betake thee
1220 To nothing but dispaire. A thousand knees,
Ten thousand yeares together, naked, fasting,
Vpon a barren Mountaine, and still Winter
In storme perpetuall, could not moue the Gods
To looke that way thou wer't.

LEONTES   Go on, go on:
Thou canst not speake too much, I haue deseru'd
All tongues to talke their bittrest.

A LORD (*to Paulina*)   Say no more;
How ere the businesse goes, you haue made fault
I'th boldnesse of your speech.

PAULINA   I am sorry for't;
All faults I make, when I shall come to know them,
1230 I do repent: Alas, I haue shew'd too much
The rashnesse of a woman: he is toucht
To th'Noble heart. What's gone, and what's past helpe
Should be past greefe: (*To Leontes*) Do not receiue
     affliction
At my petition; I beseech you, rather
Let me be punish'd, that haue minded you
Of what you should forget. Now (good my Liege)
Sir, Royall Sir, forgiue a foolish woman:
The loue I bore your Queene (Lo, foole againe)

Ile speake of her no more, nor of your Children:
Ile not remember you of my owne Lord,   1240
(Who is lost too:) take your patience to you,
And Ile say nothing.

LEONTES   Thou didst speake but well,
When most the truth: which I receyue much better,
Then to be pittied of thee. Prethee bring me
To the dead bodies of my Queene, and Sonne,
One graue shall be for both: Vpon them shall
The causes of their death appeare (vnto
Our shame perpetuall) once a day, Ile visit
The Chappell where they lye, and teares shed there
Shall be my recreation. So long as Nature   1250
Will beare vp with this exercise, so long
I dayly vow to vse it. Come, and leade me
To these sorrowes.   *Exeunt*

Enter Antigonus carrying the Babe, with a   **3.3**
Marriner   **(Sc. 8**

ANTIGONUS
Thou art perfect then, our ship hath toucht vpon
The Desarts of *Bohemia*.

MARRINER   I (my Lord) and feare
We haue Landed in ill time: the skies looke grimly,
And threaten present blusters. In my conscience
The heauens with that we haue in hand, are angry,
And frowne vpon's.

ANTIGONUS
Their sacred wil's be done: go get a-boord,   1260
Looke to thy barke, Ile not be long before
I call vpon thee.

MARRINER   Make your best haste, and go not
Too-farre i'th Land: 'tis like to be lowd weather,
Besides this place is famous for the Creatures
Of prey, that keepe vpon't.

ANTIGONUS   Go thou away,
Ile follow instantly.

MARRINER   I am glad at heart
To be so ridde o'th businesse.   *Exit*

ANTIGONUS   Come, poore babe;
I haue heard (but not beleeu'd) the Spirits o'th'dead
May walke againe: if such thing be, thy Mother
Appear'd to me last night: for ne're was dreame   1270
So like a waking. To me comes a creature,
Sometimes her head on one side, some another,
I neuer saw a vessell of like sorrow
So fill'd, and so becomming: in pure white Robes
Like very sanctity she did approach
My Cabine where I lay: thrice bow'd before me,
And (gasping to begin some speech) her eyes
Became two spouts; the furie spent, anon
Did this breake from her. Good *Antigonus*,
Since Fate (against thy better disposition)   1280
Hath made thy person for the Thrower-out
Of my poore babe, according to thine oath,
Places remote enough are in *Bohemia*,
There weepe, and leaue it crying: and for the babe
Is counted lost for euer, *Perdita*

I prethee call't: For this vngentle businesse
Put on thee, by my Lord, thou ne're shalt see
Thy Wife *Paulina* more: and so, with shriekes
She melted into Ayre. Affrighted much,
1290 I did in time collect my selfe, and thought
This was so, and no slumber: Dreames, are toyes,
Yet for this once, yea superstitiously,
I will be squar'd by this. I do beleeue
Hermione hath suffer'd death, and that
Apollo would (this being indeede the issue
Of King *Polixenes*) it should heere be laide
(Either for life, or death) vpon the earth
Of it's right Father. Blossome, speed thee well,
    He layes downe the babe and a scroll
There lye, and there thy charracter:
    He layes downe a box
                      there these,
1300 Which may if Fortune please, both breed thee (pretty)
And still rest thine.
    ⌈*Thunder*⌉
              The storme beginnes, poore wretch,
That for thy mothers fault, art thus expos'd
To losse, and what may follow. Weepe I cannot,
But my heart bleedes: and most accurst am I
To be by oath enioyn'd to this. Farewell,
The day frownes more and more: thou'rt like to haue
A lullabie too rough: I neuer saw
The heauens so dim, by day. A sauage clamor?
Well may I get a-boord: This is the Chace,
1310 I am gone for euer.   *Exit pursued by a Beare*
    Enter an Old Sheepe-heard
OLD SHEPHEARD I would there were no age betweene ten
and three and twenty, or that youth would sleep out
the rest: for there is nothing (in the betweene) but
getting wenches with childe, wronging the Auncientry,
stealing, fighting, hearke you now: would any but
these boylde-braines of nineteene, and two and twenty
hunt this weather? They haue scarr'd away two of my
best Sheepe, which I feare the Wolfe will sooner finde
then the Maister; if any where I haue them, 'tis by the
1320 sea-side, brouzing of Iuy. Good-lucke (and't be thy will.)
    He sees the Babe
What haue we heere? Mercy on's, a Barne? A very
pretty barne; A boy, or a Childe I wonder? (A pretty
one, a verie prettie one) sure some Scape; Though I
am not bookish, yet I can read Waiting-Gentlewoman
in the scape: this has beene some staire-worke, some
Trunke-worke, some behinde-doore worke: they were
warmer that got this, then the poore Thing is heere.
Ile take it vp for pity, yet Ile tarry till my sonne come:
he hallow'd but euen now. Whoa-ho-hoa.
    Enter Clowne
1330 CLOWNE Hilloa, loa.
OLD SHEPHEARD What? art so neere? If thou'lt see a thing
    to talke on, when thou art dead and rotten, come
    hither: what ayl'st thou, man?
CLOWNE I haue seene two such sights, by Sea & by Land:
    but I am not to say it is a Sea, for it is now the skie,

betwixt the Firmament and it, you cannot thrust a
bodkins point.
OLD SHEPHEARD Why boy, how is it?
CLOWNE I would you did but see how it chafes, how it
    rages, how it takes vp the shore, but that's not to the 1340
    point: Oh, the most pitteous cry of the poore soules,
    sometimes to see 'em, and not to see 'em: Now the
    Shippe boaring the Moone with her maine Mast, and
    anon swallowed with yest and froth, as you'ld thrust
    a Corke into a hogs-head. And then for the Land-
    seruice, to see how the Beare tore out his shoulder-
    bone, how he cride to mee for helpe, and said his name
    was *Antigonus*, a Nobleman: But to make an end of
    the Ship, to see how the Sea flap-dragon'd it: but first,
    how the poore soules roared, and the sea mock'd them: 1350
    and how the poore Gentleman roared, and the Beare
    mock'd him, both roaring lowder then the sea, or
    weather.
OLD SHEPHEARD Name of mercy, when was this boy?
CLOWNE Now, now: I haue not wink'd since I saw these
    sights: the men are not yet cold vnder water, nor the
    Beare halfe din'd on the Gentleman: he's at it now.
OLD SHEPHEARD Would I had bin by, to haue help'd the
    olde man.
CLOWNE I would you had beene by the ship side, to haue 1360
    help'd her; there your charity would haue lack'd
    footing.
OLD SHEPHEARD Heauy matters, heauy matters: but looke
    thee heere boy. Now blesse thy selfe: thou met'st with
    things dying, I with things new borne. Here's a sight
    for thee: Looke thee, a bearing-cloath for a Squires
    childe:
    He points to the box
    looke thee heere, take vp, take vp (Boy:) open't: so,
    let's see, it was told me I should be rich by the Fairies.
    This is some Changeling: open't: what's within, boy? 1370
CLOWNE (*opening the box*) You're a made olde man: If the
    sinnes of your youth are forgiuen you, you're well to
    liue. Golde, all Gold.
OLD SHEPHEARD This is Faiery Gold boy, and 'twill proue
    so: vp with't, keepe it close: home, home, the next
    way. We are luckie (boy) and to bee so still requires
    nothing but secrecie. Let my sheepe go: Come (good
    boy) the next way home.
CLOWNE Go you the next way with your Findings, Ile go
    see if the Beare bee gone from the Gentleman, and 1380
    how much he hath eaten: they are neuer curst but
    when they are hungry: if there be any of him left, Ile
    bury it.
OLD SHEPHEARD That's a good deed: if thou mayest
    discerne by that which is left of him, what he is, fetch
    me to th'sight of him.
CLOWNE 'Marry will I: and you shall helpe to put him
    i'th'ground.
OLD SHEPHEARD 'Tis a lucky day, boy, and wee'l do good
    deeds on't.   *Exeunt* 1390

4.1   *Enter Time, the Chorus*
(Sc. 9) TIME

I that please some, try all: both ioy and terror
Of good, and bad: that makes, and vnfolds error,
Now take vpon me (in the name of Time)
To vse my wings: Impute it not a crime
To me, or my swift passage, that I slide
Ore sixteene yeeres, and leaue the growth vntride
Of that wide gap, since it is in my powre
To orethrow Law, and in one selfe-borne howre
To plant, and ore-whelme Custome. Let me passe
1400   The same I am, ere ancient'st Order was,
Or what is now receiu'd. I witnesse to
The times that brought them in, so shall I do
To th'freshest things now reigning, and make stale
The glistering of this present, as my Tale
Now seemes to it: your patience this allowing,
I turne my glasse, and giue my Scene such growing
As you had slept betweene: *Leontes* leauing
Th'effects of his fond iealousies, so greeuing
That he shuts vp himselfe, imagine me
1410   (Gentle Spectators) that I now may be
In faire Bohemia, and remember well,
I mentioned a sonne o'th'Kings, which *Florizell*
I now name to you: and with speed so pace
To speake of *Perdita*, now growne in grace
Equall with wond'ring. What of her insues
I list not prophesie: but let Times newes
Be knowne when 'tis brought forth. A shepherds
         daughter
And what to her adheres, which followes after,
Is th'argument of Time: of this allow,
1420   If euer you haue spent time worse, ere now:
If neuer, yet that Time himselfe doth say,
He wishes earnestly, you neuer may.   *Exit*

4.2   *Enter Polixenes, and Camillo*
(Sc. 10) POLIXENES I pray thee (good *Camillo*) be no more
importunate: 'tis a sicknesse denying thee any thing:
a death to grant this.

CAMILLO It is xvi yeeres since I saw my Countrey: though
I haue (for the most part) bin ayred abroad, I desire to
lay my bones there. Besides, the penitent King (my
Master) hath sent for me, to whose feeling sorrowes I
1430   might be some allay, (or I oreweene to thinke so) which
is another spurre to my departure.

POLIXENES As thou lou'st me (*Camillo*) wipe not out the
rest of thy seruices, by leauing me now: the neede I
haue of thee, thine owne goodnesse hath made: better
not to haue had thee, then thus to want thee, thou
hauing made me Businesses, (which none (without
thee) can sufficiently manage) must either stay to
execute them thy selfe, or take away with thee the
very seruices thou hast done: which if I haue not
1440   enough considered (as too much I cannot) to bee more
thankefull to thee, shall bee my studie, and my profite
therein, the heaping friendshippes. Of that fatall
Countrey Sicillia, prethee speake no more, whose very

naming, punnishes me with the remembrance of that
penitent (as thou calst him) and reconciled King my
brother, whose losse of his most precious Queene &
Children, are euen now to be a-fresh lamented. Say to
me, when saw'st thou the Prince *Florizell* my son?
Kings are no lesse vnhappy, their issue, not being
gracious, then they are in loosing them, when they   1450
haue approued their Vertues.

CAMILLO Sir, it is three dayes since I saw the Prince:
what his happier affayres may be, are to me vnknowne:
but I haue (missingly) noted, he is of late much retyred
from Court, and is lesse frequent to his Princely exercises
then formerly he hath appeared.

POLIXENES I haue considered so much (*Camillo*) and with
some care, so farre, that I haue eyes vnder my seruice,
which looke vpon his remouednesse: from whom I
haue this Intelligence, that he is seldome from the   1460
house of a most homely shepheard: a man (they say)
that from very nothing, and beyond the imagination
of his neighbors, is growne into an vnspeakable estate.

CAMILLO I haue heard (sir) of such a man, who hath a
daughter of most rare note: the report of her is extended
more, then can be thought to begin from such a cottage.

POLIXENES That's likewise part of my Intelligence: but (I
feare) the Angle that pluckes our sonne thither. Thou
shalt accompany vs to the place, where we will (not
appearing what we are) haue some question with the   1470
shepheard; from whose simplicity, I thinke it not
vneasie to get the cause of my sonnes resort thether.
'Prethe be my present partner in this busines, and lay
aside the thoughts of Sicillia.

CAMILLO I willingly obey your command.

POLIXENES My best *Camillo*, we must disguise our selues.
                                                        Exeunt

          Enter Autolicus singing   **4.3**
AUTOLICUS   **(Sc. 1)**

When Daffadils begin to peere,
  With heigh the Doxy ouer the dale,
Why then comes in the sweet o'the yeere,
  For the red blood raigns in ye winters pale.   1480

The white sheete bleaching on the hedge,
  With hey the sweet birds, O how they sing:
Doth set my pugging tooth an edge,
  For a quart of Ale is a dish for a King.

The Larke, that tirra Lyra chaunts,
  With heigh, with heigh, the Thrush and the Iay:
Are Summer songs for me and my Aunts
  While we lye tumbling in the hay.

I haue seru'd Prince *Florizell*, and in my time wore
three pile, but now I am out of seruice.   1490

But shall I go mourne for that (my deere)
  The pale Moone shines by night:
And when I wander here, and there
  I then do most go right.

If Tinkers may haue leaue to liue,
And beare the Sow-skin Bowget,
Then my account I well may giue,
And in the Stockes auouch-it.

1500 My Trafficke is sheetes: when the Kite builds, looke to lesser Linnen. My Father nam'd me *Autolicus,* who being (as I am) lytter'd vnder Mercurie, was likewise a snapper-vp of vnconsidered trifles: With Dye and drab, I purchas'd this Caparison, and my Reuennew is the silly Cheate. Gallowes, and Knocke, are too powerfull on the Highway. Beating and hanging are terrors to mee: For the life to come, I sleepe out the thought of it. A prize, a prize.

Enter Clowne

CLOWNE Let me see, euery Leauen-weather toddes, euery tod yeeldes pound and odde shilling: fifteene hundred
1510 shorne, what comes the wooll too?

AUTOLICUS (*aside*) If the sprindge hold, the Cocke's mine.

CLOWNE I cannot do't without Compters. Let mee see, what am I to buy for our Sheepe-shearing-Feast? Three pound of Sugar, fiue pound of Currence, Rice: What will this sister of mine do with Rice? But my father hath made her Mistris of the Feast, and she layes it on. Shee hath made-me four and twenty Nose-gayes for the shearers (three-man song-men, all, and very good ones) but they are most of them Meanes and Bases;
1520 but one Puritan amongst them, and he sings Psalmes to horne-pipes. I must haue Saffron to colour the Warden Pies, Mace: Dates, none: that's out of my note: Nutmegges, seuen; a Race or two of Ginger, but that I may begge: Foure pound of Prewyns, and as many of Reysons o'th Sun.

AUTOLICUS (*grouelling on the ground*) Oh, that euer I was borne.

CLOWNE I'th'name of me.

AUTOLICUS Oh helpe me, helpe mee: plucke but off these
1530 ragges: and then, death, death.

CLOWNE Alacke poore soule, thou hast need of more rags to lay on thee, rather then haue these off.

AUTOLICUS Oh sir, the loathsomnesse of them offend mee, more then the stripes I haue receiued, which are mightie ones and millions.

CLOWNE Alas poore man, a million of beating may come to a great matter.

AUTOLICUS I am rob'd sir, and beaten: my money, and apparrell tane from me, and these detestable things put
1540 vpon me.

CLOWNE What, by a horse-man, or a foot-man?

AUTOLICUS A footman (sweet sir) a footman.

CLOWNE Indeed, he should be a footman, by the garments he has left with thee: If this bee a horsemans Coate, it hath seene very hot seruice. Lend me thy hand, Ile helpe thee. Come, lend me thy hand.

He helpes Autolicus vp

AUTOLICUS Oh good sir, tenderly, oh.

CLOWNE Alas poore soule.

AUTOLICUS Oh good sir, softly, good sir: I feare (sir) my
1550 shoulder-blade is out.

CLOWNE How now? Canst stand?

AUTOLICUS Softly, deere sir: good sir, softly:
⌈*He picks the Clowne's pocket*⌉
you ha done me a charitable office.

CLOWNE (*reaching for his Purse*) Doest lacke any mony? I haue a little mony for thee.

AUTOLICUS No, good sweet sir: no, I beseech you sir: I haue a Kinsman not past three quarters of a mile hence, vnto whome I was going: I shall there haue money, or anie thing I want: Offer me no money I pray you, that killes my heart.   1560

CLOWNE What manner of Fellow was hee that robb'd you?

AUTOLICUS A fellow (sir) that I haue knowne to goe about with Troll-my-dames: I knew him once a seruant of the Prince: I cannot tell good sir, for which of his Vertues it was, but hee was certainely Whipt out of the Court.

CLOWNE His vices you would say: there's no vertue whipt out of the Court: they cherish it to make it stay there; and yet it will no more but abide.   1570

AUTOLICUS Vices I would say (Sir.) I know this man well, he hath bene since an Ape-bearer, then a Processe-seruer (a Bayliffe) then hee compast a Motion of the Prodigall sonne, and married a Tinkers wife, within a Mile where my Land and Liuing lyes; and (hauing flowne ouer many knauish professions) he setled onely in Rogue: some call him *Autolicus.*

CLOWNE Out vpon him: Prig, for my life Prig: he haunts Wakes, Faires, and Beare-baitings.

AUTOLICUS Very true sir: he sir hee: that's the Rogue that   1580 put me into this apparrell.

CLOWNE Not a more cowardly Rogue in all *Bohemia*; If you had but look'd bigge, and spit at him, hee'ld haue runne.

AUTOLICUS I must confesse to you (sir) I am no fighter: I am false of heart that way, & that he knew I warrant him.

CLOWNE How do you now?

AUTOLICUS Sweet sir, much better then I was: I can stand, and walke: I will euen take my leaue of you, & pace   1590 softly towards my Kinsmans.

CLOWNE Shall I bring thee on the way?

AUTOLICUS No, good fac'd sir, no sweet sir.

CLOWNE Then fartheewell, I must go buy Spices for our sheepe-shearing.

AUTOLICUS Prosper you sweet sir.   *Exit the Clowne*
Your purse is not hot enough to purchase your Spice: Ile be with you at your sheepe-shearing too: If I make not this Cheat bring out another, and the sheerers proue sheepe, let me be vnrold, and my name put in   1600 the booke of Vertue.

Song

Iog-on, Iog-on, the foot-path way,
And merrily hent the Stile-a:
A merry heart goes all the day,
Your sad tyres in a Mile-a.

Exit

4.4
(Sc. 12)   *Enter Florizell as Doricles a Countreyman, and*
      Perdita as Queene of the Feast

FLORIZELL
These your vnusuall weeds, to each part of you
Do's giue a life: no Shepherdesse, but *Flora*
Peering in Aprils front. This your sheepe-shearing,
Is as a meeting of the petty Gods,
And you the Queene on't.

1610   PERDITA   Sir: my gracious Lord,
To chide at your extreames, it not becomes me:
(Oh pardon, that I name them:) your high selfe
The gracious marke o'th'Land, you haue obscur'd
With a Swaines wearing: and me (poore lowly Maide)
Most Goddesse-like prank'd vp: But that our Feasts
In euery Messe, haue folly; and the Feeders
Digest it with a Custome, I should blush
To see you so attyr'd: swound I thinke,
To shew my selfe a glasse.

    FLORIZELL   I blesse the time
1620   When my good Falcon, made her flight a-crosse
Thy Fathers ground.

    PERDITA   Now Ioue affoord you cause:
To me the difference forges dread (your Greatnesse
Hath not beene vs'd to feare:) euen now I tremble
To thinke your Father, by some accident
Should passe this way, as you did: Oh the Fates,
How would he looke, to see his worke, so noble,
Vildely bound vp? What would he say? Or how
Should I (in these my borrowed Flaunts) behold
The sternnesse of his presence?

    FLORIZELL   Apprehend
1630   Nothing but iollity: the Goddes themselues
(Humbling their Deities to loue) haue taken
The shapes of Beasts vpon them. Iupiter,
Became a Bull, and bellow'd: the greene Neptune
A Ram, and bleated: and the Fire-roab'd-God
Golden Apollo, a poore humble Swaine,
As I seeme now. Their transformations,
Were neuer for a peece of beauty, rarer,
Nor in a way so chaste: since my desires
Run not before mine honor: nor my Lusts
Burne hotter then my Faith.

1640   PERDITA   O but Sir,
Your resolution cannot hold, when 'tis
Oppos'd (as it must be) by th'powre of the King:
One of these two must be necessities,
Which then will speake, that you must change this
    purpose,
Or I my life.

    FLORIZELL   Thou deerest *Perdita*,
With these forc'd thoughts, I prethee darken not
The Mirth o'th'Feast: Or Ile be thine (my Faire)
Or not my Fathers. For I cannot be
Mine owne, nor any thing to any, if
1650   I be not thine. To this I am most constant,
Though destiny say no. Be merry (Gentle)
Strangle such thoughts as these, with any thing

That you behold the while. Your guests are comming:
Lift vp your countenance, as it were the day
Of celebration of that nuptiall, which
We two haue sworne shall come.

PERDITA   O Lady Fortune,
Stand you auspicious.

FLORIZELL   See, your Guests approach,
Addresse your selfe to entertaine them sprightly,
And let's be red with mirth.

    Enter the Old Shepheard, with Polixenes and
    Camillo, disguised, the Clowne, Mopsa, Dorcas, and
    others

OLD SHEPHEARD (*to Perdita*)
Fy (daughter) when my old wife liu'd: vpon   1660
This day, she was both Pantler, Butler, Cooke,
Both Dame and Seruant: Welcom'd all: seru'd all,
Would sing her song, and dance her turne: now heere
At vpper end o'th Table; now, i'th middle:
On his shoulder, and his: her face o'fire
With labour, and the thing she tooke to quench it
She would to each one sip. You are retyred,
As if you were a feasted one: and not
The Hostesse of the meeting: Pray you bid
These vnknowne friends to's welcome, for it is   1670
A way to make vs better Friends, more knowne.
Come, quench your blushes, and present your selfe
That which you are, Mistris o'th'Feast. Come on,
And bid vs welcome to your sheepe-shearing,
As your good flocke shall prosper.

PERDITA (*to Polixenes*)   Sir, welcome:
It is my Fathers will, I should take on mee
The Hostesseship o'th'day: (*to Camillo*) you're
    welcome sir.
Giue me those Flowres there (*Dorcas.*) Reuerend Sirs,
For you, there's Rosemary, and Rue, these keepe
Seeming, and sauour all the Winter long: 1680
Grace, and Remembrance be to you both,
And welcome to our Shearing.

POLIXENES   Shepherdesse,
(A faire one are you:) well you fit our ages
With flowres of Winter.

PERDITA   Sir, the yeare growing ancient,
Not yet on summers death, nor on the birth
Of trembling winter, the fayrest flowres o'th season
Are our Carnations, and streak'd Gilly-vors,
(Which some call Natures bastards) of that kind
Our rusticke Gardens barren, and I care not
To get slips of them.

POLIXENES   Wherefore (gentle Maiden)   1690
Do you neglect them.

PERDITA   For I haue heard it said,
There is an Art, which in their pidenesse shares
With great creating-Nature.

POLIXENES   Say there be:
Yet Nature is made better by no meane,
But Nature makes that Meane: so ouer that Art,
(Which you say addes to Nature) is an Art

That Nature makes: you see (sweet Maid) we marry
A gentler Sien, to the wildest Stocke,
And make conceyue a barke of baser kinde
1700 By bud of Nobler race. This is an Art
Which do's mend Nature: change it rather, but
The Art it selfe, is Nature.

PERDITA   So it is.

POLIXENES
Then make your Garden rich in Gilly'vors,
And do not call them bastards.

PERDITA   Ile not put
The Dible in earth, to set one slip of them:
No more then were I painted, I would wish
This youth should say 'twer well: and onely therefore
Desire to breed by me. Here's flowres for you:
Hot Lauender, Mints, Sauory, Mariorum,
1710 The Mary-gold, that goes to bed with'Sun,
And with him rises, weeping: These are flowres
Of middle summer, and I thinke they are giuen
To men of middle age. Y'are very welcome.
        She giues them flowers

CAMILLO
I should leaue grasing, were I of your flocke,
And onely liue by gazing.

PERDITA   Out alas:
You'ld be so leane, that blasts of Ianuary
Would blow you through and through. (*To Florizell*)
        Now (my fairst Friend),
I would I had some Flowres o'th Spring, that might
Become your time of day: (*to Mopsa and Dorcas*) and
        yours, and yours,
1720 That weare vpon your Virgin-branches yet
Your Maiden-heads growing: O *Proserpina*,
For the Flowres now, that (frighted) thou let'st fall
From *Dysses* Waggon: Daffadils,
That come before the Swallow dares, and take
The windes of March with beauty: Violets (dim,
But sweeter then the lids of *Iuno's* eyes,
Or *Cytherea's* breath) pale Prime-roses,
That dye vnmarried, ere they can behold
Bright Phœbus in his strength (a Maladie
1730 Most incident to Maids:) bold Oxlips, and
The Crowne Imperiall: Lillies of all kinds,
(The Flowre-de-Luce being one.) O, these I lacke,
To make you Garlands of, and my sweet friend,
To strew him o're, and ore.

FLORIZELL   What? like a Coarse?

PERDITA
No, like a banke, for Loue to lye, and play on:
Not like a Coarse: or if: not to be buried,
But quicke, and in mine armes. Come, take your
        flours,
Me thinkes I play as I haue seene them do
In Whitson-Pastorals: Sure this Robe of mine
Do's change my disposition.

1740 FLORIZELL   What you do,
Still betters what is done. When you speake (Sweet)

I'ld haue you do it euer: When you sing,
I'ld haue you buy, and sell so: so giue Almes,
Pray so: and for the ord'ring your Affayres,
To sing them too. When you do dance, I wish you
A waue o'th Sea, that you might euer do
Nothing but that: moue still, still so:
And owne no other Function. Each your doing,
(So singular, in each particular)
Crownes what you are doing, in the present deeds,   1750
That all your Actes, are Queenes.

PERDITA   O *Doricles*,
Your praises are too large: but that your youth
And the true blood which peepes so fairely through't,
Do plainly giue you out an vnstain'd Shepherd
With wisedome, I might feare (my *Doricles*)
You woo'd me the false way.

FLORIZELL   I thinke you haue
As little skill to feare, as I haue purpose
To put you to't. But come, our dance I pray,
Your hand (my *Perdita*:) so Turtles paire
That neuer meane to part.

PERDITA   Ile sweare for 'em.   1760

POLIXENES (*to Camillo*)
This is the prettiest Low-borne Lasse, that euer
Ran on the greene-sord: Nothing she do's, or seemes
But smackes of something greater then her selfe,
Too Noble for this place.

CAMILLO   He tels her something
That makes her blood looke out: Good sooth she is
The Queene of Curds and Creame.

CLOWNE   Come on: strike vp.

DORCAS *Mopsa* must be your Mistris: marry Garlick to
mend her kissing with.

MOPSA Now in good time.

CLOWNE Not a word, a word, we stand vpon our manners,   1770
Come, strike vp.
        *Musicke. Heere a Daunce of Shepheards and
        Shephearddesses*

POLIXENES
Pray good Shepheard, what faire Swaine is this,
Which dances with your daughter?

OLD SHEPHEARD
They call him *Doricles*, and boasts himselfe
To haue a worthy Feeding; but I haue it
Vpon his owne report, and I beleeue it:
He lookes like sooth: he sayes he loues my daughter,
I thinke so too; for neuer gaz'd the Moone
Vpon the water, as hee'l stand and reade
As 'twere my daughters eyes: and to be plaine,   1780
I thinke there is not halfe a kisse to choose
Who loues another best.

POLIXENES   She dances featly.

OLD SHEPHEARD
So she do's any thing, though I report it
That should be silent: If yong *Doricles*
Do light vpon her, she shall bring him that
Which he not dreames of.

Enter Seruant

SERUANT O Master: if you did but heare the Pedler at the doore, you would neuer dance againe after a Tabor and Pipe: no, the Bag-pipe could not moue you: hee
1790 singes seuerall Tunes, faster then you'l tell money: hee vtters them as he had eaten ballads, and all mens eares grew to his Tunes.

CLOWNE He could neuer come better: hee shall come in: I loue a ballad but euen too well, if it be dolefull matter merrily set downe: or a very pleasant thing indeede, and sung lamentally.

SERUANT He hath songs for man, or woman, of all sizes: No Milliner can so fit his customers with Gloues: he has the prettiest Loue-songs for Maids, so without
1800 bawdrie (which is strange,) with such delicate burthens of Dildo's and Fadings: Iump-her, and thump-her; and where some stretch-mouth'd Rascall, would (as it were) meane mischeefe, and breake a fowle gap into the Matter, hee makes the maid to answere, *Whoop, doe me no harme good man*: put's him off, slights him, with *Whoop, doe mee no harme good man.*

POLIXENES This is a braue fellow.

CLOWNE Beleeue mee, thou talkest of an admirable conceited fellow, has he any vnbraided Wares?

1810 SERUANT Hee hath Ribbons of all the colours i'th Raine-bow; Points, more then all the Lawyers in *Bohemia*, can learnedly handle, though they come to him by th'grosse: Inckles, Caddysses, Cambrickes, Lawnes: why he sings em ouer, as they were Gods, or Goddesses: you would thinke a Smocke were a shee-Angell, he so chauntes to the sleeue-hand, and the worke about the square on't.

CLOWNE Pre'thee bring him in, and let him approach singing.

1820 PERDITA Forewarne him, that he vse no scurrilous words in's tunes.   *Exit Seruant*

CLOWNE You haue of these Pedlers, that haue more in them, then youl'd thinke (Sister.)

PERDITA I, good brother, or go about to thinke.

Enter Autolicus, wearing a false beard, carrying his packe, and singing

AUTOLICUS
          Lawne as white as driuen Snow,
          Cypresse blacke as ere was Crow,
          Gloues as sweete as Damaske Roses,
          Maskes for faces, and for noses:
          Bugle-bracelet, Necke-lace Amber,
1830   *Perfume for a Ladies Chamber:*
          Golden Quoifes, and Stomachers
          For my Lads, to giue their deers:
          Pins, and poaking-stickes of steele.
          What Maids lacke from head to heele:
          Come buy of me, come: come buy, come buy,
          Buy Lads, or else your Lasses cry: Come buy.

CLOWNE If I were not in loue with *Mopsa*, thou shouldst take no money of me, but being enthrall'd as I am, it will also be the bondage of certaine Ribbons and Gloues.

MOPSA I was promis'd them against the Feast, but they   1840
come not too late now.

DORCAS He hath promis'd you more then that, or there be lyars.

MOPSA He hath paid you all he promis'd you: 'May be he has paid you more, which will shame you to giue him againe.

CLOWNE Is there no manners left among maids? Will they weare their plackets, where they should bear their faces? Is there not milking-time? When you are going to bed? Or kill-hole? To whistle of these secrets, but   1850
you must be tittle-tatling before all our guests? 'Tis well they are whispring: clamor your tongues, and not a word more.

MOPSA I haue done; Come you promis'd me a tawdry-lace, and a paire of sweet Gloues.

CLOWNE Haue I not told thee how I was cozen'd by the way, and lost all my money.

AUTOLICUS And indeed Sir, there are Cozeners abroad, therfore it behooues men to be wary.

CLOWNE Feare not thou man, thou shalt lose nothing   1860
here.

AUTOLICUS I hope so sir, for I haue about me many parcels of charge.

CLOWNE What hast heere? Ballads?

MOPSA Pray now buy some: I loue a ballet in print, a life, for then we are sure they are true.

AUTOLICUS Here's one, to a very dolefull tune, how a Vsurers wife was brought to bed of twenty money baggs at a burthen, and how she long'd to eate Adders heads, and Toads carbonado'd.   1870

MOPSA Is it true, thinke you?

AUTOLICUS Very true, and but a moneth old.

DORCAS Blesse me from marrying a Vsurer.

AUTOLICUS Here's the Midwiues name to't: one Mist. *Tale-Porter*, and fiue or six honest Wiues, that were present. Why should I carry lyes abroad?

MOPSA (*to Clowne*) 'Pray you now buy it.

CLOWNE Come-on, lay it by: and let's first see moe Ballads: Wee'l buy the other things anon.

AUTOLICUS Here's another ballad of a Fish, that appeared   1880
vpon the coast, on wensday the fourescore of April, fortie thousand fadom aboue water, & sung this ballad against the hard hearts of maids: it was thought she was a Woman, and was turn'd into a cold fish, for she wold not exchange flesh with one that lou'd her: The Ballad is very pittifull, and as true.

DORCAS Is it true too, thinke you.

AUTOLICUS Fiue Iustices hands at it, and witnesses more then my packe will hold.

CLOWNE Lay it by too; another.   1890

AUTOLICUS This is a merry ballad, but a very pretty one.

MOPSA Let's haue some merry ones.

AUTOLICUS Why this is a passing merry one, and goes to the tune of two maids wooing a man: there's scarse a Maide westward but she sings it: 'tis in request, I can tell you.

MOPSA We can both sing it: if thou'lt beare a part, thou
  shalt heare, 'tis in three parts.

DORCAS We had the tune on't, a month agoe.

1900 AUTOLICUS I can beare my part, you must know 'tis my
  occupation: Haue at it with you:

Song

AUTOLICUS *Get you hence, for I must goe*
  Where it fits not you to know.

DORCAS *Whether?*

MOPSA   *O whether?*

DORCAS   *Whether?*

MOPSA *It becomes thy oath full well,*
  Thou to me thy secrets tell.

DORCAS *Me too: Let me go thether:*

MOPSA *Or thou go'st to th'Grange, or Mill,*

DORCAS *If to either thou dost ill,*

AUTOLICUS *Neither.*

DORCAS   *What neither?*

1910 AUTOLICUS   *Neither:*

DORCAS *Thou hast sworne my Loue to be,*

MOPSA *Thou hast sworne it more to mee.*
  Then whether goest? Say whether?

CLOWNE Wee'l haue this song out anon by our selues:
  My Father, and the Gent. are in sad talke, & wee'll not
  trouble them: Come bring away thy pack after me,
  Wenches Ile buy for you both: Pedler let's haue the
  first choice; folow me girles.

                            Exit with Dorcas and Mopsa
AUTOLICUS And you shall pay well for'em.

Song

1920 *Will you buy any Tape,*
  Or Lace for your Cape?
  My dainty Ducke, my deere-a?
  Any Silke, any Thred,
  Any Toyes for your head
  Of the news't, and fins't, fins't weare-a.
  Come to the Pedler,
  Money's a medler,
  That doth vtter all mens ware-a.

                                            Exit

Enter Seruant

SERUANT Mayster, there is three Carters, three Shepherds,
1930 three Neat-herds, three Swine-herds yᵗ haue made
  themselues all men of haire, they cal themselues
  Saltiers, and they haue a Dance, which the Wenches
  say is a gally-maufrey of Gambols, because they are
  not in't: but they themselues are o'th'minde (if it bee
  not too rough for some, that know little but bowling)
  it will please plentifully.

OLD SHEPHEARD Away: Wee'l none on't; heere has beene
  too much homely foolery already. (*To Polixenes*) I know
  (Sir) wee wearie you.

1940 POLIXENES You wearie those that refresh vs: pray let's see
  these foure-threes of Heardsmen.

SERUANT One three of them, by their owne report (Sir,)
hath danc'd before the King: and not the worst of the
three, but iumpes twelue foote and a halfe by th'squire.

OLD SHEPHEARD Leaue your prating, since these good men
  are pleas'd, let them come in: but quickly now.

SERUANT Why, they stay at doore Sir.

  Heere a Dance of twelue Satyres

POLIXENES (*to the Old Shepheard*)
  O Father, you'l know more of that heereafter:
  (*To Camillo*) Is it not too farre gone? 'Tis time to part
    them,
  He's simple, and tels much.
  (*To Florizell*)   How now (faire shepheard) 1950
  Your heart is full of something, that do's take
  Your minde from feasting. Sooth, when I was yong,
  And handed loue, as you do; I was wont
  To load my Shee with knacks: I would haue ransackt
  The Pedlers silken Treasury, and haue powr'd it
  To her acceptance: you haue let him go,
  And nothing marted with him. If your Lasse
  Interpretation should abuse, and call this
  Your lacke of loue, or bounty, you were straited
  For a reply at least, if you make a care   1960
  Of happie holding her.

FLORIZELL   Old Sir, I know
  She prizes not such trifles as these are:
  The gifts she lookes from me, are packt and lockt
  Vp in my heart, which I haue giuen already,
  But not deliuer'd.
  (*To Perdita*)   O heare me breath my life
  Before this ancient Sir, who (it should seeme)
  Hath sometime lou'd: I take thy hand, this hand,
  As soft as Doues-downe, and as white as it,
  Or Ethyopians tooth, or the fan'd snow, that's bolted
  By th' Northerne blasts, twice ore.

POLIXENES   What followes this? 1970
  How prettily the yong Swaine seemes to wash
  The hand, was faire before? I haue put you out,
  But to your protestation: Let me heare
  What you professe.

FLORIZELL   Do, and be witnesse too't.

POLIXENES
  And this my neighbour too?

FLORIZELL   And he, and more
  Then he, and men: the earth, the heauens, and all;
  That were I crown'd the most Imperiall Monarch
  Thereof most worthy: were I the fayrest youth
  That euer made eye swerue, had force and knowledge
  More then was euer mans, I would not prize them 1980
  Without her Loue; for her, employ them all,
  Commend them, and condemne them to her seruice,
  Or to their owne perdition.

POLIXENES   Fairely offer'd.

CAMILLO
  This shewes a sound affection.

OLD SHEPHEARD   But my daughter,
  Say you the like to him.

PERDITA   I cannot speake

So well, (nothing so well) no, nor meane better.
By th'patterne of mine owne thoughts, I cut out
The puritie of his.
OLD SHEPHEARD   Take hands, a bargaine;
And friends vnknowne, you shall beare witnesse to't:
1990   I giue my daughter to him, and will make
Her Portion, equall his.
FLORIZELL   O, that must bee
I'th Vertue of your daughter: One being dead,
I shall haue more then you can dreame of yet,
Enough then for your wonder: but come-on,
Contract vs fore these Witnesses.
OLD SHEPHEARD   Come, your hand:
And daughter, yours.
POLIXENES   Soft Swaine a-while, beseech you,
Haue you a Father?
FLORIZELL I haue: but what of him?
POLIXENES Knowes he of this?
2000 FLORIZELL He neither do's, nor shall.
POLIXENES Me-thinkes a Father,
Is at the Nuptiall of his sonne, a guest
That best becomes the Table: Pray you once more
Is not your Father growne incapeable
Of reasonable affayres? Is he not stupid
With Age, and altring Rheumes? Can he speake? heare?
Know man, from man? Dispute his owne estate?
Lies he not bed-rid? And againe, do's nothing
But what he did, being childish?
FLORIZELL   No good Sir:
2010   He has his health, and ampler strength indeede
Then most haue of his age.
POLIXENES   By my white beard,
You offer him (if this be so) a wrong
Something vnfilliall: Reason my sonne
Should choose himselfe a wife, but as good reason
The Father (all whose ioy is nothing else
But faire posterity) should hold some counsaile
In such a businesse.
FLORIZELL   I yeeld all this;
But for some other reasons (my graue Sir)
Which 'tis not fit you know, I not acquaint
My Father of this businesse.
2020 POLIXENES   Let him know't.
FLORIZELL
He shall not.
POLIXENES   Prethee let him.
FLORIZELL   No, he must not.
OLD SHEPHEARD
Let him (my sonne) he shall not need to greeue
At knowing of thy choice.
FLORIZELL   Come, come, he must not:
Marke our Contract.
POLIXENES (remouing his disguise)
     Marke your diuorce (yong sir)
Whom sonne I dare not call: Thou art too base
To be acknowledgd. Thou a Scepters heire,

That thus affects a sheepe-hooke?
(To the Old Shepheard)   Thou, old Traitor,
I am sorry, that by hanging thee, I can but
Shorten thy life one weeke.
(To Perdita)   And thou, fresh peece
Of excellent Witchcraft, who of force must know   2030
The royall Foole thou coap'st with.
OLD SHEPHEARD   Oh my heart.
POLIXENES
Ile haue thy beauty scratcht with briers & made
More homely then thy state.
(To Florizell)   For thee (fond boy)
If I may euer know thou dost but sigh,
That thou no more shalt see this knacke (as neuer
I meane thou shalt) wee'l barre thee from succession,
Not hold thee of our blood, no not our Kin,
Farre then Deucalion off: (marke thou my words)
Follow vs to the Court.
(To the Old Shepheard)   Thou Churle, for this time
(Though full of our displeasure) yet we free thee   2040
From the dead blow of it.
(To Perdita)   And you Enchantment,
Worthy enough a Heardsman: yea him too,
That makes himselfe (but for our Honor therein)
Vnworthy thee. If euer henceforth, thou
These rurall Latches, to his entrance open,
Or hope his body more, with thy embraces,
I will deuise a death, as cruell for thee
As thou art tender to't.   Exit
PERDITA   Euen heere vndone:
I was not much a-fear'd: for once, or twice
I was about to speake, and tell him plainely,   2050
The selfe-same Sun, that shines vpon his Court,
Hides not his visage from our Cottage, but
Lookes on alike. Wilt please you (Sir) be gone?
I told you what would come of this: Beseech you
Of your owne state take care: This dreame of mine
Being now awake, Ile Queene it no inch farther,
But milke my Ewes, and weepe.
CAMILLO (to the Old Shepheard)   Why how now Father,
Speake ere thou dyest.
OLD SHEPHEARD   I cannot speake, nor thinke,
Nor dare to know, that which I know:
(To Florizell)   O Sir,
You haue vndone a man of fourescore three,   2060
That thought to fill his graue in quiet: yea,
To dye vpon the bed my father dy'de,
To lye close by his honest bones; but now
Some Hangman must put on my shrowd, and lay me
Where no Priest shouels-in dust.
(To Perdita)   Oh cursed wretch,
That knew'st this was the Prince, and wouldst aduenture
To mingle faith with him. Vndone, vndone:
If I might dye within this houre, I haue liu'd
To die when I desire.   Exit
FLORIZELL (to Perdita)   Why looke you so vpon me?
I am but sorry, not affear'd: delaid,   2070

But nothing altred: What I was, I am:
More straining on, for plucking backe; not following
My leash vnwillingly.

CAMILLO   Gracious my Lord,
You know your Fathers temper: at this time
He will allow no speech: (which I do ghesse
You do not purpose to him:) and as hardly
Will he endure your sight as yet, I feare;
Then till the fury of his Highnesse settle
Come not before him.

FLORIZELL   I not purpose it:
I thinke *Camillo*.

2080 CAMILLO   Euen he, my Lord.

PERDITA (*to Florizell*)
How often haue I told you 'twould be thus?
How often said my dignity would last
But till 'twer knowne?

FLORIZELL   It cannot faile, but by
The violation of my faith, and then
Let Nature crush the sides o'th earth together,
And marre the seeds within. Lift vp thy lookes:
From my succession wipe me (Father) I
Am heyre to my affection.

CAMILLO   Be aduis'd.

FLORIZELL
I am: and by my fancie, if my Reason
2090 Will thereto be obedient: I haue reason:
If not, my sences better pleas'd with madnesse,
Do bid it welcome.

CAMILLO   This is desperate (sir.)

FLORIZELL
So call it: but it do's fulfill my vow:
I needs must thinke it honesty. *Camillo*,
Not for *Bohemia*, nor the pompe that may
Be thereat gleand: for all the Sun sees, or
The close earth wombes, or the profound seas, hides
In vnknowne fadomes, will I breake my oath
To this my faire belou'd: Therefore, I pray you,
2100 As you haue euer bin my Fathers honour'd friend,
When he shall misse me, (as in faith I meane not
To see him any more) cast your good counsailes
Vpon his passion: Let my selfe, and Fortune
Tug for the time to come. This you may know,
And so deliuer, I am put to Sea
With her, who heere I cannot hold on shore:
And most opportune to her neede, I haue
A Vessell rides fast by, but not prepar'd
For this designe. What course I meane to hold
2110 Shall nothing benefit your knowledge, nor
Concerne me the reporting.

CAMILLO   O my Lord,
I would your spirit were easier for aduice,
Or stronger for your neede.

FLORIZELL   Hearke *Perdita*,
(*To Camillo*) Ile heare you by and by.

CAMILLO (*aside*)   Hee's irremoueable,
Resolu'd for flight: Now were I happy if
His going, I could frame to serue my turne,

Saue him from danger, do him loue and honor,
Purchase the sight againe of deere *Sicillia*,
And that vnhappy King, my Master, whom
I so much thirst to see.

FLORIZELL   Now good *Camillo*,   2120
I am so fraught with curious businesse, that
I leaue out ceremony.

CAMILLO   Sir, I thinke
You haue heard of my poore seruices, i'th loue
That I haue borne your Father?

FLORIZELL   Very nobly
Haue you deseru'd: It is my Fathers Musicke
To speake your deeds: not little of his care
To haue them recompenc'd, as thought on.

CAMILLO   Well (my Lord)
If you may please to thinke I loue the King,
And through him, what's neerest to him, which is
Your gracious selfe; embrace but my direction,   2130
If your more ponderous and setled proiect
May suffer alteration. On mine honor,
Ile point you where you shall haue such receiuing
As shall become your Highnesse, where you may
Enioy your Mistris; from the whom, I see
There's no disiunction to be made, but by
(As heauens forefend) your ruine: Marry her,
And with my best endeuours, in your absence,
Your discontenting Father, striue to qualifie
And bring him vp to liking.

FLORIZELL   How *Camillo*   2140
May this (almost a miracle) be done?
That I may call thee something more then man,
And after that trust to thee.

CAMILLO   Haue you thought on
A place whereto you'l go?

FLORIZELL   Not any yet:
But as th'unthought-on accident is guiltie
To what we wildely do, so we professe
Our selues to be the slaues of chance, and flyes
Of euery winde that blowes.

CAMILLO   Then list to me:
This followes, if you will not change your purpose
But vndergo this flight; make for *Sicillia*,   2150
And there present your selfe, and your fayre Princesse,
(For so I see she must be) 'fore *Leontes*;
She shall be habited, as it becomes
The partner of your Bed. Me thinkes I see
Leontes opening his free Armes, and weeping
His Welcomes forth: asks thee there Sonne
        forgiuenesse,
As 'twere i'th' Fathers person: kisses the hands
Of your fresh Princesse; ore and ore diuides him,
'Twixt his vnkindnesse, and his Kindnesse: th'one
He chides to Hell, and bids the other grow   2160
Faster then Thought, or Time.

FLORIZELL   Worthy *Camillo*,
What colour for my Visitation, shall I
Hold vp before him?

CAMILLO   Sent by the King your Father

To greet him, and to giue him comforts. Sir,
The manner of your bearing towards him, with
What you (as from your Father) shall deliuer,
Things knowne betwixt vs three, Ile write you downe,
The which shall point you forth at euery sitting
What you must say: that he shall not perceiue,
2170 But that you haue your Fathers Bosome there,
And speake his very Heart.

FLORIZELL   I am bound to you:
There is some sappe in this.

CAMILLO   A Course more promising,
Then a wild dedication of your selues
To vnpath'd Waters, vndream'd Shores; most certaine,
To Miseries enough: no hope to helpe you,
But as you shake off one, to take another:
Nothing so certaine, as your Anchors, who
Doe their best office, if they can but stay you,
Where you'le be loth to be: besides you know,
2180 Prosperitie's the very bond of Loue,
Whose fresh complexion, and whose heart together,
Affliction alters.

PERDITA   One of these is true:
I thinke Affliction may subdue the Cheeke,
But not take-in the Mind.

CAMILLO   Yea? say you so?
There shall not, at your Fathers House, these seuen
     yeeres
Be borne another such.

FLORIZELL   My good Camillo,
She's as forward, of her Breeding, as
She is i'th' reare' our Birth.

CAMILLO   I cannot say, 'tis pitty
She lacks Instructions, for she seemes a Mistresse
To most that teach.

2190 PERDITA   Your pardon Sir, for this,
Ile blush you Thanks.

FLORIZELL   My prettiest Perdita.
But O, the Thornes we stand vpon: (Camillo)
Preseruer of my Father, now of me,
The Medicine of our House: how shall we doe?
We are not furnish'd like Bohemia's Sonne,
Nor shall appeare so in Sicilia.

CAMILLO My Lord,
Feare none of this: I thinke you know my fortunes
Doe all lye there: it shall be so my care,
2200 To haue you royally appointed, as if
The Scene you play, were mine. For instance Sir,
That you may know you shall not want: one word.
          They speake apart.
          Enter Autolicus

AUTOLICUS Ha, ha, what a Foole Honestie is? and Trust
(his sworne brother) a very simple Gentleman. I haue
sold all my Tromperie: not a counterfeit Stone, not a
Ribbon, Glasse, Pomander, Browch, Table-booke,
Ballad, Knife, Tape, Gloue, Shooe-tye, Bracelet, Horne-
Ring, to keepe my Pack from fasting: they throng who
should buy first, as if my Trinkets had beene hallowed,
2210 and brought a benediction to the buyer: by which

meanes, I saw whose Purse was best in Picture; and
what I saw, to my good vse, I remembred. My Clowne
(who wants but something to be a reasonable man)
grew so in loue with the Wenches Song, that hee would
not stirre his Petty-toes, till he had both Tune and
Words, which so drew the rest of the Heard to me,
that all their other Sences stucke in Eares: you might
haue pinch'd a Placket, it was sencelesse; 'twas nothing
to gueld a Cod-peece of a Purse: I could haue fill'd
Keyes of that hung in Chaynes: no hearing, no feeling, 2220
but my Sirs Song, and admiring the Nothing of it. So
that in this time of Lethargie, I pickd and cut most of
their Festiuall Purses: And had not the old-man come
in with a Whoo-bub against his Daughter, and the
Kings Sonne, and scar'd my Chowghes from the Chaffe,
I had not left a Purse aliue in the whole Army.
          Camillo, Florizell, and Perdita come forward

CAMILLO
Nay, but my Letters by this meanes being there
So soone as you arriue, shall cleare that doubt.

FLORIZELL
And those that you'le procure from King *Leontes*?

CAMILLO
Shall satisfie your Father.

PERDITA   Happy be you: 2230
All that you speake, shewes faire.

CAMILLO (*seeing Autolicus*)   Who haue we here?
Wee'le make an Instrument of this: omit
Nothing may giue vs aide.

AUTOLICUS (*aside*) If they haue ouer-heard me now: why
hanging.

CAMILLO How now (good Fellow) Why shak'st thou so?
Feare not (man) Here's no harme intended to thee.

AUTOLICUS I am a poore Fellow, Sir.

CAMILLO Why, be so still: here's no body will steale that
from thee: yet for the out-side of thy pouertie, we must 2240
make an exchange; therefore dis-case thee instantly
(thou must thinke there's a necessitie in't) and change
Garments with this Gentleman: Though the penny-
worth (on his side) be the worst, yet hold thee, (*giuing
him money*) there's some boot.

AUTOLICUS I am a poore Fellow, Sir: (*aside*) (I know ye
well enough.)

CAMILLO Nay prethee dispatch: the Gentleman is halfe
fled already.

AUTOLICUS Are you in earnest, Sir? (*Aside*) (I smell the 2250
trick on't.)

FLORIZELL Dispatch, I prethee.

AUTOLICUS Indeed I haue had Earnest, but I cannot with
conscience take it.

CAMILLO Vnbuckle, vnbuckle.
          Florizell and Autolicus exchange clothes
(*To Perdita*) Fortunate Mistresse (let my prophecie
Come home to ye:) you must retire your selfe
Into some Couert; take your sweet-hearts Hat
And pluck it ore your Browes, muffle your face,
Dis-mantle you, and (as you can) disliken   2260
The truth of your owne seeming, that you may

(For I doe feare eyes) ouer to Ship-board
Get vndescry'd.

PERDITA   I see the Play so lyes,
That I must beare a part.

CAMILLO   No remedie:
(*To Florizell*) Haue you done there?

FLORIZELL   Should I now meet my Father,
He would not call me Sonne.

CAMILLO   Nay, you shall haue no Hat:

He giues the hat to Perdita
Come Lady, come: Farewell (my friend.)

AUTOLICUS   Adieu, Sir.

FLORIZELL
O *Perdita*: what haue we twaine forgot?
'Pray you a word.
          They speake aside

CAMILLO (*aside*)
2270   What I doe next, shall be to tell the King
Of this escape, and whither they are bound;
Wherein, my hope is, I shall so preuaile,
To force him after: in whose company
I shall re-view *Sicilia*; for whose sight,
I haue a Womans Longing.

FLORIZELL   Fortune speed vs:
Thus we set on (*Camillo*) to th'Sea-side.

CAMILLO The swifter speed, the better.
          Exeunt Florizell, Perdita, and Camillo

AUTOLICUS I vnderstand the businesse, I heare it: to haue
an open eare, a quick eye, and a nimble hand, is
2280   necessary for a Cut-purse; a good Nose is requisite also,
to smell out worke for th'other Sences. I see this is the
time that the vniust man doth thriue. What an
exchange had this been, without boot? What a boot is
here, with this exchange? Sure the Gods doe this yeere
conniue at vs, and we may doe any thing extempore.
The Prince himselfe is about a peece of Iniquitie (stealing
away from his Father, with his Clog at his heeles:) if I
thought it were a peece of honestie to acquaint the
King withall, I would not do't: I hold it the more
2290   knauerie to conceale it; and therein am I constant to
my Profession.
          Enter Clowne and the Old Shepheard, carrying a
          Farthell and a Box
Aside, aside, here is more matter for a hot braine:
Euery Lanes end, euery Shop, Church, Session,
Hanging, yeelds a carefull man worke.

CLOWNE See, see: what a man you are now? there is no
other way, but to tell the King she's a Changeling, and
none of your flesh and blood.

OLD SHEPHEARD Nay, but heare me.

CLOWNE Nay; but heare me.

2300 OLD SHEPHEARD Goe too then.

CLOWNE She being none of your flesh and blood, your
flesh and blood ha's not offended the King, and so your
flesh and blood is not to be punish'd by him. Shew
those things you found about her (those secret things,
all but what she ha's with her:) This being done, let
the Law goe whistle: I warrant you.

OLD SHEPHEARD I will tell the King all, euery word, yea,

and his Sonnes prancks too; who, I may say, is no
honest man, neither to his Father, nor to me, to goe
about to make me the Kings Brother in Law.   2310

CLOWNE Indeed Brother in Law was the farthest off you
could haue beene to him, and then your Blood had
beene the dearer, by I know not how much an ounce.

AUTOLICUS (*aside*) Very wisely (Puppies.)

OLD SHEPHEARD Well: let vs to the King: there is that in
this Farthell, will make him scratch his Beard.

AUTOLICUS (*aside*) I know not what impediment this
Complaint may be to the flight of my Master.

CLOWNE 'Pray heartily he be at' Pallace.

AUTOLICUS (*aside*) Though I am not naturally honest, I am   2320
so sometimes by chance: Let me pocket vp my Pedlers
excrement.
          He remoues his false Beard
How now (Rustiques) whither are you bound?

OLD SHEPHEARD To th' Pallace (and it like your Worship.)

AUTOLICUS Your Affaires there? what? with whom? the
Condition of that Farthell? the place of your dwelling?
your names? your ages? of what hauing? breeding,
and any thing that is fitting to be knowne, discouer?

CLOWNE We are but plaine fellowes, Sir.

AUTOLICUS A Lye; you are rough, and hayrie: Let me   2330
haue no lying; it becomes none but Trades-men, and
they often giue vs (Souldiers) the Lye, but wee pay
them for it with stamped Coyne, not stabbing Steele,
therefore they doe not giue vs the Lye.

CLOWNE Your Worship had like to haue giuen vs one, if
you had not taken your selfe with the manner.

OLD SHEPHEARD Are you a Courtier, and't like you Sir?

AUTOLICUS Whether it like me, or no, I am a Courtier.
Seest thou not the ayre of the Court, in these enfoldings?
Hath not my gate in it, the measure of the Court?   2340
Receiues not thy Nose Court-Odour from me? Reflect I
not on thy Basenesse, Court-Contempt? Think'st thou,
for that I insinuate, to toaze from thee thy Businesse,
I am therefore no Courtier? I am Courtier *Cap-a-pe*;
and one that will eyther push-on, or pluck-back, thy
Businesse there: whereupon I command thee to open
thy Affaire.

OLD SHEPHEARD My Businesse, Sir, is to the King.

AUTOLICUS What Aduocate ha'st thou to him?

OLD SHEPHEARD I know not (and't like you.)   2350

CLOWNE (*aside to the Old Shepheard*) Aduocate's the Court-
word for a Pheazant: say you haue none.

OLD SHEPHEARD
None, Sir: I haue no Pheazant Cock, nor Hen.

AUTOLICUS (*aside*)
How bless'd are we, that are not simple men?
Yet Nature might haue made me as these are,
Therefore I will not disdaine.

CLOWNE This cannot be but a great Courtier.

OLD SHEPHEARD His Garments are rich, but he weares
them not handsomely.

CLOWNE He seemes to be the more Noble, in being   2360
fantasticall: A great man, Ile warrant; I know by the
picking on's Teeth.

AUTOLICUS The Farthell there? What's i'th' Farthell? Wherefore that Box?

OLD SHEPHEARD Sir, there lyes such Secrets in this Farthell and Box, which none must know but the King, and which hee shall know within this houre, if I may come to th' speech of him.

AUTOLICUS Age, thou hast lost thy labour.

2370 OLD SHEPHEARD Why Sir?

AUTOLICUS The King is not at the Pallace, he is gone aboord a new Ship, to purge Melancholy, and ayre himselfe: for if thou bee'st capable of things serious, thou must know the King is full of griefe.

OLD SHEPHEARD So 'tis said (Sir:) about his Sonne, that should haue marryed a Shepheards Daughter.

AUTOLICUS If that Shepheard be not in hand-fast, let him flye; the Curses he shall haue, the Tortures he shall feele, will breake the back of Man, the heart of Monster.

2380 CLOWNE Thinke you so, Sir?

AUTOLICUS Not hee alone shall suffer what Wit can make heauie, and Vengeance bitter; but those that are Iermaine to him (though remou'd fiftie times) shall all come vnder the Hang-man: which, though it be great pitty, yet it is necessarie. An old Sheepe-whistling Rogue, a Ram-tender, to offer to haue his Daughter come into grace? Some say hee shall be ston'd: but that death is too soft for him (say I:) Draw our Throne into a Sheep-Coat? all deaths are too few, the sharpest 2390 too easie.

CLOWNE Ha's the old-man ere a Sonne Sir (doe you heare) and't like you, Sir?

AUTOLICUS Hee ha's a Sonne: who shall be flayd aliue, then 'noynted ouer with Honey, set on the head of a Waspes Nest, then stand till he be three quarters and a dram dead: then recouer'd againe with Aquauite, or some other hot Infusion: then, raw as he is (and in the hotest day Prognostication proclaymes) shall he be set against a Brick-wall, (the Sunne looking with a 2400 South-ward eye vpon him; where hee is to behold him, with Flyes blown to death.) But what talke we of these Traitorly-Rascals, whose miseries are to be smil'd at, their offences being so capitall? Tell me (for you seeme to be honest plaine men) what you haue to the King: being something gently consider'd, Ile bring you where he is aboord, tender your persons to his presence, whisper him in your behalfes; and if it be in man, besides the King, to effect your Suites, here is man shall doe it.

2410 CLOWNE (to the Old Shepheard) He seemes to be of great authoritie: close with him, giue him Gold; and though Authoritie be a stubborne Beare, yet hee is oft led by the Nose with Gold: shew the in-side of your Purse to the out-side of his hand, and no more adoe. Remember ston'd, and flay'd aliue.

OLD SHEPHEARD And't please you (Sir) to vndertake the Businesse for vs, here is that Gold I haue: Ile make it as much more, and leaue this young man in pawne, till I bring it you.

AUTOLICUS After I haue done what I promised?   2420

OLD SHEPHEARD I Sir.

AUTOLICUS Well, giue me the Moitie: (To the Clowne) Are you a partie in this Businesse?

CLOWNE In some sort, Sir: but though my case be a pittifull one, I hope I shall not be flayd out of it.

AUTOLICUS Oh, that's the case of the Shepheards Sonne: hang him, hee'le be made an example.

CLOWNE (to the Old Shepheard) Comfort, good comfort: We must to the King, and shew our strange sights: he must know 'tis none of your Daughter, nor my Sister: 2430 wee are gone else. (To Autolicus) Sir, I will giue you as much as this old man do's, when the Businesse is performed, and remaine (as he sayes) your pawne till it be brought you.

AUTOLICUS I will trust you. Walke before toward the Sea-side, goe on the right hand, I will but looke vpon the Hedge, and follow you.

CLOWNE (to the Old Shepheard) We are bless'd, in this man: as I may say, euen bless'd.

OLD SHEPHEARD Let's before, as he bids vs: he was prouided   2440 to doe vs good.   Exit with the Clowne

AUTOLICUS If I had a mind to be honest, I see Fortune would not suffer mee: shee drops Booties in my mouth. I am courted now with a double occasion: (Gold, and a means to doe the Prince my Master good; which, who knowes how that may turne backe to my aduancement?) I will bring these two Moales, these blind-ones, aboord him: if he thinke it fit to shoare them againe, and that the Complaint they haue to the King, concernes him nothing, let him call me Rogue,   2450 for being so farre officious, for I am proofe against that Title, and what shame else belongs to't: To him will I present them, there may be matter in it.   Exit

✤

Enter Leontes, Cleomines, Dion, and Paulina   **5.1**
                                                        (Sc. 13
CLEOMINES (to Leontes)

Sir, you haue done enough, and haue perform'd
A Saint-like Sorrow: No fault could you make,
Which you haue not redeem'd; indeed pay'd downe
More penitence, then done trespas: At the last
Doe, as the Heauens haue done; forget your euill,
With them, forgiue your selfe.

LEONTES   Whilest I remember
Her, and her Vertues, I cannot forget   2460
My blemishes in them, and so still thinke of
The wrong I did my selfe: which was so much,
That Heire-lesse it hath made my Kingdome, and
Destroy'd the sweet'st Companion, that ere man
Bred his hopes out of, true.

PAULINA   Too true (my Lord:)
If one by one, you wedded all the World,
Or from the All that are, tooke something good,
To make a perfect Woman; she you kill'd,
Would be vnparallell'd.

LEONTES   I thinke so. Kill'd?

2470 She I kill'd? I did so: but thou strik'st me
Sorely, to say I did: it is as bitter
Vpon thy Tongue, as in my Thought. Now, good now,
Say so but seldome.

CLEOMINES   Not at all, good Lady:
You might haue spoke a thousand things, that would
Haue done the time more benefit, and grac'd
Your kindnesse better.

PAULINA   You are one of those
Would haue him wed againe.

DION   If you would not so,
You pitty not the State, nor the Remembrance
Of his most Soueraigne Name: Consider little,
2480 What Dangers, by his Highnesse faile of Issue,
May drop vpon his Kingdome, and deuoure
Incertaine lookers on. What were more holy,
Then to reioyce the former Queene is well?
What holyer, then for Royalties repayre,
For present comfort, and for future good,
To blesse the Bed of Maiestie againe
With a sweet Fellow to't?

PAULINA   There is none worthy,
(Respecting her that's gone:) besides the Gods
Will haue fulfill'd their secret purposes:
2490 For ha's not the Diuine *Apollo* said?
Is't not the tenor of his Oracle,
That King *Leontes* shall not haue an Heire,
Till his lost Child be found? Which, that it shall,
Is all as monstrous to our humane reason,
As my *Antigonus* to breake his Graue,
And come againe to me: who, on my life,
Did perish with the Infant. 'Tis your councell,
My Lord should to the Heauens be contrary,
Oppose against their wills. (*To Leontes*) Care not for
Issue,
2500 The Crowne will find an Heire. Great *Alexander*
Left his to th' Worthiest: so his Successor
Was like to be the best.

LEONTES   Good *Paulina*,
Who hast the memorie of *Hermione*
I know in honor: O, that euer I
Had squar'd me to thy councell: then, euen now,
I might haue look'd vpon my Queenes full eyes,
Haue taken Treasure from her Lippes.

PAULINA   And left them
More rich, for what they yeelded.

LEONTES   Thou speak'st truth:
No more such Wiues, therefore no Wife: one worse,
2510 And better vs'd, would make her Sainted Spirit
Againe possesse her Corps, and on this Stage
(Where we Offendors morne) appeare Soule-vext,
And begin, why to me?

PAULINA   Had she such power,
She had iust cause.

LEONTES   She had, and would incense me
To murther her I marryed.

PAULINA   I should so:

Were I the Ghost that walk'd, Il'd bid you marke
Her eye, and tell me for what dull part in't
You chose her: then Il'd shrieke, that euen your eares
Should rift to heare me, and the words that follow'd,
Should be, Remember mine.

LEONTES   Starres, Starres,   2520
And all eyes else, dead coales: feare thou no Wife;
Ile haue no Wife, *Paulina*.

PAULINA   Will you sweare
Neuer to marry, but by my free leaue?

LEONTES
Neuer (*Paulina*) so be bless'd my Spirit.

PAULINA
Then good my Lords, beare witnesse to his Oath.

CLEOMINES
You tempt him ouer-much.

PAULINA   Vnlesse another,
As like *Hermione*, as is her Picture,
Affront his eye.

CLEOMINES   Good Madame, I haue done.

PAULINA
Yet if my Lord will marry: if you will, Sir;
No remedie but you will: Giue me the Office   2530
To chuse your Queene: she shall not be so young
As was your former, but she shall be such
As (walked your first Queenes Ghost) it should take ioy
To see her in your armes.

LEONTES   My true *Paulina*,
We shall not marry, till thou bidst vs.

PAULINA   That
Shall be when your first Queene's againe in breath:
Neuer till then.

     Enter a Seruant

SERUANT
One that giues out himselfe Prince *Florizell*,
Sonne of *Polixenes*, with his Princesse (she
The fairest I haue yet beheld) desires accesse   2540
To your high presence.

LEONTES   What with him? he comes not
Like to his Fathers Greatnesse: his approach
(So out of circumstance, and suddaine) tells vs,
'Tis not a Visitation fram'd, but forc'd
By need, and accident. What Trayne?

SERUANT   But few,
And those but meane.

LEONTES   His Princesse (say you) with him?

SERUANT
I: the most peerelesse peece of Earth, I thinke,
That ere the Sunne shone bright on.

PAULINA   Oh *Hermione*,
As euery present Time doth boast it selfe
Aboue a better, gone; so must thy Graue   2550
Giue way to what's seene now.

(*To the Seruant*)   Sir, you your selfe
Haue said, and writ so; but your writing now
Is colder then that Theame: she had not beene,
Nor was not to be equall'd, thus your Verse

Flow'd with her Beautie once; 'tis shrewdly ebb'd,
To say you haue seene a better.

SERUANT   Pardon, Madame:
The one, I haue almost forgot (your pardon:)
The other, when she ha's obtayn'd your Eye,
Will haue your Tongue too. This is a Creature,
2560   Would she begin a Sect, might quench the zeale
Of all Professors else; make Proselytes
Of who she but bid follow.

PAULINA   How? not women?

SERUANT
Women will loue her, that she is a Woman
More worth then any Man: Men, that she is
The rarest of all Women.

LEONTES   Goe Cleomines,
Your selfe (assisted with your honor'd Friends)
Bring them to our embracement.   Exit Cleomines
                              Still 'tis strange,
He thus should steale vpon vs.

PAULINA   Had our Prince
(Iewell of Children) seene this houre, he had payr'd
2570   Well with this Lord; there was not full a moneth
Betweene their births.

LEONTES   'Prethee no more; cease: thou know'st
He dyes to me againe, when talk'd-of: sure
When I shall see this Gentleman, thy speeches
Will bring me to consider that, which may
Vnfurnish me of Reason. They are come.

          Enter Florizell, Perdita, Cleomines, and others
Your Mother was most true to Wedlock, Prince,
For she did print your Royall Father off,
Conceiuing you. Were I but twentie one,
Your Fathers Image is so hit in you,
2580   (His very ayre) that I should call you Brother,
As I did him, and speake of something wildly
By vs perform'd before. Most dearely welcome,
And your faire Princesse (Goddesse) oh: alas,
I lost a couple, that 'twixt Heauen and Earth
Might thus haue stood, begetting wonder, as
You (gracious Couple) doe: and then I lost
(All mine owne Folly) the Societie,
Amitie too of your braue Father, whom
(Though bearing Miserie) I desire my life
Once more to looke on him.

2590 FLORIZELL   By his command
Haue I here touch'd Sicilia, and from him
Giue you all greetings, that a King (at friend)
Can send his Brother: and but Infirmitie
(Which waits vpon worne times) hath something
          seiz'd
His wish'd Abilitie, he had himselfe
The Lands and Waters, 'twixt your Throne and his,
Measur'd, to looke vpon you; whom he loues
(He bad me say so) more then all the Scepters,
And those that beare them, liuing.

LEONTES   Oh my Brother,
2600   (Good Gentleman) the wrongs I haue done thee, stirre
Afresh within me: and these thy offices

(So rarely kind) are as Interpreters
Of my behind-hand slacknesse. Welcome hither,
As is the Spring to th'Earth. And hath he too
Expos'd this Paragon to th'fearefull vsage
(At least vngentle) of the dreadfull Neptune,
To greet a man, not worth her paines; much lesse,
Th'aduenture of her person?

FLORIZELL   Good my Lord,
She came from Libia.

LEONTES   Where the Warlike Smalus,
That Noble honor'd Lord, is fear'd, and lou'd?   2610

FLORIZELL
Most Royall Sir, from thence: from him, whose
          Daughter
His Teares proclaym'd his, parting with her: thence
(A prosperous South-wind friendly) we haue cross'd,
To execute the Charge my Father gaue me,
For visiting your Highnesse: My best Traine
I haue from your Sicilian Shores dismiss'd;
Who for Bohemia bend, to signifie
Not onely my successe in Libia (Sir)
But my arriuall, and my Wifes, in safetie
Here, where we are.

LEONTES   The blessed Gods   2620
Purge all Infection from our Ayre, whilest you
Doe Clymate here: you haue a holy Father,
A gracefull Gentleman, against whose person
(So sacred as it is) I haue done sinne,
For which, the Heauens (taking angry note)
Haue left me Issue-lesse: and your Father's bless'd
(As he from Heauen merits it) with you,
Worthy his goodnesse. What might I haue been,
Might I a Sonne and Daughter now haue look'd on,
Such goodly things as you?

          Enter a Lord

LORD   Most Noble Sir,   2630
That which I shall report, will beare no credit,
Were not the proofe so nigh. Please you (great Sir)
Bohemia greets you from himselfe, by me:
Desires you to attach his Sonne, who ha's
(His Dignitie, and Dutie both cast off)
Fled from his Father, from his Hopes, and with
A Shepheards Daughter.

LEONTES   Where's Bohemia? speake:

LORD
Here, in your Citie: I now came from him.
I speake amazedly, and it becomes
My meruaile, and my Message. To your Court   2640
Whiles he was hastning (in the Chase, it seemes,
Of this faire Couple) meetes he on the way
The Father of this seeming Lady, and
Her Brother, hauing both their Countrey quitted,
With this young Prince.

FLORIZELL   Camillo ha's betray'd me;
Whose honor, and whose honestie till now,
Endur'd all Weathers.

LORD   Lay't so to his charge:
He's with the King your Father.

LEONTES   Who? Camillo?

LORD

    Camillo (Sir:) I spake with him: who now

2650 Ha's these poore men in question. Neuer saw I

    Wretches so quake: they kneele, they kisse the Earth;

    Forsweare themselues as often as they speake:

    Bohemia stops his eares, and threatens them

    With diuers deaths, in death.

PERDITA   Oh my poore Father:

    The Heauen sets Spyes vpon vs, will not haue

    Our Contract celebrated.

LEONTES   You are married?

FLORIZELL

    We are not (Sir) nor are we like to be:

    The Starres (I see) will kisse the Valleyes first:

    The oddes for high and low's alike.

LEONTES   My Lord,

    Is this the Daughter of a King?

2660 FLORIZELL   She is,

    When once she is my Wife.

LEONTES

    That once (I see) by your good Fathers speed,

    Will come-on very slowly. I am sorry

    (Most sorry) you haue broken from his liking,

    Where you were ty'd in dutie: and as sorry,

    Your Choise is not so rich in Worth, as Beautie,

    That you might well enioy her.

FLORIZELL (*to Perdita*)   Deare, looke vp:

    Though *Fortune*, visible an Enemie,

    Should chase vs, with my Father; powre no iot

2670 Hath she to change our Loues. Beseech you (Sir)

    Remember, since you ow'd no more to Time

    Then I doe now: with thought of such Affections,

    Step forth mine Aduocate: at your request,

    My Father will graunt precious things, as Trifles.

LEONTES

    Would he doe so, I'ld beg your precious Mistris,

    Which he counts but a Trifle.

PAULINA   Sir (my Liege)

    Your eye hath too much youth in't: not a moneth

    'Fore your Queene dy'd, she was more worth such

        gazes,

    Then what you looke on now.

LEONTES   I thought of her,

    Euen in these Lookes I made. (*To Florizell*) But your

2680   Petition

    Is yet vn-answer'd: I will to your Father:

    Your Honor not o're-throwne by your desires,

    I am friend to them, and you: Vpon which Errand

    I now goe toward him: therefore follow me,

    And marke what way I make: Come good my Lord.

                           Exeunt

5.2   *Enter Autolicus, and a Gentleman*

(Sc. 14) AUTOLICUS Beseech you (Sir) were you present at this

    Relation?

    I. GENTLEMAN I was by at the opening of the Farthell,

    heard the old Shepheard deliuer the manner how he

found it: Whereupon (after a little amazednesse) we 2690

were all commanded out of the Chamber: onely this

(me thought) I heard the Shepheard say, he found the

Child.

AUTOLICUS I would most gladly know the issue of it.

I. GENTLEMAN I make a broken deliuerie of the Businesse;

but the changes I perceiued in the King, and *Camillo*,

were very Notes of admiration: they seem'd almost,

with staring on one another, to teare the Cases of their

Eyes. There was speech in their dumbnesse, Language

in their very gesture: they look'd as they had heard of 2700

a World ransom'd, or one destroyed: a notable passion

of Wonder appeared in them: but the wisest beholder,

that knew no more but seeing, could not say, if

th'importance were Ioy, or Sorrow; but in the

extremitie of the one, it must needs be.

    Enter another Gentleman

Here comes a Gentleman, that happily knowes more:

The Newes, *Rogero*.

2. GENTLEMAN Nothing but Bon-fires: the Oracle is

fulfill'd: the Kings Daughter is found: such a deale of

wonder is broken out within this houre, that Ballad- 2710

makers cannot be able to expresse it.

    Enter another Gentleman

Here comes the Lady *Paulina's* Steward, hee can deliuer

you more. How goes it now (Sir.) This Newes (which

is call'd true) is so like an old Tale, that the veritie of

it is in strong suspition: Ha's the King found his Heire?

3. GENTLEMAN Most true, if euer Truth were pregnant by

Circumstance: That which you heare, you'le sweare

you see, there is such vnitie in the proofes. The Mantle

of Queene *Hermiones*: her Iewell about the Neck of it:

the Letters of *Antigonus* found with it, which they know 2720

to be his Character: the Maiestie of the Creature, in

resemblance of the Mother: the Affection of Noblenesse,

which Nature shewes aboue her Breeding, and many

other Euidences, proclayme her, with all certaintie, to

be the Kings Daughter. Did you see the meeting of the

two Kings?

2. GENTLEMAN No.

3. GENTLEMAN Then haue you lost a Sight which was to

bee seene, cannot bee spoken of. There might you haue

beheld one Ioy crowne another, so and in such manner, 2730

that it seem'd Sorrow wept to take leaue of them: for

their Ioy waded in teares. There was casting vp of Eyes,

holding vp of Hands, with Countenance of such

distraction, that they were to be knowne by Garment,

not by Fauor. Our King being ready to leape out of

himselfe, for ioy of his found Daughter; as if that Ioy

were now become a Losse, cryes, Oh, thy Mother, thy

Mother: then askes *Bohemia* forgiuenesse, then

embraces his Sonne-in-Law: then againe worryes he

his Daughter, with clipping her. Now he thanks the 2740

old Shepheard (which stands by, like a Weather-bitten

Conduit, of many Kings Reignes.) I neuer heard of such

another Encounter; which lames Report to follow it,

and vndo's description to doe it.

2. GENTLEMAN What, 'pray you, became of *Antigonus*, that carryed hence the Child?

3. GENTLEMAN Like an old Tale still, which will haue matter to rehearse, though Credit be asleepe, and not an eare open; he was torne to pieces with a Beare: 2750 This auouches the Shepheards Sonne; who ha's not onely his Innocence (which seemes much) to iustifie him, but a Hand-kerchiefe and Rings of his, that *Paulina* knowes.

1. GENTLEMAN What became of his Barke, and his Followers?

3. GENTLEMAN Wrackt the same instant of their Masters death, and in the view of the Shepheard: so that all the Instruments which ayded to expose the Child, were euen then lost, when it was found. But oh the Noble 2760 Combat, that 'twixt Ioy and Sorrow was fought in *Paulina*. Shee had one Eye declin'd for the losse of her Husband, another eleuated, that the Oracle was fulfill'd: Shee lifted the Princesse from the Earth, and so locks her in embracing, as if shee would pin her to her heart, that shee might no more be in danger of loosing.

1. GENTLEMAN The Dignitie of this Act was worth the audience of Kings and Princes, for by such was it acted.

3. GENTLEMAN One of the prettyest touches of all, and that which angl'd for mine Eyes (caught the Water, 2770 though not the Fish) was, when at the Relation of the Queenes death (with the manner how shee came to't, brauely confess'd, and lamented by the King) how attentiuenesse wounded his Daughter, till (from one signe of dolour to another) shee did (with an *Alas*) I would faine say, bleed Teares; for I am sure, my heart wept blood. Who was most Marble, there changed colour: some swownded, all sorrowed: if all the World could haue seen't, the Woe had beene vniuersall.

1. GENTLEMAN Are they returned to the Court?

2780 3. GENTLEMAN No: The Princesse hearing of her Mothers Statue (which is in the keeping of *Paulina*) a Peece many yeeres in doing, and now newly perform'd, by that rare Italian Master, *Iulio Romano*, who (had he himselfe Eternitie, and could put Breath into his Worke) would beguile Nature of her Custome, so perfectly he is her Ape: He so neere to *Hermione*, hath done *Hermione*, that they say one would speake to her, and stand in hope of answer. Thither (with all greedinesse of affection) are they gone, and there they intend to 2790 Sup.

2. GENTLEMAN I thought she had some great matter there in hand, for shee hath priuately, twice or thrice a day, euer since the death of *Hermione*, visited that remoued House. Shall wee thither, and with our companie peece the Reioycing?

1. GENTLEMAN Who would be thence, that ha's the benefit of Accesse? euery winke of an Eye, some new Grace will be borne: our Absence makes vs vnthriftie to our Knowledge. Let's along.   *Exeunt Gentlemen*

2800 AUTOLICUS Now (had I not the dash of my former life in me) would Preferment drop on my head. I brought the old man and his Sonne aboord the Prince; told him, I heard them talke of a Farthell, and I know not what: but he at that time ouer-fond of the Shepheards Daughter (so he then tooke her to be) who began to be much Sea-sick, and himselfe little better, extremitie of Weather continuing, this Mysterie remained vndiscouer'd. But 'tis all one to me: for had I beene the finder-out of this Secret, it would not haue rellish'd among my other discredits.   2810

Enter the Old Shepheard and Clowne, dressed as gentlemen

Here come those I haue done good to against my will, and alreadie appearing in the blossomes of their Fortune.

OLD SHEPHEARD Come Boy, I am past moe Children: but thy Sonnes and Daughters will be all Gentlemen borne.

CLOWNE (*to Autolicus*) You are well met (Sir:) you deny'd to fight with mee this other day, because I was no Gentleman borne. See you these Clothes? say you see them not, and thinke me still no Gentleman borne: You were best say these Robes are not Gentlemen 2820 borne. Giue me the Lye: doe: and try whether I am not now a Gentleman borne.

AUTOLICUS I know you are now (Sir) a Gentleman borne.

CLOWNE I, and haue been so any time these foure houres.

OLD SHEPHEARD And so haue I, Boy.

CLOWNE So you haue: but I was a Gentleman borne before my Father: for the Kings Sonne tooke me by the hand, and call'd mee Brother: and then the two Kings call'd my Father Brother: and then the Prince (my Brother) and the Princesse (my Sister) call'd my Father, Father; 2830 and so wee wept: and there was the first Gentleman-like teares that euer we shed.

OLD SHEPHEARD We may liue (Sonne) to shed many more.

CLOWNE I: or else 'twere hard luck, being in so preposterous estate as we are.

AUTOLICUS I humbly beseech you (Sir) to pardon me all the faults I haue committed to your Worship, and to giue me your good report to the Prince my Master.

OLD SHEPHEARD 'Prethee Sonne doe: for we must be gentle, now we are Gentlemen.   2840

CLOWNE Thou wilt amend thy life?

AUTOLICUS I, and it like your good Worship.

CLOWNE Giue me thy hand: I will sweare to the Prince, thou art as honest a true Fellow as any is in *Bohemia*.

OLD SHEPHEARD You may say it, but not sweare it.

CLOWNE Not sweare it, now I am a Gentleman? Let Boores and Francklins say it, Ile sweare it.

OLD SHEPHEARD How if it be false (Sonne?)

CLOWNE If it be ne're so false, a true Gentleman may sweare it, in the behalfe of his Friend: (*To Autolicus*) 2850 And Ile sweare to the Prince, thou art a tall Fellow of thy hands, and that thou wilt not be drunke: but I know thou art no tall Fellow of thy hands, and that thou wilt be drunke: but Ile sweare it, and I would thou would'st be a tall Fellow of thy hands.

AUTOLICUS I will proue so (Sir) to my power.

CLOWNE I, by any meanes proue a tall Fellow: if I do not
wonder, how thou dar'st venture to be drunke, not
being a tall Fellow, trust me not.
⌐Flourish within⌐
2860   Harke, the Kings and Princes (our Kindred) are going
to see the Queenes Picture. Come, follow vs: wee'le be
thy good Masters.   Exeunt

5.3   Enter Leontes, Polixenes, Florizell, Perdita, Camillo,
c. 15)   Paulina, Lords, &c.
LEONTES
O graue and good Paulina, the great comfort
That I haue had of thee?
PAULINA   What (Soueraigne Sir)
I did not well, I meant well: all my Seruices
You haue pay'd home. But that you haue vouchsaf'd
(With your Crown'd Brother, and these young
contracted
Heires of your Kingdomes) my poore House to visit;
It is a surplus of your Grace, which neuer
My life may last to answere.
2870   LEONTES   O Paulina,
We honor you with trouble: but we came
To see the Statue of our Queene. Your Gallerie
Haue we pass'd through, not without much content
In many singularities; but we saw not
That which my Daughter came to looke vpon,
The Statue of her Mother.
PAULINA   As she liu'd peerelesse,
So her dead likenesse I doe well beleeue
Excells what euer yet you look'd vpon,
Or hand of Man hath done: therefore I keepe it
2880   Lonely, apart. But here it is: prepare
To see the Life as liuely mock'd, as euer
Still Sleepe mock'd Death: behold, and say 'tis well.
She draws a Curtaine and reueals the figure of
Hermione, standing like a Statue
I like your silence, it the more shewes-off
Your wonder: but yet speake, first you (my Liege)
Comes it not something neere?
LEONTES   Her naturall Posture.
Chide me (deare Stone) that I may say indeed
Thou art Hermione; or rather, thou art she,
In thy not chiding: for she was as tender
As Infancie, and Grace. But yet (Paulina)
2890   Hermione was not so much wrinckled, nothing
So aged as this seemes.
POLIXENES   Oh, not by much.
PAULINA
So much the more our Caruers excellence,
Which lets goe-by some sixteene yeeres, and makes her
As she liu'd now.
LEONTES   As now she might haue done,
So much to my good comfort, as it is
Now piercing to my Soule. Oh, thus she stood,
Euen with such Life of Maiestie (warme Life,
As now it coldly stands) when first I woo'd her.

I am asham'd: Do's not the Stone rebuke me,
For being more Stone then it? Oh Royall Peece: 2900
There's Magick in thy Maiestie, which ha's
My Euils coniur'd to remembrance; and
From thy admiring Daughter tooke the Spirits,
Standing like Stone with thee.
PERDITA   And giue me leaue,
And doe not say 'tis Superstition, that
I kneele, and then implore her Blessing. Lady,
Deere Queene, that ended when I but began,
Giue me that hand of yours, to kisse.
PAULINA   O, patience:
The Statue is but newly fix'd; the Colour's
Not dry.   2910
CAMILLO (to Leontes)
My Lord, your Sorrow was too sore lay'd-on,
Which sixteene Winters cannot blow away,
So many Summers dry: scarce any Ioy
Did euer so long liue; no Sorrow,
But kill'd it selfe much sooner.
POLIXENES (to Leontes)   Deere my Brother,
Let him, that was the cause of this, haue powre
To take-off so much griefe from you, as he
Will peece vp in himselfe.
PAULINA (to Leontes)   Indeed my Lord,
If I had thought the sight of my poore Image
Would thus haue wrought you (for the Stone is mine)   2920
Il'd not haue shew'd it.
She makes to draw the Curtaine
LEONTES   Doe not draw the Curtaine.
PAULINA
No longer shall you gaze on't, least your Fancie
May thinke anon, it moues.
LEONTES   Let be, let be:
Would I were dead, but that me thinkes alreadie.
(What was he that did make it?) See (my Lord)
Would you not deeme it breath'd? and that those
veines
Did verily beare blood?
POLIXENES   'Masterly done:
The very Life seemes warme vpon her Lippe.
LEONTES
The fixure of her Eye ha's motion in't,
As we are mock'd with Art.
PAULINA   Ile draw the Curtaine: 2930
My Lord's almost so farre transported, that
Hee'le thinke anon it liues.
LEONTES   Oh sweet Paulina,
Make me to thinke so twentie yeeres together:
No setled Sences of the World can match
The pleasure of that madnesse. Let't alone.
PAULINA
I am sorry (Sir) I haue thus farre stir'd you: but
I could afflict you farther.
LEONTES   Doe Paulina:
For this Affliction ha's a taste as sweet
As any Cordiall comfort. Still me thinkes

2940 There is an ayre comes from her. What fine Chizzell
Could euer yet cut breath? Let no man mock me,
For I will kisse her.

PAULINA   Good my Lord, forbeare:
The ruddinesse vpon her Lippe, is wet:
You'le marre it, if you kisse it; stayne your owne
With Oyly Painting: shall I draw the Curtaine.

LEONTES
No: not these twentie yeeres.

PERDITA   So long could I
Stand-by, a looker-on.

PAULINA   Either forbeare,
Quit presently the Chappell, or resolue you
For more amazement: if you can behold it,
2950 Ile make the Statue moue indeed; descend,
And take you by the hand: but then you'le thinke
(Which I protest against) I am assisted
By wicked Powers.

LEONTES   What you can make her doe,
I am content to looke on: what to speake,
I am content to heare: for 'tis as easie
To make her speake, as moue.

PAULINA   It is requir'd
You doe awake your Faith: then, all stand still:
Or those that thinke it is vnlawfull Businesse
I am about, let them depart.

LEONTES   Proceed:
No foot shall stirre.

2960 PAULINA   Musick; awake her: Strike:
        Musick
(*To Hermione*) 'Tis time: descend: be Stone no more:
        approach:
Strike all that looke vpon with meruaile: Come:
Ile fill your Graue vp: stirre: nay, come away:
Bequeath to Death your numnesse: (for from him,
Deare Life redeemes you) (*to Leontes*) you perceiue she
        stirres:
        Hermione slowly descends
Start not: her Actions shall be holy, as
You heare my Spell is lawfull: doe not shun her,
Vntill you see her dye againe; for then
You kill her double: Nay, present your Hand:
2970 When she was young, you woo'd her: now, in age,
Is she become the Suitor?

LEONTES   Oh, she's warme:
If this be Magick, let it be an Art
Lawfull as Eating.

POLIXENES She embraces him.

CAMILLO She hangs about his necke,
If she pertaine to life, let her speake too.

POLIXENES
I, and make it manifest where she ha's liu'd,
Or how stolne from the dead?

PAULINA   That she is liuing,
Were it but told you, should be hooted at
Like an old Tale: but it appeares she liues,   2980
Though yet she speake not. Marke a little while:
(*To Perdita*) Please you to interpose (faire Madam)
        kneele,
And pray your Mothers blessing: turne good Lady,
Our *Perdita* is found.

HERMIONE   You Gods looke downe,
And from your sacred Viols poure your graces
Vpon my daughters head: Tell me (mine owne)
Where hast thou bin preseru'd? Where liu'd? How
        found
Thy Fathers Court? For thou shalt heare that I
Knowing by *Paulina*, that the Oracle
Gaue hope thou wast in being, haue preseru'd   2990
My selfe, to see the yssue.

PAULINA   There's time enough for that,
Least they desire (vpon this push) to trouble
Your ioyes, with like Relation. Go together
You precious winners all: your exultation
Partake to euery one: I (an old Turtle)
Will wing me to some wither'd bough, and there
My Mate (that's neuer to be found againe)
Lament, till I am lost.

LEONTES   O peace *Paulina*:
Thou shouldst a husband take by my consent,
As I by thine a Wife. This is a Match,   3000
And made betweene's by Vowes. Thou hast found mine,
But how, is to be question'd: for I saw her
(As I thought) dead: and haue (in vaine) said many
A prayer vpon her graue. Ile not seeke farre
(For him, I partly know his minde) to finde thee
An honourable husband. Come *Camillo*,
And take her by the hand: whose worth, and honesty
Is richly noted: and heere iustified
By Vs, a paire of Kings. Let's from this place.
(*To Hermione*) What? looke vpon my Brother: both
        your pardons,   3010
That ere I put betweene your holy lookes
My ill suspition: This your Son-in-law,
And Sonne vnto the King, whom heauens directing
Is troth-plight to your daughter. Good *Paulina*,
Leade vs from hence, where we may leysurely
Each one demand, and answere to his part
Perform'd in this wide gap of Time, since first
We were disseuer'd: Hastily lead away.   *Exeunt*

FINIS

CYMBELINE

OUR first reference to *Cymbeline* is a note by the astrologer Simon Forman that he saw the play, probably not long before his death on 8 September 1611. He refers to the heroine as 'Innogen', and this is her name in the sources; the form 'Imogen', found only in the Folio, appears to be a misprint. The play's courtly tone, and the masque-like quality of, particularly, the episode (5.4) in which Iupiter 'descends in Thunder and Lightning, sitting vppon an Eagle', and 'throwes a Thunder-bolt', suggest that as Shakespeare wrote he may have had in mind the audiences and the stage equipment of the Blackfriars theatre, which his company used from the autumn of 1609; and stylistic evidence places the play about 1610-11. It was first printed in the 1623 Folio, as the last of the tragedies. In fact it is a tragicomedy, or a romance, telling a complex and implausible tale of events which cause the deaths of certain subsidiary characters (Cloten, and the Queene) and bring major characters (including the heroine, Innogen) close to death, but which are miraculously resolved in the reunions and reconciliations of the closing scene.

Shakespeare's plot reflects a wide range of reading. He took his title and setting from the name and reign of the legendary British king Cymbeline, or Cunobelinus, said to have reigned from 33 BC till shortly after the birth of Christ. *Cymbeline* is no chronicle history, but Shakespeare derived some ideas, and many of his characters' names, from accounts of early British history in Holinshed's *Chronicles* and elsewhere. Drawing partially, it seems, on an old play, *The Rare Triumphs of Love and Fortune* (acted 1582, printed 1589), he gives Cymbeline a daughter, Innogen, and a wicked second Queene with a loutish, vicious son, Cloten, whom she wishes to see on the throne in her husband's place. Cymbeline, disapproving of his daughter's marriage to 'a poore, but worthy Gentleman', Posthumus Leonatus, banishes him. The strand of plot showing the outcome of a wager that Posthumus, in Rome, lays on his wife's chastity is indebted, directly or indirectly, to Boccaccio's *Decameron*. Another old play, *Sir Clyomon and Clamydes* (printed in 1599), may have suggested the bizarre scene (4.2) in which Innogen mistakes Cloten's headless body for that of Posthumus; and Holinshed's *History of Scotland* supplied the episode in which Cymbeline's two sons, Guiderius and Aruiragus, helped only by the old man (Belarius) who has brought them up in the wilds of Wales, defeat the entire Roman army.

The tone of *Cymbeline* has puzzled commentators. Its prose and verse style is frequently ornate, sometimes grotesque. Its characterization often seems deliberately artificial. Extremes are violently juxtaposed, most daringly when Innogen, supposed dead, is laid beside Cloten's headless body: the beauty of the verse in which she is mourned, and of the flowers strewn over the bodies, contrasts with the hideous spectacle of the headless corpse; her waking speech is one of Shakespeare's most thrillingly difficult challenges to his performers. The appearance of Iupiter lifts the action to a new level of even greater implausibility, preparing us for the extraordinary series of revelations by which the play advances to its impossibly happy ending. *Cymbeline* has been valued mostly for its portrayal of Innogen, ideal of womanhood to, especially, Victorian readers and theatre-goers. The play as a whole is a fantasy, an experimental exercise in virtuosity.

The Folio text was set from a scribal copy, perhaps prepared by the scrivener Ralph Crane. Either the identity of the scribe, or the nature of what he was copying, changed at line 1154.

THE NAMES OF THE ACTORS

CYMBELINE, King of Britaine

Princesse INNOGEN, his Daughter, later disguised as a Man nam'd Fidele

GUIDERIUS, known as Polidore ⎱ Cymbelines Sonnes, stolen
ARUIRAGUS, known as Cadwall ⎰ by Belarius

QUEENE, Cymbelines Wife, Step-Mother to Innogen

Lord CLOTEN, her Sonne

BELARIUS, a banish'd Lord, calling himselfe Morgan

CORNELIUS, a Physitian

Helene, a LADY attending on Innogen

Two LORDS attending on Cloten

Two GENTLEMEN

Two Britaine CAPTAINES

Two GAOLERS

POSTHUMUS Leonatus, a poore Gentleman, Innogens Husband

PISANIO, his Seruant

PHILARIO, a Friend of Posthumus

IACHIMO, an Italian ⎫
A FRENCHMAN ⎬ Friends of Philario
A DUTCHMAN ⎪
A SPANIARD ⎭

Caius LUCIUS, Ambassador from Rome, later Generall of the Roman Forces

Two Roman SENATORS

Roman TRIBUNES

A Roman CAPTAIN

Philarmonus, a SOOTHSAYER

IUPITER

Ghost of SICILIUS Leonatus, father of Posthumus

Ghost of the MOTHER of Posthumus

Ghosts of the BROTHERS of Posthumus

Lords attending on Cymbeline, Ladies attending on the Queene, Musitians attending on Cloten, Messengers, Souldiers

Cymbeline King of Britaine

Enter two Gentlemen

I. GENTLEMAN

You do not meet a man but Frownes. Our bloods
No more obey the Heauens then our Courtiers
Still seeme, as do's the King.

2. GENTLEMAN   But what's the matter?

I. GENTLEMAN

His daughter, and the heire of's kingdome (whom
He purpos'd to his wiues sole Sonne, a Widdow
That late he married) hath referr'd her selfe
Vnto a poore, but worthy Gentleman. She's wedded,
Her Husband banish'd; she imprison'd, all
Is outward sorrow, though I thinke the King
Be touch'd at very heart.

10 2. GENTLEMAN   None but the King?

I. GENTLEMAN

He that hath lost her too: so is the Queene,
That most desir'd the Match. But not a Courtier,
Although they weare their faces to the bent
Of the Kings lookes, hath a heart that is not
Glad of the thing they scowle at.

2. GENTLEMAN   And why so?

I. GENTLEMAN

He that hath miss'd the Princesse, is a thing
Too bad, for bad report: and he that hath her,
(I meane, that married her, alacke good man,
And therefore banish'd) is a Creature, such,
20 As to seeke through the Regions of the Earth
For one, his like; there would be something failing
In him, that should compare. I do not thinke,
So faire an Outward, and such stuffe Within
Endowes a man, but hee.

2. GENTLEMAN   You speake him farre.

I. GENTLEMAN

I do extend him (Sir) within himselfe,
Crush him together, rather then vnfold
His measure duly.

2. GENTLEMAN   What's his name, and Birth?

I. GENTLEMAN

I cannot delue him to the roote: His Father
Was call'd *Sicillius*, who did ioyne his Honor
30 Against the Romanes, with *Cassibelan*,
But had his Titles by *Tenantius*, whom
He seru'd with Glory, and admir'd Successe:
So gain'd the Sur-addition, *Leonatus*.
And had (besides this Gentleman in question)
Two other Sonnes, who in the Warres o'th'time
Dy'de with their Swords in hand. For which, their
      Father
Then old, and fond of yssue, tooke such sorrow
That he quit Being; and his gentle Lady
Bigge of this Gentleman (our Theame) deceast
40 As he was borne. The King he takes the Babe
To his protection, cals him *Posthumus Leonatus*,

Breedes him, and makes him of his Bed-chamber,
Puts to him all the Learnings that his time
Could make him the receiuer of, which he tooke
As we do ayre, fast as 'twas ministred,
And in's Spring, became a Haruest: Liu'd in Court
(Which rare it is to do) most prais'd, most lou'd,
A sample to the yongest: to th'more Mature,
A glasse that feated them: and to the grauer,
A Childe that guided Dotards. To his Mistris,   50
(For whom he now is banish'd) her owne price
Proclaimes how she esteem'd him; and his Vertue
By her electiō may be truly read,
What kind of man he is.

2. GENTLEMAN   I honor him,
Euen out of your report. But pray you tell me,
Is she sole childe to'th'King?

I. GENTLEMAN   His onely childe:
He had two Sonnes (if this be worth your hearing,
Marke it) the eld'st of them, at three yeares old;
I'th'swathing cloathes the other, from their Nursery
Were stolne, and to this houre, no ghesse in
      knowledge   60
Which way they went.

2. GENTLEMAN How long is this ago?

I. GENTLEMAN Some twenty yeares.

2. GENTLEMAN

That a Kings Children should be so conuey'd,
So slackely guarded, and the search so slow
That could not trace them.

I. GENTLEMAN   Howsoere, 'tis strange,
Or that the negligence may well be laugh'd at:
Yet is it true Sir.

2. GENTLEMAN   I do well beleeue you.

Enter the Queene, Posthumus, and Innogen

I. GENTLEMAN

We must forbeare. Heere comes the Gentleman,
The Queene, and Princesse.   *Exeunt two Gentlemen* 70

QUEENE

No, be assur'd you shall not finde me (Daughter)
After the slander of most Step-Mothers,
Euill-ey'd vnto you. You're my Prisoner, but
Your Gaoler shall deliuer you the keyes
That locke vp your restraint. For you *Posthumus*,
So soone as I can win th'offended King,
I will be knowne your Aduocate: marry yet
The fire of Rage is in him, and 'twere good
You lean'd vnto his Sentence, with what patience
Your wisedome may informe you.

POSTHUMUS   'Please your Highnesse,   80
I will from hence to day.

QUEENE   You know the perill:
Ile fetch a turne about the Garden, pittying
The pangs of barr'd Affections, though the King
Hath charg'd you should not speake together.   *Exit*

INNOGEN
 O dissembling Curtesie! How fine this Tyrant
 Can tickle where she wounds? My deerest Husband,
 I something feare my Fathers wrath, but nothing
 (Always reseru'd my holy duty) what
 His rage can do on me. You must be gone,
90 And I shall heere abide the hourely shot
 Of angry eyes: not comforted to liue,
 But that there is this Iewell in the world,
 That I may see againe.

POSTHUMUS   My Queene, my Mistris:
 O Lady, weepe no more, least I giue cause
 To be suspected of more tendernesse
 Then doth become a man. I will remaine
 The loyall'st husband, that did ere plight troth.
 My residence in Rome, at one *Filario's*,
 Who, to my Father was a Friend, to me
100 Knowne but by Letter; thither write (my Queene)
 And with mine eyes, Ile drinke the words you send,
 Though Inke be made of Gall.
   Enter Queene

QUEENE   Be briefe, I pray you:
 If the King come, I shall incurre, I know not
 How much of his displeasure: (*aside*) yet Ile moue him
 To walke this way: I neuer do him wrong,
 But he do's buy my Iniuries, to be Friends:
 Payes deere for my offences.   *Exit*

POSTHUMUS   Should we be taking leaue
 As long a terme as yet we haue to liue,
 The loathnesse to depart, would grow: Adieu.

110 INNOGEN Nay, stay a little:
 Were you but riding forth to ayre your selfe,
 Such parting were too petty. Looke heere (Loue)
 This Diamond was my Mothers; take it (Heart)
   She giues him a Ring
 But keepe it till you woo another Wife,
 When *Innogen* is dead.

POSTHUMUS   How, how? Another?
 You gentle Gods, giue me but this I haue,
 And seare vp my embracements from a next,
 With bonds of death. Remaine, remaine thou heere,
   He puts on the Ring
 While sense can keepe it on: And sweetest, fairest,
120 As I (my poore selfe) did exchange for you
 To your so infinite losse; so in our trifles
 I still winne of you. For my sake weare this,
   He giues her a Bracelet
 It is a Manacle of Loue, Ile place it
 Vpon this fayrest Prisoner.

INNOGEN   O the Gods!
 When shall we see againe?
   Enter Cymbeline, and Lords

POSTHUMUS   Alacke, the King.

CYMBELINE
 Thou basest thing, auoyd hence, from my sight:
 If after this command thou fraught the Court
 With thy vnworthinesse, thou dyest. Away,
 Thou'rt poyson to my blood.

POSTHUMUS   The Gods protect you,

 And blesse the good Remainders of the Court:
 I am gone.   *Exit* 130

INNOGEN   There cannot be a pinch in death
 More sharpe then this is.

CYMBELINE   O disloyall thing,
 That should'st repayre my youth, thou heap'st
 A yeares age on mee.

INNOGEN   I beseech you Sir,
 Harme not your selfe with your vexation,
 I am senselesse of your Wrath; a Touch more rare
 Subdues all pangs, all feares.

CYMBELINE   Past Grace? Obedience?

INNOGEN
 Past hope, and in dispaire, that way past Grace.

CYMBELINE
 That might'st haue had the sole Sonne of my Queene.

INNOGEN
 O bless'd, that I might not: I chose an Eagle, 140
 And did auoyd a Puttocke.

CYMBELINE
 Thou took'st a Begger, would'st haue made my Throne,
 A Seate for basenesse.

INNOGEN   No, I rather added
 A lustre to it.

CYMBELINE   O thou vilde one!

INNOGEN   Sir,
 It is your fault that I haue lou'd *Posthumus*:
 You bred him as my Play-fellow, and he is
 A man, worth any woman: Ouer-buyes mee
 Almost the summe he payes.

CYMBELINE   What? art thou mad?

INNOGEN
 Almost Sir: Heauen restore me: would I were
 A Neat-heards Daughter, and my *Leonatus* 150
 Our Neighbour-Shepheards Sonne.
   Enter Queene

CYMBELINE   Thou foolish thing;
 (*To Queene*) They were againe together: you haue done
 Not after our command. (*To Lords*) Away with her,
 And pen her vp.

QUEENE   Beseech your patience: Peace
 Deere Lady daughter, peace. Sweet Soueraigne,
 Leaue vs to our selues, and make your self some comfort
 Out of your best aduice.

CYMBELINE   Nay, let her languish
 A drop of blood a day, and being aged
 Dye of this Folly.   *Exit with Lords*

QUEENE   Fye, you must giue way:
   Enter Pisanio
 Heere is your Seruant. How now Sir? What newes? 160

PISANIO
 My Lord your Sonne, drew on my Master.

QUEENE   Hah?
 No harme I trust is done?

PISANIO   There might haue beene,
 But that my Master rather plaid, then fought,
 And had no helpe of Anger: they were parted
 By Gentlemen, at hand.

QUEENE   I am very glad on't.

INNOGEN
Your Son's my Fathers friend, he takes his part
To draw vpon an Exile. O braue Sir,
I would they were in Affricke both together,
My selfe by with a Needle, that I might pricke
The goer backe. (*To Pisanio*) Why came you from your
170   Master?

PISANIO
On his command: he would not suffer mee
To bring him to the Hauen: left these Notes
Of what commands I should be subiect too,
When't pleas'd you to employ me.

QUEENE   This hath beene
Your faithfull Seruant: I dare lay mine Honour
He will remaine so.

PISANIO I humbly thanke your Highnesse.

QUEENE Pray walke a-while.   ⌜*Exit*⌝

INNOGEN
About some halfe houre hence, pray you speake with
        me;
180   You shall (at least) go see my Lord aboord.
For this time leaue me.   *Exeunt seuerally*

1.2   *Enter Clotten, and two Lords*
(Sc. 2)   1. LORD Sir, I would aduise you to shift a Shirt; the
Violence of Action hath made you reek as a Sacrifice:
where ayre comes out, ayre comes in: There's none
abroad so wholesome as that you vent.

CLOTEN If my Shirt were bloody, then to shift it. Haue I
hurt him?

2. LORD (*aside*) No faith: not so much as his patience.

1. LORD Hurt him? His bodie's a passable Carkasse if he
190   bee not hurt. It is a through-fare for Steele if he be not
hurt.

2. LORD (*aside*) His Steele was in debt, it went o'th'Backe-
side the Towne.

CLOTEN The Villaine would not stand me.

2. LORD (*aside*) No, but he fled forward still, toward your
face.

1. LORD Stand you? you haue Land enough of your owne:
But he added to your hauing, gaue you some ground.

2. LORD (*aside*) As many Inches, as you haue Oceans
200   (Puppies.)

CLOTEN I would they had not come betweene vs.

2. LORD (*aside*) So would I, till you had measur'd how
long a Foole you were vpon the ground.

CLOTEN And that shee should loue this Fellow, and refuse
mee.

2. LORD (*aside*) If it be a sin to make a true election, she
is damn'd.

1. LORD Sir, as I told you alwayes: her Beauty & her
Braine go not together. Shee's a good signe, but I haue
210   seene small reflection of her wit.

2. LORD (*aside*) She shines not vpon Fooles, least the
reflection should hurt her.

CLOTEN Come, Ile to my Chamber: would there had beene
some hurt done.

2. LORD (*aside*) I wish not so, vnlesse it had bin the fall
of an Asse, which is no great hurt.

CLOTEN (*to 2. Lord*) You'l go with vs?

1. LORD Ile attend your Lordship.

CLOTEN Nay come, let's go together.

2. LORD Well my Lord.   *Exeunt*   220

Enter Innogen, and Pisanio   **1.3**
(Sc. 3)

INNOGEN
I would thou grew'st vnto the shores o'th'Hauen,
And question'st euery Saile: if he should write,
And I not haue it, 'twere a Paper lost
As offer'd mercy is: What was the last
That he spake to thee?

PISANIO   It was his Queene, his Queene.

INNOGEN
Then wau'd his Handkerchiefe?

PISANIO   And kist it, Madam.

INNOGEN
Senselesse Linnen, happier therein then I:
And that was all?

PISANIO   No Madam: for so long
As he could make me with this eye, or eare,
Distinguish him from others, he did keepe   230
The Decke, with Gloue, or Hat, or Handkerchife,
Still wauing, as the fits and stirres of's mind
Could best expresse how slow his Soule sayl'd on,
How swift his Ship.

INNOGEN   Thou should'st haue made him
As little as a Crow, or lesse, ere left
To after-eye him.

PISANIO   Madam, so I did.

INNOGEN
I would haue broke mine eye-strings; crack'd them,
        but
To looke vpon him, till the diminution
Of space, had pointed him sharpe as my Needle:
Nay, followed him, till he had melted from   240
The smalnesse of a Gnat, to ayre: and then
Haue turn'd mine eye, and wept. But good *Pisanio*,
When shall we heare from him.

PISANIO Be assur'd Madam,
With his next vantage.

INNOGEN
I did not take my leaue of him, but had
Most pretty things to say: Ere I could tell him
How I would thinke on him at certaine houres,
Such thoughts, and such: Or I could make him
        sweare,
The Shees of Italy should not betray   250
Mine Interest, and his Honour: or haue charg'd him
At the sixt houre of Morne, at Noone, at Midnight,
T'encounter me with Orisons, for then
I am in Heauen for him: Or ere I could,
Giue him that parting kisse, which I had set
Betwixt two charming words, comes in my Father,
And like the Tyrannous breathing of the North,
Shakes all our buddes from growing.

Enter a Lady

LADY   The Queene (Madam)
Desires your Highnesse Company.

INNOGEN (*to Pisanio*)
260   Those things I bid you do, get them dispatch'd,
       I will attend the Queene.
PISANIO   Madam, I shall.
                *Exeunt Innogen and Lady at one doore,
                                Pisanio at another*

1.4   ⌈*A Table brought out, with a Banket vpon it.*⌉ *Enter
(Sc. 4) Philario, Iachimo: a Frenchman, a Dutchman, and
         a Spaniard*

IACHIMO Beleeue it Sir, I haue seene him in Britaine; hee
       was then of a Cressent note, expected to proue so
       woorthy, as since he hath beene allowed the name of.
       But I could then haue look'd on him, without the help
       of Admiration, though the Catalogue of his endowments
       had bin tabled by his side, and I to peruse him by
       Items.
270   PHILARIO You speake of him when he was lesse furnish'd,
       then now hee is, with that which makes him both
       without, and within.
       FRENCHMAN I haue seene him in France: wee had very
       many there, could behold the Sunne, with as firme
       eyes as hee.
       IACHIMO This matter of marrying his Kings Daughter,
       wherein he must be weighed rather by her valew, then
       his owne, words him (I doubt not) a great deale from
       the matter.
280   FRENCHMAN And then his banishment.
       IACHIMO I, and the approbation of those that weepe this
       lamentable diuorce vnder her colours, are wonderfully
       to extend him, be it but to fortifie her iudgement, which
       else an easie battery might lay flat, for taking a Begger
       without lesse quality. But how comes it, he is to
       soiourne with you? How creepes acquaintance?
       PHILARIO His Father and I were Souldiers together, to
       whom I haue bin often bound for no lesse then my life.
                Enter Posthumus
       Heere comes the Britaine. Let him be so entertained
290   among'st you, as suites with Gentlemen of your
       knowing, to a Stranger of his quality. I beseech you all
       be better knowne to this Gentleman, whom I commend
       to you, as a Noble Friend of mine. How Worthy he is,
       I will leaue to appeare hereafter, rather then story him
       in his owne hearing.
       FRENCHMAN (*to Posthumus*) Sir, we haue knowne togither
       in Orleance.
       POSTHUMUS Since when, I haue bin debtor to you for
       courtesies, which I will be euer to pay, and yet pay
300   still.
       FRENCHMAN Sir, you o're-rate my poore kindnesse, I was
       glad I did attone my Countryman and you: it had
       beene pitty you should haue beene put together, with
       so mortall a purpose, as then each bore, vpon
       importance of so slight and triuiall a nature.
       POSTHUMUS By your pardon Sir, I was then a young
       Traueller, rather shun'd to go euen with what I heard,
       then in my euery action to be guided by others
       experiences: but vpon my mended iudgement (if I offend

not to say it is mended) my Quarrell was not altogether   310
slight.
FRENCHMAN Faith yes, to be put to the arbiterment of
Swords, and by such two, that would by all likelyhood
haue confounded one the other, or haue falne both.
IACHIMO Can we with manners, aske what was the
difference?
FRENCHMAN Safely, I thinke, 'twas a contention in
publicke, which may (without contradiction) suffer the
report. It was much like an argument that fell out last
night, where each of vs fell in praise of our Country-   320
Mistresses. This Gentleman, at that time vouching (and
vpon warrant of bloody affirmation) his to be more
Faire, Vertuous, Wise, Chaste, Constant, Qualified, and
lesse attemptible then any, the rarest of our Ladies in
Fraunce.
IACHIMO That Lady is not now liuing; or this Gentlemans
opinion by this, worne out.
POSTHUMUS She holds her Vertue still, and I my mind.
IACHIMO You must not so farre preferre her, 'fore ours of
Italy.   330
POSTHUMUS Being so farre prouok'd as I was in France: I
would abate her nothing, though I professe my selfe
her Adorer, not her Friend.
IACHIMO As faire, and as good: a kind of hand in hand
comparison, had beene something too faire, and too
good for any Lady in Britaine; if she went before others,
I haue seene as that Diamond of yours out-lusters many
I haue beheld, I could not but beleeue she excelled
many: but I haue not seene the most pretious Diamond
that is, nor you the Lady.   340
POSTHUMUS I prais'd her, as I rated her: so do I my Stone.
IACHIMO What do you esteeme it at?
POSTHUMUS More then the world enioyes.
IACHIMO Either your vnparagon'd Mistris is dead, or she's
out-priz'd by a trifle.
POSTHUMUS You are mistaken: the one may be solde or
giuen, or if there were wealth enough for the purchase,
or merite for the guift. The other is not a thing for sale,
and onely the guift of the Gods.
IACHIMO Which the Gods haue giuen you?   350
POSTHUMUS Which by their Graces I will keepe.
IACHIMO You may weare her in title yours: but you know
strange Fowle light vpon neighbouring Ponds. Your
Ring may be stolne too, so your brace of vnprizeable
Estimations, the one is but fraile, and the other Casuall;
A cunning Thiefe, or a (that way) accomplish'd Courtier,
would hazzard the winning both of first and last.
POSTHUMUS Your Italy, containes none so accomplish'd
a Courtier to conuince the Honour of my Mistris: if
in the holding or losse of that, you terme her fraile,   360
I do nothing doubt you haue store of Theeues,
notwithstanding I feare not my Ring.
PHILARIO Let vs leaue heere, Gentlemen?
POSTHUMUS Sir, with all my heart. This worthy Signior I
thanke him, makes no stranger of me, we are familiar
at first.
IACHIMO With fiue times so much conuersation, I should

get ground of your faire Mistris; make her go backe,
euen to the yeilding, had I admittance, and opportunitie
370 to friend.

POSTHUMUS No, no.

IACHIMO I dare thereupon pawne the moytie of my Estate,
to your Ring, which in my opinion o're-values it
something: but I make my wager rather against your
Confidence, then her Reputation. And to barre your
offence heerein to, I durst attempt it against any Lady
in the world.

POSTHUMUS You are a great deale abus'd in too bold a
perswasion, and I doubt not you sustaine what y'are
380 worthy of, by your Attempt.

IACHIMO What's that?

POSTHUMUS A Repulse though your Attempt (as you call
it) deserue more; a punishment too.

PHILARIO Gentlemen enough of this, it came in too
sodainely, let it dye as it was borne, and I pray you be
better acquainted.

IACHIMO Would I had put my Estate, and my Neighbors
on th'approbation of what I haue spoke.

POSTHUMUS What Lady would you chuse to assaile?

390 IACHIMO Yours, whom in constancie you thinke stands
so safe. I will lay you ten thousand Duckets to your
Ring, that commend me to the Court where your Lady
is, with no more aduantage then the opportunitie of a
second conference, and I will bring from thence, that
Honor of hers, which you imagine so reseru'd.

POSTHUMUS I will wage against your Gold, Gold to it: my
Ring I holde deere as my finger, 'tis part of it.

IACHIMO You are a Friend, and therein the wiser: if you
buy Ladies flesh at a Million a Dram, you cannot
400 preserue it from tainting; but I see you haue some
Religion in you, that you feare.

POSTHUMUS This is but a custome in your tongue: you
beare a grauer purpose I hope.

IACHIMO I am the Master of my speeches, and would
vnder-go what's spoken, I sweare.

POSTHUMUS Will you? I shall but lend my Diamond till
your returne: let there be Couenants drawne between's.
My Mistris exceedes in goodnesse, the hugenesse of
your vnworthy thinking. I dare you to this match:
410 heere's my Ring.

PHILARIO I will haue it no lay.

IACHIMO By the Gods it is one: if I bring you no sufficient
testimony that I haue enioy'd the deerest bodily part
of your Mistris: my ten thousand Duckets are yours,
so is your Diamond too: if I come off, and leaue her in
such honour as you haue trust in; Shee your Iewell,
this your Iewell, and my Gold are yours: prouided, I
haue your commendation, for my more free
entertainment.

420 POSTHUMUS I embrace these Conditions, let vs haue
Articles betwixt vs: onely thus farre you shall answere,
if you make your voyage vpon her, and giue me directly
to vnderstand, you haue preuayl'd, I am no further
your Enemy, shee is not worth our debate. If shee
remaine vnseduc'd, you not making it appeare

otherwise: for your ill opinion, and th'assault you haue
made to her chastity, you shall answer me with your
Sword.

IACHIMO Your hand, a Couenant: wee will haue these
things set downe by lawfull Counsell, and straight away   430
for Britaine, least the Bargaine should catch colde, and
sterue: I will fetch my Gold, and haue our two Wagers
recorded.

POSTHUMUS Agreed.   ⌈Exit with Iachimo⌉

FRENCHMAN Will this hold, thinke you.

PHILARIO Signior Iachimo will not from it. Pray let vs
follow 'em.   Exeunt. ⌈Table is remoued⌉

             Enter Queene, Ladies, and Cornelius   1.5

QUEENE   (Sc. 5)
Whiles yet the dewe's on ground, gather those Flowers,
Make haste. Who ha's the note of them?

A LADY   I Madam.

QUEENE Dispatch.   Exit Ladies   440
Now Master Doctor, haue you brought those drugges?

CORNELIUS
Pleaseth your Highnes, I: here they are, Madam:
    He giues her a boxe
But I beseech your Grace, without offence
(My Conscience bids me aske) wherefore you haue
Commanded of me these most poysonous Compounds,
Which are the moouers of a languishing death:
But though slow, deadly.

QUEENE   I wonder, Doctor,
Thou ask'st me such a Question: Haue I not bene
Thy Pupill long? Hast thou not learn'd me how
To make Perfumes? Distill? Preserue? Yea so,   450
That our great King himselfe doth woo me oft
For my Confections? Hauing thus farre proceeded,
(Vnlesse thou think'st me diuellish) is't not meete
That I did amplifie my iudgement in
Other Conclusions? I will try the forces
Of these thy Compounds, on such Creatures as
We count not worth the hanging (but none humane)
To try the vigour of them, and apply
Allayments to their Act, and by them gather
Their seuerall vertues, and effects.

CORNELIUS   Your Highnesse   460
Shall from this practise, but make hard your heart:
Besides, the seeing these effects will be
Both noysome, and infectious.

QUEENE   O content thee.
    Enter Pisanio
(Aside) Heere comes a flattering Rascall, vpon him
Will I first worke: Hee's factor for his Master,
And enemy to my Sonne. (Aloud) How now Pisanio?
Doctor, your seruice for this time is ended,
Take your owne way.

CORNELIUS (aside)   I do suspect you, Madam,
But you shall do no harme.

QUEENE (to Pisanio)   Hearke thee, a word.

CORNELIUS (aside)
I do not like her. She doth thinke she ha's   470

Strange ling'ring poysons: I do know her spirit,
And will not trust one of her malice, with
A drugge of such damn'd Nature. Those she ha's,
Will stupifie and dull the Sense a-while,
Which first (perchance) shee'l proue on Cats and Dogs,
Then afterward vp higher: but there is
No danger in what shew of death it makes,
More then the locking vp the Spirits a time,
To be more fresh, reuiuing. She is fool'd
480   With a most false effect: and I, the truer,
So to be false with her.

QUEENE   No further seruice, Doctor,
Vntill I send for thee.

CORNELIUS   I humbly take my leaue.   *Exit*
QUEENE (*to Pisanio*)
Weepes she still (saist thou?) Dost thou thinke in time
She will not quench, and let instructions enter
Where Folly now possesses? Do thou worke:
When thou shalt bring me word she loues my Sonne,
Ile tell thee on the instant, thou art then
As great as is thy Master: Greater, for
His Fortunes all lye speechlesse, and his name
490   Is at last gaspe. Returne he cannot, nor
Continue where he is: To shift his being,
Is to exchange one misery with another,
And euery day that comes, comes to decay
A dayes worke in him. What shalt thou expect
To be depender on a thing that leanes?
Who cannot be new built, nor ha's no Friends
So much, as but to prop him?
┌She drops her boxe; he takes it vp┐
Thou tak'st vp
Thou know'st not what: But take it for thy labour,
It is a thing I made, which hath the King
500   Fiue times redeem'd from death. I do not know
What is more Cordiall. Nay, I prythee take it,
It is an earnest of a farther good
That I meane to thee. Tell thy Mistris how
The case stands with her: doo't, as from thy selfe;
Thinke what a chance thou changest on, but thinke
Thou hast thy Mistris still, to boote, my Sonne,
Who shall take notice of thee. Ile moue the King
To any shape of thy Preferment, such
As thou'lt desire: and then my selfe, I cheefely,
510   That set thee on to this desert, am bound
To lqade thy merit richly. Call my women.
Thinke on my words.   *Exit Pisanio*
A slye, and constant knaue,
Not to be shak'd: the Agent for his Master,
And the Remembrancer of her, to hold
The hand-fast to her Lord. I haue giuen him that,
Which if he take, shall quite vnpeople her
Of Leidgers for her Sweete: and which, she after
Except she bend her humor, shall be assur'd
To taste of too.
    Enter Pisanio, and Ladies
So, so: Well done, well done:

The Violets, Cowslippes, and the Prime-Roses   520
Beare to my Closset: Fare thee well, *Pisanio*.
Thinke on my words *Pisanio*.

PISANIO   And shall do:
                    Exit Queene and Ladies
But when to my good Lord, I proue vntrue,
Ile choake my selfe: there's all Ile do for you.   *Exit*

    Enter Innogen alone   **1.6**
                                                       (Sc. 6
INNOGEN
A Father cruell, and a Stepdame false,
A Foolish Suitor to a Wedded-Lady,
That hath her Husband banish'd: O, that Husband,
My supreame Crowne of griefe, and those repeated
Vexations of it. Had I bin Theefe-stolne,
As my two Brothers, happy: but most miserable   530
Is the desire that's glorious. Blessed be those
How meane so ere, that haue their honest wills,
Which seasons comfort.
    Enter Pisanio, and Iachimo
                    Who may this be? Fye.

PISANIO
Madam, a Noble Gentleman of Rome,
Comes from my Lord with Letters.

IACHIMO   Change you, Madam:
The Worthy *Leonatus* is in safety,
And greetes your Highnesse deerely.
    He giues her the Letters
INNOGEN   Thanks good Sir,
You're kindly welcome.
    She reades the Letters
IACHIMO (*aside*)
All of her, that is out of doore, most rich:
If she be furnish'd with a mind so rare   540
She is alone, th'Arabian-Bird; and I
Haue lost the wager. Boldnesse be my Friend:
Arme me Audacitie from head to foote,
Or like the Parthian I shall flying fight,
Rather directly fly.

INNOGEN (*reads aloud*) *He is one of the Noblest note, to whose*
kindnesse I am most infinitely tied. Reflect vpon him
accordingly, as you value your truest   Leonatus.
(*To Iachimo*) So farre I reade aloud.
But euen the very middle of my heart   550
Is warm'd by'th'rest, and takes it thankefully.
You are as welcome (worthy Sir) as I
Haue words to bid you, and shall finde it so
In all that I can do.

IACHIMO   Thankes fairest Lady:
What are men mad? Hath Nature giuen them eyes
To see this vaulted Arch, and the rich Crop
Of Sea and Land, which can distinguish 'twixt
The firie Orbes aboue, and the twinn'd Stones
Vpon thunnumber'd Beach, and can we not
Partition make with Spectacles so pretious   560
Twixt faire, and foule?

INNOGEN   What makes your admiration?

IACHIMO
   It cannot be i'th'eye: for Apes, and Monkeys
   'Twixt two such She's, would chatter this way, and
   Contemne with mowes the other. Nor i'th'iudgment:
   For Idiots in this case of fauour, would
   Be wisely definit: Nor i'th'Appetite.
   Sluttery to such neate Excellence, oppos'd
   Should make desire vomit emptinesse,
   Not so allur'd to feed.

570 INNOGEN What is the matter trow?

IACHIMO The Cloyed will:
   That satiate yet vnsatisfi'd desire, that Tub
   Both fill'd and running: Rauening first the Lambe,
   Longs after for the Garbage.

INNOGEN   What, deere Sir,
   Thus rap's you? Are you well?

IACHIMO
   Thanks Madam well: (*To Pisanio*) Beseech you Sir,
   Desire my Man's abode, where I did leaue him:
   He's strange and peeuish.

PISANIO   I was going Sir,
   To giue him welcome.   *Exit*

INNOGEN   Continews well my Lord?
   His health beseech you?

580 IACHIMO   Well, Madam.

INNOGEN
   Is he dispos'd to mirth? I hope he is.

IACHIMO
   Exceeding pleasant: none a stranger there,
   So merry, and so gamesome: he is call'd
   The Britaine Reueller.

INNOGEN   When he was heere
   He did incline to sadnesse, and oft times
   Not knowing why.

IACHIMO   I neuer saw him sad.
   There is a Frenchman his Companion, one
   An eminent Monsieur, that it seemes much loues
   A Gallian-Girle at home. He furnaces
590 The thicke sighes from him; whiles the iolly Britaine,
   (Your Lord I meane) laughes from's free lungs: cries oh,
   Can my sides hold, to think that man who knowes
   By History, Report, or his owne proofe
   What woman is, yea what she cannot choose
   But must be: will's free houres languish
   For assured bondage?

INNOGEN   Will my Lord say so?

IACHIMO
   I Madam, with his eyes in flood with laughter,
   It is a Recreation to be by
   And heare him mocke the Frenchman: but Heauen's
      know
   Some men are much too blame.

600 INNOGEN   Not he I hope.

IACHIMO
   Not he: but yet Heauen's bounty towards him, might
   Be vs'd more thankfully. In himselfe 'tis much;
   In you, which I count his beyond all Tallents.

   Whil'st I am bound to wonder, I am bound
   To pitty too.

INNOGEN   What do you pitty Sir?

IACHIMO
   Two Creatures heartyly.

INNOGEN   Am I one Sir?
   You looke on me: what wrack discerne you in me
   Deserues your pitty?

IACHIMO   Lamentable: what
   To hide me from the radiant Sun, and solace
   I'th'Dungeon by a Snuffe.

INNOGEN   I pray you Sir,   610
   Deliuer with more opennesse your answeres
   To my demands. Why do you pitty me?

IACHIMO That others do,
   (I was about to say) enioy your—but
   It is an office of the Gods to venge it,
   Not mine to speake on't.

INNOGEN   You do seeme to know
   Something of me, or what concernes me; pray you
   Since doubting things go ill, often hurts more
   Then to be sure they do. For Certainties
   Either are past remedies; or timely knowing,   620
   The remedy then borne. Discouer to me
   What both you spur and stop.

IACHIMO   Had I this cheeke
   To bathe my lips vpon: this hand, whose touch,
   (Whose euery touch) would force the Feelers soule
   To'th'oath of loyalty: This obiect, which
   Takes prisoner the wild motion of mine eye,
   Fiering it onely heere, should I (dampn'd then)
   Slauer with lippes as common as the stayres
   That mount the Capitoll: Ioyne gripes, with hands
   Made hard with hourely falshood (falshood as   630
   With labour:) then by peeping in an eye
   Base and illustrious as the smoakie light
   That's fed with stinking Tallow: it were fit
   That all the plagues of Hell should at one time
   Encounter such reuolt.

INNOGEN   My Lord, I feare,
   Has forgot Brittaine.

IACHIMO   And himselfe, not I
   Inclin'd to this intelligence, pronounce
   The Beggery of his change: but 'tis your Graces
   That from my mutest Conscience, to my tongue,
   Charmes this report out.

INNOGEN   Let me heare no more.   640

IACHIMO
   O deerest Soule: your Cause doth strike my hart
   With pitty, that doth make me sicke. A Lady
   So faire, and fasten'd to an Emperie
   Would make the great'st King double, to be partner'd
   With Tomboyes hyr'd, with that selfe exhibition
   Which your owne Coffers yeeld: with diseas'd ventures
   That play with all Infirmities for Gold,
   Which rottennesse can lend to Nature. Such boyl'd
      stuffe

As well might poyson Poyson. Be reueng'd,
650　Or she that bore you, was no Queene, and you
Recoyle from your great Stocke.

INNOGEN　　　　　　　　　　Reueng'd:
How should I be reueng'd? If this be true,
(As I haue such a Heart, that both mine eares
Must not in haste abuse) if it be true,
How should I be reueng'd?

IACHIMO　　　　　　　　　Should he make me
Liue like *Diana's* Priest, betwixt cold sheets,
Whiles he is vaulting variable Rampes
In your despight, vpon your purse: reuenge it.
I dedicate my selfe to your sweet pleasure,
660　More Noble then that runnagate to your bed,
And will continue fast to your Affection,
Still close, as sure.

INNOGEN　　　　　　　What hoa, *Pisanio?*

IACHIMO
Let me my seruice tender on your lippes.

INNOGEN
Away, I do condemne mine eares, that haue
So long attended thee. If thou wert Honourable
Thou would'st haue told this tale for Vertue, not
For such an end thou seek'st, as base, as strange:
Thou wrong'st a Gentleman, who is as farre
From thy report, as thou from Honor: and
670　Solicites heere a Lady, that disdaines
Thee, and the Diuell alike. What hoa, *Pisanio?*
The King my Father shall be made acquainted
Of thy Assault: if he shall thinke it fit,
A sawcy Stranger in his Court, to Mart
As in a Romish Stew, and to expound
His beastly minde to vs; he hath a Court
He little cares for, and a Daughter, who
He not respects at all. What hoa, *Pisanio?*

IACHIMO
O happy *Leonatus* I may say,
680　The credit that thy Lady hath of thee
Deserues thy trust, and thy most perfect goodnesse
Her assur'd credit. Blessed liue you long,
A Lady to the worthiest Sir, that euer
Country call'd his; and you his Mistris, onely
For the most worthiest fit. Giue me your pardon,
I haue spoke this to know if your Affiance
Were deeply rooted, and shall make your Lord,
That which he is, new o're: And he is one
The truest manner'd: such a holy Witch,
690　That he enchants Societies into him:
Halfe all mens hearts are his.

INNOGEN　　　　　　　You make amends.

IACHIMO
He sits 'mongst men, like a desended God;
He hath a kinde of Honor sets him off,
More then a mortall seeming. Be not angrie
(Most mighty Princesse) that I haue aduentur'd
To try your taking of a false report, which hath
Honour'd with confirmation your great Iudgement,
In the election of a Sir, so rare,

Which you know, cannot erre. The loue I beare him,
Made me to fan you thus, but the Gods made you　　700
(Vnlike all others) chaffelesse. Pray your pardon.

INNOGEN
All's well Sir: take my powre i'th'Court for yours.

IACHIMO
My humble thankes: I had almost forgot
T'intreat your Grace, but in a small request,
And yet of moment too, for it concernes
Your Lord, my selfe, and other Noble Friends
Are partners in the businesse.

INNOGEN　　　　　　　Pray what is't?

IACHIMO
Some dozen Romanes of vs, and your Lord
(Best Feather of our wing) haue mingled summes
To buy a Present for the Emperor:　　　　　　　710
Which I (the Factor for the rest) haue done
In France: 'tis Plate of rare deuice, and Iewels
Of rich, and exquisite forme, their valewes great,
And I am something curious, being strange
To haue them in safe stowage: May it please you
To take them in protection.

INNOGEN　　　　　　　Willingly:
And pawne mine Honor for their safety, since
My Lord hath interest in them, I will keepe them
In my Bed-chamber.

IACHIMO　　　　　　　They are in a Trunke
Attended by my men: I will make bold　　　　　720
To send them to you, onely for this night:
I must aboord to morrow.

INNOGEN　　　　　　　O no, no.

IACHIMO
Yes I beseech: or I shall short my word
By length'ning my returne. From Gallia,
I crost the Seas on purpose, and on promise
To see your Grace.

INNOGEN　　　　　　　I thanke you for your paines:
But not away to morrow.

IACHIMO　　　　　　　O I must Madam.
Therefore I shall beseech you, if you please
To greet your Lord with writing, doo't to night,
I haue out-stood my time, which is materiall　　730
To'th'tender of our Present.

INNOGEN　　　　　　　I will write:
Send your Trunke to me, it shall safe be kept,
And truely yeelded you: you're very welcome.

　　　　　　　　　　　　Exeunt seuerally

✦

Enter Clotten, and the two Lords　　　　　　2.1

CLOTEN　Was there euer man had such lucke? when I kist　(Sc. 7)
the Iacke vpon an vp-cast, to be hit away? I had a
hundred pound on't: and then a whorson Iacke-an-
Apes, must take me vp for swearing, as if I borrowed
mine oathes of him, and might not spend them at my
pleasure.

1. LORD　What got he by that? you haue broke his pate　740
with your Bowle.

2. LORD (*aside*) If his wit had bin like him that broke it:
it would haue run all out.

CLOTEN When a Gentleman is dispos'd to sweare: it is not
for any standers by to curtall his oathes. Ha?

2. LORD No my Lord; (*aside*) nor crop the eares of them.

CLOTEN Whorson dog: I giue him satisfaction? would he
had bin one of my Ranke.

2. LORD (*aside*) To haue smell'd like a Foole.

750 CLOTEN I am not vext more at any thing in th'earth: a
pox on't. I had rather not be so Noble as I am: they
dare not fight with me, because of the Queene my
Mother: euery Iacke-Slaue hath his belly full of
Fighting, and I must go vp and downe like a Cock, that
no body can match.

2. LORD (*aside*) You are Cocke and Capon too, and you
crow Cock, with your combe on.

CLOTEN Sayest thou?

2. LORD It is not fit your Lordship should vndertake euery
760 Companion, that you giue offence too.

CLOTEN No, I know that: but it is fit I should commit
offence to my inferiors.

2. LORD I, it is fit for your Lordship onely.

CLOTEN Why so I say.

I. LORD Did you heere of a Stranger that's come to Court
to night?

CLOTEN A Stranger, and I not know on't?

2. LORD (*aside*) He's a strange Fellow himselfe, and knowes
it not.

770 I. LORD There's an Italian come, and 'tis thought one of
Leonatus Friends.

CLOTEN *Leonatus?* A banisht Rascall; and he's another,
whatsoeuer he be. Who told you of this Stranger?

I. LORD One of your Lordships Pages.

CLOTEN Is it fit I went to looke vpon him? Is there no
derogation in't?

2. LORD You cannot derogate my Lord.

CLOTEN Not easily I thinke.

2. LORD (*aside*) You are a Foole graunted, therefore your
780 Issues being foolish do not derogate.

CLOTEN Come, Ile go see this Italian: what I haue lost to
day at Bowles, Ile winne to night of him. Come: go.

2. LORD Ile attend your Lordship.

Exit Cloten and I. Lord

That such a craftie Diuell as is his Mother
Should yeild the world this Asse: A woman, that
Beares all downe with her Braine, and this her Sonne,
Cannot take two from twenty for his heart,
And leaue eighteene. Alas poore Princesse,
Thou diuine *Innogen*, what thou endur'st,
790 Betwixt a Father by thy Step-dame gouern'd,
A Mother hourely coyning plots: A Wooer,
More hatefull then the foule expulsion is
Of thy deere Husband, then that horrid Act
Of the diuorce, heel'd make. The Heauens hold firme
The walls of thy deere Honour: Keepe vnshak'd
That Temple thy faire mind, that thou maist stand
T'enioy thy banish'd Lord: and this great Land.   *Exit*

A Trunke ⌈and Arras⌉. A Bed is ⌈thrust forth⌉, with   **2.2**
Innogen in it reading a book; enter to her a Lady   **(Sc. 8)**

INNOGEN
Who's there? My woman: *Helene?*

LADY   Please you Madam.

INNOGEN
What houre is it?

LADY   Almost midnight, Madam.

INNOGEN
I haue read three houres then: mine eyes are weake,   800
Fold downe the leafe where I haue left: to bed.
Take not away the Taper, leaue it burning:
And if thou canst awake by foure o'th'clock,
I prythee call me: Sleepe hath ceiz'd me wholly.

⌈*Exit Lady*⌉

To your protection I commend me, Gods,
From Fayries, and the Tempters of the night,
Guard me beseech yee.   *Sleepes*

Iachimo comes from the Trunke

IACHIMO
The Crickets sing, and mans ore-labor'd sense
Repaires it selfe by rest: Our *Tarquine* thus
Did softly presse the Rushes, ere he waken'd   810
The Chastitie he wounded. *Cytherea,*
How brauely thou becom'st thy Bed; fresh Lilly,
And whiter then the Sheetes: that I might touch,
But kisse, one kisse. Rubies vnparagon'd,
How deerely they doo't: 'Tis her breathing that
Perfumes the Chamber thus: the Flame o'th'Taper
Bowes toward her, and would vnder-peepe her lids,
To see th'inclosed Lights, now Canopied
Vnder these windowes, White and Azure lac'd
With Blew of Heauens owne tinct. But my designe?   820
To note the Chamber, I will write all downe,

He writes in his Tables

Such, and such pictures: There the window, such
Th'adornement of her Bed; the Arras, Figures,
Why such, and such: and the Contents o'th'Story.
Ah, but some naturall notes about her Body,
Aboue ten thousand meaner Moueables
Would testifie, t'enrich mine Inuentorie.
O sleepe, thou Ape of death, lye dull vpon her,
And be her Sense but as a Monument,
Thus in a Chappell lying. Come off, come off;   830
As slippery as the Gordian-knot was hard.

He takes the Bracelet from her Arme

'Tis mine, and this will witnesse outwardly,
As strongly as the Conscience do's within:
To'th'madding of her Lord. On her left brest
A mole Cinque-spotted: Like the Crimson drops
I'th'bottome of a Cowslippe. Heere's a Voucher,
Stronger then euer Law could make; this Secret
Will force him thinke I haue pick'd the lock, and t'ane
The treasure of her Honour. No more: to what end?
Why should I write this downe, that's riueted,   840
Screw'd to my memorie. She hath bin reading late,
The Tale of *Tereus*, heere the leaffe's turn'd downe

Where *Philomele* gaue vp. I haue enough,
To'th'Truncke againe, and shut the spring of it.
Swift, swift, you Dragons of the night, that dawning
May bare the Rauens eye: I lodge in feare,
Though this a heauenly Angell: hell is heere.

Clocke strikes

One, two, three: time, time.

*Exit into the Trunke; ⌈the Bed
and Trunke are remoued⌉*

2.3   *Enter Clotten, and the two Lords*
(Sc. 9)
850   1. LORD Your Lordship is the most patient man in losse,
        the most coldest that euer turn'd vp Ace.

CLOTEN It would make any man cold to loose.

1. LORD But not euery man patient after the noble temper
of your Lordship; You are most hot, and furious when
you winne.

CLOTEN Winning will put any man into courage: if I could
get this foolish *Innogen*, I should haue Gold enough:
it's almost morning, is't not?

1. LORD Day, my Lord.

CLOTEN I would this Musicke would come: I am aduised
860   to giue her Musicke a mornings, they say it will
penetrate.

Enter Musitians

Come on, tune: If you can penetrate her with your
fingering, so: wee'l try with tongue too: if none will
do, let her remaine: but Ile neuer giue o're. First, a
very excellent good conceyted thing; after a wonderful
sweet aire, with admirable rich words to it, and then
let her consider.

⌈*Musicke*⌉

SONG

⌈MUSITIAN⌉

Hearke, hearke, the Larke at Heauen gate sings,
    and *Phœbus* gins arise,
870   His Steeds to water at those Springs
    on chalic'd Flowres that lyes:
And winking Mary-buds begin to ope their Golden eyes:
With euery thing that pretty is, my Lady sweet arise:
    Arise, arise.

CLOTEN So, get you gone: if this penetrate, I will consider
your Musicke the better: but if it do not, it is a vyce in her
eares which Horse-haires, and Calues-guts, nor the
voyce of vnpaued Eunuch to boot, can neuer amend.

Exeunt Musitians

Enter Cymbaline, and Queene

2. LORD Heere comes the King.

880   CLOTEN I am glad I was vp so late, for that's the reason
I was vp so earely: he cannot choose but take this
Seruice I haue done, fatherly. Good morrow to your
Maiesty, and to my gracious Mother.

CYMBELINE

Attend you here the doore of our stern daughter?
Will she not forth?

CLOTEN I haue assayl'd her with Musickes, but she
vouchsafes no notice.

CYMBELINE

The Exile of her Minion is too new,
She hath not yet forgot him, some more time
Must weare the print of his remembrance out,   890
And then she's yours.

QUEENE (*to Cloten*)   You are most bound to'th'King,
Who let's go by no vantages, that may
Preferre you to his daughter: Frame your selfe
To orderly solicits, and be friended
With aptnesse of the season: make denials
Encrease your Seruices: so seeme, as if
You were inspir'd to do those duties which
You tender to her: that you in all obey her,
Saue when command to your dismission tends,
And therein you are senselesse.

CLOTEN   Senselesse? Not so.   900

Enter a Messenger

MESSENGER (*to Cymbeline*)
So like you (Sir) Ambassadors from Rome;
The one is *Caius Lucius.*

CYMBELINE   A worthy Fellow,
Albeit he comes on angry purpose now;
But that's no fault of his: we must receyue him
According to the Honor of his Sender,
And towards himselfe, his goodnesse fore-spent on vs
We must extend our notice: Our deere Sonne,
When you haue giuen good morning to your Mistris,
Attend the Queene, and vs, we shall haue neede
T'employ you towards this Romane. Come our Queene.   910

Exeunt all but Cloten

CLOTEN
If she be vp, Ile speake with her: if not
Let her lye still, and dreame:
    ⌈*He knocks*⌉
                        by your leaue, hoa!
I know her women are about her: what
If I do line one of their hands, 'tis Gold
Which buyes admittance (oft it doth) yea, and makes
Diana's Rangers false themselues, yeeld vp
Their Deere to'th'stand o'th'Stealer: and 'tis Gold
Which makes the True-man kill'd, and saues the
    Theefe:
Nay, sometime hangs both Theefe, and True-man: what
Can it not do, and vndoo? I will make   920
One of her women Lawyer to me, for
I yet not vnderstand the case my selfe.
By your leaue.

Knockes. Enter a Lady

LADY
Who's there that knockes?

CLOTEN   A Gentleman.

LADY   No more.

CLOTEN
Yes, and a Gentlewomans Sonne.

LADY   That's more
⌈*Aside*⌉ Then some whose Taylors are as deere as yours,
Can iustly boast of: (*to him*) what's your Lordships
    pleasure?

CLOTEN
  Your Ladies person, is she ready?
LADY   I,
  ⌈Aside⌉ To keepe her Chamber.
CLOTEN   There is Gold for you,
930 Sell me your good report.
LADY
  How, my good name? or to report of you
  What I shall thinke is good.
        Enter Innogen
                        The Princesse.   ⌈Exit⌉
CLOTEN
  Good morrow fairest, Sister your sweet hand.
INNOGEN
  Good morrow Sir, you lay out too much paines
  For purchasing but trouble: the thankes I giue,
  Is telling you that I am poore of thankes,
  And scarse can spare them.
CLOTEN   Still I sweare I loue you.
INNOGEN
  If you but said so, 'twere as deepe with me:
  If you sweare still, your recompence is still
  That I regard it not.
940 CLOTEN   This is no answer.
INNOGEN
  But that you shall not say, I yeeld being silent,
  I would not speake. I pray you spare me, 'faith
  I shall vnfold equall discourtesie
  To your best kindnesse: one of your great knowing
  Should learne (being taught) forbearance.
CLOTEN
  To leaue you in your madnesse, 'twere my sin,
  I will not.
INNOGEN   Fooles cure not mad Folkes.
CLOTEN
  Do you call me Foole?
INNOGEN   As I am mad I do:
  If you'l be patient, Ile no more be mad,
950 That cures vs both. I am much sorry (Sir)
  You put me to forget a Ladies manners
  By being so verball: and learne now, for all,
  That I which know my heart, do heere pronounce
  By th'very truth of it, I care not for you,
  And am so neere the lacke of Charitie
  To accuse my selfe, I hate you: which I had rather
  You felt, then make't my boast.
CLOTEN   You sinne against
  Obedience, which you owe your Father, for
  The Contract you pretend with that base Wretch,
960 One, bred of Almes, and foster'd with cold dishes,
  With scraps o'th'Court: It is no Contract, none;
  And though it be allowed in meaner parties
  (Yet who then he more meane) to knit their soules
  (On whom there is no more dependancie
  But Brats and Beggery) in selfe-figur'd knot,
  Yet you are curb'd from that enlargement, by
  The consequence o'th'Crowne, and must not foyle
  The precious note of it; with a base Slaue,

A Hilding for a Liuorie, a Squires Cloth,
A Pantler; not so eminent.
INNOGEN   Prophane Fellow: 970
  Wert thou the Sonne of Iupiter, and no more,
  But what thou art besides: thou wer't too base,
  To be his Groome: thou wer't dignified enough
  Euen to the point of Enuie, If 'twere made
  Comparatiue for your Vertues, to be stil'd
  The vnder Hangman of his Kingdome; and hated
  For being prefer'd so well.
CLOTEN   The South-Fog rot him.
INNOGEN
  He neuer can meete more mischance, then come
  To be but nam'd of thee. His meanest Garment
  That euer hath but clipt his body; is dearer   980
  In my respect, then all the Heires aboue thee,
  Were they all made such men: How now Pisanio?
        Enter Pisanio
CLOTEN His Garment? Now the diuell.
INNOGEN (to Pisanio)
  To Dorothy my woman hie thee presently.
CLOTEN
  His Garment?
INNOGEN (to Pisanio) I am sprighted with a Foole,
  Frighted, and angred worse: Go bid my woman
  Search for a Iewell, that too casually
  Hath left mine Arme: it was thy Masters. Shrew me
  If I would loose it for a Reuenew,
  Of any Kings in Europe. I do think,   990
  I saw't this morning: Confident I am:
  Last night 'twas on mine Arme; I kiss'd it,
  I hope it be not gone, to tell my Lord
  That I kisse aught but he.
PISANIO   'Twill not be lost.
INNOGEN
  I hope so: go and search.   Exit Pisanio
CLOTEN   You haue abus'd me:
  His meanest Garment?
INNOGEN   I, I said so Sir,
  If you will make't an Action, call witnesse to't.
CLOTEN
  I will enforme your Father.
INNOGEN   Your Mother too:
  She's my good Lady; and will concieue, I hope
  But the worst of me. So I leaue you Sir,   1000
  To'th'worst of discontent.   Exit
CLOTEN   Ile be reueng'd:
  His meanest Garment? Well.   Exit

        Enter Posthumus, and Philario   2.4
POSTHUMUS   (Sc. 10)
  Feare it not Sir: I would I were so sure
  To winne the King, as I am bold, her Honour
  Will remaine her's.
PHILARIO   What meanes do you make to him?
POSTHUMUS
  Not any: but abide the change of Time,
  Quake in the present winters state, and wish

That warmer dayes would come: In these sear'd
   hopes
I barely gratifie your loue; they fayling
1010   I must die much your debtor.

PHILARIO
Your very goodnesse, and your company,
Ore-payes all I can do. By this your King,
Hath heard of Great *Augustus*: *Caius Lucius*,
Will do's Commission throughly. And I think
Hee'le grant the Tribute: send th'Arrerages,
Or looke vpon our Romaines, whose remembrance
Is yet fresh in their griefe.

POSTHUMUS   I do beleeue
(Statist though I am none, nor like to be)
That this will proue a Warre; and you shall heare
1020   The Legions now in Gallia, sooner landed
In our not-fearing-Britaine, then haue tydings
Of any penny Tribute paid. Our Countrymen
Are men more order'd, then when *Iulius Cæsar*
Smil'd at their lacke of skill, but found their courage
Worthy his frowning at. Their discipline,
(Now wing-led with their courage) will make knowne
To their Approuers, they are People, such
That mend vpon the world.

    Enter Iachimo

PHILARIO   See *Iachimo.*

POSTHUMUS (*to Iachimo*)
1030   The swiftest Harts, haue posted you by land;
And Windes of all the Corners kiss'd your Sailes,
To make your vessell nimble.

PHILARIO (*to Iachimo*)   Welcome Sir.

POSTHUMUS (*to Iachimo*)
I hope the briefenesse of your answere, made
The speedinesse of your returne.

IACHIMO   Your Lady, is
One of the fayr'st that I haue look'd vpon

POSTHUMUS
And therewithall the best, or let her beauty
Looke through a Casement to allure false hearts,
And be false with them.

IACHIMO   Heere are Letters for you.

POSTHUMUS
Their tenure good I trust.

IACHIMO   'Tis very like.

    Posthumus reads the letters

⌈PHILARIO⌉
Was *Caius Lucius* in the Britaine Court,
When you were there?

1040   IACHIMO   He was expected then,
But not approach'd.

POSTHUMUS   All is well yet,
Sparkles this Stone as it was wont, or is't not
Too dull for your good wearing?

IACHIMO   If I had lost it,
I should haue lost the worth of it in Gold,
Ile make a iourney twice as farre, t'enioy
A second night of such sweet shortnesse, which
Was mine in Britaine, for the Ring is wonne.

POSTHUMUS
The Stones too hard to come by.

IACHIMO   Not a whit,
Your Lady being so easy.

POSTHUMUS   Make not Sir
Your losse, your Sport: I hope you know that we   1050
Must not continue Friends.

IACHIMO   Good Sir, we must
If you keepe Couenant: had I not brought
The knowledge of your Mistris home, I grant
We were to question farther; but I now
Professe my selfe the winner of her Honor,
Together with your Ring; and not the wronger
Of her, or you hauing proceeded but
By both your willes.

POSTHUMUS   If you can mak't apparant
That you haue tasted her in Bed; my hand,
And Ring is yours. If not, the foule opinion   1060
You had of her pure Honour; gaines, or looses,
Your Sword, or mine, or Masterlesse leaues both
To who shall finde them.

IACHIMO   Sir, my Circumstances
Being so nere the Truth, as I will make them,
Must first induce you to beleeue; whose strength
I will confirme with oath, which I doubt not
You'l giue me leaue to spare, when you shall finde
You neede it not.

POSTHUMUS   Proceed.

IACHIMO   First, her Bed-chamber
(Where I confesse I slept not, but professe
Had that was well worth watching) it was hang'd   1070
With Tapistry of Silke, and Siluer, the Story
Proud *Cleopatra*, when she met her Roman,
And *Sidnus* swell'd aboue the Bankes, or for
The presse of Boates, or Pride. A peece of Worke
So brauely done, so rich, that it did striue
In Workemanship, and Value, which I wonder'd
Could be so rarely, and exactly wrought
Such the true life on't was.

POSTHUMUS   This is true:
And this you might haue heard of heere, by me,
Or by some other.

IACHIMO   More particulars   1080
Must iustifie my knowledge.

POSTHUMUS   So they must,
Or doe your Honour iniury.

IACHIMO   The Chimney
Is South the Chamber, and the Chimney-peece
Chaste *Dian*, bathing: neuer saw I figures
So likely to report themselues; the Cutter
Was as another Nature dumbe, out-went her,
Motion, and Breath left out.

POSTHUMUS   This is a thing
Which you might from Relation likewise reape,
Being, as it is, much spoke of.

IACHIMO   The Roofe o'th'Chamber,
With golden Cherubins is fretted. Her Andirons   1090
(I had forgot them) were two winking Cupids

Of Siluer, each on one foote standing, nicely
Depending on their Brands.

POSTHUMUS   This is her Honor:
Let it be granted you haue seene all this (and praise
Be giuen to your remembrance) the description
Of what is in her Chamber, nothing saues
The wager you haue laid.

IACHIMO   Then if you can
Be pale, I begge but leaue to ayre this Iewell: See,
He shewes the Braclet
And now 'tis vp againe: it must be married
To that your Diamond, Ile keepe them.

1100 POSTHUMUS   Ioue—
Once more let me behold it: Is it that
Which I left with her?

IACHIMO   Sir (I thanke her) that:
She stript it from her Arme: I see her yet:
Her pretty Action, did out-sell her guift,
And yet enrich'd it too: she gaue it me,
And said, she priz'd it once.

POSTHUMUS   May be, she pluck'd it off
To send it me.

IACHIMO   She writes so to you? doth shee?

POSTHUMUS
O no, no, no, 'tis true. Heere, take this too,
He giues Iachimo his Ring
It is a Basiliske vnto mine eye,
1110 Killes me to looke on't: Let there be no Honor,
Where there is Beauty: Truth, where semblance: Loue,
Where there's another man. The Vowes of Women,
Of no more bondage be, to where they are made,
Then they are to their Vertues, which is nothing:
O, aboue measure false.

PHILARIO   Haue patience Sir,
And take your Ring againe, 'tis not yet wonne:
It may be probable she lost it: or
Who knowes if one her woman, being corrupted
Hath stolne it from her.

POSTHUMUS   Very true,
1120 And so I hope he came by't: backe my Ring,
He takes his Ring again
Render to me some corporall signe about her
More euident then this: for this was stolne.

IACHIMO
By Iupiter, I had it from her Arme.

POSTHUMUS
Hearke you, he sweares: by Iupiter he sweares.
'Tis true, nay keepe the Ring; 'tis true: I am sure
She would not loose it: her Attendants are
All sworne, and honourable: they induc'd to steale it?
And by a Stranger? No, he hath enioy'd her,
The Cognisance of her incontinencie
Is this: she hath bought the name of Whore, thus
1130   deerly.
He giues Iachimo his Ring
There, take thy hyre, and all the Fiends of Hell
Diuide themselues betweene you.

PHILARIO   Sir, be patient:

This is not strong enough to be beleeu'd
Of one perswaded well of.

POSTHUMUS   Neuer talke on't:
She hath bin colted by him.

IACHIMO   If you seeke
For further satisfying, vnder her Breast
(Worthy the pressing) lyes a Mole, right proud
Of that most delicate Lodging. By my life
I kist it, and it gaue me present hunger
To feede againe, though full. You do remember   1140
This staine vpon her?

POSTHUMUS   I, and it doth confirme
Another staine, as bigge as Hell can hold,
Were there no more but it.

IACHIMO   Will you heare more?

POSTHUMUS
Spare your Arethmaticke, neuer count the Turnes:
Once, and a Million.

IACHIMO   Ile be sworne.

POSTHUMUS   No swearing:
If you will sweare you haue not done't, you lye,
And I will kill thee, if thou do'st deny
Thou'st made me Cuckold.

IACHIMO   Ile deny nothing.

POSTHUMUS
O that I had her heere, to teare her Limb-meale:
I will go there and doo't, i'th'Court, before   1150
Her Father. Ile do something.   *Exit*

PHILARIO   Quite besides
The gouernment of Patience. You haue wonne:
Let's follow, and peruert the present wrath
He hath against himselfe.

IACHIMO   With all my heart.   *Exeunt*

Enter Posthumus   2.5
POSTHUMUS   (Sc. 11)
Is there no way for Men to be, but Women
Must be halfe-workers? We are Bastards all,
And that most venerable man, which I
Did call my Father, was, I know not where
When I was stampt. Some Coyner with his Tooles
Made me a counterfeit: yet my Mother seem'd   1160
The *Dian* of that time: so doth my Wife
The Non-pareill of this. Oh Vengeance, Vengeance!
Me of my lawfull pleasure she restrain'd,
And pray'd me oft forbearance: did it with
A pudencie so Rosie, the sweet view on't
Might well haue warm'd olde Saturne; that I thought
      her
As Chaste, as vn-Sunn'd Snow. Oh, all the Diuels!
This yellow *Iachimo* in an houre, was't not?
Or lesse; at first? Perchance he spoke not, but
Like a full Acorn'd Boare, a Iarmen on,   1170
Cry'de oh, and mounted; found no opposition
But what he look'd for, should oppose, and she
Should from encounter guard. Could I finde out
The Womans part in me, for there's no motion
That tends to vice in man, but I affirme

It is the Womans part: be it Lying, note it,
The womans: Flattering, hers; Deceiuing, hers:
Lust, and ranke thoughts, hers, hers: Reuenges hers:
Ambitions, Couetings, change of Prides, Disdaine,
1180   Nice-longing, Slanders, Mutability;
All Faults that man can name, nay, that Hell knowes,
Why hers, in part, or all: but rather all.
For euen to Vice
They are not constant, but are changing still;
One Vice, but of a minute old, for one
Not halfe so old as that. Ile write against them,
Detest them, curse them: yet 'tis greater Skill
In a true Hate, to pray they haue their will:
The very Diuels cannot plague them better.   *Exit*

❀

3.1   ⌜*Flourish.*⌝ *Enter in State, Cymbeline, Queene,*
(Sc. 12)   *Clotten, and Lords at one doore, and at another,*
               Caius Lucius; and Attendants

    CYMBELINE
1190   Now say, what would *Augustus Cæsar* with vs?
    LUCIUS
       When *Iulius Cæsar* (whose remembrance yet
       Liues in mens eyes, and will to Eares and Tongues
       Be Theame, and hearing euer) was in this Britain,
       And Conquer'd it, *Cassibelan* thine Vnkle
       (Famous in *Cæsars* prayses, no whit lesse
       Then in his Feats deseruing it) for him,
       And his Succession, granted Rome a Tribute,
       Yeerely three thousand pounds; which (by thee) lately
       Is left vntender'd.
    QUEENE   And to kill the meruaile,
       Shall be so euer.
1200 CLOTEN   There will be many *Cæsars*,
       Ere such another *Iulius*: Britaine's a world
       By it selfe, and we will nothing pay
       For wearing our owne Noses.
    QUEENE   That opportunity
       Which then they had to take from's, to resume
       We haue againe. Remember Sir, my Liege,
       The Kings your Ancestors, together with
       The naturall brauery of your Isle, which stands
       As Neptunes Parke, ribb'd, and pal'd in
       With bākes vnskaleable, and roaring Waters,
1210   With Sands that will not beare your Enemies Boates,
       But sucke them vp to'th'Top-mast. A kinde of Conquest
       Cæsar made heere, but made not heere his bragge
       Of Came, and Saw, and Ouer-came: with shame
       (The first that euer touch'd him) he was carried
       From off our Coast, twice beaten: and his Shipping
       (Poore ignorant Baubles) on our terrible Seas
       Like Egge-shels mou'd vpon their Surges, crack'd
       As easily 'gainst our Rockes. For ioy whereof,
       The fam'd *Cassibelan*, who was once at point
1220   (Oh giglet Fortune) to master *Cæsars* Sword,
       Made *Luds-Towne* with reioycing-Fires bright,
       And Britaines strut with Courage.

CLOTEN Come, there's no more Tribute to be paid: our
    Kingdome is stronger then it was at that time: and (as
    I said) there is no mo such *Cæsars*, other of them may
    haue crook'd Noses, but to owe such straite Armes,
    none.
CYMBELINE Son, let your Mother end.
CLOTEN We haue yet many among vs, can gripe as hard
    as *Cassibelan*, I doe not say I am one: but I haue a   1230
    hand. Why Tribute? Why should we pay Tribute? If
    Cæsar can hide the Sun from vs with a Blanket, or put
    the Moon in his pocket, we will pay him Tribute for
    light: else Sir, no more Tribute, pray you now.
CYMBELINE (*to Lucius*) You must know,
       Till the iniurious Romans, did extort
       This Tribute from vs, we were free. *Cæsars* Ambition,
       Which swell'd so much, that it did almost stretch
       The sides o'th'World, against all colour heere,
       Did put the yoake vpon's; which to shake off   1240
       Becomes a warlike people, whom we reckon
       Our selues to be, we do say then to *Cæsar*,
       Our Ancestor was that *Mulmutius*, which
       Ordain'd our Lawes, whose vse the Sword of *Cæsar*
       Hath too much mangled; whose repayre, and franchise,
       Shall (by the power we hold) be our good deed,
       Tho Rome be therfore angry. *Mulmutius* made our
          lawes
       Who was the first of Britaine, which did put
       His browes within a golden Crowne, and call'd
       Himselfe a King.
LUCIUS   I am sorry *Cymbeline*,   1250
       That I am to pronounce *Augustus Cæsar*
       (*Cæsar*, that hath moe Kings his Seruants, then
       Thy selfe Domesticke Officers) thine Enemy:
       Receyue it from me then. Warre, and Confusion
       In *Cæsars* name pronounce I 'gainst thee: Looke
       For fury, not to be resisted. Thus defide,
       I thanke thee for my selfe.
CYMBELINE   Thou art welcome Caius,
       Thy *Cæsar* Knighted me; my youth I spent
       Much vnder him; of him, I gather'd Honour,
       Which he, to seeke of me againe, perforce,   1260
       Behooues me keepe at vtterance. I am perfect,
       That the Pannonians and Dalmatians, for
       Their Liberties are now in Armes: a President
       Which not to reade, would shew the Britaines cold:
       So *Cæsar* shall not finde them.
LUCIUS   Let proofe speake.
CLOTEN His Maiesty biddes you welcome. Make pastime
    with vs, a day, or two, or longer: if you seek vs
    afterwards in other tearmes, you shall finde vs in our
    Salt-water-Girdle: if you beate vs out of it, it is yours:
    if you fall in the aduenture, our Crowes shall fare the   1270
    better for you: and there's an end.
LUCIUS So sir.
CYMBELINE
       I know your Masters pleasure, and he mine:
       All the Remaine, is welcome.   ⌜*Flourish.*⌝ *Exeunt*

3.2   *Enter Pisanio reading of a Letter*

Sc. 13) PISANIO

How? of Adultery? Wherefore write you not
What Monsters her accuser? *Leonatus*:
Oh Master, what a strange infection
Is falne into thy eare? What false Italian,
(As poysonous tongu'd, as handed) hath preuail'd

1280   On thy too ready hearing? Disloyall? No.
She's punish'd for her Truth; and vndergoes
More Goddesse-like, then Wife-like; such Assaults
As would take in some Vertue. Oh my Master,
Thy mind to hers, is now as lowe, as were
Thy Fortunes. How? That I should murther her,
Vpon the Loue, and Truth, and Vowes; which I
Haue made to thy command? I her? Her blood?
If it be so, to do good seruice, neuer
Let me be counted seruiceable. How looke I,

1290   That I should seeme to lacke humanity,
So much as this Fact comes to?
(*Reades*)   *Doo't: The Letter,*
That I haue sent her, by her owne command,
Shall giue thee opportunitie. Oh damn'd paper,
Blacke as the Incke that's on thee: senselesse bauble,
Art thou a Feodarie for this Act; and look'st
So Virgin-like without?
          Enter Innogen
                         Loe here she comes.
I am ignorant in what I am commanded.

INNOGEN How now *Pisanio*?

PISANIO

Madam, heere is a Letter from my Lord.

INNOGEN

1300   Who, thy Lord? That is my Lord *Leonatus*?
Oh, learn'd indeed were that Astronomer
That knew the Starres, as I his Characters,
Heel'd lay the Future open. You good Gods,
Let what is heere contain'd, rellish of Loue,
Of my Lords health, of his content: yet not
That we two are asunder, let that grieue him;
Some griefes are medcinable, that is one of them,
For it doth physicke Loue, of his content,
All but in that. Good Wax, thy leaue: blest be

1310   You Bees that make these Lockes of counsaile. Louers,
And men in dangerous Bondes pray not alike,
Though Forfeytours you cast in prison, yet
You claspe young *Cupids* Tables: good Newes Gods.
          She opens and reades the Letter

Iustice and your Fathers wrath (should he take me in his
Dominion) could not be so cruell to me, as you: (oh the
deerest of Creatures) would euen renew me with your eyes.
Take notice that I am in Cambria *at Milford-Hauen: what*
your owne Loue, will out of this aduise you, follow. So he
wishes you all happinesse, that remaines loyall to his Vow,
1320   *and your encreasing in Loue*   Leonatus-Posthumus.

Oh for a Horse with wings: Hear'st thou *Pisanio*?
He is at Milford-Hauen: Read, and tell me
How farre 'tis thither. If one of meane affaires

May plod it in a weeke, why may not I
Glide thither in a day? Then true *Pisanio*,
Who long'st like me, to see thy Lord; who long'st
(Oh let me bate) but not like me: yet long'st
But in a fainter kinde. Oh not like me:
For mine's beyond, beyond: say, and speake thicke
(Loues Counsailor should fill the bores of hearing,   1330
To'th'smothering of the Sense) how farre it is
To this same blessed Milford. And by'th'way
Tell me how Wales was made so happy, as
T'inherite such a Hauen. But first of all,
How we may steale from hence: and for the gap
That we shall make in Time, from our hence-going,
Till our returne, to excuse: but first, how get hence.
Why should excuse be borne or ere begot?
Weele talke of that heereafter. Prythee speake,
How many score of Miles may we well ride   1340
Twixt houre, and houre?

PISANIO   One score 'twixt Sun, and Sun,
Madam's enough for you: and too much too.

INNOGEN

Why, one that rode to's Execution Man,
Could neuer go so slow: I haue heard of Riding
          wagers,
Where Horses haue bin nimbler then the Sands
That run i'th'Clocks behalfe. But this is Foolrie,
Go, bid my Woman faigne a Sicknesse, say
She'le home to her Father; and prouide me presently
A Riding Suit: No costlier then would fit
A Franklins Huswife.

PISANIO   Madam, you're best consider.   1350

INNOGEN

I see before me (Man); nor heere, nor heere
Nor what ensues but haue a Fog in them
That I cannot looke through. Away, I prythee,
Do as I bid thee: There's no more to say:
Accessible is none but Milford way.   *Exeunt*

Enter Belarius, followed by Guiderius, and   **3.3**
Aruiragus [from a Caue in the Woods]   **(Sc. 14)**

BELARIUS

A goodly day, not to keepe house with such,
Whose Roofe's as lowe as ours: Stoope Boyes, this gate
Instructs you how t'adore the Heauens; and bowes
          you
To a mornings holy office. The Gates of Monarchs
Are Arch'd so high, that Giants may iet through   1360
And keepe their impious Turbonds on, without
Good morrow to the Sun. Haile thou faire Heauen,
We house i'th'Rocke, yet vse thee not so hardly
As prouder liuers do.

GUIDERIUS   Haile Heauen.

ARUIRAGUS   Haile Heauen.

BELARIUS

Now for our Mountaine sport, vp to yond hill
Your legges are yong: Ile tread these Flats. Consider,
When you aboue perceiue me like a Crow,

That it is Place, which lessen's, and sets off,
And you may then reuolue what Tales, I haue told
     you,
1370 Of Courts, of Princes; of the Tricks in Warre;
That Seruice, is not Seruice; so being done,
But being so allowed. To apprehend thus,
Drawes vs a profit from all things we see:
And often to our comfort, shall we finde
The sharded-Beetle, in a safer hold
Then is the full-wing'd Eagle. Oh this life,
Is Nobler, then attending for a checke:
Richer, then doing nothing for a Bable:
Prouder, then rustling in vnpayd-for Silke:
1380 Such gaine the Cap of him, that makes em fine,
Yet keepes his Booke vncros'd: no life to ours.

GUIDERIUS
Out of your proofe you speak: we poore vnfledg'd
Haue neuer wing'd from view o'th'nest; nor know not
What Ayre's from home. Hap'ly this life is best,
(If quiet life be best) sweeter to you
That haue a sharper knowne. Well corresponding
With your stiffe Age; but vnto vs, it is
A Cell of Ignorance: trauailing a bed,
A Prison for a Debtor, that not dares
To stride a limit.
1390 ARUIRAGUS (*to Belarius*) What should we speake of
When we are old as you? When we shall heare
The Raine and winde beate darke December? How
In this our pinching Caue, shall we discourse
The freezing houres away? We haue seene nothing:
We are beastly; subtle as the Fox for prey,
Like warlike as the Wolfe, for what we eate:
Our Valour is to chace what flyes: Our Cage
We make a Quire, as doth the prison'd Bird,
And sing our Bondage freely.

BELARIUS   How you speake.
1400 Did you but know the Citties Vsuries,
And felt them knowingly: the Art o'th'Court,
As hard to leaue, as keepe: whose top to climbe
Is certaine falling: or so slipp'ry, that
The feare's as bad as falling. The toyle o'th'Warre,
A paine that onely seemes to seeke out danger
I'th'name of Fame, and Honor, which dyes i'th'search,
And hath as oft a sland'rous Epitaph,
As Record of faire Act. Nay, many times
Doth ill deserue, by doing well: what's worse
1410 Must curt'sie at the Censure. Oh Boyes, this Storie
The World may reade in me: My bodie's mark'd
With Roman Swords; and my report, was once
First, with the best of Note. Cymbeline lou'd me,
And when a Souldier was the Theame, my name
Was not farre off: then was I as a Tree
Whose boughes did bend with fruit. But in one night,
A Storme, or Robbery (call it what you will)
Shooke downe my mellow hangings: nay my Leaues,
And left me bare to weather.

GUIDERIUS   Vncertaine fauour.
BELARIUS
1420 My fault being nothing (as I haue told you oft)

But that two Villaines, whose false Oathes preuayl'd
Before my perfect Honor, swore to *Cymbeline*,
I was Confederate with the Romanes: so
Followed my Banishment, and this twenty yeeres,
This Rocke, and these Demesnes, haue bene my World,
Where I haue liu'd at honest freedome, payed
More pious debts to Heauen, then in all
The fore-end of my time. But, vp to'th'Mountaines,
This is not Hunters Language; he that strikes
The Venison first, shall be the Lord o'th'Feast,   1430
To him the other two shall minister,
And we will feare no poyson, which attends
In place of greater State: Ile meete you in the Valleyes.
                    Exeunt Guiderius, and Aruiragus
How hard it is to hide the sparkes of Nature?
These Boyes know little they are Sonnes to'th'King,
Nor *Cymbeline* dreames that they are aliue.
They thinke they are mine, and though train'd vp
     thus meanely
I'th'Caue, wherein they Bowe, their thoughts do hit,
The Roofes of Palaces, and Nature prompts them
In simple and lowe things, to Prince it, much   1440
Beyond the tricke of others. This *Polidour*,
The heyre of *Cymbeline* and Britaine, who
The King his Father call'd *Guiderius*. Ioue,
When on my three-foot stoole I sit, and tell
The warlike feats I haue done, his spirits flye out
Into my Story: say thus mine Enemy fell,
And thus I set my foote on's necke, euen then
The Princely blood flowes in his Cheeke, he sweats,
Straines his yong Nerues, and puts himselfe in posture
That acts my words. The yonger Brother *Cadwall*, 1450
Once *Aruiragus*, in as like a figure
Strikes life into my speech, and shewes much more
His owne conceyuing.
     ⌈*A Hunting Horn sounds*⌉
                         Hearke, the Game is rows'd,
Oh *Cymbeline*, Heauen and my Conscience knowes
Thou didd'st vniustly banish me: whereon
At three, and two yeeres old, I stole these Babes,
Thinking to barre thee of Succession, as
Thou rest's me of my Lands. *Euriphile*,
Thou was't their Nurse, they took thee for their
     mother,
And euery day do honor to her graue: 1460
My selfe *Belarius*, that am *Morgan* call'd
They take for Naturall Father.
     ⌈*A Hunting Horn sounds*⌉
                         The Game is vp.   *Exit*

Enter Pisanio, and Innogen in a Riding Suit   **3.4**
INNOGEN   (Sc. 1⁵
Thou told'st me when we came frõ horse, yᵉ place
Was neere at hand: Ne're long'd my Mother so
To see me first, as I haue now. *Pisanio*, Man:
Where is *Posthumus*? What is in thy mind
That makes thee stare thus? Wherefore breaks that
     sigh
From th'inward of thee? One, but painted thus

Would be interpreted a thing perplex'd
1470 Beyond selfe-explication. Put thy selfe
Into a hauiour of lesse feare, ere wildnesse
Vanquish my stayder Senses. What's the matter?
     Pisanio giues her a Letter
Why tender'st thou that Paper to me, with
A looke vntender? If't be Summer Newes
Smile too't before: if Winterly, thou need'st
But keepe that count'nance stil. My Husbands hand?
That Drug-damn'd Italy, hath out-craftied him,
And hee's at some hard point. Speake man, thy Tongue
May take off some extreamitie, which to reade
Would be euen mortall to me.
1480 PISANIO   Please you reade,
And you shall finde me (wretched man) a thing
The most disdain'd of Fortune.
INNOGEN (*reades*) *Thy Mistris (Pisanio) hath plaide the*
Strumpet in my Bed: the Testimonies whereof, lyes bleeding
in me. I speak not out of weake Surmises, but from proofe
as strong as my greefe, and as certaine as I expect my
Reuenge. That part, thou (Pisanio) must acte for me, if thy
Faith be not tainted with the breach of hers; let thine owne
hands take away her life: I shall giue thee opportunity at
1490 *Milford Hauen. She hath my Letter for the purpose; where,*
if thou feare to strike, and to make mee certaine it is done,
thou art the Pander to her dishonour, and equally to me
disloyall.
PISANIO (*aside*)
What shall I need to draw my Sword, the Paper
Hath cut her throat alreadie? No, 'tis Slander,
Whose edge is sharper then the Sword, whose tongue
Out-venomes all the Wormes of Nyle, whose breath
Rides on the posting windes, and doth belye
All corners of the World. Kings, Queenes, and States,
1500 Maides, Matrons, nay the Secrets of the Graue
This viperous slander enters. (*To Innogen*) What
     cheere, Madam?
INNOGEN
False to his Bed? What is it to be false?
To lye in watch there, and to thinke on him?
To weepe 'twixt clock and clock? If sleep charge Nature,
To breake it with a fearfull dreame of him,
And cry my selfe awake? That's false to's bed? Is it?
PISANIO Alas good Lady.
INNOGEN
I false? Thy Conscience witnesse: *Iachimo,*
Thou didd'st accuse him of Incontinencie,
1510 Thou then look'st like a Villaine: now, me thinkes
Thy fauours good enough. Some Iay of Italy
(Whose mother was her painting) hath betraid him:
Poore I am stale, a Garment out of fashion,
And for I am richer then to hang by th'walles,
I must be ript: To peeces with me: Oh!
Mens Vowes are womens Traitors. All good seeming
By thy reuolt (oh Husband) shall be thought
Put on for Villainy; not borne where't growes,
But worne a Baite for Ladies.
PISANIO   Good Madam, heare me.

INNOGEN
True honest men being heard, like false *Æneas,*   1520
Were in his time thought false: and *Synons* weeping
Did scandall many a holy teare: tooke pitty
From most true wretchednesse. So thou, *Posthumus*
Wilt lay the Leauen on all proper men;
Goodly, and gallant, shall be false and periur'd
From thy great faile: (*To Pisanio*) Come Fellow, be
     thou honest,
Do thou thy Masters bidding. When thou seest him,
A little witnesse my obedience. Looke
I draw the Sword my selfe, take it, and hit
The innocent Mansion of my Loue (my Heart:)   1530
Feare not, 'tis empty of all things, but Greefe:
Thy Master is not there, who was indeede
The riches of it. Do his bidding, strike,
Thou mayst be valiant in a better cause;
But now thou seem'st a Coward.
PISANIO   Hence vile Instrument,
Thou shalt not damne my hand.
INNOGEN   Why, I must dye:
And if I do not by thy hand, thou art
No Seruant of thy Masters. Against Selfe-slaughter,
There is a prohibition so Diuine,
That crauens my weake hand: Come, heere's my heart: 1540
Something's a-fort: Soft, soft, wee'l no defence,
Obedient as the Scabbard. What is heere,
     She takes Letters from her bosom
The Scriptures of the Loyall *Leonatus,*
All turn'd to Heresie? Away, away
Corrupters of my Faith, you shall no more
Be Stomachers to my heart: thus may poore Fooles
Beleeue false Teachers: Though those that are betraid
Do feele the Treason sharpely, yet the Traitor
Stands in worse case of woe. And thou *Posthumus,*
That didd'st set vp my disobedience 'gainst the King   1550
My Father, and make me put into contempt the suites
Of Princely Fellowes, shalt heereafter finde
It is no acte of common passage, but
A straine of Rarenesse: and I greeue my selfe,
To thinke, when thou shalt be disedg'd by her,
That now thou tyrest on, how thy memory
Will then be pang'd by me. (*To Pisanio*) Prythee
     dispatch,
The Lambe entreats the Butcher. Wher's thy knife?
Thou art too slow to do thy Masters bidding
When I desire it too.
PISANIO   Oh gracious Lady: 1560
Since I receiu'd command to do this businesse,
I haue not slept one winke.
INNOGEN   Doo't, and to bed then.
PISANIO
Ile wake mine eye-balles out first.
INNOGEN   Wherefore then
Didd'st vndertake it? Why hast thou abus'd
So many Miles, with a pretence? This place?
Mine Action? and thine owne? Our Horses labour?
The Time inuiting thee? The perturb'd Court

For my being absent? whereunto I neuer
Purpose returne. Why hast thou gone so farre
1570   To be vn-bent? when thou hast 'tane thy stand,
Th'elected Deere before thee?

PISANIO   But to win time
To loose so bad employment, in the which
I haue consider'd of a course: good Ladie
Heare me with patience.

INNOGEN   Talke thy tongue weary, speake:
I haue heard I am a Strumpet, and mine eare
Therein false strooke, can take no greater wound,
Nor tent, to bottome that. But speake.

PISANIO   Then Madam,
I thought you would not backe againe.

INNOGEN   Most like,
Bringing me heere to kill me.

PISANIO   Not so neither:
1580   But if I were as wise, as honest, then
My purpose would proue well: it cannot be,
But that my Master is abus'd. Some Villaine,
I, and singular in his Art, hath done you both
This cursed iniurie.

INNOGEN   Some Roman Curtezan?

PISANIO   No, on my life:
Ile giue but notice you are dead, and send him
Some bloody signe of it. For 'tis commanded
I should do so: you shall be mist at Court,
And that will well confirme it.

1590   INNOGEN   Why good Fellow,
What shall I do the while? Where bide? How liue?
Or in my life, what comfort, when I am
Dead to my Husband?

PISANIO   If you'l backe to'th'Court.

INNOGEN
No Court, no Father, nor no more adoe
With that harsh, churlish noble, simple nothing:
That *Clotten*, whose Loue-suite hath bene to me
As fearefull as a Siege.

PISANIO   If not at Court,
Then not in Britaine must you bide.

INNOGEN   Where then?
Hath Britaine all the Sunne that shines? Day? Night?
1600   Are they not but in Britaine? I'th'worlds Volume
Our Britaine seemes as of it, but not in't:
In a great Poole, a Swannes-nest, prythee thinke
There's liuers out of Britaine.

PISANIO   I am most glad
You thinke of other place: Th'Ambassador,
Lucius the Romane comes to Milford-Hauen
To morrow. Now, if you could weare a minde
Darke, as your Fortune is, and but disguise
That which t'appeare it selfe, must not yet be,
But by selfe-danger, you should tread a course
1610   Pretty, and full of view: yea, happily, neere
The residence of *Posthumus*; so nie (at least)
That though his Actions were not visible, yet
Report should render him hourely to your eare,
As truely as he mooues.

INNOGEN   Oh for such meanes,

Though perill to my modestie, not death on't
I would aduenture.

PISANIO   Well then, heere's the point:
You must forget to be a Woman: change
Command, into obedience. Feare, and Nicenesse
(The Handmaides of all Women, or more truely
Woman it pretty selfe) into a waggish courage,   1620
Ready in gybes, quicke-answer'd, sawcie, and
As quarrellous as the Weazell: Nay, you must
Forget that rarest Treasure of your Cheeke,
Exposing it (but oh the harder heart,
Alacke no remedy) to the greedy touch
Of common-kissing *Titan*: and forget
Your laboursome and dainty Trimmes, wherein
You made great *Iuno* angry.

INNOGEN   Nay be breefe?
I see into thy end, and am almost
A man already.

PISANIO   First, make your selfe but like one.   1630
Fore-thinking this, I haue already fit
('Tis in my Cloake-bagge) Doublet, Hat, Hose, all
That answer to them: Would you in their seruing,
(And with what imitation you can borrow
From youth of such a season) 'fore Noble *Lucius*
Present your selfe, desire his seruice: tell him
Wherein you're happy; which will make him know,
If that his head haue eare in Musicke, doubtlesse
With ioy he will imbrace you: for hee's Honourable,
And doubling that, most holy. Your meanes abroad: 1640
You haue me rich, and I will neuer faile
Beginning, nor supplyment.

INNOGEN   Thou art all the comfort
The Gods will diet me with. Prythee away,
There's more to be consider'd: but wee'l euen
All that good time will giue vs. This attempt,
I am Souldier too, and will abide it with
A Princes Courage. Away, I prythee.

PISANIO
Well Madam, we must take a short farewell,
Least being mist, I be suspected of
Your carriage from the Court. My Noble Mistris,   1650
Heere is a boxe, I had it from the Queene,
What's in't is precious: If you are sicke at Sea,
Or Stomacke-qualm'd at Land, a Dramme of this
Will driue away distemper. To some shade,
And fit you to your Manhood: may the Gods
Direct you to the best.

INNOGEN   Amen: I thanke thee.

                              Exeunt seuerally

⌈*Flourish.*⌉ *Enter Cymbeline, Queene, Cloten,*   3.5
Lucius, and Lords   (Sc. ⁊

CYMBELINE (*to Lucius*)
Thus farre, and so farewell.

LUCIUS   Thankes, Royall Sir:
My Emperor hath wrote, I must from hence,
And am right sorry, that I must report ye
My Masters Enemy.

CYMBELINE   Our Subiects (Sir)   1660

Will not endure his yoake; and for our selfe
To shew lesse Soueraignty then they, must needs
Appeare vn-Kinglike.

LUCIUS   So Sir: I desire of you
A Conduct ouer Land, to Milford-Hauen.
(*To the Queene*) Madam, all ioy befall your Grace,
⌈*to Cloten*⌉ and you.

CYMBELINE
My Lords, you are appointed for that Office:
The due of Honor, in no point omit:
So farewell Noble *Lucius*.

LUCIUS   Your hand, my Lord.

CLOTEN
Receiue it friendly: but from this time forth
I weare it as your Enemy.

1670 LUCIUS   Sir, the Euent
Is yet to name the winner. Fare you well.

CYMBELINE
Leaue not the worthy *Lucius*, good my Lords
Till he haue crost the Seuern. Happines.

                              Exit Lucius, &c

QUEENE
He goes hence frowning: but it honours vs
That we haue giuen him cause.

CLOTEN   'Tis all the better,
Your valiant Britaines haue their wishes in it.

CYMBELINE
Lucius hath wrote already to the Emperor
How it goes heere. It fits vs therefore ripely
Our Chariots, and our Horsemen be in readinesse:
1680 The Powres that he already hath in Gallia
Will soone be drawne to head, from whence he moues
His warre for Britaine.

QUEENE   'Tis not sleepy businesse,
But must be look'd too speedily, and strongly.

CYMBELINE
Our expectation that it would be thus
Hath made vs forward. But my gentle Queene,
Where is our Daughter? She hath not appear'd
Before the Roman, nor to vs hath tender'd
The duty of the day. She lookes vs like
A thing more made of malice, then of duty,
1690 We haue noted it. Call her before vs, for
We haue beene too slight in sufferance.

                              Exit one or more

QUEENE   Royall Sir,
Since the exile of *Posthumus*, most retyr'd
Hath her life bin: the Cure whereof, my Lord,
'Tis time must do. Beseech your Maiesty,
Forbeare sharpe speeches to her. Shee's a Lady
So tender of rebukes, that words are strokes;
And strokes death to her.

       Enter a Messenger

CYMBELINE   Where is she Sir? How
Can her contempt be answer'd?

MESSENGER   Please you Sir,
Her Chambers are all lock'd, and there's no answer
1700 That will be giuen to'th'lowdst of noise, we make.

QUEENE
My Lord, when last I went to visit her,
She pray'd me to excuse her keeping close,
Whereto constrain'd by her infirmitie,
She should that dutie leaue vnpaide to you
Which dayly she was bound to proffer: this
She wish'd me to make knowne: but our great Court
Made me too blame in memory.

CYMBELINE   Her doores lock'd?
Not seene of late? Grant Heauens, that which I
Feare, proue false.   *Exit*

QUEENE   Sonne, I say, follow the King.

CLOTEN
That man of hers, *Pisanio*, her old Seruant   1710
I haue not seene these two dayes.

QUEENE   Go, looke after:
                              Exit Cloten
Pisanio, thou that stand'st so for *Posthumus*,
He hath a Drugge of mine: I pray, his absence
Proceed by swallowing that. For he beleeues
It is a thing most precious. But for her,
Where is she gone? Haply dispaire hath seiz'd her:
Or wing'd with feruour of her loue, she's flowne
To her desir'd *Posthumus*: gone she is,
To death, or to dishonor, and my end
Can make good vse of either. Shee being downe,   1720
I haue the placing of the Brittish Crowne.

    Enter Cloten
How now, my Sonne?

CLOTEN   'Tis certaine she is fled:
Go in and cheere the King, he rages, none
Dare come about him.

QUEENE   All the better: may
This night fore-stall him of the comming day.

                              Exit Queene

CLOTEN
I loue, and hate her: for she's Faire and Royall,
And that she hath all courtly parts more exquisite
Then Lady, Ladies, Woman, from euery one
The best she hath, and she of all compounded
Out-selles them all. I loue her therefore, but   1730
Disdaining me, and throwing Fauours on
The low *Posthumus*, slanders so her iudgement,
That what's else rare, is choak'd: and in that point
I will conclude to hate her, nay indeede,
To be reueng'd vpon her. For, when Fooles
Shall—

    Enter Pisanio
       Who is heere? What, are you packing sirrah?
Come hither: Ah you precious Pandar, Villaine,
Where is thy Lady? In a word, or else
Thou art straightway with the Fiends.

PISANIO   Oh, good my Lord.

CLOTEN
Where is thy Lady? Or, by Iupiter,   1740
I will not aske againe. Close Villaine,
Ile haue this Secret from thy tongue, or rip
Thy heart to finde it. Is she with *Posthumus*?

From whose so many waights of basenesse, cannot
A dram of worth be drawne.

PISANIO   Alas, my Lord,
How can she be with him? When was she miss'd?
He is in Rome.

CLOTEN   Where is she Sir? Come neerer:
No farther halting: satisfie me home,
What is become of her?

1750 PISANIO Oh, my all-worthy Lord.

CLOTEN All-worthy Villaine,
Discouer where thy Mistris is, at once,
At the next word: no more of worthy Lord:
Speake, or thy silence on the instant, is
Thy condemnation, and thy death.

PISANIO   Then Sir:
This Paper is the historie of my knowledge
Touching her flight.

         He giues Cloten a Letter

CLOTEN   Let's see't: I will pursue her
Euen to *Augustus* Throne.

PISANIO ⌈*aside*⌉   Or this, or perish.
She's farre enough, and what he learnes by this,
May proue his trauell, not her danger.

1760 CLOTEN   Humh.

PISANIO (*aside*)
Ile write to my Lord she's dead: Oh *Innogen*,
Safe mayst thou wander, safe returne agen.

CLOTEN
Sirra, is this Letter true?

PISANIO   Sir, as I thinke.

CLOTEN It is *Posthumus* hand, I know't. Sirrah, if thou
would'st not be a Villain, but do me true seruice:
vndergo those Imployments wherin I should haue cause
to vse thee with a serious industry, that is, what villainy
soere I bid thee do to performe it, directly and truely,
I would thinke thee an honest man: thou should'st
1770 neither want my meanes for thy releefe, nor my voyce
for thy preferment.

PISANIO Well, my good Lord.

CLOTEN Wilt thou serue mee? For since patiently and
constantly thou hast stucke to the bare Fortune of that
Begger *Posthumus*, thou canst not in the course of
gratitude, but be a diligent follower of mine. Wilt thou
serue mee?

PISANIO Sir, I will.

CLOTEN Giue mee thy hand, heere's my purse. Hast any
1780 of thy late Masters Garments in thy possession?

PISANIO I haue (my Lord) at my Lodging, the same Suite
he wore, when he tooke leaue of my Ladie & Mistresse.

CLOTEN The first seruice thou dost mee, fetch that Suite
hither, let it be thy first seruice, go.

PISANIO I shall my Lord.   *Exit*

CLOTEN Meet thee at Milford-Hauen: (I forgot to aske him
one thing, Ile remember't anon:) euen there, thou
villaine *Posthumus* will I kill thee. I would these
Garments were come. She saide vpon a time (the
1790 bitternesse of it, I now belch from my heart) that shee
held the very Garment of *Posthumus*, in more respect,

then my Noble and naturall person; together with the
adornement of my Qualities. With that Suite vpon my
backe wil I rauish her: first kill him, and in her eyes;
there shall she see my valour, which wil then be a
torment to hir contempt. He on the ground, my speech
of insultment ended on his dead bodie, and when my
Lust hath dined (which, as I say, to vex her, I will
execute in the Cloathes that she so prais'd:) to the
Court Ile knock her backe, foot her home againe. She 1800
hath despis'd mee reioycingly, and Ile bee merry in my
Reuenge.

         Enter Pisanio with Posthumus Suite
Be those the Garments?

PISANIO   I, my Noble Lord.

CLOTEN
How long is't since she went to Milford-Hauen?

PISANIO She can scarse be there yet.

CLOTEN Bring this Apparrell to my Chamber, that is the
second thing that I haue commanded thee. The third
is, that thou wilt be a voluntarie Mute to my designe.
Be but dutious, and true preferment shall tender it selfe
to thee. My Reuenge is now at Milford, would I had 1810
wings to follow it. Come, and be true.   *Exit*

PISANIO
Thou bid'st me to my losse: for true to thee,
Were to proue false, which I will neuer bee
To him that is most true. To Milford go,
And finde not her, whom thou pursuest. Flow, flow
You Heauenly blessings on her: This Fooles speede
Be crost with slownesse; Labour be his meede.   *Exit*

         Enter Innogen alone, dressed as a man, before the   **3.6**
         Caue   (Sc.)

INNOGEN
I see a mans life is a tedious one,
I haue tyr'd my selfe: and for two nights together
Haue made the ground my bed. I should be sicke,   1820
But that my resolution helpes me: Milford,
When from the Mountaine top, *Pisanio* shew'd thee,
Thou was't within a kenne. Oh Ioue, I thinke
Foundations flye the wretched: such I meane,
Where they should be releeu'd. Two Beggers told me,
I could not misse my way. Will poore Folkes lye
That haue Afflictions on them, knowing 'tis
A punishment, or Triall? Yes; no wonder,
When Rich-ones scarse tell true. To lapse in Fulnesse
Is sorer, then to lye for Neede: and Falshood   1830
Is worse in Kings, then Beggers. My deere Lord,
Thou art one o'th'false Ones: Now I thinke on thee,
My hunger's gone; but euen before, I was
At point to sinke, for Food. But what is this?
Heere is a path too't: 'tis some sauage hold:
I were best not call; I dare not call: yet Famine
Ere cleane it o're-throw Nature, makes it valiant.
Plentie, and Peace breeds Cowards: Hardnesse euer
Of Hardinesse is Mother. Hoa? who's heere?
If any thing that's ciuill, speake: if sauage,   1840
Take, or lend. Hoa? No answer? Then Ile enter.

Best draw my Sword; and if mine Enemy
But feare the Sword like me, hee'l scarsely looke on't.
Such a Foe, good Heauens.   *Exit into the Caue*
        Enter Belarius, Guiderius, and Aruiragus
BELARIUS
You *Polidore* haue prou'd best Woodman, and
Are Master of the Feast: *Cadwall*, and I
Will play the Cooke, and Seruant, 'tis our match:
The sweat of industry would dry, and dye
But for the end it workes too. Come, our stomackes
1850   Will make what's homely, sauoury: Wearinesse
Can snore vpon the Flint, when restie Sloth
Findes the Downe-pillow hard. Now peace be heere,
Poore house, that keep'st thy selfe.
GUIDERIUS   I am throughly weary.
ARUIRAGUS
I am weake with toyle, yet strong in appetite.
GUIDERIUS
There is cold meat i'th'Caue, we'l brouz on that
Whil'st what we haue kill'd, be Cook'd.
BELARIUS (*looking into the Caue*)   Stay, come not in:
But that it eates our victualles, I should thinke
Heere were a Faiery.
GUIDERIUS   What's the matter, Sir?
BELARIUS
By Iupiter an Angell: or if not
1860   An earthly Paragon. Behold Diuinenesse
No elder then a Boy.
        Enter Innogen from the Caue, dressed as a Man
INNOGEN   Good masters harme me not:
Before I enter'd heere, I call'd, and thought
To haue begg'd, or bought, what I haue took: good
        troth
I haue stolne nought, nor would not, though I had
        found
Gold strew'd i'th'Floore. Heere's money for my Meate,
I would haue left it on the Boord, so soone
As I had made my Meale; and parted
With Pray'rs for the Prouider.
GUIDERIUS   Money? Youth.
ARUIRAGUS
All Gold and Siluer rather turne to durt,
1870   As 'tis no better reckon'd, but of those
Who worship durty Gods.
INNOGEN   I see you're angry:
Know, if you kill me for my fault, I should
Haue dyed, had I not made it.
BELARIUS   Whether bound?
INNOGEN
To Milford-Hauen.
BELARIUS   What's your name?
INNOGEN
Fidele Sir: I haue a Kinsman, who
Is bound for Italy; he embark'd at Milford,
To whom being going, almost spent with hunger,
I am falne in this offence.
BELARIUS   Prythee (faire youth)
Thinke vs no Churles: nor measure our good mindes

By this rude place we liue in. Well encounter'd,   1880
'Tis almost night, you shall haue better cheere
Ere you depart; and thankes to stay, and eate it:
Boyes, bid him welcome.
GUIDERIUS   Were you a woman, youth,
I should woo hard, but be your Groome in honesty:
I bid for you, as Ide buy.
ARUIRAGUS   Ile make't my Comfort
He is a man, Ile loue him as my Brother:
(*To Innogen*) And such a welcome as I'ld giue to him
(After long absence) such is yours. Most welcome:
Be sprightly, for you fall 'mongst Friends.
INNOGEN   'Mongst Friends,
If Brothers: (*aside*) would it had bin so, that they   1890
Had bin my Fathers Sonnes, then had my prize
Bin lesse, and so more equall ballasting
To thee *Posthumus*.
        The three men speak apart
BELARIUS   He wrings at some distresse.
GUIDERIUS
Would I could free't.
ARUIRAGUS   Or I, what ere it be,
What paine it cost, what danger: Gods!
BELARIUS   Hearke Boyes.
        They whisper
INNOGEN (*aside*) Great men
That had a Court no bigger then this Caue,
That did attend themselues, and had the vertue
Which their owne Conscience seal'd them: laying by
That nothing-guift of differing Multitudes   1900
Could not out-peere these twaine. Pardon me Gods,
I'ld change my sexe to be Companion with them,
Since *Leonatus* false.
BELARIUS   It shall be so:
Boyes wee'l go dresse our Hunt. Faire youth come in;
Discourse is heauy, fasting: when we haue supp'd
Wee'l mannerly demand thee of thy Story,
So farre as thou wilt speake it.
GUIDERIUS   Pray draw neere.
ARUIRAGUS
The Night to'th'Owle, and Morne to th'Larke lesse
        welcome.
INNOGEN Thankes Sir.
ARUIRAGUS I pray draw neere.   *Exeunt into the Caue*   1910

        Enter two Roman Senators, and Tribunes   **3.7**
1. SENATOR   (Sc. 18)
This is the tenor of the Emperors Writ;
That since the common men are now in Action
'Gainst the Pannonians, and Dalmatians,
And that the Legions now in Gallia, are
Full weake to vndertake our Warres against
The falne-off Britaines, that we do incite
The Gentry to this businesse. He creates
Lucius Pro-Consull: and to you the Tribunes
For this immediate Leuy, he commands
His absolute Commission. Long liue *Cæsar*.   1920

A TRIBUNE
   Is *Lucius* Generall of the Forces?
2. SENATOR   I.
A TRIBUNE
   Remaining now in Gallia?
1. SENATOR   With those Legions
   Which I haue spoke of, whereunto your leuie
   Must be suppliant: the words of your Commission
   Will tye you to the numbers, and the time
   Of their dispatch.
A TRIBUNE   We will discharge our duty.
                                  Exeunt

4.1   *Enter Clotten alone, in Posthumus Suite*
(Sc. 19)
CLOTEN I am neere to'th'place where they should meet,
   if *Pisanio* haue mapp'd it truely. How fit his Garments
   serue me? Why should his Mistris who was made by
1930   him that made the Taylor, not be fit too? The rather
   (sauing reuerence of the Word) for 'tis saide a Womans
   fitnesse comes by fits: therein I must play the Workman,
   I dare speake it to my selfe, for it is not Vainglorie for
   a man, and his Glasse, to confer in his owne Chamber;
   I meane, the Lines of my body are as well drawne as
   his; no lesse young, more strong, not beneath him in
   Fortunes, beyond him in the aduantage of the time,
   aboue him in Birth, alike conuersant in generall
   seruices, and more remarkeable in single oppositions;
1940   yet this imperseuerant Thing loues him in my despight.
   What Mortalitie is? *Posthumus*, thy head (which now
   is growing vppon thy shoulders) shall within this houre
   be off, thy Mistris inforced, thy Garments cut to peeces
   before thy face: and all this done, spurne her home to
   her Father, who may (happily) be a little angry for my
   so rough vsage: but my Mother hauing power of his
   testinesse, shall turne all into my commendations. My
   Horse is tyed vp safe, out Sword, and to a sore purpose:
   Fortune put them into my hand: This is the very
1950   description of their meeting place and the Fellow dares
   not deceiue me.   *Exit*

4.2   *Enter Belarius, Guiderius, Aruiragus, and Innogen*
(Sc. 20)   *dressed as a Man from the Caue*
BELARIUS (*to Innogen*)
   You are not well: Remaine heere in the Caue,
   Wee'l come to you from Hunting.
ARUIRAGUS (*to Innogen*)   Brother, stay heere:
   Are we not Brothers?
INNOGEN   So man and man should be,
   But Clay and Clay, differs in dignitie,
   Whose dust is both alike. I am very sicke.
GUIDERIUS (*to Belarius and Aruiragus*)
   Go you to Hunting, Ile abide with him.
INNOGEN
   So sicke I am not, yet I am not well:
   But not so Citizen a wanton, as
1960   To seeme to dye, ere sicke: So please you, leaue me,
   Sticke to your Iournall course: the breach of Custome,

Is breach of all. I am ill, but your being by me
Cannot amend me. Society, is no comfort
To one not sociable: I am not very sicke,
Since I can reason of it: pray you trust me heere,
Ile rob none but my selfe, and let me dye
Stealing so poorely.
GUIDERIUS   I loue thee: I haue spoke it,
   How much the quantity, the waight as much,
   As I do loue my Father.
BELARIUS   What? How? how?
ARUIRAGUS
   If it be sinne to say so (Sir) I yoake mee   1970
   In my good Brothers fault: I know not why
   I loue this youth, and I haue heard you say,
   Loue's reason's, without reason. The Beere at doore,
   And a demand who is't shall dye, I'ld say
   My Father, not this youth.
BELARIUS (*aside*)   Oh noble straine!
   O worthinesse of Nature, breed of Greatnesse!
   'Cowards father Cowards, & Base things Syre Bace;
   'Nature hath Meale, and Bran; Contempt, and Grace.
   I'me not their Father, yet who this should bee,
   Doth myracle it selfe, lou'd before mee.   1980
   (*Aloud*) 'Tis the ninth houre o'th'Morne.
ARUIRAGUS (*to Innogen*)   Brother, farewell.
INNOGEN
   I wish ye sport.
ARUIRAGUS   You health.—So please you Sir.
INNOGEN (*aside*)
   These are kinde Creatures. Gods, what lyes I haue
      heard:
   Our Courtiers say, all's sauage, but at Court;
   Experience, oh thou disproou'st Report.
   Th'emperious Seas breeds Monsters; for the Dish,
   Poore Tributary Riuers, as sweet Fish:
   I am sicke still, heart-sicke; *Pisanio*,
   Ile now taste of thy Drugge.
      ⌈*She swallowes the Drugge.*⌉ *The men speake apart*
GUIDERIUS   I could not stirre him:
   He said he was gentle, but vnfortunate;   1990
   Dishonestly afflicted, but yet honest.
ARUIRAGUS
   Thus did he answer me: yet said heereafter,
   I might know more.
BELARIUS   To'th'Field, to'th'Field:
   (*To Innogen*) Wee'l leaue you for this time, go in, and
      rest.
ARUIRAGUS (*to Innogen*)
   Wee'l not be long away.
BELARIUS (*to Innogen*)   Pray be not sicke,
   For you must be our Huswife.
INNOGEN   Well, or ill,
   I am bound to you.   *Exit*
BELARIUS   And shal't be euer.
   This youth, how ere distrest, appeares hath had
   Good Ancestors.
ARUIRAGUS How Angell-like he sings?   2000
GUIDERIUS But his neate Cookerie?

⌈BELARIUS⌉
　He cut our Rootes in Charracters,
　And sawc'st our Brothes, as *Iuno* had bin sicke,
　And he her Dieter.
ARUIRAGUS　　　　　Nobly he yoakes
　A smiling, with a sigh; as if the sighe
　Was that it was, for not being such a Smile:
　The Smile, mocking the Sigh, that it would flye
　From so diuine a Temple, to commix
　With windes, that Saylors raile at.
GUIDERIUS　　　　　　　　I do note,
2010　That greefe and patience rooted in him both,
　Mingle their spurres together.
ARUIRAGUS　　　　　　　Grow patienc,
　And let the stinking-Elder (Greefe) vntwine
　His perishing roote, with the encreasing Vine.
BELARIUS
　It is great morning. Come away: Who's there?
　　　　Enter Cloten in Posthumus Suite
CLOTEN
　I cannot finde those Runnagates, that Villaine
　Hath mock'd me. I am faint.
BELARIUS (*aside to Aruiragus and Guiderius*)
　　　　　　　　　Those Runnagates?
　Meanes he not vs? I partly know him, 'tis
　Cloten, the Sonne o'th' Queene. I feare some Ambush:
　I saw him not these many yeares, and yet
2020　I know 'tis he: We are held as Out-Lawes: Hence.
GUIDERIUS (*aside to Aruiragus and Belarius*)
　He is but one: you, and my Brother search
　What Companies are neere: pray you away,
　Let me alone with him.　　　*Exit Aruiragus and Belarius*
CLOTEN　　　　　　Soft, what are you
　That flye me thus? Some villaine-Mountainers?
　I haue heard of such. What Slaue art thou?
GUIDERIUS　　　　　　　　　A thing
　More slauish did I ne're, then answering
　A Slaue without a knocke.
CLOTEN　　　　　　Thou art a Robber,
　A Law-breaker, a Villaine: yeeld thee Theefe.
GUIDERIUS
　To who? to thee? What art thou? Haue not I
2030　An arme as bigge as thine? A heart, as bigge:
　Thy words I grant are bigger: for I weare not
　My Dagger in my mouth. Say what thou art:
　Why I should yeeld to thee?
CLOTEN　　　　　　　Thou Villaine base,
　Know'st me not by my Cloathes?
GUIDERIUS　　　　　No, nor thy Taylor, Rascall:
　Who is thy Grandfather: He made those cloathes,
　Which (as it seemes) make thee.
CLOTEN　　　　　　　Thou precious Varlet,
　My Taylor made them not.
GUIDERIUS　　　　　　Hence then, and thanke
　The man that gaue them thee. Thou art some Foole,
　I am loath to beate thee.
CLOTEN　　　　　　Thou iniurious Theefe,
　Heare but my name, and tremble.
2040　GUIDERIUS　　　　　　　　What's thy name?

CLOTEN　*Cloten*, thou Villaine.
GUIDERIUS
　Cloten, thou double Villaine be thy name,
　I cannot tremble at it, were it Toad, or Adder, Spider,
　'Twould moue me sooner.
CLOTEN　　　　　　To thy further feare,
　Nay, to thy meere Confusion, thou shalt know
　I am Sonne to'th'Queene.
GUIDERIUS　　　　　　I am sorry for't: not seeming
　So worthy as thy Birth.
CLOTEN　　　　　　Art not afeard?
GUIDERIUS
　Those that I reuerence, those I feare: the Wise:
　At Fooles I laugh: not feare them.
CLOTEN　　　　　　　Dye the death:
　When I haue slaine thee with my proper hand,　　2050
　Ile follow those that euen now fled hence:
　And on the Gates of *Luds-Towne* set your heads:
　Yeeld Rusticke Mountaineer.　　*Fight and Exeunt*
　　　Enter Belarius and Aruiragus
BELARIUS　　　　　　　No Companie's abroad?
ARUIRAGUS
　None in the world: you did mistake him sure.
BELARIUS
　I cannot tell: Long is it since I saw him,
　But Time hath nothing blurr'd those lines of Fauour
　Which then he wore: the snatches in his voice,
　And burst of speaking were as his: I am absolute
　'Twas very *Cloten*.
ARUIRAGUS　　　　In this place we left them;
　I wish my Brother make good time with him,　　2060
　You say he is so fell.
BELARIUS　　　　　　Being scarse made vp,
　I meane to man; he had not apprehension
　Of roaring terrors: For defect of iudgement
　Is oft the cause of Feare.
　　　Enter Guiderius with Clotens head
　　　　　　　　But see thy Brother.
GUIDERIUS
　This *Cloten* was a Foole, an empty purse,
　There was no money in't: Not *Hercules*
　Could haue knock'd out his Braines, for he had none:
　Yet I not doing this, the Foole had borne
　My head, as I do his.
BELARIUS　　　　　　What hast thou done?
GUIDERIUS
　I am perfect what: cut off one *Clotens* head,　　2070
　Sonne to the Queene (after his owne report)
　Who call'd me Traitor, Mountaineer, and swore
　With his owne single hand heel'd take vs in,
　Displace our heads, where (thanks ye Gods) they grow
　And set them on *Luds-Towne*.
BELARIUS　　　　　　We are all vndone.
GUIDERIUS
　Why, worthy Father, what haue we to loose,
　But that he swore to take, our Liues? the Law
　Protects not vs, then why should we be tender,
　To let an arrogant peece of flesh threat vs?
　Play Iudge, and Executioner, all himselfe?　　2080

For we do feare the Law. What company
Discouer you abroad?

BELARIUS   No single soule
Can we set eye on: but in all safe reason
He must haue some Attendants. Though his Humor
Was nothing but mutation, I, and that
From one bad thing to worse: Not Frenzie,
Not absolute madnesse could so farre haue rau'd
To bring him heere alone: although perhaps
It may be heard at Court, that such as wee
2090 Caue heere, hunt heere, are Out-lawes, and in time
May make some stronger head, the which he hearing,
(As it is like him) might breake out, and sweare
Heel'd fetch vs in, yet is't not probable
To come alone, either he so vndertaking,
Or they so suffering: then on good ground we feare,
If we do feare this Body hath a taile
More perillous then the head.

ARUIRAGUS   Let Ord'nance
Come as the Gods fore-say it: howsoere,
My Brother hath done well.

BELARIUS   I had no minde
2100 To hunt this day: The Boy *Fideles* sickenesse
Did make my way long forth.

GUIDERIUS   With his owne Sword,
Which he did waue against my throat, I haue tane
His head from him: Ile throw't into the Creeke
Behinde our Rocke, and let it to the Sea,
And tell the Fishes, hee's the Queenes Sonne, *Cloten*,
That's all I reake.   *Exit with Clotens head*

BELARIUS   I feare 'twill be reueng'd:
Would (*Polidore*) thou had'st not done't: though
          valour
Becomes thee well enough.

ARUIRAGUS   Would I had done't:
So the Reuenge alone pursu'de me: *Polidore*
2110 I loue thee brotherly, but enuy much
Thou hast robb'd me of this deed: I would Reuenges
That possible strength might meet, wold seek vs
          through
And put vs to our answer.

BELARIUS   Well, 'tis done:
Wee'l hunt no more to day, nor seeke for danger
Where there's no profit. I prythee to our Rocke,
You and *Fidele* play the Cookes: Ile stay
Till hasty *Polidore* returne, and bring him
To dinner presently.

ARUIRAGUS   Poore sicke *Fidele*.
Ile willingly to him, to gaine his colour,
2120 Il'd let a parish of such *Clotens* blood,
And praise my selfe for charity.   *Exit into the Caue*

BELARIUS   Oh thou Goddesse,
Thou diuine Nature; how thy selfe thou blazon'st
In these two Princely Boyes: they are as gentle
As Zephires blowing below the Violet,
Not wagging his sweet head; and yet, as rough
(Their Royall blood enchaf'd) as the rud'st winde,
That by the top doth take the Mountaine Pine,

And make him stoope to th'Vale. 'Tis wonder
That an inuisible instinct should frame them
To Royalty vnlearn'd, Honor vntaught,   2130
Ciuility not seene from other: valour
That wildely growes in them, but yeelds a crop
As if it had beene sow'd: yet still it's strange
What *Clotens* being heere to vs portends,
Or what his death will bring vs.
          Enter Guidereus

GUIDERIUS   Where's my Brother?
I haue sent *Clotens* Clot-pole downe the streame,
In Embassie to his Mother; his Bodie's hostage
For his returne.
          Solemn Musick

BELARIUS   My ingenuous Instrument,
(Hearke *Polidore*) it sounds: but what occasion
Hath *Cadwal* now to giue it motion? Hearke.   2140

GUIDERIUS
Is he at home?

BELARIUS   He went hence euen now.

GUIDERIUS
What does he meane? Since death of my deer'st Mother
It did not speake before. All solemne things
Should answer solemne Accidents. The matter?
Triumphes for nothing, and lamenting Toyes,
Is iollity for Apes, and greefe for Boyes.
Is *Cadwall* mad?
          Enter from the Caue Aruiragus, with Innogen dead,
          bearing her in his Armes

BELARIUS   Looke, heere he comes,
And brings the dire occasion in his Armes,
Of what we blame him for.

ARUIRAGUS   The Bird is dead
That we haue made so much on. I had rather   2150
Haue skipt from sixteene yeares of Age, to sixty:
To haue turn'd my leaping time into a Crutch,
Then haue seene this.

GUIDERIUS (*to Innogen*) Oh sweetest, fayrest Lilly:
My Brother weares thee not one halfe so well,
As when thou grew'st thy selfe.

BELARIUS   Oh Melancholly,
Who euer yet could sound thy bottome? Finde
The Ooze, to shew what Coast thy sluggish crare
Might easilest harbour in. Thou blessed thing,
Ioue knowes what man thou might'st haue made:
          but I,
Thou dyed'st a most rare Boy, of Melancholly.   2160
(*To Aruiragus*) How found you him?

ARUIRAGUS   Starke, as you see:
Thus smiling, as some Fly had tickled slumber,
Not as deaths dart being laugh'd at: his right Cheeke
Reposing on a Cushion.

GUIDERIUS   Where?

ARUIRAGUS   O'th'floore:
His armes thus leagu'd, I thought he slept, and put
My clowted Brogues from off my feete, whose rudenesse
Answer'd my steps too lowd.

GUIDERIUS   Why, he but sleepes:

If he be gone, hee'l make his Graue, a Bed:
With female Fayries will his Tombe be haunted,
(*To Innogen*) And Wormes will not come to thee.

2170 ARUIRAGUS (*to Innogen*)   With fayrest Flowers
Whil'st Sommer lasts, and I liue heere, *Fidele*,
Ile sweeten thy sad graue: thou shalt not lacke
The Flower that's like thy face, Pale-Primrose, nor
The azur'd Hare-Bell, like thy Veines: no, nor
The leafe of Eglantine, whom not to slander,
Out-sweetned not thy breath: the Ruddocke would
With Charitable bill (Oh bill sore shaming
Those rich-left-heyres, that let their Fathers lye
Without a Monument) bring thee all this,
2180 Yea, and furr'd Mosse besides, when Flowres are none
To winter-goune thy Coarse—

GUIDERIUS   Prythee haue done,
And do not play in Wench-like words with that
Which is so serious. Let vs bury him,
And not protract with admiration, what
Is now due debt. To'th'graue.

ARUIRAGUS   Say, where shall's lay him?

GUIDERIUS
By good *Euriphile*, our Mother.

ARUIRAGUS   Bee't so:
And let vs (*Polidore*) though now our voyces
Haue got the mannish cracke, sing him to'th'ground
As once our Mother: vse like note, and words,
2190 Saue that *Euriphile*, must be *Fidele*.

GUIDERIUS *Cadwall*,
I cannot sing: Ile weepe, and word it with thee;
For Notes of sorrow, out of tune, are worse
Then Priests, and Phanes that lye.

ARUIRAGUS   Wee'l speake it then.

BELARIUS
Great greefes I see med'cine the lesse: For *Cloten*
Is quite forgot. He was a Queenes Sonne, Boyes,
And though he came our Enemy, remember
He was paid for that: though meane, and mighty
      rotting
Together haue one dust, yet Reuerence
2200 (That Angell of the world) doth make distinction
Of place 'tweene high, and low. Our Foe was Princely,
And though you tooke his life, as being our Foe,
Yet bury him, as a Prince.

GUIDERIUS   Pray you fetch him hither,
Thersites body is as good as *Aiax*,
When neyther are aliue.

ARUIRAGUS (*to Belarius*)   If you'l go fetch him,
Wee'l say our Song the whil'st: *Exit Belarius*
                              Brother begin.

GUIDERIUS
Nay *Cadwall*, we must lay his head to th'East,
My Father hath a reason for't.

ARUIRAGUS   'Tis true.

GUIDERIUS
Come on then, and remoue him.

ARUIRAGUS   So, begin.

GUIDERIUS *Feare no more the heate o'th'Sun,*   2210
      Nor the furious Winters rages,
Thou thy worldly task hast don,
      Home art gon, and tane thy wages.
Golden Lads, and Girles all must,
As Chimney-Sweepers come to dust.

ARUIRAGUS *Feare no more the frowne o'th'Great,*
      Thou art past the Tirants stroake,
Care no more to cloath and eate,
      To thee the Reede is as the Oake:
The Scepter, Learning, Physicke must,   2220
All follow this and come to dust.

GUIDERIUS *Feare no more the Lightning flash.*
ARUIRAGUS   *Nor th'all-dreaded Thunderstone.*
GUIDERIUS *Feare not Slander, Censure rash.*
ARUIRAGUS   *Thou hast finish'd Ioy and mone.*
BOTH   *All Louers young, all Louers must,*
      Consigne to thee and come to dust.

GUIDERIUS *No Exorcisor harme thee,*
ARUIRAGUS *Nor no witch-craft charme thee.*
GUIDERIUS *Ghost vnlaid forbeare thee.*   2230
ARUIRAGUS *Nothing ill come neere thee.*
BOTH   *Quiet consumation haue,*
      And renowned be thy graue.

Enter Belarius with the body of Cloten in
Posthumus Suite

GUIDERIUS
We haue done our obsequies: come lay him downe.

BELARIUS
Heere's a few Flowres, but 'bout midnight more:
The hearbes that haue on them cold dew o'th'night
Are strewings fit'st for Graues: vpon therths Face.
You were as Flowres, now wither'd: euen so
These Herbelets shall, which we vpon you strew.
Come on, away, apart vpon our knees   2240
⌈   ⌉
The ground that gaue them first, ha's them againe:
Their pleasures here are past, so is their paine.
            Exeunt Belarius, Aruiragus, and Guiderius

INNOGEN (*awakes*)
Yes Sir, to Milford-Hauen, which is the way?
I thanke you: by yond bush? pray how farre thether?
'Ods pittikins: can it be sixe mile yet?
I haue gone all night: 'Faith, Ile lye downe, and sleepe.
      She sees Cloten
But soft; no Bedfellow? Oh Gods, and Goddesses!
These Flowres are like the pleasures of the World;
This bloody man the care on't. I hope I dreame: 2250
For so I thought I was a Caue-keeper,
And Cooke to honest Creatures. But 'tis not so:
'Twas but a bolt of nothing, shot of nothing,
Which the Braine makes of Fumes. Our very eyes,
Are sometimes like our Iudgements, blinde. Good faith
I tremble still with feare: but if there be
Yet left in Heauen, as small a drop of pittie

As a Wrens eye; fear'd Gods, a part of it.
The Dreame's heere still: euen when I wake it is
2260   Without me, as within me: not imagin'd, felt.
A headlesse man? The Garments of *Posthumus*?
I know the shape of's Legge: this is his Hand:
His Foote Mercuriall: his martiall Thigh
The brawnes of *Hercules*: but his Iouiall face—
Murther in heauen? How? 'tis gone. *Pisanio*,
All Curses madded *Hecuba* gaue the Greekes,
And mine to boot, be darted on thee: thou
Conspir'd with that Irregulous diuell *Cloten*,
Hath heere cut off my Lord. To write, and read,
2270   Be henceforth treacherous. Damn'd *Pisanio*,
Hath with his forged Letters (damn'd *Pisanio*)
From this most brauest vessell of the world
Strooke the maine top! Oh *Posthumus*, alas,
Where is thy head? where's that? Aye me! where's
        that?
Pisanio might haue kill'd thee at the heart,
And left thy head on. How should this be, *Pisanio*?
'Tis he, and *Cloten*: Malice, and Lucre in them
Haue laid this Woe heere. Oh 'tis pregnant, pregnant!
The Drugge he gaue me, which hee said was precious
2280   And Cordiall to me, haue I not found it
Murd'rous to'th'Senses? That confirmes it home:
This is *Pisanio's* deede, and *Cloten*: Oh!
Giue colour to my pale cheeke with thy blood,
That we the horrider may seeme to those
Which chance to finde vs.
        ⌜*She smears her face with blood*⌝
                            Oh, my Lord! my Lord!
        ⌜*She faints.*⌝
        Enter Lucius, Roman Captaines, and a Soothsayer
A ROMAN CAPTAINE (*to Lucius*)
To them, the Legions garrison'd in Gallia
After your will, haue crost the Sea, attending
You heere at Milford-Hauen, with your Shippes:
They are hence in readinesse.
LUCIUS   But what from Rome?
A ROMAN CAPTAINE
2290   The Senate hath stirr'd vp the Confiners,
And Gentlemen of Italy, most willing Spirits,
That promise Noble Seruice: and they come
Vnder the Conduct of bold *Iachimo*,
Syenna's Brother.
LUCIUS   When expect you them?
A ROMAN CAPTAINE
With the next benefit o'th'winde.
LUCIUS   This forwardnesse
Makes our hopes faire. Command our present numbers
Be muster'd: bid the Captaines looke too't.
                            ⌜*Exit one or more*⌝
(*To Soothsayer*)   Now Sir,
What haue you dream'd of late of this warres purpose.
SOOTHSAYER
Last night, the very Gods shew'd me a vision
2300   (I fast, and pray'd for their Intelligence) thus:

I saw Ioues Bird, the Roman Eagle wing'd
From the spungy South, to this part of the West,
There vanish'd in the Sun-beames, which portends
(Vnlesse my sinnes abuse my Diuination)
Successe to th'Roman hoast.
LUCIUS   Dreame often so,
And neuer false.
        He sees Clotens body
                    Soft hoa, what truncke is heere?
Without his top? The ruine speakes, that sometime
It was a worthy building. How? a Page?
Or dead, or sleeping on him? But dead rather:
For Nature doth abhorre to make his bed   2310
With the defunct, or sleepe vpon the dead.
Let's see the Boyes face.
A ROMAN CAPTAINE   Hee's aliue my Lord.
LUCIUS
Hee'l then instruct vs of this body: Young one,
Informe vs of thy Fortunes, for it seemes
They craue to be demanded: who is this
Thou mak'st thy bloody Pillow? Or who was he
That (otherwise then noble Nature did)
Hath alter'd that good Picture? What's thy interest
In this sad wracke? How came't? Who is't?
What art thou?
INNOGEN   I am nothing; or if not,   2320
Nothing to be were better: This was my Master,
A very valiant Britaine, and a good,
That heere by Mountaineers lyes slaine: Alas,
There is no more such Masters: I may wander
From East to Occident, cry out for Seruice,
Try many, all good: serue truly: neuer
Finde such another Master.
LUCIUS   'Lacke, good youth:
Thou mou'st no lesse with thy complaining, then
Thy Maister in bleeding: say his name, good Friend.
INNOGEN
Richard du Champ: (*Aside*) If I do lye, and do   2330
No harme by it, though the Gods heare, I hope
They'l pardon it. (*Alowd*) Say you Sir?
LUCIUS   Thy name?
INNOGEN   *Fidele* Sir.
LUCIUS
Thou doo'st approue thy selfe the very same:
Thy Name well fits thy Faith; thy Faith, thy Name:
Wilt take thy chance with me? I will not say
Thou shalt be so well master'd, but be sure
No lesse belou'd. The Romane Emperors Letters
Sent by a Consull to me, should not sooner
Then thine owne worth preferre thee: Go with me.
INNOGEN
Ile follow Sir. But first, and't please the Gods,   2340
Ile hide my Master from the Flies, as deepe
As these poore Pickaxes can digge: and when
With wild-wood leaues & weeds, I ha' strew'd his graue
And on it said a Century of prayers
(Such as I can) twice o're, Ile weepe, and sighe,

And leauing so his seruice, follow you,
So please you entertaine mee.

LUCIUS   I good youth,
And rather Father thee, then Master thee: My
    Friends,
The Boy hath taught vs manly duties: Let vs
2350   Finde out the prettiest Dazied-Plot we can,
And make him with our Pikes and Partizans
A Graue: Come, Arme him: Boy hee is preferr'd
By thee, to vs, and he shall be interr'd
As Souldiers can. Be cheerefull; wipe thine eyes,
Some Falles are meanes the happier to arise.
                                Exeunt with Clotens body

4.3   *Enter Cymbeline, Lords, and Pisanio*
(Sc. 21)   CYMBELINE
Againe: and bring me word how 'tis with her,
                                Exit one or more
A Feauour with the absence of her Sonne;
A madnesse, of which her life's in danger: Heauens,
How deeply you at once do touch me. *Innogen*,
2360   The great part of my comfort, gone: My Queene
Vpon a desperate bed, and in a time
When fearefull Warres point at me: Her Sonne gone,
So needfull for this present? It strikes me, past
The hope of comfort. (*To Pisanio*) But for thee, Fellow,
Who needs must know of her departure, and
Dost seeme so ignorant, wee'l enforce it from thee
By a sharpe Torture.

PISANIO   Sir, my life is yours,
I humbly set it at your will: But for my Mistris,
I nothing know where she remaines: why gone,
2370   Nor when she purposes returne. Beseech your Highnes,
Hold me your loyall Seruant.

A LORD   Good my Liege,
The day that she was missing, he was heere;
I dare be bound hee's true, and shall performe
All parts of his subiection loyally. For *Cloten*,
There wants no diligence in seeking him,
And will no doubt be found.

CYMBELINE   The time is troublesome:
(*To Pisanio*) Wee'l slip you for a season, but our iealousie
Do's yet depend.

A LORD   So please your Maiesty,
The Romaine Legions, all from Gallia drawne,
2380   Are landed on your Coast, with a supply
Of Romaine Gentlemen, by the Senate sent.

CYMBELINE
Now for the Counsaile of my Son and Queen,
I am amaz'd with matter.

A LORD   Good my Liege,
Your preparation can affront no lesse
Then what you heare of. Come more, for more you're
    ready:
The want is, but to put those Powres in motion,
That long to moue.

CYMBELINE   I thanke you: let's withdraw
And meete the Time, as it seekes vs. We feare not

What can from Italy annoy vs, but
We greeue at chances heere. Away.   2390
                        Exeunt Cymbeline and Lords

PISANIO
I heard no Letter from my Master, since
I wrote him *Innogen* was slaine. 'Tis strange:
Nor heare I from my Mistris, who did promise
To yeeld me often tydings. Neither know I
What is betide to *Cloten*, but remaine
Perplext in all. The Heauens still must worke:
Wherein I am false, I am honest: not true, to be true.
These present warres shall finde I loue my Country,
Euen to the note o'th'King, or Ile fall in them:
All other doubts, by time let them be cleer'd,   2400
Fortune brings in some Boats, that are not steer'd.
                                                        Exit

4.4   *Enter Belarius, Guiderius, & Aruiragus*
(Sc. 22)   GUIDERIUS
The noyse is round about vs.

BELARIUS   Let vs from it.

ARUIRAGUS
What pleasure Sir, finde we in life, to locke it
From Action, and Aduenture.

GUIDERIUS   Nay, what hope
Haue we in hiding vs? This way the Romaines
Must, or for Britaines slay vs, or receiue vs
For barbarous and vnnaturall Reuolts
During their vse, and slay vs after.

BELARIUS   Sonnes,
Wee'l higher to the Mountaines, there secure vs.
To the Kings party there's no going: newnesse   2410
Of *Clotens* death (we being not knowne, not muster'd
Among the Bands) may driue vs to a render
Where we haue liu'd; and so extort from's that
Which we haue done, whose answer would be death
Drawne on with Torture.

GUIDERIUS   This is (Sir) a doubt
In such a time, nothing becomming you,
Nor satisfying vs.

ARUIRAGUS   It is not likely,
That when they heare the Roman horses neigh,
Behold their quarter'd Files; haue both their eyes
And eares so cloyd importantly as now,   2420
That they will waste their time vpon our note,
To know from whence we are.

BELARIUS   Oh, I am knowne
Of many in the Army: Many yeeres
(Though *Cloten* then but young) you see, not wore him
From my remembrance. And besides, the King
Hath not deseru'd my Seruice, nor your Loues,
Who finde in my Exile, the want of Breeding;
The certainty of this heard life, aye hopelesse
To haue the courtesie your Cradle promis'd,
But to be still hot Summers Tanlings, and   2430
The shrinking Slaues of Winter.

GUIDERIUS   Then be so,
Better to cease to be. Pray Sir, to'th'Army:

I, and my Brother are not knowne; your selfe
So out of thought, and thereto so ore-growne,
Cannot be question'd.

ARUIRAGUS   By this Sunne that shines
Ile thither: What thing is't, that I neuer
Did see man dye, scarse euer look'd on blood,
But that of Coward Hares, hot Goats, and Venison?
Neuer bestrid a Horse saue one, that had
2440   A Rider like my selfe, who ne're wore Rowell,
Nor Iron on his heele? I am asham'd
To looke vpon the holy Sunne, to haue
The benefit of his blest Beames, remaining
So long a poore vnknowne.

GUIDERIUS   By heauens Ile go,
If you will blesse me Sir, and giue me leaue,
Ile take the better care: but if you will not,
The hazard therefore due fall on me, by
The hands of Romaines.

ARUIRAGUS   So say I, Amen.

BELARIUS
No reason I (since of your liues you set
2450   So slight a valewation) should reserue
My crack'd one to more care. Haue with you Boyes:
If in your Country warres you chance to dye,
That is my Bed too (Lads) and there Ile lye.
Lead, lead; (aside) the time seems long, their blood
        thinks scorn
Till it flye out, and shew them Princes borne.   Exeunt

❁

5.1   Enter Posthumus alone, dress'd as an Italian
(Sc. 23)   Gentleman, carrying a bloody cloth

POSTHUMUS
Yea bloody cloth, Ile keep thee: for I onc wisht
Thou should'st be colour'd thus. You married ones,
If each of you should take this course, how many
Must murther Wiues much better then themselues
2460   For wrying but a little? Oh Pisanio,
Euery good Seruant do's not all Commands:
No Bond, but to do iust ones. Gods, if you
Should haue 'tane vengeance on my faults, I neuer
Had liu'd to put on this: so had you saued
The noble Innogen, to repent, and strooke
Me (wretch) more worth your Vengeance. But alacke,
You snatch some hence for little faults; that's loue
To haue them fall no more: you some permit
To second illes with illes, each elder worse,
2470   And make them dread il, to the dooers thrift.
But Innogen is your owne, do your blest willes,
And make me blest to obey. I am brought hither
Among th'Italian Gentry, and to fight
Against my Ladies Kingdome: 'Tis enough
That (Britaine) I haue kill'd thy Mistris-peace,
Ile giue no wound to thee: therefore good Heauens,
Heare patiently my purpose. Ile disrobe me
Of these Italian weedes, and suite my selfe
As do's a Britaine Pezant:
        ⌜He disrobes himselfe⌝
                so Ile fight

Against the part I come with: so Ile dye   2480
For thee (O Innogen) euen for whom my life
Is euery breath, a death: and thus, vnknowne,
Pittied, nor hated, to the face of perill
My selfe Ile dedicate. Let me make men know
More valour in me, then my habits show.
Gods, put the strength o'th'Leonati in me:
To shame the guize o'th'world, I will begin
The fashion, lesse without, and more within.   Exit

⌜A March.⌝ Enter Lucius, Iachimo, and the Romane   5.2
Army at one doore: and the Britaine Army at   (Sc. 24)
another: Leonatus Posthumus following like a poore
Souldier. They march ouer, and goe out. ⌜Alarums.⌝
Then enter againe in Skirmish Iachimo and
Posthumus: he vanquisheth and disarmeth Iachimo,
and then leaues him

IACHIMO
The heauinesse and guilt within my bosome,
Takes off my manhood: I haue belyed a Lady,   2490
The Princesse of this Country; and the ayre on't
Reuengingly enfeebles me, or could this Carle,
A very drudge of Natures, haue subdu'de me
In my profession? Knighthoods, and Honors borne
As I weare mine) are titles but of scorne.
If that thy Gentry (Britaine) go before
This Lowt, as he exceeds our Lords, the oddes
Is, that we scarse are men, and you are Goddes.   Exit

The Battaile continues. ⌜Alarums. Excursions. The   5.3
Trumpets sound a Retreat:⌝ the Britaines fly,   (Sc. 25)
Cymbeline is taken: Then enter to his rescue,
Bellarius, Guiderius, and Aruiragus

BELARIUS
Stand, stand, we haue th'aduantage of the ground,
The Lane is guarded: Nothing rowts vs, but   2500
The villany of our feares.

GUIDERIUS and ARUIRAGUS   Stand, stand, and fight.
Enter Posthumus like a poore Souldier, and seconds
the Britaines. They Rescue Cymbeline, and Exeunt

⌜The Trumpets sound a Retreat.⌝ Then enter Lucius,   5.4
Iachimo, and Innogen   (Sc. 26)

LUCIUS (to Innogen)
Away boy from the Troopes, and saue thy selfe:
For friends kil friends, and the disorder's such
As warre were hood-wink'd.

IACHIMO   'Tis their fresh supplies.

LUCIUS
It is a day turn'd strangely: or betimes
Let's re-inforce, or fly.   Exeunt

Enter Posthumus like a poore Souldier, and a   5.5
Britaine Lord   (Sc. 27)

LORD
Cam'st thou from where they made the stand?

POSTHUMUS   I did,
Though you it seemes come from the Fliers?

LORD   I.

POSTHUMUS

No blame be to you Sir, for all was lost,
2510 But that the Heauens fought: the King himselfe
Of his wings destitute, the Army broken,
And but the backes of Britaines seene; all flying
Through a strait Lane, the Enemy full-hearted,
Lolling the Tongue with slaught'ring: hauing worke
More plentifull, then Tooles to doo't: strooke downe
Some mortally, some slightly touch'd, some falling
Meerely through feare, that the strait passe was damm'd
With deadmen, hurt behinde, and Cowards liuing
To dye with length'ned shame.

LORD   Where was this Lane?

POSTHUMUS

2520 Close by the battell, ditch'd, & wall'd with turph,
Which gaue aduantage to an ancient Soldiour
(An honest one I warrant) who deseru'd
So long a breeding, as his white beard came to,
In doing this for's Country. Athwart the Lane,
He, with two striplings (Lads more like to run
The Country base, then to commit such slaughter,
With faces fit for Maskes, or rather fayrer
Then those for preseruation cas'd, or shame)
Made good the passage, cryed to those that fled.
2530 Our *Britaines* harts dye flying, not her men,
To darknesse fleete soules that flye backwards; stand,
Or we are Romanes, and will giue you that
Like beasts, which you shun beastly, and may saue
But to looke backe in frowne: Stand, stand. These
      three,
Three thousand confident, in acte as many:
For three performers are the File, when all
The rest do nothing: With this word stand, stand,
Accomodated by the Place; more Charming
With their owne Noblenesse, which could haue turn'd
2540 A Distaffe, to a Lance, guilded pale lookes;
Part shame, part spirit renew'd, that some turn'd
      coward
But by example (Oh a sinne in Warre,
Damn'd in the first beginners) gan to looke
The way that they did, and to grin like Lyons
Vpon the Pikes o'th'Hunters. Then beganne
A stop i'th'Chaser; a Retyre: Anon
A Rowt, confusion thicke: forthwith they flye
Chickens, the way which they stoopt Eagles: Slaues
The strides they Victors made: and now our Cowards
2550 Like Fragments in hard Voyages became
The life o'th'need: hauing found the backe doore open
Of the vnguarded hearts: heauens, how they wound,
Some slaine before some dying; some their Friends
Ore-borne i'th'former waue, ten chac'd by one,
Are now each one the slaughter-man of twenty:
Those that would dye, or ere resist, are growne
The mortall bugs o'th'Field.

LORD   This was strange chance:
A narrow Lane, an old man, and two Boyes.

POSTHUMUS

Nay, do not wonder at it: yet you are made

Rather to wonder at the things you heare,   2560
Then to worke any. Will you Rime vpon't,
And vent it for a Mock'rie? Heere is one:
'Two Boyes, an Oldman (twice a Boy) a Lane,
'Preseru'd the Britaines, was the Romanes bane.

LORD

Nay, be not angry Sir.

POSTHUMUS   Lacke, to what end?
Who dares not stand his Foe, Ile be his Friend:
For if hee'l do, as he is made to doo,
I know hee'l quickly flye my friendship too.
You haue put me into Rime.

LORD   Farewell, you're angry.

                                             Exit

POSTHUMUS

Still going? This a Lord: Oh Noble misery   2570
To be i'th'Field, and aske what newes of me:
To day, how many would haue giuen their Honours
To haue sau'd their Carkasses? Tooke heele to doo't,
And yet dyed too. I, in mine owne woe charm'd
Could not finde death, where I did heare him groane,
Nor feele him where he strooke. Being an vgly
      Monster,
'Tis strange he hides him in fresh Cups, soft Beds,
Sweet words; or hath moe ministers then we
That draw his kniues i'th'War. Well I will finde him:
For being now a Fauourer to the Britaine,   2580
No more a Britaine, I haue resum'd againe
The part I came in. Fight I will no more,
But yeeld me to the veriest Hinde, that shall
Once touch my shoulder. Great the slaughter is
Heere made by'th'Romane; great the Answer be
Britaines must take. For me, my Ransome's death,
On eyther side I come to spend my breath;
Which neyther heere Ile keepe, nor beare agen,
But end it by some meanes for *Innogen*.

      Enter two Britaine Captaines, and Soldiers

1. CAPTAINE

Great Iupiter be prais'd, *Lucius* is taken,   2590
'Tis thought the old man, and his sonnes, were Angels.

2. CAPTAINE

There was a fourth man, in a silly habit,
That gaue th'Affront with them.

1. CAPTAINE   So 'tis reported:
But none of 'em can be found. Stand, who's there?

POSTHUMUS A Roman,
Who had not now beene drooping heere, if Seconds
Had answer'd him.

2. CAPTAINE (*to Souldiers*) Lay hands on him: a Dogge,
A legge of Rome shall not returne to tell
What Crows haue peckt them here: he brags his seruice
As if he were of note: bring him to'th'King.   2600

      ⌈Flourish.⌉ Enter Cymbeline ⌈and his traine,⌉
      Belarius, Guiderius, Aruiragus, Pisanio, and
      Romane Captiues. The Captaines present Posthumus
      to Cymbeline, who deliuers him ouer to a Gaoler.
      Exeunt. Manet Posthumus, and two Gaolers, ⌈who
      lock Gyues on his legges⌉

GAOLER

You shall not now be stolne, you haue lockes vpon
  you:
So graze, as you finde Pasture.

2. GAOLER   I, or a stomacke.

Exeunt Gaolers

POSTHUMUS

Most welcome bondage; for thou art a way
(I thinke) to liberty: yet am I better
Then one that's sicke o'th'Gowt, since he had rather
Groane so in perpetuity, then be cur'd
By'th'sure Physitian, Death; who is the key
T'vnbarre these Lockes. My Conscience, thou art fetter'd
More then my shanks, & wrists: you good Gods giue
  me
2610   The penitent Instrument to picke that Bolt,
Then free for euer. Is't enough I am sorry?
So Children temporall Fathers do appease;
Gods are more full of mercy. Must I repent,
I cannot do it better then in Gyues,
Desir'd, more then constrain'd, to satisfie
If of my Freedome 'tis the maine part, take
No stricter render of me, then my All.
I know you are more clement then vilde men,
Who of their broken Debtors take a third,
2620   A sixt, a tenth, letting them thriue againe
On their abatement; that's not my desire.
For *Innogens* deere life, take mine, and though
'Tis not so deere, yet 'tis a life; you coyn'd it,
'Tweene man, and man, they waigh not euery stampe:
Though light, take Peeces for the figures sake,
(You rather) mine being yours: and so great Powres,
If you will make this Audit, take this life,
And cancell these cold Bonds. Oh *Innogen*,
Ile speake to thee in silence.

> *He sleepes. Solemne Musicke. Enter (as in an*
> *Apparation) Sicillius Leonatus, Father to*
> *Posthumus, an old man, attyred like a warriour,*
> *leading in his hand an ancient Matron (his wife, &*
> *Mother to Posthumus) with Musicke before them.*
> *Then after other Musicke, followes the two young*
> *Leonati (Brothers to Posthumus) with wounds as*
> *they died in the warrs. They circle Posthumus*
> *round as he lies sleeping*

SICILIUS

2630   No more thou Thunder-Master shew
  thy spight, on Mortall Flies:
With Mars fall out with *Iuno* chide,
  that thy Adulteries
Rates, and Reuenges.
Hath my poore Boy done ought but well,
  whose face I neuer saw:
I dy'de whil'st in the Wombe he staide,
  attending Natures Law.
Whose Father then (as men report,
  thou Orphanes Father art)
2640   Thou should'st haue bin, and sheelded him,
  from this earth-vexing smart.

MOTHER

Lucina lent not me her ayde,
  but tooke me in my Throwes,
That from me was *Posthumus* ript,
  came crying 'mong'st his Foes.
A thing of pitty.

SICILIUS

Great Nature like his Ancestrie,
  moulded the stuffe so faire:
That he deseru'd the praise o'th'World,   2650
  as great *Sicilius* heyre.

1. BROTHER

When once he was mature for man,
  in Britaine where was hee
That could stand vp his paralell?
  or fruitfull obiect bee?
In eye of *Innogen*, that best
  could deeme his dignitie.

MOTHER

With Marriage wherefore was he mockt
  to be exil'd, and throwne
From *Leonati* Seate, and cast   2660
  from her, his deerest one:
Sweete *Innogen*?

SICILIUS

Why did you suffer *Iachimo*,
  slight thing of Italy,
To taint his Nobler hart & braine,
  with needlesse ielousy,
And to become the gecke and scorne
  o'th'others vilany?

2. BROTHER

For this, from stiller Seats we come,
  our Parents, and vs twaine,   2670
That striking in our Countries cause,
  fell brauely, and were slaine,
Our Fealty, & *Tenantius* right,
  with Honor to maintaine.

1. BROTHER

Like hardiment *Posthumus* hath
  to *Cymbeline* perform'd:
Then Iupiter, yᵘ King of Gods,
  why hast yᵘ thus adiourn'd
The Graces for his Merits due,
  being all to dolors turn'd?   2680

SICILIUS

Thy Christall window ope; looke out,
  no longer exercise
Vpon a valiant Race, thy harsh,
  and potent iniuries:

MOTHER

Since (Iupiter) our Son is good,
  take off his miseries.

SICILIUS

Peepe through thy Marble Mansion, helpe,
  or we poore Ghosts will cry
To'th'shining Synod of the rest,
  against thy Deity.   2690

BROTHERS

    Helpe (Iupiter) or we appeale,
        and from thy iustice flye.

    Iupiter descends in Thunder and Lightning, sitting
    vppon an Eagle: hee throwes a Thunder-bolt. The
    Ghostes fall on their knees

IUPITER

    No more you petty Spirits of Region low
      Offend our hearing: hush. How dare you Ghostes
    Accuse the Thunderer, whose Bolt (you know)
      Sky-planted, batters all rebelling Coasts.
    Poore shadowes of Elizium, hence, and rest
      Vpon your neuer-withering bankes of Flowres.
    Be not with mortall accidents opprest,
2700   No care of yours it is, you know 'tis ours.
    Whom best I loue, I crosse; to make my guift
      The more delay'd, delighted. Be content,
    Your low-laide Sonne, our Godhead will vplift:
      His Comforts thriue, his Trials well are spent:
    Our Iouiall Starre reign'd at his Birth, and in
      Our Temple was he married: Rise, and fade,
    He shall be Lord of Lady *Innogen*,
      And happier much by his Affliction made.
    This Tablet lay vpon his Brest, wherein
2710   Our pleasure, his full Fortune, doth confine,
    He giues the Ghostes a Tablet, which they lay vpon
    Posthumus Brest
    And so away: no farther with your dinne
      Expresse Impatience, least you stirre vp mine:
    Mount Eagle, to my Palace Christalline.
                  Ascends into the Heauens

SICILIUS

    He came in Thunder, his Celestiall breath
    Was sulphurous to smell: the holy Eagle
    Stoop'd, as to foote vs: his Ascension is
    More sweet then our blest Fields: his Royall Bird
    Prunes the immortall wing, and cloyes his Beake,
    As when his God is pleas'd.

ALL THE GHOSTES   Thankes Iupiter.

SICILIUS

2720   The Marble Pauement clozes, he is enter'd
    His radiant Roofe: Away, and to be blest
    Let vs with care performe his great behest.
                  The Ghostes vanish

    Posthumus awakes

POSTHUMUS

    Sleepe, thou hast bin a Grandsire, and begot
    A Father to me: and thou hast created
    A Mother, and two Brothers. But (oh scorne)
    Gone, they went hence so soone as they were borne:
    And so I am awake. Poore Wretches, that depend
    On Greatnesse, Fauour; Dreame as I haue done,
    Wake, and finde nothing. But (alas) I swerue:
2730   Many Dreame not to finde, neither deserue,
    And yet are steep'd in Fauours; so am I
    That haue this Golden chance, and know not why:
    What Fayeries haunt this ground? A Book? Oh rare
      one,

Be not, as is our fangled world, a Garment
Nobler then that it couers. Let thy effects
So follow, to be most vnlike our Courtiers,
As good, as promise.
(*Reades*) *When as a Lyons whelpe, shall to himselfe*
vnknown, without seeking finde, and bee embrac'd by a
peece of tender Ayre: And when from a stately Cedar shall 2740
be lopt branches, which being dead many yeares, shall after
reuiue, bee ioynted to the old Stocke, and freshly grow,
then shall Posthumus end his miseries, Britaine be
fortunate, and flourish in Peace and Plentie.
'Tis still a Dreame: or else such stuffe as Madmen
Tongue, and braine not: either both, or nothing,
Or senselesse speaking, or a speaking such
As sense cannot vntye. Be what it is,
The Action of my life is like it, which Ile keepe
If but for simpathy.   2750
    Enter Gaoler

GAOLER Come Sir, are you ready for death?

POSTHUMUS Ouer-roasted rather: ready long ago.

GAOLER Hanging is the word, Sir, if you bee readie for
  that, you are well Cook'd.

POSTHUMUS So if I proue a good repast to the Spectators,
  the dish payes the shot.

GAOLER A heauy reckoning for you Sir: But the comfort
  is you shall be called to no more payments, fear no
  more Tauerne Bils, which are as often the sadnesse of
  parting, as the procuring of mirth: you come in faint 2760
  for want of meate, depart reeling with too much drinke:
  sorrie that you haue payed too much, and sorry that
  you are payed too much: Purse and Braine, both empty:
  the Brain the heauier, for being too light; the Purse too
  light, being drawne of heauinesse. Of this contradiction
  you shall now be quit: Oh the charity of a penny Cord,
  it summes vp thousands in a trice: you haue no true
  Debitor, and Creditor but it: of what's past, is, and to
  come, the discharge: your necke (Sir) is Pen, Booke,
  and Counters; so the Acquittance followes.   2770

POSTHUMUS I am merrier to dye, then thou art to liue.

GAOLER Indeed Sir, he that sleepes, feeles not the Tooth-
  Ache: but a man that were to sleepe your sleepe, and
  a Hangman to helpe him to bed, I think he would
  change places with his Officer: for, look you Sir, you
  know not which way you shall go.

POSTHUMUS Yes indeed do I, fellow.

GAOLER Your death has eyes in's head then: I haue not
  seene him so pictur'd: you must either bee directed by
  some that take vpon them to know, or take vpon your 2780
  selfe that which I am sure you do not know: or iump
  the after-enquiry on your owne perill: and how you
  shall speed in your iournies end, I thinke you'l neuer
  returne to tell one.

POSTHUMUS I tell thee, Fellow, there are none want eyes,
  to direct them the way I am going, but such as winke,
  and will not vse them.

GAOLER What an infinite mocke is this, that a man shold
  haue the best vse of eyes, to see the way of blindnesse:
  I am sure hanging's the way of winking.   2790

Enter a Messenger

MESSENGER Knocke off his Manacles, bring your Prisoner
    to the King.

POSTHUMUS Thou bring'st good newes, I am call'd to bee
    made free.

GAOLER Ile be hang'd then.

POSTHUMUS Thou shalt be then freer then a Gaoler; no
    bolts for the dead.

GAOLER (*aside*) Vnlesse a man would marry a Gallowes, &
    beget yong Gibbets, I neuer saw one so prone: yet on
2800   my Conscience, there are verier Knaues desire to liue,
    for all he be a Roman; and there be some of them too
    that dye against their willes; so should I, if I were one.
    I would we were all of one minde, and one minde
    good: O there were desolation of Gaolers and Galowses:
    I speake against my present profit, but my wish hath
    a preferment in't.   *Exeunt*

5.6
(Sc. 28)   ⌈*Flourish.*⌉ *Enter Cymbeline, Bellarius, Guiderius,*
        Aruiragus, Pisanio, and Lords

CYMBELINE (*to Belarius, Guiderius, and Aruiragus*)
    Stand by my side you, whom the Gods haue made
    Preseruers of my Throne: woe is my heart,
    That the poore Souldier that so richly fought,
    Whose ragges, sham'd gilded Armes, whose naked
2810   brest
    Stept before Targes of proofe, cannot be found:
    He shall be happy that can finde him, if
    Our Grace can make him so.

BELARIUS   I neuer saw
    Such Noble fury in so poore a Thing;
    Such precious deeds, in one that promist nought
    But beggery, and poore lookes.

CYMBELINE   No tydings of him?

PISANIO
    He hath bin search'd among the dead, & liuing;
    But no trace of him.

CYMBELINE   To my greefe, I am
    The heyre of his Reward, which I will adde
    (*To Belarius, Guiderius, and Aruiragus*)
2820   To you (the Liuer, Heart, and Braine of Britaine)
    By whom (I grant) she liues. 'Tis now the time
    To aske of whence you are. Report it.

BELARIUS   Sir,
    In Cambria are we borne, and Gentlemen:
    Further to boast, were neyther true, nor modest,
    Vnlesse I adde, we are honest.

CYMBELINE   Bow your knees:
    They kneel. He knights them
    Arise my Knights o'th'Battell, I create you
    Companions to our person, and will fit you
    With Dignities becomming your estates.
    Belarius, Guiderius, and Aruiragus rise.
    Enter Cornelius and Ladies
    There's businesse in these faces: why so sadly
2830   Greet you our Victory? you looke like Romaines,
    And not o'th'Court of Britaine.

CORNELIUS   Hayle great King,

    To sowre your happinesse, I must report
    The Queene is dead.

CYMBELINE   Who worse then a Physitian
    Would this report become? But I consider,
    By Med'cine life may be prolong'd, yet death
    Will seize the Doctor too. How ended she?

CORNELIUS
    With horror, madly dying, like her life,
    Which (being cruell to the world) concluded
    Most cruell to her selfe. What she confest,
    I will report, so please you. These her Women   2840
    Can trip me, if I erre, who with wet cheekes
    Were present when she finish'd.

CYMBELINE   Prythee say.

CORNELIUS
    First, she confest she neuer lou'd you: onely
    Affected Greatnesse got by you: not you:
    Married your Royalty, was wife to your place:
    Abhorr'd your person.

CYMBELINE   She alone knew this:
    And but she spoke it dying, I would not
    Beleeue her lips in opening it. Proceed.

CORNELIUS
    Your daughter, whom she bore in hand to loue
    With such integrity, she did confesse   2850
    Was as a Scorpion to her sight, whose life
    (But that her flight preuented it) she had
    Tane off by poyson.

CYMBELINE   O most delicate Fiend!
    Who is't can read a Woman? Is there more?

CORNELIUS
    More Sir, and worse. She did confesse she had
    For you a mortall Minerall, which being tooke,
    Should by the minute feede on life, and ling'ring,
    By inches waste you. In which time, she purpos'd
    By watching, weeping, tendance, kissing, to
    Orecome you with her shew; and in fine   2860
    (When she had fit you with her craft, to worke
    Her Sonne into th'adoption of the Crowne:
    But fayling of her end by his strange absence,
    Grew shamelesse desperate, open'd (in despight
    Of Heauen, and Men) her purposes: repented
    The euils she hatch'd, were not effected: so
    Dispayring, dyed.

CYMBELINE   Heard you all this, her Women?

⌈LADIES⌉
    We did, so please your Highnesse.

CYMBELINE   Mine eyes
    Were not in fault, for she was beautifull:
    Mine eares that heard her flattery, nor my heart,   2870
    That thought her like her seeming. It had beene vicious
    To haue mistrusted her: yet (Oh my Daughter)
    That it was folly in me, thou mayst say,
    And proue it in thy feeling. Heauen mend all.
    Enter Lucius, Iachimo, Soothsayer and other Roman
    prisoners, Leonatus behind, and Innogen dressed as
    a Man, all guarded by Britaine souldiers
    Thou comm'st not *Caius* now for Tribute, that

The Britaines haue rac'd out, though with the losse
Of many a bold one: whose Kinsmen haue made suite
That their good soules may be appeas'd, with slaughter
Of you their Captiues, which our selfe haue granted,
2880 So thinke of your estate.

LUCIUS

Consider Sir, the chance of Warre, the day
Was yours by accident: had it gone with vs,
We should not when the blood was cool, haue threatend
Our Prisoners with the Sword. But since the Gods
Will haue it thus, that nothing but our liues
May be call'd ransome, let it come: Sufficeth,
A Roman, with a Romans heart can suffer:
Augustus liues to thinke on't: and so much
For my peculiar care. This one thing onely
I will entreate,

He presents Innogen to Cymbeline

2890   my Boy (a Britaine borne)
Let him be ransom'd: Neuer Master had
A Page so kinde, so duteous, diligent,
So tender ouer his occasions, true,
So feate, so Nurse-like: let his vertue ioyne
With my request, which Ile make bold your Highnesse
Cannot deny: he hath done no Britaine harme,
Though he haue seru'd a Roman. Saue him (Sir)
And spare no blood beside.

CYMBELINE   I haue surely seene him:
His fauour is familiar to me: Boy,
2900 Thou hast look'd thy selfe into my grace,
And art mine owne. I know not why, wherefore,
To say, liue boy: ne're thanke thy Master, liue;
And aske of *Cymbeline* what Boone thou wilt,
Fitting my bounty, and thy state, Ile giue it:
Yea, though thou do demand a Prisoner
The Noblest tane.

INNOGEN   I humbly thanke your Highnesse.

LUCIUS

I do not bid thee begge my life, good Lad,
And yet I know thou wilt.

INNOGEN   No, no, alacke,
There's other worke in hand: I see a thing
2910 Bitter to me, as death: your life, good Master,
Must shuffle for it selfe.

LUCIUS   The Boy disdaines me,
He leaues me, scornes me: briefely dye their ioyes,
That place them on the truth of Gyrles, and Boyes.
Why stands he so perplext?

CYMBELINE (*to Innogen*)   What would'st thou Boy?
I loue thee more, and more: thinke more and more
What's best to aske. Know'st him thou look'st on?
    speake
Wilt haue him liue? Is he thy Kin? thy Friend?

INNOGEN

He is a Romane, no more kin to me,
Then I to your Highnesse, who being born your vassaile
Am something neerer.

2920 CYMBELINE   Wherefore ey'st him so?

INNOGEN

Ile tell you (Sir) in priuate, if you please
To giue me hearing.

CYMBELINE   I, with all my heart,
And lend my best attention. What's thy name?

INNOGEN

Fidele Sir.

CYMBELINE Thou'rt my good youth: my Page
Ile be thy Master: walke with me: speake freely.

Cymbeline and Innogen speake apart

BELARIUS (*aside to Guiderius and Aruiragus*)

Is not this Boy reuiu'd from death?

ARUIRAGUS   One Sand another
Not more resembles: that sweet Rosie Lad
Who dyed, and was *Fidele*: what thinke you?

GUIDERIUS The same dead thing aliue.   2930

BELARIUS

Peace, peace, see further: he eyes vs not, forbeare,
Creatures may be alike: were't he, I am sure
He would haue spoke to vs.

GUIDERIUS   But we see him dead.

BELARIUS

Be silent: let's see further.

PISANIO (*aside*)   It is my Mistris:
Since she is liuing, let the time run on,
To good, or bad.

CYMBELINE (*to Innogen*) Come, stand thou by our side,
Make thy demand alowd. (*To Iachimo*) Sir, step you
    forth,
Giue answer to this Boy, and do it freely,
Or by our Greatnesse, and the grace of it
(Which is our Honor) bitter torture shall   2940
Winnow the truth from falshood. (*To Innogen*) One
    speake to him.

INNOGEN

My boone is, that this Gentleman may render
Of whom he had this Ring.

POSTHUMUS (*aside*)   What's that to him?

CYMBELINE (*to Iachimo*)

That Diamond vpon your Finger, say
How came it yours?

IACHIMO

Thou'lt torture me to leaue vnspoken, that
Which to be spoke, wou'd torture thee.

CYMBELINE   How? me?

IACHIMO

I am glad to be constrain'd to vtter that
Torments me to conceale. By Villany
I got this Ring: 'twas *Leonatus* Iewell,   2950
Whom thou did'st banish: and which more may
    greeue thee,
As it doth me: a Nobler Sir, ne're liu'd
'Twixt sky and ground. Wilt thou heare more my Lord?

CYMBELINE

All that belongs to this.

IACHIMO   That Paragon, thy daughter,

For whom my heart drops blood, and my false spirits
Quaile to remember. Giue me leaue, I faint.
CYMBELINE
    My Daughter? what of hir? Renew thy strength,
    I had rather thou should'st liue, while Nature will,
    Then dye ere I heare more: striue man, and speake.
IACHIMO
2960   Vpon a time, vnhappy was the clocke
    That strooke the houre: it was in Rome, accurst
    The Mansion where: 'twas at a Feast, oh would
    Our Viands had bin poyson'd (or at least
    Those which I heau'd to head:) the good *Posthumus*,
    (What should I say? he was too good to be
    Where ill men were, and was the best of all
    Among'st the rar'st of good ones) sitting sadly,
    Hearing vs praise our Loues of Italy
    For Beauty, that made barren the swell'd boast
2970   Of him that best could speake: for Feature, laming
    The Shrine of *Venus*, or straight-pight *Minerua*,
    Postures, beyond breefe Nature. For Condition,
    A shop of all the qualities, that man
    Loues woman for, besides that hooke of Wiuing,
    Fairenesse, which strikes the eye.
CYMBELINE   I stand on fire.
    Come to the matter.
IACHIMO   All too soone I shall,
    Vnlesse thou would'st greeue quickly. This *Posthumus*,
    Most like a Noble Lord, in loue, and one
    That had a Royall Louer, tooke his hint,
2980   And (not dispraising whom we prais'd, therein
    He was as calme as vertue) he began
    His Mistris picture, which, by his tongue, being made,
    And then a minde put in't, either our bragges
    Were crak'd of Kitchin-Trulles, or his description
    Prou'd vs vnspeaking sottes.
CYMBELINE   Nay, nay, to'th'purpose.
IACHIMO
    Your daughters Chastity, (there it beginnes)
    He spake of her, as *Dian* had hot dreames,
    And she alone, were cold: Whereat, I wretch
    Made scruple of his praise, and wager'd with him
2990   Peeces of Gold, 'gainst this, which then he wore
    Vpon his honour'd finger) to attaine
    In suite the place of's bed, and winne this Ring
    By hers, and mine Adultery: he (true Knight)
    No lesser of her Honour confident
    Then I did truly finde her, stakes this Ring,
    And would so, had it beene a Carbuncle
    Of *Phœbus* Wheele; and might so safely, had it
    Bin all the worth of's Carre. Away to Britaine
    Poste I in this designe: Well may you (Sir)
3000   Remember me at Court, where I was taught
    Of your chaste Daughter, the wide difference
    'Twixt Amorous, and Villanous. Being thus quench'd
    Of hope, not longing; mine Italian braine,
    Gan in your duller Britaine operate
    Most vildely: for my vantage excellent.
    And to be breefe, my practise so preuayl'd

That I return'd with simular proofe enough,
To make the Noble *Leonatus* mad,
By wounding his beleefe in her Renowne,
With Tokens thus, and thus: auerring notes   3010
Of Chamber-hanging, Pictures, this her Bracelet
(Oh cunning how I got it) nay some markes
Of secret on her person, that he could not
But thinke her bond of Chastity quite crack'd,
I hauing 'tane the forfeyt. Whereupon,
Me thinkes I see him now.
POSTHUMUS (*comming forward*) I so thou do'st,
    Italian Fiend. Aye me, most credulous Foole,
    Egregious murtherer, Theefe, any thing
    That's due to all the Villaines past, in being
    To come. Oh giue me Cord, or knife, or poyson,   3020
    Some vpright Iusticer. Thou King, send out
    For Torturors ingenious: it is I
    That all th'abhorred things o'th'earth amend
    By being worse then they. I am *Posthumus*,
    That kill'd thy Daughter: Villain-like, I lye,
    That caus'd a lesser villaine then my selfe,
    A sacrilegious Theefe to doo't. The Temple
    Of Vertue was she; yea, and she her selfe.
    Spit, and throw stones, cast myre vpon me, set
    The dogges o'th'street to bay me: euery villaine   3030
    Be call'd *Posthumus Leonatus*, and
    Be villain lesse then 'twas. Oh *Innogen*!
    My Queene, my life, my wife: oh *Innogen*,
    Innogen, Innogen.
INNOGEN (*approaching him*) Peace my Lord, heare, heare.
POSTHUMUS
    Shall's haue a play of this? Thou scornfull Page,
    There lye thy part.
            He strikes her downe
PISANIO (*comming forward*) Oh Gentlemen, helpe,
    Mine and your Mistris: Oh my Lord *Posthumus*,
    You ne're kill'd *Innogen* till now: helpe, helpe,
    (*To Innogen*) Mine honour'd Lady.
CYMBELINE   Does the world go round?
POSTHUMUS
    How comes these staggers on mee?
PISANIO (*to Innogen*)   Wake my Mistris.   3040
CYMBELINE
    If this be so, the Gods do meane to strike me
    To death, with mortall ioy.
PISANIO (*to Innogen*) How fares my Mistris?
INNOGEN Oh get thee from my sight,
    Thou gau'st me poyson: dangerous Fellow hence,
    Breath not where Princes are.
CYMBELINE   The tune of *Innogen*.
PISANIO
    Lady, the Gods throw stones of sulpher on me, if
    That box I gaue you, was not thought by mee
    A precious thing, I had it from the Queene.
CYMBELINE
    New matter still.
INNOGEN   It poyson'd me.
CORNELIUS   Oh Gods!   3050

I left out one thing which the Queene confest,
(*To Pisanio*) Which must approue thee honest. If *Pisanio*
Haue (said she) giuen his Mistris that Confection
Which I gaue him for Cordiall, she is seru'd,
As I would serue a Rat.

CYMBELINE   What's this, *Cornelius*?

CORNELIUS
The Queene (Sir) very oft importun'd me
To temper poysons for her, still pretending
The satisfaction of her knowledge, onely
In killing Creatures vilde, as Cats and Dogges
3060   Of no esteeme. I dreading, that her purpose
Was of more danger, did compound for her
A certaine stuffe, which being tane, would cease
The present powre of life, but in short time,
All Offices of Nature, should againe
Do their due Functions. (*To Innogen*) Haue you tane
        of it?

INNOGEN
Most like I did, for I was dead.

BELARIUS (*aside to Guiderius and Aruiragus*) My Boyes,
There was our error.

GUIDERIUS   This is sure *Fidele*.

INNOGEN (*to Posthumus*)
Why did you throw your wedded Lady frō you?
Thinke that you are vpon a locke, and now
Throw me againe.

        She throwes her armes about his necke

3070   POSTHUMUS   Hang there like fruite, my soule,
Till the Tree dye.

CYMBELINE (*to Innogen*) How now, my Flesh? my Childe?
What, mak'st thou me a dullard in this Act?
Wilt thou not speake to me?

INNOGEN (*kneeling*)   Your blessing, Sir.

BELARIUS (*aside to Guiderius and Aruiragus*)
Though you did loue this youth, I blame ye not,
You had a motiue for't.

CYMBELINE   My teares that fall
Proue holy-water on thee;
        ⌈*He raises her*⌉
                        Innogen,
Thy Mothers dead.

INNOGEN   I am sorry for't, my Lord.

CYMBELINE
Oh, she was naught; and long of her it was
That we meet heere so strangely: but her Sonne
Is gone, we know not how, nor where.

3080 PISANIO   My Lord,
Now feare is from me, Ile speake troth. Lord *Cloten*
Vpon my Ladies missing, came to me
With his Sword drawne, foam'd at the mouth, and
        swore
If I discouer'd not which way she was gone,
It was my instant death. By accident,
I had a feigned Letter of my Masters
Then in my pocket, which directed him
To seeke her on the Mountaines neere to Milford,
Where in a frenzie, in my Masters Garments
3090   (Which he inforc'd from me) away he postes

With vnchaste purpose, and with oath to violate
My Ladies honor, what became of him,
I further know not.

GUIDERIUS   Let me end the Story:
I slew him there.

CYMBELINE   Marry, the Gods forefend.
I would not thy good deeds, should from my lips
Plucke a hard sentence: Prythee valiant youth
Deny't againe.

GUIDERIUS I haue spoke it, and I did it.

CYMBELINE He was a Prince.

GUIDERIUS
A most inciuill one. The wrongs he did mee   3100
Were nothing Prince-like; for he did prouoke me
With Language that would make me spurne the Sea,
If it could so roare to me. I cut off's head,
And am right glad he is not standing heere
To tell this tale of mine.

CYMBELINE   I am sorrow for thee:
By thine owne tongue thou art condemn'd, and must
Endure our Law: Thou'rt dead.

INNOGEN   That headlesse man
I thought had bin my Lord.

CYMBELINE (*to souldiers*)   Binde the Offender,
And take him from our presence.

BELARIUS   Stay, Sir King.
This boy is better then the man he slew,   3110
As well descended as thy selfe, and hath
More of thee merited, then a Band of *Clotens*
Had euer scarre for. Let his Armes alone,
They were not borne for bondage.

CYMBELINE   Why old Soldier:
Wilt thou vndoo the worth thou art vnpayd for
By tasting of our wrath? How of descent
As good as we?

ARUIRAGUS   In that he spake too farre.

CYMBELINE ⌈*to Belarius*⌉
And thou shalt dye for't.

BELARIUS   We will dye all three,
But I will proue that two one's are as good
As I haue giuen out him. My Sonnes, I must   3120
For mine owne part, vnfold a dangerous speech,
Though haply well for you.

ARUIRAGUS   Your danger's ours.

GUIDERIUS
And our good his.

BELARIUS   Haue at it then, by leaue
Thou hadd'st (great King) a Subiect, who
Was call'd *Belarius*.

CYMBELINE   What of him? He is
A banish'd Traitor.

BELARIUS   He it is, that hath
Assum'd this age: indeed a banish'd man,
I know not how, a Traitor.

CYMBELINE (*to souldiers*)   Take him hence,
The whole world shall not saue him.

BELARIUS   Not too hot;
First pay me for the Nursing of thy Sonnes,   3130

1335

And let it be confiscate all, so soone
As I haue receyu'd it.

CYMBELINE   Nursing of my Sonnes?

BELARIUS

I am too blunt, and sawcy: (*kneeling*) heere's my knee:
Ere I arise, I will preferre my Sonnes,
Then spare not the old Father. Mighty Sir,
These two young Gentlemen that call me Father,
And thinke they are my Sonnes, are none of mine,
They are the yssue of your Loynes, my Liege,
And blood of your begetting.

CYMBELINE   How? my Issue.

BELARIUS

3140 So sure as you, your Fathers: I (old *Morgan*)
Am that *Belarius*, whom you sometime banish'd:
Your pleasure was my meere offence, my punishment
It selfe, and all my Treason: that I suffer'd,
Was all the harme I did. These gentle Princes
(For such, and so they are) these twenty yeares
Haue I train'd vp; those Arts they haue, as I
Could put into them. My breeding was (Sir)
As your Highnesse knowes: Their Nurse *Euriphile*
(Whom for the Theft I wedded) stole these Children
3150 Vpon my Banishment: I moou'd her too't,
Hauing receyu'd the punishment before
For that which I did then. Beaten for Loyaltie,
Excited me to Treason. Their deere losse,
The more of you 'twas felt, the more it shap'd
Vnto my end of stealing them. But gracious Sir,
Heere are your Sonnes againe, and I must loose
Two of the sweet'st Companions in the World.
The benediction of these couering Heauens
Fall on their heads like dew, for they are worthie
To in-lay Heauen with Starres.

3160 **CYMBELINE**   Thou weep'st, and speak'st:
The Seruice that you three haue done, is more
Vnlike, then this thou tell'st. I lost my Children,
If these be they, I know not how to wish
A payre of worthier Sonnes.

BELARIUS ⌜*rising*⌝   Be pleas'd awhile;
This Gentleman, whom I call *Polidore*,
Most worthy Prince, as yours, is true *Guiderius*:
        ⌜*Guiderius kneeles*⌝
This Gentleman, my *Cadwall*, *Aruiragus*,
Your yonger Princely Son,
        ⌜*Aruiragus kneeles*⌝
                              he Sir, was lapt
In a most curious Mantle, wrought by th'hand
3170 Of his Queene Mother, which for more probation
I can with ease produce.

CYMBELINE   *Guiderius* had
Vpon his necke a Mole, a sanguine Starre,
It was a marke of wonder.

BELARIUS   This is he,
Who hath vpon him still that naturall stampe:
It was wise Natures end, in the donation
To be his euidence now.

CYMBELINE   Oh, what am I

A Mother to the byrth of three? Nere Mother
Reioyc'd deliuerance more: Blest, pray you be,
That after this strange starting from your Orbes,
You may reigne in them now:
        ⌜*Guiderius and Aruiragus rise*⌝
                              Oh *Innogen*,   3180
Thou hast lost by this a Kingdome.

INNOGEN   No, my Lord:
I haue got two Worlds by't. Oh my gentle Brothers,
Haue we thus met? Oh neuer say heereafter
But I am truest speaker. You call'd me Brother
When I was but your Sister: I you Brothers,
When ye were so indeed.

CYMBELINE   Did you ere meete?

ARUIRAGUS

I my good Lord.

GUIDERIUS   And at first meeting lou'd,
Continew'd so, vntill we thought he dyed.

CORNELIUS

By the Queenes Dramme she swallow'd.

CYMBELINE   O rare instinct!
When shall I heare all through? This fierce
        abridgment,   3190
Hath to it Circumstantiall branches, which
Distinction should be rich in. Where? how liu'd you?
And when came you to serue our Romane Captiue?
How parted with your Brothers? How first met them?
Why fled you from the Court? And whether? these
And your three motiues to the Battaile? with
I know not how much more should be demanded,
And all the other by-dependances
From chance to chance? But nor the Time, nor Place
Will serue our long Intergatories. See,   3200
Posthumus Anchors vpon *Innogen*;
And she (like harmlesse Lightning) throwes her eye
On him: her Brothers, Me, her Master hitting
Each obiect with a Ioy: the Counter-change
Is seuerally in all. Let's quit this ground,
And smoake the Temple with our Sacrifices.
(*To Belarius*) Thou art my Brother, so wee'l hold thee
        euer.

INNOGEN (*to Belarius*)
You are my Father too, and did releeue me:
To see this gracious season.

CYMBELINE   All ore-ioy'd
Saue these in bonds, let them be ioyfull too,   3210
For they shall taste our Comfort.

INNOGEN (*to Lucius*)   My good Master,
I will yet do you seruice.

LUCIUS   Happy be you.

CYMBELINE

The forlorne Souldier, that so Nobly fought
He would haue well becom'd this place, and grac'd
The thankings of a King.

POSTHUMUS   I am Sir
The Souldier that did company these three
In poore beseeming: 'twas a fitment for
The purpose I then follow'd. That I was he,

Speake *Iachimo*, I had you downe, and might
Haue made you finish.

3220 IACHIMO (*kneeling*)   I am downe againe:
But now my heauie Conscience sinkes my knee,
As then your force did. Take that life, beseech you
Which I so often owe: but your Ring first,
And heere the Bracelet of the truest Princesse
That euer swore her Faith.

POSTHUMUS (*raising him*)   Kneele not to me:
The powre that I haue on you, is to spare you:
The malice towards you, to forgiue you. Liue
And deale with others better.

CYMBELINE   Nobly doom'd:
Wee'l learne our Freenesse of a Sonne-in-Law:
Pardon's the word to all.

3230 ARUIRAGUS (*to Posthumus*) You holpe vs Sir,
As you did meane indeed to be our Brother,
Ioy'd are we, that you are.

POSTHUMUS
Your Seruant Princes. (*To Lucius*) Good my Lord of
Rome
Call forth your Sooth-sayer: As I slept, me thought
Great Iupiter vpon his Eagle back'd
Appear'd to me, with other sprightly shewes
Of mine owne Kindred. When I wak'd, I found
This Labell on my bosome; whose containing
Is so from sense in hardnesse, that I can
3240 Make no Collection of it. Let him shew
His skill in the construction.

LUCIUS   *Philarmonus*.

SOOTHSAYER
Heere, my good Lord.

LUCIUS   Read, and declare the meaning.

SOOTHSAYER (*reades the Tablet*) *When as a Lyons whelpe,
shall to himselfe vnknown, without seeking finde, and bee
embrac'd by a peece of tender Ayre: And when from a
stately Cedar shall be lopt branches, which being dead many
yeares, shall after reuiue, bee ioynted to the old Stocke,
and freshly grow, then shall Posthumus end his miseries,
Britaine be fortunate, and flourish in Peace and Plentie.*
3250 Thou *Leonatus* art the Lyons Whelpe,
The fit and apt Construction of thy name
Being *Leonatus*, doth import so much:
(*To Cymbeline*) The peece of tender Ayre, thy vertuous
Daughter,
Which we call *Mollis Aer*, and *Mollis Aer*

We terme it *Mulier*; (*to Posthumus*) which *Mulier* I
diuine
Is this most constant Wife, who euen now
Answering the Letter of the Oracle,
Vnknowne to you vnsought, were clipt about
With this most tender Aire.

CYMBELINE   This hath some seeming.

SOOTHSAYER
The lofty Cedar, Royall *Cymbeline*   3260
Personates thee: And thy lopt Branches, point
Thy two Sonnes forth: who by *Belarius* stolne
For many yeares thought dead, are now reuiu'd
To the Maiesticke Cedar ioyn'd; whose Issue
Promises Britaine, Peace and Plenty.

CYMBELINE   Well,
My Peace we will begin: And *Caius Lucius*,
Although the Victor, we submit to *Cæsar*,
And to the Romane Empire; promising
To pay our wonted Tribute, from the which
We were disswaded by our wicked Queene,   3270
Whom heauens in Iustice both on her, and hers,
Haue laid most heauy hand.

SOOTHSAYER
The fingers of the Powres aboue, do tune
The harmony of this Peace: the Vision
Which I made knowne to *Lucius* ere the stroke
Of this yet scarse-cold-Battaile, at this instant
Is full accomplish'd. For the Romaine Eagle
From South to West, on wing soaring aloft
Lessen'd her selfe, and in the Beames o'th'Sun
So vanish'd; which fore-shew'd our Princely Eagle   3280
Th'Imperiall *Cæsar*, should againe vnite
His Fauour, with the Radiant *Cymbeline*,
Which shines heere in the West.

CYMBELINE   Laud we the Gods,
And let our crooked Smoakes climbe to their Nostrils
From our blest Altars. Publish we this Peace
To all our Subiects. Set we forward: Let
A Roman, and a Brittish Ensigne waue
Friendly together: so through *Luds-Towne* march,
And in the Temple of great Iupiter
Our Peace wee'l ratifie: Seale it with Feasts.   3290
Set on there: Neuer was a Warre did cease
(Ere bloodie hands were wash'd) with such a Peace.
                          ⌜*Flourish.*⌝ *Exeunt* ⌜*in Triumph*⌝

FINIS

THE TEMPEST

THE King's Men acted *The Tempest* before their patron, James I, at Whitehall on 1 November 1611. (It was also chosen for performance during the festivities for the marriage of James's daughter, Princess Elizabeth, to the Elector Palatine during the winter of 1612-13). Shakespeare's play takes place on a desert island somewhere between Tunis and Naples; he derived some details of it from his reading of travel literature, including accounts of an expedition of nine ships taking five hundred colonists from Plymouth to Virginia, which set sail in May 1609. On 29 July the flagship, the *Sea-Adventure*, was wrecked by a storm on the coast of the Bermudas. She was presumed lost, but on 23 May 1610 those aboard her arrived safely in Jamestown, Virginia, having found shelter on the island of Bermuda, where they were able to build the pinnaces in which they completed their journey. Accounts of the voyage soon reached England; the last-written that Shakespeare seems to have known is a letter by William Strachey, who was on the *Sea-Adventure*, dated 15 July 1610; though it was not published until 1625, it circulated in manuscript. So it seems clear that Shakespeare wrote *The Tempest* during the later part of 1610 or in 1611. It was first printed in the 1623 Folio, where it is the opening play.

Though other items of Shakespeare's reading—including both Arthur Golding's translation and Ovid's original *Metamorphoses* (closely echoed in Prospero's farewell to his magic), John Florio's translation of essays by Michel de Montaigne, and (less locally but no less pervasively) Virgil's *Aeneid*—certainly fed Shakespeare's imagination as he wrote *The Tempest*, he appears to have devised the main plot himself. Many of its elements are based on the familiar stuff of romance literature: the long-past shipwreck after a perilous voyage of Prospero and his daughter Miranda; the shipwreck, depicted in the opening scene, of Prospero's brother, Anthonio, with Alonso, King of Naples, and others; the separation and estrangement of relatives—Anthonio usurped Prospero's dukedom, and Alonso believes his son, Ferdinand, is drowned; the chaste love, subjected to trials, of the handsome Ferdinand and the beautiful Miranda; the influence of the supernatural exercised through Prospero's magic powers; and the final reunions and reconciliations along with the happy conclusion of the love affair. Shakespeare had employed such conventions from the beginning of his career in his comedies, and with especial concentration, shortly before he wrote *The Tempest*, in *Pericles*, *The Winters Tale*, and *Cymbeline*. But whereas those plays unfold the events as they happen, taking us on a journey through time and space, in *The Tempest* (as elsewhere only in *The Comedie of Errors*) Shakespeare gives us only the end of the story, concentrating the action into a few hours and locating it in a single place, but informing us about the past, as in the long, romance-type narrative (1.2) in which Prospero tells Miranda of her childhood. The supernatural, a strong presence in all Shakespeare's late plays, is particularly pervasive in *The Tempest*; Prospero is a 'white' magician—a beneficent one—attended by the spirit Ariel and the sub-human Caliban, two of Shakespeare's most obviously symbolic characters; and a climax of the play is the supernaturally induced wedding masque that Prospero conjures up for the entertainment and edification of the young lovers, and which vanishes as he remembers Caliban's plot against his life.

The text was set from a transcript apparently prepared by the scrivener Ralph Crane.

THE NAMES OF THE ACTORS

PROSPERO, 'the right Duke of Millaine'

MIRANDA, 'daughter to Prospero'

ANTHONIO, 'his brother, the vsurping Duke of Millaine'

ALONSO, 'K. of Naples'

SEBASTIAN, 'his Brother'

FERDINAND, 'Son to the King of Naples'

GONZALO, 'an honest old Councellor' of Naples

ADRIAN
FRANCISCO } 'Lords'

ARIELL, 'an ayrie spirit' attendant vpon Prospero

CALIBAN, 'a saluage and deformed' natiue of the Island,
    Prosperoes 'slaue'

TRINCULO, Alonsoes 'Iester'

STEPHANO, Alonsoes 'drunken Butler'

The MASTER of a Ship

BOATE-SWAINE

MARINERS

SPIRITS

The Masque

Spirits appearing as:

IRIS

CERES

IUNO

Nimphes, Reapers

The Tempest

*A tempestuous noise of Thunder and Lightning
heard: Enter ⌈seuerally⌉ a Ship-master, and a
Boteswaine*

MASTER Bote-swaine.

BOTESWAINE Heere Master: What cheere?

MASTER Good: Speake to th'Mariners: fall too't, yarely,
or we run our selues a ground, bestirre, bestirre.   *Exit*

Enter Mariners

BOTESWAINE Heigh my hearts, cheerely, cheerely my
harts: yare, yare: Take in the toppe-sale: Tend to
th'Masters whistle: Blow till thou burst thy winde, if
roome enough.

*Enter Alonso, Sebastian, Anthonio, Ferdinando,
Gonzalo, and others*

ALONSO Good Boteswaine haue care: where's the Master?
10 (*To the Mariners*) Play the men.

BOTESWAINE I pray now keepe below.

ANTHONIO Where is the Master, Boson?

BOTESWAINE Do you not heare him? you marre our labour,
Keepe your Cabines: you do assist the storme.

GONZALO Nay, good be patient.

BOTESWAINE When the Sea is: hence, what cares these
roarers for the name of King? to Cabine; silence:
trouble vs not.

GONZALO Good, yet remember whom thou hast aboord.

20 BOTESWAINE None that I more loue then my selfe. You
are a Counsellor, if you can command these Elements
to silence, and worke peace of the present, wee will
not hand a rope more, vse your authoritie: If you
cannot, giue thankes you haue liu'd so long, and make
your selfe readie in your Cabine for the mischance of
the houre, if it so hap. (*To the Mariners*) Cheerely good
hearts: (*to Gonzalo*) out of our way I say.   *Exit*

GONZALO I haue great comfort from this fellow: methinks
he hath no drowning marke vpon him, his complexion
30 is perfect Gallowes: stand fast good Fate to his hanging,
make the rope of his destiny our cable, for our owne
doth little aduantage: If he be not borne to bee hang'd,
our case is miserable.   *Exeunt ⌈Courtiers⌉*

Enter Boteswaine

BOTESWAINE Downe with the top-Mast: yare, lower, lower,
bring her to Try with Maine-course.

A cry within

A plague vpon this howling: they are lowder then the
weather, or our office:

Enter Sebastian, Anthonio & Gonzalo

Yet againe? What do you heere? Shal we giue ore and
drowne, haue you a minde to sinke?

40 SEBASTIAN A poxe o'your throat, you bawling, blasphe-
mous incharitable Dog.

BOTESWAINE Worke you then.

ANTHONIO Hang cur, hang, you whoreson insolent Noyse-
maker, we are lesse afraid to be drownde, then thou
art.   *⌈Exeunt Mariners⌉*

GONZALO I'le warrant him for drowning, though the Ship
were no stronger then a Nutt-shell, and as leaky as an
vnstanched wench.

BOTESWAINE Lay her a hold, a hold, set her two courses,
off to Sea againe, lay her off.   50

Enter Mariners wet

MARINERS All lost, to prayers, to prayers, all lost.

⌈Exeunt Mariners⌉

BOTESWAINE What must our mouths be cold?

GONZALO
The King, and Prince, at prayers, let's assist them,
For our case is as theirs.

SEBASTIAN   I'am out of patience.

ANTHONIO
We are meerly cheated of our liues by drunkards,
This wide-chopt-rascall, would thou mightst lye
          drowning
The washing of ten Tides.

GONZALO   Hee'l be hang'd yet,
Though euery drop of water sweare against it,
And gape at widst to glut him.

A confused noyse within

MARINERS (*within*)   Mercy on vs.
We split, we split, Farewell my wife, and children,   60
Farewell brother: we split, we split, we split.

⌈Exit Boteswaine⌉

ANTHONIO
Let's all sinke with' King.

SEBASTIAN   Let's take leaue of him.

Exit Anthonio and Sebastian

GONZALO Now would I giue a thousand furlongs of Sea,
for an Acre of barren ground: Long heath, Broume,
firrs, any thing; the wills aboue be done, but I would
faine dye a dry death.   *Exit*

*Enter Prospero ⌈in his magicke Cloake, with a
staffe⌉, and Miranda*

MIRANDA
If by your Art (my deerest father) you haue
Put the wild waters in this Rore; alay them:
The skye it seemes would powre down stinking pitch,
But that the Sea, mounting to th' welkins cheeke,   70
Dashes the fire out. Oh! I haue suffered
With those that I saw suffer: A braue vessell
(Who had no doubt some noble creature in her)
Dash'd all to peeces: O the cry did knocke
Against my very heart: poore soules, they perish'd.
Had I byn any God of power, I would
Haue suncke the Sea within the Earth, or ere

It should the good Ship so haue swallow'd, and
The fraughting Soules within her.
PROSPERO   Be collected,
80 No more amazement: Tell your pitteous heart
There's no harme done.
MIRANDA   O woe, the day.
PROSPERO   No harme:
I haue done nothing, but in care of thee
(Of thee my deere one; thee my daughter) who
Art ignorant of what thou art, naught knowing
Of whence I am: nor that I am more better
Then *Prospero*, Master of a full poore cell,
And thy no greater Father.
MIRANDA   More to know
Did neuer medle with my thoughts.
PROSPERO   'Tis time
I should informe thee farther: Lend thy hand
And plucke my Magick garment from me:
         Miranda remoues Prospero's cloake, ⌈*and he laies it*
         on the ground⌉
90   So,
Lye there my Art: wipe thou thine eyes, haue comfort,
The direfull spectacle of the wracke which touch'd
The very vertue of compassion in thee:
I haue with such prouision in mine Art
So safely ordred, that there is no soule
No not so much perdition as an hayre
Betid to any creature in the vessell
Which thou heardst cry, which thou saw'st sinke: Sit
         downe,
For thou must now know farther.
         Miranda sits
MIRANDA   You haue often
100 Begun to tell me what I am, but stopt
And left me to a bootelesse Inquisition,
Concluding, stay: not yet.
PROSPERO   The howr's now come
The very minute byds thee ope thine eare,
Obey, and be attentiue. Canst thou remember
A time before we came vnto this Cell?
I doe not thinke thou canst, for then thou was't not
Out three yeeres old.
MIRANDA   Certainely Sir, I can.
PROSPERO
By what? by any other house, or person?
Of any thing the Image, tell me, that
Hath kept with thy remembrance.
110 MIRANDA   'Tis farre off:
And rather like a dreame, then an assurance
That my remembrance warrants: Had I not
Fowre, or fiue women once, that tended me?
PROSPERO
Thou hadst; and more *Miranda*: But how is it
That this liues in thy minde? What seest thou els
In the dark-backward and Abisme of Time?
Yf thou remembrest ought ere thou cam'st here,
How thou cam'st here thou maist.
MIRANDA   But that I doe not.

PROSPERO
Twelue yere since (*Miranda*) twelue yere since,
Thy father was the Duke of *Millaine* and   120
A Prince of power:
MIRANDA   Sir, are not you my Father?
PROSPERO
Thy Mother was a peece of vertue, and
She said thou wast my daughter; and thy father
Was Duke of *Millaine*, and his onely heire,
And Princesse; no worse Issued.
MIRANDA   O the heauens,
What fowle play had we, that we came from thence?
Or blessed was't we did?
PROSPERO   Both, both my Girle.
By fowle-play (as thou saist) were we heau'd thence,
But blessedly holpe hither.
MIRANDA   O my heart bleedes
To thinke oth' teene that I haue turn'd you to,   130
Which is from my remembrance, please you, farther.
PROSPERO
My brother and thy vncle, call'd *Anthonio*:
I pray thee marke me, that a brother should
Be so perfidious: he, whom next thy selfe
Of all the world I lou'd, and to him put
The mannage of my state, as at that time
Through all the signories it was the first,
And *Prospero*, the prime Duke, being so reputed
In dignity; and for the liberall Artes,
Without a paralell; those being all my studie, 140
The Gouernment I cast vpon my brother,
And to my State grew stranger, being transported
And rapt in secret studies, thy false vncle
(Do'st thou attend me?)
MIRANDA   Sir, most heedefully.
PROSPERO
Being once perfected how to graunt suites,
How to deny them: who t'aduance, and who
To trash for ouer-topping; new created
The creatures that were mine, I say, or chang'd 'em,
Or els new form'd 'em; hauing both the key,
Of Officer, and office, set all hearts i'th state 150
To what tune pleas'd his eare, that now he was
The Iuy which had hid my princely Trunck,
And suckt my verdure out on't: Thou attend'st not?
MIRANDA
O good Sir, I doe.
PROSPERO   I pray thee marke me:
I thus neglecting worldly ends, all dedicated
To closenes, and the bettering of my mind
With that, which but by being so retir'd
Ore-priz'd all popular rate: in my false brother
Awak'd an euill nature, and my trust
Like a good parent, did beget of him   160
A falsehood in it's contrarie, as great
As my trust was, which had indeede no limit,
A confidence sans bound. He being thus Lorded,
Not onely with what my reuenew yeelded,
But what my power might els exact. Like one

Who hauing into truth, by telling oft,
Made such a synner of his memorie
To credite his owne lie, he did beleeue
He was indeed the Duke, out o'th' Substitution
170 And executing th'outward face of Roialtie
With all prerogatiue: hence his Ambition growing:
Do'st thou heare?
MIRANDA   Your tale, Sir, would cure deafenesse.
PROSPERO
To haue no Schreene between this part he plaid,
And him he plaid it for, he needes will be
Absolute *Millaine*, Me (poore man) my Librarie
Was Dukedome large enough: of temporall roalties
He thinks me now incapable. Confederates
(So drie he was for Sway) with King of *Naples*
To giue him Annuall tribute, doe him homage,
180 Subiect his Coronet to his Crowne and bend
The Dukedom yet vnbow'd (alas poore *Millaine*)
To most ignoble stooping.
MIRANDA   Oh the heauens.
PROSPERO
Marke his condition, and th'euent, then tell me
If this might be a brother.
MIRANDA   I should sinne
To thinke but Noblie of my Grand-mother,
Good wombes haue borne bad sonnes.
PROSPERO   Now the Condition.
This King of *Naples* being an Enemy
To me inueterate, hearkens my Brothers suit,
Which was, That he in lieu o'th' premises,
190 Of homage, and I know not how much Tribute,
Should presently extirpate me and mine
Out of the Dukedome, and confer faire *Millaine*
With all the Honors, on my brother: Whereon
A treacherous Armie leuied, one mid-night
Fated to th' purpose, did *Anthonio* open
The gates of *Millaine*, and ith' dead of darkenesse
The ministers for th' purpose hurried thence
Me, and thy crying selfe.
MIRANDA   Alack, for pitty:
I not remembring how I cride out then
200 Will cry it ore againe: it is a hint
That wrings mine eyes too't.
PROSPERO ⌈sitting⌉   Heare a little further,
And then I'le bring thee to the present businesse
Which now's vpon's: without the which, this Story
Were most impertinent.
MIRANDA   Wherefore did they not
That howre destroy vs?
PROSPERO   Well demanded, wench:
My Tale prouokes that question: Deare, they durst
     not,
So deare the loue my people bore me: nor set
A marke so bloudy on the businesse; but
With colours fairer, painted their foule ends.
210 In few, they hurried vs a-boord a Barke,
Bore vs some Leagues to Sea, where they prepared

A rotten carkasse of a Butt, not rigg'd,
Nor tackle, sayle, nor mast, the very rats
Instinctiuely haue quit it: There they hoyst vs
To cry to th' Sea, that roard to vs; to sigh
To th' windes, whose pitty sighing backe againe
Did vs but louing wrong.
MIRANDA   Alack, what trouble
Was I then to you?
PROSPERO   O, a Cherubin
Thou was't that did preserue me; Thou didst smile,
Infused with a fortitude from heauen,   220
When I haue deck'd the sea with drops full salt,
Vnder my burthen groan'd, which rais'd in me
An vndergoing stomacke, to beare vp
Against what should ensue.
MIRANDA How came we a shore?
PROSPERO By prouidence diuine,
Some food, we had, and some fresh water, that
A noble *Neopolitan Gonzalo*
Out of his Charity, (who being then appointed
Master of this designe) did giue vs, with   230
Rich garments, linnens, stuffs, and necessaries
Which since haue steeded much, so of his gentlenesse
Knowing I lou'd my bookes, he furnishd me
From mine owne Library, with volumes, that
I prize aboue my Dukedome.
MIRANDA   Would I might
But euer see that man.
PROSPERO   Now I arise,
     ⌈He stands and puts on his cloake⌉
Sit still, and heare the last of our sea-sorrow:
Heere in this Iland we arriu'd, and heere
Haue I, thy Schoolemaster, made thee more profit
Then other Princesse can, that haue more time   240
For vainer howres; and Tutors, not so carefull.
MIRANDA
Heuens thank you for't. And now I pray you Sir,
For still 'tis beating in my minde; your reason
For raysing this Sea-storme?
PROSPERO   Know thus far forth,
By accident most strange, bountifull *Fortune*
(Now my deere Lady) hath mine enemies
Brought to this shore: And by my prescience
I finde my *Zenith* doth depend vpon
A most auspitious starre, whose influence
If now I court not, but omit; my fortunes   250
Will euer after droope: Heare cease more questions,
Thou art inclinde to sleepe: 'tis a good dulnesse,
And giue it way: I know thou canst not chuse:
     Miranda sleepes
Come away, Seruant, come; I am ready now,
Approach my *Ariel*. Come.
     Enter Ariel
ARIELL
All haile, great Master, graue Sir, haile: I come
To answer thy best pleasure; be't to fly,
To swim, to diue into the fire: to ride

On the curld clowds: to thy strong bidding, taske
Ariel, and all his Qualitie.

260 PROSPERO   Hast thou, Spirit,
Performd to point, the Tempest that I bad thee.

ARIELL To euery Article.
I boorded the Kings ship: now on the Beake,
Now in the Waste, the Decke, in euery Cabyn,
I flam'd amazement, sometime I'ld diuide
And burne in many places; on the Top-mast,
The Yards and Bore-spritt, would I flame distinctly,
Then meete, and ioyne. *Ioues* Lightning, the
      precursers
O'th dreadfull Thunder-claps more momentarie
270 And sight out-running were not; the fire, and cracks
Of sulphurous roaring, the most mighty *Neptune*
Seeme to besiege, and make his bold waues tremble,
Yea, his dread Trident shake.

PROSPERO   My braue Spirit,
Who was so firme, so constant, that this coyle
Would not infect his reason?

ARIELL   Not a soule
But felt a Feauer of the madde, and plaid
Some tricks of desperation; all but Mariners
Plung'd in the foaming bryne, and quit the vessell,
Then all a fire with me; the Kings sonne *Ferdinand*
280 With haire vp-staring (then like reeds, not haire)
Was the first man that leapt; cride hell is empty,
And all the Diuels are heere.

PROSPERO   Why that's my spirit:
But was not this nye shore?

ARIELL   Close by, my Master.

PROSPERO
But are they (*Ariell*) safe?

ARIELL   Not a haire perishd:
On their sustaining garments not a blemish,
But fresher then before: and as thou badst me,
In troops I haue dispersd them 'bout the Isle:
The Kings sonne haue I landed by himselfe,
Whom I left cooling of the Ayre with sighes,
290 In an odde Angle of the Isle, and sitting
His armes in this sad knot.

PROSPERO   Of the Kings ship,
The Marriners, say how thou hast disposd,
And all the rest o'th' Fleete?

ARIELL   Safely in harbour
Is the Kings shippe, in the deepe Nooke, where once
Thou calldst me vp at midnight to fetch dewe
From the still-vext *Bermoothes*, there she's hid;
The Marriners all vnder hatches stowed,
Who, with a Charme ioynd to their suffred labour
I haue left asleep: and for the rest o'th' Fleet
300 (Which I dispers'd) they all haue met againe,
And are vpon the *Mediterranian* Flote
Bound sadly home for *Naples*,
Supposing that they saw the Kings ship wrackt,
And his great person perish.

PROSPERO   *Ariel*, thy charge

Exactly is perform'd; but there's more worke:
What is the time o'th'day?

ARIELL   Past the mid season.

PROSPERO
At least two Glasses: the time 'twixt six & now
Must by vs both be spent most preciously.

ARIELL
Is there more toyle? Since y^u dost giue me pains,
Let me remember thee what thou hast promis'd,   310
Which is not yet perform'd me.

PROSPERO   How now? moodie?
What is't thou canst demand?

ARIELL   My Libertie.

PROSPERO
Before the time be out? no more.

ARIELL   I prethee,
Remember I haue done thee worthy seruice,
Told thee no lyes, made thee no mistakings, serv'd
Without or grudge, or grumblings; thou did promise
To bate me a full yeere.

PROSPERO   Do'st thou forget
From what a torment I did free thee?

ARIELL   No.

PROSPERO
Thou do'st: & thinkst it much to tread ye Ooze
Of the salt deepe;   320
To run vpon the sharpe winde of the North,
To doe me businesse in the veines o'th' earth
When it is bak'd with frost.

ARIELL   I doe not Sir.

PROSPERO
Thou liest, malignant Thing: hast thou forgot
The fowle Witch *Sycorax*, who with Age and Enuy
Was growne into a hoope? hast thou forgot her?

ARIELL
No Sir.

PROSPERO Thou hast: where was she born? speak: tell me.

ARIELL
Sir, in *Argier*.

PROSPERO   Oh, was she so: I must
Once in a moneth recount what thou hast bin,   330
Which thou forgetst. This damn'd Witch *Sycorax*
For mischiefes manifold, and sorceries terrible
To enter humane hearing, from *Argier*
Thou know'st was banish'd: for one thing she did
They wold not take her life: Is not this true?

ARIELL I, Sir.

PROSPERO
This blew ey'd hag, was hither brought with child,
And here was left by th' Saylors; thou my slaue,
As thou reportst thy selfe, was then her seruant,
And for thou wast a Spirit too delicate   340
To act her earthy, and abhord commands,
Refusing her grand hests, she did confine thee
By helpe of her more potent Ministers,
And in her most vnmittigable rage,
Into a clouen Pyne, within which rift
Imprison'd, thou didst painefully remaine

A dozen yeeres: within which space she di'd,
And left thee there: where thou didst vent thy groanes
As fast as Mill-wheeles strike: Then was this Island
350 (Saue for the Son, that she did littour heere,
A frekelld whelpe, hag-borne) not honour'd with
A humane shape.
ARIELL   Yes: *Caliban* her sonne.
PROSPERO
Dull thing, I say so: he, that *Caliban*
Whom now I keepe in seruice, thou best know'st
What torment I did finde thee in; thy grones
Did make wolues howle, and penetrate the breasts
Of euer-angry Beares; it was a torment
To lay vpon the damn'd, which *Sycorax*
360 Could not againe vndoe: it was mine Art,
When I arriu'd, and heard thee, that made gape
The Pyne, and let thee out.
ARIELL   I thanke thee Master.
PROSPERO
If thou more murmur'st, I will rend an Oake
And peg-thee in his knotty entrailes, till
Thou hast howl'd away twelue winters.
ARIELL   Pardon, Master,
I will be correspondent to command
And doe my spryting, gently.
PROSPERO Doe so: and after two daies
I will discharge thee.
ARIELL   That's my noble Master:
What shall I doe? say what? what shall I doe?
PROSPERO
370 Goe make thy selfe like to a Nymph o'th' Sea, be subiect
To no sight but thine, and mine: inuisible
To euery eye-ball else: goe take this shape
And hither come in't: goe: hence with diligence.
                                        Exit Ariell
Awake, deere hart awake, thou hast slept well,
Awake.
MIRANDA (*awaking*) The strangenes of your story, put
Heauinesse in me.
PROSPERO   Shake it off: Come on,
Wee'll visit *Caliban*, my slaue, who neuer
Yeelds vs kinde answere.
MIRANDA   'Tis a villaine Sir,
I doe not loue to looke on.
PROSPERO   But as 'tis
380 We cannot misse him: he do's make our fire,
Fetch in our wood, and serues in Offices
That profit vs: What hoa: slaue: *Caliban*:
Thou Earth, thou: speake.
CALIBAN (*within*)   There's wood enough within.
PROSPERO
Come forth I say, there's other busines for thee:
Come thou Tortoys, when?
        Enter Ariel like a water-Nymph
Fine apparision: my queint *Ariel*,
Hearke in thine eare.
        He whispers
ARIELL   My Lord, it shall be done.   *Exit*

PROSPERO
Thou poysonous slaue, got by yᵉ diuell himselfe
Vpon thy wicked Dam; come forth.
        Enter Caliban
CALIBAN
As wicked dewe, as ere my mother brush'd   390
With Rauens feather from vnwholesome Fen
Drop on you both: A Southwest blow on yee,
And blister you all ore.
PROSPERO
For this be sure, to night thou shalt haue cramps,
Side-stitches, that shall pen thy breath vp, Vrchins
Shall forth at vast of night, that they may worke
All exercise on thee: thou shalt be pinch'd
As thicke as hony-combe, each pinch more stinging
Then Bees that made 'em.
CALIBAN   I must eat my dinner:
This Island's mine by *Sycorax* my mother,   400
Which thou tak'st from me: when thou cam'st first
Thou stroakst me, & made much of me: wouldst giue
    me
Water with berries in't: and teach me how
To name the bigger Light, and how the lesse
That burne by day, and night: and then I lou'd thee
And shew'd thee all the qualities o'th' Isle,
The fresh Springs, Brine-pits; barren place and fertill,
Curs'd be I that did so: All the Charmes
Of *Sycorax*: Toades, Beetles, Batts light on you:
For I am all the Subiects that you haue,   410
Which first was min owne King: and here you sty-me
In this hard Rocke, whiles you doe keepe from me
The rest o'th' Island.
PROSPERO   Thou most lying slaue,
Whom stripes may moue, not kindnes: I haue vs'd thee
(Filth as thou art) with humane care, and lodg'd thee
In mine owne Cell, till thou didst seeke to violate
The honor of my childe.
CALIBAN
Oh ho, oh ho, would't had bene done:
Thou didst preuent me, I had peopel'd else
This Isle with *Calibans*.
MIRANDA   Abhorred Slaue,   420
Which any print of goodnesse wilt not take,
Being capable of all ill: I pittied thee,
Took pains to make thee speak, taught thee each houre
One thing or other: when thou didst not (Sauage)
Know thine owne meaning; but wouldst gabble, like
A thing most brutish, I endow'd thy purposes
With words that made them knowne: But thy vild race
(Tho thou didst learn) had that in't, which good natures
Could not abide to be with; therefore wast thou
Deseruedly confin'd into this Rocke,   430
Who hadst deseru'd more then a prison.
CALIBAN
You taught me Language, and my profit on't
Is, I know how to curse: the red-plague rid you
For learning me your language.
PROSPERO   Hag-seed, hence:

Fetch vs in Fewell, and be quicke thou'rt best
To answer other businesse: shrug'st thou (Malice)
If thou neglectst, or dost vnwillingly
What I command, Ile racke thee with old Crampes,
Fill all thy bones with Aches, make thee rore,
That beasts shall tremble at thy dyn.

440 CALIBAN   No, 'pray thee.
    (Aside) I must obey, his Art is of such pow'r,
    It would controll my Dams god *Setebos*,
    And make a vassaile of him.

PROSPERO   So slaue, hence.
                                        Exit Caliban

    Enter Ferdinand, and Ariel ⌈like a water-Nymph⌉,
    inuisible playing & singing.
    ⌈Prospero and Miranda stand aside⌉

                        Song

ARIELL   *Come vnto these yellow sands,*
                And then take hands:
            Curtsied when you haue, and kist:
                The wilde waues whist:
            Foote it featly heere, and there,
                And sweete Sprights beare
450   *The burthen. Harke, harke,*
⌈SPIRITS⌉ (*dispersedly within*)
                Bowgh wawgh:
⌈ARIELL⌉   *The watch-Dogges barke,*
⌈SPIRITS⌉ (*within*) *Bowgh-wawgh.*
ARIELL   *Hark, hark, I heare,*
                The straine of strutting Chanticlere
                Cry cockadidle-dowe.

FERDINAND
    Where shold this Musick be? I'th aire, or th'earth?
    It sounds no more: and sure it waytes vpon
    Some God 'oth'lland, sitting on a banke,
460 Weeping againe the King my Fathers wracke,
    This Musicke crept by me vpon the waters,
    Allaying both their fury, and my passion
    With it's sweet ayre: thence I haue follow'd it
    (Or it hath drawne me rather) but 'tis gone.
    No, it begins againe.

                        Song

ARIELL   *Full fadom fiue thy Father lies,*
                Of his bones are Corrall made:
            Those are pearles that were his eies,
                Nothing of him that doth fade,
470   *But doth suffer a Sea-change*
            Into something rich, & strange:
                Sea-Nimphs hourly ring his knell.
⌈SPIRITS⌉ (*within*) *Ding dong.*
ARIELL   *Harke now I heare them,*
SPIRITS (*within*)   *Ding-dong bell. ⌈etc.⌉*
FERDINAND
    The Ditty do's remember my drown'd father,
    This is no mortall busines, nor no sound
    That the earth owes.
                        ⌈Musicke⌉
                I heare it now aboue me.

PROSPERO (*to Miranda*)
    The fringed Curtaines of thine eye aduance,
    And say what thou see'st yond.
MIRANDA   What is't a Spirit?
    Lord, how it lookes about: Beleeue me sir,   480
    It carries a braue forme. But 'tis a spirit.
PROSPERO
    No wench, it eats, and sleeps, & hath such senses
    As we haue: such. This Gallant which thou seest
    Was in the wracke: and but hee's something stain'd
    With greefe (that's beauties canker) yᵘ might'st call him
    A goodly person: he hath lost his fellowes,
    And strayes about to finde 'em.
MIRANDA   I might call him
    A thing diuine, for nothing naturall
    I euer saw so Noble.
PROSPERO (*aside*)   It goes on I see
    As my soule prompts it: (*to Ariell*) Spirit, fine spirit,
        Ile free thee   490
    Within two dayes for this.
FERDINAND ⌈*aside*⌉   Most sure the Goddesse
    On whom these ayres attend: (*To Miranda*) Vouchsafe
        my pray'r
    May know if you remaine vpon this Island,
    And that you will some good instruction giue
    How I may beare me heere: my prime request
    (Which I do last pronounce) is (O you wonder)
    If you be Mayd, or no?
MIRANDA   No wonder Sir,
    But certainly a Mayd.
FERDINAND   My Language? Heauens:
    I am the best of them that speake this speech,
    Were I but where 'tis spoken.
PROSPERO   How? the best?   500
    What wer't thou if the King of *Naples* heard thee?
FERDINAND
    A single thing, as I am now, that wonders
    To heare thee speake of *Naples*: he do's heare me,
    And that he do's, I weepe: my selfe am *Naples*,
    Who, with mine eyes (neuer since at ebbe) beheld
    The King my Father wrack't.
MIRANDA   Alacke, for mercy.
FERDINAND
    Yes faith, & all his Lords, the Duke of *Millaine*
    And his braue sonne, being twaine.
PROSPERO (*aside*)   The Duke of *Millaine*
    And his more brauer daughter, could controll thee
    If now 'twere fit to do't: At the first sight   510
    They haue chang'd eyes: Delicate *Ariel*,
    Ile set thee free for this. (*To Ferdinand*) A word good
        Sir,
    I feare you haue done your selfe some wrong: A
        word.
MIRANDA (*aside*)
    Why speakes my father so vngently? This
    Is the third man that ere I saw: the first
    That ere I sigh'd for: pitty moue my father
    To be enclin'd my way.
FERDINAND   O, if a Virgin,

1346

And your affection not gone forth, Ile make you
The Queene of *Naples*.
PROSPERO   Soft sir, one word more.
520 (*Aside*) They are both in eythers pow'rs: But this swift busines
I must vneasie make, least too light winning
Make the prize light. (*To Ferdinand*) One word more: I charge thee
That thou attend me: Thou do'st heere vsurpe
The name thou ow'st not, and hast put thy selfe
Vpon this Island, as a spy, to win it
From me, the Lord on't.
FERDINAND   No, as I am a man.
MIRANDA
Ther's nothing ill, can dwell in such a Temple,
If the ill-spirit haue so fayre a house,
Good things will striue to dwell with't.
PROSPERO (*to Ferdinand*)   Follow me.
(*To Miranda*) Speake not you for him: hee's a Traitor:
530 (*to Ferdinand*) come,
Ile manacle thy necke and feete together:
Sea water shalt thou drinke: thy food shall be
The fresh-brooke Mussels, wither'd roots, and huskes
Wherein the Acorne cradled. Follow.
FERDINAND   No,
I will resist such entertainment, till
Mine enemy ha's more power.
   He drawes, and is charmed from mouing
MIRANDA   O deere Father,
Make not too rash a triall of him, for
Hee's gentle, and not fearfull.
PROSPERO   What I say,
My foote my Tutor? Put thy sword vp Traitor,
Who mak'st a shew, but dar'st not strike: thy
540 conscience
Is so possest with guilt: Come, from thy ward,
For I can heere disarme thee with this sticke,
And make thy weapon drop.
MIRANDA   Beseech you Father.
PROSPERO
Hence: hang not on my garments.
MIRANDA   Sir haue pity,
Ile be his surety.
PROSPERO   Silence: One word more
Shall make me chide thee, if not hate thee: What,
An aduocate for an Impostor? Hush:
Thou think'st there is no more such shapes as he,
(Hauing seene but him and *Caliban*:) Foolish wench,
550 . To th'most of men, this is a *Caliban*,
And they to him are Angels.
MIRANDA   My affections
Are then most humble: I haue no ambition
To see a goodlier man.
PROSPERO (*to Ferdinand*) Come on, obey:
Thy Nerues are in their infancy againe,
And haue no vigour in them.
FERDINAND   So they are:
My spirits, as in a dreame, are all bound vp:
My Fathers losse, the weaknesse which I feele,

The wracke of all my friends, nor this mans threats,
To whom I am subdude, are but light to me,
Might I but through my prison once a day 560
Behold this Mayd: all corners else o'th'Earth
Let liberty make vse of: space enough
Haue I in such a prison.
PROSPERO (*aside*) It workes: (*To Ferdinand*) Come on.
(*To Ariell*) Thou hast done well, fine *Ariell*: (*to Ferdinand*) follow me,
(*To Ariell*) Harke what thou else shalt do mee.
MIRANDA (*to Ferdinand*)   Be of comfort,
My Fathers of a better nature (Sir)
Then he appeares by speech: this is vnwonted
Which now came from him.
PROSPERO (*to Ariell*)   Thou shalt be as free
As mountaine windes; but then exactly do
All points of my command. 570
ARIELL To th'syllable.
PROSPERO (*to Ferdinand*)
Come follow: (*to Miranda*) speake not for him. *Exeunt*

        ✱

  Enter Alonso, Sebastian, Anthonio, Gonzalo, 2.1
   Adrian, and Francisco (Sc. 3)
GONZALO (*to Alonso*)
Beseech you Sir, be merry; you haue cause,
(So haue we all) of ioy; for our escape
Is much beyond our losse; our hint of woe
Is common, euery day, some Saylors wife,
The Masters of some Merchant, and the Merchant
Haue iust our Theame of woe: But for the miracle,
(I meane our preseruation) few in millions
Can speake like vs: then wisely (good Sir) weigh 580
Our sorrow, with our comfort.
ALONSO   Prethee peace.
SEBASTIAN (*to Anthonio*) He receiues comfort like cold porredge.
ANTHONIO The Visitor will not giue him ore so.
SEBASTIAN Looke, hee's winding vp the watch of his wit,
By and by it will strike.
GONZALO (*to Alonso*) Sir.
SEBASTIAN (*to Anthonio*) One: Tell.
GONZALO (*to Alonso*)
When euery greefe is entertaind, that's offer'd
Comes to th'entertainer.
SEBASTIAN A dollor. 590
GONZALO Dolour comes to him indeed, you haue spoken truer then you purpos'd.
SEBASTIAN You haue taken it wiselier then I meant you should.
GONZALO (*to Alonso*) Therefore my Lord.
ANTHONIO (*to Sebastian*) Fie, what a spend-thrift is he of his tongue.
ALONSO (*to Gonzalo*) I pre-thee spare.
GONZALO Well, I haue done: But yet
SEBASTIAN (*to Anthonio*) He will be talking. 600
ANTHONIO Which, of he, or Adrian, for a good wager, first begins to crow?
SEBASTIAN The old Cocke.

ANTHONIO The Cockrell.

SEBASTIAN Done: The wager?

ANTHONIO A Laughter.

SEBASTIAN A match.

ADRIAN (*to Gonzalo*) Though this Island seeme to be desert.

610 ⌈ANTHONIO⌉ (*to Sebastian*) Ha, ha, ha.

⌈SEBASTIAN⌉ So: you'r paid.

ADRIAN Vninhabitable, and almost inaccessible.

SEBASTIAN (*to Anthonio*) Yet

ADRIAN Yet

ANTHONIO (*to Sebastian*) He could not misse't.

ADRIAN It must needs be of subtle, tender, and delicate temperance.

ANTHONIO (*to Sebastian*) *Temperance* was a delicate wench.

SEBASTIAN I, and a subtle, as he most learnedly deliuer'd.

620 ADRIAN (*to Gonzalo*) The ayre breathes vpon vs here most sweetly.

SEBASTIAN (*to Anthonio*) As if it had Lungs, and rotten ones.

ANTHONIO Or, as 'twere perfum'd by a Fen.

GONZALO (*to Adrian*) Heere is euery thing aduantageous to life.

ANTHONIO (*to Sebastian*) True, saue meanes to liue.

SEBASTIAN Of that there's none, or little.

GONZALO (*to Adrian*) How lush and lusty the grasse lookes?

630 How greene?

ANTHONIO The ground indeed is tawny.

SEBASTIAN With an eye of greene in't.

ANTHONIO He misses not much.

SEBASTIAN No: he doth but mistake the truth totally.

GONZALO (*to Adrian*) But the rariety of it is, which is indeed almost beyond credit.

SEBASTIAN (*to Anthonio*) As many voucht rarieties are.

GONZALO (*to Adrian*) That our Garments being (as they were) drencht in the Sea, hold notwithstanding their

640 freshnesse and glosses, being rather new dy'de then stain'd with salte water.

ANTHONIO (*to Sebastian*) If but one of his pockets could speake, would it not say he lyes?

SEBASTIAN I, or very falsely pocket vp his report.

GONZALO (*to Adrian*) Me thinkes our garments are now as fresh as when we put them on first in Affricke, at the marriage of the kings faire daughter *Claribel* to the king of *Tunis*.

SEBASTIAN 'Twas a sweet marriage, and we prosper well

650 in our returne.

ADRIAN *Tunis* was neuer grac'd before with such a Paragon to their Queene.

GONZALO Not since widdow *Dido's* time.

ANTHONIO (*to Sebastian*) Widow? A pox o'that: how came that Widdow in? Widdow *Dido*!

SEBASTIAN What if he had said Widdower *Æneas* too? Good Lord, how you take it?

ADRIAN (*to Gonzalo*) Widdow *Dido* said you? You make me study of that: She was of *Carthage*, not of *Tunis*.

660 GONZALO This *Tunis* Sir was *Carthage*.

ADRIAN *Carthage*?

GONZALO I assure you *Carthage*.

ANTHONIO (*to Sebastian*) His word is more then the miraculous Harpe.

SEBASTIAN He hath rais'd the wall, and houses too.

ANTHONIO What impossible matter wil he make easy next?

SEBASTIAN I thinke hee will carry this Island home in his pocket, and giue it his sonne for an Apple.

ANTHONIO And sowing the kernels of it in the Sea, bring 670 forth more Islands.

GONZALO (*to Adrian*) I.

ANTHONIO (*to Sebastian*) Why in good time.

GONZALO (*to Alonso*) Sir, we were talking, that our garments seeme now as fresh as when we were at *Tunis* at the marriage of your daughter, who is now Queene.

ANTHONIO And the rarest that ere came there.

SEBASTIAN Bate (I beseech you) widow *Dido*.

ANTHONIO O Widdow *Dido*? I, Widdow *Dido*.

GONZALO (*to Alonso*) Is not Sir my doublet as fresh as the 680 first day I wore it? I meane in a sort.

ANTHONIO (*to Sebastian*) That sort was well fish'd for.

GONZALO (*to Alonso*) When I wore it at your daughters marriage.

ALONSO

You cram these words into mine eares, against

The stomacke of my sense: would I had neuer

Married my daughter there: For comming thence

My sonne is lost, and (in my rate) she too,

Who is so farre from *Italy* remoued,

I ne're againe shall see her: O thou mine heire 690

Of *Naples* and of *Millaine*, what strange fish

Hath made his meale on thee?

FRANCISCO   Sir he may liue,

I saw him beate the surges vnder him,

And ride vpon their backes; he trod the water

Whose enmity he flung aside: and brested

The surge most swolne that met him: his bold head

'Boue the contentious waues he kept, and oared

Himselfe with his good armes in lusty stroke

To th'shore; that ore his waue-worne basis bowed

As stooping to releeue him: I not doubt 700

He came aliue to Land.

ALONSO   No, no, hee's gone.

SEBASTIAN (*to Alonso*)

Sir you may thank your selfe for this great losse,

That would not blesse our Europe with your daughter,

But rather loose her to an Affrican,

Where she at least, is banish'd from your eye,

Who hath cause to wet the greefe on't.

ALONSO   Pre-thee peace.

SEBASTIAN

You were kneel'd too, & importun'd otherwise

By all of vs: and the faire soule her selfe

Waigh'd betweene loathnesse, and obedience, at

Which ende o'th'beame should bow: we haue lost

your son, 710

I feare for euer: *Millaine* and *Naples* haue

Mo widdowes in them of this businesse making,
Then we bring men to comfort them: The faults your
    owne.

ALONSO
So is the deer'st oth'losse.

GONZALO   My Lord *Sebastian*,
The truth you speake doth lacke some gentlenesse,
And time to speake it in: you rub the sore,
When you should bring the plaister.

SEBASTIAN (*to Anthonio*) Very well.

ANTHONIO And most Chirugeonly.

GONZALO (*to Alonso*)
It is foule weather in vs all, good Sir,
When you are cloudy.

SEBASTIAN (*to Anthonio*) Fowle weather?

ANTHONIO   Very foule.

GONZALO (*to Alonso*)
Had I plantation of this Isle my Lord.

ANTHONIO (*to Sebastian*)
Hee'd sow't with Nettle-seed.

SEBASTIAN   Or dockes, or Mallowes.

GONZALO
And were the King on't, what would I do?

SEBASTIAN (*to Anthonio*)
Scape being drunke, for want of Wine.

GONZALO
I'th'Commonwealth I would (by contraries)
Execute all things: For no kinde of Trafficke
Would I admit: No name of Magistrate:
Letters should not be knowne: Riches, pouerty,
And vse of seruice, none: Contract, Succession,
Borne, bound of Land, Tilth, Vineyard none:
No vse of Mettall, Corne, or Wine, or Oyle:
No occupation, all men idle, all:
And Women too, but innocent and pure:
No Soueraignty.

SEBASTIAN (*to Anthonio*) Yet he would be King on't.

ANTHONIO The latter end of his Common-wealth forgets
the beginning.

GONZALO (*to Alonso*)
All things in common Nature should produce
Without sweat or endeuour: Treason, fellony,
Sword, Pike, Knife, Gun, or neede of any Engine
Would I not haue: but Nature should bring forth
Of it owne kinde, all foyzon, all abundance
To feed my innocent people.

SEBASTIAN (*to Anthonio*) No marrying 'mong his subiects?

ANTHONIO None (man) all idle; Whores and knaues.

GONZALO (*to Alonso*)
I would with such perfection gouerne Sir:
T'Excell the Golden Age.

SEBASTIAN   'Saue his Maiesty.

ANTHONIO
Long liue *Gonzalo*.

GONZALO (*to Alonso*) And do you marke me, Sir?

ALONSO
Pre-thee no more: thou dost talke nothing to me.

GONZALO I do well beleeue your Highnesse, and did it to

minister occasion to these Gentlemen, who are of such
sensible and nimble Lungs, that they alwayes vse to
laugh at nothing.

ANTHONIO 'Twas you we laugh'd at.

GONZALO Who, in this kind of merry fooling am nothing
to you: so you may continue, and laugh at nothing
still.

ANTHONIO What a blow was there giuen?

SEBASTIAN And it had not falne flat-long.

GONZALO You are Gentlemen of braue mettal: you would
lift the Moone out of her spheare, if she would continue
in it fiue weekes without changing.
            Enter Ariell inuisible, playing solemne Musicke

SEBASTIAN We would so, and then go a Bat-fowling.

ANTHONIO (*to Gonzalo*) Nay good my Lord, be not angry.

GONZALO No I warrant you, I will not aduenture my
discretion so weakly: Will you laugh me asleepe, for I
am very heauy.

ANTHONIO Go sleepe, and heare vs.
        Gonzalo, Adrian, and Francisco sleepe

ALONSO
What, all so soone asleepe? I wish mine eyes
Would (with themselues) shut vp my thoughts, I finde
They are inclin'd to do so.

SEBASTIAN   Please you Sir,
Do not omit the heauy offer of it:
It sildome visits sorrow, when it doth,
It is a Comforter.

ANTHONIO   We two my Lord,
Will guard your person, while you take your rest,
And watch your safety.

ALONSO   Thanke you: Wondrous heauy.
        He sleepes. ⌈*Exit Ariell*⌉

SEBASTIAN
What a strange drowsines possesses them?

ANTHONIO
It is the quality o'th'Clymate.

SEBASTIAN   Why
Doth it not then our eye-lids sinke? I finde
Not my selfe dispos'd to sleep.

ANTHONIO   Nor I, my spirits are nimble:
They fell together all, as by consent,
They dropt, as by a Thunder-stroke: what might
Worthy *Sebastian*? O, what might? no more:
And yet, me thinkes I see it in thy face:
What thou should'st be, th'occasion speakes thee, and
My strong imagination see's a Crowne
Dropping vpon thy head.

SEBASTIAN   What? art thou waking?

ANTHONIO
Do you not heare me speake?

SEBASTIAN   I do, and surely
It is a sleepy Language; and thou speak'st
Out of thy sleepe: What is it thou didst say?
This is a strange repose, to be asleepe
With eyes wide open: standing, speaking, mouing:
And yet so fast asleepe.

ANTHONIO   Noble *Sebastian*,

Thou let'st thy fortune sleepe: die rather: wink'st
Whiles thou art waking.

SEBASTIAN   Thou do'st snore distinctly,
There's meaning in thy snores.

ANTHONIO
I am more serious then my custome: you
Must be so too, if heed me: which to do,
Trebbles thee o're.

SEBASTIAN   Well: I am standing water.

ANTHONIO
Ile teach you how to flow.

800 SEBASTIAN   Do so: to ebbe
Hereditary Sloth instructs me.

ANTHONIO   O!
If you but knew how you the purpose cherish
Whiles thus you mocke it: how in stripping it
You more inuest it: ebbing men, indeed
(Most often) do so neere the bottome run
By their owne feare, or sloth.

SEBASTIAN   'Pre-thee say on,
The setting of thine eye, and cheeke proclaime
A matter from thee; and a birth, indeed,
Which throwes thee much to yeeld.

ANTHONIO   Thus Sir:
810 Although this Lord of weake remembrance; this
Who shall be of as little memory
When he is earth'd, hath here almost perswaded
(For hee's a Spirit of perswasion, onely
Professes to perswade) the King his sonne's aliue,
'Tis as impossible that hee's vndrown'd,
As he that sleepes heere, swims.

SEBASTIAN   I haue no hope
That hee's vndrown'd.

ANTHONIO   O, out of that no hope,
What great hope haue you? No hope that way, Is
Another way so high a hope, that euen
820 Ambition cannot pierce a winke beyond
But doubt discouery there. Will you grant with me
That Ferdinand is drown'd.

SEBASTIAN   He's gone.

ANTHONIO   Then tell me,
Who's the next heire of Naples?

SEBASTIAN   Claribell.

ANTHONIO
She that is Queene of Tunis: she that dwels
Ten leagues beyond mans life: she that from Naples
Can haue no note, vnlesse the Sun were post:
The Man i'th Moone's too slow, till new-borne chinnes
Be rough, and Razor-able: She that from whom
We all were sea-swallow'd, though some cast againe,
(And by that destiny) to performe an act
830 Whereof, what's past is Prologue; what to come
In yours, and my discharge.

SEBASTIAN   What stuffe is this? How say you?
'Tis true my brothers daughter's Queene of Tunis,
So is she heyre of Naples, 'twixt which Regions
There is some space.

ANTHONIO   A space, whose eu'ry cubit
Seemes to cry out, how shall that Claribell

Measure vs backe to Naples? keepe in Tunis,
And let Sebastian wake. Say, this were death
That now hath seiz'd them, why they were no worse
Then now they are: There be that can rule Naples   840
As well as he that sleepes: Lords, that can prate
As amply, and vnnecessarily
As this Gonzallo: I my selfe could make
A Chough of as deepe chat: O, that you bore
The minde that I do; what a sleepe were this
For your aduancement? Do you vnderstand me?

SEBASTIAN
Me thinkes I do.

ANTHONIO   And how do's your content
Tender your owne good fortune?

SEBASTIAN   I remember
You did supplant your Brother Prospero.

ANTHONIO   True:
And looke how well my Garments sit vpon me,   850
Much feater then before: My Brothers seruants
Were then my fellowes, now they are my men.

SEBASTIAN But for your conscience.

ANTHONIO
I Sir: where lies that? If 'twere a kybe
'Twould put me to my slipper: But I feele not
This Deity in my bosome: 'Twentie consciences
That stand 'twixt me, and Millaine, candied be they,
And melt ere they mollest: Heere lies your Brother,
No better then the earth he lies vpon,
If he were that which now hee's like (that's dead)   860
Whom I with this obedient steele (three inches of it)
Can lay to bed for euer: whiles you doing thus,
To the perpetuall winke for aye might put
This ancient morsell: this Sir Prudence, who
Should not vpbraid our course: for all the rest
They'l take suggestion, as a Cat laps milke,
They'l tell the clocke, to any businesse that
We say befits the houre.

SEBASTIAN   Thy case, deere Friend
Shall be my president: As thou got'st Millaine,
I'le come by Naples: Draw thy sword, one stroke   870
Shall free thee from the tribute which thou paiest,
And I the King shall loue thee.

ANTHONIO   Draw together:
And when I reare my hand, do you the like
To fall it on Gonzalo.

They draw

SEBASTIAN   O, but one word.

Enter Ariell inuisible, with Musicke

ARIELL (*to Gonzalo*)
My Master through his Art foresees the danger
That you (his friend) are in, and sends me forth
(For else his proiect dies) to keepe them liuing.

Sings in Gonzaloes eare
        While you here do snoaring lie,
        Open-ey'd Conspiracie
            His time doth take: 880
        If of Life you keepe a care,
        Shake off slumber and beware.
            Awake, awake.

ANTHONIO (*to Sebastian*)
  Then let vs both be sodaine.
GONZALO (*awaking*)   Now, good Angels
  Preserue the King.
ALONSO (*awaking*)
  Why how now hoa; awake?
     The others awake
  (*To Anthonio and Sebastian*) why are you drawn?
  (*To Gonzalo*) Wherefore this ghastly looking?
GONZALO   What's the matter?
SEBASTIAN
  Whiles we stood here securing your repose,
  (Euen now) we heard a hollow burst of bellowing
890 Like Buls, or rather Lyons, did't not wake you?
  It strooke mine eare most terribly.
ALONSO   I heard nothing.
ANTHONIO
  O, 'twas a din to fright a Monsters eare;
  To make an earthquake: sure it was the roare
  Of a whole heard of Lyons.
ALONSO   Heard you this *Gonzalo*?
GONZALO
  Vpon mine honour, Sir, I heard a humming,
  (And that a strange one too) which did awake me:
  I shak'd you Sir, and cride: as mine eyes opend,
  I saw their weapons drawne: there was a noyse,
  That's verily: 'tis best we stand vpon our guard;
900 Or that we quit this place: let's draw our weapons.
ALONSO
  Lead off this ground & let's make further search
  For my poore sonne.
GONZALO   Heauens keepe him from these Beasts:
  For he is sure i'th Island.
ALONSO   Lead away.
                   Exeunt; manet Ariell
ARIELL
  Prospero my Lord, shall know what I haue done.
  So (King) goe safely on to seeke thy Son.   *Exit*

2.2   *Enter Caliban, wearing a Gaberdine, and with a*
(Sc. 4)   *burthen of Wood*
CALIBAN ⌈*throwing downe his burthen*⌉
  All the infections that the Sunne suckes vp
  From Bogs, Fens, Flats, on *Prosper* fall, and make him
  By ynch-meale a disease:
    ⌈*A noyse of Thunder heard*⌉
                His Spirits heare me,
  And yet I needes must curse. But they'll nor pinch,
910 Fright me with Vrchyn-shewes, pitch me i'th mire,
  Nor lead me like a fire-brand, in the darke
  Out of my way, vnlesse he bid'em; but
  For euery trifle, are they set vpon me,
  Sometime like Apes, that moe and chatter at me,
  And after bite me: then like Hedg-hogs, which
  Lye tumbling in my bare-foote way, and mount
  Their pricks at my foot-fall: sometime am I
  All wound with Adders, who with clouen tongues
  Doe hisse me into madnesse:
    Enter Trinculo
                Lo, now Lo,

Here comes a Spirit of his, and to torment me   920
For bringing wood in slowly: I'le fall flat,
Perchance he will not minde me.
  He lies downe
TRINCULO Here's neither bush, nor shrub to beare off any
  weather at all: and another Storme brewing, I heare
  it sing ith' winde: yond same blacke cloud, yond huge
  one, lookes like a foule bumbard that would shed his
  licquor: if it should thunder, as it did before, I know
  not where to hide my head: yond same cloud cannot
  choose but fall by paile-fuls. (*Seeing Caliban*) What haue
  we here, a man, or a fish? dead or aliue? a fish, hee   930
  smels like a fish: a very ancient and fish-like smell: a
  kinde of, not of the newest poore-Iohn: a strange fish:
  were I in *England* now (as once I was) and had but
  this fish painted; not a holiday-foole there but would
  giue a peece of siluer: there, would this Monster, make
  a man: any strange beast there, makes a man: when
  they will not giue a doit to relieue a lame Begger, they
  will lay out ten to see a dead *Indian*: Leg'd like a man;
  and his Finnes like Armes: warme o' my troth: I doe
  now let loose my opinion; hold it no longer; this is no   940
  fish, but an Islander, that hath lately suffered by a
  Thunderbolt:
    ⌈*Thunder*⌉
  Alas, the storme is come againe: my best way is to
  creepe vnder his Gaberdine: there is no other shelter
  hereabout: Misery acquaints a man with strange
  bedfellowes: I will here shrowd till the dregges of the
  storme be past.
  He hides vnder Calibans Gaberdine.
  Enter Stephano singing, with a wooden bottle in his
  hand
STEPHANO   *I shall no more to sea, to sea,*
            Here shall I dye ashore.
This is a very scuruy tune to sing at a mans Funerall: 950
  well, here's my comfort.
  He drinkes, then sings
  The Master, the Swabber, the Boate-swaine & I;
    The Gunner, and his Mate
  Lou'd Mall, Meg, and Marrian, and Margerie,
    But none of vs car'd for Kate.
    For she had a tongue with a tang,
    Would cry to a Sailor goe hang:
  She lou'd not the sauour of Tar nor of Pitch,
  Yet a Tailor might scratch her where ere she did itch.
    Then to Sea Boyes, and let her goe hang.   960
    Then to Sea, etc.
This is a scuruy tune too: But here's my comfort.
  He drinks
CALIBAN (*to Trinculo*) Doe not torment me: oh.
STEPHANO What's the matter? Haue we diuels here? Doe
  you put trickes vpon's with Saluages, and Men of Inde?
  ha? I haue not scap'd drowning, to be afeard now of
  your foure legges: for it hath bin said; as proper a man
  as euer went on foure legs, cannot make him giue
  ground: and it shall be said so againe, while *Stephano*
  breathes at' nostrils.   970

CALIBAN The Spirit torments me: oh.

STEPHANO This is some Monster of the Isle, with foure legs; who hath got (as I take it) an Ague: where the diuell should he learne our language? I will giue him some reliefe if it be but for that: if I can recouer him, and keepe him tame, and get to *Naples* with him, he's a Present for any Emperour that euer trod on Neates-leather.

CALIBAN (*to Trinculo*) Doe not torment me 'prethee: I'le
980 bring my wood home faster.

STEPHANO He's in his fit now; and doe's not talke after the wisest; hee shall taste of my Bottle: if hee haue neuer drunke wine afore, it will goe neere to remoue his Fit: if I can recouer him, and keepe him tame, I will not take too much for him; hee shall pay for him that hath him, and that soundly.

CALIBAN (*to Trinculo*) Thou do'st me yet but little hurt; thou wilt anon, I know it by thy trembling: Now *Prosper* workes vpon thee.

990 STEPHANO Come on your wayes: open your mouth: here is that which will giue language to you Cat; open your mouth; this will shake your shaking, I can tell you, and that soundly: you cannot tell who's your friend; open your chaps againe.

Caliban drinkes

TRINCULO I should know that voyce: It should be, But hee is dround; and these are diuels; O defend me.

STEPHANO Foure legges and two voyces; a most delicate Monster: his forward voyce now is to speake well of his friend; his backward voice, is to vtter foule speeches,
1000 and to detract: if all the wine in my bottle will recouer him, I will helpe his Ague: Come:

Caliban drinkes

Amen, I will poure some in thy other mouth.

TRINCULO *Stephano.*

STEPHANO Doth thy other mouth call me? Mercy, mercy: This is a diuell, and no Monster: I will leaue him, I haue no long Spoone.

TRINCULO *Stephano*: if thou beest *Stephano*, touch me, and speake to me: for I am *Trinculo*; be not afeard, thy good friend *Trinculo.*

1010 STEPHANO If thou bee'st *Trinculo*: come forth: I'le pull thee by the lesser legges: if any be *Trinculo's* legges, these are they:

He pulls out Trinculo by the legs

Thou art very *Trinculo* indeede: how cam'st thou to be the siege of this Moone-calfe? Can he vent *Trinculo's*?

TRINCULO (*rising*) I tooke him to be kil'd with a thunder-strok; but art thou not dround *Stephano*? I hope now thou art not dround: Is the Storme ouer-blowne? I hid mee vnder the dead Moone-Calfes Gaberdine, for feare of the Storme: And art thou liuing *Stephano*? O *Stephano*,
1020 two *Neapolitanes* scap'd?

⌈*He dances Stephano round*⌉

STEPHANO 'Prethee doe not turne me about, my stomacke is not constant.

CALIBAN

These be fine things, and if they be not sprights:

That's a braue God, and beares Celestiall liquor: I will kneele to him.

⌈*He kneels*⌉

STEPHANO (*to Trinculo*) How did'st thou scape? How cam'st thou hither? Sweare by this Bottle how thou cam'st hither: I escap'd vpon a But of Sacke, which the Saylors heaued o're-boord, by this Bottle which I made of the barke of a Tree, with mine owne hands, since I was 1030 cast a'shore.

CALIBAN I'le sweare vpon that Bottle, to be thy true subiect, for the liquor is not earthly.

STEPHANO (*offering Trinculo the Bottle*) Heere: sweare then how thou escap'dst.

TRINCULO Swom ashore (man) like a Ducke: I can swim like a Ducke i'le be sworne.

STEPHANO Here, kisse the Booke.

Trinculo drinkes

Though thou canst swim like a Ducke, thou art made like a Goose. 1040

TRINCULO O *Stephano*, ha'st any more of this?

STEPHANO The whole But (man) my Cellar is in a rocke by th'sea-side, where my Wine is hid:

⌈*Caliban rises*⌉

How now Moone-Calfe, how do's thine Ague?

CALIBAN Ha'st thou not dropt from heauen?

STEPHANO Out o'th Moone I doe assure thee. I was the Man ith' Moone, when time was.

CALIBAN

I haue seene thee in her: and I doe adore thee: My Mistris shew'd me thee, and thy Dog, and thy Bush.

STEPHANO Come, sweare to that: kisse the Booke: I will 1050 furnish it anon with new Contents: Sweare.

Caliban drinkes

TRINCULO By this good light, this is a very shallow Monster: I afeard of him? a very weake Monster: The Man ith' Moone? A most poore creadulous Monster: Well drawne Monster, in good sooth.

CALIBAN (*to Stephano*)

Ile shew thee euery fertill ynch 'oth Island: And I will kisse thy foote: I prethee be my god.

TRINCULO By this light, a most perfidious, and drunken Monster, when's god's a sleepe he'll rob his Bottle.

CALIBAN (*to Stephano*)

Ile kisse thy foot. Ile sweare my selfe thy Subiect. 1060

STEPHANO Come on then: downe and sweare.

⌈*Caliban kneeles*⌉

TRINCULO I shall laugh my selfe to death at this puppi-headed Monster: a most scuruie Monster: I could finde in my heart to beate him.

STEPHANO (*to Caliban*) Come, kisse.

⌈*Caliban kisses his foote*⌉

TRINCULO But that the poore Monster's in drinke: An abhominable Monster.

CALIBAN (*to Stephano*)

I'le shew thee the best Springs: I'le plucke thee Berries:

I'le fish for thee; and get thee wood enough.

A plague vpon the Tyrant that I serue; 1070

I'le beare him no more Stickes, but follow thee,
Thou wondrous man.

TRINCULO A most rediculous Monster, to make a wonder
of a poore drunkard.

CALIBAN (*to Stephano*)
I 'prethee let me bring thee where Crabs grow;
And I with my long nayles will digge thee pig-nuts;
Show thee a Iayes nest, and instruct thee how
To snare the nimble Marmazet: I'le bring thee
To clustring Philbirts, and sometimes I'le get thee
1080   Young Seamels from the Rocke: Wilt thou goe with me?

STEPHANO I pre'thee now lead the way without any more
talking. *Trinculo*, the King, and all our company else
being dround, wee will inherit here: Here; beare my
Bottle: Fellow *Trinculo*; we'll fill him by and by againe.

CALIBAN (*singing drunkenly*) Farewell Master; farewell,
farewell.

TRINCULO A howling Monster: a drunken Monster.

CALIBAN (*sings*)
        No more dams I'le make for fish,
           Nor fetch in firing,
1090   At requiring,
        Nor scrape trenchering, nor wash dish,
           Ban' ban' Cacalyban
        Has a new Master, get a new Man.
Freedome, high-day, high-day freedome, freedome high-
day, freedome.

STEPHANO O braue Monster; lead the way.   *Exeunt*

3.1   *Enter Ferdinand (bearing a Log)*
(Sc. 5) FERDINAND
There be some Sports are painfull; & their labor
Delight in them sets off: Some kindes of basenesse
Are nobly vndergon; and most poore matters
1100   Point to rich ends: this my meane Taske
Would be as heauy to me, as odious, but
The Mistris which I serue, quickens what's dead,
And makes my labours, pleasures: O She is
Ten times more gentle, then her Father's crabbed;
And he's compos'd of harshnesse. I must remoue
Some thousands of these Logs, and pile them vp,
Vpon a sore iniunction; my sweet Mistris
Weepes when she sees me worke, & saies, such
        basenes
Had neuer like Executor: I forget:
1110   But these sweet thoughts, doe euen refresh my labours,
Most busielest, when I doe it.
        Enter Miranda, and Prospero following at a distance
MIRANDA   Alas, now pray you
Worke not so hard: I would the lightning had
Burnt vp those Logs that you are enioynd to pile:
Pray set it downe, and rest you: when this burnes
'Twill weepe for hauing wearied you: my Father
Is hard at study; pray now rest your selfe,
Hee's safe for these three houres.

FERDINAND   O most deere Mistris,

The Sun will set before I shall discharge
What I must striue to do.

MIRANDA   If you'l sit downe
Ile beare your Logges the while: pray giue me that,   1120
Ile carry it to the pile.

FERDINAND   No precious Creature,
I had rather cracke my sinewes, breake my backe,
Then you should such dishonor vndergoe,
While I sit lazy by.

MIRANDA   It would become me
As well as it do's you; and I should do it
With much more ease: for my good will is to it,
And yours it is against.

PROSPERO (*aside*)   Poore worme thou art infected,
This visitation shewes it.

MIRANDA (*to Ferdinand*)   You looke wearily.

FERDINAND
No, noble Mistris, 'tis fresh morning with me
When you are by at night: I do beseech you   1130
Cheefely, that I might set it in my prayers,
What is your name?

MIRANDA   *Miranda*, O my Father,
I haue broke your hest to say so.

FERDINAND   Admir'd *Miranda*,
Indeede the top of Admiration, worth
What's deerest to the world: full many a Lady
I haue ey'd with best regard, and many a time
Th'harmony of their tongues, hath into bondage
Brought my too diligent eare: for seuerall vertues
Haue I lik'd seuerall women, neuer any
With so full soule, but some defect in her   1140
Did quarrell with the noblest grace she ow'd,
And put it to the foile. But you, O you,
So perfect, and so peerlesse, are created
Of euerie Creatures best.

MIRANDA   I do not know
One of my sexe; no womans face remember,
Saue from my glasse, mine owne: Nor haue I seene
More that I may call men, then you good friend,
And my deere Father: how features are abroad
I am skillesse of; but by my modestie
(The iewell in my dower) I would not wish   1150
Any Companion in the world but you:
Nor can imagination forme a shape
Besides your selfe, to like of: but I prattle
Something too wildely, and my Fathers precepts
I therein do forget.

FERDINAND   I am, in my condition
A Prince (*Miranda*) I do thinke a King
(I would not so) and would no more endure
This wodden slauerie, then to suffer
The flesh-flie blow my mouth: heare my soule speake.
The verie instant that I saw you, did   1160
My heart flie to your seruice, there resides
To make me slaue to it, and for your sake
Am I this patient Logge-man.

MIRANDA   Do you loue me?

FERDINAND

O heauen; O earth, beare witnes to this sound,
And crowne what I professe with kinde euent
If I speake true: if hollowly, inuert
What best is boaded me, to mischiefe: I,
Beyond all limit of what else i'th world
Do loue, prize, honor you.

MIRANDA (*weeping*)   I am a foole
To weepe at what I am glad of.

1170 PROSPERO (*aside*)   Faire encounter
Of two most rare affections: heauens raine grace
On that which breeds betweene 'em.

FERDINAND (*to Miranda*)   Wherefore weepe you?

MIRANDA

At mine vnworthinesse, that dare not offer
What I desire to giue; and much lesse take
What I shall die to want: But this is trifling,
And all the more it seekes to hide it selfe,
The bigger bulke it shewes. Hence bashfull cunning,
And prompt me plaine and holy innocence.
I am your wife, if you will marrie me;

1180 If not, Ile die your maid: to be your fellow
You may denie me, but Ile be your seruant
Whether you will or no.

FERDINAND ⌈*kneeling*⌉   My Mistris (deerest)
And I thus humble euer.

MIRANDA My husband then?

FERDINAND I, with a heart as willing
As bondage ere of freedome: heere's my hand.

MIRANDA

And mine, with my heart in't; and now farewel
Till halfe an houre hence.

FERDINAND   A thousand, thousand.
      Exeunt seuerally Miranda and Ferdinand

PROSPERO

So glad of this as they I cannot be,

1190 Who are surpriz'd with all; but my reioycing
At nothing can be more: Ile to my booke,
For yet ere supper time, must I performe
Much businesse appertaining.   *Exit*

3.2
(Sc. 6)   *Enter Caliban, Stephano, and Trinculo*

STEPHANO (*to Caliban*) Tell not me, when the But is out
we will drink water, not a drop before; therefore beare
vp, & boord em' Seruant Monster, drinke to me.

TRINCULO Seruant Monster? the folly of this Iland, they say
there's but fiue vpon this Isle; we are three of them, if
th' other two be brain'd like vs, the State totters.

1200 STEPHANO Drinke seruant Monster when I bid thee, thy
eies are almost set in thy head.

TRINCULO Where should they bee set else? hee were a
braue Monster indeede if they were set in his taile.

STEPHANO My man-Monster hath drown'd his tongue in
sacke: for my part the Sea cannot drowne mee, I swam
ere I could recouer the shore, fiue and thirtie Leagues
off and on, by this light thou shalt bee my Lieutenant
Monster, or my Standard.

TRINCULO Your Lieutenant if you list, hee's no standard.

STEPHANO Weel not run Monsieur Monster.   1210

TRINCULO Nor go neither: but you'l lie like dogs, and yet
say nothing neither.

STEPHANO Moone-calfe, speak once in thy life, if thou
beest a good Moone-calfe.

CALIBAN

How does thy honour? Let me licke thy shooe:
Ile not serue him, he is not valiant.

TRINCULO Thou liest most ignorant Monster, I am in case
to iustle a Constable: why, thou debosh'd Fish thou,
was there euer man a Coward, that hath drunk so
much Sacke as I to day? wilt thou tell a monstrous lie,   1220
being but halfe a Fish, and halfe a Monster?

CALIBAN (*to Stephano*) Loe, how he mockes me, wilt thou
let him my Lord?

TRINCULO Lord, quoth he? that a Monster should be such
a Naturall?

CALIBAN (*to Stephano*)
Loe, loe againe: bite him to death I prethee.

STEPHANO *Trinculo*, keepe a good tongue in your head: If
you proue a mutineere, the next Tree: the poore
Monster's my subiect, and he shall not suffer indignity.

CALIBAN

I thanke my noble Lord. Wilt thou be pleas'd   1230
To hearken once againe to the suite I made to thee?

STEPHANO Marry will I: kneele, and repeat it, I will stand,
and so shall *Trinculo*.
      ⌈*Caliban kneeles.*⌉
      Enter Ariell inuisible

CALIBAN As I told thee before, I am subiect to a Tirant,
a Sorcerer, that by his cunning hath cheated me of the
Island.

ARIELL Thou lyest.

CALIBAN (*to Trinculo*)
Thou lyest, thou iesting Monkey thou:
I would my valiant Master would destroy thee.
I do not lye.   1240

STEPHANO *Trinculo*, if you trouble him any more in's tale,
by this hand, I will supplant some of your teeth.

TRINCULO Why, I said nothing.

STEPHANO Mum then, and no more: (*to Caliban*) proceed.

CALIBAN

I say by Sorcery he got this Isle.
From me, he got it. If thy Greatnesse will
Reuenge it on him, (for I know thou dar'st)
But this Thing dare not.

STEPHANO That's most certaine.

CALIBAN

Thou shalt be Lord of it, and Ile serue thee.   1250

STEPHANO How now shall this be compast? Canst thou
bring me to the party?

CALIBAN

Yea, yea my Lord, Ile yeeld him thee asleepe,
Where thou maist knocke a naile into his head.

ARIELL Thou liest, thou canst not.

CALIBAN

What a py'de Ninnie's this? (*To Trinculo*) Thou scuruy
patch:

(*To Stephano*) I do beseech thy Greatnesse giue him
        blowes,
And take his bottle from him: When that's gone,
He shall drinke nought but brine, for Ile not shew him
1260   Where the quicke Freshes are.
STEPHANO *Trinculo*, run into no further danger: Interrupt
    the Monster one word further, and by this hand, Ile
    turne my mercie out o'doores, and make a Stockfish of
    thee.
TRINCULO Why, what did I? I did nothing: Ile go farther
    off.
STEPHANO Didst thou not say he lyed?
ARIELL Thou liest.
STEPHANO Do I so? (*Striking Trinculo*) Take thou that, as
1270   you like this, giue me the lye another time.
TRINCULO I did not giue the lie: Out o'your wittes, and
    hearing too? A pox o'your bottle, this can Sacke and
    drinking doo: A murren on your Monster, and the
    diuell take your fingers.
CALIBAN Ha, ha, ha.
STEPHANO Now forward with your Tale: (*to Trinculo*)
    prethee stand further off.
CALIBAN
    Beate him enough: after a little time
    Ile beate him too.
STEPHANO (*to Trinculo*)
            Stand farther: (*To Caliban*) Come proceede.
CALIBAN
1280   Why, as I told thee, 'tis a custome with him
    I'th afternoone to sleepe: there thou maist braine him,
    Hauing first seiz'd his bookes: Or with a logge
    Batter his skull, or paunch him with a stake,
    Or cut his wezand with thy knife. Remember
    First to possesse his Bookes; for without them
    Hee's but a Sot, as I am; nor hath not
    One Spirit to command: they all do hate him
    As rootedly as I. Burne but his Bookes,
    He ha's braue Vtensils (for so he calles them)
1290   Which when he ha's a house, hee'l decke withall.
    And that most deeply to consider, is
    The beautie of his daughter: he himselfe
    Cals her a non-pareill: I neuer saw a woman
    But onely *Sycorax* my Dam, and she;
    But she as farre surpasseth *Sycorax*,
    As great'st do's least.
STEPHANO   Is it so braue a Lasse?
CALIBAN
    I Lord, she will become thy bed, I warrant,
    And bring thee forth braue brood.
STEPHANO Monster, I will kill this man: his daughter and
1300   I will be King and Queene, saue our Graces: and
    Trinculo and thy selfe shall be Vice-royes: Dost thou
    like the plot *Trinculo*?
TRINCULO Excellent.
STEPHANO Giue me thy hand, I am sorry I beate thee: But
    while thou liu'st keepe a good tongue in thy head.
CALIBAN
    Within this halfe houre will he be asleepe,
    Wilt thou destroy him then?

STEPHANO I on mine honour.
ARIELL (*aside*) This will I tell my Master.
CALIBAN
    Thou mak'st me merry: I am full of pleasure,   1310
    Let vs be iocond. Will you troule the Catch
    You taught me but whileare?
STEPHANO At thy request Monster, I will do reason, any
    reason: Come on *Trinculo*, let vs sing.
    (*Sings*)   Flout 'em, and cout 'em:
                    And skowt 'em, and flout 'em,
                        Thought is free.
CALIBAN That's not the tune.
        Ariell plaies the tune on a Tabor and Pipe
STEPHANO What is this same?
TRINCULO This is the tune of our Catch, plaid by the   1320
    picture of No-body.
STEPHANO (*calling towards Ariell*) If thou beest a man, shew
    thy selfe in thy likenes: If thou beest a diuell, take't as
    thou list.
TRINCULO O forgiue me my sinnes.
STEPHANO He that dies payes all debts: (*Calling*) I defie
    thee; Mercy vpon vs.
CALIBAN Art thou affeard?
STEPHANO No Monster, not I.
CALIBAN
    Be not affeard, the Isle is full of noyses,   1330
    Sounds, and sweet aires, that giue delight and hurt
        not:
    Sometimes a thousand twangling Instruments
    Will hum about mine eares; and sometime voices,
    That if I then had wak'd after long sleepe,
    Will make me sleepe againe, and then in dreaming,
    The clouds methought would open, and shew riches
    Ready to drop vpon me, that when I wak'd
    I cri'de to dreame againe.
STEPHANO This will proue a braue kingdome to me, where
    I shall haue my Musicke for nothing.   1340
CALIBAN When *Prospero* is destroy'd.
STEPHANO That shall be by and by: I remember the storie.
                    Exit Ariell, playing Musicke
TRINCULO The sound is going away, lets follow it, and
    after do our worke.
STEPHANO Leade Monster, wee'l follow: I would I could
    see this Taborer, he layes it on.
TRINCULO (*to Caliban*) Wilt come? Ile follow *Stephano*.
                                            Exeunt

    Enter Alonso, Sebastian, Anthonio, Gonzallo,   3.3
    Adrian, and Francisco   (Sc. 7)
GONZALO (*to Alonso*)
    By'r lakin, I can goe no further, Sir,
    My old bones ake: here's a maze trod indeede
    Through fourth-rights, & Meanders: by your patience, 1350
    I needes must rest me.
ALONSO   Old Lord, I cannot blame thee,
    Who, am my selfe attach'd with wearinesse
    To th'dulling of my spirits: Sit downe, and rest:
    Euen here I will put off my hope, and keepe it
    No longer for my Flatterer: he is droun'd

Whom thus we stray to finde, and the Sea mocks
Our frustrate search on land: well, let him goe.
⌜*They sit*⌝

ANTHONIO (*aside to Sebastian*)
I am right glad, that he's so out of hope:
Doe not for one repulse forgoe the purpose
That you resolu'd t'effect.

1360 SEBASTIAN (*aside to Anthonio*) The next aduantage
Will we take throughly.

ANTHONIO (*aside to Sebastian*) Let it be to night,
For now they are oppress'd with trauaile, they
Will not, nor cannot vse such vigilance
As when they are fresh.

SEBASTIAN (*aside to Anthonio*) I say to night: no more.
*Solemne and strange Musicke: Enter Prosper on the
top (inuisible)*

ALONSO
What harmony is this? my good friends, harke.

GONZALO Maruellous sweet Musicke.
*Enter Spirits in seuerall strange shapes, bringing in
a Table and a Banket; and dance about it with
gentle actions of salutations, and inuiting the King,
&c. to eate, they depart*

ALONSO
Giue vs kind keepers, heauẽs: what were these?

SEBASTIAN
A liuing *Drolerie*: now I will beleeue
That there are Vnicornes: that in *Arabia*
1370 There is one Tree, the Phœnix throne, one Phœnix
At this houre reigning there.

ANTHONIO   Ile beleeue both:
And what do's else want credit, come to me
And Ile be sworne 'tis true: Trauellers nere did lye,
Though fooles at home condemne 'em.

GONZALO   If in *Naples*
I should report this now, would they beleeue me?
If I should say I saw such Islanders;
(For certes, these are people of the Island)
Who though they are of monstrous shape, yet note
Their manners are more gentle, kinde, then of
1380 Our humaine generation you shall finde
Many, nay almost any.

PROSPERO (*aside*)   Honest Lord,
Thou hast said well: for some of you there present;
Are worse then diuels.

ALONSO   I cannot too much muse:
Such shapes, such gesturė, and such sound expressing
(Although they want the vse of tongue) a kinde
Of excellent dumbe discourse.

PROSPERO (*aside*)   Praise in departing.

FRANCISCO
They vanish'd strangely.

SEBASTIAN   No matter, since
They haue left their Viands behinde; for wee haue
stomacks.
Wilt please you taste of what is here?

ALONSO   Not I.

GONZALO
Faith Sir, you neede not feare: when wee were Boyes   1390
Who would beleeue that there were Mountayneeres,
Dew-lapt, like Buls, whose throats had hanging at'em
Wallets of flesh? or that there were such men
Whose heads stood in their brests? which now we finde
Each putter out of fiue for one, will bring vs
Good warrant of.

ALONSO ⌜*rising*⌝   I will stand to, and feede,
Although my last, no matter, since I feele
The best is past: brother: my Lord, the Duke,
Stand too, and doe as we.
⌜*Alonso, Sebastian, and Anthonio approach the Table.*⌝
*Thunder and Lightning. Ariell ⌜descends⌝ (like a
Harpey) claps his wings vpon the Table, and with a
quient deuice the Banquet vanishes*

ARIELL
You are three men of sinne, whom destiny   1400
That hath to instrument this lower world,
And what is in't: the neuer surfeited Sea,
Hath caus'd to belch vp you; and on this Island,
Where man doth not inhabit, you 'mongst men,
Being most vnfit to liue: I haue made you mad;
And euen with such like valour, men hang, and
drowne
Their proper selues:
Alonso, Sebastian, and Anthonio draw
          you fooles, I and my fellowes
Are ministers of Fate, the Elements
Of whom your swords are temper'd, may as well
Wound the loud windes, or with bemockt-at-Stabs   1410
Kill the still closing waters, as diminish
One dowle that's in my plumbe: My fellow ministers
Are like-invulnerable: if you could hurt,
Your swords are now too massie for your strengths,
And will not be vplifted:
Alonso, Sebastian, and Anthonio stand amazed
          But remember
(For that's my businesse to you) that you three
From *Millaine* did supplant good *Prospero*,
Expos'd vnto the Sea (which hath requit it)
Him, and his innocent childe: for which foule deed,
The Powres, delaying (not forgetting) haue   1420
Incens'd the Seas, and Shores; yea, all the Creatures
Against your peace: Thee of thy Sonne, *Alonso*
They haue bereft; and doe pronounce by me
Lingring perdition (worse then any death
Can be at once) shall step, by step attend
You, and your wayes, whose wraths to guard you
from,
Which here, in this most desolate Isle, else fals
Vpon your heads, is nothing but hearts-sorrow,
And a cleere life ensuing.
*He ⌜ascends and⌝ vanishes in Thunder: then (to soft
Musicke.) Enter the Spirits againe, and daunce
(with mockes and mowes) and carrying out the
Table they depart*

PROSPERO

1430 Brauely the figure of this *Harpie*, hast thou
Perform'd (my *Ariell*) a grace it had deuouring:
Of my Instruction, hast thou nothing bated
In what thou had'st to say: so with good life,
And obseruation strange, my meaner ministers
Their seuerall kindes haue done: my high charmes
        work,
And these (mine enemies) are all knit vp
In their distractions: they now are in my powre;
And in these fits, I leaue them, while I visit
Yong *Ferdinand* (whom they suppose is droun'd)

1440 And his, and mine lou'd darling.   *Exit*
⌈*Gonzalo, Adrian, and Francisco go towards the others*⌉

GONZALO

I'th name of something holy, Sir, why stand you
In this strange stare?

ALONSO   O, it is monstrous: monstrous:
Me thought the billowes spoke, and told me of it,
The windes did sing it to me: and the Thunder
(That deepe and dreadfull Organ-Pipe) pronounc'd
The name of *Prosper*: it did base my Trespasse,
Therefore my Sonne i'th Ooze is bedded; and
I'le seeke him deeper then ere plummet sounded,
And with him there lye mudded.   *Exit*

SEBASTIAN   But one feend at a time,
Ile fight their Legions ore.

1450 ANTHONIO   Ile be thy Second.
                Exeunt Sebastian and Anthonio

GONZALO

All three of them are desperate: their great guilt
(Like poyson giuen to worke a great time after)
Now gins to bite the spirits: I doe beseech you
(That are of suppler ioynts) follow them swiftly,
And hinder them from what this extasie
May now prouoke them to.

ADRIAN   Follow, I pray you.
                Exeunt omnes

✿

4.1   *Enter Prospero, Ferdinand, and Miranda*
(Sc. 8) PROSPERO (*to Ferdinand*)
If I haue too austerely punish'd you,
Your compensation makes amends, for I
Haue giuen you here, a third of mine owne life,

1460 Or that for which I liue: who, once againe
I tender to thy hand: All thy vexations
Were but my trials of thy loue, and thou
Hast strangely stood the test: here, afore heauen
I ratifie this my rich guift: O *Ferdinand*,
Doe not smile at me, that I boast of her,
For thou shalt finde she will out-strip all praise
And make it halt, behinde her.

FERDINAND   I doe beleeue it
Against an Oracle.

PROSPERO

Then, as my guift, and thine owne acquisition
1470 Worthily purchas'd, take my daughter: But

If thou do'st breake her Virgin-knot, before
All sanctimonious ceremonies may
With full and holy right, be ministred,
No sweet aspersion shall the heauens let fall
To make this contract grow; but barraine hate,
Sower-ey'd disdaine, and discord shall bestrew
The vnion of your bed, with weedes so loathly
That you shall hate it both: Therefore take heede,
As Hymens Lamps shall light you.

FERDINAND   As I hope
For quiet dayes, faire Issue, and long life,   1480
With such loue as 'tis now, the murkiest den,
The most opportune place, the strongst suggestion,
Our worser *Genius* can, shall neuer melt
Mine honor into lust, to take away
The edge of that dayes celebration,
When I shall thinke, or *Phœbus* Steeds are founderd,
Or Night kept chain'd below.

PROSPERO   Fairely spoke;
Sit then, and talke with her, she is thine owne;
        Ferdinand and Miranda sit and talk together
What *Ariell*; my industrious seruāt *Ariell*.
        Enter Ariell

ARIELL

What would my potent master? here I am.   1490

PROSPERO

Thou, and thy meaner fellowes, your last seruice
Did worthily performe: and I must vse you
In such another tricke: goe bring the rabble
(Ore whom I giue thee powre) here, to this place:
Incite them to quicke motion, for I must
Bestow vpon the eyes of this yong couple
Some vanity of mine Art: it is my promise,
And they expect it from me.

ARIELL   Presently?

PROSPERO I: with a twincke.

ARIELL   Before you can say come, and goe,   1500
        And breathe twice; and cry, so, so:
        Each one, tripping on his Toe,
        Will be here with mop, and mowe.
        Doe you loue me Master? no?

PROSPERO

Dearely, my delicate *Ariell*: doe not approach
Till thou do'st heare me call.

ARIELL   Well: I conceiue.   *Exit*

PROSPERO (*to Ferdinand*)

Looke thou be true: doe not giue dalliance
Too much the raigne: the strongest oathes, are straw
To th'fire ith' blood: be more abstenious,
Or else good night your vow.

FERDINAND   I warrant you, Sir,   1510
The white cold virgin Snow, vpon my heart
Abates the ardour of my Liuer.

PROSPERO   Well.
Now come my *Ariell*, bring a Corolary,
Rather then want a Spirit; appear, & pertly.
        Soft musick
(*To Ferdinand and Miranda*) No tongue: all eyes: be silent.

Enter Iris

IRIS

    Ceres, most bounteous Lady, thy rich Leas

    Of Wheate, Rye, Barley, Fetches, Oates and Pease;

    Thy Turphie-Mountaines, where liue nibling Sheepe,

    And flat Medes thetchd with Stouer, them to keepe:

1520   Thy bankes with pioned, and twilled brims

    Which spungie *Aprill*, at thy hest betrims;

    To make cold Nymphes chast crownes; & thy broome-

        groues;

    Whose shadow the dismissed Batchelor loues,

    Being lasse-lorne: thy pole-clipt vineyard,

    And thy Sea-marge stirrile, and rockey-hard,

    Where thou thy selfe do'st ayre, the Queene o'th Skie,

    Whose watry Arch, and messenger, am I,

    Bids thee leaue these, & with her soueraigne grace,

        Iuno ⌈appeares in the ayre⌉

    Here on this grasse-plot, in this very place

1530   To come, and sport: her Peacocks flye amaine:

    Approach, rich *Ceres*, her to entertaine.

        Enter ⌈Ariell as⌉ Ceres

CERES

    Haile, many-coloured Messenger, that nere

    Do'st disobey the wife of *Iupiter*:

    Who, with thy saffron wings, vpon my flowres

    Diffusest hony drops, refreshing showres,

    And with each end of thy blew bowe do'st crowne

    My boskie acres, and my vnshrubd downe,

    Rich scarph to my proud earth: why hath thy Queene

    Summond me hither, to this short gras'd Greene?

IRIS

1540   A contract of true Loue, to celebrate,

    And some donation freely to estate

    On the bles'd Louers.

CERES   Tell me heauenly Bowe,

    If *Venus* or her Sonne, as thou do'st know,

    Doe now attend the Queene? since they did plot

    The meanes, that duskie *Dis*, my daughter got,

    Her, and her blind-Boyes scandald company,

    I haue forsworne.

IRIS   Of her societie

    Be not afraid: I met her deitie

    Cutting the clouds towards *Paphos*: and her Son

1550   Doue-drawn with her: here thought they to haue done

    Some wanton charme, vpon this Man and Maide,

    Whose vowes are, that no bed-right shall be paid

    Till *Hymens* Torch be lighted: but in vaine,

    Marses hot Minion is returnd againe,

    Her waspish headed sonne, has broke his arrowes,

    Swears he will shoote no more, but play with Sparrows,

    And be a Boy right out.

        ⌈*Musicke. Iuno descends to the Stage*⌉

CERES   Highest Queene of State,

    Great *Iuno* comes, I know her by her gate.

IUNO

    How do's my bounteous sister? goe with me

1560   To blesse this twaine, that they may prosperous be,

    And honourd in their Issue.

⌈*Ceres ioynes Iuno, and*⌉ *they sing*

IUNO   *Honor, riches, marriage, blessing,*

    Long continuance, and encreasing,

    Hourely ioyes, be still vpon you,

    Iuno sings her blessings on you.

⌈CERES⌉   *Earths increase, and foyzon plentie,*

    Barnes, and Garners, neuer empty.

    Vines, with clustring bunches growing,

    Plants, with goodly burthen bowing:

    Spring come to you at the farthest,   1570

    In the very end of Haruest.

    Scarcity and want shall shun you,

    Ceres blessing so is on you.

FERDINAND

    This is a most maiesticke vision, and

    Harmonious charmingly: may I be bold

    To thinke these spirits?

PROSPERO   Spirits, which by mine Art

    I haue from their confines call'd to enact

    My present fancies.

FERDINAND   Let me liue here euer,

    So rare a wondred Father, and a wise

    Makes this place Paradise.

        Iuno and Ceres whisper, and send Iris on employment

PROSPERO   Sweet now, silence: 1580

    Iuno and *Ceres* whisper seriously,

    There's something else to doe: hush, and be mute

    Or else our spell is mar'd.

IRIS

    You Nimphs cald *Nayades* of yᵉ windring brooks,

    With your sedg'd crownes, and euer-harmelesse lookes,

    Leaue your crispe channels, and on this greene-Land

    Answere your summons, *Iuno* do's command.

    Come temperate Nimphes, and helpe to celebrate

    A Contract of true Loue: be not too late.

        Enter Certaine Nimphes

    You Sun-burn'd Sicklemen of August weary,   1590

    Come hether from the furrow, and be merry,

    Make holly day: your Rye-straw hats put on,

    And these fresh Nimphes encounter euery one

    In Country footing.

        Enter certaine Reapers (properly habited:) they ioyne

        with the Nimphes, in a gracefull dance, towards the

        end whereof, Prospero starts sodainly and speakes

PROSPERO *(aside)*

    I had forgot that foule conspiracy

    Of the beast *Calliban*, and his confederates

    Against my life: the minute of their plot

    Is almost come: *(To the spirits)* Well done, auoid: no

      more.

        To a strange hollow and confused noyse, the spirits

        in the Pageant heauily vanish.

        ⌈*Ferdinand and Miranda rise*⌉

FERDINAND *(to Miranda)*

    This is strange: your fathers in some passion

    That workes him strongly.

MIRANDA   Neuer till this day   1600

    Saw I him touch'd with anger, so distemper'd.

PROSPERO

You doe looke (my son) in a mou'd sort,
As if you were dismaid: be cheerefull Sir,
Our Reuels now are ended: These our actors,
(As I foretold you) were all Spirits, and
Are melted into Ayre, into thin Ayre,
And like the baselesse fabricke of this vision
The Clowd-capt Towres, the gorgeous Pallaces,
The solemne Temples, the great Globe it selfe,
1610 Yea, all which it inherit, shall dissolue,
And like this insubstantiall Pageant faded
Leaue not a racke behinde: we are such stuffe
As dreames are made on; and our little life
Is rounded with a sleepe: Sir, I am vext,
Beare with my weakenesse, my old braine is troubled:
Be not disturb'd with my infirmitie,
If you be pleas'd, retire into my Cell,
And there repose, a turne or two, Ile walke
To still my beating minde.

FERDINAND *and* MIRANDA   We wish your peace.
                              Exit Ferdinand and Miranda

PROSPERO

1620 Come with a thought; I thank thee *Ariell*: come.
     Enter Ariell

ARIELL

Thy thoughts I cleaue to, what's thy pleasure?

PROSPERO   Spirit:

We must prepare to meet with *Caliban*.

ARIELL

I my Commander, when I presented *Ceres*
I thought to haue told thee of it, but I fear'd
Least I might anger thee.

PROSPERO

Say again, where didst thou leaue these varlots?

ARIELL

I told you Sir, they were red-hot with drinking,
So full of valour, that they smote the ayre
For breathing in their faces: beate the ground
1630 For kissing of their feete; yet alwaies bending
Towards their proiect: then I beate my Tabor,
At which like vnback't colts they prickt their eares,
Aduanc'd their eye-lids, lifted vp their noses
As they smelt musicke, so I charm'd their eares
That Calfe-like, they my lowing follow'd, through
Tooth'd briars, sharpe firzes, pricking gosse, & thorns,
Which entred their fraile shins: at last I left them
I'th' filthy mantled poole beyond your Cell,
There dancing vp to th'chins, that the fowle Lake
Ore-stunck their feet.

1640 PROSPERO   This was well done (my bird)
Thy shape inuisible retaine thou still:
The trumpery in my house, goe bring it hither
For stale to catch these theeues.

ARIELL   I go, I goe.   *Exit*

PROSPERO

A Deuill, a borne-Deuill, on whose nature
Nurture can neuer sticke: on whom my paines
Humanely taken, all, all lost, quite lost,
And, as with age, his body ouglier growes,
So his minde cankers: I will plague them all,
Euen to roaring.
     Enter Ariell, loaden with glistering apparell, &c.
                Come, hang them on this line.
     Ariell hangs vp the apparell; ⌈*Exeunt Prospero and
     Ariell.*⌉
     Enter Caliban, Stephano, and Trinculo, all wet

CALIBAN

Pray you tread softly, that the blinde Mole may   1650
Not heare a foot fall: we now are neere his Cell.

STEPHANO Monster, your Fairy, wᶜ you say is a harmles
Fairy, has done little better then plaid the Iacke with vs.

TRINCULO Monster, I do smell all horse-pisse, at which
my nose is in great indignation.

STEPHANO So is mine. Do you heare Monster: If I should
take a displeasure against you: Looke you.

TRINCULO Thou wert but a lost Monster.

CALIBAN

Good my Lord, giue me thy fauour stil,
Be patient, for the prize Ile bring thee too   1660
Shall hudwinke this mischance: therefore speake softly,
All's husht as midnight yet.

TRINCULO I, but to loose our bottles in the Poole.

STEPHANO There is not onely disgrace and dishonor in
that Monster, but an infinite losse.

TRINCULO That's more to me then my wetting: Yet this
is your harmlesse Fairy, Monster.

STEPHANO I will fetch off my bottle, though I be o're eares
for my labour.

CALIBAN

Pre-thee (my King) be quiet. Seest thou heere   1670
This is the mouth o'th Cell: no noise, and enter:
Do that good mischeefe, which may make this Island
Thine owne for euer, and I thy *Caliban*
For aye thy foot-licker.

STEPHANO   Giue me thy hand,
I do begin to haue bloody thoughts.

TRINCULO (*seeing the apparell*) O King *Stephano*, O Peere:
O worthy *Stephano*, looke what a wardrobe heere is for
thee.

CALIBAN

Let it alone thou foole, it is but trash.

TRINCULO (*putting on a gowne*) Oh, ho, Monster: wee know   1680
what belongs to a frippery, O King *Stephano*.

STEPHANO Put off that gowne (*Trinculo*) by this hand Ile
haue that gowne.

TRINCULO Thy grace shall haue it.

CALIBAN

The dropsie drowne this foole, what doe you meane
To doate thus on such luggage? let't alone
And doe the murther first: if he awake,
From toe to crowne hee'l fill our skins with pinches,
Make vs strange stuffe.

STEPHANO Be you quiet (Monster) Mistris line, is not this   1690
my Ierkin? now is the Ierkin vnder the line: now Ierkin
you are like to lose your haire, & proue a bald Ierkin.
     Stephano and Trinculo take garments

TRINCULO Doe, doe; we steale by lyne and leuell, and't
like your grace.

STEPHANO I thank thee for that iest; heer's a garment
for't: Wit shall not goe vn-rewarded while I am King
of this Country: Steale by line and leuell, is an excellent
passe of pate: there's another garment for't.

TRINCULO Monster, come put some Lime vpon your
1700   fingers, and away with the rest.

CALIBAN
I will haue none on't: we shall loose our time,
And all be turn'd to Barnacles, or to Apes
With foreheads villanous low.

STEPHANO Monster, lay to your fingers: helpe to beare
this away, where my hogshead of wine is, or Ile turne
you out of my kingdome: goe to, carry this.

TRINCULO And this.

STEPHANO I, and this.

They load Caliban with apparell.
A noyse of Hunters heard. Enter diuers Spirits in
shape of Dogs and Hounds, hunting them about:
Prospero and Ariel setting them on

PROSPERO
Hey *Mountaine*, hey.

ARIELL   *Siluer*: there it goes, *Siluer*.

PROSPERO
1710   Fury, Fury: there Tyrant, there: harke, harke.
                            Exeunt Stephano, Trinculo, and
                            Caliban, pursued by Spirits
(*To Ariel*) Goe, charge my Goblins that they grinde
their ioynts
With dry Convultions, shorten vp their sinewes
With aged Cramps, & more pinch-spotted make them,
Then Pard, or Cat o' Mountaine.
                Cries within

ARIELL   Harke, they rore.

PROSPERO
Let them be hunted soundly: At this houre
Lies at my mercy all mine enemies:
Shortly shall all my labours end, and thou
Shalt haue the ayre at freedome: for a little
Follow, and doe me seruice.   *Exeunt*

❀

5.1   *Enter Prospero (in his Magicke robes) and Ariel*
(Sc. 9)   PROSPERO
1720   Now do's my Proiect gather to a head:
My charmes cracke not: my Spirits obey, and Time
Goes vpright with his carriage: how's the day?

ARIELL
On the sixt hower, at which time, my Lord
You said our worke should cease.

PROSPERO   I did say so,
When first I rais'd the Tempest: say my Spirit,
How fares the King, and's followers?

ARIELL   Confin'd together
In the same fashion, as you gaue in charge,
Iust as you left them; all prisoners Sir
In the *Line-groue* which weather-fends your Cell,
1730   They cannot boudge till your release: The King,

His Brother, and yours, abide all three distracted,
And the remainder mourning ouer them,
Brim full of sorrow, and dismay: but chiefly
Him that you term'd Sir, the good old Lord *Gonzallo*,
His teares run downe his beard like winters drops
From eaues of reeds: your charm so strongly works 'em
That if you now beheld them, your affections
Would become tender.

PROSPERO   Dost thou thinke so, Spirit?

ARIELL
Mine would, Sir, were I humane.

PROSPERO   And mine shall.
Hast thou (which art but aire) a touch, a feeling   1740
Of their afflictions, and shall not my selfe,
One of their kinde, that rellish all as sharpely
Passion as they, be kindlier mou'd then thou art?
Thogh with their high wrongs I am strook to th'quick,
Yet, with my nobler reason, gainst my furie
Doe I take part: the rarer Action is
In vertue, then in vengeance: they, being penitent,
The sole drift of my purpose doth extend
Not a frowne further: Goe, release them *Ariell*,
My Charmes Ile breake, their sences Ile restore,   1750
And they shall be themselues.

ARIELL   Ile fetch them, Sir. *Exit*
⌈*Prospero drawes a circle with his staffe*⌉

PROSPERO
Ye Elues of hils, brooks, stãding lakes & groues,
And ye, that on the sands with printlesse foote
Doe chase the ebbing-*Neptune*, and doe flie him
When he comes backe: you demy-Puppets, that
By Moone-shine doe the greene sowre Ringlets make,
Whereof the Ewe not bites: and you, whose pastime
Is to make midnight-Mushrumps, that reioyce
To heare the solemne Curfewe, by whose ayde
(Weake Masters though ye be) I haue bedymn'd   1760
The Noone-tide Sun, call'd forth the mutenous windes,
And twixt the greene Sea, and the azur'd vault
Set roaring warre: To the dread ratling Thunder
Haue I giuen fire, and rifted *Ioues* stowt Oke
With his owne Bolt: The strong bass'd promontorie
Haue I made shake, and by the spurs pluckt vp
The Pyne, and Cedar. Graues at my command
Haue wak'd their sleepers, op'd, and let 'em forth
By my so potent Art. But this rough Magicke
I heere abiure: and when I haue requir'd   1770
Some heauenly Musicke (which euen now I do)
To worke mine end vpon their Sences, that
This Ayrie-charme is for, I'le breake my staffe,
Bury it certaine fadomes in the earth,
And deeper then did euer Plummet sound
Ile drowne my booke.

Solemne musicke. Heere enters Ariel before, inuisible:
Then Alonso with a franticke gesture, attended by
Gonzalo. Sebastian and Anthonio in like manner
attended by Adrian and Francisco: They all enter
the circle which Prospero had made, and there stand
charm'd: which Prospero obseruing, speakes

(*To Alonso*) A solemne Ayre, and the best comforter,

To an vnsetled fancie, Cure thy braines
(Now vselesse) boild within thy skull:
(*To Sebastian and Anthonio*)   there stand
1780   For you are Spell-stopt.
Holy *Gonzallo*, Honourable man,
Mine eyes ev'n sociable to the shew of thine
Fall fellowy drops: (*Aside*) The charme dissolues apace,
And as the morning steales vpon the night
(Melting the darkenesse) so their rising sences
Begin to chace the ignorant fumes that mantle
Their cleerer reason. O good *Gonzallo*
My true preseruer, and a loyall Sir,
To him thou follow'st; I will pay thy graces
1790   Home both in word, and deede: Most cruelly
Didst thou *Alonso*, vse me, and my daughter:
Thy brother was a furtherer in the Act,
Thou art pinch'd for't now *Sebastian*.
(*To Anthonio*)   Flesh, and bloud,
You, brother mine, that entertaind ambition,
Expelld remorse, and nature, whom, with *Sebastian*
(Whose inward pinches therefore are most strong)
Would heere haue kill'd your King: I do forgiue thee,
Vnnaturall though thou art: (*Aside*) Their vnderstanding
Begins to swell, and the approching tide
1800   Will shortly fill the reasonable shores
That now ly foule, and muddy: not one of them
That yet lookes on me, or would know me: *Ariell*,
Fetch me the Hat, and Rapier in my Cell,
I will discase me, and my selfe present
As I was sometime *Millaine*: quickly Spirit,
Thou shalt ere long be free.
        Ariell sings, and helps to attire him as Duke of Millaine
ARIELL   *Where the Bee sucks, there suck I,*
            In a Cowslips bell, I lie,
            There I cowch when Owles doe crie,
1810   *On the Batts backe I doe flie*
            After Sommer merrily.
            Merrily, merrily, shall I liue now,
            Vnder the blossom that hangs on the Bow.
            Merrily, merrily, shall I liue now,
            Vnder the blossom that hangs on the Bow.
PROSPERO
Why that's my dainty *Ariell*: I shall misse thee,
But yet thou shalt haue freedome: so, so, so.
To the Kings ship, inuisible as thou art,
There shalt thou finde the Marriners asleepe
1820   Vnder the Hatches: the Master and the Boat-swaine
Being awake, enforce them to this place;
And presently, I pre'thee.
ARIELL
I drinke the aire before me, and returne
Or ere your pulse twice beate.   *Exit*
GONZALO
All torment, trouble, wonder, and amazement
Inhabits heere: some heauenly power guide vs
Out of this fearefull Country.
PROSPERO   Behold Sir King
The wronged Duke of *Millaine*, *Prospero*:

For more assurance that a liuing Prince
Do's now speake to thee, I embrace thy body,   1830
And to thee, and thy Company, I bid
A hearty welcome.
        He embraces Alonso
ALONSO   Where thou bee'st he or no,
Or some inchanted trifle to abuse me,
(As late I haue beene) I not know: thy Pulse
Beats as of flesh, and blood: and since I saw thee,
Th'affliction of my minde amends, with which
I feare a madnesse held me: this must craue
(And if this be at all) a most strange story.
Thy Dukedome I resigne, and doe entreat
Thou pardon me my wrongs: But how shold *Prospero*   1840
Be liuing, and be heere?
PROSPERO (*to Gonzalo*)   First, noble Frend,
Let me embrace thine age, whose honor cannot
Be measur'd, or confin'd.
        He embraces Gonzalo
GONZALO   Whether this be,
Or be not, I'le not sweare.
PROSPERO   You doe yet taste
Some subtleties o'th'Isle, that will not let you
Beleeue things certaine: Wellcome, my friends all,
(*Aside to Sebastian and Anthonio*)
But you, my brace of Lords, were I so minded
I heere could plucke his Highnesse frowne vpon you
And iustifie you Traitors: at this time
I will tell no tales.
SEBASTIAN (*to Anthonio*) The Diuell speakes in him:
PROSPERO   No: 1850
(*To Anthonio*) For you (most wicked Sir) whom to call
        brother
Would euen infect my mouth, I do forgiue
Thy rankest fault; all of them: and require
My Dukedome of thee, which, perforce I know
Thou must restore.
ALONSO   If thou beest *Prospero*
Giue vs particulars of thy preseruation,
How thou hast met vs heere, whom three howres since
Were wrackt vpon this shore? where I haue lost
(How sharp the point of this remembrance is)
My deere sonne *Ferdinand*.
PROSPERO   I am woe for't, Sir.   1860
ALONSO
Irreparable is the losse, and patience
Saies, it is past her cure.
PROSPERO   I rather thinke
You haue not sought her helpe, of whose soft grace
For the like losse, I haue her soueraigne aid,
And rest my selfe content.
ALONSO   You the like losse?
PROSPERO
As great to me, as late, and supportable
To make the deere losse, haue I meanes much weaker
Then you may call to comfort you; for I
Haue lost my daughter.
ALONSO   A daughter?
Oh heauens, that they were liuing both in *Naples*   1870

The King and Queene there, that they were, I wish
My selfe were mudded in that oo-zie bed
Where my sonne lies: when did you lose your
    daughter?

PROSPERO
In this last Tempest. I perceiue these Lords
At this encounter doe so much admire,
That they deuoure their reason, and scarce thinke
Their eies doe offices of Truth: Theis words
Are naturall breath: but howsoeu'r you haue
Beene iustled from your sences, know for certain
1880 That I am *Prospero*, and that very Duke
Which was thrust forth of *Millaine*, who most strangely
Vpon this shore (where you were wrackt) was landed
To be the Lord on't: No more yet of this,
For 'tis a Chronicle of day by day,
Not a relation for a break-fast, nor
Befitting this first meeting: Welcome, Sir;
This Cell's my Court: heere haue I few attendants,
And Subiects none abroad: pray you looke in:
My Dukedome since you haue giuen me againe,
1890 I will requite you with as good a thing,
At least bring forth a wonder, to content ye
As much, as me my Dukedome.
    Here Prospero discouers Ferdinand and Miranda,
    playing at Chesse

MIRANDA
Sweet Lord, you play me false.

FERDINAND No my dearest loue,
I would not for the world.

MIRANDA
Yes, for a score of Kingdomes, you should wrangle,
And I would call it faire play.

ALONSO   If this proue
A vision of the Island, one deere Sonne
Shall I twice loose.

SEBASTIAN   A most high miracle.

FERDINAND (*comming forward*)
1900 Though the Seas threaten they are mercifull,
I haue curs'd them without cause.
    He kneels

ALONSO   Now all the blessings
Of a glad father, compasse thee about:
Arise, and say how thou cam'st heere.
    Ferdinand rises

MIRANDA (*comming forward*)   O wonder!
How many goodly creatures are there heere?
How beauteous mankinde is? O braue new world
That has such people in't.

PROSPERO   'Tis new to thee.

ALONSO (*to Ferdinand*)
What is this Maid, with whom thou was't at play?
Your eld'st acquaintance cannot be three houres:
Is she the goddesse that hath seuer'd vs,
And brought vs thus together?

1910 FERDINAND   Sir, she is mortall;
But by immortall prouidence, she's mine;

I chose her when I could not aske my Father
For his aduise: nor thought I had one: She
Is daughter to this famous Duke of *Millaine*,
Of whom, so often I haue heard renowne,
But neuer saw before: of whom I haue
Receiu'd a second life; and second Father
This Lady makes him to me.

ALONSO   I am hers.
But O, how odly will it sound, that I
Must aske my childe forgiuenesse?

PROSPERO   There Sir stop,   1920
Let vs not burthen our remembrance, with
A heauinesse that's gon.

GONZALO   I haue inly wept,
Or should haue spoke ere this: looke downe you gods
And on this couple drop a blessed crowne;
For it is you, that haue chalk'd forth the way
Which brought vs hither.

ALONSO   I say Amen, *Gonzallo*.

GONZALO
Was *Millaine* thrust from *Millaine*, that his Issue
Should become Kings of *Naples*? O reioyce
Beyond a common ioy, and set it downe
With gold on lasting Pillers: In one voyage   1930
Did *Claribell* her husband finde at *Tunis*,
And *Ferdinand* her brother, found a wife,
Where he himselfe was lost: *Prospero*, his Dukedome
In a poore Isle: and all of vs, our selues,
When no man was his owne.

ALONSO (*to Ferdinand and Miranda*) Giue me your hands:
Let griefe and sorrow still embrace his heart,
That doth not wish you ioy.

GONZALO   Be it so, Amen.
    Enter Ariell, with the Master and Boatswaine
    amazedly following
O looke Sir, looke Sir, here is more of vs:
I prophesi'd, if a Gallowes were on Land
This fellow could not drowne: (*To the Boat-swaine*)
    Now blasphemy,   1940
That swear'st Grace ore-boord, not an oath on shore,
Hast thou no mouth by land? What is the newes?

BOTESWAINE
The best newes is, that we haue safely found
Our King, and company: The next: our Ship,
Which but three glasses since, we gaue out split,
Is tyte, and yare, and brauely rig'd, as when
We first put out to Sea.

ARIELL (*aside to Prospero*) Sir, all this seruice
Haue I done since I went.

PROSPERO (*aside to Ariell*)   My tricksey Spirit.

ALONSO
These are not naturall euents, they strengthen
From strange, to stranger: say, how came you hither? 1950

BOTESWAINE
If I did thinke, Sir, I were well awake,
I'ld striue to tell you: we were dead of sleepe,
And (how we know not) all clapt vnder hatches,

Where, but euen now, with strange, and seuerall
    noyses
Of roring, shreeking, howling, gingling chaines,
And mo diuersitie of sounds, all horrible,
We were awak'd: straight way, at liberty;
Where we, in all her trim, freshly beheld
Our royall, good, and gallant Ship: our Master
1960   Capring to eye her: on a trice, so please you,
Euen in a dreame, were we diuided from them,
And were brought moaping hither.

ARIELL (*aside to Prospero*)   Was't well done?

PROSPERO (*aside to Ariell*)
Brauely (my diligence) thou shalt be free.

ALONSO
This is as strange a Maze, as ere men trod,
And there is in this businesse, more then nature
Was euer conduct of: some Oracle
Must rectifie our knowledge.

PROSPERO   Sir, my Leige,
Doe not infest your minde, with beating on
The strangenesse of this businesse, at pickt leisure
1970   (Which shall be shortly) single I'le resolue you,
(Which to you shall seeme probable) of euery
These happend accidents: till when, be cheerefull
And thinke of each thing well: (*Aside to Ariell*) Come
    hither Spirit,
Set *Caliban*, and his companions free:
Vntye the Spell: *Exit Ariell*
(*To Alonso*)   How fares my gracious Sir?
There are yet missing of your Companie
Some few odde Lads, that you remember not.
        Enter Ariell, driuing in Caliban, Stephano, and
        Trinculo in their stolne Apparell

STEPHANO Euery man shift for all the rest, and let no man
take care for himselfe; for all is but fortune: *Coragio*
1980   Bully-Monster *Coragio*.

TRINCULO If these be true spies which I weare in my head,
here's a goodly sight.

CALIBAN
O *Setebos*, these be braue Spirits indeede:
How fine my Master is? I am afraid
He will chastise me.

SEBASTIAN
Ha, ha: What things are these, my Lord *Anthonio*?
Will money buy em?

ANTHONIO   Very like: one of them
Is a plaine Fish, and no doubt marketable.

PROSPERO
Marke but the badges of these men, my Lords,
1990   Then say if they be true: This mishapen knaue;
His Mother was a Witch, and one so strong
That could controle the Moone; make flowes, and ebs,
And deale in her command, without her power:
These three haue robd me, and this demy-diuell;
(For he's a bastard one) had plotted with them
To take my life: two of these Fellowes, you
Must know, and owne, this Thing of darkenesse, I
Acknowledge mine.

CALIBAN   I shall be pincht to death.

ALONSO
Is not this *Stephano*, my drunken Butler?

SEBASTIAN
He is drunke now; Where had he wine?   2000

ALONSO
And *Trinculo* is reeling ripe: where should they
Finde this grand Liquor that hath gilded 'em?
(*To Trinculo*) How cam'st thou in this pickle?

TRINCULO I haue bin in such a pickle since I saw you last,
that I feare me will neuer out of my bones: I shall not
feare fly-blowing.

SEBASTIAN Why how now *Stephano*?

STEPHANO O touch me not, I am not *Stephano*, but a
Cramp.

PROSPERO You'ld be King o'the Isle, Sirha?   2010

STEPHANO I should haue bin a sore one then.

ALONSO (*pointing to Caliban*) This is a strange thing as ere
I look'd on.

PROSPERO
He is as disproportion'd in his Manners
As in his shape: (*To Caliban*) Goe Sirha, to my Cell,
Take with you your Companions: as you looke
To haue my pardon, trim it handsomely.

CALIBAN
I that I will: and Ile be wise hereafter,
And seeke for grace: what a thrice double Asse
Was I to take this drunkard for a god?   2020
And worship this dull foole?

PROSPERO   Goe to, away.
                                    Exit Caliban

ALONSO (*to Stephano and Trinculo*)
Hence, and bestow your luggage where you found it.

SEBASTIAN Or stole it rather.
                    Exeunt Stephano and Trinculo

PROSPERO (*to Alonso*)
Sir, I inuite your Highnesse, and your traine
To my poore Cell: where you shall take your rest
For this one night, which part of it, Ile waste
With such discourse, as I not doubt, shall make it
Goe quicke away: The story of my life,
And the particular accidents, gon by
Since I came to this Isle: And in the morne   2030
I'le bring you to your ship, and so to *Naples*,
Where I haue hope to see the nuptiall
Of these our deere-beloued, solemnized,
And thence retire me to my *Millaine*, where
Euery third thought shall be my graue.

ALONSO   I long
To heare the story of your life; which must
Take the eare strangely.

PROSPERO   I'le deliuer all,
And promise you calme Seas, auspicious gales,
And saile, so expeditious, that shall catch
Your Royall fleete farre off: (*Aside to Ariell*) My *Ariel*;
    chicke   2040
That is thy charge: Then to the Elements
Be free, and fare thou well: *Exit Ariell*
                please you draw neere.
                Exeunt ⌈all but Prospero⌉

Epilogue

PROSPERO

Now my Charmes are all ore-throwne,
And what strength I haue's mine owne,
Which is most faint: now 'tis true
I must be heere confinde by you,
Or sent to Naples, Let me not
Since I haue my Dukedome got,
And pardon'd the deceiuer, dwell
In this bare Island, by your Spell,
But release me from my bands
With the helpe of your good hands:

Gentle breath of yours, my Sailes
Must fill, or else my proiect failes,
Which was to please: Now I want
Spirits to enforce: Art to inchant,
And my ending is despaire,
Vnlesse I be relieu'd by praier
Which pierces so, that it assaults
Mercy it selfe, and frees all faults.
As you from crimes would pardon'd be,
Let your Indulgence set me free.

He awaits applause, then exit

CARDENIO
A SHORT ACCOUNT

MANY plays acted in Shakespeare's time have failed to survive; they may easily include some that he wrote. The mystery of *Loues labours won* is discussed elsewhere (p. 349). Certain manuscript records of the seventeenth century suggest that at least one other play in which he had a hand may have disappeared. On 9 September 1653 the London publisher Humphrey Moseley entered in the Stationers' Register a batch of plays including 'The History of Cardenio, by Mr Fletcher & Shakespeare'. Cardenio is a character in Part One of Cervantes' *Don Quixote*, published in English translation in 1612. Two earlier allusions suggest that the King's Men owned a play on this subject at the time that Shakespeare was collaborating with John Fletcher (1579-1625). On 20 May 1613 the Privy Council authorized payment of £20 to John Heminges, as leader of the King's Men, for the presentation at court of six plays, one listed as 'Cardenno'. On 9 July of the same year Heminges received £6 13s. 4d. for his company's performance of a play 'called Cardenna' before the ambassador of the Duke of Savoy.

No more information about this play survives from the seventeenth century, but in 1728 Lewis Theobald published a play based on the story of Cardenio and called *Double Falsehood, or The Distrest Lovers*, which he claimed to have 'revised and adapted' from one 'written originally by W. Shakespeare'. It had been successfully produced at Drury Lane on 13 December 1727, and was given thirteen times up to 1 May 1728. Other performances are recorded in 1740, 1741, 1767 (when it was reprinted), 1770, and 1847. In 1770 a newspaper stated that 'the original manuscript' was 'treasured up in the Museum of Covent Garden Playhouse'; fire destroyed the theatre, including its library, in 1808.

Theobald claimed to own several manuscripts of an original play by Shakespeare, and remarked that some of his contemporaries thought the style was Fletcher's, not Shakespeare's. When he himself came to edit Shakespeare's plays he did not include either *Double Falsehood* or the play on which he claimed to have based it; he simply edited the plays of the First Folio, not adding either *Pericles* or *The Two Noble Kinsmen*, though he believed they were partly by Shakespeare. It is quite possible that *Double Falsehood* is based (however distantly) on a play of Shakespeare's time; if so, the play is likely to have been the one performed by the King's Men and ascribed by Moseley in 1653 to Fletcher and Shakespeare.

Double Falsehood is a tragicomedy; the characters' names differ from those in *Don Quixote*, and the story is varied. Henriquez rapes Violante, then falls in love with Leonora, loved by his friend Julio. Her parents agree to the marriage, but Julio interrupts the ceremony. Leonora (who had intended to kill herself) swoons and later takes sanctuary in a nunnery. Julio goes mad with desire for vengeance on his false friend; and the wronged Violante, disguised as a boy, joins a group of shepherds, and is almost raped by one of them. Henriquez's virtuous brother, Roderick, ignorant of his villainy, helps him to abduct Leonora. Leonora and Violante both denounce Henriquez to Roderick. Finally Henriquez repents and marries Violante, while Julio (now sane) marries Leonora.

Some of the motifs of *Double Falsehood*, such as the disguised heroine wronged by her lover and, particularly, the reuniting and reconciliation of parents with children, recall Shakespeare's late plays. But most of the dialogue seems un-Shakespearian. Though the play deserved its limited success, it is now no more than an interesting curiosity.

ALL IS TRUE

(HENRY VIII)

BY WILLIAM SHAKESPEARE AND JOHN FLETCHER

ON 29 June 1613 the firing of cannon at the Globe Theatre ignited its thatch and burned it to the ground. According to a letter of 4 July the house was full of spectators who had come to see 'a new play called all is triewe, wch had beene acted not passinge 2 or 3 times before'. No one was hurt 'except one man who was scalded wth the fier by aduenturing in to saue a Child wch otherwise had beene burnte'. This establishes the play's date with unusual precision. Though two other accounts of the fire refer to a play 'of'—which may mean simply 'about'—Henry VIII, yet another two unequivocally call it *All is True*; and these words also end the refrain of a ballad about the fire. When the play came to be printed as the last of the English history plays—all named after kings—in the 1623 Folio it was as *The Famous History of the Life of King Henry the Eight*. We restore the title by which it was known to its first audiences.

No surviving account of the fire says who wrote the play that caused it. In 1850, James Spedding (prompted by Tennyson) suggested that Shakespeare collaborated on it with John Fletcher (1579-1625). We have external evidence that the two dramatists worked together in or around 1613 on the lost *Cardenio* and on *The Two Noble Kinsmen*. For their collaboration in *All is True* the evidence is wholly internal, stemming from the initial perception of two distinct verse styles within the play; later, more rigorous examination of evidence provided by both the play's language and its dramatic technique has convinced most scholars of Fletcher's hand in it. The passages most confidently attributed to Shakespeare are Act 1, Scenes 1 and 2; Act 2, Scenes 3 and 4; Act 3, Scene 2 to line 1697; and Act 5, Scene 1.

The historical material derives, often closely, from the chronicles of Raphael Holinshed and Edward Hall, supplemented by John Foxe's *Book of Martyrs* (1563, etc.) for the Cranmer episodes in Act 5. It covers only part of Henry's reign, from the opening description of the Field of the Cloth of Gold, of 1520, to the christening of Princess Elizabeth, in 1533. It depicts the increasing abuse of power by Cardinall Wolsey; the execution, brought about by Wolsey's machinations, of the Duke of Buckingham; the King's abandonment of his Queen, Katherine of Arragon; the rise to the King's favour of Anne Bullen; Wolsey's disgrace; and the birth to Henry and Anne of a daughter instead of the hoped-for son.

Sir Henry Wotton, writing of the fire, said that the play represented 'some principal pieces of the Reign of *Henry* the 8*th*, which was set forth with many extraordinary Circumstances of Pomp and Majesty'. It has continued popular in performance for the opportunities that it affords for spectacle and for the dramatic power of certain episodes such as Buckingham's speeches before execution (2.1), Queene Katherine's defence of the validity of her marriage (2.4), Wolsey's farewell to his greatness (3.2), and Katherine's dying scene (4.2). Though the play depicts a series of falls from greatness, it works towards the birth of the future Elizabeth I, fulsomely celebrated in the last scene (not attributed to Shakespeare) along with her successor, the patron of the King's Men.

The Folio text appears to derive from a scribal transcript.

THE NAMES OF THE ACTORS

PROLOGUE

KING Henry the Eight

Duke of BUCKINGHAM
Lord ABURGAUENNY
Earle of SURREY   } his Sonnes in Law
Duke of NORFOLKE
Duke of SUFFOLKE
Lord CHAMBERLAINE
Lord CHANCELLOUR
Lord SANDS (also called Sir William Sands)
Sir Thomas LOUELL
Sir Anthony DENNY
SIR HENRY GUILFORD

CARDINALL Wolsey
Two SECRETARIES
Buckinghams SURUEYOR
Cardinall CAMPEIUS
GARDINER, the Kings new Secretary, later Bishop of Winchester
His PAGE
Thomas CROMWELL
CRANMER, Archbishop of Canterbury

QUEENE, later KATHERINE Princesse Dowager
GRIFFITH, her Gentleman Vsher
PATIENCE, her woman
Other WOMEN
Sixe Personages, who Dance in a Vision
A MESSENGER
Lord CAPUCHIUS

ANNE Bullen
An OLD LADY

BRANDON
SERGEANT at Armes   } who arrest Buckingham and
                       Aburgauenny
Sir Nicholas VAUX
Tipstaues
Halberds   } after Buckinghams Arraignment
Common people

Two Vergers
Two SCRIBES in the habite of Doctors
Archbishop of Canterbury
BISHOP OF LINCOLNE
Bishop of Ely
Bishop of Rochester   } Appearing in the
Bishop of S. Asaph   Legantine Court
Two Priests
Sergeant at Armes
Two Noblemen
A CRIER

Three GENTLEMEN
Two Iudges
Qirristers
Lord Maior of London
Garter
Marquesse Dorset   } Appearing in the Coronation
Foure Barons of the Cinque-Ports
Stokesley, Bishop of London
Olde Duchesse of Norfolke
Countesses

A KEEPER
Doctor BUTS, the Kings Physitian   } At Cranmers
Purseuants, Pages, Foot-Boyes, and Groomes   Trial

A PORTER
His MAN
Two Aldermen
Lord Maior of London
GARTER   } At the
Sixe Noblemen   Christening
Olde Dutchesse of Norfolke, Godmother
The Childe Princesse Elizabeth
Marchionesse Dorset, Godmother

EPILOGUE

Ladies, Gentlemen, a SERUANT, Guard, Attendants, Trumpets

All is true

Prologue *Enter Prologue*

PROLOGUE

I come no more to make you laugh, Things now,
That beare a Weighty, and a Serious Brow,
Sad, high, and working, full of State and Woe:
Such Noble Scœnes, as draw the Eye to flow
We now present. Those that can Pitty, heere
May (if they thinke it well) let fall a Teare,
The Subiect will deserue it. Such as giue
Their Money out of hope they may beleeue,
May heere finde Truth too. Those that come to see
10 *Onely a show or two, and so agree,*
The Play may passe, if they be still, and willing,
Ile vndertake may see away their shilling
Richly in two short houres. Onely they
That come to heare a Merry, Bawdy Play,
A noyse of Targets: Or to see a Fellow
In a long Motley Coate, garded with Yellow,
Will be deceyu'd. For gentle Hearers, know
To ranke our chosen Truth with such a show
As Foole, and Fight is, beside forfeyting
20 *Our owne Braines, and the Opinion that we bring*
To make that onely true, we now intend,
Will leaue vs neuer an vnderstanding Friend.
Therefore, for Goodnesse sake, and as you are knowne
The First and Happiest Hearers of the Towne,
Be sad, as we would make ye. Thinke ye see
The very Persons of our Noble Story,
As they were Liuing: Thinke you see them Great,
And follow'd with the generall throng, and sweat
Of thousand Friends: Then, in a moment, see
30 *How soone this Mightinesse, meets Misery:*
And if you can be merry then, Ile say,
A Man may weepe vpon his Wedding day. *Exit*

1.1 ⌐*A Cloth of State throughout the Play.*⌐ *Enter the*
(Sc. 1) *Duke of Norfolke at one doore. At the other, the*
Duke of Buckingham, and the Lord Aburgauenny

BUCKINGHAM (*to Norfolke*)

Good morrow, and well met. How haue ye done
Since last we saw in France?

NORFOLKE   I thanke your Grace:
Healthfull, and euer since a fresh Admirer
Of what I saw there.

BUCKINGHAM   An vntimely Ague
Staid me a Prisoner in my Chamber, when
Those Sunnes of Glory, those two Lights of Men
Met in the vale of Andren.

NORFOLKE   'Twixt Guynes and Arde,
40 I was then present, saw them salute on Horsebacke,
Beheld them when they lighted, how they clung
In their Embracement, as they grew together,

Which had they, what foure Thron'd ones could haue
    weigh'd
Such a compounded one?

BUCKINGHAM   All the whole time
I was my Chambers Prisoner.

NORFOLKE   Then you lost
The view of earthly glory: Men might say
Till this time Pompe was single, but now married
To one aboue it selfe. Each following day
Became the next dayes master, till the last
Made former Wonders, it's. To day the French,   50
All Clinquant all in Gold, like Heathen Gods
Shone downe the English; and to morrow, they
Made Britaine, India: Euery man that stood,
Shewd like a Mine. Their Dwarfish Pages were
As Cherubins, all gilt: the Madams too,
Not vs'd to toyle, did almost sweat to beare
The Pride vpon them, that their very labour
Was to them, as a Painting. Now this Maske
Was cry'de incompareable; and th'ensuing night
Made it a Foole, and Begger. The two Kings   60
Equall in lustre, were now best, now worst
As presence did present them: Him in eye,
Still him in praise, and being present both,
'Twas said they saw but one, and no Discerner
Durst wagge his Tongue in censure, when these
    Sunnes
(For so they phrase 'em) by their Heralds challeng'd
The Noble Spirits to Armes, they did performe
Beyond thoughts Compasse, that former fabulous
    Storie
Being now seene, possible enough, got credit
That *Beuis* was beleeu'd.

BUCKINGHAM   Oh you go farre.   70
NORFOLKE
As I belong to worship, and affect
In Honor, Honesty, the tract of eu'ry thing,
Would by a good Discourser loose some life,
Which Actions selfe, was tongue too. All was Royall,
To the disposing of it nought rebell'd,
Order gaue each thing view. The Office did
Distinctly his full Function.

BUCKINGHAM   Who did guide,
I meane who set the Body, and the Limbes
Of this great Sport together, as you guesse?

NORFOLKE
One certes, that promises no Element   80
In such a businesse.

BUCKINGHAM   I pray you who, my Lord?
NORFOLKE
All this was ordred by the good Discretion
Of the right Reuerend Cardinall of Yorke.

BUCKINGHAM
  The diuell speed him: No mans Pye is freed
  From his Ambitious finger. What had he
  To do in these fierce Vanities? I wonder,
  That such a Keech can with his very bulke
  Take vp the Rayes o'th'beneficiall Sun,
  And keepe it from the Earth.

NORFOLKE   Surely Sir,
90 There's in him stuffe, that put's him to these ends:
  For being not propt by Auncestry, whose grace
  Chalkes Successors their way; nor call'd vpon
  For high feats done to'th'Crowne; neither Allied
  To eminent Assistants; but Spider-like
  Out of his Selfe-drawing Web, a giues vs note,
  The force of his owne merit makes his way;
  A guift that heauen giues for him, which buyes
  A place next to the King.

ABURGAUENNY   I cannot tell
  What Heauen hath giuen him: let some Grauer eye
100 Pierce into that, but I can see his Pride
  Peepe through each part of him: whence ha's he
        that?
  If not from Hell, the Diuell is a Niggard,
  Or ha's giuen all before, and he begins
  A new Hell in himselfe.

BUCKINGHAM   Why the Diuell,
  Vpon this French going out, tooke he vpon him
  (Without the priuity o'th'King) t'appoint
  Who should attend on him? He makes vp the File
  Of all the Gentry; for the most part such
  To whom as great a Charge, as little Honor
110 He meant to lay vpon: and his owne Letter,
  The Honourable Boord of Councell out,
  Must fetch him in, he Papers.

ABURGAUENNY   I do know
  Kinsmen of mine, three at the least, that haue
  By this, so sicken'd their Estates, that neuer
  They shall abound as formerly.

BUCKINGHAM   O many
  Haue broke their backes with laying Mannors on 'em
  For this great Iourney. What did this vanity
  But minister communication of
  A most poore issue.

NORFOLKE   Greeuingly I thinke,
120 The Peace betweene the French and vs, not valewes
  The Cost that did conclude it.

BUCKINGHAM   Euery man,
  After the hideous storme that follow'd, was
  A thing Inspir'd, and not consulting, broke
  Into a generall Prophesie; That this Tempest
  Dashing the Garment of this Peace, aboaded
  The sodaine breach on't.

NORFOLKE   Which is budded out,
  For France hath flaw'd the League, and hath attach'd
  Our Merchants goods at Burdeux.

ABURGAUENNY   Is it therefore
  Th'Ambassador is silenc'd?

NORFOLKE   Marry is't.

ABURGAUENNY
  A proper Title of a Peace, and purchas'd   130
  At a superfluous rate.

BUCKINGHAM   Why all this Businesse
  Our Reuerend Cardinall carried.

NORFOLKE   Like it your Grace,
  The State takes notice of the priuate difference
  Betwixt you, and the Cardinall. I aduise you
  (And take it from a heart, that wishes towards you
  Honor, and plenteous safety) that you reade
  The Cardinals Malice, and his Potency
  Together; To consider further, that
  What his high Hatred would effect, wants not
  A Minister in his Power. You know his Nature, 140
  That he's Reuengefull; and I know, his Sword
  Hath a sharpe edge: It's long, and't may be saide
  It reaches farre, and where 'twill not extend,
  Thither he darts it. Bosome vp my counsell,
  You'l finde it wholesome. Loe, where comes that Rock
  That I aduice your shunning.

     Enter Cardinall Wolsey, the Purse borne before him,
     certaine of the Guard, and two Secretaries with
     Papers: The Cardinall in his passage, fixeth his eye
     on Buckingham, and Buckingham on him, both full
     of disdaine

CARDINALL (*to a Secretary*)
  The Duke of *Buckinghams* Surueyor? Ha?
  Where's his Examination?

SECRETARY   Heere so please you.

CARDINALL
  Is he in person, ready?

SECRETARY   I, please your Grace.

CARDINALL
  Well, we shall then know more, & *Buckingham* 150
  Shall lessen this bigge looke.

           Exeunt Cardinall, and his Traine

BUCKINGHAM
  This Butchers Curre is venome-mouth'd, and I
  Haue not the power to muzzle him, therefore best
  Not wake him in his slumber. A Beggers booke,
  Out-worths a Nobles blood.

NORFOLKE   What are you chaff'd?
  Aske God for Temp'rance, that's th'appliance onely
  Which your disease requires.

BUCKINGHAM   I read in's looks
  Matter against me, and his eye reuil'd
  Me as his abiect obiect, at this instant
  He bores me with some tricke; He's gone to'th'King: 160
  Ile follow, and out-stare him.

NORFOLKE   Stay my Lord,
  And let your Reason with your Choller question
  What 'tis you go about: to climbe steepe hilles
  Requires slow pace at first. Anger is like
  A full hot Horse, who being allow'd his way
  Selfe-mettle tyres him: Not a man in England
  Can aduise me like you: Be to your selfe,
  As you would to your Friend.

BUCKINGHAM   Ile to the King,

And from a mouth of Honor, quite cry downe
170 This *Ipswich* fellowes insolence; or proclaime,
There's difference in no persons.

NORFOLKE   Be aduis'd;
Heat not a Furnace for your foe so hot
That it do sindge your selfe. We may out-runne
By violent swiftnesse that which we run at;
And lose by ouer-running: know you not,
The fire that mounts the liquor til't run ore,
In seeming to augment it, wasts it: be aduis'd;
I say againe there is no English Soule
More stronger to direct you then your selfe;
180 If with the sap of reason you would quench,
Or but allay the fire of passion.

BUCKINGHAM   Sir,
I am thankfull to you, and Ile goe along
By your prescription: but this top-proud fellow,
Whom from the flow of gall I name not, but
From sincere motions, by Intelligence,
And proofes as cleere as Founts in *Iuly*, when
Wee see each graine of grauell; I doe know
To be corrupt and treasonous.

NORFOLKE   Say not treasonous.

BUCKINGHAM
To th'King Ile say't, & make my vouch as strong
190 As shore of Rocke: attend. This holy Foxe,
Or Wolfe, or both (for he is equall rau'nous
As he is subtile, and as prone to mischiefe,
As able to perform't) his minde, and place
Infecting one another, yea reciprocally,
Only to shew his pompe, as well in France,
As here at home, suggests the King our Master
To this last costly Treaty: Th'enteruiew,
That swallowed so much treasure, and like a glasse
Did breake ith'wrenching.

NORFOLKE   Faith, and so it did.

BUCKINGHAM
200 Pray giue me fauour Sir: This cunning Cardinall
The Articles o'th'Combination drew
As himselfe pleas'd; and they were ratified
As he cride thus let be, to as much end,
As giue a Crutch to th'dead. But our Count-Cardinall
Has done this, and tis well: for worthy *Wolsey*
(Who cannot erre) he did it. Now this followes,
(Which as I take it, is a kinde of Puppie
To th'old dam Treason) *Charles* the Emperour,
Vnder pretence to see the Queene his Aunt,
210 (For twas indeed his colour, but he came
To whisper *Wolsey*) here makes visitation,
His feares were that the Interview betwixt
England and France, might through their amity
Breed him some preiudice; for from this League,
Peep'd harmes that menac'd him. Priuily he
Deales with our Cardinal, and as I troa
Which I doe well; for I am sure the Emperour
Paid ere he promis'd, whereby his Suit was granted
Ere it was ask'd. But when the way was made

And pau'd with gold: the Emperor thus desir'd,   220
That he would please to alter the Kings course,
And breake the foresaid peace. Let the King know
(As soone he shall by me) that thus the Cardinall
Does buy and sell his Honour as he pleases,
And for his owne aduantage.

NORFOLKE   I am sorry
To heare this of him; and could wish he were
Somthing mistaken in't.

BUCKINGHAM   No, not a sillable:
I doe pronounce him in that very shape
He shall appeare in proofe.
    Enter Brandon, a Sergeant at Armes before him,
    and two or three of the Guard

BRANDON
Your Office Sergeant: execute it.

SERGEANT   Sir,   230
(*To Buckingham*) My Lord the Duke of *Buckingham*, and
    Earle
Of *Hereford, Stafford* and *Northampton*, I
Arrest thee of High Treason, in the name
Of our most Soueraigne King.

BUCKINGHAM ⌈*to Norfolke*⌉   Lo you my Lord,
The net has falne vpon me, I shall perish
Vnder deuice, and practise.

BRANDON   I am sorry,
To see you tane from liberty, to looke on
The busines present. Tis his Highnes pleasure
You shall to th'Tower.

BUCKINGHAM   It will helpe me nothing
To plead mine Innocence; for that dye is on me   240
Which makes my whit'st part, black. The will of
    Heau'n
Be done in this and all things: I obey.
O my Lord *Aburgany*: Fare you well.

BRANDON
Nay, he must beare you company.
(*To Aburgauenny*)   The King
Is pleas'd you shall to th'Tower, till you know
How he determines further.

ABURGAUENNY   As the Duke said,
The will of Heauen be done, and the Kings pleasure
By me obey'd.

BRANDON   Here is a warrant from
The King, t'attach Lord *Mountacute*, and the Bodies
Of the Dukes Confessor, *Iohn de la Car*,   250
One *Gilbert Perke*, his Chancellour.

BUCKINGHAM   So, so;
These are the limbs o'th'Plot: no more I hope.

BRANDON
A Monke o'th'*Chartreux*.

BUCKINGHAM   O *Nicholas Hopkins?*

BRANDON He.

BUCKINGHAM
My Surueyor is falce: The ore-great *Cardinall*
Hath shew'd him gold; my life is spand already:
I am the shadow of poore *Buckingham*,

Whose Figure euen this instant Clowd puts on,
By Darkning my cleere Sunne. (*To Norfolke*) My Lord
  farewell.

> *Exeunt ⌈Norfolke at one doore, the rest*
> *(Buckingham and Aburgauenny vnder Guard)*
> *at another⌉*

1.2
(Sc. 2)
> *Cornets. Enter King Henry, leaning on the Cardinals*
> *shoulder, the Cardinalls two Secretaries, the*
> *Nobles, and Sir Thomas Louell: the King takes his*
> *Seate; the Cardinall places himselfe vnder the*
> *Kings feete on his right side*

KING ⌈*to the Cardinall*⌉
260 My life it selfe, and the best heart of it,
Thankes you for this great care: I stood i'th'leuell
Of a full-charg'd confederacie, and giue thankes
To you that choak'd it. Let be cald before vs
That Gentleman of *Buckinghams*, in person,
Ile heare him his confessions iustifie,
And point by point the Treasons of his Maister,
He shall againe relate.

> *A noyse within crying roome for the Queene,*
> *vsher'd by the Duke of Norfolke. Enter the Queene,*
> *Norfolke and Suffolke: she kneels. King riseth from*
> *his State, takes her vp, and kisses her*

QUEENE KATHERINE
Nay, we must longer kneele; I am a Suitor.

KING
Arise, and take place by vs;
> *He placeth her by him*
                   halfe your Suit
270 Neuer name to vs; you haue halfe our power:
The other moity ere you aske is giuen,
Repeat your will, and take it.

QUEENE KATHERINE   Thanke your Maiesty.
That you would loue your selfe, and in that loue
Not vnconsidred leaue your Honour, nor
The dignity of your Office; is the poynt
Of my Petition.

KING   Lady mine proceed.

QUEENE KATHERINE
I am solicited not by a few,
And those of true condition; That your Subiects
Are in great grieuance: There haue beene Commissions
280 Sent downe among 'em, which hath flaw'd the heart
Of all their Loyalties; wherein, although
My good Lord Cardinall, they vent reproches
Most bitterly on you, as putter on
Of these exactions: yet the King, our Maister
Whose Honor Heauen shield from soile; euen he
  escapes not
Language vnmannerly; yea, such which breakes
The sides of loyalty, and almost appeares
In lowd Rebellion.

NORFOLKE   Not almost appeares,
It doth appeare; for, vpon these Taxations,
290 The Clothiers all not able to maintaine

The many to them longing, haue put off
The Spinsters, Carders, Fullers, Weauers, who
Vnfit for other life, compeld by hunger
And lack of other meanes; in desperate manner
Daring th'euent too th'teeth, are all in vprore,
And danger serues among them.

KING   Taxation?
Wherein? and what Taxation? My Lord Cardinall,
You that are blam'd for it alike with vs,
Know you of this Taxation?

CARDINALL   Please you Sir,
I know but of a single part in ought   300
Pertaines to th'State; and front but in that File
Where others tell steps with me.

QUEENE KATHERINE   No, my Lord?
You know no more then others? But you frame
Things that are knowne alike, which are not wholsome
To those which would not know them, and yet must
Perforce be their acquaintance. These exactions
(Whereof my Soueraigne would haue note) they are
Most pestilent to th'hearing, and to beare 'em,
The Backe is Sacrifice to th'load; They say
They are deuis'd by you, or else you suffer   310
Too hard an exclamation.

KING   Still Exaction:
The nature of it, in what kinde let's know,
Is this Exaction?

QUEENE KATHERINE I am much too venturous
In tempting of your patience; but am boldned
Vnder your promis'd pardon. The Subiects griefe
Comes through Commissions, which compels from
  each
The sixt part of his Substance, to be leuied
Without delay; and the pretence for this
Is nam'd, your warres in France: this makes bold
  mouths,
Tongues spit their duties out, and cold hearts freeze   320
Allegeance in them; their curses now
Liue where their prayers did: and it's come to passe,
This tractable obedience is a Slaue
To each incensed Will: I would your Highnesse
Would giue it quicke consideration; for
There is no primer busenesse.

KING   By my life,
This is against our pleasure.

CARDINALL   And for me,
I haue no further gone in this, then by
A single voice, and that not past me, but
By learned approbation of the Iudges: If I am   330
Traduc'd by ignorant Tongues, which neither know
My faculties nor person, yet will be
The Chronicles of my doing: Let me say,
'Tis but the fate of Place, and the rough Brake
That Vertue must goe through: we must not stint
Our necessary actions, in the feare
To cope malicious Censurers, which euer,
As rau'nous Fishes doe a Vessell follow
That is new trim'd; but benefit no further

340 Then vainly longing. What we oft doe best,
By sicke Interpreters (once weake ones) is
Not ours, or not allow'd; what worst, as oft,
Hitting a grosser quality, is cride vp
For our best Act: if we shall stand still,
In feare our motion will be mock'd, or carp'd at,
We should take roote here, where we sit;
Or sit State-Statues onely.

KING   Things done well,
And with a care, exempt themselues from feare:
Things done without example, in their issue
350 Are to be fear'd. Haue you a President
Of this Commission? I beleeue, not any.
We must not rend our Subiects from our Lawes,
And sticke them in our Will. Sixt part of each?
A trembling Contribution; why we take
From euery Tree, lop, barke, and part o'th' Timber:
And though we leaue it with a roote, thus hackt,
The Ayre will drinke the Sap. To euery County
Where this is question'd, send our Letters, with
Free pardon to each man that has deny'de
360 The force of this Commission: pray looke too't;
I put it to your care.

CARDINALL (to a Secretary) A word with you.
Let there be Letters writ to euery Shire,
Of the Kings grace and pardon:
(Aside to the Secretary)   the greeued Commons
Hardly conceiue of me. Let it be nois'd,
That through our Intercession, this Reuokement
And pardon comes: I shall anon aduise you
Further in the proceeding.   Exit Secretary
          Enter Surueyor

QUEENE KATHERINE (to the King)
I am sorry, that the Duke of Buckingham
Is run in your displeasure.

KING   It grieues many:
370 The Gentleman is Learn'd, and a most rare Speaker,
To Nature none more bound; his trayning such,
That he may furnish and instruct great Teachers,
And neuer seeke for ayd out of himselfe: yet see,
When these so Noble benefits shall proue
Not well dispos'd, the minde growing once corrupt,
They turne to vicious formes, ten times more vgly
Then euer they were faire. This man so compleat,
Who was enrold 'mongst wonders; and when we
Almost with rauish'd listning, could not finde
380 His houre of speech, a minute: He, (my Lady)
Hath into monstrous habits put the Graces
That once were his, and is become as blacke,
As if besmear'd in hell. Sit by Vs, you shall heare
(This was his Gentleman in trust) of him
Things to strike Honour sad. (To the Cardinall) Bid him
          recount
The fore-recited practises, whereof
We cannot feele too little, heare too much.

CARDINALL (to the Surueyor)
Stand forth, & with bold spirit relate what you

Most like a carefull Subiect haue collected
Out of the Duke of Buckingham.

KING (to the Surueyor)   Speake freely.   390

SURUEYOR
First, it was vsuall with him; euery day
It would infect his Speech: That if the King
Should without issue dye; hee'l carry it so
To make the Scepter his. These very words
I'ue heard him vtter to his Sonne in Law,
Lord Aburgany, to whom by oth he menac'd
Reuenge vpon the Cardinall.

CARDINALL (to the King)   Please your Highnesse note
His dangerous conception in this point,
Not frended by his wish to your High person;
His will is most malignant, and it stretches   400
Beyond you to your friends.

QUEENE KATHERINE   My learn'd Lord Cardinall,
Deliuer all with Charity.

KING (to the Surueyor)   Speake on;
How grounded hee his Title to the Crowne
Vpon our faile; to this poynt hast thou heard him,
At any time speake ought?

SURUEYOR   He was brought to this,
By a vaine Prophesie of Nicholas Hopkins.

KING
What was that Hopkins?

SURUEYOR   Sir, a Chartreux Fryer,
His Confessor, who fed him euery minute
With words of Soueraignty.

KING   How know'st thou this?

SURUEYOR
Not long before your Highnesse sped to France,   410
The Duke being at the Rose, within the Parish
Saint Laurence Poultney, did of me demand
What was the speech among the Londoners,
Concerning the French Iourney. I replide,
Men feard the French would proue perfidious
To the Kings danger: presently, the Duke
Said, 'twas the feare indeed, and that he doubted
'Twould proue the verity of certaine words
Spoke by a holy Monke, that oft, sayes he,
Hath sent to me, wishing me to permit   420
Iohn de la Car, my Chaplaine, a choyce howre
To heare from him a matter of some moment:
Whom after vnder the Confessions Seale,
He sollemnly had sworne, that what he spoke
My Chaplaine to no Creature liuing, but
To me, should vtter, with demure Confidence,
This pausingly ensu'de; neither the King, nor's
          Heyres
(Tell you the Duke) shall prosper, bid him striue
To win the loue o'th'Commonalty, the Duke
Shall gouerne England.

QUEENE KATHERINE   If I know you well,   430
You were the Dukes Surueyor, and lost your Office
On the complaint o'th' Tenants; take good heed
You charge not in your spleene a Noble person,

And spoyle your nobler Soule; I say, take heed;
Yes, heartily beseech you.

KING   Let him on:
(*To the Surueyor*) Goe forward.

SURUEYOR   On my Soule, Ile speake but truth.
I told my Lord the Duke, by th'Diuels illusions
The Monke might be deceiu'd, and that 'twas
        dangerous
To ruminate on this so farre, vntill
440   It forg'd him some designe, which being beleeu'd
It was much like to doe: He answer'd, Tush,
It can do me no damage; adding further,
That had the King in his last Sicknesse faild,
The Cardinals and Sir *Thomas Louels* heads
Should haue gone off.

KING   Ha? What, so rancke? Ah, ha,
There's mischiefe in this man; canst thou say
        further?

SURUEYOR
I can my Liedge.

KING   Proceed.

SURUEYOR   Being at *Greenwich*,
After your Highnesse had reprou'd the Duke
About Sir *William Bulmer*.

KING   I remember
450   Such a time, being my sworn seruant,
The Duke retein'd him his. But on: what hence?

SURUEYOR
If (quoth he) I for this had beene committed,
As to the Tower, I thought; I would haue plaid
The Part my Father meant to act vpon
Th'Vsurper *Richard*, who being at *Salsbury*,
Made suit to come in's presence; which if granted,
(As he made semblance of his duty) would
Haue put his knife into him.

KING   A Gyant Traytor.

CARDINALL (*to the Queene*)
Now Madam, may his Highnes liue in freedome,
And this man out of Prison.

460   QUEENE KATHERINE   God mend all.

KING (*to the Surueyor*)
Ther's somthing more would out of thee; what
        say'st?

SURUEYOR
After the Duke his Father, with the knife
He stretch'd him, and with one hand on his dagger,
Another spread on's breast, mounting his eyes,
He did discharge a horrible Oath, whose tenor
Was, were he euill vs'd, he would outgoe
His Father, by as much as a performance
Do's an irresolute purpose.

KING   There's his period,
To sheath his knife in vs: he is attach'd,
470   Call him to present tryall: if he may
Finde mercy in the Law, 'tis his; if none,
Let him not seek't of vs: By day and night
Hee's Traytor to th'height.   ⌈*Flourish.*⌉ *Exeunt*

Enter L. Chamberlaine and L. Sandys   1.3
                                                    (Sc.

CHAMBERLAINE
Is't possible the spels of France should iuggle
Men into such strange mysteries?

SANDS   New customes,
Though they be neuer so ridiculous,
(Nay let 'em be vnmanly) yet are follow'd.

CHAMBERLAINE
As farre as I see, all the good our English
Haue got by the late Voyage, is but meerely
A fit or two o'th' face, (but they are shrewd ones)   480
For when they hold 'em, you would sweare directly
Their very noses had been Councellours
To *Pepin* or *Clotharius*, they keepe State so.

SANDS
They haue all new legs, and lame ones; one would
        take it,
That neuer see 'em pace before, the Spauen
Or Spring-halt rain'd among 'em.

CHAMBERLAINE   Death my Lord,
Their cloathes are after such a Pagan cut too't,
That sure th'haue worne out Christendome:
        Enter Sir Thomas Louell
                                        how now?
What newes, Sir *Thomas Louell*?

LOUELL   Faith my Lord,
I heare of none but the new Proclamation,   490
That's clapt vpon the Court Gate.

CHAMBERLAINE   What is't for?

LOUELL
The reformation of our trauel'd Gallants,
That fill the Court with quarrels, talke, and Taylors.

CHAMBERLAINE
I'm glad 'tis there; now I would pray our Monsieurs
To thinke an English Courtier may be wise,
And neuer see the *Louure*.

LOUELL   They must either
(For so run the Conditions) leaue those remnants
Of Foole and Feather, that they got in France,
With all their honourable points of ignorance
Pertaining thereunto; as Fights and Fire-workes,   500
Abusing better men then they can be
Out of a forreigne wisedome, renouncing cleane
The faith they haue in Tennis and tall Stockings,
Short blistred Breeches, and those types of Trauell;
And vnderstand againe like honest men,
Or pack to their old Playfellowes; there, I take it,
They may *Cum Priuilegio*, wee away
The lag end of their lewdnesse, and be laugh'd at.

SANDS
Tis time to giue 'em Physicke, their diseases
Are growne so catching.

CHAMBERLAINE   What a losse our Ladies   510
Will haue of these trim vanities?

LOUELL   I marry,
There will be woe indeed Lords, the slye whorsons
Haue got a speeding tricke to lay downe Ladies.
A French Song, and a Fiddle, ha's no Fellow.

SANDS
    The Diuell fiddle 'em, I am glad they are going,
    For sure there's no conuerting of 'em: now
    An honest Country Lord as I am, beaten
    A long time out of play, may bring his plaine song,
    And haue an houre of hearing, and by'r Lady
    Held currant Musicke too.
520 CHAMBERLAINE   Well said Lord *Sands*,
    Your Colts tooth is not cast yet?
SANDS   No my Lord,
    Nor shall not while I haue a stumpe.
CHAMBERLAINE (*to Louell*)   Sir *Thomas*,
    Whither were you a going?
LOUELL   To the Cardinals;
    Your Lordship is a guest too.
CHAMBERLAINE   O, 'tis true;
    This night he makes a Supper, and a great one,
    To many Lords and Ladies; there will be
    The Beauty of this Kingdome Ile assure you.
LOUELL
    That Churchman beares a bounteous minde indeed,
    A hand as fruitfull as the Land that feeds vs,
    His dewes fall euery where.
530 CHAMBERLAINE   No doubt hee's Noble;
    He had a blacke mouth that said other of him.
SANDS
    He may my Lord, ha's wherewithall; in him
    Sparing would shew a worse sinne, then ill Doctrine,
    Men of his way, should be most liberall,
    They are set heere for examples.
CHAMBERLAINE   True, they are so;
    But few now giue so great ones: my Barge stayes;
    Your Lordship shall along: (*To Louell*) Come, good Sir
       Thomas,
    We shall be late else, which I would not be,
    For I was spoke to, with Sir *Henry Guilford*
    This night to be Comptrollers.
540 SANDS   I am your Lordships.
            Exeunt

1.4   *Hoboies. ⌈Enter Seruants with⌉ a small Table ⌈which*
(Sc. 4) *they place⌉ vnder the Cloth of State for the*
   Cardinall, and a longer Table for the Guests. Then
   Enter Anne Bullen, and diuers other Ladies, &
   Gentlemen, as Guests at one Doore; at an other
   Doore enter Sir Henry Guilford
SIR HENRY GUILFORD
    Ladyes, a generall welcome from his Grace
    Salutes ye all; This Night he dedicates
    To faire content, and you: None heere he hopes
    In all this Noble Beuy, has brought with her
    One care abroad: hee would haue all as merry:
    As feast, good Company, good wine, good welcome,
    Can make good people.
      Enter L. Chamberlaine L. Sands, and Louell
    (*To the Chamberlaine*) O my Lord, y'are tardy;
    The very thought of this faire Company,
    Clapt wings to me.
CHAMBERLAINE   You are young Sir *Harry Guilford*.

SANDS
    Sir *Thomas Louell*, had the Cardinall   550
    But halfe my Lay-thoughts in him, some of these
    Should finde a running Banket, ere they rested,
    I thinke would better please 'em: by my life,
    They are a sweet society of faire ones.
LOUELL
    O that your Lordship were but now Confessor,
    To one or two of these.
SANDS   I would I were,
    They should finde easie pennance.
LOUELL   Faith how easie?
SANDS
    As easie as a downe bed would affoord it.
CHAMBERLAINE
    Sweet Ladies will it please you sit; Sir *Harry*
    Place you that side, Ile take the charge of this: 560
      They sit about the longer Table. ⌈A noyse within⌉
    His Grace is entring. Nay, you must not freeze,
    Two women plac'd together, makes cold weather:
    My Lord *Sands*, you are one will keepe 'em waking:
    Pray sit betweene these Ladies.
SANDS   By my faith,
    And thanke your Lordship:
      He sits between Anne and another
            by your leaue sweet Ladies,
    If I chance to talke a little wilde, forgiue me:
    I had it from my Father.
ANNE   Was he mad Sir?
SANDS
    O, very mad, exceeding mad, in loue too;
    But he would bite none, iust as I doe now,
    He would Kisse you Twenty with a breath.
      Kisses her
CHAMBERLAINE   Well said my Lord: 570
    So now y'are fairely seated: Gentlemen,
    The pennance lyes on you; if these faire Ladies
    Passe away frowning.
SANDS For my little Cure,
    Let me alone.
      Hoboyes. Enter Cardinall Wolsey, and takes his
      State
CARDINALL
    Y'are welcome my faire Guests; that noble Lady
    Or Gentleman that is not freely merry
    Is not my Friend. This to confirme my welcome,
    And to you all good health.
      He drinkes
SANDS   Your Grace is Noble,
    Let me haue such a Bowle may hold my thankes, 580
    And saue me so much talking.
CARDINALL   My Lord *Sands*,
    I am beholding to you: cheere your neighbours:
    Ladies you are not merry; Gentlemen,
    Whose fault is this?
SANDS   The red wine first must rise
    In their faire cheekes my Lord, then wee shall haue 'em,
    Talke vs to silence.
ANNE   You are a merry Gamster

My Lord *Sands*.

SANDS   Yes, if I make my play:
Heer's to your Ladiship, and pledge it Madam:
For tis to such a thing.

ANNE   You cannot shew me.

SANDS (*to the Cardinall*)
I told your Grace, they would talke anon.
        Drum and Trumpet, Chambers dischargd

590 CARDINALL   What's that?

CHAMBERLAINE (*to the Seruants*)
Looke out there, some of ye.   *Exit a Seruant*

CARDINALL   What warlike voyce,
And to what end is this? Nay, Ladies, feare not;
By all the lawes of Warre y'are priuiledg'd.
        Enter Seruant

CHAMBERLAINE
How now, what is't?

SERUANT   A noble troupe of Strangers,
For so they seeme; th'haue left their Barge and landed,
And hither make, as great Embassadors
From forraigne Princes.

CARDINALL   Good Lord Chamberlaine,
Go, giue 'em welcome; you can speake the French
        tongue
And pray receiue 'em Nobly, and conduct 'em
600 Into our presence, where this heauen of beauty
Shall shine at full vpon them. Some attend him.
        Exit Chamberlaine, attended
        All rise, and Tables remou'd ⌐*by Seruants*⌐
You haue now a broken Banket, but wee'l mend it.
A good digestion to you all; and once more
I showre a welcome on yee: welcome all.
        Hoboyes. Enter King and others as Maskers, habited
        like Shepheards, vsher'd by the Lord Chamberlaine.
        They passe directly before the Cardinall, and
        gracefully salute him
A noble Company: what are their pleasures?

CHAMBERLAINE
Because they speak no English, thus they praid
To tell your Grace: That hauing heard by fame
Of this so Noble and so faire assembly,
This night to meet heere they could doe no lesse,
610 (Out of the great respect they beare to beauty)
But leaue their Flockes, and vnder your faire Conduct
Craue leaue to view these Ladies, and entreat
An houre of Reuels with 'em.

CARDINALL   Say, Lord *Chamberlaine*,
They haue done my poore house grace: for which I
        pay 'em
A thousand thankes, and pray 'em take their pleasures.
        Choose Ladies, King and Anne Bullen

KING (*to Anne*)
The fairest hand I euer touch'd: O Beauty,
Till now I neuer knew thee.
        Musicke, Dance

CARDINALL (*to the Chamberlaine*) My Lord.

CHAMBERLAINE Your Grace.

620 CARDINALL Pray tell 'em thus much from me:

There should be one amongst 'em by his person
More worthy this place then my selfe, to whom
(If I but knew him) with my loue and duty
I would surrender it.

LORD CHAMBERLAINE   I will my Lord.
        ⌐*Whispers Maskers*⌐

CARDINALL
What say they?

CHAMBERLAINE   Such a one, they all confesse
There is indeed, which they would haue your Grace
Find out, and he will take it.

CARDINALL ⌐*standing*⌐   Let me see then,
By all your good leaues Gentlemen; heere Ile make
My royall choyce.
        ⌐*Bows before the King*⌐

KING ⌐*vnmasking*⌐   Ye haue found him Cardinall,
You hold a faire Assembly; you doe well Lord: 630
You are a Churchman, or Ile tell you Cardinall,
I should iudge now vnhappily.

CARDINALL   I am glad
Your Grace is growne so pleasant.

KING   My Lord Chamberlaine,
Prethee come hither, (*aside to the Chamberlaine,*
        gesturing towards Anne) what faire Ladie's that?

CHAMBERLAINE
An't please your Grace, Sir *Thomas Bullens* Daughter,
The Viscount *Rochford*, one of her Highnesse women.

KING
By Heauen she is a dainty one. (*To Anne*) Sweet heart,
I were vnmannerly to take you out,
And not to kisse you ⌐*kisses her*⌐. A health Gentlemen,
        ⌐*He drinkes*⌐
Let it goe round.   640

CARDINALL
Sir *Thomas Louell*, is the Banket ready
I'th' Priuy Chamber?

LOUELL   Yes, my Lord.

CARDINALL (*to the King*)   Your Grace
I feare, with dancing is a little heated.

KING I feare too much.

CARDINALL There's fresher ayre my Lord,
In the next Chamber.

KING
Lead in your Ladies eu'ry one: (*To Anne*) Sweet Partner,
I must not yet forsake you: (*To the Cardinall*) Let's be
        merry,
Good my Lord Cardinall: I haue halfe a dozen healths,
To drinke to these faire Ladies, and a measure   650
To lead 'em once againe, and then let's dreame
Who's best in fauour. Let the Musicke knock it.
        Exeunt with Trumpets

❀

Enter two Gentlemen at seuerall Doores   2.1
                                                  (Sc. 5)
I. GENTLEMAN
Whether away so fast?

2. GENTLEMAN   O, God saue ye:

Eu'n to the Hall, to heare what shall become
Of the great Duke of Buckingham.

1. GENTLEMAN   Ile saue you
That labour Sir. All's now done but the Ceremony
Of bringing backe the Prisoner.

2. GENTLEMAN   Were you there?

1. GENTLEMAN
Yes indeed was I.

2. GENTLEMAN   Pray speake what ha's happen'd.

1. GENTLEMAN
You may guesse quickly what.

2. GENTLEMAN   Is he found guilty?

1. GENTLEMAN
660   Yes truely is he, and condemn'd vpon't.

2. GENTLEMAN I am sorry fort.

1. GENTLEMAN So are a number more.

2. GENTLEMAN But pray how past it?

1. GENTLEMAN
Ile tell you in a little. The great Duke
Came to the Bar; where, to his accusations
He pleaded still not guilty, and alleadged
Many sharpe reasons to defeat the Law.
The Kings Atturney on the contrary,
Vrg'd on the Examinations, proofes, confessions
670   Of diuers witnesses, which the Duke desir'd
To him brought *viua voce* to his face;
At which appear'd against him, his Surueyor
Sir *Gilbert Perke* his Chancellour, and *Iohn Car*,
Confessor to him, with that Diuell Monke,
Hopkins, that made this mischiefe.

2. GENTLEMAN   That was hee
That fed him with his Prophecies.

1. GENTLEMAN   The same,
All these accus'd him strongly, which he faine
Would haue flung from him; but indeed he could not;
And so his Peeres vpon this euidence,
680   Haue found him guilty of high Treason. Much
He spoke, and learnedly for life: But all
Was either pittied in him, or forgotten.

2. GENTLEMAN
After all this, how did he beare himselfe?

1. GENTLEMAN
When he was brought agen to th' Bar, to heare
His Knell rung out, his Iudgement, he was stir'd
With such an Agony, he sweat extreamly,
And somthing spoke in choller, ill, and hasty:
But he fell to himselfe againe, and sweetly,
In all the rest shew'd a most Noble patience.

2. GENTLEMAN
I doe not thinke he feares death.

690 1. GENTLEMAN   Sure he does not,
He neuer was so womanish, the cause
He may a little grieue at.

2. GENTLEMAN   Certainly,
The Cardinall is the end of this.

1. GENTLEMAN   Tis likely,
By all coniectures: First *Kildares* Attendure;
Then Deputy of Ireland, who remou'd,

Earle *Surrey* was sent thither, and in hast too,
Least he should helpe his Father.

2. GENTLEMAN   That tricke of State
Was a deepe enuious one.

1. GENTLEMAN   At his returne,
No doubt he will requite it; this is noted
(And generally) who euer the King fauours,   700
The Cardnall instantly will finde imployment,
And farre enough from Court too.

2. GENTLEMAN   All the Commons
Hate him perniciously, and o' my Conscience
Wish him ten faddom deepe: This Duke as much
They loue and doate on: call him bounteous *Buckingham*,
The Mirror of all courtesie.

> *Enter Buckingham from his Arraignment, Tipstaues*
> *before him, the Axe with the edge towards him,*
> *Halberds on each side, accompanied with Sir*
> *Thomas Louell, Sir Nicholas Vaux, Sir William*
> *Sands, and common people*

1. GENTLEMAN   Stay there Sir,
And see the noble ruin'd man you speake of.

2. GENTLEMAN
Let's stand close and behold him.

> *They stand apart*

BUCKINGHAM (*to the Common People*) All good people,
You that thus farre haue come to pitty me;
Heare what I say, and then goe home and lose me.   710
I haue this day receiu'd a Traitors iudgement,
And by that name must dye; yet Heauen beare witnes,
And if I haue a Conscience, let it sincke me,
Euen as the Axe falls, if I be not faithfull.
The Law I beare no mallice for my death,
T'has done vpon the premises, but Iustice:
But those that sought it, I could wish more Christians:
(Be what they will) I heartily forgiue 'em;
Yet let 'em looke they glory not in mischiefe;
Nor build their euils on the graues of great men;   720
For then, my guiltlesse blood must cry against 'em.
For further life in this world I ne're hope,
Nor will I sue, although the King haue mercies
More then I dare make faults. You few that lou'd me,
And dare be bold to weepe for *Buckingham*,
His Noble Friends and Fellowes; whom to leaue
Is only bitter to him, only dying:
Goe with me like good Angels to my end,
And as the long diuorce of Steele fals on me,
Make of your Prayers one sweet Sacrifice,   730
And lift my Soule to Heauen. (*To the Guard*) Lead on a
Gods name.

LOUELL
I doe beseech your Grace, for charity
If euer any malice in your heart
Were hid against me, now to forgiue me frankly.

BUCKINGHAM
Sir *Thomas Louell*, I as free forgiue you
As I would be forgiuen: I forgiue all.
There cannot be those numberlesse offences

Gainst me, that I cannot take peace with: no blacke
    Enuy
Shall marke my Graue. Commend mee to his Grace:
740 And if he speake of *Buckingham*; pray tell him,
You met him halfe in Heauen: my vowes and prayers
Yet are the Kings; and till my Soule forsake,
Shall cry for blessings on him. May he liue
Longer then I haue time to tell his yeares;
Euer belou'd and louing, may his Rule be;
And when old Time shall lead him to his end,
Goodnesse and he, fill vp one Monument.

LOUELL
To th' water side I must conduct your Grace;
Then giue my Charge vp to Sir *Nicholas Vaux*,
Who vndertakes you to your end.

750 VAUX (*to an Attendant*)   Prepare there,
The Duke is comming: See the Barge be ready;
And fit it with such furniture as suites
The Greatnesse of his Person.

BUCKINGHAM   Nay, Sir *Nicholas*,
Let it alone; my State now will but mocke me.
When I came hither, I was Lord High Constable,
And Duke of *Buckingham*: now, poore *Edward Bohun*;
Yet I am richer then my base Accusers,
That neuer knew what Truth meant: I now seale it;
And with that bloud will make 'em one day groane
    for't.
760 My noble Father *Henry* of *Buckingham*,
Who first rais'd head against Vsurping *Richard*,
Flying for succour to his Seruant *Banister*,
Being distrest; was by that wretch betraid,
And without Tryall, fell; Gods peace be with him.
Henry the Seauenth succeeding, truly pittying
My Fathers losse; like a most Royall Prince
Restor'd me to my Honours: and out of ruines
Made my Name once more Noble. Now his Sonne,
Henry the Eight, Life, Honour, Name and all
770 That made me happy; at one stroake ha's taken
For euer from the World. I had my Tryall,
And must needs say a Noble one; which makes me
A little happier then my wretched Father:
Yet thus farre we are one in Fortunes; both
Fell by our Seruants, by those Men we lou'd most:
A most vnnaturall and faithlesse Seruice.
Heauen ha's an end in all: yet, you that heare me,
This from a dying man receiue as certaine:
Where you are liberall of your loues and Councels,
780 Be sure you be not loose; for those you make friends,
And giue your hearts to; when they once perceiue
The least rub in your fortunes, fall away
Like water from ye, neuer found againe
But where they meane to sinke ye: all good people
Pray for me, I must now forsake ye; the last houre
Of my long weary life is come vpon me:
Farewell; and when you would say somthing that is
    sad,
Speake how I fell. I haue done; and God forgiue me.
                  Exeunt Buckingham and Traine

The two Gentlemen come forward
1. GENTLEMAN
O, this is full of pitty; Sir, it cals
I feare, too many curses on their heads   790
That were the Authors.
2. GENTLEMAN   If the Duke be guiltlesse,
'Tis full of woe: yet I can giue you inckling
Of an ensuing euill, if it fall,
Greater then this.
1. GENTLEMAN   Good Angels keepe it from vs:
What may it be? you doe not doubt my faith Sir?
2. GENTLEMAN
This Secret is so weighty, 'twill require
A strong faith to conceale it.
1. GENTLEMAN   Let me haue it:
I doe not talke much.
2. GENTLEMAN   I am confident;
You shall Sir: Did you not of late dayes heare
A buzzing of a Separation   800
Betweene the King and *Katherine*?
1. GENTLEMAN   Yes, but it held not;
For when the King once heard it, out of anger
He sent command to the Lord Mayor straight
To stop the rumor; and allay those tongues
That durst disperse it.
2. GENTLEMAN   But that slander Sir,
Is found a truth now: for it growes agen
Fresher then e're it was; and held for certaine
The King will venture at it. Either the Cardinall,
Or some about him neere, haue out of malice
To the good Queene, possest him with a scruple 810
That will vndoe her: To confirme this too,
Cardinall *Campeius* is arriu'd, and lately,
As all thinke for this busines.
1. GENTLEMAN   Tis the Cardinall;
And meerely to reuenge him on the Emperour,
For not bestowing on him at his asking,
The Archbishopricke of *Toledo*, this is purpos'd.
2. GENTLEMAN
I thinke you haue hit the marke; but is't not cruell,
That she should feele the smart of this: the Cardinall
Will haue his will, and she must fall.
1. GENTLEMAN   'Tis wofull.
Wee are too open heere to argue this: 820
Let's thinke in priuate more.   *Exeunt*

Enter Lord Chamberlaine   **2.2**
CHAMBERLAINE (*reading this Letter*) *My Lord, the Horses your* **(Sc. 6)**
Lordship sent for, with all the care I had, I saw well chosen,
ridden, and furnish'd. They were young and handsome, and
of the best breed in the North. When they were ready to set
out for London, a man of my Lord Cardinalls, by Commission,
and maine power tooke 'em from me, with this reason: his
maister would bee seru'd before a Subiect, if not before the
King, which stop'd our mouthes Sir.
I feare he will indeede; well, let him haue them;   830
Hee will haue all I thinke.

Enter to the Lord Chamberlaine, the Dukes of
Norfolke and Suffolke

NORFOLKE Well met my Lord *Chamberlaine*.

CHAMBERLAINE Good day to both your Graces.

SUFFOLKE
How is the King imployd?

CHAMBERLAINE   I left him priuate,
Full of sad thoughts and troubles.

NORFOLKE   What's the cause?

CHAMBERLAINE
It seemes the Marriage with his Brothers Wife
Ha's crept too neere his Conscience.

SUFFOLKE   No, his Conscience
Ha's crept too neere another Ladie.

NORFOLKE   Tis so;
This is the Cardinals doing: The King-Cardinall,
840 That blinde Priest, like the eldest Sonne of Fortune,
Turnes what he list. The King will know him one day.

SUFFOLKE
Pray God he doe, hee'l neuer know himselfe else.

NORFOLKE
How holily he workes in all his businesse,
And with what zeale? For now he has crackt the League
Between vs & the Emperor (the Queens great Nephew)
He diues into the Kings Soule, and there scatters
Dangers, doubts, wringing of the Conscience,
Feares, and despaires, and all these for his Marriage.
And out of all these, to restore the King,
850 He counsels a Diuorce, a losse of her
That like a Iewell, ha's hung twenty yeares
About his necke, yet neuer lost her lustre;
Of her that loues him with that excellence,
That Angels loue good men with: Euen of her,
That when the greatest stroake of Fortune falls
Will blesse the King: and is not this course pious?

CHAMBERLAINE
Heauen keep me from such councel: tis most true
These newes are euery where, euery tongue speaks 'em,
And euery true heart weepes for't. All that dare
860 Looke into these affaires, see this maine end,
The French Kings Sister. Heauen will one day open
The Kings eyes, that so long haue slept vpon
This bold bad man.

SUFFOLKE And free vs from his slauery.

NORFOLKE We had need pray,
And heartily, for our deliuerance;
Or this imperious man will worke vs all
From Princes into Pages: all mens honours
Lie like one lumpe before him, to be fashion'd
Into what pitch he please.

870 SUFFOLKE   For me, my Lords,
I loue him not, nor feare him, there's my Creede:
As I am made without him, so Ile stand,
If the King please: his Curses and his blessings
Touch me alike: th'are breath I not beleeue in.
I knew him, and I know him: so I leaue him
To him that made him proud; the Pope.

NORFOLKE   Let's in;

And with some other busines, put the King
From these sad thoughts, that work too much vpon him:
(To the Chamberlaine)
My Lord, youle beare vs company?

CHAMBERLAINE   Excuse me,
The King ha's sent me otherwhere: Besides   880
You'l finde a most vnfit time to disturbe him:
Health to your Lordships.

NORFOLKE   Thanks my good Lord *Chamberlaine*.
                                    Exit Lord Chamberlaine
The King drawes the Curtaine and sits reading
pensiuely

SUFFOLKE
How sad he lookes; sure he is much afflicted.

KING
Who's there? Ha?

NORFOLKE   Pray God he be not angry.

KING
Who's there I say? How dare you thrust your selues
Into my priuate Meditations?
Who am I? Ha?

NORFOLKE
A gracious King, that pardons all offences
Malice ne're meant: Our breach of Duty this way,
Is businesse of Estate; in which, we come   890
To know your Royall pleasure.

KING   Ye are too bold:
Go too; Ile make ye know your times of businesse:
Is this an howre for temporall affaires? Ha?
Enter Cardinall Wolsey and Campeius with a
Commission
Who's there? my good Lord Cardinall? O my *Wolsey*,
The quiet of my wounded Conscience;
Thou art a cure fit for a King; *(to Campeius)* you'r
welcome
Most learned Reuerend Sir, into our Kingdome,
Vse vs, and it: *(To Wolsey)* My good Lord, haue great
care,
I be not found a Talker.

CARDINALL   Sir, you cannot;
I would your Grace would giue vs but an houre   900
Of priuate conference.

KING *(to Norfolke and Suffolke)* We are busie; goe.
Norfolke and Suffolke speake priuately to one
another as they depart

NORFOLKE
This Priest ha's no pride in him?

SUFFOLKE   Not to speake of:
I would not be so sicke though for his place:
But this cannot continue.

NORFOLKE   If it doe,
Ile venture one haue at him.

SUFFOLKE   I another.
                            Exeunt Norfolke and Suffolke

CARDINALL *(to the King)*
Your Grace ha's giuen a President of wisedome
Aboue all Princes, in committing freely
Your scruple to the voyce of Christendome:

Who can be angry now? What Enuy reach you?
910 The Spaniard tide by blood and fauour to her,
Must now confesse, if they haue any goodnesse,
The Tryall, iust and Noble. All the Clerkes,
(I meane the learned ones in Christian Kingdomes)
Haue their free voyces. Rome (the Nurse of Iudgement)
Inuited by your Noble selfe, hath sent
One generall Tongue vnto vs. This good man,
This iust and learned Priest, Cardnall *Campeius*,
Whom once more, I present vnto your Highnesse.

KING (*embracing Campeius*)
And once more in mine armes I bid him welcome,
920 And thanke the holy Conclaue for their loues,
They haue sent me such a Man, I would haue wish'd
      for.

CAMPEIUS
Your Grace must needs deserue all strangers loues,
You are so Noble: To your Highnesse hand
I tender my Commission;
      He giues the Commission to the King
(*to the Cardinall*)   by whose vertue,
The Court of Rome commanding, you my Lord
Cardinall of *Yorke*, are ioyn'd with me their Seruant,
In the vnpartiall iudging of this Businesse.

KING
Two equall men: The Queene shall be acquainted
Forthwith for what you come. Where's *Gardiner*?

CARDINALL
930 I know your Maiesty, ha's alwayes lou'd her
So deare in heart, not to deny her that
A Woman of lesse Place might aske by Law;
Schollers allow'd freely to argue for her.

KING
I, and the best she shall haue; and my fauour
To him that does best, God forbid els: Cardinall,
Prethee call *Gardiner* to me, my new Secretary.
      The Cardinall goes to the dore and cals Gardiner
I find him a fit fellow.
      Enter Gardiner

CARDINALL (*aside to Gardiner*)
Giue me your hand: much ioy & fauour to you;
You are the Kings now.

GARDINER (*aside to the Cardinall*) But to be commanded
940 For euer by your Grace, whose hand ha's rais'd me.

KING Come hither *Gardiner*.
      Walkes and whispers

CAMPEIUS (*to the Cardinall*)
My Lord of *Yorke*, was not one Doctor *Pace*
In this mans place before him?

CARDINALL   Yes, he was.

CAMPEIUS
Was he not held a learned man?

CARDINALL   Yes surely.

CAMPEIUS
Beleeue me, there's an ill opinion spread then,
Euen of your selfe Lord Cardinall.

CARDINALL   How? of me?

CAMPEIUS
They will not sticke to say, you enuide him;
And fearing he would rise (he was so vertuous)
Kept him a forraigne man still, which so greeu'd him,
That he ran mad, and dide.

CARDINALL   Heau'ns peace be with him: 950
That's Christian care enough: for liuing Murmurers,
There's places of rebuke. He was a Foole;
For he would needs be vertuous.
(*Gesturing towards Gardiner*)   That good Fellow,
If I command him followes my appointment,
I will haue none so neere els. Learne this Brother,
We liue not to be grip'd by meaner persons.

KING (*to Gardiner*)
Deliuer this with modesty to th' Queene.
                              Exit Gardiner
The most conuenient place, that I can thinke of
For such receipt of Learning, is Black-Fryers:
There ye shall meete about this waighty busines. 960
My *Wolsey*, see it furnish'd, O my Lord,
Would it not grieue an able man to leaue
So sweet a Bedfellow? But Conscience, Conscience;
O 'tis a tender place, and I must leaue her.   *Exeunt*

            Enter Anne Bullen, and an old Lady   2.3
ANNE   (Sc. 7
Not for that neither; here's the pang that pinches.
His Highnesse, hauing liu'd so long with her, and she
So good a Lady, that no Tongue could euer
Pronounce dishonour of her; by my life,
She neuer knew harme-doing: Oh, now after
So many courses of the Sun enthroaned,   970
Still growing in a Maiesty and pompe, the which
To leaue, a thousand fold more bitter, then
'Tis sweet at first t'acquire. After this Processe
To giue her the auaunt, it is a pitty
Would moue a Monster.

OLD LADY   Hearts of most hard temper
Melt and lament for her.

ANNE   Oh Gods will, much better
She ne're had knowne pompe; though't be temporall,
Yet if that quarrell, Fortune, do diuorce
It from the bearer, 'tis a sufferance, panging
As soule and bodies seuering.

OLD LADY   Alas poore Lady,   980
Shee's a stranger now againe.

ANNE   So much the more
Must pitty drop vpon her; verily
I sweare, tis better to be lowly borne,
And range with humble liuers in Content,
Then to be perk'd vp in a glistring griefe,
And weare a golden sorrow.

OLD LADY   Our content
Is our best hauing.

ANNE   By my troth, and Maidenhead,
I would not be a Queene.

OLD LADY   Beshrew me, I would,

And venture Maidenhead for't, and so would you
990   For all this spice of your Hipocrisie:
You that haue so faire parts of Woman on you,
Haue (too) a Womans heart, which euer yet
Affected Eminence, Wealth, Soueraignty;
Which, to say sooth, are Blessings; and which guifts
(Sauing your mincing) the capacity
Of your soft Chiuerell Conscience, would receiue,
If you might please to stretch it.

ANNE   Nay, good troth.

OLD LADY
Yes troth, & troth; you would not be a Queen?

ANNE
No, not for all the riches vnder Heauen.

OLD LADY
1000   Tis strange; a threepence bow'd would hire me
Old as I am, to Queene it: but I pray you,
What thinke you of a Dutchesse? Haue you limbs
To beare that load of Title?

ANNE   No in truth.

OLD LADY
Then you are weakly made; plucke off a little,
I would not be a young Count in your way,
For more then blushing comes to: If your backe
Cannot vouchsafe this burthen, tis too weake
Euer to get a Boy.

ANNE   How you doe talke;
I sweare againe, I would not be a Queene,
For all the world.

1010   OLD LADY   In faith, for little England
You'ld venture an emballing: I my selfe
Would for *Carnaruanshire*, although there long'd
No more to th'Crowne but that: Lo, who comes here?
        Enter Lord Chamberlaine

CHAMBERLAINE
Good morrow Ladies; what wer't worth to know
The secret of your conference?

ANNE   My good Lord,
Not your demand; it values not your asking:
Our Mistris Sorrowes we were pittying.

CHAMBERLAINE
It was a gentle businesse, and becomming
The action of good women, there is hope
All will be well.

1020   ANNE   Now I pray God, *Amen*.

CHAMBERLAINE
You beare a gentle minde, & heau'nly blessings
Follow such Creatures. That you may, faire Lady
Perceiue I speake sincerely, and high notes
Tane of your many vertues; the Kings Maiesty
Commends his good opinion of you; and
Doe's purpose honour to you no lesse flowing,
Then Marchionesse of *Pembrooke*; to which Title,
A Thousand pound a yeare, Annuall support,
Out of his Grace, he addes.

ANNE   I doe not know
1030   What kinde of my obedience, I should tender;
More then my All, is Nothing: Nor my Prayers

Are not words duely hallowed; nor my Wishes
More worth, then empty vanities: yet Prayers & Wishes
Are all I can returne. 'Beseech your Lordship,
Vouchsafe to speake my thankes, and my obedience,
As from a blushing Handmaid, to his Highnesse;
Whose health and Royalty I pray for.

CHAMBERLAINE   Lady;
I shall not faile t'approue the faire conceit
The King hath of you. (*Aside*) I haue perus'd her well,
Beauty and Honour in her are so mingled,   1040
That they haue caught the King: and who knowes yet
But from this Lady, may proceed a Iemme,
To lighten all this Ile. (*To Anne*) I'le to the King,
And say I spoke with you.

ANNE My honour'd Lord.   *Exit Lord Chamberlaine*

OLD LADY Why this it is: See, see,
I haue beene begging sixteene yeares in Court
(Am yet a Courtier beggerly) nor could
Come pat betwixt too early, and too late
For any suit of pounds: and you, (oh fate)   1050
A very fresh Fish heere; fye, fye vpon
This compel'd fortune: haue your mouth fild vp,
Before you open it.

ANNE   This is strange to me.

OLD LADY
How tasts it? Is it bitter? Forty pence, no:
There was a Lady once (tis an old Story)
That would not be a Queene, that would she not
For all the mud in Egypt; haue you heard it?

ANNE
Come you are pleasant.

OLD LADY   With your Theame, I could
O're-mount the Larke: The Marchionesse of *Pembrooke*?
A thousand pounds a yeare, for pure respect?   1060
No other obligation? by my Life,
That promises mo thousands: Honours traine
Is longer then his fore-skirt; by this time
I know your backe will beare a Dutchesse. Say,
Are you not stronger then you were?

ANNE   Good Lady,
Make your selfe mirth with your particular fancy,
And leaue me out on't. Would I had no being
If this salute my blood a iot; it faints me
To thinke what followes.
The Queene is comfortlesse, and wee forgetfull   1070
In our long absence: pray doe not deliuer,
What heere y'haue heard to her.

OLD LADY   What doe you thinke me—
                Exeunt

Trumpets: Sennet. Cornets. Enter two Vergers, with   **2.4**
short siluer wands; next them two Scribes in the   (Sc. 8)
habite of Doctors; after them, the Archbishop of
Canterbury alone; after him, the Bishops of Lincolne,
Ely, Rochester, and S. Asaph: Next them, with some
small distance, followes a Gentleman bearing the
Purse, with the great Seale, and a Cardinals Hat:
Then two Priests, bearing each a Siluer Crosse:

Then a Gentleman Vsher bare-headed, accompanyed
with a Sergeant at Armes, bearing a Siluer Mace:
Then two Gentlemen bearing two great Siluer
Pillers: After them, side by side, the two
Cardinals (Wolsey and Campeius), two
Noblemen, with the Sword and Mace. The King
takes place vnder the Cloth of State. The two
Cardinalls sit vnder him as Iudges. The Queene,
attended by Griffith her Gentleman Vsher,
takes place some distance from the King. The
Bishops place themselues on each side the Court
in manner of a Consistory: Below them the
Scribes. The Lords sit next the Bishops. The rest
of the Attendants stand in conuenient order about
the Stage

CARDINALL
  Whil'st our Commission from Rome is read,
  Let silence be commanded.

KING   What's the need?
  It hath already publiquely bene read,
  And on all sides th'Authority allow'd,
  You may then spare that time.

CARDINALL   Bee't so, proceed.

SCRIBE (*to the Crier*)
  Say, *Henry* K. of England, come into the Court.

CRIER
  Henry King of England, come into the Court.

1080 KING Heere.

SCRIBE (*to the Crier*)
  Say, *Katherine* Queene of England, come into the Court.

CRIER
  Katherine Queene of England, come into the Court.
    The Queene makes no answer, rises out of her
    Chaire, goes about the Court, comes to the King,
    and kneeles at his Feete. Then speakes

QUEENE KATHERINE
  Sir, I desire you do me Right and Iustice,
  And to bestow your pitty on me; for
  I am a most poore Woman, and a Stranger,
  Borne out of your Dominions: hauing heere
  No Iudge indifferent, nor no more assurance
  Of equall Friendship and Proceeding. Alas Sir:
  In what haue I offended you? What cause
1090 Hath my behauiour giuen to your displeasure,
  That thus you should proceede to put me off,
  And take your good Grace from me? Heauen
     witnesse,
  I haue bene to you, a true and humble Wife,
  At all times to your will conformable:
  Euer in feare to kindle your Dislike,
  Yea, subiect to your Countenance: Glad, or sorry,
  As I saw it inclin'd. When was the houre
  I euer contradicted your Desire?
  Or made it not mine too? Or which of your Friends
1100 Haue I not stroue to loue, although I knew
  He were mine Enemy? What Friend of mine,
  That had to him deriu'd your Anger, did I
  Continue in my Liking? Nay, gaue notice

  He was from thence discharg'd? Sir, call to minde,
  That I haue beene your Wife, in this Obedience,
  Vpward of twenty yeares, and haue bene blest
  With many Children by you. If in the course
  And processe of this time, you can report,
  And proue it too, against mine Honor, aught;
  My bond to Wedlocke, or my Loue and Dutie   1110
  Against your Sacred Person; in Gods name
  Turne me away: and let the fowl'st Contempt
  Shut doore vpon me, and so giue me vp
  To the sharp'st kinde of Iustice. Please you, Sir,
  The King your Father, was reputed for
  A Prince most Prudent; of an excellent
  And vnmatch'd Wit, and Iudgement. *Ferdinand*
  My Father, King of Spaine, was reckon'd one
  The wisest Prince, that there had reign'd, by many
  A yeare before. It is not to be question'd,   1120
  That they had gather'd a wise Councell to them
  Of euery Realme, that did debate this Businesse,
  Who deem'd our Marriage lawful. Wherefore I
     humbly
  Beseech you Sir, to spare me, till I may
  Be by my Friends in Spaine, aduis'd; whose Counsaile
  I will implore. If not, i'th'name of God
  Your pleasure be fulfill'd.

CARDINALL   You haue heere Lady,
  (And of your choice) these Reuerend Fathers, men
  Of singular Integrity, and Learning;
  Yea, the elect o'th'Land, who are assembled   1130
  To pleade your Cause. It shall be therefore bootlesse,
  That longer you desire the Court, as well
  For your owne quiet, as to rectifie
  What is vnsetled in the King.

CAMPEIUS   His Grace
  Hath spoken well, and iustly: Therefore Madam,
  It's fit this Royall Session do proceed,
  And that (without delay) their Arguments
  Be now produc'd, and heard.

QUEENE KATHERINE (*to Wolsey*)   Lord Cardinall,
  To you I speake.

CARDINALL   Your pleasure, Madam.

QUEENE KATHERINE   Sir,
  I am about to weepe; but thinking that   1140
  We are a Queene (or long haue dream'd so) certaine
  The daughter of a King, my drops of teares,
  Ile turne to sparkes of fire.

CARDINALL   Be patient yet.

QUEENE KATHERINE
  I will, when you are humble; Nay before,
  Or God will punish me. I do beleeue
  (Induc'd by potent Circumstances) that
  You are mine Enemy, and make my Challenge,
  You shall not be my Iudge. For it is you
  Haue blowne this Coale, betwixt my Lord, and me;
  (Which Gods dew quench) therefore, I say againe,   1150
  I vtterly abhorre; yea, from my Soule
  Refuse you for my Iudge, whom yet once more

I hold my most malicious Foe, and thinke not
At all a Friend to truth.

CARDINALL   I do professe
You speake not like your selfe: who euer yet
Haue stood to Charity, and displayd th'effects
Of disposition gentle, and of wisedome,
Ore-topping womans powre. Madam, you do me wrong.
I haue no Spleene against you, nor iniustice
1160 For you, or any: how farre I haue proceeded,
Or how farre further (Shall) is warranted
By a Commission from the Consistorie,
Yea, the whole Consistorie of Rome. You charge me,
That I haue blowne this Coale: I do deny it,
The King is present: If it be knowne to him,
That I gainsay my Deed, how may he wound,
And worthily my Falsehood, yea, as much
As you haue done my Truth. If he know
That I am free of your Report, he knowes
1170 I am not of your wrong. Therefore in him
It lies to cure me, and the Cure is to
Remoue these Thoughts from you. The which before
His Highnesse shall speake in, I do beseech
You (gracious Madam) to vnthinke your speaking,
And to say so no more.

QUEENE KATHERINE   My Lord, My Lord,
I am a simple woman, much too weake
T'oppose your cunning. Y'are meek, & humble-mouth'd:
You signe your Place, and Calling, in full seeming,
With Meekenesse and Humilitie: but your Heart
1180 Is cramm'd with Arrogancie, Spleene, and Pride.
You haue by Fortune, and his Highnesse fauors,
Gone slightly o're lowe steppes, and now are mounted
Where Powres are your Retainers, and your words
(Domestickes to you) serue your will, as't please
Your selfe pronounce their Office. I must tell you,
You tender more your persons Honor, then
Your high profession Spirituall. That agen
I do refuse you for my Iudge, and heere
Before you all, Appeale vnto the Pope,
1190 To bring my whole Cause 'fore his Holinesse,
And to be iudg'd by him.

She Curtsies to the King, and offers to depart
CAMPEIUS   The Queene is obstinate,
Stubborne to Iustice, apt to accuse it, and
Disdainfull to be tride by't; tis not well.
Shee's going away.

KING (*to the Crier*)   Call her againe.

CRIER
Katherine. Q. of England, come into the Court.

GRIFFITH (*to the Queene*) Madam, you are cald backe.

QUEENE KATHERINE
What need you note it? pray you keep your way,
When you are cald returne. Now the Lord helpe,
They vexe me past my patience, pray you passe on;
1200 I will not tarry: no, nor euer more
Vpon this businesse my appearance make,
In any of their Courts.

Exit Queene, and her Attendants
KING   Goe thy wayes *Kate*,

That man i'th' world, who shall report he ha's
A better Wife, let him in naught be trusted,
For speaking false in that; thou art alone
(If thy rare qualities, sweet gentlenesse,
Thy meeknesse Saint-like, Wife-like Gouernment,
Obeying in commanding, and thy parts
Soueraigne and Pious els, could speake thee out)
The Queene of earthly Queenes: Shee's Noble borne;   1210
And like her true Nobility, she ha's
Carried her selfe towards me.

CARDINALL   Most gracious Sir,
In humblest manner I require your Highnes,
That it shall please you to declare in hearing
Of all these eares (for where I am rob'd and bound,
There must I be vnloos'd, although not there
At once, and fully satisfide) whether euer I
Did broach this busines to your Highnesse, or
Laid any scruple in your way, which might
Induce you to the question on't: or euer   1220
Haue to you, but with thankes to God for such
A Royall Lady, spake one, the least word that might
Be to the preiudice of her present State,
Or touch of her good Person?

KING   My Lord Cardinall,
I doe excuse you; yea, vpon mine Honour,
I free you from't: You are not to be taught
That you haue many enemies, that know not
Why they are so; but like to Village Curres,
Barke when their fellowes doe. By some of these
The Queene is put in anger; y'are excus'd: 1230
But will you be more iustifi'de? You euer
Haue wish'd the sleeping of this busines, neuer desir'd
It to be stir'd; but oft haue hindred, oft,
The passages made toward it; on my Honour,
I speake my good Lord Cardnall, to this point;
And thus farre cleare him. Now, what mou'd me too't,
I will be bold with time and your attention:
Then marke th'inducement. Thus it came; giue heede
    too't:
My Conscience first receiu'd a tendernes,
Scruple, and pricke, on certaine Speeches vtter'd   1240
By th'Bishop of *Bayon*, then French Embassador,
Who had beene hither sent on the debating
A Marriage 'twixt the Duke of *Orleance*, and
Our Daughter *Mary*: I'th'Progresse of this busines,
Ere a determinate resolution, hee
(I meane the Bishop) did require a respite,
Wherein he might the King his Lord aduertise,
Whether our Daughter were legitimate,
Respecting this our Marriage with the Dowager,
Sometimes our Brothers Wife. This respite shooke   1250
The bosome of my Conscience, enter'd me;
Yea, with a spitting power, and made to tremble
The region of my Breast, which forc'd such way,
That many maz'd considerings, did throng
And prest in with this Caution. First, me thought
I stood not in the smile of Heauen, who had
Commanded Nature, that my Ladies wombe

If it conceiu'd a male-child by me, should
Doe no more Offices of life too't; then
1260 The Graue does yeeld to th' dead: For her Male Issue,
Or di'de where they were made, or shortly after
This world had ayr'd them. Hence I tooke a thought,
This was a Iudgement on me, that my Kingdome
(Well worthy the best Heyre o'th' World) should not
Be gladded in't by me. Then followes, that
I weigh'd the danger which my Realmes stood in
By this my Issues faile, and that gaue to me
Many a groaning throw: thus hulling in
The wild Sea of my Conscience, I did steere
1270 Toward this remedy, whereupon we are
Now present heere together: that's to say,
I meant to rectifie my Conscience, which
I then did feele full sicke, and yet not well,
By all the Reuerend Fathers of the Land,
And Doctors learn'd. First I began in priuate,
With you my Lord of *Lincolne*; you remember
How vnder my oppression I did reeke
When I first mou'd you.

BISHOP OF LINCOLNE   Very well my Liedge.

KING
I haue spoke long, be pleas'd your selfe to say
How farre you satisfide me.

1280 BISHOP OF LINCOLNE   So please your Highnes,
The question did at first so stagger me,
Bearing a State of mighty moment in't,
And consequence of dread, that I committed
The daringst Counsaile which I had to doubt,
And did entreate your Highnes to this course,
Which you are running heere.

KING (*to Canterbury*)   I then mou'd you,
My Lord of *Canterbury*, and got your leaue
To make this present Summons. Vnsolicited
I left no Reuerend Person in this Court;
1290 But by particular consent proceeded
Vnder your hands and Seales; therefore goe on,
For no dislike i'th'world against the person
Of the good Queene; but the sharpe thorny points
Of my alleadged reasons, driues this forward:
Proue but our Marriage lawfull, by my Life
And Kingly Dignity, we are contented
To weare our mortall State to come, with her,
(*Katherine* our Queene) before the primest Creature
That's Parragon'd o'th' World.

CAMPEIUS   So please your Highnes,
1300 The Queene being absent, 'tis a needfull fitnesse,
That we adiourne this Court till further day;
Meane while, must be an earnest motion
Made to the Queene to call backe her Appeale
She intends vnto his Holinesse.

KING (*aside*)   I may perceiue
These Cardinals trifle with me: I abhorre
This dilatory sloth, and trickes of Rome.
My learn'd and welbeloued Seruant *Cranmer*,
Prethee returne: with thy approch, I know,

My comfort comes along: (*aloud*) breake vp the Court;
I say, set on.   *Exeunt, in manner as they enter'd* 1310

❁

Enter Queene and her Women as at worke   **3.1**
                                                        (Sc. 9)
QUEENE KATHERINE
Take thy Lute wench, my Soule growes sad with
    troubles,
Sing, and disperse 'em if thou canst: leaue working.

                    SONG.

WOMAN   *Orpheus with his Lute made Trees,*
          And the Mountaine tops that freeze,
              Bow themselues when he did sing.
          To his Musicke, Plants and Flowers
          Euer sprung; as Sunne and Showers,
              There had made a lasting Spring.

          Euery thing that heard him play,
          Euen the Billowes of the Sea,   1320
              Hung their heads, & then lay by.
          In sweet Musicke is such Art,
          Killing care, & griefe of heart,
              Fall asleepe, or hearing dye.

Enter ⌈Griffith⌉ a Gentleman

QUEENE KATHERINE How now?
⌈GRIFFITH⌉
And't please your Grace, the two great Cardinals
Wait in the presence.

QUEENE KATHERINE   Would they speake with me?
⌈GRIFFITH⌉
They wil'd me say so Madam.

QUEENE KATHERINE   Pray their Graces
To come neere: ⌈*Exit Griffith*⌉
                    what can be their busines
With me, a poore weake woman, falne from fauour? 1330
I doe not like their comming, now I thinke on't;
They should bee good men, their affaires as righteous:
But all Hoods, make not Monkes.

Enter the two Cardinalls, Wolsey & Campeius
⌈*vsher'd by Griffith*⌉

CARDINALL   Peace to your Highnesse.

QUEENE KATHERINE
Your Graces find me heere part of a Houswife,
(I would be all) against the worst may happen:
What are your pleasures with me, reuerent Lords?

CARDINALL
May it please you Noble Madam, to withdraw
Into your priuate Chamber; we shall giue you
The full cause of our comming.

QUEENE KATHERINE   Speake it heere.
There's nothing I haue done yet o' my Conscience 1340
Deserues a Corner: would all other Women
Could speake this with as free a Soule as I doe.
My Lords, I care not (so much I am happy
Aboue a number) if my actions
Were tri'de by eu'ry tongue, eu'ry eye saw 'em,
Enuy and base opinion set against 'em,

I know my life so euen. If your busines
Seeke me out, and that way I am Wife in;
Out with it boldly: Truth loues open dealing.

CARDINALL
1350 *Tanta est erga te mentis integritas Regina serenissima.*
QUEENE KATHERINE O good my Lord, no Latin;
I am not such a Truant since my comming,
As not to know the Language I haue liu'd in:
A strange Tongue makes my cause more strange,
      suspitious:
Pray speake in English; heere are some will thanke
      you,
If you speake truth, for their poore Mistris sake;
Beleeue me she ha's had much wrong. Lord Cardinall,
The willing'st sinne I euer yet committed,
May be absolu'd in English.
CARDINALL   Noble Lady,
1360 I am sorry my integrity should breed,
(And seruice to his Maiesty and you)
So deepe suspition, where all faith was meant;
We come not by the way of Accusation,
To taint that honour euery good Tongue blesses;
Nor to betray you any way to sorrow;
You haue too much good Lady: But to know
How you stand minded in the waighty difference
Betweene the King and you, and to deliuer
(Like free and honest men) our iust opinions,
And comforts to your cause.
1370 CAMPEIUS   Most honour'd Madam,
My Lord of Yorke, out of his Noble nature,
Zeale and obedience he still bore your Grace,
Forgetting (like a good man) your late Censure
Both of his truth and him (which was too farre)
Offers, as I doe, in a signe of peace,
His Seruice, and his Counsell.
QUEENE KATHERINE (*aside*)   To betray me.
  (*Aloud*) My Lords, I thanke you both for your good wills,
Ye speake like honest men, (pray God ye proue so)
But how to make ye sodainly an Answere
1380 In such a poynt of weight, so neere mine Honour,
(More neere my Life I feare) with my weake wit;
And to such men of grauity and learning;
In truth I know not. I was set at worke,
Among my Maids, full little (God knowes) looking
Either for such men, or such businesse;
For her sake that I haue beene, for I feele
The last fit of my Greatnesse; good your Graces
Let me haue time and Councell for my Cause:
Alas, I am a Woman frendlesse, hopelesse.
CARDINALL
1390 Madam, you wrong the Kings loue with these feares,
Your hopes and friends are infinite.
QUEENE KATHERINE   In England,
But little for my profit: can you thinke Lords,
That any English man dare giue me Councell?
Or be a knowne friend 'gainst his Highnes pleasure,
(Though he be growne so desperate to be honest)
And liue a Subiect? Nay forsooth, my Friends,

They that must weigh out my afflictions,
They that my trust must grow to, liue not heere,
They are (as all my other comforts) far hence
In mine owne Countrey Lords.
CAMPEIUS   I would your Grace   1400
Would leaue your greefes, and take my Counsell.
QUEENE KATHERINE   How Sir?
CAMPEIUS
Put your maine cause into the Kings protection,
Hee's louing and most gracious. 'Twill be much,
Both for your Honour better, and your Cause:
For if the tryall of the Law o'retake ye,
You'l part away disgrac'd.
CARDINALL (*to the Queene*)   He tels you rightly.
QUEENE KATHERINE
Ye tell me what ye wish for both, my ruine:
Is this your Christian Councell? Out vpon ye.
Heauen is aboue all yet; there sits a Iudge,
That no King can corrupt.
CAMPEIUS   Your rage mistakes vs.   1410
QUEENE KATHERINE
The more shame for ye; holy men I thought ye,
Vpon my Soule two reuerend Cardinall Vertues:
But Cardinall Sins, and hollow hearts I feare ye:
Mend 'em for shame my Lords: Is this your comfort?
The Cordiall that ye bring a wretched Lady?
A woman lost among ye, laugh't at, scornd?
I will not wish ye halfe my miseries,
I haue more Charity. But say I warn'd ye;
Take heed, for heauens sake take heed, least at once
The burthen of my sorrowes, fall vpon ye.   1420
CARDINALL
Madam, this is a meere distraction,
You turne the good we offer, into enuy.
QUEENE KATHERINE
Ye turne me into nothing. Woe vpon ye,
And all such false Professors. Would you haue me
(If you haue any Iustice, any Pitty,
If ye be any thing but Churchmens habits)
Put my sicke cause into his hands, that hates me?
Alas, ha's banish'd me his Bed already,
His Loue, too long ago. I am old my Lords,
And all the Fellowship I hold now with him   1430
Is onely my Obedience. What can happen
To me, aboue this wretchednesse? All your Studies
Make me acurst, like this.
CAMPEIUS   Your feares are worse.
QUEENE KATHERINE
Haue I liu'd thus long (let me speake my selfe,
Since Vertue findes no friends) a Wife, a true one?
A Woman (I dare say without Vainglory)
Neuer yet branded with Suspition?
Haue I, with all my full Affections
Still met the King? Lou'd him next Heau'n? Obey'd
      him?
Bin (out of fondnesse) superstitious to him?   1440
Almost forgot my Prayres to content him?
And am I thus rewarded? 'Tis not well Lords.

Bring me a constant woman to her Husband,
One that ne're dream'd a Ioy, beyond his pleasure;
And to that Woman (when she has done most)
Yet will I adde an Honor; a great Patience.

CARDINALL
Madam, you wander from the good we ayme at.

QUEENE KATHERINE
My Lord, I dare not make my selfe so guiltie,
To giue vp willingly that Noble Title
1450   Your Master wed me to: nothing but death
Shall e're diuorce my Dignities.

CARDINALL   Pray heare me.

QUEENE KATHERINE
Would I had neuer trod this English Earth,
Or felt the Flatteries that grow vpon it:
Ye haue Angels Faces; but Heauen knowes your
      hearts.
What will become of me now, wretched Lady?
I am the most vnhappy Woman liuing.
(To her Women) Alas (poore Wenches) where are now
      your Fortunes?
Shipwrack'd vpon a Kingdome, where no Pitty,
No Friends, no Hope, no Kindred weepe for me?
1460   Almost no Graue allow'd me? Like the Lilly
That once was Mistris of the Field, and flourish'd,
Ile hang my head, and perish.

CARDINALL   If your Grace
Could but be brought to know, our Ends are honest,
Youl'd feele more comfort. Why shold we (good Lady)
Vpon what cause wrong you? Alas, our Places,
The way of our Profession is against it;
We are to Cure such sorrowes, not to sowe 'em.
For Goodnesse sake, consider what you do,
How you may hurt your selfe: I, vtterly
1470   Grow from the Kings Acquaintance, by this Carriage.
The hearts of Princes kisse Obedience,
So much they loue it. But to stubborne Spirits,
They swell and grow, as terrible as stormes.
I know you haue a Gentle, Noble temper,
A Soule as euen as a Calme; Pray thinke vs,
Those we professe, Peace-makers, Friends, and
      Seruants.

CAMPEIUS
Madam, you'l finde it so: you wrong your Vertues
With these weake Womens feares. A Noble Spirit
As yours was, put into you, euer casts
1480   Such doubts as false Coine from it. The King loues you,
Beware you loose it not: For vs (if you please
To trust vs in your businesse) we are ready
To vse our vtmost Studies, in your seruice.

QUEENE KATHERINE
Do what ye will, my Lords: and pray forgiue me;
If I haue vs'd my selfe vnmannerly,
You know I am a Woman, lacking wit
To make a seemely answer to such persons.
Pray do my seruice to his Maiestie,
He ha's my heart yet, and shall haue my Prayers
1490   While I shall haue my life. Come reuerend Fathers,

Bestow your Councels on me. She now begges
That little thought when she set footing heere,
She should haue bought her Dignities so deere.

                                    Exeunt

Enter the Duke of Norfolke, Duke of Suffolke, Lord   **3.2**
Surrey, and Lord Chamberlaine   (Sc. 10

NORFOLKE
If you will now vnite in your Complaints,
And force them with a Constancy, the Cardinall
Cannot stand vnder them. If you omit
The offer of this time, I cannot promise,
But that you shall sustaine moe new disgraces,
With these you beare alreadie.

SURREY   I am ioyfull
To meete the least occasion, that may giue me   1500
Remembrance of my Father-in-Law, the Duke,
To be reueng'd on him.

SUFFOLKE   Which of the Peeres
Haue vncontemn'd gone by him, or at least
Strangely neglected? When did he regard
The stampe of Noblenesse in any person
Out of himselfe?

CHAMBERLAINE   My Lords, you speake your pleasures:
What he deserues of you and me, I know:
What we can do to him (though now the time
Giues way to vs) I much feare. If you cannot
Barre his accesse to'th'King, neuer attempt   1510
Any thing on him: for he hath a Witchcraft
Ouer the King in's Tongue.

NORFOLKE   O feare him not,
His spell in that is out: the King hath found
Matter against him, that for euer marres
The Hony of his Language. No, he's setled
(Not to come off) in his displeasure.

SURREY   Sir,
I should be glad to heare such Newes as this
Once euery houre.

NORFOLKE   Beleeue it, this is true.
In the Diuorce, his contrarie proceedings
Are all vnfolded: wherein he appeares,   1520
As I would wish mine Enemy.

SURREY   How came
His practises to light?

SUFFOLKE   Most strangely.

SURREY   O how? how?

SUFFOLKE
The Cardinals Letters to the Pope miscarried,
And came to th'eye o'th'King, wherein was read
How that the Cardinall did intreat his Holinesse
To stay the Iudgement o'th'Diuorce; for if
It did take place, I do (quoth he) perceiue
My King is tangled in affection, to
A Creature of the Queenes, Lady *Anne Bullen.*

SURREY
Ha's the King this?

SUFFOLKE   Beleeue it.

SURREY   Will this worke?   1530

CHAMBERLAINE
The King in this perceiues him, how he coasts
And hedges his owne way. But in this point
All his trickes founder, and he brings his Physicke
After his Patients death; the King already
Hath married the faire Lady.

SURREY   Would he had.

SUFFOLKE
May you be happy in your wish my Lord,
For I professe you haue it.

SURREY   Now all my ioy
Trace the Coniunction.

SUFFOLKE   My Amen too't.

NORFOLKE   All mens.

SUFFOLKE
1540   There's order giuen for her Coronation:
Marry this is yet but yong, and may be left
To some eares vnrecounted. But my Lords
She is a gallant Creature, and compleate
In minde and feature. I perswade me, from her
Will fall some blessing to this Land, which shall
In it be memoriz'd.

SURREY   But will the King
Digest this Letter of the Cardinals?
The Lord forbid.

NORFOLKE   Marry Amen.

SUFFOLKE   No, no:
There be moe Waspes that buz about his Nose,
Will make this sting the sooner. Cardinall *Campeius*,
1550   Is stolne away to Rome, hath 'tane no leaue,
Ha's left the cause o'th'King vnhandled, and
Is posted as the Agent of our Cardinall,
To second all his plot. I do assure you,
The King cry'de Ha, at this.

CHAMBERLAINE   Now God incense him,
And let him cry Ha, lowder.

NORFOLKE   But my Lord
When returnes *Cranmer*?

SUFFOLKE
He is return'd in his Opinions, which
Haue satisfied the King for his Diuorce,
Together with all famous Colledges
1560   Almost in Christendome: shortly (I beleeue)
His second Marriage shall be publishd, and
Her Coronation. *Katherine* no more
Shall be call'd Queene, but Princesse Dowager,
And Widdow to Prince *Arthur*.

NORFOLKE   This same *Cranmer*'s
A worthy Fellow, and hath tane much paine
In the Kings businesse.

SUFFOLKE   He ha's, and we shall see him
For it, an Arch-byshop.

NORFOLKE   So I heare.

SUFFOLKE   'Tis so.
Enter Cardinall Wolsey and Cromwell
The Cardinall.

NORFOLKE   Obserue, obserue, hee's moody.
*They stand aloofe and obserue the Cardinall and
Cromwell*

CARDINALL (*to Cromwell*)
The Packet Cromwell, gau't you the King?

CROMWELL
To his owne hand, in's Bed-chamber.

CARDINALL   Look'd he   1570
O'th'inside of the Paper?

CROMWELL   Presently
He did vnseale them, and the first he view'd,
He did it with a Serious minde: a heede
Was in his countenance. You he bad
Attend him heere this Morning.

CARDINALL   Is he ready
To come abroad?

CROMWELL I thinke by this he is.

CARDINALL Leaue me a while.   *Exit Cromwell*
(*Aside*) It shall be to the Dutches of Alanson,
The French Kings Sister; He shall marry her.   1580
Anne Bullen? No: Ile no *Anne Bullens* for him,
There's more in't then faire Visage. *Bullen*?
No, wee'l no *Bullens*: Speedily I wish
To heare from Rome. The Marchionesse of Pembroke?
The Nobles speake among themselues

NORFOLKE
He's discontented.

SUFFOLKE   Maybe he heares the King
Does whet his Anger to him.

SURREY   Sharpe enough,
Lord for thy Iustice.

CARDINALL (*aside*)
The late Queenes Gentlewoman? A Knights Daughter
To be her Mistris Mistris? The Queenes, Queene?
This Candle burnes not cleere, 'tis I must snuffe it,   1590
Then out it goes. What though I know her vertuous
And well deseruing? yet I know her for
A spleeny Lutheran, and not wholsome to
Our cause, that she should lye i'th'bosome of
Our hard rul'd King. Againe, there is sprung vp
An Heretique, an Arch-one; *Cranmer*, one
Hath crawl'd into the fauour of the King,
And is his Oracle.
The Nobles speake among themselues

NORFOLKE   He is vex'd at something.
Enter King, reading of a Scedule, and Louell with him

SURREY
I would 'twer somthing y\(^t\) would fret the string,
The Master-cord on's heart.

SUFFOLKE   The King, the King.   1600

KING ⌈*aside*⌉
What piles of wealth hath he accumulated
To his owne portion? And what expence by'th'houre
Seemes to flow from him? How, i'th'name of Thrift
Does he rake this together? (*To the Nobles*) Now my
Lords,
Saw you the Cardinall?

NORFOLKE   My Lord, we haue
Stood heere obseruing him. Some strange Commotion
Is in his braine: He bites his lip, and starts,
Stops on a sodaine, lookes vpon the ground,
Then layes his finger on his Temple: straight

1610 Springs out into fast gate, then stops againe,
Strikes his brest hard, and anon, he casts
His eye against the Moone: in most strange Postures
We haue seene him set himselfe.

KING   It may well be,
There is a mutiny in's minde. This morning,
Papers of State he sent me, to peruse
As I requir'd: and wot you what I found
There (on my Conscience put vnwittingly)
Forsooth an Inuentory, thus importing
The seuerall parcels of his Plate, his Treasure,
1620 Rich Stuffes and Ornaments of Houshold, which
I finde at such proud Rate, that it out-speakes
Possession of a Subiect.

NORFOLKE   It's Heauens will,
Some Spirit put this paper in the Packet,
To blesse your eye withall.

KING   If we did thinke
His Contemplation were aboue the earth,
And fixt on Spirituall obiect, he should still
Dwell in his Musings, but I am affraid
His Thinkings are below the Moone, not worth
His serious considering.

        King takes his Seat, whispers Louell, who then goes
        to the Cardinall

CARDINALL   Heauen forgiue me,
(*To the King*) Euer God blesse your Highnesse.

1630 KING   Good my Lord,
You are full of Heauenly stuffe, and beare the Inuentory
Of your best Graces, in your minde; the which
You were now running o're: you haue scarse time
To steale from Spirituall leysure, a briefe span
To keepe your earthly Audit, sure in that
I deeme you an ill Husband, and am glad
To haue you therein my Companion.

CARDINALL   Sir,
For Holy Offices I haue a time; a time
To thinke vpon the part of businesse, which
1640 I beare i'th'State: and Nature does require
Her times of preseruation, which perforce
I her fraile sonne, among'st my Brethren mortall,
Must giue my tendance to.

KING   You haue said well.

CARDINALL
And euer may your Highnesse yoake together,
(As I will lend you cause) my doing well,
With my well saying.

KING   'Tis well said agen,
And 'tis a kinde of good deede to say well,
And yet words are no deeds. My Father lou'd you,
He said he did, and with his deed did Crowne
1650 His word vpon you. Since I had my Office,
I haue kept you next my Heart, haue not alone
Imploy'd you where high Profits might come home,
But par'd my present Hauings, to bestow
My Bounties vpon you.

CARDINALL (*aside*)   What should this meane?

The Lord increase this businesse.

KING   Haue I not made you
The prime man of the State? I pray you tell me,
If what I now pronounce, you haue found true:
And if you may confesse it, say withall
If you are bound to vs, or no. What say you?

CARDINALL
My Soueraigne, I confesse your Royall graces   1660
Showr'd on me daily, haue bene more then could
My studied purposes requite, which went
Beyond all mans endeauors. My endeauors,
Haue euer come too short of my Desires,
Yet fill'd with my Abilities: Mine owne ends
Haue beene mine so, that euermore they pointed
To'th'good of your most Sacred Person, and
The profit of the State. For your great Graces
Heap'd vpon me (poore Vndeseruer) I
Can nothing render but Allegiant thankes,   1670
My Prayres to heauen for you; my Loyaltie
Which euer ha's, and euer shall be growing,
Till death (that Winter) kill it.

KING   Fairely answer'd:
A Loyall, and obedient Subiect is
Therein illustrated, the Honor of it
Does pay the Act of it, as i'th'contrary
The fowlenesse is the punishment. I presume,
That as my hand ha's open'd Bounty to you,
My heart drop'd Loue, my powre rain'd Honor, more
On you, then any: So your Hand, and Heart,   1680
Your Braine, and euery Function of your power,
Should, notwithstanding that your bond of duty,
As 'twer in Loues particular, be more
To me your Friend, then any.

CARDINALL   I do professe,
That for your Highnesse good, I euer labour'd
More then mine owne: that am, haue, and will be
(Though all the world should cracke their duty to you,
And throw it from their Soule, though perils did
Abound, as thicke as thought could make 'em, and
Appeare in formes more horrid) yet my Duty,   1690
As doth a Rocke against the chiding Flood,
Should the approach of this wilde Riuer breake,
And stand vnshaken yours.

KING   'Tis Nobly spoken:
Take notice Lords, he ha's a Loyall brest,
For you haue seene him open't.
(*To the Cardinall*)   Read o're this,
        He giues him a Paper
And after this (*giuing him another Paper*), and then to
        Breakfast with
What appetite you haue.

        Exit King, frowning vpon the Cardinall,
        the Nobles throng after him smiling, and
        whispering

CARDINALL   What should this meane?
What sodaine Anger's this? How haue I reap'd it?

He parted Frowning from me, as if Ruine
1700 Leap'd from his Eyes. So lookes the chafed Lyon
Vpon the daring Huntsman that has gall'd him:
Then makes him nothing. I must reade this paper:
I feare the Story of his Anger.

He reades one of the Papers

'Tis so:
This paper ha's vndone me: 'Tis th'Accompt
Of all that world of Wealth I haue drawne together
For mine owne ends, (Indeed to gaine the Popedome,
And fee my Friends in Rome.) O Negligence!
Fit for a Foole to fall by: What crosse Diuell
Made me put this maine Secret in the Packet
1710 I sent the King? Is there no way to cure this?
No new deuice to beate this from his Braines?
I know 'twill stirre him strongly; yet I know
A way, if it take right, in spight of Fortune
Will bring me off againe. What's this?

He reades the other Paper

To th'Pope?
The Letter (as I liue) with all the Businesse
I writ too's Holinesse. Nay then, farewell:
I haue touch'd the highest point of all my Greatnesse,
And from that full Meridian of my Glory,
I haste now to my Setting. I shall fall
1720 Like a bright exhalation in the Euening,
And no man see me more.

*Enter to Cardinall Woolsey, the Dukes of Norfolke
and Suffolke, the Earle of Surrey, and the Lord
Chamberlaine*

NORFOLKE
Heare the Kings pleasure Cardinall, who commands
    you
To render vp the Great Seale presently
Into our hands, and to Confine your selfe
To Asher-house, my Lord of Winchesters,
Till you heare further from his Highnesse.

CARDINALL   Stay:
Where's your Commission, Lords? Words cannot carrie
Authority so weighty.

SUFFOLKE   Who dare crosse 'em,
Bearing the Kings will from his mouth expressely?

CARDINALL
1730 Till I finde more then will, or words to do it,
(I meane your malice) know, Officious Lords,
I dare, and must deny it. Now I feele
Of what course Mettle ye are molded, Enuy,
How eagerly ye follow my Disgraces
As if it fed ye, and how sleeke and wanton
Ye appeare in euery thing may bring my ruine?
Follow your enuious courses, men of Malice;
You haue Christian warrant for 'em, and no doubt
In time will finde their fit Rewards. That Seale
1740 You aske with such a Violence, the King
(Mine, and your Master) with his owne hand, gaue
    me:
Bad me enioy it, with the Place, and Honors

During my life; and to confirme his Goodnesse,
Ti'de it by Letters Patents. Now, who'll take it?

SURREY
The King that gaue it.

CARDINALL   It must be himselfe then.

SURREY
Thou art a proud Traitor, Priest.

CARDINALL   Proud Lord, thou lyest:
Within these fortie houres, Surrey durst better
Haue burnt that Tongue, then saide so.

SURREY   Thy Ambition
(Thou Scarlet sinne) robb'd this bewailing Land
Of Noble Buckingham, my Father-in-Law,   1750
The heads of all thy Brother-Cardinals,
(With thee, and all thy best parts bound together)
Weigh'd not a haire of his. Plague of your policie,
You sent me Deputie for Ireland,
Farre from his succour; from the King, from all
That might haue mercie on the fault, thou gau'st him:
Whil'st your great Goodnesse, out of holy pitty,
Absolu'd him with an Axe.

CARDINALL   This, and all else
This talking Lord can lay vpon my credit,
I answer, is most false. The Duke by Law   1760
Found his deserts. How innocent I was
From any priuate malice in his end,
His Noble Iurie, and foule Cause can witnesse.
If I lou'd many words, Lord, I should tell you,
You haue as little Honestie, as Honor,
That in the way of Loyaltie, and Truth,
Toward the King, my euer Roiall Master,
Dare mate a sounder man then Surrie can be,
And all that loue his follies.

SURREY   By my Soule,
Your long Coat (Priest) protects you, thou should'st
    feele   1770
My Sword i'th'life blood of thee else. My Lords,
Can ye endure to heare this Arrogance?
And from this Fellow? If we liue thus tamely,
To be thus Iaded by a peece of Scarlet,
Farewell Nobilitie: let his Grace go forward,
And dare vs with his Cap, like Larkes.

CARDINALL   All Goodnesse
Is poyson to thy Stomacke.

SURREY   Yes, that goodnesse
Of gleaning all the Lands wealth into one,
Into your owne hands (Card'nall) by Extortion:
The goodnesse of your intercepted Packets   1780
You writ to'th'Pope, against the King: your goodnesse
Since you prouoke me, shall be most notorious.
My Lord of Norfolke, as you are truly Noble,
As you respect the common good, the State
Of our despis'd Nobilitie, our Issues,
(Whom if he liue, will scarse be Gentlemen)
Produce the grand summe of his sinnes, the Articles
Collected from his life. *(To the Cardinall)* Ile startle you
Worse then the Sacring Bell, when the browne Wench
Lay kissing in your Armes, Lord Cardinall.   1790

CARDINALL
    How much me thinkes, I could despise this man,
    But that I am bound in Charitie against it.
NORFOLKE (*to Surrey*)
    Those Articles, my Lord, are in the Kings hand:
    But thus much, they are foule ones.
CARDINALL   So much fairer
    And spotlesse, shall mine Innocence arise,
    When the King knowes my Truth.
SURREY   This cannot saue you:
    I thanke my Memorie, I yet remember
    Some of these Articles, and out they shall.
    Now, if you can blush, and crie guiltie Cardinall,
    You'l shew a little Honestie.
1800 CARDINALL   Speake on Sir,
    I dare your worst Obiections: If I blush,
    It is to see a Nobleman want manners.
SURREY
    I had rather want those, then my head; haue at you.
    First, that without the Kings assent or knowledge,
    You wrought to be a Legate, by which power
    You maim'd the Iurisdiction of all Bishops.
NORFOLKE (*to the Cardinall*)
    Then, That in all you writ to Rome, or else
    To Forraigne Princes, *Ego & Rex meus*
    Was still inscrib'd: in which you brought the King
    To be your Seruant.
SUFFOLKE (*to the Cardinall*)
1810   Then, that without the knowledge
    Either of King or Councell, when you went
    Ambassador to the Emperor, you made bold
    To carry into Flanders, the Great Seale.
SURREY (*to the Cardinall*)
    Item, You sent a large Commission
    To *Gregory de Cassado*, to conclude
    Without the Kings will, or the States allowance,
    A League betweene his Highnesse, and *Ferrara*.
SUFFOLKE (*to the Cardinall*)
    That out of meere Ambition, you haue caus'd
    Your holy-Hat to be stampt on the Kings Coine.
SURREY (*to the Cardinall*)
1820   Then, That you haue sent inumerable substance,
    (By what meanes got, I leaue to your owne conscience)
    To furnish Rome, and to prepare the wayes
    You haue for Dignities, to the meere vndooing
    Of all the Kingdome. Many more there are,
    Which since they are of you, and odious,
    I will not taint my mouth with.
CHAMBERLAINE   O my Lord,
    Presse not a falling man too farre: 'tis Vertue:
    His faults lye open to the Lawes, let them
    (Not you) correct him. My heart weepes to see him
    So little, of his great Selfe.
1830 SURREY   I forgiue him.
SUFFOLKE
    Lord Cardinall, the Kings further pleasure is,
    Because all those things you haue done of late
    By your power Legãtine within this Kingdome,

    Fall into'th'compasse of a Premunire;
    That therefore such a Writ be sued against you,
    To forfeit all your Goods, Lands, Tenements,
    Cattles, and whatsoeuer, and to be
    Out of the Kings protection. This is my Charge.
NORFOLKE (*to the Cardinall*)
    And so wee'l leaue you to your Meditations
    How to liue better. For your stubborne answer   1840
    About the giuing backe the Great Seale to vs,
    The King shall know it, and (no doubt) shal thanke
    you.
    So fare you well, my little good Lord Cardinall.
            Exeunt all but Cardinall Wolsey
CARDINALL
    So farewell, to the little good you beare me.
    Farewell? A long farewell to all my Greatnesse.
    This is the state of Man; to day he puts forth
    The tender Leaues of hopes, to morrow Blossomes,
    And beares his blushing Honors thicke vpon him:
    The third day, comes a Frost; a killing Frost,
    And when he thinkes, good easie man, full surely   1850
    His Greatnesse is a ripening, nippes his roote,
    And then he fals as I do. I haue ventur'd
    Like little wanton Boyes that swim on bladders:
    This many Summers in a Sea of Glory,
    But farre beyond my depth: my high-blowne Pride
    At length broke vnder me, and now ha's left me
    Weary, and old with Seruice, to the mercy
    Of a rude streame, that must for euer hide me.
    Vaine pompe, and glory of this World, I hate ye,
    I feele my heart new open'd. Oh how wretched   1860
    Is that poore man, that hangs on Princes fauours?
    There is betwixt that smile we would aspire too,
    That sweet Aspect of Princes, and their ruine,
    More pangs, and feares then warres, or women haue;
    And when he falles, he falles like Lucifer,
    Neuer to hope againe.
       Enter Cromwell, standing amazed
              Why how now *Cromwell*?
CROMWELL
    I haue no power to speake Sir.
CARDINALL   What, amaz'd
    At my misfortunes? Can thy Spirit wonder
    A great man should decline.
       Cromwell begins to weepe
              Nay, and you weep
    I am falne indeed.
CROMWELL   How does your Grace.
CARDINALL   Why well: 1870
    Neuer so truly happy, my good *Cromwell*,
    I know my selfe now, and I feele within me,
    A peace aboue all earthly Dignities,
    A still, and quiet Conscience. The King ha's cur'd me,
    I humbly thanke his Grace: and from these shoulders
    These ruin'd Pillers, out of pitty, taken
    A loade, would sinke a Nauy, (too much Honor.)
    O 'tis a burden *Cromwel*, 'tis a burden
    Too heauy for a man, that hopes for Heauen.

CROMWELL

1880 I am glad your Grace, ha's made that right vse of it.

CARDINALL

I hope I haue: I am able now (me thinkes)
(Out of a Fortitude of Soule, I feele)
To endure more Miseries, and greater farre
Then my Weake-hearted Enemies, dare offer.
What Newes abroad?

CROMWELL   The heauiest, and the worst,
Is your displeasure with the King.

CARDINALL   God blesse him.

CROMWELL

The next is, that Sir *Thomas Moore* is chosen
Lord Chancellor, in your place.

CARDINALL   That's somewhat sodain.
But he's a Learned man. May he continue
1890 Long in his Highnesse fauour, and do Iustice
For Truths-sake, and his Conscience; that his bones,
When he ha's run his course, and sleepes in Blessings,
May haue a Tombe of Orphants teares wept on him.
What more?

CROMWELL   That *Cranmer* is return'd with welcome;
Install'd Lord Arch-byshop of Canterbury.

CARDINALL

That's Newes indeed.

CROMWELL   Last, that the Lady *Anne*,
Whom the King hath in secrecie long married,
This day was view'd in open, as his Queene,
Going to Chappell: and the voyce is now
1900 Onely about her Corronation.

CARDINALL

There was the waight that pull'd me downe. O *Cromwell*,
The King ha's gone beyond me: All my Glories
In that one woman, I haue lost for euer.
No Sun, shall euer vsher forth mine Honors,
Or gilde againe the Noble Troopes that waighted
Vpon my smiles. Go get thee from me *Cromwel*,
I am a poore falne man, vnworthy now
To be thy Lord, and Master. Seeke the King
(That Sun, I pray may neuer set) I haue told him,
1910 What, and how true thou art; he will aduance thee:
Some little memory of me, will stirre him
(I know his Noble Nature) not to let
Thy hopefull seruice perish too. Good *Cromwell*
Neglect him not; make vse now, and prouide
For thine owne future safety.

CROMWELL ⌈*weeping*⌉   O my Lord,
Must I then leaue you? Must I needes forgo
So good, so Noble, and so true a Master?
Beare witnesse, all that haue not hearts of Iron,
With what a sorrow *Cromwel* leaues his Lord.
1920 The King shall haue my seruice; but my prayres
For euer, and for euer shall be yours.

CARDINALL (*weeping*)

Cromwel, I did not thinke to shed a teare
In all my Miseries: But thou hast forc'd me
(Out of thy honest truth) to play the Woman.
Let's dry our eyes: And thus farre heare me *Cromwel*,
And when I am forgotten, as I shall be,

And sleepe in dull cold Marble, where no mention
Of me, more must be heard of: Say I taught thee;
Say *Wolsey*, that once trod the wayes of Glory,
And sounded all the Depths, and Shoales of Honor,   1930
Found thee a way (out of his wracke) to rise in:
A sure, and safe one, though thy Master mist it.
Marke but my Fall, and that that Ruin'd me:
Cromwel, I charge thee, fling away Ambition,
By that sinne fell the Angels: how can man then
(The Image of his Maker) hope to win by it?
Loue thy selfe last, cherish those hearts that hate thee;
Corruption wins not more then Honesty.
Still in thy right hand, carry gentle Peace
To silence enuious Tongues. Be iust, and feare not;   1940
Let all the ends thou aym'st at, be thy Countries,
Thy Gods, and Truths. Then if thou fall'st (O *Cromwell*)
Thou fall'st a blessed Martyr.
Serue the King: And prythee leade me in:
There take an Inuentory of all I haue,
To the last peny, 'tis the Kings. My Robe,
And my Integrity to Heauen, is all,
I dare now call mine owne. O *Cromwel*, *Cromwel*,
Had I but seru'd my God, with halfe the Zeale
I seru'd my King: he would not in mine Age   1950
Haue left me naked to mine Enemies.

CROMWELL

Good Sir, haue patience.

CARDINALL   So I haue. Farewell
The Hopes of Court, my Hopes in Heauen do dwell.

Exeunt

❖

Enter two Gentlemen, meeting one another. The   **4.1**
First holds a Paper   **(Sc. 11)**

1. GENTLEMAN

Y'are well met once againe.

2. GENTLEMAN   So are you.

1. GENTLEMAN

You come to take your stand heere, and behold
The Lady *Anne*, passe from her Corronation.

2. GENTLEMAN

'Tis all my businesse. At our last encounter,
The Duke of Buckingham came from his Triall.

1. GENTLEMAN

'Tis very true. But that time offer'd sorrow,
This generall ioy.

2. GENTLEMAN   'Tis well: The Citizens   1960
I am sure haue shewne at full their Royall minds,
As let 'em haue their rights, they are euer forward
In Celebration of this day with Shewes,
Pageants, and Sights of Honor.

1. GENTLEMAN   Neuer greater,
Nor Ile assure you better taken Sir.

2. GENTLEMAN

May I be bold to aske what that containes,
That Paper in your hand.

1. GENTLEMAN   Yes, 'tis the List
Of those that claime their Offices this day,
By custome of the Coronation.

1970   The Duke of Suffolke is the first, and claimes
        To be high Steward; Next the Duke of Norfolke,
        He to be Earle Marshall: you may reade the rest.
            He giues him the Paper
        2. GENTLEMAN
        I thanke you Sir: Had I not known those customs,
        I should haue beene beholding to your Paper:
        But I beseech you, what's become of *Katherine*
        The Princesse Dowager? How goes her businesse?
        1. GENTLEMAN
        That I can tell you too. The Archbishop
        Of Canterbury, accompanied with other
        Learned, and Reuerend Fathers of his Order,
1980   Held a late Court at Dunstable; sixe miles off
        From Ampthill, where the Princesse lay, to which
        She was often cyted by them, but appear'd not:
        And to be short, for not Appearance, and
        The Kings late Scruple, by the maine assent
        Of all these Learned men, she was diuorc'd,
        And the late Marriage made of none effect:
        Since which, she was remou'd to Kymmalton,
        Where she remaines now sicke.
        2. GENTLEMAN   Alas good Lady.
            Flourish of Trumpets within
        The Trumpets sound: Stand close, the Queene is
        comming.
            Enter the Coronation Procession, passing ouer the
            Stage in Order and State. Ho-boyes within ⌈sound
            the while⌉

The Order of the Coronation.

1 A liuely Flourish of Trumpets.

2 Then, two Iudges.

3 Lord Chancellor, with Purse and Mace before him.

4 Quirristers singing. Musicke.

5 Maior of London, bearing the Mace. Then
    Garter, in his Coate of Armes, and on his head
    he wore a Gilt Copper Crowne.

6 Marquesse Dorset, bearing a Scepter of Gold, on
    his head, a Demy Coronall of Gold. With him,
    the Earle of Surrey, bearing the Rod of Siluer
    with the Doue, Crowned with an Earles
    Coronet. Collars of Esses.

7 Duke of Suffolke, in his Robe of Estate, his
    Coronet on his head, bearing a long white
    Wand, as High Steward. With him, the Duke of
    Norfolke, with the Rod of Marshalship, a
    Coronet on his head. Collars of Esses.

8 A Canopy, borne by foure of the Cinque-Ports,
    vnder it Anne the new Queene in her Robe, in
    her haire, richly adorned with Pearle, Crowned.
    On each side her, the Bishops of London, and
    Winchester.

9 The Olde Dutchesse of Norfolke, in a Coronall of
    Gold, wrought with Flowers bearing the
    Queenes Traine.

10 Certaine Ladies or Countesses, with plaine
    Circlets of Gold, without Flowers.

The two Gentlemen comment on the Procession as it
passes ouer the Stage

2. GENTLEMAN
A Royall Traine beleeue me: These I know: 1990
Who's that that beares the Scepter?
1. GENTLEMAN   Marquesse Dorset,
And that the Earle of Surrey, with the Rod.
2. GENTLEMAN
A bold braue Gentleman. That should bee
The Duke of Suffolke.
1. GENTLEMAN   'Tis the same: high Steward.
2. GENTLEMAN
And that my Lord of Norfolke?
1. GENTLEMAN   Yes.
2. GENTLEMAN (*seeing Anne*)   Heauen blesse thee,
Thou hast the sweetest face I euer look'd on.
Sir, as I haue a Soule, she is an Angell;
Our King ha's all the Indies in his Armes,
And more, and richer, when he straines that Lady,
I cannot blame his Conscience.
1. GENTLEMAN   They that beare   2000
The Cloath of Honour ouer her, are foure Barons
Of the Cinque-Ports.
2. GENTLEMAN Those men are happy,
And so are all, are neere her.
I take it, she that carries vp the Traine,
Is that old Noble Lady, Dutchesse of Norfolke.
1. GENTLEMAN
It is, and all the rest are Countesses.
2. GENTLEMAN
Their Coronets say so. These are Starres indeed.
⌈1. GENTLEMAN⌉
And sometimes falling ones.
2. GENTLEMAN   No more of that.
            Exit the last of the Procession, and then,
                A great Flourish of Trumpets within
        Enter a third Gentleman ⌈in a sweate⌉
1. GENTLEMAN
God saue you Sir. Where haue you bin broiling?   2010
3. GENTLEMAN
Among the crow'd i'th'Abbey, where a finger
Could not be wedg'd in more: I am stifled
With the meere ranknesse of their ioy.
2. GENTLEMAN
You saw the Ceremony?
3. GENTLEMAN   That I did.
1. GENTLEMAN How was it?
3. GENTLEMAN
Well worth the seeing.
2. GENTLEMAN   Good Sir, speake it to vs?
3. GENTLEMAN
As well as I am able. The rich streame
Of Lords, and Ladies, hauing brought the Queene
To a prepar'd place in the Quire, fell off
A distance from her; while her Grace sate downe   2020
To rest a while, some halfe an houre, or so,
In a rich Chaire of State, opposing freely
The Beauty of her Person to the People.

Beleeue me Sir, she is the goodliest Woman
That euer lay by man: which when the people
Had the full view of, such a noyse arose,
As the shrowdes make at Sea, in a stiffe Tempest,
As lowd, and to as many Tunes. Hats, Cloakes,
(Doublets, I thinke) flew vp, and had their Faces
Bin loose, this day they had beene lost. Such ioy
I neuer saw before. Great belly'd women,
That had not halfe a weeke to go, like Rammes
In the old time of Warre, would shake the prease
And make 'em reele before 'em. No man liuing
Could say this is my wife there, all were wouen
So strangely in one peece.

2030

2. GENTLEMAN   But what follow'd?

3. GENTLEMAN
At length, her Grace rose, and with modest paces
Came to the Altar, where she kneel'd, and Saint-like
Cast her faire eyes to Heauen, and pray'd deuoutly.
Then rose againe, and bow'd her to the people:
When by the Arch-byshop of Canterbury,
She had all the Royall makings of a Queene;
As holy Oyle, *Edward* Confessors Crowne,
The Rod, and Bird of Peace, and all such Emblemes
Laid Nobly on her: which perform'd, the Quire
With all the choysest Musicke of the Kingdome,
Together sung *Te Deum*. So she parted,
And with the same full State pac'd backe againe
To Yorke-Place, where the Feast is held.

2040

I. GENTLEMAN   Sir,
You must no more call it Yorke-place, that's past:
For since the Cardinall fell, that Titles lost,
'Tis now the Kings, and call'd White-Hall.

2050

3. GENTLEMAN   I know it:
But 'tis so lately alter'd, that the old name
Is fresh about me.

2. GENTLEMAN   What two Reuerend Byshops
Were those that went on each side of the Queene?

3. GENTLEMAN
Stokesley and *Gardiner*, the one of Winchester,
Newly preferr'd from the Kings Secretary:
The other London.

2. GENTLEMAN   He of Winchester
Is held no great good louer of the Archbishops,
The vertuous *Cranmer*.

2060 3. GENTLEMAN   All the Land knowes that:
How euer, yet there is no great breach, when it comes
Cranmer will finde a Friend will not shrinke from him.

2. GENTLEMAN
Who may that be, I pray you.

3. GENTLEMAN   *Thomas Cromwell*,
A man in much esteeme with th'King, and truly
A worthy Friend. The King ha's made him
Master o'th'Iewell House,
And one already of the Priuy Councell.

2. GENTLEMAN
He will deserue more.

3. GENTLEMAN   Yes without all doubt.

Come Gentlemen, ye shall go my way,
Which is to'th Court, and there ye shall be my Guests: 2070
Something I can command. As I walke thither,
Ile tell ye more.

I. *and* 2. GENTLEMEN You may command vs Sir.

Exeunt

⌈*Three Chaires.*⌉ *Enter Katherine Dowager, sicke,*   **4.2**
lead betweene Griffith, her Gentleman Vsher, and   (Sc. 12)
Patience her Woman

GRIFFITH
How do's your Grace?

KATHERINE   O *Griffith*, sicke to death:
My Legges like loaden Branches bow to'th'Earth,
Willing to leaue their burthen: Reach a Chaire,
    A Chaire is reached. She sits
So now (me thinkes) I feele a little ease.
Did'st thou not tell me *Griffith*, as thou lead'st mee,
That the great Childe of Honor, Cardinall *Wolsey*
Was dead?

GRIFFITH   Yes Madam: but I thinke your Grace
Out of the paine you suffer'd, gaue no eare too't.   2080

KATHERINE
Pre'thee good *Griffith*, tell me how he dy'de.
If well, he stept before me happily
For my example.

GRIFFITH   Well, the voyce goes Madam,
For after the stout Earle Northumberland
Arrested him at Yorke, and brought him forward
As a man sorely tainted, to his Answer,
He fell sicke sodainly, and grew so ill
He could not sit his Mule.

KATHERINE   Alas poore man.

GRIFFITH
At last, with easie Rodes, he came to Leicester,
Lodg'd in the Abbey; where the reuerend Abbot   2090
With all his Couent, honourably receiu'd him;
To whom he gaue these words. O Father Abbot,
An old man, broken with the stormes of State,
Is come to lay his weary bones among ye:
Giue him a little earth for Charity.
So went to bed; where eagerly his sicknesse
Pursu'd him still, and three nights after this,
About the houre of eight, which he himselfe
Foretold should be his last, full of Repentance,
Continuall Meditations, Teares, and Sorrowes,   2100
He gaue his Honors to the world agen,
His blessed part to Heauen, and slept in peace.

KATHERINE
So may he rest, his Faults lye gently on him:
Yet thus farre *Griffith*, giue me leaue to speake him,
And yet with Charity. He was a man
Of an vnbounded stomacke, euer ranking
Himselfe with Princes. One that by suggestion
Ty'de all the Kingdome. Symonie, was faire play,
His owne Opinion was his Law. I'th'presence
He would say vntruths, and be euer double   2110

Both in his words, and meaning. He was neuer
(But where he meant to Ruine) pittifull.
His Promises, were as he then was, Mighty:
But his performance, as he is now, Nothing:
Of his owne body he was ill, and gaue
The Clergy ill example.

GRIFFITH   Noble Madam:
Mens euill manners, liue in Brasse, their Vertues
We write in Water. May it please your Highnesse
To heare me speake his good now?

KATHERINE   Yes good *Griffith*,
I were malicious else.

2120 GRIFFITH   This Cardinall,
Though from an humble Stocke, vndoubtedly
Was fashion'd to much Honor. From his Cradle
He was a Scholler, and a ripe, and good one:
Exceeding wise, faire spoken, and perswading:
Lofty, and sowre to them that lou'd him not:
But, to those men that sought him, sweet as Summer.
And though he were vnsatisfied in getting,
(Which was a sinne) yet in bestowing, Madam,
He was most Princely: Euer witnesse for him
2130 Those twinnes of Learning, that he rais'd in you,
Ipswich and Oxford: one of which, fell with him,
Vnwilling to out-liue the good that did it.
The other (though vnfinish'd) yet so Famous,
So excellent in Art, and still so rising,
That Christendome shall euer speake his Vertue.
His Ouerthrow, heap'd Happinesse vpon him:
For then, and not till then, he felt himselfe,
And found the Blessednesse of being little.
And to adde greater Honors to his Age
2140 Then man could giue him; he dy'de, fearing God.

KATHERINE
After my death, I wish no other Herald,
No other speaker of my liuing Actions,
To keepe mine Honor, from Corruption,
But such an honest Chronicler as *Griffith*.
Whom I most hated Liuing, thou hast made mee
With thy Religious Truth, and Modestie,
(Now in his Ashes) Honor: Peace be with him.
(*To her Woman*) *Patience*, be neere me still, and set me
        lower,
I haue not long to trouble thee. Good *Griffith*,
2150 Cause the Musitians play me that sad note
I nam'd my Knell; whil'st I sit meditating
On that Cœlestiall Harmony I go too.
        Sad and solemne Musicke. Katherine sleepes

GRIFFITH (*to the Woman*)
She is asleep: Good wench, let's sit down quiet,
For feare we wake her. Softly, gentle *Patience*.
        They sit

                The Vision.
Enter solemnely tripping one after another, sixe
Personages, clad in white Robes, wearing on their
heades Garlands of Bayes, and golden Vizards on their
faces, Branches of Bayes or Palme in their hands.
They first Conge vnto Katherine, then Dance:

and at certaine Changes, the first two hold a spare
Garland ouer her Head, at which the other foure
make reuerend Curtsies. Then the two that held
the Garland, deliuer the same to the other next
two, who obserue the same order in their
Changes, and holding the Garland ouer her head.
Which done, they deliuer the same Garland to the
last two: who likewise obserue the same Order.
At which (as it were by inspiration) she makes
(in her sleepe) signes of reioycing, and holdeth
vp her hands to heauen. And so, in their Dancing
vanish, carrying the Garland with them. The
Musicke continues

KATHERINE (*waking*)
Spirits of peace, where are ye? Are ye all gone?
And leaue me heere in wretchednesse, behinde ye?
        Griffith and Patience rise and come forward

GRIFFITH
Madam, we are heere.

KATHERINE   It is not you I call for,
Saw ye none enter since I slept?

GRIFFITH   None Madam.

KATHERINE
No? Saw you not euen now a blessed Troope
Inuite me to a Banquet, whose bright faces   2160
Cast thousand beames vpon me, like the Sun?
They promis'd me eternall Happinesse,
And brought me Garlands (*Griffith*) which I feele
I am not worthy yet to weare: I shall
Assuredly.

GRIFFITH
I am most ioyfull Madam, such good dreames
Possesse your Fancy.

KATHERINE   Bid the Musicke leaue,
They are harsh and heauy to me.
        Musicke ceases

PATIENCE (*to Griffith*)   Do you note
How much her Grace is alter'd on the sodaine?
How long her face is drawne? How pale she lookes,   2170
And of an earthy colo^r? Marke her eyes?

GRIFFITH
She is going Wench. Pray, pray.

PATIENCE   Heauen comfort her.
        Enter a Messenger

MESSENGER (*to Katherine*)
And't like your Grace—

KATHERINE   You are a sawcy Fellow,
Deserue we no more Reuerence?

GRIFFITH (*to the Messenger*)   You are too blame,
Knowing she will not loose her wonted Greatnesse
To vse so rude behauiour. Go too, kneele.

MESSENGER (*kneeling before Katherine*)
I humbly do entreat your Highnesse pardon,
My hast made me vnmannerly. There is staying
A Gentleman sent from the King, to see you.

KATHERINE
Admit him entrance *Griffith*. But this Fellow   2180
Let me ne're see againe.   *Exit Messenger*
        Enter Lord Capuchius ⌜vsher'd by Griffith⌝
                        If my sight faile not,

1394

You should be Lord Ambassador from the Emperor,
My Royall Nephew, and your name *Capuchius*.
CAPUCHIUS
Madam the same. ⌜*Bowing*⌝ Your Seruant.
KATHERINE   O my Lord,
The Times and Titles now are alter'd strangely
With me, since first you knew me. But I pray you,
What is your pleasure with me?
CAPUCHIUS   Noble Lady,
First mine owne seruice to your Grace, the next
The Kings request, that I would visit you,
2190   Who greeues much for your weaknesse, and by me
Sends you his Princely Commendations,
And heartily entreats you take good comfort.
KATHERINE
O my good Lord, that comfort comes too late,
'Tis like a Pardon after Execution;
That gentle Physicke giuen in time, had cur'd me:
But now I am past all Comforts heere, but Prayers.
How does his Highnesse?
CAPUCHIUS   Madam, in good health.
KATHERINE
So may he euer do, and euer flourish,
When I shall dwell with Wormes, and my poore name
Banish'd the Kingdome. (*To her Woman*) *Patience*, is
2200   that Letter
I caus'd you write, yet sent away?
PATIENCE   No Madam.
KATHERINE (*to Capuchius*)
Sir, I most humbly pray you to deliuer
This to my Lord the King.
          The Letter is giuen to Capuchius
CAPUCHIUS   Most willing Madam.
KATHERINE
In which I haue commended to his goodnesse
The Modell of our chaste loues: his yong daughter,
The dewes of Heauen fall thicke in Blessings on her,
Beseeching him to giue her vertuous breeding.
She is yong, and of a Noble modest Nature,
I hope she will deserue well; and a little
2210   To loue her for her Mothers sake, that lou'd him,
Heauen knowes how deerely. My next poore Petition,
Is, that his Noble Grace would haue some pittie
Vpon my wretched women, that so long
Haue follow'd both my Fortunes, faithfully,
Of which there is not one, I dare auow
(And now I should not lye) but will deserue
For Vertue, and true Beautie of the Soule,
For honestie, and decent Carriage
A right good Husband (let him be a Noble)
2220   And sure those men are happy that shall haue 'em.
The last is for my men, they are the poorest,
(But pouerty could neuer draw 'em from me)
That they may haue their wages, duly paid 'em,
And something ouer to remember me by.
If Heauen had pleas'd to haue giuen me longer life
And able meanes, we had not parted thus.
These are the whole Contents, and good my Lord,
By that you loue the deerest in this world,

As you wish Christian peace to soules departed,
Stand these poore peoples Friend, and vrge the King   2230
To do me this last right.
CAPUCHIUS   By Heauen I will,
Or let me loose the fashion of a man.
KATHERINE
I thanke you honest Lord. Remember me
In all humilitie vnto his Highnesse:
Say his long trouble now is passing
Out of this world. Tell him in death I blest him
(For so I will) mine eyes grow dimme. Farewell
My Lord. *Griffith* farewell. (*To her Woman*) Nay *Patience*,
You must not leaue me yet. I must to bed,
Call in more women. When I am dead, good Wench,   2240
Let me be vs'd with Honor; strew me ouer
With Maiden Flowers, that all the world may know
I was a chaste Wife, to my Graue: Embalme me,
Then lay me forth (although vnqueen'd) yet like
A Queene, and Daughter to a King enterre me.
I can no more.
          Exeunt ⌜*Capuchius and Griffith at one doore,*
            Patience⌝ *leading Katherine* ⌜*at another*⌝

          Enter ⌜*at one doore*⌝ *Gardiner Bishop of Winchester,*   5.1
          a Page with a Torch before him   (Sc. 13)
GARDINER
It's one a clocke Boy, is't not.
PAGE   It hath strooke.
GARDINER
These should be houres for necessities,
Not for delights: Times to repayre our Nature
With comforting repose, and not for vs   2250
To waste these times.
          Enter ⌜*at another doore*⌝ *Sir Thomas Louell, meeting*
          them
                              Good houre of night Sir *Thomas*:
Whether so late?
LOUELL   Came you from the King, my Lord?
GARDINER
I did Sir *Thomas*, and left him at Primero
With the Duke of Suffolke.
LOUELL   I must to him too
Before he go to bed. Ile take my leaue.
GARDINER
Not yet Sir *Thomas Louell*: what's the matter?
It seemes you are in hast: and if there be
No great offence belongs too't, giue your Friend
Some touch of your late businesse: Affaires that walke
(As they say Spirits do) at midnight, haue   2260
In them a wilder Nature, then the businesse
That seekes dispatch by day.
LOUELL   My Lord, I loue you;
And durst commend a secret to your eare
Much waightier then this worke. The Queens in Labor,
They say in great Extremity, and fear'd
Shee'l with the Labour, end.
GARDINER   The fruite she goes with
I pray for heartily, that it may finde

Good time, and liue: but for the Stocke Sir *Thomas*,
I wish it grubb'd vp now.

LOUELL   Me thinkes I could

2270   Cry the Amen, and yet my Conscience sayes
Shee's a good Creature, and sweet-Ladie do's
Deserue our better wishes.

GARDINER   But Sir, Sir,

Heare me Sir *Thomas*, y'are a Gentleman
Of mine owne way. I know you Wise, Religious,
And let me tell you, it will ne're be well,
'Twill not Sir *Thomas Louell*, tak't of me,
Till *Cranmer*, *Cromwel*, her two hands, and shee
Sleepe in their Graues.

LOUELL   Now Sir, you speake of two

The most remark'd i'th'Kingdome: as for *Cromwell*,
2280   Beside that of the Iewell-House, is made Master
O'th'Rolles, and the Kings Secretary. Further Sir,
Stands in the gap and Trade of moe Preferments,
With which the time will loade him. Th'Archbyshop
Is the Kings hand, and tongue, and who dare speake
One syllable against him?

GARDINER   Yes, yes, Sir *Thomas*,

There are that Dare, and I my selfe haue ventur'd
To speake my minde of him: and indeed this day,
Sir (I may tell it you I thinke) I haue
2290   Incenst the Lords o'th'Councell, that he is
(For so I know he is, they know he is)
A most Arch-Heretique, a Pestilence
That does infect the Land: with which, they moued
Haue broken with the King, who hath so farre
Giuen eare to our Complaint, of his great Grace,
And Princely Care, fore-seeing those fell Mischiefes,
Our Reasons layd before him, hath commanded
To morrow Morning to the Councell Boord
He be conuented. He's a ranke weed Sir *Thomas*,
2300   And we must root him out. From your Affaires
I hinder you too long: Good night, Sir *Thomas*.

LOUELL

Many good nights, my Lord, I rest your seruant.

                    Exit Gardiner and Page at one doore
           Enter King and Suffolke at another doore

KING (*to Suffolke*)

Charles, I will play no more to night,
My mindes not on't, you are too hard for me.

SUFFOLKE

Sir, I did neuer win of you before.

KING But little *Charles*,

Nor shall not when my Fancies on my play.
Now *Louel*, from the Queene what is the Newes.

LOUELL

I could not personally deliuer to her
What you commanded me, but by her woman,
2310   I sent your Message, who return'd her thankes
In the great'st humblenesse, and desir'd your Highnesse
Most heartily to pray for her.

KING   What say'st thou? Ha?

To pray for her? What is she crying out?

LOUELL

So said her woman, and that her suffrance made
Almost each pang, a death.

KING   Alas good Lady.

SUFFOLKE

God safely quit her of her Burthen, and
With gentle Trauaile, to the gladding of
Your Highnesse with an Heire.

KING   'Tis midnight *Charles*,

Prythee to bed, and in thy Prayres remember
Th'estate of my poore Queene. Leaue me alone,   2320
For I must thinke of that, which company
Would not be friendly too.

SUFFOLKE   I wish your Highnesse

A quiet night, and my good Mistris will
Remember in my Prayers.

KING   *Charles* good night.

                              Exit Suffolke
           Enter Sir Anthony Denny
Well Sir, what followes?

DENNY

Sir, I haue brought my Lord the Arch-byshop,
As you commanded me.

KING   Ha? Canterbury?

DENNY

I my good Lord.

KING   'Tis true: where is he *Denny*?

DENNY

He attends your Highnesse pleasure.

KING   Bring him to Vs.

                              Exit Denny

LOUELL (*aside*)

This is about that, which the Byshop spake,   2330
I am happily come hither.

           Enter Cranmer the Archbishop and Denny

KING (*to Louell and Denny*) Auoyd the Gallery.

           ⌈*Denny offers to depart.*⌉ *Louel seemes to stay*
Ha? I haue said. Be gone.
What?   *Exeunt Louell and Denny*

CRANMER (*aside*)

           I am fearefull: Wherefore frownes he thus?
'Tis his Aspect of Terror. All's not well.

KING

How now my Lord? You do desire to know
Wherefore I sent for you.

CRANMER (*kneeling*)   It is my dutie

T'attend your Highnesse pleasure.

KING   Pray you arise

My good and gracious Lord of Canterburie:
Come, you and I must walke a turne together: 2340
I haue Newes to tell you. Come, come, giue me your
           hand.

           ⌈*Cranmer rises. They walke*⌉
Ah my good Lord, I greeue at what I speake,
And am right sorrie to repeat what followes.
I haue, and most vnwillingly of late
Heard many greeuous, I do say my Lord

Greeuous complaints of you; which being consider'd,
Haue mou'd Vs, and our Councell, that you shall
This Morning come before vs, where I know
You cannot with such freedome purge your selfe,
2350 But that till further Triall, in those Charges
Which will require your Answer, you must take
Your patience to you, and be well contented
To make your house our Towre: you, a Brother of vs
It fits we thus proceed, or else no witnesse
Would come against you.

CRANMER *(kneeling)*   I humbly thanke your Highnesse,
And am right glad to catch this good occasion
Most throughly to be winnowed, where my Chaffe
And Corne shall flye asunder. For I know
There's none stands vnder more calumnious tongues,
Then I my selfe, poore man.

2360 KING   Stand vp, good Canterbury,
Thy Truth, and thy Integrity is rooted
In vs thy Friend. Giue me thy hand, stand vp,
Prythee let's walke.
          Cranmer rises. They walke
                    Now by my Holydame,
What manner of man are you? My Lord, I look'd
You would haue giuen me your Petition, that
I should haue tane some paines, to bring together
Your selfe, and your Accusers, and to haue heard you
Without indurance further.

CRANMER   Most dread Liege,
The good I stand on, is my Truth and Honestie:
2370 If they shall faile, I with mine Enemies
Will triumph o're my person, which I waigh not,
Being of those Vertues vacant. I feare nothing
What can be said against me.

KING   Know you not
How your state stands i'th'world, with the whole
     world?
Your Enemies are many, and not small; their practises
Must beare the same proportion, and not euer
The Iustice and the Truth o'th'question carries
The dew o'th'Verdict with it; at what ease
Might corrupt mindes procure, Knaues as corrupt
2380 To sweare against you: Such things haue bene done.
You are Potently oppos'd, and with a Malice
Of as great Size. Weene you of better lucke,
I meane in periur'd Witnesse, then your Master,
Whose Minister you are, whiles heere he liu'd
Vpon this naughty Earth? Go too, go too,
You take a Precepic for no leape of danger,
And woe your owne destruction.

CRANMER   God, and your Maiesty
Protect mine innocence, or I fall into
The trap is laid for me.

KING   Be of good cheere,
2390 They shall no more preuaile, then we giue way too:
Keepe comfort to you, and this Morning see
You do appeare before them. If they shall chance
In charging you with matters, to commit you:
The best perswasions to the contrary

Faile not to vse, and with what vehemencie
Th'occasion shall instruct you. If intreaties
Will render you no remedy, ⌈*giuing his Ring*⌉ this Ring
Deliuer them, and your Appeale to vs
There make before them.
          Cranmer weeps
                    Looke, the goodman weeps:
He's honest on mine Honor. Gods blest Mother,   2400
I sweare he is true-hearted, and a soule
None better in my Kingdome. Get you gone,
And do as I haue bid you.   *Exit Cranmer*
                    He ha's strangled
His Language in his teares.
          Enter Olde Lady
⌈LOUELL⌉ *(within)*   Come backe: what meane you?
          ⌈*Enter Louell following*⌉
OLD LADY
Ile not come backe, the tydings that I bring
Will make my boldnesse, manners.
(To the King)   Now good Angels
Fly o're thy Royall head, and shade thy person
Vnder their blessed wings.

KING   Now by thy lookes
I gesse thy Message. Is the Queene deliuer'd?
Say I, and of a boy.

OLD LADY   I, I my Liege,   2410
And of a louely Boy: the God of heauen
Both now, and euer blesse her: 'Tis a Gyrle
Promises Boyes heereafter. Sir, your Queen
Desires your Visitation, and to be
Acquainted with this stranger; 'tis as like you,
As Cherry, is to Cherry.

KING   Louell.

LOUELL   Sir.

KING
Giue her an hundred Markes. Ile to the Queene.
                              Exit King
OLD LADY
An hundred Markes? By this light, Ile ha more.
An ordinary Groome is for such payment.
I will haue more, or scold it out of him.   2420
Said I for this, the Gyrle was like to him? Ile
Haue more, or else vnsay't: and now, while 'tis hot,
Ile put it to the issue.   *Exeunt Ladie and Louell*

          Enter ⌈*Purseuants, Pages, Foot-boyes, and Groomes.*   **5.2**
          Then enter⌉ *Cranmer, Archbyshop of Canterbury*   (Sc. 14)
CRANMER
I hope I am not too late, and yet the Gentleman
That was sent to me from the Councell, pray'd me
To make great hast. All fast? What meanes this?
          (Calling at the doore) Hoa?
Who waites there?
          Enter Keeper
                    Sure you know me?
KEEPER   Yes, my Lord:
But yet I cannot helpe you.
CRANMER   Why?

⌈*Enter Doctor Buts, passing ouer the Stage*⌉

KEEPER

Your Grace must waight till you be call'd for.

CRANMER   So.

BUTS (*aside*)

2430 This is a Peece of Malice: I am glad
I came this way so happily. The King
Shall vnderstand it presently.   *Exit Buts*

CRANMER (*aside*)   'Tis *Buts*,
The Kings Physitian. As he past along
How earnestly he cast his eyes vpon me:
Pray heauen he found not my disgrace: for certaine
This is of purpose laid by some that hate me,
(God turne their hearts, I neuer sought their malice)
To quench mine Honor; they would shame to make me
Wait else at doore: a fellow Councellor
2440 'Mong Boyes, Groomes, and Lackeyes. But their pleasures
Must be fulfill'd, and I attend with patience.

Enter the King, and Buts, at a Windowe aboue

BUTS

Ile shew your Grace the strangest sight.

KING   What's that *Buts*?

BUTS

I thinke your Highnesse saw this many a day.

KING

Body a me: where is it?

BUTS (*pointing at Cranmer, below*) There my Lord:
The high promotion of his Grace of *Canterbury*,
Who holds his State at dore 'mongst Purseuants,
Pages, and Foot-boyes.

KING   Ha? 'Tis he indeed.
Is this the Honour they doe one another?
'Tis well there's one aboue 'em yet; I had thought
2450 They had parted so much honesty among 'em,
At least good manners; as not thus to suffer
A man of his Place, and so neere our fauour
To dance attendance on their Lordships pleasures,
And at the dore too, like a Post with Packets:
By holy *Mary* (*Butts*) there's knauery;
Let 'em alone, and draw the Curtaine close:
We shall heare more anon.

⌈*Cranmer and the Keeper stand to one side.*
Exeunt the Lackeyes⌉
Aboue, Buts ⌈*partly*⌉ *drawes the Curtaine close.*
Below, a Councell Table brought in with Chayres
and Stooles, and placed vnder the State. Enter Lord
Chancellour, places himselfe at the vpper end of the
Table, on the left hand: A Seate being left void
aboue him, as for Canterburies Seate. Duke of
Suffolke, Duke of Norfolke, Surrey, Lord
Chamberlaine, Gardiner, seat themselues in
Order on each side. Cromwell at lower end,
as Secretary

CHANCELLOUR (*to Cromwell*)

Speake to the businesse, M. Secretary;
Why are we met in Councell?

CROMWELL   Please your Honours,
2460 The chiefe cause concernes his Grace of *Canterbury*.

GARDINER

Ha's he had knowledge of it?

CROMWELL   Yes.

NORFOLKE (*to the Keeper*)   Who waits there?

KEEPER ⌈*comming forward*⌉

Without my Noble Lords?

GARDINER   Yes.

KEEPER   My Lord Archbishop:
And ha's done halfe an houre to know your pleasures.

CHANCELLOUR

Let him come in.

KEEPER (*to Cranmer*) Your Grace may enter now.

Cranmer approches the Councell Table

CHANCELLOUR

My good Lord Archbishop, I'm very sorry
To sit heere at this present, and behold
That Chayre stand empty: But we all are men
In our owne natures fraile, and capable
Of our flesh, few are Angels; out of which frailty
And want of wisedome, you that best should teach vs, 2470
Haue misdemean'd your selfe, and not a little:
Toward the King first, then his Lawes, in filling
The whole Realme, by your teaching & your Chaplaines
(For so we are inform'd) with new opinions,
Diuers and dangerous; which are Heresies;
And not reform'd, may proue pernicious.

GARDINER

Which Reformation must be sodaine too
My Noble Lords; for those that tame wild Horses,
Pace 'em not in their hands to make 'em gentle;
But stop their mouthes with stubborn Bits & spurre 'em, 2480
Till they obey the mannage. If we suffer
Out of our easinesse and childish pitty
To one mans Honour, this contagious sicknesse;
Farewell all Physicke: and what followes then?
Commotions, vprores, with a generall Taint
Of the whole State; as of late dayes our neighbours,
The vpper *Germany* can deerely witnesse:
Yet freshly pittied in our memories.

CRANMER

My good Lords; Hitherto, in all the Progresse
Both of my Life and Office, I haue labour'd,   2490
And with no little study, that my teaching
And the strong course of my Authority,
Might goe one way, and safely; and the end
Was euer to doe well: nor is there liuing,
(I speake it with a single heart, my Lords)
A man that more detests, more stirres against,
Both in his priuate Conscience, and his place,
Defacers of a publique peace then I doe:
Pray Heauen the King may neuer find a heart
With lesse Allegeance in it. Men that make   2500
Enuy, and crooked malice, nourishment;
Dare bite the best. I doe beseech your Lordships,
That in this case of Iustice, my Accusers,
Be what they will, may stand forth face to face,
And freely vrge against me.

SUFFOLKE   Nay, my Lord,

That cannot be; you are a Counsellor,
And by that vertue no man dare accuse you.

GARDINER *(to Cranmer)*

My Lord, because we haue busines of more moment,
We will be short with you. 'Tis his Highnesse pleasure
2510 And our consent, for better tryall of you,
From hence you be committed to the Tower,
Where being but a priuate man againe,
You shall know many dare accuse you boldly,
More then (I feare) you are prouided for.

CRANMER

Ah my good Lord of *Winchester*: I thanke you,
You are alwayes my good Friend, if your will passe,
I shall both finde your Lordship, Iudge and Iuror,
You are so mercifull. I see your end,
'Tis my vndoing. Loue and meekenesse, Lord
2520 Become a Churchman, better then Ambition:
Win straying Soules with modesty againe,
Cast none away: That I shall cleere my selfe,
Lay all the weight ye can vpon my patience,
I make as little doubt as you doe conscience,
In doing dayly wrongs. I could say more,
But reuerence to your calling, makes me modest.

GARDINER

My Lord, my Lord, you are a Sectary,
That's the plaine truth; your painted glosse discouers
To men that vnderstand you, words and weaknesse.

CROMWELL *(to Gardiner)*

2530 My Lord of *Winchester*, y'are a little,
By your good fauour, too sharpe; Men so Noble,
How euer faulty, yet should finde respect
For what they haue beene: 'tis a cruelty,
To load a falling man.

GARDINER   Good M. Secretary,
I cry your Honour mercie; you may worst
Of all this Table say so.

CROMWELL   Why my Lord?

GARDINER

Doe not I know you for a Fauourer
Of this new Sect? ye are not sound.

CROMWELL   Not sound?

GARDINER

Not sound I say.

CROMWELL   Would you were halfe so honest:
2540 Mens prayers then would seeke you, not their feares.

GARDINER

I shall remember this bold Language.

CROMWELL   Doe.
Remember your bold life too.

CHANCELLOUR   This is too much;
Forbeare for shame my Lords.

GARDINER   I haue done.

CROMWELL   And I.

CHANCELLOUR *(to Cranmer)*

Then thus for you my Lord, it stands agreed
I take it, by all voyces: That forthwith,
You be conuaid to th'Tower a Prisoner;

There to remaine till the Kings further pleasure
Be knowne vnto vs: are you all agreed Lords.

ALL THE COUNCELL

We are.

CRANMER Is there no other way of mercy,
But I must needs to th'Tower my Lords?

GARDINER   What other,   2550
Would you expect? You are strangely troublesome:
Let some o'th'Guard be ready there.
        Enter the Guard

CRANMER   For me?
Must I goe like a Traytor thither?

GARDINER *(to the Guard)*   Receiue him,
And see him safe i'th'Tower.

CRANMER   Stay good my Lords,
I haue a little yet to say. Looke there my Lords,
        He shewes the Kings Ring
By vertue of that Ring, I take my cause
Out of the gripes of cruell men, and giue it
To a most Noble Iudge, the King my Maister.

CHAMBERLAINE

This is the Kings Ring.

SURREY   'Tis no counterfeit.

SUFFOLKE

'Tis the right Ring, by Heau'n: I told ye all,   2560
When we first put this dangerous stone a rowling,
'Twold fall vpon our selues.

NORFOLKE   Doe you thinke my Lords
The King will suffer but the little finger
Of this man to be vex'd?

CHAMBERLAINE   Tis now too certaine;
How much more is his Life in value with him?
Would I were fairely out on't.
                    ⌈*Exit King with Buts aboue*⌉

CROMWELL   My mind gaue me,
In seeking tales and Informations
Against this man, whose honesty the Diuell
And his Disciples onely enuy at,
Ye blew the fire that burnes ye: now haue at ye.   2570
        *Enter, below, King frowning on them, takes his
        Seate*

GARDINER

Dread Soueraigne, how much are we bound to
        Heauen,
In dayly thankes, that gaue vs such a Prince;
Not onely good and wise, but most religious:
One that in all obedience, makes the Church
The cheefe ayme of his Honour, and to strengthen
That holy duty out of deare respect,
His Royall selfe in Iudgement comes to heare
The cause betwixt her, and this great offender.

KING

You were euer good at sodaine Commendations,
Bishop of *Winchester*. But know I come not   2580
To heare such flattery now, and in my presence
They are too thin, and base to hide offences,
To me you cannot reach. You play the Spaniell,

And thinke with wagging of your tongue to win me:
But whatsoere thou tak'st me for; I'm sure
Thou hast a cruell Nature and a bloody.
(*To Cranmer*) Good man sit downe:
   Cranmer takes his Seate at the Councell Table
       Now let me see the proudest,
Hee, that dares most, but wag his finger at thee.
By all that's holy, he had better starue,
2590 Then but once thinke this place becomes thee not.

SURREY

May it please your Grace;—

KING   No Sir, it doe's not please me,
I had thought, I had had men of some vnderstanding,
And wisedome of my Councell; but I finde none:
Was it discretion Lords, to let this man,
This good man (few of you deserue that Title)
This honest man, wait like a lowsie Foot-boy
At Chamber dore? and one, as great as you are?
Why, what a shame was this? Did my Commission
Bid ye so farre forget your selues? I gaue ye
2600 Power, as he was a Counsellour to try him,
Not as a Groome: There's some of ye, I see,
More out of Malice then Integrity,
Would trye him to the vtmost, had ye meane,
Which ye shall neuer haue while I liue.

CHANCELLOUR   Thus farre
My most dread Soueraigne, may it like your Grace,
To let my tongue excuse all. What was purpos'd
Concerning his Imprisonment, was rather
(If there be faith in men) meant for his Tryall,
And faire purgation to the world then malice,
I'm sure in me.

2610 KING   Well, well my Lords respect him,
Take him, and vse him well; hee's worthy of it.
I will say thus much for him, if a Prince
May be beholding to a Subiect; I
Am for his loue and seruice, so to him.
Make me no more adoe, but all embrace him;
Be friends for shame my Lords: (*To Cranmer*) My Lord
  of *Canterbury*
I haue a Suite which you must not deny mee.
That is, a faire young Maid that yet wants Baptisme,
You must be Godfather, and answere for her.

CRANMER
2620 The greatest Monarch now aliue may glory
In such an honour: how may I deserue it,
That am a poore and humble Subiect to you?

KING Come, come my Lord, you'd spare your spoones;
You shall haue two noble Partners with you: the old
Duchesse of *Norfolke*, and Lady Marquesse *Dorset*? will
these please you?
(*To Gardiner*) Once more my Lord of *Winchester*, I
  charge you
Embrace, and loue this man.

GARDINER   With a true heart,
And Brother-loue I doe it.
   ⌈*Gardiner and Cranmer embrace*⌉

CRANMER (*weeping*)   And let Heauen
2630 Witnesse how deare, I hold this Confirmation.

KING

Good Man, those ioyfull teares shew thy true heart,
The common voyce I see is verified
Of thee, which sayes thus: Doe my Lord of *Canterbury*
A shrewd turne, and hee's your friend for euer:
Come Lords, we trifle time away: I long
To haue this young one made a Christian.
As I haue made ye one Lords, one remaine:
So I grow stronger, you more Honour gaine. *Exeunt*

  Noyse and Tumult within: Enter Porter ⌈*with* **5.3**
  Rushes⌉ *and his man* ⌈*with a broken Cudgell*⌉ (Sc. 15

PORTER (*to those within*)
You'l leaue your noyse anon ye Rascals: doe you take
The Court for Parish Garden: ye rude Slaues, 2640
Leaue your gaping.

ONE (*within*)
Good M. Porter I belong to th'Larder.

PORTER
Belong to th'Gallowes, and be hang'd ye Rogue:
Is this a place to roare in?
(*To his Man*)
Fetch me a dozen Crab-tree staues, and strong ones;
⌈*Raising his Rushes*⌉ These are but switches to 'em:
(*To those within*)   Ile scratch your heads;
You must be seeing Christenings? Do you looke
For Ale, and Cakes heere, you rude Raskalls?

MAN
Pray Sir be patient; 'tis as much impossible,
Vnlesse wee sweepe 'em from the dore with Cannons, 2650
To scatter 'em, as 'tis to make 'em sleepe
On May-day Morning, which will neuer be:
We may as well push against Powles as stirre 'em.

PORTER How got they in, and be hang'd?

MAN
Alas I know not, how gets the Tide in?
As much as one sound Cudgell of foure foote,
  He raises his Cudgell
(You see the poore remainder) could distribute,
I made no spare Sir.

PORTER   You did nothing Sir.

MAN
I am not *Sampson*, nor Sir *Guy*, nor *Colebrand*,
To mow 'em downe before me: but if I spar'd any 2660
That had a head to hit, either young or old,
He or shee, Cuckold or Cuckold-maker:
Let me ne're hope to see a Chine againe,
And that I would not for a Cow, God saue her.

ONE (*within*) Do you heare M. Porter?

PORTER
I shall be with you presently,
Good M. *Puppy*, (*to his Man*) keepe the dore close Sirha.

MAN
What would you haue me doe?

PORTER   What should you doe,
But knock 'em downe by th' dozens? Is this More fields
to muster in? Or haue wee some strange Indian with 2670
the great *Toole*, come to Court, the women so besiege
vs? Blesse me, what a fry of Fornication is at dore? On

my Christian Conscience this one Christening will beget
a thousand, here will bee Father, God-father, and all
together.

MAN The Spoones will be the bigger Sir: There is a fellow
somewhat neere the doore, he should be a Brasier by
his face, for o' my conscience twenty of the Dog-dayes
now reigne in's Nose; all that stand about him are
2680 vnder the Line, they need no other pennance: that
Fire-Drake did I hit three times on the head, and three
times was his Nose discharged against mee; hee stands
there like a Morter-piece to blow vs. There was a
Habberdashers Wife of small wit, neere him, that rail'd
vpon me, till her pinck'd porrenger fell off her head,
for kindling such a combustion in the State. I mist the
Meteor once, and hit that Woman, who cryed out
Clubbes, when I might see from farre, some forty
Truncheoners draw to her succour, which were the
2690 hope o'th' Strond where she was quartered; they fell
on, I made good my place; at length they came to th'
broome staffe to me, I defide 'em stil, when sodainly a
File of Boyes behind'em, loose shot, deliuer'd such a
showre of Pibbles, that I was faine to draw mine
Honour in, and let 'em win the Worke, the Diuell was
amongst 'em I thinke surely.

PORTER These are the youths that thunder at a Playhouse,
and fight for bitten Apples, that no Audience but the
tribulation of Tower Hill, or the Limbes of Limehouse,
2700 their deare Brothers are able to endure. I haue some
of 'em in *Limbo Patrum*, and there they are like to
dance these three dayes; besides the running Banquet
of two Beadles, that is to come.

Enter Lord Chamberlaine

CHAMBERLAINE
Mercy o' me: what a Multitude are heere?
They grow still too; from all Parts they are comming,
As if we kept a Faire heere? Where are these Porters?
These lazy knaues? (*To the Porter and his Man*) Y'haue
    made a fine hand fellowes?
Theres a trim rabble let in: are all these
Your faithfull friends o'th'Suburbs? We shall haue
2710 Great store of roome no doubt, left for the Ladies,
When they passe backe from the Christening?

PORTER   And't please your Honour,
We are but men; and what so many may doe,
Not being torne a pieces, we haue done:
An Army cannot rule 'em.

CHAMBERLAINE   As I liue,
If the King blame me for't; Ile lay ye all
By th'heeles, and sodainly: and on your heads
Clap round Fines for neglect: y'are lazy knaues,
And heere ye lye baiting of Bombards, when
Ye should doe Seruice.

Flourish of Trumpets within
                                Harke the Trumpets sound,
2720 Th'are come already from the Christening,
Go breake among the preasse, and finde a way out
To let the Troope passe fairely; or Ile finde
A Marshallsey, shall hold ye play these two Monthes.

⌐As they leaue, the Porter and his Man call within⌐
PORTER
Make way there, for the Princesse.
MAN   You great fellow,
Stand close vp, or Ile make your head ake.
PORTER
You i'th'Chamblet, get vp o'th'raile,
Ile pecke you o're the pales else.   *Exeunt*

Enter Trumpets sounding: Then two Aldermen, L.   5.4
Maior, Garter, Cranmer, Duke of Norfolke with his   (Sc. 16)
Marshals Staffe, Duke of Suffolke, two Noblemen,
bearing great standing Bowles for the Christening
Guifts: Then foure Noblemen bearing a Canopy,
vnder which the Dutchesse of Norfolke, Godmother,
bearing the Childe Elizabeth richly habited in a
Mantle. Traine borne by a Lady: Then followes the
Marchionesse Dorset, the other Godmother,
and Ladies. The Troope passe once about the Stage,
and Garter speakes

GARTER Heauen from thy endlesse goodnesse, send prosperous life, long, and euer happie, to the high and
Mighty Princesse of England *Elizabeth*.   2730

Flourish. Enter King and Guard

CRANMER (*kneeling*)
And to your Royall Grace, & the good Queen,
My Noble Partners, and my selfe thus pray
All comfort, ioy in this most gracious Lady,
Heauen euer laid vp to make Parents happy,
May hourely fall vpon ye.

KING   Thanke you good Lord Archbishop:
What is her Name?

CRANMER   *Elizabeth*.

KING   Stand vp Lord,

Cranmer rises

(*To the Childe*) With this Kisse, take my Blessing:

He kisses the Childe

                                God protect thee,
Into whose hand, I giue thy Life.

CRANMER   Amen.

KING (*to Cranmer, old Dutchesse, and Marchionesse*)
My Noble Gossips, y'haue beene too Prodigall;
I thanke ye heartily: So shall this Lady,   2740
When she ha's so much English.

CRANMER   Let me speake Sir,
For Heauen now bids me; and the words I vtter,
Let none thinke Flattery; for they'l finde 'em Truth.
This Royall Infant, Heauen still moue about her;
Though in her Cradle; yet now promises
Vpon this Land a thousand thousand Blessings,
Which Time shall bring to ripenesse: She shall be,
(But few now liuing can behold that goodnesse)
A Patterne to all Princes liuing with her,
And all that shall succeed: *Saba* was neuer   2750
More couetous of Wisedome, and faire Vertue
Then this pure Soule shall be. All Princely Graces
That mould vp such a mighty Piece as this is,
With all the Vertues that attend the good,

Shall still be doubled on her. Truth shall Nurse her,
Holy and Heauenly thoughts still Counsell her:
She shall be lou'd and fear'd. Her owne shall blesse her;
Her Foes shake like a Field of beaten Corne,
And hang their heads with sorrow: Good growes with
    her.
2760   In her dayes, Euery Man shall eate in safety,
Vnder his owne Vine what he plants; and sing
The merry Songs of Peace to all his Neighbours.
God shall be truely knowne, and those about her,
From her shall read the perfect ways of Honour,
And by those claime their greatnesse; not by Blood.
Nor shall this peace sleepe with her: But as when
The Bird of Wonder dyes, the Mayden Phoenix,
Her Ashes new create another Heyre,
As great in admiration as her selfe,
2770   So shall she leaue her Blessednesse to One,
(When Heauen shal call her from this clowd of darknes)
Who, from the sacred Ashes of her Honour
Shall Star-like rise, as great in fame as she was,
And so stand fix'd. Peace, Plenty, Loue, Truth, Terror,
That were the Seruants to this chosen Infant,
Shall then be his, and like a Vine grow to him;
Where euer the bright Sunne of Heauen shall shine,
His Honour, and the greatnesse of his Name,
Shall be, and make new Nations. He shall flourish,
2780   And like a Mountaine Cedar, reach his branches,
To all the Plaines about him: Our Childrens Children
Shall see this, and blesse Heauen.
KING   Thou speakest wonders.
CRANMER
She shall be to the happinesse of England,
An aged Princesse; many dayes shall see her,
And yet no day without a deed to Crowne it.
Would I had knowne no more: But she must dye,

She must, the Saints must haue her; yet a Virgin,
A most vnspotted Lilly shall she passe
To th' ground, and all the World shall mourne her.
KING O Lord Archbishop   2790
Thou hast made me now a man, neuer before
This happy Child, did I get any thing.
This Oracle of comfort, ha's so pleas'd me,
That when I am in Heauen, I shall desire
To see what this Child does, and praise my Maker.
I thanke ye all. To you my good Lord Maior,
And your good Brethren, I am much beholding:
I haue receiu'd much Honour by your presence,
And ye shall find me thankfull. Lead the way Lords,
Ye must all see the Queene, and she must thanke ye,   2800
She will be sicke els. This day, no man thinke
'Has businesse at his house; for all shall stay:
This Little-One shall make it Holy-day.
                              ⌈Flourish.⌉ Exeunt

        Enter Epilogue   Epilogue
EPILOGUE
Tis ten to one, this Play can neuer please
All that are heere: Some come to take their ease,
And sleepe an Act or two; but those we feare
W'haue frighted with our Trumpets: so 'tis cleare,
They'l say tis naught. Others to heare the City
Abus'd extreamly, and to cry that's witty,
Which wee haue not done neither; that I feare   2810
All the expected good w'are like to heare
For this Play at this time, is onely in
The mercifull construction of good women,
For such a one we shew'd 'em: If they smile,
And say twill doe; I know within a while,
*   All the best men are ours; for 'tis ill hap,*
*   If they hold, when their Ladies bid 'em clap.*   Exit

                      FINIS

THE TWO NOBLE KINSMEN

BY JOHN FLETCHER AND WILLIAM SHAKESPEARE

WHEN it first appeared in print, in 1634, *The Two Noble Kinsmen* was stated to be 'by the memorable Worthies of their time; Mr John Fletcher, and Mr William Shakspeare'. There is no reason to disbelieve this ascription: many plays of the period were not printed till long after they were acted, and there is other evidence that Shakespeare collaborated with Fletcher (1579-1625). The morris dance in Act 3, Scene 5, contains characters who also appear in Francis Beaumont's *Masque of the Inner Temple and Grayes Inn* performed before James I on 20 February 1613. Their dance was a great success with the King; probably the King's Men—some of whom may have taken part in the masque—decided to exploit its success by incorporating it in a play written soon afterwards, in the last year of Shakespeare's playwriting life.

The Two Noble Kinsmen, a tragicomedy of the kind that became popular during the last years of the first decade of the seventeenth century, is based on Chaucer's *Knight's Tale*, on which Shakespeare had already drawn for episodes of *A Midsommer nights dreame*. It tells a romantic tale of the conflicting claims of love and friendship: the 'two noble kinsmen', Palamon and Arcite, are the closest of friends until each falls in love with Emilia, sister-in-law of Theseus, Duke of Athens. Their conflict is finally resolved by a formal combat with Emilia as the prize, in which the loser is to be executed. Arcite wins, and Palamon's head is on the block as news arrives that Arcite has been thrown from his horse. Dying, Arcite commends Emilia to his friend, and Theseus rounds off the play with a meditation on the paradoxes of fortune.

Studies of style suggest that Shakespeare was primarily responsible for the rhetorically and ritualistically impressive Act 1; for Act 2, Scene 1; Act 3, Scenes 1 and 2; and for most of Act 5 (Scene 4 excepted), which includes emblematically spectacular episodes related to his other late plays. Fletcher appears mainly to have written the scenes showing the rivalry of Palamon and Arcite along with the sub-plots concerned with the Iailors Daughter's love for Palamon and the rustics' entertainment for Theseus.

Though the play was adapted by William Davenant as *The Rivals* (1664), its first known performances since the seventeenth century were at the Old Vic in 1928; it has been played only occasionally since then, but was chosen to open the Swan Theatre in Stratford-upon-Avon in 1986. Critical interest, too, has been slight; but Shakespeare's contributions are entirely characteristic of his late style, and Fletcher's scenes are both touching and funny.

This edition is printed from the 1634 quarto, which appears to be based on the foul papers of both authors annotated by a bookkeeper, and considerably modified in the printing-house.

THE NAMES OF THE ACTORS

PROLOGUE

THESEUS, Duke of Athens

HIPOLITA, Queene of the Amazons, later Wife of Theseus

EMILIA, her Sister

PIRITHOUS, friend of Theseus

PALAMON ⎫ the Two Noble Kinesmen, Cosens, Nephewes to
ARCITE ⎭ Creon, the King of Thebes

Hymen, god of marriage

A BOY, who singes

ARTESIUS, an Athenian Souldier

3. QUEENES, Widdowes of Kings killed in the Siege of Thebes

VALERIUS, a Theban

A HERALD

WOMAN, attending Emilia

An Athenian GENTLEMAN

MESSENGERS

6. KNIGHTES, 3. attending Arcite and 3. Palamon

A SERUANT

A IAYLOR, in charge of Theseus prison

The Iaylors DAUGHTER

The Iaylors BROTHER

The WOOER of the Iaylors Daughter

2. FRIENDS of the Iaylor

A DOCTOR

6. COUNTRYMEN, 1. dressed as a Bavian

Gerrold, a SCHOOLEMASTER

NEL, a Country Wench

4. Other Country Wenches: Friz, Maudline, Luce, and Barbery

Timothy, a TABOROUR

EPILOGUE

Nimphs, Attendants, Maides, Executioner, Gard

The Two Noble Kinsmen

Prologue

Florish. Enter Prologue

PROLOGUE

New Playes, and Maydenheads, are neare a kin,
Much follow'd both, for both much mony g'yn,
If they stand sound, and well: And a good Play
(Whose modest Sceanes blush on his marriage day,
And shake to loose his honour) is like hir
That after holy Tye, and first nights stir
Yet still is Modestie, and still retaines
More of the maid to sight, than Husbands paines;
We pray our Play may be so; For I am sure
It has a noble Breeder, and a pure,
A learned, and a Poet never went
More famous yet twixt Po and silver Trent.
Chaucer (of all admir'd) the Story gives,
There constant to Eternity it lives;
If we let fall the Noblenesse of this,
And the first sound this child heare, be a hisse,
How will it shake the bones of that good man,
And make him cry from under ground, O fan
From me the witles chaffe of such a wrighter
That blastes my Bayes, and my fam'd workes makes
  lighter
Then Robin Hood? This is the feare we bring;
For to say Truth, it were an endlesse thing,
And too ambitious to aspire to him;
Weake as we are, and almost breathlesse swim
In this deepe water. Do but you hold out
Your helping hands, and we shall take about,
And something doe to save us: You shall heare
Sceanes though below his Art, may yet appeare
Worth two houres travell. To his bones sweet sleepe:
Content to you. If this play doe not keepe,
A little dull time from us, we perceave
Our losses fall so thicke, we must needs leave.

          Florish. Exit

1.1
(Sc. 1)

*Musike. Enter Hymen with a Torch burning: a Boy,
in a white Robe before singing, and strewing
Flowres: After Hymen, a Nimph, encompast in her
Tresses, bearing a wheaten Garland. Then Theseus
betweene two other Nimphs with wheatan Chaplets
on their heades. Then Hipolita the Bride, lead by
Pirithous, and another holding a Garland over her
head (her Tresses likewise hanging.) After her
Emilia holding up her Traine. Then Artesius ⌈and
other Attendants⌉*

The Song

BOY   Roses their sharpe spines being gon,
      Not royall in their smels alone,
       But in their hew.

Maiden Pinckes, of odour faint,
Dazies smel-lesse, yet most quaint
  And sweet Time true.

Prim-rose first borne child of Ver,
Merry Spring times Herbinger,
  With harbels dimme.
Oxlips, in their Cradles growing,
Mary-golds, on death beds blowing,
  Larkes-heeles trymme.

All deere natures children sweete:
Ly fore Bride and Bridegroomes feete

He strews Flowers

   Blessing their sence.
Not an angle of the aire,
Bird melodious, or bird faire,
  Is absent hence.

The Crow, the slaundrous Cuckoe, nor
The boding Raven, nor Chough hor,
  Nor chattring Pie,
May on our Bridehouse pearch or sing,
Or with them any discord bring
  But from it fly.

*Enter 3. Queenes in Blacke, with vailes staind, with
imperiall Crownes. The 1. Queene fals downe at the
foote of Theseus; The 2. fals downe at the foote of
Hypolita. The 3. before Emilia*

1. QUEENE (*to Theseus*)
For pitties sake and true gentilities,
Heare, and respect me.

2. QUEENE (*to Hipolita*)   For your Mothers sake,
And as you wish your womb may thrive with faire
  ones,
Heare and respect me.

3. QUEENE (*to Emilia*)
Now for the love of him whom *Iove* hath markd
The honour of your Bed, and for the sake
Of cleere virginity, be Advocate
For us, and our distresses: This good deede
Shall raze you out o'th Booke of Trespasses
All you are set downe there.

THESEUS (*to 1. Queene*)
  Sad Lady rise.

HIPOLITA (*to 2. Queene*) Stand up.

EMILIA (*to 3. Queene*)   No knees to me.
What woman I may steed that is distrest,
Does bind me to her.

THESEUS (*to 1. Queene*)
What's your request? Deliver you for all.

1. QUEENE ⌈*kneeling still*⌉
We are 3. Queenes, whose Soveraignes fel before

1405

The wrath of cruell *Creon*; who endured
The Beakes of Ravens, Tallents of the Kights,
And pecks of Crowes, in the fowle feilds of Thebs,
He will not suffer us to burne their bones,
To urne their ashes, nor to take th' offence
Of mortall loathsomenes from the blest eye
Of holy *Phœbus*, but infects the windes
With stench of our slaine Lords. O pitty Duke,
80   Thou purger of the earth, draw thy feard Sword
That does good turnes to'th world; give us the Bones
Of our dead Kings, that we may Chappell them;
And of thy boundles goodnes take some note
That for our crowned heades we have no roofe,
Save this which is the Lyons, and the Beares,
And vault to every thing.

THESEUS   Pray you kneele not,
I was transported with your Speech, and suffer'd
Your knees to wrong themselves; I have heard the
            fortunes
Of your dead Lords, which gives me such lamenting
90   As wakes my vengeance, and revenge for'em:
King *Capaneus*, was your Lord: the day
That he should marry you, at such a season,
As now it is with me, I met your Groome,
By *Marsis Altar*, you were that time faire;
Not *Iunos Mantle* fairer then your Tresses,
Nor in more bounty spread her. Your wheaten
            wreathe
Was then nor threashd, nor blasted; Fortune at you
Dimpled her Cheeke with smiles: *Hercules* our
            kinesman
(Then weaker than your eies) laide by his Club,
100   He tumbled downe upon his Nemean hide
And swore his sinews thawd: O greife, and time,
Fearefull consumers, you will all devoure.

1. QUEENE ⌈*kneeling still*⌉ O I hope some God,
Some God hath put his mercy in your manhood
Whereto heel infuse powre, and presse you forth
Our undertaker.

THESEUS   O no knees, none Widdow,
    ⌈*The 1. Queene rises*⌉
Vnto the Helmeted-Belona use them,
And pray for me your Souldier. Troubled I am.
    He turnes away

2. QUEENE ⌈*kneeling still*⌉ Honour'd *Hypolita*
110   Most dreaded *Amazonian*, that ha'st slaine
The Sith-tuskd-Bore; that with thy Arme as strong
As it is white, wast neere to make the male
To thy Sex captive; but that this thy Lord
Borne to uphold Creation, in that honour
First nature stilde it in, shrunke thee into
The bownd thou wast ore-flowing; at once subduing
Thy force, and thy affection: Soldiresse
That equally canst poize sternenes with pitty,
Whom now I know hast much more power on him
120   Then ever he had on thee, who ow'st his strength,
And his Love too: who is a Servant for
The Tenour of thy Speech. Deere Glasse of Ladies

Bid him that we whom flaming war doth scortch,
Vnder the shaddow of his Sword, may coole us:
Require him he advance it ore our heades;
Speak't in a womans key: like such a woman
As any of us three; weepe ere you faile;
Lend us a knee;
But touch the ground for us no longer time
Then a Doves motion, when the head's pluckt off: 130
Tell him if he i'th blood cizd field, lay swolne
Showing the Sun his Teeth; grinning at the Moone
What you would doe.

HIPOLITA   Poore Lady, say no more:
I had as leife trace this good action with you
As that whereto I am going, and never yet
Went I so willing, way. My Lord is taken
Hart deepe with your distresse: Let him consider:
Ile speake anon.
    ⌈*The 2. Queene rises*⌉

3. QUEENE (*kneeling* ⌈*still*⌉ *to Emilia*) O my petition was
Set downe in yce, which by hot greefe uncandied
Melts into drops, so sorrow wanting forme   140
Is prest with deeper matter.

EMILIA   Pray stand up,
Your greefe is written in your cheeke.

3. QUEENE   O woe,
You cannot reade it there; there through my teares,
Like wrinckled peebles in a glassie streame
You may behold 'em.
    ⌈*The 3. Queene rises*⌉
                (Lady, Lady, alacke)
He that will all the Treasure know o'th earth
Must know the Center too; he that will fish
For my least minnow, let him lead his line
To catch one at my heart. O pardon me,
Extremity that sharpens sundry wits   150
Makes me a Foole.

EMILIA   Pray you say nothing, pray you,
Who cannot feele, nor see the raine being in't,
Knowes neither wet, nor dry, if that you were
The ground-peece of some Painter, I would buy you
T'instruct me gainst a Capitall greefe, indeed
Such heart peirc'd demonstration; but alas
Being a naturall Sister of our Sex
Your sorrow beates so ardently upon me,
That it shall make a counter reflect gainst
My Brothers heart, and warme it to some pitty   160
Though it were made of stone: pray have good comfort.

THESEUS
Forward to'th Temple, leave not out a Iot
O'th sacred Ceremony.

1. QUEENE   O This Celebration
Will longer last, and be more costly then,
Your Suppliants war: Remember that your Fame
Knowles in the eare o'th world: what you doe quickly,
Is not done rashly; your first thought is more,
Then others laboured meditance: your premeditating
More then their actions: But oh Iove, your actions
Soone as they moove as Asprayes doe the fish,   170

Subdue before they touch, thinke, deere *Duke* thinke
What beds our slaine Kings have.

2. QUEENE   What greifes our beds
That our deere Lords have none.

3. QUEENE   None fit for'th dead:
Those that with Cordes, Knives, drams, precipitance,
Weary of this worlds light, have to themselves
Beene deaths most horrid Agents, humaine grace
Affords them dust and shaddow.

1. QUEENE   But our Lords
Ly blistring fore the visitating Sunne,
And were good Kings, when living.

THESEUS   It is true,
And I will give you comfort, to give your dead Lords
180   graves:
The which to doe, must make some worke with
          Creon.

1. QUEENE
And that worke presents it selfe to'th doing:
Now twill take forme, the heates are gone to morrow.
Then, booteles toyle must recompence it selfe,
With it's owne sweat; Now he's secure,
Not dreames, we stand before your puissance
Wrinching our holy begging in our eyes
To make petition cleere.

2. QUEENE   Now you may take him,
Drunke with his victory.

3. QUEENE   And his Army full
Of Bread, and sloth.

190 THESEUS   *Artesius* that best knowest
How to draw out fit to this enterprise,
The prim'st for this proceeding, and the number
To carry such a businesse, forth and levy
Our worthiest Instruments, whilst we despatch
This grand act of our life, this daring deede
Of Fate in wedlocke.

1. QUEENE (*to the other 2. Queenes*)
                    Dowagers, take hands:
Let us be Widdowes to our woes, delay
Commends us to a famishing hope.

ALL 3. QUEENES   Farewell.

2. QUEENE
We come unseasonably: But when could greefe
200 Cull forth as unpang'd judgement can, fit'st time
For best solicitation.

THESEUS   Why good Ladies,
This is a service, whereto I am going,
Greater then any war; it more imports me
Then all the actions that I have foregone,
Or futurely can cope.

1. QUEENE   The more proclaiming
Our suit shall be neglected, when her Armes
Able to locke *Iove* from a Synod, shall
By warranting Moone-light corslet thee, oh when
Her twyning Cherries shall their sweetnes fall
210 Vpon thy tastefull lips, what wilt thou thinke
Of rotten Kings or blubberd Queenes, what care
For what thou feelst not? what thou feelst being able

To make *Mars* spurne his Drom. O if thou couch
But one night with her, every howre in't will
Take hostage of thee for a hundred, and
Thou shalt remember nothing more, then what
That Banket bids thee too.

HIPOLITA (*to Theseus*)   Though much unlike
You should be so transported, as much sorry
I should be such a Suitour; yet I thinke
Did I not by th'abstayning of my joy   220
Which breeds a deeper longing, cure their surfeit
That craves a present medcine, I should plucke
All Ladies scandall on me. ⌈*Kneeles*⌉ Therefore Sir
As I shall here make tryall of my prayres,
Either presuming them to have some force,
Or sentencing for ay their vigour dombe,
Prorogue this busines, we are going about, and hang
Your Sheild afore your Heart, about that necke
Which is my ffee, and which I freely lend
To doe these poore Queenes service.

ALL 3. QUEENES (*to Emilia*)   Oh helpe now   230
Our Cause cries for your knee.

EMILIA (*kneeles to Theseus*)   If you grant not
My Sister her petition in that force,
With that Celerity, and nature which
Shee makes it in: from henceforth ile not dare
To aske you any thing, nor be so hardy
Ever to take a Husband.

THESEUS   Pray stand up.
          ⌈*They rise*⌉
I am entreating of my selfe to doe
That which you kneele to have me; *Pyrithous*
Leade on the Bride; get you and pray the Gods
For successe, and returne, omit not any thing   240
In the pretended Celebration: Queenes
Follow your Soldier: (*to Artesius*) (*as before*) hence
          you
And at the banckes of Aulis meete us with
The forces you can raise, where we shall finde
The moytie of a number, for a busines,
More bigger look't;   *Exit Artesius*
(*To Hipolita*)   since that our Theame is haste
I stamp this kisse upon thy currant lippe,
Sweete keepe it as my Token; (*To the wedding party*) Set
          you forward
For I will see you gone.
(*To Emilia*) Farewell my beauteous Sister: *Pyrithous*   250
Keepe the feast full, bate not an howre on't.

PIRITHOUS   Sir
Ile follow you at heeles; The Feasts solempnity
Shall want till your returne.

THESEUS   Cosen I charge you
Boudge not from Athens; We shall be returning
Ere you can end this Feast; of which I pray you
Make no abatement; once more farewell all.
          Exeunt Hipolita, Emilia, Pirithous, and train
                                towards the Temple

1. QUEENE
Thus do'st thou still make good the tongue o'th world.

2. QUEENE
  And earnst a Deity equal with Mars,
3. QUEENE If not above him, for
260   Thou being but mortall mak'st affections bend
       To Godlike honours; they themselves some say
       Grone under such a Mastry.
THESEUS   As we are men
       Thus should we doe, being sensually subdude
       We loose our humane tytle; good cheere Ladies.
       Now turne we towards your Comforts.
                                    ⌈Florish.⌉ Exeunt

1.2   Enter Palamon, and Arcite
(Sc. 2) ARCITE
       Deere *Palamon*, deerer in love then Blood
       And our prime Cosen, yet unhardned in
       The Crimes of nature; Let us leave the Citty
       Thebs, and the temptings in't, before we further
270   Sully our glosse of youth,
       And here to keepe in abstinence we shame
       As in Incontinence; for not to swim
       I'th aide o'th Current, were almost to sincke,
       At least to frustrate striving, and to follow
       The common Streame, twold bring us to an Edy
       Where we should turne or drowne; if labour through,
       Our gaine but life, and weakenes.
PALAMON   Your advice
       Is cride up with example: what strange ruins
       Since first we went to Schoole, may we perceive
280   Walking in Thebs? Skars, and bare weedes
       The gaine o'th Martialist, who did propound
       To his bold ends, honour, and golden Ingots,
       Which though he won, he had not, and now flurted
       By peace for whom he fought, who then shall offer
       To *Marsis* so scornd *Altar*? I doe bleede
       When such I meete, and wish great *Iuno* would
       Resume her ancient fit of *Ielouzie*
       To get the Soldier worke, that peace might purge
       For her repletion, and retaine anew
290   Her charitable heart now hard, and harsher
       Then strife, or war could be.
ARCITE   Are you not out?
       Meete you no ruine, but the Soldier in
       The Franckes, and turnes of Thebs? you did begin
       As if you met decaies of many kindes:
       Perceive you none, that doe arowse your pitty
       But th'un-considerd Soldier?
PALAMON   Yes, I pitty
       Decaies where ere I finde them, but such most
       That sweating in an honourable Toyle
       Are paide with yce to coole 'em.
ARCITE   Tis not this
300   I did begin to speake of: This is vertue
       Of no respect in Thebs, I spake of Thebs
       How dangerous if we will keepe our Honours,
       It is for our resyding, where every evill
       Hath a good cullor; where eve'ry seeming good's
       A certaine evill, where not to be ev'n Iumpe

       As they are, here were to be strangers, and
       Such things to be, meere Monsters.
PALAMON   Tis in our power,
       (Vnlesse we feare that Apes can Tutor's) to
       Be Masters of our manners: what neede I
       Affect anothers gate, which is not catching
       Where there is faith, or to be fond upon
       Anothers way of speech, when by mine owne
       I may be reasonably conceiv'd; sav'd too,
       Speaking it truly; why am I bound
       By any generous bond to follow him
       Followes his Taylor, haply so long untill
       The follow'd, make pursuit? or let me know,
       Why mine owne Barber is unblest, with him
       My poore Chinne too, for tis not Cizard iust
       To such a Favorites glasse: What Cannon is there
       That does command my Rapier from my hip
       To dangle't in my hand, or to go tip toe
       Before the streete be foule? Either I am
       The fore-horse in the Teame, or I am none
       That draw i'th sequent trace: these poore sleight
            sores,
       Neede not a plantin; That which rips my bosome
       Almost to'th heart's,
ARCITE   Our Vncle *Creon*.
PALAMON   He,
       A most unbounded Tyrant, whose successes
       Makes heaven unfeard, and villany assured
       Beyond its power, there's nothing: almost puts
       Faith in a feavour, and deifies alone
       Voluble chance, who onely attributes
       The faculties of other Instruments
       To his owne Nerves and act; Commands mens service,
       And what they winne in't, boot and glory; on
       That feares not to do harm; good, dares not; Let
       The blood of mine that's sibbe to him, be suckt
       From me with Leeches, Let them breake and fall
       Off me with that corruption.
ARCITE   Cleere spirited Cozen
       Lets leave his Court, that we may nothing share,
       Of his lowd infamy: for our milke,
       Will relish of the pasture, and we must
       Be vile, or disobedient, not his kinesmen
       In blood, unlesse in quality.
PALAMON   Nothing truer:
       I thinke the Ecchoes of his shames have dea'ft
       The eares of heav'nly Iustice: widdows cryes
       Descend againe into their throates, and have not
            Enter Valerius
       Due audience of the Gods: *Valerius*.
VALERIUS
       The King cals for you; yet be leaden footed
       Till his great rage be off him. *Phebus* when
       He broke his whipstocke and exclaimd against
       The Horses of the Sun, but whisperd too
       The lowdenesse of his Fury.
PALAMON   Small windes shake him,
       But whats the matter?

VALERIUS

Theseus (who where he threates appals,) hath sent
Deadly defyance to him, and pronounces
Ruine to Thebs, who is at hand to seale
The promise of his wrath.

ARCITE   Let him approach;
But that we feare the Gods in him, he brings not
360   A jot of terrour to us; Yet what man
Thirds his owne worth (the case is each of ours)
When that his actions dregd, with minde assurd
Tis bad he goes about.

PALAMON   Leave that unreasond.
Our services stand now for Thebs, not *Creon*,
Yet to be neutrall to him, were dishonour;
Rebellious to oppose: therefore we must
With him stand to the mercy of our Fate,
Who hath bounded our last minute.

ARCITE   So we must;
Ist sed this warres afoote? or it shall be
On faile of some condition.

370   VALERIUS   Tis in motion,
The intelligence of state came in the instant
With the defier.

PALAMON   Lets to the king, who, were he
A quarter carrier of that honour, which
His Enemy come in, the blood we venture
Should be as for our health, which were not spent,
Rather laide out for purchase: but alas
Our hands advanc'd before our hearts, what will
The fall o'th stroke doe damage?

ARCITE   Let th'event,
That never erring Arbitratour, tell us
380   When we know all our selves, and let us follow
The becking of our chance.   *Exeunt*

1.3   *Enter Pirithous, Hipolita, Emilia*
(Sc. 3)   PIRITHOUS
No further.

HIPOLITA   Sir farewell; repeat my wishes
To our great Lord, of whose succes I dare not
Make any timerous question, yet I wish him
Exces, and overflow of power, and't might be
To dure ill-dealing fortune; speede to him,
Store never hurtes good Gouernours.

PIRITHOUS   Though I know
His Ocean needes not my poore drops, yet they
Must yeild their tribute there: (*To Emilia*) My precious
Maide,
390   Those best affections, that the heavens infuse
In their best temperd peices, keepe enthroand
In your deare heart.

EMILIA   Thanckes Sir; Remember me
To our all royall Brother, for whose speede
The great Bellona ile sollicite; and
Since in our terrene State petitions are not
Without giftes understood: Ile offer to her
What I shall be advis'd she likes; our hearts
Are in his Army, in his Tent.

HIPOLITA   In's bosome:

We have bin Soldiers, and wee cannot weepe
When our Friends don their helmes, or put to sea,   400
Or tell of Babes broachd on the Launce, or women
That have sod their Infants in (and after eate them)
The brine, they wept at killing 'em; Then if
You stay to see of us such Spincsters, we
Should hold you here for ever.

PIRITHOUS   Peace be to you
As I pursue this war, which shall be then
Beyond further requiring.   *Exit Pirithous*

EMILIA   How his longing
Followes his Friend; since his depart, his sportes
Though craving seriousnes, and skill, past slightly
His careles execution, where nor gaine   410
Made him regard, or losse consider, but
Playing one busines in his hand, another
Directing in his head, his minde, nurse equall
To these so diffring Twyns; have you observ'd him,
Since our great Lord departed?

HIPOLITA   With much labour:
And I did love him fort, they two have Cabind
In many as dangerous, as poore a Corner,
Perill and want contending, they have skift
Torrents whose roring tyranny and power
I'th least of these was dreadfull, and they have   420
Fought out together, where Deaths-selfe was lodgd,
Yet fate hath brought them off: Their knot of love
Tide, weau'd, intangled, with so true, so long,
And with a finger of so deepe a cunning
May be outworne, never undone. I thinke
Theseus cannot be umpire to himselfe
Cleaving his conscience into twaine, and doing
Each side like Iustice, which he loves best.

EMILIA   Doubtlesse
There is a best, and reason has no manners
To say it is not you: I was acquainted   430
Once with a time, when I enjoyd a Play-fellow;
You were at wars, when she the grave enrichd,
Who made too proud the Bed, tooke leave o'th Moone
(Which then lookt pale at parting) when our count
Was each a leven.

HIPOLITA   Twas *Flauina*.

EMILIA   Yes:
You talke of *Pirithous* and *Theseus* love;
Theirs has more ground, is more maturely seasond,
More buckled with strong Iudgement, and their
needes
The one of th'other may be said to water
Their intertangled rootes of love, but I   440
And shee (I sigh and spoke of) were things innocent,
Lou'd for we did, and like the Elements
That know not what, nor why, yet doe effect
Rare issues by their operance; our soules
Did so to one another; what she lik'd,
Was then of me approov'd, what not condemd
No more arraignement, the flowre that I would
plucke
And put betweene my breasts, oh (then but beginning
To swell about the blossome) she would long

450　Till shee had such another, and commit it
To the like innocent Cradle, where *Phenix* like
They dide in perfume: on my head no toy
But was her patterne, her affections (pretty
Though happely, her careles were, I followed
For my most serious decking, had mine eare
Stolne some new aire, or at adventure humd on
From musicall Coynadge; why it was a note
Whereon her spirits would sojourne (rather dwell on)
And sing it in her slumbers; This rehearsall
460　(Which sely innocenc wots well, comes in
Like old importments bastard) has this end,
That the true love tweene Mayde, and mayde, may be
More then in sex dividuall.

HIPOLITA　　　　　　　　Y'are out of breath
And this high-speeded-pace, is but to say
That you shall never (like the Maide *Flavina*)
Love any that's calld Man.

EMILIA I am sure I shall not.

HIPOLITA Now alacke weake Sister,
I must no more beleeve thee in this point
470　(Though, in't I know thou dost beleeve thy selfe,)
Then I will trust a sickely appetite,
That loathes even as it longs, but sure my Sister
If I were ripe for your perswasion, you
Have saide enough to shake me from the Arme
Of the all noble *Theseus*, for whose fortunes,
I will now in, and kneele with great assurance,
That we, more then his *Pirithous*, possesse
The high throne in his heart.

EMILIA　　　　　　　　I am not
Against your faith, yet I continew mine.　　　*Exeunt*

1.4　　*Cornets: A Battaile strooke within: Then a Retrait:*
(Sc. 4)　*Florish. Then Enter Theseus (victor), the three*
Queenes meete him, and fall on their faces before
him. ⌈*Also enter a Herald and Attendants bearing*
Palamon and Arcite on 2. hearses⌉

I. QUEENE (*to Theseus*)
To thee no starre be darke.

480　2. QUEENE (*to Theseus*)　　　　Both heaven and earth
Friend thee for ever.

3. QUEENE (*to Theseus*) All the good that may
Be wishd upon thy head, I cry Amen too't.

THESEUS
Th'imparciall Gods, who from the mounted heavens
View us their mortall Heard, behold who erre,
And in their time chastice: goe and finde out
The bones of your dead Lords, and honour them
With treble Ceremonie, rather then a gap
Should be in their deere rights, we would suppl'it.
But those we will depute, which shall invest
490　You in your dignities, and even each thing
Our hast does leave imperfect; So adiew
And heavens good eyes looke on you.
　　　　　　　　　　　　　　Exeunt Queenes
　　　　　　　　What are those?

HERALD
Men of great quality, as may be judgd

By their appointment; Some of Thebs have told's
They are Sisters children, Nephewes to the King.

THESEUS
By'th Helme of Mars, I saw them in the war,
Like to a paire of Lions, smeard with prey,
Make lanes in troopes agast. I fixt my note
Constantly on them; for they were a marke
Worth a god's view: what prisoner was't that told me　500
When I enquir'd their names?

HERALD　　　　　　　　　　Wi leave, they'r called
Arcite and *Palamon*.

THESEUS　　　　　Tis right, those, those.
They are not dead?

HERALD
Nor in a state of life, had they bin taken
When their last hurts were given, twas possible
They might have bin recover'd; Yet they breathe
And haue the name of men.

THESEUS　　　　　　　　Then like men use'em:
The very lees of such (millions of rates)
Exceed the wine of others. All our Surgions
Convent in their behoofe, our richest balmes　　　　510
Rather then niggard wast, their lives concerne us,
Much more then Thebs is worth, rather then have'em
Freed of this plight, and in their morning state
(Sound and at liberty) I would 'em dead,
But forty thousand fold, we had rather have 'em
Prisoners to us, then death; Beare 'em speedily
From our kinde aire, to them unkinde, and minister
What man to man may doe: for our sake more,
Since I have knowne frights, fury, friends beheastes,
Loves provocations, zeale, a mistris Taske,　　　　520
Desire of liberty, a feavour, madnes,
Hath set a marke which nature could not reach too
Without some imposition, sicknes in will
Or wrastling strength in reason, for our Love
And great *Appollos* mercy, all our best,
Their best skill tender. Leade into the Citty,
Where having bound things scatterd, we will post
To Athens for our Army.　　　　　　*Florish. Exeunt*

Musicke. Enter the 3. Queenes with the Hearses of　**1.5**
their Knightes, in a Funerall Solempnity, with　　**(Sc. 5)**
Attendants

　　　　　　　　Song
Vrnes, and odours, bring away,
Vapours, sighes, darken the day;　　　　　　　530
*　Our dole more deadly lookes than dying.*
Balmes, and Gummes, and heavy cheeres,
Sacred vials fill'd with teares,
*　And clamors through the wild ayre flying.*

Come all sad, and solempne Showes,
That are quick-eyd pleasures foes;
We convent nought else but woes.
We convent nought else but woes.

3. QUEENE
This funeral path, brings to your housholds grave:
Ioy ceaze on you againe: peace sleepe with him.　　540

2. QUEENE
And this to yours.

1. QUEENE   Yours this way: Heavens lend
A thousand differing waies, to one sure end.

3. QUEENE
This world's a Citty full of straying Streetes,
And Death's the market place, where each one
        meetes.   *Exeunt severally*

❈

2.1
(Sc. 6)   *Enter Iailor, and Wooer*

IAYLOR I may depart with little, while I live, some thing
I may cast to you, not much: Alas the Prison I keepe,
though it be for great ones, yet they seldome come;
Before one *Salmon*, you shall take a number of
Minnowes: I am given out to be better lyn'd then it
550   can appeare to me report is a true speaker: I would I
were really, that I am deliverd to be: Marry, what I
have (be it what it will) I will assure upon my daughter
at the day of my death.

WOOER Sir I demaund no more then your owne offer, and
I will estate your Daughter in what I have promised.

IAYLOR Wel, we will talke more of this, when the
solemnity is past; But have you a full promise of her?

        Enter Daughter with rushes

When that shall be seene, I tender my consent.

WOOER I have Sir; here shee comes.

560 IAYLOR (*to Daughter*) Your Friend and I have chanced to
name you here, upon the old busines: But no more of
that now; so soone as the Court hurry is over, we will
have an end of it: I'th meane time looke tenderly to
the two Prisoners. I can tell you they are princes.

DAUGHTER These strewings are for their Chamber; tis pitty
they are in prison, and twer pitty they should be out:
I doe thinke they have patience to make any adversity
asham'd; the prison it selfe is proud of 'em; and they
have all the world in their Chamber.

570 IAYLOR They are fam'd to be a paire of absolute men.

DAUGHTER By my troth, I think Fame but stammers 'em,
they stand a greise above the reach of report.

IAYLOR I heard them reported in the Battaile, to be the
only doers.

DAUGHTER Nay most likely, for they are noble suffrers; I
mervaile how they would have lookd had they beene
victors, that with such a constant Nobility, enforce a
freedome out of Bondage, making misery their mirth,
and affliction, a toy to jest at.

580 IAYLOR Doe they so?

DAUGHTER It seemes to me they have no more sence of
their captivity, then I of ruling Athens: they eate well,
looke merrily, discourse of many things, but nothing
of their owne restraint, and disasters: Yet sometime a
devided sigh, martyrd as twer i'th deliverance, will
breake from one of them. When the other presently
gives it so sweete a rebuke, that I could wish my selfe
a Sigh to be so chid, or at least a Sigher to be comforted.

WOOER I never saw'em.

590 IAYLOR The Duke himselfe came privately in the night,
        Palamon, and Arcite appear ⌈at a window⌉ above

and so did they, what the reason of it is, I know not:
Looke yonder they are; that's *Arcite* lookes out.

DAUGHTER No Sir, no, that's *Palamon*: *Arcite* is the lower
of the twaine; (*pointing at Arcite*) you may perceive a
part of him.

IAYLOR Goe too, leave your pointing; they would not
make us their object; out of their sight.

DAUGHTER It is a holliday to looke on them: Lord, the
diffrence of men.   *Exeunt*

      Enter Palamon, and Arcite in prison ⌈in shackles,   **2.2**
      above⌉   **(Sc. 7)**

PALAMON
How doe you Noble Cosen?

ARCITE   How doe you Sir?   600

PALAMON
Why strong inough to laugh at misery,
And beare the chance of warre, yet we are prisoners
I feare for ever Cosen.

ARCITE   I beleeve it,
And to that destiny have patiently
Laide up my houre to come.

PALAMON   Oh Cosen *Arcite*,
Where is Thebs now? where is our noble Country?
Where are our friends, and kindreds? never more
Must we behold those comforts, never see
The hardy youthes strive for the Games of honour
(Hung with the painted favours of their Ladies)   610
Like tall Ships under saile: then start among'st 'em
And as an Eastwind leave 'em all behinde us,
Like lazy Clowdes, whilst *Palamon* and *Arcite*,
Even in the wagging of a wanton leg
Out-stript the peoples praises, won the Garlands,
Ere they have time to wish 'em ours. O never
Shall we two exercise, like Twyns of honour,
Our Armes againe, and feele our fyry horses
Like proud Seas under us, our good Swords, now
(Better the red-eyd god of war nev'r wore)   620
Ravishd our sides, like age must run to rust,
And decke the Temples of those gods that hate us,
These hands shall never draw'em out like lightning
To blast whole Armies more.

ARCITE   No *Palamon*,
Those hopes are Prisoners with us, here we are
And here the graces of our youthes must wither
Like a too-timely Spring; here age must finde us,
And which is heaviest (*Palamon*) unmarried,
The sweete embraces of a loving wife
Loden with kisses, armd with thousand Cupids   630
Shall never claspe our neckes, no issue know us,
No figures of our selves shall we ev'r see,
To glad our age, and like young Eagles teach'em
Boldly to gaze against bright armes, and say
Remember what your fathers were, and conquer.
The faire-eyd Maides, shall weepe our Banishments,
And in their Songs, curse ever-blinded fortune
Till shee for shame see what a wrong she has done
To youth and nature; This is all our world;
We shall know nothing here but one another,   640

Heare nothing but the Clocke that tels our woes.
The Vine shall grow, but we shall never see it:
Sommer shall come, and with her all delights;
But dead-cold winter must inhabite here still.

PALAMON
Tis too true *Arcite*. To our Theban houndes,
That shooke the aged Forrest with their ecchoes,
No more now must we halloa, no more shake
Our pointed Iavelyns, whilst the angry Swine
Flyes like a parthian quiver from our rages,
650 Strucke with our well-steeld Darts: All valiant uses,
(The foode, and nourishment of noble mindes,)
In us two here shall perish; we shall die
(Which is the curse of honour) lastly,
Children of greife, and Ignorance.

ARCITE   Yet Cosen,
Even from the bottom of these miseries
From all that fortune can inflict upon us,
I see two comforts rysing, two meere blessings,
If the gods please, to hold here a brave patience,
And the enjoying of our greefes together.
660 Whilst *Palamon* is with me, let me perish
If I thinke this our prison.

PALAMON   Certeinly,
Tis a maine goodnes Cosen, that our fortunes
Were twyn'd together; tis most true, two soules
Put in two noble Bodies, let'em suffer
The gaule of hazard, so they grow together,
Will never sincke, they must not, say they could,
A willing man dies sleeping, and all's done.

ARCITE
Shall we make worthy uses of this place
That all men hate so much?

PALAMON   How gentle Cosen?

ARCITE
670 Let's thinke this prison, holy sanctuary,
To keepe us from corruption of worse men,
We are young and yet desire the waies of honour,
That liberty and common Conversation,
The poyson of pure spirits, might like women
Wooe us to wander from. What worthy blessing
Can be but our Imaginations
May make it ours? And heere being thus together,
We are an endles mine to one another;
We are one anothers wife, ever begetting
New birthes of love; we are father, friends,
680   acquaintance,
We are in one another, Families,
I am your heire, and you are mine: This place
Is our Inheritance: no hard Oppressour
Dare take this from us; here with a little patience
We shall live long, and loving: No surfeits seeke us:
The hand of war hurts none here, nor the Seas
Swallow their youth: were we at liberty,
A wife might part us lawfully, or busines,
Quarrels consume us, Envy of ill men
690 Crave our acquaintance, I might sicken Cosen,
Where you should never know it, and so perish

Without your noble hand to close mine eies,
Or praiers to the gods; a thousand chaunces
Were we from hence, would seaver us.

PALAMON   You have made me
(I thanke you Cosen *Arcite*) almost wanton
With my Captivity: what a misery
It is to live abroade? and every where:
Tis like a Beast me thinkes: I finde the Court here,
I am sure a more content, and all those pleasures
That wooe the wils of men to vanity,   700
I see through now, and am sufficient
To tell the world, tis but a gaudy shaddow,
That old Time, as he passes by takes with him,
What had we bin old in the Court of *Creon*,
Where sin is Iustice, lust, and ignorance,
The vertues of the great ones: Cosen *Arcite*,
Had not the loving gods found this place for us
We had died as they doe, ill old men, unwept,
And had their Epitaphes, the peoples Curses,
Shall I say more?

ARCITE   I would heare you still.

PALAMON   Ye shall.   710
Is there record of any two that lov'd
Better then we doe *Arcite*?

ARCITE   Sure there cannot.

PALAMON
I doe not thinke it possible our friendship
Should ever leave us.

ARCITE   Till our deathes it cannot

*Enter Emilia and her woman [below]. Palamon sees
Emilia and is silent*

And after death our spirits shall be led
To those that love eternally. Speake on Sir.

EMILIA (*to her woman*)
This garden has a world of pleasure in't.
What Flowre is this?

WOMAN   Tis calld Narcissus Madam.

EMILIA
That was a faire Boy certaine, but a foole,
To love himselfe, were there not maides enough?   720

ARCITE (*to Palamon*)
Pray forward.

PALAMON   Yes.

EMILIA (*to her woman*) Or were they all hard hearted?

WOMAN
They could not be to one so faire.

EMILIA   Thou wouldst not.

WOMAN
I thinke I should not, Madam.

EMILIA   That's a good wench:
But take heede to your kindnes though.

WOMAN   Why Madam?

EMILIA
Men are mad things.

ARCITE (*to Palamon*)   Will ye goe forward Cosen?

EMILIA (*to her woman*)
Canst not thou worke such flowers in silke wench?

WOMAN   Yes.

EMILIA
Ile have a gowne full of'em and of these,
This is a pretty colour, wilt not doe
Rarely upon a Skirt wench?

WOMAN   Deinty Madam.

ARCITE (*to Palamon*)
730   Cosen, Cosen, how doe you Sir? Why *Palamon*?

PALAMON
Never till now was I in prison *Arcite*.

ARCITE
Why whats the matter Man?

PALAMON   Behold, and wonder.

        Arcite sees Emilia
By heaven shee is a Goddesse.

ARCITE   Ha.

PALAMON   Doe reverence.
She is a Goddesse *Arcite*.

EMILIA (*to her woman*)   Of all Flowres,
Me thinkes a Rose is best.

WOMAN   Why gentle Madam?

EMILIA
It is the very Embleme of a Maide.
For when the west wind courts her gently
How modestly she blowes, and paints the Sun,
With her chaste blushes? When the North comes
        neere her,
740   Rude and impatient, then, like Chastity
Shee lockes her beauties in her bud againe,
And leaves him to base briers.

WOMAN   Yet good Madam,
Sometimes her modesty will blow so far
She fals for't: a Mayde
If shee have any honour, would be loth
To take example by her.

EMILIA   Thou art wanton.

ARCITE (*to Palamon*)
She is wondrous faire.

PALAMON   She is all the beauty extant.

EMILIA (*to her woman*)
The Sun grows high, lets walk in, keep these flowers,
Weele see how close Art can come neere their
        colours;
750   I am wondrous merry hearted, I could laugh now.

WOMAN
I could lie downe I am sure.

EMILIA   And take one with you?

WOMAN
That's as we bargaine Madam.

EMILIA   Well, agree then.
        Exeunt Emilia and woman

PALAMON
What thinke you of this beauty?

ARCITE   Tis a rare one.

PALAMON
Is't but a rare one?

ARCITE   Yes a matchles beauty.

PALAMON
Might not a man well lose himselfe and love her?

ARCITE
I cannot tell what you have done, I have,
Beshrew mine eyes for't, now I feele my Shackles.

PALAMON You love her then?

ARCITE Who would not?

PALAMON And desire her?   760

ARCITE Before my liberty.

PALAMON
I saw her first.

ARCITE   That's nothing

PALAMON   But it shall be.

ARCITE
I saw her too.

PALAMON   Yes, but you must not love her.

ARCITE
I will not as you doe; to worship her;
As she is heavenly, and a blessed Goddes;
(I love her as a woman, to enjoy her)
So both may love.

PALAMON   You shall not love at all.

ARCITE
Not love at all. Who shall deny me?

PALAMON
I that first saw her; I that tooke possession
First with mine eye of all those beauties   770
In her reveal'd to mankinde: if thou lou'st her,
Or entertain'st a hope to blast my wishes,
Thou art a Traytour *Arcite* and a fellow
False as thy Title to her: friendship, blood
And all the tyes betweene us I disclaime
If thou once thinke upon her.

ARCITE   Yes I love her,
And if the lives of all my name lay on it,
I must doe so, I love her with my soule,
If that will lose ye, farewell *Palamon*,
I say againe,   780
I love her, and in loving her maintaine
I am as worthy, and as free a lover
And have as just a title to her beauty
As any *Palamon* or any living
That is a mans Sonne.

PALAMON   Have I cald thee friend?

ARCITE
Yes, and have found me so; why are you mov'd
        thus?
Let me deale coldly with you, am not I
Part of your blood, part of your soule? you have told
        me
That I was *Palamon*, and you were *Arcite*.

PALAMON   Yes.

ARCITE
Am not I liable to those affections,   790
Those joyes, greifes, angers, feares, my friend shall
        suffer?

PALAMON
Ye may be.

ARCITE   Why then would you deale so cunningly,
So strangely, so vnlike a noble kinsman

To love alone? speake truely, doe you thinke me
Vnworthy of her sight?

PALAMON   No; but unjust,
If thou pursue that sight.

ARCITE   Because an other
First sees the Enemy, shall I stand still
And let mine honour downe, and never charge?

PALAMON
Yes, if he be but one.

ARCITE   But say that one
Had rather combat me?

800 PALAMON   Let that one say so,
And use thy freedome: els if thou pursuest her,
Be as that cursed man that hates his Country,
A branded villaine.

ARCITE   You are mad.

PALAMON   I must be,
Till thou art worthy, *Arcite*, it concernes me,
And in this madnes, if I hazard thee
And take thy life, I deale but truely.

ARCITE   Fie Sir.
You play the Childe extreamely: I will love her,
I must, I ought to doe so, and I dare,
And all this justly.

PALAMON   O that now, that now
810 Thy false-selfe and thy friend, had but this fortune
To be one howre at liberty, and graspe
Our good Swords in our hands, I would quickly teach
    thee
What tw'er to filch affection from another:
Thou art baser in it then a Cutpurse;
Put but thy head out of this window more,
And as I have a soule, Ile naile thy life too't.

ARCITE
Thou dar'st not foole, thou canst not, thou art feeble.
Put my head out? Ile throw my Body out,
And leape the garden, when I see her next
    Enter Iaylor ⌈above⌉
820 And pitch between her armes to anger thee.

PALAMON
No more; the keeper's comming; I shall live
To knocke thy braines out with my Shackles.

ARCITE   Doe.

IAYLOR
By your leave Gentlemen.

PALAMON   Now honest keeper?

IAYLOR
Lord *Arcite*, you must presently to'th Duke;
The cause I know not yet.

ARCITE   I am ready keeper.

IAYLOR
Prince *Palamon*, I must awhile bereave you
Of your faire Cosens Company.
                    Exeunt Arcite, and Iaylor

PALAMON   And me too,
Even when you please of life; why is he sent for?
It may be he shall marry her, he's goodly,
830 And like enough the Duke hath taken notice

Both of his blood and body: But his falsehood,
Why should a friend be treacherous? If that
Get him a wife so noble, and so faire;
Let honest men ne're love againe. Once more
I would but see this faire One: Blessed Garden,
And fruite, and flowers more blessed that still blossom
As her bright eies shine on ye, would I were
For all the fortune of my life hereafter
Yon little Tree, yon blooming Apricocke;
How I would spread, and fling my wanton armes   840
In at her window; I would bring her fruite
Fit for the Gods to feed on: youth and pleasure
Still as she tasted should be doubled on her,
And if she be not heavenly I would make her
So neere the Gods in nature, they should feare her.
    Enter Iaylor ⌈above⌉
And then I am sure she would love me: how now
    keeper
Wher's *Arcite*?

IAYLOR   Banishd: Prince *Pirithous*
Obtained his liberty; but never more
Vpon his oth and life must he set foote
Vpon this Kingdome.

PALAMON ⌈aside⌉   Hees a blessed man,   850
He shall see Thebs againe, and call to Armes
The bold yong men, that when he bids 'em charge,
Fall on like fire: *Arcite* shall have a Fortune,
If he dare make himselfe a worthy Lover,
Yet in the Feild to strike a battle for her;
And if he lose her then, he's a cold Coward;
How bravely may he beare himselfe to win her
If he be noble *Arcite*; thousand waies.
Were I at liberty, I would doe things
Of such a vertuous greatnes, that this Lady,   860
This blushing virgine should take manhood to her
And seeke to ravish me.

IAYLOR   My Lord for you
I have this charge too,

PALAMON   To discharge my life.

IAYLOR
No, but from this place to remoove your Lordship,
The windowes are too open.

PALAMON   Devils take 'em
That are so envious to me; pre'thee kill me.

IAYLOR
And hang for't afterward.

PALAMON   By this good light
Had I a sword I would kill thee.

IAYLOR   Why my Lord?

PALAMON
Thou bringst such pelting scuruy news continually
Thou art not worthy life; I will not goe.   870

IAYLOR
Indeede you must my Lord.

PALAMON   May I see the garden?

IAYLOR
Noe.

PALAMON Then I am resolud, I will not goe.

IAYLOR

I must constraine you then; and for you are dangerous
Ile clap more yrons on you.

PALAMON   Doe good keeper.

Ile shake'em so, ye shall not sleepe,
Ile make ye a new Morrisse, must I goe?

IAYLOR

There is no remedy.

PALAMON   Farewell kinde window.

May rude winde never hurt thee. O my Lady
If ever thou hast felt what sorrow was,
880 Dreame how I suffer. Come; now bury me.

Exeunt Palamon, and Iaylor

2.3   *Enter Arcite*
(Sc. 8)   ARCITE

Banishd the kingdome? tis a benefit,
A mercy I must thanke 'em for, but banishd
The free enjoying of that face I die for,
Oh twas a studdied punishment, a death
Beyond Imagination: Such a vengeance
That were I old and wicked, all my sins
Could never plucke upon me. *Palamon*;
Thou ha'st the Start now, thou shalt stay and see
Her bright eyes breake each morning gainst thy
        window,
890 And let in life into thee; thou shalt feede
Vpon the sweetenes of a noble beauty,
That nature nev'r exceeded, nor nev'r shall:
Good gods? what happines has *Palamon*?
Twenty to one, hee'le come to speake to her,
And if she be as gentle, as she's faire,
I know she's his, he has a Tongue will tame
Tempests, and make the wild Rockes wanton.
Come what can come,
The worst is death; I will not leave the Kingdome,
900 I know mine owne, is but a heape of ruins,
And no redresse there, if I goe, he has her.
I am resolu'd an other shape shall make me,
Or end my fortunes. Either way, I am happy:
Ile see her, and be neere her, or no more.

Enter .4. Country people, & one with a Garlond
before them. Arcite stands a loofe

1. COUNTRYMAN

My Masters, ile be there that's certaine.

2. COUNTRYMAN And Ile be there.

3. COUNTRYMAN And I.

4. COUNTRYMAN

Why then have with ye Boyes; Tis but a chiding,
Let the plough play to day, ile tick'lt out
Of the Iades tailes to morrow.

910 1. COUNTRYMAN   I am sure

To have my wife as jealous as a Turkey:
But that's all one, ile goe through, let her mumble.

2. COUNTRYMAN

Clap her aboard to morrow night, and stoa her,
And all's made up againe.

3. COUNTRYMAN   I, doe but put

A feskue in her fist, and you shall see her
Take a new lesson out, and be a good wench.
Doe we all hold, against the Maying?

4. COUNTRYMAN

Hold? what should aile us?

3. COUNTRYMAN   *Arcas* will be there.

2. COUNTRYMAN And *Sennois*. And *Rycas*, and 3. better
lads nev'r dancd under green Tree, and yee know what   920
wenches: ha? But will the dainty Domine, the
Schoolemaster keep touch doe you thinke: for he do's
all ye know.

3. COUNTRYMAN Hee'l eate a hornebooke ere he faile: goe
too, the matter's too farre driven betweene him, and
the Tanners daughter, to let slip now, and she must
see the Duke, and she must daunce too.

4. COUNTRYMAN Shall we be lusty.

2. COUNTRYMAN All the Boyes in Athens blow wind i'th
breech on's, and heere ile be and there ile be, for our   930
Towne, and here againe, and there againe: ha, Boyes,
heigh for the weavers.

1. COUNTRYMAN This must be done i'th woods.

4. COUNTRYMAN O pardon me.

2. COUNTRYMAN By any meanes our thing of learning sed
so: where he himselfe will edifie the Duke most parlously
in our behalfes: hees excellent i'th woods, bring him
to'th plaines, his learning makes no cry.

3. COUNTRYMAN Weele see the sports, then every man to's
Tackle: and sweete Companions lets rehearse by any   940
meanes, before the Ladies see us, and doe sweetly, and
God knows what may come on't.

4. COUNTRYMAN Content; the sports once ended, wee'l
performe. Away Boyes and hold.

ARCITE *(comming forward)*

By your leaves honest friends: pray you whither goe
        you.

4. COUNTRYMAN Whither? why, what a question's that?

ARCITE Yet tis a question,
To me that know not.

3. COUNTRYMAN   To the *Games* my Friend.

2. COUNTRYMAN

Where were you bred you know it not?

ARCITE   Not farre Sir,

Are there such *Games* to day?

1. COUNTRYMAN   Yes marry are there: 950

And such as you neuer saw; The *Duke* himselfe
Will be in person there.

ARCITE   What pastimes are they?

2. COUNTRYMAN

Wrastling, and Running; *(To the others)* Tis a pretty
        Fellow.

3. COUNTRYMAN *(to Arcite)*

Thou wilt not goe along.

ARCITE   Not yet Sir.

4. COUNTRYMAN   Well Sir

Take your owne time, *(to the others)* come Boyes.

1. COUNTRYMAN   My minde misgives me

This fellow has a veng'ance tricke o'th hip,
Marke how his Bodi's made for't.

2. COUNTRYMAN   Ile be hangd though

If he dare venture, hang him plumb porredge,
He wrastle? he rost eggs. Come lets be gon Lads.

Exeunt 4. Countrymen

ARCITE

960   This is an offerd oportunity
I durst not wish for. Well I could have wrestled,
The best men calld it excellent, and run
Swifter, then winde upon a feild of Corne
(Curling the wealthy eares) never flew: Ile venture,
And in some poore disguize be there, who knowes
Whether my browes may not be girt with garlands?
And happines preferre me to a place,
Where I may ever dwell in sight of her.   *Exit Arcite*

2.4

(Sc. 9)   *Enter Iailors Daughter alone*

DAUGHTER

Why should I love this Gentleman? Tis odds
970   He never will affect me; I am base,
My Father the meane Keeper of his Prison,
And he a prince; To marry him is hopelesse;
To be his whore, is witles; Out upon't;
What pushes are we wenches driven to
When fifteene once has found us? First I saw him,
I (seeing) thought he was a goodly man;
He has as much to please a woman in him,
(If he please to bestow it so) as ever
These eyes yet lookt on; Next, I pittied him,
980   And so would any young wench o'my Conscience
That ever dream'd, or vow'd her Maydenhead
To a yong hansom Man; Then I lov'd him,
(Extreamely lov'd him) infinitely lov'd him;
And yet he had a Cosen, faire as he too.
But in my heart was *Palamon*, and there
Lord, what a coyle he keepes? To heare him
Sing in an evening, what a heaven it is?
And yet his Songs are sad-ones; Fairer spoken,
Was never Gentleman. When I come in
990   To bring him water in a morning, first
He bowes his noble body, then salutes me, thus:
Faire, gentle Mayde, good morrow, may thy goodnes,
Get thee a happy husband; Once he kist me,
I lov'd my lips the better ten daies after,
Would he would doe so ev'ry day; He greives much,
And me as much to see his misery.
What should I doe, to make him know I love him,
For I would faine enjoy him? Say I ventur'd
To set him free? what saies the law then? Thus much
1000   For Law, or kindred: I will doe it,
And this night, or to morrow he shall love me.   *Exit*

2.5

(Sc. 10)   *Short florish of Cornets and Showtes within. Enter*
Theseus, Hipolita, Pirithous, Emilia: Arcite
disguised, with a Garland, and Attendants

THESEUS

You have done worthily; I have not seene
Since *Hercules*, a man of tougher synewes;
What ere you are, you run the best, and wrastle,
That these times can allow.

ARCITE   I am proud to please you.

THESEUS
What Countrie bred you?

ARCITE   This; but far off, Prince.

THESEUS
Are you a Gentleman?

ARCITE   My father said so;
And to those gentle uses gave me life.

THESEUS
Are you his heire?

ARCITE   His yongest Sir.

THESEUS   Your Father
Sure is a happy Sire then: what prooves you?   1010

ARCITE
A little of all noble Quallities:
I could have kept a Hawke, and well have holloa'd
To a deepe crie of Dogges; I dare not praise
My feat in horsemanship: yet they that knew me
Would say it was my best peece: last, and greatest,
I would be thought a Souldier.

THESEUS   You are perfect.

PIRITHOUS
Vpon my soule, a proper man.

EMILIA   He is so.

PIRITHOUS (*to Hipolita*)
  How doe you like him Ladie?

HIPOLITA   I admire him,
I have not seene so yong a man, so noble
(If he say true,) of his sort.

EMILIA   Beleeve,   1020
His mother was a wondrous handsome woman,
His face me thinkes, goes that way.

HIPOLITA   But his Body
And firie minde, illustrate a brave Father.

PIRITHOUS
Marke how his vertue, like a hidden Sun
Breakes through his baser garments.

HIPOLITA   Hee's well got sure.

THESEUS (*to Arcite*)
  What made you seeke this place Sir?

ARCITE   Noble *Theseus*,
To purchase name, and doe my ablest service
To such a well-found wonder, as thy worth,
For onely in thy Court, of all the world
Dwells faire-eyd honor.

PIRITHOUS   All his words are worthy.   1030

THESEUS (*to Arcite*)
Sir, we are much endebted to your travell,
Nor shall you loose your wish: *Perithous*
Dispose of this faire Gentleman.

PIRITHOUS   Thankes *Theseus*.
(*To Arcite*) What ere you are y'ar mine, and I shall
    give you
To a most noble service, to this Lady,
This bright yong Virgin; pray observe her goodnesse;
You have honourd hir faire birth-day, with your
    vertues,
And as your due y'ar hirs: kisse her faire hand Sir.

ARCITE
Sir, y'ar a noble Giver: (*to Emilia*) dearest Bewtie,

Thus let me seale my vowd faith:
            He kisses her hand
1040   when your Servant
(Your most unworthie Creature) but offends you,
Command him die, he shall.
EMILIA   That were too cruell.
If you deserve well Sir; I shall soone see't:
Y'ar mine, and somewhat better than your rancke Ile
            use you.
PIRITHOUS (*to Arcite*)
Ile see you furnish'd, and because you say
You are a horseman, I must needs intreat you
This after noone to ride, but tis a rough one.
ARCITE
I like him better (Prince) I shall not then
Freeze in my Saddle.
THESEUS (*to Hipolita*)   Sweet, you must be readie,
1050 And you *Emilia*, ⌈*to Perithous*⌉ and you (Friend) and all
To morrow by the Sun, to doe observance
To flowry May, in *Dians* wood: (*to Arcite*) waite well
            Sir
Vpon your Mistris: *Emely*, I hope
He shall not goe a foote.
EMILIA   That were a shame Sir,
While I have horses: (*to Arcite*) take your choice, and
            what
You want at any time, let me but know it;
If you serve faithfully, I dare assure you
You'l finde a loving Mistris.
ARCITE   If I doe not,
Let me finde that my Father ever hated,
Disgrace, and blowes.
1060 THESEUS   Go leade the way; you have won it:
It shall be so; you shall receave all dues
Fit for the honour you have won; Twer wrong else.
(*To Emilia*) Sister, beshrew my heart, you have a
            Servant,
That if I were a woman, would be Master,
But you are wise.
EMILIA   I hope too wise for that Sir.
                    Florish. Exeunt omnes

2.6   *Enter Iaylors Daughter alone*
(Sc. 11) DAUGHTER
Let all the Dukes, and all the divells rore,
He is at liberty: I have venturd for him,
And out I have brought him: to a little wood
A mile hence, I have sent him, where a Cedar
1070 Higher than all the rest, spreads like a plane
Fast by a Brooke, and there he shall keepe close,
Till I provide him Fyles, and foode, for yet
His yron bracelets are not off. O Love
What a stout hearted child thou art! My Father
Durst better have indur'd cold yron, than done it:
I love him, beyond love, and beyond reason,
Or wit, or safetie: I have made him know it:
I care not, I am desperate, If the law
Finde me, and then condemne me for't; some wenches,

Some honest harted Maides, will sing my Dirge,   1080
And tell to memory, my death was noble,
Dying almost a Martyr: That way he takes,
I purpose is my way too: Sure he cannot
Be so unmanly, as to leave me here,
If he doe, Maides will not so easily
Trust men againe: And yet he has not thank'd me
For what I have done: no not so much as kist me,
And that (me thinkes) is not so well; nor scarcely
Could I perswade him to become a Freeman,
He made such scruples of the wrong he did   1090
To me, and to my Father. Yet I hope
When he considers more, this love of mine
Will take more root within him: Let him doe
What he will with me, so he use me kindly,
For use me so he shall, or ile proclaime him
And to his face, no-man: Ile presently
Provide him necessaries, and packe my cloathes up,
And where there is a patch of ground Ile venture
So hee be with me; By him, like a shadow
Ile ever dwell; within this houre the whoobub   1100
Will be all ore the prison: I am then
Kissing the man they looke for: farewell Father,
Get many more such prisoners, and such daughters,
And shortly you may keepe your selfe. Now to him.
                                        Exit

                    ❀

⌈*A Bush in place.*⌉ *Cornets in sundry places. Noise*   **3.1**
and hallowing as people a Maying: (Sc. 12)
Enter Arcite alone
ARCITE
The Duke has lost Hypolita; each tooke
A severall land. This is a solemne Right
They owe bloomd May, and the *Athenians* pay it
To'th heart of Ceremony: O Queene *Emilia*
Fresher then May, sweeter
Then hir gold Buttons on the bowes, or all   1110
Th'enamelld knackes o'th Meade, or garden, yea
(We challenge too) the bancke of any Nymph
That makes the streame seeme flowers; thou o Iewell
O'th wood, o'th world, hast likewise blest a pace
With thy sole presence, in thy ⌈
                    ⌉ rumination
That I poore man might eftsoones come betweene
And chop on some cold thought, thrice blessed chance
To drop on such a Mistris, expectation
Most giltlesse on't: tell me O Lady Fortune   1120
(Next after *Emely* my Soveraigne) how far
I may be prowd. She takes strong note of me,
Hath made me neere her; and this beuteous Morne
(The prim'st of all the yeare) presents me with
A brace of horses, two such Steeds might well
Be by a paire of Kings backt, in a Field
That their crownes titles tride: Alas, alas
Poore Cosen *Palamon*, poore prisoner, thou
So little dream'st upon my fortune, that
Thou thinkst thy selfe, the happier thing, to be   1130

So neare *Emilia*, me thou deem'st at *Thebs*,
And therein wretched, although free; But if
Thou knew'st my Mistris breathd on me, and that
I ear'd her language, livde in her eye; O Coz
What passion would enclose thee.

> *Enter Palamon as out of a Bush, with his Shackles:*
> *bends his fist at Arcite*

PALAMON   Traytor kinseman,
Thou shouldst perceive my passion, if these signes
Of prisonment were off me, and this hand
But owner of a Sword: By all othes in one
I, and the iustice of my love would make thee
1140   A confest Traytor, o thou most perfidious
That ever gently lookd, the voyd'st of honour,
That eu'r bore gentle Token; falsest Cosen
That ever blood made kin, call'st thou hir thine?
Ile prove it in my Shackles, with these hands,
Void of appointment, that thou ly'st, and art
A very theefe in love, a Chaffy Lord
Not worth the name of villaine: had I a Sword
And these house clogges away.

ARCITE   Deere Cosin *Palamon*,
PALAMON
Cosoner *Arcite*, give me language, such
As thou hast shewd me feate.

1150   ARCITE   Not finding in
The circuit of my breast, any grosse stuffe
To forme me like your blazon, holds me to
This gentlenesse of answer; tis your passion
That thus mistakes, the which to you being enemy,
Cannot to me be kind: honor, and honestie
I cherish, and depend on, how so ev'r
You skip them in me, and with them faire Coz
Ile maintaine my proceedings; pray be pleas'd
To shew in generous termes, your griefes, since that
1160   Your question's with your equall, who professes
To cleare his owne way, with the minde and Sword
Of a true Gentleman.

PALAMON   That thou durst *Arcite*.
ARCITE
My Coz, my Coz, you have beene well advertis'd
How much I dare, y'ave seene me use my Sword
Against th'advice of feare: sure of another
You would not heare me doubted, but your silence
Should breake out, though i'th Sanctuary.

PALAMON   Sir,
I have seene you move in such a place, which well
Might justifie your manhood, you were calld
A good knight and a bold; But the whole weeke's not
1170   faire
If any day it rayne: Their valiant temper
Men loose when they encline to trecherie,
And then they fight like compelld Beares, would fly
Were they not tyde.

ARCITE   Kinsman, you might as well
Speake this, and act it in your Glasse, as to
His eare, which now disdaines you.

PALAMON   Come up to me,

Quit me of these cold Gyves, give me a Sword
Though it be rustie, and the charity
Of one meale lend me; Come before me then
A good Sword in thy hand, and doe but say   1180
That *Emily* is thine, I will forgive
The trespasse thou hast done me, yea my life
If then thou carry't, and brave soules in shades
That have dyde manly, which will seeke of me
Some newes from earth, they shall get none but this
That thou art brave, and noble.

ARCITE   Be content,
Againe betake you to your hawthorne house,
With counsaile of the night, I will be here
With wholesome viands; these impediments
Will I file off, you shall have garments, and   1190
Perfumes to kill the smell o'th prison, after
When you shall stretch your selfe, and say but *Arcite*
I am in plight, there shall be at your choyce
Both Sword, and Armour.

PALAMON   Oh you heavens, dares any
So noble beare a guilty busines! none
But onely *Arcite*, therefore none but *Arcite*
In this kinde is so bold.

ARCITE   Sweete *Palamon*.
PALAMON
I doe embrace you, and your offer, for
Your offer doo't I onely, Sir your person
Without hipocrisy I may not wish   1200

> *Winde hornes of: Cornets*

More then my Swords edge ont.

ARCITE   You heare the Hornes;
Enter your Musitte least this match between's
Be crost, er met, give me your hand, farewell.
Ile bring you every needfull thing: I pray you
Take comfort and be strong.

PALAMON   Pray hold your promise;
And doe the deede with a bent brow, most certaine
You love me not, be rough with me, and powre
This oile out of your language; by this ayre
I could for each word, give a Cuffe: my stomach
Not reconcild by reason.

ARCITE   Plainely spoken,   1210
Yet pardon me hard language, when I spur

> *Winde hornes within*

My horse, I chide him not; content, and anger
In me have but one face. Harke Sir, they call
The scatterd to the Banket; you must guesse
I have an office there.

PALAMON   Sir your attendance
Cannot please heaven, and I know your office
Vnjustly is atcheev'd.

ARCITE   Tis a good title,
I am perswaded this question sicke between's,
By bleeding must be cur'd. I am a Suitour,
That to your Sword you will bequeath this plea,   1220
And talke of it no more.

PALAMON   But this one word:

You are going now to gaze upon my Mistris,
For note you, mine she is.
ARCITE   Nay then.
PALAMON   Nay pray you,
You talke of feeding me to breed me strength,
You are going now to looke upon a Sun
That strengthens what it lookes on, there you have
A vantage ore me, but enjoy it till
I may enforce my remedy. Farewell.
                    Exeunt severally: ⌈*Palamon as into the Bush*⌉

3.2   *Enter Iaylors daughter alone, with a File*
(Sc. 13) DAUGHTER
         He has mistooke the Brake I meant, is gone
1230   After his fancy, Tis now welnigh morning,
         No matter, would it were perpetuall night,
         And darkenes Lord o'th world, Harke tis a woolfe:
         In me hath greife slaine feare, and but for one thing
         I care for nothing, and that's *Palamon.*
         I wreake not if the wolves would jaw me, so
         He had this File; what if I hallowd for him?
         I cannot hallow: if I whoop'd; what then?
         If he not answeard, I should call a wolfe,
         And doe him but that service. I have heard
1240   Strange howles this live-long night, why may't not be
         They have made prey of him? he has no weapons,
         He cannot run, the Iengling of his Gives
         Might call fell things to listen, who have in them
         A sence to know a man unarmd, and can
         Smell where resistance is. Ile set it downe
         He's torne to peeces, they howld many together
         And then they fedd on him: So much for that,
         Be bold to ring the Bell; how stand I then?
         All's char'd when he is gone, No, no I lye,
1250   My Father's to be hang'd for his escape,
         My selfe to beg, if I prizd life so much
         As to deny my act, but that I would not,
         Should I try death by dussons: I am mop't,
         Foode tooke I none these two daies.
         Sipt some water. I have not closd mine eyes
         Save when my lids scowrd off their brine; alas
         Dissolue my life, Let not my sence unsettle
         Least I should drowne, or stab, or hang my selfe.
         O state of Nature, faile together in me,
1260   Since thy best props are warpt: So which way now?
         The best way is, the next way to a grave:
         Each errant step beside is torment. Loe
         The Moone is down, the Cryckets chirpe, the
              Schreichowle
         Calls in the dawne; all offices are done
         Save what I faile in: But the point is this
         An end, and that is all.   *Exit*

3.3   *Enter Arcite, with a bundle containing Meate,*
(Sc. 14)   *Wine, and Files*
         ARCITE
         I should be neere the place, hoa. Cosen *Palamon.*
              Enter Palamon ⌈*as from the Bush*⌉

PALAMON
Arcite.
ARCITE   The same: I have brought you foode and files,
Come forth and feare not, her'es no *Theseus.*
PALAMON
Nor none so honest *Arcite.*
ARCITE   That's no matter,   1270
Wee'l argue that hereafter: Come take courage,
You shall not dye thus beastly, here Sir drinke
I know you are faint, then ile talke further with you.
PALAMON
Arcite, thou mightst now poyson me.
ARCITE   I might.
But I must feare you first: Sit downe, and good now
No more of these vaine parlies; let us not
Having our ancient reputation with us
Make talke for Fooles, and Cowards, To your
     health, Sᵣ.
PALAMON
Doe.
     ⌈*Arcite drinkes*⌉
ARCITE Pray sit downe then, and let me entreate you
By all the honesty and honour in you,   1280
No mention of this woman, t'will disturbe us,
We shall have time enough.
PALAMON   Well Sir, Ile pledge you.
     Palamon drinkes
ARCITE
Drinke a good hearty draught, it breeds good blood
     man.
Doe not you feele it thaw you?
PALAMON   Stay, Ile tell you
After a draught or two more.
     Palamon drinkes
ARCITE   Spare it not,
The Duke has more Cuz: Eate now.
PALAMON   Yes.
     Palamon eates
ARCITE   I am glad
You have so good a stomach.
PALAMON   I am gladder
I have so good meate too't.
ARCITE   Is't not mad lodging,
Here in the wild woods Cosen?
PALAMON   Yes, for them
That have wilde Consciences.
ARCITE   How tasts your vittails?   1290
Your hunger needs no sawce I see.
PALAMON   Not much.
But if it did, yours is too tart: sweete Cosen:
What is this?
ARCITE   Venison.
PALAMON   Tis a lusty meate:
Giue me more wine; here *Arcite* to the wenches
We have known in our daies. ⌈*Drinking*⌉ The Lord
     Stewards daughter.
Doe you remember her?
ARCITE   After you Cuz.

PALAMON
> She lov'd a black-haird man.

ARCITE   She did so; well Sir.

PALAMON
> And I have heard some call him *Arcite*, and

ARCITE
> Out with't faith.

PALAMON   She met him in an Arbour:
1300 What did she there Cuz? play o'th virginals?

ARCITE
> Something she did Sir.

PALAMON   Made her groane a moneth for't;
> Or 2. or 3. or 10.

ARCITE   The Marshals Sister,
> Had her share too, as I remember Cosen,
> Else there be tales abroad, you'l pledge her?

PALAMON   Yes.

> ⌈*They drinke*⌉

ARCITE
> A pretty broune wench t'is. There was a time
> When yong men went a hunting, and a wood,
> And a broade Beech: and thereby hangs a tale:
> Heigh ho.

PALAMON   For *Emily*, upon my life; Foole
> Away with this straind mirth; I say againe
1310 That sigh was breathd for *Emily*; base Cosen,
> Dar'st thou breake first?

ARCITE   You are wide.

PALAMON   By heaven and earth,
> Ther's nothing in thee honest.

ARCITE   Then Ile leave you:
> You are a Beast now.

PALAMON   As thou makst me, Traytour.

ARCITE (*pointing to the bundle*)
> Ther's all things needfull, files and shirts, and,
>   perfumes:
> Ile come againe some two howres hence, and bring
> That that shall quiet all.

PALAMON   A Sword and Armour.

ARCITE
> Feare me not; you are now too fowle; farewell.
> Get off your Trinkets, you shall want nought.

PALAMON   Sirha:

ARCITE
> Ile heare no more.   *Exit*

PALAMON   If he keepe touch, he dies for't.

> *Exit* ⌈*as into the Bush*⌉

3.4   *Enter Iaylors daughter*
(Sc. 15) DAUGHTER
1320 I am very cold, and all the Stars are out too,
> The little Stars, and all, that looke like aglets:
> The Sun has seene my Folly: *Palamon*;
> Alas no; hees in heaven; where am I now?
> Yonder's the sea, and ther's a Ship; how't tumbles
> And ther's a Rocke lies watching under water;
> Now, now, it beates upon it; now, now, now,
> Ther's a leak sprung, a sound one, how they cry?
> Open her before the winde, you'l loose all els:

Vp with a course or two, and take about Boyes.
> Good night, good night, y'ar gone; I am very hungry,   1330
> Would I could finde a fine Frog; he would tell me
> Newes from all parts o'th world, then would I make
> A Carecke of a Cockle shell, and sayle
> By east and North East to the King of *Pigmes*,
> For he tels fortunes rarely. Now my Father
> Twenty to one is trust up in a trice
> To morrow morning, Ile say never a word.

(*Sing*)
> *For ile cut my greene coat, a foote above my knee,*
> *And ile clip my yellow lockes, an inch below mine eie.*
> *Hey, nonny, nonny, nonny,*   1340
> *He's buy me a white Cut, forth for to ride*
> *And ile goe seeke him, throw the world that is so wide*
> *Hey, nonny, nonny, nonny.*

O for a pricke now like a Nightingale,
> To put my breast against. I shall sleepe like a Top else.
>   *Exit*

> *Enter Gerrold (a Schoole master) .4. Countrymen:*   **3.5**
> *and .1. as a Bavian, 5. wenches, with Timothy (a*   (Sc. 1
> *Taborer), all as morris dancers*

SCHOOLEMASTER Fy, fy,
> What tediosity, & disensanity
> Is here among ye? have my Rudiments
> Bin labourd so long with ye? milkd unto ye,
> And by a figure even the very plumbroth   1350
> And marrow of my understanding laid upon ye?
> And do you still cry where, and how, & wherfore?
> You most course freeze capacities, ye jane Iudgements,
> Have I saide thus let be, and there let be,
> And then let be, and no man understand mee,
> *Proh deum, medius fidius,* ye are all dunces:
> For why here stand I. Here the Duke comes, there are
>   you
> Close in the Thicket; the Duke appeares, I meete him
> And unto him I utter learned things,
> And many figures, he heares, and nods, and hums,   1360
> And then cries rare, and I goe forward, at length
> I fling my Cap up; marke there; then do you
> As once did *Meleager*, and the *Bore*
> Break comly out before him: like true lovers,
> Cast your selves in a Body decently,
> And sweetly, by a figure, trace and turne Boyes.

1. COUNTRYMAN
> And sweetly we will doe it Master *Gerrold*.

2. COUNTRYMAN
> Draw up the Company, Where's the Taborour.

3. COUNTRYMAN
> Why *Timothy*.

TABOROUR   Here my mad boyes, have at ye.

SCHOOLEMASTER
> But I say where's theis women?

4. COUNTRYMAN   Here's *Friz* and *Maudline*.   1370

2. COUNTRYMAN
> And little *Luce* with the white legs, and bouncing
>   *Barbery*.

1. COUNTRYMAN
And freckeled *Nel*; that never faild her Master.

SCHOOLEMASTER
Wher be your Ribands maids? swym with your Bodies
And carry it sweetly, and deliverly
And now and then a fauour, and a friske.

NEL
Let us alone Sir.

SCHOOLEMASTER   Wher's the rest o'th Musicke.

3. COUNTRYMAN
Dispersd as you commanded.

SCHOOLEMASTER   Couple then
And see what's wanting; wher's the *Bavian*?
(*To the Bavian*) My friend, carry your taile without
    offence
1380   Or scandall to the Ladies; and be sure
You tumble with audacity, and manhood,
And when you barke doe it with judgement.

BAVIAN   Yes Sir.

SCHOOLEMASTER
Quo usque tandem. Here is a woman wanting.

4. COUNTRYMAN
We may goe whistle: all the fat's i'th fire.

SCHOOLEMASTER We have,
As learned Authours utter, washd a Tile,
We have beene *fatuus*, and labour'd vainely.

2. COUNTRYMAN
This is that scornefull peece, that scurvy hilding
That gave her promise faithfully, she would be here,
1390   Cicely the Sempsters daughter:
The next gloves that I give her shall be dog skin;
Nay and she faile me once, you can tell *Arcas*
She swore by wine, and bread, she would not breake.

SCHOOLEMASTER An Eele and woman,
A learned Poet sayes: unles by'th taile
And with thy teeth thou hold, will either faile,
In manners this was false position.

1. COUNTRYMAN
A fire ill take her; do's she flinch now?

3. COUNTRYMAN   What
Shall we determine Sir?

SCHOOLEMASTER   Nothing,
1400   Our busines is become a nullity
Yea, and a woefull, and a pittious nullity.

4. COUNTRYMAN
Now when the credite of our Towne lay on it,
Now to be frampall, now to pisse o'th nettle,
Goe thy waies, ile remember thee, ile fit thee.
    Enter Iaylors daughter

DAUGHTER (*sings*)
        The George alow, came from the South,
            From the coast of Barbary a.
        And there he met with brave gallants of war
            By one, by two, by three, a.
        Well haild, well haild, you jolly gallants,
1410   *And whither now are you bound a?*
        O let me have your company
            Till I come to the sound a.

There was three fooles, fell out about an howlet:

        The one he sed it was an owle
            The other he sed nay,
        The third he sed it was a hawke,
            And her bels wer cut away.

3. COUNTRYMAN
Ther's a dainty mad woman M^r.
Comes i'th Nick as mad as a march hare:
If wee can get her daunce, wee are made againe: 1420
I warrant her, shee'l doe the rarest gambols.

1. COUNTRYMAN
A mad woman? we are made Boyes.

SCHOOLEMASTER (*to the Daughter*)
And are you mad good woman?

DAUGHTER   I would be sorry else,
Give me your hand.

SCHOOLEMASTER   Why?

DAUGHTER   I can tell your fortune.
    ⌈*She examines his hand*⌉
You are a foole: tell ten, I have pozd him: Buz.
Friend you must eate no white bread, if you doe
Your teeth will bleede extreamely, shall we dance ho?
I know you, y'ar a Tinker: Sirha Tinker
Stop no more holes, but what you should.

SCHOOLEMASTER   *Dij boni.*
A Tinker Damzell?

DAUGHTER   Or a Conjurer: 1430
Raise me a devill now, and let him play
Quipassa, o'th bels and bones.

SCHOOLEMASTER   Goe take her,
And fluently perswade her to a peace:
Et opus exegi, quod nec Iouis ira, nec ignis.
Strike up, and leade her in.

2. COUNTRYMAN   Come Lasse, lets trip it.

DAUGHTER Ile leade.

3. COUNTRYMAN Doe, doe.

SCHOOLEMASTER
Perswasively, and cunningly:
    Winde Hornes within
                        away boyes,
I heare the hornes: give me some meditation,
And marke your Cue;   *Exeunt all but Schoolemaster*
                    Pallas inspire me.   1440
    Enter Theseus, Pirithous, Hipolita, Emilia, Arcite:
    and traine

THESEUS This way the Stag tooke.

SCHOOLEMASTER Stay, and edifie.

THESEUS What have we here?

PIRITHOUS
Some Countrey sport, upon my life Sir.

THESEUS (*to the Schoolemaster*)
Well Sir, goe forward, we will edifie.
Ladies sit downe, wee'l stay it.
    They sit: ⌈*Theseus*⌉ *in a chaire, the others on stooles*

SCHOOLEMASTER
Thou doughtie Duke all haile: all haile sweet Ladies.

THESEUS This is a cold beginning.

SCHOOLEMASTER

If you but favour; our Country pastime made is,
1450   We are a few of those collected here
That ruder Tongues distinguish villager,
And to say veritie, and not to fable;
We are a merry rout, or else a rable
Or company, or by a figure, *Choris*
That fore thy dignitie will dance a Morris.
And I that am the rectifier of all
By title Pedagogus, that let fall
The Birch upon the breeches of the small ones,
And humble with a Ferula the tall ones,
1460   Doe here present this Machine, or this frame,
And daintie Duke, whose doughtie dismall fame
From *Dis* to *Dedalus*, from post to pillar
Is blowne abroad; helpe me thy poore well willer,
And with thy twinckling eyes, looke right and
    straight
Vpon this mighty Morr—of mickle waight—
Is now comes in, which being glewd together
Makes Morris, and the cause that we came hether.
The body of our sport of no small study
I first appeare, though rude, and raw, and muddy,
1470   To speake before thy noble grace, this tenner:
At whose great feete I offer up my penner.
The next the Lord of May, and Lady bright,
The Chambermaid, and Servingman by night
That seeke out silent hanging: Then mine Host
And his fat Spowse, that welcomes to their cost
The gauled Traveller, and with a beckning
Informes the Tapster to inflame the reckning:
Then the beast eating Clowne, and next the foole,
The *Bavian* with long tayle, and eke long toole,
1480   *Cum multis alijs* that make a dance,
Say I, and all shall presently advance.

THESEUS

I, I by any meanes, deere Domine.

PIRITHOUS   Produce.

SCHOOLEMASTER (*knocke for the Dance*)
Intrate filij, Come forth, and foot it,

⌐*He flings up his Cap.*⌐ *Musicke.*
⌐*The Schoolemaster ushers in*

May Lord,   *May Lady.*
Servingman,   *Chambermaide.*
A Countrey Clowne,
  or Shepheard,   *Countrey Wench.*
An Host,   *Hostesse.*
A Hee Bavian,   *Shee Bavian.*
A Hee Foole,   *The Iaylors Daughter as*
                Shee Foole.

*All these persons apparelled to the life, the Men
issuing out of one doore, and the Wenches from the
other. They dance a morris*⌐

Ladies, if we have beene merry
And have pleasd yee with a derry,
And a derry, and a downe
Say the Schoolemaster's no Clowne:

Duke, if we have pleasd thee too
And have done as good Boyes should doe,
Give us but a tree or twaine   1490
For a Maypole, and againe
Ere another yeare run out,
Wee'l make thee laugh and all this rout.

THESEUS

Take 20. Domine; (*to Hipolita*) how does my sweet
    heart.

HIPOLITA

Never so pleasd Sir.

EMILIA   Twas an excellent dance,
And for a preface I never heard a better.

THESEUS

Schoolemaster, I thanke you, One see'em all rewarded.

PIRITHOUS

And heer's something to paint your Pole withall.
    He gives them money

THESEUS Now to our sports againe.

SCHOOLEMASTER

May the Stag thou huntst stand long,   1500
And thy dogs be swift and strong:
May they kill him without lets,
And the Ladies eate his dowsets:
    *Exeunt Theseus and traine. Winde Hornes
                          within*
Come we are all made. *Dij Deæq; omnes,*
Ye have danc'd rarely wenches.   *Exeunt*

Enter Palamon from the Bush   **3.6**

PALAMON   (Sc. 1?

About this houre my Cosen gave his faith
To visit me againe, and with him bring
Two Swords, and two good Armors; if he faile
He's neither man, nor Souldier; when he left me
I did not thinke a weeke could have restord   1510
My lost strength to me, I was growne so low,
And Crest-falne with my wants: I thanke thee *Arcite*,
Thou art yet a faire Foe; and I feele my selfe
With this refreshing, able once againe
To out dure danger: To delay it longer
Would make the world think when it comes to hearing,
That I lay fatting like a Swine, to fight
And not a Souldier: Therefore this blest morning
Shall be the last; and that Sword he refuses,
If it but hold, I kill him with; tis Iustice: 1520
So love, and Fortune for me:
    Enter Arcite with two Armors and two Swords
                  O good morrow.

ARCITE

Good morrow noble kinesman.

PALAMON   I have put you
To too much paines Sir.

ARCITE   That too much faire Cosen,
Is but a debt to honour, and my duty.

PALAMON

Would you were so in all Sir; I could wish ye
As kinde a kinsman, as you force me finde

A beneficiall foe, that my embraces
Might thanke ye, not my blowes.

ARCITE   I shall thinke either
Well done, a noble recompence.

PALAMON   Then I shall quit you.

ARCITE

1530   Defy me in these faire termes, and you show
More then a Mistris to me, no more anger
As you love any thing that's honourable;
We were not bred to talke man, when we are arm'd
And both upon our guards, then let our fury
Like meeting of two tides, fly strongly from us,
And then to whom the birthright of this Beauty
Truely pertaines (without obbraidings, scornes,
Dispisings of our persons, and such powtings
Fitter for Girles and Schooleboyes) will be seene

1540   And quickly, yours, or mine: wilt please you arme Sir,
Or if you feele your selfe not fitting yet
And furnishd with your old strength, ile stay Cosen
And ev'ry day discourse you into health,
As I am spard, your person I am friends with,
And I could wish I had not saide I lov'd her
Though I had dide; But loving such a Lady
And justifying my Love, I must not fly from't.

PALAMON
Arcite, thou art so brave an enemy
That no man but thy Cosen's fit to kill thee,
I am well, and lusty, choose your Armes.

1550   ARCITE   Choose you Sir.

PALAMON
Wilt thou exceede in all, or do'st thou doe it
To make me spare thee?

ARCITE   If you thinke so Cosen,
You are deceiv'd, for as I am a Soldier,
I will not spare you.

PALAMON   That's well said.

ARCITE   You'l finde it.

PALAMON
Then as I am an honest man and love,
With all the justice of affection
Ile pay thee soundly:
    He chooses an armour
                This ile take.

ARCITE (*indicating the remaining armour*)
                            That's mine then,
Ile arme you first.

PALAMON   Do:
    Arcite arms Palamon
                pray thee tell me Cosen,
Where gotst thou this good Armour.

ARCITE   Tis the Dukes,
And to say true, I stole it; doe I pinch you?

1560   PALAMON   Noe.

ARCITE
Is't not too heavie?

PALAMON   I have worne a lighter,
But I shall make it serve.

ARCITE   Ile buckl't close.

PALAMON
By any meanes.

ARCITE   You care not for a Grand guard?

PALAMON
No, no, wee'l use no horses, I perceave
You would faine be at that Fight.

ARCITE   I am indifferent.

PALAMON
Faith so am I: good Cosen, thrust the buckle
Through far enough.

ARCITE   I warrant you.

PALAMON   My Caske now.

ARCITE
Will you fight bare-armd?

PALAMON   We shall be the nimbler.

ARCITE
But use your Gauntlets though; those are o'th least,
Prethee take mine good Cosen.

PALAMON   Thanke you *Arcite*.   1570
How doe I looke, am I falne much away?

ARCITE
Faith very little; love has usd you kindly.

PALAMON
Ile warrant thee, Ile strike home.

ARCITE   Doe, and spare not;
Ile give you cause sweet Cosen.

PALAMON   Now to you Sir,
    Palamon arms Arcite
Me thinkes this Armo'rs very like that, *Arcite*,
Thou wor'st that day the 3. Kings fell, but lighter.

ARCITE
That was a very good one, and that day
I well remember, you outdid me Cosen,
I never saw such valour: when you chargd
Vpon the left wing of the Enemie,   1580
I spurd hard to come up, and under me
I had a right good horse.

PALAMON   You had indeede
A bright Bay I remember.

ARCITE   Yes but all
Was vainely labour'd in me, you outwent me,
Nor could my wishes reach you; yet a little
I did by imitation.

PALAMON   More by vertue,
You are modest Cosen.

ARCITE   When I saw you charge first,
Me thought I heard a dreadfull clap of Thunder
Breake from the Troope.

PALAMON   But still before that flew
The lightning of your valour: Stay a little,   1590
Is not this peece too streight?

ARCITE   No, no, tis well.

PALAMON
I would have nothing hurt thee but my Sword,
A bruise would be dishonour.

ARCITE   Now I am perfect.

PALAMON
Stand off then.

ARCITE   Take my Sword, I hold it better.

PALAMON

    I thanke ye: No, keepe it, your life lyes on it,
    Here's one, if it but hold, I aske no more,
    For all my hopes: My Cause and honour guard me.

ARCITE

    And me my love:
        They bow severall wayes: then advance and stand
                Is there ought else to say?

PALAMON

    This onely, and no more: Thou art mine Aunts Son.
1600   And that blood we desire to shed is mutuall,
    In me, thine, and in thee, mine: My Sword
    Is in my hand, and if thou killst me
    The gods, and I forgive thee; If there be
    A place prepar'd for those that sleepe in honour,
    I wish his wearie soule, that falls may win it:
    Fight bravely Cosen, give me thy noble hand.

ARCITE

    Here *Palamon*: This hand shall never more
    Come neare thee with such friendship.

PALAMON   I commend thee.

ARCITE

    If I fall, curse me, and say I was a coward,
1610   For none but such, dare die in these just Tryalls.
    Once more farewell my Cosen.

PALAMON   Farewell *Arcite*.
        Fight. Hornes within: they stand

ARCITE

    Loe Cosen, loe, our Folly has undon us.

PALAMON   Why?

ARCITE

    This is the Duke, a hunting as I told you,
    If we be found, we are wretched, O retire
    For honours sake, and safely presently
    Into your Bush agen; Sir we shall finde
    Too many howres to dye; in, gentle Cosen:
    If you be seene you perish instantly
    For breaking prison, and I, if you reveale me,
1620   For my contempt; Then all the world will scorne us,
    And say we had a noble difference,
    But base disposers of it.

PALAMON   No, no, Cosen
    I will no more be hidden, nor put off
    This great adventure to a second Tryall:
    I know your cunning, and I know your cause,
    He that faints now, shame take him, put thy selfe
    Vpon thy present guard.

ARCITE   You are not mad?

PALAMON

    Or I will make th'advantage of this howre
    Mine owne, and what to come shall threaten me,
1630   I feare lesse then my fortune: know weake Cosen
    I love *Emilia*, and in that ile bury
    Thee, and all crosses else.

ARCITE   Then come, what can come
    Thou shalt know *Palamon*, I dare as well
    Die, as discourse, or sleepe: Onely this feares me,

    The law will have the honour of our ends.
    Have at thy life.

PALAMON   Looke to thine owne well *Arcite*.
    Fight againe.
    Hornes. Enter Theseus, Hipolita, Emilia, Perithous
    and traine. ⌈*Theseus*⌉ *separates Palamon and Arcite*

THESEUS

    What ignorant and mad malicious Traitors,
    Are you? That gainst the tenor of my Lawes
    Are making Battaile, thus like Knights appointed,
    Without my leave, and Officers of Armes?   1640
    By *Castor* both shall dye.

PALAMON   Hold thy word *Theseus*,
    We are certainly both Traitors, both despisers
    Of thee, and of thy goodnesse: I am *Palamon*
    That cannot love thee, he that broke thy Prison,
    Thinke well, what that deserves; and this is *Arcite*
    A bolder Traytor never trod thy ground
    A Falser neu'r seem'd friend: This is the man
    Was begd and banish'd, this is he contemnes thee
    And what thou dar'st doe; and in this disguise
    Against thīe owne Edict followes thy Sister,   1650
    That fortunate bright Star, the faire *Emilia*
    Whose servant, (if there be a right in seeing,
    And first bequeathing of the soule to) justly
    I am, and which is more, dares thinke her his.
    This treacherie like a most trusty Lover,
    I call'd him now to answer; if thou bee'st
    As thou art spoken, great and vertuous,
    The true descider of all injuries,
    Say, Fight againe, and thou shalt see me *Theseus*
    Doe such a Iustice, thou thy selfe wilt envie,   1660
    Then take my life, Ile wooe thee too't.

PIRITHOUS   O heaven,
    What more then man is this!

THESEUS   I have sworne.

ARCITE   We seeke not
    Thy breath of mercy *Theseus*, Tis to me
    A thing as soone to dye, as thee to say it,
    And no more mov'd: where this man calls me Traitor,
    Let me say thus much; if in love be Treason,
    In service of so excellent a Beutie,
    As I love most, and in that faith will perish,
    As I have brought my life here to confirme it,
    As I have seru'd her truest, worthiest,   1670
    As I dare kill this Cosen, that denies it,
    So let me be most Traitor, and ye please me:
    For scorning thy Edict Duke, aske that Lady
    Why she is faire, and why her eyes command me
    Stay here to love her; and if she say Traytor,
    I am a villaine fit to lye unburied.

PALAMON

    Thou shalt have pitty of us both, o *Theseus*,
    If unto neither thou shew mercy, stop,
    (As thou art just) thy noble eare against us,
    As thou art valiant, for thy Cosens soule   1680
    Whose 12. strong labours crowne his memory,
    Lets die together, at one instant Duke,

Onely a little let him fall before me,
That I may tell my Soule he shall not have her.

THESEUS
I grant your wish, for to say true, your Cosen
Has ten times more offended, for I gave him
More mercy then you found, Sir, your offenses
Being no more then his: None here speake for'em
For ere the Sun set, both shall sleepe for ever.

HIPOLITA (to Emilia)
1690   Alas the pitty, now or never Sister
Speake not to be denide; That face of yours
Will beare the curses else of after ages
For these lost Cosens.

EMILIA   In my face deare Sister
I finde no anger to'em; nor no ruyn,
The misadventure of their owne eyes kill'em;
Yet that I will be woman, and have pitty,
     ⌐She kneeles⌐
My knees shall grow to'th ground but Ile get mercie.
Helpe me deare Sister, in a deede so vertuous,
The powers of all women will be with us,
     Hipolita kneeles
Most royall Brother.

1700 HIPOLITA   Sir by our tye of Marriage.

EMILIA
By your owne spotlesse honour.

HIPOLITA   By that faith,
That faire hand, and that honest heart you gave me.

EMILIA
By that you would have pitty in another,
By your owne vertues infinite.

HIPOLITA   By valour,
By all the chaste nights I have ever pleasd you.

THESEUS
These are strange Conjurings.

PIRITHOUS   Nay then Ile in too:
     ⌐He kneeles⌐
By all our friendship Sir, by all our dangers,
By all you love most, warres; and this sweet Lady.

EMILIA
By that you would have trembled to deny
A blushing Maide.

1710 HIPOLITA   By your owne eyes: By strength
In which you swore I went beyond all women,
Almost all men, and yet I yeelded Theseus.

PIRITHOUS
To crowne all this; By your most noble soule
Which cannot want due mercie, I beg first.

HIPOLITA
Next heare my prayers.

EMILIA   Last let me intreate Sir.

PIRITHOUS
For mercy.

HIPOLITA   Mercy.

EMILIA   Mercy on these Princes.

THESEUS
Ye make my faith reele: Say I felt
Compassion to'em both, how would you place it?

⌐They rise⌐

EMILIA
Vpon their lives: But with their banishments.

THESEUS
You are a right woman, Sister; you have pitty,   1720
But want the vnderstanding where to use it.
If you desire their lives, invent a way
Safer then banishment: Can these two live
And have the agony of love about 'em,
And not kill one another? Every day
The'yld fight about you; howrely bring your honour
In publique question with their Swords; Be wise then
And here forget 'em; it concernes your credit,
And my oth equally: I have said they die,
Better they fall by'th law, then one another.   1730
Bow not my honor.

EMILIA   O my noble Brother,
That oth was rashly made, and in your anger,
Your reason will not hold it, if such vowes
Stand for expresse will, all the world must perish.
Beside, I have another oth, gainst yours
Of more authority, I am sure more love,
Not made in passion neither, but good heede.

THESEUS
What is it Sister?

PIRITHOUS (to Emilia) Vrge it home brave Lady.

EMILIA
That you would nev'r deny me any thing
Fit for my modest suit, and your free granting: 1740
I tye you to your word now, if ye fall in't,
Thinke how you maime your honour;
(For now I am set a begging Sir, I am deafe
To all but your compassion) how their lives
Might breed the ruine of my name, Opinion;
Shall any thing that loves me perish for me?
That were a cruell wisedome, doe men proyne
The straight yong Bowes that blush with thousand
     Blossoms
Because they may be rotten? O Duke Theseus
The goodly Mothers that have groand for these,   1750
And all the longing Maides that ever lov'd,
If your vow stand, shall curse me and my Beauty,
And in their funerall songs, for these two Cosens
Despise my crueltie, and cry woe worth me,
Till I am nothing but the scorne of women;
For heavens sake save their lives, and banish 'em.

THESEUS
On what conditions?

EMILIA   Sweare'em never more
To make me their Contention, or to know me,
To tread upon thy Dukedome, and to be
Where ever they shall travel, ever strangers   1760
To one another.

PALAMON   Ile be cut a peeces
Before I take this oth, forget I love her?
O all ye gods dispise me then: Thy Banishment
I not mislike, so we may fairely carry
Our Swords, and cause along: else never trifle,

But take our lives Duke, I must love and will,
And for that love, must and dare kill this Cosen
On any peece the earth has.

THESEUS   Will you *Arcite*
Take these conditions?

PALAMON   H'es a villaine then.

PIRITHOUS   These are men.

ARCITE

1770   No, never Duke: Tis worse to me than begging
To take my life so basely, though I thinke
I never shall enjoy her, yet ile preserve
The honour of affection, and dye for her,
Make death a Devill.

THESEUS
What may be done? for now I feele compassion.

PIRITHOUS
Let it not fall agen Sir.

THESEUS   Say *Emilia*
If one of them were dead, as one must, are you
Content to take the other to your husband?
They cannot both enjoy you; They are Princes
1780   As goodly as your owne eyes, and as noble
As ever fame yet spoke of; looke upon'em,
And if you can love, end this difference,
I give consent, (*to Palamon and Arcite*) are you content
    too Princes?

PALAMON *and* ARCITE
With all our soules.

THESEUS   He that she refuses
Must dye then.

PALAMON *and* ARCITE Any death thou canst invent Duke.

PALAMON
If I fall from that mouth, I fall with favour,
And Lovers yet unborne shall blesse my ashes.

ARCITE
If she refuse me, yet my grave will wed me,
And Souldiers sing my Epitaph.

THESEUS (*to Emilia*)   Make choice then.

EMILIA

1790   I cannot Sir, they are both too excellent:
For me, a hayre shall never fall of these men.

HIPOLITA ⌈*to Theseus*⌉
What will become of'em?

THESEUS   Thus I ordaine it,
And by mine honor, once againe it stands,
Or both shall dye. (*To Palamon and Arcite*) You shall
    both to your Countrey,
And each within this moneth accompanied
With three faire Knights, appeare againe in this place,
In which Ile plant a Pyramid; and whether
Before us that are here, can force his Cosen
By fayre and knightly strength to touch the Pillar,
1800   He shall enjoy her: the other loose his head,
And all his friends; Nor shall he grudge to fall,
Nor thinke he dies with interest in this Lady:
Will this content yee?

PALAMON   Yes: here Cosen *Arcite*
I am friends againe, till that howre.

ARCITE   I embrace ye.

THESEUS (*to Emilia*)
Are you content Sister?

EMILIA   Yes, I must Sir,
Els both miscarry.

THESEUS (*to Palamon and Arcite*)
                    Come shake hands againe then,
And take heede, as you are Gentlemen, this Quarrell
Sleepe till the howre prefixt, and hold your course.

PALAMON
We dare not faile thee *Theseus*.

THESEUS   Come, Ile give ye
Now usage like to Princes, and to Friends: 1810
When ye returne, who wins, Ile settle heere,
Who looses, yet Ile weepe upon his Beere.
            Exeunt. ⌈*In the Act Time the Bush is remooved*⌉

            ✿

        Enter Iailor, and his friend   4.1
                                              (Sc. 1
IAYLOR
Heare you no more, was nothing saide of me
Concerning the escape of *Palamon*?
Good Sir remember.

FRIEND   Nothing that I heard,
For I came home before the busines
Was fully ended: Yet I might perceive
Ere I departed, a great likelihood
Of both their pardons: For *Hipolita*,
And faire-eyd *Emilie*, upon their knees   1820
Begd with such hansom pitty, that the Duke
Me thought stood staggering, whether he should
    follow
His rash oth, or the sweet compassion
Of those two Ladies; and to second them,
That truely noble Prince *Perithous*
Halfe his owne heart, set in too, that I hope
All shall be well: Neither heard I one question
Of your name, or his scape.
        Enter 2. Friend

IAYLOR   Pray heaven it hold so.

2. FRIEND
Be of good comfort man; I bring you newes,
Good newes.

IAYLOR   They are welcome.

2. FRIEND   *Palamon* has cleerd you, 1830
And got your pardon, and discoverd how,
And by whose meanes hee scapt, which was your
    Daughters,
Whose pardon is procurd too, and the Prisoner
Not to be held ungratefull to her goodnes,
Has given a summe of money to her Marriage,
A large one ile assure you.

IAYLOR   Ye are a good man
And ever bring good newes.

1. FRIEND   How was it ended?

2. FRIEND
Why, as it should be; they that nev'r begd
But they prevaild, had their suites fairely granted,
The prisoners have their lives.

1. FRIEND   I knew t'would be so. 1840

2. FRIEND
But there be new conditions, which you'l heare of
At better time.

IAYLOR   I hope they are good.

2. FRIEND   They are honourable,
How good they'l prove, I know not.
          Enter Wooer

1. FRIEND   T'will be knowne.

WOOER
Alas Sir, wher's your Daughter?

IAYLOR   Why doe you aske?

WOOER
O Sir when did you see her?

2. FRIEND   How he lookes?

IAYLOR
This morning.

WOOER   Was she well? was she in health?
Sir, when did she sleepe?

1. FRIEND   These are strange Questions.

IAYLOR
I doe not thinke she was very well, for now
You make me minde her, but this very day
1850   I ask'd her questions, and she answer'd me
So farre from what she was, so childishly,
So sillily, as if she were a foole,
An Inocent, and I was very angry.
But what of her Sir?

WOOER   Nothing but my pitty;
But you must know it, and as good by me
As by an other that lesse loves her.

IAYLOR
Well Sir.

1. FRIEND Not right?

WOOER   No Sir not well.

2. FRIEND   Not well?

WOOER
Tis too true, she is mad.

1. FRIEND   It cannot be.

WOOER
Beleeve you'l finde it so.

IAYLOR   I halfe suspected
1860   What you told me: the gods comfort her:
Either this was her love to *Palamon*,
Or feare of my miscarrying on his scape,
Or both.

WOOER   Tis likely.

IAYLOR   But why all this haste Sir?

WOOER
Ile tell you quickly. As I late was angling
In the great Lake that lies behind the Pallace,
From the far shore, thicke set with reedes, and Sedges,
As patiently I was attending sport,
I heard a voyce, a shrill one, and attentive
I gave my eare, when I might well perceive
1870   T'was one that sung, and by the smallnesse of it
A boy or woman. I then left my angle
To his owne skill, came neere, but yet perceivd not
Who made the sound; the rushes, and the Reeds
Had so encompast it: I laide me downe

And listned to the words she song, for then
Through a small glade cut by the Fisher men,
I saw it was your Daughter.

IAYLOR   Pray goe on Sir?

WOOER
She sung much, but no sence; onely I heard her
Repeat this often. *Palamon* is gone,
Is gone to'th wood to gather Mulberies,   1880
Ile finde him out to morrow.

1. FRIEND   Pretty soule.

WOOER
His shackles will betray him, hee'l be taken,
And what shall I doe then? Ile bring a beavy,
A hundred blacke eyd Maides, that love as I doe
With Chaplets on their heads of Daffadillies,
With cherry-lips, and cheekes of Damaske Roses,
And all wee'l daunce an Antique fore the Duke,
And beg his pardon; Then she talk'd of you Sir;
That you must loose your head to morrow morning,
And she must gather flowers to bury you,   1890
And see the house made handsome, then she sung
Nothing but Willow, willow, willow, and betweene
Ever was, *Palamon*, faire *Palamon*,
And *Palamon*, was a tall yong man. The place
Was knee deepe where she sat; her careles Tresses,
A wreath of bull-rush rounded; about her stucke
Thousand fresh water flowers of severall cullors.
That she appeard me thought like the faire Nimph
That feedes the lake with waters, or as Iris
Newly dropt downe from heaven; Rings she made   1900
Of rushes that grew by, and to 'em spoke
The prettiest posies: Thus our true love's tide,
This you may loose, not me, and many a one:
And then she wept, and sung againe, and sigh'd,
And with the same breath smil'd, and kist her hand.

2. FRIEND
Alas what pitty it is?

WOOER   I made in to her.
She saw me, and straight sought the flood, I sav'd
          her,
And set her safe to land: when presently
She slipt away, and to the Citty made,
With such a cry, and swiftnes, that beleeve me   1910
Shee left me farre behinde her; three, or foure,
I saw from farre off crosse her, one of 'em
I knew to be your brother, where she staid,
And fell, scarce to be got away: I left them with her,
          Enter Iaylors Brother, Iaylors Daughter, and others
And hether came to tell you: Here they are.

DAUGHTER (*singes*)
May you never more enjoy the light, &c.
Is not this a fine Song?

BROTHER   O a very fine one.

DAUGHTER
I can sing twenty more.

BROTHER   I thinke you can.

DAUGHTER
Yes truely can I, I can sing the Broome,
And Bony Robin. Are not you a tailour?   1920

BROTHER
  Yes.

DAUGHTER Wher's my wedding Gowne?

BROTHER   Ile bring it to morrow.

DAUGHTER
  Doe, very rarely, I must be abroad else
  To call the Maides, and pay the Minstrels
  For I must loose my Maydenhead by cocklight
  Twill never thrive else. (*Singes*) *O faire, oh sweete, &c.*

BROTHER ⌜*to the Iaylor*⌝
  You must ev'n take it patiently.

IAYLOR   Tis true.

DAUGHTER
  Good'ev'n, good men, pray did you ever heare
  Of one yong *Palamon*?

IAYLOR   Yes wench we know him.

DAUGHTER
  Is't not a fine yong Gentleman?

IAYLOR   Tis, Love.

BROTHER
1930 By no meane crosse her, she is then distemperd
  For worse then now she showes.

I. FRIEND (*to Iaylors Daughter*)   Yes, he's a fine man.

DAUGHTER
  O, is he so? you have a Sister.

I. FRIEND   Yes.

DAUGHTER
  But she shall never have him, tell her so,
  For a tricke that I know, y'had best looke to her,
  For if she see him once, she's gone, she's done,
  And undon in an howre. All the young Maydes
  Of our Towne are in love with him, but I laugh at'em
  And let 'em all alone, Is't not a wise course?

I. FRIEND   Yes.

DAUGHTER
1940 There is at least two hundred now with child by him,
  There must be fowre; yet I keepe close for all this,
  Close as a Cockle; and all these must be Boyes,
  He has the tricke on't, and at ten yeares old
  They must be all gelt for Musitians,
  And sing the wars of *Theseus*.

2. FRIEND   This is strange.

⌜BROTHER⌝
  As ever you heard, but say nothing.

I. FRIEND   No.

DAUGHTER
  They come from all parts of the Dukedome to him,
  Ile warrant ye, he had not so few last night
  As twenty to dispatch, hee'l tickl't up
  In two howres, if his hand be in.

IAYLOR   She's lost
  Past all cure.

1950 BROTHER   Heaven forbid man.

DAUGHTER (*to the Iaylor*)
  Come hither, you are a wise man.

I. FRIEND   Do's she know him?

2. FRIEND
  No, would she did.

DAUGHTER   You are master of a Ship?

IAYLOR
  Yes.

DAUGHTER Wher's your Compasse?

IAYLOR   Heere.

DAUGHTER   Set it too'th North.
  And now direct your course to'th wood, wher *Palamon*
  Lyes longing for me; For the Tackling
  Let me alone; Come waygh my hearts, cheerely all.
  Owgh, owgh, owgh, tis up, the wind's faire, top the
    bowling,
  Out with the maine saile, wher's your whistle Master?

BROTHER Lets get her in.

IAYLOR
  Vp to the top Boy.

BROTHER   Wher's the Pilot?

I. FRIEND   Heere.   1960

DAUGHTER
  What ken'st thou?

2. FRIEND   A faire wood.

DAUGHTER   Beare for it master:
  Take about:
  (*Singes*) *When Cinthia with her borrowed light, &c.*
                         Exeunt

⌜*Enter Emilia alone, with 2. Pictures*⌝   **4.2**
                                        (Sc. 1⌐

EMILIA
  Yet I may binde those wounds up, that must open
  And bleed to death for my sake else; Ile choose,
  And end their strife: Two such yong hansom men
  Shall never fall for me, their weeping Mothers,
  Following the dead cold ashes of their Sonnes
  Shall never curse my cruelty: Good heaven,
  What a sweet face has *Arcite*? if wise nature   1970
  With all her best endowments, all those beuties
  She sowes into the birthes of noble bodies,
  Were here a mortall woman, and had in her
  The coy denialls of yong Maydes, yet doubtles,
  She would run mad for this man: what an eye?
  Of what a fyry sparkle, and quick sweetnes,
  Has this yong Prince? Here Love himselfe sits smyling,
  Iust such another wanton *Ganimead*,
  Set Iove a fire once, and enforcd the god
  Snatch up the goodly Boy, and set him by him   1980
  A shining constellation: What a brow,
  Of what a spacious Majesty he carries?
  Arch'd like the great eyd *Iuno's*, but far sweeter,
  Smoother then *Pelops* Shoulder? Fame and honour
  Me thinks from hence, as from a Promontory
  Pointed in heaven, should clap their wings, and sing
  To all the under world, the Loves, and Fights
  Of gods, and such men neere 'em. *Palamon*,
  Is but his foyle, to him, a meere dull shadow,
  Hee's swarth, and meagre, of an eye as heavy   1990
  As if he had lost his mother; a still temper,
  No stirring in him, no alacrity,
  Of all this sprightly sharpenes, not a smile;
  Yet these that we count errours may become him:
  Narcissus was a sad Boy, but a heavenly:
  Oh who can finde the bent of womans fancy?

I am a Foole, my reason is lost in me,
I have no choice, and I have ly'd so lewdly
That women ought to beate me. On my knees
2000 I aske thy pardon: *Palamon*, thou art alone,
And only beutifull, and these the eyes,
These the bright lamps of beauty, that command
And threaten Love, and what yong Mayd dare crosse
    'em?
What a bold gravity, and yet inviting
Has this browne manly face? O Love, this only
From this howre is Complexion: Lye there *Arcite*,
Thou art a changling to him, a meere Gipsey,
And this the noble Bodie: I am sotted,
Vtterly lost: My Virgins faith has fled me.
2010 For if my brother but even now had ask'd me
Whether I lov'd, I had run mad for *Arcite*,
Now if my Sister, More for *Palamon*;
Stand both together: Now, come aske me Brother,
Alas, I know not: aske me now sweet Sister,
I may goe looke; What a meere child is *Fancie*,
That having two faire gawdes of equall sweetnesse,
Cannot distinguish, but must crie for both.
        ⌈*Enter a Gentleman*⌉
How now Sir?
GENTLEMAN   From the Noble Duke your Brother
Madam, I bring you newes: The Knights are come.
EMILIA
    To end the quarrell?
GENTLEMAN   Yes.
2020 EMILIA   Would I might end first:
What sinnes have I committed, chast *Diana*,
That my unspotted youth must now be soyld
With blood of *Princes*? and my Chastitie
Be made the Altar, where the lives of Lovers,
Two greater, and two better never yet
Made mothers joy, must be the sacrifice
To my unhappy Beautie?
        Enter Theseus, Hipolita, Perithous and attendants
THESEUS   Bring 'em in
Quickly, by any meanes, I long to see'em.
                    Exit one or more
(*To Emilia*) Your two contending Lovers are return'd,
And with them their faire Knights: Now my faire
2030   Sister,
You must love one of them.
EMILIA   I had rather both,
So neither for my sake should fall untimely.
        Enter a Messenger
THESEUS
Who saw'em?
PIRITHOUS   I a while.
GENTLEMAN   And I.
THESEUS (*to the Messenger*)
  From whence come you Sir?
MESSENGER   From the Knights.
THESEUS   Pray speake
You that have seene them, what they are.
MESSENGER   I will Sir,
And truly what I thinke: Six braver spirits

Then these they have brought, (if we judge by the
    outside)
I never saw, nor read of: He that stands
In the first place with *Arcite*, by his seeming
Should be a stout man, by his face a Prince,   2040
(His very lookes so say him) his complexion,
Nearer a browne, than blacke; sterne, and yet noble,
Which shewes him hardy, fearelesse, proud of dangers:
The circles of his eyes show fire within him,
And as a heated Lyon, so he lookes;
His haire hangs long behind him, blacke and shining
Like Ravens wings: his shoulders broad, and strong,
Armd long and round, and on his Thigh a Sword
Hung by a curious Bauldricke; when he frownes
To seale his will with, better o'my conscience   2050
Was never Souldiers friend.
THESEUS Thou ha'st well describde him.
PIRITHOUS   Yet a great deale short
Me thinkes, of him that's first with *Palamon*.
THESEUS
Pray speake him friend.
PIRITHOUS   I ghesse he is a Prince too,
And if it may be, greater; for his show
Has all the ornament of honour in't:
Hee's somewhat bigger, then the Knight he spoke of,
But of a face far sweeter; His complexion
Is (as a ripe grape) ruddy: he has felt   2060
Without doubt what he fights for, and so apter
To make this cause his owne: In's face appeares
All the faire hopes of what he undertakes,
And when he's angry, then a setled valour
(Not tainted with extreames) runs through his body,
And guides his arme to brave things: Feare he cannot,
He shewes no such soft temper, his head's yellow,
Hard hayr'd, and curld, thicke twind like Ivy tods,
Not to undoe with thunder; In his face
The liverie of the warlike Maide appeares,   2070
Pure red, and white, for yet no beard has blest him.
And in his rowling eyes, sits victory,
As if she ever ment to court his valour:
His Nose stands high, a Character of honour.
His red lips, after fights, are fit for Ladies.
EMILIA
Must these men die too?
PIRITHOUS   When he speakes, his tongue
Sounds like a Trumpet; All his lyneaments
Are as a man would wish 'em, strong, and cleane,
He weares a well-steeld Axe, the staffe of gold,
His age some five and twenty.
MESSENGER   Ther's another,   2080
A little man, but of a tough soule, seeming
As great as any: fairer promises
In such a Body, yet I never look'd on.
PIRITHOUS
O, he that's freckle fac'd?
MESSENGER   The same my Lord,
Are they not sweet ones?
PIRITHOUS   Yes they are well.
MESSENGER   Me thinkes,

Being so few, and well disposd, they show
Great, and fine art in nature, he's white hair'd,
Not wanton white, but such a manly colour
Next to an aborne, tough, and nimble set,
2090 Which showes an active soule; his armes are brawny
Linde with strong sinewes: To the shoulder peece,
Gently they swell, like women new conceav'd,
Which speakes him prone to labour, never fainting
Vnder the waight of Armes; stout harted, still,
But when he stirs, a Tiger; he's gray eyd,
Which yeelds compassion where he conquers: sharpe
To spy advantages, and where he finds 'em,
He's swift to make 'em his: He do's no wrongs,
Nor takes none; he's round fac'd, and when he smiles
2100 He showes a Lover, when he frownes, a Souldier:
About his head he weares the winners oke,
And in it stucke the favour of his Lady:
His age, some six and thirtie. In his hand
He beares a charging Staffe, embost with silver.

THESEUS
 Are they all thus?

PIRITHOUS   They are all the sonnes of honour.

THESEUS
 Now as I have a soule I long to see'em,
 (*To Hipolita*) Lady you shall see men fight now.

HIPOLITA   I wish it,
2110 But not the cause my Lord; They would show
 Bravely about the Titles of two Kingdomes;
 Tis pitty Love should be so tyrannous:
 (*To Emilia*) O my soft harted Sister, what thinke you?
 Weepe not, till they weepe blood; Wench it must be.

THESEUS (*to Emilia*)
 You have steel'd'em with your Beautie:
 (*To Perithous*)   honord Friend,
 To you I give the Feild; pray order it,
 Fitting the persons that must use it.

PIRITHOUS   Yes Sir.

THESEUS
 Come, Ile goe visit 'em: I cannot stay,
 Their fame has fir'd me so; Till they appeare,
 Good Friend be royall.

PIRITHOUS   There shall want no bravery.

EMILIA ⌈*aside*⌉
 Poore wench goe weepe, for whosoever wins,
2120 Looses a noble Cosen, for thy sins. *Exeunt*

4.3   *Enter Iailor, Wooer, Doctor*
(Sc. 20)
DOCTOR Her distraction is more at some time of the Moone,
 then at other some, is it not?

IAYLOR She is continually in a harmelesse distemper,
 sleepes little, altogether without appetite, save often
 drinking, dreaming of another world, and a better; and
 what broken peece of matter so'ere she's about, the
 name *Palamon* lardes it, that she farces ev'ry busines
   Enter Daughter
 withall, fyts it to every question; Looke where shee
 comes, you shall perceive her behaviour.
   They stand a loofe
2130 DAUGHTER I have forgot it quite; The burden on't, was

downe a downe a, and pend by no worse man, then
Giraldo, Emilias Schoolemaster; he's as fantasticall too,
as ever he may goe upon's legs, for in the next world
will *Dido* see *Palamon*, and then will she be out of love
with *Eneas*.

DOCTOR What stuff's here? pore soule.

IAYLOR Ev'n thus all day long.

DAUGHTER Now for this Charme, that I told you of, you
must bring a peece of silver on the tip of your tongue,
or no ferry: then if it be your chance to come where 2140
the blessed spirits ar: the'rs a sight now; we maids
that have our Lyvers, perish'd, crakt to peeces with
love, we shall come there, and doe nothing all day long
but picke flowers with Proserpine, then will I make
Palamon a Nosegay, then let him marke me,—then.

DOCTOR How prettily she's amisse? note her a little further.

DAUGHTER Faith ile tell you, sometime we goe to Barly
breake, we of the blessed; alas, tis a sore life they have
i'th tother place, such burning, frying, boyling, hissing,
howling, chattring, cursing, oh they have shrowd 2150
measure, take heede; if one be mad, or hang or drowne
themselves, thither they goe, *Iupiter* blesse us, and there
shall we be put in a Caldron of lead, and Vsurers
grease, amongst a whole million of cutpurses, and there
boyle like a Gamon of Bacon that will never be enough.

DOCTOR How her braine coynes?

DAUGHTER Lords and Courtiers, that have got maids with
Child, they are in this place, they shall stand in fire up
to the Nav'le, and in yce up to'th hart, and there
th'offending part burnes, and the deceaving part 2160
freezes; in troth a very greevous punishment, as one
would thinke, for such a Trifle, belebe me one would
marry a leaprous witch, to be rid on't Ile assure you.

DOCTOR How she continues this fancie? Tis not an
engraffed madnesse, but a most thicke, and profound
mellencholly.

DAUGHTER To heare there a proud Lady, and a proud Citty
wiffe, howle together: I were a beast and il'd call it
good sport: one cries, o this smoake, th'other this fire;
One cries, o, that ever I did it behind the arras, and 2170
then howles; th'other curses a suing fellow and her
garden house.
 (*Sings*) *I will be true, my stars, my fate*, &c.
         Exit Daughter

IAYLOR (*to Doctor*) What thinke you of her Sir?

DOCTOR I think she has a perturbed minde, which I cannot
minister to.

IAYLOR Alas, what then?

DOCTOR Vnderstand you, she ever affected any man, ere
she beheld *Palamon*?

IAYLOR I was once Sir, in great hope, she had fixd her 2180
liking on this gentleman my friend.

WOOER I did thinke so too, and would account I had a
great pen-worth on't, to give halfe my state, that both
she and I at this present stood unfainedly on the same
tearmes.

DOCTOR That intemprat surfeit of her eye, hath distemperd
the other sences, they may returne and settle againe
to execute their preordaind faculties, but they are now

2190 in a most extravagant vagary. This you must doe,
Confine her to a place, where the light may rather
seeme to steale in, then be permitted; take vpon you
(yong Sir her friend) the name of *Palamon*, say you
come to eate with her, and to commune of Love; this
will catch her attention, for this her minde beates vpon;
other objects that are inserted tweene her minde and
eye, become the prankes and friskins of her madnes;
Sing to her, such greene songs of Love, as she sayes
Palamon hath sung in prison; Come to her, stucke in
as sweet flowers, as the season is mistres of, and thereto
2200 make an addition of som other compounded odours,
which are gratefull to the sence: all this shall become
Palamon, for *Palamon* can sing, and *Palamon* is sweet,
and ev'ry good thing, desire to eate with her, carve
her, drinke to her, and still among, intermingle your
petition of grace and acceptance into her favour: Learne
what Maides have beene her companions, and play-
pheeres, and let them repaire to her with *Palamon* in
their mouthes, and appeare with tokens, as if they
suggested for him, It is a falsehood she is in, which is
2210 with falsehoods to be combated. This may bring her to
eate, to sleepe, and reduce what's now out of square
in her, into their former law, and regiment; I have
seene it approved, how many times I know not, but to
make the number more, I have great hope in this. I
will betweene the passages of this project, come in with
my applyance: Let us put it in execution; and hasten
the successe, which doubt not will bring forth comfort.

Exeunt

❀

5.1   ⌈*An Altar prepared.*⌉ *Florish. Enter Thesius,*
(Sc. 21)   *Perithous, Hipolita, attendants*

PIRITHOUS

THESEUS
Now let'em enter, and before the gods
Tender their holy prayers: Let the Temples
2220 Burne bright with sacred fires, and the Altars
In hallowed clouds commend their swelling Incense
To those above us: Let no due be wanting,
Florish of Cornets
They have a noble worke in hand, will honour
The very powers that love 'em.
Enter Palamon with his 3. Knights ⌈*at one door*⌉,
and Arcite with his 3. Knights ⌈*at the other door*⌉
PIRITHOUS   Sir they enter.
THESEUS
You valiant and strong harted Enemies
You royall German foes, that this day come
To blow that nearenesse out that flames betweene ye;
Lay by your anger for an houre, and dove-like
Before the holy Altars of your helpers
2230 (The all feard gods) bow downe your stubborne bodies,
Your ire is more than mortall; So your helpe be,
And as the gods regard ye, fight with Iustice,
Ile leave you to your prayers, and betwixt ye
I part my wishes.
PIRITHOUS   Honour crowne the worthiest.
Exit Theseus, and his traine

PALAMON (*to Arcite*)
The glasse is running now that cannot finish
Till one of us expire: Thinke you but thus,
That were there ought in me which strove to show
Mine enemy in this businesse, wer't one eye
Against another: Arme opprest by Arme:
I would destroy th'offender, Coz, I would   2240
Though parcell of my selfe: Then from this gather
How I should tender you.
ARCITE   I am in labour
To push your name, your auncient love, our kindred
Out of my memory; and i'th selfe same place
To seate something I would confound: So hoyst we
The sayles, that must these vessells port even where
The heavenly Lymiter pleases.
PALAMON   You speake well;
Before I turne, Let me embrace thee Cosen
This I shall never doe agen.
ARCITE   One farewell.
PALAMON
Why let it be so: Farewell Coz.
ARCITE   Farewell Sir;   2250
Exeunt Palamon and his 3. Knights
Knights, Kinsemen, Lovers, yea my Sacrifices
True worshippers of Mars, whose spirit in you
Expells the seedes of feare, and th'apprehension
Which still is father off it; Goe with me
Before the god of our profession: There
Require of him the hearts of Lyons, and
The breath of Tigers, yea the fearcenesse too,
Yea the speed also, to goe on, I meane:
Else wish we to be Snayles; you know my prize
Must be drag'd out of blood, force and great feate   2260
Must put my Garland on me, where she stickes
The Queene of Flowers: our intercession then
Must be to him that makes the Campe, a Cestron
Brymd with the blood of men: give me your aide
And bend your spirits towards him.
They kneele before the altar, ⌈*fall on their faces,*
then on their knees againe⌉
(*Praying to Mars*)   Thou mighty one,
That with thy power hast turnd greene Neptune into
purple,
Whose havocke in vaste Feild comets prewarne,
Vnearthed skulls proclaime, whose breath blowes
downe,
The teeming Ceres foyzon, who dost plucke
With hand armypotent from forth blew clowdes,   2270
The masond Turrets, that both mak'st, and break'st
The stony girthes of Citties: me thy puple,
Yongest follower of thy Drom, instruct this day
With military skill, that to thy lawde
I may advance my Streamer, and by thee,
Be stil'd the Lord o'th day, give me great Mars
Some token of thy pleasure.
Here they fall on their faces as formerly, and there
is heard clanging of Armor, with a short Thunder
as the burst of a Battaile, whereupon they all rise
and bow to the Altar

O Great Corrector of enormous times,
Shaker of ore-rank States, thou grand decider
2280   Of dustie, and old tytles, that healst with blood
The earth when it is sicke, and curst the world
O'th pluresie of people; I doe take
Thy signes auspiciously, and in thy name
To my designe, march boldly; (*to his Knights*) let us
     goe.   *Exeunt*

5.2   *Enter Palamon and his Knights, with the former*
(Sc. 22)   *observance*

PALAMON (*to his Knights*)
Our stars must glister with new fire, or be
To daie extinct; our argument is love,
Which if the goddesse of it grant, she gives
Victory too, then blend your spirits with mine,
You, whose free noblenesse doe make my cause
2290   Your personall hazard; to the goddesse *Venus*
Commend we our proceeding, and implore
Her power unto our partie.
     Here they kneele before the altar, ⌈fall on their
     faces, then on their knees againe⌉
(*Praying to Venus*) Haile Soveraigne Queene of secrets,
     who hast power
To call the feircest Tyrant from his rage;
And weepe unto a Girle; that ha'st the might
Even with an ey-glance, to choke *Marsis* Drom
And turne th'allarme to whispers, that canst make
A Criple florish with his Crutch, and cure him
Before *Apollo*; that may'st force the King
2300   To be his subjects vassaile, and induce
Stale gravitie to daunce, the pould Bachelour
Whose youth like wanton Boyes through Bonfyres
Have skipt thy flame, at seaventy, thou canst catch
And make him to the scorne of his hoarse throate
Abuse yong laies of love; what godlike power
Hast thou not power upon? To *Phœbus* thou
Add'st flames, hotter then his; the heavenly fyres
Did scortch his mortall Son, thine him; the huntresse
All moyst and cold, some say began to throw
2310   Her Bow away, and sigh: take to thy grace
Me thy vowd Souldier, who doe beare thy yoke
As t'wer a wreath of Roses, yet is heavier
Then Lead it selfe, stings more then Nettles;
I have never beene foule mouthd against thy law,
Nev'r reveald secret, for I knew none; would not
Had I kend all that were; I never practised
Vpon mans wife, nor would the Libells reade
Of liberall wits: I never at great feastes
Sought to betray a Beautie, but have blush'd
2320   At simpring Sirs that did: I have beene harsh
To large Confessors, and have hotly ask'd them
If they had Mothers, I had one, a woman,
And women t'wer they wrong'd. I knew a man
Of eightie winters, this I told them, who
A Lasse of foureteene brided; twas thy power
To put life into dust, the aged Crampe
Had screw'd his square foote round,

The Gout had knit his fingers into knots,
Torturing Convulsions from his globie eyes,
Had almost drawne their spheeres, that what was life   2330
In him seem'd torture: this Anatomie
Had by his yong faire pheare a Boy, and I
Beleev'd it was his, for she swore it was,
And who would not beleeve her? briefe, I am
To those that prate and have done, no Companion;
To those that boast and have not, a defyer;
To those that would and cannot, a Rejoycer;
Yea him I doe not love, that tells close offices
The fowlest way, nor names concealements in
The boldest language, such a one I am,   2340
And vow that lover never yet made sigh
Truer then I. O then most soft sweet goddesse
Give me the victory of this question, which
Is true loves merit, and blesse me with a signe
Of thy great pleasure.
     Here Musicke is heard, Doves are seene to flutter,
     they fall againe upon their faces, then on their knees
O thou that from eleven, to ninetie raign'st
In mortall bosomes, whose chase is this world
And we in heards thy game; I give thee thankes
For this faire Token, which being layd unto
Mine innocent true heart, armes in assurance   2350
My body to this businesse: (*To his Knights*) Let us rise
And bow before the goddesse:
     They rise and bow
                 Time comes on.   *Exeunt*

Still Musicke of Records. Enter Emilia in white, her   5.3
haire about her shoulders, with a wheaten wreath: (Sc. 23)
One in white holding up her traine, her haire stucke
with flowers: One before her carrying a silver
Hynde, in which is conveyd Incense and sweet
odours, which being set upon the Altar her maides
standing a loofe, she sets fire to it, then they
curtsey and kneele
EMILIA (*praying to Diana*)
O sacred, shadowie, cold and constant Queene,
Abandoner of Revells, mute contemplative,
Sweet, solitary, white as chaste, and pure
As windefand Snow, who to thy femall knights
Alow'st no more blood than will make a blush,
Which is their orders robe. I heere thy Priest
Am humbled fore thine Altar, O vouchsafe
With that thy rare greene eye, which never yet   2360
Beheld thing maculate, looke on thy virgin,
And sacred silver Mistris, lend thine eare
(Which nev'r heard scurrill terme, into whose port
Ne're entred wanton sound,) to my petition
Seasond with holy feare; This is my last
Of vestall office, I am bride habited,
But mayden harted, a husband I have pointed,
But doe not know him, out of two, I should
Choose one, and pray for his successe, but I
Am guiltlesse of election; of mine eyes,   2370
Were I to loose one, they are equall precious,

I could doombe neither, that which perish'd should
Goe too't unsentenc'd: Therefore most modest Queene,
He of the two Pretenders, that best loves me
And has the truest title in't, Let him
Take off my wheaten Gerland, or else grant
The fyle and qualitie I hold, I may
Continue in thy Band.
        Here the Hynde vanishes under the Altar: and in
        the place ascends a Rose Tree, having one Rose
        upon it
(*To her women*) See what our Generall of Ebbs and
        Flowes
2380   Out from the bowells of her holy Altar
With sacred act advances: But one Rose,
If well inspird, this Battaile shal confound
Both these brave Knights, and I a virgin flowre
Must grow alone unpluck'd.
        Here is heard a sodaine twang of Instruments, and
        the Rose fals from the Tree
The flowre is falne, the Tree descends: (*To Diana*) O
        Mistris
Thou here dischargest me, I shall be gather'd,
I thinke so, but I know not thine owne will;
Vnclaspe thy Misterie: ⌈*To her women*⌉ I hope she's
        pleas'd,
Her Signes were gratious.   *They curtsey and Exeunt*

5.4   *Enter Doctor, Iaylor and Wooer, in habite of*
(Sc. 24) *Palamon*
2390 DOCTOR Has this advice I told you, done any good upon
      her?
      WOOER O very much; The maids that kept her company
      have halfe perswaded her that I am *Palamon*; within
      this halfe houre she came smiling to me, and asked me
      what I would eate, and when I would kisse her:
      I told her presently, and kist her twice.
      DOCTOR
        Twas well done; twentie times had bin far better,
        For there the cure lies mainely.
      WOOER   Then she told me
        She would watch with me to night, for well she knew
        What houre my fit would take me.
2400 DOCTOR   Let her doe so,
        And when your fit comes, fit her home,
        And presently.
      WOOER   She would have me sing.
      DOCTOR
        You did so?
      WOOER   No.
      DOCTOR   Twas very ill done then,
        You should observe her ev'ry way.
      WOOER   Alas
        I have no voice Sir, to confirme her that way.
      DOCTOR
        That's all one, if yee make a noyse,
        If she intreate againe, doe any thing,
        Lye with her if she aske you.
      IAYLOR   Hoa there Doctor.

DOCTOR
  Yes in the waie of cure.
IAYLOR   But first by your leave
  I'th way of honestie.
DOCTOR   That's but a nicenesse,   2410
  Nev'r cast your child away for honestie;
  Cure her first this way, then if shee will be honest,
  She has the path before her.
IAYLOR   Thanke yee *Doctor*.
DOCTOR
  Pray bring her in and let's see how shee is.
IAYLOR
  I will, and tell her her *Palamon* staies for her:
  But *Doctor*, me thinkes you are i'th wrong still.
                                      Exit Iaylor
DOCTOR
  Goe, goe: you Fathers are fine Fooles: her honesty?
  And we should give her physicke till we finde that.
WOOER
  Why, doe you thinke she is not honest Sir?
DOCTOR
  How old is she?
WOOER   She's eighteene.
DOCTOR   She may be,   2420
  But that's all one, tis nothing to our purpose,
  What ere her Father saies, if you perceave
  Her moode inclining that way that I spoke of
  Videlicet, the *way of flesh*, you have me.
WOOER
  Yes very well Sir.
DOCTOR   Please her appetite
  And doe it home, it cures her *ipso facto*,
  The mellencholly humour that infects her.
WOOER I am of your minde *Doctor*.
        Enter Iaylor, Daughter ⌈Madde⌉
DOCTOR
  You'l finde it so; she comes, pray humour her.
        ⌈*Doctor and Wooer stand a loofe*⌉
IAYLOR (*to Daughter*)
  Come, your Love *Palamon* staies for you childe,   2430
  And has done this long houre, to visite you.
DAUGHTER
  I thanke him for his gentle patience,
  He's a kind Gentleman, and I am much bound to him,
  Did you nev'r see the horse he gave me?
IAYLOR   Yes.
DAUGHTER
  How doe you like him?
IAYLOR   He's a very faire one.
DAUGHTER
  You never saw him dance?
IAYLOR   No.
DAUGHTER   I have often.
  He daunces very finely, very comely,
  And for a Iigge, come cut and long taile to him,
  He turnes ye like a Top.
IAYLOR   That's fine indeede.
DAUGHTER
  Hee'l dance the Morris twenty mile an houre,   2440

And that will founder the best hobby-horse
(If I have any skill) in all the parish,
And gallops to the tune of *Light a'love*,
What thinke you of this horse?
IAYLOR   Having these vertues
I thinke he might be broght to play at Tennis.
DAUGHTER
Alas that's nothing.
IAYLOR   Can he write and reade too.
DAUGHTER
A very faire hand, and casts himselfe th'accounts
Of all his hay and provender: That Hostler
Must rise betime that cozens him; you know
The Chestnut Mare the Duke has?
2450 IAYLOR   Very well.
DAUGHTER
She is horribly in love with him, poore beast,
But he is like his master coy and scornefull.
IAYLOR
What dowry has she?
DAUGHTER   Some two hundred Bottles,
And twenty strike of Oates; but hee'l ne're have her;
He lispes in's neighing able to entice
A Millars Mare, hee'l be the death of her.
DOCTOR What stuffe she utters?
IAYLOR Make curtsie, here your love comes.
WOOER (*comming forward*) Pretty soule
How doe ye?
            She curtsies
2460   that's a fine maide, ther's a curtsie.
DAUGHTER
Yours to command ith way of honestie;
How far is't now to'th end o'th world my Masters?
DOCTOR
Why a daies Iorney wench.
DAUGHTER (*to Wooer*)   Will you goe with me?
WOOER
What shall we doe there wench?
DAUGHTER   Why play at stoole ball,
What is there else to doe?
WOOER   I am content
If we shall keepe our wedding there.
DAUGHTER   Tis true
For there I will assure you, we shall finde
Some blind Priest for the purpose, that will venture
To marry us, for here they are nice, and foolish;
2470 Besides my father must be hang'd to morrow
And that would be a blot i'th businesse:
Are not you *Palamon*?
WOOER   Doe not you know me?
DAUGHTER
Yes, but you care not for me; I have nothing
But this pore petticoate, and too corse Smockes.
WOOER
That's all one, I will have you.
DAUGHTER   Will you surely?
WOOER
Yes by this faire hand will I.
DAUGHTER   Wee'l to bed then.

WOOER
Ev'n when you will.
    He kisses her
DAUGHTER (*rubbing off the kiss*)
                    O Sir, you would faine be nibling.
WOOER
Why doe you rub my kisse off?
DAUGHTER   Tis a sweet one,
And will perfume me finely against the wedding.
(*Indicating the Doctor*) Is not this your Cosen *Arcite*?
DOCTOR   Yes sweet heart,   2480
And I am glad my Cosen *Palamon*
Has made so faire a choice.
DAUGHTER   Doe you thinke hee'l have me?
DOCTOR
Yes without doubt.
DAUGHTER (*to Iaylor*) Doe you thinke so too?
IAYLOR   Yes.
DAUGHTER
We shall have many children: ⌜*To the Doctor*⌝ Lord,
    how y'ar growne,
My *Palamon* I hope will grow too finely
Now he's at liberty: Alas poore Chicken
He was kept downe with hard meate, and ill lodging
But ile kisse him up againe.
    Enter a Messenger
MESSENGER
What doe you here, you'l loose the noblest sight
That ev'r was seene.
IAYLOR   Are they i'th Field?
MESSENGER   They are: 2490
You beare a charge there too.
IAYLOR   Ile away straight,
⌜*To the others*⌝ I must ev'n leave you here.
DOCTOR   Nay wee'l goe with you,
I will not loose the sight.
IAYLOR   How did you like her?
DOCTOR
Ile warrant you within these 3. or 4 daies
Ile make her right againe.
            ⌜*Exit Iaylor with Messenger*⌝
(*To Wooer*)   You must not from her
But still preserve her in this way.
WOOER   I will.
DOCTOR
Lets get her in.
WOOER (*to Daughter*) Come sweete wee'l goe to dinner
And then weele play at Cardes.
DAUGHTER   And shall we kisse too?
WOOER
A hundred times
DAUGHTER   And twenty.
WOOER   I and twenty.
DAUGHTER
And then wee'l sleepe together.
DOCTOR (*to Wooer*)   Take her offer.   2500
WOOER (*to Daughter*)
Yes marry will we.
DAUGHTER   But you shall not hurt me.

WOOER
   I will not sweete.

DAUGHTER   If you doe (Love) ile cry.   *Exeunt*

5.5   *Florish. Enter Theseus, Hipolita, Emilia, Perithous:*
(Sc. 25)   *and some Attendants*

EMILIA
   Ile no step further.

PIRITHOUS   Will you loose this sight?

EMILIA
   I had rather see a wren hawke at a fly
   Then this decision; ev'ry blow that falls
   Threats a brave life, each stroake laments
   The place whereon it fals, and sounds more like
   A Bell, then blade: I will stay here,
   It is enough my hearing shall be punishd,
2510   With what shall happen, gainst the which there is
   No deaffing, but to heare; not taint mine eye
   With dread sights, it may shun.

PIRITHOUS (*to Theseus*)   Sir, my good Lord
   Your Sister will no further.

THESEUS   Oh she must.
   She shall see deeds of honour in their kinde,
   Which sometime show well pencild. Nature now
   Shall make, and act the Story, the beleife
   Both seald with eye, and eare; (*to Emilia*) you must be
      present,
   You are the victours meede, the price, and garlond
   To crowne the Questions title.

EMILIA   Pardon me,
   If I were there, I'ld winke.

2520   THESEUS   You must be there;
   This Tryall is as t'wer i'th night, and you
   The onely star to shine.

EMILIA   I am extinct,
   There is but envy in that light, which showes
   The one the other: darkenes which ever was
   The dam of horrour, who do's stand accurst
   Of many mortall Millions, may even now
   By casting her blacke mantle over both
   That neither could finde other, get her selfe
   Some part of a good name, and many a murther
   Set off wherto she's guilty.

2530   HIPOLITA   You must goe.

EMILIA
   In faith I will not.

THESEUS   Why the knights must kindle
   Their valour at your eye: know of this war
   You are the Treasure, and must needes be by
   To give the Service pay.

EMILIA   Sir pardon me,
   The tytle of a kingdome may be tride
   Out of it selfe.

THESEUS   Well, well then, at your pleasure,
   Those that remaine with you, could wish their office
   To any of their Enemies.

HIPOLITA   Farewell Sister,
   I am like to know your husband fore your selfe

By some small start of time, he whom the gods   2540
Doe of the two know best, I pray them he
Be made your Lot.

                Exeunt Theseus, Hipolita, Perithous, and
                        Attendants. Manet Emilia
         ⌜*Emilia takes out the 2. Pictures: one from her*
         right side and one from her left⌝

EMILIA
Arcite is gently visagd; yet his eye
Is like an Engyn bent, or a sharpe weapon
In a soft sheath; mercy, and manly courage
Are bedfellowes in his visage: *Palamon*
Has a most menacing aspect, his brow
Is grav'd, and seemes to bury what it frownes on,
Yet sometime tis not so, but alters to
The quallity of his thoughts; long time his eye   2550
Will dwell upon his object. Mellencholly
Becomes him nobly; So do's *Arcites* mirth,
But *Palamons* sadnes is a kinde of mirth,
So mingled, as if mirth did make him sad,
And sadnes, merry; those darker humours that
Sticke misbecomingly on others, on them
Live in faire dwelling.
         Cornets. Trompets sound as to a charge
Harke how yon spurs to spirit doe incite
The Princes to their proofe, *Arcite* may win me,
And yet may *Palamon* wound *Arcite* to   2560
The spoyling of his figure. O what pitty
Enough for such a chance; if I were by
I might doe hurt, for they would glance their eies
Toward my Seat, and in that motion might
Omit a ward, or forfeit an offence
Which crav'd that very time: it is much better
         (*Cornets. A great cry and noice within crying a*
         Palamon)
I am not there, oh better never borne
Then minister to such harme,
         Enter Servant
                        what is the chance?

SERVANT The Crie's a *Palamon*.

EMILIA
Then he has won: Twas ever likely,   2570
He lookd all grace and successe, and he is
Doubtlesse the prim'st of men: I pre'thee run
And tell me how it goes.
         Showt, and Cornets: Crying a Palamon

SERVANT   Still *Palamon*.

EMILIA
Run and enquire,   *Exit Servant*
         ⌜*She speakes to the Picture in her right hand*⌝
                  poore Servant thou hast lost,
Vpon my right side still I wore thy picture,
Palamons on the left, why so, I know not,
I had no end in't; else chance would have it so.
         Another cry, and showt within, and Cornets
On the sinister side, the heart lyes; *Palamon*
Had the best boding chance: This burst of clamour
Is sure the end o'th Combat.   2580

Enter Servant

SERVANT

   They saide that *Palamon* had *Arcites* body
   Within an inch o'th Pyramid, that the cry
   Was generall a *Palamon*: But anon,
   Th'Assistants made a brave redemption, and
   The two bold Tytlers, at this instant are
   Hand to hand at it.

EMILIA   Were they metamorphisd

   Both into one; oh why? there were no woman
   Worth so composd a Man: their single share,
   Their noblenes peculier to them, gives

2590   The prejudice of disparity (values shortnes)
   To any Lady breathing—

     Cornets. Cry within, Arcite, Arcite

                more exulting?

   Palamon still?

SERVANT   Nay, now the sound is *Arcite*.

EMILIA

   I pre'thee lay attention to the Cry.

     Cornets. A great showt and cry, Arcite, victory

   Set both thine eares to'th busines.

SERVANT   The cry is

   Arcite, and victory, harke *Arcite*, victory,
   The Combats consummation is proclaim'd
   By the wind Instruments.

EMILIA   Halfe sights saw

   That *Arcite* was no babe: god's lyd, his richnes
   And costlines of spirit look't through him, it could

2600   No more be hid in him, then fire in flax,
   Then humble banckes can goe to law with waters,
   That drift windes, force to raging: I did thinke
   Good *Palamon* would miscarry, yet I knew not
   Why I did thinke so; Our reasons are not prophets
   When oft our fancies are: They are comming off:
   Alas poore *Palamon*.

     ⌈*She puts away the Pictures.*⌉
     Cornets. Enter Theseus, Hipolita, Pirithous, Arcite
     as victor, and attendants

THESEUS

   Lo, where our Sister is in expectation,
   Yet quaking, and unsetled: Fairest *Emily*,
   The gods by their divine arbitrament

2610   Have given you this Knight, he is a good one
   As ever strooke at head: ⌈*To Arcite and Emilia*⌉ Give
     me your hands;
   (*To Arcite*) Receive you her, (*to Emilia*) you him, (*to*
     both) be plighted with
   A love that growes, as you decay.

ARCITE   *Emilia*,

   To buy you, I have lost what's deerest to me,
   Save what is bought, and yet I purchase cheaply,
   As I doe rate your value.

THESEUS (*to Emilia*) O loved Sister,

   He speakes now of as brave a Knight as ere
   Did spur a noble Steed: Surely the gods

2620   Would have him die a Batchelour, least his race

   Should shew i'th world too godlike: His behaviour
   So charmd me, that me thought *Alcides* was
   To him a sow of lead: if I could praise
   Each part of him to'th all I have spoke, your *Arcite*
   Did not loose by't; For he that was thus good
   Encountred yet his Better, I have heard
   Two emulous Philomels, beate the eare o'th night
   With their contentious throates, now one the higher,
   Anon the other, then againe the first,
   And by and by out breasted, that the sence   2630
   Could not be judge betweene'em: So it far'd
   Good space betweene these kinesmen; till heavens did
   Make hardly one the winner: (*to Arcite*) weare the
     Girlond
   With joy that you have won: For the subdude,
   Give them our present Iustice, since I know
   Their lives but pinch'em; Let it here be done:
   The Sceane's not for our seeing, goe we hence,
   Right joyfull, with some sorrow. (*To Arcite*) Arme your
     prize,
   I know you will not loose her: *Hipolita*
   I see one eye of yours conceives a teare   2640
   The which it will deliver.

     Florish

EMILIA   Is this wynning?

   Oh all you heavenly powers where is your mercy?
   But that your wils have saide it must be so,
   And charge me live to comfort this unfriended,
   This miserable Prince, that cuts away
   A life more worthy from him, then all women;
   I should, and would die too.

HIPOLITA   Infinite pitty

   That fowre such eies should be so fixd on one
   That two must needes be blinde fort.

THESEUS   So it is.   *Exeunt*

     Enter Palamon and his 3. Knightes pyniond: Iaylor,   **5.6**
     Executioner with Blocke and Axe, Gard   **(Sc. 26**

PALAMON

   Ther's many a man alive, that hath out liv'd   2650
   The love o'th people, yea i'th selfesame state
   Stands many a Father with his childe; some comfort
   We have by so considering: we expire
   And not without mens pitty. To live still,
   Have their good wishes, we prevent
   The loathsome misery of age, beguile
   The Gowt and Rheume, that in lag howres attend
   For grey approachers; we come towards the gods
   Yong, and unwapper'd, not halting under Crymes
   Many and stale: that sure shall please the gods   2660
   Sooner than such, to give us Nectar with 'em,
   For we are more cleare Spirits. My deare kinsemen,
   Whose lives (for this poore comfort) are laid downe,
   You have sould 'em too too cheape.

I. KNIGHT   What ending could be

   Of more content? ore us the victors have
   Fortune, whose title is as momentary,

As to us death is certaine: A graine of honour
They not ore'-weigh us.

2. KNIGHT   Let us bid farewell;
And with our patience, anger tottring Fortune,
Who at her certain'st reeles.

2670 3. KNIGHT   Come? who begins?

PALAMON
Ev'n he that led you to this Banket, shall
Taste to you all: (*to the Iailor*) ah ha my Friend, my
    Friend,
Your gentle daughter gave me freedome once;
You'l see't done now for ever: pray how do'es she?
I heard she was not well; her kind of ill
Gave me some sorrow.

IAYLOR   Sir she's well restor'd,
And to be married shortly.

PALAMON   By my short life
I am most glad on't; Tis the latest thing
I shall be glad of, pre'thee tell her so:

2680 Commend me to her, and to peece her portion
Tender her this.
    He gives his purse

I. KNIGHT   Nay lets be offerers all.

2. KNIGHT
Is it a maide?

PALAMON   Verily I thinke so,
A right good creature, more to me deserving
Then I can quight or speake of.

ALL 3. KNIGHTS   Commend us to her.
    They give their purses

IAYLOR
The gods requight you all, and make her thankefull.

PALAMON
Adiew; and let my life be now as short,
As my leave taking.
    He lies on the Blocke

I. KNIGHT   Leade couragious Cosin.

2. *and* 3. KNIGHTS Wee'l follow cheerefully.
    A great noise within crying, run, save hold:
    Enter in hast a Messenger

MESSENGER Hold, hold, O hold, hold, hold.
    Enter Pirithous in haste

PIRITHOUS
2690 Hold hoa: It is a cursed hast you made
If you have done so quickly: noble *Palamon*,
The gods will shew their glory in a life,
That thou art yet to leade.

PALAMON   Can that be,
When *Venus* I have said is false? How doe things fare?

PIRITHOUS
Arise great Sir, and give the tydings eare
That are most rarly sweet, and bitter.

PALAMON   What
Hath wakt us from our dreame?

PIRITHOUS   List then: your Cosen
Mounted upon a Steed that *Emily*
Did first bestow on him, a blacke one, owing
2700 Not a hayre worth of white, which some will say

Weakens his price, and many will not buy
His goodnesse with this note: Which superstition
Heere findes allowance: On this horse is *Arcite*
Trotting the stones of *Athens*, which the *Calkins*
Did rather tell, then trample; for the horse
Would make his length a mile, if't pleas'd his Rider
To put pride in him: as he thus went counting
The flinty pavement, dancing as t'wer to'th Musicke
His owne hoofes made; (for as they say from iron
Came Musickes origen) what envious Flint,   2710
Cold as old *Saturne*, and like him possest
With fire malevolent, darted a Sparke
Or what feirce sulphur else, to this end made,
I comment not; the hot horse, hot as fire
Tooke Toy at this, and fell to what disorder
His power could give his will, bounds, comes on end,
Forgets schoole dooing, being therein traind,
And of kind mannadge, pig-like he whines
At the sharpe Rowell, which he freats at rather
Then any jot obaies; seekes all foule meanes   2720
Of boystrous and rough Iadrie, to dis-seate
His Lord, that kept it bravely: when nought serv'd,
When neither Curb would cracke, girth breake nor
    diffring plunges
Dis-roote his Rider whence he grew, but that
He kept him tweene his legges, on his hind hoofes
On end he stands
That *Arcites* leggs being higher then his head
Seem'd with strange art to hang: His victors wreath
Even then fell off his head: and presently
Backeward the Iade comes ore, and his full poyze 2730
Becomes the Riders loade: yet is he living,
But such a vessell tis, that floates but for
The surge that next approaches: he much desires
To have some speech with you: Loe he appeares.
    Enter Theseus, Hipolita, Emilia: Arcite in a chaire,
    borne by Attendants

PALAMON
O miserable end of our alliance:
The gods are mightie *Arcite*, if thy heart,
Thy worthie, manly heart be yet unbroken:
Give me thy last words, I am *Palamon*,
One that yet loves thee dying.

ARCITE   Take *Emilia*
And with her, all the worlds joy: Reach thy hand, 2740
Farewell: I have told my last houre; I was false,
Yet never treacherous: Forgive me Cosen:
One kisse from faire *Emilia*: (*They kiss*) Tis done:
Take her: I die.   *He dies*

PALAMON   Thy brave soule seeke *Elizium*.

EMILIA (*to Arcites Body*)
Ile close thine eyes Prince; blessed soules be with thee,
Thou art a right good man, and while I live,
This day I give to teares.

PALAMON   And I to honour.

THESEUS
In this place first you fought: ev'n very here
I sundred you, acknowledge to the gods

2750 Our thankes that you are living:
His part is playd, and though it were too short
He did it well: your day is lengthned, and
The blissefull dew of heaven do's arowze you.
The powerfull *Venus*, well hath grac'd her Altar,
And given you your love: Our Master *Mars*
Hath vouch'd his Oracle, and to *Arcite* gave
The grace of the Contention: So the Deities
Have shewd due justice: Beare this hence.

⌜*Exeunt Attendants with Arcites Body*⌝

PALAMON   O Cosen,
That we should things desire, which doe cost us
2760 The losse of our desire; That nought could buy
Deare love, but losse of deare love.

THESEUS   Never Fortune
Did play a subtler Game: The conquerd triumphes,
The victor has the Losse: yet in the passage,
The gods have beene most equall: *Palamon*,
Your kinesman hath confest the right o'th Lady
Did lye in you, for you first saw her, and
Even then proclaimd your fancie: He restord her
As your stolne Iewell, and desir'd your spirit
To send him hence forgiven; The gods my justice
2770 Take from my hand, and they themselves become
The Executioners: Leade your Lady off;
And call your Lovers from the stage of death,
Whom I adopt my Frinds. A day or two
Let us looke sadly, and give grace unto
The Funerall of *Arcite*, in whose end
The visages of Bridegroomes weele put on
And smile with *Palamon*; for whom an houre,

But one houre since, I was as dearely sorry,
As glad of *Arcite*: and am now as glad,
As for him sorry. O you heavenly Charmers,   2780
What things you make of us? For what we lacke
We laugh, for what we have, are sorry, still
Are children in some kind. Let us be thankefull
For that which is, and with you leave dispute
That are above our question: Let's goe off,
And beare us like the time.   *Florish. Exeunt*

EPILOGUE
I would now aske ye how ye like the Play,
But as it is with Schoole Boyes, cannot say,
I am cruell fearefull: pray yet stay a while,
And let me looke upon ye: No man smile?   2790
Then it goes hard I see; He that has
Lov'd a yong hansome wench then, show his face:
Tis strange if none be heere, and if he will
Against his Conscience let him hisse, and kill
Our Market: Tis in vaine, I see to stay yee,
Have at the worst can come, then; Now what say ye?
And yet mistake me not: I am not bold
We have no such cause. If the tale we have told
(For tis no other) any way content ye,
(For to that honest purpose it was ment ye)   2800
We have our end; and ye shall have ere long
I dare say many a better, to prolong
Your old loves to us: we, and all our might,
Rest at your service, Gentlemen, good night.

Florish. Exit

FINIS

A SELECT GLOSSARY

Because of the wide range of spellings in the early texts, this glossary is in modern spelling, with limited cross-reference to variant forms.

a, (as pronoun) familiar, unstressed form of 'he'

abate, to shorten, take from, deprive, except, blunt

abatement, reduction, depreciation

abhor, disgust, protest against

abide, await the issue of, pay the penalty for

able, to vouch for

abode, delay, stay; to foretell

about, irregularly, indirectly; be on the move

abram, auburn

abridgement, reduction, pastime

abroad, away, apart, on foot, current

abrogate, abstain from

abruption, breaking off

absolute, complete, certain, positive, beyond doubt

Absyrtus, see MEDEA

abuse, wrong, ill-usage, deception; to deceive, dishonour

aby, pay the penalty for

accident, occurrence, event, incident

accite, summon

accommodate, equip, adapt itself to

accommodation, comfort, entertainment

accomplish, equip, obtain

accountant, accountable

accoutred, dressed, equipped

acerb, bitter

Acheron, river of the underworld

achieve, make an end, finish, win, obtain

Achilles' spear, a mythical spear: rust scraped from it cured a wound that it had inflicted

acknow, acknowledge

acknown, *be acknown,* confess knowledge

aconitum, poison

acquit, atone for, repay, release

Actaeon. Diana turned him into a stag because he saw her bathing; he was torn to pieces by his dogs.

acture, action

adamant, impenetrably hard stone; magnet

addition, mark of distinction, title

admiration, wonder, astonishment, marvel

admire, wonder, marvel

admittance, fashion, reception

adoptious christendoms, fond nicknames

advantage, opportunity, interest on money; to profit

adventure, chance, hazard, to risk

advertise, inform

advertisement, information, advice

advice, consideration, forethought

advised, cautious, aware, carefully considered

Aeneas, a Trojan prince who carried his father, Anchises, from the blazing city. Dido, Queen of Carthage, received him and his son, Ascanius. She fell in love with him, but he left Carthage at the gods' command, and Dido committed suicide.

Aeolus, god of the winds

Aesculapius, god of medicine

affect, affection, tendency, disposition; love, like, imitate

affected, disposed, in love

affection, passion, desire, disposition, affectation

affeer, confirm

affiance, confidence

affined, related, obliged

affront, meet, confront

affy, trust, betroth

after, according to, at the rate of

against, in expectation of, in preparation for the time when, in time for

Agenor, father of Europa

aglet-baby, tag in shape of a tiny figure

agnize, confess, acknowledge

aim, target, guess

Ajax, a strong, dim-witted Greek hero; mad with anger at not being given the arms of the dead Achilles he slaughtered a flock of sheep as if they were human enemies and killed himself

alarum, call to arms, assault

Alcides, Hercules

alder-liefest, dearest of all

Alecto, one of the three fates; her head was wreathed with serpents

allay, relief; to qualify

All-hallond eve, Halloween, the eve of All Saints' Day

Allhallowmas, All Saints' Day (1 November)

All-hallown summer, fine weather in late autumn

allowance, admission of a claim, reputation

alter, exchange

Althaea. Her son, Meleager, was fated to live until a brand of fire burned away. After he killed her brothers she burned it.

amerce, punish with a fine

ames ace, two aces, lowest possible throw at dice

amort, spiritless, dejected

and, an, if, though, whether, as if

anatomize, dissect, lay bare

anatomy, skeleton

Anchises, see AENEAS

anchor, hermit

ancient, ensign

Anna, sister of Dido of Carthage

anon, soon, 'coming'

Anthropophagi, cannibals

antique, grotesque pageant, clown; fantastic

antre, cave

ape, to lead apes in hell, an old maid's function

Apollo, god of the sun, music and poetry. Daphne, escaping from his pursuit, was changed to a laurel.

appaid, contented, satisfied

apparently, openly

appeach, inform against

appeal, accusation; to accuse

apple-john, apple eaten when shrivelled

appliance, service, remedy, treatment

appointment, equipment, instruction

apprehensive, lively, quick-witted

approof, proof, trial, approval

approve, prove, show to be true, confirm, put to the proof, test, convict

apt, willing, impressionable

Aquilon, north wind

Arabian bird, phoenix

are, ere, before

argo, see ERGO

argosy, large merchant ship

argue, prove, show

argument, proof, subject of debate, subject-matter, summary

Ariadne, deserted by her lover, Theseus

Arion, a singer carried ashore by a dolphin

arm, reach, take in one's arms

arm-jaunced, jolted by armour

armipotent, powerful in arms

aroint thee, be gone

arras, wall-tapestry

articulate, arrange terms, specify

artificial, made by art, skilled, skilful

artist, scholar, doctor

Ascanius, see AENEAS

asinico, ass

aspect, look, glance, position and influence of a planet, sight

aspersion, sprinkling

asprey, osprey

assay, trial, attempt

assubjugate, debase

assurance, pledge, deed of conveyance, guarantee

assure, betroth, convey property

Astraea, goddess of justice

Atalanta, maiden huntress who killed the suitors she outraced

Ate, goddess of mischief and destruction

atomy, atom, mote

atone, reconcile, unite, agree

atonement, reconciliation

Atropos, one of the three fates; her duty was to cut the thread of life

attach, arrest, seize

attachment, arrest, stop

attaint, conviction, infection; infect, convict of treason, disgrace

attone, see ATONE

attribute, reputation, credit

attribution, praise

aught, anything

aunt, old woman, bawd, girl friend

austringer, falconer

avoid, get rid of, get out of

awkward, oblique, not straightforward

back friend, pretended friend

baffle, disgrace

bait, set dogs on, worry, persecute, entice with bait, feed, feast

balk, let slip, quibble, heap

ballow, cudgel

ban, to curse

Banbury cheese, proverbially thin

bandog, fierce chained dog

banket, dessert, light meal of fruit and sweetmeats

bases, skirt-like garment worn by a knight

Basilisco-like, like Basilisco, a braggart knight in the play Soliman and Perseda

basilisk, fabulous reptile whose look was fatal, large cannon

basta, enough!

bastard, sweet Spanish wine

bastinado, beating

bate, trouble; beat wings ready for flight, blunt, reduce, grow less, deduct

bateless, not to be blunted

bat-fowling, catching birds at night

batlet, bat used in washing clothes

bauble, jester's stick

bavin, brush-wood

bawd, procurer (male or female)

beadle, parish officer with power to punish

beadsman, one who prays for another

bearherd, bear-keeper

bearing cloth, christening garment

beaver, visor, helmet

bedlam, lunatic hospital, lunatic

beetle, heavy hammer-like tool; overhang

begin, see BIGGIN

beldam, grandmother, hag

bell-wether, castrated ram with a bell round its neck

be-mete, measure

bemoiled, covered with mud

bench, raise to authority, sit as judge

bench-hole, privy

bend, look, glance; to turn, incline, direct, strain, submit

bent, inclination, direction, tension, force, range, aim

berayed, defiled

bergamask, a rustic dance

besonian, beggar, scoundrel

besort, suitable company; to suit

beteem, pour over, grant

bewray, reveal

bias, in bowls, weight which makes a

bowl swerve; natural bent, inclination, compelling influence

bigamy, marriage with widow(er)

biggin, nightcap

bilbo, finely-tempered sword

bilboes, shackles

bile, boil

bill, halberd, pike, note, catalogue, label

burbolt, blunt-headed arrow for shooting birds

bisson, partly blind, blinding

blank, blank page or charter, white mark in centre of target, aim, range; to make pale

blazon, coat of arms, description, proclamation; to proclaim, praise

blood-baltered, stained with clots of blood

blow, swell, blossom, (of flies) deposit eggs (on), defile

blowse, chubby girl

bluecap, Scotsman

blurt, make light of

board, to address, make advances to, mount sexually

bob, taunt, mock, cheat, get by trickery, pummel

bodkin, dagger, hair-pin or ornament

boll'n, swollen

bolt, broad-headed arrow, shackle; to sieve, fetter

bolter, sieve

bolting-hutch, sifting-bin

bombard, leather jug or bottle

bombast, cotton-wool padding for clothes, bombastic

bona roba, well dressed prostitute

bone-ache, syphilis

boot, booty, profit, advantage, help, use, avail, addition; to be of use, profit, present in addition

Boreas, north wind

borrow, receive, assume, counterfeit

bosky, wooded

botchy, ulcerous

bots, disease of horses caused by worms

bottom, ship, valley, bobbin; to wind on a bobbin

bounce, bang

brabble, brawl

brace, suit of armour, readiness

brach, hound, bitch

braid, deceitful; to reproach

branched, patterned as with branches

brave, finely dressed, splendid, excellent; bravado or threat; to adorn, challenge, defy, swagger, taunt

bravery, bravado, finery, splendour, ostentation, defiance

brawl, French dance; quarrel

break-neck, ruinous course of action

breast, voice

breathe, speak, exercise, rest

breathed, exercised, valiant, inspired

breese, gadfly

Briareus, hundred-handed giant

brief, letter, summary

broke, bargain

broken, (of music) in parts, scored for different instruments

broker, agent, go-between

Brownist, member of a Puritan sect founded by Robert Browne

bruit, rumour, report; to announce

bubuncle, facial eruption

buck, washing, dirty clothes for washing

buckler, shield

Bucklersbury, street of apothecaries' and druggists' shops off Cheapside

budget, wallet, bag

buff, strong leather used for coats of bailiffs and legal officers

bug, bogey, terror

bugle, bead, hunting-horn

bulk, body, stall in front of a shop

bully, friend, fine fellow

bung, pickpocket

burgonet, helmet

burn, infect with venereal disease

buss, kiss

cabin, den

cabinet, dwelling

cacodemon, evil spirit

caddis, woollen tape

cade, barrel

caduceus, Mercury's magic wand entwined by two serpents

caitiff, wretch, miserable person

caliver, light musket

callet, whore

Cambyses, hero of a bombastic tragedy

can, to know, be skilled in

canary, lively dance, light sweet wine

cantle, segment

canvass, toss (as in a blanket)

capable, able to receive, feel, or understand

cap-à-pie, from head to foot

capitulate, specify terms

captious, capacious

carbonado, meat scored across for cooking

carcanet, necklace

card, playing card, compass card; mix, debase

carl, carlot, peasant

carnation, flesh-colour

carrack, galleon

carriage, ability to bear

carve, cut, shape, invite with look and gesture

case, vagina

cast, throw of dice, tinge, founding; to throw, vomit, reckon, add

casual, accidental, subject to accident

cataplasm, poultice

catastrophe, end, outcome, rear

caterpillar, extortioner, parasite

cates, food, delicacies

catling, catgut string

cautel, trick, deceit

cautelous, deceitful

censure, judgement, blame; judge, estimate

centre, centre of the earth or the universe

Cerberus, three-headed dog of the underworld

cerecloth, cerements, winding-sheet

Ceres, goddess of agriculture

certain, fixed

cess, death; out of all cess, beyond all measure

challenge, claim, accuse

chamber-lye, urine
chamblet, light fabric
champaign, open country
changeling, waverer
chape, sheath
chapman, merchant, customer
chaps, jaws
character, writing, hand-writing; to write
charactery, writing
charneco, Portuguese wine
Charon, ferryman of the underworld
chaudron, entrails
cheapen, bargain, bid for
cheater, officer appointed to look after property forfeited to the King
cherry-pit, game of throwing cherry stones into a little hole
cheverel, kid leather, pliant and easily stretched
child, baby girl, youth of noble birth
childing, fertile
chopine, shoe with high platform-sole
cicatrice, scar, impression
cinquepace, lively dance
cipher, zero, nought; to express, decipher
cittern, wire-stringed instrument
civil, of the city, well-ordered
clack-dish, begging bowl
clapperclaw, maul, thrash
clepe, call
clerk, scholar
clew, ball of thread
climate, region, dwell
cling, shrivel
clinquant, glittering
clip, embrace
closure, bound, enclosure, conclusion
clown, rustic, jester
clyster, enema
cockney, milksop, squeamish or affected woman
cod, testicle
codpiece, bag-shaped flap on breeches, covering the genitals, tied with laces, often embroidered and padded
coffin, pastry case
cog, cheat, flatter
coign, corner-stone, corner
coil, noisy disturbance, fuss, trouble
Colbrand, legendary Danish giant
collection, inference, understanding
collied, darkened
collop, slice, offspring
colour, pretext, excuse
colours, military ensigns
colt, young fool; to make a fool of; to have sexual intercourse with
co-mart, agreement, bargain
commodity, commercial privileges, expediency, advantage, consignment
companion, knave
comparative, proportionate, full of comparisons; one who assumes equality
competitor, associate, partner
complexion, bodily habit or constitution, temperament, appearance, colour
complot, conspiracy
composition, consistency, agreement
comptible, sensitive
con, learn by heart
conceit, idea, device, apprehension, under-

standing, opinion, judgement, fancy, imagination, fancy trifle; to think, estimate
conceited, full of imagination, ingenious, having a certain opinion
conclusion, experiment, riddle
condolement, mourning
conference, conversation, talk, discussion
confiner, inhabitant
congree, harmonize
conscience, knowledge, understanding, scruple
conscionable, ruled by conscience
consign, agree, yield up possession
consist, insist
conspectuity, sight
contain, keep
continent, container, sum; restrained, temperate
controller, detractor
convenience, fitness, advantage
convent, convene, summon
conversation, intercourse, behaviour
convert, turn, change
convey, lead away, carry
conveyance, underhand dealing
convince, overcome
convive, feast together
convoy, means of conveyance
cony, rabbit
cony-catch, cheat
copatain, highcrowned
cope, sky; have to do with, encounter, recompense
copped, peaked
copy, original; subject-matter, copyhold-tenure
coranto, a dance
Corinthian, reveller
corky, withered
Cornelia, mother of the Gracchi, model of Roman motherhood
cornett, a brass instrument, capable of great brilliance
cornuto, cuckold, deceived husband
corollary, surplus
costard, an apple; the head
cote, cottage; pass by; and see QUOTE
cotquean, 'old woman', man who interferes in housekeeping
couch, hide, lie hidden, make crouch
counsel, secret, secret purpose or thought
Counter, debtors' prison
counterpoint, quilt, counterpane
countervail, equal, counter-balance
court-cupboard, sideboard
cousin, nephew, kinsman, relative
cowl-staff, pole on which a 'cowl' (or basket) is carried
coy, scorn, stroke
cozen, cheat
cozier, cobbler
crackhemp, gallows-bird, one born (or deserving) to be hanged
crank, twist; wind
crant, wreath
crare, small trading vessel
craze, break
credent, believing, credible
credit, credibility, reputation, report
cresset, fire-basket, torch

crow-keeper, one employed to drive away crows
crusado, Portuguese coin
cry, pack of hounds; yelp in following scent
cubiculo, bedroom
cullion, testicle (term of abuse)
culverin, large cannon
cunning, knowledge, skill; ingenious
Cupid, god of love, son of Venus and Mars (or Mercury), usually thought of as a boy armed with bow and arrows
curate, parish priest
curiosity, exactness, over-scrupulousness, delicacy
curious, anxious, needing care, fastidious, difficult to please, delicate, beautifully made; delicately
curst, shrewish, cross, cantankerous, malignant, fierce
curtal, having the tail docked
curtle-axe, cutlass
customer, prostitute
cut, docked or gelded horse; vulva
Cyclops, one of a race of one-eyed giants, workmen for Vulcan the smith
cyme, medicinal plant
Cynthia, goddess of the moon
cypress, fine lawn fabric
Cytherea, Venus, goddess of love

Daedalus, with his son Icarus, escaped from imprisonment on home-made wings. Icarus flew too high, the sun melted the wax, and he was drowned. Daedalus escaped.
danger, harm, injury, power to harm, range (of a weapon), debt
Daphne, see APOLLO
dare, dazzle
date, time, term, term of life, end
daub, cover with false show; daub it, pretend
dear, important, energetic, dire
debile, weak
Deborah, prophetess who inspired Israel to victory
decimation, execution of every tenth man
decoct, heat
defeat, destruction; to ruin, destroy, disfigure, defraud
defeature, disfigurement
defend, forbid
defunction, death
defunctive, funereal
delightsome, delightful, delighted
demerit, merit, sin
denier, copper coin of little value
denunciation, formal declaration
deplore, tell with grief
depose, swear, examine on oath
deprave, defame
deputation, office of deputy
deracinate, uproot
derive, inherit, descend, bring down on, draw
dern, dark, drear
determinate, fix; ended, decisive, intended
determination, ending, decision, intention
determine, end, settle, decide
Deucalion, the Greek Noah
dexter, right

dey-woman, dairy-woman

Diana, goddess of hunting, the moon, and chastity

diaper, table napkin

dich, attach to

Dido, see AENEAS

diffidence, distrust, suspicion

diffused, confused, disordered

dilate, relate, express at length

dildo, penis, phallus; used in ballad refrains

dime, tenth man

Dis, god of the underworld

disable, impair, disparage

disappointed, unprepared

discase, undress

discourse, reasoning, talk, conversational power, familiarity

discover, uncover, reveal, make known, recognize, spy out, reconnoitre

disease, trouble, annoyance; to disturb

disedge, dull the appetite, sate

disgracious, disliked, out of favour

dishabit, dislodge

dishonest, dishonourable, unchaste, immoral

dishonesty, dishonour, immorality

dislike, disagreement, disapproval; to displease

disliken, disguise

dismiss, forgive

dismission, dismissal

dismount, lower, draw from sheath

dispiteous, pitiless

dispose, disposal, control, disposition, temperament, manner; to control, direct, incline, come to terms

disputable, argumentative

distain, stain, defile

distemper, ill humour, illness of mind or body, intoxication; disturb, disorder

distemperature, intemperateness of weather, illness, ailment, disturbance of mind

distinction, discrimination

distinctly, separately, individually

distract, divide, perplex, drive mad; distraught

distrain, seize

distressful, hard-earned

dive-dapper, dabchick, little grebe

division, variation, modulation, disposition

divulge, proclaim

do, copulate (with)

doctrine, lesson, learning

document, lesson

dogged, cruel

doit, coin worth half a farthing, a minute sum

dole, portion, share, grief, sorrow

dolphin, dauphin

domineer, feast riotously

dominical, red-printed letter in calendar marking the Sundays

doom, judgement

double, false, deceitful; wraith

doubt, suspicion, fear; to suspect, fear

dout, extinguish

dowlas, coarse linen

dowle, downy feather

doxy, beggar's wench

draff, pigwash

draught, cesspool, privy

draw, withdraw, empty, search for game, track by scent

drawer, tapster

dressing, trimming

dribbling, falling short or wide of the mark

drift, purpose, plot, shower

drollery, puppet-show, comic picture

drumble, move slowly

drybeat, beat soundly

dudgeon, hilt of a dagger

duello, duelling code

dump, mournful tune or song

dun, dark; dun horse

dup, open

durance, durability, strong and durable cloth, imprisonment

eager, sour, bitter

ean, to bring forth (lambs)

eanling, young lamb

ear, plough

ecstasy, excitement, trance, madness

edge, appetite, desire

effectual, pertinent, to the point

eftest, easiest

eftsoons, soon

egg, epitome of worthlessness; *take eggs for money*, accept injury tamely

eisel, vinegar

eld, old age, ancient time

elder gun, pop-gun made from elder wood

element, sky, *pl.* atmospheric powers

elf, tangle

eliad, see OEILLADE

embarquement, embargo, prohibition

emboss, to drive (a hunted animal) to extremity

embossed, swollen, foaming at the mouth

embowel, disembowel

empiric, quack

emulation, ambitious rivalry, grudge, envy

emulator, disparager

encompassment, winding course, 'talking round' a subject

enew, drive into water

engine, artifice, plot, mechanical contrivance, rack

engross, write out in a fair hand; collect, monopolize, fatten

enlarge, set free

enlargement, release, liberty

enormous, disordered, irregular

ensconce, shelter, hide

enseamed, defiled with sweat

ensear, dry up

enshield, concealed, emblazoned

ensteeped, lying under water

entreat, treat, negotiate, intercede

entreatment, entering into negotiation

envy, malice, enmity; show malice towards

Ephesian, boon companion

epicurism, luxury, excess

Erebus, place of darkness, hell

ergo, therefore

eringo, aphrodisiac sweetmeat

erne, grieve

erst, formerly

escot, support financially

espial, spy

estimable, appraising

estimate, valuation, value, repute

estimation, value, thing of value, esteem, reputation, conjecture

estridge, goshawk, ostrich

Europa, carried away by Jupiter who had taken the form of a bull

event, outcome, issue, result

evitate, avoid

exception, objection, dissatisfaction

exclamation, loud reproach

excrement, growth (of hair)

excursion, rush, passage of arms

exempt, cut off

exhalation, meteor

exhale, draw forth

exhaust, draw out

exhibit, to submit, present

exhibition, allowance of money, gift

expectancy, hope

expedience, speed, expedition

expedient, speedy, direct

experimental, of experience

expiate, end

extend, be lavish in praise, exaggerate the worth of, take by force

extent, seizure of property in execution of a writ, attack

extirp, root out

extracting, distracting

extravagancy, wandering

extravagant, straying, vagrant

eyas, young hawk

eyas-musket, young sparrow-hawk

eye-glass, retina, eye's lens

eyestrings, muscles or nerves of eye

face, appearance, appearance of right; to put on a false appearance, brave, bully, brazen, trim

facinorous, vile

fact, deed, crime

factious, seditious

factor, agent

faculty, disposition, quality

fadge, be suitable, succeed

fading, refrain of a song

fail, failure, fault; to offend, die

fain, glad, obliged

fairing, gift

faithed, believed

faitor, cheat, rogue

falchion, sword, scimitar

falling sickness, epilepsy

falsing, deceptive

fame, rumour, report, reputation; make famous

familiar, attendant spirit

fancy, love, whimsicality; to love, fall in love with

fang, seize

fangled, foppish

fantastic, imaginary, fanciful, extravagant

fantasy, delusion, imagination, fancy, whim

fap, drunk

farce, to cram, stuff

farced, stuffed out

fardel, bundle, burden

farm, lease

farthingale, hooped petticoat

fashions, disease of horses

fat, vat

fault, lack, (in hunting) break in the scent

favour, leniency, something given as a mark of favour, badge, charm, appearance, look, face, feature

feat, dexterous, graceful; show to advantage; deed

feature, shape, form, comeliness

fedary, federary, confederate, accomplice

feed, pasture

feeder, servant, parasite, shepherd

fee-farm, fixed rent for perpetual tenancy

fee-grief, individual sorrow

fee-simple, estate belonging to owner and his heirs for ever, absolute possession

felicitate, happy

fell, fierce, cruel, enraged; skin, covering of hair or wool, fleece

felly, section of rim of wooden wheel

fence, art of fencing, defence; to defend

fere, spouse

fernseed, believed to be invisible and to confer invisibility

ferret, worry

festinate, hasty

fetch, stratagem, trick; to draw, derive, strike a blow

fettle, make ready

fia, see VIA

fichew, polecat

fig, to insult with a 'figo'

fig of Spain, figo, fico, scornful gesture made by thrusting the thumb between two of the closed fingers or into the mouth.

fight, screen for protection of crew in sea battle

figure, vigour

file, catalogue, list, roll, rank, number; to smooth, polish, defile

fill, fulfil

fill-horse, shaft horse

fills, shafts

fine, end; to end, pay, fix as sum payable, punish

fire-drake, fiery dragon, meteor

firk, thrash

fitment, fit equipment, fitting office

fives, strangles, a disease of the horse

flap-dragon a raisin in burning brandy; to swallow as a flap-dragon

flapjack, pancake

flatness, completeness

flaw, flake of snow, gust, fragment, fault, outburst; to crack, break

fleckled, dappled

fledge, fledged, covered with down

fleer, mock, sneer; to gibe

flesh, initiate in bloodshed, inflame, gratify

fleshment, excitement resulting from a first success

flewed, having large chaps

flirt-jill, woman of loose character

float, sea

flourish, gloss, embellishment, florid decoration, fanfare of trumpets

flush, full, lusty

flux, discharge, flowing, stream

fob, cheat, trick

foin, thrust

foison, harvest, plentiful crop

fond, foolish, silly, trivial, eager, desirous

fool, professional jester, term of endearment or pity, plaything

foot, see FOUTRE

footcloth, saddle cloth

fop, to dupe, fool

foppery, folly, deceit

foppish, foolish

forage, preying

forbid, cursed

fordo, kill, destroy

fordone, exhausted

forecast, foresight

forehorse, first in team

forespent, previously spent, past

forestall, condemn in advance

forgetive, inventive

fork, forked tongue, barbed arrow-head

forked, horned

formal, traditional, dignified, sane

former, foremost

forsake, refuse, reject, renounce

forslow, delay

forspent, exhausted

fortitude, strength

forwhy, because

foutre, strong expression of contempt, a fuck (French)

fox, kind of sword

fracted, broken

fraction, discord, quarrel, fragment

frame, contriving, structure, plan; to prepare, go, bring to pass, perform

frampold, disagreeable

franchise, freedom, privilege

franchised, free

frank, unrestrained, generous, free; sty; to pen up in a sty

franklin, yeoman

fray, frighten

free, generous, magnanimous, innocent, untroubled; to absolve, banish

French crown, French coin, baldness produced by venereal disease

frequent, addicted, familiar

friend, lover, mistress

frieze, coarse woollen cloth

frippery, old-clothes' shop

front, forehead, face, foremost line of battle, beginning; to confront, oppose

frontlet, band worn on forehead

froward, perverse, wilful, rebellious

frush, smash

fullam, false dice

fulsome, pregnant, loathsome, filthy

furnishings, externals

furniture, equipment, harness

fury, rage, passion, poetic passion, goddess of vengeance

fustian, coarse cloth, bombastic gibberish

gaberdine, loose-fitting coat or cloak

gage, pledge; to stake, bind, engage

gain-giving, misgiving

Galen, famous physician of second century

gall, resentment, bitterness; to rub sore, chafe, graze, wound, harass, scoff

galliard, lively dance

galliass, large, heavy ship

galloglasses, heavily-armed foot-soldiers of Ireland or the Western Isles

gallow, frighten

gallows, gallows-bird, one born (or deserving) to be hanged

gamut, musical scale

garboil, disturbance, quarrel

Gargantua, large-mouthed giant in Rabelais

garland, royal crown, glory

garnish, dress; to adorn, equip

gaskins, breeches

gaud, plaything, showy ornament; to ornament

gear, stuff, talk, matter, business

geck, dupe

gender, kind, sort, offspring

generosity, high birth

generous, high-born

genius, spirit, good or bad angel, embodied spirit

gentle, of noble birth; to ennoble

gentry, rank by birth, good breeding, courtesy

George, jewel bearing figure of the saint, part of insignia of Order of the Garter

germen, seed

gest, deed, time allotted to stage of journey

gesture, bearing

ghasted, frightened

ghastness, terror

ghostly, spiritual

gig, whipping-top

gigloet, wanton

gimmaled, jointed, hinged

ging, gang

gird, gibe; taunt, besiege

give, fetter

glance (at), hint at, cast a slight on

glass, mirror, sand-glass

glaze, stare

gleek, gibe; to gibe, jest

glib, castrate

glut, swallow

go, walk

go to! expression of disapproval, protest, or disbelief

goatish, lustful

good, financially sound, rich

good-brother, brother-in-law

goodman, husband, yeoman, master

goose, smoothing iron

goose of Winchester, prostitute

gorbellied, fat-bellied

gore, to defile, wound

gorge, what has been swallowed

gorget, piece of armour for the throat

Gorgon, woman whose look turned the beholder to stone

gossip, god-father or -mother, sponsor; make merry

gourd, kind of false dice

gout, drop

government, control, self-command, evenness of temper

grained, ingrained, showing grain of the wood, lined, forked

gramercy, thank you

grange, outlying farmhouse

gratify, thank, reward, pay, do honour to

gratulate, pleasing; greet, express joy at

greasily, obscenely

grece, step, stair, degree

gree, agree

groat, fourpenny piece

groundlings, those who stood in the cheapest part of the theatre

grow, be or become due

guard, caution, border, trimming; to ornament

guidon, pennant

guiled, treacherous

guinea-hen, prostitute

guise, custom, habit

gules, red (heraldry)

gull, unfledged bird, dupe, fool, trick; to cheat

gummed, stiffened with gum

gust, taste, relish

Guy, Guy of Warwick, slayer of the giant Colbrand

habit, dress, appearance

habitude, temperament

hackney, prostitute

haggard, wild hawk

haggle, to hack, gash

hag-seed, child of a witch

hai, home-thrust in fencing

hair, kind, character

halcyon, kingfisher

half, partner

half-blooded, of noble blood by one parent only

half-cheek, profile

half-cheeked, with a piece missing or broken on one side

half-face, thin face

half-faced, showing half the face

half-sword, half a sword's length

halidom, holy relic

Hallowmas, All Saints' Day, 1 November

handfast, firm hold, marriage contract

handy-dandy, choose which you please (in a children's game)

haply, happily, perhaps, by chance

happiness, handsomeness, appropriateness, opportunity

hardiment, bold exploit

hardness, difficult, hardship

harlot, man or woman of promiscuous life

harlotry, harlot, silly wench

hatch, engrave, inlay, lower half of a divided door

hatchment, memorial tablet with coat of arms

hautboy, wood-wind instrument, ancestor of the oboe

havoc, devastation; *cry havoc*, give the signal to an army to plunder

hazard, game at dice, chance, venture

head, headland, topic, army

head borough, parish officer

heap, crowd

heavy, important, dull, sluggish, sleepy, grievous

hectic, wasting fever

Hector, Trojan hero

Hecuba, Queen of Troy, wife of Priam and mother of Hector

hedge-pig, hedgehog

Helen, most beautiful woman of her world, wife of the Greek Menelaus, carried off to Troy by Paris

Helicon, mountain of Greece sacred to the Muses

hemp-seed, gallows-bird, one born (or deserving) to be hanged

Hercules, as a baby strangled two serpents; performed twelve great labours, including the obtaining of the golden apples of the Hesperides and the overcoming of Cerberus, the three-headed dog of the underworld

Hero, see LEANDER

Hesperus, the evening star

hest, command

heyday, excitement

high-lone, quite alone, without support

high-proof, in the highest degree

high-stomached, haughty

hight, called

hilding, contemptible, good-for-nothing, baggage

him, male, (dog)

hint, occasion, reason, opportunity

hipped, lame in the hip

hit, succeed, agree

hive, hive-shaped hat

hoar, grow mouldy

hobby-horse, figure of a horse used in morris dances, etc., buffoon, prostitute

holding, consistency, burden of a song

holp, helped

honest, worthy, virtuous, chaste

honesty, honour, decency, chastity

honour, chastity

hoodman-blind, blind man's buff

horn, the mark of a cuckold

horn-book, child's first reader

horn-mad, ready to gore the enemy, enraged at being cuckolded

hose, stockings, breeches

host, lodge

hot-house, brothel

housekeeper, householder, watch-dog, stay-at-home

hox, hamstring

hoy, a small vessel

hugger-mugger, secrecy

hull, float, drift with sails furled

humorous, moist, capricious, moody

humour, moisture; bodily fluid supposedly composed of blood, phlegm, choler, and melancholy, the proportions determining personal temperament; temperament, mood, whim, caprice, inclination

Hungarian, hungry, needy

hunt's-up, morning-song to arouse huntsmen

hurricano, waterspout

hurry, commotion, disorder

husband, one who keeps house; to farm, till

husbandry, management, thrift

Hybla, mountain in Sicily famous for fragrant flowers and honey

Hydra, many-headed snake whose heads grew again as they were cut off

Hymen, god of marriage

Hyperion, sun god

Icarus, see DAEDALUS

idea, image

Ides of March, according to the old Roman calendar, 15 March

idle, empty, trifling, worthless, useless, foolish, out of one's mind

ignis fatuus, will-o'-the-wisp

Ilion, Ilium, citadel of Troy

image, likeness, copy, representation, sign, embodiment, idea

imbecility, weakness

imbrue, pierce, shed blood of

immanity, cruelty

imminence, impending evil

immodest, arrogant, immoderate

immoment, insignificant

imp, young shoot, child; to engraft feathers into a bird's wing

impart, afford, make known

impartment, communication

impeach, accusation, reproach; to accuse, challenge, discredit

impeachment, accusation, detriment, hindrance

impertinency, irrelevancy, ramblings

impertinent, irrelevant

imply, involve

import, involve, imply, express, be important, concern, portend

importance, matter, meaning, importunity

importancy, significance

important, importunate, urgent

importless, meaningless, trivial

imposition, imputation, accusation, command

impostume, abscess

impress, impression, to stamp

imputation, reputation

incapable, unable to receive or realize

inclining, compliant; party, inclination

incomprehensible, boundless

incontinently, immediately

incorpsed, made one body

incorrect, unchastened, rebellious

incredulous, incredible

index, table of contents, preface

indifferency, impartiality, moderate size

indifferent, impartial, ordinary; tolerably, fairly

indigest, unformed, unformed mass

indign, unworthy

indirection, roundabout method, dishonest practice

indirectly, wrongfully, evasively, by suggestion, inattentively

indiscreet, lacking judgement

indiscretion, want of judgement

indisposition, disinclination

indistinguishable, mongrel

indrenched, waterlogged

infect, affect with some feeling

influence, supposed flowing from the heavens of an ethereal fluid acting on human character and destiny, inspiration

inform, take shape, inspire, instruct

infuse, shed, imbue

ingenious, talented, intelligent, discerning, skilfully contrived

ingling, engaging in sexual play

inhabitable, uninhabitable

inherit, possess

inhibit, prohibit

inhibition, prohibition

injurious, insulting, malicious

inkle, linen tape, thread, or yarn

inland, of the central, more cultured, part of a country

innocent, idiot, half-wit

inoculate, engraft by budding

insensible, imperceptible to senses

insinuate, ingratiate, suggest

insinuation, ingratiation, hint

instance, cause, detail, proof, mark, presence

intellect, meaning, content

intelligence, communication, information, news, obtaining of secret information, spy; to pass information

intelligencer, agent

intelligencing, informative

intelligent, giving information, open, informative

intemperature, wildness, intemperance

intenable, unretentive

intendment, purpose, intention

intercept, interrupt

interressed, invested right or share

interest, right, title, share

interlude, entertainment, play

intrenchant, invulnerable

intrinse, intrinsicate, closely entwined

investments, vestments, clothes

irreconciled, unexpiated

irregular, irregulous, lawless

iterance, repetition

iwis, indeed, certainly

Jack, jack, fellow, scoundrel, figure striking the bell on a clock; key of a virginal, smaller bowl aimed at, quarter of a pint

Jack-a-Lent, puppet set up as target during Lent

jade, horse of poor condition or vicious temper, term of contempt; to wear out, make a fool of

jakes, privy

jaunce, prance, trudge up and down

jay, a flashy whore

jealous, suspicious, afraid, apprehensive, doubtful

jealousy, suspicion, apprehension, mistrust

jennet, small Spanish horse

jerk, see YERK

jess, strap attached to the leg of a trained hawk

jet, strut, encroach

jig, quick lively dance, short lively comic entertainment

jointress, dowager

jollity, finery

jolthead, block-head

jordan, chamber-pot

journal, daily

journey-bated, exhausted with travel

Jove, poetic form of JUPITER

jowl, strike, knock

jump, just, precisely; hazard; to hazard, agree, coincide

junket, sweetmeat, delicacy

Juno, queen of the gods and wife of Jupiter; goddess of marriage

Jupiter, ruler of the gods. He was thought to hurl thunderbolts at mortals who displeased him, but otherwise was best known for his many amorous adventures.

just, true, honourable, exact

justicer, judge

justify, maintain the innocence of, vindicate, prove, corroborate

justly, with good reason

jut, encroach

keech, fat of slaughtered animal rolled into a lump

keel, skim

ken, range of sight; to see, recognize, know

kennel, pack, gutter

kern, light-armed Irish foot-soldier

kersey, homely; coarse woollen material

kibe, chilblain

kind, natural, tender, courteous, affectionate; nature, way, race, sort

kindle, bring forth

kindly, naturally, properly, exactly

knack, trifle, knick-knack

knap, nibble, strike

knot, fancifully laid-out flower bed or garden plot

laager, camp

label, slip of paper, strip of paper or parchment by which a seal is attached; to add as a codicil

laboured, worn out, highly finished

laboursome, elaborate

lace, to ornament

lag, last, late

lampass, disease of the horse in which flesh swells behind front teeth

land-damn, damn in this world

lank, become thin

lantern, window-turret

lard, fatten, garnish

large, generous, lavish, free, improper

latch, strike, catch, receive, bewitch

laund, glade

lavolt, lavolta, high-leaping dance

lay, wager

lazar, leper, sick beggar

leading, command, direction, generalship

leaguer, see LAAGER

Leander, lover of Hero of Sestos, he swam the Hellespont nightly to visit her in her tower, and was drowned in a storm

learn, teach

leasing, lying

leather-coat, russet apple

lecture, lesson, instruction

leer, appearance, complexion

leese, lose

leet, court held by lord of the manor

leman, sweetheart, lover

lengthen, delay, postpone

lenity, gentleness

leno, pimp, pander

lenten, meagre

let, hindrance; to hinder, forbear, cause

Lethe, river in Hades; to drink its waters gave forgetfulness

level, aim, line of fire, range; to aim, guess

liable, subject, suitable

liberal, accomplished, humane, abundant, free in speech, unrestrained, gross

lie, to lodge, stay, be still, in prison or in defensive posture

lief, dear

liege, sovereign lord

light, frivolous, unchaste, swift, easy, merry, trivial, delirious

like, please, be in good condition

liking, bodily condition

limbeck, distilling vessel

limber, flexible

lime, cement, catch with birdlime

limit, prescribed time, time of rest after childbearing, region; to appoint

limitation, allotted time

line, rank, Equator, cord for taking measurements; copulate with

linger, prolong, defer

link, torch, lamp-black

linsey-woolsey, woven material of wool and flax, hence medley, nonsense

linstock, forked stick holding a gunner's match

list, limit, bound, barriers enclosing tilting ground, desire; to please, choose

lither, yielding

livelihood, liveliness, animation

liver, supposedly the seat of love and strong emotion

lob, bumpkin

lockram, linen cloth

lodge, flatten, beat down

loggats, game of aiming small logs at a fixed stake

long, belong

loose, unattached, negligent; moment of arrow's discharge, last moment

lose, to ruin, forget

lover, friend, mistress

luce, pike as heraldic device

luggage, baggage of an army

lune, fit of temper, of frenzy

lurch, lurk, rob

lure, dummy bird for recalling hawk

lust, pleasure, desire

lustihood, vigour

lusty, merry, lustful

luxurious, lustful, lecherous

luxury, lust

lym, bloodhound

maculate, stained, impure

maculation, stain, impurity

mainly, with force, greatly, perfectly

majority, pre-eminence

make, mate, husband or wife

making, form, appearance

malapert, saucy

malkin, servant wench, slut

mammer, hesitate

mammock, tear to bits

manage, art of horsemanship

mandrake, poisonous plant believed to shriek when pulled up

mankind, resembling a man, violent, ferocious

manner, stolen goods found on a thief

mansionry, dwelling-place

map, picture, embodiment

mappery, map-making

marches, border country next to Scotland or Wales

marry, (as an exclamation) by (the Virgin) Mary

Mars, god of war and patron of soldiers

mate, rival, checkmate, destroy, stupefy

material, important, forming the substance, full of sense

maugre, in spite of

maund, basket

mazzard, head

meacock, coward, weakling

meal, spot, stain

mean, something between or intervening, middle, medium position, tenor, alto; to lament

measurable, suitable

measure, a stately dance; tune; to measure

mechanic, labourer

mechanical, mean, vulgar; labourer

Medea, escaping with Jason she tore to pieces her brother Absyrtus, scattering his limbs in her father's path to delay him; restored the youth of Jason's father, Aeson

medicinable, healing, medicinal

medlar, fruit eaten soft and pulpy; prostitute

meed, reward, gift, merit

meiny, company of retainers, multitude

mell, to meddle

memorize, make memorable

memory, memorial, memento, remembrance

Mercury, messenger of the gods

mere, sure, absolute, unqualified, only

merely, simply, entirely

merit, reward

mess, dish, portion, group originally of four persons eating together, set of four

metaphysical, supernatural

mete, measure, aim

metheglin, spiced mead

methinks, it seems to me

method, table of contents

micher, truant

mickle, great

microcosm, little world, man considered as epitome of the universe

milch, in milk, tearful

mince, to extenuate, moderate, affect

mineral, mine

Minerva, goddess of wisdom

minimus, creature of tiniest size

minion, favourite, darling, harlot, saucy creature

Minotaur, devouring monster dwelling in labyrinth of Crete

mirable, wonderful

mirror, model, pattern

mischief, misfortune, injury, disease

misdread, fear of evil

miser, miserable wretch

misgoverned, unruly

misgovernment, misconduct

misgrafted, badly matched

misprision, contempt, mistake, misunderstanding

misproud, arrogant

missive, messenger

mistake, take, undertake or deliver wrongly, misjudge, blunder, feel misgiving about

misthink, think evil of

mistress, the jack at bowls

mobled, muffled

mockery, imitation, futile action

model, architect's plan, mould, copy

modern, everyday, commonplace

modest, moderate, satisfactory, becoming

modestly, without exaggeration

modesty, moderation, avoidance of exaggeration

moiety, half, share, small part

moldwarp, mole

mome, blockhead

moment, cause

monster, make a monster of, show as monstrous

monument, sepulchre, effigy, portent

monumental, memorial, commemorating

mood, anger, outward appearance, mode

mooncalf, misshapen creature

moonish, changeable

mop, grimace

mope, move blindly and stupidly, be bewildered

moralize, interpret, explain

mort, note on a horn at the death of the deer

mortified, dead to the world, deadened, destroyed

mortifying, mortal

mose in the chine, suffer from glanders

mot, motto

moth, mote

mother, hysteria

motion, motive, puppet show, puppet; to propose

motive, cause, instigator, instrument, moving limb or organ

mould, earth

mouse, tear, bite

mouse-hunt, woman-chaser

mow, grimace

mulled, thick, heavy

mummy, dead flesh, medicinal or magical preparation from this

muniments, furnishings

mure, wall

murrain, plague

muse, wonder

muset, gap

muss, scramble

mutine, mutineer; rebel

mutiny, strife, quarrel

mutual, common, intimate

mutually, in return, together

mystery, trade, profession, skill

naked, unarmed, plain

Naso, family name of the poet Ovid

native, source, origin; natural, kindred, closely related, rightful

natural, that is so by birth, related by blood, kind, tender; half-wit

naturalize, familiarize

naught, wickedness, wicked, ruined, ruin

naughty, bad, wicked, good-for-nothing

nave, nub, navel

neaf, fist

neat, animal of the ox kind, cattle

neb, mouth

Nebuchadnezzar, king of Babylon, driven out to eat grass like cattle

neeze, sneeze

neglect, cause of neglect

nephew, cousin, grandson

Neptune, god of the sea

Nereides, sea-nymphs

Nero, Roman emperor, responsible for the assassination of his mother; believed to have played on the lyre and recited while watching the burning of the city set on fire by his orders

nerve, sinew

nervy, sinewy

Nessus, centaur killed by Hercules for trying to rape Deianira; a tunic dyed with his blood poisoned Hercules

Nestor, oldest and wisest of the Greeks at the siege of Troy

next, nearest, quickest

nice, wanton, delicate, shy, difficult to please, fastidious, scrupulous, subtle, needing precision, delicately balanced, intricate, exact, skilful, trivial

nicely, elegantly, scrupulously, sophistically, exactly

niceness, coyness, fastidiousness

nicety, coyness

Nicholas, patron saint of scholars; Saint Nicholas' clerks, highwaymen

nickname, name wrongly

niggard, to act in a miserly way, supply sparingly

night-gown, dressing gown

night-rule, disorder by night

nine-men's morris, cutting in turf for game played with nine pegs or discs

Niobe, overboastful of her children, who were slain; she was herself turned to stone.

noise, rumour, music, band of musicians; clamour, spread by rumour

noll, head

nonsuit, to refuse to listen to or grant the suit of

nook-shotten, having a very uneven outline

notedly, precisely

nothing, vulva

notion, understanding, mind

novum, dice-game in which chief throws are nine and five

noyance, injury, harm

nuncio, messenger

nursery, nursing, care

nut-hook, beadle, constable

oathable, fit to take an oath

ob., abbreviation of 'obolus', halfpenny

objection, charge, accusation

obligation, contract

obliged, pledged

obsequious, dutiful, dutiful in funeral rites

observant, obsequious servant

observe, humour

occasion, opportunity, pretext, cause, course of events

occulted, hidden

occupation, business, handicraft, trade

occupy, have to do with sexually

occurrent, event

oddly, unevenly

oeillade, inviting glance, ogling

o'erblow, blow away

o'ercount, outnumber

o'ercrow, triumph over

o'erdyed, dyed with a second colour

o'ereaten, left after most has been eaten

o'erflourished, decorated on the outside

o'erlook, examine, bewitch, despise

o'ermaster, possess

o'erparted, having too difficult a part

o'er-peer, rise above

o'erpost, get over easily

o'er-raught, overtook

o'er-teemed, worn out by child-bearing

o'er-watch, stay awake too long

o'erwhelm, overhang

o'erwrested, strained

offend, harm, hurt

offer, act on the offensive, venture

office, function, service

offices, parts of a house devoted to household matters

omit, neglect, disregard, lay aside

omittance, postponement

open-arse, medlar

operant, effecting, effective

operation, effect, efficacy

opinion, censure, public judgement, self-conceit, self-confidence

opposeless, irresistible

opposite, antagonist, opponent; hostile, adverse

oppress, suppress, distress

oppression, burden, distress

oppugnancy, conflict

orb, circle, sphere, sphere in which a star moves, heavenly body, earth

ordinance, what is ordained, established rule, decree, rank

ordinary, fixed-price tavern meal, 'ordinary run'

orgulous, proud

orifex, aperture

orison, prayer

ort, fragment, scrap

ostent, appearance, show

ostentation, appearance, show, spectacle

othergates, in another way

otherwhiles, at times

ouch, jewel

ounce, lynx

ouph, elf

ousel, blackbird

outbrave, to surpass in beauty or valour

outlandish, foreign

outlive, survive

outpeer, surpass

outsell, exceed in value

outward, outward appearance

overhear, hear over again

overhold, overestimate

overlook, overtop, look down on from above, read through

overpeer, rise above, look down on

over-scutched, made haggard with beating, worn out

overture, disclosure; formal opening, first indication

Ovid, Roman poet who was sent into exile

owe, own, possess

pace, train (a horse) to pace

pack, gang; conspire, shuffle (cards), to cheat, be off

packing, plotting

paddock, toad

pageant, show, spectacle

pain, trouble, punishment

painful, laborious, toilsome

pale, fence, enclosure; enclose, encircle

palisado, staked fence

pall, fail

palliament, white robe of a candidate for the Roman consulship

palmer, pilgrim

palter, equivocate, use trickery

pander, go-between in a love affair, pimp

Pandion, see PHILOMEL

pantaloon, foolish old man

pantler, servant in charge of the pantry

paper, notice specifying offence committed; write down

paragon, compare, excel, show as a model

Parca, one of the three fates who prepared and cut the thread of human life

parcel, part, item, group

parcel-gilt, partly gilded

pard, panther or leopard

pardie, certainly, indeed

Paris ball, tennis ball

paritor, official who summoned offenders to an ecclesiastical court

parlous, perilous, cunning, dreadful

part, action, side

partage, freight, cargo

partake, impart, take sides

partaker, confederate, supporter

parted, divided, gifted

partialize, make partial

particular, detail, individual, personal interest, intimacy; private, personal

partisan, footsoldier's weapon, a long-handled spear with a blade

pash, head; to strike violently, smash

passado, a forward thrust in fencing

passant, heraldic term of beast stepping; surpassing

passenger, traveller on foot

passion, suffering, affliction, fit of disease, overpowering emotion, passionate speech, sorrow; feel deep emotion

passionate, express with passion; compassionate, sorrowful

patch, fool

patchery, trickery

paten, thin circular metal plate

patent, title, privilege, authority

patience, permission, leave

patronage, uphold, defend

pattern, precedent, model; to give an example, be a pattern or precedent for

pax, tablet kissed by priest and congregation in celebration of mass

peach, denounce, turn informer

peat, spoilt girl

peck, pitch

peculiar, individual, private, belonging to one person

pedant, schoolmaster

peeled, tonsured

Pegasus, winged horse

peise, balance, weight, suspend

pelf, property, possessions

pelican, believed to feed its young with its own blood

pelt, rage, scold

pelting, paltry, worthless

pencil, paintbrush

pendulous, impending, suspended

pensioners, royal bodyguard

Penthesilea, Amazon queen

peradventure, by chance, perhaps

perdie, see PARDIE

perdition, ruin, loss, damnation

perdurable, everlasting

peregrinate, travelled, foreign in style

perfect, fully informed, equipped, ready; accomplish, instruct

perfection, performance, completion

periapt, amulet

period, end, goal, highest point, full pause, full stop; to end

perjure, perjurer; corrupt

perniciously, to destruction

perpend, consider

persistive, steadfast

perspective, optical device for producing fantastic images; picture of figure producing a distorted or unexpected effect

pert, lively

pervert, turn aside

pester, throng, obstruct

pestiferous, pernicious

phantasim, fantastic being

Philomel, Philomela, daughter of Pandion, raped by Tereus (husband of her sister Progne), who cut out her tongue; she wove her story into a tapestry. Progne feasted Tereus on their murdered son; Philomela was changed into a nightingale

phere, see FERE

Phoebe, Diana, goddess of the moon

Phoebus, Apollo, god of the sun

phoenix, unique Arabian bird which, dying, is recreated from its own ashes

phraseless, inexpressible

phthisic, consumptive cough

physical, beneficial to health

pia mater, brain

picked, refined, fastidious

Pickt-hatch, London district noted for brothels

pie, magpie

piece, cask of liquor, masterpiece; add to, augment

pied, parti-coloured

pike, spike in centre of buckler

pill, plunder, rob, strip (of bark), make bald

pillicock, penis

pin and web, disease of the eye

pinch, bite, pang; to bite, harass, distress

pismire, ant

placket, petticoat, opening, slit

planched, made of boards

plant, sole of the foot

plantage, plants

plash, pool

plausible, pleasing

plausibly, with applause

plausive, deserving of applause

Plautus, Roman writer of comedy

pleached, formed by intertwined over-arched boughs, folded

pleasant, merry, jokey

pleurisy, abundance, excess

plight, pledge

Pluto, ruler of the underworld

Plutus, god of riches

poach, to thrust, stab

point, highest point, conclusion, lace with tags (for attaching hose to doublet, etc.), full stop

poking-stick, rod used for pleating ruffs

polecat, prostitute

policy, government, administration, prudence in managing public or private affairs, cunning, craftiness, trick

politic, dealing with government and administration, crafty

politician, schemer, scheming statesman

pomewater, large juicy kind of apple

pomp, procession, pageant

Pontic sea, Black Sea

poop, swamp, overwhelm

poor-john, salted fish

popular, plebeian, vulgar

popularity, common pledge

porridge, porrage, soup

porringer, basin

port, gate, bearing, style of living

portable, bearable, endurable

portage, portholes

portance, behaviour

posied, inscribed with a motto

possess, inform, acquaint

posset, drink of hot milk curdled with ale or wine; curdle, thicken

post, post set up for notices, etc., doorpost on which tavern reckoning was kept, courier, messenger, post-horse; to hasten, carry swiftly

poster, swift traveller

posy, motto inscribed inside a ring

potable, able to be drunk

potato, sweet potato, supposedly aphrodisiac

potency, power, authority

potent, potentate

potential, powerful

potting, tippling

pouncet-box, small box for perfumes

powder, preserve meat with salt or spice

powdering-tub, pickling-tub, sweating-tub used in cure of venereal disease

power, army

pox, syphilis, venereal disease

practice, trickery, conspiracy, plot

practisant, one who carries out a trick

practise, plot, conspire

praemunire, writ for maintaining papal jurisdiction in England

praetor, Roman magistrate

praise, appraise, value

prank, adorn

precedent, former; original from which a copy is made, sign

precisian, puritan

precurrer, forerunner

precurse, heralding

predicament, situation

prefer, present, advance, introduce, recommend

pregnancy, quickness of wit

pregnant, clear, fertile, compelling, resourceful, receptive

prejudicate, influence beforehand

prejudice, injury; injure

premised, sent before

preparation, accomplishment

preposterous, inverting the natural order of things, monstrous

prerogative, precedence, pre-eminence

presage, omen, prognostication, foreboding

presence, presence-chamber, company, person

present, immediate, instant; ready money, to show, represent, bring a charge against

presently, immediately

presentment, dedication

press, crowd, crowding, printing-press, cupboard, authority to enlist men compulsorily; to crowd, oppress, force into military service

pressure, impression, character impressed

pretence, expressed aim, intention, pretext

prevent, anticipate, escape, avoid

prick, mark made by pricking, dot, point, spot in centre of target, prickle, penis; to mark by making a dot, etc., pierce, fix, point, spur

pricket, buck in its second year

prick-song, music sung from notes

pride, magnificence, splendid adornment, highest state, mettle, sexual desire

prig, thief

prime, first, chief, sexually excited; springtime

primogenitive, first-born's right to inherit

principal, superior, abettor, principal rafter

princox, pert youth

Priscian, Roman grammarian

prithee, please

private, private person

privates, sexual organs

prize, contest; to value, esteem

prizer, prize-fighter, wrestler

probal, *to,* able to bear the probe or examination of

probation, trial, proof

proceeder, one proceeding to a university degree

procurator, proxy

prodigious, ominous, portentous, monstrous, abnormal

proditor, traitor

proface, 'may it do you good', formula of welcome before a meal

profited, proficient

progeny, lineage, race

project, notion, idea; set forth, exhibit

projection, plan

prolixious, prolonged

prolong, postpone

Prometheus, stole fire from heaven and was chained to Mount Caucasus

prone, ready, eager

proof, test, trial, experience, issue, result

propend, incline

proper, (one's) own, private, peculiar, excellent, handsome

property, identity, particular quality, take

possession of, endow with qualities, make a tool of

proportion, portion, division, relative size, proportioning, rhythm

propose, put forward, set before one's mind, suppose, converse

propriety, identity, proper state

propugnation, defence

prorogue, prolong, postpone

prosecution, pursuit

Proserpina, daughter of Ceres, carried away by Pluto to become queen of hell

prosperous, favourable

Proteus, a sea-god, able to assume different shapes

protractive, consisting in delay

proud, elated, giving cause for pride, lofty, splendid, spirited, swollen, over-luxuriant, sexually excited

prove, try, test, find by experience, experience

publish, make known, proclaim, denounce

pucelle, virgin, maid, slut

puck, pixy, mischievous spirit

pudding, sausage, stuffing

pudency, modesty

puissance, strength, armed force

puissant, strong, powerful

pumpion, pumpkin

punk, prostitute, harlot

punto reverso, back-handed thrust in fencing

purblind, quite blind, partially blind

purchase, booty, prize, annual rent from land; to strive, gain, acquire otherwise than by inheritance

purgation, clearing from accusation or suspicion

purlieu, tract of land bordering on a forest

purpose, proposal, conversation

pursuivant, junior attendant on heralds, herald, messenger

pursy, short-winded, fat

purveyor, steward going ahead to make provision

putter on, instigator

puttock, bird of prey, kite, buzzard

quail, prostitute; to fail, faint, overpower

quaint, skilful, clever, dainty, fine, beautiful, elaborate

qualification, calm and controlled condition

qualify, moderate, mitigate, appease, control, dilute

quality, accomplishment, rank, profession, party, side, manner, cause

quarry, heap of slaughtered game

quarter, part, watch, relations with and conduct towards another

quat, pimple

quatch, word of unknown meaning

quean, hussy, whore

queasy, hazardous, squeamish

quell, slaughter

quest, jury, inquest, search party

questant, seeker

questionable, inviting question

questrist, seeker

quick, flowing, fresh, impatient

quiddity, subtlety, equivocation

quietus, clearing of accounts

quintain, object or figure to practise tilting at

quirk, quibble, clever expression, peculiarity of behaviour, fit, start

quit, set free, rid, acquit, acquit oneself of, revenge, repay, requite

quittal, requital

quittance, discharge from debt, requital; requite

quoif, close-fitting cap

quondam, former

quote, give marginal references to, set down in writing, note, observe, regard

quoth, said

quotidian, (of an intermittent fever) returning every day

race, root (of ginger), lineage, breed, natural disposition

rack, driving cloud; to torture, extend, stretch, strain

rage, madness, angry disposition, sexual passion; to enrage

ramp, loose woman

rampallian, riotous woman

rampire, barricade

rank, growing too luxuriantly, swollen, grown too fat, rebellious, high, full, lustful, in heat, coarse, festering; closely

rankle, cause a festering wound

rankness, overflowing, insolence

rascal, inferior deer

rate, estimate, value, expense

ravel, become entangled, disentangle

raven, devour greedily

rayed, bespattered, fouled

read, teach, discover the meaning of, expound a riddle

re-answer, compensate for

reason, speech, remark; to talk, discuss, explain

reasonable, needing the use of reason

reave, deprive, take away

rebate, make dull, blunt

rebato, stiff collar

receipt, what is received, receptacle, receiving, capacity, recipe

receiving, understanding, reception

recheat, notes sounded on a horn to call hounds together in stag-hunting

reck, to care (for), mind

reclaim, tame, subdue

recognizance, bond, token

recomfort, console

record, witness, memory; to witness, sing

recordation, memorial, impression on the memory

recourse, access, admission, flowing

recover, reconcile, reach, rescue

recovery, process by which entailed estate was transferred from one party to another

rector, ruler, head

rectorship, rule

recure, restore, heal

reduce, bring, bring back

reechy, smoky, dirty, stinking

reek, smoke, steam

refel, refute

reflect, shine

regiment, authority, rule

region, upper air, air

regreet, greeting, contract

reguerdon, reward

rehearsal, account

rehearse, describe, tell

reins, kidneys

rejoindure, reunion

rejourn, adjourn

relative, able to be related and believed

religion, strict fidelity, religious duty

religious, exact, conscientious, strict

remember, mention, commemorate, remind

remit, pardon, give up

remonstrance, demonstration

remorse, pity, tenderness, moderation, qualification, mitigation

remorseful, compassionate

remotion, departing

removed, remote, secluded, separated by time or space

removedness, absence

remover, one who changes

render, surrender, rendering of an account, statement; to give back, represent, describe as being, declare, state, surrender

rendezvous, refuge, last resort

renege, deny, renounce

repair, restoring, coming; go, come, return

repairing, able to renew the attack

repasture, food

repeal, recall from exile; recall as from banishment, call back into favour

repetition, recital, mention

repine, vexation

replenished, perfect

replication, reply, echo

reprisal, prize

reprobance, damnation, rejection by God

reprobate, depraved

reproof, disgrace, disproof, refutation

reprove, disprove, refute

repugn, oppose

repugnancy, resistance

repugnant, refractory

rescue, freeing from legal custody by force

resemblance, appearance, likelihood

resist, affect with distaste

resolve, dissolve, answer (a question), solve (a problem), convince, inform

resolvedly, answering all questions

respect, relationship, discrimination, consideration, esteem; to regard, care for, esteem

respective, careful, worthy of being cared for, discriminating

respectively, respectfully

respite, delay, date to which something is postponed, limit

responsive, suited

rest, place to rest, restored strength, resolution, stakes kept in reserve

restrain, draw tight, withhold

resty, restive, sluggish

retention, detention, reserve, power to hold or retain

retentive, confining, restraining

retire, return

retort, to reflect (heat), reject (an appeal)

retreat, recall of pursuing force

retrograde, contrary, seeming to move in a backward course

reverb, resound

revolt, revulsion, change; rebel

revolution, alteration, change produced by time

revolve, consider

rhapsody, confused medley

rheum, mucus from nose or throat, cold in the head, rheumatism

riggish, wanton

rigol, ring, circle

rim, belly, membrane lining the abdomen

ring-carrier, go-between

ringlet, little circle

riot, loose living, debauchery

rivage, shore

rival, partner

rive, split

rivelled, wrinkled

road, riding, period of riding, stage (of journey), roadstead, highway

robustious, boisterous

roguing, roaming

roguish, vagrant

roisting, blustering, bullying

rondure, circle

ropery, knavery

Roscius, famous Roman actor

rote, fix by memory

round, plain, plain-spoken, severe; round dance, roundabout way, rung of a ladder; surround, become round

roundel, round dance

rouse, full draught of liquor, drinking bout

royal, gold coin of the value of ten shillings (fifty pence)

royalty, prerogative enjoyed, or granted, by the sovereign

roynish, scurvy

rub, in bowls an obstacle hindering or turning aside the bowl, obstacle, hindrance, roughness, unevenness; to turn aside, hinder

rubious, ruby-red

ruddock, robin

rude, ignorant, barbarous, violent, rough

rudeness, violence, roughness

rudesby, rough unmannerly brute

ruffle, bustle; swagger, bear oneself proudly, bluster, be turbulent

rugged, shaggy, frowning

rug-headed, having shaggy hair

ruinous, brought to ruin

rumour, fame, tumult, uproar

runagate, deserter, vagabond

runnion, wretch (a term of abuse)

russet, homely, simple

sable, black

sack, white wine

sackbut, trumpet resembling a trombone

sad, steadfast, grave, serious, dismal

sadly, gravely, seriously

sadness, seriousness

safe, make safe

safety, custody, safeguard

sain, said

salamander, lizard-like animal supposed to live in fire

sale-work, ready-made goods not of the highest quality

sallet, light helmet, something mixed or savoury

salt, lecherous

salute, touch, affect

sample, example

sanctimony, holiness, sanctity

sanctuarize, give sanctuary to

sand-blind, half-blind

sanguine, red

sans, without

sapient, wise

sarcenet, fine soft silk material

sauce, over-charge, rebuke

saucy, insolent, presumptuous, wanton

savagery, wild growth

savour, smell, perfume, style, character

saw, saying, maxim, proverb

say, finely woven cloth, taste, saying

scab, rascal, scurvy fellow

scald, scabby, mean

scale, weigh

scandalize, disgrace

scantling, specimen, sample

scantly, slightingly

scape, escapade, transgression; escape

scarf, officer's sash, sling, streamer; blindfold, deck with streamers

scathe, harm; to injure

schedule, document

school, university, instruction, learning; reprimand, discipline

science, knowledge

scion, shoot, slip for grafting

sconce, head, small fort or earthwork

scope, object, aim, purpose, theme, liberty

score, notch cut in stock or tally in keeping accounts, account; to notch

scorn, taunt, insult, object of contempt

scotch, cut, gash

scour, hasten

scrimer, fencer

scrip, small bag, piece of paper with writing on

scrippage, contents of scrip

scripture, writing

scrubbed, stunted

scruple, tiny part, doubt, difficulty

scurril, coarsely abusive

scut, deer's tail

scutcheon, shield with coat of arms; tablet showing armorial bearings of a dead man

seam, fat, grease

sectary, dissenter, one who pursues a particular study

secure, free from care, confident, unsuspicious; make confident or overconfident

securely, confidently, without suspicion

security, confidence, overconfidence

seed, mature, run to seed

seedness, sowing

seeing, appearance

seel, make blind, close (a person's eyes)

seely, foolish, innocent, harmless

seen, skilled

seld, seldom

self, one's own, same

semblable, similar, like, equal

semblative, like, resembling

Seneca, Roman tragic dramatist

sennight, week

sense, physical feeling, sensuality, sexual desire, mental apprehension, mind, opinion

senseless, without feeling or perception, free from sensual sin

sensible, perceptible, tangible, substantial, having sensation, sensitive, endowed with feeling

sensibly, having sensation, feelingly

sentence, sententious saying, maxim

septentrion, north

sequel, series

sequent, succeeding, following

sequester, separation; to separate

sequestration, separation, seclusion

sere, dry, withered

serpigo, a skin disease

servanted, subject

service, what is placed on the table for a meal

several, distinct, different, individual, respective, various

severally, separately, at different entrances or exits

sewer, attendant in charge of service at a meal

shadow, shade; to hide, shelter

shame, to be ashamed

shard, piece of broken pottery, patch of cow-dung

shark, gather hastily together

shearman, one who shears woollen cloth

sheaved, made of straw

sheep-biter, sneaking rascal

sheep-biting, sneaking

shent, blamed, rebuked, reproved

shift, expedient, resource, trick; for (a) shift, to serve a turn; make (a) shift, contrive, manage

ship-tire, kind of head-dress

shive, slice

shoal, shallow, sand-bar

shock, to meet with force

shog, go, shift

shotten, that has spawned, lean

shoulder-shotten, having a dislocated shoulder

shove-groat, shovel-board

shrewd, wicked, mischievous, badtempered, dangerous, evil, difficult

shrewdly, sharply, grievously, intensely, very much

shrieve, sheriff

shrift, confession and absolution, penance

shrill-gorged, shrill-throated

shrive, to hear confession and absolve

shroud, protection, sailropes; shelter, hide

shuffle, use trickery, smuggle, shift

siege, seat, rank, turd

sight, visor

sightless, unseen, unsightly

silly, see SEELY

simple, medicinal herb, single ingredient in a compound

simpleness, innocence, simplicity, foolishness

simplicity, ignorance, silliness

simular, pretended, plausible; counterfeiter

sinfully, with sins unatoned for

single, slight, trivial, sincere, simple

singularity, eccentricity, own person

sinister, left (hand), unfavourable, unjust

sink, cause to fall, ruin; sewer, drain

Sinon, a Greek who by guile persuaded the Trojans to take the Grecians' wooden horse into Troy

sirrah, form of address used mainly to inferiors

sith, sithence, since

size, allowance

skill, judgement, reason, ability; to make a difference, matter

skilless, ignorant

skimble-skamble, confused, rubbishy

skipper, flighty youth

skirr, fly, scour

slab, half-solid

slander, ill-repute, disgrace, discredit; bring into disgrace, reproach

slanderous, shameful, disgraceful

slave, enslave, make subservient to oneself

sleave, floss-silk, silk untwisted into fine threads

sleeve-hand, cuff

sleided, (of silk) floss, untwisted into fine threads

sliding, slip

slipper, shifty

slippery, unstable, fickle

slipshod, in slippers

slobbery, sloppy, slovenly

slops, wide breeches

slovenly, nasty, disgusting

slubber, sully, hurry over

smatch, taste

smatter, chatter

smock, woman's undergarment, woman

smooth, flatter, gloss over

smother, suffocating smoke

smug, trim, spruce

sneap, snub, pinch with cold

snuff, resentment

sob, opportunity for a horse to recover his wind, respite

sod, steeped, boiled

soiled, fed with fresh-cut green fodder

soilure, sullying, defilement

sole, unique, mere, alone

solely, alone, entirely

solemnity, ceremony, festivity

solicit, urging, entreaty; move, stir, bring something about

sometime, at some time, sometimes, once, formerly

sonance, sounding, signal

sonties, saints

sooth, truth, flattery

soothe, humour, flatter

soother, flatterer

sop, bread or wafer dipped in wine, etc

sophister, one using false arguments

sore, buck, deer, in its fourth year

sorel, buck, deer, in its third year

sort, lot, rank, company, group, way, state; allot, ordain, come about, turn out, be suitable, correspond, adapt, fit, classify, choose, contrive, go in company

sortance, agreement, suitableness

sound, utter, proclaim, keep sound; swoon

souse, swoop on, pickle

span-counter, game in which counters are thrown to lie within a hand's span

spavin, disease of horses consisting of swelling of joints, producing lameness

specialty, special characteristic, possession, special contract under seal

spectacles, organs of sight

speculation, watcher, power of seeing, sight, looking on

speculative, seeing

speed, fortune, outcome, protection, assistance; to fare (well or ill), turn out, be successful, assist, favour

speeding, successful, fruitful; lot, outcome, success

spend, consume, waste

sphere, orbit of a planet, one of the concentric globes supposed to revolve round the earth with a harmonious sound

spherical, planetary

spial, spy

spigot, peg in faucet of a barrel

spill, destroy

spilth, spilling

spin, spurt

spinner, spider

spinster, spinner

spital, hospital

spleen, bodily organ regarded as the seat of emotions

spoil, plundering, prey, ruin; plunder, seize, destroy

spot, stain, disgrace, embroidered pattern

spring, fountain, source, shoot of a plant

springe, snare for birds

springhalt, disease of horse characterized by twitching and lameness

spurn, kick, insult, blow; to kick, oppose scornfully

square, fair, just; carpenter's set-square, measure, rule; body of troops in square formation, square of material in bosom of a dress; to regulate, quarrel (among), be at variance

squarer, quarreller

squash, unripe peapod

squiny, look asquint

staff, shaft of lance, lance, stanza

stagger, hesitate, waver

staggers, giddiness

stain, tinge, to eclipse, dim, be obscured

stair-work, furtive love-making

stale, decoy, bait, prostitute, laughing-stock, urine (of horses)

stall, install, keep, dwell, bring (a hunted animal) to a stand

stamp, stamping tool, coin, medal, distinguishing mark, imprint; to impress, mark with an impression, give approval to

stanch, satisfy

stanchless, insatiable

stand, place where one stands in ambush or in hiding; confront, oppose, stand firm; *stand at a guard with,* be fully protected against; *stand on, upon,* insist on, persist in, depend on, rely on, concern, be the duty or interest of; *stand to,* have an erection, support, maintain,

be firm in, persist in; *stand to it,* maintain a cause, take a stand

standard, standard-bearer

staniel, kestrel

stare, (of hair) stand on end

start, sudden invasion, sudden flight, impulse; to startle, rush

starting-hole, refuge, loop-hole

starve, die, die of cold, kill or benumb with cold

state, condition, condition of health or prosperity, rank, dignity, chair of state, throne, nobles, ruling body, government

station, way of standing, attitude

statist, statesman

statute, bond, mortgage

statute-cap, woollen cap ordered in 1571 to be worn on Sundays and holy days by all below a certain rank

stay, obstacle; detain, stand, stand firm, wait (for), attend on

stead, to be of use to, help

stell, to fix, portray

stern, rudder

stew, brothel, stewpan

stick, stab, be fastened or fixed, hesitate

stickler-like, like an umpire

stigmatic, deformed person

stigmatical, deformed

still, always, continually

stillitory, apparatus for distillation

stilly, softly

sting, sexual desire

stint, stop

stithy, forge

stoccado, thrust with a rapier

stock, block of wood, person without feeling, stocking, dowry; set in the stocks

stockfish, dried cod or other fish, beaten before cooking

stockish, blockish, unfeeling

stomach, appetite, inclination, temper, courage, pride, anger; resent

stomacher, ornamental front over which the bodice was laced

stone, mirror, thunderbolt, testicle; turn to stone

stone-bow, cross-bow used for shooting stones

stoop, (of a bird of prey) swoop

stop, hole in a wind-instrument, stopped to produce a difference in pitch, fingering of musical chords, fret of a lute; staunch, heal

store, breeding, increase; to populate

stout, bold, strong, proud

stoutness, stubborn pride

stover, fodder for cattle

strain, race, character, kind, class, tune; clasp, force, constrain, urge

strait, narrow, tight-fitting, strict, niggardly; narrow place, difficulty

strange, foreign, new, not knowing, unfriendly, cold, shy

strange-achieved, gained at a distance and for others

strange-disposed, of unusual character

strangely, coldly, without greeting, as a stranger, to an extraordinary degree, in an unusual way

strangeness, behaving as a stranger, aloofness, reserve

strappado, torture in which victim was hoisted up by his arms, which were tied behind his back, then let down halfway with a jerk

stratagem, deed of violence

straw, *wisp of straw,* mark of disgrace for a scolding woman

stray, body of stragglers; lead astray

strength, authority, legal power, body of troops

strewment, strewing of flowers

stricture, strictness

strike, to lower (sail), blast, destroy, tap (a cask)

strossers, trousers

stubborn, inflexible, stiff, rude, harsh, ruthless

stuff, semen

style, title

subduement, conquest

subjection, duty as, or of, a subject

submission, confession of error

subscribe, sign, write down, assent, acknowledge, admit, submit, yield up, answer

subscription, submission

substractor, slanderer

subtle, thin, fine, cunning, treacherous, tricky

subtlety, illusion

success, outcome, result, good or bad fortune, succession

successfully, likely to succeed

succession, following on, successors, success

successive, hereditary, descending by succession

successively, by inheritance

sufferance, suffering, damage, patient endurance

suffice, content, satisfy

sufficient, able, able to meet liabilities, solvent

suggest, tempt, prompt to evil, insinuate to

suggestion, prompting to evil, temptation

sumless, incalculable

summoner, officer who summoned offenders to an ecclesiastical court

sumpter, driver of pack-horse, pack-horse

superflux, superabundance, surplus

supernal, heavenly

superscript, superscription, address or direction on letter

superstitious, idolatrously devoted

supervise, perusal; look over

suppliance, pastime

supply, help, reinforcements

supposal, opinion

suppose, supposition, expectation; believe, imagine, guess

supposition, doubt

surcease, cessation; cease

sure, safe, beyond power of doing harm, reliable, united

surety, confidence of safety, certainty, stability, warrant

sur-reined, overridden

suspect, suspicion

suspire, breathe, draw breath

sutler, one who sells provisions to soldiers
swagger, rant, bluster, quarrel
swaggerer, blusterer, quarreller
swart, dark, swarthy
swasher, blustering ruffian
swashing, swaggering, slashing
sway, direction, control, sovereignty; to rule, move
swayed, curved in
swear, *swear out,* forswear
sweat, sweating sickness, sweating cure; take a sweating cure
sweet, scented; scent
sweeting, sweet variety of apple, term of endearment
swim, float
swinge, thrash
swinge-buckler, roisterer
sworder, cut-throat, gladiator
'Swounds, by God's wounds (a strong oath)
sympathize, to be similarly affected, agree (with), match

table, tablet for an inscription, writing-tablet, flat surface on which a picture is painted, quadrangular space between chief lines on palm of hand
table-book, notebook
tables, backgammon
tabor, small drum
tackled stair, rope ladder
tag, tag-rag, rabble
tailor, ? sex organ
take, strike, strike with disease or enchantment, catch, take effect, reckon, measure, write down, accept as true, catch fire, perceive, understand, esteem, take away, conclude; *take head,* deviate, run off its course; *take in,* capture; *take me with you,* speak so that I can understand you; *take it on,* assume authority; *take on,* rage, show great distress, pretend; *take out,* make a copy of; *take up* lift, enlist, arrest, buy on credit, rebuke, reprimand, oppose, encounter, make up (a quarrel)
taking, blasting; state of great excitement or alarm, malignant influence
tale, numbering one after another, talk, story, falsehood
talent, treasure, measure for a large sum of money
tall, long, lofty, goodly, fine, brave
tally, stick marked with notches for keeping accounts
'tame, broach (a cask)
tang, ring out
tardy, delay
targe, light shield
tarre, urge, incite
tarriance, delay, waiting
tarry, wait, await, remain, delay
task, tax, impose a task on, occupy, put a strain on, put to proof
tasking, challenge
tassel-gentle, tercel, male hawk
tawdry-lace, silk lace or ribbon for the neck
tax, accusation; blame, accuse, charge
taxation, claim, demand, slander
teem, conceive, bring forth, bear children, be fruitful

teen, affliction, grief, sorrow
tell, count
temper, disposition, temperament, mental balance, hardness and elasticity imparted to steel; to compound, mix, persuade
temperance, mildness of temperature, calmness, chastity
temperate, chaste, secular
temporary, secular
tempt, test, risk
tenant, vassal
tend, listen, watch over, attend on, wait (for)
tendance, attending to, service, people in attendance
tender, offer, thing offered, care; to exhibit, pay down, care for; sensitive, compassionate
tender-hefted, tender-hested, gently framed
tent, probe; to probe, cure (a wound), lodge
Tereus, see PHILOMEL
Termagant, violent character, supposedly god of the Mohammedans, in old miracle plays
termination, expression, term
termless, indescribable
tertian, fever returning every third day
tester, sixpenny piece
tetter, skin disease
text, capital letter
thane, Scottish title or rank, somewhat lower than earl
thankful, deserving thanks
theoric, theory
therefor, for that
Thetis, a sea-goddess, the sea
thews, bodily parts, strength
thick, rapid, dim
thills, shafts of a cart
thing, sexual organ
think, seem
this, these
thought, anxiety, sorrow
thrasonical, boastful
three-farthings, thin silver coin, having a profile of Queen Elizabeth with a rose behind the ear
three-nooked, three-cornered
threne, threnos, dirge
thrift, profit, gain, advantage
thriftless, profitless
thrum, thread left at end of a warp
thunder-stone, thunderbolt
tickle, unstable, precarious; please, provoke
tick-tack, game in which pegs were put into holes; fornication
tide, time, course
tidy, plump
tight, sound, able
tilt, thrust, fight, encounter
timeless, untimely, premature
timely, early, in due season
tinct, colour, elixir of the alchemists
tire, equipment, dress, head-dress; attire, prey (on), feed greedily
tis, this (dialectal)
tisick, consumptive cough
Titan, god of the sun, the sun
tithe, tenth; to take the tenth part

tithing, district
tittle, dot
to, in addition to, against, appropriate to, in comparison with, in respect of, as to
tod, 28 lb. weight of wool; to yield this amount of wool
tofore, previously
toge, Roman toga
toil, net, snare; to cause to work hard, weary with work
token, spot of infection, plague-spot
toll, exact toll or tribute
tool, weapon, penis
top, head, forelock, highest point; to surpass, copulate with
top-gallant, highest mast, summit
topless, supreme
tortive, twisted
toss, impale, toss on a pike
tottered, tattered
tottering, ragged
touch, touchstone, taint; sound, test, wound
touse, pull out of joint
trace, follow, pass (through)
tract, trace, track, course
trade, coming and going, path, habit, business
traded, practised
trade-fallen, out of work
traditional, bound by tradition
train, tail, troop, bait; draw, entice, lead astray
traject, ferry
trammel, bind with the corpse, entangle
transfix, remove
translate, change, transform
transpose, change
trash, check, hold in leash
traverse, march, move from side to side
treatise, tale, talk
treble-dated, living three times as long as man
trench, cut
trencher, wooden plate
trencher-friend, parasite
trenchering, plates
trencher-knight, hanger-on
tribunal, dais
trick, custom, way, knack, touch (of a disease), toy; to adorn, blazon
tricking, adornment
trill, trickle
triple, third
triple-turned, three times faithless
tristful, sorrowful
triumph, public festivity, tournament, trump card
triumphant, triumphal, celebrating a triumph
triumphantly, in celebration
Trojan, good fellow
troll, sing
troll-my-dames, troll-madams game resembling bagatelle
trophy, token of victory, memorial, monument
tropically, figuratively
trot, bawd
troth, truth, faith, word of honour
trow, believe, think, know

truepenny, honest fellow

trull, prostitute, wench

truncheon, staff carried as a symbol of office

try, test; purify, refine, prove

tub, sweating-tub used in the treatment of venereal disease

tuck, rapier

tucket, signal, flourish on a trumpet

tun-dish, funnel

turtle, turtle-dove, symbol of chaste and faithful love

tushes, tusks

twire, twinkle

type, distinguishing sign, stamp

tyrannically, vehemently

tyranny, violence, outrage

tyrant, usurper

umbrage, shadow

unaccommodated, unprovided

unacquainted, unfamiliar

unadvised, rash, without consideration or knowledge

unagreeable, unsuited

unaneled, not having received extreme unction

unapproved, unconfirmed by proof

unaptness, disinclination

unattainted, without infection, un-prejudiced

unattempted, untempted

unavoided, inevitable

unbarbed, unarmed

unbated, unabated, not blunted (with a button)

unbent, with bow unbent, unprepared, unfrowning

unbid, unexpected

unbitted, unbridled

unbolted, unsifted, coarse

unbookish, unskilled, inexperienced

unbreathed, unpractised

uncase, strip, lay bare

uncharge, acquit of guilt

uncharged, unattacked

unchary, carelessly

unchecked, not contradicted

unclasp, reveal

unclew, undo, ruin

uncomprehensive, unplumbable

unconfirmed, uninstructed, ignorant

uncovered, open, bare-headed

uncrossed, not crossed through because bill still unpaid

unction, salve, ointment

uncurrent, not current, not permisible

undercrest, wear as a device of honour

undergo, undertake, come under, support, carry, bear

underhand, unobtrusive

underskinker, under-tapster, assistant barman

undertake, take charge of, assume, have to do with, venture

undertaker, one who takes on himself another's quarrel, one who settles with

underwrite, subscribe, submit to

uneath, with difficulty, scarcely

unexperient, inexperienced

unexpressive, inexpressible

unfair, rob of beauty

unfashionable, badly formed

unfenced, defenceless

unfold, disclose, display, reveal, release from the fold

unfurnished, unprovided, unprepared

ungalled, uninjured

ungenitured, impotent

ungored, unwounded

unhandsome, unskilled, nasty

unhappily, unfavourably, evilly

unhappiness, evil nature

unhappy, ill-fated, wretched, mischievous

unhouseled, not having received the sac-rament

union, pearl

unkind, unnatural

unluckily, with foreboding

unmanned, not trained, not broken in

unowed, having no owner

unpaved, without testicles, castrated

unpitied, unmerciful

unplausive, unapproving

unpregnant, unapt

unprevailing, unavailing

unprizable, without value, invaluable

unprized, not valued, beyond value

unproper, not belonging to one person, indecent

unprovide, make unprepared

unquestionable, not inviting conversation

unraked, not covered with fuel to keep it burning

unrecalling, past recall

unreclaimed, untamed

unrecuring, past cure

unrespective, heedless, held back by no consideration, undiscriminating

unrolled, struck off the register

unscanned, unconsidered

unseasoned, ill-timed, inexperienced

unseminared, without seed

unsifted, untried

unsorted, ill-chosen

unspeakable, indescribable, inexpressible

unspeaking, unable to speak

unsquared, inappropriate

unstanched, unquenchable, freely men-struating

unstate, deprive of rank and state

untainted, unaccused

untempering, unwinning

untented, unable to be treated, incurable

untoward, perverse, unruly

untowardly, unluckily

untraded, not customary

untrimmed, undressed

untrussing, undoing hose, undressing

unwarily, unexpectedly

unweighed, hasty, unconsidered

unwrung, not pinched or rubbed

up, in arms, in rebellion, in prison; *up and down,* completely, exactly

upon, because of, in consequence of

urchin, hedgehog, goblin

urinal, glass to hold urine

usance, interest on money

use, habit, custom, usual experience, advantage, profit, lending at interest, interest on something lent, need; to be

accustomed, continue, make a practice of, deal with, treat, go often

usurp, take or hold what belongs to another, supplant, assume

utterance, utmost extremity

uttermost, latest

vail, gratuity, tip, setting (of the sun); lower, let fall, do homage

vain, foolish, silly, unreal

valanced, fringed with hair

validity, strength, value

value, estimate, be worth

valued, denoting the value

vantage, advantage, gain, superiority, vantage-ground, opportunity

varletry, rabble

vastidity, immensity

vaulty, arched, hollow

vaunt, beginning

vaunt-courier, herald, harbinger

vengeance, harm, injury

vent, emission, utterance, outlet for en-ergy; let out, emit, utter, make known

ventage, aperture, finger-hole

ventricle, cavity of the brain

Venus, goddess of love and beauty; wife of Vulcan, the smith-god, but more often associated with her lover Mars

verge, compass, circle

vexation, agitation, torment, grief

via, away

vice, character in a morality play repres-enting a vice, jester, buffoon, gripping tool; to screw

vicegerent, deputy, representative

vicious, blameworthy, blemished

vie, add one to another

villein, peasant, servant

vinewed'st, most mouldy

violent, to rage, storm

virginalling, fingering as on the virginals—a keyed musical instrument

virtue, courage, merit, accomplishment, power, efficacy, essence, essential characteristic

virtuous, powerful, beneficial

visitor, one who visits to offer spiritual comfort

voice, speech, words, common talk, rumour, report, expressed opinion, judgement, vote, approval, authority to be heard; to acclaim, vote

voiding lobby, anteroom

voluntary, volunteer

votaress, woman who has taken a vow

votarist, votary one who has taken a vow

vouch, assertion, testimony; affirm, guarantee, bear witness

Vulcan, the smith-god, whose wife, Venus, was unfaithful

vulgar, of the common people, commonly known, common, public, mean; com-mon people, vernacular

waft, to convey by water, beckon, turn

waftage, passage by water

wafture, wave

wage, to wager, hazard, attempt, carry on war, pay

waist, girdle

wake, remain awake, be up late for revelry or on guard, wear out with lack of sleep, arouse

walk, tract of forest

wall-eyed, white-eyed, having glaring eyes

want, lack, miss

wanton, frolicsome, lawless, capricious, luxurious, luxuriant, lustful, unchaste; spoilt child, pampered darling, roguish, sportful, unruly or lustful creature

wappered, worn out

ward, guard, custody, prison-cell, defensive position in fencing; guard, protect

warden, kind of cooking pear

warp, distort, deviate

war-proof, war-tested, courage

warrant, guarantee, assure

warrantize, surety, authorization

warranty, sanction, authorization

warren, game enclosure

warrener, gamekeeper

wassail, drinking, revelling, feast

waste, spend, consume

watch, wakefulness, sleeplessness, watchfulness; be awake, keep from sleep, catch in the act

watchful, sleepless

water, lustre

water-gall, secondary rainbow

watering, drinking

water-standing, tearful

wave, waver

waxen, increase

weal, welfare, commonwealth

wear, fashion; carry, possess, be fashionable, weary

weather, storm

weed, garment, dress

week, *to be in by the,* be caught, ensnared, deeply in love

ween, expect, hope

weet, know

welkin, sky

well-liking, plump

well-respected, well-considered

well to live, prosperous

wharf, river bank

wheel, spinning wheel, tread-wheel on which a dog was harnessed to turn a roasting-spit

whelk, pimple

where, whereas

whiffler, officer who keeps the way clear for a procession

while, whiles, whilst, till

whipstock, whip-handle

whist, become silent

whiting-time, bleaching time

whitster, bleacher

whittle, small clasp-knife

wide, missing the mark, astray

widgeon, to cheat

wight, creature

wild, reckless, distracted, (of sea) open

wilderness, wildness of character, licentiousness

wildly, without cultivation, naturally

wildness, madness

will, sexual desire, sexual organ (male or female)

wimpled, hooded, blinkered

wince, kick

Winchester goose, sufferer from syphilis, prostitute

windgall, soft tumour on horse's leg

windlass, circuit made to intercept game, crafty device

wink, sleep, close one's eyes

wintered, used in winter

wipe, scar

wistly, intently, closely

wit, mental power, mind, sense, wisdom, imagination, one who has such qualities; know

withal, with this, with it, as well, at the same time, with

without, beyond

wittol, a man aware of and tolerating his wife's adultery

witty, wise, cunning

woman-tired, henpecked

wonder, admiration; admire, marvel

wondered, performing wonders

wondering, admiration

wood, mad

woodcock, dupe

woodman, hunter

woolward, wearing wool next to the skin

world, *to go to the,* marry; *a woman of the,* married woman

worm, serpent, snake

worn, exhausted, past

worship, dignity, honour, authority; to honour

wort, vegetable, unfermented beer

worthy, excellent, valuable, deserved, well-founded, fitting

wot, know

wrack, ruin, destruction

wreak, vengeance, revenge

wrest, tuning-key; take by force

wring, wrest, force, writhe, press painfully on

writ, document, writing, mandate, written command, scripture

writhled, wrinkled

wry, to swerve

Xantippe, scolding wife of the philosopher Socrates

yard, yard measure, penis

yare, ready, quick, moving lightly

yaw, sail out of course, lose direction

yellowness, jealousy

yellows, jaundice

yerk, thrust suddenly

yerne, see ERNE

younker, fine young man, novice, greenhorn

zany, comic performer awkwardly imitating a clown or mountebank

Zouns, Zounds, see 'SWOUNDS

INDEX TO FIRST LINES OF
SONNETS